written and researched by

Harry Adès, Danny Aeberhard, Nicky Agate, Andrew Benson, David Cleary, Jonathan Franklin, Joshua Goodman, Melissa Graham, Dilwyn Jenkins, Oliver Marshall, Anja Mutic, Lucy Phillips, James Read, Paul Smith, Ross Velton and Brad Weiss

NEW YORK • LONDON • DELHI

www.roughguides.com

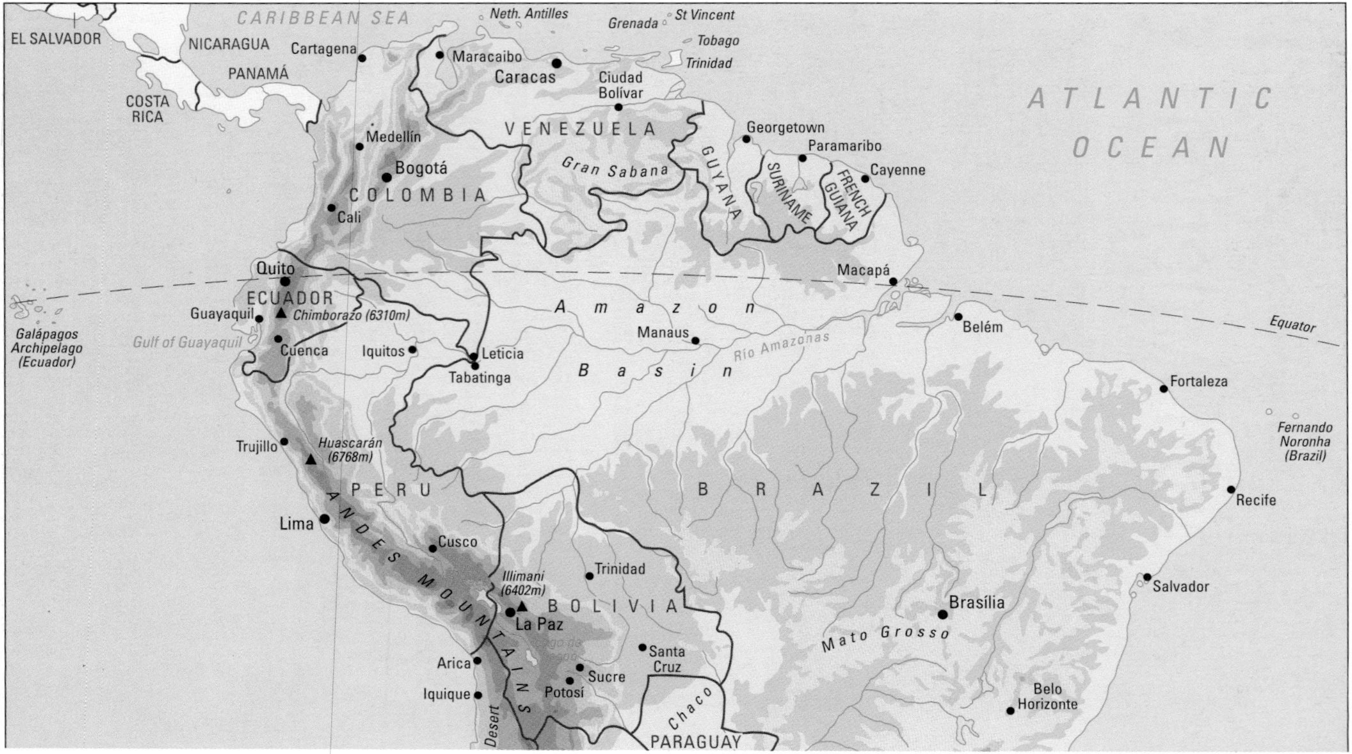

CARIBBEAN SEA
Neth. Antilles
Grenada
St Vincent
Tobago
Trinidad
EL SALVADOR
NICARAGUA
COSTA RICA
PANAMÁ
Cartagena
Maracaibo
Caracas
Ciudad Bolívar
ATLANTIC OCEAN
VENEZUELA
Gran Sabana
GUYANA
Georgetown
SURINAME
Paramaribo
FRENCH GUIANA
Cayenne
Medellín
Bogotá
COLOMBIA
Cali
Quito
ECUADOR
Guayaquil
Chimborazo (6310m)
Gulf of Guayaquil
Cuenca
Galápagos Archipelago (Ecuador)
Macapá
Amazon
Manaus
Río Amazonas
Belém
Equator
Iquitos
Leticia
Tabatinga
Basin
Fortaleza
Fernando Noronha (Brazil)
Trujillo
Huascarán (6768m)
PERU
Lima
ANDES MOUNTAINS
BRAZIL
Recife
Cusco
Illimani (6402m)
Trinidad
BOLIVIA
La Paz
Brasília
Salvador
Mato Grosso
Arica
Iquique
Desert
Santa Cruz
Sucre
Potosí
Chaco
PARAGUAY
Belo Horizonte

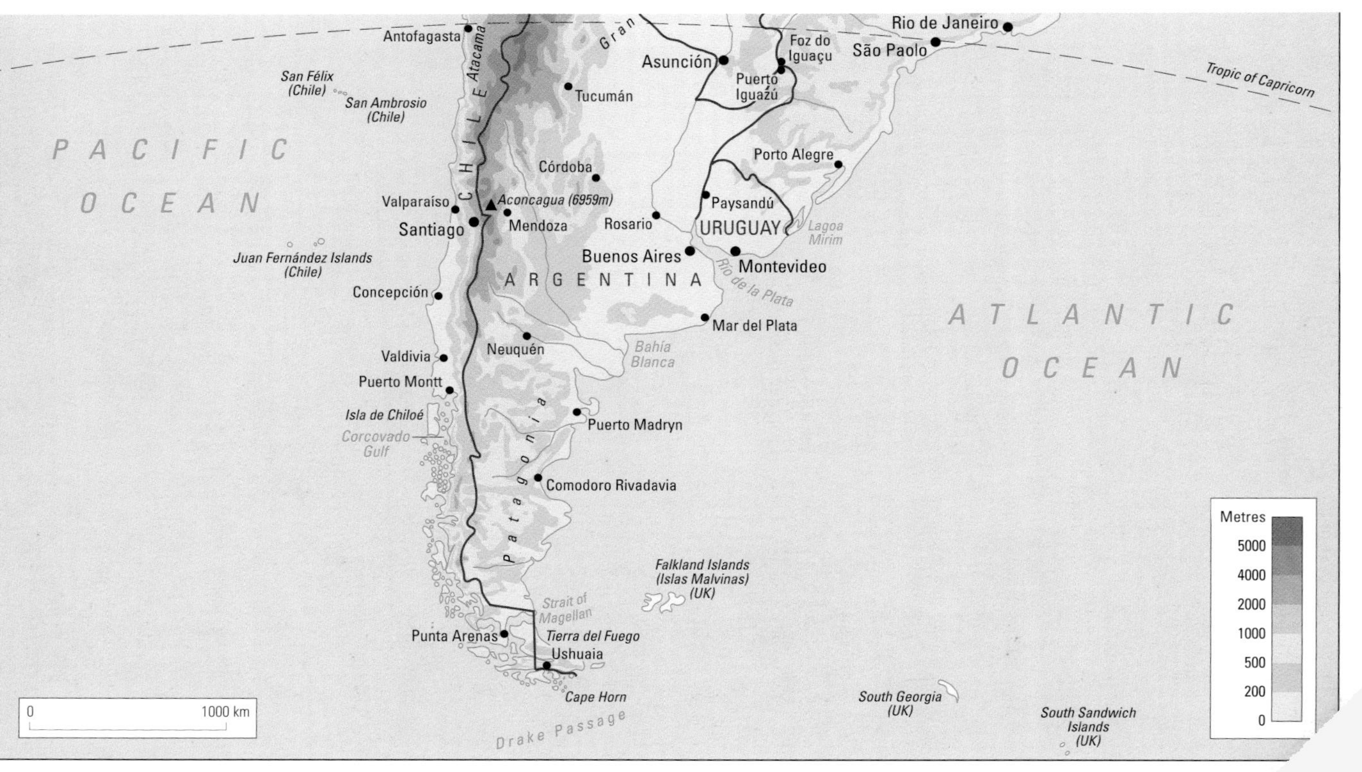

Easter Island (Chile)
Antofagasta
Atacama
Gran
Rio de Janeiro
São Paolo
Foz do Iguaçu
Asunción
Puerto Iguazú
Tropic of Capricorn
San Félix (Chile)
San Ambrosio (Chile)
Tucumán
PACIFIC OCEAN
CHILE
Córdoba
Porto Alegre
Valparaíso
Aconcagua (6959m)
Paysandú
Santiago
Mendoza
Rosario
URUGUAY
Lagoa Mirim
Juan Fernández Islands (Chile)
Buenos Aires
Montevideo
ARGENTINA
Río de la Plata
Concepción
Mar del Plata
ATLANTIC OCEAN
Neuquén
Bahía Blanca
Valdivia
Puerto Montt
Isla de Chiloé
Puerto Madryn
Corcovado Gulf
Patagonia
Comodoro Rivadavia
Metres
5000
4000
2000
1000
500
200
0
Falkland Islands (Islas Malvinas) (UK)
Strait of Magellan
Punta Arenas
Tierra del Fuego
Ushuaia
Cape Horn
South Georgia (UK)
South Sandwich Islands (UK)
0
1000 km
Drake Passage

Introduction to

South America

Stretching from the shores of the Caribbean to the icy waters off Tierra del Fuego, South America is a vast and remarkable mosaic of climates, landscapes and peoples. Almost twice the size of Europe, the continent takes in an enormous geographic and cultural diversity, comprising enormous primeval rainforests, vibrant metropolises, stunning mountain ranges, vast desert plains and remote indigenous villages.

The thirteen countries that make up South America are fascinating in equal parts for their supranational commonalities and for their differences within individual borders.Geographic realities, earlysettlement patterns, French, Dutch, English and, especially Spanish and Portuguese colonization and their legacies of independent states, have moulded a continent where differences within countries can appear greater than between them. Brazil's huge northern region, for example, has far more in common – language aside – with the neighbouring portions of the Amazon basin located within Peru or Colombia than it does, say, with Rio de Janeiro. Extreme social and economic disparities are striking, nowhere more so than in the cities where extreme wealth can exist side by side with extreme poverty, the once burgeoning middle classes being squeezed out of existence. South America shares a common history based on its original Amerindian population, European colonization, slavery and immigration. **Indigenous peoples** – whose ancestors migrated to South America thousands of years ago and went on to develop complex societies and rich cultures – are still presences in many parts of the continent, in particular in the central Andes, the Amazon basin and Paraguay.

At the beginning of the sixteenth century Spanish and Portuguese explorers established settlements in South America, and soon the continent was divided between **European powers** – mainly by Spain and Portugal, but with England, France and Holland also staking small territorial claims. To Europe, South America was a land of fabled wealth, but it was seen to lack a sufficient or suitable supply of labour. The colonizing powers soon turned to Africa, and by the mid-nineteenth century millions of **enslaved Africans** had been introduced to toil in South America's mines and sugar plantations.

With the independence of the former Spanish and Portuguese colonies in the early nineteenth century followed by the gradual suppression of the slave trade and the emancipation of slaves, South America became a target of mass **immigration**. Irish and German farmers were placed on Argentina's and Chile's "Indian frontiers", Italian and Japanese were directed to Brazil's expanding coffee plantations, while tin, copper and gold mines throughout the continent attracted Cornish miners. Meanwhile, skilled and unskilled workers from throughout Europe headed for burgeoning cities, playing vital roles in the development of South America's transportation, power and banking networks and industrial capacity. Immigration even played a vital role in the Guianas – the continent's last European colonies – with the importation by sugar plantations of tens of thousands of East Indian, Javanese and indentured labourers from other lands.

Where to go

Each of South America's countries has, of course, its own special attractions, and your choice of what to do on a trip is virtually unlimited. There are cities with fine dining and the most sophisticated cultural offerings, quiet colonial-era villages, ancient monuments, mountain trails, gorgeous beaches, nature reserves and vast

primeval forests. With a little time, it's easy to visit several countries during a single trip as cross-border air, road and river links are in most cases excellent. While transport infrastructure within individual countries does vary, all have well-developed plane and bus networks, while river boats and railways can also sometimes be effective – and enjoyable – means of transportation. With tourism becoming increasingly important, most places have accommodation to suit all budgets ranging from the most basic of hostels where you can sling your hammock to luxurious boutique hotels and nature lodges.

In the north of the continent lies **Venezuela**, a country little visited because of lack of tourist development and recent social strife; it boasts many of the features associated with South America. The beaches on its long Caribbean shore are some of the finest anywhere in the continent, with the best protected within national parks. The Andean city of Mérida has a perpetual spring-like climate and makes a delightful prelude to visiting Los Llanos, a vast grassland plain offering outstanding birdwatching opportunities. In the south of the country lies the Amazon region of Guayana, slowly luring more adventurous travellers intent on exploring the huge expanse of forest and its amazing mountainous terrain and waterfalls, of which Angel Falls is the most dramatic.

As a result of decades of civil war,

Wildlife

South America's diversity of wildlife stems from its wide range of habitats in a continent of rivers, tropical forests, mountains, grasslands and deserts. Human encroachment has devastating consequences on wildlife, but an increase in environmental consciousness in recent years has led to the development throughout the continent of national and state parks, as well as private nature reserves. Many of these as yet contain absolutely no infrastructure to receive visitors, but an ever increasing number have access by road or river and accommodation that ranges from the utmost basic to incredibly luxurious.

Especially rich in wildlife are, of course, the dense forests of the Amazon which contain a wealth of insects, birds, reptiles and mammals. Wildlife can, however, be more easily spotted in other parts of tropical South America. The Pantanal swamp of Brazil (see p.417) and the Llanos plains of Venezuela (see p.1049) offer amazing possibilities of viewing wildlife: in the wet season these regions are alive with migratory birds heading to or from North America or southern South America, while in the dry season creatures such as capybara (the world's largest rodent), boar, tapir monkeys and even the occasional jaguar or other large cats can easily be seen congregating alongside riverbanks or pools of water.

Geography and terrain

South America's most prominent physical feature is the Andes mountain chain, which extends from Venezuela down to Argentina and Chile. The range includes lush tropical valleys on the northern and eastern slopes; the high, semi-arid Altiplano plateau that drains into Lago Titicaca between Peru and Bolivia; active and recently extinct volcanoes reaching classic proportions in Ecuador; the Mediterranean-like climate of Chile's Central Valley; the cloudforest of northwest Argentina; and the dramatically contrasting conditions that include temperate rainforests, virtual desert and awe-inspiring glaciers.

To the east of the Andes are four well-defined lowland zones. The Orinoco basin (which includes some of the Llanos region of eastern Venezuela) is an area of high rainfall that supports both a savanna-like vegetation and dense tropical forest. The vast Amazon basin is very similar and is the largest area of surviving equatorial rainforest in the world. Further south can be found an area of swamp (most notably the Pantanal of Brazil), savanna grasslands and thorn scrub of the Chaco. The extremely fertile grasslands of the Argentine pampas have rainfall throughout the year, peaking in the summer and diminishing westwards towards the margins of the Andes.

Eastern South America comprises two ancient geological formations – the Guiana Highlands and the Brazilian Shield – divided by the lower Amazon basin. The area to the south of the Amazon and towards the Atlantic coast is extremely varied, both in terms of climate and physical appearance including Araucaria pine forests in the south of Brazil, the coffee-supporting valleys in southeast Brazil and the desert-like *sertão* of the Brazilian northeast. The coast too is varied: flat and fertile in the northeast, but characterized by a steep escarpment known as the Serra do Mar, which extends from Rio to the south.

Colombia is even more overlooked by visitors. The tourist potential, however, is enormous, and much of the country is relatively safe to visit – though caution should still the byword. Bogotá, the capital located high up in the Andes, offers a vivacious nightlife and music scene where Caribbean, Pacific and Andean sounds meet. On the Caribbean coast, the Spanish colonial walled-city of Cartagena is beautifully preserved, with excellent beaches close by. In the far southwest of the country stand the mysterious ancient statues at San Agustín, near the charming colonial town of Popayán. Although particular caution should be taken if venturing into

Colombia's large portion of the Amazon basin, the sleepy town of Leticia makes a good jumping-off point for travels into Brazil or Peru.

Perhaps **Ecuador**'s diminutive size makes its contrasts feel heightened. Within the course of a single day, it's possible to pass through coastal lowlands, high sierra and into dense Amazonian forests. Quito, high in the Andes, is one of the continent's most instantly appealing capitals, featuring both a stunning colonial centre and attractive modern suburbs where most visitor-oriented services are located. Ecuador's portion of the Amazon rainforest is easily accessible, and it's possible to arrange to stay with an indigenous community or take a trek into the jungle. Nearly a thousand kilometres from the mainland, the Galápagos Islands are less accessible, yet their unique collection of wildlife makes them one the continent's major draws.

For many visitors, **Peru** is quintessential South America, embracing an astonishing array of coastal, mountain and Amazon landscapes, important archeological sights and vibrant cultures based on indigenous, *mestizo*, Spanish and African peoples. There's little to delay tourists in Lima, the capital city, or other parts of coastal Peru, with the country's highlights instead lying deep inland. Cusco, the ancient Inca capital, offers a fascinating blend of Inca and colonial Spanish architecture, and an excellent base from which to explore the surrounding region. An essential excursion is to the citadel of Machu Picchu, arguably the single most impressive monument in South America.

Remote **Bolivia** has gradually become one of the more alluring countries of South America, in large measure owing to the persistence of strong indigenous cultures, in particular of the Quechua- and Aymara-speaking peoples of the Altiplano, the bleak high plateau of the Andes mountains. La Paz, Bolivia's de facto capital, serves as a transport hub for most parts of the country. The city of Potosí, in the Altiplano south of La Paz, bears particular witness to the country's era of good fortune in silver mining, and is studded with gorgeous, if dilapidated, colonial buildings. The awe-inspiring valleys of the Yungas can be easily reached from La Paz, while for wildlife a visit to the Reserva de la Biósfera del Beni is well worth the effort.

Stretching thousands of kilometres, long and narrow

Chile too is a land of astonishing natural variety. To the south of the busy and not overly appealing capital, Santiago, is the picture postcard Lake District, surrounded by snowcapped volcanoes, while further south is the mystical Chiloé archipelago, beyond which lies the primeval temperate rainforest of northern Patagonia stretching into the deep fjords of the coast. Southern Patagonia's windswept plains are largely given over to sheep farms, but the lakes, glaciers and granite massif of the majestic Parque Nacional Torres del Paine combine to create an incredibly dramatic setting. North of Santiago, the land grows increasingly parched, with the bone-dry Atacama Desert displaying a unique desolate beauty.

Moving across the Andes, **Argentina** offers a kaleidoscope of panoramas ranging from subtropical rainforests to sub-Antarctic conditions. Sophisticated Buenos Aires, Argentina's sprawling capital, has museums, parks, theatres, restaurants and nightlife that compare to the best almost anywhere in the Americas. To the immediate west and the south are the grasslands of the pampa where it's possible to arrange a stay at a working cattle estancia. The rest of the country abounds with natural wonders, including the mighty waterfalls of Iguazú (shared with Brazil) in the northeast and, in Patagonia, the Glaciar Perito Moreno, a huge wall of ice that tumbles into the lake below. The Argentine Andes, too, are attractive, with captivating colonial towns in the north, vineyards in the foothills of the central portion, and a range of simple and elegant mountain resorts further south offering excellent skiing in winter and hiking in the summer.

Wedged between Argentina and Brazil, **Uruguay** usually gets overlooked in favour of its giant neighbours. The smallest Spanish-speaking republic in South America, it can hardly lay claim to being the continent's most exciting destination, but it does have an immensely likeable capital, Montevideo. To the east of the city are a series of resorts, with by far the most up-scale being Punta del Este, popular with wealthy Argentine tourists attracted by the area's varied Atlantic beaches and vibrant nightlife. Inland, Uruguay is largely made up of rolling grasslands given over to cattle and sheep estancias, many of which have opened their doors to guests wanting a taste of gaucho life.

Landlocked **Paraguay** is rarely high on the list of destinations for South America, but this helps to preserve an untrammelled feel. The capital, Asunción, is

Music

Whether it's a simple rhythm produced by tapping a tin can against a counter top in a Rio bar, street musicians playing melodic tunes with panpipes in Cusco, a tape of an overly amplified salsa being played on long-distance buses in Venezuela, or the Anglo-Caribbean and Indian "Bollywood" sounds that compete for Guyana's airwaves, music can often appear to be a South American obsession.

The music on the continent derives from three major sources: the indigenous Amerindian population, the Spanish and Portuguese colonizers and the transported African slaves. Elements of all three are found in many combinations within musical form, instrumentation, vocal and performing style, rhythm and melody and in many places there is a fusion into **culturally mixed forms** linking traditional and modern societies. In Peru, Bolivia and Chile, for example, panpipes of the Aymara and Quechua peoples are played alongside stringed instruments such as the *charango* (a kind of a mandolin made from the shell of an armadillo) and guitar to melodies restructured to suit a modern urban and European aesthetic.

Beyond the Andes, African influences are most prevalent. Even **tango** (see p.103), a music so linked with Argentina's immigrant history, is infused with African *candomblé* and percussion. Musical styles that emerged from coastal Peru, Colombia and Venezuela as well as widely in Brazil and even Uruguay feature more obvious African influences. For example, **cumbia** – born on Colombia's Atlantic coast and for many people the quintessential "Latin" sound that's hugely in popular clubs from Cali to New York – offered a rhythmic template of pronounced African and Indigenous Indian origins that could be studio remixed for the dancefloor. In Brazil, **samba** – the sound synonymous with Carnaval (see p.339) – has even purer African roots, having first emerged in the nineteenth century in downtown Rio de Janeiro's so-called "Little Africa". The Africanness of samba's drums was hated by the elite for being so "primitive" – but that didn't stop it from becoming the dominant form of Brazilian music.

pleasant enough, but it's rural Paraguay that is the country's greatest draw. To the south of the capital stand the eighteenth-century Jesuit ruins of Trinidad and Jesús, while the northern half of the country is the immense Chaco, a region of scrub and marshland, whose sparse population includes indigenous peoples clinging to traditional ways of life and, intriguingly, German-speaking Mennonite farmers.

Sharing a border with every South American country apart from Ecuador and Chile, **Brazil**, the largest, most populated and only Portuguese-speaking country in South America, is fairly easy to visit in conjunction with its neighbours. Rio de Janeiro, an exciting metropolis in a truly gorgeous setting, is an almost essential destination on any Brazilian itinerary. In the northeast, the city of Salvador is very much the Brazil of many people's imagination with an exotic overlay of Portuguese and African influences. With the lion's share of the Amazon basin, Brazil boasts a stunning array of wildlife and eco-tourism opportunities, and its long coastline should satisfy even the most jaded travellers.

Finally, and all too often overlooked, are **the Guianas** – the former British and Dutch colonies of Guyana and Suriname as well as the French overseas *département* of French Guiana. Although the region's history and diverse ethnic make-up give the Guianas something of a Caribbean feel, in particular on the coast where most of the population is concentrated, the interior – tropical rainforest and savanna only now being opened up to tourism – is unmistakably South America.

When to go

Most of South America enjoys a tropical or a subtropical **climate** that entices visitors all year round. Roughly two-thirds of the continent is in some proximity to the equator or the tropic of Capricorn, ensuring that temperatures seldom – if ever – drop too far below 20° Celsius, while the rainforest areas have average maximum temperatures of around 30° Celsius through the year. As you head further south, South America offers increasingly sharp winters – June to August – and milder summers – December to February; visits to Tierra del Fuego, at the southern tip of the continent, can be extremely cold from April to October.

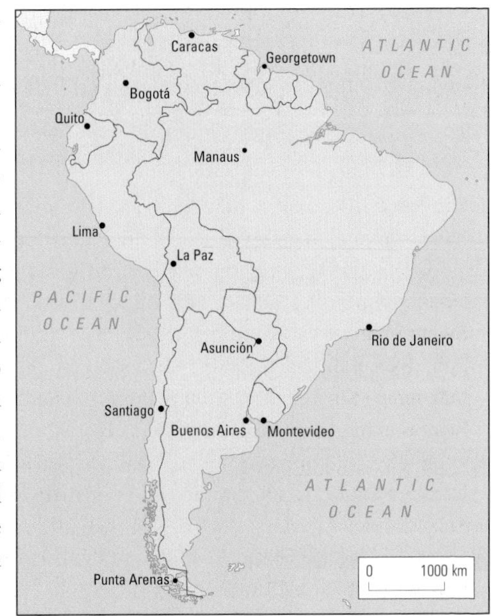

When planning a visit, you should also take into account local **rainy seasons**, particularly when travelling in the Andes. Roads in Bolivia and Peru can be extremely hard to negotiate from November to April. For further details on weather and seasonal changes, please see the "When to go" section of each chapter.

Average temperatures and rainfall

	Jan	Feb	Mar	Apr	May	Jun	Jul	Aug	Sep	Oct	Nov	Dec
Asunción												
Max temp. (°C)	33	33	31	27	23	22	22	24	26	30	32	34
Rainfall (mm)	147	146	146	147	128	75	51	40	78	149	148	150
Bogotá												
Max temp (°C)	18	18	19	18	18	17	17	17	18	18	18	18
Rainfall (mm)	33	41	80	110	100	50	40	50	50	150	110	50
Buenos Aires												
Max temp (°C)	29	28	26	22	18	14	14	16	18	21	24	28
Rainfall (mm)	79	71	109	89	76	61	56	61	79	86	84	99
Caracas												
Max temp (°C)	25	26	27	28	28	27	26	27	27	26	26	25
Rainfall (mm)	17	14	12	55	78	140	124	126	119	124	74	47
Georgetown												
Max temp (°C)	28	28	30	30	30	30	31	32	32	32	31	30
Rainfall (mm)	196	151	110	200	308	394	298	195	105	102	175	248
La Paz												
Max temp (°C)	13	13	13	14	14	13	13	14	14	14	15	14
Rainfall (mm)	130	105	70	37	12	8	10	12	30	46	51	90
Lima												
Max temp (°C)	26	27	27	24	22	21	19	18	19	21	22	24
Rainfall (mm)	0	0	0	0	0	3	5	3	3	3	0	0
Manaus												
Max temp (°C)	30	30	30	30	31	31	32	33	33	33	32	31
Rainfall (mm)	220	210	256	208	177	95	55	25	25	108	125	200
Montevideo												
Max temp (°C)	28	28	26	21	18	14	13	14	18	20	24	26
Rainfall (mm)	70	55	100	100	80	78	75	78	75	60	76	81
Punta Arenas												
Max temp (°C)	14	14	12	10	7	5	4	6	8	11	12	14
Rainfall (mm)	38	23	33	36	33	41	28	31	23	28	18	36
Quito												
Max temp (°C)	19	19	19	19	19	19	19	19	20	19	9	19
Rainfall (mm)	114	130	152	175	24	48	20	25	79	127	109	104
Rio de Janeiro												
Max temp (°C)	30	30	27	29	26	25	25	25	25	26	28	28
Rainfall (mm)	120	118	120	105	82	51	24	24	75	90	100	132
Santiago												
Max temp (°C)	29	29	27	23	18	14	15	17	19	22	26	28
Rainfall (mm)	3	3	5	13	64	84	76	56	31	15	8	5

things not to miss

It's not possible to see everything that South America has to offer in one trip – and we don't suggest you try. What follows is a selective taste of the continent's highlights: stunning landscapes, vibrant cities and spectacular wildlife. They're arranged in five colour-coded categories, which you can browse through to find the very best things to see and experience. All highlights have a page reference to take you straight into the guide, where you can find out more.

01 Boat trip down the Amazon Page **398** • Taking a slow boat journey on the Amazon is the most leisurely way to experience the mighty river and luxuriate in the lush jungle atmosphere.

02 Mountain biking in Bolivia Page **242** • The deep valleys of the Yungas are perfect terrain for mountain biking.

03 Colca Canyon Page **920** • The terraces of Peru's Colca Canyon, one of the deepest in the world, are home to indigenous villages, while its skies are rife with condors.

04 Football Page **54** • From the Caribbean to Tierra del Fuego, El Fútbol is something of a religion and attending a match should not be missed.

05 Ceviche Page **853** • Savour the national dish of Peru, fresh fish soaked briefly in lime juice and chillies, one of the continent's culinary delights.

06 Parque Nacional Torres del Paine Page 572 • One of the most alluring sights in southern Chile, the park's granite towers are as stunning from afar as they are up close.

07 The Amazon Page 392 • Easily the planet's largest rainforest, the Amazon covers more than six million square kilometres and boasts a fifth of the world's bird and plant species.

08 The architecture of Brasília Page 412 • A futurist's dream, Brazil's capital is singular in its otherwordly buildings, such as the Aztec-inspired Teatro Nacional.

09 Plaza de los Héroes Page 825 • Sleepy Asunción is centred on the monumental Plaza de los Héroes, dominated by the Pantheón de los Héroes.

10 Galápagos wildlife Page **736** • The scarred volcanic Galápagos Islands that inspired Darwin offer an unparalleled wildlife diversity as well as insight into the mechanics of nature at work.

11 Rocket launch Page **803** • Catch a rocket launch in the jungle at the Centre Spatial Guyanais in Kourou, French Guiana.

12 Andean festivals Page **250** • The villages of the Andes afford numerous opportunities for carousing, such as the Oruro Carnaval, pictured above.

13 Sugar Loaf mountain Page **333** • No trip to Rio is complete without taking the cable car up Sugar Loaf mountain to catch the awe-inspiring panoramic view of the city and the surrounding bay.

14 Iguazú Falls Pages **130 & 448** • The world's largest waterfalls, Iguazú spans Argentina and Brazil and can be visited on a network of trails and catwalks leading above and below the roaring rapids.

15 Buenos Aires cafe culture Page **101** • One of the most seductive of the Argentine capital's many *barrios*, San Telmo features some of its most atmospheric cafés.

16 Scenic winter-sports Page **494** • Easily accessible from Santiago, the Chilean Andes offer some of the finest skiing and snowboarding in South America.

17 Kogi village huts Page **622** • Of the myriad indigenous peoples in South America, the cocoa-chewing Kogi Indians of Colombia's Parque Nacional Tayrona are among the least touched by modernity.

18 Nazca Lines Page **909** • Theories abound behind these mysterious animal shapes and geometric figures embedded in the landscape of southern Peru, but there is no disputing their impressiveness.

19 Tango Page **103** • If watching the celebrated Argentine dance at a *milonga* is inspiring, its intricate steps can be learned – or at least, better appreciated – with tango classes.

20 Volcán Cotopaxi Page **687** • One of the tallest active volcanoes in the world, Cotopaxi is but one of Ecuador's many mountains that can challenge specialists and complete novices.

21 Angel Falls Page **1063** • Venezuela's Angel Falls tumble dramatically off the edge of the enormous Auyantepui tabletop mountain and into the verdant jungle below.

22 La Paz's Mercado de Hechiceria Page **226** • The most colourful of Bolivia's street markets, the Mercado de Hechiceria (witches' market) offers a fascinating glimpse into the world of Aymara mysticism and herbal medicine.

23 The floating villages of Lago Titicaca Page **926** • One of Titicaca's many treasures, these man-made villages have been floating on the lake since Inca times.

24 Tiwanaku Page **231** • One of the cradles of Andean civilization – and once the centre of a massive empire, Tiwanaku in Bolivia is among the most intriguing and monumental archeological sites in South America.

25 Capybara Page **1049** • The immense plains of Venezuela's Los Llanos region are known for the llaneros cowboys as well as an impressive array of wildlife, including the capybara, the world's largest rodent.

26 **The Copacabana** Page **333** • The world's most famous beach, Rio's three-kilometre-long Copacabana is ideal for sunbathing, volleyball and people-watching.

27 **Parilla** Page **74** • Carnivores can sample the internationally renowned – and enormous – steaks of Argentina's pampa, barbecued on a grill.

28 Mercado del Puerto Page **983** • This former nineteenth-century Montevideo meat market now comprises an impressive array of grills and restaurants.

29 Carnaval Page **339** • The most vibrant of Brazil's festivals, Carnaval is famously celebrated in Rio, Salvador and Olinda.

30 Driving across Salar de Uyuni Page **258** • Drive across the world's biggest salt lake, one of Bolivia's most extraordinary landscapes.

31 Salsa Club Page **635** • Day or night, the streets of Cali pulse with the sounds of Cuban-style salsa music blaring from the numerous clubs.

32 Trekking Page **542** • Get away from it all with a trek among the pristine lakes and snowcapped volcanoes of Chile's Lake District.

33 Machu Picchu Page **900** • This citadel at the end of Peru's Inca Trail lives up to its reputation thanks to its mysterious temples, palaces and breathtaking setting.

34 Otavalo market Page **678** • Even hardened skinflints won't be able to resist the fabulous Ecuadoran handicrafts on offer at one of the largest and most colourful *artesanía* markets on the continent.

35 Glaciar Perito Moreno Page **187** • Witness the titanic struggle of Patagonia's Perito Moreno, one of only a handful of the advancing glaciers on the planet, as it tries to reach the Península de Magallanes.

36 Chilean wine Page **535** • Taste some of Chile's beefy red and elegant white vintages and tour one of the country's celebrated vineyards.

Contents

Using this Rough Guide

We've tried to make this Rough Guide a good read and easy to use. The book is divided into five main sections, and you should be able to find whatever you want in one of them.

Colour section

The front colour section offers a quick tour of South America. The **introduction** aims to give you a feel for the place, with suggestions on where to go. We also tell you what the weather is like and give an overview of the continent's geography and terrain. Next, our authors round up their favourite aspects of South America in the **things not to miss** section – whether it's great food, amazing sights or a unique activity. Right after this comes a full **contents** list.

Basics

The Basics section covers all the **pre-departure** nitty-gritty to help you plan your trip. This is where to find out which airlines fly to your destination, what paperwork you'll need, what to do about money and insurance, about internet access, food, security, public transport, car rental – in fact just about every piece of **general practical information** you might need.

Guide

This is the heart of the Rough Guide, divided into user-friendly chapters, each of which covers a specific country. Every chapter starts with a list of **highlights** and an **introduction** that helps you to decide where to go, depending on your time and budget. Likewise, introductions to the various towns and smaller regions within each chapter should help you plan your itinerary. We start most town accounts with information on arrival and accommodation, followed by a tour of the sights, and finally reviews of places to eat and drink, and details of nightlife. Longer accounts also have a directory of practical listings.

Language

The **language** section gives useful guidance for speaking Spanish and Portuguese and pulls together all the vocabulary you might need on your trip, including a comprehensive menu reader. Here you'll also find a glossary of words and terms peculiar to the region.

Index + small print

Apart from a **full index**, which includes maps as well as places, this section covers publishing information, credits and acknowledgements, and also has our contact details in case you want to send in updates and corrections to the book – or suggestions as to how we might improve it.

Map and chapter list

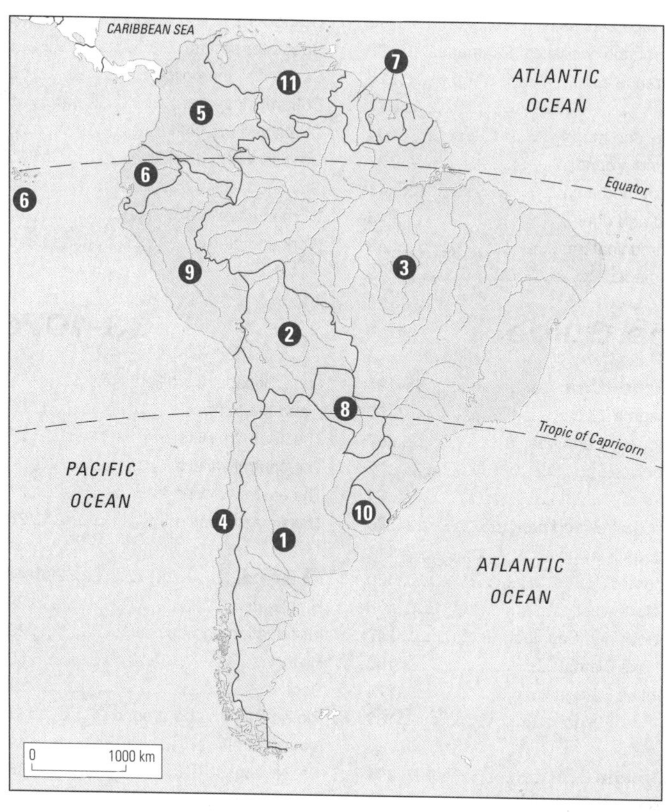

Contents

Colour section i–xxiv

Basics 9–62

The Guide 63–1076

Language 1077–1090

Index and small print 1091–1102

Map symbols

maps are listed in the full index using coloured text

International boundary
State/province boundary
Chapter boundary
Equator/tropic line
Highway
Major road
Minor road
Unpaved road/track
4-wheel drive
Pedestrianized street
Steps
Path
Railway
Funicular railway
Cable car
Tram line
Metro line
Ferry route
Waterway
International airport
Domestic airport
Point of interest
Mountain range
Mountain peak
Volcano
Crater
Cave
Ruins
Spring
Waterfall
Mountain pass
Ranger station
Lodge/refuge

Customs post
Church (regional maps)
Synagogue
Viewpoint
Lighthouse
Statue
Campsite
Accommodation
Vineyard
Ski area
Harbour/port
Gate
Bus/taxi stop
Metro station
Ecovia stop
Trole stop
Post office
Information office
Telephone office
Internet access
Hospital
Swimming pool
Bank
Building
Church (town maps)
Stadium
Market
Christian cemetery
Park
Beach
Swamp
Salt flats

Basics

Basics

Getting there

The easiest way to reach South America is by air via the US, usually through an East Coast hub such as Miami and with one of the national South American airlines, such as Varig or LanChile, particularly if you want a reasonable choice of schedules and routes. Many customs departments in South America insist that you have an onward or return ticket, but such stipulations are seldom checked or enforced.

Airfares always depend on the **season**, with the highest being around July, August and mid-December to mid-January; you'll get the best prices during the dry **winter** (May, June and late September) and the wet **summer** (February to April). Note also that flying on weekends – unless there are only a few flights a week – is usually more expensive; price ranges quoted below assume midweek travel.

You can often cut costs by going through a **specialist flight agent** – either a consolidator, who buys up blocks of tickets from the airlines and sells them at a discount, or a **discount agent** who, in addition to dealing with discounted flights, may also offer special student and youth fares and a range of other travel-related services such as travel insurance, rail passes, car rentals, tours and the like. Booking flights well in advance, or taking advantage of Web-only offers and airline frequent-flyer programs, can often knock a couple of hundred dollars off the price of your flight.

Another way to reduce the price of your South American holiday vastly is to book with a tour operator who can put together a **package deal** including flights and accommodation at a specially arranged price, and perhaps tours as well. If you are starting your flight in mainland Europe – or can get there cheaply from Ireland or the UK – it may be wise to investigate some of the **charter flights** offered by French airlines. A further possibility is to see if you can arrange a **courier flight**, although you'll need to be flying from a major city such as New York or London, will require a flexible schedule, and will preferably be travelling alone with very little luggage. In return for shepherding a parcel through customs, you can expect to get a deeply discounted ticket – maybe as little as US$250 to Rio from mainland USA. However, you'll probably be restricted in the duration of your stay.

If you intend to take in South America as part of a world trip, a **round-the-world ticket (RTW)** offers the greatest flexibility. Many international airlines are now aligned with one of two globe-spanning networks: the "Star Alliance", which includes Air New Zealand, Lufthansa, SAS, Singapore Airlines, Thai, Varig and Air Canada; or "One World", which combines routes run by American, British Airways, Cathay Pacific, LanChile and Quantas, among others. Both networks offer RTW deals requiring a minimum number of stopovers. Fares depend on your point of origin, the class you fly and the number of continents or the distance you travel.

Booking flights online

Many airlines and discount travel websites offer you the opportunity to book tickets online, cutting out the costs of agents and middlemen. Good deals can often be found through discount or auction sites, as well as through the airlines' own websites.

Online booking agents and general travel sites

ⓦwww.cheapflights.com Bookings from the UK and Ireland only. Flight deals, travel agents, plus links to other travel sites.

ⓦwww.cheaptickets.com Discount flight specialists.

ⓦwww.expedia.com Discount airfares, all-airline search engine and daily deals.

ⓦwww.flyaow.com Online air travel info and reservations site.

ⓦwww.gaytravel.com Gay online travel agent,

concentrating mostly on accommodation but with cruises and flight offers too.

@www.hotwire.com Bookings from the US only. Last-minute savings of up to forty percent on regular published fares. Travellers must be at least 18 and there are no refunds, transfers or changes allowed. Log-in required.

@www.lastminute.com Bookings from the UK only. Offers good last-minute holiday package and flight-only deals.

@www.priceline.com Name-your-own-price website that has deals at around forty percent off standard fares. You cannot specify flight times (although you do specify dates) and the tickets are non-refundable, non-transferable and non-changeable.

@www.skyauction.com Bookings from the US only. Auction tickets and travel packages using a "second bid" scheme. The best strategy is to bid the maximum you're willing to pay, since if you win you'll pay just enough to beat the runner-up regardless of your maximum bid.

@www.travelocity.com Destination guides, hot web fares and best deals for car hire, accommodation and lodging as well as fares. Provides access to the travel agent system SABRE, the most comprehensive central reservations system in the US.

@www.travelshop.com.au Australian website offering discounted flights, packages, insurance and online bookings.

Flights from the US and Canada

Most airlines departing North America operate their South American **flights** from New York or Miami, except for Japan Air, which flies from Los Angeles. Flying from Miami tends to afford you greater flexibility in travel planning and cheaper prices. From Canada it's best to transfer at a US hub.

Airfares **peak** around Christmas and New Year, when they can reach US$900 from Miami to Buenos Aires, for example, and US$1200 to Rio or São Paulo, even if bought well in advance. For most other times, airlines tend to offer reasonable year-round fares, and it costs around US$850 to fly from New York and US$745 from Miami to Buenos Aires; or US$760 from New York or Los Angeles and US$625 from Miami to Rio de Janeiro in Brazil. Lima costs around US$530 from New York or Los Angeles, US$450 from Miami; while Santiago will set you back US$740 from LA, US$680 from New York and US$730 from Miami. Flights from New York or Los Angeles to Quito can usually be found for around US$650, from Miami for around US$500. Bolivia's La Paz can be reached for around US$620 from Miami, US$800 from New York and US$870 from Los Angeles; while flights to Caracas cost US$650 from LA, US$590 from New York and US$400 from Miami. Finally; if you're hoping to go to Bogota, expect to pay around US$480 from Miami, US$650 from Los Angeles and US700 from New York.

Airlines

Aces Airlines ⓣ1-800/846-2237, @www.avianca.com. Flights to Colombia from the US, operated under Avianca.

Aero California ⓣ1-800/237-6225, @www.abstravel.com/aerocalifornia. Flights to a variety of South American locations.

Aero Continente ⓣ1-888/232-4125, @www.aerocontinente.com. Flights from Miami to Peru twice weekly.

Aerolineas Argentinas US ⓣ1-800/333-0276 or 305/648-4100, Canada ⓣ1-800/688-0008, @www.aeroargentinas.com. Flights to Argentina from New York and Miami.

Aeromexico ⓣ1-800/237-6639, @www.aeromexico.com. Flights from the US to South America via Mexico.

Air Canada ⓣ1-888/247-2262, @www.aircanada.ca. Flights from Toronto to Argentina and Brazil.

American Airlines ⓣ1-800/433-7300, @www.aa.com. Flights to most South American countries via New York and Miami.

Avianca ⓣ1-800/284-2622, @www.avianca.com. Colombia's national airline specializes in flights to Bogotá.

Continental Airlines ⓣ1-800/231-0856, @www.continental.com. Flights to Brazil, Colombia, Ecuador, Peru and Venezuela from the US.

Delta Air Lines ⓣ1-800/241-4141, @www.delta.com. Flies to Brazil, Chile, Colombia, Peru and Venezuela.

Japan Air Lines ⓣ1-800/525-3663, @www.japanair.com. Flights from Los Angeles and New York to Brazil.

LanChile ⓣ1-800/735-5526, @www.lanchile.com. Frequent flights from many US locations to many South American countries.

Lloyd Aereo Boliviano ⓣ1-800/337-0918, @www.labairlines.com. Three flights weekly from Miami to Brazil and Bolivia.

Northwest ⓣ1-800/447-4747, ⓦwww.nwa.com. Flights to Brazil, Colombia and Peru from the US.
United Airlines ⓣ1-800/538-2929, ⓦwww.ual.com. Flies to Argentina, Brazil and Uruguay.
Varig ⓣ1-800/468-2744, ⓦwww.varigbrasil.com. Specializes in flights to its native Brazil.

Courier flights

Air Courier Association ⓣ1-800/282-1202, ⓦwww.aircourier.org. Courier flight broker. Membership (3 months/US$19, 1yr/US$29, 3yr/US$58, 5yr/US$87) also entitles you to twenty percent discount on travel insurance and name-your-own-price non-courier flights.
International Association of Air Travel Couriers ⓣ308/632-3273, ⓦwww.courier.org. Courier flight broker with membership fee of US$45/yr or US$80/two years.

Discount travel companies

Air Brokers International ⓣ1-800/883-3273, ⓦwww.airbrokers.com. Consolidator and specialist in round-the-world and Circle Pacific tickets.
Airtech ⓣ212/219-7000, ⓦwww.airtech.com. Standby seat broker; also deals in consolidator fares and courier flights.
Airtreks.com ⓣ1-877-AIRTREKS or 415/912-5600, ⓦwww.airtreks.com. Round-the-world and Circle Pacific tickets. The website itself features an interactive database that lets you build and price your own round-the-world itinerary.
Educational Travel Center ⓣ1-800/747-5551 or 608/256-5551, ⓦwww.edtrav.com. Student/youth discount agent.
STA Travel US ⓣ1-800/781-4040, Canada 1-888/427-5639, ⓦwww.sta-travel.com. Worldwide specialists in independent travel; also student IDs, travel insurance, car rental, rail passes, etc.
Travac ⓣ1-800/TRAV-800, ⓦwww.thetravelsite.com. Consolidator and charter broker with offices in New York City and Orlando.
Travel Avenue ⓣ1-800/333-3335, ⓦwww.travelavenue.com. Full-service travel agent that offers discounts in the form of rebates.
Travel Cuts Canada ⓣ1-800/667-2887, US ⓣ1-866/246-9762, ⓦwww.travelcuts.com. Canadian student-travel organization.
Travellers Advantage ⓣ1-877/259-2691, ⓦwww.travellersadvantage.com. Discount travel club; annual membership fee required (currently US$1 for three months' trial).
Worldtek Travel ⓣ1-800/243-1723, ⓦwww.worldtek.com. Discount travel agency for worldwide travel.

Specialist tour operators

4th Dimension Tours Miami, FL ⓣ1-800/343-0020, ⓦwww.4thdimension.com. South American tour specialist, who will organize an itinerary tailored to your needs.
Abercrombie & Kent International, Inc. Oak Brook, IL ⓣ630/954-2944 or 1-800/323-7308, ⓦwww.abercrombiekent.com. Upmarket South America packages plus independent travel service.
Above the Clouds ⓣ1-800/233-4499 or 802/482-4848, ⓦwww.aboveclouds.com. Hiking specialists featuring trips to Patagonia.
Adventure Center ⓣ1-800/228-8747 or 510/654-1879, ⓦwww.adventurecenter.com. Hiking and "soft adventure" specialists with trips deep into most South American countries as well as the Galápagos Islands.
Adventures Abroad ⓣ1-800/665-3998 or 360/775-9926, ⓦwww.adventures-abroad.com. Specialists featuring most major South American locations.
Adventures on Skis/Adventure Sport Holidays ⓣ1-800/628-9655 or 413/568-2855, ⓦwww.advonskis.com. Summer ski trips to Chile and Argentina.
Backroads ⓣ1-800/462-2848 or 510/527-1555, ⓦwww.backroads.com. Cycling, hiking and multi-sport tours to Argentina, Ecuador and the Galápagos Islands, Chile and Peru.
Classic Journeys ⓣ1-800/200-3887 or 858/454-5004, ⓦwww.classicjourneys.com. Cultural walking tours to Peru.
Cosmos ⓣ1-800/276-1241, ⓦwww.cosmosvacations.com. Planned vacation packages taking in Brazil, Argentina and Chile, with an optional extension to Peru.
Delta Vacations ⓣ1-800/221-2216, ⓦwww.deltavacations.com. Highly organized trips to Chile, Argentina and Brazil.
Global Exchange ⓣ1-800/497-1994 or 415/255-7296, ⓦwww.globalexchange.org. Self-styled "Reality tours" for the socialist-leaning to Argentina, Brazil and Venezuela.
Himalayan Travel ⓣ1-800/225-2380 or 203/743-2349, ⓦwww.himalayantravelinc.com. Well-organized wilderness trips to most South American countries.
Holidaze Ski Tours ⓣ1-800/526-2827 or 732/280-1120, ⓦwww.holidaze.com. Summer ski trips to Argentina and Chile with optional add-on city breaks to the capitals of each.
International Market Place ⓣ1-800/441-1339, ⓦwww.imp-world-tours.com. Educational cruises to Galápagos, Argentina, Chile and Peru.
Journeys International ⓣ1-800/255-8735 or

734/665-4407, ⓦwww.journeys-intl.com. Year round luxury eco-tourism to most South American destinations.

Mountain Travel Sobek ⓣ1-888/MTSOBEK or 510/527-8100, ⓦwww.mtsobek.com. Hiking trips to Suriname, Peru, Chile, Argentina, Bolivia and Ecuador.

Nature Expeditions International ⓣ1-800/869-0639, ⓦwww.naturexp.com. Varied educational adventure vacations to most of the region.

Overseas Adventure Travel ⓣ1-800/955-1925, ⓦwww.oattravel.com. People with tight schedules as well as older customers favour these trips to Peru and the Galápagos Islands.

REI Adventures ⓣ1-800/622-2236, ⓦwww.rei.com/travel. Climbing, cycling, hiking, cruising, paddling and multi-sport tours to many countries in the continent.

Safaricentre Manhattan Beach, CA ⓣ310/546-4411 or 1-800/624-5342, rest of US ⓣ1-800/223-6046, Canada ⓣ1-800/233-6046, ⓦwww.safaricentre.com. Wide range of packages, including a four-day cruise of the Patagonian lakes.

Saga Road Scholar Tours Boston, MA ⓣ1-800/621-2151. Adventures for senior travellers, including "South American Odyssey" – eighteen nights starting in Brazil and ending in Peru, with stops in Argentina and Chile along the way.

Wilderness Travel ⓣ1-800/368-2794 or 510/558-2488, ⓦwww.wildernesstravel.com. Adventure travel and wildlife tours throughout South America.

Worldwide Quest Adventures ⓣ1-800/387-1483 or 416/633-5666, ⓦwww.worldwidequest.com. Expedition cruises to Galápagos and the Amazon.

Flights from the UK and Ireland

If you book your flight well in advance flying to South America **from the UK** can be a bargain. Generally, returning within thirty days of your departure will enable you to find a cheaper fare than if you stay in South America for two or three months. All the airlines listed below operate out of London, though several will include connections from regional airports in the UK for no extra cost. British Airways operates direct flights to both Rio de Janeiro and São Paulo in Brazil and Buenos Aires in Argentina, but fares tend to be at least £100 more than those of their European and South American rivals. The best value-for-money airline depends on the country you are flying to, but generally taking a flight with a European airline such as Alitalia or Air France, via their mainland hub, will be the cheapest option.

Fares are fairly consistent year round, with the exception of July, August and December, when they can more than double. The following prices presume travel booked well in advance and out of high season – they also include tax: you can fly from London to Buenos Aires for as little as £450 or £350 to Caracas, Venezuela, but these are special deals. Fares to Bogota, Colombia, sometimes come as low as £640, while Quito, Ecuador, and Lima, Peru, can be good value at around £550. Fights to Santiago, Chile, Asunción, Paraguay, and Montevideo, Uruguay, can be found for around £650. Bolivia is the most expensive country to reach in the region – expect fares to La Paz be between £840 and £1000. Flying from London to Brazil should cost no more than £600, while Paramaribo in Suriname and Georgetown, Guyana, can be reached for £680; Cayenne in French Guiana for £550.

There are no direct flights **from Ireland** to South America. If you're trying to keep costs down, consider flying to London with an economy airline such as Ryanair and making a connection there. For less hassle, though, and only a fraction more money, you'd be better flying direct to New York, or making a connection to Miami and then catching a plane from the US.

Airlines

Unless otherwise specified all phone numbers work within the UK only.

Aerolineas Argentinas UK ⓣ0845/601 1915 or 020/7494 1009, ⓦwww.aerolineas.com.ar/. Flights to all over the region, via Buenos Aires, from London Gatwick.

Air Europa UK ⓣ0870/240 1501, ⓦwww.aireuropa.co.uk. Flights to Ecuador and Peru via Madrid from London.

Air France UK ⓣ0845/084 5111, Republic of Ireland ⓣ01/605 0383, ⓦwww.airfrance.co.uk, ⓦwww.airfrance.ie. Regional flights in the UK and Ireland connect to Paris and then go on to most countries in the area.

Alitalia UK ⓣ0870/544 8259, Republic of Ireland ⓣ01/677 5171, ⓦwww.alitalia.co.uk. Flights from

London to Argentina and Brazil via Italy.

American Airlines UK ⓣ0845/778 9789 or 020/85725555, Republic of Ireland ⓣ01/602 0550, ⓦwww.aa.com. Flights to all countries in the continent, bar Guyana, French Guiana and Suriname, via the US.

Avianca ⓣ0870/576 7747, ⓦwww.avianca.co.uk. Flights from London via Madrid to Argentina, Colombia, Brazil, Chile and Peru.

British Airways UK ⓣ0845/773 3377, Republic of Ireland ⓣ1800/626 747, ⓦwww.britishairways.com. Flights from all UK regional hubs to Argentina, Brazil, Chile, Colombia, Peru and Venezuela.

BWIA International ⓣ020/8577 1100, ⓦwww.bwee.com. Flights to Suriname and Guyana via the US.

Caribbean Star Airlines ⓣ020/8571 7533, ⓦwww.flycaribbeanstar.com. Flights to Guyana via Barbados.

Continental UK ⓣ0800/776464, Republic of Ireland ⓣ1890/925252, ⓦwww.flycontinental.com. Flights from UK and Ireland regional hubs via New York to Peru; via New York and to Peru and Brazil via Houston.

Delta UK ⓣ0800/414767, Republic of Ireland ⓣ1800-768-080 or 01/407 3165, ⓦwww.delta.com. Flights to Chile, Peru, Brazil, Colombia and Venezuela from London and Dublin via the US.

Iberia Airlines UK ⓣ0845/5601 2854, Republic of Ireland ⓣ01/407 3017, ⓦwww.iberiaairlines.co.uk. Flights from regional UK hubs to Chile, Peru, Brazil, Colombia, Argentina, Ecuador, Uruguay, Venezuela and Paraguay via London and Madrid.

KLM UK ⓣ08705/074074, Ireland ⓣ353/212 4331, ⓦwww.klmuk.com. Flights to Ecuador, Peru, Suriname and Venezuela from regional UK hubs via London and Amsterdam.

LanChile ⓣ01293/596607, ⓦwww.lanchile.com/english/un. Flights from London to Chile via Madrid, with further route offered by code-share partners.

Lufthansa UK ⓣ0845/773 7747, Republic of Ireland ⓣ01/844 5544, ⓦwww.lufthansa.com. Flights to Venezuela via regional hubs in the UK and Ireland and Germany.

TAM ⓣ0118/903 4003, ⓦwww.tam.co.br. Flights to several major cities in Brazil from London.

TAP Air Portugal UK ⓣ0845/601 0932, Republic of Ireland ⓣ01/679 8844, ⓦwww.tap-airportugal.co.uk. Flights from London to Venezuela and Brazil via Lisbon. Regional connections available in the UK.

United Airlines UK ⓣ0845/844 4777, ⓦwww.unitedairlines.co.uk. Flights to Argentina, Brazil, Chile, Uruguay and Venezuela from Manchester or London via the US; code-share connections available with bmi.

Varig UK ⓣ020/8321 7170, ⓦwww.varig.co.uk, Ireland ⓣ01/189 1089. Flights from Dublin and the UK via Portugal to most countries in South America.

Courier flights

International Association of Air Travel Couriers UK ⓣ0800/074 6481 or 01305/216920, ⓦwww.aircourier.co.uk. Agent for lots of companies.

Travel agents

Apex Travel Ireland ⓣ01/241 8000, ⓦwww.apextravel.ie. Specialists in flights to all countries in South America.

Aran Travel International Ireland ⓣ091/562595, ⓦwww.iol.ie/~arantvl/aranmain. Good-value flights to all parts of the world.

Bridge the World UK ⓣ0870/443 2399, ⓦwww.bridgetheworld.com. Specializing in round-the-world tickets, with good deals aimed at the backpacker market.

Co-op Travel Care UK ⓣ0870/112 0085, ⓦwww.travelcare.co.uk. Cheap flights and holidays to Brazil.

ebookers ⓣ01/241 5689, ⓦwww.ebookers.com/ie. Ireland-based online booking agency that trawls all major airlines for the best fares, with a special "student zone".

Flightbookers UK ⓣ0870/010 7000, ⓦwww.ebookers.com. Low fares on an extensive selection of scheduled flights.

Flights 4 Less UK ⓣ0871/222 3423, ⓦwww.flights4less.com. Good discount airfares to most countries in the region.

Joe Walsh Tours Ireland ⓣ01/872 2555 or 676 3053, ⓦwww.joewalshtours.ie. General budget fares agent.

Journey Latin America UK ⓣ020/8747 8315, ⓦwww.journeylatinamerica.co.uk. Knowledgeable and helpful staff, good at sorting out stopovers and open-jaw flights. Also does package tours.

Lee Travel Ireland ⓣ021/277111, ⓦwww.leetravel.ie. Flights and holidays worldwide.

McCarthy's Travel Ireland ⓣ021/427 0127, ⓦwww.mccarthystravel.ie. General flight agent.

North South Travel ⓣ & ⓕ01245/608291, ⓦwww.northsouthtravel.co.uk. Friendly, competitive travel agency, offering discounted fares worldwide – profits are used to support projects in the developing world, especially the promotion of sustainable tourism.

Premier Travel Northern Ireland ⓣ028/7126 3333, ⓦwww.premiertravel.uk.com. Discount flight specialists.

Rosetta Travel Northern Ireland ⓣ028/9064 4996, ⓦwww.rosettatravel.com. Flight and holiday agent.
Scott Dunn South America ⓣ020/8767 8989, ⓦwww.scottdunn.com/latinamerica/index. Very good South American specialist, offering low-cost fares and helpful advice.
South American Experience ⓣ020/7976 5511, ⓦwww.southamericanexperience.co.uk. Mainly a discount flight agent but also offers a range of tours, plus a very popular "soft landing package", which includes a couple of nights' accommodation and airport transfer on arrival.
STA Travel UK ⓣ08701/600599, ⓦwww.statravel.co.uk. Low-cost flights and tours for students and under-26s, though other customers welcome.
Trailfinders UK ⓣ020/7628 7628, ⓦwww.trailfinders.co.uk, Republic of Ireland ⓣ01/677 7888, ⓦwww.trailfinders.ie. One of the best-informed and most efficient agents for independent travellers.
Travel Cuts UK ⓣ020/7255 2082, ⓦwww.travelcuts.co.uk. Canadian company specializing in budget, student and youth travel, and round-the-world tickets.
usit NOW Republic of Ireland ⓣ01/602 1600, Northern Ireland ⓣ028/9032 7111, ⓦwww.usitnow.ie. Student and youth specialists for flights and overland adventure.

Specialist tour operators

Adventure Bound ⓣ0800/316 2717, ⓦwww.adventurebound.co.uk. Impressive selection of overland expeditions and adventure holidays to South America.
Austral Tours ⓣ020/7233 5384, ⓦwww.latinamerica.co.uk. Small company offering tailor-made itineraries and some brochure packages to South America. Especially good at organizing special-interest holidays, based around wine tours, fishing, trekking and archeology.
Blue Green Adventures ⓣ020/8947 2756. The leading specialist in horse-riding expeditions in Patagonia and the Chilean and Argentine Lake Districts, mostly on ten-day tours.
Dragoman UK ⓣ01728/861133, ⓦwww.dragoman.co.uk. A range of South American overland trips, including a new line with all accommodation in hotels rather than in tents. Regular slide shows in London.
Encounter Overland UK ⓣ020/7370 6845, ⓦwww.encounter.co.uk. Overland tours ranging in length from five nights to six months.
Exodus ⓣ020/8675 7996. Rather more upmarket overland tours of varying lengths throughout the region.
Explore Worldwide UK ⓣ01252/319448, ⓦwww.explore.co.uk. Overland tours to Chile, Ecuador, Argentina and Peru.
Footprint Adventures UK ⓣ01552/804929, ⓦwww.footprint-adventures.co.uk. Established specialists in trekking, wildlife and overland adventure tours.
Guerba Expeditions UK ⓣ01373/826611, ⓦwww.guerba.co.uk. British branch of Canadian GAP Adventures, with an emphasis on responsible, sustainable adventure tourism.
Hayes & Jarvis UK ⓣ0870/898 9890, ⓦwww.hayes-jarvis.com. Specialists in long-haul holidays, particularly with diving destinations. Exotic weddings organized, accommodation in upmarket hotels.
Jagged Globe UK ⓣ0114/276 3322, ⓦwww.jagged-globe.co.uk. Well-established climbing company offering Aconcagua expedition (24 days), which includes the option to try the Polish Glacier route.
Kuoni Travel UK ⓣ01306/742888, ⓦwww.kuoni.co.uk. Flexible package holidays with extensive presence and good family offers.
Kumuka Expeditions UK ⓣ0800/068 0855, ⓦwww.kumaka.co.uk. Responsible tourism, extensive overland tours and adventure packages.
Last Frontiers UK ⓣ01296/653000, ⓦwww.lastfrontiers.com. Very knowledgeable Latin America specialists with a wide range of tailor-made tours.
Thomas Cook UK ⓣ08705/666222, ⓦwww.thomascook.co.uk. Long-established one-stop 24-hour travel agency for package holidays or scheduled flights.
Trips Worldwide ⓣ0117/311 4400, ⓦwww.tripsworldwide.co.uk. "Alternative" tailor-made holidays to Latin America include rainforests, culture, birdwatching and plenty of activities. The website lets you create your own itinerary.
World Expeditions 4 Northfields Prospect, Putney Bridge Rd, London SW18 1PE ⓣ020/8870 2600, ⓦwww.worldexpeditions.co.uk. UK branch of the very professional Australian tour company, offering a range of trekking, climbing and photographic tours in South America.
Worldwide Adventures Abroad Unit H/04, Staniforth Estates, Main St, Hackenthorpe, Sheffield, Yorkshire S12 4LB ⓣ0114/247 3400, ⓦwww.adventures-abroad.com. Culturally sensitive tour operator specializing in small group expeditions.

Flights from Australia and New Zealand

Not surprisingly, the best deals to South America are offered by the major South American airlines Aerolíneas Argentinas, Varig and LanChile in conjunction with Qantas and Air New Zealand. **Aerolineas Argentinas** flies from Sydney via Auckland and Buenos Aires and then on to other countries in the continent; Qantas flies with **Varig** and **LanChile** via Auckland and Santiago onwards.

There are also plenty of flights **via the US**, but most are not scheduled all the way through to South America and therefore tend to offer much more time-consuming and expensive routings, as each sector has to be priced separately. Often airlines will charge more if you wish to stay in South America for longer than a month, but recently several have begun to offer comparatively priced fares with between two and six months' validity.

On **direct routes** to most major South American airports you should be able to get a return fare starting around A$2035/NZ$2350. Special offers with Aerolíneas Argentinas and LanChile to Buenos Aires and Santiago respectively sometimes bring fares for these cities down as low as A$1800/NZ$2050. Flights via the US can – with much forward thinking and flexibility – be found for A$2360/NZ$2700 but are more likely to be around A$3150/NZ$3600.

If you plan to do a fair amount of travelling within South America think about buying an **airpass** with your main ticket. These passes offer substantial savings, but can be bought only outside South America with your international ticket. See p.38 for more information.

Round-the-world tickets

One option you might want to consider, since you're travelling so far in the first place, is a **round-the-world** ticket. Choice is actually somewhat limited and most fares are mileage based, making routes via South America more expensive than other round-the-world options but, in comparison with the fares and routings of standard return deals to Argentina, they are still definitely worth exploring. Star Alliance allows you to take in US, European and Asian destinations as well as South America from around A$3200/NZ$3300 for a maximum of 29,000 miles, A$3800/NZ$3800 for up to 34,000 miles, and up to A$4300/NZ$4500 for 39,000 miles.

Airlines

Aerolíneas Argentinas Sydney ⓣ02/9283 3660, Auckland ⓣ09/379 3675, ⓦwww.aerolineas.com.
Air New Zealand Sydney ⓣ13/2476, Auckland ⓣ0800/737000 or 09/357 3000 ⓦwww.airnz.co.nz
BWIA International Australia ⓣ02/9285 6811, ⓦwww.bwee.com.
LanChile Sydney ⓣ02/9244 2333 or 1800/221572, Brisbane ⓣ07/3407 7188, ⓦwww.lanchile.com.
Qantas Australia ⓣ13/1211, New Zealand ⓣ09/357 8900 or 0800/808767, ⓦwww.qantas.com.au.
Varig Brazilian Australia ⓣ02/9321 9179, New Zealand ⓣ09/379 4455, ⓦwww.varig.com.br/english.

Travel agents

Anywhere Travel Australia ⓣ02/9663 0411, ⓦwww.anywheretravel.com.au. Worldwide fare discount agent close to the airport.
Budget Travel New Zealand ⓣ09/366 0061 or 0800/808040, ⓦwww.budgettravel.co.nz. Established airfare discounter.
Destinations Unlimited New Zealand ⓣ09/373 4033, ⓦwww.destinations-unlimited.co.nz. Worldwide fare discounts plus a good selection of brochures.
Flight Centres Australia, plus branches nationwide ⓣ02/9235 3522, nearest branch ⓣ13/1600, ⓦwww.flightcentre.com.au; New Zealand ⓣ0800/243 544 or 09/358 4310, ⓦwww.flightcentre.co.nz. Friendly service with competitive discounts on airfares plus wide range of travel brochures.
Northern Gateway Australia ⓣ1800/174800, ⓦwww.northerngateway.com.au.
STA Travel Australia ⓣ1300/733035, ⓦwww.statravel.com.au; New Zealand ⓣ0508/782872, ⓦwww.statravel.co.nz. Fare discounts for students and under-26s, student cards and travel insurance.
Student Uni Travel Australia ⓣ02/9232 8444, ⓦwww.sut.com.au; New Zealand ⓣ09/379 4224, ⓦwww.sut.co.nz.

Student/youth discounts and travel advice.
Thomas Cook Australia: Sydney ⓣ02/9231 2877, ⓦwww.thomascook.com.au, Melbourne plus branches in other state capitals local branch ⓣ13/1771, Thomas Cook Direct telesales ⓣ1800/801002; New Zealand: Auckland ⓣ09/379 3920. Discounts on fares, travellers' cheques, bus and rail passes.
Trailfinders Australia ⓣ02/9247 7666, ⓦwww.trailfinders.com.au. Independent travel advice, good discounts on fares.
travel.com.au ⓣ02/9262 3555, ⓦwww.travel.com.au. Online worldwide fare discounter.

Specialist tour operators

Adventure Associates Adventure Associates Australia ⓣ02/9389 7466, ⓦwww.adventureassociates.com.au. Tours and cruises to South America, including the Amazon and Galápagos.
Adventure Specialists Australia ⓣ02/9261 2927. Overland specialist. Agent for Encounter Overland's five- and nine-week expeditions.
Adventure World Australia ⓣ02/8913 0755, ⓦwww.adventureworld.com.au, New Zealand ⓣ09/524 5118, ⓦwww.adventureworld.co.nz. Agent for a vast array of international adventure travel companies.
Austral Tours Australia ⓣ1800/620833 or 03/9600 1733, ⓦwww.australtours.com. Central and South American specialist covering the region from Ecuador to Easter Island and Tierra del Fuego, with special tours to Machu Picchu and the Amazon.
Australian Andean Adventures Australia ⓣ02/9235 1889, ⓦwww.andeanadventures.com.au. Trekking specialist for Argentina, Peru, Bolivia and Chile.
Birding Worldwide Australia ⓣ03/9899 9303, ⓦwww.birdingworldwide.com.au. Organizes group trips to Ecuador and Galápagos for those wanting to glimpse typical, unique and rare species.
Earthwatch Australia 3205 ⓣ03/9682 6828, ⓦwww.earthwatch.org. Organizes volunteer work throughout the region on scientific, wildlife and cultural projects.
Journeys Worldwide Australia ⓣ07/3221 4788, ⓦwww.journeysworldwide.com.au. Personalized and escorted tours to Latin America.
Kumuka Expeditions Australia ⓣ1800/804277 or 02/9279 0491, ⓦwww.kumuka.com.au. Independent tour operator specializing in overland expeditions, as well as local and private transport tours.
Latin Link Adventure New Zealand ⓣ03/525 9945, ⓦwww.latinlink.co.nz. "Semi-independent" adventure tours to Latin America.
South America Travel Centre Australia ⓣ1800/655051 or 03/9642 5353, ⓦwww.satc.com.au. Big selection of tours and city accommodation packages throughout the region.
South American Adventure Travel Australia ⓣ07/3854 1022. Independent and group travel specialists.
Silke's Travel Australia ⓣ1800/807 860 or 02/8347 2000, ⓦwww.silkes.com.au. Gay and lesbian specialist travel agent.

Red tape and visas

Country-specific advice about visas and entry requirements is given at the beginning of each chapter, where necessary. As a broad guide, citizens of the US, Canada, UK, Ireland, Australia and New Zealand do not need a visa for stays of up to ninety days in most South American countries, with the exception of Bolivia and Colombia where you can stay for only thirty days without a visa. US citizens do need visas for Brazil, and all nationalities for Suriname; all other countries require that your passport be valid for at least six months from your date of entry and that you have proof of onward travel. As all visa requirements, prices and processing times are subject to change, it's definitely worth double-checking with the relevant embassies or consulates.

South American embassies and consulates abroad

Argentina

Australia Embassy: PO Box 4835, Kingston, ACT 2604 ⓣ02/6273 9111, ⓦwww.argentina.org.au; Consulate: Level 20, 44 Market St, Sydney, NSW 2000 ⓣ02/9262 2933, ⓔconargen@ram.net.au.
Canada Embassy: 90 Sparks St, Suite 910, Ottawa, ON K1P 5B4 ⓣ613/236-2351, ⓔembargentina@argentina-canada.com; Consulates: Montreal, 2000 Peel St, Suite 600, Montreal, QC H3A 2W5 ⓣ514/842-6582, ⓦwww.consargenmtl.com;
Toronto, 5001 Yonge St, Toronto, ON, M2N 6P6 ⓣ416/955 9075, ⓦwww.consargtoro.ca.
Ireland 15 Ailesbury Drive, Ballsbridge, Dublin 4 ⓣ01/269 1546.
New Zealand Sovereign Assurance Building, Level 14–142 Lambton Quay, PO Box 5430, Wellington ⓣ04/472 8330, ⓦwww.arg.org.nz.
UK 27 Three Kings Yard, London W1Y 1FL ⓣ020/7318 1340, ⓦwww.argentine-embassy-uk.org.
US Embassy: 1600 New Hampshire NW, Washington, DC 20009 ⓣ202/238-6400; Consulates: 205 N Michigan Ave, Suite 4208/9, Chicago, IL 60601 ⓣ312/819-2610, ⓦwww.consulateargentina-chicago.org; 245 Peachtree Center Ave, Suite 2101, Atlanta, Georgia 30303 ⓣ404/880-0805, ⓦwww.consuladoargentinoatlanta.org; 3050 Post Oak Blvd, Suite 1625, Houston, TX 77056 ⓣ713/993-0315, ⓔfchous@mrecic.gov.ar; 5055 Wilshire Blvd, Suite 210, Los Angeles, CA 90036 ⓣ323/954-9155, ⓦwww.consuladoargentino-losangeles.org; 800 Brickwell Ave, Suite PH-1, Miami, FL 33131 ⓣ305/358-0530, ⓦwww.consuladoargentinoenmiami.org; 12 W 56th St, New York, NY 10019 ⓣ212/603-0445, ⓦwww.consuladoargentinoennuevayork.com.

Bolivia

Australia Suite 1102, Level 11, 4 Bridge St, Sydney, NSW 2000 ⓣ02/9247 4235.
Canada 130 Albert St, Suite 416, Ottawa, Ontario K1P 5G4 ⓣ613/236-5730, ⓦwww.boliviaemb.ca.
New Zealand No.38 Kowa Building, 8th Floor, Room 804, 4-12-24 Nishi-Azabu, Mianto-Ku, Tokyo 106-0031 ⓣ8133/499 5441, ⓔemboltk4@ad.i124.net.
UK 106 Eaton Square, London SW1W 9AD ⓣ020/7235 4248, ⓦwww.embassyofbolivia.co.uk.
US Embassy (Consular Section): 3014 Mass. Ave, NW Washington, DC 20008 ⓣ202/232-4827; Consulate: 211 E 43 St, Suite 702, New York, NY 10017 ⓣ212/499-7401.

Brazil

Australia Embassy: 19 Forster Crescent, Yarralumla, Canberra, ACT 2600 ⓣ02/6273 2372; Consulate: 31 Market St, Sydney ⓣ02/9267 4414.
Canada Embassy: 450 Wilbrod St, Ottawa, ON K1N 6M8 ⓣ613/237-1090;
Consulates: 3630 Kempt Road, Halifax, NS B3K 4X8 ⓣ902/455-9638; 2000 Mansfield St, Suite 1700, Montreal, QC H3A 3A5 ⓣ514/499-0968; 77 Bloor St West, Suite 1109, Toronto, ON M5S 1M2 ⓣ415/922-2503; 837 West Hastings St, Vancouver, BC V6C 3NH.

Ireland Europa House, Block 9, Harcourt Centre, 41–45 Harcourt House, Dublin 2 ⓣ01/475 6000.
New Zealand 10 Brandon St, Level 9, PO Box 5432, Wellington ⓣ04/473 3516, ⓦwww.brazil.org.nz.
UK 32 Green S, Mayfair, London W1Y 4AT ⓣ020/7499 0877, ⓦwww.brazil.org.uk.
US Embassy: 3006 Massachusetts Ave NW, Washington, DC 20008 ⓣ202/238-2700, ⓦwww.brasilemb.org;
Consulates: The Stattler Building, 20 Park Plaza, Suite 810, Boston, MA 02116 ⓣ617/542-4000, ⓦwww.consulatebrazil.org; 401 North Michigan Ave, Suite 3050, Chicago, IL 60611 ⓣ312/464-0245, ⓔcgchgo@ix.netcome.com; 1233 West Loop South, Park Tower North, Suite 1150, Houston, TX 77027 ⓣ713/961-3063, ⓦwww.brazilhouston.org; 8484 Wilshire Blvd, Suites 711–730, Beverly Hills, CA 90211 ⓣ323/651-2664, ⓦwww.brazilian-consulate.org; 2601 South Bayshore Drive, Suite 800, Miami, FL 33133 ⓣ305/285-6200, ⓦwww.brazilmiami.org; 1185 Ave of the Americas, 21st Floor, New York, NY 10036 ⓣ212/827-0976, ⓦwww.brasilny.org; 300 Montgomery St, Suite 1160, San Francisco, CA 94104 ⓣ415/981-8170, ⓦwww.brazilsf.org.

Chile

Australia Embassy: PO Box 69, Red Hill, ACT 2603 ⓣ02/6286-2430, ⓦwww.embachile-australia.com;
Consulates: Level 18, 44 Market St, Sydney, NSW 2000 ⓣ02/9299 2533 ⓦwww.consul-chile-sydney.net; 87 Lyndale St, Daisy Hill, QLD 4127 ⓣ07/3208 8444 ⓔhonconchilebne@hotmail.com; Unit 32, The Silo's, 1 Castray Esplanade, Battery Point, Tas 7004 ⓣ03/6223 2160 ⓔmkentam@hotmail.com; Level 43, Nauru House, 80 Collins St, Melbourne, Vic 3000 ⓣ03/9654 4479, ⓦwww.chile.com.au; 55 Broadway, Nedlands, WA 6909 ⓣ08/9389 4702, ⓦwww.chile.com.au.
Canada Embassy: 50 O'Connor St, Suite 1413, Ottawa ON, K1P 6I2 ⓣ613/235-4402, ⓦwww.chile.ca;
Consulates: 421 Seventh Ave, SW Trust Tower, Suite 1200, Calgary, AB T2P 4K9 ⓣ780/439-9839; 4612 99th St, Edmonton, AB T6E 5H5; 1010 Sherbrooke St W, Suite 710, Montreal, QC H3A 2R7; 2 Bloor St West, Suite 1801, Toronto, ON M4W 3E2; 1250–1185 West Georgia St, Vancouver, BC V6E 4E6 ⓣ604/681-9162; 810 Sherbrooke St, Room R.S. 404, Respiratory Bldg, Winnipeg, MB R3A 1R8.
Ireland 40 Ailesbury Road, Ballsbridge, Dublin 4 ⓣ01/269 1707.
New Zealand Embassy: 19 Bolton St, PO Box 3861, Wellington ⓣ04/271 6270, ⓦwww.embchile.co.nz;
Consulates: PO Box 612, Auckland ⓣ64/9373 4602, ⓔpbex@ihug.co.nz; PO Box 359, Christchurch ⓣ64/3366 5096, ⓔpetert@cecc.org.nz.
UK12 Devonshire St, London W1N 2DS ⓣ020/7580 6392, ⓔechileuk@demon.co.uk.
US Embassy: 1732 Massachusetts Ave NW, Washington, DC 20036 ⓣ202/785-1746, ⓦwww.chile-usa.org;
Consulates: 875 North Michigan Ave, Suite 3352, Chicago, IL 60611 ⓣ312/654-8780; 1900 Ave of the Stars, Suite 2450, Century City, CA 90067 ⓣ310/785-0047; 800 Brickell Ave, Suite 1230, Miami, FL 33131 ⓣ305/373-8623.

Colombia

Australia Level 2, Colombia House, 101 Northbourne Ave, Turner, Canberra, ACT 2612 ⓣ02/6257 2027 ⓔemaustralia@iprimus.com.au.
Canada Embassy: 360 Albert St, Suite 1002, Ottawa, ON K1R 7X7 ⓣ613/230-3760, ⓦwww.embajadacolombia.ca;
Consulates: 505 8th Ave, Suite 310, Calgary, AB T2P 1G2 ⓣ403/266-1881; 1010 Sherbrooke St W, Suite 420, Montreal, QC H3A 2R7 ⓣ514/849-4852; 1 Dundas St W, Suite 2108, Toronto, ON M5G 1Z3 ⓣ416/977-0098; 789 West Prender St, Suite 890, Vancouver, BC V6C 1H2.
New Zealand PO Box 17072, Karori, Wellington 5 ⓣ04/476 9857, ⓔpbl@ecodyne.co.nz.
UK 3rd Floor, 15–19 Great Titchfield St, London W1N 7FB ⓣ020/7589 9177, ⓔcolumbia@columbia.demon.co.uk.
US Embassy: 2118 Leroy Place NW, Washington, DC 20008 ⓣ202/387-8338, ⓦwww.colombiaemb.org;
Consulates: 5901-C Peachtree Dunwoody Rd, Suite 375, Atlanta, GA 30328 ⓦwww.miavenida.com/consulcol; 535 Boylston St, 11th Floor, Boston, MA 02116 ⓣ617/536-6222, ⓔconboston@aol.com; 500 North Michigan Ave, Suite 2040, Chicago, IL 60611 ⓣ312/923-1196, ⓔchicag95@aol.com; 5851 San Felipe, Suite 300, Houston, TX 77057 ⓣ713/527-8919, ⓦwww.colhouston.org; 8383 Wilshire Blvd, Suite 420, Beverly Hills, CA 90211 ⓣ323/653-9863, ⓦwww.conangeles.org; 280 Aragon Ave, Coral Gables, FL 33134 ⓣ305/448-5558, ⓔchcmiami@bellsouth.net; 10 E 46 St, New York, NY 10017 ⓣ212/949-9898, ⓦcolombia.nosotros .com; 595 Market St, Suite 2130, San Francisco, CA 94105 ⓣ415/495-7195, ⓔcolombia@pacbell.net.

Ecuador

Australia First Floor, Law Society Building, 11 London Circuit, Canberra, ACT 2601 ⓣ02/6262 5282, ⓔembecu@hotkey.net.au.
Canada 151 Bloor St West, Suite 470, Toronto, ON M5S 1S4 ⓣ416/968-2077.
New Zealand Ferry Building, 2nd Floor, Quay St, Auckland ⓣ09/309-0229.
UK 3 Hans Crescent, London SW1X 0LS ⓣ020/7584 2468 or 09/377 4321, ⓔjmorlaconsulecuador@xtra.co.nz.
US Embassy: 2535 15th St, NW, Washington, DC 20009 ⓣ202/234-7200, ⓦwww.ecuador.org; Consulates: 800 Second Ave, Suite 601, New York, NY 10017 ⓣ212/808-0170; 300 Montgomery St, Suite 1020, Jersey City, NJ 07302 ⓣ201/985-1700; B.I.V. Tower, 1101 Brickell Ave, Suite M-102, Miami, FL 33131 ⓣ305/539-8214; 4200 Westheimer, Suite 118 2535, Houston, TX 77027 ⓣ713/622-8105; World Trade Center, Suite 1312, 2 Canal St, New Orleans, LA 70130 ⓣ504/523-3229; 500 N Michigan Ave, Suite 1510, Chicago, IL 60611 ⓣ312/329-0266; 8484 Wilshire Blvd, Suite 540, Beverly Hills, CA 90211 ⓣ323/658-1934; 455 Market St, Suite 980, San Francisco, CA 94105 ⓣ415/957-5921.

French Guiana

Australia Level 26, St Martins Tower, 31 Market St, Sydney, NSW 2000 ⓣ02/9261 5779, ⓦwww.consulfrance-sydney.org.
Canada Embassy: 42 Sussex Drive, Ottawa, ON K1M 2C9, ⓦwww.ambafrance-ca.org; Consulates: 1 Place Ville Marie, Suite 2061, Montreal, QC H3B 4S3 ⓣ514/878-4385, ⓦwww.consulfrance-montreal.org; Kent House, 25 Saint Louis St, Quebec City, QC G1R 3Y8 ⓣ418/694-2294, ⓦwww.consulfrance-quebec.org; 130 Bloor St W, Suite 400, Toronto, ON M5S 1N5, ⓦwww.consulfrance-toronto.org; 1130 West Pender St, Suite 1100, Vancouver, BC V6E 4A4 ⓣ604/681-4345, ⓦwww.consulfrance-vancouver.ca.
Ireland 36 Ailesbury Road, Dublin 4 ⓣ01/260-1666.
New Zealand 34–42 Manners St, PO Box 11-343, Wellington ⓣ04/384–2555, ⓦwww.ambafrance.net.nz.
UK 58 Knightsbridge, London SW1X 7JT ⓣ020/7073 1000, ⓦwww.ambafrance-uk.org.
US Embassy: 4101 Reservoir Rd, NW, Washington, DC 20007 ⓣ202/944 6211, ⓦwww.france-consulat.org; Consulates: 3475 Piedmont Road, NE, Suite 1840, Atlanta, GA 30305 ⓣ404/495-1660, ⓦwww.consulfrance-atlanta.org; Park Square Building, Suite 750, 31 Saint James Ave, Boston, MA 02116 ⓣ617/542-7374, ⓦwww.consulfrance-boston.org; 205 North Michigan Ave, Suite 2020, Chicago, IL 60601 ⓣ312/787-5359, ⓦwww.consulfrance-chicago.org; 1 Biscayne Tower, Suite 1710, 2 Biscayne South Blvd, Miami, FL 33131 ⓣ305/372-9799, ⓦwww.consulfrance-miami.org; Post Oak Blvd, Suite 600, Houston, TX 77056 ⓣ713/572-2788, ⓦwww.consulfrance-houston.org; 10990 Wilshire Blvd, Suite 300, Los Angeles, CA 90024 ⓣ310/235-3294, ⓦwww.consulfrance-losangeles.org; 1340 Poydras St, Suite 1710, New Orleans, LA 70112 ⓣ504/523-5772, ⓦwww.consulfrance-nouvelleorleans.org; 934 Fifth Ave, New York, NY 10021 ⓣ212/606-3680, ⓦwww.consulfrance-newyork.org; 540 Bush St, San Francisco, CA 94108 ⓣ415/396-4330, ⓦwww.consulfrance-sanfrancisco.org.

Guyana

Canada 505 Consumers Road, Suite 206, Willowdale, Toronto, ON M2J 4V8 ⓣ416/494-6040.
UK 3 Palace Court, Bayswater Road, London W2 4LP ⓣ020/7229 7684.
US Embassy: 2490 Tracy Pl, NW, Washington, DC 20008 ⓣ202/265-6900;
Consulate: 866 UN Plaza, Third Floor, New York, NY 10017 ⓣ212/527-3215.

Paraguay

Canada 151 Slater St, Suite 501, Ottawa, ON K1P 5H3 ⓣ613/567-1283, ⓦwww.paraguayembassy.ca.
UK 344 High St Kensington, 3rd Floor, London W14 8NS ⓣ020/7937 1253, ⓔembapar@londresdy.freeserve.co.uk.
US 2400 Massachusetts Ave, NW, Washington, DC 20008 ⓣ202/483-6960.

Peru

Australia Embassy: PO Box 106, Red Hill, ACT 2603 ⓣ02/6273 8752, ⓦwww.embaperu.org.au; Consulates: 36 Main St, Croydon, Melbourne ⓣ03/9725-4908; Level Three, 30 Clarence St, Sydney ⓣ02/9262-6464.
Canada Embassy: 130 Albion St, Suite 1901, Ottawa, ON K1P 5GA ⓣ613/238-1777, ⓔemperuca@sprint.ca;
Consulates: 550 Sherbrooke West, Suite 970, West Tower, Montreal, QC H3A 1B9 ⓣ514/844-5123;

250 Grande Allée West, Suite 1507, Quebec City, QC G1R 2H4 ⓣ418/529-7473; 10 Saint Mary St, Suite 301, Toronto, ON, M4Y 1P9 ⓣ416/963-9696; 260–505 Burrard St, Vancouver, BC V7X 1M3 ⓣ604/662-3564, ⓦwww.perunited.bc.ca; 145 Elm St, Winnipeg, MB R3M 3N4 ⓣ204/488-5041.
New Zealand Level Eight, Cigna House, 40 Mercer St, Wellington ⓣ04/499 8087, ⓔembperu@xtra.co.nz.
UK 52 Sloane St, London SW1X 9SP ⓣ020/7235 1917. ⓦwww.peruembassy-uk.com.
US Embassy: 1700 Massachusetts Ave, NW, Washington, DC 20036-1903 ⓣ202/833-9860, ⓦwww.peruemb.org;
Consulates: 870 Market St, Suite 482, San Francisco, CA 94102 ⓣ415/362-7136; 180 N Michigan Ave, Suite 1830, Chicago, IL 6-601 ⓣ312/853-6170; 5177 Richmond Ave, Suite 695, Houston, TX 77056 ⓣ713/355-9517; 3460 Wilshire Blvd, Suite 1005, Los Angeles, CA 90010 ⓣ213/252-5910; 444 Brickell Ave, Suite M135, Miami, FL 33131 ⓣ305/374-1305; 100 Hamilton Plaza, Twelfth Floor, Paterson, NJ 07505 ⓣ973/278-3324; 215 Lexington Ave, 21st Floor, New York, NY 10016 ⓣ212/481-7410.

Suriname

Canada Van Ness Center, Suite 460, 4301 Connecticut Ave, NW, Washington, DC 20008, USA ⓣ202/244-7488, ⓔembsur@erols.com.
UK Alexander Gogelweg 2, The Hague 2517JH ⓣ70 36 50 899.
US Embassy: 4301 Connecticut Ave, NW, Suite 460, Washington, DC 20008 ⓣ202/244-7488, ⓦwww.surinameembassy.org;
Consulate: 7235 NW 19th St, Suite A, Miami, FL 33126 ⓣ305/593-2697, ⓔcgsurmia@bellsouth.net.

Uruguay

Australia PO Box 5058, Kingston, ACT 2604 ⓣ02/6273 9100, ⓔurucan@austarmetro.com.au.
Canada Embassy: 130 Albert St, Suite 1905, Ottawa, ON K10 5G4 ⓣ613/234-2727, ⓔuruott@iosphere.net;
Consulates: 1117 Ste Catherine St W, Suite 512, Montreal, QC H3B 1H9 ⓣ514/288-0990; 1710-1040 West Georgia St, Suite 1710, Vancouver, BC V6E 4H1 ⓣ604/602-1717 Ext 301.
New Zealand c/o Kingett Mitchell Ltd, Level 3, 79 Cambridge Terrace, Christchurch 8051 ⓣ03/374 6774, ⓔecassells@kma.co.nz.
UK 2nd Floor, 140 Brompton Road, London SW3 1HY ⓣ020/7589 8835, ⓔemb@urubri.demon.co.uk.
US Embassy: 2715 M St, NW, 3rd Floor, Washington, DC 20007 ⓣ202/331-4219, ⓦwww.embassy.org/uruguay;
Consulates 67 Union St., Natick, Boston, MA 01760 ⓣ508/653-4874; 875 N. Michigan Ave, Suite 1422, Chicago, IL 60611 ⓣ312/642-3430; 1077 Ponce de Leon Blvd, Coral Gables, Florida 33134 ⓣ305/443-9764; 540 World Trade Center, 2nd Canal St, New Orleans, LA 70130 ⓣ504/525-8354; 747 Third Ave, 21st Floor, New York, NY 10017 ⓣ212/753-8581; 564 Market St, Suite 221, San Francisco, CA 94014 ⓣ415/986-5222; Lane Powell Pears Lubersky, 1420 Fifth Ave, Suite 1400, Seattle, Washington 98101.

Venezuela

Australia 5 Culgoa Circuit, O'Malley, ACT 2606 ⓣ02/6290 2900.
Canada Embassy: 32 Range Road, Ottawa, K1N 8J4 ⓣ613/235-5151, ⓔembavene@travel-net.com;
Consulates: 2055 Peel St, Suite 400, Montreal, QC H3A 1V4 ⓣ514/842-3417; 365 Bloor St East, Suite 1904, Toronto, ON M4W 3L4 ⓣ416/960-6070.
UK 1 Cromwell Road, London SW7 2HR ⓣ020/7584 4206, ⓦwww.venezlon.demon.co.uk.
US Embassy: 1099 30th St, NW, Washington, DC 20007 ⓣ202/342-2214, ⓦwww.embavenez-us.org;
Consulates: 545 Boylston St, Third Floor, Boston, MA 02116 ⓣ617/266-9355; 20 N, Wacker Drive, Suite 1925, Chicago, IL 60606 ⓣ312/236-9659; 2925 Briarpark Drive, Suite 900, Houston, TX 77042 ⓣ713/974-0028; 1101 Brickell Ave, North Tower, Suite 901, Miami, FL 33131 ⓣ305/577-3834; 1908 World Trade Center, 2 Canal St, New Orleans, LA 70130 ⓣ504/522-3284; 7 East 51st St, New York, NY 10222 ⓣ212/826-1660; 311 California St, Suite 620, San Francisco, CA 94104 ⓣ415/955-1982.

Information, websites and maps

Advance information about most South American countries can be obtained from the tourist information offices listed below. If there is not an information centre for your destination in your home country, your best bet is to look on the Internet (see p.24) or contact one on the tour companies specializing in Latin America mentioned on p.40. Once you've arrived at your destination, you'll find most airports and cities have visitor centres of some description that will give out detailed information on the local area and can often help with finding accommodation.

Tourist offices

There are very few official tourist offices abroad for Latin American countries. Some embassies or consulates (see p.19 for addresses) might be willing to send you information; otherwise, you could consider contacting the **national tourist information offices** of your destination.

Argentina

Argentina Centro de Información Turística, Av Santa Fe 883 (C1059ABC) Buenos Aires, Argentina ⓣ0800/555-0016, ⓦwww.sectur.gov.ar/eng/menu
UK 65 Brooke St, London W1K 4AH ⓣ020/7318 1399
USA 12 West 56th St, New York, NY 10009 ⓣ212/603-0443, ⓦwww.sectur.gov.ar/eng/menu; 5055 Wilshire Blvd, Suite 210, Los Angeles, CA 90036 ⓣ213/930-0681;
2655 Le Jeune Rd, Ph. 1, Miami, FL 33134 ⓣ305/442-1366, ⓕ305/441-7029.

Bolivia

Bolivia Viceministerio de Turismo, Ministerio de Comercio Exterior, Inversión y Turismo, A. Mcal. Santa Cruz, Palazio de las Comunicaciones, Piso 16 ⓣ591/2236-7463, ⓦwww.boliviaweb.com/travel

Brazil

Brazil Embratur, Instituto Brasileiro de Turismo, Setor Comercial Norte, Quadra 2, Bloco "G", Brasilia/DF, Brasil 70712-907 ⓣ61/429-7777, ⓦwww.embratur.gov.br
UK Brazilian Tourist Information Office, 32 Green St, London W1K 7AT ⓣ020/7629 6909, ⓦwww.brazil.org.uk
USA Brazilian Tourism Office, 3006 Massachusetts Ave, NW, Washington, DC 20008 ⓣ1800/727-2945, ⓦwww.braziltourism.org

Chile

Chile SERNATUR, Providencia 1550, PO Box 14082, Santiago, Chile ⓣ562/696-7141, ⓦwww.sernatur.cl, ⓦwww.visit-chile.org
UK Embassy of Chile, 12 Devonshire St, London W1N 2DS ⓣ020/7580 6392, ⓔechileuk@demon.co.uk
USA Embassy of Chile, 1732 Massachusetts Ave, NW, Washington, DC 20036 ⓣ202/785-1746, ⓦwww.chile-usa.org, ⓔofitour@embassyofchile.org;
LanChile Tourism Offic, 6500 NW 22nd St, Miami, FL 33122 ⓣ1-800/244-5366

Colombia

Colombia Fondo de Promoción Turística Colombia, Carrera 16A No. 78–55 Oficina 604, Bogotá, Colombia ⓣ571/611-4330, ⓦwww.turismocolombia.com/home

Ecuador

Ecuador Ministerio de Turismo, Eloy Alfaro N32–300 Carlos Tobar, Quito, Ecuador ⓣ593/2250-7559, ⓦwww.vivecuador.com

French Guiana

French Guiana Comité du Tourisme de la Guyane, 12 rue Lallouette, BP 801, 97338 Cayenne Cedex ⓣ05 94 29 65 00
France Bureau parisien du Comité du Tourisme de la Guyane, 1 rue Clapeyron, 75008 Paris, France ⓣ01 42 94 15 16

Guyana

Guyana Ministry of Tourism, Industry and Commerce of the Cooperative Republic of Guyana, 229 South Road, Lacytown, Georgetown, Guyana ⓣ592/226-2505, ⓦwww.sdnp.org.gy/mtti/guyana

Paraguay

Paraguay SENATUR, Palma 468 c/Chile, Centro, Asunción, Paraguay ⓣ595/2144-1530, ⓦwww.senatur.gov.py

Peru

Peru Jorge Basadre 610, San Isidro, Lima ⓣ01/421-1627, ⓦwww.peru.org.pe, ⓔiperulima@promperu.gob.pe

Suriname

Suriname Suriname Tourism Foundation, Dr JF Nassylaan, 2 Paramaribo, Suriname ⓣ597/410-357, ⓦwww.parbo.com/tourism

Uruguay

Uruguay Ministerio de Turísmo del Uruguay, Av Del Libertador 1409, Colonía 1013, Montevideo, Uruguay ⓣ0598/2901-3243, ⓦwww.turismo.gub.uy
USA Tourist Information of Uruguay, PO Box 144531, Coral Gables, FL 33114 ⓣ305/443-7431

Venezuela

Venezuela Corpoturismo, Parque Central, Torre Oeste, Pisos 35–37, Parque Central Caracas, DC 1010 Venezuela ⓣ582/507 8800
USA Venezuala Tourism Association, Box 3010, Sausalito, CA 94966 ⓣ415/331-0100

Websites

There is a lot of information about South America on the **Web** that will help you plan your trip and answer all sorts of questions about history, language and current goings-on. We've listed websites wherever pertinent throughout the guide; the following is a general list of places to begin your wanderings. For details of Internet access within the continent, see p.48.

ⓦwww.amerispan.com/lata/ The newly digitized version of the excellent Latin American Travel Advisor publishes detailed reports about public safety, current political climate, weather, travel costs and health risks for the whole continent.

ⓦwww.clarin.com The largest Spanish-language daily newspaper in the world, printed in Buenos Aires.

ⓦwww.buenosairesherald.com English-language newspaper, updated weekly.

ⓦwww.latinnews.com Real-time newsfeed with major stories from all over South America in English.

ⓦwww.latinamericanlinks.com Good site for traveller information, with links for each country in the continent.

ⓦwww.lafi.org/magazine/magazine Website of the Latin American Folk Institute and the cyber-version of their arts and culture journal, *Clave*.

ⓦwww.narconews.com Up-to-date site dealing with the so-called Drug War and democracy in the continent.

ⓦwww.zonalatina.com/Zlmusic Excellent directory of regional music links and information, covering everything from Mariachi and Sertaneja to Christina Aguilera and Shakira.

ⓦwww.latinomale.com Gay Latino site with good links.

ⓦwww.planeta.com/south Excellent selection of online eco-travel and tourism resources for South America.

ⓦwww.planeta.com/schoolist Great, frequently updated information about Spanish language schools in South America.

ⓦwww.roughguides.com Not only has complete text from relevant guidebooks on the site, but links to travel journals and photos, and a catalogue to lead you to an easy place to buy the guides and maps themselves.

ⓦwww.samexplo.org The website of the South American Explorers, a non-profit organization with the latest research, travel and adventure information.

Travel bookshops and map outlets

Recommended **maps** of individual countries are given at the beginning of the relevant chapter; Rough Guides also publishes a series of detailed, indestructible country maps, including the major South American countries such as Argentina. The most detailed map of the entire continent is the 1: 5,000,000 South America map, published by International Travel Maps.

In the US and Canada

Complete Traveller Bookstore 199 Madison Ave, NY ⓣ212/685-9007

Distant Lands 56 S Raymond Ave, Pasadena, CA 91105 ⓣ1-800/310-3220, ⓦwww.distantlands.com

Elliot Bay Book Company 101 S Main St, Seattle, WA 98104 ⓣ1-800/962-5311, ⓦwww.elliotbaybook.com

Globe Corner Bookstore 28 Church St, Cambridge, MA 02138 ⓣ1-800/358-6013, ⓦwww.globecorner.com

GORP Books & Maps ⓣ1-877/440-4677, ⓦwww.gorp.com/gorp/books/main

Map Link 30 S La Patera Lane, Unit 5, Santa Barbara, CA 93117 ⓣ805/692-6777, ⓦwww.maplink.com

Rand McNally ⓣ1-800/333-0136, ⓦwww.randmcnally.com. Around thirty stores across the US; dial ext 2111 or check the website for the nearest location.

Travel Books and Language Center 4437 Wisconsin Ave, NW, Washington, DC 20016 ⓣ1-800/220-2665, ⓦwww.bookweb.org/bookstore/travelbks

The Travel Bug Bookstore 2667 W Broadway, Vancouver, BC V6K 2G2 ⓣ604/737-1122, ⓦwww.swifty.com/tbug

World of Maps 1235 Wellington St, Ottawa, ON K1Y 3A3 ⓣ1-800/214-8524, ⓦwww.worldofmaps.com

In the UK and Ireland

Blackwell's Map and Travel Shop 50 Broad St, Oxford OX1 3BQ ⓣ01865/793550, ⓦmaps.blackwell.co.uk/index

Easons Bookshop 40 O'Connell St, Dublin 1 ⓣ01/873 3811, ⓦwww.eason.ie

Heffers Map and Travel 20 Trinity St, Cambridge CB2 1TJ ⓣ01223/568568, ⓦwww.heffers.co.uk

Hodges Figgis Bookshop 56-58 Dawson St, Dublin 2 ⓣ01/677 4754, ⓦwww.hodgesfiggis.com

James Thin Booksellers 53–59 South Bridge, Edinburgh EH1 1YS ⓣ0131/622 8222, ⓦwww.jthin.co.uk

John Smith & Son 100 Cathedral St, Glasgow G4 0RD ⓣ0141/552 3377, ⓦwww.johnsmith.co.uk

National Map Centre 22–24 Caxton St, London SW1H 0QU ⓣ020/7222 2466, ⓦwww.mapsnmc.co.uk

Ordnance Survey Ireland Phoenix Park, Dublin 8 ⓣ01/802 5349, ⓦwww.irlgov.ie/osi

Ordnance Survey of Northern Ireland Colby House, Stranmillis Ct, Belfast BT9 5BJ ⓣ028/9025 5761, ⓦwww.osni.gov.uk

Stanfords 12–14 Long Acre, London WC2E 9LP ⓣ020/7836 1321, ⓦwww.stanfords.co.uk. Maps available by mail, phone order, or email. Other branches within British Airways offices at 156 Regent St, London W1R 5TA ⓣ020/7434 4744 and 29 Corn St, Bristol BS1 1HT ⓣ0117/929 9966

The Travel Bookshop 13–15 Blenheim Crescent, London W11 2EE ⓣ020/7229 5260, ⓦwww.thetravelbookshop.co.uk

In Australia and New Zealand

The Map Shop 6–10 Peel St, Adelaide, SA 5000 ⓣ08/8231 2033, ⓦwww.mapshop.net.au

Mapland 372 Little Bourke St, Melbourne, Victoria 3000, ⓣ03/9670 4383, ⓦwww.mapland.com.au

MapWorld 173 Gloucester St, Christchurch ⓣ03/374 5399 or 0800/627967, ⓦwww.mapworld.co.nz

Perth Map Centre 1/884 Hay St, Perth, WA 6000, ⓣ08/9322 5733, ⓦwww.perthmap.com.au

Specialty Maps 46 Albert St, Auckland 1001 ⓣ09/307 2217, ⓦwww.ubdonline.co.nz/maps

Insurance

It is always sensible, and often necessary, to take out an insurance policy before travelling to cover against theft, loss and illness or injury. Before spending on a new policy, however, it's worth checking whether you are already covered: some all-risks home insurance policies may cover your possessions when overseas, and many private medical schemes include cover when abroad. In Canada, provincial health plans usually provide partial cover for medical mishaps overseas, while holders of official student/teacher/youth cards in Canada and the US are entitled to meagre accident coverage and hospital in-patient benefits. Students will often find that their student health coverage extends during the vacations and for one term beyond the date of last enrolment.

Rough Guides travel insurance

Rough Guide offers its own low-cost **travel insurance**, especially customized for our statistically low-risk readers by a leading British broker, provided by the American International Group (AIG) and registered with the British regulatory body GISC (the General Insurance Standards Council).

There are five main Rough Guides insurance plans: **No Frills** for the bare minimum for secure travel; **Essential**, which provides decent all-round cover; **Premier** for comprehensive cover with a wide range of benefits; **Extended** Stay for cover lasting two months to a year; and **Annual Multi-Trip**, a cost-effective way of getting Premier cover if you travel more than once a year. Premier, Annual Multi-Trip and Extended Stay policies can be supplemented by a "Hazardous Pursuits Extension" if you plan to indulge in sports considered dangerous, such as scuba diving or trekking. For a policy quote, call the Rough Guide Insurance Line: toll-free in the UK ⓣ0800/015 0906 or ⓣ+44 1392/314665 from elsewhere. Alternatively, get an online quote at ⓦwww.roughguides.com/insurance.

After exhausting the possibilities above, you might want to contact a specialist travel insurance company, or consider the travel insurance deal we offer (see box below). A typical travel insurance policy usually provides cover for the loss of baggage, tickets and – up to a certain limit – cash or cheques, as well as cancellation or curtailment of your journey. Most of them exclude so-called dangerous sports unless an extra premium is paid: in the Caribbean this can mean scuba-diving, white-water rafting, windsurfing and trekking, though probably not kayaking or jeep safaris. Many policies can be chopped and changed to exclude coverage you don't need – for example, sickness and accident benefits can often be excluded or included at will. If you do take medical coverage, ascertain whether benefits will be paid as treatment proceeds or only after your return home, and whether there is a 24-hour medical emergency number. When securing baggage cover, make sure that the per-article limit – typically under US$730/£500 – will cover your most valuable possession. If you need to make a claim, you should keep receipts for medicines and medical treatment and, in the event you have anything stolen, you must obtain an official statement from the police.

Health

Catching a nasty bug – there are plenty to chose from – or worse is the nightmare of a South American trip. However, with a few precautions – such as watching what you eat and drink (see below), avoiding mosquitoes (see p.28) and getting the necessary inoculations (see below), you should be fine. Jungle and heavily forested areas, as well poverty-stricken rural neighbourhoods, are much more likely to harbour diseases than major cities.

Inoculations

If you are travelling to South America, there are several inoculations that the Center for Disease Control (@www.cdc.gov) recommends you get 4–6 weeks before you leave: **hepatitis A** and **B** – especially if you could be exposed to blood, sexual contact with locals, or are planning to stay in the continent for more than six months; **rabies**, particularly if you risk exposure to wild or domestic animals during your trip; **typhoid** – especially if you plan to travel to less-developed areas in South America; **yellow fever**, if you are travelling outside urban areas generally or anywhere at all in Colombia, Brazil, Bolivia, Peru and Ecuador. Infants and children up to the age of 12 who did not complete courses of tetanus-diptheria, measles and hepatitis B vaccines as infants should receive booster injections for these diseases.

Food and water

Taking a few common-sense **precautions** will lessen the chances of contracting a stomach bug greatly. Steer clear of unpasteurized dairy products and unrefrigerated food, prepared salads and uncooked vegetables; wash and peel fresh fruit and vegetables. When buying street food, stick to obviously popular food vendors and restaurants, and wash your hands well before you eat. You're unlikely to escape a prolonged stay in South America without at least suffering from diarrhoea, and maybe stomach cramps and vomiting too. Usually it will pass (if you'll excuse the pun) in a couple of days. For more information on what to do, see p.32.

Drink only bottled or boiled **water**, or carbonated drinks in cans or bottles. Avoid tap water, fruit juices made with water, fountain drinks and ice cubes. If you are outside of cities and this is not possible, make water safer by both passing it through an "absolute 1-micron or less" filter as well as adding iodine tablets to the filtered water – remember, though, that iodine can be harmful to pregnant women, babies and people with thyroid complaints. You can also purify it, by boiling it for at least ten minutes (longer at high altitude). Filters – a rather cumbersome

A traveller's first-aid kit

Items you would be wise to pack for a trip anywhere in South America include:

- Insect repellent
- Anti-fungal cream
- Antiseptic cream
- Bandaids
- Hydrocortisone cream (for bites and stings)
- Moisturizing lotion
- Plasters
- Scissors
- Lint
- Sealed bandages
- Surgical tape
- Emergency diarrhoea treatment (such as Immodium)
- Paracetamol
- Multivitamins
- Rehydration sachets/tablets
- Water sterilization/purification tablets
- Skin wipes

option, especially if you are hiking – and tablets are available from travel clinics and good outdoor equipment stores. For information on food-and-water-borne diseases, such as **dysentery** and **giardia**, see p.30.

Bites and stings

Bites and stings can lead to infection, so keep wounds clean and wash with antiseptic soap. Wear a generous layer of bug spray during the day and remain in well-screened areas at night; in cheaper hotels, use a **mosquito net** (with the finest mesh available, at least eighteen holes per inch, pre-treated or sprayed with a permethrin product such as Pemanone if possible); in an emergency, wear clothes that cover as much of your body as possible. You should also bring insect **repellent** (preferably containing DEET, or diethylmethyloluamide) and use it on exposed areas of skin at all times, though especially from dusk until dawn when **malarial mosquitoes** are active. Sprays and mosquito coils – containing a pyrethoid insecticide – are also available and can be used to clear rooms of flying insects quickly.

Spiders, **scorpions** and venomous **snakes** do exist throughout the continent, and bites from these – while rare – are very painful and even fatal. Before dressing you should check your shoes, socks and clothes; your bedclothes before retiring for the night; and under the lavatory seat. If you are trekking in the rainforest, avoid leaning against trees and watch where you put your hands and feet – never, ever walk around barefoot in the forest.

Snakes are more scared of you than you are of them, it's true, but this is of little consolation when you're faced with one. If you do get bitten, stay calm and still. Get someone to kill the snake if you can (for species identification) and seek medical attention immediately. If you are miles from any town, remember that rainforest communities will be full of local know-how, and that village remedies and antidotes, especially when dispensed by **curanderos** (village doctors) may be much more efficient than waiting for hours until you can get to a hospital.

Sun

The South American **sun** is not be taken lightly. The continent's position near the equator means that the sun's rays are very strong – use a high-factor **sunblock** (SPF 15 or more) and apply it liberally at least every two hours and after swimming or exercise. Keep sun exposure to a minimum, especially between the hours of 11am and 4pm; wear a hat and a shirt, drink plenty of water or other liquids – but not alcohol – and make sure children are well covered up. Always make sure you have a sufficient supply of water when embarking on any kind of outdoor activity – it's best to take more than you think you will need.

Dizziness, headache and nausea are symptoms of **dehydration** and should be treated by lying down in a shaded place and sipping water or other hydrating fluids. Should symptoms persist, or if you are suffering from hot, dry (but not sweaty) skin – potentially a sign of **heatstroke** – seek medical assistance immediately.

Altitude sickness

Visitors to the mountainous regions of Chile, Peru, Bolivia, Argentina, Peru, Venezuela Ecuador and Colombia may encounter **altitude sickness**, a potentially – though rarely – fatal condition. It may occur at anything over 2000m, but is likeliest and most serious at altitudes of 4000m and above. It can cause severe difficulties – but a little preparation should help avoid the worst of its effects. In many South American countries, it is known by the Quechua word **soroche**, but in Argentina is most commonly called **puna** (the local word for altiplano or high Andean steppes).

If you're **driving**, make sure that your vehicle's engine has been properly adjusted. All engines labour because of the low oxygen levels, and when you start walking you'll empathize, so don't try to force the pace and stay in low gears. To avoid the effects of altitude sickness yourself, don't rush anywhere, but instead walk slowly and breathe steadily – and make things easier on yourself by not smoking.

Whenever possible, **acclimatize yourself**: it's better to spend a day or two at around 2000m and then 3000–3500m before climbing to 4000m or more, allowing the body to produce more red blood corpuscles rather than forcing it to cope with a sudden reduction in oxygen levels. And make sure you're fully rested; an all-night party isn't exactly the best preparation for a trip up into the mountains. As for drinking, alcohol is best avoided, before or during high-altitude travel, and the best thing to drink is plenty of still water – never fizzy because it froths over or can even explode at high altitudes – or tea. Eating, too, needs some consideration: digestion uses up considerable quantities of oxygen, so snacking is preferable to copious lunches and dinners.

Be sure to carry supplies of non-salty high-energy cereal bars, chocolate, dried fruit (the local raisins, prunes and dried apricots are delicious), walnuts or cashews, crackers and biscuits, avoiding anything that ferments in the stomach such as milk, fresh fruit and juices, vegetables or acidic food, as they're guaranteed to make you throw up if you're affected; the best – because it's the least acidic – form of sugar to ingest is honey. Grilled meat is fine, but don't overindulge. As an extra precaution against *soroche*, you could try *mate de coca* (coca-leaf tea) – the local preventative cure-all.

Minor **symptoms** of altitude sickness (such as headaches or a strange feeling of pressure inside the skull, nausea, loss of appetite, insomnia or dizziness) are nothing to worry about. However, more severe problems, such as persistent migraines, repeated vomiting, severe breathing difficulties, excessive fatigue and a marked reduction in the need to urinate are of more concern. If you suffer from any of these, seek **medical advice** at once and consider returning to a lower altitude. Severe respiratory problems should be treated immediately with oxygen, carried by tour operators on excursions to 3000m or more, as a legal requirement, but you're unlikely ever to need it.

The higher you go, the more risk you run of getting altitude sickness, and those travelling to heights above 4000m should also be aware of two of its more serious forms – **high altitude pulmonary oedema (HAPO)** and **high altitude cerebral oedema (HACO)**. HAPO is caused by a build-up of liquid in the lungs and symptoms include fever, racing pulse, and coughing up white fluid. If you find yourself suffering from any of these, you should immediately descend to a lower level. HACO is more serious yet (and, fortunately, rarer) and is caused when fluid floods the brain. Symptoms of HACO include severe weariness, listlessness and apathy, loss of balance, weakness or numbness on one side of the body and mental confusion. If you or anyone around you seems to be suffering from these conditions, descend and seek medical help straight away, as HACO can be fatal in just 24 hours.

Hypothermia

Of all mishaps or illnesses, **hypothermia** causes the most deaths among climbers and trekkers every year in South America. It is brought on when the body is exposed to extreme or prolonged cold, starts to lose heat and cannot generate more heat at a fast enough rate to counteract the loss. The likelihood of catching hypothermia is exacerbated if you are wet and tired or in the wind, as clothing – especially cotton, denim or down – loses its purpose as an insulator when wet. The first **symptoms** of hypothermia include a quasi-euphoric sense of **disorientation** and **weariness** that are often not recognized for what they are – this means that your body temperature can become dangerously low before you even realize that you might be at risk. Later symptoms include strange, unpredictable behaviour, **severe shivering**, **slurred speech**, **loss of coordination** and **drowsiness** – because your brain slows down and gets confused. If you suspect that you or someone around you has hypothermia, there are several measures you can take. Make a fire in which to warm rocks and place these near major blood vessels (under the arms and knees; near the crotch); make sure the sufferer has warm, dry clothes and is wrapped in a dry sleeping bag. Make them drink warm liquids, but slowly, and try to keep them awake as falling asleep will make their body temperature drop even further. In more serious cases, the best way to restore body temperature in a hypothermic person is to take off their clothes, your clothes (and even the clothes of a third person) and squeeze into a sleeping bag together, warming the victim with your bodies on both sides.

Diseases

While South America is host to a range of **diseases** that can be quite debilitating, if you take the necessary precautions, look out for symptoms and – if necessary – get medical treatment immediately, you should be all right.

Dysentery and giardia

Food-and-water-borne diseases include **bacterial dysentery**, giardia, amoebic dysentery and cholera. The former can be treated by following a course of antibiotics such as Ciprofloxacin, but you should always check with a medical professional first, and request a stool sample (cheap; reassuring) in the nearest town. **Amoebic dysentery** is indicated by bloody stools and fever and should be treated only with medical advice. Usually, you will be prescribed a course of metronidazole or tinidazole such as Flagyl or Fasigyn. These drugs are also often prescribed for **giardia**, a water-borne disease that induces watery, foul-smelling diarrhoea, bloating, wind and fatigue – symptoms that, left untreated, can last on and off for weeks. Cholera tends to break out only in rural areas with poor sanitation, often places where no tourist would dare to tread. However, if you find yourself suffering from chronic watery diarrhoea, fever and intense vomiting you should see a doctor immediately and drink plenty of boiled or bottled water. There is a cholera vaccine available, however the germ has developed an immunity to it and it therefore no longer serves a purpose.

Yellow fever

Yellow fever is a very serious mosquito-borne viral disease that occurs in subtropical and tropical forested regions, particularly where there are monkeys. There has been a dramatic upsurge in cases in South America recently, some of which seem to have occurred in urban as well as rural areas. **Symptoms** range from flu-like chills and fever to severe hepatitis and haemorrhage. Colombia, Brazil, Bolivia, Peru and Ecuador are the worst effected areas in the continent, with Venezuela, Guyana, Suriname and French Guiana also reporting incidences of the disease.

The disease occurs primarily in young men and rarely in travellers, although there have been fatal cases in some unvaccinated travellers to rural areas. A **preventative vaccine** is available and recommended to all travellers to the above regions; you should also follow the general guidelines for avoiding insect bites and stings (see p.28). In urban areas, mosquitoes that transmit yellow fever generally feed during the day.

River blindness

Caused by the bite of female black flies, **river blindness** (*onchocerciasis*) is usually found by day near fast-flowing rivers and streams, particularly in Brazil, Colombia, Ecuador and Venezuela. It can result in dermatitis, lymphadenitis, visual impairment and even blindness. Short-term travellers seem to be at low risk of infection but those who plan to stay longer than three months should be on their guard. There is no vaccine available, so you should make sure you are aware of **black fly habitats** in the continent, and follow the general guidelines for avoiding insects bites (see p.28). If you do contract river blindness, you will need to take repeat annual doses of **ivermectin** because the disease can lie dormant and then recur.

Chagas' disease

Chagas' disease is transmitted by a microscopic parasite, the *Trypanosome cruzi*, transported by a small beetle, the *vinchuca* or *chinche gaucha*. The parasite-bearing beetle bites its victim and then defecates next to the wound – and scratching of the bite thus causes the parasite to be borne into the bloodstream. The immediate **symptoms** – a fever, a hard swelling on the skin and occasionally around the eyes – last two to three weeks, are mild and may even be imperceptible; but the disease is treatable at this stage. In around twenty percent of untreated cases, however, potentially fatal cardiac problems caused by a gross enlargement of the heart can appear twenty or thirty years later, with no other symptoms suffered in between. Though it can be extremely serious, the disease isn't widespread and travellers should be aware of, but not unduly worried about, catching it. Contact is most likely to occur in poorer rural regions, particularly in dwellings with adobe walls. Where possible you should avoid camping in such areas and if you do sleep in an adobe hut, you should use a mosquito net and sling your hammock as far away from the walls as possible. If you suspect you have been bitten by a *vinchuca*, avoid scratching the wound; bathe it with alcohol instead and get a blood test as soon as possible.

Hantavirus

A rare, incurable viral disease transmitted by long-tailed wild mice, **hantavirus** is present throughout the Americas and produces haemorrhagic fever and severe respiratory problems caused by the accumulation of liquid in the lungs. Initial symptoms are similar to influenza – with fever, headache, stomach ache and muscle pain – and the fatality rate is around fifty percent. The virus is present in the excrement, urine and saliva of the mouse and is transmitted to humans through breathing in contaminated air, consuming contaminated food or water, or by being bitten by or handling a virus-bearing mouse. It cannot survive sunlight, detergent or disinfectant, and the best way to avoid contamination is by being scrupulously clean when camping, particularly in rural areas. **Recommended precautions** are using tents with a proper floor, good fastenings and no holes; keeping food in sealed containers and out of reach of mice (hanging a knotted carrier bag from a tree is a standard precaution) and cleaning up properly after eating. If staying in a *cabaña* which looks as though it hasn't been used for a while, let the place ventilate for a good thirty minutes before checking (while covering your mouth and nose with a handkerchief) for signs of mouse excrement. If any is found, all surfaces should be disinfected then swept and aired. Despite the severity of hantavirus, you should not be unduly worried about the disease. In the unlikely case that there is an outbreak in the area you are visiting you will be well-informed by the local authorities of the virus's presence.

Malaria and dengue fever

Malaria is a very serious disease transmitted to humans via mosquito bites, usually between dusk and dawn. The worst-affected areas are below 1500m; your chances of contracting malaria are much less at higher altitudes than this and nonexistent above 2500m, at which altitude the malarial mosquito cannot survive. Because symptoms do not occur until at least 7–9 days after you have been bitten by an infected mosquito, travellers should be aware that a fever in the first week of travel in the area is unlikely to be malarial. **Symptoms** of malaria include fever and flu-like illness, including chills, wooziness, muscle aches and fatigue. They can occur any time up to a year after you have been bitten, so if you recognize these symptoms even after you return home, you should seek medical help immediately and ensure that you inform your doctor about your travel history.

Malaria **prevention** is twofold: everyone should take every precaution possible to avoid mosquito bites (see p.28), and travellers should be sure to take a prescription anti-malarial drug: chloroquine for visitors to Paraguay, and atovanquone, doxycycline or mefloquine – although ask your physician about side effects – to those travelling in the rest of tropical South America. Do not wait until you reach your destination to take anti-malarial medication – many South American countries use a drug called halfantrine (Halfan) to treat the disease, and the drug has been linked with serious cardiac side effects and death.

Dengue fever is another mosquito-borne illness, this time transmitted by the buggers during the day. Symptoms resemble those of malaria but include extreme aches and pains in the bones and joints, along with fever and dizziness. The only cure for dengue fever is rest and painkillers, and the only precaution you can take is to avoid mosquito bites (for details, see p.28).

Leishmaniasis

Leishmaniasis is found all over South America, and is more common in rural areas and the outskirts of cities, making adventure travellers particularly prone. It is carried by some sandflies, usually between dusk and dawn but also during the day if resting sandflies are disturbed. The disease manifests in external skin sores that develop weeks to months after infection, or in visceral forms such as fever, anemia and enlargement of the liver and spleen that may take years to appear. Preventative measures can be taken in the form of avoiding outdoor activities at night in areas populated by sand flies (see p.28) and following general instructions for avoiding insect bites. If you do suspect that you may have contracted leishmaniasis, contact a tropical medicine specialist immediately.

Travellers' diarrhoea

Food-and-water-borne diseases are the main cause of illness in travellers to Latin America, and of these diseases **travellers' diarrhoea** is the most common of all. It can be caused by bacteria, viruses and parasites found in contaminated food and water throughout the continent. Typical symptoms usually last from three to seven days and include bloating, nausea, urgency and diarrhoea. The best way to prevent travellers' diarrhoea is to watch what you eat and drink and where you get your food and water from (see p.27). If you do fall ill, though, rest up and replace the fluids you've lost by drinking plenty of water or – for persistent diarrhoea – an oral rehydration solution, readily available from your home pharmacy, should do the trick. Barring that, you can make a homemade solution by dissolving a teaspoon of salt and eight teaspoons of sugar in a litre of boiling water. An anti-diarrheal drug such as **Immodium** can alleviate the symptoms somewhat, but it won't really cure the problem. Try to drink at least three litres of liquids a day. Fruit juices and caffeine-free beverages are also an option, but avoid all dairy products, as these may exacerbate symptoms. If you are still suffering after a week, if your symptoms are accompanied by chills or fever, if there is blood or if you are too ill to drink, seek medical help immediately.

AIDS and HIV

The spread of **AIDS** (or **SIDA**, as it is known in Spanish) throughout Latin America has been highly diverse, with the highest rates of infection being on the Caribbean side of the continent and in Brazil, where the disease has reached an epidemic level among heterosexual, homosexual and injecting drug-user communities alike. Cases are less widespread in Argentina and Chile and the Western coast. A few of the governments of the larger countries have implemented a program of antiretroviral therapy for all people infected with HIV, but prevention is still a key issue. With regard to sex, the same common-sense rule applies here as anywhere else: condomless sex is a serious health risk, and it's worth bringing (latex) **condoms** from home as those sold in many areas in South America (*preservativos* or *condones* in Spanish-speaking countries; *camisinhas* in Brazil) are of poor quality. You should bring some sterilized disposable syringes in your first-aid kit too, as some hospitals are less than fastidious about blood screening or needle sterilizing.

Medical resources for travellers

Before going to South America, travellers seeking health advice should consult the websites and organizations listed below.

Websites

@www.cdc.gov/travel/ US Department of Health and Human Services travel health and disease control department, listing precautions, diseases and preventative measures by region, as

Prescriptions

Be aware that even in cities with good medical facilities and well-stocked pharmacies you may not be able to find the exact medication that you take at home, or even a viable alternative. To be safe, bring any prescribed medicine in its original container and make sure you have enough for the length of your trip, as well as a copy of the prescription itself. The US State Department also advises bringing a letter from the prescribing doctor explaining why the drugs are needed.

well as a summary of cruise ship sanitation levels.
@**www.fitfortravel.scot.nhs.uk** British National Health Service website carrying information about travel-related diseases and how to avoid them.
@**www.istm.org** The website of the International Society for Travel Medicine, with a full list of clinics specializing in international travel health.
@**www.masta.org** Comprehensive website for medical advisory services for travel abroad (see also under medical resources in the UK and Ireland).
@**www.tmvc.com.au** Contains a list of all Travellers Medical and Vaccination Centres throughout Australia, New Zealand and Southeast Asia, plus general information on travel health.
@**www.travelvax.net** Website detailing everything you could ever want to know about diseases and travel vaccines.
@**www.tripprep.com** Travel Health Online provides an online comprehensive database of necessary vaccinations for most countries, as well as destination and medical service provider information.

In the US and Canada

Canadian Society for International Health 1 Nicholas St, Suite 1105, Ottawa, ON K1N 7B7 ⓣ613/241-5785, @www.csih.org. Distributes a free pamphlet, "Health Information for Canadian Travellers", containing an extensive list of travel health centres in Canada.
Center for Disease Control 1600 Clifton Rd NE, Atlanta, GA 30333 ⓣ404/639-3534 or 1-800/311-3435, @www.cdc.gov. Publishes outbreak warnings, suggested inoculations, precautions and other background information for travellers. Useful website plus International Travellers Hotline on ⓣ1-877/FYI-TRIP.
International Association for Medical Assistance to Travellers 417 Center St, Lewiston, NY 14092 ⓣ716/754-4883, @www.sentex.net/~iamat, and 40 Regal Rd, Guelph, ON N1K 1B5 ⓣ519/836-0102. A non-profit organization, IAMAT provides a list of English-speaking doctors in the Caribbean, climate charts and leaflets on various diseases and inoculations.
International SOS Assistance Eight Neshaminy Interplex Suite 207, Trevose, US 19053-6956 ⓣ1-800/523-8930, @www.intsos.com. Members receive pre-trip medical referral info, as well as overseas emergency services designed to complement travel insurance coverage.
Travel Medicine ⓣ1-800/872-8633, @www.travmed.com. Sells first-aid kits, mosquito netting, water filters, reference books and other health-related travel products.

In the UK and Ireland

British Airways Travel Clinics Twenty-eight regional clinics (call ⓣ01276/685040 for the nearest, or consult @www.britishairways.com). All clinics offer vaccinations, tailored advice from an online database and a complete range of travel healthcare products.
Communicable Diseases Unit Brownlee Centre, Glasgow G12 0YN ⓣ0141/211 1074. Travel vaccinations including yellow fever.
Dun Laoghaire Medical Centre 5 Northumberland Ave, Dun Laoghaire, Co Dublin ⓣ01/280 4996. Advice on medical matters abroad.
Hospital for Tropical Diseases Travel Clinic 2nd floor, Mortimer Market Centre, off Capper Street, London WC1E 6AU ⓣ020/7388 9600. Consultations cost £15, which is waived if you have your injections here. Also offer a recorded Health Line (ⓣ09061/337733, 50p per min) gives tips on hygiene and illness prevention as well as listing appropriate immunizations.
Liverpool School of Tropical Medicine Pembroke Place, Liverpool L3 5QA ⓣ0151/708 9393. Walk-in clinic Mon–Fri 1–4pm; appointment required for yellow fever inoculation, but not for other jabs.
Medical Advisory Service for Travellers Abroad London School of Hygiene and Tropical Medicine. MASTA operates a recorded 24-hour Travellers' Health Line (UK ⓣ0906/822 4100, 60p per min; Republic of Ireland ⓣ01560/147000, 75p per min) and givies written information tailored to your journey by return of post.
Travel Health Centre Department of International Health and Tropical Medicine, Royal College of Surgeons in Ireland, Mercers Medical Centre, Stephen's St Lower, Dublin ⓣ01/402 2337. Expert pre-trip advice and inoculations.
Travel Medicine Services PO Box 254, 16 College St, Belfast 1 ⓣ028/9031 5220. Offers medical advice before a trip and help afterwards in the event of a tropical disease.

In Australia and New Zealand

Travellers' Medical and Vaccination Centres @www.tmvc.com.au; 27–29 Gilbert Place, Adelaide ⓣ08/8212 7522; 1/170 Queen St, Auckland ⓣ09/373 3531; 5/247 Adelaide St, Brisbane ⓣ07/3221 9066; 5/8–10 Hobart Place, Canberra ⓣ02/6257 7156; 147 Armagh St, Christchurch ⓣ03/379 4000; 5 Westralia St,

Darwin ☎08/8981 2907; 270 Sandy Bay Rd, Sandy Bay, Hobart ☎03/6223 7577; 2/393 Little Bourke St, Melbourne ☎03/9602 5788; 5 Mill St, Perth ☎08/9321 1977, plus branch in Fremantle; 7/428 George St, Sydney ☎02/9221 7133, plus branches in Chatswood and Parramatta; Shop 15, Grand Arcade, 14–16 Willis St, Wellington ☎04/473 0991.

Costs and money

When travelling to most Latin American countries it's wise to obtain local currency before you set off, particularly if you plan to visit Venezuela, where it is extremely difficult to obtain.

ATM availability is reasonable in most large cities, but you should not rely solely on using international debit cards to access funds. Make sure, therefore, that you are carrying alternative forms of payment, such as **US dollars** to exchange (including notes in small denominations) and **credit cards**. Another option is **travellers' cheques**, although they are not as widely accepted. Travellers should be aware that credit card fraud is a problem in the continent, particularly in Brazil and Venezuela; be sure to retain your copy of the transaction slip, along with the carbon paper. Beware, also, that in many countries credit cards will not be accepted anywhere but the biggest hotels and shops, and banks will sometimes refuse to offer cash advances against them. When exchanging money, you should only use authorized bureaux de change, such as banks, *cambios* and tourist facilities, rather than deal with moneychangers on the streets. For details on each country, consult the "Costs and money" section at the beginning of each chapter.

Costs

Your **daily budget** in South America depends, of course, on where you are travelling and how comfortable you want to be. Many people still labour under the delusion that South America is very cheap indeed, only to be rudely awakened when they arrive. Many countries are really not that much cheaper than Europe or America, especially in their major cities. Argentina, Uruguay and Chile are the most expensive places in the region to visit, and travellers should count on spending US$400/£250 per week here in order to have a little more breathing room, including the occasional museum, nice restaurant meal or adventure activity. Some travellers can get by on much less than this, but if you try to do so you may find yourself regretting that you did not allow for a little more freedom once you are there. Remember that **incidentals** such as car rental, room and departure tax, local driving permits and guides – never mind country-hopping, rainforest trips, fancy dinners or scuba diving – really add up but are some of the most enjoyable facets of a South American holiday. Solo travellers should also keep in mind that costs will be more if you are travelling alone. Ecuador is at the cheaper end of the scale, and you can get by on as little as US$100/£60 per week, as long as you sleep in hostels or camp, take public transport and eat from street stalls and cheap cafés. In between are Bolivia and Colombia, which cost the budget traveller around US$175–200/£110–120 per week, to live reasonably well; and Brazil, Chile, Peru and Venezuela, which can be enjoyed for around US$230/week.

Youth and student discounts

Once obtained, various official and quasi-official **youth/student ID cards** soon pay for themselves in savings. Full-time students are eligible for the International Student ID Card (ISIC, ⓦwww.isiccard.com), which entitles the bearer to special air, rail and bus fares and discounts at museums, theatres and other attractions. For Americans, there's also a health benefit, providing up to US$3000 in emergency medical coverage and US$100 a day for sixty days in the hospital, plus a 24-hour hotline to call in the event of a medical, legal or financial emergency. The card costs US$22 in the US; Can$16 in Canada; AUS$16.50 in Australia; NZ$20 in New Zealand; £7 in the UK; and €12.70 in the Republic of Ireland.

You only have to be 26 or younger to qualify for the **International Youth Travel Card**, which costs US$22/£7 and carries the same benefits. Teachers qualify for the **International Teacher Card**, offering similar discounts and costing US$22, Can$16, AUS$16.50 and NZ$20. All these cards are available in the US from STA, Travel Cuts and, in Canada, Hostelling International (see p.43 for addresses); in Australia and New Zealand from STA or Campus Travel; and in the UK from STA.

Several other travel organizations and accommodation groups also sell their own cards, good for various discounts. A university photo ID might open some doors, but is not easily recognizable, as are the ISIC cards. However, the latter are often not accepted as valid proof of age, for example in bars or liquor stores.

Impuesto al Valor Agregado (IVA)

This twelve percent tax is added to the marked price of most goods and services in **South America**. It includes restaurants and the pricier hotels, although some budget accommodation may also quote you pre-tax prices and then bill you for a vastly inflated sum that includes tax and a 10 percent service charge. If in doubt as to whether or not IVA is included in the price quoted to you, ask.

Cash and travellers' cheques

If you are going to be away from urban or tourist centres at all or shopping in local markets and stalls, **cash** is a necessity – preferably in small denominations of local currency although some countries in the continent, such as Argentina and Brazil, may accept US dollars. The US dollar is the official currency of Ecuador. To avoid hassles regarding change with street vendors or local businesses, ask for small denominations when exchanging money or cashing cheques, break large notes in service environments such as post offices and hotels, and withdraw odd amounts from ATMs to avoid getting your cash dispensed in large denominations only.

As a general rule, US **travellers' cheques** are accepted in hotels in the main cities, but outside of hotels you may have trouble cashing them, as they have become an obsolete method of payment.

If you are in doubt, though, or simply want some peace of mind, you can generally cash travellers' cheques in bureaux de change in city centres and airports. Remember, though, that unless you are willing to seek out an exchange office every day, you will still end up carrying a fair amount of cash on your person once you have cashed the cheques – a risk in Latin American countries whose economic crises have lead to an increase in crime.

The usual fee for travellers' cheque sales is one or two percent, though this fee may be waived if you buy the cheques through your bank. Some outlets offer better rates for cheques than for cash and most charge a commission. Keep the purchase agreement and a record of cheque serial numbers safe and separate from the cheques themselves. In the event that they're lost or stolen, you'll need to report the loss to the issuing company; refer to the list of phone numbers provided with the cheques; some companies claim to replace lost or stolen cheques within 24 hours.

Credit and debit cards

Credit cards are a handy back-up and can be used either at ATMs or over the counter at banks. **MasterCard** and **Visa** are the most commonly accepted in the region; other cards may not be recognized at all. Remember that if you use your credit card to obtain **cash advances**, you'll pay credit-card rates of interest on the cash from the date of withdrawal; there may be a transaction fee on top of this.

If you plan to travel only to major cities and want the security of travellers' cheques without the hassle of carrying large amounts of cash or waiting for exchange offices to open, consider using your ATM card – many ATMs in Latin America now take US and European **debit cards** (linked to Cirrus, Plus or Maestro) at a minimal fee – check with your bank for details. Make sure you have a personal identification number (PIN) that lets you access your account from overseas. A complete list of ATMs on the Cirrus and Maestro networks can be found at Ⓦwww.mastercard.com; for those on the Visa Plus network, log on to Ⓦwww.visa.com/atms.

A compromise between travellers' cheques and plastic is **Visa Travel Money**, a disposable prepaid debit card. Load up your account with funds before leaving home and when they run out, simply throw the card away. You can buy up to nine cards to access the same funds – useful for couples or families travelling together – and it's a good idea to buy at least one extra as a back-up in case of loss or theft.

The card is available in most countries from branches of **Thomas Cook** and **Citicorp**. For more information, check the Visa TravelMoney website at Ⓦwww.usa.visa.com /personal/cards/visa_travel_money.

Wiring money

Having money wired from home using one of the companies listed below is never convenient or cheap, and should be considered a last resort. It's also possible to have money wired directly from a bank in your home country to a South American bank, although this is somewhat less reliable because it involves two separate institutions. If you go this route, your home bank will need the address of the branch bank where you want to pick up the money and the address and telex number of its main island office. Money wired this way normally takes two working days to arrive, and costs around US$40/£25 per transaction.

Money-wiring companies

American Express
Ⓦwww.moneygram.com
Australia Ⓣ1800/230100
New Zealand Ⓣ09/379 8243 or 0800/262 263l
UK and Republic of Ireland Ⓣ0800/6663 9472
US and Canada Ⓣ1-800/926-9400

Thomas Cook/Travelex
Ⓦwww.us.thomascook.com
Australia Ⓣ02/9223 6633
Canada Ⓣ1-888/823-4732
Republic of Ireland Ⓣ01/677 1721
New Zealand Ⓣ06/359 1655
UK Ⓣ01733/318922 or Ⓣ028/9055 0030
US Ⓣ1-800/287-7362

Western Union
Ⓦwww.westernunion.com
Australia Ⓣ1800/649565
New Zealand Ⓣ09/270 0050
Republic of Ireland Ⓣ1800/395395
UK Ⓣ0800/833833
US and Canada Ⓣ1-800/325-6000

Getting around

South American roads, especially outside the major cities, are notorious for their bumpy, pothole-riddled and generally poor condition. Many car rental companies in South America do not allow their vehicles to be driven across borders, or permit very restricted border crossing only, making independent exploring the whole continent by car a rather difficult proposition.

Most South Americans travel by **bus** and this is the recommended mode of transport for shorter distances, as there is a reliable bus network throughout most of the region. This certainly makes for cost-effective transport too. In more remote areas such as Patagonia, though, there are few bus and no train services, and car rental may be your only option. Remember, though, that inter-country distances are huge and you may end up spending much time sitting and sweating rather than exploring. If you have a little spare cash and limited time, your best bet may be to use one of the **airpasses** detailed on p.38. These offer reasonable value for money, flights are frequent, and the time saving is well worth the extra cash.

By car

If you are determined to go it alone and drive around South America, you will find car hire companies at all airports and in most major cities. Hotels should be able to alert you to better value local places, but often you can get a reasonable deal by booking far enough in advance and over the Internet (see p.24). Costs are high due to skyrocketing insurance rates, but the independence granted you by a car may be worth any amount. Be sure to verify if the car is covered and, if so, for which incidences it is insured as car theft, vandalism and general security are renowned problems in some parts of South America, especially Argentina, Chile and Brazil, and you may not be covered. Rental charges range from a pricey US$50/day to an extortionate US$100/day; you may be required to present a credit card and you will need an International Driving License or an Inter-American Driving Permit as well as your licence from back home.

Rules of the road

There are established road rules in South America, although in some countries – Argentina, say, or Brazil – you would be forgiven for thinking that none of the locals had ever heard of the Highway Code. A certain machismo reigns here, so beware other drivers, especially at night. When driving in hilly or twisty terrain, a good rule of thumb seems to be to honk your horn before going round any corner – the locals do this with great gusto, so rest assured that no one will find you rude. South Americans drive on the right, except in Suriname and Guyana.

Car rental agencies

In North America

Avis US ⓣ1-800/331-1084, Canada ⓣ1-800/272-5871, ⓦwww.avis.com
Budget US ⓣ1-800/527-0700, ⓦwww.budgetrentacar.com
Dollar US ⓣ1-800/800-4000, ⓦwww.dollar.com
National ⓣ1-800/227-7368, ⓦwww.nationalcar.com

In Britain

Avis ⓣ0870/606 0100, ⓦwww.avis.co.uk
Budget ⓣ0800/181181, ⓦwww.budget.co.uk
National ⓣ0870/536 5365, ⓦwww.nationalcar.co.uk
Hertz ⓣ0870/844 8844, ⓦwww.hertz.co.uk

In Ireland

Avis Northern Ireland ⓣ028/9024 0404, Republic of Ireland ⓣ01/605 7500, ⓦwww.avis.ie
Budget Republic of Ireland ⓣ0903/27711, ⓦwww.budget.ie
Hertz Republic of Ireland ⓣ01/676 7476, ⓦwww.hertz.ie

In Australia

Avis ⓣ136333 or 02/9353 9000, ⓦwww.avis.com.au
Budget ⓣ1300/362848, ⓦwww.budget.com.au
Dollar ⓣ02/9223 1444, ⓦwww.dollarcar.com.au
Hertz ⓣ133039 or 03/9698 2555, ⓦwww.hertz.com.au
National ⓣ131045, ⓦwww.nationalcar.com.au.

In New Zealand

Avis ⓣ09/526 2847 or 0800/655111, ⓦwww.avis.co.nz
Budget ⓣ09/976 2222, ⓦwww.budget.co.nz
Hertz ⓣ0800/654321, ⓦwww.hertz.co.nz
National ⓣ0800/800115, ⓦwww.nationalcar.co.nz

Motoring organizations

In North America

AAA ⓣ1-800/AAA-HELP, ⓦwww.aaa.com. Each state has its own club – check the phone book for local address and phone number.
CAA ⓣ613/247-0117, ⓦwww.caa.ca. Each region has its own club – check the phone book for local address and phone number.

In the UK and Ireland

AA UK ⓣ0870/600 0371, ⓦwww.theaa.com
AA Ireland Dublin ⓣ01/617 9988, ⓦwww.aaireland.ie
RAC UK ⓣ0800/550055, ⓦwww.rac.co.uk

In Australia and New Zealand

AAA Australia ⓣ02/6247 7311, ⓦwww.aaa.asn.au
New Zealand AA New Zealand ⓣ09/377 4660, ⓦwww.nzaa.co.nz

Shipping or buying a car

Some travellers to South America, especially those who plan to be in the continent for a long amount of time, either ship their car from the mainland United States or Europe, or buy an old car when they arrive and sell it on again (at a vastly reduced price) before they leave.

The process of **buying a car** is beset with bureaucracy, though, so be prepared to trawl through miles of red tape before you get to set off into the great unknown. It's a good idea to get a notarized document stating that you are the new owner of the car, as you may need something to present to authority figures on demand. Chile has the reputation for being the best place to buy a car in the continent, and Asunción in Paraguay the best place to sell one.

If you want to **bring your own vehicle** to South America, you will need to sort out shipping arrangements around a month or so in advance. Costs are high – count on at least US$1500 each way from the East Coast of the US – and you will have to provide the shipper with three notarized copies of the vehicle's title. If you plan to drive from North America, remember that you cannot drive any further south than Panama (there are no roads) and that you will have to get your car shipped across to Colombia once you arrive here, over the Darien Gap. Make sure to bargain with shippers – you should be able to ship with somebody reliable for around US$1000.

All travellers who plan to take a vehicle across borders should have a *libreta de pasos por aduana / carnet de passage* to present to customs officials at checkpoints. Legally you are required to carry one of these, though you may not be asked for it every time you cross a country line. Further details and the *carnets de passages* themselves are available from the relevant motoring organization in your home country (see above); US residents should contact the Canadian Automobile Association for information, as the AAA does not issue the *carnet*.

By air

If you plan to be doing a fair amount of travelling around Latin America, you might want to consider one of the reasonable **airpasses** on offer in the region. These are a godsend if you want to see as much as possible in a limited time, and – given the size of the continent – can make all the difference between arriving at your destination exhausted and frayed and arriving fresh and ready to explore.

The **All America Airpass** is valid for ninety days and offers special fares throughout Latin America on more than thirty airlines. It comprises of individual segment passes that combine to make a multi-sector trip up to a value of US$1800, although you can just buy one sector if you so desire. Fares range from US$180 for a one-way ticket from Santiago to Lima with TACA to US$420 for a journey from Lima to Cuzco to Quito. The passes are only available to travellers with a scheduled international return ticket and must be bought in the traveller's country of origin. Should you need to cancel before you travel, you will be refunded save for a US$60 administration fee; after you have used the first sector on your pass the ticket is non-refundable. Remember that many Latin American countries charge a **departure tax** when leaving their airports on international flights – this tax is payable locally and is not included in the airpass price. For more information, contact one of the travel agents on p.40 or go to ⓦwww.allairpass.com.

The **Mercosur Airpass** covers travel in and between Argentina, Brazil, Chile, Paraguay and Uruguay. Prices are calculated on a miles-flown basis, regardless of how many countries you visit. There is a maximum of two stopovers and four flight coupons for each country, and the pass is valid for a minimum of seven and a maximum of thirty days. Prices start at US$225 for 1200–1900 miles, then are US$285 for 1901–2500 miles; US$345 for 2501–3200 miles; US$420 for 3201–4200 miles; US$530 for 4201–5200 miles; US$645 for 5201–6200 miles; US$755 for 6201–7200 miles and US$870 for more than 7201 miles. The pass covers substantial reductions on standard air travel in the continent, with a flight from Santiago to Buenos Aires to Asunción to Rio de Janeiro costing just US$285, and one from Santiago to Calama to Mendoza to Buenos Aires to Rio de Janeiro costing US$420. You can rebook to change dates (but not reroute).

By bus

Buses are the primary mode of transport for South Americans and are by far the cheapest – if not the most time efficient – way to see the continent. While you can technically travel all the way from the tropical north of the continent to Argentina by bus, there are few direct international services and you will usually have to disembark at the border, cross it, then get on another bus to a large city in the new country, from whence you can travel pretty much anywhere within that country. The process is repeated at most border crossings – it's not a particularly expedient way to travel, but it is by far the least expensive, averaging just 5¢/km, in the region.

Terminals are usually situated somewhat out of town – follow the signs to the *terminal de autobuses*, the *terminal terrestre* (in Ecuador) or the *rodoviária* (in Brazil). Levels of comfort very madly, from rickety, dilapidated buses that leave only when every seat – and most of the aisle – is taken, that are rarely on time, and from which you will emerge needing a massage-and-sauna session, to beautiful modern machines with reclining seats, snack and beverage service, and movies shown en route. The most luxurious of all is the bus *cama*, which has beds for the longest journeys – in the latter two situations, your seats will normally be assigned in advance.

By train

Trains are much less frequent, expensive and efficient than South American buses, but if you have a little time to spare they provide a wonderful way to see the countryside and wildlife, as they tend to travel much more exotic routes than the more functional buses. There are several types of train, including the fast and efficient *ferrotren*, stopping at major stations only; the average *tren rápido*; the slower *expreso*, which stops at most stations; and the super-slow and amazingly cheap *mixto*, which stops for every Tom, Dick and Harry – and their livestock too.

By boat

There are several **ferry** and **catamaran** services providing travel on South America's lakes, especially those in Chile, Argentina, Peru and Bolivia, allowing some of the finest scenic experiences in the region. Those relevant to a single country are explored in the relevant chapter but there are two cross-border crossings that are particularly recommended: the **Southern Lakes Crossing** (p.170) between Argentina and Chile and the

Lake Titicaca Crossing (see p.238) between Bolivia and Peru.

One of the finest ways to soak in South American atmosphere and get a taste for the slowed-down pace of life is to travel some of the continent's rivers by boat. Unfortunately, the **riverboat** industry is one in decline, especially on the Amazon, as increased air services have facilitated speedier transportation for the time-pressed but moneyed traveller and cargo-only tugs have brought about the demise of several passenger-friendly services. There are, however, still several riverboat services available, and this is a recommended activity for anyone – particularly on the narrower, less-frequented rivers – with the time and patience for the slow life. One rule of thumb is to shop around, as boats vary hugely in quality and you want to be sure that you will have a somewhat decent home for the next four to ten days. Your ticket will include hammock space and rudimentary food, but beverages are extra and will probably be expensive on board – it's best to bring your own supplies. You should also bring a hammock, rope, insect repellent, a sleeping bag (it gets cold) and aim to be on board well before departure to ensure that you don't get the hammock space right next to the toilets.

By bicycle

If you're fit and hardy enough to consider **cycling** in South America – and it certainly is a beautiful way to see the land – there are a few common-sense rules to follow before you go. Given the nature of the terrain, a mountain bike is invariably best, unless you're planning to stick to paved roads and well-travelled routes, in which case a (good quality) touring or road bike would suffice. Bikes and bike parts tend to be of a lesser quality in South America than in other parts of the world, so it's a good idea to bring your own bicycle and to give it a thorough maintenance overhaul before you go, carry a basic repair kit and to check your machine daily when you arrive. Weather can be a problem, especially in Patagonia, where winds can reach 50mph, and be aware that bicycle theft – particularly in larger towns and cities – is common; it's probably best to pay someone local to mind your bike if you want to sightsee.

Finally, remember that South American drivers can be a hazard, so try to avoid major roads and motorways if at all possible.

Hitchhiking

Hitchhiking is still fairly common in South America, and you shouldn't find it too hard to get a ride with a truck driver or another morning traveller if you're on the road early enough. Be aware, though, that an annoying sidebar to the availability of rides means that many drivers now expect to be paid for their services – it's only in Argentina, Brazil, Chile and Uruguay that hitchhiking seems to be understood to be free. Prices are usually around that of a bus fare, but if you head to the local truck park or refuelling station (most towns have one), you can ask around to get a good idea of the going rate. Hitchhiking in South America, like anywhere in the world, is a somewhat perilous enterprise – travellers should be aware that they do so at their own risk. Couples and groups are safest; women should never, ever, hitchhike alone.

Overland tours

Sometimes the best way to ensure that you see a good part of the region is to take part in an organized tour, at least for part of your stay in South America. Tour operators offer everything from exuberant all-inclusive bus trips, where you stay in hostels and camp, to specialist excursions for those interested in eco-tourism, mountain biking, hiking, canoeing or other forms of cultural or adventure travel. A brief selection of specialist tours is listed in the box below – for more information, see the relevant country chapter.

Specialist overland tours in South America

In North America

Above the Clouds ⓣ1-800/233-4499 or 802/482-4848, ⓦwww.aboveclouds.com
Adventure Center ⓣ1-800/228-8747 or 510/654-1879, ⓦwww.adventurecenter.com
Backroads ⓣ1-800/462-2848 or 510/527-1555, ⓦwww.backroads.com
Himalayan Travel ⓣ1-800/225-2380 or

203/743-2349, Ⓦwww.himalayantravelinc.com
Wilderness Travel Ⓣ1-800/368-2794 or 510/558-2488, Ⓦwww.wildernesstravel.com

In the UK

Adventure Bound Ⓣ0800/316 2717, Ⓦwww.adventurebound.co.uk
Blue Green Adventures Ⓣ020/8947 2756
Dragoman, Ⓣ01728/861133, Ⓦwww.dragoman.co.uk
Encounter Overland Ⓣ020/7370 6845, Ⓦwww.encounter.co.uk
Footprint Adventures Lincoln Ⓣ01552/804929, Ⓦwww.footprint-adventures.co.uk
Guerba Expeditions Wiltshire Ⓣ01373/826611, Ⓦwww.guerba.co.uk

In Australia and New Zealand

Adventure Specialists Australia Ⓣ02/92612927
Austral Tours Australia Ⓣ1800/620833 or 03/9600 1733, Ⓦwww.australtours.com
Kumuka Expeditions Australia Ⓣ1800/804277 or 02/9279 0491, Ⓦwww.kumuka.com.au
Latin Link Adventure New Zealand Ⓣ03/525 9945, Ⓦwww.latinlink.co.nz

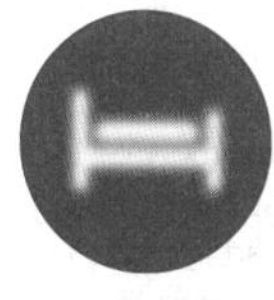

Accommodation

The range of accommodation available in South America – and the range of price and quality that goes with it – is enormous, and should you be leaving on a multi-country tour, you'll find that the US$4/£2.50 that buys you a night's rest in Ecuador or Peru won't even stretch to breakfast in the Southern cone or French Guiana.

Most tourist offices will happily provide a list of available accommodation but bear in mind that establishments often have to pay to be included on these lists and that they may have little to offer outside the main tourist hotspots. Generally, however, tourist boards will not recommend specific accommodation, nor will they book it – for this, you either have to go through a travel agent or do it yourself, and some Spanish or Portuguese will be necessary if you leave it until you get there – the **Web** is a great place to look for accommodation choices in advance, as you can often check out rates, photographs of properties and rooms, and special offers and amenities before you decide on a place.

Usually there is no shortage of places to stay, but use common sense if you plan to be somewhere at the time of a local **festival**, such as in Rio for Carnaval. Obviously, accommodation fills up really quickly at these times, and it's best to book accommodation well in advance.

While the types of lodging described below offers an overview of your options in Latin America, names, classifications and prices vary from country to country. For information regarding the nomenclature in a specific country, check the "Accommodation" section of the relevant chapter.

Hospedajes, residencias, albergues and pensiónes

These categories of accommodation are all used throughout South America, and are pretty much interchangeable terms although **pensiónes** (known as *pensoes* in Portuguese) and **residenciales** are officially the most basic forms of accommodation. Generally, the Andean countries are the least expensive, and you should be able to find a decent *residenciale* or *pensión* for under

Accommodation price codes

All accommodation listed in this guide has been graded according to the following **price categories**. Rates are generally for the **least expensive double or twin room in high season**, and do not include tax, except where this is explicitly stated. For ease of comparison, local prices have been converted to **US dollars**.

- ❶ up to US$5
- ❷ US$5–10
- ❸ US$10–15
- ❹ US$15–25
- ❺ US$25–40
- ❻ US$40–60
- ❼ US$60–90
- ❽ US$90–120
- ❾ US$120+

US$5, for which you should get a bed and maybe a desk and chair, but little else – you will have to share a bathroom, and the water may or may not be hot, or may be hot for just a few hours a day. In Brazil, the room cost will usually also include breakfast but most other places are room only. In the south of Argentina and Chile, you can expect to spend around US$35 a night – check out the quality of the local *casas familiares* (family houses where you stay with a local family in a room in their house), which can also be the best value for money in these areas.

Hoteles, hosterías and haciendas

Hostales tend to fill the gap between the totally basic *pensión* and the rather more classy hotel and come in many architectural shapes, sizes and forms. Usually they include private bathrooms and hot water, clean towels and maybe a television and cost from $5 to $15/night.

Hosterías and **haciendas** are lovely examples of South American architecture, often old, sprawling estates converted into hotels in the middle of nowhere, and are perhaps the grandest places to stay in the continent. They are often furnished in period style and offer excellent home-cooked meals, fires and hot water and maybe a swimming pool. Be aware that *hostería* can also refer to a family-style hotel complex out of town, usually an anything-but-charming experience – be sure to check which kind of *hostería* you're getting first.

Camping

Camping is most popular in the southern region of Latin America, particularly in the cone areas of Argentina and Chile. Where no official campsite is available, "wild" camping is practised, and often people set up their tents on football pitches, fields or gas stations. If you decide to take the unofficial route, you're best to check with the landowner or a town official to make sure they don't mind you being there. Apart from pissing off the locals, you should be wary of making your presence too well known, as thieves are attracted to unsecured valuables and vulnerable foreigners. Never set up camp on a beach – quite apart from the fact that they tend to be deserted and thus will make you easy prey for any local *ladrón*, they are inhabited by sandflies, whose bites can carry all kinds of nasty diseases.

Most official sites are usually well equipped, with hot, running water, toilets, firepits and maybe even a laundry for around $5/night. Some places – like those in Chile for example – charge a four- or five-person minimum, which can make camping a costly venture if you're travelling solo or as a couple. Camping is not really a popular or viable option in the northern countries, and is practically nonexistent in Colombia, French Guiana and Paraguay – in the more remote areas, though, you can set up your tent just about anywhere. It's best to bring your tent and accessories from home, as they can be hard to get outside major cities and national park areas.

If you plan to cook your own food on a **camping stove**, the best idea is to bring one that burns different types of fuel including unleaded petrol and *benzina blanca* (kerosene) which is readily available from most *ferreterías* (hardware stores). An alternative is an alcohol-burning stove, but be sure to carry a lot of fuel with you if you bring one of these; gas stoves are possibly the worst option, as gas cylinders are not widely available. Be sure to know whether you use butane or propane gas.

Youth hostels

Youth hostels are not usually the cheapest or most viable option in South America, but they do exist and can be an excellent place to meet other young travellers, and a good way to ward off loneliness if you're going it alone. Prices average around US$6–10/night and most hostels are open year round, although some only open in January and February, for the South American summer. The IYHF has hostels in Argentina, Brazil, Chile, Colombia (Bogotá only), Peru and Uruguay.

Hostelling organizations

Hostelling International Argentina / Red Argentina se Alojamiento para Jóvenes (RAAJ) Florida 835, piso 3, Buenos Aires ⓣ011/4511-8712, ⓦwww.hostels.org.ar
Asociación Argentina de Albergues de la Juventud (AAAJ) Oficina 6, piso 2, Talcahuano 214, Buenos Aires ⓣ011/4476-1001
Federação Brasileira dos Albergues de Juventude (FBAJ) R da Assambleia 10, room 1211 ⓣ531-1129, ⓦwww.hostel.org.br
Asociación Chilena de Albergues Turísticos Juveniles Hernando de Aguirre 201, Providencia, Santiago ⓣ233-3220, ⓔachatj@hostelling.co.cl
Asociación Peruana de Albergues Turísticos Juveniles Avenida Casimiro Ulloa 328, Miraflores, Lima ⓣ446-5488
Asociación de Alberguistas del Uruguay Calle Pablo de María 1583, Montevideo ⓣ400-4245

Food and drink

As you would expect from a continent of this size, food varies from country to country and region to region. You can count on beans and rice being prevalent in most cheap street cuisine, excellent fresh seafood in coastal areas and the best steak in the world in Argentina. A hearty snack from a street vendor should rarely set you back more than a couple of US dollars.

South America is not as difficult as you might think for **vegetarians** – most towns have a central market selling cheap fruit and vegetables – and all but the snootiest restaurants will probably adapt something on the menu for you. Be sure to know how to say "I don't eat meat" (*No como carne* in Spanish and *Eu nao como carne* in Portuguese) and "I am a vegetarian" (*Soy vegetariano/a* or *Sou vegetariano/a*).

Meals and snacks

Some accommodation – especially in Brazil – will include **breakfast** (*desayuno*) in the price of a night's stay, which can be anything from coffee or tea and rolls (the usual) to fruit, eggs, cheese, meat and juice. **Lunch** (*almuerzo*) is generally the cheapest meal of the day, as well as the largest, with most restaurants offering enormous lunch specials for very reasonable prices. Expect to pay no more than US$5 for this, usually called the *menú del día*. Those craving fast food will often find it near bus stations, and should try and find some of the local pizza – the offerings in Argentina and Uruguay are particularly good. **Dinner** (*cena*) is the most varied meal, with some of the larger, more cosmopolitan cities offering cuisines from all over the world. In some countries, such as Argentina, it is not uncommon for dinner to

Tipping

You should tip **at least ten percent** for most services in South America although in restaurants this may be included in the bill. If you really want to ensure your waiters – and not the restaurant management – get the money, though, you should tip them personally as well.

begin until around 10 or 11pm. If you have a sweet tooth, pastries and chocolate items are usually excellent, as is *manjarblanco* or *arequipe*, a delicious fudge-like candy.

Fruits and vegetables

The variety of fruit and vegetables is amazing, and travellers have no excuse for not getting their RDA of vitamin C. If you're eating **fruit** raw, try to avoid anything that you can't peel – the same goes for vegetables, and you should avoid uncooked vegetable dishes such as salads as a general rule. *Plátanos* (bananas) are pretty ubiquitous, and often get served up in the most unexpected places, often as a sort of savoury side dish to your main meal. Apart from bananas, tropical fruits such as mango, custard apple, passion fruit (*maracuyó* in Spanish, *maracujá* in Portuguese) and guava are common, as well as several less famous fruits, which vary from area to area.

Vegetables include delicious avocados (*paltas* in Spanish, *abacates* in Portuguese), used as a central element to much cooking; *palmitos*, or palm hearts.

Black beans are plentiful in South America, and especially good in Brazil, where meat eaters should make sure to try the *feijoada completa*, wherein the beans are cooked with spices, herbs and a hodgepodge of many meats including smoked sausage and jerked beef. Potatoes are known as *papas* and are also common – one of the best ways to have them is in *lacro de papas*, a potato and cheese soup. Similar to potatoes are *yuca* (cassava) and sweet potatoes, fellow tubular vegetables used for stews, soups, roasting, grilling and generally filling up.

Meat and seafood

Chicken and rice is something of a continental speciality here, and is often one of the cheapest things you can eat. Each country seems to prepare it a little differently – look for *arroz con pollo* in any Spanish-speaking country and see what you think. Argentina is renowned for the quality of its beef, and rightly so. Here, and throughout much of Latin America, you can walk into any **parilla** (or steakhouse) and sample a juicy steak, cooked to your preference, for as little as US$5 and rarely more than US$10. There are different cuts of meat, from the standard *bife de costilla* (T-bone steak) to a *bife de chorizo* (sirloin) and they can be prepared *a punto* (medium) or *jugoso* (rare) – don't even bother asking for anything else. At the other end of the scale, the cheapest meats are usually the least appealing, and include *cordero* (mutton), *cabrito* (goat) and *llama* (um, llama). *Cuy* is a local delicacy and may be offered to you whole and roasted on a plate. It allegedly tastes like a mixture between chicken and rabbit – just be aware that that's a guinea pig you're about to scoff.

Empanadas (*empadão* in Brazil) are great for a late afternoon snack if you're hungry before the late dinner hour kept by most restaurants. The standard *empanada* is basically a meat pie, while *empanadas de humita* are vegetarian versions with sweetcorn, cheese and squash. Similar are *salteñas* and *salgados*, chicken or meat pasties popular in Bolivia and Brazil.

Fish is excellent along coastal areas, less fresh in inland cities. Some of the most popular fishes are prawns (*langostinos* in Spanish, *camarãos* in Portuguese), one of the safest forms of seafood, as they are usually cooked long before they are prepared. *Parihuela* and *cazuela* are delicious fish stews, kind of like a hearty bouillabaisse, and no visit to the Northeast of Brazil is complete without trying *moqueca*, a seafood

Additional local **specialities** and particular eating habits of individual countries are listed under "Food and drink" in each country's Basics section; a Spanish and Portuguese **menu reader** can be found on pp.1081 and 1087.

stew cooked in palm-oil-based *dende* sauce.

Remember that meat can carry bacteria and disease – it's not really a good idea to buy meat dishes from street vendors, and pork and llama meat often contains parasites. Ensure that your food is well cooked and that it is still hot when you eat it. Another word of caution – it may be wise to avoid mussels and seafood from vendors, as they can carry *marea roja*, which kills humans.

Alcohol

Chile and Argentina produce world-class **wines**, and these are inexpensive in most of the region, and far superior to their continental counterparts. *Cerveza/cerveja* (**beer**) is everywhere; locally brewed offerings are inevitably cheaper than national or international ones, and draught beers are usually cheaper than bottled ones. *Caña* or *aguardiente* is a spirit made from sugarcane, and potent it is too. *Ron* (**Rum**) is produced throughout much of the continent, and tends to be very acceptable, while Brazilians prefer a sugarcane-based rum called *cachaça*. Imported **spirits** are available in most large towns and cities, but tend to be very expensive.

Non-alcoholic beverages

Coffee seems to be the national drink of South America, and is popular throughout. It can often be instant or made from a liquid concentrate, though, so ask for *café puro* if you want the real thing, and request *café negro* (*cafézinho* in Brazil) if you want it black. Names for white coffee vary hugely from country to country – check the separate chapters for local information. *Café con leche* tends to be very milky indeed, often closer to a mug of coffee-like milk than milky coffee. *Mate de coca* a delicious alternative to coffee; it is a tea made from the leaf of the coca plant. *Tés de hierba* (herbal **teas**) are usually much better than the standard black variety (*té*), and more readily available.

Unsurprisingly, *zumos* (**fruit juices**, *sucos* in Brazil) are excellent, and also form the basis for more exotic *batidos* or *licuados*, smoothie-like drinks often made with fruit juice and milk. A *vitamina* is similar, but made with vegetables too. Other tasty beverages include coconut water, a deliciously refreshing drink from the green coconut; and *agua de panela* or *mosto*, sugared water often straight from the sugarcane.

It's best not to drink tap water at all, unless you purify it – *agua minerale* (bottled **mineral water**) is available pretty much everywhere, and comes either *con gaz* (carbonated) or *sin gaz*. Similarly, steer clear of ice – ask for drinks *sin hielo*. **Soft drinks** are also ubiquitous, and often the word *cola* simply refers to any kind of canned, carbonated, sugary drink.

Endangered species

Be wary of some of the local delicacies offered to you in South America. These can include turtle eggs, monkey (*mono*) and lobster, which any conscientious traveller should avoid.

Communications

It's easy enough in the more developed South American countries to keep in contact while you're there. What follows is general advice about communications across South America; country-specific information on phone, mail and Internet facilities is given at the beginning of each chapter.

Mail

Post offices in cities and major towns offer a wide range of services; those in villages are much more basic, with shorter opening hours and often infuriatingly slow service. Most hotels in capital cities sell stamps and have a postbox – if you are staying in such an establishment, this can often be the most convenient way to send a letter home. Expect airmail to take up to one week to Western Europe and the USA from Peru, Venezuela and Ecuador, 3–4 days from Bolivia, Uruguay and Chile, 4–6 days from Brazil and Paraguay, 5–7 days from Colombia, Guyana and French Guiana and a week to ten days from Argentina. Travellers can receive mail via **poste restante** throughout the region, but should be aware that in some countries, such as Argentina, it can cost up to US$1.50 to pick up mail. The system is efficient enough but tends to be available only at the main post office in cities, or even only in the capital, and not in small towns and villages. Most post offices hold letters for a maximum of one month, though some hold them for up to three.

Telephones

You can make **direct-dial** calls from public telephones in most Latin American countries, apart from some of the more remote areas, where calls must be made through an operator. **Public phone boxes** can be found in shops and restaurants, and local calls can be made very cheaply using coins or – in larger cities – cards, available from newspaper kiosks, where you will also find metal discs, sometimes needed for older phone boxes.

In general, calls are cheaper between the hours of 7pm and 5am and at weekends, although some countries in the region may start their cheap rates before or after this. See individual country chapters for details. International phone calls are, in general, expensive from South America. A three-minute daytime call to the UK from Brazil, for example, will cost around £6, while the same call would cost US$7.50 to the USA or Canada.

Avoid calling long distance from hotels unless you have a cheap long-distance

Calling Latin America

To **phone abroad** from home, you must first dial the international access code followed by the country code, the area code and then the phone number.

IDD codes for calling from home

Australia ☎0011
Canada ☎011
Ireland ☎00
New Zealand ☎00
UK ☎00
US ☎011

Country codes for South America

Argentina ☎54
Bolivia ☎591
Brazil ☎55
Chile ☎56
Colombia ☎57
Ecuador ☎593
French Guiana ☎594
Guyana ☎592
Paraguay ☎595
Peru ☎51
Suriname ☎597
Uruguay ☎598
Venezuela ☎58

phone card with a free or local access number; even then check to see if the establishment charges for such calls.

Calling home from abroad

One of the most convenient ways of phoning home from abroad is via a **telephone charge card** from your phone company back home. Using a PIN number, you can make calls from most hotel, public and private phones that will be charged to your account. Since most major charge cards are free to obtain, it's certainly worth getting one at least for emergencies; enquire first though whether your destination is covered, and bear in mind that rates aren't necessarily cheaper than calling from a public phone. In some countries, such as Ecuador, these phonecards will only work from residential lines.

In the **US and Canada**, AT&T, MCI, Sprint, Canada Direct and other North American long-distance companies all enable their customers to make credit-card calls while overseas, billed to your home number. Call your company's customer service line to find out if they provide service from the countries you intend to visit and, if so, what the toll-free access code is.

In **the UK and Ireland**, British Telecom (Ⓣ0800/345144, Ⓦwww.chargecard.bt.com) will issue free to all BT customers the BT Charge Card, which can be used in 116 countries; AT&T (dial Ⓣ0800/890011, then 888/641-6123 when you hear the AT&T prompt to be transferred to the Florida Call Centre, free 24 hours) also has the Global Calling Card.

To call **Australia and New Zealand** from overseas, telephone charge cards such as Telstra Telecard or Optus Calling Card in Australia and Telecom NZ's Calling Card can be used to make calls abroad, which are charged back to a domestic account or credit card. Apply to Telstra (Ⓣ1800/038000), Optus (Ⓣ1300/300937) or Telecom NZ (Ⓣ04/801 9000).

Calling home from overseas

To **phone abroad** from the following countries, you must first dial the **international access code** followed by the **country code**, the area code and then the phone number.

Note that the initial zero is omitted from the area code when dialling the UK, Ireland, Australia and New Zealand from abroad.

Country codes

Australia international access code + 61 + city code
New Zealand international access code + 64 + city code
Republic of Ireland international access code + 353 + city code
UK international access code + 44 + city code
USA and Canada international access code + 1 + area code

International access codes

Argentina Ⓣ00
Bolivia Ⓣ0010 (Entel) Ⓣ0011 (AES) Ⓣ0012 (Teledata) Ⓣ0013 (Boliviatel)
Brazil Ⓣ0014 (Brasil Telecom) Ⓣ0015 (Telefonica) Ⓣ0021 (Embratel) Ⓣ0023 (Intelig) Ⓣ0031 (Telemar)
Chile Ⓣ00
Colombia Ⓣ009 (Telecom) Ⓣ007 (ETB/Mundo) Ⓣ005 (Orbitel)
Ecuador Ⓣ00
French Guiana Ⓣ00
Guyana Ⓣ001
Paraguay Ⓣ00
Peru Ⓣ00
Suriname Ⓣ002
Uruguay Ⓣ00
Venezuela Ⓣ00

Mobile phones

If you want to use your **mobile phone** abroad, you'll need to check with your phone provider whether it will work overseas, and what the call charges are. Unless you have a tri-band phone, it is unlikely that a mobile bought for use outside the US will work inside the States and vice versa – for details of which mobiles will work outside the US, contact your mobile service provider.

Most mobiles in Australia and New Zealand use **GSM**, which works well in many South American countries.

In the UK and Ireland, for all but the very top-of-the-range packages, you'll have to inform your phone provider before going abroad to get international access switched on. You may get charged extra for this depending on your existing package and where you are travelling to. You are also likely to be charged extra for incoming calls when abroad, as the people calling you will be paying the usual rate. If you want to retrieve messages while you're away, you'll have to ask your provider for a new access code, as your home one is unlikely to work abroad.

Most UK mobiles use GSM too, which gives access to most countries in the region. Tri-band phones will automatically switch to the US frequency, but these can be pricey. For further information about using your phone abroad, check out ⓦwww.telecomsadvice.org.uk/features/using_your_mobile_abroad.

Mobile phone networks in South America

Peru, Chile and Bolivia operate a **GSM** 1900 network, as do Argentina and Paraguay (urban areas only). Brazil has recently implemented a GSM 1800 network and many IS-style networks are also in place. In French Guiana and Venezuela, there is a GSM 900 network although coverage tends to be limited to major cities and their suburbs; Suriname has a new GSM 900/1800 network in place but coverage is really only available in Paramaribo. Colombia, Uruguay and Ecuador only operate US-style AMPS networks and GSM phones will not work in these countries. Guyana still has a tri-band network in use.

Email

One of the best ways to keep in touch while travelling is to sign up for a **free Internet email address** that can be accessed from anywhere, for example YahooMail or Hotmail – accessible through ⓦwww.yahoo.com and ⓦwww.hotmail.com. Once you've set up an account, you can use these sites to pick up and send mail from any Internet café, or hotel with Internet access.

ⓦwww.kropla.com is a useful website giving details of how to plug your laptop in when abroad, phone country codes around the world, and information about electrical systems in different countries.

Internet access in South America

Main cities in Peru, Bolivia, Brazil and Argentina have both **Internet cafés** and public Internet booths, as do Chile, Uruguay, Venezuela and Colombia, albeit to a lesser extent. In smaller towns in Brazil you may be able to access the Internet at a post office. Large hotels in the region often supply Internet service also. There are fewer Internet services in Ecuador and Paraguay, just a few in Georgetown, Guyana, and in French Guiana they are limited mainly to Cayenne.

The media

In addition to the information available on the Internet (see p.24), an innumerable array of newspapers and magazines offers local, regional and national news and listings for visitors once they've arrived. These will, of course, be largely incomprehensible if you are unfamiliar with Spanish or Portuguese, but if you need to find out the latest goings on in the world, rest assured that most large cities carry the major foreign newspapers.

There is also a decent range of English-language media in South America and, if your radio has decent reception, you'll be able to pick up English-language radio in most regions.

English-language radio in South America

The **BBC** world service (Ⓦwww.bbc.co.uk/worldservice), **Radio Canada** (Ⓦwww.rcinet.ca) and **Voice of America** (Ⓦwww.voa.gov) all have frequencies around the globe, listed on their respective websites.

English-language press in South America

Among the major English-language publications in South America are:
Argentina *Buenos Aires Herald*
Bolivia *The Bolivian Times*
Brazil *The Brazil Herald*
Colombia *The Colombian Post*
Guyana *The Guyana Chronicle*
Peru *The Lima Times*

Public holidays and festivals

Travelling through South America entails negotiating a variety of public holidays that change from country to country. The essential ones are listed in the "Opening hours and public holidays" section of each chapter, but bear in mind that, particularly in more remote areas, some towns and villages celebrate saints' days and other local holidays that shut down businesses and make travel difficult. Check with local tourist information offices for more details.

South Americans are not known to shy away from an excuse to celebrate, and we have included the finer **festivals** in the relevant chapters. Among them are Venezuela's *Diablos Danzantes*, held throughout the country on Corpus Christi; November's bullfighting festivals in Lima, Peru; Pwadwah, the Hindu spring festival celebrated in Guyana; Ecuador's Yamor festival, held in Otavalo in the first two weeks of September and costume, masks and dance and the Rio Film Festival, in September. For more specific information, see the relevant chapter.

Carnaval

Every country in Latin America has some form of carnival (known in Spanish and

Portuguese as **Carnaval**); the exact time varies, but the official celebrations usually take place on the days before Ash Wednesday and Lent, with the months and weeks beforehand almost as lively as excitement fills the air. There are national variations of course: in Ecuador, for instance, the festivities are most visibly represented by the water fights taking place everywhere in the country. There are a couple of locations where Carnaval has become legendary, such as Oruro in Bolivia.

The most famous Carnaval of all, however, has to be the one that takes place in **Rio de Janeiro**, Brazil. This variegated orgy lasts for weeks before and after the "official" Carnaval time and is an extravagant, heady mix of dance, sweat, drink, laughter and colour. Brazilians go all out to make their festivities the best in the world, and visitors from all over flock to see the mass of flesh, dress and fun on display. For a detailed account of Rio's Carnaval, see p.339.

Outdoors and eco-tourism

South America has long been a popular destination for outdoor types, and there's a wide range of challenging and more intermediate options available. The mountains provide particularly fun opportunities, with climbing and skiing both being well represented. All those ups and downs also make for challenging hiking and mountain biking. Scuba diving is good off the Caribbean coast, in Venezuela and spectacular in the Galápagos while white-water rafting is a high-thrill activity available mainly in Chile, but also in Peru and Venezuela.

Climbing

South America has to have some of the best and most challenging peaks in the world, but offers a lot to amateur and professional alike. The highest mountain in all of Latin America is **Aconagua** in Argentina, whose Fitz Roy range also offers some very exciting mountaineering opportunities. Other popular places to climb include the **Cordillera Blanca** in Peru and the **Cordillera Real** in Bolivia. Ecuador's "avenue of the volcanoes" also offers ample opportunity for mountain climbing. If you're planning to climb snow peaks, you'll need a full set of mountaineering equipment. Anyone planning to climb in South America needs to have worked on their physical strength, fitness and stamina – as well as their determination – long before setting off for the continent. Some peaks demand a certain level of technical expertise as well – check the relevant country chapter for more information.

Even if you are an experienced climber at home, you should consider climbing with an accredited local guide. Climbing is a risky enterprise, and guides have an intimate knowledge of climate, topographical features such as glaciers and potential avalanches and crevasses, and route options available to you. Guides also provide all equipment and food (bring your own unsalty, energy-packed nibbles and always have a full water bottle handy).

Finally, be sure to acclimatize before climbing any of the South American mountains. You should count on about a week's worth of acclimatization before you even attempt the highest peaks – several days spent at a height around 2500m or 3000m; then four or five days at between 3500 and 3800 metres, including some day hikes here and at a slightly higher altitude (up to 4200m, say). For more information on **altitude sickness** see p.28.

Climbing specialists

Adventure Consultants Limited 58 McDougall St, PO Box 97, Lake Wanaka, New Zealand ⓣ03/443 8711, US ⓣ970/453-1407, ⓦwww.adcenture.co.nz. Very professional climbing trips in the Andes.
Andes 37a St. Andrew Street, Castle Douglas, Kirkcudbrightshire, DG7 1EN, Scotland ⓣ01556/503929, ⓦwww.andes.co.uk. Mountain climbing, trekking and biking tours to the Andean countries.
Climb Ecuador 47 West 79th St, #1D, New York, NY 10024, ⓣ212/362-4721, ⓦwww.climbecuador.com. Organized Andean tours to Bolivia, Ecuador and Peru with a guaranteed maximum client guide ratio of 2:1.
Ecuadorian Alpine Institute Ramírez Dávalos 136 y Amazonas 1er Piso, Oficina 102, Quito, Ecuador ⓣ5932/256-5465, ⓦwww.volcanoclimbing.com. Climbing excursions and tailor-made activities in Ecuador, Peru and Bolivia.

Cycling

The variety of terrain in Latin America makes it a favourite for mountain bikers, many of whom come to **cycle** around a country or two while others attempt the entire continent. If you're planning to take on the Andes, make sure your bike is of excellent quality and in good shape before you travel; if you really want to rent a bike, go for a reputable brand such as Cannondale or Trek. Most airlines will let you check your bike on board, but make sure to phone them well in advance of your departure to notify them of your plans and check any regulations regarding removal of tyres or taking apart the frame. Some airlines don't charge at all for bicycle transportation; others charge up to US$100 or more, so be sure to factor this in when shopping around for a ticket (see p.11).

Cycling Specialists

Backroads 801 Cedar St, Berkeley, CA 94710 ⓣ510/527-1555 or 1-800/462-2848, ⓦwww.backroads.com. Biking and multi-sport tours to Argentina, Chile, Peru and Ecuador.
MTB Tours 3 de febrero 945 Capital Federal, Buenos Aires 1426, Argentina ⓣ011/477-6372, ⓦwww.mtbtours.com. Established, environmentally conscious mountain-biking specialist in Argentina offering tours to Patagonia, Chile, Uruguay and Brazil.
PAC Tour 202 Prairie Pedal Lane Sharon, WI 53585 ⓣ262/736-2453. Rated "the toughest tour in the world" these Peruvian jungle tours are not for the amateur or faint of heart, but the tough days of cycling are complemented by gourmet dinners and five star hotels.
Pacific Cycle Tours 17 Bay Heights Governors Bay, Lyttleton, 8033 New Zealand ⓣ03/329 9913. Bike tours of Chile, Argentina and Bolivia from this acclaimed New Zealand based company.

Diving

Diving is most popular on the Caribbean Coast of the continent, especially at the **Archipiélago Los Roques** and **Henri Pittier National Park** in Venezuela. It is also a favourite pastime in Colombia as well as at the Galápagos Islands – the latter is recommended for experienced drivers, although some dive outfits offer more gentle dives for beginners.

Diving specialists

Atlantis Centro Comercial Turistico Playa El Agua, Avenida 31 de Julio, Playa El Agua, Isla Margarita, Venezuela ⓣ295/2491325. Dive school at Venezuela's Margarita Island.
Caribbean Divers Carrera 2 #11A-98, El Rodadero, Santa Maria, Colombia ⓣ575/422-7015, ⓦwww.caribbeandiverscol.com. Diving in the vicinity of Colombia's Tayrona National Park.
Reef and Rainforest 1 The Plains, Totnes, Devon TQN 5DR, ⓣ01803/866965, ⓦwww.reefrainforest.co.uk. Company specializing in trips to natural history sites offers dive trips to the Galápagos for the more experienced diver.
Scuba Iguana Av Amazonas 1004 y Wilson, Oficina 4, Quito, Ecuador ⓣ5932/290-6666, ⓦwww.scubaiguana.com. Very professional dive outfit operating in the Galápagos. Staff speak good English.

Hiking

The entire continent is a gift to **trekkers**, and perhaps more so in the Andean region than anywhere else, where excellent trails form a network of breathtaking and challenging hikes. Well-laid trail paths wend their

Responsible tourism

Tourism is a mixed blessing for many poorer countries which, while they desperately need the money brought in by the industry – money that often enables endangered sites and species to remain protected – suffer terribly from the impact of irresponsible travellers and careless or rogue tour operators. There are many fragile eco-systems in South America that risk being set off balance and even destroyed by an influx of thoughtless tourists and guides. If you travel to South America you should be aware of **responsible tourism** as a concept and realize that you will have an impact wherever you go – the important thing is to minimize that impact and ensure that you don't support industries or companies that do environments or cultures more harm than good.

Ways in which you can impact negatively upon a country include upsetting cultural values, damaging eco-systems, and encouraging industries that unnecessarily destroy local livelihood, such as dynamite fishing, fast food and hotel chains. There are many micro-steps you can make to ensure that you don't add to the damage already wrought in Latin America. If you're booking an adventure holiday, check to see if the company employs local guides, respects community privacy and if they have been recognized by one of the watchdogs for environmental travel, such as **Green Stop** (Ⓦwww.greenstop.net), **Responsible Traveling**, PO Box 827, San Aselmo, CA 94979 Ⓣ415/258-6594 or **Tourism Concern**, Stapleton House, 277–281 Holloway Road, London N7 8HN Ⓣ020/7753 3330, Ⓦwww.tourismconcern.org.uk. The **Green Year Book** (Ⓦwww.greenyearbook.org) is also a good reference point. On a more local level, make sure you leave the great outdoors as you found it. Don't run down sand dunes or leave trash in national parks; use locally produced goods and services; accept local standards and don't complain when they don't "match up" to Western ideals. Be sure to ask locals if it's OK to take their photograph (or a photograph of their house) before you take them, and be prepared to offer something in exchange; respect people's privacy; don't eat endangered species – even if they are produced as a local "delicacy".

way across the southern countries, especially in the national parks of Argentina, Chile and Venezuela. Some travellers might prefer to explore beyond the set trail paths – if you want to do this, stick to Bolivia, Ecuador and Peru, where it is a very acceptable and common practice. The weather in South America can change rapidly – particularly in mountainous areas, where nights can be really cold – so pack for variable climates. Remember to bring plenty of water, a hat, a spare pair of socks, a jumper, a good topographical map, compass and first-aid kit, sunblock, a sandwich and some high-energy snack foods, insect repellent, sunglasses, a camera, quick-drying trousers, gloves, over-trousers, a light Gore-Tex style jacket...you get the idea. If you're planning to stay overnight, you should also have a waterproof tent, a warm sleeping bag, a reliable stove, waterproof matches and candles. Travellers who wish to hike in the Andes should remember that the heights are very high indeed and they will need a few days to acclimatize so as to avoid altitude sickness (see p.28). Never set off on a hike – no matter how short – without lots of water and a first-aid kit. The best plan is to start early in the morning and cover plenty of distance before the midday heat sets in, or else choose a hike that goes through forests.

Hiking specialists

Andean Trails The Clockhouse, Bonnington Mill Business Centre, 72 Newhaven Rd, Edinburgh EH6 5QG, Ⓣ0131/467 7086, Ⓦwww.andeantrails.co.uk. Hiking adventures in Peru, Bolivia and Patagonia.

Bike Hike Adventures 97 Markham St.,Toronto, ON M6G 2L7 Ⓣ416/534-7401, Ⓦwww.bikehike.com. Biking and hiking all over the continent.

Rio Hiking Tours Rua Coelho Neto, 70/401, Laranjeiras, Rio de Janeiro, RJ, 22231-110 Brazil, Ⓣ5521/9874-3698, Ⓦwww.riohiking.com.br. Hiking tours in the Amazonian rainforest.

The Adventure Climbing and Trekking Company of South America PO Box 100, Salida, CO 81201, ⓣ719/530-9053, ⓦwww.adventureco.com. Trips to Argentina, Peru, Bolivia and Ecuador.

White-water rafting

One of the biggest attractions of **white-water rafting** is the facility with which it enables you to see parts of the country that would be simply invisible by any other means. The most important country in the region for any white-water rafting enthusiast has to be Chile, with its dramatic rivers – some of them tributaries of the mighty Amazon – and beautiful scenery. The **Futaleufú**, **Maipó** and **Trancura** rivers are recommended for rafting and kayaking. Argentina and Ecuador also offer some river rafting – on the **Manso** and other Andean rivers in the former country, and in **Baños** and **Teno** in Ecuador. You could also try the **Apurimac**, **Tambopata** or **Urubamba** rivers in Peru and the **Orinoco** in Venezuela.

Usually, a white-water raft will carry six to eight people plus a guide. Runs are graded on a five-point scale, with anything up to a three being fine for beginners (except after heavy rains, when difficulty increases) and a five being strictly for weathered rafters only. Make sure that the company you decide to raft with is a professional outfit, with good quality life jackets and helmets, fully trained and accredited guides, and a safety kayak that accompanies the rafts on their trip.

White-water rafting specialists

Earthquest Adventure 2400 NW 80th St #114, Seattle, WA 98117 ⓣ206/334-3404, ⓦwww.earthquestadventure.com.

Earth River Expeditions 180 Towpath Road, Accord, NY 12404, ⓣ1800/643-2784, ⓦwww.earthriver.com. Rafting specialists with trips to Patagonia, Chile and Ecuador.

Mountain Travel-Sobek 6420 Fairmount Ave, El Cerrito, CA 94530 ⓣ1-888/687-6235 and 67 Verney Ave, High Wycombe, Bucks HP12 3ND, UK ⓣ01494/448901. ⓦwww.mtsobek.com. Multiactivity holidays with days spent rafting in Chile, Ecuador, Peru and Argentina.

Northwest Passage 1130 Greenleaf Ave, Wilmette, IL 60091 ⓣ847/256-4409, ⓦwww.nwpassage.com. Kayak and rafting adventures in Patagonia and on the Futaleufú.

Skiing and snowboarding

The South American **ski season** lasts from late May/early June to September and is centred mainly in Chile and Argentina. Theoretically, you can also ski in the Andes, but most visitors prefer to head to the less-treacherous slopes in the south.

Snow holiday operators

Adventures on Skis / Adventure Sport Holidays ⓣ1-800/628-9655 or 413/568-2855, ⓦwww.advonskis.com. Summer ski trips to Chile and Argentina.

Chilean Andean Snow Adventures CASA Tours, 187 Purdue Ave, Kensington, CA 94708 ⓣ1-888/449-2272, ⓦwww.casatours.com. Just like the name says – snow adventures in the Chilean and Argentine Andes.

Holidaze Ski Tours ⓣ1-800/526-2827 or 732/280-1120, ⓦwww.holidaze.com. Summer ski trips to Argentina and Chile with optional add-on city breaks to the capital of each.

Powderquest Tours ⓣ1-888/565-7158, ⓦwww.powderquest.com. Guided adventure skiing and snowboarding tours in the Andes and Patagonia.

Surfing

Surfing is one of the greatest pleasures afforded by South America's coastlines, and the keenest surfers head to the consistent waves at **Punta Hermosa**, near Lima in Peru, or to the southeast of Brazil. This is by no means the only place to catch a few waves though – other surfer havens can be found in Argentina, Chile and Uruguay. The best time to surf tends to be winter – between June and August.

Surf holiday operators

Surf Express 568 Highway AIA, Satellite Beach, FL 32937 ⓣ321/779-2124, ⓦwww.surfex.com. Specialist surfer holidays dedicated to finding the best waves in Peru, Galápagos and Ecuador.

Surfing Adventures ⓣ1-800/796-9110, ⓦwww.surfingadventures.com. Budget adventure travel specialists offering surf trips to Peru.

Waterways Surf Adventures 22611 Pacific Coast Highway, Malibu, CA 90265 ⓣ1-888/669-SURF, ⓦwww.waterwaystravel.com. Devoted solely to surfing, these folks say head for Peru.

Parks and reserves

There is an immense range of gorgeous vegetation and all manner of natural wonders – from mountains to waterfalls to volcanoes to rainforest – in South America's national parks, some of which allow you to camp, particularly those in Argentina and Chile. Some to look out for include **Parque Nacional Henri Pittier**, the oldest park in Venezuela and one famous for its rich variety of wildlife, thanks to the range of eco-systems; the Chilean **Parque Nacional Torres del Paines**, a beautiful and extremely popular spot for trekking, replete with waterfalls, rivers and lush forest; **Parque Nacional Machalilla**, the only national park situated on Ecuador's coastline; and the junglish **Parque Nacional Tayrona** on Columbia's Caribbean coast. There are more specific details on national and state parks in the relevant country chapters.

Spectator sports

The biggest spectator sports down this way are football, football, and football, followed by tennis, in Argentina, Chile and Paraguay, and basketball, which is played with particular devotion in Argentina and Paraguay. South America boasts some of the finest football teams in the world, and every fan knows the ferocious glory of the Argentine side, say, or the beauty displayed by Brazil. Perhaps because of its proximity to the teams of the West Indies, Guyana's national sport is cricket, whereas the least football-friendly nation in the continent, Venezuela, prefers baseball.

There are **soccer pitches** throughout the towns and villages in the continent, and you will see young men, old men, women and dogs all kicking a ball around and looking like they were born to play the beautiful game. The two most famous footballing countries in Latin America have to be **Argentina** and **Brazil**, but the sport is also hugely popular in Chile, Peru, Uruguay, Colombia, Suriname and Paraguay. The Argentine side has won the World Cup twice, in 1978 and 1986, while the reigning champs from Brazil won in 1958, 1962, 1970, 1994 and 2002. The football season officially runs from July to December, but there are matches all year round, and you should be able to secure tickets for a mind-blowing game for under US$10.

Safety and the police

South America is a continent categorized by poverty and attendant crime levels which, while much magnified by tales in the foreign news media, certainly exist. Be sure to consult the relevant "Safety and the police" section of each chapter.

In general, cities are more dangerous than rural areas, although the very deserted mountain plains can harbour bandits and hungry refugees. Many of the *barrios* of big cities are "no go" areas for tourists, as are the marginal areas near them. One of the biggest problems in the urban parts of the region is **theft**, with bag snatching, handbag slitting and even armed robbery being problems in cities such as Buenos Aires, Lima, Rio, Salvador, Georgetown and Cusco. Take particular care on the street, in taxis, and in restaurants. Any unsolicited approach from a stranger should be treated with the utmost suspicion, no matter how well dressed or trustworthy they may look – assailants have been known to slip drugs into food, drink or cigarettes and then proffer them to strangers. The drugs last for long enough for the attackers to rob (or worse) the victim and then escape. Always exercise common sense.

In some countries, notably **Guyana** and **Colombia**, crime levels can be particularly high, and indiscriminate shootings, kidnapping and armed robberies of foreigners have been reported. Tourists can make obvious targets, and it's best to try and avoid travelling after dark; if you have to go out then, make liberal use of taxis.

Drugs

In a word, don't. **Drug trafficking** is a huge, ugly and complicated enterprise in South America, and large-scale dealers love to prey on lost-looking foreigners. Make sure that you don't let anyone else touch your luggage, pack it yourself and don't carry anything – no matter how innocuous it may seem – for anyone else.

You will find that drugs, particularly marijuana and cocaine, are fairly ubiquitous in the region, but should be aware that they are very illegal – and severely punished – everywhere. Beware of anyone who offers you drugs or even a cigarette – these may be laced, and often these substances, once taken, suffice to render the tourist incapable while they are robbed, blackmailed or worse. Tourists are likely to come off much worse than locals at the hands of the South American police, something of which the dealers and pushers are very aware. If you happen to be visiting a region famed for drug trafficking, stay well away from anything that looks (or smells) like trouble.

The only legal drugs on sale in South America are the leaves of **coca**, which are only available in Bolivia and Peru. They are usually used to make *mate de coca*, a

Political upheaval in Colombia

Some countries are more risky for the traveller than others, with Colombia perhaps being the worst. Political and criminal violence, urban terrorism and kidnapping are all problems in Colombia, especially in Bogotá. Outside the capital, the dangers lie in **guerrilla and paramilitary activity**, and even backpackers have been kidnapped and caught up in terrorist activity – some have even been killed. The most dangerous areas of all are not actually open to foreigners – under the direct command of the armed forces, they have been somewhat euphemistically designated "Zones of rehabilitation and consolidation". Travellers to countries bordering Colombia should also take especial care and if possible avoid these border areas, which have become hide-outs for kidnappers and guerrillas focusing on foreign nationals. For more information, see p.592.

hugely popular tea in the Andes, and one that's claimed to cure altitude sickness (among other things). Some people chew the leaves as this is meant to produce a mildly intoxicated state, but the taste and texture involved in such an enterprise may well convince you that you can do without the alleged high. If you want to try *mate de coca* or chewing on coca leaves, fine, but be aware that there is a possibility that you could test positive for cocaine use in the weeks following your trip.

Preventative measures

There are obvious **preventative measures** you can take to avoid being mugged: avoid isolated and poorly lit areas, especially at night; never walk along a beach alone, or even – if you're women – in a pair. Keep a particular eye out in heavily touristed areas and watch out on public transport and at bus stations, where pickpocketing is rife. If you need to hail a taxi, get someone at your hotel to recommend one, or hail a moving one – never get into a "taxi" that just happens to be parked at the curbside. Avoid wearing expensive or flashy jewellery and watches, dress down, and keep cameras out of sight.

Car jackings can also be a problem, particularly in certain areas of Brazil. When driving in the city, keep doors locked and windows closed, particularly at night, and be especially vigilant at traffic lights.

In case you are **mugged** or **robbed**, you should make sure that you have a photocopy of all your documents – passport, tickets, etc – in a safe place. Call the local police immediately and tell them what happened.

Cultural hints

There are certain rules you should observe while travelling to ensure that you don't distress or offend local populations. Remember that you will be seen to be in a position of privilege (you could afford to come here, after all) and that you should respect rather than abuse local customs, habits and hospitality.

People generally shake hands upon introduction throughout the continent, and express pleasure at having made the acquaintance – no matter how briefly – of others. It is common to wish people you meet on the street "*Buenos días*" ("*bom dia*" in Brazil) or "*buenos tardes*" ("*boa tarde*" in Brazil). Politeness is generally a way of life in South America, and pleasantries are always exchanged before getting to any kind of business. You should also be polite to street vendors, no matter how annoyed you get with their peddling of their wares. Remember that this is their livelihood and smile, saying "*no, gracias*" or "*não*, *obrigado*", but if you decide to buy something, remember also to be firm – ask the price and then confirm it before proffering any cash. Dress with respect **in official or religious buildings**.

Crafts and markets

Shops and markets in South America tend to offer a wide range of beautifully crafted goods and antiques for the visitor. Prices are usually very reasonable; you can bargain a little in markets and outside the main tourist drags, but only do so if you really think the item is worth less than its asking price. Make sure to check that you are not purchasing objects that have been plundered from the jungle or that are made from endangered species – remember, tourism can harm as well as help.

Each country – and many regions – have their own specialities in the marketplace. As a rule of thumb, native crafts are usually of the best quality – and cheapest – when bought close to the source. Buying such items, rather than mass produced alternatives, is a good way to help local **artesania** and give something back to the communities you're visiting. In Bolivia, for example, look for llama blankets while Chile is a good bet for a poncho and Peru for an alpaca sweater; Brazil has excellent handmade silver, jewellery and hammocks, while Chile is good for copper work and French Guiana for gold. Gems – especially emeralds – are to be found in Brazil and Colombia; semi-precious stones such as agate and jade abound in Chile. For beautiful jewellery using local gold, silver and precious stones, Guyana is hard to beat. Textiles, too, are remarkable: the unique *ñandutí* lace of Paraguay; Uruguayan suede clothing; the *shigra* bags of Ecuador and the Javanese *batik* and cotton hammocks of Suriname are among some of the discoveries to be made.

If, however, it's western-style shopping you're really hankering for, Buenos Aires is known to be the most upscale marketplace in Latin America; what it displays in variety it usually matches in price.

Travellers with disabilities

South America is not the friendliest of destinations for travellers with disabilities and many places are downright inaccessible. As a rule, though, the more modern the society, the more likely you are to find services for physically challenged travellers – this means that while Bolivia and Paraguay are pretty impenetrable, much of inhabitable Chile and Argentina, as well as several cities in Brazil, may prove accessible.

Unfortunately, though, you may need to compromise over destination – big hotels in major cities that are very much on the tourist trail are much more likely to have facilities to cater to your needs than idyllic *cabañas* in the middle of nowhere. You might be limited as regards mobility, too, as local buses will probably prove difficult and you might need to settle for taxi services or internal flights. In any case, check with one of the agencies below before planning anything – if anyone knows how to get over inaccessibility hiccups, it is these agents.

Contacts for travellers with disabilities

In the US and Canada

Directions Unlimited 123 Green Lane, Bedford Hills, NY 10507 ⓣ914/241-1700 or 1-800/533-5343. Tour operator specializing in custom tours for people with disabilities.

Mobility International USA 451 Broadway, Eugene, OR 97401, voice and TDD ⓣ541/343-1284, ⓦwww.miusa.org. Information and referral services, access guides, tours and exchange programmes. Annual membership US$35 (includes quarterly newsletter).

Society for the Advancement of Travelers with Handicaps 347 Fifth Ave, New York, NY 10016 ⓣ212/447-7284, ⓦwww.sath.org. SATH is a non-profit educational organization that has actively represented travellers with disabilities since 1976.

Travel Information Service Moss Rehabilitation Hospital, 1200 West Tabor Rd, Philadelphia, PA 19141 ⓣ215/456-9600. Information and referral service for disabled travellers – they cannot book accommodation, and only accept queries by mail or telephone.

Twin Peaks Press Box 129, Vancouver, WA 98661 ⓣ360/694-2462 or 1-800/637-2256, ⓦwww.twinpeak.virtualave.net. Publisher of the *Directory of Travel Agencies for the Disabled* (US$19.95), listing more than 370 agencies worldwide; *Travel for the Disabled* (US$19.95); the *Directory of Accessible Van Rentals* (US$12.95) and *Wheelchair Vagabond* (US$19.95), loaded with personal tips.

Wheels Up! (no address) ⓣ1-888/389-4335, ⓦwww.wheelsup.com. Provides discounted airfare, tour and cruise prices for disabled travellers; also publishes a free monthly newsletter and has a comprehensive website.

In the UK and Ireland

Access Travel 6 The Hillock, Astley, Lancashire M29 7GW ⓣ01942/888844, ⓦwww.access-travel.co.uk. Small tour operator that can arrange flights, transfer and accommodation. Personally checks out places before recommendation and can guarantee accommodation standards in many countries – for places they do not cover, they can arrange flight-only deals.

Disability Action Group 2 Annadale Ave, Belfast BT7 3JH, ⓣ028/9049 1011. Provides information about access for disabled travellers abroad.

Holiday Care 2nd floor, Imperial Building, Victoria Rd, Horley, Surrey RH6 7PZ ⓣ0845/124 9971, Minicom ⓣ0845/124 9976, ⓦwww.holidaycare.org.uk. Providers of a £5 booklet about accessible cruise holidays and information about financial help for holidays.

Irish Wheelchair Association Aras Cuchulainn, Blackheath Drive, Clontarf, Dublin 3 ⓣ01/833 8241, ⓦwww.iwa.ie. Lots of help and advice for wheelchair-bound travellers abroad.

Tripscope Alexandra House, Albany Rd, Brentford, Middlesex TW8 0NE ⓣ08457/585641, ⓦwww.justmobility.co.uk/tripscope. This registered charity provides a national telephone information service offering free advice on UK and international transport for those with a mobility problem.

In Australia and New Zealand

Australian Council for Rehabilitation of the Disabled PO Box 60, Curtin, ACT 2605 ⓣ02/6282 4333; 24 Cabarita Rd, Cabarita, NSW 2137 ⓣ02/9743 2699. ACROD furnishes lists of travel agencies and tour operators for people with disabilities.

Disabled Persons Assembly 4/173–175 Victoria St, Wellington, New Zealand ⓣ04/801 9100. Resource centre with lists of travel agencies and tour operators for people with disabilities.

Disabled travel advice on the web

Access-Able ⓦwww.access-able.com. Online resource for travellers with disabilities, including detailed information on cruise lines that cater to disabled travellers.

Allgohere Airline Directory ⓦwww.everybody.co.uk/airindex. Online guide to the services different airlines provide for mobility-challenged customers.

Emerging Horizons ⓦwww.emerginghorizons.com. Consumer-oriented magazine about accessible travel, with lots of features and regularly updated columns.

Jim Lubin's Disability Resource ⓦwww.makoa.org/index. Extensive database of links for disabled travel around the world.

Gay and lesbian travellers

Rural, Catholic South America is not overly welcoming to homosexuality. Homosexual acts are even technically illegal in some countries (such as Chile), but this usually just means that local gay couples tend to keep themselves to themselves and avoid flaunting their orientation in front of others. Gay and lesbian travellers would probably be safest following their example – public displays of affection between two men or two women will be frowned upon in much of the continent's countryside.

Things are generally easier in the big cities, though, and there are a couple of major destinations where anything goes. **Brazil** boasts most of them – Rio de Janeiro, Salvador and São Paulo providing safe and welcoming havens for any sexual orientation, as do Buenos Aires and Santiago. If you are looking for thumping night life and a very "out scene", then these cities are the best in the continent.

Contacts for gay and lesbian travellers

In the US and Canada

Alyson Adventures PO Box 180129, Boston, MA 02118 ⓣ1-800/825-9766, ⓦwww.alysonadventures.com. Adventure holidays all over the world, including gay scuba-diving packages to the Caribbean.

Damron Company PO Box 422458, San Francisco, CA 94142 ⓣ415/255-0404 or 1-800/462-6654, ⓦwww.damron.com. Publisher of the *Men's Travel Guide*, a pocket-sized yearbook full of listings of hotels, bars, clubs and resources for gay men; the *Women's Traveler*, which provides similar listings for lesbians; the *Road Atlas*, which covers lodging and entertainment in major US cities; and *Damron Accommodations*, which lists over 1000 places of accommodation for gays and lesbians worldwide.

Envoy Resorts and Tours 1649 N Wells St, Suite 201, Chicago, IL 60614 ⓣ312/787-2400 or 1-800/44ENVOY, ⓦwww.envoytravel.com/rainbow. Gay-specific information and travel services, including gay cruise ship bookings.

Ferrari Publications PO Box 37887, Phoenix, AZ 85069 ⓣ602/863-2408 or 1-800/962-2912, ⓦwww.ferrariguides.com. Publishes *Ferrari Gay Travel A to Z*, a gay and lesbian guide to international travel; *Inn Places*, a worldwide accommodation guide; the guides *Men's Travel in Your Pocket*, and *Women's Travel in Your Pocket*, and the quarterly *Ferrari Travel Report*. Also has gay guides to Paris and Mexico.

International Gay & Lesbian Travel Association 4331 N Federal Hwy, Suite 304, Ft Lauderdale, FL 33308 ⓣ1-800/448-8550, ⓦwww.iglta.org. Trade group that can provide a list of gay- and lesbian-owned or -friendly travel agents, accommodation and other travel businesses.

Out and About Travel Providence, RI ⓣ1-800/842-4753, ⓦwww.outandaboutravel.com. Gay- and lesbian-oriented cruises, tours and packages.

In the UK

ⓦwww.gaytravel.co.uk Online gay and lesbian travel agent, offering good deals on all types of holidays. Also lists gay- and lesbian-friendly hotels around the world.

Dream Waves Redcot High Street, Child Okeford, Blandford, DT22 8ET ⓣ01258/861149, ⓔdreamwaves@aol.com. Specializes in exclusively gay holidays, including skiing trips and summer sun packages.

Madison Travel 118 Western Rd, Hove, East Sussex NN3 1DB ⓣ01273/202532, ⓦwww.madisontravel.co.uk. Established travel agents specializing in packages to gay- and lesbian-friendly mainstream destinations.

In Australia and New Zealand

Gay and Lesbian Travel PO Box 208, Darlinghurst, NSW 1300 ⓣ02/9380 4115, ⓦwww.galta.com.au. Directory and links for gay and lesbian travel worldwide.

Parkside Travel 70 Glen Osmond Rd, Parkside, SA 5063 ⓣ08/8274 1222 or 1800/888501,

Ⓔhwtravel@senet.com.au. Gay travel agent associated with local branch of Hervey World Travel; covers all aspects of gay and lesbian travel worldwide.

Silke's Travel 263 Oxford St, Darlinghurst, NSW 2010 Ⓣ02/9380 6244 or 1800/807860, Ⓔsilba@magna.com.au. Long-established gay and lesbian specialist, with the emphasis on women's travel.

Tearaway Travel 52 Porter St, Prahan, VIC 3181 Ⓣ03/9510 6344, Ⓔtearaway@bigpond.com. Gay-specific business dealing with international and domestic travel.

Gay resources on the web

Gay and Lesbian Travel Ⓦwww.galta.com.au. Directory and links for gay and lesbian travel in Australia and worldwide.

Gay Caribbean Ⓦwww.gaycaribbean.net. Covers accommodations, meetings and social events throughout the Caribbean region and South America.

Gay Dive Ⓦwww.gaydive.com/home. Provides summaries about attitudes on individual islands as well as information on dive sites and gay-friendly accommodation.

Gay Places to Stay Ⓦwww.gayplaces2stay.com. Information about gay-friendly accommodation worldwide.

Gay Travel Ⓦwww.gaytravel.com. The most helpful site for trip planning, bookings and general information about international travel.

Out and About Ⓦwww.outandabout.com. Gay travel newsletter with back issues on gay life in Argentina and Brazil.

Viajar Travel Ⓦwww.viajartravel.com. Adventure travel specialists with lots of information about the continent.

Women travellers

Though violent attacks against women travellers are not very common – except in some of the particularly crime-laden cities (see p.551) – many women find that the barrage of hisses, hoots and comments in certain parts of South America comes close to spoiling their vacation.

It's unlikely that **women travelling alone** will leave the continent without a little harassment, some of which can be threatening and scary, some of which is just amazement that a woman would be travelling alone, anyway. Latin American men are not renowned for their forward-thinking attitudes towards women's emancipation, and genuinely see nothing wrong with the heady sense of machismo that rules much of the continent. You may find that attitudes ARE less polarized in *campesino* communities.

Of course, there are measures you can take to avoid being hassled constantly. Don't go to bars or nightclubs alone, for one – this is an activity only undertaken by the most brazen prostitutes in the region, and you will be considered fair game. Don't be sarcastic or scream, as the man in question may feel that you are showing him up in front of his friends and get more macho and aggressive. However, don't be afraid to seem rude; even the mildest polite response will be considered an indication of serious interest. In any event, watch how the local women behave and where they go, and never be afraid to ask for help if you feel lost or threatened.

Solo women travellers should also avoid going off to remote locations alone, and if you are going as part of an organized visit, it's always best to **check the credentials** of the tour company. Your safety may be in their hands, so a little asking around doesn't seem too much to ask.

There are emergency numbers given in individual chapters of this book. However, if you are attacked or raped, you should contact tourist police, your country's embassy and also get medical attention as well as go to the regular police.

Work and study

Studying Spanish or Portuguese is a great way to get to know the continent and its people, and to get beyond the tourist facade. Spanish-language courses are extremely popular in Peru, Ecuador and Argentina, and many students – particularly Americans – take a semester or a summer to improve their language skills here.

Those wishing to **volunteer** (and who are willing to pay for the privilege) have no shortage of options available to them throughout Latin America, and a great many people come here to help with environmental and social charities. Other, paid work is available but it's hard to get, especially if you don't have a visa. English teaching and tutoring are the most promising paths to try.

Language study

Latin America has long been a hugely popular destination for people wishing to brush up on their **Spanish-language skills**. Cusco in Peru, Buenos Aires in Argentina, Sucre in Bolivia and Quito in Ecuador seem to be the most popular destinations, and all offer a huge variety of courses and levels for the foreign student. You can also learn some of the indigenous languages here – **Quechua** in Bolivia, for example. Most of Brazil's large cities, but particularly Rio and São Paulo, are great locations for learning **Brazilian Portuguese**.

Language schools

Academía Latinoamericana de Español ⓣ1-801/268-2468, ⓦwww.alespanish.com. Spanish classes in Ecuador, Peru and Bolivia.

Amerispan PO Box 58129, Philadelphia, PA 19102 ⓣ1-800/879-6640, ⓦwww.amerispan.com. Spanish courses and volunteer opportunities

Bridge Linguatec ⓣ1-800/724-4210, ⓦwww.bridgelinguatec.com. Spanish and Portuguese classes in Argentina, Chile and Brazil.

Don Quijote ⓦwww.donquijote.org. A multi-media approach to Spanish classes in the heart of Cusco. Classes cost around US$100/week. Class/volunteer work combinations available.

Escuela Runawasi ⓣ00591/4424-8923, ⓦwww.runawasi.org. Quechua and Spanish language and literature lessons in Cochabamba, Bolivia.

Working

Opportunities for **volunteer and non-profit work** abound, but be prepared to pay something towards your own upkeep. The organziations listed below specialize in placing volunteers with organizations throughout the continent. You will need to have a good basic level of Spanish – or Portuguese if you want to communicate in Brazil – and often some kind of specialist knowledge to separate you from the herd.

If you're looking for paid work, though, you might have a little more trouble as almost all such efforts will be illegal. Qualified English teachers should usually be able to find something, but unqualified teachers may have to forfeit several months' pay while they are being trained and tutoring services – while they may help eventually – take a while to establish. The most reputable employers will require that you have a **work permit**; contact the embassy or consulate (p.19) of the relevant country for details. If you are determined to find some work, you're probably best looking in the major cities, especially the ones more frequented by tourists.

Volunteer organizations

Alliance Abroad ⓣ1866/5ABROAD, ⓦwww.internshipsaborad.com. Wide choice of activities throughout the continent.

Amerispan PO Box 58129, Philadelphia, PA 19102 ⓣ1-800/879-6640, ⓦwww.amerispan.com. One of the best-known volunteer organziations with opportunities throughout Latin America.

Association of American Schools in South America ⓣ305/821-0345, ⓦwww.aassa.com. Volunteer teaching work throughout Latin America.

Australian Volunteers International ⓣ61 392/791829, ⓦwww.ozvol.org.au. Opportunities for Australians in Colombia, Ecuador and Guyana.

Concordia ⓣ44 1473/422218, ⓦwww.concordia-iye.org.uk. Environmental, archeological and arts projects are among some of the wide range offered by this UK company.

Earthwatch Institute ⓣ1-800/776-0188, ⓦwww.earthwatch.org. Long-established research company offering environmental and social volunteer programs throughout the continent.

Global Vision International ⓣ1582/831300, ⓦwww.gvi.co.uk. Conservation projects to the Amazon.

I to I International Projects ⓦwww.i-to-i.com.Volunteer as a special needs tutor or a youth development counsellor in Ecuador or Bolivia.

RefugioBolivia ⓦwww.geocities.com/refugiobolivia, ⓔdave_gould@hotmail.com. An animal rehabilitation centre in the Inti Wara Yassi community in Bolivia. Volunteers just turn up and spend between two weeks and two months at the refuge.

WorldTeach ⓦwww.worldteach.org. Summer and year-long teaching opportunities in Ecuador.

Guide

Guide

Argentina

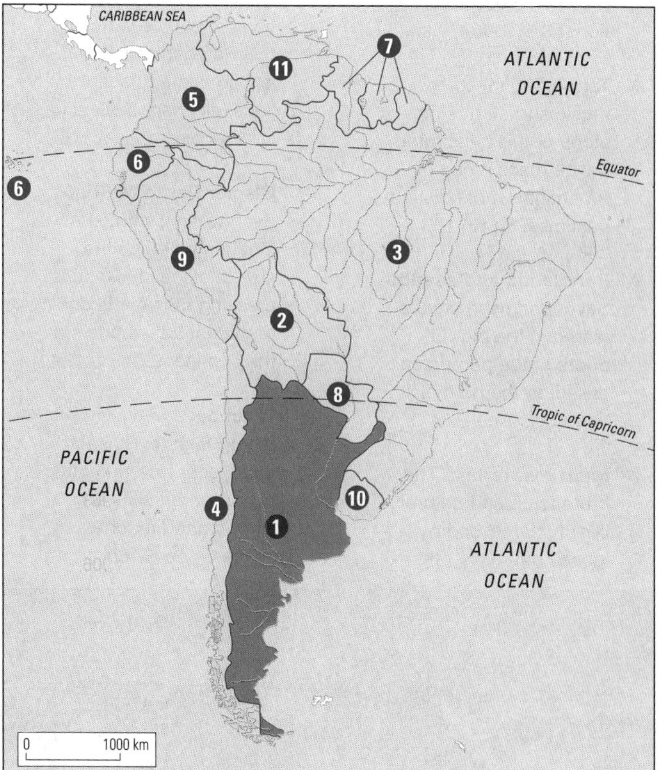

CARIBBEAN SEA
ATLANTIC OCEAN
Equator
Tropic of Capricorn
PACIFIC OCEAN
ATLANTIC OCEAN
0 1000 km

Argentina highlights

* **Buenos Aires** Dynamic yet laid-back, South America's most alluring capital city combines cosmopolitan sophistication with deep-seated neighbourhood traditions. See p.86

* **Tango** The mesmerizing music and staggering steps of this celebrated dance make it one of Argentina's most distinct pastimes. See p.103

* **Parrilladas and asados** Savour crimson steaks reared in the big outdoors of the pampa and grilled on the perfect barbecue. See p.74

* **Iguazu waterfalls** The brute force and natural beauty harnessed by Iguazu put every other falls to shame and make an unforgettably moving (not to mention wet) experience. See p.130

* **Península Valdés** One of the world's top locations for whale-watching, this Patagonian isthmus is also home to sea lions, elephant seals and killer whales. See p.176

* **Glacier Perito Moreno** Even when it's not shedding lumps of ice the size of office blocks, this creaking monster is one of the natural wonders of the continent. See p.187

* **Talampaya and Ischigualasto** These parks offer towering otherworldly red cliffs and wind-crafted moonscapes. See p.160

Introduction and basics

Even without the titanic wedge of Antarctica that cartographers include in its national territory, **Argentina** ranks as the world's eighth largest country. Standing between the tropic of Cancer and the most southerly reaches of the planet's landmass, it encompasses a staggering diversity of climates and landscapes. The mainland points down from the hot and humid **jungles of its northeast** and the **bone-dry highland steppes of its northwest** through windswept **Patagonia** to the end-of-the-world archipelago of **Tierra del Fuego**, a territory that is shared with Chile.

Argentina is less obviously exotic than its neighbours to the north, and its inhabitants will tell you how great an influence Europe has been on their nation. Yet it's a country with a very special character all of its own, distilled into the national ideal of **Argentinidad** – an elusive identity the country's Utopian thinkers and practical doers have never quite agreed upon. And while there's some truth to the clichés about Argentinians (their passions *are* dominated by the national religion of **football**, politics and living life in the fast lane), not everyone here dances the **tango**, or is obsessed with **Evita**, or gallops around on a horse, **gaucho style**.

Where to go

Argentina has many natural wonders of the world, including the majestic waterfalls of **Iguazú** (shared with Brazil), the spectacular **Perito Moreno Glacier**, whose towering sixty-metre walls carve icebergs into the lake below, and the fascinating whale colonies off the **Península Valdés**. Yet many of the country's most noteworthy sights are also its least known, such as the **Reserva Natural del Iberá**, a huge reserve of swamps and floating islands offering unforgettably close-up encounters with cayman, monkeys, capybara and hundreds of brightly plumed birds.

Buenos Aires is likely to be your point of entry, and only inveterate city-haters will resist the capital's charm. The country's gastronomic mecca and transport hub, it also boasts a frenzied nightlife that makes it one of the world's great round-the-clock cities.

Due north stretches **El Litoral**, a region of subtropical riverine landscapes featuring the photogenic Iguazú waterfalls and the much-visited Jesuit Missions whose once-noble ruins are crumbling into the tangled jungle, with the notable exception of well-preserved **San Ignacio Miní**. Tucked away in the country's landlocked **Northwest**, the historic cradle of present-day Argentina is the polychrome **Quebrada del Toro** gorge, best viewed in comfort from the **Tren a las Nubes**, one of the world's highest railways. In the **Valles Calchaquíes** stunningly beautiful valleys with high-altitude vineyards produce the delightfully flowery *torrontés* wine.

West and immediately south of Buenos Aires is pampa, pampa and more **pampa**. This is where you'll still glimpse signs of the traditional *gaucho* culture, most famously celebrated in **San Antonio de Areco**. Here, too, you'll find some of the classiest **estancias**, offering a combination of understated luxury and horseback adventure activities. On the Atlantic coast lie a string of fun beach resorts, including long-standing favourite **Mar del Plata**, while the farther west you go, the larger the Central Sierras loom on the horizon: within reach of **Córdoba**, the country's vibrant second city, are some of the oldest resorts on the continent. The regional capital of **Mendoza** is also the country's wine capital, and from here, the scenic Alta Montaña route climbs steeply to the Chilean border, passing **Cerro Aconcagua**, well established as a dream challenge for mountaineers from around the world. San Juan and La Rioja provinces are relatively uncharted territory but their star attractions are **Parque Nacional Talampaya**, with its giant red cliffs, and the nearby **Parque Provincial Ischigualasto**, usually known the Valle de la Luna on account of its intriguing moonscapes.

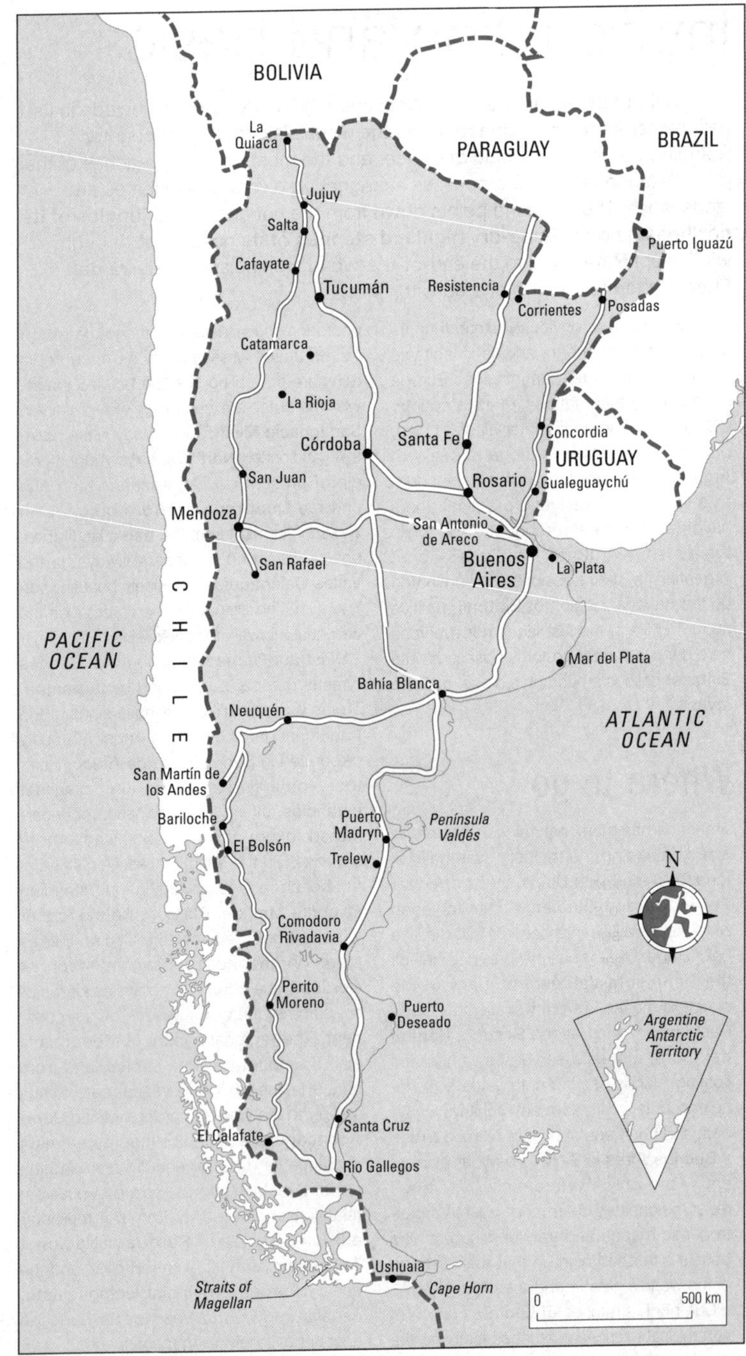
BOLIVIA
PARAGUAY
BRAZIL
La Quiaca
Jujuy
Salta
Cafayate
Tucumán
Resistencia
Corrientes
Posadas
Puerto Iguazú
Catamarca
La Rioja
Córdoba
Santa Fe
Concordia
URUGUAY
San Juan
Rosario
Gualeguaychú
Mendoza
San Antonio de Areco
Buenos Aires
La Plata
San Rafael
CHILE
PACIFIC OCEAN
Mar del Plata
Bahía Blanca
Neuquén
ATLANTIC OCEAN
San Martín de los Andes
Bariloche
Puerto Madryn
Península Valdés
El Bolsón
Trelew
N
Comodoro Rivadavia
Perito Moreno
Puerto Deseado
Argentine Antarctic Territory
Santa Cruz
El Calafate
Río Gallegos
Ushuaia
Straits of Magellan
Cape Horn
0
500 km

Argentina claims the lion's share of the wild, sparsely populated expanses of **Patagonia** and the archipelago of **Tierra del Fuego**. An almost unbroken chain of national parks along these Patagonian and Fuegian cordilleras make for some of the best trekking anywhere on the planet – certainly include the savage granite peaks of the **Parque Nacional Los Glaciares** in your itinerary. For wildlife enthusiasts the **Peninsula Valdés** is another must-see, famous above all else as a breeding ground for southern right whales.

When to go

Roughly falling in September to November, the Argentine **spring** is perfect just about everywhere except in parts of the South, where icy gales may blow, while **autumn** (March and April) is great for the wine-harvest in the Mendoza and San Juan provinces and the red and orange hues of the beeches down south. Above all, you're best off not being in the far south in the coldest months (April to October), or in the Chaco and some lowland parts of the northwest in the height of **summer** (December to February). On the other hand, summer's the only time to climb the highest Andean peaks and the most reliable time of year to head for Tierra del Fuego. Buenos Aires can get unbearably hot and sticky in midsummer and may come across as somewhat bleak in **midwinter**. You should, however, aim to be in the skiing resorts in July and August.

A point to bear in mind: the **national holidays** are roughly January, Easter and July, when transport and accommodation can get booked up and many resorts, especially in Patagonia and along the coast, are packed out.

Red tape and visas

At press time, citizens of the USA, Canada, Australia, New Zealand, South Africa, Britain, Ireland and other Western European nations did not need a visa for tourist trips of up to ninety days. However, always verify this in advance with your local consulate, as the situation can change.

You will need a valid **passport** and must fill in a **landing card** on arrival; you will be given a stamp for stays of thirty, sixty or (most often) ninety days. Fasten your duplicate of the landing card to your passport, preferably next to your entrance stamp, as you'll need it to leave the country and police may check it. If you do lose it, it's rarely a serious problem, but you'll have to fill in a new form at the border control.

On entering the country, you will also be given a **customs declaration form**. Duty is not charged on used personal effects, booksand other articles for non-commercial purposes. Make sure you declare any valuable electronic items such as laptop computers, as customs officers can be suspicious that you may be bringing them into the country to sell.

You can **extend your stay** for a further sixty days by presenting your passport to the main immigration department: **Dirección de Migraciones**, at Av Antártida Argentina 1350, Retiro, in Buenos Aires (☎011/4312-3288 or 4311-4118). When leaving the country, you must obtain an **exit stamp**.

Visitors are legally obliged to carry their **passports as ID**. You might get away with carrying a photocopy, but don't forget to copy your entrance stamp and landing card as well.

Costs and money

The Argentine **peso** is divided into one hundred **centavos**. In Argentina, it's represented by the dollar sign ($) but to avoid confusion we have used the symbol **AR$** throughout this section. Notes come in 2, 5, 10, 20, 50 and 100 peso denominations, and 1 peso and 5, 10, 25 and 50 centavo coins are also in circulation. You may get handed parallel currency notes, such as Lecops (though people often politely ask if you mind them); these may be phased out, so check the latest situation to avoid being lumbered with worthless paper.

Argentina still has a relatively healthy economy, by South American standards, even since the crisis in early 2002, when the peso was sharply devalued. It has since settled at around 3 to the US dollar. Although the **cost** of basic products rocketed following the devaluation, the price of most services has remained surprisingly low, turning Argentina into a reasonably economical country to visit for the first time in years. It will still seem expensive if you arrive from Peru or Bolivia, and the far South still tends to eat up money, partly owing to the huge distances to be covered.

Eating out is on the pricey side by South American standards, but quantities are generous and quality is reliable; you can usually save money by having your main meal at lunchtime, when set menus (sometimes called *menú ejecutivo*) are really quite reasonable. Long-distance **transport** will also eat up a huge chunk of your expenses and hitchhiking is not always an option; you may have to budget for some internal flights. Many places, especially hotels, restaurants and big stores, ask for a huge handling fee for credit-card payments (as high as twenty percent); remember that many businesses – hotels in particular – will give you a fair-sized **discount for cash payments** (*efectivo* or *contado*) on the quoted price, though they may need prompting.

ATMs (*cajeros automáticos*) are plentiful in Argentina, though you can sometimes be caught out in very remote places, especially in the northwest, so never rely completely on them. **Travellers' cheques**, however, are not really a viable option as fewer and fewer banks seem to accept them.

Roughly speaking, you'll need to reckon on spending at least US$50 a week on a shoestring budget, US$200 to satisfy creature comforts, by staying in mid-range accommodation and not stinting, while if you are set on a luxury holiday allow at least US$1000.

Be aware that many services – especially air travel and hotels – operate **dual pricing**, one price for Argentine residents and another, often as much as three times more, for foreign visitors. Hotels and other types of commerce, especially at the luxury end of the market, may charge foreigners in US dollars, rather than Argentine pesos, as a covert but perfectly legal way of charging more. This practice is mostly found, of course, in more touristy locations, such as Ushuaia and Bariloche.

Information, maps and websites

Argentina's main **National Tourist Office** is at Santa Fe 883 (Mon–Fri 9am–5pm; ⓣ011/4312-2232), and offers maps of the country and general information about getting around. Every province maintains a **Casa de Provincia** in Buenos Aires, where you can pick up information about what there is to see or do, prior to travelling. The standard of information you'll glean from them varies wildly, often reflecting the comparative wealth of a given province.

One of the main sources of information for Argentina is the **Internet**. Useful sites include ⓦwww.turismo.gov.ar, the official government tourist website; ⓦwww.mercotour.com, for reliable region-by-region information on a variety of tourism-related issues, from skiing to adventure tours to farm holidays, and ⓦwww.wam.com.ar/tourism /homepage, a multilingual site that puts you in touch with tour operators catering for foreigners in Argentina. Finally, ⓦwww.buenosairesherald.com is a condensed but interesting overview of local, national and international news in English, with plenty of articles on culture and eating out.

The clearest and most accurate **map** of the whole country is the one you can get free from the national tourist office in Buenos Aires; it's called **Rutas de la Argentina** and has small but clear inset maps of twenty towns and cities as well as a 1:2,500,000 national map, the ideal scale for most travellers. The **ACA** (Automóvil Club) produces individual maps for each province, which vary enormously in detail and accuracy; the regional maps or route planners the club publishes may be enough for most travellers.

Accommodation

Accommodation in Argentina runs the gamut from campsites and youth hostels to international five-star hotels. In the middle, there is everything from distinguished old colonial houses with balconies to dark and seedy hotels, which lack so much as a window. The vast majority of places, however, are pretty anonymous, albeit acceptable, hotels with so little to distinguish one from another that when you find a place that stands out you feel like cheering.

Prices are relatively high, especially in Patagonia and at the luxury end in general, particularly in comparison with the very low prices of some other Latin America countries; however you can, in general, expect to pay rather less than in many European countries.

Hotels and estancias

You can often tell by a hotel's name what kind of place to expect: the use of the term **posada** for example usually suggests a slightly rustic feel, but generally comfortable or even luxurious. In a similar vein, **hostería** is often used for smallish, upmarket hotels – oriented towards the tourist rather than the businessman. **Hostal** is sometimes used too – but doesn't seem to refer reliably to anything – there are youth hostels called *hostales* as well as high-rise modern hotels.

Residenciales and **hospedajes** are basically simple hotel-style accommodation, graded accorded to a different system (A, B or C is used instead of stars). Most are reasonably clean and comfortable and a few of them stand out as some of Argentina's best budget accommodation.

A very different experience from staying in a hotel is provided by Argentina's **estancias**, as the country's large ranches are called. Estancia accommodation is generally luxurious, and with a lot more character than hotels of a similar price; for between US$100 and US$200 per person a day you are provided with four meals, invariably including a traditional *asado*; at working estancias you will have the chance to observe or join in ranch activities such as cattle herding and branding; and at all of them horse riding and often swimming are also included in the price. To **book estancia accommodation**, either approach individual estancias directly or try travel agencies, at no extra cost: the two main agencies are both based in Buenos Aires: Comarcas, Laprida 1380 (☎011/4821-1876, ©comarcas@tournet.com.ar) and José de Santis, Diag. Roque Sáenz Peña 616, 5th Floor (☎011/4342-8417).

Hostels and campsites

Youth hostels are known as *albergues juveniles* or *albergues de la juventud* in Argentina. There are two hostelling organizations, both recognizing Hostelling International (HI) cards at their separate networks of hostels: the Asociación Argentina de Albergues de la Juventud (AAAJ) is at Talchahuano 214, 2nd Floor (☎011/4372-1001); and the more dynamic Red Argentina de Albergues Juveniles (RAAJ) is at Florida 835, 3rd Floor (☎011/4511-8712). Accommodation at either is generally in **dormitories**, though most places also have one or two double **rooms**, often excellent value. Facilities vary from next to nothing to Internet access, washing machines, cable TV and patios with barbecue facilities.

There are plenty of **campsites** (*campings*), with most towns and villages having their own municipal campsite, but standards vary wildly. At the major resorts, there are usually plenty of privately owned, well-organized sites, with facilities ranging from provisions stores to volleyball courts and TV rooms. In non-touristy towns, municipal sites can be rather desolate and sometimes not particularly secure places: it's usually a good idea to check with locals before pitching your tent.

Getting around

Distances are immense in Argentina, and you are likely to spend a considerable proportion of your budget on travel expenses. Most people travel **by bus**, but a domestic **airpass** is often the best way of seeing a lot of the country if your time is limited. **Car rental** is useful in places, but still too expensive for most budget travellers, unless they can share the cost; and in fact, many backpackers on a tight budget might be forced to hitch. Finally, most **boat trips** and some ferry crossings are incredibly scenic, and are well worth working into your itinerary if at all possible.

By bus

There are hundreds of private **bus** companies, most of which concentrate on one particular region, although a few, such as **TAC**, run pretty much nationwide. A high proportion of buses are modern, plush models designed for long-distance travel, and your biggest worry will be what video the driver or conductor has chosen. On longer journeys, snacks and even hot meals are served (included in the ticket price), although these vary considerably in quality. Some of the more luxurious services have waiter service and are usually worth the extra money for long night-rides: *coche cama* and *pullman* services have wide, fully reclinable seats, and *semi-cama* services are not far behind in terms of seat comfort.

Buying tickets is normally a simple on-the-spot matter, but you must plan in advance if travelling in peak summer season (mid-December to February), especially if you're taking a long-distance bus from Buenos Aires or any other major city to a particularly popular holiday destination.

By plane

Argentina's most important domestic airport by far is Buenos Aires' **Aeroparque Jorge Newbery**. There are connections to most provincial capitals and major tourist centres of the country. Some cut-price deals booked in advance can work out to be little more expensive than the bus. One of the best deals is the "Visit Argentina" **airpass** sold by Aerolíneas Argentinas and valid for domestic flights on Aerolíneas and its subsidiary, Austral. This pass must be bought in conjunction with your international flight, and it is not for sale within Argentina. The pass is valid for up to two months.

Domestic **departure taxes** tend to hover at around AR$5 to AR$13 (check to see whether or not this has been included in the price before buying your ticket). Many smaller airports are not served by public transport, though some airline companies run shuttle services to connect with flights; otherwise, you're stuck with taxis.

By train

Argentina's **train network**, developed with British investment from the late nineteenth century, collapsed in the 1990s with the withdrawal of government subsidies. Certain long-distance services were maintained by provincial governments, but these tend to be slower and less reliable than buses.

You're far less likely to want to use Argentine trains as a method of getting around, however, than you are to try one of the country's famous **tourist trains**, where the aim is simply to travel for the sheer fun of it. There are two principal stars: **La Trochita**, the Old Patagonian Express from Esquel; and the **Tren a los Nubes**, one of the highest railways in the world, which climbs through the mountains from Salta towards the Chilean border.

By boat

The two **ferry services** you are most likely to use are the comfortable ones from Buenos Aires to Colonia del Sacramento in Uruguay; and the much more spartan, functional Chilean ones that transport foot passengers and vehicles across the Magellan Straits into Tierra del Fuego at Punta Delgada and Porvenir. There are also several practical river crossings throughout the Litoral region. Tigre, just to the northwest of the capital, tends towards the pleasure-trips end of the market, and offers boat trips around the Delta. In Patagonia, most lacustrine **boat trips** are designed purely for their scenic value. Chief among these are the different options to behold the polar scenery of the Parque Nacional Los Glaciares near El Calafate at close quarters, especially the renowned Perito Moreno Glacier.

By car

You are unlikely to want or need a **car** for your whole stay in Argentina, but you'll find one pretty indispensable if you want to explore some of the more isolated areas of Patagonia, Tierra del Fuego, the Northwest, and Mendoza and San Juan provinces.

To **rent a car**, you need to be over 21 (25 with some agencies) and to hold an **International Driving Licence**. Bring your passport as well as a credit card for the **deposit**. Before you drive off, check that you've been given insurance, tax and ownership papers. Check too for dents and paintwork damage, and get hold of a 24-hour emergency telephone number. Also, pay close attention to the small print, most notably what you're liable for in the event of an accident: excess normally doesn't cover you for the first AR$5000 or so if you flip the car, nor for the cost of a smashed windscreen or headlight – a particularly common occurrence if driving on unsurfaced roads. Look for **unlimited mileage** deals if you're using it for more than just a runaround, as the per-kilometre charge can otherwise exceed your daily rental cost many times over.

Mail and communications

Postal charges to North America, Europe and Australasia via Argentina's postal service **Correo Argentino** are astronomical (at least AR$5.50 for a postcard). You should send any important letters or packets registered (*certificado*), as this increases the likelihood of them reaching their destination (though registered items also go missing).

For sending **packages within Argentina**, your best bet it to use the *encomienda* services offered by bus companies (seal boxes in brown paper to prevent casual theft by tampering). This isn't a door-to-door service like the post: the recipient must collect the package from its end destination (bring ID). By addressing the package to yourself, this system makes an excellent and remarkably good-value way of reducing the weight in your pack whilst travelling, but be aware that companies usually keep an *encomienda* for only one month before returning it to its original destination.

By far the most common way to make calls and send **faxes** is from public call centres (*centros de llamadas*), known as **locutorios** (Telefónica) or **telecentros** (Telecom). You'll be assigned a cabin, and most have meters with which you can monitor your expenditure; make as many calls as you want and then pay at the counter. Off-peak rates generally apply from 10pm for international calls until 7am the next morning, usually fifteen to twenty percent less than peak rates. In some of the more out-of-the-way places, **public telephones** take coins only (AR$0.10 coins upwards).

Argentina is fast catching on to the **Internet** and is one of the best developed of the Latin American countries in terms of using it as a business tool. Most reasonably sized towns now have at least one or two public places for accessing the Net, with rates varying considerably, from AR$1 to AR$8 an hour (the highest rates being at tourist centres in the south).

Food and drink

Argentine food could be summed up by one word: "**beef**". Not just any beef, but the best in the world: succulent, cherry-red, healthy meat raised on some of the greenest, most extensive pastures known to cattle. The barbecue or *asado* is an institution, but it's not the whole story. In general, you nearly always eat well in Argentina and you seldom have a bad meal, portions are always generous and the raw ingredients are of an amazingly high quality.

Argentinians love dining out, and in Buenos Aires especially eateries stay open all day and till very late. By South American standards the quality of **restaurants** is high, with prices to match. If you eat à la carte, you'll be hard put to find a main dish for under AR$10 but you can keep costs down by eating at the market or taking advantage of the **menú del día** or **menú ejecutivo** – usually good-value set meals for as little as AR$8–10. In the evening **tenedor libre** or **diente libre** restaurants are just the place if your budget's tight. Here, you can eat as much as you like, they're usually self-service (cold and hot buffets plus grills) and the food is fresh and well prepared, if a little dull.

Cheaper hotels and more modest accommodation often skimp on **breakfast**: you'll be lucky to be given more than tea or coffee, and some bread, jam and butter, though the popular *media lunas* (small, sticky croissants) are sometimes also served. The sacred national delicacy **dulce de leche** is often provided for spreading on toast or bread, as is top-notch honey. Hardly any restaurant opens for **dinner** before 8pm, and in the hotter months – and all year round in Buenos Aires – few people turn up before 10 or 11pm.

If you're feeling hungry during the day there are plenty of **minutas** or snacks to choose from. The **lomito** is a nourishing sandwich filled with a juicy slice of steak, often made with delicious *pan árabe*, while the **chivito** is made with a less tender cut. At cafés a popular snack is the **tostado**, a toasted cheese-and-ham sandwich, sometimes called a **carlitos**. **Milanesas**, in this context, refer to breaded veal escalopes in a sandwich, hamburger-style.

The variety of cuisines reflects the mosaic of different communities who have migrated to Argentina over the decades: Italian, Spanish, Chinese, Middle Eastern, German and even Welsh. Japanese and Thai food have become fashionable in Buenos Aires, where nearly every national cuisine is available, but such variety is almost unheard of in the provinces.

Parrilla, pizza and pasta are the mainstays of Argentine cuisine. The **parrilla** is a barbecue, the national dish, served at restaurants known as *parrillas*. Usually there's a set menu, the **parrillada**, but the establishments themselves vary enormously. Traditionally, you start off by eating the offal before moving on to the choicer cuts, but you can choose to head straight for the steaks and fillets. Either way, these places are not for the faint-hearted: everything comes with heaps of salads and mountains of chips. Although mustard (*mostaza*) is usually available, the lightly salted meat is usually best served with nothing on it, but the traditional condiments are **chimichurri**, olive oil shaken in a bottle with salt, garlic, chilli pepper, vinegar and bayleaf, and **salsa criolla**, similar but with onion and tomato as well – everyone jealously guards their secret formulae for both these "magic" dressings.

Asian or Middle Eastern food (things like stir-fries, hummus and tabbouleh) may be the answer to vegetarians' prayers; in such a carnivorous land, real **vegetarian** food is very hard to come by, though vegetarian restaurants are on the increase.

Excellent local-style fast food is available in the form of **empanadas**, turnovers or pasties that come with a bewildering array of non-traditional fillings, including tuna, roquefort cheese and pineapple. The conventional fillings are beef, cheese and chicken. **Humitas** are made of steamed creamed sweetcorn, usually served in neat parcels made from the outer husk of corn cobs. **Tamales** are maize-flour balls, stuffed with minced beef and onion, wrapped in maize leaves and simmered. While the typical main dish, **locro**, is a warming, substantial stew based on maize, with onions, beans, meat, chicken or sausage thrown in. Less common but worth trying if you see it on the menu is **guaschalocro**, similar to *locro* but based on pumpkin.

Drinks

Fizzy drinks (*gaseosa*) are popular with people of all ages and are often drunk to accompany a meal, in this country where fewer and fewer people drink alcohol (even if wine consumption is relatively high). All the big brand names are available, along with local brands such as Paso de los Toros whose fizzy grapefruit drinks (*pomelo*) are becoming increasingly popular.

Although few beans are grown in the country, good, if expensive, **coffee** is easy to come by in Argentina. In the cafés of most towns and cities you will find very decent espressos, or delicious *café con leche* for breakfast (except in hotels). **Mate**, the bitter national drink, is a whole world unto itself, with special rules of etiquette and ritual involved.

Argentina's **beer** is more thirst-quenching than alcoholic and mostly comes as fairly bland lager. The Quilmes brewery dominates the market with ales such as Cristal, while in Mendoza, the Andes brand crops up all over the place while Salta's own brand is also good, and a kind of stout (*cerveza negra*) can sometimes be obtained in the northwest. If you want draught beer you must ask for a *chopp*.

Argentine **wine** is excellent and not too expensive, though in restaurants the predictable corkage hikes the price up considerably. The locally distilled **aguardientes** or firewaters are often deliciously grapey. There is no national alcoholic drink or cocktail, but a number of Italian vermouths and digestives are made in Argentina. **Fernet Branca** is the most popular, a demonic-looking brew the colour of molasses with a rather medicinal taste, invariably combined with cola, whose colour it matches, and consumed in huge quantities – it's generally regarded as the gaucho's favourite tipple.

Safety and the police

Argentina is one of the continent's **safest countries** and, as long as you take a few basic precautions, you are unlikely to encounter any problems during your stay. Indeed, you'll find many of the more rural parts of the country pretty much risk-free: people leave doors unlocked, windows open and bikes unchained. More care should be taken in large cities and some of the border towns, particularly the northeastern ones, where poverty and easily available arms and drugs make opportunistic crime a more common occurrence. Some potential pitfalls are outlined here, not to induce paranoia but on the principle that to be forewarned is to be forearmed.

By Argentine standards, **Buenos Aires** is currently suffering something of a crime wave, and incidents of violence and armed robbery are definitely on the increase. It's sometimes difficult to know how much local anxiety is due to a genuine increase in crime and how much to middle-class paranoia but, in general, serious crime tends to affect locals more than tourists. Nevertheless, you should not take unofficial taxis from the airport and you're advised to be wary when taking a taxi from areas where serious money circulates (the new casino for example). Though Buenos Aires doesn't really have any "no go" areas, avoid walking around the quieter neighbourhoods after dark. In the rare event of being held up at gunpoint, don't play the hero. Locals warn that this is especially the case if your mugger is a kid, since they know that, as minors, they can't be jailed even if they shoot someone.

Theft from **hotels** is rare but, as anywhere else in the world, do not leave valuables lying round the room. Some hostels have lockers (it's worth having a padlock of your own but, in any case, reports of theft from these places are rare.

Drugs are frowned upon in general. They attract far more stigma here than in most European countries, for example, and Argentine society at large draws very little in the way of a line between "acceptable" soft drugs and "unacceptable" hard drugs. You're very much advised to steer clear of buying or partaking yourself – the penalties are stiff if you get caught.

Useful numbers

Ambulance ⓣ107
Fire ⓣ100
Police ⓣ101

Opening hours, public holidays and fiestas

Most shops and services are open Monday to Friday 9am to 7pm, and Saturday 9am to 2pm. They may close at some point during the day for between one and five hours – as a rule the further north you go, the longer the midday break or **siesta**, sometimes offset by later closing times in the evening, especially in the summer. Supermarkets seldom close during the day and are generally open much later, often until 8 or even 10pm, and on Saturday afternoons. Large shopping malls don't close before 10pm and their food and drink sections (*patios de comida*) may stay open as late as midnight. Many of them open on Sundays, too. Banks tend to be open only on weekdays, from 10am to 4pm, but *casas de cambio* more or less follow shop hours. However, in the northeast, bank opening hours tend to be more like 7am–noon, to avoid the hot, steamy afternoons.

In addition to the **national holidays** listed below, some local anniversaries or **saints' days** are also public holidays when everything in a given city may close down, taking you by surprise. Festivals of all kinds, both religious and profane, celebrating local patrons such as Santa Catalina or the Virgin Mary, or showing off produce such as handicrafts, olives, goats or wine, are good excuses for much partying and pomp.

Calendar of public holidays

January 1 New Year's Day (*Año Nuevo*).
Good Friday (*Viernes Santo*). The whole of *Semana Santa* or Holy Week, from Palm Sunday to Easter weekend, is a big event and traditionally a time when people go on the last vacation of the summer. Accommodation and restaurants stay open to take advantage of this. The Friday, and sometimes the Thursday, but not Easter Monday, are official public holidays.
May 1 Labour Day (*Día del Trabajo*).
May 25 May 1810 Revolution (*Revolución de Mayo*).
June 10 Malvinas Day (*Día de las Malvinas*). The anniversary of the unilateral treaty establishing military rule by Argentina over the Falkland Islands in 1829 (only exercised briefly in 1982; coincidentally the South Atlantic conflict ended on June 10, 1982).
June 20 Flag Day (*Día de la Bandera*).
July 9 Independence Day (*Día de la Independencia*).
August 17 San Martín's Day (*Día de San Martín*). The anniversary of San Martín's death in Boulogne-sur-Mer, France, in 1850.
October 12 Columbus Day (*Día de la Raza*). Controversial commemoration of the "discovery" of the Americas in 1492.
December 25 Christmas Day (*Navidad*).

Outdoor activities

Argentina is a highly exciting destination for outdoors enthusiasts, whether you're keen to tackle radical rock faces or prefer to appreciate the vast open spaces at a more gentle pace, hiking or on horseback. World-class fly-fishing, horse riding, trekking and rock climbing options abound, as do opportunities for white-water rafting, skiing, ice climbing, and even – for those with sufficient stamina and preparation, expeditions onto the Southern Patagonian Icecap. The Patagonian Andes provide the focus for most of these activities, most particularly the area of the central Lake District around Bariloche and El Calafate/El Chaltén, but Mendoza and the far northwest of the country, around Salta and Jujuy, are also worth considering for their rugged mountain terrain. If you're keen on any of the above activities (bar angling, of course), ensure you have taken out appropriate insurance cover before leaving home.

Hiking and climbing

Argentina offers some truly marvellous **hiking** possibilities, and it is still possible to find areas where you can trek for days without seeing a soul. Most of the best treks are found in the national parks – especially the ones in Patagonia – but you can often find lesser-known but equally superb options in the lands bordering the parks. Most people head for the savage granite spires of the **Fitz Roy** region around El Chaltén, an area whose fame has spread so rapidly over the last ten years that it now holds a similar status to Chile's renowned Torres del Paine, not far away, and is packed in the high season (late Dec to Feb). The other principal trekking destination is the mountainous area of **Nahuel Huapi National Park** which lies to the south of Bariloche, centring on the Cerro Catedral massif and Cerro Tronador.

For **climbers**, the Andes offer incredible variety – from volcanoes to shale summits, from the continent's loftiest giants to some of its fiercest technical walls. You do not have to be a technical expert to reach the summit of some of these and, though you must always take preparations seriously, you can often arrange your climb close to the date through local agencies – though it's best to bring as much high-quality gear with you as you can. The climbing season is fairly short – November to March in some places, though December to February is the best time. The best-known, if not the most technical, challenge is South America's highest peak, **Aconcagua** (6962m), accessed from the city of Mendoza. The altitude and storms

National park information

The **National Park Headquarters** at Santa Fe 680 in Buenos Aires (Mon–Fri 10am–5pm; ⓣ011/4311-0303) has an information office on the lower ground floor, with introductory leaflets on the nation's parks, though some are occasionally out of stock. A wider range of free leaflets is often available at each individual park, but these are of variable quality and limited funding means that many parks give you only ones with a basic map and a brief park description. Contact the headquarters well in advance if you are interested in voluntary or scientific projects.

claim several victims a year, some of whom are experienced climbers. Permission to climb must be obtained in advance from the Subsecretaría de Turismo in Mendoza, in person or through a tour company, and climbing fees are high (as much as US$120 in peak season). In the far south are the **Fitz Roy** massif and **Cerro Torre**, which have few equals on the planet in terms of sheer technical difficulty and grandeur of the scenery. On all of these climbs, but especially those over 4000m, you must acclimatize thoroughly, and be fully aware of the dangers of **puna** or **altitude sickness**.

Skiing

The main **skiing** months are July and August (late July is peak season), although in some resorts it is possible to ski from late May to early October. Snow conditions vary wildly from year to year, but you can often find excellent powder snow. The most prestigious resort for downhill skiing is modern **Las Leñas**, which offers the most challenging skiing and once hosted the World Cup; followed by the **Bariloche** resorts of **Cerro Catedral** and **Cerro Otto**, which are the longest-established in the country and are still perhaps the classic Patagonian ski centres, with their wonderful panoramas of the Nahuel Huapi region. For updates on conditions and resorts, check out the Andesweb **website** (ⓦwww .andesweb.com).

History

What sets Argentina apart from the rest of South America is its overwhelmingly European population, representing all four corners of the Old World, and its relatively successful economy until decline set in around the middle of the twentieth century. Since then its potential wealth has been criminally squandered by incompetent or corrupt politicians. Whereas between the two world wars Argentina was one of the richest countries on the globe it now struggles to keep afloat. Yet visitors to most of the country will find a modern, sophisticated nation with a remarkably high standard of living.

Pre-Columbian Argentina

Over the millennia that preceded the arrival of Europeans, widely varying cultures developed. The most complex of these emerged in the Andean northwest, where sedentary agricultural practices developed from about 500 BC. Trade networks were vastly increased once the area came under the sway of pan-Andean empires, especially the

Incas, who incorporated the area into Kollasuyo, their southernmost administrative region, from 1480 on.

By the early sixteenth century, before the arrival of Europeans, Argentina's indigenous population was probably in the region of 400,000, an estimated two-thirds of whom lived in the northwest. The first group to encounter the Spanish were probably the nomadic Querandí of the Pampas region – the northernmost group of the wider Tehuelche culture. Though they put up determined resistance to the Spanish for several decades, their culture was eliminated during the subsequent colonial period.

Early colonization

After **Juan Díaz de Solís** led a small crew to the shores of the River Plate in the search of a trade route to the Far East in 1516 and **Ferdinand Magellan** passed by in 1520 on the way to discovering the straits that now bear his name, the most significant expedition to this part of the world was made by **Sebastian Cabot**. He reached the River Plate in 1526 and built a small, short-lived fort near modern Rosario and misleadingly christened the river Río de la Plata (the River of Silver), after finding bullion amongst the indigenous groups of Paraguay and believing deposits to be nearby. This was not the case – this silver had probably been brought there by the Portuguese – but its lasting legacy is in the word "**Argentina**" itself, which derives from the metal's Latin name, *argentum*. Another result of his expedition was that, in 1535, Pedro de Mendoza was authorized by the Spanish Crown to found Buenos Aires.

From 1543, the new Viceroyalty of Peru was given authority over all of southern Spanish South America. The northwestern Andean region of Argentina was first tentatively explored from the north in the mid 1530s, but the impetus for colonizing this region really came with the discovery, in 1545, of enormous **silver deposits** in **Potosí**, in Upper Peru. This led to the establishment of the **Governorship of Tucumán**, covering a region far larger than the modern province of that name. In 1553, Francisco de Aguirre founded Santiago del Estero, Argentina's earliest continually inhabited town, while other Spaniards soon established the settlements of Mendoza, San Juan and Córdoba.

The Jesuits first arrived in the Paraná area in the late sixteenth century. The first **missions** to the **Guaraní** were established in the upper Paraná from 1609. After raids in the region by roaming **Portuguese slavers** in the 1630s, the Jesuits established their own indigenous militias for protection. Thereafter, Jesuit activity thrived: there were as many as thirty missions, such as San Ignacio Miní, here by the beginning of the eighteenth century, with a total indigenous population exceeding 50,000. In the seventeenth century, the Crown revoked its tax concessions to the Jesuits and their communities were forced to enter the colonial economy. They did so with characteristic vigour, becoming exporters of **yerba mate**, sugar and tobacco. But in 1767, King Charles III ordered their **expulsion** from all Spanish territories – an order carried out the following year.

Towards independence

The **British** had caught wind of the commercial tensions in Buenos Aires and, in June 1806, a force of 1600 men stormed into the city unchecked. The people of Buenos Aires regrouped and ousted their invaders during the **Reconquista** of August 12. One consequence of the victory over the British was to make the people of Buenos Aires aware of the extent to which they could manage their own affairs, and on May 25, they gathered in front of the *cabildo*, proudly wearing rosettes made from sky-blue and white ribbons, the colours that were later to make up the Argentine flag. Inside, the **Primera**

Junta was sworn in to become the first independent government of the region. However, many proclaimed loyalty to Ferdinand VII, imprisoned heir to Charles IV, and this schism heralded two decades of turbulence, involving **independence struggles** with Spain, and **civil war** between Buenos Aires and the interior provinces of the old viceroyalty in the attempt to develop a new order to replace the old. It was not until the late 1820s that the confederation that provided the nucleus of modern Argentina began to stabilize.

The royalist factions in Buenos Aires had, by 1812, effectively been crushed, and a front led by **José de San Martín**, the Sociedad Patriótica, sought full emancipation from foreign powers. However, unitarist and Federalist interests continued to battle for control of the capital, and struggles with pro-royalist forces continued to flare up across the old viceroyalty. The struggles after 1810 saw the emergence in the interior of Federalist **caudillos**, powerful local warlords with their own militias. They press-ganged their rank and file from among the slaves, indigenous peoples and gauchos of the countryside. At the second of two congresses convened to discuss the future of the former viceroyalty, on **July 9, 1816**, in the city of Tucumán, the independence of the **United Provinces of the River Plate** was formally declared. July 9 has since come to be recognized as Argentina's official **independence day.**

The Argentine Republic

In 1862, Bartolomé Mitre was elected to the first presidency of the newly titled **Argentine Republic**; other constitutional provisions included ending trade restrictions throughout the country and promoting the colonization of the interior, one result of which was the sponsorship of the small **Welsh settlements** in Patagonia. Mitre aimed for the rapid modernization of the country, and his achievements included promoting administrational efficiency, creating a national army and overseeing the expansion of a **railway network**. These initiatives were financed by foreign investment from Britain, which contributed the capital to build railroads, and greater export earnings as a result. The first **railway**, built in 1854, connected Buenos Aires to the farms and estancias in its vicinity. By 1880, the railway network carried over three million passengers and over one million tonnes of cargo. Wool production became such a strong sector of the economy in the second half of the nineteenth century that exports dwarfed those of hides, and sheep outnumbered people by thirty to one. The countryside was further altered by the boom in **export crops** such as wheat, oats and linseed, while the invention of **refrigerator ships** in 1876 enabled Argentina to start exporting enormous quantities of meat to the urban centres of newly industrialized Britain and Europe.

Between 1880 and 1918, an astounding six million **immigrants** came to Argentina. Half of these were Italians, a quarter Spaniards while other groups included French, Portuguese, Russians, Ottomans, Irish and Welsh. Many came in search of land but settled for work either as sharecroppers in estancias and *latifundios* or as shepherds, labourers and artisans.

Radicalism and Peronism

As the twentieth century wore on, power still remained in the hands of a tiny minority of the landed and urban elite, leaving the professional and working classes of the rapidly expanding cities unrepresented; a new party, the **Radical Civic Union**, agitated for reform but was excluded from power. A sea change came with the introduction of **universal manhood suffrage** and secret balloting by the reformist conservative president, Roque Sáenz Peña, in 1912. This saw the victory of the first radical president, **Hipólito Yrigoyen**, in 1916, and ushered in thirteen unbroken years of radicalism, under him and Marcelo T. de Alvear.

Soon after World War I, economic growth continued, with the expansion of manufacturing industry, but the benefits were far from equally distributed. By the end of the 1920s, Argentina was the **seventh richest nation** in the world. Britain remained the country's major investor and market. Within fifty years, however, Argentina had fallen to the status of a Third World power, and the loss of this golden dream of prosperity has haunted and perplexed the Argentine conscience ever since. The world **depression** that followed the Wall Street Crash of 1929 marked one of the first serious blows. The affects of the crash and the collapse of export markets left the radical regime reeling and precipitated a **military takeover** in 1930 – an inauspicious omen of what was to come. The military restored power to the old, oligarchic elite, who ruled through a succession of coalition governments that gained a reputation for fraud and electoral corruption.

The first important real watershed of the twentieth century was the rise of **Juan Domingo Perón**, a charismatic military man of relatively modest origins who had risen through the ranks to attain the status of colonel. Perón's involvement with politics intensified after a **military coup** in 1943. During an earlier spell as military attaché in Mussolini's Italy at the outbreak of war, he'd seen for himself the political momentum that could be generated by combining dynamic personal leadership with well-orchestrated mass rallies. His military superiors arrested him in 1945 but this move backfired – Perón's wife, **Evita**, helped organize the mass demonstrations that secured his release, generating the momentum that swept him to the **presidency** in the 1946 elections. His first term in government signalled a programme of radical social and political change.

Certainly, Perón's brand of fierce **nationalism** plus an **authoritarian cult of the leader** resembled Fascism, but he assumed power by overwhelming democratic vote and was seen as a saviour for the labour movement. Perón saw strong **state intervention** as a way of melding the interests of labour and capital, and propounded the doctrine of **Peronism**. His administration passed a comprehensive programme of social welfare legislation, established house-building programmes and supported **nationalization** and **industrialization**, in an attempt to render Argentina less dependent on foreign capital.

The military in politics

Against a background of strikes and civil unrest, factions within the military rebelled in 1955, with the tacit support of the Church and the oligarchy. In the **Revolución Libertadora** Perón was ousted from power and went into exile. There followed eighteen years of alternate military and short-lived civilian regimes that lurched from one crisis to another with little in the way of effectual long-term policies. In 1966, a **military coup** led by General Juan Carlos Onganía saw the imposition of austere measures to stabilize the economy. Onganía's position was becoming less and less tenable and, with unrest spreading throughout the country and an economic crisis provoking devaluation, he was deposed by the army.

It was about this time that society saw the emergence of **guerrilla** organizations: the People's Revolutionary Army (Ejército Revolucionario del Pueblo or **ERP**), committed to radical international revolution in the style of Trotsky or Che Guevara; and the **Montoneros**, a more urban movement that espoused revolution on a more distinctly national model. Multinationals, landed oligarchies and the security forces were favoured Montonero targets.

By 1973, the army seemed to have recognized that its efforts to engineer national unity had failed. General Lanusse risked calling an election, and permitted the Peronist party – but not

Perón himself – to stand. Perón, then living in Spain, nominated a proxy candidate, **Héctor Cámpora**, to stand in his place. Cámpora won, but resigned almost immediately, allowing Perón to return to stand in new elections. As his running mate, Perón chose a former actress from Venezuela – his third wife, María Estela Martínez de Perón, commonly known as **Isabelita**. Perón was now 78, and his health was failing. Though he won the elections with ease, his third term was to last less than nine months, ending with his death in July 1974. Power devolved to Isabelita, who thus became the world's first woman president. Rudderless, out of her depth as regards policy, and with no bedrock of support, she clung increasingly desperately to the advice of José López Rega. Rega's prime notoriety stems from having founded the feared right-wing **death squads** that targeted left-wing intellectuals and guerrilla sympathizers. The long-expected **military coup** finally came in March 1976. Under **General Jorge Videla**, a military junta initiated what it termed the Process of National Reorganization (usually known as the **Proceso**), more often referred to as the Guerra Sucia, or **Dirty War**. In the minds of the military, there was only one response to guerrilla opposition: an iron fist. To that end, they suspended the Constitution, unleashing a campaign of systematic violence with the full apparatus of the state at their disposal. They invoked the Doctrine of National Security to justify what they saw as part of the war against international Communism, and the generals received covert CIA support. Apart from guerrillas and anyone suspected of harbouring guerrilla sympathies, those who were targeted included liberal intellectuals, journalists, psychologists, Jews, Marxists, trade unionists and atheists.

The most notorious tactic was to send hit squads to make people "disappear". Once seized, these **desaparecidos** simply ceased to exist. In fact, the *desaparecidos* were taken to secret detention camps where they were subjected to torture, rape and, usually, execution. Many victims were taken up in planes and thrown, drugged and weighted with concrete, into the River Plate. In the midst of this, the armed forces had the opportunity to demonstrate its "success" to the world, by hosting the **1978 World Cup**. Though victory of the Argentine team stoked nationalist pride, few were fooled into seeing this as a reflection of the military's achievements. Indeed, the vast expense of hosting the project compounded the regime's economic problems. Moreover, it provided a forum for human-rights advocates, including a courageous new group called the **Madres de Plaza de Mayo**, to bring the issue of the *desaparecidos* to the attention of the international media. The Mothers were one of the few groups to challenge the regime directly, organizing silent weekly demonstrations in Buenos Aires' historic central square demanding to know the whereabouts of missing family members. Their protests continue to the present day.

The military's grip on the country was beginning to look increasingly shaky, with the economy in severe recession, skyrocketing interest rates and the first mass demonstrations against the regime. In April 2, 1982, **General Leopoldo Galtieri**, who had seized power in 1981, had no other cards left to play and played his trump: an **invasion of the Falkland Islands**, or **Islas Malvinas**. The population reacted with ecstatic delight but it soon turned to dismay when Argentine forces were defeated by mid-June. For Argentina, the sole positive thing to come out of the war was that it enabled Argentina to throw off an unwanted military regime.

The return to democracy

Democracy was finally restored with the elections of October 1983, won by the radical, **Raúl Alfonsín** who faced two great challenges: to build some sort of national concord and to restore a shattered economy, where inflation was running at over 400 percent. The issue of prosecuting those responsible for crimes during the dictatorship proved an intractable one that could not be resolved to everyone's satisfaction. Alfonsín set up a **National Commission** to investigate the alleged atrocities and its report *Nunca Más* – "Never Again" – documented 9000 cases of torture and disappearance, although it is generally accepted that the number of deaths during the Dirty War was closer to 30,000. Those tried and sentenced to life imprisonment in the first wave of **trials** after the report's initial findings included the reviled Videla, Galtieri and Admiral Emilio Massera.

Alfonsín managed to restructure the national debt and, in 1985, introduced stringent austerity measures known as the **Plan Austral** in reference to the new currency to be introduced. The government continued to be crippled by **hyperinflation**, however, even after the introduction of a second raft of belt-tightening measures, the *Australito*, in 1987. The inflationary crisis turned to meltdown in 1989 when the World Bank suspended all loans: many shops remained closed, preferring to keep their stock rather than selling it for a currency whose value disappeared before their eyes. Elections were called in 1989 but, with severe **civil unrest** breaking out across the country, Alfonsín stood down early, handing control to his elected successor, **Carlos Saúl Menem**.

The 1990s were dominated by Menem and characterized by radical reforms and hefty doses of controversy. Menem's **Justicialist Party** (*Partido Justicialista* or PJ) was Peronist in name but not in nature, and he was to embark on a series of sweeping **neo-Liberal reforms** that reversed virtually all planks of traditional Peronism. His most lauded achievement is that he finally slew inflation in 1991–92. With the backing of international finance organizations, Menem and his Finance Minister, **Domingo Cavallo**, introduced the **Convertibility Plan** in 1992, pegging a **new currency** (the new Argentine peso, worth 10,000 australes) at parity with the US dollar. As a result, inflation remained in single figures throughout the Nineties, which also saw the **privatization** of all the major nationalized utilities and industries.

In August 1994, Menem secured a **constitutional amendment** that allowed a sitting president to stand for a second term, although the mandate was reduced from six years to four. Voters, trusting Menem's economic record, elected him to a second term, one of the hallmarks of which was the increasing **venality** of an administration that had lost much of its earlier reforming impetus. In 1996, Menem sacked Domingo Cavallo and the economic situation remained on a knife edge, with austerity measures seeming to apply to anyone not in government, and a foreign debt that continued to balloon. When, at the beginning of 1999, Brazil's currency was devalued, the government had to resist acute pressure to devalue the peso. As the end of his second term approached, the president mooted the possibility of running for a third consecutive term of office, by arguing that he had only enjoyed one full term of government since the two-term constitutional amendment had been passed. **Fernando de la Rúa**, mayor of the city of Buenos Aires, won the candidacy of the **Alianza** (Alliance Party), a coalition between the radicals (UCR), of which he was leader, and **FREPASO**, itself a coalition party of left-wingers and disaffected Peronists that rose to prominence in the 1995 election. De la Rúa won a clear mandate.

The De la Rúa government

Upon taking office in 1999 De la Rúa seemed to represent the **fiscal and**

moral probity that Argentinians felt their country needed above all else, but it was soon evident that the ruling Alianza would have to seek some pragmatic compromise with the Peronists to govern effectively. Once in charge, the Alianza coalition was hit by severe infighting. De la Rúa's economy minister reached an agreement with the **IMF** to meet stiff budgetary targets in exchange for a "financial shield". When he resigned in March 2001, claiming he lacked De la Rúa's support to carry out the requisite spending and wage cuts and his successor's budget cuts sparked the wrath of progressive sectors of the Radical Party, De la Rúa summoned Domingo Cavallo.

Menem's erstwhile economy minister announced an unrealistic "**zero deficit**" drive to meet stiff IMF targets and protect convertibility, but the country was failing to pull out of recession, with exports and industrial production dismally low, unemployment growing rapidly and financial confidence on the wane. Then, in the national elections of October 2001, the Peronists gained control of both houses of Congress. Soon afterwards, private depositors began to pull their money out of banks, afraid the peso–dollar peg would be abolished but, although under severe pressure to abandon convertibility and devalue the peso, Cavallo stood firm. In early December 2001, he announced restrictions severely limiting access to private deposits, including salaries. This measure, known as the ***corralito*** or "playpen", understandably riled Argentinians of all classes, though the wealthiest managed to get their money out and into accounts abroad. To cap it all, shortly afterwards, the IMF announced the withdrawal of financial support.

On December 13, a general strike was staged against the *corralito* by the Peronist-controlled unions and acts of looting were reported in Greater Buenos Aires. Despite De la Rúa's announcement of a state of siege to deal with the crisis, on 19 December tens of thousands of protestors bashing pots and pans (the first of many noisy "cacerolazos", or saucepan protests) marched on the Plaza de Mayo. More demonstrations took place the following day, and De la Rúa found himself politically isolated and brutal efforts by the police to clear the plaza and halt demonstrations in other major cities ended in a bloodbath, with as many as 33 believed dead. De la Rúa finally left office, ignominiously leaving Government House by helicopter.

The caretaker presidents

Ramón Puerta took over as caretaker president and a congressional assembly was arranged to appoint a new Head of State. On December 23, 2001, the Peronist-controlled assembly appointed San Luis Governor, **Adolfo Rodríguez Saá**. Street demonstrations erupted when Rodríguez Saá appointed an unpopular former Buenos Aires city mayor as his advisor, and the other Peronist governors forced Rodríguez Saá to quit after just a week in office. Puerta took charge again briefly but the lower house Speaker summoned another provincial assembly, and **Eduardo Duhalde** (the Peronist candidate defeated by De la Rúa in 1999) was sworn in as president on January 1, 2002, the fourth in two weeks; he devalued the peso within days. After militant jobless groups clashed with police, leaving two people dead in June 2002, he announced early presidential elections for April 2003, promising not to stand for office. His economy minister, **Roberto Lavagna**, was soon credited with calming financial markets, avoiding hyperinflation and stabilizing the US dollar exchange rate at around three pesos, after a peak of nearly four. He also reached a short-term agreement with the IMF and, by early 2003, signs of economic recovery began to show – the downside being a sharp rise in **poverty** across the country as the price of basic products and imports soared.

The Peronist party, meanwhile, failed to unite, allowing the warring factions to field three separate contenders in the presidential elections, former Presidents Menem and Rodríguez Saá and Duhalde's favourite, **Néstor Kirchner**. Weak candidates and memories of the disastrous De la Rúa administration meant, however, that none of the opposition parties could oust the Peronists from power. On April 27 Argentinians unenthusiastically went to the polls and, as expected, the result was close, with Menem and Kirchner winning just over twenty percent of the vote each. A second round was due in mid-May, to decide between the two leading candidates. When opinion polls gave Kirchner a two-to-one lead over the former president, the latter withdrew from the race. This unexpected move was seen as a spiteful ploy aimed at undermining the new president's authority, depicting him as the "20 percent president". As Kirchner took office at the end of the month, with Duhalde's economy minister in his cabinet, all eyes were on the peso and Argentina's economic recovery.

Books

There's a fair number of books on Argentina available in English, ranging from specialist academic publications to travelogues. Most major bookstores will have an historical work or two while secondhand bookstores are often a goldmine for finding quirky and obscure works by travellers in the nineteenth and early twentieth centuries.

Jorge Luis Borges, *Labyrinths* (Penguin/W.W. Norton & Co). A good introduction to the short stories and essays of Argentina's most famous writer, with selections from various of his major collections, including the seminal *Ficciones*, first published in 1945. Borges is sometimes regarded as the founding father of magic realism, but his complex, highly original works are really in a class of their own.

Nick Caistor, *Argentina in Focus: a Guide to the People, Politics and Culture* (Latin America Bureau, UK). A highly accessible and concise introduction to the country, with chapters dedicated to the economy, culture, society, history and politics, and land and people.

Bruce Chatwin, *In Patagonia* (Vintage/Penguin). For many travellers, *the* Argentine travel book; really a series of self-contained tales (most famously of the Argentine adventures of Butch Cassidy and the Sundance Kid) strung together by their connection with Patagonia. Also see Chatwin and Paul Theroux's, *Patagonia Revisited* (Picador), published in the US as *Nowhere is a Place* (Sierra Club Books).

Julio Cortázar, *Hopscotch* (Harvill Press/Pantheon). In this fantastically complex work, Cortázar defies traditional narrative structure, inviting the reader to "hop" between chapters (hence the name), which recount the interweaving of lives of a group of friends in Paris and London. Cortázar is also well regarded for his enigmatic short stories; try the collections *Bestiary: Selected Stories* (Harvill, UK) and *Blow Up and Other Stories* (Random House).

Che Guevara, *The Motorcycle Diaries* (Verso, UK). A lively counterpoint to the weighty biographies of Argentina's greatest revolutionary, this is Che's own account of his epic motorcycle tour around Latin America, beginning in Buenos Aires and heading south to Patagonia and then up through Chile. Che undertook the tour when he was just 23 and the resulting diary is an intriguing blend of travel anecdotes and an insight into the mind of a nascent revolutionary.

Tomás Eloy Martínez, *The Perón Novel* (Anchor/Vintage) and *Santa Evita* (Anchor/Vintage). In a compelling book that darts between fact and fiction, Martínez intersperses his account of the events surrounding Perón's return to Argentina in 1973 with anecdotes from his past. Perón emerges as a strange and manipulative figure, pragmatic in all his relationships and still irked by Evita's popularity thirty years after her death. The companion volume to *The Perón Novel*, *Santa Evita* recounts the fascinating, morbid and at times farcical true story of Evita's life and – more importantly – afterlife, during which her corpse is hidden, hijacked and smuggled abroad.

Alicia Dujovne Ortiz, *Eva Perón: a Biography* (Warner/St Martin's Press). A biography of Argentina's most famous female icon from an Argentine author, who places her subject firmly within the context of national culture. As colourful as its subject, mixing fact, gossip and rumour, the book lets you judge the woman for yourself.

Manuel Puig, *Kiss of the Spiderwoman* (Vintage, UK). Mixing film dialogue and popular culture with more traditional narrative, this is an absorbing tale of two cellmates, worlds apart on the outside but drawn ever closer together by gay protagonist Molina's recounting of films to his initially cynical companion, left-wing guerrilla Valentín.

Jacobo Timerman, *Prisoner Without A Name, Cell Without A Number* (Vintage). A gruelling tale of detention under the 1976–83 military dictatorship, as endured by Timerman, then the editor of leading liberal newspaper of the time, *La Opinión*. The author is Jewish, and his experiences lead to a wider consideration of anti-Semitism and the nature of totalitarian regimes.

1.1

Buenos Aires and around

Argentina's vibrant, wonderfully idiosyncratic capital, **BUENOS AIRES**, is the third largest city in Latin America, after Brazil's Rio de Janeiro and São Paulo, yet it is a resolutely human kind of place. Famous for its tango, football and European-style architecture, it also holds hidden gems, including picturesque cobbled neighbourhoods, sophisticated shopping and some of the best and most varied cuisine in the whole continent. Cinemas and art galleries, jazz clubs and theatres, atmospheric cafés and antiques markets abound, while exercising or just lazing around in beautifully landscaped parks filled with subtropical vegetation are part of the dynamic yet laid-back *porteño* lifestyle.

Arrival, information and city transport

All international **flights**, with the exception of a few from neighbouring countries, arrive 35km west of the city centre at **Ezeiza International Airport**. The tourist information stand (daily 8am–8pm) is friendly and helpful, with good information on accommodation in the city. If you're determined to take a **taxi** into the city, head for an official taxi stand – a taxi or *remise* (radio-cab) to the centre will set you back around AR$40. Considerably less expensive, the **tourist buses** run by Manuel Tienda Léon and San Martín depart every thirty minutes between 4am and 9pm and drop you at the respective company's central office, both in the downtown area; Manuel Tienda Léon is at Av Santa Fe 790 (☎011/43150-0489), while San Martín is at Av Santa Fe 1158 (☎011/4314-4747). Buenos Aires' domestic airport (also used for shorter-distance international connections) is **"Aeroparque" Jorge Newbery** on the Costanera Norte, around six kilometres north of the city centre. Local bus #33 runs along the Costanera past the airport and will take you to Paseo Colón, on the fringe of the microcentro. Alternatively, Manuel Tienda Léon runs a minibus service though, to most central parts of the city a taxi would not cost much more than the AR$5 they charge.

If you arrive in Buenos Aires by **bus** from domestic points, or on international services from neighbouring countries, you will be dropped off at Buenos Aires' huge bus terminal, **Retiro**, on Avenida Antártida and Ramos Mejía. Taxis are plentiful and the Retiro subte (metro) station just a block away, outside the adjoining train station. Bus #5 or #50 will take you to Congreso and the upper end of Avenida de Mayo, a good hunting ground for accommodation if you don't have anything booked.

Few tourists arrive in Buenos Aires by **train** these days; the only long-distance services arriving in the capital are from Tucumán, Rosario and various cities in the provinces of Buenos Aires and La Pampa. Trains from the Atlantic Coast and La Plata arrive at **Constitución**, in the south of the city at General Hornos 11; those from Mercedes and Lobos in the province of Buenos Aires and Santa Rosa at **Once**, in the west of the city at Avenida Pueyrredón and Calle Bartolomé Mitre. Partly renovated **Retiro** on Avenida Ramos Mejía, just to the east of Plaza San Martín, is the arrival point for trains from Tigre and the northern suburbs. All three terminals have subte stations and are served by numerous local bus routes. Additionally, there are **ferry** services from Uruguay (see p.986).

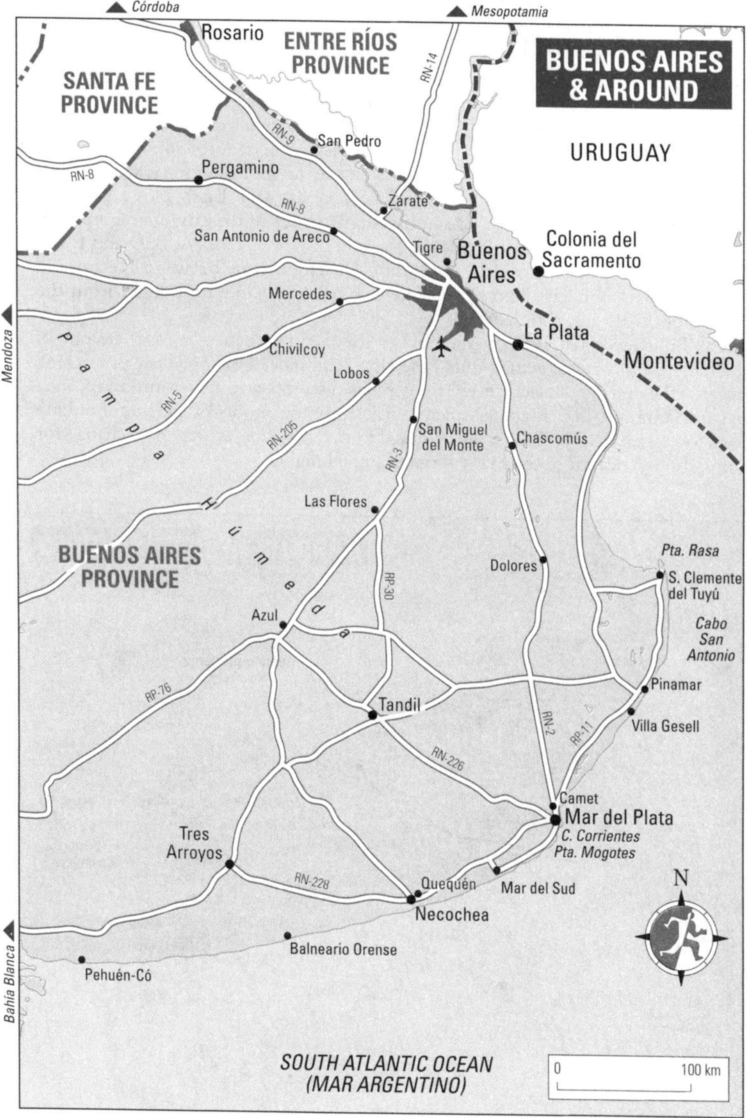

For **tourist information**, head to the city's Secretaría de Turismo at Balcarce 360, 2nd floor (Mon–Fri 9am–5pm; ⓣ011/4114-5791, ⓦwww.buenosaires.gov.ar), a useful port of call for specialized enquiries; otherwise the information on offer at the various **kiosks** – the most useful of these is at Avenida Diagonal Roque Sáenz Peña and Florida (Mon–Fri 9am–5pm) – in the city centre is more than adequate. You can also pick up local (and national) information from the very well-organized **National Tourist Office** at Santa Fe 883 (Mon–Fri 9am–5pm; ⓣ011/4312-2232), which also has details of the **provincial tourist offices** within the capital.

City transport

Buenos Aires is served by an extensive, cheap and efficient **public transport** service. The easiest part of this system to come to grips with is undoubtedly the underground railway or **subte**, which serves most of the city centre and the north of the city from 7am to 11pm. The first in Latin America, Buenos Aires' subte is a reasonably efficient system, and certainly the quickest way to get from the centre to points such as Caballito, Plaza Italia or Chacarita. There are **five lines**, plus a so-called "premetro" system serving the far southwestern corner of the city, linking up with the subte at the Plaza de los Virreyes, at the end of line E. Lines A, B, D and E run from the city centre outwards, while line C, which runs between Retiro and Constitución, connects them all. Tickets cost AR$0.80 and are bought from the ticket booths at each station.

Peak hours excepted, Buenos Aires' **buses** (Ⓦwww.locolectivos.com.ar) are one of the most useful ways of getting round the city – and indeed the only way of reaching many of the outlying districts. Invest in a combined **street- and bus-route map**, such as Guía Lumi or Guía "T", both widely available from street kiosks, and you shouldn't have too much trouble. Tickets are acquired from a machine, which gives change for coins, though not for notes. Many services run all night.

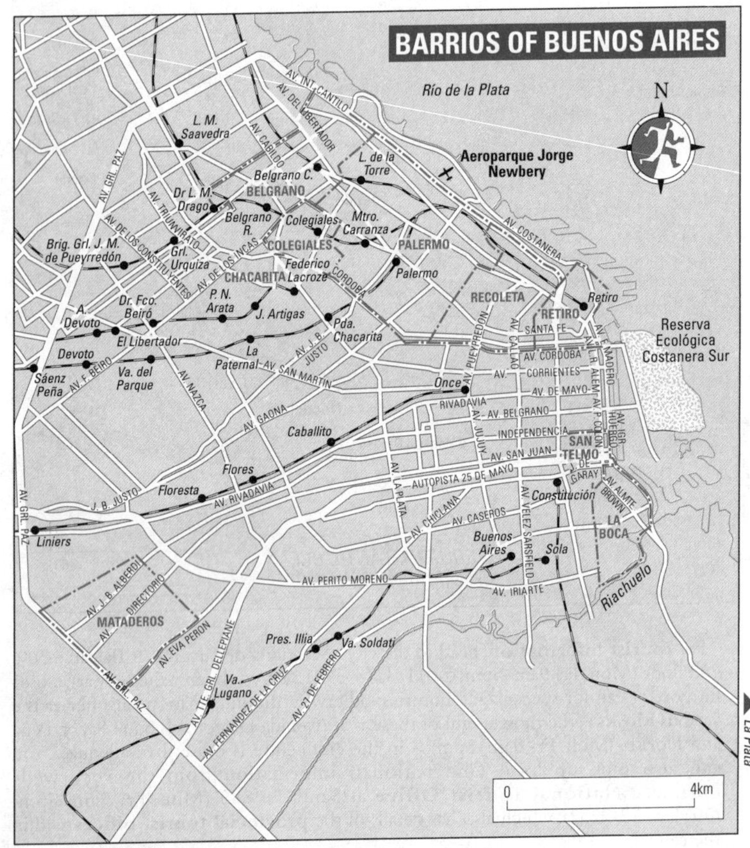

The sheer volume of black and yellow **taxis** touting their business on Buenos Aires' streets is one of the city's most notable sights, and it's rare that it takes more than a few minutes to flag down a cab. The meter starts at just over AR$1 (charges increase at night), and you should calculate on a ride costing around AR$4 per twenty blocks. Taxis are generally a safe form of transport, though you should be aware of the existence of fake taxis, particularly in the vicinity of the financial district or Puerto Madero. **Remises** are radio cabs, plain cars booked through an office (and therefore preferred by some wary locals). Though not particularly economical for short journeys, they're cheaper than taxis for getting to the airport and for early morning starts you may prefer to book one; try Remises Uno (ⓣ011/4638-8318).

Accommodation

Finding **accommodation** in Buenos Aires is rarely a problem – almost half of all the hotels in the country are to be found in the capital. A fan, or air conditioning, is pretty much an essential requirement in summer, and heating is a big plus in winter. **Discounts** can sometimes be negotiated, particularly if you are staying for more than a few days.

All hotels are in the centre unless indicated.

Hotels

Alvear Palace Hotel Av Alvear 1891, Recoleta ⓣ011/4804-7777, ⓦwww.alvearpalace.com. One of the most stylish and traditional of Buenos Aires' luxury hotels, it offers well-appointed and tastefully decorated rooms and extras such as cellular phones, newspapers delivered to each room and a private email address at the hotel. There are floors offering non-smoking rooms and access to the hotel's business centre and gym. ❾

Hotel Alcázar Av de Mayo 935 ⓣ011/4345-0926. This old hotel with a lovely central staircase features attractive, recently refurbished rooms all with heating, a fan and private bathroom. There's a fifteen percent discount for stays over ten days. ❹

Hotel Castelar Av de Mayo 1152 ⓣ011/4381-7873, ⓦwww.castelarhotel.com. A Buenos Aires institution, this pleasant, old-fashioned hotel offers attractive rooms with big comfortable beds and good soundproofing for rooms overlooking noisy Avenida de Mayo. There's also a glamorous bar downstairs. ❻

Hotel Chile Av de Mayo 1297 ⓣ011/4383-7877, ⓦwww.hotelchile.com. Recently refurbished, exceptionally friendly Art Deco hotel; some rooms with pleasant balconies overlooking a side street. Spacious rooms, all with central heating, air conditioning and TV. ❺

Hotel de los Dos Congresos Rivadavia 1777 ⓣ011/4371-0072, ⓦwww.hoteldoscongresos.com. Some of the promotions offered here make the hotel's luxurious suites (the best of which have a spiral staircase and windows overlooking Congreso) excellent deals. All rooms are a good size and decorated in a clean, modern style with air conditioning, TV and minibar. ❻

Hotel Europa Bartolomé Mitre 1294 ⓣ011/4381-9629. Immaculately maintained hotel with pleasingly decorated and comfortable rooms; all with TV and private bathroom, some overlooking the street. One of the best in its price range. ISIC discounts available. ❹

Hotel Maipú Maipú 735 ⓣ011/4322-5142. The old-fashioned *Maipú* is a bit scruffy but has reasonably comfortable rooms and is friendly and eternally popular with foreigners who have left behind a small library of travel guides and novels. Rooms are available with or without private bathroom. ❸

Hotel Phoenix San Martín 780 ⓣ011/4312-4845, ⓦwww.hotelphoenix.com.ar. A pretty hotel in an elegant late-nineteenth-century building, whose central wrought-iron stairwell is illuminated by light filtering through exquisite glass domes. Rooms are large and furnished with a mixture of antiques and modern facilities such as air conditioning and cable TV. Just one block from the more exclusive end of Florida, *Hotel Phoenix* is fairly quiet given its central location. Buffet breakfast. ❻

Hotel Roma Av de Mayo 1413 ⓣ011/4381-4921. A good deal, given its pleasant and central location, the *Roma* has some nice if slightly noisy rooms with balconies looking onto Avenida de Mayo. ❹

Hotel San Martín Av Callao 327, 1st Floor ⓣ&ⓕ011/4371-6450. A comfortable and friendly – if very slightly scruffy – hotel. All rooms have TV and fan and some have balconies – although, as always on Buenos Aires' busy central streets, this can be a mixed blessing. ❹

Marriott Plaza Hotel Florida 1005, Retiro ⓣ011/4318-3000, ⓦwww.marriotplaza.com.ar. Long-established luxury hotel recently taken over by the Marriott chain, who've given it a slightly corporate feel. Top-notch, very plush rooms with plenty of attention to detail; the nicest rooms have a stunning view over Plaza San Martín. Elegant Thirties-style bar and good restaurant. ❾

NH Hotels ⓦwww.nh-hoteles.com. Four extremely well-located, comfortable and stylishly decorated hotels dotted around the central area of the city, all charging reasonable rates especially at weekends. ❺–❼

Sheraton Hotel San Martín 1225, Retiro ⓣ011/4318-9000, ⓦwww.sheraton.com/bue. High-rise hotel with glamorous views over the city from the front and slightly less glamorous – though still impressive – views over the port and railway tracks from the back. Neatly decorated modern and spacious rooms with all the trimmings you'd expect. Oriented towards the needs of business travellers; there's also an outdoor swimming pool, tennis courts and a gym. ❾

Hostels

Buenos Ayres Hostel Pasaje San Lorenzo 320, San Telmo ⓣ011/4361-0694, ⓦwww.buenosayreshostel.com. This newish hostel is a smart modern place with bright, attractively decorated small dormitories and some double rooms. Agreeable communal space with cable TV, Internet access and laundry facilities, plus a terrace with a barbecue. AR$15 per person.

Che Lagarto Youth Hostel Combate de los Pozos 1151, Constitución ⓣ011/4304-7618, ⓔchelagarto@hotmail.com. Laid-back hostel run by a young team. A bit of a squash but very friendly and the owners are expert guides to the city's nightlife. The three-tiered bunk-bed dormitories take some getting used to; or you could try for the one double room. Be warned that the hostel can be pretty noisy, particularly when large contingents from the interior arrive. AR$10 per person.

El Hostal de San Telmo Carlos Calvo 614 ⓣ011/4300-6899, ⓔelhostal@satlink.com. Very well located in one of the prettiest parts of San Telmo, this small hostel is friendly, well kept and bordering on the luxurious: there's Internet access and a fax machine, a laundry, terrace and barbecue area. Most accommodation is in four-bed dormitories (AR$15 per person) but there are also a handful of very small double rooms (AR$20 per room).

Recoleta Youth Hostel Libertad 1216 ⓣ011-4812-4419, ⓔrecoletayouthhostel@libertel.com.ar. Smart new hostel in an attractively modernized and spacious old mansion. Accommodation is in a mixture of dormitories and double rooms and there is a large terrace area and good facilities including TV and Internet access. AR$15 per person.

V&S Youth Hostel Viamonte 887 ⓣ&ⓕ011/4322-0994, ⓦwww.hostelclub.com. This fantastic new youth hostel is the most luxurious in Buenos Aires. In a stylish 1910 French-style mansion, it features a bar, giant TV and even a small gym. There's dormitory accommodation ($20 per person) and a beautiful double room with a balcony and private bathroom (book well in advance; AR$50).

The City

Lending itself perfectly to aimless wandering, **BUENOS AIRES** is primarily is a city of **barrios** (neighbourhoods). For many people, these are Buenos Aires' best sights, more intriguing than most museums, churches or monuments, and requiring nothing more than a bit of time to be enjoyed. More important than the divisions between *barrios* is the one that exists between the **north**, where you'll find Buenos Aires' moneyed classes, and the **south**, which is largely working class – yet for the tourist, all these areas of the city have much to offer.

The main draw in the north, along with the glamour of **Recoleta**'s galleries and boutiques, are the city's best **museums**, and the **landscaped parks** of Buenos Aires' largest and greenest *barrio*, **Palermo**. The microcentro, or downtown, is a transitional zone, beset by a sometimes hectic atmosphere but mellowed by countless welcoming cafés, bookstores and cultural centres. The south features the cultivated charm of **San Telmo**, setting for the city's popular Sunday antique market, as well as the highly idiosyncratic **La Boca**, the city's famously colourful southern

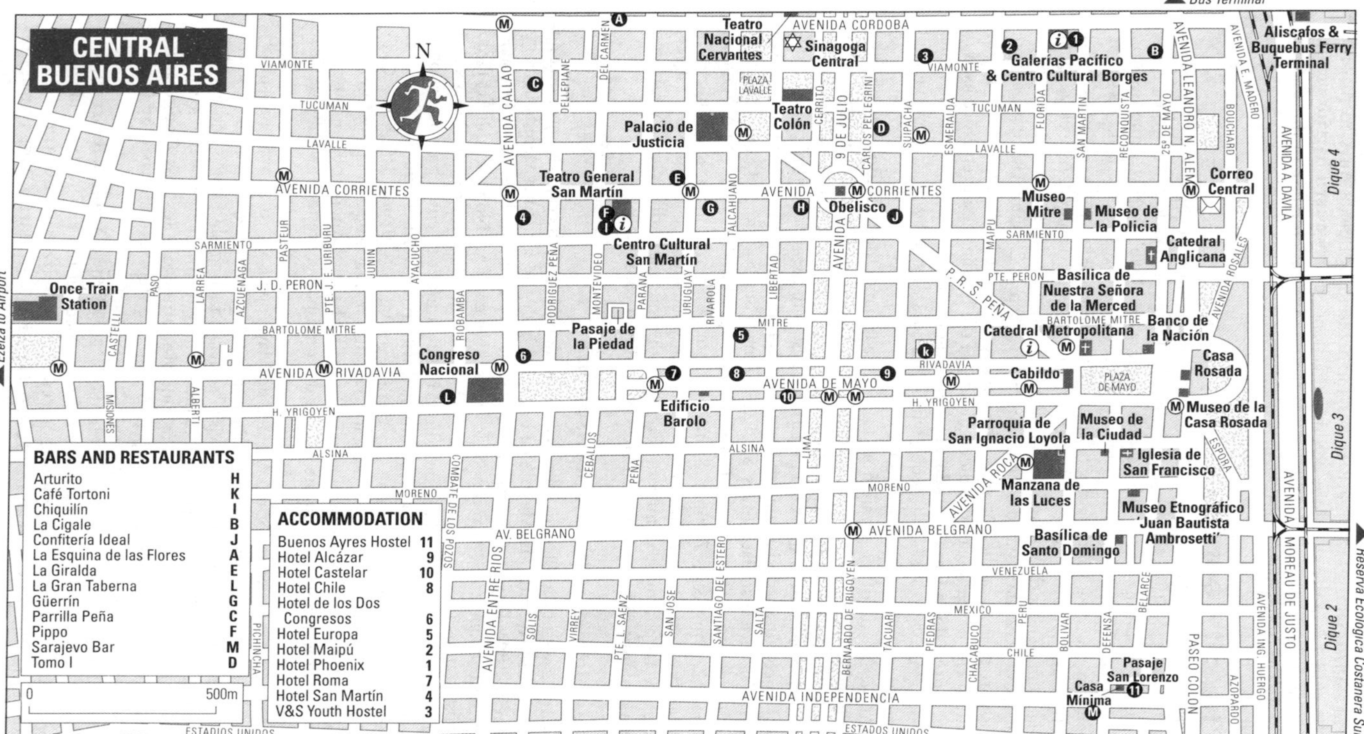
CENTRAL BUENOS AIRES
N
Bus Terminal
Ezeiza to Airport
Reserva Ecológica Costanera Sur
Aliscafos & Buquebus Ferry Terminal
Teatro Nacional Cervantes
Sinagoga Central
Galerías Pacífico & Centro Cultural Borges
Palacio de Justicia
Teatro Colón
Teatro General San Martín
Correo Central
Obelisco
Museo Mitre
Museo de la Policia
Catedral Anglicana
Centro Cultural San Martín
Basílica de Nuestra Señora de la Merced
Once Train Station
Pasaje de la Piedad
Banco de la Nación
Catedral Metropolitana
Congreso Nacional
Casa Rosada
Cabildo
Plaza de Mayo
Plaza Lavalle
Edificio Barolo
Museo de la Casa Rosada
Parroquia de San Ignacio Loyola
Museo de la Ciudad
Iglesia de San Francisco
Manzana de las Luces
Museo Etnográfico 'Juan Bautista Ambrosetti'
Basílica de Santo Domingo
Pasaje San Lorenzo
Casa Mínima
Dique 4
Dique 3
Dique 2
AVENIDA CORDOBA
VIAMONTE
TUCUMAN
LAVALLE
AVENIDA CORRIENTES
SARMIENTO
J. D. PERON
BARTOLOME MITRE
AVENIDA RIVADAVIA
AVENIDA DE MAYO
H. YRIGOYEN
ALSINA
MORENO
AV. BELGRANO
AVENIDA BELGRANO
VENEZUELA
MEXICO
CHILE
AVENIDA INDEPENDENCIA
ESTADOS UNIDOS
AVENIDA CALLAO
AVENIDA ENTRE RIOS
COMBATE DE LOS POZOS
AVENIDA 9 DE JULIO
AVENIDA LEANDRO N. ALEM
AVENIDA E. MADERO
BOUCHARD
AVENIDA A. DAVILA
AVENIDA MOREAU DE JUSTO
AVENIDA ING. HUERGO
AZOPARDO
PASEO COLON
AVENIDA ROSALES
AVENIDA ROCA
P. R. S. PEÑA
BARS AND RESTAURANTS
Arturito H
Café Tortoni K
Chiquilín I
La Cigale B
Confitería Ideal J
La Esquina de las Flores A
La Giralda E
La Gran Taberna L
Güerrín G
Parrilla Peña C
Pippo F
Sarajevo Bar M
Tomo I D
ACCOMMODATION
Buenos Ayres Hostel 11
Hotel Alcázar 9
Hotel Castelar 10
Hotel Chile 8
Hotel de los Dos Congresos 6
Hotel Europa 5
Hotel Maipú 2
Hotel Phoenix 1
Hotel Roma 7
Hotel San Martín 4
V&S Youth Hostel 3
0 500m

port district, which gives the Porteños, the denizens of Buenos Aires, their name. Less visited than the rest of the city, the attractions of the **western barrios** include one of the city's most enjoyable events, the Sunday **gaucho fair** in the outlying *barrio* of **Mataderos**.

The city centre

Most of Buenos Aires' historical moments and monuments lie around the **Plaza de Mayo**. The plaza's been bombed, filled by Evita's *descamisados* (or manual workers) and is still the site of the Madres de Plaza de Mayo's weekly demonstration. The square itself is one of the most attractive in the city, largely thanks to its stupendous towering palm trees, which give the plaza a wonderfully subtropical feel, particularly when the whole place is bathed in evening sunlight. As well as Evita, Maradona, Galtieri and Perón have all addressed the crowds from the balcony of the **Casa Rosada** (guided tours Mon–Fri 11.15am & 2.15pm; AR$5; bring your passport to leave at the entrance), the pink governmental palace that occupies the eastern end of the square. On the south side of the building, a side entrance leads to the **Museo de la Casa Rosada**, Hipólito Yrigoyen 219 (Mon–Fri 10am–6pm Sun 2–6pm; AR$1; ⓣ011/4344-3600), which provides a carefully neutral overview of Argentina's turbulent political history.

At the far end of the square from Casa Rosada stands the **Cabildo**, the only civil building to have survived from colonial times. Despite Italianate remodelling at the end of the last century, its simple unadorned lines, green and white shuttered facade and colonnaded front still stand in stark contrast with the more ornate public buildings since constructed around it. The interior of the Cabildo houses a small **museum** of historical artefacts (Tues–Sat 12.30–7pm & Sun 3–7pm; AR$1). To the right is the columned facade of the **Catedral Metropolitana** (Mon–Fri 8am–7pm, Sat 9am–12.30pm & 5–7.30pm, Sun 9am–2pm & 4–7.30pm; free guided tours Mon–Fri 1pm, Sat 11.30am, Sun 10am), a sturdy and rather severe Neoclassical edifice. By far the most significant feature of the interior is the solemnly guarded **mausoleum** to Independence hero, **General San Martín**.

Avenida de Mayo and around

Heading west from Plaza de Mayo takes you along one of the capital's most striking streets, the **Avenida de Mayo**. The city's first high-rise structures were built along here in 1894. Part of a project to remodel the city along the lines of Haussmann's Paris, the Avenida de Mayo is notable for its melange of Art Nouveau and Art Deco constructions. On the corner of Perú and Avenida de Mayo is **Perú station**, second stop on Line A of the subte. You'll need to buy a ticket to enter, but the station is well worth a visit, having been refurbished with old advertisements and fittings to reflect the history of the line. At Avenida de Mayo 829, you'll find the **Café Tortoni**. Going for over 150 years, it is famous for its artistic and literary connections (Borges was among its patrons); inside, heavy brown columns and Art Nouveau mirrored walls create an elegant atmosphere, presided over by discreet white-coated waiters.

At its western extremity, the Avenida de Mayo opens up to encircle the spindly **Plaza del Congreso**, whose western end is dominated by the Greco–Roman-style **Congress** building (guided visits available in English, French and Spanish; enquire at Hipólito Yrigoyen 1864, to the south of the main entrance). The square's most striking monument is the exuberant **Monumento a los dos Congresos**, a series of sculptural allegories atop heavy granite steps and crowned by the triumphant figure of the Republic.

Four blocks to the north of Avenida de Mayo runs **Avenida Corrientes**. Immortalized in several tangos and long the focus of the city's cultural life, it's a broad avenue lined by cafés, bookshops, cinemas and pizzerias. At Corrientes 1500, you'll find the glass front of the **Teatro General San Martín** with a small free gallery at the back of the building, which often has some worthwhile photographic exhibitions showcasing Argentine photographers. In the same building, the **Centro Cultural San Martín** houses the Museo de Arte Moderno's Ignacio Pirovano Collection on the ninth floor, with a strong selection on Arte Concreto, Argentina's major abstract art movement, which was founded in 1945 and counted Tomás Maldonado, Ennio Iommi and Lidy Prati anoong its members. Looking east along the avenue, you won't miss the **Obelisco**, a 67-metre tall obelisk that dominates the busy intersection between Corrientes and Avenida 9 de Julio and features on the city's most clichéd postcards. It was erected in 1936 and is a magnet for car-loads of celebrating fans after a major football victory.

One block to the north of Corrientes, on **Plaza Lavalle**, sandwiched between calles Libertad and Talcahuano, stands the handsome **Teatro Colón** (see p.104 for booking details), its grand but restrained French Renaissance exterior painted a muted pinkish beige. Most of the twentieth century's major opera and ballet stars have appeared here, from Caruso and Callas to Nijinsky and Nureyev. There are regular, very informative **guided visits** to the theatre (Mon–Fri 11am–4pm hourly; AR$5) in both Spanish and English.

Calle Florida and around

A brisk walk five blocks east from the Teatro Colón will brng you to the pedestrianized **Calle Florida**, which bisects the lower reaches of Corrientes and runs due north from Avenida de Mayo. There's a lively buzz about this commercial street and always a handful of street performers doing their best to charm passers-by into digging into their pockets. Towards the northern end, the **Galerías Pacífico** shopping centre offers a glitzy bit of retailing within a vaulted and frescoed building constructed by Paris department store Bon Marché at the end of the nineteenth century. On the first floor is the entrance to the **Centro Cultural Borges** (Mon–Sat 10am–9pm, Sun noon–9pm; AR$2; Ⓦwww.ccborges.org.ar), a surprisingly large space offering photography or painting exhibitions, from both Argentine and foreign artists.

A short way southeast of Galerías Pacífico, running north–south from Avenida Córdoba to Avenida Juan de Garay, **Puerto Madero** is Buenos Aires' newest *barrio*. The port was constructed in 1882 and consists of four enormous docks running parallel to the River Plate and lined by sturdy red-brick warehouse buildings. Its transformation has undoubtedly opened up a long-ignored space in the city, but it's a rather elitist development – good for a stroll, but created with little regard as to the potential of the dock area as a recreational space for all the city's inhabitants.

The southern barrios

The **south** of the city is perhaps its most distinctive part, featuring the historic monuments of **Montserrat**, the atmospheric streets and squares of **San Telmo** and colourful **La Boca**, whose run-down port is fringed by some of the city's most photographed and brightly painted houses.

Montserrat

MONTSERRAT is the oldest part of the city and, together with neighbouring San Telmo, one of the most interesting parts to explore on foot. A good starting point for delving into its grid of narrow streets and historic buildings is **Calle Defensa**, named in honour of residents who slowed the pace of British troops by pouring boiling water on them during the British Invasions of 1806 and 1807. On the corner of Alsina and Defensa, the eclectic, Neo-Baroque **Iglesia de San Francisco** (Mon–Fri 6.30am–noon & 4.30–7pm, Sat 7.30–11am & 4.30–7pm, Sun 7.30–11am) is one of the churches burnt by angry Peronists in March 1955 after the navy had bombed a trade union demonstration in Plaza de Mayo, killing several hundred people. Half a block west of the church, the **Museo de la Ciudad**, at Alsina 412 (Mon–Fri 11am–7pm, Sun 3–7pm; AR$1, free on Wed), an imaginative though small museum, offers regularly changing exhibitions designed to illustrate everyday aspects of *porteño* life. Taking up the block bounded by Alsina, Perú, Moreno and Bolívar – one block west of Defensa – is the complex of buildings known as the **Manzana de las Luces**, or block of enlightenment (for guided visits, ask at Perú 272: daily 3pm, Sat & Sun also 4.30 and 6pm; AR$2). Dating from 1662, the complex originally housed a Jesuit community, and has been home to numerous official institutions throughout its history. Today, the block encompasses the elite Colegio Nacional as well as Buenos Aires' oldest church, **San Ignacio** (Mon–Fri 8am–1.30pm & 5–8.30pm, Sat & Sun 8am–1.30pm), begun in 1675, on the corner of Bolívar and Alsina. Offering a break from all the colonial architecture, the **Museo Etnográfico Juan Bautista Ambrosetti**, at Moreno 350 (Wed–Sun 2.30–6.30pm; guided visits Sat & Sun 3.30pm & 5pm; AR$1), runs some good temporary exhibitions on mostly indigenous themes.

San Telmo

It's impossible not to be seduced by the crumbling decorative facades and cobbled streets of **SAN TELMO**, one of Buenos Aires' most atmospheric neighbourhoods. Calle Defensa runs through the heart of the *barrio* all the way to Parque Lezama: on weekdays it's a busy thoroughfare, with buses tearing recklessly along it, but at the weekends you've plenty of space to stand back and admire the elegant mansions that line it. At the bottom of Pasaje San Lorenzo, a narrow side street off Defensa between Chile and Av Independencia, you'll encounter a cluster of **tango bars**, or *tanguerías,* of which the most famous, on the corner of Independencia and Balcarce, is *El Viejo Almacén* (see p.103). Continue along Defensa to tiny **Plaza Dorrego**, San Telmo's main square, surrounded by some elegant two-storeyed mansions. On Sunday it becomes the setting for the city's long-running antique market, the **Feria de San Pedro Telmo** (Sun 10am–5pm; buses #9, #10, #24, #28 and #86 easily picked up downtown). Almost theatrically set up and overflowing with antique *mates*, jewel-coloured soda syphons, watches and old ticket machines, the stalls offer fascinating browsing and you'll be entertained – weather permitting – by a free but dazzling display of **tango**. In addition to the many **antique shops** clustered around the plaza are a number of tempting bars, but watch out for prices; the most traditional of all is the lovely *Plaza Dorrego Bar* (see p.102), at Defensa 1098.

Heading south of Plaza Dorrego, along Defensa, you'll come to the **Pasaje de la Defensa**, at no. 1179, a converted nineteenth-century residence, with a typical tiled courtyard inside and stairs leading up to a gallery now housing yet more antique shops and cafés. Half a block further south, the old-world charm of San Telmo's most prettified quarter is rather abruptly curtailed by busy Avenida San Juan, on which you'll find the **Museo de Arte Moderno de Buenos Aires** at no. 350 (Tues–Fri 10am–8pm, Sat & Sun 11am–8pm; AR$1, free on Wed; Ⓦwww.mam-ba.org). Housed in an old tobacco factory, the museum stages some interesting temporary exhibitions in its vast and well-laid-out galleries. Still another three blocks south along Defensa will bring you to **Parque Lezama**, one of Buenos Aires' most beautiful and underrated parks. Within the park, though entered via Defensa 1600, the **Museo Histórico Nacional** (Tues–Fri 11am–2pm, Sat 3–6pm, Sun 2–6pm; guided visits Sat & Sun 2pm; AR$1) is housed in a magnificent colonial building, painted an almost startling deep red and covered with elaborate white mouldings that look almost like piped icing. Inside, there is a well-organized exposition of the country's past dating from the pre-Spanish period to 1950. A high point is the absolutely stunning **Tarja de Potosí**, an elaborate silver and gold shield given to General Belgrano in 1813 by the women of Potosí, Bolivia, in recognition of his role in the struggle for independence from Spain.

La Boca

In the capital's southeastern corner, **LA BOCA** is most renowned for its brightly coloured wooden and corrugated-iron houses and its football team, **Boca Juniors**, who, much to the pique of fierce rivals, River Plate, are the most legendary Argentine team abroad, partly thanks to Diego Maradona. By far the most visited area is the huddle of three or four streets around the **Vuelta de Rocha**, an acute bulge in the river's course. La Boca has gained an unfortunate reputation for being, if not unsafe, at least slightly risky for tourists; there's no need to be paranoid about visiting, but you should avoid wandering around visibly touting a camera. La Boca is easily reached on foot from Parque Lezama or by **bus** #29 from Corrientes or Plaza de Mayo, #86 from Plaza de Mayo or #53 from Constitución.

The major landmark in La Boca, **La Bombonera** makes a good place to start your tour of the neighbourhood. Boca Juniors' stadium stands at Brandsen 805 (Ⓣ011/4362-2050), three blocks west of Avenida Almirante Brown. Even if you're not lucky enough to catch a game here, it's free to visit the stadium (you'll need ID). A close second behind La Bombonera in the monumental stakes is, oddly enough, a former railway siding now transformed into a pedestrian street and open-air art museum: **Caminito**. It's only a short street, running diagonally between the riverfront and Calle Olavarría, three blocks away form the soccer stadium. It was "founded" by the *barrio*'s most famous artist, **Benito Quinquela Martín**, who painted epic and expressive scenes of daily life in the neighbourhood. He encouraged the immigrants' tradition of painting their houses in bright colours and took the name for the street from a 1926 tango. There's almost something of the pastiche about Caminito these days – its houses seem almost too colourful, too perfectly photogenic – but these bold blocks of rainbow-coloured walls set off with contrasting window frames and iron-railed balconies are still absolutely stunning. Down the middle of the street, there's an open-air **arts and crafts fair** (daily 10am–6pm), dominated by garish paintings of the surrounding area.

The southern end of Caminito leads down to the riverfront; the **Riachuelo** bulges dramatically at this point, creating a kind of inlet known as the **Vuelta de Rocha** whose contours are followed by **Avenida Don Pedro de Mendoza**. A wide pedestrian walkway runs alongside the river in a rather ambitious attempt to lure passers-by closer to the notoriously evil-smelling Riachuelo. The view from Pedro de Mendoza is of a jumbled mass of boats, factories and bridges: directly south lies the largely industrial suburb of Avellaneda, while to your left stands one of Buenos Aires' major landmarks, the massive iron **Puente Transbordador** or transporter bridge, built in the early years of the twentieth century and now out of use. Away from the riverbank, half a block south of the intersection between Caminito and Pedro de Mendoza, you'll find one of Buenos Aires' newest and best art galleries, the **Fundación Proa** at no. 1929 (Tues–Sun 11am–7pm; AR$3; Ⓣ011/4303-0909, Ⓦwww.proa.org). Housed within a strikingly converted white mansion Proa has no permanent collection but hosts some fascinating and diverse exhibitions.

The northern barrios

Buenos Aires' finest **museums**, containing the country's principal collections of colonial, Spanish, folk, decorative and plastic art since independence, are concentrated in its northern residential *barrios* of **Retiro**, **Recoleta**, **Palermo** and **Belgrano**, which stretch for kilometres along wide avenues beyond Avenida Córdoba. Like the rest of the city's neighbourhoods, each has a distinctive character while being true to the city as a whole – broadly speaking a combination of extravagant elegance and an authentic lived-in feel pervades each of them.

Retiro

At the far northern end of Calle Florida, **Plaza San Martín**, the focal point of **RETIRO**, is one of the city's most enticing green spaces. It is flanked by opulent patrician buildings, such as Palacio Paz, now a military museum, as well as one of Buenos Aires' top hotels, and the lavish Basílica del Santísimo Sacramento. Its leafy

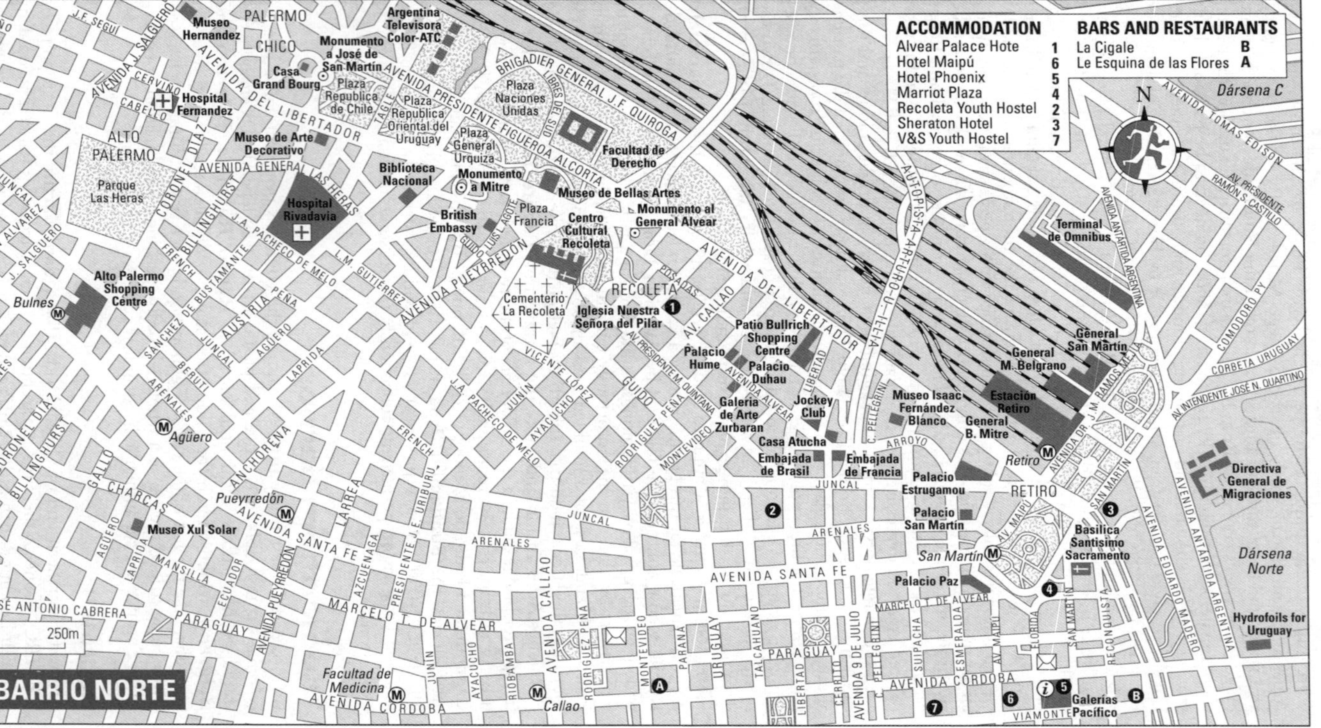
BARRIO NORTE
ACCOMMODATION
Alvear Palace Hote 1
Hotel Maipú 6
Hotel Phoenix 5
Marriot Plaza 4
Recoleta Youth Hostel 2
Sheraton Hotel 3
V&S Youth Hostel 7
BARS AND RESTAURANTS
La Cigale B
Le Esquina de las Flores A
Malba & Belgrano
PALERMO CHICO
ALTO PALERMO
RECOLETA
RETIRO
Museo Hernandez
Hospital Fernandez
Casa Grand Bourg
Monumento a José de San Martín
Argentina Televisora Color-ATC
Plaza Republica de Chile
Plaza Republica Oriental del Uruguay
Plaza General Urquiza
Plaza Naciones Unidas
Facultad de Derecho
Museo de Arte Decorativo
Biblioteca Nacional
Monumento a Mitre
Museo de Bellas Artes
Hospital Rivadavia
Parque Las Heras
British Embassy
Plaza Francia
Centro Cultural Recoleta
Monumento al General Alvear
Cementerio La Recoleta
Iglesia Nuestra Señora del Pilar
Alto Palermo Shopping Centre
Bulnes
Agüero
Pueyrredón
Museo Xul Solar
Patio Bullrich Shopping Centre
Palacio Hume
Palacio Duhau
Galeria de Arte Zurbaran
Jockey Club
Casa Atucha
Embajada de Brasil
Embajada de Francia
Museo Isaac Fernández Blanco
Palacio Estrugamou
Palacio San Martín
Palacio Paz
San Martín
Estación Retiro
General B. Mitre
General M. Belgrano
General San Martín
Terminal de Omnibus
Retiro
Basilica Santisimo Sacramento
Directiva General de Migraciones
Dársena C
Dársena Norte
Hydrofoils for Uruguay
Galerías Pacífico
Facultad de Medicina
Callao
AUTOPISTA ARTURO U. ILLIA
AVENIDA DEL LIBERTADOR
AVENIDA PRESIDENTE FIGUEROA ALCORTA
AVENIDA SANTA FE
AVENIDA CALLAO
AVENIDA 9 DE JULIO
AVENIDA CÓRDOBA
AVENIDA PUEYRREDÓN
AVENIDA ALVEAR
AVENIDA ANTÁRTIDA ARGENTINA
AVENIDA EDUARDO MADERO
AVENIDA TOMÁS EDISON
0 250m

southern half is a romantic meeting place, office-workers' picnic area, children's playground and many people's arrival point in downtown Buenos Aires, since the airport shuttle-buses drop you off here, at the far eastern end of Avenida Santa Fe. It was created specially for a **monument to General San Martín**, moved here in 1910 for the country's centenary. Aligned with Avenida Santa Fe, the imposing bronze equestrian statue stands proudly on a high marble pedestal decorated with scenes representing national liberation. The more open, northern half of the plaza is dominated by the seventy-metre **Torre Monumental** (formerly known as the Torre de los Ingleses), the Anglo-Argentine community's contribution to the 1910 centenary celebrations; during and after the 1982 South Atlantic conflict, there was talk of demolishing it.

Immediately to the northwest of Plaza San Martín, **Palacio San Martín** (guided tours Thurs 11am & noon, Fri 3pm, 4pm, 5pm & 6pm, last Sat of month 11am, noon, 3pm, 4pm, 5pm & 6pm; free; ⓣ011/4819-8092) is a particularly extravagant example of the ostentatious palaces that many of the city's rich and famous commissioned in the early twentieth century. It was built in 1905 for one of Argentina's richest and most influential land-owning clans, the aristocratic **Anchorena family** – who gave rise to the Argentine expression "as rich as an Anchorena". The overall structure is based on a nineteenth-century Parisian banker's mansion, with its slate mansard roofs, colonnades and domed attics, while the neo-Baroque interior is inspired by the eighteenth-century *Hôtel de Condé*, also in Paris.

Three irregular blocks away from the Palacio San Martín, at Suipacha 1422, is the **Museo de Arte Hispanoamericano Isaac Fernández Blanco** (Tues–Sun 2–7pm; guided tours in Spanish and English Sat & Sun 4pm; closed Jan; AR$1, free on Thurs), one of the city's cultural highlights. It's housed in the Palacio Noel, a stunning 1920s house in a style imitating eighteenth-century Lima Baroque. It's the perfect home for a superb collection of Spanish-American art, which was merged from several private collections and is highlighted by a huge display of colonial silverware.

Recoleta

A *barrio* almost synonymous with its world-famous cemetery, **RECOLETA** extends northwestwards from Retiro, together with which it forms the prestigious Barrio Norte, once the city's most aristocratic neighbourhood. **La Recoleta Cemetery** at Av Quintana and Junín (daily 8am–6pm, 3rd Sun of month 8am–2.30pm; guided tours last Sun of month at 2.30pm; free) exerts a magnetic attraction on locals and foreigners, principally because it's where **Evita** is buried. Created in 1822, in the gardens of the Franciscan monastery, the necropolis features great monuments of dark granite, white marble and gleaming bronze, decorated with countless stone angels and statues of the Virgin Mary. A haven of peace and quiet within its high walls, it's a great place to wander, exploring its narrow streets and wide avenues of yews and cypress trees, where dozens of feral cats prowl among the graves. Evita's family's plain, polished black granite vault is now her final resting place, but unlike many other graves it's not signposted, so follow the signs to President Sarmiento's, over to the left when you come in, then count five alleyways farther away from the entrance, and look out for the pile of bouquets by the vault. Her full name, María Eva Duarte de Perón, and some poignant quotes from her speeches are inscribed on several bronze plaques.

North of the cemetery gates is the stark white silhouette of the **Basílica Nuestra Señora del Pilar** (daily 9am–7pm; guided tours Tues, Thurs & Sat 10.30am, Sun 2.30pm & 6.15pm; free). Built in the early eighteenth century by Jesuits, it's the second oldest church in Buenos Aires. The sky-blue Pas-de-Calais ceramic tiles atop its single slender turret were then painstakingly restored, along with the plain facade, using eighteenth-century watercolours as a guide. Inside, the magnificent Baroque silver altarpiece, embellished with an Inca sun and other pre-Hispanic details, was made by craftsmen from Jujuy.

The **Centro Cultural de Recoleta** (Tues–Fri 2–9pm, Sat & Sun 10am–9pm; guided visits Sat & Sun 4pm; AR$1), immediately north of the basílica, at Junín 1930, is one of the city's leading arts centres. It stages several exhibitions simultaneously in the various galleries; some are mainstream, others more avant-garde, but all have an emphasis on local talent. From the roof terrace you can enjoy views of the surrounding parkland and part of the cemetery.

Argentina's principal art museum, the **Museo Nacional de Bellas Artes** (Tues–Fri 12.30–7.30pm, Sat & Sun 9.30am–7.30pm; free; Ⓦwww.startel.com.ar/bellasartes/mnba) is housed in an unassuming building at Av del Libertador 1473, half a kilometre north of the cemetery. Like the *barrio*'s architecture, the museum's contents are resoundingly European, and the European influences on the Argentine art on display are clearly evident. On the ground floor is a modest but refined collection of mostly European art, while the upper floor galleries contain a selection of major Argentine artists, some of whom studied in Europe. A large collection of works by one of the artists on display here can be seen at the unusual **Museo Xul Solar** (Tues–Fri noon–8pm, Sat noon–7pm; AR$3), at Laprida 1212 near the corner of Calle Mansilla, tucked away in a residential area, 1.5km southwest of the Museo de Bellas Artes. The artist's house was remodelled in the 1990s and its design is as exciting as the display of paintings and other works by Solar spanning nearly five decades.

Palermo

Associated more than any other part of the city with Borges – he lived in the neighbourhood's historic core of **Palermo Viejo** – **PALERMO** is a huge expanse of middle-class homes and leafy parkland, dotted with bombastic monuments and some of the city's best museums. Along Avenida del Libertador, which sweeps past the eastern reaches of the *barrio*, are two outstanding yet distinctive museums. With its remarkable collection of mostly European art and furniture, the **Museo de Arte Decorativo**, at no. 1902 (Tues–Sat 2–7pm; AR$2, free Tues; Ⓦwww.mnad.org), is housed in Palacio Errázuriz, one of the city's most original private mansions, albeit of typically French design. At no. 2373, you'll find the quaint **Museo Hernández** (Wed–Sun 1–7pm; AR$1) and its permanent exhibition about the Argentine folk heritage is housed in two buildings separated by a shady patio. The first section is a display of mostly nineteenth-century rural silverware, while the second, across the courtyard, comprises a number of beautiful ponchos, the inevitable reconstructed *pulpería* (rural inn) and other miscellany related to gaucho customs and rituals.

A few blocks away towards the river, at Av Figueroa Alcorta 3415, stands a welcome newcomer to Buenos Aires' museum scene, the impressive **Museo de Arte Latinamericano de Buenos Aires** or "**Malba**" (Mon & Thurs–Sun noon–8pm, Wed noon–9pm; AR$4, free Wed, free for students and pensioners; Ⓦwww.malba.org.ar). The smart, glass-dominated building houses a magnificent collection of Latin American art from the twentieth century onwards. Sumptuously set off in beautifully lit, spacious galleries on the middle floor, the remarkably varied permanent exhibition guides you through three major periods of Latin American art from several countries, though Argentine artists account for the lion's share. The museum also boasts one of the city's best art bookshops and an airy café serving varied fare and excellent wines (Mon & Thurs–Sun 9am–9pm, Wed 9am–midnight).

The cultural and social focal point of atmospheric **Palermo Viejo** is Plaza Serrano, officially named **Plaza Cortázar** after the Argentine novelist Julio Cortázar, who frequented this part of the city on his rare visits to Buenos Aires from his adoptive Paris in the 1960s. This lively plaza is now surrounded by trattorias, cafés and trendy bars, some of them doubling as extremely active arts centres and galleries. The stretch of Calle Serrano leading due east from this plaza, to Avenida Santa Fe, has been officially renamed Calle J.L. Borges. The writer's home, a two-storey villa with its own mill, used to stand at no. 2135, but **Borges** pilgrims will have to make do with a commemorative plaque at no. 2108.

A short way to the northwest, at the corner of Avenida del Libertador and Avenida Sarmiento, **Parque 3 de Febrero** is one of the biggest and most popular parks in the city. Designed at the end of the nineteenth century, it was originally planned by environmentally conscious **President Sarmiento**. He named the park after the date of the 1852 Battle of Monte Caseros when his archrival General Rosas was defeated and overthrown. After decades of neglect by the municipal authorities, the park has recently been cleaned up, and its massive rubber trees, palms and jacarandas, where parrots squawk, are surrounded by well-tended lawns.

Belgrano

The principal attraction of mainly residential **BELGRANO**, to the north of Palermo, stands on the northern side of central Plaza Belgrano. The **Museo de Arte Español** at Juramento 2291 (Mon & Wed–Fri 2–8pm, Sat & Sun 3–8pm; guided visits Sun 4pm & 6pm; AR$2, free on Thurs; for English tours call ⓣ011/4783-2640). Housed in the well-restored, whitewashed colonial building is a priceless collection of Spanish art, from the Renaissance to the early twentieth century, collected by the aristocratic Uruguayan exile **Enrique Larreta**. In 1900, Larreta (1873–1961) married Josefina Anchorena, the daughter of Mercedes Castellanos de Anchorena, and her dowry was a Greco-Roman villa, built in 1882 as a summerhouse for the architects' parents-in-law. Larreta had the house transformed into an Andalucian-style mansion, now the museum, with the help of his friend, the leading architect and aesthete Martín Noel. From around 1900 to 1916, the dandyish Larreta spent a lot of time in Spain, visiting churches and monasteries and buying up artworks for his Belgrano home, mostly from the Renaissance – statues and paintings of saints, but also furniture, porcelain, silverware and tapestries, all of which are displayed in the magnificent setting of this house. A huge *ombú* dominates the oasis-like garden next door, a profusion of magnolias, hydrangeas and agapanthus.

The western barrios: Chacarita and Mataderos

Taking its name from the days when the *barrio* was home to a small farm (*chacra*) run by Jesuits, **CHACARITA** is nowadays synonymous with its enormous cemetery, containing the city's most-visited tomb. Lying at the northern end of Avenida Corrientes (subte station Federico Lacroze), due west from Palermo, the **Cementerio de Chacarita** (daily 7am–6pm; free), whose main entrance is at Av Guzmán 780, covers a good third of the neighbourhoud. By far the best sight in the cemetery is the tomb of **Carlos Gardel**, Argentina's most famous tango singer, which lies on the corner of streets 6 and 33, to the left of the entrance. It is topped by a life-sized statue of the singer in typical rakish pose – hand in pocket, hair slicked back and characteristic wide grin. Every inch of the surrounding stoneworks is plastered with plaques of gratitude and flowers, placed there by the singer's devotees for whom he has become a kind of saint. In comparison with Gardel's much-visited grave, **General Perón**'s final resting place – a low-key family mausoleum on the corner of street 34, two blocks to the right of the entrance – is very restrained

MATADEROS, one of the *barrios* in the southwestern corner of the city, has a gory past. In the nineteenth century, people went there to drink the fresh blood of animals killed in the slaughterhouses from which the area takes its name, in the belief that this would cure such illnesses as tuberculosis. The slaughterhouses have long gone, but Mataderos is still home to the **Mercado Nacional de Hacienda**, or livestock market, set back from the intersection of Lisandro de la Torre and Avenida de los Corrales, whose faded pink walls and arcades provide the backdrop for one of Buenos Aires' most fabulous events: the **Feria de Mataderos** (Sun

11am–8pm; buses #36, #92 & #126; ⊕011/4687-5602). A celebration of Argentina's rural traditions, this busy fair attracts thousands of locals and tourists. The highpoint is the display of **gaucho skills** in which riders participate in events such as the *sortija* in which, galloping at breakneck speed and standing rigid in their stirrups, they attempt to spear a small ring strung on a ribbon.

Eating

Buenos Aires is arguably Latin America's gastronomic capital. As well as the excellent and ubiquitous **pizza** and **pasta** restaurants common to the country as a whole, the capital offers an ever-increasing number of **cosmopolitan** cuisines. The city's crowning glory, however, are its **parrillas**. While the centre and the south are best for the city's most traditional restaurants, the north is the place to head for if you're looking for more innovative or exotic cooking. You'll find a crop of original restaurants around the hugely popular and trendy **Las Cañitas** area in Palermo (subte station Ministro Carranza) and, increasingly, in **Palermo Viejo** (especially Palermo "Hollywood"), where the establishments are given added charm by being in elegant late nineteenth- and early twentieth-century constructions. Though most restaurants open at around 8pm, bear in mind that most Porteños don't go out to eat much before 10pm (often dining after midnight, particularly in hot weather). All restaurants are in the centre, unless indicated.

Arturito Av Corrientes 1124 ⊕011/4382-0227. An old-fashioned oasis reigned over by courteous white-jacketed waiters, *Arturito* is a Corrientes landmark, and its *bife de chorizo con papas* (rump steak and chips) is an unquestionably good deal at just AR$5.

La Cancha Brandsen 697, La Boca ⊕011/4362-2975. A great place to spend a weekend lunch – in the shadow of Boca Juniors' legendary football stadium. Good fresh seafood including excellent *pulpo a la gallega* (octopus with oil and paprika) to share between two.

Chiquilín Sarmiento 1599 ⊕011/4373-5163. A classic *porteño* restaurant serving traditional dishes at moderate prices such as *pollo al verdeo* (chicken with spring onions) in a friendly and stylish atmosphere.

Club del Vino Cabrera 4737, Palermo ⊕011/4833-0048. With a modern Argentine menu including duck, lamb and seafood, this small and elegant restaurant shares the space with a music venue (tango and jazz) and a wine bar. Evenings only; closed Sun.

La Esquina de las Flores Av Córdoba 1587 ⊕011/4813-3630. Reliable vegetarian and macrobiotic restaurant serving a variety of cold and hot dishes (including a good *carbonada de vegetales*, a vegetarian version of the popular *criollo* stew). Closed Sat evening and all day Sun.

Freddo Buenos Aires' best ice-cream chain – *dulce de leche* fans will be in heaven and the unusual *pomelo* (grapefruit) flavour is superb. Many branches throughout the city.

La Giralda Corrientes and Uruguay, Centre. Brightly lit and austerely decorated Corrientes café, famous for its *chocolate con churros*. A perennial hangout for students and intellectuals and a good place to observe the *porteño* passion for conversation.

La Gran Taberna Combate de los Pozos 95, Montserrat ⊕011/4951-7586. A popular, bustling and down-to-earth restaurant a block from Congreso. The vast, reasonably priced menu offers a mixture of Spanish dishes, including a good selection of seafood, and *porteño* staples as well as a sprinkling of more exotic dishes such as *ranas a la provenzal* (frogs' legs with parsley and garlic). Many dishes are large enough to share.

Güerrín Av Corrientes 1368. If you want a traditional *porteño* pizza experience look no further than this Corrientes institution. The usual order is a portion of *muzzarella* and *fainá* eaten at the counter and accompanied by a glass of sweet *moscato*. Some *porteños* hold that the pizzas served in the proper dining area are a notch above the counter versions; however, all are inexpensive.

Las Nazarenas Reconquista 1132, Retiro ⊕011/4312-5559. Superb *parrilla* cooked gaucho-style on the *asador criollo*, where meat is staked around an open barbecue. Moderate to expensive.

El Obrero Caffarena 64, La Boca ⊕011/4362-9912. With the Boca Juniors souvenirs on the walls, and tango musicians moving from table to table at weekends, the atmosphere at the hugely popular and moderately priced *El Obrero* is as much a part of the attraction as the simple home-cooked food. Closed Sun.

Parrilla 1880 Defensa 1665, San Telmo ☎011/4305-1746. Extremely good joint right opposite Parque Lezama, its walls are lined with photos and drawings from the restaurant's famous and mostly bohemian clients, and the very friendly owner makes sure everyone is happy. Prices are reasonable, too. Daily until about 12.30am.

Parrilla Peña Rodríguez Peña 682 ☎011/4371-5643. Excellent *parrilla* at a reasonable price in a bustling atmosphere. Avoid the downstairs tables if you want to prevent your clothes from reeking of grilled meat.

Pippo Montevideo 341 ☎011/4374-0762. Despite fairly indifferent pasta and *parrillada*, *Pippo* has established itself as a Buenos Aires institution: it's worth paying this inexpensive, glaringly lit restaurant a visit for a glimpse of *porteño* dining in all its noisy, gesticulating glory. The thick *vermicelli mixto*, with bolognese sauce and pesto, is a good deal.

La Popular corner of Lavalle and Mario Bravo, Almagro. Decorated in the style of a *fonda*, the walls and ceilings of this attractive restaurant are strewn with football flags from around the world (there's usually a game showing too). The meat is very good and there's also *verduras a las brasas*, a delicious and unusual dish of grilled peppers, tomatoes, cucumbers, squash and aubergines, for a reasonable AR$6 or so.

Rimini Necochea 1234, La Boca ☎011/4302-6900. One of the oldest of Necochea's renowned *cantinas*, serving up a *menú fijo* of the usual chicken and pasta for AR$15, plus lively music until 4am. Evenings only (ring first).

Sarkis Thames 1101, Villa Crespo ☎011/4772-4911. Excellent tabbouleh, *keppe crudo* (raw meat with onion – much better than it sounds) and falafel at this popular restaurant serving a fusion of Armenian, Arab and Turkish cuisine. Close to one of Buenos Aires' nicest *barrios*, Palermo Viejo.

Tomo 1 Carlos Pellegrini 525, in *Hotel Crowne Plaza Panamericano* ☎011/4326-6698. Considered by many to be Buenos Aires' best *haute cuisine* restaurant, this is an elegant but refreshingly unpretentious place where all the emphasis is on the exquisitely cooked food. Lunch and evening set menus for around AR$50 offer dishes such as a terrine of zucchini with almonds and an à la carte menu, with a superb *magrets* of duck accompanied by pears and rosemary.

Drinking and nightlife

There's no excuse for staying in on any night in Buenos Aires: *porteños* are consummate night owls and though **nightlife** peaks from Thursday to Saturday, you'll find plenty of things to do during the rest of the week too. Venues are to be found all over the city, but there are certain key areas. The daily paper *Clarín* and *Vía Libre*, *La Nación*'s Friday supplement, have topical listings sections. Also worth looking out for is the tiny magazine *wipe* (Ⓦwww.wipe. com.ar), given out in some bars or on sale in kiosks, which is particularly good for the trendy end of the city's cultural events and nightlife.

Bars and live music

Buenos Aires has some great **bars**, ranging from noisy Irish pubs to drop-dead cool places where the young and moneyed sip on cocktails. There are also plenty of places offering live music including jazz, tango and rock music, hugely popular in Argentina. *El bajo*, as the streets around Reconquista and 25 de Mayo are known, offers a walkable circuit of trendy **bars** and restaurants, while San Telmo harbours some eclectic and interesting bars in amongst the tango spectacles.

Bar Británico corner of Defensa and Brasil, San Telmo. Old men, bohemians and night owls while away the small hours in this traditional wood-panelled bar overlooking Parque Lezama. Open 24 hours.

Café París Rodríguez Peña 1032. One of Buenos Aires' coolest hangouts, a trendily decorated but refreshingly unpretentious bar attracting a hardcore of late night clubbers after a hard night's clubbing. Daily from 8pm to very late – or very early, depending on how you look at it.

Café Tortoni Av de Mayo 825, Centre ☎011/4342-4328. Buenos Aires' most famous café offers pure elegance. Live jazz and tango in

La Bodega downstairs.

La Cigale 25 de Mayo 722, Centre. One of Buenos Aires' hippest bars attracting a young crowd. Regular live music and DJs on Thursdays (free). Happy hour with two drinks for the price of one Mon–Fri 6–9pm.

Plaza Dorrego Bar Defensa 1098, San Telmo. Most traditional of the bars around Plaza Dorrego, a sober wood-panelled place where the names of countless customers have been etched on its wooden tables and walls, and piles of empty peanut shells adorn the tables.

Sarajevo Bar Defensa 827, San Telmo. Apocalyptically named and eclectically decorated bar offering quintessential neighbourhood mix of poetry nights, tango and rock music. Popular with students and an alternative crowd.

El Taller Serrano 1595, Palermo Viejo ⓣ011/4831-5501. Bars and restaurants have sprouted around it, but *El Taller* still has the best outside seating in one of Buenos Aires' prettiest plazas. It also hosts regular jazz events.

Tobago Alvarez Thomas 1368, Chacarita ⓣ011/4553-5530. Off the beaten track in Chacarita, this popular bar hosts regular live music, particularly jazz.

Voodoo Báez 340, Palermo. One of the places to be seen in Las Cañitas, *Voodoo* is a lively bar with room to dance and comfy armchairs. Closed Mon.

Nightclubs

Club **music** tends towards the commercial dance variety, interspersed in some places with salsa or rock, though there are also a growing number of places playing more cutting-edge dance music. At the other end of the spectrum, **bailantas** are truly democratic events where the predominant music is home-grown *cumbia*, Argentina's favourite "tropical" sound – a very basic but infectious version of Colombia's famous rhythm. Some places issue tickets, which are stamped when you get your free drink, and which you must hand in on leaving the nightclub hours later or pay an exorbitant "fine" of around AR$100.

Buenos Aires has a multitude of bars, restaurants and discos for **gay men and lesbians**, a couple of which are listed below. Buenos Aires can be very cruisy, making its streets and parks likelier places for meeting people than bars or discos, where people tend to go out in groups of friends. News of events and venues can all be found in *NX*, *Corazones Bizarros* or *La Otra Guía*, the three national gay and lesbian publications, easily available at downtown kiosks or in gay establishments. The standard entrance charge for discos is AR$15, but some pre-discos give you discount vouchers.

Ave Porco Av Corrientes 1980, Centre. Consciously avant-garde club with a wild mix of music and a wild crowd. Thurs–Sat from midnight.

Club 69 Av Corrientes 1218, Centre. Friendly club attracting a relaxed and diverse crowd. The DJs play a mixture of soul, funk and hip-hop. Open Thurs–Sun.

Contramano Rodriguez Peña 1082, Centre. Late Wed to Sat and evenings on Sunday. Currently one of the city's leading – and sometimes most outrageous – gay nightclubs.

El Dorado Hipólito Yrigoyen 947, Centre. Current favourite of Buenos Aires' growing legion of dance-music fans, with popular night on Friday.

Fantástico Bailable Rivadavia and Sánchez de Loria, Once. The city's trendiest *bailanta* – and a good place for your first taste of the heady mix of non-stop dancing and full-on flirting that comes with the territory. Open Fri & Sat from midnight.

El Living M. T. de Alvear 1540, Centre. Laid-back club in a rambling old building with two bars and a coffee stand and a long, narrow dancefloor that gets very packed. Plays a fun, danceable mix of funk, disco and rock music. Open Thurs–Sat.

Maluco Beleza Sarmiento 1728, Centre. Long-running Brazilian club, playing a mix of lambada, afro, samba and reggae to a lively crowd of Brazilians and Brazilophiles.

Morocco Hipólito Yrigoyen 851, Centre. Theatre, nightclub and (expensive) restaurant. Arty, alternative – and seemingly popular with transvestites. Tues poetry evening, Tues, Wed drum'n'bass.

La Morocha Dorrego 3307, Palermo. Currently one of most popular mainstream clubs where an energetic crowd works up a sweat to dance on the main floor and jig about a bit to funk and rock music on a smaller floor next door. Friday and Saturday nights are packed.

Palacio Buenos Aires, Alsina 940, Centre. Popular gay venue in truly palatial surroundings, on Friday nights and Sunday evening from 7pm.

La Terraza Rivadavia 4307, Caballito. Saturday late night pub for lesbians only.

Milongas

Tango, once regarded as the preserve of older couples, or merely a tourist attraction, has recently gained a new audience, with an increasing number of young people filling the floors of social clubs, *confiterías* and traditional dancehalls for regular events known as **milongas**. Even if you don't dance, it's still worth going: the spectacle of couples slipping almost trance-like around the dancefloor, as if illustrating the oft-quoted remark "tango is an emotion that is danced", is captivating. Watching real tango danced makes people long to do it themselves, but a *milonga* is not the best place to take your first plunge; unlike, say, salsa, even the best partner in the world will find it hard to carry a complete novice through a tango. In short, if you can't bear the thought of attending a *milonga* without dancing, the answer is to take some **classes**. There are innumerable places in Buenos Aires offering dance classes, including cultural centres, bars and *confiterías* and, for the impatient or shy, there are private teachers advertising in the specialized publications *El Tangauta* and *Buenos Aires Tango*. The following places offer classes only: Academia Nacional del Tango, Av de Mayo 833, 1st Floor (☎011/4345-6967); Centro Cultural La Florcita, Sarmiento 4106, Almagro (☎011/4865-8995); and La Escuela del Tango, San José 364, 3rd Floor, Montserrat (☎011/4981-9626).

La Trastienda Balcarce 460, San Telmo. Live music including rock, jazz and tango, salsa dancing on Saturday nights and massively popular salsa classes on Wed evenings at 8.30pm.

Tango

The most obvious face of **tango** in Buenos Aires is that of the tango *espectáculos* offered by places such as *El Viejo Almacén*. Often referred to by *porteños* as tango for export, these generally rather expensive shows are performed by professionals who put on a highly skilled and choreographed display. If you want to dance – or would prefer to see the tango as a social phenomenon – you're better off heading to one of the city's dancehalls to experience the popular **milongas** (see box above). Note that the days, times and locations of *milongas* change frequently, so it's advisable to consult the listings in the *El Tangauta* and *Buenos Aires Tango* freesheets.

Bar Sur Estados Unidos 299, San Telmo ☎011/4362-6086. One of San Telmo's most reasonably priced tango shows. The quality can vary but this is an intimate space where audience participation (singing and dancing) is encouraged towards the end of the evening. Mon–Sat 9pm–4am.

El Chino Beazley 3566, Pompeya ☎011/4911-0215. *El Chino* is the eponymous owner of this atmospheric bar and *parrilla* in traditional Pompeya – probably the most authentic place to hear tango, sung by the talented staff and a crowd of locals and regulars. Fri & Sat from 10pm.

Club Almagro Medrano 522, Almagro ☎011/4774-7454; Medrano subte station. This sports centre in Almagro is the setting for various *milongas* (Tues 10pm, Fri 11pm, Sat 11pm, Sun 10pm) – the Tuesday night dance in particular is rated by many serious tango dancers as the best *milonga* in town. The club offers classes most days.

Confitería Ideal Suipacha 384, 1st Floor, Centre ☎011/4326-1515. An oasis of elegance just a few blocks from busy Corrientes, the Ideal has a stunning salon that is undoubtedly one of the most atmospheric places to dance. Wed & Thurs 4pm, Fri 1pm; classic "La Milonga Ideal" Sat 9pm, Sun 3–9pm.

Niño Bien Centro Región Leonesa, Humberto 1° 1462, Constitución ☎011/4496-3053; San José subte station. Appears to be particularly popular with a growing number of foreign "tango tourists" but there are plenty of locals, too, and a great atmosphere. They also serve food. Classes Thursday 8.30–10.30pm and *milongas* on Thursday and Saturday from 11pm.

El Viejo Almacén Av Independencia and Balcarce, Centre ☎011/4307-6689, ⓦwww.viejo-almacen.com.ar. The most famous of San Telmo's *tanguerías*, housed in an attractive nineteenth-century building. Occasionally hosts nationally famous tango singers of the stature of Susana Rinaldi, otherwise slickly executed dinner and dance shows daily from 9.30pm. Transport is available to and from central hotels.

The arts and entertainment

There's a superb range of cultural events on offer in Argentina's capital, ranging from avant-garde theatre to blockbuster movies and grand opera with a wealth of options in between. There are a plethora of **listings** in the entertainment sections of both *Clarín* and *La Nación*; the latter's Friday supplement, *Vía Libre*, is particularly good. You can buy tickets at discounted prices for theatre, cinema and music events, at the various centralized **ticket agencies** (*carteleras*) in the centre. Try Cartelera, Lavalle 835, local 27 (Mon–Fri 10am–10pm, Sat 11am–11pm, Sun 3–9pm; ⓣ011/4322-9263); Cartelera Baires, Av Corrientes 1382, local 24 (Mon–Thurs 10am–10pm, Fri 10am–11pm, Sat 10am–midnight, Sun 2–10pm; ⓣ011/4372-5058); Cartelera de Espectáculos, Lavalle 742 (Mon–Fri 10am–11pm, Sat noon–midnight, Sun noon–11pm; ⓣ011/4322-1559); Cartelera Vea Más, Av Corrientes 1660, Paseo La Plaza, local 26 (daily 10am–10pm; ⓣ011/4384-5319, ⓦwww.veamas.com).

Cultural centres, cinemas and galleries

British Arts Centre Suipacha 1333, Centre ⓣ011/4393-0275. The place to head for if you're nostalgic for a bit of Hitchcock – regular film and video showings, also English-language plays by playwrights such as Harold Pinter.

Centro Cultural Borges corner of Viamonte and San Martín, Centre ⓣ011/4319-5449. Large space above the Galerías Pacífico shopping centre, with several galleries showing a mixture of photography and painting, also a theatre. Daily 10am–9pm; AR$2.

Centro Cultural General San Martín Sarmiento 1551, Centre ⓣ011/4374-1251. Tucked behind the Teatro General San Martín, the centre features a varied selection of free painting, sculpture, craft and photography exhibitions, and an art-house cinema. Also hosts free tango recitals by the Orquesta de Tango de la Ciudad de Buenos Aires on Tuesdays at noon.

Centro Cultural Recoleta Junín 1930, Recoleta ⓣ011/4803-1040. One of the city's best cultural centres, constructed around a pretty patio with a number of art galleries showing an imaginative range of contemporary, mostly Argentine work, an auditorium and theatre. Great café and roof terrace, too. Tues–Fri 2–9pm, Sat & Sun 10am–9pm; AR$1; free guided visits Sat & Sun 4pm.

Centro Cultural Ricardo Rojas Av Corrientes 2038, Centre ⓣ011/4953-0390. Affiliated to the University of Buenos Aires, this friendly cultural centre offers free events including live music and bargain film showings, usually alternative/art house. Also a gallery space.

Ruth Benzacar Gallery C Florida 1000, Centre ⓣ011/4313-8480. Rather unexpectedly reached through an underground entrance at the end of Florida, this prestigious gallery has temporary exhibitions featuring international artists as well as Argentine artists of the stature of sculptor Enio Iommi, one of the most important figures in the Asociación Arte Concreto-Invención, Argentina's major abstract art movement. Mon–Fri 11.30am–8pm, Sat 10.30am–1.30pm.

Classical music venues

Teatro Coliseo M.T. de Alvear 1155, Centre ⓣ011/4816-6115. Major venue for ballet and classical music; also has occasional free recitals.

Teatro Colón Libertad 621, Centre ⓣ011/4382-5414. One of the world's great opera houses – acoustically on a par with La Scala in Milan. Opera, ballet and classical music from March to December. Buenos Aires' most glamorous night out. Tickets from AR$5 standing to more than AR$100 for boxes. Also free recitals in the Salón Dorado from Tuesday to Friday (5.30pm).

Listings

Airlines Aerolíneas Argentinas, Perú 2 ⓣ011/4340-7777; Aeroperú, Av Santa Fé 840 ⓣ011/4311-4115; Air France, Paraguay 610, 14th Floor ⓣ011/4317-4747; Alitalia, Suipacha 1111, 28th Floor ⓣ011/4310-9910; American Airlines, Av Santa Fe 881 ⓣ011/4318-1111; Austral, Paraná 590 y San Martín 427 ⓣ011/4340-7777; British Airways, Viamonte 570, 1st Floor ⓣ011/4320-6600; Canadian Airlines, Av Córdoba 656 ⓣ011/4322-3632; Cubana, Sarmiento 552, 11th Floor ⓣ011/4326-5291; KLM, Reconquista 559, 5th Floor ⓣ011/4312-1200; LAER, Maipú

935 P.B. ☎011/4311-5237; LADE, Perú 714 ☎011/4361-0853; Lan Chile, Paraguay 609 ☎011/4311-5334; LAPA, Carlos Pellegrini 1075 ☎011/4819-5272; Lufthansa, Marcelo T. de Alvear 636 ☎011/4319-0600; Southern Winds, Florida 868, 13th Floor ☎011/4312-2811; Swissair, Av Santa Fe 846, 1st Floor ☎011/4319-0000; United Airlines, Av Madero 900, 9th Floor Torre Catalinas Plaza ☎011/4316-0777.

Car rental Avis, Tucuman 633 ☎011/4378-9640; Dollar, Marcelo T. Alvear 449 ☎011/4315-8800; Localiza, Maipú 924 ☎011/4315-8384.

Embassies and consulates Australia, Villanueva 1400; Bolivia, Av Corrientes 545, 2nd Floor; Brazil, Carlos Pellegrini 1363, 5th Floor; Canada, Tagle 2828; Chile, San Martín 439, 9th Floor; Ireland, Av del Libertador 1068, 6th Floor; New Zealand, Carlos Pellegrini 1427, 5th Floor; UK, Dr Luis Agote 2412; United States, Av Colombia 4300; Uruguay, Av Las Heras 1097.

Post office Correo Central, Sarmiento 189 (Mon–Fri 10am–8pm).

Travel agents and tours Agreste, Viamonte 1636 (☎011/4373-4442) offers adventurous camping trips across the country to destinations such as the Saltos de Moconá and the Valle de la Luna. Buenos Aires Tur, Lavalle 1444, Office 16 (☎011/4371-2304), offers city tours of Buenos Aires, including tango shows, and visits to Tigre and nearby estancias. ASATEJ, Florida 835, 3rd Floor, is a young and dynamic travel agency, affiliated to STA Travel and offering the cheapest flight deals in the city – be prepared to wait as the office gets very busy. Lihué Expediciones, Maipú 926, 1st Floor (☎011/4311-9610), offers imaginative literary walks through the city, based around the writings of Borges, Cortázar and others.

Around Buenos Aires

Visitors to the metropolis have ample opportunity to get away from the bustle of the city for a day or two. **Tigre**, a riverside resort along the Paraná Delta, offers plenty of historical associations and a colourful fruit market and is served by regular train and bus services. Lying on the River Plate, **La Plata** is often treated as a day-trip from the capital and houses one of Latin America's most famous museums, the Museo de Ciencias Naturales. Just across the river, the Uruguayan town of **Colonia del Sacramento** (see p.994) makes an excellent overnight trip, and Argentina's premier coastal resort, **Mar del Plata**, boasts some interesting historical buildings; otherwise the beach is the main reason to visit. Inland, the huge province of Buenos Aires is dominated by the vast **Pampa**, a region almost synonymous with Argentina itself and whose main attraction is **San Antonio de Areco**, a charmingly old-fashioned town of cobbled streets and well-preserved nineteenth-century architecture. Nearby you'll find some of the most traditional and luxurious **estancias** (ranches) – great places to spend a night or two if you fancy a taste of the high life.

Tigre

Just a few kilometres to the north of Buenos Aires' Avenida General Paz lies the exotic **Paraná Delta**, a wonderfully seductive maze of lushly vegetated islands separated by rivers and streams, lined by traditional houses on stilts. By far the most visited area lies within an hour and a half's boat trip from the pretty town of **TIGRE**, around 20km northwest of the capital. As a departure point for **excursions to the delta** (see below), the town itself is sometimes overlooked by tourists, however; it offers an appealing mix of faded glamour, and the bars and restaurants around its recently refurbished riverside provide perfect vantage points for contemplation of the comings and goings of delta life. A good place to begin a tour is around the river terminal, the **Estación Fluvial**, on the eastern side of town, immediately north of the bridge over the Río Tigre. The point of contact between island and mainland life, the Estación bustles with activity, particularly at weekends, when holiday-makers and locals pass their luggage to the crew of the waiting boats, who pile it on to the roofs of the low wooden vessels. Alongside the Río Luján is the **Puerto de Frutos** (daily 10am–6pm) where crafts, particularly wickerwork, are steadily taking over from fruit as the market's chief product.

Over the bridge, the **Museo Naval**, at Paseo Victorica 602 (Mon–Thurs 8am–12.30pm, Fri 8am–5.30pm, Sat & Sun 10am–6.30pm; AR$2), is housed in the old naval workshops and holds exhibits – such as scale models and navigational instruments – relating to general maritime history, as well as to Argentine naval history from the British invasions of 1806 and 1807 to the Malvinas conflict. At the end of Paseo Victorica, you'll find the vast turreted and balustraded **Tigre Club**, modelled on the grand European hotels of the nineteenth century. From here, the road merges with Avenida Liniers, which leads back towards the bridge and is flanked by fine, if sometimes slightly decaying, examples of the town's grand nineteenth-century mansions, interspersed with equally luxurious modern residences. At no. 818, the reconstructed colonial Casa de Goyechea houses the **Museo de la Reconquista** (Wed–Sun 10am–6pm; free), which displays documents and objects relating to the recapture of Buenos Aires, including a number of English caricatures from the time, satirizing the poor performance of British troops.

Practicalities

The hour-long **train** journey departs regularly for Tigre from Buenos Aires' central Retiro station (Línea Mitre), terminating at Tigre's new **train station** on the riverbank, just to the south of Avenida Cazón. Or you could take the #60 (marked "Bajo") **bus** from Constitución station, which also stops along Avenida Callao and takes you into the centre of Tigre but the journey can be well over an hour. Tigre's helpful **tourist office** is on the western side of the Río Tigre, on the corner of Lavalle and R. Fernández (daily 10am–5pm; ⓣ011/4512-4498, ⓦwww.tigre.gov.ar/turismo). There are plenty of **restaurants** in Tigre, the best along Paseo Victorica, while on the delta itself there's the rather swanky *Gato Blanco*, on the Río Capitán (ⓣ011/4728-0390). One of the nicest places, though, is the simple and pretty *Riviera* (ⓣ011/4728-0177) just by the jetty at Tres Bocas.

For delta tours, make for Tigre's **Estación Fluvial** on General Bartolomé Mitre, one block north of the main train station. From here, frequent regular passenger services, known as *lanchas colectivas*, run by various companies including Interisleña (ⓣ011/4749-0900) and Delta (ⓣ011/4731-1236), leave for all points in the delta. On the opposite side of the river, at Lavalle 520, you'll find the **international terminal**, from where boats depart for Uruguay.

La Plata

When Buenos Aires was made Federal Capital in 1880, its province was left without a centre of government, a void filled when **LA PLATA**, some thirty miles east, became the new provincial capital. The new city's layout, based on rationalist concepts and characterized by an absolutely regular numbered street plan within a five-kilometre square, was designed by French architect Pedro Benoit. In the northeastern part of the city you'll find the **Paseo del Bosque**, home to the city's **Museo de Ciencias Naturales** (Tues–Sun 10am–6pm; AR$2), the first purpose-built museum in Latin America, and something of a relic in itself. Room VI is dedicated to the beginnings of the Cenozoic Period, or the Age of Mammals, and houses the museum's most important collection: the **megafauna**, a group of giant herbivorous mammals that evolved in South America when the region was separated from the other continents. The room's impressive skeletons include the gliptodon, forerunner of today's armadillos, and the enormous megatherium, largest of the megafauna which, when standing upright on its powerful two hind legs, would have reached almost double its already impressive six metres.

Over in the southwestern sector **Plaza Moreno**, is a vast open square covering four blocks and dominated, on the southern side, by the vast and rather forbidding **Catedral**. Heavily neo-Gothic in style, it has a pinkish stone facade and steep slate roofs and was not finally completed until 1932, its two principal towers being finished only at the end of the twentieth century. Its soaring interior is tremendously imposing, punctuated by austere ribbed columns. The **museum in the crypt** (Mon 9am–1pm, Tues–Sat 9am–6pm, Sun 9am–1pm & 3–7pm; AR$2, free Tues) features some excellent photographs documenting the cathedral's construction.

Avenidas 51 and 53 lead from Plaza Moreno to **Plaza San Martín**, the real hub of city life. **Pasaje Dardo Rocha**, on its western side is an elegant pitched-roof building, whose three-storeyed facade mixes French and Italian influences. Built in 1883 as the city's first train station, it now functions as an important **cultural centre** (daily 8am–10pm or later; free) comprising a small cinema and various art museums, including the new **Museo de Arte Contemporáneo Latinoamericano**.

Practicalities

The **bus terminal** – on the corner of calles 4 and 42, but at the time of writing it is due to move a couple of blocks – receives frequent buses from the capital, and elsewhere. Housed in the beautiful Palácio Campodónico at the corner of calles 5 and 56, with diagonal 79, the city's **tourist office** (Mon–Fri 9am–6pm; Ⓣ0221/422-9764, Ⓦwww.vivalaspampas.gov.ar) has limited information.

The bulk of La Plata's **bars and restaurants** can be found around the intersection of calles 10 and 47. Among the best meeting places are *La Trattoria*, a restaurant and café whose tables command the best view of local life and, two blocks away, on the corner of 8 and 47, *La Esquina*, a popular spot for an evening beer. One block west of Plaza San Martín there's La Plata's most celebrated – and most atmospheric – bar and restaurant, *Cervecería Modelo* on the corner of calles 5 and 54. Diagonally opposite is the smart *La Alternativa*, with vegetarian options plus huge platters of cold meats and cheese and the standard carnivorous fare.

Mar del Plata

If the thought of queuing for a restaurant makes you shudder, big, busy and brash **MAR DEL PLATA** in the height of summer is best avoided. However, if you prefer to mix your sunbathing and swimming with a spot of culture, nightlife or shopping, you'll find it one of Argentina's most appealing resorts. With the notable exception of its landmark Rambla Casino and Grand Hotel Provincial, Mar del Plata's coastline is dominated by modern high-rise developments, but here and there are quirky buildings, built in a decorative – even fantastical – style, known as *pintoresco*, an eclectic brew of mostly mock-Norman and Tudor architecture.

The city's official centre is **Plaza San Martín**, which covers four blocks and is bounded by calles San Martín, 25 de Mayo, H.Yrigoyen and San Luis. At the southern end of the square stands the **Catedral de los Santos Pedro y Cecilia** (free guided tours Wed at 11am; meet at Mitre 1780), designed by Pedro Benoit, chief architect of the provincial capital La Plata and notable for its beautiful and decorative stained-glass windows. To the immediate south of the square lies the hectic **microcentro**, dominated by pedestrianized **Calle San Martín**, which becomes a claustrophobe's nightmare in the evening when it is so packed it becomes difficult to weave your way through the assembled mass of holiday-makers and street performers.

Some nine blocks to the southeast of Plaza San Martín is **Playa Bristol**, Mar del Plata's most famous beach. Together with neighbouring Playa Popular, just to the north, these are the city's busiest beaches, and in high season their blanket coverage of beach tents and shades is reminiscent of a strange nomadic settlement. At the centre of the bay formed by these two beaches you will find the **Rambla Casino** whose monumental red and white buildings – a casino and the former **Hotel Provincial** – vie with Buenos Aires' Obelisco for Argentina's most recognizable cityscape. Follow the bay round to the southeast and you will come to a promontory, known as Punta Piedras, crowned by the **Torreón del Monje**, a perfect example of Mar del Plata's peculiar brand of fantasy architecture, this "monk's tower" at times makes the city look like a toy village. Built as a folly in 1904 by Ernesto Tornquist, the tower looks a little overwhelmed by its neighbours these days, but you can still get a great view of Playa Bristol and the Rambla Casino from its *confitería*.

Heading north from Plaza San Martín takes you through the quieter neighbourhood of **La Perla**, home to the stunning **La Cuadrada** café (see opposite), one block from the Plaza on Mitre and 9 de Julio. Following Mitre another two blocks will bring you to **La Perla beach**, almost as busy as the central beaches but regarded as slightly more upmarket. One block to the south of Mitre there is a monument by Luis Perlotti to the poetess **Alfonsina Storni**.

The bustling **port area** is also worth a visit, not only for its the striking yellow fishing fishing boats, but for a close encounter with the area's noisy colony of **sea lions**. At the far end of the wharf, around eight hundred males can be observed from only one metre or so all year round, though the colony is much smaller in summer when they head to the Uruguayan coast to mate. There are a number of good seafood restaurants around the port itself, as well as on the streets to the east. Various **buses** head here, including #551, #552 and #553, all of which can be caught along Avenida Luro.

Practicalities

The **airport** (ⓣ0223/478-0744) is around 8km northwest of the city centre along the RN2. Local bus #542 will take you from the airport into town, passing along Avenida Pedro Luro all the way to the seafront. **Trains** from Buenos Aires (Constitución) arrive at Estación Norte to the northwest of the town centre, at Luro and Italia (ⓣ0223/475-6075), and various local buses, including #511, #512 and #542, run between the station and the town centre. The **bus** terminal, at Alberti 1602, is right in the centre of things. The main office for Emtur, Mar del Plata's **tourist information** service, is centrally located at Belgrano 2740 (Mon–Fri 9am–8pm, Sat & Sun 9am–1pm & 4–8pm; ⓣ0223/495-1777, ⓦwww.mardelplata.com).

It's advisable to book ahead if you plan to stay in Mar del Plata during high season. Most **budget accommodation** is to be found around the bus terminal, although you can also find some good deals in La Perla, north of the town centre. The only **hostel** in town is the *Pergamino*, Tucumán 2728 (ⓣ0223/491-9872; AR$20 per person with HI card); more of a budget hotel than a hostel, it has bunk beds squeezed into small rooms, and things can be pretty cramped. *Hermitage*, on Boulevard Marítimo 2657 (ⓣ0223/451-9081, ⓔhermitage@lacapitalnet.com.ar; ❼), is a classically elegant hotel, almost lost amidst the surrounding modern buildings. More financially accessible are the *Hotel Bayo*, Alberti 2056 (closed Easter–Oct, ⓣ0223/495-6546; ❹), a pretty hotel that stands out from its rather dingy neighbours near the bus terminal, and *Hotel Storni*, 11 de Septiembre 2642 (ⓣ&ⓕ0223/491-6200, ⓔstorni@argenet.com.ar; ❹), which is very close to La Perla beach, has fairly simple ground-floor rooms – all have TV and private bathrooms – and more luxurious rooms with minibar and bathtub upstairs. Popular, central and with a lively atmosphere, thanks to the restaurant downstairs, *Residencial San Miguel*, Tucumán 2383 (ⓣ0223/495-7226; ❹), features pleasant rooms with private bathrooms.

There's a huge concentration of reasonable **restaurants** in the **microcentro**, though less crowded spots can be found southwest in the quieter streets bounded roughly by Avellaneda, Alberti, Independencia and Santiago del Estero. *Trenque Lauquen,* Mitre 2807 (ⓣ0223/4937149), offers some of the best meat you're likely to eat, serving wonderful *parrillada* on traditional wooden *tablas* at around AR$20 a head; be sure to book ahead. Mar del Plata's most famous café, *Cabaña del Bosque* can be found in a wooden building on Bosque Peralta Ramos set in lush grounds within this residential district around 10km south of the city centre (take bus #526). The wildly exotic and rambling interior, decorated with fossils, carved wooden sculptures and stuffed animals, is worth a visit on its own, though the café's fantastic cakes are enticing too. Another café-bar (and theatre) worth a visit for its decor, *La Cuadrada,* 9 de Julio and Mitre, is built around a patio with a fountain and huge spreading palm tree, its interior lavishly decorated with paintings, sculptures, antiques and wood carvings. It's a mesmerizing place to while away an hour or two and the food, though not cheap, is excellent and served with great style. *Manolo de la Costa* Castelli 15 offers good sea views and does upmarket fast food such as pizzas and a delicious *brochette mixto*, a kebab of beef and chicken served with chips, salad and aubergine. Be prepared to queue in the evening – the sister branch at Rivadavia 2371 is busy, too, and a popular spot for *chocolate con churros* after a hard night's clubbing.

San Antonio de Areco

Some 113km northwest of Buenos Aires, the charming town of **SAN ANTONIO DE ARECO** is the recognized centre of pampa tradition, with a popular gaucho festival, some highly respected artisans and an extremely attractive and unusually well-preserved town centre. San Antonio also has a prestigious literary connection: the town was the setting for Ricardo Güiraldes' classic, *Don Segundo Sombra* (1926), one of the first novels to celebrate the gaucho – previously regarded as a undesirable outlaw – as a symbol of national values. San Antonio has retained a surprisingly authentic feel and while you may not find the town full of galloping gauchos outside the annual festival, you still have a good chance of spotting estancia workers on horseback, sporting traditional berets and rakishly knotted scarves.

The main square, **Plaza Ruiz de Arellano** is named after the man who built San Antonio's founding chapel, the Iglesia Parroquial San Antonio de Padua, on the south side of the square. Among the elegant *fin de siècle* residences that flank the square, the Italianate **municipalidad** to the north is painted a particularly delicate version of the pink that characterizes so many of Areco's buildings. A block north, along Valentin Alsina, the **Centro Cultural Usina Vieja** (Mon–Fri 8am–2pm, Sat & Sun 11am–5pm; free) is a restored building that originally housed Areco's first electrical generator. Now housing a cultural centre, the building also contains the **Museo de la Ciudad**, an eclectic collection of everyday items, from clothing to record players and even the town's old telephone switchboard; an exhibition of the works of local artisans; and occasional temporary exhibitions, focusing mainly on subjects related to rural Argentine life.

Beyond the cultural centre, wide Calle Zerboni separates the town centre from the grassy banks of the Río Areco. If you are travelling by car, you must cross via the **Puente Gabino Tapia** to the right, but if on foot, cross straight over the simple brick **Puente Viejo**, which begins at the foot of M. Moreno, two blocks west of Alsina and leads to the rather scrubby **Parque Criollo**. Less a park than a kind of exhibition ground, it is used in November during the **Día de la Tradición** as the setting for the main displays of gaucho skills. It also houses, in a rather drab 1930s reproduction of an old estancia, the **Museo Gauchesco Ricardo Güiraldes** (Mon–Fri 8am–2pm, Sat & Sun 11am–5pm; AR$2). The collection's confusion is soon forgotten next to the fantastic collection of works by **Pedro Figari**, a Uruguayan artist who settled in Buenos Aires in 1921 and worked with Güiraldes. Figari was best known, though, for his dreamlike and deceptively primitive portrayals of gauchos, *candomble* (Afro-Brazilian religious rituals) and the distinctive urban and rural landscapes of the pampa. The **museum shop**, close to the *pulpería*, is worth a visit for its small but superior collection of souvenirs.

Practicalities

Buses from Buenos Aires stop six blocks east of Areco's town centre, along Avenida Dr Smith. There's no terminal as such – ticketing and bus information are dealt with in *Bar Don Segundo*, on the corner of Segundo Sombra and Avenida Dr Smith. Taxis are easily available, but it's an easy and enjoyable stroll (ten minutes) into town along Calle Segundo Sombra, which brings you to Plaza Ruiz de Arellano, the town's main square. The main **tourist office** is a short walk from the main square towards the river, on the corner of Arellano and Zerboni (Mon–Fri 8am–2pm, Sat 8am–8.30pm, Sun 8am–5pm; ⓣ02326/453165, ⓦwww.areconet.com.ar).

Though San Antonio is easily visited on a day-trip from Buenos Aires, staying overnight gives you the chance to explore the town at a more leisurely pace. Practically all **hotels** increase their prices at weekends and public holidays. The *Posada del Café de las Artes*, at Bolívar 70 (ⓣ02326/456371, ⓔgonzalom@areconet.com.ar; ❹), has a few simple but charmingly decorated rooms with big old-fashioned beds and en-suite bathrooms. The best option if you're on a tight budget is the simple but comfortable and well-kept *Hotel San Cayetano* on Segundo Sombra 515 (ⓣ02326/456393; ❸). *Los Abuelos*, on Zapiola and Zerboni (ⓣ02326/456390; ❹), is a bit pricier than the *Posada* but is very friendly, and a good deal if you prefer a more modern hotel. The tourist office can provide information on **staying with families**, a particularly useful option during the Día de la Tradición celebrations, when accommodation can otherwise be hard to come by. There are also several **campsites** within easy reach of San Antonio, including the spacious municipal site on the riverbank to the northeast of the town centre; it charges AR$5 per tent. There's a smaller site just across the river – ask for directions to "Lo de Miriam" (AR$5 per tent).

There are surprisingly few **places to eat** in San Antonio, but some are very good. The excellent *Almacén de Ramos Generales*, at Zapiola 143, serves delicious traditional food for exceptional value: the low-priced *picada* alone will be enough for most people. The *asado* at *La Costa*, on the corner of Zerboni and Belgrano, is popular with the locals, as is the pasta at *El Colonial* on Zerboni and Alsina. There are a handful of lively **bars** in town, mostly grouped a few blocks south of Plaza Arellano between General Paz and Além. The noisy *Gualicho*, popular with a young crowd, is on General Paz between Alsina and Arellano, while the *Barril*, at San Martín 377, attracts a slightly older clientele and has occasional live music.

The estancias

The countryside around San Antonio is home to several of the province's most traditional **estancias**. The closest of the overnight options to San Antonio is **La Porteña** (ⓣ02326/453770; ❽), named in honour of the Argentina's first steam locomotive, introduced to the country by the grandfather of Ricardo Güiraldes. To get to *La Porteña* head southeast along the RN8 towards Buenos Aires, and turn left on to the RP41 just past the police post. After about one kilometre, turn right onto the unsealed road signposted to *La Porteña*. After a short distance the road forks; take the road to the left. Arguably the most luxurious of all San Antonio's estancias, **El Ombú**, Cuartel 6 (ⓣ02326/4793-2454; ❼) contains sumptuously decorated rooms, and a lovely tiled and ivy-covered veranda that runs round the exterior of the building. To reach *El Ombú* from San Antonio, head southeast along the RN8 towards Buenos Aires, and turn left on to the RP41 just past the police post. After about 5km, you'll come to another intersection where there is an aerodrome: turn right onto the unsealed RP31, from where it is another 5km to the estancia. **La Bamba** (ⓣ02326/456293, ⓦwww.la-bamba.com.ar; ❼), a couple of kilometres beyond the turn-off for *El Ombú*, is one of Argentina's most distinctive estancias. The elegantly simple deep-rose facade of the *casco*, presided over by a *mirador*, or watchtower, is a particularly beautiful example of early eighteenth-century rural architecture. A less exclusive, but much more affordable, estancia experience is offered by **La Cinacina** in Areco itself; follow Bartolome Mitre five blocks west of the main plaza to the end of the street (ⓣ02326/452773, ⓦwww.lacinacina.com.ar). It offers a full day of *asado*, horse riding, and a display of gaucho skills.

1.2

Córdoba Province

The western border of one of Argentina's biggest and most densely populated provinces, **CÓRDOBA PROVINCE**, is traced by the **Central Sierras**, the highest **mountain ranges** in Argentina away from the Andean cordillera. The sierras stretch across some 100,000 square kilometres, peaking at **Cerro Champaquí**, its 2884-metre summit often encircled by cloud.

Colonized at the end of the sixteenth century, the region's first city, **Córdoba**, is now a vibrant, thrusting metropolis as befits the country's second city. The Society of Jesus and its missionaries played a major part in the city's foundation, at a strategic point along the Camino Real, the Spanish route from Alto Peru to the Crown's emerging Atlantic trading posts on the River Plate. You can still see their handsome temple in the city centre, among other well-preserved examples of colonial architecture. Further reminders of the Jesuits' heyday, **Santa Catalina and Jesús María** are two of Argentina's best-preserved Jesuit estancias, between Córdoba city and the province's northern border, promoted locally as the **Camino de la Historia**. Directly south of Córdoba, the **Calamuchita Valley** is also famed for a Jesuit estancia, that of **Alta Gracia**, along with a string of popular holiday spots, principally Germanic **Villa General Belgrano**.

The province is well served by **public transport**, but you can renti a car or a mountain bike. Nearly everywhere is within striking distance from the city of Córdoba, which can be used as a base for day excursions.

Córdoba

CÓRDOBA, Argentina's second city, guards some of the country's finest colonial architecture in its compact historic centre. The jagged silhouettes visible at the western end of its broad avenues announce that the cool heights of the **Sierras** are not far away, and it's in these, or in the lower hills nearer the city centre, that many of the million-plus Cordobeses take refuge from the sweltering heat of the valley. The capital of one of Argentina's largest provinces, Córdoba is nationally renowned for its hospitable, elegant population, of predominantly Italian descent, and its people have a pronounced sense of civic pride, reflected in initiatives such as the country's first ever urban cycle-paths or the careful restoration of many of the oldest buildings. Many people spend only an hour or two here before sprinting off to the nearby resorts, yet the city's plentiful accommodation and lively ambience make it an ideal base for exploring the area.

On July 6, 1573, **Jerónimo Luis de Cabrera** founded the city at the fork in the main routes from Chile and Alto Peru to Buenos Aires, calling it Córdoba la Llana de la Nueva Andalucía, after the city of his Spanish ancestors. Almost from the outset, the **Society of Jesus** played a crucial role in Córdoba's development, founding a college here that was to become South America's second university, the Universidad San Carlos, in 1621. Indeed, the Jesuits dominated life in Córdoba until King Charles III of Spain's order to expel them from the Spanish Empire in 1767. Seventeen year later, a forward-looking governor expanded Córdoba to the west of La Cañada, providing the growing city with secure water supplies. Like so

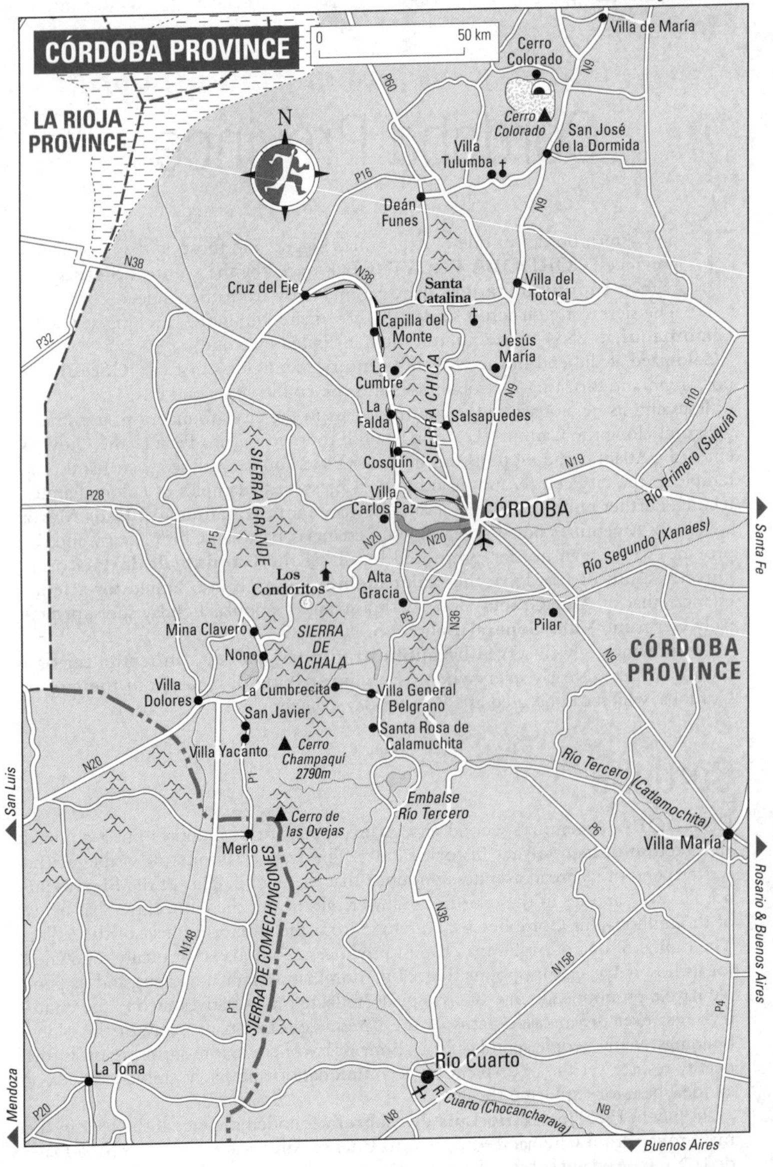

many Argentine cities, Córdoba benefited from the arrival of the British-built railways in 1870, its station acting as a hub for its expanding eastern districts. A period of prosperity followed, still visible in some of the city's lavishly decorated banks and theatres. The city has always vehemently opposed the country's dictatorships, including the 1976–83 military regime, with mass demonstrations and civil disobedience and was also a hive of anti-Menemism and, appropriately enough, produced Carlos Menem's ill-fated successor, Fernando de la Rúa.

Arrival, information and getting around

Córdoba's refurbished **Aeropuerto Internacional Taravella** (☎0351/425-5804) is at Pajas Blancas, 13km north of the city centre. A regular **minibus** service privately run by Transfer Express, the Travellers Airport Service (☎0351/475-9201/2), picks passengers up and sets them down in the city centre and at a selection of hotels for AR$4. A **taxi** ride to downtown will set you back AR$10.

The long-distance **bus station** (☎0351/423-4199 or 423-0532), at 300 Blvd Perón (known to locals as Avenida Reconquista), boasts an impressive array of **facilities** on four levels including banks and ATMs. Tickets for destinations throughout the country are sold in the basement, and advance booking is advisable during busy periods. It is several blocks to the east of the city centre, so you might need to take a bus or a taxi (AR$2 to most central places); stops for city buses and taxi ranks are close to the exit. Local buses serving some provincial destinations leave from the cramped **Terminal de Minibuses** behind the Mercado Sur market on Boulevard Arturo Illia, between calles Buenos Aires and Ituzaingó.

The main **tourist office** (including the **provincial information service**) is in the Recova del Cabildo (daily 8am–8pm; ☎0351/428-5856), on Plaza San Martín, at the corner of calles Deán Funes and San Martín. Staff at the **information centre** in the bus station (☎0351/433-1980) are very helpful – they have stacks of **maps** and leaflets plus travel information and online accommodation details, but they cannot book rooms.

Informative, two-hour **walking tours** of selected downtown sights start from the city tourist office at Rosario de Santa Fe 39 (daily 9.30am & 4.30pm, the latter in English upon request; AR$5–15; ☎0351/428-5600). Privately run City Tour (Mon–Wed 6pm, Thurs–Sat 10am & 6pm, Sun 10.30am; AR$9; ☎0351/424-6605) offers fun introductory **city tours**, lasting ninety minutes, in a London-style red double-decker bus, starting from the Plaza San Martín.

Accommodation

Córdoba has plenty of centrally located and reasonably priced **hotels**. The **cheapest places**, some of them squalid, are mostly gathered at the eastern end of calles Entre Ríos and Corrientes, towards the bus station, but there is now a good HI **youth hostel** too. There's a decent **campsite** (☎0351/433-8011/2; AR$3 per tent), offering free parking and a range of facilities, at Av General San Martín, behind the Fair Complex, on the banks of the Río Suquía, 10km northwest of the city centre. The #31 bus from Plaza San Martín runs there.

Hostel Ituzaingó 1070 ☎0351/468-7359, Ⓦwww.cordobahostel.com.ar. Brand new HI hostel in a great Nueva Córdoba location. AR$8–16 per person, depending on size of dorm and HI membership.

Hotel Dorá Entre Ríos 70 ☎0351/421-2031, Ⓔreservas@hoteldora.com. In a central location, the *Hotel Dorá* offers a wide range of facilities including a swimming pool and garage, and big, smart bedrooms. ❹

Hotel Quetzal San Jerónimo 579 ☎0351/422-9106. Appealing hotel features bright summery decor, en-suite bathrooms and ultra-friendly English-speaking staff. Avoid the street-facing bedrooms – otherwise it's quiet. ❸

Hotel Royal Blvd Presidente Perón 180 ☎0351/421-5000, Ⓔinfo@hotelmontecarlo.com.ar. The freshest-looking, least squalid of all the hotels near the bus terminal. Rooms are plain but comfortable. Breakfasts are generous. ❸

Hotel Windsor Buenos Aires 214 ☎&Ⓕ0351/422-4012, Ⓔreserves@windsortower.com. One of the few hotels with charm in this category, going for a resolutely British style complete with Beefeater doormen; in the classy new wing, rooms are more expensive, and the bathrooms are more modern. Sauna, heated pool and gym, plus the pretentious *Oxford* restaurant. ❻

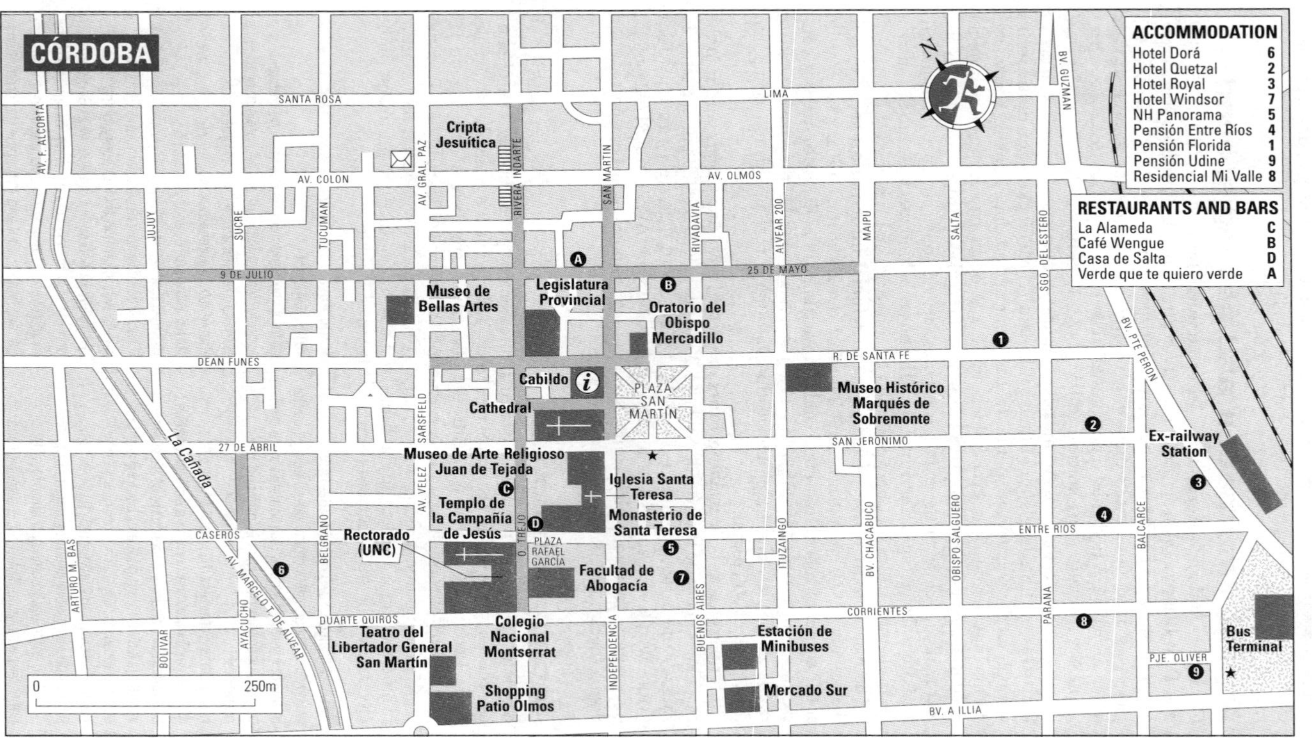
CÓRDOBA
ACCOMMODATION
Hotel Dorá 6
Hotel Quetzal 2
Hotel Royal 3
Hotel Windsor 7
NH Panorama 5
Pensión Entre Ríos 4
Pensión Florida 1
Pensión Udine 9
Residencial Mi Valle 8
RESTAURANTS AND BARS
La Alameda C
Café Wengue B
Casa de Salta D
Verde que te quiero verde A
N
Cripta Jesuítica
Museo de Bellas Artes
Legislatura Provincial
Oratorio del Obispo Mercadillo
Cabildo
Cathedral
PLAZA SAN MARTÍN
Museo Histórico Marqués de Sobremonte
Ex-railway Station
Museo de Arte Religioso Juan de Tejada
Templo de la Campañía de Jesús
Iglesia Santa Teresa
Monasterio de Santa Teresa
Rectorado (UNC)
PLAZA RAFAEL GARCÍA
Facultad de Abogacía
Colegio Nacional Montserrat
Teatro del Libertador General San Martín
Shopping Patio Olmos
Estación de Minibuses
Mercado Sur
Bus Terminal
La Cañada
SANTA ROSA
LIMA
AV. COLON
AV. OLMOS
9 DE JULIO
25 DE MAYO
DEAN FUNES
R. DE SANTA FE
27 DE ABRIL
SAN JERONIMO
CASEROS
ENTRE RIOS
DUARTE QUIROS
CORRIENTES
BV. A ILLIA
AV. F. ALCORTA
JUJUY
SUCRE
TUCUMAN
AV. GRAL. PAZ
RIVERA INDARTE
SAN MARTIN
RIVADAVIA
ALVEAR 200
MAIPU
SALTA
SGO. DEL ESTERO
BV. GUZMAN
BV. PTE PERON
SARSFIELD
AV. VELEZ
O. TREJO
INDEPENDENCIA
BUENOS AIRES
ITUZAINGO
BV. CHACABUCO
OBISPO SALGUERO
PARANA
BALCARCE
PJE. OLIVER
ARTURO M. BAS
BOLIVAR
AYACUCHO
AV. MARCELO T. DE ALVEAR
BELGRANO
0 250m

NH Panorama Hotel Marcelo T. de Alvear 251 ⓣ0351/410-3900, ⓔinfo@nh_panorama.com.ar. As the name suggests, the hotel enjoys fine views from its rooms, roof garden and pool. It also has luxurious but understated bedrooms and en-suite bathrooms, with smart stainless-steel washbasins. ❻
Pensión Entre Ríos Entre Ríos 567 ⓣ0351/423-0311. A simple family-run B&B in the vicinity of the bus station; safe, clean and quiet with plenty of hot water. ❷
Pensión Florida Rosario de Santa Fe 459 ⓣ0351/422-8373. The rooms with air conditioning are brighter and more appealing; the others only have fans. The decor is plain and fresh, mattresses are firm, and the bathrooms functional. ❷
Pensión Udine Pasaje Tomas Oliver 666 (no phone). Very small, spartan but clean rooms; the pick of the places near the bus station. ❷
Residencial Mi Valle Corrientes 586 (no phone). A small, family-run place without much character but scrupulously clean, tidy and hospitable; most rooms have a bathroom. ❷

The City

Córdoba's more about soaking up atmosphere than traipsing around tourist attractions, and you can see most of the sights in a couple of days. The city's historic core, or **microcentro**, wrapped around the leafy Plaza San Martín, contains all the major colonial buildings that sealed the city's importance in the seventeenth and eighteenth centuries.

Originally used for military parades, **Plaza San Martín** was granted its recreational role in the 1870s when the Italianate cast-iron fountains were installed and semitropical shrubbery was planted. Recumbent on the traffic-free western side of the square, the **Cabildo**, or colonial headquarters, is a sleekly elegant two-storey building whose white **façade** dates back to the late eighteenth century. The original *cabildo* was built on this very spot at the end of the sixteenth century. Nowadays, the building and its courtyards are mainly used for exhibitions, official receptions, the occasional concert and regular summer tango evenings (*Patio de Tango*: Fri midnight; AR$5); in cold or wet weather, the musicians and dancers take refuge in the Cripta Jesuítica. Inside, the **Museo de la Ciudad** (Mon 4–9pm, Tues–Sun 9am–1pm; AR$1) displays all kinds of **archeological** remains and other artefacts and exhibits about the city's past.

Immediately to the south of the *cabildo*, stands Córdoba's eighteenth-century **Catedral**, Argentina's oldest. Part Baroque, part Neoclassical, its imposing, immense **cupola** is surrounded by stern Romanesque turrets, yet today looks like a huge scorched meringue. The highly porous, pale cream-coloured stone has suffered badly from the ambient pollution and, scrubbed clean only a few years back, it has already begun to blacken again. The cathedral's **clock towers** are decorated at each corner with angelic trumpeters dressed in skirts of exotic plumes, like those worn by the Guaraní craftsmen who carved them. Inside, the first thing you notice is the almost tangible gloom: scant daylight filters through small, stained-glass windows onto an ornate but subdued floor of Valencian tiles; the ornate Rococo pulpit, in the left-hand aisle, momentarily lifts the otherwise oppressive atmosphere, as does the richly painted decoration of the ceiling and chancel.

Immediately southwest of Plaza San Martín, across Calle 27 de Abril from the cathedral, lies a set of buildings dedicated to St Teresa, including the lavish pink and cream-coloured **Monasterio de las Carmelitas Descalzadas de Santa Teresa de Jesús**, completed in 1770. Of the working nunnery, only the soberly decorated **Iglesia Santa Teresa**, built in 1717, is open to the public (Matins: daily 8am) – the entrance is at Independencia 146. It was designed by Portuguese architects brought over from Brazil, as can be seen from the typical ornate cross and gabled shape of the church's two-dimensional bell tower, like a cardboard cut-out stuck next to the main facade. Housed in the northern side of the complex, in a part no longer used by the holy order is the **Museo de Arte Religioso Juan de Tejeda**, Independencia 122 (Wed–Sat 8.30am–12.30pm; AR$1), entered through an intricate, cream-coloured Baroque doorway. Informative guides will show you around the partly restored **courtyards**, the garden of hydrangeas, orange trees, jasmine and pomegranates, and the rooms and cells of the former nuns' quarters. On display alongside all manner of religious artefacts and sacred relics are a very fine polychrome wooden statue of St Peter, a lavish silver-embroidered banner made for Emperor Charles V and some striking paintings from Cusco.

Two blocks southwest of Plaza San Martín, the **Manzana de los Jesuitas** was apportioned to the Society of Jesus a decade after the founding of Córdoba. Set back only slightly from Plazoleta Rafael García, the **Templo de la Compañía de Jesús** was built by Felipe de Lamer in 1640 and is Argentina's oldest surviving Jesuit temple. The almost rustic simplicity of its restored façade is a foretaste of the severe, single-naved interior, with its precious roof of Paraguayan cedar in the shape of an upturned ship. Fifty painted canvas panels huddled around the ceiling, darkened by time, depict the figures and legends of the Society of Jesus. Even more striking is the handsome Cusqueño altarpiece and the floridly decorated **pulpit**.

East of Plaza San Martín, at Rosario de Santa Fe 218, the well-preserved and carefully restored **Museo Histórico Provincial Marqués de Sobremonte** (Tues–Fri 10am–1pm & 4–7pm, Sat & Sun 10am–1pm; AR$1) is the city's last private colonial house, built at the beginning of the eighteenth century. The calm, leafy patio is shaded by enormous jasmine bushes and pomegranate trees, supposedly planted when the first owner lived here. Best of the exhibits displayed on the ground floor are an outstanding set of paintings of the **Cusco School**, housed in the first two rooms on the right, and a fascinating collection of period **musical instruments**.

To see some Argentine art from the nineteenth and twentieth centuries, head for the **Museo de Bellas Artes Dr Genaro Pérez**, a block west of the Legislatura Provincial at Av General Paz 33 (Tues–Fri 9.30am–1.30pm & 4.30–9pm, Sat & Sun 10am–8pm; free). The municipal art gallery is housed in a handsome late nineteenth-century building, built to a French design. Impeccably restored in the late 1990s, along with its fine iron and glass details including an intricate **lift**, the museum is worth a visit for its interior alone. Most of the paintings on permanent display belong to the **Escuela Cordobesa**, a school whose leading master was Genaro Pérez himself – mostly brooding portraits and local landscapes. Temporary exhibitions, usually of local artists, are also held from time to time.

Beyond the microcentro, boulevards San Juan and Presidente Illia mark the northern limits of **Nueva Córdoba**. This trendy neighbourhood, awash with bars and restaurants, sliced through by diagonal Avenida Hipólito Yrigoyen, which leads from Plaza Vélez Sarsfield to the Parque Sarmiento, one of the city's open, green spaces, built on an isolated hill. A bigger park, Parque General San Martín, stretches alongside the leafy suburban neighbourhood of **Cerro de las Rosas**, on high ground to the northwest of the centre; head here to sample the restaurants or the fashionable nightlife.

Eating, drinking and entertainment

Córdoba has a wide selection of **restaurants**, with something to please nearly all tastes. The best places for eating and drinking are concentrated in Nueva Córdoba and on the cooler heights of the Cerro de las Rosas. Much of the nightlife has moved to the outlying district of El Abasto, a revitalized former warehouse district close to the centre on the northern banks of the Río Suquía, that buzzes with **bars**, **discos** and **live music venues**, including a couple of gay nightspots. The even trendier Chateau Carreras area, just south of Cerro de las Rosas, has several more upmarket **nightclubs** to choose from, including *Complejo Lola* and *Shark*.

Al Salam Rondeau 711. Delicious hummus, tabbouleh, kebabs and *baklawa* are the order of the day at this atmospheric, reasonably priced Middle Eastern restaurant, complete with hookahs and belly dancers. Closed Mon.

La Alameda Obispo Trejo 170. A slightly hippie ambience, with wooden benches to sit on. Reasonably priced food including great *empanadas* and *humitas*. Patrons leave scribbled notes and minor works of art pinned to the walls. Closed Sunday lunch.

El Arrabal Fructuoso Rivera and Belgrano (☎0351/428-2495). Good-value meals but the main reason to come is for the entertainment – regular, and brilliant, tango shows.
Café Wengue 25 de Mayo and Rivadavia. Smart modern café favoured by locals; excellent coffee.
Casa de Salta Caseros 84. A taste of the Argentine Northwest, serving typical Salta dishes (at low prices), such as *locro* (maize-based stew) and delicious *empanadas*. Closed Sun.
Estación Victorino Av Rafael Núñez 4005, Cerro de las Rosas. An atmospheric café-bar in the Cerro de las Rosas, serving hearty, moderately priced meals and huge cocktails. A rusty locomotive and an old red British telephone box on the forecourt serve as landmarks.
Rancho Grande Av Rafael Núñez 4142, Cerro de las Rosas. Generous pastas and enormous barbecues – all very good value – are served by trendy staff in a large barn-like structure, often rented out by parties.
Las Rías de Galicia Montevideo 271 (☎0351/428-1333). At this swish, expensive restaurant you can choose from top-quality Spanish-influenced seafood and meat dishes; the weekday lunch *menú ejecutivo* is great value at AR$9.
Rock&Fellers Av Hipólito Yrigoyen 320, Nueva Córdoba and Av Rafael Núñez 4791, Cerro de la Rosas branches. These identical twins are trendy cocktail-bar-cum-restaurants and popular meeting places, with live rock music most weekends. Student discount for drinks and meals.
Verde que te quiero Verde 9 de Julio 36. Appetizing pizzas, quiches, soya burgers and fresh salads served by weight (and at very little cost) in cool surroundings; Córdoba's only real vegetarian restaurant.

Listings

Airlines Aerolíneas Argentinas, Av Colón 520 ☎0351/410-7690; Lan Chile, Av Colón 564 ☎0351/425-3447; Lapa, Av Colón 534 ☎0351/428-3784; Southern Winds, Av F Alcorta 152 ☎0351/446-7800; Varig, 9 de Julio 40 ☎0351/426-3315.
Car rental Avis, airport ☎0351/475-0815; Hertz, airport ☎0351/475-0581; Localiza, airport ☎0800/999-2999.
Post office Av General Paz 201.

The Camino de la Historia

The 150km stretch of the RN9 running north of Córdoba city is promoted as the **CAMINO DE LA HISTORIA**, or history route. One of the country's finest Jesuit estancias, now the well-presented Museo Jesuítico Nacional San Isidro Labrador can be visited in **Jesús María**, while beautiful **Santa Catalina**, lying off the main road to the north, is still inhabited by direct descendants of the family who moved there at the end of the eighteenth century. Further north, in **Villa Tulumba**, the nondescript parish church houses a masterpiece of Jesuit art, an altarpiece that, until the early nineteenth century, adorned Córdoba cathedral.

Jesús María

Just off the busy RN9, 50km north of Córdoba, **JESÚS MARÍA** is a sleepy little market town on whose northern outskirts stands the **Museo Jesuítico Nacional San Isidro Labrador** (Mon–Fri 8am–noon & 2–7pm, Sat & Sun 2–6pm; AR$2), housed in the former residence and the *bodega*, or wineries, of a well-restored Jesuit estancia. In contrast to the bare, rough-hewn granite of the outside walls, a white courtyard lies beyond a gateway to the right of the spartan church. The U-shaped *residencia* contains the former missionaries' cells, storehouses and communal rooms, now used for temporary exhibits and various permanent displays of archeological findings, colonial furniture, sacred relics and religious artwork from the seventeenth and eighteenth centuries, along with farming and wine-making equipment.

Santa Catalina and Villa Tulumba

The RN156 to the west of Jesús María leads to Ascochinga, where a dirt road heads 20km northwest to **SANTA CATALINA**. Almost hidden among the wooded hills, Santa Catalina is an outstanding example of colonial architecture in the Spanish Americas and is a UNESCO world heritage site. A harmonious set of early eighteenth-century buildings, it's dominated by its church, with its elegant white silhouette and symmetrical towers. On arrival, head straight for the little *confitería*, accessible to the right of the church; at least one member of the Díaz family – direct descendants of Antonio Díaz, who acquired it in the 1770s – should be on hand to serve you some delicious home-cured ham, open up the church (AR$1, closed lunch) and show you around the estancia. You can also stay overnight in beautifully restored **rooms** (ⓣ03525/493134, ⓔrancheria@cop5.com.ar; ④). Dedicated to St Catherine of Alexandria, the church features an austere single nave decorated with a gilded wooden retable, housing an image of the saint, and a fine carob-wood pulpit.

Some 70km north, along the RN9, at San José de la Dormida, a signposted road heads west to **VILLA TULUMBA**, 22km beyond, a tiny hamlet that's home to a Baroque masterpiece: you'll find the subtly crafted seventeenth-century tabernacle, complete with polychrome wooden cherubs and saints, inside the parish church.

The Calamuchita Valley

The green **CALAMUCHITA VALLEY** begins 30km south of Córdoba city at the Jesuit estancia town of **Alta Gracia** – a popular day-trip destination from Córdoba – and stretches due south for over 100km, between the undulating Sierras Chicas and the steep Sierra de Comechingones. A good base for exploring the range, **Villa General Belgrano** is a chocolate-box resort with a predominantly Germanic population. Frequent **buses** and minibuses run along the arterial RP5 some stopping at Alta Gracia.

Alta Gracia

Forty kilometres south of Córdoba, historic **ALTA GRACIA** lies at a hilly spot between Córdoba and the mountains, which once made it popular with the wealthy bourgeoisie, who built holiday homes here. Regular **buses** from Córdoba stop at the corner of avenidas Sarmiento and Vélez Sarsfield, and leave equally regularly for Villa General Belgrano. The municipal **tourist office** is in the clock tower at Luís Sáenz Peña and Calle del Molino (daily 9am–5pm; ⓣ03547/423455).

In 1643, Alta Gracia was chosen as the site for a **Jesuit estancia** around which the town grew up; after the Jesuits' expulsion in 1767, it fell into ruin but was inhabited for a short time in 1810 by Viceroy Liniers. The **Museo Histórico Casa del Virrey Liniers** is housed in the Jesuits' original living quarters and workshops (Dec–Easter Tues–Fri 9am–1pm 4–8pm, Sat, Sun & public holidays 9.30am–12.30pm & 5–8pm; Easter–Nov Tues–Fri 9am–1pm & 3–7pm, Sat, Sun & public holidays 9.30am–12.30pm & 3.30–6.30pm; AR$2, free on Wed; guided tours in English). Exhibits consist mainly of period furniture and art, mostly dating from the early nineteenth century, but the most interesting sections are the painstakingly re-created **kitchen** and the toilets, from which the waste was channelled into a cistern used to irrigate and fertilize the estancia's crops.

Avenida Sarmiento leads up a slope into **Villa Carlos Pellegrini**, a residential district of quaint timber and wrought-iron dwellings. One of these, Villa Beatriz, at Avellaneda 501, was in the 1930s home to **Ernesto "Che" Guevara**, sent here as an adolescent in the vain hope of curing his debilitating asthma. Nearby another villa, Los Espinillos, at Av Carlos Pellegrini 1011, was home to Spanish composer

Manuel de Falla until his death on November 14, 1946. It is now the **Museo Manuel de Falla** (Dec–Easter Tues–Fri 3–8pm, Sat, Sun & holidays 10am–noon & 3–8pm; Easter–Nov Tues–Fri 2–7pm, Sat, Sun & holidays 10am–noon & 3–8pm; AR$1), exhibiting his personal effects, and occasionally hosting piano and other recitals.

Villa General Belgrano

Fifty kilometres south of Alta Gracia is the demure resort of **VILLA GENERAL BELGRANO**, from where alpine trails climb into the nearby Comechingones Range, an excellent place to observe **condors**. The unspoiled alpine scenery of its backcountry, the folksy architecture and decor, and the Germanic traditions of the local population all give the place a distinctly Mitteleuropean feel. Some of the townsfolk are descended from escapees from the *Graf Spee*, a U-boat sunk off the Uruguayan coast on December 13, 1939. The town is an excellent base for the region if you'd rather avoid the city of Córdoba but it suddenly shifts up a gear or two during one of its many festivals: the annual climax is the nationally famous **Oktoberfest**, held during the second week of October. Stein after stein of foaming Pilsener is knocked back, after which merry revellers stagger down Villa Belgrano's normally genteel streets to their hotels. **Avenida Julio Roca**, the town's main drag, lined with shops, cafés, restaurants and hotels, many of them replicas of Swiss chalets or German beer houses, runs south from Plaza José Hernández, where the Oktoberfest takes place. Frankly, the town's three museums – one containing some vintage carriages, another housing a jumble of pre-Hispanic ceramics and the third with an exhibit about UFOs, supposedly a common phenomenon hereabouts – are not worth the candle.

Practicalities

Buses arrive at the small **terminal** on Avenida Vélez Sarsfield, five minutes northwest of Plaza José Hernández. The **tourist office** is at Avenida Julio Roca 168 (Mon–Fri 8am–8.30pm, Sat & Sun 8.30am–8.30pm; Ⓣ03546/6121, Ⓦwww.elsitiodelavilla.com). Banks and **ATMs** can also be found along the main avenue.

Most of the **hotels** are relatively expensive but of a high standard; book ahead in the high season. Those offering the best-value are the very Teutonic *Bremen*, at Cerro Negro 173 (Ⓣ03546/461133, Ⓦwww.hotelbremen.com; ❻), and the humbler, but extremely comfortable and centrally located *Posada Nehuen*, at San Martín 17 (Ⓣ03546/461412, Ⓔnehuen@elsitiodelavilla.com; ❺). The excellent **youth hostel**, *El Rincón* at Calle Alexander Fleming s/n, fifteen minutes' walk northwest of the bus station and very laid-back (Ⓣ03546/461323, Ⓔrincon@calamuchitanet.com.ar; ❷), has dorms, rooms with private bath, and you can pitch your tent. **Cabañas**, mostly rustic but upmarket, are an excellent alternative, especially for groups of four or five: try the differently priced *Aufenthalt* complexes (Ⓣ03546/461687, Ⓔaufenthalt@elsitiodelavilla.com; ❻–❼), just outside the town centre, or set among woods the well-spaced *Am Bach*, at Lago di Como s/n (Ⓣ03546/461543, Ⓔambach3@calamuchitanet.com.ar; ❻–❼). The *San José* (Ⓣ03546/462496) and *La Florida* (Ⓣ03546/461298) **campsites**, along the RP5 east of the town centre, are both spotless and set in beautiful wooded locations with swimming pools.

The town's plentiful **places to eat** specialize in Germanic fare, such as the *Ciervo Rojo*, at Julio Roca 210, good for schnitzels and wurst, washed down with tankards of home-brewed beer; *Café Rissen* at Av Julio Roca 36 is the place to go for Black Forest gateau, strudel and fruit crumbles.

1.3

El Litoral

Lying either side of the huge Paraguay and Uruguay rivers and stretching from the lower reaches of the Paraná Delta to Argentina's border with Brazil and Paraguay, **EL LITORAL** is a region defined by its proximity to water. Its major attraction by far is the **Iguazú Falls** (shared with Brazil) in Misiones Province, whose claim to the title of the world's most spectacular waterfalls has few serious contenders. Apart from them and **San Ignacio Miní** – one of the best-preserved ruins of all the Jesuit Missions – the region is little exploited in terms of tourism. Few travellers make the very worthwhile detour to one of Argentina's most unusual attractions: the **Esteros del Iberá**, a vast wetland reserve stretching across the centre of Corrientes Province that offers outstanding opportunities for observing birds and animals. Provincial capital **Corrientes** boasts one of the best preserved historic centres in Argentina while urbanites will enjoy the region's biggest city, **Rosario**, home to a vibrant cultural life and some exquisite turn-of-the-century architecture. Entre Ríos is perhaps the gentlest of Argentina's provinces, whose best attraction is probably the **Parque Nacional El Palmar**, an enormous protected grove of dramatically tall yatay palms near the delightful river-side town of **Colón**.

For most Argentinians, El Litoral means two things: **mate** and **chamamé**. The *litoraleños* are fanatical consumers of Argentina's national drink, while *chamamé* is perhaps Argentina's most infectious folk music, with a lively danceable rhythm. Note that summers are invariably hot and humid in El Litoral, with temperatures regularly reaching 40°C and above in the north.

Rosario

A major port, **ROSARIO** enjoys a close relationship with the **River Paraná**; its attractive riverfront area runs for some 20km along the city's eastern edge, flanked by parks, bars and restaurants and, to the north, beaches. The city's trump card, however, is the splendidly undeveloped **delta islands** with wide sandy beaches, which lie just minutes away from the city centre. Many of Argentina's most famous artists and musicians hail from the city and Rosario is noted for its lively nightlife, known as *la movida*. It is also famous for being the birthplace of one of the twentieth-century's greatest icons: **Che Guevara**. Some particularly attractive examples of a worldly architecture – **stylish bars**, mansions and old department stores – make it a rewarding city to simply wander around.

Arrival and information

Rosario's international **airport** lies around 10km northwest of the city centre, along the RN9 (☎0341/456-7997). There is no bus service to the centre from the airport – the half-hour taxi ride will cost around AR$10; alternatively you can take a taxi to the nearby neighbourhood of Fisherton, from where buses #115 and #116 run to the bus terminal. Buses arrive at Rosario's clean and attractive **Terminal de Omnibus Mariano Moreno**, some twenty blocks west of the city centre, at Santa Fe and Cafferata (☎0341/437-2384). There's a very helpful information kiosk,

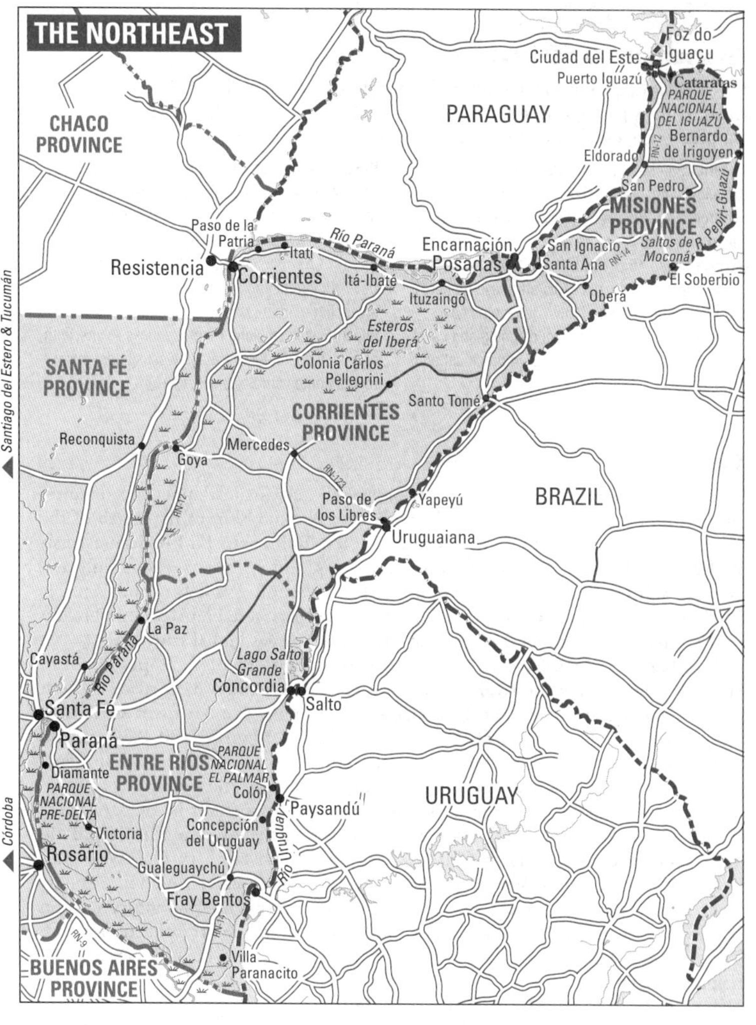

which can provide you with a list of hotels and a map. Plenty of taxis pull up outside the front entrance or you can walk one block north along Cafferata to catch a bus (#116, #107) to the centre from San Lorenzo. The **Estación Fluvial**, which you need for getting to the Delta islands, lies just 500 metres east of central Plaza 25 de Mayo.

There's a **tourist information office** down by the riverfront, on the corner of Avenida Belgrano and Calle Buenos Aires (daily 9am–7pm; ⓣ0341/480-2230, ⓦwww.rosario.com.ar/turismo).

Accommodation

Rosario is adequately catered for as far as hotels go, though decent budget **accommodation** is pretty thin on the ground, while most of the more expensive places are pretty faceless. Discounts are often available at weekends.

Britania San Martín 364 ⓣ0341/440-6036. An old, slightly chaotic hotel one block from the riverfront, the *Britania* has very basic rooms, but is cheap and central. ❷

Garden Callao 45 ⓣ0341/437-0025, ⓔgardenh@citynet.net.ar. This attractive modern hotel is in a quiet area of town. It's rooms have large, comfortable beds, air conditioning and cable TV. Spacious bar area. ❺, including breakfast and parking. ❺

Plaza del Sol San Juan 1055 ⓣ0341/421-9899, ⓦwww.rosario.com.ar/plaza. This hotel has attractive rooms, with an excellent buffet breakfast and a nice swimming pool. ❼

Savoy Hotel San Lorenzo 1022 ⓣ0341/448-0071. Beautiful and atmospheric old hotel with a sweeping marble staircase and a grandly anachronistic smoking room. Spotless rooms, with original wooden furniture and washstands; many rooms come with balconies. ❹–❺

The City

Rosario's **Costanera**, or riverfront, is one of the city's most appealing features, offering numerous green spaces and river views. Around 8km to the north of the centre lies Rosario's most popular mainland beach, **Balneario La Florida** (accessible by bus #101), packed on summer weekends, and with bars, restaurants and shower facilities. At the southern end of the *balneario* you'll find the Rambla Catalunya and Avenida Carrasco, lined with glitzy bars, restaurants and nightclubs which, during the summer, become the focus of Rosario's famed **movida**.

The **Plaza 25 de Mayo** sits on the edge of the city before it slopes down to Avenida Belgrano and the river. The plaza itself is a pleasantly shady space laid out very formally around its central marble monument, the **Monumento a la Independencia**. The **Catedral** (Mon–Sat 7.30am–12.30pm & 4.30–8.30pm, Sun 7.30–1pm & 5–9.30pm) is a late nineteenth-century construction in which there's a fine Italianate altar carved from Carrara marble and, in the crypt, the colonial wood-carved image of the Virgin of Rosario, brought from Cádiz in 1773. At Santa Fe 748 on the southern side of the plaza, you'll find the **Museo Municipal de Arte Decorativo Firma y Odilio Estévez** (mid-March to Dec Wed–Sun 5–9pm & 4–8pm; AR$1; ⓦwww.rosario.gov.ar/museoestevez). Housed in a fantastically ornate mansion, whose facade reflects the early twentieth-century fashion for heavily ornamented moulding, the museum exhibits the art collection of the Estévez family, which covers everything from Egyptian glass to Flemish tapestry and includes a striking portrait by Goya.

Your first sight of the **Monumento a la Bandera** is likely to be through the gap between the cathedral and the Palacio de los Leones on the main plaza, from where the Pasaje Juramento leads down to the monument itself. Basically a huge allegorical sculpture based on the idea of a ship sailing towards a glorious future, it is well worth taking the lift to the top of the tower (Mon 2–7pm, Tues–Sun 9am–7pm; AR$1), from where there's a commanding **view** of the river and the city.

Dissected by various avenues and containing several museums, a football stadium and a racetrack, the **Parque de la Independencia**, nearly 3km southwest of Plaza 25 de Mayo, feels like a neighbourhood in itself. At Av Pellegrini 2202, which runs through the park, you'll find the **Museo Municipal de Bellas Artes Juan B. Castagnino** (Tues–Sat noon–8pm, Sun 10am–8pm; ⓣ0341/480-2542), regarded as the country's second most important fine arts museum after the Museo de Bellas

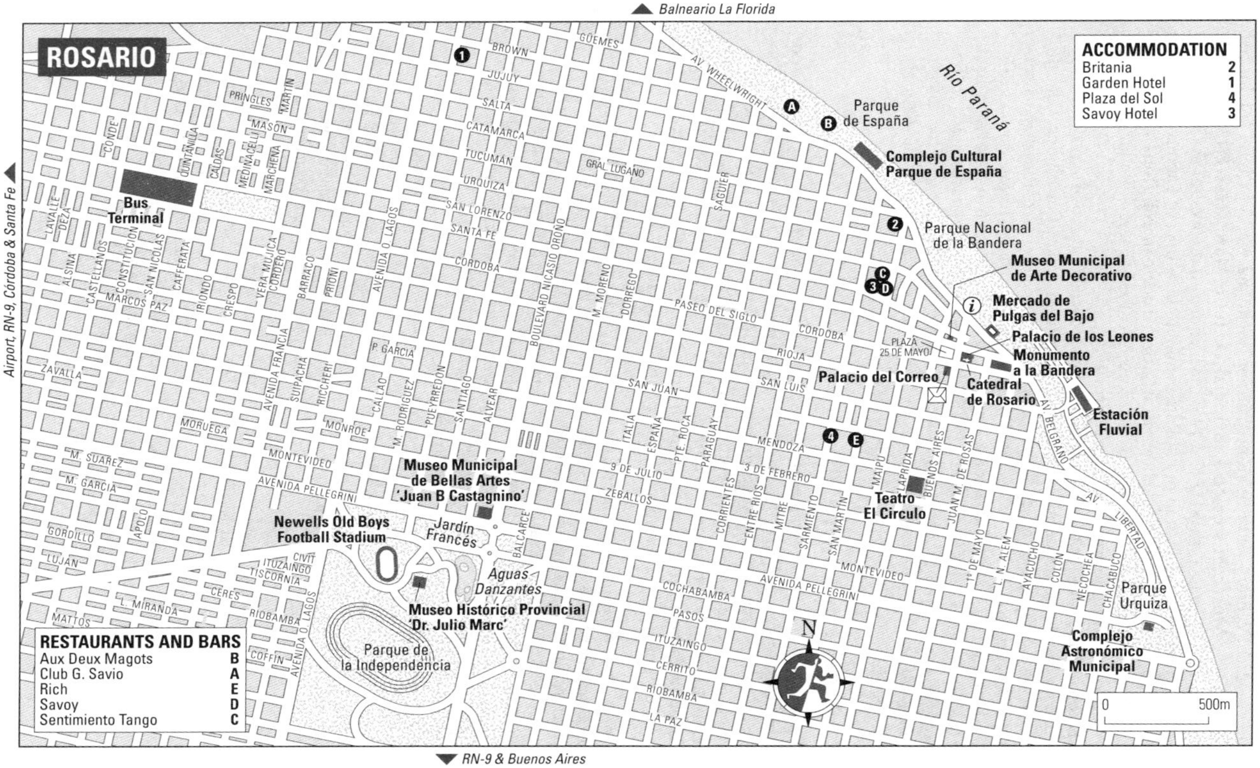

ROSARIO

▲ Balneario La Florida

◄ Airport, RN-9, Córdoba & Santa Fe

▼ RN-9 & Buenos Aires

ACCOMMODATION

Britania	2
Garden Hotel	1
Plaza del Sol	4
Savoy Hotel	3

RESTAURANTS AND BARS

Aux Deux Magots	B
Club G. Savio	A
Rich	E
Savoy	D
Sentimiento Tango	C

Río Paraná

Parque de España

Complejo Cultural Parque de España

Parque Nacional de la Bandera

Museo Municipal de Arte Decorativo

Mercado de Pulgas del Bajo

Palacio de los Leones

Monumento a la Bandera

Catedral de Rosario

Palacio del Correo

Plaza 25 de Mayo

Estación Fluvial

Teatro El Círculo

Parque Urquiza

Complejo Astronómico Municipal

Bus Terminal

Museo Municipal de Bellas Artes 'Juan B Castagnino'

Jardín Francés

Aguas Danzantes

Newells Old Boys Football Stadium

Museo Histórico Provincial 'Dr. Julio Marc'

Parque de la Independencia

Brown, Jujuy, Salta, Catamarca, Tucumán, Urquiza, San Lorenzo, Santa Fe, Córdoba, Güemes, Av. Wheelwright, Gral. Lugano, Saguier, Paseo del Siglo, Rioja, San Luis, San Juan, Mendoza, 3 de Febrero, 9 de Julio, Zeballos, Italia, España, Pte. Roca, Paraguay, Corrientes, Entre Ríos, Mitre, Sarmiento, San Martín, Maipú, Laprida, Buenos Aires, Juan M. de Rosas, 1º de Mayo, L. N. Alem, Ayacucho, Colón, Necochea, Chacabuco, Av. Belgrano, Av. Libertad, Montevideo, Avenida Pellegrini, Cochabamba, Pasos, Ituzaingo, Cerrito, Riobamba, La Paz, Balcarce, Alvear, Santiago, Pueyrredón, M. Rodríguez, Callao, P. García, Monroe, Richieri, Suipacha, Avenida Francia, Prioni, Barraco, Cordero, Vera Mujica, Avenida O. Lagos, Boulevard Nicasio Oroño, M. Moreno, Dorrego, Pringles, Martín, Masón, Medinacelli, Marchena, Caldas, Quintanilla, Conde, Lavalle, Deza, Alsina, Castellanos, Constitución, San Nicolás, Marcos Paz, Cafferata, Iriondo, Crespo, Zavalla, Morueña, M. Suárez, M. García, Apolo, Gordillo, Luján, L. Miranda, Mattos, Ceres, Civit, Ituzaingo, Tiscornia, Coffin

N

0 500m

Artes in Buenos Aires (see p.98). Arranged on two floors with large and well-lit rooms, its two permanent collections cover European art from the Renaissance to the twentieth century and Argentine painting, including works by local lad, Lucio Fontana. The **Museo Histórico Provincial Dr Julio Marc** (Tues–Fri 9am–5pm, Sat & Sun 2–5pm; free; ☎0341/472-1457), which lies to the west of the lake in the park, features a vast collection of exhibits spanning the whole of Latin America. Its most notable collections are dedicated to **Latin American religious art**, with a stunning eighteenth-century silver altar from Alto Perú. There's also an important collection of **indigenous American ceramics**.

Known as the Alto Delta, the low-lying **islands** that sit off Rosario's coast actually fall under the jurisdiction of the neighbouring province, Entre Ríos. Like the islands of the Tigre Delta (see p.105) in Buenos Aires Province, they have a subtropical vegetation fed by sediment from Misiones Province. If you can afford it, the best way of seeing the delta is on an **excursion**, which will set you back AR$30-50; try Carlos Vaccarezza (☎0341/449-1921) or El Holandés (☎156-415880). Alternatively, there are various islands offering camping facilities, accommodation and restaurants which you can reach by one of the regular passenger services from the Estación Fluvial (see above).

Eating and nightlife

Rosario has plenty of **restaurants** to suit all budgets, both in the city centre and along the Costanera. What the city really excels in, however, are **bars** – there are so many stylishly revamped establishments around the city centre that you're pretty much spoilt for choice when it comes to drinking. In comparison, Rosario's **clubs** are a little disappointing and in summer, when all the action moves to the Rambla Catalunya, a beachfront avenue at the northern end of town, you're pretty much limited to one or two very popular but pretty faceless mega-discos.

Cafes, bars and restaurants

Aux Deux Magots Entre Ríos 2. Spacious café-bar serving excellent coffee overlooking the river – a lovely spot for a leisurely Sunday breakfast.

Club G. Savio right by the river, at the end of Calle Paraguay; access via Calle Corrientes ☎0341/426-7157. Popular fish restaurant with lovely wooden terrace overlooking the river. Try the simple grilled *boga al limón*.

Rancho Av Carrasco 2765. Popular summer bar along the Rambla Catalunya and a good place to pick up free invites for one of the area's clubs. Vast outside seating area and a range of beers, cocktails and fast food.

Rich San Juan 1031 ☎0341/440-8657. Rosario's most venerable restaurant, a lovely old-fashioned place with a vast mouth-watering menu mixing traditional dishes such as *puchero* with more elaborate creations like sea bass with champagne sauce or sirloin steak with shallots, mushrooms, bacon and red wine. Among the vegetarian choices are pasta with tomato pesto, cream and mushrooms, and asparagus omelette. Expensive, but well worth it.

Savoy San Lorenzo and San Martín. Definitely the best deal in town with plenty of fish, meat and pasta dishes for around AR$3. The spaghetti with home-made pesto and fresh parmesan for only AR$1.30 is unbelievably cheap and delicious. A good place for breakfast, too, with coffee and croissants for AR$1.

Clubs and tango bars

Catalinas Av Colombres 2600. *The* club in the summer; a big, mainstream disco along the Rambla Catalunya with outside bar area and a young, lively, Alvear and Catamarca. Attractive wood-panelled bar on a pretty corner of Pichincha. Good range of beers as well as fruity non-alcoholic drinks.

Sentimiento Tango San Martín 580. A slightly down-at-heel but atmospheric tango bar attracting a handful of dancers every night except Monday. The atmosphere is anything but intimidating, which makes it a good place to take your first tango steps; classes Tues, Thurs, Sat & Sun from 9pm.

Colón and around

COLÓN is the most appealing of Entre Ríos' resorts and, thanks to its lovely riverside setting and attractive hotels and restaurants, a good place to stop over before heading on to **Parque Nacional El Palmar**, 50km to the north. The town sits along the Río Uruguay and has a narrow strip of beach running for several kilometres alongside its handsome riverside avenue, the **Costanera Gobernador Quirós**, flanked by a pretty balustrade. Ten blocks inland, the town's central square, Plaza Washington, where you will find the *municipalidad*, covers four blocks, but far more elegant **Plaza San Martín**, lies to the east along Colón's main commercial street, Avenida 12 de Abril. Immediately to the north of Plaza San Martín, the sleepy **port area** is a small quarter lined with a clutch of pretty colonial-style buildings that slope down to the riverbank.

In the middle of the river lie some lushly vegetated **islands** flanked with spectacularly pristine sandbanks. Fascinating and fun excursions to the islands in motorised dinghies, or visits to the area around Colón, can be made with *Ita I Cora* (Ⓣ&Ⓕ 03447/423360, Ⓦwww.itaicora.com), whose lively English-speaking owner can usually be found at the office at San Martín 97, unless he is out on an excursion.

Practicalities

Colón's **bus terminal** (Ⓣ03447/421716) lies some fifteen blocks northwest of Plaza San Martín, on the corner of Paysandú and Sourigues. The busy **tourist office** (Ⓣ03447/421233) is down in the port area, two blocks north of the plaza, on the corner of the Avenida Costanera and Gouchón, and is a useful place to get accommodation information. The town can be very busy for long weekends, so it's a good idea to book **accommodation** ahead of time. Easily the most attractive hotel is the stunning *Hostería del Puerto* (Ⓣ03447/422698, Ⓦwww.colonentrerios.com.ar/hosteria; ❹), a pretty, pink colonial building just one block from the port at Alejo Peyret 158. The huge, beautifully decorated rooms are around a central courtyard; the best rooms are upstairs with large balconies and a view over the river. Breakfast is included and there is a twenty-percent discount during the week. A good option near the bus terminal is the *Hotel Paysandú* (Ⓣ03447/421140; ❸), on the corner of Maipú and Paysandú, a spruce modern place with clean and comfortable rooms, parking and very friendly owners; breakfast is included. Colón's dynamic new HI-affiliated hostel at Laprida 128 (Ⓣ03447/422385, Ⓔcasamate@casamate.com.ar; ❷) is the best budget accommodation by far. There are plenty of **campsites**, spread out along the length of Colón's beaches. At the northern end is the simple *Camping Municipal Norte* (Ⓣ03447/421917; AR$3 per person), on the beach at the foot of Calle Paysandú, with showers, electric light and barbecue facilities.

There are some good **restaurants** in Colón, mostly within a few blocks of Plaza San Martín. On the corner of Calles 12 de Abril and Alejo Peyret, the *Plaza* is a lively pizzeria and *parrilla* and is also a good place for a drink. Another good choice is the *Viejo Almacén*, on the corner of Calles Urquiza and J.J. Paso, one block southeast of the plaza, a stylishly old-fashioned place which does excellent river fish.

Parque Nacional El Palmar

The first sign that you are approaching **PARQUE NACIONAL EL PALMAR,** fifty kilometres north of Colón along the RN14, is a sprinkling of tremendously tall palm trees towering above the flat lands that border the highway. This 85-square-kilometre park was set up in 1966 to conserve examples of the **yatay palm**, which once covered large areas of Entre Ríos, Uruguay and Southern Brazil. Intensive cultivation of the region almost wiped out the palm, and the Parque Nacional El Palmar is now the largest remaining reserve of the yatay, as well as one of the southernmost palm groves in the world. The sheer proliferation of the majestic yatay – with many examples over 300 years old and growing up to 18 metres in height – makes for a wonderfully exotic landscape. Well-signposted trails in the park take you along the streams and through palm forests. There are great views from **La Glorieta**, a gentle bluff from where you can take in the surrounding sea of palms. The park's wildlife includes *ñandúes*, armadillos, foxes and capybaras and, particularly around the campsite, vizcachas and monitor lizards.

From the *guardaparques'* post at the entrance, where you pay a AR$12 entrance fee, it's a hefty ten-kilometre or so walk to the visitor centre and campsite, though at all but the quietest times it should be possible to get a lift with someone else entering the park. The only place to stay within the park is at **Los Loros campground** (☎03447/493031; AR$6 per tent, plus AR$4 per person), a spacious and shady site with showers and a provisions store.

Corrientes

A sultry, subtropical city sitting on a bend in the Río Paraná, **CORRIENTES** is one of El Litoral's oldest and most attractive cities. If you visit in summer, though, be aware that both temperatures and humidity can be very high.

All the major points of interest lie within the streets to the north of Avenida 3 de Abril, which runs east–west through the city towards Puente General Belgrano. A lovely old-fashioned leafy square surrounded by some of Corrientes' most striking architecture, **Plaza 25 de Mayo** encapsulates the city's sleepy subtropical ambience. One of the most striking buildings is the pretty pink **Casa de Gobierno**, on the eastern side, constructed in 1886 in the ornate Italianate style. On the corner of Fray José de la Quintana and Salta, you'll find the **Museo de Artesanía** (Mon–Fri 7am–noon & 4–7pm) and the Taller de Artesanos (same hours), housed within a typical colonial Corrientes building; a low whitewashed residence constructed around a central patio flanked by a gallery, providing shade from the fierce summer sun. Inside you'll find an interesting selection of leather, ceramics and basketwork. At the southern end of the square, the nineteenth-century **Iglesia de Nuestra Señora de la Merced** (daily 7am–noon & 4–8pm) houses a handsome hand-carved wooden retable with twisted wooden pillars and rich golden inlay work. Lined with fine examples of native trees, Corrientes' riverside avenue, the **Avenida Costanera General San Martín**, is a lovely spot on summer evenings, when the heat dissipates a little and locals pack its promenades for a jog or a stroll, or simply sit sipping *mate* or *tereré* on stone benches.

The city has an important Mardi Gras **Carnival**, a very Brazilian-influenced affair held in the Corsódromo – a kind of open-air stadium specially constructed for the event at Avenida Centenario 2800. Visitors seeking a more locally authentic affair will enjoy the **Festival del Chamamé**, a celebration of the region's most popular folk music with plenty of live music and dancing, held on the second weekend in December.

Practicalities

Corrientes' **airport**, the Aeropuerto Fernando Piragine Niveyro (☎03783/458340), lies some 10km northeast of the city, along the RN12. Coinciding with the arrival of its flights from Buenos Aires, Austral runs a shuttle service for its passengers from the airport to the city. The city's **bus terminal** (☎03783/442149) is about 4km southeast of Plaza 25 de Mayo, along one of the city's main access roads, the Avenida Maipú, and various local buses, including the #103, run between the terminal and the centre; a taxi from the terminal to the centre costs around AR$5. Local buses from Resistencia arrive at a smaller bus terminal on the Costanera, opposite the northern end of La Rioja, within walking distance of most accommodation. Corrientes' **tourist office** is centrally located at 25 de Mayo 1330 (daily 7am–1pm & 3–9pm; ⓣ03783/427200, ⓦwww.planetacorrientes.com).

Corrientes' **hotels** are pitched towards businessmen and while there are some good upmarket places, simple residential accommodation is pretty thin on the ground. Corrientes' particularly hot and humid summers make air conditioning almost a necessity – though a shady room with a good fan can be acceptable. By far, the best hotel in town, the *Hotel Plaza*, on Junín 1549 (ⓣ03783/466500; ❺), features beautifully renovated en-suite rooms, a smart bar and a large swimming pool. In a modern block facing the river, the *Hostal del Pinar*, on Plácido Martínez 1098 (ⓣ&ⓕ03783/29726; ❹), has slightly bland but spacious rooms, with cable TV and good air conditioning. It has a small outdoor swimming pool, and its very efficient staff speaks some English. The best of the cheaper hotels, *Hospedaje San Lorenzo*, on San Lorenzo 1136 (no phone; ❷), is a friendly place offering basic, well-kept rooms on a quiet central street. Rooms have fans and private bathrooms. There's a good **campsite**, with showers, electricity and barbecue facilities around 10km northeast of town at Laguna Soto; get there on local bus #109 from the terminal.

Corrientes isn't overly endowed with interesting places to **eat** and **drink**, but there are a few good places both in the city centre (mostly around the *centro comercial*) and along the Costanera. At San Lorenzo 830, there's an excellent buffet-style restaurant, *El Solar*, providing plenty of appetizing fresh salads, fruit juices and a variety of hot dishes. A popular **nightlife** option is a *chamamé* folk music show held at various restaurants – try *Parrilla El Quincho* on Avenida Juan Pujol and Pellegrini and *La Peña Puente Pesoa* at the intersection of the RN12 with Avenida P. Ferrer (the continuation of Avenida 3 de Abril). Both do a *tenedor libre parrilla* for AR$5 a head and have live shows on Fridays and Saturdays from about 10pm.

The Reserva Natural del Iberá

Covering nearly 13,000 square kilometres, the **RESERVA NATURAL DEL IBERÁ** is a vast system of wetlands with some of the best opportunities for close-up observation of wildlife in the whole of Argentina. The reserve is composed of a series of lakes, *esteros* (marshes) and wonderful floating islands formed by a build-up of soil on top of densely intertwined waterlilies. For many years, the **Esteros del Iberá** was one of Argentina's wildest and least-known regions, but since the creation of the reserve, in 1983 hunting in the area has been prohibited and many locals have been employed as highly specialized guides and park rangers. There has been an upsurge in the region's abundant bird and animal population including caymans, capybaras, marsh deer, howler monkeys, boas, the rare-maned wolf and over three hundred species of birds. **Boat trips** afford incredibly close contact with many of the species.

The reserve is best reached from the village of **Colonia Carlos Pellegrini**, a charming semi-rural settlement beside one of the system's major lakes, the Laguna Iberá; the best access to the village is from **Mercedes**, 118km to the southwest.

Mercedes

A quiet little agricultural town given a distinctive flavour by a mix of old-fashioned adobe and galleried roof buildings and elegant nineteenth-century town architecture, **MERCEDES** is built on a regular grid pattern centred on **Plaza 25 de Mayo**, a densely planted square with little fountains. At its southern end stands the town's rather unusual church, the **Iglesia Nuestra Señora de las Mercedes**, a lofty late nineteenth-century red-brick construction. Avenida San Martín runs east–west along the northern side of the square, connecting with the bus terminal and the major access routes in and out of town. Three blocks to the east of the square, on the corner of San Martín and Batalla de Salta, is a beautifully preserved example of the local building style: a low whitewashed adobe-walled construction with a gently sloping red-tiled roof that overhangs the pavement, supported on simple wooden posts. The building houses the **Fundación Manos Correntinas**, a non-profit enterprise that functions as an outlet for locally produced crafts. Mercedes' **bus terminal**, with regular services to Colonia Carlos Pellegrini (see below) and Buenos Aires, is on the corner of Avenida San Martín and El Ceibo.

Colonia Carlos Pellegrini and the esteros

The heart of the Reserva Natural del Iberá is the village of **COLONIA CARLOS PELLEGRINI**, accessed via the unsealed – and sometimes trying – RP40. It sits on a peninsula, on the edges of the Laguna Iberá, a 53 square-kilometre expanse of water spread with acres of waterlilies, most notably the striking mauve and yellow *aguapé*, and dotted with floating islands, or *embalsados*. Before you cross the narrow bridge to the village, there's a small **visitor centre** immediately to the left, with a small photographic display on the *esteros*. To the south of the visitors' centre, a short trail leads through a small forested area, a densely packed mix of palms, jacarandas, *lapachos* and willows. This is a good place to spot the black and brown howler monkeys that typically slouch in a ball shape amongst the branches or swing from tree to tree on lianas.

The village itself is composed of a small grid of sandy streets, centred on a grassy **Plaza San Martín**. There's only one public phone, used by the whole village to receive calls, and nothing in the way of banking facilities. so make sure you bring enough cash with you for your stay. The best **accommodation** in the village is provided by three posadas. The pioneering *Posada de la Laguna*, on a quiet lakeside spot at the eastern edge of the village (Ⓣ03773/1562-9532 or 9827, Ⓔposadadelalaguna@ibera.net; ❽ full board) has elegant and spacious en-suite rooms in a galleried building whose veranda provides a good vantage point, and the food is delicious. A couple of blocks west, *Posada Aguapé* (Ⓣ03773/1562-9759 or 011/4742-3015, Ⓔaguape@interserver.com.ar; ❽ full board) is set in spacious grounds with very pretty en-suite rooms overlooking the lake. The newest *posada* is the *Ñanderetá*, towards the western end of the village (Ⓣ154-629536 or 011/4811-2005, Ⓦwww.nandereta.com; ❼ full board).

Trips to the marshes (including horse riding) are organized through the posadas, who take visitors out on small motorboats. Around the reed beds at the edges of the lake you may see snakes, such as the handsome yellow anaconda, and *chajás* (southern screamers), large grey birds with a startling patch of red around the eyes. You soon find yourself amongst a wonderful landscape of waterlilies and verdant floating islands, teeming with bird and animal life. Easiest to spot are the birds, most commonly neotropic cormorants, storks and herons. As you approach the edges of the islands, seemingly static caymans suddenly slip into the water and observe you with their prehistoric eyes peeking above the water. Listen, too, for the sudden splash of a capybara – one of the world's most unlikely aquatic mammals – diving into the water.

San Ignacio

After the Iguazú Falls, Misiones' major tourist attractions are the **Jesuit Missions** to the north of the provincial capital Posadas. The largest of these, **San Ignacio Miní**, 60km to the north of Posadas, is the best preserved in the entire mission region, which extended beyond the Paraguay and Uruguay rivers to Paraguay and Brazil, and also into the province of Corrientes. Far less well preserved – and much less visited – are the ruins of **Santa Ana** (daily 7am–6pm; AR$1) and **Loreto** (same hours and price), just to the south of San Ignacio, though these crumbling monuments, set amongst thick jungle vegetation, have a mysterious appeal of their own. Near the pretty village of San Ignacio, there's a stunning area of forest and beaches to the southwest of the village with a good campsite and perhaps the finest stretch of river scenery in the whole littoral region.

Considering it's home to such a major attraction, the town of **SAN IGNACIO** is remarkably tranquil. Away from the huddle of restaurants and souvenir stands around the ruins themselves, the town has few tourist amenities. San Ignacio is laid out on the usual grid pattern; it's a rather long thin shape, dissected east–west by broad Avenida Sarmiento and north–south by Bolívar. The western extremity is bounded by Avenida Horacio Quiroga. Heading south along the avenue for a kilometre or so, you'll come to the **Casa de Horacio Quiroga** (daily 8am–7pm; AR$2; ⓣ03752/470130), a museum to the Uruguayan writer famed for his rather gothic short stories, who made his home here in the early twentieth century.

Continuing south past the museum, the unsealed road winds down for another 2km or so to the stunning **Puerto Nuevo**, where there's a lovely strip of sandy beach and, best of all, a fantastic view across the curves of the Paraná to the Paraguayan border – all rolling wooded slopes tumbling down to the water. It is also enjoyable to take the trip from San Ignacio to the **Parque Provincial Teyú Cuaré**, some 10km south of the village via a good unsealed road accessed from the southern end of Bolívar. The park's most famous feature is its high rocky cliff, the **Peñón Reina Victoria**, named for its supposed similarity to the profile of the British queen. There is a wild **campsite** within the park.

San Ignacio Miní

The most famous of all the *reducciones*, **SAN IGNACIO MINÍ** (daily 7am–7pm; AR$2.50) was originally founded in 1610 in the Guayrá region in what is now Brazil. After the *bandeirantes* attacked the mission in 1631, the Jesuits moved southwards for thousands of miles through the jungle, stopping several times en route at various temporary settlements before finally re-establishing the *reducción* on its present site in 1696. Today, the ruins occupy some six blocks at the northeastern end of the village of San Ignacio. At the entrance, there's an excellent **Centro de Interpretación Regional** (same times as for site; ⓣ03752/470186) with a series of themed rooms depicting various aspects of Guaraní and mission life. Upon entering the settlement itself, along a wide grassy path, you'll come first to rows of simple *viviendas* or living quarters; a series of six to ten adjoining one-roomed structures, each one of which housed a Guaraní family. Like all the mission settlements, these are constructed in a mixture of basaltic rock and sandstone. Between the *viviendas*, you'll find the spacious Plaza de Armas, whose emerald grass provides a stunning contrast with the rich red hues of the sandstone. At the southern end of the plaza, and dominating the entire site, stands the magnificent facade of San Ignacio's **church**, designed – like Santa Ana's – by the Italian architect Brazanelli. The roof and much of the interior have long since crumbled away, but two large chunks of wall on either side of the entrance still remain, rising out of the ruins like two great Baroque wings. Though somewhat eroded, many fine details can still be made out: two columns flank either side of the doorway, and much of the walls' surface is covered with decorative bas-relief sculpture executed by Guaraní craftsmen.

Practicalities

Buses to San Ignacio all arrive at the western end of Avenida Sarmiento. It's not a terminal as such, but there's a kiosk here whose friendly owner may agree to look after left luggage for a few hours. **Accommodation** options in the town are limited but agreeable. The largest hotel, the *Residencial San Ignacio* (ⓣ03752/470047; ❸), on the corner of San Martín and Sarmiento, is a slick modern place with comfortable en-suite rooms, all with air conditioning. Eternally popular with foreign travellers on a budget is the *Hospedaje Los Alemanes*, on Avenida Horacio Quiroga, 50m west of the bus terminal (☎03752/470362; AR$15 per person with shared bathroom). Tents can also be pitched for AR$3 per day. Towards the outskirts of the village, *Hospedaje El Descanso*, at Pellegrini 270, around ten blocks south of the bus terminal (☎03752/470207; ❷) offers smart little *cabañas* with private bathrooms. The best **campsite** in town is at the *Club de Pesca y Deportes Acuáticos*, down at Puerto Nuevo (☎03752/1568-3411; AR$2.50 per tent plus AR$2 per person); tents can be pitched here on a bluff with an absolutely stunning view over the river and the Paraguayan coast. On Puerto Nuevo's beach itself, tents can be pitched behind the *cantina* (AR$2.50 per tent plus AR$1 per person).

Iguazú Falls

Composed of over 250 separate falls and straddling the Argentina–Brazil border, the **IGUAZÚ FALLS**, or *Cataratas*, as they are known locally, are quite simply the world's most dramatic waterfalls. Set amongst the exotic subtropical forests of the **Parque Nacional Iguazú** in Argentina, and the **Parque Nacional do Iguaçu** in Brazil (see p.448), the falls tumble for some 2km from the Río Iguazú superior over a 70m cliff to the Río Iguazú inferior below. At their heart, the dizzying **Garganta del Diablo** is a powerhouse display of natural forces in which 1800 cubic metres of water per second hurtles over a 3km semicircle of rock into the boiling river canyon below. The surrounding subtropical **forest** is packed with exotic animals, birds and insects – even on the busy catwalks and paths that skirt the edges of the falls you've a good chance of seeing gorgeously hued bright blue butterflies as big as your hand.

March to November is regarded as the **best time to visit** the park, when temperatures are not too high – although the combination of steamy heat, intense blue skies and sparkling spray in summer has a pretty undeniable appeal too. The rainy season runs from May to July, and the falls are at their most spectacular after heavy rain.

The Parque Nacional Iguazú and the Falls

The vast majority of the **Iguazú Falls** lie on the Argentine side of the border, within the **Parque Nacional Iguazú**, 18km southeast of Puerto Iguazú along RN12. This side offers the most extensive experience of the falls, thanks to its well-thought-out system of trails and catwalks taking you both below and above them – most notably to the Garganta del Diablo. (New catwalks have made **wheelchair access** possible to all of the Paseo Superior and much of the Paseo Inferior.) The surrounding forest also offers excellent opportunities to discover the region's wildlife.

Without a doubt, the best place to begin your tour of Iguazú is on the **Argentine side** (for the Brazilian side and Foz do Iguaçu, see p.448). As you get off the bus within the park, you're greeted by the sound of rushing water from the falls. There's a **visitor centre** to the left of the bus stop, where you can pick up maps and information leaflets. From the visitor centre, two well-signposted trails take you along a series of catwalks and paths past the falls. The best approach is probably to tackle the **Paseo Superior** first, a short trail which takes you along the top of the first few waterfalls. For more drama, head along the **Paseo Inferior**, which winds down through the forest before taking you to within metres of some of the smaller but still spectacular falls – notably **saltos Ramírez** and **Bosetti**. Around the falls, look out for the swallow-like *vencejo*, a remarkable small bird that makes its nest behind the gushing torrents of water. Along the lower reaches of the paseo, a regular free boat service leaves for **Isla San Martín**, a rocky island in the

middle of the river. From the departure point, Iguazú Jungle Explorer (☎03757/421600) also offers short **boat trips**, starting from AR$25 and taking you up close to the falls, where the crew take special delight in getting you really soaked.

To visit the **Garganta del Diablo**, you must return to the visitor centre and pick up the Cataratas bus (hourly, last bus 5.05pm) for Puerto Canoas, some 4km south-east. From Puerto Canoas launches take you to the remains of a catwalk where a small viewing platform takes you to within just a few metres of the staggering, sheer drop of water formed by the union of several immensely powerful falls around a kind of horseshoe. Heading west from the visitor centre, a well-marked trail leads to the start of the **Sendero Macuco**, a four-kilometre nature trail down to the lower banks of the Río Iguazú, past a waterfall, the **Salto Arrechea** where

△ A gaucho on horseback

there is a lovely secluded bathing spot. Commonly spotted species along the trail include various species of toucans and shy capuchin monkeys.

Crossing into Brazil

To round off your trip to Iguazú, however, you should also visit the **Brazilian side** (see p.448), where the view is more panoramic, and photography opportunities are excellent. A bus (AR$5.60 return) runs to the park every hour from the bus terminal in town with the first one leaving at 7.30am and the last one returning at 8pm. The bus stops at the entrance to the park, where you have to get off and pay an admission fee of AR$30, before it leaves you at the visitors' centre. International buses leave every 45mins from Puerto Iguazú to Foz do Iguaçu between about 6.20am and 7pm (a taxi will cost around AR$30 or its Brazilian equivalent). Immigration formalities take place on the Brazilian side of the bridge, and officially everyone, apart from locals, must acquire the necessary stamps and visas; it's worth taking the trouble to get stamped in and out. Note that from October to March, Brazil is one hour ahead of Argentina – something to keep in mind when making sure you catch the last bus back into town.

Puerto Iguazú

PUERTO IGUAZÚ is a strange kind of place. Potentially it's a far more attractive town to base yourself than Foz – its tropical vegetation and quiet streets seem more in keeping with the region than the high-rise concrete of the Brazilian city. Yet while the town's tranquil atmosphere provides a restful contrast to the goings-on just over the border, Puerto Iguazú really lacks anything that would make you want to stay there any longer than necessary. You wouldn't exactly call Iguazú's **town centre** bustling, but most of what goes on goes on around the intersection of Avenida Aguirre, Calle Brasil and Calle Ingeniero Gustavo Eppens. From this intersection the Avenida Tres Fronteras runs west for some one and a half kilometres to the **Hito Tres Fronteras**, a vantage point over the rivers with views over to Brazil and Paraguay and marked by an obelisk painted in the colours of the Argentine flag.

Some 4km along the RN12 towards the park, rustic signposts direct you to **La Aripuca** (8am–sunset; ☎03757/423488; AR$3). An *aripuca* is an indigenous wooden trap used in the region to catch birds and La Aripuca is a giant replica of the trap, standing some 10m high and constructed out of 29 different species of trees native to Misiones Province (all obtained through unavoidable felling or victims of thunderstorms).

Practicalities

Puerto Iguazú's international **airport** lies around 20km southeast of the town, along the RN12 just past the entrance to the park. Aristóbulo del Valle (☎03757/421996) runs a bus service between the airport and the bus terminal. The **bus terminal** is on the corner of avenidas Córdoba and Misiones; the most helpful of the numerous kiosks offering **information** is probably the friendly *Agencia Noelia* (☎03757/422722), which also sells the tickets for the bus to the national park. There's a good restaurant in the terminal, a *locutorio* and a **left-luggage** service (AR$2 large bag, AR$1 small bag), which opens from 7am to 9pm; if you need to pick your bag up later, arrange with staff to collect the key for the luggage deposit from the toilet attendant. The **tourist office** is at Av Aguirre 311 (daily 7am–10pm; ☎03757/420800).

Puerto Iguazú has a good range of fairly priced **accommodation**, with some particularly good deals at the cheaper end of the price range. The greatest concentration of hotels is around the bus terminal, the most convenient area to stay for catching the bus to the falls as well as over the border to Brazil. Reservations are a good idea at any time of year if you want to be sure of getting your first choice –

during high season (July and Easter) they're a must. *The* place to stay for film-star glamour, the *Iguazú Grand Hotel* RN12, at Km 1640 (Ⓣ03757/498050, Ⓔjuanfperesbreton@usa.net; ❾), is a fabulously luxurious hotel with enormous suites supplied with everything from CD players to glossy picture books on Misiones. It has a landscaped outdoor pool and two very good restaurants. On the other end of the scale, the best deal is *Residencial Noelia* Fray Luis Beltrán 119 (Ⓣ03757/420729; ❶), a friendly, family-run place largely catering to backpackers. It is scrupulously maintained and has three- and four-bed rooms with fans and private bathroom and breakfast of toast, fruit and coffee brought to your room or the shady patio outside. Of Iguazú's mid-range hotels, the best is *Saint George* Av Córdoba 148 (Ⓣ03757/420633; ❺), a recently revamped and courteous hotel with some exceptionally light and attractive first-floor rooms with balconies overlooking the swimming pool. It has a good restaurant downstairs and buffet breakfast with fresh fruit included in room rate. *Residencial Lilian*, Fray Luis Beltrán 183 (Ⓣ03757/420968; ❷), offers spotless light and airy rooms with good fans and modern bathrooms. The best-organized **campsite** is the large and well-equipped *Camping Viejo Americano* (Ⓣ03757/420190; AR$4 per tent, plus AR$4 per person), about 5km out of town along the RN12 towards the national park, with showers, provisions store, telephone and swimming pool. The campsite can be reached on the Cataratas bus or by taxi (around AR$3 from terminal).

Puerto Iguazú doesn't have a particularly exciting range of **restaurants** and most of them seem fond of regaling customers with either television or live music – possibly to drown out the lack of atmosphere. Most of the better places to eat are grouped near the bus terminal. The *Jardín Iguazú*, on the corner of Avenida Misiones and Córdoba must be one of Argentina's better bus terminal restaurants, serving a mixture of *parrillada*, fish, Chinese food and fast food. Iguazú's not the best place in Argentina for meat but there's reasonably priced *parrillada* in *Charo*, at Av Córdoba 106, and *El Quincho del Tío Querido*, on Calle Bompland; both restaurants also offer grilled river fish. The bright and modern *Pizza Color*, at Av Córdoba 135, does excellent *pizza a la piedra* and good salads.

1.4

The northwest

The **NORTHWEST** is a region of ochre deserts where flocks of llamas roam, charcoal-grey lava-flows devoid of any life form, blindingly white salt flats and sooty-black volcano cones, pristine limewashed colonial chapels set against striped mountainsides, lush citrus groves and emerald-green sugar plantations, impenetrable jungles populated by toucans and tapirs. One of the many colonial cities, **Salta**, is indisputably the region's tourism capital, with some of the country's best hotels and finest colonial architecture, matchless services and a well-earned reputation for hospitality. To the northwest you can meander up the **Quebrada del Toro** on a safari or, for the slightly less adventurous, on the **Tren a las Nubes**, one of the world's highest railways. Alternatively, you can head for the jungle-clad **cloudforests**, which poke out of the flat, fertile plains into the rain cloud that gives them their name. Three of them, notably **El Rey**, are protected, along with their prolific flora and fauna, by national park status. Capital of secluded Jujuy Province, **Jujuy** is the best starting-point for exploring one of the country's most photogenic features, the multicoloured **Quebrada de Humahuaca**. Further south, mountain roads scale the verdant **Cuesta del Obispo** and the vividly hued **Quebrada de Cafayate** from Salta to the **Valles Calchaquíes**, dry, sunny valleys along which high-altitude vineyards somehow thrive, around the airy regional capital of **Cafayate**. Much of the Northwest region is accessible by **public transport** but organized tours or, even better, exploring in a 4WD are generally more rewarding ways of discovering the area, and at times are the only way of getting around. Should you choose to go it alone, take into account the mind-boggling distances involved, the challenging road and climatic conditions and, above all, the sheer remoteness of it all.

Salta

SALTA, historic capital of one of Argentina's largest and most beautiful provinces, easily lives up to its well-publicized nickname of Salta the Fair (*Salta la Linda*), thanks to its festive atmosphere, handsome buildings and dramatic setting. The city is squeezed between steep, rippling mountains, 1500km northwest of Buenos Aires; it enjoys a relatively balmy climate, thanks to its location at 1190m above sea level. In addition to a cable car and a tourist railway, its sights include a striking Neoclassical church, several museums and a generous sprinkling of well-preserved or well-restored colonial architecture.

Many visitors to Salta speed around the city and then head off to the major attractions of the Quebrada del Toro – often on the Tren a las Nubes – and the Valles Calchaquíes, perhaps staying over in Cafayate. An alternative excursion destination is the cloudforest national park of **El Rey**, to the east.

Arrival and information

Salta's **Airport** (☎0387/424-2904) is about 10km southwest of the city centre. Airbus (☎0387/156-832-897; AR$4) runs between the airport and central Salta whereas a taxi would set you back about AR$10. Buses from all across the region

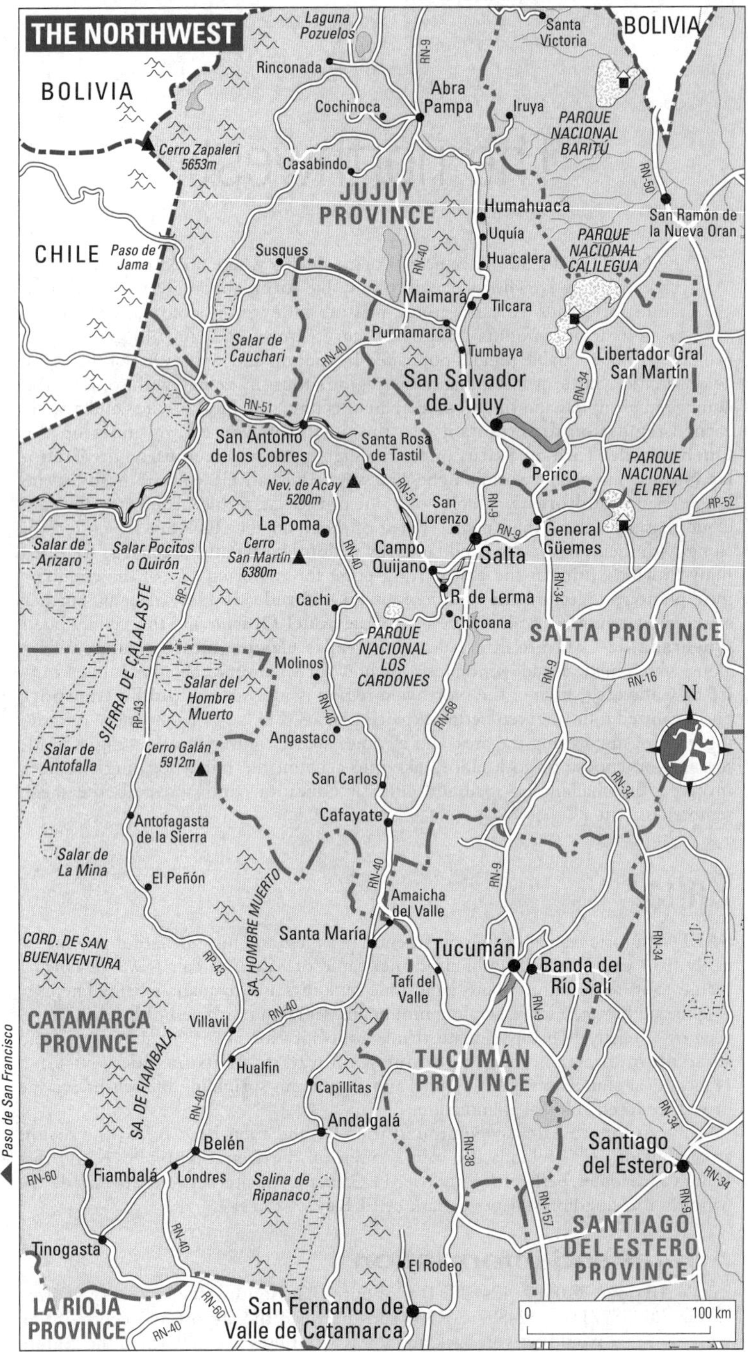
La Quiaca & Yavi
THE NORTHWEST
BOLIVIA
Laguna Pozuelos
Santa Victoria
BOLIVIA
Rinconada
Abra Pampa
Cochinoca
Iruya
PARQUE NACIONAL BARITÚ
Cerro Zapaleri 5653m
Casabindo
JUJUY PROVINCE
Humahuaca
San Ramón de la Nueva Oran
Uquía
PARQUE NACIONAL CALILEGUA
CHILE
Paso de Jama
Susques
Huacalera
Maimará
Tilcara
Purmamarca
Salar de Cauchari
Tumbaya
Libertador Gral San Martín
San Salvador de Jujuy
RN-51
San Antonio de los Cobres
Santa Rosa de Tastil
Perico
PARQUE NACIONAL EL REY
Nev. de Acay 5200m
San Lorenzo
RP-52
La Poma
General Güemes
Salar de Arizaro
Salar Pocitos o Quirón
Cerro San Martín 6380m
Campo Quijano
Salta
R. de Lerma
Cachi
Chicoana
SALTA PROVINCE
PARQUE NACIONAL LOS CARDONES
Molinos
SIERRA DE CALALASTE
Salar del Hombre Muerto
RN-16
N
Salar de Antofalla
Cerro Galán 5912m
Angastaco
San Carlos
Cafayate
Antofagasta de la Sierra
Salar de La Mina
El Peñón
Amaicha del Valle
SA. HOMBRE MUERTO
Santa María
CORD. DE SAN BUENAVENTURA
Tucumán
Banda del Río Salí
Tafí del Valle
CATAMARCA PROVINCE
Villavil
Hualfin
TUCUMÁN PROVINCE
Capillitas
SA. DE FIAMBALÁ
Andalgalá
Paso de San Francisco
Belén
Santiago del Estero
Fiambalá
Londres
Salina de Ripanaco
SANTIAGO DEL ESTERO PROVINCE
Tinogasta
El Rodeo
LA RIOJA PROVINCE
San Fernando de Valle de Catamarca
0
100 km
RN-9
RN-40
RN-34
RN-50
RN-68
RP-17
RP-43
RN-38
RN-157
RN-60

and throughout the country use the scruffy but user-friendly **bus terminal** at Avenida Hipólito Yrigoyen (ⓣ0387/431-5227), just east of the Parque San Martín, five blocks south and eight east of central Plaza 9 de Julio. Bus #5 links the bus terminal with the **train station**, at Ameghino 690, via Plaza 9 de Julio. The only trains serving Salta apart from the privately run tourist train, the Tren a las Nubes (see box, p.140), are the infrequent goods and passenger trains to the Chilean border.

The excellent, dynamic and well-equipped provincial **tourist office** is at Buenos Aires 93 (Mon–Fri 8am–9pm, Sat, Sun & public holidays 9am–8pm; ⓣ0387/431-0950, ⓦwww.turismosalta.com). The **city tourist office** is farther down Buenos Aires at the corner of Av San Martín (daily 8am–9pm; ⓣ0387/437-3341).

Accommodation

Salta has a wide range of **places to stay**, ranging from a couple of the few boutique hotels in the country to a fun youth hostel, plus plenty of decent middle-range hotels and excellent-value *residenciales* in between. The **Backpackers Hostel** is at Buenos Aires 930 (ⓣ0387/423-5910, ⓔbackpack@hostels.org.ar) and has double rooms (❷) as well as very cramped dorms (AR$12). Facilities are not great but there's a very friendly, international atmosphere. Salta's enormous municipal **campsite**, *Carlos Xamena* (ⓣ0387/423-1341), in the Parque Municipal, 3km to the south of the centre, is a little noisy but well equipped, with a huge swimming pool, hot showers, *balneario* and a supermarket. It costs AR$3 per tent and AR$2 per person.

Hotel Cristian Islas Malvinas 160 ⓣ0387/431-9600. Very pleasant rooms, mostly quiet, with private bath, and fresh decoration. ❹

Hotel Cumbre Ituzaingo 585 ⓣ0387/421-4747, ⓔcumbre@salnet.com.ar. Not luxurious, *Cumbre* is smarter than most of the mid-range places and features modern plumbing. It has large bedrooms, all with private bath. ❺

Hotel El Lagar 20 de Febrero 877 ⓣ0387/421-7943, ⓔellagar@arnet.com.ar. A wonderful boutique hotel, where the decor forms an exquisite art collection; it's exclusive but not snobbish. Rooms must be booked in advance. ❼

Hotel Petit Hipólito Yrigoyen 225 ⓣ0387/421-3012. From the swimming pool and café terrace, and the rooms at the back, you get wonderful mountain views. Good service and plush rooms. ❹

Hotel Regidor Buenos Aires 10 ⓣ0387/421-1305. Charming place, with a rustic *confitería* and very pleasant rooms. Rooms overlooking the square tend to be noisy. ❹

Hotel Solar de la Plaza Luiguizamón 669 ⓣ0387/431-5111, ⓦwww.solardelaplaza.com.ar). A converted neocolonial mansion on the shady Plaza Güemes, this luxury boutique hotel offers impeccable service in tasteful rooms and an unforgettable buffet breakfast plus a small rooftop pool. ❼

Residencial Elena Buenos Aires 256 ⓣ0387/421-1529. Large bedrooms with en-suite bathrooms, in a Spanish-run guesthouse built around a leafy patio. ❷

Residencial Galleguillos Mendoza 509 ⓣ0387/431-8985. One of the best budget *pensiónes* in town; the rooms are basic, but the breakfast is generous, and you could not want for kinder hospitality. ❷

Residencial Kelly O'Higgins 440 ⓣ0387/422-4721. Convenient for the train station, *Residencial Kelly* is small and basic but the rooms are more than adequate and very good value. ❷

The City

Surrounded on all four sides by graceful, shady arcades, under which several café terraces lend themselves to idle people-watching, **Plaza 9 de Julio** is a pleasant spot to while away an hour or two. On the northern side of the Plaza, the cream-coloured **Catedral** dates from 1882, the city's third centenary. It's an Italianate Neoclassical pile, with some well-executed interior frescoes – the one of the Four Apostles around the cupola is particularly fine. Opposite the cathedral, on the southern side of the plaza at Caseros 549, stands the white-facaded **Cabildo** which houses the highly eclectic **Museo Histórico del Norte** (Tues–Sat 9.30am–1.30pm & 3.30–8.30pm, Sun 9.30am–1pm; AR$2). Its collections range from coins and eighteenth-century paintings through wooden saints and archeological finds to wonderful horse-drawn carriages parked in the atmospheric cobbled courtyards; the superb views across the plaza from the upper-storey veranda alone make a visit worthwhile. More colonial and neocolonial buildings are clustered in a few blocks to the west of Plaza 9 de Julio. The **Museo Provincial de Bellas Artes Arías Rengel**, at La Florida 20 (Tues–Sat 9am–1pm & 5–9pm, Sun 9am–1pm; AR$1), houses the city's rich fine art collection. Highlights include a *St Matthew* of the **Cusco school**, and some fine engravings by nineteenth-century artists Basaldúa, Spilimbergo and Quinquela Martín.

Calle Caseros takes you past a number of striking neocolonial buildings to a city landmark and one of the most beautiful religious buildings in the country, the **Iglesia y Convento San Francisco**. An extravaganza of Italianate exuberance by architect Luigi Giorgi, it displays a textbook compliance with architectural principles combined with clever idiosyncrasies. The first thing that strikes you is the colour: pure ivory-white columns stand out from the vibrant oxblood walls. The church's imposing **campanile** towers over the **facade** of the church, lavishly decorated behind a suitably austere statue of St Francis, but the most original features are the organza-like **stucco curtains** that billow down from each of the three archways, nearly touching the elegant wrought-iron gates below. Another convent, the **Convento San Bernardo**, stands three blocks further east along Caseros, on a large, open square. Its sturdy lime-washed facade, punctuated by the tiniest of windows and a couple of dainty lamps on simple iron brackets, contrasts pleasingly with the backdrop of chocolate-brown mountains, the stark plaza in front and two heavily ornate **Rococo-style doors**. The centrepiece of the right hand entrance is a lavishly carved **cedar-wood door**, dating from 1762 and transferred from a patrician house elsewhere in the city.

If you have more time you should certainly try and get over to the modern **Museo Antropológico Juan Martín Leguizamón**, which stands at Ejército del Norte and Polo Sur (Mon–Fri 8am–1pm & 2–6pm, Sun 10am–1pm; AR$1). The varied collection could be better presented, but many of the items on display are well worth seeing, such as a well-preserved **mummy**, found on Cerro Lullaillaco, on the Chilean border, bearing signs that it may have been a human sacrifice. The centrepiece of the extensive ceramics collection is a set of finds from Tastil, along with a petroglyph known as the **Bailarina de Tastil**, a delightful dancing figure painted onto rock, removed from a *pukará* or pre-Columbian fortress. Immediately behind the museum, a steep path zigzags up the overgrown flanks of **Cerro San Bernardo** (1458m), but you might prefer to take the **teleférico**, or cable car, from Avenida Hipólito Yrigoyen, between Urquiza and Avenida San Martín, at the eastern end of Parque San Martín (daily 10am–7.30pm; AR$4 each way, AR$3 for children). The smooth cable-car gondolas, running in a continuous loop, take you to the summit in less than ten minutes, and from the small garden at the top you can admire panoramic **views** of the city and the mountains to the west; a **café** with terrace serves drinks and simple meals.

Eating, drinking and entertainment

Salta has plenty of **eating** places to suit all pockets, ranging from simple **snack bars** where you can savour the city's famous **empanadas**, to a couple of classy **restaurants**, where people dress up to go out for dinner. The most atmospheric **cafés** huddle together around the Plaza 9 de Julio, while the city's many lively **peñas**, informal folk-music clubs, also serve food and drinks, so you can kill two birds.

Restaurants

La Casona Virrey Toledo 1017; and at 25 de Mayo and Santiago del Estero. Both branches, open round the clock, churn out a never-ending supply of *empanadas*, including the best cheese pasties in town.

El Corredor de las Empanadas Caseros 117. Pleasant decor and a large patio are the setting for outstanding *empanadas*, *humitas*, *tamales* and other northwestern dishes.

La Estrella Oriental San Juan 137. If you fancy a change from *empanadas* and steaks, this Middle Eastern restaurant can help out with hummus and lamb kebabs, rounded off with *baklawa*.

Mamá Gaucha Gurruchaga 225. This *parrilla* serves gaucho-style steaks in a friendly ambience.

Mercado Central La Florida and San Martín. A number of small stalls serving all the local fare at very low prices. Particularly great for a lunch snack.

El Palacio de la Pizza Caseros 427. Living up to its name, *El Palacio de la Pizza* serves the best pizzas in Salta by far. Also features good *empanadas*.

El Solar del Convento Caseros 444 ⓣ0387/421-5124. Elegant surroundings, classical music and a free glass of champagne set the tone for this high-class restaurant, serving juicy steaks and providing an excellent wine list. Salta's top restaurant, without a doubt.

Trattoria Mamma Mia Pasaje Zorrilla 1. Delicious fresh pasta, pizzas, soups, grilled meats, tiramisu and a good wine list.

Bars, cafés and peñas

Boliche de Balderrama San Martín 1126 ⓣ0387/421-1542. One of the most popular *peñas*; well known as a bohemian hang-out in the 1950s, nowadays it's a more conventional place, attracting tourists and local folk singers. Some nights an additional charge is added to the bill for the music.

La Casona del Molino Luis Burela and Caseros 2500 ⓣ0387/434-2835. *Empanadas*, *locro*, *guaschalocro*, *tamales*, *humitas*, sangria and improvised live music much later on, all in an atmospherically dilapidated mansion.

El Farito Caseros 509, Plaza 9 de Julio. Tiny *empanada* joint, dishing out piping-hot cheese and meat pasties all day long.

Van Gogh Plaza 9 de Julio. The best coffee in town, excellent cakes, quick meals, appetizing snacks and the local glitterati are the attractions, plus live music late at weekends.

Listings

Airlines Aerolíneas Argentinas at the airport ⓣ0387/424-1185, and at Caseros 475 ⓣ0387/431-1331; Lloyd Aéreo Boliviano, at the airport ⓣ0387/424-1181, and at Deán Funes 29 ⓣ0387/431-9388; Lapa, at the airport ⓣ0387/424-2333, and at Buenos Aires 24 ⓣ0387/431-7080; Southern Winds, Caseros 434 ⓣ0387/421-0808.

Car rental Rent a Truck, Buenos Aires 1 ⓣ0387/431-0740.

Post office Deán Funes 170.

Travel agents Ricardo Clark Expediciones, Caseros 121 ⓣ0387/421-5390, ⓦwww.clarkexpediciones.com; MoviTrack Safaris, Buenos Aires 68 ⓣ0387/431-6749, ⓦwww.movitrack.com.ar; Marina Turismo, Buenos Aires 1 ⓣ0387/431-0740, ⓦwww.salnet.com.ar/marinaturismo; Norte Trekking, Los Juncos 173 ⓣ0387/439-6957, ⓔfede@nortetrekking.com; Martin Pekarek, España 45, Chicoana ⓣ0387/490-7009, ⓔmartinpek@impsat1.com.ar; Salta Rafting Ruta 47, km 34, Cabra Corral ⓣ0387/156-856-085, ⓦwww.saltarafting.com.

Parque Nacional El Rey

Cloudforests are peculiar to southern Bolivia and northwestern Argentina, and the nearest one to Salta, nearly 200km by road, is the **PARQUE NACIONAL EL REY**. Like the other cloudforest parks of the Northwest, it is an upland enclave draped in exuberant vegetation, sticking up from a low-lying plain, and characterized by clearly distinct dry and wet seasons, winter and summer, but relatively high year-round precipitation. The peaks are often shrouded in cloud and mist – hence the name cloudforest – keeping most of the varied plant life lush even in the drier, cooler months.

El Rey (9am–dusk; free) nestles in a natural horseshoe-shaped amphitheatre, hemmed in by the curving **Crestón del Gallo** ridge to the northwest, and the higher crest of the **Serranía del Piquete**, to the east, peaking at around 1700m. The handsome **toucan** is the park's striking and easily recognizable mascot, but other birdlife abounds, totalling over 150 varieties. The park's only access road is the RP20, branching to the left from the RP5 that leads eastwards from the RN9, near the village of Lumbrera halfway between Metán and Güemes. The RP20 fords several rivers, but cars will have no problem except during summer flash floods. **Guardaparques** at the park entrance can advise you on how to get around in your vehicle.

The only **accommodation** option is to pitch your tent in the clearing in the middle of the park. A road of sorts follows the **Río Popayán**, while more marked trails through the park are currently being planned to add to the two-hour climb from the rangers' station to **Pozo Verde**, where birds come to drink. An **organized trip** is the best option, for which two operators can be recommended: Norte Trekking and Ricardo Clark Expediciones (see "Listings", p.139).

Quebrada del Toro

Whether you travel up the magnificent gorge called the **QUBRADA DEL TORO** by train – along one of the highest railways in the world (see box) – in a tour operator's jeep, by rented car or, as the pioneers did centuries ago, on horseback, the experience will be unforgettable, thanks to the constantly changing dramatic mountain scenery and multicoloured rocks. The gorge is named after the **Río El Toro**, normally a meandering trickle, but occasionally a raging torrent and as bullish as its name suggests, especially in the spring. It swerves up from the tobacco fields of the Valle de Lerma, 30km southwest of Salta, through dense thickets of **ceibo**, Argentina's national tree, ablaze in October and November with their fuchsia-red spring blossom, past **Santa Rosa de Tastil** and the pre-Incan site of **Tastil**, to the desiccated highlands of the Puna Salteña, Salta's Altiplano, focused on the ghostly mining village of **San Antonio de los Cobres**. Between this highest point

The train to the clouds

Travelling through the Quebrada del Toro gorge on the Tren a las Nubes, or **Train to the clouds**, is an unashamedly touristic – and not cheap – experience. The smart train, with its comfortable, leather-upholstered interior, shiny wooden fittings and spacious seats was custom-built for this purpose. As the train begins to climb into the gorge, coca-tea is brought round to help you combat *puna*, or altitude sickness. Clambering from the station in Salta to the magnificent Meccano-like La Polvorilla Viaduct, high in the Altiplano, the train line was originally built to service the borax mines in the salt flats of Pocitos and Arizaro, 300km beyond La Polvorilla. The viaduct lies 219km away from Salta, and on the way the train crosses 29 bridges and 12 viaducts, threads through 21 tunnels, swoops round two gigantic 360° loops and chugs up two switchbacks. Seen on many posters and in all tour operators' brochures, the viaduct is 224m long, 64m high and weighs over 1600 tonnes; built in Italy it was assembled here in 1930. The highest point of the whole line, just 13km west of the viaduct, is at Abra Chorrillos, 4475m. Brief stopovers near the LA Polvorilla Viaduct, where the train doubles back, and in San Antonio de los Cobres, allow you to stretch your legs and meet some locals, keen on selling you llama-wool scarves and posing for photos. Folk groups and solo artists interspersed with people selling arts, crafts, cheese, honey and souvenirs galore help while the time away on the way down.

The trip, run by a company called La Veloz, leaves Salta's Ferrocarril Belgrano station punctually at 7.05am – several times a week, during the high season, from April to October, with plans to extend the service throughout the year. The train returns to Salta at around 10pm, after a long, exhilarating but potentially tiring trip. Tickets should be reserved in advance, especially during the most popular periods, such as July weekends, through ⓦwww.lavelozturismo.com.ar. The Ferrocarril Belgrano station is at Ameghino 690, ten blocks due north of the central Plaza 9 de Julio.

and **Campo Quijano**, in the valley bottom, the RN51 road and the railway wind, loop and zigzag side by side for over 100km, joining two distinct worlds: the fertile, moist lowlands of Salta's populous central valleys, and the waterless highland wastes at over 3000m altitude. Many operators in Salta offer **tours by road** (see Listings", p.139), many of which ironically follow the train for much of the way, offering their passengers the chance to photograph the handsome locomotive and wave at it frantically, expecting passengers to reciprocate.

San Salvador de Jujuy

Just over 90km north of Salta by the direct, scenic RN9, **SAN SALVADOR DE JUJUY** – "Jujuy" – is the highest provincial capital in the country (1260m above sea level), and enjoys an enviably temperate climate. Dramatically located, Jujuy sits in a fertile natural bowl, with the fabulous multicoloured gorge of the **Quebrada de Humahuaca** immediately to the north, a major reason for coming in the first place. Scratch its lacklustre surface, and you'll unearth some real treasures, among them one of the finest pieces of sacred art to be seen in Argentina, the **pulpit** in the **Catedral** – and the interior of **Iglesia San Francisco** is almost as impressive. However, you'll soon want to start exploring the rich hinterland, its polychrome gorges and typical Altiplano villages of adobe houses.

Arrival and information

Jujuy's **airport** (Ⓣ0388/491-1102), is over 30km southeast of the city, along the RN66 motorway. TEA Turismo (Ⓣ0388/423-6270 or 156-857913) runs a shuttle service to and from the city centre for AR$5; the **taxi** fare is around AR$30. The rudimentary **bus terminal**, at Iguazú and Av Dorrego (Ⓣ0388/422-6299), just south of the centre, across the Río Chico, serves all local, regional and national destinations, and also runs an erratic service to Chile.

For **tourist information**, head for the Dirección Provincial de Turismo at Belgrano and Gorriti (Mon–Fri 7am–9pm, Sat, Sun & public holidays 8am–9pm; Ⓣ0388/422-1325, Ⓦwww.jujuy.gov.ar/turismo).

Accommodation

Apart from two excellent **campsites** near the city – *Los Vertientes* (Ⓣ0388/498-0030; AR$4 per person) and *El Carmen* (Ⓣ0388/493-3117; AR$2 per person) – Jujuy's limited but decent accommodation covers the range from squalid *residenciales*, best avoided, to a couple of top-notch five-star **hotels**.

Finca Los Lapachos RP42, Perico Ⓣ0388/491-1291, Ⓔlapachos@jujuytel.com.ar. Some 25km outside the city yet conveniently close to the airport, this is definitely the place if you're looking for charm, luxury, peace and quiet, as well as an authentic *finca* experience, with horse riding and a beautiful swimming pool. The Leach family, which calls this place home, prefers that you book ahead instead of turning up on their doorstep. ❻

Hotel Altos de la Viña Pasquini López, La Viña Ⓣ0388/426-1666, Ⓦwww.hotelaltosdelavina.com.ar. On the heights of La Viña, 4km northeast of the city centre, this recently refurbished hotel, with large, comfortable rooms and a shady garden, commands fabulous views of the valley and mountains. Shuttle service available to and from downtown. ❺

Hotel Augustus Belgrano 715 Ⓣ0388/423-0203, Ⓔhotelaugustus@arnet.com.ar. An extremely friendly place, *Hotel Augustus* offers clean rooms, spacious bathrooms and good breakfasts. Its snack bar serves delicious sandwiches and *lomitos*. ❹

Hotel Jujuy Palace Belgrano 1060 Ⓣ0388/423-0433, Ⓔpalace@imagine.com.ar. One of the two top-range hotels actually in central Jujuy, this one has the edge in terms of stylish decor and charm. Professionally run, with a pleasant restaurant. ❺

Hotel Panorama Belgrano 1295 Ⓣ0388/423-0433, Ⓔhotelpanorama@arnet.com.ar. The other top-range downtown hotel, enjoying great views from its upper rooms, but blander. Generous breakfasts in the stylish *confitería*, though. ❹

Hotel Sumay Otero 232 ☎0388/423-5065. By far the best lower-range hotel, it's roomy, comfortable, and very popular, so book ahead. Can be noisy. ❹

Residencial San Antonio Lisandro de la Torre 993 ☎0388/422-5998. The only non-squalid place in the vicinity of the bus terminal, *Residencial San Antonio* is small but modern. ❷

The City

Jujuy is not a beautiful city, but its central streets, with their women in brightly coloured shawls with their babies strapped to their backs huddling in groups and whispering in Quechua, have a certain atmosphere. **Plaza General Belgrano**, at the eastern extremity of the compact microcentro, is the city's hub, partly occupied by craftsmen, mainly potters, displaying their wares. To the west stands Jujuy's late eighteenth-century **Catedral** (Mon–Fri 7.30am–1pm & 5–9pm, Sat & Sun 8am–noon & 5–9pm), topped by an early twentieth-century tower and extended by an even later Neoclassical atrium. The exterior is unremarkable, while the interior, a layer of painted Bakelite concealing the original timber structure, is impressively naive: a realistic mock-fresco of sky and clouds soars over the altar. Two original doors and two confessionals, Baroque masterpieces from the eighteenth century, immediately catch the eye, with their profusion of vivid red and sienna paint, picked out with gilt, but the undisputed highlight – and the main attraction of the whole city – is the magnificent **pulpit**. Decorated in the eighteenth century by local artists, it rivals those of **Cusco**, Peru (see p.877), its apparent inspiration, with its harmonious compositions and the finesse of its carvings. Its various tableaux movingly depict subjects such as Jacob's ladder and St Augustine along with Biblical genealogies. Also inspired by the pulpits of Cusco, the Spanish Baroque **pulpit** in **Iglesia San Francisco**, two blocks west at Belgrano and Lavalle, and almost certainly carved by craftsmen in eighteenth-century Bolivia. It drips with detail, with a profusion of little Franciscan monks peeking out from row upon row of tiny columns, all delicately gilded.

Eating

Jujuy is no gastronomic paradise but its **restaurants** will give you more than enough variety between local specialities and *parrilladas*.

La Candelaria Alvear 1346. This very stylish *parrilla*, ten blocks or so out to the west of the city, serves mountains of meat until you burst. The desserts are heavenly, too.

Madre Tierra Belgrano 619. Delightful, airy vegetarian lunch-only spot, serving an unbeatable menu at AR$7; even if you're not a vegetarian you'll find the fresh salads and delicious fruit juices a great change from the meat overdose. Closed Sun.

Manos Jujeñas Senador Pérez 222. Absolutely fabulous inexpensive northwestern food, including memorable *locro* and delicious *empanadas*, accompanied from time to time by folk music. Incredibly friendly, too. Closed Sun lunch & Mon evening.

Quebrada de Humahuaca

The intense beauty of the **QUEBRADA DE HUMAHUACA** gorge is an unforgettable and moving, offering some stunning, varied scenery all the way up from the valley bottom, just to the northwest of Jujuy, to the town of **Humahuaca** that gives the gorge its name, 125km north of the provincial capital. From there you can continue along the same road, crossing bleak but incredibly beautiful Altiplano landscapes, all the way to La Quiaca on the Bolivian border nearly 2000m higher, and 150km farther on. On the way to Humahuaca you'll see the hauntingly beautiful graveyard at **Maimará** and the impressive pre-Columbian site at **Tilcara**, where you'll find places to spend the night.

Maimará and Tilcara

From Jujuy the RN9 winds past Purmamarca, and from there it continues to climb through the Quebrada de Humahuaca past coloured mountainsides, ornamented with rock formations like organ-pipes or elephants' feet with painted toes. The extraordinary cemetery at **MAIMARÁ**, 75km from Jujuy, is a highly photogenic sight, surrounded by rough-hewn walls and a jumble of tombs of all shapes and sizes, and laid with bouquets of artificial flowers. Behind it, the rock formations at the base of the mountain resemble multicoloured oyster-shells.

Only 5km further on you are treated to your first glimpse of the great pre-Incan *pukará* or fortress of **TILCARA**. Just beyond it is the side road off to the village itself. At an altitude of just under 3000m, and yet still dominated by the dramatic mountains that surround it, this is one of the biggest settlements along the Quebrada. The pleasant, easygoing village is always very lively, but even more so during **carnival**. Like the rest of the Quebrada, it also celebrates **El Enero Tilcareño**, a religious and popular procession and feast held during the latter half of January, and **Pachamama**, or the Mother Earth festival, in August, with remarkable festivities, and accommodation is booked up in advance. The impressively massive colonial church, **Nuestra Señora del Rosario**, stands one block back from the main square, Plaza C. Alvarez Prado, where you'll find the **Museo Arqueológico** (daily 9am–7pm public holidays 9am–8pm; AR$2, Tues free), on the south side of the square in a beautiful colonial house. Well presented, the collection includes a mummy from San Pedro de Atacama. Keep your ticket to visit the **pukará** (daily 9am–6pm; AR$2, Tues free), a kilometre or so southwest of the plaza. The University of Buenos Aires has reconstructed many of the houses, and the whole magnificent fortress is spiked with a grove of cacti and, with the backdrop of imposing mountains on all sides, it affords marvellous panoramic views in all directions.

Practicalities

Frequent **buses** from Humahuaca and Jujuy stop at Tilcara's main square. **Accommodation** is seldom hard to come by: *Albergue Malka*, a very well-run youth hostel, 400m up a steep hill, to the east of Plaza Alvarez Prado, at San Martín s/n (ⓣ0388/495-5200, ⓔmalka@hostels.org.ar; ❷) is extremely comfortable and serves excellent breakfasts. Rather less charming but slightly more lavish is the *Hotel de Turismo* at Belgrano 590 (ⓣ0388/495-5002, ⓔtilcahot@imagine.com.ar; ❹). *Casa de la Nona*, a traditional mountain-house at Belgrano 553 (ⓣ0388/495-5068, ⓔccaliari@imagine.com.ar; ❺) is much more luxurious. *Residencial El Antigal* (ⓣ0388/495-5020; ❷) at Rivadavia and Belgrano has a picturesque tearoom that doubles up as a bar in the evening. *El Jardín* (ⓣ0388/495-5128; AR$4 per person) is Tilcara's main **campsite**, well run and in an attractive riverside location 1km to the northwest of the village. Apart from facilities provided by the hotels, the only **place to eat** is the *Ruta 9*, on the main road near the turn-off to the village. It serves cheap and cheerful meals based on local delicacies such as goat and trout.

Humahuaca

The main town in the area, **HUMAHUACA**, 125km north of Jujuy, spills across the Río Grande from its picturesque centre on the west bank of the gorge. Its enticing cobbled streets, lined with colonial-style or rustic adobe houses, lend themselves to gentle ambling – at an altitude of just below 3000m. Most of the organized tours arrive here for lunch and then double back to Jujuy or Salta, but you may like to stay over; the town's also an excellent springboard for trips up into the desolate but hauntingly beautiful landscapes of the **Puna Jujeña**. Most tours to and around the town aim to deliver you at the beautifully lush main square at midday on the dot, in time to see a kitsch **statue of San Francisco Solano** emerge from a niche in the equally kitsch tower of the whitewashed **Municipalidad**. On the western side of the square, and far more impressive, the **Catedral**, the Iglesia de Nuestra Señora de la Candelaria y San Antonio, was built in the seventeenth century and much restored since. Within its immaculate white walls is a late seventeenth-century retable, and another on the north wall by Cosmo Duarte, dated 1790, depicting the Crucifixion. The remaining artworks include a set of exuberantly Mannerist paintings the *Twelve Prophets*, signed by leading Cusqueño artist Marcos Sapaca and dated 1764. Looming over the church and the whole town is the **Monumento a la Independencia**, a bombastic concoction of stone and bronze, by local artist Ernesto Soto Avendaño, and built from 1940 to 1950. Triumphal steps lead up to it from the plaza, but the best thing about it is the view across the town and valley to the noble mountainside to the east.

Practicalities

Buses from Jujuy, Salta, La Quiaca and Iruya arrive at the small bus terminal a couple of blocks southeast of the main square. Apart from the run-down and overpriced *Hotel de Turismo* at Buenos Aires 650 (ⓣ03887/421154; ❹), **accommodation** in Humahuaca is on the basic side. The cheapest option, and just about commendable, is *Albergue El Portillo* at Tucumán 69 (ⓣ03887/421288, ⓔelportillo@cootepal.com.ar; ❶). The unofficial youth hostel, *Albergue Juvenil* at Buenos Aires 447 (ⓣ03887/421064, ⓔtoqohumahuaca@yahoo.com; ❷), has some rooms with baths, and is passable. Slightly better, and clean, with hot water and also with some en-suite rooms are *Hostería Colonial*, at Entre Ríos 110 (ⓣ03887/421007; ❷–❸), and *Residencial Humahuaca* at Córdoba 401 (ⓣ03887/421141; ❷). Regional **food** is delicious and plentiful at *La Cacharpaya*, at Jujuy 295, and accompanied by live folk music, aimed at tourists, at the *Peña del Fortunato*, San Luis and Jujuy.

Valles Calchaquíes

Named after the Río Calchaquí, the **VALLES CALCHAQUÍES** is a series of beautiful highland valleys, enjoying a dry climate and much cooler summers than the lowland plains around Salta. The fertile land, irrigated with canals and ditches that capture the plentiful snowmelt from the high mountains to the west, is mostly given over to vineyards – among the world's highest – which produce the characteristic *torrontés* grape as well as cabernet. The most rewarding way to see the Valles Calchaquíes is under your own steam, by climbing the amazing **Cuesta del Obispo**, through the Parque Nacional Los Cardones, a protected forest of gigantic *cardón* cacti, to the picturesque village of **Cachi**, then following the valley south through some memorable scenery to **Cafayate**, where plentiful accommodation facilitates a stopover. Regular **public transport** to Salta and Tucumán makes travelling around the valleys straightforward even without your own transport, though it is less frequent along the northern reaches around Cachi.

Up to Cachi

CACHI sits 170km southwest of Salta via the partly sealed RP33, a scenic road that squeezes through the dank Quebrada de Escoipe, before climbing the **Cuesta del Obispo**, a dramatic 20km mountain road of hairpin bends that offers views of the rippling Sierra del Obispo. These fabulously beautiful mountains, blanketed in olive-green vegetation and heavily eroded by countless brooks, are at their best in the morning light. The picturesque village, 2280m above sea level, is overshadowed by the permanently snowcapped **Nevado del Cachi** (6380m), whose peak looms 15km to the west. The village is centred on the delightful Plaza Mayor, shaded by palms and orange trees. On the north side, stands the much-restored **Iglesia San**

José, with its plain white facade, fine wooden floor and unusual cactus-wood altar, pews and confessionals. To the east, in a neocolonial house around an attractive whitewashed patio, the **Museo Arqueológico Pío Pablo Díaz** (daily 8am–6pm; AR$1) displays a run-of-the-mill collection of locally excavated items. Apart from that, there's little in the way of sights in Cachi – it's simply a place to wander, investigate various local crafts, including ponchos and ceramics, or climb to the **cemetery** for wonderful mountain views and a panorama of the pea-green valley, every arable patch filled with vines, maize and capsicum plantations. Farther afield, the scenic track to **Cachi Adentro**, 6km west of the village, takes you through the fertile farmland where, in late summer (March–May), the fields are carpeted with drying paprika peppers, a dazzlingly display of bright red.

Practicalities

Buses from Salta (and local buses from various villages) arrive at Cachi's little unnamed square next to *Hotel Nevado de Cachi*, on Ruíz de los Llanos (ⓣ03868/491004; ❶), a good **place to stay**, with basic rooms, cactus-wood furniture but erratic hot water. Hill-top *Hostería ACA Sol del Valle*, at General Güemes (ⓣ03868/491105; ❹–❺), is by far the village's most comfortable accommodation especially since a fantastic makeover, but nearby *Hospedaje El Cortijo* (ⓣ03868/491-034; ❺), in a colonial house at the bottom of the hill, is incredibly good value. Along the road to **Cachi Adentro**, a hamlet some 10km away into the mountains, the luxurious *Finca El Molino* (ⓣ03868/491094 or 0387/4219368; ❼) commands stunning mountain views through a huge picture window and features very comfortable rooms and a designer interior.

Apart from the *ACA*, with its unusual menu served in smart surroundings, the only decent **place to eat** in Cachi itself is *El Jagüel* on Av General Güemes (ⓣ03868/491135) serving memorable *locro* and *empanadas*.

From Cachi to Cafayate

The mostly unsealed RN40 from Cachi to Cafayate takes you along some stupendous corniche roads that wind alongside the Río Calchaquí itself, offering views on either side of sheer mountainsides and snowcapped peaks. It's only 180km from one to the other but allow plenty of time as the narrow track slows your progress and you'll want to stop to admire the views, take photographs and visit the picturesque valley settlements en route, oases of greenery in an otherwise stark landscape. **Molinos**, 60km south of Cachi, lies a couple of kilometres west of the main road, in a bend of the Río Molinos, and is worth the side-trip for a peek at its lovely adobe houses and the eighteenth-century **Iglesia de San Pedro Nolasco**. Currently undergoing restoration, its expansive façade is topped with two sturdy turrets and shored up with props. Opposite, in Finca Isasmendi, the eighteenth-century residence of the last Royalist governor of Salta is the beautiful *Hostal Provincial de Molinos* (ⓣ03868/494002; ❻), well-furnished rooms around a shady patio; nearby the unnamed *hospedaje* run by nuns charges only AR$10 per person; ask around. Just beyond Angastaco, the already impressive scenery becomes even more spectacular: after 10km you enter the surreal **Quebrada de las Flechas**, where the red sandstone cliffs form a backdrop for the flinty arrowhead-like formations on either side of the road that give the gorge its name. For 10km, weird rocks like desert roses dot the landscape and, beyond the natural stone walls of **El Cañón**, over 20m high, the road squeezes through **El Ventisquero**, the "wind-tunnel".

Nearly 190km from Salta, and almost as far from Cachi, **CAFAYATE** is the self-appointed capital of the Valles Calchaquíes and certainly the main settlement hereabouts. It's also the centre of the province's wine industry and the main tourist base for the area, thanks to its wide range of accommodation and convenient location. Straddling the RN40, called the Avenida Güemes within the village limits, it's a lively, modern village. Apart from exploring the surroundings on foot, by bike or on horseback, or tasting wine at the *bodegas,* there's not actually a lot to do here; the late nineteenth-century **Iglesia Catedral de Nuestra Señora del Rosario** dominates the main plaza but its interior is disappointingly nondescript. About 2km south, on the RN40 to Santa María, you'll find the workshop and salesroom of one of the region's finest artisans: Oscar Hipaucha sells wonderfully intricate wood and metal boxes, made of quebracho, algarrobo and copper, at justifiably high prices.

Practicalities

Frequent **buses** from Salta and less frequent ones from Cachi, via Molinos, arrive at the cramped terminus just along Belgrano, half a block east of the plaza, or sometimes deposit passengers wherever they want to get off in the village. A kiosk (Mon–Fri 9am–8pm, Sat, Sun & public holidays 7am–1pm & 3–9pm) on the plaza dispenses **information** about where to stay, what to do and where to rent bikes or hire horses. A popular **folk festival**, the Serenata Cafayateña, is held here on the first weekend of Lent, when accommodation is hard to find. Otherwise, you're spoiled for choice when it comes to **accommodation**, starting with the unofficial but decent youth hostel at Av Güemes Norte 441 (Ⓣ03868/421440; ❷). *Hospedaje Familiar Basla* at Nuestra Señora del Rosario 165(Ⓣ03868/421098; ❷), just south of the square, has basic rooms around a cheerful patio, while *Hotel Confort* at Av Güemes Norte 232 (Ⓣ03868/421091; ❸) lives up to its name. At the top end of the price bracket, *Hotel Asturias* at Av Güemes 154 (Ⓣ03868/421328, Ⓔasturias@infonoa.com.ar; ❹) has a swimming pool, a reliable restaurant, and tasteful rooms decorated with beautiful photographs of the region. For **eating**, the choice is more limited. *Europa Centro* on the north side of the plaza is an excellent pizzeria. Opposite it, *Quijote* specializes in regional cooking, as does the popular and well-priced *Carreta de Don Olegario* on the east side of the plaza. The ice creams at *Heladería Miranda*, on Avenida Güemes half a block north of the plaza, are outstanding; try the wine sorbets.

1.5

Mendoza and San Juan

Argentina's midwestern provinces of **MENDOZA** and **SAN JUAN** stretch all the way from the chocolate-brown pampas of **La Payunia**, on the northern borders of Patagonia, to the remote highland steppes of the altiplano, nearly a thousand kilometres to the north. They extend across vast, thinly populated territories of bone-dry desert dotted with vibrant oases where fertile farmland and the region's famous **vineyards** are to be found. To the west loom the world's loftiest peaks outside the Himalayas, culminating in the defiant **Aconcagua**, whose summit is only a shade less than 7000 metres. The region's urban centre, the sophisticated metropolis of **Mendoza**, is extremely well geared to the tourist industry, as are **San Rafael** and **Malargüe**, further south, while the charming provincial capital of **San Juan** is a backwater by comparison.

The regional dynamics really revolve about the highly varied **landscapes** and **wildlife**. Ranging from the snowy peaks of the Andes to totally flat pampas in the east, from green, fertile valleys to dark barren volcanoes, and from sand dunes to highland marshes, the scenery includes two of the country's most photographed national parks, declared world heritage sites by UNESCO: the sheer red sandstone cliffs of **Talampaya** (in neighbouring La Rioja Province) and the nearby canyons and moonscapes of **Ischigualasto**. European settlers have wrought changes to the environment, bringing the **grapevine** and all kinds of fruit trees with them, but the thousands of kilometres of irrigation channels that water the region existed long before Columbus reached America. Winter sports can be practised at one of the continent's most exclusive resorts, **Las Leñas**, where the season is July to September. Other activities on offer are rock climbing, mountaineering and white-water rafting and, if you're tempted by more demanding challenges, the ascension of Aconcagua.

Mendoza

Home to nearly a million Mendocinos, **MENDOZA** is a mostly low-rise city, spread across a wide valley, less than 100km to the east of the highest section of the Andean cordillera – whose perennially snowcapped peaks are clearly visible from downtown. Its airy microcentro is less compact than that of most comparable cities, partly because the streets, squares and avenues were deliberately widened when the city was rebuilt in the late nineteenth century. Where Mendoza really comes into its own is as a base for some of the world's most thrilling **mountain-climbing** opportunities; treks and ascensions can be organized through a number of specialized operators in the city. In quite a different vein, you could also go on a **wine-tasting tour** of the many **bodegas** in or near the city, some traditional, some state of the art.

Arrival and information

Mendoza's **airport** (Ⓣ0261/430-7837), only 7km north of the city centre, has regular domestic flights, including several daily to and from Buenos Aires, as well as a

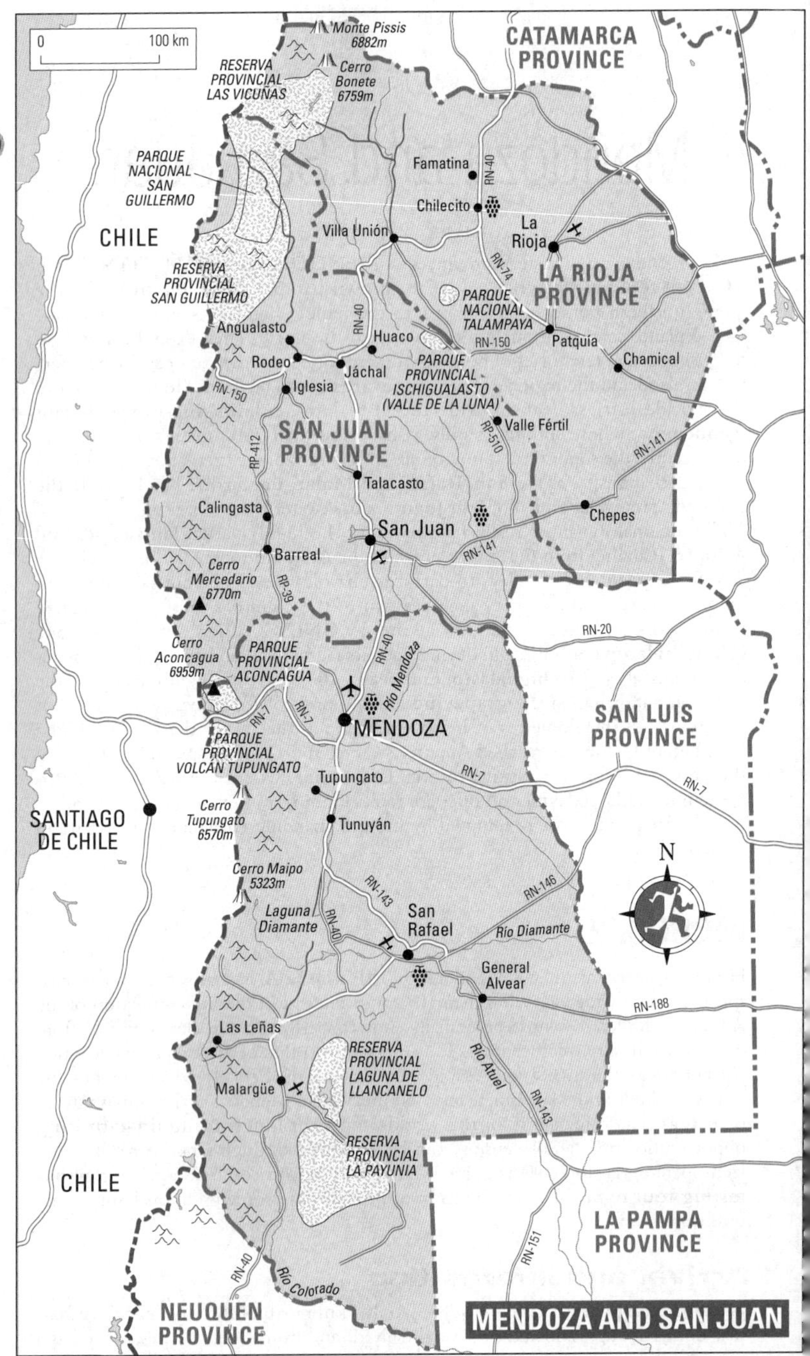
0
100 km
Monte Pissis
6882m
RESERVA
PROVINCIAL
LAS VICUÑAS
Cerro
Bonete
6759m
CATAMARCA
PROVINCE
PARQUE
NACIONAL
SAN
GUILLERMO
Famatina
RN-40
Chilecito
CHILE
Villa Unión
La
Rioja
RESERVA
PROVINCIAL
SAN GUILLERMO
RN-74
LA RIOJA
PROVINCE
PARQUE
NACIONAL
TALAMPAYA
RN-40
Angualasto
Huaco
RN-150
Patquía
Rodeo
Jáchal
PARQUE
PROVINCIAL
ISCHIGUALASTO
(VALLE DE LA LUNA)
Chamical
Iglesia
RN-150
Valle Fértil
RP-510
SAN JUAN
PROVINCE
RP-412
RN-141
Talacasto
Calingasta
Chepes
San Juan
Barreal
RN-141
Cerro
Mercedario
6770m
RP-39
RN-20
Cerro
Aconcagua
6959m
PARQUE
PROVINCIAL
ACONCAGUA
RN-40
Río Mendoza
RN-7
RN-7
MENDOZA
SAN LUIS
PROVINCE
PARQUE
PROVINCIAL
VOLCÁN TUPUNGATO
RN-7
RN-7
Tupungato
SANTIAGO
DE CHILE
Cerro
Tupungato
6570m
Tunuyán
N
Cerro Maipo
5323m
RN-143
RN-146
Laguna
Diamante
RN-40
San
Rafael
Río Diamante
General
Alvear
RN-188
Las Leñas
RESERVA
PROVINCIAL
LAGUNA DE
LLANCANELO
Río Atuel
Malargüe
RN-143
RESERVA
PROVINCIAL
LA PAYUNIA
CHILE
LA PAMPA
PROVINCE
RN-151
RN-40
Río Colorado
NEUQUEN
PROVINCE
MENDOZA AND SAN JUAN

couple of flights a day to and from Santiago de Chile. **Taxis** or *remises* are in plentiful supply; the trip to downtown will set you back AR$10. Mendoza's modern, efficient and very busy **bus station** (☎0261/431-3001) is due east of the microcentro, on the edge of the suburb of Guaymallén, at the corner of avenidas Gobernador Videla and Acceso Este (RN7); a taxi to the centre costs about AR$2.

While the city's main **tourist information centre** is at San Martín and Garibaldi (daily 8am–8pm; ☎0261/420-1333, ⓦwww.turismo.mendoza.gov.ar), the **provincial tourist office** can be found at San Martín 1143 (daily 8am–9pm; ☎0261/420-2656, 420-2357 or 420-2800), with material on the rest of the province.

Accommodation

Mendoza has more than enough beds for its needs, except during the Fiesta de la Vendimia in early March, when they're in short supply. The city also has several outstanding **youth hostels**. Campers should head for the cool heights of El Challao, 6km to the northwest, where **campsite** *El Suizo* rests among shady woods, on Av Champagnat (☎0261/444-1991; AR$4 per person). It has a swimming pool, a small restaurant and even an open-air cinema. **Bus** #110 runs out to El Challao from the corner of Salta and Avenida Além.

Hostel Campo Base Mitre 946 ☎0261/429-0707, ⓔmendoza2@hostels.org.ar. The youth hostel preferred by Aconcagua climbers, as the owners organize their own treks. Clean, friendly and very laid-back atmosphere, though some of the dorms are slightly cramped. Lots of events, barbecues, parties and general fun. ❷

Hostel International España 343 ☎0261/424-0018, ⓔinfo@hostelmendoza.net. The most inviting of the three hostels, *Hostel International* has a bright patio, stimulating ambience, small dorms with private bathroom, an excellent kitchen, and fixes you up with tours and sports activities in the whole region. ❷

Hotel Aconcagua San Lorenzo 545 ☎0261/420-4499, ⓦwww.hotelaconcagua.com.ar. Professionally run modern hotel, with small but comfortable rooms, with TV and minibar. A swimming pool, sauna and massage are welcome facilities. ❻

Hotel Balbi Av Las Heras 340 ☎0261/423-3500. Glitzy place with a lavish reception area, huge dining room, and spacious, fresh rooms. Swimming pool and terrace. ❻

Hotel Cervantes Amigorena 65 ☎0261/420-1782, 420-0131 or 420-0737, ⓦwww.hotel.cervantes. Traditional-style, comfortable hotel, with pleasant rooms, *Cervantes* has one of the best hotel restaurants in town, the *Sancho*. ❻

Hotel Crillon Perú 1065 ☎0261/429-8494 or 423-8963, ⓦwww.hcrillon.com.ar. One of the smartest, most charming hotels in its category, the *Crillon* has stylish furniture and new bathrooms. ❺

Hotel Park Hyatt Chile 1124 ☎0261/441-1234, ⓦwww.mendoza.park.hyatt.com. Housed in a historically important building on Mendoza's central plaza, this *Hyatt* lives up to the chain's reputation for luxury, with everything from one of the city's top restaurants to a spa and swimming pool where you will be pampered into submission. ❼

Hotel Petit Perú 1459 ☎0261/423-2099 or 429-7537, ⓔpetit@slatinos.com.ar. Clean, airy rooms and bathrooms. Very Seventies decor, with candlewick bedspreads, but the young owners know the latest places to go at night. ❸

Hotel Princess 25 de Mayo 1168 ☎0261/423-5666. Extremely smart rooms, with simple decor, and modern bathrooms. There's a swimming pool, too, and a part-shaded patio. ❺

NH Hotel Av España 1324 ☎0261/441-6464, ⓦwww.nh-hotels.com. Beautiful, well-located modern hotel, with a decent restaurant and excellent service. Cheaper at weekends. ❻

Quinta Rufino Rufino Ortega 142 ☎0261/420-4696 ⓦwww.quintarufino.com.ar. Excellent new bed and breakfast in a converted villa near the trendy nightlife area, with spacious, smart rooms and a shared kitchen. ❸

The City

Plaza Independencia lies at the nerve-centre of the post-earthquake city and at the crossroads of two of Mendoza's main streets, east–west Avenida Sarmiento and north–south Avenida Mitre. It's the modern city's recreational and cultural focus,

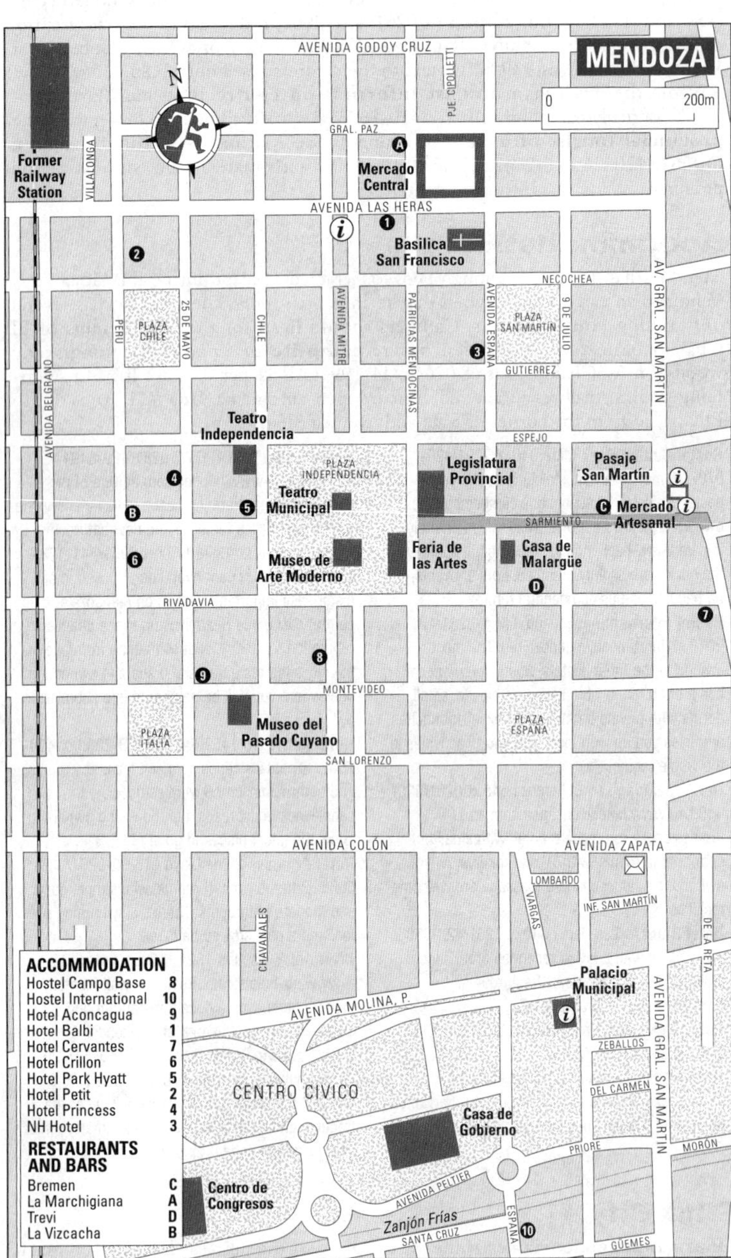
MENDOZA
0
200m
N
AVENIDA GODOY CRUZ
PJE. CIPOLLETTI
GRAL. PAZ
Former Railway Station
VILLALONGA
Mercado Central
AVENIDA LAS HERAS
Basilica San Francisco
NECOCHEA
PLAZA CHILE
PERU
25 DE MAYO
CHILE
AVENIDA MITRE
PATRICIAS MENDOCINAS
AVENIDA ESPAÑA
PLAZA SAN MARTÍN
9 DE JULIO
AV. GRAL. SAN MARTIN
GUTIERREZ
AVENIDA BELGRANO
Teatro Independencia
ESPEJO
PLAZA INDEPENDENCIA
Legislatura Provincial
Pasaje San Martín
Teatro Municipal
Mercado Artesanal
SARMIENTO
Museo de Arte Moderno
Feria de las Artes
Casa de Malargüe
RIVADAVIA
MONTEVIDEO
PLAZA ITALIA
Museo del Pasado Cuyano
PLAZA ESPAÑA
SAN LORENZO
AVENIDA COLÓN
AVENIDA ZAPATA
LOMBARDO
VARGAS
INF. SAN MARTÍN
CHAVANALES
DE LA RETA
Palacio Municipal
AVENIDA MOLINA, P.
AVENIDA GRAL. SAN MARTIN
ZEBALLOS
DEL CARMEN
CENTRO CIVICO
Casa de Gobierno
PRIORE
MORÓN
Centro de Congresos
AVENIDA PELTIER
ESPAÑA
Zanjón Frías
SANTA CRUZ
GÜEMES
ACCOMMODATION
Hostel Campo Base 8
Hostel International 10
Hotel Aconcagua 9
Hotel Balbi 1
Hotel Cervantes 7
Hotel Crillon 6
Hotel Park Hyatt 5
Hotel Petit 2
Hotel Princess 4
NH Hotel 3
RESTAURANTS AND BARS
Bremen C
La Marchigiana A
Trevi D
La Vizcacha B

planted with shady acacias, magnolias and sycamores among others. The small plaza a block east and south of Independencia's southeast corner is **Plaza España**, the most beautiful of Mendoza's plazas – its benches are decorated with brightly coloured Andalucian ceramic tiles and its paths are lined with luxuriant trees and shrubs. The mellow terracotta flagstones, picked out with smaller blue and white tiles, and the lily ponds and fountains set off the monument to the Spanish discovery of South America, standing at the southern end of the plaza.

Half a block east of the plaza's northeast corner, the **Museo del Pasado Cuyano** (Mon–Fri 9am–12.30pm; AR$1), at Montevideo 544, is the city's history museum, housed in part of an aristocratic late nineteenth-century mansion. The adobe house contains a large amount of General San Martín memorabilia and eighteenth-century furniture, artworks and weapons. The most valuable exhibit is a fabulous fifteenth-century polychrome **wooden altarpiece**, with a liberal dose of rosy cherubim, that somehow turned up here from Sant Andreu de Socarrats in Catalonia, housed in the mansion's chapel.

Just over 1km due west of Plaza Independencia by Avenida Sarmiento, on a slope that turns into a steep hill overlooking the city, **Parque General San Martín** is one of the most beautiful parks in the country. The main entrance is through magnificent bronze and wrought-iron gates, topped with a rampant condor, at the western end of Avenida Emilio Civit. You can rent a bike, take a horse and cart or catch a bus to the farthest points in the park. At the southern tip of the park's one-kilometre-long serpentine rowing-lake, in its southeastern corner, is the **Museo de Ciencias Naturales y Antropológicas Juan Cornelio Moyano** (Tues–Fri 8am–1pm & 2–7pm, Sat & Sun 3–7pm; AR$1). The museum is a series of mostly private collections of stuffed animals, ancient fossils, indigenous artefacts and mummies.

Eating, drinking and nightlife

Mendoza's leading restaurants serve seafood from the Pacific Coast or delicious local produce accompanied by the outstanding local wines. As a result, Mendoza's many, varied and often highly sophisticated **restaurants** and **wine bars** are usually full, and serve some of the best food and drink in the country. Its bars are lively, it has a well-developed café-terrace culture and **nightlife** is vibrant, mostly concentrated in outlying places such as El Challao, to the northwest, Las Heras, to the north, and most fashionably Chacras de Coria, to the south.

Restaurants

Date Cuenta Monte Caseros 1177. The best vegetarian restaurant in the city, *Date Cuenta*'s bright decor and friendly staff are added bonuses to the food, which is more imaginative than in most veggie places: try the stuffed vegetables, vegetarian *locro* and wonderful fruit dishes.

Don Mario 25 de Mayo and Paso de los Patos, Guaymallén. An institutional *parrilla*, frequented by Mendocino families in search of comforting decor and an old-fashioned *parrillada*.

Francis Mallmann 1884 Belgrano 1188, Godoy Cruz ☎0261/424-2698 & 424-3336. This ultra-chic wine bar and restaurant named after its chef, with fashion-model staff, swish decor and crystal wine-glasses – rare in Argentina – is next to the sumptuous Bodega Escorihuela and serves the *bodega*'s fine wines with an expensive yet balanced menu.

La Marchigiana Patricias Mendocinas 1550 ☎0261/423-0751. This is *the* Italian restaurant in the city, run by the same family for decades. For a reasonable price you can eat fresh asparagus from the oasis, have delicious cannelloni, and finish with one of the best tiramisus in the country.

Trevi Las Heras 68. You could be in Bologna or Genoa in this home-style northern Italian restaurant with old-fashioned, discreet service, dowdy decor and delicious food. The *menú ejecutivo* is one of the best-value lunches in the city at AR$8.

La Vizcacha Av Sarmiento and Av Perú. Extremely commendable *parrilla*, serving decent pasta as well as top-notch grills, in very pleasant surroundings.

Bars and cafés

La Aldea Av Arístides Villanueva 495. A lively

pub-style bar that does great sandwiches and *lomitos*.

Bremen Paseo Sarmiento and 9 de Julio. As you'd expect, this German-style beer-house serves up large steins of foaming Pilsener and can rustle up a mean ham sandwich.

Chini España and Las Heras. One of the best ice-creameries in the city, doing dozens of flavours, but the best are the range of *dulce de leche*-based ones.

Dunga Dunga Palmares Open Mall, Ruta Panamericana 2650. Very popular meeting place for young people, happy to make one Corona last all evening, with top-rate salsa music, and live bands at weekends.

Iguana Pub Av Arístides Villanueva and Coronel Oloscoaga. Funky decor and good music, enormous cocktails and hunky sandwiches at this fun bar.

Listings

Airlines Aerolíneas/Austral, Paseo Sarmiento 82 ⓣ0261/420-4100; Air New Zealand, Espejo 183 ⓣ0261/423-4683; American Airlines, Av España 943 ⓣ0261/425-9078; Avianca, Espejo 183 ⓣ0261/438-1643; Iberia, Rivadavia 180 ⓣ0261/429-5608; LanChile, Rivadavia 138 ⓣ0261/425-7900; Lapa, España 100 ⓣ0261/423-1000; Lufthansa 9 de Julio 928 ⓣ0261/429-6287; Southern Winds, España 943 ⓣ0261/429-3200; Varig, Rivadavia 209 ⓣ0261/429-5898.

Car rental Andina, Sarmiento 129 ⓣ0261/438-0480; Aramendi, San Lorenzo 245 ⓣ0261/429-1857; Aruba, Primitivo de la Reta 936 ⓣ0261/423-4071; Avis, Primitivo de la Reta 914 ⓣ0261/429-6403; Herbst, Chile 1124 ⓣ0261/423-3000; Localiza, Gutiérrez 470 ⓣ0261/444-9149; Thrifty, Colón 241 ⓣ0261/425-3947.

Post office San Martín and Colón ⓣ0261/424-9777.

Tour operators Argentina Rafting, Potrerillos ⓣ02624/482037, ⓔarg_rafting@hotmail.com; Aymará, 9 de Julio 983 ⓣ0261/420-0607, ⓔaymara@satlink.com; Campo Base Adventures and Expeditions, Av Mitre 946 ⓣ0261/429-0707, ⓦwww.campo-base.com.ar; El Cristo, Espejo 228 ⓣ0261/429-1911; Exploradores, ⓣ0261/425-6181, ⓔjasanchi@lanet.com.ar; Holding, Av España 1030 ⓣ0261/423-1352, ⓔholdinviajes@arnet.com.ar; Mendoza Viajes, Sarmiento 129 ⓣ0261/438-0480, ⓔmdzviajes@lanet.losandes.com.ar; Ritz, Perú 1008 ⓣ0261/423-5115.

Argentine wine

The heart of **Argentina's wine industry** has always been Mendoza. Some wine experts think that, within a few years, Argentina's vintages will outstrip Chile's, in terms of quality, reflecting the sunnier climate, cleaner air and richer soil. Although the most attractive wineries to visit (ask at the tourist office for a list of them, plus opening hours) are the old-fashioned ones, with atmospheric musty cellars crammed with ancient oak barrels, some of the finest wines are now produced by growers who've invested in the latest equipment. The main grape varieties in Mendoza are Riesling, Chenin Blanc and Chardonnay, for whites, and Pinot Noir, Cabernet Sauvignon and Malbec, for reds – Argentine reds tend to be better than whites. Malbec is often regarded as the Argentine grape par excellence, giving rich fruity wines, with overtones of blackcurrant and prune, which are the perfect partners for a juicy steak. Moreover, very convincing sparkling wines are being made locally by the *méthode champenoise*. Winegrower names to look for are **Bianchi, Chandon**, **Etchart**, **Graffigna**, **Navarro Correas**, **Norton** and **Weinert**.

Mendoza's main festival is the giant **Fiesta de la Vendimia**, or Wine Harvest Festival, which reaches its climax during the first weekend of March every year. Wine seems to take over the city – bottles even decorate boutique windows – and the tourist trade shifts into top gear. On the Saturday evening, the Acto Central is held in an amphitheatre in the Parque San Martín; it's a gala performance of song, dance and general kitschorama, compered by local TV celebs and eventually leading up to a drawn-out vote to elect the queen of the festival. The same show is rerun, minus the election and therefore for a much lower entrance price – and less tedium – on the Sunday evening.

Alta Montaña

The Andean cordillera, including some of the world's tallest mountains, loom a short distance west of Mendoza. You'll want to head up into them before long, even if you don't feel up to climbing the highest peak in the Americas, **Aconcagua**, ironically out of sight behind the high precordillera – the scenery is fabulous, and skiing, trekking and highland walks are all possible, or you can simply enjoy the views on an organized excursion. The **ALTA MONTAÑA ROUTE**, the RN7, is also the international highway to **Santiago de Chile**. The tunnel under the Andes is one of the major border crossings between Argentina and Chile, blocked by snow only on rare occasions in July and August. The old mountain pass is no longer used but can be visited from Mendoza, weather permitting, to see the **Cristo Redentor**, a huge statue of Christ and a sign of peace between the old rivals, and for the fantastic mountain views.

Los Penitentes and Puente del Inca

Beyond the crossroads town of Uspallata, the RN7 swings round to the west and rejoins the Río Mendoza, whose valley it shares with the now disused rail line all the way to its source at Punta de Vacas. You are following an ancient Inca trail; in the mountains to the south, several mummified corpses have been found that are displayed in Mendoza at the Museo de Ciencias Naturales y Antropológicas Juan Cornelio Moyano (see p.151). You'll pass through narrow canyons, where stripes of different coloured rock decorate the steep walls of the cordillera peaks. Some 65km from Uspallata lies the small ski resort of **LOS PENITENTES**. The resort's 21 pistes vary from nursery slopes to the black Las Paredes, with most of the runs classified as difficult and the biggest total drop being 700m. The modern ski lifts also run at weekends in the summer, so you can enjoy the fabulous mountain and valley views from the top of Cerro San Antonio (3200m); the fissured peak looming over it all is the massive Cerro Leña (4992m).

Just 6km west of Los Penitentes, **PUENTE DEL INCA** is a compulsory stop for anyone heading along the Alta Montaña route; it is also near the track that leads north towards the Aconcagua base camp. At just over 2700m this natural **stone bridge**, featured on many a postcard, is still especially impressive to visit, if only because you can walk across it. Formed by sediment deposited by the Río de las Cuevas, it nestles in an arid valley, overlooked by majestic mountains; just beneath the bridge are the remains of a once sophisticated spa resort, built in the 1940s but swept away by a flood. The ruins, the bridge itself and the surrounding rocks are all stained a nicotine-yellow by the very high sulphur content of the warm waters which gurgle up nearby from beneath the earth's surface.

Aconcagua

At 6959m, **CERRO ACONCAGUA** is the highest peak in both the western and southern hemispheres – or outside the Himalayan Range. Its glacier-garlanded summit dominates the Parque Provincial Aconcagua, even though it is encircled by several other mountains that exceed 5000m. The discovery in 1985 of an Incan mummy – now in the Museo del Área Fundacional, Mendoza – at 5300m on the southwest face suggests that it was a holy site for the Incas (and no doubt for pre-Incan peoples, too) and that ceremonies including burials and perhaps sacrifices took place at these incredible heights.

The three most important requisites for climbing Aconcagua are fitness, patience and acclimatization and, unless you're an experienced climber, you shouldn't even consider going up other than as part of an organized climb. Of the three approaches – south, west or east – the western route from the Plaza de Mulas (4230m) is the easiest and known as the Ruta Normal. For more details of the different routes, advice on what to take with you and how to acclimatize, consult the Aconcagua website (Ⓦwww.aconcagua.com.ar) or the excellent *Bradt Guide to Backpacking in Chile and Argentina*. For more specialist information, especially for serious climbers who are considering one of the harder routes, the best publication is R.J. Secor's *Aconcagua, A Climbing Guide* (1994).

Practicalities

Unless you are having everything arranged by a tour operator, the first place you need to go to is the **Dirección de Recursos Naturales Renovables** (daily 8am–1pm & 4–8pm), whose offices are in Mendoza's Parque General San Martín (see p.151). Not only can you get good maps of the park here but this is where you must apply for compulsory permits to climb Aconcagua in the first place. These cost US$30 for foreign trekkers inside the park (valid for a week) or AR$120–200 to climb the mountain (valid for three weeks). To get to either of the base camps at Los Horcones or to Punta de Vacas, you can get the twice-daily **buses** from Mendoza, run by Uspallata, or get off a bus to Santiago de Chile. It's definitely preferable though, whether trekking or climbing, to go on an **organized trip**, if only because of the treacherous weather – local guides know the whims of the mountain and its sudden storms. Several outfits in Mendoza specialize in these tours, including Campo Base Adventures and Expeditions at Av Mitre 946 (Ⓣ0261/429-0707); Aconcagua Trek at Güiraldes 246, San José (Ⓣ0261/424-2003); Aymará Viajes at 9 de Julio 983 (Ⓣ0261/420-0607); Fernando Grajales, José Moreno 898 (Ⓣ0261/429-3830, Ⓔgrajales@satlink.com); and Rumbo al Horizonte at Caseros 1053, Godoy Cruz (Ⓣ0261/452-0641). Mules are in short supply and heavy demand; it's around US$120 for the first mule to Plaza de Mulas, though prices are lower if you hire several (only viable if you're in a group). Fernando Grajales and Aconcagua Trek are the two main outfits dealing in mule-hire. If you need **somewhere to stay** near the base camps, the only possibilities are at Puente del Inca or at Las Cuevas. There are only a couple of possibilities for **accommodation** at Puente del Inca: the fairly luxurious *Hostería Puente del Inca* (Ⓣ0262/442-0222; ❹) with dormitory-style rooms at much lower rates (❷) and the *Refugio La Vieja Estación* (Ⓣ0261/432-1485; ❷) with basic bunk beds and shared baths. At Las Cuevas the best bet is *Refugio Paco Ibañez* (❷) run by *Hostel Campo Base* in Mendoza (see p.149). Most people camp at the Plaza de Mulas – that's the only way to overnight up on the mountain-trail – and the hotels' hot water and meals are invariably welcome after the climb.

San Rafael and around

The small city of **SAN RAFAEL**, some 230km south of the provincial capital, is a kind of mini-Mendoza, complete with wide avenues, irrigation channels along the gutters and scrupulously clean public areas. It built its prosperity on vineyards, olives and tree-fruit, grown in the province's second biggest oasis, and its industry has always been agriculture-based: fruit preserving, olive oil and fine wines. In all, there are nearly eighty **bodegas** in San Rafael department, most of them tiny, family-run businesses, some of which welcome visitors (ask at the tourist office for details). Tourism has been a big money-spinner over the past couple of decades, especially since adventure tourism has taken off. The **Cañon del Atuel**, a short way to the southwest, is one of the best places in the country to try out **white-water rafting**.

Arrival and information

San Rafael's small **airport**, serving Buenos Aires, is 5km west of the town centre, along the RN143 towards Mendoza. There are no buses, so just hop into a taxi (AR$3) if you don't fancy the long hike into town. The **bus terminal** – buses arrive here from Mendoza, Malargüe, San Juan and places farther afield – is wedged in between calles Almafuerte and Avellaneda, at Coronel Suárez. It's extremely central, so you shouldn't need transport to get anywhere.

The very helpful **tourist information office** is at the corner of avenidas Hipólito Yrigoyen and Balloffet (daily 8am–9pm; ⓣ02627/424217, ⓦwww.sanrafael-tour.com), where you can get information about tour operators, pick up a map and fix up somewhere to stay.

Accommodation

San Rafael has no shortage of **places to stay**, ranging from basic refuges to luxurious *apart-hotels*, while one of the country's best youth hostels lies in very attractive grounds just outside the town. The best **campsite** hereabouts is *Camping El Parador*, on the Isla Río Diamante, 6km to the south of the centre; it has excellent facilities, is in a beautiful wooded location and charges AR$6 per tent per day.

Hospedaje Andino Coronel Campos 197 ⓣ02627/421877. This small, family-style place has some very attractive, spacious rooms with impeccable bathrooms, plus a common kitchen for guests. ❸

Hostel Puesta del Sol Deán Funes 998 ⓣ02627/434881, ⓔmendoza3@hostels.org.ar or puestaso@hostels.org.ar. One of the newest and most beautiful hostels in the country, with modern facilities, a huge swimming pool amid landscaped grounds, and a lively atmosphere. ❷

Hotel Jardín Hipólito Yrigoyen 259 ⓣ02627/434621. Very comfy rooms, all en suite, arranged around a lush patio shaded by an impressive palm tree. ❺

Hotel Regine Independencia 623 and Colón ⓣ02627/421470 or 430274, ⓔregine@infovia.com.ar. All the rooms here are well furnished and charming, while the rustic dining room serves reliably good food; there's also a beautiful garden dominated by a ceibo tree. ❹

Hotel San Rafael Coronel Day 30 ⓣ02627/430128. An extremely smart place with very stylish but unpretentious rooms, *Hotel San Rafael* features lovely bathrooms and a very good restaurant. ❻

The City

Although San Rafael lends itself to a gentle stroll, the town is essentially a base for visiting the surrounding area. The main drag with most of the shops, cafés and many of the hotels, a continuation of the RN143 Mendoza road, is called Avenida Hipólito Yrigoyen west of north–south axis Avenida General San Martín, and Avenida Bartolomé Mitre to the east. Two blocks north of Avenida Hipólito Yrigoyen and one west of Avenida San Martín is the town's main square, leafy and peaceful **Plaza San Martín**, dominated by the modern cathedral. To fill an hour or so with something "cultural", take a taxi or a bus marked "Isla Diamante" from Avenida Hipólito Yrigoyen to the **Museo de Historia Natural** (daily 7am–1pm & 2–8pm; AR$1). On the upper floor, you'll find some poorly displayed but fabulous pre-Columbian ceramics, the best of which are statues from Ecuador; there's also a small collection of crafts from Easter Island. In addition to some particularly fine ceramics from northwestern Argentina, you'll see a mummified child dating from 40 AD and a gorgeous multicoloured leather bag decorated with striking, very modern-looking geometric designs, found in the Cañón del Atuel.

Eating

Most of San Rafael's restaurants line Hipólito Yrigoyen; the food tends to be of good value but unimaginative.

La Fusta Hipólito Yrigoyen 538. By far the town's best *parrilla*, serving succulent steaks and full *parrilladas* at very reasonable rates; the local wines are recommended.

La Fusta II Hipólito Yrigoyen and Beato Marcelino Champagnat. Sister restaurant to the above in ultra-modern surroundings with fine decor and a large terrace.

Jockey Club Belgrano 330. Good old-fashioned service and hearty food, with a very good-value *menú turista* at lunch for AR$8.

Tienda del Sol Hipólito Yrigoyen 1663. One of a cluster of trendy, post-modern bars, serving cocktails and other drinks at slightly inflated prices.

Las Leñas

LAS LEÑAS is where the *porteño* jet set comes to show off its winter fashions, to get photographed for society magazines and to have a good time. Skiing and, increasingly, snowboarding is all part of it, but as in the most exclusive Swiss and American winter resorts, the *après ski* is just as important if not more. The Argentine, Brazilian and South American skiing championships are all held here in August, while other events include snow-polo matches, snow-rugby, snow-volleyball and fashion shows. Las Leñas is also trying to branch out into summertime adventure travel, making the most of its splendid upland setting, with some amazingly beautiful trekking country nearby.

The road to Las Leñas heads due west from the RN40 Mendoza to Malargüe road, 28km south of the crossroads settlement of El Sosneado. It climbs past the weird **Pozo de las Animas**, a set of two well-like depressions, each several hundred metres in diameter, caused by underground water erosion, with a huge pool of water in the bottom. The resort of Las Leñas lies 50km from the RN40, a total of nearly 200km southwest of San Rafael. If you are booked at the resort, you might get a transfer from Mendoza or San Rafael, otherwise you either need your own transport or, during the ski season, take the daily **bus** run by TAC from Mendoza, a seven-hour journey. Las Leñas resort has made an effort to come up with inoffensive architecture, and aesthetically it compares well with many European ski resorts. The skiing is often excellent, and the craggy mountaintops make for a breathtaking backdrop. Equipment-rental service is pricey but of tip-top quality, and the twelve lifts are state of the art.

Practicalities

The ski-village's **accommodation** varies considerably in price, and ranges from the utterly luxurious to the functional. The *Club de la Nieve* (❹), housed in an Alpine-style chalet, has its own reasonable restaurant and spacious, functional rooms. More economical options can be found at the edge of the village in the so-called "dormy houses": *Laquir*, *Lihuén*, *Milla* and *Payén* (all ❸). Booking is organized centrally through Las Leñas resort at Reconquista 559, Buenos Aires (ⓣ011/4313-1300, ⓦwww.laslenas.com). For **eating** at the ski village, there's the *confitería* and popular meeting place *El Nuevo Innsbruck*, which serves beer and expensive snacks on its terrace with piste views. *Bacus* is an on-piste snackbar, while *Elurra* serves lunch and is accessible by the Minerva chairlift. *La Cima* is a pizzeria by day and a more chic restaurant by night, while delicious, huge-portioned fondues and raclettes are served with the best Argentine white wines at the *El Refugio*, in the central Pirámide building.

Malargüe and around

MALARGÜE is a small, laid-back little town, lying 186km south of San Rafael by the RP144 and RN40. It is a good spot for exploring some of the least known, but most spectacular landscapes in Argentina, let alone Mendoza Province, as well as for dabbling in a spot of fishing. As yet, however, accommodation is the town's weak point, with less variety and quality than in San Rafael. Nevertheless, the town's within day-trip distance of the black and red pampas of **La Payunia**, a nature reserve where flocks of guanacos and *ñandúes* roam over lava-flows. Far nearer to hand – double as half-day outings – are some remarkable underground caves, the **Caverna de las Brujas** and **Laguna Llancanelo**, a shining lagoon flecked pink with flamingoes and crammed with other aquatic birdlife.

The core of the town lies either side of the RN40, called Avenida San Martín within the town's boundaries, a wide rather soulless avenue along which many of the hotels are located, as well as a couple of cafés, the bank and telephone centres. **Plaza General San Martín** is the focal point, but it's nothing to get excited about. Being totally flat and compact, however, the town is extremely easy to find your way around, and in any case its handful of attractions are clustered together at the northern reaches, beyond the built-up area. Conveniently close to the tourist office, the beautiful landscaped **Parque del Ayer**, or "Park of Yesteryear", is planted with native and imported tree varieties. The **Centro Pierre Auger**, opposite, is named after a French physicist who discovered the energy-producing potential of cosmic rays, and was built with international funding as the southern hemisphere element in a worldwide project to harness those rays. Housed in a fine colonial building, the impeccably refurbished **Museo Regional** (daily 9am–1pm & 5–9pm, Sat, Sun & public holidays 9am–noon & 4–8pm; free) offers a beautifully displayed collection of ammonites, clay pipes for religious ceremonies, a mummified corpse, jewellery, dinosaur remains and even a set of vehicle registration plates dating from the 1950s, when the town was temporarily renamed Villa Juan Domingo Perón.

Practicalities

Buses from Mendoza, San Rafael and Neuquén go all the way to the bus terminal at Esquibel Aldao and Fray Luis Beltrán, four blocks south and two west of central Plaza San Martín, but will also drop off and collect passengers at the plaza en route. Malargüe's excellent **tourist office** (daily 7am–10pm; ⓣ02627/471659, ⓔturismun@slatinos.com.ar), in a rustic building on the RN40 four blocks north of the plaza, has loads of information on what to see and do, and where to stay.

Accommodation is limited. The *Hotel Portal del Valle,* RN40 Norte (ⓣ02627/471294; ❹), has a small indoor pool, a sauna, bar and decent restaurant and organizes excursions; rooms are modern and very pleasant. Next door, the *Río Grande Hotel* (ⓣ02627/471589; ❻) offers tastefully decorated rooms in a British style, very friendly owners and delicious food in its restaurant. *Hotel Llancanelo*, at Av Rufino Ortega 158 (ⓣ02627/470689, ⓔllancane@slatinos.com.ar; ❸), has attractive double and triple bedrooms; the Alpine-style, pine-clad bar-cum-*confitería* serves very decent food. Otherwise you could **camp** at *Camping Polideportivo* at Capdeval and Esquibal Aldao (ⓣ02627/470691; AR$4) or in a wonderful setting at Castillos de Pincheiras, 27km southwest of the town.

Apart from the *Hotel Río Grande*, the best place **to eat** in town is *La Posta*, an excellent *parrilla* serving goat and trout, at Av Roca 374. For the best trout, though, head out of town to El Dique, 8km west of Malargüe, where at the trout farm *Cuyam-Co* you can even catch your own fish if you want; it is then perfectly cooked and served with an excellent local rosé.

All of the **tour operators**, offering excursions in the region to places like La Payunia and Cueva de las Brujas, are of a very high standard. Check out Karen Travel at San Martín 1056 (ⓣ02627/470342, ⓦwww.karentravel.com.ar); who can also fix you up with a vehicle, preferably a 4WD.

La Caverna de las Brujas

The **CAVERNA DE LAS BRUJAS** is a marvellous cave that plunges deep into the earth at an altitude of just under 2000m, just 73km southwest of Malargüe, 8km off the RN40 along a marked track. The name, literally "witches' cave", is thought to be linked to local legends that it was used as a meeting place for sorcerers. The

Caverna lies within a provincial park, and a small *guardería*, manned by a couple of *guardaparques*, stands nearby; they have the key to the padlocked gates that protect the grotto (AR$10). It's compulsory to enter accompanied by a guide (numbers are limited), and the best option in any case is to go on an organized tour from Malargüe. Take pocket torches, though miners' helmets are also supplied – but don't rely on their batteries; a highlight inside the cave is experiencing the total darkness by turning out all lights and getting used to the spooky atmosphere. Las Brujas is filled with amazing rock formations, including some impressive **stalactites and stalagmites**; typically, they have been given imaginative names such as the Virgin's Chamber, the Pulpit, the Flowers and the Crystals. Wear good walking shoes and take a sweater as the difference in temperature between inside and out can be as much as 20°C.

La Payunia

The highlight of any trip to southernmost Mendoza Province, **LA PAYUNIA**, or the Reserva Provincial El Payén, is a fabulously wild area of staggering beauty, sometimes referred to as the Patagonia Mendocina. Dominated by Cerro Payún or Payén (3690m) and inactive Volcán Payún Matrú (2900m), it is utterly unspoiled apart from some remnants of old fluorite and manganese mines plus some petrol-drilling derricks, whose nodding-head pump-structures are locally nicknamed "guanacos", after the member of the llama family they vaguely resemble in shape. "Fresh" trails of lava debris can be seen at various points throughout the park, and enormous boulders of igneous rock are scattered over these dark plains, also ejected during the violent volcanic activity. The only vegetation is flaxen grass, whose golden colour stands out against the treacle-coloured hillsides. Another section of the reserve is the aptly named **Pampa Roja**, where reddish oxides in the lava give the ground a henna-like tint. The threatening hulk of Volcán Pihuel looms at the western extremity of the reserve – its top was blown off by a particularly violent explosion that occurred when the mountain was beneath the sea. The approach to the park from Malargüe is farther along the RN40 from the Caverna de las Brujas, and the actual entrance to the reserve is at a place called El Zampal. There isn't really any viable alternative to one of the excellent day-trips run out of Malargüe (see p.157).

San Juan

Some 165km north of Mendoza and nearly 1150km northwest of Buenos Aires, the city of **SAN JUAN** basks in the sun-drenched valley of the Río San Juan, which twists and turns between several steep mountain ranges. Periodic tremors, some of them alarmingly high on the Richter scale, remind Sanjuaninos that they live along one of the world's most slippery seismic faults; the Big One is dreaded as much here as in California but, as they do there, people just live their lives, trusting the special construction techniques of the city's modern buildings. One of South America's strongest recorded earthquakes, around 8.5 on the Richter scale, and Argentina's worst ever, flattened the city in 1944, claiming over ten thousand lives. Broad pavements, grand avenues and long boulevards shaded by rows of flaky-trunked plane trees lend the city a feeling of spaciousness and openness. None of the sights amounts to much, but San Juan is a comfortable starting point for touring some of the country's finest scenery.

Arrival and information

The **airport** is 12km east of the city, just off the RN141 (ⓣ0264/425-0487); a taxi or *remise* to the centre from here will set you back around AR$10. The city's user-friendly, spacious **bus station**, with regular services all over the province, region and country, is eight blocks east of the central Plaza 25 de Mayo, at Estados Unidos 492 sur (☎0264/422-1604). En-Pro-Tur, the **provincial (and municipal) tourist office**, can be found at Sarmiento 24 sur (daily 7am–9pm; ☎0264/422-7219, Ⓦwww.ischigualasto.com).

Accommodation

San Juan's central accommodation ranges from basic *residenciales* to a swanky hotel aimed at the commercial traveller; however, on the outskirts is a great new place if you're looking for something a bit classier.

Hotel Alkazar Laprida 84 este ☎0264/421-4961. This is San Juan's only luxury hotel to date; albeit on the impersonal side, it does have extremely smart, well-kept rooms, with ultra-modern bathrooms, and sweeping views across the city. Swimming pool. ❺

Hotel América 9 de Julio 1052 este ☎0264/421-4514. Pleasant, traditional, small hotel, popular with foreign visitors, so call first to reserve. All rooms have en-suite bathroom. ❹

Hotel Jardín Petit 25 de Mayo 345 este ☎0264/421-1825. *Hotel Jardín Petit* offers small, functional rooms with bath, and a bright patio overlooked by the breakfast room. ❸

Hotel Nuevo San Francisco Av España 284 sur ☎0264/422-3760. Extremely reliable place, with smart, pleasant rooms, new bathrooms and friendly service. ❹

Hotel Viñas del Sol Ruta 20 and Gal Roca ☎0264/425-3924, Ⓦwww.vinasdelsol.com.ar. Just outside the city but conveniently near the airport, this is a welcome newcomer with smart en-suite rooms. ❹

Residencial La Toja Rivadavia 494 este ☎0264/422-2584. This *residencial* has cramped but very clean rooms and offers a friendly welcome. ❸

The City

Plaza 25 de Mayo is the epicentre, surrounded by cafés with terraces and some shops, as well as the *Club Español*, on the northern side, a city institution but not the best place to eat or drink. The **Catedral**, too modern for many tastes, on the northwest edge of the plaza, has a fifty-metre brick campanile that takes its inspiration from the tower of St Mark's in Venice. You can climb almost to the top of the **bell tower** (daily 9am–1pm & 5–9.30pm; AR$1) – which plays a Big Ben chime, and the Argentine national anthem for special occasions – for panoramic views of the city and the surrounding countryside. Two blocks west and one north, opposite the tourist office, is the only museum of any interest in the city, the **Museo Casa de Sarmiento** (Tues–Fri 8.30am–1.30pm & 3.30–8pm, Mon & Sat 8.30am–1.30pm; AR$1; guided tours half-hourly, in Spanish only) at Sarmiento 21 sur. The beautiful, simple whitewashed house where Sarmiento, Argentine president and Renaissance man, was born in 1811, was only slightly damaged in the 1944 earthquake, thanks to its sturdy adobe walls and sandy foundations, and has since been restored several times. The rooms contain Sarmiento relics and personal effects, plenty of portraits and signs of sycophancy.

Of San Juan's several other museums, the best is the **Museo de Ciencias Naturales** (Tues–Sun 9am–1pm; AR$2), housed in the former train station at avenidas España and Maipú, seven blocks west and five north of the central plaza. It contains an incipient, state-of-the-art exhibition focusing on the remarkable **dinosaur skeletons** unearthed at Parque Provincial Ischigualasto (see p.161). You can see the scientific workshop, where the finds are examined and analyzed, while the collections of semiprecious stones extracted from the province's mines are for once imaginatively displayed, using modern techniques. Round off your exploration with a visit to one of the city's **bodegas**, one of the most alluring being the **Antigua Bodega Chirino** at Salta 782 norte (Mon–Sat 8.30am–12.30pm & 4.30–8.30pm; free; ☎0264/421-4327), housed in a beautiful brick reconstruction of the pre-quake winery; its wines are among the best in the province.

Eating and nightlife

San Juan has a wide range of **places to eat**, including one of the region's best vegetarian restaurants – so good it can be recommended for non-veggies too. You can also find excellent Middle Eastern, Spanish and French cuisine in addition to the usual pizzerias, *parrillas* and *tenedor libre* joints. Most of the best places are in the western, residential part of the city, away from the microcentro. **Café** life is all part of the *paseo* tradition, imported lock, stock and barrel from Spain, but later in the evening most Sanjuaninos seem to entertain themselves in their gardens, round a family *asado*. You'll also find a couple of decent **discos**, mostly in the outskirts.

Antonio Gómez Supermercado, General Acha and Córdoba. Stupendous paellas and other Spanish fare are served at this extremely popular market-stall. Lunch only.

Las Leñas Av San Martín 1670 oeste. Cavernous dining room often packed out with large parties; the meat here is particularly delicious.

La Nonna María Av San Martín 1893 oeste and P. Moreno. Top-quality pizzeria, serving wonderful creations cooked in wood ovens.

Rigoletto Paula A. de Sarmiento 418 sur. Cosy atmosphere and friendly service, as well as delicious pizzas and pasta.

Soychú Av José Ignacio de la Roza 223 oeste. Delightful vegetarian restaurant serving fabulous dishes, in a bright, airy space; office workers flock here, taking food away, too, so come early.

Parque Provincial Ischigualasto and Parque Nacional Talampaya

San Juan and La Rioja provinces boast two of the most photographed protected areas in the country. In San Juan, the **Parque Provincial Ischigualasto** is better known as Valle de la Luna (Moon Valley) because of its eerily out-of-this-world landscapes and apocryphal legends. **Parque Nacional Talampaya** is another vulnerable biotope, home to several rare varieties of flora and fauna, including condors, but it's best known for its giant red sandstone cliffs, which are guaranteed to impress even the jaded traveller. Both parks are within reach of the delightful little town of **San Agustín de Valle Fértil**, high in the mountains of eastern San Juan Province. Most visitors take in both parks in the same day, though each merits a longer visit.

San Agustín de Valle Fértil

Set among enticing mountainside landscapes, some 250km northeast of San Juan, by the RN141 and mostly unpaved RP510, the oasis town of **SAN AGUSTÍN DE VALLE FÉRTIL** is the best place to spend the night in eastern San Juan Province. The fertile valley that gives it its name is a patchwork of maize fields, olive-groves and pasture for goats and sheep. Valle Fértil's *raison d'être* for the traveller is as a base for visiting the twin parks of Talampaya and Ischigualasto; it is an attractive town, built around a mirror-like reservoir, the Dique San Agustín; cacti and gorse grow on its banks, and a small peninsula juts artistically into the waters.

Buses from San Juan (three daily) and La Rioja (two weekly) arrive at Mitre and Entre Ríos. The **tourist office** (Mon–Fri 7am–1pm & 5–9pm, Sat 8am–1pm; no phone) at Plaza San Agustín is extremely helpful, and can fix you up with guides and transport both to Ischigualasto and to other less dramatic sites in the nearby mountains, including pre-Hispanic petroglyphs. Note that there are no ATMs in town.

Practicalities

The best **place to stay** is the comfortable *Hostería Valle Fértil* on a hilltop overlooking the Dique, at Rivadavia (☎02646/420015; ❺). It has a decent restaurant, delightfully modern, bright rooms – the more expensive ones with lake views – but the bathrooms are cramped. Both *Hospedaje San Agustín* at Rivadavia and Juan Rojas (☎02646/420004; ❷) and *Hospedaje Los Olivos* at Santa Fe (☎02646/420115; ❷) are basic, lackadaisically run pensions, but their clean rooms are fine for a night. There are two **campsites**: the *Campismo Municipal* (☎02646/420192) on the banks of the Dique charges AR$8 per tent, but *Camping Valle Fértil* (no phone), at the lower end of the road leading up to the Hostería Valle Fértil, at AR$10 per tent, is generally better kept and more appealing. Apart from the restaurant at the *hostería*, the best **places to eat** are the traditional *parrillas Los Olivos* and *Rancho Criollo*, both a block south of Plaza San Agustín.

Parque Provincial Ischigualasto

Just under 100km north of Valle Fértil, the **PARQUE PROVINCIAL ISCHIGUALASTO**, also known as the Valle de la Luna (Moon Valley), is San Juan's most famous feature by far. It can be visited only by vehicle, whether your own, that of your tour operator or one rented for the duration from the park authorities, though don't count on the latter – you might be put with other visitors who can squeeze you into theirs. A rich burial ground of some of the Earth's most enigmatic inhabitants, the dinosaurs, the park is unique as all stages of the 45-million-year Triassic era are represented in its rocks. Most visitors, however, come simply to admire the spectacular lunar landscapes, which give the park its popular nickname, and the much publicized and alarmingly fragile rock formations. Tours follow set **circuits**, beginning in the more lunar landscapes to the south; a segmented row of rocks is known as **El Gusano** (The Worm); a huge set of vessel-like boulders, including one resembling a funnel, is known as **El Submarino**; and a sandy field dotted with cannon-ball-shaped stones is dubbed the **Cancha de Bolas** (The Ball-court). These are the typical moonscapes, but they look uncannily like the famous landscapes of Cappadocia, with their Gaudí-esque pinnacles and curvaceous mounds. Then you head north, where sugary white fields are scattered with petrified tree-trunks and weird and wonderful rocks. One famous formation, painfully fragile on its slender stalk, is **El Hongo** (The Mushroom), beautifully set off against the orange sandstone cliffs behind. This whole tour needs at least a couple of hours to be done at all comfortably; be warned that sudden summer storms can cut off the tracks for a day or two, in which case you may not be able to see all the park.

Park practicalities

The **guardería** (daily 9am–dusk), staffed by ultra-friendly *guardaparques*, lies at the entrance to the park, along a well-signposted lateral road, off the RP510 at Los Baldecitos. You must pay AR$5 per person, which entitles you to a guided tour. While you can **camp** for free next to the **visitors' centre** (which has a few photographs and sketchy information about the park's geology and wildlife), most people stay at either Villa Unión or, preferably, Valle Fértil (see above). You could also visit on an **organized tour** from San Juan – Fascinatur at Ramón y Cajal 232 norte (☎0264/422-7709, ©raphaeljolat@speedy.com.ar) is by far the best operator in the city. Triassic Tour at Hipólito Yrigoyen 294 sur, San Juan (☎0264/423-0358), specializes in trips to the park, as its name suggests. As for **public transport**, the infrequent Vallecito bus from San Juan to La Rioja could drop you at Los Baldecitos, about 5km from the park entrance. The optimal time of day for visiting the park is in the mid- to late afternoon, when the light is the most flattering.

Parque Nacional Talampaya

The entrance to **PARQUE NACIONAL TALAMPAYA**, known as the Puerta de Talampaya, is 55km down the RP26 from Villa Unión, a nondescript town in La Rioja Province, and then 12km along a signposted track to the east. Coming from the south, it's 93km north of Ischigualasto and 190km from Valle Fértil. The park's main feature is a wide-bottomed canyon flanked by 180-metre-high, rust-coloured sandstone cliffs, so smooth and sheer that they look as if they were sliced through by a giant cheese-wire. The only feature interrupting this smooth perfection is the **Chimenea** ("chimney"), a rounded vertical groove stretching all the way up the cliff-side; guides revel in demonstrating its extraordinary echo, which sends condors flapping as it ricochets off the rock face. Another section of the canyon is made up of rock formations that seem to have been created as part of a surreal Gothic cathedral. Added attractions are the presence of several bird species, including **condors** and **eagles**, as well as rich flora and some pre-Columbian **petroglyphs** etched on the natural walls of rock. The national park, covering 215 square kilometres, was created in 1997; geologically it's part of the Sierra Los Colorados, whose rippling mass you can see in the distance, to the east, along with the giant snowcapped range of the Sierra de Famatina, to the north.

Park practicalities

The **guardería** (daily 9am–5pm; AR$5; no phone) is staffed throughout the year and stands at the end of the trail off the RP26, at the Puerta de Talampaya. To get to the park without your own transport or without going on an **organized tour** from La Rioja or San Juan, you can be dropped off on the main road by the buses from Villa Unión to La Rioja and Valle Fértil, or you can take the regular bus from Villa Unión to the village of **Pagancillo** 27km north of the park entrance. There you can stay at the basic but clean *Cabañas Adolfo Páez* (☎03825/470397; ❷); the owner might even take you to the park and guide you around. It's also possible to **camp** in the open, next to the *guardería*, but bear in mind that it's often windy and can get extremely cold at night for much of the year. There's also a *confitería* serving basic, reasonably priced snacks and small meals.

Whatever the rangers tell you, you are allowed to use your own vehicle, but you need a 4WD and must take a guide. Alternatively you can negotiate a fee to use one of their pick-up trucks, which give you an open-air view of the canyon as you drive along – but this should be avoided if it's windy. The best time of day by far to visit is soon after opening, when the dawn light deepens the red of the sandstone; in the afternoon and evening the canyon is shaded and the colours are less intense.

1.6

The Lake District

One of Argentina's most popular holiday destinations, the **LAKE DISTRICT** is famous for the series of easily accessible national parks strung along the Andean cordillera. A land of immense glacial lakes – hence its name – but also dense forests, jagged peaks and extinct volcanoes, it was controlled, until a little over a century ago, by the Mapuche people. The mountains in the south of Neuquén Province are covered in dense Andean forest, best seen in the **Parque Nacional Lanín**, accessed via **Junín de los Andes** which, with more touristy **San Martín de los Andes**, provide good bases for exploring the whole northern half of the region, including the **Parque Nacional Los Arrayanes**, a wood of myrtle trees at the end of the Peninsula Quetrihué. This tiny park is surrounded by a goliath: **Parque Nacional Nahuel Huapi**, perhaps the most famous, and one of the most visited, of all Argentina's national parks. Argentine holiday-makers pack out nearby towns such as the archetypal Patagonian holiday resort, **Bariloche**, both in summer and for skiing in winter. Further south, in the province of Chubut, the major holiday destination is **Esquel**. From here, you can visit another classic Patagonian park, **Parque Nacional Los Alerces**, home to some exceptional lakes and the best place to see threatened, majestic **alerce** trees, some of them thousands of years old.

Parque Nacional Lanín

The most northerly of Patagonia's great national parks, **PARQUE NACIONAL LANÍN** has three trademark features. The presence of various Mapuche communities who live in and around the park; its geographical centrepiece – the fabulous

The Mapuche

Knowing themselves as the people (*che*) of the earth (*Mapu*), **the Mapuche** were, before the arrival of the Spanish in the sixteenth century, a loose confederation of tribal groups who lived exclusively on the western, Chilean side of the cordillera. The Spanish were forced to abandon attempts to subjugate this fiercely proud nation, opting instead for a policy of containment, but their encroachments into Araucania sparked a series of Mapuche migrations eastwards into territory that is now Argentina. These invasions, in turn, displaced ethnic groups such as the northern Tehuelche and, in time, Mapuches became the dominant force in northern Patagonia to the east of the Andes; their cultural and linguistic influence spread far beyond the areas they actually controlled.

Today, the Mapuche remains one of Argentina's principal indigenous nations, with a population of some 40,000 people who live in communities dotted around the provinces of Buenos Aires, La Pampa, Chubut, Río Negro and, above all, Neuquén. Increasingly, Mapuche communities are setting up tourist-related projects. When visiting Mapuche communities, especially outside a tourist environment, remember that cameras can be a tourists' worst enemy at times: use them sensitively and always ask permission first.

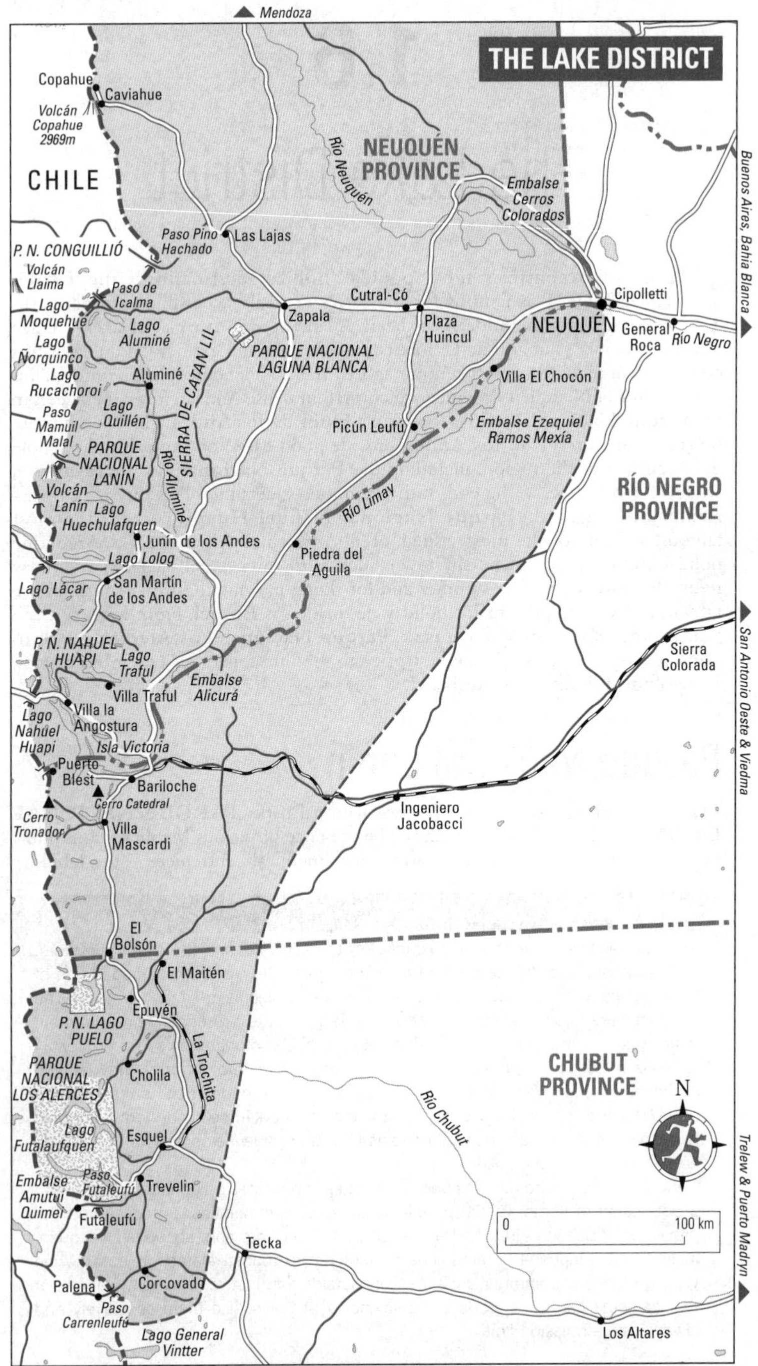
THE LAKE DISTRICT
Mendoza
Copahue
Caviahue
Volcán Copahue 2969m
CHILE
NEUQUÉN PROVINCE
Río Neuquén
Embalse Cerros Colorados
Buenos Aires, Bahia Blanca
Paso Pino Hachado
Las Lajas
P. N. CONGUILLIÓ
Volcán Llaima
Paso de Icalma
Lago Moquehue
Lago Aluminé
Lago Ñorquinco
Zapala
Cutral-Có
Plaza Huincul
NEUQUÉN
Cipolletti
General Roca
Río Negro
SIERRA DE CATAN LIL
PARQUE NACIONAL LAGUNA BLANCA
Lago Rucachoroi
Aluminé
Villa El Chocón
Paso Mamuil Malal
Lago Quillén
Picún Leufú
Embalse Ezequiel Ramos Mexía
PARQUE NACIONAL LANÍN
Río Aluminé
Volcán Lanín
Lago Huechulafquen
Río Limay
RÍO NEGRO PROVINCE
Junín de los Andes
Piedra del Aguila
Lago Lolog
Lago Lácar
San Martín de los Andes
San Antonio Oeste & Viedma
P. N. NAHUEL HUAPI
Lago Traful
Villa Traful
Embalse Alicurá
Sierra Colorada
Lago Nahuel Huapi
Villa la Angostura
Isla Victoria
Puerto Blest
Bariloche
Cerro Catedral
Cerro Tronador
Villa Mascardi
Ingeniero Jacobacci
El Bolsón
El Maitén
Epuyén
P. N. LAGO PUELO
La Trochita
PARQUE NACIONAL LOS ALERCES
Cholila
CHUBUT PROVINCE
Río Chubut
N
Lago Futalaufquen
Esquel
Embalse Amutui Quimei
Paso Futaleufú
Trevelin
Futaleufú
Trelew & Puerto Madryn
0
100 km
Tecka
Palena
Corcovado
Paso Carrenleufú
Lago General Vintter
Los Altares
RN-40 South

cone of **Volcán Lanín**, rising to 3776m and dominating the scenery around; and a species of tree – the araucaria or *pehuén*. Araucarias can be found in isolated stands as far south as Lago Curruhue Grande, but are especially prevalent in the northern sector of the park around Quillén, Rucachoroi and Ñorquinco. The southern sector of the park and the famous Seven Lakes Route through the north of Parque Nacional Nahuel Huapi towards Villa La Angostura and Bariloche are covered in the section on **San Martín de los Andes** (see below). The park reputedly protects a population of *huemules*, although their status is precarious. You have a very slim chance of seeing a *pudu*, the tiny native deer, a puma or a *gato huiña* wildcat, but better chances exist of spotting a coipu or a grey fox. However, some of the likeliest creatures you'll come across are the ones introduced for hunting a century ago: the wild boar and the red deer that roam the semi-arid steppes and hills of the eastern margin of the park.

The park can be covered in snow from May to October, but it can snow in the higher mountain regions at almost any time of year. The **best time to visit** is in spring (especially Oct–Nov) – or autumn (March to mid-May), when the deciduous trees adopt a spectacular palette, particularly in the Pehuenia area; the contasts of rusts, golds and dark greens is irresistible.

Junín de los Andes

Favoured by anglers, **JUNÍN DE LOS ANDES** is well placed for trips to the central sector of Parque Nacional Lanín, especially for exploring the **Lago Huechulafquen** area and if you plan to climb Volcán Lanín itself. The RN234, called Boulevard J.M. Rosas for this stretch, cuts across the western side of town, and all you'll need is to the east of this. Chapelco **airport** (Ⓣ02972/428388) lies halfway between Junín and San Martín and is shared by both; it's 19km out of Junín (*remise* into town AR$15–20); the **bus terminal** is one block to the east, at Olavarría and F.S. Martín. Continue east along Olavarría for two blocks and turn right (south) for one block along Calle San Martín to reach the main square, Plaza San Martín, where all life centres. Diagonally opposite, at Padre Milanesio and Coronel Suárez, is the **tourist office** (daily April–Nov 8am–9pm; Dec–March 8am–10pm; Ⓣ&Ⓕ02972/491160, Ⓔturismo@jandes.com.ar). Part of the same building acts as an excellent **park information office** (Mon–Fri 9am–1pm & 7–10pm).

Hotel tariffs rise slightly in summer, when it's worth reserving a little in advance. Conveniently just round the corner from the terminal, *Residencial Marisa*, J.M. Rosas 360 (Ⓣ&Ⓕ02972/491175, Ⓔresidencialmarisa@com.ar; ❸), is a neat, amiable place, and not too noisy, despite some rooms facing the main road. A rare gem, combining excellent value with a distinct personality that engenders great loyalty amongst its regular guests, *Hostería Chimehuín*, at Coronel Suárez and 25 de Mayo (Ⓣ02972/491132; ❹), offers a fine home-made breakfast included in the price. One and a half blocks east of the main square, *Posada Pehuén*, Coronel Suárez 560 (Ⓣ02972/491569, Ⓔposadapehuen@hotmail.com; ❹), is a peaceful place with its own garden that features two-course evening meals for AR$10. Reserve three weeks ahead in high season. Within easy reach of the centre, the *Municipal* **campsite**, at the eastern end of Coronel Suárez, is a pleasant, shady site by the larger channel of the Río Chimehuín. (AR$5 per person).

There are not many **places to eat** in Junín de los Andes. *Ruca Hueney*, at Padre Milanesio y Coronel Suárez (Ⓣ02972/491113), is a good first port of call; trout is its speciality (AR$15 for a huge portion), but it also serves Middle Eastern food and has inexpensive tourist menus.

San Martín de los Andes and around

One of the most beautiful of all Patagonian towns, **SAN MARTÍN DE LOS ANDES** is a small resort of chalets and low-key architecture set in a flat, sheltered valley at the eastern end of **Lago Lácar**, compressed between steep-sided slopes covered in native cypress and forestry pine. Expansion here has been rapid, but by no means as uncontrolled as in its much larger rival resort, Bariloche. And whereas Bariloche caters to the young party crowd, San Martín has deliberately set itself up for a more sedate type of small-town tourism, pitching for families rather than students.

There is little to do in town itself, bar shopping, sunning yourself on the small beach by the lake, or popping in to the tiny **Museo de los Primeros Pobladores** (Tues–Fri 10am–7pm, Sat & Sun 3–8pm; AR$1) on the main square, which offers exhibits on archeology and skiing. San Martín is the northern terminus of the **Ruta de Los Siete Lagos**; the seven principal lakes by the roadside are, from north to south: Lácar, Machónico, Falkner, Villarino, Correntoso, Espejo and Nahuel Huapi.

Practicalities

Chapelco **airport** lies 25km away in the direction of Junín de los Andes, and Caleuche minibuses connect the airport with the town (Ⓣ02972/422115 for hotel pick-up, AR$10). The **bus terminal** is scenically located in the southwest of town, across the road from the Lago Lácar **pier**, handy for the tourist launches across the lake. On the main square, you'll find the **tourist office** (mid-Dec to Easter 8am–10pm; rest of year 8am–9pm; Ⓣ&Ⓕ02972/427347, Ⓦwww.smandes.gov.ar). At the **Intendencia of Parque Nacional Lanín**, on the Plaza San Martín at Emilio Frey 749 (Mon–Fri 8am–1pm), you can get maps, leaflets and various information on trekking.

During the peak summer and skiing seasons it is essential to **reserve rooms** as far in advance as possible; out of season, rooms can be as little as half price. Commanding one of the finest hotel views in Patagonia, *Hostería Ayelén*, postal address Pasaje Arrayanes, Casilla de Correo 21 (Ⓣ&Ⓕ02972/425660, Ⓔjanetdickinson@smandes.com.ar; ❹), is owned by an English-speaking couple. While prices include an excellent breakfast, dinner is an optional extra. *Residencial Casa Alta*, Gabriel Obeid 659 (Ⓣ&Ⓕ02972/427456; ❹), has homely, wood-panelled rooms for up to five people, most with private bathrooms, The personable, English-speaking owners allow use of their impressive private library, but it is closed mid-Sept to Nov & Easter–June. An excellent family-run residence, *Residencial Los Pinos* Almirante Brown 420 (Ⓣ02972/427207; ❸; closed May & June), has a pleasant garden, inexpensive rooms and shared bathroom for single budget travellers. Breakfast is included in the price of the room. *Hostería Hueney Ruca*, at Obeid and Coronel Pérez (Ⓣ02972/427499, ❹), features a garden and free parking; all rooms have a private bathroom, and breakfast is included in the price. There's one **hostel** in town, the *Puma*, Fosberry 535 (Ⓣ02972/422443, Ⓦwww.pumahostel.com.ar; AR$11 HI members, otherwise AR$13); a small, well-scrubbed, modern place, with a couple of double rooms (❸), kitchen and washing facilities. For **camping**, there's a choice of three sites, the best of which is probably *Camping Lolen* (AR$6 per person), a lakeside site with superb views, run by the Curruhuinca Mapuche community, 4km southwest of town and 1km off the main RN234, down a very steep track to Playa Catritre.

For **eating**, pride of place in town goes to *Avataras*, Teniente Ramayón 765 (Ⓣ02972/427104), an ambitious venture with an exquisite menu offering a select choice of gourmet foods from around the world, in a sympathetically lit venue. There are Thai, Moroccan, and Indian offerings, with freshwater fish sushi on Fridays, and live jazz and blues on Thursdays. At *Panquequería El Amanecer de Carlitos*, San Martín 1371 (Ⓣ02972/425990), three hundred varieties of sweet and savoury crepes – many vegetarian, and all surprisingly inexpensive – are served in a down-home atmosphere, while *Pura Vida* Villegas, 745 (Ⓣ02972/429302), serves freshly prepared vegetarian quiches, bursting with flavour, as well as trout and chicken for non-vegetarians.

Parque Nacional Los Arrayanes

A park within a park, **PARQUE NACIONAL LOS ARRAYANES** (daylight hours; AR$12) was created to protect the world's best stand of myrtle woodland, the **Bosque de los Arrayanes**, found at the far tip of the Península Quetrihué. This narrow-necked peninsula juts out into Lago Nahuel Huapi from **Villa La Angostura**. Quetrihué in Mapudungun means "place of the *arrayanes*", and the peninsula is a legacy from the glaciation of the Pleistocene era, as its rock proved more resilient to erosion than that which surrounded it.

The Bosque itself can be reached by hiking or cycling the trail from Villa La Angostura (12km one way), or by boat from Villa La Angostura or Bariloche. Boulevard Nahuel Huapi begins in Villa La Angostura with the stretch that connects the two bays on either side of the peninsula's narrow neck. **Bahía Mansa** ("Peaceful Bay"), on the eastern side, is where you'll find the Intendencia of the park and the Puerto Angostura **jetty** for boats to the Bosque; and **Bahía Brava** ("Wild Bay") on the western side, which is used only by fishing boats. The park entrance is halfway between the two. When seen from the lake, the Bosque doesn't look much different from the surrounding forest, but it's when you're underneath the canopy that its magic envelops you. If you're **hiking**, count on a five- to six-hour round trip (2hr 15min one-way). Start early to enjoy the wildlife of the peninsula and to get to the myrtle forest by 10am (before the arrival of the first boat). Walk around the 600-metre **boardwalk** at your leisure while the contorted corkscrew trunks creak against each other in the breeze and the light plays like a French Impressionist's dream.

Villa La Angostura

Spread haphazardly along the northernshore of Lago Nahuel Huapi, **VILLA LA ANGOSTURA** (ⓦwww.villalaangostura.net.ar) is a relaxed but expensive holiday town that caters mainly for better-off Argentinians. Though the area has plenty of outdoor possibilities, the main reason for over-nighting here is to see the Bosque de los Arrayanes in the Parque Nacional Quetrihué. From here, too, the Ruta de Los Siete Lagos heads north to San Martín de los Andes. It's in poor condition, so be prepared for some hellish dust, yet the views of indigo lakes reflecting wooded crags form some of the finest scenery in the country. If you arrive in winter, there's **skiing** on the slopes of Cerro Bayo, 10km to the northeast of the village.

The town is actually divided into two main settlements: **El Cruce** ("The Crossroads") is the first you'll come across, being built around the main RN231 – called Avenida Siete Lagos at its western end and Avenida Los Arrayanes, the main commercial street, from Bariloche to the east – while Villa La Angostura proper is next to the national park entrance, 3km south down the Boulevard Nahuel Huapi spur road. These three roads converge on the ACA service station in El Cruce. The **bus terminal** is a block west of ACA, on Avenida Siete Lagos. The oldest, most traditional **accommodation** in Villa La Angostura is at *Hotel Angostura*, Nahuel Huapi s/n (ⓣ&ⓕ02944/494224, ⓔhotel-angostura@cybersnet.com.ar; ❺), a comfortable, family-run establishment with calming lakeside views and a decent restaurant. Spotless *Río Bonito* is two blocks northwest of the terminal at Topa Topa 260 (ⓣ02944/494110; ❹). All along the lakeside a huge of number of new places have sprung up, mostly catering for the longer-term, upper-scale market; details from the tourist information service. The most convenient **campsite** is *Camping Unquehué* (ⓣ02944/494688; AR$6 per person), 500m west of the bus terminal on Avenida Siete Lagos.

Bariloche

Approaching from the north, you can appreciate the mountain backdrop of the holiday capital of Argentine Patagonia, **BARILOCHE**, or San Carlos de Bariloche, to give it its full title, spread along the dry southeastern shores of Lago Nahuel Huapi. Everything in town faces the lake, Northern Patagonia's heavyweight; it is an impressive expanse of water that can seem like a benign Mediterranean lake one moment and a froth of seething whitecaps the next, lashed by the icy winds that sometimes whip off it into town. This is a place of pilgrimage for the nation's students, who flood here in January and February. The area's main attraction is a large one: the Parque Nacional Nahuel Huapi that surrounds town, although in winter it's specifically the **ski-resort** of Cerro Catedral nearby – one of the country's most important. At peak times of year, you may find that the excesses of commercialization and crowds of tourists will spoil elements of your visit. Nevertheless, the place does work well in giving remarkably painless access to many beautiful, and some genuinely wild, areas of the cordillera and, out of season, the town is still big enough to retain some life.

Arrival and information

Bariloche's **airport** (ⓣ02944/422555) is 14km to the east of town, and a shuttle bus runs in to town (daily 9.30am–5.30pm; AR$3); a *remise* into the centre will cost about AR$5. The main **bus terminal** is next door to the **train station** (ⓣ02944/423172), 3km east of the city centre along the main RN237. The best local buses for the centre are #10, #20 and #21 (every 15–20min; 10min; AR$1), running along Calle Moreno and dropping you at the corner of Calle Morales near the **centro cívico**; a cab to here will cost around AR$4.

The **tourist office** (daily 8am–9pm; ⓣ&ⓕ02944/426784 or 423122, ⓔsecturismo@bariloche.com.ar) is in the *centro cívico*. Just to the south of the tourist office, the Club Andino Bariloche, 20 de Febrero 30, is a vital port of call for trekkers; and the **Intendencia** of the Parque Nacional Nahuel Huapi, Av San Martín 24 (8am–4pm; ⓣ02944/423111), has pamphlets on all the sectors of the park.

Accommodation

During peak periods – mid-December to February, Easter, and July and August – it's best to reserve **accommodation** in advance. The *Albergue Patagonia Andina*, Morales 564 (ⓣ02944/422783, ⓔelalbergue@bariloche.com.ar; dorm beds AR$10, rooms AR$24), is a popular and pleasant **hostel** in the centre, though the double rooms are cramped. Facilities include Internet access, kitchen, laundry and luggage store. *Casa de Familia Arko*, at Guërres 691, Barrio Belgrano (ⓣ02944/423109; AR$12), is run by a helpful, multilingual couple who have exceptional regional historical and mountaineering knowledge. There's a luggage store, a kitchen, and space in the garden for tents.

Hostería El Ciervo Rojo Elflein 115 ⓣ&ⓕ02944/435241, ⓔciervorojo@mailcity.com. One of the best mid-range options, *El Ciervo Rojo* is a tastefully remodelled and centrally located townhouse that successfully fuses modest old-style charm with modern comforts. It has light and airy rooms, with continental breakfast included in the price. ❺

Hostería Güemes Güemes 715 ⓣ02944/424785. Some rooms at this simple, clean two-star lodging have private bathrooms; the use of a large living room is open to all. ❸

Hotel Edelweiss San Martín 202 ⓣ02944/426165, ⓔreservas@edelweiss.com.ar. A cultivated five-star hotel in the downtown area with lakeside views. All rooms come with private bath, plus there's an excellent restaurant and indoor pool. The service is attentive, and English is spoken. ❾

Hotel Milan Beschtedt 120 ⓣ02944/422624. A smart, modern hotel near the lakeside. Some rooms hold up to five people. ❺

Hotel Plaza Vice Almirante O'Connor 431 ⓣ & ⓕ02944/424100. Nothing flashy, but good value for its lakeside location and a simple breakfast is included in the price – served in the dining room, which has panoramic views over the lake. Popular with students, particularly in the winter. ❹

The Town

The **centro cívico**, dating from 1939, is a noble architectural statement of permanence: an ensemble of buildings constructed out of timber and local greenish-grey stone that are grouped around a plaza and resolutely face the lake. The Alpine design is the work of Ernesto de Estrada, who collaborated with Argentina's most famous architect, Alejandro Bustillo, in the development of a style that has come to represent the region. In the centre of the main plaza, around which these buildings are grouped, is an equestrian **statue** of General Roca, whose horse looks suitably hang-dog after the Campaign of the Desert. On the lake shore in front of the plaza is the **Puerto San Carlos**, where boats depart for various excursions across Nahuel Huapi. Of the attractions around the plaza, the most interesting is the **Museo de la Patagonia** (Mon & Sat 10am–1pm, Tues–Fri 10am–12.30pm & 2–7pm; AR$2.50), which rates as one of the very best museums in Patagonia. Running due east from *centro cívico* is Bariloche's main commercial street, the busy **Calle Mitre**, full of ice-cream parlours, shops selling regional smoked specialities and the much-lauded palaces devoted to chocoholics.

Restaurants, bars and clubs

El Boliche de Alberto Villegas 347 ⓣ02944/431433 and Bustillo 8800 (ⓣ02944/462285). The juiciest and largest *parrilla* in town: prepare to gorge yourself

Chachao Bistró Bustillo Km 3.8 ⓣ02944/520574. Fantastic little bistro specializing in cuisine inspired by pre-Columbian dishes.

Familia Weiss Palacios and O'Connor ⓣ02944/435788. Try the *ciervo a la cazadora* (venison in a creamy mushroom sauce) or a *picada* selection of smoked specialities. Evening shows range from salsa to cheesy Julio Iglesias covers. Open 8am–3am.

La Marmite Mitre 329 ⓣ02944/423685. The intimate, old-fashioned *La Marmite* is no bargain, but recommended for its regional and Swiss specialities, especially its fondues. Closed Sun lunch.

Vegetariano Elflein and Morales. Pleasant atmosphere, and well-prepared vegetarian and fish dishes.

El Viejo Matías Elflein 47 ⓣ&ⓕ02944/434466. A cheerful, no-frills eatery. *Tenedor libre* of *parrilla* with salads and dessert.

The Circuito Chico and Cerro Catedral

Bariloche's most popular excursion is along the **CIRCUITO CHICO**, a 65-kilometre circuit along the lakeshore to the west of town. You could join one of the organized tours (4hr) or visit the highlights via public transport. **Buses** (3 de Mayo) leave from the terminal and from Moreno and Rolando: #20 for Puerto Pañuelo and Llao Llao and #10 for Colonia Suiza. One of the attractions is the magnificent sight of the **Llao Llao**, Argentina's most famous hotel (ⓣ02944/448530, ⓔllaollao@datamarkets.com.ar; ⑨), from the very Germanic-looking timber Capilla San Eduardo (closed most of the time). Guarding the neck of the peninsula from its verdant knoll, the palatial hotel is sited like some country chateau, backed up by a centurion guard of mountains. Yet, despite the hotel's size, Alejandro Bustillo's alpine design sits harmoniously with the scene. State-owned until 1991, the place itself is now owned by a private company and can be visited as part of a **guided tour** (Thurs only, book in advance; ⓣ02944/445709). The wildest scenery of the circuit is found along the road that runs through the forested sector beyond *Llao Llao*.

Some 20km south of Bariloche, **CERRO CATEDRAL** is named after the Gothic spires of rock that make up this craggy massif's summits (2405m). In summer, the village of **Villa Catedral** at the foot of the bowl (just over 1000m) is the starting point for several fantastic treks, and you can take a cable car and then a chairlift to reach *Refugio Lynch* near the summit (1870m; AR$20). Views from here and from the ridge above are superb. In winter, the village serves the main ski resort, with amenities that include hotels, restaurants and shops offering ski rental.

There are 67km of pistes, and descents of up to 4km in length. July and August are the busiest months to visit. Buses (3 de Mayo) leave from Moreno 470 in Bariloche; you could also take a half-day organized trip to the village (4hr 30min; AR$15).

Crossing by boat into Chile from Bariloche

From Bariloche, you can reach Puerto Montt in Chile, making the spectacular journey across lagos Huapi, Frieas and Todos os Santos by boat and the in-between overland parts by bus. The trip, arranged by Catedral Turismo, Mitre 399 (ⓣ02944/425444, ⓔcattur@bariloche.com.ar), is quite spectacular and can be done in a day in spring and summer over 13.5 hours; alternatively there are two optional overnight stops on the way, at Petrohué and Peulla. The crossing costs around US$126, excluding overnight stops, and can be done in either direction.

Parque Nacional Nahuel Huapi

The mother of the Argentine national park system, **PARQUE NACIONAL NAHUEL HUAPI** protects a glorious chunk of the northern Patagonian cordillera and its neighbouring steppe. Most of the park falls within the watershed of **Lago Nahuel Huapi** (770m above sea level) and drains to the Atlantic. Of glacial origin, the lago is 557 square kilometres in area and forms the centrepiece of the park, with its peninsulas, islands and attenuated, fjord-like tentacles that sweep down from the thickly forested border region. Another important habitat is the high Alpine environment above the treeline, including some summits that retain snow all year round. The dominant massif of the park is an extinct volcano, **Cerro Tronador**, whose three peaks (all around 3500m) straddle the Argentine–Chilean border in the south. The "thundering" in its Spanish name does not refer to anything volcanic, but rather the echoing roar heard when vast chunks of ice break off its hanging glaciers and plunge down to impact on the slopes below.

Parque Nacional Nahuel Huapi is a famous and spectacular destination for hikers, and the **trekking season** is generally between December and March. All prospective trekkers should visit the **Club Andino Bariloche**, at 20 de Febrero 30, in Bariloche. Their information office and shop is in the wooden hut alongside the main building (Jan & Feb 9am–1pm & 4–9pm; rest of year 11am–1pm & 6–9pm; ⓣ02944 422266). They sell a series of trekking **maps**: the standard one is the *Carta de Refugios, Sendas y Picadas* (1:100,000), which has been expanded into three larger-scale (1:50,000) maps. These are very useful and include stage times, but the route descriptions are in Spanish only, and not all topographical details are accurate. Snow can occur into December and as early as March at higher altitudes: for this reason, it's not advisable to hike certain trails in the park outside the main high season. Average temperatures are 18°C in summer and 2°C in winter months. The strongest winds blow in spring, but these months otherwise make for a **good time to visit**, as do the calmer **autumn** months, when the deciduous trees wear their spectacular late-season colours.

Park practicalities

North to south, the park is divided into three zones. The **zone to the north** of Lago Nahuel Huapi centres around **Lago Traful**, but tends to be visited more for the Seven Lakes Route, which runs north from Villa La Angostura, passes through spectacular forested mountain scenery and enters the contiguous Parque Nacional Lanín before reaching San Martín de los Andes (see p.165). *Guardaparques* stationed at points along the way are helpful when it comes to recommending treks in their particular sectors. In the far south of this zone is the main overland pass through to Chile – **Paso Cardenal Samoré**, formerly called Paso Puyehue (Argentine immigration open 8am–8pm; Chilean side open 8am–7pm). The **central zone** is centred on Lago Nahuel Huapi itself, and embraces the "park within a park", Parque Nacional Los Arrayanes (see p.167) on the Península Quetrihué. Visits to this central zone are dependent, for the most part, on boat trips from Bariloche. One of these trips heads to **Isla Victoria**, the elongated, thickly forested island to the northwest. The focus of the **southern zone** is V-shaped **Lago Mascardi**, whose rock-fringed banks are popular with bathers and divers in the warmer months.

The three most important **hosterías** in the area are the *Posada Lago Hess* near the Cascada Los Alerces (reservations in Bariloche at Morales 439; ⓣ&ⓕ02944/462249, ⓔpiccino@bariloche.com.ar; ❻); the upmarket *Hotel Tronador*, at the northwestern end of hook-shaped Lago Mascardi (ⓣ02944/468127; ❽, half board); and *Hostería Pampa Linda*, at the base of Tronador (ⓣ02944/442038; ❺). There are also **campsites** at all major destinations: *Lago Roca* near the Cascada Los Alerces (AR$3 per person), *Los Rápidos* (ⓣ02944/461861; AR$3 per person) and *La Querencia* (ⓣ02944/426225; AR$6 per person) at Lago Mascardi and *Pampa Linda* (AR$3 per person). Check, too, with the Intendencia in Bariloche as to the current status of the other authorized sites.

Esquel

For a place so close to the exuberant Andean forests of Parque Nacional Los Alerces, **ESQUEL**, 340km south of Bariloche, can surprise you on arrival for the aridity of its setting. Enclosed in a bowl of dusty ochre mountains, it has something of the feel of a cowboy town, but a pleasant one nonetheless. The reason why most people make the trip to Esquel, however, is to visit the nearby **Parque Nacional Los Alerces**, with the trip on the Trochita (see box) as the next biggest attraction.

Practicalities

The town's **airport** is 21km east of the centre; Esquel Tours, Fontana 754 (ⓣ02945/452704), runs minibus services. The **bus terminal** is handily situated in the centre of town, on the corner of Fontana and the main boulevard, **Avenida Alvear**. The *La Trochita* **train station** (see box) is at Roggero and Brun, nine blocks northeast of the terminal. The proficient **tourist office** is 100m to the right of the bus terminal, just past the post office, at Av Alvear y Sarmiento (March–Nov Mon–Sat 7.30am–8pm; Dec also Sun 9am–noon & 4–7pm; Jan & Feb daily 7.30am–10.30am; ⓣ&ⓕ02945/451927, ⓦwww.esquel.gov.ar).

La Trochita: the Old Patagonian Express

A trip on the **Old Patagonian Express** is one of South America's classic train journeys. This steam train puffs, judders and lurches across the arid, rolling steppe of northern Chubut between Esquel and El Maitén, like a drunk on the well-worn route home, running on a track with a gauge of a mere 75cm. You'll see guanacos, rheas, hares and even condors as you pass through the giant estate of Estancia Leleque.

Referred to as **La Trochita**, the line was closed in 1993, but the Province took over the running of the 165km section between Esquel and El Maitén soon thereafter, and its future now seems secure. *La Trochita* is not only a tourist train but the only means of transport for locals living in isolated outposts along the line. For most people, a trip on *La Trochita* means the half-day trip from Esquel to Nahuel Pan, 22km away (high season Mon–Wed, Fri & Sat 10am & 2pm; rest of year Sat only same times; 2hr; AR$15; further information on ⓣ02945/451403).

If you need a **place to stay**, *Sol del Sur*, 9 de Julio 1086 (Ⓣ&Ⓕ02945/452189; ❹), is the best of the three-stars, with fairly standard amenities. It has spacious bathrooms, and breakfast is included – but mind the step by the lift. *Hostería Arrayán*, Antártida Argentina 767 (Ⓣ02945/451051; ❸), is a tidy place with personable atmosphere that's worth the extra walk from the centre, while *Argentino*, 25 de Mayo 862 (Ⓣ02945/452237; ❷), is a basic budget hotel popular with young party crowd that gets noisy in the evenings owing to a pumping bar. *Lago Verde*, Volta 1081 (Ⓣ02945/452251, Ⓔlagoverd@hostels.org.ar; ❷), run by a hard-working family who speak English, is a peaceful, welcoming home with spotless little rooms and a small garden, which honours a hostelling price (AR$11) for those with HI cards, but otherwise charges a standard hotel rate. Reserve in advance in high season.

Eating options consist of *Cassis*, Sarmiento 120 (Ⓣ02945/450576), the best cuisine in town offering succulent Patagonian specialities, such as trout and lamb, from 9pm. *Don Chiquino*, 9 de Julio 964 (Ⓣ02945/451508), features Italian food in a cosy atmosphere yet is always packed in season, while *El Lomo del Abuelo*, Av Alvear 1360, is popular for straightforward pasta, *milanesas* and pizzas, with the emphasis on value for money. *La Trochita*, 25 de Mayo 633, is a good bet for carnivores, with a *parrilla* on the go, while *La Tour D'Argent*, San Martín 1063, serves cheap and filling tourist menus of pastas and chicken. More adventurous, appetizing à la carte selection includes trout with cheese and mushrooms (AR$13). Closed Tues lunch.

Parque Nacional Los Alerces

Established in 1937, the big **PARQUE NACIONAL LOS ALERCES**, some 30km west of Esquel, protects some of the most biologically important habitats and scenic landscapes of the central Patagonian cordillera. Its lakes are famous for both their rich colours and their fishing; while most have a backdrop of sumptuous forests that quilt the surrounding mountain slopes. In the northeast of the park these lakes form a network, centring on **Lagos Rivadavia**, **Menéndez** and **Futalaufquen**, whose waters drain south to the dammed reservoir of **Lago Amutui Quimei**, and from here into the Río Futaleufú (or Río Grande).

As in other parks in this region, the vegetation changes considerably as you move east from the Chilean border into the area affected by the rain shadow cast by the cordillera. Up against the border, rainfall exceeds 3000mm a year, enough to support the growth of dense **Valdivian temperate rainforest**, and most particularly the species for which the park is named: the **alerce.** This is one of the oldest species of tree in the world, some of them have been living for over four thousand years. The **northeastern section** of the park is the most interesting for the visitor, especially around the area of beautiful **Lago Verde**, which works as a useful base for camping and trekking. The must-see of the park, irrespective of time or budgetary concerns, is the transcendental **Río Arrayanes** that drains Lagos Menéndez and Verde. A **pasarela**, or suspension bridge, 34km from the Intendencia, offers access to a delightful hour-long loop walk that takes you along the riverbank to Puerto Chucao. Another highlight – unless the weather really closes in and is only for those whose budget allows – is the trip from Puerto Chucao across Menéndez to see **El Abuelo**, a titanic millennial *alerce*.

There are 130km of public trails in the park, which are generally well maintained and marked at intervals with red spots. For several you are required you to **register** with the nearest *guardaparque* before setting off (remember to check back in afterwards). In times of drought, some trails are closed, while others must be undertaken only with a guide.

Park practicalities

Los Alerces is fast growing more popular as holiday-makers explore further afield from the often saturated Bariloche area. If possible, visit the park off-peak: **March and April** are perhaps the best months, as the deciduous trees put on a blaze of colour; but spring (October and November) is also very beautiful, if subject to some fierce winds. Year-round access is possible, although the main route through the park, the RP71, can, on rare occasions, be cut off by snow for a day or so. If you come in winter, remember that many places close outside the fishing season (mid-Nov to Easter), so you'll have to be more self-sufficient.

Entrance to the park costs AR$12. Those who don't have their own transport can get around the park with Transportes Esquel (ⓣ02945/453529), which has a twice-daily service along the RP71 in summer. Plans to pave the RP71 from the Futalaufquen lakehead to Rivadavia have been thwarted up to now by budgetary and environmental concerns: walk this road in summer and you'll get coated in dust from passing vehicles. Set on manicured lawns alongside the bus stop in **Villa Futalaufquen** is the Intendencia (ⓣ02945/471020; open daily 8am–2pm); the **visitors' centre** here (daily Easter–Nov 9am–1pm; Dec–Easter 8am–9pm) is staffed by volunteers who give information on hikes and fishing, and sell fishing permits. They'll give you a useful map marking the myriad campsites and lodgings in the park, and up-to-date prices per person. There is a good range of services in the village – including a fuel station, post office and general stores – but it's much cheaper to pick up everything you need in Esquel.

In season, you have a wide choice of **accommodation** in the park, especially along Lago Futalaufquen's easternshore. Just over 4km north of the Intendencia, 400m beyond Puerto Limonao, is the *Hostería Futalaufquen* (ⓣ02945/471008; ❽; closed Easter–Sept), a solid, granite-block and log lodge designed by Bustillo. It's in an attractive setting by the lake, but the atmosphere is spoilt somewhat by the "ambient" piped music; the restaurant has a limited choice and is overpriced. On the easternshore of Futalaufquen from the Intendencia is *Hostería Quimei Quipan* (ⓣ02945/454134; ❼ for six people). *Los Maitenes* (ⓣ02945/451003; AR$4 per person plus AR$5 one-off tent charge; closed Easter to mid-Nov) is the closest **campsite** to Villa Futalaufquen (400m from the Intendencia) and is generally good, although packed.

1.7

Argentine Patagonia

As a place of extreme contrasts, **PATAGONIA** has few equals in the world: from the biting winds that howl off the gigantic Southern Patagonian Icecap to the comforting warmth of Patagonian hospitality; from the lowest point on the South American continent, the Gran Bajo de San Julián, to the high peaks of the **Fitz Roy Massif**. Allow time to see the world-famous wildlife reserve at **Península Valdés**, usually accessed from the seaside town of **Puerto Madryn**; to investigate Patagonia's Welsh legacy in the Chubut valley near **Trelew**; and to break the journey south with a stopover in beautiful **Puerto Deseado**, blessed by significant populations of marine wildlife. The region's principal artery, the RN3, runs south from the historic town of Carmen de Patagones all the way to **Río Gallegos**, providing access to the vast central steppe, a desiccated area, covered by tough *coirón* grassland and scrub. The second main route is the **RN40**, which runs parallel to the Andes. Two of the region's star attractions, a long way south, are the trekkers' and climbers' paradise of the **Fitz Roy** sector of the **Parque Nacional Los Glaciares**, accessed from El Chaltén; and the craggy blue face of the **Glacier Perito Moreno**, regularly cited as one of the world's natural wonders, situated near the town of El Calafate.

High season runs from December to the end of February, but March and April can be the most rewarding months for travel: you'll avoid the crowds, while the Patagonian forests assume their autumnal colours and the winds drop. It is worth noting that a group of estancia owners runs the Estancias de Santa Cruz, which produces an excellent booklet promoting their establishments, available at Suipacha 1120, Buenos Aires (Ⓣ&Ⓕ011/5325 3098, Ⓦwww.estanciasdesantacruz.com). Room prices are generally too high for budget travellers, although some places also run campsites on their land.

Puerto Madryn

Spread out along the beautiful sweep of the Golfo Nuevo Bay, the neat town of **PUERTO MADRYN** is promoted as a Patagonian **summer resort**, centred along a fun beachfront boulevard, though its real pull is as a base for trips to the ecological treasure-trove of the Península Valdés.

Arrival and information

The new El Telhuelche **airport** (served by Lapa, Lade and American Falcon airlines with flights to Buenos Aires and one or two other destinations) lies 7km to the west, and a taxi to the town centre should come to around AR$9. Madryn's **bus terminal** can be found in one of the town's most attractive buildings, the old train station of 1889. From here, the **tourist office** is only five or six blocks away, at Avenida Julio Roca 223 (Jan & Feb daily 7am–1am; March–Dec Mon–Fri 7am–2pm & 3–9pm, Sat & Sun 8.30am–8.30pm; Ⓣ&Ⓕ02965/453504 or 452148, Ⓦwww.madryn.gov.ar).

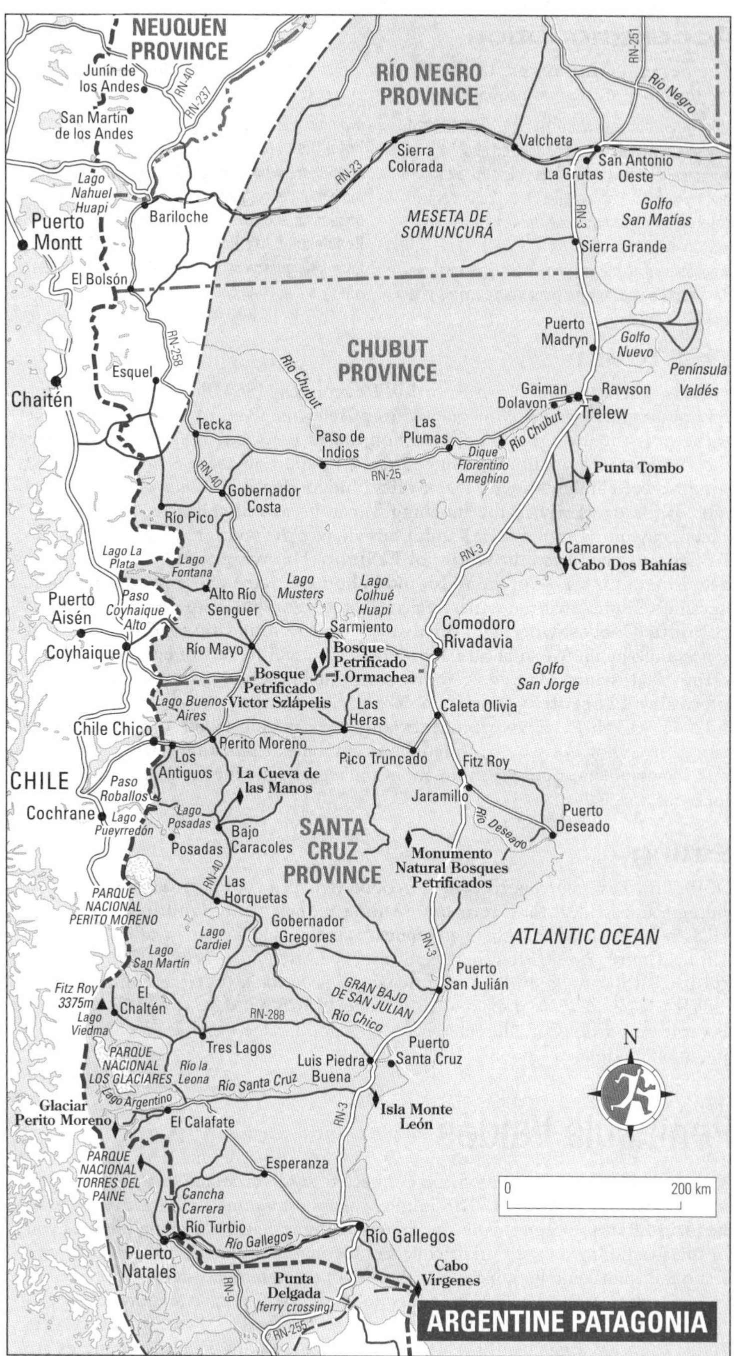
ARGENTINE PATAGONIA
NEUQUÉN PROVINCE
RÍO NEGRO PROVINCE
CHUBUT PROVINCE
SANTA CRUZ PROVINCE
CHILE
ATLANTIC OCEAN
Junín de los Andes
San Martín de los Andes
RN-40
RN-237
Lago Nahuel Huapi
Puerto Montt
Bariloche
El Bolsón
RN-258
Esquel
Chaitén
Sierra Colorada
RN-23
Valcheta
RN-251
Río Negro
San Antonio Oeste
La Grutas
RN-3
Golfo San Matías
MESETA DE SOMUNCURÁ
Sierra Grande
Puerto Madryn
Golfo Nuevo
Península Valdés
Río Chubut
Gaiman
Dolavon
Rawson
Trelew
Tecka
Paso de Indios
Las Plumas
Dique Florentino Ameghino
RN-25
Punta Tombo
Gobernador Costa
Río Pico
Camarones
Cabo Dos Bahías
Lago La Plata
Lago Fontana
Alto Río Senguer
Lago Musters
Lago Colhué Huapi
Sarmiento
Comodoro Rivadavia
Puerto Aisén
Paso Coyhaique Alto
Coyhaique
Río Mayo
Bosque Petrificado J.Ormachea
Bosque Petrificado Victor Szlápelis
Golfo San Jorge
Lago Buenos Aires
Las Heras
Caleta Olivia
Chile Chico
Perito Moreno
Pico Truncado
Los Antiguos
La Cueva de las Manos
Fitz Roy
Jaramillo
Río Deseado
Puerto Deseado
Paso Roballos
Cochrane
Lago Pueyrredón
Lago Posadas
Posadas
Bajo Caracoles
Monumento Natural Bosques Petrificados
PARQUE NACIONAL PERITO MORENO
Las Horquetas
Gobernador Gregores
Lago Cardiel
Lago San Martín
Puerto San Julián
GRAN BAJO DE SAN JULIAN
Río Chico
Fitz Roy 3375m
El Chaltén
Lago Viedma
RN-288
Tres Lagos
PARQUE NACIONAL LOS GLACIARES
Río la Leona
Río Santa Cruz
Luis Piedra Buena
Puerto Santa Cruz
N
Lago Argentino
Glaciar Perito Moreno
El Calafate
Isla Monte León
PARQUE NACIONAL TORRES DEL PAINE
Esperanza
0
200 km
Cancha Carrera
Río Turbio
Río Gallegos
Puerto Natales
RN-9
Punta Delgada (ferry crossing)
Cabo Vírgenes
RN-255

Accommodation

The nearest **campsites** are by the El Indio statue, round the bay (*colectivo* #2 from the terminal or the main square will take you to within easy walking distance).

Albergue Huefur B. Mitre 798 ⓣ02965/453224, ⓔhuefur245@hotmail.com. Relaxed and recommended hostel, with free pick-up, plus laundry and cooking facilities. AR$12 per person.

Hotel Aguas Mansas José Hernández 51 ⓣ&ⓕ02965/473103, ⓔaguasmansa@cpsarg.com. Warm, pricey three-star near the beach, with comfortable rooms and a swimming pool. ❹

Hotel Bahía Nueva Roca 67 ⓣ&ⓕ02965/451677 or 450045, ⓔhotel@bahianueva.com.ar. A smart, modern hotel on the seafront with ample buffet breakfasts and covered parking. ❺

Residencial Jo's Bolivar 75 ⓣ02965/471433. Cosy little guesthouse with good prices for singles, run by a charming couple. ❸

The Town

The site where the Welsh first landed in Patagonia in 1865, Puerto Madryn didn't develop until the arrival of the railway from Trelew in 1889, when it began to serve as the port for the agricultural communities in the Chubut Valley. Madryn has experienced very rapid growth since the 1970s and now rates as one of the most important of Chubut's towns. The **Golfo Nuevo Bay** is best seen at the opposite ends of the day. Early in the morning, it can be as still and glassy smooth as a millpond, while at sunset there's a glorious view of the wide arc of the gulf back to the lights of town from the **statue of El Indio**. This was placed here to mark the centenary of the arrival of the Welsh and in homage to the native Tehuelche whose assistance ensured that the settlers survived. Just before the statue, a signpost points to **Punta Cuevas**, where the three-metre-square foundations of the very first houses built by the Welsh lie, just above the high-water mark. Just beyond it, at Julio Verne 3784, stands Madryn's newest and most impressive attraction, the highly informative **Ecocentro** (Thurs–Sun 3-7pm; closed first two weeks of June; AR$8; ⓣ02965/457470–3, ⓦwww.ecocentro.org.ar). Enjoying fabulous bay views and housed in a glorious wooden building, it combines fascinating scientific displays with hands-on, interactive sections about the region's marine fauna. The cafeteria is gorgeous, too.

Eating

Of the town's restaurants *El Barco*, on Boulevard Brown, Punta Cuevas, is one of the best and is ideal for a romantic seafood dinner: a meal with wine will cost AR$15–20 per head, and there are delicious paellas and a mixed seafood grill that will feed three. Even better, but relatively expensive, *Taska Beltza*, 9 de Julio 345 (ⓣ02965/1566-8085), does a mouth-watering *merluza* (hake) accompanied by chilled Chablis. *Café de la Ciudad*, 28 de Julio and 25 de Mayo (ⓣ02965/455783), serves large portions of affordable pasta or a good-value *menú del día*, served in a fun, unpretentious café popular with the locals.

Península Valdés

A sandy-beige, treeless hump of land connected to the mainland by a 35-kilometre isthmus, **PENÍNSULA VALDÉS** is one of the most significant marine reserves on the planet. Except in spring, the land here is extremely arid – nothing prepares you for the astonishing diversity and richness of the marine environment that surrounds it, and the animal colonies that live at the feet of the peninsula's steep, unstable cliffs.

Most **tours to the Península Valdés** follow a standard route, visiting the look-out point for Isla de los Pájaros, Puerto Pirámides, Punta Delgada and/or Caleta Valdés. Tours are long (10–12hr), so bring picnic provisions. The best **agencies** are

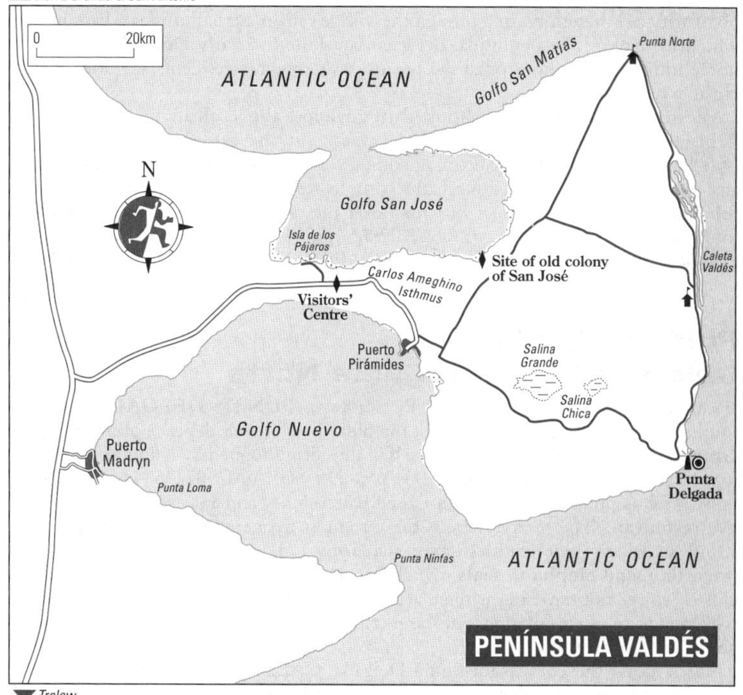

found in Puerto Madryn and include Tito Bottazzi, Mitre 80 (☎02965/474110); South Patagonia, 25 de Mayo 226 (☎02965/455053); Argentina Vision, Roca 536 (☎02965/451427); Nievemar at Roca 549 (☎02965/455544); and Sur Turismo, Roca and Sáenz Peña (☎02965/455714) – all have tours for around AR$60. Agencies also offer tours to the penguin colony at Punta Tombo, but it's better to arrange these in Trelew, which is much closer.

If you want to visit the peninsula independently, the 28 de Julio **bus service** links Madryn with Puerto Pirámides (Nov–Easter: Tues, Thurs, Sat & Sun, and twice daily in Jan; Easter–Oct: Thurs & Sun; AR$5). On days when there's no bus, Dino Ramírez runs a service with his traffic minibus (☎02965/454413 or 473988). The most flexible way to see the peninsula, however, is to **rent a car** – quite affordable for groups, especially if you look for unlimited mileage offers – try Localiza at Roca 536 (☎02965/456300). A word of warning, however: **do not rush** – serious crashes and fatalities happen with alarming regularity on the peninsula, especially after rain. There's a huge excess on rental cars in case of overturning and, more importantly, it'll be hours before they can get you to hospital in the only (primitive) ambulance available.

Puerto Pirámides

Some 75km out of Madryn, after entering the **reserve** (AR$7) and crossing the isthmus, you pass a signposted turn-off north that takes you 5km to the lookout point for the **Isla de los Pájaros** (Bird Island), a strictly controlled area where access is only permitted for the purposes of scientific research. At the end of the asphalt road, 105km from Madryn, lies the tiny settlement of

PUERTO PIRÁMIDES. It has an attractive fringe of sand and is growing in popularity as a **beach resort**, though the village's main attraction is as a base from which to explore the peninsula. Between late June and early December it's also home to the most famous of all the peninsula's temporary residents, the **southern right whales**.

Accommodation is best booked in advance, above all in the January to February peak season. *Hostería The Paradise*, at the far end of the village (Ⓣ02965/495030, Ⓔparadise@satlink.com; ❺), is the most luxurious option, with airy, modern rooms and en-suite bathrooms. Its restaurant serves well-priced fresh fish and pasta till late. *Cabañas El Cristal* over the road has small cabins for two to four people, also with sea views (Ⓣ&Ⓕ02965/495033; ❹). Budget options include *Hospedaje Médanos* across the road (Ⓣ02965/495032; ❷), whose double room will sleep three for the same price.

Punta Delgada, Caleta Valdés and Punta Norte

It's another 70km on from Puerto Pirámides to **PUNTA DELGADA**, at the southeasterly tip of the peninsula, past the pinkish-white salt deposits of the **Salina Grande** depression. Punta Delgada itself is a headland topped by a lighthouse next to which are an upmarket **hotel**, *Faro Punta Delgada*, (Ⓣ02965/458444 or 1540-6304, Ⓔfaro@puntadelgada.com; ❺ closed Easter–June), and a decent if unimaginative **restaurant**. The reserve here is the one most frequented by tour groups and affords excellent opportunities to see **sea lions** and, in high season, a colony of seven thousand **elephant seals**, which lie on the beach at the foot of the high cliffs. If you're not travelling with an accredited guide, time your arrival to coincide with one of the free, escorted, one-hour trips to the beach – you're not allowed to go unaccompanied.

North along the coast from Punta Delgada, **CALETA VALDÉS** (8am–8pm; closed for two months after Easter) is elephant seal heaven. The best time to visit is from late September until early November, when the bull elephant seals face off and slam their blubbery bulks together like overweight armless wrestlers, trying to impress the largely uninterested females. For the rest of the year, they're likely to be fairly inactive, lying dolloped on the shingle like grey sausage-skins stuffed with silicone. From September to November, killer whales (*orcas*) may be sighted off Caleta.

The road north to wild **PUNTA NORTE** can get very rough if the levelling machines haven't passed recently, and very muddy if it has recently rained. It's famous for the **killer whale attacks** on baby sea lions during March and April. These remarkable events are rare, and the attack channels where they occur are mostly quite a distance from the public viewing points. To stand even a chance of witnessing an attack, time your arrival to coincide with the hour either side of high tide, but the scenery at low tide is also very beautiful. There's a **café** where the personable owner prepares filling snacks and an interesting visitors' centre and **museum**.

Trelew and the Welsh villages

The Welsh of Chubut, like the indigenous Tehuelche, have been absorbed almost seamlessly into the diverse cultural hybrid that is Argentina. Under the surface, however, there remain vestiges of the pioneering culture as well as a real pride in the historical legacy and the current cultural connection that goes well beyond the touristy trappings. Halting Welsh is still spoken by some of the third- or fourth-generation residents in **Trelew** and **Gaiman**, even if it isn't the language of common usage and, whereas it once seemed doomed to die out, the tongue now appears to be enjoying a limited renaissance.

Trelew

An industrial and commercial centre, **TRELEW** is also the self-proclaimed "Capital of the Penguin" – not because it has any of these birds but thanks to its relative proximity to the famous penguin colony at Punta Tombo (see p.180). Its urban centrepiece is its beautiful main square, the **Plaza de la Independencia**, with flourishing trees and an elegant gazebo, built by the Welsh to honour the centenary of Argentine Independence. In the second half of October, the most important of the province's **eisteddfodau** (Welsh folk festivals) is celebrated here. Trelew's name, in Welsh, means the "Village of Lewis", in honour of Lewis Jones, its founder. The settlement rose to prominence after the completion, in 1889, of the rail link to Puerto Madryn, which allowed easy export of the burgeoning agricultural yields. The railway has since disappeared, and the old station, on 9 de Julio and Fontana, is now used to house the **Museo Regional Pueblo de Lewis** (Mon–Fri 8am–8pm; Sat & Sun 5–8pm; AR$2). One of two fine museums in Trelew, it contains some illuminating exhibits on the coexistence of the Welsh and the Tehuelche, some gruesome photos of the sea lion hunt at Punta Norte on the Península Valdés and items on the Eisteddfodau. Across the road is the excellent modern **Museo Paleontológico Egidio Feruglio**, Fontana and Lewis Jones (Mon–Fri 10am–6pm, Sat & Sun 10am–8pm; AR$8), one of South America's most important paleontological collections, which contains rarities like beautifully preserved clutches of dinosaur eggs and skeletons from the region.

Practicalities

Trelew's **airport** is situated 5km northeast from the town. Taxis cost AR$8 to the town centre. The **bus terminal** is centrally located, and Mar y Valle buses head to Puerto Madryn via the airport every hour; 28 de Julio buses depart for Gaiman and Dolavon every half-hour and for the full provincial capital, Rawson, every fifteen minutes. The helpful main **tourist office** is at San Martín 171 (Mon–Fri 8am–8pm, Sat 10am–1pm & 6–8pm; Ⓣ&Ⓕ02965/420139).

The least expensive **accommodation** in town, *Hotel Avenida,* Lewis Jones 49 (Ⓣ02965/434172; ❷), is good for single budget travellers. It is friendly and well situated but spartan with shared bathrooms. *Hotel Rayentray*, San Martín 101 (Ⓣ02965/434702; ❹) is very 1970s in style, but upper rooms have bathtubs and good city views. It's also equipped with swimming pool, gym and sauna. *Residencial Rivadavia*, Rivadavia 55 (Ⓣ02965/434472; ❸), has clean, centrally heated rooms.

El Viejo Molino, Avenida Gales 250, is a renovated mill hosting concerts and cultural events, and a civilized place to enjoy a coffee, a Welsh tea or a delicious **meal** at moderate prices.

Gaiman

Leaving Trelew, the RN25 strikes west for 16km, before coming to the most frequently visited of the Welsh villages, **GAIMAN**, lying among poplar trees in the irrigated centre of the valley and full of **tearooms** (*casas de té*) and other memorials to its Celtic heritage. Gaiman hosts mini **eisteddfodau** in mid-September and the first week of May. Gaiman's most individual and surprising monument has nothing whatever to do with tradition, Welsh or otherwise. **El Desafío** ("The Challenge"; daily 10–6pm; AR$5), on Almirante Brown, is a backyard where **tin cans** and plastic bottles have been recycled and reincarnated: "A place where rubbish is beauty, and perhaps even art."

Practicalities

The **bus** from Trelew stops outside the **tourist office** (Mon–Fri 8am–3pm, Sun 3–7pm; Aug–March daily 8am–6pm; Ⓣ02965/491152) in the Casa de Cultura on the corner of Rivadavia and Belgrano, one block up from the modest main street, Avenida Tello.

If you want **to stay** here, there are a couple of decent choices. The *Plas y Coed casa de té*, on the main square (T&F 02965/491133; ❸ with huge breakfast), offers upstairs rooms with private bathroom, and there's a spacious living room for guests. Otherwise, try the *Hostería Gwesty Tywi*, at Miguel Jones 342 (T&F 02965/491292, E gwestywi@infovia.com.ar; ❸, ❹ with private bathroom), an immaculately clean bed and breakfast. There's also an inexpensive **campsite**, Los Doce Nogales, across the river to the southeast, near the Ty Té Caerdydd teahouse.

The **casas de té** in Gaiman do a thriving trade – some of them are owned and run by descendants of the original Welsh settlers, and all serve similar arrays of cake, toast, scones and home-made jam (AR$10–15 per person). The most typical cake of all is the *torta negra* (Welsh black cake). *Ty Nain*, H. Irigoyen 283 (closed May and June), is one of the most authentic, and bang in the centre, next to the plaza; have tea surrounded by the mementoes of the owners' museum.

Punta Tombo

From Trelew it's around 360km south along a paved road to Comodoro Rivadavia. En route, it's worth making a side-trips to the coastal nature reserve of **Punta Tombo**, the largest single colony of black and white **Magellanic penguins** (or any variety, in fact) on the continent, with a population of more than a million birds. It's an unmissable experience to wander around this scrubland avian metropolis amid an urban cacophony of braying, surrounded on all sides by waddling clowns as they totter about their business. The penguins nest behind the beach in scrapes underneath the bushes, eyeing you as you approach. Entry to the reserve costs AR$12, and any time between August and early April is a good time to visit, although **November** is the best month of all, as there are plenty of young chicks.

Southern Chubut and northern Santa Cruz

Encompassing some pretty dreary towns and some of the most desolate scenery in the whole of the country, the region along this stretch of the RN3 possesses two natural gems: the **Río Deseado estuary** at **Puerto Deseado**, with its beautiful porphyry cliffs and tremendous opportunities to view photogenic wildlife at close quarters, and the tremendous trunks of fossilized araucaria monkey puzzles in the **Monumento Natural Bosques Petrificados**.

The largest of all Patagonian towns, with a population of 130,000, **Comodoro Rivadavia** is not a place you're likely to want to stay for longer than it takes to make your bus connection; the bus terminal is slap-bang in the centre. Leaving the terminal, walk one block towards Cerro Chenque to reach the main thoroughfare, Avenida Rivadavia, with the helpful tourist office, half a block away at no. 430 (daily mid-March to mid-Dec 8am–5pm; mid-Dec to mid-March 8am–9pm; T 0297/446-2376).

Puerto Deseado

PUERTO DESEADO, a straggly but engaging fishing port on the estuary of the Río Deseado, is blessed with spectacular coastal scenery and some remarkable colonies of marine wildlife that thrive within sight of the town. A bus service connects the town with Caleta Olivia, but Deseado's **bus terminal** is inconveniently sited at the far end of town. Try to disembark in the centre or, if leaving town, flag down the bus as it passes along Avenida España. The **tourist office** is at San Martín 1120 (Dec–Easter 9am–9pm; Easter–Nov 9am–4pm; T 0297/487-2261, E turismo@pdeseado.com.ar). The staff will give you a useful town plan.

The cheapest **accommodation** is the clean *Albergue Municipal "La Ría"* (☎0297/487-0260; ③, or AR$10 per person in twelve-bed dorms), in the *gimnasio* on Colón and Belgrano, near the Museo Regional. Two upper-end hotels are *Isla Chaffers*, bang in the centre of town on San Martín and Moreno (☎&Ⓕ0297/487-2246; ④); and, occupying the bluff as you come into town, the better *Los Acantilados* (☎&Ⓕ0297/487-2167 or 487-2007; ⑤), at España and Pueyrredón, whose comfortable rooms command estuary views. Always full of locals, the best **restaurant** in town is *El Pingüino*, Piedrabuena 958 (closed Thurs), with prompt, cheerful service. The *platos del día* are excellent value, and the *pejerrey* fish is always extremely fresh.

The Ría Deseado

Stretching 42km inland from Puerto Deseado is the **Ría Deseado** (Deseado Estuary), an astonishing sunken river valley, flooded by the sea. Opposite the town, its purple cliffs are smeared with guano from five different types of **cormorant**. Most **trips** round the estuary stop at the **Isla de los Pájaros** (Bird Island), so passengers can disembark and photograph the penguins. If the tide is high, they enter the **Cañon Torcida**, a narrow and steep-sided channel of the estuary. Tours, lasting around two hours, leave from the pier at the entrance to town and tend to depart at 10am and 3pm; morning ones are generally better for the light. In summer, later evening tours are also excellent. Arrange them with Darwin Expediciones (at their office on the pier or on ☎0297/1562-47554). They also have other interesting options, the most regular of which is the "Ruta de Darwin" day excursion, retracing the journey made by the scientist in 1834 to the end of the submerged estuary.

The Monumento Natural Bosques Petrificados

The **Monumento Natural Bosques Petrificados** (8am–8pm; free) is found down a branch road 50km off the RN3, some 256km from Puerto Deseado and 280km north of San Julián. The sheer magnitude of the **fossilized trunks** here is astonishing, measuring some 35m long and up to 3m wide. The primeval Jurassic forest grew here 150 million years ago – sixty million years before the Andean cordillera was forced up, forming the rain barrier that has such a dramatic effect on the scenery we know now. **Day-trips** to the park can be organized with travel agents from Comodoro or Puerto Deseado – ask at the respective tourist offices. You're not permitted to pitch a tent in the park; the only **camping** nearby is at La Paloma, 24km before the administration (☎0297/444-3503; AR$5 per person). Otherwise, the best option is to continue on to San Julián or Puerto Deseado.

Río Gallegos

Few people hang around long in the provincial capital, **RÍO GALLEGOS**, heading out instead to Calafate, south to Ushuaia or northwards with as little delay as possible. However, one thing that does attract people to Gallegos from as far away as North America, Europe and Japan, is its incredible **fly fishing**. As with the Río Grande in Tierra del Fuego (see p.687), the **Río Gallegos** (the river that the town is named after) is the haunt of some of the most spectacularly sized, sea-going **brown trout** anywhere in the world.

Practicalities

The town's **airport** is 5km west of the bus terminal, 7km from the town. A taxi into town will cost around AR$7; there are no buses to the town centre, though (perversely) you can take a bus to El Calafate, some 300km away. From the **bus terminal**, situated near the edge of town on the RN3, it's best to take a cab the

2km into the centre; alternatively, buses #1 or #12 will drop you in Avenida Roca in the heart of town. The **provincial tourist office** is at Roca 863 (Easter–Oct Mon–Fri 9am–8pm; Nov–Easter Mon–Fri 9am–9pm, Sat & Sun 10am–8pm; ⓣ02966/422702, ⓦwww.scruz.gov.ar/turismo).

If you plan **to stay**, *Sehuen*, Rawson 160 (ⓣ02966/425683; ❹), is Gallegos' best hotel, a refreshing combination of bright, modern rooms and economical prices. It has en-suite bathrooms with bath and good shower. *Santa Cruz*, Roca 701 (ⓣ02966/420601, ⓔhtlscruz@infovia.com.ar; ❹), is very central and clean, with cable TV, cramped bathrooms and a restaurant.

El Horreo, Roca 862 (02966/426462; open till 1.30am), is a popular **place to eat** bang in the centre, in the attractive Casa España. It has good wood-fired pizzas and Iberian dishes, including *pollo a la portuguesa* (chicken in a pepper sauce). *El Ancla*, at Magallanes 353, serves delicious à la carte seafood. Try the *cazuela de marisco* (AR$10) or the sea bass, *róbalo con roquefort*. For well-priced and imaginative food, head to *Club Británico* Roca 935. Its *pulpo en escabeche* (marinated octopus) is just one dish that will excite a jaded palate. The bar remains the favoured hangout for the declining community of those of British descent.

Crossing into Chile and the Tierra del Fuego

It can take up to a day to get from Río Gallegos to San Sebastían, the first settlement in Argentine Tierra del Fuego (see p.189), a journey that involves crossing two borders and the Magellan Straits. The **Monte Aymond border crossing** is 67km south of Gallegos. Formalities are fairly straightforward, but don't try to bring fresh vegetables, fruit or meat products into Chile, as they'll be confiscated. On the Chilean side, the road improves and heads to **Punta Arenas** (see p.566) and **Puerto Natales** (see p.570). Alternatively, you can make for **Tierra del Fuego** by turning onto the RN257 at Kimiri Aike, 42km from the border. This takes you to the Primera Angostura (the First Narrows) of the straits, and the Punta Delgada **ferry** that plies across them (see p.189). Heading for Ushuaia (see p.189), the road then crosses Chilean Tierra del Fuego to the border settlements of San Sebastián.

Perito Moreno and around

With a whopping 3000 inhabitants, **PERITO MORENO** is the most populous town for miles around. It's a typically featureless, spread-out Patagonian settlement, built on a grid system and is of use to the visitor only as a base for excursions to the Cueva de las Manos, or for its transport services to Posadas, along the RN40, and to the Chilean border at Los Antiguos and Chile Chico.

The new **bus terminal** is located to the north of town on the RP43, by the Eg3 fuel station. **Accommodation** is overpriced, especially for single rooms. The only places in town that offer reasonable value for money are the homely bed and breakfast, the *Posada del Caminante* (ⓣ02963/432204, ⓔmatejedor@interlap.com.ar; ❹) at Rivadavia 937, and the sociable municipal **campsite**, conveniently situated a few minutes' walk south from the centre along Avenida San Martín. The site also has a couple of **cabins** for hire – the cheapest option in town for those with sleeping bags but without tents. For those heading south, Perito Moreno is the best place until El Calafate to stock up on **food** and **cash**. If heading into Chile, change excess Argentine pesos into dollars, as these get better rates across the border.

△ The pampa plains

South to the Cueva de las Manos Pintadas

Follow the RN40 south of Perito Moreno to reach the turn-off to Estancia Telken (open Sept–April; ⓣ02963/432079; ❼), renowned for the hospitable welcome offered by its owners. This is one of the best estancias to visit for a taste of what it means to live on a working ranch. As with other farms in the area, it was particularly hard hit by the explosion of Volcán Hudson in 1991.

The **CUEVA DE LAS MANOS PINTADAS** (Cave of the Painted Hands) can be approached either via 45km of gravel road from Bajo Caracoles or, better, by walking or riding up the canyon it overlooks, the impressive **Cañón de Río Pinturas**. The *cueva* itself is less a cave than a series of overhangs: natural cutaways at the foot of a towering ninety-metre cliff face overlooking the canyon below. The collage of black, white, red and ochre **handprints**, mixed with gracefully flowing vignettes of guanaco hunts, still makes for an astonishing spectacle. Of the trademark 829 handprints, most are male, and only 31 are right-handed. Interspersed with these are human figures, as well as the outlines of puma paws and rhea prints, and creatures such as a scorpion. The earliest paintings date as far back as 7300 BC, but archeologists have identified four later cultural phases, ending with depictions by early Tehuelche groups from approximately 1000 AD. Whether they were connected to religious ceremonies that preceded the hunt will probably never be known.

Parque Nacional Los Glaciares

Declared a world heritage site by UNESCO, the wild expanse of the **PARQUE NACIONAL LOS GLACIARES** encompasses environments ranging from the enormous sterile glaciers that flow down from the heights of the Southern Continental Icecap, to thick, sub-Antarctic woodland of deciduous *lenga* and *ñire*; from savage unclimbed crags where 5000mm of precipitation falls annually, to billiard-table Patagonian *meseta* that receives little more than 100mm annually. The vast majority is off limits to the public, and most will visit only the northern Fitz Roy sector (see below), for trekking, as well as the sightseeing area around the **Glaciar Perito Moreno** (see p.187), one of the world's most famous glaciers.

El Chaltén and the Fitz Roy Massif

The northernmost section of the Parque Nacional Los Glaciares, the **FITZ ROY** sector, contains some of the most breathtakingly beautiful mountain peaks on the planet. Two concentric jaws of jagged teeth puncture the Patagonian sky, with the 3445-metre incisor of **Monte Fitz Roy** at the centre of the massif. It was known to the Tehuelche as El Chaltén, "The mountain that smokes", an allusion to the almost perpetual presence of a scarf of cloud attached to its summit. Alongside Monte Fitz Roy rise **Cerro Poincenot** and **Aguja Saint Exupéry**, while set behind them is the forbidding needle of **Cerro Torre**.

EL CHALTÉN, the Tehuelche name for Fitz Roy, has undergone a convulsive expansion since it was established in 1985. In fact, this thriving tourist centre is showing signs of uncontrolled development and, whereas certain buildings have been built in a style sympathetic to the mountain surroundings, others would look more at ease in the beach resort of Mar del Plata. Nonetheless, the atmosphere is relaxed, with a friendly mix of young Argentinians and foreign visitors. Between Easter and mid-October many establishments are closed; conversely, in high season, especially January, it is advisable to book accommodation in advance.

Practicalities

The **national park information centre** (8am–8pm; Ⓣ&Ⓕ02962/493004), less than 1km before the village, is a necessary point of call where volunteers advise visitors of the park's regulations. Inside are wildlife exhibits, a message board, and a useful information book for climbers, all of whom must register here, as should anyone planning to stay at the Lago Toro refuge and campsite to the south. The **tourist office** is in the Comisión de Fomento at Güemes 21 (Nov–March daily 8am–7pm; July-Oct 9–7pm; Ⓣ02962/493011, Ⓦwww.elchalten.com), one of the first buildings as you enter the village. Despite having a relatively small population, the village is quite spread out. Unless you ask otherwise, **buses** from Calafate will drop you off at their respective offices or hotels; it's better to try to get them to drop you off in the centre if that's where you plan to stay. Fitzroy Expediciones (Ⓣ&Ⓕ02962/493017, Ⓔfroyexp@internet.siscotel.com), at Lionel Terray 545, rents harnesses and organizes trekking on Glaciar Torre, teaching basic ice-climbing techniques, and much more serious and expensive expeditions onto the continental ice-cap.

Accommodation is to be found in the centre or on and around Avenida San Martín, north of the village. Camping Madsen, 1km from centre at the far north of town where Avenida San Martín ends, is the best of the free **campsites**, at the trail-head for Laguna Capri and with a scenic setting. It has no showers and only one latrine; you should only use fallen wood for fires. El Refugio, San Martín s/n (Oct–April; AR$8 per person), next to Río de las Vueltas, has 24hr hot showers and barbecue facilities. *Albergue Cóndor de los Andes*, on Río de las Vueltas and Halvorsen (Ⓣ02962/493101, Ⓦwww.condordelosandes.com; ❷), is the newest HI-affiliated hostel with very pleasant four- or six-bedded rooms, a kitchen and reading area; they organize good excursions and treks. *Albergue Patagonia*, San Martín 493 (Ⓣ&Ⓕ02962/493019; ❷), is the most homely of the HI-affiliated hostels, offering cooking facilities, a cheap laundry service, a book exchange, and a snug living room with videos. It also serves hearty three-course meals. Some of the best-value rooms (for two to four people) in El Chaltén are at *La Base* at Lago del Desierto s/n (Ⓣ02962/493031; ❸; closed Oct some years.), several featuring mountain views. Its owners are hospitable, and it has kitchen facilities and free video showings in the attic sitting room. The knowledgeable geologist owner of *Casa de Piedra*, Lago del Desierto s/n (Ⓣ&Ⓕ02962/493015; ❹), also works as a guide and rents neat bungalows and rooms, with great beds, good private bathrooms and plentiful hot water – some rooms have the village's best views of the high peaks. *Posada Poincenot*, at San Martín 693 (Ⓣ02962/493022; ❹; Nov–March) is a peaceful, spacious, cabin-style guesthouse run by a welcoming couple. It also has triples and quadruples, a laundry service, and serves a good-value three-course dinner. Finally, *Rancho Grande*, at San Martín 635 (Ⓣ&Ⓕ02962/493005, Ⓔrancho@cotecal.com.ar; ❷), is a large, modern YHA-affiliated hostel with clean, clinical four-bed rooms, and one double (❸). It has a lively bar-restaurant, kitchen facilities, left luggage and a good laundry service. It's also the agent for Chaltén Travel buses.

Restaurants tend to be pricey but *La Casita* on the main drag does a mean roast lamb for lower prices than most. *La Chocolatería*, in a fun, funky wooden cabin at the western end of Lago del Desierto, cooks reasonable pizzas, and has well-chilled beers and slabs of chocolate. About the only **nightlife** option in the village, along with *Zafarrancho*, the bar-restaurant of the Rancho Grande youth hostel, is *Cervecería El Bodegón*, San Martín, known for its hop-flavoured home-brewed ales.

Trekking in the park

The area's claim to be the **trekking capital of Argentina** is justified, and the closer you get to the mountains, the clearer their beauty becomes. Unlike in Torres del Paine (see p.572), one of the beauties of this park is that those with limited time can still make worthwhile **day walks**, using El Chaltén as a base. For those who enjoy camping, the quintessential Monte Fitz Roy/Cerro Torre loop at the centre of the park makes a good three-day option, given good weather; the longer interlocking circuit to the north will add at least another two or three days. The advantage of going anticlockwise is that you avoid the steep climb up to Lagunas Madre y Hija from the valley, and have the wind at your back when returning down that valley to Chaltén. However, the biggest gamble is always what the weather will be like around Cerro Torre, so if this most unpredictable of peaks is visible on day one, you might like to head for it first. The blanket **ban on lighting campfires** in the park must be observed, so if you need your food hot, please make careful use of gas stoves. The best trekking **map** available is the 1:50,000 Monte Fitz Roy & Cerro Torre published by Zagier & Urruty, on sale in the village, which includes a 1:100,000 scale map of the Lago del Desierto area.

El Calafate

EL CALAFATE is one of the country's most-visited tourist destinations. The nearby attractions cluster around the tremendous **Lago Argentino**, the greatest of all exclusively Argentine lakes, and the third largest in all South America. By any standards, the town isn't cheap, although it does offer some decent budget hostel accommodation and a couple of well-stocked, reasonably priced supermarkets. The best **months to visit** are those in spring and autumn (Nov to mid-Dec, and March to Easter/early April), when there's a balance between having enough visitors to keep services running but not too many for the place to seem overcrowded.

Practicalities

Calafate's international **airport** lies over 15km east of town, and is connected to town by **taxis** (AR$22) and infrequent Aerobus **shuttles** (AR$8). All **buses** stop at the terminal on Avenida Julio Roca, on the hillside one block above the main thoroughfare, Avenida Libertador, to which it's connected by a flight of steps. The **tourist office** is situated in the terminal (daily April–Oct 8am–10pm; Nov–March 8am–11pm; Ⓣ&Ⓕ02902/491090 or 492884, Ⓦwww.calafate.com). They can help you track down a room in a *casa de familia* (AR$15–20 per person) if you can't find accommodation (a real possibility in January and February). The **national park information office**, at Libertador 1302 (Mon–Fri 8am–9.30pm, Sat & Sun 1.30–9.30pm; Ⓣ02902/491005), has some useful maps, sell fishing licences, and will give you the latest information on campsites near the glacier.

High season runs from November until Easter. Prices are considerably reduced in low season, when the upper-end **hotels** become much more affordable. If you don't care to stay in the town itself, there are other options at the tourist estancias and near the glacier. The most exclusive and expensive of these, the *Estancia Alta Vista* (Ⓣ&Ⓕ02902/491247, in Buenos Aires 011/4343-8883, Ⓔaltavista@cotecal.com.ar; ❾), plays host to those seeking discretion and peace, with airy, intimate rooms with tasteful, restrained decor; non-intrusive, professional service; and a delightful garden filled with lupins. It serves simple, classically prepared regional cuisine. *Hotel Los Alamos*, at Gob. Moyano and Bustillo (Ⓣ02902/491144 or 491146, Ⓔposadalosalamos@posadalosalamos.com; ❾), is the most luxurious of the town's hotels, modestly posing as a posada, but with the feel of a village complex. It has wood-panelled rooms with bright bathrooms, an excellent restaurant, gardens, tennis courts and even a Lilliputian golf course. A helpful if rather crowded place close to bus terminal, *Residencial Buenos Aires*, at Buenos Aires 296 (Ⓣ&Ⓕ02902/491399; ❺), offers a free luggage store and a cheap laundry service. *Calafate Hostel*, on 25 de Mayo and Gob. Moyano (Ⓣ02902/492212, Ⓔcalafatehostel@cotecal.com.ar; ❹–❺), is a brand-new and fully equipped hostel only blocks from the bus terminal, with kitchen, living room and Internet services, while the *Albergue del Glaciar*, Los Pioneros s/n (Ⓣ&Ⓕ02902/491243, offseason Ⓣ&Ⓕ0488-69416, Ⓔinfo@glaciar.com), is a popular, YHA-affiliated hostel with clean, four-bed rooms, plus kitchen, free luggage store, shuttle to and from bus terminal, a multilingual reception, Internet access, travel services and a good-value restaurant.

Camping options include the pleasant Camping Municipal, José Pantín s/n (Ⓣ02902/491829; AR$5 per person plus AR$5 per tent), with restaurant and shower block, conveniently situated one block behind the YPF station at the entrance to town; Jorgito, Gob. Moyano 943 (Ⓣ02902/491323; AR$5 per person), in the garden of the owner's house; and Los Dos Pinos, 9 de Julio 358 (Ⓣ&Ⓕ02902/491271; AR$7 per person).

Top **restaurants** include *Bordeaux*, Julio Roca and 1° de Mayo (Ⓣ02902/492118), an intimate place specializing in fondues for two or more (AR$22), with Swiss side dishes; in the off-season, it's only open on weekends. *La Posta*, in the grounds of the *Los Alamos* hotel (Ⓣ02902/491144), has a spacious dining room looking out over a manicured setting. It has an exotic international menu, with an inventive range of sauces and good use of local ingredients – the rolled lamb with rose-hip sauce is excellent (AR$18). By far the best of the low-budget feeds, *Quincho Don Raúl*, on Libertador 1472, features a hands-on gaucho owner who isn't called "Raúl", but who is otherwise the genuine article. His place offers all-day AR$5 *tenedor libre* and AR$12 *asado tenedor libre* and is well worth the walk to the outskirts of town. *Don Diego de la Noche* Libertador 1603 (Ⓣ02902/491270) is the only place in town with a lively nightlife buzz, especially in high season – but don't turn up till midnight. Moustachioed Don Diego himself frequently provides the live music.

Los Glaciares: the southern sector

In the southern sector of the national park there are two main destinations. First the **glacier** itself, which lies in front of the **Península de Magallanes**, which is not a part of the park, apart from the fringe of land around the lake channels. The park's **main gate** is here and from there it is 30km, past several campsites, picnic spots and one hotel, to the **boardwalks** in front of the glacier. The second is **Puerto Bandera**, from where boat trips depart to Upsala and the other northern glaciers.

The **entrance charge** for this section of the park is AR$20 per person, which you must pay at the respective gates. Within the boundaries, be especially aware of the dangers of fire and extinguish any campfire with plenty of water. The national park authorities are trying gradually to withdraw facilities close to the glacier in order to reduce visual and aquatic pollution, so check at the gate or the park office which **campsites** are open.

Glaciar Perito Moreno

GLACIAR PERITO MORENO has a star quality that none of the others in this part of the world rival, performing for its public, who come to enjoy the spectacle of its titanic struggle with Lago Argentino as the glacier tries to reach the Península de Magallanes. Vast blocks of ice, some weighing hundreds of tonnes, detonate off the face of the glacier with the report of a small cannon and come crashing down into the waters below. Moreno is one of only two **advancing glaciers** in South America, and one of the very few on the planet. Above all, the glacier became famous for the way it would periodically push right across the channel, forming a massive dyke of ice that cut the Brazo Rico and Brazo Sur off from the main body of Lago Argentino. Cut off from their natural outlet, the water in the *brazos* would build up against the flank of the glacier, flooding the surrounding area, until eventually the pressure forced open a passage into the Canal de los Témpanos (Iceberg Channel) once again. Occurring over the course of several hours, such a rupture was, for those lucky enough to witness it, one of nature's most awesome spectacles – it's said that the roars of breaking ice could be heard in Calafate, 80km away. The glacier then settled into a fairly regular cycle, completely blocking the channel approximately every three to seven years until the last time, in 1988. The glacier tends to be more active in sunny weather and in the afternoon, but early morning can also be beautiful, as the light strikes the ice cliffs.

Practicalities

Guided day excursions to the glacier are offered by virtually all agencies in El Calafate, allowing for between two and three hours at the ice face, though many find this is too little to appreciate the spectacle fully. Enquire at the tourist office for details of tour companies or alternative ways of getting to the glacier. The tour with the Albergue del Glaciar (see p.186) and the more expensive one with Chaltén Travel are recommended. Several bus companies offer their own tours (book at the terminal), leaving every day, year round.

If you don't want to be restricted to a tour, you have several options. Several private minibus operators run reasonably flexible transport-only services, where you phone up to arrange times and be collected. Things work out best if you can form a group of four or so first; enquire at the tourist office. Otherwise, you could rent a car, or hire a *remise* taxi (AR$80 for two passengers, AR$100 for four), but agree on a waiting time before setting out, since drivers normally calculate on a two-hour stay. Alternatively, you could hitch. Remember that the glacier lies a long way from the park entrance itself (over 30km), in the event that your potential lift is only going that far.

Driving, you have two choices: either take the RP15 towards Lago Roca or continue straight down Libertador along the RP11. The first route has the advantage of passing historical Estancia Anita and the tourist estancia of Alta Vista, with the shark-fin of Cerro Moreno (1640m) ahead of you in the background.

Once there, do not stray from the boardwalks: as notices tell you, 32 people were killed by ice falls between 1968 and 1988, either being hit by lethal richocheting chunks of ice or swept off the rocks into the freezing water by the subsequent wave surge. **Boat trips** can be made from either Puerto Bandera or the much nearer Bahía Bajo de las Sombras. Hielo y Aventura, Libertador 935 (Ⓣ&Ⓕ02902/491053), organizes fun "mini-trekking" excursions where you get **to walk on the glacier**.

1.8

Tierra del Fuego

TIERRA DEL FUEGO, the "Land of Fire", is where South America finally funnels into the icy waters of the southern oceans, at the end of the inhabited globe. It gets its Spanish name from the fires that these people lit when Magellan and his crew first sailed fearfully through the newly discovered straits later to be named after him. Strictly, it comprises the entire archipelago to the south of Patagonia but the term is more commonly applied solely to the main, most developed island of the group, the **Isla Grande**, the biggest island in South America. Its eastern section, roughly a third of the island, along with a few islets, belong to Argentina, the rest being **Chilean territory**.

By far and away the leading tourist attraction is the well-known city of **Ushuaia**, a round-the-year resort on the south coast. Beautifully located, backed by distinctive jagged mountains, it is *the* base for visiting the **Beagle Channel**, rich in **marine wildlife**, and the wild, forested peaks of the **Cordillera Darwin**. With the lakes, forests and tundra of **Parque Nacional Tierra del Fuego**, just 12km to the west, and historic **Estancia Harberton** an easy half-day excursion, this is where you'll spend the most time.

You won't miss much, on the other hand, if you leave the windswept plains and scrubby *coirón* grasslands in the north of the island to the sheep that thrive there. The main Argentine town up there is **Río Grande**, a bleak place but a useful overnight stop for travellers exploring the island's heartland or for those entering the island by one of the ferry crossings. It's especially popular with fly fishermen who come here from all over the world hoping to outwit the seagoing **brown trout** of the río Grande, regarded as the world's premier river for that species.

People tend to visit Tierra del Fuego between December and February, but in March and April the countryside is daubed with the spectacular autumnal colours of the southern beech, while springtime from October to mid-November, before the tourist season gets going, is also a great time to come, though it can be even windier than normal.

Ushuaia and around

USHUAIA, Fuego's undisputed tourist hub, lies in the far south of the island. Dramatically located between the mountains and the sea, the town tumbles down the hillside to the wide, encircling arm of land that protects its bay from the south-westerly winds and occasional thrashing storms of the icy **Beagle Channel**. It's a convenient base for discovering the rugged beauty of the lands that border this historically important sea channel, or for taking boat trips along the channel itself.

In 1869, Reverend Stirling became Tierra del Fuego's first white settler when he founded his **Anglican mission** amongst the Yámana here. Stirling stayed for six months, before being recalled to the Falklands Islands to be appointed Anglican bishop for South America. Thomas Bridges, his assistant, returned to take over the mission in 1871, after which time Ushuaia began to figure on mariners' charts as a place of refuge in the event of shipwreck. In 1896, in order to consolidate its sovereignty and open up the region to wider colonization, the Argentine State used a

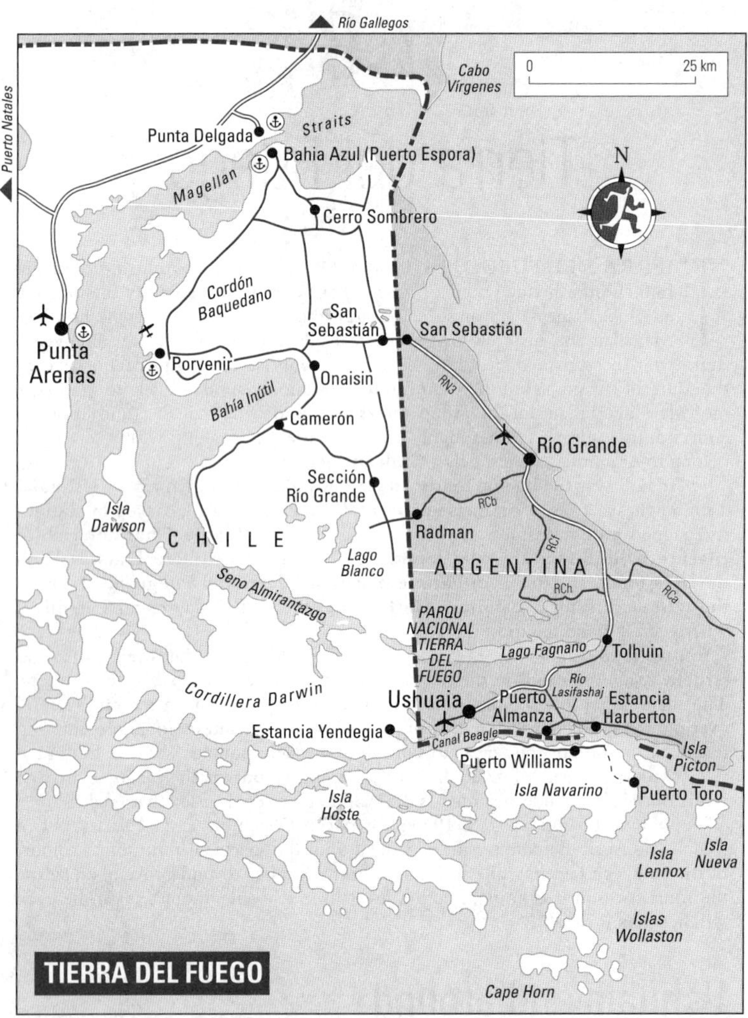

popular nineteenth-century tactic and established a **penal colony** here, eventually closed by Perón in 1947.

Arrival and information

The international **airport**, Malvinas Argentinas, is 4km southwest of town; a **taxi** to the centre costs about AR$6. **Buses** usually arrive and depart from their companies' respective offices (see "Listings" p.192).

Avenida San Martín is the main thoroughfare; at no. 674 you'll find the **tourist office** (Mon–Fri 8am–10pm, Sat & Sun 9am–8pm; ⓣ2901/432000, ⓔmuniush@speedy.com.ar), with English speaking staff and a free illustrated guide to the region.

Accommodation

Ushuaia has a lot of **hotels** and hostels, most of which are found along the first four streets parallel to the bay, but they remain expensive by Argentine standards especially in the short summer season when they can get booked up well in advance. **Campsites** include the well-equipped *Club Andino*, Alem 2873 (T&F02901/422335; AR$6 per person) and the *Camping Municipal*, 8km from the centre, which is basic but free.

Cap Polonio San Martín 746 T&F02901/422140, Ecappolonio@tierradelfuego.org.ar. A well-located hotel, with comfortable, spruce rooms, pleasant bathrooms, the *Cap Polonio* also runs the *Marcopolo* restaurant next door. 5

"La Casa" Gob. Paz 1380 T02901/423202, Ecasalaga@satlink.com. A highly recommended, spotlessly clean B&B with great views from the breakfast room, and worth reserving in advance. Rooms have shared bathrooms. Often closed between May and August. 5

Las Hayas Resort Luis Martial 1650 T02901/430710-18, Elashayas@overnet.com.ar. Five-star hotel: luxurious, quiet and high up, 4km from centre. Most of the stylish commodious rooms enjoy sea views; singles almost same price as doubles, no triples. Facilities include a health spa and indoor pool. Shuttle bus to port and centre. 9

Hostería América Gob. Paz 1665 T02901/423358, Ehosteriaamerica@arnet.com.ar. A competitively priced, mid-range hostel, quite a walk from the centre. 6

La Posada Hotel San Martín 1299 T&F02901/433330 or 433222. One of the best-value mid-range hotels, with bright, slightly cramped rooms for two to four people, and panoramic views from the second floor. 6

Residencial Linares Gob. Deloqui 1522 T02901/423594. An excellent B&B, in a cosy, split-level house with sterling views of the Beagle Channel. You can use the living room after 4pm. 6

Torre al Sur Hostel Gob. Paz 1437 T02901/430745, Etorrealsur@impsat1.com.ar. A popular, friendly HI-affiliated hostel that gets extremely busy in summer, when it can be cramped and noisy. It has great views, a small kitchen, good-value meals, and cheap Internet access. 2 (reductions for HI cardholders)

The Town

Start your wanderings down by the pier, the Muelle Turístico, where Lasserre joins the seafront avenue, Maipú. The 1920s **Provincial Legislature** overlooking the sea here is one of the town's most stately buildings. Northeast of here at Maipú 175 is the small, recommended **Museo del Fin del Mundo** (April–Sept Mon–Sat 3–7pm; Oct–March daily 10am–1pm & 3–7.30pm; AR$5), with exhibits on the region's history and wildlife. At the former **prison** two blocks further along the front and two more inland, at Yaganes and Gobernador Paz, you'll see the **Museo del Presidio**, also called Museo Marítimo (daily 9am–8pm; AR$13). This museum houses a motley collection of exhibits, with the central draw being the sprawling prison building itself, whose wings radiate out like spokes from a half-wheel. The best exhibits are the painstakingly made scale models of famous **ships** from the island's history; and a much cruder, if equally painstaking, reconstruction of a Yámana canoe, complete with video of the archeologists' attempts to make it according to authentic techniques.

Head 7km behind the town to the hanging **Glaciar Martial**, good for first-rate views of the Beagle Channel and the islands of Chile. To get there, walk or take the Pasarela bus (AR$5) from Maipú up to the *Hotel Del Glaciar*, and then climb or take the **chair lift** (AR$7) from behind the hotel. Take sun protection: the ozone hole affects these latitudes and solar radiation can be fierce.

Eating, drinking and entertainment

Casa Tía 12 de Octubre and Karukinka. Cheap snacks and light meals, including good breakfasts, are the attraction at this Ushuaia institution.

Ideal San Martín 393. Housed in one of Ushuaia's more venerable buildings, the *Ideal* serves king crab *thermidor* at a price while grilled trout and

other dishes are less pricey (AR$15–25).
Marcopolo San Martín 748. Breakfasts, lunch, tea and dinner are all served in this bright restaurant, also the dining room for the *Cap Polonio* hotel. Food is well cooked and presented, and includes trout stuffed with crab, and juicy *parrillas*.
Rancho Argentino San Martín 237 ⓣ02901/430100. Beautiful mock-rustic decor and attentive service mark the *Rancho Argentino*, whose fresh salad bar, huge *parrillas* and decent selection of wines, make it one of the best newcomers in town.
Shelknam San Martín 273. A decent *confitería*-café on the main drag, with a lively buzz throughout the day.
Té para Dos San Martín 1485. Deliciously kitsch tearoom, in a chintzy house, serving wonderful home-made cakes, to accompany select teas and creamy hot chocolate.
Tía Elvira Maipú 349. Fine selection of fresh seafood, excellent mussels and a delicious *merluza negra a la Marquery* (black hake in a seafood sauce). Main courses from AR$10. *Tía Elvira* also has a good list of Argentine wines.
El Turco San Martín 1440. Sizeable, hearty portions of pizza, home-made pasta and meat dishes. Excellent AR$7 lunch menu; good-humoured service. Closed Sunday lunch.

Listings

Airlines Aerolíneas Argentinas, Roca 116 ⓣ02901/421218; DAP, 25 de Mayo 64 ⓣ02901/432112; LADE, San Martín 542 ⓣ02901/421123; Lapa, 25 de Mayo 64 ⓣ02901/432112; Transporte Aeronaval, airport: ⓣ02901/421607.
Banks and exchanges ATMs at most banks, nearly all of which are along San Martín, as is the main *casa de cambio*, no 877.
Bus companies Lider, Gob. Paz 921 ⓣ02901/430264; Tecni Austral, Roca 157 ⓣ02901/431408; Tolkeyen, Maipú 237 ⓣ&ⓕ02901/437073; Transportes Montiel, Marcos Zar 330 ⓣ02901/421366; Transportes Tolhuin, Kuanip 579 ⓣ02901/434273.
Car rental Avis, San Martín 1195 ⓣ02901/422744; Dollar, Maipú & Sarmiento ⓣ02901/432134; Localiza, San Martín 1222 ⓣ02901/430739.
Post office San Martín 301.
Travel agencies All Patagonia, Juana Fadul 54 ⓣ02901/433622; Canal Fun & Nature, Rivadavia 82 ⓣ02901/437610; Témpanos, San Martín 626 ⓣ02901/436020; Turismo del Campo, 25 de Mayo 34 ⓣ02901/437351.

Trips along the Beagle Channel

No trip to Ushuaia is complete without a trip on the **BEAGLE CHANNEL**, the majestic, mountain-fringed sea passage to the south of the city. Most **boat trips** start and finish in Ushuaia, and you get the best views of town looking back at it from the straits. The main purpose of these excursions is to see the **marine wildlife** – notably sea lions and cormorants – that lives along the channel, all or part of the year. Boats depart from the pier, **Muelle Turístico**, where you'll find a huddle of agents' booking huts. Try the *Barracuda*, offering good-value three-hour tours (9.30am & 3pm; AR$50); or Héctor Monsalve's trips for small groups on the quiet motorized sailboat, *Tres Marías* (ⓣ02901/421897; Nov–Easter 9.30am & 3pm; 4hr; AR$70), which includes a stop at Islas Bridges to see Yámana shell middens.

Estancia Harberton and the RCj

The unsealed **RCj** is one of the most interesting branch roads on the island, offering spectacular views of the Beagle Channel. The turn-off for the RCj is 40km south of Ushuaia on the RN3. Twenty-five kilometres from the turn-off, you emerge from the forested route by a delightful lagoon and can look right across the Beagle Channel to the Chilean naval town of Puerto Williams (see p.577). A few hundred metres beyond here, the road splits: take the left-hand fork heading eastwards across rolling open country and past a clump of **banner trees**, swept back in exaggerated quiffs by the unremitting wind.

Ten kilometres beyond the turn-off and 85km east of Ushuaia, **ESTANCIA HARBERTON** is an ordered assortment of whitewashed buildings on the shores of a sheltered bay (10am–4pm; ☎02901/422742). This farmstead was a place of voluntary refuge for groups of Yámana, Selk'nam and Mannekenk. Built by the Reverend Thomas Bridges, author of the Yámana–English dictionary, it is now run by his great grandson, Tommy Goodall, and his American biologist wife who have created a wonderfully educational **marine wildlife museum** near the estancia proper (same opening hours, see below; AR$4). Entrance is by **guided tour** only (45min–1hr 30min; mid-Oct to mid-April 10am–7pm; last tour 5.30pm; AR$10). You will be shown the copse on the hill, the family cemetery, and the old shearing shed. The *Mánacatush* **tearoom** is the only part of the main estancia building open to the public: here you can enjoy afternoon tea, with large helpings of cake and delicious home-made jams, or – if you book two days in advance – a generous three-course lunch. It is possible to spend a night at one of the estancia's three **campsites**: all are free, but you must first register at the tearoom and obtain a permit. For anyone seeking a more comfortable and probably drier pioneer experience, **rooms** are also available in the converted out-sheds, but are quite basic and rather overpriced at US$110–150 for two. **Buses** (several companies) leave Ushuaia several times daily, costing AR$40–50 return; check the time of the last bus back.

Parque Nacional Tierra del Fuego

The **PARQUE NACIONAL TIERRA DEL FUEGO**, a mere 12km west of Ushuaia, protects 630 square kilometres of jagged mountains, intricate lakes, southern beech forest, swampy peat bog, sub-Antarctic tundra and verdant coastline. The park stretches along the frontier with Chile, from the Beagle Channel to the **Sierra de Injugoyen** north of Lago Fagnano, but only the southernmost quarter of this is open to the public, accessed by the RN3 from Ushuaia. Fortunately, this area contains much of the park's most beautiful scenery, if also some of the wettest, so bring your raingear.

It is broken down into three main sectors: Bahía Ensenada and Río Pipo in the east; Lago Roca further to the west; and the Lapataia area to the south of Lago Roca, which includes Lago Verde and, at the end of RN3, Bahía Lapataia on the Beagle Channel. While here you may see **birds** such as Magellanic woodpeckers, condors, torrent ducks, steamer ducks, upland geese and buff-necked ibises; as well as **mammals** like the guanacos, the rare sea otter, Patagonian grey foxes and their larger, endangered cousin, the native Fuegian fox. The park offers several relatively unchallenging though beautiful **trails**, many of which are completed in minutes rather than hours or days. The Senda Costera (Coastal Path), connecting Bahía Ensenada with Lago Roca or Bahía Lapataia, and the comparatively tough Cerro Guanaco climb from Lago Roca are both recommended.

Park highlights

Bahía Ensenada, situated 2km south of the crossroads by the train station, is a small bay with little of intrinsic interest, save the jetty for boats to Lapataia and the Isla Redonda. It's also the trailhead for one of the most pleasant of the park's walks, the highly recommended **Senda Costera** (7km; 3hr). The route is not too strenuous and allows you to experience dense coastal forest of evergreen beech, Winter's bark, and *lenga*, while affording spectacular views from the Beagle Channel shoreline. On the way, you'll pass grass-covered mounds that are the ancient campsite **middens** of the Yámana. These mounds are protected archeological sites and should not be disturbed.

Another worthy, if tiring trek, is the climb up **Cerro Guanaco** (970m; 8km; 3hr), the mountain ridge on the north side of **Lago Roca**. Remember that, at any time of the year, the weather can turn capricious with little warning, so bring adequate clothing even if you set out in glorious sunshine. Take the Hito XXIV path from the car park at Lago Roca and after ten minutes you'll cross a small bridge over a stream. Immediately afterwards, the path forks: left to Hito XXIV and right up the slope to the Cerro. The path up the forested mountainside is not hazardous, but after rain you're sure to encounter some slippery tree roots and muddy patches.

Above the tree line, the **views** are spectacular, but the path becomes increasingly difficult to follow in the boggy valley, especially after snowfalls. The view from the crest to the south is spectacular: the tangle of islands and rivers of the Archipélago Cormoranes, Lapataia's sinuous curves, the Isla Redonda in the Beagle Channel, and across to the Chilean islands, Hoste and Navarino, separated by the Murray Narrows.

The **Lapataia** area of the park is accessed by way of the final four-kilometre stretch of the RN3, as it winds south from the Lago Roca junction, past **Lago Verde**, and on to **Lapataia** itself, on the bay of the same name. In the space of a few hours, you can take a network of short trails that enable you to see an incredible variety of scenery, which includes bog land, river islets, wooded knolls and sea coast. A few hundred metres past the Lago Roca junction, you cross the Río Lapataia over a bridge that's a favoured haunt of ringed kingfishers. Not far beyond the bridge the road passes through an area known as the **Archipiélago Cormoranes** (Cormorant Archipelago). Signposted left off the road here is a short (20min) circuit trail, the **Paseo de la Isla**, which heads through this scenery of tiny, enchanting humped islets that would not look out of place in a miniaturist Japanese garden.

Next you pass Lago Verde, which is not a lake but actually a sumptuous, sweeping bend of the Río Ovando. Here you'll find *Camping Lago Verde* and *Camping Los Cauquenes*. From Lago Verde, it's only 2km to Lapataia. On the way, you pass several brief, easy nature trails that you can stroll along in twenty minutes or so. A little further along the RN3 – about 1km from Lago Verde – is a turn-off along Circuito Lenga, which takes you to a lookout over Lapataia Bay. This whole area to the left (east) of the RN3 is crisscrossed by trails through peat bog scenery, including the **Paseo del Turbal** (Peat-Bog Walk). Just past the Circuito Lenga turn-off along the RN3, is the start of the **Castorera** path, heading only a couple of hundred metres off the road to a **beaver dam**. You stand a good chance of spotting beavers if you time your arrival to coincide with early morning or dusk.

Practicalities

The most common and cheapest way to access the park is along the good dirt road from Ushuaia (sometimes cut off briefly by snowfalls, late May to early Oct). A AR$12 entrance fee must be paid at the main park gate except in the winter. Virtually all travel agencies in Ushuaia (see p.192) offer **tours** of the park (around AR$40); most last four hours and stop at the major places of interest – be sure to book on a minibus and try to avoid the big tour buses.

There are four main areas for **camping** in the park; Bahía Ensenada and Río Pipo are currently free, but you're better off heading to the paying sites of the Lago Roca and Lago Verde areas, the latter of which has the two most beautiful campsites in the park, right next door to each other. *Camping Lago Verde* (Ⓣ02901/421433, Ⓔlagunaverde@tierradelfuego.ml.org; AR$4 per person), has a tiny toilet block and sink, a shop, and rents tents (AR$10 a day, sleeping bags included), and *Camping Los Cauquenes* (pay at *Lago Verde*; AR$4 per person) lies just across the road.

Río Grande and around

RÍO GRANDE is a drab, sprawling city, which grew up on the river of the same name as a port for exporting sheep products but lost its prominence as a result of the

Border crossings

The only operative land border crossing between the Chilean and Argentine halves of Tierra del Fuego's Isla Grande is at **San Sebastián** in the north of the island. The respective customs posts (April–Oct 8am–10pm; Nov–March open 24hr) are some way apart, 16km west of the Argentine village of the same name. Formalities are straightforward if somewhat lengthy at times. You may not take any fresh fruit, meat or dairy products into Chile, and Argentine officers sometimes reciprocate. Note that Argentina is one hour ahead of Chile from March to October.

frequently treacherous tides along this stretch of the coast. The lone monument worth visiting is the **Candelaria Salesian Mission**, 11km to the north on the RN3, a smart collection of whitewashed buildings grouped around a modest but elegant chapel – and the first Rio Grande mission. To reach the mission from town, take the Línea B **bus** "Misión" from Avenida San Martín (hourly; 25min; AR$1).

The most comfortable **accommodation** is at the restful *Posada de los Sauces*, El Cano 839 (Ⓣ&Ⓕ02964/430672, Ⓔposadadelossauces@arnet.com.ar; ❻), across the road from the bus terminal, with a relaxed lounge bar and a high-quality *à la carte* restaurant.

South of Río Grande, a few kilometres before you cross the Río Grande river, you pass the turn-off for **RCb**, worth detouring along for 1km to see the tiny village of **Estancia José Menéndez**, whose shearing shed is emblazoned by the tremendous head of a prize ewe, its face obscured by an over-effusive wig of curls. The estancia was founded as Estancia Primera Argentina in 1896 by the powerful sheep magnate, Menéndez. The RCb continues across the steppe for 70km to the Chilean frontier at **Radman**, where there's a little-used **border crossing** (Nov–March 8am–9pm), providing a route to **Porvenir**, Chile.

2

Bolivia

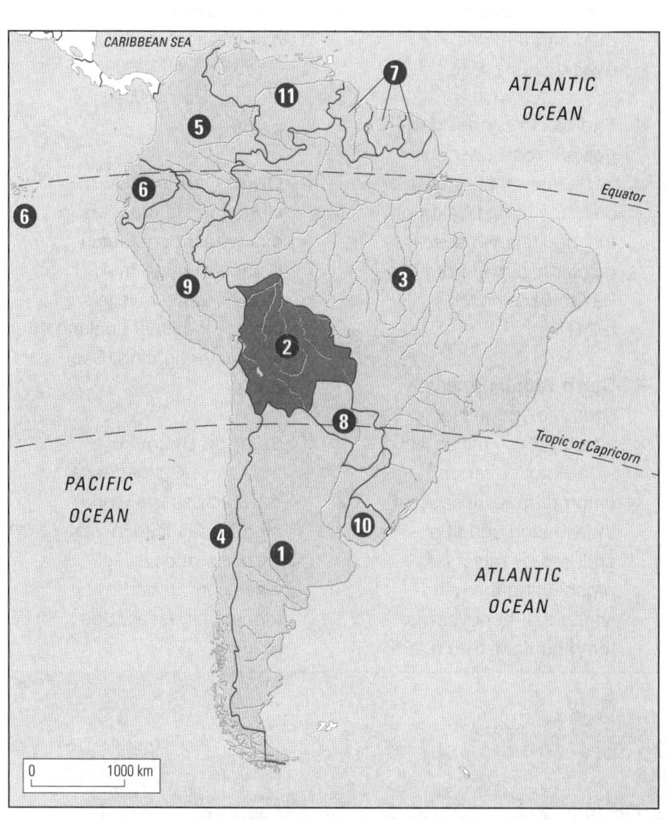
CARIBBEAN SEA
ATLANTIC
OCEAN
Equator
PACIFIC
OCEAN
Tropic of Capricorn
ATLANTIC
OCEAN
0
1000 km
1
2
3
4
5
6
6
7
8
9
10
11

Bolivia highlights

* **Isla del Sol** This island on Lago Titicaca is the spiritual centre of the Andean world, revered as the place where the Sun and Moon were created and the Inca dynasty born. See p.236

* **The world's most dangerous road** Descend more than 3500m over a distance of just 64km on this perilous yet spectacular highway from La Paz to Coroico. See p.241

* **Cerro Rico** Formerly a source of immense wealth, these mines outside Potosí offer an unforgettable glimpse of the working conditions endured by miners prospecting the mineshafts that honeycomb the mountain. See p.255

* **Andean mountain climbing** With six peaks over 6000m high, Bolivia is a paradise for experienced mountaineers, while complete novices can arrange a guided climb up to the 6090m Huayna Potosí. See p.239

* **Oruro Carnaval** At this vibrant fiesta, dancers in extravagant costumes parade through the streets, while revellers indulge in heavy drinking and water fighting. See p.250

* **Salar de Uyuni** For a truly surreal experience, drive across the world's biggest salt lake, a vast expanse of dazzling white surrounded by mountain passes. See p.258

Introduction and basics

Surrounded by Brazil, Paraguay, Argentina, Chile and Peru, Bolivia lies at the heart of South America. Stretching from the majestic icebound peaks and bleak high-altitude deserts of the Andes to the exuberant rainforests and vast savannas of the Amazon basin, it embraces an astonishing range of landscapes and climates. Bolivia encompasses everything outsiders find most exotic and mysterious about the continent.

While three centuries of Spanish colonial rule have left their mark on Bolivia's language, religion and architecture, this European influence is essentially no more than a thin veneer overlying indigenous cultural traditions that stretch back long before the conquest. Though Spanish is the language of business and government, more than thirty indigenous languages are spoken across a country covering an area the size of France and Spain combined. Bolivia is home to less than nine million people, the majority living in a handful of cities founded by the Spanish and graced by some of the finest colonial architecture on the continent.

Bolivia is dominated by the mighty Andes, which march through the west of the country along two parallel chains; between them stretches the Altiplano, a bleak and virtually treeless plateau historically home to most of Bolivia's population. Northeast of the Altiplano, the Andes plunge abruptly into the tropical rainforests and savannas of the Amazon lowlands, a seemingly endless wilderness dominated by the major rivers that flow north to the Brazilian border and beyond. East of the Altiplano, the Andes march down more gradually through a drier region of fertile highland valleys that give way eventually to the Eastern Lowlands, a vast and sparsely populated plain covered by a variety of ecosystems, from dense Amazonian rainforest in the north to the dry thornbrush and scrub of the Chaco to the south. This immensely varied topography supports an extraordinary diversity of plant and animal life, and the country's underdevelopment and lack of tourism have been blessings in disguise for the environment. Owing to its remoteness, Bolivia remains one of South America's least-visited countries despite its myriad attractions.

Where to go

Most visitors spend a few days in the fascinating city of **La Paz**, Bolivia's de facto capital, which combines a dramatic high-altitude setting with a compelling intermingling of traditional indigenous and modern urban cultures. It is also close to magical **Lago Titicaca**, the massive high-altitude lake that straddles the border with Peru, and serves as a good base for trekking, climbing or mountain biking in the **Cordillera Real**, a magnificent range of high Andean peaks that runs north of the city. Just north of La Paz, the Andes plunge precipitously down into the Amazon basin through the deep valleys of the **Yungas**, a region of dramatic scenery and sudden transformations in climate and vegetation. The best base for visiting the **Bolivian Amazon** further north is **Rurrenabaque**, but more adventurous travellers can head east via the **Reserva de la Bíosfera del Beni** – another good place to observe wildlife – to the regional capital Trinidad. This is the start of exciting trips north along the Río Mamoré towards Brazil or south towards Cochabamba.

South of La Paz, the **southern Altiplano** – the bleak, high plateau that stretches between the eastern and western chains of the Andes – is home to some of Bolivia's foremost attractions. The legendary and tragic city of **Potosí**, whose silver mines were the source of fabulous wealth and the scene of terrible cruelty in the colonial era, merits a visit for its treasure-trove of colonial architecture and the opportunity to experience underground life in the mines of Cerro Rico. Further south, **Uyuni** is the jumping-off point for expeditions into the astonishing landscapes of the **Salar de Uyuni** and the **Reserva de Fauna Andina Eduardo Avaroa**, a remote

N
0
200km
BRAZIL
PERU
PANDO
BENI
BOLIVIA
THE YUNGAS
CORDILLERA APOLOBAMBA
CORDILLERA
Llanos de Moxos
Río Madre de Dios
Río Beni
Río Mamore
Río Guaporé
Lago Titicaca
Brasileia
Cobija
Guayaramerín
Guajará-Mirim
Riberalta
Santa Ana del Yacuma
Rurrenabaque
San Borja
San Ignacio
Trinidad
Yucumo
Pelechuco
Mapiri
Sorata
Caranavi
Achacachi
Coroico
Coripata
Chulumani
Copacabana
LA PAZ
Concepción

Tiwanaku
Illimani 6439m
REAL
CORDILLERA ORIENTAL
CHAPARE
Cochambamba
Quillacollo
Totora
Buena Vista
San Javier
San Ignacio
San Miguel
Santa Ana
San Rafael
San Matías
ALTIPLANO
Oruro
Volcán Sajama
CORDILLERA OCCIDENTAL
Lagó Poopó
Aiquile
Samaipata
Santa Cruz
San José de Chiquitos
Vallegrande
Sucre
Tarabuco
Potosí
Salar de Coipasa
Salar de Uyuni
Uyuni
CHACO
Puerto Suárez
Corumbá
Volcán Ollagüe
Tupiza
Villamontes
Tarija
Yacuiba
Villazón
Laguna Colorado
Laguna Verde
CHILE
PARAGUAY
ARGENTINA

region of high-altitude deserts and half-frozen, mineral-stained lakes, populated by great flocks of pink flamingoes and herds of vicuñas. A few hours north of Potosí by road, **Sucre** boasts similarly fine colonial architecture, but is very different in character: a charming and refined city of students and lawyers set in a warm Andean valley in the midst of a region noted for its traditional weaving villages. The market city of **Cochabamba** has less obvious appeal, but enjoys a similar spring-like climate and a warm and friendly outlook that makes it a pleasant place to hang out. Northeast from here are the rainforests and coca fields of the **Chapare** region, but for most travellers Cochabamba is just somewhere to break the journey between La Paz and **Santa Cruz**. A brash, modern and lively tropical metropolis, Santa Cruz makes the best base for exploring the diverse attractions of the **Eastern Lowlands**, including the rainforests of the Parque Nacional Amboró and the idyllic town of Samaipata. Scattered across the forested lowlands east of Santa Cruz, the immaculately restored Jesuit missions of **Chiquitos** provide one of Bolivia's most unusual attractions, while a train line heads east to the Brazilian border. For those with the time or money to spare, Santa Cruz is also the jumping-off point for trips to the remote and beautiful **Parque Nacional Noel Kempff Mercado**, Bolivia's most spectacular protected area.

When to go

Climate varies much more as a result of altitude and topography – often over very short distances – than it does between different seasons. Winter, between May and October, is the **dry season**, and in many ways the best time to visit Bolivia, though it's also the high season for tourism. In the **highlands** it's noticeably colder at night, particularly in June and July, but the days are usually bright and sunny, making this the best time of year for trekking and climbing. Winter is also the best time for visiting the hot and humid **lowlands**, when temperatures are generally slightly (but pleasantly) lower, although the dry season is less pronounced and rain remains a possibility all year round. Usually, between July and August the country is swept by cold fronts coming up from Patagonia, which can send temperatures plunging even in the Amazon. In late August and September, when farmers set fire to cleared forest areas across much of Bolivia, heavy smoke can obscure views and cause respiratory problems.

The summer is the **rainy season**, which runs roughly from November to March and is much more pronounced in the lowlands. Rain affects the condition of roads throughout the country, making journey times much longer or blocking roads altogether. In much of the **lowlands**, particularly the Amazon, road transport becomes pretty much impossible and river transport more frequent. Heat, humidity and mosquitoes are also much worse during the rainy season. In the **highlands**, particularly the Altiplano, it rains much less and travel is far less restricted, though delays and road closures still occur. Despite this, the rainy season is also a very beautiful time in the Andes, with the parched Altiplano and mountainsides being briefly transformed into lush grassland and wild flowers proliferate as the earth comes to life.

Red tape and visas

Many visitors to Bolivia do not need a visa, although the situation does change periodically, so always check with your local embassy or consulate a month or two before travelling. Note, however, that some nationalities, including citizens of the Republic of Ireland, do need to acquire a **visa** and prior authorization from the Bolivian Ministry of Foreign Affairs; this can be arranged through any Bolivian embassy or consulate and takes up to five weeks; the fee varies according to nationality.

On arrival, you'll be issued with a **tourist card** (*tarjeta de turismo*) valid for thirty or ninety days, depending on your nationality. Before entry, check on the number of days you're allowed to stay and make sure the border officials give you the stamp with maximum days; if not, you can request it on the spot or go to the Immigration office and receive another stamp.

To **stay on** in Bolivia beyond the thirty/ninety-day limit, it's best to leave the country overland and return the next day, when you'll be issued with a new tourist card. You can also purchase a thirty-day extension for US$20, or overstay and be fined US$1.40 per each extra day. There have been recent reports of immigration officials illegally fining travellers; you can try to object, bargain the fine or simply leave the country. If you're leaving Bolivia by a particularly remote border crossing, you may need to get an exit stamp in advance from the *migración* in the nearest major town.

Costs and money

The Bolivian currency is the **boliviano**, sometimes referred to as the peso. It's usually written "Bs." and is subdivided into 100 centavos. Notes come in denominations of 10, 20, 50, 100 and 200 bolivianos; coins in denominations of 1, 2 and 5 bolivianos, and of 5, 10, 20 and 50 centavos.

The boliviano has been relatively stable in recent years, devaluing only gradually against the US dollar, though because of the weakness of the Bolivian economy it still remains extremely vulnerable to devaluation. Apart from tour operators and many hotels, which take US dollars and won't accept anything else, most businesses use bolivianos. Because of the likelihood of devaluation, however, **prices in this chapter are quoted in US dollars**. At the time of writing the exchange rate was roughly Bs7.58 = US$1. US dollars can be changed at banks, hotels or shops and by street moneychangers almost everywhere in the country, and are a good way of carrying emergency back-up funds.

One of the least expensive countries in South America, Bolivia is considerably cheaper than neighbouring Chile, Brazil and Argentina. Imported goods are expensive, but food, accommodation and transport are all relatively cheap, and travellers on a tight budget should be able to get around on US$15–20 per day, staying in basic hotels and eating set meals in local restaurants. For US$30–40 per day you can enjoy more comfortable hotels and good food, take taxis when necessary and go on the occasional guided tour.

The easiest way to access funds in cities and larger towns is using **plastic**; Visa and MasterCard are most widely accepted. Banks in all major cities and larger towns are connected to the nationwide Enlace network of **ATMs**, from which you can withdraw cash in US dollars or bolivianos using a credit or debit card. In rural areas, it's important to carry plenty of cash as plastic and travellers' cheques are fairly useless.

Information, maps and websites

Most major cities have a regional **tourism office**, either run by the city municipality or by the departmental prefecture. Local Bolivian tour operators are generally a good source of information, and many are happy to answer queries, often in English, though obviously their main aim is to sell you one of their tours.

Some of the best **websites** devoted to Bolivia are Ⓦwww.boliviaweb.com, with links to related web pages and general background information on subjects such as Bolivian art, history and food; Ⓦwww.boliviangeographic.com, an online magazine with heaps of useful travel info and quarterly articles on adventure sports, local economy, culture and traditional customs; Ⓦwww.enjoybolivia.com, a user-friendly site with information on Bolivia's main cities and regions; and Ⓦlanic.utexas.edu/la/sa/Bolivia, an excellent resource with links to a massive range of Bolivia-related sites.

It's worth buying a good **map** of the country to take with you, as these are rarely available in Bolivia itself. A reasonably good national road map, entitled *Bolivia Highlights*, can be had from the municipal tourist office in La Paz (see p.220), and from bookshops and tour agencies in La Paz and other major cities. The best general map of Bolivia is the *Travel Map of Bolivia* (1:2,200,000), produced by O'Brien Cartographics; it can be purchased online from Ⓦwww.saexplorers.org or Ⓦwww.boliviaweb.com. If you're planning to do any **trekking** or **climbing** in the Cordillera Real, O'Brien Cartographics also produces the excellent *Cordillera Real Recreation Map*, which you should try to get hold of before you travel. In addition, the

Bolivian Instituto Geográfico Militar (IGM) produces maps at a scale of 1:50,000 and 1:250,000 that cover about three-quarters of the country.

Accommodation

While accommodation in Bolivia is generally good value, the standard is not particularly high. In larger cities you'll find a broad range of places to stay, up to and including luxurious international hotels charging over US$100 a night. In smaller towns, however, there's not much choice, particularly in the mid- and upper price ranges, though there are usually plenty of decent but totally unexceptional budget places.

Room rates vary according to **season**, rising during the May to September high tourist season and on weekends in popular resort towns and doubling or tripling during major fiestas. Accommodation in big cities tends to cost more, whereas smaller towns that see a lot of budget travellers tend to have a good range of inexpensive places to stay.

Budget travellers will almost always be able to find a double room, often with a private bathroom, in a clean and reasonably comfortable hotel for around US$10. Smaller and cheaper **hostales, alojamientos** or **residenciales** tend to offer basic rooms with shared bathrooms only, with rates charged per person rather than per room. **Cabañas** are self-contained cabins or bungalows, usually found away from big cities, particularly in resort towns popular with Bolivians. Note that a **motel** is not an inexpensive roadside hotel, but a place where unmarried couples go to have sex, while a **pension** is a cheap place to eat, rather than somewhere to stay.

Mid-range accommodation (US$15 and upwards for a double room) should offer greater comfort, pleasant decor, efficient hot water, towels and soap, and extras like television. For US$25 or so you'll find some very pleasant hotels indeed, while at the **top end** of the scale (US$50 and upwards) there are some beautiful old colonial mansions that have been converted into delightful hotels, as well as more staid modern places aimed primarily at business people.

Even in the coldest **highland** cities, heating is found only in the more expensive hotels; in the **lowlands**, heat rather than cold is often a problem. All but the cheapest rooms are equipped with a fan, and many places offer the option of air conditioning. In the lowlands, you should also check whether the windows of your room are screened against **mosquitoes** or if the bed is equipped with a net. All but the cheapest places have hot water, but the reliability and effectiveness of water-heating systems varies considerably. Most common are the individual electric heaters that you'll find attached to the tops of showers; don't touch the apparatus while the water is running unless you want an electric shock. These electric heaters work in inverse proportion to the amount of water flowing – the less water, the warmer it is – and so require a delicate balance to get right.

Camping

With so few designated campsites in the country and budget accommodation so inexpensive, few travellers bother **camping** in Bolivia unless exploring the country's wilderness areas. Outside cities and towns, you can camp almost everywhere, usually for free; make sure you ask for permission from the nearest house first. On the more popular trekking routes you may be asked for a small fee of a dollar or two by local villagers; though not official, refusing this can lead to problems and disputes. Though **attacks** on trekkers are rare, it's best to camp with at least one other person, and women shouldn't camp unless accompanied by men.

In some **national parks** and other protected wilderness areas you'll find shelters – called *albergues* or *refugios* – where you can stay for a small fee, often in the *campamentos* used by the park guards. These range from relatively comfortable rooms with beds, mosquito nets and bathrooms, to very basic huts where you can stretch out your sleeping bag or string a hammock. Rudimentary cooking facilities and running water are usually available.

Getting around

Bolivia's topography, size and lack of basic infrastructure mean that getting around is often a challenge. Only about five percent of Bolivia's road network is paved – most highways are in a very poor condition and are kept open only through constant labour against floods, landslides and mud, and by the determination, skill and sheer bloody-mindedness of bus and lorry drivers.

By bus and lorry

Known as *buses* or *flotas*, Bolivia's **buses** are run by a variety of private companies and ply all the main routes in the country, moving passengers at low cost over great distances despite often appalling road conditions. Cities and larger towns have **bus terminals**, which usually have some kind of **information** office, but even so the number of different companies operating the same route can make it difficult at times to work out departure times and frequencies. Remember that departing passengers usually have to pay a small fee just for the use of the terminal. For less frequently used routes it's worth buying a **ticket** in advance, but there's no need on busier routes: ticket touts will usually hustle you onto the next departing bus or point you in the direction of the company that serves your destination.

Some routes are served by comparatively luxurious overnight **sleeper buses** (*buscamas*), which cost about fifty percent more but have extra legroom and reclining seats. More local routes are served by smaller buses and minibuses known as **micros**; on some you also have the choice of travelling in **collective taxis**, which charge slightly more but are faster, more comfortable and depart with greater frequency. Most buses stop anywhere for anyone until every available crack has been filled. Because of the poor conditions of most roads and many vehicles, **journey times** are unpredictable, and you should always be prepared for major delays, especially in the rainy season.

When travelling in the **highlands**, you should have warm clothing and a blanket or sleeping bag to hand, as it can get bitterly cold and heated buses are virtually unheard of. If you can, avoid sitting at the back of the bus, as this is where you'll get bounced around the most. In **the Andes**, be prepared for hair-raising turns dotted with crosses marking the many accidents that occur on these roads. These stomach-churning, often very long journeys are not for the faint-hearted but are sometimes the only means of transportation. Unless it's small enough to keep with you inside the bus, your **luggage** will be put on the roof, at the back or in a locked compartment underneath the vehicle. This is usually pretty safe, but it's still worth keeping an eye out at each stop.

The heavy-goods **lorries** (*camiones*) and smaller pick-up trucks, known as **camionetas**, are the other mainstay of Bolivian land transport, and sometimes the only option in remote or little-visited regions. They're cheaper, but also slower and generally more dangerous and uncomfortable than buses. The best place to find one is around any town's market areas or at the police checkpoints (*trancas*) at the edge of town; most also stop for passengers who flag them down at the side of the road. This is the closest you'll get to **hitching** in Bolivia, and you will always be expected to pay something for the ride.

By train

Bolivia's **railway** network, like the mining industry that spawned it, is now a shadow of its former self. At the moment only two networks still function, each run by a different private company. The **Ferrocarril Occidental** runs passenger trains from Oruro south across the Altiplano via Uyuni and Tupiza to Villazón on the Argentine border. From Uyuni, another line, served twice a week, runs southeast to Calama in Chile. The scenery on both these Altiplano routes is magnificent, but will sadly be missed as all journeys are overnight.

The **Ferrocarril Oriental** runs two lines: one from Santa Cruz east to the Brazilian border at Quijjaro; the other from Santa Cruz south to Yacuiba in the Chaco on the Argentine border. Trains on both these long routes are slow and unreliable, and the lowlands scenery is monotonous.

By plane

Flying in Bolivia is a good way of avoiding exhausting overland journeys and saving time; it's also relatively inexpensive, with most internal flights costing US$40–100, and offers splendid bird's-eye views of the high Andes or the endless green expanse of the Amazon. La Paz, Santa Cruz, Sucre and Cochabamba are all connected by daily flights, and there are also frequent services to Tarija, Trinidad, Rurrenabaque and a number of remote towns in the Amazon and the eastern lowlands.

There are three main commercial carriers: **Lloyd Aéreo Boliviano** (ⓦwww.labairlines.com), **AeroSur** (ⓦwww.aerosur.com) and Amaszonas. LAB offers a thirty-day pass (Vibolpass) which allows you to visit four destinations for US$250; you are not allowed to visit the same city twice unless it's a stopover. The Bolivian air force also operates passenger services under its commercial arm **Transportes Aereo Militar** (TAM), which is almost as reliable and somewhat cheaper than the three commercial airlines, and flies to some out-of-the-way places as well as the major towns. All four airlines have offices in the cities they serve, though you can also buy tickets from almost any travel agency for only a small extra charge, which is often faster and more convenient (especially in La Paz). The busier routes should be booked at least several days in advance, and it's important to reconfirm a couple of days before departure. Flights are often cancelled or delayed, and sometimes even leave earlier than scheduled, especially in the Amazon, where the weather can be a problem. If passengers haven't shown up twenty minutes or so before departure, their seats can be given to someone else. For domestic travel, there are **passenger taxes** of up to US$2. For international travel, you'll be charged a hefty tax of US$25, payable at check-in.

By boat

Although Bolivia is a landlocked country, there are still several regions – particularly Lago Titicaca and the Amazon – where water is still the best way of getting around. Several upmarket tour agencies run hydrofoil and catamaran cruises on **Lago Titicaca**, and smaller passenger launches run between Copacabana and the Isla del Sol.

There are two main forms of river transport in the Bolivian **Amazon**. Dugout canoes powered by outboard motors are used by tour agencies to take groups into protected areas like the Parque Nacional Madidi or available for hire with a boatman for a few days if you search for one around the riverbank and negotiate a decent price. The more economic but far from comfortable **cargo boats** ply the two main water routes not yet supplanted by roads – the Río Mamoré, between Trinidad and Guayaramerín on the Brazilian frontier, and the Río Ichilo, between Trinidad and Puerto Villaroel in the Chapare.

By car

If you're short on time or want to get to some really out of the way destinations, **renting a car** is a possibility, though it's often easier and not much more expensive to hire a taxi or *camioneta* to drive you around for a day or longer.

Outside towns, most roads are unpaved and in very poor condition, so **four-wheel drive** (4WD) is essential. **Petrol** stations are few and far between and breakdown services even scarcer, so you should fill your tank whenever you can, carry extra fuel, and take food, drink and warm clothing in case you get stuck. Always carry your passport, driving licence and the registration documents of the vehicle when driving, as **police checks** are frequent, and any infringement will usually result in an on-the-spot fine, whether official or not. **Speed limits** are irregularly posted, but the speed is usually dictated by the state of the road.

Virtually none of the major international **car rental companies** are represented in Bolivia, but you'll find local rental companies in all the major cities: see the relevant listings section in each city account for details. Generally, you'll pay a flat fee of US$25–40 per day, plus about US50¢ extra for each kilometre you drive; 4WDs cost about double. You'll need to be over 25 to rent a car, and to leave a major credit card or large cash deposit as security; you'll also require some kind of insurance.

Organized tours

Although relatively expensive, **organized tours** offer a quick and effortless way to see some of Bolivia's popular attractions and experience adventures ranging from mountain climbing and wildlife safaris to less strenuous city tours and countryside excursions. They're also a good way of visiting remote sites that are otherwise difficult to reach. Tours tend to cost US$25–50 per person per day, depending on the nature of the trip, the degree of comfort and the number of people going along.

Most **agencies** are based in La Paz, where you can arrange almost any trip in the country or buy internal **airline tickets** for a small commission. Check whether you'll get an **English-speaking guide** – most operators can arrange this, though it may cost more. For the more popular wilderness excursions it's often easier, cheaper and more reliable to arrange things with local operators.

Akhamani Trek Linares 888 ⓣ02/237-5680, ⓔandeaninfo@mail.com. Well-organized and moderately priced trekking agency with knowledgeable and enthusiastic English-speaking guides specializing in the Cordillera Apolobamba and the Choro, Takesi and Yunga Cruz trails.

America Tours ground floor office 9, Edificio Avenida, Av 16 de Julio 1490 ⓣ02/237-4204, ⓦwww.america-ecotours.com. Efficient and reliable travel agency: they're the main booking agent for Chalalán Ecolodge in Parque Nacional Madidi, and are a good place to book internal flights, as well as trips to the Pampas del Yacuma and the Salar de Uyuni.

Fremen Av Mariscal Santa Cruz, Galeria Handal, Oficina 13 ⓣ02/240-8200, ⓦwww.andes-amazonia.com. La Paz branch of the excellent and highly respected Cochabamba-based agency offering a wide range of excellent tailor-made tours throughout Bolivia, including river trips on the Río Mamoré on their own luxury floating hotel, the *Reina de Enín*.

Gravity Assisted Mountain Biking Ground floor office 10, Edificio Avenida, Av 16 de Julio 1490 ⓣ02/231-3849, ⓦwww.gravitybolivia.com. The original and best downhill mountain-bike operator, offering daily trips to Coroico or the Zongo Valley with excellent US-made bikes and experienced and enthusiastic English-speaking guides.

Mail and communications

Airmail (*por avión*) to Europe and North America tends to take between one and two weeks to arrive; mail to the rest of the world outside the Americas and Europe takes longer. Letters cost about US$1 to Europe, a little less to the US and Canada, and about US$1.20 to Australia and New Zealand. For a small extra charge, you can send letters certified (*certificado*), which is more reliable, but even then it's not a good idea to send anything you can't afford to lose. Also, there's no point sending anything from small town post offices, as you'll almost certainly reach the nearest city or large town before your letter or package does.

To phone Bolivia from abroad, dial the international access code followed by the **Bolivian country code** (ⓣ591) and the relevant area code, minus the initial zero, followed by the number. To phone national long-distance within Bolivia, dial ⓣ010 followed by the area code and the number. The **area code** for La Paz, Oruro and Potosí is ⓣ02; for Beni, Pando and Santa Cruz ⓣ03; and for Cochabamba, Chuquisaca and Tarija ⓣ04.

Substantial funds have been invested in modernizing the Bolivian **phone system** in recent years, and it's now fairly efficient. The Bolivian national telephone company, **ENTEL**, has offices in all cities and most towns where you can make local, national and international calls. Local calls are very cheap, and long-distance national calls are moderately priced, but international calls are relatively expensive: it costs about US0.55¢ per minute to North America, about US$1.10

per minute to Europe, and even more to anywhere else in the world outside the Americas.

For the same price, you can either get the clerk in an ENTEL office to dial the number for you or you can purchase a **phone card** (*tarjeta telefonica*) for the cardphones in ENTEL offices and on the streets of most towns. Confusingly, there are two different kinds of phone card – magnetic and chip – each work only in some phone booths. You'll also find a small number of **coin-operated phones** in most towns. Most major cities also have their own **regional telephone co-operatives** and private companies, such as Viva and Aes in La Paz, with their own networks of cardphones.

Telephone numbers have changed several times recently in Bolivia and, though the new system is supposed to be definitive, things could change again. If a number you call doesn't work, call ⓣ**104** to check if it's changed and get the new number.

Internet cafés tend to charge about US$0.70–1 an hour, though this can double in remote areas where competition is thin on the ground. The speed of machines and servers usually isn't very fast, but with a little patience you'll get a connection eventually.

Food and drink

The style of eating and drinking varies considerably between Bolivia's three main geographical regions – the Altiplano, the highland valleys and the tropical lowlands – differences that reflect the variety of produce commonly available in each region and the different cultural traditions of their inhabitants. Each region has *comidas típicas* (traditional dishes).

All larger towns in Bolivia have a fair selection of **restaurants**; almost all offer enormously filling good-value set lunches, or **almuerzos**, usually costing between US$1 and US$3, while many offer a set dinner, or **cena**, in the evening and also have a range of a la carte main dishes (*platos extras*), rarely costing more than US$3–4. For US$5 you should expect a very good meal in more upmarket restaurants, while about US$10 will get you most dishes even in the best restaurants in La Paz or Santa Cruz. **Tipping** is not generally expected, and no additional tax is charged on meals, although there is sometimes a cover charge in restaurants with live music performances, known as **peñas**.

Although Bolivia is obviously not the place to come for seafood, **fish** features regularly on menus, especially the succulent *trucha* (trout) and *pejerrey* (kingfish) around Lago Titicaca and the juicy white river fish known as *surubí* and *pucú* in the lowlands. Most cities have at least one Chinese restaurant, many pizzerias and cheap chicken restaurants known as *pollos spiedo*, *pollos broaster* or *pollos a la brasa*. Ordinary restaurants rarely offer much in the way of **vegetarian food**; the situation changes a great deal in popular travellers' haunts, where salads, vegetarian dishes and pancakes are widely available.

Few restaurants and cafés open much before 8am for **breakfast**. A good and cheap alternative is to head to the markets, which open around 6am and sell cheap and filling snacks and meals for less than US$1. These are the best places to try regional specialities and delicious fruit juices blended with milk or boiled water and costing about US$0.25 for a glass and a half.

The most popular snack throughout Bolivia is the **salteña**, a pasty filled with a spicy, juicy stew of meat or chicken with chopped vegetables, olives and hard-boiled egg, usually sold from street stalls and eaten in the mid-morning accompanied by a cold drink and a spoonful or two of chilli sauce if desired. The best *salteñas* are found in Sucre, where they're also sold in specialist cafés called *salteñerias*. Also commonly available are **tucumanes,** deep-fried and with a higher potato content than *salteñas,* and **empanadas**, simpler pasties filled with meat, chicken or cheese and either baked or (particularly in the lowlands, where the humidity makes baking difficult) fried.

In the **Altiplano**, traditional Aymara cuisine is dominated by the potato in all its manifold guises, featuring in the many thick hearty **soups**. The most common meat in the Altiplano is **mutton**, closely followed by **llama**, which is lean and tasty and often eaten in a dried form known as *charque*. If you like your food with a kick, douse your dish in **llajua** – a hot sauce made from tomatoes, small chilli peppers (*locotos*) and herbs.

In the *comida típica* of the **valley regions**, maize features strongly, often used as the basis for thick soups known as *laguas* or boiled on the cob and served with fresh white cheese – a classic combination known as *choclo con queso*. Meat and chicken are often cooked in spicy sauces known as *picantes,* and pork and beef are served widely in the popular valley mainstay known as *pique a lo macho*, a massive plate of chopped beef and sausage fried together with potatoes, onions, tomatoes and chillies.

In the **tropical lowlands**, plantains and yucca generally take the place of potatoes alongside rice. Classic staples are *masaco*, mashed plantain or yucca mixed with shredded *charque*, fried and eaten for breakfast, and beef in all shapes and forms – the lowlands are cattle-ranching regions, so beef is of good quality and relatively low price – try *pacumutus,* massive kebabs cooked on skewers or fried steaks.

Drinks

Known as **refrescos**, bottled fizzy drinks from processed fruit juices or home-made from fruit juices and sold from street stalls, can be found all over Bolivia. **Mineral water** is fairly widely available in large plastic bottles, as is less expensive purified water labelled "Naturagua" – a good thing, as it's best not to the drink tap water. The delicious variety of tropical fruits grown in Bolivia are available as **juices** from market stalls throughout the country, and freshly squeezed orange and grapefruit juice is also sold on the streets from handcarts for about US$0.15 a glass. **Tea** and **coffee** are available almost everywhere, as well as *mates*, or herbal teas – *mate de coca* is the best known and a good remedy for altitude sickness, but many others are usually available, including *anis* and *manzanilla* (camomile), as well as *trimate* (combination of the three and great for digestion). Locally produced **alcoholic drinks** are widely available in Bolivia, and drinking is a serious past time. **Beer** is available in shops, restaurants and bars almost everywhere and Bolivians consume it in large quantities, especially at fiestas – Paceña, produced in La Paz, is the most popular and widely available, followed by Huari, made by the same company but with a slightly saltier taste. Although not widely consumed, Bolivia also produces a growing variety of **wines** (*vinos*), mostly from the Tarija Valley – the best labels are Concepción, Kohlberg and Aranjuez.

When Bolivians really want to get drunk they turn to spirits, in particular a white grape brandy called **singani**, produced in the Tarija valley and usually mixed with Sprite or Seven-Up, a fast-acting combination known as **Chufflay**. Finally, no visit to the Cochabamba is complete without a taste of **chicha cochabambina**, a thick, mildly alcoholic yeasty-flavoured beer made of fermented maize and considered sacred by the Incas. It is available throughout the region wherever you see a white flag or bunch of flowers raised on a pole outside a house.

Safety and the police

In recent years, Bolivia's crime levels have risen partly in response to the country's worsening economic situation. If you apply common sense precautions, however, there's no need to be paranoid: the vast majority of crime against tourists is opportunistic theft, and violence is extremely rare.

With any luck, most of your contact with the **police** will be at frontiers and road checkpoints. Sometimes, particularly near borders and in remote regions, you may have to register with them, so carry your passport at all times.

If you are the victim of theft, you'll probably need to go to the police to make a report (*denuncia*) and get a written report for insurance purposes. In La Paz you should go to the **tourist police** if you are the victim of any crime – their offices (open 24hr; ⓣ02/222-5016) are at Edificio Olimpia 1314, Plaza Tejada Sorzano, opposite the stadium in Miraflores and on Calle Sucre, two blocks up from Plaza de Armas (ⓣ110). Occasionally, the police may search your bags. If they do, watch carefully, and ideally get a witness to

Useful numbers

Police	ⓣ110
Ambulance	ⓣ118
Directory assistance	ⓣ104

watch with you, to make sure nothing is planted or stolen – a rare but not impossible occurrence.

Possession of **drugs** is a serious offence in Bolivia, usually leading to a long jail sentence. The main **cocaine**-producing region of the Chapare is the scene of ongoing, sometimes violent, confrontations between the security forces and coca-growers. Towns on the main Chapare road are generally safe to visit, but be wary of going off the beaten track, as you may be mistaken for a drug trafficker, undercover CIA or drug-enforcement agent.

In recent years, **road blockades** by indigenous communities have become a feature of Bolivian political life, particularly in the Altiplano between La Paz and Peru, the Chapare and the Yungas. If you get caught up in the blockades, keep your head down and get out of the area. The army has killed several protesters in recent years, and tempers can run high, with blockade-breaking buses sometimes getting stoned or torched. **Political unrest** is a constant in Bolivia, and demonstrations are a regular event in La Paz and other major cities. These are usually fairly peaceful events and interesting to watch, but keep your distance and get out of the area if the tear-gas grenades start to fly.

Opening hours, public holidays and fiestas

Public offices in Bolivia have adopted a new system, *horario continuo*, whereby they work Monday to Friday straight through from 8.30am to 4pm without closing for lunch.

Banks' opening hours are generally Monday to Friday from 8.30am to noon and 2.30pm to 6pm; some bank branches are also open on Saturdays from 9am until noon. ENTEL **telephone offices** usually open daily from around 8am to 8pm, sometimes later. Public offices tend to often open later and close earlier than they are supposed to; conversely, private businesses, particularly those connected with tourism, often work longer hours than advertised and open on Sundays.

Bolivians welcome any excuse for a party, and the country enjoys a huge number of national, regional and local **fiestas**, which are taken very seriously, often involving lengthy preparation and substantial expense. In addition to the major national and regional celebrations, almost every town and village has its own annual **local fiesta** (some have several), usually held on the day of its patron saint. The occasional visitor will usually be warmly welcomed to local fiestas, but these are often fairly private affairs, and crowds of

Calendar of public holidays

January 1 New Year's Day
February/March Carnaval. Celebrated throughout the country in the week before Lent. The Oruro Carnaval (see box on p.250) is the most famous, but Santa Cruz, Sucre and Tarija also stage massive fiestas.
March/April Semana Santa (Easter) is celebrated with religious processions throughout Bolivia. Good Friday is a public holiday.
May 1 Labour Day (movable public holiday).
May/June Corpus Christi (public holiday). La Paz stages the Señor del Gran Poder, its biggest and most colourful folkloric dance parade.
July 16 Virgen del Carmen. Processions and dances in honour of the Virgen del Carmen, the patron saint of many towns and villages across Bolivia.
August 6 Independence Day (public holiday). Parades and parties throughout the country, notably in Copacabana.
November 1–2 All Saints and Day of the Dead (public holiday).
December 25 Christmas Day (public holiday).

camera-wielding tourists may provoke a hostile reaction – sensitivity is the key.

Outdoor activities

Dominated by the dramatic high mountain scenery of the Andes and home to some of the most pristine wilderness areas in South America, Bolivia has the potential to become one of the world's top destinations for outdoor enthusiasts. As yet, though, its enormous potential has scarcely been tapped, and organized facilities are few and far between. To the true outdoor enthusiast, however, this should simply add to the appeal.

Whether you want to stroll for half a day, take a hardcore hike for two weeks over high passes down into remote Amazonian valleys or climb one of the hundred peaks over 5000m, Bolivia is ideal for **trekking and climbing.** The best **season** is between May and September, while the most pleasant and reliable weather is between June and August. During the rainy season between December and March or April, rain turns paths and roads to mud and streams to impassable torrents, while cloud covers the high passes and blocks many of the best views.

The most popular region for these activities is the **Cordillera Real**, crisscrossed by paths and mule trains used by local people. The shores of **Lago Titicaca** and the Isla del Sol are also excellent for hiking, combining awesome scenery with gentle gradients. People looking for more seclusion should head for the remote and beautiful **Cordillera Apolobamba**, which is traversed by one of Bolivia's finest trekking routes, the Trans-Apolobamba Trek.

The easiest way to go trekking or climbing is on an **organized trip** with a local tour operator. There are dozens of these in La Paz (see box on p.207) and in several other cities, with treks costing between US$20 and $40 per person per day, depending on what's included and how many people are in the group. Things are much cheaper if you have all your own equipment, organize the logistics yourself, and just hire a **guide**. You can get good advice and find fully qualified mountaineering guides through the **Club Andino Boliviano** (☎02/231-2875) in La Paz at Calle Mexico 1638, just up from Plaza del Estudiante. In rural towns and villages you can usually find local *campesinos* who know all the trails and will act as a guide for a relatively small fee (on treks of more than one day you'll also need to provide them with food and possibly a tent).

In the highlands it's often a good idea to hire a **pack animal**, most commonly a mule, to carry your gear. These cost about US$6–8 a day and can carry over 100kg with relative ease; donkeys and llamas carry less, move slowly but should be proportionally cheaper to hire. You'll also need to pay for the *arriero* who handles the animals, and who can usually double as an effective guide. If you plan to go trekking over longer distances without a guide, you should be competent at route-finding and map-reading, carry a compass and/or Global Positioning System, and equip yourself with the relevant topographical maps, where available. Really, though, it's much better to trek with a **guide**: getting lost in remote mountain or forested regions is easy and can be very dangerous, and rescue services are pretty much nonexistent.

Bolivia is home to some of the finest **mountain bike** routes in the world, and travelling by bike is one of the best ways to experience the Andes. In recent years a number of tour companies in La Paz have set up **downhill mountain biking** trips; Gravity Assisted Mountain Biking (see p.207) has the best reputation for its experienced guides, well-maintained and high-quality bikes and adequate safety equipment. The most popular route by far is down the road from **La Paz to Coroico** in the Yungas (see p.241), a stunning 3500m descent that many travellers rate as one of the highlights of South America. You don't need any previous mountain-biking experience to do this ride, which is easy to organize as a day-trip from La Paz.

History

Landlocked Bolivia has frequently been subjected to the expansionist aspirations of its neighbours – returning the dubious favour on several occasions. Following the mysterious demise of the indigenous Tiwanaku, the Aymara tribe emerged, only to be invaded by the Incas, who were in turn overrun by the Spanish. Following a nearly two-decade-long war for independence, Bolivia spent much of the nineteenth century engaged in various territorial struggles with Peru, Chile, Brazil and Paraguay. While Bolivia has embraced democracy and civilian rule since the military relinquished power in 1982, national tensions are now internal, taking the form of urban demonstrations and roadblocks in the countryside.

Pre-Columbian Bolivia

The first major civilization to develop on the Bolivian Altiplano was the **Tiwanaku** culture, centred on the city of the same name, which was founded on the southern shores of Lago Titicaca around 1000 BC. At the height of its power, the city was a sophisticated religious and urban centre with distinct classes of peasants, priests, warriors, artisans and aristocrats, and an economy based on mining, llama and alpaca herding and, above all, the cultivation of potatoes and other crops. From around 700 AD Tiwanaku's influence spread across the Andes and it became the centre of a vast empire of colonies and religious centres linked by paved stone roads served by huge llama caravans and comprising much of modern Bolivia, southern Peru, northeast Argentina and northern Chile. Some time after 1000 AD, however, the Tiwanaku Empire collapsed as dramatically as it had risen, its population dispersed and its great cities of stone were abandoned and fell into ruin. The reasons for the empire's sudden downfall remain unclear: possible explanations include a cataclysmic earthquake or foreign invasion, though the most likely is that a prolonged drought from about 1000 AD wiped out the intensive agriculture on which Tiwanaku depended.

The Altiplano around the shores of Lago Titicaca fell under the control of the **Aymara**, who probably migrated to the region from the highlands to the west sometime after the collapse of Tiwanaku. Aymara lived in fortified settlements (*pucaras*) some distance from the lakeshore, relied on large-scale llama and alpaca herding rather than intensive cultivation and followed a much more localized religion, building few ceremonial sites other than the stone tombs (*chulpas*), where important individuals were buried.

By the mid-fifteenth century the Aymara kingdoms found themselves in growing competition with the expansionist **Incas**, whose capital was at Cusco in southern Peru. The Aymara kingdoms were gradually incorporated into the *Collasuyo*, one of the richest and most populous of the Inca Empire's four quarters, or *suyus*. With the conquest of the *Collasuyo* the Incas confirmed their status as the most powerful Andean Empire since Tiwanaku. In the space of a century, the Incas had become masters of the greatest empire yet seen in the Americas, stretching over five thousand kilometres from southern Colombia to northern Chile and boasting a population of perhaps twenty million. It was ruled by a god-emperor who claimed direct descent from the sun.

The Spanish conquest and the colonial era

Within eighty years of their conquest of the Altiplano, the Inca Empire was brought to a catastrophic end by a small band of Spaniards led by Francisco Pizarro, who landed on the coast of northern Peru and set about a war of conquest that would change the Andean world forever. The first **conquistadors** arrived in 1532 to find the Inca Empire weakened by a devastating epidemic, – probably smallpox – and increasing rivalries between the Inca rulers. Pizarro and his followers began their steady conquest by occupying Cusco without a fight and installing a puppet emperor. In 1537, Spanish abuses prompted a massive Inca rebellion, ending after a series of bloody battles with the Spanish conquest of **Alto Peru**. With its dense indigenous population and rich mineral wealth – the two resources that the conquistadors were keenest to exploit – Alto Peru was a rich prize.

The first Spanish city founded in Alto Peru was **La Plata** (now Sucre), strategically located in a temperate valley southeast of the Altiplano. In 1545, the continent's richest deposit of silver was discovered southwest of La Plata at what became known as **Cerro Rico** (Rich Mountain) and the mining city of **Potosí** sprung up at the foot of the mountain. A second city, **La Paz**, was founded in 1548 just east of Lago Titicaca, followed by **Cochabamba** and **Tarija** (both 1574) in the well-populated, temperate and fertile inter-Andean valleys. La Plata was confirmed as the **capital of Alto Peru** in 1558, when it was made the seat of an independent royal court and administration – the Audiencia de Charcas – with judicial and executive power over the entire region. The city of **Santa Cruz de la Sierra** was founded in 1561 in the midst of the Eastern Lowlands.

The colonial society was conceived of as consisting of two separate communities, the Spanish and the *Republica de Indios*, with the latter clearly subject to the former. During the colonial era, the Spanish introduced a variety of measures to subjugate the indigenous population, convert them to Catholicism through missionary efforts and generally "civilize" them. In the highlands, the conquerors took indigenous wives and concubines and within a few decades, they were surrounded by an ever-increasing number of mixed-race *mestizos*, or *chollos*. A complex system of class and caste developed, with Spanish-born *peninsulares* at the top, followed by Spaniards born in the Americas, the so-called *criollos*, the *mestizo* classes in the middle and the oppressed indigenous majority at the bottom.

Independence

Indigenous discontent with Spanish rule remained strong throughout the colonial period and resulted in a massive indigenous **rebellion in 1780–82**, which shook the Spanish colonial regime to its foundations. The war was characterized by great brutality on both sides, with massive destruction of property and loss of life, and ended with the Spanish comprehensively crushing the revolt.

By the early nineteenth century, growing resentment with Spanish rule had spread amongst the white *criollo* and *mestizo* population of Alto Peru, the result of severe economic depression, their exclusion from high-level administrative jobs (reserved for Spanish-born immigrants) and regulations preventing trade with any country other than Spain. The first move towards open revolt against Spanish rule took place in La Plata on May 25, 1809, with the judges of the Audiencia de Charcas rejecting the demands of the president of Audiencia that they recognize the authority of the Junta Central. In July, the citizens of La Paz went a step further, declaring an independent government – the first declaration of independence by a Spanish colony in America. These revolts were quickly crushed by armies sent by the viceroys in Lima and Buenos Aires, but this only fuelled the growing *criollo* enthusiasm for independence. Struggles for independence swept South America – the citizens of Buenos Aires successfully rebelled against Spain in 1810, the Argentine General José de San Martín crossed the Andes to liberate Chile in 1817, and by 1821 the great Venezuelan independence leader Simón Bolívar – known as "El Libertador" – was advancing south through Ecuador having finally liberated Venezuela and Colombia. The two forces converged on Peru, the last major centre of Spanish power and, in 1824, Bolívar's most brilliant general, Antonio José de Sucre, destroyed the last Spanish army at the Battle of Ayacucho in the southern Peruvian Andes, securing Alto Peru's freedom early the following year. Bolívar handed control of the region over to Sucre. On August 6, 1825, the delegates unanimously rejected union with either Peru or Argentina and adopted a declaration of independence. Five days later, they resolved to name the new republic Bolivia.

Post-independence Bolivia

Sixteen years of war had devastated the country's infrastructure and severely disrupted the economy. The country's first president, General Sucre, sought to organize the Bolivian state along classic liberal lines, radically attacked the Catholic Church and confiscated most of its wealth and property, a revolutionary act from which the Bolivian church never really recovered. After surviving a coup and assassination attempt by former comrades, he left office in 1829 and went into voluntary exile.

His successor, **General Andrés de Santa Cruz**, intervened decisively in a civil war in Peru and sought to join Bolivia and Peru together in a confederation, a move seen as a threat by Chile, which sent aid to rebels and then an entire army to Peru. In 1839, Santa Cruz was finally defeated at the **Battle of Yunguyo** and went into exile, and the Peru–Bolivia confederation was dissolved. For the next forty years the country was characterized by political chaos, presided over by a series of military strongmen, or *caudillos*.

The late nineteenth and early twentieth centuries were marked by a series of **wars**. The lucrative industry of exporting guano and nitrates (both used as fertilizer) found on Bolivia's desert coastal strip prompted president Hilarión Daza to increase export taxes in 1878 despite protests by Chilean and British companies who controlled the industry. Pursuing a longstanding expansionist aim, Chilean forces began the **War of the Pacific** early next year, occupying the entire Bolivian coastline and then invading Peru, then allied with Bolivia. Both countries were defeated, and Bolivia officially ceded the territory to Chile in 1904. The loss of the coast – and with it direct access to the outside world – was perceived as a national tragedy.

Towards the end of the nineteenth century, the explosion of the rubber boom in the Amazon lowlands owing to the massive increase in the international demand for rubber led to yet another war with a neighbouring country, Brazil. After three years of sporadic fighting – the **Acre War** – the region was annexed by Brazil, an act later recognized by Bolivia in return for compensation.

Around the same time, as the price of silver collapsed and the international demand for tin rose, the new tin-mining elite and the growing urban professional classes became dissatisfied with Sucre's conservative government. In 1899, they successfully rebelled in the bloody **Federal Revolution**, making La Paz the seat of a centralized government; Sucre, however, remained the capital in name.

By 1931, the Bolivian army began aggressively probing the disputed frontier with Paraguay in the thorny wilderness of the Chaco. Border clashes escalated and, by July 1932, the **Chaco War** had broken out and lasted for the next two years, resulting with terrible loss of life and the Bolivian army driven out of all the disputed territory.

Modern era

The most important of the many new political parties that emerged in the period following the Chaco War was the **Movimiento Nacionalista Revolucionario** (MNR), which advocated nationalization of the mines and, with other left-wing groups, quickly came to dominate the national congress. The MNR-organized **National Revolution** began in La Paz on April 9, 1952, and lasted for three days, after which its leader **Víctor Paz Estenssoro** took power. He introduced a series of new measures: universal suffrage, nationalization of the big mining companies and radical agrarian reforms under which hacienda lands in the highlands were given back to the indigenous peasants. In 1956, **Hernán Siles** took over as president and turned to the US for financial aid, which stabilized the economy to a degree but opened factional rifts within the party. Paz Estenssoro was re-elected in 1960 and again in 1964, the second time with **General René Barrientos** as his vice-president who, within months of the vote, led a military junta and ousted him from power.

A succession of military regimes followed Barrientos' death in a helicopter crash in 1969. **General Juan José Torres** sought to move military government to the left, even turning to the Soviet Union for financial aid, but was ousted by right-wing army colleagues backed by the US. This coup in 1971 brought to power **Colonel Hugo Banzer**, who banned all political parties and trade unions during a right-wing regime that lasted for the next seven years until he stepped down amid widening protests and strikes. In 1978 elections were held then annulled after massive fraud by Banzer's chosen successor, General Juan Pereda. In the elections of 1980, the centre-left coalition led by Hernán Siles emerged victorious, but before he could take office, hardline officers launched yet another military coup, bringing to power General **Luis Garcia Meza**. Presiding over the most brutal and corrupt military regime in modern Bolivian history, Meza's rule was enforced by paramilitary death squads used ruthlessly against opponents of the regime and funded by his government's direct involvement in the emerging international cocaine trade.

The return to democracy

Garcia Meza was deposed in an army revolt in 1980 and two years later the last military junta was forced to resign following massive protests. The recalled congress elected Hernán Siles as president, marking a **return to democratic rule** that has lasted ever since. Siles stepped down in 1985 and Víctor Paz Estenssoro won his fourth presidential term. To the surprise of all, Paz Estenssoro turned his back on the traditional MNR approach and adopted the **New Economic Plan** – a raft of orthodox liberal shock policies backed by the three main parties – the MNR, Banzer's ADN and the centre-left MIR led by Jaime Paz Zamora and designed to rescue the economy and combat hyperinflation. Although it succeeded in ending hyperinflation, its immediate effect was to plunge Bolivia into a recession which was eased only by a growing trade in the production and export of **cocaine**, in response to the rising demand in the US. The enormous wealth generated by the cocaine industry created enormous corruption at every level of Bolivian society. Elections in 1989 saw the MNR win a majority of votes, but horse trading in the congress led to the third-placed candidate, MIR leader **Jaime Paz Zamora**, becoming president with the backing of the ADN. By the end of the 1970s, a new generation of radical Aymara leaders had formed a powerful new national peasant union, the **CSUTCB**. Inspired by a new ideology of Aymara resurgence known as **Katarismo** (after the nineteenth-century rebel Tupac Katari), these peasant leaders demanded recompense for the unequal treatment meted out to indigenous peasants by successive governments and the redefining of Bolivia's national identity to reflect its indigenous majority. When the MNR returned to power in 1993, president **Gonzalo Sánchez de Lozada** recognized Bolivian multi-cultural society and introduced a series of far-reaching reforms, as well as inviting the moderate Katarista leader **Víctor Hugo Cárdenas** to serve as vice-president, the first time an Aymara Bolivian had occupied so high an official position.

In 1997, Hugo Banzer was elected president and, under pressure from the US, made the eradication of illegal coca, the so-called **Coca Zero** campaign, a priority – a particular irony given the known links of most of his government to drug traffickers. The campaign provoked massive resistance from the well-organized *campesino* syndicates and an escalating death toll as the Bolivian army was sent in to clear roadblocks and tear up coca plantations. As well as the human cost, the loss of coca dollars had a knock-on effect on the Bolivian economy, which in the late 1990s slid into recession following financial crises in Brazil and Argentina.

Bolivia today

With the economy in crisis, Banzer approached the end of his democratic term in familiar style, declaring a state of emergency in 2000 and sending troops in to clear roads blocked in a combined national protest by coca-growers, Aymara peasants, and residents of Cochabamba outraged at the sale of their water supplies to foreign corporations. The following year, Banzer was diagnosed with cancer and forced to retire, leaving his successor, the technocrat **Jorge Quiroga**, to serve out the rest of his party's term.

In the August 2002 elections, the centre-right Gonzalo Sánchez de Lozada won a victory over his major opponent **Evo Morales**, the radical leader of indigenous coca growers, and proposed various solutions to the country's fundamental social and economic problems, such as setting up a public works campaign to bring down the harrowing unemployment rates. His austerity policies led to a proposed income tax hike in Feb 2003, which caused violent protests in La Paz, as well as other parts of Bolivia, resulting in a number of casualties. Though he quickly withdrew the tax raise plan in response to the demonstrations, in the fall of 2003, massive protests against a proposed scheme to export natural gas shook the country, resulting in more deaths and Sánchez de Lozada's **resignation** that October.

Books

There are few books published exclusively about Bolivia, and even fewer Bolivian writers make it into English. That said, the works listed below offer a good range of background material on Bolivian history, culture, society and the natural world.

Jon Lee Anderson *Che Guevara: A Revolutionary Life* (Bantam/Grove Press). Absorbing and exhaustively researched account of Latin America's most famous guerrilla, by the journalist whose investigations led to the discovery of Che's secret grave in Vallegrande.

Yossi Brain *Bolivia: A Climbing Guide* (Cordee/Mountaineers Books) and *Trekking in Bolivia: A Traveller's Guide* (Menasha Ridge

Press/Mountaineers Books). Both are musts for all serious climbers, with expert route descriptions and excellent logistical advice and information by the man who was the leading climbing guide in Bolivia.

Richard Gott *Land Without Evil: Utopian Journeys Across the South American Watershed* (Verso). Wonderful account of a journey through the former Jesuit mission towns of Brazil and Eastern Bolivia, interspersed with finely researched histories of the many fruitless journeys and forgotten expeditions across the same region of swamp and trackless scrub made by travellers through the centuries.

Ernesto "Che" Guevara *The Motorcycle Diaries* (Verso). Amusing account of Che's motorcycle trip through South America in the 1950s, providing an intimate portrait of a young beatnik traveller and romantic idealist undergoing some of the experiences – particularly in revolutionary Bolivia – that would later transform him into a ruthless guerrilla leader.

Susanna Hecht and Alexander Cockburn *The Fate of the Forest: Developers, Destroyers and Defenders of the Amazon* (o/p in the US/Penguin). Comprehensive and highly readable account of the threat to the Amazon rainforest, with detailed description of the political and social conflicts that underlie the destruction of the rainforest and a heartfelt and well-argued plea for its survival.

Herbert S. Klein *Bolivia, the Evolution of a Multi-Ethnic Society* (Oxford). The best standard English-language history of Bolivia from the arrival of early man to the present day: concise, detailed and clearly written, if a little dry.

John C. Kricher *A Neotropical Companion* (Princeton University Press). Enjoyable general introduction to the flora, fauna and ecology of the tropical lowlands of South and Central America, well written and packed with detail.

Steve J. Stern (ed) *Resistance, Rebellion and Consciousness in the Andean Peasant World* (Wisconsin). Absorbing collection of richly detailed historical essays on Quechua and Aymara insurrections and uprisings, ranging from the Great Rebellion of the late eighteenth century to the radical peasant politics of today.

2.1

La Paz and around

Few cities have a setting as spectacular as **LA PAZ**. Over 3500m above sea level, the city cowers in a narrow canyon gouged from the high Altiplano, the cluster of church spires and office blocks at its centre dwarfed by the magnificent icebound peak of Mount Illimani, which rises imperiously to the southeast. On either side, the steep slopes of the valley are covered by the ramshackle homes of the city's poorer inhabitants, which cling precariously to even the harshest gradients.

With a population of just over a million, La Paz is the political and commercial hub of Bolivia and the capital in all but name (technically, that honour belongs to Sucre, the seat of the supreme court). But for all that it retains the feel of a provincial city, holding off the tides of globalization by its isolation and unique cultural make-up. Despite an underlying bustle and frenetic energy, the exigencies of the high altitude make the pace of life quite slow.

Most visitors find La Paz's compelling street life and tremendous cultural vitality worthy of a few days' exploration – you'll brush shoulders with well-dressed office workers on mobile phones and colourfully dressed Aymara women selling dried llama foetuses. The city also makes an excellent base for trekking in the surrounding mountains and exploring the rest of the country.

Some history

Founded in 1548, **La Ciudad de Nuestra Señora de la Paz** – the City of Our Lady of Peace – prospered as a waystation on the route between the mines of Potosí and the coast and between Lima and Buenos Aires, the two great centres of colonial rule in South America. By 1665 some five hundred Spaniards – many of them missionaries bent on converting the densely populated surrounding area – were living in La Paz, while a much larger indigenous population was housed in the three parishes that sprang up on the other side of the Río Choqueyapu, clearly separated from the Spanish city.

La Paz's importance as a centre of colonial power made it an obvious target during the great rebellion that swept the Andes in 1780–81. In 1781 an indigenous army led by **Tupac Katari** twice laid siege to the city, unsuccessfully. The relative tranquillity that followed lasted only until 1809, when the leading citizens of La Paz became the first South American group to declare their complete independence from Spain, launching a fourteen-year civil war. By the time Bolivia's independence was finally secured in 1825, La Paz was the biggest city in the country, with a population of some 40,000. The growing rivalry between the capital of Sucre and the politically powerful city of La Paz culminated in a short but bloody **civil war** in 1899 that left La Paz the seat of the government, home to the president and the congress, and Sucre the seat of the supreme court.

In 1952 La Paz was the scene of the fierce street fighting, which ushered in the **revolution** led by the MNR (see p.215). Post-revolutionary changes triggered a mass migration of Aymara peasants to the city, quadrupling La Paz's population to over a million and transforming it into a predominantly Aymara city. Today, as the poor indigenous neighbourhoods have crept up the steep slopes around the centre and to El Alto, so the wealthier, European-descended residents have retreated to the new residential suburbs of the Zona Sur, maintaining to some extent the city's old duality.

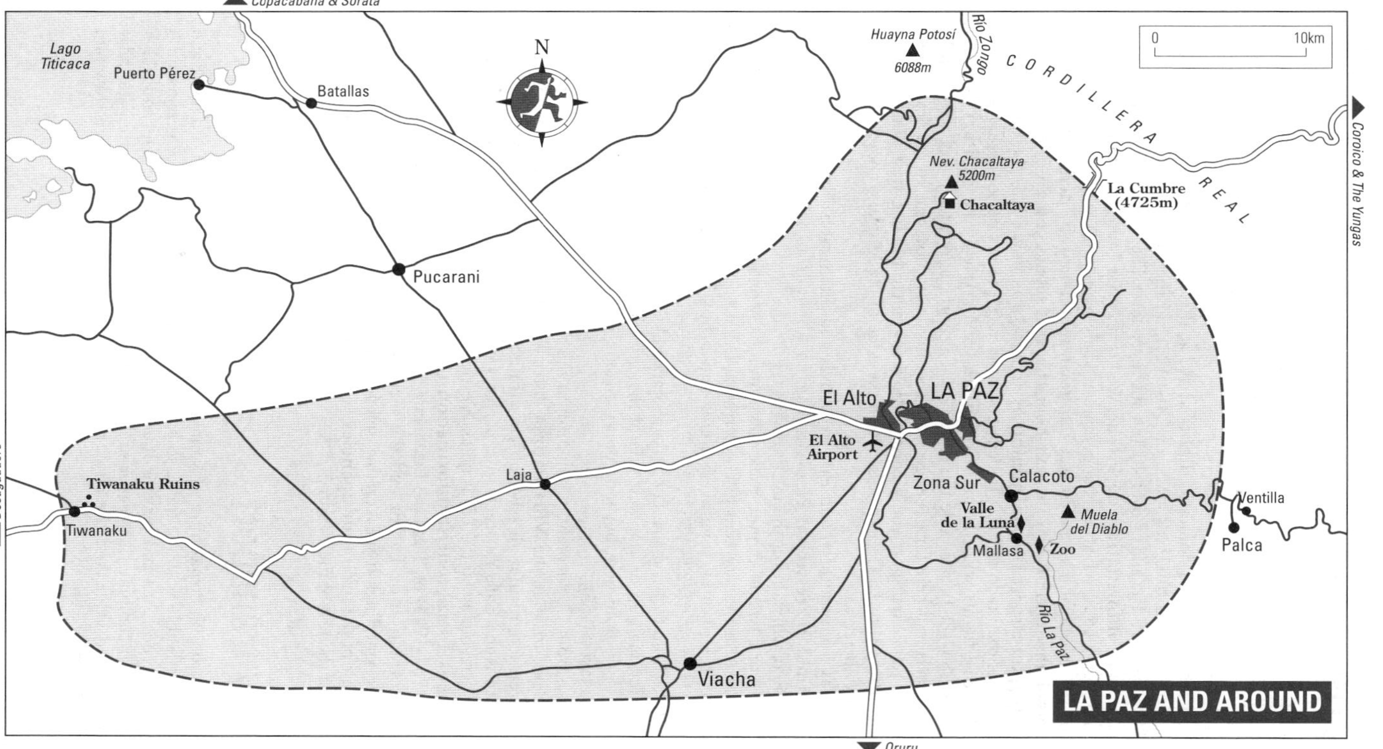
LA PAZ AND AROUND
Copacabana & Sorata
Lago Titicaca
Puerto Pérez
Batallas
N
Huayna Potosí
6088m
Río Zongo
CORDILLERA REAL
0
10km
Coroico & The Yungas
Nev. Chacaltaya
5200m
Chacaltaya
La Cumbre (4725m)
Pucarani
El Alto
LA PAZ
El Alto Airport
Desaguadero
Tiwanaku Ruins
Tiwanaku
Laja
Zona Sur
Calacoto
Valle de la Luna
Mallasa
Zoo
Muela del Diablo
Ventilla
Palca
Río La Paz
Viacha
Oruru

Arrival and information

Arriving in La Paz by **bus** or **plane** is a relatively painless experience: the city's small size makes it fairly easy to find your way around and there are inexpensive taxis and still cheaper public transport, though the latter isn't always easy to travel in with big bags.

International and domestic **flights** arrive at the small **El Alto airport** (flight information on ⓣ02/281-0122 or 281-0123), on the rim of the Altiplano about 11km from La Paz and at over 4000m above sea level. The airport's limited facilities include an **information desk** (Tue, Wed, Fri & Sat 5am–11.30pm, other days 5am–9pm), an ATM, an exchange bureau (daily 5am–9pm), phone booths and an Internet terminal. The easiest way into town from here is by **taxi**, they wait right outside the terminal and the half-hour ride that should cost $6–7. Alternatively, Cotranstur airport **shuttle minibuses** (micros) run down into the city and the length of the Prado to Plaza Isabella La Católica ($0.55 per person; every 10 min).

Internal flights with the military airline TAM arrive at the **military airport** (ⓣ02/284-1884), alongside the commercial airport on Avenida Juan Pablo II in El Alto. Taxis wait here for passengers, but the shuttle bus does not; to get down to La Paz by public transport you'll need to catch any micro heading west along Avenida Juan Pablo II to La Ceja, the district on the edge of the Altiplano above La Paz, and change there.

Buses from southern and eastern Bolivia and international buses arrive at the **Terminal Terrestre** on Plaza Antofagasta, about 1km northeast of Plaza San Francisco, which lies at the north end of the Prado. From here, it's a short taxi ride ($0.90) or a twenty-minute walk down Avenida Montes to the main accommodation areas in the city centre. The terminal has snack bars, luggage storage, a post office, telephones, several agencies and a bus **information office** (daily 7am–11pm; ⓣ02/228-0551).

Buses from Copacabana, Tiwanaku, Sorata and Charazani arrive in the **cemetery district**, high up on the west side of the city. Plenty of micros head down to the city centre from here, but it's a pretty chaotic part of town, so it's a good idea to take a taxi ($0.85).

Buses from Coroico and Chulumani in the Yungas, and from Rurrenabaque and the Beni, arrive in the **Villa Fátima** district, in the far northeast of the city. The different companies all have offices around the intersection of Avenida de las Americas and Calle Yanacachi. Again, plenty of micros head down to the city centre from here, but a taxi ($0.85) is quicker, easier and more secure.

There's a small **tourist information office** (Mon–Fri 9am–noon & 3–7pm; ⓣ02/237-1044) on Plaza del Estudiante at the end of the Prado, which has plenty of information on La Paz and the surrounding area. The helpful staff usually includes one English-speaker; they sell good city and regional maps and offer flyers for most of the main **tour agencies**, which are the best places to go for information on the rest of the country.

City transport

You'll probably spend most of your time in the city centre, which is compact and easily **walkable** with the traffic so congested that the quickest way to get around is often on foot. That said, beware of unruly drivers, the lack of traffic rules and take it easy when climbing the steeper streets at this altitude. **Taxis** are plentiful and relatively good value, and the city's **public transport** network, though slow and chaotic, is very cheap.

Taxis

Unlicensed taxis charge about $0.55 per passenger for journeys anywhere in the centre of town – there are no meters so it's best to agree on the fare at the beginning of the journey. The more reliable, marked **radio taxis** charge a flat rate of about $0.80 for anywhere in the city centre regardless of the number of passengers; try Alfa (Ⓣ02/241-2525), Diplomatico (Ⓣ02/222-4343) or Ideal (Ⓣ02/222-2425). Taxi fares increase for longer journeys by both unlicensed and radio taxis. For trips outside the city there's a **long-distance taxi** office (Ⓣ02/235-8336) outside the *Radisson* hotel on Avenida Arce.

Buses, micros and trufis

There are two main forms of public transport in La Paz: **city buses** and privately owned minibuses, known as **micros**. Though quicker and more numerous than the big buses, micros can be incredibly cramped and their routes very confusing. The names of the micro's destinations are written on signs inside the windscreen and bellowed incessantly by the driver's assistants so it's usually enough to wait by any major intersection until you hear the name of your destination shouted out; alternatively, ask a driver's assistant where to catch the relevant micro. Your third option is a **trufi** – basically a car operating as a micro with a maximum of four passengers and following fixed routes. Trufis charge a flat rate of about $0.25 in the city centre and micros about $0.20; city buses cost slightly less. All charge extra if your luggage fills a space that might otherwise be occupied by another passenger.

Accommodation

There's plenty of accommodation in La Paz to suit most budgets, though things get busier and pricier in the peak tourist season from June to August. Most places to stay are in the **city centre** within a few blocks of **Plaza San Francisco**, close to or in the midst of the colourful market district and within walking distance of most of the city's main attractions. As this is where most tourist services are concentrated, it's convenient for booking tours, changing money and sorting out other practicalities. The other option is to stay in one of the more upmarket places down the **Prado**, towards the peaceful neighbourhood of **San Pedro**, midway between the city centre and the middle-class suburb of **Sopocachi** to the south, where most of the city's better restaurants and nightspots are.

City Centre

Alojamiento El Solario Murillo 776 Ⓣ02/236-7963, Ⓔelsolariohotel@yahoo.com. Very good budget option, close to Plaza San Francisco, with welcoming staff and a friendly atmosphere. Rooms feature comfortable beds, shared bathrooms, Internet access, laundry and kitchen facilities. ❷

Angelo Colonial Hotel Mariscal Santa Cruz 1058 Ⓣ02/212-5067, Ⓔhostalangelocolonial@yahoo.com. Very good central budget option, with clean rooms, each with shared bath and kitchen facilities, set around a colonial courtyard. Try to get a room in the back, as the front ones overlook the noisy Prado. Internet access available. ❸

Gran Hotel Paris Plaza Murillo Ⓣ02/220-3030 231-9170, 236-2547 Ⓔparishot@ceibo.entelnet.bo, Ⓦwww.granparishotel.com. The oldest hotel in La Paz, built in 1911 in delightful Belle Epoque style and recently refurbished. The spacious rooms come with period furniture and are set around a glass-roofed patio, while the suites with balconies looking onto Plaza Murillo are well worth the extra cost. Heating, cable TV, Internet access and a buffet breakfast are included. Rooms ❽, suites ❾

Hostal Naira Sagárnaga 161 Ⓣ02/235-5645, Ⓔhnaira@ceibo.entelnet.bo, Ⓦwww.cafe-monet.com/hostal_naira. Perhaps the best value in its price range and excellently located just up from Plaza San Francisco with bright, modern rooms with TV and phone set around a lovely colonial courtyard. Internet access is available and breakfast is included in the downstairs café. ❺

Hostal Republica Comercio 1455 ⓣ02/220-2742 or 220-3448, ⓔmarynela@ceibo.entelnet.bo, ⓦwww.angelfire.com/wv/hostalrepublica. Pleasant rooms (with or without bath; triples and quadruples available) in a beautifully restored old mansion set around two quiet courtyards and a sunny garden, with cafeteria and laundry facilities. It's just three blocks from Plaza Murillo, but a steep climb up from the Prado. ❹

Hostal Señorial Yanacocha 540 ⓣ02/240-6042. A block down from Plaza Murillo, this friendly hostel has a set of clean pleasant albeit dark rooms, with shared and private bath, kitchen and laundry facilities. ❸

Hostería Blanquita Calle Santa Cruz 242, between Illampu and Murillo ⓣ02/245-7495, ⓔcindysuarezz@yahoo.es. Newly renovated colonial mansion in the heart of the market district, with clean pleasant rooms, all with private bath, set around a plant-filled patio. Rooms in the front get noisy. Tourist info and breakfast available. ❸

Hotel Gloria Calle Potosí 909 ⓣ02/240-7070, ⓔgloriatr@ceibo.entelnet.bo, ⓦwww.hotelgloriabolivia.com. Uninspiring high-rise hotel with central location and comfortable modern rooms equipped with cable TV, heat, and a fridge and nice city views. It also features a great vegetarian restaurant. ❼

Hotel Torino Socabaya 457 ⓣ02/240-6003. Former backpackers' favourite and still always busy, offering basic rooms with or without bath set around an elegant colonial courtyard; pick one of the more comfortable rooms in the new wing. The rather dour staff and noisy restaurant have dented its popularity. ❷

Residencial Latino Junín 857 ⓣ02/228-5463. Cheap central establishment, just a couple of blocks up from Plaza Murillo, with basic but clean rooms (with or without bath) set around a quiet colonial patio. ❷

El Prado, San Pedro and Sopocachi

El Rey Palace Hotel Av 20 de Octubre 1947, Sopocachi ⓣ02/241-8541, ⓔhotelrey@caoba.entelnet.bo or info@hotel-rey-palace-bolivia.com, ⓦwww.hotel-rey-palace-bolivia.com. One of the best value upmarket options in La Paz, with big, comfortable and stylishly decorated rooms boasting the full range of facilities, including heating, cable TV, American buffet breakfast and parking. ❼

Hostal Sucre Calle Colombia 340, Plaza San Pedro, San Pedro ⓣ02/249-2038. Friendly and well-located hostel, with basic rooms with or without bath set around a pleasant courtyard. Breakfast available. ❸–❹

Hotel Europa Tiahuanacu 64, Sopocachi ⓣ02/231-5656, ⓔunico@hotel-europa-bolivia.com. La Paz's most luxurious and expensive hotel, decorated in style and boasting all the features you could wish for, including heating and humidifiers, Internet access, bars and restaurants, along with a swimming pool, Jacuzzi, sauna and gymnasium. ❾

The City

In terms of conventional tourist attractions La Paz's appeal is modest. There are still some fine **colonial palaces** and **churches** in the centre of town, but in general the architecture is drab and functional, while the city's few **museums** scarcely do justice to Bolivia's fascinating history and culture. Most visitors are enthralled by the energy of La Paz's **street life** and its rich cultural heritage, while the absence of green areas is more than redeemed by the sight of Illimani, the majestic mountain whose permanently snow-covered 6439-metre peak dominates the landscape.

El Prado, La Paz's main commercial thoroughfare, runs southeast through the city, its official name changing from Avenida Mariscal Santa Cruz to Avenida 16 de Julio as it heads south before ending at Plaza del Estudiante. The boulevard – one of the city's few flat and spacious areas – is punctuated with statues of historical figures and features a central promenade with pleasant gardens and benches, a popular place for strolling and socializing.

To the east of the Prado, the **colonial city centre** is still the main commercial and government district, dominated by banks, ministries and the men in grey suits who run them. To the west of the Prado, the main **indigenous neighbourhoods** sweep up the steep slopes of the valley, their narrow, winding streets filled with the colour and ceaseless bustle of seemingly endless street markets.

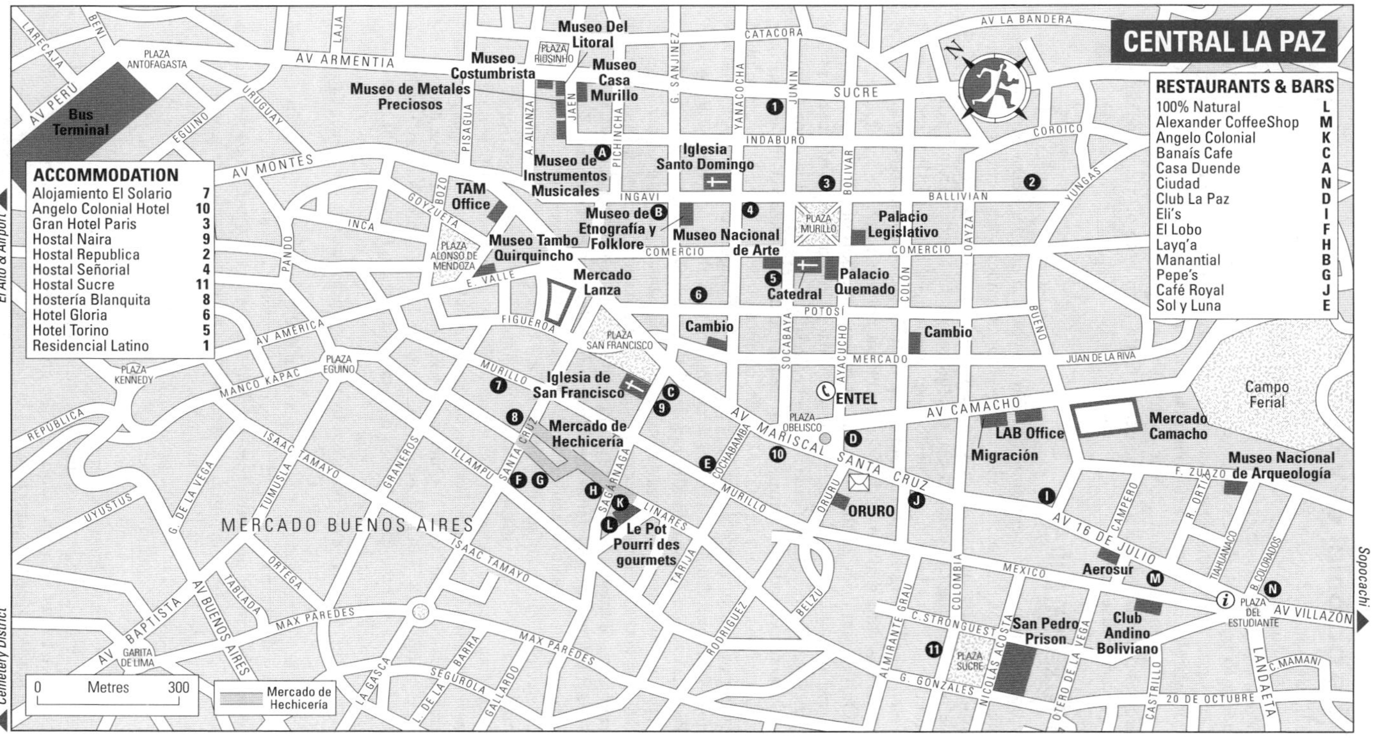
CENTRAL LA PAZ
RESTAURANTS & BARS
100% Natural L
Alexander CoffeeShop M
Angelo Colonial K
Banaís Cafe C
Casa Duende A
Ciudad N
Club La Paz D
Eli's I
El Lobo F
Layq'a H
Manantial B
Pepe's G
Café Royal J
Sol y Luna E
ACCOMMODATION
Alojamiento El Solario 7
Angelo Colonial Hotel 10
Gran Hotel Paris 3
Hostal Naira 9
Hostal Republica 2
Hostal Señorial 4
Hostal Sucre 11
Hostería Blanquita 8
Hotel Gloria 6
Hotel Torino 5
Residencial Latino 1
Bus Terminal
Museo Del Litoral
Museo Costumbrista
Museo Casa Murillo
Museo de Metales Preciosos
Museo de Instrumentos Musicales
Iglesia Santo Domingo
TAM Office
Museo de Etnografía y Folklore
Museo Nacional de Arte
Palacio Legislativo
Museo Tambo Quirquincho
Mercado Lanza
Catedral
Palacio Quemado
Cambio
Cambio
ENTEL
Iglesia de San Francisco
Mercado de Hechicería
Le Pot Pourri des gourmets
ORURO
LAB Office
Migración
Mercado Camacho
Campo Ferial
Museo Nacional de Arqueología
Aerosur
Club Andino Boliviano
San Pedro Prison
MERCADO BUENOS AIRES
PLAZA ANTOFAGASTA
PLAZA RIOSINHO
PLAZA MURILLO
PLAZA ALONSO DE MENDOZA
PLAZA SAN FRANCISCO
PLAZA OBELISCO
PLAZA EGUINO
PLAZA KENNEDY
PLAZA SUCRE
PLAZA DEL ESTUDIANTE
GARITA DE LIMA
AV LA BANDERA
AV ARMENTIA
AV PERU
AV MONTES
AV AMERICA
AV CAMACHO
AV MARISCAL SANTA CRUZ
AV 16 DE JULIO
AV VILLAZON
AV BUENOS AIRES
AV BAPTISTA
SUCRE
COMERCIO
MERCADO
MURILLO
MAX PAREDES
ISAAC TAMAYO
El Alto & Airport
Cemetery District
Sopocachi
0 Metres 300
Mercado de Hechicería

The colonial city centre

The well-ordered streets of the colonial city centre still preserve the neat grid pattern laid out by the city founders in accordance with Spanish laws governing the laying out of settlements in the Indies. At its centre stands the **Plaza Murillo**, home to both the Palacio Presidential and the parliament building, the Palacio Legislativo. A fair number of colonial buildings still survive, though most are in a poor state of repair, their crumbling facades and dilapidated balconies obscured by tangled phone lines and electric cables. The exceptions are concentrated on and around the Plaza Murillo and the nearby **Calle Jaen**, both of which are also home to several **museums**.

Plaza Murillo

Though it remains the epicentre of Bolivia's political life, the **Plaza Murillo** – the main square of the colonial city centre – has an endearingly provincial feel, busy with people feeding pigeons and eating ice cream in the shade. Known as the Plaza de Armas during the colonial era, the square was renamed after independence in honour of Pedro Domingo Murillo, who was hanged here in 1810 after leading a failed rebellion against the colonial authorities, one of several bloody scenes the square has witnessed during Bolivia's turbulent political past.

On the south side of the plaza stand two great symbols of political and spiritual power in Bolivia, the Cathedral and the Palacio Presidential. With its broad but rather plain Neoclassical facade and vaulted relatively unadorned interior, the twin-belltowered **Catedral** is remarkable more for the time in took to complete than for its aesthetic value. Built in 1835 (when its colonial predecessor had to be demolished owing to structural problems), it wasn't actually inaugurated until 1925, and was finally completed only in 1989 in a last-minute rush ahead of a visit by Pope John Paul II. Its most unusual feature is a detailed stained-glass window behind the altar depicting former presidents Mariscal Andrés de Santa Cruz and General José de Ballivián and their families receiving blessings from on high, a surprisingly explicit expression of the historic conflation in Bolivia of church, military and state.

Next to the cathedral stands the distinguished **Palacio Presidencial** (Presidential Palace), with its yellow facade, thin elegant columns and ceremonial guards in red nineteenth-century uniforms from the War of the Pacific discreetly backed up by military policemen with more modern equipment. The palace isn't open to the public, but the guards may let you have a look at a rather nondescript central courtyard when the president is not in residence. Completed in 1852, the palace is generally known as the "Palacio Quemado" (the Burnt Palace) after it was badly damaged by fire in 1875 during one of the more violent of Bolivia's many revolutionary episodes. On the east side of the plaza is the Palacio Legislativo, the seat of the Bolivian parliament, built in a similar Neoclassical style in the early twentieth century on the site previously occupied by the Jesuit headquarters until their expulsion from the Spanish Empire in 1767.

On the southwest corner of the plaza on Calle Socabaya, the **Palacio de Los Condes de Arana**, one of La Paz's finest surviving colonial palaces, houses the **Museo Nacional de Arte** (Tues–Fri 9am–12.30pm & 3–7pm, Sat 9am–1pm, Sun 10am–1pm; $1.40, under 18 free). Well worth visiting for its comprehensive collection of works by major Bolivian painters, it was completed in 1775, when La Paz was at the peak of its colonial prosperity. The palace (also known as the Palacio de Diez Medina) is a magnificent example of Baroque architecture, with a grand portico opening onto a central patio overlooked by three floors of arched walkways, all elaborately carved from pink granite in a rococo style with stylized shells, flowers and feathers. The emphasis of the museum's art collection is firmly on colonial religious art, featuring several works by the great master of Andean colonial painting, Melchor Pérez de Holguín, as well as by contemporary Bolivian artists.

Along Calle Ingavi

A block northeast from the plaza along Calle Ingavi on the corner with Yanacocha, the **Iglesia Santo Domingo** boasts a richly detailed eighteenth-century facade carved from soft white stone in Mestizo-Baroque style, exemplifiying the intimate combination of Spanish and indigenous symbolism characteristic of Andean colonial architecture, with delicately carved trees, grapes and pomegranates (typical Spanish Baroque devices representing the Eucharist) intermingled with New World fruits and parrots. The interior was remodelled in the nineteenth century in rather anodyne Neoclassical style.

A little further down Calle Ingavi is the small but rewarding **Museo de Etnografía y Folklore** (Tues–Fri 9am–12.30pm & 3–7pm, Sat & Sun 9am–1pm; free; Ⓦwww.bcb.gov.bo/8fundacion/index), housed in an elegant colonial seventeenth-century mansion built for the Marques de Villaverde, whose coat of arms looks down on the central patio from an exquisite Mestizo-Baroque portico, complete with floral designs, parrots and feline figures. Through a variety of costumes and artefacts, the display explains three of Bolivia's most distinctive indigenous cultures: the **Ayorea** culture formed of thirty ethnic groups of the Cordillera Oriental, the **Uru-Chipayas** who subsist in the Altiplano around Oruro and the Quechua-speaking **Tarabuqueños** from the highlands east of Sucre.

Calle Jaen and its museums

A short walk uphill from Calle Ingavi on Calle Gerardo Sanjinez and then left along Calle Indaburo brings you to the foot of **Calle Jaen**, the best preserved colonial street in La Paz and home to no fewer than four **municipal museums** (all Tues–Fri 9.30am–12.30pm & 3–7pm, Sat & Sun 10am–1pm; $0.55), all accessed on a single ticket, sold at the **Museo Costumbrista Juan de Vargas** at the top of the street (the entrance is just around the corner on Calle Sucre). Set inside a renovated colonial mansion, this museum gives a good introduction to the folkloric customs of the Altiplano and history of La Paz, through a series of richly detailed ceramic dioramas of colonial scenes and a colourful display of costumes and masks worn in traditional dances and fiestas. Housed in the same building but accessed from Calle Jaen, the **Museo del Litoral** is dedicated to one of Bolivia's national obsessions: the loss of its coastline to Chile during the nineteenth century War of the Pacific (see p.214). Unless you share that obsession, however, the collection of old uniforms, photos of the lost ports, and maps justifying Bolivia's claim to the coast is not very inspiring. Next door, the **Museo de Metales Preciosos**, also known as the Museo del Oro, has a small but impressive hoard of Inca and Tiwanaku gold ornaments, housed in a steel vault, and informative displays explaining the techniques used by pre-Columbian goldsmiths. On the other side of the road, inside the sumptuous mansion which was once the home of the venerated independence martyr after whom it's now named, the **Museo Casa Murillo** houses an eclectic collection, ranging from colonial religious art and portraits of former presidents to artefacts used in witchcraft, Kallawaya herbal medicine.

Set around yet another pretty colonial courtyard a little further down Calle Jaen, the independently owned, delightful **Museo de Instrumentos Musicales** (daily 9.30am–1pm & 2.30–6.30pm; $0.70) features an astonishing variety of handmade musical instruments from all over Bolivia, including the indigenous *charangos*, some of which you can pick up and play.

Plaza San Francisco and the market district

At the north end of the Prado, **Plaza San Francisco** is the gateway to the main Aymara neighbourhoods of La Paz, which climb up the slopes of the valley to the west. Founded in the colonial era as the *parroquias de Indios* (the Indian parishes) and neatly separated from the Spanish city by the Río Choqueyapu, these neighbourhoods were where the Aymara population from the surrounding countryside was encouraged to settle around churches built as part of the effort to convert them to Christianity and expected to serve as a pool of cheap labour. Today, the area retains a very strong Aymara identity, and its narrow, winding and at times almost vertical streets are filled with lively markets that make it one of the most vibrant and distinctive parts of the city. The **Mercado de Hechicería** is without doubt one of the most extraordinary sights in La Paz.

Plaza San Francisco and around

Though the frenetic traffic running alongside detracts from its charm, the **Plaza San Francisco** is the focal point for the city's Aymara population. It is one of the liveliest plazas in La Paz, busy with people enjoying snacks and juices or crowding around the many comedians, storytellers, magicians and sellers of miracle cures who come to ply their trade. It's also the usual focus of the city's frequent **political protests**, and if you're in La Paz for more than a few days, you're likely to witness a march – not uncommonly broken up by police using liberal amounts of tear gas – by whatever social or political group has taken to the streets that week.

On the south side of the plaza stands the **Iglesia de San Francisco**, the most beautiful colonial church in La Paz, first constructed in 1549 and rebuilt in the mid-seventeenth century. The richly decorated facade is a classic example of the Mestizo-Baroque style, showing clear indigenous influence, with carved anthropomorphic figures reminiscent of pre-Columbian sculpture as well as more common birds and intertwined floral designs. Inside, the walls of the church are lined with extravagantly carved altarpieces featuring smiling angels, abundant gold leaf and gruesome depictions of the crucifixion or of individual saints that are the principal objects of veneration for those who come here to pray.

To your right as you face the church, the plaza is overlooked by a bizarre modern statue known as the **Pucara**, crowned by abstract figures of huddled Aymara women and with a massive carving of the head of the Mariscal Andrés de Santa Cruz at its foot.

To the left of the Iglesia San Francisco, **Calle Sagárnaga**, La Paz's main tourist street, is crowded with hotels, tour agencies, restaurants, handicraft shops and stalls. Sometimes referred to rather dismissively as "Gringo Alley", the street has catered to travellers' needs since colonial times.

The Mercado de Hechicería and Museo de la Coca

Two blocks up Sagárnaga on Calle Linares, the **Mercado de Hechicería**, or Witches' Market, offers a fascinating window on the usually secretive world of Aymara mysticism and herbal medicine. The stalls here are heavily laden with a colourful cornucopia of ritual and medicinal items, ranging from herbal cures for minor ailments like rheumatism or stomach pain to incense, coloured sweets, protective talismans and dried llama foetuses. The area abounds with great photo opportunities, but remember to ask permission; buying a memento will make vendors more receptive to your camera-snapping.

Also on Calle Linares, a block south of Sagárnaga, is the excellent **Museo de la Coca** (daily 10am–6pm; $1; Ⓦwww.cocamuseum.com), inaugurated in 1997 and dedicated to the small green leaf that is both the central religious and cultural sacrament of the Andes and the raw material for the manufacture of cocaine. Crammed into a couple of small rooms, the museum gives a good overview of the history, chemistry, cultivation and uses of this most controversial of plants, imaginatively illustrated and explained in several languages.

The Mercado Buenos Aires

Three blocks further up Sagárnaga, a right turn along Calle Max Paredes takes you into the heart of the **Mercado Buenos Aires**, also known as the Huyustus.

Centred on the intersection of Max Paredes and Calle Buenos Aires, this vast open-air market sprawling over some thirty city blocks is where La Paz's Aymara conduct their daily business. Street after street is lined with stalls piled high with sacks of sweet-smelling coca leaf and great mounds of brightly coloured tropical fruit from the Yungas; enormous heaps of potatoes from the Altiplano; piles of smelly, silver-scaled fish from Lago Titicaca; smuggled stereos and televisions; and endless racks of the latest imitation designer clothes. In the last week of January, the area, as well as most of the rest of the city, is taken over by stalls selling all manner of miniature items during the **Feria de Alasitas**, which is centred on representations of Ekeko, the diminutive mustachioed household god of abundance.

Museo Tambo Quirquincho

Just northwest of Plaza San Francisco, **Plaza Alonso de Mendoza** is a pleasant square named after the founder of La Paz, whose statue stands at its centre. On the southern side of the square on Calle Evaristo Valle, the **Museo Tambo Quirquincho** (Tues–Fri 9.30am–12.30pm & 3–7pm, Sat & Sun 10am–1pm; $0.15) is one of the most varied and interesting in La Paz, with an eclectic collection focusing on the city's culture and history. Exhibits include an extensive collection of grotesque yet beautiful folkloric masks; several rooms full of quaint old photos of La Paz, which give a good impression of life in the city in the late nineteenth and early twentieth centuries; and a room dedicated to the city's quintessential icons, the **cholas**, the ubiquitous Aymara and *mestiza* women dressed in voluminous skirts and bowler hats who dominate much of the day-to-day business in the city's endless markets.

San Pedro and Sopocachi

South of Plaza San Francisco, the busy, tree-lined Prado passes between the peaceful suburb of **San Pedro** – whose **prison** attracts travellers jaded by the more traditional tourist attractions – before reaching the relatively wealthy suburb of **Sopocachi**, home to the modest **Museo Nacional de Arqueología**, as well as some of the city's best restaurants and a lively nightlife.

Plaza Sucre and the San Pedro Prison

Two blocks southwest of the Prado along Calle Colombia, **Plaza Sucre** lies at the centre of **San Pedro**, one of the city's oldest suburbs. Also known as the Plaza San Pedro, the square's tranquil and well-tended gardens surround a statue of Bolivia's first president, the Venezuelan General Antonio José de Sucre, and are popular with portrait photographers with ancient box-cameras.

On the southeast side of the square rises the formidable bulk of the **Cárcel de San Pedro**, which has become one of La Paz's most unusual attractions. Though it's not officially allowed, if you turn up with your passport on Thursday or Sunday mornings, the guards will sometimes admit you for a brief tour. For about $7–10, an English-speaking prisoner will show you around for about half an hour, accompanied by a couple of bodyguards. The interior is like a microcosm of Bolivian society – there are shops, restaurants and billiard halls, and prisoners with money can live quite well in luxurious accommodation complete with cellphones and satellite television, while those without any income sleep in the corridors and struggle to survive on the meagre official rations. Note that, at the time of writing, tourist visits have been banned by the authorities, although it is worth trying, as people have been known to get in even during these "blackout" periods and there's also talk of reopening the prison to visitors.

Sopocachi and around

Shortly before the Prado ends at Plaza del Estudiante, a left turn down the steps and two blocks along Calle Tiahuanaco brings you to the **Museo Nacional de**

Arqueología (Mon–Fri 9am–12.30pm & 3–7pm, Sat 10am–12.30pm & 3–6.30pm, Sun 10am–1pm; $1.40; Ⓦwww.bolivian.com/arqueologia/), also known as Museo Tiahuanaco. Set inside a bizarre Neo-Tiwanaku building, it houses a reasonable collection of textiles, ceramics and stone sculptures from the Inca and Tiwanaku cultures, though the exhibits are poorly explained.

To the south of the Plaza del Estudiante at the end of the Prado lies the middle-class suburb of **Sopocachi**, the city's most pleasant residential area and home to many of its more upmarket restaurants and nightlife spots – the centre is around the parallel Avenues 6 de Agosto and 20 de Octubre.

Eating

La Paz has an excellent range of **restaurants**, **cafés** and **street stalls** to suit pretty much all tastes and budgets – from traditional eateries that dish up local meat-based delicacies to the more exotic ethnic restaurants and tourist-orientated spots with international menus. For those whose stomachs have adjusted to basic local food, the cheapest places to eat are the city's **markets**, where you can get entire meals for less than $1. **Street food** is another good low-cost option: the ubiquitous *salteñas* and *tucumanes* – delicious pastries filled with meat or chicken with vegetables – make excellent mid-morning snacks, especially if washed down by the freshly squeezed orange and grapefruit juice which is sold from wheeled stalls all over the city.

Cafés

Alexander Coffee Shop Av 16 de Julio 1832, Calle Potosí 1091, Calle Montenegro in Zona Sura and El Alto airport. Very fashionable but expensive chain café with several locations in the city, with extremely good coffee, juices, salads and sandwiches, and fantastic home-made cakes and cookies.

Angelo Colonial Linares, just off Sagárnaga. Popular and often packed gringo hangout set around a colonial courtyard and imaginatively decorated with masks and antiques. Serves reasonable sandwiches and drinks, as well as some more substantial meals, and also offers tourist information, post office services, a book exchange and plenty of Internet terminals.

Banaís Café Sagárnaga 161. Adjacent to *Hostal Naira* (see p.221), this pleasant, colourful café, popular with travellers, dishes up the standard fare of crepes, omelettes, salads and sandwiches. Internet access available in the basement.

Café Royal Mariscal Santa Cruz and Grau. Cosy little corner café serving excellent strong coffee and snacks; a perfect spot for reading papers and observing street protests along the Prado.

Ciudad Plaza del Estudiante. Lively and long-established café that's open 24 hours a day and is always busy, even though the coffee and food are hardly the best.

Club La Paz Av Camacho, just beyond the corner with the Prado. Atmospheric, smoke-filled café with wood-panelled walls and an old-world feel where the great and the good of La Paz – mostly old men in grey suits – come to discuss Bolivia's latest political crises. Once popular with escaped Nazis, it still has bratwurst on the menu, as well as *salteñas* and good strong coffee.

Pepe's Jimenez 894, just off Linares between Sagárnaga and Santa Cruz. Friendly little place with colourful decor and the usual menu of sandwiches, omelettes, crepes and great organic coffee.

Restaurants

100% Natural Sagárnaga 345. Largely vegetarian health-food restaurant serving a good range of salads, fruit juices, breakfasts and main courses like trout and soya steaks, all at moderate prices.

Café Montmartre Fernando Guachalla 399. Authentic French food and drinks in a lively bistro atmosphere. Crepes and omelettes are particularly tasty and, at $4, the *almuerzo* is very good value. Live music Thurs–Sat evenings. Closed Sun.

California Av Camacho, just off the Prado. Spacious, moderately priced café-restaurant serving decent sandwiches, snacks, ice cream, and Bolivian beef and chicken mainstays. Open until midnight for drinking to music from La Paz's largest and most eclectic record collection. Closed Sun.

Churrasqueria El Gaucho Av 20 de Octubre 2041, near the corner with Aspiazu Ⓣ02/231-0440. First-class Argentine steak house with attentive service, good wine and excellent meat dishes – it's decorated with football memorabilia. Closed Sun.

Eli's El Prado with Bueno. Cosy film-themed corner bistro in business since 1942, with a great selection of cakes and pastries and an extensive good-value menu of delicious American staples such as burgers and Philly cheese steaks.

Layq'a On the first floor above the corner of Linares and Sagárnaga. Although touristy and overpriced, this is a good place to try traditional Altiplano dishes, including llama steaks and *crema de chuño* – a delicious soup made from freeze-dried potatoes. There's also a good salad bar, and the set *almuerzo* is a challenge to even the biggest appetite.

Le Pot-Pourri des Gourmets Linares 906. In the same courtyard as the Coca Museum (see p.226), this popular restaurant with wood-heavy decor and a cosy open-air patio serves an excellent all-day set menu of traditional and international dishes, such as curries, pastas and crepes, for $2 only.

El Lobo Illampu with Santa Cruz. The most popular hangout for Israelis in La Paz, with cheap and tasty vegetarian and Middle Eastern dishes as well as burgers, sandwiches, salads, pasta and pizza; good value buffet lunch charged by kilogram. Internet access available.

Manantial Inside the *Hotel Gloria* at Potosí 909. At around $2.50, the set *almuerzo* is probably the best vegetarian food in La Paz, with four excellent courses including salad. In the evenings you can choose your own ingredients for Chinese stir-fry. Closed Sun.

Nuevo Hong Kong Belisario Salinas 355, between 6 de Agosto and 20 de Octubre, Sopocachi. Excellent value Chinese food; for a special treat, try the platters with shiitake mushrooms, bamboo shoots and other Asian delicacies.

El Vagon Pedro Salazar 384, off Plaza Avaroa. Quiet, reasonably priced restaurant popular with locals, serving deliciously prepared Bolivian staples, such as *picante surtido*, *chuño* and *charque*.

Vienna Federico Zuazo 1905 ⓣ02/244-1660. Probably the best restaurant in La Paz, with exquisite Austrian cuisine and immaculate service, though it's still surprisingly good value, with main courses from about $6. Closed Sat; open Sun for lunch only.

Wagamama Pasaje Pinilla 2557, just off Av Arce ⓣ02/243-4911. Upmarket and authentic Japanese restaurant with a varied menu including sublime sushi and sashimi. Closed Mon.

Nightlife and entertainment

La Paz is generally fairly quiet on weekday evenings, but explodes into life on **Friday** nights when much of the city's male population goes out drinking. In the city centre – and above all in the market district along Max Paredes and Avenida Buenos Aires – there are countless rough and ready **whiskerías** and **karaoke bars**. Going out to one of these bars is certainly a very authentic Bolivian experience, but is best avoided for women.

With one or two exceptions, the more upmarket nightspots – where as a foreigner you'll probably feel more at home – are concentrated in the suburb of **Sopocachi**, where you'll find a good variety of bars and restaurants, many with live music and dancing to Latin American pop, cumbia, salsa, rock and house. For more traditional entertainment, head to one of the folk music venues known as **peñas**, where you'll see Andean folk dancing to traditional music.

Bars and nightclubs

Casa Duende Indaburo 848. Great little bohemian hideaway featuring modern artwork and a dark, cosy atmosphere. A steep climb from the centre, it's a great alternative to the touristy bars around Calle Sagárnaga. Open late Thurs–Sat; closed Sun & Mon.

Dead Stroke Av 6 de Agosto 2460. Stylishly seedy US-owned late-night bar and pool hall with good tables and a fair share of hustlers.

Diesel Av 20 de Octubre with Rosendo Gutierrez. Lively and very stylish bar with an extraordinary post-apocalyptic design complete with aircraft engines hanging from the ceiling and bathrooms straight out of a science-fiction movie.

Mongo's Hermanos Manchego 2444. Lively and fashionable bar-restaurant where televised sports and decent food give way to serious drinking, live music and raucous dancing as the evening wears on. Despite super slow service, it's hugely popular with Bolivians, travellers and expats alike, and packed on weekends. Opens at 7pm daily, until wee hours.

La Salsa del Loro Rosendo Gutiérrez, just up the

steps from Av 6 de Agosto. Lively salsa nightclub where serious *salseros* dance the night away to throbbing Latin beats. Open Thurs–Sat.
Sol y Luna Cochabamba with Murillo. Groovy bar-café serving strong coffee and cold beer in a mellow, candlelit atmosphere. It's conveniently close to the main accommodation area and a good place to meet other travellers.
Thelonious Jazz Bar Av 20 de Octubre 2172. The best jazz bar in town, with an intimate basement atmosphere and live music Tues–Sat. $3.50 cover charge. Closed Sun and Mon.

Peñas

Los Escudos Av Santa Cruz with Camacho ⓣ02/232-2028. Cavernous folk music venue popular with tour groups. $4 cover charge; closed Sun.
Peña Marka Tambo Jaen 710 ⓣ02/228-0041. Perhaps the most authentic traditional music and dance show in La Paz, with an ideal setting in an old colonial mansion, though the food is mediocre. $4 cover charge; shows start at 10.30pm.

Listings

Airlines For flights with the military airline TAM, it's easiest to book through a travel agent. Aerolineas Argentinas, Reyes Ortiz 73 ⓣ02/235-1711; AeroMexico, Capitán Ravelo 2101 ⓣ02/244-3306; AeroSur, Av 16 de Julio 616 ⓣ02/243-0430 or 231-3233; Amaszonas, Av Saavedra 1649 ⓣ02/222-0848 or 224-4705; American Airlines, Plaza Venezuela 1440 ⓣ02/277-1970; British Airways, Ayachucho 378 ⓣ02/220-3885; Continental Airlines, Alto de la Alianza 664 ⓣ02/228-0232; Iberia, Ayacucho 378 ⓣ02/220-3869; KLM, Plaza del Estudiante 1931 ⓣ02/244-1595; LanChile, Av 16 de Julio 1566 ⓣ02/235-8377; Lloyd Aero Boliviano (LAB), Av Camacho 1456–60 ⓣ02/236-7707; Lufthansa, Av 6 de Agosto 2512 ⓣ02/243-1717; Grupo TACA, Paseo del Prado 1479 ⓣ02/231-3132; Transporte Aero Militar (TAM), Av Montes 738 ⓣ02/212-1585 or 212-1582; Varig, Av Mariscal Santa Cruz 1392 ⓣ02/231-4040.
Banks and exchange There are plenty of banks with ATMs in the centre of town, especially on Av Camacho, and a growing number of freestanding ATMs. The best places to change cash and travellers' cheques include Money Exchange International, Mercado 990 with Yanacocha (Mon–Fri 8.30am–12.30pm & 2.30–7pm, Sat 9am–12.30pm) and Casa de Cambios, Colon 330 between Mercado and Potosí (Mon–Fri 9.30am–noon & 2.30–4.30pm).
Car rental American, Av Camacho 1574 ⓣ02/220-2933; Dollar ⓣ02/243-0043; Imbex, Av Montes 522 ⓣ02/231-6895; Oscar Crespo Maurice, Av Simón Bolívar 1865 ⓣ02/222-0989; Localiza, at Hotel Radisson ⓣ02/244-1011.
Embassies and consulates Argentina, Av Sánchez Lima 497 ⓣ02/241-7737; Australia, Av Arce with Montevideo ⓣ02/244-0459; Brazil, Av Arce, Edificio Multicentro ⓣ02/244-0202; Canada, Plaza España with Sanjinez ⓣ02/241-5021; Colombia, C 9 Calacoto 7835 ⓣ02/278-4491; Chile, Av Hernando Siles 5873 ⓣ02/278-5275; Ecuador, Av 16 de Julio 1440 Edificio Hermann ⓣ02/231-9739; Paraguay, Edificio Illimani, Av 6 de Agosto ⓣ02/243-2201; Peru, Av 6 de Agosto 2190, Edificio Alianza ⓣ02/244-0631; US, Av Arce 2780 ⓣ02/243-0251; UK, Av Arce 2732 ⓣ02/243-3424; Venezuela, Av Arce 2678 ⓣ02/243-1365.
Immigration Migración office is on Avenida Camacho, ⓣ02/211-0960.
Internet access There are Internet cafés all over the city and their number is growing very quickly. Most charge about $0.70 an hour. Try Punto Entel, Potosí 1110 (Mon–Sat 8am–9.30pm); MicroNet, Mariscal Santa Cruz 1088, Ed. Sagrados Corazones (Mon–Fri 9am–9pm); Banaís Café, Sagárnaga 161 (daily 7am–10pm); or Angelo Colonial, Linares, just off Sagárnaga (daily 9am–11pm).
Post office Correo Central, Av Mariscal Santa Cruz with Oruro (Mon–Fri 8am–8pm, Sat 8am–6pm, Sun 9am–noon).
Shopping With its many markets, La Paz is a great place for shopping, with a wide range of *artesanía* (handicrafts) on sale from all over the country. You'll find dozens of shops and stalls along Calle Sagárnaga and the surrounding streets, selling traditional textiles, leather items, silver jewellery and talismans. Beware that most fossils sold on this street are fake.
Telephones The main ENTEL office is at Ayacucho 267, just below Mercado (daily 7am–midnight). There are phone booths all over the city which accept cards available from any stall – the most expensive card costs about $7, for which you can make a short international call. Directory enquiries are on ⓣ104.
Tourist police ⓣ02/222-5016.

Tiwanaku

The most worthwhile attraction within a few hours of La Paz is the mysterious ruined city of **Tiwanaku**, Bolivia's most impressive archeological site.

Set on the Altiplano 71km west of La Paz, the ancient ruined city of **TIWANAKU** (also spelt **Tiahuanaco**) was declared a cultural patrimony site by UNESCO in 2000. Founded some three millennia ago, Tiwanaku became the capital of a massive empire that lasted almost a thousand years, developing into a sophisticated urban-ceremonial complex that, at its peak, was home to some 50,000 people. And though the society that built it disappeared many centuries before the first Europeans arrived in the Andes, Tiwanaku remains a place of exceptional symbolic meaning for the Aymara of the Altiplano, who come here to make ceremonial offerings to the *achachilas*, the gods of the mountains. The most spectacular of these, the **Aymara New Year**, takes place each June 21 (the winter solstice), when hundreds of *yatiris* (traditional priests) congregate to watch the sun rise and celebrate with music, dancing, elaborate rituals and copious quantities of coca and alcohol.

Though the city of Tiwanaku originally covered several square kilometres, only a fraction of the site has been excavated, and the main **ruins** (daily 9am–5pm; $3.50) occupy a fairly small area which can easily be visited in half a day. Two **museums** by the entrance house many of the smaller archeological finds, as well as several large stone monoliths. The main ruins cover the area which was once the ceremonial centre of the city, a jumble of tumbled pyramids and ruined palaces and temples made from megalithic stone blocks, many weighing over a hundred tons. It requires a leap of the imagination to visualize Tiwanaku as it was at its peak: a thriving city whose great pyramids and opulent palaces were painted in bright colours and inlaid with gold, surrounded by extensive residential areas built largely from mud brick (of which little now remains) and set amid lush green fields, rather than the harsh, arid landscape you see today.

Minibuses to Tiwanaku depart from the corner of Aliaga and Eyzaguirre in the cemetery district in La Paz (every 30min; 1hr 30min; $1.40 round-trip); on the way back they leave from the square in Tiwanaku town. You can hire a **guide** outside the museum to show you around the ruins for about $7, but if you want a guided tour you're better off coming with an agency from La Paz (see box on p.207); most run one-day **tours** to the site for about $15 to $20 per person.

2.2

Lago Titicaca, Cordillera Real and the Yungas

The region immediately around La Paz is sometimes known as "Little Bolivia", because the variety of landscapes it encompasses can seem like a microcosm of the entire country. The vast high-altitude **Lago Titicaca**, its deep waters a vivid blue against the parched grasslands, lies northwest of La Paz, with the small charming town of **Copacabana** as the base for exploring the Bolivian side of the lake and the **Isla del Sol** and **Isla de la Luna**, two idyllic islands dotted with the ruins of Inca temples and shrines. Just east of Lago Titicaca the **Cordillera Real** is the highest and most spectacular section of the eastern chain of the Andes within Bolivia, and can be easily explored from La Paz. Some of the best treks starting close to the city, or from the delightful colonial town of **Sorata** at the northeastern edge of the range. East of La Paz, the northeastern slopes of the Andes plunge down into the Amazon lowlands in a series of deep valleys called the **Yungas**, where the pleasant resort town of **Coroico** is the best launching point for exploring the region's rugged, forest-covered mountains, rushing rivers and warm, fertile valleys.

Lago Titicaca

Some 75km northwest of La Paz, **LAGO TITICACA**, an immense, sapphire-blue lake, easily the largest high-altitude body of water in the world, sits astride the border with Peru at the northern end of the Altiplano. The area around the lake is the heartland of the **Aymara**, whose distinct language and culture have survived centuries of domination, first by the Incas, then by the Spanish. The Aymara continue to cultivate maize on ancient mountainside terraces around the lake; grow barley, *quinoa* and potatoes on the fertile plains; and raise herds of llamas, alpacas, cattle and sheep.

Titicaca has always played a dominant role in Andean religious conceptions, and is considered a powerful female deity that controls climate and rainfall. The Incas, who believed the creator god Viracocha rose from its waters to call forth the sun and moon to light up the world, also claimed their own ancestors came from here. The remains of their shrines and temples can still be seen on the **Isla del Sol** and the nearby **Isla de la Luna**, whose serene beauty is a highlight of any visit to the lake. Nor did Lago Titicaca lose its religious importance with the advent of Christianity: it's no coincidence that the Bolivia's most important Catholic shrine can be found in **Copacabana**, the lakeside town closest to the Isla del Sol.

Copacabana

Just a few kilometres from the Peruvian border, the pleasant little town of **COPACABANA** overlooks the deep blue waters of Lago Titicaca. As well as being within easy walking distance of a series of mysterious **Inca ruins** that show this

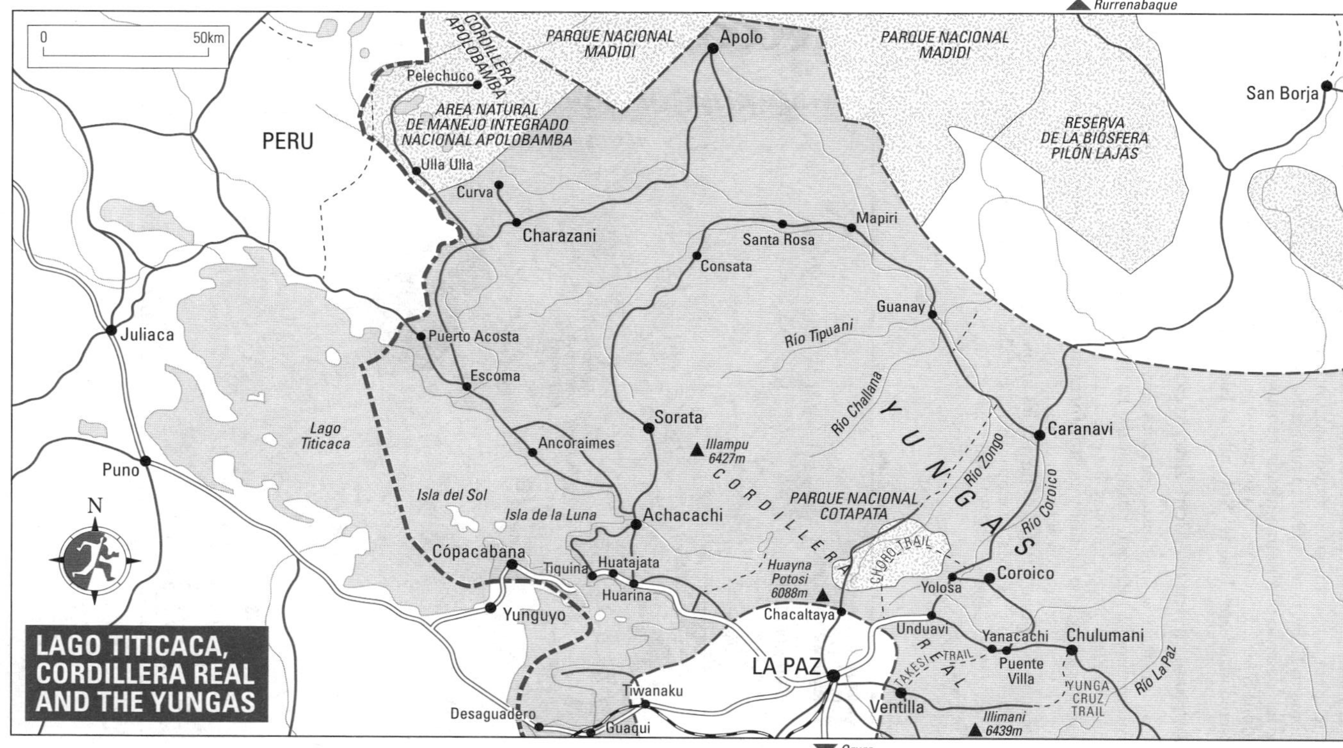
LAGO TITICACA, CORDILLERA REAL AND THE YUNGAS
0
50km
N
PERU
Rurrenabaque
Oruro
PARQUE NACIONAL MADIDI
PARQUE NACIONAL MADIDI
CORDILLERA APOLOBAMBA
AREA NATURAL DE MANEJO INTEGRADO NACIONAL APOLOBAMBA
RESERVA DE LA BIOSFERA PILÓN LAJAS
PARQUE NACIONAL COTAPATA
San Borja
Apolo
Pelechuco
Ulla Ulla
Curva
Charazani
Santa Rosa
Mapiri
Consata
Guanay
Juliaca
Puerto Acosta
Escoma
Río Tipuani
Río Challana
Caranavi
Y U N G A S
Sorata
Lago Titicaca
Ancoraimes
Puno
Illampu 6427m
C O R D I L L E R A
Río Zongo
Río Coroico
Isla del Sol
Isla de la Luna
Achacachi
Cópacabana
Tiquina
Huatajata
Huarina
CHORO TRAIL
Huayna Potosi 6088m
Yolosa
Coroico
Chacaltaya
Yunguyo
Unduavi
Yanacachi
Chulumani
R E A L
TAKESI TRAIL
Puente Villa
LA PAZ
Río La Paz
YUNGA CRUZ TRAIL
Tiwanaku
Ventilla
Desaguadero
Guaqui
Illimani 6439m

was a site of great spiritual importance long before Christianity reached the Andes, the town is also the most important Catholic pilgrimage site in the country, as home to Bolivia's most revered image, the **Virgen de Copacabana**; hordes of pilgrims descend on the city in early Febraury and early August for the two main religious fiestas. This town is also the jumping-off point for visits to Titicaca's two sacred islands, the **Isla del Sol** and the **Isla de la Luna**.

Arrival, information and accommodation

Copacabana is a small place, and it's easy to find your way around. **Buses** and **micros** from La Paz and Kasani at the Peruvian border arrive and depart from and just off Plaza Sucre, midway between the lake shore and the central Plaza 2 de Febrero. There's no formal tourist **information** office in Copacabana, but staff in the cluster of tour agencies on and around the Plaza Sucre can tell you all you need to know about how to get to the islands or on to Peru.

There are no **ATMs** in Copacabana, but the Banco Cooperativo Multiactivo (Mon–Fri 9am–noon & 2.30–6pm, Sat & Sun 9am–1pm) next to the *Hotel Playa*

Azul on Avenida 6 de Agosto changes US dollars and **travellers' cheques**, as do several of the *artesanía* shops on Plaza 2 de Febrero; the Banco Uníon on Avenida 6 de Agosto gives advance on credit cards for a three percent commission.

Accommodation

Owing to its role as a pilgrimage centre, Copacabana has an enormous number of **places to stay**, though they fill up fast and prices double or triple during the main fiestas.

Hostal Colonial del Lago Av 6 de Agosto with Av 16 de Julio ⓣ02/862-2270, ⓦwww.titicacabolivia.com. Comfortable mid-range hostel with decent open-air patio restaurant, sunny rooftop terrace and clean rooms, sporting beautiful views of Titicaca and private baths. ❷

Hostal Emperador Murillo 235 ⓣ02/862-2083. Good budget option, popular with backpackers, with clean, simple rooms (with or without bath) around a bright courtyard. Staff are friendly and full of great tourist info, and there are kitchen and laundry facilities and breakfast is available. At the time of writing, they were about to open a more comfortable *Hostal La Sonia* across the street, with lake views, a rooftop terrace and comparable prices. ❶

Hostal La Cúpula Michel Pérez 1–3 ⓣ02/862-2029, ⓔbolivia@hotelcupula.com. ⓦwww.hotelcupula.com. Delightful hotel built in a neo-Moorish style on a hillside overlooking the town and lake, with 20 pleasant rooms (with or without bath), one suite with the most spectacular lake views and a nice garden with hammocks. Staff are helpful, and facilities include a kitchen and laundry, game room, and a good vegetarian restaurant where breakfast is included. Reserve minimum two days ahead. ❸–❺

Hostal Wara Av 6 de Agosto ⓣ02/862-2346. Great budget choice, steps from the waterfront, with clean basic rooms (with or without bath), friendly staff, plenty of hot water and laundry service. Triples and quadruples are also available, and the adjacent *Café Bistrot* serves great English breakfasts and deliciously strong coffee. ❶–❷

The Town

Copacabana is a fairly untidy collection of red-tiled houses and modern concrete buildings nestled between two steep hills that provide some shelter from the winds occasionally sweeping across the lake. Though without the attractions of its more famous namesake in Brazil (which was named in honour of the shrine here), Copacabana's **beach** is a pleasant place for a lakeside stroll and a bite to eat.

The focal point of Copacabana is the imposing **Catedral** (daily 7.30am–8pm; free), also known as the "Moorish Cathedral", set on the Plaza 2 de Febrero six blocks east of the waterfront. Inside the bright vaulted interior, a door beside the massive gold altarpiece leads upstairs to a small chapel that houses the beautiful **Virgen de Copacabana** herself. Encased in glass, the lavishly dressed statue is only taken out of the sanctuary during fiestas: locals believe moving her at any other time might trigger catastrophic floods.

Another interesting religious site is **Cerro Calvario**, the hill that rises steeply above the town to the north. It's a half-hour walk up to the top along a trail that begins beside the small church at the north end of Calle Bolívar, five or so blocks up from Plaza Sucre. The trail follows the stations of the cross up to the summit dotted with ramshackle stone altars where pilgrims light candles, burn offerings and pour alcoholic libations to ensure their prayers are heard.

Eating and drinking

There's no shortage of **restaurants** in Copacabana, most catering to travellers and pilgrims, and some also doubling as bars and evening hangouts.

Café Bistrot Av 6 de Agosto. Pleasant café inside *Hostal Wara*, with friendly multilingual owners, book exchange, tourist info, full English breakfasts, excellent strong coffee, vegetarian food and barbecues upon request. Opens early morning and closes for siesta between 3 and 5.30 pm.

Chuquiago Marka Av Costanera and 6 de Agosto. One of several inexpensive beachfront restaurants serving up trout, beef and chicken, as well as decent breakfasts – a good place to hang out if you're waiting for a boat departure.

La Cúpula Inside the hotel of the same name on Michel Pérez. Cosy restaurant overlooking the lake and serving mostly vegetarian food, with good breakfasts, fruits and salads and tasty meat-free main courses ($3–5), served up in a bright room with views over the lake; great packed lunches for island trips. Closed Tues morning.

La Orilla Av 6 de Agosto. Travellers' favourite, with intimate atmosphere warmed up by a fireplace, delicious international and Bolivian dishes and a great wine list; their pepper steak is an absolute hit. Closed Mon.

Sol y Luna Beside the *Hotel Gloria* on Av 16 de Julio. Cosy candlelit bar-café serving the best coffee in town, as well as cold beer, cocktails and good but pricey meals and snacks. There's also a book exchange, a decent CD collection and it's open late.

Isla del Sol

Just off the northern tip of the Copacabana Peninsula about 12km northwest of Copacabana, the **Isla del Sol** (Island of the Sun) has been attracting pilgrims and visitors for many hundreds of years. Now a quiet rural backwater, the island was one of the most important religious sites in the Andean world in the sixteenth century, revered as the place where the sun and moon were created and where the Inca dynasty was born. Scattered with enigmatic ancient ruins and populated by traditional Aymara communities, Isla del Sol is an excellent place to spend some time hiking and contemplating the magnificent scenery. Surrounded by the azure expanse of Lago Titicaca, with the imperious peaks of the Cordillera Real rising above the shore on the mainland to the east, the island is a place of great natural beauty and tranquillity.

Measuring 9.5km long and 6.5km across at its widest point, the Isla del Sol is the largest of the forty or so islands in Lago Titicaca, with three main settlements – **Yumani**, **Ch'alla** and **Ch'allapampa**. You can visit the island (along with nearby Isla de la Luna, see opposite) on a day- or even half-day trip from Copacabana, but it's really worth spending at least one night on the island to appreciate its serene beauty fully.

Around the island

The best way to see the Isla del Sol is to walk the length of the island from Yumani in the south to Ch'allapampa in the north, or the other way round – a four-hour hike. At Ch'allapampa, you can either catch a boat back to Copacabana immediately (via Isla de la Luna and Yumani), spend the night on the island and return the next morning, or get a boat across to the mainland at Yampupata, from where an eighteen-kilometre trail leads back to Copacabana.

All the boats make their first stop at **YUMANI**, the largest village on the island. Boats from Copacabana dock here on their way to Ch'allapampa and pick up passengers on their way back in the afternoon. There are occasionally smaller boats available to take you over to the Isla de la Luna and back (about $10), or across to the mainland at Yampupata. From the lakeshore a functional Inca stairway, the **Escalera del Inca**, runs steeply up to the village through a natural amphitheatre covered by some of the finest Inca agricultural terracing on the island, irrigated by bubbling stone canals fed by a natural spring believed to have magic powers.

Two different paths – an inland ridge-top one that provides great views and another that runs along the island's east coast – head from Yumani in the south to Ch'allapampa at the other end of the island. About an hour and a half north of Yumani on the coastal path you reach the quiet village of **CH'ALLA**, which sits above a calm bay. Close to the waterfront beside the football pitch is a small **Museo Etnografico** (daily 6.30am–7pm; although it may appear closed during these times, stick around and someone will assist you; donation suggested), set up by the local community to preserve and explain some of their cultural traditions, with a modest display of intriguing dance costumes, elaborate masks and handmade musical instruments. From here, the path drops to **Playa Ch'alla**, a picturesque stretch of sand on a wide bay.

About an hour's walk from Ch'aalla is the island's northernmost settlement, **CH'ALLAPAMPA**, founded by the Incas as a centre for the nearby ceremonial complexes. Set on a narrow spit of land between two large bays on the east coast of the island, the pleasant village has a small but interesting **Museo de Oro** (daily 8am–12.30pm & 2–6pm; $1.40; occasionally closed owing to administrative problems), which houses artefacts found both on the island and offshore. In 1992, archeologists discovered the underwater site of Marka Pampa off the coast of the Isla del Sol, where offerings were dropped into the water, and tales of a lost sunken city persist to this day.

From Ch'allapampa it's a forty-minute walk northwest along an easy-to-follow path to the **Chincana** (8am–6pm; $1.40, on the same ticket as Museo de Oro), the ruined Inca complex of rambling interlinked rooms, plazas and passageways built around the sacred rock where the creator god Viracocha is believed to have created the sun and moon.

Practicalities

Full- and half-day boat **tours** to the Isla del Sol leave every morning from the beach at the end of Avenida Jaúregui in Copacabana – one boat usually departs at around 8am for a full day ($3.40 round-trip), another at around 1.30pm for a half day ($2 round-trip). Tours are run by several agencies: try Titicaca Tours (Ⓣ02/862-2060, Ⓦwww.titicacabolivia.com) with offices on Avenida 6 de Agosto and a kiosk on the beach, where you can buy tickets in advance, or Wara Tours on Calle Jaúregui and Av 6 de Agosto (Ⓣ02/862-2600). The La Paz-based Transturin agency, with an office on Av 6 de Agosto (Ⓣ02/8622284, Ⓦwww.turismo-bolivia.com), runs luxurious catamaran cruises to the Isla del Sol; a half-day tour will set you back $45 and a full-day one $55.

Yumani is home to most of the islands **accommodation**; the best of the basic bunch (all serve meals upon request and have sporadic running water) is the *Hostal Puerta del Sol* (Ⓣ07/195-5181; ❷) on the ridge above the village with excellent views. More pleasant and expensive options include the *Ecolodge La Estancia* (book through Magri Tours in La Paz at Ⓣ02/244-2727 or Ⓔmagri_emete@megalink.com; ❼), which has delightful community-run traditional-style cottages a fifteen-minute walk away from the village with solar electricity, heated water, a decent restaurant and fantastic views over the lake, and *Hostal Isla del Sol*, also known as *Don Ricardo's*, a beautifully decorated B&B on top of the ridge, with cosy rooms, all with private bath and outstanding lake vistas (Ⓣ07/193-4427, Ⓔbirdyzehnder@hotmail.com; ❹, includes breakfast).

There are also a couple of simple but friendly places to stay in Ch'allapampa. The *Hostal San Francisco* (no phone; ❶) is to your left as you enter the village from Ch'alla and the new *Hostal Las Kantutas* (Ⓣ02/213-4010; ❶), with the helpful, informative owner, is further down the main beach road. *Restaurant Chincana* across from the boat landing serves basic **meals.**

Isla de la Luna

About 8km west of the Isla del Sol, the far smaller **Isla de la Luna** (Island of the Moon) was another important pre-Columbian religious site. For much of the twentieth century, the island was used as a prison for political detainees, yet for the Incas it was a place of great spiritual importance. Known as Coati ("Queen Island"), it was associated with the moon, considered the female counterpart of the sun, and a powerful deity in her own right. The main site on the island – and one of the best-preserved Inca complexes in Bolivia – is a temple on the east coast known as **Iñak Uyu** (8am–7pm; $0.70), the "Court of Women", probably dedicated to the moon and staffed entirely by women. From the beach a series of broad Inca agricultural terraces lead up to the temple complex, a series of stone buildings with facades containing eleven massive external niches still covered in mud stucco, all around a broad central plaza.

To reach the island **by boat**, it takes about an hour from the Isla del Sol; there's a boat that arrives from Ch'allapampa daily at 2pm, docking for about 30min before it sets off for Yumani, and from there to Copacabana at 4pm.

Crossing into Peru

Crossing into Peru from Copacabana is easy. Micros to the border at **Kasani**, fifteen minutes away, leave from Plaza Sucre every half-hour or so when full. At Kasani you can get your exit stamp at the passport control (8am–9pm) and then walk across to Peru, where you micros and taxis wait for passengers to take them to **Yunguyo**, which has regular departures for **Puno** and on to **Cusco**. Alternatively you can catch one of the **tourist micros** which travel direct from Copacabana to Puno several times a day; these are run by all the companies that have an office around Plaza Sucre and, at around $3, cost just a little more than the public micros.

It is also possible to reach Peru by **crossing the lake**. The best way to do this is by the bus and catamaran tours from La Paz to Puno – or vice versa – with Transturin. The trip, which pauses at the Isla del Sol, costs around US$150 and takes about eleven hours. Transturin's offices are located in Mariscal Santa Cruz 1295 (Ⓣ02/310-442, Ⓔsales@turismo-bolovia.com) in La Paz.

The Cordillera Real

Stretching for about 160km along the northeastern edge of the Altiplano, the **Cordillera Real** – the "Royal Range" – is the loftiest and most dramatic section of the Cordillera Oriental in Bolivia, with six peaks over 6000m high and many more over 5000m forming a jagged wall of soaring, ice-bound peaks separating the Altiplano from the tropical lowlands of the Amazon Basin. Easily accessible from La Paz, the mountains are perfect for climbing and trekking (see box opposite) – indeed, the only way to really appreciate the overwhelming splendour of the Andean landscape. Populated by isolated Aymara communities that cultivate the lower slopes and valleys and raise llamas and alpacas on the high pastures, the cordillera is a largely pristine natural environment, where the mighty Andean condor is still a common sight, pumas, though rarely seen, still prowl the upper reaches, while the elusive Andean spectacled bear roams the high cloudforest that fringes the mountains' upper eastern slopes.

To locals, the high mountain peaks are more than just breathtaking natural phenomena – they're considered living beings inhabited by powerful spirits. As controllers of weather and the source of vital irrigation water, these mountain gods must be appeased with constant offerings and worship. At almost every high pass you'll see stone cairns known as **apachetas**, which serve as both markers for the pass and shrines to the mountain gods. Travellers carry stones up to the pass to add to the *apachetas*, thereby securing the good will of the *achachilas* and leaving the burden of their worries behind.

Sorata and around

Set at an altitude of 2695m, **SORATA** is a placid and enchanting little town that's the most popular base for trekking and climbing in the Cordillera Real. Hemmed in on all sides by steep mountain slopes, often shrouded in clouds and with a significantly warmer climate than La Paz, it was compared by Spanish explorers to the Garden of Eden.

During the colonial era Sorata was an important trade and gold-mining centre with a large Spanish population. In republican times, Sorata prospered as one of the main routes into the Yungas from the Altiplano. Today, the town's fortunes increasingly depend on its growing popularity with Bolivians and foreigners alike. Indeed,

Trekking and climbing in the Cordillera Real

The easiest base from which to explore the Cordillera Real is **La Paz**. Many of the best and most popular treks start close to the city, including the three so-called "Inca trails", which cross the cordillera, connecting the Altiplano with the warm, forested valleys of the Yungas. Two of these ancient paved routes – the **Choro Trail** and the **Takesi Trail** – are relatively easy to follow without a guide; the third, the **Yunga Cruz Trail**, is more difficult. You can do all three of these treks, as well as many other more challenging routes, with any of the adventure tour agencies based in La Paz (see box on p.207).

The other major starting point for trekking is the small town of **Sorata**, nestled at the north end of the range at the foot of the mighty Illampu massif. From here, numerous trekking routes take you high up amongst the glacial peaks, while others plunge down into the remote forested valleys of the Yungas. Local *campesinos* in Sorata have organized a co-operative, the **Sorata Guides and Porters Association** (see p.240), which provides trekking guides, mules and porters. Further afield, the remote and beautiful **Cordillera Apolobamba** (see p.240), a separate range of the Cordillera Oriental north of Lago Titicaca with almost no tourist infrastructure, offers excellent trekking possibilities for the more adventurous traveller.

Unless you're going on a fully organized trip with a tour agency you'll need all your own **camping equipment**, including tent, sleeping bag, warm and waterproof clothing, cooking stove and fuel. If you're an experienced hiker, able to communicate effectively with local *campesinos* in Spanish (though many locals speak only Aymara) and have maps, detailed directions and a compass and/or GPS, you can try doing some of these treks without a guide, although that is not advisable due to unpredictable weather conditions and the region's remoteness. Most of the trekking routes are covered in the excellent *Cordillera Real Recreation Map*, published in the US by O'Brien Cartographics.

Really, it's much better to go with a **local guide**. Getting lost in this isolated region is easy and can be very dangerous, and rescue services are pretty much nonexistent. A guide can help avoid misunderstandings with the communities you pass through, and hiring one is also a good way to ensure locals see some economic benefit from tourism. Don't go trekking in these mountains alone, as the consequences of a minor fall or a twisted ankle can quickly prove disastrous if there's no one around to help. You may also want to hire a mule to carry your pack, either for your entire trip or for that first gruelling ascent to a high pass.

With so many high peaks, the Cordillera Real is obviously an excellent place for **mountain climbing**. While serious climbers should bring all their own equipment from home, inexperienced climbers can also scale some of these high peaks with help from specialist agencies in La Paz, which will take you up for not much over $100 per person; you should check carefully that the guide they provide is qualified and experienced and the equipment adequate. **Huayna Potosí** (6090m), near La Paz, is one of the few peaks in South America over 6000m that can be climbed by someone with no mountaineering experience.

there's not a lot to do in Sorata itself but hang out and relax while preparing for or recovering from some hard trekking or climbing, or less strenuous walks in the surrounding countryside.

Practicalities

Buses from La Paz pull up every hour starting at 5am until 4pm in front of the bus company, Transportes Unificada, on the Plaza Enrique Peñaranda. **Wagonetas** arriving from Santa Rosa in the Yungas (see p.241) also stop in the plaza on their way through to La Paz, usually in the early hours of the morning.

For **information** and advice on trekking in the surrounding mountains, try the Sorata Guides and Porters Association, whose office, opposite the *Residencial Sorata*, just off the plaza on Calle Sucre (Ⓣ02/213-6698, Ⓔbolivia@hotelcupula.com or guiasorata@hotmail.com), is a good place to meet up with other people if you want to form a group to share costs. They can arrange guides for all the main trekking routes around Sorata for about $12–15 a day (per group) plus food; they also organize the hire of **mules**, which cost about $8–10 a day plus food for the handler and have a limited amount of camping equipment available for rent, though don't count on what you need being available. The long-established **Club Sorata** travel agency (Ⓣ02/213-5042, Ⓦwww.khainata.com/sorata), based in the *Hotel Copacabana*, also organize treks along the main routes – these cost twice as much but include food, mules, tents and other equipment, plus the services of an experienced guide. The agency can also organize climbing expeditions with experienced and qualified guides, though you'll need to book these in advance.

There's a good choice of finding inexpensive **places to stay** in Sorata, as well as a couple of mid-range options with creature comforts that grow more alluring the longer you've spent climbing or trekking in the surrounding mountains. Set in the delightful, rambling nineteenth-century Casa Gunther, the *Residencial Sorata*, on Plaza Enrique Peñaranda (Ⓣ02/213-6672, Ⓔresorata@ceibo.entelnet.bo; ❸), features pleasant, moderately priced rooms (with or without bath) and a restaurant. The best budget place in town, the *Hostal El Mirador*, Calle Muñecas (Ⓣ02/213-5052; ❷), offers small but clean rooms with or without bath, a pleasant terrace and unbeatable views across the valley, while *Hotel Paraíso*, Calle Villavicencio (Ⓣ02/213-6671; ❸) is a small, modern hotel with a rooftop terrace and clean, comfortable rooms with private bath and breakfast available. The most elegant place in town is the comfortable German-owned *Hotel Landhaus Copacabana*, Av 9 de Abril (Ⓣ02/213-6670, Ⓦwww.khainata.com/sorata; ❹), below the football pitch on the edge of town, with big, well-equipped rooms offering good views, more expensive suites with Jacuzzis and two fully equipped cabins on the other side of the valley.

There are also two good **campsites** outside town (about $1 per person per night): the campsite at the *Café Illampu*, noted for its delicious pastries, is fifteen to twenty minutes' walk across the valley on the road leading to the Gruta de San Pedro; *Camping Altai Oasis* is slightly closer to town, down by the river, and has a vegetarian restaurant on site.

By far the best **place to eat** in Sorata is *Pete's Place* on Plaza Enrique Peñaranda, which has excellent vegetarian food (including breakfast and a different set *almuerzo* every day) and curries served in a warm and welcoming atmosphere. The best of three restaurants with near-identical names and similar menus on the southeast corner of the same plaza is *Pizzeria Italia*, which serves up good pizza and pasta from about $3, as well as decent breakfasts, juices, cold beer and wine by the glass.

The Cordillera Apolobamba

North of Lago Titicaca flush with the Peruvian border rises the **Cordillera Apolobamba**, the remote northern extension of the Cordillera Oriental. The splendour of the high mountain scenery and the pristine environment in this isolated range equals or even exceeds that of the Cordillera Real. The region is now protected by the recently established **Area Natural de Manejo Integrado Nacional Apolobamba**, which covers nearly 5000 square kilometres and is home to a small number of mostly Quechua- and Aymara-speaking farmers and herders. The range is still rich in Andean wildlife rarely found elsewhere – condors, caracaras and other big birds are frequently seen; pumas and spectacled bears still roam the most isolated regions; and large herds of vicuña are visible from the road crossing the plain of **Ulla Ulla**, which runs along the western side of the range. The Cordillera Apolobamba is also home to Bolivia's most mysterious indigenous culture, the **Kallawayas**, itinerant herbalists famous throughout the Andes, who preserve secret healing techniques handed down over generations and still speak an arcane language that may have come to them from the Incas.

Tourist facilities are virtually nonexistent in this isolated region, but for the adventurous it offers perhaps the best high-mountain trekking in Bolivia. The only real towns in the Cordillera Apolobamba are **Pelechuco** and **Charazani**, both of which can be reached by tough but spectacular bus journeys from La Paz; buses from La Paz to Pelechuco leave from the cemetery district on Tues, Fri and Sat at 5am. Between the two runs the fabulous four- or five-day **Trans-Apolobamba Trek**, which takes you through the heart of the range, past glacier-covered peaks and through traditional indigenous villages.

It is not advisable to explore the area independently, mainly because there are no maps of this remote region and it is easy to get lost. To find a guide in Pelechuco to accompany you on your trek, you can contact SERNAP (Servicio Nacional de Áreas Protegidas) at their La Paz office at Avenida 20 de Octubre 2659 (☎02/243-0881 or 243-0420); they have a list of park rangers who offer their services for free. For organized treks, Akhamani Trek (see box on p.207) has the best reputation.

The Yungas

East of La Paz, the Cordillera Real drops precipitously into the Amazon lowlands, plunging down through a region of rugged, forest-covered mountains and deep subtropical valleys known as **THE YUNGAS**, abundant with crops of coffee, tropical fruit and coca. Three of the well-built stone roads that linked the agricultural outposts of the Yungas to the main population centres before the Spanish conquest, the so-called "Inca" trails – the **Takesi**, **Choro** and **Yunga Cruz trails** – are still in good condition, and make excellent three- to four-day hikes from La Paz. Even if you don't hike, the journey down to the Yungas from the Altiplano is truly spectacular. Beware that the **road from La Paz to Coroico** is widely considered the most dangerous – and amongst the most scenic – in the world, hugging the forest-covered mountain slopes as it winds above fearsome precipices.

The most frequently visited Yungas town is the idyllic resort of **Coroico**, set amidst spectacular scenery and exuberant tropical vegetation. From Coroico, the road continues north towards Rurrenabaque and the Bolivian Amazon (see p.286). Alternatively, you can avoid Coroico and head to **Chulumani**, a less-touristed Yungas market town that's the centre of the equally scenic but less frequently visited **South Yungas**.

La Paz to Coroico

Few highways in the world have as intimidating a reputation as the road linking La Paz with Coroico in the North Yungas. A rough, narrow track chiselled out of near-vertical mountainsides that descends more than 3500m over a distance of just 64km, it's widely referred to as the **world's most dangerous road**, a title bestowed on it by the Inter-American Development Bank. Statistically, the label is

Coca in the Yungas

The Yungas is one of Bolivia's major **coca**-producing regions, a role it has played since the colonial era. Considered sweeter and better for chewing than that produced in the Chapare region, Yungas coca still dominates the Andean market, and remains legal for traditional use. It's worth checking on the coca-eradication situation before travelling anywhere off the beaten track in the Yungas; if an eradication campaign starts up before you arrive, strange gringos wandering around the back-country might easily be misidentified as undercover US drug-enforcement agents.

difficult to dispute: every year dozens of vehicles go off the road and, with vertical drops of up to 1000m over the edge, annual fatalities often reach into the hundreds. Despite the heavy traffic it receives – it's the main link between the Altiplano and the Amazon, and between Brazil and the Pacific coast – this is worrying stuff.

What the statistics don't tell you, however, is that this is also one of the most beautiful roads in the world. Starting amidst the icebound peaks of the Cordillera Real, it plunges down through the clouds into the humid valleys of the Yungas, winding along deep, narrow gorges where dense cloudforest clings to even the steepest slopes. So spectacular is the descent that travelling the Yungas road by **mountain bike** is fast becoming one of Bolivia's most popular tourist attractions, an exhilarating ride that's easy to organize as a day-trip with tour companies in La Paz. (Gravity Assisted Mountain Biking – see p.207 – has the best reputation; keep in mind that mountain-bike trips are suspended in the rainy months of December and January.)

The journey from La Paz to Coroico takes about three and a half hours. Shortly beyond Unduavi, approximately two hours from La Paz, on the Coroico branch the tarmac ends – the next 40km from here are the most perilous and spectacular of the entire route. For the most hair-raising views, sit on the left of your vehicle. At times the road is only 3m wide, and trucks and buses appear to lean out over precipices more than a kilometre deep. To make matters worse, the road is often swathed in cloud, and in places waterfalls crash down onto its surface.

A new, asphalted two-lane road from Chuspipata to Yolosa is currently under construction, and due to open sometime in 2004. Once it's completed, the plan is to keep the old road to Yolosa open for mountain bikers only.

Coroico

Rightly considered one of the most beautiful spots in the Yungas, the peaceful little town of **COROICO** is perched on a steep mountain slope around 600m above the river of the same name, with panoramic views across the forest-covered Andean foothills to the icy peaks of the Cordillera Real beyond. Founded in the colonial era as a gold-mining outpost, the town is still an important market centre for the surrounding agricultural communities. At an altitude of 1760m, it enjoys a warm and pleasantly humid climate, and this, combined with the dramatic scenery and good facilities, makes it an excellent place to relax and recuperate. It also makes a great stop-off if you're attempting the tough overland journey from La Paz to Rurrenabaque or elsewhere in the Amazon lowlands, and if you're heading in the opposite direction it's ideal for acclimatizing to the higher altitude.

Arrival and information

Buses and **micros** from La Paz drop passengers off outside the offices of the three bus companies, either right in the centre of town on Plaza Principal or just off it on Calle Sagárnaga, the road that leads up to Coroico from Yolosa. If you're coming to Coroico from anywhere else, you'll have to catch a pick-up truck for the fifteen-minute ride up from the main road at Yolosa – these drop passengers off outside the Mercado Municipal, also on Sagárnaga.

Almost everything is within easy walking distance of the plaza, where you can also usually find a taxi to take you to the more outlying hotels. There's a small **tourist office** on the plaza (Mon–Sun 9am–noon & 2–7pm), which usually has a selection of fliers and maps of the town and can give limited advice in Spanish on accommodation and the attractions in and around Coroico. Vagantes Eco Aventuras agency (Tues–Sat 8.30am–12.30pm & 2.30–7pm, Sun 8.30am–12.30pm; ⓣ07/191-2981, ⓔvagantesguias@yahoo.es) with a kiosk on the plaza with Linares has informative staff and offers a variety of jeep and trekking half-day or day tours around the countryside. You can also get useful information – often in English – by checking the websites ⓦwww.coroico-info.net and www.coroicoparaiso.com.

Accommodation

For a small town Coroico has a good range of **places to stay**, aimed primarily at visitors from La Paz. At weekends and on public holidays everywhere gets very full and prices go up, so it's worth booking in advance. Conversely, things are pretty quiet midweek, when prices are much more reasonable.

Las Hamacas A block away from the main plaza on Pando with Pinilla ⓣ07/196-2755, ⓔrichardrojasfernandez@hotmail.com. Friendly and central budget option, with three basic double rooms and a dormitory for five people, all with shared bath. ❶

Hostal Kory Linares ⓣ07/156-4050, in La Paz ⓣ02/243-1311, ⓔkoryhostalcelia@hotmail.com. Longstanding backpacker favourite, with plenty of small but clean rooms (with or without bath) around a series of terraces and a large swimming pool, with fantastic views across the valley. There's also a reasonable restaurant, a kitchen for guest use and laundry facilities are available. ❷–❸

Hostal Sol y Luna Just under 1km outside town uphill on Julio Zuazo Cuenca, beyond the *Hotel Esmeralda* ⓣ07/156-1626, in La Paz ⓣ02/236-2099, ⓦwww.solyluna-bolivia.com. Peaceful hideaway with six delightful rustic cabins, with cooking facilities and private showers, spread out in a beautiful hillside garden, with hammocks, fire pits, a hot bath and plunge pools. There are also several basic rooms with shared bath (2/$3.50 per person) in the main building, and camping space is available for $2 per person. Staff are friendly and welcoming, there's a meditation room and a small restaurant serving a variety of dishes and excellent home-grown and roasted Yungeña coffee. You can also get a wonderful shiatsu massage for $10–12. ❸–❺

Hotel Esmeralda 400m above town up Julio Zuazo Cuenca ⓣ02/213-6017, ⓦwww.hotelesmeralda.com, ⓔinfo@hotelesmeralda.com. A large hotel favoured by mountain bikers yet lacking in service. If offers good views across the valley, an attractive garden with a swimming pool, a sauna and a reasonable restaurant. The more expensive rooms have private baths, hammocks on each balcony and incredible vistas; the cheaper ones have neither and are rather cramped. There's an Internet connection and happy hour. ❸–❺

Residencial La Casa Linares ⓔlacasa@ceibo.entelnet.bo. Efficient, European-run place with small but comfortable and reasonably priced rooms with or without bath, plus a small swimming pool and a very good restaurant. ❷

The Town

There are no sights as such in Coroico, and it's hardly surprising that most visitors spend much of their time relaxing on the peaceful **Plaza Principal**, lounging by a swimming pool, sipping a cold drink and enjoying the fantastic views. For those with a bit more energy, there are some pleasant walks through the surrounding countryside, whose forested mountain slopes are covered in a lush patchwork of coffee and coca plantations and banana and orange groves. Coroico gets very busy at weekends and during Bolivian public holidays, when it's transformed by large numbers of Paceños on vacation.

Around October 20 each year, Coroico celebrates its biggest annual **fiesta** with several days of drinking, processions and costumed dances. The fiesta commemorates the day in 1811 when the statue of the Virgin in the church – brought here from Barcelona in 1680, when Coroico was founded – supposedly summoned a ghost army to drive off a force of indigenous rebels that were besieging the town.

Eating and drinking

There's no lack of variety when it comes to **places to eat**, including everything from pizza and Mexican food to quality French cuisine, German pastries and even Swiss fondue, as well as plenty of places serving inexpensive standard Bolivian food. During the week, **nightlife** tends to involve drinking beer in the town's bar-restaurants or poolside in the better hotels. On weekends, however, several bars and discos – *La Tropicana*, on the edge of town on the road down to Yolosa and *Safari* on Zuazo Cuenca off the main plaza – cater for the many young visiting Paceños.

Back-Stube Linares off the main plaza. German café-bakery serving excellent soups, snacks and sandwiches, and deliciously decadent home-made cakes. The terrace has wonderful views of the valleys below. Closed Tues.

Bamboo's Café Iturralde. Candlelit hideaway open in the evenings for reasonable Mexican staples like burritos, enchiladas and tacos at about $3.50 a plate, as well as ice-cold beers and mean margaritas. It's open late, with live music at weekends.

El Cafetal Beside the hospital about 15min walk southeast of the town centre. Small French-run restaurant with panoramic views and an extensive menu of crepes, soufflés, fish and meat dishes, as well as great coffee, though the service is slow and spotty. Sometimes closed Mon.

La Casa In *Residencial La Casa*, Linares. Swiss-run restaurant serving authentic cheese, meat or chocolate fondues for a minimum of two people at about $5 each. They feature other European dishes like *raclette* or goulash.

Esmeralda *Hotel Esmeralda*. Efficient restaurant with indoor and outdoor seating and great views, and decent buffet meals with a wide range of meat, fish and vegetarian courses.

Chulumani

From Unduavi on the road from La Paz to the Yungas, a side road heads east off the main highway towards the provincial capital of **CHULUMANI**, providing a dramatic ride as it plunges down from the high Andes into the lush vegetation of the Yungas, though it's neither as spectacular nor as dangerous as the road from La Paz to Coroico. Today, Chulumani is a very tranquil little town, set on a steep hillside overlooking a broad river valley, where life is taken at an easy pace and, though some locals have attempted to turn it into a resort like Coroico, it's never really caught on as a retreat for wealthy Paceños. With its palm-shaded plaza and steep and narrow cobbled streets, lined with neat houses with red-tiled roofs, Chulumani is a typical Yungas town. Now the capital of the Sur Yungas province and the market centre for an extensive rural hinterland, in the 1950s it was notorious as a hideout for fugitive Nazi war criminals, such as Klaus Barbie, the "Butcher of Lyon", who some say once sold fruit juices on the plaza. The main attractions of Chulumani are the surrounding peaceful hamlets, splendid scenery and exuberant tropical vegetation of the countryside.

Practicalities

Buses from La Paz arrive outside the bus offices on Plaza Libertad, the main square. There's a small tourist office on the main square (sporadic opening hours) with skimpy information. English-speaking Javier Sarabia, owner of the *Hostal Country House*, is a mine of information on hikes from Chulumani and also runs guided excursions and camping trips on foot or by jeep and can arrange bicycle and motorbike rental.

Accommodation options are rather limited. Apart from the *Hostal Country House*, it comes down to a choice between budget *alojamientos* and rather overpriced hotels with swimming pools aimed at weekenders from La Paz. The best of the budget places is *Alojamiento Daniel,* uphill from the plaza on Bolívar (Ⓣ02/213-6359; ❷) with simple but clean rooms with shared bath; those upstairs have balconies and nice views. More pleasant options include *Hotel Panorama* on Murillo (Ⓣ02/213-6109; ❸), with cosy rooms set around a flower-filled garden and small swimming pool, friendly staff and a reasonable restaurant where breakfast is included and *Hostal Country House* (no phone; ❸), a quirky little guesthouse 1km southeast of town beyond the mirador with a welcoming, homely feel and comfortable rooms (with private bath and breakfast included) around a lovely garden with a small swimming pool.

The selection of **places to eat** in Chulumani is also disappointing, and the better places are usually open only at weekends. The most reliable restaurants are in the *Monarcha* and *Panorama* hotels, which serve decent set *almuerzos* and standard main courses including fresh local trout. Less expensive set *almuerzos* and *cenas* are available at *El Mesón* and *Restaurant Chulumani*, on Plaza Libertad.

2.3

The southern Altiplano

South of La Paz, the **SOUTHERN ALTIPLANO** – a high, bleak plateau that lies between the eastern and western chains of the Andes, swept by unforgiving winds and illuminated by harsh sunshine – stretches 800km to the Chilean and Argentine borders. Set at an average altitude of around 3700m, this starkly beautiful landscape is the image most frequently associated with Bolivia: a barren and treeless expanse whose arid steppes stretch to the horizon, where snowcapped mountains shimmer under deep-blue skies.

Since the Spanish conquest, the Altiplano's prime importance has lain in the rich **mineral deposits** found in the Cordillera Oriental, the mountain range on its eastern range. Mines established here to exploit first silver and then tin were for centuries the basis of the Bolivian economy, and the two biggest cities in the region are both formerly rich mining centres fallen on hard times. The unavoidable transport nexus of the Altiplano is the unattractive tin-mining city of **Oruro**, 230km south of La Paz, a grim monument to industrial decline that comes alive once a year during the Carnaval. Some 310km further southeast of Oruro is the legendary silver-mining city of **Potosí**. Once the richest jewel in the Spanish Empire, it's now a city of sublime colonial architecture, marooned at 4100m above sea level and filled with monuments to a glorious but tragic past.

The Altiplano grows more desolate still as it stretches south towards the Argentine border. From the forlorn railway town of **Uyuni**, 323km due south of Oruro by road and rail, you can venture into the dazzling white **Salar de Uyuni**, the world's largest salt lake. Beyond the Salar in the far southwestern corner of the country is the **Reserva de Fauna Andina Eduardo Avaroa**, a bleak-looking nature reserve of lunar landscapes and home to a surprising array of wildlife.

Southwest of Uyuni, the Altiplano changes character. The pleasant little mining town of **Tupiza** is surrounded by arid red mountains and cactus-strewn badlands eroded into deep gullies and rock pinnacles. In the far south of the country lies the provincial capital of **Tarija**, a remote yet welcoming city set in a deep and fertile valley that enjoys a much warmer climate than the Altiplano.

The region is bitterly **cold** at night, with temperatures often falling well below zero, particularly between May and July. Even during the day temperatures can drop sharply when the sun slips behind a cloud, and the wind makes things colder still although you'll also need to protect yourself from the fierce, high-altitude sunshine. **Travel** around the region is painfully slow, as none of the roads south of Oruro are paved; trains between Oruro and Villazón on the Argentine border offer a faster and more comfortable alternative.

Parque Nacional Sajama

Southwest of La Paz, the road to Chile passes through a desert plain from the middle of which rises the perfect snowcapped cone of **Volcán Sajama**. At 6542m, Sajama is the tallest mountain in Bolivia and the centre of the country's oldest national park, the **PARQUE NACIONAL SAJAMA**, established in 1939 to protect the local population of **vicuñas**, a wild Andean relative of the llama hunted

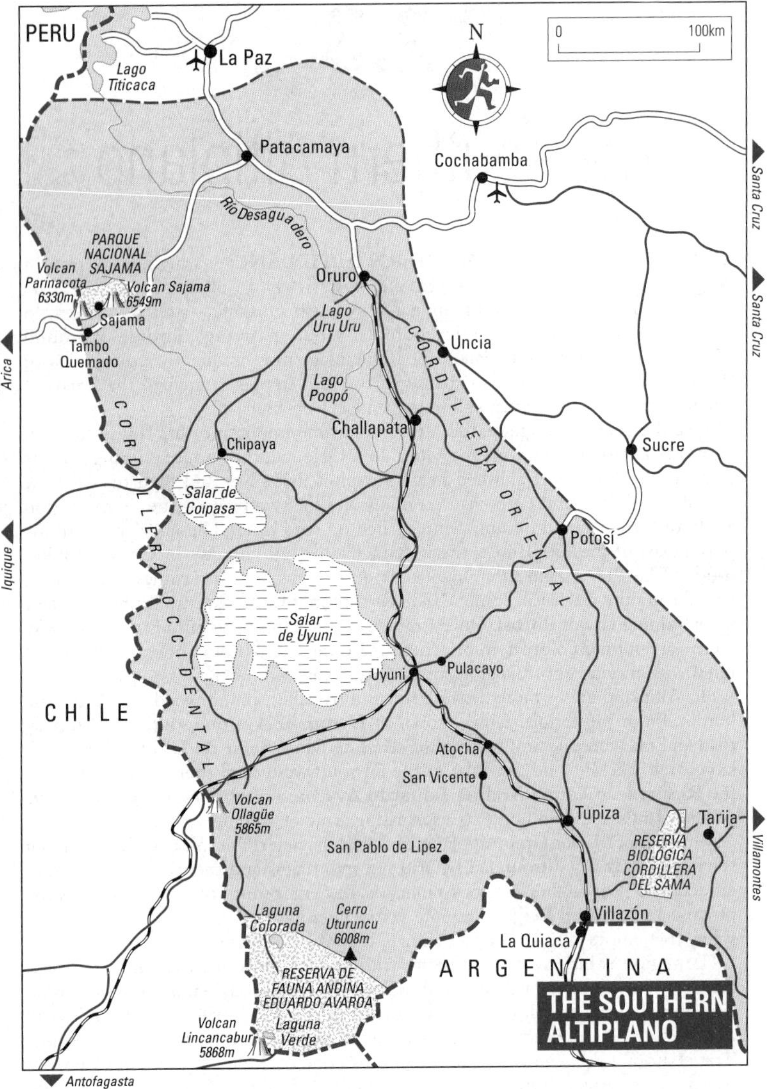

almost to extinction for its highly prized wool. The park encompasses the entire mountain, the slopes of which support the **highest forest in the world**, as well as much of the surrounding desert, where pumas, rare Andean deer and the rarely seen, flightless, ostrich-like rheas. **Mountain climbers** are drawn by the peak's relative ease of ascension – it is only allowed between April and October, when the ice is sufficiently frozen – and the mountain's lower slopes, containing bubbling geysers and hot springs, make for excellent **hiking**. The administrative centre of the park, where you can register to climb Sajama and arrange guides, mules and porters, is the village of **SAJAMA**, a small cluster of simple adobe houses and a crumbling white-washed colonial church huddled at the foot of the volcano. The routes to nearby attractions – including the forest, the **geyser field** and **aguas termales** (hot springs) – are marked with signposts and easy to find.

Practicalities

There are two ways to reach Sajama by **public transport** from La Paz. The first, and more scenic, is to take any Oruro-bound bus as far as the crossroads town of **Patacamaya**, from where a micro goes directly to Sajama every day at about 1pm, returning to Patacamaya at 7am the next day. The other way of reaching the park is to get on a bus from La Paz (2 daily; 3hr 30min–4hr) headed for Arica in Chile and alight at the turn-off to Sajama on the main road. Jeeps from the village usually wait there to collect passengers arriving from La Paz – they charge about $6 per vehicle for the twelve-kilometre drive back to the village.

If you want information before the trip, contact SERNAP at Av 20 de Octubre 2659 in La Paz (Ⓣ02/243-0420 or 243-0881, Ⓦwww.sernap.gov.bo). On arrival in Sajama village you must register at the **park office** (daily 8am–noon & 2.30–7pm) and pay the $2 entrance fee. The usually helpful park rangers can answer most questions about the reserve and will help you arrange **accommodation** in one of the very basic *alojamientos* (❶) run by several people in the village. There are also various **places to eat** in the village, where you can get simple and inexpensive set *almuerzos*, cenas and breakfasts for about $1, though it's best to order a few hours in advance.

Crossing into Chile at Tambo Quemado

The **border between Chile and Bolivia** is 9km west of the turn-off to Sajama at **Tambo Quemado**. Crossing into Chile is straightforward: there's a Bolivian *migración* where you get your exit stamp and a couple of restaurants catering mainly to truck drivers. A couple of kilometres further on from Tambo Quemado is the Chilean border post of Chungará, open daily from 8am till 9pm, where you'll have your passport stamped for entry to Chile. If you're coming from La Paz, the bus will take you all the way through to Arica on Chile's Pacific Coast. If you're heading to Chile from Sajama, you can get to the border on the 7am micro to Patacamaya, which comes to Tambo Quemado to pick up passengers, then walk across the frontier and pick up transport on the Chilean side. For more information on entering Chile, see p.469.

Oruro

Huddled on the bleak Altiplano some 230km south of La Paz, the grim mining city of **ORURO** was the economic powerhouse of Bolivia for much of the twentieth century because of the enormous mineral wealth found in the rugged, ochre-coloured mountains that rise to the east of the city and the tin mines established there in the late nineteenth century. Since the fall of world tin prices in 1985, however, Oruro's fortunes have plummeted and, though it's still the biggest city in the Altiplano after La Paz and El Alto, with a population of about 170,000, two decades of economic decline have made it a shadow of its former self.

Oruro is a cold and rather sombre place, with the melancholic air of a city forever looking back on a golden age that is unlikely to return. Every year in late February or early March, however, Oruro explodes into life, celebrating its **Carnaval** (see box on p.250) in what is without doubt one of the most spectacular cultural events in all South America. At any other time of year, there's not much reason to stop here for more than a day, though given its importance as a transport hub you're almost certain to pass through the city at some stage during your travels in Bolivia.

There's relatively little in Oruro to remind you that this was once the industrial centre of Bolivia. There are a few exceptions, however. At the centre, the **Plaza 10 de Febrero** is a pleasant enough square shaded by cypress trees. Five blocks east of the plaza stands the **Santuario del Socavón** (Sanctuary of the Mineshaft), home to the image of the **Virgin del Socavón**, the patron saint of miners, in whose honour the Carnaval celebrations are staged. The abandoned mineshaft beneath the church is now home to the **Museo Etnográfico Minero** (daily 9am–noon & 3–6pm; $0.50) with an interesting display of equipment that explains the history of mining, as well as two fearsome-looking statues of **El Tío**, the devil-like figure worshipped by Bolivian miners as the king of the underworld and owner of all minerals.

Practicalities

Almost all long-distance **buses** pull in at the Terminal Terrestre, ten blocks north-east of the city centre on Avenida Rajka Bakovic. A **taxi** into town from here should cost $0.50 per person, the flat rate for journeys within the city; alternatively, take any micro heading south along Avenida 6 de Agosto. The **train station** (☎02/527-4605) is a short walk east of the city centre on Avenida Galvarro.

Surprisingly, there are two tourist information offices in Oruro: the **Caseta de Información** (Mon–Fri 8am–noon & 2–6pm) kiosk on Plaza Manuel Castro de Padilla with helpful staff and the less informative **Unidad de Turismo Prefectural** (Mon–Fri 8am–noon & 2–6pm; ☎02/525-0144), on the east side of Plaza 10 de Febrero. Another good source of information are tour operators; Viajeros del Tiempo at Soria Galvarro 1232 (☎02/527-1166) offers half-day city tours and day-trips to various attractions just outside the city.

There are several banks in Oruro which change cash and travellers' cheques and have ATMs. Try Banco Bisa, on Bolívar between Montes and La Plata, or Banco Union, at Mier and La Plata. The city centre, especially on 6 de Octubre, abounds with Internet shops; try Infocomp on Bolívar between La Plata & Galvarro, inside Galería Onasis.

There's a fairly good range of places **to stay** in Oruro; during Carnaval prices go up by as much as five times, and most places will only rent rooms for the entire weekend. There are several places to stay near the train station; *Residencial San Salvador* on Av Galvarro 6325 (☎02/527-6771; ❷) is recommended for its good-value, simple and clean although gloomy rooms with or without bath. Also by the bus terminal is the recently built *Hotel Samay Wasy* at Av Brasil 232 (☎02/527-6737; ❹) featuring functional but bland rooms, all with private bath and continental breakfast included. In the city centre, the distinguished *Hotel Gran Sucre* on Sucre 510 (☎02/527-6800 or 527-6320; ❷–❺) preserves some of the grandeur of Oruro's heyday, with elegant wood-panelled corridors and a glass-roofed ballroom, and offers accommodation to suit most budgets: simple rooms with shared bath or well-appointed modern rooms with private bath.

Oruro has a fairly diverse selection of **places to eat**, though most don't open until mid-morning. There are plenty of cheap roast-chicken **restaurants and snack bars** on 6 de Octubre, where late on Friday and Saturday night stalls serve the local speciality *rostro asado*, roasted sheep's head, from which the face is peeled off and served along with the eyeballs. By far the best restaurant in town is *Nayjama* on the corner of Pagador and Aldana, serving huge portions of deliciously cooked local food for $4–5 a plate, with specialities including sublime roast lamb and *criadillos*, prairie oysters, not for the faint-hearted. The small peaceful Hare Krishna-run *Govinda* on 6 de Octubre and Bolívar provides healthy, tasty and inexpensive vegetarian alternatives to the meat-based Orureño cuisine, including muesli and yoghurt, delicious samosas and pastas; it's closed on Sundays. For simple, filling meals and snacks, head to *Oggy* on Bolívar 615, a spacious local hangout with a big-screen TV serving coffee, juices, snacks and ice cream, as well as a reasonable set

ORURO
0
200m
AYACUCHO
JUNIN
A. MIER
BOLIVAR
SUCRE
WASHINGTON
PDTE. MONTES
LA PLATA
S. GALVARRO
Catedral
Banco Uníon
Migración
PLAZA 10 DE FEBRERO
PLAZA MANUEL CASTRO DE PADILLA
Police
ENTEL
Banco de Crédito
SANTA CRUZ
SOTOMAYOR
LIRA
OBLITAS
VILLARROEL
AROMA
RODRÍGUEZ
LEÓN
1 DE NOVEMBRE
HERRERA
MONTECINOS
CARO
COCHABAMBA
AV LA PAZ
AV 6 DE AGOSTO
AV DEL FOLKLORE
Bus Terminal
Faro de Conchupata
HT Viajeros del Tiempo
Casa de Cultura Simón I. Patiño
Santuario del Socavón
PLAZA DEL FOLKLORE
AV CIVICA
LINARES
PETOT
CAMACHO
6 DE OCTUBRE
POTOSI
PEGADOR
V. GALVARRO
R. BAKOVIC
BRASIL
Mercado Campero
See Inset
Train Station
MURGUÍA
ALDANA
BALLIVIÁN
SAN FELIPE
ARCE
ACCOMMODATION
Hotel Gran Sucre 2
Hotel Samay Wasy 1
Residencial San Salvador 3
RESTAURANTS & BARS
Bar Huari B
Govinda C
Nayjama D
Oggy A
Museo Antropológico Eduardo López Rivas & Museo de Mineralógia

Dancing with the Devil: the Oruro Carnaval

A moveable feast celebrated a week before Lent each year – usually late February or early March – the **Oruro Carnaval** attracts tens of thousands of visitors who come to enjoy what is by far the most raucous and spectacular fiesta in Bolivia. During the week-long party, thousands of costumed dancers parade through the streets in a vibrant and bizarre celebration of the sacred and profane that combines Christian beliefs with Andean folklore, with a good deal of heavy drinking and chaotic water-fighting thrown in for good measure.

At the centre of the festivities are two events: the **Entrada** on the Saturday before Ash Wednesday, with a massive procession of more than fifty different troups of costumed dancers passing through the streets, and the **Diablada**, or Dance of the Devils, led by two lavishly costumed dancers representing Lucifer and St Michael, followed by hundreds of devil dancers who leap and prance through the streets. Even though the number of Bolivian and foreign visitors coming to Oruro increases every year, you can still turn up a day or two before the Saturday Entrada and find somewhere to sleep and a seat on the route of the procession.

almuerzo. Once the most fashionable bar in Oruro, the sadly run-down *Bar Huari* on the corner of Junín and Galvarro is still a lively place for a beer and a bite to eat at weekends; legend has it that Bolivia's national cocktail, the *chufflay* (a mixture of *singani* and Seven-Up), was invented here by British mining engineers.

Potosí and around

Set on a desolate, windswept plain amid barren mountains at almost 4100m above sea level and 330km from Oruro, **POTOSÍ** is the highest city in the world, and at once the most fascinating and tragic place in Bolivia. Given its remote and inhospitable location, it's difficult to see at first glance why it was ever built here at all. The answer lies in **Cerro Rico** ("Rich Mountain"), the conical peak that rises imperiously above the city to the south and was, quite simply, the richest source of silver the world had ever seen. Potosí's legacy reflected both the magnificence and the horror of its colonial past. The city is a treasure-trove of **colonial art and architecture**, with hundreds of well-preserved buildings, including some of the finest churches in Bolivia. However, its tragic history weighs heavily on the shoulders of the living.

Some history

The silver rush of Cerro Rico was started in 1545 by a llama herder who was caught out after dark on the mountain's slopes, started a fire to keep warm, and was amazed to see a trickle of molten silver run out from the blaze. News of this discovery soon reached the Spaniards, and the rush was soon underway. Over the next twenty years the new city of Potosí became the richest single source of silver in the world, and its population mushroomed to over 100,000, making it easily the largest metropolis in the Americas.

By the beginning of the seventeenth century Potosí was home to more than 160,000 people – far bigger than contemporary Madrid – and boasted dozens of magnificent churches, as well as theatres, gambling-houses, brothels and dancehalls. For the **indigenous workers and African slaves** who produced this wealth, however, the working conditions were appalling and the consequences catastrophic. Estimates of the total number who died over three centuries of colonial mining in Potosí run as high as nine million, making the mines of Potosí a central factor in the demographic collapse that swept the Andes under Spanish rule.

Like all such booms, the silver bonanza at Potosí eventually cooled. After around 1650, silver production entered a century-long decline that saw the population of Potosí dwindle to just 30,000, as people sought opportunity elsewhere; by independence in 1825, Potosí's population was just nine thousand. From the end of the nineteenth century Potosí came to rely more and more on the mining of **tin**, but the town never recovered from the decline of silver production, much less the crash of the tin market in the mid-1980s. Today, the city's many fine churches are all that remains of the immense wealth that once flowed from its mines.

Arrival and information

All **buses** (except those from Uyuni) arrive at the Terminal de Buses on Avenida Universitario, on the way out of town towards Oruro. Buses from Uyuni pull in at the various bus company offices on the corner of Avenida Universitario and Sevilla, two blocks up from the terminal, which has a restaurant, phone boxes, post office, luggage storage and a small **bus information office** (daily 9am–noon & 2–8pm; ⓣ02/624-3361). From the terminal, a **taxi** into the city centre costs $0.60 per person (the basic rate for journeys throughout the city), or you can catch **micro** "A" heading up Avenida Universitario, which will take you to Plaza 10 de Noviembre, the central square.

The best place for information is the **Oficina de Turismo Municipal** (Mon–Fri 8am–noon & 2–6pm; ⓣ02/622-6408) in the striking modern mirrored building through the arch of Torre de la Compañía on Calle Ayacucho, a block west of Plaza 10 de Noviembre. English is spoken, and there are maps and small city guides for sale ($0.70).

Accommodation

With night-time temperatures often falling below zero, the main consideration when choosing where to stay in Potosí is warmth. A couple of the more upmarket places have central heating, but otherwise try to find a room that gets some sun during the day.

Hostal Carlos V Linares 42 ⓣ02/622-5121. Charming converted colonial house with simple but clean rooms looking out onto a glass-roofed central patio. Surly staff and a midnight curfew. Breakfast available. ❷–❸

Hostal Colonial Hoyos 8 ⓣ02/622-4265 or 622-4809, ⓔbolivia@hotelcupula.com or colonial_hostal@hotmail.com. Beautifully restored colonial mansion featuring a centrally heated modern interior and comfortable, well-furnished rooms (each with private bath), set around two peaceful tiled courtyards with fountains. Breakfast available. ❻

Hostal Compañía de Jesœs Chuquisaca 445 ⓣ02/622-3173. Delightful converted colonial building in the centre of town with clean, cosy rooms, good hot showers and a welcoming family atmosphere. Simple breakfast included. ❸

Hostal Hacienda Caraya Caraya ⓣ02/622-6380. Set in lush farmland in a warm valley 20km outside town and 500m lower, this wonderfully restored and opulently furnished colonial hacienda and is an ideal place if you find the altitude of Potosí too punishing. Transport to the city by taxi (about $11 return) can be organized and meals are available on request. Guests also have full use of a living room with a wood fire and an extensive library. Reserve through the office on Calle Cochabamba 32 (Mon–Fri 8.30am–1pm & 2.30–7pm, Sat 8.30am–1pm). Breakfast included. ❻

Hostal Santa Teresa Ayacucho 43 ⓣ02/623-0092 or 622-5270. New centrally located hostel, featuring clean, modern rooms with heating and private bathrooms, a decent restaurant and a rooftop terrace with great vistas. Simple breakfast included. ❺

Hotel Central Bustillo 1230 ⓣ02/622-2207. This crumbling colonial mansion is in a good central location and has basic rooms with shared bathrooms and limited hot water, plus the use of a kitchen. Breakfast available. At the time of writing, they were adding new rooms with private bath. ❷

Koala Den Junín 56 ⓣ02/622-6467, ⓔk_tours_potosi@hotmail.com. A travellers' favourite, this charming, friendly hostel owned and run by Koala Tours features basic but clean rooms, shared bathrooms with gas-powered showers, kitchen for use, and a communal area with games and book exchange. There's a dorm room with 8 beds, $2 each. ❷

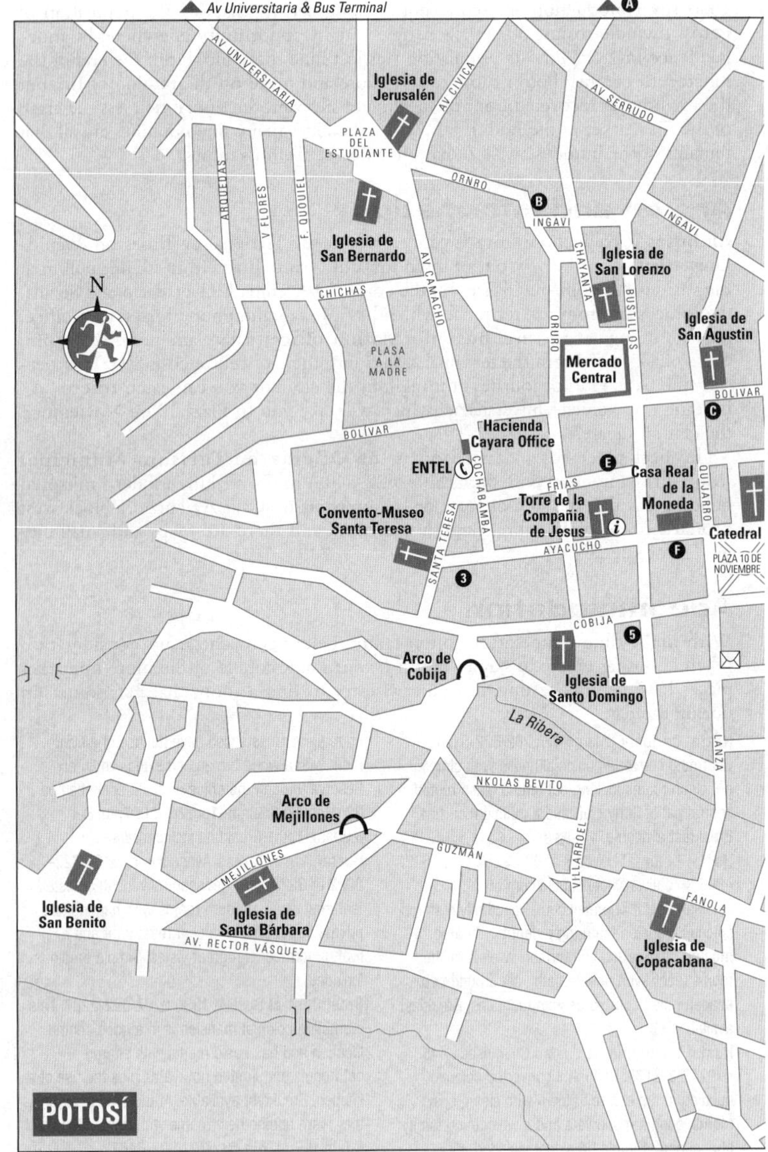

The City

The centre of the city is the **Plaza 10 de Noviembre**, a pleasant tree-shaded square with a broken fountain and a small replica of the Statue of Liberty, erected in 1926 to commemorate Bolivian independence. On the north side of the square, the site of the original church (which collapsed in 1807) is now occupied by the twin-

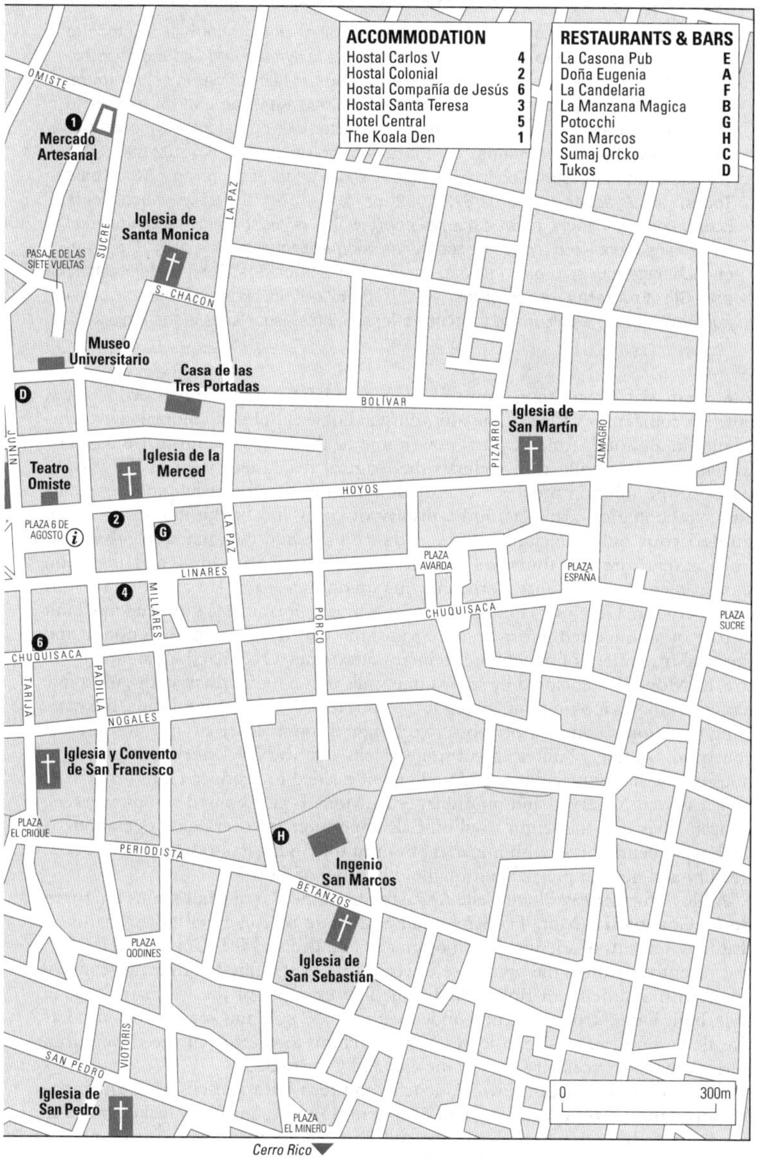

towered **Catedral**, completed in Neoclassical style in 1836. To the east of the square lies the **Plaza 6 de Agosto**, at the centre of which is a column commemorating the Battle of Ayacucho in 1824, which secured Bolivian independence early the following year.

Half a block west of the Plaza 10 de Noviembre on Calle Ayacucho stands the unmissable **Casa Real de la Moneda**, or Royal Mint (Tues–Fri 9am–noon &

Organized tours in Potosí

There are a growing number of **tour operators**, all of whom offer half-day trips to the mines of **Cerro Rico** (see opposite). These are fairly standard and supposed to cost a fixed $10 per person. Most companies also run half- or one-day **city tours**, and some also organize hiking trips in the Cordillera Kari-Kari and excursions to other attractions outside Potosí. Some of the better tour operators are the upmarket **Andean Salt Expeditions**, on Plaza Alonso de Ibañez 3 (ⓣ02/622-5175, ⓔturismo_potosi@hotmail.com), who has a wide range of tours on offer; **Koala Tours**, on Ayacucho 5 ⓣ02/622-2092 or ⓣ02/622-4708, ⓦwww.koalatoursbolivia.com, ⓔk_tours_potosi@hotmail.com), which is most highly recommended for its mine tours – run by experienced ex-miner multilingual guides, with 15 percent of each mine tour sold going toward improving health-care facilities for the miners; and **Sin Fronteras** on Bustillos 1092 ⓣ02/622-4058, ⓦwww.organizacionsinfronteras.com), a small, friendly agency offering all the usual tours in the region.

2–6.30pm, Sat & Sun 9am–1pm; $3, cameras $1.50, video cameras $3, ⓦwww.bolivian.com/cnm/). One of the most outstanding examples of colonial civil architecture in all South America, it is now home to the best museum in Bolivia. The vast and eclectic collection includes the original machinery used in the various stages of the minting process, some of Bolivia's finest colonial religious art, militaria, archeological artefacts, and a display of coins and banknotes. Visits are by **guided tour** only – included in the entrance price and conducted in Spanish or English; there are two tours daily, usually beginning each morning and afternoon shortly after opening, so it's worth showing up on time; tours last about two hours. Built between 1759 and 1773, La Moneda is a truly formidable construction, built as part of a concerted effort by the Spanish crown to reform the economic and financial machinery of the empire to increase revenues. Over 7500 square metres in size, La Moneda is enclosed by stout stone walls over a metre thick with only a few barred windows looking out, giving it the appearance of a fortress. Inside, the rambling two-storey complex of about two hundred rooms is set around five internal courtyards, all finely built with cut stone blocks and neat brickwork. In addition to housing the heavy machinery and equipment needed to produce coins – much of which is well preserved and on display – La Moneda also housed troops, workers, African slaves and the senior royal officials responsible for overseeing operations. A vital nerve centre of Spanish imperial power in the Andes, it also served as a prison, treasury and near-impregnable stronghold in times of disorder.

A block further east along Calle Ayacucho from the Royal Mint stands **La Torre de la Compañia** (Mon–Fri 8am–noon & 2–6pm; $0.70), a bell tower that is all that now remains of a Jesuit church originally founded in 1581. Completed in 1707 and recently restored, the grandiose tower is one of the finest eighteenth-century religious monuments in Bolivia and a sublime example of the Mestizo-Baroque style, built with a triumphal arch underneath and 32 columns carved with decorative flowers and grape-laden leaves. You can climb to the top of the tower, from where there are excellent views of the city and Cerro Rico.

Walk another block east down Ayacucho and turn left to reach the **Convento-Museo Santa Teresa** (daily 9–11am & 3–5pm; $3), a beautiful colonial church and convent worth visiting both for its fine collection of colonial religious painting and sculpture, and for a somewhat disturbing insight into the bizarre lifestyle of nuns in the colonial era. Visits are by guided tour only, so you need to get here at least an hour before closing.

Cerro Rico

Immediately south of Potosí the near-perfect cone of **Cerro Rico** (*Sumaj Orko* in Quechua) rises above the city, its slopes stained in startling hues of red and yellow by centuries of mining waste, and pockmarked with the entrances to the thousands of mines that lead deep into its entrails. All the agencies listed in the box opposite run regular **tours** of the mines. Groups should be no bigger than eight people, and you should be provided with rubber boots, a mining jacket or overalls, safety helmet and headlamp. Be warned, though, that this is an unpleasant and highly dangerous environment, where **safety precautions** are largely left to fate; anyone suffering from claustrophobia, heart or breathing problems is advised against entering. The air inside is fetid with dust and gases, including arsenic, and the chances of being hit by falling rocks or a speeding mine trolley are real. Owing to these obvious and real dangers, you'll be asked to sign a release form upon booking your tour. Some question the ethics of making a tourist attraction of a workplace where conditions are so appalling and life expectancy is about fifteen years, with most miners falling victim to silicosis, a deadly lung disease caused by inhaling silicon dust. However, most visitors find the experience one of the most unforgettable in Bolivia; seeing 13-year-old boys working in these inhuman conditions is a wake-up call that you will never forget.

Tours of the mines begin with a visit to the **miners' market** on and around Plaza El Calvario, where you can buy coca leaves, dynamite, black-tobacco cigarettes, pure cane alcohol and fizzy soft drinks – you should take a selection of these as gifts for the miners you'll be visiting. The miners are generally proud of their work and the hardship they endure, and are usually happy to talk about their lives with visitors.

Eating and drinking

Potosí's popularity with travellers is reflected in the city's growing variety of **places to eat**, with more and more cafés and restaurants offering vegetarian food and travellers' favourites like pizza and pasta.

La Candelaria Ayacucho 5. Mellow first-floor travellers' café opposite the Case Real de la Moneda serving up a combination of traditional Bolivian dishes and international favourites. It opens early for breakfast and also has a book exchange, tourist information, Internet access ($0.45 per hour) and a cosy covered terrace on the second floor.

La Casona Pub Frias 41. The liveliest nightspot in town, housed in an eighteenth-century mansion whose inside walls are decorated with contemporary graffiti. The atmosphere is friendly, with ice-cold beer and good but expensive food, including excellent trout. Live folk music on Thurs nights.

Doña Eugenia Opposite the cemetery just off Av Santa Cruz with Hermanos Ortega. Popular and inexpensive little restaurant on the outskirts of the town worth visiting as it's about the only place you can still get *kala phurka*, a thick, spicy maize soup served in earthenware bowls. A hot stone is plunged just before serving, so it stays piping hot and bubbles like a volcano as you eat it.

La Manzana Magica Calle Bustillos 1094. Welcoming hole-in-the-wall vegetarian restaurant serving hearty breakfasts, good-value set *almuerzos* and a wide variety of salads and snacks, as well as seven different kinds of veggie-burger. Closed Sun evening.

Potocchi Millares 13. Small café-restaurant serving reasonable traditional Bolivian and international food – it's worth visiting for the live folkloric music shows it hosts several nights a week, when there's a small cover charge.

San Marcos Inside the Ingenio San Marcos museum, La Paz with Betanzos. One of the best restaurants in town, with glass tables mounted on restored pieces of nineteenth-century industrial machinery and a menu of hearty Bolivian traditional dishes like llama steak for about $5, plus an excellent set *almuerzo* for just under $3.

Sumaj Orco Quijarro 46. Inexpensive restaurant popular with travellers and locals alike, serving large portions of hearty regional cuisine and good-value set *almuerzos*. Regional specialities worth trying here include *picante de viscacha* – a large Andean rabbit-like animal cooked in a spicy sauce – and *perdiz* – a partridge-like game bird.

Tukos Third floor, Junín 9. This self-styled "highest

cyber café in the world" serves coffee, juices, beer, snacks, good breakfasts and main courses like pasta and pizza in a warm and friendly atmosphere. There are also Internet terminals ($0.45 per hour), a pool table, chess, books and newspapers, and occasional live music.

Listings

Banks and exchange The Banco Nacional de Bolivia on Junín changes cash and travellers' cheques, and several shops along Bolívar change US dollars cash. There are several ATMs where you can withdraw cash on Visa or Mastercard, including the Banco Mercantil, on Padilla and Hoyos, and Banco de Crédito, on Bolívar and Sucre.
Buses to Cochabamba, La Paz, Oruro, Sucre, Tarija, Tupiza and Villazón depart regularly from the Terminal de Buses (Ⓣ02/622-7354) on Avenida Universitario. Buses for Uyuni leave from the various bus company offices on the corner of Avenida Universitario and Sevilla, two blocks up from the terminal.
Post office Correo Central, a block south of Plaza 10 de Noviembre on Lanza and Chuquisaca.
Telephone office ENTEL, Cochabamba and Plaza Arce.
Trains One each Monday morning to Uyuni departing from Estacion Central on Av Sevilla (info on Ⓣ02/622-4211 or 622-3101).

Uyuni

Set on the bleak southern Altiplano 212km southwest of Potosí, the cold railway town of **UYUNI** has little to recommend it except its usefulness as a jump-off point for expeditions into the beautiful and remote landscapes of the far southwest. Founded in 1889 at the junction of the railways that enter Bolivia from Chile and Argentina, Uyuni in its heyday was Bolivia's main gateway to the outside world and a symbol of modernity and industrial progress. Today, its streets are lined with a collection of shabby, tin-roofed houses and semi-abandoned railway yards filled with the decaying skeletons of redundant trains. A small town, it holds everything you might need within a few blocks; the effective centre is the nineteenth-century **clocktower** at the intersection of avenidas Arce and Potosí. That Uyuni hasn't become a ghost town is due to the ever-growing number of travellers who come here to visit the spectacular scenery of the **Salar de Uyuni** and the **Reserva de Fauna Andina Eduardo Avaroa**, which are usually visited together on a four-day tour from Uyuni.

Practicalities

The **train station** is on Avenida Ferroviaría, right in the centre of town. **Buses** from Potosí, Oruro and Tupiza pull up in front of the various bus company offices (an area optimistically described as "the terminal"), three blocks north of the train station along the partly pedestrianized Avenida Arce.

There are a couple of **tourist information offices** in Uyuni. The most useful is run by the Reserva Eduardo Avaroa inside the clocktower (Mon–Fri 9am–12.30pm & 2.30–6.30pm; Ⓣ02/693-2400). Just across the road on the corner of Arce and Potosí is the Oficina Municipal de Turismo with erratic opening hours and not particularly helpful staff. The **tour agencies**, all situated within a few blocks of Avenida Arce, are a better source of information, though their main aim is to sell you a trip to the Salar and the reserve (see p.259).

There's a limited range of **accommodation** in Uyuni, and most of it is pretty basic, though a couple of more upmarket places now exist where you'll get a warm room and a comfortable bed – most places stay open late for train passengers arriving in the middle of the night. The most comfortable and friendly option in town is *Toñito Hotel*, Av Ferroviaria 48 (Ⓣ02/693-3186, Ⓦwwwbolivianexpeditions.com; ❹), featuring wonderfully decorated rooms with private bath set around a bright covered courtyard; continental breakfast is included in the popular restaurant on site

△ The highway to Coroico, the world's most dangerous road

and there are cheaper cabins in the back for $5 per person, with basic but cosy rooms and shared bathrooms. The best budget options in town are *Hotel Avenida*, Av Ferroviaria 11 (☎02/693-2078; ❷), conveniently located right by the train station, with clean functional rooms without or without bath; and *Hotel Kutimuy*, Potosí and Avaroa (☎02/693-2391; ❷–❸), popular with big tour groups, with clean, modern, parquet-floored rooms (with or without bath) and a sunny rooftop cafeteria with good views over the town.

As with accommodation, the range of **places to eat** in Uyuni is pretty limited. There are a few restaurants concentrated around the pedestrianized Plaza Arce, offering generally overpriced and mediocre gringo-oriented food; try *16 de Julio*, a warm, glass-fronted restaurant serving up a good, filling four-course set *almuerzo* for just over $2, and *Arco Iris*, popular with travellers despite the very slow service for its decent pizza and pasta. Highly recommended is *Minuteman Pizza* in the *Toñito Hotel*, with cosy atmosphere, great decor and by far the best pizza in town, heavily laden with imaginative toppings, and also serving pasta dishes, creative salads and delicious muffins and pancakes.

Crossing into Chile from Uyuni

There are two ways of **crossing into Chile** from Uyuni. Twice a week, on Wednesday and Sunday at 4am, a passenger train travels from Uyuni to **Calama** in Chile via the Bolivian border post of **Avaroa**. If you're travelling this way you'll need to get an exit stamp ($2) at the *migración* in Uyuni on Av Potosí. A more popular route into Chile is across the border at **Laguna Verde** in the far south of the Reserva Eduardo Avaroa, which can be arranged through one of the tour agencies in Uyuni; most agencies have daily departures. The officials at this border post have been known to charge small unauthorized fees for letting you cross. See p.469 for information on entering Chile.

The far southwest: the Salar de Uyuni and Reserva de Fauna Andina Eduardo Avaroa

One of Bolivia's most extraordinary attractions, the **Salar de Uyuni**, covering some 9000 square kilometres of the Altiplano west of Uyuni, is by far the largest salt lake in the world. The Salar is not a lake in any conventional sense of the word – though below the surface it is largely saturated by water, its uppermost layer consists of a thick, hard crust of salt, easily capable of supporting the weight of a car. The surface is mostly covered by water between December and April, but even then it's rarely more than a metre deep, and usually much less. Driving across the perfectly flat white expanse of the Salar, with the unbroken chains of snowcapped mountains lining the far horizon, it's easy to believe you're on another planet, so harsh and inhospitable is the terrain.

The southwesternmost corner of Bolivia is covered by the **Reserva de Fauna Andina Eduardo Avaroa**, a 7147-square-kilometre wildlife reserve, ranging between 4000m and 6000m in altitude and encompassing some of the most startling scenery in Bolivia. Like the Salar de Uyuni, the desolate landscapes of this remote region possess an otherworldly beauty. This is a land of glacial salt lakes whose icy waters are stained bright red or emerald green by micro-organisms or mineral deposits. It features snowcapped volcanic peaks and frozen, high-altitude deserts; rock outcrops scoured by the unremitting wind into strange, Dalí-esque formations; and a wide range of rare **Andean wildlife**, including the world's largest population of the James flamingo, the elusive Andean fox and herds of graceful vicuñas.

Visiting the Salar and the reserve

Pretty much the only way to visit the Salar de Uyuni and Reserva Eduardo Avaroa is on an **organized tour**, which can be easily arranged from Uyuni. Even if you have your own 4WD complete with supplies and navigational aids, you should be very cautious about venturing onto the Salar – it's easy to get lost in the uniform white landscape, while the hard crust on the surface can occasionally give way under the weight of vehicles and the consequence of breakdown can be grave.

In Uyuni, avenidas Arce, Ferroviaria and Potosí are lined with some two-dozen **tour agencies**, all of which run combined trips to the Salar and the reserve. The **standard trip** (usually between $70 and $110, including food, accommodation, transport and Spanish-speaking guide) is a four-day tour by 4WD around a circuit comprising the Salar de Uyuni and Lagunas Colorada and Verde in the reserve; three-day trips are also available, if you find enough people who are interested. Bear in mind that wind-chill temperatures can drop to anything from -25°C to -40°C and that you should bring sun block and sunglasses to counter the very real possibility of snow blindness, as well as a good sleeping bag and plenty of warm clothing.

It's difficult to recommend any particular agency: all offer pretty much identical tours, but are prone to the same problems – late departures, dangerous (and often drunk) drivers, insufficient food prepared in unsanitary conditions, inadequate accommodation and vehicle breakdowns are all possibilities no matter which agency you choose. The best advice is to talk to travellers just returned from a tour and to request a written contract detailing exactly what you are paying for. Despite all the hassles and potential pitfalls, however, these tours are well worth the trouble.

Into the Salar de Uyuni and Reserva Eduardo Avaroa

Tours invariably enter the Salar via **Colchani**, a salt-processing village on its eastern shores about 20km north of Uyuni. Side by side a few kilometres west of Colchani are two **salt hotels**: the extravagant **Palacio del Sal** and the simpler, cosier **Hotel de Sal Playa Blanca** built from greyish blocks of raw salt cut from the surface of the Salar. Both have been shut down in October 2002 owing to poor sanitation that has caused considerable environmental damage; they're worth looking around for the novelty value and great photo opportunities – someone is usually around to let you in for a small entrance free.

From the salt hotels, all tours head 60km or so west across the Salar to the **Isla de Pescado** (Fish Island), one of several small islands, where you pay a $1 entrance fee. More properly known by the traditional name of Inca Wasi, or "Inca House" in Quechua, it manages to support a delicate but extremely tenacious ecosystem despite the harsh climate – its entire surface is covered by **giant cacti**, some of which are more than ten metres tall and thought to be hundreds of years old. From the island's peak, a short, sharp climb up from the shore on a well-marked trail, the views across the immense white expanse of the Salar are unforgettable.

From the village of Colcha K, just south of the Salar de Uyuni, it's a 160-kilometre drive down to the **entrance** to the reserve. The rough track climbs above 4000m and runs past a series of snow-frosted volcanoes and ancient lava fields straddling the border. One of these, the 5865-metre **Ollagüe**, is Bolivia's only active volcano, and you can usually make out thin plumes of smoke rising from just below its peak.

The trail then climbs still higher to over 4500m and across the **Pampa Siloli**, a high-altitude desert of volcanic ash and gravel scattered with rock outcrops that have been sand-blasted into surreal shapes by the constant, howling winds. The strangest of these is the **Arbol de Piedra** (Stone Tree), a massive boulder eight metres high that balances on a narrow stem.

Shortly after the Arbol de Piedra, the trail enters the Reserva Eduardo Avaroa and drops down to the extraordinary blood-red waters of **Laguna Colorada**, the biggest lake in the reserve. The lake owes its bizarre red colour, which changes in intensity during the day, to the natural pigments of the algae that live in its shallow, mineral-laden water. The **park office**, where you have to pay the $4.20 entrance fee, is beside the lake, and there are several very basic huts and refuges where almost all tour groups spend the night. Be warned that it gets bitterly cold here, with temperatures often dropping below –20°C.

You need to set off before dawn the next morning in sub-zero temperatures to enjoy the full spectacle of the **Sol de Mañana geyser**. Set at an altitude of 5000m amid boiling pools of mud and sulphur, the geyser's high-pressure jet of steam shoots out from the earth to a great height, but diminishes in power once the air temperature rises later in the day. After the geyser the trail drops down to **Laguna Polques**, which has a series of **hot springs** on its southern shore. No matter how cold you may feel, don't miss out on the chance to bathe here, or at least dip your feet – the deliciously warm waters are the perfect antidote to the high-altitude chill.

The next stop, about 30km further on, is **Laguna Verde**, a striking green lake – the colour is due to the arsenic and other minerals suspended in its waters – set at over 4300m in the southeasternmost corner of the reserve. You can cross into **Chile** at the manned border post about 7km away – make sure you get your exit stamp in Uyuni (see p.258). If you want to continue into Chile you should let your tour company know before leaving Uyuni, as the staff should be able to arrange onward transport to **San Pedro de Atacama**, 35km away, which otherwise may be hard to come by.

From Laguna Verde, tours make the 360km or so return trip to Uyuni by a more easterly route, stopping overnight at one of the few scattered llama-herding hamlets or mining camps along the way; three-day tours return from here directly to Uyuni. As you head out of the reserve look out for good views of Laguna Colorada below you in the distance to the west, and for the white peak of the highest mountain in the region, the 6006-metre **Cerro Uturuncu**, to the east.

Tupiza and around

Some 200km southwest of Uyuni, the isolated mining town of **TUPIZA** nestles in a narrow, fertile valley that cuts through the harsh desert landscape of the Cordillera de Chichas, with its cactus-strewn badlands, deep canyons and strangely shaped rock formations and pinnacles. Sheltered from the bitter winds of the Altiplano by the jagged mountains that rise steeply on either side of the valley, the town draws visitors largely because of its dramatic surrounding **desert landscape** that is ideal for hiking, horse riding or just touring by jeep. All these activities are easily arranged in this friendly town, which features a fledgling but well-organized tourist industry.

Founded in 1535, Tupiza was the home of one of Bolivia's biggest mining barons in the late nineteenth and early twentieth centuries. The mines were rich enough to attract the attention of the infamous North American gunslingers **Butch Cassidy** and the **Sundance Kid**, who are believed to have died in a shoot-out in the town of San Vicente, some 100km to the northwest. Today, though, the mineral deposits are largely exhausted, and Tupiza's economy depends more on its role as a market centre for the agricultural communities of the surrounding region and, increasingly, on tourism.

Practicalities

Tupiza is a small town, and it's easy to find your way around it. The **bus terminal** (Ⓣ02/694-2901; for info, also try Expreso Tupiza on Ⓣ02/694-4116) is on Avenida

Arraya, three blocks south and two blocks east of the main square, Plaza Independencia. The **train station** (ⓣ02/694-2529 or 694-2527) is three blocks east of the main plaza on Plazuela Adolfo Torres del Carpio, just off Avenida Serrudo. There's no formal **tourist information** office in the town, but the two main tour operators – Tupiza Tours, inside the *Hotel Mitru* on Avenida Chichas, and Valle Hermoso, inside *Hostal Valle Hermoso* – can tell you all you need to know.

Several *cambios* east of the plaza on Calle Avaroa will change **travellers' cheques**, as well as US dollars and Argentine pesos. Tupiza Tours, inside the *Hotel Mitru*, and the *Hostal Valle Hermoso* also change US dollars, Argentine pesos and travellers' cheques, and may also give cash advances on credit cards. There's expensive **Internet access** at Cyber Snack Heladería ($0.70/hr) on Chorolque, and at Full Internet ($1/hr) on the plaza. The **post office** and the **ENTEL** office are just west of Plaza Independencia on Plazuela Gualberto Villaroel.

There's only a small range of **accommodation** in Tupiza, all of it inexpensive and relatively simple, and aimed specifically at backpackers on limited budgets. The best budget option is *Residencial El Rancho* Av Pedro Arraya 86 (ⓣ02/694-3116; ❶–❷), with basic but clean and spacious rooms (with or without bath) set around a green patio. More pleasant places to stay include *Hotel Mitru*, Av Chichas 187 (ⓣ02/694-3001, ⓔtpztours@cedro.pts.entelnet.bo; suites: ❺/doubles ❷–❸, breakfast included), a friendly place popular with travellers and great for organizing group tours, featuring clean, simple rooms with or without bath, and recently added suites with great vistas, all set around a leafy sunny central courtyard with a swimming pool ($1.40 per day) and *Hostal Valle Hermoso* Av Pedro Arraya 478 (ⓣ02/694-2370 or 694-2592, ⓔhostalvh@hotmail.com; ❸), a welcoming and helpful establishment with a cosy rooftop terrace, a comfortable common room and recently refurbished clean and sunny rooms (with or without bath), all around a small patio shaded by a giant fig tree.

There's only a small choice of places **to eat and drink** in Tupiza. As usual, the cheapest place for food is the **market**, on the first floor of the corner of calles Chichas and Florida. Local specialities include *asado de cordero* (roast lamb), usually served on weekends, and *tamales* stuffed with dehydrated llama meat – the best are to be found outside the Mercado Negro on Av Chichas. For delicious *salteñas* and other morning snacks, try *El Bambino* on the corner of calles Florida and Santa Cruza, also serving reasonable set *almuerzo*, and pizza, meat and chicken dishes in the evening. The best food place is *El Rinconcito Quilmes* on Avaroa and Chichas, popular with locals for its filling set *almuerzos* ($1), excellent meat dishes (including delicious Argentine-style steaks; $2) and special lamb roasts on the weekend. For gringo favourites at gringo prices, try *Los Helechos* on the corner of Av Avaroa and Chichas, with a wide range of vegetarian dishes.

Organized tours from Tupiza

Tupiza's three **tour agencies** all offer broadly similar guided excursions into the desert landscapes around the town in 4WDs or on horseback, as well as longer but not terribly rewarding trips to **San Vicente**, where Butch Cassidy and the Sundance Kid are thought to have died. Horse-riding trips cost $2.75 per person per hour, half-day jeep excursions are about $7 per person, while a day-trip costs between $12 and $19 per person, depending on the itinerary (usually there's a four-person minimum and lunch is included). The agencies can also organize trips to the **Reserva de Fauna Andina Eduardo Avaroa** and the **Salar de Uyuni**, a four-day circuit that should cost about $100 per person in a jeep with at least four passengers. Tupiza's agencies are: **Explore Andina Tours**, Av Chichas 220, inside the *Hotel Roca Colorada* ⓣ02/694-3016, **Tupiza Tours**, Av Chichas 187, inside the *Hotel Mitru* ⓣ02/694-3001, ⓦwww.tupizatours.com, and **Valle Hermoso Tours**, Av Pedro Arraya 478, inside the *Hostal Valle Hermoso* ⓣ02/694-2370, ⓦwww.bolivia.freehosting.net.

Crossing into Argentina at Villazón

The main **border crossing** between Bolivia and Argentina is at the dusty ramshackle frontier town of **Villazón**, about 92km south of Tupiza by road or rail. There's no reason to stay overnight, so you're better crossing into Argentina, which couldn't be easier. Just walk south from the plaza down to the frontier along Avenida Internacional and get an exit stamp at the Bolivian *migración* office (daily 6am–8pm), then walk across the bridge into Argentina, where immigration is open 24 hours a day. From the Argentine border town of **La Quiaca** there are regular buses to the city of Jujuy, from where there are connections to the rest of the country. Accommodation and food in La Quiaca are much better than in Villazón, but cost a bit more. See p.69 for more information on entering Argentina.

Tarija and around

In the far south of the country, hemmed in by the high Altiplano to the west and by the cactus-choked hills that drop down into the impenetrable forests of the Chaco to the east, the isolated city of **TARIJA** is in many ways a world apart from the rest of Bolivia. Set in a broad, fertile valley at an altitude of 1924m, Tarija is famous for its **wine** production, and the valley's rich soils and fecund climate attracted large numbers of Andalucían farmers. Known as **Chapacos**, the largely *mestizo* Tarijeños take considerable pride in their distinct cultural identity.

Though it doesn't boast much in the way of formal tourist attractions, Tarija is a great place to hang out for a few days and relax. The surrounding countryside is beautiful without being spectacular, particularly in the spring (Jan–April), when the vineyards come to fruit and the whole valley blooms.

Arrival and information

The **bus terminal**, ten blocks or so southeast of the city centre on Avenida Las Américas, has a helpful bus information office (daily 6.30am–noon & 3–9.30pm; ⓣ04/663-6508). It's about twenty minutes into the city centre on foot from here, or a short **taxi** ride ($0.50). Alternatively, catch one of the frequent **micros** that run along Avenida Las Américas from the stop opposite the terminal. The **airport** (ⓣ04/664-3135) is on the outskirts of town a few kilometres further east along Avenida Las Américas. A taxi into the town centre from here should cost about $2.50, and there are also frequent micros from the Avenida into the centre ($0.50).

There are two **tourist information offices** in Tarija, but sadly they compete with each other for the title of worst in the country; for free maps and leaflets, try the Oficina Departmental de Turismo (Mon–Fri 8am–noon & 2.30–6.30pm; ⓣ04/663-1000) on the Plaza Luis de Fuentes, or the Oficina Municipal de Turismo (Mon–Fri 8.30am–12.30pm & 3–7pm, Sat 8.30am–12.30pm; ⓣ04/663-3581) on the corner of Bolívar and Sucre. Better sources of information are the city's two **tour operators**; see Listings.

The closest **border crossing into Argentina** is at Bermejo (10 daily, in the afternoon; 7hr), a gas- and sugar-producing town just over 200km south of Tarija.

Accommodation

Tarija has a good range of **accommodation**, almost all in the very centre of town – the exceptions are around the bus terminal, though there's no point staying down there unless you're just passing the night before continuing your journey.

Hostal Carmen Ingavi 784 ⓣ04/664-3372 or 664-4341, ⓔvtb@olivo.tja.entelnet.bo. Recently refurbished hostel with warm, well-decorated rooms set around a glass-roofed central patio and boasting plentiful hot water and cable TV – there's also a small apartment with kitchen for longer stays, and slightly cheaper shabby rooms in the old wing. Breakfast and transfer in from airport included. ❸

Hostal Costanera Av Las Américas with Saracho ⓣ04/664-2851 or 664-4817, ⓔcostnera@olivo.tja.entelnet.bo. Pleasant, clean option four blocks from the main square, with quiet rooms with private bath, phone and cable TV, set around a leafy backyard overlooking the city rooftops. Breakfast is included, there's free Internet service and good-value vegetarian buffet lunch Mon–Sat. ❺

Hostal Miraflores Sucre 920 ⓣ04/664-3355 or 664-4976. Converted colonial house with a sunny central courtyard, helpful and efficient staff, and a choice between comfortable rooms with cable TV, private bath and breakfast, or small, spartan rooms without. ❷–❸

Hostal Segovia Angel Calabi, right by the bus terminal ⓣ04/663-2965. Pleasant friendly hostel with clean rooms, with or without bath, conveniently located right by the bus terminal. ❷

The City

Laid out in the classic grid pattern of Spanish colonial cities, Tarija has few obvious attractions – its appeal lies more in the easy charm of its citizens and the warm, balmy climate. The centre of town is the tranquil, palm-lined **Plaza Luis de Fuentes**, named after the city's founder, whose statue stands in the middle.

A block south of the plaza on the corner of Virginio Lema and Trigo, the outstanding **Museo Paleontológico** (Mon–Fri 8am–noon & 3–6pm, Sat 9am–noon & 3–6pm; free) offers a fantastic collection of **fossils** from the Tarija Valley, including bones from the extinct Andean elephant, or mastodon, and an enormous skull and many bones of the *megatherium*, or giant sloth, at five metres long one of the biggest land mammals ever to exist. Most of the fossils on display are of mammals from the Pleistocene era, between a million and 250,000 years ago, many of them from species similar to ones that still exist today, such as horses, bears and llamas.

Also worth visiting is the **Casa Dorada** (Mon–Fri 8.30am–noon & 2.30–6pm; $0.50), also known as Casa de la Cultura, on the corner of Ingavi and Trigo. Built in the nineteenth century in the Art Nouveau style by a wealthy merchant, the house has been restored and declared a national monument. You can wander through its rooms with photo displays depicting the history of Tarija, or check out one of the many cultural events hosted here, including concerts and dance performances.

The charming small **Plaza Sucre**, two blocks southeast of the main plaza, is a great place to while away an afternoon sitting in one of the many cafés and enjoying the city's laid-back and gregarious Mediterranean flavour.

Eating and drinking

Nowhere is Tarija's strong Argentine influence more evident than in its **restaurants**. Good-quality grilled beef features strongly, ideally accompanied by a glass of local wine, while Tarijeños are also justly proud of their distinctive traditional cuisine featuring chicken and meat dishes cooked in delicious spicy sauces – try *ranga-ranga*, *saice* or *chancao de pollo*.

El Amigo Lema with Ballivián. Popular restaurant with generous portions of meat dishes and delicious salads for $2.50. Open evenings only, with folkloric shows every Fri ($2 entrance).

Baghdad Café Plaza Sucre. Cosy little bar-café with a bohemian atmosphere – it attracts a lively young crowd who come here for coffee in the afternoon and wine and hot snacks in the evening.

Mateos Trigo and Madrid. Superior restaurant with indoor and outdoor seating and a refined ambience, serving a superb four-course *almuerzo* ($3.50), as well as a la carte meat, fish and pasta dishes and a very good salad bar.

El Solar Campero with Virginio Lemo. A welcome vegetarian alternative, this New Age oasis serves a healthy yet tasty four-course *almuerzo* for $1.50, as well as a range of salads, snacks, juices and herbal teas. Lunchtime only.

El Tropero Virginio Lema and Daniel Campos. Authentic Argentine steakhouse with outdoor seating serving excellent grilled beef and chicken as well as a filling *almuerzo* for $2.

Wine in the Tarija Valley

There are some worthwhile excursions close to Tarija in the warm and fertile **Tarija Valley**, which is notable as Bolivia's prime wine-producing region. A visit to one of the Tarija Valley **bodegas** (wineries) to see how the wines are produced (and sample a few glasses at source) makes an excellent half-day excursion from the city. Generally, you can only visit the closest *bodegas* on an organized trip with a Tarija-based agency (about $6 per person for a half-day tour), but you can independently visit the **Concepción-Rugero** *bodega* (Ⓣ04/613-2008; closed Sat afternoon and Sunday), which arguably produces the best wine in Bolivia about 35km from Tarija. A micro marked "V" from Plaza Sucre will drop you off in the village of Concepción, from where it's a twenty-minute walk to the *bodega* along a track heading out across a bridge to the right of the main road – ask the driver or anyone in the village for directions.

Listings

Airlines AeroSur, Ingavi and Sucre Ⓣ04/663-0893; LAB, Trigo and Lemo Ⓣ04/664-5706 or 664-2195; TAM, Madrid and Trigo Ⓣ04/664-2734.
Banks and exchange The Banco Nacional de Bolivia, opposite the *Hotel Gran Tarija* on Sucre, changes cash and travellers' cheques and has an ATM that takes Visa and Mastercard. There are several other ATMs in town, including at the Banco de Santa Cruz on Trigo and Lema.
Consulate The Argentine consulate is on Ballivián and Bolívar Ⓣ04/663-7706 or 663-7707.
Internet access There are plenty of places to surf the web in the city centre; try Consultel on Plaza Sucre ($0.60/hr).
Post office The Correo Central is on Lema, between Sucre and Trigo.
Radio taxis 4 de Julio Ⓣ04/663-8860 or 663-8890; Sur Ⓣ04/664-1616.
Telephone office The ENTEL office is on Lema and Daniel Campos.
Tour operators VTB Turismo Receptivo, inside the *Hostal Carmen* at Ingavi 784 Ⓣ04/664-3372 or 664-4341, Ⓔvtb@olivo.tja.entelnet.bo, and Viva Tours, just off the Plaza Luis de Fuentes on Sucre Ⓣ04/663-8325, Ⓔvivatour@cosett.com.bo, both run one-day tours of the city and around the vineyards and *bodegas* of the Tarija Valley with experienced English-speaking guides.

2.4

The central valleys

East of the Altiplano, the Andes march gradually down towards the eastern lowlands in a series of rugged mountain ranges, scarred with long, narrow valleys formed by rivers draining to the east. Blessed with rich alluvial soils, and midway in climate and altitude between the cold of the Altiplano and the tropical heat of the lowlands, these **CENTRAL VALLEYS** have historically been among the most fertile and habitable areas in Bolivia.

The administrative, political and religious centre of all Bolivia during Spanish rule, and still officially the capital of the republic, **Sucre** is a masterpiece of immaculately preserved colonial architecture, filled with elegant churches and mansions, and home to some of Bolivia's finest museums. The charms of **Cochabamba**, on the other hand, are more prosaic and lacking in conventional tourist attractions – while most travellers view it as no more than a place to break a journey between La Paz and Santa Cruz in the eastern lowlands, those who do spend some time here find it one of the most pleasant cities in Bolivia. It is also the jumping off point for an adventurous journey south into the harsh, arid mountain scenery of the remote Northern Potosí province, where the diverse attractions of the **Parque Nacional Torotoro**, Bolivia's smallest national park, include labyrinthine limestone caves, deep canyons and waterfalls, dinosaur footprints and ancient ruins.

East of Cochabamba, the main road to Santa Cruz passes through the **Chapare**, a beautiful region of rushing rivers and dense tropical forests, where the last foothills of the Andes plunge down into the Amazon basin. The area has become notorious in recent decades as the source of most of Bolivia's coca crop. As such, it's hardly an ideal area for travellers, but some areas remain safe to visit and provide a frontline insight into the war on drugs, one of the great dramas of contemporary Bolivia.

Sucre and around

Set in a broad highland valley on the eastern edge of the Altiplano about 162km north of Potosí, **SUCRE** is widely considered the most sophisticated and beautiful city in Bolivia, with some of the finest Spanish colonial architecture in South America and a pleasant, spring-like climate all year round. The city is the administrative and market centre for a mountainous rural hinterland inhabited by the Quechua-speaking **indigenous communities**, particularly renowned for their beautiful weavings, considered amongst the finest in all the Andes. They can be seen – and bought – in the city itself or on a day-trip to **Tarabuco**, a rural town about 60km southeast of Sucre that hosts a colourful Sunday market.

Founded some time between 1538 and 1540 and initially named Chuquisaca, Sucre's official title changed to **Villa de la Plata** (City of Silver) after the discovery of significant quantities of silver nearby. The first half of the seventeenth century was La Plata's golden age, as the wealth from the nearby Potosí mines funded the construction of lavish churches and monasteries, extravagant palaces and administrative buildings. After independence, it was made the **capital** of the new Republic of Bolivia and renamed **Sucre**, but the city's economic importance declined. When the seat of both congress and the presidency was moved to La Paz after the civil

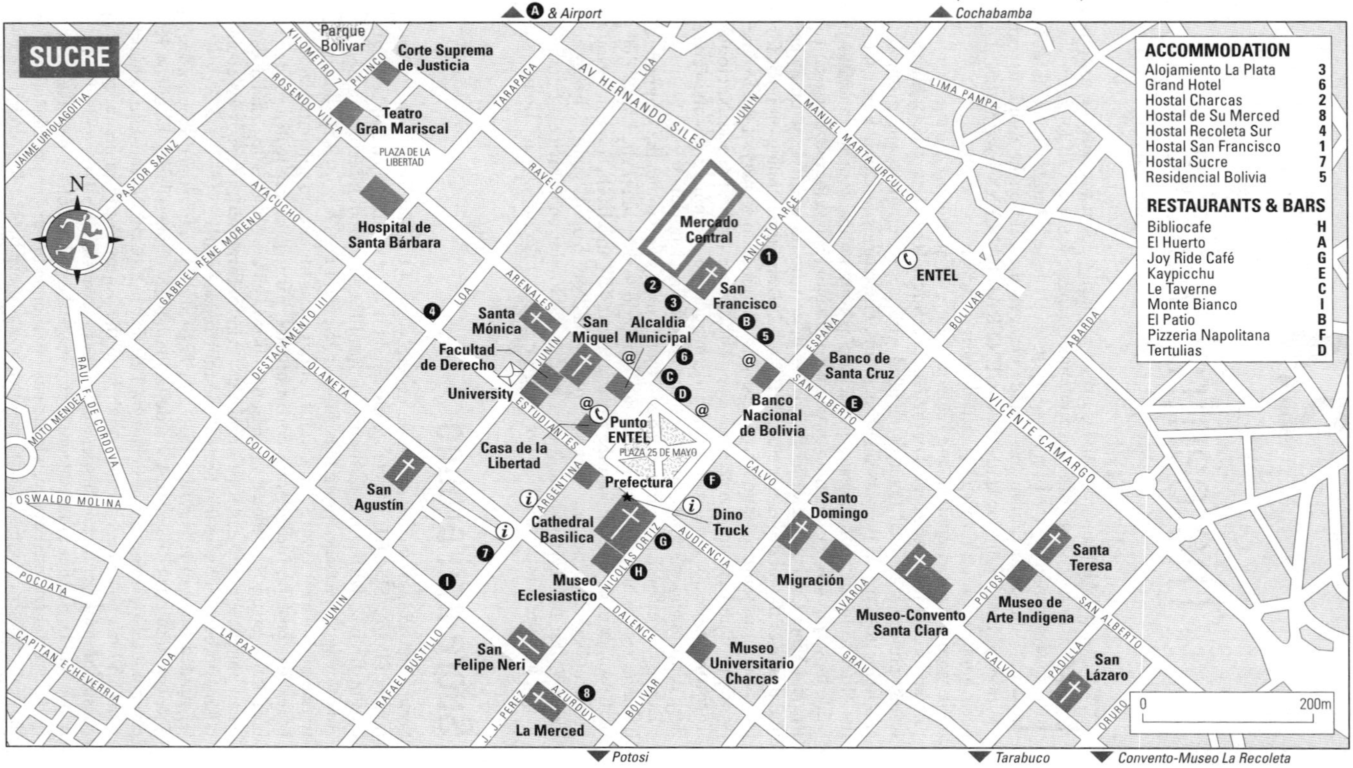

SUCRE

ACCOMMODATION

Alojamiento La Plata	3
Grand Hotel	6
Hostal Charcas	2
Hostal de Su Merced	8
Hostal Recoleta Sur	4
Hostal San Francisco	1
Hostal Sucre	7
Residencial Bolivia	5

RESTAURANTS & BARS

Bibliocafe	H
El Huerto	A
Joy Ride Café	G
Kaypicchu	E
Le Taverne	C
Monte Bianco	I
El Patio	B
Pizzeria Napolitana	F
Tertulias	D

A & Airport
Cochabamba
Potosi
Tarabuco
Convento-Museo La Recoleta
N
0 200m
Parque Bolivar
Corte Suprema de Justicia
Teatro Gran Mariscal
PLAZA DE LA LIBERTAD
Hospital de Santa Bárbara
Mercado Central
San Francisco
ENTEL
Santa Mónica
San Miguel
Alcaldia Municipal
Banco de Santa Cruz
Banco Nacional de Bolivia
Facultad de Derecho
University
Punto ENTEL
PLAZA 25 DE MAYO
Casa de la Libertad
Prefectura
Dino Truck
San Agustín
Cathedral Basilica
Santo Domingo
Migración
Museo Eclesiastico
Museo-Convento Santa Clara
Museo de Arte Indigena
Santa Teresa
San Lázaro
Museo Universitario Charcas
San Felipe Neri
La Merced
KILOMETRO 7
PILINCO
ROSENDO VILLA
TARAPACA
AV HERNANDO SILES
LOA
JUNIN
MANUEL MARTA URCULLO
LIMA PAMPA
JAIME URIOLAGOITIA
PASTOR SAINZ
AYACUCHO
RAVELO
ANICETO ARCE
GABRIEL RENE MORENO
ARENALES
ESPAÑA
BOLIVAR
ABARDA
DESTACAMENTO III
OLANETA
SAN ALBERTO
VICENTE CAMARGO
RAUL F. DE CORDOVA
MOTO MENDEZ
ESTUDIANTES
COLON
CALVO
ARGENTINA
OSWALDO MOLINA
NICOLAS ORTIZ
AUDIENCIA
AVAROA
POTOSI
POCOATA
DALENCE
GRAU
CAPITAN ECHEVERRIA
LA PAZ
RAFAEL BUSTILLO
J. J. PEREZ
AZURDUY
PADILLA
ORURO

war between the two cities in 1899, the transfer merely confirmed long-established realities. Sucre remained the seat of the supreme court and was allowed to retain the title of official or constitutional capital, an honorary position it still holds today. This unusual state of affairs preserves Sucre's capital status and an exaggerated sense of its own importance, while giving the feel of a provincial backwater basking in past glories, frozen in time in the late nineteenth century.

Arrival and information

Sucre is a small, compact city, and other than the bus terminal and airport everything is within easy walking distance of the historic city centre, where all the accommodation is located. The **airport** (Ⓣ04/645-4445) is about 8km northwest of the city; Micros I and F run from there into the centre of town along Avenida Siles (30min); alternatively, a taxi should cost about $3. All long-distance buses arrive and depart from the **bus terminal** (Ⓣ04/645-2029 or 644-1292), about 3km northwest of the town centre on Ostria Gutiérrez. From here it's a $0.50 taxi ride into the centre of town, or you can catch Micro A, which runs down to the Mercado Central, a block north of the main Plaza 25 de Mayo. Collective **taxis** arriving from Potosí will drop you off outside your hotel or anywhere else in the centre of town.

The main municipal **tourist office** (Mon–Fri 8am–noon & 2–6pm; Ⓣ04/645-1083 or 642-7102) is on the first floor of the Casa de Cultura, a block southeast of Plaza 25 de Mayo on Calle Argentina, and there's also an information **kiosk** (Mon–Fri 8.30am–noon & 2.30–6pm, Sat 9am–noon) on the corner of calles Bustillos and Olañeta, and an Oficina Universitaria de Turismo (Mon–Fri 9am–noon & 3–6pm) on Calle Estudiantes, just off the Plaza 25 de Mayo, run by enthusiastic student guides who sometimes volunteer to show you around for free, although a tip is always welcome.

Accommodation

Sucre has a pretty good range of **accommodation**, almost all of it conveniently located in the heart of the old city centre.

Alojamiento La Plata Ravelo 32 Ⓣ04/645-2102. Popular budget option offering small and basic but clean rooms with shared bath around a sunny courtyard, as well as recently added (and more comfortable) rooms in the back. ❷

Grand Hotel Arce 61 Ⓣ04/645-1704. Good-value mid-range option with comfortable and well-decorated rooms, all with private bath, set around two peaceful colonial patios, the innermost of which overflows with lush tropical vegetation. Suites and triples available, and breakfast is included. ❹

Hostal Charcas Ravelo 62 Ⓣ04/645-3972, Ⓔhostalcharcas@yahoo.com. Modern and efficient establishment, with helpful, welcoming staff, abundant hot water and sunny rooftop terrace. Rooms are scrupulously clean but rather cramped, and those with private bathrooms lack ventilation. Breakfast available. ❷–❸

Hostal de Su Merced Azurduy 16 Ⓣ04/644-2706 or 644-5150, Ⓦwww.boliviaweb.com/companies/sumerced. Immaculately restored and converted eighteenth-century house with a charming central patio and two delightful rooftop sun terraces with panoramic views of the city. Rooms combine opulent antique furniture with a full range of modern comforts, including cable TV. Elaborate buffet breakfast included. ❻

Hostal Recoleta Sur Ravelo 205 Ⓣ04/645-4789. Modern carpeted rooms with cable TV and private bath in a converted colonial house with a glass-roofed patio and a classic stone-pillar corner doorway. Breakfast included. ❹

Hostal San Francisco Arce 191 Ⓣ04/645-2117. Modern, colonial-style building with pleasant rooms opening onto sunny balconies around the usual central patio. Excellent value, with breakfast available. ❸

Hostal Sucre Bustillos 113 Ⓣ04/645-1411 or 646-1928, Ⓔhosucre@mara.scr.entelnet.bo. Converted colonial mansion with period decor and pleasant if slightly gloomy rooms set around two charming flower-filled courtyards. Breakfast included. ❹

Residencial Bolivia San Alberto 42 Ⓣ04/645-4346, Ⓔres_bol@cotes.net.bo. Friendly and good-value *residencial*, with spacious, airy rooms (with or without bathroom) set around a bright courtyard with plenty of plants. A meagre breakfast is included. ❷–❸

The City

Laid out in the classic grid pattern required by Spanish imperial ordinances, Sucre is a jewel of colonial and nineteenth-century architecture, its splendid churches, monasteries and mansions a reminder of the wealth and power the city once enjoyed. The historic city centre was declared a UNESCO world heritage site in 1991, and strict building codes mean most of it has been preserved much as it was a hundred years ago. Neon signs are banned, and a municipal regulation requires all buildings to be whitewashed once a year, maintaining the characteristic that earned Sucre another of its many grandiose titles: "La Ciudad Blanca de Las Americas" – the White City of the Americas.

Plaza 25 de Mayo

The centre of Sucre is the spacious **Plaza 25 de Mayo**, shaded by tall palms and dotted with benches where people of all social classes – from eminent lawyers to humble *campesinos* – pass the time of day chatting, reading newspapers or greeting passing acquaintances. It's a great place to watch the world go by while having your shoes shined or enjoying a hot *salteña* and a cool glass of the orange juice sold from handcarts by ever-present street vendors.

On the northwest side of the square stands the simple but well-preserved colonial facade of the original seventeenth-century Jesuit University, with carved wooden balconies overlooking the square and an elegant stone portico bearing the university's coat of arms. Now known as the **Casa de La Libertad** (Mon–Fri 9am–noon & 2.30–6.30pm, Sat 9.30am–noon; $1.40; guided tours in Spanish and English; Ⓦwww.bcb.gov.bo/8fundacion/index), this was where the Bolivian act of independence was signed on August 6, 1825, and it now houses a small but interesting museum dedicated to the birth of the republic. Inside, the original signed document proclaiming a sovereign and independent state is on display in the assembly room, as well as a gallery of portraits of almost all Bolivia's presidents, plus paintings of pro-independence guerrillas and their royalist foes and a collection of captured royalist swords, guns and bloodstained banners.

Half a block northwest of Plaza 25 de Mayo along Calle Arenales, the modest whitewashed Baroque facade of the **Iglesia de San Miguel** (sporadic opening hours; best to visit during Sunday mass between 6.30 and 8pm), completed in 1621, conceals one of the most lavish church interiors in Sucre, with glorious carved Baroque altarpieces covered in gold leaf and an exquisite panelled *mudejár* ceiling of intricate interlocking geometric shapes.

South of Plaza de Mayo

Housed in an elegant colonial building three blocks southeast of Plaza 25 de Mayo on the corner of calles San Alberto and Potosí, the fascinating **Museo de Arte Indigena** (Mon–Fri 8.30am–noon & 2.30–6pm, Sat 9.30am–noon & 2.30–6pm, open on Sat afternoon only in low season; $2, includes complimentary tea service and free books to guide you around the museum; Ⓦwww.bolivianet.com/asur) is dedicated to the distinctive weavings of two local Quechua-speaking indigenous groups, the **Jalq'a** and the **Tarabuqueños**. The museum was initially a great project that brought about a renaissance of indigenous art and turned the weaving craft into a source of income for hundreds of desperately poor *campesino* families but it has sadly declined over the years, with the artists seeing less and less of the profits. Nevertheless, the expertly laid out collection of tools, colour photos and maps that explain the weaving techniques and the plants used to make natural dyes, as well as the weavings themselves, provide an excellent insight into a distinctly Andean artistic expression.

Three blocks south of Calle Potosí and two blocks toward the centre on Dalence on the corner with Bolívar is the rambling but worthwhile **Museo Universitario**

Charcas (Mon–Fri 8.30am–noon & 2.30–6pm, Sat 9am–noon & 3–6pm; $1.40), housed in a delightful seventeenth-century mansion. It is really four museums in one, combining the university's archeological, anthropological, colonial and modern art collections, all set around a series of colonial flower-filled patios. Visits are by guided tour only, mostly in Spanish, and last at least an hour.

Two blocks north on Bolívar, Calle Calvo climbs steeply uphill towards Plaza Pedro de Anzures, on the southeast side of which stands the **Convento-Museo La Recoleta** (Mon–Fri 9–11.30am & 2.30–4.30pm; $1.10), a tranquil Franciscan monastery that now houses an interesting little museum of colonial religious art and materials related to the missionary work of the Franciscan order in Bolivia. Visits are by guided tour in Spanish only, so it's best to show up shortly after opening, or wait for the next tour in *Café Mirador* across the square and enjoy the scenic views of the city below.

The footprints at Cal Orko

Five kilometres outside Sucre on the road to Cochabamba, the low mountain of **Cal Orko** is home to the world's largest collection of **dinosaur footprints**, discovered in 1994 by workers at a local cement works and limestone quarry. The site has been declared a national monument, and has become a major tourist attraction for its 5000 or so prints from at least 150 different types of dinosaur that cover an area of around 30,000 square metres of near-vertical rock face; it requires a good guide and some imagination to appreciate the footprints, as they're not easy to spot at first sight. You can only visit the site on a guided tour in the Dino-Truck, a painted pick-up run by the Abbey Path tour agency (Ⓣ04/645-1863), which leaves Mon–Sat at 9.30am, noon and 2.30pm from outside the cathedral. Tours cost $3.50, which includes transfer and admission, and last one to two hours.

Eating and drinking

Sucre is home to a good variety of **restaurants** where you can get everything from the spicy local cuisine to authentic French, Italian and vegetarian food at reasonable prices. Don't miss out on *salteñas*, rightly considered the best in Bolivia and available from stalls, handcrafts and specialist *salteñerias*, which are only open from mid-morning to noon.

Bibliocafé N. Ortíz 50. Bohemian bar-café attracting a good mix of locals and travellers from early evening until late at night with its mellow music and intimate atmosphere. Also serves snacks and light meals, and gets packed on weekends.

El Huerto Ladislao Cabrera 86. Ask a local for the best restaurant in town, and the chances are they'll direct you here. The menu features excellent meat, chicken and fish dishes cooked to both traditional Bolivian and sophisticated international recipes for about $4–5, served outdoors in a beautiful garden. It's some distance from the city centre, but well worth the taxi fare. Lunchtimes only.

Joy Ride Café N. Ortíz 14. Trendy Dutch-run bar-café serving tasty breakfasts, meals and snacks as well as excellent coffee, cocktails and cold beer; there's a charming small patio upstairs. Opens at 7.30am on weekdays and 9am on weekends, until late; gets particularly busy on Friday and Saturday nights. Also the place to book one of the popular mountain biking or motorbike tours, through Joy Ride Bolivia agency on site.

Kaypichu San Alberto 168. Popular vegetarian restaurant offering a wide range of tasty and healthy dishes including muesli, fruit and yoghurt for breakfast, good soups, salads and pastas, and a decent set *almuerzo* for $1.50. Open 7am–2pm & 5–7pm; closed Mon.

La Taverne Arce 35. Authentic French restaurant serving classic dishes like *coq au vin*, *boeuf bourguignon* and rabbit for about $4, as well as excellent home-made pâté and delicious chocolate gateaux. Closed Mon all day and Sun 3–6pm.

Monte Bianco Colón 149. Wonderful little Italian-owned restaurant with a warm, cosy atmosphere and delicious pasta and pizza for about $3. The *penne a la vodka* is particularly good, and the tiramisu irresistible. Evenings only. There's been talk of closing the restaurant in which case *Monte Rosso* on Bolívar between Calvo and San Alberto is a great alternative.

El Patio San Alberto 18. Popular *salteñeria* dishing

up rich, juicy *salteñas* in a beautiful colonial patio filled with bougainvillea and other flowering plants. Open until noon only and always packed; order and pay at the entrance booth.

Pizzeria Napolitana Plaza 25 de Mayo 30. Sucre's longest-established Italian restaurant, serving reasonable pizza and pasta, home-made ice cream, strong coffee and a daily choice of six different set lunches for $2–3.

Tertulias Plaza 25 de Mayo 59. Popular night-time drinking hideaway for Sucre's artists and intellectuals, dimly lit and decorated with a bizarre mix of colonial religious and surrealist art; they also serve tasty but expensive food.

Listings

Airlines AeroSur, Arenales 31 ⓣ04/646-2141; LAB, España 105–109 ⓣ04/645-2666; TAM, Junín 744 ⓣ04/645-2213.

Banks and exchange Casa de Cambios Ambar, San Alberto 7, and El Arca, España 134, both change travellers' cheques and cash dollars at reasonable rates. There are also plenty of ATMs around town where you can withdraw cash on Visa or Mastercard, including at the Banco de Santa Cruz and Banco Nacional de Bolivia, opposite each other at San Alberto with España.

Car rental Auto Cambio Chuquisaca, Av Jaime Mendoza 1106 ⓣ04/646-0984; Imbex, Serrano 165 ⓣ04/646-1222.

Emergencies Dial ⓣ118 for medical help or ⓣ110 for police assistance.

Hospital Hospital Universitario Santa Bárbara, Plaza de la Libertad ⓣ04/645-1900 or 645-1064.

Internet access There are Internet cafés all over the city, most of which charge about $0.50 an hour: try Cyber-Station on the east side of the plaza or Café Internet Maya on Arenales 5.

Language courses Academia Latinoamericana de Español, Dalence 109 with N. Ortiz (ⓣ04/646-0537, ⓦwww.latinoschools.com).

Post office Correo Central, Junín with Ayacucho.

Telephone office The main ENTEL office is at España 271 with Camargo, and there are smaller Punto ENTEL offices on the northeast side of Plaza 25 de Mayo and on the corner of Ravelo with Junín, plus numerous card-operated phone booths on Plaza 25 de Mayo and at major intersections around the city.

Tour operators Sur Andes, Ortíz 6 with Audiencia (ⓣ04/645-2632); Candelaria Tours, Audiencia 1 (ⓣ04/646-1661, ⓦwww.candelariatours.com); Joy Ride Bolivia inside the Joy Ride Café at Ortíz 14 (ⓣ04/642-5544, ⓦwww.joyridebol.com); and Turismo Sucre, Bustillos 117 (ⓣ04/646-0349, ⓦwww.entelnet.bo/turismosucre).

Tarabuco and Hacienda Candelaria

By far the most popular excursion from Sucre is to the small rural town of **TARABUCO**, set amid crumpled brown mountains about 60km southeast of the city. The town itself is an unremarkable collection of red-tiled adobe houses and cobbled streets, but its real claim to fame is the **Sunday market**. This is the focus for the indigenous communities of the surrounding mountains, the **Tarabuqueños**, who come to sell the beautiful weavings for which they're famous throughout Bolivia. The market is actually a bit of a tourist trap, and the stalls selling weavings and other handicrafts to tourists are still far outnumbered by those selling basic supplies such as dried foodstuffs, agricultural tools, sandals made from tyres, big bundles of coca and pure alcohol in great steel drums. The market provides plenty of perfect photo-snapping opportunities, but make sure you either ask before you take people shots, buy something from the vendors in return or simply be very discreet.

Buses and trucks to Tarabuco from Sucre (2hr; $1) leave most mornings from Plaza Huallparimachi in the east of the city, returning in the afternoon; however, it's much more convenient and only slightly more expensive to go in one of the **tourist buses** (they usually charge around $3 for the return trip) organized by hotels and tour agencies in Sucre, which will pick you up outside the Mercado Central on Calle Ravelo in the morning and bring you back in the afternoon.

Another delightful and little-known excursion from Sucre is a trip to **Hacienda Candelaria**, 82km from Sucre, which provides a unique opportunity to interact with an indigenous community. Owned and run by Candelaria Tours (see above), the seventeenth-century hacienda lies in a weaving village of Candelaria, amidst quiet countryside of apple orchards, lush forests and a mountainous backdrop. **Visits** have to be booked with the agency, and tours range from full-day excursions from Sucre ($50–80 per person, including private transport, bilingual guide and meals) to overnight stays with activities ($80–120 per person, with basic accommodation), such as visits to the peasants' houses and partaking in their daily activities of weaving, spinning wool, baking bread and cooking traditional foods.

Cochabamba

Set at the geographical centre of Bolivia, midway between the Altiplano and the eastern lowlands, **COCHABAMBA** is one of the country's most welcoming cities and the commercial hub of the country's richest agricultural region, the Cochabamba Valley, known as the breadbasket of Bolivia. It's a friendly and unpretentious city, also known as the "City of Eternal Spring" for its year-round sunny climate matched by the warmth and openness of its population, and a good base for exploring the understated attractions of the surrounding valley.

The **Incas** were quick to spot the agricultural potential when they conquered the region in the mid-fifteenth century, moving Quechua-speaking agricultural colonists here from across the empire to cultivate maize. Inca control of the area was ended by the arrival of the **Spanish**, who founded the city on January 1, 1574. They soon established haciendas to produce grain for the silver mines of Potosí, but when the mines went into decline towards the end of the colonial period and the early republican era, many of the hacienda lands were rented out. What followed was the emergence of a class of independent Quechua-speaking **peasant farmers**, who played a central role in Bolivia's radical peasant political organizations during the 1950s and 1960s, and, as migrants to the Chapare, have assumed a key role in the more recent coca-growers' movement.

Arrival and information

Almost all long-distance buses arrive and depart from Cochabamba's **bus terminal**, on Avenida Ayacucho just south of Avenida Aroma. The terminal has a bus **information kiosk** (daily 5am–11pm; toll-free ⓣ155 or 04/423-4600), post office, ENTEL office and plenty of phone booths, a left-luggage store, a 24-hour café-restaurant and a number of ATMs outside. Many of the city's hotels are within easy walking distance of the terminal; otherwise, a taxi to anywhere in the city centre should cost about $0.50 per person. Buses from the **Chapare** region east of Cochabamba arrive around the junction of Avenida Oquendo and Avenida 9 de Abril to the southeast of the city centre. Cochabamba's extremely modern but underused Jorge Wilsterman **airport** (ⓣ04/459-1820) is a few kilometres outside town to the southwest; a taxi into the city centre should cost about $3; alternatively, take micro B, which goes up Avenida Ayacucho to Plaza 14 de Septiembre, the city's main square. The regional **tourist office** (Mon–Fri 8.30am–noon & 2.30–6pm, Sat 8.30am–noon; ⓣ04/422-1793) is in a kiosk on Calle Achá, half a block west of Plaza 14 de Septiembre, and distributes free maps and leaflets on tours to the surrounding attractions.

Accommodation

Accommodation in Cochabamba reflects the nature of the city: though functional and reasonably priced, it's unexceptional and generally not aimed at tourists (the city sees few). The only time accommodation is difficult to find is in mid-August during the **Fiesta de la Virgen de Urkupiña** in nearby Quillacollo; it's best to book in advance during this period.

Gran Hotel Cochabamba Plaza Ubaldo Anze E-0415 ⓣ04/411-9986 or 428-2553, ⓔcbbhotel@bo.net. Luxurious Art Deco country-club–style hotel with spacious, fully equipped and stylishly decorated rooms looking out over a swimming pool and extensive palm-filled garden.

There's also a bar, a classy restaurant and a tennis court, and breakfast is included. ❼

Hostal Colonial Junín N-0134 ⓣ04/422-1791. Friendly and good-value family-run place offering clean but slightly dilapidated rooms on two floors, overlooking a charming garden with lush tropical vegetation. Breakfast is included. ❷

Hostal Elisa Lopéz S-0834 ⓣ04/425-4406, ⓔhelisa@supernet.com.bo. Helpful and friendly little place just a block away from the bus terminal. It's much nicer than it appears from outside, with small but clean rooms (with or without bath) around a pleasant central garden with outdoor seating. There's also a cafeteria, and Internet access is available. ❷–❸

Hostal Florida 25 de Mayo S-0583 ⓣ04/425-7911 or 423-5617, ⓔfloridah@elsitio.com. Justly popular backpackers' favourite halfway between the bus terminal and the city centre. The simple but clean rooms (with or without bath) are set around a sunny central courtyard, and breakfast is available. ❷–❸

Hostal Jardín Hamiraya N-0248 ⓣ04/424-7844. Small but reasonably comfortable rooms (with or without bath) opening onto a peaceful garden with outdoor seating. Breakfast available. ❸

Hotel Americana Arce S-0788 ⓣ04/425-0552 or 425-0553. Good-value modern high-rise hotel with attentive staff and comfortable, well-equipped rooms with private bath and good views but rather garish pink decor. Breakfast is included. ❺

Residencial San Sebastian Lopéz N-0837 ⓣ04/425-1435. Decent no-frills budget option, with reasonably clean rooms, with or without bath – pick only if you're strapped for choice. ❷

The City

Among the most vibrant and youthful cities in Bolivia, Cocha, as it is known to locals, is perfect for relaxing in one of its many cafés and bohemian hideaways around Calle España. For all its charm, Cochabamba has little to offer in terms of conventional tourist attractions and not much remains of the original colonial city centre other than a few old but unspectacular churches.

The centre of Cochabamba is **Plaza 14 de Septiembre**, a placid and pleasant square with flower-filled ornamental gardens, a colonial stone fountain and plenty of benches where Cochabambinos sit under the shade of tall palm trees. A block south of the plaza on the corner of calles Aguirre and Jordán stands the extensive **Museo Archeológico** (Mon–Fri 8am–6pm; $2), which explains the evolution of pre-Hispanic culture in the Cochabamba region with its collection of small stone idols, bronze Inca axeheads, ceremonial knives, star-shaped stone maces and well-preserved Tiwanaku woven skull caps made specially for ritual trepanation.

The commercial heart of this market city is the south, with its massive rambling street markets. About nine blocks south of the plaza, an entire block between calles Tarata and Pulucayo on the east side of Avenida Barrientos is occupied by the massive covered street market known as **La Cancha** (Quechua for walled enclosure), where *campesinos* and merchants come to buy and sell their produce. Wandering through the market's sprawling labyrinth of stalls is the best way to get a feel for the vibrant commercial culture of the city and the surrounding region. The buzz of Quechua fills the air, the traditional costumes of different *campesino* groups are very much in evidence and the range of fruits and vegetables on sale reflects the full diversity of Bolivia's different ecological zones.

About 1km north of the city centre, with its entrance off Avenida Potosí, the **Palacio Portales** (visits by guided tour only; Mon–Fri 5pm – Spanish, 5.30pm – English; Sat 11am – Spanish, 11.30am – English; $2) is the luxurious former house of the Cochabamba-born "King of Tin" Simón Patiño. Built between 1915 and 1922 in a bizarre mix of architectural styles, including French Neoclassical and Mudejár, the palace's interior is decorated with astonishing opulence: marble fireplaces and statues or Roman emperors, Venetian crystal chandeliers and Louis XV furniture. If anything, it's the magnificent lush garden (Mon–Fri 2.30–6.30pm, Sat & Sun 10.30am–12.30pm; admission included with Palace entrance) that really impresses, laid out in perfect proportion by Japanese specialists and featuring a beautiful and rare ginko tree.

Eating and drinking

The best places **to eat** if you're on a tight budget are Cochabamba's many **markets**, and the choice of **restaurants** in the city is broad, with some very good meals available at relatively low prices. As elsewhere in Bolivia, many restaurants stay open late at weekends and double as bars.

Café Francés Les Temps Modernes España with Colombia. Sophisticated French bar-café serving good coffee, imaginative mixed juices, sweet and savoury crepes, and various other snacks and pastries. Open 3–9pm; closed Sun.
Canguro Colombia with España. Popular, no-nonsense *salteñeria* serving delicious beef, chicken and pork *fricasé salteñas*, with indoor and outdoor seating.
La Casa de Campo Boulevard Recoleta. Excellent restaurant with a pleasant leafy courtyard, serving generous portions of delicious local specialities, such as *pique macho*, *pacumutu* and *churrasco*, all for about $6.50 a head, including appetizer and desert. Out of the centre, but worth the taxi fare.
Casablanca España with Ecuador. Trendy Hollywood-themed bar serving cold beer, good cocktails and pretty much the same food as *Metropolis* (see below), across the street. The first-floor balcony is great for people-watching, and they sometimes show classic films in an upstairs movie theatre as well as host jazz gigs and art exhibits.
Gopal España with Ecuador. Inexpensive Hare Krishna-run wholefood restaurant serving up cheap and tasty vegetarian meals and snacks, including a filling buffet *almuerzo* for just under $1.50. Closed Sat & Sun evenings.
Metrópolis España with Ecuador. Cosy corner café popular with trendy students and travellers alike for its savoury German pancakes, massive salads and varied pasta dishes – the latter (about $3.50) are so big they're usually enough for two. They also serve good strong coffee, fruits juices and cocktails in the evening, and host occasional music performances. Open late; closed Sunday morning.
La Pimienta Verde Ballivían and La Paz. The wildest nightclub of the moment, popular with travellers for its raucous atmosphere and loud music. Open Thurs–Sat only.

Listings

Banks and exchange Casa de Cambio Exprinter, on the west side of Plaza 14 de Septiembre, changes cash dollars and travellers' cheques, and there are street moneychangers at all the major intersections in the centre of town. There are also plenty of ATMs in the city centre where you can withdraw cash in dollars or bolivianos on Visa or Mastercard.
Internet access Internet cafés abound and most charge around $0.40 per hour. Some of the best with late-night hours are Black Cat, on Achá, just off the main square, Cliksmania, on España with Colombia and ENTEL on Av Ayacucho with Achá.
Post office Correo Central, Av Ayacucho with Av Heroínas.
Taxis America ⓣ04/424-0460; Panamericana ⓣ04/424-3333; Diplomat ⓣ04/456-2277.
Tour operators Fremen at Tumulsa N-0245 (ⓣ04/425-9392, ⓦwww.andes-amazonia.com), Turismo Santa Rita, Buenos Aires 866 ⓣ04/428-0305, ⓦwww.camind.com/s_rita, Caxia Tours, Arze S-0559 ⓣ04/422-6148.

Parque Nacional Torotoro

Some 139km south of Cochabamba, the **PARQUE NACIONAL TOROTORO** protects a remote and sparsely inhabited stretch of the arid, scrubby landscape characteristic of the eastern foothills and valleys of the Andes. Covering just 165 square kilometres around the small town of the same name, Torotoro is Bolivia's smallest national park, but what it lacks in size it makes up for with its powerful scenery and varied attractions. The park encompasses a high, hanging valley and deep eroded canyons, ringed by low mountains whose twisted geological formations are strewn with fossils, dinosaur footprints and labyrinthine limestone cave complexes. The park's cactus and scrubby woodland supports considerable wildlife – including flocks of parakeets and the rare and beautiful red-fronted macaw, found only in this particular region of Bolivia – while ancient rock paintings and pre-Inca ruins reveal a longstanding human presence. The main attractions are the limestone caves of **Umajallanta**, the beautiful, waterfall-filled **Torotoro Canyon**, and hiking expeditions to the pre-Inca ruined fortress of **Llama Chaqui**.

Though reached from Cochabamba, Parque Nacional Torotoro actually lies within Northern Potosí department, a region noted as a repository of traditional

Andean culture and the focus of frequent uprisings during the colonial era and long after independence. Founded in the late colonial period by *mestizo* migrants from Cochabamba, Torotoro's main annual celebration is the **Fiesta de Tata Santiago**. It is held on July 25 each year, when the *ayllus* descend on the town to drink, dance and stage Tinku fights, ritualized hand-to-hand combats that take place on certain feast days in small indigenous rural communities, mainly in the northern areas of Potosí department.

Buses ($3.25) to Torotoro leave Cochabamba from the corner of Avenida 6 de Agosto and Avenida Republica several times per week. The bus ride lasts about seven hours in the dry season, a rough and dusty trip along unpaved roads and dry riverbeds – in the rainy season it takes much longer and the route can become impassable when rivers are too high to cross.

On arrival you should head to the **tourist office** (daily 8am–noon & 2–5pm), on the main street of the village, where you'll need to pay the $2.50 park admission fee. The office has basic information about the park and can find you a **guide** for about $7 a day for groups of up to five people (slightly more for larger groups). There's one **place to stay**, the *Alojamiento Charcas* (ⓣ04/413-3927; ❶), which has plenty of simple but clean rooms with shared toilet and shower, though there's no hot water and rarely any electricity. Torotoro doesn't have any real restaurants, but a couple of women prepare basic **meals** for about $1 if you order a few hours in advance – just ask around to find out who's cooking.

The Chapare

Northeast of Cochabamba, the main road to Santa Cruz crosses the last ridge of the Andes and drops down into the **CHAPARE**, a broad, rainforest-covered plain in the Upper Amazon Basin, which has been heavily settled by peasant migrants from the highlands. Over the last few decades, they have turned the region into Bolivia's largest provider of coca grown to make **cocaine**. For the traveller, the ongoing conflict between coca farmers and Bolivian government troops trying to eradicate their crops means the Chapare is not the place for expeditions far off the beaten track – you're likely to be mistaken for a US agent or a narco-trafficker if you set out to explore the area on your own. For all the region's troubles, however, it's worth a visit for its natural beauty and the peaceful towns along the main Cochabamba to Santa Cruz road, which are perfectly safe to visit, unless you go during one of the sporadic road blockades by protesting *cocaleros*; these are usually announced in advance, so make sure to look through the local newspapers before your trip.

The small laid-back town of **Villa Tunari**, a one-time narco-traffickers playground, is a good place to break a journey between Cochabamba and Santa Cruz and also to get a brief introduction to the Amazon lowlands. Now at the centre of efforts to promote the Chapare as a tourist destination, its main street is lined with large restaurants and moderately priced hotels – once frequented by the movers and shakers of the cocaine. Buses from Cochabamba arrive and depart from the office of Trans Tours 7 de Junio on the main road; you can also flag down buses passing through on their way to Cochabamba from elsewhere in the Chapare. Through buses from Santa Cruz will drop you off at the police control *tranca* at the west end of town, and buses heading to Santa Cruz sometimes pick up passengers here if they have room, though most pass through in the middle of the night. The best **place to stay** is the *Hotel El Puente* (book through Fremen in Cochabamba on ⓣ04/425-9392; ❺, including breakfast), about 4km east of town, with modern, comfortable rooms for up to four people set amid a patch of rainforest with a private swimming pool, fourteen natural river pools close by and a restaurant. To get there either take a taxi ($2–3) or walk out of town along the main road to the east, then take the track that leads off it to the right after the second bridge. On the south side of the main road are a couple of rather overpriced mid-range country club-style hotels with small swimming pools. The best **restaurants** in town are the *San Silvestre*, on the main road, and the restaurant in the *Hotel Las Palmas*, on the main plaza.

A few kilometres south of Villa Tunari, some 6226 square kilometres of the forested northern slopes of the Andes are protected by the **Parque Nacional Carrasco**, which adjoins the Parque Nacional Amboró (see p.280) to the east. Plunging steeply down from high mountain peaks, the park encompasses a variety of ecosystems from high Andean grasslands and cloudforest to dense tropical rainforest and also supports a great range of wildlife, including all the major Amazonian mammals, among them jaguar, tapir and peccary, and over 700 species of bird, including several which are endemic to the region.

2.5

The eastern lowlands

Stretching from the last foothills of the Andes east to Brazil and south to Paraguay and Argentina, Bolivia's **EASTERN LOWLANDS** – the Llanos Orientales – were until recently amongst the least-known and least-developed regions in the country. Rich in natural resources, in recent decades the region has undergone astonishingly rapid development, while its economy has grown to become the most important in the country, fuelled by oil and gas, cattle-ranching and massive agricultural development.

At the centre of this unprecedented economic boom is the regional capital of **Santa Cruz**. Though it has little to detain you, it is a crucial transport hub and the ideal base for exploring the many attractions of the surrounding area, where much of the region's beautiful natural environment survives, despite the ravages of deforestation and development. Just an hour and a half's drive west of the city are the pristine and exceptionally biodiverse rainforests protected by the **Parque Nacional Amboró**; the beautiful cloudforest that covers the upper regions of the park can be visited from the idyllic resort town of **Samaipata**. From Samaipata, you can also head further southwest through the Andean foothills to the town of **Vallegrande** and the nearby hamlet of **La Higuera**, where the iconic Argentine revolutionary Ernesto "Che" Guevara was killed in 1967.

East of Santa Cruz, the railway to Brazil passes through the broad forested plains of **Chiquitos**, whose beautiful Jesuit mission churches bear witness to one of the most extraordinary episodes in Spanish colonial history, when a handful of priests established a semi-autonomous theocratic state in the midst of the wilderness. In the far north of the region, accessible only by air or by an arduous overland journey, the **Parque Nacional Noel Kempff Mercado** is perhaps the most beautiful and untouched of all Bolivia's protected rainforest areas. Finally, south of Santa Cruz, the vast and inhospitable **Chaco**, an arid wilderness of dense thorn and scrub, stretches south to Argentina and Paraguay.

Santa Cruz

Set among the steamy, tropical lowlands just beyond the last Andean foothills, **SANTA CRUZ** has emerged in recent decades as the economic powerhouse of Bolivia. An isolated frontier town until the middle of the twentieth century, the city has grown in the last fifty years – a new road and railway link in the 1950s and the booming 1970s Bolivian cocaine industry helping to fuel that growth – to become the second biggest in the country, a sprawling metropolis that rivals La Paz for power and influence, with a booming economy based on oil and gas, timber and cattle, and large-scale agro-industry.

Largely because most of it is so new, Santa Cruz has little to match the colonial charm of highland cities like Sucre and Potosí, and few conventional tourist sights beyond several mediocre museums and an architecturally unexciting cathedral. While some travellers find its unapologetic modernity, commercialism and pseudo-Americanism unappealing, others enjoy its blend of dynamism and tropical insouciance.

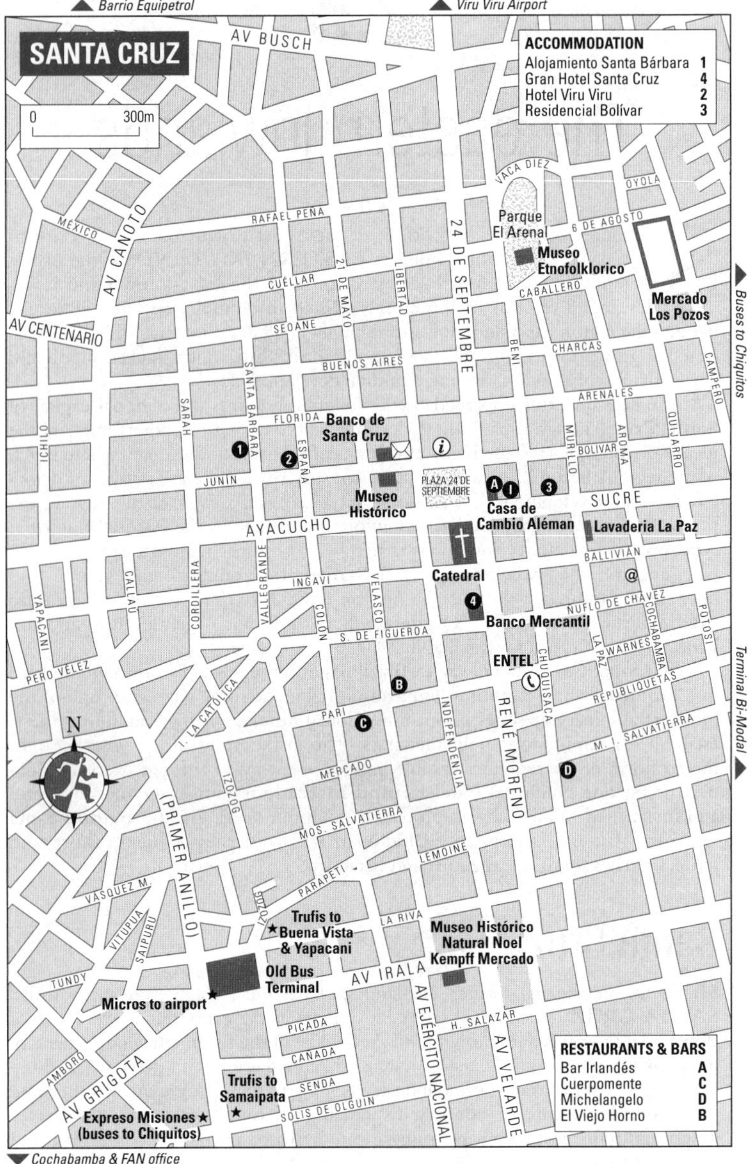

Arrival and information

Santa Cruz is divided into concentric rings by successive ring roads called **anillos**; when travelling outside the central area, which comprises the first two *anillos*, you'll need to know which *anillo* you want when giving directions. **Long-distance**

buses and all **trains** arrive and depart from the recently completed **Terminal Bi-Modal de Transporte**, the combined bus and train terminal (information on ⓣ03/346-3388 or 346-3900) about 2km west of the city centre just outside the Segundo Anillo at the end of Avenida Brasil. There are always plenty of taxis outside (a trip to most city hotels will cost you about $1); otherwise, you can get into the city centre by catching any micro heading east along Avenida Brasil and marked "Plaza 24 de Septiembre". For getting around the city, **taxis** charge just under $1 within the Primer Anillo, plus an additional $0.14 for each extra *anillo* you cross.

Santa Cruz's main airport is the modern **Aeropuerto Viru-Viru** (ⓣ03/385-2400 or 181), 17km north of the city centre, from where it's a $7 flat-fare taxi ride into the centre of town; alternatively, you can catch a micro (every 15min; $0.65) to the corner of avenidas Irala and Cañoto, outside the old bus terminal. The city's second airport, the smaller **Aeropuerto El Trompillo** (ⓣ03/352-6600), is used by the military airline, TAM, which operates weekly flights to San Ignacio.

Santa Cruz's tourist information office, the **Unidad de Turismo** (Mon–Fri 8am–4pm; ⓣ03/336-9595 ext 17), is inside the Prefectura building on the north side of Plaza 24 de Septiembre and gives out helpful information in English and German.

Accommodation

Most **mid-range** and **budget accommodation** is conveniently located in or close to the old city centre, while there's an oversupply of top-range accommodation in Santa Cruz's wealthy Barrio Equipetrol.

Alojamiento Santa Bárbara I Santa Bárbara 151 ⓣ03/332-1817 or 332-1928, ⓔalojstabarbara@yahoo.com. No-frills budget option with basic but clean rooms with cool tiled floors and shared bath (but no fans) around a small courtyard. ❷

Gran Hotel Santa Cruz Moreno 269 ⓣ03/334-8811, ⓦwww.granhotelsantacruz.com, ⓔhotelsantacruz@cotas.com.bo. One of the few top-range hotels in the city centre, built in grandiose style with lashings of marble and spacious and opulently furnished rooms and suites. Facilities include a swimming pool, sauna and gym, plus a good restaurant and bar. Breakfast and free Internet use included. ❼

Hotel Viru-Viru Junín 338 ⓣ03/333-5298 or 336-2922. Excellent, centrally located mid-range option boasting comfortable modern a/c rooms with cable TV and balconies overlooking a large central courtyard with a swimming pool. Ten percent discount for three-night or longer stays, and breakfast is included. ❺

Residencial 7 de Mayo Av Brasil ⓣ03/348-9634. Sparkling new establishment directly opposite the new Terminal Bi-Modal de Transporte, and thus convenient if you're arriving late, leaving early or just passing through. The clean and modern rooms come in a variety of prices depending on whether or not you want a private bath and a/c or fan. ❷–❸

Residencial Bolívar Sucre 131 ⓣ03/334-2500. Longstanding backpackers' favourite with helpful staff and small but immaculately clean rooms (with fan and private or shared bath) around a cool, leafy patio with hammocks. Often fills up, so worth phoning in advance to reserve a room if you're arriving late. Breakfast available. ❸

The City

At the centre of Santa Cruz is **Plaza 24 de Septiembre**, a spacious, lively square with well-tended gardens shaded by tall trees that are home to a small population of three-toed sloths. The plaza is named after the day in 1810 when Santa Cruz declared independence and joined the struggle against Spanish rule. On the south side of the plaza stands the salmon-pink **Cathedral** (daily 7am–8pm), or Basílica Mayor de San Lorenzo, a hulking brick structure with twin belltowers that was built between 1845 and 1915 on the site of an original church dating back to 1605. The cool, vaulted interior boasts some fine silverwork around the altar, but the best religious art, including sculpture and exquisite silverwork decorated in a florid Baroque riot, is tucked away in the adjacent **Museo de Arte Sacro** (Tues & Thurs

10am–noon & 4–6pm, Sun 10am–noon & 6–8pm; $0.75); the entrance is just to the right as you face the altar. Four blocks north and a block east of Plaza 24 de Septiembre inside the Parque Arenal (a little park with an artificial lake), the **Museo Etno-folklórico** (Mon–Fri 8am–noon & 2.30–6.30pm; free) houses a small but varied collection of artefacts that furnishes a good introduction to the different indigenous ethnic groups of the Eastern Lowlands. It also hosts all-day cultural events with food, concerts and dancing every Sunday between 10am and 7pm.

Eating and drinking

Santa Cruz's relative wealth and cosmopolitanism are fairly well reflected in the city's wide variety of **restaurants** and vibrant **bar and nightclub** scene.

Bar Irlandés Plaza 24 de Septiembre. On the first-floor of the Bolívar shopping centre, with tables overlooking the plaza, this upmarket Irish-themed bar is a great place to enjoy a beer, cocktail or coffee while watching the world go by outside. Gets very lively with locals and travellers in the evenings, and especially on weekends.

La Casa del Camba Av Cristóbal de Mendoza 539. The best of the many traditional Cruceño restaurants on this stretch of the Segundo Anillo, and a great place to enjoy moderately priced *parillada* (barbecued meat), *majao de charque* (rice with beef jerky, fried egg and bananas) and *pacumutu* (massive shish kebab).

Cuerpomente Pari 228. Busy vegetarian restaurant offering a varied self-service buffet priced by weight (good value at around $2.30 a kilo) as well as soups, juices and *empanadas*. The food is tasty and wholesome, as long as the overzealous healthy-living mantras posted on the wall don't put you off.

Michelangelo Chuquisaca 502. One of the finest restaurants in Bolivia offering superb, authentic Italian cuisine and immaculate service in an intimate atmosphere. It's not cheap, with main courses from around $5, but an excellent place to splash out, especially if you've just hit town after a spell in the wilderness. Closed Sun.

El Viejo Horno Velasco with Pari. No-nonsense restaurant serving up filling set *almuerzos* for less than $1 as well as La Paz favourites like *fricase* (pork stew) and *riñon al jugo* (kidneys in sauce) to impecunious Altiplano migrants.

Listings

Banks and exchange You can change US dollars and travellers' cheques at the Casa de Cambio Aleman (Mon–Fri 8.30–noon & 2.30–6pm, Sat 8.30–noon), on the east side of Plaza 24 de Septiembre, and there are plenty of banks with ATMs where you can make cash withdrawals on Visa or Mastercard – try Banco Santa Cruz on Junín or Banco Ganadero on Bolívar with Beni.

Car rental Barron's, Av Alemana 50 ⓣ03/342-0160; Localiza, Carretera al Norte 3km ⓣ03/343-3939.

Internet access There are numerous Internet cafés around the city centre, especially along Calle Murillo between Ballivián and Parque Arenal; most charge around $0.50 per hour. Try Light-Soft Internet on Junín 333, Web Boli on Ballivián 267, between La Paz and Cochabamba, or the small shop inside the Bolívar shopping complex on the main plaza.

Tour operators The following companies are all well established and have good reputations: Cambatur, Sucre 8 ⓣ03/334-9999, ⓔcambatur@cotas.com.bo; Fremen, Beni 79, Edificio Libertador ⓣ03/333-8535, ⓔfremen@cotas.com.bo, ⓦwww.andes-amazonia.com; Rosario Tours, Arenales 193 ⓣ03/336-9977, ⓔaventura@cotas.com.bo.

Parque Nacional Amboró

Forty kilometres east of Santa Cruz, the **Parque Nacional Amboró** covers some 4300 square kilometres of a great forest-covered spur of the Andes that juts out into the eastern plains. Situated at the confluence of three major bio-geographic regions – the Andes, the Amazon rainforest, and the Northern Chaco – and ranging in altitude from 3300m to just 300m above sea level, Amboró's steep, densely forested slopes support an astonishing biodiversity, including over 830 different types of **bird** and pretty much the full range of rainforest **mammals**, including jaguars, giant anteaters, tapirs and several species of monkey, while its enormous range of plant and insect species is still largely unexplored.

The northern gateway to the park is the picturesque and peaceful town of **BUENA VISTA**, some 100km northwest of Santa Cruz along the main road to Cochabamba. Raised slightly above the plains, the town is aptly named, enjoying good views to the densely forested mountain slopes of Amboró. There are two ways to visit the park from Buena Vista. The easiest is to go on an organized trip with one of the **tour operators** in town. For about $45 per person (4 person minimum) they offer two-day trips into the park, camping overnight or staying in one of the refuges in the park ($5 per person extra), with all meals, a Spanish-speaking guide, camping equipment and transport included. They can also arrange longer trips and treks deeper into the park. Amboró Tours (Ⓣ03/932-2093, Ⓔamborotours@yahoo.com), opposite the church just off the plaza in Buena Vista, is the most professional outfit; Amboró Adventures, on the plaza, is also good.

You can also visit the park **independently**, camping or staying overnight at the refuges in La Chonta or Macuñuco (although both tend to be closed sporadically, especially during the rainy season). However, you'll need to bring camping equipment, a sleeping bag and your own food, and make arrangements with the park office (Mon–Fri 8am–noon & 3–6pm), which is a block southwest from the main plaza in Buena Vista, in advance. It's best to avoid visiting the park on your own during the rainy season when the crossing of the Río Surutú, usually possible by walking or driving, or with a raft, becomes a real challenge. A **micro** from the plaza in Buena Vista runs daily along the boundary of the park via Huaytú and Santa Rosa, returning the next day – times vary so ask around to see when the micro passes through, and check the return time with the driver so you don't get stuck on the way out.

Samaipata

Some 120km west of Santa Cruz on the old mountain road to Cochabamba, the tranquil little town of **SAMAIPATA** is enjoying growing popularity as a tourist destination amongst Bolivians and foreign travellers alike. Nestled in an idyllic valley surrounded by rugged, forest-covered mountains, the town has emerged as a popular weekend resort for people from Santa Cruz – appropriately enough, since its Quechua name means "rest in the highlands". With its sixteen nationalities of residents, this *micromundo* is the kind of place where many travellers arrive planning to stay a couple of days and end up staying a week or longer. Innumerable good walking trails run through the surrounding countryside, the beautiful cloudforests of the Parque Nacional Amboró are within easy reach, and just 9km outside town stands one of Bolivia's most intriguing archeological sites – the mysterious, ruined pre-Hispanic ceremonial complex known as **El Fuerte** (see box on p.282).

At the centre of town lies the small **Plaza Principal**, the core of the grid of tranquil streets lined with whitewashed houses under red-tiled roofs. A few blocks north on Bolívar, the small **Museo Archeológico** (Mon–Sat 8.30am–12.30pm & 2.30–6.30pm, Sun 8.30am–4.30pm; $2.80, combined with El Fuerte, or $0.70 separately) offers a small collection of archeological finds from all over Bolivia, including beautiful Inca carved wooden ceremonial *chicha*-drinking cups, Inca stone axes and mace heads and a range of pottery from various cultures.

Practicalities

Micros and **trufis** from Santa Cruz arrive in the Plaza Principal; trufis should drop you off wherever you want – convenient if you want to stay in one of the out-of-town places. For **information** on Samaipata and the surrounding area, the best place to go is the helpful and enthusiastic English, German and Spanish-speaking Roadrunners (ⓣ03/944-6193 or 6153, ⓦwww.samaipata.info/roadrunners/, ⓔdustyroad99@hotmail.com or brocoli63@hotmail.com), in the *Café Hamburg* on Calle Bolívar. Amboró Tourist Services (ⓣ03/944-6293), on the same street, is also helpful.

There are no **banks** or ATMs in Samaipata, but La Cooperativa La Merced on Calle Sucre, a block east of the plaza, will change dollars; you can also try Roadrunners in the *Café Hamburg* who will sometimes change cash and travellers' cheques for a small commission. The **ENTEL** office is two blocks north of the Museo Archeológico on Ponce Sanjinés, and there are also phone booths at *Heladería Dany* on the western side of the Plaza Principal. **Internet access** is available at the *Café Hamburg* (weekday evenings only; $2) and at *Heladería Dany* on the square (daily until 11pm; $1.70). **Taxis** can be found by the gas station on Calle Santa Cruz at the town exit, or called at ⓣ03/944-6133 or 944-6016.

Accommodation in Samaipata comes in two categories: simple budget *alojamientos* in the centre of town along Bolívar and around the plaza, where you can get a basic double room for less than $10; check out *Hostería Mi Casa* on Bolívar 96 (no phone; ❸) or *Residencial Don Jorge* on Bolívar opposite *Café Hamburg* (ⓣ03/944-6086; ❷). More expensive, rustic, chalet-style *cabañas* can be found on the outskirts of town, many of them family-size, with a kitchen and fireplace; try the friendly *Guesthouse La Víspera* (ⓣ03/944-6082, ⓔvispera@entelnet.bo; ❷–❸), which features comfortable lodgings, idyllic location amidst orchards and terraced herb, vegetable and flower gardens, and friendly owners who will happily share their immense knowledge of the region with you, as well as book tailor-made trips to other parts of Bolivia. Everything fills up (and prices go up) at weekends and public holidays, particularly between October and April.

Samaipata's status as a resort town and its significant international community ensure a varied range of **restaurants and cafés**, though some only open at weekends; try *Café Hamburg*, a block north and three blocks east of the plaza on Bolívar, a lively restaurant with good coffee, tasty food, helpful staff and occasional live music in the evenings, or *La Chakana* on Plaza Principal, a small European-run café with cosy decor, a book exchange, a wide range of herbal teas and good-value vegetarian *almuerzos*.

Vallegrande and La Higuera

Some 68km west of Samaipata on the old road from Santa Cruz to Cochabamba, a side road leads 53km south to **VALLEGRANDE**, a pleasant market town set in a broad valley at an altitude of just over 2000m. A peaceful backwater founded as a

El Fuerte

Located 10km east of Samaipata, **El Fuerte** (daily 9am–5pm; $2.80) is a striking and enigmatic ancient site with a great sandstone rock at its centre, carved with a fantastic variety of abstract and figurative designs and surrounded by the remains of more than fifty Inca buildings. It's thought that the first rock carvings were made before 1000BC by an ancient lowland people, while the Incas later on altered and embellished the rock. The easiest way to reach El Fuerte is by taxi from Samaipata (about $5 one way, or $8 return with an hour's waiting time), or to join a guided tour with one of the tour agencies in town. Otherwise, you can walk to the ruins in about two hours – just follow the road out of town toward Santa Cruz for a few kilometres, then turn right up the marked side road that climbs to the site.

Spanish outpost in 1612, Vallegrande leapt briefly to the world's attention in 1967, when the arid region to the south of the town became the scene of a doomed guerrilla campaign led by Cuban revolutionary hero, **Ernesto "Che" Guevara**. Vallegrande served as the headquarters of the Bolivian army's successful counter-insurgency campaign, and after Che was captured and executed on October 9 in the hamlet of La Higuera, his body was flown here strapped to the skids of a helicopter and put on display in the town hospital. Twenty-eight years later, it was revealed that **Che's body** – minus his hands, amputated for identification purposes – had been buried by night in an unmarked pit near the airstrip, to prevent his grave from becoming a place of pilgrimage. Today, Che's erstwhile grave – his remains were exhumed in 1997 – and the hamlet of La Higuera, where his dreams of leading a continent-wide revolution ended, attract a steady trickle of pilgrims, but unless you share their veneration of the revolutionary icon, there's little reason to come here. For Che aficionados, there's a small **museum** (Mon–Fri 10am–noon, 3–5pm & 7–9pm, Sat 10am–noon; $0.80) in the municipal Casa de Cultura on the central Plaza 26 de Enero, which houses an unexciting collection of local archeological finds and an upstairs room filled with photographs of Che.

The best **places to stay** are the good value *Residencial Ganadera* (☎03/942-2176; ❷), a block northeast of the main plaza on Bolívar, with clean, spacious, modern rooms with private bath and breakfast and the more basic *Residencial Vallegrande* (☎03/942-2112; ❷) off the plaza on calles Sucre and Escalante. The best **restaurants** are the German-run *El Mirador* (evenings only; closed Mon), which offers a daily selection of tasty beef, pork chicken and trout dishes and the *Churasqueria El Gaucho* that dishes out massive slabs of Argentine-style steak.

LA HIGUERA, the hamlet where Che Guevara met his end, lies about 50km south of Vallegrande and can be reached from Vallegrande by **taxi** (around $25 round trip) or by **lorry** ($3 return) – these leave most days from Calle Señor de Malta early in the morning, returning the next day. It's a miserable collection of simple adobe houses with tiled roofs, many of them scrawled with revolutionary slogans, and a one-room **Museo Historico del Che** (Thurs & Sun; $0.80, free if you're arriving in the curator's lorry; open only when the curator is in town, which can be checked by calling him on ☎03/942-2003), with the atmosphere of a shrine, complete with relics including Che's machete, bullets, ammo clips and a rifle used by the other guerrillas or their military pursuers.

Chiquitos: the Jesuit missions

East of Santa Cruz stretches a vast, sparsely populated plain broken by occasional low rocky ridges and covered in scrub and fast-disappearing dry tropical forest, which gradually gives way to swamp as it approaches the border with Brazil. Named **CHIQUITOS** by the Spanish (apparently because the indigenous inhabitants lived in houses with low doorways – chiquito means small), this region was the scene of one of the most extraordinary episodes in Spanish colonial history. In the eighteenth century, a handful of Jesuit priests established a series of flourishing mission towns, where previously hostile indigenous Chiquitanos converted to Catholicism, adopting European agricultural techniques and building some of the most magnificent colonial churches in South America. Of all the cultural influences brought by the Jesuits, music was the one most enthusiastically embraced by the Chiquitanos, and the choirs and orchestras of the settlements were said to have matched anything in Spanish America at the time. This theocratic socialist utopia ended in 1767, when the Spanish crown expelled the Jesuits from the Americas, allowing their indigenous charges to be exploited by settlers from Santa Cruz, who seized the Chiquitanos's lands and placed many of them into forced servitude. While the region has been in a state of economic decline ever since, six of the ten Jesuit mission churches have been restored and are recognized as UNESCO World

Heritage Sites. Their incongruous splendour in the midst of the wilderness is one of the most remarkable sights in Bolivia.

The six missions can be visited in a five to seven-day loop by road and rail from Santa Cruz. A rough road runs northeast to **San Javier** and **Concepción**, then continues to San Ignacio (from where the churches of **San Miguel**, **San Rafael** and **Santa Ana** can all be visited by taxi in a day). From San Ignacio, the road heads south to **San José**, the easternmost of the surviving missions, which is on the railway line between Santa Cruz and the Brazilian border at Quijjaro. Buses connect all these mission towns as far as San José, from where you can get the train back to Santa Cruz or continue east to the Brazilian border. Transport links are slightly more convenient in a counter-clockwise loop, for you avoid having to catch a bus in the middle of the night from Concepción to San Ignacio, as well as the hassle of getting a seat on the train back to Santa Cruz from San José.

Parque Nacional Noel Kempff Mercado

Occupying 16,000 square kilometres of Bolivia's far northeast, on the border with Brazil, the **PARQUE NACIONAL NOEL KEMPFF MERCADO** is the most isolated, pristine and spectacular national park in the country, and one of the most remote wildernesses in all South America. Encompassing a range of different ecosystems, including different types of Amazon rainforest, dry and seasonally inundated savanna and scrubby woodlands, the park supports an astonishing range and abundance of wildlife, including eleven species of monkey, all the major Amazonian mammals, over 630 species of birds (among them twenty different types of parrot and seven different macaws), multicoloured tanagers and toucans, and such rarities as the mighty harpy eagle.

The park's remote location inevitably means that it's expensive and difficult to visit. The southern border of the park is over 200km from the nearest town, San Ignacio de Velasco in Chiquitos, which is itself another 400km by road from Santa Cruz. The park is administered by the Santa Cruz–based conservation organization, Fundación Amigos de la Naturaleza (FAN), whose main office is 7.5km out of town on the old road to Cochabamba (ⓣ03/355-6800, ⓦwww.fan-bo.org). There is also an office in San Ignacio (ⓣ03/692-2194), just off the plaza on Calle 31 de Julio. To visit the park, contact the office first for information and permission to enter; entry costs $30, irrespective of how long you stay. FAN maintains two "camps" (*campamentos*) with accommodation for visitors in the park: **Los Fierros**, towards the southern end, which can be reached by light aircraft or overland along a rough logging trail; and the more luxurious **Flor de Oro**, on the banks of the Río Iteñez, which can be reached either by light aircraft or by a circuitous overland route via Brazil.

Only a few hundred people visit the park each year, and almost all of those arrive by chartered light aircraft from Santa Cruz, a spectacular **flight** across hundreds of kilometres of virtually uninhabited rainforest. This can be arranged either by FAN or by a handful of tour agencies in Santa Cruz (see p.280). A return flight to Flor de Oro costs several hundred dollars per person depending on the size of the plane, whether or not all the seats are full, and how long you spend at the park; flights to Los Fierros cost slightly less. A typical five-day all-inclusive package with a Santa Cruz-based tour agency visiting both camps by plane should cost about $1000 – a high price for Bolivia, but one which few visitors regret paying.

East from Santa Cruz to the Brazilian border

From Santa Cruz, the railway line runs some 680km east to the Brazilian border across a seemingly endless expanse of forest and tangled scrub, gradually giving way to the vast swamplands of the **Pantanal** as the border draws near – it's known as the Train of Death, not because of any danger, but because the interminably slow journey across the hot, monotonous plain can become so boring.

The region's main towns are both close to the Brazilian border. **PUERTO SUÁREZ** is a half-forgotten lakeside outpost but the place to book your walking, 4WD or boat tour into the Pantanal, either on the Bolivian side, which is more expensive but less tourist-ridden, or the Brazilian or Paraguayan sides; this can be done with most tour operators, the best of which is the non-profit Centro Ecológico El Tumbador (ⓣ03/762-8699, ⓔeltumbador@yahoo.com). The **train station** is a couple of kilometres from town, a short ride in one of the collective taxis that meet every train. There's no great reason **to stay** unless you're waiting for a train or plane to Santa Cruz, but the best place is the *Hotel Sucre* on the main plaza (ⓣ03/976-2069; ④), which offers small but comfortable air-conditioned rooms around a pleasant courtyard garden, and also has a decent restaurant. A cheaper option is the basic *Hotel Beby* (ⓣ03/976-2270; ②–③), a few blocks northwest of the plaza along Avenida Bolívar, which has simple, box-like rooms with fan or air conditioning.

The last stop on the railway line in Bolivia is **QUIJARRO**, a dismal collection of shacks and dosshouses surrounding the station – if you're heading on to Brazil, you're better off pushing on to the border at Arroyo Concepción. If you end up having to **spend the night** here, the best budget option is the basic but clean *Residencial Ariane* (ⓣ03/978-2129; ①–②), directly opposite the station. A more upmarket option, the *Hotel Santa Cruz* (ⓣ03/978-2113; ④–⑤) is two blocks east of the station and offers comfortable rooms with TV and air conditioning.

The Chaco

South of the Santa Cruz–Quijarro railway line, the tropical dry forest gradually gives way to **the Chaco**, a vast and arid landscape of dense scrub and virtually impenetrable thornbrush that stretches beyond the Paraguayan border, inhabited only by isolated cattle ranchers and occasional communities of Guaraní and semi-nomadic Ayoreo. The Chaco is one of the last great wildernesses of South America and supports plenty of wildlife, including jaguars, peccaries and deer – much of it now protected by the **Parque Nacional Kaa-Iya del Gran Chaco**, the largest protected area in all South America. The park covers over 34,000 square kilometres southeast of Santa Cruz adjacent to the Paraguayan border. There are no organized tourist facilities in the Chaco so, unless you have your own 4WD and are prepared to organize a wilderness adventure, your view of the region will be limited to what you can see from the window of a bus or train: a wall of dense, scrubby vegetation broken only occasionally where farms or ranches have been hacked out of the bush.

There are two routes through the Bolivian Chaco, both starting from Santa Cruz. The first and less taxing is the route by road or railway down the region's western edge to the towns of **Villamontes**, the biggest settlement in the Bolivian Chaco, and **Yacuiba** on the Argentine border. The second and more strenuous is along the rough **trans-Chaco road**, which splits off from the road and rail route to Yacuiba at Boyuibe, heading east to the Paraguayan border at Hito Villazón, from where it runs across the heart of this great wilderness to Asunción. This arduous and adventurous journey (served by daily buses from Santa Cruz) takes 24 hours in the May to September dry season, when conditions are good, and much longer after rain, when the road turns to mud.

2.6

The Amazon basin

About a third of Bolivia lies within the **AMAZON BASIN**, a vast, sparsely populated and largely untamed lowland region of swamp, savanna and tropical rainforest (known as *selva*), which supports a bewildering diversity of plant and animal life. Though generally hot and humid all year round, the region is subject to occasional cold snaps, or *surazos*, when the temperature drops suddenly and dramatically. Roads are poor in the best of conditions and in the rainy season between November and April are often completely impassable; even in the dry season sudden downpours can quickly turn roads to quagmires.

Linked by road to Santa Cruz, the capital of the Beni is **Trinidad,** a bustling frontier city with few obvious attractions, though for the adventurous it's the start-

ing point for slow boat journeys down the Río Mamoré to the Brazilian border or south into the Chapare. From Trinidad, a long and rough road heads east across the Llanos de Moxos, passing through the **Reserva del Biosfera del Beni**, which is an excellent place to get close to the wildlife of the savanna, before joining the main road down into the region from La Paz at Yucumo. Just north of Yucumo, the small town of **Rurrenabaque**, on the banks of the Río Beni, is the obvious destination for anyone wanting a taste of the Amazon, given its proximity to the pristine forests of the **Parque Nacional Madidi**, one of Bolivia's most stunning protected areas, and the savannas of the Llanos de Moxos along the wildlife-rich **Río Yacuma**. From Rurrenabaque, the road continues north to the city of **Riberalta**, a centre for rubber and Brazil nut collection, and on to the Brazilian border and the remote, forest-covered department of **Pando**.

Trinidad

Close to the Río Mamoré, some 500km northwest of Santa Cruz, the city of **TRINIDAD** is the capital of the Beni and the commercial and administrative centre of a vast wilderness of swamp, forest and savanna where rivers remain the main means of transport and cattle-ranching is the biggest industry. Like most towns in the region, Trinidad was originally a Jesuit mission, but few signs of it remain, and it's now a modern commercial city dominated by a vigorous cattle-ranching culture and economy. Hot and humid, with few real attractions, Trinidad doesn't really merit a visit in its own right. It is, however, the jumping-off point for adventurous trips to the rainforest and savannah that surround it.

Arrival, information and getting around

Buses from Santa Cruz, Guayaramerín and Rurrenabaque arrive at the Terminal Terrestre on Av Romulo Mendoza between calles Viador Pinto Saucedo and Beni. Buses from San Borja arrive just behind the terminal on Av Beni. **Trucks and buses** from San Ignacio de Moxos arrive at the ticket office on Calle Mamoré opposite the ice factory. The **airport**, on the outskirts of town to the northeast, has frequent flights to La Paz, Santa Cruz and elsewhere in the Beni. The easiest way to get around is by **motorcycle taxi**, which costs $0.30 for rides within the city and $0.85 to or from the airport. If you are arriving by **boat** along the Río Mamoré from Guayaramerín to the north or Puerto Villaroel in the Chapare to the south you will dock at **Puerto Barador**, Trinidad´s river port, about 13km west of town. Frequent trucks run between the port and the intersection of Av Pedro Ignacio Muiba with the ring road on the outskirts of town, from where you can get a motorbike taxi into the centre.

There's a **tourist information office** (Mon–Fri 8am–4pm; ⓣ03/462-1305) of sorts in the Prefectura building on the corner of calles Joaquín de Sierra and La Paz.

Accommodation

There's a good range of **accommodation** in Trinidad, most of it a short distance from the Plaza Ballivián.

Hotel Beni Av 6 de Agosto ⓣ03/462-2788 or 462-0522. A block away from the main plaza, clean and pleasant, with well-furnished rooms equipped with a/c or fans. ❹

Hotel La Hostería Av Ganadera s/n ⓣ03/462-2911, ⓔletty_hosteria@hotmail.com. A rambling old hacienda ten minutes' taxi ride out of town, with pleasant clean rooms with a/c or fan and a lush patio with a swimming pool. Price includes use of gym, sauna and pool, and breakfast is included. Cheaper triples with fans are available for $10 per person. ❺–❻

Hotel Mi Residencia M. Limpias 76. ⓣ03/465-2235 or 462-1529, ⓔmiresidencia@hotmail.com.

Good upmarket option, with quiet kitschy rooms with a/c, cable TV, fridge and modest breakfast. The hotel's annex, a few blocks away on Felix Pinto Saucedo, is more modern and features a swimming pool. ❼

Residencial 18 de Noviembre Av 6 de Agosto with Santa Cruz, two blocks west of the plaza ⓣ03/462-1272. Basic, good value place, with a small snackbar, patio with hammocks and rooms with private or shared bathrooms. ❷

The Town

Though most of its buildings are modern, Trinidad maintains the classic layout of a Spanish colonial town, its streets set out in a neat grid around a central square, the **Plaza Ballivián**. Shaded by tall trees hiding three-toed sloths and with well-maintained gardens, the plaza is the most popular hangout in town. The buildings around the plaza and the surrounding streets are all built with eaves overhanging the pavement designed to protect pedestrians from the harsh tropical sun and torrential Amazonian rain, while the pavements are raised up to two feet above the ground to escape flooding in the rainy season. In addition, the streets are lined with open sewers that, while necessary for drainage, emit a horrible stench, provide an ideal breeding ground for the mosquitoes that plague the town, and represent a dangerous obstacle to unwary pedestrians.

Eating

There are some pretty good **restaurants** on and around Plaza Ballivián. The beef in Trinidad is excellent and very good value; the local speciality is *pacumutu*, great chunks of meat and chicken marinated and grilled on a skewer.

Carlitos Plaza Ballivián. The best restaurant in town, serving up surprisingly sophisticated Bolivian and international meat, fish and pasta dishes for $4–5.

La Casona Plaza Ballivián. Lively and popular place with great atmosphere, good *almuerzos*, *pacumutu*, pizza and pasta, as well as steak and fried river fish.

Club Social 18 de Noviembre Plaza Ballivián. A vast, elegant dining hall with a rather old-fashioned feel, serving up good-value *almuerzos* and standard Bolivian dishes like *milanesa* and *pique macho*.

Don Pedrito Calle Manuel Maraza. Out of the centre, but worth a taxi ride for its great variety of local river fish served on a cosy narrow patio underneath mango trees; try *pacu* or *surubí*.

Heladeria Kivon Plaza Ballivián. Ice-cream parlour right on the plaza serving good cakes, sandwiches and main dishes. The breakfasts are disappointing, however.

Reserva de la Biosfera del Beni

Covering some 1350 square kilometres of savanna and rainforest to the east of the mission town of **San Borja**, the **RESERVA DE LA BIOSFERA DEL BENI** (Beni Biosphere Reserve) was one of the first protected areas established in Bolivia. Standing at the intersection of two important geographical zones, the reserve is exceptionally biodiverse, hosting some 500 species of birds and 100 species of mammals – these include almost half the protected species in Bolivia, among them the rare swamp deer and armadilloes.

Unusually for Bolivia, the reserve also has very well-organized facilities for visitors, based at the **Beni Biological Station** at El Porvenir, a former ranch about 100km west of San Ignacio on the road to San Borja. Though most of the reserve is actually rainforest, the area immediately around El Porvenir is largely savanna, a seemingly endless sea of natural grasses up to two metres high, dotted with islands of forest. The reserve is open all year round, but during the rainy season the whole area becomes flooded and the road is impassable, so you can really only visit between May and October.

Rainforest trips from Trinidad

A couple of **tour operators** run trips into the wilderness around Trinidad. **Turismo Moxos**, Avenida 6 de Agosto 114 (ⓣ03/462-1141, ⓔturmoxos@sauce.ben.entelnet.bo), organizes popular birdwatching excursions with the star attraction of spotting rare blue-bearded macaws. They also offer various one- to three-day trips into the rainforest by motorized canoe along the Río Ibare, a tributary of the Mamoré, with plenty of opportunity for seeing wildlife and visiting indigenous communities. Trips cost around $20 per person per day. The highly professional **Fremen** agency, Av 6 de Agosto 140 (ⓣ03/462-2276, ⓦwww.andes-amazonia.com, ⓔfremenfl@entelnet.bo), operates similar excursions, as well as four- to six-day cruises on the Mamoré aboard its luxury floating hotel, the *Reina de Enín*, starting at $349 per person. It also offers more adventurous six-day camping trips into the enormous Parque Naciónál y Territorio Indigena Isiboro-Sécure at $550 per person (for a group of 9); make sure you book in advance.

If you're travelling in a big group it's probably worth phoning the reserve office in San Borja (ⓣ03/895-3898) a day in advance to let them know you're coming, but otherwise it's fine to arrive at El Porvenir unannounced. To reach the biological station take any bus or truck heading east from San Borja or west from San Ignacio and ask the driver to let you off at El Porvenir. **Admission** to the reserve costs $5 per person and **accommodation** in basic but clean barrack-like rooms with shared bathrooms costs $12 per person, including three meals a day, or $9 a day if you bring your own equipment and **camp**. Moving on from El Porvenir can be tricky: your only option is to try to flag down one of the few passing vehicles.

Rurrenabaque

Set on the banks of the Río Beni some 430km by road north of La Paz, the small town of **RURRENABAQUE** has recently emerged as the most popular ecotourism destination in the Bolivian Amazon. Standing between the last forest-covered foothills of the Andes and the great lowland plains, Rurrenabaque, or "Rurre," is close to some of the best-preserved and most accessible wilderness areas in the region. These include the spectacular rainforests of the **Parque Nacional Madidi** and the **Reserva de Biosfera y Territorio Indígena Pilón Lajas**, as well as the wildlife-rich pampas along the **Río Yacuma**, all of which are easily visited with one of Rurrenabaque's numerous tour agencies.

There's not much to see here. Most commercial activity is concentrated along the first few blocks of **calles Avaroa** and **Comercio**, which run north from the pleasant **Plaza 2 de Febrero** and parallel to the river. They are lined with ramshackle stores selling all manner of goods, from dried fish and tropical fruit to plastic chairs and brand-name cosmetics. The riverside itself is quite a nice place to watch canoes arrive and haul in bananas or freshly caught fish.

Practicalities

All **flights** arrive at the gravel airstrip a short distance north of the town, and are met by free hotel minibuses for those with reservations and airline shuttle buses that charge a small fee for transport to their offices in the centre of town. You can also catch a motorbike taxi to the centre for $0.70, although the journey along the unpaved bumpy roads with luggage on your back might be quite a challenge; rides around the centre cost about $0.20. **Buses** arrive at the Terminal Terrestre (daily 6.30am–7.30pm; ⓣ03/892-2112) a few blocks away from the centre of town on

△ The Arbol de Piedra, south of the Salar de Uyuni

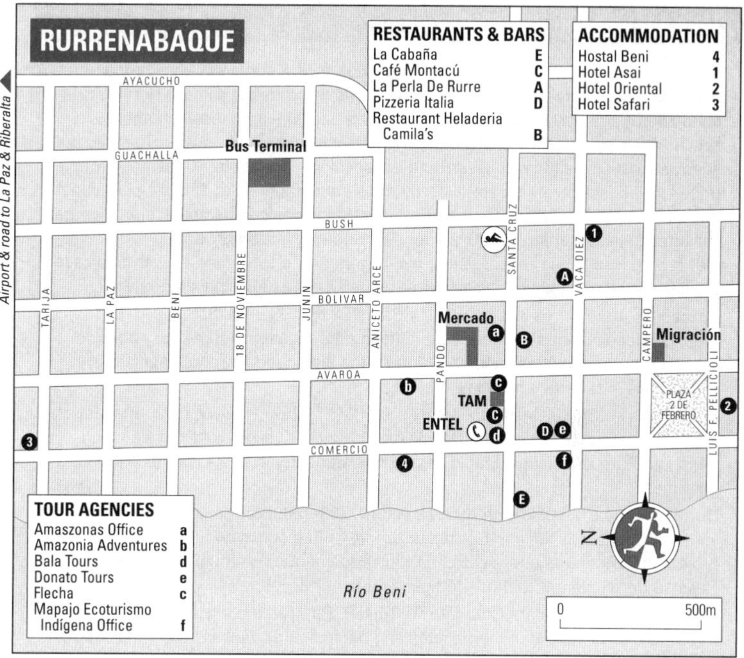

the corner of calles Guachalla and 18 de Noviembre; you can get a motorbike taxi into the centre for about $0.25. When the road is closed in the rainy season, **motorized canoes** occasionally carry passengers between Rurrenabaque and Guanay (6–8 hours; $139–195 per boat carrying up to six people) and Riberalta (8–10 days; $42 per person). These have to be booked in advance; try Tacanita Tours with the office on the corner of calles Avaroa and Aniceto Arce (ⓣ07/114-9543).

There are no banks in Rurrenabaque. Some tour agencies accept payment with **travellers' cheques** and credit cards, and there are a couple of place where you may change cheques or get advance cash on credit cards, though only for a large commission: try Amazonas on Calle Santa Cruz, Cooperativa Cactri one block towards the river on the same side of the street or Moskkito Bar on Calle Comercio.

For a small town, Rurrenabaque has an impressive number of places **to stay**, though rooms can still be difficult to find in high season (May–Aug). Unless otherwise mentioned, everywhere listed has hot water and fans, though the water and electricity supply is less reliable in the cheaper places. The best well-priced options are *Hostal Beni*, Comercio and Aniceto Arce (ⓣ03/892-2408; ❷, ❹ with a/c), with clean and modern rooms, some with a/c and private bath, around a peaceful patio with cool, tiled floors; and *Hotel Oriental*, Plaza 2 de Febrero (ⓣ03/892-2401; ❶–❷), with cool, comfortable rooms (with or without bathroom) set around a peaceful courtyard garden with hammocks. A touch classier and more expensive is *Hotel Asai*, Vaca Diez and Bush (ⓣ07/114-7729; ❸), with spacious singles, doubles and triples around a tranquil shaded courtyard. The only upmarket option in town is *Hotel Safari*, Final Comercio (ⓣ03/892-2210 or 892-2410; ❺, breakfast included), ten minutes' walk from the town centre, with comfortable and spacious cabins set around a swimming pool and a restaurant overlooking the river, with occasional karaoke nights.

Tour agencies in Rurrenabaque

A growing number of **tour agencies** offer trips to the rainforest and the pampas, generally lasting three nights. The tour agencies listed below all have good reputations and offer pretty similar packages, but the best way to choose an agency is to talk to other travellers returning from trips. Most guides only speak Spanish, but agencies can usually arrange an English-speaking interpreter for larger groups. Prices for all-inclusive trips are fixed by the local authorities at $30 per person per day for the *selva*, and $35 per person per day for the pampas, although agencies are still offering trips starting at $20–25 per day. **Security** is also an issue owing to several rape cases in the recent years; avoid going on a trip alone or with freelance guides who don't hold an official licence issued by the municipal authorities.

Amazonia Adventures Avaroa with Av Santa Cruz ⓣ03/892-2333, ⓔamazoniaadventures@hotmail.com. Offering the most environmentally conscious three- to four-day pampas and *selva* tours, and also good for longer specialist expeditions into Parque Nacional Madidi.

Bala Tours Av Santa Cruz with Comercio ⓣ03/892-2527, ⓦwww.mirurrenabaque.com, ⓔbalatours@yahoo.com. Specializes in longer five- to eight-day camping tours into Parque Nacional Madidi, as well as standard *selva* and pampas programmes.

Donato Tours Comercio with Vaca Diez ⓣ01/793-1660, ⓔdonatotours@hotmail.com. Specialists in *Turismo Ecologico Social*, or Ecological and Social Tourism, a project that organizes one-day tours to four indigenous communities in the Reserva de Biosfera y Territorio Indígena Pilón Lajas.

Flecha Avaroa with Santa Cruz ⓣ07/150-5450. Popular, friendly agency offering three- to four-day tours of the pampas and rainforest, as well as longer trips into Parque Nacional Madidi.

Mapajo Ecoturismo Indígena Comercio with Vaca Diez ⓣ03/892-2317, ⓦwww.mapajo.com, ⓔmapajo_eco@yahoo.com. Indigenous community-run agency specializing in five-, four- and three-night lodge-based trips into the Reserva de Biosfera y Territorio Indígena Pilón Lajas; the lodge is fully operated and owned by the Río Quiquibey communities.

A large number of **restaurants** have sprung up in Rurrenabaque to cater to the eco-tourism boom, with most serving Bolivian dishes – often using the delicious local river fish – along with gringo favourites like pizza and pasta. For great views of the river at sunset and large meat and fish dishes and filling *almuerzos*, try *La Cab*aña at the bottom of Av Santa Cruz. The moderately priced *La Perla de Rurre* on the corner of Bolívar and Vaca Diez dishes up mouthwatering lowland river fish specialities, including the delicious *surubí a la plancha* in the house sauce, in a plant-filled patio shaded by tall mango trees. For travellers' favourites, try *Pizzeria Italia* on Comercio with Av Santa Cruz, with its imaginative range of pizza and pasta dishes, *Café Montacú* on Av Santa Cruz next to the TAM office (open 8.30am–noon & 6.30–9.30pm; closed Tues afternoon & Sun), with a standard menu of vegetarian meals and snacks, along with home-made cakes, fruit salads, excellent coffee and book exchange, or *Restaurant Heladeria Camila's* on Av Santa Cruz with Avaroa, popular for its delicious ice cream, filling portions of standard mainstays and reliable but expensive Internet access.

Around Rurrenabaque

Rurrenabaque is the best place in the Bolivian Amazon to organize a trip into the wilderness, either to the **rainforests** of the **Parque Nacional Madidi** and the **Reserva de Biosfera y Territorio Indígena Pilón Lajas**, or into the **pampas** along the **Río Yacuma** to the north. A five- or four-night stay at *Albergue Ecologico Chalalán* in the Parque Nacional Madidi has become a tourist favourite in recent years (although the lodge has an office in Rurrenabaque on Calle Comercio, it's best to book in advance through America Tours in La Paz, see box on p.207). A more grassroots and cheaper alternative to *Chalalán* is a visit to the indigenous community-run *Albergue Ecologico Mapajo* in the Reserva de Biosfera y Territorio Indígena Pilón Lajas. See the box opposite for tour operators.

The northern Amazon frontier

Now a remote economic backwater, just over a hundred years ago Bolivia's **NORTHERN AMAZON FRONTIER** was in the midst of an unprecedented economic boom generated by the region's richest forests of rubber trees. Great fortunes were made by the so-called "rubber barons", who controlled production, but for the indigenous peoples of the Amazon – forced to work under appallingly brutal conditions – the rubber boom was an unmitigated disaster, reducing their population catastrophically. When the boom ended in the early twentieth century, the region slipped back into the economic torpor which characterizes it today, with collection of wild Brazil nuts – known as *castañas* – as the main export industry.

From Rurrenabaque a dirt road continues north across a wide savanna-covered plain towards the Brazilian frontier, more than 500km away. As the road draws near to **Riberalta**, the largest city in the region, the savanna gives way to dense Amazonian rainforest. East of Riberalta, the road continues 100km to **Guayaramerín**, on the banks of the Río Mamoré, which is the main border crossing point if you're heading north into Brazil.

Riberalta and Guayaramerín

Set on a bluff above a great sweep of the Río Madre de Dios just after its silt-laden waters are joined by those of the Beni, sleepy, sun-baked **RIBERALTA** is the second biggest town in the Amazon lowlands, with a population of about 40,000, largely employed in the processing and export of Brazil nuts. At least twelve hours by road from Rurrenabaque when conditions are good in the dry season, there's no great reason to stop unless you're heading for Cobija (see p.294) and want to break your journey. **Buses** arrive and depart from the offices of various transport companies in the centre of town, and the **airport** is about ten minutes' walk along Avenida Ochoa from the town centre. The best **place to stay** is the *Hotel Colonial* (Ⓣ03/852-3018; ❸), just off the plaza on Calle Placido Méndez, which has pleasant rooms set around a cool courtyard garden. The best budget option is the basic but clean *Hotel Lazo* (Ⓣ03/852-2352; ❷), a couple of blocks from the plaza on Calle Nicolas Salvatierra, which has cheaper rooms with shared bathrooms. There are plenty of **places to eat** on the Plaza Principal; *Snack Tom*, on the southeast corner of the plaza, has decent *almuerzos* as well as the two Beni stalwarts: beef steaks and river fish. Away from the plaza on the riverfront Parque Costanera, the *Club Social Nautico* serves good Bolivian food and cheap *almuerzos*; you can also cool off in the **swimming pool** for $1.50.

On the banks of the Río Mamoré some 86km east of Riberalta, **GUAYARAMERÍN** is the main crossing point on Bolivia's northern border, a modern and prosperous frontier town with a distinctly Brazilian flavour and a thriving economy based on duty-free sales. Most people who make it to Guayaramerín only come here to cross the border. **Buses** from Riberalta and beyond arrive at the Terminal de Buses, about 3km from the centre of town along Calle Beni; a **motorbike taxi** from here should cost about $0.50. Everything you might need is concentrated around the Plaza Principal, a few blocks south of the river. The **airport** is just four blocks east of the plaza along Calle 25 de Mayo. The *Hotel San Carlos*, a block north and east from the Plaza on Avenida 6 de Agosto, changes **travellers' cheques** – the only place in town that does – and also changes dollars and Brazilian reais. There are no ATMs in town. The **post office** is on Calle Oruro, three blocks south of the plaza. The **ENTEL** office is on Calle Mamoré, two blocks north of the plaza. There are several good **accommodation** options in town. The cheapest is the *Hotel Central* (Ⓣ03/855-3911; ❷) on Avenida Santa Cruz, a block north of the plaza, which has small, basic rooms with shared bathrooms. The *Hotel Litoral* (Ⓣ03/855-3895; ❷), just east of the plaza on Avenida 25 de Mayo, is a bit more spacious and comfortable. The best **places to eat** are on and around the plaza; the two *heladerías* are good for ice cream, coffee, juices and snacks.

Crossing into Brazil: Guajaré-Mirim

From the port at the bottom of Avenida Federico Roman, regular passenger **boats** (every 15min; $1; $1.65 to return) make the ten-minute crossing to **Guajará-Mirim** in Brazil. The Bolivian **migración** (Mon–Fri 8–11am & 2–6pm, Sat 8am–noon) is to the right of the port as you face the river; you should get an exit stamp here if you're continuing into Brazil but it's not necessary if you're just making a day-trip across the river. If you need a visa, the **Brazilian Consulate** (Mon–Fri 11am–3pm) is on the corner of Calles Beni and 24 de Septiembre, a block east of the plaza. Note that to enter Brazil, you need to have an international certificate of **yellow fever vaccination**; if you don't there's a clinic beside the immigration office in Guajará-Mirim where you can get vaccinated. From Guajará-Mirim there are frequent buses to Porto Velho, from where there are connections to other destinations in Brazil.

Cobija and the Pando

The northwestern-most tip of the Bolivia is covered by the department of **PANDO**, a remote and sparsely populated rainforest region where logging and the collection of wild rubber and Brazil nuts are the main economic activities. Until recently the Pando was accessible only by boat along the Madre de Dios, Tahuamanu and Orthon rivers, which flow into the region from Peru, but now a rough road cut through the rainforest runs from just south of Riberalta to **Cobija**, the departmental capital, on the Brazilian border.

With a population of just 15,000, **COBIJA** is the smallest departmental capital in Bolivia, an isolated border town with a distinctly Brazilian flavour. The town's busiest area is around the **central plaza**, close to the **Río Acre**, which forms the border with Brazil. The Bolivian **immigration office** (open daily 24hr) is on the main border crossing, the international bridge over the Río Acre at the end of Avenida Internacional. **Taxis** from the town centre across the bridge to the federal police office (where you'll need to clear immigration) in the Brazilian town of **Brasiléia** charge a steep $10; otherwise it's a twenty-minute walk or you can take a cheaper motorbike taxi or a canoe. Be aware that you need an international yellow-fever vaccination certificate to enter Brazil here. If you need a visa go to the **Brazilian Consulate** (Mon–Fri 8am–1pm), just off the plaza on Calle Ayacucho. From Brasiléia, there are regular buses to **Río Branco**, from where you can get further connections.

3

Brazil

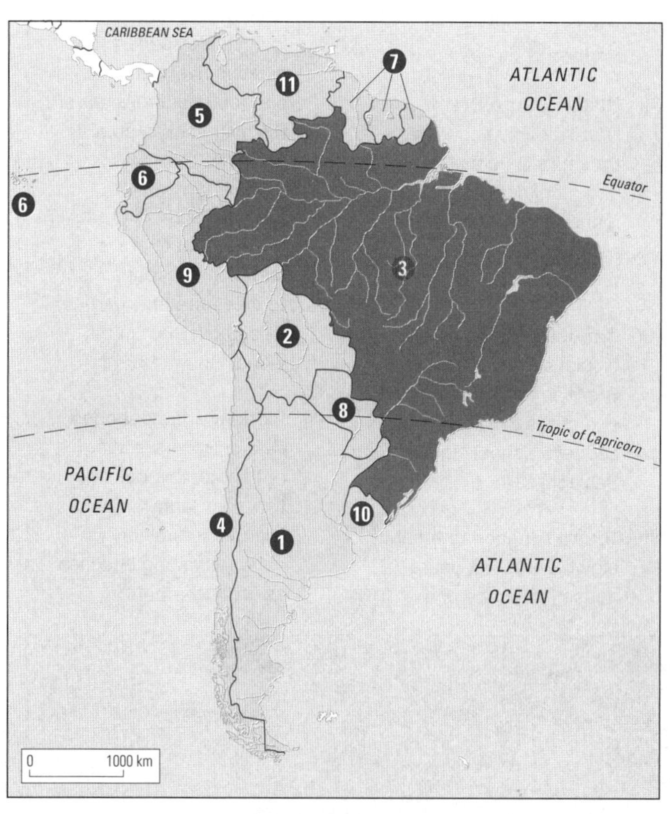
CARIBBEAN SEA
ATLANTIC OCEAN
Equator
PACIFIC OCEAN
Tropic of Capricorn
ATLANTIC OCEAN
0 1000 km
1
2
3
4
5
6
6
7
8
9
10
11

Brazil highlights

* **Museu de Arte Contemporânea** One of Oscar Niemeyer's most beautiful futuristic creations, this museum offers dazzling views across the bay to Rio. See p.341

* **Historic Ouro Preto** Brazil's richest concentration of Baroque art and architecture can be found in this eighteenth-century gold-mining centre. See p.357

* **Capoeira** Watch nimble displays of this Afro-Brazilian martial art at one of the organized *capoeira* schools in Salvador. See p.373

* **Teatro Amazonas** A full-blown European opera house in the one of the least likely locations – in the middle of the Amazon jungle. See p.404

* **Amazon River trips** The best way to take in the lush jungle scenery, fascinating river settlements and the beautiful sight of the river itself is on a boat trip. See p.434

* **Iguaçu Falls** No trip to the south of Brazil is complete without a visit to these breathtaking falls, the largest in the world. See p.448

* **Florianópolis beaches** One of Brazil's surfing hot spots, this peaceful town on Santa Catarina Island offers plenty of calm swimming beaches as well. See p.451

Introduction and basics

Brazilians often say they live in a continent rather than a country, and that's an excusable exaggeration. The landmass is bigger than the United States if you exclude Alaska. Brazil has no mountains to compare with its Andean neighbours, but in every other respect it has all the scenic – and cultural – variety you would expect from so vast a country.

Despite the immense expanses of the interior, roughly two-thirds of Brazil's **population** live on or near the coast; and well over half live in cities – even in the Amazon. In Rio and São Paulo, Brazil has two of the world's great metropolises, and nine other cities have over a million inhabitants. Yet Brazil still thinks of itself as a frontier country, and certainly the deeper into the interior you go, the thinner the population becomes.

Brazilians are one of the most **ethnically diverse** peoples in the world: in the extreme south, German and Italian immigration has left distinctive European features; São Paulo has the world's largest Japanese community outside Japan; there's a large black population concentrated in Rio and Salvador; while the Indian influence is most visible in the people of Amazônia and the Northeastern interior.

Brazil is a land of profound **economic contradictions**. Rapid postwar industrialization made Brazil one of the world's ten largest economies and put it among the most developed of Third World countries. But this has not improved the lot of the vast majority of Brazilians. The cities are dotted with **favelas**, shantytowns that crowd the skyscrapers, and the contrast between rich and poor is one of the most glaring anywhere. Brazil has enormous natural resources but their exploitation so far has benefited just a few. The IMF and the greed of First World banks must bear some of the blame for this situation, but institutionalized corruption and the reluctance of the country's large middle class to do anything that might jeopardize its comfortable lifestyle are also part of the problem.

These difficulties, however, rarely seem to overshadow everyday life in Brazil. Nowhere in the world do people know how to enjoy themselves more – most famously in the annual orgiastic celebrations of **Carnaval**, but reflected, too, in the lively year-round nightlife that you'll find in any decent-sized town. This national hedonism also manifests itself in Brazil's highly developed **beach culture**, the country's superb **music** and dancing, rich regional **cuisines**, and in the most relaxed and tolerant attitude to **sexuality** – gay and straight – that you'll find anywhere in South America.

Where to go

The most heavily populated and economically advanced part of the country is the southeast, where the three largest cities – **São Paulo**, **Rio de Janeiro** and **Belo Horizonte** – form a triangle around which the economy pivots. All are worth visiting in their own right, though Rio, one of the world's most stupendously sited cities, stands head and shoulders above the lot. The **South**, encompassing the states of Paraná, Santa Catarina and Rio Grande do Sul, stretches down to the borders with Uruguay and northern Argentina, and westwards to Paraguay. The spectacular **Iguaçu Falls** (at the northernmost point where Brazil and Argentina meet) are one of the great natural wonders of South America.

Brasília, the country's space-age capital, built from nothing in the late 1950s, is the gateway to a vast interior, notably the mighty **Pantanal** swampland, the richest wildlife reserve on the continent. North and west, the interior shades into the **Amazon**, a mosaic of jungle, rivers, savanna and marshland that also contains two major cities – **Belém**, at the mouth of the Amazon itself, and **Manaus**, some 1600km upstream.

The other major sub-region of Brazil is the **Northeast**, the part of the country that curves out into the Atlantic Ocean. This was the first part of Brazil to be settled by the

VENEZUELA
COLOMBIA
SURIN
Rio Branco
Boa Vista
GUYANA
ECUADOR
Rio Negro
Óbidos
Manaus
Rio Amazonas
Rio Solimões
(Amazon)
Tabatinga
Rio Tapajós
Cruzeiro
do Sul
Porto
Velho
Rio Branco
PERU
Cuiabá
BOLIVIA
Corumbá
PACIFIC
OCEAN
PARAGUAY
CHILE
Rio Paraguay
Uruguaiana
ARGENTINA
Livramento
URUGUAY

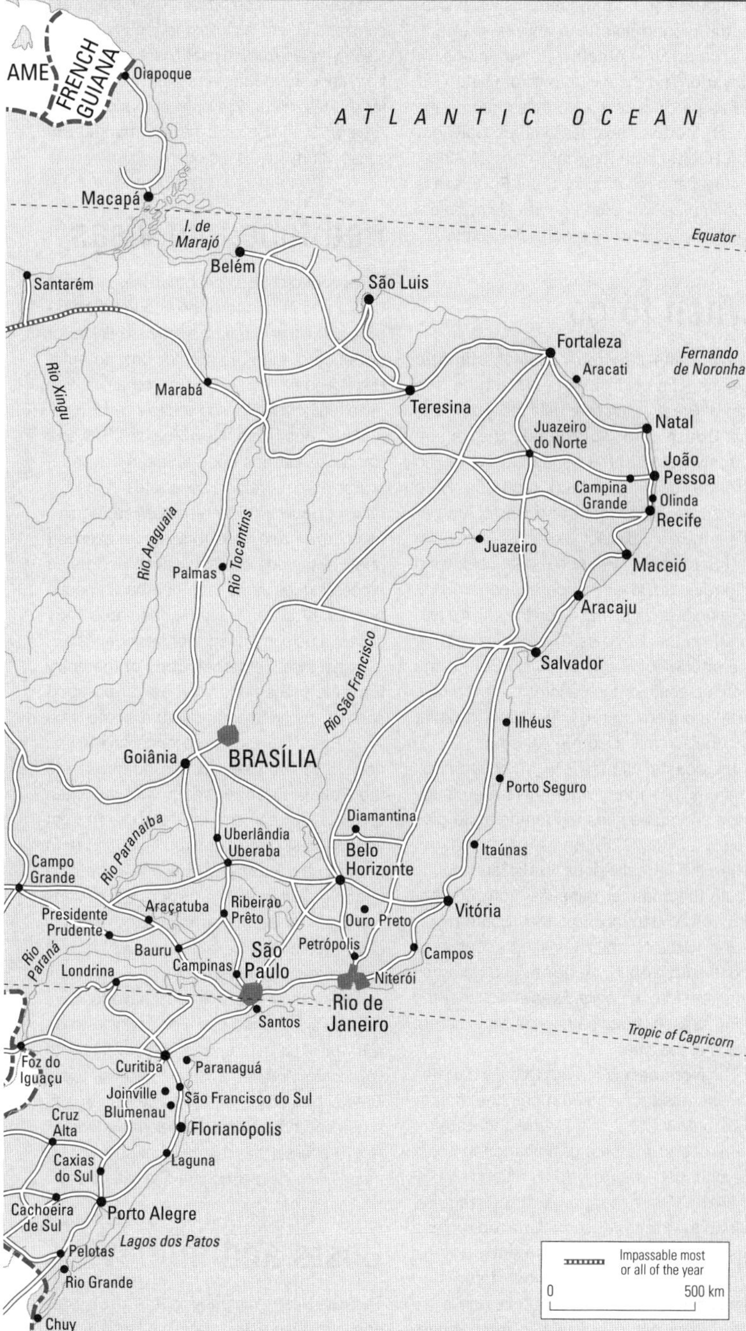
ATLANTIC OCEAN
FRENCH GUIANA
AME
Oiapoque
Macapá
Equator
I. de Marajó
Belém
Santarém
São Luis
Rio Xingu
Marabá
Teresina
Fortaleza
Aracati
Fernando de Noronha
Natal
Juazeiro do Norte
João Pessoa
Campina Grande
Olinda
Recife
Rio Araguaia
Rio Tocantins
Palmas
Juazeiro
Maceió
Aracaju
Rio São Francisco
Salvador
Ilhéus
BRASÍLIA
Goiânia
Porto Seguro
Rio Paranaiba
Diamantina
Uberlândia
Uberaba
Belo Horizonte
Itaúnas
Campo Grande
Vitória
Araçatuba
Ribeirao Prêto
Presidente Prudente
Ouro Preto
Rio Paraná
Bauru
São Paulo
Petrópolis
Campos
Londrina
Campinas
Niterói
Rio de Janeiro
Santos
Tropic of Capricorn
Foz do Iguaçu
Curitiba
Paranaguá
Joinville
São Francisco do Sul
Blumenau
Cruz Alta
Florianópolis
Caxias do Sul
Laguna
Cachoeira de Sul
Porto Alegre
Lagos dos Patos
Pelotas
Rio Grande
Chuy
Impassable most or all of the year
0
500 km

Portuguese and colonial remains are thicker on the ground here than anywhere else in the country – notably in the cities of **Salvador** and the lovely town of **Olinda**. All the major cities of the Northeast are on the coast; the two most famous are Salvador and **Recife**, both magical blends of Africa, Portugal and the Americas, but **Fortaleza** is also impressive, bristling with skyscrapers and justly proud of its progressive culture.

When to go

Brazil splits into four distinct **climatic** regions. The coldest part – in fact the only part of Brazil which ever gets really cold – is the **South and Southeast**, the region roughly from central Minas Gerais to Rio Grande do Sul, which includes Belo Horizonte, São Paulo and Porto Alegre. Here, there's a distinct winter between June and September, with occasional cold, wind and rain. However, temperatures rarely hit freezing overnight, and when they do it's featured on the TV news. The coldest part is the interior of Rio Grande do Sul, in the extreme south of the country, but even here there are many warm, bright days in winter and the summer (Dec–March) is hot.

The **coastal climate** is warm and tropical. There is a "winter", when there are cloudy days and sometimes the temperature dips below 25°C (77°F), and a rainy season, when it can really pour. In Rio and points south **the summer rains** last from October through to January, but they come much earlier in the Northeast, lasting about three months from April in Fortaleza and Salvador, and from May in Recife. Even in winter or the rainy season, the weather will be excellent much of the time.

The **Northeast** is too hot to have a winter. Nowhere is the average monthly temperature below 25°C (77°F) and the interior, semi-arid at the best of times, often soars beyond that – regularly to as much as 40°C (104°F). Rain is sparse and irregular, although violent. Much of **Amazônia** has a distinct dry season – apparently getting longer every year in the most deforested areas of east and west Amazônia. And in the large expanses of savanna in the northern and central Amazon basin, rainfall is far from constant. Belém is closest to the image of a steamy tropical city: it rains there an awful lot from January to May, and merely quite a lot for the rest of the year. Manaus and central Amazônia, in contrast, have a marked dry season from July to October.

Red tape and visas

Citizens of most European nations, including Britain and Ireland, only need a **valid passport** and either a return or onward ticket, or evidence of funds to pay for one, to enter Brazil. You fill in an entry form on arrival and get a tourist visa allowing you to stay for ninety days. Australian, New Zealand, US and Canadian citizens need **visas** in advance, available from Brazilian consulates abroad; a return or onward ticket is usually a requirement. You'll also need to submit a passport photo with your visa application and pay a processing fee in the form of a bank cheque or money order (some consulates may accept a personal cheque or bank deposit).

Try not lose the **carbon copy of the entry form** the police hand you back at passport control; you are meant to return it when you leave Brazil, but you are no longer fined if you don't. If you do lose your passport, report to the **Polícia Federal** (see p.306) and then obtain a replacement travel document from your nearest consulate. You'll then have to return to the Polícia Federal who will put an endorsement in your passport. EU citizens can extend a tourist permit for another ninety days if you apply at least fifteen days before it expires, but it will only be extended once; if you want to stay longer you'll have to leave the country and re-enter. For anything to do with entry permits and visas you deal with the federal police, the Policía Federal. Every state capital has a federal police station with a visa section: ask for the *delagacia federal*. A $10 charge, payable in local currency, is made on tourist permit and visa extensions.

Costs and money

The Brazilian currency is the **real** (pronounced "hey-al"), plural reais (pronounced "hey-ice"). The real is made up of one hundred centavos. Notes are for 1, 2, 5, 10, 20, 50 and 100 reais; coins are 1, 5, 10, 25, 50 centavos and 1 real. At the time of writing, the Brazilian real was worth R$3.50 to US$1 – this was the basis for the price calculations in this edition. Given the current instability of the *real*, we quote prices in this book in **US dollars**; this should give an approximate idea of what you'll be paying on the spot although sometimes considerable fluctuations can be expected.

The **cost of living** in Brazil is cheap – similar to that of neighbouring Argentina but more expensive than Bolivia. The cheapness of food and budget hotels – and the fact that some of the best attractions, like the beaches, are free – makes it possible to have a very enjoyable time for under $50 a day. Staying in good hotels, travelling by comfortable buses and not stinting on the extras will cost around $100 a day.

You'll find life much easier if you bring only **US dollar banknotes and plastic**. Euros notes are slowly being recognized, but generally only in *casas de câmbio* in Rio and São Paulo will you be able to change other currencies – and then only at very poor rates of exchange. Changing money in Brazil is simple; just take your bank or credit card with PIN and use **ATMs** – look for a sign saying *Cartão* or *Saques por Cartão*. Only Visa cards can be used to withdraw cash advances at the ATMs of Banco do Brasil and Banco Bradesco; only MasterCard at HSBC, Itaú and Banco Mercantil. Do not, however, completely count on being able to find a compatible ATM. For security reasons, between 10pm and 6am ATMs only allow the withdrawal of the equivalent of $15.

The main **credit cards** are widely accepted by shops, hotels and restaurant throughout Brazil, even in rural areas. MasterCard and Visa are the most prevalent, with Diners Club and American Express also widespread.

Given the ease of using plastic, **travellers' cheques** are not recommended, unless you want a small emergency reserve. Only the head offices of major **banks** (Banco do Brasil, HSBC, Banco Itaú, Banespa) will have an exchange department (ask for the *câmbio*). Exchange departments of banks often close early, sometimes at 1pm, although more often at 2pm or 3pm, and it can take up to two hours to complete all the necessary paperwork. Airport banks are open seven days a week, others only Monday to Friday.

Information, websites and maps

In Brazil, tourist information facilities vary greatly. Popular destinations like Rio, Salvador, the Northeast beach resorts and towns throughout the South have efficient and helpful **tourist offices** (addresses given in the text), but anywhere off the beaten track has nothing at all. As a rule, only the airport tourist offices have **hotel-booking services**, yet none of them is very good on advising about budget accommodation. There are EMBRATUR offices in a few of the major centres, but the local tourist offices are usually more helpful; these are run by the different state and municipal governments, so you have to learn a new acronym every time you cross a state line.

Websites

Of the numerous **websites** on Brazil, the following are the most helpful. The official site of the Brazilian Tourist Office in the US, ⓦwww.braziltourism.org, features up-to-date information on visa requirements, while ⓦwww.brazil.org.uk, run by the Brazilian Embassy in London, offers a link to its extremely efficient and knowledgable tourism department. Run by the Student Travel Bureau, ⓦwww.stb.com.br provides information on student discounts, air tickets and cultural exchanges, and ⓦwww.alberguesp.com.br is an information and booking service for the official youth hostel association in Brazil.

The official site of EMBRATUR, the Brazilian government's national tourist service, ⓦwww.embratur.gov.br, is only in Portuguese.

Detailed **maps** are surprisingly hard to get hold of outside Brazil, and are rarely very good. The six regional maps in the *Mapa Rodoviário Touring* series (1:2,500,000), which mark all the major routes clearly, are difficult to find even in Brazil. A useful compendium of **city maps** and **main road networks**, published by Guias Quatro Rodas, which also has maps to Rio, São Paulo and other cities, states and regions, are easy to find in bookstores, newsagents and magazine stalls. Very clear maps of individual states are published by Polimapas, and are usually available in Brazilian bookstores and newspaper kiosks.

Accommodation

At the bottom end of the scale, in terms of both quality and price, are **dormitórios**, small and very basic (to put it mildly) hotels, situated close to bus stations and in the poorer parts of town. Extremely cheap, they are usually unsavoury and sometimes positively dangerous. You could stay for not much more, in far better conditions, in a **youth hostel**, an *albergue de juventude*, also sometimes called a *casa de estudante*, where the cost per person is between $5 and $10 a night. There's an extensive network of these hostels, with at least one in every state capital, and they are very well maintained. It helps to have an IYHF card with a recent photograph – you're not usually asked for one, but every so often you'll find an *albergue* that refuses entry unless it's produced.

Pensões, pousadas and hotels

In a slightly higher price range are the small, family-run hotels, called either a **pensão** (*pensões* in the plural) or a *hotel familiar*. Varying a great deal, *Pensões* tend to be better in small towns than in large cities, but are also usefully thick on the ground in some of the main tourist towns, where conventional hotels are pretty well nonexistent. You will also come across the **pousada**, which can just be another name for a *pensão*, but can also be a small hotel, running up to luxury class but usually less expensive than a hotel proper. In the Amazon and the Pantanal in particular, pousadas tend to be purpose-built **fazenda** lodges geared towards the growing eco-tourist markets and are not aimed at budget travellers.

Hotels proper run from dives to luxury apartments. There is a Brazilian classification system, from one to five stars; the star system depends on bureaucratic requirements as much as on the standard of accommodation, and many perfectly good hotels don't have stars.

Hotels offer a range of different rooms, with significant price differences: a **quarto** is a room without a bathroom, an **apartamento** with (actually a shower – Brazilians don't use baths); an **apartamento de luxo** is normally just an *apartamento* with a fridge full of (marked-up) drinks; a **casal** is a double room; and a **solteiro** a single. In a starred hotel, an *apartamento* upwards would normally come with telephone, air conditioning (*ar condicionado*) and a TV; a *ventilador* is a fan. **Rates** for rooms vary tremendously between different parts of Brazil, but start at around $5 in a one-star hotel, around $15 in a two-star hotel, and around $25 in a three-star place. Generally speaking, for $25–30 a night you could expect to stay in a reasonable mid-range hotel, with bathroom and air conditioning. During the off-season most hotels in tourist areas offer hefty **discounts**, usually around 25–35 percent, but when discounts are offered credit cards are not accepted.

There are a fair number of **campsites** in Brazil and almost all of them are on the coast near the bigger beaches. They will usually have basic facilities – running water and toilets, perhaps a simple restaurant – and are popular with young Argentines and Brazilians.

Getting around

Local travel in Brazil is always easy. Public transport outside the Amazon is generally by bus or plane, though there are a few passenger trains, too. However you travel, services will be crowded, plentiful and, apart from planes, cheap.

Car rental is also possible, but driving in Brazil is not for the faint-hearted.

Hitchhiking, over any distance, is not recommended.

By bus

Intercity **buses** leave from a station called a **rodoviária**, usually built on city outskirts. Buses are operated by hundreds of private companies, but **prices** are standardized, even when more than one firm plies the same route, and are very reasonable. Long-distance buses are comfortable enough to sleep in, and have on-board toilets. Buses stop every two or three hours, but it's not a bad idea to bring along water and some food to last the journey.

There are luxury buses, too, called **leitos**, which do nocturnal runs between the major cities, with fully reclining seats in curtained partitions. They cost about a third of the price of an air ticket, and need to be booked a few days in advance. Going any distance, it's best to **buy your ticket** at least a day in advance, from the rodoviária or, in some cities, from travel agents. An exception is the Rio–São Paulo route, where a shuttle service means you can always turn up without a ticket. If you cross a state line you will get a small form with the ticket, which asks for the number of your seat (*poltrona*), the number of your ticket (*passagem*), the number of your passport (*identidade*) and your destination (*destino*). You have to fill it in and give it to the driver before you'll be let on board.

By plane

It's hardly surprising that a country the size of Brazil relies on **air travel** a good deal. The main domestic carriers are **VASP**, **Varig** and **TAM**; important regional airlines include the Varig subsidiaries **RioSul** (mainly serving the South) and **RioNordeste** (covering the Amazon region), together with **Viabrasil**, which connects São Paulo with Fortaleza, Natal, João Pessoa and Recife in the Northeast. A recent phenomenon is the appearance of budget airlines, of which the biggest is **GOL** (Ⓣ0800/701 2131, Ⓦwww.voegol.com.br), known to have an extensive network and cheap seats, but also for very long check-in lines and flight delays. Also be aware that credit cards issued outside Brazil are not accepted on its website.

Prices are very reasonable, but tickets are almost always much cheaper when purchased in Brazil rather than abroad, and you can benefit from special promotions. If you plan on flying a lot in a relatively short time, then consider buying an **airpass** from Varig (along with its regional subsidiaries RioSul and RioNordeste), VASP or TAM. Passes can only be bought **outside Brazil** in advance of your trip with a return air ticket to the country.

Departure tax for international flights is $36, payable in local currency or dollars when you check in – tickets sold in Brazil include the tax, as increasingly do tickets sold outside the country.

By Amazon riverboat

Amazon river travel is slow and can be tough going, but it's a fascinating experience. On longer journeys there are a number of classes; in general it's better to avoid *cabine*, where you swelter in a cabin, and choose *primeiro* (first class) instead, sleeping in a hammock on deck. *Segundo* (second class) is usually hammock space in the lower deck or engine room. Take plenty of provisions, and expect to practise your Portuguese.

The **range of boat transport** in the Amazon runs from luxury tourist boats and large three-level riverboats to smaller one- or two-level boats (the latter normally confining their routes to main tributaries and local runs) and covered launches operated by tour companies. As a rule, most local boats cost about $10 a day (including food), more for the tourist boats and tour-based launches. The popular **Belém–Manaus trip** costs $35–55 (hammock space), taking four to six days.

By car

Driving standards in Brazil hover between the abysmal and the appalling. Brazil has one of the highest death tolls from driving-related accidents in the world. While most cities are fairly well signposted, outside urban areas, Brazilian roads are death-traps at night; poorly lit, in bad condition and lightly policed. Service stations in rural areas do not always accept international credit cards, so make sure you always have sufficient cash on a long trip. Especially worth avoiding at night are the **Via Dutra**, linking Rio and São Paulo, because of the huge numbers of trucks and the treacherous ascent and descent of the Serra do Mar, and the **Belem-Brasilia highway**, whose potholes and uneven asphalt make it difficult enough to drive even in daylight. Where possible, avoid driving after dark in the Mato Grosso and Amazon regions as well; though rare, armed roadside robberies have been known to happen there.

Renting a car in Brazil is straightforward. Hertz, Avis and other big-name international companies operate here, and there are plenty of Brazilian alternatives, such as Interlocadora, Nobre and Localiza. Unidas is also represented throughout the country and is highly recommended, as their cars are always in excellent condition, service is efficient and – if you take out their comprehensive insurance policy – there is no excess payable if your car is stolen or damaged. Car rental offices (*locadoras*) can be found at every airport and in most towns regardless of size.

An **international driving licence** is recommended: although foreign licences are accepted for visits of up to six months, you may have a hard time convincing a police officer of this. Occasionally the police can be quite intimidating as they point to trumped up contraventions – what they are probably angling for is a bribe and an on-the-spot *multa*, or fine, may be suggested. It's a personal judgement whether to stand one's ground or just pay up. No matter how certain you are of the righteousness of your position, stay calm and bend over backwards to appear polite. If your passport is confiscated, demand to be permitted to phone your consulate – there should always be a duty officer available.

Mail and communications

These days, public phones are operated mostly by **phonecards** (*carta telefônico*) which are on sale from newspaper stands, street sellers' trays and most cafés. For local calls, a 5 reis card will last for several conversations; for long-distance or international calls, higher-value phonecards come in 10, 20, 50 or 100 reis denominations. Calls to the US or Europe cost about $1.50 per minute. Before dialling direct, lift the phone from the hook, insert the phonecard and listen for a dialling tone. Note that long-distance calls are cheaper after 8pm.

Before making a national or international call you must select the telephone company you wish to use by inserting a **two-digit code** between the zero and the area code or country code of the number you are calling. To call Rio, for example, from anywhere else in the country, you would dial 0xx21 (zero + phone company code + city code) followed by the seven-digit number. For local calls you simply dial the seven- or eight-digit number.

As different phone companies are responsible for different areas of the country, pay phones will display which company code should be used from that particular phone, or the hotel receptionist will let you know the correct code to be used if calling from your hotel. Only two companies (Embratel – code 21; and Intelig – code 23) allow you to make **international calls** from Brazil – one of these numbers will be an option from most phones.

Long-distance and international calls can also be made from a **posto telefônico**, which all operate in the same way: you ask at the counter for a *chave* and are given a numbered key. You go to the booth, insert the key and turn it to the right, and can then make up to three completed calls. You are billed when you return the key – around $1.50 a minute to the US or Europe. For international calls, ask for *chamada internacional*; a reverse-charge call is a *chamada a cobrar*.

A **post offices** – *correios* – are identifiable by their bright yellow postboxes and signs. A foreign postage stamp costs around 40¢ for either a postcard or a letter up to 10 grammes. **Airmail** letters to Europe and North America usually take about a week or sometimes even less. **Surface mail** takes about a month to North America, and three to Europe. Although the postal system is generally very reliable, it is not advisable to send valuables through the mail.

Food and drink

There are four main **regional cuisines**: **comida mineira** (see box on p.355) from Minas Gerais ; **comida baiana** (see box on p.375) from Bahia; **comida do sertão** from the interior of the Northeast, which relies on rehydrated dried or salted meat and the fruit, beans and tubers of the region; and **comida gaúcha** from Rio Grande do Sul, the most carnivorous diet in the world, revolving around every imaginable kind of meat grilled over charcoal.

Alongside the regional restaurants, there is a **standard fare** available everywhere that can soon get dull unless you cast around: steak (**bife**) or chicken (**frango**), served with **arroz e feijão**, rice and beans, and often with salad, fries and **farinha**, dried **manioc** (cassava) flour that you sprinkle over everything. *Farofa* is toasted *farinha*, and usually comes with onions and bits of bacon mixed in.

Feijoada is the closest Brazil comes to a national dish: a stew of pork, sausage and smoked meat cooked with black beans and garlic, garnished with slices of orange. Eating it is a national ritual at weekends, when restaurants serve *feijoada* all day.

Some of the **fruit** is familiar – *manga* (mango), *maracujá* (passion fruit), *limão* (lime) – but most of it has only Brazilian names: *jaboticaba*, *fruta do conde*, *sapoti* and *jaca*. The most exotic fruits are Amazonian: try *bacuri*, *açaí* and the extraordinary *cupuaçu*, the most delicious of all.

Restaurants

Restaurants – *restaurantes* – are ubiquitous, portions are very large and prices are extremely reasonable. A *prato comercial* is around $3, while a good full meal can usually be had for about $10, even in expensive-looking restaurants. One of the best options offered by many restaurants, typically at lunchtime only, is self-service **comida por kilo**, where a wide choice of food is priced according to the weight of the food on your plate. Specialist restaurants to look out for include a **rodízio**, where you pay a fixed charge and eat as much as you want; most **churrascarias** – restaurants specializing in charcoal-grilled meat of all kinds, especially beef – operate this system, too, bringing a constant supply of meat on huge spits to the tables.

While the bill normally comes with a ten percent service charge, you should still **tip**, as waiters rely more on tips than on their very low wages.

Drinks

Coffee is often a great disappointment in Brazil: most of the good stuff is exported, and what's available often comes so stiff with sugar that it's almost undrinkable. You are never far from a **cafézinho** (as these small cups of coffee are known; *café* refers to coffee in its raw state). Tea (*chá*) is surprisingly good. Try **chá mate**, a strong green tea with a noticeable caffeine hit, or one of the wide variety of herbal teas, most notably that made from *guaraná*. The great variety of fruit in Brazil is put to excellent use in **sucos**: fruit is popped into a liquidizer with sugar and crushed ice to make a deliciously refreshing drink. Made with milk rather than water it becomes a **vitamina**.

Beer is mainly of the lager type. Brazilians drink it ice-cold and it comes mostly in 600ml bottles: ask for a *cerveja*. Many places only serve beer on draught – called *chopp*. Generally acknowledged as the best brands are the regional beers of Pará and Maranhão, Cerma and Cerpa, but the best nationally available beers are Skol and Brahma. Despite the undoubted improvement in the quality of Brazilian **wines** in recent years, imported wines from Chile and Argentina (or Europe) remain more reliable and can be cheaper than the best that Brazil produces.

As for **spirits**, you should stick to what Brazilians drink, **cachaça**, which is sugarcane rum. The best way to drink it is in a **caipirinha**, along with football and music one of Brazil's great gifts to world civilization – rum mixed with fresh lime, sugar and crushed ice: it may not sound like much, but it is the best cocktail you're ever likely to drink.

Safety and the police

Brazil reputation as a rather dangerous place is not entirely undeserved, but it is often overblown, and many visitors arrive with a wildly exaggerated idea of the perils lying in wait for them. While you would be foolish to ignore them, don't allow worries about safety to interfere with your enjoyment of the country.

Remember that while being a gringo can attract unwelcome attention, it can also provide an important measure of protection. The Brazilian police can be extremely violent, and law enforcement tends to take the form of periodic crackdowns. Therefore, criminals know that any injury to a foreign tourist is going to mean a heavy clampdown, which in turn means no pickings for a while. So unless you resist, nothing is likely to happen to you. That said, having a knife or a gun held on you, as anyone who's had the experience will know, is something of a shock: it's very difficult to think rationally. But if you are unlucky enough to be the victim of an **assalto**, a hold-up, try to remember that it's your possessions rather than *you* that's the target. Your money and anything you're carrying will be snatched, your watch will get pulled off your wrist, but within a couple of seconds it will be over. On no account resist: it isn't worth the risk.

Most *assaltos* take place at night, in back streets of cities with few people around, so stick to busy, well-lit streets; in a city, it's always a lot safer to **take a taxi** than walk.

You're at your most vulnerable when travelling and though the luggage compartments of buses are pretty safe – remember to get a **baggage check** from the person putting it in and don't throw it away – the overhead racks inside are less safe; keep an eye on things you stash there, especially on night journeys. On a city beach, never leave things unattended while you take a dip; any beachside bar will stow things for you. Most hotels (even the cheaper ones) will have a **safe**, a *caixa*, and unless you have serious doubts about the place you should lock away your most valuable things: the better the hotel, the more secure it's likely to be. In cheaper hotels, where rooms are shared, the risks are obviously greater – some people take along a small padlock for extra security and many wardrobes in cheaper hotels have latches fitted for this purpose.

If you are robbed or held up, it's not necessarily a good idea to go to the **police**. Except with something like a theft from a hotel room, they're very unlikely to be able to do anything, and reporting something can take hours even without the language barrier. You may have to do it for insurance purposes, when you'll need a local police report; this could take an entire, and very frustrating, day to get, so think first about how badly you want to be reimbursed. If your passport is stolen, go to your consulate first and they'll smooth the path. If you decide to go to the police in a city where there is a consulate, get in touch with the consulate first and do as they tell you.

You should be very, very careful about **drugs**. **Marijuana** – *maconha* – is common, but you are in serious trouble if the police find any on you. **Cocaine** is not as common as you might think as most of it passes through Brazil from Bolivia or Colombia for export.

Opening hours, public holidays and fiestas

Basic hours for most stores and businesses are from 9am to 6pm, with an extended lunch hour from around noon to 2pm. Banks don't open until 10am, stay open all day, but usually stop changing money at either 2pm or 3pm; except for those at major airports, they're closed at weekends and on public holidays. Museums and monuments more or less follow office hours but many are closed on Monday.

Although plane and bus **timetables** are kept to whenever possible, in the less developed parts of the country – most notably Amazônia but also the interior of the Northeast – delays often happen. Turn up at the arranged time, but don't be surprised at all if you're kept waiting. Waiting times are especially long if you have to deal with any part of the state bureaucracy, like extending a visa. There is no way out of this; just take a good book.

Calendar of public holidays

There are plenty of local and state holidays, but on the following **national holidays** just about everything in the country will be closed:

January 1 New Year's Day
Carnaval The five days leading up to Ash Wednesday
Good Friday
April 21 Remembrance of Tiradentes
May 1 Labour Day
Corpus Christi
September 7 Independence Day
October 12 Nossa Senhora Aparecida
November 2 Dia dos Finados (the Day of the Dead)
November 15 Proclamation of the Republic
December 25 Christmas Day

Carnaval

Carnaval is the most important festival in Brazil, but there are other holidays, too, from saints' days to celebrations based around elections or the World Cup.

When Carnaval comes, the country gets down to some of the most serious partying in the world. The most familiar and most spectacular is in **Rio** (see p.339), one of the world's great sights, and televized live to the whole country.

Salvador's less commercialized Carnaval (see p.375) is, in many ways, the antithesis of Rio, with several parades around the old city centre.

Football

Brazilian football (*futebol*) is revered the world over and it is a privilege to experience it at first hand. Games are usually enthralling; the stadiums are often spectacular sights in their own right; and Brazilian crowds are fantastic – wildly enthusiastic, and bringing along their own excellent live music. The only downside is a recent upsurge of crowd violence, provoked by small but highly organized hooligan groups. It is not a good idea to wear a local team shirt to a match, although foreign team shirts will guarantee you a friendly conversation with curious fans.

The best grounds are the temples of Brazilian football, Maracanã in Rio and the Art Deco Pacaembú in São Paulo, one of the most beautiful football stadiums in the world. Even the small cities have international-class stadiums – in essence, symbols of municipal virility. **Tickets** are cheap – less than a couple of dollars to stand on the terraces (*geral*), around $5 for stand seats (*arquibancada*); championship and international matches cost a little more. Grounds are large, and stadiums usually well below their enormous capacities except for important matches, which means that you can almost always turn up and pay at the turnstile rather than having to get a ticket in advance.

Good teams are thickest on the ground in Rio and São Paulo. In Rio, **Flamengo** and **Fluminense** have historically had the most intense rivalry in Brazilian club football, though the latter are currently in steep decline and their place has been taken by **Vasco**; together with **Botafogo** they dominate *carioca* football. In São Paulo there is similar rivalry between **São Paulo** and **Coríntians**, whose pre-eminence is challenged by **Guaraní**, **Palmeiras**, **Portuguesa** and **Santos**, the last of these now a shadow of the team that Pelé led to glory in the 1960s. The only clubs elsewhere that come up to the standards of the best of Rio and São Paulo are **Internacional** and **Grêmio** in Porto Alegre, **Atlético Mineiro** in Belo Horizonte, **Vitória** and **Bahia** in Bahia, and **Sport** in Recife.

History

Brazil's recorded history begins with the arrival of the Portuguese in 1500, although the country had obviously been discovered and settled by Indians centuries before. The importation of millions of African slaves over the next four centuries completed the rich blend of European, Indian and African influences that formed modern Brazil and its people. The eternal "Land of the Future" is still a prisoner of its past, as industrialization turned Brazil into the economic giant of South America, but sharpened social divisions. After a twenty-year interlude of military rule, the civilian "New Republic" has struggled, with some success, against deep-rooted economic crisis and has managed to consolidate democracy. Although social divisions remain, the current economic and political outlook is the best it has been for a generation.

Pre-Columbian Brazil

Little is known about the thousands of years that Brazil was inhabited exclusively by **Indians**. The first chroniclers who arrived with the Portuguese saw large villages, but nothing resembling the huge Aztec and Inca cities the Spanish encountered. The material traces left by Brazil's earliest inhabitants have for the most part not survived. The few exceptions come from cultures that have vanished so completely that not even a name records their passing. It is thought the total number of Indians was probably around five million when the Portuguese arrived; today, there are about two hundred thousand.

Conquest

A year after **Pedro Alvares Cabral** was blown off course on his way to Calcutta, and landed in southern Bahia on April 23, 1500, King Manuel I of Portugal sent **Amerigo Vespucci** to explore further. Reserving the name of the continent for himself, he spent several months sailing along the coast, calendar in hand, baptizing places after the names of saints' days: entering Guanabara Bay on New Year's Day 1502, he called it Rio de Janeiro. He named the land Terra do Brasil, after a tropical redwood that was its first export; the scarlet dye it yielded was called *brasa*, "a glowing coal".

In 1532, King João III divided up the coastline into **sesmarias**, captaincies fifty leagues wide and extending indefinitely inland, distributing them to aristocrats and courtiers in return for undertakings to found settlements.

In 1548, irritated by the lack of progress, King João repossessed the captaincies and brought Brazil under direct royal control. By the closing decades of the century increasing numbers of Portuguese settlers were flowing in, and the import of slaves from the Portuguese outposts on the African coast began, as **sugar plantations** sprang up around Salvador and Olinda. When Europe's taste for sugar took off in the early seventeenth century, the Northeast of Brazil quickly became very valuable real estate – and a tempting target for the expanding maritime powers of northern Europe, jealous of the Iberian monopoly in the New World. War was fought with the Dutch ending in 1654, when they were driven out of Recife.

The bandeirantes: gold and God

The toughness of the early Brazilians was readily apparent in the penetration and settling of **the interior** during the seventeenth and eighteenth centuries. Every few months, expeditions set out to explore the interior, following rumours of gold and looking for Indians to enslave. They carried an identifying banner, a *bandeira*, which gave the name

bandeirantes to the adventurers; they became the Brazilian version of the Spanish *conquistadores*. São Paulo, thanks to its position on the Rio Tietê, one of the few natural highways that flowed east–west into the deep interior, became the main *bandeirante* centre.

It was the *bandeirantes* who pushed the borders of Brazil way inland; they explored the Amazon, Paraná and Uruguai river systems, but the most important way they shaped the future of Brazil was in locating the Holy Grail of the New World: gold.

Gold was first found by *bandeirantes* in 1695, in Minas Gerais. As towns sprang up around further gold strikes in Minas, gold was discovered deeper in the Brazilian the interior. By the mid-eighteenth century, the flow of gold from Brazil was keeping the Portuguese Crown afloat, temporarily halting its long slide down the league table of European powers. In Brazil, the rush of migrants to the gold areas changed the regional balance, as the new interior communities drew population away from the Northeast. The shift was recognized in 1763, when the capital was transferred from Salvador to Rio, and that filthy, disease-ridden port began its transformation into one of the great cities of the world.

The Jesuits

Apart from the *bandeirantes*, the most important agents of the colonization of the interior were the **Jesuits**. The first missionaries arrived in 1549 and, thanks to the influence they held over successive Portuguese kings, they acquired power in Brazil second only to that of the Crown. In Salvador, they built the largest Jesuit college outside Rome, and set in motion a crusade to convert the Indian population. The usual method was to congregate the Indians in **missions**, where they worked under the supervision of Jesuit fathers. After 1600, dozens of were founded in the interior, especially in the Amazon and in the grasslands of the Southeast.

The role the Jesuits played in the conversion of the Indians was ambiguous. Mission Indians were often released by Jesuits to work for settlers, where they died like flies; and the missionaries' intrepid penetration of remote areas resulted in the spread of diseases that wiped out entire tribes. On the other hand, many Jesuits distinguished themselves in protecting Indians against the settlers.

Seeing the Jesuits as a threat to Crown control, the **Marquis de Pombal** expelled the Order from Brazil in 1760. The Jesuits may have been imperfect protectors, but from this time on the Indians were denied even that.

Independence

Almost unique among South American countries, Brazil achieved a peaceful transition to independence. Brazilian resentment at their exclusion from government, and at the Portuguese monopoly of foreign trade, grew steadily during the eighteenth century. It culminated, in 1789, in the **Inconfidência Mineira**, a plot hatched by twelve prominent citizens of Ouro Preto to proclaim Brazilian independence. The rebels, however, were betrayed almost before they started – their leader, **Tiradentes**, was executed and the rest exiled.

Just as tensions mounted in Brazil, **Napoleon** invaded Portugal in 1807. With the French army poised to take Lisbon, the British navy hurriedly evacuated **King João VI** to Rio, which was declared the temporary capital of the Portuguese Empire and seat of the government-in-exile. João was entranced by his tropical kingdom, unable to pull himself away even after Napoleon's defeat. Finally, in 1821, he was faced with a liberal revolt in Portugal that threatened to topple the monarchy, and he was unable to delay his return any longer. In April 1822 he appointed his son, **Dom Pedro**, as prince regent and governor of Brazil; when he sailed home, his last words to his son were "Get your hands on this kingdom, before some adventurer does."

Pedro, young and arrogant, grew increasingly irritated by the strident demands of the Côrtes, the Portuguese assembly, that he return home to his father and allow Brazil to be ruled from Portugal once again. On September 7, 1822, Pedro was out riding on the plain of Ypiranga, near São Paulo. Buttoning himself up after an attack of diarrhoea, he was surprised by a messenger with a bundle of letters from Lisbon. Reading the usual demands for him to return, his patience snapped, and he declared Brazil independent with the cry "Independence or death!" With overwhelming popular support for the idea, he had himself crowned **Dom Pedro I**, Emperor of Brazil, on December 1, 1822. The Portuguese, preoccupied by political crises at home and demoralized by Pedro's defection, put up little resistance and by the end of 1823 no Portuguese forces remained.

Early empire: revolt in the regions

Headstrong and autocratic, Dom Pedro became increasingly estranged from his subjects, devoting more attention to scandalous romances than affairs of state. In April 1831, he abdicated, in a fit of petulance, in favour of the heir apparent, **Dom Pedro II**, and returned to Portugal. Pedro II would later prove an enlightened ruler, but as he was only five at the time there were limits to his capacity to influence events. With a power vacuum at the centre of the political system, long-standing tensions in the outlying provinces erupted into **revolt**.

The crisis led to Dom Pedro II being declared emperor four years early, in 1840, when he was only fourteen. His instincts were conservative, but he regularly appointed liberal governments and was respected even by republicans. With government authority restored, the provincial rebellions had by 1850 either blown themselves out or been put down. And with **coffee** beginning to be planted on a large scale in Rio, São Paulo and Minas, and the flow of European immigrants rising from a trickle to a flood, the economy of southern Brazil began to take off in earnest.

The War of the Triple Alliance

With the rebellions in the provinces, the **army** became increasingly important in Brazilian political life. Pedro insisted they stay out of domestic politics, but his policy of diverting the generals by allowing them to control foreign policy ultimately led to the disaster of the war with Paraguay (1864–70). The **War of the Triple Alliance** was the bloodiest war in South American history, with a casualty list almost as long as that of the American Civil War: Brazil alone suffered over 100,000 casualties. It pitted, in unequal struggle, the landlocked republic of Paraguay, under the dictator **Francisco Lopez**, against the combined forces of Brazil, Argentina and Uruguay. Although the Paraguayans started the war, by invading Uruguay and parts of Mato Grosso in 1864, they had been sorely provoked by Brazilian meddling in Uruguay. The generals in Rio, with no more rebels to fight within Brazil, wanted to incorporate Uruguay into the empire; they were confident of victory as the Paraguayans were heavily outnumbered and outgunned. Yet the Paraguayans demonstrated the military prowess that would mark their history. It turned into a war of extermination and six terrible years were only ended by the killing of Lopez in 1870.

The end of slavery

From the seventeenth to the nineteenth century around ten million Africans were transported to Brazil as **slaves** – ten times as many as were shipped to the United States – yet the death rate in Brazil was so great that in 1860 Brazil's black population was half the size of that in the US. Slavery was always contested: slaves fled from the cities and plantations to form refugee communities called *quilombos*.

But it was not until the nineteenth century that slavery was seriously challenged. Abolition was regarded with horror by the large landowners in Brazil, and a combination of racism and fear of economic dislocation led to a determined rearguard action to preserve slavery. The slave trade was finally **abolished** in 1854 but, to the disgust of the abolitionists, slavery itself remained legal. Ultimately it was a passionate campaign within Brazil itself, led by the fiery lawyer **Joaquim Nabuco**, that finished slavery off. The growing liberal movement, increasingly republican and anti-monarchist, squared off against the landowners, with Dom Pedro hovering indecisively somewhere in between. By the time full **emancipation** came, in the "Golden Law" of May 13, 1888, Brazil had achieved the shameful distinction of being the last country in the Americas to abolish slavery.

From empire to republic

The end of slavery was also the death knell of the monarchy. Since the 1870s the intelligentsia, deeply influenced by French liberalism, had turned against the emperor and agitated for a republic. By the 1880s they had been joined by the officer corps, who blamed Dom Pedro for lack of backing during the Paraguayan war. When the large landowners withdrew their support, furious that the emperor had not prevented emancipation, the **monarchy collapsed** very suddenly in 1889.

Once again, Brazil managed a bloodless transition. The push came from the army, detachments led by **Marechal Deodoro da Fonseca** meeting no resistance when they occupied Rio on November 15, 1889. They invited the royal family to remain, but Dom Pedro insisted on exile. Deodoro began a Brazilian tradition of ham-fisted military autocracy. Ignoring the clamour for a liberal republic, he declared himself dictator in 1891, but was forced to resign three weeks later when even the army refused to support him. His deputy, **Marechal Floriano de Peixoto**, took over, but proved even more incompetent; Rio was actually shelled in 1893 by rebellious warships, demanding Peixoto's resignation. Finally, in 1894 popular pressure led to Peixoto stepping down in favour of the first elected civilian president, **Prudente de Morais**.

Immigration and urbanization

The years from 1890 to 1930 were politically undistinguished, but saw Brazil rapidly transformed economically and socially by large-scale **immigration** from Europe and Japan; they were decades of swift growth and swelling cities, which saw a very Brazilian combination of a boom-bust-boom economy and corrupt pork-barrel politics.

The boom was led by **coffee** and **rubber**, which – at opposite ends of the country – had entirely different labour forces. Millions of *nordestinos* moved into the Amazon to tap rubber, but the coffee workers swarming into São Paulo in their hundreds of thousands came chiefly from Italy. Between 1890 and 1930 over four million migrants arrived from Europe and another two hundred thousand from Japan. Most went to work on the coffee estates of southern Brazil, but enough remained to turn São Paulo into the fastest-growing city in the Americas. **Urban industrialization** appeared in Brazil for the first time, taking root in São Paulo to supply the voracious markets of the young cities springing up in the *paulista* interior. By 1930, São Paulo had displaced Rio as the leading industrial centre.

The Vargas years

The revolution of 1930 brought to power the populist **Getúlio Vargas**, who dominated Brazilian politics for the next quarter-century; the Vargas years were a time of radical change, marking a decisive break with the past.

Vargas had much in common with his Argentinian contemporary, Juan Perón: both were charming, but cunning and ruthless with it, and rooted their power base in the new urban working class.

When the **Great Depression** hit, the government spent millions protecting coffee growers by buying crops at a guaranteed price; the coffee was then burnt, as the export market had collapsed. Workers in the cities and countryside were appalled, and as the economic outlook worsened the pressure started building up from other states to end the São Paulo and Minas grip on power.

In 1926, **Washington Luis** was made president without an election, as the elite contrived an unopposed nomination. When Luis appeared set to do the same thing in 1930, an unstoppable **mass revolution** developed, first in Vargas's home state of Rio Grande do Sul, then in Rio, then in the Northeast. There was some resistance in São Paulo, but the worst fighting was in the Northeast, where street battles left scores dead. The shock troops of the revolution were the young army officers who led their units against the *ancien régime* in Minas and Rio, and the gaucho cavalry that accompanied Vargas on his triumphant procession to Rio.

Vargas played the nationalist card with great success, nationalizing the oil, electricity and steel industries, and setting up a health and social welfare system that earned him unwavering working-class support which continued even after his death. Reforms this fundamental could not be carried out under the old constitutional framework. Vargas simplified things by declaring himself **dictator** in 1937 and imprisoning political opponents – most of whom were in the trade union movement or the Communist Party, or were Brazilian fascists. He called his regime the "New State", the **Estado Novo**, and certainly its reforming energy was something new. Although he cracked down hard on dissent, Vargas was never a totalitarian dictator. He was massively popular and his great political talents enabled him to outflank most opponents.

The result was both political and economic success. The ruinous coffee subsidy was abolished, industry encouraged and agriculture diversified: by 1945 São Paulo had become the largest industrial centre in South America. With the federal government increasing its powers at the expense of state rights, regional government power was wrested out of the hands of the oligarchs for the first time.

At first Brazil stayed neutral in **World War II**, reaping the benefits of increased exports, but when the United States offered massive aid in return for bases and Brazilian entry into the war, Vargas joined the Allies. Brazil was the only country in South America to play an active part in the war. A **Brazilian Expeditionary Force**, 5000-strong, fought in Italy from 1944 until the end of the war; when it returned, the military High Command was able to exploit the renewed prestige of the army, forcing Vargas to stand down. It argued that the armed forces could hardly fight for democracy abroad and return home to a dictatorship and, in any case, after fifteen years a leadership change was overdue. In the election that followed in 1945, Vargas grudgingly endorsed the army general **Eurico Dutra**, who duly won.

JK and Brasília

Juscelino Kubitschek, "JK" to Brazilians, president from 1956 to 1961, proved just the man to fix Brazil's attention on the future rather than the past. "Fifty years in five!" was his election slogan, and his economic programme lived up to its ambitious billing. His term saw a spurt in growth rates that was the platform for the "economic miracle" of the next decade; the economic boom led to wider prosperity and renewed national confidence. Kubitschek drew on both in the flight of inspired imagination that led to **the building of Brasília**.

It could so easily have been an expensive disaster, a purpose-built capital miles from anywhere, the personal brainchild of a president anxious to make his mark. But Kubitschek implanted the idea in the national imagination by portraying it as a renewed statement of faith in the interior, a symbol of national integration and a better future for all Brazilians, not just those in the South. He brought it off with great panache, bringing in the extravagantly talented **Oscar Niemeyer**, whose brief was to come up with a revolutionary city layout and the architecture to go with it. Kubitschek spent almost every weekend on the huge building site that became the city, consulted on the smallest details and had the satisfaction of handing over to his successor, **Jânio Quadros**, in the newly inaugurated capital.

Military rule

At the time, the **military coup of 1964** was considered a temporary hiccup in Brazil's postwar democracy, but it lasted 21 years and left a very bitter taste. The coup itself, in the tradition of Brazilian coups, was swift and bloodless. On March 31, troops from Minas Gerais moved on Rio; when the commanders there refused to oppose them, the first in a line of generals, **Humberto Castelo Branco**, became president.

The military moved swiftly to dismantle democracy. Congress was dissolved, then reconvened with only two parties, an official government and an official opposition. The Peasant Leagues and trade unions were repressed, with many of their leaders tortured and imprisoned.

The political climate worsened steadily during the 1960s. An **urban guerrilla campaign** took off but it only served as an excuse for the hardliners to crack down even further. General **Emílio Garrastazú Médici**, leader of the hardliners, took over the presidency in 1969 and the worst period of military rule began. Torture became routine, censorship was strict and thousands were driven into exile: this dark chapter in Brazilian history lasted for five agonizing years, until Médici gave way to **Ernesto Geisel** in 1974.

The economic miracle

Despite the cold winds blowing on the political front, the Brazilian economy forged ahead from the mid-1960s to 1974, the years of the **economic miracle** – and the combination of high growth and low inflation indeed seemed miraculous to later governments. The military welcomed foreign investment, and the large pool of cheap but skilled labour was irresistible. Cities swelled, industry grew, and by the mid-1970s Brazil was the economic giant of South America, São Paulo state alone having a GNP higher than any South American country.

The problem, though, was uneven development. Even miraculous growth rates could not provide enough jobs for the hordes migrating to the cities, and the squalid **favelas** expanded even faster than the economy. The problem was worst in the Northeast and the Amazon, where industry was less developed, and drought combined with land conflict to push the people of the interior into the cities. The miracle years also saw the origins of the **debt crisis**, a millstone around the neck of the Brazilian economy in the 1980s and 1990s.

Anxious to set this new capital to work, international banks and South American military regimes fell over themselves in their eagerness to organize deals. The military needed money for a series of huge development projects that were central to its trickle-down economic policy, and a **nuclear power programme**. By the end of the 1970s the debt was at $50 billion; by 1990 it had risen to $120 billion, and the interest payments were crippling the economy.

The road to the New Republic

Soon debt, rising inflation and unemployment were turning the economy from a success story into a joke, and the military was further embarrassed by an unsavoury chain of corruption scandals. Slow though the process was, the return to democracy would have been delayed even longer had it not been for two events along the way: the **metalworkers' strikes** in São Paulo in 1977 and the mass **campaign for direct elections** in 1983–84.

The São Paulo strikes began in the car industry and soon spread throughout the industrial belt of São Paulo. Led by still illegal unions, and the charismatic young factory worker **Lula (Luís Inácio da Silva)**, the strikers had a tense stand-off with the army, until the military realized that having São Paulo on strike would be worse for the economy than conceding the right to free trade unions.

Reforms in the early 1980s lifted censorship, brought the exiles home and allowed normal political life to resume. But the military's control of Congress allowed them to pass a resolution that the president due to take office in 1985 would be elected not by direct vote, but by an electoral college, made up of congressmen and senators, where the military party had the advantage.

The democratic opposition responded with a counter-amendment proposing a direct election. It needed a two-thirds majority in Congress to be passed, and a campaign began for **diretas-já**, "elections now". The campaign culminated in huge rallies of over a million people in Rio and São Paulo; however, when the vote came in March 1984, the amendment just failed. The military still nominated a third of Senate seats, and this proved decisive.

The moment found the man in **Tancredo Neves**, who put himself forward as opposition candidate in the electoral college. By now it was clear what the public wanted, and Tancredo's unrivalled political skills enabled him to stitch together an alliance that included dissidents from the military's own party. In January 1985 he romped home in the electoral college, to great national rejoicing, and military rule came to an end. Tancredo proclaimed the civilian **Nova República** – the "New Republic".

Cardoso: stability and reform

Uniquely among modern Brazilian presidents, **Fernando Henrique Cardoso**, an ex-academic from São Paulo who became president in 1995, proved able and effective. He pushed through a privatization programme in the teeth of fierce nationalist opposition, cutting tariff barriers, opening up the economy to competition and making Brazil the dominant member of **Mercosul**, a regional trade organization which also includes Argentina, Uruguay and Paraguay, with Bolivia and Chile in the queue to join. During his first term the result was healthy growth, falling unemployment and low inflation, an achievement without precedent in modern Brazilian history. Politically, he steered a skilful middle course between dinosaurs of right and left, corrupt *caudilhos* and their patron–client politics on the one hand, and time-warped nationalists still clinging to protectionism and suspicious of the outside world on the other.

Cardoso's second term, which began in 1998, proved more difficult, however. The Asian financial collapse of that year brought down much of Latin America with it, including Brazil; there was a sharp recession for a year, and GDP growth during Cardoso's second term ran at an anaemic annual average of just under two percent, barely ahead of population growth. But despite devaluations of the real foreign investment kept coming and inflation remained low, an important break with the economic patterns of the 1980s and

1990s, and a sign that some at least of Cardoso's reforms were working.

Corruption, social inequality and regional imbalances still plagued Brazil, although growing public impatience was reflected in a newly aggressive and powerful federal prosecutors system, which started to take on powerful vested interests. Cardoso's reliance on a broad centrist coalition, however, limited his ability to deal with rural inequalities or really get to grips with environmental issues, and the public finances remained perennially in deficit because of a bloated public sector pensions system extraordinarily resistant to reform.

Lula: left turn?

"Historic" is an over-used word, but it is the only one to describe the **2002 election of Lula** to the presidency of Brazil, at the fourth attempt. It represented the final consolidation and maturing of Brazilian democracy, as the generation that had been tear-gassed by the military and opted for armed struggle suited up and became ministers – there are four ex-guerrilla ministers in the Lula government, and his right-hand man, **José Dirceu**, had plastic surgery in Cuba and lived underground for five years.

Lula is the first Brazilian president not to be a member of the country's elite, and the story of his life is extraordinary. Born in desperate poverty in the Pernambuco *sertão*, like millions of northeasterners he made the journey as a child to Sao Paulo, ten days on the back of a truck, and worked as a shoeshine boy before becoming a factory worker at a car plant.

He gradually rose to the leadership of the strike movement in the early 1980s and founded of the **Partido dos Trabalhadores** (Workers' Party), which allied the union movement to the liberal middle class and evolved into what is now the largest political party in Brazil. The charismatic Lula's victory, with over sixty percent of the popular vote, was crushing.

Lula's is a government of pragmatists with principles, inexperienced in government but competent and likely to learn fast. Although the general economic and international outlook is grim, there is scope – or at least hope – for finding resources for social programmes by cracking down hard on corruption and maladministration. And given that this government will need to borrow money abroad to keep the public finances going, it will quickly learn it has to reform the public sector if it wants to concentrate spending on reducing poverty. With that justification, and its roots in the union movement, it seems possible at the time of writing that Lula and the PT are well placed to push reform through.

It was a long twentieth century for Brazil, but as the country advances into the new millennium, Brazilians have good reason to extend their traditional optimism to fields other than the football pitch.

Books

The recent flood of books on the Amazon masks the fact that Brazil is not well covered by books in English. With some exceptions, good books on Brazil either tend to be fairly expensive or are out of print. Easily available paperbacks are given here, together with a selection of others that a good bookshop or library will have in stock or will be able to order.

Alex Bellos *Futebol: The Brazilian Way of Life* (Bloomsbury). Long overdue, accessible, literate and interesting analysis of Brazilian football, from early history to the present compulsive mixture of world-beating players on the pitch and equally world-beating levels of corruption and shenanigans off it. Thankfully written by a journalist rather than an academic; essential reading.

Sue Branford and Bernardo Kucinski *Politics Transformed: Lula and the Workers' Party in Brazil* (Latin America Bureau). An impassioned and easy-to-digest look at the rise of the PT, the most powerful and most representative socialist party in the Americas, charting its development out of trade union resistance to the military regime in São Paulo to the election of Lula as president in 2002.

Sue Branford and Jan Rocha *Cutting the Wire: The Story of the Landless Movement in Brazil* (Latin America Bureau). Written by journalists with long experience of Brazil, this book tells the story of one of the most remarkable popular movements of modern times, the MST – the gathering of Brazilian landless rural workers. A much needed book.

Darién J. Davis *Afro-Brazilians: Time for Recognition* (Minority Rights Group, UK). A valuable introduction to the role of blacks in Brazilian society. Scholarly, impassioned and essential reading for anyone wanting to understand the often contradictory nature of Brazilian racial ideology and politics.

Warren Dean *With Brandaxe and Firestorm* (California UP). Brilliant and very readable environmental history that tells the story of the almost complete destruction of the Mata Atlântica, the coastal rainforest of southern Brazil, from colonial times to the twentieth century.

Boris Fausto *A Concise History of Brazil* (Cambridge UP). The best single-volume introductory history of Brazil, written by an eminent historian from São Paulo. The author successfully demonstrates how Brazil has changed, both politically and socio-economically, despite being so often characterized by apparent historical inertia.

Claude Lévi-Strauss *Tristes Tropiques* (Picador o/p; Penguin). In the best book ever written about the country by a foreigner, the great French anthropologist describes his four years spent in 1930s Brazil. There are great descriptions of sojourns with Nambikwara and Tupi-Kawahib Indians, epic journeys and a remarkable eyewitness account of São Paulo exploding into a metropolis.

Richard Parker *Bodies, Pleasures and Passions* (Beacon Press, US). A provocative analysis of the erotic in Brazilian history and popular culture, written by an American anthropologist resident in Brazil. It offers fascinating insight into sexual behaviour, combining insider and outsider perspectives.

3.1

Rio de Janeiro and around

The citizens of the ten-million-strong city of **RIO DE JANEIRO** call it the *Cidade Marvilhosa* – and there can't be much argument about that. Rio sits on the southern shore of a landlocked harbour within the magnificent natural setting of Guanabara Bay. Extending for twenty kilometres along an alluvial strip, between an azure sea and jungle-clad mountains, the city's streets and buildings have been moulded around the foothills of the mountain range which provides its backdrop, while out in the bay there are innumerable rocky islands fringed with white sand. The panoramic view over Rio is breathtaking, and even the concrete skyscrapers that dominate the city's skyline add to the attraction.

Although riven by inequality, Rio de Janeiro has great style. Its international renown is bolstered by a series of symbols that rank as some of the greatest landmarks in the world: the **Corcovado** mountain supporting the great statue of Christ the Redeemer; the rounded incline of the **Sugar Loaf** mountain, standing at the entrance to the bay; and the famous sweep of **Copacabana beach**, probably the most notable length of sand on the planet. It's a setting enhanced by the annual, frenetic sensuality of **Carnaval**, an explosive celebration which – for many people – sums up Rio and her citizens, the **cariocas**. The major downside in a city given over to conspicuous consumption is the rapacious development that is engulfing Rio de Janeiro. As the rural poor, escaping drought and poverty in other regions of Brazil, flock to swell Rio's population, the city is being squeezed like a toothpaste tube between mountains and sea, pushing its human contents out along the coast in either direction. Rio's **favelas** cling precariously to the hillsides, and although not exclusive to the capital, these slums seem all the more harsh here because of the plenty and beauty surrounding them.

The **state of Rio de Janeiro**, surrounding the city, was established in 1975. Fairly small by Brazilian standards, it is both beautiful and accessible; it is possible to make easy trips either east along the **Costa do Sol** or west along the **Costa Verde**, taking in unspoilt beaches, which are washed by a relatively unpolluted ocean. **Inland** routes make a welcome change from the sands, especially the trip to **Petrópolis**, the nineteenth-century mountain retreat of Rio's aristocracy.

Some history

On January 1, 1502, a **Portuguese** captain, André Gonçalves, steered his craft into Guanabara Bay, thinking he was heading into the mouth of a great river. The city takes its name from this event – Rio de Janeiro means the "River of January". When **gold** was discovered in the neighbouring state of Minas Gerais in the 1690s, the city became the nerve and taxation centre for the gold trade, and the **sugar-cane** economy brought further wealth to Rio. The city's strategic importance also grew, and in 1763 it replaced Bahia (now Salvador) as Brazil's capital. By the eighteenth century, the majority of Rio's inhabitants were **African** slaves, and virtually nothing in Rio remained untouched by African customs, beliefs and behaviour – a state of affairs that clearly influences today's city, too, with its mixture of Afro-Brazilian music, spiritualist cults and cuisine. In March 1808, **Dom João VI** of Portugal arrived in Rio (see p.309), and became so enamoured of Brazil that he proclaimed it "The United Kingdom of Portugal, Brazil and the Algarves, of this side and the far side of the sea, and the Guinea Coast of Africa", with Rio as its capital. During Dom João's reign, the city's streets were paved and lit, and Rio acquired a new prosperity based on **coffee**. By the late nineteenth century, Rio started to develop as a modern city: trams and trains replaced sedans, the first sewerage system was inaugurated in 1864, and a tunnel was excavated opening the way to Copacabana, as people left the crowded centre and looked for new living space. During the **1930s** Rio enjoyed international renown, buttressed by Hollywood images and the patronage of the first-generation jet set. It became the nation's commercial centre, and a new wave of modernization swept the city, leaving little more than the Catholic churches as monuments to the past. Even the removal of the country's political administration to the new federal capital of Brasília in 1960 did nothing to discourage the developers. Today, with the centre rebuilt many times since colonial days, most interest lies not in Rio's buildings and monuments but firmly in the **beaches** to the south of the city.

Arrival and information

You're most likely to fly in to Rio or arrive by bus; the city's train station is now only used for commuter services. Be warned that opportunistic thieves are active at all points of arrival, so don't leave baggage unattended or valuables exposed.

By air

Rio de Janeiro is served by two airports. **Santos Dumont** (Ⓣ21/3814-7070) handles shuttle services to and from São Paulo, Brasília and Belo Horizonte, and is at the north end of the Parque de Flamengo, immediately east of Centro. Every 40 minutes an air-conditioned **executivo bus** ($2) will take you from here through

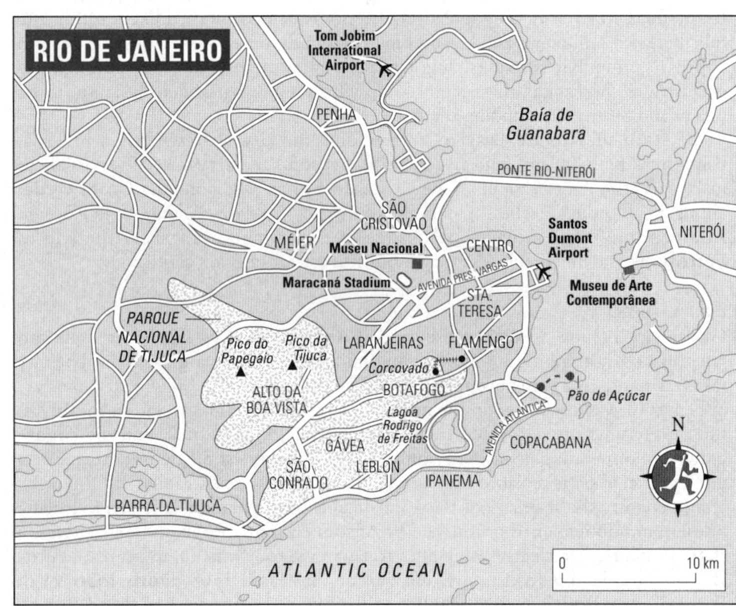

the Zona Sul, stopping wherever passengers want to get off along the beaches of Copacabana, Ipanema, Leblon and São Conrado. Ordinary **taxis** (yellow with a blue stripe) are readily available outside the terminal but beware of overcharging – the fare should amount to around $9 to Copacabana. A less stressful option is to purchase a voucher from one of the many radio-taxi stands within the terminal; you'll be charged a flat rate of around $14 to Copacabana. Alternatively, cross the pedestrian walkway in front of the airport terminal and catch an ordinary bus from Avenida Marechal Câmara: #438 to Ipanema and Leblon via Botafogo; #442 to Urca; #472 to Leme. For Copacabana, #484 goes from Avenida General Justo.

The Tom Jobim **international airport** (☎21/3398-4526), which serves most Brazilian destinations, lies 14km north of the city. If arriving from abroad, make sure that your passport is stamped and that you retain your immigration form, as failure to do so can cause problems come departure. In the arrivals hall, consult one of the official **tourist information** desks – Riotur, TurisRio or EMBRATUR. To reach your hotel, catch one of the air-conditioned **executivo buses** ($2), which run every half-hour between 5.20am and 11pm, either via Centro to Santos Dumont, or along the coast, via Centro, to Copacabana and on to São Conrado. Outside these hours, a **taxi** ride is the only alternative. Buy a ticket at either the Cootramo, Coopertramo or Transcoopass desks, near the arrivals gate, and give it to the driver at the taxi rank; to Flamengo costs about $15, Copacabana $17. Again, be wary of the ordinary taxis and don't accept a lift from one of the unofficial drivers hanging about in the airport.

Heading out to the international airport, ask your hotel to arrange for a fixed-fare taxi to pick you up, or take the air-conditioned bus which follows the Zona Sul coastline and can be picked up on Avenida Delfim Moreira (Leblon), Avenida Vieira Souto (Ipanema), Avenida Atlântica (Copacabana), Avenida Beira Mar (Flamengo) or on the Avenida Rio Branco in Centro – allow at least an hour from the beaches.

By bus

All major intercity and international bus services arrive at the **Novo Rio Rodoviária** (☎21/2291-5151), 3km north of Centro at the corner of Avenida Rodrigues Alves and Avenida Francisco Bicalho. The rodoviária has two sides, one for departures, the other for arrivals: once through the gate at arrivals, either grab a taxi ($4 to Centro, $8-15 to the Zona Sul), catch an *executivo* air-conditioned bus along the coast towards Copacabana and Leblon ($1.50; every half-hour from directly outside the arrivals side of the station), or cross the road to the ordinary bus terminal in Praça Hermes. Alternatively, head first for the **tourist office** desk (daily 8am–8pm) at the bottom of the stairs, in the middle of the foyer in front of the main exit – they'll help with hotels, and advise which buses to catch.

A more central terminal, the **Menezes Cortes Rodoviária** in Rua São José (☎21/2533-8819), handles services from some in-state towns such as Petrópolis and Teresópolis, but mainly operates buses to and from the suburbs and Zona Sul.

Leaving Rio by bus and travelling out of the state, it's best to book two days in advance; you can reach the rodoviária on bus #104 from Centro, #127 or #128 from Copacabana, and #456, #171 or #172 from Flamengo.

Information

Information about Rio itself is available from **Riotur**, which distributes maps and brochures and has a helpful English-speaking telephone information service Alô Rio (daily 8am–8pm; ☎0800/707-1808). Riotur's main office is in Centro at Rua da Assembléia 10 (Mon–Fri 9am–6pm; ☎21/3217-7575), and it also has a branch in Copacabana at Av Princesa Isabel 18 (daily 8am–8pm). Most of Riotur's information can also be picked up at their booths at the rodoviária (6am–midnight) and

Galeão and Santos Dumont airports (6am–midnight). Information about the state of Rio is available from **TurisRio**, at Rua da Assembléia 10 (☎21/3215-0011) and the most basic information about the rest of Brazil from **EMBRATUR**, also in Centro at Rua Uruguaina 174 (Mon–Fri 9am–6pm; ☎21/509-6017).

City transport

Most places can be reached cheaply by *Metrô*, bus or taxi, or a combination of these, while for getting about the state you might want to rent a car – though driving in the city itself is not recommended unless you have nerves of steel.

The safest and most comfortable way to travel is by using Rio's **Metrô** system (Mon–Sat 6am–11pm). There are just two lines: **Linha 1** runs from central Copacabana (Siqueira Campos station), north through Centro and then out to the Sãens Pena station in the *bairro* of Maracanã; **Linha 2** comes in from Maria de Graça, to the north of the city, via the Maracanã stadium, and meets Linha 1 at Estação Central, by Dom Pedro II train station. The system is well designed and efficient, the stations bright, cool, clean and secure, and the trains gently air conditioned. Tickets are sold as singles (*ida*; 50¢), returns (*duplo*; $1) or ten-journey tickets (*dez*; $5), which save time, but cost the same and can't be shared.

While it's true that some of Rio's **bus** drivers have a somewhat erratic driving style – to say the least – it's well worth mastering the system: with over three hundred routes and six thousand buses, you never have to wait more than a few moments for a bus, they run till midnight and it's not that easy to get lost. **Numbers** and **destinations** are clearly marked on the front of buses, and there are plaques at the front and by the entrance detailing the route. You get on at the back, pay the seated conductor (the price is on a card behind his head) and then push through the turnstile and find yourself a seat.

Taxis in Rio come in two varieties: **yellow** with a blue stripe which cruise the streets; or the larger, more comfortable **radio cabs**, white and with a red and yellow stripe, ordered by phone. Both have meters and, unless you have prepaid at the airport, you should insist that they are activated, and check that it has been cleared after the last fare. The flag, or *bandeira*, over the meter denotes the tariff. Normally this will read "1", but after 10pm, and on Sundays, holidays and throughout December, you have to pay twenty percent more; then the *bandeira* will read "2".

From Praça XV de Novembro **ferries** transport passengers across Guanabara Bay to the city of Niterói (see p.341). Ferries are cheap and the view of Rio they afford is well worth the effort. The thirty-minute crossings to Niterói are very frequent and cost 50¢; just turn up and buy a ticket. The CONERJ company ferries (Companhia de Navegação do Estado de Rio de Janeiro; ☎21/2533-6661) run Monday to Saturday, every fifteen minutes from 6am to 11pm; Sunday and public holidays, every thirty minutes from 7am to 11pm. Also from Praça XV de Novembro, Transtur (☎21/2533-4343) operates **hydrofoils** to Niterói every fifteen minutes from 6.35am to 9pm; the journey takes ten minutes and costs $2.

Rio's last remaining electric **trams**, the *bondes* (pronounced "bonjis"), climb from near Largo Carioca, across the eighteenth-century Aqueduto da Carioca, to the inner suburb of Santa Teresa and on to Dois Irmãos. Two lines run every fifteen minutes between 5am and midnight: the one for Dois Irmãos permits you to see more of Santa Teresa; the other line terminates at Largo do Guimarães. The trams still serve their original purpose of transporting locals, and haven't yet become a tourist service. The views of Rio are excellent, but beware of the young men who jump onto the tram and attempt to relieve you of your possessions.

Accommodation

December to February is **high season**, so if you arrive then without an advance booking, make one through a tourist office. Prices rise particularly steeply over Carnaval, when accommodation is hard to find. During low season, hotels usually lower their prices by around thirty percent. There is often keen competition for tourists and you should be able to find a reasonable double room for $30–50, normally with air conditioning. The highest concentration of budget places is in Catete, but reasonably priced accommodation can be found just about anywhere.

There are some excellent **hostels** in Botafogo, Copacabana and Ipanema (see below); remember, however, that the universities are on holiday between December and March, when these places will be packed out. For **apartments**, try *Rio Star Imóveis Ltda* in Copacabana (Ⓣ21/3275-8393) or Rio Flat Service (Ⓣ21/3512-9922), which has apartment buildings in Copacabana, Leblon and Lagoa – from $50 a day for a studio or one-bedroom apartment, with swimming pool. If you want to be in Ipanema, call Ipanema Sweet (Ⓣ21/3239-1819), who has one- and two-bedroom apartments near the beach from $60 per day.

The city centre: Centro and Lapa

Ambassador Rua Senador Dantas 25, Centro Ⓣ21/2215-2910, Ⓔambassador@uol.com.br. Popular with Brazilian business executives, although this hotel has seen better days. Offers high standards of comfort in the heart of Cinelândia, near the Biblioteca Nacional. ❺

Bragança Av Mem de Sá 117, Lapa Ⓣ21/2242-8116, Ⓔhotelbraganca@rj.sol.com.br. Busy, well-equipped place where rooms come with *frigobar*, telephones and TV. Ideally situated near Lapa's nightlife. ❺

Guanabara Palace Av Presidente Vargas 392, Centro Ⓣ21/2518-0333, Ⓦwww.windsorhoteis.com.br. The only luxury hotel in the centre, the recently renovated *Guanabara Palace* is the haunt of expense-account visitors. Although utterly soulless, it has the added bonus of a pool. ❼

Marajó Rua São Joaquim da Silva 99, Lapa Ⓣ21/2224-4134. Comfy beds and efficient showers make this probably the best choice in the area. Also has some singles for around $7. ❸

Glória, Catete, Flamengo and Botafogo

Chave do Rio Hostel Rua General Dionísio 63, Botafogo Ⓣ21/2286-0303, Ⓦwww.riohostel.com.br. Comfortable and friendly Hostelling International–associated hostel in a beautiful house just off Voluntaríos da Patria in Botafogo. Beds, in dorms, go for $10 per head (including breakfast), and not all rooms are air conditioned. There are cooking and laundry facilities available as well. Book ahead at peak periods.

Flórida Rua Ferreira Viana 81, Flamengo Ⓣ21/2555-6000, Ⓦwww.windsorhoteis.com.br. Highly recommended for its spacious, modern rooms and excellent facilities, including a pool and free Internet usage. Popular with Brazilian business travellers, the hotel offers reduced rates at weekends. ❻

Glória Rua do Russel 632, Glória Ⓣ21/2555-7272, Ⓦwww.hotelgloriario.com.br. Built in the 1920s, this is one of Rio's most traditional hotels. Rooms are spacious and most offer tremendous views, and there are two excellent pools and a fine restaurant. By far the best hotel within easy reach of downtown, the *Glória* is just 15min from Ipanema by taxi. Room rates vary enormously, with heavy discounts often available. ❼

Imperial Rua do Catete 186, Catete Ⓣ21/2556-5212, Ⓦwww.imperialhotel.com.br. Spacious and comfy rooms in an attractive, renovated 1880s building, well located near to both the *Metrô* station and park. There's also parking and a decent pool, unusual for a hotel in this price category. ❺

Real Rua Real Grandeza 122, Botafogo Ⓣ21/2579-3863. No-frills but good value hotel in an area that's a bit of a trek from the *Metrô* (convenient for buses), though close to good restaurants. Rooms are clean if rather dilapidated, but all have air conditioning. ❺

Turístico Ladeira da Glória 30, Glória Ⓣ21/2557-7698. From the Glória *Metrô* station, climb up round to the right of the Igreja da Glória and through the Largo da Glória to reach this hotel. Friendly, clean and cheap, with spacious, air-conditioned rooms which come with bath and balconies. Though a bit overpriced, it's a firm favourite with backpackers and usually busy, so try and book ahead. Highly recommended. ❺

Copacabana, Leme and Ipanema

Acapulco Copacabana Rua Gustavo Sampaio 854, Leme ⓣ21/2275-0022, ⓦwww.acapulcopacabanahotel.com.br. Very comfortable hotel in a quiet location handy for both Copacabana and Ipanema. Rooms are spacious and well decorated and some of the balconies even manage a beach view. Highly recommended. ❻

Arpoador Inn Rua Francisco Otaviano 177, Arpoador ⓣ21/2523-0060, ⓔarpoador@unisys.com.br. In a peaceful location on the edge of Ipanema (bordering Copacabana), this popular hotel is reasonable for the area, but room rates don't fluctuate much during the year and in low season the basic rooms (some sleeping three people) may seem overpriced. You'll pay double for a beachfront room. ❻

Che Lagarto Youth Hostel Rua Barão de Jaguaripe 208, Ipanema ⓣ21/2247-4582, ⓦwww.chelagarto.com. In a great location just a block from the Lagoa and fifteen minutes' walk from Ipanema beach, with helpful staff, its own bar and occasional live music. Facilities include laundry, a kitchen and Internet access. $13 per person (including breakfast) in a dorm which sleeps four.

Copacabana Chalet Hostel Rua Pompeu Loureiro 99, Copacabana ⓣ21/2236-0047, ⓦwww.geocities.com/thetropics/cabana/7617. Just a short walk from the beach, this is a long-established, small and extremely welcoming hostel. Always popular, so advance booking at peak holiday periods is essential. $8 per head in six-bed dorms.

Copacabana Palace Av Atlântica 1702, Copacabana ⓣ21/2548-7070, ⓦwww.copacabanapalace.com.br. A glorious Art Deco landmark that, despite Copacabana's general decline, remains a firm favourite. Although every possible facility is on offer, apart from the large pool in a central courtyard, there's a curious lack of communal areas. All in all, this is a great place to end a trip to Brazil if you can possibly afford it. ❾

Copacabana Praia Hostel Rua Tenente Marones de Gusmão 85, Copacabana ⓣ21/22547-5422, ⓦwww.wcenter.com.br/copapraia. Set several blocks back from the beach, off Rua Figueiredo Magalhães. This efficiently run but rather institutional hostel, by far the largest in Rio, charges $8 per head in a six-bed dorm. Rooms sleeping two to four people (including a private bathroom and basic cooking facilities) are also available. ❺

Hostel Ipanema Rua Barão da Torre 175, Casa 14, Ipanema ⓣ21/2268-0565, ⓔjustfly@justfly.com.br. The most basic of Rio's hostels, three blocks from the beach in a quiet area, but with laundry and bike rental facilities. The hostel's owner also runs Rio's most reliable hang-gliding operation (see p.335) and offers discounts to hostel guests. $10 per person in dorms sleeping two to six people. Airport pick-up can be arranged.

Ipanema Plaza Rua Farme de Amoedo 34, Ipanema ⓣ21/3687-2000, ⓦwww.ipanemaplazahotel.com. Excellent location in the middle of Ipanema. This discreetly luxurious hotel is small enough that it provides individual attention. Rooms and suites are well appointed and there's a small rooftop pool with breathtaking views towards the beach. ❾

Praia Leme Av Atlântica 866, Leme ⓣ21/2275-3322. This cosy two-storey hotel offers the best value for a beachfront location. Owing to its popularity an advance reservation is highly recommended. ❻

Santa Clara Rua Décio Vilares 316, Copacabana ⓣ21/2256-2650, ⓦwww.hotelsantaclara.com.br. This cosy, well-maintained hotel is excellent value and very friendly. Situated in a tranquil location five blocks from the beach, and close to the Túnel Velho leading to Botafogo's restaurants and museums. ❺

São Marco Rua Visconde de Pirajá 524, Ipanema ⓣ21/2540-5032. A good deal for its location, on the main shopping street just a few minutes from the beach. Although air conditioned, rooms are small and basic and there's quite a lot of street noise. ❻

Vermont Rua Visconde de Pirajá 254, Ipanema ⓣ21/2522-0057. Simple, though perfectly adequate, rooms (including some that sleep three people), in a central location. The rooms are air conditioned but not likely to suit those bothered by street noise. ❻

The City

Though enormous, Rio is easily broken down for visitors into three major sectors. While the **city centre** features the financial district that crowds the last vestiges of the metropolis's colonial past, the **Zona Sul**, or southern sector, contains its legendary beaches as well as Sugerloaf Mountain. To the north, the largely run-down **Zona Norte** holds little for the visitor beyond the Museu Nacional, and can easily be covered in a day. The *bairro* of **Santa Teresa** and the celebrated Christ the Redeemer stature atop **Corcovado** each easily repay the effort of a day-trip.

Central Rio

Much of historical Rio is concentrated in **Centro**, with pockets of interest, too, in the neighbouring **Saúde** and **Lapa** quarters of the city. You'll find you can tour the centre fairly easily on foot, yet it's worth noting that it's not the most exciting city in Brazil to explore. Lots of the old historical squares, streets and buildings disappeared in the twentieth century under a torrent of redevelopment, and fighting your way through the traffic – the reason many of the streets were widened in the first place – can be quite a daunting prospect. However, although a lot of what remains is decidedly low-key, there are enough churches and interesting museums to keep anybody happy for a day or two.

Praça XV de Novembro and around

PRAÇA XV DE NOVEMBRO is the obvious place to start. Once the hub of Rio's social and political life, it takes its name from the day (November 15) in 1899 when Marechal Deodoro de Fonseca, the first president, proclaimed the Republic of Brazil. One of Rio's oldest **markets** is held here on Thursday and Friday (8am–6pm), its stalls packed with typical foods, handicrafts and ceramics, and there are paintings and prints for sale, as well as a brisk trade in stamps and coins.

Built in 1743, the imposing **Paço Imperial** (Tues–Sun noon–6.30pm; free) has served variously as the Governor's Palace, the headquarters of the Portuguese government in Brazil until 1791 and, later, of the Department of Post and Telegraph. It was here, in 1808, that the Portuguese monarch, Dom João VI, established his court in Brazil (later shifting to the Palácio da Quinta da Boa Vista, now the Museu Nacional), and the building continued to be used for royal receptions and special occasions: on May 13, 1888, Princess Isabel proclaimed the end of slavery in Brazil from here. Today, the building is a popular meeting point, and its first floor houses the Biblioteca Paulo Santos, which specializes in books and journals on Portuguese and Brazilian architecture. On the northern side of the square, the **Arco de Teles**, named after the judge and landowner who ordered its construction on the site of the old *pelourinho* (pillory) in around 1755, links the Travessa do Comércio to the Rua Ouvidor. At the back of Praça XV de Novembro, where Rua VII de Setembro meets Rua I de Março, the **Igreja de Nossa Senhora do Carmo da Antigá Sé** (Mon–Fri 9am–5pm) served until 1980 as Rio's cathedral. Building started in 1749 and continued right into the twentieth century as structural collapse and financial difficulties necessitated several delays. Inside, the high altar is detailed in silver and boasts a beautiful work by the painter Antônio Parreires. Below, in the **crypt**, rest the supposed remains of Pedro Alvares Cabral, Portuguese discoverer of Brazil; in actual fact, he was almost certainly laid to rest in Santarem in Portugal.

Along Rua I de Março

Heading up **RUA I DE MARÇO** from the *praça*, you'll pass the late eighteenth-century **Igreja da Ordem Terceira do Monte do Carmo** (Mon–Fri 8am–3.30pm, Sat 8am–noon), whose seven altars each bear an image symbolizing a moment from the Passion of Christ. The church and adjacent convent are linked by a small public chapel, dedicated to Our Lady of the Cape of Good Hope, and decorated in *azulejos* tiling.

A little further along Rua I de Março is the museum and church of **Santa Cruz dos Militares** (Mon–Fri 9am–3pm), its name hinting at its curious history. In 1628, a number of army officers organized the construction of the first church here, on the site of an early fort. It was used for the funerals of serving officers until, in 1703, the Catholic Church attempted to take over control of the building. The proposal met stiff resistance, and it was only in 1716 that the Fathers of the Church of São Sebastião, which had become severely dilapidated, succeeded in installing themselves in Santa Cruz. Sadly, they were no more successful in the maintenance of this church, either, and by 1760 it had been reduced to a state of ruin – only

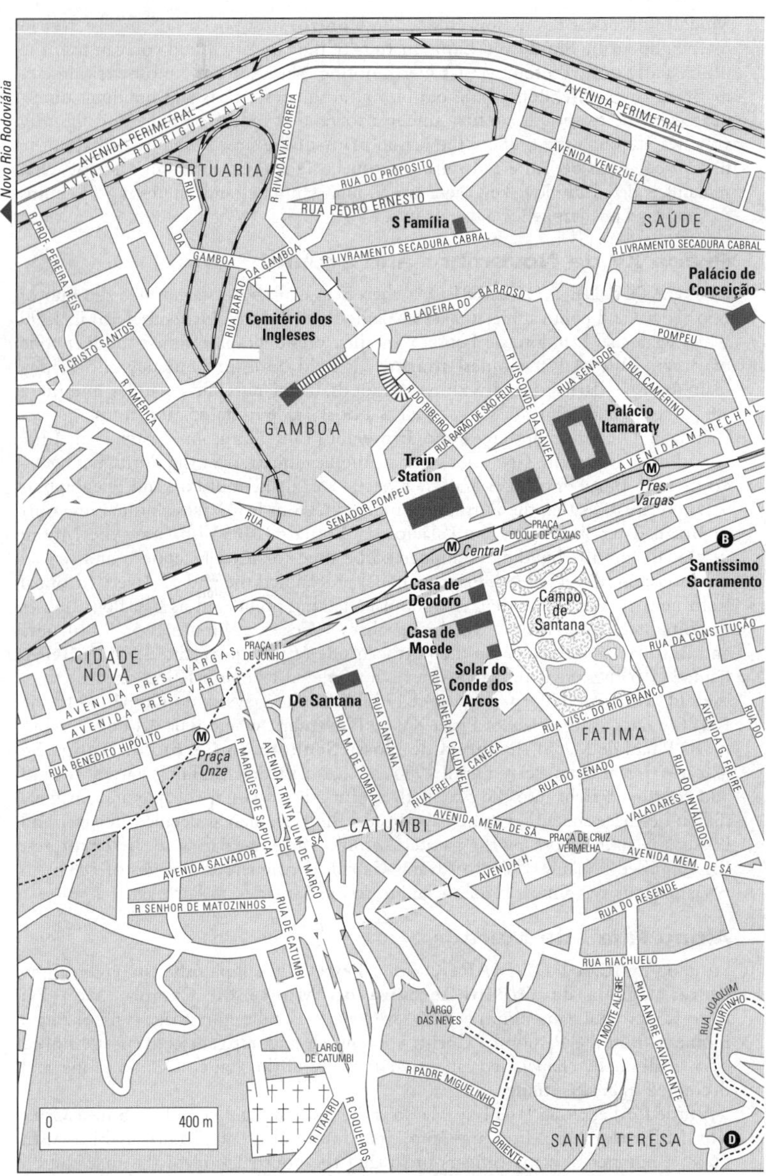

reversed when army officers again took control of the reconstruction work in 1780, completing the granite and marble building that survives today.

From São Bento to the Largo da Carioca

Heading north, on the continuation of Rua I de Março, the Ladeira de São Bento leads to the **IGREJA E MOSTEIRO DE SÃO BENTO** (Mon–Fri 8–11am &

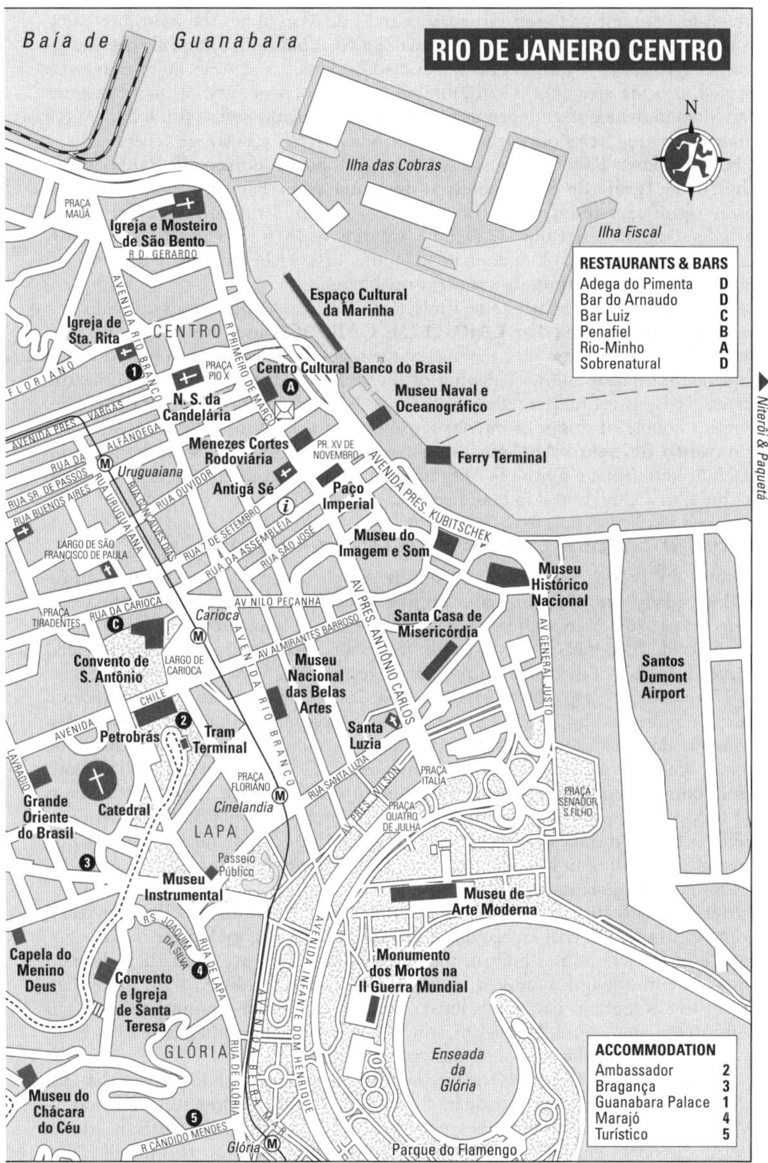

2.30–5.30pm, Sat from 7.15am, Sun from 8.15am). The monastery was founded by Benedictine monks, and building started in 1633, finishing nine years later. The facade displays a pleasing simplicity, its twin towers culminating in pyramid-shaped spires, while the interior is richly adorned. The altars and walls are covered by images of saints, and there are statues representing various popes and bishops, work executed by the deft hand of Mestre Valentim. The late seventeenth-century panels and paintings are valuable examples of colonial art.

Cross Avenida Presidente Vargas and continue down **Rua Uruguaiana**. In the streets to your left (between Uruguaiana and I de Março) lies the most interesting concentration of shops in Rio, in the area known as **Saara**. Traditionally the cheapest place to shop, it was originally peopled by Jewish and Arab merchants, who moved into the area after a ban prohibiting their residence within the city limits was lifted in the eighteenth century. In the maze of narrow streets you'll find everything from basic items of beachware and handicrafts to expensive jewellery.

Halfway down Rua Uruguaiana is **Largo de São Francisco de Paula**, whose church, the **Igreja de São Francisco de Paula** (Mon–Fri 9am–1pm), has hosted some significant moments in Brazil's history. Behind the monumental carved wooden entrance door the "Te Deum" was sung in 1816 to celebrate Brazil's promotion from colony to kingdom; in 1831, the mass celebrating the "Swearing-in" of the Brazilian Constitution was performed here.

From Largo de São Francisco de Paula, Rua Ramalho Ortigão leads the short distance to **Rua Carioca**. The **LARGO DE CARIOCA** itself has undergone considerable transformation since the turn of the nineteenth century, many of its buildings demolished to allow widening of the square and the improving of nearby streets. Today street traders selling leather goods dominate the centre of the square, while a couple of things of interest remain, most notably the cloistered **Igreja e Convento de Santo Antônio** (Mon–Sat 2–5pm). Known as St Anthony of the Rich (to differentiate it from St Anthony of the Poor, located elsewhere in the city), it's the oldest church in Rio built between 1608 and 1620.

From the Nova Catedral to Praça Floriano

Behind the Largo da Carioca, the unmistakeable shape of the **NOVA CATEDRAL** (daily 7am–5.30pm) rises up like some futuristic teepee. Built between 1964 and 1976, it's an impressive piece of modern architecture and a considerable engineering feat, whatever you think of the style. Resembling the blunt-topped Mayan pyramids of the Mexican Yucatán, the cathedral is 83m high with a diameter of 104m and has a capacity of 25,000 people. Inside, it feels vast, a remarkable sense of space enhanced by the absence of supporting columns. Four huge stained-glass windows dominate, each measuring 20m by 60m and corresponding to a symbolic colour scheme – ecclesiastical green, saintly red, Catholic blue and apostolic yellow. From outside, you'll be able to see the **Aqueduto da Carioca**, which carries trams up to Santa Teresa, the beautiful *bairro* on the hill opposite (see p.328); the tram terminal is between the cathedral and the Largo da Carioca, behind what is certainly the ugliest building in Rio, the glass, steel and concrete hulk that is the headquarters of Petrobrás, the state oil company.

Along Avenida República de Chile, and right down **Avenida Rio Branco**, you'll come to Praça Marechal Floriano and the area known as **Cinelândia**, named after long-gone movie houses built in the 1930s. Old photos of Avenida Rio Branco show its entire length bordered by Neoclassical-style buildings of no more than three storeys high, its pavements lined with trees, and with a promenade that ran right down the centre. Nowadays, however, the once graceful avenue has been swamped by ugly office buildings and traffic pollution.

The **PRAÇA FLORIANO** is the one section of Avenida Rio Branco that still impresses. In the centre of the square is a bust of **Getúlio Vargas**, still anonymously decorated with flowers on the anniversary of the ex-dictator's birthday, March 19. At the north end of the square the **Teatro Municipal**, opened in 1909, was modelled on the Paris Opera – all granite, marble and bronze, with a foyer decorated in the white and gold characteristic of Louis XV style. The theatre has a decent restaurant and bar, the *Café do Teatro* (Mon–Fri 11am–4pm), which is richly adorned with elaborate Assyrian-inspired mosaics.

On the opposite side of the road, the **Museu Nacional das Belas Artes** (Tues–Fri 10am–6pm, Sat & Sun 2–6pm; $2.50, Sun free) is a grandiose construction built in 1908 to imitate the Louvre in Paris. The European collection includes Boudin, Tournay and Franz Post amongst many others, but it's the **Brazilian collection** that is of most interest. The last building of note on the Praça Floriano is the **Biblioteca Nacional** (Mon–Fri 9am–8pm, Sat 9am–3pm), whose stairway was decorated by some of the most important artistic names of the nineteenth century, including Modesto Brocas, Eliseu Visconti, Rodolfo Amoedo and Henrique Bernadelli.

Lapa and around

Continuing south, Avenida Rio Branco passes Praça Mahatma Gandhi, which borders the **Passeio Público** park (daily 7.30am–9pm), well into **LAPA** *bairro*. A little past its best, and neglected by the authorities these days, the park is, nevertheless, a green oasis away from the hustle and bustle of the city. Opened in 1783, it was designed in part by Mestre Valentim, Brazil's most important late eighteenth-century sculptor, its trees providing shade for busts of famous figures from the city's history – including Mestre Valentim de Fonseca e Silva himself.

The rest of **Lapa** has much the same faded charm as the park, though it would be wise not to wander the streets unaccompanied at night. From Lapa you can walk east to the Avenida Beira Mar and the glass and concrete **Museu de Arte Moderna** (Tues–Fri noon–5.30pm, Sat & Sun noon–6.30pm; $2.50; Ⓦwww.mamrio.com.br). The museum's collection was devastated by a fire in 1978 and only reopened in 1990 following restoration. The permanent collection is of little artistic significance, but the museum hosts visiting exhibitions, which are occasionally worth checking out.

The nearby **Museu Histórico Nacional** (Tues–Fri 10am–5.30pm, Sat & Sun 2–6pm; $1.50, free Sun; Ⓦwww.museuhistoriconacional.com.br) is uncomfortably located in the shadow of the Presidente Kubitschek flyover that runs into the Parque do Flamengo. The large **collection** contains some pieces of great value – from furniture to nineteenth-century firearms and locomotives – but it's not very well presented. Nevertheless, the displays on the second floor, a documentation of Brazilian history since 1500, make this museum a must.

Zona Norte

The parts of the **ZONA NORTE** you'll have seen on the way in from the transport terminals aren't very enticing, and they're a fair reflection of the general tenor of northern Rio. But well worth a visit is the **Museu Nacional** in the Quinta da Boa Vista, to the immediate northwest of Centro, which you reach by *Metrô* (get off at Estação São Cristovão) or by bus #472, #474 or #475 from Copacabana or Flamengo, or #262 from Praça Mauá.

The Quinta da Boa Vista

The area covered by the **QUINTA DA BOA VISTA** (daily 7am–6pm) was once incorporated in a *sesmaria* held by the Society of Jesus in the sixteenth and seventeenth centuries. Long used the area as a sugar plantation, in 1808 it became a country seat of the Portuguese royal family. The park, with its wide open expanses of greenery, tree-lined avenues, lakes, sports areas and games tables, is an excellent place for a stroll, though weekends can get very crowded.

In the centre of the park, on a small hill, stands the imposing Neoclassical structure of the **Museu Nacional** (Tues–Sun 10am–4pm; Ⓦacd.ufrj.br/museu; $1.50), certainly one of the most important scientific institutions in Brazil. Its **archeological** section deals with the human history of Latin America. In the Brazilian room, exhibits of Tupi-Guarani and Marajó ceramics lead on to the indigenous **ethnographical** section, uniting pieces collected from the numerous tribes that once populated Brazil. The genocidal practices of Brazil's European settlers, together with the ravages of disease, reduced the indigenous population from an estimated six million in 1500 to the present-day total of less than two hundred thousand. The ethnology section has a room dedicated to Brazilian folklore, centred on an exhibition of the ancient Afro- and Indo-Brazilian cults that still play an important role in modern Brazilian society.

Santa Teresa and the Corcovado

Before you hit the beaches of the Zona Sul, two of the most pleasant city excursions are to *bairros* to the southwest of Centro. **SANTA TERESA**, a leafy *bairro* composed of labyrinthine, cobbled streets and steps (*ladeiras*), with stupendous vistas of the city and bay below, makes a refreshing contrast to the city centre. Although it clings to the side of a hill, Santa Teresa is no *favela*: it's a slightly dishevelled residential area dominated by the early nineteenth-century mansions and walled gardens of a prosperous community that still enjoys something of a Bohemian reputation. In recent years, it has developed into an important artistic centre, and twice a year (the last weekend in May and November), about a hundred artists open their studios, offering the public an opportunity to buy or simply to look.

Trams run from Centro, from the terminal behind the massive Petrobrás building, up to Santa Teresa. They take you across the mid-eighteenth-century **Arcos da Lapa**, a monumental Roman-style aqueduct, high over Lapa. As you climb, the panoramic view of Guanabara Bay drifts in and out of view between the trees that line the streets. On your right, you'll pass the **Bar do Arnaudo** (see p.336), a traditional meeting place of artists and intellectuals; when the tram reaches the terminus at the top, you can stay on (and pay again) to descend for something to eat. From here, it's an enjoyable ten-minute walk downhill to the **Museu Chácara do Céu** (daily except Tues 1–5pm; 70¢) at Rua Murtinho Nobre 93, in a modernist stone building set in its own grounds – one of Rio's better museums. It holds a good, eclectic collection twentieth-century Brazilian and European art, its displays regularly changing. A pathway links the museum to the **Parque das Ruínas** (Wed–Fri & Sat 10am–10pm, Sun 10am–5pm), an attractive public garden containing the ruins of a mansion that was once home to a Brazilian heiress around whom artists and intellectuals gathered in the first half of the twentieth century. After her death in 1946, the mansion was allowed to fall into disrepair, but in the 1990s it was partially renovated as a cultural centre, and today houses art exhibitions. There's also a pleasant café and a small stage where jazz concerts are held most Thursday evenings.

The most famous of all images of Rio de Janeiro is that of the vast statue of **Christ the Redeemer** gazing across the bay from the **CORCOVADO** ("hunchback") hill, arms outstretched in welcome, or as if preparing for a dive into the waters below. The **statue** (daily 8.30am–7pm), 30m high and weighing over 1000 metric tons, was first planned for completion in 1922 as part of Brazil's centenary independence celebrations. In fact, it wasn't finished until nine years later. The French sculptor Paul Landowski was responsible for the head and hands, and the rest was erected by the engineers Heitor Silva Costa and Pedro Viana. In clear weather, fear no anticlimax: climbing to the statue is a stunning experience by day, and nothing short of miraculous at night. In daylight the whole of Rio and Guanabara Bay is laid out before you; after dark, the floodlit statue can be seen from everywhere in the Zona Sul.

All major hotels organize **excursions** to the Corcovado. Alternatively, the easiest way to get there yourself is by **taxi** – about $7 from the Zona Sul, a little more from Centro. You can also **drive** up to a car park near the top if you wish, but if you want to **walk** go in a group, as reports of assaults and robberies are becoming ever more frequent. However you choose to get there, keep an eye on the weather before setting out: what ought to be one of Rio's highlights can turn into a great disappointment if the Corcovado is shrouded in cloud.

Zona Sul

From Rio's Bay of Guanabara to the Bay of Sepetiba, to the west, there are approximately 90km of sandy **beaches**. Uniquely, Rio's identity is closely linked to the beaches of **ZONA SUL**, which shape the social life of all the city's inhabitants, who use them as a source of recreation and inspiration. For many, the beach provides a source of livelihood, and a sizeable service industry has developed, providing for the needs of those who regard the beach as a social environment – as significant, say, as the pub is in England.

The most renowned of the beaches, **Copacabana**, was originally an isolated area, cut off from the city by mountains, until 1892 when the Túnel Velho link with **Botafogo** was inaugurated. The open sea and strong waves soon attracted beachgoers, though Copacabana remained a quiet, sparsely populated *bairro* until the splendid Neoclassical *Copacabana Palace Hotel* opened its doors, its famous guests publicizing the beach and alerting enterprising souls to the commercial potential of the area. Rapid growth followed and a landfill project was undertaken, along which the two-lane **Avenida Atlântica** now runs.

Prior to Copacabana's rise, it was the beaches of **Guanabara Bay** – **Flamengo**, Botafogo, **Urca** and **Vermelha** – that were the most sought after. Today, the most fashionable beaches are those of **Ipanema** and **Leblon**, residential areas where the young, wealthy and beautiful have only to cross the road to flaunt their tans.

The beaches of Rio: some warnings

• Many of the beaches are **dangerous**. The sea bed falls sharply away, the waves are strong, and currents can pull you down the beach. Mark your spot well before entering the water, or you'll find yourself emerging from a paddle twenty or thirty metres from where you started – which, when the beaches are packed at weekends, can cause considerable problems when it comes to relocating your towel and coconut oil. Copacabana is particularly dangerous, even for strong swimmers. However, the beaches are well served by **lifeguards**, whose posts are marked by a white flag with a red cross; a **red flag** indicates that bathing is prohibited.

• **Pollution** is another problem to bear in mind. Although much has been done in recent years to clean up Guanabara Bay, it is still not safe to swim in the water from Flamengo or Botafogo beaches. While usually the water beyond the bay at Copacabana and Ipanema is clean, there are times when it and the beaches themselves are not, especially following a prolonged period of heavy summer rain when the city's strained drainage system is unable to cope. Unfortunately, these periods are increasingly common – if you've chosen Rio essentially as a beach vacation, you may well be in for a major disappointment.

• Giving your passport, money and **valuables** the chance of a sun tan, rather than leaving them in the hotel safe, is madness. Take only the clothes and money that you'll need; it's quite acceptable to use public transport while dressed for the beach. Don't be caught out either by the young lad who approaches you from one side, distracting your attention with some request, while his mate approaches from the other side and whips your bag: it's the most common and efficient method of relieving you of things you shouldn't have brought with you in the first place.

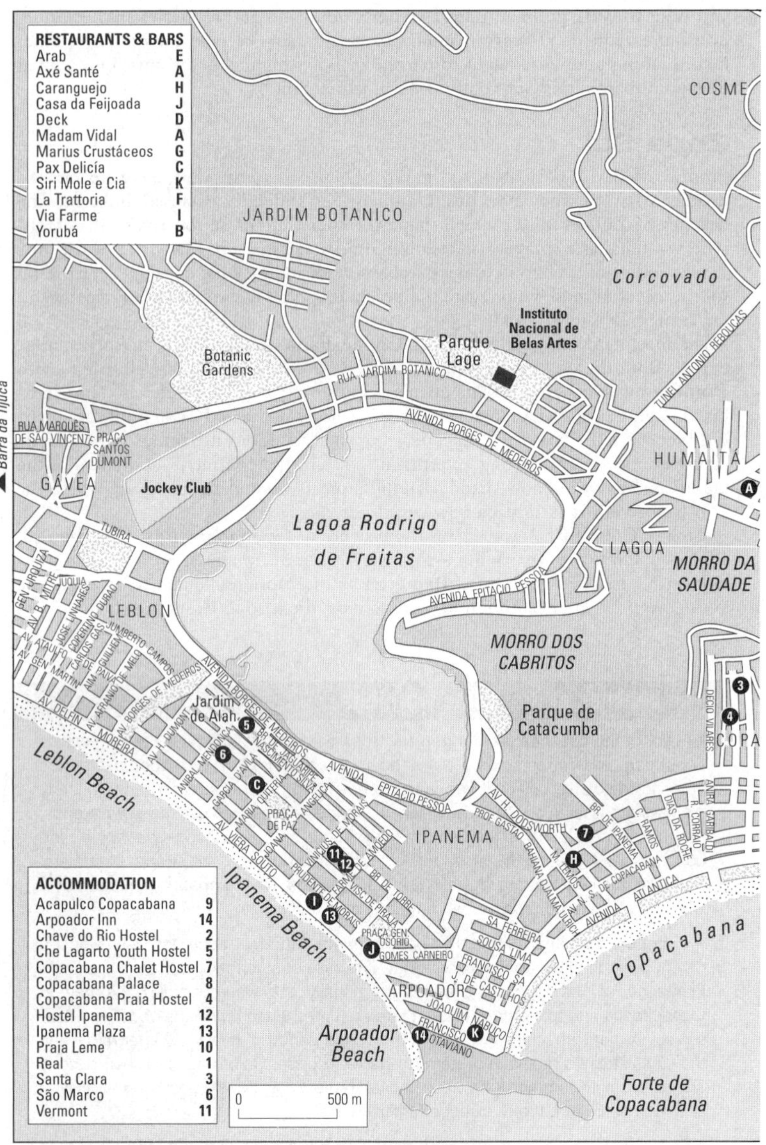

Glória, Catete and Flamengo

The nearest beach to the city centre is at **FLAMENGO**, and although it's not the best in Rio you might end up using it more than you think, since the neighbouring *bairros*, **CATETE** and **GLÓRIA**, are useful and cheap **places to stay** (see p.321). The streets away from the beach – especially around Largo do Machado and along

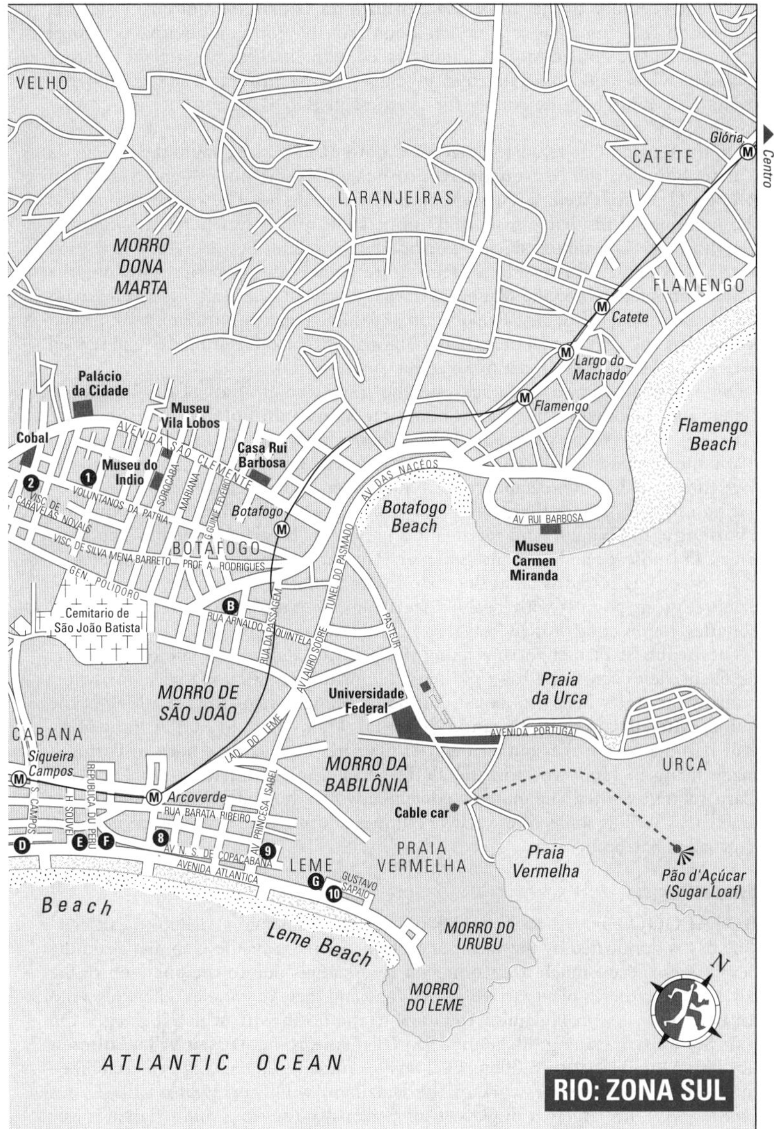

Rua do Catete – are full of inexpensive hotels, and there's a pleasant atmosphere to this part of town. Busy during the day, the tree-lined streets are alive at night with residents eating in the local restaurants; and though the nightlife is nothing special, it's tranquil enough to encourage sitting out on the pavement at the bars, beneath the palm trees and apartment buildings.

Across from the **Glória** *Metrô* station, on top of the Morro da Glória, stands the eighteenth-century **Igreja de Nossa Senhora da Glória do Outeiro** (Tues–Fri 9am–noon & 1–5pm, Sat & Sun 9am–noon), notable for its innovative octagonal ground plan and domed roof, the latter decked with excellent seventeenth-century blue-and-white *azulejos* and nineteenth-century marble masonry. Painstakingly renovated, the church, quite simply the prettiest in Rio, is an absolute gem, easily worth a quick detour.

On the Rua do Catete, adjacent to the **Catete** *Metrô* station, stands the Palácio do Catete, home to the **Museu da República** (Tues–Fri noon–5pm, Sat & Sun 2–6pm; $1.50, free Wed; ⓦwww.museudarepublica.org.br). The palace was used as the presidential residence from 1897 until 1960, and it was here, in 1954, that Getúlio Vargas committed suicide. The building was built between 1858 and 1866 as the Rio home of a wealthy coffee *fazenda* owner. As a historical museum, the *palácio* continues where the Museu Histórico Nacional (see p.327) leaves off, with the establishment of the first Republic in 1888. The collection features both period furnishings and presidential memorabilia, though it's the opulent marble and stained glass of the building itself that make a visit so worthwhile.

Divided between two buildings, one also inside the grounds of the Palácio do Catete and the other in an adjacent house, the **Museu de Folclore Edison Cruz** (Tues–Fri 11am–6pm, Sat & Sun 3–6pm; 70¢) is a fascinating folkloric collection that unites pieces from all over Brazil – leatherwork, musical instruments, ceramics, toys, Afro-Brazilian cult paraphernalia, photographs and *ex votos*.

If you follow Avenida Beira Mar away from Centro you enter the **Parque do Flamengo**, the biggest land reclamation project in Brazil, designed by the great Brazilian landscape architect and gardener, Roberto Burle Marx, and completed in 1960. Sweeping round as far as Botafogo Bay, it comprises 1.2 square kilometres of prime seafront, popular with local residents who use it mostly for sports – there are countless tennis courts (open 9am–11pm) and football pitches.

The **beach** at Flamengo runs along the park for about a kilometre and offers excellent views across the bay to Niterói. Unfortunately, it's not a place for swimming as the water here is polluted. Instead, you might want to take a look at the quirky **Museu Carmen Miranda** (Tues–Fri 11am–5pm; $1.50), in front of Av Rui Barbosa 560, at the southern end of the park. Carmen was born in Portugal, made it big in Hollywood in the 1940s and became the patron saint of Rio's Carnaval transvestites. The museum contains a wonderful collection of kitsch memorabilia, as well as some of the star's costumes and personal possessions including fruit-laden hats and posters.

Botafogo

BOTAFOGO curves around the 800m between Flamengo and Rio's yacht club. The bay is dominated by the yachts and boats moored near the club, and again the beach doesn't have much to recommend it to bathers due to the pollution of the bay. However, there's plenty to see in Botafogo and there're some excellent places to eat here, as well as in **Humaitá**, the *bairro* to the north with which it merges. On Rua Sorocaba, a turning off Avenida São Clemente, is the **Museu Villa-Lobos** at no. 200 (Mon–Fri 10am–5.30pm; 70¢; ⓦwww.museuvillalobos.org.br). Established in 1960 to celebrate the work of the Brazilian composer, Heitor Villa-Lobos (1887–1959), it's largely a display of his personal possessions and original music scores, but you can also buy tapes and records of his music here. Botafogo's other museum, the **Museu do Índio** (Tues–Fri 10am–5pm, Sat & Sun 1–5pm; 70¢; ⓦwww.museudoindio.org.br), lies in the next street along, at Rua das Palmeiras 55. Housed in an old colonial building, the museum boasts a broad and interesting collection, containing utensils, musical instruments, tribal costumes and ritual devices from many of Brazil's dwindling indigenous peoples.

Urca and the Sugar Loaf

The best bet for swimming this close to the centre is around **URCA**. There are small beaches on each side of the promontory on which this wealthy *bairro* stands, its name an acronym of the company that undertook its construction – Urbanizador Construção. Facing Botafogo, the **Praia da Urca**, only 100m long, is frequented almost exclusively by the small *bairro*'s inhabitants, while in front of the cable car station (see below), beneath the Sugar Loaf mountain, **Praia Vermelha** is a cove sheltered from the South Atlantic, whose relatively gentle waters are popular with swimmers.

You should come to Urca at least once during your stay to take the cable car up the **Pão de Açúcar**, which rises where Guanabara Bay meets the Atlantic Ocean. In Portuguese the name means **SUGAR LOAF**, referring to the ceramic or metal mould used during the refining of sugarcane. The base station of **cable car** (daily 8am–10pm, every 30min; $8) is at Praça General Tibúrcio, which can be reached by buses marked "Urca" or "Praia Vermelha" from Centro, #107 from Centro, Catete and Flamengo; or #511 and #512 from Zona Sul. The 1400-metre journey is made in two stages, first to the summit of **Morro da Urca** (215m), where there is a theatre, restaurant and shops, and then on to the top of Pão de Açúcar itself (394m). The cable cars have glass walls and once on top the view is as glorious as you could wish. Facing inland, you can see right over the city, from Centro and the Santos Dumont airport all the way through Flamengo and Botafogo; face Praia Vermelha and the cable car terminal, and to the left you'll see the sweep of Copacabana and on into Ipanema, while back from the coast the mountains around which Rio was built rise to the Tijuca National Park. Try to avoid the busy times between 10am and 3pm: it's best of all at sunset on a clear day, when the lights of the city are starting to twinkle.

Leme and Copacabana

LEME and **COPACABANA** are different stretches of the same four-kilometre beach. Avoid walking through the Túnel Novo that links Botafogo with Leme as it's a favourite place for tourists to be relieved of their wallets. The **Praia do Leme** extends for a kilometre, between the Morro do Leme and Avenida Princesa Isabel, by the *Meridien Hotel*, which maintains a hawkish security watch on the part of the beach nearest the hotel and is thus a good place to park your towel.

From there, the Praia de **Copacabana** runs a further 3km to the military-owned Forte de Copacabana. The beach is amazing, the over-the-top atmosphere apparent even in the mosaic pavements, designed by Burle Marx to represent images of rolling waves. The seafront is backed by a line of prestigious, high-rise hotels and luxury apartments that have sprung up since the 1940s, while a steady stream of noisy traffic patrols the two-lane **Avenida Atlântica**. Scattered around the *bairro* are some fine examples of Art Deco architecture, none more impressive than the *Copacabana Palace Hotel* on Avenida Atlântica, built in 1923 and considered one of Rio's best hotels.

Arpoador, Ipanema and Leblon

On the other side of the point from Forte de Copacabana, the lively waters off the **ARPOADOR** are popular with families and the elderly as the ocean here is slightly calmer than at Ipanema. From here, as far as the unkempt and balding greenery of the Jardim de Allah, a couple of kilometres away, you're in **IPANEMA**; thereafter lies **LEBLON**. Much calmer than Copacabana, the beaches here are stupendous, though there's not much in the way of bars and restaurants near the beach: in fact, the only bar-restaurant on the front is *Caneco*, at the far end of Leblon. As with Copacabana, Ipanema's beach is unofficially divided according to the supposed interest of the beach users. Thus the stretch of sand east from Rua Farme de Amoedo to Rua Teixeira de Melo is where gay men are concentrated, while *posto 9* is where artists and intellectuals ponder life. On Sunday, the seafront roads – Avenida Vieira Souto in Ipanema, Avenida Delfim Moreira in Leblon – are closed to traffic, and given over to strollers, skateboarders and rollerbladers.

Since the 1960s, Ipanema has developed a reputation as a fashion centre second to none in Latin America and the place is packed with bijou little boutiques, flogging the very best names in fine threads. If you do go shopping here, go on Friday and take in the large **food and flower market** on the Praça de Paz.

Lagoa

Back from Ipanema's plush beaches is the Lagoa Rodrigo de Freitas, always referred to simply as **LAGOA**. A lagoon linked to the ocean by a narrow canal that passes through Ipanema's Jardim de Allah, Lagoa is fringed by apartment buildings where Rio's most seriously rich and status-conscious live. Until recently, the lagoon's water was seriously polluted, but a programme to clean it up has been remarkably successful and the lagoon's mangrove swamps are now recovering. On Sundays, the shore surrounding the lagoon (which forms the Parque Tom Jobin, named in memory of Rio's famed *bossa nova* composer who died in 1994) comes alive as people walk, rollerblade, jog or cycle the 7.5km perimeter pathway, or just watch the passers-by. Summer evenings are especially popular when, on the west side of the lagoon in the Parque dos Patins (Skaters' Park), there are food stalls, live music and *forró* dancing.

Jardim Botânico and Gávea

To the northwest of the Lagoa lies **Jardim Botânico** *bairro*, whose **Parque Lage** (daily 9am–5pm), designed by the English landscape gardener John Tyndale, in the early 1840s, consists of half a million square metres of forest, with a labyrinthine path network and seven small lakes. A little further along the Rua Jardim Botânico is the **JARDIM BOTÂNICO** itself (Tues–Sun 8am–5pm; $1.50), half of it natural jungle, half laid out in impressive avenues lined with immense imperial palms that date from the garden's inauguration in 1808. There are also a number of sculptures throughout the garden, notably the Greek mythology-inspired *Ninfa do Eco* and *Caçador Narciso* (1783) by Mestre Valentim, the first two metal sculptures cast in Brazil. The **entrance** is at Rua Jardim Botânico 1008.

On the **GÁVEA** side of Lagoa lies the **Jockey Club,** which can be reached on any bus marked "via Jóquei" – get off at Praça Santos Dumont at the end of Rua Jardim Botânico. **Races** take place four times a week, every week of the year (Mon 6.30–11.30pm, Fri 4–9.30pm, Sat & Sun 2–8pm). Remember, no one in shorts is admitted. On alternate weekends throughout the year, part of the club is taken over by an arts and crafts market, the **Babilônia Feira Hype** (2–11pm; $1.50). Apart from the clothes, jewellery and handicrafts on sale, there are food stalls, music and dance.

About 3km northwest of the Jockey Club, at Rua Marquês de São Vicente 476, is the **Instituto Moreira Salles** (Tues–Fri 1–8pm, Sat & Sun 1–6pm; ⓣ21/2512-6448, ⓦwww.ims.com.br; free), one of Rio's most beautiful cultural centres. Completed in 1951, the house is stunningly beautiful – one of the finest examples of modernist domestic architecture in Brazil – and the gardens, landscaped by Roberto Burle Marx, are also attractive; the centre itself hosts temporary art exhibitions. Take bus #170 from Centro (Av Rio Branco), Botafogo or Jardim Botânico, or #174 from Copacabana, Ipanema or Leblon.

The coast west of Leblon

Back on the coast, to the west of Leblon, lies kilometre after kilometre of white sand. **Praia do Vidigal**, tucked under the Morro Dois Irmãos, is only about 500m long, and used to be the preserve of the inhabitants of the **Favela do Vidigal** – one of the biggest shantytowns in Rio – until they lost their beach with the construction of the *Rio Sheraton Hotel*. Further west is the beautiful beach at **São Conrado**, dominated by up-market apartment buildings.

Above São Conrado, on the slopes between the Tijuca Mountains and the peak of Pedra dos Dois Irmãos, sits **Favela Roçinha** – spuriously picturesque and glistening in the tropical sun. Here, over 160,000 Brazilians live, for whom a salary of around $40 a month is about as much as an entire family can expect. It is not safe to enter Roçinha unless accompanied by someone who knows the favela well. For most people the best option is to take a **tour**, with the most insightful run by Marcelo Armstrong (ⓣ21/3322-2727, ⓦwww.favelatour.com.br; $25), who picks you up at your hotel. Marcelo, who speaks excellent English, is widely known and respected in the *favelas* that are visited and has made a point of getting community approval. If you're worried about voyeurism, you shouldn't be: residents are eager that outsiders understand that *favelas* are not in fact terrifying and lawless ghettos, but inhabited by people as decent as anywhere else, eager to improve the local quality of life.

Parque Nacional da Tijuca

If you look up from the streets of Zona Sul, the mountains running southwest from the Corcovado are covered with exuberant forest. This is the periphery of the **PARQUE NACIONAL DA TIJUCA** (daily 7am–9pm; free), which covers an area of approximately 120 square kilometres, and is maintained by Brazil's State Institute of Forestry (IBDF). The forest is home to insects and reptiles, ocelots, howler monkeys, agoutis, three-toed sloths and other animals. The park offers lots of walks and some excellent views of Rio, and though areas of it have been burnt by forest fires it remains an appealing place to get away from the city for a few hours. If you have the energy for an all-day climb, you can go all the way to the **Pico do Papagaio** (975m) or **Pico da Tijuca** (1021m) – peaks in the far north of the forest, above the popular picnic spot known as **Bom Retiro**.

Buses don't enter the park, so a **car** is useful if you plan to do an extensive tour: you can go in via Cosme Velho *bairro*, near the **Entrada dos Caboclos**, and follow Estrada Heitor da Silva Costa. An alternative entrance is at Rua Leão Pacheco, which runs up the side of the Jardim Botânico (off Rua Jardim Botânico) and leads to the **Entrada dos Macacos** and on to the **Vista Chinesa**, above the Museu Histórico da Cidade in Gávea. From here there's a marvellous view of Guanabara Bay and the Zona Sul. If you're intent upon **walking**, you should be warned that even the shorter trip from the Entrada dos Macacos will mean a hot, dehydrating climb for more than 20km.

Alternatively, you can join an **organized tour** of the park. The best are run by Rio Hiking (ⓣ021/2552-9420, ⓦwww.riohiking.com.br), which take small groups of people on half- or full-day hikes along the park's many trails. For a bird's-eye view of the forest, you can take off with an experienced pilot on a tandem **hang-glider** flight from the Pedra Bonita ramp on the western edge of the park, 520m above the beach at São Conrado. The most experienced and reliable operator, **Just Fly** (ⓦwww.justfly.com.br), offers flights daily (usually 10am–3pm) when weather permits, and the cost is $80 per person, which includes pick-up and drop-off from your hotel.

Eating and drinking

As one of the world's most exotic tourist resorts and with (for Brazil) a relatively large middle-class population, Rio is well served by restaurants offering a wide variety of cuisines – from traditional Brazilian to French and Japanese. In general, eating out in Rio is not cheap – and it can be very expensive – but there's no shortage of low-priced places to grab a lunchtime meal which serve very cheap combined plates of meat, beans and rice, as well as other snacks. *Cariocas* dine late, and restaurants don't start to fill up until after 9pm. Generally, last orders will be taken around midnight in most places, but there are others where you can get a meal well after 2am.

The City Centre

Bar Luiz Rua Carioca 39. Near Largo da Carioca, this manic, but essentially run-of-the-mill restaurant and bar, serving German-style food and ice-cold *chopp*, is considered quite an institution and still a popular meeting place for journalists and intellectuals. Closed Sun.

Cosmopolita Travessa do Mosqueira 4, Lapa. An excellent Portuguese restaurant established in 1926 with a loyal, rather bohemian, clientele. Fish dishes are the firm favourites here. Closed Sun.

Penafiel Rua Senhor dos Passos 121. Superb – and amazingly inexpensive – Portuguese dishes have been served here since 1912. Fish dishes and stews (such as bean, tongue and tripe) are the speciality. Lunch only, closed Sat & Sun.

Rio–Minho Rua do Ouvidor 10. Tasty Brazilian food at fair prices. The kitchen concentrates on seafood – try *badejo* fish, lobster in butter, prawn in coconut milk or the fried fish with red peppers, rice and broccoli. Lunch only, closed Sat & Sun.

Santa Teresa

Adega do Pimenta Rua Almirante Alexandrino 296. Moderately priced German cooking – most people go for the sausage and sauerkraut, but the duck with red cabbage is excellent.

Bar do Arnaudo Rua Almirante Alexandrino 316. Just up from the *Adega do Pimenta*, an excellent mid-priced place to sample traditional food from Brazil's Northeast, such as *carne do sol* (sun-dried meat), *macaxeira* (sweet cassava) and *pirão de bode* (goat meat soup). Sat–Sun closed from 8pm & closed all Mon.

Sobrenatural Rua Almirante Alexandrino 432. Basically a fish restaurant, where the highlights are the *moquecas* and the catch of the day. Deliberately rustic looking, this is an inviting place for a leisurely meal. Closed Mon.

Flamengo, Botafogo and Humaitá

A Mineira Rua Duque de Caxias, Humaitá. A perfect introduction to the *comida mineira* of Minas Gerais, with all the standard dishes on offer as part of the excellent value ($6 per person) all-you-can-eat buffet.

Axé Santé Rua Capitão Solomão 55, Botafogo. A nicely decorated French-Bahian restaurant with live music. The food's both well presented and tasty – try the salad with mango and nuts, or the *carne do sol* with banana purée.

Lamas Rua Marquês de Abrantes 18, Flamengo This 130-year-old restaurant serves well-prepared Brazilian food (the Oswaldo Aranha steak – pan fried with lots of garlic – is a popular choice) to artist and journalist types. Always busy, with a vibrant atmosphere, *Lamas* is a good example of *carioca* middle-class tradition, and highly recommended. Open until 4am.

Madam Vidal Rua Capitão Solomão 69, Botafogo. This gay-friendly music club and restaurant serves tasty dishes that incorporate Brazilian, European and Japanese influences. The jazz nights with Leila Maria, a critically acclaimed singer, are a treat. Mon–Sat until 3am; closed Sun.

Majórica Rua Senador Vergueiro 11–15, Flamengo. A long-established, better-than-average place to tuck into some meat – the *picanha especial* (special rump steak) is the favourite. If you're not in the mood for beef, try the excellent grilled trout from near Petrópolis.

Yorubá Rua Arnaldo Quintela 94, Botafogo ⊕21/2541-9387. Friendly restaurant serving up moderately priced Bahian cooking with its strong African influences. Meals always take a long time to appear, but the *bobó* (a dish based on mandioca purée), *moquecas* and other Bahian specialities are all well worth the wait. Beautifully presented food in an attractive setting. Closed Mon & Tues; lunch only Sun.

Copacabana, Leme, Ipanema and Leblon

Arab Av Atlântica 1936, Copacabana. One of the very few good restaurants on Avenida Atlântica, this reasonably priced Lebanese restaurant is where you can opt for a cold beer and snack on the terrace or a full meal inside (the *por kilo* lunch is excellent value). Though the menu is rather heavy on meat choices, vegetarians certainly won't go hungry.

Caranguejo Rua Barata Ribeiro 771, corner of Rua Xavier da Silveira, Copacabana. Excellent, inexpensive seafood – especially the *caranguejos* (crabs) – served in an utterly unpretentious environment packed with locals and tourists alike. Closed Mon.

Casa da Feijoada Rua Prudente de Morais 10, Ipanema. Usually served only on Saturdays, *feijoada* is served seven days a week here, along with other traditional, moderately priced and extremely filling Brazilian dishes.

Deck Av Atlântica 2316, corner of Rua Siqueira Campos, Copacabana. Until 5pm, this always-busy restaurant serves an all-you-can-eat Brazilian buffet for just $5 per person, after which the offerings include *rodizio de galeto* (mouthwatering thyme-and-garlic chicken with polenta fried in palm oil) and all-you-can-eat pasta for $4.

Garcia & Rodriques Av Ataulfo de Paiva 1251, Leblon. A foodies paradise: although the French restaurant is unimaginative and stuffy, there's an excellent bistro, wine shop, ice-cream parlour, bakery and deli. This is one of the few places in Rio where you can buy genuinely good bread and there's an excellent choice of take-out salads and other prepared meals. Open Sun–Fri 8am–midnight, Sat 8am–1am.

La Trattoria Rua Fernando Mendes 7, Copacabana. Cheap and cheerful place serving the best Italian food in the neighbourhood. Among the excellent range of pasta dishes, the fettuccine doused in a mixed seafood sauce is especially recommended.

Marius Crustáceos Av Atlântica 290, Leme ⊕21/2543-6363. Definitely the place to come for oysters, crabs, crayfish, prawns and other seafood choices. The menu is varied, though Italian–Brazilian styles dominate. Expensive, but quite a treat.

Pax Delicía Rua Quitéria 99, at Praça de Nossa Senhora da Paz, Ipanema. Equally suitable for a light lunch or drawn-out evening meal, this moderately priced comfortable restaurant specializes in modern Brazilian cooking with dishes such as duck in a *jabuticaba* sauce, as well as excellent salads and pastas. Do save space for the desserts: the guava cheesecake is delicious.

Siri Mole e Cia Rua Francisco Otaviano 50, Copacabana. ⊕21/2267-0894. A rarity in Rio – an excellent Bahian restaurant, serving beautifully presented dishes (many of them spicy) in an upmarket, yet comfortable, setting. Inside, the restaurant is quite formal, but there are also a few tables outside where you can munch on *acarajé* and other Bahian snacks.

Via Farme Rua Farme de Amoedo 47, Ipanema. Good Italian food – especially the pizzas and seafood. Choose from air-conditioned dining upstairs or open-air downstairs. Not cheap, but reasonable for the area.

Zuka Rua Dias Ferreira 233, Leblon ⊕21/3205-7154. Food is grilled in front of your eyes, then doused in amazing sauces by a chef capable of creating unforgettable fusion cuisine: one of his specialities is seared tuna in a cashew crust, served with a potato-horseradish sauce. Around $25 per person.

Nightlife and entertainment

The best way to find out what's on and where in Rio is to consult *Caderno B*, a separate section of the *Jornal do Brasil*, which lists cinema, arts events and concerts; *O Globo*, too, details sporting and cultural events in the city. *Veja*, Brazil's answer to *Newsweek*, includes an excellent weekly Rio supplement with news of concerts, exhibitions and other events; the magazine reaches the newsstands on Sunday. Alternatively, ⓦwww.guiarj.com.br has up-to-date listings of entertainment possibilities.

Samba and other live music

Samba shows are tourist affairs, where members of Rio's more successful samba schools perform glitzy music and dance routines. Still, some are worth catching. Every Monday night at 10pm, the Beija Flor (⊕21/791-1353) school performs at the Morro da Urca, halfway up Pão d'Açúcar; the $30 entrance fee includes dinner from 8pm, a well-executed show and spectacular city views, though the event is a tad snooty. On Thursday and Friday live music shows start at 10pm, and you can eat and drink till 2am. For a less touristy experience of a samba school, you can easily arrange to watch rehearsals held from August to February (see box on p.340).

If you're not in search of Carnaval glitz, you're better off making for the bars and clubs of Lapa, where samba and other local rhythms play to an enthusiastic and overwhelmingly local crowd. Especially recommended there is *Carioca da Gama* (Mon–Sat from 6pm) at Avenida Mem de Sá 79: look out for Teresa Cristina who brings the house down with her steamy samba. Excellent samba artists also perform on Friday and Saturday at *Bar Semente* at Rua Joaquim Silva 138. Visitors to Lapa should take particular care at night, when it's advisable to take a taxi even from one block to the next. If you feel uncomfortable going alone – or simply want company – contact Rio Hiking (ⓣ021/2552-9420, ⓦwww.riohiking.com.br), which regularly takes small groups bar-hopping in Lapa ($35 per person – excluding drinks). Visitors interested in other forms of live music should try the following bars and clubs.

Bar Semente at Rua Joaquim Silva 138, Lapa. Friday and Saturday nights are basically reserved for samba, but on Monday through Thursday other traditional-rooted styles of Brazilian music, in particular *choró*, are performed at this easy-going bar. From 8.30pm.

Café Cultural Sacrilégio Av Mem de Sá 81, Lapa. A small old town house with a terrific atmosphere and killer *batidas* as well as other drinks. The place attracts some popular performers such as, on Thursdays, Nilze Carvalho, a great young *choro* singer who performs the great classical works of this musical genre. Mon–Sat from 6pm until early morning.

Rio Scenarium Rua do Lavradio 20, Lapa ⓣ21/2233-3239. One of the liveliest places in Lapa, more to listen to music, rather to dance, in old baronial town house filled with antiques and specialising in *choro*, where visitors can sit on one of the several landings and watch the daily shows on the stage below. Reservations recommended on weekends.

Discos

Although Rio's discos attempt sophistication, the end result is generally bland and unpalatable. Discos, particularly, too often pump out a steady stream of British and American hits, interspersed with examples from Brazil's own dreadful pop industry.

Gay Rio

If you're expecting **gay nightlife** to rival San Francisco's or Sydney's, you may well be disappointed. In general nightlife is pretty integrated with gay men, lesbians and heterosexuals tending to share the same venues and there are few areas of concentration: apart from transvestites who hang out on street corners and are visible during Carnaval, the scene is unexpectedly discreet.

A good starting point for an evening out is Rua Visconde Silva in Botafogo, which is lined with numerous gay and lesbian cafés, bars and restaurants. The classic introduction to Rio's more traditional male gay society is *Le Ball*, a bar in the Travessa Cristiano Lacorte, just off Rua Miguel Lemos, at the Ipanema end of Copacabana. Opposite this, the *Teatro Brigitte Blair* hosts a gay transvestite show from around 10pm. Also in Copacabana, *Inc*, a bar and nightclub at Praça Serzedelo Correia 15, next to Rua Siquera Campos, is open nightly and very popular, mainly with tourists. In Lapa, at Rua Mem de Sá 25, behind a pink facade under the Aqueduto da Carioca, the *Casanova*, Rio's oldest and most interesting gay bar, features drag shows, lambada and samba music. The most popular gay nightclub at the moment is undoubtedly *Le Boy* (ⓣ21/2513-4993, ⓦwww.leboy.com.br) at Rua Raul Pompéia 102 (in Copacabana, towards Ipanema). This huge club is open nightly apart from Mondays and features dancefloors, drag shows and much more besides.

In the daytime, the beach area in front of the *Copacabana Palace Hotel* is frequented by gay bathers, and the café next door, *Maxims*, is a fun gay place to hang out. Nearby on Avenida Atlântica, at the junction with Rua Siqueira Campos, is the Gay Kiosk Rainbow, a summer-time **information point** for gay visitors – ask about circuit parties, usually held in Centro. The strip of beach between Rua Farme de Amoedo and Rua Teixeira do Melo in Ipanema is another well-known gay meeting point. For the post-beach gay crowd, there's *Boofetada*, a bar and café at Rua Farme de Amoedo 87. See the "Carnaval" section opposite for information about Rio's gay balls.

00 Av Padre Leonel Franca 240, Gávea ☎21/2540-8041. The nightclub of the moment, frequented by a rich and trendy crowd, where some of Brazil's top DJs play an eclectic mix of music; like most places it doesn't really get going until after 11pm, though on Sunday the best time to go is 7pm, immediately after returning from the beach.

Arco Imperial Travessa do Comércio 13, Lapa ☎21/2242-2695. Always packed from the early hour of 10pm, this dance club plays a mix of European and Brazilian disco.

Mess Club, Rua Francisco Otaviano 20, Copacabana ☎21/2227-0419, ⓦwww.messclub.com.br. New, very hip, but without a trace of snobbishness. Mainly popular with twenty-somethings, though pretty mixed. Music alters nightly, with Tuesday's 'Afro Rio' – DJs playing hip-hop, soul, reggae and other black music styles accompanied by live percussion – is especially recommended.

Six Electro Rua das Marrecas 38, Lapa ☎21/2510-3230. An old house renovated to give a rustic-chic air to the place. There are three dance floors featuring hip-hop and soul, trance and drum 'n' bass. A good place to end up after some Lapa bar hopping.

Carnaval

Carnaval is celebrated in all of Brazil's cities, but Rio's is the biggest and most flash. From the Friday before Ash Wednesday to the following Thursday, the city shuts up shop and throws itself into the world's most famous manifestation of unbridled hedonism. Rio's Carnaval has never become stale, owing to its status as the most important celebration on the Brazilian calendar, easily outstripping either Christmas or Easter. In a city riven by poverty, Carnaval represents a moment of release, when the aspirations of *cariocas* can be expressed in music and song.

The action

Rio's street celebrations centre on the **evening processions** that fill **Avenida Rio Branco** (*Metrô* to Largo do Carioca or Cinelândia). Be prepared for the crowds and beware of pickpockets. The processions include rival samba schools (though not the best), *blocos* and loudspeaker-laden floats blasting out the frenetic dance music.

The **samba schools**, each representing a different neighbourhood or social club, are divided into three leagues, each allowing promotion and relegation, and the proceedings all start in the year preceding Carnaval, as each school mobilizes thousands of supporters who will create the various parts of the display. A theme is chosen, music written, costumes created, while the dances are choreographed by the **carnavelesco**, the school's director. By December, rehearsals have begun and, in time for Christmas, the sambas are recorded and released to record stores.

The main procession of Division 1 schools – the **Desfile** – takes place on the Sunday and Monday nights of Carnaval week in the purpose-built **Sambódromo**, further along the avenue beyond the train station, a concrete structure 1700m long which can accommodate 90,000 spectators. The various schools – involving some 50,000 people – take part in a spectacular piece of theatre: no simple parade, but a competition between schools attempting to gain points from their presentation composed of song, story, dress, dance and rhythm. The schools pass through the Passarela da Samba, the Sambódromo's parade ground, and the judges allocate points according to a number of criteria. Each school must parade for between 85 and 95 minutes, no more and no less, with the **bateria**, or percussion section, sustaining the cadence that drives the school's song and dance. Costumes are judged

Carnaval dates

The four days of Carnaval for the next few years are as follows:
21–24 Feb 2004
5–8 Feb 2005
25–28 Feb 2006
17–20 Feb 2007

Samba schools

If you can't make Carnaval, give the fake shows in the Zona Sul a miss and get a taste of the samba schools at the *ensaios* (rehearsals) below. They take place at weekends from August to February; phone to confirm times and days. After New Year, Saturday nights are packed solid with tourists and prices triple. Instead, go to one on a mid-week evening or, better still, on Sunday afternoon when there's no entrance fee and locals predominate. Most of the schools are in distant *bairros*, often in, or on the edge of, a *favela*, but there's no need to go accompanied by a guide. It's easy, safe and not too expensive to take a taxi there and back.

Beija-Flor Rua Pracinha Wallace Paes Leme 1652, Nilopolis ⓣ21/2253-2860, ⓦwww.beija-flor.com.br. Founded 1948; blue and white.
Mangueira Rua Visconde de Niterói 1072, Mangueira ⓣ21/2567-4637, ⓦwww.mangueira.com.br. Founded 1928; green and pink.
Moçidade Independente de Padre Miguel Rua Cel. Tamarindo 38, Padre Miguel ⓣ21/3332-5823. Founded 1952; green and white.
Portela Rua Clara Nunes 81, Madureira ⓣ21/3390-0471. Founded 1923; blue and white.
Salgueiro Rua Silva Telles 104, Tijuca ⓣ21/2238-5564, ⓦwww.salgueiro.com.br. Founded 1953; red and white.

on their originality; their colours are always the traditional ones adopted by each school. Potentially big point scorers are the **carros alegóricos**, or the gigantic, richly decorated floats that carry some of the prominent figures, among them the **Porta-Bandeira** ("flag bearer") – a woman who carries the school's symbol. The bulk of the procession behind is formed by the **alas**, the wings or blocks consisting of hundreds of costumed individuals each linked to a part of the school's theme.

The **parade** of schools starts at 7.30pm, with eight schools parading on each of the two nights, and goes on till noon the following day. Two stands (7 & 9) in the Sambódromo are reserved for foreign visitors and **seats** cost over $60 per night. Though much more expensive than other areas, they are more comfortable and have good catering facilities. Other sections of the Sambódromo cost from $3 to $25 and the seating options are: the high stands (*arquibancadas*), lower stands (*geral*) and the ringside seats (*cadeiras de pista*) – these last the best, consisting of a table, four chairs and full bar service. Unless you have a very tough backside, you will find sitting through a ten-hour show an intolerable test of endurance. Most people don't turn up until 11pm, by which time the show is well under way and hotting up considerably. **Tickets** are available principally from Riotur (see p.319), or through the Banco do Brasil, with offices in most major capital cities. Book well in advance if you can, or try local travel agents, who often have tickets available.

Listings

Airlines Aerolíneas Argentinas ⓣ21/3398-3520; Air Canada ⓣ21/2220-5343; Air France ⓣ21/2532-3642; Alitalia ⓣ21/2292-4424; American Airlines ⓣ21/2210-3126 or 3398-4093; British Airways ⓣ21/2259-6144 or 3398-3888; Continental Airlines ⓣ21/2531-1142; Delta Airlines ⓣ21/2507-7227; Gol ⓣ21/3398-5131; Iberia ⓣ21/2282-1336; Japan Airlines ⓣ21/2220-6414; KLM ⓣ21/2544-7744; Lan Chile ⓣ800-55-4900; Lloyd Aéreo Boliviano ⓣ21/2220-9548; Lufthansa ⓣ21/2217-6111 or 3398-3855; Pluna ⓣ21/2240-8217 or 3398-2000; TAP ⓣ212/210-1278 or 3393-1411; United Airlines ⓣ21/2532-1212 or 3398-4050; Varig ⓣ21/2220-3821 or 3398-3522; VASP ⓣ800-998-277.

Banks and exchange Main bank branches are concentrated in Av Rio Branco in Centro and Av N.S. de Copacabana in Copacabana. It's worth remembering that although most banks remain open until 4.30pm you can usually exchange money only until 3pm or 3.30pm. There are ATMs throughout the city.

Car rental Avis, Av Princesa Isabel 150, Copacabana ⓣ21/2542-3392; Hertz, Av Princesa

Isabel 334, Copacabana ☎21/2275-3245 & 800/701-7300; Localiza-National, Av Princesa Isabel 214, Copacabana ☎800/99-2000. Prices start at about $40 per day and you'll need a credit card to rent the car.

Consulates Argentina, Praia de Botafogo 228, Botafogo ☎21/2553-1646; Australia, Rua Rio Branco 1, Centro ☎21/2518-3351; Canada, Rua Lauro Müller 116, Botafogo ☎21/2542-9297; Peru, Av Rui Barbosa 314, Flamengo ☎21/2551-6296; UK, Praia do Flamengo 284, 2nd floor, Flamengo ☎21/2553-9600; US, Av Presidente Wilson 147, Centro ☎21/2292-7117; Uruguay, Praia de Botafogo 242, Botafogo ☎21/2552-6699; Venezuela, Praia de Botafogo 242, Botafogo ☎21/2551-5398.

Departure tax $4 for internal flights or $28 for international flights, payable in either US or Brazilian currency (but not a mix of the two). Often the fee is already covered by your ticket.

Health matters For medical emergencies, English-speakers should try a private clinic such as Sorocaba Clinic, Rua Sorocaba 464, Botafogo (☎21/2286-0022) or Centro Médico Ipanema, Rua Anibal Mendonça 135, Ipanema (☎21/2239-4647). Your best bet for any non-emergency problems is the Rio Health Collective, Banco Nacional building (room 303), Avdas Américas 4430, Barra de Tijuca; a non-profit organization, its phone-in service (☎21/3325-9300, ext 44) is free, and provides names of qualified professionals who speak foreign languages.

Police Emergency number ☎190. The beach areas have police posts at regular intervals. The special Tourist Police are at Avenida Afrânio de Melo Franco (opposite the Teatro Casa Grande), Leblon (☎21/2511-5112); they are very helpful, speak English and efficiently process reports of theft or other incidents.

Rio de Janeiro state

It's easy to get out of Rio city, something you'll probably want to do at some stage during your stay. There are good **bus** services to all the places mentioned below, while the easiest trips are by ferry just over the bay to **Niterói**, whose Museu de Arte Contemporânea has become an essential sight for visitors to Rio. After that, the choice is a simple one: either head east along the **Costa do Sol** to Búzios, or west along the **Costa Verde** to Ilha Grande and Parati; both coasts offer endless good beaches and little holiday towns, developed to varying degrees. Or strike off **inland** to Petrópolis and Teresópolis, where the mountainous interior provides a welcome, cool relief from the frenetic goings-on back in Rio.

If you planning on **renting a car** (see opposite for addresses in Rio), this is as good a state as any to brave the traffic: the coasts are an easy drive from the city and stopping off at more remote beaches is easy, while your own wheels would let you get to grips with the extraordinary scenery up in the mountains.

East: Niterói and the Costa do Sol

Across the strait at the mouth of Guanabara Bay lies **Niterói**, founded in 1573 and until 1975 the capital of the old state of Guanabara. Though lacking the splendour of the city of Rio, Niterói has a busy commercial centre and a renowned museum. It is also the gateway to the **COSTA DO SOL** to the east, which features plenty of resorts, most notably **Búzios**. Buses out of Niterói head east along the **Costa do Sol**, which is dominated by three large **lakes** – Maricá, Saquerema and Araruama, separated from the ocean by long, narrow stretches of white sandy beach – and flecked with small towns bearing the same names as the lakes.

Niterói

Cariocas have a tendency to sneer at **NITERÓI**, typically commenting that the only good thing about the city is the views back across Guanabara Bay to Rio. While it's certainly true that the views are absolutely gorgeous on a clear day, Niterói has more to offer, though only the Oscar Niemeyer–designed **Museu de Arte Contemporânea** (Tues–Fri 11am–6pm, Sat 1–9pm & Sun 11am–6pm; 70¢), or MAC as it is more commonly called, typically lures visitors from Rio. Opened in 1996, and located just south of the centre on a promontory by the Praia da Boa Viagem, the spaceship-shaped building offers 360-degree views of Niterói and across the bay to Rio. MAC boasts a worthy, though hardly exciting, permanent display of Brazilian art from the 1950s to the 1990s and also hosts temporary exhibitions, but the real work of art is the building itself, which even hardened critics of Niemeyer find it difficult to dismiss. The curved lines of the building are simply beautiful, and the views of the headland, nearby beaches and Guanabara Bay as you walk around inside it breathtaking.

You can reach Niterói either by car or **bus** across the 14km of the Ponte Costa e Silva, the Rio–Niterói bridge (bus #999 from the Menezes Cortes bus terminal), or, much more fun, by catching the **ferry** or hydrofoil (see p.320). Although MAC is just 1.5km from the ferry terminal, do not attempt to walk there as tourists have been robbed along the route. A taxi won't cost much, or take a bus to Praia de Icaraí and walk from there.

Búzios

ARMAÇÃO DOS BÚZIOS, or Búzios as it's more commonly known, was "discovered" by none other than Brigitte Bardot, who stumbled upon it by accident while touring the area in 1964. Now, between December and February, the population of "Brazil's St Tropez" swells from 20,000 to 150,000, the fishing boats that once ferried the catch back to shore take pleasure-seekers island-hopping and scuba diving, and the roads connecting the town with the outlying beaches have been paved. If a crowded resort full of high-spending beautiful people is your thing then you're sure to fall for Búzios, but if not give it a miss – at least during the summer high season. Direct buses run from Rio at least five times a day.

Accommodation

Hibiscus Beach Rua 1, Praia de João Fernandes ⓣ22/2623-6221, ⓦwww.hibiscusbeach.com.br. Spacious bungalows, each with a small terrace and wonderful sea views, make up this welcoming British-owned and -run pousada. There's a good-sized pool, and the area's best snorkelling beach is just seconds away, while Armaçao's nightlife is a five-minute taxi ride (or half-hour walk). 7

Meu Sonho Av José Bento Ribeiro Dantas 1289, Ossos ⓣ22/2623-0902, ⓦwww.meusonho-buzios.8k.com. One block from the beach, this pousada has clean, basic rooms and a plunge pool, with the only Internet café in Búzios next door. 5

Morombo Av José Bento Ribeiro Dantas 1242, Armação ⓣ22/2623-1532. An extremely hospitable Argentine owner, good rooms and an attractive terrace combine to make the *Morombo*, on the waterfront road leading to Ossos, an appealing place to stay. 6

Solar do Peixe Vivo Rua José Bento Ribeiro Dantas 999, Armação ⓣ22/2623-1850, ⓦwww.solardopeixevivo.com.br. The main reception building is one of the oldest structures in Búzios. The guestrooms, in cabins in the garden, are simple but spacious; the atmosphere friendly and relaxed. The beach is directly across the road, and there's a pool in the garden. 7

The Town and its beaches

Búzios consists of three main settlements, each with its own distinct character. **Manguinos**, on the isthmus, is the main service centre with a 24-hour tourist office (ⓣ0800/249-999), a medical centre, banks and petrol stations. Midway along the peninsula, linked to Manguinos by a road lined with brash hotels, is **Armação**, an attractive village where cars are usually banned from the cobbled roads. Most of Búzio's best restaurants and boutiques are concentrated here, along with some of the resort's nicest pousadas, and there's also a helpful tourist office on the main square, Praça Santos Dumont (daily 9am–8pm; ⓣ022/2623-2099). A fifteen-minute walk along the coast from Armação, passing the lovely seventeenth-century Igreja Nossa Senhora de Sant'Ana on the way, you reach **Ossos**, the oldest settlement, with a pretty harbour, a quiet beach and a few bars, restaurants and pousadas.

Within walking distance of all the settlements are beautiful white-sand **beaches**, 27 in total, cradled between rocky cliffs and promontories, and bathed by crystal blue waters. It doesn't matter which you choose – Brava, Ossos, Ferradura, Geribá – as each is charming, the ocean offshore studded with little islands. There are good minibus services between Armação and the beaches, and hitching lifts is also widely accepted. The Brava, Ferradura and João Fernandes beaches all have *barracas*, which serve cold beer and expensive fried fish. You can rent kayaks or pedalos, or indulge in a little windsurfing or diving.

Eating and drinking

Restaurants are, predictably, either fairly expensive or very expensive, with cheaper options including the *barracas* selling grilled fish on the beaches or the numerous pizza places in outlying parts of Búzios.

Bananaland Rua Manoel Turíbio de Farias 50. On a parallel street to Rua das Pedras, this is the best *por kilo* restaurant in Búzios and one of the cheapest for a good meal. The choice amongst the buffet of salads and hot dishes is outstanding.

Chez Michou Crêperie Rua das Pedras 90. Belgian-owned, this has long been Armação's most popular hangout thanks to its open-air bar, cheap drinks and authentic crêpes. Open until dawn, when it serves breakfast to the patrons pouring out of the nearby *Fashion Café*.

Esotância Don Juan Rua das Pedras 178. An airy moderately priced Argentine restaurant serving first-rate meat to a demanding (mainly Argentine) clientele. If cuts of beef mean little to you, opt for the *bife de chorizo*, the Argentine standard cut.

Sawasdee Av José Bento Ribeiro Dantas 422. Excellent, spicy Thai food based around vegetables and seafood at reasonable prices. Next door, *Shiitake* is a good attempt at pan-Asian cooking, drawing on Thai, Chinese, Japanese, Vietnamese and Indian cuisine.

West: the Costa Verde

One of Brazil's truly beautiful landscapes, the **COSTA VERDE** has been made much more accessible by the **Rio–Santos BR-101 Highway** – something, however, that has led to an increase in commercial penetration of this region. The fate of this 280-kilometre stretch of lush vegetation, rolling hills and tropical beaches hangs in the balance between rational development and ecological destruction, and so far the signs augur badly. Enjoy your trip; you may be amongst the last to have the privilege to visit the beaches of **Ilha Grande** or the colonial architecture of **Parati**. There are two ways to reach the Costa Verde from Rio. By **car**, drive through the Zona Sul by way of Barra de Tijuca, to Barra de Guaratiba. Alternatively, take one of the **buses** from Rio's rodoviária which leave the city by the Zona Norte and follow the BR-101 to Itacuruçá and beyond.

Ilha Grande

ILHA GRANDE comprises 193 square kilometres of mountainous jungle, historic ruins and beautiful beaches, excellent for some scenic tropical rambling. The entire island, lying about 150kn of Rio, is a state park and the authorities have been successful at limiting building development and in maintaining a ban on motor vehicles, whether owned by visitors or locals. The main drawback is the ferocity of the insects, especially during the summer, so come equipped with repellent.

Ilha Grande offers lots of beautiful **walks** along well-maintained and fairly well-signposted trails, but it's sensible to take some basic precautions. Be sure to set out as early as possible and always inform people at your pousada where you are going, if possible in writing. Carry plenty of water with you and remember to apply sunscreen and insect repellent at regular intervals. Darkness comes suddenly, and even on a night with a full moon the trails are likely to be pitch-black due to the canopy formed by the overhanging foliage; if possible, carry a flashlight with you – most pousadas will be happy to lend you one. Whatever you do, avoid straying from the trail: not only could you easily get hopelessly lost, but there are also rumours of booby traps primed to fire bullets, left over from the days when the island hosted a high-security prison.

As you approach the low-lying, whitewashed colonial port of **Vila do Abraão**, the mountains rise dramatically from the sea, and in the distance there's the curiously shaped summit of Bico do Papagaio ("Parrot's Beak"), which rises to a height of 980m and can be reached in about three hours. There's really very little to see in Abraão itself, but it's a pleasant enough base from which to explore the rest of the island. A half-hour walk along the coast west from Abraão are the ruins of the **Antigo Presídio**. Originally built as a hospital, it was converted to a prison for political prisoners in 1910 and was finally dynamited in the early 1960s. Among the ruins, you'll find the *cafofo*, the containment centre where prisoners who had failed in escape attempts were immersed in freezing water. Just fifteen minutes inland from Abraão, and overgrown with vegetation, stands the **Antigo Aqueduto**, which used to channel the island's water supply. There's a fine view of the aqueduct from the **Pedra Mirante**, a hill near the centre of the island and, close by, a waterfall provides the opportunity for a cool bathe on a hot day.

For the most part the **beaches** – Aventureiro, Lopes Mendes, Canto, Júlia and Morcegoare to name a few – are still wild and unspoilt and are most easily reached by **boat**. A typical day-long excursion costs $7–10 per person, and departs from Abraão's jetty at 10.30am, stopping for snorkelling (equipment provided) before continuing on to a beach where you'll be picked up later in the day to arrive back in Abraão at around 4.30pm.

Practicalities

There are **boats** from both Mangaratiba and Angra dos Reis to Vila do Abraão on Ilha Grande, each taking an hour or so. From **Mangaratiba** to Abraão, the boat leaves at 9am and returns at noon. From **Angra dos Reis**, boats leave at 3.15pm on Monday, Friday, Saturday and Sunday, returning at 10am on the same days. Tickets cost $3 from both Mangaratiba and Angra; if you miss the ferry you can usually count on finding a small launch to do the crossing, charging around $5 per person and taking around ninety minutes. During the summer there's a constant flow of these launches from both mainland towns, but at other times Angra is the best bet. Be sure to come with plenty of **cash**: changing dollars or travellers' cheques is impossible on the island, there's no ATM and few pousadas and restaurants accept credit cards.

Accommodation is mainly around Vila do Abraão where there are quite a few pousadas, most of which are simple but fairly expensive. Reservations in the high season, especially at weekends, are absolutely essential; try to come in the off-season when prices are halved. One of the nicest pousadas is the cosy and friendly *Pousada Oásis* (☎24/3361-5549; ❻), peacefully located on the far end of the beach, a ten-minute walk from the jetty. More hotel-like is the *Pousada Água Viva* (☎21/3361-5166; ❼), amid a busy strip of shops and restaurants. There's an appealing **youth hostel** – the always popular *Pousada do Holandês* (☎24/3361-5034; ❸) – behind the beach next to the Assembléia de Deus.

Parati

About 300km from Rio on the BR-101 is the Costa Verde's main attraction, the town of **PARATI**. Inhabited since 1650, Parati has remained fundamentally unaltered since its heyday as a staging post for the eighteenth-century trade in Brazilian gold, passing from Minas Gerais to Portugal. As trade was diverted to Rio, Parati's fortunes declined and, apart from a short-lived coffee-shipping boom in the nineteenth century, it remained hidden away off the beaten track. Today, UNESCO considers Parati one of the world's most important examples of Portuguese colonial architecture, and the city has been named a national monument.

Arrival, information and accommodation

The **rodoviária** is about half a kilometre from the old town; turn right out of the bus station and walk straight ahead. The helpful **tourist office** (daily 8am–7pm; ⓣ24/3371-1266), on the corner of Avenida Roberto Silveira and Praça Macedo Soares, can supply a map, local bus times and a list of hotels and restaurants.

Most of the best **pousadas** are in the old Portuguese colonial centre, five minutes' walk from the bus station. From late December to after Carnaval, however, this entire area is packed, and hotel space becomes hard to find. Your best hope will be to find a room outside the historic centre, in a hotel used by tour groups – ask the tourist office for advice.

Hotel Coxixo Rua do Comércio 362 ⓣ24/3371-1460, ⓦwww.hotelcoxixo.com.br. Comfortable rooms, a beautiful garden and a good-size pool. One of the larger hotels in the historic centre, where you'll have a chance of securing a last-minute room. Apart from babies under 12 months, only children over the age of 10 are accepted. ❻

Pousada da Marquesa Rua Dona Geralda 69 ⓣ24/3371-2163. The least expensive luxury pousada in town, boasting wonderful views from the bedrooms, an attractive pool and all the comfort you could need. ❻

Pousada da Matriz Rua da Matriz ⓣ24/3371-1610. Small, basic but clean rooms in one of the cheapest pousadas in the old town (❹). Very similar, and located just next door, is the *Pousada Ramiro* (ⓣ24/3371-1361; ❹).

Pousada do Ouro Rua Dr Pereira 145 ⓣ24/3371-1378. Discreet luxury pousada offering a range of tastefully furnished rooms – the nicest are in the main building, while those in the annex across the road are rather dark. There's a pretty walled garden and a good-size pool, too. ❼

Solar dos Gerânios Praça da Matriz ⓣ24/3371-1550. Beautiful Swiss-owned and -run pousada filled with rustic furniture and curios. The rooms are spartan but impeccably kept; most have a balcony and all have a private bathroom. Superb value (prices remain much the same throughout the year) and rightly popular, and reservations are always advised – request a room overlooking the beautiful *praça*. ❹

The Town

The town centre was one of Brazil's first planned urban projects, and its narrow cobbled streets, out of bounds to motorized transport, are bordered by houses built around courtyards, adorned with brightly coloured flowers and alive with hummingbirds. The cobbles of the streets are arranged in channels to drain off storm water and allow the sea to enter and wash the streets at high tides and full moon.

As with most small colonial towns in Brazil, Parati's churches traditionally each served a different sector of the population. Dating back to 1646, **Nossa Senhora dos Remédios** (daily 9am–5pm) on the Praça da Matriz is Parati's main church and the town's most imposing building. Parati's aristocracy had their own church built in 1800, the graceful **Igreja das Dores** (daily 1–5pm) with its own small cemetery, three blocks from the main church by the sea. Along Rua do Comércio is the smallest church, the **Igreja do Rosário** (Mon–Fri 9am–noon), built in 1725 and used by the slaves. Finally, at the southern edge of the town is the **Igreja de Santa Rita** (Wed–Sun 10am–noon & 2–5pm), the oldest and most architecturally significant of the town's churches. Built in 1722 for the freed mulatto population, the elaborate facade is done in Portuguese Baroque style.

Beaches and islands

From the **Praia do Pontal** on the other side of the Perequé-Açu River from town, and from the **port quay**, *baleiras* and *saveiros* (whaling and fishing boats) leave for the beaches of Paraty-Mirim, Jurumirim, Lula and Picinguaba. In fact, there are 65 islands and about 200 beaches to choose from, and anyone can tell you which are the current favourites. Hotels and travel agents sell tickets for trips out to the islands, typically at a cost of $10 per person, leaving Parati at noon, stopping at three or four islands giving time for a swim and returning at 6pm.

Best of all the beaches are those near the village of **Trinidade**, 21km south of Parati and reached by a steep, but good winding road (7 buses daily; 45min).

Sandwiched between the ocean and Serra do Mar, Trinidade has reached the physical limits of growth, the dozens of inexpensive pousadas, holiday homes, camping sites, bars and restaurants crammed with tourists in the peak summer season. The main beach is nice enough, but you're better off walking away from the village across the rocky outcrops to Praia Brava or Praia do Meio, where the only signs of development on what are some of the most perfect mainland beaches on this stretch of coast are just a few beach bars.

Eating, drinking and entertainment

The town has a good choice **restaurants** in all price brackets, though often the expensive-looking ones can be surprisingly reasonable, thanks to portions big enough for two people. Predictably, fish is the local speciality, but there are many other options, with the restaurants listed here being the more noteworthy.

Banana da Terra Rua Dr Samuel Costa 198. Possibly Parati's most interesting restaurant, emphasizing local ingredients (most notably bananas) and regional cooking. The grilled fish with garlic-herb butter and served with banana is delicious, as are the wonderful banana desserts. Evenings only except Sat & Sun, when lunch is also served; closed Wed.

Beija Flor Rua Dr Pereira, no number. A Lebanese-Portuguese café in a quiet corner of the historic centre – a good place for a cold beer or *caipirinha* and some savoury snacks. From 4pm, closed Wed.

Margarida Café Praça Chafariz. Well-prepared, imaginative modern Brazilian cooking. There's a nice bar, plus remarkably good live music on most nights. Expensive.

Merlin o Mago Rua do Comércio 376. Overly formal for laid-back Parati, but the French-influenced fish dishes are excellent if expensive. Evenings only, closed Wed.

Sabor da Terra Av Roberto Silveira 180. Outside the historic centre, next to the Banco do Brasil, the inexpensive *Sabor da Terra* is Parati's best *por kilo* restaurant, offering a wide variety of hot and cold dishes, including excellent seafood.

Inland: Petrópolis

Excellent bus services from Rio de Janeiro make the **interior** of the state easily accessible, and its mountainous wooded landscape and relatively cool climate are a pleasant contrast to the coastal heat. Sixty-six kilometres directly to the north of Rio de Janeiro, high in the mountains, stands the imperial city of **PETRÓPOLIS**. Buses leave Rio for Petrópolis every fifteen minutes and, in fine weather, the journey is glorious. Be sure to sit on the left-hand side of the bus; the scenery is dramatic, climbing among forested slopes that give way suddenly to ravines and gullies, while clouds shroud the surrounding mountains.

You can easily tour Petrópolis in a day. The **Palácio Imperial** on Avenida VII de Setembro (Tues–Sun & holidays 11am–5.30pm; $1.50; ⓣ24/2237-8000, ⓦwww.museuimperial.gov.br) is a fine structure, set in beautifully maintained gardens. Upon entry, you're given felt overshoes with which to slide around the polished floors of this royal residence, and inside there's everything from Dom Pedro II's crown (639 diamonds, 77 pearls, all set in finely wrought gold) to the regal commode. The cathedral of **São Pedro de Alcântara** (Tues–Sun 8am–noon and 2–6pm) blends with the rest of the architecture around, but is much more recent than its rather overbearing neo-Gothic style suggests – it was only finished in 1939. Inside, on the walls, are ten relief sculptures depicting scenes from the Crucifixion; in the mausoleum lie the tombs of Dom Pedro himself, Princess Regent Dona Isabel and several other royal personages.

Practicalities

Petrópolis has an extremely helpful **tourist office** (ⓣ800/241-516) at the entrance to town at Quitandinha (Mon–Thurs & Sun 8am–7pm, Fri & Sat 8am–8pm), with a branch at the Casa do Barão de Maurá, Praça da Confluência 3 (Mon–Sat 9am–6.30pm, Sun and holidays 9am–5pm).

There are some reasonable low-budget **hotels** in town, with the nicest being *Pousada 14 Bis* at Rua Santos Dumont 162 (Ⓣ24/2231-0946, Ⓦwww.pousada14bis.com.br; ❹), its simple rooms all with colonial-style furnishings. A number of former mansions have been converted into hotels: the *Bragança*, behind the cathedral at Rua Raul de Leon 109 (Ⓣ24/2242-0434; ❻), maintains some of the residence's former style, while the *Casablanca*, next to the Palácio Imperial at Rua da Imperatriz 286 (Ⓣ24/2242-6662, Ⓦwww.casablancahotel.com.br; ❻), which has a pool, is far more institutional in feel. By far the most attractive, having the air of a country inn rather than a city hotel, is the *Pousada Monte Imperial* (Ⓣ24/2237-1664; ❼), on a hilltop at Rua José Alencar 27, which, although central, is a stiff walk from the town's attractions. Rooms are quite small but appealing, and there's a nice garden with a pool, too; the English-speaking owner is extremely friendly.

Restaurants are surprisingly lacklustre in Petrópolis, most of the best being some distance from town. However, there's a good and moderately priced Portuguese restaurant in the *Hotel Bragança*, and an excellent *por kilo* choice, *Rink Marowil*, at Praça Rui Barbosa 27. Much more atmospheric is the *Arte Temperada* (Wed–Sun lunch only, Fri & Sat also dinner; Ⓣ24/2237-2133), in a converted stable of a beautiful nineteenth-century mansion at Rua Ipiranga 716; the modern Brazilian offerings include local trout and salads

3.2

Minas Gerais

The discovery of gold and diamonds in the hills and mountains of **MINAS GERAIS** at the end of the seventeenth century unleashed a wave of migration from Rio and São Paulo, which shifted the centre of gravity of the country's economy and population decisively to the south. While the state capital, **Belo Horizonte**, is a thriving metropolis in the centre of the rich mining and agricultural hinterland, the eighteenth-century mining settlements of Minas Gerais are now quiet and beautiful colonial towns, with a fraction of the population they had two hundred years ago. Known as the **cidades históricas**, "the historic cities", and are the only colonial survivals in southern Brazil that stand comparison with the Northeast. Most importantly, they're the repository of a great flowering of Baroque **religious art** that took place here in the eighteenth century. The most

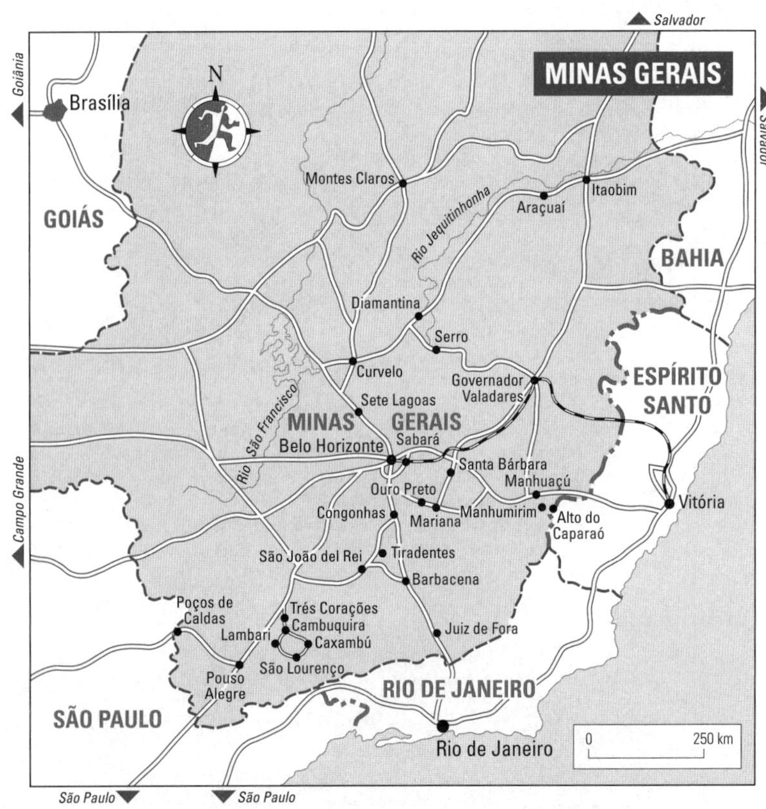

important of the *cidades históricas* are **Ouro Preto** and **Mariana**, both within easy distance of Belo Horizonte, and **São João del Rei**, **Tiradentes** and **Diamantina**, a little further afield.

Belo Horizonte

The best way to approach **BELO HORIZONTE** is from the south, over the magnificent hills of the Serra do Espinhaço, on a road that winds back and forth before finally cresting a ridge where the entire city is set spectacularly out before you. Belo Horizonte sprawls in an enormous bowl surrounded by hills, a sea of skyscrapers, *favelas* and industrial suburbs. From the centre, the jagged rust-coloured skyline of the Serra do Espinhaço, which gave the city its name, is always visible on the horizon.

Laid out in the early 1890s and shaped by the new ideas of "progress" that emerged with the new Republic, Belo Horizonte was the first of Brazil's planned cities and arguably the most successful. As late as 1945 it had only 100,000 inhabitants; now it has well over twenty times that number (forty times if one includes the city's metropolitan hinterland), an explosive rate of growth even by Latin American standards. And while it may not be as historic as the rest of the state, Belo Horizonte's central location and proximity to some of the most important *cidades históricas* make it a good base for exploring Minas Gerais.

Arrival and information

The nearer of Belo Horizonte's two **airports** is Pampulha (☎31/3689-2700), 9km from the centre and connected by bus #1202. All short-haul flights and an increasing number of flights from further afield arrive here. Aeroporto Tancredo Neves (☎31/3490-2001), usually referred to as Confins, the name of a nearby town, was designed to take most air traffic away from Pampulha, but its distance from the city (well over 30km) has made it unpopular. Confins is linked to the centre by **airport buses** that leave you either at the rodoviária (the *ônibus convencional*; 75¢) or at the tourist centre, Terminal Turístico JK, west along Avenida Amazonas (the faster, air-conditioned *ônibus executivo*; $3). Both buses have rather erratic timetables (every 20min at best, every 2hr at worst); if you're departing by plane, phone in advance to check departure times (*convencional* ☎31/3271-1335; *executivo* ☎31/3271-4522). **Taxis** to the city centre cost around $10 from Pampulha or $25 from Confins; there are desks in the arrivals areas from where you can purchase vouchers at rates fixed according to your destination.

The **rodoviária** is on Praça Rio Branco, an easy walk from the commercial centre of the city, and offers direct bus services to most significant destinations in the country. The information desk (☎31/3201-8933) can provide details of times and fares. Nearby is the **train station** (☎31/3273-5976) on Praça da Estação (also called Praça Rui Barbosa). Apart from the local commuter service, only one line out of Belo Horizonte has survived the post-privatization cuts of the 1990s, namely the daily connection with Vitória on the coast.

Information

The municipal BELOTUR organization is very knowledgeable about the city and the rest of the state, and publishes a useful, free monthly guide-booklet, the *Guia Turística*, which contains a good map. You'll find it in the city's better hotels and in the **tourist offices** at the Palácio das Artes (see below; Mon–Sat 9am–7pm), at both airports (daily 8am–10pm), and the rodoviária (Mon–Fri 8am–8pm, Sat & Sun 8am–4pm). Belotur also has a phone number ("Alô Turismo") for specific queries: ☎31/3277-9777 (daily 8am–10pm). The Minas Gerais state tourist office,

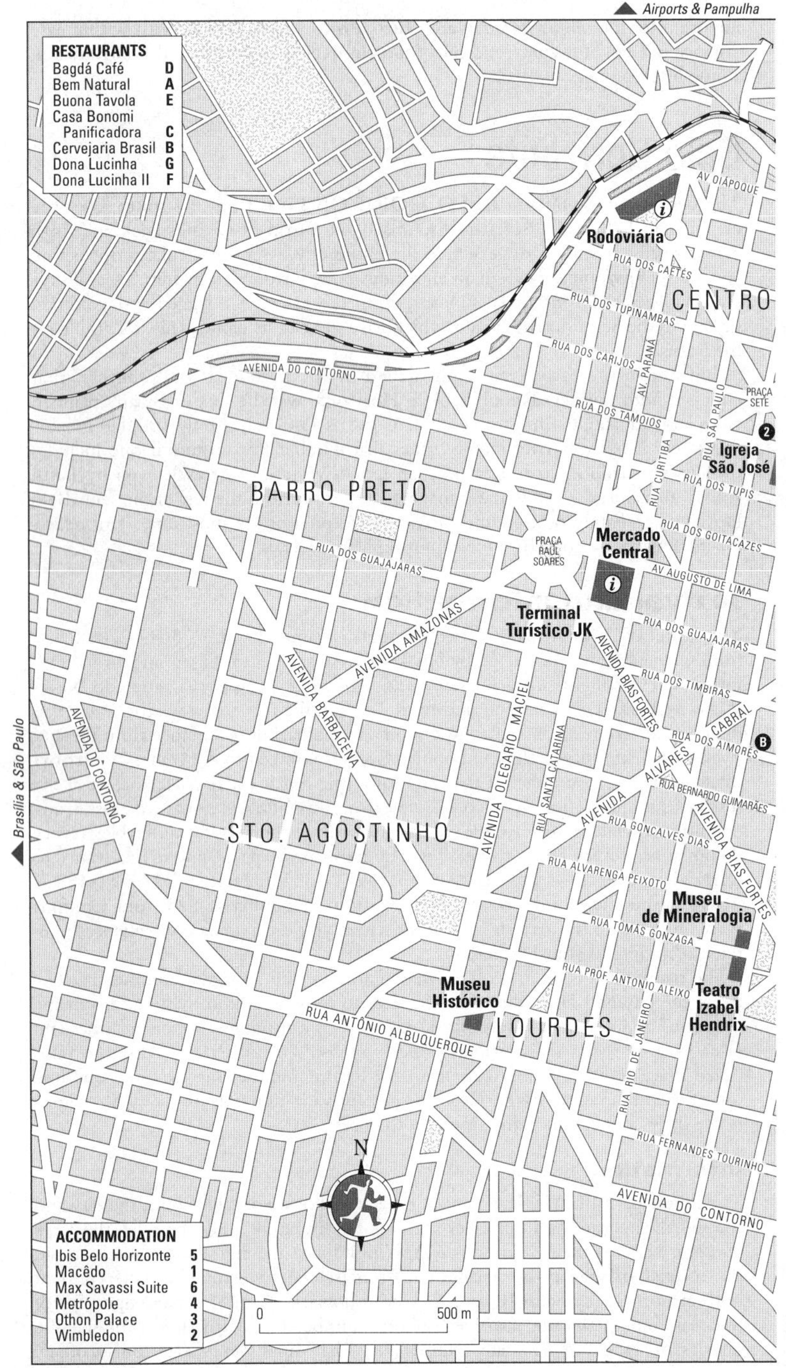
Airports & Pampulha
RESTAURANTS
Bagdá Café D
Bem Natural A
Buona Tavola E
Casa Bonomi Panificadora C
Cervejaria Brasil B
Dona Lucinha G
Dona Lucinha II F
AV OIÁPOQUE
Rodoviária
RUA DOS CAETÉS
CENTRO
RUA DOS TUPINAMBAS
RUA DOS CARIJOS
AV. PARANÁ
AVENIDA DO CONTORNO
PRAÇA SETE
RUA DOS TAMOIOS
RUA SÃO PAULO
Igreja São José
RUA CURITIBA
RUA DOS TUPIS
BARRO PRETO
RUA DOS GOITACAZES
PRAÇA RAUL SOARES
Mercado Central
RUA DOS GUAJAJARAS
AV AUGUSTO DE LIMA
Terminal Turístico JK
AVENIDA AMAZONAS
AVENIDA BARBACENA
AVENIDA BIAS FORTES
RUA DOS TIMBIRAS
AVENIDA OLEGARIO MACIEL
RUA SANTA CATARINA
AVENIDA ÁLVARES CABRAL
RUA DOS AIMORÉS
RUA BERNARDO GUIMARÃES
Brasília & São Paulo
AVENIDA DO CONTORNO
STO. AGOSTINHO
RUA GONÇALVES DIAS
RUA ALVARENGA PEIXOTO
Museu de Mineralogia
RUA TOMÁS GONZAGA
RUA PROF. ANTONIO ALEIXO
Museu Histórico
Teatro Izabel Hendrix
RUA ANTÔNIO ALBUQUERQUE
LOURDES
RUA RIO DE JANEIRO
RUA FERNANDES TOURINHO
N
AVENIDA DO CONTORNO
ACCOMMODATION
Ibis Belo Horizonte 5
Macêdo 1
Max Savassi Suite 6
Metrópole 4
Othon Palace 3
Wimbledon 2
0
500 m

Vitória
RUA GUAICURUS
AV SANTOS DUMONT
PRAÇA DA ESTAÇÃO
Train Station & Museu de Artes e Ofícios
AVENIDA DO CONTORNO
AV ASSIS CHATEAUBRIAND
AVENIDA FRANCISCO SALES
RUA AQUILES LOBO
R. ESPIRITO SANTO
AVENIDA
Bahia Shopping
TELEMIG
Prefeitura
Parque Municipal
Palácio da Justica
AVENIDA DOS ANDRADAS
RUA DOMINGOS VIEIRA
AL. ALVARO CELSO
STA. EFIGÊNIA
AV. PROF. ALFREDO BALENA
Centro Cultural Belo Horizonte
AFONSO PENA
Escola da Música
Palácio das Artes
RUA DA BAHIA
RUA JOÃO PINHEIRO
RUA SERGIPE
RUA ALAGOAS
PERNAMBUCO
RUA PARAIBA
Central Shopping
RUA RIO GRANDE DO NORTE
AVENIDA BERNARDO MONTEIRO
AVENIDA BRASIL
AVENIDA CARANDAÍ
AVENIDA DO CONTORNO
S. LUCAS
Museu Mineiro
Catedral da Boa Viagem
RUA CEARA
RUA PIAUI
RUA MARANHAO
FUNCIONÁRIOS
AVENIDA BRASIL
AVENIDA AFONSO PENA
RUA GONCALVES DIAS
RUA CLAUDIO MANOEL
AVENIDA GETULIO VARGAS
PRAÇA DE LIBERDADE
Edifício Niemeyer
RUA STA. RITA DURAO
AV CRISTOVÃO COLOMBO
RUA DOS INCONFIDENTES
Palácio da Liberdade
SAVASSI
PRAÇA SAVASSI
SÃO PEDRO
SION
BELO HORIZONTE
Rio de Janeiro & Ouro Preto
Mangabeiras

Sectur, is at Praça Rio Branco 56 (Mon–Fri 9am–6pm; ⓣ31/3272-8585), and is well worth a visit for help planning routes in the interior.

The *Estado de Minas* **newspaper** features a daily *Espetáculo* section, listing ongoing events in the city and previewing new shows. By far the most comprehensive information source, however, with detailed reviews of restaurants, films and nightlife of all sorts, is the *Roteiro Cultural* supplement of the free *Pampulha* paper, published every Saturday and available in the city's hotels.

Accommodation

You don't need to stray far from the centre for **accommodation**, as there are scores of hotels, most extremely reasonable, within easy reach of the rodoviária. There are also some good hotel options in the pleasant Savassi area, an easy taxi or bus ride (or a half-hour walk) from the centre. For those on a tight budget, the city's **youth hostel**, the *Albergue de Juventude Chalé Mineiro*, Rua Santa Luzia 288 (ⓣ31/3467-1576; $6 per person), is just a short taxi ride (or bus #2701) from the centre in the *bairro* of Santa Efigênia, 3km away; the hostel has its own garden and pool and is always very popular, so phone ahead to check that they have space.

Ibis Belo Horizonte Av João Pinheiro, Centro ⓣ0800/703-7000, ⓦwww.accorhotels.com.br. A renovated old house with a modern extension behind, this efficient hotel on the edge of Funcionários is typical of the French-owned chain. The no-frills rooms are small, but each has a shower and all are air conditioned. ❹

Macêdo Praça da Estação 123, Centro ⓣ31/3222-9255. By far the best of the cheaper options, with good clean rooms (though some of the furniture has clearly seen better days), even cheaper *quartos*, and a basic breakfast. Some rooms have excellent views across the *praça* and train station, but those overlooking Avenida Amazonas can be noisy at night. ❸

Max Savassi Suite Rua Antôniode Albuquerque 335, Savassi ⓣ31/3225-6466, ⓦwww.maxsavassi.com.br. This excellent-value apartment hotel is on a pleasant tree-lined street. All the apartments have a bedroom, a living room and a small kitchen, and the whole building shares a pool. ❺

Metrópole Rua da Bahia 1023, Centro ⓣ31/3273-1544. A splendid Art Deco edifice that wouldn't appear out of place in Miami's South Beach. A very central location, but the most attractive rooms (those at the front of the hotel with balconies) are very noisy during the day. The rooms are clean and well equipped, with air conditioning, cable TV and *frigobar*. ❹

Othon Palace Av Afonso Pena 1050, Centro ⓣ31/3273-3844, ⓦwww.othon.com.br. Huge and newly refurbished 1970s skyscraper, with friendly and highly professional staff, well-equipped rooms and a fine rooftop pool. Be sure to request a room on one of the upper floors facing the front of the building – the views across the Parque Municipal and onwards to the Serra do Curral are absolutely spectacular. ❻

Wimbledon Av Afonso Pena 772, Centro ⓣ0800/318-383, ⓦwww.wimbledon.com.br. Good mid-range hotel in the heart of downtown. The rooms are small and simply furnished, but all have a *frigobar*, cable TV and air conditioning. Ask for a room overlooking Avenida Afonso Pena as these are much brighter. The hotel has a very small pool. ❺

The City

Even the most patriotic *mineiro* would make few claims for the architecture of Belo Horizonte, dominated as it is by nondescript 1960s and 1970s high-rises. Nonetheless, there are a few notable exceptions, notably around **Praça da Liberdade**. And if you stand in the heart of the city, in **Praça Sete**, and look down the broad Avenida Afonso Pena towards the Parque Municipal, or along the graceful palm-lined Avenida Amazonas, it's hard to call the city ugly.

A good place to begin one's wanderings through downtown Belo Horizonte is the **train station** on Praça da Estação, one of the city's prettiest buildings. The 1922 Neoclassical yellow building is one of Brazil's finest examples of tropical Edwardiana although, these days, the station's platforms are used only by passengers on the once daily Vitória-bound service or commuters using the city's *Metrô*. Beautifully renovated in 2002, the building's primary function is as the **Museu de**

△ The Teatro Amazonas, Manaus

Artes e Ofícios (Tues–Fri 1–6pm, Sat & Sun 10am–4pm; $1). Although the stained-glass windows, decorative iron and plaster work inside the building repay examination, the museum's collection of agricultural, handicraft and industrial implements is somewhat disappointing.

Graced on both sides by imperial palms, Avenida Amazonas, one of the city's main arteries, leads up from Praça da Estação into the **Praça Sete**. Humming with activity, Praça Sete is full of office workers and also the main venue of street draughts tournaments, when rows of hustlers set up boards on the pavement and play all comers for money. A ten-minute stroll further along on Avenida Amazonas, at the intersection of Rua Goitacazes and Rua Santa Catarina, brings you to the **Mercado Central** (Mon–Sat 7am–6pm, Sun 7am–noon), a sprawling indoor market of almost four hundred stalls. There's an incredible range of goods on offer, ranging from the usual fruit, vegetables, cheeses and meats, to *cachaças*, spices and herbs, parakeets, kitchen equipment, rustic handicrafts, and *umbanda* and *candomblé* accessories.

Running southeast from Praça Sete, the broad Avenida Afonso Pena bisects the city and is lined by some of the city's showcase buildings. The 1906 **Igreja São José**, midway between Rua Tamoios and Rua Espírito Santo at the top of a flight of steps, was the first church in the new capital; its eclectic Manueline and Gothic style is characteristically Brazilian. Further south along the avenue between Rua da Bahia and Avenida Álvares Cabral is the Art Deco-influenced **Prefeitura** (town hall), built in the 1930s, while just a short distance on is the imposing **Palácio da Justiça** and the **Escola da Música** with its Corinthian columns.

On the other side of the avenue is one of the very few large-scale areas of relief from the traffic and noise of downtown: the green and shade of the **Parque Municipal** (Tues–Sun 6am–6pm). Beautifully laid out by the French landscape artist Paul Villon, the park encompasses a boating lake, two thousand species of tree, shaded walks, aviaries, a permanent fairground and exercise yards. It also contains the main arts complex in the city, the **Palácio das Artes** (entrance on Avenida Afonso Pena), one of the finest modern buildings in the city. When parts of the *palácio* burned down in March 1997, reconstruction began barely a week later. Now fully restored, the *palácio* is divided into a number of well-laid-out **galleries** (daily 9am–9pm; free), with exhibitions concentrating on modern Brazilian art, a couple of small **theatres** and one big one, the **Grande Teatro**, which suffered most in the fire.

Though it's hard to believe in such a large city, the *palácio* has one of the few shops in Belo Horizonte where you'll come across a really good display of the distinctive *artesanato* of the state. The **Centro de Artesanato Mineiro** (Mon 1–6pm, Tues–Fri 9am–9pm, Sat 9am–1pm, Sun 10am–2pm), a large shop rather than a gallery proper, is a great place you can wander around and look without being pressured to buy. Although there's a lot of dross here, there is also some excellent pottery – stubby figurines and realistic clay tableaux. More *artesanato* is available every Sunday morning at the **Feira de Arte e Artesanato**. One of the best of its kind anywhere in the country, with buyers and sellers coming from all over Brazil, this massive market takes over the Avenida Afonso Pena bordering the Parque Municipal. It's always packed, and by mid-morning moving through the narrow avenues between rows of stalls gets difficult; by 2pm, stallholders are packing up and leaving.

One of the few museums in the city really worth a visit is the **Museu Histórico Abílio Barreto** (Tues, Wed, Fri–Sun 10am–5pm, Thurs 10am–9pm; free) at Rua Bernardo Mascarenhas in Cidade Jardim. To get there, you need to take the #5901 bus (marked "Nova Floresta/Santa Lúcia"); from the centre, you can catch the bus along Avenida Amazonas between Rua Espírito Santo and Rua dos Caetés. The museum was once a *fazenda*, built in 1883, comfortable but not luxurious, and typical of the ranches of rural Minas. Though now swamped by the burgeoning city, it once stood on its own, a few kilometres away from the church and hovels of the hamlet of Curral del Rey. The *fazenda* has been perfectly preserved and now houses the usual collection of old furniture and mediocre paintings, upstairs, and in the garden an old tram and turn-of-the-century train used in the construction of Belo Horizonte. Easily the most interesting part of the museum is the **galeria de fotografias**, juxtaposing the sleepy village before it was obliterated – mules, mud huts and oxcarts – with views of the modern city through the decades; there are a couple of well-designed maps to help you get your bearings.

Pampulha

Some distance north of the centre is the luxurious district of **Pampulha**, built around an artificial lake which is overlooked by some of the finest modern buildings in the city. The construction of the **Igreja de São Francisco de Assis** (daily 8am–6pm), with its striking curves and *azulejo* frontage, provides a roll call of the greatest names of Brazilian modernism: Robert Burle Marx laid out its grounds, Oscar Niemeyer designed the church, Cândido Portinari did the tiles and murals and João Ceschiatti (best known for his gravity-defying angels in Brasília's cathedral) contributed the bronze baptismal font. Decades ahead of its time, it's astonishing to realize that the church dates from the 1940s. To get there, take bus #2004 (marked "Bandeirantes/Olhos d'Água") from Avenida Afonso Pena, between Avenida Amazonas and Rua Tupinambás.

The **Museu de Arte da Pampulha** (Tues–Sun & holidays 9am–7pm, ⓣ31/3443-4533, ⓦwww.map.art.br; $1.50) is more difficult to reach. Take the #2215 bus from Rua dos Caetés and get off when you see a sign for the *museu* to the left – you then have to walk down to the lakeside Avenida Otacílio Negrão de Lima, turn right, and the museum is on a small peninsula jutting out into the lake. It's worth the trip, although the small collection of modern art it holds isn't at all compelling in itself. The building itself, however, is a product of two geniuses at the height of their powers. Niemeyer offered a virtuoso effort, all straight lines and

Comida mineira

Minas Gerais' delicious (if somewhat heavy) **regional food**, *comida mineira*, is one of Brazil's most distinctive – based mainly on pork, the imaginative use of vegetables, *couve*, a green vegetable somewhere between spinach and cabbage, and the famous *tutu*, a thick bean sauce made by grinding uncooked beans with manioc flour and cooking the mixture. Many of the dishes originate from the early mule trains and *bandeirante* expeditions of the eighteenth century, when food had to keep for long periods and be easily prepared without elaborate ingredients. Among the **typical dishes** are:

Tutu a mineira Most common of all dishes, found on every menu; roasted pork served with lashings of *tutu*, garnished with steamed *couve* and *torresmo* (an excellent salted pork crackling).

Feijão tropeiro ("Mule driver's beans") A close relative to *tutu a mineira*, with a name that betrays its eighteenth-century origins; it features everything that is in a *tutu* but also has beans fried with *farinha* (manioc flour) and egg, often with onion, thrown into the mix.

Frango com quiabo Chicken roasted with okra and served sizzling with a side plate of *anju*, a corn porridge that *mineiros* eat with almost anything.

Frango ao molho pardo Definitely one for hardened carnivores only: essentially chicken cooked in its own blood. It's better than it sounds, but rather bitter in taste.

Carne picadinha A straightforward, rich stew of either beef or pork, cooked for hours until tender.

Dobradinha Tripe stew cooked with sweet potatoes. Stews (including the two above) often include the excellent Minas sausages, smoked and peppery.

right angles at the front but melting into rippling curves at the back, with a marvellous use of glass; Burle Marx set the whole thing off beautifully, with a sculpture garden out back and an exquisite garden framing the building from the front.

Eating, drinking and nightlife

You can eat well in Belo Horizonte and prices are generally quite reasonable, though outside the immediate downtown area, **restaurants** and **bars** tend to be more upmarket. Savassi has a particularly good range of places. The monthly *Guia Turístico* and the weekly paper *Pampulha* both contain up-to-date listings of Belo Horizonte's better restaurants.

The best area for cheaper eating places is **downtown**, around Praça Sete and towards the train station, where many of the *lanchonetes* serve good, simple and cheap *comida mineira*. Rua Pernambuco in **Funcionários** is also a good place for reasonable *comida mineira por kilo* restaurants, especially popular at lunchtime with workers from nearby government offices.

Bagdá Café Rua Getúlio Vargas 1621, Savassi ⊕31/3223-7535. Inexpensive and attractive Lebanese cooking – the *cordeiro* (lamb) dishes are especially good. Evenings only.

Bem Natural Av Afonso Pena 941, Edifício Sulacap, 2 blocks east of Praça Sete. Excellent vegetarian food, as well as some chicken and fish dishes, are served in a restaurant, which is combined with a health-food shop and alternative bookstore. Inexpensive and highly recommended. Open Mon–Fri; full menu at lunchtime, soup only 5–8pm.

Buona Tavola Rua Santa Rita Durão 309, Funcionários ⊕31/3227-6155. Near the intersection with Av Afonso Pena, this is a relatively simple and quite authentic Italian restaurant. Expect to pay around $15 per person.

Casa Bonomi Panificadora Rua Cláudio Manoel 460, Funcionários ⊕31/3261-3460. Located in a burgundy-coloured building without a sign near Av Afonso Pena, this "bakery" serves excellent light meals (salads, pasta, soups and sandwiches), wonderful cakes and superb bread.

Cervejaria Brasil Rua dos Aimorés 90, Funcionários ⊕31/3287-3299. One of the best centrally located *churrascarias* with a selection of meat likely to bewilder the most dedicated of carnivores. Pleasant surroundings and moderate prices.

Dona Lucinha II Rua Sergipe 811, Funcionários ⊕31/3261-5930. This and its sister restaurant (*Dona Lucinha*, Rua Padre Odorico 38, São Pedro; ⊕31/3227-0562) offer a first rate *comida mineira* buffet for just $6 per person. The vast range of meat and vegetables dishes, and the wonderful desserts, are all helpfully labelled in English, and excellent home-made liqueurs are available to sample. If you have time for just one meal in Belo Horizonte, this is the place to go. Closed Sun evening.

Mala e Cuia Av Antônio Carlos 8305, Pampulha ⊕31/3441-2993. Situated by the lake near Aeroporto de Pampulha and decorated in typical Mineiro rustic country style. You'll get a filling meal of regional cuisine here from around $6 a head. Live music Thursday to Sunday.

Nightlife and entertainment

There are several areas in the central part of city where the **bars** spring to life once it gets dark. Most days of the week, the bottom end of **Rua da Bahia** between Avenida Afonso Pena and Praça da Estação is lively: the bars put out tables under the palm trees and the action goes on until the small hours. The area around the intersection of **Rua Rio de Janeiro** and **Avenida Augusto de Lima** is also good, but more student-like. There are a couple of small theatres and cinemas close by, and a group of bars and restaurants: *Mateus* on the corner is a good one. It's also worth checking out the bars along **Rua Guajajaras** between Rua Espírito Santo and Rua da Bahia. The more sophisticated bars are in **Savassi**, a pleasant place in which to spend an evening. One of the few unpretentious places along Rua Alagoas is *Diário da Noite*, on the corner with Rua Cláudio Manoel, with infectiously danceable music (daily from 4pm). *Chopperia Margherita Ville* and *Sausalito Point* at the intersection of ruas Tomé de Souza and Pernambuco are always busy, and most people end up drinking their beer on the street outside (both open till

4am). A far more gritty scene is to be found in **Barro Preto**, centre of the city's garment industry. Along Avenida Raja Gabáglia there are lots of nightclubs, simple *mineiro* restaurants and small bars where you can listen to live *setaneja* (Brazilian country music).

Listings

Airlines Aerolíneas Argentinas, Rua Tupis 204, sala 209, Centro ☎31/3224-7466; Air Canada, Av Prudente de Moraís 135, Cidade Jardim ☎31/3344-8355; American Airlines, Av Bernardo Monteiro 1539, Funcionários ☎31/3274-3166; British Airways, Rua São Paulo 1106, sala 305, Centro ☎31/3274-6211; Continental Airlines, Rua Espírito Santo 466, sala 1801, Centro ☎31/3274-3177; Delta Airlines, Rua Ceará 1709, sala 1202, Funcionários ☎31/3287-0001; Gol ☎31/3490-2073; Pluna, Av Getúlio Vargas 840, Funcionários ☎31/3291-9292; TAM, Pampulha airport ☎31/3689-2233; TAP, Rua Timbiras 1200, sala 311, Funcionários ☎31/3213-1611; United Airlines, Av Getúlio Vargas 874, 13th Floor, Savassi ☎31/3269-3939; Varig/Nordeste/Rio-Sul, Av Getúlio Vargas 840, Funcionários ☎31/3339-6000; VASP, Av Getúlio Vargas 1492, Funcionários ☎0800/988-277.

Banks and exchange Banks are concentrated downtown on Av João Pinheiro, between Rua dos Timbiras and Avenida Afonso Pena. ATMs are common throughout the city.

Car rental Hertz, at the airports and Av João Pinheiro 341 ☎31/3224-5166 or 224-1279; Interlocadora, at the airports and Rua dos Timbiras 2229 ☎31/3275-4090; Localiza, at the airports and Av Bernardo Monteiro 1567 ☎0800/312-121; Unidas, at the airports and Av Santa Rosa 100 ☎0800/121-121.

Consulates Argentina, Rua Ceará 1566, 3rd floor, Funcionários ☎31/3281-5288; Paraguay, Rua Guandaus 60, apto. 102, Santa Lúcia ☎31/3344-6349; UK, Rua Inconfidentes 1075, sala 1302, Savassi ☎31/3261-2072; Uruguay, Av do Contorno 6777, 13th floor, salas 1301–4, Funcionários ☎31/3296-8293.

Health matters For an ambulance, phone ☎192. Hospital das Clínicas da UFMG is attached to the university, Av Alfredo Badalena 190, Santa Efigênia ☎31/3239-7100.

Police ☎190. For visa or tourist permit extension, go to the Polícia Federal at Rua Nascimento Gurgel 30, Guiterrez ☎31/3330-5200.

Post office The main post office is at Av Afonso Pena 1270 (Mon–Fri 9am–7pm, Sat & Sun 9am–1pm). Collect poste restante round the back at Rua Goiás 77.

Taxis ☎31/3443-2288.

The cidades históricas

The **CIDADES HISTÓRICAS** of Minas Gerais – small enough really to be towns rather than cities – were founded within a couple of decades of each other in the early eighteenth century. Rough and violent mining camps in their early days, they were soon transformed by mineral wealth into treasure houses, not merely of gold, but also of Baroque art and architecture. Well preserved and carefully maintained, together the towns form one of the most impressive sets of colonial remains in the Americas, comparable only to the silver-mining towns that flourished in Mexico at roughly the same time. In Brazil, they are equalled only by the remnants of the plantation culture of the Northeast, to which they contributed much of the gold you see in the gilded churches of Olinda and Salvador.

Two hours southeast of Belo Horizonte, **Ouro Preto** is the ex-capital of the state and the largest of the historic cities, with **Mariana** a short distance away. A two-hour bus ride further south brings you to **São João del Rei**, which rather unfairly overshadows nearby **Tiradentes**. Six hours north by bus from the capital, **Diamantina** is nestled in the wild scenery of the Serra do Espinhaço.

Ouro Preto

The first thing that strikes you about **OURO PRETO**, 100km southeast of Belo Horizonte, is how small the town is, considering that until 1897 it was the capital of Minas – its population is still only around 65,000. That said, you can see at a glance why the capital had to be shifted to Belo Horizonte: the steep hills the town is built around, straddling a network of creeks, severely limit space for expansion. Today, the hills and vertiginous streets are vital ingredients in what is one of the loveliest towns in Brazil, albeit one that can no longer in all honesty lay claim to being the unspoilt eighteenth-century jewel that it was able to just a few years back. There's enough to keep you going for days, however, including thirteen colonial churches, seven chapels and six museums.

Avoid coming on Monday if you want to see the sights, as all the churches and most of the museums close for the day. Ouro Preto has an extremely popular street **Carnaval** that attracts visitors from far afield: be sure to reserve accommodation long in advance. Likewise, at **Easter** time, the town becomes the focus of a spectacular series of plays and processions lasting for about a month before Easter Sunday, during which the last days of the life of Christ are played out in open-air theatres throughout the town.

Arrival and information

Arriving from Mariana, the bus passes through the main square, Praça Tiradentes – where you should get off – before continuing to the **rodoviária**, some fifteen minutes' walk westwards on Rua Padre Rolim. Belo Horizonte buses proceed straight to the rodoviária, from where there are regular buses to the *praça*.

On the east side of Praça Tiradentes at no. 41 is the **municipal tourist office** (Mon–Fri 8am–6pm; ⓣ31/3559-3269), which sells an excellent city map for $2 (and has a smaller version for free); it can also provide details of some spectacular walks in the surrounding countryside. The tourist office has details and prices of even the cheapest hotels, and will phone round for you if you have problems, or keep an eye on your luggage while you search. There are ATMs at Bradesco on Praça Tiradentes, HSBC at Rua São José 105 and at the Banco do Brasil, Rua São José 189; the Banco do Brasil also changes money over the counter from Monday to Friday between 11am and 4pm.

Accommodation

The price codes below are based on weekend (Fri–Sun) and high-season prices; midweek and in low season, Ouro Preto's hotels usually offer discounts of around 20–30 percent.

Albergue de Juventude Brumas Ladeira de São Francisco de Paula 68 ⓣ31/3551-2944, ⓦwww.brumasonline.hpg.ig.com.br). Part of the Hostelling International network, this youth hostel offers fairly basic dorms, kitchen and laundry facilities. Reached by a steep 10-minute trek, with commanding views overlooking Ouro Preto's historic centre. $8 per person.

Grande Hotel de Ouro Preto Rua Senador Rocha Lagoa 164 ⓣ31/3551-1488, ⓦwww.hotelouropreto.com.br. Opened in 1940, this is one of Oscar Niemeyer's earliest creations, though not one of his best. If you like airport lounges, you'll love this three-star hotel. Central, with good service and a small pool in the Burle Marx-designed gardens. ❺

Pousada do Mondego Largo de Coimbra 38 (ⓣ31/3551-2040, ⓕ3551-3094). An excellent place in a beautiful restored eighteenth-century building with a modern annex beside the Igreja de São Francisco de Assis, with period furniture in all rooms – ask for one with a balcony. ❼

Pouso Chico Rei Rua Brigador Mosqueira 90 (ⓣ31/3551-1274). The best of the many fine places to stay in town, this small eighteenth-century house converted into a stunningly beautiful *pensão* is filled with a collection of relics that would do credit to a museum. It affords a wonderful view from the reading room on the first floor, excellent breakfasts and a tranquil atmosphere. There are only six rooms, so book in advance. ❺

Solar Nossa Senhora do Rosário Rua Getúlio Vargas 270 (ⓣ31/3551-5200, ⓦwww.hotelsolardorosario.com.br). A nineteenth-century mansion transformed into the city's most luxurious hotel. The hotel's restaurant is one of the best in the city serving fine Franco-mineiro dishes. ❼

Pensão Vermelha Largo de Coimbra, at the corner with Rua Antônio Pereira (ⓣ31/3551-1138). Quiet, family-run place, with clean if simple rooms, some overlooking the magnificent facade of the São Francisco church. ❸

The Town

Right on the **Praça Tiradentes** stands the mining school, the **Escola de Minas**, now housed in the old governor's palace. It's still the best mining school in the country, and its students, with their bars and motorbikes, lend a Bohemian air to the town. The white turrets make the building itself look rather like a fortress: the exterior, with a fine marble entrance, dates from the 1740s, but the interior was gutted during the nineteenth century and not improved by it. Attached to the school is the **Museu de Mineralogia** (daily noon–5pm; 75¢), founded in 1877 from the collection of the French geologist Henri Gorceix. Although most of the exhibits are of interest only to geologists, there is one fascinating room where gold and precious stones are beautifully displayed, in contrast with the chaos of the rest of it. Also in the square are the old city chambers, the **Paço Municipal** (Tues–Sun noon–5.30pm; 75¢), a glorious eighteenth-century building that provides a perfect example of the classical grace of Minas colonial architecture. Like many colonial town halls it was also a jail, and many of the huge rooms, so well suited to the display of *arte sacra*, were once dungeons. The building contains the **Museu da Inconfidência** (same hours as Paço Municipal), housing relics of eighteenth-century daily life, from sedan chairs and kitchen utensils (including the seal the bishop used to stamp his coat of arms on his cakes) to swords and pistols.

Next door to the Paço Municipal is one of the finest churches in Ouro Preto, the **Igreja de Nossa Senhora do Carmo** (Tues–Sat noon–4.45pm, Sun 9.30–11am & 1–4.45pm). It was designed by Manoel Francisco Lisboa, Aleijadinho's father, and construction began just before his death in 1766. **Aleijadinho** himself then took over the building of the church and finished it six years later. He contributed the carving of the exterior, and worked on the interior, on and off, for four decades. The baptismal font in the sacristy is a masterpiece, as are the carved doors leading to the pulpits. Two of the side chapels in the main church (São João and Nossa Senhora da Piedade) were among the last commissions he was able to complete, in 1809.

It's a lovely walk from Praça Tiradentes to Ouro Preto's oldest church. **Rua Brigador Mosqueira**, which runs downhill from the square, is one of the quietest and most beautiful streets in Ouro Preto, almost every building worth savouring. Wander down, bear left at the bottom, and you come out onto the incredibly steep Rua do Pilar, from where you can glimpse the towers of the **Igreja do Pilar** (Tues–Sun 9–10.45am & noon–4.45pm) well before the plunging, cobbled path deposits you in front of it. With an exterior ornate even by Baroque standards, the church is the finest example anywhere of early Minas-Baroque architecture. It was begun in the 1720s and the interior is the opposite of the Carmo's restraint, a wild explosion of glinting Rococo, liberally plastered with gold. The best carving was done by Francisco Xavier de Brito, who was responsible for the astonishing arch over the altar, where the angels supporting the Rococo pillars seem to swarm out of the wall on either side.

Retrace your steps to Praça Tiradentes and follow Rua Cláudio Manoel downhill. Ahead, on the right, is arguably the most beautiful church in Ouro Preto, the **Igreja de São Francisco de Assis** (Tues–Sun 8.30–11.45am & 1.30–5pm). The small square that sets it off – Largo do Coimbra – plays host to a food **market** in the morning and a mediocre arts and crafts market in the afternoon. The church was begun in 1765, and no other in Ouro Preto contains more work by Aleijadinho. The magnificent exterior soapstone panels are his, as is virtually all of the virtuoso carving, in both wood and stone, inside; and to top it off, Aleijadinho also designed the church and supervised its construction. You would think the church commissioners would have left it at that, but in 1801 they contracted the best painter of the *barroco mineiro*, **Manoel da Costa Athayde**, to decorate the ceilings.

Returning to Rua Cláudio Manoel, follow the winding Rua Bernardo de Vasconcelos to the left – this is the back way down to the last of the major churches in Ouro Preto, **Matriz de Nossa Senhora da Conceição** (Tues–Sat

9–11.45am & 1.30–5pm, Sun noon–5pm), and it's a steep descent. Coming this way, you're leaving the main tourist area and everything looks just as it did the day Aleijadinho died; the Matriz is celebrated as the church he belonged to and where he is buried, yet Despite Aleijadinho's connection with the church, he never worked on this one. All the same, it is an impressive example of mid-period Minas-Baroque, and the painting and carving are very fine, especially the figures of saints in the side altars. Aleijadinho is buried in a simple **tomb** on the right of the nave, marked "Antônio Francisco Lisboa" and covered by nothing more elaborate than a plain wooden plank. A side door by the main altar of the church leads to the sacristy and the fascinating **Museu do Aleijadinho** (Tues–Sat 8.30–11.45am & 1.30–5pm, Sun noon–5pm; 50¢), which is worth lingering over: it is not so much a museum of Aleijadinho's work as of his life and times. What work there is by him is in the basement, and is quite something – four magnificent lions that once served as supports for the plinth on which coffins were laid. Aleijadinho, never having seen a lion, drew from imagination and produced medieval monsters with the faces of monkeys. The ground floor is taken up by a high-quality collection of religious art, but the highlight is upstairs, in a room dedicated not just to Aleijadinho but to all the legendary figures of Ouro Preto's golden age.

Eating and drinking

During term-time, at the weekend, the steep Rua Conde de Bobadela (also called Rua Direita), leading up to Praça Tiradentes, is packed with students spilling out of the **bars** and cafés; more congregate in the square itself, though most of the bars there have been turned into expensive restaurants. The modern wing of the mining school on the square contains a bar and a **live music** venue (see the posters in the lobby). If you prefer a quiet drink away from the crowds, try *Bar Sena*, a local dive on the corner outside the Igreja do Pilar.

There is no shortage of **restaurants**, either; the better-value ones are clustered at the bottom of the hill on Rua São José, of which the best is unquestionably *Restaurante Chafariz* at no. 167, which does a superb *mineiro* buffet for about $7. Established in 1929, the restaurant has become something of a local institution, with pleasantly rustic decor and smooth service – altogether highly recommended. More expensive places are clustered at the top of Rua Direita (Rua Conde de Bobadela), where you'll get good regional food in uniformly beautiful surroundings for $6–15 per person: a particularly appealing choice is the rather elegant *Restaurante Casa do Ouvidor*, Rua Direita 42. For a splurge, try *Le Coq D'Or* (☎31/3551-1032), a Franco-Mineiro restaurant in the *Hotel Solar do Rosário*, Rua Vargas 270. Although one of the best restaurants in Minas Gerais, it's surprisingly reasonable (around $20 a head). If you don't want a substantial meal, the delightful *Café Geraes* at Rua Direita 122 is well worth trying for delicious sandwiches, soups, cakes and wine.

Mariana

MARIANA is one of the major colonial towns, and in the first half of the eighteenth century was grander by far than its younger rival, Ouro Preto, 12km to the west. Mariana was the administrative centre of the gold mines of central Minas until the 1750s. The first governors of Minas had their residence here and the first bishops their palace, and the town proudly celebrated its tercentenary in 1996. Yet today Mariana's churches are far less grand than its illustrious neighbour's, and it's really no more than a large village, albeit one that is steadily expanding. It does, however, have a perfectly preserved colonial centre, mercifully free of steep climbs, that is less crowded and commercialized than Ouro Preto. It's only a twenty-minute bus ride away and if you can't stand the crowds in Ouro Preto you could always stay here instead. There are also at least seven daily buses direct from Belo Horizonte.

Although it has been overshadowed by its neighbour for over two centuries, you can still get a good idea of Mariana's early flourishing in one of the best museums in Minas Gerais, the **Museu Arquidiocesano** in the old bishop's palace, on Rua Frei Durão (Tues–Sun 8.30am–noon & 1.30–5pm; 75¢). The **building** itself is magnificent, with parts dating from the first decade of the eighteenth century, when it began life, bizarrely, as a prison for erring churchmen. Between 1720 and 1756 the jail was extended into a palace; the door and window frames are massive, built in beautifully worked local soapstone. Inside, the **collection** is predictable – *arte sacra* and colonial furniture – but is distinguished by its quality and age.

Mariana's colonial churches are smaller and less extravagant than Ouro Preto's. The oldest church is the **Catedral de Nossa Senhora da Assunção** on Praça Cláudio Manoel (Tues–Sun 7am–7pm), begun in 1709 and choked with gilded Rococo detail. This is very much an Aleijadinho family venture: his father, Manoel Francisco Lisboa, designed and built it, while Aleijadinho contributed the carvings in the sacristy and a font. The interior is dominated by a massive German organ dating from 1701 and donated by the king of Portugal in 1751.

The two churches on Praça João Pinheiro, around the corner, show how tastes had changed by the end of the century. Their ornate facades and comparatively restrained interiors are typical of the third phase of *barroco mineiro*. The **Igreja de São Francisco de Assis** (daily 8am–5pm), finished in 1794, has the finest paintings of any Mariana church, as befits the place where Athayde is buried.

Practicalities

The local **buses from Ouro Preto** leave you right in the centre at Praça Tancredo Neves, opposite an excellent **tourist information post**, the Terminal Turístico (daily 8am–5pm; ⓣ31/3557-1158), which sells a good map for $1.50 and supplies guides for tours in the region (around $20 a day). If you're coming from further afield, you'll arrive at the new **rodoviária** (ⓣ31/3557-1122), on the main road a couple of kilometres from the centre; if you can't be bothered to walk, catch one of the buses from Ouro Preto, which pass through the rodoviária every twenty minutes or so.

All the **places to stay** are within easy walking distance of Praça Tancredo Neves. One of the nicest is the *Pousada Solar dos Corrêa*, Rua Josafá Macedo 70 (ⓣ31/3557-2080; ❺), one block up from the Terminal Turístico on the corner with Rua Direita. The hotel has fifteen very different rooms done up with mock-colonial furniture. It pays to come mid-week to secure the room of your choice, as at weekends you'd be lucky to get one at all. Similar in style, but slightly more expensive, is the *Pousada Typographia* at Praça Gomes Freire 220 (ⓣ31/3557-1577; ❺), an eighteenth-century mansion restored in period detail. The rooms are spacious and comfortable and the location especially attractive. Cheaper options include the basic *Hotel Central* (ⓣ31/3557-1630; ❸), a beautiful but run-down colonial building at Rua Frei Durão 8, overlooking the Praça Gomes Freire, and the clean and tidy *Hotel Providência*, Rua Dom Silvério 233 (ⓣ31/3577-1444; ❸), along the road that leads up to the Basílica, which has use of the neighbouring school's pool when classes finish at noon.

Mariana has some decent **restaurants** with nice views across Praça Gomes Freire (all open daily until midnight). The cosy *Restaurante Pizzeria Senzala* serves good food at lunchtime and turns into a lively and very friendly bar in the evenings; and *Mangiare della Mamma*, three doors up at Rua Dom Viçoso 27, does a top-notch *mineiro comida à kilo* ($4 per kg), presented in heavy iron casseroles sizzling on a hot, wood-fired iron stove. Just up from Praça Gomes Freire at Travessa João Pinheiro 26, next to the Igreja São Francisco, is arguably the town's best *mineiro* restaurant, *Tambau* (ⓣ31/3557-1406). For bargain lunches, a good place to try is the self-service *Panela de Pedra*, a restaurant attached to the Terminal Turístico.

São João del Rei

SÃO JOÃO DEL REI is the only one of the historic cities to have adjusted successfully to life after the gold rush. It has all the usual trappings of the *cidades* *históricas* – gilded churches, well-stocked museums, colonial mansions – but it's also a thriving market town, easily the largest of the historic cities, with a population of around 80,000. If possible, stay over on a Friday, Saturday or Sunday when you can take a ride on the "Smoking Mary", a lovingly restored nineteenth-century steam train, to the nearby village of **Tiradentes**.

Arrival and information

The centre of town is fifteen minutes' walk southwest from the **rodoviária**, or you can take a local bus in; the stop isn't the obvious one immediately outside the rodoviária's main entrance – instead you need to turn left and take any bus from the stop on the other side of the road. Local buses enter the old part of town along **Avenida Tancredo Neves**, with its small stream and grassy verges to your left, then turn right to leave you at the **tourist office** (daily 8am–6pm), where you can pick up a tourist booklet with a helpful map. **Money changing** is quick at the BEMGE bank, Av Tancredo Neves 213 (Mon–Fri 11am–4pm); should you need an ATM, the Banco do Brasil and Banespa have branches on the same avenue.

Accommodation

Finding somewhere to stay is rarely a problem as **accommodation** in São João is plentiful and often excellent value. Bear in mind, however, that the town is a popular spot to spend Carnaval in, and Easter celebrations also attract huge numbers of visitors; at these times hotel reservations are essential. The *Hotel Brasil* (Ⓣ32/3371-2804; ❹) at Av Tancredo Neves 395, facing the train station, is a favourite budget choice, though its high-ceilinged rooms are rather shabby. Very similar accommodation is offered by the *Pousada Portal del Rey* at Praça Severiano Resende 134 (Ⓣ32/3371-8820; ❸), above a restaurant.

Of the medium-range places, the best value is the *Pousada Casarão*, Rua Ribeiro Bastos 94 (Ⓣ32/3371-7447; ❹), a wonderful converted mansion near São Francisco church, with the added attraction of a small swimming pool. Top of the range, with a very good pool, is the very comfortable, but somewhat impersonal, three-star *Pousada do Bispo* (Ⓣ32/3371-8844, Ⓦwww.becodobispo.com.br; ❺), just outside the historic centre at Beco do Bispo 93.

The Town

São João's colonial sections are complemented by some fine buildings of more recent eras, notably the end of the nineteenth century, when the town's prosperity and self-confidence were high. The 1920s and 1930s were also good times – some of the vaguely Art Deco buildings combine surprisingly well with the colonial ones. The main public buildings line the south bank of the stream, best viewed from Avenida Tancredo Neves on the north side; there's a sumptuous French-style **theatre** (1893), and the graceful blue **Prefeitura** with an imposing Banco do Brasil building facing it.

The most impressive of the town's colonial churches is the **Igreja de São Francisco de Assis** (daily 8am–noon & 1.30–5pm), one block off the western end of Avenida Eduardo Magalhães. Overlooking a square with towering palms the church, finished in 1774, is exceptionally large, with an ornately carved exterior by a pupil of Aleijadinho. The master himself contributed the intricate decorations of the side chapels, which can be seen in all their glory now that the original paint and gilding has been stripped off. From the plaques, you'll see that the church has been visited by some illustrious guests, including President Mitterand of France, who came to pay homage at the **grave of Tancredo Neves**, in the cemetery behind the church.

Over on the other side of the stream, one block north from Avenida Tancredo Neves, lies the main street of the other colonial area, **Rua Getúlio Vargas**. The western end is formed by the small early eighteenth-century **Igreja da Nossa**

Senhora do Rosário (Tues–Sun noon–6pm), which looks onto a cobbled square dominated by two stunning colonial mansions. The one nearest the church is the Solar dos Neves, the family home of the Neves clan for over two centuries, the place where Tancredo was born and lived.

A couple of buildings east along from the Solar dos Neves is an excellent **Museu de Arte Sacra** (Tues–Sun noon–5pm; 75¢), contained within another sensitively restored house. The collection is small but very good; highlights are a finely painted St George and a remarkable figure of Christ mourned by Mary Magdalene, with rubies representing drops of blood. Almost next door to the museum on Avenida Getúlio Vargas is a magnificent early Baroque church, the **Catedral Basílica de Nossa Senhora de Pilar** (Tues–Sun noon–6pm), completed in 1721. The interior is gorgeous; the gilding is seen to best effect over the altar, a riot of Rococo pillars, angels and curlicues. The ceiling painting is all done with vegetable dyes, and there's a beautiful tiled floor.

More or less on a level with the cathedral, just off Avenida Tancredo Neves on Praça Severiano de Rezende, is an excellent museum, the **Museu Regional** (Tues–Sun noon–5.30pm; $1), housed in a magnificently restored colonial mansion. Perhaps the most fascinating pieces here are the eighteenth-century *ex votos* on the ground floor, their vivid illustrations detailing the pickles that both masters and slaves got themselves into – José Alves de Carvalho was stabbed in the chest while crossing a bridge on the way home in 1765; a slave called Antônio had his leg broken and was half buried for hours in a mine cave-in. On the first floor are several figures of saints made by ordinary people in the eighteenth century; they have a simplicity and directness that makes them stand out.

Eating and drinking

On the **north side** of the Lenheiro stream, on Praça Severiano de Rezende, you'll find two of the town's swishest **restaurants**: the *Churrascaria Ramon*, which does a good-value *churrasco*, and the *Quinta do Ouro*, which serves the best *mineiro* food in São João. On the same *praça*, is the cheaper perfectly adequate *por kilo Restaurante Rex* (11am–4pm).

The best places, however, combining good food with lively atmosphere, are on the **south side**, where trippers from Belo Horizonte, as well as young townsfolk and families flock to drink, eat and go to the cinema. Almost all of the action is concentrated on Avenida Tiradentes, and the **bars** are bunched both at Tiradentes' western end near São Francisco. Here *Cabana do Zotti* at no. 805 (9pm onwards) is always packed and does good snacks – and halfway along Tiradentes at the junction with Rua Gabriel Passos (the road which runs in from the blue Prefeitura). *Miaxôu Bar*, at Rua Gabriel Passos 299 (5pm onwards), has charming *dona*, excellent food (try the *bolinhos de queijo* or the pizzas) and efficient service. It gets very animated at weekends when whole families get up and shimmy to the live music (around 8pm–3am), often old sambas.

Tiradentes

Founded as early as 1702, **TIRADENTES** had already been overshadowed by São João by the 1730s and is now no more than a sleepy village, with a population of only 5000. The core is much as it was in the eighteenth century, straggling down the side of a hill crowned by the twin towers of the **Igreja Matriz de Santo Antônio** (Tues–Sun noon–4pm). Completed around 1730, it's one of the earliest and largest of the major Minas-Baroque churches, and in 1732 began to acquire the gilding for which it is famous, becoming in the process one of the richest churches in any of the mining towns. It was decorated with the special extravagance of the newly rich, using more gold, locals say, than any other in Brazil save the Capela Dourada in Recife (see p.381). Whether this is true or not – and Pilar in Ouro Preto is probably as rich as either – the glinting and winking of the gold around the altar is certainly impressive.

If you had to take one photograph to summarize Minas Gerais, it would be from the steps of the church down an unspoilt colonial street – the old town hall with the veranda has a restored eighteenth-century jail – framed by the crests of the hills. Before descending, check out the **Museu Padre Toledo** (Mon, Wed–Fri, 1–4.40pm, Sat & Sun 9am–4.40pm), to the right of Santo Antônio as you're standing on the steps. Padre Toledo, who built the mansion that is now the museum, obviously didn't let being a priest stand in the way of enjoying the pleasures of life – the two-storey *sobrado* must have been very comfortable, and even though the ceiling paintings are dressed up as classical allegories, they're not the sort of thing you would expect a priest to commission. The museum comprises the usual mixture of furniture and religious art, but the interesting part is the yard out back, now converted into toilets but once the old slave quarters.

There could be a no more eloquent reminder of the harsh divisions between masters and slaves than the **Igreja da Nossa Senhora do Rosário dos Pretos** (Tues–Sun 9am–noon & 2–5pm), down the hill and along the first street to the right. This small chapel was built by slaves for their own worship, and there is gilding even here – some colonial miners were freed blacks working on their own account. Two fine figures of the black St Benedict stand out, but overall the church is moving precisely because it is so simple and dignified.

Practicalities

Finding **accommodation** is rarely a problem, as a good proportion of the town's population have turned their homes into pousadas. Nevertheless, during *Carnaval*, over Easter and in July, advanced reservations are pretty much essential, and most will only accept bookings of at least four nights. You'll find a selection along the road leading into the village from the train station, around the lovely Praça das Mercês it leads into, or on the main square, the Largo das Forras; the staff at the **tourist office**, Largo das Forras 71 (Mon–Fri 9am–12.30pm & 1.30–5.30pm, Sat & Sun 9am–5pm), will help you find available rooms.

The cheapest – and one of the friendliest – places to stay is the *Pousada da Bia*, Rua Frederico Ozanan 330 (☎32/3355-1173; ❸). Rooms here are simple, but clean, there's a kitchen for the use of guests and a helpful English-speaking owner. Slightly more expensive options are the large and impersonal *Hotel Ponta do Morro*, Largo das Forras 2 (☎32/3355-1342; ❹), with a pool, or, across the square at no. 48, the very pleasant *Pousada do Largo* (☎32/3355-1166; ❺).

The best **restaurant** in Tiradentes is *Viradas do Largo*, Rua do Moinho 11 (☎32/3355-1111), which sets itself apart from other Mineiro restaurants with the delicacy of its cooking; a full meal costs around $20. For a break from Mineiro food, try *Mandalun*, Rua Padre Toledo 172, an attractive and very good Lebanese place or the *Royal Dansk*, Largo das Forras 66, one of Brazil's very few Danish restaurants, which is especially strong on trout dishes.

Diamantina

DIAMANTINA is the only historic city to the north of Belo Horizonte and, at six hours by bus, is by some way the furthest from it. Yet the **journey** itself is one of the reasons for going there, as the road heads into the different landscapes of northern Minas on its way to the *sertão mineiro*. The second half of the 288-kilometre journey is much the most spectacular, so to see it in daylight you need to catch either the 5.30am, 9am or 11.30am bus from Belo Horizonte.

Scattered down the steep side of a rocky valley, Diamantina itself faces escarpments the colour of rust; the setting has a lunar quality you also come across in parts of the Northeastern *sertão*. In fact, in Diamantina you're not quite in the *sertão* – that begins roughly at Araçuaí, some 300km to the north – but in the uplands of the **Serra do Espinhaço**, the highlands that form the spine of the state.

The central square in the old town is **Praça Conselheiro Mota**, which has the

Catedral Metropolitana de Santo Antônio built in the middle of it – everyone calls the cathedral and the square "Sé". Most of the sights and places to stay are within a stone's throw of here. The **Museu do Diamante** (Tues–Sat noon–5.30pm, Sun & holidays 9am–noon; $1) on the cathedral square is the best place to get an idea of what *garimpagem* has meant to Diamantina. An excellent local museum, not so much for the glories of its exhibits but for the effort it makes to give you an idea of daily life in old Diamantina.

Despite the comparative ugliness of the **Catedral Metropolitana de Santo Antônio**, built in 1940 on the site of an old colonial church, the cathedral square is worth savouring. It's lined with *sobrados*, many of them with exquisite ornamental bronze- and ironwork, often imported from Portugal – look closely and you'll see iron pineapples on the balconies. Most impressive of all are the serried windows of the massive Prefeitura, and the ornate Banco do Brasil building next to it.

For the **other churches**, you're faced with two problems. Some are closed for restoration, which is taking years, and though the workmen are usually happy to let you in, you're not seeing them at their best. Also, in recent years, a rash of thefts of artworks from churches in and around Diamantina has made people very reluctant to open them up for visitors. The one church worth trying to see the inside of, if at all possible, is the **Igreja de Nossa Senhora do Carmo** (Tues–Sat 2–6pm, Sun 8am–noon) on Rua Bonfim, built between 1760 and 1765. Legend has it that the heir of Diamantina's richest miner made sure the tower was built at the back of the church rather than the front, as was usual, so the bells didn't disturb his wife's beauty sleep. You'll find the interior atypically florid, its two main features being a rich, intricately carved altar screen and a gold-sheathed organ, which was actually built in Diamantina.

On the cobbled street leading down the hill from here is a local curiosity. The church at the bottom, **Igreja de Nossa Senhora do Rosário** (Tues–Sat 2–6pm, Sun 8am–noon), has a tree growing in front of it; look closely and you can see a large distorted wooden cross embedded in the trunk and lower branches. The year the old Sé church was knocked down, in 1932, the padre of Rosário planted a wooden cross outside his church to commemorate the chapel that old Diamantina had originally been built around. A fig tree sprouted up around it so that at first the cross seemed to flower – there's a photo of it at this stage in the Museu do Diamante – and eventually, rather than knocking it down, the tree grew up around the cross and ended up absorbing it. Inside the church itself is a marvellous Baroque altar and a simple, yet stunning, painted ceiling.

The old **Mercado dos Tropeiros** on Praça Barão do Guaicuí, just a block downhill from the cathedral square, is the focus of Diamantina's trade, and worth seeing for the building alone, an interesting tiled wooden structure built in 1835 as a trading station by the Brazilian army. Its frontage, a rustic but very elegant series of shallow arches, played a significant role in modern Brazilian architecture. Niemeyer, who lived in Diamantina for a few months in the 1950s to build the *Hotel do Tijuco*, was fascinated by it, and later used the shape for the striking exterior of the presidential palace in Brasília, the Palácio da Alvorada. The market itself (Saturdays only) has a very Northeastern feel, with its cheeses, *doces* made of sugar and fruit, blocks of salt and raw sugar, and mules and horses tied up alongside the pick-ups. The **artesanato** section of the market is small and uninspiring, which is unfortunate since the most distinctive products of the Jequitinhonha Valley are its beautiful clay and pottery figures.

Practicalities

Although the **rodoviária** is not far from the centre of town, it's on a steep hill, and the only way back to it once in the centre is by taxi (around $3), unless you have the legs and lungs of a mountain goat.

Maps are free from the **tourist office** in the Casa da Cultura, tucked away behind the Largo do Rosário on Rua Farinha Seca (Mon–Fri 8am–6pm, Sat

9am–5pm, Sun 8am–noon; ⓣ38/3531-1636). There's also a **tourist post** in the rodoviária (daily 8–11am & 1–6pm), but it's often shut because of staff shortages.

Hotels are plentiful. The largest and priciest is the *Pousada do Garimpo*, a five-minute walk from the town centre at Av da Saudade 265, on the western continuation of Rua Direita (ⓣ38/3531-1044, ⓦwww.pousadadogarimpo.com.br; ❺); the hotel is friendly and well equipped (with pool), but has a somewhat soulless feel to it. Much more interesting, and cheaper too, is the town's 1951 Niemeyer creation, the *Hotel do Tijuco*, Rua Macau do Meio 211 (ⓣ38/3531-1022; ❹), where it's worth splashing out on one of the more expensive "luxo" rooms, which are larger and brighter than the others and have balconies offering wonderful views across Diamantina. Just up from the cathedral, at Rua Macau de Baixo 104, is the *Pousada Relínquias do Tempo* (ⓣ38/3531-1627; ❹), in a wonderfully converted nineteenth-century house filled with period furnishings and decorated with handicrafts from the Jequitinhonha valley. The *Dália Hotel*, Praça J Kubitschek 25 (ⓣ38/3531-1477; ❸), just down from the cathedral, is possibly the best value in town. Housed in a lovely two-storey building, it has bags of character, good rooms and fine views over the square.

The streets around the cathedral are the heart of the town, and there's no shortage of simple bars and *mineiro* **restaurants** here, though the food on offer is rather uninspiring. Best of all is *Cantinha do Marinho* on Rua Direita 113, in front of the cathedral: the food is good and offers the best value for money in town; try a *doce de limão* to round off your meal. Reasonable options include the *Capistrana* on Praça Antônio Eulálio and *Espeto de Prata* on Beco da Pena just off Rua Direita, a sophisticated *churrasco* joint with live music Thursdays to Sundays. The main focus of weekend **nightlife** activity is Rua Direita; the busiest bar is *Oasis Clube* at no. 132 (daily 8am–late), which has live music upstairs on Friday and Sunday evenings and a disco on Saturdays.

3.3

The Northeast

The Northeast (*nordeste*) of Brazil covers an immense area and features a variety of climates and scenery, from the dense equatorial forests of western Maranhão, only 200km from the mouth of the Amazon, to the parched interior of Bahia, some 2000km to the south. It takes in all or part of the nine states of Maranhão, Piauí, Ceará, Rio Grande do Norte, Paraíba, Pernambuco, Alagoas, Sergipe and Bahia, which together form roughly a fifth of Brazil's land area

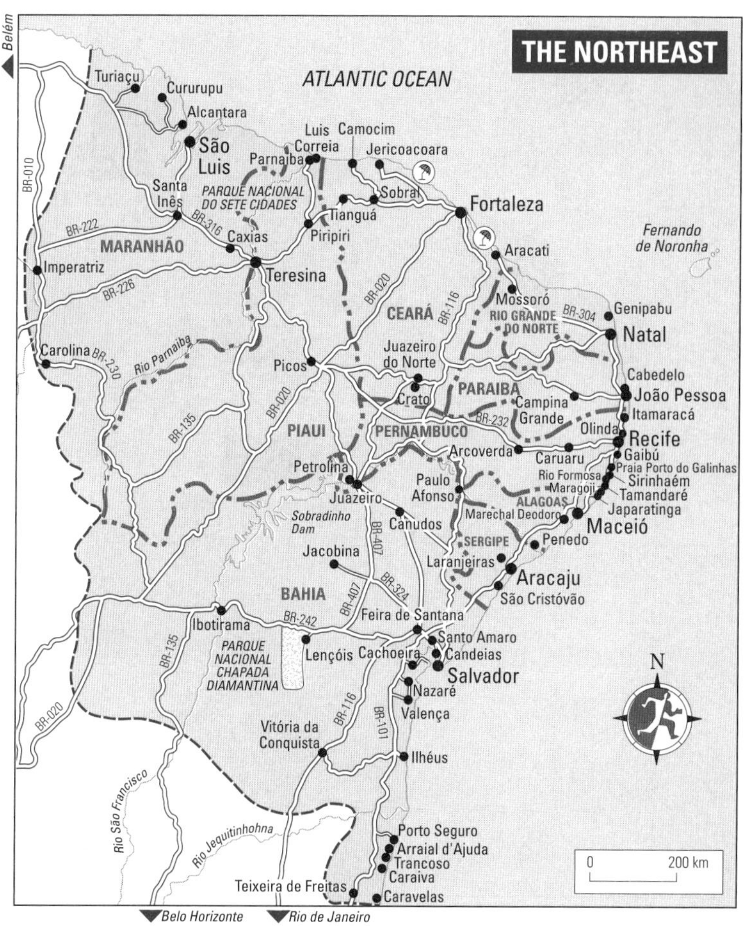

and have a combined population of 36 million. When *nordestinos* living outside the region are included, they make up about a third of Brazil's total population. Notorious for its poverty within Brazil, it has been described as the largest concentration of poor people in the Americas. Yet it's also one of the most rewarding areas of Brazil to visit, with a special identity and culture nurtured by fierce regional loyalties, shared by rich and poor alike. The Northeast has the largest concentration of black people in Brazil, most of whom live on or near the coast, concentrated around Salvador and Recife, where **African influences** are very obvious – in the cuisine, music and religion. In the *sertão*, though, Portuguese and Indian influences predominate in popular culture and racial ancestry.

As far as specific attractions go, the region has a lot to offer. The **coastline** is over two thousand kilometres of practically unbroken beach, much of it just as you imagine

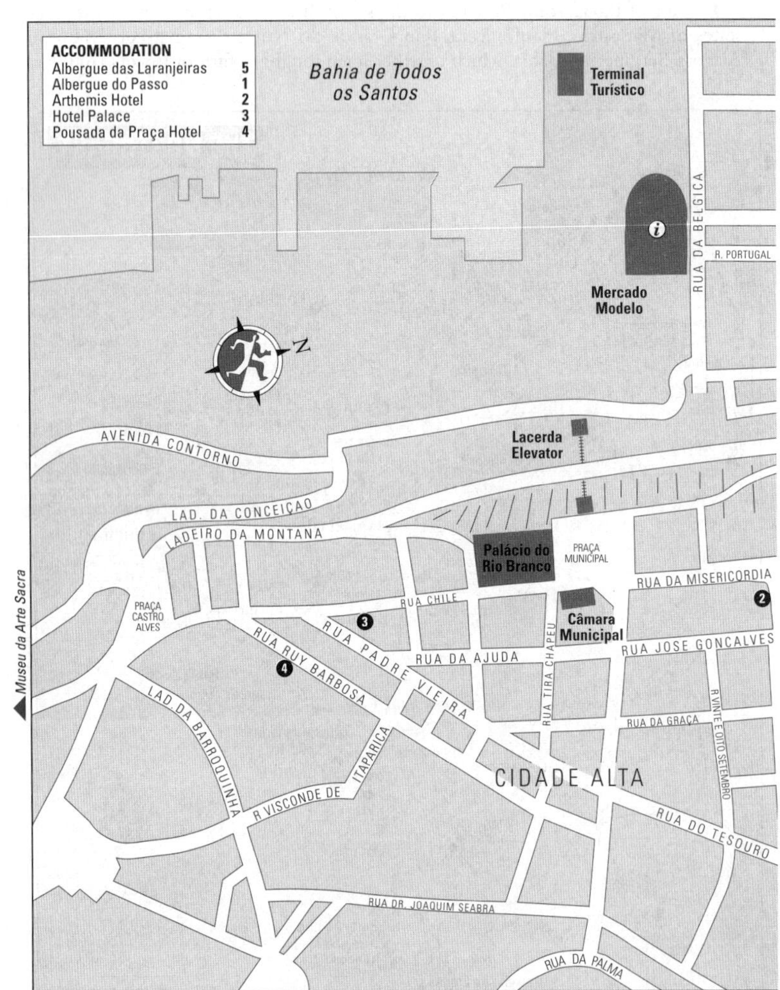

tropical beaches to be: white sands, blue sea, palm trees. The **colonial heritage** survives in the Baroque churches and cobbled streets of **Salvador** and **Olinda**. And in Salvador and **Recife**, with populations of around two million each, the Northeast has two of Brazil's great **cities**. Head **inland**, and the bustling market towns of the **agreste** and the enormous jagged landscapes of the **sertão** more than repay the journeys.

Getting around the Northeast is straightforward thanks to the region's extensive bus network. However, even the main highways can be a little bumpy at times, and minor roads are often precarious. This is especially true in the rainy season: in Maranhão the rains come in February, in Piauí and Ceará in March, and points east in April, lasting for around three months. These are only general rules, though: Maranhão can be wet even in the dry season, and Salvador's skies are liable to give you a soaking at any time of year.

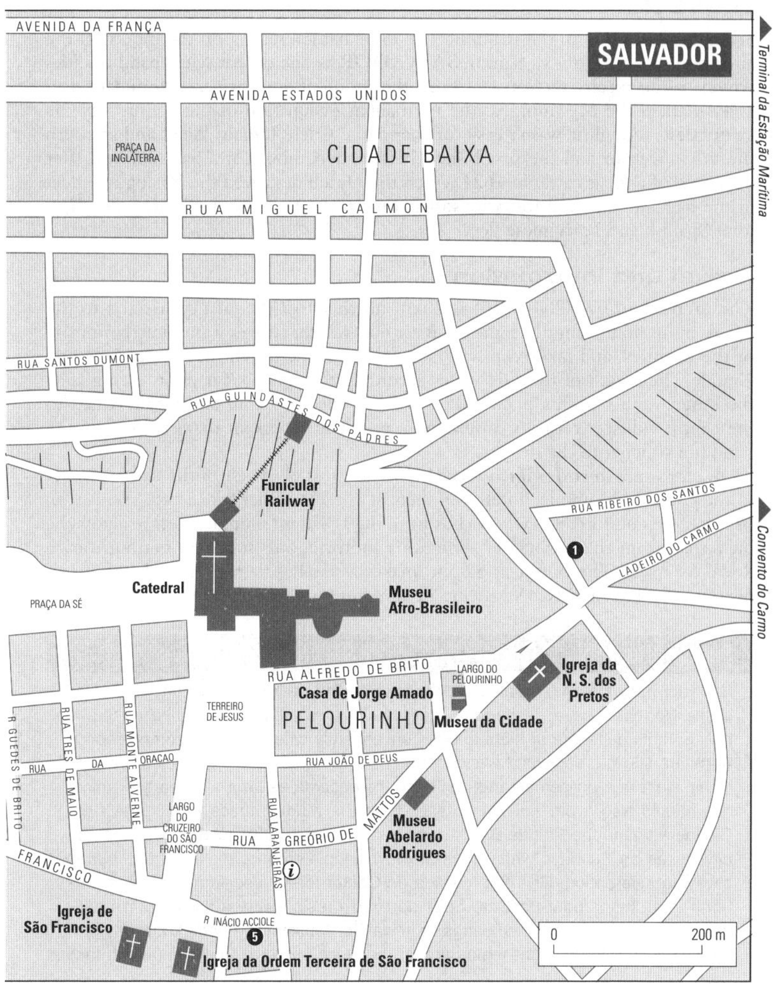

Bahia

Bahia itself has over 1200kms of the most delightful coastline, high levels of sunshine and an average temperature of around 27 degrees centigrade. Cruise ships frequently visit the three most historic port towns of Salvador, Ilhéus and Porto Seguro. The oldest and most historic city in Brazil, **Salvador**, the largest city in Bahia state, possesses one of the largest collections of colonial architecture in Latin America and was the national capital for over two centuries, before relinquishing the title to Rio in 1763. The countryside changes to the south of Salvador, with mangrove swamps and fast-developing island resorts around the town of **Valença**, before reverting to a spectacular coastline typical of the Northeast. Inland, the Bahian **sertão** is massive, a desert-like land which supports a few interesting frontier towns.

Salvador

Second only to Rio in the magnificence of its natural setting on the mouth of the enormous bay of Todos os Santos, **SALVADOR** is one of that select band of cities which has an electricity you feel from the moment you arrive. Its foundation in 1549 marked the beginning of the permanent occupation of the country by the Portuguese, though it wasn't easy for them. The Caeté Indians killed and ate both the first governor and the first bishop before succumbing, and Salvador was later the scene of a great battle in 1624, when the Dutch destroyed the Portuguese fleet in the bay and took the town by storm, only to be forced out within a year by a joint Spanish and Portuguese fleet.

Arrival and information

The **airport** (☎071/204-1010) is 20km northeast of the city, connected to the centre by an hourly shuttle express bus service ($2) that leaves from directly in front of the terminal, and takes you to Praça da Sé via the beach districts and Campo Grande. The length of the ride varies according to traffic, but if you're going back the other way to catch a plane make sure you allow an hour and a half. A taxi to the centre will set you back around $15; pay at the kiosk in the arrivals area and hand the voucher to the driver.

Salvador's superb **rodoviária** (☎071/358-4970) is 8km east of the centre. To get to the Cidade Alta and its hotels from here, it's best to either take a taxi (about $10) or catch the comfortable *executivo* bus from the Iguatemi shopping centre across the busy road from the rodoviária – there's a footbridge to stop you getting mown down by traffic. The bus costs $2 and makes a stately progress through the beach districts of Pituba and Rio Vermelho before dropping you in the Praça da Sé.

Personal safety

Salvador has more of a problem with **robberies** and **muggings** than anywhere else in the Northeast save Recife. The main tourist area around Pelourinho is heavily policed until quite late at night and is consequently safe. However, some **precautions** are still in order. Don't wander down ill-lit sidestreets at night unless you are within sight of a policeman and don't use the Lacerda elevator after early evening. You should also avoid walking up and down the winding roads that connect the Cidade Alta and the Cidade Baixa, and you should be careful about using ordinary city buses on Sundays when there are few people around; the *executivo* bus is always a safe option. Give the Avenida do Contorno – the seafront road that runs north from the harbour past the *Solar do Unhão* restaurant – a miss too; it's dangerous even in daylight when gangs lie in wait for tourists who don't know any better; if you want to go to the restaurant, or the Museu de Arte Moderna near it, take a taxi.

The state tourist agency, **Bahiatursa**, is used to foreigners; most offices have English-speakers; and there are a variety of maps and handouts on the city: the best two are the *Mapa Turístico de Salvador da Bahia* ($1.50) and the free *Guia do Pelourinho*. If you're travelling on to other parts of Bahia, you should also ask for whatever material they have on the rest of the state, as elsewhere the service is nothing like as good.

There are **information posts** on arrival at the airport (daily 7.30am–11pm; ⓣ071/204-1244) and the rodoviária (daily 8am–11pm; ⓣ071/450-3871). Bahiatursa's **main office** is in Cidade Alta at Rua das Laranjeiras 12 (daily 8.30am–9pm or until 10pm at weekends; ⓣ071/321-2133 or 321-2463), and there are other offices at the Mercado Modelo (Mon–Sat 9am–6pm, Sun 9am-2pm; ⓣ071/241-0242); in Barra Shopping, Av Centenario 2992 (Mon–Sat 10am–10pm; ⓣ071/264-0242); and in Iguatemi Shopping, Av Tancredo Neves 148 (Mon–Fri 9am–11pm, Sat 9am–2pm; ⓣ071/480-5511). An additional source of information is the **tourist hotline**, "Disque Turismo" – just ring ⓣ0800/716-622 from any telephone and you should find an English-speaker on the other end.

City transport

Conveniently, many of the museums, churches and historic buildings are concentrated within **walking** distance of each other in Cidade Alta. Failing that, **taxis** are plentiful, although all the beach areas except Barra are a long ride from the centre. There are three **local bus terminals**, and the bus system is efficient and easy to use. To reach the centre, any bus with "Sé", "C. Grande" or "Lapa" on the route card will do.

Accommodation

Salvador is the second most popular tourist destination in Brazil and consequently full of **hotels**. Unless you want to stay on a beach, the best area to head for is **Cidade Alta**, not least because of the spectacular view across the island-studded bay. **Camping** is permitted at a city run site *Camping Ecológica Stella Maris* (ⓣ071/374-3506), with shower and restaurant facilities and enough space for motorhomes too; located at Itapuá beach, near the *farol*, at Alameda da Praia (no number).

City centre

Albergue das Laranjeiras Rua Inácio Acciole 13, Pelhourinho ⓣ& ⓕ071/321-1366, ⓦwww.alaranj.com.br. Excellent and lively youth hostel in the heart of the historic centre; very relaxed and also offers Internet access and inexpensive laundry, and has a trendy café. ❷

Albergue do Passo Rua do Passo 3 ⓣ071/326-1951 or 243-1820, ⓕ351-3285, ⓔpassoyouthhostel@yahoo.com, ⓦwww.passoyouthhostelH.P.G.com.br. Another good Pelourinho hostel in an attractive building; rooms with showers, good breakfasts, communal room with cable TV and the staff speak English, French and Spanish. Prices go up twenty-fold for carnival. ❷

Arthemis Hotel Praca da Se 398, Edf. Themis, 7th floor ⓣ071/322-0724, ⓔartemis@artemishotel.com.br, ⓦwww.artemishotel.com.br. An odd but fun place to stay, right in the heart of the historic centre; run by a Frenchman, it has tremendous views, a patio bar and café as well as comfortable enough rooms for the price. ❷–❸

Hotel Palace Rua Chile 20 ⓣ71/322-1155, ⓔpalace@e-net.com.br. If you want a bit more comfort than a no-frills room for a bit more money, this is a good bet; all rooms are cosy but the ones with air conditioning are easily the best. ❹

Pousada da Praça Hotel Rua Rui Barbosa 5 ⓣ071/321-0642, ⓔgifc@zaz.com.br. A highly recommended budget hotel offering great service, more than adequate bedrooms and a magnificent breakfast just off Praça Castro Alves. ❸

The beaches

Âmbar Pousada Rua Afonso Celso 485, Barra ⓣ071/264-6956, ⓕ264-3791, ⓔambarpousada@ambarpousada.com.br, ⓦwww.ambarpousada.com.br. A very friendly pousada close to Praia do Porto da Barra. Basic but clean and cosy rooms on two stoeys set around a pleasant courtyard. Popular with a range of travellers. ❸

Bahia Othon Palace Hotel Av Presidente Vargas 2456, Ondina ⓣ071/203-2000, ⓦwww.othon.com.br. Superb luxury hotel standing on the seafront at the Praia Ondina; has 280 apartments all with minibars, TVs, many with great views; there's a pool, sauna and a very good restaurant. ❼.

Hotel Porto da Barra Av Sete de Setembro 3783, Praia do Porto da Barra ⓣ071/264-7711, ⓕ264-2619, ⓔhpbarra@bol.com.br, ⓦwww.hotelportodabarra.com.br. Good-value, no-frills and no-nonsense hotel right by the beach; all rooms have either air conditioning or fan. ❸.

The City

Salvador is built around the craggy, fifty-metre-high bluff that dominates the eastern side of the bay, and splits the central area into upper and lower sections. The heart of the old city, **Cidade Alta** (or simply Centro), is strung along its top, linked to the **Cidade Baixa**, below, by precipitous streets, a funicular railway and the towering Art Deco lift shaft of the Carlos Lacerda elevator, the city's largest landmark. Cidade Alta is the administrative and cultural centre of the city, Cidade Baixa the financial and commercial district.

The best spot to begin a walking tour is at the **Praça Municipal**, the square dominated by the impressive **Palácio do Rio Branco**, the old governor's palace. It was burnt down and rebuilt during the Dutch wars, and the regal plaster eagles were added by nineteenth-century restorers, who turned a plain colonial mansion into an imposing palace. The interior is fine, a blend of Rococo plasterwork, polished wooden floors, and painted walls and ceilings. There is also a museum inside, the **Memorial dos Governadores** (Mon 2–6pm, Tues–Fri 10am–noon & 2–6pm; free), which houses period pieces from the colonial era, but the building itself is the most interesting part. Also facing the square is the **Câmara Municipal**, the seventeenth-century city hall, graced by a series of elegant but solid arches.

To the east, Rua Chile becomes Rua da Misericórdia and leads into **Praça da Sé**, the heart of Cidade Alta, where the *executivo* buses terminate. The **Terreiro de Jesus** lies to the south in front of the plain **Catedral Basílica** (Mon-Sat 8-11.30am & 2-5.30pm, Sun 10.30am-12.30pm), once the chapel of the largest Jesuit seminary outside Rome. Its interior is one of the most beautiful in the city, particularly the stunning panelled ceiling of carved and gilded wood, which gives the church a light, airy feel that's an effective antidote to the overwrought Rococo altar and side chapels. To the left of the altar is the tomb of **Mem de Sá**, third viceroy of Brazil from 1556 to 1570, and the most energetic and effective of all Brazil's colonial governors. It was he who supervised the first phase of building in Salvador, in the process destroying the Caeté Indians. Look in on the restored sacristy, too, while you're here – portraits of Jesuit luminaries, set into the walls and ceiling, gaze down intimidatingly on intruders.

Next to the cathedral stands one of the best museums in the city, the **Museu Afro-Brasileiro** (Mon–Fri 9am–5pm; $2). The main building houses three different collections, one on each of the storeys. Largest and best is on the **ground floor**, recording and celebrating the black contribution to Brazilian culture. Four rooms are dedicated to different aspects of black culture – popular religion, *capoeira*, weaving, music and Carnaval – and everything, for once, is very well laid out. The section on *capoeira*, the balletic martial art the slaves developed (see box opposite), is fascinating, supported by photos and old newspaper clippings. Other highlights include the gallery of large photographs of *candomblé* leaders, some dating from the nineteenth century, most in full regalia and exuding pride and authority; and the famous carved panels by Carybé, in the exhibition room past the photo gallery. The **basement**, containing the **Museu Arqueológico e Etnológico**, is largely given over to fossils and artefacts from ancient burial sites and incorporates the only surviving part of the old Jesuit college, a section of the cellars, in the arched brickwork at the far end. It was from here that the conversion of the Brazilian Indians was organized. After the Jesuits were expelled in 1759, most of the college was

Capoeira

Capoeira, which began in Angola as a ritual fight to gain the nuptial rights of women when they reached puberty, and has evolved into a graceful semi-balletic art form somewhere between fighting and dancing, is not difficult to find in Salvador. It's usually accompanied by the characteristic rhythmic twang of the *berimbau*, and takes the form of a pair of dancers/fighters leaping and whirling in stylized "combat" – which, with younger *capoeiristas*, occasionally slips into a genuine fight when blows land by accident and the participants lose their temper. There are regular displays, largely for the benefit of tourists but interesting nevertheless, on Terreiro de Jesus and near the entrances to the Mercado Modelo in Cidade Baixa, where contributions from onlookers are expected. The best *capoeira*, however, can be found in the **academias de capoeira**, organized schools that have classes that anyone can watch free of charge. The first and most famous *academia*, the Associação de Capoeira Mestre Bimba, is still the best; it's on the first floor of Rua das Laranjeiras 1, Terreiro de Jesus, and sometimes has classes open to tourists.

demolished by the rich for building material for their mansions, part of the site used to found a university, and the rest parcelled out and sold for redevelopment.

Terreiro de Jesus has more than its fair share of churches; there are two more fine sixteenth-century examples on the square itself. But outshining them both, on nearby **Largo do Cruzeiro de São Francisco**, are the superb carved stone facades of two ornate Baroque buildings in a single, large complex dedicated to St Francis: the **Igreja de São Francisco** and the **Igreja da Ordem Terceira de São Francisco** (Mon-Fri 8am-5pm). Of the two, the latter has the edge: it's covered with a wild profusion of saints, virgins, angels and abstract patterns. Remarkably, the facade was hidden for 150 years, until in 1936 a painter knocked off a chunk of plaster by mistake and revealed the original frontage, Brazil's only example of high-relief facade carved in ashlar (square cut stones). It took nine years of careful chipping before the facade was returned to its original glory, and today the whole church is a strong contender for the most beautiful single building in the city. Its **reliquary**, or *ossuário*, is extraordinary, the entire room redecorated in the 1940s in Art Deco style, one of the most unusual examples you're ever likely to come across. From here, there's a door into a pleasant garden at the back.

To get into the centre of the complex, you have to go via the Igreja de São Francisco (the entrance is by a door to the right of the main doors). The small cloister in this church is decorated with one of the finest single pieces of *azulejo* work in Brazil. Running the entire length of the cloister, this **tiled wall** tells the story of the marriage of the son of the king of Portugal to an Austrian princess; beginning with the panel to the right of the church entrance. The vigour and realism of the incidental detail in the street scenes is remarkable: beggars and cripples display their wounds, dogs skulk, children play in the gutter; and the panoramic view of Lisbon it displays is an important historical record of how Lisbon looked before the calamitous earthquake of 1755.

Heading down the narrow Rua Alfredo de Brito, next to the Museu Afro-Brasileiro, brings you to the beautiful, cobbled **Largo do Pelourinho**, still much as it was during the eighteenth century. Lined with solid colonial mansions, it's topped by the Asian-looking towers of the **Igreja da Nossa Senhora dos Pretos** (Mon–Fri 9.30am-6pm, Sat 9.30am–5pm, Sun 10am–noon), built by and for slaves and still with a largely black congregation. Across from here is the **Casa da Cultura Jorge Amado** (Mon noon–6pm, Tues–Sat 9am–6pm; free), a museum given over to the life and work of the hugely popular novelist, who doesn't number modesty among his virtues; you can have fun spotting his rich and famous friends in the collection of photographs.

Next door, the **Museu da Cidade** (Mon & Wed–Fri 9.30am–6.30pm, Sat 1–5pm, Sun 9.30am–1pm; free), is housed in an attractive Pelourinho mansion. The lower levels are given over to paintings and sculpture by young city artists, some startlingly good and some pretty dire, while luxuriously dressed dummies show off Carnaval costumes from years gone by. There are models of *candomblé* deities and, on the first floor, a room containing the personal belongings of the greatest Bahian poet, Castro Alves, with some fascinating photographs from the beginning of the twentieth century. Completing the constellation of museums around Pelourinho is the **Museu Abelardo Rodrigues** (Tues–Sun noon–6pm; $0.50c) at Rua Gregório de Mattos 45, which has a good collection of Catholic art from the sixteenth century onwards, well displayed in a restored seventeenth-century mansion.

From Largo do Pelourinho, a steep climb up Ladeira do Carmo rewards you with two more exceptional examples of colonial architecture: the **Convento da Ordem Primeira do Carmo** (Mon–Sat 9am–noon & 2–6pm) and on the right the **Igreja da Ordem Terceira do Carmo** (Mon–Sat 9am-1pm & 2–6pm; $0.50). Both are on the right of the street and built around large and beautiful cloisters, with a fine view across the old city at the back. Both also have chaotic but interesting museums attached. The convent museum is very eclectic, mostly religious but including collections of coins and furniture, with hundreds of unlabelled exhibits jumbled together in gloomy rooms. The highlight is a superbly expressive statue of Christ at the whipping post by Salvador's greatest colonial artist, the half-Indian slave **Francisco Manuel das Chagas**, whose powerful religious sculpture broke the formalistic bonds of the period – most of Chagas' work was completed in the 1720s. Unfortunately, Chagas died young of tuberculosis, leaving only a small body of work; this statue is appallingly displayed, jumbled together with much inferior work in a glass case in a corner of the rear gallery. In the church museum next door is another Chagas statue, a life-size body of Christ, this time sensibly displayed alone and, if anything, even more powerful. If you look closely at both statues, you'll find that the drops of blood are small rubies inlaid in the wood.

Eating and drinking

Eating out is one of the major pleasures Salvador has to offer, and the local cuisine (*comida baiana*) is deservedly famous. There's a huge range of restaurants and, although Cidade Alta has an increasing number of stylish, expensive places, it's still quite possible to eat well for significantly less than $10, though easier to spend $20.

Aquárius Restaurant Rua Ribeiro dos Santos 37. Inexpensive Pelourinho restaurant which does good *carne do sol* and has a lovely view over the old city.

Café Odean Rua Joao de Deus 01, 1st floor, Pelourinho ⓣ071/321-5725. A trendy, very modern arty café; large and spacious with loads of weird organic material and objects woven into the fabric of the furniture. Right in the middle of the action, it gets very busy on Friday and Saturday nights when there's a $3 minimum consumption charge.

Casa da Gamboa Rua João de Deus 32 ⓣ071/321-3393. One of Pelourinho's top restaurants and worth a splurge, serving mainly Bahian dishes. Expect to pay at least $20 per head. Closed Sundays.

Jardim Delicias Café Rua João de Deus 12. Fantastic Bahian and international cuisine and a lovely garden where you'll sometimes catch live music sessions in the heart of Pelourinho; salads are especially good.

Maria Mata Mouro Rua Inacio Acioly 08, Pelourinho ⓣ071/326-7330. One of the finest Bahian restaurants in Pelourinho district; whatever you chose from the menu, such as the grilled sea bass, will be divine and lovingly presented. It gets very busy at weekends, so it's best to book a table in advance.

Restaurante Contos dos Réis Rua do Carmo 66. If you want maximum indulgence for both your eyes and your tastebuds, try this restaurant, beyond Pelourinho and on the way to the fort of Santo Antônio Além do Carmo. It's by no means cheap but the setting – with the whole of the bay spread out beneath you – is breathtaking.

Restaurante do SENAC Largo do Pelourinho, opposite the Casa da Cultura Jorge Amado ⓣ071/321-5502. Municipal restaurant school in a finely restored colonial mansion. It looks very expensive from the outside, but it's good value for what you get. You pay a set charge – about $15 – and take as much as you want from a quality buffet of around fifty dishes, all labelled so that you know what you're eating. If you go for dinner, try to finish before 10pm, when there's a rather touristy folklore show. Mon–Wed lunch only; closed Sun.

Comida baiana: dishes and ingredients

The secret to Bahian cooking is twofold: a rich seafood base, and the abundance of traditional West African **ingredients** like palm oil, nuts, coconut and ferociously strong peppers. Many ingredients and dishes have African names: most famous of all is *vatapá*, a bright yellow porridge of palm oil, coconut, shrimp and garlic, which looks vaguely unappetizing but is delicious. Other dishes to look out for are *moqueca*, seafood cooked in the inevitable palm-oil based sauce; *caruru*, with many of the same ingredients as *vatapá* but with the vital addition of loads of okra; and *acarajé*, deep-fried bean cake stuffed with *vatapá*, salad and (optional) hot pepper. Bahian cuisine also has good **desserts**, less stickily sweet than elsewhere: *quindim* is a delicious small cake of coconut flavoured with vanilla, which often comes with a prune in the middle.

Some of the best food is also the cheapest, and even gourmets could do a lot worse than start with the street-corner *baianas*, women in traditional white dress. Be careful of the *pimenta*, the very hot pepper sauce, which newcomers should treat with respect, taking only a few drops. The *baianas* serve *quindim*, *vatapá*, slabs of maize pudding wrapped in banana leaves, fried bananas dusted with icing sugar, and fried sticks of sweet batter covered with sugar and cinnamon – all absolutely wonderful.

Nightlife

Salvador's most distinctive **nightlife** is to be found in Pelourinho. The whole area is always very lively, and there are any number of bars where you can sit and while the evening away. The Rua das Laranjeiras, Cruzeiro de São Francisco and Rua Castro Rabelo are all good places to head for. However, undoubtedly the biggest attraction of the area is the chance to hear **live music**. Salvador marches to a different beat from the rest of the country, and instead of being connected to a single style – as Rio is to samba and Recife is to *frevo* – it has spawned several and still claims to become the most creative centre of Brazilian music. Some of the best music in the city comes from organized cultural groups, who work in the communities and have clubhouses and an *afoxé* – Salvador's Africanized version of a *bloco* – or two for Carnaval. They are overwhelmingly black and a lot of their music is political. In the weeks leading up to Carnaval, their *afoxés* have public rehearsals around the clubhouses, and the music is superb.

Carnaval in Salvador

Having steadfastly resisted commercialization, Carnaval in Salvador has remained a street event of mass participation. From December onwards Carnaval groups hold **public rehearsals** and dances all over the city. The most famous are Grupo Cultural Oludum: they rehearse on Sunday nights from 6.30pm onwards in the Largo do Pelourinho itself and on Tuesdays from 7.30pm in the Teatro Miguel Santana on Rua Gregório de Mattos. On Friday night, it's the turn of Ara Ketu, who start their show at 7pm in Rua Chile, and Ilê Aiyê rehearse on Saturdays from 8pm near the fort of Santo Antônio Além do Carmo. These rehearsals get very crowded, so be careful with your belongings.

Information about Carnaval is published in special supplements in the local papers on Thursday and Saturday. Bahiatursa and EMTURSA offices also have schedules, route maps, and sometimes sell tickets for the Campo Grande grandstands. One point worth bearing in mind is that all-black *blocos* may be black culture groups who won't appreciate being joined by non-black Brazilians, let alone gringos, so look to see who's dancing before leaping in.

Listings

Airlines Air France, Rua Portugal 17, Ed. Regente Feijó, Cidade Baixa ⓣ071/351-6631; Lufthansa, Av Tancredo Neves 805, Sala 601, Iguatemi ⓣ071/341-5100; TAP Air Portugal, Av Estados Unidos 137, Ed. Cidade de Ilhéus, Cidade Baixa ⓣ071/243-6122; Transbrasil, Rua Portugal 3, Cidade Baixa ⓣ071/326-1044; Varig, Rua Carlos Gomes 6, Cidade Alta ⓣ071/343-3100 or 204-1050, or Rua Miguel Calmon 19, Cidade Baixa ⓣ071/243-9311; VASP, Rua Chile 27, Edifício Chile, Cidade Alta ⓣ071/204-1304, Rua Miguel Calmon 27, Cidade Baixa, or Rua Marquês de Leâo 455, Barra.
Banks and exchange There are several places where you can change money in the Pelourinho area, including Olímpio Turismo on Largo do Cruzeiro de São Francisco and Vert-Tour on Rua das Laranjeiras.
Car rental Avis Rentacar, Av Sete de Setembro 1796 (ⓣ071/377-2276); Localiza, based at the airport ⓣ071/332-1999; Nobre Rent a Car, Av Oceânica 409 ⓣ071/245-8022.
Consulates Canada, Av Presidente Vargas 2400, Sala 311, Ondina Apart Hotel, Ondina ⓣ071/331-0064; UK, Av Estados Unidos 4, 18-B 8th floor, Cidade Baixa ⓣ071/243-7399; USA, Rua Pernambuco 51, Pituba ⓣ071/354-3312.
Post office At the airport; Marquês de Caravelas 101, Barra; Shopping Barra (3rd floor); Av Amaralina 908, Amaralina; Rua J. Seabra 234; the rodoviária; Rua Rui Barbosa 19, Cidade Alta; and at the Praça da Inglaterra, Cidade Baixa. Opening hours are Mon–Fri 8am–6pm.
Taxis Chame Táxi ⓣ071/241-2266; Teletáxi ⓣ071/341-9988.
Telephones You can make international collect calls from a booth on Terreiro de Jesus; other *postos telefônicos* are in the airport, the rodoviária, in Campo da Pôlvora in Cidade Alta, and in the Iguatemi shopping centre.
Travel and tour companies Ceu e Mar Turismo, Rua Fonte do Boi 12, Rio Vermelho ⓣ071/334-7566, ⓔceuemar@e-net.com.br is a good travel agent and also represents the Student Travel Bureau. LR Turismo, Rua Marques de Leao 172, Barra ⓣ071/264-0999, ⓔlrturismo@e-net.com.br runs several exciting tours, from historic Bahia to boat trips to the tropical islands in the Bahia de Todos os Santos; Tours Bahia, Cruzeiro de Sao Francisco 4, Centro Historic ⓣ071/322-3676, ⓔtbi@compos.com.br, offers a range of services, including city tours, airline tickets, money exchange and tours; Privé Tur, Av Sete de Setembro 2068, Vitória ⓣ071/336-7522, operates a range of city tours, beach trips and schooner cruises.

Morro de São Paulo

The island of **Tinharé**, about 75km south west of Salvador, is home to the world famous beaches at **MORRO DE SÃO PAULO**, where there's always a great atmosphere, with reggae bars, hippy dives, real divers, surfers and great seafood restaurants. With no roads on the island, it's still relatively peaceful and undeveloped, though at the weekends, especially between December and March, Morro de São Paulo can get unbearably crowded. The island itself is quite large, around 30kms by an average of 8kms. At the northwest end there's the main settlement and resort of Morro de São Paulo, while at the diagonally opposite end sits the much smaller and less developed fishing village of Garapua. The more remote island of Boipeba lies just across a channel from the southern tip of Tinharé. Much closer to Morro and normally seen when arriving at the island from Valença is the relatively quiet beach of Porto Gamboa. There are several **boats** a day from Valença to Tinharé (more than one an hour generally), which cost about $3 and take ninety minutes, plus a quicker and more expensive *lancha rapida* ($8).

The small settlement of Morro de São Paulo sits on a hill between the port and the first of the beaches, Primeira Praia. If you don't mind being a few minutes' walk from the beach, it's a pleasant place to stay, close to the shops and restaurants. From beside the *Pousada Natureza*, a trail leads up some steps to the lighthouse affording viewing points from top of the hill. From the port, by following the coastal path (clockwise if you were going round the island) you come to an old fortification, semi-ruined but still atmospheric and well worth exploring with its impressive battlements. There's still a rusting canon and a Moorish looking gun turret jutting out over the ocean. The **tourist information** office (ⓣ075/483-1083, ⓦwww

.morrosp.com.br) is on Paraca Aureliano Lima just as you enter the island from the top of the port steps. Good **pousadas** here include the *Pousada Natureza* (ⓣ075/483-1361, ⓦwww.hotelnatureza.com; ④), on the left at the top of the harbour steps, behind the massive amendoeira tree, with commanding views over the bay and lovely rooms with hammock verandas, a pool, some apartments with Jacuzzis as well as a lovely patio bar for breakfast and evening meals surrounded by attractive gardens with fine statues of local Afro-Brazilian gods and godesses. The *Pizzaria Forno a Lenha* on Praça Aureliano is a good **restaurant** and one of the best places to meet people in the evenings and find out where the parties are. More restaurants and ice-cream parlours line the track from the square down to Primeira Praia, where you'll find *Restaurante Da Dona Elda* (ⓣ075/483-1041) and some excellent seafood dishes, including delicious *moqueca de peixe* and *bobó de camarão*, on their airy upstairs patio.

There are four main beaches on the populated corner of the island, all linked by paths. **Diving** enthusiasts or anyone wishing to dive ($30 a day for certificated divers) or seriously learn how to scuba dive and get certificated ($200 for a six-day course) should contact the Companhia do Mergulho, Primeira Praia (ⓣ075/483-1200, ⓦwww.ciamergulho.com.br). They go out in fast boats by day and night to the clear water areas of the sea around the island.

Pernambuco

Recife, capital of the state of **Pernambuco**, wasn't founded by the Portuguese: when they arrived in the 1530s, they settled just to the north, building the beautiful colonial town of **Olinda** and turning most of the surrounding land over to sugar. A century later, the Dutch, under Maurice of Nassau, took Olinda and burned it down, choosing to build a new capital, Recife, on swampy land to the south, where there was the fine natural harbour that Olinda had lacked. The Dutch, playing to their strengths, drained and reclaimed the low-lying land, and the main evidence of the Dutch presence today is not so much their few surviving churches and forts dotted up and down the coast, as the reclaimed land on which the core of Recife is built.

Recife

RECIFE, the Northeast's second-largest city, appears rather dull on first impressions, but it's lent a colonial grace and elegance by Olinda, 6km to the north and considered part of the same conurbation. Recife itself has long since burst its original colonial boundaries and much of the centre is now given over to uninspired modern skyscrapers and office buildings. But there are still a few quiet squares, where an inordinate number of impressive churches lie cheek by jowl with the uglier urban sprawl of the past thirty years. North of the centre are some pleasant leafy suburbs, dotted with museums and parks, and to the south there is the modern beachside district of **Boa Viagem**.

Tourists wandering around Recife should be particularly careful with their possessions and it's best, too, to use taxis to get home after an evening out. Recife is one of Brazil's most violent cities, an unsurprising statistic given the immediately obvious disparity of wealth and stark poverty, and the large number of homeless people on the streets. On Sundays in the old centre of Recife, the streets often seem deserted except for beggars; everyone else seems to be on the beach at Boa Viagem. Tourists tend to hang out in the much pleasanter environment of laid-back Olinda.

Arrival, information and city transport

The **airport** is fairly close to the city centre, at the far end of Boa Viagem. A taxi to Boa Viagem itself shouldn't be more than $6–7, to the neighbouring island of Santo

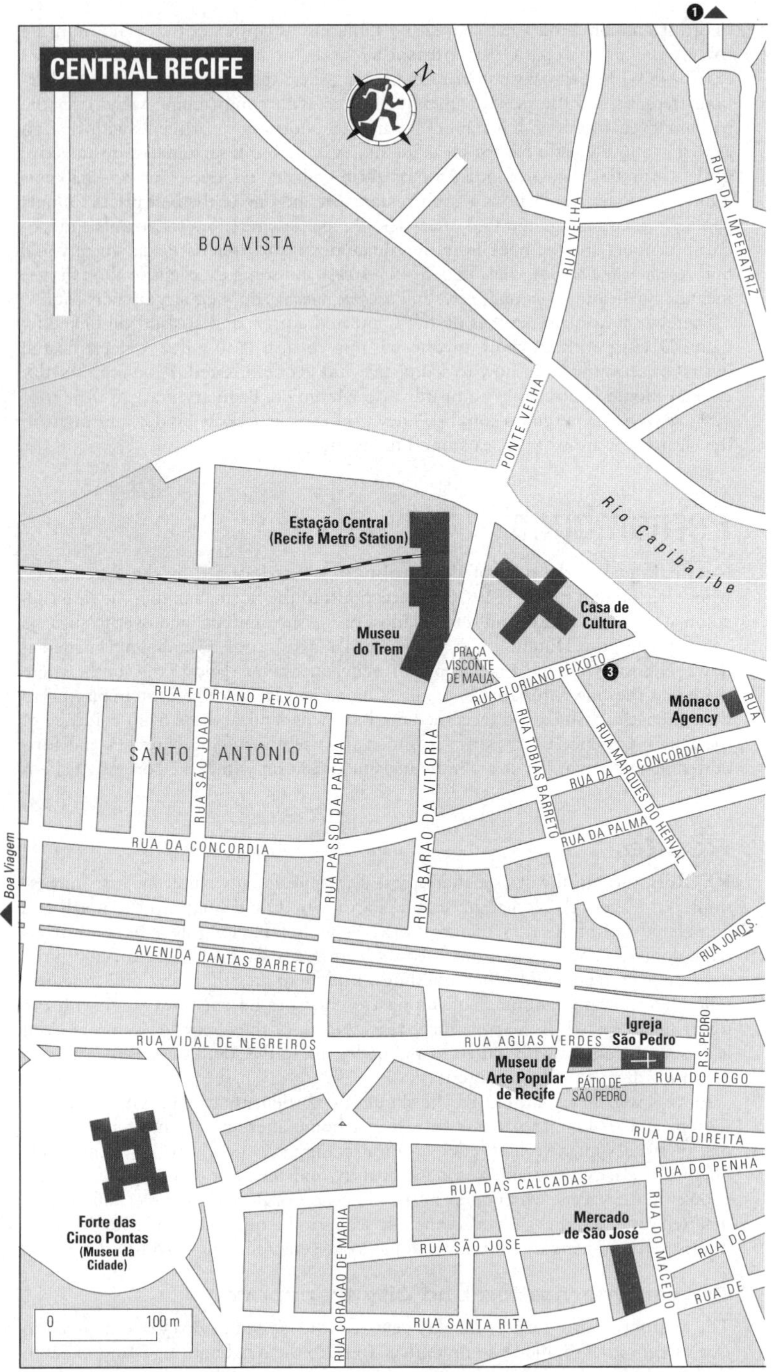
CENTRAL RECIFE
BOA VISTA
RUA VELHA
RUA DA IMPERATRIZ
PONTE VELHA
Rio Capibaribe
Estação Central
(Recife Metrô Station)
Casa de Cultura
Museu do Trem
PRAÇA VISCONTE DE MAUÁ
RUA FLORIANO PEIXOTO
Mônaco Agency
SANTO ANTÔNIO
RUA SÃO JOAO
RUA PASSO DA PATRIA
RUA BARAO DA VITORIA
RUA TOBIAS BARRETO
RUA MARQUES DO HERVAL
RUA DA CONCORDIA
RUA DA PALMA
Boa Viagem
AVENIDA DANTAS BARRETO
RUA JOAO S.
RUA VIDAL DE NEGREIROS
RUA AGUAS VERDES
Igreja São Pedro
R.S. PEDRO
Museu de Arte Popular de Recife
PÁTIO DE SÃO PEDRO
RUA DO FOGO
RUA DA DIREITA
RUA DO PENHA
RUA DAS CALCADAS
Forte das Cinco Pontas
(Museu da Cidade)
RUA CORACAO DE MARIA
RUA SÃO JOSE
Mercado de São José
RUA DO MACEDO
RUA DO
RUA DE
RUA SANTA RITA
0 100 m

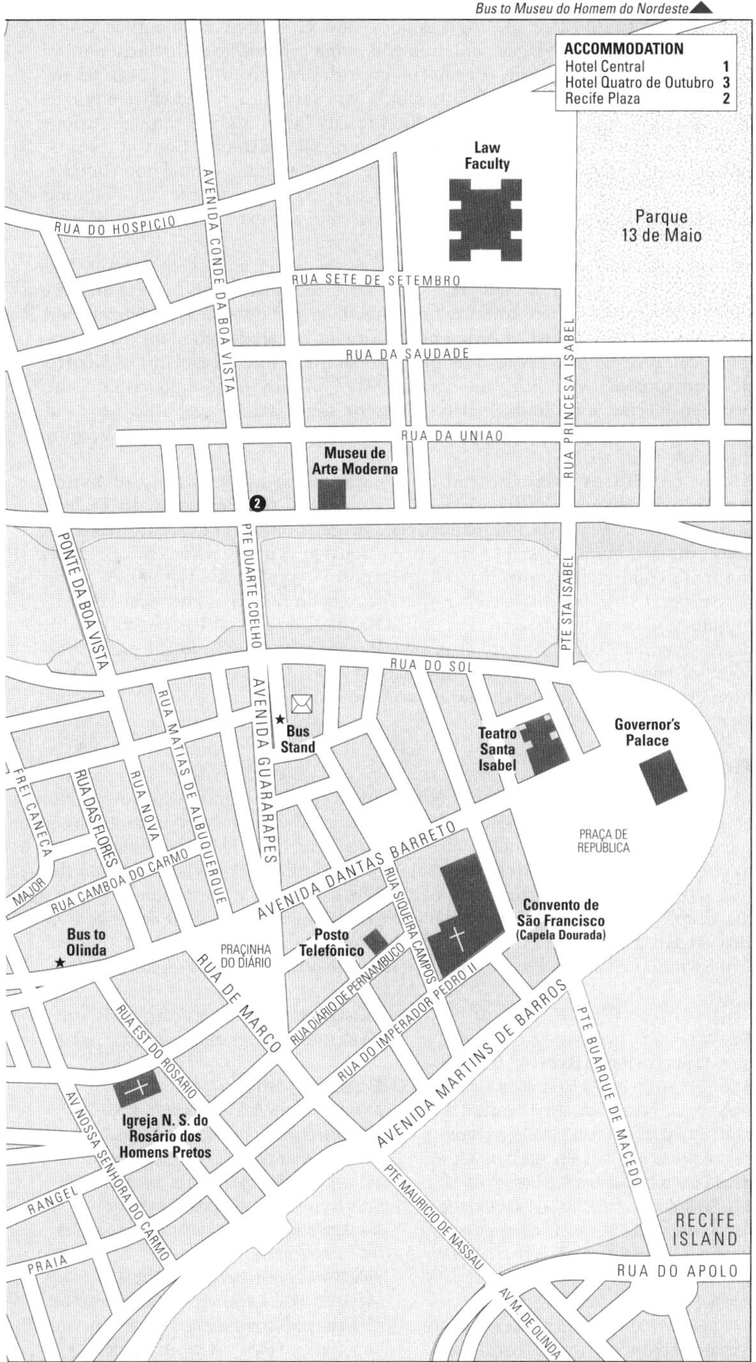
Bus to Museu do Homem do Nordeste
ACCOMMODATION
Hotel Central 1
Hotel Quatro de Outubro 3
Recife Plaza 2
Law Faculty
Parque 13 de Maio
RUA DO HOSPICIO
AVENIDA CONDE DA BOA VISTA
RUA SETE DE SETEMBRO
RUA DA SAUDADE
RUA PRINCESA ISABEL
RUA DA UNIAO
Museu de Arte Moderna
2
PONTE DA BOA VISTA
PTE DUARTE COELHO
PTE STA ISABEL
RUA DO SOL
AVENIDA GUARARAPES
Bus Stand
Teatro Santa Isabel
Governor's Palace
RUA MATIAS DE ALBUQUERQUE
RUA NOVA
RUA DAS FLORES
FREI CANECA
PRAÇA DE REPÚBLICA
AVENIDA DANTAS BARRETO
RUA SIQUEIRA CAMPOS
RUA CAMBOA DO CARMO
MAJOR
Convento de São Francisco
(Capela Dourada)
Bus to Olinda
PRAÇINHA DO DIÁRIO
Posto Telefônico
RUA DE MARCO
RUA DIÁRIO DE PERNAMBUCO
RUA DO IMPERADOR PEDRO II
AVENIDA MARTINS DE BARROS
PTE BUARQUE DE MACEDO
RUA EST DO ROSARIO
Igreja N. S. do Rosário dos Homens Pretos
AV NOSSA SENHORA DO CARMO
PTE MAURICIO DE NASSAU
RANGEL
PRAIA
RECIFE ISLAND
RUA DO APOLO
AV M. DE OLINDA

Antônio about $10–12; or take the Aeroporto bus ($2.50) from right outside, which will drive through Boa Viagem and drop you in the centre. The **rodoviária** is miles out, though this is not really a problem since the **Metrô** (☎081/3424-1662 for information), an overground rail link, whisks you very cheaply and efficiently into the centre, giving you a good introduction to city life as it glides through various *favelas*. It will deposit you at the old train station, called **Estação Central** (or simply "Recife"). To get to your hotel from there, whether in the central hotel district, Boa Viagem or even Olinda, you're best off taking a **taxi** – Recife is a confusing city even when you've been there a few days, and the extra money will be well spent.

Tourist information is directed mainly at the upper end of the market. The state tourist office, EMPETUR, runs a 24-hour information post at the **airport** (☎081/3462-4533), where you may find English-speaking staff and a few maps and calendars of events. They'll also ring hotels for you, but are no good for the cheapest places. EMPETUR has its headquarters inconveniently located at the **Centro de Convenções** (Mon–Fri 9am–6pm; ☎081/3427-8183), more or less en route between Recife and Olinda. In **Boa Viagem**, there is a Delegacia do Turista at Praca do Boa Viagem (☎081/3463-3621; 8am–8pm) which can help with accommodation at the beach.

Most city **buses** originate and terminate on the central island of **Santo Antônio**, on Avenida Dantas Barreto, either side of the **Pracinha do Diário** (also known as Praça da Independência). To get from the city centre **to Boa Viagem**, take buses marked "Aeroporto", "Iguatemi" or "Boa Viagem", or catch the more comfortable *frescão* marked "Aeroporto", just outside the offices of the newspaper, *Diário de Pernambuco*, on the Pracinha do Diário; it goes every twenty minutes and costs about $2.50. To get to **Olinda** from central Recife, walk south down Avenida Dantas Barreto from the Pracinha do Diário to the last of the series of bus stops, and catch the bus marked "Casa Caiada". Alternatively, a taxi from central Recife to Olinda should cost around $8–10 and will take about fifteen minutes.

Accommodation

It's cheapest to stay right in the rather run-down centre, and most expensive in the beach district of Boa Viagem, where finding a hotel is the least of your problems: it sometimes seems as if they outnumber apartment buildings. The other obvious area to consider staying is Olinda (see p.385), where prices fall somewhere between the two and, although there's not much of a beach, it has a lot more culturally to offer the visitor. Recife's **youth hostel**, the *Albergue da Juventude Maracatus do Recife*, is in Boa Viagem at Rua Maria Carolina 185 (☎081/3326-1964), and is superb. Complete with swimming pool and free breakfast, it's excellent value at $15 a night.

The centre: Boa Vista and Santo Antônio

Hotel Central Av Manoel Borba 209, Boa Vista ☎081/3423-6411 or 423-6604. As its name suggests, this hotel is central and is located on what remains one of Recife's quieter and more elegant streets. Also does a superb breakfast. ❸

Hotel Quatro de Outubro Rua Floriano Peixoto 141, Santo Antônio ☎081/3224-4900. Close to Recife's main metrô station, it's run-down but reasonable value; all rooms have air conditioning and TV. ❸

Recife Plaza Rua da Aurora 225, Boa Vista ☎081/3231-1200. Nondescript place close to the central river bridge, the Ponte do Coelho. Rooms are reasonable, with air conditioning and TV, and there's a restaurant, sauna and swimming pool. ❹

Boa Viagem

Atlante Plaza Av Boa Viagem 5426 ☎081/3302-3333, freephone for reservations ☎081/3302-3344, www.atlanteplaza.com.br. Large, modern and well located in the centre of beach and night life, this upmarket hotel boasts panoramic elevators, bar, restaurant, swimming pool, saunas and fitness suite. ❼

Hotel Park Rua dos Navegantes 9 (☎ & ℉ 081/3465-4666). Large, modern and upmarket but still quite good value in the centre of action just a block from the beach, and with its own pool. ❹

Pousada Aconchego Rua Felix de Brito 382 ⓣ081/3326-2989, ⓦwww.hotelaconchego.com.br. This small and comfortable hotel has a swimming pool and good restaurant open 24 hours a day. ❸

Recife Monte Hotel Rua dos Navegantes 363 ⓣ081/3465-7422, ⓦwww.recifemontehotel .com.br. A glorified apartment building with all mod cons and the claim to fame that Chico Buarque and Charles Aznavour once stayed here. ❼

The City

Modern Recife sprawls onto the mainland, but the heart of the city is three small **islands**, Santo Antônio, Boa Vista and Recife proper, connected with each other and the mainland by more than two dozen bridges over the rivers Beberibe and Capibaribe.

The broad **Avenida Dantas Barreto** forms the spine of the central island of Santo Antônio. In southern Brazil, avenues like this are lined with skyscrapers, but, although some have sprouted in Recife's financial district, generally the centre is on a human scale, with crowded, narrow lanes lined with stalls and shops opening out directly onto the streets. Dantas Barreto, the main thoroughfare, ends in the fine **Praça da República**, lined with majestic palms and surrounded by Recife's grandest public buildings – the governor's palace (not open to visitors) and an ornate theatre.

Perhaps the most enticing of the central buildings is the seventeenth-century Franciscan complex known as the **Santo Antônio do Convento de São Francisco**, on Rua do Imperador – a combination of church, convent and museum. Outside, you'll be besieged by crowds of beggars displaying sores and stumps, but negotiate your way through to the entrance of the museum (Mon–Fri 8–11.30am & 2–5pm, Sat 2–5pm), pay the nominal fee, and you'll find yourself in a cool and quiet haven. Built around a beautiful small cloister, the museum contains some delicately painted statues of saints and other artwork rescued from demolished or crumbling local churches. But the real highlight here is the **Capela Dourada** (Golden Chapel), a rather vulgar demonstration of colonial prosperity. Finished in 1697, the Rococo chapel is the usual wall-to-ceiling-to-wall ornamentation, except that everything is covered with gold leaf.

Just off the Avenida Dantas Barreto, the church of **São Pedro** (Mon–Fri 8–11am & 2–4pm, Sat 8–10am) is situated on the Pátio de São Pedro. The impressive facade is dominated by a statue of St Peter that was donated to the church in 1980 by a master sculptor from the ceramics centre of Tracunhaém in the interior. Inside the church there's some exquisite woodcarving and a trompe l'oeil ceiling, and on another corner of the Pátio is the **Museu de Arte Popular de Recife** (Mon–Fri 9am–7pm; free), which has some interesting exhibits, including pottery and wooden sculpture. If you've missed the church's opening hours, content yourself with the exterior views, best seen with a cold beer in hand from one of the several bars which set up tables in the square outside. The whole of the Pátio has in fact been beautifully restored, which lends this part of the city a charm of its own.

Recife is probably the best big Brazilian city to find **artesanato**, and the area around São Pedro is the best place to look for it. If you shop around, even tight budgets can stretch to some wonderful bargains. There are stalls all over the city, but they coagulate into a bustling complex of winding streets, lined with beautiful but dilapidated early nineteenth-century tenements, which begins on the Pátio de São Pedro. The streets are choked with people and goods, all of which converge on the market proper, the **Mercado de São José**, an excellent place for *artesanato*.

Determined culture vultures could also make the hop from here to Recife's most central museum, the **Museu da Cidade** (Mon–Sat 9am–6pm, Sun 1–5pm; free), in the star-shaped fort, the Forte das Cinco Pontas, off the western end of Avenida Dantas Barreto; the best view of it is coming in by bus from Boa Viagem. Built in

1630 by the Dutch, the fort was the last place they surrendered when they were expelled in 1654. The building is actually far more interesting than the museum itself, which is dedicated entirely to the history of the city, with old engravings and photographs.

Right opposite the Estação Central, in Rua Floriano Peixoto, the forbidding **Casa da Cultura de Pernambuco** (Mon–Sat 9am–7pm, Sun 10am–5pm; free) was once the city's prison and is now an essential stop for visitors. It's cunningly designed, with three wings radiating out from a central point, so that a single warder could keep an eye on all nine corridors. The whole complex has been turned into an arts and crafts centre, the cells converted into little boutiques and one or two places for refreshment. The quality of the goods on offer here is good, but the prices are a lot higher than elsewhere in the city, so go to look rather than buy. The Casa da Cultura is also the best place to get information on cultural events in the city, providing a monthly *Agenda Cultural* with listings of plays, films and other entertainment.

The **Museu de Arte Moderna Aloisio Magalhães**, located in Boa Vista just over the river from Santo Antônio at Rua da Aurora 256 (Tues–Sun noon–6pm; free), houses prestigious changing exhibitions of mainly Brazilian modern artists, many amongst Pernambuco's best. The **Museu do Homem do Nordeste** (Tues, Wed & Fri 11am–5pm, Thurs 8am–5pm, Sat & Sun 1–5pm; $1.50) was assembled by anthropologists and is one of Brazil's great museums and the best introduction there is to the history and culture of the Northeast. It's quite a way out of central Recife in Casa Forte at Avenida 17 de Agosto 2223 (☎081/3441-5500). Take the "Dois Irmãos" bus from outside the post office or from Parque 13 de Maio, at the bottom of Rua do Hospício; there are two "Dois Irmãos" services, but the one marked "via Barbosa" is the one to get, a pleasant half-hour drive through leafy northern suburbs. The museum is not very easy to spot, on the left-hand side, so ask the driver or conductor where to get off.

Boa Viagem: the beach

Regular buses make it easy to get down to **BOA VIAGEM** and the beach, an enormous skyscraper-lined arc of sand that constitutes the longest stretch of urbanized seafront in Brazil. As you'd expect of a city of islands, Recife was once studded with beaches, but they were swallowed up by industrial development, leaving only Boa Viagem within the city's limits – though there are others a short distance away to the north and south. Much of Boa Viagem is only three or four blocks deep, so it's easy to find your way around.

The **beach** is longer and (claim the locals) better even than Copacabana, with warm natural rock pools to wallow in just offshore when the tide is out. It's also rather narrow, however, and more dominated by the concrete culture around it than most in the Northeast. It gets very crowded at the weekends, but weekdays are relatively relaxed. There's a constant flow of people selling fresh coconut milk, iced beers, ready-mixed *batidas* (rum cocktails), pineapples, watermelon, shrimp, crabs, oysters, ice creams, straw hats and suntan lotion. The usual **cautions** apply about not taking valuables to the beach or leaving things unattended while you swim. There have also been a small number of shark attacks over the years, but they have almost always involved surfers far from shore.

Eating

Eating out is cheapest in Santo Antônio, more expensive in Recife Island and Boa Viagem, with Olinda (see p.385) somewhere in between. Recifense cuisine revolves around **fish** and **shellfish**. Try *carangueijo mole*, crabs cooked in a spicy sauce until shells and legs are soft and edible, which solves the problem of digging out the meat; small crabs called *guaiamum*; and *agulhas fritas*, fried needle fish.

Well worth the visit is the classy *Restaurante Leite*, Praça Joaquim Nabuco 147

(☎081/3224-7977), close to the *Hotel Quatro de Outubro*, which serves good local dishes in a very stylish nineteenth-century interior. **Recife Island** has plenty of restaurants, and you may want to eat there as a prelude to going on to a bar or a nightclub. The emphasis here is on sophistication rather than good old-fashioned hearty Brazilian cooking. *Buon Gustaio*, on Rua do Bom Jesus, does superb Italian food, and *Gambrinus*, at Rua Marquês de Olinda 263, is one of the places where you can get some local dishes. There's also a branch of the vegetarian restaurant, *O Vegetal*, on Rua do Brum (lunchtime only).

In **Boa Viagem** itself the best value is to be found at the seafood places on the promenade near the city-centre end of the beach, and in the dining rooms of the cheaper hotels, all of which are open to non-residents. *Peixada do Lula*, at Av Boa Viagem 244, is a reasonably priced seafood restaurant; *Bargaço*, on the same street at no. 670, does a mixture of seafood and spicier Bahian dishes.

Bars and nightlife

As night falls and the rest of the city centre shuts down, **Recife Island** comes to life. There are all kinds of bars here, including quiet places where middle-aged professionals sit and discuss the events of the day. But the scene is mainly young and noisy: **Rua do Apolo** in particular has a string of bars with names like *Armazém da Cerveja* and *Arsenal do Chopp*, which gives you some idea of the spirit of the place. In the same street, the *Moritzstad* club frequently holds live concerts of the Manue Beat bands, one of Pernambuco's modern musical movements. You should certainly sample the atmosphere here at least once just to get an idea of how seriously young Recifenses take enjoying themselves.

In **Boa Viagem**, bars open and close with bewildering speed, which makes it difficult to keep track of them. The liveliest area, though, is around Praça de Boa Viagem (quite a long way down the beach from the city centre, near the junction of Avenida Boa Viagem and Rua Bavão de Souza Leão); the *Lapinha* bar and restaurant is a popular meeting place, as is the *Caktos* bar, Av Conselheiro Aguiar 2328.

As elsewhere in Brazil, **nightlife** in Recife starts late, after 10pm. The variety of music and dances is enormous, and Recife has its own frenetic carnival music, the **frevo**, as well as **forró**, which you hear all over the Northeast. The dancing to *forró* can be really something, couples swivelling around the dancefloors with ball bearings for ankles. In the past couple of years, Recife Island has become the most happening place in the city centre, but there's also plenty of action in Boa Viagem as well as in Olinda. For a taste of strongly regional music of all types it's worth trying out an **espaço cultural** or two. The Espaço Nodaloshi, at Estrada dos Remédios 1891 in Madalena (☎081/3228-3511), frequently brings together large numbers of musicians from all over Pernambuco, generally starting the shows around 10pm or later. The Espaço Cultural Alberto Cunha Melo, at Rua Leila Félix Karan 15 in Bongi (☎081/3228-6846), runs similar live music shows.

Listings

Airlines Aerolíneas Argentinas, Av Mn. Borba 324 ☎081/3423-4188; Air France, Rua Sete de Setembro 42, Boa Vista ☎081/3231-7735; Air Portugal, Avenida Conselheiro de Aguiar 1472 ☎081/3465-8800; TAM, Praça Min. Salgado ☎081/3462-4466; Transbrasil, Av Conde de Boa Vista 1546 ☎081/3423-2566; United Airlines, Rua Progresso 465 ☎081/3423-2444; Varig, Avenida Conselheiro de Aguiar 456 ☎081/3464-4440; VASP, Rua Dr Nilo Dornelas Cámara 90, Loja 4, Boa Viagem ☎081/3421-3611.

Banks and exchange Banco do Brasil has branches at the airport (daily 10am–9pm), at Av Dantas Barreto 541, at Av Rio Branco 240 (4th floor), and on Rua Sete de Setembro in Boa Vista, all charging commission. You're much better off going to a *casa de câmbio* or a travel agency: the Mônaco agency at Praça Joaquim Nabuco 159 (☎081/3224-4289) in Santo Antônio will change dollars or cheques free of charge. Don't at any time change money with people who approach you on the street.

△ The Museu de Arte Contemporânea, Niteroi

Car rental Hertz at the airport ⓣ081/3800-8900 and at Av Conselheiro Aguiar 4214, Boa Viagem ⓣ081/3325-2907; Avis ⓣ081/3462-5069; Budget ⓣ081/3341-2505.
Consulates UK, Av Eng. Domingos Ferreira 4150, Boa Viagem (Mon–Fri 8–11.30am, Tues & Thurs also 2–4.30pm; ⓣ081/3325-0247); USA, Rua Gonçalves Maia 163, Boa Vista (Mon–Fri 8am–5pm; ⓣ081/3421-2441).
Health matters Albert Sabin, Rua Senador José Henrique 141, Ilha do Leite ⓣ081/3421-5411.
Post office The main post office is the Correio building on Avenida Guararapes in Santo Antônio (Mon–Fri 9am–5pm).
Taxis Disk Taxis Recife ⓣ081/3424-5030 and Teletaxi ⓣ081/3429-4242 are safe.
Telephones Inter-urban and international telephone offices are located at the Telemar office, Praça do Carmo (next to Praça Maxambomba; daily 6am–11pm) in Olinda.
Travel and tour companies Among the best tour companies in and around Recife are Soltur, Rua Matias de Albuquerque 233 ⓣ081/3424-1965; Káritas Turismo e Ecologia, Rua Ribeiro do Brito 1002 ⓣ081/3466-5447; and Crystal Tour, Rua Capitão Zuzinha 22 ⓣ081/3462-4485.

Olinda

OLINDA is, quite simply, one of the largest and most beautiful complexes of **colonial architecture** in Brazil: a maze of cobbled streets, hills crowned with brilliant white churches, pastel-coloured houses, Baroque fountains and graceful squares. Not surprisingly, in 1982 it was designated a cultural heritage site by UNESCO. Founded in 1535, the old city is spread across several small hills looking back towards Recife, but it belongs to a different world. It's here that many of the larger city's artists, musicians and liberal professionals live, and it's also the centre of Recife's gay scene. Olinda is most renowned, though, for its **Carnaval**, famous throughout Brazil, which attracts visitors from all over the country, as well as sizeable contingents from Europe to see over 480 huge, artistically created puppets among the celebrations.

A city in its own right, Olinda is far larger than it first appears. The old colonial centre is built on the hills, slightly back from the sea, but arching along the seafront and spreading inland behind the old town is a modern Brazilian city of over 300,000 people – known as Novo Olinda, the usual bland collection of suburbs and main commercial drags. Like Recife, Novo Olinda has a growing reputation for robberies, but the heart of colonial Olinda is safe enough. There's a calm, almost sleepy atmosphere about the place, and wandering around at night is pretty safe. Despite its size, Olinda has become effectively a neighbourhood of Recife: a high proportion of the population commutes into the city, which means that **transport links** are good, with buses leaving every few minutes.

Arrival and information

Buses from Recife follow the seafront road; get off in the Praça do Carmo, just by Olinda's main post office, from where it's a two-minute walk up into the old city.

A reasonable town map is available from the Secretaria de Turismo in the **Biblioteca** (daily 9am–5pm) at the start of Rua Pruden De Moraes. The **municipal tourist office** in Rua São Bento can help with information about accommodation during Carnaval, but it's not geared up for much more than this. There's also an information kiosk on Praça do Carmo, where the buses stop, but it's not particularly useful. To find out what's happening in the art scene check out the Olinda arts web site ⓦwww.arte.olinda.info.

Accommodation

Prices vary enormously throughout the year – high-season prices are given below, but bear in mind that if you go between March and June or between August and November it will be cheaper. During Carnaval it's virtually impossible to get a room unless you've booked months in advance. There's a **campsite**, *Camping Olinda*, just inside the old city at Rua do Bom Sucesso 262, Amparo (ⓣ081/3429-1365), but do watch your valuables.

Hostal Albergue de Olinda Rua do Sol 233, Carmo ⓣ081/3429-1592, ⓕ3439-1913, ⓔalberguedeolinda@alberguedeolinda.com.br, ⓦwww.alberguedeolinda.com.br. An excellent youth hostel, very comfortable and with a nice hammock area and a small swimming pool; it's also close to the seafront, though right on a busy road. $6 per person.

Hotel Sete Colinas Ladeira de São Francisco 307, Carmo ⓣ081/3439-6055, ⓦwww.hotel7colinasolinda.com.br. Fabulous hotel right in the centre of Olinda, set in beautiful gardens with modern sculptures and a fine swimming pool. There's a range of rooms, suites and luxury apartments, and a good restaurant too. ❺–❼

Pousada do Amparo Rua do Amparo 199 ⓣ081/3439-1749. Quality place combining excellent rooms, an art gallery and a restaurant in a colonial mansion; sauna and pool, too. ❹

Pousada dos Quatro Cantos Rua Prudente de Morais 441 ⓣ081/3429-0220, ⓕ3429-1845, ⓦwww.pousada4cantos.com.br. Beautiful small mansion with a lovely leafy courtyard, right in the heart of the old city. A range of rooms and suites is available, the cheapest with shared bathrooms. ❸

Pousada Peter Rua do Amparo 215 ⓣ081/3439-2171, ⓦwww.pousadapeter.com.br. Located among other art galleries, this is a comfortable gallery-cum-lodging situated in a colonial-style building. ❸

The Town

Olinda's hills are steep, and you'll be best rewarded by taking a leisurely stroll around the town. A good spot to have a drink and plan your attack is the **Alto da Sé**, the highest square in the town, not least because of the stunning view of Recife's skyscrapers shimmering in the distance, framed in the foreground by the church towers, gardens and palm trees of Olinda. There's always an arts and crafts **market** going on here during the day, peaking in the late afternoon; a lot of the things on offer are pretty good, but the large numbers of tourists have driven prices up, and there's little here you can't get cheaper in Recife or the interior.

The **churches** you see are not quite as old as they look. The Dutch burnt them all down, except one, in 1630; they built none of their own, and left the Portuguese to restore them during the following centuries. There are eighteen churches dating from the seventeenth and eighteenth centuries left today, seemingly tucked around every corner and up every street. Very few of them have set opening times, but they're usually open during weekday mornings, and even when they're closed you can try knocking on the door and asking for the *vigia*, the watchman.

If you have time to see only one church it should be the **Convento Franciscano** (Mon–Fri 8–11.30am & 2.30–5pm, Sat 8am–5.30pm), tucked away on Rua São Francisco. Built in 1585, the complex of convent, chapel and church has been stunningly restored to its former glory; particular highlights are the tiled cloister depicting the lives of Jesus and St Francis of Asissi, and the sacristy's beautiful Baroque furniture carved from jacaranda wood. In the north wing there's an elaborate two-tiered altarpiece in gold leaf and white, and behind the convent there's a grand patio with even grander panoramas across the ocean.

Among other churches, the **Igreja da Misericórdia**, built right at the top of an exhaustingly steep hill, has a fine altar and rear walls covered in blue *azulejo*, while the **Mosteiro de Sâo Bento** (Mon–Fri 8am–noon & 2–6pm, Sat 8am–noon, Sun 10am–5pm) looks quite wonderful from the outside with palm trees swaying in the courtyard, though the interior is less striking. The **Igreja da Sé**, on the *praça* of the same name, is rather bland and austere inside – more of a museum than a living church – but is worth a look if only to see the eighteenth-century sedan chair and large wooden sculptures in the small room at the northeast wing. It's also notable for being at the highest point in the region's landscape, making it visible from all the other churches for many miles around. It's the most important temple in Recife area, and all other churches are oriented facing towards the Igreja da Sé. This can be partially appreciated from the viewing patio at the back right hand side of the church.

There's also a good sampling of religious art on display in the **Museu de Arte Sacra de Pernambuco** (Mon–Fri 8am–1pm; free), in the seventeenth-century bishop's palace by the Alto da Sé, while modern art is on display in the **Museu de Arte Contemporânea**, on Rua 13 de Maio next to the market (Tues–Fri 9am–noon & 2–5pm, Sat & Sun 2–5pm; free). The latter is a fine eighteenth-century building that was once used as a jail by the Inquisition, though the exhibits themselves are a bit disappointing. Much more interesting is the **Museu do Mamulengo** (Tues–Fri 9am–5pm, Sat & Sun 2–5pm; free) at Rua do Amparo 59, which houses an excellent collection of traditional puppets.

Eating and drinking

The best place to go for crowds and serious eating and drinking is the **Alto da Sé**. The good, cheap **street food** here, cooked on charcoal fires, can't be recommended too highly; try *acarajé*, which you get from women sitting next to sizzling wok-like pots – bean-curd cake, fried in palm oil, cut open and filled with green salad, dried shrimps and *vatapá*, a yellow paste made with shrimps, coconut milk and fresh coriander. It's absolutely delicious and very cheap.

Olinda is extremely well off for **restaurants**. If you want to eat for less than $5, try the *comida por kilo* places along the seafront and in the new part of town. However, for just a little bit more, you can eat far better in the old town. *Blues Bar*, in the garden of an old house at Rua do Bonfim 66 (Tues–Thurs 6pm–1am, Fri & Sat 6pm–3am and Sun 11am–8pm; ⓣ081/9156-6415) is moderately priced and makes excellent, if unique, meat dishes and plays great, authentic blues music much of the time. *Goya Restaurant*, Rua do Amparo 157, is hard to beat for imaginative Brazilian and French cuisine, while the *Creperia*, Praça João Alfredo 168 (ⓣ081/3429-2935), serves great salads as well as the obvious. The Restaurante Flor do Coco, Rua do Amparo 199, also serves excellent cuisine but with more of a regional flavour. Other good spots at the higher end of the price range are the *Porta D'Italia*, Rua do Bonfim – which serves surprisingly good Italian food and has a good range of wines – and the *Oficina do Sabor*, Rua do Amparo 365, which is excellent for local cuisine – try the shrimps in mango sauce. If it's just good coffee you're after, try the *Café Adego*, at Rua 27 de Janeiro 70.

Fortaleza

FORTALEZA, which means "fortress", is a sprawling city of over two million inhabitants, the centre bristling with offices and apartment blocks. For well over a century, it has been the major commercial centre of the northern half of the Northeast and recently has poured resources into expanding its tourist trade, lining the fine city beaches with gleaming luxury hotels and a developing the city centre.

The first Portuguese settlers arrived in 1603 and were defeated initially by the Indians, who killed and ate the first bishop (a distinction the city shares with Belém), and then by the Dutch, who drove the Portuguese out of the area in 1637. It wasn't until well into the eighteenth century that the Indians were finally overwhelmed by the determined blazing of cattle trails into the interior. In 1816, the Fortaleza de Nossa Senhora da Assunção was built by the Portuguese on the site of an earlier Dutch one. The city did well in the **nineteenth century**, as the port city of a hinterland where ranching was expanding rapidly. While it's not a beautiful city, the beaches and weather make up for that, and Fortaleza has something of the same atmosphere as Rio, especially when it comes to the good things in life like food, beaches and nightlife.

Arrival, city transport and information

The **rodoviária** and **airport** are some way from the centre in the southern suburb of Fátima, but getting into town is easy thanks to the comfortable *frescão* service operated by the Top Bus company ($3). The buses will stop to let you off – or can be flagged down – wherever you want along their circular route, which winds its way through the crowded city centre to the beach areas; it's supposed to run throughout the night, but the service is less frequent then, and you should check with the tourist office if you're relying on it to catch an early morning bus or plane. It might be cheaper to take a taxi, which costs around $8 to the airport from most places.

Fortaleza also has plenty of **local buses**. Useful routes that take you out to the main beach areas and back to the city centre are those marked "Grande Circular", "Caça e Pesca", "Mucuripe" and "P. Futuro". Two buses, the "Circular 1" and "Circular 2", run services that cover the outskirts and central part of Fortaleza respectively. There are loads of taxis, too, which are essential for getting around late at night; cabs are available from Cooperttur (Ⓣ085/224-6206). You can walk around Fortaleza quite easily: the city is heavily policed and feels much safer than many other Brazilian cities, though the usual basic precautions are still in order.

The **main information office** of the state tourist office, SETUR (Mon–Sat 8am–6pm, Sun 8am–noon; Ⓣ085/488-7411), is in the Centro de Turismo in the centre, at Rua Senador Pompeu 350, and should be your first port of call; the staff know their stuff, and are especially good on the complicated bus journeys that are often necessary to get to the out-of-town beaches. The best maps of Fortaleza are usually to be obtained from the municipal tourist organization, **FORTUR**, which has an information post (daily 8am–5pm; Ⓣ085/252-1444) on Praça do Ferreira in the centre.

There are a number of **tour agencies** in town, notably *Ernaitur*, Avenida Barao de Studart 1165 (1st floor), Conjunto 101–107, Aldeota (Ⓣ085/244-9363, Ⓕ261-6782, Ⓦwww.ernanitur.com.br) and *Wall Street*, Aveniuda Santos Dumont 3000, Aldeota (Ⓣ085/486-3900) or Aveinda Beira Mar 2982, Loja 02 (Ⓣ085/242-2235), which offers trips to Jericoacoara ($50), Canoa Quebrada ($12), Lagoinha ($10) as well as city tours ($10). *Praia Turismo* (Ⓣ085/9989-6685), which parks its sales van by the beach on Beira Mar at the Praia Iracema end most mornings, runs similar tours at very slightly cheaper prices and will also pick up from hotels. **Car rental** is available from RCA (Ⓣ085/219-7000) and RHP (Ⓣ085/257-7533), Ⓦwww.rhprentacar.com.br.

Accommodation

The budget hotels, as ever, tend to be in the **centre**, which hums with activity during the day but empties at night, and the more expensive ones are generally out by the **beaches**, notably Iracema and Meireles. Remember that Fortaleza can get very hot, and either air conditioning or a fan is essential.

The city centre

Hotel Sol Rua Barão do Rio Branco 829 Ⓣ085/211-9166, Ⓕ262-1021. A classy option with airy rooms and a swimming pool. ④

Lidia Hotel Rua Rufino de Alencar 300 Ⓣ085/252-4174. Friendly, very small modern conversion of a house into a hotel, it meets all the basic requirements for comfort and cleanliness. ②

Pousada Toscana Rua Rufino de Alenar 272 Ⓣ085/231-6378, Ⓔfabriziostasi@yahoo.com.br, Ⓦwww.pousadatoscana.hpg.com.br. Very close to the central market and the Centro Dragão, this exceptionally clean and well-run hostel is located in an attractive, modest-sized house; rooms are bright and airy, beds comfortable. ②

Praia da Iracema area

Pousada Atalaia Av Beira Mar 814 Ⓣ085/219-0658, Ⓔalberguedajuventude@task.com.br, Ⓦwww.pousadaatalaia.com.br. This must be one of the best-located youth hostels in the Americas, right opposite the beach on the Praia Iracema and within shouting distance of the best nightlife spots in Fortaleza. Accommodation mostly in dormitories, some private rooms available too. ①–③

Pousada Portal de Iracema Rua dos Ararius 2, Praia de Iracema Ⓣ085/219-0066, Ⓕ219-3411, Ⓔpousada@ultranet.com.br. Well-located pousada, very close to the sea and beside the heart of the nightlife district, yet surprisingly quiet; clean and bright rooms with TVs and minbars, good English spoken, very friendly and conscientious service and lovely breakfasts. ③.

Turismo Praia Av Beira Mar 894, Praia de Iracema Ⓣ085/219-6133 Ⓕ219-1638. Small, good-value hotel with functional rooms, tiny pool,

OK restaurant but great location right opposite the beach. ❸

Praia Meireles area

Hotel Beira-Mar Av Beira Mar (Av Presidente Kennedy) 3130, Praia de Meireles ⓣ085/242-5000 ⓕ242-5659, ⓦwww.hotelbeiramar.com.br. Luxury hotel with pool, right next to the Praia de Meireles. ❺.

Hotel La Maison Av Desembarador Moreira 201 ⓣ085/242-7017, ⓦwww.hotellamaison.com.br. This thirteen-room pousada is based in a tastefully converted family house just a few blocks from the beach; the rooms are pleasant and have air conditioning, TVs, telephone. French and English spoken; parking spaces available. ❸.

Hotel Marina Praia Rua Paula Barros 44 ⓣ085/242-7734, ⓕ242-5275, ⓔreservas@hotelmarinapraia.com.br, ⓦwww.hotelmarinapraia.com.br. A small hotel, little bigger than a house, the Marina Praia is less than a block from the beach in the Nautico section of Praia Meireles; incredibly spick and span, it somehow fits 25 apartments into its comfortable and colourful interior. There's also a small patio for taking the afternoon sunshine outfront. Staff are very pleasant. ❸

The City

While not the most visually attractive of Brazilian city centres, there is enough going on in the heart of Fortaleza to merit more attention than it usually gets from visitors. It certainly can't be faulted for being boring: the streets are very crowded, with shops and hawkers colonizing large areas of pavement and squares, so that much of the centre often seems like a single large market.

The **Igreja da Sé** cathedral is unmistakable in the centre of town, near the Fortaleza and central market. Quite ugly at first glance, it almost shocks with its dark batman-like Neogothic yet eclectic architectural style. Megalithic flying buttresses lift the weird building from the ground, all black and grey with age and city grime. Set right next to the cathedral on Rua Conde d'Eu, the striking new **Mercado Central**, a huge complex holding hundreds of small stores, dominates the skyline. The market, and the nearby shops on the other side of the cathedral, is the best place to buy a hammock in the city: if you're going to use one on your travels, purchase it with care. Cloth ones are the most comfortable, but are heavier, bulkier and take longer than nylon ones to dry out if they get wet. Less comfy in the heat, but more convenient, much lighter and more durable are nylon hammocks.

Right opposite the Mercado Central, the nineteenth-century **Fortaleza de Nossa Senhora da Assunção** – the city's namesake – is easily identified by its thick, plain white walls and old black cannons. It belongs to the Tenth Military Regiment of the Brazilian army, but is open to visitors on request (Mon–Fri 9am–5pm; ⓣ085/255-1600); visits are best organized the day before.

The brand-new **Centro Dragão do Mar de Arte e Cultura**, a couple of blocks east of the market, marks a strident modernist landmark in the city; its steel and glass curves blend unusually with the attractive old terraced buildings over and around which it is built. Within the complex, there's a small, shiny-domed planetarium, cinemas, an auditorium, a couple of museums – one dedicated to contemporary art – information hall and bookshop, toilets and a good coffee bar, the *Torre do Café*, in the tower that supports the covered walkway between the two main sections of the Centro.

Overlooking the sea at the bottom of Rua Senador Pompeu is the **Centro de Turismo**, housed in the city's old prison – a perfect place to stop and have a beer in the bar in the one-time exercise yard, shaded by mango trees. The centre is also the location of the best museum in the city, the **Museu de Arte e Cultura Popular** (Mon–Fri 8am–6pm, Sat 8am–noon; free). Well laid out in a single huge gallery on the first floor, this is a comprehensive collection of Cearense *artesanato* of all kinds, together with a sample of the painting and sculpture produced by the best of the state's modern artists. What distinguishes the museum is the imaginative juxtaposition of more traditional popular art with modernism. Both collections are of very high quality.

The nerve centre of this part of the city, however, is its largest square, **Praça José de Alencar**, four blocks inland from the train station. In the late afternoon and early evening, the crowds here attract *capoeira* groups, street sellers of all kinds and especially *repentistas*. These street poets gather an audience with great skill and wit, improvising a verse or two about those standing around watching, passing round a hat for you to show your appreciation. If you refuse, or give what they consider too little, the stream of innuendo and insults is unmistakeable, even if you don't understand a word. On the square you'll also find the one truly impressive building in the city, the beautiful **Teatro José de Alencar**, named after the great nineteenth-century novelist and poet, a native of the city. Built in the first decade of the twentieth century, the fine tropical Edwardian exterior is in fact only an elegant facade, which leads into an open courtyard and the main body of the theatre. It is built in ornate and beautifully worked cast-iron sections, which were brought over complete from Scotland and reassembled in 1910. It is extremely cool and pleasant to be in, even when the sun is at its height, for the ironwork is open and lets in the air without trapping heat, a masterly example of Scottish design in the least Scottish setting imaginable. In 1991 it was superbly restored and is now a key venue for theatrical performances and concerts.

The city beaches

The main city beaches are the **Praia de Iracema** and the adjacent **Praia do Meireles**, both major foci for Fortaleza's nightlife; in terms of nightlife, the former has a slightly younger, wilder edge, while the latter appeals to a broader cross section of the local and tourist populations. In terms of beach, the Praia do Meireles wins hands down, though the water is not as clean as out of town beaches, owing to the proximity of docks both east and west. The further away from the centre, the better for swimming. By day there are surfers on the waves and beach parties at the *barracas*, and in the early evening it seems everyone in the city turns out to stroll or rollerblade down the boulevard, which has replaced the city's squares as the favoured meeting place. In the early evenings, the promendade at the Praia do Meireles in particular comes alive with thronging crowds of friends and familes,

Forró: dancing and clubs

Fortaleza is justly famous for its **forró**. Nowhere is it so popular as in Fortaleza, and there is no better way to see what Cearenses do when they want to enjoy themselves than to spend a night there in a *dancetaria*. Although most *dancetarias* open at 10pm, people don't really start arriving until around midnight, and peak time is in the early hours of the morning. One of the busiest nightspot areas is the streets around the Ponte dos Ingleses, where you'll find the *Pirata* club and the *Disco Bar Desigual* (see below) as well as the *Pantera Africas Bar,* half a block inland from the pier, at Rua Almi 83, which has live shows of music and sometimes comedy.

Pirata (Ⓣ085/219-8030, Ⓦwww.pirata.com.br) one of the most easily accessible nightclubs in Fortaleza, has live music from Tuesday through Saturday at Rua dos Tabajaras 325. Music encompasses rock and pop to *forró* with live accordion playing and, later, the acclaimed Banda do Pirata usually takes the audience through a medley of *axe*, *salsa*, *baiao*, *pagode* and *zouk* styles of Brazilian popular music. Entrance costs about $4. *Subindo ao Céu*, at Av Zezé Diogo out on Praia do Futuro, is a popular venue on Tuesday nights. On Wednesdays the scene shifts to the *Clube do Vaqueiro* (Ⓣ085/276-2014), a taxi ride away out on the periphery of the city along the BR-116 highway leading east to Natal. Most weekends, the *Disco Bar Desigual*, on the seafront between the pier and Paraiso do Praia Hotel, blasts out live music and is popular with the younger Fortaleza set. For the middle-aged, the *Circulo Militar* offers a more traditional though still lively show and couples dancing on Saturday nights (11pm–3am) at Rua Canuto de Aguiar 425 (Ⓣ085/242-7979).

joggers, people looking for somewhere nice to eat, revellers and street-sellers with everything from sunglasses to cashew nuts.

Eating, drinking and nightlife

Most of what Fortaleza has to offer your palate is to be found on the beaches, especially around **Rua dos Tabajaras** on Praia de Iracema. Rua dos Tabajaras itself is a joy to wander around, with its brightly coloured bars and **restaurants**, and glamorous young people out enjoying themselves. A stone's throw from the pier there's the airy and very pleasant split-level *Restaurant Belas Artes* (Ⓣ085/219-0330) at Rua dos Tabajaras 179, with a good range of Brazilian and international dishes and an excellent bar. Nearby, the impressive wooden – almost boat-like – structure of the *Restaurant Sobre o Mar*, Rua dos Tremembes 2 (Ⓣ085/219-7999), has a larger floor on two storeys and a cover charge of $1 for the frequent live music shows; it serves good lobster and has a good range of wines. A little closer towards the pier, the attractive low-lying older building of the *Restaurante Estoril* (Ⓣ085/219-8389) makes the best of its setting at Rua dos Tabajaras 397, serving excellent if pricey *Cearense* cuisine, offering shows at weekends, and comedy on Tuesday nights. Much further south along the seafront, past Praia do Futuro at Av Beira Mar 4566, the *Marquinhos Restaurante* (Ⓣ085/263-1204) serves excellent seafood (try the skewered lobster); it's not cheap but the service is good and the restaurant open and airy.

3.4

The Amazon

The Amazon is a vast forest – the largest on the planet – and a giant river system. It covers over half of Brazil and a large portion of South America. The forest extends into Brazil's neighbouring countries, Venezuela, Colombia, Peru and Bolivia, where the river itself begins life among thousands of different headwaters. In Brazil only the stretch between Manaus and Belém is actually known as the **Rio Amazonas**: above Manaus the river is called the **Rio Solimões** up to the border with Peru, where it once again becomes the Amazonas. The daily flow of the river is said to be enough to supply a city the size of New York with water for nearly ten years, and its power is such that the muddy Amazon waters stain the Atlantic a silty brown for over 200km out to sea. This was how its existence was first identified by the Spaniard, Vicente Yanez Pinon, sailing the Atlantic in search of El Dorado. He was drawn to the mouth of the Amazon by the sweet freshness of the ocean or, as he called it, the Mar Dulce.

Eastern Amazônia

Politically divided between the states of Pará and Amapá, the **EASTERN AMAZON** is essentially a vast area of forest and savanna plains centred on the final seven hundred miles or so of the giant river's course. Belém, an Atlantic port near the mouth of the estuary, is the elegant capital of Pará and a worthwhile place to spend some time. It overlooks the river and the vast Ilha de Marajó, a marshy island in the estuary given over mainly to cattle farming, but with a couple of good beaches. **Amapá**, in the northeastern corner of the Brazilian Amazon, is a poor and little-visited area, nevertheless offering the possibility of an adventurous overland route to French Guiana and on into Surinam, Guyana and Venezuela. It's possible to do much of this journey by ocean-going boat.

Connections in the region are pretty straightforward, in that you have very few choices. The main throughway is still the Amazon, with stops at **Santarém** – a sleepy town entirely dominated by the river – and **Óbidos**, far less enticing. As far as roads go there are good highways south from Belém towards Brasília (the BR-010) and east into the state of Maranhão (the BR-316). In the north there's just one road from **Macapá**, the capital of Amapá, up towards the border with French Guyana. The BR-010 crosses the powerful Rio Tocantins near Estreito (in Maranhão) close to the start of the **Transamazônica**.

Belém

Strategically placed on the Amazon River estuary close to the mouth of the mighty Rio Tocantins, **BELÉM** was founded by the Portuguese in 1616 as the City of Our Lady of Bethlehem (Belém). Its original role was to protect the river mouth and establish the Portuguese claim to the region, but it rapidly became established as an Indian slaving port and a source of cacao and spices from the Amazon. Owing to the Amazon rubber boom, by the end of the nineteenth century, Belém was a very rich town, accounting for close to half of all Brazil's rubber exports. After the crash of 1914, the city suffered a disastrous decline – but it kept afloat, just about, on the back of Brazil nuts and the lumber industry. Belém remains the economic centre of the North, and the chief port for the Amazon.

Arrival and information

Belém's **rodoviária** is situated some 2km from the centre on Avenida Governador José Malcher; any bus from the stops opposite the entrance to the rodoviária will take you downtown. If you want Praça da República, catch the #316 or #904, or take one with "P. Vargas" on its route card; for the port area take the #318. There are excellent facilities and services at the rodoviária, including a Parátur information office (not always open, even when it's meant to be). If you're coming by scheduled airline, you'll arrive at Belém **airport**, 15km out of town (☎091/210-6039). Walk to the opposite end of the terminal where you'll find the taxi stand for ordinary city cabs, which are much cheaper than the co-op taxis. **Boats** dock on the river near the town centre, from where you can easily catch a taxi. For information on boat services see "Listings", p.398.

As well as the somewhat erratic Belémtur offices at Avenida Gov. Jose Malcher 592 (8am-6pm Mon-Fri; ☎91/242-0033) and the airport (supposedly daily 8am-11pm; ☎91/210-6330) **tourist information** is also available at Parátur offices downtown at the Feira de Artesanato do Estado on Praça Maestro Waldemar Henrique (previously Praça Kennedy; Mon–Fri 8am–5pm; ☎091/212-0575). There are also tourist information points operated at the Solar da Beira (daily 8am–7pm; ☎91/212-8484) in the *Ver o Peso* complex as well as at the *Hidroviário* on Praça Princesa Isabel (daily 8am–7pm; ☎91/249-6250). **Maps** and town guides can be bought cheaply from the newspaper stands on Avenida Presidente Vargas or in the shop inside the foyer of the *Belém Hilton*.

Accommodation

The more expensive and mid-price hotels are on Avenida Presidente Vargas. Other, more basic hotels tend to be found in the narrow streets behind, between Avenida Presidente Vargas and the old heart of town by Avenida Portugal, the government palace and the fort.

Belém Hilton Av Presidente Vargas 882 ☎91/217-7000, ⓔbelemhil@amazon.com.br, ⓦwww.amazon.com.br/hilton. Belém's best and most expensive hotel dominates the Praça da República. The rooms are really swish, with excellent air conditioning and some with superb views across the city and watery forests. Although usually exorbitant, the *Hilton* occasionally has radical price reductions at slack times of year. ❽

Canto do Rio Av Castilhos Franca ☎91/224-7473. Situated very close to the port, this hotel has friendly staff but offers very basic accommodation, sometimes quite grubby, in a dubious neighbourhood more or less opposite one end of the Ver o Peso market. The *Canto do Rio* also acts as an agent for boats going upstream. ❶

Central Av Presidente Vargas 290 ☎91/241-4800. Probably the best value in town, this well-situated hotel is a splendid, if somewhat down-at-heel old building with a wide range of comfortable, spacious rooms and a refreshing rooftop breakfast. Some of the rooms have windows opening onto corridors, so put valuables in the hotel safe. ❷

Fortaleza Rua Frutuoso Guimaraes 275 ☎91/212-1050 or 283-0688. Undoubtedly the best of the very cheapest places – a safe, very friendly and family-run establishment with large shared rooms in a modest and pleasant colonial house in a bustling backstreet of the commercial sector. Breakfast is quite good value at an extra $1.50. Just a few streets behind Avenida Presidente Vargas, the *Fortaleza* can also organize boat trips. ❶

Vidonho's Rua O. de Almeida 476 ☎91/242-1444. Good value, central and modern, with air conditioning in all rooms, good showers and well located, if a bit noisy, just off the Avenida Presidente Vargas. ❸

The City

The **Praça da República**, an attractive central park with plenty of trees affording valuable shade, is a perfect place from which to get your bearings and start a walking tour of Belém's downtown and riverfront attractions. The *praça* itself is

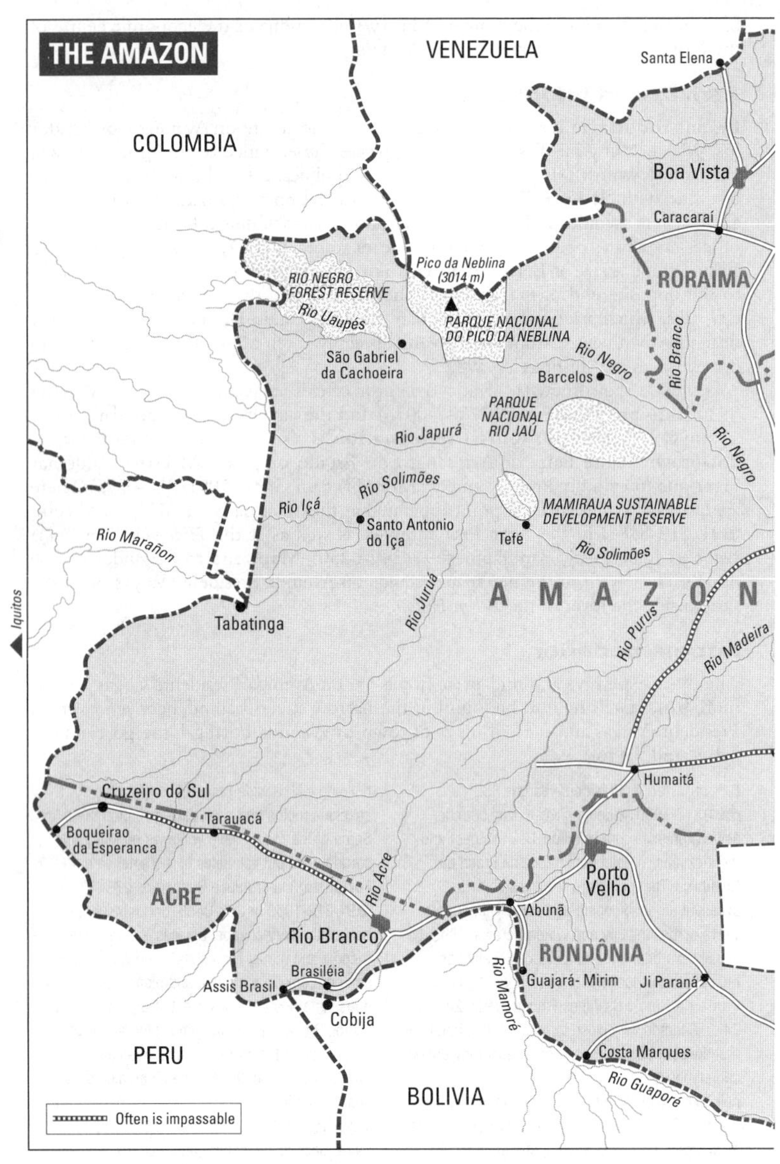

sumptuously endowed with fine statues and columns focusing on its fountain centrepiece. Overlooking it is the most obvious sign of Belém's rubber fortunes: the nineteenth-century Rococo **Theatro da Paz**, dripping with Neoclassical fixtures, this fine opera house influenced by Milan's La Scala, and the hottest place Anna Pavlova ever danced, was built on the profits of the rainforest back in 1878. Recently restored, it's open for free visits Mon–Fri 9am–6pm.

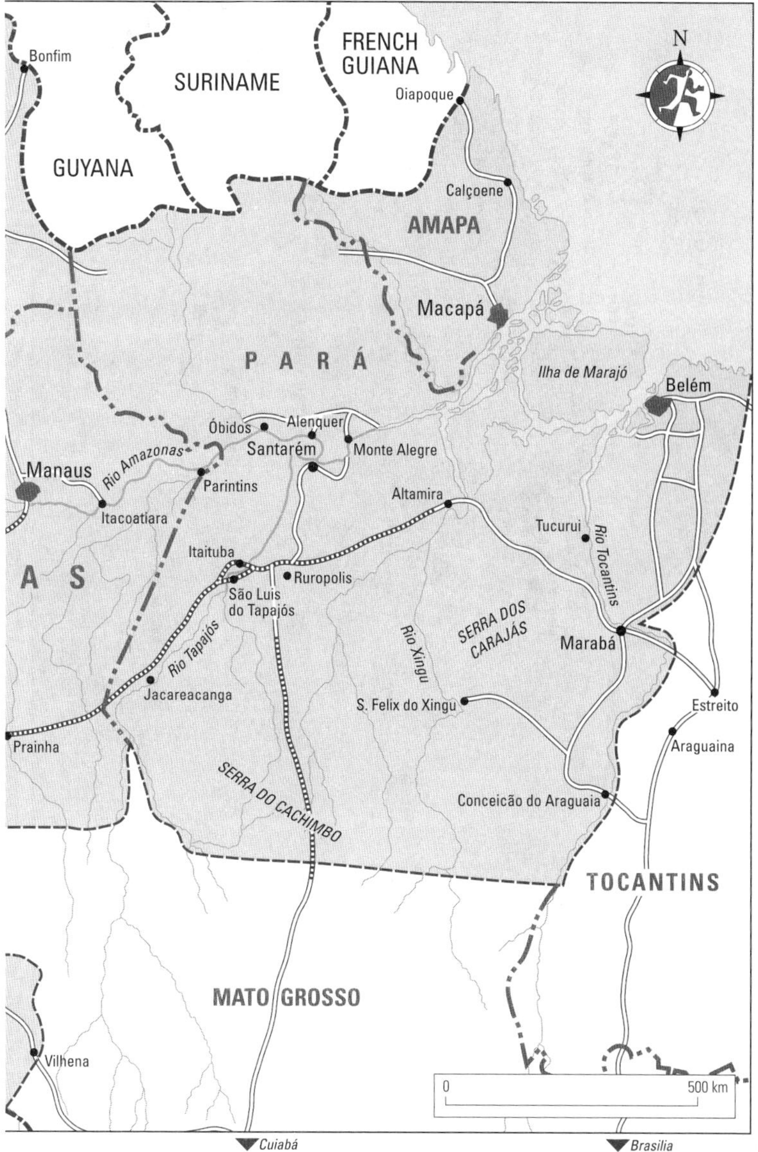

Heading down Presidente Vargas towards the river, the old part of town – the **Cidade Velha** – lies off to the left, full of crumbling Portuguese colonial mansions and churches. The oldest church of all is the **Igreja das Mercês**, Rua Frutuoso Guimarães 31. Architecturally it's nothing special, but as a living, working relic it's totally fascinating, full of quaint little touches. The holy water, for example, is dispensed from an upside-down rum bottle with the label half torn off.

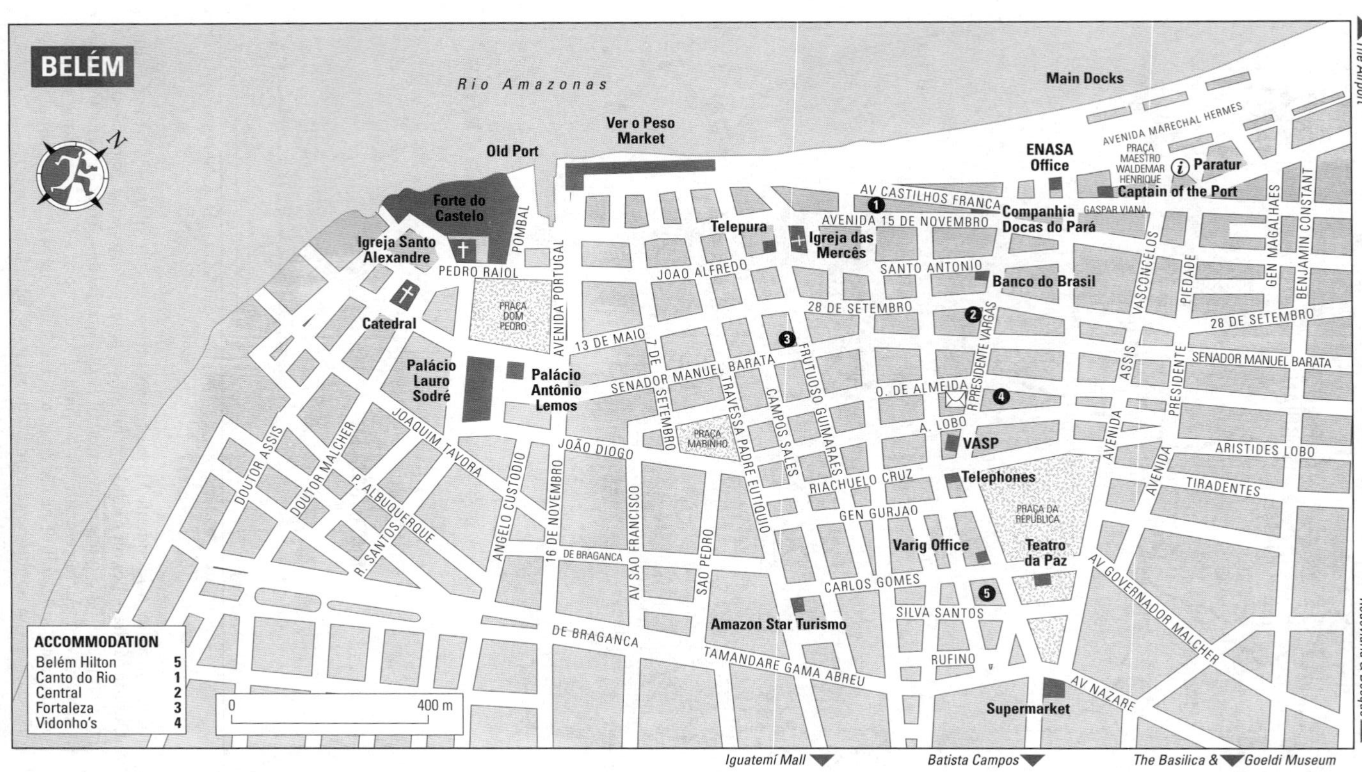
BELÉM
N
Rio Amazonas
Main Docks
Ver o Peso Market
Old Port
ENASA Office
Paratur
Captain of the Port
PRAÇA MAESTRO WALDEMAR HENRIQUE
AVENIDA MARECHAL HERMES
GASPAR VIANA
AV CASTILHOS FRANCA
AVENIDA 15 DE NOVEMBRO
Companhia Docas do Pará
Forte do Castelo
Igreja Santo Alexandre
Catedral
Telepura
Igreja das Mercês
Banco do Brasil
PEDRO RAIOL
POMBAL
AVENIDA PORTUGAL
PRAÇA DOM PEDRO
JOAO ALFREDO
SANTO ANTONIO
28 DE SETEMBRO
13 DE MAIO
7 DE SETEMBRO
SENADOR MANUEL BARATA
TRAVESSA PADRE EUTIQUIO
CAMPOS SALES
FRUTUOSO GUIMARAES
R PRESIDENTE VARGAS
O. DE ALMEIDA
A. LOBO
VASP
Telephones
Palácio Lauro Sodré
Palácio Antônio Lemos
PRAÇA MARINHO
JOÃO DIOGO
RIACHUELO CRUZ
GEN GURJAO
Varig Office
PRAÇA DA REPÚBLICA
Teatro da Paz
CARLOS GOMES
SILVA SANTOS
RUFINO
Amazon Star Turismo
Supermarket
AV NAZARE
AV GOVERNADOR MALCHER
TIRADENTES
ARISTIDES LOBO
AVENIDA PRESIDENTE
ASSIS
AVENIDA
VASCONCELOS
PIEDADE
GEN MAGALHAES
BENJAMIN CONSTANT
JOAQUIM TAVORA
ANGELO CUSTODIO
16 DE NOVEMBRO
DE BRAGANCA
AV SAO FRANCISCO
SAO PEDRO
TAMANDARE GAMA ABREU
P. ALBUQUERQUE
R. SANTOS
DOUTOR MALCHER
DOUTOR ASSIS
ACCOMMODATION
Belém Hilton 5
Canto do Rio 1
Central 2
Fortaleza 3
Vidonho's 4
0 400 m
The Airport
Rodoviária & Bosque
Iguatemí Mall
Batista Campos
The Basilica & Goeldi Museum

At the river docks, the hectic and anarchic market sells Amazonian produce, overlooked closely by the old fort. **Ver o Peso market** is not quite the colourful spectacle it once was, but it remains the liveliest spot in town early in the morning. Ver o Peso ("see the weight") was originally a slave market, but these days its main commodities are fish, fruit and vegetables, manioc flour, nuts and other jungle produce. Next to the open market stands the proud **Iron Market** or *Mercado de Ferro,* supplied and built by British engineers in the nineteenth century. The whole Ver o Peso sector doesn't have that much aimed at tourists, but nevertheless this is one of the most lively and varied traditional markets in all South America and is arguably reason enough in itself to visit Belém. It can be a dangerous place, so leave your valuables somewhere safe, and it's not a good idea to go to the market area at any time other than the morning. In recent years, the riverfront promenade northeast of the market has been cleaned up and turned into an attractive pedestrian walkway and, more recently still, an old storage building at the docks close to the end of Aveinda President Vargas has been transformed into a cultural centre called the **Estação das Docas** (Tues–Thurs 10am–1pm, Fri–Sun 9am–3pm) on the Boulevard Castilhos França; inside there are *artesania* stalls as well as excellent local dishes and a theatre space.

Near the Fort do Castelo (closed at the time of writing) there are two important churches: the eighteenth-century **Igreja Santo Alexandre**, which now houses a small religious art museum, and the finer **Catedral de Nossa Senhora da Graça** (Mon 3–6pm, Tues–Fri 8–11am & 3–6pm), on Praça Frei Caetano Brandão. The cathedral was built in 1748, though it has been renovated many times since, including in the nineteenth century when the original wooden altar was replaced by one of marble and alabaster, over 10m high.

The architectural highlights of Cidade Velha, however, dominate the square behind the old port and Ver O Peso. Together with the Opera House in Manaus, the magnificent **palaces** of Lauro Sodré and Antônio Lemos are the finest buildings left by the rubber boom. Until recently the seat of the mayor and state governor respectively, and more than a little run-down, they have been sensitively restored, with the addition of museums, and thrown open to the public for under $1.50 each. The **Palácio Lauro Sodré** (Mon–Fri 9am–6pm, Sat 10am–6pm), completed in the 1890s, has a dazzling white Neoclassical colonnaded exterior and a series of airy arched courtyards which are occasionally used as galleries for travelling exhibitions. Upstairs, the Salão Nobre, a huge suite of reception rooms runs the entire length of the frontage with crystal chandeliers, beautiful inlaid wooden floors and Art Nouveau furniture, marred only by a few grim paintings. A separate section of the palace houses the **Museu do Estado do Pará** (Mon–Fri 9am–6pm, Sat 10am–6pm, Sun & holidays 9am–1pm), which has an archive of around 6000 historical pieces plus collections of Art Nouveau and modern art. Next door, painted a delightful blue and white, is the **Palácio Antônio Lemos** (Tues–Fri 9am–noon & 2–6pm, Sat 9am–1pm), built in the 1770s by Antônio Landí, a talented emigré Italian, who was also an artist and sketched the first scientifically accurate drawings of Amazonian fauna.

Two of the most important and worthwhile sights in Belém lie about fifteen minutes' walk inland from the Praça da República along Avenida Nazaré. The **Basílica de Nossa Senhora de Nazaré** (daily 6.30–11.30am & 2.30–7pm) on Praça Justo Chermont was created in 1908 and, supposedly modelled on St Peter's in Rome, it rates – internally at least – with the most beautiful temples in South America. Most importantly, however, it is home to one of the most revered images in Brazil, **Nossa Senhora de Nazaré**, said to have been originally sculpted in Nazareth in the early years of Christianity, from where it found its way to Spain, then Portugal, before getting lost and rediscovered in the Brazilian jungle in 1700 by a rancher. He built a rough shrine to house the Virgin, and word of its miraculous properties rapidly spread; today that shrine has grown to an impressive church, and the cult of Nossa Senhora de Nazaré is stronger than ever.

At the annual **Círio de Nazaré** (Festival of Candles), something approaching a million people flock to Belém on the second Sunday in October. A copy of the image is carried in a vast parade made up of thousands of young people, who between them also carry an old 380-metre-long anchor rope that weighs well over a ton, to receive the blessing of Our Lady.

Eating and drinking

Belém is a great place to eat out given the wide range of delicious Amazonian cuisine which emanates from the city, offering an opportunity to get acquainted with the distinctive dishes.

Avenida Av Nazaré 1086 ⓣ91/223-4015. One of Belém's best restaurants with a great setting overlooking the basilica, excellent food and air conditioning – though it's fairly expensive and a bit short on atmosphere; try the *piraruco ao leite de coco.* Usually open until midnight but closed on Mondays.

Casa Portuguesa Rua Senador Manuel Barata 897 ⓣ91/242-4871. Directly behind *Restaurant Inter* with surprisingly inexpensive but superb-quality local and Portuguese food, *cabaña*-style decor and a quiet atmosphere.

Inter 28 de Setembro 304. Superb value, large delicious helpings and local specialities, frequented mostly by Belém's office workers at lunchtime for its self-service buffet.

Lá em Casa Av Gov. José Malcher 247 ⓣ091/223-1212. Good, moderately priced food, eaten underneath an enormous mango tree, with a retractable roof in case of rain. Regional dishes are recommended (the menu has a helpful English translation); this has one of the best reputations in the city for its local cuisine.

Nectar Av Gentil Bittencourt, Travesa Padre Eutiquio 248. Best vegetarian lunches in the city; get there early because the best choices are often finished before 2pm. Closed on Sundays.

Restó das Docas Blvd Castilhos França ⓣ91/212-3737. In the lively Estacao das Docas building at the end of Avenida Presidente Vargas, this air-conditioned restaurant is one of the best new places in town, serving excellent self-service buffets at lunch. Closed Mondays.

Sabor da Terra Av Souza Franco (also called Docas) 600. The food is nothing special but the highlight is the floor show afterwards, which is touristy but very good as these things go: regional dances and music, well staged, with especially good dancers. Reasonably priced: around $15–20 a head, excluding drinks.

Listings

Airlines Taba, Av Dr. Feitas 1191, office at the airport ⓣ91/257-4000; TAM, Av Assis de Vasconcelos 265 ⓣ91/212-2166; Tavaj ⓣ91/210-6257; Transbrasil, Av Presidente Vargas 780 ⓣ091/212-6977; Varig, Av Presidente Vargas 768 ⓣ91/210-6262; VASP, Av Presidente Vargas 345 ⓣ91/257-0944.

Banks and exchange Banco da Amazônia, Av Presidente Vargas; Banco do Brasil, 2nd Floor, Av Presidente Vargas 248; HSBC Bank, Av Presidente Vargas 670.

Boats Boats leave Belém regularly for upstream Amazon River destinations, even as far as Porto Velho (at least one a day to Macapá, Santarém and Manaus) and for coastal cities such as Salvador and Rio; there are also boats every day to the port of Souré on the Ilha de Marajó (4hr). However, boats don't have set times of departure, and there are a huge number of different companies, with no central place where you can get information. Any travel agent will book a ticket for you, or speak to the captains on the docks. It's easy enough to find what boats are going when and select which suits your needs by going down to the Portobrás docks themselves, starting at the bottom end of Avenida Presidente Vargas (ask along the waterfront by the warehouses Amazém numbers 3 and also 10 where the best boats usually dock). For Santarem, Manaus and Macapa, the Agencia Amazonas at Avenida Castilho Franca 548 can sell most tickets – try to catch one of the Mareques Pinto Navegaco boats if they're available, since they are one of the best operators and most comfortable charter boats.

Car hire Avis, Rua Sen. Lemos 121 ⓣ91/257-2277; Dallas, Av Bras de Aguiar 621 ⓣ91/212-2237; Localiza, Av Gov. José Malcher 1365 ⓣ91/257-1541. The Forest Off Road Club, Av Marquês de Herval 948, Pedreira ⓣ91/266-1423, hires a variety of jeeps and pick-ups with driver.

Hospital Hospital Guadalupe (private), Rua Arcipreste Manoel Teodoro 734 (ⓣ091/241-8940).

Post office The central post office (Mon–Sat 9.30am–6pm) is an impressive building at Av Presidente Vargas 498. However, as this is frequently crowded, it's often quicker to walk to the small post office at Av Nazaré 319, three blocks beyond the Praça da República.

Shopping Belém is one of the best places in the world to buy hammocks (essential if you go upriver) – look in the street markets between Avenida Presidente Vargas and Ver o Peso, starting in Rua Santo Antônio, or try the one at Frutuoso Guimarães 273, near the *Hotel Fortaleza*.

Taxis Aguia ⓣ91/276-4000, or Comista ⓣ91/276-0108.

Telephones Telemar operates indoor public kiosks on the corner of Av Presidente Vargas and Rua Riachuelo; there is also a *poste telefônico* on the third block of João Alfredo (Mon–Fri 10am–7pm, Sat 10am–4pm).

Travel and tour companies Mundial Turismo, Av Presidente Vargas 780 ⓣ91/223-1981 is one of the main travel agents in Belém and the best place to buy air tickets. More personal service, and a greater choice of tours around Belém, is offered by Amazon Star Turismo, Rua Henrique Gurjão 236 (ⓣ91/212-6244, ⓔamazonstar@interconect.com.br), an excellent French-run agency specializing in eco-tours, including visits to Cotijuba, Icoaraçi, Mosqueiro island and Ilha de Marajó. Gran Para, Av Presidente Vargas 676 (ⓣ91/212-3233), operates city tours, and can also organize flights; Gaia Terra (ⓣ91/276-3362, ⓔgaia@amazon.com.br, ⓦwww.amazon.com.br/~gaia), runs very good boat eco-oriented trips to and around the *bairro* of Guamá, where they take visitors on forest trails with expert guides, as well as a range of tours deeper into the rainforest.

Ilha do Marajó

The **ILHA DO MARAJÓ** is a vast island of some 40,000 square kilometres of largely uninhabited mangrove swamps and beaches in the Amazon River delta opposite Belém. Created by the accretion of silt and sand over millions of years, it's a wet and marshy area, the western half covered in thick jungle, the east flat savanna, swampy in the wet season (Jan–June), brown and firm in the dry season (June–Dec). Originally inhabited by the Marajoara Indians, famed for their ceramics, the savanna is dominated by *fazendas* where huge water buffalo are ranched; some 60,000 of them roam the island, and supplying meat and hides to the markets in Belém is Marajó's main trade. The island is also famous for its giant *pirarucu* fish, which, at over 180kg, are the largest freshwater breed in the world. Other animal life abounds, including numerous snakes, alligators and venomous insects, so be careful where you walk. There are also some beautiful sandy beaches, and the island has become a popular resort for sunseekers and eco-tourists alike.

The island's earliest inhabitants have left behind burial mounds, 1000 years old and more, in which many examples of the distinctive geometric Marajó pottery were found. The best examples are in the Museu Goeldi in Belém.

Practicalities

The main port of **SOURÉ** is a growing resort offering pleasant beaches where you can relax under the shade of ancient mango trees. The *Hotel Souré*, just a few blocks from the docks in the town centre (❶), is very basic, while the *Hotel Marajó*, Praça Inhangaiba (ⓣ091/741-1396; ❹), and the *Hotel Ilha do Marajó*, Av Assis de Vasconcelos 199 (ⓣ091/224-5966, ⓦwww.dadoscon.com.br/himarajo; ❺), both offer more comfort and a pool. One of the best restaurants in Souré is the *Delícias da Nalva*, Quarta Rua 1051, whose *marajoara* banquet includes a *filé a marajoara* (buffalo meat covered with cheese), a *filhote* with crab sauce, fried shrimp and more.

Other magnificent empty **beaches** can be found all around the island – the **Praia do Pesqueiro**, about 13km from Souré, is one of the more accessible and well served with places to eat, such as the *Restaurant Maloca*. If you want to see the interior of the island – or much of the wildlife – you have to be prepared to camp or pay for a room at one of the *fazendas*: book with travel agents in Belém or take your chance on arrival. One of the best rural lodgings, the *Pousada dos Guarás* (ⓣ&ⓕ 91/765-1133, ⓦwww.pousadadosguaras.com.br; ❻), is situated close to Praia Grande de Salvaterra, and has a pool, eco-trails and buffalo riding.

While organized trips can be booked at most travel agencies in the city (see "Listings" above), it is also easy enough to get to Marajó yourself. By river – a four-

or five- hour trip each way – boats leave weekday mornings from Belém port (Amazém 4 on at the docks at the bottom end of Avenida Presidente Vargas). Be at the port before 6am (boats leave at 6.30am, return at 3pm) to be sure of finding an early one if you don't want to stay overnight. There are also larger **boats**, usually leaving Wednesday and Friday at 8pm and Saturday around 2pm. Tickets are best bought a day in advance.

Crossing through Amapá into French Guiana

The main reason to pass through Amapá is to get to Guynane (previously French Guiana). The key road in the state connects Macapá, on the north side of the Amazon across from Ilha do Marajó, with **OIAPOQUE**, on the river of the same name which delineates the frontier. The road isn't asphalted all the way, but even where it's dirt road it's usually of pretty good quality; if you want to make it in one run, the regular buses (about $10) to Oiapoque can take as little as twelve hours, though they can take nearer twenty in the worst periods of the rainy season.

A more leisurely option is to go **by boat** from Macapá to Oiapoque, a journey of two days ($20); boats depart once a week or so, but there's no regular schedule.

If you are not a citizen of a European Union country, the USA or Canada, you will need a **visa** to enter Guynane. There is an EU (French) consulate in Macapá at the Pousada Ekinox, Rua Jovina Dinoa 1693 (☎096/222-4378), though it's better to arrange visas before you leave home. Buy **Euros** in Belém or Macapá; you can get them in Oiapoque but the rates are worse, and you can't depend on changing either Brazilian currency or US dollars for francs in Saint-Georges-de-l'Oyapok.

Dug-out taxis are the usual means of transport between Oiapoque and Saint-Georges-de-l'Oyapok (see p.808), about ten minutes downriver. Brazilian **exit stamps** can be obtained from the *Polícia Federal* at the southern road entrance into Oiapoque; on the other side you have to check in with the *gendarmes* in Saint-Georges.

Most travellers, in fact, cross the border the easy way – by **flying** from Macapá to the capital at Cayenne (from around $200). Once you're across the border you'll probably want to fly from the border settlement of Saint-Georges to Cayenne in any case – or else catch a boat – since overland transport is atrocious.

Western Amazônia

Encompassing the states of **Amazonas**, **Rondônia**, **Acre** and **Roraima**, the western Amazon is dominated even more than the east by the Amazon and Solimões rivers and their tributaries. To the north, the forest is centred on the Negro and Branco rivers, before phasing into the wooded savannas of Roraima. To the south, the Madeira, Purús and Juruá rivers meander through the forests from the prime rubber region of Acre and the recently colonized state of Rondônia.

The hub of this area is **Manaus**, more or less at the junction of three great rivers – the Solimões/Amazonas, the Negro and the Madeira – which between them support the world's greatest surviving forest. There are few other settlements of any real size. **Travel** is never easy or particularly comfortable in the western Amazon. **From Manaus**, it's possible to go by **bus** to Boa Vista and Venezuela: currently it takes just twelve hours or so to Boa Vista on the recently tarmacked BR-174 through the stunning tropical forest zone of the Waimiris tribe. To the south of this region, **from Porto Velho** a well-used road continues into Acre and **Rio Branco**, from where overland routes on to Peru are possible, although really only in the dry season.

Manaus and around

MANAUS is the capital of Amazonas, a tropical forest state covering around one and a half million square kilometres. Manaus isn't actually on the Amazon at all, but lies on the Rio Negro, six kilometres from the point where that river meets the Solimões to form (as far as Brazilians are concerned) the Rio Amazonas. Just a few hundred metres away from the tranquil life on the rivers, the centre of Manaus perpetually buzzes with energy: always noisy, crowded and confused. Escaping from the frenzy is not easy, but there is the occasional quiet corner, and the sights of the port, markets, **Opera House** and some of the museums make up for the hectic pace in the downtown area.

Some history

The city you see today is primarily a product of the **rubber boom** and in particular the child of visionary state governor **Eduardo Ribeiro**, who from 1892 transformed Manaus into a major city. Under Ribeiro, the Opera House was completed, and whole streets were wiped out in the process of laying down broad Parisian-style avenues, interspersed with Italian piazzas centred on splendid fountains. In 1899, Manaus was the first Brazilian city to have trolley buses and only the second to have electric lights in the streets. However, this heyday lasted barely thirty years, and by 1914 the rubber market was collapsing fast. Today's prosperity is largely due to the creation of a **Free Trade Zone**, the *Zona Franca*, in 1966. Over the following ten years the population doubled, from 250,000 to half a million, and many new industries moved in, especially electronics companies. Today, with over three million inhabitants, Manaus is an aggressive commercial and industrial centre for an enormous region – the Hong Kong of the Amazon.

Arrival and information

Try to avoid arriving on a Sunday, when the city is very quiet, with few places open. If you arrive in Manaus by river, your **boat** will dock right in the heart of the city, either by the Mercado Municipal or a short way along in the floating port. In addition to the thousands of riverboats, there were over twenty ocean-going cruise boats that arrived and spent time in Manaus last year. If you're arriving from Peru or Colombia, don't forget to have your passport stamped at the Customs House, if you haven't already done so in Tabatinga. The **rodoviária** (☎92/642-6644) is some 10km north of the centre: #306 buses run every twenty minutes down Avenida Constantino Nery, two streets from the bus station, to Praça da Matriz in the heart of town, or taxis cost around $10. The **airport** (Aeroporto de Eduardo Gomes; ☎092/652-1212 or 654-2044) is on Avenida Santos Dumont, 17km from town in the same direction. It is also served by bus #306 (first bus 5.30am, last bus around midnight; 40min); alternatively, take a taxi (around $15). Many tour operators will offer airport pickup if you're booked with them; and Geraldo Mesquita (☎92/232-9416, mobile 9983-6273) also offers airport pickup (approx. $11 for up to four passengers).

The most central **tourist office** is close to the back of the Opera House at Avenida Eduardo Ribeira 666 (Mon–Fri 8am–6pm, Sat 8am–1pm; ☎92/231-1998); it has friendly staff who can direct you or supply town maps and other informative brochures on the cultural sites and city's entertainment itinerary. This is the best place to ask for reports on complaints that might exists against a particular tour operator, if you feel the need to check out the background of any operators trying to sell you a tour. The main SEC office, however, is at the side of the Palácio da Cultura at Av Sete de Setembro 1546 (Mon–Fri 8am–6pm; ☎92/633-2850), and has a range of brochures, maps and information packs about Manaus and Amazonas.

Accommodation

There's a wide range of places to stay in Manaus, with a number of perfectly reasonable **cheap hotels**, especially in the area around Avenida Joaquim Nabuco and

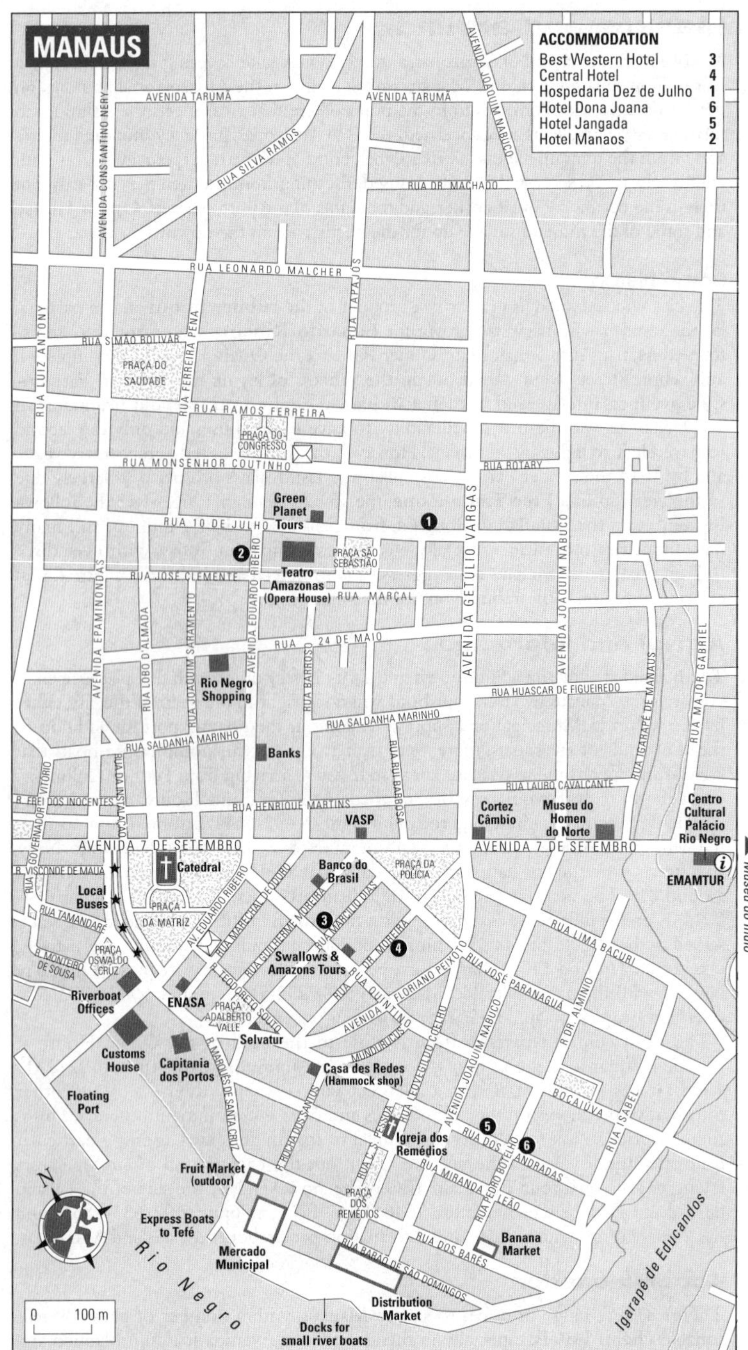
MANAUS
ACCOMMODATION
Best Western Hotel 3
Central Hotel 4
Hospedaria Dez de Julho 1
Hotel Dona Joana 6
Hotel Jangada 5
Hotel Manaos 2
Green Planet Tours
Teatro Amazonas (Opera House)
Rio Negro Shopping
Banks
VASP
Cortez Câmbio
Museu do Homen do Norte
Centro Cultural Palácio Rio Negro
EMAMTUR
Museu do Indio
Catedral
Local Buses
Banco do Brasil
Swallows & Amazons Tours
Riverboat Offices
ENASA
Selvatur
Customs House
Capitania dos Portos
Casa des Redes (Hammock shop)
Floating Port
Igreja dos Remédios
Fruit Market (outdoor)
Express Boats to Tefé
Mercado Municipal
Banana Market
Distribution Market
Docks for small river boats
Rio Negro
Igarapé de Educandos
0 100 m

Rua dos Andradas. The downtown centre is just a few blocks from here, with the docks for boats up and down the Amazon and Rio Negro. If you want to **camp**, the only secure option is beyond the *Tropical Hotel* at the sites around Praia Ponta Negra.

Best Western Hotel Rua Marcílio Dias 217 ⓣ92/622-7700 or 622-2844, ⓦwww.bestwestern.com.br/manaus. Very plush, with apartments and suites; the best value hotel in central Manaus and some with views over the city centre, but no pool. ❺

Central Hotel Rua Dr Moreira 202 ⓣ92/622-2600, ⓔhcentral@terra.com.br. Wide choice of comfortable rooms, all with TV, *frigobar* and air conditioning; it has a good restaurant, too, and 24-hour room service. Excellent value at the price. ❸

Hospedaria Dez de Julho Rua Dez de Julho 679 ⓣ092/232-6280, ⓔhtdj@internext.com.br. A modernized, clean place, popular with travellers and extending into next door; it has very good breakfasts and is a small family-run hotel near the Opera House in a pleasant part of the city. The hotel also runs trips out of the city (see p.408). ❸–❹

Hotel Dona Joana Rua dos Andradas 553 ⓣ92/233-7553. Their rooms are large and well looked after, many with superb views over the river, something that most other budget hotels lack. ❶–❷

Hotel Jangada Rua dos Andradas 473 ⓣ92/622-0264. This place has reasonably friendly staff, a decent little restaurant, and always seems busy. Rooms have air conditioning and guests can use their kitchen and laundry; TVs are available. ❶–❷

Hotel Manaos Avenida Eduardo Ribeiro 881 ⓣ92/633-5744. A large, modern, well-air-conditioned hotel very close to Teatro Amazonas; the service is cheerful and the ambience clean and efficient but unpretentious. Rooms have all mod cons. ❹–❺

The City

Since it's the docks that have created Manaus, it's logical to start your exploration here. The **port** itself is an unforgettable spectacle, a constant throng of activity stretching along the riverfront, while the ships tied up at the docks bob serenely up and down. People cook fish at stalls to sell to the hungry sailors and their passengers, or to the workers once they've finished their shift of carrying cargo from the boats to the distribution market. Hectic and impossibly complex and anarchic as it appears to the unaccustomed eye, the port of Manaus is in fact very well organized, if organically so. During the day, there's no problem wandering around, and it's easy enough to find out which boats are going where just by asking around. At night, however, this can be a dangerous area and is best avoided: many of the river men carry guns.

From the Praça Adalberto Valle, the impressive **Customs House** (Mon–Fri 8am–1pm), known locally as *Alfândega*, stands between you and the floating docks. Erected in 1906, the building was shipped over from Britain in prefabricated blocks. The tower here once acted as a lighthouse guiding vessels in at night. The floating docks, too, were built by a British company, at the beginning of the twentieth century. To cope with the river rising over a 14m range, the concrete pier is supported on pontoons which rise and fall to allow even the largest ships to dock here all year round (the highest recorded level of the river so far was in 1953, when it rose some 30m above sea level).

Following Rua Marquês de Santa Cruz down towards the new docks will bring you to the covered **Mercado Municipal Adolfo Lisboa** (Mon–Sat 5am–6pm, Sun 5am–noon) whose elegant Art Nouveau roof was designed by Eiffel during the rubber boom and is a copy of the former Les Halles market in Paris. Inaugurated in 1882, it now offers tropical fruit and vegetables, jungle herbs, scores of different fresh fishes and Indian craft goods jumbled together on sale. Just to the east of this market is the wholesale port distribution market, whose traders buy goods from incoming boats and sell them on wholesale to shops, market stall-holders and restaurants. It's at its busiest first thing in the morning; by the afternoon most of the merchants have closed shop, and the place looks abandoned.

Over the main road from the port you come to the **Praça Terreira Araña** where there are several craft stalls selling indigenous Amazon tribal *artesania*, leather sandals and jungle souvenirs. There's also a small semi-covered café serving drinks and snacks, open in the daytime only. From here you enter the commercial area, evolved out of the Free Trade Zone era, which is full of shops selling everything from electronic appliances to shoes.

In the midst of this rampant commercialism, the city's most famous building, the **Teatro Amazonas**, or Opera House (Mon–Sat 9am–4pm; $4 including guided tour; ⓣ92/622-2420), seems even more extraordinary coming. The whole incongruous, magnificent thing, designed in a pastiche of Italian Renaissance style by a Lisbon architectural firm, cost in the region of $3 million. After twelve years of building, with virtually all the materials – apart from the regional wood – brought from Europe, the Opera House was finally completed in 1896. Its main feature, the fantastic **cupola**, was created from 36,000 tiles imported from Alsace. The chandeliers are of Italian crystal and French bronze, and the theatre's seven hundred seats and its main columns and the balconies are made of English cast iron. By no means a mere relic, the Opera House hosts regular concerts, including in April the **Festa da Manaus**, initiated in 1997 to celebrate thirty years of the Zona Franca.

In front of the Teatro, the wavy black and white mosaic designs of the **Praça São Sebastião** are home to the "Monument to the Opening of the Ports", a marble and granite creation with four ships that represent four continents – America, Europe, Africa and Asia/Australasia – and children who symbolize the people of those continents. Also on the *praça,* the beautiful little **Igreja de São Sebastião** was built in 1888; like many other churches in Brazil it has only one tower owing to the nineteenth-century tax payable by churches with two towers. Appropriately, nearby on Avenida Eduardo Ribeiro, over the road from the SEC Tourist offices you'll find the **Palácio da Justiça** (Mon–Fri 8am–1pm), which was supposedly modelled on the Neoclassical lines of Versailles, but was only inaugurated in 1900, obviously during the rubber boom. Functioning today as the main state court. It's famous for a statue of the Greek goddess Temis, which, unlike the standard, does not have her eyes blindfolded.

The excellent **Museu do Índio**, Rua Duque de Caxias 356 (Mon–Fri 8am–noon & 2–5pm, Sat 8am–noon; $2), lies along Avenida Sete de Setembro. Run by the Salesian Sisters, who have long-established missions along the Rio Negro, especially with the Tukano tribe, it features excellent, carefully presented exhibits ranging from sacred ritual masks and inter-village communication drums to fine ceramics, superb palm-frond weavings and even replicas of Indian dwellings.

Out of the centre

The most popular and most widely touted day-trip around Manaus is to the **meeting of the waters**, some 10km downstream, where the Rio Negro and the Rio Solimões meet to form the Rio Amazonas. For several kilometres beyond the point where they join, the waters of the two rivers continue to flow separately, the muddy yellow of the Solimões contrasting sharply with the black of the Rio Negro. If you're going under your own steam, take the "Vila Burity" **bus** (#713) from Praça da Matriz to the end of the line, where there is a free half-hourly government ferry over the river, passing the meeting of the waters. Alternatively, book a tour (from around $50 upwards) with one of the agents in the "Listings" below.

Most **tours** to the meeting of the waters leave the docks at Manaus and pass by the shantytown of Educandos and the Rio Negro riverside industries before heading out into the main river course. Almost all will also stop in at the **Parque Ecólogico Janauary**, an ecological park some 7km from Manaus on one of the main local tributaries of the Rio Negro. Usually you'll be transferred to smaller motorized canoes to explore its creeks (*igarapés*), flooded forest lands (*igapós*) and abundant vegetation. One of the highlights of the area is the abundance of *Victoria Amazonica*, the extraordinary giant floating lily for which Manaus is famous. At weekends, the river beach at **Praia Ponta Negra**, about 13km northwest of Manaus, is packed with locals. Once the home of the Manaos Indians, today it boasts a massive modern amphitheatre where regular concerts and other events take place. It's also an enjoyable place to go for a swim, with plenty of bars and restaurants serving freshly cooked river fish nearby. Soltur's Ponta Negra bus (#120) leaves every half-hour; catch it by the cathedral on Praça da Matriz.

Eating and drinking

There are very few places in Manaus where you can sit down and enjoy any peace, and even the cafés and bars are too full to give you much elbow room. One advantage of the crowds is that there's **street food** everywhere: especially around the docks, the Mercado Municipal and in busy downtown locations like the Praça da Matriz, where a plate of rice and beans with a skewer of freshly grilled meat or fish costs well under $2. One traditional dish you should definitely try here is **tacacá** – a soup that consists essentially of yellow manioc root juice in a hot, spicy dried-shrimp sauce. It's often mixed and served in traditional gourd bowls, *cuias*, and is usually sold in the late afternoons by *tacacazeiras*.

African House Praça São Sebastião. A really pleasant, recently renovated café with a vaguely Parisian feel, opening out onto the square in front of the Opera House; it serves snacks like burgers, chicken and juices with vitamins or *guarana*.

Canto da Peixada Rua Emilio Moreira 1677 ☎92/234-3021. Considered by many to be Manaus's best regional and river-fish restaurant, *Canto da Peixada* prepares its *tambaqui*, *pirarucu*, *jaraqui* and *tucunare* in the traditional way, with lemon, salt, herbs and spices, then grilled and sometimes served in a sauce. Closed Sundays, but usually open until 11.30pm.

Churrascaria Búfalo Av Joaquim Nabuco 628A. Excellent *rodízio* and one of the best meat restaurants in downtown Manaus, but expensive at $12 a head.

Fiorentina Praça da Polícia. Upmarket Italian restaurant right in the heart of town – the menu ranges from local river fish dishes to traditional pastas and steaks.

Himawari Rua 10 de Julho 618 ☎92/233-2208. A quality Japanese restaurant, spacious and with both food and service very good; conveniently located on the Praça São Sebastião. Closed Mondays.

Mandarim Av Eduardo Ribeiro 650, at the corner of Rua 24 de Maio. Excellent and reasonably priced Chinese restaurant, with a *comida por kilo* system for lunch and à la carte evenings (6–10.30pm). Their *chopa* (sizzling platter) dishes are recommended.

O Naturalista Rua Sete de Setembro 752, 2nd floor. A large, clean and enjoyable vegetarian restaurant one block east of the cathedral. Open Mon–Fri lunchtime.

Scarola Pizzaria Rua Dez de Julho 739. Away from the action a little, this is a pleasant pizzeria, with a nice patio, good service and reasonable food.

Listings

Airlines Lloyd Aereo Boliviano Avenida 7 de Setembro 993 ☎92/6334200 or at the airport ☎92/652-1182; Penta, Rua Barroso 352 ☎92/234-1046 and at the airport ☎92/652-1161, covering the eastern Amazon; Tavaj, at the airport ☎92/652-1486; Transbrasil, Rua Guilherme Moreira 150 ☎92/621-1705; Varig, Rua Marcílio Dias 284 ☎92/652-1551; VASP, Av Sete de Setembro 993 ☎92/622-3470 or 652-1448.

Banks and exchange Câmbio e Turismo Cortez (Mon–Fri 9am–5pm, Sat 9am–12.30pm), at the corner of Av Getúlio Vargas #88 and Av Sete de Setembro, has good rates and a fast service for both cash and travellers' cheques, unlike the Banco do Brasil, Rua Guilherme Moreira 315. There are several banks on Avenida Eduardo Ribeiro, just a block or two down the street from the SEC Tourist Information offices.

Boats There are regular passenger boat services to: Belém, Santarém and all ports along the Rio Amazonas; along the Rio Solimões to Tabatinga; and up the Rio Madeira to Porto Velho. Less frequent services go up the Rio Negro to São Gabriel da Cachoeira and up the Rio Branco to Caracaraí. Tickets for the regular services can be bought from the ticket windows inside the port building off Praça da Matriz, next to where the boat departure list is posted. Before buying your ticket, ask for a paper pass (*papel do permissão*), which allows you into the docks (you'll need your passport, too) where the bigger, long-distance riverboats are moored; here you can have a look at the boats before deciding which you want to travel on. It's sensible to buy tickets in advance, for which you can often get a reasonable discount, and always get on your boat a good two hours or more before it's due to depart. Standard boats from Manaus to Belém can cost anything from $40 to $80 and take three to five days, often stopping off in Santarém. Smaller boats with no regular schedules, and those serving local settlements up the Rio Negro, are found to the east of the Mercado Municipal. They usually display signs with their destinations marked up. The main ENASA ticket office is at Rua Marechal Deodoro 61 ☎92/633-3280. See also the "River Journeys" box pp.408–409. For a fast boat to Tefé , it's best to take the Expreso Barcos service (13hr; $40) from the Hidroviaria near the Mercado Municipal.

Car rental Avis ☎92/652-1579; Interlocadora ☎92/233-5288; Rede Brasil, Av Constantino Nery 572 ☎92/233-6473; Unidas ☎92/652-1575.

Consulates Bolivia, Avenida Engenio Sales 2226, Quadrant B-20 ☎92/236-9988; Colombia, Rua 24 de Maio ☎92/234-6777; Peru, Rua A – C/19 – Conj. Aristocratico, Chapada ☎92/656-3267 or 656-1015; UK, Rua Paraque 240 ☎92/237-7869; USA, Rua Recife 1010 – CCI – Adrianópolis ☎92/633-4907; Venezuela, Rua Ferreira Pena 179 ☎92/233-6004.

FUNAI Av Joaquim Nabuco 294 ☎92/633-3132 or 233-7103. This is where you'll need to get (rarely given) authorization to visit any Indian reserves.

Health matters For tropical complaints the best is the Instituto de Medicina Tropical, Avenida Pedro Teixeira 25 ☎92/656-1441 or 656-4573. The Drogueria Nossa Senhor de Nazare, 7 de Setembro 1333, is a reasonably well-stocked pharmacy.

Police ☎190.

Post office The main one, with a reliable poste restante service (first floor), is just off the Praça da Matriz on Rua Marechal Deodoro at the corner with Rua Teodoreto Souto (Mon–Fri 9am–5pm, Sat 8am–noon). There's a smaller, quieter post office just beyond the top of Avenida Eduardo Ribeiro on the right hand side of the small leafly square Praca do Congresso.

Shopping *Artesanato* is available from the Museu do Índio (see p.404) and several shops around the square in front of the Teatro Amazonas. The best selection (and the most fun way to shop) is at the Sunday morning street market that appears out of nowhere in the broad Avenida Eduardo Ribeira, behind the Teatro Amazonas. Indian crafts are also sold at the Mercado Municipal. Interesting *macumba* and *umbanda* items, such as incense, candles, figurines and bongos, can be found at Cabana São Jorge at Rua da Instalação 36. A good hammock shop is Casa des Redes on Rua dos Andradas.

Taxis Amazonas ☎92/232-3005; Rádio Táxi ☎92/633-3211; Tocantins ☎92/656-1330.

Telephones National and international calls can be made with phonecards in public booths around the city; alternatively, the Telmar office (Mon–Fri 8am–6pm, Sat 8am–noon) is on Av Getúlio Vargas 950, close to the junction with Rua Ramos Ferreira.

Jungle trips from Manaus

The amount and nature of the **wildlife** you get to see on a standard **jungle tour** depends mainly on how far away from Manaus you go and how long you can devote to the trip. Birds like macaws, jabarus and toucans can generally be spotted, and you might see alligators, snakes and a few species of monkey on a three-day trip. For a reasonable chance of glimpsing wild deer, tapirs, armadillos or wild cats then a more adventurous trip is required of a week or more. On any trip, make sure that you'll get some time in the smaller channels in a canoe, as the sound of a motor is a sure way of scaring every living thing out of sight. The Rio Negro region has water with high acidity because of the geology of its main sources in the Guyana Shield. Because of the acid water, it tends to have fewer mosquitoes which is an obvious bonus; but it also tends to have less abundant wildlife than some of the lakes and channels around the Rio Solimoes. You can still see much the same species in both regions, it's just that the densities are lower on the Rio Negro and many of its tributaries. Plenty of tours combine both the Solimoes and Negro rivers in their itineraries.

If you want to forgo organized tours entirely and travel independently, **milk boats** are a very inexpensive way of getting about on the rivers around Manaus. The best place to look for these is down on Flutuante Três Estrelas, one of the wooden wharves behind the distribution market, further along the river edge from the Hidroviario at the back of the Mercado Municipal.

Tour itineraries

The **one-day river trip**, usually costing around $60 per person, generally includes an inspection of the famous meeting of the waters, some 10km downriver from Manaus (see p.404). The other most popular jungle river trips tend to be the **three- to five-day expeditions**. If you want to sleep in the forest, either in a lodge, riverboat or, for the more adventurous (and perhaps those with a low budget), swinging in a hammock outside in a small jungle clearing, it really is worth taking as many days as you can to get as far away from Manaus as possible. The usual price for guided tours, including accommodation and food, should be between $40 and $100 a day per person (no matter the sales pitch), more again if you opt for an upmarket jungle lodge or a decent riverboat. As well as tour itinerary, make sure that you're getting what you need in terms of security, health and safety, food, sleeping arrangements, guide quality and transfers.

The most commonly operated tours are three-day trips combining both the **Rio Negro** and **Rio Solimões**, although some trips only cover the former, as it is more accessible from Manaus. Four-day trips should ideally also include the **Anavilhanas Archipelago** on the Rio Negro, the second-largest freshwater archipelago in the world with around four hundred isles, as well as a good day's walk through the jungle. On the Solimões, some of the three- to five-day options include trips to Lago Mamori or Manacapuru.

The Rio Solimões and crossing into Peru and Colombia

The stretch of river upstream from Manaus, as far as the pivotal frontier with **Peru** and **Colombia** at Tabatinga, is known to Brazilians as the **RIO SOLIMõES**. Once into Peru it again becomes the Rio Amazonas. Although many Brazilian maps show it as the Rio Marañón on the Peru side, Peruvians don't call it this until the river forks into the Marañón and Ucayali headwaters, quite some distance beyond Iquitos.

From Manaus to **Iquitos** in Peru (see p.951), the river remains navigable by large ocean-going boats, though few travel this way any more. Since the collapse of the rubber market and the emergence of air travel, the river is left to smaller, more locally oriented riverboats. Many travellers do come this way, however; and, although some complain about the food and many get upset stomachs (especially on the Peruvian leg), it can be a really pleasant way of moving around – lying in your hammock, reading and relaxing, or drinking at the bar. Against this, there are all the inherent dangers of travelling by boat on a large river, especially at night. Boats do frequently break down, causing long delays, and many captains seem to take great pleasure in overloading boats with both cargo and passengers. In spite of the discomforts, however, the river journey remains popular; and it's unarguably an experience that will stick in the memory.

The river journey is also, of course, by far the cheapest way of travelling between Brazil and Peru. There are reasonable facilities for visitors in the border town of **Tabatinga** and the adjacent Colombian town of **Leticia** (see p.642). All boats have to stop at one of these ports, and most will terminate at the border whichever direction they've come from.

The boat trip from Manaus to **Tabatinga** – five to eight days upstream – costs around $65 inclusive of food (though bring some treats, as the fare on board, though good, does get a bit monotonous). The downstream journey, which is often very crowded, takes three to four days and costs upward of $45. If you want to break the journey, you can do so at **Tefé**, around halfway; but the main reason to stop here is to visit the **Mamiraua Sustainable Development Reserve**, an accessible, beautiful and wild area of rainforest upstream from the town. An alternative reason for stopping here might be if you really can't face the boat

Jungle tour operators and lodges in Manaus

There are scores of different **jungle tour companies** in Manaus offering very similar services and the competition is intense. Tourist regularly get hassled by touts all over town, and the sales patter is unrelenting. By playing them off against each other, you may be able to bargain the price down a bit (groups can always get a better deal than people travelling alone), but your best bet is really to shop around, talk to other tourists who have already been on trips and to be wary of parting with wads of cash before you know exactly what you'll be getting in return (see below). Better still is to book through one of the more established outfits, with the security of an office and, ideally, registration with EMBRATUR as an operator.

Tour operators

Amazon Nut Safaris Av Beira Mar 43, São Raimundo ⓣ92/234-5860, ⓔamazonnut@horizon.com.br, ⓦwww.amazonnut.com. This tour company runs upmarket ecological expeditions to the Anavilhanas Archipelago. It also operates a fleet of boats and a small nine-room lodge, *Apurissawa*, on the Rio Cuieiras (Rio Negro area), 4hr by boat from Manaus. Tours include the meeting of the waters, or – further afield – alligator- and birdwatching as well as visits to the local *caboclos* (traditional river dwellers) communities. They also have a sales kiosk at the airport.

Gero's Tour ⓣ92/232-9416, mobile 9983-6273, ⓔgeromesquita@hotmail.com or via the *Hospedaria Dez de Julho* (see above). An independent, reliable and pleasant guide, Geraldo Neto Mesquita speaks English and Portuguese, as well as organizing tours. A wide range of tours are available through Gero's Tour, including boat and canoe trips, jungle hiking and visits to native people, with accommodation in hammocks, overnight in the bush or at local family houses. Mainly visits the Mamori and Juma areas; Rio Negro on request. Tours can be combined with luxury lodge accommodations. Prices start at $50–80 depending on size of group.

Green Planet Tours Rua Dez de Julho 481 ⓣ92/232-1398, mobile 989-4889, ⓔinfo@planettours.com.br, ⓦwww.planettours.com.br. A popular operator, Green Planet specializes in a range of trips starting at $50 a day (sleeping in hammocks, or from $60 a day in "bedrooms"). Most of their trips use the company's own Rio Negro floating base camp; trips can include the meeting of the waters, alligator spotting, piranha fishing and jungle walks. Travel is generally by motorized canoe; there is also a covered twin-decked riverboat, but it's not a houseboat with cabin accommodation. Tours sometimes go to the Mamori Lake (50km south of Manaus).

Swallows and Amazons Rua Quintino Bocaiúva 189, 1st floor, sala 13 ⓣ92/622-1246, ⓔswallows@internext.com.br, ⓦwww.swallowsandamazonstours.com. A family-run company, combining Brazilian and US expertise and organization, it spe-

journey any longer (there are several weekly flights from Tefé to Manaus and Tabatinga if you're really fed up). There's also an express boat service (13 hr; $40) connecting Tefé with Manaus.

Five large boats currently ply the river upstream from Manaus regularly, all pretty similar and with good facilities (toilets with paper, showers, mineral water and enough food). Smaller boats also occasionally do the trip, but more often terminate at Tefé, from where other small boats continue. On the other side of the border, the boat trip to Iquitos from Tabatinga costs around $30–50 and takes three or four

cializes in private and small-group houseboat, riverboat, jungle lodge and rainforest adventure tours. These can be customized to suit requirements but most trips explore the Rio Negro and its tributaries and rainforest around the Anavilhanas Archipelago. Swallows and Amazons also runs its own jungle lodge, *Over Look Lodge*, 50km from Manaus on the Rio Negro for shorter budget tours. Rates range from $75 to $150 per person per day depending on accommodation desired.

Lodges and camps

Jungle lodges offer travellers the opportunity to experience the rainforest while maintaining high levels of comfort, even elegance. There are scores of lodges in and around the Manaus area, most operated by tour companies.

Acajatuba Jungle Lodge Rua Lima Bacuri 345 ⓣ92/233-7642, ⓔacajatuba@acajatuba.com.br, ⓦwww.acajatuba.com.br. A lodge with large communal areas and spacious clean cabins, Acajatuba offers trips from one to four nights. It's located in the Anavilhanas Archipelago islands and has wooden elevated footbridges joining the various parts of the site. Night-time lighting is from battery powered bulbs, so there's rarely any generator noise to disturb the exciting night sounds of the jungle.

Amazon Lodge Nature Safaris, Rua Santa Quitéria 15, Presidente Vargas ⓣ92/656-5464, ⓦwww.natsafaris.com. Powerful motorboats take you 80km upriver to Lago Juma and its comfortable floating lodge with fourteen double rooms and a restaurant. Expensive at $250 for three days and two nights.

Ariau Amazon Towers Rio Amazonas Turismo, Hotel Monaco, Rua Silva Ramos 41 ⓣ92/234-7308 or 232-4160, ⓦwww.ariautowers.com. Just 65km up the Rio Negro from Manaus (3hr by boat) by Ariau lake, this is one of the largest and most developed of the jungle lodges, with a helicopter pad, swimming pool, almost 100 rooms, mostly in wooden chalets, and a 35-metre viewing tower from which you get an exceptionally close and breathtaking view of the forest canopy. It's a must if your budget isn't restricted (from $300 per person for three days and two nights).

Hotel Ecológico Terra Verde (Green Land Lodge) Rua Silva Ramos 20, Sala 305 ⓣ92/622-7305, ⓔterraverde@internext.com.br). Located in the Forest of Life 10,000-hectare ecological reserve, on the Fazenda São Francisco 50km from Manaus beyond Manacapuru on the Tiririca River, this lodge has five relatively luxurious cabins, a floating swimming pool and horse-riding facilities. A comfortable and interesting place, but probably a bit tame for the adventurous traveller. $80 per person for two days and one night. Can be reached with daily boat departures from the pier at the Tropical Hotel (8am and 2pm departures).

days, sometimes more, rarely less. Coming downstream from Iquitos to Tabatinga ($20–30) gives you one and a half days on the river. Again, it's advisable to take your own food and water – all normal supplies can be bought in Tabatinga. There are also more popular super-fast sixteen-seater powerboats connecting Tabatinga and Leticia with Iquitos. They cost upwards of $50 and take roughly ten to twelve hours. Small planes also connect Iquitos with Santa Rosa, an insignificant Peruvian border settlement just a short boat ride over the river from Tabatinga and Leticia; there is at least one flight a week operated by the Peruvian airline TANS.

3.5

Brasília

Almost 1000km from Rio and located in the rolling savanna-like *cerrado* of the central Brazilian highlands, **BRASÍLIA** is the largest and most fascinating of the world's "planned cities". Declared the national capital in 1960 and a UNESCO World Heritage Site in 1995, the futuristic city was the vision of **Juscelino Kubitschek**, who made good on an election promise to build it if elected president in 1956. Designed by **Oscar Niemeyer**, South America's most able student of Le Corbusier, it is located in a federal zone of its own – Brasília D.F. (Distrito Federal) – right in the centre of Goiás state. Until the city's construction this was one of Brazil's most isolated regions.

Originally intended for a population of half a million by the year 2000, Brasília and the area around it today has close to four million people, and is the fastest growing city in the country. Looking at the gleaming government buildings or zooming down the city's excellent roads, you'll think Brasília is the modern heart of a new world superpower – an illusion quickly dispelled by driving ten minutes in any direction, once you hit the miles and miles of low-income housing of the millions who commute from the so-called *cidades satélites*, the satellite cities.

Arrival and information

The central **rodoviária** is the main hub of movement within Brasília, with the Eixo Monumental passing around it and the Eixo Rodoviário crossing over the top of it. The **airport** (☎61/365-1941) is 12km south of the centre, and bus #102 runs every hour from there into Brasília, dropping you at the downtown rodoviária. *Lotação* minibuses run more frequently, or a taxi will cost you between $8 and $10. Intercity and long-distance buses use the **rodoferroviária**, the bus and former train station at the far western end of the Eixo Monumental (☎61/233-7200). From here, the #131 bus covers the 5km of the Eixo Monumental to the downtown rodoviária. The best place for **tourist information** is the kiosk at the airport (daily 8am–8pm; ☎61/365-1024), which stocks a range of leaflets, maps and brochures, and also has a surprisingly useful touch-screen computer terminal. There's also a helpful tourist office on the Praça dos Três Poderes (Mon 1.30–6pm, Tues–Sun 8am–6pm; ☎61/325-5730). The state tourist office, SETUR, on the third floor of the unusual and futuristic Centro de Convenções Dr Ulisses Guimarães, Eixo Monumental (☎61/321-3318, Ⓦwww.setur.df.gov.br), may just about be able to help you if you have a special request, but it is short on brochures and more mundane information.

Getting around

There are two **circular bus routes** which are very handy for a cheap overview of the city: buses #105 and #106 leave from and return to the downtown rodoviária (☎61/223-0557) after a long outer city tour; just try to avoid these routes between 4pm and 6pm on weekdays when the buses are particularly crowded. The city has a

good **taxi** service, which costs a minimum of $2 even for the shortest ride. Flag a taxi down when you want one, or pick one up at the many ranks throughout the city. Most hotels in Brasília are keen to offer **city tours** to their guests, as they take a percentage of the fee for themselves, or you can book direct with one of the tour organizers: Power Turismo (ⓣ61/332-6699); AeroVan Turismo (ⓣ61/340-9251); or Monserat Turismo (ⓣ61/326-1407, ⓔmonserrat@conectanet.com.br). Tours cost from $20 to $60 per person, and range from a variety of three-hour programmes covering commercial, banking and residential sectors as well as prominent buildings, to the night-time tour ($70–90), which ends with an evening meal. If you want to hire your personal English-speaking guide to the city, Waldeck Costa, Caixa Postal 2983 (ⓣ61/384-1909 or mobile 964-8673) is reliable and knows his stuff.

Accommodation

Medium- and upper-range hotels post prices that are considerably more than they really charge, so ask for rates when you check in. If you're on a tight budget, $8–10 will get you a bed at a *pousada*; these cluster on W3 Sul, starting at *quadra* 703 to around 708. Most are squalid and none too secure; the ones recommended below are the pick of the bunch, but are still below the standards of the worst of the hotels. Staying in campsites or in the satellite cities is definitely not recommended; besides being dangerous, you can get accommodation in Brasília for much the same price anyway.

Central hotel sectors

Aristus SHN Q.2 ⓣ61/328-8675. One of the cheapest options in this good location, offering a choice of slightly cheaper basement rooms. ❷

Bonaparte Hotel Résidence SHS Q.2 ⓣ61/322-2288 or 0800/619-991, ⓦwww.bonapartehotel.com.br. A top-notch hotel, with a large convention facility and all mod cons. ❺

Bristol SHS Q.4 ⓣ61/321-6162. Comfortable and with a rooftop swimming pool, this is a good value hotel without being top of the range; highly recommended. ❸

Carlton SHS Q.5 ⓣ61/226-8109, ⓦwww.carltonhotel.com.br. Older upmarket hotel, with great 1960s decor, but slightly expensive compared with similar places. ❻

Casablanca SHN Q.3 ⓣ61/328-8586. Close to the Eixo Monumental and within sight of the TV Tower, a small and friendly hotel with excellent rooms and a nice restaurant. Good value at the lower end of this price bracket. $15.

Nacional SHS Q.1 ⓣ61/321-7575, ⓦwww.hotelnacional.com.br. The oldest of the big hotels, reflected in fine retro-1960s kitsch decor. Well run with the added advantage of having all of the major airline offices out front. ❺

Natal 708 Norte, Bloco B ⓣ61/340-1984. Most comfortable of the pousadas; breakfast included. ❷

Planalto Bittar SHS Q.3 ⓣ61/322-217. Just about the best of cheaper hotels, slightly more expensive but better quality than others in this market. Good location. ❸

The City

Brasília is neatly divided into sectors: there are residential neighbourhoods – each with their own shopping and other facilities – hotel districts, embassy areas and banking and commercial zones. Roads are numbered, rather than named, with digits representing their position and distance north or south of the **Eixo Monumental**, and east or west of the other main axis, the **Eixo Rodoviário**.

The commercial centres and the downtown *rodoviária* are separated by the Brazilian government complex known as the **Esplanada dos Ministérios**, which is focused on the unmistakable twin towers of the Congress building. Entrance to all the buildings is free, and they can all be seen in half a day. Each was designed by **Niemeyer**, and they are rightly regarded as among the best modernist buildings in the world. The combination of white marble, water pools, reflecting glass and the airy, flying buttresses on the presidential palace and Supreme Court lends these buildings an unmistakable elegance. At night, floodlighting and internal lights make them even more impressive; a slow taxi or bus ride around the Esplanada in the early evening, when people are still working and the buildings glow like Chinese lanterns, is a must.

At the centre of the complex is the **Praça dos Três Poderes** (Square of Three Powers), representing the Congress, judiciary and the presidency. The **Congresso Nacional** is the heart of the legislative power and one of the most obvious landmarks in Brasília – in a way, everything else flows from here. If you accept the analogy of the city built as a bird, then the Congresso is its beak, something it clearly resembles with its twin 28-storey towers. The two large "bowls" on each side of the towers house the Senate Chamber (the smaller, inverted one) and the House of Representatives; they were designed so that the public could climb and play on them, though only patrolling soldiers of the Polícia Militar are allowed here now. The chambers themselves are a hoot – as Sixties as the Beatles, though they haven't aged as well. To see them, you must take one of the guided tours that leave every half-hour on weekdays and hourly at weekends. Most guides speak some English and there is a strict dress code – long trousers, shirt and shoes for men, smart casual for women (Senate tours Mon–Fri 1.30–5.30pm, Sat & Sun 10am–2pm; ⓣ61/311-2149; House of Representatives tours Mon–Fri 1–5pm, Sat & Sun 9am–2pm; ⓣ61/318-5092).

The **Palácio da Justiça** (Mon–Fri 10am–noon & 3–5pm; same dress code as above) is beside the Congresso building, on the northern side of the Esplanada dos

Ministerios. Created in 1960 with a concrete facade, the building was covered with fancy – and, to many, elitist – marble tiles by the military government during the dictatorship. With the return to democracy the tiles were removed, laying bare the concrete waterfalls between the pillars, but the water has been shut off for years as the pools proved to be a perfect breeding ground for the dengue mosquito. The structure is much less interesting inside than any of the other buildings, and without the waterfalls the exterior is more than a little bleak. Much more worthwhile is the **Palácio Itamarati** (Mon–Fri 2–4.30pm, Sat & Sun 10am–3.30pm, no guided tours but visitors are restricted to certain areas, with same dress code as above; ⓣ61/411-6159), the vast Foreign Office structure. Combining modern and classical styles, it's built around elegant courtyards, sculptures and gardens, and inside its airiness and sense of space is breathtaking, well set off by a carefully chosen selection of modern art and wall-hangings. Outside, the marble *Meteor* sculpture by Bruno Giorgi is a stunning piece of work, its five parts representing the five continents.

Behind the Congresso Nacional, on the northern side, the **Palácio do Planalto** houses the president's office (Sun 9.30am–1.30pm; formal dress code), which is viewable only by guided tour. The interior is dominated by sleek columns and a glorious, curving ramp, down into the reception area. On weekdays, however, visitors will have to content themselves with a changing of the guard out front at 8.30am and 5.30pm daily. Nearby in Praça dos Três Poderes, the **Museu Histórico de Brasília** (Mon–Sat 9am–1pm & 2–5pm; free) tells the tale of the transfer of the capital from Rio; the large-scale architectural model of the entire city, with lights for points of interest, is fun and useful to the newly arrived.

To complete your tour of Niemeyer gems, take a short taxi or bus ride from here to the president's official residence two miles away, the **Palácio da Alvorada** (bus #104, leaves from stand 13 of Platform A at the rodoviária), which some consider the most beautiful of Niemeyer's buildings. The residence is nestled behind an emerald green lawn and beautifully sculpted gardens, which perfectly set off the brilliant white of its exterior – note the architect's distinctive slender buttresses – and its blue-tinted glass. If you go by taxi, make sure it waits for you in the car park to the right – taxis rarely pass by here. Guards will shout at you if you sit in the car in the left parking lot, the only one with the clear view, owing to heightened security concerns, as everywhere else.

Between the ministries and the downtown rodoviária, and within walking distance of either, the striking **Catedral Metropolitana Nossa Senhora Aparecida** (daily 7am–6.30pm; no shorts allowed) marks the spot where the city of Brasília was inaugurated in 1960 and is built in the form of an inverted chalice and crown of thorns; its sunken nave puts most of the interior floor below ground level. Some of the glass roof panels in the interior reflect rippling water from outside, adding to the sense of airiness in the cathedral, while the statues of St Peter and the angels suspended from the ceiling help create a feeling of elevation. Nevertheless, although some 40m in height and with a capacity of 2000, the cathedral seems surprisingly small inside.

About ten minutes' walk away, on the northern side of the Eixo Monumental, is the **Teatro Nacional**. Built in the form of an Aztec temple, it's a marvellous, largely glass-covered pyramid set at an angle to let light into the lobby, where there are often good art exhibitions with futuristic and environmental themes. Inside are three halls: the Martins Pena, the Villa-Lobos (the largest, seating 1200) and the much smaller Alberto Nepomuceno. Most theatre productions are in Portuguese, but all three venues are also used for **music concerts** – Brasília has a symphony orchestra, and popular music stars often play here as well.

The **Torre de Televisão** (TV Tower) on Eixo Monumental, an obvious city landmark, is easily reached on foot or by bus (#131 from the rodoviária). The 218-metre-high tower's viewing platform (Tues–Sun 9am–9pm) is a great place from which to put Brasília into perspective, and there is no better place to watch the sunset though, frustratingly, there is no bar to watch it from. Lower down, above its weird concrete supports, the **Museu Nacional das Gemas** (Tues–Fri 3–8.30pm, Sat & Sun 10.30am–6.30pm; $1) is actually little more than a glorified and quite expensive gem shop. At the weekend the tower is also popular for its craft market, held around the base – a good place to pick up cheap clothes.

Further up the Eixo is the famous **Juscelino Kubitschek (JK) Memorial** (Tues–Sun 9am–5.45pm; $2), best reached by one of the shoals of buses heading up the Eixo as it's too far to walk. Here, a rather Soviet-like statue of Brasília's founder stands inside an enormous question mark, pointing down the Eixo towards the heart of government, while more interesting is the museum below, which reverently reproduces JK's library and study. The man himself lies in state in a black marble sarcophagus, backlit by an extraordinary combination of purple, violet and orange lights – the only thing missing is a sound system piping in "The Age of Aquarius". All around is a fascinating display of personal mementoes of JK's career and the founding and construction of the city, including video clips of his funeral and dedication of the Memorial.

Across the road from the JK Memorial is another Niemeyer building, the white and curving **Memorial dos Povos Indígenas** (Tues–Fri 10am–4pm; free), which houses one of the best collections of indigenous art in Brazil, much of it from the *planalto* itself and produced by the indigenous groups who inhabit the headwaters of the Xingú River. Highlights are the extraordinary ceramic pots of the Warao, the Xingú's ceramic specialists, beautifully adorned with figures of birds and animals, and vivid, delicate featherwork. The gallery itself is set in a long, downward curve around a circular courtyard, the smoked glass set against Niemeyer's trademark brilliant white exterior. At the lower end is a café, virtually never open but where Indians up from the Xingú often leave artwork for the museum staff to sell for them. Run by the chronically hard-up state government, the museum's opening hours are largely theoretical. If you arrive on the weekend or Monday and find the main entrance at the top of the ramp shut, slip down to the large metal door at ground level, to the right of the ramp, and bang hard. It's definitely worth making the effort.

Eating and drinking

One of the best things about Brasília is the wide variety of **bars and restaurants**; in fact, a combination of the government, the university and diplomats supports one of the densest concentrations of good restaurants in the country. People dine late, hanging around in bars until at least 10pm before heading off to eat. Moreover, bars and restaurants aren't always easily distinguishable – a place that looks and feels like a bar sometimes can serve substantial meals, so the listings are somewhat arbitrary. With some deserving exceptions, the following list concentrates on the best places within easy reach of the hotel sectors. If you're walking, you should have no problems with safety at most places in Asa Norte and Asa Sul, but W3 and the deserted central area should be walked around with caution at night. Most restaurants close on Monday night rather than Sunday.

Restaurants

A Tribu 105 Norte. Best vegetarian food in the city, imaginative and full of flavour. Offers a lunchtime buffet, and open at night too.

Carpe Diem 104 Sul. Deservedly the best-known bar-restaurant in town: great atmosphere, renowned politico hangout and very reasonably priced. Famous among locals for the best salad bar and lunch buffet in the city (you pick the salad ingredients, they whip it up for you) and the Saturday *feijoada*; food and drinks served practically 24/7, apart from a few hours in the morning. The high quality S&M erotica in the bathrooms is an added bonus.

Feitiço Mineiro 306 Norte. Even without the live music at weekends (see below), this spot is worth patronizing for the food alone; a buffet of *comida mineira*, heavy on the pork, bean sauce and sausages, served the traditional way on a wood-fired stove. Dinner only.

Fratello 103 Sul Best pizza in town: wood-fired kiln and original ingredients. Try the eponymous Fratello, based on sweet pickled aubergine.

Ichiban 405 Sul. Good sushi, sashimi and whatever other Japanese food you fancy; divided into western and Japanese seating sections, the latter can be hard on the knees if you're not used to it.

Patu Anú Setor dos Mansões Lago Norte (SMLN), ML12, Conjunto 1, Casa 71, near the Paranoá dam ⓣ1/369-2788 or 922-8930. The very best of Brazilian cuisine, served in a fantastic lakeside location. The menu is exclusively game – wild boar, alligator, *capivara* (the largest rodent in the world, which actually tastes great) and more, cooked with mouth-watering sauces, and regional fruits and vegetables. Dinner and drinks cost about $40 a head, plus $25 each way for the taxi. Get a taxi via your hotel and make sure you show this address to the driver before you set out. Reservations are a good idea (English spoken), and the restaurant will get you a cab for the return trip.

Sabor do Brasil 302 Sul. On a strict budget, this place offers the best meal in town – for around $5 a head. A soup buffet with trimmings, very traditional Brazilian fare, good vegetarian option but soups for carnivores too. Open for lunch and at night. Good place to line the stomach before heading out for a night on the town, or to sober up coming back from one.

Taverna di Giorgio 216 Norte. Tucked away behind Bloco A but worth the trip for the very cheap home-made pasta served with delicious sauces by the friendly proprietor and his large collection of Brazilian friends. Impromptu live music drifting upwards from the bar below on Saturday nights is an occasional bonus.

Universal Diner 210 Sul. Take your pick: the lively, crowded and loud bar downstairs or the very good restaurant upstairs, serving Brazilian and international food.

Bars

Armazém do Ferreira 202 Norte. Noted politico hangout, best late night when it gets very crowded. The tables outside are very pleasant, huddled under trees; *Café do Brasil* next door is also good.

Bar Brasília 506 Sul. Successful re-creation of an old-style Brazilian bar, complete with surly waiters; as a bar it's very good, but the view out across a car park leaves something to be desired.

Café Cassis 214 Sul. Specializes in weekend brunches for homesick Americans – they make bagels for the American embassy – but also open in the evening and weekday lunchtime; very civilized, cheaper than it looks and feels.

Daniel Briand 104 Norte; side of Bloco A. Essential, highly recommended spot, especially for a late breakfast on weekends or afternoon tea any day. French-owned patisserie and teahouse serving the best quiche and cakes in town. Nowhere better for coffee and reading; the only problem is early and rigidly enforced closing at 10pm – both un-French and un-Brazilian.

Libanus 206 Sul. Perennially crowded spot serving up excellent-value, hearty Lebanese food; the playground makes it a good place for families in the afternoons, but it turns into a young and humming scene at night.

Listings

Airlines Nordeste, airport ⓣ61/365-1022; TAM, SHS 1, Galeria Hotel Nacional 61 ⓣ61/223-5168, and at the airport ⓣ61/365-1000; Varig/Cruzeiro, ground floor of the Conjunto Empresarial Varig building opposite Brasilia Shopping mall ⓣ61/329-1169, and at the airport ⓣ61/364-9583, 24-hour reservations, English spoken on ⓣ800/99-7000; VASP, SHS 1, Galeria Hotel Nacional 53–54 ⓣ61/2225-5915; Air France, SHS 1, Galeria Hotel Nacional 39–40 ⓣ61/223-4152; Alitalia, SHS, Galeria Hotel Nacional, Loja 36–37 ⓣ61/321-5266; British Airways, SHS, Galeria Hotel Nacional, Loja 18 ⓣ61/226-4164; KLM, SHS 1, Galeria Hotel Nacional 51 ⓣ61/321-3636; Lan Chile, SCS, Q8, Bloco B-60, Edifício Venâncio ⓣ61/226-0318; Lufthansa, SHS 1, Galeria Hotel Nacional, Loja 1 ⓣ61/223-5002.

Car rental The usual suspects all line the airport road: Avis ⓣ61/365-2991, Localiza ⓣ800/992-000; Hertz ⓣ61/365-4747, Unidas ⓣ800/121-121. Avoid paying a hefty surcharge at the airport by heading into town by taxi and renting from there; highly recommended is Via Rent-A-Car ⓣ61/322-3181 or 9985-4717, SHS Q6 Conjunto A Bloco F loja 50, or, more comprehensibly, the side of the *Hotel Melia*.

Consulates Argentina, SHIS QI 01, Cj. 01, Casa 19 ⓣ61/365-3000; Australia, SHIS QI 9, Cj. 16, Cs 1 ⓣ61/248-5569; Bolivia, SHIS QL 10, Cj. 1, Cs 6 ⓣ61/364-3362; Canada, SES Av das Nações 803, Lote 16, sala 130 ⓣ61/321-2171; Colombia, SES Av das Nações 803, Lote 10 ⓣ61/226-8997;

Ecuador, SHIS Q1 11, Cj. 09, Cs. 24 ☎61/248-5560; Paraguay, SES Av das Nações 811, Lote 42 ☎61/242-3732; Peru, SES Av das Nações 811, Lote 43 ☎61/242-9435; UK, SES Av das Nações 801 ☎61/225-2710; US, SES Av das Nações 801, Lote 3 ☎61/321-7272; Venezuela, SES Av das Nações 803, Lote 13 ☎61/223-9325.

Emergencies Medical ☎192; police ☎197; fire brigade ☎193.

Exchange Cash and travellers' cheques are accepted at Banco do Brasil, SBS, Edifício Sede 1, Terreo (Mon–Fri 10am–5pm). Reasonable rates with no commission apply at the *câmbio* in the *Hotel Nacional* (Mon–Fri 9am–6pm).

Health matters Dr C. Menecucci, Centro Medico, Av. W3 Sul 716, Bloco D, sala 16, speaks good English. Hospitals are: Da Base do Distrito Federal, SMHS 101 ☎61/325-5050; and Santa Lúcia, SHLS 716, Bloco C ☎61/245-3344.

Post office Brasília's main post office (Mon–Sat 9am–6pm) is the small, white building in the open grassy space behind the *Hotel Nacional.*

Taxis Cidade ☎61/321-8181, Coobras ☎61/224-1000, Radiotaxi ☎61/325-3030.

3.6

The Pantanal

An open swampland larger than France, extending deep into the states of Mato Grosso and Mato Grosso do Sul, **THE PANTANAL** is a slightly daunting region to visit, one of the many, but perhaps one of the best, places in Brazil where you're more likely to find wildlife than nightlife. In fact, you see so many birds and animals that you start to think you're in a well-stocked wildlife park – the wildlife is wild, but not at all shy. *Jacarés* (alligators), jaguar, anacondas and *tuiui* (giant red-necked storks) are all quite common sights in the Pantanal, and it's probably the best place for wild mammals and exotic birds in the whole of the Americas. Having said that, it's only fair to mention that you'll still see more cattle than any other creature.

As no road or rail track crosses the swamp it's a tricky place to travel. The easiest and one of the best ways to experience the Pantanal is by taking an **organized tour**, perhaps spending a night or two at a **fazenda-lodge** (called **pousadas** in the northern Pantanal). The *fazenda*-lodges are generally reached by jeep; those that require access by boat or plane are usually deeper into the swamp, increasing your chances of spotting the more elusive wildlife. At least one night in the swamp is essential if you want to see or do anything other than sit in a bus or jeep the whole time; three- or four-day excursions will give you a couple of full days in the swamp. Without an organized trip, unless you've got bags of money or are travelling in a large group, you're dependent on local **cargo boats**, which inevitably take much longer than expected. **Renting a car** is also a slim possibility, though without 4WD you're limited only to a few tracks on the fringes of the swamp where the wildlife makes itself scarce.

Most organized tours enter the Pantanal by road and spend a couple of days exploring in canoes, small motorboats or on horseback from a land base. The most obvious initial target is **Corumbá**. There's lots of accommodation here and no end of agencies and operators running trips into the swamp. Other routes into the swamp are from **Campo Grande** in the east or **Cuiabá**, to the north, through settlements like **Porto Jofre** and **Cáceres**. The **best time** to explore the Pantanal is towards the end of the rainy season, around April, when there's high chance of seeing both mammals and reptiles, still crowded onto islands. In 2002, the dry season was exceptionally long, causing drought and loss of livestock as well as river life.

Some background

The Pantanal occupies an arguably unique ecological niche as an unparalleled biogenetic reservoir. It's almost unnerving spending the afternoon on the edge of a remote lagoon in the swamp surrounded by seemingly endless streams of flying and wading birds – toucans, parrots, red and even the endangered hyacinth macaws, blue herons and the symbol of the Pantanal, the magnificent *jabiru*, or giant red-throated storks, known locally as *tuiuiú*. Unlike most other areas of wilderness, the birdsong and density of wildlife in the Pantanal frequently lives up to the soundtrack of Hollywood jungle movies, and in the middle of the swamp it's actually possible to forget that there are other people in the world – though it's very difficult to forget the **mosquitoes**. (Malaria is supposedly absent in the Pantanal, so you'll only have the insufferable itching to worry about.) The mosquitoes should be no surprise,

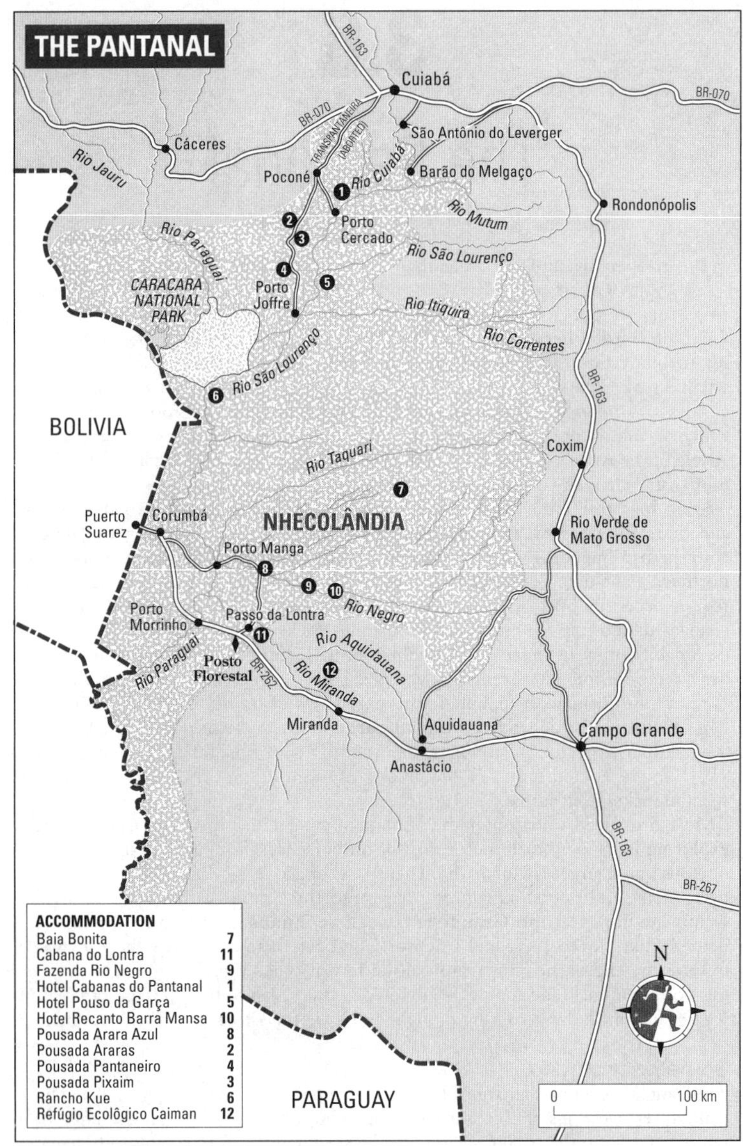

given that it's the biggest inland swamp in the world, covering some 230,000 square kilometres of the upper Rio Paraguai basin, over 140,000 of which are flooded annually. The Pantanal acts as an immense sponge, seasonally absorbing the swollen waters of three large rivers – the Paraguai, Taquari and Cuiabá.

During the **rainy season** from November to March, river levels rise by up to 3m producing a vast flooded plain with islands of scrubby forest amidst oceans of floating vegetation. Transport is necessarily dominated by the rivers, natural water channels and hundreds of well-hidden lagoons. The small islands of vegetated land created during the rains crawl with wild jaguar, tapirs, capybaras (the world's largest rodents) and wild boar living side by side with domesticated cattle.

At other times of the year, much of the Pantanal is still very boggy though interspersed with open grassy savannas studded with small wooded islands of taller vegetation, mainly palm trees. The **dry season**, from April to October, with its peak normally around September, transforms the swamp into South America's most exciting natural wildlife reserve. Its infamous piranha and alligator populations crowd into relatively small pools and streams, while the astonishing array of aquatic birds follows suit, forming very dense colonies known here as *viveiros*. Treeless bush savanna alternates with wet swamp, while along the banks of the major rivers grow belts of rainforest populated with colonies of monkeys (including spider monkeys and noisy black gibbons). Note, however, that the previously metronomic regularity of the seasons has become most unpredictable of late, with the onset of global warming.

History and development

At the time of the first unsuccessful attempts at populating the region by the Spanish in the sixteenth century, the region was dominated by three main tribes. In the south lived the horse-riding **Guaicuru**, who adopted stray or stolen horses and cattle from the advancing white settlers, making the tribe an elite group amongst Indians. Wearing only jaguar skins as they rode into battle, they were feared by the neighbouring **Terena** (Guana) tribe, who lived much of their lives as servants to Guaicuru families. To the north lived another powerful people, the **Paiaguá**, masters of the main rivers, lagoons and canals of the central Pantanal.

It wasn't until the **discovery of gold** in the northern Pantanal and around Cuiabá during the early eighteenth century that any genuine settlement schemes were undertaken. A rapid influx of colonists, miners and soldiers led to several bloody battles.

The decline of the gold mines during the nineteenth century brought development in the Pantanal to a standstill and the population began to fall. The twentieth century saw the establishment of unrestricted **cattle-grazing** ranches – *fazendas* – and today over twenty million head of cattle roam the swamp. To the east, the BR-163 between Campo Grande and Cuiabá skirts the Pantanal, and Ministry of Transport plans for a *Transpantaneira* road from Cuiabá to Corumbá have been shelved for the sake of the region's ecological balance. For all that, tourism has developed greatly in the region over the last few years, which has coincided with a slump in the price for cattle. Some *fazendeiros* have been quick to realize the potential of converting their farms and land into ecological reserves.

The Pantanal, however, is still **under threat** from the illegal exploitation of skins, fish and rare birds, and even gold panning. The chemical fertilizers and pesticides used on the enormous *fazendas* to produce cash crops such as soya beans are also beginning to take their toll. **Eco-tourism** has been heralded as a potential saviour for the swamp, but this will only work if sufficient money is ploughed back into conservation. The Pantanal has its own Polícia Florestal who try to enforce the environment-friendly regulations now being strictly applied to visitors and locals alike: no disposal of non-biodegradable rubbish, no noise pollution, no fishing without a licence (it costs $100) or between November and January during the breeding season, no fishing with nets or explosives and no removal of rocks, wildlife or plant life. Fishing is, in fact, one of the Pantanal's greatest attractions, for both the huge variety and ease of catching it; apart from piranhas, these rivers and lakes contain Dourado, Tucunaré, Pintado, Pacu, Piraputanga – all local delicacies in their own right.

Practicalities

Locals will almost certainly recommend going into the Pantanal by road, which is usually cheaper and quicker than renting a boat or going on one of the cruises. The main problem, though, is knowing where and how to go, and which company or lodge to choose. This section gives a rough overview of the various options, together with a box listing a selection of recommended **tour operators**. The following sections describe some possible **routes**, from Corumbá and from Cuiabá, together with details of **accommodation** in *fazenda*-lodges and pousadas. The box on pp.422–423 describes the options for **boat trips** from Cáceres and Corumbá.

If you want to go **independently** remember that the Pantanal is a difficult and dangerous place to travel in. There are very few roads and, although hundreds of tracks sneak their way into the swamp, they are only used by *fazenda* workers who know them inside out. An inexperienced driver or hiker could easily get lost – or worse. That said, there's no better way to see the wildlife than to camp or stay on a boat deep in the swamp, away from roads, tracks or *fazenda*-lodges, but to do this you will need a local **guide**; these are generally available only at lodges or in end-of-the-track settlements like Porto Jofre. Also, it's important to take all the **equipment** you need with you if you're going it alone like this in the Pantanal – food, camping gear, a first-aid kit and lots of mosquito repellent. It's possible to take **buses** and **boats** from Cuiabá and Corumbá to places such as Cáceres, Coxim, Porto Jofre or Aquidauana, and then it's a matter of finding a boat going your way deeper into the swamp or paying a local guide or *fazendeiro* to take you on a trip. This will cost around $20–50 per person per day, including canoe or vehicle transport and a guide/boatman/driver. Local guides and *fazendeiros* usually prefer to use the road networks to reach *fazenda*-lodges within the swamp, and explore in canoes or on horseback from there. Cheaper still, and certainly the most unusual alternative, is to buy a passage (around $10–20 a day; hammock essential) on one of the few **trading boats** still crossing the Pantanal between Corumbá and Cáceres, and occasionally Porto Jofre (both connected by road to Cuiabá).

Most people, however, go on **organized tours**, entering the swamp in jeeps or trucks and following one of the few rough roads that now connect Corumbá, Aquidauana, Coxim and Cuiabá (via Poconé or Cáceres) with some of the larger *fazenda* settlements of the interior. Otherwise you can seek out **small boat trips**

Upmarket Pantanal agents and operators

The following is a selection of the more upmarket Pantanal operators who deal with both complete packages and bookings for boats and or lodges.

Aguas do Pantanal Av Afonso Pena 367, Miranda ⓣ067/242-1242. This company owns and runs several pousadas around Miranda, Passo do Lontra and Porto Morrinho on the Rio Paraguai.

Anaconda Rua Marechal Deodoro, Cuiabá 2142 ⓣ065/624-4142. Short but well-organized and comfortable tours in the Pantanal and elsewhere in the Brazilian wilderness.

Corumbá Tur Rua Antônio Maria Coelho 852, Corumbá ⓣ & ⓕ067/231-1532. Corumbá's leading upmarket agency, dealing with all the main *fazendas* and luxury boat cruises, as well as organizing its own fishing and photography tours (anything from $120 per person per day). Prices for the fishing cruises (departing Sun on a variety of boats) range from $675 to $1300 per person per week.

Pantanal Express Av Afonso Pena 2081, Campo Grande ⓣ067/382-5333. Agents for some of the more upmarket tour operators and *fazenda* experiences.

SuperPesca Pantanal Rua Marechal Cândido Rondon 2300, Campo Grande ⓣ067/721-5713. Specialists in angling tours, and particularly knowledgeable about which boats go down which rivers, which could be useful in hitching a ride.

(around $40–80 a day, from Corumbá, Porto Jofre or Cáceres; there are no agencies for this, so just ask around), or a **combination of jeep and boat**, over four or five days, which would certainly give the trip a taste of adventure.

Swamping it **upmarket** at one of an increasing number of **fazenda-lodges** well away from towns and main roads is much easier. Most of the *fazenda*-lodges are located east and northeast of Corumbá, and also on either side of the Rio Cuiabá in the north, accessible for the most part via the aborted *Transpantaneira* road between Poconé and Porto Jofre. With few exceptions these lodges cost upwards of $100 a night per person, and $200 is not uncommon; prices always include various activities, including trips by boat or jeep, horse riding, guided walks or fishing expeditions, as well as meals. Prices are generally more reasonable in the northern Pantanal (accessible from Cuiabá) than in the south (Corumbá, Miranda and Aquidauana). *Fazenda*-lodges offer **all-inclusive package tours**, though their prices vary wildly, sometimes undercutting the official lodge price, at other times almost doubling it – it's worth shopping around and bargaining (the tour operators listed in the box opposite all have a selection). As a general rule, however, you'll pay less if you deal direct with a *fazenda*-lodge owner in Porto Jofre, Cáceres, Aquidauana and even Corumbá, rather than through their agents.

Into the swamp: routes from Corumbá and Campo Grande

Of the three main Pantanal towns, **Corumbá** is best placed for getting right into the Pantanal by bus or jeep, and has a welter of guides and agencies to choose from, as well as boats for hire. Campo Grande has better hotels and communications with the rest of Brazil, so it is probably used as much as a point for entry as Corumbá. Currently the most popular *fazenda*-lodges are those in Nhecolândia, roughly speaking the area between the *rios* Negro and Taquari east of Corumbá. These benefit from a well-established dirt access road, the MS-184/MS-228, which loops off from the main BR-262 highway 300km from Campo Grande near Passo do Lontra (it's well signposted), and crosses through a large section of the swamp before rejoining the same road some 10km before Corumbá.

Ecological Expeditions, at Rua Joaquim Nabuco 185, Campo Grande (Ⓣ067/382-3504, Ⓔecoexpeditionsbr@hotmail.com, Ⓦwww.pantanaltrekking.com), offers the cheapest option for going deep into the swamp area; they make the swamp more accessible by offering mainly camping facilities. Buraco das Piranhas is their Pantanal entry point and main roadhead for their base camp fairly deep into the swamp another couple of hours into the swamp. Tours are kitted out with igloo tents with mattresses, mosquito nets and hammocks, and the main activities are bush walking, horse riding, vehicle safaris, canoeing in the wet season, piranha fishing, bird and wildlife spotting. The base camp has a fair range of facilities but the temporary bush camp, frequently located on the banks of the caiman-infested Rio Negro under the protective shade of a large tree, is cooler and usually more popular. This is a good place for experiencing the wilderness of the Pantanal, meeting local people and enjoying the comradeship of the fellow Pantanal visitors. Most of the guides are indigenous to the Pantanal and some of the best are local *gaúchos* by upbringing, more cowboy than conventional tour guide. Tour prices are also reasonable, with a three day tour at around $90 (4 days $100 and 5 days $120). Given a few days you should get to see a fair selection of wildlife, including caiman, capaybara, coati mundi, rheas (emus), wild pigs and marsh deer. Ecological Expeditions also has an office in Corumba as well as close contacts with the youth hostel in Bonito.

Fazenda-lodges in the southern Pantanal

The following *fazenda*-lodges are accessible from Corumbá, Miranda or Aquidauana, offer full-board accommodation and swamp trips, and can be booked

Pantanal boat tours

At present, inexpensive **soya** and **cattle barges** cross the swamp between Cáceres and Corumbá fairly regularly. Neither has fixed schedules or itineraries, so it's a matter of checking on departure dates when you arrive in either town. The trip usually takes about six to ten days upstream from Corumbá, three to six downstream, with plenty of time for relaxing and looking out for wildlife. The barges, though, do tend to keep to the main channel of the Rio Paraguai, which obviously doesn't give you a very good chance of spotting anything particularly shy or rare. As well as your hammock, take some extra food (tins, biscuits, bottled drinks etc), insect repellent and a few good books. And a bottle of whisky or good *cachaça* wouldn't go amiss with the captain.

Travelling on the barges hasn't been strictly legal since 1985, when the son of a naval minister accidentally died while on board one of the cement barges that used to ply the same route. Passengers have consequently been "smuggled" aboard in dinghies, under cover of darkness. However, you might find it's still possible to buy a ride simply by asking the *comandante* of Portobras, one of the barge companies – offices on the waterfront in both Corumbá and Cáceres (☎065/222-1728). The cattle barge between Corumbá and Cáceres run by Serviço de Navegação da Bacia da Prata often picks up passengers from the ports at either end, but leaves at irregular intervals.

Luxury fishing boats are the other option and an ideal way to meet the swamp's wildlife on the end of a line and ultimately on your plate. Essentially floating hotels designed with the Brazilian passion for angling in mind, one of these for a week costs anything from $500 to 2000 a head, though the price is full board and usually includes ample drink, food and unlimited use of their small motorboat tenders for exploring further afield. Note that for **families with small children**, any river trip is inadvisable as none of the boats currently in use has guardrails safe enough to keep a toddler from falling in.

Most of the boats are based in Corumbá, with some others in Cáceres, Barão do Melgaço and Cuiabá, and all can be booked through the upmarket agents listed in the box on p.420. In high season, they tend to run pre-scheduled trips, departing and returning on Sundays; routes are mentioned where they remain fixed from year to year. Out of season, they're up for rent, with a minimum number of passengers and days invariably demanded, though bargaining is possible.

Luxury boats from Caceres

Botel Pantanal Explorer II ☎065/682-2800. Mainly covering the Rio Paraguai, this

through the addresses given below or through the upmarket Pantanal operators listed in the box on p.420.

Baia Bonita Nhecolândia ☎067/231-9600, Ⓔbaiabonita@pantanalnet.com.br, Ⓦwww.pantanalnet.com.br/baiabonita. On reasonably dry land approximately 160km northeast of Passo do Lontra (turn right before you reach Porto Manga), this two-storey block beside a ranch house has a homely atmosphere and features safari-style tours on foot, in 4's or on horseback. Minimum two people for two nights. ❼

Cabana do Lontra Passo do Lontra ☎067/987-3311 or 383-4532. Situated near where the MS-184 crosses the Rio Miranda, some 100km southeast of Corumbá and 7km off the main BR-262. With over twenty rooms and its own motorboats, this is a good spot for most wildlife; excellent for fishing. ❺

Fazenda Rio Negro Rio Negro, Rua Antônio Correa 1161, Bairro Monte Libano, Campo Grande ☎067/351-5191, Ⓔrionegro@conservation.org.br, Ⓦwww.fazendarionegro.com.br. This is one of the Pantanal's oldest ranches, founded in 1895. Now owned by Orlando Rondon, it is located up the Rio Negro with access from Aquidauana. It is a small, upmarket place with boats, horses and good guides. Air transfer from Campo Grande or Aquidauana is $100 return. ❽

Hotel Recanto Barra Mansa Rio Negro ☎067/383-5088, Ⓔbmansa@terra.com.br,

boat is very small with only three quadruple cabins. Upwards of $130 per person per day.

Cobra Grande ⓣ065/223-4203. Small boat with five cabins and an adequate dining room. Need to book well in advance.

Rei do Rio and Velho do Rio, contact Moretti Serviços Fluviais, Cuiabá ⓣ065/361-2082. A couple of Louisiana-style houseboats intended primarily as bases for fishing expeditions.

Luxury boats from Corumbá

Arara Tur Rua Manoel cavassa 47, by the port, Corumbá ⓣ067/231-4851, ⓔararatur@pantanalnet.com.br, ⓦwww.araratur.com.br. This company has a fine boat – the *Albatroz* – beautifully furnished with bars and cosy but very comfortable cabins. Wide range of short and longer boat tours in the Pantanal; specializes in photo safaris on the Rio Paraguai. $200 per person per day, five days minimum.

Barco Hotel Falcão Rodrigues Turismo, Rua Manoel Cavassa 331, Corumbá ⓣ067/231-5186. For six to eight passengers, conceived as a floating base for sports anglers. There's a five-day minimum rent, $180 per person per day. The *Falcão* is also available for return trips along the Rio Paraguai to Cáceres, at $2000 per person (the trip takes around eight days upriver, five days down).

Cabexy I & II Pantanal Tours, Rua Manoel Cavassa 61, Corumbá ⓣ067/231-4683 or 231-1559, ⓦwww.pantanaltours.tur.br. Two two-tiered riverboats for rent, similar in style to the *Kalypso* but, with a maximum of eight passengers each, rather more exclusive. Motorboats and fishing accessories provided. Five-day minimum period, $200 per person per day. Reservations and $3000 deposit required.

Cidade Barão do Melgaço book direct on ⓣ067/231-1460 or through Fish World. This converted tour boat with eight double cabins is only for rent from Corumbá: five days and eight people minimum, starting at $180 per person per day.

Kalypso book direct on ⓣ067/231-1460 or through agents Corumbá Tur, Mutum Turismo or Pan Tur. Brazil's answer to Nile cruisers, the *Kalypso* is a spacious three-tier affair with berths for 120 passengers, and looks for all the world like a pile of portacabins on a barge (which is what it once was). The interior is wood-panelled, the restaurant is self-service, and there's a pool on top in which to escape the mosquitoes and the heat. Originally designed as a base for fishing trips, it has a number of small motorboats and a giant fridge in which you can keep your catch. Prices start at $120 per person per day, with a minimum stay of six nights.

ⓦwww.hotelbarramansa.com.br. Further east from *Fazenda Rio Negro* on the north shore of the river, 130km from Aquidauana, this new place owned by Guilherme Rondon has room for twelve guests. It specializes in game and fly fishing. Daily buses from Corumbá. ❽

Pousada Arara Azul Rio Negrinho ⓣ067/384-6114, ⓔterrasms@uol.com.br, ⓦwww.pousadaararaazul.com.br. Close to the Rio Negro in Nhecolândia 38km up the MS-184 past Passo do Lontra, this pousada offers all the comforts you could want, plus amazing guaranteed access to virtually all the bird and mammalian wildlife apart from the rarer jaguars and wolves. Excellent for piranha fishing, night-time *jacarés* observation and horse riding. Camping allowed, too ($10 a night), though owners may require a minimum stay of two days in the lodge. ❼

Refúgio Ecolôgico Caiman Rio Aquidauana. They have a Reservation Center in São Paulo at R. Campos Bicudo, 98, cj. 112, Itaim – CEP 04536-010, São Paulo – SP ⓣ3079-6622, ⓔcaiman@caiman.com.br, ⓦwww.caiman.com.br) with agents in Campo Grande (ⓣ067/382-5197). This is the luxurious Pantanal jungle lodge experience. The *Refúgio* is located some 240km west of Campo Grande, 36km north of Miranda, and covers over 530 square kilometres. It has its own airstrip and offers transfer services leaving from Campo Grande four times a week. Full board, all activities and bilingual guide services are included in the daily rate of $200 per person per night in a double room.

Into the swamp: routes from Cuiabá

One of the simplest ways into the swamp is to take a three-hour **bus** from Cuiabá south **to BARÃO DO MELGAÇO**, a small, quiet village on the banks of the Rio Cuiabá. Although not quite in the true swamp, and therefore with less in the way of wildlife, Barão is perfect if you're short on time and just want a taste of the Pantanal. There's a reasonable hotel by the river in town, the *Barão Tour Pantanal Hotel*, bookings at Rua Joaquim Murtinho 1213, Cuiabá (☎065/713-1166; ❸), which also has boats for hire; while the exclusive *Pousada do Rio Mutum* is just an hour away by boat, in a stunning location on the Baía de Siá Mariana bay near the Rio Mutum (☎065/623-7022; or book through Eldorado Exec. Centre, Av Rubens de Mendonça 917, sala 301, Cuiabá ☎065/321-7995; ❻). Although Barão is no longer served by regular boats from Corumbá, it might still be worth asking around should a shallow-draught vessel be covering the journey – an unforgettable experience right through the centre of the swamp.

The most exploited option from Cuiabá is to follow the route south to Poconé and Porto Jofre. There are daily **buses** from Cuiabá's rodoviária as far as **POCONÉ** along a paved and fairly smooth hundred-kilometre stretch of road. Like Barão, Poconé is not real Pantanal country, but it's a start and there are plenty of **hotels in town** if you need to stay over. On the main square, Praça Rondon, the *Hotel Skala* at no. 64 (☎065/721-1407; ❸) and a couple of restaurants take most of the trade.

The swamp proper begins as you leave the town going south, along the aborted *Transpantaneira* Road. In fact, it's just a bumpy track, often impassable during the rains, but you'll see plenty of wildlife from it, as well as signs marking the entrances to a number of *fazenda*-lodges and pousadas set back from the road around various tributaries of the Rio Cuiabá, notably the Pixaim. Although pricey, they're cheaper than the ones in the southern Pantanal, and all have restaurants and facilities for taking wildlife day-trips into the swamp by boat, on horseback or on foot. Another track from Poconé, in an even worse state, trails off southeast to Porto Cercado on the banks of the Rio Cuiabá, and also has a few pousadas.

After 145km, having crossed around a hundred wooden bridges in varying stages of dilapidation, the track eventually arrives at **PORTO JOFRE**. After Cuiabá, Porto Jofre appears as little more than a small fishing hamlet, literally the end of the road. This is as far as the *Transpantaneira* route has got – or ever looks like getting, thanks to technical problems and the sound advice of ecological pressure groups. As far as **accommodation in town** goes, the *Hotel Porto Jofre* (☎065/322-6322; ❻; closed Nov–Feb) has the monopoly and therefore charges through the nose. If you have a hammock or a tent, it's usually all right to sleep outside somewhere, but check with someone in authority first (ask at the port) and don't leave your valuables unattended.

From Porto Jofre, there are irregular cargo **boats** to Corumbá (about twice a month), normally carrying soya or cattle from Cáceres, and the journey takes between two and five days, depending on whether the boats sail through the night. It's also possible to arrange a day or two's excursion up the Piquiri and Cuiabá rivers from Porto Jofre.

Northern Pantanal

All of the following can be booked directly or through upmarket travel agents in Cuiabá (see box on p.420); some lodges insist on advance reservation and won't let you in unannounced. All the lodges offer full-board accommodation, with swamp trips included in the price; they're listed in loose geographical order, from northeast to southwest.

Hotel Cabanas do Pantanal ☎065/345-1887 or Confiança Turismo, Rua Cândido Mariano 434, Cuiabá ☎065/623-4141. Situated 50km from Poconé on the Rio Piraim, left off the Porto Cercado track. Confiança prefers you take one of their various three- to five-day packages, including trips to Aguas Quentes and Chapada dos Guimarães. ❺–❻

Pousada Araras office at Cuiabá airport, or Av Ponce de Arruda 670, Várzea Grande ☎065/682-2800, www.araraslodge.com.br. At Km 32 of the *Transpantaneira*, this long-established pousada is an old brick ranch building, more atmospheric than most of the more modern pousadas, with a pool, as well as boats and horses, but its fourteen rooms are likely to be full in high season. ❺

Pousada Pantaneiro (c/o Anaconda Pantanal Operator, Rua Comandante Costa 649 ☎065/624-4142 or 624-5128. Approximately 100km south of Poconé, a small place (five rooms) and one of the more reasonably priced pousadas which, although not on a river itself, offers swamp trips on horseback. It should be OK to camp here, too, and they also have tents for hire. ❸–❹.

Pousada Pixaim ☎065/721-2091, reservations ☎065/721-1172. At Km 64 on the Rio Pixaim, and not always reachable by road (this and the more southerly pousadas are often cut off in the rains, but all have airstrips). Ten wooden three-bed rooms on stilts, with motorboats for hire and a number of swamp tracks to follow on foot. ❺

Hotel Pouso da Garça ☎065/322-8823 or 322-4916; bookings at Rua Miranda Reis 38, Cuiabá, or through ☎011/299-5353 or 267-9966. On the Rio São Lourenço near its confluence with the Rio Cuiabá (access by light aircraft), with a pool, motorboats and horses at the service of visitors. ❻

Rancho Kue ☎067/241-1875. This is one of the best-located *fazendas*, right in the centre of the swamp and close to the confluence of the big *rios* Paraguai and São Lourenço. Access available by plane. ❼

3.7

São Paulo

In 1554, the two priests established a mission station on the banks of the Rio Tietê in an attempt to bring Christianity to the Tupi-Guarani Indians. Called **São Paulo dos Campos de Piratininga**, it was 70km inland and 730m up, in the sheer, forest-covered inclines of the Serra do Mar, above the port of São Vicente. The gently undulating plateau and the proximity to the Paraná and Plata rivers facilitated traffic into the interior and, with São Paulo as their base, roaming gangs of *bandeirantes* set out in search of loot. Around the mission school, a few adobe huts were erected and the settlement soon developed into a trading post and a base from which to secure mineral wealth. In 1681, **SÃO PAULO** – as the town became known – became a seat of regional government and, in 1711, it was made a municipality by the king of Portugal, the cool, healthy climate helping to attract settlers from the coast.

With the mid-nineteenth-century expansion of **coffee** plantations westwards from Rio de Janeiro, São Paulo's fortunes looked up. The region's rich soil was ideally suited to coffee cultivation, and from about 1870 the city underwent a rapid transformation into a bustling regional centre. In the 1890s, enterprising "coffee barons" began to place some of their profits in local industry, hedging their bets against a possible fall in the price of coffee, with textile factories being a favourite area for investment. As the local population could not meet the ever-increasing demands of plantation owners, factories looked to **immigrants** (see box on p.434) to meet their labour requirements. By 1950, it had reached 2.2 million and São Paulo had clearly established its dominant role in Brazil's urbanization: today the city's population stands at around ten million, rising to at least sixteen million when the sprawling metropolitan area is included.

As industry, trade and population developed at such a terrific pace, buildings were erected with little time to consider their aesthetics; in any case, they often became cramped as soon as they were built, or had to be demolished to make way for a new avenue. However, some grand **public buildings** were built in the late nineteenth and early twentieth centuries, and a few still remain, though none is as splendid as those found in Buenos Aires, a city that developed at much the same time. São Paulo lays claim to have long surpassed Rio as Brazil's **cultural** centre, and is home to a lively music and arts world. The city's **food**, too, is often excellent, in part thanks to immigrants from so many parts of the world.

Arrival and information

You'll probably **arrive** in São Paulo by plane or bus, though there are train connections with Bauru and Campinas in the interior of the state. Watch your belongings at all times, as thieves thrive in the confusion of airports and stations.

By air

Just to the south of the centre, the always congested **Congonhas** (☎11/5090-9000 or 5090-9195) handles services within the state of São Paulo, but also operates the shuttle service (the *ponte aérea*) to Rio and some flights to other neighbouring states. Other domestic and all international flights use the much newer **Guarulhos** airport (☎11/6445-2945), 30km from the city.

Congonhas and Guarulhos are connected to each other by air-conditioned *executivo* **buses** leaving at roughly half-hourly intervals (5.30am–11pm; $5). At similar intervals, buses link both airports with the western side of Praça da República (7am–9pm; $5). From Guarulhos there are more options: every 35 minutes there are buses to the Rodoviária Tietê (5.40am–10.10pm); and there's also a bus service ($5) to the *Maksoud Plaza Hotel*, which stops off at the other top hotels around Avenida Paulista. Even cheaper, but only really practical if you have little luggage, is to take a bus to the Bresser *Metrô* station (5am–11pm; 70c) where you can catch a train into the city centre. **Taxis** from Congonhas to the centre is around $12, from Guarulhos about $20. At both airports there are taxi desks in the arrivals halls and you pay a fixed price depending on the distance of your destination.

SET (Secretaria de Esportese Turismo) maintains helpful state **tourist information** desks at the airports (daily 7.30am–10.30pm); there are also banks with exchange facilities and ATMs at both airports.

By bus and train

Intercity bus services arrive at one of four **rodoviárias**. To the south of the centre, **Jabaquara** (☎11/5581-0856) is mainly used for buses to and from the Santos region. **Barra Funda** (☎11/3666-4682), northwest of the centre, serves destinations in southern São Paulo state and Paraná. **Bresser** (☎11/6692-5191) is for buses to Minas Gerais. The largest bus station, serving all state capitals as well as destinations in neighbouring countries, is the **Tietê** terminal to the north (☎11/3235-0322). All four rodoviárias are on the *Metrô* system, and a night bus (#510M) runs between the Jabaquara and Tietê, passing through the centre at Praça da Sé.

There are very few train services now to São Paulo's **Estação da Luz**. The train still runs to Bauru in the interior of the state of São Paulo, but the connection on to Campo Grande for Corumbá has been suspended. To get to the city centre from the station, take the *Metrô* (from the Luz station) or a taxi, which will cost $5–10.

Information

Anhembi Turismo, the city's tourism department (☎11/6971-5511), maintains several **information booths** scattered about the city whose English-speaking staff are helpful for general directions. Booths can be found on Praça da República, across from Rua Sete de Abril (daily 9am–6pm); at Praça da Liberdade (daily 9am–6pm); at the Teatro Municipal (Mon–Fri 9am–6pm, Sat 9am–1pm); and at Avenida Paulista (across from MASP; daily 9am–6pm). A good map, and information on the state of São Paulo, is available from the state **tourist office** at Avenida São Luís 97 (Mon–Fri 10am–5pm).

For up-to-date **listings** of what's going on in the city, the São Paulo edition of the weekly magazine *Veja* contains an excellent entertainment guide, and the daily newspaper *Folha de São Paulo* lists cultural and sporting events and, on Friday, contains a useful entertainment guide.

City transport

São Paulo's **public transport** network is extensive but traffic congestion and a seemingly perpetual rush hour can make travelling by bus or taxis frustratingly slow going. As a **safety precaution**, when using public transport always make sure you have some small notes at hand, so as not to attract attention to yourself when fumbling through your wallet or bag for change.

Traffic congestion rarely allows São Paulo's **buses** to be driven at the same terrifying speeds as in Rio, though drivers do their best to compete. Despite everything,

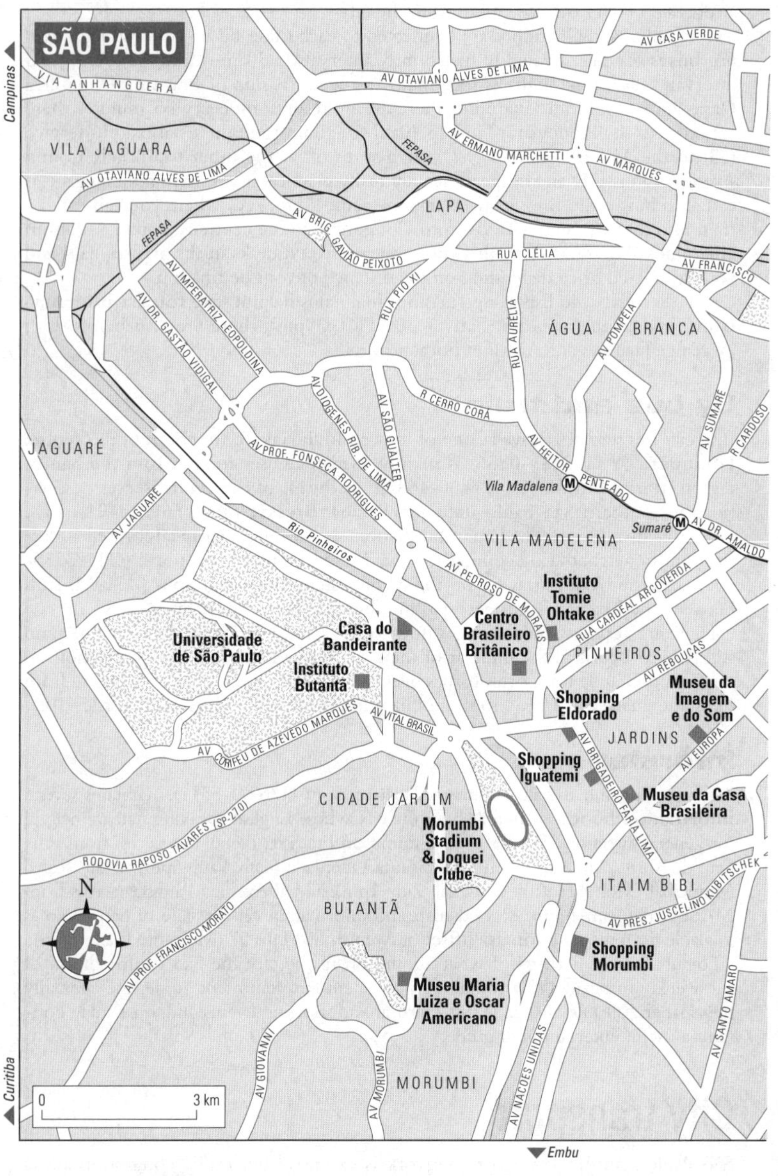

the network is remarkably efficient and includes trolley buses as well as ordinary buses; there is a flat fare of 35¢. The number of the bus is clearly marked at the front, and there are cards at the front and the entrance (towards the back) that indicate the route. At **bus stops** you'll have to flag down the buses you want: be attentive or they'll speed by. Buses run between 4am and midnight, but avoid travelling

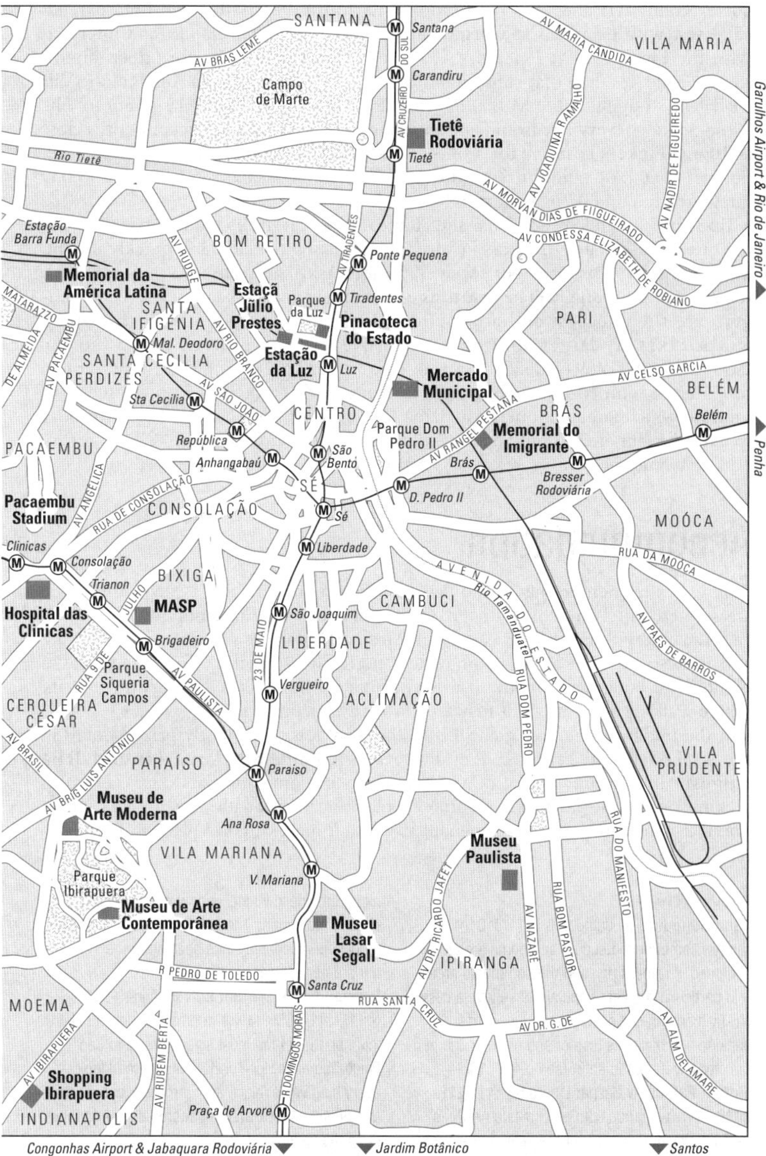

during the height of the evening rush hour (around 5–7pm) when they are overflowing with passengers.

Quiet, comfortable and fast, São Paulo's **Metrô** would be by far the easiest way to move around the city were it not limited to just three lines. The north–south **Linha Azul** (blue line) has terminals at Tucuruvi in the far north of the city and

Jabaquara (the rodoviária from where buses to Santos depart) and also serves the Tietê Rodoviária and Luz train station. The **Linha Vermelha** (red line) extends east–west with terminals at Corinthians–Itaquera and Barra Funda, and intersects with the Linha Azul at Praça da Sé. There's also the **Linha Verde** (green line), a shorter east–west line that runs underneath Avenida Paulista from Ana Rosa to Vila Madalena stopping at the Museu de Arte de São Paulo (Trianon-Masp station). The *Metrô* operates every day from 5am until midnight, although the ticket booths close at 10pm. **Tickets** cost 45¢ for a one-way journey and come either as singles (*ida*), doubles (*dople*), or valid for ten journeys (*bilhete com dez unidades*). You can also buy integrated bus and *Metrô* tickets.

Taxis in São Paulo are reliable and abundant but, given the volume of traffic and the often considerable distances involved in navigating the city, fares quickly mount. With irregular – or no – bus services at night, taxis are really the only means of transport after midnight. The **comuns**, generally small cars that carry three passengers, are the cheapest and are found at taxi ranks or hailed from the street. **Rádiotáxis** are larger and more expensive, and are ordered by phone: try Coopertax (☎11/6941-2555) or Ligue Táxi (☎11/3262-2633). Both types of taxi have meters with two fare rates, and a flag, or *bandeira*, is displayed on the meter to indicate which fare is in operation: fare "1" is charged from 6am to 10pm Monday to Saturday, but after 10pm and on Sunday and public holidays, fare "2" is charged, costing twenty percent more.

Accommodation

Finding somewhere to stay in São Paulo is rarely a problem and, as there are several areas where hotels are concentrated, you should get settled in quite quickly.

Compared with Europe or North America, top hotels are very reasonably priced, and it's also possible to find somewhere perfectly satisfactory for around $50 a night. Most budget and medium-priced places are in rather seedy parts of the city where walking alone at night may feel distinctly uncomfortable.

In the traditional centre of São Paulo, there are lots of modestly priced hotels in the streets around Praça da República and Avenida São Luís. **Around Rua Augusta** in the direction of downtown, there are some affordable options worth seeking out, while **Jardins** has some excellent accommodation; as an area where one feels safe both in the daytime and at night, it makes a good place to base oneself.

Downtown

Cambridge Av 9 de Julho 216 ☎11/3101-4376, ⓦwww.cambridgehotel.com.br. Rooms are well equipped, if rather tatty, and the communal areas – in particular the very popular bar – have a cosy old-fashioned feel. Located near the central banking and business district and on the edge of the city's lively "Little Italy" (see p.437). ❺

Marian Palace Av Cáspar Libero 65 ☎11/228-8433, ⓦwww.marian.com.br. This late Art Deco gem has been updated over the years but retains many of its original features in its rooms and public areas. A nice pool and garden terrace help compensate for the location, which can be dodgy at night. ❻

Municipal Av São João 354 ☎11/228-7833. In a busy part of the centre that feels safe day and night, this friendly hotel is now protected as a historic monument. The hotel's simple rooms have hardly been updated since opening in the 1940s, but are perfectly adequate. ❹

Normandie Design Hotel Av Ipiranga 1187 ☎11/3311-9855, ⓦwww.normandiedesignhotel.com.br. One of the most stylish hotels in São Paulo. You either love or hate the general look – everything white, black and chrome – but the staff are all enthusiastic and the bedrooms comfortable (if on the small side). ❼

São Sebastião Rua Sete de Abril 364 ☎11/257-4988. Quiet but dark and rather musty rooms, all with shower, just minutes from the entrance to the Praça da República *Metrô* station. A popular choice with European backpackers, with safe night-time access. ❹

Rua Augusta and around

Cá d'Oro Rua Augusta 129 ⓣ11/3256-4300, ⓦwww.cadoro.com.br. An easy stroll from Avenida Paulista, this excellent hotel offers a full range of facilities – including a business centre and a pool – in a more tasteful environment than is generally the case with São Paulo's luxury hotels. The large and simply furnished rooms are extremely comfortable and also excellent value. ⑦

Maksoud Plaza Alameda Campinas 150 ⓣ11/3145-8000, ⓦwww.maksoud.com.br. Up against severe competition in recent years, the *Maksoud Plaza* clings nervously to its reputation as the city's most distinguished hotel. The rooms are as comfortable as you'd expect, the staff are efficient and welcoming and there's a pool and several decent on-site restaurants. Hardly cheap, but a comparative bargain. ⑧

Pousada dos Franceses Rua dos Franceses 100 ⓣ11/3262-4026, ⓦwww.pousadadosfranceses.com.br. In a quiet location a couple of blocks from both Bixiga and Avenida Paulista, this small property has been newly converted into a simple pousada. Guests have use of the kitchen, and breakfast is available at a small extra cost. Rates vary from $6 per person per night in a dorm, to $15 for a double room with private bathroom.

Jardins

Emiliano Rua Oscar Freire 384 ⓣ11/3069-4369, ⓦwww.emiliano.com.br. São Paulo's most trendy – and most expensive – hotel. With just 57 rooms, the *Emiliano* prides itself on providing discreet individual attention. For an extra charge you can arrange to be transferred to and from Guarulhos airport by helicopter. If you can't afford to stay here but are curious, stop by at the bar for a drink and to people watch. ⑨

Formule 1 São Paulo Paraiso Rua Vergueiro 1571 ⓣ11/5085-5699, ⓦwww.hoteis-accor.com.br. This extremely simple French-owned hotel offers a double bed with a single bunk bed above, a shower and toilet, and TV (but no telephone) in all rooms. A popular choice, thanks to a good location by the Paraiso *Metrô* station and rates that are the same whether single, double or triple occupancy: reservations are highly recommended. ④

Metropolitan Plaza Alameda Campinas 474 ⓣ0800/553-600 and 11/3288-0369, ⓦwww.metropolitanplaza.com.br. There are attractive rooms, all with fully equipped kitchenette, and a smallish pool at this hotel, where rates are very reasonable given the amenities and the neighbourhood. De-luxe rooms are only $5 more but have a separate living room and a larger bathroom. ⑥

Pousada Dona Ziláh Alameda Franca 1621 ⓣ11/3062-1444, ⓦwww.zilah.com. This large house, converted into a simple, but pretty pousada, is the only one in Jardins, and the cheapest place to stay in an otherwise upmarket neighbourhood. The atmosphere is friendly but unintrusive, and there's always someone on hand to offer local advice. ④

The City

In the nineteenth century, most of colonial São Paulo was levelled and replaced by a disorganized patchwork of wide avenues and large buildings, the process repeating itself ever since. Today, not only has the city's colonial architectual heritage all but vanished, but there's little physical evidence of the coffee boom decades either.

Nevertheless, a few relics have, somehow, escaped demolition and offer hints of São Paulo's bygone eras. What remains is hidden away discreetly in corners, scattered throughout the city, often difficult to find but all the more thrilling when you do.

Around Praça da Sé

PRAÇA DA SÉ is the most convenient starting point for the very brief hunt for **colonial São Paulo**. The square itself is a large expanse of concrete and fountains, dominated by the **Catedral Metropolitana**, a huge, but otherwise unremarkable, neo-Gothic structure. During the day the square outside bustles with activity, always crowded with hawkers and people heading towards the commercial district on its western fringes. At night it's transformed into a campsite for homeless children, who survive as best they can by shining shoes, selling chewing gum or begging.

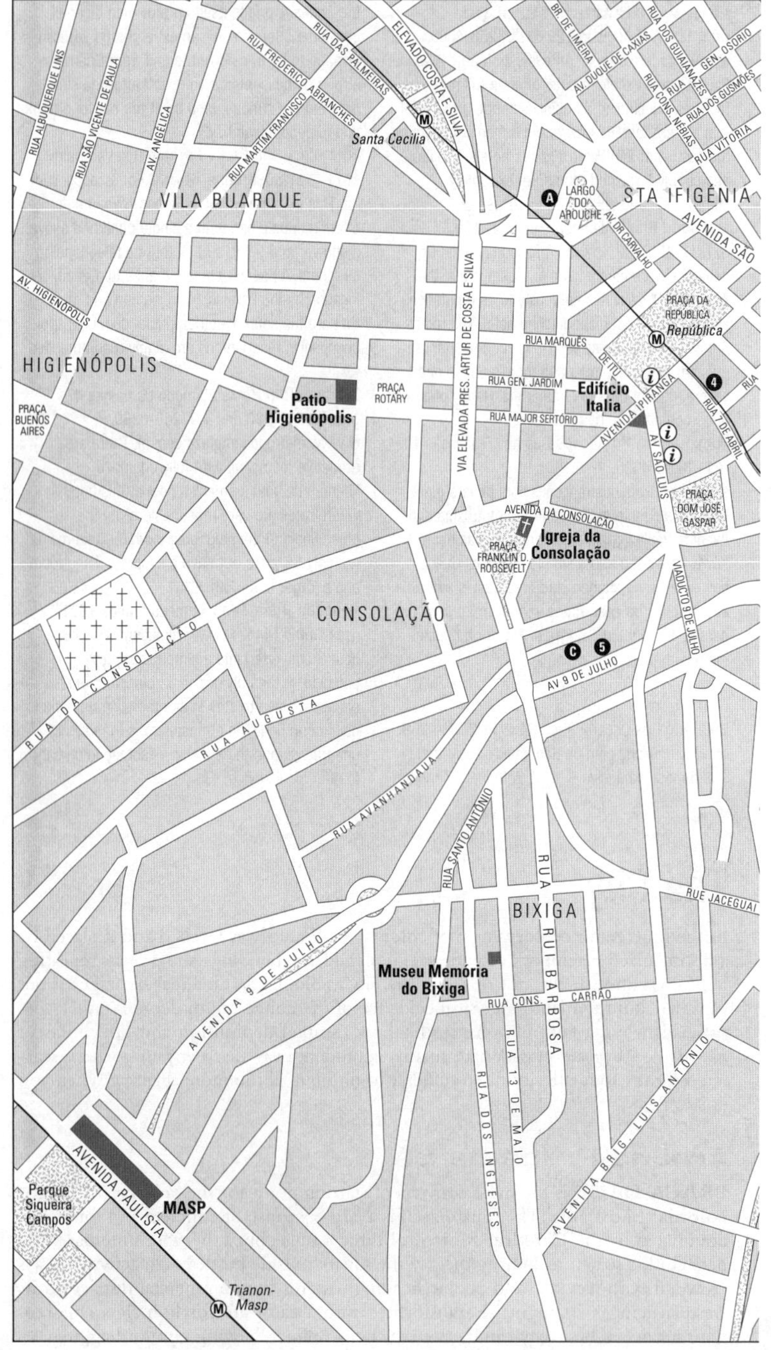
VILA BUARQUE
STA IFIGÉNIA
HIGIENÓPOLIS
CONSOLAÇÃO
BIXIGA
Santa Cecilia
República
Trianon-Masp
LARGO DO AROUCHE
PRAÇA DA REPÚBLICA
PRAÇA DOM JOSÉ GASPAR
PRAÇA FRANKLIN D. ROOSEVELT
PRAÇA ROTARY
PRAÇA BUENOS AIRES
Patio Higienópolis
Edifício Italia
Igreja da Consolação
Museu Memória do Bixiga
MASP
Parque Siqueira Campos
RUA ALBUQUERQUE LINS
RUA SÃO VICENTE DE PAULA
AV. ANGÉLICA
RUA MARTIM FRANCISCO
RUA FREDERICO ABRANCHES
RUA DAS PALMEIRAS
ELEVADO COSTA E SILVA
BR. DE LIMEIRA
AV. DUQUE DE CAXIAS
RUA DOS GUAIANAZES
RUA GEN. OSORIO
RUA DOS GUSMÕES
RUA CONS. NÉBIAS
RUA VITORIA
AVENIDA SÃO
AV. DR CARVALHO
AV. HIGIENÓPOLIS
VIA ELEVADA PRES. ARTUR DE COSTA E SILVA
RUA MARQUÊS DE ITU
RUA GEN. JARDIM
RUA MAJOR SERTÓRIO
AVENIDA IPIRANGA
AV SÃO LUIS
RUA 7 DE ABRIL
AVENIDA DA CONSOLAÇÃO
VIADUCTO 9 DE JULHO
AV 9 DE JULHO
RUA DA CONSOLAÇÃO
RUA AUGUSTA
RUA AVANHANDAUA
RUA SANTO ANTÔNIO
RUA RUI BARBOSA
RUE JACEGUAI
AVENIDA 9 DE JULHO
RUA CONS. CARRÃO
RUA 13 DE MAIO
RUA DOS INGLESES
AVENIDA BRIG. LUIS ANTÔNIO
AVENIDA PAULISTA

3

3.7 | BRAZIL | São Paulo

Along Rua Boa Vista, on the opposite side of the square from the cathedral, is where the city of São Paulo originated. The whitewashed Portuguese Baroque **Pátio do Colégio** is a replica of the college and chapel that formed the centre of the Jesuit mission founded here in 1554. Although built in 1896 (the other buildings forming the Pátio were constructed in the twentieth century), the chapel (Mon–Fri 8am–5pm) is an accurate reproduction, but it's in the Pátio's **Museu Padre Anchieta** (Tues–Sun 9am–5pm; free) that the most interesting sixteenth- and early seventeenth-century relics – mostly old documents – are held.

Virtually around the corner from the Pátio do Colégio at Rua Roberto Simonsen 136 is the **Museu da Cidade** (Tues–Sun 9am–5pm; free). More interesting than the museum's small collection chronicling the development of São Paulo is the building that it's housed in, the **Solar da Marquesa de Santos**, an eighteenth-century manor house that represents the sole remaining residential building in the city from this period. A couple of hundred metres from here, at Av Rangel Pestana 230, is the well-preserved **Igreja do Carmo** (Mon–Fri 7–11am & 1–5pm, Sat & Sun 7–11am), which was built in 1632 and still retains many of its seventeenth-century features, including a fine Baroque high altar.

Over the other side of Praça da Sé, a two-minute walk down Rua Senado Feijó to the Largo de São Francisco is the **Igreja de São Francisco** (Mon–Fri 7.30am–8pm & Sat–Sun 7–10am), a typical mid-seventeenth-century Portuguese colonial church that features intricately carved ornaments and an elaborate Baroque altar. Before leaving this area, you should visit the **Igreja de Santo Antônio** at Praça do Patriarca, by the Viaduto do Chá (the pedestrian bridge linking the two parts of the commercial centre). Built in 1717, its yellow and white facade has been beautifully restored; the interior has been stripped of most of its eighteenth-century accoutrements, though its simple painted wooden ceiling deserves a glance.

Since the early twentieth century, the Italian immigrant population of the *bairro* of **Bixiga**, lying to the southwest of Praça da Sé, has given it the name "Little Italy" (it's also known as Bela Vista). Calabrian stonemasons built their own homes with leftover materials from the building sites where they were employed, and the narrow streets are still lined with such houses. In an otherwise ordinary house at Rua dos Ingleses 118, the **Museu Memória do Bixiga** (Wed–Sun 2–5.30pm; 70¢) enthusiastically documents the history of the *bairro*, and has a small collection of photographs and household items. The central Rua 13 de Maio, and the streets

Immigration and São Paulo

São Paulo is a city built by **immigrants** whose arrival is largely responsible for making it the country's second-largest city by 1950. Mass immigration didn't begin until the late 1870s, and conditions were initially appalling for the immigrants, many of whom succumbed to malaria or yellow fever while waiting in the port of Santos to be transferred inland to the plantations. In response to criticisms, the government opened the Hospedaria dos Imigrantes in 1887, a hostel in the eastern suburb of Moóca. Now open to the public as the **Memorial do Imigrante**, Rua Visconde de Paraíba 1316 (Tues–Sun 10am–5pm; $1; ⓦwww.memorialdoimigrante.sp.gov.br), the hostel buildings house an immigration research centre and one of the best museums in São Paulo.

The museum has a permanent collection of period furniture, documents and photographs, and regularly hosts temporary exhibits relating to particular aspects of immigration history. The main building itself is the most interesting feature of the complex, however, with vast dormitories and its own rail siding and platform for unloading immigrants and their baggage. Designed to hold 4000 people, the hostel housed as many as 10,000 at times, the immigrants treated little better than cattle. On Sundays and holidays, a beautiful nineteenth-century train connects the complex with Bresser *Metrô* station (10am–5pm) and succeeds in drawing larger crowds.

running off it, are lined with *cantinas*, pizzerias and bars, and at night this normally quiet neighbourhood springs to life, though it's become increasingly run-down in recent years.

Just east of Bixiga is the *bairro* of **Liberdade**, traditional home of the city's large Japanese community. Rua Galvão Bueno and intersecting streets are largely devoted to Japanese restaurants and shops selling semiprecious stones and Japanese food. The **Museu da Imigração Japonesa**, Rua São Joaquim 381 (Wed–Sun 1.30–5.30pm; 70¢) has a Japanese-style rooftop garden and excellent displays on the contribution of the Japanese community to Brazil since their arrival in 1908 to work on the coffee plantations. In recent years, Liberdade's ethnic character has been changing and, although the area is still Japanese-dominated, an increasing number of Chinese, Korean and Vietnamese immigrants are settling in the area and introducing new restaurants and food shops.

North of Praça da Sé

To the north of Praça da Sé, at Rua da Cantareira 306, you'll find the **Mercado Municipal**, an imposing, vaguely German neo-Gothic hall, completed in 1933. Apart from the phenomenal display of fruit, vegetables, cheese and other produce, the market (Mon–Sat 4am–4pm) is celebrated for its enormous stained-glass windows depicting scenes of cattle raising, market gardening and coffee and banana plantations. Just across the Viaduto do Chá, in the direction of Praça da República, stands the **Teatro Municipal**, São Paulo's most distinguished public building, an eclectic mixture of Art Nouveau and Italian Renaissance styles. The theatre is still the city's main venue for classical music, and the auditorium, lavishly decorated and furnished with Italian marble, velvet, gold leaf and mirrors, can be viewed only if you're attending a performance.

Further north, the once affluent *bairro* of Luz is home to São Paulo's two main train stations, around which one of the city's seediest red-light districts has sprung up. At the intersection of Rua Duque de Caxias and Rua Mauá lies the **Estação Júlio Prestes**, built between 1926 and 1937 and drawing on late nineteenth-century French and Italian architectural forms. The building's most beautiful features are its large stained-glass windows, which depict the role of the train in the expansion of the Brazilian economy in the early twentieth century. Although part of the building still serves as a train station for suburban services, its Great Hall was transformed in the late 1990s into the Sala São Paulo, a 1500-seat concert hall – home of the world-class Orquestra Sinfônica de Estado de São Paulo, and centrepiece of the **Complexo Cultural Júlio Prestes** (☎11/3337-5414). Further along Rua Mauá, towards Avenida Tiradentes, is the **Estação da Luz**, part of the British-owned rail network that did much to stimulate São Paulo's explosive growth in the late nineteenth century. Built in 1901, its materials were imported from Britain for the construction, from the design of the project to the smallest of screws. Although the refined decoration of its chambers was destroyed by fire in 1946, interior details – iron balconies, passageways and grilles – bear witness to the majestic structure's original elegance.

One block north on Avenida Tiradentes, the **Parque da Luz** (daily 10am–6pm) dates back to 1800 and is São Paulo's first public garden. Its intricate wrought-iron fencing, Victorian bandstands, ponds and rich foliage offer evidence of its former glory. Until very recently, the park was considered off limits, but security is now excellent and, as one of the very few centrally located patches of greenery in the city. Adjoining the park, at Av Tiradentes 141, is the **Pinacoteca do Estado** (Tues–Sun 10am–6pm; $1.50), the state of São Paulo gallery. One of the most pleasant and professionally maintained galleries in Brazil, it contains an extensive collection of beautifully displayed nineteenth- and twentieth-century Brazilian art, including works by Larsar Segall, Di Cavalcanti, Cândido Portinari, Tarsilla do Amaral and Almeida Junior.

Around Praça da República

Once home to the lavish mansions of the coffee-plantation owners who took up residence in the city after 1870, the streets surrounding **Praça da República** are now given over to office buildings, hotels and shops. Southeast of the *praça* lies the **Triângulo**, the traditional banking district and a zone of concentrated vertical growth. At the Triângulo's northern edge, on Avenida São João, stands the thirty-storey **Edifício Martinelli**, the city's first skyscraper. Modelled on New York's Empire State Building, Martinelli was inaugurated in 1929 and remains an important landmark, only dwarfed by Latin America's tallest office building, the 42-storey **Edifício Itália**, built in 1965 on Avenida São Luís, the street leading south from the *praça*. On cloud- and smog-free days, the Itália's 41st-floor restaurant, the *Terraço Itália*, is a good vantage point from which to view the city; the food's expensive and not very good, so you're best off just having afternoon tea or an early evening drink at the bar. In the 1940s and 1950s, **Avenida São Luís** itself was São Paulo's version of New York's Fifth Avenue, lined with high-class apartment buildings and offices, and, though no longer fashionable, it still retains a certain degree of elegance. Admirers of the Brazilian architect Oscar Niemeyer will immediately pick out the serpentine Edifício Copan, the largest of the apartment and office buildings on the avenue.

Along Avenida Paulista

By 1900, the coffee barons had built new mansions, set in spacious gardens stretching, along the three-kilometre-long **Avenida Paulista**. In the late 1960s, and throughout the 1970s, Avenida Paulista resembled a giant building site, with banks and other companies competing to build ever-taller buildings. There was little time for creativity, and along the entire length of the avenue it would be difficult to single out more than one example of decent modern architecture. There are, however, about a dozen Art Nouveau or Art Deco mansions along Avenida Paulista, afforded official protection from the developers' bulldozers. One mansion that is well worth visiting is the French-style **Casa das Rosas**, Av Paulista 35 (Tues–Sun noon–8pm; ⓦwww.casadasrosas.sp.gov.br), near Brigadeiro *Mêtro* station at the easterly end of the *avenida*. Set in a rose garden with a beautiful Art Nouveau stained-glass window, it contrasts stunningly with the mirrored-glass and steel office building behind it. The Casa das Rosas is now a cultural centre owned by the state of São Paulo, where diverting art exhibitions are often held.

One of the few interesting modern buildings along Avenida Paulista is the **Museu de Arte de São Paulo** at no. 1578 (Tues–Sun 11am–6pm; $2, free on Thurs; ⓦwww.masp.art.br). The huge concrete 1968 structure appears to float above the ground, supported only by remarkably delicate pillars. MASP is the great pride of São Paulo's art lovers, and is considered to have one of the most important collections of Western art in Latin America, featuring the work of great European artists from the last five hundred years. For most North American and European visitors, the highlights of the collection are likely to be the few seventeenth- to nineteenth-century landscapes of Brazil by European artists. MASP's excellent and very reasonably priced restaurant (Mon–Fri 11.30am–3pm, Sat, Sun & holidays noon–4pm) is a great escape from the crowds, exhaust fumes and heat of Avenida Paulista outside.

The Jardins and the Parque do Ibirapuera

Avenida Paulista marks the southwestern boundary of downtown São Paulo; beyond that are the **Jardins**, laid out in 1915 and styled after the British idea of the garden suburb. These exclusive residential neighbourhoods have long since taken over from the city centre as the location of most of the city's best restaurants and shopping streets, and many residents never stray from their luxurious ghettos. At the northeastern edge of the Jardins suburb, and falling mostly within it, the district of

Cerqueira César straddles both sides of Avenida Paulista and is dominated by a mixed bag of hotels, offices and apartment buildings interspersed with shops and restaurants geared towards the city's upper middle class.

The **Parque do Ibirapuera** (daily 6am–9pm), southeast of the Jardins, is the most famous of São Paulo's parks and is the city's main sports centre. It's a ten-minute bus ride from the bus stops on Avenida Brigadeiro Luís Antônio. Opened in 1954, the park was created to mark the 400th anniversary of the founding of the city of São Paulo.

The park is also home to the **Museu de Arte Contemporânea** (Tues, Wed & Fri 10am–7pm, Sat, Sun & holidays 10am–4pm; $2; ⓦwww.mac.usp.br), located in the Pavilhão da Bienal. Although the collection includes work by important twentieth-century European and Brazilian artists, the pieces actually on display can be disappointing. Next door to the Pavilhão da Bienal in the Marquise do Parque do Ibirapuera, the **Museu de Arte Moderna** (Tues, Wed & Fri noon–6pm, Sat, Sun & holidays 10am–6pm; $3, free Tues; ⓦwww.mam.org.br), is a much smaller museum that mainly hosts temporary exhibits of the work of Brazilian artists. There's an excellent restaurant here serving light meals and snacks, and a good bookshop.

If you're on the art-gallery trail, there are two other museums nearby well worth seeking out. The *bairro* due east of the Parque do Ibirapuera, Vila Mariana, contains the wonderful **Museu Lasar Segall** at Rua Afonso Celso 388 (Tues–Sun 2–7pm; $2). As most of Lasar Segall's work is contained in this museum (his home and studio from 1932 until his death in 1957), the Latvian-born naturalized-Brazilian painter is relatively little known outside Brazil. Originally a member of the German Expressionist movement at the beginning of the twentieth century, his later work was influenced by the exuberant colours of his adopted homeland. East of here in the *bairro* of Ipiranga, the **Museu do Ipiranga** – also known as the Museu Paulista – (Tues–Sun 9am–4.45pm; 70¢; ⓦwww.mp.usp.br), at the intersection of *avenidas* Nazareth and Dom Pedro in the Parque da Independência, is worthwhile if you have a passing interest in Brazilian history. The museum is especially strong on the nineteenth century, featuring many paintings, furniture and other items that belonged to the Brazilian royal family.

Eating

Locals like to claim that São Paulo's range of restaurants is second only to New York's. Certainly, the variety of eating options is one of the great joys of São Paulo, though the quality is often disappointing, not least at the more expensive end of the scale. São Paulo's "Little Italy", the Bixiga *barrio*, is good for a fun night out, with countless inexpensive eateries, but the food there is nothing special, and you'll find better fare elsewhere in the city. With the largest Japanese community outside Japan, São Paulo also has many excellent Japanese restaurants that serve food as good as that in Japan itself. Vegetarians will have no problem in São Paulo as most restaurants offer a good range of suitable choices.

Asian and Middle Eastern

Arabe Rua Com. Abdo Schahin 102, Centro. Crowded at lunchtime with Lebanese diners, for the rest of the day the inexpensive restaurant is a focus for dawdling, elderly Arabs who live nearby.

Jun Sakamoto Rua José Maria Lisboa 55, Jardim Paulista ⓣ11/3088-6019. This expensive restaurant stands out amongst São Paulo's many Japanese eateries, with its attractive steel and wood setting and a daring chef who adds modern twists to otherwise classic dishes. The sushi is creatively presented, and the tempura, in a light batter with sesame seeds, is excellent. Very popular at weekends when a reservation is advisable. Evenings only.

Korea House Rua Galvão Bueno 43, Liberdade. One of the very few Korean restaurants in the city, despite the large Korean community. Many dishes are prepared at the table, and the often spicy meals are very different from Chinese or Japanese cooking. Around $6 per person.

Yamaga Rua Tomás Gonzaga 66, Liberdade. Small, mainly attracting Japanese diners who drop by for some sushi and a drink; a meal with a full range of Japanese specialities will cost around $20 a head.

Brazilian

Andrade Rua Artur de Azevedo 874, Pinheiros. Moderately priced restaurant specializing in Northeastern food, in particular *carne do sol* (sun-dried meat served with manioc flour).

Cantaloup Rua Manoel Guedes, Itaim Bibi ☎11/3846-6445. Known for simply placing tropical Brazilian ingredients alongside French and Italian ones, always with mouthwatering results. Lush foliage and efficiently friendly service create an intimate atmosphere in this converted warehouse. Fairly expensive but excellent.

Dona Lucinha Rua Bela Cintra 2325, Jardim Paulista. The best *mineiro* food that you're likely to taste in São Paulo, this is a branch of a highly regarded restaurant with the same name in Belo Horizonte (see p.356). Inexpensive, with an excellent fixed-price buffet.

Templo da Bahia Alameda Campinas 720, Jardim Paulista. Hugely popular Bahian restaurant with beautifully presented – and extremely tasty – dishes. If you're new to Bahian food, choose one of the many *moquecas* (stews) or try the Festival do Templo, a large platter of seafood and fish and tasty street food such as *acarajé* (fried bean cakes) and *bolinhos de bacalhau* (small cod pastries). Expect to pay around $25 for a meal for two people.

Tucupy Rua Bela Cintra 1551, Jardins. If you don't make it to the Amazon, this is your opportunity to try the food of the state of Pará. Distinctive fish and duck dishes. Helpful waiters take you through the unusual menu. Closed Mon.

Churrascarias

Baby Beef Rubaiyat Av Brigadeiro Faria Lima 2954, Itaim Bibi ☎11/3849-9488. Airy, modern surroundings and meat of the highest quality has helped to make this a firm favourite of the city's more upmarket *churrascarias*. The menu is bewildering, but if in doubt choose the house speciality – the exceptionally tender baby beef, sourced from the restaurant's own ranch.

Esplanada Grill Rua Haddock Lobo 1682, Jardins. An upmarket and expensive place, but still one of the best *churrascarias* in the city.

Grill da Villaa Rua Inácio Pereira da Rocha 422, Vila Madalena. Good meat and pleasant surroundings in this restaurant, in a neighbourhood that's fast becoming the city's most fashionable area for nightlife. Moderate. Closed Mon–Thurs lunch.

Italian

Famiglia Mancini, Rua Avanhandava 81, Centro. Great atmosphere, especially late at night when it's crowded with young people. There are often long queues for a table, though the food is rather mediocre apart from the fabulous cold buffet.

Fasano Rua Taiarana 78, Cerqueira César ☎11/3062-4000. Rated the best Italian restaurant in São Paulo, this elegant (and very expensive – expect to pay over $50 per person) restaurant is a place to go to for very special occasions. Renowned for its fine ingredients and unusual vinegar marinades, interesting pastas and simple but delicious vegetable and meat dishes.

Gero Rua Haddock Lobo 1629, Cerqueira César ☎11/3064-0005. With the same owners as *Fasano* (see above), this restaurant features a menu that is less extensive but still very good. Comparatively, the food is moderately priced (but still expect to pay at least $25 per person); the atmosphere is relaxed, the diners rather trendy.

Other European

Antiquarius Alameda Lorena 1884, Cerqueira César. Excellent – but wildly expensive – Portuguese food and wine, though uncomfortably formal, not to say vulgar. Closed Mon lunch & Sun evening.

Cecília Rua Tinhorão 122, Higienópolis. The restaurant serves authentic Polish-Jewish dishes and on weekends a Central European version of *feijoada* made with white beans, beef and potato. Tues–Fri & Sun lunch only, Sat lunch and dinner; closed Mon.

La Casserole Largo do Arouche 346, Centro. An old favourite for a romantic evening out, with ever-reliable – though fairly expensive – French food. Closed Sat lunch and Mon.

Presidente Rua Visconde de Parnaíba 2424, Brás. Very good food in an area which once had a large Portuguese community. Closes daily at 9.30pm and all day Sun; Sat lunch only.

Roanne Rua Henrique Martins 631, Jardim Paulista. *Nouvelle cuisine* of a high standard in this relaxed, yet sophisticated French restaurant. Closed Sat lunch and Sun.

Seafood

Amadeus Rua Haddock Lobo 807, Cerqueiro César ☎11/3061-2859. The best and probably the most expensive seafood in the city, known for the high quality of its supplies. The oysters are especially good, but prawns and fish dishes can all also be relied on. Expect to pay over $40 per person.

Crab Rua Wisard 193, Vila Madalena. As the name suggests, this restaurant's menu has a rather narrow focus. However, depending on availability, different types of crabs are served, all creatively prepared and presented. Open Tues–Fri dinner only, Sat lunch and dinner, Sun lunch only.

Mr Fish Grill Alameda Lorena 1430, Cerqueiro César. Simply prepared but extremely fresh fish served with a choice of sauces and accompaniments. Somewhat sterile atmosphere, but prices are reasonable – around $15 per person.

Bars, nightlife and entertainment

Whether you're after "high culture", live music, a disco or just a bar to hang out in, you won't have much of a problem in São Paulo. There are four main centres for nightlife in São Paulo: **Bixiga**, with good bars and live music; **Jardins**, with some good neighbourhood bars; **Itaim Bibi** and **Vila Olímpia**, best known for its flashy nightclubs; and **Vila Madalena** and adjoining **Pinheiros**, fast becoming known for its trendier, slightly "alternative" scene.

São Paulo has a large gay population but clubs and bars tend to be mixed rather than specifically gay, with the scene mainly in the Jardins area. The bars that you'll find scattered throughout the city depend largely upon the neighbourhoods that they're in for their character. Some of the liveliest, a few with live music, are found around Rua 13 de Maio in Bixiga, and in fashionable Vila Madalena and Pinheiros.

All of Jazz Rua João Cachoeira 1366, Vila Madalena. Nice, intimate place with excellent live jazz.

Barnaldo Lucrecia Rua Abilio Soares 207, Paraíso. An instantly recognizable yellow house, this place attracts a young crowd. Especially lively on Fridays, and live music most evenings.

Café do Bixiga Rua 13 de Maio 76, Bixiga. Excellent *chopp* and a carefully nurtured Bohemian atmosphere.

Fidalga Rua Fidalga 32, Jardins. Live jazz and Brazilian music during the week, and its own small bookstore.

Finnegan's Alameda Itú 1529, Jardins, and Rua Cristiano Viana 358, Pinheiros. Irish-theme bars, busy late into the evening, often with live blues and jazz. Hugely popular with English-speaking residents.

Quinta do Mandioca Rua Oscar Freire, Jardim Paulista. This rustic bar and café opens out somewhat incongruously onto one of São Paulo's most chic shopping streets. The menu features good snacks (including fired *mandioca*) and light meals.

Live music and dancing

São Paulo has quite an imaginative **jazz** tradition. The *Bourbon Street Music Club*, Rua dos Chanés 127, Moema, has a consistently good, though very expensive (entrance is $17), programme including visiting international artists and frequent festivals. In newly fashionable Vila Madalena, there are several jazz venues, probably the best being *Blen Blen Brasil*, Rua Inácio Pereira da Rocha 520. In Bixiga, the *Café Piu-Piu* (closed Mon), at Rua 13 de Maio 134, is a lively venue for some very good jazz and *choro*, as well as the most appalling rock and country-and-western music.

If it's more obviously **Brazilian music** that you're seeking, check the newspaper entertainment listings for touring artists or, if feeling slightly adventurous, you could go to a **gafieira**, a dancehall that's the meeting place of working-class and Bohemian chic. A *gafieira* that's always packed to the rafters with migrants from the Northeast dancing to *forró* is *Pedro Sertanejo*, Rua Catumbi 183, Brás (Sat 9pm–4am, Sun 8pm–midnight). Be warned that *gafieiras* tend to be out of the centre and can seem rather alien and disconcerting places if you've only just arrived in Brazil.

Cinema, theatre and classical music

Most cinemas are on Avenida Paulista, but there are also several downtown on Avenida São Luís. Keep a special eye out for what's on at CineSesc, Rua Augusta 2075 (Cerqueira César); Bixiga, Rua 13 de Maio (Bixiga); Espaço Unibanco de Cinema, Rua Augusta 1475 (Cerqueira César); and the Centro Cultural de São Paulo, Rua Vergueiro 1000, by the Vergueiro *Metrô* station – all of which are devoted to Brazilian and foreign art films.

São Paulo is Brazil's theatrical centre and boasts a busy season of classical and avant-garde productions; a visit to the **theatre** is worthwhile even without any knowledge of Portuguese. The Brasileiro de Comédia, Rua Major Diorgo 311, and the Teatro Sérgio Cardoso, Rua Rui Barbosa, both in Bixiga, have particularly good reputations.

The traditional focal point for São Paulo's vibrant **opera** and **classical music** season is the Teatro Municipal (☎11/222-8698; see also p.435), in Praça Ramos de Azevado in the city centre, where in the 1920s Villa-Lobos himself performed. The beautifully renovated Estação Júlio Prestes (☎11/3337-5414; see also p.435) in the *bairro* of Luz is the home of the world-class Orquestra Sinfônica de Estado de São Paulo and has a new 1500-seat concert hall.

Listings

Airlines Aerolíneas Argentinas ☎11/3214-4233 & 6445-3806; Air Canada ☎11/3259-9066; Air France ☎11/3049-0900 & 6445-2211; Alitalia ☎11/3218-7600 & 6445-2324; American Airlines ☎11/3214-4000 & 6445-3234; British Airways ☎11/3145-9700 & 6445-2021; Continental ☎0800/554-777; Delta ☎0800/221-121 and 11/6445-4153; GOL ☎0800/701-2131 and 11/4331-6885; Iberia ☎11/3218-7130 & 6445-2060; Japan Airlines (JAL) ☎11/3251-5222; KLM ☎11/3457-3230 & 6445-2887; Lan Chile ☎11/3259-2900 & 6445-3532; Lloyd Aéreo Boliviano ☎11/3258-8111 & 6445-2425; Lufthansa ☎11/3048-5800 & 6445-2220; Pluna ☎11/3231-2822 & 6445-2130; Qantas ☎11/3145-9700; SAS ☎11/3259-4300 & 6445-3934; South African Airways ☎11/3065-5115 & 6445-4151; Swiss Air ☎11/3251-4000 & 6445-2535; TAM ☎0800/123-100; TAP ☎11/3255-5366 & 6445-3215; United Airlines ☎0800/162-323; Varig ☎11/5091-7000; VASP ☎11/5532-3838.

Car rental Avis, Rua da Consolação 335, Centro ☎0800/118-066; Hertz, Rua da Consolação 439, Centro ☎0800/147-300; Localiza, Rua da Consolação 419, Centro ☎0800/312-121; Unidas, Rua da Consolação 347, Centro ☎0800/121-121.

Consulates Argentina, Av Paulista 1106, 9th floor Cerqueira César ☎11/3284-1355; Australia, Rua Tenente Negrão 140, 12th floor, Chácara Itaim ☎11/3829-6281; Bolivia, Rua da Consolação 37, 3rd floor, Centro ☎11/881-1688; Canada, Av Paulista 1106, 1st floor, Cerqueira César ☎11/3253-4944; Colombia, Rua Peixoto Gomide 996, 10th floor, Cerqueira César ☎11/3285-6350; Ireland, Av Paulista 2006, 5th floor, Cerqueira César ☎11/3287-6362; New Zealand, Al. Campinas, 15th floor, Cerqueira César ☎11/3148-0616; Paraguay, Rua Bandeira Paulista 600, 15th floor, Itaim Bibi ☎11/3020-1412; Peru, Rua Votuverava 350, Morumbi ☎11/3870-1793; South Africa, Av Paulista 1754, 12th floor, Cerqueira César, ☎11/3285-0433; UK, Rua Ferreira de Araújo 741, Pinheros ☎11/3094-2700; Uruguay, Al. Santos 905, 10th floor, Cerqueira César ☎11/3284-0998; US, Rua Padre João Manoel 933, Jardim Paulista ☎11/3081-6511; Venezuela, Rua Veneza 878, Jardim Europa ☎11/3087-2318.

Health matters The private Albert Einstein Clinic, Av Albert Einstein 627, Morumbi (☎11/3747-1233) is considered to be the best hospital in Brazil.

Police Emergencies ☎190. DEATUR, a special police unit for tourists (☎11/3214-0209), is at Av São Luís 91, one block from Praça da República. To extend your visa, visit the Polícia Federal, Av Prestes Maia 700, Centro (Mon–Fri 10am–4pm; ☎11/3223-7177 ext 231).

Shopping centres Ibirapuera Av Ibirapuera 3103, Moema (bus from *Metrô* Ana Rosa, or Praça da República); Iguatemi Av Brigadeiro Faria Lima 1191, Jardim Europa (bus from Av Ipiranga); and Patio Higienópolis Av Higienópolis 615 (bus from Praça da República or Av Paulista).

3.8

The South

The states forming the **South** of Brazil – **Paraná**, **Santa Catarina** and **Rio Grande do Sul** – are generally considered to be the most developed part of the country. The smallest of Brazil's regions, the South maintains an economic influence completely out of proportion to its size, largely the result of an agrarian structure that is primarily based on highly efficient small and medium-sized units, and an economically over-active population that produces a per capita output considerably higher than the national average. With little of the widespread poverty found elsewhere in the country, Brazilians tend to dismiss the South as being a region that has more in common with Europe or the United States than with South America.

For the tourist the region offers much that's attractive. The **coast** has a subtropical climate that in the summer months (November to March) attracts people who want to avoid the oppressive heat of northern resorts, and the vegetation and atmosphere feels more Mediterranean than Brazilian. Much of the Paranaense coast is still unspoilt by the ravages of mass tourism, and building development is virtually forbidden on the beautiful islands of the **Bay of Paranaguá**. By way of contrast, tourists have encroached along Santa Catarina's coast, but only a few places have been allowed to develop into a concrete jungle. Otherwise, resorts such as most of those on the **Ilha de Santa Catarina** around **Florianópolis** remain small and do not seriously detract from the region's natural beauty.

Despite the attractions of the coast, the spectacular **Iguaçu Falls** are the South's most visited attraction, the powerful waters set against a background of unspoiled rain forest. The rest of the **interior** is less frequently visited. Much of it is mountainous, the home of people whose way of life seems to have altered little since the arrival of the European pioneers last century. Cities in the interior that were founded by Germans, Italians and Ukrainians have lost much of their former ethnic character, but only short distances from them are villages and hamlets where time appears to have stood still. The highland areas and the grasslands of southern and western Rio Grande do Sul are largely given over to vast cattle ranches, where the modern gaúchos keep alive many of the skills of their forebears.

Paraná

PARANÁ is the northernmost of Brazil's southern states and one of the wealthiest in all Brazil. Its economy is based on small- and medium-sized land holdings, modern industries which, unlike those of neighbouring São Paulo, have been subject to at least limited planning controls, and a population comprised largely of the descendants of immigrants. Unless you're heading straight for the **Iguaçu** waterfalls, **Curitiba** makes a good base. Transport services fan out in all directions from the state capital and there's plenty to keep you occupied in the city between excursions. The **Bay of Paranaguá** can be visited as a day-trip from Curitiba, but the bay's islands, such as the **Ilha do Mel** and colonial towns could also easily take up a week or more of your time.

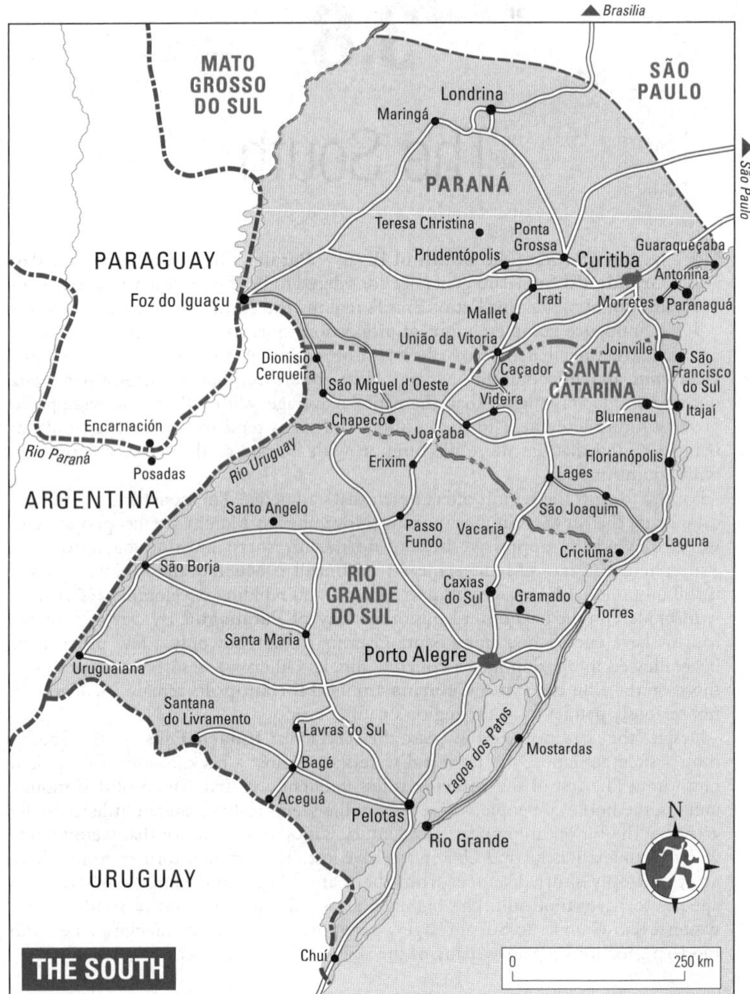

Curitiba

Founded in 1693 as a gold-mining camp, **CURITIBA** was of little importance until 1853 when it was made capital of Paraná. Since then, the city's population has steadily risen from a few thousand, reaching 140,000 in 1940 and some 1.5 million today, its inhabitants largely descendants of Polish, German, Italian and other immigrants. On average, *curitibanos* enjoy Brazil's highest standard of living: the city boasts health, education and public transport facilities that are the envy of other parts of the country. There are *favelas*, but they're well hidden and, because of the cool, damp winters, sturdier than those in cities to the north.

Arrival and information

Flights to most major Brazilian cities as well as to Argentina arrive and depart from the ultramodern **airport** (☎41/381-1515), about thirty minutes from the city centre. Taxis from the airport to the centre charge about $15, or take a bus marked "Aeroporto" (in the centre, they leave about every hour from outside the *Hotel Presidente* on Rua Westphalen by Praça Rui Barbosa).

The main bus (☎41/320-3000) and train (☎041/323-4008) stations – the **rodoferroviária** – are located adjacent to one another, about ten blocks from the city centre. There's a minibus from almost in front of the station – catch it at the intersection of Avenida Presidente Afonso Camargo and Avenida Sete de Setembro, to the left of the entrance to the station's drive.

The Secretaria Especial do Esporte e Turismo (SETUR), the state **tourist information** organization, has its headquarters near the Palácio Iguaçu at Rua Deputado Mário de Barros 1290, on the third floor of Edifício Caetano Munhoz da Rocha (Mon–Fri 9am–6pm). It keeps up-to-date information on changes to rail and boat schedules and provides useful maps of trails in state parks; many of the employees speak English. For information specifically on Curitiba, go to the well-organized tourist office on Rua da Glória 362 (Mon–Fri 8am–noon & 2–6pm).

City transport

Curitiba is small enough to be able to **walk** to most places within the city centre. **Taxis** are easy to come by and, as distances are generally small, they're not too expensive. If you have limited time in Curitiba, an excellent way to view the city's main attractions is to take a **bus tour**. Buses of the Linha Turismo depart from Praça Tiradentes every half-hour (Tues–Sun, first bus leaves 9am, last bus 5.30pm; $2.50) and stop at 22 attractions around the city centre and suburbs. The bus takes just over two hours to complete the itinerary, but tickets allow passengers to get off at three of the stops and rejoin the tour on a later bus.

Accommodation

If your sole reason for being in Curitiba is to catch the dawn train to the coast, there are numerous cheap **hotels** within a few minutes' walk of the rodoferroviária. Otherwise, places to stay in the city centre are within walking distance of most attractions and are generally excellent value. Curitiba's **youth hostel** is at Rua Padre Agostinho 645 (☎41/233-2746; $7 per person). It's friendly but is located twenty minutes' walk from the city centre in the up-scale residential suburb of Mercês, and on the opposite side of town from the rodoferroviária.

Bourbon Rua Cândido Lopes 102 ☎41/322-4001, ⓦwww.bourbon.com.br. Widely considered the best hotel in the city, with an atmosphere of traditional elegance combined with every modern facility, including a pool, business centre and very good restaurants. ❼

Elo Hotel Universidade Rua Amintas de Barros 383 ☎41/3028-9400, ⓦwww.hoteiselo.com.br. Modern, rather characterless hotel with a pool, situated next to the university's main administrative building. The rooms are clean and comfortable and the staff are very helpful. ❹

Ibis Curitiba Rua Mateus Leme 358 ☎41/324-0469, ⓦwww.ibis-brasil.com.br. The reception and restaurant is in an attractive, German-style early twentieth-century house, with the small but well-appointed guestrooms located in a modern tower behind. Superb value and central location near the historic centre and the Shopping Mueller. ❹

Jaraguá Av Presidente Afonso Camargo 279 ☎41/362-2022. Directly opposite the rodoferroviária, this has the best facilities of all hotels in the vicinity. The rooms are comfortable and clean, the service efficient. ❹

Nikko Rua Barão do Rio Branco 546 ☎41/322-1808, ⓦwww.hotelnikko.com.br. Modern hotel set behind a pretty nineteenth-century facade. The small rooms are simply and attractively furnished, with mineral water supplying the bath and shower, and there's a small Japanese-style garden, a tiny swimming pool and a sushi bar. ❺

The City

The **Rua das Flores** – a pedestrianized precinct section of the Rua XV de Novembro lined with graceful, well-maintained, pastel-coloured early twentieth-century buildings – is the centre's main late afternoon and early evening meeting point, its bars, tearooms and coffee shops crammed with customers. Few of the surrounding streets are especially attractive, but the former city hall, at Praça José Borges across from the flower market, is well worth a look. Built in 1916, the building is a magnificent Art Nouveau construction that until recently housed the Museu Paranaense, its collections now relocated to the historic quarter (see below) and the future use of the building still undecided. A couple of blocks north from Rua das Flores is Praça Tiradentes, where the **Catedral Metropolitana** is located. Inaugurated in 1893, it's a totally unremarkable neo-Gothic construction.

Near the cathedral, a pedestrian tunnel leads to Curitiba's **historic quarter**, an area of impeccably preserved eighteenth- and nineteenth-century buildings. While most would not be out of place in a small village in Portugal, some point more towards a central European heritage. Today the buildings all have state preservation orders on them and do duty as bars, restaurants, art and craft galleries and cultural centres.

Two of Curitiba's oldest churches physically dominate the historic quarter. Dating from 1737, with the bell tower added in the late nineteenth century, the **Igreja da Ordem Terceira de São Francisco das Chagas**, on Largo da Ordem, is the city's oldest surviving building and one of the best examples of Portuguese ecclesiastical architecture in southern Brazil. Plain outside, the church is also simple within, its only decoration being typically Portuguese blue and white tiling and late Baroque altars. The church contains the **Museu de Arte Sacra** (Tues–Fri 9am–noon & 1–6pm, Sat & Sun 9am–2pm; 50c), with relics gathered from Curitiba's churches. Opposite the church is the mid-eighteenth-century **Casa Romário Martins**, Curitiba's oldest surviving house, now the site of a cultural foundation and exhibition centre for Paranaense artists. A short distance uphill from here, on the same road, the church of **Nossa Senhora do Rosário** dates back to 1737, built by and for Curitiba's slave population. However, after falling into total disrepair, the church was completely reconstructed in the 1930s and remains colonial in style only.

Further up the hill, the newly installed Museu Paranaense on Praça João Cândido (Tues–Fri 9am–noon & 2–6pm, Sat & Sun 10am–4pm; $1) contains work by mainly Paranaense artists of the nineteenth and early twentieth centuries, who were important if only for documenting the local landscape of their time and a limited but attractive collection of artefacts charting the history of Paraná from pre-colonial times into the twentieth century.

Eating and drinking

Given Curitiba's prosperity and its inhabitants' diverse ethnic origins, it's not surprising that there's a huge range of **restaurants**. There are also numerous **cafés**, and a fair amount of evening **entertainment**, too, based around the usual bars, cinemas and theatres.

Restaurants

Durski Rua Jaime Reis 254. Curitiba's only Ukrainian restaurant, located in a renovated house the heart of the historic centre looking onto Largo da Ordem. The food (including Polish and Brazilian dishes) is attractively presented and very tasty. Closed Sun evening.

Estrela da Terra Rua Kellers 95 (corner with Praça Garibaldi). An excellent and moderately priced restaurant, providing Paranaense cooking at its most varied. For lunch there's an always tasty *por kilo* buffet, while in the evenings the menu include *barreado* and *charque* (dried salted beef), as well as dishes representing the Italian, Dutch and Polish immigrant traditions. Closed Sun evening.

Famiglia Caliceti (Bologna) Rua Carlos de Carvalho 1367. One of the few decent Italian restaurants close to the downtown area. The moderate-to-expensive food is quite good and served in pleasant surroundings. Closed Sun evening and all Tues.

No Kafé Fest Rua Duque de Caxias 4. Located along an alley next to the Igreja do Rosário in the historic centre, *No Kafé Fest* offers an excellent and reasonably priced *por kilo* buffet of hot and cold dishes at lunch. A German-style high tea is served in the afternoon in a very pleasant building shared with an art gallery.

Schwarzwald Rua Claudino dos Santos 63. Excellent German food served with cold beer – a popular evening student meeting point in the Largo da Ordem. Daily 5pm to late.

Listings

Airlines Aerolíneas Argentinas ☎41/232-9012; Gol ☎41/381-1744; Rio-Sul ☎41/381-1644; TAM ☎41/323-5201; Varig ☎41/381-1588; VASP ☎41/381-1727.

Banks and exchange Main offices of banks are concentrated at the Praça Osório end of Rua das Flores.

Car rental Avis ☎41/381-1381; Hertz ☎41/269-8000; Localiza ☎41/253-0330; Unidas ☎41/332-1080.

Consulates Argentina, Rua Benjamin Constant 67, 15th floor ☎41/222-9589; UK, Rua Presidente Faria 51, 2nd floor ☎41/322-1202.

Health matters In emergencies use the Pronto-Socorro Municipal hospital at Av São José 738 ☎41/262-1121. Otherwise, go to Nossa Senhora das Graças hospital at Rua Alcides Munhoz 433 ☎41/222-6422.

Post office The main office is at Rua XV de Novembro 700, by Praça Santos Andrade.

Shopping On Sundays (9am–2pm) the Feira de Artesanato takes over the Largo da Ordem and Praça Garibaldi, with stalls selling handicrafts produced in Curitiba and elsewhere Paraná – look out for Polish and Ukrainian items, including simple embroideries and intricately painted eggs. There's a surprisingly good selection of handicrafts, T-shirts and other souvenirs available at the airport.

Telephones The telephone office is next to the main post office on Praça Santos Andrade.

Paranaguá

Propelled into the position of Brazil's second most important port for exports within the last couple of decades, **PARANAGUÁ**, 96 kilometres from Curitiba, has now lost most of its former character. It was founded in 1585, and is one of Brazil's oldest cities, but only recently have measures been undertaken to preserve its colonial buildings. What is worth seeing is conveniently concentrated in quite a small area, allowing the possibility of spending a few interesting hours between boats, trains or buses.

Left out of the train station, it's three blocks or so to Rua XV de Novembro. Here, on the corner, is the **Teatro da Ordem**, housed in the very pretty former **Igreja São Francisco das Chagras**, a small and simple church built in 1741 and still containing its eighteenth-century Baroque altars. Along Rua XV de Novembro, the **Mercado Municipal do Café** is a turn-of-the-century building that used to serve as the city's coffee market. Today the Art Nouveau structure contains handicraft stalls and simple restaurants serving excellent and very cheap seafood.

Just beyond the market, Paranaguá's most imposing building, the fortress-like **Colégio dos Jesuítas**, the old Jesuit college, overlooks the waterfront. Construction of the college began in 1698, sixteen years after the Jesuits were invited by Paranaguá's citizens to establish a school for their sons. Because it lacked a royal permit, however, the authorities promptly halted work on the college until 1738, when one was at last granted and building recommenced. In 1755 the college finally opened, only to close four years later with the Jesuits' expulsion from Brazil. The building was then used as the headquarters of the local militia, then as a customs house, and today is home to the **Museu de Arqueologia e Etnología** (Tues–Sun noon–5pm; 80c). None of the museum's exhibits relates to the Jesuits, concentrating instead on prehistoric archeology, Indian culture and popular art.

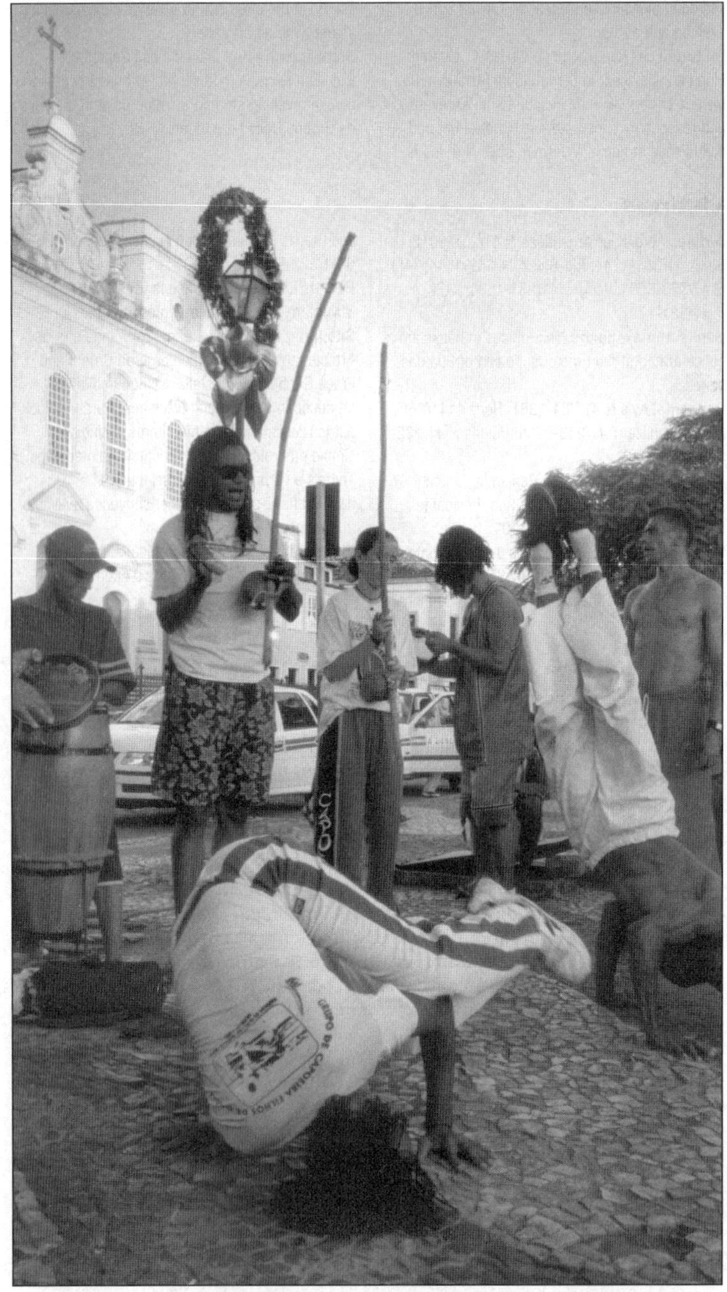

△ A capoiera display

Practicalities

The **train station,** three blocks from the waterfront on Avenida Arthur de Abreu, houses a very helpful **tourist office** (☎041/423-2155), which has useful maps of the city, hotel lists and boat, bus and train information. The **rodoviária** is located on the waterfront, a few hundred metres beyond the Jesuit college.

Paranaguá remains basically a place to pass through – it's worth getting details about leaving immediately you get here, and only later setting out to explore the city. If you find you have no alternative but to spend a night, there are several inexpensive and centrally located **hotels**, including the rudimentary *Pousada Itiberê*, just a few blocks back from the waterfront at Rua Princesa Isabel 24 (☎41/423-2485; ❷), and the more comfortable *Monte Líbano*, nearby at Rua Júlia da Costa 152 (☎041/422-2933; ❸). The best hotel in town is the *Camboa*, on Rua João Estevão (☎041/423-2121, Ⓦwww.hotelcamboa.com.br; ❻), which has large, well-equipped rooms and a pool. There are numerous **restaurants** specializing in seafood and *barreado*, the best of which is the *Casa do Barreado* at Rua Antonio da Cruz 9 (weekend lunches only), which offers an excellent buffet of regional dishes at a remarkably low price or, for lunch only, try the excellent and inexpensive seafood restaurants in the Mercado Municipal do Café.

The Ilha do Mel

The **ILHA DO MEL** is reached by hourly buses from Paranaguá to **Pontal do Sul**; the last stop is the beach, where small boats depart for the island. As there are no shops on the island, it is worth coming supplied with a flashlight and candles (electric current is available for only a few hours a day), mosquito coils, fruit and fruit juices. The **boat crossing** to Encantada (also referred to as Prainha) or Nova Brasília, the only villages on the island, takes between twenty and forty minutes, with boats departing hourly from 8am to 5pm ($2).

Livelier than Encantada, but lacking its intimate fishing-village atmosphere, **Nova Brasília** is where the bulk of the island's 1200 inhabitants are concentrated. Stretched between two gently curving, sheltered bays on a narrow strip of land linking the flat western section of the island to the rugged, smaller, eastern portion, this is the area of the island where most tourist facilities (such as they are) are located. Close to the jetty where the passenger boats land, there's a **campsite**, the ecological station, a police, medical and telephone post, and beyond this an immense beach along which are several pousadas, **restaurants** and **bars** which are crowded with young people in the evenings. These are not always immediately visible, as many are hidden along paths leading from the beach, up to a 45-minute walk from Nova Brasília's "centre". For a pleasant and undemanding stroll, wander along the beach towards the ruins of **Fortaleza**, the Portuguese fort (built in 1769 to guard the entrance of the Bay of Paranaguá), in the opposite direction from the clearly visible lighthouse. The most beautiful part of the island is the series of **beaches** along its mountainous southeast side, between Encantada's Praia de Fora and the lighthouse at Nova Brasília – an area of quiet coves, rocky promontories and small waterfalls. It takes about three hours to walk between the two settlements but the journey should only be undertaken at low tide. As the tide comes in, be extremely careful on the rocks: it's easy to slip or get pulled into the ocean by a wave. Let someone where you're staying know where you're going, and carry a bottle of water (there's a clean mountain stream about halfway for a refill) and enough money to be able to return by boat if need be.

If you plan to visit in the height of summer, it's best to arrive during the week and as early as possible in the morning as **accommodation** is scarce. The island is always filled to capacity over New Year and Carnaval when reservations are essential and are accepted only for minimum stays of four or five nights. There's only one genuine **hotel**, the *Park Hotel Ilha do Mel* (☎041/223-2585; ❹ including dinner), a 45-minute walk out towards Fortaleza – staff will meet you in Nova Brasília and carry your luggage. Following the trail leading from the jetty, one of the first **pousadas** is the justly popular *Pousadinha* (☎41/978-3662 or 455-2304; ❺). The young, multilingual employees are friendly, and rooms (with or without a bathroom) are simple but comfortable.

Foz do Iguaçu

The **Iguaçu Falls** are, unquestionably, one of the world's great natural phenomena. To describe their beauty and power is a tall order, but for starters cast out any ideas that Iguaçu is some kind of Niagara Falls transplanted south of the equator – compared with Iguaçu, with its total of 275 falls that cascade over a precipice 3km wide, Niagara is a ripple. But it's not the falls alone that make Iguaçu so special: the vast surrounding subtropical **nature reserve** – in Brazil the Parque Nacional do Iguaçu, in Argentina the much larger Parque Nacional Iguazú (see p.130) – is a timeless haunt that even the hordes of tourists fail to destroy.

Foz do Iguaçu

The Iguaçu Falls are a short distance from the towns of **Foz do Iguaçu** in Brazil, **Puerto Iguazú** (see p.133) in Argentina and **Ciudad del Este** (see p.832) in Paraguay – which makes the practical details of getting in and out that bit trickier. Foz do Iguaçu and Puerto Iguazú are both about 20km northwest of the entrances to the Brazilian Parque Nacional do Iguaçu and the Argentine Parque Nacional Iguazú, while Ciudad del Este is 7km northwest of Foz do Iguaçu. Most tourists choose to stay in Foz do Iguaçu, much the largest of the three towns, though many visitors prefer the relative tranquillity and frontier atmosphere of Puerto Iguazú.

The forest can only really be approached by tourists in the Argentine park, and a day is sufficient in the Brazilian park from where you best capture the general magnifance of the falls.

Arrival and information

The **airport** at **FOZ DO IGUAÇU** is served by flights from Curitiba, São Paulo, Rio de Janeiro, Brasília, Salvador and Belém. Regular buses (5am–midnight, Mon–Sat every 15min, Sun every 50min; 35c) head to the **local bus terminal** in the centre of town on Avenida Juscelino Kubitschek. If you want to go straight to Argentina, get off the bus at the *Hotel Bourbon* and then cross the road for a bus to Puerto Iguazú (80c). By taxi, the fixed fare into Foz is $8, or $15 to Puerto Iguazú (see p.133). Arriving by bus, Foz do Iguaçu's **rodoviária** (☎45/522-3633) is located on the northern outskirts of town and is served by buses from throughout southern Brazil, as well as Asunción and Buenos Aires. Buses #01, #02 and #03 link the rodoviária with the local bus terminal in town; taxis cost around $5.

There are **tourist offices** at the airport (daily 9am–11pm), at the rodoviária (daily 6am–6pm) and on the Brazilian side of the Ponte Tancredo Neves (daily 8am–6pm). In town, there are offices at the local bus terminal (daily 9am–6pm), on Rua Barão do Rio Branco (daily 7am–10pm) and at Rua Almirante Barroso 1300 (Mon–Fri 9am–5pm). For information by phone, call the Foz tourist office, Teletur on ☎0800/451-516.

Accommodation

Finding **somewhere to stay** in Foz do Iguaçu is usually easy, and as occupancy rates are generally low you are likely to be offered a knock-down rate, especially outside the peak tourist months of January, February and July and over Easter. Many of the **hotels**, including some of the best, lie some distance from town on the road leading to the falls, and most of the cheaper ones in town cater largely to shoppers bound for Paraguay. There's an excellent **campsite** run by the *Camping Club do Brazil* (☎45/529-6034 and 0800/22-7050) situated alongside the visitors' centre of Brazilian *parque nacional*; at $4 per person, facilities are very good (including a laundry area and a clean swimming pool), and the experience of sleeping surrounded by jungle is unforgettable.

Albergue da Juventude Paudimar Av das Cataratas km 12.5 ⓣ45/529-6061, ⓦwww.paudimar.com.br. An excellent international hostelling establishment with superb facilities. Cabins (each with a private bathroom) sleep five to eight people and there are family rooms with private facilities. The grounds are extensive and include a swimming pool. Dinner is served ($2) or you can use the kitchen. Located near the airport, it's very easy here to flag down a bus going to the Brazilian *parque nacional*, and arrangements can be made to be taken to the Argentine *parque nacional*. $7 per person.

Continental Inn Hotel Av Paraná 1089 ⓣ45/523-5000, ⓦwww.continentalinn.com.br. Excellent value for a centrally located and high-quality – if somewhat anonymous – hotel. The well-equipped rooms are spacious, breakfasts are ample, the staff are efficient and there's a good pool. ❻

Hotel Rafain Centro Rua Marechal Deodoro 984 ⓣ45/523-1213, ⓦwww.rafaincentro.com.br. The rooms are large here, with balconies, and the service friendly. Ask for a room overlooking the pool at the rear of the building. ❺

Pousada Evelina Navarrete Rua Kalichewski 171 ⓣ45/574-3817. An extremely friendly place with a youth hostel atmosphere that mainly attracts foreign backpackers. Rooms are simple but spotless, breakfasts are adequate, there's Internet access and multilingual Evelina goes out of her way to be helpful. Well located for buses to the falls. ❹

Pousada da Laura Rua Naipi 629 ⓣ45/574-3628. Laura is incredibly friendly and her small and simple bed-and-breakfast-style accommodation has become a favourite for backpackers. Although the house is in a very central, apparently pleasant residential neighbourhood, particular care should be taken as young men from the neighbouring *favela* have been known to be on the lookout for arriving and departing tourists to rob. $9 per person.

Tropical das Cataratas Eco Resort Parque Nacional do Iguaçu ⓣ45/521-7000 and 0800/701-2670, ⓦwww.tropicalhotel.com.br. The only hotel within the Brazilian national park, discreetly located just out of sight from the falls. The rooms are comfortable with colonial-style furnishings. Even if you can't afford to stay here, you can wander around the hotel's grounds or eat in the restaurant (see below). Reservations are usually required; do not expect discounted rates. ❾

The Falls

The **Iguaçu Falls** are formed by the Rio Iguaçu, which has its source near Curitiba. Starting at an altitude of 1300m, the river snakes westward, picking up tributaries and increasing in size and power during its 1200-kilometre journey. About 15km before joining the Rio Paraná, the Iguaçu broadens out, then plunges precipitously over an eighty-metre-high cliff, the central of the over 250 interlinking cataracts that extend nearly 3km across the river. There is no "best time" to visit since the falls are impressive and spectacularly beautiful whatever the season. That said, the rainy season is during the winter months of May to July, and at this time the volume of water is at its greatest. The one time to avoid at all costs is Easter, when the area attracts vast throngs of Argentine and Brazilian tourists.

Although many people arrive at Iguaçu in the morning and depart the same evening, the falls should really be viewed from both the Brazilian and the Argentine sides of the river: at least two days are needed to do them justice and you could easily spend longer. Crossing the **frontier** to see both sides is easy, and if you're of a nationality that normally requires a visa to visit either Argentina or Brazil you won't need one just for a day-trip. If, however, you're not returning to Foz do Iguaçu or Puerto Iguazú the same day, you'll have to go through normal **immigration** formalities on either side of the **Ponte Presidente Tancredo Neves**, the bridge that crosses the Rio Iguaçu between the two towns. There are good bus services between the two cities and onwards to the falls, but consider renting a car if your time is limited; see "Listings", below, for details.

If the Argentine side of the falls is more extensive, the finest overall view of the falls is obtained from the Brazilian side, best seen in the morning when the light is much better for photography. You'll only need about half a day here (longer if you're also visiting the Parque das Aves – see below), since, although the view is magnificent and it's from here that you get the clearest idea as to the size of the falls, the area from which to view them is fairly limited.

From the local bus terminal in central Foz do Iguaçu, there are **buses** every half-hour (daily 8am–7pm) to the "Parque Nacional", which cost around 80¢ and take about 45 minutes. Buses stop at the park entrance where, after paying the $2.50 entrance fee, you transfer directly onto another bus to take you to the falls or first visit the **Parque das Aves** (daily 8.30am–6.30pm; $8), just across the road. The bird park maintains both small breeding aviaries and enormous walk-through aviaries, still surrounded by dense forest. There's also a large walk-through butterfly cage – butterflies are bred throughout the year and released when mature. All the butterflies and eighty percent of the birds are Brazilian, most of them endemic to the Atlantic forests, the main exception being those in the Pantanal aviary. Buses stop on the road beneath the renowned hotel, the *Tropical das Cataratas* (see p.449), where you're only a couple of minutes' walk from the first views of the falls.

From the bus stop, there's a stairway that leads down to a 1.5-kilometre cliff-side **path** near the rim of the falls. From spots all along the path there are excellent views, at first across the lower river at a point where it has narrowed to channel width. At the bottom of the path, where the river widens again, there's a catwalk leading out towards the falls themselves. Depending on the force of the river, the spray can be quite heavy, so if you have a camera be sure to carry a plastic bag. From here, you can either walk back up the path or take the elevator to the top of the cliff and the road leading to the hotel.

Every fifteen minutes or so you'll hear the buzzing from a **helicopter** flying overhead. It takes off just outside the park's entrance, and offers eight-minute flights over the falls for $60, or a 35-minute flight over the falls and Itaipu for $150. In recent years the helicopter has been the cause of a minor rift between Brazil and Argentina: the Argentines refuse to allow it to fly over their side of the falls as they claim that it disturbs the wildlife. Whether this is in fact true is a matter of fierce debate, but certainly the view from above is spectacular and the ride exhilarating.

Eating and drinking

Foz do Iguaçu is certainly no gastronomic paradise, but it's possible to **eat** well without paying too much. On Rua Marechal Deodoro there are numerous buffet-style *por kilo* restaurants, and if you're really on a tight budget follow the Ciudad del Este-bound shoppers to dinner.

Bier Kastell Av Jorge Schimmelpfeng (corner with Rua Marechal Deodoro). A lively beer garden where you can enjoy ice-cold *chopp* and German-style sausage and other light meals.

Churrascaria Bianco Rua Quintino Bocaiúva 839. Excellent quality all-you-can-eat meals for $6 per person make this popular with visitors and locals alike.

Clube Maringá Porto Meira ⓣ45/527-3472; reservations advised on Sun. Justly popular amongst locals for its superb *rodízio de peixe* lunch and stunning views of the Iguaçu river. Apart from a selection of local freshwater fish, there's an excellent salad bar and you can pay a little extra for some of the freshest sashimi you're likely to come across. Expect to pay $8–10 per person. Take the "Porto Meira" bus and ask for directions, or a taxi ($3).

As Portugalios Av das Cataratas 569. Friendly and attractive place serving excellent Portuguese food at surprisingly reasonable prices. Evenings only.

Recanto Gaúcho Av Cataratas, km 15 – near the Brazilian park entrance ⓣ45/572-2358. A favourite Sunday outing for locals: the atmosphere's lively, the meat's excellent and cheap ($5 for all you can eat) and the owner (who dresses in full gaúcho regalia) is a real character. Turn up soon after 11am; food is served until 3pm. It's advisable to phone ahead. Closed Dec and Jan.

Trigo & Cia Rua Almirante Barroso 1750. Adjoining the *Hotel Internacional Foz*, this busy café serves tasty savoury snacks, good coffee and the best cakes in Foz.

Tropical das Cataratas Parque Nacional do Iguaçu. The only hotel restaurant worth trying. In peak season an excellent buffet lunch of typical Brazilian dishes is available for $10.

Listings

Airlines TAM ☎45/523-8500; Varig/Rio-Sul ☎45/529-6601; VASP ☎45/529-7161.
Banks and exchange Dollars (cash or travellers' cheques) can be easily changed in travel agents and banks along Avenida Brasil, which also have ATMs.
Car rental Avis ☎45/529-6160, Localiza ☎45/529-6300 and Yes ☎45/522-2956 are all represented at the airport and will deliver a car to your hotel. If you are just travelling between Foz do Iguaçu and Puerto Iguazú or the two national parks, no special car documentation is required to cross the Brazilian–Argentine border. If, however, you intend taking your rental car to the Paraguayan or Argentine Jesuit missions (see p.837 and p.128) or anywhere else south of Puerto Iguazú, you will need to request the correct papers (an extra $5 per day is charged), or you will be turned back by customs officers.
Consulates Argentina, Rua Dom Pedro II 28 ☎45/574-2969; Paraguay, Rua Bartolomeu de Gusmão 777 ☎45/523-2898.
Post office Praça Getúlio Vargas near Rua Barão do Rio Branco.
Travel and tour companies Martin Travel, Rua Jorge Sanways 835 ☎45/523-4959, is a reliable local travel agency that specializes in eco-tourism and puts together groups to go mountain biking through forest trails, and canoeing. Many travel agents organize day-trips to the Argentine Jesuit ruins of San Ignacio Miní (see p.129) for around $45 per person.

Santa Catarina

SANTA CATARINA shares a similar pattern of settlement with other parts of southern Brazil, the indigenous Indians rapidly being displaced by outsiders. In the eighteenth century the state received immigrants from the Azores who settled along the coast; cattle herders from Rio Grande do Sul spread into the higher reaches of the mountainous interior; and European immigrants and their descendants made new homes for themselves in the fertile river valleys. Even today, small communities on the **island of Santa Catarina**, and elsewhere on the coast, continue a way of life that has not changed markedly over the generations. Most people call the island of Santa Catarina **Florianópolis**, which is actually the name of the state capital – also situated on the island.

The island of Santa Catarina

The **island of SANTA CATARINA** is noted throughout Brazil for its Mediterranean-like scenery, attractive fishing villages and the city of **Florianópolis**, the state's small and prosperous capital. The island has a subtropical climate, rarely cold in winter and with a summer heat tempered by refreshing South Atlantic breezes; the vegetation is much softer than that further north. Joined to the mainland by two suspension bridges (the longest, British-designed, has been closed for several decades to all but cyclists and pedestrians), the island is served by frequent **bus** services connecting it with the rest of the state, other parts of Brazil, Buenos Aires, Ascunción and Santiago. During January and February the island is extremely popular with Argentine and Uruguayan tourists as the beaches here are far nicer than the ones at home.

Florianópolis

FLORIANÓPOLIS was founded in 1700 and settled fifty years later by immigrants from the Portuguese mid-Atlantic islands of the Azores. Since then, it's gradually developed from being a sleepy provincial backwater into a sleepy state capital. With the construction of the bridges linking the island with the mainland, Florianópolis as a port has all but died, and today it thrives as an administrative, commercial and tourist centre. Land reclamation for a multi-laned highway and new bus terminals has totally eliminated the character of the old seafront and, with it, vanished much of the city's former charm. Despite all the changes, though, the late nineteenth-century pastel-coloured, stuccoed buildings still recall faint "old world" images.

Arrival and information

Buses arrive at the modern **rodoviária** (☎48/224-2777) situated between the two bridges that link the island to the mainland. Outside the main entrance, beyond the car park and dual carriageway, stands one of the **municipal bus terminals** from where frequent buses (50¢) set out for most parts of the city as well as to all points in the south of the island. Otherwise, buses to the northern and eastern beach resorts depart from the corner of Rua José da Costa Moelmann and Avenida Mauro Ramos, a fifteen-minute walk around the hillside. These buses run to a surprisingly accurate timetable (check times at the information booths) and are cheap, though generally crowded. Alternatively, from both terminals there are faster, more comfortable and more expensive *executivo* minibuses ($1.50) to most of the beaches. The **airport** (☎48/331-4000) is 12km south of the city and is served by taxis ($12) and "Aeroporto" buses (50¢).

In Praça XV de Novembro, there's a **tourist information kiosk** (Dec–March Mon–Sat 7am–10pm, Sun 7am–7pm; April–Nov Mon–Sat 8am–6pm; ☎48/223-7796), where very good, free maps of the island and city are available. Listings of events in Florianópolis and elsewhere in Santa Catarina can be found in the daily newspaper *Diário Catarinense*.

Accommodation

Most tourists choose to stay at the beaches and resorts around the island (see below), but staying in Florianópolis itself has the benefit of a concentration of reasonably priced hotels, and direct bus services to all parts of the island. Try to arrive early in the day as **accommodation** is snapped up quickly during peak holiday periods; it's especially difficult to get a bed at the well-cared-for **youth hostel** at Rua Duarte Schutel 227 (☎048/225-3781, ⓦwww.albuerguedajuventurafpolis.com.br; open year-round; $12 per person).

Colonial Rua Conselheiro Mafra 399 ☎048/222-2302. Simple, good-sized rooms, often none too clean, but the staff are friendly. ❸

Felipe Rua João Pinto 26, at the intersection with Rua Antônio Luz ☎048/222-4122. The rooms here are clean and small, with ten percent discounts offered to Youth Hostel Association card-holders. ❸

Florianópolis Palace Rua Artista Bittencourt 2 ☎048/222-9633. The only luxury hotel in the city centre, with excellent facilities. The hotel has a minibus service to its private beach at Canasvieras. ❼

Valerim Center Rua Felipe Schmidt 554 ☎048/225-1100, ⓦwww.hotelvalerim.com.br. The largest of the budget hotels, the rooms (some of which sleep up to six people) are perfectly comfortable, all air conditioned with TV and minibar. ❹

The City

With the notable exception of *Carnaval*, few tourists visit the island for the limited charm and attractions of Florianópolis itself. However, being so centrally located, the city does make a good base for exploring the rest of the island, as most points are easily reached within an hour by bus. On the former waterfront, you'll find two ochre-coloured buildings: the **Mercado Público** (Mon–Fri 8am–9pm & Sat 8am–4pm), which contain some excellent bars and small restaurants, and the **Alfândega** (Mon–Fri 8am–7pm), a former customs house which has been converted for use as a crafts market.

From here, there's a steep walk up to the Praia de Fora, the "new town", centred on the main, tree-filled square, **Praça XV de Novembro**. On one side of the square is the **Palácio Cruz e Souza**, an imposing pink building built between 1770 and 1780 as the seat of provincial government. Now open to the public, it houses the **Museu Histórico de Santa Catarina** (Tues–Fri 10am–6pm, Sat–Sun 10am–4pm; free) whose nineteenth-century interior decoration is more engaging than the unexciting collection of guns, swords and official scrolls. Overlooking the square is the utterly unremarkable **Catedral Metropolitana**, originally constructed between 1753 and 1773, but enlarged and totally remodelled in 1922, so you'd be hard-pressed to identify any original features. The only church in the city centre dating back to the colonial era is the mid-eighteenth-century **Igreja de Nossa**

Senhora do Rosário, higher up from the cathedral and best approached by a flight of steep steps from Rua Marechal Guilherme.

Eating and drinking

On Rua Victor Meirellas behind the main post office, *Kaffa* offers huge portions of good and very reasonably priced Lebanese food. Good vegetarian meals are available at *Vida*, Rua Visconde de Ouro Preto 62 (Mon–Sat lunch only). There are several excellent bars and simple restaurants in the Mercado Público, serving cold beer, light meals and tasty snacks: *Box 32* (Mon–Fri 10am–10pm, Sat 10am–3pm) is especially good and is known as a meeting point for local politicians and artists, while *Pirão do Mercado* (Mon–Sat lunch only) specializes in local dishes of Azorean origin.

In the streets off the far end of Beira Mar Norte (take any bus which reads "via Beira Mar Norte"), *La Pergoletta* (open Tues–Sat evening and all Sun) at Travessa Carreirão 62 serves pretty good Italian food, while *Sushimasa* at Travessa Harmonia 2 (open Mon–Sat evenings) is a fine Japanese place. Also around here, the Beira Mar Norte Shopping Center (Mon–Sat 10am–10pm) features a dozen fast-food outlets including the usual hamburgers as well as seafood and a decent vegetarian restaurant. The best Japanese food on the island is at *Miyoshi* (Rodovia SC401, km 3.5), located yet further north, in the suburb of Saco Grande; a taxi there will cost around $7. The best times to go are Tuesday and Friday evenings when there's a very reasonably priced *por kilo* buffet that includes an excellent sushi and sashimi selection – other evenings the restaurant is much more expensive.

Listings

Airlines Aerolíneas Argentinas ⓣ48/224-7835; Gol ⓣ48/331-4127; Varig/RioSul/Pluna ⓣ048/331-4154; VASP ⓣ048/236-3033.
Banks and exchange Banks are located on Rua Felipe Schmidt and by Praça XV de Novembro.
Car rental Avis ⓣ48/236-1426, Hertz ⓣ48/236-9955, Localiza ⓣ48/236-1244, Unidas ⓣ48/236-0607 and YES ⓣ048/284-4656. During the peak summer season advance reservations are strongly recommended.
Consulates Argentina, Rua Saldanha Marinho 392, 5th floor ⓣ48/216-4903; Uruguay, Rua Tenente Silveira 94, 10th floor ⓣ48/216-8800.
Post office The main post office is on Praça XV de Novembro.

The rest of the island

Most people arriving in Florianópolis head straight for the beaches, undoubtedly the best of which are found on the **north** and **west** coasts. With 42 beaches around the island to choose from, even the most crowded are rarely unbearably so, and they're all suited to a few days' winding down. Despite the existence of a good **bus network**, this is one place where **renting a car** (see "Listings" above) should be seriously considered, especially if you have limited time and want to see as much of the island as possible: the roads are excellent, though extremely crowded in midsummer, and the drivers fairly civilized.

The island's built-up **north coast** offers safe swimming in calm, warm seas and, as such, is particularly popular with families. The long, gently curving bay of **Canasvieras** is the most crowded of the northern resorts, largely geared towards Argentine families who own or rent houses near the beach. By walking away from the concentration of bars at the centre of the beach, towards the east and Ponta das Canas, it's usually possible to find a relatively quiet spot. Unless you're renting a house for a week or more (agencies abound), finding **accommodation** is difficult, as the unappealing hotels are usually booked solid throughout the summer months. The local **restaurants** mostly offer the same menu of prawn dishes, pizza and hamburgers.

The **Lagoa da Conceição** is popular for swimming, canoeing and windsurfing. **Centro da Lagoa**, a bustling little town at the southern end of the lagoon, is both an attractive and convenient place to stay: there are good bus services from here into Florianópolis and to the east coast beaches, a post office, a branch of Banco do Brasil (with an ATM), grocery stores and numerous restaurants and bars on the main road. This is one of the most lively nightspots on the island during the summer and at weekends throughout the year, with restaurants always crowded and people overflowing into the street from the bars. The lagoon's beaches are close by; cross the small bridge on the road leaving Centro da Lagoa and it's a ten-minute walk. **Accommodation** is scarce, however: try the rather spartan *Pousada A'guia Pequena*, a couple of minutes' walk from the bridge that crosses the lagoon, at Rua Rita Lourenço da Silveira 114 (☎48/232-2339; ❺), or the very similar *Pousada do Grego* at Rua Antônio da Silveira 58 (☎048/232-0734; ❹). The largest place in Lagoa is the *Hotel Samuka*, Travessa Pedro Manuel Fernandes 96, at the intersection with Av Das Rendeiras (☎48/232-5024, ⓦwww.hotelsamuka.cjb.net; ❺) with a rather institutional feel but where the odd room may be available when other places are fully booked.

Of the east coast beaches, **PRAIA MOLE** (a few kilometers from Centro da Lagoa) is particularly beautiful, slightly hidden beyond sand dunes and beneath low-lying cliffs. Mole is extremely popular with young people but, rather surprisingly, commercial activity has remained low-key, probably because there's a deep drop-off right at the water's edge. Approached by a road passing between gigantic dunes, the next beach is at **JOAQUINA**, attracting serious surfers. The water's cold, however, and the sea rough, only really suitable for strong swimmers. If you have the energy, climb to the top of the dunes where you'll be rewarded with the most spectacular views in all directions.

The principal places of interest on the **west coast** are Santo Antônio **de Lisboa** to the north of Florianópolis, and **Ribeirão da Ilha** to the south. As the island's oldest and least spoilt settlements, the houses in these places are almost all painted white and have dark blue sash windows – in typical Azorean style – and both villages have a simple colonial church. Fishing, rather than catering to the needs of tourists, remains the principal activity of the three villages, and the waters offshore from Santo Antônio are used to farm mussels and oysters, considered the best anywhere in the island. Because the beaches are small and face the mainland, tourism has remained minimal, the few visitors who are about on day-trips, staying no longer than to sample some oysters at a local bar. **Accommodation** is limited, your best hope being in Santo Antônio: the *Pousada Caminho dos Açores* (☎48/235-1363; ❺) is set in a lovely garden where there's an attractive pool, or there's the *Pousada Mar de Dentro* (☎48/235-1521; ❻), very similar, with a tiny pool, but right on the beach. In the heart of Ribeirão da Ilha, try the simple *Pousada do Museu* (☎48/237-8148; ❹).

The north coast to São Francisco do Sul

If you're going to travel by bus on Santa Catarina's coastal highway (the BR-101) **north of Florianópolis** in the Brazilian summer you're best off keeping your eyes firmly closed. The bumper-to-bumper traffic moves at terrifying speeds, and the wrecked cars littering the highway are enough to make you get out and walk to your destination – something that, at times, might be faster anyway. But worse, if you don't have a car of your own, is that much of the BR-101 passes alongside absolutely stunning beaches, some of which have remained totally devoid of buildings and people. If you're on the bus, there's no hope of stopping for a refreshing dip, and you'll just have to make do with the idyllic images out of the window.

The Ilha de São Francisco

North of the town of Itajaí, some 90 kilometers from Florianópolis, the highway gradually turns inland towards Joinville, but 45km east of here is the **ILHA DE SÃO FRANCISCO**, a low-lying island separated from the mainland by a narrow strait which is spanned by a causeway. As Joinville's port and the site of a major Petrobras oil refinery, it might be reasonable to assume that São Francisco should be avoided, but this isn't the case. Both the port and refinery keep a discreet distance from the main town, **São Francisco do Sul**, and the beaches, and the surprisingly few sailors who are around blend perfectly with the slightly dilapidated colonial setting.

São Francisco do Sul

While the island was first visited by European sailors as early as 1504, it was not until the middle of the following century that the town of **SÃO FRANCISCO DO SUL** was established. One of the oldest settlements in the state, it is also one of the very few places in Santa Catarina where colonial and nineteenth-century buildings survive concentrated together. In the nineteenth century, with the opening of nearby areas to immigrants from Germany, the town grew in importance as a transhipment point for people and produce. Merchants established themselves in town, building grand houses and dockside warehouses, many of which remain today – protected from demolition and gradually undergoing restoration. Dominating the city's skyline is the **Igreja Matriz**, the main church, originally built in 1665 by Indian slaves, but completely reconstructed in 1884, losing all of its original features. The **Museu Nacional do Mar** on Rua Manoel Lourenço de Andrade (Tues–Fri 9am–6pm, Sat & Sun 11am–6pm; $1) has a collection relating to the technology of ocean travel and the people who make their living from the sea, with an emphasis on southern Brazil.

The prettiest beaches, **Paulos** and **Ingleses**, are also the nearest to town, just a couple of kilometres to the east. Both are small, and have trees to provide shade, and surprisingly few people take advantage of the protected sea, ideal for weak swimmers. On the east coast, **Praia de Ubatuba** and the adjoining **Praia de Enseada**, about 15km from town, offer enough surf for you to have fun but not enough to be dangerous. A ten-minute walk across the peninsula from the eastern end of Enseada leads to **Praia da Saúde** (or just Prainha), where the waves are suitable for only the most macho surfers.

Most of the island's visitors bypass the town altogether and head straight for the beaches to the east, so, even in midsummer, there's rarely any difficulty in finding a **hotel** with room. Quite comfortable, and with sea views, is the *Hotel Kontiki* (☎47/444-0232; ❸) at Rua Camacho 33, near the market or, if you want a pool, there's the relatively luxurious *Hotel Zibamba* (☎47/444-2020; ❺) at Rua Fernandes Dias 27. Eating out holds no great excitement, with the *Hotel Zibamba*'s restaurant the best of a generally poor bunch.

From the market in the town centre, there are **buses** to the rodoviária, beyond the town's limits, from where there are hourly connections to Joinville as well as daily services to São Paulo and Curitiba. **Buses** to Enseada and Ubatuba leave from the market in the town centre, with the last buses in both directions departing at about 9.30pm.

Rio Grande do Sul

For many people the state of **RIO GRANDE DO SUL**, bordering Argentina and Uruguay, is their first or last experience of Brazil. More than most parts of the country, it has an extremely strong regional identity. Central government's authority over Brazil's southernmost state has often been weak: in the colonial era, the territory was virtually a no-man's-land separating the Spanish and Portuguese empires. Out of this emerged a strongly independent people, mostly pioneer farmers and the descendants of European immigrants, isolated fishing communities and, best known, the gaúchos, the cowboys of southern South America whose name is now used for all inhabitants of the state, whatever their origins.

The **road and bus network** is excellent and it's easy to zip through the state without stopping if need be. However, Rio Grande do Sul is as Brazilian as Bahia or Rio and it would be foolish to ignore the place. The capital, **Porto Alegre**, is southern Brazil's most important cultural and commercial centre but, like all the other cities in Rio Grande do Sul, has little to detain tourists. However, it's also the state's transportation axis and at some point you're likely to pass through the city. For a truer flavour of Rio Grande do Sul, visit the **Serra Gaúcha**, a range a couple of hours north of Porto Alegre that is populated with the descendants of German and Italian immigrants and which offers several national parks. And for the classic image, head for the cattle country of *campanha* where old **gaúcho traditions** still linger.

Porto Alegre

The capital of Rio Grande do Sul, **PORTO ALEGRE**, lies on the eastern bank of the Rio Guaiba, at the point where five rivers converge to form the **Lagoa dos Patos**, a giant freshwater lagoon navigable by even the largest of ships. Founded in 1755 as a Portuguese garrison, to guard against Spanish encroachment into this part of the empire, it wasn't until Porto Alegre became the port for the export of beef that it developed into Brazil's leading commercial centre south of São Paulo.

The city has considerable life, if not much visible history, and you'll find many ways to occupy yourself, particularly if your visit coincides with one of the main festivals: *Semana Farroupilha* (Sept 13–20) features traditional local folk dancing and singing, while the highlight of *Festa de Nossa Senhora dos Navegantes* (Feb 2) is a procession of fishing boats.

Arrival and information

There's hardly an airport in southern Brazil that doesn't serve Porto Alegre, and there are international services to Buenos Aires, Montevideo and Santiago, too. The **airport** (☎51/3358-2000) is linked by *Metrô* to the Mercado Público, in the city centre, or take the L.05 bus, which links the airport with Praça Parobe (next to the Mercado Público). Taxis into the city cost about $8.

Buses from throughout Brazil and neighbouring countries stop at Porto Alegre's **rodoviária** (☎51/3210-0101), which is within walking distance of the centre; however, because the rodoviária is virtually ringed by a mesh of highways and overpasses, it's far less confusing, and safer, to use the *Metrô* from here

The **Metrô** (Mon–Fri 6am–11pm, Sat & Sun 5am–10pm; 50¢) has its city centre terminal at the Mercado Público, but as the system is very limited in extent it's only really of use when you arrive and leave Porto Alegre.

The city's **tourist office** (☎0800/51-7686), which hands out excellent free maps of Porto Alegre, has very helpful branches at the airport (7am–midnight), at the rodoviária (7am–10pm), the Usina do Gasômetro (Tues–Sun 10am–6pm) and at the Mercado Público (Mon–Sat 9am–6pm). For up-to-date **listings**, consult the monthly *Programa*, or the events listings in the newspaper *Zero Hora*.

Accommodation

Most **hotels** are scattered around the city centre, but distances are small and it's possible to walk to most places, although great care should be taken at night when the area is usually eerily quiet.

Lancaster Travessa Acelino de Carvalho 67 ☎51/3224-4630, ⓦwww.hotel-lancaster-poa.com.br). Located in one of the livliest commercial areas of downtown Porto Alegre, this modern hotel is set behind an imposing 1940s façade. The rooms are small but well equipped, and offer excellent value for money. ❹

Palácio Rua Vigário José Inácio 644 (☎51/3225-3467). One of the city's oldest hotels and which is friendly, secure and popular with budget travellers. Situated on a busy lane in the commercial district, the small rooms (sleeping 2–4 people, with and without bathrooms) are somewhat noisy. ❹

Plaza São Rafael Av Alberto Bins 514 ☎51/3221-5767, ⓦwww.plazahoteis.com.br. All the features you'd expect in the city's best downtown hotel, including an efficient business centre. Rates are usually heavily discounted, especially at weekends, and include an evening meal in the hotel's reasonable, though hardly exciting, restaurant. Ask for a room overlooking the river. ❼

Praça da Matriz Largo João Amorim do Albuquerque ☎51/3225-5772. Located in an early nineteenth-century house on a large tree-lined square near the cathedral and a few blocks back from the main commercial district, this hotel has clearly seen better days. However, the ornate building retains its original grace and there's an attractive

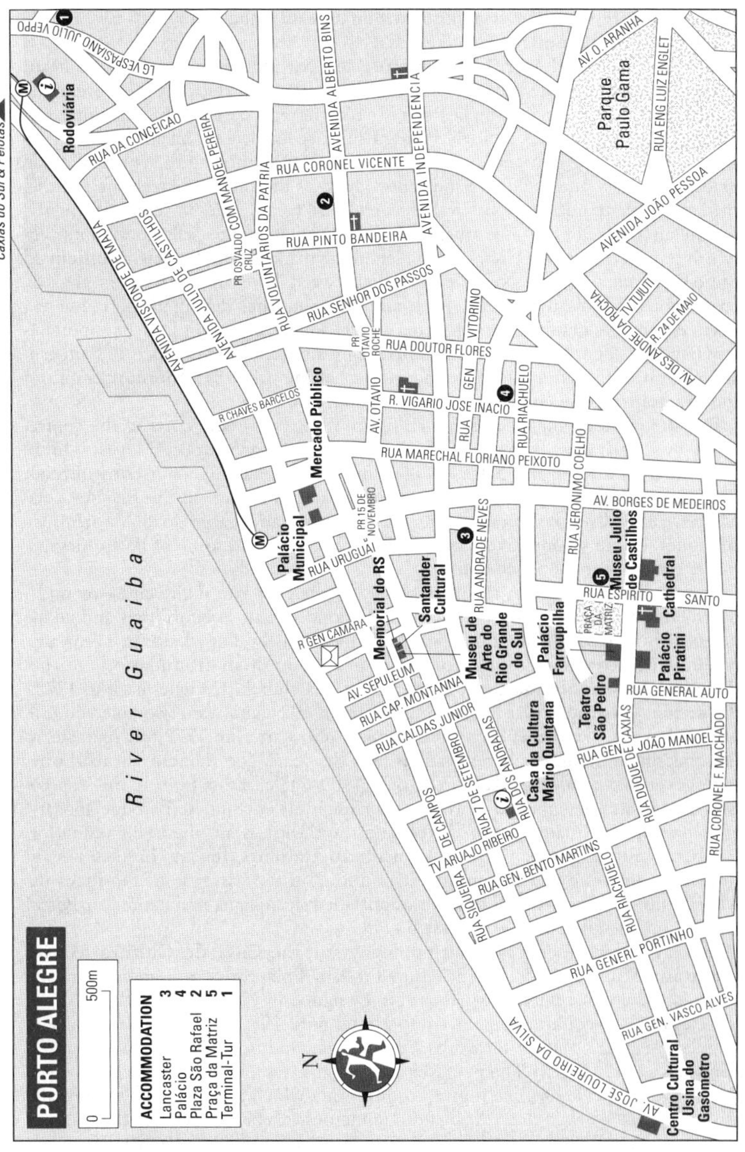

courtyard. The basic rooms are very simple, with the "luxo" being a bit larger, having a more pleasant aspect as well as a telephone and minibar. ❹

Terminal-Tur Largo Vespasiano Júlio Veppo 125 ⓣ51/3227-1656. Small rooms but with air conditioning, very important for a Porto Alegre summer. This is the cheapest secure hotel near the rodoviária. ❹

The City

Porto Alegre sprawls out over a series of hills with the centre spread between two levels, the older residential area on the higher level and the commercial area below.

In the city centre itself, everything is within an easy walk, and a half-day or so is enough to visit most places of interest.

The ochre-coloured **Mercado Público** (Mon–Sat 9am–5pm) stands at the heart of the lower town, located alongside Praça Rui Barbosa and Praça XV de Novembro. Dating back to 1869 and a replica of Lisbon's Mercado da Figueira, this imposing building, with its intricate, typically Portuguese, stuccoed detail, contains an absorbing mix of stalls selling household goods, food, a vast variety of herbs, *erva maté* of all grades of quality and regional handicrafts. Much of the maze of streets around the market is pedestrianized; the bar and restaurant on Praça XV de Novembro, formerly the meeting place of the city's artists and intellectuals, is an especially good spot from which to watch everyone pass by. To the left of the market is the **Palácio Municipal**, the old *prefeitura*, built in Neoclassical style between 1898 and 1901, its impressive proportions an indication of civic pride and self-confidence during the period when Porto Alegre was developing from being a mere southern outpost into an important city. Between about 1880 and 1930, Porto Alegre attracted large numbers of southern and eastern European immigrants, and in front of the palace is a **fountain**, a gift to the city from its once considerable Spanish community.

The streets along the steep slope rising from the low-lying parts of the centre (Rua dos Andradas, Rua General Vitorino and Rua Andrade Neves, which becomes Avenida Senador Salgado Filho) mark Porto Alegre's main **commercial district** of clothing stores, travel agents and banks. Further up the hill Praça da Matriz (officially called Praça Marechal Deodoro) and Largo João Amorim do Albuquerque are where the former legislative assembly and some of Porto Alegre's oldest buildings are concentrated.

Despite the buildings in this part of the city having late eighteenth- to mid-nineteenth-century origins, they have undergone so many renovations and additions over the past couple of centuries that only vaguely, if at all, do they bear any resemblance to their colonial predecessors. Though the foundations of the **Catedral Metropolitana** are built over those of a church that dates back to 1772, the present Italianate structure was only begun in 1921, and wasn't completed until 1986. Work on the former legislative assembly also started in 1772 but, likewise, it has undergone innumerable renovations over the years. The **Palácio Piratini** (the state governor's residence) dates from only 1909 while, across from it, the **Teatro São Pedro** was inaugurated in 1858. Surprisingly, its Portuguese Baroque appearance has remained largely unmolested, and the theatre is an important venue for local and visiting companies. The **Consulado Italiano** (Italian consulate) is an impressive mansion and its prominent position, on the east side of the Praça da Matriz (no. 134), is a symbol of the important role Italians maintained in Porto Alegre and elsewhere in Rio Grande do Sul.

Porto Alegre's museum's are disappointing, but the **Casa de Cultura Mário Quintana**, Rua dos Andradas 736 (Tues–Fri 9am–9pm, Sat & Sun noon–9pm), an important cultural centre, is worth a visit. Designed in Neoclassical style in 1923, the elegant rose-coloured building was a hotel until 1980 and as such was once a popular meeting point for local artists, intellectuals and politicians, including presidents Vargas and Goulart. The poet Mário Quintana was a long-time resident, hence the name, and pride of place is given to his room, which is maintained in the state as it was while he lived there. Apart from numerous exhibition galleries, the Casa de Cultura houses a library, a bookshop, a cinema, a decent restaurant and a café.

Eating and drinking

As you'd expect, meat dominates menus here and *churrascarias* abound. However, the city centre has only a limited selection of **restaurants** of any sort, with the best located in the suburbs – which, fortunately, are rarely more than a $5 taxi-fare away. Although during the daytime you can walk around most places in the city with reasonable safety, take care after dark, as Porto Alegre is developing a reputation for street crime to rival the worst of Brazilian cities.

Al Al Dente Rua Mata Bacelar 210. There are several very good Italian restaurants in the suburb of Auxiliadora, 3km northeast of the centre, and this is one of the best. Fairly expensive northern Italian food served in attractive surroundings. Reservations advised at weekends. Evenings only, closed Sun.
Bistô do Museu Praça da Alfândega. In the Museu de Arte do Rio Grande do Sul and with tables on the *praça* itself, this is one of the few restaurants in the area. Food is simple – pastas, steak, and salads – but pretty good. Open Tues–Sun 11am–10pm.
Café do Porto Rua Padre Chagas 293. Excellent light meals, sandwiches, wine and cakes are served in this pleasant Moinhos do Vento café in an area where there are plenty of similar places to choose from.
Galpão Crioulo Parque da Harmonia. An excellent and very reasonably priced city-centre *churrascaria* offering a bewildering selection of meats in its *rodízio*, along with a good range of salad and vegetable selections. In the evenings there's gaúcho music and dance performances.
I Puritani Rua Hilário Ribeiro 208. A rather plush bistro in Moinhos de Vento serving a mix of French-, Italian- and Brazilian-influenced dishes such as artichoke rissoto, wild boar in an apricot sauce and passion fruit mousse served with a *jabuticaba coulis*.
Koh Pee Pee Rua Schiller 83. A brave – and rather successful – attempt to introduce Thai food to Porto Alegre. A good assortment of dishes, pleasant surroundings and reasonable prices. Mon–Sat evenings only.
Via Fettuccine Largo Visconde de Cairú 17, 7th floor. An excellent-value buffet of hot and cold Brazilian and international dishes helps to draw business diners to this anonymous downtown office block. But what's really special is the stunning view out towards the lake and beyond. Mon–Fri lunch only.

Nightlife and entertainment

Bars, some with live music and most with a predominantly young and trendy clientele with Bohemian pretensions, are spread out along, and just off, Avenida Osvaldo Aranha, alongside the Parque Farroupilha and near the Federal University. Favourites change constantly, but the *Ocidente*, on Avenida Osvaldo Aranha itself, can be relied on for being lively and for dancing. Be warned, though, that things don't get going until around 11pm. Another popular area for bars is the upscale residential suburb of Moinhos do Vento, especially places along Rua Padre Chagas and Rua Fernando Gomes, near the Moinhos do Vento Shopping.

Porto Alegre boasts a good popular **music scene** and a considerable **theatrical** tradition. Foreign performers of all kinds usually include Porto Alegre on any Brazilian or wider South American tour. The *Sala Jazz Tom Jobim* at Rua Santo Antônio 421 (☎51/225-1229) features the city's best **jazz**, or there are live afternoon jazz sessions at the *Café Concerto* within the Casa de Cultura (see opposite), which also has a good art-house **cinema**. There are three more screens at the Espaço Unibanco, Rua dos Andradas 736 (☎51/221-7147), another art-house cinema. Finally, the Centro Cultural Usina do Gasômetro, a converted 1920s power station on the banks of the river just west of the centre, is well worth a visit; there's always something going on in its cinema, theatre and galleries, and it also has a café and a good bookshop.

Listings

Airlines Aerolíneas Argentinas ☎51/3221-3300; Gol ☎51/3358-2028; TAP ☎51/3226-1211; Varig and Rio-Sul ☎51/3358-2595; VASP ☎51/3358-2233.
Banks and exchange There are banks and *casas de câmbio* (Mon–Fri 10am–4.30pm) along Rua dos Andradas and Avenida Senador Salgado Filho near Praça da Alfândega and ATMs everywhere. The *casa de câmbio* at the rodoviária changes travellers' cheques and dollar cash.
Boats Two-hour excursions on the Rio Guaiba leave from the tour-boat berth (Doca Turística) on Avenida Mauá, near the train station. Schedules vary, so check with the tourist office. There are also boat excursions from the Centro Cultural Usina do Gasômetro (see above).
Car rental Avis ☎51/3358-2354; Hertz ☎51/3337-7755; Localiza ☎51/3358-2045; Unidas ☎51/3358-2375.
Consulates Argentina, Rua Coronel Bordini 1033 ☎51/3321-1360; South Africa, Rua Bororó 496 ☎51/3249-2497; Uruguay, Av Cristóvão Colombo 2999 ☎51/3325-6200; UK, Rua Itapeva 110 ☎51/3341-0720; USA, Rua Riachuelo 1257 ☎51/3226-3344.
Health matters Pronto-Socorro Municipal hospital is on Av Osvaldo Aranha at the intersection with Venâncio Aires ☎51/231-5900.
Post offices At Rua Siqueira Campos 1100, Rua Sete de Setembro 1020 and Rua General Camara, near the waterfront Avenida Mauá.

The Serra Gaúcha

North of Porto Alegre is the **SERRA GAÚCHA**, a range of hills and mountains populated mainly by the descendants of German and Italian immigrants. To the **east** are the high-altitude resort towns of **Gramado** and Canela, where unspoilt landscapes, mountain trails, refreshing temperatures, the *cafe colonial* – a vast selection of cakes, jams, cheeses, meats, wine and other drinks produced by the region's *colonos* – and luxurious hotels attract visitors from cities throughout Brazil. Canela is a good base for visting the **Parque Estadual do Caracol** as well as the **Parque Nacional dos Aparados da Serra**, two of the highlights of the Serra Gaúcha.

Gramado

One hundred and thirty kilometres north of Porto Alegre, **GRAMADO** is Brazil's best-known mountain resort. At 825m you're unlikely to suffer from altitude sickness, but Gramado is high enough to be refreshingly cool in summer and positively chilly in winter. Architectually, Gramado tries hard to appear Swiss, with "alpine" chalets and flower-filled window boxes the norm. It's a mere affectation, though, since hardly any of the inhabitants are of Swiss origin – and only a small minority are of German extraction. The most pleasant time to visit the area is during the spring (Oct and Nov) when the parks, gardens and roadsides are full of flowers, but the hydrangeas remain in bloom well into January.

For most visitors, drawn from throughout Brazil, Gramado's attractions lie mainly within the town itself: some excellent hotels, pretty good restaurants and shopping. There really isn't much to do in town, but a stroll around the large and very pretty flower-filled **Parque Knorr** (daily 9am–6pm) and the secluded Lago Negro, which is surrounded by attractive woodland, help to fill the hours between meals.

The surrounding region is magnificent, and the **Vale do Quilombo**, settled in the nineteenth century by German and Italian farmers, is especially beautiful. Although just six kilometers from town, it's a difficult trek and you'll need a good map to identify the incredibly steep unpaved approach road, Linha 28. Due to the incline, much of the original forest cover has survived intact and can be best appreciated at the Sítio da Família Sperry where you'll be guided ($6) along forest trails, past waterfalls, by the English-speaking owner who's incredibly knowledgeable on the subject of the local flora. A neighbouring family-owned cantina, the *Quinta dos Conte*, can also be visited. Arrangements to visit both should be made in advance and together – call ⓣ54/504-1649. Tours are available to both places; as the backroads are unpaved and treacherous following heavy rain, the Casa da Montanha Adventures (ⓣ54/286-2544, ⓦwww.hotelcasadamontanha.com.br), which uses Land Rovers, is recommended.

Practicalities

Gramado can easily be reached by bus from Porto Alegre. The **rodoviária** (ⓣ54/286-1302) is on the main street, Avenida Borges de Medeiros, a couple of minutes' walk from the town centre. The **tourist office** (Mon–Thurs 9am–6pm and Fri–Sun 9am–8pm) at no. 1674 of the avenue, is extremely well organized and provides reasonable maps and comprehensive lists of local hotels and restaurants.

Most **hotels** offer steep discounts outside the peak summer and winter months, especially during the week, though accommodation is hard to during the Festival de Cinema. There's an excellent new **youth hostel** (ⓣ54/295-1020) 1.5km from the centre at no. 3880 of Avenida das Hortências, towards Canela; most beds in small dorms ($8 per person) but there are also some double rooms (❹). The lowest-priced hotel in the centre is the *Dinda*, Rua Augusto Zatti 160, at the corner with Av Borges de Medeiros (ⓣ054/286-2810; ❸), with simple but homely rooms. There's no lack of more expensive places to stay: the *Estalagem St Hubertus*, at Rua da Carriere 974, overlooking Lago Negro (ⓣ54/286-1273, ⓦwww.sthubertus.com; ❻), offers pleasingly luxurious rooms, attractive grounds and a heated pool.

Gramado some reasonably good **restaurants**. The *Tarantino Ristorante*, at Av das

Hortênsias 1522 by Praça Major Nicoleti, serves fairly authentic and very reasonably priced northern Italian dishes, but the most interesting restaurant is *La Caceria* (evenings only, closed Mon–Weds) in the *Hotel Casa da Montanha*, Av Borges de Medeiros 3166. Game dishes are the specialities at this rather expensive restaurant, and unusual tropical fruits sauces go well with the often strong-tasting meat.

Parque Nacional dos Aparados da Serra

The dominant physical feature of south central Brazil is a **highland plateau**, the result of layer upon layer of ocean sediment piling up and the consequent rock formations being lifted to form the Brazilian Shield. Around 150 million years ago, lava slowly poured onto the surface of the shield, developing into a thick layer of basalt rock. At the edge of the plateau, cracks puncture the basalt and it is around the largest of these that the **Parque Nacional dos Aparados da Serra** (Wed–Sun 9am–5pm; $2), 100km east of Canela, was created.

Approaching the park from any direction, you pass through rugged cattle pasture, occasionally interrupted by the distinctive umbrella-like Paraná pine trees and solitary farm buildings. As the dirt road enters the park itself, forest patches appear, suddenly and dramatically interrupted by a canyon of breathtaking proportions, **Itaimbezinho**. Some 5800m in length, between 600 and 2000m wide and 720m deep, Itaimbezinho is a dizzying sight. The canyon and the area immediately surrounding it have two distinct climates and support very different types of vegetation. On the higher levels, with relatively little rainfall, but with fog banks moving in from the nearby Atlantic Ocean, vegetation is typical of a cloudforest, while on the canyon's floor a mass of subtropical plants flourishes. The park has abundant birdlife and is home to over 150 different species.

In the park, there's a **visitors' centre** (☎54/251-1262) and a **snack bar**. From here, you can hire a guide to lead you down the steep trail (including a five-metre vertical incline, which you have to negotiate by rope) to the canyon floor. You'll need to be physically fit, have good hiking boots and be prepared for flash floods. Most visitors, however, follow the well-marked paths keeping to the top of Itaimbezinho, enjoying views either into the canyon (a two-and-a-half-hour walk from the visitors' centre) or out, towards the sea (a 45min walk).

Visiting the park

The Parque Nacional dos Aparados da Serra can be visited throughout the year, but spring (Oct and Nov) is the best time for flowers. In the winter, June through August, it can get very cold, though visibility tends to be clearest. Summers are warm, but heavy rainfall sometimes makes the roads and trails impassable and fog and low-level cloud often completely obscure what should be spectacular views. Avoid April, May and September, the months with the most sustained rain. Without your own transport, or if you're not travelling as part of an organized tour, the park is difficult to reach. As only 1000 visitors are permitted to enter the park each day, it's advisable to phone the visitors' centre in advance to reserve a place.

To get to the park, take a bus from Porto Alegre, Gramado or Canela to **São Francisco de Paula**, 69km from the park's entrance. From São Francisco, you need to take another bus northeast to **Cambará do Sul** and ask to be let off at the entrance to the park. From here it's a further 15km to Itaimbezinho. Buses occasionally run between São Francisco or Cambará and Praia Grande (which has a couple of basic hotels, one on the main square and the other at the rodoviária), on the Santa Catarina side of the state line. These will drop you just 3km from Itaimbezinho. In São Francisco, you may be able to join a tour group headed for the park. Coming from Cambará, the park entrance is only 3km away and you should be able to get a taxi to take you. Visiting the park as a day-trip from Canela or Gramado is also perfectly feasible: Casa da Montanha Adventures (see p.460) escorts individuals or groups for around $35 per person including an excellent lunch.

Gaúcho country: Lavras do Sul

If you want to witness the everyday working life of the pampas close up, **LAVRAS DO SUL** is the place to head for. Located some 300km southwest of Porto Alegre, there's nothing to mark out the town from countless others in the region, dedicated to raising cattle, horses and sheep. What makes Lavras different is the local **fazenda** owners who have started taking guests, turning part of either the main house or their outhouses into pousadas. On arrival at a *fazenda*, you first have to show whether you can handle a horse. If you can't, you're quickly coached to develop some basic equestrian skills. Guests then join the *fazenda*'s workers in their day-to-day duties minding the livestock around the property. There are natural pools and streams for cooling off in on hot summer days, while the extremely comfortable *fazenda* buildings all have open fires for the often bitterly cold winter evenings.

Three *fazendas* (all ❻ full board) in Lavras do Sul accept guests: *Fazenda do Sobrado* (☎51/282-1239), *Fazenda Quero-Quero* (☎51/282-1223) and *Fazenda São Crispin* (☎51/282-1207). **Reservations** are essential as the *fazendas* only have room for between six and eight guests each and will need some notice if you need collecting from the rodoviária in town. The *fazendas* are very similar in style and operation, but *Sobrado* is particularly attractive, the house being one of the oldest of its kind in the region, dating back to the mid-nineteenth century.

Crossing into Uruguay at Chuí

Unless you're shopping for cheap Scotch whisky or visiting the casino, there's absolutely nothing in **CHUÍ** (or "Chuy" on the Uruguayan side of the frontier, see p.992), 527 kilometres from Porto Alegre, to stick around for. **Buses** entering and leaving Brazil stop at an immigration office a short distance from town for passports to be stamped. The Brazilian **rodoviária** ((☎053/265-1498; frequent services from Pelotas, Rio Grande and Porto Alegre), on Rua Venezuela, is just a couple of blocks from Avenida Brasil, which divides the Brazilian and Uruguayan sides of town; you can cross back and forth quite freely. Onda, one of Uruguay's main bus companies, stops on the Uruguayan side of Avenida Brasil and has frequent departures for Punta del Este and Montevideo. If you are travelling to or from western Uruguay and Treinta y Tres, you will have to walk 3km down Calle General Artigas (follow the signs to Montevideo) to the Uruguayan immigration post for an entry or exit stamp in your passport.

Change money at a Uruguayan *casa de câmbio* as you will receive the equivalent of the best rates available in Brazilian cities, though you'll find ATMs in Chuí. If you can, try to avoid **staying** in Chuí as hotels are overpriced and unpleasant; as a rule, those on the Brazilian side of the common avenue are cheaper, those on the Uruguayan side cleaner and more comfortable. **Restaurants** – even the most simple – are better on the Uruguayan side of the avenue.

The border towns

Apart from Chuí (see box on p.461), the most commonly used **border crossing** into Uruguay is at **Santana do Livramento**. Most buses cross into Argentina via **Uruguaiana**, and rarely do people remain in the border towns longer than it takes to go through immigration formalities, but, if you're trying to get a taste of gaúcho life, check to see if there's a *rodeio* about to be held somewhere around. Alternatively, use a smaller border crossing point, like **Aceguá**, near **Bagé**, where at least your first impressions of Uruguay or Brazil will be of cattle and ranch hands rather than duty-free shops and casinos.

Bagé and Aceguá

Of all the towns on or very near Rio Grande do Sul's border with Argentina and Uruguay, **BAGÉ** is the only one with any charm, remaining first and foremost a cattle and commercial centre, rather than a transit point. Like all towns in the *campanha*, Bagé has its own lively events, which attract people from the surrounding cattle ranches. The most important **festival**, held in January in odd-numbered years, is the **Semana Crioula Internacional**, but the *Semana de Bagé* (a folklore festival held annually from July 10 to 17), or even the *Exposição* (first half of Oct), will give you a taste of the *campanha*. For details of these and other events ask at the **tourist office** at Praça Silveira Martins (Mon–Fri 9–11.30am & 2–6pm, Sat 9am–noon). For an understanding of the region's history, a visit to the **Museu Dom Diogo de Souza**, Av Guilayn 5759 (Tues–Fri 8.30–11.30am & 1.30–5.30pm, Sat & Sun 1.30–5.30pm; 80c), is a must. Also worth visiting is the **Museu da Gravura Brasileira** at Rua Coronel Azambuja 18 (Mon–Fri 1.30–7.30pm, Sat 1.30–6pm; closed Jan; $1), which has a small but important collection of engravings. Rio Grande do Sul has a long tradition of this art form and some of the most important artists worked in Bagé.

Arriving from the Uruguayan border (Melo is the nearest Uruguayan town), ask to be let off at the **Polícia Federal**, a few blocks from the main square, Praça General Osório, at Rua Barão do Trunfo 1572. It's here, not at Aceguá, where you'll need to have your passport stamped. Arriving in Bagé from elsewhere, take a "Santa Tecla" bus into the centre from the main road next to the **rodoviária** (ⓣ53/242-8122; three daily buses from Santa Maria and Porto Alegre, one each from Santo Ângelo and, via Curitiba, São Paulo). If you're leaving Brazil, have your passport stamped; failing to report to the Polícia Federal here will mean that you're likely to have difficulties entering or leaving Brazil later on.

Hotels in Bagé are plentiful, with the clean and friendly *Mini*, Avenida Sete de Setembro, near Praça General Osório (❷), the centre's cheapest. If you want something more refined, there's the *Hotel Fenícia* at Rua Juvêncio Lemos 45 (ⓣ053/242-8222; ❸), while the best, largest and, dating from 1850, oldest hotel in town is the *Obinotel*, at Av Sete de Setembro 901 (ⓣ053/242-8211; ❺).

ACEGUÁ, 60km south and the actual frontier crossing point, is very much a back door into Brazil and Uruguay, with only a Uruguayan immigration post (remember to be stamped in or out of the country) and a few houses and stores – certainly not a place to spend a night. However, as the four buses a day in each direction between Bagé and Aceguá connect with others to and from Melo, this shouldn't be a problem – but check bus times carefully before setting out.

Changing money is best done at a *casa de câmbio* in Melo, but in Aceguá there are always plenty of men milling about offering reasonable rates for dollar bills. In Bagé, if you can't wait for the border, you can change dollars at Bradesco and many of the other banks in town are equipped with an ATM.

Santana do Livramento

Apart from Brazilians attracted to the casino and the duty-free shopping in Rivera, the Uruguayan border town into which **SANTANA DO LIVRAMENTO** merges (see p.1005), few people stay here long. Unless you're in pursuit of gaúchos and intent upon taking local buses to outlying villages, the only time when Livramento is actually worth visiting in its own right is when there's a livestock exhibition, *rodeio* or cultural event on – check with the **tourist office** at Rua Tamandaré (Mon–Sat 7am–1pm & 3–6pm, Sun 3–8pm). Livramento is also a very good place to purchase **gaúcho clothing and accessories**, with Correaria Gaúcha, Rua Rivadávia Correia 184, and Correaria Nova Esperança, Rua Duque de Caxias and Rua 24 de Maio, offering good selections.

Otherwise, the only possible reason not to move straight on would be a visit to the surrounding *campanha*, the rolling countryside traditionally given over to the raising of cattle and, to a lesser extent, sheep. For a more authentic gaúcho experience, visit the *Fazenda Palomas* (ⓣ55/505-6417 and 9118-2640), 20km from Livramento with the access road at km 480 of BR-158 in the direction of Porto Alegre. The 1000 hectare *fazenda* receives visitors during the daytime for horse riding along the trails that crisscross the property or to particpate in cattle round-ups and other day-to-day activities. Alternatively, you can stay over in one of the four very comfortable guestrooms (❹–❺) of the late-nineteenth-century *fazenda* house.

Practicalities

Livramento's **rodoviária**, at Rua Sen. Salgado Filho 335, serves most points in Rio Grande do Sul, while the **ferroviária**, in Praça Castello Branco, receives three trains a week from Santa Maria and Porto Alegre.

If you need to stay, **hotels** are cheapest in Livramento. The *Laçador* (❶) near the park, at Rua Uruguai 1227, is good, or try the *Livramento*, opposite the rodoviária (Ⓣ55/242-5444; ❷). Should you want somewhere more comfortable, try the *Jandaia* at Rua Uruguai 1452 (Ⓣ55/242-2288, Ⓦwww.jandaiah.com.br; ❺) which has been *the* place to stay in Livramento since 1896. There's a **youth hostel** at Rua Manduca Rodrigues 615 (Ⓣ55/242-3340; $7 per person), about five blocks from the rodoviária.

Before **leaving** Livramento and Rivera, you'll need a Brazilian exit (or entry) passport stamp from the Polícia Federal, Rua Uruguai 1177, near the central park, and a stamp from Uruguay's Dirección Nacional de Migración, Calle Suarez 516 (three blocks from Plaza General José Artigas, Rivera's main square). If you have problems, Uruguay's consulate is at Av Tamandaré 2110 (Ⓣ55/242-1416). **Change money** at a *casa de câmbio* or bank in Rivera, where exchange rates are as good as you'll find in Brazil and the process much faster, or use a Brazilian ATM.

Uruguaiana

The busiest crossing point on Rio Grande do Sul's border with Argentina, **URUGUAIANA** is also one of the state's most important cattle centres. However, unless you're around while there's a livestock show or folklore festival, there's little incentive to remain here: ask about festival dates at the **tourist office** (Mon–Sat 8.30am–6pm) in the Prefeitura, Praça Barão do Rio Branco. Otherwise, the **Museu Crioulo, Histórico e Artístico** (Mon–Fri 8.30am–noon & 2–5.30pm), in the cultural centre on the corner of *ruas* Santana and Duque de Caxias (by the main square), is worth a look for its wide-ranging collection of gaúcho-related items.

Uruguaiana is connected to Argentina and the town of Paso de los Libres by a 1400-metre-long bridge spanning the Rio Uruguai. Frequent **local buses** connect the train and bus stations, and the centres of each city, and **immigration** formalities take place on either side of the bridge. If you have problems entering Argentina, visit the **consulate** in Uruguaiana at Rua Santana 2496 (Ⓣ055/412-1925). The Brazilian consulate in Paso de los Libres is at Calle Mitre 918. You're best off **changing money** in Paso de los Libres, but failing this there are plenty of banks with ATMs in Uruguaiana. If you need **accommodation**, simple hotels in Uruguaiana include the *Wamosy* (Ⓣ55/412-1326; ❷) and *Mazza Tur* (Ⓣ55/412-3404; ❸), at Rua Sete de Setembro, nos 1973 and 1088 respectively, while for greater comfort your best bet is the new *Elyt* at Av Presidente Vargas 3718 (Ⓣ55/411-8800; ❺). **Restaurants** (for carnivores only) are better (but more expensive) over the border in Argentina but, in Uruguaiana, the *Casa d'Itália* at Rua Dr Maia 3112 has a varied menu to choose from.

Bus services from Uruguaiana are excellent, and you can get to or from most of the important centres, from Rio southwards. From Paso de los Libres, there are equally good services to points within Argentina, including Buenos Aires, Posadas and Puerto Iguazú. Finally, there are three **trains** a week to and from Santa Maria and Porto Alegre. There are daily **air services** from Uruguaiana to Porto Alegre and from Paso de los Libres to Buenos Aires.

4

Chile

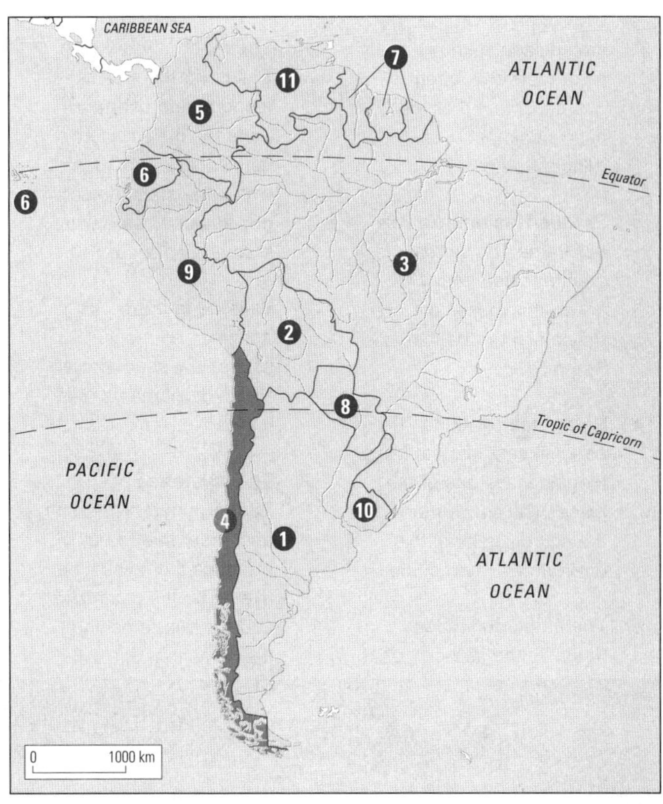
CARIBBEAN SEA
ATLANTIC OCEAN
Equator
PACIFIC OCEAN
Tropic of Capricorn
ATLANTIC OCEAN
0 1000 km
7
11
5
6
6
9
3
2
8
10
4
1

Chile Highlights

* **Pisco** Try a pisco sour and visit a distillery at Pisco Elqui, where the brandy is made. **See p.514**

* **Churches of Chiloé** The archipelago is known for its attractive wooden churches, found at the heart of almost every village. **See p.552**

* **Parque Nacional Torres del Paine** The surreal granite towers that crown this massif are truly a sight to behold. **See p.572**

* **Patagonian wildlife** The penguin sanctuary at Isla Magdalena is one of the places you can witness the rich diversity of this environment. **See p.569**

* **The altiplano wilderness** To the far north of the country, near Parque Nacional Lauca, you can see wild vicuña as well as salt flats, volcanoes and flamingo colonies. **See p.531**

* **The night sky** Beneath Chile's northern skies – among the most transparent in the southern hemisphere – you can watch the stars at such observatories as Cerro Mamalluca. **See p.514**

* **Valle de la Luna** An aptly named moonscape, just south of San Pedro de Atacama. **See p.523**

* **The mysteries of Easter Island** It's remote and expensive to get to, but once there you'll be riveted by the giant *moai* and the puzzle behind their creation. **See p.580**

Introduction and basics

Seen in the pages of an atlas, Chile's outline seems aberrant, even fantastical: almost 4000km in length and with an average width of just 180km, the very idea of it seems absurd. Once on Chilean soil, however, you'll be impressed by the country as a physical geographic entity. While the formidable barrier of rock and ice formed by the **Andes** cuts the country off from Argentina and Bolivia, the **Atacama Desert**, a thousand-kilometre stretch of parched wasteland, separates it from Peru to the north. And to the west, only a few islands dotted in the Pacific Ocean break the waves that roll onto **Chile's coast** from Australasia.

All this has created a country distinct from much of the rest of South America. It is Westernized, relatively affluent, and – with the exception of the infamous military Pinochet regime of the 1970s and 1980s – boasts a long tradition of political stability and orderly government. Above all, though, it is its remote and dizzyingly beautiful landscapes that lure visitors to Chile. Much of the country is covered by vast tracts of barely touched **wilderness** – places where you can be days from the nearest tarred road, and where you can have steaming hot springs, gleaming white salt flats or emerald lakes all to yourself. Few countries can match the astounding contrasts of scenery, ranging from the driest desert in the world to immense ice fields and glaciers. In between these extremes is a kaleidoscope of panoramas: sun-baked scrubland, lush vineyards and orchards, virgin temperate rainforest, dramatic fjords and bleak **Patagonian steppes**. Towering over it all is the long spine of the Andes, punctuated by colossal peaks and smouldering volcanoes.

You can experience this wilderness in whichever style you choose – Chile is not a poor country, and you don't have to slum it while you're here. Whatever your budget, you'll probably want to take advantage of the numerous possibilities for outdoor activities, all offered by an increasing number of local outfitters. If you have less active plans in mind, you can sit back and take in Chile's scenery from various ferry rides in the south, reliable flights, or on organized bus tours from most of the main cities.

Where to go

Most visitors tend to choose between heading either north or south of Santiago. Most of Chile's cities are not that exciting and are best used as jumping-off points to get out into the backcountry.

Santiago, while boasting some fine monuments, museums and restaurants, is not to everyone's taste, yet it's handy for visiting some of the country's oldest **vineyards**; the romantic port of **Valparaíso** and fashionable resort of **Viña del Mar** also sit on its doorstep.

North of Santiago, highlights include the handsome colonial city of **La Serena**, the lush **Elqui Valley**, and some idyllic beaches, the dazzling fringe of the **Norte Chico,** a region that mostly comprises semi-arid landscapes and brittle vegetation. At the northern edge of this region, **Copiapó** serves as a springboard for excursions to the white sands and turquoise waters of **Bahía Inglesa**, and east into the cordillera, where you'll find the mineral-streaked volcanoes of **Parque Nacional Nevado de Tres Cruces**, and the dazzling Laguna Verde. Further north, the barren **Atacama Desert** presents an unforgettable landscape, whose attractions include ancient petroglyphs, abandoned nitrate ghost towns and a scattering of fertile oases. Up in the Andes, the vast, high plateau known as the **altiplano** encompasses snow-capped volcanoes, bleached-white salt flats, lakes speckled pink with flamingos, grazing llamas, alpacas and vicuñas and tiny whitewashed churches. The best points to head for up here are **Parque Nacional Lauca** and **Parque Nacional Volcán Isluga**.

PERU
Tacna
Arica
BOLIVIA
Iquique
PARAGUAY
5
Calama
San Pedro de Atacama
Antofagasta
Copiapó
CHILE
La Serena
Vicuña
ARGENTINA
Los Vilos
Viña del Mar
Valparaíso
Santiago
Rancaqua
Juan Fernandez Archipelago (Chile)
Talca
Chillán
Concepción
5
PACIFIC OCEAN
Temuco
Valdivia
Osorno
Puerto Varas
Puerto Montt
Chiloé
Chaitén
Arch. de los Chonos
ATLANTIC OCEAN
Puerto Aisén
Coyhaique
Golfo de Penas
Cochrane
I. Wellington
Puerto Natales
Straits of Magellan
Punta Arenas
Tierra del Fuego
Ushuaia
Puerto Williams
Cape Horn
0 500 km

Earthquakes

You can expect to experience a few mild tremors during your stay in Chile. If you feel the ground move slightly, don't be alarmed – it's highly unlikely to be a fully fledged earthquake. If, however, you're unlucky enough to be caught in one, don't panic (remember that buildings in this country are designed to withstand earthquakes). Whatever you do, don't run out into the street, as this is how most injuries and fatalities are caused. Instead, stand under a doorway, which is the strongest part of a building. Note that lights will automatically go off if the quake is over 5 on the Richter scale.

South of Santiago is the lush **Central Valley**, with its swaths of orchards and vineyards, while further south, the famous, much-visited **Lake District** presents a picture-postcard landscape of perfectly conical volcanoes (such as **Volcán Osorno**), iris-blue lakes and dense native forests, perfect for hiking. A short ferry ride from **Puerto Montt**, at the southern edge of the Lake District, the **Chiloé** archipelago is a quiet, rural backwater, famous for its rickety houses on stilts and old wooden churches.

Back on the mainland, south of Puerto Montt, the **Carretera Austral** carves its way through virgin temperate rainforest, and past dramatic fjords, one of which is the embarkation point for a boat trip out to the sensational **Laguna San Rafael glacier**. Beyond the Carretera Austral lies **Southern Patagonia**, a country of bleak windswept plains bordered by the magnificent granite spires of the **Torres del Paine** massif, a magnet for hikers and climbers. Across the Magellan Strait, **Tierra del Fuego**, shared with Argentina, is a remote land of harsh, desolate beauty.

Finally, there are distant **Easter Island**, famed for its mysterious statues and fascinating ancient culture; and the little-visited **Isla Robinson Crusoe**, part of the Juan Fernández Archipelago, sporting dramatic volcanic peaks covered with dense vegetation.

When to go

The **north** of the country can be comfortably visited at any time of year. However, if you're planning to rent a 4WD and tour the altiplano, note that the unpredictable weather phenomenon known as the **Bolivian Winter** (or *invierno altiplánico*) can produce heavy, sporadic rainfall between December and February (the height of summer), washing away roads and disrupting communications.

In the **centre** and **south** of the country, you should avoid the months of June to September (unless you plan to go skiing), when heavy snowfall often blocks access to the mountains, including many national parks. The peak summer months are January and February, but as accommodation rates and crowds increase in equal measure, you'd be better off coming in November, December or March, when the weather is often just as good.

Red tape and visas

Most foreign visitors to Chile do not need a **visa**, with the exception of citizens of **New Zealand** (at a cost of NZ$90) and a small number of other countries. Visitors of all nationalities are issued a **tourist card** (*Tarjeta de Turismo*) on arrival in Chile, which is valid for ninety days, and can be extended once for an additional ninety days. It will be checked by the International Police at the airport or border post when you leave Chile – if it's expired you won't be allowed to leave the country until you've paid the appropriate fine at the nearest **Intendencia** (up to US$100, depending on the number of days past the expiry date). If this happens when you're trying to fly out of the international airport in Santiago, you'll have to go back downtown to Moneda 1342 (Mon–Fri 9am–1pm; ⓣ2/672-5320).

If you **lose** your tourist card, ask for a duplicate immediately, either from the Fronteras department of the Policía Internacional, General Borgoño 1052,

Santiago (Ⓣ2/698-2211), or from the Extranjer's department of the Intendencia, Moneda 1342, Santiago (Ⓣ2/672-5320).

If you want to **extend** your tourist card, you've got two choices. You can either pay US$100 at the Intendencia of Santiago or any provincial capital, or you can simply leave the country and re-enter, getting a brand-new ninety-day *Tarjeta de Turismo* for free. The latter option is usually cheaper, not to mention easy, given the many opportunities for border crossing up and down Chile.

Costs and money

The basic unit of currency is the **peso**, usually represented by the $ sign (and by **CH$** in this chapter, for clarity). Notes come in 1000, 5000, 10,000 and 20,000 (rare) denominations. There's a chronic shortage of change in Chile, and trying to pay for something small with a CH$10,000 note (sometimes even a CH$5000 note) invariably results in the shopkeeper scurrying around, desperately trying to beg change from his neighbours. It's a good idea to break up these larger notes whenever you can – in big supermarkets and post offices, for instance – and keep a stock of loose change and small notes on you at all times.

We've given prices in **US dollars** below, to help you get an idea of basic costs before you're familiar with the local currency. Note, however, that you'll use Chilean pesos to pay for just about everything in Chile, with the exception of some hotels that also accept US dollars.

For many goods and services, prices are closer to those in Europe and North America than in neighbouring Andean countries, but road transport and eating out are still far less expensive. Typical **accommodation** prices are usually around US$15 per night for a bottom-end double room, US$40 for a mid-range double with private bath, and US$70 and up per room in a smart, attractive hotel. **Eating** out can be pricey in the evening, especially in big cities and more sophisticated restaurants, but a typical beefsteak and French fries plus mineral water in an ordinary local restaurant still only costs around US$7. Thankfully, **transport** is still relatively inexpensive, with long-distance buses offering particularly good value – for instance, the 2000km journey from Santiago to Arica costs around US$40.

In general, then, you'll need to allow at least US$180 a week to get by on a tight budget; at least US$300 a week to live a little more comfortably, staying in mid-range hotels and eating in restaurants most days; and from US$700 a week to live in luxury.

While there are numerous *casas de cambio* in Santiago for exchanging **traveller's cheques**, and usually one or two in the larger provincial cities, they're by no means in all towns and cities, which is fairly limiting. Note that it's normally either impossible or prohibitively expensive to change cash and travellers' cheques at banks. **Credit cards** can be used either in ATMs or over the counter. MasterCard, Visa and American Express are accepted just about everywhere, but other cards may not be recognized. You may be able to make withdrawals from ATMs in Chile using your **debit card**.

Information, websites and maps

Chile's government-run tourist board is called **Sernatur** (short for Servicio Nacional de Turismo). There's a large and very helpful office in Santiago (see p.488), as well as branches in every provincial capital in Chile. They produce a huge amount of material, including themed booklets on camping, skiing, national parks, beaches, thermal springs and so on; for some reason these are often kept out of sight, so you'll have to ask specifically to see everything they've got. Another source of information is the excellent series of **TurisTel** guidebooks, published annually by the Chilean phone company, CTC.

Chile has embraced the **Internet** with much enthusiasm, and any Web search on "Chile" will produce thousands of matches. Make Ⓦwww.chiptravel.cl your first stop to check out its vast range of useful information, from bus timetables to nightlife listings. Ⓦwww.chile-hotels.com offers a long list of Chilean hotels, with online booking facilities, plus brief descriptions of the towns and cities, while LanChile's site Ⓦwww.lanchile.cl features timetables and fares for the national flight network. Ⓦwww.turismochile.cl has good descriptions of the major attractions in each region, with some historical and cultural background, and Ⓦwww.chileaustral.com is dedicated to tourism in Chilean Patagonia, including city guides, national parks, hotels, weather forecasts and lots more. Finally, Ⓦwww.samexplo.org is an excellent site, giving travel advice and warnings, trip reports, a bulletin board and sensibly indexed links with other sites.

No two **road maps** of Chile are identical. The most reliable and complete road map is probably the one produced by **Turistel**, printed in the back of its guides to Chile (see opposite) and also published in a separate booklet. **Sernatur** produces a good fold-out map of the whole of Chile, called the *Gran Mapa Caminero de Chile*. The best ones to use for hiking are the new series of JLM maps (Ejmattassi@interactiva.cl), which cover some of the main national parks. They're available in bookshops and some souvenir or outdoor stores.

Accommodation

On the whole, the standard of accommodation in Chile is not great, and many visitors feel that prices are high for what you get, especially in mid- and upper-range hotels. Bottom-end accommodation starts at around US$15 for a double room, while you'll have to pay around US$40 for a double room with private bath in a decent mid-range hotel and anything from US$70 up for a smart, upmarket hotel. Note that the price of accommodation in the main tourist centres increases dramatically in **high season** – January and February – particularly in seaside resorts, where it can be as much as double.

Hotels and motels

Chilean hotels are given a one- to five-star rating by Sernatur (the national tourist board), but this only reflects facilities and not standards, which vary widely from hotel to hotel. In general, mid-range **hotels** fall into two main categories: large, old houses with spacious, but sometimes tired, rooms; and modern, purpose-built hotels, usually with smaller rooms, no common areas and better facilities.

Finally, a word of note on **motels**, which are usually not economical roadside hotels, but places where couples go to have sex. Motel rooms are rented for three hours at very reasonable rates. Though you may get a few strange stares if you show up with your backpack, they are a cheap and, usually, perfectly safe place to escape for a few hours.

Residenciales, cabañas and refugios

Residenciales are the most widely available, and widely used, accommodation option in Chile. As with hotels, standards can vary enormously, but in general *residenciales* offer simple, modestly furnished rooms, usually off a corridor in the main house, or else in a row arranged around the backyard or patio.

Cabañas are very popular in Chile, and you'll find them in tourist spots up and down the country, particularly by the coast. They are basically holiday chalets and are geared towards families, usually with a fully equipped kitchen area, a sitting/dining area, one double bedroom and a second bedroom with bunks. They range from the very rustic to the distinctly grand, complete with daily maid service. Many *cabañas* are in superb locations, right by the ocean, and it can be wonderfully relaxing to self-cater for a few days in the off-season – cooking the fresh fish you bought in the local market, sipping your cabernet on the veranda looking out to sea.

Many of the ranger stations in the national parks have a limited number of bunk beds available for tourists, at a charge of around US$8 per person. Known as **refugios**, these places are very rustic – often a small, wooden hut – but they usually have flushable toilets, hot running water, clean sheets and heavy woollen blankets. Most *refugios* are open year-round, but if you're travelling in winter or during other extreme weather conditions it's best to check with the regional forestry (Conaf) office in advance.

Hostels and camping

Hostels are increasingly banding together to provide a link among Chile's major cities. Unfortunately, news on the ground tends to be word of mouth, as new spots are being organized monthly – usually by Europeans who have travelled the world and are now seeing the business and personal opportunities in becoming a hostel owner in Chile. For the latest updates, the best information is found on the Web. Try one of the major search engines like Google, type in "hostelling and Chile", and then start sorting your way through the increasing number of options.

There are lots of opportunities for **camping** in Chile, though it's not always the cheapest way to sleep. If you plan to do a lot of camping, the first thing you should do is equip yourself with the annual camping guide published by Turistel, which has details of every campsite in Chile. Published only in Spanish, this guide is titled Turistel Rutero Camping and has plenty of maps, prices and information.

Getting around

Travelling in Chile is easy, comfortable and, compared with Europe or North America, inexpensive. Most of the population travels by bus, and it's such a reliable, affordable option that you'll probably do likewise. However, internal airlines, catering primarily to business passengers, are handy for covering long distances in a hurry. Thanks to a very manageable online ticket purchase system, last-minute flights on LanChile cost as little as US$29 (round-trip) in 2003.

By plane

Flying is definitely the quickest and most convenient way of taking in both its northern and southern regions in a single trip. It's also a surprisingly inexpensive way of getting about, thanks to fierce competition between LanChile and the constantly shuffling cast of other airlines – many of which seem to arrive with a splash and evaporate within the next eighteen months – that serve the country's numerous regional airports.

Far and away the leading airline is **LanChile/Lanexpress** (Ⓣ2/526-2000, in regions Ⓣ600/526-2000, US toll-free Ⓣ1-800-735-5526; Ⓦwww.lanchile.com), which besides offering the widest choice of domestic flights has a fantastic website that takes nearly all the hassle out of organizing even last minute flights. Another good-value option is LanChile's **"Visit Chile"** airpass, which can be used on three internal flights within a one-month period. Note that the pass can only be bought outside Chile – for details, see their website.

By bus

Chile's long-distance **buses** offer an excellent service, far better than their European or North American counterparts – thanks largely to the enormous amount of legroom, frequent departures and flexible itineraries (you can stop a bus at nearly any point of the route). When it comes to **boarding**, make sure that the departure time written on your ticket corresponds exactly to the time indicated on the little clock on the bus's front window, as your ticket is valid only on the bus it was booked for. Your luggage will be safely stored in lockers under the bus and the conductor will issue you a numbered stub for each article. Soon after departure – and it cannot be stressed forcefully enough that Chilean buses leave punctually – the conductor will check your ticket and leave you with a stub that must be kept until the end of your journey.

Be warned that if you're travelling north of Santiago on a very long-distance route, or crossing an international border, the bus and all luggage will be searched by Ministry of Agriculture officials, and all sandwiches, fresh fruit and vegetables will be destroyed – while you stand waiting, usually in the cold night.

Local buses, often called **micros**, connect city centres with residential outskirts and nearby villages. For some journeys, a faster alternative is provided by **colectivos**, which are shared taxis operating along a fixed route with fixed fares.

By car

Many remote attractions are visited by tour companies operating out of the nearest

Ferry companies

Andina del Sud Varas 437, Puerto Montt ⓣ65/257797; Del Salvador 72, Puerto Varas ⓣ65/232811.
Navimag ⓦwww.australis.com. Angelmo 2187, Puerto Montt ⓣ65/432300; Puerto Montt 262, Puerto Natales ⓣ61/414300; Av Independencia 830, Punta Arenas ⓣ61/200200; Av El Bosque Norte 0440, eleventh floor, Santiago ⓣ442-3120.
TransMarChilay ⓣ600/600-8687, ⓦwww.transmarchilay.cl. 21 de Mayo 417, second floor, Coyhaique ⓣ67/231971; Angelmo 2187, Puerto Montt ⓣ65/270411; Av Providencia 2653 local 24, Santiago ⓣ600/600-8688.

major city, but for more independence, your best bet is **to rent a vehicle**. To do this, you need to be at least 21 years old and have a major credit card so you can leave a blank voucher as a guarantee. You're allowed to use your national driver's licence.

Several international car-rental companies have offices throughout Chile, including Hertz, Avis, Budget and First. The cost of car rental is much higher in Chile than in North America, and more on a par with European prices. Your rental contract will almost certainly be in (legal and convoluted) Spanish – get the company to take you through it and explain everything. In most cases your liability, in the event of an accident, is normally around the US$500 mark and costs over this amount will be covered in total by the company.

You'll probably find that many places you want to get to are reached by dirt road, for which it's essential to rent a suitable vehicle, namely a **jeep** or **pick-up truck**. On regular dirt roads you rarely need a 4WD vehicle. Make sure, too, that you take two spare tyres, not just one, and that you always carry a funnel or tube for siphoning and more than enough petrol. (Work it out yourself then add lots – don't rely on what the guys in the rental shop say.) Also pick up several five-litre water jugs for a driving in the altiplano – it may be necessary for either the passengers or the engine at some point. Finally, a general point on **tyre punctures**: This is such a common occurrence in Chile that even the smallest towns have special workshops (bearing signs with a tyre painted white) where they are quickly and cheaply repaired.

Taxis are black with a yellow roof, and in the bigger cities can be flagged down very quickly on the street. As Chilean taxi drivers are often eager to charge foreigners too much, it's worth checking to see that the meter has been turned on before you start a journey and get an estimate for the fare to the nearest CH$500. Fares are clearly shown on the windscreen.

Hitching

While we don't recommend **hitching** as a safe way of getting about, there's no denying that it's widely practised by Chileans themselves. In the summer it seems as though all the students in Chile are sitting beside the road with their thumb out, and in rural areas it's not uncommon for entire families to hitch a lift whenever they need to get into town.

By ferry

South of Puerto Montt, where the mainland breaks up into an archipelago, a network of **ferries** operates through the fjords, inlets and channels of Chile's far south, providing a far more scenic and romantic alternative to flights and long-distance buses. Two ferries in particular are very popular with tourists: one from Puerto Montt to Chacabuco and the San Raphael glacier, the other between Puerto Montt and Puerto Natales.

Mail and communications

Chile's postal service, **Correos de Chile**, is somewhat dependable and efficient, and overseas mail sent even from remote areas generally reaches its destination within a couple of weeks. Do not send any gifts to Chile using regular post; theft is extremely

Carrier codes

One Telcom (119)
Entel (123)
Telefónica Mundo (188) (best overall)

common for incoming shipments. For important shipping to Chile use express services such as FedEx and DHL.

Chilean **phone services** are the best on the continent, with excellent lines and cheap rates that include calls to the US for as little as 10¢ a minute. However, the system is also bewildering to visitors. In Chile, there's no single national telecommunications company, but roughly a dozen telecoms, known as carriers (*portadores*). Stiff competition among the companies means that prices are low and constantly changing.

Each carrier has its own access code (see box). This will be the first three digits of the call from cell phones, private lines and public telephones. In nearly all cases, dial your chosen carrier's code, add "0", then the number. For example, to call England you would dial 119 (or another company's code), then 0, then 44 and the number. For calls within Chile the "0" is dropped. So to call Valparaíso from Santiago you would dial carrier code 119 (or whichever you choose), then 32 (for Valparaíso area), and the six- or seven-digit number.

There are a huge variety of public phones – avoid them all, few work. Instead, use call centres, or *centros de llamadas*. There are dozens of these in most cities, and some of them offer cheap rates – particularly the small private ones, which are more likely to have promotions and special offers. The catch, however, is that in most *centros de llamadas* you can't set a time limit for the call, so you have to be really careful about not talking too long, as you can quickly run up a huge bill.

One of the best ways to keep in touch while travelling is to sign up for a free **email** account that can be accessed from anywhere; among the free email services are YahooMail (ⓦwww.yahoo.com) and Hotmail (ⓦwww.hotmail.com).

Chile is far and away the most wired Latin American nation. **Cybercafés** are everywhere, and broadband access is quite common in cities. **Internet access** typically costs about CH$200 for fifteen minutes. If you have multiple options, it is always good to ask for "banda ancha", which means a high-speed and not a dial-up connection. Even in many remote parts of Chile, this is now available.

Food and drink

Given the vast range and superior quality of the country's raw produce, Chilean food is a disappointment. The main problem is a lack of variety and imagination, as so many restaurants, up and down the country, offer the same boring, limited menu of fried chicken, boiled beef and fried fish, usually served with chips or mashed potatoes.

The best trick is to join the Chileans and make your main meal of the day **lunch**, when many restaurants offer a fixed-price *menú del día*. It is always much better value than the à la carte options. Many travellers only figure this out after several weeks of overspending. Learn how to ask for the "menu", and the same food is instantly available for half the price.

As for the other meals of the day, **breakfast** at most *residenciales* and hotels is usually a disappointing affair. Except during annual holidays or at weekends, relatively few Chileans go out to dinner, which leaves most restaurants very quiet through the week. Note, also, that most places don't open for dinner before 8 or 9pm.

One notable exception to the general dreariness of Chilean restaurant food is the country's **fish and seafood**, which rank among the best in the world. The widest choice is available on the coast of the *litoral central* and Norte Chico, where a string of fishing villages serve the day's catch in the little **marisquerías** (fish restaurants) clustered around the *caleta* (fish quay). Here, you'll find, depending on the season, *albacora* (albacore), *corvina* (sea bass), *congrio* (a firm-fleshed, white fish), *lenguado* (sole), *reineta* (similar to lemon sole) and *merluza* (hake), as well as *almejas* (clams), *choritos* (mussels), *camarones* (prawns), *jaiva* (crab) and *ostras* (oysters), to mention some of the more familiar types of shellfish. Even if you're not normally adventurous with seafood, you should persuade yourself to experiment; one of the most delicious dishes, and a good one to start with, is *machas a la parmesana* – pink clams, lightly baked in their shells and covered with parmesan cheese. Another typical – and very tasty – dish is *ceviche* (raw fish marinaded in lemon juice).

Drinks

Soft drinks (*bebidas*) can be found everywhere in Chile, particularly Coca-Cola, Sprite and Fanta. Bottled mineral water, too, is widely available, both with fizz (*con gas*) and without (*sin gas*). Coffee, in Chile, is usually instant Nescafé, although in the upmarket restaurants it's increasingly easy to find good, real coffee (ask for *café de grano*).

Chilean **beer** doesn't come in many varieties, with Crystal and Escudo dominating the choice of bottled lagers, and Kuntsman being the only speciality brand to make a national mark. There's always a good selection of **wine**, on the other hand. Regarded as the Chilean national drink, **pisco sour** is a tangy, refreshing aperitif made from *pisco* (a white brandy made from distilled Moscatel grapes), freshly squeezed lemon juice and sugar.

Safety and the police

Chile is probably the safest South American country to travel in, and violent crime against tourists is rare. The kind of sophisticated tactics used by thieves in neighbouring Peru and Bolivia are very uncommon in Chile, and the fact that you can walk around without being gripped by paranoia is one of the country's major bonuses. Out of the cities, there's no fear of banditry or general lawlessness, as there is in many parts of South America. Chile's **police** force, the *carabineros*, have the whole country covered, with stations in even the most remote areas, particularly in border regions.

Useful numbers

Air rescue ⓣ138 (for mountaineering accidents)
Ambulance ⓣ131
Police ⓣ133
Coast Guard ⓣ137
Fire ⓣ132
Investigaciones ⓣ134 (for serious crimes)

Opening hours, public holidays and fiestas

Most shops and services are open Monday through Friday from 9am to 1pm and 3pm to

Calendar of public holidays

January 1 New Year's Day (*Año nuevo*)
Easter (*Semana Santa*) with national holidays on Good Friday, Easter Saturday and Easter Sunday
May 1 Labour Day (*Día del Trabajo*)
May 21 *Combáte Naval de Iquique*. A Remembrance Day celebrating the end of the War of the Pacific after the naval victory at Iquique
June 15 Corpus Christi
June 29 San Pedro y San Pablo
August 15 Assumption of the Virgin
September 11 Public holiday marking the military coup which deposed the democratic government in 1973
September 18 National Independence Day (*Fiestas Patrias*), in celebration of the first provisional government of 1810
September 19 Armed Forces Day (*Día del Ejército*)
October 12 Columbus Day (*Día de la Raza*), marking the discovery of America
November 1 All Saints' Day (*Todos los Santos*)
December 8 Feast of the Immaculate Conception
December 25 Christmas Day (*Navidad*)

6 or 7pm, and on Saturday from 10 or 11am until 2pm. Banks have more limited hours, generally Monday through Friday from 9am to 2pm, but *casas de cambio* tend to use the same opening hours as shops. Museums are nearly always shut on Mondays, and are often free on Sundays. Post offices don't close at lunchtime on weekdays and are open on Saturdays from 9am to 1pm.

Apart from the statutory public holidays which are recognized nationwide, shops and offices will be closed for certain local festivals and on national and local election days when the country comes to an almost complete standstill for 24 hours from midnight to midnight.

Sports and entertainment

Compared with their Argentine neighbours, Chileans are not a particularly exuberant people, and the country's entertainment scene sits firmly on the tame side of the fence. **El fútbol**, introduced by British immigrants in the early 1800s, reigns supreme as Chile's favourite sport. Tickets to games in Santiago (the best place to see a match) tend to cost around US$10–15, and the games themselves have a great atmosphere, with rarely any trouble and whole families coming along to enjoy the fun.

Even though ranching has long declined in Chile, organized **rodeos** remain wildly popular, with many free competitions taking place in local stadiums (known as *medialunas*)

Adventure tourism operators and outfitters

Below is a selection of operators and outfitters for various outdoor activities. The list is by no means comprehensive, and new companies are constantly springing up to add to it – you can get more details from the relevant regional Sernatur office.

All-rounders

Altue Expediciones Encomenderos 83, Las Condes, Santiago ⓣ2/232-1103. Reliable, slick operation whose options include rafting the Río Maipo, Aconcagua and Ojos del Salado expeditions, and three- to seven-day horse treks.

Azimut 360 Arzobispo Casanova 3, Providencia, Santiago ⓣ62/735-8034. Franco-Chilean outfit with a young, dynamic team of guides and a wide range of programmes, including mountain biking in the altiplano, Aconcagua expeditions and climbs up Chile's highest volcanoes.

Cascada Expediciones Orrego Luco 054, Providencia, Santiago ⓣ2/234-2274, ⓔcascada@ibm.net. One of the early pioneers of adventure tourism in Chile, with a particular emphasis on activities in the Andes close to Santiago, where it has a permanent base in the Cajón del Maipo. Programmes include rafting and kayaking the Río Maipo, horse treks in the high cordillera, hiking and one-day mountain biking excursions.

Climbing

See also Azimut 360 and Altue Expediciones in "All-rounders", above for details of tours up Volcán Osorno and Volcán Villarica.

Concepto Indigo Ladrilleros 105, Puerto Natales ⓣ61/410678, ⓔamerindi@entelchile.net. A range of mountaineering and ice-climbing programmes in the Torres del Paine region, plus mountaineering courses. A very good company.

Mountain Service Paseo Las Palmas 2209, Providencia, Santiago ⓣ2/233-0913. An experienced, specialist company, dedicated to climbing Aconcagua, the major volcanoes and Torres del Paine.

Fly-fishing

Bahía Escocia Fly Fishing Lago Rupanco ⓣ64/371515. Small, beautifully located

throughout the season, which runs from September to April. Taking in a rodeo not only allows you to watch the most dazzling equestrian skills inside the arena, but also to see the *huasos* (a sort of gentleman cowboy) decked out in all their traditional gear: ponchos, silver spurs and all.

Huasos are also the chief performers of **cueca**, Chile's national dance – a curious cross between thigh-slapping English morris dancing and smouldering *Sevillanas*. The men are decked out in their finest *huaso* gear; the women wear wide skirts and shawls. In the background, guitar-strumming musicians sing romantic ballads full of patriotic sentiments. If you are going to a fiesta and want to take part in a *cueca*, remember to take along a clean white handkerchief.

Outdoor activities

The range of outdoor activities on offer in Chile is enormous, taking in skiing, surfing, volcano-climbing, white-water rafting, fly-fishing and horse riding. Although Chile's tourism industry was traditionally geared towards Argentine holidaymakers who came to lie on the beaches, an increasing number of operators and outfitters are wising up to the potential of organized adventure tourism, offering one- or multi-day guided excursions.

Many of these companies are based in either Puerto Varas or Pucón, with a good sprinkling of other outfitters spread throughout the south. If you plan to do any adventurous activities, be sure to check that you're covered by your **travel insurance** (see p.26), or take out specialist insurance where necessary.

lodge with fly-fishing excursions run by a US–Chilean couple. Can also book with English-run Travellers in Puerto Montt ⓣ65/262099, ⓔgochile@entelchile.net.
Cumilahue Lodge PO Box 2, Llifen ⓣ63/481015. Very expensive packages at a luxury Lake District lodge run by Adrian Dufflocq, something of a legend on the Chilean fly-fishing scene.

Horse trekking

See also Cascada Expediciones and Altue Expediciones in "All-rounders", above.
Campo Aventura ⓣ65/232910, ⓦwww.campo-adventura.com. Dynamic young outfit based in Puerto Varas, specializing in two- to twelve-day horse-trekking tours of the Cochamo Valley, also known as Chile's Yosemite Valley. Excellent food including veggie options.
Chile Nativo ⓣ61/414367, ⓦwww.chilenativo.com. Dynamic young outfit based in Puerto Natales, specializing in five- to twelve-day horse-trekking tours of the region, visiting out-of-the-way locations in addition to the Parque Nacional Torres del Paine.
Hacienda de los Andes Río Hurtado, near Ovalle ⓣ53/691822, ⓦwww.haciendalosandes.com. Beautiful newly built ranch in a fantastic location in the Hurtado valley, between La Serena and Ovalle, offering exciting one- to four-day mountain treks on some of the finest mounts in the country.

Kayaking

Al Sur Expediciones Del Salvador 100, Puerto Varas ⓣ65/232300, ⓔalsur@telsur.cl. One of the foremost adventure tour companies in the Lake District, and the first one to introduce sea kayaking in the fjords south of Puerto Montt.
Onas Patagonia Blanco Encalada 599, Casilla 78, Puerto Natales ⓣ61/412707, ⓦwww.chileaustral.com/onas. Sea-kayaking excursions in the remote, bleak waters of Patagonia.

Skiing

Full details of the resorts near Santiago are given in the box on pp.494–495.

Rafting and kayaking

Numerous narrow rivers hurtling down from the Andes to the ocean provide Chile with some excellent **white-water rafting** opportunities. These include two top "world class" rafting rivers: the great **Bío Bío**, on the southern edge of the Central Valley, and, down by the Carretera Austral, the **Futaleufú**, the venue of the Rafting World Championships in 2000. Both rivers feature class III to V rapids (out of a grading system of I to VI, with VI being commercially unraftable), as well as a spectacular backdrop of volcanoes, waterfalls and lush native forest.

Hiking

For the most part, Chile is a very empty country with vast swaths of wilderness offering potential for fantastic **hiking** (and concealing no dangerous animals or snakes). However, Chile isn't particularly geared up to the hiking scene, with relatively few long-distance trails (given the total area) and a shortage of decent trekking maps. That said, what is on offer is superb, and ranks among the country's most rewarding attractions.

By far the most popular destination for hiking is **Torres del Paine** in the far south, which offers magnificent scenery but fairly crowded trails, especially in January and February. Many quieter, less well-known alternatives are scattered between Santiago and Tierra del Fuego, ranging from narrow paths in the towering, snow-streaked central Andes, to hikes up to glaciers off the Carretera Austral.

Federación de Andinismo Almirante Simpson 77, Providencia, Santiago ⓣ2/222-0799 is a friendly organization that runs mountaineering courses, sells equipment, and can put you in touch with guides. It also helps out foreigners trying to arrange climbing authorization.

Fly-fishing

Chile is one of the world's great **fly-fishing** destinations, its crystal-clear waters teeming with rainbow, brown and brook trout, and silver and Atlantic salmon. These fish are not native, but were introduced for sport in the late nineteenth century; since then, the wild population has flourished and multiplied, and is also supplemented by generous numbers of escapees from local fish farms. The fishing season varies slightly from region to region, but in general runs from November to May.

Costs range from a reasonable US$70 per person for a day in the more visited waters of the Lake District (including full equipment hire and boat transport), to around US$400 per day to fish the scarcely touched waters of Aisén with top-notch guides. For more details contact the excellent website ⓦwww.flyfishchile.com.

Skiing

Chile has the best **skiing** in South America and, on high-altitude slopes, many argue that the very dry powder snow – known as "champagne snow" – is of a quality found nowhere else. Conditions near Santiago are frequently sunny as well. The **season** runs from June 15 to early October, with August marking the busiest period. Conveniently, the best slopes and resorts are just 40km from Santiago: neighbouring **El Colorado**, **La Parva** and **Valle Nevado** can easily be skied on a day-trip from the capital, while classy **Portillo**, 149km north, is a comfortable distance for a weekend visit. One-week all-inclusive packages at these places start at around US$800 per person in low season and about twice that much in high season; for more details on these ski centres, see box on pp.494–495.

Mountain biking

For most of Chile's length there are extremely good and little-used dirt roads perfect for **cycling** – although the numerous potholes mean it's only worth attempting them on a **mountain bike**. For a serious trip, you should bring your own bike or buy one in Santiago – renting something of the quality required can be difficult to arrange. An alternative is to go on an organized biking excursion, where all equipment, including tents, will be provided.

The most popular cycling route is the **Carretera Austral** from Puerto Montt to Cochrane, which takes you through awe-inspiring scenery – but be prepared for spells of dismal weather along the way.

History

Chile has remained relatively, if not entirely, undisturbed by the turbulence of the rest of South American history. From its early days as an independent republic Chile took on its own political shape, distinct from that of its neighbours. The repressive military regime of General Pinochet sadly brought Chile to the attention of the outside world but, today, with democracy firmly back in place, Chile is an outward-looking, stable country, albeit with some social inequalities lurking beneath the surface.

Pre-Columbian Chile

Much more is known of Chile's **pre-Columbian cultures** of the north – where the dryness of the Atacama Desert preserved remains for thousands of years – than of the south. One of the earliest groups of people to leave its mark was the **Chinchorro culture**, a collection of nomadic fishing communities that lived along the desert coast from 6000 BC. By 5000 BC they had developed the practice of mummifying their dead – two thousand years earlier than the Egyptians. Their technique, which involved removing internal organs and tissues and replacing them with vegetable fibres and mud, survived for four thousand years and is the oldest known in the world.

The Inca and Spanish conquests

In 1463 the Incan emperor, Pachacuti, initiated the massive conquest of lands stretching south as far as the Río Maule in Chile, where its progress was halted by the fierce resistance of the native Mapuche. While the **Incas** tolerated indigenous cults, they required their subjects also to adopt the **cult of the sun**. Remains of Inca worship sites have been found on numerous mountains in Chile, the most famous being **Cerro El Plomo**, near Santiago, where the frozen body of a small child, undoubtedly a sacrifice, was discovered in 1954. The Inca occupation of Chile spanned a relatively short period of time, interrupted first by civil war in Cusco. Then, in 1532, the **Spanish** arrived in Peru, marking the beginning of the end of the Inca Empire.

Diego de Almagro was given the mission of carrying the Conquest beyond Peru to the region named **Chile**, spoken of as a land rich in gold and silver. In 1535 he set off from Cusco and embarked on a long journey as far as the Aconcagua Valley but he found none of the riches spoken of. Bitterly disappointed, he returned to Cusco, where his deteriorating relations with Pizarro led to his death. Three years later, **Pedro de Valdivia** was granted a licence to colonize Chile. Owing to its lack of gold and the miseries of the first expedition, Chile was not an attractive destination, and so it was with a tiny party that Valdivia set off from Cusco in 1540. Almost a year later, Valdivia reached the Río Mapocho in the Aconcagua Valley, where he officially founded **Santiago de la Nueva Extremadura** on February 12, 1541.

The new colony was a marginal, isolated and unprofitable addition to Spain's empire. The need to maintain a standing army to guard La Frontera, and the absence of large quantities of precious metals, meant that Chile ran at a deficit. Growth was very slow, amounting to no more than five thousand settlers by 1600. At the same time, large "grants" of indigenous people were given to the colonists in what was known as the **encomienda** system. In theory, the *encomenderos* were supposed to look after the well-being of their charges and convert them to Christianity; in practice, the system simply provided the colonists with a large slave workforce that they could treat however they pleased.

Independence and the early republic

Chile entered the **nineteenth century** with a burgeoning sense of its own identity. The **criollo elite** was becoming increasingly alienated from the *peninsulares* dispatched from Spain to administer the colony. Criollo aspirations to play a more active role in government were given a sudden opportunity for fulfilment when Napoleon invaded Spain. In Chile, over four hundred leading citizens gathered in Santiago on September 18, 1810, and elected a six-man **junta**.

Over time, it became clear that a minority of *criollos* sought a far greater degree of autonomy for the colony. This was given impetus in 1811, when **José Miguel Carrera** appointed himself head of a more radical junta, creating a Chilean flag and drafting a provisional constitution that declared all rulings issued outside Chile illegitimate. The viceroy was greatly alarmed by these subversive measures and sent troops to Chiloé and Valdivia to prepare for an assault on Santiago. In response, Carrera charged down to confront them and war was effectively declared. When Carrera's military leadership did not produce results, he was replaced by **Bernardo O'Higgins**, who proved far more adept at holding off the Royalist forces. In October 1813, Royalist troops began to advance on Santiago; O'Higgins mounted a desperate and heroic defence at Rancagua, but the Patriots were overwhelmingly defeated.

The **Disaster of Rancagua**, as it is known, marked the end of La Patria Vieja (the name given to the fledgling independent nation) and its leaders fled across the Andean border to Mendoza in Argentina, as the Royalist troops marched triumphantly into Santiago. Meanwhile **José de San Martín**, the Argentine general, devised his plan for South American emancipation from his base in Mendoza. With O'Higgins placed in command of the Chilean division, San Martín's army scaled the cordillera in 1817. The Royalists fled to the south, and the Patriots entered the capital in triumph. San Martín inflicted devastating losses on their army at the Battle of Maipú in April 1818, and the final seal was set on Chilean **independence**. Leadership of the new country was offered to San Martín, but he declined – instead, the job went to Bernardo O'Higgins.

During its first thirteen years of independence, Chile got through five constitutions and eleven governments. In 1829 the Conservatives, with the support of the army, imposed an authoritarian-style government that ushered in a long period of political stability. The chief architect of the regime was **Diego Portales**, but he was not, however, without his detractors, and in 1837, he was brutally gunned down by political opponents. Nevertheless, the growing self-confidence of the nation created conditions that were favourable to growth. International trade took off rapidly, with a **silver- and copper-mining boom** in the Norte Chico.

The War of the Pacific

From the 1860s, when two enterprising Chileans started exploiting the nitrate deposits of the Atacama Desert, Chilean capital and labour dominated the industry. Most activity took place around Antofagasta, which Chile had formally acknowledged as Bolivian territory in 1874 in exchange for an assurance that export tariffs would not be raised. Many of Chile's most prominent politicians had shares in the nitrate companies, so when Bolivia raised export taxes in 1878 they were determined to take action.

A year later, after Chilean troops invaded Antofagasta and took control of the surrounding coastal strip, Chile and Bolivia were soon **at war**, with Peru drawn into the conflict on Bolivia's side. It soon became clear that success would depend on **naval supremacy** –

Bolivia did not have a navy, leaving Peru and Chile pitted against each other, and fairly evenly matched. Chile secured an overwhelming maritime victory in August 1879, when it captured Peru's principal warship, the *Huáscar*. By mid-1880 Chile had secured control of the region with a resounding victory at El Morro, Arica.

1900–1970

The first leader in the twentieth century committed to dealing with Chile's social polarization, labour unrest and mounting unemployment was **Arturo Alessandri**, elected in 1920. The weakness of his position, however, in the face of an all-powerful and obstructive Congress, prevented him from putting any of his plans into action. Then, in 1924, a strange set of events was set in motion after the relationship between the president and his military cabinet began to unravel and Alessandri fled to exile in Argentina. The following year, however, a rival junta led by Colonel **Carlos Ibañez** staged a coup and invited Alessandri to return. Alessandri, with Ibañez's support, then drafted the **1925 Constitution**, which represented a radical departure from the one of 1833, incorporating protective welfare measures among other reforms. Despite this victory tensions between Ibañez and Alessandri led to the president's resignation. The way was now clear for Ibañez to get himself elected as president in May 1927. During his early years he brought about improvements in living standards and stimulated national prosperity. But in 1929, Chile's economy virtually collapsed overnight, producing deep social unrest that forced Ibañez to resign in 1931. His departure was followed by eighteen months of chaos. The task of restoring stability to the nation fell to the old populist, Alessandri, who was re-elected in 1932.

From 1938 the government was dominated by the centre-right **Radicals**. In the 1950s left-wing groups gained considerable ground, but old-guard landowners controlled the votes of the thousands of peasants who depended on them. Nonetheless, Socialist **Salvador Allende** was only narrowly defeated by the Conservative Jorge Alessandri in 1958, causing widespread alarm among the wealthy elite. The upper classes soon threw all their efforts into securing the 1964 election of **Eduardo Frei**, of the **Christian Democrat** party. Frei turned out to be more progressive than his right-wing supporters imagined, initiating bold **agrarian reforms** that allowed the expropriation of all the biggest farms.

Allende and Pinochet

In 1970, **Salvador Allende** was narrowly elected as Chile's first socialist president, at the head of the **Unidad Popular** (UP). His government pledged to nationalize Chilean industries, redistribute the nation's wealth and speed up agrarian reform. Within a year, over eighty major companies had been nationalized, including the copper mines. The following year, over sixty percent of irrigated land was taken into government hands for redistribution among the rural workforce.

However, government expenditure exceeded income by a huge margin, creating an enormous deficit. The looming economic crisis was accelerated when the world copper price fell. Inflation began to rocket and before long food shortages became commonplace. Panic was fuelled by the right-wing press and reinforced by the CIA. Strikes broke out and, by 1973, with the country rocked by civil disorder, it was clear that the government could not survive for much longer. On September 11, 1973, tanks surrounded the presidential palace, and Salvador Allende was offered, and refused, a safe passage to exile. He was found dead in the palace ruins, clutching a submachine gun.

The coup was headed by a four-man junta, of whom **General Augusto Pinochet**, chief of the army, quickly emerged as the dominant figure. In the days and weeks following the takeover, at least seven thousand people – journalists, politicians, socialists, trades union organizers and so on – were herded into the national football stadium, where many were executed, and still more were tortured. Congress was dissolved, opposition parties and trade unions banned, and thousands of Chileans fled the country. Pinochet saw his mission as being that of rescuing Chile from the economic and political chaos into which it had undoubtedly fallen. His key strategy was to be the adoption of a radical **free-market economy**, which resulted in soaring unemployment, plummeting wages and a neglected social welfare system. It wasn't until the late 1980s that the economy really recovered and Pinochet's free-market policies achieved the results he sought.

Pinochet's economic experiment had only been possible with the tools of ruthless repression at his disposal. His chief instrument was the brutal secret police known as the **DINA**. Pinochet held the country in such a tight, personal grip that it became difficult for him to conceive of an end to his authority. The Constitution that he had drawn up in 1980 guaranteed him power until 1988, at which point the public would be given the chance either to accept military rule for another eight years or else to call for elections. In the promised **plebiscite of October 1988**, 55 percent of the nation voted against military rule. Pinochet hastily prepared **amnesty laws** to protect himself from facing charges of human rights abuses. A year later, the Christian Democrat **Patricio Aylwin**, at the head of a seventeen-party centre-ground coalition called the **Concertación**, became Chile's first democratically elected president in seventeen years.

The return of democracy

The handover of power was smooth. Aylwin was in the fortunate position of inheriting a robust economy. Pinochet's **economic** model was vigorously applied, with some protectionist modifications, in an effort to promote "growth with equity". Economic growth remained at levels that gave Chile international prestige. One of the new government's first actions was the establishment of a **National Commission for Truth and Reconciliation** to investigate and document the abuses committed by the military regime. The commission's report, published in 1991, confirmed 2279 executions, disappearances and deaths caused by torture, and listed a further 641 suspected cases.

After a successful four-year term, the Concertación was re-elected in 1993, this time headed by Christian Democrat **Eduardo Frei**. Frei's policies were essentially a continuation of his predecessor's, with a firmer emphasis on tackling human rights issues and eradicating severe poverty. In 1995, there were breakthrough convictions of members and employees of the Pinochet regime. But in its final couple of years, Frei's government ran into unexpected problems. Pinochet took up a seat in Congress as life senator. A few months after the protests had died down, he was arrested in a London hospital, following a request for his **extradition** to Spain to face charges of murder and torture. The arrest provoked strong reactions in Chile: families of Pinochet's victims rejoiced euphorically; supporters of the general were outraged, burning British flags in the streets. Meanwhile the government, in a difficult position, denounced the arrest as an affront to national sovereignty and demanded Pinochet's immediate return to Chile – whereupon, they claimed, his alleged crimes would be dealt with in the Chilean courts.

Socialist **Ricardo Lagos** pulled off an eleventh-hour victory in the presidential elections on January 16, 2000, beating his right-wing opponent narrowly. After Pinochet's eventual return to

Chile, a protracted and complex legal battle followed and these events polarized Chilean public opinion once more, but at least proved that Chile's democracy was capable of dealing with such disturbances, with the general's detainment prompting no military or civil unrest. Lagos has implemented an ambitious programme based on reforming the State. Indigenous people's rights are likely to be a fiery issue in Chilean politics over the coming decades and threaten to blot the president's otherwise rather clean copybook. The same goes for some major corruption scandals that rocked the administration in early 2003. But no doubt when the next elections are held in late 2005, Lagos will mainly be judged on his performance in the economy.

Books

Unfortunately, there are relatively few up-to-date general histories of Chile in English, with those available focusing more on the academic market than the general reader. Chilean fiction, meanwhile, is not very widely translated into English, with the exception of a handful of the country's more famous authors. Its poetry, on the other hand, or more specifically the poetry of its famous Nobel laureate, Pablo Neruda, has been translated into many languages and is widely available abroad.

Isabel Allende *The House of the Spirits* (Black Swan/Bantam Books). This baroque, fantastical and best-selling novel chronicles the fortunes of several generations of a rich, landowning family in an unnamed but thinly disguised Chile, culminating with a brutal military coup and the murder of the president. The author was a relative of Salvador Allende.

Simon Collier and William Sater *A History of Chile, 1801–1994* (CUP). Probably the best single-volume history of Chile from independence to the 1990s; thoroughly academic but enlivened by colourful detail along with the authors' clear fondness for the country and its people.

José Donoso *Curfew* (Picador/Grove Atlantic). Gripping novel about an exiled folk singer's return to Santiago during the military dictatorship, by one of Chile's most outstanding twentieth-century writers. Other works by Donoso include *Hell Has No Limits* (Sun and Moon Press), about the strange existence of a transvestite and his daughter in a Central Valley brothel, and *The Obscene Bird of Night* (Godine), a dislocated, fragmented novel narrated by a deaf-mute old man as he retreats into madness.

Ariel Dorfman *Heading South, Looking North* (Hodder & Stoughton/Penguin). Recently published memoirs of one of Chile's most famous writers, in which he reflects on themes such as language, identity, guilt and politics. Intelligent and illuminating, with some interesting thoughts on the causes of the Unidad Popular's failures.

Joan Jara *Víctor: An Unfinished Song* (Bloomsbury; o/p). Poignant memoir written by the British wife of the famous Chilean folksinger Víctor Jara, describing their life together, the Nueva Canción movement, and their optimism for Allende's new Chile. The final part, detailing Jara's imprisonment, torture and execution in Santiago's football stadium, is almost unbearably moving.

Brian Loveman *Chile: The Legacy of Hispanic Capitalism* (OUP). Solid analysis of Chile's history from the arrival of the Spanish in the 1540s to the 1973 military coup.

Pablo Neruda *Twenty Love Poems and a Song of Despair* (Jonathan Cope/Penguin); *Canto General* (French & European Publications/ University of California Press); *Captain's Verses* (New Directions). The doyen of Chilean poetry seems to be one of those poets people love or hate – his work is extravagantly lyrical, frequently verbose, but often very tender, particularly his love poetry. Neruda has been translated into many languages, and is widely available. And though the occasional displays of vanity and compulsive name-dropping in his *Memoirs* (Penguin) can be irritating, the book makes plain the extraordinary man and his fascinating life. It also serves as a useful outline of Chile's political movements from the 1930s to the 1970s.

4.1

Santiago and around

Set on a wide plain near the foot of the Andes, the capital **Santiago** boasts one of the most dazzling backdrops of any capital city in the world. Unfortunately, these same mountains prevent winds from shifting the air trapped over the valley, leaving it thickly polluted with diesel and dust, and ensuring spectacular vistas of the Andes are few and far between. The worst months for **smog** are May through August.

Most travellers stay here for just a few days before launching into far-flung trips to the north or south, but if you've time to spare you'd do well to use Santiago as a base while exploring the surrounding region. Some destinations make easy day-trips, while others demand a couple of days or so. With the Andes so close and so accessible, you can get to the mountains in an hour or two. In winter, people often go **skiing** for the day, with special buses laid on to and from the resorts. Finally, there are many excellent **beaches** about an hour and a half's bus ride away (for more on these, see the Valparaiso and Viña del Mar section). On the whole, Santiago is a good introduction to Chile and its people, offering a pleasing choice of museums, markets, restaurants and nightspots, wrapped up in a friendly, if noisy, environment.

Santiago

A sprawling metropolis of five million people, **SANTIAGO** largely comprises squat, flat suburbs stretching from the centre ever further out. Architecturally, the city is a bit of a hodgepodge, thanks to a succession of earthquakes and a spate of undisciplined rebuilding in the 1960s and 1970s. Ugly office blocks and dingy *galerías* compete for space with beautifully maintained colonial buildings. It's not a place of excesses, however – homelessness is minimal compared with many other cities of this size, and there's no tension in the air or threat of violence.

How much time you actually spend in the capital depends on the length of your stay in the country. It's by no means the highlight of Chile, and if time is really short a couple of days should suffice before you head off to the spectacular landscapes of the north or south.

Arrival and information

Santiago is undoubtedly one of the easiest and least intimidating South American capitals to **arrive** in. Connections from the airport, bus terminals and train station to downtown are frequent and straightforward, and while you should take normal precautions you're unlikely to be hassled or feel threatened while you're finding your feet.

International and domestic **flights** arrive at Arturo Merino Benítez airport (Ⓣ2/601-9709) in Pudahuel, 26km northwest of Santiago. The cheapest way to get to the city centre is by the blue Centropuerto **bus** (CH$1000), which parks at the far left or far right ends of the curb and runs frequently (7am–11.30pm; every 10–30min); it drops you off at Los Héroes on **the Alameda** (the city's main thoroughfare), where you can join the metro, catch numerous buses or flag down a taxi.

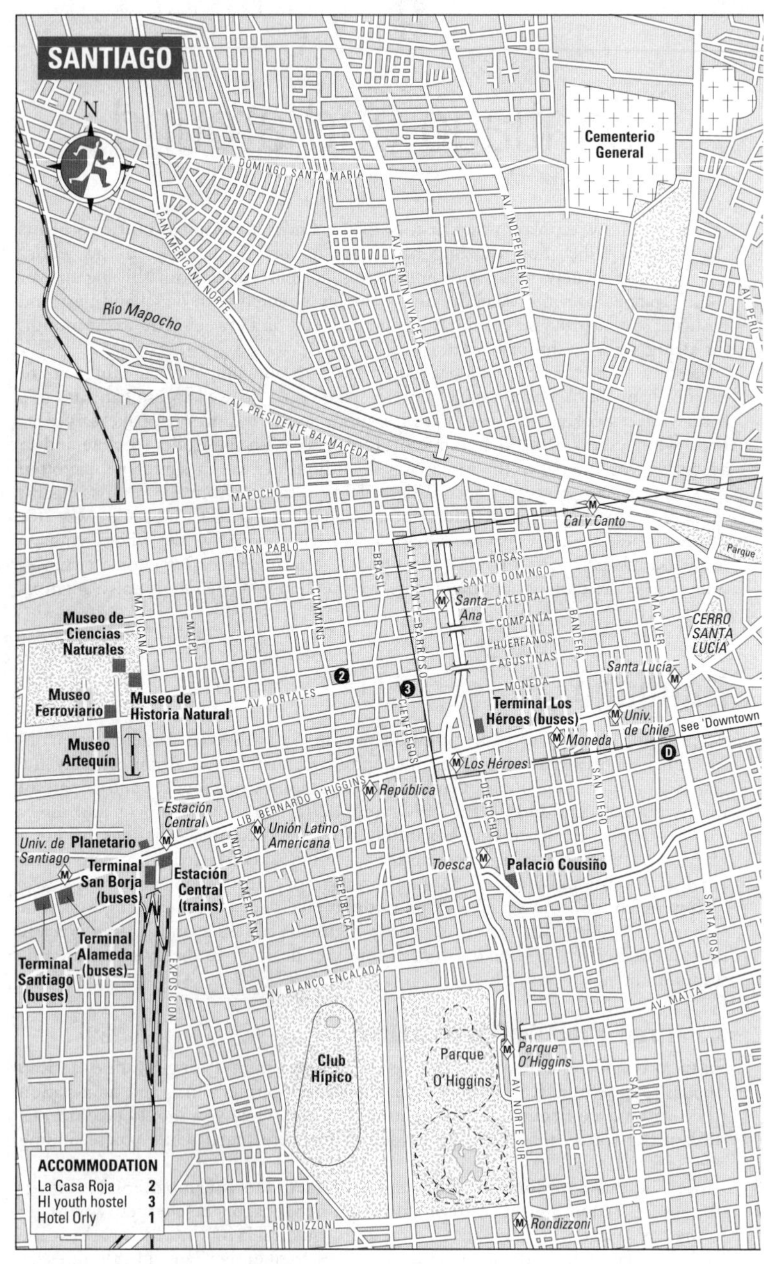
SANTIAGO
N
Cementerio General
AV. DOMINGO SANTA MARIA
PANAMERICANA NORTE
AV. FERMIN VIVACETA
AV. INDEPENDENCIA
AV. PERU
Río Mapocho
AV. PRESIDENTE BALMACEDA
MAPOCHO
Cal y Canto
Parque
SAN PABLO
BRASIL
ALMIRANTE BARROSO
ROSAS
SANTO DOMINGO
CATEDRAL
Santa Ana
COMPAÑIA
HUERFANOS
AGUSTINAS
MONEDA
BANDERA
MAC IVER
CERRO SANTA LUCIA
Santa Lucía
CUMMING
MATUCANA
MAIPU
Museo de Ciencias Naturales
Museo Ferroviario
Museo de Historia Natural
Museo Artequín
AV. PORTALES
CIENFUEGOS
Terminal Los Héroes (buses)
Univ. de Chile
see 'Downtown
Moneda
Los Héroes
SAN DIEGO
DIECIOCHO
República
LIB. BERNARDO O'HIGGINS
Estación Central
Unión Latino Americana
UNION AMERICANA
REPUBLICA
Univ. de Santiago
Planetario
Terminal San Borja (buses)
Estación Central (trains)
Toesca
Palacio Cousiño
SANTA ROSA
Terminal Alameda (buses)
Terminal Santiago (buses)
EXPOSICION
AV. BLANCO ENCALADA
AV. MATTA
Club Hípico
Parque O'Higgins
AV. NORTE SUR
ACCOMMODATION
La Casa Roja 2
HI youth hostel 3
Hotel Orly 1
RONDIZZONI
Rondizzoni

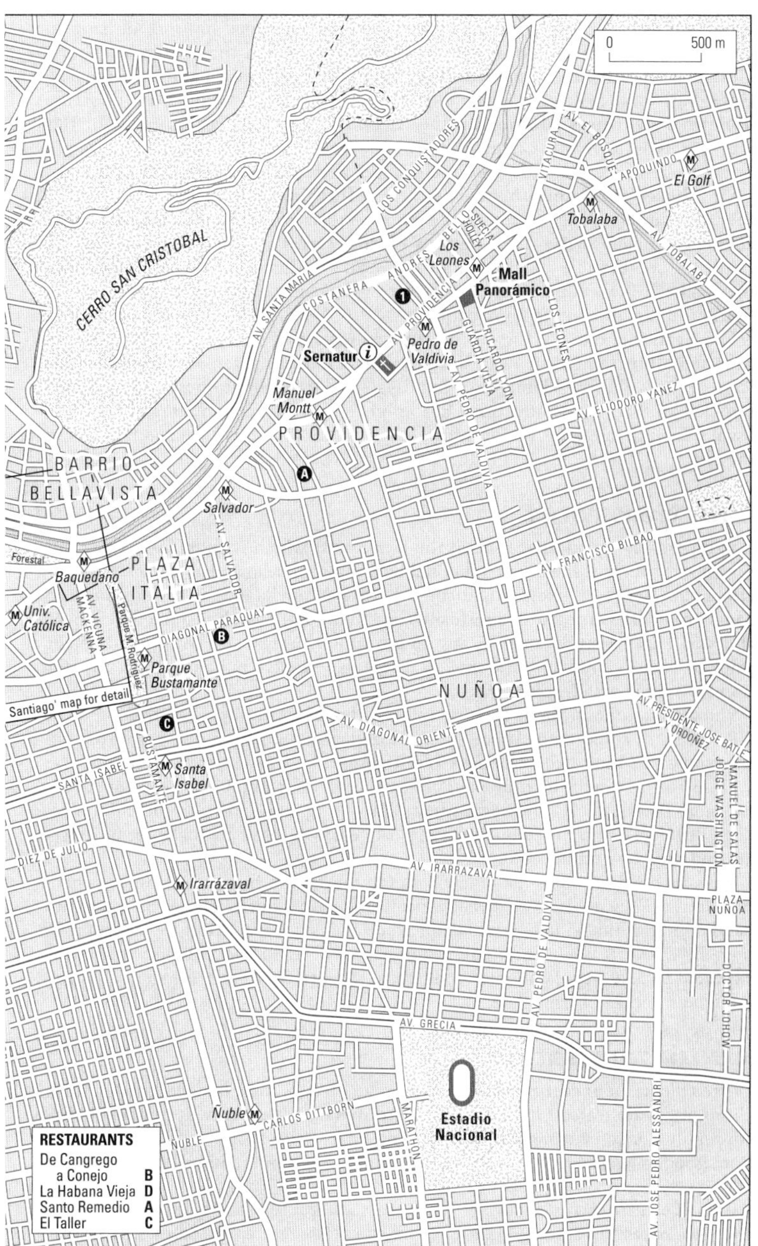
0 500 m
CERRO SAN CRISTOBAL
AV. SANTA MARIA
COSTANERA ANDRES BELLO
LOS CONQUISTADORES
AV. EL BOSQUE
VITACURA
APOQUINDO
El Golf
Tobalaba
AV. TOBALABA
SUECIA
HOLLEY
Los Leones
Mall Panorámico
AV. PROVIDENCIA
Pedro de Valdivia
Sernatur
RICARDO LYON
GUARDIA VIEJA
LOS LEONES
AV. PEDRO DE VALDIVIA
Manuel Montt
PROVIDENCIA
AV. ELIODORO YANEZ
BARRIO BELLAVISTA
Salvador
AV. SALVADOR
Forestal
Baquedano
PLAZA ITALIA
AV. FRANCISCO BILBAO
Univ. Católica
AV. VICUNA MACKENNA
Parque M. Rodríguez
DIAGONAL PARAGUAY
Parque Bustamante
NUÑOA
Santiago' map for detail
AV. DIAGONAL ORIENTE
AV. PRESIDENTE JOSE BATLE Y ORDOÑEZ
JORGE WASHINGTON
MANUEL DE SALAS
BUSTAMANTE
SANTA ISABEL
Santa Isabel
DIEZ DE JULIO
AV. IRARRAZAVAL
Irarrázaval
PLAZA NUÑOA
AV. PEDRO DE VALDIVIA
DOCTOR JOHOW
AV. GRECIA
Estadio Nacional
Ñuble
CARLOS DITTBORN
MARATHON
ÑUBLE
AV. JOSE PEDRO ALESSANDRI
RESTAURANTS
De Cangrego a Conejo B
La Habana Vieja D
Santo Remedio A
El Taller C

A **taxi** from the airport should cost CH$8000–14,000 to most parts of Santiago. Get a fixed price before leaving.

Santiago has four bus terminals serving a highly developed network of national and international buses. Most **international buses**, and those from **southern Chile**, arrive at the **Terminal de Buses Santiago** (also known as the Terminal de Buses Sur) on the Alameda, a few blocks west of the train station. Next door, the **Terminal de Buses Alameda** is the terminal for all Pullman Bus and Tur Bus journeys. From here, you can get to the centre by metro (Universidad de Santiago), or catch any of the numerous local buses and taxis hurtling east down the Alameda.

Most **buses from the north** arrive at the **Terminal San Borja**, right next to the train station and again handy for the metro (Estación Central) and buses to the centre. The much smaller **Terminal los Héroes** serves a mixture of buses from the north and south, and a few international ones; it's on Tucapel Jiménez, just north of the Alameda (near Los Héroes metro station) and is a short and cheap taxi ride from most downtown accommodation.

The **Sernatur** office is east of the city centre at Av Providencia 1550, between Manuel Montt and Pedro de Valdivia metro stations (Dec–March, Mon–Fri 9am–6.30pm, Sat 9am–2pm, closed Sunday; ⓣ2/731-8336). It offers a range of free booklets on Santiago's attractions, accommodation and restaurants, and the staff, usually English-speaking, can answer most questions about services and facilities in the city.

City transport

You'll probably spend most time in the city centre, which is entirely walkable, but for journeys further afield you'll find public transport cheap and abundant. For trips along the main east–west axis formed by the Alameda and its extensions, use Santiago's spotless **metro** system (daily 6am–10.30pm), which is modern, efficient and safe. **Fares** are the same for any length of journey, but fall into two different price brackets according to the time of day. Single tickets can be bought at any station for approximately CH$300.

Santiago has one of the highest densities of **buses** in the world, with more than 8000 of them choking the streets – and citizens. City buses are called **micros**, and are yellow. The most widely used form of transport in Santiago, they're very cheap – CH$310 a ride – and run from 5am until well past midnight. Unless you are staying for more than a week, however, it's best to avoid the buses; they're uncomfortable, dirty, bewildering to the uninitiated, and dangerous (they rarely brake for pedestrians and obey few traffic laws).

Santiago has more **taxis** than New York City – you can flag one almost anywhere downtown. They're black with yellow roofs, and have a small light in the top right-hand corner of the windscreen that's lit when the taxi is available. Fares are approximately CH$150 when the meter's started and CH$80 every 200m; you're not expected to add a tip. While not dangerous, taxi drivers are often eager to charge foreigners double or triple fare.

Accommodation

There's plenty of **accommodation** in Santiago to suit most budgets, though *really* cheap places are scarce. Upmarket hotels are abundant, especially in centrally located, highly convenient neighbourhood known as Providencia. Offers here range from good-value independent apartments to luxurious international chains.

Central Santiago

City Hotel Compañía 1063 ⓣ2/695-4526. Despite its location in the heart of downtown, right next to the Plaza de Armas, the *City* is very quiet and pleasant. The rooms, some small, are clean and well kept. Some have a view of an airshaft, others of the street and the cathedral. Best feature (by far) is the central location. Near Plaza de Armas metro; free parking. ❸

HI youth hostel Cienfuegos 151 ⓣ2/671-8532. Highly recommended hostel offers single dorm beds and four-person rooms. English-speaking staff is very helpful. A five-minute walk from Los Héroes metro. ❷

Hotel Carrera Teatinos 180 ⓣ2/698-2011, ⓦwww.carrera.cl. Chile's oldest hotel and one of its most luxurious. On the Plaza de la Constitución, it offers privileged views of La Moneda, the presidential palace and several ministries. There's an outdoor pool on the roof. One of the three exclusive hotel restaurants, the *Jardín Secreto*, is a favourite among Santiago's elite. Stop in at the bar (open to non-guests) for fantastic sunset views. Moneda metro. ❼

Hotel París Nuevo París 813 ⓣ2/639-4037. New addition to the original hotel next door, with smart, comfortable rooms and immaculate bathrooms. Best-value hotel in Santiago in this price range, and a good choice for a couple of nights' comfort at the start or end of your trip. ❸

Residencial Londres Londres 54 ⓣ2/638-2215, ⓔunico54@ctcInternet.cl. The ideal place for travellers on a shoestring budget. It's an ancient, atmospheric house in the quiet *Londres* neighbourhood, just a block from Alameda. Breakfast is included, but the one TV is in a common room and there's one phone per floor. No restaurant, bar or parking. Reservations recommended for double rooms. Universidad de Chile metro. ❷–❸

West of downtown: Barrio Brasil

La Casa Roja Agustinas 2113 Barrio Brasil ⓣ2/696-4241. Opened in 2002, this Aussie-owned place immediately made a name for itself as a backpackers' nexus. Huge remodelled mansion accommodates eighty in its various refurbished bunks and suites; there's also often live music played in the large backyard. ❶–❷

Providencia

Hotel Orly Pedro de Valdivia 027 ⓣ2/231-8947, ⓦwww.orlyhotel.com. Immaculate and highly recommended, *Orly* feels like a small-town bed and breakfast. Warm and cosy, it seems almost out of place in the heart of Providencia. The hotel has a bar and a fun little Internet café. Breakfast and parking are included. Pedro de Valdivia metro. ❻

The City

Santiago isn't a city that demands major sightseeing, and you can get round many of its attractions on foot in two days. A tour of the compact downtown core might include visits to the **Palacio de la Moneda**, the excellent **Museo Chileno de Arte Precolombino** and a climb up **Cerro Santa Lucía**. A less strenuous option might be lunch at the exhilarating **Mercado Central** or just sitting in the **Plaza de Armas** with an ice cream and a book.

North of downtown, on the other side of the Río Mapocho, it's an easy funicular ride up **Cerro San Cristóbal**, whose summit provides unrivalled views for miles around. At its foot, **Barrio Bellavista** is Santiago's "Latin Quarter", replete with small cafés, *salsatecas* and restaurants. It is also the site of the former **house of poet Pablo Neruda**, now an intriguing museum.

Plaza de Armas and around

The **Plaza de Armas** is the epicentre of Santiago, both literally – it's where all distances to the rest of Chile are measured from – and symbolically. This is where the young capital's most important seats of power – the law courts, the governor's palace and the cathedral – were built, and where its markets, bullfights, festivals and other public activities took place. These days the open market space has been replaced by flower gardens and numerous trees; palms, poplars and eucalyptus tower over benches packed with Peruvian job-hunters, giggling schoolchildren, gossiping old men, lovers, tourists, indulgent grandmothers and packs of uniformed shopgirls on their lunch break.

The west side of the square is dominated by the grandiose stone bulk of the **Cathedral** (Mon–Sat 9am–7pm, Sun 9am–noon). A combination of Neoclassical and Baroque styles, with its orderly columns and pediment and its ornate bell towers, the cathedral bears the mark of **Joaquín Toesca**, who was brought from Italy in 1780 to oversee its completion.

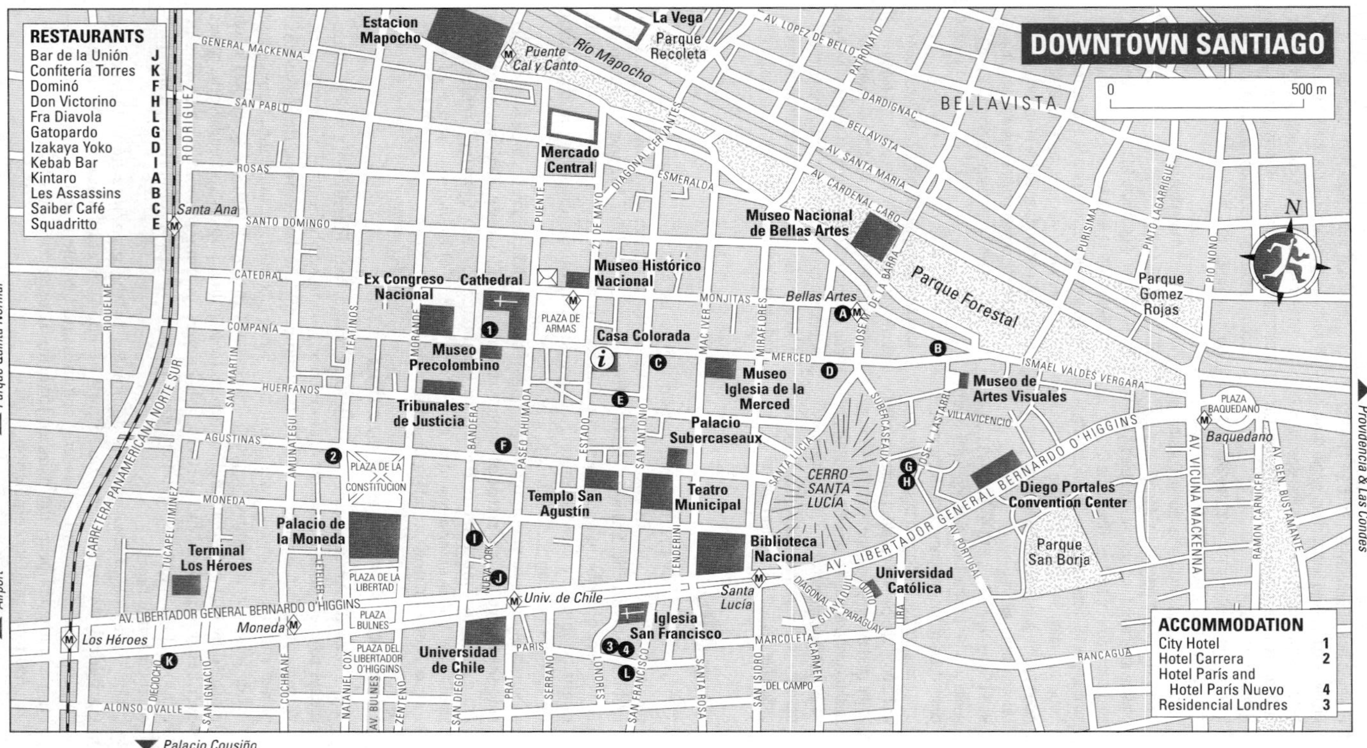
DOWNTOWN SANTIAGO
0
500 m
N
RESTAURANTS
Bar de la Unión J
Confitería Torres K
Dominó F
Don Victorino H
Fra Diavola L
Gatopardo G
Izakaya Yoko D
Kebab Bar I
Kintaro A
Les Assassins B
Saiber Café C
Squadritto E
ACCOMMODATION
City Hotel 1
Hotel Carrera 2
Hotel París and Hotel París Nuevo 4
Residencial Londres 3
Estacion Mapocho
La Vega
Parque Recoleta
Puente Cal y Canto
Río Mapocho
BELLAVISTA
Mercado Central
Museo Nacional de Bellas Artes
Parque Forestal
Parque Gomez Rojas
Museo Histórico Nacional
Ex Congreso Nacional
Cathedral
PLAZA DE ARMAS
Casa Colorada
Museo Precolombino
Tribunales de Justicia
Museo Iglesia de la Merced
Palacio Subercaseaux
Museo de Artes Visuales
CERRO SANTA LUCÍA
Templo San Agustín
Teatro Municipal
Biblioteca Nacional
Palacio de la Moneda
PLAZA DE LA CONSTITUCIÓN
PLAZA DE LA LIBERTAD
PLAZA BULNES
PLAZA DEL LIBERTADOR O'HIGGINS
Terminal Los Héroes
Universidad de Chile
Iglesia San Francisco
Universidad Católica
Diego Portales Convention Center
Parque San Borja
PLAZA BAQUEDANO
Baquedano
Bellas Artes
Santa Lucía
Univ. de Chile
Moneda
Los Héroes
Santa Ana
AV. LIBERTADOR GENERAL BERNARDO O'HIGGINS
AV. VICUNA MACKENNA
AV. GEN. BUSTAMANTE
RAMON CARNICER
AV. PORTUGAL
CARRETERA PANAMERICANA NORTE SUR
AV. LOPEZ DE BELLO
PATRONATO
DARDIGNAC
BELLAVISTA
AV. SANTA MARIA
AV. CARDENAL CARO
PURISIMA
PINTO LAGARRIGUE
PIO NONO
GENERAL MACKENNA
SAN PABLO
ROSAS
SANTO DOMINGO
CATEDRAL
COMPAÑIA
HUERFANOS
AGUSTINAS
MONEDA
RODRIGUEZ
RIQUELME
SAN MARTIN
TEATINOS
AMUNATEGUI
MORANDE
BANDERA
PASEO AHUMADA
ESTADO
SAN ANTONIO
PUENTE
21 DE MAYO
DIAGONAL CERVANTES
ESMERALDA
MAC IVER
MIRAFLORES
MONJITAS
MERCED
JOSE M. DE LA BARRA
ISMAEL VALDES VERGARA
SUBERCASEAUX
JOSE V. LASTARRI
VILLAVICENCIO
SANTA LUCIA
TUCAPEL JIMINEZ
LETELLER
NUEVA YORK
TENDERINI
DIAGONAL PARAGUAY
GUAYAQUIL
QUITO
LIRA
CARMEN
MARCOLETA
DEL CAMPO
RANCAGUA
PARIS
LONDRES
SAN FRANCISCO
SANTA ROSA
SAN ISIDRO
SERRANO
PRAT
SAN DIEGO
ZENTENO
AV. BULNES
NATANIEL COX
COCHRANE
SAN IGNACIO
DIECIOCHO
ALONSO OVALLE
Parque Quinta Normal
Airport
Palacio Cousiño
Providencia & Las Condes

A stone's throw from the southwest corner of the Plaza de Armas, on the corner of Compañía and Bandera, stands the beautifully restored Real Casa de la Aduana (the old royal customs house, built in 1807) which now houses the **Museo Chileno de Arte Precolombino** (Tues–Sat 10am–6pm & Sun 10am–2pm; CH$2000, Sun free; ⓣ2/688-7348). Unquestionably Chile's best museum, it brings together over three thousand pieces representing some one hundred pre-Columbian peoples of Latin America. The very manageable collection spans a period of about ten thousand years and covers regions from present-day Mexico down to southern Chile, brilliantly illustrating the artistic wealth and diversity of the continent's many pre-Columbian cultures. The permanent collection is displayed in seven rooms arranged around two courtyards, each room dedicated to a different cultural area.

From La Moneda to Cerro Santa Lucía

Follow Compañía into Morande and turn south for the best approach to the **Palacio de la Moneda** is from the northern side of the vast, Plaza de la Constitución. From here you can appreciate the symmetry and compact elegance of this low-lying Neoclassical building, spread across the entire block. The inner courtyards are now open to the public; approach from the north side (away from Alameda) from 10am to 6pm and stroll through. One ceremony worth watching is the **changing of the guard**, held in front of the palace at 10am on alternate days, involving dozens of green-uniformed police officers, all remarkably similar in height. In front of the Justice Ministry is one of Chile's few monuments to President **Salvador Allende**, with his arm outstretched. This work of public art pays homage to the man who committed suicide in La Moneda during the artillery and rocket siege that led to the installation of the military government on September 11, 1973.

From La Moneda, go east along the Avenida del Libertador Bernardo O'Higgans, universally known as **la Almeda**, a "word meaning poplar-lined avenue with areas for recreation." After six blocks along Santiago's most vital east–west artery, you'll arrive at the lushly terraced **Cerro Santa Lucía**, the most imaginative and exuberant piece of landscaping in Santiago. It's hard to believe that for the first three centuries of the city's development this was nothing more than a barren, rocky outcrop, completely ignored despite its historical importance – it was at the foot of this hill that Santiago was officially founded by Valdivia, on February 12, 1541. Almost Gaudíesque in appearance, with its swirling pathways and baroque terraces and turrets, this is a great place to come for panoramic views across the city, even when they're veiled behind a layer of smog.

Along the Río Mapocho

Besides the Alameda, the other major axis binding the old city is the **Río Mapocho**, filled with the muddy brown waters from the melted snow of the Andes. There are few historic buildings along here, as frequent floodings deterred riverside development until the Mapocho was canalized in 1891. Nonetheless, several city landmarks stand out, including the flamboyant Mercado Central and the elegant Palacio de Bellas Artes.

If you follow Calle Puente north from the Plaza de Armas you'll reach the **Mercado Central** (daily 6am–4pm), close to the river's southern bank. This huge metal structure, prefabricated in England and erected in Santiago in 1868, contains a very picturesque fruit, vegetable and fish market that's worth a place on everyone's itinerary. The highlight is the fish stalls, packed with glistening eel, sharks and salmon, buckets of salt-crusted oysters, mussels and clams, and unidentifiable shells out of which live things with tentacles make occasional appearances. The best time to come here is at lunchtime, when you can feast at one of the many **fish restaurants** dotted around the market.

The **Parque Forestal**, stretching along the southern bank of the Mapocho between Puente Recoleta and Puente Pío Nono, was created at the turn of the century on land that was reclaimed from the river after it was channelled. Lined with long rows of trees and lampposts, it provides a picturesque setting for the **Palacio de Bellas Artes** (Tues–Sun 10am–7pm; CH$600), built to commemorate the centenary of Chilean independence. The *palacio* houses the **Museo de Bellas Artes**, featuring predominantly Chilean works from the beginning of the colonial period onwards, and the **Museo de Arte Contemporáneo**. The quality of the work is mixed, and it could be argued that none of the paintings equals the beauty of the building's vast white hall with its marble statues bathing in the natural light pouring in from the glass and iron ceiling.

Barrio Bellavista and Cerro San Cristóbal

Head across the Pío Nono bridge at the eastern end of the Parque Forestal and you'll find yourself on Pío Nono, the main street of **Barrio Bellavista**. Nestling between the northern bank of the Mapocho and the steep slopes of Cerro San Cristóbal, Bellavista is a warren of quiet, leafy streets lined with ideosyncratic restaurants, steeped in a village-like atmosphere. Now a centre for restaurants, pubs, dancing and lofts, it has a reputation for being the capital's bohemian quarter, thanks in part to the fact that Pablo Neruda lived here, along with several other artists, writers and intellectuals. While the neighbourhood is safe during the day, watch for roaming drunks at night, especially after 2am on weekends, require a good deal of leeway and attention.

Tucked away on a tiny street at the foot of Cerro San Cristóbal – at Márquez de la Plata 0192 – you'll find **La Chascona**, the house that the poet Pablo Neruda shared with his third wife, Matilde Urrutia, from 1955 until his death in 1973 (guided tours Tues–Sun 10am–1pm & 3–6pm; CH$1500 in Spanish, CH$2500 in English or French). It was named La Chascona ("tangle-haired woman") by Neruda, as a tribute to his wife's thick red hair. Today it's the headquarters of the Fundación Neruda, which has painstakingly restored this and the poet's two other houses – La Sebastiana in Valparaíso (see p.502) and Isla Negra, about 90km down the coast – to their original condition.

A trip up to the summit of **Cerro San Cristóbal** is one of the highlights of a stay in Santiago, particularly on clear, sunny days when the views over the city and to the Andes are stunning. The easiest way to get up is to take the **funicular** from the station at the north end of Pío Nono in Bellavista (Tues–Sun 10am–8.30pm; CH$1000 return, CH$2500 return including cable-car trip, see below). The funicular trolley stops at the Terraza Bellavista where you get out. From here it's a short but steep walk up to the huge white Virgin, where you'll be rewarded with fine views over Santiago's suburbs vanishing into hazy mountains.

For an afternoon picnic and swimming in the summer months, there is no better place in Santiago than the two huge pools atop the hill. The jointly run Piscina Tupahue and Piscina Antilén (Nov 15–March 15, Tues–Sun 10am–6pm; CH$5000) offer cool, clean swimming and, at 736m above the city, wonderful views.

El barrio alto: Providencia, Las Condes and beyond

The *barrios* east of the city centre spreading into the foothills of the Andes are home to Santiago's moneyed elite; the further you go and higher you get, the richer the people, bigger the houses and higher the gates. The one you're most likely to visit is **Providencia**, as it's home to Sernatur, various adventure tourism and skiing outfits and a thriving nightlife scene.

Eating

Santiago could make a serious bid for the title of fast-food capital of the world, with a proliferation of uninviting **chains** like *McDonald's*, *Kentucky Fried Chicken*,

Lomito'n and *Pollo Stop* spread around the city. However bland those international brands are, they are often more inviting than the hundreds of **fuentes de soda** offering beer, TV and cheap snacks – usually *un completo,* which is a blanket of mayonnaise atop a hot dog or the more basic broiled horse-meat sandwich.

Most of Santiago's **restaurants** are concentrated in Old Downtown, Barrio Lastarria, Bellavista, Providencia and El Bosque Norte. The first three areas more or less comprise central Santiago, thus are most accessible, but the others are conveniently on the metro line and not too terrible a trek. There are also some imaginative places springing up in Nuñoa, centred on the Plaza Nuñoa in the southeast part of town, and Vitacura. Perhaps the most memorable place for lunch in all of Santiago is the Mercado Central, whose central hall is lined with *marisquerías*, the most famous and expensive being *Donde Augusto*. Note that nearly all restaurants serve dinner until midnight Tuesday through Saturday. Some are closed on Monday, and on Sunday, when almost all the other restaurants are closed, your best bet is to hit *Santo Remedio*, for its legendary Sunday evenings with DJ, wine and a lively crowd.

Old Downtown

Bar de la Unión Nueva York 11, near the Bolsa. Old wooden floors, shelves of dusty wine bottles and animated, garrulous old men make this an atmospheric place to pop in for a glass of wine (CH$500) served in cafeteria glasses or for a leisurely lunch. The food's tasty (lots of fish) and good value, and the servings are generous. Closed Sun.

Confitería Torres corner of Alameda and Dieciocho, near Los Héroes. Open since 1879, this is the oldest restaurant in Santiago; don't come here for the food (overpriced meat and fish) but for the dark, wood-panelled walls, the old, tarnished mirrors, the sagging chairs and the fabulous atmosphere. At weekends there's live music from around 10.30pm. Closed Sun.

Dominó 1016 Agustinas. The most popular sandwich bar in Santiago, distinguished by its fresh, good-quality fillings. Closed Sun.

Fra Diavola París 836, near *Residencial Londres.* Busy canteen sort of place offering superb-value fixed-price lunches with a daily changing menu (usually Italian-influenced). No dinner; closed Sat & Sun.

La Habana Vieja Tarapacá 755, between Santa Rosa and San Francisco. Large hall containing a restaurant, a small dancefloor and a stage, best at the weekend when there's live salsa music with dancing. The mid-priced menu includes Cuban staples like cassava, yellow rice and black beans, and fried plantains. Closed Sun.

Izakaya Yoko Merced 456, near corner with Mosqueto. Attractive Japanese canteen offering good, authentic food at unbeatable prices. Try one of the enormous bowls of soup with noodles, or the superb sushi that melts in your mouth. Closed Sun.

Kebab Bar La Bolsa 67 ⓣ2/569-0642. This tiny restaurant has excellent Greek salads, fresh fruit juices and thick meat sandwiches with Middle Eastern flavours. Blues music, too. Mon–Fri until 8.30pm; closed Sat & Sun.

Saiber Café San Antonio 333. Probably the only place in Chile that offers the massive old-fashioned *completo* (hot dog) and a broadband Internet package deal. CH$1500 buys you lunch and 30min on the Net.

Barrio Lastarria

Don Victorino Lastarria 138. The food (pastas, fish and meat) is not the best on this street, but it's one of the prettiest and most intimate places to dine, especially at the tables next to the little fountain on the terrace. Closed Sat lunch and Sun dinner.

Gatopardo Lastarria 192, just two blocks off the Alameda ⓣ2/633-6420. Very classy restaurant with a beautiful interior featuring lots of modern art and an atrium supported by eight tree trunks from the south of Chile. Good, imaginatively prepared food, including a range of Mediterranean specialities and an excellent lunchtime salad bar. Closed Sat lunch and Sun.

Kintaro Monjitas 460. A Japanese gem, with great-value fixed-price lunches. If you want to choose from the menu, they've got a book full of photos to help you out. Closed Sun.

Les Assassins Merced 297B, near corner of Lastarria ⓣ2/638-4280. Small, informal restaurant with lots of charm, serving traditional French food at reasonable prices. Very popular, so you'd be wise to reserve at weekends. Closed Sun.

Squadritto Rosal 332, on east side of Cerro Santa Lucía. Superb and pricey Italian food in a very stylish, slightly formal restaurant. Closed Sat lunch and Sun.

Bellavista

Eladio Pío Nono 241. One of the best places in the city for a big hearty steak. A good variety of reasonably priced meats, plus very expensive seafood specialities, including lobsters from the Robinson Crusoe Islands. Friendly, relaxed and eternally popular. Closed Sun dinner.

Etnico Constitución 172, at Lopez de Bello ⓣ2/732-0119. Chic restaurant specializing in fresh Chilean seafood bound into sushi and sashimi packets. Meals are moderately priced. It attracts the beautiful people and gets buzzing most every night around 11pm. Great stop for pisco sours, a sushi platter and people watching. Closed Sun.

Galindo Corner of Constitución and Dardignac. Cheap food, strong drinks and tradition all line up at the bar until all hours. In summer the tables spill out onto the street and invite many nearby copycats, but the young bohemian crowd definitely looks for this classic Bellavista hang-out.

La Divina Comedia Purísima 215. A friendly, reasonably priced Italian restaurant, extravagantly decorated with frescoes corresponding to whichever room you're in: Hell, Heaven or Purgatory. The salmon *carpaccio* is well worth a try. Closed Sun.

Skiing near Santiago

Santiago is only ninety minutes from some of the best **skiing** in South America. You don't need equipment to take advantage of this – rental skis, clothes and transport to the slopes are easily arranged – and the runs are close enough to the capital to make day-trips perfectly feasible. Sunshine is abundant and lift queues are practically nonexistent during weekdays. The season normally lasts from mid-June to early October, with snow virtually guaranteed from mid-July to the first week in September. The most expensive and crowded periods of the year are the Chilean winter vacation, during the last weeks of July, and the national holidays in the week of September 18. There are various options for **day-trips from Santiago**: either the two-hour highway drive to Portillo near the Argentine border, or the ninety-minute serpentine road to the service village of **Farellones**, where three resorts are increasingly linked together.

Farellones itself, sitting high in the Andes at the foot of Cerro Colorado, is a straggling collection of hotels and apartments. It's connected by paved roads to the ski resorts of El Colorado (4km north), La Parva (2km further on) and the chic Valle Nevado (a winding 14km east). **El Colorado** – also reached from Farellones by ski lift – has fifteen lifts and 22 runs, covering a wide range of levels. Elevations range from 2430m to 3333m. The resort's base is known as Villa El Colorado, and includes several apart-hotels, restaurants and pubs. Neighbouring **La Parva** has moderate terrain, huge swaths of backcountry skiing and an aged but classy feel. The skiing here is excellent, with some very long intermediate cruising runs and a vertical drop of nearly 1000m. The resort has thirty pistes and fourteen lifts, but limited accommodation facilities, as most people who come here have their own chalet or rent one. **Valle Nevado**, connected to both El Colorado and La Parva by ski runs, is a luxury resort with three first-class hotels and some very good restaurants. It has 27 runs and eight lifts and is the clear favourite for snowboarders.

Set just off the international road from Los Andes, 7km short of the border with Argentina, **Portillo** is a classy place, with no condominiums and just one hotel – the restored 1940s *Hotel Portillo* (ⓣ2/263-0606; ❺–❼), perched by the shores of the Laguna del Inca. This all-inclusive resort offers the most relaxing, hip ski scene in South America. **Sun, snow and sex** seem to be the themes at this home to the US, Austrian and Spanish national ski teams. Being further from Santiago (149km), the hotel is designed for weekend or weeklong bookings, with an extensive range of package deals. While most rooms are expensive, there are a wide variety of options, including bunks. The rates include four meals a day and use of the outdoor heated pool and disco. Expect an eclectic crowd of Brazilians, Argentines and world-famous actors and business leaders quietly relaxing at this American-

Venezzia Pío Nono 200. A former haunt of Pablo Neruda, this old-fashioned bar-restaurant has been around for decades and has more charm and atmosphere than many of its smarter rivals. The food is mainly grills, sandwiches and other traditional snacks at reasonable prices. Closed Sun.

Drinking and nightlife

Santiago is no Buenos Aires or Río. It is not a seven-nights-a-week party town, and compared to other Latin capitals can seem rather tame. That said, Thursdays, Fridays and Saturdays get pretty lively (perhaps to compensate for the lack of activity during the week), and huge, buzzing crowds pour into the streets and bars of the nightlife *zonas*. These fall into three main areas – Bellavista, Providencia and Nuñoa – each with a distinct flavour and clientele.

owned resort. The ski runs at Portillo are world-class, and off-piste options are endless. Elevation ranges from 2510m to 3350m. There are twelve lifts, as well as extensive snow-making equipment. Portillo is avidly kid-friendly and its ski school is routinely ranked one of the world's best.

All of the resorts described above have ski schools with English-speaking instructors, and equipment rental outlets.

Practicalities

A number of **minibus** companies offer daily services to the resorts during the ski season, including Ski Total (☎2/246-0156, Ⓦwww.skitotal.cl), which also rents out equipment, glasses and clothes. It's based at Oficina 46 in the lower-ground level of the Omnium shopping mall at Av Apoquindo 4900, four blocks east of Estación Militar metro (any micro to Las Condes or Apoquindo will drop you there). Buses leave at 8.15am daily for El Colorado, La Parva and Valle Nevado, returning to Santiago at 7.30pm; advance reservations are essential. A return ticket costs around CH$6000, hotel pickup CH$12,000, full equipment rental an additional CH$13,000.

If you intend to drive up yourself, note that traffic is only allowed up the road to Farellones until noon, and back down to Santiago from 2pm onwards; tyre chains are often required but seldom used, and can be rented on the way up. Each resort has its own **lift ticket**, the price of which ranges from CH$10,000 on weekdays to CH$17,000 at weekends.

If you want to stay, you've got several **accommodation** options. At Farellones you could try cosy *Hotel Tupungato* (☎2/321-1033; ⑥) or the *Refugio Club Andino* (☎2/242-5453; ④). The choices in El Colorado include upmarket *Hotel Posada Farellones* (☎2/201-3704; ⑥) and *Edificio Villa Palomar* (☎2/3621-111; ⑥). The only commercial place to stay in La Parva is at the *Condominio Nueva La Parva* (☎2/264-1574; ⑥). For rentals by the week it is much more economical to negotiate with private owners – one broker is Cecilia Wilson Propiedades, Apoquindo 5555, Oficina 905 (☎2/207-3700) who has a full roster of pricey ski chalets available year-round. Valle Nevado's hotels are all very upscale, and include the grand *Hotel Valle Nevado* (☎2/206-0027, Ⓦwww.vallenevado.com; ⑦). Ski Total (see above) can give advice on accommodation, and make bookings for you. Your only lodging option in Portillo is the *Hotel Portillo* (see above).

All of the ski resorts have their administrative offices in Santiago: El Colorado is at the Omnium, Oficina 47, Av Apoquindo 4900, Las Condes (☎2/246-3344, Ⓦwww.elcolorado.cl); La Parva is at La Concepción 266, Oficina 301, Providencia (☎2/264-1466. Ⓦwww.skilaparva.cl); Valle Nevado is at Gertrudis Echeñique 441, Las Condes (☎2/698-0103, Ⓦwww.vallenevado.com); and Portillo is at Renato Sanchez 4270, Vitacura (☎2/263-0595, Ⓦwww.skiportillo.com).

Bear in mind that at the weekend things don't liven up until quite late in Santiago – from around 10 or 11pm in restaurants, and from about midnight to 1am in clubs. Also be aware that the English word "**nightclub**" in Chile means "brothel". Prostitution is very common here: at least a dozen highly publicized brothels thrive throughout Santiago, and newspapers run pages of advertisements for "saunas". While Chilean health officials contend that doctors check the women every month, that is probably an exaggeration.

For details of who's playing where and when, check the listings section (under "Recitales") of Friday's *El Mercurio* or *La Tercera*, or visit *la Feria del Disco* at Ahumada 286, where performances are advertised and tickets are sold at the Ticketmaster counter. Excellent national bands to see live are classics Inti Illimani and Las Jaivas. Newer acts worth catching include La Floripondio, La Ley and Pozze Latina.

Batuta Jorge Washington 52, Plaza Nuñoa, Nuñoa. Dark room with a bar and a dancefloor; no trendy decor but a great, grungy atmosphere. Hosts established and new bands (usually Fridays). It's a disco on Saturday. Don't dress smart. CH$3000.

Boomerang Holley 2285, Providencia. Chile's top beer joint is owned by an Australian who mixes moderately priced drinks, tasty bar food and rocking weekend parties. Popular with foreigners and young Chilenas, this is a good place to drink and dance until the wee hours of the morning.

Flannery's Irish Pub Encomenderos 83, just off El Bosque Norte, Providencia. Irish pub with huge gringo clientele. Bar food is moderately priced and surprisingly good. One of Chile's better beer joints.

Las Lanzas Humberto Trucco 25, Plaza Nuñoa, Nuñoa. This traditional old bar-restaurant, with its tables spilling onto the pavement, is *the* classic drinking spot in Nuñoa. It's also a good place to eat, offering a range of fish dishes at amazingly low prices. The drinks are cheap, too.

Liguria Av Providencia 1373, Providencia. One of the most popular and packed bars in Santiago. Open late, excellent food, this is the place for a 3am Greek salad or round of pisco sours. Plenty of room in back if the street tables are full.

La Maestra Vida Pío Nono 380, Bellavista. Small, crowded *salsoteca* with a friendly atmosphere – no need to feel shy about practising your salsa here. All-age crowd, including plenty of ageing Latin American revolutionaries. Cover is CH$2500.

Listings

Airlines Aerolíneas Argentinas, Moneda 756 ⓣ2/639-3922; Air France, sixth floor, Alcantara 44 ⓣ2/290-9300; Alitalia, Oficina 21, Av El Bosque Norte 0107 ⓣ2/378-8230; American Airlines, Huérfanos 1199 ⓣ2/679-0000; Avianca, Office 101–106, Santa Magdalena 116 ⓣ2/270-6600; British Airways, third floor, Isidora Goyenechea 2934 ⓣ2/330-8600; Copa Airlines, Oficina 703, Fidel Oteiza 1921 ⓣ2/200-2100; Iberia, eighth floor, Bandera 206 ⓣ2/870-1070; KLM, second floor, San Sebastián 2839 ⓣ2/233-0011; Lacsa, second floor, Dr Barros Borgoño 105 ⓣ2/235-5500; LanChile, Agustinas 640 ⓣ2/526-2000; Lloyd Aero Boliviano ⓣ600/200-2015; Lufthansa, sixteenth floor, Moneda 970 ⓣ2/630-1655; Pluna, ninth floor, Av El Bosque Norte 0177 ⓣ2/707-8000; Swissair, Oficina 810, Av Barros Errázuriz 1954 ⓣ2/244-2888; Tame, sixteenth floor, Moneda 970 ⓣ2/630-1681; United Airlines, Tenderini 171 ⓣ2/337-0000; Varig, ninth floor, Av El Bosque Norte 0177 ⓣ2/707-8000.

Banks, cambios and ATMs ATM machines can be found all over downtown, especially along Moneda, on Huérfanos between Ahumada and Mac Iver, on Miraflores and along Alameda itself. Note that banks are open only from 9am to 2pm. Many commercial establishments all over the city also have ATMs in the entryway; look for the maroon Redbanc signs. The best place to change cash and travellers' cheques is the cluster of change houses on Agustinas between Ahumada and Bandera. There is also a cluster of change houses on Pedro de Valdivia Norte. Few Chilean banks are useful for changing dollars, but Citibank (many branches, including Huérfanos 770, Ahumada 40, Teatinos 180 and La Bolsa 64) charges no commission for changing US dollars into pesos.

Car rental Automóvil Club de Chile ⓣ2/431-1106 or 431-1107; Avis, airport and San Pablo 9900 ⓣ600/601-9966; Budget, Francisco Bilbao 1439 ⓣ2/362-3200; Chilean Rent a Car, Bellavista 0183 ⓣ2/737-9650; Diamond, airport ⓣ2/211-2682 and Manquehue Sur 841 ⓣ2/212-1523; Dollar, Av Kennedy 8292 ⓣ2/202-5510; Hertz, airport ⓣ2/601-0477 and Av Andrés Bello 1469 ⓣ2/420-5200; Just, Helvecia 228 ⓣ2/232-0900;

Lacroce, Oficina 68, Av Apoquindo 6415 ⓣ2/821-4243; Lys, Miraflores 537 ⓣ2/633-7600.
Embassies and consulates Argentina, Miraflores 285 ⓣ2/633-1076; Australia, Gertrudis Echenique 420 ⓣ2/228-5065; Bolivia, Santa María 2796 ⓣ2/232-8180; Brazil, Alonso Ovalle 1665 ⓣ2/698-2486; Canada, twelfth floor, World Trade Centre, Nueva Tajamar 481 ⓣ2/362-9660; New Zealand, Ofinica 703, El Golf 99 ⓣ2/290-9802; Peru, Av Andrés Bello 1751 ⓣ2/235-6451; South Africa, sixteenth floor, Av 11 de Septiembre 2353 ⓣ2/231-2862; UK, Av El Bosque Norte 0125 ⓣ2/370-4100; US, Av Andrés Bello 2800 ⓣ2/232-2600.
Emergencies Ambulance ⓣ131; fire department (*bomberos*) ⓣ132; police (*carabineros*) ⓣ133.
Hospitals Clínica Indisa, Av Santa María 01810 ⓣ2/362-5555; Clínica Las Condes, Lo Fontecilla 441 ⓣ2/210-4000; Clínica Las Lilas, Eleodoro Yánez 2887 ⓣ2/410-6666; Clínica Santa María, Av Santa María 0410 ⓣ2/410-2000; Clínica Universidad Católica, Lira 40, downtown ⓣ2/369-6000.
Internet access Internet cafés have boomed all over Santiago, so it's never very hard to find one, especially in commercial areas. Some well-known places are: Café.com, Alameda 143; Ciber Librería Internacional, Merced 324 ⓣ2/638-6245; Cyber Café Internet, Pedro de Valdivia 037 ⓣ2/233-3083; Easy@net, Las Palmas 2213 ⓣ2/333-7112; Sicosis Pub basement, José Miguel de la Barra 544 ⓣ2/632-4462; Sonnets Internet Café, Londres 43.
Post offices Correo Central, Plaza de Armas 559 (Mon–Fri 8.30am–7pm, Sat 8.30am–1pm). Other branches at Moneda 1155, near Morandé; Local 17, Exposición 57 Paseo Estación; Av 11 de Septiembre 2092.
Telephone centres Entel's biggest branch is at Morandé, between Huérfanos and Compañía (ⓣ2/360-9447); it's air conditioned, quiet, has plenty of phones and Internet access. You can also send and receive faxes here; they'll keep them for a month. Smaller Entel offices are at Huérfanos 1141, near corner of Morandé, and Mall del Centro Puente 689, near Mercado Central. Telefónica CTC Chile has *centros de llamadas* at Local 15, Universidad de Chile metro; Local 10 and 12, Moneda metro; and Local 145B and 167B, Mall Panorámico, Av 11 de Septiembre 2155.
Travel agents There are countless travel agents downtown, among them: Andina del Sud, second floor, Av El Golf 99 (ⓣ2/388-0101), very friendly and professional, good for international flights and package holidays inside and outside Chile; Andy Tour, Agustinas 1056 (ⓣ2/671-6592), for good-value packages in South America, especially to Peru and Argentina; and Rapa Nui, ninth floor, Huérfanos 1160 (ⓣ2/672-1050), mainly for international flights (not Easter Island specialists as the name suggests). There are plenty in Providencia as well, including Turismo Cocha, Av El Bosque Norte 0430 (ⓣ2/464-1000), Chile's largest and most prestigious chain. All the above offer city tours and regional excursions.

4.2

Valparaíso, Viña del Mar and around

Of Chile's 4000-kilometre **coastline**, the brief central strip between Santo Domingo and Papudo is the most visited and most developed. Known as **El Litoral Central** by Chileans, this 140-kilometre stretch boasts bay after bay lined with gorgeous, white-sand beaches and a string of coastal resort towns of varying size and character.

Valparaíso ("Valpo" for short) and **Viña del Mar** sit next door to each other on the northern third of the strip. They are geographical neighbours but centuries apart in look and feel. Viña is Chile's largest beach resort and one of its ritziest – a dose of modernity along the generally undeveloped coast. Valparaíso, on the other hand, has a much more natural and offhand style. With its ramshackle, brightly painted houses spilling chaotically down the hills to the sea, this is Chile's second biggest port and is wonderfully atmospheric, though bereft of decent beaches. For these, you need to head north or south where you can find anything from disco-packed pleasure grounds to tiny, secluded coves – if you know where to go. Many travellers make *Valpo* their base from which they take day-trips, including to Viña.

Heading **north up the coast**, the main spots of interest are **Zapallar**, the most architecturally graceful of all the resorts, and **Papudo**, a small fishing town dramatically hemmed in by steep, green hills.

Most Chilenos take their annual holiday in February, during which time all the resort towns, large and small, are unbearably crowded. They also get busy on weekends in December and January, but outside these times are remarkably quiet. November and March are probably the **best months** to be here, as the weather is usually perfect and the beaches virtually deserted, especially midweek, though winter can be even more romantic when the resorts wear a forlorn, abandoned look and you can go for walks along the empty, blustery beaches.

Valparaíso

Spread over an amphitheatre of hills encircling a wide bay, **VALPARAÍSO** is perhaps the most memorable city in Chile. Its most striking feature is its mad, colourful tangle of houses tumbling down the hills to a narrow shelf of land below. Few roads make it up these gradients and most people get up and down on the city's fifteen "lifts", or *ascensores*, a collection of ancient-looking funiculars that slowly haul you up to incredible viewpoints. The lower town, known as *el plan*, is a series of narrow, traffic-choked streets packed with shops, banks, offices and abandoned warehouses, crowded round the quays and port that once made Valparaíso's fortune. Still, it's a fortune that ebbed long ago, and there's a certain faded air to the town.

Arrival, information and orientation

Buses from Santiago (leaving every 10min from the Terminal Alameda) and other major cities pull in at the **Terminal Rodoviario** on the eastern end of Avenida Pedro Montt, opposite the two connected towers that make up the Congreso Nacional building. There are **left luggage** lockers (buy a token from the adjacent news kiosk), though your bus company will probably store bags in its office. From here it's about a twenty-minute walk west to the old town centre; plenty of micros and *colectivos* also go into the centre from right outside the station. There's also a regional **train** service to Valparaíso from Viña del Mar, dropping you right next door to the port.

The well-run municipal **Oficina de Turismo** hands out lists of accommodation and will sometimes ring to see if there are vacancies. There's a helpful branch with English-speaking attendants at the **bus station** (Dec 15–March 15, daily 10am–2pm & 3–7pm; March 16–Dec 14 Tues–Sun 10am–6pm; no phone), while in the centre the main branch is at the **town hall**, Condell 1490.

Countless **micros** run east and west through the city: those displaying "Aduana" on the window will take you west through the centre, past the port, while those marked "P. Montt" will take you back to the bus station. To climb the hills to the neighbourhoods of the upper town, the easiest thing to do is use the **ascensores**; some bus routes also take you to the upper town, and you can take **colectivos** from Plazuela Ecuador. **Taxis** are numerous and inexpensive and can easily be flagged down on the street.

Accommodation

There's plenty of **accommodation** in Valparaíso, the bulk of it simple and inexpensive. If you're on a short visit it's probably easiest to stay near the bus terminal and get buses in and out of the centre; otherwise, it's worth seeking out a room with a view up on the hills.

Alojamiento Mónica Venegas Av Argentina 322B ⓣ32/215673. Basic, immaculate rooms with the smell of fresh bread wafting in from the bakery next door. Those on the top floor are very quiet. Handy for the bus station. ❷

Brighton Bed & Breakfast Pasaje Atkinson 151, Cerro Concepción ⓣ32/223513, ⓔbrighton-valpo@entelchile.net. Stylish decor and fantastic

Tours

Sernatur, the Chilean government's tourism bureau, has organized and modernized Valparaíso tour companies. Below you will find a select group of operators, most with offices in town, which offer tours that run the gamut from the five-hour "bohemia tour" (that allows you to drink and party and still find your way home) to day-trips to the beaches all the way up to Zapallar. Per-person prices range from US$25 for a half day to US$50 for a full day.

Andekat Chile Prat 725, Oficina 105 ⓣ32/593834. City tours ranging from a three-hour excursion, which includes a visit to Pablo Neruda's home and several great hill-top views, to full-day wine tours in neighbouring valleys. Also good for trips to near-by coastal resorts.

Enlace Turístico ⓣ32/232313 or 9/814-5855 (mobile), ⓔenlaceturistico @hotmail.com. Customized tours with options for families and elderly tourists, including historic, artistic and archeological looks at Valpo.

Marin Tour Pasaje Ross no. 149, Oficina 511 ⓣ9/433-7575 or 32/214534. Helpful tour agency that can arrange city tours focusing on Pablo Neruda or evening pub tours as well as airport shuttles and car rental, and provides local information.

Ruta Valparaíso ⓣ32/911972 or 9/844-3958 (mobile). Guided bilingual city tours for groups or individuals. Trips on offer include a full-day tour to Isla Negra or a five-hour evening bar-hopping tour.

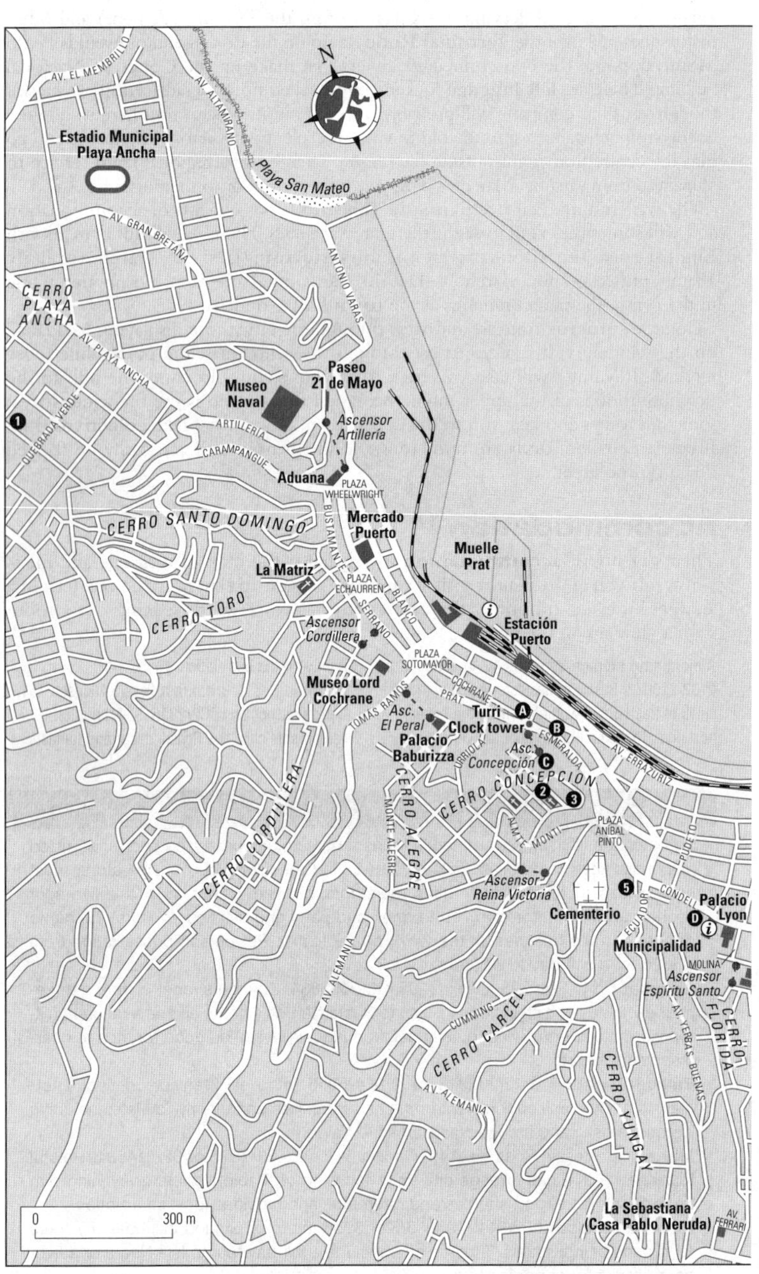
N
AV. EL MEMBRILLO
AV. ALTAMIRANO
Estadio Municipal
Playa Ancha
Playa San Mateo
AV. GRAN BRETAÑA
ANTONIO VARAS
CERRO
PLAYA
ANCHA
AV. PLAYA ANCHA
Paseo
21 de Mayo
Museo
Naval
QUEBRADA VERDE
ARTILLERÍA
Ascensor
Artillería
CARAMPANGUE
Aduana
PLAZA
WHEELWRIGHT
BUSTAMANTE
CERRO SANTO DOMINGO
Mercado
Puerto
Muelle
Prat
La Matriz
PLAZA
ECHAURREN
BLANCO
SERRANO
CERRO TORO
Ascensor
Cordillera
Estación
Puerto
PLAZA
SOTOMAYOR
Museo Lord
Cochrane
COCHRANE
PRAT
TOMÁS RAMOS
Asc.
El Peral
Turri
Clock tower
ESMERALDA
Palacio
Baburizza
URRIOLA
Asc.
Concepción
AV. ERRÁZURIZ
CERRO CONCEPCIÓN
CERRO ALEGRE
MONTE ALEGRE
CERRO CORDILLERA
ALMTE. MONTT
PLAZA
ANÍBAL
PINTO
PUDETO
Ascensor
Reina Victoria
Cementerio
CONDELL
Palacio
Lyon
ECUADOR
Municipalidad
MOLINA
Ascensor
Espíritu Santo
AV. ALEMANIA
CUMMING
CERRO CÁRCEL
AV. YERBAS BUENAS
CERRO
FLORIDA
CERRO YUNGAY
AV. ALEMANIA
0
300 m
La Sebastiana
(Casa Pablo Neruda)
AV.
FERRARI

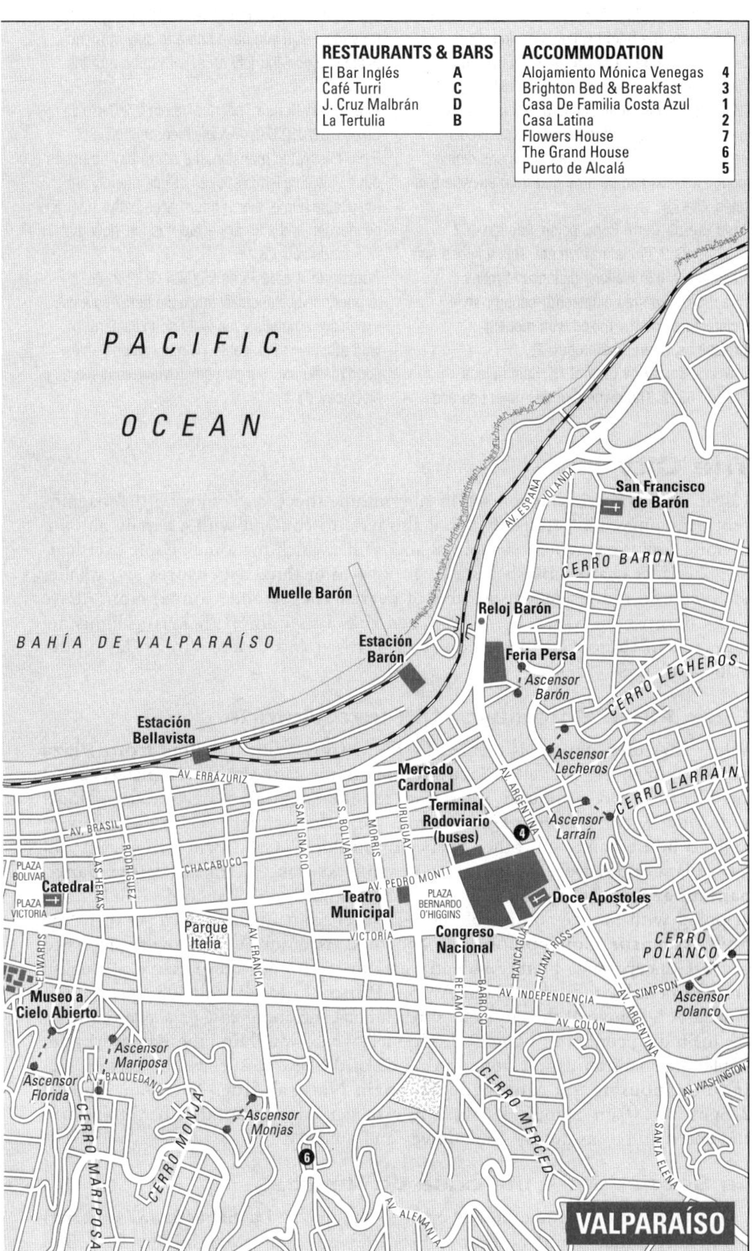
RESTAURANTS & BARS
El Bar Inglés A
Café Turri C
J. Cruz Malbrán D
La Tertulia B
ACCOMMODATION
Alojamiento Mónica Venegas 4
Brighton Bed & Breakfast 3
Casa De Familia Costa Azul 1
Casa Latina 2
Flowers House 7
The Grand House 6
Puerto de Alcalá 5
PACIFIC
OCEAN
BAHÍA DE VALPARAÍSO
Muelle Barón
Estación Barón
Estación Bellavista
Reloj Barón
Feria Persa
Ascensor Barón
San Francisco de Barón
CERRO BARON
CERRO LECHEROS
Ascensor Lecheros
CERRO LARRAIN
Ascensor Larraín
Mercado Cardonal
Terminal Rodoviario (buses)
Doce Apostoles
CERRO POLANCO
Ascensor Polanco
Catedral
PLAZA BOLIVAR
PLAZA VICTORIA
Parque Italia
Teatro Municipal
PLAZA BERNARDO O'HIGGINS
Congreso Nacional
Museo a Cielo Abierto
Ascensor Mariposa
Ascensor Florida
Ascensor Monjas
CERRO MONJA
CERRO MARIPOSA
CERRO MERCED
AV. ERRÁZURIZ
AV. BRASIL
CHACABUCO
AV. PEDRO MONTT
VICTORIA
AV. INDEPENDENCIA
AV. COLÓN
AV. ARGENTINA
AV. ESPAÑA
YOLANDA
AV. FRANCIA
AV. BAQUEDANO
AV. ALEMANIA
AV. WASHINGTON
SANTA ELENA
SIMPSON
RANCAGUA
JUANA ROSS
RETAMO
BARROSO
SAN IGNACIO
S. BOLIVAR
MORRIS
URUGUAY
RODRIGUEZ
LAS HERAS
EDWARDS
7 (1 km)
VALPARAÍSO

views at this small British-run hotel in one of the prettiest parts of town, with an outdoor terrace looking onto the bay. Take Ascensor Concepción and head for the bright yellow building. ❺

Casa de Familia Costa Azul P. Aguirre Cerda 1079, Cerro Playa Ancha Ⓣ9/889-8641 or 32/494601. This small bed and breakfast has English-speaking staff, a pool and spectacular views of the bay from the bedrooms and dining room. Pick-ups can be arranged from anywhere in Valpo. ❸–❹

Casa Latina Cerro Concepción, Papudo 462 Ⓣ32/494622, Ⓔclatina@vtr.net. This tiny bed and breakfast (within walking distance of many attractions) features nineteenth-century-style architecture smartly mixed with modern furnishings. Shared bathroom. ❸

Flowers House Av Central 15, Santa Elena Ⓣ32/376382. The owners of this quiet bed and breakfast in a peaceful residential neighbourhood will pick you up from anywhere in town. Has lawn and yard for relaxing and views of the city. This truly feels as if you have come to stay at friend's place in a non-touristy area, with full run of the home. ❸

The Grand House Federico Varela 27, Cerro La Cruz Ⓣ32/212376, Ⓦwww.thegrandhouse.cl. From this hilltop mansion, the entire bay stretches out below. English is spoken at this friendly and hospitable home, which has shared baths, Internet connection and a library – but it is the view that will dazzle you. ❹

Puerto de Alcalá Piramide 524 Ⓣ32/227478, Ⓔpuertodealcalahotel@entelchile.net. About as expensive a hotel as you will find in Valparaíso, with attentive staff, cable TV, minibar, and a very good restaurant. But no pool or view, so it seems a bit pricey. ❻

The City

Valparaíso is about losing yourself in labyrinthine streets and enjoying the magnificent panoramas. Unfortunately you'll also have to contend with a certain amount of noise, pollution, general shabbiness and crime, which for some people overshadows the city's charms. But be sure to go up two or three **ascensores** and wander the colourful old residential quarters of **cerros Alegre** and **Concepción**. Above all, don't miss the views by night, when the city's million flickering lights are reflected in the ocean like a basket of pearls – and you're sure to fall under Valparaíso's spell.

From Plaza Sotomayor to Plaza Victoria

Valparaíso's **city centre** is formed by the narrow strip stretching **from Plaza Sotomayor** in the west and **Plaza Victoria** in the east. Almost completely devastated by the 1906 earthquake, it has evolved into a mixture of ugly, modern blocks and many elegant buildings left over from the early twentieth century, which were built to house banks and other financial institutions. Calle Prat, which runs east from Plaza Sotomayor, has some good examples – take a look inside the **Banco Santander** opposite the Turri clock tower, originally the Banco de Londres and dripping with bronze and marble brought over from England. Next door to the bank, **Ascensor Concepción** (also known as Ascensor Turri) provides access to Cerro Concepción, a pretty, residential area that was once the preserve of English businessmen. Further east, **Plaza Aníbal Pinto** is a lovely cobbled square overlooked by a couple of the city's oldest restaurants, including *El Cinzano*. From here, the main drag continues along Calle Condell, where you'll find the **Palacio Lyon**, a splendid mansion dating from 1881 (one of the few to survive the earthquake) and now housing the **Museo de Historia Natural** (Tues–Sat 10am–1pm & 2–6pm, Sun 10am–2pm; CH$600). This cash-starved museum tries hard to inform and entertain but its displays look dowdy and outdated.

La Sebastiana – the casa de Neruda

Of Pablo Neruda's three houses open to the public, **La Sebastiana**, at Ferrari 692, off Avenida Alemania (Jan & Feb 10.30am–6pm, March–Dec Tues–Sun 10.30am–2pm & 3.30–6pm; CH$1800), offers the most informal look at the poet, not least because it attracts the fewest crowds and you aren't forced to take a guided

Los ascensores de Valparaíso

Most of Valparaíso's fifteen *ascensores*, or funicular "lifts", were built between 1883 and 1916 to provide a link between the lower town and the new residential quarters that were spreading up the hillsides. Appearances would suggest that they've scarcely been modernized since, but despite their rickety frames and alarming noises they've so far proved safe and reliable. What's more, nearly all drop off passengers at a panoramic viewpoint. The *ascensores* operate every few minutes from 7am to 11pm, and cost CH$70 to $120 one way. Here are a few of the best, listed from east to west:

Ascensor Barón This *ascensor* has windows on all sides, so you get good views as you go up. Inaugurated in 1906, it was the first to be powered by an electric motor, still in perfect working order. At the top, you're allowed into the machinery room where you can watch the giant cogs go round as they haul the lift up and down. There's also a display of photos of all of Valpo's *ascensores*. The entrance is hidden away at the back of a clothes market, Feria Persa el Barón, off the seaward end of Avenida Argentina. The *mirador* itself gives you a sense of how many homes are packed into the hillsides.

Ascensor Polanco The most picturesque *ascensor*, and the only one that's totally vertical. It's approached through a cavernous, underground tunnel and rises 80m through a yellow wooden tower to a balcony that gives some of the best views in the city. A narrow bridge connects the tower to Cerro Polanco with its flaking, pastel houses in varying states of repair. Ascensor Polanco is on Calle Simpson, off Avenida Argentina (opposite Independencia).

Ascensor Concepción (also known as Ascensor Turri) Hidden in a small passage opposite the Turri clock tower, at the corner of Prat and Almirante Carreño, this was the first *ascensor* to be built, in 1883, and was originally powered by steam. It takes you up to the beautiful residential area of Cerro Concepción, well worth a visit (see opposite); just by the upper entrance you'll find *Café Turri* on Paseo Gervasoni, a great place to sit and admire the views over a coffee or a meal.

Ascensor El Peral Next door to the Tribunales de Justicio, just off Plaza Sotomayor, this *ascensor* leads to one of the most romantic corners of the city: Paseo Yugoslavo, a little esplanade looking west onto some of Valparaíso's most beautiful houses, and backed by a flamboyant mansion housing the Museo de Bellas Artes. It's worth walking from here to Ascensor Concepción – see map on pp.500–501.

Ascensor Artillería Always busy with tourists, but highly recommended for the stunning vistas at the top, from the Paseo 21 de Mayo. It was built in 1893 to transport cadets to and from the naval school at the top of the hill, now the site of the very impressive Museo Naval y Marítimo.

tour. Neruda moved into this house in 1961 with his third wife. Perched high on a hill, giving dramatic views over the bay, it was his "*casa en el aire*" and although he spent less time here than in his other homes, he imprinted his style and enthusiasms on every corner of the house. Its narrow, sinuous passages and bright colours seem to mirror the spirit of Valparaíso, and the countless bizarre objects brought here by the poet are simply astonishing, from the embalmed Venezuelan coro-coro bird hanging from the ceiling of the dining room to the wooden horse in the living room, taken from a merry-go-round in Paris. After the 1973 coup the house was repeatedly vandalized by the military but has been meticulously restored by the Fundación Neruda, which opened it as a museum in 1992. To get here, take a three-minute ride in a *colectivo* (CH$200) from the Plaza Aníbal Pinto.

Eating, drinking and entertainment

Valparaíso's eating and drinking scene is one of the city's highlights, especially if you catch it in full swing on a Thursday, Friday or Saturday night. With one or two exceptions, its **restaurants** aren't notable for their food, but rather for their old-fashioned charm and warm, informal atmosphere. **Bars** are concentrated in one main area: the relatively safe **subida Ecuador**, which climbs up from Plazuela Ecuador and is lined with cheap bars, pubs and restaurants, where the partying lasts all night. Most places are closed on Sunday night and tend to be very quiet Monday to Wednesday; at the weekend, bars and restaurants don't start to fill up until after 10pm, and many stay open until 5am or later.

Restaurants

El Bar Inglés Cochrane 851 (rear entrance at Blanco 870). Longstanding favourite since the early 1900s, and very popular for lunch though more expensive than its old-fashioned, crumbling decor might suggest. Check out wall map with listings of incoming boats, which come from all over.

Café Turri Paseo Gervasoni, by upper exit of Ascensor Concepción ☎32/252091. Classy restaurant with an outdoor terrace and superb, panoramic views, especially magical at night. Excellent traditional meat and fish dishes (main courses around CH$7000); also operates as a café throughout the day. Highly recommended.

J. Cruz Malbrán Condell 1466, in side alley next to Municipalidad ☎32/211225. An extraordinary place, more like a museum than a restaurant, packed to the gills with china, old clocks, musical instruments, crucifixes and more. Famous for its filling, inexpensive *pan con carne mechada* (steak sandwiches) – not to be missed on any account.

La Tertulia Esmeralda 1083, near Turri clock tower. Stylish restaurant-bar-café with polished floors, bright yellow walls and high ceilings. Serves Spanish food and generously filled hot sandwiches (*bocas calientes*); quite frantic at lunchtime but very mellow by night.

Pubs and bars

Bar Azul Ecuador 167. Dark, blue-walled place full of candlelit tables and a very laid-back crowd. Inexpensive drinks, and live jazz at the weekend.

Barparaíso Errázuriz 1041. Funky bar with a dance area downstairs overlooked by a dimly lit balcony where you can hang out and drink. Plays a mixture of rock, Latin and dance music; popular with students. Cover CH$4000.

Valparaíso Liverpool Ecuador 130. Disco-bar with pictures of the Beatles and live bands doing Britpop covers – feels very out of place but it seems to go over well. Cover CH$3000.

Listings

Airlines LanChile/Lanexpress, Esmeralda 1048 ☎32/251441; United, Urriola 87, piso 3 ☎32/216569.

Banks and exchange The main financial street is Prat, where you'll find plenty of banks with ATMs and *cambios*, including Exprinter at no. 895 and New York at no. 659. Of the banks, the Banco de Santiago is the best for currency exchange. There is an ATM machine at the bus station.

Car rental Mach Viña, Las Heras 428 ☎32/217762; Unión Rent a Car, Esmeralda 940 ☎32/226570; Bert Rent a Car, Victoria 2682 ☎32/212885.

Hospital Van Buren Colón and San Ignacio ☎32/254074.

Post office Correo Central on Plaza Sotomayor, between Cochrane and Prat.

Telephone offices Entel, Pedro Montt 1940 and Condell 149, opposite the Municipalidad; Telefónica, Plaza Victoria (daily 8.30am–midnight) and Sotomayor 55. Also cheap call centres around the bus station.

Viña del Mar

A fifteen-minute bus ride is all it takes to exchange the colourful and chaotic alleys of Valparaíso for the tree-lined avenues and ostentatious apartment high-rises of **VIÑA DEL MAR**. Unless you adore the summer crowds, avoid Viña in February during the pop music festival that brings thousands of 12 year olds and their latest

△ An *ascensor* funicular, Valparaiso

idols together. For the remainder of the year, Viña is a clean, easy to navigate and relaxing beachfront town.

Arrival and information

Intercity buses from Santiago (every 10min from Terminal de Buses Alameda) and elsewhere arrive at the **bus terminal** at the eastern end of Avenida Valparaíso in the southern part of town. It's best to take a taxi to wherever you're staying, or a micro from the back of the terminal along Arlegui towards the centre and the sea. The most convenient place to go for tourist **information** is the **Oficina de Turismo**, just off the northwest corner of Plaza Vergara, in front of the *Hotel O'Higgins* on Av Marina (Mon–Fri 9am–2pm & 3–7pm; ⓣ800/800830, ⓦwww.vinadelmarchile.cl); it has many maps and comprehensive lists of hotels and *residenciales*.

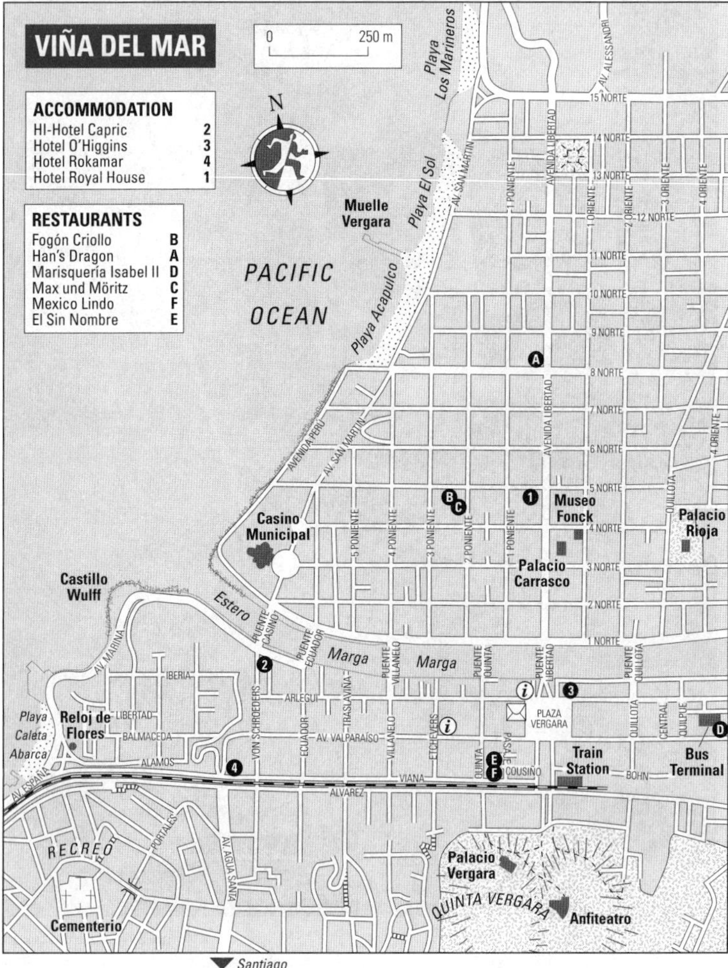

Accommodation

Viña offers an enormous choice of places to stay, from dingy hovels to five-star hotels. All the **budget accommodation** is in the southern part of town, particularly on Agua Santa and Von Schroeders, and the side streets off Avenida Valparaíso. **Smarter options**, though spread all over town, are especially abundant on the northern side. Prices drop significantly outside January and February. If you are coming in high season, book well in advance.

HI-Hotel Capric Von Schroeders 39 ⓣ32/978295, ⓔhotelcapric@yahoo.com. Probably the cheapest clean beds in Viña, this HI hostel offers simple rooms off a courtyard and smarter ones with private bath in the adjacent *Hotel Capric*, where you'll also find the reception. ❸

Hotel O'Higgins Plaza Vergara ⓣ32/882016, ⓦwww.chile-hotels.com/vohiggin.htm. Grand, 1930s hotel with nearly three hundred rooms, a sumptuous lobby and dining room. Has every possible amenity from disco to babysitters. ❼

Hotel Rokamar Viana 107 ⓣ32/690019, ⓦwww.hotelrokamar.cl. This spacious 28-room hotel in a refurbished 100-year-old mansion offers many extras, like customized meals, not usually found in this price range. Excellent value. ❸

Hotel Royal House 5 Norte 683 ⓣ32/681965. This is one of the best clean, cheap and centrally located places in Viña. Very popular, and reservations are recommended in high season. ❸

The City

Most people come to Viña for its 3.5km of beaches, though they are crowded in January and February. There are also a number of appealing distractions from the sand and sea: the **Quinta Vergara,** an extravagant subtropical park, and the Conaf-run **Jardín Botánico**, a short bus ride from the centre, more than justify the town's sobriquet of "Ciudad Jardín" (Garden City).

Plaza Vergara and Avenida Valparaíso

Viña's centre is marked by the large, green **Plaza Vergara**, full of tall, stately trees and surrounded by some fine, early twentieth-century buildings including the **Teatro Municipal** (the imposing Neoclassical building with a sweeping flight of steps leading to a grand entrance), the stately **Hotel O'Higgins** and the Italian Renaissance-style **Club de Viña**, an exclusive gentlemen's dining club (opposite department store Fallabella). You'll also find a string of ponies and traps hanging around the square, on which you can take tours of the town (CH$8000 for 30min). The south side of the square borders **Avenida Valparaíso**, Viña's main commercial street, lined with shops, malls and fast-food outlets, and constantly bustling with people. Most of its activity is in the five blocks between the plaza and Calle Ecuador, boasting modern, attractive shops and *galerías* far better than those in downtown Santiago.

The beaches and around

Viña's most central beach, and the only one south of the Marga Marga, is the **Playa Caleta Abarca**, a sheltered, sandy bay at the eastern end of Calle Viana. The **Casino Municipal** offers the usual slot machines, card games and performances by Chilean singers and artistes. But it is also useful for its loos, the air-conditioned restaurant and the all-night disco in the basement. The Casino sits in the middle of finely landscaped gardens, skirted by the coast road, **Avenida Perú**. A few blocks north, Avenida Perú swerves inland to make way for the long unbroken strip of sand stretching for over 3km towards Reñaca.

Quinta Vergara

If you make only one detour from the beach, head to the **Quinta Vergara** (daily 9am–6pm; closed on rainy days). Located two blocks south of Plaza Vergara, across the railway tracks, this exceptionally beautiful park is filled with exotic, subtropical trees and surrounded by wooded hills. Designed in the early days of the colony, this was the site of the *casa patronal* (main estate) of the Hacienda Las Siete Hermanas, owned by the prominent Carerra family. Around 1840, the hacienda was bought by a rich Portuguese businessman, Francisco Alvarez, whose wife – an amateur botanist – set out to fill her gardens with rare plants and trees. Their son, Salvador Alvarez, was a seaman and brought back exotic species from his voyages to the Far East, many of which still survive in the immaculately maintained gardens.

Eating, drinking and entertainment

Viña's **restaurants** are among the most varied outside the capital, and while many are geared towards tourists, the quality is usually good, and they offer some welcome alternatives to the *comida típica* you're restricted to in most other towns. Most, however, are fairly expensive, and if you're on a tight budget you'll have to make do with the fast-food outlets on avenidas Valparaíso and San Martín. Viña's **nightlife** tends to be seasonal, reaching a heady peak in January and February when young dancers flocks to the nightclubs and bars of **Reñaca**, a suburb further up the coast. During the summer months, micros run to and from Reñaca right through the night. In winter the partying dies out, and the focus shifts back to Viña.

Restaurants

Fogón Criollo 5 Norte 476, near corner with 2 Poniente. Upmarket "*comida típica Chilena*" is a replica of a rural Chilean country restaurant. The food, though, is outstanding – try the spicy pork *arollados* or the *conejo escabechado* (rabbit casserole).

Han's Dragon corner of Libertad and 8 Norte. Excellent Chinese restaurant specializing in sizzling *platos estilo Hong Kong*. Extremely good-value fixed-price meals, beginning at CH$1600.

Marisquería Isabel II Calle Mercado, opposite the Mercado Municipal. Local restaurant serving authentic, inexpensive fish dishes. Try the huge fish stew known as *paila marina*.

Max und Möritz 2 Poniente 377, near corner with 5 Norte. Large, tavern-style restaurant stuffed with German wine bottles, beer mats, maps and posters, and serving the most succulent meat dishes imaginable.

Mexico Lindo Cousiño 136, second floor ⓣ32/692144. Innovative Mexican food, including a number of medium-priced specialties that combine Chilean seafood with Mexican flavours.

El Sin Nombre Pasaje Cousiño 12, off Av Valparaíso. Inexpensive bar-restaurant that specializes in cheap grills and fried fish, and live music or comedy at weekends.

Bars and nightclubs

El Burro Pasaje Cousiño, off Av Valparaíso. Large, dark pub that turns into a disco after midnight on Fri and Sat. Hugely popular with a mixed crowd of foreigners and local students. Cheap beer.

Gala Restaurant Arlegui 273. Stylish hotel bar good for sipping cocktails to soothing jazz sounds.

Gato Luna Arlegui 396. Local bar with a good atmosphere; live Latin jazz and dancing at weekends.

Journal Agua Santa and Alvarez. Viña's university hang-out, serving pitchers of beer around the clock (or so it seems).

Scratch At the end of Bonn Street. This long-time favourite for dancing – one of the Viña's few discotecas – it is packed until sunrise most weekends.

Listings

Banks and exchange Most banks and *cambios* are on Arlegui: of the *cambios*, try Afex at no. 641, Cambio Andino at no. 644. Banks on Arlegui (all with ATMs) include Banco Bhif at no. 665; Scotiabank, Plaza Vergara 103; BCI at Valparaíso 193; and Citibank at 1 Norte 633.

Car rental Hertz, Quillota 766 ⓣ32/689918; March Rent a Car, Libertad 1080 ⓣ32/381080.

Internet *Cyber Blues Café*, Av Valparaíso 196, offers Internet access at CH$700 per hour.

Post office Correos de Chile is next to the Oficina de Turismo, between Plaza Vergara and Puente Libertad.

North to Papudo

North of Viña, a good road meanders up the coast to the small coastal towns of **Zapallar** and **Papudo** and beyond, hugging the oceanside in some stretches, dipping inland in others. It's far quieter than the southern coast road, and very beautiful in some parts, particularly the northern reaches towards Papudo as you approach the parched hills and rugged outlines of the Norte Chico.

Zapallar

Among the classiest and most attractive of the Litoral's resorts, **ZAPALLAR**, about sixty kilometres north of Viña del Mar, is set on a sheltered, horseshoe-shaped bay backed by lushly wooded hills where luxurious holiday homes and handsome old mansions nestle between the pine trees. Relaxing on the beach is the principal attraction, but you could also spend half an hour strolling along the coastal path around the bay, walking up Avenida Zapallar, admiring its turn-of-the-century mansions or, more strenuously, climbing 692-metre-high **Cerro Higuera**, which rises sharply between Zapallar and Papudo; the path, starting across the main road behind the tennis club, is very difficult to find, but the views from the top are superb.

If you feel like splashing out, the stylish *Hotel Isla Seca* (☎33/741224; ❻) up by the main road, at the northern end of the bay, offers good-quality **rooms**, its own pool and magnificent views, while *Residencial Villa Alicia*, Moisés Chacón 280 (☎33/741176; ❹), is a good deal simpler but comfortable enough. For **dining**, there's an excellent and pricey restaurant at the *Hotel Isla Seca*, which now has a beautiful rooftop terrace where you can feast on their special crab cakes.

Papudo

PAPUDO is the northernmost resort of the Litoral Central, giving way to deserted coves and sporadic fishing villages scattered up the coast of the Norte Chico. The steep hills that loom dramatically behind the town are undeniably beautiful, and the place has a friendly atmosphere, particularly outside high season. The best beach is the long **Playa Grande**, which boasts dunes and sheltered sunbathing on the northern part. In fine weather you can hire horses here and go for exhilarating rides across the sands.

Papudo has a wealth of good-value **accommodation** centred mainly around the town square and on Fernández Concha, branching off from it, including *Residencial Armandini* at Fernández Concha 525 (☎33/791139; ❹) and *Hotel Moderno* at Fernández Concha 150 (☎33/791114; ❹), where the rooms in the main building are best. Papudo is also home to the most offbeat **restaurant** along the entire coast: *El Barco Rojo* on Playa Grande, owned by a hip young Parisian who arranges funky jazz and Latin concerts in his restaurant by night. The seafood menu is inexpensive and fantastic.

4.3

El Norte Chico

A land of rolling, sun-baked hills streaked with sudden river valleys that cut across the earth in a flash of green, the **NORTE CHICO**, or "Little North", of Chile is what geographers call a "transitional zone". Its semi-arid scrubland and sparse vegetation mark the transformation from the country's fertile heartland to the barren deserts in the far north. A series of rivers flow year-round from the Andes to the coast, allowing the surrounding land to be irrigated and cultivated. The result is spectacular: lush, emerald-green terraces snake between the brown, parched walls of the valleys, forming a sensational visual contrast. The most famous product of these valleys is **pisco**, a pale, aromatic brandy treasured by Chileans as their national drink.

The largest population centre – and one of the country's most fashionable seaside resorts – is **La Serena**, its attractive, colonial-style architecture and lively atmosphere making it one of the few northern cities worth visiting for its own sake. It also makes a good base for exploring the beautiful **Elqui Valley**, home to luxuriant vines and idyllic riverside hamlets. Skies that are guaranteed cloudless almost year-round and very little air pollution have made the region the obvious choice for some of the world's major **astronomical observatories**. They range from the state-of-the art facility at dazzling-white **Cerro Tololo** to the modest municipal installation at **Cerro Mamalluca**, near the picturesque village of **Vicuña**.

Perhaps the most seductive attraction of the region is its string of superb **beaches**, many of them tantalizingly visible from the Panamericana as you head north from Santiago. Beyond La Serena the highway veers inland for the next 350km, coming back to the coast near **Bahía Inglesa**, famous throughout Chile for its turquoise waters. About 70km inland from here, tidy, compact **Copiapó** is the northernmost major city in the region. It serves as a useful springboard for excursions up into the high cordillera, where the **Parque Nacional Nevado de Tres Cruces**, the **Volcán Ojos de Salado** and **Laguna Verde** present some of Chile's most magnificent yet least-visited landscapes. A couple of hours to the north, near the towering cliffs and empty beaches of **Parque Nacional Pan de Azúcar**, a small island is home to colonies of seals, countless pelicans and thousands of penguins.

Ovalle

Most visitors to the region give **OVALLE** town a miss; frankly, this is a shame. The town's centre is marked by the lively **Plaza de Armas**, dominated on the eastern side of the square by the striking white and mustard yellow, **Iglesia San Vicente Ferrer**, a large, colonial-style church built in 1849, with thick adobe walls and a diminutive tower. The streets around the square are narrow, traffic-choked and flanked by typical single-storey adobe houses. One, Libertad, has a couple of good traditional **leather shops** where you'll find finely crafted belts, wallets, bags and *huaso* (cowboy) gear. Ovalle's excellent **Museo del Limarí** (Tues–Fri 9am–1pm & 3–7pm, Sat & Sun 10am–1pm; CH$600, free Wed) stands on the northeast edge of town in the former train station. Part of the eighteen-hundred-piece collection of **Diaguita pottery** was damaged, some of it severely, in the 1997 earthquake, but the small amount on display, beautifully restored and shown to great effect in modern cases, shows few signs of suffering. Not far from the museum, about ten blocks east of the plaza, you'll find a huge, ramshackle iron hangar that houses the **Feria Modelo de Ovalle** (Mon, Tues, Fri & Sat 6am–4pm). Lively and colourful, this is the largest fresh-produce market in the north of Chile and is definitely worth a visit.

Practicalities

If you arrive by **bus**, you'll be dropped at either the northern terminal, at Maestranza 443, or at the southern terminal at Ariztia Oriente 769 (Ⓣ53/626612). Most bus companies also have offices and stops on the central Avenida Ariztía (known locally as the "Alameda"), three blocks east of the Plaza de Armas. For **tourist information**, try the small *turismo* kiosk on the west side of the plaza (no fixed hours) or the Municipalidad, round the corner at Vicuña Mackenna 441 (Mon–Fri 8.30am–2pm; Ⓣ53/620955).

Ovalle has plenty of **accommodation**, though most of it has seen better days. Notable exceptions are the spruce *Hotel El Turismo*, at Victoria 295 (Ⓣ53/623536; ❻), offering spacious, well-kept rooms in a handsome old building with its own restaurant and parking; and the very similar *Gran Hotel*, at Vicuña Mackenna 210 (Ⓣ53/621084; ❺), albeit minus the restaurant and car park. For something more economical, your best bet is *Hotel Roxy* at Libertad 155 (Ⓣ53/620080; ❹), with comfortable rooms ranged around a large, brightly painted patio filled with flowers, chairs and a cageful of blackbirds. Most of Ovalle's **restaurants** limit themselves to the standard dishes you find everywhere else in Chile but you can try the local river prawns and other carefully prepared dishes at *El Castillo*, Av Romeral 10 (Ⓣ53/630584; closed Sun), in a handsome Art Nouveau villa not far from the Feria Modelo. Second best is the *Los Braseros del Angello*, at the corner ofVicuña Mackenna and Santiago, serving delicious, if unoriginal, fare, including juicy *parrillas*.

La Serena

Sitting by the mouth of the Río Elqui, **LA SERENA**, about 75km north of Ovalle, is for many visitors their first taste of northern Chile. Three kilometres in from the modern, brassy coast, lined with the apart-hotels and *cabañas* of Avenida del Mar, the city centre is an attractive mix of pale colonial-style houses, carefully restored churches, crafts markets tucked away on hidden squares and bustling crowds. La Serena's main appeal lies in just strolling, admiring the grand old houses, browsing through the numerous crafts markets, wandering in and out of its many churches and hanging out in the plaza. Entered through an imposing nineteenth-century portico on the corner of Cordovez and Cienfuegos, La Serena's **Museo Arqueológico** (Tues–Fri 9.30am–5.30pm, Sat 10am–1pm & 4–7pm, Sun 10am–1pm; CH$600, Sun free) boasts two outstanding treasures, though most of the displays could do with improving. First is its large collection of **Diaguita pottery**, considered by many to be among the most beautiful pre-Columbian ceramics in South America. The museum's second gem is the giant stone statue, or **moai**, from Easter Island, "donated" to La Serena at the behest of President González Videla in 1952.

Practicalities

La Serena's **bus terminal** is a half-hour walk south of the centre. There's no direct bus from the terminal into town, but there are plenty of taxis, charging about CH$1000; alternatively, you can flag down a micro from the Panamericana, a five-minute walk west. If you've flown in, you'll land at the **Aeropuerto La Florida**, some 5km to the east of town and served by taxis and transfers plus micros on the main road (ranging from CH$500 to CH$2000). **Sernatur** has a tourist office on the west side of the Plaza de Armas at Matta 461 (Jan & Feb Mon–Fri 8.45am–8pm, Sat 10am–2pm & 4–8pm, Sun 10am–2pm; March–Dec Mon–Fri 8.45am–6pm; Ⓣ51/225199, Ⓔinfocoquimbo@sernatur.cl).

If you need a **place to stay** in La Serena, *Casa Valentina* on Brasil 271 (Ⓣ51/223142, ⓔfampintz@hotmail.com; ❸) is a superb bed and breakfast in a brightly decorated family home. It is run by an ultra-friendly, multilingual couple who serve excellent breakfasts and make cooking and laundry facilities available to guests. La Serena's plushest hotel is the *Hotel Francisco de Aguirre,* on Cordovez 210 (Ⓣ51/222991; ❽), featuring stylish rooms in a handsome old building and a pool-side restaurant in summer. *Hotel Pacífico*, on Av de la Barra 252 (Ⓣ51/225674; ❹), is an ancient, rambling hotel with clean, basic rooms (some with bath, some without) and friendly staff, while *Hotel El Cid*, on O'Higgins 138 (Ⓣ51/212692; ❻) is a great hotel run by a Scots-Chilean couple, with a few well-furnished rooms around a flower-filled terrace. For **camping**, try *Sol di Mare*, Parcela 66 (Ⓣ51/312531), a lovely, grassy campsite down at the quieter end of the beach, with good facilities and lots of shade at CH$10,000 per site.

There's a wide choice of **eating options** in downtown La Serena, most of them unpretentious, unexceptional and not too expensive; **cafés** seem to congregate along Balmaceda. Restaurants on the Avenida del Mar, on the other hand, tend to be more select and overpriced, though some offer excellent views and a lively holiday atmosphere. La Serena's most atmospheric café-bar is *Café del Patio* on Prat 470,

Observatories

Thanks to the exceptional transparency of its skies, northern Chile is home to the largest concentration of astronomical **observatories** in the world. The region around La Serena, in particular, has been chosen by a number of international astronomical research institutions as the site of their telescopes, housed in white, futuristic domes that loom over the valleys from their hilltop locations. **Cerro Tololo** is 70km east of La Serena, reached by a side road branching south of the Elqui Valley road. Tours take place every Saturday (9.30am–noon & 1–4pm) and need to be booked several days in advance (Ⓣ51/205200, Ⓦwww.ctio.noao.edu); quote the registration number of the vehicle you'll be arriving in. You'll be told to pick up your visitor's permit from the observatory's offices in La Serena (up the hill behind the university, at Colina El Pino) the day before the tour, but ask to pick it up directly at the observatory gates; alternatively, take a prebooked tour from La Serena (see box opposite), which takes care of all the details.

Some 150km northeast of La Serena, reached by a side road branching east from the Panamericana, **La Silla** is the site of the European Southern Observatory's fourteen telescopes, including two 3.6-metre optical reflectors; they are open to the public every Saturday from September to June, with advance bookings through the observatory's Santiago offices (Ⓣ2/228-5006, Ⓦwww.eso.org); you could also contact the observatory directly (Ⓣ51/224932). The observatory's La Serena office is at El Santo 1538 (Ⓣ51/225387).

Thirty kilometres north of La Silla, the Carnegie Institute's observatory at **Las Campanas** contains four telescopes, with two 6.5-metre telescopes under construction as part of its Magellan Project. It can be visited on Saturdays (2.30–5.30pm). Contact the observatory's offices in La Serena to make reservations (Ⓣ51/207301, Ⓦwww.lco.cl); they're located next to Cerro Tololo's offices on Colina El Pino.

All of these tours take place during the day and are free of charge but are strictly no-touching; a more hands-on night-time experience is provided by the Municipalidad de Vicuña's small but user-friendly observatory on **Cerro Mamalluca**, 5km north of the town – for details, see p.514.

with tables dotting a little patio and live jazz at weekends. It's a good, mellow place to spend an evening. The best *parrilladas* in La Serena can be found at *Donde el Guatón* on Brazil 750, a lively, friendly and intimate, colonial-style restaurant that offers live, romantic *boleros*, the Latin answer to the waltz, at weekends.

At the popular, tastefully decorated *La Creperie*, on O'Higgins 635, delicious crepes and snacks and a lively atmosphere are the attractions, while on the corner of Cienfuegos and Cantournet, dozens of good-value *marisquerías* (seafood stalls) are found on the upper gallery of the handicrafts market, all good places for lunch.

The Elqui Valley

Quiet, rural and extremely beautiful, the **ELQUI VALLEY** pans east from La Serena and climbs into the Andes. Irrigated by canals fed by the Puclara and La Laguna dams, the valley floor is given over entirely to cultivation – of papayas, custard apples (*chirimoyas*), oranges, avocados and, most famously, the vast expanses of grape vines grown to produce **pisco**. It's the fluorescent green of these vines that makes the valley so stunning, forming a spectacular contrast with the charred, brown hills that rise on either side. To get the full visual impact of the valley you need to visit between September and March, but this is a gorgeous region to spend a couple of days at any time of year.

Some 60km east of La Serena, **Vicuña** is the main town and transport hub of the Elqui valley. The road from La Serena is paved for 105km as far as **Pisco Elqui**, a very pretty village that makes a great place to unwind for a couple of days.

Vicuña

VICUÑA, an hour by bus inland from La Serena, is a neat and tidy agricultural town laid out around a large, luxuriantly landscaped square. It's a pleasant, easygoing place with a few low-key attractions, a good choice of places to stay and eat and a major new public observatory on its doorstep. Life revolves firmly around the **plaza,** which has at its centre a huge stone replica of the **death mask** of Nobel prize-winning poet **Gabriela Mistral**, the Elqui Valley's most famous daughter. Just out of town, across the bridge by the filling station, you'll find the **Planta Capel**, the largest pisco distillery in the Elqui Valley. It offers free and very slick guided tours in English and Spanish every half an hour (daily 10am–12.30pm & 2.30–6pm; also during lunchtime in summer and on winter holidays and long weekends), with free tastings and the chance to buy bottles and souvenirs at the end.

Nine kilometres northeast of Vicuña, the recently opened **Cerro Mamalluca observatory** is the only observatory in Chile built specifically for public use. Run by the Municipalidad de Vicuña and featuring a 30cm Smith-Cassegrain telescope donated by the Cerro Tololo team, it runs two-hour **evening tours** (CH$3500) that start with a high-tech audiovisual talk on the history of the universe, and end with the chance to look through the telescope. If you are lucky, you might see a dazzling display of stars, planets, galaxies, nebulas and clusters. The observatory's administrative office is in Vicuña, at Gabriela Mistral 260 (Mon–Sat 9am–10pm, Sun 10am–10pm; ⓣ51/411352, ⓦwww.mamalluca.org), from where transport is provided to Cerro Mamalluca (CH$1500 return); reservations are essential, either by phone, fax, email or in person at the office.

Practicalities

Buses drop off at the small terminal at the corner of O'Higgins and Prat, one block south of the Plaza de Armas. Vicuña's **Oficina de Turismo** (Mon–Fri 9am–1pm & 2–5.30pm; ⓣ51/411359) is on the northwest corner of the plaza, beneath the Torre Bauer. There's plenty of good **accommodation**. The *Hostal Valle Hermoso*, a handsome old building at Gabriela Mistral 706 (ⓣ51/411206; ❹), has clean, spacious rooms with private bath (although some have no windows), and parking. For something more upmarket, *Hotel Halley* at Gabriela Mistral 404 (ⓣ412070; ❺) comes highly recommended, with large, impeccably decorated rooms in a colonial-style building, and access to a pool. Vicuña's poshest hotel, the *Hostería Vicuña*, at the western end of Gabriela Mistral (ⓣ51/411301; ❼), is overpriced but has a fabulous pool and probably Vicuña's best restaurant, with an unadventurous but good-quality meat- and fish-based menu.

For **eating**, you could do worse than the *Club Social* at Gabriela Mistral 445, which serves typical Chilean meat and fish dishes, or *Halley*, across the road at no. 404, which has a large, attractive dining room and is a good place for Sunday lunch.

Pisco Elqui

PISCO ELQUI was known as La Unión until 1939, when it was to thwart Peru's efforts to gain exclusive rights to the name "Pisco". An idyllic village with fewer than five hundred inhabitants, it boasts a beautiful square filled with lush palm trees and flowers, overlooked by a colourful church with a tall, wooden tower. Locals sell home-made jam and marmalade in the square, and its abundant shade provides a welcome relief from the sun. Down by the main road, the **Solar de Pisco Elqui** is Chile's oldest pisco distillery, which today (considerably modernized) produces the famous Tres Erres brand. There are free **guided tours** (daily 10am–7pm) around the old part of the plant, with tastings at the end.

Copiapó

Overlooked by rippling mountains, the prosperous city of **COPIAPÓ** sits in the flat basin of the **Río Copiapó**, some 60km from the coast and 145km north of

Pisco

The fruity, aromatic brandy known as **pisco** is Chile's undisputed national drink. Made from the distilled wine of Muscatel grapes, it's produced in the transverse valleys of northern Chile, particularly the Elqui Valley, where consistently high temperatures, light, alkaline soil and brilliant sunshine combine to produce grapes with a high sugar content and low acidity, perfect for distillation. Some believe its name derives from the Quechua word "Pisku", which means "flying bird"; others say that the drink was named for the small Peruvian port from which it was shipped, illegally, during colonial times. It's most commonly drunk as a tangy, refreshing aperitif known as **pisco sour**, an ice-cold mix of pisco, lemon juice and sugar – sometimes with whisked eggwhite for a frothy head and angostura bitters for an extra zing. A visit to one of the distilleries in the region is not to be missed – if only for the free tasting at the end.

Vallenar. There isn't a great deal to do here, however, and Copiapó's main use to travellers tends to be as a springboard for excursions into the surrounding region. The nucleus of Copiapó is the large, green **Plaza Prat**, lined with 84 towering old pepper trees planted in 1880. On the southwest corner of the square stands the mid-nineteenth-century **Iglesia Catedral**, designed by the English architect William Rogers, sporting a Neoclassical three-door portico and topped by an unusual tiered wooden tower. Just off the northwest corner of the square, at the corner of Colipí and Rodriguez, the University of Atacama's excellent **Museo Mineralógico** (Mon–Fri 10am–1pm & 3.30–7pm, Sat 10am–1pm; CH$300) displays a glittering collection of over two thousand mineral samples from around the world, including huge chunks of malachite, amethyst, quartz, marble and onyx.

Practicalities

Copiapó's main **bus terminal** is centrally located on the corner of Freire and Chacabuco, three blocks south of Plaza Prat. Next door, also on Chacabuco, is the **Tur Bus terminal**, while one block east, on the corner of Freire and Colipí, is the gleaming new **Pullman Bus terminal**. The **airport** is 15km northwest of the city. There are no buses from the airport into the centre, but there's always a **minibus** there to meet arriving planes; it will take you into town for around CH$2000.

There's a **Sernatur** office on the north side of Plaza Prat, at Los Carrera 691 (mid-Dec to Feb Mon–Fri 8.30am–8pm, Sat 10am–2pm & 4–7pm; March to mid-Dec Mon–Fri 8.30am–6pm; ⓣ52/212838). **Conaf**, at Atacama 898 (Mon–Fri 9am–1pm & 2.30–5.30pm; ⓣ52/213404), will give you information on protected areas in Region IV, including Pan de Azúcar and Nevado de Tres Cruces national parks; it's also good source of information on road conditions in the altiplano.

For **accommodation**, try the small, charming and impeccably decorated *Hotel La Casona*, on O'Higgins 150 (ⓣ52/217277; ❻); it has an English-speaking owner and offers excellent breakfasts included in the rate, while other meals are available. Also on O'Higgans, the *Hotel Chagall* at no. 760 (ⓣ52/213775; ❼), is a North American-style hotel with an attractive lobby and bar, spacious, new-looking rooms, smart baths, a good restaurant and private parking. The *Hotel Montecatini I*, on Infante 766 (ⓣ52/211363; ❻), has its own parking as well as bright, spacious rooms falling into two classes: smart, new "ejecutivo" and older but cheaper "turista", both with private bath. Finally, the *Residencial Ben Bow*, on Rodriguez 541 (ⓣ52/217634; ❸), features cramped but perfectly fine little rooms, among the cheapest in town.

Among Copiapó's **restaurants** are the old-fashioned *El Corsario*, on Atacama 245, with tables around the interior patio of an old adobe house. It offers basic traditional Chilean dishes such as *pastel de choclo* and *humitas*. The elegant restaurant of the *Hotel Miramonti* Ramón Freire 731, opposite the Pullman Bus terminal, serves decent but quite expensive Italian food – then spoils it all with appalling music, while *La Pizza di Tito*, at Chacabuco 710, is an intimate Italian restaurant offering pizzas, pastas and good service.

Around Copiapó

The region around Copiapó offers some of the most striking and varied landscapes in Chile. High up in the Andes, Chile is transformed into a world of salt flats, volcanoes and lakes, encompassed by the **Parque Nacional Nevado de Tres Cruces**, the **Volcán Ojos de Salado** and the blue-green **Laguna Verde**. To the west, **Bahía Inglesa**, near the port of **Caldera**, could be a little chunk of the Mediterranean, with pristine sands and odd-shaped rocks rising out of the sea. Further south, reached only in a 4WD, the coast is lined with wild, deserted **beaches** lapped by turquoise waters.

Parque Nacional Nevado de Tres Cruces

The bumpy road up to **PARQUE NACIONAL NEVADO DE TRES CRUCES** takes you through a brief stretch of desert before twisting up narrow canyons flanked by mineral-stained rocks. As you climb higher, the colours of the scoured, bare mountains become increasingly vibrant, ranging from oranges and golds to greens and violets. Some 165km from Copiapó, at an altitude of around 3700m, the road (following the signs to Mina Marta) reaches the first sector of the park, skirting the pale-blue **Laguna Santa Rosa**, home to dozens of pink flamingoes. A track branching north of the road leads to a tiny wooden **refugio** maintained by Conaf on the western shore of the lake. It's a basic but convenient place to camp (no bunk beds, floor space only), with its own private views of the lake backed by the snowcapped **Volcán Tres Cruces**.

Laguna Verde and Volcán Ojos de Salado

The first, sudden sight of **LAGUNA VERDE** takes your breath away. The intense colour of its waters – green or turquoise, depending on the time of day – almost leaps out at you from the muted browns and ochres of the surrounding landscape. The lake is situated at an altitude of 4500m, about 250km from Copiapó on the "international road" to Argentina. At the western end of the lake, a small shack contains a fabulous **hot-spring bath**, where you can soak and take blissful refuge from the biting wind outdoors. The best place to camp is just outside the bath, where a stone wall offers some protection from the wind, and hot streams provide useful washing-up water. Laguna Verde is surrounded by huge volcanoes: Mulas Muertas, Incahuasi and the monumental **OJOS DE SALADO**. At 6893m, this is the highest peak in Chile and the highest active volcano in the world; its last two eruptions were in 1937 and 1956.

Caldera

Just over 70km west from Copiapó, **CALDERA** is a small, easygoing seaside town with a smattering of nineteenth-century buildings, a beach, a pier and a few good fish restaurants. The town itself is nothing special, its only landmarks the Gothic-towered **Iglesia de San Vicente** on the main square, built by English carpenters in 1862, and the former **train station** by the pier, dating from 1850 and looking a little sorry for itself these days. The **pier**, down by the beach, makes a nice place for a stroll and is the starting point for **boat rides** around the bay in summer. Caldera's main **beach** is the sheltered, mid-sized Copiapina, while to the west of the pier, the large, windswept Playa Brava stretches towards the desert sands of the Norte Grande.

Practicalities

Caldera is a one-hour **bus** ride from Copiapó; buses arrive at a small terminal at the corner of Cifuentes and Ossa Varas. The town has a reasonable spread of

accommodation. The cheapest rooms – basic but clean and quiet – are at *Sra Marta's*, at Ossa Varas 461 (☎52/315222; ❸), while the nicest budget choice is probably *Residencial Millaray*, on the plaza at Cousiño 331 (☎52/315528; ❸), which offers simple, airy rooms (without bath) looking onto a leafy patio. Caldera's best hotel, the *Puerta del Sol*, at Wheelwright 750 (☎52/31505; ❼), has a mix of smart and dowdy rooms, and an attractive outdoor restaurant and pool area.

Caldera's **restaurants**, specializing in fish and shellfish, offer better quality than its hotels. Best in town is the down-to-earth *Il Pirón de Oro* at Cousiño 218, which serves imaginatively prepared dishes, including exquisite dressed crab. No-frills *El Macho* is inexpensive and always busy with locals.

Bahía Inglesa

The **beaches** of **BAHÍA INGLESA** are probably the most photographed in Chile, adorning wall calendars up and down the country. More than their white, powdery sands – which, after all, you can find the length of Chile's coast – it's the exquisite clarity of the turquoise sea, and the curious rock formations that rise out of it, that sets these beaches apart. The problem with staying here is that **accommodation** tends to be ridiculously overpriced, but you should be able to bargain the rates down outside summer. *Cabañas Villa Alegre*, at the corner of El Morro and Valparaíso (☎52/315074; ❼), offers humble but well-equipped cabins – and discounts of up to fifty percent outside high season. Neighbouring *El Coral* (☎52/315331; ❽) has comfortable rooms, two of them with good sea views, and an excellent, unpretentious fish **restaurant**. *Camping Bahía Inglesa* (☎52/315424; CH$15,000 per site) is an expensive **campsite** just off Playa Las Machas.

Parque Nacional Pan de Azúcar

North of Copiapó and Caldera, the first stop on the Panamericana is **Chañaral**, a drab, uninviting town useful principally as a base for visiting **Parque Nacional Pan de Azúcar**, 30km up the coast. The park, with its towering cliffs and pristine beaches, certainly deserves a visit.

Chañaral

Some 167km north of Copiapó, sitting by a wide, white bay and the Panamericana, **CHAÑARAL** is a rather sorry-looking town of houses staggered up a hillside. It makes a useful base for visiting the far more appealing **Parque Nacional Pan de Azúcar**, just 30km north. There are a number of **accommodation** choices, including the basic (no hot water or private bath) but clean *Hotel La Marina* on the main street at Merino Jarpa 562 (no phone; ❷); and the good-value *Residencial Sutivan* at Comercio 365 (☎52/489123; ❹), with comfortable rooms at the back looking down to the ocean. The smartest place to stay is the *Hostería Chañaral*, at Müller 268 (☎52/480055; ❺), which also has a pleasant restaurant offering good-quality meat and fish dishes. More economical options for **eating** include *Nuria* on the main square, opposite the church, and busy *El Rincón Porteño* at Merino Jarpa 567; both serve basic Chilean staples like fried fish and *lomo con papas* (steak and chips).

Parque Nacional Pan de Azúcar

PARQUE NACIONAL PAN DE AZÚCAR is a forty-kilometre strip of desert containing the most stunning coastal scenery in the north of Chile. Steep hills and cliffs rise abruptly from the shore, which is lined with a series of pristine sandy beaches, some of them of the purest white imaginable. The only inhabited part of the park is **CALETA PAN DE AZÚCAR**, 30km north of Chañaral, where you'll find a cluster of twenty or so fishermen's shacks as well as the Conaf information centre and a campsite. Opposite the village, 2km off shore, the **Isla Pan de Azúcar** is a small island sheltering a huge collection of marine wildlife. Another highlight is the **Mirador Pan de Azúcar**, a lookout point 10km north of the village, giving fabulous panoramic views up and down the coast.

Park practicalities

There are two **access roads** to the park, both branching off the Panamericana: approaching from the south, the turn-off is at the north end of Chañaral, just past the cemetery; from the north, take the turn-off at Las Bombas, 45km north of Chañaral. Both roads are bumpy but passable in a saloon car. There is no **public transport** to the park, but Chango Turismo (Ⓣ52/480668 or 480484) runs a twice-daily **bus** (CH$2000) to Caleta Pan de Azúcar from Chañaral; it leaves at 8am and 3pm from opposite the Pullman Bus terminal, at Freire 493, and returns from the park at 10am and 5pm (phone to confirm times). Chango Turismo also runs **jeep tours** to the Mirador Pan de Azúcar (CH$7000) and Las Lomitas (CH$15,000). Alternatively you could get a **taxi** (CH$6000 each way from Chañaral but worth it if there are several in your group), or you could also come on a **day-trip** from Copiapó.

The **Conaf information centre** (daily 8.30am–12.30pm & 2–6pm), near the village, offers maps, leaflets and souvenirs. This is where you pay your park fee (CH$1500). A single concessionaire (Ⓣ52/480539) provides **camping** areas (CH$6000 per site) on the beaches around the village and at Playa Piqueros, further south, as well as two beautifully located *cabañas* (❺) on a secluded beach north of the village. Rough camping is not allowed in the park. **Boat trips** to the island depart from the *caleta* and cost CH$4000 per person (minimum six people) or CH$24,000 per boat trip.

4.4

El Norte Grande

Austerely beautiful, inhospitably arid and overwhelmingly vast, the **NORTE GRANDE** of Chile occupies almost a quarter of the country's mainland territory but contains barely five percent of its population. Its single most outstanding feature is the **Atacama Desert**, stretching all the way down from the Peruvian border for over 1000km; the driest desert in the world, it contains areas where no rainfall has ever been recorded. To the west, the plain is lined by a range of coastal hills that drop abruptly to a narrow shelf of land where most of the region's towns and cities – chiefly **Antofagasta**, **Iquique** and **Arica** – are scattered, hundreds of kilometres apart. East, the desert climbs towards the cordillera, which rises to the **altiplano**: a high, windswept plateau composed of lakes and salt flats ringed with snowcapped volcanoes, forming a fabulous panorama.

For several millennia, the Norte Grande has been home to indigenous peoples and the excessive dryness of the climate has left countless relics of these people almost perfectly intact – most remarkably the **Chinchorro mummies**, buried on the desert coast near Arica some seven thousand years ago. It wasn't until the nineteenth century that much attention was given to the Atacama, when it became apparent that the desert was rich in **nitrates** that could be exported at great commercial value.

The Pacific seaboard is lined by vast tracts of stunning **coastal scenery** while inland the **desert pampa** itself impresses not only with its out-of-this-world geography, but also with a number of fascinating testimonies left by man. One of these is the trail of decaying nitrate **ghost towns**, most notably **Humberstone**, easily reached from Iquique. Up in the Andes, the altiplano is undoubtedly one of the country's highlights, with its dazzling **lakes**, **salt flats and volcanoes**, its abundance of **wildlife** and its tiny, whitewashed villages inhabited by native Aymara. The main altiplano tourist base is **San Pedro de Atacama**, a pleasant oasis 315km northeast of Antofagasta, where numerous tour companies offer excursions to attractions like the famous **El Tatio geysers** and the **Valle de la Luna**. Further north, the stretch of altiplano within reach of Iquique and Arica is home to countless wild vicuña and spectacular scenery, preserved in **Parque Nacional Lauca** and several adjoining parks and reserves.

Many of the region's attractions can be reached by **public transport**, though to explore the region in depth you'll need to book some tours or, better still, rent a 4WD vehicle. Bear in mind the **Bolivian winter**, when sporadic heavy rains between December and February can wash roads away and seriously disrupt communications and access.

Antofagasta

While the lacklustre desert city of **ANTOFAGASTA** does not rank high on Chile's list of highlights, it boasts plenty of useful facilities and is a major transport hub. Sitting on a flat shelf between the ocean and the hills, Antofagasta has a compact downtown core, made up of dingy, traffic-choked streets that sport a few handsome old public buildings, and a modern stretch spread along the coastal avenue.

Arrival and information

Buses drop off at one of two main terminals, at opposite corners of Bolívar and Latorre. The Aeropuerto Cerro Moreno is 25km north of the city. For **tourist information**, head for the excellent **Sernatur** office at Prat 384, on the ground floor of the Intendencia at the corner of the central plaza (Mon–Fri 8.30am–5.30pm; ⓣ55/451818–20, ⓔsernatur_antof@entelchile.net).

Accommodation

Frontera Hotel Bolívar 558 ⓣ55/281219. Best mid-range choice, offering spotless, modern rooms with private bath and cable TV. Some rooms can be noisy. ⑤

Holiday Inn Express Av Grecia 1490 ⓣ800/808080 or 55/228888. Modern, super-clean American chain hotel, with pool and parking – a good place to pamper yourself if the desert is getting to you. It's on the coast road, out of town, but is connected to the centre by plenty of *micros*. ⑧

Hotel Ciudad de Ávila Condell 2840 ⓣ55/221040. Simple, no-frills accommodation; most rooms have private bath and external windows. ④

Hotel Colón San Martín 2434 ⓣ55/261851. Reasonable-value, clean and fairly comfortable rooms with private bath. ⑤

The City

Antofagasta's centre is marked by the large, green **Plaza Colón**, dominated by a tall clock tower whose face is supposedly a replica of London's Big Ben. The square is surrounded by the city's administrative and public buildings, including the Neo-Gothic **Iglesia Catedral**, built between 1906 and 1917. A couple of blocks northwest towards the port, spread along Bolívar, you'll find the magnificently restored nineteenth-century offices and railway terminus. Opposite, at the corner of Bolívar and Balmaceda, the old customs house, or **Aduana**, was built in 1866, making it the oldest building in the city. Inside, the **Museo Regional** (Tues–Sat 10am–1pm & 3.30–6.30pm, Sun 11am–2pm; CH$500; ⓦwww.dibam.cl) houses an impressive mineral display downstairs and, upstairs, a collection of clothes, furniture and general paraphernalia dating from the nitrate era. At the opposite end of town, at the corner of Ossa and Maipú, the **Mercado Central** is a huge, crumbling pink and cream building selling fresh food and *artesanía*.

Eating, drinking and entertainment

Antofagasta's **restaurants** tend to be busy and lively, with a couple of classy establishments standing out among the grillhouses and pizzerias. The nightlife scene, thanks mainly to the number of university students around town, is surprisingly vibrant, with some good **bars** to choose from. Antofagasta also has that rarity in Chile, a **gay disco**, the only one in the whole of the north: *Underboys* is at Av Edmundo Pérez Zujovic 4800 (the northern coast road).

La Portada

Sixteen kilometres north along the coast road, and an obligatory day-trip from Antofagasta, **La Portada** is a huge eroded arch looming out of the sea. Declared a national monument in 1990, it's something of a regional symbol, and its picture graces postcards and wall calendars all over Chile. To get there, take micro #15 from the Terminal Pesquero; or one of the Mejillones-bound minibuses leaving from Bazar Acuario at Latorre 2733, Bazar Mariela at Latorre 2727, or Bazar Mejillones, Latorre 2715 – all near the Tur Bus terminal. If you're driving, follow the coast road north and take the turn-off to Juan López, from where La Portada is well signed.

El Arriero Condell 2644. Lively atmosphere provided by two brothers who play old jazz tunes on the piano every night. Excellent, moderately priced *parrilladas* and an interesting Spanish-inn-style decor, complete with hanging hams.
Club de la Unión Prat 474. The building is attractive, with a balcony, and the service is efficient, but the food is standard Chilean fare, though moderately priced.
Club de Yates Balmaceda 2705, at the corner with Sucre. Elegant restaurant on the waterfront with ocean views and an expensive seafood-based menu, more imaginative than most.
La Pizzería d'Alfredo Condell 2539. Popular, inexpensive pizzeria with a little outdoor balcony where you can eat your meal alfresco.

San Pedro de Atacama and around

About three hundred kilometres east of Antofagasta, **SAN PEDRO DE ATACAMA** is a little oasis village of narrow dirt streets and adobe houses that has transformed itself, over the last ten years or so, into the travel centre of northern Chile. Sitting at an altitude of 2400m between the desert and the altiplano, or *puna* (the high basin connecting the two branches of the cordillera), this has been an important settlement since pre-Hispanic times, originally as a major stop on the trading route connecting the llama herders of these highlands with the fishing communities of the Pacific. Later, during the nitrate era, it was the main rest stop on the cattle trail from Salta in Argentina to the nitrate *oficinas*, where the cattle were driven to supply the workers with fresh meat. Now it's a small, friendly and laid-back place offering an excellent range of accommodation and restaurants, albeit with an increasingly trendy feel and more than a few visitors to pack them in. And for sheer convenience and ease of access into spectacular wilderness areas, San Pedro can't be beaten.

Arrival, information and orientation

Several **bus** companies have regular services from Calama to San Pedro; they all have different drop-off points, but these are all within a couple of blocks of the main square, mostly along Licancábur. Head for the plaza if you want to visit the **Oficina de Turismo** (Jan–March daily 10am–2pm & 3–9pm, but erratic; ⓣ55/851126); if it's closed, try the Municipalidad, also on the square, but do not expect very much help. Note that there are **no banks or ATMs** in the village, though you can change money at a couple of *cambios*. Many but not all places accept credit cards, so check first.

Accommodation

There are more than two dozen places offering **rooms** in San Pedro, including a number of good-value, comfortable *residenciales* plus some classy, upmarket places for those on a more generous budget. There are also several **campsites** within easy reach of the village centre: *Camping Cunza* at Gustavo Le Paige s/n (no phone), a fairly hard-ground campsite, with shade provided by a straw roof over each site (around CH$2000 per person); and *Edén Atacameño* Tocanao (ⓣ55/851154), the best campsite in San Pedro (around CH$2000 per person), with lots of trees, water and an outdoor kitchen. Note that San Pedro has electricity only until midnight, and that, as a rule, only the more expensive hotels have their own generators.

Casa Corvatsch Gustavo Le Paige s/n ⓣ55/851101. Swiss-owned *residencial* offering simple but immaculate rooms, including four singles, and reliable shared showers (hot water evenings only). A good budget choice. ❹
Casa de Don Tomás Tocopilla s/n ⓣ55/851055, ⓔdontomas@rdc.cl. Rustic, well-established hotel verging on the old-fashioned, with spacious rooms, a pool, good breakfasts and a friendly welcome. Located away from the buzz of central San Pedro, 300m south of the crossroads with Caracoles. ❽
Hostal Katarpe Domingo Atienza ⓣ55/851033. Excellent-value, comfortable rooms, most with private bath and fluffy towels and all-night light (thanks to on-site generator). ❺
Hostal Takha Takha Caracoles ⓣ55/851038. Small but tidy and quiet rooms giving onto a

pleasant garden. A good bet for singles. Also has spaces for camping. ❺

Hotel Altiplánico Domingo Atienza 282 ⓣ55/851212, ⓦwww.altiplanico.cl. Gorgeous new hotel complex in typical San Pedro adobe-style, with fantastic views, tasteful decor, comfortable en-suite rooms, a swimming pool, Internet access, a café-bar and bicycle rental. Located in a calm spot 250m from the centre, on the way to the Pukará de Quitor. ❽

Hotel Kimal Domingo Atienza ⓣ55/851030. Spacious, light and very attractive rooms, combining contemporary, spartan architecture with soft, warm rugs and plants. ❼

Hotel Tulor Domingo Atienza s/n ⓣ55/851248, ⓦwww.tulor.cl. This place has comfortable but small rooms, and a friendly archeologist owner. There's a nice bar-restaurant attached. ❽

Residencial Chiloé Domingo Atienza ⓣ55/851017. Good simple rooms kept very clean by the friendly owner. ❹

Residencial Juanita Plaza ⓣ55/851039. Pleasant and popular *residencial* on the square, with an agreeable terrace-restaurant attached. ❸

The Town

The focus of San Pedro is the little **plaza** at its centre, dotted with pepper trees and wooden benches. On its western side stands the squat white **Iglesia de San Pedro**, one of the largest Andean churches in the region. It's actually San Pedro's second church, built in 1744, just over a hundred years after the original church was erected near the present site of the archeological museum. Opposite the church, on the other side of the square, the lopsided colonial-looking house known as the **Casa Incaica** is San Pedro's oldest building, thought to date from the earliest days of the colony. A narrow alley full of **artesanía** stalls, where you can buy alpaca knitwear and other souvenirs, links the square to the main bus stops to the north.

Just off the northeast corner of the square, the outstanding **Museo Arqueológico Gustavo Le Paige** (Jan & Feb daily 10am–1pm & 3–7pm; March–Dec Mon–Fri 9am–noon & 2–6pm, Sat & Sun 10am–noon & 2–6pm; CH$1000) should not be missed. It possesses more than 380,000 artefacts, from Neolithic tools to sophisticated ceramics, gathered from the region around San Pedro, of which the best examples are displayed in eight "naves" arranged around a central hall. The most arresting and compelling exhibits are the prehistoric mummies, most famously that of a young woman sitting with her knees huddled up to her chest, her skin all withered and leathery, but her hair still thick and black. She is known affectionately as "Miss Chile".

Eating, drinking and entertainment

San Pedro's **eating and drinking** scene is usually quite lively, thanks to the steady flow of young travellers passing through town. Many eating places double up as bars, sometimes with live music, while a couple of places also have **dancing**. Partying in San Pedro reaches a climax on **June 29**, when the village celebrates its saint's day with exuberant dancing and feasting.

Café Etnico Tocopilla s/n. Excellent place for breakfast, a quick lunch or afternoon tea complete with scrummy cakes, fruit juices, Internet connection and a funky ambience.

Café Export Caracoles and Tocanao. Real (not instant) coffee, snacks and sandwiches in a building and patio with striking decor, including Valle de la Luna-inspired tables, hand-crafted using adobe.

La Casona Caracoles s/n. Informal and inexpensive, but arguably the best restaurant in San Pedro. The dining room is very elegant, inside a large, colonial-style house, and the menu is fairly imaginative.

La Estaka Caracoles 259. Rustic-looking restaurant-cum-bar with trendy young waiters and waitresses and loud music, open from breakfast-time until 1am. Very popular, though not cheap.

La Florida Tocopilla s/n. Unpretentious little restaurant serving simple but very good and inexpensive Chilean meals.

Tierra Caracoles 46. Tiny café specializing in low-priced home-made vegetarian food, including wholemeal bread, *empanadas*, fruit pancakes, yoghurt, salads and cakes.

Tours around San Pedro

There is now a bewildering number of **tour companies** based in San Pedro, most offering pretty much the same tours at similar prices. Tours usually take place in minibuses, though smaller groups may travel in jeeps. Competition keeps prices relatively low – you can expect to pay from around CH$4000 to visit the Valle de la Luna, CH$12,000 for a tour to the Tatio geysers, and around CH$20,000 for a full-day tour of the local lakes and oases. If a company does not appear on this list, it doesn't mean it's not worth checking out, it may just be new on the block. Website Ⓦwww.sanpedroatacama.com offers more information and links.

Tour operators

Atacama Inca Tour Toconao s/n Ⓣ55/851062. Long established and recommended.
Azimut 360 Caracoles 195 Ⓣ55/851469, Ⓔbase-spa@netline.cl. The best operator for mountain ascents (plus the usual tours).
Cunza Ecoturismo Caracoles 205 Ⓣ55/851183. The standard tours, with an ecological slant.
Desert Adventure Caracoles s/n Ⓣ55/851067, and also Latorre 1815, Calama (Ⓣ55/344894, Ⓦwww.desertadventure.cl.) Professional and reliable outfit.
Pirka Expediciones Caracoles 233 Ⓣ55/851526, Ⓔpirkaexpediciones @hotmail.com. An operator specializing in unusual tours such as trips to the rock-paintings at Los Altos del Loa, with never more than four people per tour.
Tara Exploraciones Tocopilla and Gustavo Le Paige Ⓣ55/851228, Ⓔtaraexploraciones@yahoo.com. They offer a visit to Salar de Tara and a tour taking in the mine at Cuquicamata.
Turismo Colque Caracoles s/n Ⓣ55/851109. The only company in San Pedro regularly offering trips across the border into Bolivia, to see the fabulous Salar de Uyuni; it has a mixed reputation.

Around San Pedro

The landscape around San Pedro is really quite spectacular: vast desolate plains spread out for miles around, cradling numerous **volcanoes** of the most delicate colours imaginable and beautiful **lakes** speckled pink with flamingoes. You'll also find the lunar landscape of the **Valle de la Luna**, the **Salar de Atacama** (the largest **salt flat** in Chile), a whole field full of fuming **geysers** at **El Tatio** and a scattering of fertile oasis villages. You might prefer to explore these marvels by yourself, but several companies in San Pedro trip over themselves to take you on guided tours.

Valle de la Luna

About 14km west of San Pedro, the **VALLE DE LA LUNA**, or Valley of the Moon, presents a dramatic lunar landscape of wind-eroded hills surrounding a crust-like valley floor, once the bottom of a lake. An immense sand dune sweeps across the valley, easy enough to climb and a great place to sit and survey the scenery. If you're prepared to battle your way through the flying sand, you can even walk along the dune's crest. The valley is at its best at sunset, when it's transformed into a spellbinding palette of golds and reds, but you'll have to share this view with a multitude of fellow visitors, as all San Pedro tour operators offer daily sunset trips here. A more memorable experience would be to get up before day breaks and cycle to the valley, arriving at sunrise. The way here is straightforward: take Caracoles west out of San Pedro and at the end take the left-hand turn, following the old road to Calama directly to the valley. Remember to take plenty of water and sunscreen.

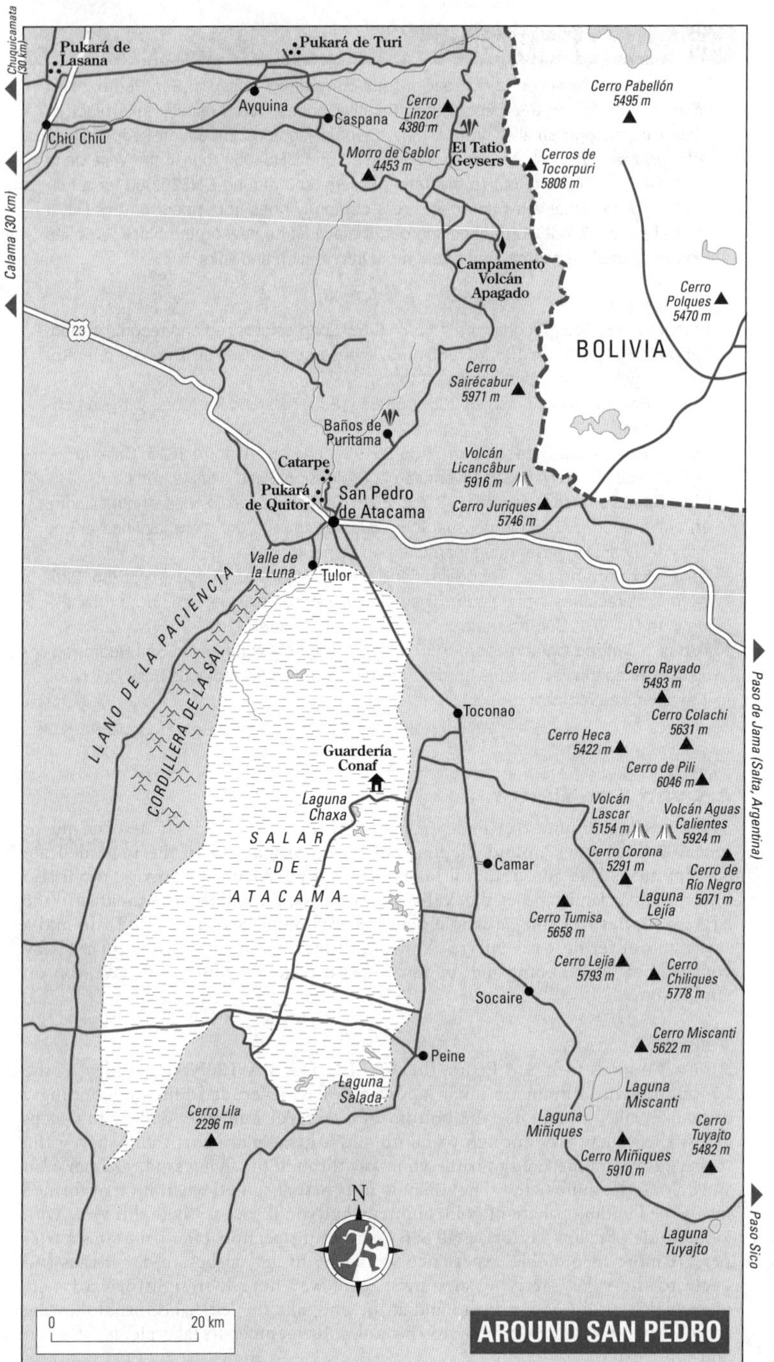

Chuquicamata (30 km)
Calama (30 km)
Pukará de Lasana
Pukará de Turi
Ayquina
Caspana
Chiu Chiu
Cerro Linzor 4380 m
Morro de Cablor 4453 m
El Tatio Geysers
Cerro Pabellón 5495 m
Cerros de Tocorpuri 5808 m
Campamento Volcán Apagado
Cerro Polques 5470 m
BOLIVIA
23
Cerro Sairécabur 5971 m
Baños de Puritama
Catarpe
Pukará de Quitor
San Pedro de Atacama
Volcán Licancâbur 5916 m
Cerro Juriques 5746 m
Valle de la Luna
Tulor
LLANO DE LA PACIENCIA
CORDILLERA DE LA SAL
Toconao
Paso de Jama (Salta, Argentina)
Cerro Rayado 5493 m
Cerro Colachi 5631 m
Cerro Heca 5422 m
Cerro de Pili 6046 m
Guardería Conaf
Laguna Chaxa
Volcán Lascar 5154 m
Volcán Aguas Calientes 5924 m
SALAR DE ATACAMA
Camar
Cerro Corona 5291 m
Cerro de Río Negro 5071 m
Laguna Lejía
Cerro Tumisa 5658 m
Cerro Lejía 5793 m
Cerro Chiliques 5778 m
Socaire
Peine
Cerro Miscanti 5622 m
Laguna Salada
Laguna Miscanti
Cerro Lila 2296 m
Laguna Miñiques
Cerro Miñiques 5910 m
Cerro Tuyajto 5482 m
Paso Sico
N
Laguna Tuyajto
0 20 km
AROUND SAN PEDRO

The Salar de Atacama

Some 10km south of San Pedro you reach the northern edge of the **SALAR DE ATACAMA**, a three-thousand-square-kilometre basin covered by a vast crust of saline minerals. The largest salt flat in Chile, it's formed by waters flowing down from the Andes which, unable to escape from the basin, are forced to evaporate, leaving salt deposits on the earth. The *salar* contains several small lakes, including **Laguna Chaxa**, home to dozens of flamingoes.

The Tatio geysers

Getting to the **TATIO GEYSERS**, 95km north of San Pedro, is quite an ordeal but hardly anyone who makes the trip regrets it. At 4300m above sea level, El Tatio is the highest geyser field in the world. It's essentially a large, flat field containing countless blowholes full of bubbling water that, between around 6 and 8am, send billowing clouds of steam high into the air. At the same time, the geysers' spray forms pools of water on the ground that are streaked with silver as they catch the first rays of the sun. It's really a magnificent spectacle. You should take great care, however, when walking around the field; the crust of earth is very thin in some parts, and serious accidents can happen. You should also remember that it will be freezing cold when you arrive, though once the sun's out the place warms up quite quickly. There's a swimming pool near the geysers, visited by most tour companies, so remember to take your bathing suit. On the way back, some tour companies also pay a visit to the **Baños de Puritama** (CH$5000), a rocky pool filled with warm thermal water, 60km south of the geysers and run by a local community but owned and maintained by a San Pedro hotel.

Iquique and around

Dramatically situated at the foot of the eight-hundred-metre coastal cordillera, with an enormous sand dune looming precariously above one of its *barrios*, **IQUIQUE**, 390km north of Calama, is a sprawling, busy city and the capital of Region I. With the abrupt end of the nitrate era after World War I, Iquique's boom was over, and the grand mansions were left to fade and crumble as the industrialists took themselves back to Santiago. Fishing stepped in to fill the economic gap, at least partially, and over the years Iquique has transformed itself into the world's leading exporter of fishmeal. The central square and main avenue conserve some splendid **buildings from the nitrate era**, which, along with the city's beaches, are for many people a good enough reason to visit. Seizing upon this, Iquique authorities have invested in an ambitious restoration scheme aimed at enhancing the beauty of this historic part of the city. Still more people, mainly Chileans, head here for the duty-free shopping at Iquique's Zona Franca, or "Zofri", just north of the centre, in an industrial area.

Iquique is a convenient place to arrange excursions into the interior, whose attractions include several nitrate ghost towns, such as **Humberstone**, and the stunning altiplano scenery of **Parque Nacional Volcán Isluga**.

Arrival and information

Iquique's main **bus terminal** is in a rather run-down quarter at the northern end of Patricio Lynch, several blocks from the centre – best take a taxi to the centre, or wait for a *colectivo*. **Tur Bus**, however, has its own terminal in a beautifully converted townhouse, at the corner of Ramírez and Esmeralda. This saves you a couple of blocks' walk and is in a more agreeable neighbourhood, so don't get out at the main terminal even though Tur Bus buses stop there, too. If you're arriving **by air**, you'll land at Diego Arecena airport, a whacking 40km south of the city. From here, you can get to the centre by bus (Transfer ⓣ57/410250; CH$2500), *colectivo* or regular taxi (CH$6000).

For **tourist information**, head for the Sernatur office at Aníbal Pinto 436 (March 16–Dec 14 Mon–Thur 9am–5pm, Fri 9am–4.30pm; Dec 15–March 15

Mon–Sat 9am–8pm, Sun 9am–2pm; sometimes closed for lunch; ⓣ57/312238, ⓔesernaturiquiq@entelchile.net).

Accommodation

Iquique is a popular holiday resort and offers an abundance of **accommodation**. The widest choice is in the centre, where you'll find cheap *residenciales* and smart hotels alike, while the hotels by the beaches are almost unanimously expensive – but worth it, perhaps, if you want a couple of days by the ocean.

Hostal Sol del Norte Juan Martínez 852 ⓣ57/421546. Simple but clean rooms (with shared bath) off a long corridor, with a very friendly *señora*. Recommended. ❸

Hotel Arturo Prat Aníbal Pinto 695 ⓣ57/411067. Plush city-centre hotel with an elegant period front section containing the reception and restaurant, and modern rooms in tall blocks behind. Also has a small rooftop pool. ❼

Hotel Intillanka Obispo Labbé 825 ⓣ57/311104. Friendly and efficiently run hotel offering thirty spacious, light rooms with private bath. Shows its age a little, but very clean. ❹

Residencial José Luis Ramírez 402. Bright, airy and fairly spacious rooms with shared bath – a good budget choice. ❸

The City

The focus of town is the large, partly pedestrianized **Plaza Prat**, dominated by the gleaming white **Teatro Municipal** (daily 9am–1pm & 3–8pm; CH$400), whose magnificent facade features Corinthian columns and statues representing the four seasons – spoiled at night by criminally hideous fairy lights. It was built in 1890 as an opera house and was visited by some of the most distinguished divas of its time. Opposite the theatre, in the centre of the square, the **Torre Reloj** is a tall white clock tower with Moorish arches, adopted by Iquique as the city's symbol. On the northeast corner of the square, the **Casino Español** – formerly a gentlemen's club, now a restaurant – features an extravagant Moorish-style interior with oil paintings depicting scenes from *Don Quijote* hanging from the walls; it is definitely worth a visit.

Leading south from here, **Calle Baquedano** is lined with an extraordinary collection of turn-of-the-century timber houses, all with porches and balconies and fine wooden balustrades, and many undergoing loving restoration. The street has been pedestrianized from the plaza all the way down to Zegers, using noble materials such as fine stone for the paving and polished timber for the sidewalks. Three buildings on this street are open to the public: the **Sala de Artes Collahuasi** at no. 930 (open every evening till late; free), an impeccably restored building used for temporary art exhibitions, usually of outstanding quality; the **Museo Regional** at no. 951 (Mon–Fri 8.30am–4pm, Sat 10.30am–1pm; free), which houses an eclectic collection of pre-Hispanic and natural history artefacts, including deformed skulls and a pickled two-headed shark; and the **Palacio Astoreca** (Tues–Fri 10am–1pm & 4–7.30pm, Sat 10am–1.30pm, Sun 11am–2pm; CH$400; entrance on O'Higgins), a glorious, though deteriorating, mansion featuring a massive wood-panelled entrance hall with a painted glass Art Nouveau ceiling.

The beaches

There are two beaches within striking distance of the city centre: **Playa Cavancha**, the nearest and most popular, and **Playa Brava**, larger, less crowded and more windswept. You can just about walk to Playa Cavancha, which begins at the southern end of Amunategui, but it's far easier, and very cheap, to take one of the numerous taxis constantly travelling between the plaza and the beach; many continue to Playa Brava, as well, for a slightly higher fare. Both beaches, particularly Cavancha, are lined with modern hotels and apartment blocks, but the construction is fairly low-level, and not too ugly. Further south, between Playa Brava and the airport, there's a series of attractive sandy beaches including **Playa Blanca**, 13km south of the centre, **Playa Lobito**, at km 22, and the fishing cove of **Los Verdes**, at km 24. You can get to these on the airport bus or *colectivo*.

Eating

Barracuda Gorostiaga 601, at the corner with Ramírez. Very popular wood-panelled pub serving wine by the glass, pisco sour, foreign beers, tea, coffee, milkshakes and delicious snacks, plus reasonably priced full-blown meals in the evening. Soft jazz music, lovely mellow atmosphere and top-notch service.

Boulevard Baquedano 790. Beautiful French-style bistro with a stylish terrace offers a wonderful change from Chilean fare, if you are prepared to pay a little extra. The French chef rustles up fantastic fish and seafood dishes, crepes, pasta, pizzas and even *tajines* (a Moroccan speciality of meat or fish cooked with herbs and spices in an earthenware pot). Excellent wines and delicious desserts, too.

Casino Español Plaza Prat 584. Huge, fabulous dining room decorated like a mock Moorish palace. The food is unexceptional, and a little overpriced, but this is a must-visit.

Mercado Centenario Barros Arana, between Latorre and Sargento Aldea. Cheap fish lunches available upstairs at the ten or so bustling *marisquerías*.

Humberstone

Some 45km inland from Iquique, sitting by Ruta 16 just before it meets the Panamericana, **HUMBERSTONE** (daily 8am–8pm; CH$1000) is a former nitrate *oficina*, abandoned in 1960 and now the best-preserved ghost town in Chile. It began life in 1862 and was renamed in 1925 in honour of its British manager, James Humberstone, an important nitrate entrepreneur. In its time it was one of the busiest *oficinas* on the pampas; today it is an eerie, empty ghost town, slowly crumbling beneath the desert sun. What sets Humberstone apart from other ghost towns is the fact that just about all of it is still standing – from the terraced workers' houses and the plaza with its bandstand, to the church and company store. The **theatre**, in particular, is highly evocative, with its rows of dusty seats staring at the stage. You should also seek out the **hotel**, and walk through to the back where you'll find a huge, empty **swimming pool** with a diving board – curiously the pool is made from the sections of a ship's iron hull.

Parque Nacional Volcán Isluga

PARQUE NACIONAL VOLCÁN ISLUGA, lying in the heart of the altiplano, is named after the towering, snowcapped volcano whose 5500-metre peak dominates the park's landscape. Its administrative centre is in **ENQUELGA**, a dusty, tumbledown hamlet – 3850m above sea level – home to a small Aymara community. Many of its inhabitants, particularly the women, still dress in traditional, brightly coloured clothes, and most live from tending llamas and cultivating potatoes and barley. There's a **Conaf refugio** in the village, with **accommodation** for five people (CH$5500 per person); it's supposed to be open year-round, but sometimes isn't. Two kilometres on from Enquelga, **Aguas Calientes** is a long, spring-fed pool containing warm (but not hot) waters, set in an idyllic location with terrific views of the volcano. The pool is surrounded by pea-green *bofedal* – a spongy grass, typical of the altiplano – and drains into a little stream, crossed every morning and evening by herds of llamas driven to and from the sierra by Aymara shepherdesses. There's a stone changing-hut next to it, and a few **camping** spaces and picnic areas, protected from the evening wind by thick stone walls.

Arica and around

ARICA, Chile's northernmost city, only 19km south of the Peruvian border, is blessed with a mild climate, which, along with its sandy beaches, makes it a popular holiday resort for Chileans and Bolivians. The city's compact, tidy centre sits proudly at the foot of the Morro cliff, the site of a major Chilean victory in the War of the Pacific. It was this war that delivered Arica into Chilean hands, in 1883, and while the city is emphatically Chilean today, there's no denying the strong presence of *mestizo* and Quechua Peruvians on the streets. Arica is more colourful, more ethnically diverse and a good deal more vibrant than most northern Chilean cities, although the early years of the new millennium have seen an economic slump. A short taxi ride out of town, in the Azapa Valley, the marvellous **Museo Arqueológico** is one of Chile's best and certainly deserves a visit. A few hours east, up in the cordillera, **Parque Nacional Lauca** has become one of the most popular attractions in the north of Chile.

Arrival and information

Coming in **by bus**, you'll arrive at Arica's Terminal Rodoviario, quite a distance from the centre on Avenida Diego Portales. From here, it's easy to get a *colectivo* or *micro* into the centre. Arica's **airport** is 18km north of the city and is connected to the centre by reasonably priced airport taxis (CH$4000). For tourist information, head for the **Sernatur** office at San Marcos 101 (Mon–Fri 8.30am–1pm & 3–7pm; ⓣ58/252054, ⓔsernatur_arica@entelchile.net). The regional **Conaf** office, at Vicuña Mackenna 820 (Mon–Fri 8.30am–5pm; ⓣ58/250750), is where you can pick up basic maps and information on Parque Nacional Lauca and adjoining protected areas. You can also try and reserve beds at the Conaf *refugíos* in these areas, if you know exactly when you'll be arriving.

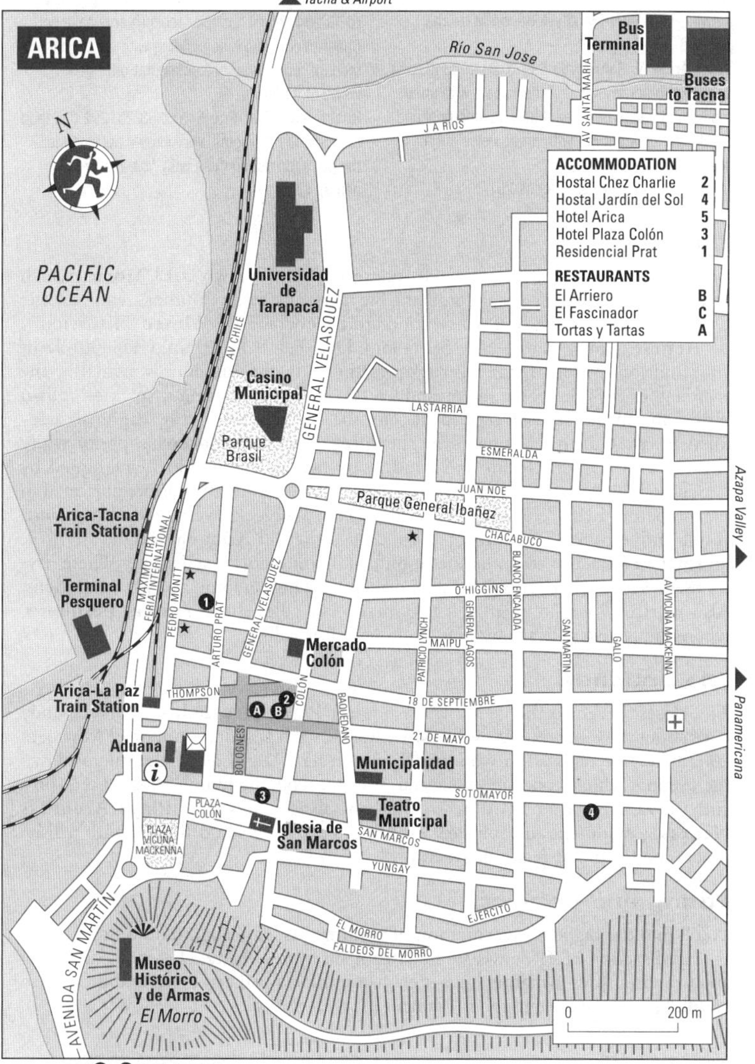

Accommodation

In the centre, there's no shortage of *residenciales*, ranging from the dirt-cheap to the polished and comfortable. Typically for these parts, however, there's a lack of decent mid-range accommodation. **Camping** options are limited to *El Refugio* (☎58/227545; CH$8000 per site), a shady, grassy campsite with a pool 1.5km up the Azapa Valley, reached by frequent *colectivos*.

Hostal Chez Charlie Thompson 236 ☎58/250007. Spacious rooms with shared bathrooms on a quiet pedestrian street. ❸

Hostal Jardín del Sol Sotomayor 848 ☎58/232795. Small, tidy rooms with private bath off a flower-filled courtyard with tables, chairs and a swing-sofa. Very friendly, too – great for the price. ❹

Hotel Arica Av San Martín 599 ⓣ58/254540. Upmarket hotel overlooking the ocean, with smart rooms and *cabañas*, a beautifully located pool and an elegant dining room with great views out to sea. ❽

Hotel Plaza Colón San Marcos 261 ⓣ58/254424, ⓔhotelplazacolon@entelchile.net. Cheerful pink and blue building with small, clean, modern rooms with balconies that offer good views of the plaza. ❻

Residencial Prat Prat 545 ⓣ58/251292. Thirteen spruce and tidy rooms, very simple but good for the price (do not confuse with *hostal* of same name). ❹

The City

Arica's most visible feature is the 110-metre-high cliff known as **El Morro**, which signals the end of the coastal cordillera. Steps starting at the southern end of Calle Colón lead you to the top, where panoramic views and the **Museo Histórico y de Armas** (daily: March–Nov 8am–8pm; Dec–Feb 8am–10pm; CH$400) await you. Built on top of a former Peruvian fortification, this museum is owned by the army, rather than the government, and has clearly had more money spent on it than most Chilean museums. Down in the city, the centre is marked by the small, tree-filled **Plaza Colón**, dominated by the **Iglesia de San Marcos**, a pretty white church with a high, Gothic spire and many tall, arched windows. Designed by Gustave Eiffel, this curious church is made entirely of iron and was prefabricated in France before being erected in Arica in 1876. Two blocks west, towards the port, you'll find another Eiffel-designed building – the old **Aduana**, erected in 1874, sporting an attractive stone facade of pink and white horizontal stripes. These days it's used as a cultural centre and puts on regular photographic and art exhibitions. Also worth a look-in, nearby, is the smelly but colourful **terminal pesquero**, where inquisitive pelicans wander around the fish stalls.

The beaches

The closest beach to the centre is the popular **Playa El Laucho**, a curved, sandy cove about a twenty-minute walk down Avenida San Martín, south of El Morro; in 2002 extensive renovation work was going on here. You can also get micros down the avenue, which continue to several other beaches, including **Playa La Lisera** and **Playa Brava**, both attractive, and the usually deserted **Playa Arenillas Negras**, a wide expanse of dark sand backed by low sand dunes, with a fish-processing factory at its southern end.

Eating and drinking

You'll find the biggest concentration of **restaurants**, **cafés** and **bars** on the pedestrianized section of 21 de Mayo, the city's main thoroughfare. The choice of eating and drinking spots is marginally better than in most northern cities, and there are a couple of places nice enough to return to several times.

Restaurants

El Arriero 21 de Mayo 385. Mid-price grillhouse serving good fillet steaks and other meat dishes; often has live folk music at weekends.

El Fascinador Av San Martín 1010, Playa La Lisera ⓣ58/231890. Good-value *parrilladas* served right by the beach in a wacky, jungle-themed dining room with fake leopard-skin chairs and a bamboo roof. To get here, take any *colectivo* south down the coastal avenue; they'll call a taxi for you when you want to get back.

Tortas y Tartas 21 de Mayo 233. With a terrace strategically located on the main drag and bright, stylish decor, this godsend serves real coffee, excellent breakfasts, a range of sandwiches, snacks and crisp salads, some hot dishes and delicious cakes (such as raspberry cheesecake). It offers a good selection of beers, wines and cocktails, too.

Bars

Bar Barrabas 18 de Septiembre 520, corner with Lynch. Trendy, popular pub with much wrought iron and odd architectural salvage pieces. Good music, good drinks, good atmosphere. Has a disco attached next door that fills up after midnight.

Cantaverdi Bolognesi 453. Attractive, much frequented pub-bar with a pleasant buzz, serving snacks and pizzas along with a wide range of drinks.

Listings

Airlines LanChile, 21 de Mayo 345 ⓣ58/251641; Lloyd Aereo Boliviano, 21 de Mayo 423 ⓣ58/251919; Sky Airlines, Edificio Parque Colón, Chacabuco between Colón and Baquedano ⓣ58/251816 or 290768 at airport.
Car rental American Rent-a-Car, General Lagos 559 ⓣ58/252234; Budget, Av San Martín 599 ⓣ58/258911; Hertz, Baquedano 999 ⓣ58/231487; Klasse, Velásquez 760 ⓣ58/254498.
Post office Arturo Prat 305.

Out to the Azapa Valley and the Museo Arqueológico

Avenida Diego Portales extends out of the city centre into the green **Azapa Valley**. Thirteen kilometres along the road, the outstanding **Museo Arqueológico** (daily: Jan & Feb 9am–8pm; March–Dec 10am–6pm; closed Jan 1, May 1 and Dec 25; CH$1000), part of the University of Tarapacá, houses an excellent collection of regional pre-Columbian artefacts, including four extraordinary Chinchorro mummies – of a man, a woman and two children – buried over four thousand years ago.

Up to Parque Nacional Lauca

Some 160km east of Arica, **Parque Nacional Lauca** is the perfect microcosm of the Chilean altiplano. The journey there takes you through some beautiful and varied scenery, ranging from deep-green vegetation to rippling desert hills. The busy little mountain town of **Putre** makes for a popular overnight stop en route to the higher altitudes of the park.

Putre

At 3500m above sea level, **PUTRE** is surrounded by a patchwork of green fields and Inca terraces. Putre's rustic houses are clustered around a large, green square, overlooked by the Municipalidad, which provides basic **tourist information** (Mon–Fri 8.30am–12.30pm & 3–6pm). Nearby, off the northeast corner of the square, you'll find the **church**, built in 1670 after an earthquake destroyed the original church, which, according to old Spanish chronicles, was clad in gold and silver. Putre has limited options for eating and sleeping. On Calle Baquedano, you'll find small, tidy **rooms** off a sunny backyard at *Residencial Cali* (no phone; ❸), and basic but reasonable rooms in a large, covered yard at *Residencial La Paloma* (no phone; ❸), where breakfasts are frugal. Across the bridge and up the track, *Hostería Las Vicuñas* (ⓣ58/228564; ❼) is the smartest, and most expensive, place to stay, offering slightly faded-looking en-suite bungalow rooms. Most of Putre's few **restaurants** are dire, with the exception of *Kuchu Marka* on Baquedano, where you can get alpaca stew and other hearty mountain dishes like *picante de conejo*.

Parque Nacional Lauca

As you continue up the main road, at a 4400-metre-high mountain pass, you cross the boundary into **PARQUE NACIONAL LAUCA**. By now the air is thin and cold, and the road is flanked by light-green *bofedal* where herds of wild vicuña come to feed in the mornings. Ten kilometres into the park, you reach the Conaf hut at **Las Cuevas**, a good place to stop to check on weather and road conditions and observe the comical antics of vizcachas, cuddly chinchilla-like rodents with curly tails and a spring-like leap. From here the road continues through a wide, green plain filled with grazing llamas and alpacas, passing the turn-off for Parinacota, 19km on from the Conaf hut, and Lago Chungará, a further 18km along the road.

Parinacota

The park's headquarters are in **PARINACOTA**, an idyllic *pueblo altiplánico* composed of fifty or so crumbling, whitewashed houses huddled around a beautiful little **church**. Built in 1789, this is one of Chile's most assiduously maintained Andean churches, sporting brilliant white walls and a bright-blue wooden door, trimmed with yellow and green. Like most churches of the altiplano, it has thick stone and adobe walls and a sloping straw roof, and is enclosed within a little white wall incorporating the bell tower into one of its corners. Inside, you'll find a series of faded, centuries-old friezes depicting the Stations of the Cross and vivid scenes of sinners suffering in hell. Opposite the church, in the plaza, local women sell alpaca knitwear and other **artesanía**. The **Conaf** administration centre nearby is a large, chalet-style building making a valiant attempt at informing the public about the park and its wildlife, possibly with space for **camping** out the back; ask around for very basic **rooms** without hot water (❷). Parinacota can be reached by **bus** from Arica, with Buses Martínez, Pedro Montt 620 (Thurs & Sat; Ⓣ58/232265) and, a few doors along at no. 662, Buses Humire (Tues & Fri; Ⓣ58/253497).

Lago Chungará

Eighteen kilometres on from Parinacota, at an altitude of 4600m, **LAGO CHUNGARÁ** is a wide blue lake spectacularly positioned at the foot of a snow-capped volcano that rises over its rim like a giant Christmas pudding covered in cream. This is 6330-metre-high **Volcán Parinacota**, one of the highest peaks in Chile and the park's most challenging climb. When the lake is mill-pond calm, in other words when there is no wind, the reflection of the volcano is one of the most memorable views in the whole region. On the southern shore of the lake, right by the highway, there's a small stone **Conaf refugio** with five beds (CH$5500 per person), a kitchen, **camping** spaces (CH$5000 per site) and unbeatable views. This is unquestionably the best place to stay in the park, allowing you to observe the changing colours of the lake and volcano at different times of day.

4.5

The Central Valley

Extending south from Santiago as far as the Río Bío Bío, Chile's **CENTRAL VALLEY** is a long, narrow plain hemmed in by the Andes to the east and the coastal range to the west. This is the most fertile land in Chile, and the immense orchards, vineyards and pastures that cover the valley floor form a dazzling patchwork of greenery. The kernel of the Central Valley is **Chillán**, some 400km south. Further south, the busy city of **Concepción** guards the mouth of the **Bío Bío**, the mighty river that for over three hundred years was the boundary between conquered, colonial Chile and unconquered **Mapuche territory**.

Many visitors bypass the Central Valley altogether, certainly the agricultural towns dotted along the highway – **Rancagua**, **San Fernando**, **Curicó**, **Talca** and **Los Angeles** – are, on the whole, rather dull, offering little to tempt tourists off the bus or out of their car. After a strenuous day in the mountains, there are numerous **hot springs** at hand to relax in: the **Termas de Chillán** are at the base of a booming ski and adventure resort, among the most famous and visited in Chile.

Getting down the Central Valley by **public transport** is easy, with hundreds of **buses** ploughing down the Panamericana. The amount of annual rainfall picks up steadily as you head south; by the time you reach the Bío Bío there is a significant amount of rain every month. While winter is never too cold and snowfall is plentiful in the foothills, most visits are planned between October and March.

Rancagua

Zipping down the Panamericana from Santiago, you can reach the prosperous agricultural town of **RANCAGUA**, 87km south, in less than an hour. Once in town, you'll find little to hold your interest for more than a few hours beyond the well-preserved colonial building occupied by the **Museo Regional de Rancagua** at Estado 685 (Tues–Fri 10am–6pm, Sat & Sun 9am–1pm; CH$600; ⓣ72/221524), dating from the late eighteenth century. Rancagua is a stopover town. Arriving by **bus**, you'll be dropped at the terminal at Salinas 1165 (ⓣ72/236938); a couple of blocks south, the **train station** (ⓣ72/230361) is served by both the fast *metrotrén* (hourly) and the slow train from Santiago. There's an extremely helpful **Sernatur** office one block east of the plaza at Germán Riesco 277 (Mon–Fri 8.30am–5.15pm; ⓣ72/230413, ⓔsernatur_rancag@entelchile.net).

San Fernando and the Colchagua Valley

Fifty-five kilometres south of Rancagua, **SAN FERNANDO** is a busy little town sitting in the valley of the Río Tinguiririca, known locally as the **Colchagua Valley** after the province through which it runs. The town itself is short on sights. Buses pull in at the **bus terminal** (ⓣ72/713912) on the corner of Avenida Manso de Velasco and Rancagua. Of San Fernando's four **hotels**, three are on Manuel Rodríguez. The best is at no. 770, second floor, where friendly *Hotel Imperial* (ⓣ72/714595; ❸) has comfortable rooms and a pleasant dining area. Places to eat include the *Club Social*, Manuel Rodríguez 787, where you'll find typical, filling meat dishes such as *pollo asado* and *lomo*.

Hacienda Los Lingues

Twenty kilometres northeast of San Fernando, **HACIENDA LOS LINGUES** (☎2/2355446, Ⓦwww.loslingues.com) is one of the oldest and best-preserved haciendas in Chile. It dates from 1599, when King Philip III of Spain presented it as a gift to the first mayor of Santiago. Since then, the hacienda has remained in the same family and is today presided over by the elderly and redoubtable don Germán Claro-Lira. Outside, the hacienda's grounds take in sumptuous, mature gardens, a *medialuna* and the stables where thoroughbred "Aculeo" horses are bred, reputed to be among the finest in South America. The high rates (❼) deter most people from staying overnight, but you can visit the hacienda on a short **tour** (US$19), lasting about forty minutes, or for the day (US$54), which includes lunch, cocktails and the chance to watch a horse show.

Curicó

Back on the Panamericana, 54km south of San Fernando, the prosperous, manicured town of **Curicó** makes an appealing route to the nearby **wineries**, or further west to **Lago Vichuquén**, near the coast, or the **Siete Tazas waterfalls**, southwest towards the mountains. While you're in town, you could also make an easy excursion 5km south to the **winery** of Miguel Torres (Mon–Fri 9am–3pm & 4–6pm; Sat 10am–2pm; free; ☎75/310455), the innovative Spanish vintner who revolutionized the Chilean wine industry in the 1980s. Other wine tours are arranged by an organization called Ruta del Vino del Valle – Curicó, an office in front of the Plaza de Armas at Merced 321, second floor (☎75/328972).

Practicalities

Arriving in Curicó by bus, you'll pull in at the **bus terminal** (☎75/328575) on the corner of Avenida Camilo Henríquez and Carmen, three blocks north of the plaza. The **train station** (☎75/310028) is on Prat, four blocks west of the Plaza de Armas. You can pick up a map of the town and other **tourist information** in the Municipalidad, opposite the Plaza de Armas. Reasonably priced **accommodation** is available at *Hotel Prat*, a large *residencial* at Peña 427 (☎75/311069; ❸) offering dark but spotless rooms. Options for **eating** include the unpretentious straw-roofed *El Fogón Chileno*, at Yungay 802, serving good-value *parilladas*.

Reserva Nacional Radal Siete Tazas

Of all the natural phenomena in Chile, the **Siete Tazas**, 73km southeast of Curicó, must be one of the most extraordinary. In the depths of the native forest, a crystal-clear mountain river drops down a series of seven waterfalls, each of which has carved a sparkling *taza* – literally, a "teacup" – out of the rock. The falls are set within the Conaf-administered **Reserva Nacional Radal Siete Tazas** (April–Nov 8.30am–6pm; Dec–March 8.30am–8pm; CH$1000, camping CH$8000), reached by a poor dirt road from the village of Molina, 18km southwest of Curicó – be sure to fill up with petrol there.

Accommodation can be found near the administration at *Hosteria La Flor de la Canela* (☎75/491613; ❸). There are also various options for camping in this area, including *Radal Eco Adventure,* 1km before the town of Radal, on the right (☎9/333-8719; CH$12,000 per site). You can get to the Siete Tazas on **public transport** from Curicó with Buses Hernández, which has two services daily throughout the year. The best time of year to visit this park is from December to March, as the winter months are frequently snowy.

Talca

As the capital of Region VII, **TALCA** boasts its fair share of services and commercial activity, most of it centred on the main shopping street, **Calle 1 Sur**. Buses to

San Javier and the wineries

Twenty kilometres south of Talca is a massive iron bridge over the Río Maule, followed by the turn-off to **SAN JAVIER**. Today the town's main interest lies in its proximity to two dozen local **vineyards**. Tours – of what is now called the **Ruta del Vino Valle del Maule** – are half-day or full-day bilingual tours and can be arranged at C Sargento Aldea 2491 (Ⓣ73/246460, Ⓦwww.chilewineroute.com); 48 hours' notice is recommended. The concept of letting visitors taste and tour is only just catching on, so check first. One notable exception is **Viña Balduzzi**, at Av Balmaceda 1189 in San Javier (Mon–Sat 9am–6pm; CH$1000; Ⓣ73/322138, Ⓦwww.enoteca.cl).

Talca pull in at the **Terminal de Buses** (Ⓣ71/243270) on 2 Sur and 12 Oriente, ten blocks east of the Plaza de Armas. There's a friendly and helpful **Sernatur** office just north of the plaza at 1 Poniente 1281 (Mon–Fri 8.30am–5.30pm; Ⓣ71/233669, Ⓔsernaturtalca@entelchile.net), while **Conaf** is on the corner of 2 Poniente and 3 Sur (71/228029).

One block east of the square, on the corner of 1 Norte and 2 Oriente, the **Museo O'Higgiano** (Tues–Thurs 9.15am–1.45pm & 2.30–6.45pm, Fri 9.15am–1pm & 3–7pm, Sat & Sun 10am–1pm; CH$500) occupies a handsome colonial house that hosted some of the most important developments of the independence movement: here it was that Bernardo O'Higgins, future "Liberator" of Chile, lived as a nine-year-old, where the Carrera brothers established the first *Junta de Gobierno* in 1813, and where O'Higgins signed the final Act of Independence in 1818. Today, the museum houses copious (and rather dull) historical documents relating to Chilean independence, along with an eclectic assortment of oil paintings, sculpture, nineteenth-century furniture, pre-Columbian spearheads, old coins and more. A few blocks southwest at 2 Sur 1172 (near the corner with 5 Oriente), the **Museo Bomberil Benito Riquelme** (variable times) is crammed full of shiny red antique fire engines, hoses and other firefighting equipment, and is enjoyable to browse in.

There is little reason **to stay**, but if you do a cluster of places can be found on 2 Sur, a few blocks west of the bus terminal.

Chillán and the Itata Valley

Back on the Panamericana, a hundred and fifty kilometres – punctuated by the nondescript towns of Linares and Parral – separate Talca from the busy city of **Chillán**, sitting in the middle of the **Itata Valley**. Though lush and very beautiful, the valley is short on specific attractions, which amount to a **naval museum** in the village of Ninhue, 50km northwest of Chillán, and the hot-springs resort and ski centre of the **Termas de Chillán**, 80km east, high in the cordillera.

Chillán

The busy city of **CHILLÁN** is famous throughout Chile as the birthplace of Bernardo O'Higgins, the founding father of the republic. Unlike most of the towns staggered down the highway, it is, moreover, a place worth visiting in its own right – principally for its vast **handicrafts market** and fascinating **Mexican murals** – and not just as a staging post to arrange transport to neighbouring attractions.

Arrival and information

Many **long-distance buses** use the new Terminal María Teresa at Av O'Higgins 010 (Ⓣ42/272149), on the northern edge of town. You can pick up tourist information at **Sernatur**, 18 de Septiembre 455 (Mon–Fri 8.30am–6pm; Ⓣ71/223272, Ⓔinfochillan@sernatur.cl) and at the **Oficina de Turismo** in the Municipalidad on the Plaza de Armas (Mon–Fri 8.30am–12.30pm & 3–6pm; sporadic hours

May–Aug; ⓣ42/214117). Chillán has a wide range of accommodation, although the upper- and mid-range hotels cater primarily to business travellers and tend to be functional rather than intimate. Budget accommodation is plentiful, but not of a great standard.

Accommodation

Casa Pensión Itata 288 ⓣ42/214879. A friendly, popular family house offering excellent-value rooms and kitchen facilities. Note that solo travellers might have to share rooms when it gets busy. ❷

Gran Hotel Isabel Riquelme Arauco 600 ⓣ42/213663. Old-fashioned hotel with large en-suite rooms and a restaurant with a good international menu and cheaper set meals. ❼

Hostal Canadá Libertad 269, second floor ⓣ42/234515. Small and clean, with bright, airy rooms and a rooftop terrace. A good budget choice. ❷

Hotel Javiera Carrera Carrera 481 ⓣ42/221175. Neat and comfortable, with good facilities and fair-size rooms. ❷

Hotel Las Terrazas Constitución 664 ⓣ42/227000. On the fifth floor of a modern office block, this is an attractively decorated hotel with bright, comfortable, well-equipped rooms. ❺

Residencial 18 18 de Septiembre 317 ⓣ42/211102. An immaculate *residencial* complete with pool table and games room. Inexpensive meals are available. ❷

The Town

Thanks to periodic earthquakes and regular Mapuche attacks, Chillán has seen itself repeatedly rebuilt since its founding in 1550. The last major earthquake was in 1939, and most of Chillán's present architecture dates from the reconstruction of the city during the 1940s. The focal square is the **Plaza Bernardo O'Higgins**, dominated by a giant, 36-metre concrete cross, erected to commemorate the thirty thousand inhabitants who died in the 1939 earthquake. A few blocks northwest, the **Escuela México**, a school built with money donated by the Mexican government following the 1939 disaster, looks out over the leafy **Plaza de los Héroes de Iquique**. On Pablo Neruda's initiative, two renowned Mexican artists, David Alfaro Siqueiros and Xavier Guerrero, decorated the school's main staircase and library with fabulous murals depicting pivotal figures of Mexican and Chilean history.

Eating

For a cheap bite and a great, buzzing atmosphere, head one block north of the Feria de Chillán to the hectic **Mercado Cubierto**, crammed with butchers' stands and boisterous food stalls, and the slightly more restrained **Mercado Modelo**, with its good-value restaurants and lines of communal tables. Next door, the **Roble Mall** has plenty of fast-food outlets that are another inexpensive option. The best place in Chillán for coffee, rich cakes and hot meat sandwiches is *Fuente Alemana* at Arauco 661, while *Restaurante Vegetariano Arcoiris*, El Roble 525, serves good-value vegetarian lunches, including delicious omelettes and salads.

Termas de Chillán

Eighty kilometres east of Chillán, nestled at the foot of the 3122-metre **Volcán Chillán**, the all-season tourist complex of the **Termas de Chillán** is the most famous and most developed mountain resort south of Santiago (information from Chillán at Libertad 1042; ⓣ42/223887; from Santiago at Pío X 2460, Oficina 508; ⓣ2/233-1313). The hot baths and spa function year-round, but in winter the emphasis shifts to the resort's excellent **skiing** facilities, which include nine lifts and 28 runs, one of which is 2500m, the longest in South America. A full variety of ski packages and pricing options is available (ⓣ2/233-1313, ⓦwww.termaschillan.cl). Summer activities are now burgeoning in the area, with hiking, tennis and mountain biking becoming very popular.

On the way up to the resort you'll pass several **campsites** along the road between Km 50 and 57. Crowded on summer weekends, these pleasant sites sit near the riverbank and offer basic facilities. Further along, between Km 68 and 75, a growing number of **lodging places** have sprung up; a good listing of the cabins is available on the Web at Ⓦwww.vallelastrancas.cl and Ⓦwww.nevadosdechillan.cl.

Concepción and the Bío Bío Valley

South of Chillán and the Itata Valley, Chile is intersected by the great **Río Bío Bío**, generally considered to mark the southern limit of the Central Valley. One of Chile's longest rivers, it cuts a 380km diagonal slash across the country, emptying into the ocean by the large city of **Concepción**, over 200km north of its source in the Andean mountains. These days the river is best known as a world-class **white-water rafting** destination, but for more than three hundred years the Bío Bío was simply "La Frontera", forming the border beyond which Spanish colonization was unable to spread, fiercely repulsed by the native **Mapuche** population.

Concepción

Sitting at the mouth of the Bío Bío, 112km southwest of Chillán along a fast motorway, the sprawling, fast-paced metropolis of **CONCEPCIÓN** is the region's administrative capital and economic powerhouse and Chile's second-largest city. The city is surrounded by some of the ugliest industrial suburbs in the country. This lack of civic splendour reflects the long series of catastrophes that have punctuated Concepción's growth – from the incessant Mapuche raids during the city's days as a Spanish garrison, guarding La Frontera, to the devastating earthquakes that have razed it to the ground dozens of times since its founding in 1551.

Arrival and information

Most **buses** arrive at the Terminal Collao, northeast of the centre at Tegualda 860, just off the Autopista General Bonilla (Ⓣ41/749000); from here, plenty of *colectivos* and taxis will take you into town. If you arrive with Tur Bus, you'll be dropped either at the smaller Terminal Chillancito, also called the Terminal Henríquez, off the Autopista General Bonilla at Av Henríquez 2565 (Ⓣ41/315036), or at its downtown office at Tucapel 530. **Trains** from Santiago and Chillán arrive at the train station on Av Arturo Prat 501, six blocks west of the plaza (Ⓣ41/226925). If you're **flying** to Concepción, you'll land at Aeropuerto Carriel Sur, 5km northwest of town, from where you can get a taxi or minibus transfer directly to your hotel (Ⓣ42/732000).

You can pick up maps, brochures and other tourist information at **Sernatur**'s office on the central square at Aníbal Pinto 460 (April–Nov Mon–Fri 9am–1pm & 3–6pm; Dec–March Mon–Fri 8.30am–8pm, Sat 9am–2pm; Ⓣ41/227976, Ⓔserna08@entelchile.net). **Conaf** has an office at Serrano 529 (Ⓣ42/237202).

Accommodation

Concepción is well endowed with upmarket, expensive hotels catering to business travellers, but budget accommodation is very hard to find, with no rock-bottom options at all.

Hotel Bío Bío Barros Arana 751, second floor Ⓣ41/230463. Bright and cheerful hotel with all the rooms looking onto a central lightwell. ❸

Hotel Carrera El Araucano Caupolicán 521 Ⓣ41/740606, Ⓔguests.concepcion@carrera.cl. Top-notch luxury hotel with an indoor pool and a very good restaurant with a terrace over the Plaza de Armas. ❼

Residencial Central Rengo 673, second floor Ⓣ41/227309. An old building with lots of character and large rooms, a few with outside windows. ❷

Residencial O'Higgins O'Higgins 457 Ⓣ41/228303. A small B&B with basic but adequate rooms off a long corridor, among the cheapest places in town. ❸

The Town

The focal point of Concepción is its busy **Plaza de la Independencia**, though there's little to detain you here once you've called into the Sernatur office. For a better introduction to the city, head for the **Galería de la Historia** (Tues–Sun 10am–1.30pm & 3–6.30pm; free) at the southern end of Lincoyán, in Parque Ecuador, where you'll find a series of impressive dioramas, some with sound and light effects, depicting the long and troubled history of Concepción. If you walk up to the far end of the park and on to Calle Larenas, you'll reach the **university**, set in splendid, landscaped gardens surrounded by thickly wooded hills. Chile's second largest university, it has the curious distinction of being funded by the local lottery. It houses one of Chile's largest national art collections, displayed in the **Casa del Arte** (Tues–Fri 10am–6pm, Sat 10am–4pm, Sun 10am–2pm; free). The bulk of the collection consists of nineteenth-century landscapes and portraits by Chilean artists, but the showpiece is the magnificent mural in the entrance hall, *Presencia de América Latina*, painted by the Mexican artist Jorge González Camarena in 1964. Dominating the mural is the giant face of an *indígena*, representing all the indigenous peoples of the continent, while the many faces of different nationalities superimposed onto it indicate the intrusion of outside cultures and fusion of races that characterize Latin America. Woven into the densely packed images are the flags of every Latin American country, and several national icons like Chile's condor and the feathered serpent, Quetzalcoatl, the Mexican symbol of culture.

Eating, drinking and nightlife

Concepción has a good range of **eating** places to suit all pockets, and boasts the liveliest **nightlife** in the Central Valley, fuelled by the large student population. The **Barrio Estación** has a vibrant night scene, concentrated on Calle Prat, that revolves mainly around a string of small, intimate restaurants that double up as bars on Friday and Saturday night, Calle Prat is also the site of numerous drinking holes, including *Comanche Pub*, at no. 442. If you want to go **clubbing**, head for the steamy *Hot House* at O'Higgins 2002, a short taxi ride out of town

Chela's Barros Arana 405. Tasty and inexpensive Chilean dishes like *empanadas* and *pastel de choclo* as well as good desserts and ice cream. Great for people-watching. Very cheap fixed menu.

L'Angolo Barros Arana 494. Large, moderate-priced and very popular café, full of young couples, families and frantic waiters serving delicious light meals and beer.

Tequila Mezcal Prat 532. Colourfully decorated Mexican restaurant, serving tasty *fajitas* and *burritos*, accompanied by lots of raucous margarita- and tequila drinking at the weekend. Moderately priced.

Vegetariano Arcoiris Barros Arana 244. An interesting healthfood shop-cum-restaurant, owned by a dentist who speaks English and German and never puts sugar in his food. It's not expensive, and you eat in a large old barn-like building that closes at 6pm.

Listings

Airlines American Airlines, Barros Arana 340, Local 2 ⓣ41/521616; LanChile/Lanexpress, Barros Arana 600 ⓣ41/248824; TAN, Aeropuerto Carriel Sur ⓣ41/480337.

Banks and exchange There are many banks with ATMs, most of them on O'Higgins, by the plaza. You'll find *casas de cambio* Cambio Fides and Afex inside the small shopping centre at Barros Arana 565. Another is Varex, at O'Higgins 537.

Car rental Avis, Chacabuco 726 ⓣ41/235837; Budget, Chacabuco 175 ⓣ41/12438; First, Cochrane 862 ⓣ42/223121; Hertz, Prat 248 ⓣ41/230341.

Consulates Argentina, O'Higgins 420, Oficina 82 ⓣ41/230257.

Hospital San Martín and Lautaro ⓣ42/208500.

Post office Corner of O'Higgins and Colo Colo.

Telephone centres Entel, Barros Arana 541 and O'Higgins 920.

Travel agents There's a cluster of travel agents in an office block at O'Higgins 630, including Turismo Cocha, Oficina 309 (ⓣ41/237303) and Aventuratur, Ejército 599 (ⓣ41/819634).

Down the Panamericana to the Salto del Laja and Los Angeles

Heading south from Concepción, the first major town you reach **Los Angeles**, some 50km down the highway; halfway along this route, the Panamericana crosses the Río Laja. Until recently the highway passed directly by the **SALTO DEL LAJA**, which ranks among the most impressive waterfalls in Chile. It is still a good break spot on the long drive from Santiago, but beware of old maps that show the highway cruising by the falls. To actually get to the Salto del Laja, you'll need to follow the turn-off signs for the "Salto", which lead to the old highway. From there you will see the falls; cascading almost 50m from two crescent-shaped cliffs down to a rocky canyon, they appear as a broad white curtain of foam, almost like a miniature Niagara Falls.

There are parking spaces around the bridge (surrounded by tacky souvenir stalls), and a short path passes through the cabins and campground of the *Complejo Turístico Los Manantiales* (ⓣ43/314275; ❹) to a closer viewpoint. Other options include the rooms at *Hotel Salto del Laja*, Panamericana km 480, about 30km north of Los Angeles (ⓣ43/321706, ⓦwww.saltodellaja.cl; ❺), which has sixty acres of parks, delightful swimming holes, Jacuzzis and waterfall views. For low-budget camping, there are numerous places convenient to public transport. One kilometre south of the falls, the road east (by the church) holds two year-round campsites, jointly run. The first, *Salta Chica* (ⓣ43/314772 or 318220; ❹) is 800m from the highway and has beautiful, but noisy, campsites. Up the road 1.5km is *Playa Caliboro* (ⓣ43/318220; ❷) which sports a mini beach and a good natural swimming pool. Both are CH$8000 for up to five people, including hot water all day.

Los Angeles

LOS ANGELES itself is an easygoing agricultural town, pleasant enough with its leafy Plaza de Armas and bustling commercial core, but without any great attractions to grab your interest. **Arriving** in Los Angeles by bus, you'll be dropped at the terminal on Avenida Sor Vicenta, the northern access road from the Panamericana; from here, plenty of *colectivos* go into the centre. You can get **tourist information** from the Oficina de Turismo in the Municipalidad, on the southeast corner of the Plaza de Armas (Mon–Fri 8.30am–1pm & 3–5.30pm; ⓣ43/409400), and from Cayaqui Turismo, Lautaro 252 (ⓣ43/322248). Los Angeles is short on inexpensive **accommodation**, but you could try *Hotel Central* at Almagro 377 (ⓣ43/323381; ❷) for basic, adequate rooms off a courtyard. Moving up the scale, *Hotel Winser*, at Rengo 138 (ⓣ43/320348; ❸–❹), is a small, neat hotel with en-suite rooms, while *Hotel Mariscal Alcázar*, Lautaro 385 (ⓣ43/311725, ⓔhalcazar@entelchile.net; ❼), is modern and well equipped. One of the best **restaurants** in town is at the *Club de la Union*, at Colón 285 – next door to the tourist office.

Parque Nacional Laguna del Laja

Ninety-three kilometres east of Los Angeles, **PARQUE NACIONAL LAGUNA DEL LAJA** (daily: April–Nov 8am–6pm; Dec–March 8am–9pm; CH$700; ⓣ43/321086) takes its name from the great green lake formed by the 1752 eruption of **Volcán Antuco** (2985m), set in an otherworldly volcanic landscape of lava flows and honeycombed rock. The road from Los Angeles is paved for the 66km to **Antuco**; after there, the road surface is gravel but in decent condition (4WD not necessary) for the 30km to the park entrance.

The park boundary is 4km east of the village of **El Abanico**, but the Conaf hut, where you pay your entrance fee, is 12km on from the and the **Centro de Informaciones**, which offers talks and videos about the park, another kilometre beyond the hut. From here, an easy path leads a couple of kilometres to a pair of large, thundering waterfalls, **Saltos las Chilcas** and **Saltos del Torbellino**. Hikes to the summit ofVolcán Antuco are not particularly technical, but allow four to five hours for the trip up and three hours for the hike down, and wear strong boots as the volcanic rocks will shred light footwear. Ask at the hostel for seasonal conditions and other information. Getting to the park by **public transport** is very difficult.

Angol and around

ANGOL is the final major town before Temuco, the gateway to the Lake District, and serves as a useful base for visiting the nearby **Parque Nacional Nahuelbuta**. The town's Plaza de Armas is one of the liveliest and most attractive in the region, full of kids on roller skates, toddlers on pedal cars and watchful grandparents sitting beneath the shade of the numerous elms, cypresses and cedars.

Practicalities

The *Hostal El Vergel* (☎45/712103 or 712403; ❸), Angol's best **place to stay**, is out in the suburbs, 5km south down Avenida Bernardo O'Higgins, reached by *colectivo* from the Plaza de Armas. This hostal has large rooms in an old wooden house, and a good restaurant. In the centre, there's not a lot to choose from: *Residencial Olimpia*, at Caupolicán 625 (☎45/711162; ❷), has reasonable rooms in a family home, while a couple of blocks along at no. 498, the *Hotel Club Social* (☎45/711103; ❹) has light, airy rooms, an outdoor pool and a wood-panelled games room with fine old billiards tables. It also has a decent **restaurant**. Another place to try is *Josánh Paecha*, at Caupolicán 579, where you can eat in the attractive garden in fine weather. Angol's long-distance **bus terminal** is conveniently located on the corner of Caupolicán 200 and Chorillos (☎45/711100), one block north of the plaza, while rural services operate from the far end of Lautaro, three blocks east of the plaza. There's a very helpful **Oficina de Turismo** at the fork of O'Higgins and Bonilla (Mon–Fri 8.30am–1pm & 2.30–6pm; ☎45/201556), just over the river from the town centre. You can get information on Parque Nacional Nahuelbuta at Conaf's office at Prat 191 (Mon–Fri 9am–2pm; ☎45/711870).

Parque Nacional Nahuelbuta

From Angol, a dirt road (difficult to pass after rain) climbs 35km west to the entrance of **PARQUE NACIONAL NAHUELBUTA** (daily: April–Nov 8am–6pm; Dec–March 8am–8pm; CH$2000), spread over the highest part of the Cordillera de Nahuelbuta. The park was created in 1939 to protect the last remaining araucaria trees in the coastal mountains, after the surrounding native forest had been wiped out and replaced with thousands of radiata pines for the pulp and paper industry. Today it's a 68-square-kilometre enclave of mixed evergreen and deciduous forest, providing the coastal cordillera's only major refuge for wildlife such as foxes, pumas and *pudús* (pygmy deer). You can find out more about the park's flora and fauna at the **Centro de Informaciones**, 5km west along the road from the entrance. From here, an easy one-hour, four-kilometre footpath leads through the forest (look out for the giant araucaria about five minutes' walk along the path, estimated to be 1800 years old) up to the **Piedra de Aguila**. Another rewarding walk leads up the gentle slopes of **Cerro Anay**, 4km north of the information centre, reached by a jeep track followed by a short path. Its 1400-metre peak is the best place to take in the whole of the park, with the distribution of the different types of tree clearly standing out.

Park practicalities

There's no regular **public transport** to Parque Nacional Nahuelbuta for most of the year. The park is open year-round, but expect snow and 4WD conditions from June to September. There are two **camping** areas (CH$5500 per site), one next to the information centre, with showers and toilets, and a more rustic one, with no facilities, about a twenty-minute walk away in Sector Coimallín. Bring all food, as there's nowhere to buy supplies in the park.

Parque Nacional Tolhuaca

Back on the Panamericana, 40km south of the turn-off to Angol, a detour into the Andean foothills will take you to another area of protected native forest, **PARQUE NACIONAL TOLHUACA** (daily: May–Nov 8am–6pm; Dec–April 8am–9pm; CH$1700), a pristine landscape offering some of the finest hiking in the region. The park covers a long and relatively narrow strip of land stretching through the valley of the Río Malleco, hemmed in by steep, thickly wooded hills. Dominating the bottom of the valley is the wide and shallow **Laguna Malleco**, bordered by tall reeds rich in bird life, while other attractions include waterfalls, small lakes and hundreds of araucaria trees. The best **approach** to the park is along the 57-kilometre dirt road (via the village of Inspector Fernández) branching east from the Panamericana, a couple of kilometres north of **Victoria** (a small, ramshackle town of no interest). This leads directly to the Conaf administration on the southeastern shore of Laguna Malleco, where you'll also find **camping** (CH$7200 per site) and picnic areas. From here, a footpath follows the northern shore of the lake for about 3km, through lush evergreen forest to the **Salto Malleco**, where the lake's waters spill down into the Río Malleco.

Termas de Tolhuaca

From the Conaf office, a bouncy nine-kilometre dirt road leads to the **Termas de Tolhuaca** (daily 8.30am–6pm; CH$1700; ⓣ45/881164, ⓦwww.termasdetolhuaca.co.cl), just outside the park's boundaries. It can get very busy here in January and February, especially at weekends, but outside these months the place is blissfully quiet.

The road to Lonquimay

At the dreary little town of **Victoria**, a good paved road branches east from the Panamericana to the small agricultural town of **Lonquimay**, 115km away, passing the entrance to the **Reserva Nacional Malalcahuello-Nalcas** en route. There's nothing especially appealing about Lonquimay itself, but the road there – running through a narrow valley overlooked by towering volcanoes – is spectacular, particularly the stretch across the **Cuesta de Las Raíces**. Fifty-six kilometres out of Victoria, the road passes through the logging town of **CURACAUTÍN**. There's little to make you want to stay in town, however, and a better option is to carry on to the more dramatic scenery further along the road – including the sixty-metre waterfall, **Salto del Indio**, just off the road, 14km out of Curacautín, and 7km beyond, the fifty-metre **Saltos de la Princesa**. A full 27km east of town is a well-furnished and very popular youth hostel, *La Suiza Andina* (ⓣ9/884-9541, ⓦwwwsuizaandina.com; ❷–❸), which provides up-to-date hiking information, horse and bike rentals, camping and laundry facilities.

4.6

The Lake District

The landscape gradually softens as you travel south along the Panamericana, and as you pass beyond the Central Valley this is the **LAKE DISTRICT**, which stretches 339km from **Temuco** in the north to **Puerto Montt** in the south, a region of lush farmland, dense forest, snowcapped volcanoes and deep, clear lakes, hidden for the most part in the mountains. Until the 1880s, these forests were inhabited by the tenacious **Mapuche** (literally "people of the land"), who fought off the Incas and resisted Spanish attempts at colonization for 350 years before finally falling to the Chilean Army in the 1880s. The traditional centre of tourism is the adventure sports capital **Pucón**, on the shores of **Lago Villarrica**. Further south, the town of **Puerto Varas** on **Lago Llanquihue** is steadily mounting a challenge to Pucón. It offers the chance to take a boat to Argentina across the emerald-coloured **Lago Todos Los Santos**. The serenity of the sleeping volcanoes, and the blackened earth scorched by active ones, characterize this unique corner of the world. You can feel a more benevolent side of this volcanic power – for example, in the **thermal springs** near **Puyehue** or **Liquiñe**, where you can soak your bones in steaming hot mineral waters.

Travelling around the main resorts of the Lake District is fast improving as the Panamericana is now a divided highway with tolls every hour or so. Buses run regularly north and south along here, and east and west from the main transport hubs of Temuco, Osorno and Puerto Montt. Getting to more remote areas, however, can be a challenge and a car is very useful.

Temuco

Once a Mapuche stronghold, **TEMUCO**, 677km south of Santiago, is the largest city in southern Chile. Most visitors use it solely as a transport hub, but the city itself has a certain charm, not least being its rich **Mapuche heritage**, evident in and around the colourful **markets**, among the best places in the country to hear the Mapuche language spoken.

A few blocks northeast of the central **Plaza Aníbal Pinto**, at the corner of Portales and Aldunate, the sprawling **Mercado Municipal** (Mon–Sat 8am–8pm & Sun 8.30am–3pm), built in 1929, is one of the best covered markets in the country. Festooned with strings of sausages and salamis, the stalls around the edge are all occupied by butchers and fishmongers, loud with the din of whirring bandsaws cutting through bones. In contrast, the centre of the market is a pleasant, peaceful retreat with benches and gurgling fountains, a choice of restaurants and countless craft stalls selling silver Mapuche jewellery, baskets, musical instruments, woven ponchos and more.

Ten blocks west of the centre (bus #1 or *colectivo* #11 from Manuel Montt) is the solid **Museo Regional de la Araucanía**, Av Alemána 84 (Mon–Fri 10am–5.30pm, Sat 11am–5.30pm, Sun 11am–noon; CH$500), in a fine 1920s house with a garden full of stately palms and totem poles of fat-faced people with buck teeth.

The most striking exhibit in the museum is the collection of silver **Mapuche jewellery**. Still worn by Mapuche women today, this ornamentation was originally an overt display of wealth, then a means of keeping treasure portable in times of crisis, and is now a distinct art form.

Practicalities

The **train station** (☎45/233522 or 233416) is eight blocks east of the town centre. If you're coming from a nearby town by **bus**, you'll be dropped at the rural bus terminal on Pinto and Balmaceda (☎54/210494). For general tourist information, visit the **Sernatur** office on the north side of Plaza Aníbal Pinto at Claro Solar 899 (Mon–Fri 9am–1pm & 3–5pm; ☎45/211969).

Temuco is filled with **hotels**, ranging from luxury to well below basic. The *Hotel Espelette*, Claro Solar 492 (☎45/234805; ❸), is chock-a-block with colourful arts and crafts, the bedrooms are pleasantly bright, quiet and airy. Facing each other across the street on Bulnes 726 are two hotels, the *Nuevo* and the *Clásico* (☎45/200400, Ⓦwww.hotelfrontera.cl; ❹) that share many facilities. The *Nuevo* has the edge, as it's slightly more modern and has a decent restaurant and piano bar. Temuco is not short of good **places to eat** – especially the lively and colourful *El Fogón*, Aldunate 288, and the vegetarian-friendly fast-food restaurant *Quick Bliss*, Antonio Varas 755 – but it *is* a bit short on things to do afterwards.

Lago Villarrica and around

There's not much of interest on the central plain south of Temuco, and the next logical stop is **Lago Villarrica**. The draw is the presence of **Pucón**, one of Patagonia's prime outdoor adventure centres. At the other end of the lake from Pucón is **Villarrica**, a less aesthetically pleasing but functional town with cheap rooms for rent and a beautiful view. About thirty kilometres northeast of Pucón, **Parque Nacional Huerquehue** is home to several beautiful lakes surrounded by lush and mountainous forests.

Villarrica

Despite sitting on the southwestern edge of the lake with a beautiful view of the volcano, **VILLARRICA** the town has a distinct lack of holiday atmosphere. Villarrica isn't short of **accommodation**. At the cheaper end of the scale there's *La Torre Suiza*, Francisco 969 (☎45/411213, Ⓔinfo@torresuiza.com; ❷), run by two world cyclists who've finally hung up their pedals. It offers accommodation in double rooms, dorm rooms or two tents, plus an open kitchen, bike rental, broadband Internet access and a book exchange. **Camping** is also an option; it's recommended to buy your supplies in Villarrica where prices are better. Villarrica's **restaurants** are reasonably priced, many with far superior views to any in Pucón. A pricey but fantastic Chilean meal of meat or seafood is guaranteed at *El Tabor*, Epulef 1187, while *Las Brasas*, Pedro de Valdivia 529, which specializes in char-grilled meat, is a carnivore's delight. *El Rey del Marisco*, Valentín Letelier 1030, has moderately priced and highly recommended seafood. The most popular lunch spot in town is *Treffpunkt*, Pedro de Valdivia 640, which has good-value set meals.

Pucón

Nature smiled on **PUCÓN**. Every year, thousands of people flock here to climb Volcán Villarrica, to ride horses on the volcano's slopes in Parque Nacional Villarrica, to raft the Río Trancura rapids, to hike in the remote forested corners of Parque Nacional Huerquehue, to fish in the crystal-clear rivers or to soak their bones in the many thermal spas surrounding the town.

Pucón has none of the authenticity of, say, San Pedro de Atacama or Valparaíso. Still, this probably won't stop you from enjoying yourself in Pucón, whether you arrive at the height of the crowded high season or during the more peaceful shoulder seasons (Sept–Nov and March–April).

Arrival and information

Pucón doesn't have a main bus terminal. Buses JAC and Tur Bus have their own purpose-built large terminals, the former at Palguín 605 (☎45/443963; buses from

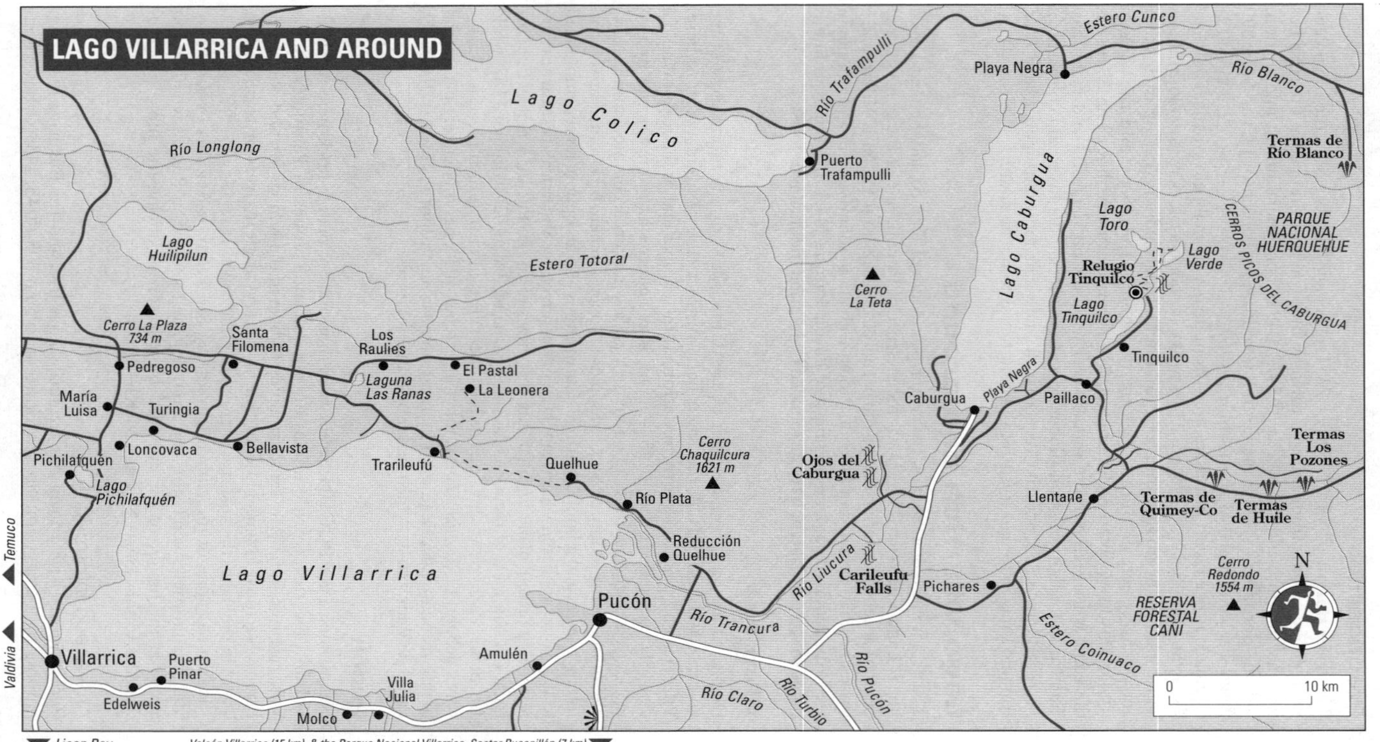
LAGO VILLARRICA AND AROUND
Lago Colico
Río Longlong
Lago Huilipilun
Estero Totoral
Cerro La Plaza 734 m
Santa Filomena
Los Raulíes
Pedregoso
Laguna Las Ranas
El Pastal
La Leonera
María Luisa
Turingia
Loncovaca
Bellavista
Pichilafquén
Lago Pichilafquén
Trarileufú
Quelhue
Río Plata
Cerro Chaquilcura 1621 m
Reducción Quelhue
Lago Villarrica
Pucón
Río Trancura
Río Claro
Río Turbio
Río Pucón
Río Liucura
Carileufu Falls
Ojos del Caburgua
Cerro La Teta
Río Trafampulli
Puerto Trafampulli
Playa Negra
Estero Cunco
Río Blanco
Termas de Río Blanco
Lago Caburgua
Lago Toro
Relugio Tinquilco
Lago Verde
Lago Tinquilco
Tinquilco
PARQUE NACIONAL HUERQUEHUE
CERROS PICOS DEL CABURGUA
Caburgua
Playa Negra
Paillaco
Llentane
Termas Los Pozones
Termas de Quimey-Co
Termas de Huile
Cerro Redondo 1554 m
RESERVA FORESTAL CANI
Estero Coinuaco
Pichares
N
0 10 km
Villarrica
Puerto Pinar
Edelweis
Molco
Villa Julia
Amulén
Temuco
Valdivia
Lican Ray
Volcán Villarrica (15 km), & the Parque Nacional Villarrica, Sector Rucapillán (7 km)

Temuco every 20min), the latter on O'Higgins 910 on the outskirts of town (Ⓣ45/443328). The **Cámara de Turismo** has a well-stocked kiosk on the corner of Caupolicán and Brasil, where the road from Villarrica enters town (Mon–Sat 10am–2pm & 3–7pm, Sun 10am–2pm & 3–7pm; Ⓣ45/441671, Ⓦwww.puconturismo.cl). The very good **Oficina de Turismo Municipal** is at O'Higgins 488 (Mon–Fri 8.30am–7pm, Sat & Sun 9am–7pm; Ⓣ45/293002). For information about national parks, **Conaf** is at Lincoyán 336 (Mon–Fri 8.30am–noon & 2pm–6.30pm; Ⓣ45/443781).

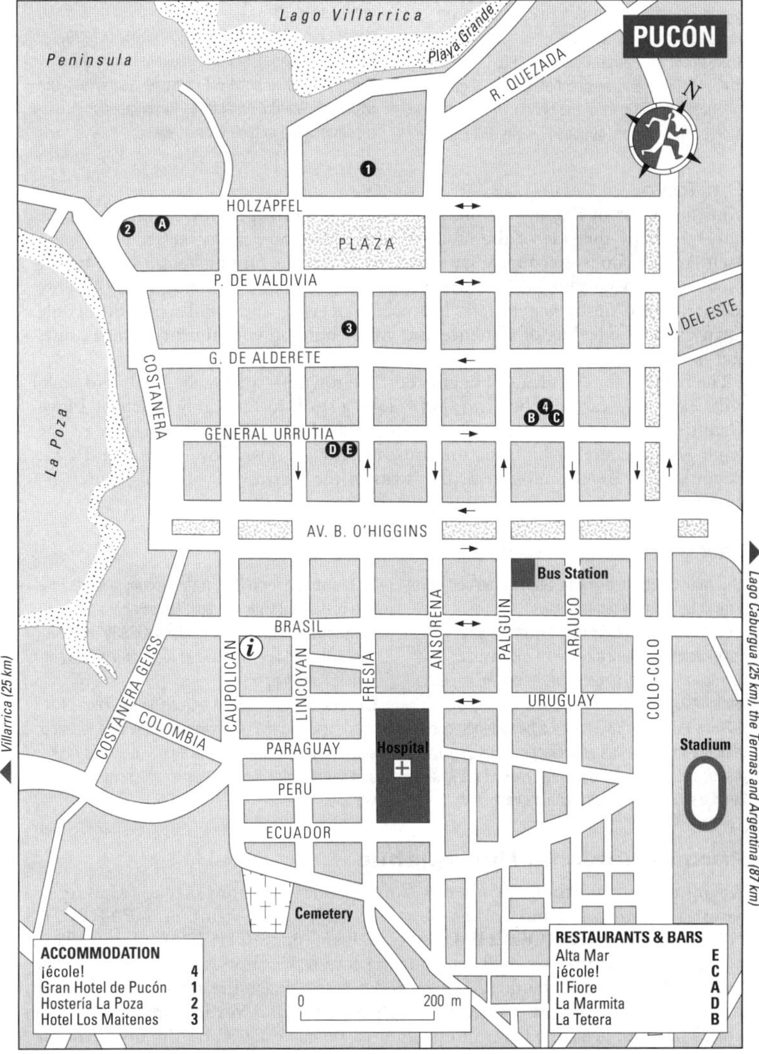

Accommodation

One of the advantages in Pucón's meteoric rise in popularity is that competition at the lower end of the market has kept prices relatively stable. At the upper end, though, prices double from Christmas to the end of February, and you need to book in advance.

¡école! Urrutia 592 ⓣ45/441675, ⓦwww.ecole-adventures.com. With owners who are deeply involved in conservation projects throughout southern Chile, this excellent *residencial* offers a wealth of fantastic traveller information. The rooms are good and often booked, so reserve well in advance. Many travellers come for the fine vegetarian restaurant with a charming trellised courtyard covered in vines. ❷

Gran Hotel de Pucón Holzapfel 190 ⓣ45/441001, ⓦwww.granhotelpucon. Right on the most popular part of the beach, the *Gran Hotel* is probably the most famous hotel in Chile, and in the summer both it and its beach get very busy. It rested on its laurels for years until a major fire forced the owners to bring it into the twentieth century. ❼

Hostería La Poza Holzapfel 11 ⓣ45/441320. This traditional old house in the quieter section of town is a very comfortable place to stay. All rooms are en suite. ❹

Hotel Los Maitenes Fresia 354 ⓣ45/441820, ⓦwww.puconturismo.cl/losmaitenes. A clean, centrally located hotel with parquet floors, helpful staff and plentiful breakfasts. Reservations recommended in high season. ❹

The Town

Your first sight of Pucón will probably be the bright paper flowers for sale, stuck into bushes by the side of the road – not real, but very pretty, rather like Pucón itself. And Pucón is very pretty, set in the shadow of the fuming volcano and by the shore of the deep-blue lake, whose waters are often cut by slashing lines of white foam churned up by waterskiers. The streets are wide and regular, and the whole town gives off a feeling of affluence and youth, bustling with tourist agencies, cafés and hotels.

The main street, Avenida O'Higgins, cuts the town in two, a wide boulevard lined with expensive cars and bustling shops. Take a stroll to the sandy beach of **Playa Grande**, packed with oiled and sweating sunbathers lying in the shadow of the *Gran Hotel*, where in high season you can rent jet skis. Move on to **La Poza**, Pucón's other beach, and gaze at the boats in the marina. Beyond this, there isn't much to see.

Eating

Alta Mar Urrutia and Fresia. Superb seafood, all of it fresh but somewhat expensive.

¡école! Urrutia 592. Tasty, inexpensive and imaginative vegetarian dishes – moussaka, burritos and large, large salads – served in peace and quiet in a vine-covered courtyard.

Il Fiore Holzapfel 83. There's a bewildering choice of home-made pastas and sauces on this upscale menu, including three different types of lasagne, but if it's busy the service can be very slow.

La Marmita Fresia 300. A rare example in Pucón of a restaurant with candlelit tables and atmosphere. Two-person fondues (US$30) are the speciality; indulge your sweet tooth and wallow in a chocolate one.

La Tetera Urrutia 580. A refreshing selection of teas, including the otherwise unobtainable lapsang souchong, properly made in a pot. They also make and serve fine cakes, not just confections of whipped cream.

Parque Nacional Huerquehue

Rising almost two thousand metres from the eastern shore of Lago Caburgua forest-clad hills and peaks that form the 125-square-kilometre **PARQUE NACIONAL HUERQUEHUE** (daily 8.30am–6pm; CH$2200), about 30km northeast of Pucón. Crowned by araucaria forests, the horseshoe-shaped Cerros Picos de Caburgua (Caburgua Mountains) enclose a dozen breathtakingly beautiful lakes of which the largest – **Tinquilco**, **Chico**, **Toro** and **Verde** – are easily accessible. The most acclaimed accommodation is *Trinquilco Lodge*, on the northeastern shores of Lake Tinquilco (Ⓣ2/777-7673, Ⓔpatriciolanfranco@entelchle.net; ❷–❸). This airy, hostel offers both en-suite doubles and bunks; pluses include a sauna, use of a kitchen and loads of good advice on exploring the park.

Valdivia

Although **Valdivia** is fifty kilometres off the Panamericana, so many long-distance buses pass through the city that it is almost impossible not to come here. The highly efficient **bus terminal** (Ⓣ63/212212), surrounded by *hospedajes*, is on the corner of Anwandter and Muñoz, five blocks from the city centre. Valdivia's **airport** lies 32km northeast of town in the village of Pichoy.

Sernatur, with the usual full complement of leaflets and information, is at Prat 555, next to the river between the cruise boats and the Mercado Fluvial (Mon–Fri 9am–5pm; Ⓣ63/342300, Ⓔinfovaldivia@sernatur.cl). For information on parks and treks, contact **Conaf** at Ismael Valdés 431 (Mon–Fri 9am–1pm & 3–5pm; Ⓣ63/245200).

Unlike most Chilean towns, Valdivia's heart is not its plaza but its bustling **waterfront**, where the Río Calle Calle and the Río Cau Cau meet the Río Valdivia. Valdivia has a couple of excellent restaurants, serving Chilean food with a Germanic twist. Like most university towns, it also has a number of lively bars and discotheques.

Practicalities

In January and February, when Valdivia's student population is on holiday, the city has some of the cheapest **accommodation** in the Lake District. An enormous old mansion near the bus terminal, *Hostal Casagrande*, at Carlos Anwandter 880 (Ⓣ63/202035; ❸), has a view of the river. Rooms have cable TV and the house is nicely maintained – good laundry facilities are another plus. The smart, refurbished *Hostal Prat*, Av Prat 595 (Ⓣ63/222020; ❸), also overlooks the river and features en-suite rooms and cable TV. Right in the centre of the city, the *Hotel Pedro de Valdivia*, Carampangue 190 (Ⓣ63/212931, Ⓦwww.hotelpedrodevaldivia.telsur.cl; ❻), is a large traditional old hotel that is well run with a very good international restaurant, attractive gardens and a pool.

Dining opitions include *Bacarana*, at Arauco 379, a student hang-out that delivers hearty sandwiches and local brew at low prices while, on the road to Niebla, the *Cervecería Kuntsmann* (Ⓣ63/292969, Ⓦwww.cerveza-kuntsmann.cl) is Chile's premiere local brewery offering guided tours of the plant, with tastings, lunch and German food. The celebrated *Chocolatería Entre Lagos* on Vicente Pérez Rosales 622–640 is connected to a *salón de té* that sells giant veggie sandwiches, a wide range of ice creams and freshly made natural fruit juices.

Lago Ranco

Back on the Panamericana and heading south, the next temptation off the highway is pretty **LAGO RANCO**, 91km east of Valdivia, surrounded by dozens of distant mountains on a high and rugged skyline. The lake is big – the second largest in the region, covering over four hundred square kilometres – and is bordered to the west by flat land, and to the east by the rising Andes. Around the lake's edge is a 121-kilometre dirt road, passing the village of **Futrono** – small and tidy but boring – and leading to **Llifén** on the eastern shore, a small village with good fishing. Beyond Llifén, hidden away in the mountains, is **Lago Maihue**, untouched and almost unvisited, while on the southeast shore is **Lago Ranco Village**, undeveloped and shabby. In the middle of the lake is **Isla Huapi**, a Mapuche *reducción*, which you can visit from Futrono.

Osorno and around

OSORNO is an agricultural city and it has little for the tourist – except **buses**, which, as transport hub for the southern Lake District and starting point for the region's main road into Argentina, it has aplenty. Most visitors will only stop here on the way to **Parque Nacional Puyehue**.

Osorno's two **bus terminals** are less than a block from each other on Calle Errázuriz and close to the city centre. The long-distance terminal is at Errázuriz 1400 (Ⓣ64/234149), and the rural terminal is at Mercado Municipal, Errázuriz 1300 (Ⓣ64/232073). Rail services no longer run to Osorno. Sernatur's **information office**, O'Higgins 667, first floor (Mon–Fri 8.30am–1pm & 2.30–6.30pm; Ⓣ64/237575), is in the Gobernación building on the west side of the Plaza de Armas and is filled with maps and leaflets.

Practicalities

Osorno's **accommodation** is largely aimed at travelling salesmen and businessmen, so the mid-range is good but the low end is a bit thin on the ground. An old colonial house, the *Apart Hotel Ñiltaihuen*, Los Carrera 951 (Ⓣ64/234960, Ⓔtnilque@telsur.cl; ❹), has been converted into double and triple suites with cooking facilities, while *Residencial Schulz*, on Freire 530 (Ⓣ64/237211; ❸), offers rooms that are clean and cheerful.

The **food** in Osorno has a strong Germanic flavour, a legacy of the nineteenth-century settlers, so don't miss out on the Germanic cakes (*küchen*), tarts (*tortas*) and chocolates. Visit *Café Central* on O'Higgins 610 for American breakfasts, hamburgers, sandwiches and good service or *Restaurant Club de Artesanos*, on Mackenna 634, which serves inexpensive Chilean food, particularly fish and seafood, served in an informal setting.

Parque Nacional Puyehue

PARQUE NACIONAL PUYEHUE (daily 8.30am–6pm; CH$1000; Ⓣ64/236988 & 232881), 81km from Osorno, is one of Chile's busiest national parks, largely because of the traffic on the international road that runs through its middle. It's part of a massive, fifteen-thousand-square-kilometre area of protected wilderness, one of the largest in the Andes; it borders the Parque Nacional Vicente Pérez Rosales to the south and some Argentinean parks that stretch all the way to Pucón's Parque Nacional Villarrica in the north. The land is high temperate rainforest spread over two volcanoes: Volcán Puyehue (2240m), to the north, and Volcán Casablanca (1990m) on the west slope of which is the Antillanca ski resort.

Lago Llanquihue and around

The Panamericana from Osorno passes through some unremarkable scenery, but after about 55km is **Lago Llanquihue**. Far across the lake is one of the icons of the Lake District, the symmetrical perfection of the Mount Fuji-like **Volcán Osorno** (2661m). Bustling **Puerto Varas**, on the southern edge of the lake, is fast challenging Pucón as the Lake District's adventure tourism centre.

The magical green waters of **Lago Todos Los Santos** offer a spectacular trip to Argentina using a combination of ferries across the lake and buses leaving from Puerto Montt.

Puerto Varas

PUERTO VARAS is a spruce little town with wide streets, grassy lawns and exquisite views over two volcanoes, Osorno and Calbuco. Like Pucón there's not much to see in the town itself – the reason you come is for its tourist facilities. Puerto Varas is built on a long bay that curves from southeast to northwest, and the heart of town is clustered around a small pier to the northwest. The biggest draw is the **waterfront** where you can admire Volcán Osorno's perfection glimmering above the waves. (From the docks you can rent motorboats for any imaginable tour of the lake.)

Practicalities

The only public transportation to Puerto Varas is by **bus**. The top spot for **tourist information** is on the wharf at the Casa del Turista, Piedraplén s/n, Muelle de Puerto Varas (daily 9am–1.30pm & 3–7pm; Ⓣ65/237956 or 237272, Ⓦwww.puertovaras.org).

There are a number of private houses that let **rooms** during the summer, particularly along San Francisco, and the tourist office will have an up-to-date list of them. Try the popular *Casa Azul*, on El Mirador 18 (Ⓣ65/232904, Ⓔcasazyk@telsur.cl; ❷), for spacious rooms, plenty of fellow travellers, a reading room, kitchen and garden.

The beautifully restored *Guest House* mansion, on O'Higgins 608 (Ⓣ65/231521; ❸), has many extras ranging from yoga to massage to Internet access. Its rooms are sunny and large. An oversized Swiss chalet, the *Hotel Licarayén*, on San José 114 (Ⓣ65/232305; ❹), overlooks the lake. All rooms are clean and most have a view, but the Jacuzzi suites on the top floor offer a lake view and excellent service.

The food is good in Puerto Varas and most of the **restaurants** are in the centre. The *Café Mamusia*, on San José 316, offers a complete menu ranging from lasagne to salmon, all at great prices – but the cakes and bread are best. *Kika Restaurant*, on Walker Martínez 584, specializes in seafood and has huge lunches on the cheap; ask for the set menu. Finally, *La Olla*, on San Bernardo and Martinez, is the place to go if you're looking for a local hang-out. It features inexpensive meals, with plenty of soups, steaks, *empanadas* and mashed potatoes.

Lago Todos Los Santos and ferries to Argentina

The road from Puerto Varas passes through the forgettable village of Ensenada before arriving at in the town of **Petrohué** on the western shore of the lake. There are five **buses** daily to Petrohué from Puerto Montt via Puerto Varas, run by Buses JM year-round, and by Fierro and Buses Adriazola in summer. Ten kilometres past Ensenada are the **Saltos de Petrohué** (CH$1700), a series of rapids formed by an extremely hard layer of lava that has been eroded into small channels. At the end of the road you reach **LAGO TODOS LOS SANTOS**, deep green and incredibly clear, one of the most beautiful in the Lake District. The boat trip here is fantastic, either for a day-trip or as part of a trip to Bariloche in Argentina. On the other side of the lake is a road that leads to the Argentine border. Two-hour ferry **crossings to Peulla**, at the far end of the lake, leave at 10.30am and cost CH$16,000. At Peulla, there's little except the border post (daily: Jan–March 8am–9pm; April–Dec 8am–8pm) and the *Hotel Peulla* (Ⓣ2/196-4182; ❽). Argentinean customs is 23km east, at Laguna Frias.

Puerto Montt and around

After Puerto Varas, the Panamericana begins to run out of land. It approaches the city of **PUERTO MONTT**, 17km south of Puerto Varas. Puerto Montt looks like a run-down port at the end of the road. It was exactly that for many years, when both the Panamericana and the railway from Santiago ended here. For tourists it's an important, albeit ugly, launchpad.

Arrival and information

If you're arriving by **bus**, you'll pitch up at the bus terminal, which is on the seafront (Av Portales s/n), six blocks to the west of the town centre. The **ferry**

terminal is a further half-kilometre out of town, southwest towards the suburb of Angelmó. Again, taxis and *colectivos* run frequently into town. The **airport** (Ⓣ65/486200) is 16km northwest of Puerto Montt; flights are met by the ETM bus company, which will take you to the bus terminal for CH$1000. A taxi from the airport to town costs CH$12,000.

Puerto Montt **tourist information** is on the main Oficina de Turismo, on the eastern side of the Plaza de Armas in a seafront park (mid-March to mid-Dec Mon–Fri 9am–6.30pm & Sat 9am–1pm; mid-Dec to mid-March daily 9am–9pm; Ⓣ65/261700 ext. 823).

Accommodation

There's no shortage of cheap **accommodation** in Puerto Montt, and it's generally a buyer's market.

HI Hotel Don Teo Andrés Bello 990, second floor Ⓣ65/251625. This HI-property has a friendly staff, a nice environment and a good location next to the bus station. Private rooms; breakfast included. ❸

Hotel Viento Sur Ejército 200 Ⓣ65/258701, Ⓔreservas@hotelvientosur.cl. The best-positioned hotel in the city, on the hill overlooking the bay. It's beautifully decorated with woods, and there's a small restaurant that specializes in fish and home-made pasta. ❽

The City

Puerto Montt is strung out along the bay. To the east, around a headland, is the beach and university district of Pelluco, and a kilometre to the west, down past the port and opposite Isla Tenglo, is the best local fishing district – **Angelmó**, where the *costanera* (coastal road) is lined with a **feria artesanal**, or crafts market. At the end of the road, a pleasant path along the water from the centre of town, past the mountain of shredded native forests, leads to a thriving **fish market**.

Eating and drinking

In addition to Angelmó, which is known for its (not inexpensive) seafood, other districts around Puerto Montt have become famous for their food.

Ferries from Puerto Montt

One of the main reasons people travel to Puerto Montt is to catch a **ferry** south. From Puerto Montt you can sail to Quellón on the island of Chiloé, Chaitén and Puerto Chacabuco on the Carretera Austral, the Laguna San Rafael far south in the fjords of the southern coast and Puerto Natales in Magallanes. These ferry trips are almost always fully booked in summer, and you must **reserve ahead** if you want to be certain of travelling.

Navimag at Av Angelmó 2187 (Ⓣ65/270416, Ⓦwww.navimag.com) is the busiest of Puerto Montt's ferry companies, and it's recommended that you book ahead at least a month before travel. The short-distance *Alejandrina* serves Chaitén and Quellón and costs CH$10,000 from Puerto Montt to Chaitén (9hr). It sails from Puerto Montt on Thursdays, Fridays, Saturdays and Sundays, returning on Fridays, Saturdays, Sundays and Mondays. The middle-distance *Evangelista* serves Puerto Chacabuco and the Laguna San Rafael; it costs CH$135,000 for a round-trip from Puerto Montt to Laguna San Rafael (5 days, 4 nights) and CH$18,000 for a one-way to Puerto Chacabuco (24hr). It sails from Puerto Montt every four days in summer. The long-distance *Puerto Edén* heads all the way down to Puerto Natales; it costs from CH$140,000 to Puerto Natales (3 days, price includes food), sailing from Puerto Montt about once a week.

Balzac Urmeneta 305. You'll recognize this restaurant from its logo: a chef in whites rowing out to sea. The dining room is painted in attractive primary colours; the seafood menu varies daily and is pricey but excellent.

El Bodegón Antonio Varas 931. An old-fashioned workers' restaurant where set lunches cost CH$2000.

Club de Yates Juan Soler Manfredini 200, Pelluco ⓣ65/284000. On a pier sticking out into the ocean, with a bright neon light on top, the *Club de Yates* is hard to miss. It's less ostentatious on the inside, and is one of the best seafood restaurants in Puerto Montt – but expensive. Booking is advisable.

4.7

Chiloé

Immediately to the south of the Lake District, the Chilean mainland narrows even further, and the straight Pacific coastline splinters into a seemingly never-ending series of islands continuing all the way down to Cape Horn. The first group of isles is the fascinating **CHILOÉ** archipelago, whose main island is **Isla Grande**, South America's second largest. Exposed to the ocean on its moist westward flank, Isla Grande is separated from the mainland by the Golfo de Ancud, across which are scattered the lesser Chilote islands. A verdant rectangle of rolling hills, Isla Grande is sliced in half lengthways by the Panamericana as it tears past the two main towns, **Ancud** and **Castro**; the latter, the island's colourful capital, makes the best base for exploration, especially if you have no transport of your own. Regular buses trundle up and down the highway, and the lesser roads are generally served by at least one bus a day. However, the ideal way to explore is by going on an organized tour, or to drive or cycle along the islands' minor roads. It's well worth heading west into the densely forested **Parque Nacional Chiloé**, the most accessible part of the almost pristine wilderness of the coastal rainforest, which can be visited on all-too-brief excursions from Castro.

More than 150 eighteenth- and nineteenth-century **wooden churches and chapels**, with their characteristic arched porticoes and towers, dot the land; sixteen of them are protected by UNESCO's world heritage status. Chiloé is also one of the few places in the country where you can still see **palafitos**, precarious but picturesque timber houses built on stilts on the edge of the sea or estuaries.

Arriving in Chiloé

Although there are controversial plans to build a **bridge** across the narrow straits that separate Chiloé's Isla Grande from the mainland south of Puerto Montt – a project that could be completed by 2004–2005 if it goes ahead – at present you must take one of the regular **ferries** to get to the island. Scheduled ferry and catamaran services also crisscross the gulf, linking Puerto Montt, Chaitén, Castro and Quellón, and making it relatively straightforward to combine a visit to both the island and the nearby mainland; Chaitén is the main northerly entry point to the dramatic Carretera Austral. The ferry from Pargua, 59km southwest of Puerto Montt on the mainland (daily every 15–30min; 30min; cars CH$5000, foot passengers free), arrives at **Chacao** on the Isla Grande's northern shore. There's not much here to detain you, except perhaps the excellent **tourist kiosk** half a kilometre along the road to Ancud (Jan–March daily 9am–9pm; ⓣ65/262811 ext 237). If you've no transport you can pick up one of the **buses** coming off the ferry, which run every fifteen minutes to Ancud (CH$800) or Castro (CH$1500). Most people take one of the frequent buses from Puerto Montt; the fare includes the ferry ride, and your bus takes you on to your Chiloé destination.

Ancud

ANCUD is a pretty little seaside town and lively fishing port, built on a small, square promontory jutting into the Canal de Chacao and the Golfo de Quetalmahue. The town is spread along two hilly sides of an old riverbed, a chaotic mass of streets and one-way systems.

Arrival and information

Long-distance buses **arrive** in the terminal on Calle Aníbal Pinto, a five-minute taxi ride (CH$1000) from the Plaza de Armas towards Ruta 5. The local bus terminal is on Pedro Montt, opposite Dieciocho. Ancud's tourist information office is **Sernatur**, on the Plaza de Armas at Libertad 665 (Jan–March Mon–Fri 8.30am–8pm, Sat & Sun 9.30am–1.30pm & 3–6.30pm; April–Dec Mon–Fri 9.30am–1pm & 2.30–6pm; ⓣ65/622800). It has information on the entire archipelago and is far better than the information hut in Castro (see p.554).

Accommodation

There's much more accommodation in Ancud in the summer, when many private houses open their doors to offer bed and breakfast, but there's enough to go around even in winter. For rooms in private houses (④) in the nearby countryside, contact the **Oficina de Agroturismo** (ⓣ65/628333).

Hospedaje O'Higgins 6 ⓣ65/622266. With an almost life-size bronze statue facing the front door, and well-proportioned, pale-wood-panelled bright rooms with views over the bay, this is the best budget accommodation in Ancud. Closed April–Dec. ③

Hostal Lluhay Lord Cochrane 458 ⓣ65/622656; ⓔlluhay@entelchile.net. This marvellous *hostal* looks modest from the outside, but inside you'll discover a 200-year-old French rosewood piano, a collection of antique gramophones and one of the best-stocked bars in Ancud. The rooms have private baths, and the friendly owners will arrange private tours. Credit cards are accepted. ⑤

Hostería Ahui Av Costanera 906 ⓣ65/622415. A two-storey beachfront building, with good views from the comfortable en-suite rooms, all of which makes it a popular mid-range choice. ⑤

Hostería Ancud San Antonio 30 ⓣ65/622340. Built up on the peninsula just to the north, this is the best hotel in town, with a luxurious log-cabin feel and large picture windows overlooking the sea. ⑧

The Town

The centre is the **Plaza de Armas**, a pretty little square which, in summer, is filled with the temporary crafts stalls that spill out of the colourful **Mercado Municipal**, one block to the north. There are some more stalls a block to the west, down near the hectic little **fishing harbour**, a great place to hang around and watch the catch being landed. Just south, a crushed-shell promenade leads past half a dozen intriguing pieces of **sculpture**. Perched above the promenade is the **Museo Regional** (officially and more poetically known as the Museo Azul de las Islas de Chiloé), a fort-like building with a blue façade. Its entrance is on Libertad, one block south of the Plaza de Armas (Jan–Feb Mon–Fri 10.30am–7.30pm, Sat & Sun 10am–7.30pm; March–Dec Mon–Fri 9.30am–5.30pm, Sat & Sun, holidays 10am–2pm; CH$600, children CH$300). Outside, on an untidy patio, you can inspect a traditional **fogón**, a type of hut introduced into Chiloé by the first Spanish missionaries three hundred years ago. Don't miss the collection of rustic **carved demons** from Chilote mythology. Inside the museum is an excellent, partly interactive exhibit, covering various aspects of life in the archipelago, with an emphasis on domesticity and arts and crafts.

Eating and drinking

Being a fishing town, Ancud has a sizeable collection of good **seafood restaurants**, albeit with similar menus. Most huddle around the sheltered courtyard in the Mercado Municipal, where it can get so busy that at times it's difficult to tell who's supposed to be serving you.

Kurantón Prat 94. All kinds of excellent dishes, meat and fish, on offer in trendy surroundings, with prices to match, but the speciality is the eponymous *curanto* (with a "c"), a fish and shellfish stew.

Pastelería Pederson Lord Cochrane 470. Enjoy unbeatable harbour views as you tuck in to a delicious, reasonably priced lunch or *once*. The *küchen* are unforgettable, especially the raspberry cream cake (in season).

La Pincoya Prat 61. One of the best places to eat *curanto* and *ceviche*, with a family-run atmosphere, low prices and excellent service.

Castro

Built on a small promontory at the head of a twenty-kilometre fjord, **CASTRO** occupies an unusual position both physically and historically. Founded in 1567, it's the third-oldest city in Chile, but it never became strategically important because it's a terrible harbour for sailing ships. Life here is now placid and slow but a series of disasters have taken their toll, burning, shaking or washing away most of old Castro, though some buildings have miraculously survived, such as the garishly painted **Iglesia San Francisco** on the Plaza de Armas, and the groups of brightly coloured *palafitos* (houses on stilts) on the waterfront to the north and south of town.

Arrival and information

Castro has two **bus terminals**, the long-distance terminal at San Martín 486, a block north of the Plaza de Armas, and the rural terminal at San Martín 667, down an alley four blocks north of the plaza. Both are within walking distance of anywhere you might be heading.

There's a **tourist information** kiosk on the Plaza de Armas, but it's erratically open and pretty useless, run by the local hotels as a means of advertising. Conaf is at Gamboa 424 (Mon–Fri 10am–12.30pm & 2.30–4pm; ⓣ65/632289).

Accommodation

There's plenty of cheap accommodation in Castro, and almost every other house seems to have a "*Hospedaje*" sign in the window – the chances are you'll be met by a tout at the bus station, so play the field.

Hospedaje Lillo 204 (no phone). If you want to wake up to the sound of seagulls and the smell of the sea, then this traditional old house, perched on the edge of the shore, is the place to stay. It's a bit scruffy though. ❸

Hospedaje Matilde Barros Arana 146 ⓣ65/633614. The downstairs rooms are the best, cut off from the rest of the house and with their own private balcony overlooking the port. The beds sag a bit. ❸

Hospedaje El Molo Barros Arana 140 ⓣ65/635026. Sharing the great views – and tricky access – of other guesthouses on this steep stairway, it edges ahead of the field with its warm, comfortable rooms, kitchen, Internet access and hospitable welcome. ❸

Hotel Unicornio Azul Av Pedro Montt 228 ⓣ65/632359, ⓦwww.chiloeweb.com/unicornioazul. In stiff competition with the Iglesia San Francisco for the virulence of its colour scheme, this unmissable hotel down by the port is the most luxurious place to stay in town. Its small, quaint rooms offer marvellous views. ❼

The Town

Castro has the feel of an isolated town on the edge of the modern mainstream, like the west coast of Ireland. The promontory on which it's centred is small, and fringed on the north and south by the town's *palafitos*, which the authorities are torn between preserving as national monuments and condemning as unsanitary slums. The centre of town is the **Plaza de Armas**, a block and a half from the southern tip of the promontory. On the northeastern corner is the **Iglesia San Francisco**, painted bright orangey-pink and purple. The impressive interior is a harmonious blend of the island's native hardwoods, lit with a soft light that brings out their warm hues.

Just off the southeast corner of the Plaza de Armas, on Calle Esmeralda, is the **Museo Regional** (Jan–Feb Mon–Sat 9.30am–1pm & 3–6.30pm, Sun

10.30am–1pm; March–Dec Mon–Sat 9.30am–noon, Sun 10.30am–noon; free), a small but well-laid-out museum containing artefacts from the various aboriginal tribes that inhabited the Chiloé archipelago before the arrival of the Spanish. Two blocks east of the plaza, down by the water, is the **feria artesanal**, a large covered market building where hand-knitted woollens vie for space with home-grown vegetables. Next to the market there's a line of *palafitos* on the sea, used today as restaurants. They're a great place to come and eat, but they get packed at lunchtime, so it's much more relaxed to wait until the afternoon.

Eating and drinking

Castro's menus are dominated by seafood plucked fresh from the fjord by the town's fleet of fishermen. The nightlife here is quiet.

Años Luz San Martín 399. This modern, sophisticated café with a dazzling yellow façade is *the* place to be seen in Castro. Excellent coffee and drinks are served from a fishing boat converted into a bar. The food, including delicious salads and cakes, is good too, if a little overpriced, as is the Internet access.

Restaurant Palafito Lillo 30. The main *palafito* restaurant by the market, serving standard Chilean seafood at reasonable prices in a beautiful setting over the placid waters of Castro's fjord.

Restaurant Sacho Thompson 213 ⓣ65/632079. The best restaurant in Castro. It's slightly dingy downstairs, but the upstairs dining area offers views across the fjord. The service can be a little frosty and the prices are higher than elsewhere, but even this cannot detract from the heavenly seafood, such as *carapacho* (crab). It's worth booking an upstairs table in the evening.

Listings

Airlines LanChile, Blanco Encalada 299 ⓣ65/635254.

Car rental Automotriz del Sur, Esmeralda 260 (ⓣ65/637777), and Salfa Sur, Gabriela Mistral 499 (ⓣ65/632704), are both cheaper than outfits in Puerto Montt.

Post office Plaza de Armas, at O'Higgins 326.

Tour operators Pehuén Expediciones, Blanco Encalada 229 (ⓣ65/632484), is an experienced outfit; its office is where you book catamaran tickets for Chaitén. In summer it runs boat trips, lasting from a day to a week, to the small, uninhabited islands of the Chilote archipelago. Pehuén Expediciones also offers city tours (CH$7000), trips to Isla Quinchao (CH$18,500) and excursions to the Parque Nacional Chiloé (CH$18,500). Turismo Quelcun, San Martín 581 (ⓣ65/632396), runs reliable tours of the Chilote archipelago at competitive prices (CH$10–15,000 for day-long outings, often with food included).

Parque Nacional Chiloé, Sector Anay

Every summer, unperturbed by the infamously changeable weather along this particularly exposed stretch of seaboard, hordes of Chilean backpackers descend on **PARQUE NACIONAL CHILOÉ, SECTOR ANAY** (daily 9am–7pm; CH$1000; ⓦwww.parquechiloe.com), 45km southwest of Castro, keen to camp on its twenty kilometres of white-sand beach and to explore its dense forest. This more accessible section of the national park covers 350 square kilometres of the Cordillera de Piuchen, rising up to 800m above sea level. It's reached by a 25-kilometre road that shoots west from a junction on the Panamericana, 20km south of Castro. At the end of the road is the gateway to the park, the picturesque but ramshackle village of **CUCAO**. Near to the sea, straddling a sluggish, murky river and with two lakes, Lago Cucao and Lago Huillinco, which almost bisect the island at this point, the village is dominated by water, and its few streets of tumbledown wooden huts are littered with whalebones, fishing floats and flotsam and jetsam from the Pacific. Cucao's basic **accommodation** is in houses near the bridge: *La Paloma* (no phone; ❷) has floor space that you can sleep on, a garden in which you can camp, hot showers and a communal kitchen. Just across the river is the German-owned *Posada Darwin* (closed June & July; messages ⓣ65/6333040; ❸) with small *cabaña* rooms and a small restaurant. Out of season, the best place to stay is *Hospedaje Paraiso* (no phone; ❷), when the snug little kitchen provides respite from the wind and rain. A converted barn next door serves fried fish and boiled potatoes. You can camp in the gardens of most of these places, and there's also a spot for wild camping by the river mouth, with a freshwater spring nearby. Across Cucao's suspension bridge and at the northern end of the wide, sandy beach is the Conaf **Cucao ranger post** (also known as the Chanquin ranger post). There's a **visitor centre** here that explains the various environments you'll find in the park, and you can also look at the display of wonderful old Chilote wooden contraptions. Close to the visitor centre (ask there for directions) there are some short nature walks in the forest, but to experience fully the beauty of the park, you have to cross about 5km of beach. There are a couple of short **hikes** that start from here. At least three **buses** a day go to Cucao from Castro, leaving from the rural bus station. They drive along a new road carved out of the southern shore of the two lakes and stop on the village football field by the suspension bridge.

4.8

The Carretera Austral

From Puerto Montt, the **Carretera Austral**, or "Southern Highway", stretches over 1000km south, ending its mammoth journey at the tiny settlement ofVilla O'Higgins, a long, long way from anywhere. Carving its path through tracts of untouched wilderness, the route takes in soaring, snowcapped mountains, Ice Age glaciers, bottle-green fjords, turquoise lakes and rivers and one of the world's largest swaths of temperate rainforest. The attractions kick in from the very beginning: less than 120km down the road from Puerto Montt is **Parque Nacional Hornopirén**, with its perfect, conical volcano. The next stop is privately owned **Parque Pumalín**, where the Carretera cuts a passage through virgin temperate rainforest, on one of the loveliest stretches of the entire road. Further south, a couple of hours' drive beyond the small town and ferry terminal of **Chaitén**, a side road branches east to the border village of **Futaleufú**, a growing centre for white-water rafting and other activities. Continuing down the Carretera Austral, you come to **Parque Nacional Queulat** whose extraordinary hanging glacier and excellent trails make this one of the most rewarding places to get off the road. Don't miss the chance to soak your bones in the secluded hot pools of the nearby **Termas de Puyuhuapi**, the most luxurious thermal resort in Chile. Further south, you come to the regional capital of **Coyhaique**, a thriving city with a wide range of useful services, including the region's main airport at Balmaceda. West of here, Puerto Chacabuco is the principal starting point for boat excursions to the sensational **San Rafael Glacier**, a 15km tongue of ice spilling into a lagoon. The final stretch of the Carretera winds its way down to the isolated hamlet of **Villa O'Higgins**.

"Doing" the Carretera Austral requires a certain amount of forward planning, and time should always be allowed for unexpected delays. A limited **bus** service does exist between the few main towns along the road (see box overleaf), but it's very sporadic and, more importantly, provides little opportunity for getting off along the way and exploring the back-country. If you really want to get the most out of the region, you'll need your own transport, which for a growing number of visitors is a **mountain bike**, but for most people still means a **rented vehicle**. The road has a hard dirt covering which even in heavy rainfall rarely turns muddy. The layer of loose gravel on top, however, can make the surface very slippery, and by the far the best option is a sturdy pick-up truck which will hold the road well; 4WD is a bonus, but not essential. There are sufficient **petrol** stations along the way to get by without carrying your own fuel, but it's always worth keeping a spare supply in case you get stuck.

Hornopirén

The sheltered, sandy cove of **La Arena** is the departure point of a **ferry** (7–10 per day; CH$5000 per car, passengers free) for tiny **Caleta Puelche**, from where the road winds through thickly forested hills, before arriving at the village of **HORNOPIRÉN** where you catch another **ferry**, TransMarChilay's *Mailén*, plugging the gaps between stretches of road (Jan & Feb only; 1 daily at 3pm; 5hr; CH$10,000 for passengers, CH$50,000 for cars). The village enjoys a spectacular location on the shore of a wide fjord, at the foot of **Volcán Hornopirén**. The

The Carretera Austral: practicalities overview

Ferries

It's always a good idea to book your ticket at least a week in advance, particularly in January and February. For details on services to the Laguna San Rafael, see box on p.563, and for more information on the ferry companies, see box on p.473.

La Arena–Caleta Puelche (see p.557): 30min. Seven to ten crossings per day in each direction, operated year-round by TransMarChilay; CH$5000 per car, passengers free.

Hornopirén–Caleta Gonzalo (see below): 5hr. One daily in each direction, operated only in January and February by TransMarChilay; cars CH$50,000, passengers CH$10,000.

Puerto Montt–Chaitén: 10hr. TransMarChilay departs from Puerto Montt on Fridays, and from Chaitén on Wednesdays. Between December and March Navimag runs three to four crossings per week in each direction. Fares are from CH$15,000 per person, plus CH$50,000 for a vehicle.

Quellón–Chaitén: 5hr. TransMarChilay makes one or two crossings a week in each direction throughout the year; Navimag makes four crossings per week between December and March. Fares are from CH$10,000 per person and CH$50,000 per vehicle.

Puerto Montt–Puerto Chacabuco: 24hr. Three or four crossings per week in each direction with TransMarChilay and Navimag. Fares are around CH$20,000 for passengers and CH$75,000 for vehicles.

Quellón–Puerto Chacabuco: TransMarChilay departs from Quellón on Saturdays and from Puerto Chacabuco on Mondays; fares are around CH$10,000 per passenger and CH$55,000 per vehicle.

Bus services

The following is an outline of the main bus links down the Carretera Austral; fuller details are given in relevant parts of the section.

Puerto Montt–Hornopirén: 3 daily; 5hr (Buses Fierro ⓣ65/253600).
Caleta Gonzalo–Chaitén: buses meet ferry arrivals.
Chaitén–Futaleufú: 6 or 7 per week; 4hr.
Chaitén–Coyhaique: 1 or 2 daily; 12hr.
Coyhaique–Cochrane: 4 per week; 10hr.
Cochrane–Villa O'Higgins: 1 or 2 per week; 6–7hr.

most charming **place to stay** is *Hotel Hornopirén* at Ignacio Carrera Pinto 388 (ⓣ65/217256; ❹), an old wooden building on the edge of the sea. The cheapest option is probably the friendly *Hospedaje Chuchito* on O'Higgins (ⓣ65/217210; ❷), while *Central Plaza*'s timber *cabañas*, down from the square on Lago Pinto Concha (ⓣ65/217247; ❻), are a good deal for groups. The attached **restaurant** is one of Hornopirén's best, with a huge *quincho* (a cement base topped with a grill), over which meat and fish are barbecued on skewers. You could also try *Monteverde*, on O'Higgins, an inexpensive choice serving typical Chilean fried fish and meat.

Parque Pumalín

After five hours of sailing through the island-studded channel between Chiloé and the mainland, the ferry from Hornopirén enters the steep-sided Reñihué fjord and unloads its passengers at **Caleta Gonzalo**, where the Carretera Austral resumes its course. Getting off the boat, you'll find yourself at the main arrival point of **PARQUE PUMALÍN**, the world's largest privately owned conservation area. The Pumalín Project, founded by North American millionaire Douglas Tompkins to protect one of the world's last strongholds of temperate rainforest, has generated a considerable amount of controversy over the past five years. But, standing at Caleta Gonzalo, faced with the jungle-like vegetation covering every inch of visible land, few would deny that the park represents a magnificent environmental achievement. It's a place of overwhelming natural beauty, with hauntingly calm lakes reflecting stands of alerce trees, ferocious waterfalls gushing through chasms of dark rock and high, snowy-peaked mountains off which glaciers dangle precariously. At Caleta Gonzalo, a wooden bridge across the river leads to a "**demonstration farm**", where visitors can get a close-up view of the kind of small-scale, ecologically friendly farming and animal husbandry that the project is promoting in the local community. Nearby, close to the ferry ramp, the **Sendero Cascadas** is a steep trail through a canopy of overhanging foliage up to a 15m waterfall (3hr roundtrip). Three other trails have been carved out of the forest, branching off from the Carretera Austral as it heads south through the park.

Practicalities

Immediately beyond the ferry ramp is the park's **information centre** (daily 8am–8pm). English-speaking staff hand out leaflets explaining the project's aims and detailing the trails in the park, and there's a range of locally produced *artesanía* for sale. Opposite the information centre is a **café** (daily 7.30am–11pm) that serves delicious organic food; if you plan to camp call in here for a supply of firewood and food. The café is also the place to enquire about available **accommodation** in the handsome four-person *cabañas* (❼) lining the edge of the shore. There are also several **camping** areas, the main one just a few hundred metres from the information centre, with basic sites (CH$650 per person), covered areas with picnic tables (CH$1300 per person) and an octagonal wooden hut with bunk beds and a log fire. There are barbecue facilities, and if you phone in advance the park staff will slaughter a lamb for your arrival, which you roast on skewers over the *fogón*. The two other camping areas in the park are 12km and 14km down the road.

Chaitén

Just beyond the southern limit of Parque Pumalín, 25km south of Caleta Gonzalo, the Carretera Austral skirts the pale, calm expanse of **Lago Blanco**, which reflects Chile's most southerly stands of alerce trees in its smooth surface, before turning west towards the coast. Farther south, you reach the little town of **CHAITÉN**, whose ferry terminal is the starting point for journeys south along the Carretera Austral outside January and February, when the Hornopirén–Caleta Gonzalo ferry doesn't function. Chaitén is beautifully located but rather charmless, made up of squat, modern houses and wide, grid-laid streets.

As the provincial capital, Chaitén does offer a number of extremely useful **services**, including supermarkets, a petrol station, a public telephone, tour companies and plenty of places to stay and eat, prompting most people travelling down the Carretera to spend a night or two here. The town's only **ATM** does not normally work with non-Chilean cards; the next ATM that does is way down at Puerto Aisén. The town's **tourist office** (mid-Dec to mid-March 9am–9pm) is at the far end of O'Higgins.

Practicalities

The cheapest **accommodation** option is probably *Hospedaje Rita Gutierrez* (☎65/731502; ❸) on the corner of Almirante Riveros and Prat. Beside it, slightly sprucer *Residencial Ancud* at Libertad 105 (☎65/731535; ❸) is a good alternative. Best in the mid-range is well-run *Hostería Llanos*, down on the esplanade at Corcovado 378 (☎65/731332; ❺), where you can get decent meals, including breakfast. Better value in this price range is the *Hotel Schilling* on the seafront at Corcovado 230 (☎65/731295; ❻), with comfortable en-suite rooms. The Pumalín

Project runs a beautifully furnished *hostería*, the *Puma Verde*, offering delicious food, at O'Higgins 54 (Ⓣ65/731184, Ⓔpumaverde@telsur.cl; ❻). Places to **eat** include the good-value *Brisas del Mar* at Av Corcovado 278, with basic fish and meat dishes, and the smarter *Canasto de Agua* at Prat 65, which does hearty *parrilladas*. Best of all is the *Flamengo* at Corcovado 218, with unbeatable seafood dishes served with a little more style than anywhere else in town. Real coffee and cakes can be had at *Mely's Café*, tucked away at Libertad 641.

Futaleufú

The eighty-kilometre side trip up the Futaleufú River Valley is one of the most enjoyable diversions off the Carretera Austral. Heading east from Villa Santa Lucía, you first skirt the southern shore of Lago Yelcho before coming to a fork, 30km along the road. The left branch follows the turquoise **Río Futaleufú** for 17km through towering gorges, lush forests and snow-streaked mountain peaks. A growing number of Chilean and US operators offer **rafting** trips down the river, which boasts over forty class IV–V rapids with alarming names like *Purgatorio*, *Infierno* and *Terminador*.

The pretty pastel-painted village of **FUTALEUFÚ** ("Fu" or "Futa") sits on the Futaleufú River, near its confluence with the Espolón River, surrounded by forested, snowy peaks. Various outfits offer **outdoor activities**, such as Centro Aventura Futaleufú, operating out of the *Hostería Río Grande*, and the equally professional Club de Rafting y Kayak at Cerda 545 (Ⓣ65/721298). Expect to pay between CH$25,000 and CH$60,000 per river trip, significantly less for the more low-key activities such as horse riding or biking.

Practicalities

In the summer an **Oficina de Información Turística** operates on the south side of the Plaza de Armas. Twice-weekly buses take you up to the **Argentine border** at Paso Futaleufú (customs post open daily 8am–10pm), 10km from Futaleufú. One of the best **places to stay** for miles around, the *Hostería Río Grande*, on O'Higgins 397 (Ⓣ65/721320; ❻), is a modern, timber-built hotel, with chic-rustic decor, quality en-suite rooms and fine restaurant and bar. Sitting in a beautiful garden, the charming *Posada Campesina La Gringa*, on the corner of Aldea and Carrera, (Ⓣ65/721260; ❻), away from the bustle of the centre, has the best view of the surrounding countryside. The *Lodge Frontera Patagónica*, 5km south of town (Ⓣ65/721320, Ⓔfronterapatagonica@hotmail.com; ❽), is a Dutch–Chilean-owned complex of handsome four-person cabins with wood-burning stoves. It is a good bet for groups. Breakfast is included and other meals are available; fishing, kayaking and rafting trips can be organized. Most hotels and *hospedajes* in this area also offer **meals**; the best choice is cosmopolitan *Hostería Río Grande* (see above), which offers a European-influenced menu, stylish decor and young crowd. On the corner of Cerda and Sargento Aldea, *Restaurant Futaleufú* is a bright and airy place that features inexpensive but hearty meat and fish dishes, while *Sur Andes*, on Cerda 308, is a good bet for snacks, and a great place for fruit juices and other drinks.

Puyuhuapi and around

Squatting at the head of the narrow Ventisquero fjord, surrounded by steep, wooded hills, the quaint little village of **PUYUHUAPI** is a great place to break your journey along the Carretera Austral in either direction – not only for the wild beauty of its setting, but also for its proximity to a couple of the most compelling attractions in the whole region, the homonymous **spa** and the **Parque Queulat**. Puyuhuapi's rambling streets and old timber houses make a pleasing contrast to the utilitarian "villages" installed along the Carretera in the 1980s after the completion of the road.

Practicalities

The best place to **stay** in Puyuhuapi itself is the *Casa Ludwig* at Av Otto Uebel s/n (Ⓣ67/325220, Ⓦwww.contactchile.cl/casaludwig; ❹ shared bath, ❺ en suite), a delightful yellow chalet with comfortable rooms, run by a charming lady who even lets people camp in the house or its grounds. A good budget choice is *Residencial Elizabeth*, Circunvalación s/n (Ⓣ67/325106; ❸), which offers simple rooms and filling home-cooking. All of these are economical alternatives to staying at the *Termas de Puyuhuapi* lodge (see below), where the first-class facilities and comfort are not matched by the food. In the village excellent **meals** are available at the twee *Café Rossbach*, where wild berries are used in the mouthwatering *küchen*. An alternative is *Kermes*, at Circunvalación 14, where simple dishes and equally delicious *küchen* are on offer – the CH$3000 full lunch is unbeatable value. Best of all, though, is the excellent *Lluvia Marina*, next to Casa Ludwig, where you can get real coffee, delicious cakes and meals of unbeatable value.

Termas de Puyuhuapi

The luxurious **TERMAS DE PUYUHUAPI** (Santiago, Fidel Oteiza 1921, oficina 1006: Ⓣ2/225-6489; Puyuhuapi: Ⓣ67/325103 & 325117, Ⓦwww.patagoniaconnex.cl; ❾) enjoy a fantastic location marooned on the edge of a peninsula on the opposite side of the fjord to the Carretera; behind is a steep jungle of rainforest, making the resort inaccessible by land and reachable only by boat. Therefore, four times a day (Dec–March 10am, 12.30pm 3.30pm & 7pm), less frequently off-season, a motor launch collects passengers from the signposted wooden jetty, 15km south of the village, and whisks them across the water on a ten-minute ride to the Lodge. The thermal baths used to be a handful of ramshackle cabins nobody had heard of. Today they are housed in low-lying, beautifully designed buildings made out of reddish-brown alerce timber and lots of glass. The main reason to come here is to soak in the steaming **hot springs**, channelled into three outdoor pools reached by a short walk through the forest. There's a large indoor pool, too, part of the new state-of-the-art **spa** centre (closed Mon). You don't need to be a staying guest to visit, though day visits are limited when the lodge is full, so you should phone ahead to book; a **day visit** costs CH$12,000 for the outdoor pools and CH$5000 for the return boat ride. If you're considering a splurge somewhere along the Carretera there are few better places to do so; **staying** at the lodge costs from US$220 a night per double room.

Parque Nacional Queulat

Puyuhuapi conveniently sits right on the doorstep of **PARQUE NACIONAL QUEULAT**, a vast expanse of virgin forest, towering granite peaks and rumbling glaciers. The Carretera Austral runs through or along the edge of the park for 70km, entering the northern boundary 15km north of Puyuhuapi and crossing the southern limit 55km south of the village. Along the way, a number of trails lead off from the road into the park, while several scenic highlights can easily be reached from parking areas just off the highway. By far the most popular attraction is the incredible **Ventisquero Colgante**, or "hanging glacier", 36km south of Puyuhuapi. Wedged between two peaks, forming a V-shaped mass of blue-white ice, the glacier indeed seems to hang suspended over a sheer rock face. Long fingers of ice feed two thundering waterfalls that plummet 150m down to Laguna Los Témpanos below. Adding to the spectacle, large blocks of ice periodically calve off the glacier and crash down the rocks to the lake. The easiest way to get a look at the glacier is from the **viewpoint** at the end of a signed two-kilometre road branching off the Carretera Austral, about 24km south of Puyuhuapi; Conaf charges a CH$1500 fee to visit this sector of the park (daily: April–Nov 8.30am–6.30pm; Dec–March 8.30am–8pm), which you pay at the hut en route to the parking area.

△ A *moai* statue, Easter Island

There's also a **camping** area (CH$7000 per site) by the river, on a fairly hard ground with toilets and cold showers.

To the San Rafael Glacier

Still heading south, the Carretera Austral follows the Río Cisnes along the foot of a massive granite outcrop known as the **Piedra del Gato**, where several simple crosses honour the workmen killed while blasting through the rock. Just over 100km south of the turn-off to Puerto Cisnes, you reach a fork in the road; to the left a road leads to the regional capital of **Coyhaique**, while to the right a paved section of the Carretera Austral heads west to the small town of **Puerto Aisén**, from where more paved roads link up with Coyhaique, and with the port and ferry terminal at **Puerto Chacabuco**.

This is the departure point for the two-hundred-kilometre boat ride through the labyrinthine fjords of Aisén to the dazzling **SAN RAFAEL GLACIER**, spilling into the broad Laguna San Rafael. The journey – four to sixteen hours, depending on type of craft – is a spectacle in itself, as boats edge their way through narrow channels hemmed in by precipitous cliffs dripping with vegetation. After sailing

Visiting the San Rafael glacier

The glacier is accessible *only* by boat or plane. **Flights** from Coyhaique (see below) in five-seater planes are offered by three companies (see below), last ninety minutes each way and cost US$150–200 per person – usually requiring a full plane. Flying over the ice field is indeed an unforgettable experience, but the most sensational views of the glacier are from the small **dinghies** that thread through the icebergs towards its base, usually included as part of a visit to the *laguna* **by sea**. Scheduled departures leave from Puerto Chacabuco and Puerto Montt (via Puerto Chacabuco) throughout the warmer months. Some only operate in January and February, others run from September to March.

Catamarans

Catamaranes del Sur Isidora Goyenechea 3250, Oficina 802, Santiago ⓣ2/333-7127, ⓦwww.catamaranesdelsur.cl; Av Diego Portales 510, Puerto Montt ⓣ65/267533.

Iceberg Expedition Providencia 2331, Oficina 602 ⓣ2/335-0579, ⓔhotelsa@chilesat.net.

Patagonia Express Fidel Oteiza 1921, Oficina 1006, Santiago ⓣ2/225-6489, ⓦwww.patagoniaconnex.cl. These excursions may be combined with a stay at the *Termas de Puyuhuapi* (see p.561) on multiple-day packages (from US$1500).

Cruise ships and ferries

Navimag Av El Bosque Norte 0440, Santiago ⓣ2/203-5030, ⓦwww.australis.com; Angelmó 2187, Puerto Montt ⓣ65/253318. Ferries.

Skorpios Agusto Leguia Norte 118, Las Condes, Santiago ⓣ2/231-1030, ⓔskorpios@tmm.cl; Angelmó 1660, Puerto Montt ⓣ65/256619, ⓦwww.skorpios.cl. Cruise ships.

TransMarChilay Agustinas 715, Oficina 403, Santiago ⓣ2/633-5959; Angelmó 2187, Puerto Montt ⓣ65/270416; O'Higgins s/n, Puerto Chacabuco ⓣ67/351144. Ferries.

Flights

Aero Don Carlos Subteniente Cruz 63 ⓣ67/231981, ⓦwww.doncarlos.cl.

Aerohein Baquedano 500, Coyhaique ⓣ67/232772, ⓦwww.aerohein.cl.

Transportes San Rafael 18 de Septiembre 469, Coyhaique ⓣ67/232048.

down the long, thin Golfo de Elefantes, the boat enters the seemingly unnavigable Río Témpanos, or "Iceberg River", before emerging into the Laguna San Rafael. Floating in the lagoon are dozens of **icebergs**. Sailing around these icy phantoms, you approach the giant **glacier** at the far end of the lagoon. Over 4km wide, and rearing out of the water to a height of 70m, it really is a dizzying sight. While the cruise boat keeps at a safe distance, to avoid being trapped by icebergs, you'll probably be given the chance to get a closer look on board an inflatable motor dinghy – but not too close, as the huge blocks of ice that, with a deafening roar, calve off into the water create dangerous, crashing waves. What you can see from the boat is in fact just the tip of the glacier's "tongue", which extends some 15km from its source. If you look at the rocks that encircle the lagoon, either side of this tongue, you'll see a series of white markers, painted by scientists since the 1980s to monitor the position of the glacier's edge. It is, unmistakeably, retreating fast. It is estimated that by the year 2030 or so the glacier will be gone.

Coyhaique

From Puerto Chacabuco, a good paved section of the Carretera heads 15km east to Puerto Aisén, from where it continues 67km to the city of Coyhaique. It's a very scenic route, holding fast to the Río Simpson as it rushes through the **Reserva Nacional Río Simpson**, sandwiched between tall, craggy cliffs. **COYHAIQUE** is the only place along the Carretera that offers a wide range of services. Although resolutely urban, it's also a good launch pad for some great **day-trips** that will give you a taste of the region's wilderness – for more details see box on p.563.

Arrival and information

Most **buses** pull in at the centrally located terminal on the corner of Lautaro and Magallanes, though a few arrive at and depart from their respective company offices, separate from the terminal. Flights land at the **Aeropuerto de Balmaceda**, 55km south, and are met by **minibuses** that take passengers to their hotels (CH$3000–4000). You can pick up information on the city and the region at the very helpful **Sernatur** office, at Bulnes 35 (Dec–Feb Mon–Fri 8.30am–9pm, Sat & Sun 11am–8pm; March–Nov Mon–Fri 8.30am–1pm & 2.30–7pm; ⓣ67/231752, ⓔsernatur_coyhai@entelchile.net), which produces printed lists of Coyhaique's accommodation (with prices), restaurants, transport facilities and tour operators.

Accommodation

Coyhaique offers a wide choice of places to stay, from simple *hospedajes* to upmarket hotels. **Camping** facilities are available at *Ogana*, on Avenida Ogana, Pasaje 8, set in a small orchard with a hut for cooking and hot showers (CH$2000 per person), and at *HI Albergue Las Salamandras* (listed below; CH$5000 per site).

HI Albergue Las Salamandras Carretera Teniente Vidal, km 1.5 ⓣ67/234700. Set in a wood by a river 1.5km along the road to Teniente Vidal, this popular Spanish-run hostel offers the use of a kitchen, laundry facilities, mountain-bike rental and a range of excursions, including cross-country skiing in Coyhaique's long winter. ❹

Hospedaje Lautaro Lautaro 269 ⓣ67/238116. An attractive old house in a quiet garden with single, double and triple rooms and a bunk dormitory. The helpful owners have their own minibus and organize local tours, including horse trekking. ❹

Hotel Luis Loyola Prat 455 ⓣ67/234200. A modern hotel with eighteen en-suite rooms, all with cable TV and central heating. Probably the best choice in this price range. ❺

El Reloj Baquedano 828 ⓣ67/231108. Better than ever in its new location (a tastefully converted lumberyard), *El Reloj* is spotlessly clean with comfortable en-suite rooms and Coyhaique's best restaurant (see opposite). ❼

Sra Herminia Mansilla 21 de Mayo 60 ⓣ67/231579. Neat and tidy *casa de familia*, slightly out of the centre, with light, airy rooms and a friendly owner who is very proud of the long list of foreign visitors in her guest book. ❸

The Town

At the centre is the large, five-sided **Plaza de Armas**, from which the main streets radiate. On the southwest corner with Horn, the small **Feria de Artesanos** sells jewellery and leather goods, while, just across the plaza on the corner with Montt, the **Galería Artesanal de Cema Chile** has a wide range of handicrafts. Continue up Montt, walking away from the plaza, and you'll come to Baquedano, the city's main thoroughfare. Immediately to your right stands one of Coyhaique's quirkiest landmarks, the **Monumento al Ovejero**, a large sculpture of a shepherd and a flock of sheep. Almost opposite the monument is the **Museo Regional de la Patagonia** (Jan & Feb daily 9am–9pm; March–Dec Mon–Fri 8.30am–1pm & 2.30–6.30pm; voluntary donation), with an informative collection of black and white photographs.

Eating and drinking

Although Coyhaique's **restaurants** are, on the whole, no more adventurous than those in most other Chilean cities, they're a real treat after the limited choice along the rest of the Carretera Austral.

Loberías de Chacabuco Prat 387. An unassuming little café-restaurant whose owner prides himself on the freshness of his seafood, and more often than not cooks and serves it himself – at a rather unhurried pace.

La Olla Prat 176 ⓣ67/234700. Run by a charming man from Extremadura, this cosy, old-fashioned restaurant does excellent paellas every Sunday (and through the week if you phone in advance), and first-class *estofado de cordero* (lamb stew) all at reasonable prices.

El Reloj Baquedano 828. Some of the tastiest – and most expensive – food in town is served in this sophisticated dining room tended by the friendly hoteliers. Specialities include lamb with rosemary.

Ricer Horn 48. Just off the plaza, this bright and cheerful café, charging moderate prices, attracts a lot of gringos, partly for its vegetarian dishes, and is a good meeting place.

Listings

Airlines Aero Don Carlos, Subteniente Cruz 63 ⓣ67/231981, ⓦwww.doncarlos.cl; LanChile, General Parra 211 ⓣ67/231188.

Car rental AGS, Av Ogana 1298 ⓣ67/235354; Aisén, Bilbao 926 ⓣ67/231532; Andes Patagónicos, Horn 48 ⓣ67/216711; Arriendo de Jeep, O'Higgins 501 ⓣ67/411461; Automóvil Club de Chile, Bolívar 194 ⓣ67/231649; Automundo, Bilbao 510 ⓣ67/231621; Travel Car, Colón 190-B ⓣ67/236840.

The end of the road: Villa O'Higgins

Tiny **VILLA O'HIGGINS** is reached via the very final 100km stretch of the Carretera beyond Puerto Yungay: the road seems to fly over the crags. It sits at the head of a narrow arm of Lago O'Higgins, a beautiful Andean lake squeezed by mountainous peninsulas. Several glaciers, including Ventisquero O'Higgins, spill down into Lago O'Higgins and can be visited by boat from the concrete jetty at **Bahía Bahamondez**, just south of town. Immediately north is the entrance to the **Reserva Natural Shoën** (daylight hours for most of the year; free), which has a number of viewpoints affording magnificent views across the village and its surroundings, including the peaks of the Campo de Hielo. Given its remoteness and harsh conditions, Villa O'Higgins is not a place to turn up on spec; call the Municipalidad on ⓣ67/211849 or try one of two informative websites ⓦwww.ohiggins.cl or www.turismoohiggins.cl. The most reliable **accommodation** is to be found at *Hospedaje Apocalipsis 1:3* at Pasaje Lago El Salto (ⓣ67/216927; ④), with pleasant rooms, or the more impersonal and slightly more expensive *Hospedaje Patagonia* at Calle Río Pascua 1956 (ⓣ67/234813; ⑤). **Bus** services run once or twice a week between Cochrane and Villa O'Higgins (at least 6 hours; CH$8000).

4.9

Southern Patagonia

Patagonia is cursed by a persistent wind, its winters are cold and summers short. These days large numbers of Chileans and non-Chilean visitors come to Patagonia principally to hike in the country's most famous and arguably most stunning national park, **Parque Nacional Torres del Paine**, a massif crowned with otherworldly granite towers. Others want to follow in the footsteps of the region's famous travellers, such as the navigator Ferdinand Magellan, the naturalist Charles Darwin and, more recently, the author Bruce Chatwin. Others still just want to look at the **glaciers** that calve icebergs into the sea, or see **penguins**, or simply discover what it's like down here, at the very foot of the world. The Chileans call the area the province of **Magallanes**, in the explorer's honour, and it's one of the least inhabited areas in Chile. The provincial capital is the lively city of **Punta Arenas** and the only other town of any size is superbly located little **Puerto Natales** to the northwest, gateway to Torres del Paine. Both settlements seem to huddle patiently with their backs against the elements. Since the whole of this region is physically cut off from the rest of Chile by two vast icecaps, the only links with territory to the north are by air, water or through **Argentina**. Across the Magellan Strait lies the huge main island of **Tierra del Fuego**, the most interesting part of which lies in Argentine territory (see p.189), though the Isla Navarino and its welcoming naval base of **Puerto Williams** are worth a visit.

Punta Arenas and around

Seen from the air, **PUNTA ARENAS** seems lost in the flat barren plains and vast expanses of water that surround it, a sprawling patchwork of galvanized tin roofs struggling up from the shores of the Magellan Strait. On the ground, however, the city looks much more substantial and modern, especially in the centre where glass and concrete office buildings have replaced the ramshackle wooden houses, paid for in part by the oil that's been flowing into the city since the first wells started gushing in the 1940s. Set on a bleak, windy edge of the strait, Punta Arenas faces eastward to the ocean, an unusual orientation for a Chilean city.

Arrival and information

Most travellers arrive at the user-friendly **airport**, 20km north of town. Taxis to the centre charge CH$5000, minibuses CH$1500–2000 and buses – run by a company called Transfer (Ⓣ61/223205) – charge CH$1500; they all meet incoming flights. Many people make directly for **Puerto Natales** and **Torres del Paine**, a headlong rush partly catered for by the local bus companies, which sometimes stop at the airport in both directions.

Punta Arenas doesn't have a bus terminal as such, so different **bus companies** drop passengers at various points around town, though all within five blocks of the main Plaza Muñoz Gamero. You might also arrive at Punta Arenas by **ferry** from Porvenir, in Tierra del Fuego. The ferry terminal is a shortish taxi ride (CH$1000) from downtown, along the Natales road to the north.

The town has an excellent **Sernatur** office at the northwestern corner of the Plaza Muñoz Gamero, just along Waldo Seguel (April–Oct Mon–Fri 8am–1pm &

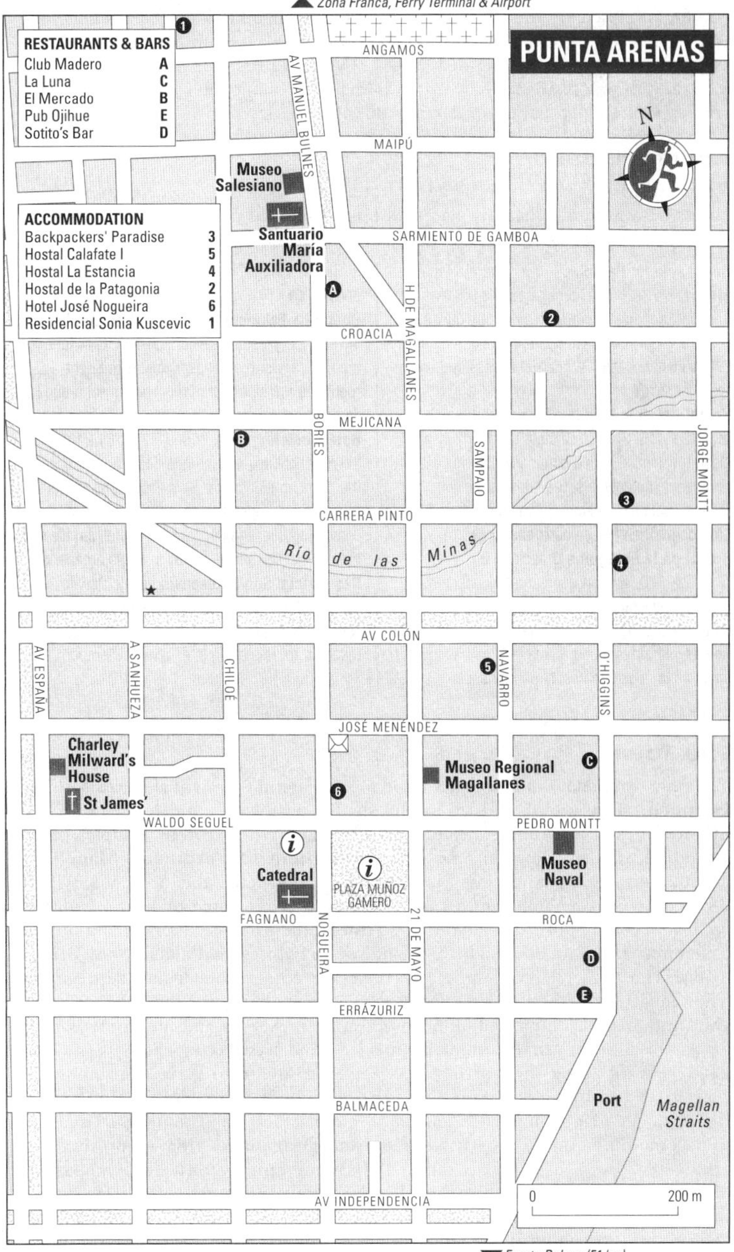

4

4.9 | CHILE | Southern Patagonia

3–6.30pm; Nov–March Mon–Fri 8am–8pm; ⓣ61/221644, ⓦwww.puntaarenas.cl), with helpful staff and lots of information on both the city and the region. Should you find it closed, try the city tourist office, housed in a kiosk on the southern side of the plaza (Nov–March Mon–Fri 8am–8pm, Sat 9am–7pm & Sun 9am–3pm). **Conaf** is at José Menéndez 1147 (Mon–Thurs 8.30am–5.50pm, Fri 8.30am–4.50pm; ⓣ61/223420) – it is informative about the area's national parks and reserves, though rather surprisingly doesn't have any maps.

Accommodation

Punta Arenas boasts a wide range of hotels, hostels and *residenciales* in all price ranges. However, the cheapest places fill up quickly and don't take bookings, so to be sure of a budget room try and arrive early in the day.

Backpackers' Paradise Ignacio Carrera Pinto 1022 ⓣ61/222554. The most popular backpackers' hostel in town, with thirty bunks (CH$3500 per person) in two open-plan rooms. Extras include cable TV, Internet access and use of the kitchen. ❷

Hostal Calafate I Lautaro Navarro 850 ⓣ61/248415, ⓦwww.calafate.tie.cl. A pleasant, clean townhouse with a commodious living room and personable owners. Breakfast is included, English spoken, and some rooms have their own bathroom. Often full, so book ahead. ❹

Hostal de la Patagonia Croacia 970 ⓣ61/249970, ⓦwww.ecotourpatagonia.com. A snug, friendly home that offers welcoming, spruce rooms with beds that have good mattresses. Rooms with private bathrooms cost half as much again as the basic rooms, but breakfast is included, and they offer hefty discounts off-season. ❻

Hostal La Estancia O'Higgins 765 ⓣ61/249130, ⓔreservas_laestancia@hotmail.com. Excellent little place, warm and hospitable, with bright rooms on the first floor of a house, all set around a communal landing. ❸

Hotel José Nogueira Bories 959 ⓣ61/248840, ⓦwww.hotelnogueira.com. A beautiful location on the plaza, in the Palacio Sara Braun. The rooms are a little cramped because of the restrictions of converting this old building into a hotel, but it's still the most stylish place to stay in Punta Arenas. ❾

Residencial Sonia Kuscevic Pasaje Darwin 175 ⓣ61/248543. A compact, long-established *residencial* in a 1970s building with parking. Discount for Hostelling International members. ❹

The Town

The centre of town is quite compact, and focused around the central **Plaza Muñoz Gamero**, a tranquil place, with shady pathways under magnificent hundred-year-old Monterey cypresses, thronged with strolling couples of an evening. In the middle is an imposing **monument to Ferdinand Magellan**, donated by the sheep baron José Menéndez. You'll notice that the toe of one stylized Ona Indian has been polished to a shine – if you touch it (some say kiss it), tradition has it that you'll return to Punta Arenas. Around the plaza are several grand houses dating from the wool boom. The only one you can visit is the **Palacio Sara Braun** (Mon–Fri 3–6pm; CH$500), on the northwestern corner, now divided between the Club de la Unión and the *Hotel José Nogueira*. It was built over the course of nine years from materials imported from Europe at great expense, and after forty years of renovation is once again full of marble fireplaces and crystal chandeliers.

If you walk along the northern edge of the square to Calle Hernando de Magallanes and turn north, you'll find the glorious **Palacio Braun Menéndez**. It's no longer a family residence, having been donated to the nation some years ago to become the home of the **Museo Regional Magallanes** (May–Sept Mon–Fri 10.30am–2pm; Oct–April Mon–Sat 10.30am–5pm & Sun 10.30am–2pm; CH$800, free on Sun and holidays). The beautifully preserved private quarters, a time-capsule turn-of-the-century French family home, is lavishly decorated and filled with European furniture and paintings; the dining room, bedrooms and sitting rooms recall a wealthy middle-class lifestyle achieved by few who came to Patagonia in search of it.

Seven blocks north of the plaza is the **Museo Salesiano Maggiorino Borgatello** (Tues–Sun 10am–1pm & 3–6pm; CH$500). Among the cases of geological samples, jars of pickled marine animals and trays of mounted insects, displays vividly depict the daily life of the extinct Fuegian Indians. One room of the museum is completely taken up by a full-size copy of the **Cave of Hands**, the original of which is near Chile Chico, 1600km north of Punta Arenas. The 11,000-year-old rock paintings are typical of the nomadic art found throughout Patagonia.

Two blocks north of the Museo Salesiano, on the other side of Avenida Bulnes, is the city's magnificent **cemetery** (daily 7.30am–10pm; free), which covers four city blocks and for many is the most fascinating sight in Punta Arenas. Crisscrossed by a network of footpaths lined with immaculately clipped cypresses, this eclectic necropolis reflects the turbulent history of Patagonia in marble and stone.

Eating and drinking

It's an affordable pleasure to eat out in Arenas, and the local speciality, king crab (*centolla*) is a delight, either on its own or in a gratin or chowder (*chupe*). Many of the country's excellent wines are widely available and, owing to the Zona Franca, imported lagers are easier to find in Punta Arenas than elsewhere, should you want a change from Chilean brews.

Club Madero Bories 655. This mock Alpine hut, complete with a roaring fire in cool weather, is a great place for a drink and a reasonably priced snack. You'll also be entitled to free entrance at the *Kamikaze* disco down below.

La Luna O'Higgins 974. Fine fare, a bright blue and yellow decor, Latin rhythms and wonderfully friendly service make this one of Arenas' best eateries. After a perfect pisco sour you can try the *chupe del día* or other well-cooked dishes (around CH$3000). Don't forget to pin your place of origin on the map provided.

El Mercado Mejicana 617, second floor. First-class seafood served until late, for a moderate outlay. There's a full-size *centolla* mounted on the wall, so you can see just how big these crustacean monsters really are.

Pub Ojihue Errázuriz 970. A cosy atmospheric pub with wooden panelling and a no-smoking area, great for drinks and snacks. Open from 7pm until late, it is *the* place to be seen in Arenas.

Sotito's Bar O'Higgins 1138 ⓣ61/221061. The bare brick walls and starched linen tablecloths are an attempt to make this relatively expensive restaurant resemble a New York or London brasserie. Attentive waiters serve large portions of meat and seafood – *the milanesa de pollo* is a good value. During the high season, booking is recommended Friday to Sunday.

Listings

Airlines DAP, O'Higgins 891 ⓣ61/223340, ⓦwww.aeroviasdap.cl; LanChile, Lautaro Navarro 999, on the corner of Pedro Montt ⓣ61/241232 or 247079.

Car rental Avis (Emsa), Roca 1044 ⓣ61/241182; Budget, O'Higgins 964 ⓣ61/241696; Hertz, O'Higgins 987 ⓣ61/248742; International, Waldo Seguel 443 ⓣ61/228323. Because there are so many loose stones on Patagonian roads, you are almost guaranteed to get a shattered windscreen or headlight, so it's a good idea to ask how much you'll have to pay if the car's glass gets damaged. Some companies (such as, International) charge a fixed fee per crack and don't ask you to pay for a whole new windscreen.

Post office Bories 911.

Tour operators To visit the Torres del Paine national park, you're better off travelling up to Puerto Natales and visiting a tour operator there (see box on p.572). To visit the penguin sanctuaries or any of the sights near Punta Arenas, it's cheaper to take one of the bus companies' tours or ask in your hotel – trips cost around CH$5000 for a half-day. For a large, well-established general operator, contact Aventur, José Nogueira 1255 (ⓣ61/241197) or Turismo Yamana, Av Colón 568 (ⓣ61/221130).

Monumento Natural Isla Magdalena

Thirty-five kilometres northeast of Arenas, two hours away by boat and easily visible from the city in clear weather, sits the penguin sanctuary of **MONUMENTO**

NATURAL ISLA MAGDALENA, one of the largest penguin colonies in southern Chile, home to an estimated 120,000 **Magellanic penguins**. It's a small island, just one square kilometre, topped by a pretty red lighthouse and surrounded by fifteen-metre-high cliffs. The cliffs are covered in tufts of grass, under which the penguins dig their burrows. In September or October each year, the birds migrate back here and find their mate. They start burrowing, and the female lays two eggs in the nest. When the chicks hatch, both parents nurture the young, one adult remaining with the chick, the other going fishing. In late January the ground is covered with drifts of white down, as the chicks shed their baby feathers and get ready for their first trips into the ocean. You can get surprisingly close to the birds as they half hide in the waving grass, but if they start to cock their heads from side to side you're disturbing them; try not to upset the chicks in particular. The birds are well protected by Conaf *guardaparques*, and their nests are fenced off, so you can't get too close to the chicks in any case. Isla Magdalena is reached by the *Melinka*, a passenger ferry operated by Turismo COMAPA. It departs at 4pm every Tuesday, Thursday and Saturday in season (Dec–Feb). The five-hour round-trip costs CH$20,000, half-price for children, and is worth it for the ride alone.

Puerto Natales

Just under 250km north of Punta Arenas, Chilean Patagonia's second city, **PUERTO NATALES**, enjoys a stunning location at the edge of the pampa, sitting by a body of water fringed by tall peaks. There's not much in the town itself except tour operators, restaurants and accommodation, but its usefulness as a base for visiting the **Parque Nacional Torres del Paine** and, across the border in Argentina, the **Parque Nacional Los Glaciares** (see p.184), means it's flush with tourist dollars and filled with nylon-clad, Gore-tex-booted hikers. "Natales" is also a good transport hub, home to the terminal of the **Navimag** ferry from Puerto Montt in the Lake District, and linked to Punta Arenas by a good, regular bus service. Daily buses head up to Torres del Paine, and there are also regular services to Argentina and frequent tourist boats to the glaciers.

Arrival and information

The Navimag ferry terminal is on the coastal road, or *costanera*, five blocks west of the Plaza de Armas (☎61/411421). There's no bus terminal, so each bus pulls in outside its company's offices, all a couple of blocks from the Plaza de Armas. The helpful **Sernatur** office is in a prime location on the coast road (April–Nov Mon–Fri 8.30am–8pm, Sat & Sun 9.30am–12.30pm; Dec–March Mon–Fri 8.30am–8pm, Sat & Sun 9am–7pm; ☎61/412125). The **Conaf** office, O'Higgins 584 (Mon–Fri 8.30am–6pm; ☎61/411438), is often woefully ill equipped, so for information about Torres del Paine, visit Path@gone, the travel agent that runs the park's refuges (see box on p.572).

Accommodation

Accommodation in Natales is not normally a problem, as many people let out rooms in their houses – you'll be offered half a dozen as you step off the bus. There's a good choice of more expensive hotels, too. Even so, it's wise to book ahead, especially for stays in January.

Casa Dickson Bories 307 ☎61/411871. A well-heated lodging house, with a large kitchen open to guests, and decent bathrooms. It offers a minibus service to the Parque Nacional Torres del Paine. ❹

Costaustralis Av Pedro Montt 262 ☎61/412000, ⓦwww.australis.com. The most luxurious hotel in town, right on the waterfront, with modern rooms and all mod cons. Off-season discounts available. ❾

Hospedaje Cecilia Tomás Rogers 54 ☎61/411797, ⓔredcecilia@entelchile.net. A warm, cosy *hospedaje* kept to a Swiss standard of hygiene, with good beds, a decent breakfast and tasty, home-baked bread. Also runs tours and acts as a travel agent. Bike rental is available. ❹

Hotel Martín Gusinde Bories 278 ☎61/229512. Extremely friendly, comfortable hotel, with luxurious bathrooms and smart (though busily decorated) rooms with TV. Also boasts one of the best restaurants in town (see below). Same owners as *Hostería Lago Grey* in Parque Nacional Torres del Paine (see below); joint bookings possible. ❼

Niko's Residencial Ramirez 669 ☎61/412810. A firm favourite with backpackers, this is a good place to meet other travellers and a handy alternative if *Patagonia Adventure* is full. ❸

Patagonia Adventure Tomás Rogers 179 ☎61/411028. A truly excellent hostel, right on the plaza, with comfortable beds, warm rooms (private and dorm) and friendly young owners who are into hiking. ❹

The Town

Puerto Natales is beautifully sited on **Seno Ultima Esperanza** ("Last Hope Sound"), a narrow turquoise channel that regularly gets whipped up with white horses. Grey mountains line the other side, coated with ice and snow, a contrast with the flat pampa to the east of the town. Natales is a centred on a few blocks surrounding its **Plaza de Armas**. While hardly packed with distractions, it's a pleasant spot to prepare for a trek or unwind after it. Its most interesting feature is the **church** on the plaza, a bit uninspiring from the outside, but with a very beautiful altarpiece inside, occupying one entire wall and showing local Indians, dignitaries, the Madonna and Child and, behind their shoulders, a delicate painting of the Torres del Paine. A couple of blocks west of the plaza there's a small but well-laid-out **Museo Histórico Municipal**, at Bulnes 285 (Mon–Fri 8.30am–1pm & 3–8pm, Sat & Sun 2.30–6pm; CH$500). One room is full of photos of Aonikenk and Kaweshkar Indians, the area's original inhabitants. Another holds a collection of memorabilia relating to the region's first settler, a rather fierce-looking German called Herman Eberhard – look out for his ingenious collapsible boat. In a shed out the back there's the usual collection of stuffed animals.

Eating, drinking and nightlife

Natales has a number of **restaurants** catering for the thousands of tourists passing through each year. The quality of food is for the most part better than in other similar-sized towns in Chile. Natales isn't blessed with bars and clubs – exhausted trekkers seem to collapse into bed rather than drink and dance.

Cristal Bulnes 433–440. Pleasantly decorated in yellow and green, this is a good fish restaurant that offers, remarkably for Chile, fish prepared in ways other than frying. The salmon in butter is particularly good, and not that expensive.

Evasion Ladrilleros 105. In a somewhat trendy ambience, *Evasion* serves sandwiches on wholemeal baps as big as dinner plates, vegetarian dishes and, in the evening, good pizzas – though all at higher-than-average prices.

El Living Prat 156. Smart wooden tables, soothing decor and well-chosen music create a perfect setting for a drink and a snack or a light meal. Cocktails, selected wines, yoghurt drinks, real tea, coffee, cake, moderately priced salads and vegetarian dishes, and even banana sandwiches are available.

El Marítimo Pedro Montt 214. The best place to come and refuel after a long trek, with truly enormous *lomo a la pobre* (steak with a fried egg on top) and a glorious view to stare at while you digest.

Martín Gusinde Bories 278. Chic restaurant serving conventional but well-prepared food, at a price, accompanied by a good selection of wines. Attentive service.

La Tranquera Bulnes 579. The walls are covered with junk-shop paraphernalia at this place, where standard, inexpensive Chilean fare is served by surly staff. It's one of the few places in town that's open on Sundays in the offseason.

Listings

Airlines DAP, Bulnes 100 ☎61/415100; LanChile, Rogers 78 ☎61/411236.

Car rental Andes Patagónicos, Blanco Encalada 266 ☎61/411594; EMSA at the *Hotel Martín Gusinde*, Bories 278 ☎61/410775.

Post office Eberhard 429.

Puerto Natales tour operators

Aventur Bulnes 698 ⓣ61/410825. A Punta Arenas company that's recently expanded into Puerto Natales and is now running one of the catamarans.

Baquedano Zamora Cerro Castillo ⓣ61/412911. Based in the village of Cerro Castillo, near the Torres del Paine park, these people can arrange horse trekking in Torres del Paine from a couple of hours (at around CH$30,000 an hour) to longer hikes of up to four days.

Big Foot Bories 206 ⓣ61/414611, ⓦwww.bigfootpatagonia.com. This tour operator specializes in climbing. A day's ice climbing costs CH$40,000; a day's mountaineering from CH$95,000. It also offers three days' kayaking down the Río Serrano for CH$500,000, and a five-hour ice-hike on Glaciar Grey (see p.577) for CH$40,000.

Chile Nativo ⓣ61/414367, ⓦwww.chilenativo.com. Dynamic young outfit specializing in five- to twelve-day horse trekking tours of the region, visiting out-of-the-way locations.

Path@gone Eberhard 595 ⓣ61/41 3291, ⓔpathgone@entelchile.com. The shared office of three of the biggest companies in Puerto Natales. **Andescape** and **Fantastico Sur** run the *refugios* in the Torres del Paine park and are the first stop if you want to book a bed there. The third company, **Onas Patagonia** (ⓦwww.onaspatagonia.com), specializes in water-based activities, especially trips up the Serrano River in a Zodiac inflatable boat (CH$60,000) and a two-day sea kayaking excursion (CH$150,000).

Servitur Arturo Prat 353 ⓣ61/411858. An established local company, which specializes in tours to Torres del Paine.

Parque Nacional Torres del Paine

Fifty-six kilometres after Cerro Castillo, rising above the flat brown pampa, is a small range of mountains topped by weird twisted peaks and unfeasibly smooth towers. This is the **Paine Massif**, centrepiece of the **PARQUE NACIONAL TORRES DEL PAINE** (daily 8.30am–8pm; CH$6500 for foreigners, CH$2500 for Chileans) and one of the world's stunning geographical features. Wandering around the giants' castles and demons' lairs of this mountain is one of the highlights of any trip to Chile. on the eastern side are the soaring, unnaturally elegant **Torres del Paine** ("Paine Towers"), the icon of the park, and, further west, the dark-capped, sculpted **Cuernos del Paine** ("Paine Horns"), which rise above the moonscape of the **Valle del Francés** ("French Valley"). To the east of the park is the broad ice river of **Glaciar Grey**, and on the plains at the mountains' feet large herds of **guanacos** and the odd *ñandú* still run wild.

Arrival and information

The only entrance to the park for those coming by bus is 117km from Natales at **Laguna Amarga**. The Conaf station (*guardería*) here isn't much more than a hut with a map on the wall where you pay your entrance fee and give your name, but a regular bus (CH$1500) connects it with the *Hostería Las Torres*, 7km to the west, the starting point of the two most important trails. The buses from Natales continue along to the south of the massif and arrive at the **Lago Pehoé** *guardería* after another 19km, near the impressive cataract of Salto Grande (Large Waterfall). After 18km the bus reaches the **park administration** building, around which there's a visitor centre, a refuge, a grocery store, a *hostería* and even a post office. On the map, it looks as if you can continue on along this road and eventually return to Puerto Natales, but you can't because the road's not open to the public. You can also enter the park on the **inflatable boats** that travel up the Río Serrano (see Onas Patagonia, under Path@gone, in box opposite). These arrive opposite *Hostería Cabañas del Paine*, where they're met by a minibus that takes passengers 9km north to the park administration building, where you catch a bus.

The best place for general **information** is the park administration building, although all the *guarderías* can provide information about the state of the trails. Most also have a large map of the park to help you get your bearings, but it's a good idea to carry one of your own: *Torres del Paine*, number 13 in the JLM/Entel series, covers the area in detail and is widely available in Puerto Natales.

In January and February the park is crammed with holidaymakers, so the **best months to visit** are November and December or March and April. Although from June to September temperatures can fall to −10° Celsius, or even lower, freezing lakes and icing over trails, and there's the possibility of snow (though it's surprisingly rare), the small numbers of visitors, lack of wind and often clear visibility can also make this another good time to come – just wrap up warmly.

Accommodation

There are several different types of accommodation in the park: unserviced (free) campsites, serviced campsites, *refugios* and *hosterías*. Wild camping isn't permitted. The park's *hosterías* are expensive in comparison with those in Puerto Natales or Punta Arenas – the rooms are mostly decent enough but unimaginative, and the same goes for the food in the restaurants.

Hostería Lago Grey ⓣ61/140220, ⓦwww.chileaustral.com/grey. This *hostería* has a beautiful view of Glaciar Grey, across a lake dotted with floating icebergs. They also run boat trips (CH$140,000 per person) and dinghy runs (CH$70,000) on Lago Grey as well as dinghy runs down the *ríos* Pingo and Grey (CH$40,000 per person). The guides are excellent. 9

Hostería Las Torres ⓣ61/411572, ⓦwww.lastorres.com. Spread out across a couple of fields, *Las Torres* has the feel of an *estancia*, with good views up to the Torres del Paine. It sometimes arranges sheep-shearing exhibitions followed by barbecues, so you can shave your meal before you eat it. 9

Hostería Mirador del Payne ⓣ61/226930, ⓦwww.chileaustral.com/vientosur. This colonial-style house features a veranda and eight *cabañas* near Laguna Verde, in a quiet corner of the park. 9

Hostería Pehoé ⓣ61/411390; ⓔgerencia@pehoe.com. Beautifully sited on a small island in Lago Pehoé looking out to the highest peaks of the Paine Massif. There's a warm bar and restaurant. 9

Posada Río Serrano ⓣ61/410684. The cheapest *hostería* in the park, in an attractive old structure near the park administration building, on the site of the first *estancia*. There are no en-suite rooms.

Refugios and campsites

The **refugios** in the park are open from September to May and are generally closed by the weather during the rest of the year. Most are run by two companies, Fantástico Sur (ⓣ61/226054, ⓦwww.lastorres.com) and Andescape (ⓣ61/412592, ⓔandescape@terra.cl), who share an office in Puerto Natales, at Eberhard 595 (ⓣ61/413290 or 413291, ⓔpathgone@chileaustral.com; see box opposite). Buildings range from a bare hut with nothing but a wood-fired stove (usually free) to modern chalets with a restaurant, which charge around CH$10,000 per person for a bed and CH$7000 for a cooked meal. None comes with bedding, although you can rent a sleeping bag at the flashier places. Most of the year you can just turn up and get a bunk, but in January and February everywhere gets very busy, so you'll need to book in advance.

The unserviced **campsites** are free and are just a flat patch of land and a *fogón*. Serviced campsites cost money (around CH$2500 per person, unless otherwise stated below), but they provide firewood and have ablution blocks and sometimes even a small shop.

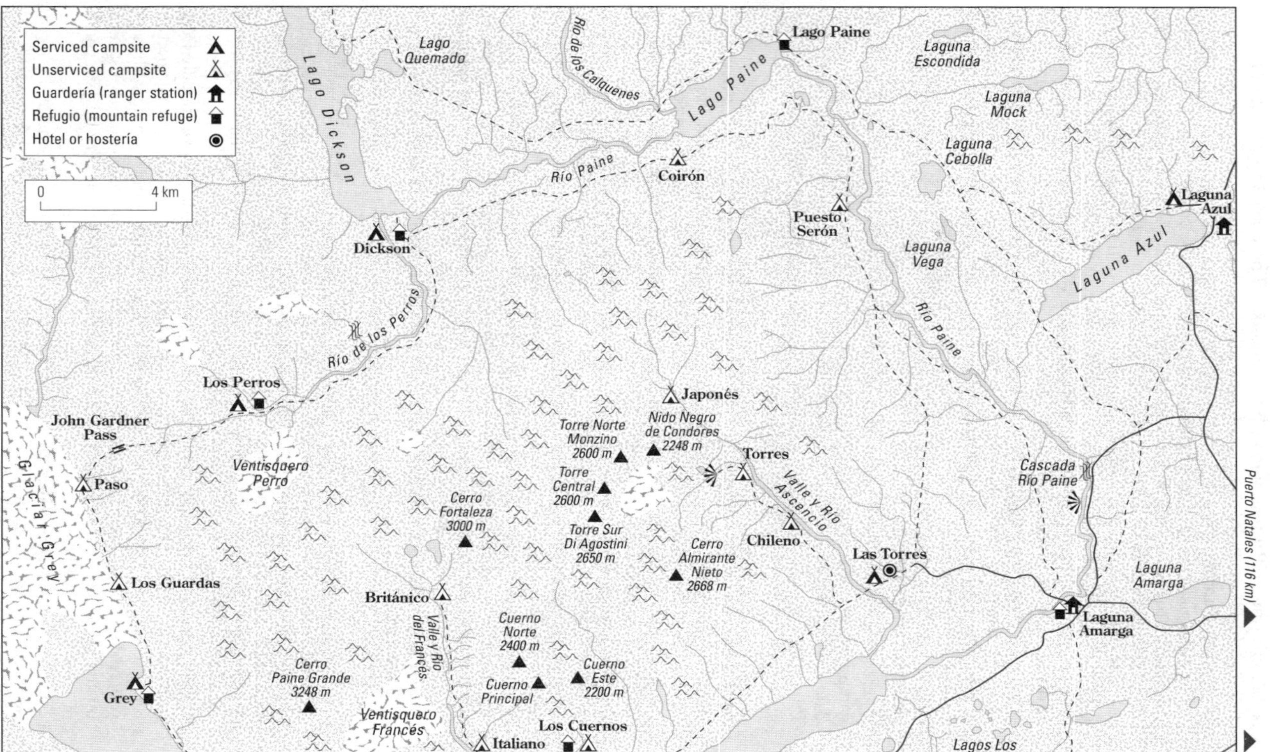
Serviced campsite
Unserviced campsite
Guardería (ranger station)
Refugio (mountain refuge)
Hotel or hostería
0
4 km
Lago Dickson
Lago Quemado
Río de los Calquenes
Lago Paine
Lago Paine
Laguna Escondida
Laguna Mock
Laguna Cebolla
Laguna Azul
Laguna Azul
Río Paine
Coirón
Puesto Serón
Laguna Vega
Río Paine
Dickson
Río de los Perros
Los Perros
Japonés
John Gardner Pass
Nido Negro de Condores 2248 m
Torre Norte Monzino 2600 m
Torres
Valle y Río Ascencio
Cascada Río Paine
Ventisquero Perro
Paso
Glaciar Grey
Torre Central 2600 m
Cerro Fortaleza 3000 m
Torre Sur Di Agostini 2650 m
Chileno
Cerro Almirante Nieto 2668 m
Las Torres
Los Guardas
Británico
Valle y Río del Francés
Laguna Amarga
Laguna Amarga
Puerto Natales (116 km)
Cuerno Norte 2400 m
Cuerno Este 2200 m
Cuerno Principal
Cerro Paine Grande 3248 m
Grey
Ventisquero Francés
Los Cuernos
Italiano
Lagos Los

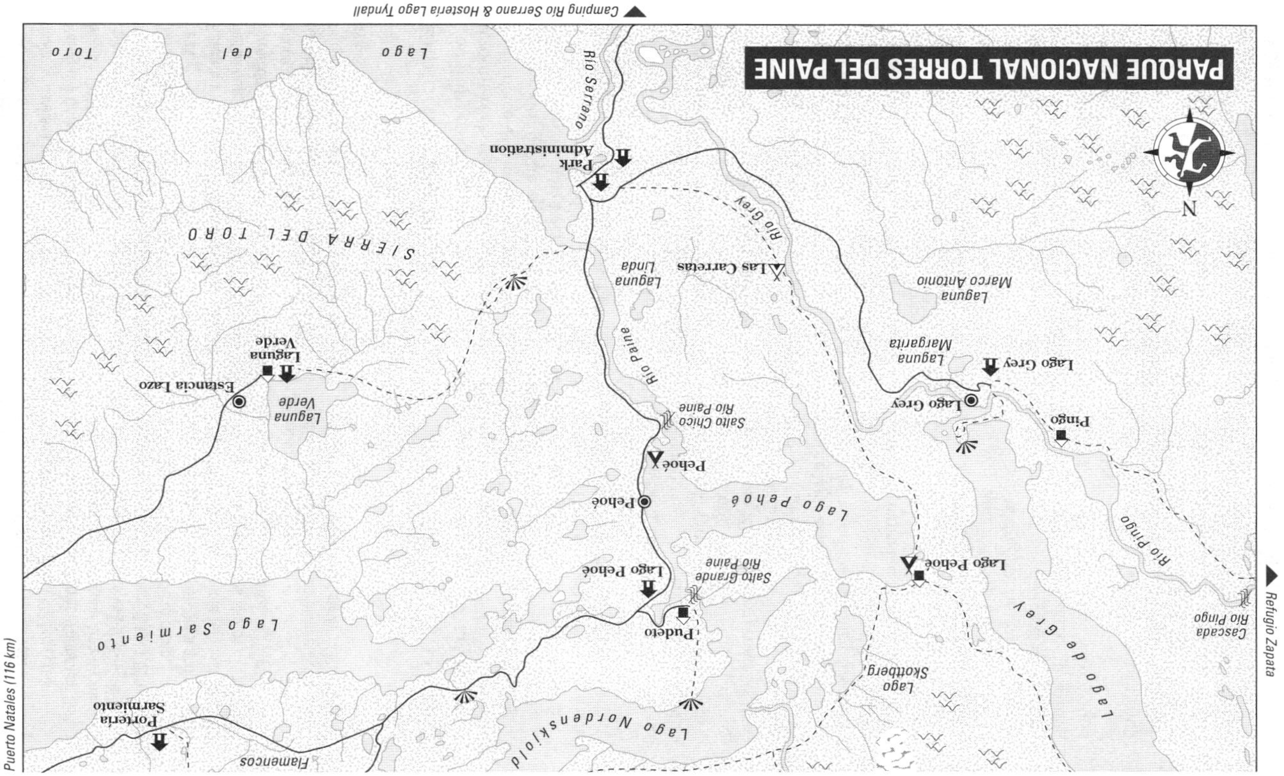

PARQUE NACIONAL TORRES DEL PAINE

Puerto Natales (116 km)
Refugio Zapata
Camping Río Serrano & Hostería Lago Tyndall

Flamencos
Portería Sarmiento
Lago Nordenskjold
Lago Sarmiento
Lago de Grey
Lago Skottberg
Cascada Río Pingo
Río Pingo
Pudeto
Salto Grande Río Paine
Lago Pehoé
Lago Pehoé
Lago Pehoé
Pehoé
Pehoé
Salto Chico Río Paine
Río Paine
Pingo
Lago Grey
Lago Grey
Laguna Margarita
Laguna Marco Antonio
Las Carretas
Laguna Linda
Río Grey
Laguna Verde
Laguna Verde
Estancia Lazo
SIERRA DEL TORO
Park Administration
Río Serrano
Lago del Toro
N

Campamento Los Perros (Andescape). Last campsite before the John Garner pass – there used to be a *refugio* here, too but it was burnt down by careless trekkers.
Refugio y Campamento Pehoé (Andescape). The *refugio* (CH$9000 per person) is many people's favourite, for its scenic location and delicious food. Camping is allowed in the adjoining grassy fields (CH$12,000 per site), and there's a small shop nearby.
Refugio y Camping Chileno (Fantástico Sur). It's halfway up the Valle Ascencio, at the foot of the Torres del Paine. CH$11,000 per person at the refuge, CH$3000 at the campsite.
Refugio y Camping Grey (Andescape). A popular *refugio* (CH$9000 per person) thanks to its position by Glaciar Grey.
Refugio y Camping Los Cuernos (Fantástico Sur). An isolated modern hut (CH$11,000 per person) in a forest beneath the Cuernos del Paine, with a restaurant and campsite (CH$3000 per person).
Refugio y Camping Los Torres (Fantástico Sur). Near the park entrance at Laguna Amarga and the *Hostería Las Torres*, this place is a first-night stop for those who are taking it easy. CH$11,000 per person in the refuge, CH$3000 to camp.
Refugio Dickson (Andescape). Quiet and peaceful, this is the most remote refuge (CH$9000 per person) in the park, on the shores of Lago Dickson. Camping also possible.
Refugio Lago del Toro (no phone). The Conaf-run *refugio* near the park administration building (ask there), just a hut with a wood stove. CH$5000 per bed.

Exploring the park

You'll have seen photographs of the park long before you visit, as the pristine-smooth rock towers that are the actual **Torres del Paine** feature on just about every piece of tourist literature produced in Chile, and beautify calendars the length and breadth of the country. And yet nothing really prepares you for your first sight of it all. As you travel across the barren featureless expanses of Patagonia, your eye gets accustomed to dreary flatness, then suddenly the **Paine Massif** rises up from the grasslands like a mirage. The finest views are from the south bank of Lago Nordenskjöld, whose waters act as a great reflecting mirror.

There are several extremely popular **hikes**, of which the "**W**" is the current favourite. The route you follow looks like a "W", up three valleys and along the bottom of the southern face of the massif. On average it takes four to five days to complete all three valleys. Anyone set on seeing more, or getting away from the madding crowds, especially in the January high season, can explore lesser-known trails such as the walk to Laguna Azul and on to Lago Paine, or the climb to Mirador Zapata.

From the *Hostería Las Torres*, you start the "W" by heading west along the foot of the massif. Just after a bridge you head uphill, up the Valle Ascencio, and it's possible to spend the first night in the *Refugio y Camping Chileno*, and leave your pack there if you want. It's a hard climb, but rest assured that the very worst bit is at the beginning and just about anyone can manage it if they pace themselves. If you find yourself at *Chileno* with time to burn, press on through *lenga* brush, fording a stream, to the *Campamento Torres*, a free, unserviced campsite by another stream, ninety minutes up the valley from *Chileno* at the foot of the track up to the **Torres** themselves. From *Campamento Torres* most people turn west and head up the small valley to the foot of the peaks, much of the route involving a thigh-aching clamber up uneven boulders. After thirty to forty minutes you arrive: if the clouds clear you are treated to a stunning postcard view across Laguna Torres, a grey tarn, up to the three strange statuesque towers that give the massif and park their name. Give yourself some time, after the stiff climb, to take in the sheer majesty of them.

An alternative trek from *Campamento Torres* is to press on north for an hour or so, guided by cairns, to the *Campamento Japonés*, another free and unserviced site. Along the way the path crosses a couple of icy brooks and some massive rock falls, so have your wits about you. At *Japonés* you'll find a hidden valley, aptly called the **Valle del Silencio**, that also heads west. It's much less visited than the Torres and a great place to escape the crowds.

For the middle arm of the "W", the **Valle del Francés**, head downhill again towards the *Hostería Las Torres*, but, after you reach the bridge where you turned up the Valle Ascencio, turn right (west) and continue along the foot of the massif. After three hours of trekking along the northwest banks of deep-blue Lago Nordenskjöld, you'll reach the *Refugio y Camping Los Cuernos*, an excellent place to stay the night (see above). Alternatively you can press on another two hours to the free *Campamento Italiano* (unserviced except for toilets), which has two sections, one higher up the valley. From the *Italiano*, head due north up the Valle del Francés. It takes three hours of hiking, some of it rather steep, but with great views of **Glaciar Francés** along the way, to reach another campsite, *Campamento Británico* (free, with drinking water but no toilets). Allow another hour or two to trudge up granite scree and reach a viewpoint at the head of the valley, taking time if possible on the way to admire Paine Grande, the massif's highest peak at 3050m, to your west. You should also be able to see the characteristically fin-shaped Aleta del Tiburón (1850m) to the north, and the twisted Cuernos to the southeast, plus the castle-like Fortaleza ("Fortress"), peaking at 2800m, ahead of you. In truly clear weather you should spy the backside of the Torres. Now turn around and head south again.

Back down at *Campamento Italiano*, carry on to the west, and after two hours you'll reach *Refugio Pehoé* and *Campamento Pehoé*, where you should spend the night. From the refuge–campsite head northwest through *ñire* glens, up the northern side of **Lago Grey**, the third arm of the "W", to *Refugio Grey* and *Camping Grey*, snug by Glaciar Grey, a three-hour walk away. About a third of the way up the aptly named **Quebrada de los Vientos** ("Windy Gorge") is a marked viewpoint over Lago Grey, just after the much smaller **Laguna Roca**, home to duck colonies. The route up to the *refugio* and campsite, past waterfalls and striped cliffs, is not one steady climb, but a roller-coaster of valleys, streams and *lenga* copses. Once you're at the top, don't miss the nearby *mirador,* affording great views of the glacier.

From *Grey*, you should go back the way you came, to *Pehoé*. Here, apart from walking back to *Hostería Las Torres*, there are two options. One is to pick up a **boat** across Lago Pehoé (three times daily; CH$6000, tickets sold at the shop in the campsite) to *Refugio Pudeto*, half a kilometre from the main road, from where you can catch a bus to Puerto Natales (they wait for the boat crossing). The boat normally makes three half-hour trips a day across the lake, but if there's a wind it can't sail. The alternative way out is the four- to five-hour hike to the park administration building along the long, flat pampa to the south of Lago Pehoé. From the park administration there are regular buses to Puerto Natales, the last leaving at 6.30pm.

Tierra del Fuego

The main town in the Chilean half of **TIERRA DEL FUEGO** (for the Argentine part and an introduction to the whole archipelago, see p.189) is Porvenir, a nondescript settlement huddled on the Magellan Strait across from Punta Arenas. However, to the south of Isla Grande, across the Beagle Channel, is **Isla Navarino**; here quirky little **Puerto Williams** is the southernmost permanently inhabited city in the world.

Puerto Williams

Nestled in a small bay on the north shore of Isla Navarino, 82km due east and ever so slightly south of Ushuaia along the Beagle Channel, is **PUERTO WILLIAMS**. Founded as a military outpost and officially the capital of Chilean Antarctica, the town looks tranquil and idyllic on a fine day, colourful roofs surrounded by the jagged peaks of **Los Dientes**. Williams is a tiny place, with a centre not much bigger than a single square kilometre. The only thing to visit as such is the **Museo Martín Gusinde**, Comandante Aragay 1 (Mon–Fri 10am–1pm & 3–6pm, Sat & Sun 3–6pm; CH$1500), at the far western end of town, where well-laid-out photographs and maps chart the history and exploration of the region, from the days of the Fuegian Indians to the commercial shipping of today. There's also an informative display of the island's flora and fauna illustrated by the usual array of stuffed creatures and dried vegetation. The true purpose of any visit to Williams is, however, to fulfil a desire to come this far south and this far away from "civilization".

Practicalities

On **arrival** at the tiny airport, you'll be met by at least one private car acting as a makeshift taxi that will take you into town. The trip is further than it looks, as the peninsula on which the airfield is built is separated from Puerto Williams by a long, narrow channel. You stop in at the **Oficina de Turismo**, not far from the museum at Ibáñez (Dec–March Mon–Fri 10am–1pm & 3–6pm; ⓣ61/621011), for copies of maps, but not much else is available there. Banco de Chile, Yelcho s/n, gives cash advances on credit cards and changes money. You can also change money in the **bank** on the main plaza or "Centro Comercial", where there is also a **post office**. A CTC **telephone centre** is on the main plaza as well.

Accommodation, mostly basic but decent, is clustered around the centre. Try *Pensión Flor Cañuñán*, Lewaia 107 (ⓣ61/621163; ❷), which has rooms in a rather basic but warm hut, with the bathroom in the main house, or the excellent *Refugio Coirón*, Maragaño 168 (ⓣ61/621150; ❺), which has shared rooms with bunks, a kitchen open to guests and space for camping. The *Camblor*, Subtenente Patricio Capdeville 4 (ⓣ61/621033; ❺), offers private bathrooms and boasts a fine restaurant. The best value are two welcoming places with shared bathroom on Piloto Pardo: *Pensión Temuco*, at no. 224 (ⓣ61/621113; ❹), where a little extra gets you a private bathroom and use of the kitchen, and highly promising newcomer *Hostal Pusaki*, next door at no. 222 (ⓣ61/621116; ❹), where use of the kitchen is free, within reason, and delicious meals are laid on for overnight guests.

Another place to eat is *Los Dientes del Navarino*, a small, friendly **restaurant** in the centre, where you'll probably have to go into the kitchen and point out what you want to eat. At the excellent *Supermercado Simón y Simón* you can buy delicious bread, *empanadas* and amazingly good wine, along with everything else you might need for a picnic. There is no **nightlife** as such here: the only place to while away your evening is the *Club de Yates Micalvi*, an ex-Navy supply ship with a well-stocked bar where you can chat and drink until the early hours.

The main **tour agency** is SIM (Sea and Ice and Mountains Adventures) on the main plaza (ⓣ61/621150, ⓦwww.simltd.com) – it also runs the *Refugio Coirón*. Ask staff for details of treks around the island and boat trips down to Cape Horn. DAP has its offices in the Centro Comercial (ⓣ61/621114 or 621051).

Around Puerto Williams

The seventy-kilometre **Los Dientes Circuit** leaves from the statue of the Virgin Mary, about one kilometre **west** of town on the road to the airport. There you'll find a turning uphill, which leads to a waterfall and a dammed stream, to the left of which is a marked trail. Allow at least four and as many as seven days to complete the circuit, taking plentiful supplies and decent outdoor gear and anticipating bad weather, even snow in summer; inform people in town before leaving too, in case you need to be rescued. An easy stroll 2km to the **east** of Puerto Williams is the straggly hamlet of **Ukika**, a small collection of houses where a dozen or so people of Yámana descent live. You can buy reed baskets and replica canoes, but do not take photographs unless invited to do so. Beyond, the road continues, giving beautiful views across the Beagle Channel before ducking into the forest and heading inland. It emerges once again at **Puerto Toro**, the end of the last road in South America, looking out at **Picton Island** and beyond, into the endless seas of the Atlantic Ocean.

4.10

Chile's Pacific Islands

Chile is the proud possessor of two remote island territories, **Easter Island** and the **Juan Fernández Archipelago**, known collectively as the **Islas Esporádicas** (or "Far Flung Isles") as they are so far from the mainland, way, way out in the Pacific Ocean. Both are classified as national parks and have been singled out by UNESCO for special protection. While it is unlikely visitors to South America on a multi-country tour will make it out this far, those that do will be amply rewarded by the spectacular beauty of these isolated spots.

The Juan Fernández Archipelago

The **JUAN FERNÁNDEZ ARCHIPELAGO** is formed by the peaks of a submerged volcanic mountain range rising from the sea bed. It's made up of two principal islands, a third, much smaller, island and numerous rocky islets. The archipelago is named for João Fernandes, the Portuguese sailor who discovered it on November 22, 1574, while straying out to sea to avoid coastal winds and currents in an attempt to shorten the journey between Lima and Valparaíso.

Isla Robinson Crusoe is the archipelago's only inhabited island, and most of the five hundred or so islanders live in the little village of **San Juan Bautista**, on the sheltered Bahía Cumberland. The island's two principal attractions are the sites associated with the famous castaway **Alexander Selkirk** – from the replica of his cave dwelling to his real-life lookout point – and the abundant **plant life** that covers the soaring peaks in a dense layer of vegetation. Only a few hundred tourists make it out here each year, most of them arriving between October and March, when the climate is warm and dry, and the sea water is perfect for bathing.

There's not a lot to do in **San Juan Bautista**, the island's only village, and for most people it's just a base from which to explore the island's interior and the coast. The **Fuerte Santa Barbara** is a small stone fort, perched on a hillside just north of the plaza. Heavily restored in 1974, it was originally built by the Spanish in 1749 in an attempt to prevent enemy buccaneers from using the island as a watering point. Down on the shore, follow the path to the north end of the bay and you'll reach the cliffs of the **Punta San Carlos**, embedded with unexploded shells fired by British warships at the German *Dresden* during World War I. The Germans surrendered, but sank their ship rather than let it go to the British, and the wreck still lies 70m under the sea in Bahía Cumberland.

Striking out from San Juan Bautista, the first place to head for is the **Mirador Alejandro Selkirk**, the famous lookout point where Selkirk lit his daily smoke signals and scoured the horizon for ships. It's a three-kilometre uphill hike from the village, taking about ninety minutes; the path starts north of the plaza, extending from Subida El Castillo, snaking through lush native forest, dense with overhanging ferns. At the top you'll be rewarded with stunning panoramic views of almost all of the island. Just south of the airstrip, **Playa Arenal** is the island's only sandy beach. It's a glorious place to spend a couple of days, with its warm, transparent waters. Two hours and thirty minutes by boat through islets and seal colonies, it can also be reached on foot near the end of the trail to the airstrip from the *mirador*.

Island practicalities

Getting to Isla Robinson Crusoe is an adventure in itself, involving a **flight** on a small plane – four to eighteen seats – that judders and wobbles for most of the two to two and a half hours it takes to get there. Two companies fly out to the island, both imposing a strict ten-kilo luggage allowance. Transportes Aéreos Isla Robinson Crusoe (or TAIRC), Av Pajaritos 3030, Oficina 604, Maipú, Santiago (Ⓣ2/534-4650, Ⓦwww.tairc.cl), flies daily from December to February, and three or four times a week in October and November and from early March until Easter, departing from Aerodromo Los Cerrillos, 8km southwest of Santiago (Ⓣ2/533-1424). The island's little airstrip is 13km from the village of San Juan Bautista; most passengers opt for the fifty- to ninety-minute ride by **motor launch** (usually included in the price of your flight); taking motion sickness tablets is a sensible precaution.

The Municipalidad (Mon–Fri 9am–1pm & 3–6pm; Ⓣ32/701045 or 751067), off the southwest corner of San Juan Bautista's main plaza, hands out tourist **information**, including maps and leaflets. **Accommodation**, on the whole, is simple and overpriced. On the west side of the plaza, *Residencial Villa Green* (Ⓣ32/751039; ❻) offers clean, comfortable doubles with private bath. *Aldea Daniel Defoe*, Larraín Alcalde 449 (Ⓣ32/751075; ❻), has a few weather-beaten but spacious and well-equipped *cabañas* overlooking the ocean. Further south along the shoreline, *Hostal Charpentier*, at Ignacio Carrera Pinto 256 (Ⓣ32/751020; ❻), has a few decent rooms with lovely views. Most visitors **eat** at their hotel, but if you're camping, or fancy a change, try *La Bahía* on Larraín Alcalde for first-rate lobster and fish (it's a good idea to get your orders in a few hours before you plan to eat). There's a **post office** just off the plaza, next to the Municipalidad (don't go home without getting a couple of Isla Robinson Crusoe stamps), with a direct-dial public **telephone**. Be sure to take plenty of cash with you as there are no **banks** or *cambios* on the island, and cheques and credit cards are not usually accepted.

Easter Island

One of the loneliest places on earth, tiny **EASTER ISLAND**, or **Rapa Nui** as it is known by its people, is home to some 2700 islanders, of whom around seventy percent are native *pascuenses*, with the rest being mainly *continentales* (Chilean immigrants). The *pascuenses* speak their own Polynesian-based language, Rapanui, although Spanish is the official language. Virtually the entire population is confined to the island's single settlement, **Hanga Roa**, and just about all the islanders make their living from tourism.

Post-contact history

Easter Island clearly enjoyed a long, rich history before it was "discovered" and named by the Dutch naval commander **Jacob Roggeveen** on Easter Sunday, 1722, but it was another 48 years before Easter Island was revisited, this time by the Spanish commander **Felipe González**, who mapped the island and claimed it for

Getting to Easter Island

The only way to reach Easter Island is with LanChile, which flies here from Santiago's international airport three times a week. The **airport** is about 1km from the southern edge of Hanga Roa. **Fares** are much cheaper if you buy your ticket in conjunction with a long-haul LanChile flight to Chile. There's no ideal time to visit the island; the **weather** is fairly constant year-round. February is the busiest month, but is also the most exciting, when the islanders put on an extravagant display of singing, dancing and feasting in their annual festival, "Tapati Rapa Nui".

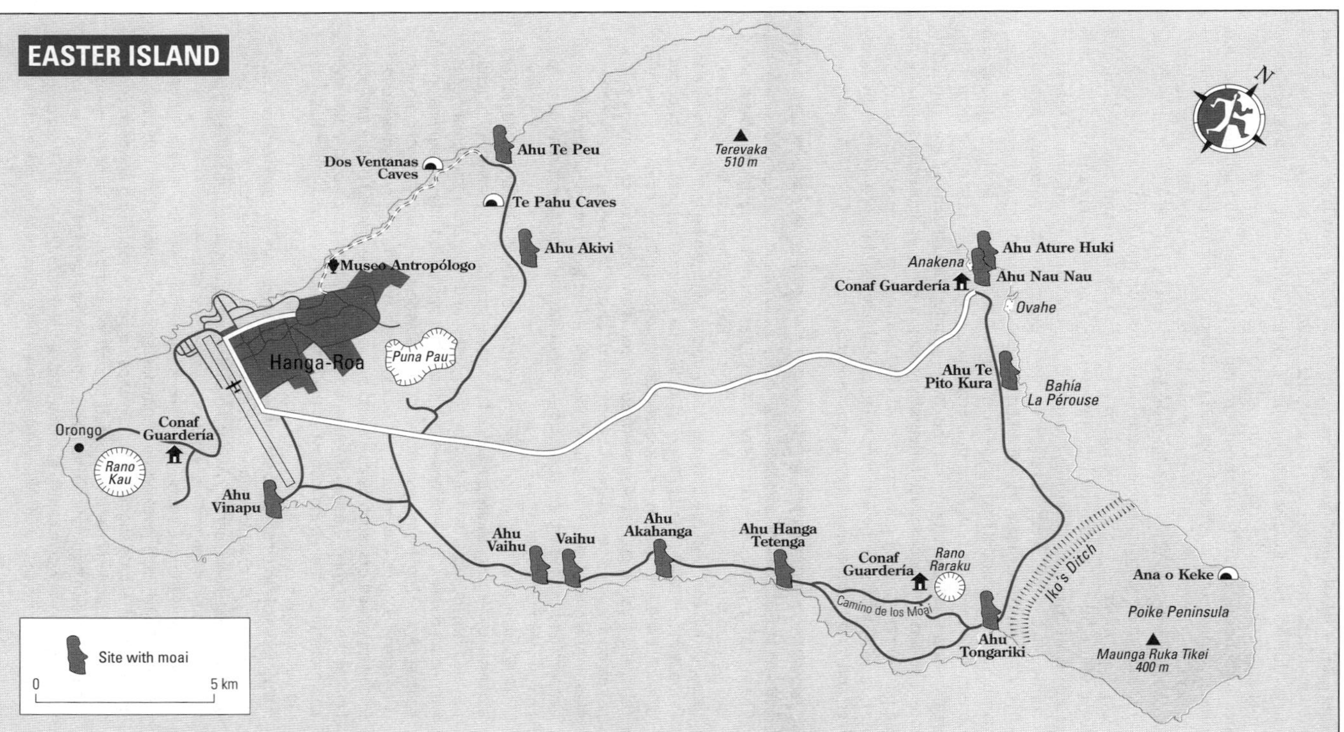
EASTER ISLAND
N
Ahu Te Peu
Dos Ventanas Caves
Te Pahu Caves
Terevaka 510 m
Ahu Akivi
Museo Antropólogo
Ahu Ature Huki
Anakena
Ahu Nau Nau
Conaf Guardería
Ovahe
Hanga-Roa
Puna Pau
Ahu Te Pito Kura
Bahía La Pérouse
Orongo
Conaf Guardería
Rano Kau
Ahu Vinapu
Ahu Vaihu
Vaihu
Ahu Akahanga
Ahu Hanga Tetenga
Conaf Guardería
Rano Raraku
Camino de los Moai
Iko's Ditch
Ana o Keke
Poike Peninsula
Ahu Tongariki
Maunga Ruka Tikei 400 m
Site with moai
0
5 km

King Carlos III of Spain during his six-day stay. Four years later, **Captain Cook** anchored here in the hope of restoring the health of his crew, who had developed scurvy during their long search for the "southern continent". As there were few provisions to be found, Cook stayed only four days, but observed with incredulity the "stupendous figures", or **moai**, erected on the island, though he noted that some lay strewn on the ground, toppled from their platforms. Later visitors reported an increasing number of fallen statues and, by 1825, all the ones on Hanga Roa bay had been destroyed. When the English doctor Linton Palmer visited in 1868, he confirmed there wasn't a single statue left standing on the island.

On September 9, 1888, the Chilean navy officially **annexed** Easter Island, and declared it Chilean territory. Chile, however, took no real interest in the place, and leased it off to a wool-trading company, which virtually governed the island according to its own needs and interests, an arrangement that continued until 1953 when the company's lease was revoked and the navy stepped in to resume command. Still the islanders were given no say in the running of their affairs, and seemed to be regarded more as property than as citizens – it was not until 1966, eighty years after annexation, that they were granted full citizenship and entitled to vote. The last few decades have thankfully seen a more enlightened approach on the part of the Chilean government, which has finally transferred the management of most local affairs to the islanders. Many inhabitants still feel badly done by, however, and land rights remain a contentious issue.

The moai of Easter Island

The enduring symbol of Easter Island always has been, and doubtless always will be, the monolithic **statues** that line its shores. The *moai* astonish for a good many reasons, not least because they are utterly unique, and can be found nowhere else in the world. How did this stone-age people, with no cross-cultural contact or outside influence, create such a specialized and advanced carving industry? There are some 400 finished statues scattered around the island, and almost as many in the statue quarry, in varying stages of completion. Clearly the people of Easter Island were in the grip of an extraordinary obsession – that led them, it would seem, to accomplish towering artistic achievements, but also, ultimately, to wreak devastation on their own society.

The Easter Island *moai* range in height from 2m to almost 10m, and while no two statues are identical, all are carved in the same highly stylized manner, with gently rounded bellies, arms held tightly by their sides, and long and rectangular heads, with pointed chins, angular noses and thin, tight lips curled into an expression of disdain. According to the assertions of the islanders, which are consistent with widespread Polynesian tradition, it would seem that these figures represented important **ancestors**, such as chiefs and priests, and were erected on the ancestral land of the kin-group these individuals belonged to, which they would watch over and protect with their *mana* (almost all the *moai* are looking inland, rather than gazing out to sea).

It's impossible to establish exactly when the first were carved, as radiocarbon dating works only on organic material, but archeologists have proposed tentative dates of around the seventh century AD for the early statues, and around the fifteenth century for the bulk of the statues, when production was at its peak.

Quite clearly, the mass production, the transportation and the erection of these monoliths must have involved an enormous amount of work. Oral traditions and archeological records suggest that there was no central controlling power on Easter Island, and that its society was based around independent clans, or **kin-groups**, each with its own high-ranking members. Presumably, then, the statue-carvers were not forced to work by a central authority, but worked voluntarily for their kin group – indeed, it seems they were highly revered members of a privileged class who were

Island highlights

Nestled in the southwest corner of the island, the village of **Hanga Roa** is somewhat low on attractions but high on accommodation and other services; unless you're camping, it is almost certainly where you'll be based. However, the **loop** from Hanga Roa to Anakena lends itself to a convenient sightseeing route that takes in some of the island's most impressive sights.

From Hanga Roa, follow Avenida Hotu Matu'a down to the southern coast road then turn right, just after the oil containers, and you'll reach **Vinapu**, the site of two large *ahus*. Anyone who's seen Peru's Macchu Pichu or other Inca ruins won't fail to be startled by the masonry ofVinapu's main *ahu*.

Back on the coast road, heading northeast towards Poike, you'll pass site after site of toppled *moai*, all knocked from their *ahu* and lying prostrate on the ground. The first site you pass is **Vaihu**, where eight tall statues lie facedown on the ground, their red stone topknots strewn along the coast. Three kilometres further along, **Ahu Akahanga** presents an equally mournful picture of a row of fallen *moai*; according to some oral traditions, it's also the burial place of Hotu Matu'a, the island's first settler and king. Further up the coast, **Ahu Hanga Tetenga** is the site of the largest moai – 9.94m – ever transported to a platform. It's not clear if the statue was successfully erected, as its eye sockets were never carved (usually the finishing touch). In any event, it now lies shattered at the foot

exempt from food production, and were supported by farmers and fishermen on the island. Such a system must have involved a great deal of economic cooperation, which appears to have been successfully maintained for hundreds of years. Then, in the later stages of the island's prehistory, something went wrong and the system collapsed. Groups that had worked peacefully, if competitively, alongside each other at Rano Raraku withdrew from the quarry and exchanged their tools for weapons, as the island became engulfed by internal strife and warfare. The island's archeological record reveals a sudden, dramatic proliferation of obsidian weapons during the eighteenth century, as well as the remains of violently beaten skulls, and evidence of the widespread use of caves as refuges. The Spanish expedition, under González, reported no toppled statues in 1770 after a fairly thorough exploration of the island, but just four years later, Captain Cook saw many overturned figures lying next to their platforms. Almost a century later, in 1868, a visiting English doctor found that not a single statue remained standing on the island.

It seems likely that the seeds of **social collapse** lay, paradoxically, in the statue cult – or rather the extremes it was taken to by the islanders. The impulse to produce *moai* apparently required more and more hands, destroying the delicate balance between food distribution and statue carving. This situation was profoundly aggravated by the growing scarcity of food brought about possibly by overpopulation, and certainly by deforestation, following centuries of logging for boat-building, fuel consumption and statue-transportation. By the time the Europeans arrived in the eighteenth century, there was scarcely a tree left on the island, and the large palm, shown by pollen samples to have been once abundant, had become extinct. This must have had a catastrophic effect on the islanders' ability to feed themselves: deep-sea fishing became increasingly difficult, and eventually impossible, owing to the lack of wood available for new canoes, and even land cultivation was affected, as the deforestation caused soil erosion. In this climate of encroaching deprivation, it begins to be clear why the system broke down, and why the farmers and fishermen were no longer willing or able to pool their spoils – and why the Easter Island civilization descended into anarchy, dragging its majestic monuments with it.

of its *ahu*, leaving no clues as to whether it fell during erection or was toppled at a later date.

Just beyond Ahu Hanga Tetenga, the road forks. The left-hand branch, known as the **Camino de los Moai**, leads to the quarry of Rano Raraku. The right-hand branch continues up the coast to the magnificent Ahu Tongariki. North of Tongariki, **Rano Raraku** rises from the land in a hulking mass of volcanic stone. This is where almost all of the island's statues were produced, carved directly from the "tuff" (compacted volcanic ash) of the crater's outer slopes. The first surprise, on approaching the crater from the car park, is the dozens of **giant heads** sprouting from the ground. They are, in fact, finished *moai* brought down from the quarry, and were probably placed in shallow pits (which gradually built up) until they could be transported to their *ahu*. Clearly these were the last of the *moai* to be completed, and one of them bears an image on its chest of a three-masted sailing ship, suggesting that they were carved *after* European contact.

Island practicalities

Accommodation on Easter Island is very expensive for what you get – a typical double room in a *residencial* costs around US$50–60 (almost always with private bath), while a smart hotel room costs up to US$120. There are over thirty **residenciales** on the island – most of them family homes (invariably bungalows) with a few extra rooms added on – and about ten proper **hotels**, which tend to earn their living from package-tour block bookings. Try *Chez Joseph*, on Av Avareipua ⓣ32/100281; ❺), a small, family-run hotel with light, spacious rooms and a pleasant dining area. There's no sign by the drive; look out for the *moai* carving by the door. *O'Tai*, on Av Pito Te Henua (ⓣ32/100250; ❻–❼), has smart, well-furnished bungalow rooms with patio doors set in a large, flower-filled garden in a central location.

There isn't a large concentration of **eating** options on Easter Island, as so many tourists eat at their *residencial* or hotel, which means demand isn't that high. That said, what's on offer is pretty good, including several excellent, though expensive, fish restaurants, and a number of cheaper outlets serving quick snacks like pizzas, *empanadas* and burgers. There's a small but lively local **nightlife** scene, focused on a couple of **bar-discos** – namely *Piriti*, on Avenida Hotu Matu'a, near the airport, and *Toroko*, north of the *caleta*. These are good places to meet the islanders, as they're geared more towards young Rapa Nui than tourists, though the strong local feel can be slightly daunting when you first walk in. Less authentic, but more exotic, entertainment is offered in the form of regular **hula dances** (beautiful women, grass skirts, swaying hips) held at various restaurants and hotels – keep your eye open for fliers, or ask at Sernatur. These are tame, soulless offerings, however, compared with the genuine hulas you'll see for free at **Tapatai Rapa Nui**, the annual festival held in the first two weeks of February.

5

Colombia

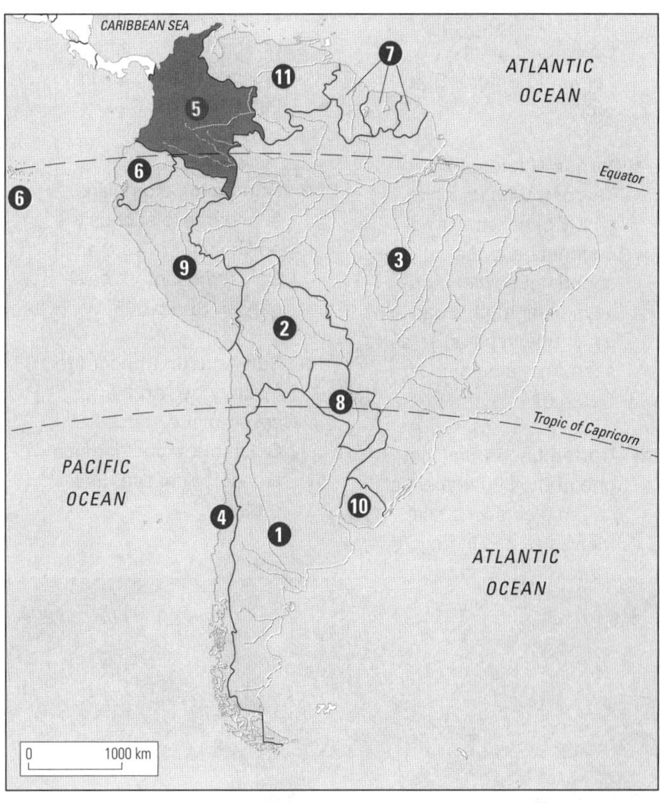
CARIBBEAN SEA
ATLANTIC OCEAN
Equator
PACIFIC OCEAN
Tropic of Capricorn
ATLANTIC OCEAN
0 1000 km
1
2
3
4
5
6
6
7
8
9
10
11

Colombia highlights

* **Donación Botero** This Bogotá museum contains one of Latin America's largest collections of modern and Impressionist art as well as the work of Colombian artist Fernando Botero. See p.602

* **Parque Nacional Tayrona** With its white sandy beaches, falling coconuts and the sounds of howler monkeys at night, this park is a Caribbean paradise as seen from a hammock. See p.621

* **Coffee fincas** Stay on one of the 300 authentic coffee plantations near Manizales and indulge in caffeine-propelled activities, such as horseback riding. See p.632

* **Cartagena's Old City** This immaculately preserved walled city is one of Spain's most enduring architectural legacy in Latin America. See p.615

* **Rumbear** Colombians take partying seriously – nowhere more so than in Cali, the country's salsa capital. See p.635

* **San Agustín** Ponder the mystery behind the seven-metre statues at Colombia's most famous archeological site. See p.639

Introduction and basics

Home to a rich history, stunning natural scenery and some of the continent's friendliest and most sophisticated people, **Colombia** offers many reasons to visit. Unfortunately, the threat of violence hangs over every aspect of Colombian life – and not only for those involved in the country's drug trade or its four-decade-long civil war. There's every reason to be cautious about a trip to Latin America's fourth largest nation – as Uruguayan writer Eduardo Galeano has pointed out, there are more homicides in any given weekend in Cali or Medellín than in an entire year in Norway. If that weren't bad enough, Colombia is also the kidnapping capital of the world.

Colombians like to call their country *Locombia*, or the "mad country", a nickname that alludes not only to their self-destructive streak but also their penchant for revelry. This exuberance is among Colombians' greatest charms, as though they are compensating for their country's poor reputation abroad by being some of the warmest and friendliest hosts anywhere. Perhaps this warmth owes itself to their **diverse roots** – more than any other country in the Andes, the mixture of the European with the African and indigenous is more complete. The result is a rich culture and a nation of proud citizens anxious to show their country off.

There's certainly plenty to put on display. In an area roughly the size of France, Colombia – the only country in South America to border both the Pacific and the Caribbean – offers every eco-system imaginable, from the Amazon **rainforest** near Leticia to the snow-capped **mountains** of the Sierra Nevada de Santa Marta. The same rugged landscape that has long fragmented economic and political power could still contribute to Colombia's future prosperity should the war end and tourism follow its natural course.

For now, though, **tourism** is barely even an industry. Only about 750,000 foreigners arrived to Colombia in 2002, most of them to do business or visit family. Perhaps that's why experienced travellers rightfully refer to the country as Latin America's best-kept secret.

Where to go

Nestled smack in the middle of the country some 2800 metres above sea level, **Bogotá** is the obligatory stop for visitors arriving by air. Like most capitals, it's a busy commercial centre, yet it also boasts a unique and vibrant cultural scene and festive nightlife. Colombia's two other major cities, **Medellín** to the north and **Cali** to the south, are also lively but less overwhelming and, despite recent histories of violence, their populations are friendlier.

Outside Bogotá, most tourists head north to the Caribbean for the sun. Just a stone's throw away from a couple of Colombia's most spectacular **beaches**, the walled-city of **Cartagena** is the biggest Spanish colonial port in South America. A short drive east, the less-scenic **Santa Marta** is near **Parque Nacional Tayrona** whose beach-combing is unrivalled. Santa Marta is also the base for a six-day trek to the beclouded archeological ruins of **La Ciudad Perdida**, the Lost City, an experience as overwhelming as being in Peru's Macchu Pichu, but more frequented by Kogi Indians than gringo backpackers.

In the southeast corner of the country, Colombia's stake of the **Amazon**, centred on the charming backwater town of **Leticia**, may not be as well known as Peru's or Brazil's but it's just as lush and far more peaceful. Heading south towards Ecuador, tranquillity also reigns in the colonial town of **Popayán**, which is close to the enigmatic archeological ruins of **San Agustín** and **Tierradentro**. Both sites are surrounded by some of the country's most breathtaking scenery, great for hiking.

Colombia's coffee-growing region, the **zona cafetera** of the central highlands near Medellín, is the country's newest tourist attraction, offering walks in the foothills

where the bean is grown, accommodation in authentic **fincas** and such activities as horseback riding and trekking. This unique experience is a potential goldmine should tourism ever prosper.

When to go

Colombia's proximity to the equator keeps regional temperatures stable throughout the year, around 24°C along the coast and 7–17°C as you move higher inland. Instead, seasons do vary in response to rainfall. In the **Andean region** there are two dry and two wet seasons per year, the driest months being December through March and then July and August. In low-lying areas, especially **southern Colombia**, rainfall is more constant but showers never last too long. The **Amazon** climate is uniformly wet the entire year. The number of tourists to Colombia is so small that it cannot be said to have a high or a low season.

Arrival

Colombia's national airline Avianca has a direct service from London and other

European cities to Bogotá at least three times a week. Round-trip fares start around £550. From the US, the competition among carriers is more intense and daily flights from Miami start around US$500. It's also possible to fly from Miami directly to Barranquilla, Cartagena and Medellín. In South America Avianca also flies to Buenos Aires, Caracas, Gyayaquil, Lima, Mexico City, Panama City, Quito, Río de Janeiro, Santiago (Chile) and Sao Paulo.

There are two official overland **border crossings** to neighbouring countries, one **to Ecuador** (Ipiales-Tulcán) and another to **Venezuela** (Cúcuta-San Antonio), both of which are open daily and don't charge taxes for entry into the country. The overland crossing into Venezuela is quite **dangerous** and really not recommended. One bus company (Ormeño) covers several international routes from Bogotá, including Quito (US$80), Caracas (US$75) and Lima (US$130). In general, though, it's cheaper to take buses at the border and travel on more frequent national lines. From the Amazon region it's also possible to cross **into Brazil and Peru** by hiring a sea ferry from Leticia. But be sure to have your passport stamped at Leticia's airport before departing.

Red tape and visas

A passport and onward ticket are the sole entry requirements of all nationals of English-speaking countries except for **residents of Ireland**, who must request a visa (£16) before arrival from any Colombian consulate; to do so, they need to produce three photos.

Upon arrival, you'll normally be given a sixty-day **tourist visa**, though it's possible to request up to ninety days if you have proof that you plan to stay that long. Once in the country, you can stay a maximum of ninety days continuously and 180 days in any single calendar year. Thirty-day extensions cost US$20 and can be obtained at any DAS immigration office in Colombia.

An **airport tax** of US$28 or US$45 – depending on whether you stayed sixty days or more – will be levied upon your departure.

Information, websites and maps

Colombia's official tourist board has been contracted out to the privately owned **El Fondo de Promoción Touristica**. The dearth of visitors to Colombia means that the Fondo's sole office in Bogotá, at Cra 16A No 78–55, office 604 (Ⓣ01/611-4330), focuses more on promoting Colombia abroad than it does assisting tourists inside the country. Still, its staff is helpful and visitors who show up during weekday office hours will be rewarded with plentiful brochures and a free copy of an English-language guidebook and road atlas. Almost every town boasts a tourist office, though quality varies widely and, in some cases, require long treks during restricted hours.

Because Colombia is not so set up for tourism, it can be difficult finding up-to-date and reliable information on the Net. One of the best **websites** devoted to the country is Ⓦwww.turismocolombia.com, Colombia's official tourism site, which has plenty of photos as well as good background on the country's main tourist pulls. You might also try the privately run Ⓦwww.colombia.com, a mega-portal with links to the most popular Colombian websites; Ⓦwww.poorbuthappy.com, an expat website with answers to all the questions you were afraid to ask and bulletin boards that are open forums for travellers to exchange recommendations; Ⓦwww.colombiareport.org, a huge database of information on Colombia and updated articles on the civil war; or Ⓦwww.eltiempo.com, a searchable website (in Spanish) to Colombia's largest and main newspaper of record.

For a country where most of the people are afraid of driving, there are a good number of quality **roadmaps** available. The *Auto Guia,* updated annually, and available in bookstores for US$8, has detailed departmental maps with hotels and attractions listed.

Costs and money

Colombia's national currency is the **peso**, divided into 100 centavos. You'll find in circulation coins of 50, 100, 200, 500 and 1000 pesos and notes of 1000, 2000, 5000 10,000, 20,000 and 50,000 pesos. As elsewhere in Latin America, changing large bills can be problematic.

The easiest way to obtain cash is through **ATM machines**, available in even small towns, which recognize foreign bank cards. For exchanging dollars or other currencies, **casas de cambio** offer similar rates, have more flexible hours and provide quicker service than most banks. Travellers' cheques can be exchanged at *casas de cambios* and banks – though sometimes only in the morning – but are generally frowned upon by most businesses other than hotels. Changing money on the street is not recommended. A byproduct of Colombia's burgeoning drug trade is the glut of illegally laundered dollars circulating in the country, a phenomenon that has lowered the demand for cash dollars. You're likely to get a better exchange rate paying with a credit card than you are exchanging dollars.

Although more expensive than its neighbours, Colombia remains cheap by Western standards. Your largest expense is likely to be **transportation**, as Colombia is a big country. Still, there's stiff competition in road transport and the wide use of air travel by the country's middle class, who fear travelling by road, has kept domestic airfares in check.

Food is generally inexpensive, especially if your stomach can withstand the *comida corriente* served at cheaper restaurants. A typical meal costs no more than US$2, but for lighter, healthier meals expect to pay more. For a nice meal, modest lodging and sightseeing, it's possible to survive on less than US$25 a day.

Accommodation

Accommodation ranges considerably, but given the country's relative prosperity you'll be pleasantly surprised at the bargains available. Backpacker **hostels** start around US$4 a night and more comfortable but still modest lodgings will rarely cost you more than US$12. The exception is Cartagena and Santa Marta, just about the only part of Colombia that survives on tourism, where there are a few low-end rundown joints, a plethora of overpriced high-rise hotels and almost nothing in between.

In the coffee-growing region, you can stay on one of the stately **fincas**, coffee-growing plantations that have barely changed over the decades. These offer luxurious accommodation for a moderate price, as well as numerous outdoor activities (see p.593).

Getting around

As in most aspects of daily life, Colombians prioritize security over price and comfort when considering their travel options. You should do the same. One golden rule is to never travel at night or on rural roads whose security status you aren't absolutely sure of. Another rule is to use **air travel** whenever possible.

By plane

There are two domestic commercial **airlines** – Avianca, serving more than twenty cities, and the newer AeroRepublica. Avianca offers a five-stop **airpass** called Discover Colombia for travel within the country over a thirty-day period. Prices start at US$240 (US$300 in the June to August and December high seasons) when bought in combination with an international ticket on Avianca, nearly double in conjunction with another carrier. Although theoretically a good deal, the cumbersome restrictions and high penalties charged for changes make it worthwhile only if you plan to keep to a rigid itinerary. At the time of writing, Avianca was in the process of reviewing this promotion and possibly streamlining it.

Although booking in advance is the best guarantor of a low fare, the large public served by air travel keeps rates low. For example, a one-way fare between Santa Marta and Bogotá purchased a day in advance costs about US$65 outside high season. When travelling by plane, be sure to arrive at the airport well in advance as vigilant security controls tend to extend check-in times. A **departure tax** of US$2.50 is usually included in the ticket price; if not, it needs to be paid at the airport.

By bus

Learning how to travel by **bus** in Colombia is an art perfected only over time and not really necessary for short visits. In addition to the wide range of options in comfort and quality to familiarize yourself with, there are the inevitable false promises of punctuality.

Generally, the Pullman or lujo categories denote larger, long-distance buses with reclining seats, air conditioning, toilets, a video and possibly even a meal. Service is usually direct and the ride comfortable, though prices tend to be higher and service less frequent. Some recommended companies are Expreso Bolivariano, Copetran and Flota Magdalena.

For shorter trips, you're better off sacrificing comfort and price for speed by buying a ticket on a *buesta*, *colectivo* or any similarly sized minibus or minivan that departs on demand. Within this category prices and quality fluctuate but at a minimum are the same price as Pullman service. Velotax and Taxiverde are two companies with a nationwide presence and a reputation for modern vehicles.

By car

Renting a car is a good option for short distances, especially touring small towns around Bogotá, where the roads are generally safe. However, for the most part the risks of getting lost on a country road and stuck in unsafe surrounding aren't worth the hassle. Several international chains operate in Bogotá and other major cities and tend to offer the same prices, starting at US$35 a day for unlimited mileage, as less reliable local companies. If you are driving, be prepared for frequent roadblocks by police and the military. Although primarily there to keep the roads safe and free of guerrillas, they're not above a little highway robbery themselves when it comes to honing in on picayune violations and then trying to settle them on the spot. Driving with a foreign licence is allowed, though it's highly advisable to have an **international driver's licence** handy to avoid harassment.

Mail and communications

Sending a postcard or a letter abroad can be done for about US$1 from almost anywhere in the country, using Colombia's **Correos de Colombia**. Standard service isn't reliable, however, and packages or important documents should be sent *certificado* (certified mail) or through one of the international couriers available in major cities.

Local phone calls cost around five cents, and **phonecards** are commonly sold at local kiosks in denominations of as little as US$1. Long-distance calls are best made from call centres called *telecentros* – you can choose between Orbitel (code 05), ETB (07) and Telecom (09) before dialling the country code or national area code (*indicitavo*) followed by the local number.

Cybercafés can be found even in small towns, though fast **Internet** connections are only available in big cities. Rates start around US$1 per hour.

Food and drink

Whether it's a platter full of starch or a suckling pig stuffed with rice, **Colombian cuisine** is anything but light. Not even the heat of the coast seems to infringe on the country's obsession with fried foods.

The carbo-doping begins with **breakfast**, which usually consists of *huevos pericos*, scrambled eggs with onion and tomatoes, accompanied by a fried maize pancake known as an *arepa* or a *tamale* stuffed with chopped pork, rice potatoes and anything else under the sun.

The most important meal of the day is the midday **almuerzo** or **comida corriente**, consisting of soup, a main course and dessert. Dinners, after 6pm, are somewhat lighter but also consist of chicken or meat.

In Bogotá and other major cities there's a surprisingly high supply of fashionable restaurants of the same quality you'd expect in any major European or US city but at a fraction of the price. Bogotá also offers an excellent array of Western and international cuisine, especially Arabic foods.

Local specialities

Traditionally each region in Colombia had its own local speciality, though now many are available across the country. One of the most widespread is the **bandeja paisa**, which consists of a cafeteria-sized tray filled to the brim with ground beef, *chorizo* sausage, beans (*frijoles*), rice, fried green banana (*platano*), a fried egg, avocado and fried pork. You can usually find one served at inexpensive market eating stalls known as **fondas**.

One of the tastiest Colombian dishes is **ajiaco**, a thick chicken stew replete with vegetables, maize, three types of potato, cream, capers and sometimes avocado. Despite its peppery-sounding name (*aji* is Spanish for chilli peppers), it's a surprisingly mild dish, ideally suited for the high Andean climate around Bogotá. **Mazamorra** is a similar meat and vegetable soup but with beans and corn flour. Both are often served with a *patacon*, a mashed and heavily salted cake of baked *platano*. Don't leave Colombia without trying one.

The most sophisticated of the regional specialities, not for the fainthearted, is called **hormigas culonas**, which consists of fried black ants and comes from Bucaramanga and the Santander area. In Cali and southern Colombia, **grilled guinea pig**, known as *cuy* or *curí*, is popular. On the coast, **fish** – especially shellfish and whitefish – is more common but far less popular than *arroz con coco*, rice with coconut, or barbecued chicken.

Drinking

Surprisingly for a country that produces some of the world's finest grinds, **coffee** is of a remarkably poor quality in most places other than speciality cafés. In any case, the only thing Colombians have adopted from the art of espresso making is the *demitasse* cup, from which they drink watered-down black coffee known as *tinto*. Colombians also consume large amounts of herbal infusions, called **aromáticas**, made from plants like *yerbabuena* (mint) and *manzanilla* (camomile). A good combatant against altitude sickness is *agua de panela*, hot water with unrefined sugar.

If there's one item your stomach will pine for when you've returned home it's Colombia's exotic variety of **fresh fruit juices**, found especially on the coast at as little as 25 cents a glass. Many are completely foreign to western palates and lack English translations. Worth trying are *guanábana*, *lulo*, mango, *fraijoa*, *maracuyá*, *mora* and *guayaba*.

While **beer** is reasonably good and inexpensive in Colombia (try brands like Dorado, Club and Aguila), the locally produced **wine** tends to be of the boxed variety. Far more popular among locals is **aguardiente**, pure grain alcohol, and **rum** (called *ron*), both of which are drunk straight-up. Brave souls won't want to pass up any offer to try *chicha*, a frothy moonshine found in rural areas whose fermenting enzyme is saliva.

Crime and safety

Without a doubt, **safety** is rightfully the top concern of any traveller in Colombia. On top of the typical street crime endemic to major Latin American cities, there's the additional threat posed by guerrillas, right-wing paramilitary groups, and narcotraffickers.

The statistics speak for themselves: the world's highest **kidnapping** rate with more than 3000 abductions in 2002 alone; a per-capita **homicide** rate thirteen times higher than the US's; a throng of vigilante justice **militias** armed to the teeth; **hijackings** of domestic flights; random firebombing of buses – it's no surprise Colombia ranks in the top ten in Robert Young Pelton's *The World's Most Dangerous Places*.

These risk are enough to convince most to skip Colombia altogether, especially when there are so many other, safer countries in Latin America to visit. Indeed, after a spate of high-profile politically motivated kidnappings targeting business and diplomatic interests, the US State Department warned citizens in February 2003 against travel to the country. Slightly toned-down warnings are also on the books for UK residents. (For up-to-date travel advice check ⓦwww.travel.state.gov/colombia or ⓦwww.fco.gov .uk.)

The situation has deteriorated since 1998, with the implementation of the US-backed

Plan Colombia and the election of hardliner president Álvaro Uribe, whose law and order policies have only intensified **guerrilla activity**. As part of the guerrilla strategy to wrest authority from the government, large cities are increasingly being targeted. Bogotá, which had until recently been largely unscathed by the civil war, experienced its worst attack in years when the exclusive (and highly fortified) *El Nogal* country club was ripped apart by a car bomb in February 2003, killing 36 people and injuring 160.

And while it's a small reassurance, most tourists have not been targeted specifically by any of the actors in the country's civil war. Both the **FARC** and **ELN**, the country's two largest guerrilla groups, are incredibly sensitive to bad press. Still, unless you're a soldier of fortune, certain areas should be avoided altogether, including the departments of Choco, Meta, Caqueta, Putumayo and Arauca. Rural areas of Anioquia, Cauca, Nariño and Norte de Santander were also considered dangerous at press time. Most guerrilla activity is confined to rural areas near the border with Panama and Venezuela, as well as the low-lying *Llanos* dominating the country's eastern half. Heading too far off the beaten path poses additional risks – be sure to stay abreast of current events and consult local authorities to assess the safety of any planned excursion.

One silver lining is that **drug-related violence** has all but disappeared. Rather than be caught in the crossfire of rival gangs, the only contact you're likely to have with Colombia's drug war is if your hotel room is raided by police or during a random interrogation before boarding your plane home. To protect yourself, don't transport any sealed packages for your new Colombian friends. Still, common sense and standard procedures for avoiding theft apply.

Opening hours and fiestas

Most stores open early at 8am until 6pm Monday through Friday. Businesses also often open Saturday until mid-afternoon. Outside Bogotá it's common for businesses to close at noon for a two- or three-hour siesta. Commercial hours in cities in warmer areas such as Cali often get started and end earlier. Government offices often follow the same pattern. Banks tend to open around 9am and close at 4pm, though *casas de cambio* stay open later.

Barranquilla's two-week long **Carnaval**, second in importance in Latin America after Río's, kicks off in the last half of February.

Sports, outdoor and ocean activities

Adventurers begin to hyperventilate in ecstasy when they discover Colombia. From almost every vantage point in Colombia there's a snowcapped peak to climb, an untamed river to ride or some sunken coral reef to explore. Though many of the country's most impressive cliffs and shorelines are

Calendar of public holidays

Note that when holidays do not fall on a Monday, the public holiday is often moved to the following Monday.

January 1 New Year's Day
January 6 Día de Reyes
March 21 St Joseph's Day
March or April Easter
May 1 Labour Day
May 9 Ascension Day
May 30 Corpus Christi
June 29 Saint Peter and Saint Paul
July 20 Independence Day
August 7 Battle of Boyacá
August 15 Assumption
October 12 Columbus's arrival in the New World
November 1 All Saints' Day
November 11 Independence of Cartagena
December 8 Immaculate Conception
December 25 Christmas

off limits because of the ongoing civil war, the areas open to the public should provide more than enough adventure to satisfy even the most hardened adrenaline addict.

Football is the national sport and Colombians have a reputation as being some of South Americans most skilled if untidy players. Going to see any of the big teams play in Bogotá, Medellín or Cali is an unforgettable experience.

Living in the clouds in a land studded with so many mountains has made Colombians crazy for **cycling**. After coffee and drugs, cyclists are probably Colombia's best-known export and Santiago Botero, a consistent top ten finisher in the Tour de France, is a national hero even though he must now train in Spain because of repeated kidnapping threats.

Among the most popular activities for adventure travellers is **scuba diving**. Colombia's waters may not be the most impressive place in the world to learn but they might be around the cheapest. All across its 3000 kilometres of coastline, but especially near Santa Marta and the Caribbean islands, operators offer week-long PADI certification courses, enabling you to dive anywhere in the world, for under US$200. **Snorkelling** and **sailing** are two other popular water-borne activities.

History

Ever since its settlement by three rival gold-seeking armies, the country's disjointed geography has fragmented political and economic authority and hamstrung the process of nation-building. Living in the mythic land of El Dorado, it would seem, has only made the struggle to control Colombia's bountiful resources – coffee, emeralds, gold, oil and, more recently, cocaine – all the more fierce. With the country's ongoing civil war now in its fourth decade, Colombia continues to pay dearly for its historical lack of consolidation.

Pre-Columbian Colombia

Before the Spanish conquest Colombia was a potpourri of **indigenous cultures** – including the Tayrona, Calimas, Sinú, Muisca, Pastos, Nariño, Tierradentro and San Agustín – scattered across the country's narrow valleys and isolated cloud forests. Unlike the Incas or Aztecs, who formed through war an amalgam culture dominant over vast regions, the reach of these groups was severely reduced by the country's mountainous terrain, endless gullies and narrow valleys.

The Spanish conquest and the colonial era

The one thing uniting these disparate tribes with one another – and the Spanish *conquistadores* – was their common appetite for **gold**. Soon after Rodrigo de Bastides established the first Spanish settlement in **Santa Marta**, in 1525, the hunt for El Dorado, a majestic city shimmering in auriferous metals, was on. The lure of the sacred metal captured the fantasies of dozens of explorers who were to lead near-suicidal expeditions over the next century into the central highlands near Bogotá, where the **Musica** lived. Although the mythical city itself was never found, a bottomless booty of more than several hundreds of thousands of tons was, and it was duly hauled back to the motherland.

The three centres of Spanish control in the sixteenth- and seventeenth-century Colombia – **Cartagena**, **Popayán** and **Santafé de Bogotá** – were settled independently and developed largely self-sufficient local economies. With the growth of the Spanish Empire the area today comprising Colombia, Ecuador, Panama and Venezuela was excised, released or freed from its dependence on royal flacks in Peru in 1717 to create the new **Viceroyalty of New Granada**; Santafé de Bogotá was made its capital.

By the end of the eighteenth century, the American-born creole elite had grown discontented with their scant influence in the Spanish-run economy, and the political system erupted into open rebellion. When Napoleon invaded Spain and arrested King Ferdinand VII, he kickstarted the drive for independence. Venezuelan-born **Simón Bolívar** landed in Cartagena in 1813 to lead the military campaign against the Spanish armies. This insurrection was thwarted, however; with the restoration of the Spanish monarch, some 10,000 loyalist forces rapidly regained control of its territories in 1817. The **patria boba** (or foolish fatherland) ended in utter failure.

Independence

By 1819, though, Bolívar's rag-tag army of scruffy horsemen from the Venezuelan and Colombian *llanos* returned. Supported by a British legion, the guerrillas' decisively defeated royalist forces at the **Battle of Boyacá** on August 7, 1819; **independence** was won. Two years later, a constitutional Congress at Cúcutua euphorically declared El Libertador president of the newly created **Gran Colombia**.

The ambitious undertaking didn't last long. With Bolívar away liberating the future states of Peru in 1824 and Bolivia a year later, his delegates back in Bogotá were powerless to arrest the encroachments of El Libertador's many rivals. Administering such a vast territory, which encompassed three socially and economically different countries, proved impossible even following his return. Venezuela broke away in 1829 and Ecuador the following year. Bolívar's dream of a Pan-American union, founded on republican principles and strong enough to resist the imperial ambitions of the world's great powers, was in shambles. In May 1830, the distraught hero left the capital for good and died seven months later in Santa Marta en route to exile in Europe.

Civil war

Bolívar's death unlocked a fierce rivalry for political and economic power among the country's elite. It was during this struggle that Colombia's modern-day political parties, the federalist leaning **Liberals** and centralist, arch-Catholic **Conservatives**, were born. Separated less by ideology than an irreconcilable lust for power among local strongmen known as *caudillos*, the two factions engulfed the country in no fewer than **eight violent civil wars** over the next seventy years. The bloodiest conflict was the **War of a Thousand Days**, from 1899 to 1902, which left a toll of 120,000 dead. The chaos of the war was also the backdrop by which Panama, under the protection of the United States Navy, seceded from Colombia in 1903.

Into the twentieth century

The demoralizing loss of Panama ushered in a period of reconciliation and economic prosperity. Spurred by the export of **coffee** – of which Colombia was the world's largest producer after Brazil – development took off, and the task of nation building began in earnest. Until 1950, all changes of government occurred within the framework of the constitution.

But political violence returned with a vengeance in the late 1940s as working classes began to agitate for a larger share of the country's wealth. The assassination of their greatest advocate, Bogotá's populist mayor, Jorge Eliécer Gaitán, in 1948, sparked off weeks of riots, with more than 1500 deaths, which came to be known as **El Bogotazo**. In the wake of Gaitan's death Liberals took up arms against the Conservative government to defend their martyred leader. The result was a decade of intense bloodletting known as **La Violencia** in which more than 300,000 people were killed, making it the deadliest conflict in the Americas after the US Civil War and Mexican Revolution.

Order was restored by the 1953 military coup of General Rojas Pinilla. Four years later Liberals and Conservatives put aside their difference to form the **Frente Nacional coalition**, by which power alternated with every presidential election until 1970.

The emergence of the guerrillas

However, it was too late to contain the revolutionary sentiment engendered by La Violencia. Peasant militias that formerly responded to Liberal or Conservative sponsors were infiltrated by communists or devolved into bandit mercenaries. In 1954, peasant refugees organized in self-defence groups became the nuclei of what would become the Communist-linked **Fuerzas Armadas Revolucioanrios Colombianos (FARC)**, Colombia's largest guerrilla group.

In the aftermath of the 1959 Cuban revolution, dozens more insurgent groups emerged. Two of the most important were the **Ejército de Liberación Nacional (ELN)** and the **Movimiento 19 de Abril (M-19)**, which took its name from the date of the fraudulent 1970 elections in which Frente Nacional candidate Misael Pastrana stole the presidency from a left-leaning Rojas Pinilla.

Attempts to disarm the guerrillas have preoccupied governments ever since. While the M-19 successfully demobilized in 1990, and its leaders have been incorporated into the political system, the remaining guerrilla groups have only grown stronger in the last decade, expanding their ranks to 25,000, a large percentage of them still minors. At the same time, they've grown fat on the country's burgeoning **drug trade**, which has enhanced their military might even while the collapse of the Communist bloc has sapped them ideologically.

The self-perpetuating link between drugs and revolution has hampered the success of even the most genuine peace efforts. The last olive branch extended by the government, the much-criticized 1998 concession of a massive **demilitarized zone** the size of Switzerland and located in the unpopulated llanos area, ended with almost no progress after it proved incapable of stemming the violence. Complicating a settlement even further is the growing presence of some 10,000 right-wing paramilitary troops defending landed interests and employing equally ruthless tactics, often in collusion with the army.

The Uribe government

The election in 2002 of **Álvaro Uribe** on a law-and-order platform has rekindled hopes that the government may yet put an end to the cycle of violence. The Colombian government has turned to the US for help in tipping the military balance in their favour in the hopes of negotiating a settlement from a position of strength. Under **Plan Colombia**, launched in 1999 but intensified under Uribe, the US has committed US$1.6 billion in foreign aid, most of it to the military, to root out illegal drug trafficking and the guerrilla protectors that allow it to blossom.

Uribe's strategy has proved immensely popular, both at home with war-weary Colombians and with the US, which has even taken the unusual step of providing their staunch ally in the War on Drugs with a 24-hour security entourage (some US$7 million is spent by the US government on his personal security alone).

So far, however, Plan Colombia has only led guerrillas to broaden their reach and intensify their strikes, leading to a situation of heightened alert for the country as a whole. At the same time, the high cost of fighting the war is sapping scarce resources from the government coffers and forcing Uribe to adopt some unpopular economic belt tightening, including laying off some 10,000 public employees in 2003. It remains to be seen how long Uribe can retain popular faith in his leadership without inciting his backers to take an even more heavy-handed, unilateral approach.

Books

While the work of Nobel Prize-winning Gabriel García Márquez is internationally celebrated, there is a small treasure of literature on Colombia that has been translated into English. The books listed below offer a good range of background material on Colombian fiction history, culture and society.

Mark Borden *Killing Pablo* (Penguin). The gripping tale of the rise and fall of Pablo Escobar, from small-time thief to ruthless cocaine godfather. The bulk of the book deals with the hunting down of the drug lord by US-backed forces.

Walter Broderick *Camilo Torres: A Biography of the Priest Guerrillero* (o/p). This out-of-print book is not only the biography of one of Colombia's most famous guerrillas but also an observant account of the socially indifferent politics of the 1960s that led even Catholic priests to take up arms against the state.

Wade Davis *One River* (Touchstone Books). A vivid chronicle of Harvard botanist Richard Evans Schultes' epic-like search for hallucinogenic plants in the Colombian Amazon during the 1940s. It's based on the mind-altering adventures in 1975 of the author, a former student.

Gabriel García Márquez *100 Years of Solitude* (Penguin). The 1982 Nobel Prize winner's masterpiece was the progenitor of the magical realism literary style that swept across South America in the 1960s and 1970s. Also of interest: *Love in the Time of Cholera* and the novellas *Chronicle of a Death Foretold* and *No One Writes to the Colonel*.

John Hemming *The Search for El Dorado* (The Phoenix Press). This well-researched and beautifully illustrated book brings to life the story of the world's first gold diggers and the justifying myth behind so much pillage and cruelty.

Jorge Isaacs *María* (iUniverse.com). Colombia's answer to *Gone with the Wind* is the story of cousinly love on a slave-owning sugar plantation near Cali. Considered the apogee of nineteenth-century Latin American romanticism.

Charles Nicholl *The Fruit Palace* (Vintage Books). Gonzo journalism meets the early 1980s cocaine underworld; a side-splitting tribute to the open road, Colombia style.

Frank Safford and Marco Palacios *Colombia: Fragmented Land, Divided Society* (Oxford University Press). Easily the most comprehensive history book on Colombia; traces the geographically hamstrung country's struggle for national unity from pre-Colombian times to the present.

Fernando Vallejo *Our Lady of the Assassins* (Consortium Book Sales). A gay, coming-of-age romance between a washed-up novelist and one of the god-fearing, teenager mercenaries that rampaged through Medellín in the early 1990s. The book was made into a movie by the same name.

5.1

Bogotá and around

At first glance Colombia's capital, **SANTAFÉ DE BOGOTÁ**, looks as drab and unwelcoming as any other ringed-in Andean capital. Name your urban ill – poverty, gridlock traffic, crime and choking smog – and this overcrowded city of seven million suffers from it in excess. But within this otherwise grim snapshot of modern-day Latin America lies one of the continent's most resplendent repositories of colonial architecture and art, and a cultural scene among the most vibrant in South America.

Situated on the **sabana de Bogotá**, Colombia's highest plateau at 2600 metres, the city was founded on August 6, 1538, by Gonzalo Jiménez de Quesada in what was a former citadel belonging to the Muisca king **Bacatá**, for whom the city's name is derived. Bogotá owes its colonial splendour to its status as the capital of the new Viceroyalty of Nueva Granada in 1740. After Independence, it remained the seat of authority of the Gran Colombia confederation and, after it dissolved in 1830, of Colombia proper.

Despite its political influence, Bogotá was long neglected. Scarce transport links with the rest of the country kept the population down throughout the early republic era, and as late as the 1940s the city had just 300,000 inhabitants. The balance tipped in the 1940s and 1950s with the advent of civil war and the mass exodus of peasant families from the war-torn countryside. Industrialization was a further magnet.

Today, Bogotá is South America's fourth largest city as well as one of its most modern and cosmopolitan. Apart from Buenos Aires, there may be no other place on the continent with such a wide variety of gourmet restaurants and chic, all-night clubs. Moreover, because so few visitors come to Bogotá, residents go out of their way to be hospitable – this even though within Colombia, *cachacos*, as residents of Bogotá are known, have somewhat of a reputation for being cold, uptight and arrogant.

Arrival and information

Most international flights land at **El Dorado International Airport** though some use **Puente Aereo** domestic terminal, a kilometre away. A taxi downtown costs about US$4.50 – be sure to buy a ticket at one of the authorized stands instead of arranging directly with the driver, who's likely to charge you more. Bus rides into town cost less than US$1 and can take about an hour. The "Germania" bus goes through the centre to La Candelaria, but just beyond the baggage claim in El Dorado there's a city-run tourist stand that can supply you with brochures and advice on buses.

The mammoth-sized long-distance bus terminal, **Terminal de Transportes**, is on the southwest edge of Bogotá near Avenida Boyacá (Carerra 72) between El Dorado (Avenida 26) and Avenida Centenario (Calle 13). It's divided into four hubs, serving destinations north, south, east or west of the city. To the centre, a taxi costs about US$3.50 and takes about half an hour. You can also get into town by hailing any **buseta** from Carerra 10, marked "Terminal terrestre".

Bogotá's professional tourist bureau produces helpful guides, many in English, to the city's main churches, museums and other historical attractions. There are small informational stands at the airport and bus station, but your best resource is the main office of the **Instituto Distrital de Cultura y Turismo** (Mon–Fri 8am–7pm, Sat 8am–5pm; ⓣ1/336-6511, ⓦwww.idct.gov.co), at the **Casa de los Comuneros** at Cra 8 No. 9–83 in La Candelaria. Be sure to pick up a copy of *Qué en Bogotá*, a monthly publication listing cultural events, restaurants, theatres and the like. On Fridays, Bogotá's leading newspaper, *El Tiempo*, publishes a twelve-page weekend guide. For up-to-date safety information on Colombia's 46 national parks and protected areas, visit the eco-tourism office of **Ministerio del Medio Ambiente** (the government organ administering the parks) at Cra 10 No. 20–30 fourth floor ⓣ1/243-3095.

City transport

Most sightseeing can be done **by foot**, as the bulk of Bogotá's tourist attractions are in or near one neighbourhood: La Candelaria. Otherwise, for moving around the city your best option is the clean and efficient **TransMilenio**, an electrically driven bus system that costs US$0.35 no matter the journey. The most popular line follows Avenida Caracas from La Candelaria all the way to the city's northern edge, El Portal del Norte. Crowded and more confusing to the uninitiated, but covering a wider range of routes, are gas-guzzling **busetas**, which charge around US$0.30 per ride. **Taxis** in Bogotá are relatively inexpensive, with a trip across the city costing about US$5. They operate on a metered system and levy a small surcharge at night; be sure to check the green fare table before paying as most drivers overcharge. At night, it's better to use a radio taxi (see "Listings", p.607); when you call, the dispatcher will give you a confirmation number that you must verify with the driver.

Accommodation

Lodgings in Bogotá are abundant and varied. Swanky, upscale accommodation and international chains can be found in North Bogotá, while more inexpensive options are concentrated in La Candelaria. Many hotels offer discounts for cash payment.

Casa Medina Cra 7, No. 69A–22, North Bogotá ⓣ1/217-0288 or 312-0299, ⓦwww.hoteles-charleston.com. Part of the Relais & Châteaux chain of luxury hotels. Every room of the *Casa Medina* has a chimney, while the oak-wood bar and restaurant make for an memorable stay. ❾

La Casona del Patio Amarillo Cra 8 No. 69–24, North Bogotá ⓣ1/212-8805. Yellow is the dominant theme in this cosy B&B close to Bogotá's financial centre and busy nightlife. The quiet indoor patio is great for relaxing. ❹

Dann Colonial C 14 No. 4–21, La Candelaria ⓣ1/341-1680. Despite its name, this is a very modern hotel offering quality service and located near most tourist sties. ❸

Hotel Aragon Cra 3 No. 14–13, La Candelaria ⓣ1/342-5239 or 284-8325. Cheap; popular with young travellers who can't find a room at the *Platypus*. ❶

Platypus C 16, No. 2–43, La Candelaria ⓣ1/352-0127 or 341-3104, ⓦwww.platypusbogota.com. An institution – some even say the best hostel in all South America, mostly because English–German speaking owner German warmly shares knowledge accumulated from extensive travels. An around the clock lounge serves free coffee. Comfortable shared and private rooms with kitchen facilities. Easy to miss because no sign, just a platypus, pegged to green-coloured colonial house. ❶

Saint Simon Cra 14, No. 81–34, North Bogotá ⓣ1/621-8188, ⓔprohtss@uolpremium.net.co. Boutique hotel in the heart of the Zona Rosa. It features recently remodelled rooms, with kitchenette. ❻

Taquendama Inter Continental Cra 10, No. 26–21, Downtown Bogotá ⓣ1/382-0300, ⓦwww.inter-tequendama.com.co. The lobby's disco-era decor attests to this high-rise's one-time fame as the preferred meeting spot for gringo drug dealers and their Colombian counterparts. It offers all the comforts and services you'd expect from an international chain, including a business centre. ❻

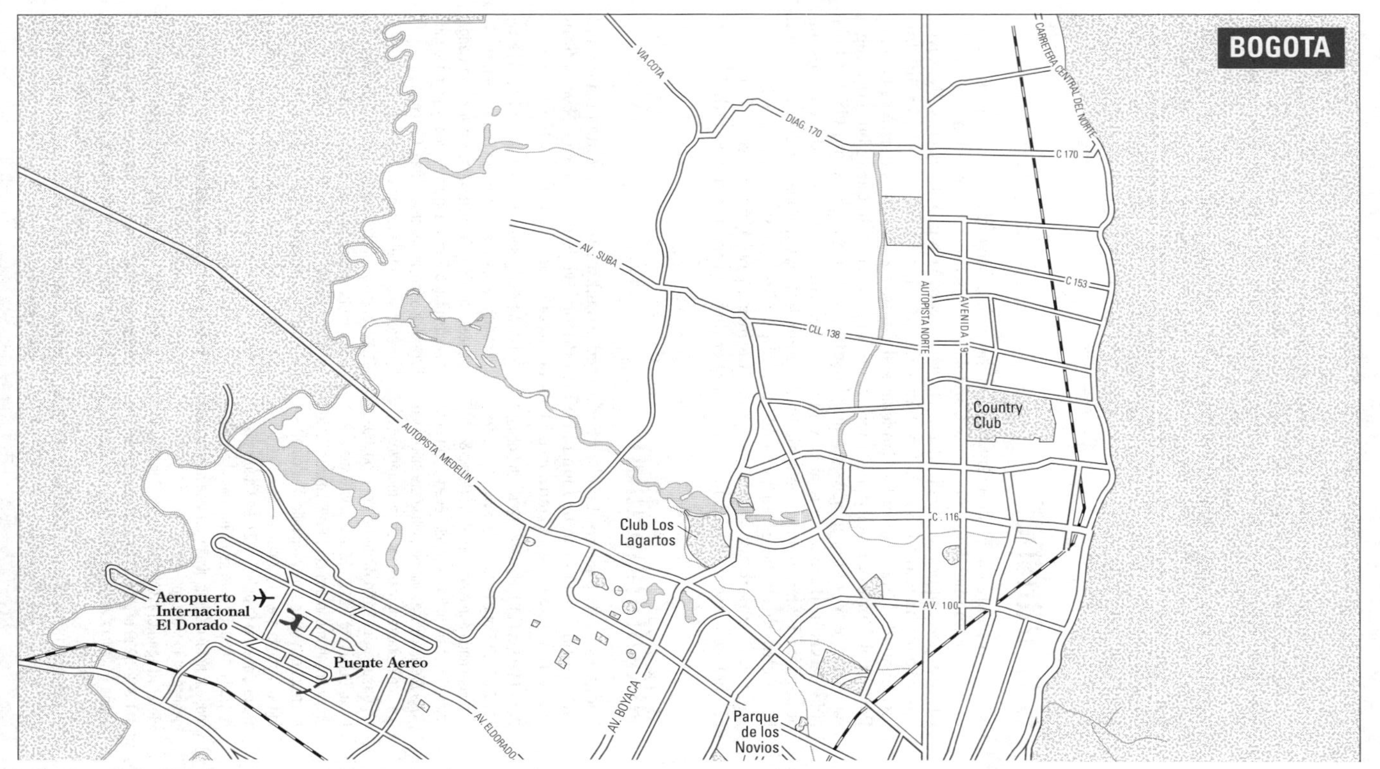
BOGOTA
CARRETERA CENTRAL DEL NORTE
C 170
DIAG. 170
VIA COTA
C 153
AV. SUBA
CLL. 138
AUTOPISTA NORTE
AVENIDA 19
Country Club
AUTOPISTA MEDELLIN
C. 116
Club Los Lagartos
AV. 100
Aeropuerto Internacional El Dorado
Puente Aereo
AV. BOYACA
Parque de los Novios
AV. ELDORADO

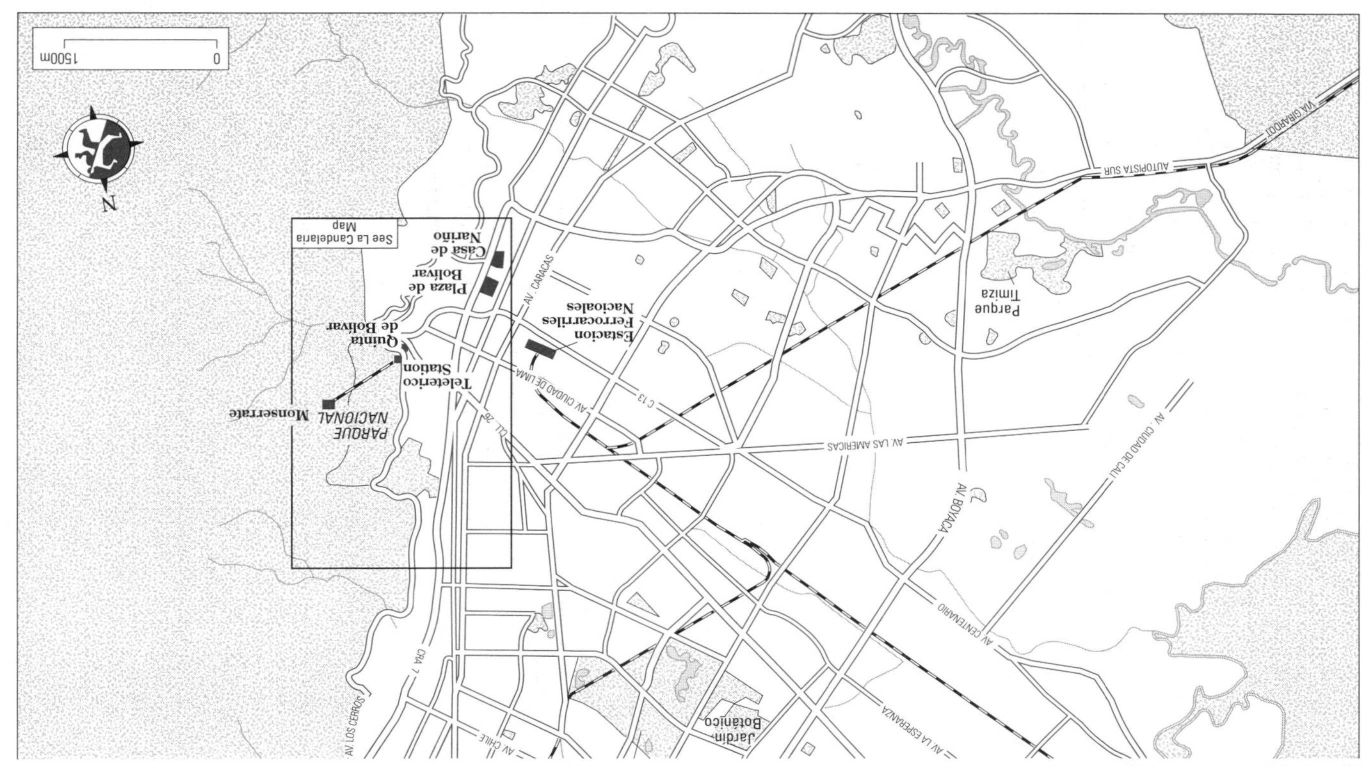
0 1500m
N
Monserrate
PARQUE NACIONAL
Teleterico Station
Quinta de Bolívar
Plaza de Bolívar
Casa de Nariño
See La Candelaria Map
Estacion Ferrocarriles Nacioales
Parque Timiza
Jardín Botánico
AV. LOS CERROS
CRA 7
AV. CHILE
CLL. 26
AV. CARACAS
AV. CIUDAD DE LIMA
C 13
AV. LAS AMERICAS
AV. LA ESPERANZA
AV. BOYACA
AV. CENTENARIO
AV. CIUDAD DE CALI
AUTOPISTA SUR
VIA GIRARDOT

The City

The city's historic colonial centre, **La Candelaria**, occupies an area that begins at Plaza de Bolívar and stretches northward to Avenida Jiménez de Quesada and is bordered by Carerra 10 to the west and the mountains to the east. **Downtown Bogotá** is the waning commercial centre, with several museums and office buildings, while **North Bogotá**, a catchall term for the wealthier neighbourhoods at the north of the centre, offers tonier shopping districts and gourmet ghettos.

Getting around Bogotá – and all Colombian cities for that matter – is facilitated by a foolproof numbering system, derived from the original Spanish grid layout, that makes finding an address virtually arithmetic. The names of the streets indicate their direction: **calles** run perpendicular to the hills, from east to west, while **carreras** run from north to south. Addresses are a function of both with the prefix indicating the cross street. For example, the address Cra 73 No. 12–20 can be found on Carerra 73 between calles 12 and 13.

La Candelaria

The heart of **LA CANDELARIA** is **Plaza de Bolívar**, between calles 10 and 11 and carerras 7 and 8, the site of a number of monumental buildings and disparate architectural styles spanning more than four centuries. The district is renowned for its churches (see box on p.604), few more historic than Bogotá's **Catedral**, bordering the concrete plaza, which was built between 1807 and 1823. The current model is the fourth on this site since the city's first Mass was said in a small chapel here in 1539. Restored in 1998, its opulent gold-laced interior is a tribute to the Baroque religious art popular during the colonial era. Among Colombia's many forefathers buried inside are city founder Gonzalo Jiménez de Quesado, independence hero Antonio Nariño and the colonial era's most famous ecclesiastic artist, Gregorio Vázquez de Arce y Ceballos. To the cathedral's left stands the Neoclassical **Capital**, which took a full 79 years to build. While its imposing colonnaded stone facade is impressive, the interior is now strictly off limits to tourists because of security concerns – congress meets here. On the plaza's north side, the modern **Palacio de Justicia** was reconstructed in 1999 after the original was damaged during the Army's much-criticized storming of the building in 1985 after the M19 guerrilla group had taken it over. More than a hundred people, including twelve supreme court justices, were killed in the raid. Engraved above the new building's **portal** is a somewhat ironic reminder of the episode, Santander's admonition to his compatriots that "arms will make you free, but laws will give you liberty".

Around Plaza de Bolívar

A block south of the plaza on Carerra 8 brings you to the **Palacio (or Casa) de Nariño**, the heavily fortified presidential palace and compound built in the style of Versailles. Because of security concerns, the palace's gaudy interior is only open to the public on the **last Sunday of September**, when some 80,000 visitors converge on it. However, it's possible to watch the ceremonial changing of the guard four times a week at 5.30pm from the adjacent streets.

East of Plaza de Bolívar, the streets become narrower and full of colourfully painted colonial residences. Nowhere is La Candelaria's grittier, bohemian side better captured then while walking the streets surrounding the **Plazoleta del Chorro de Quevedo**, at C 13 and Cra 2. Scholars say the tiny plaza was the site of the first Spanish settlement, though the tiled-roof colonial chapel on the southwest corner was built much later. Downhill a few blocks, housed in a fine colonial mansion, the **Donación Botero** at C 11 No. 4–41 (Mon–Sat 9am–7pm, Sun 10am–5pm; free; ⓣ1/343-1212) contains one of Latin America's largest collections of modern and Impressionist art, generously donated by Colombian artist Fernando Botero. Among

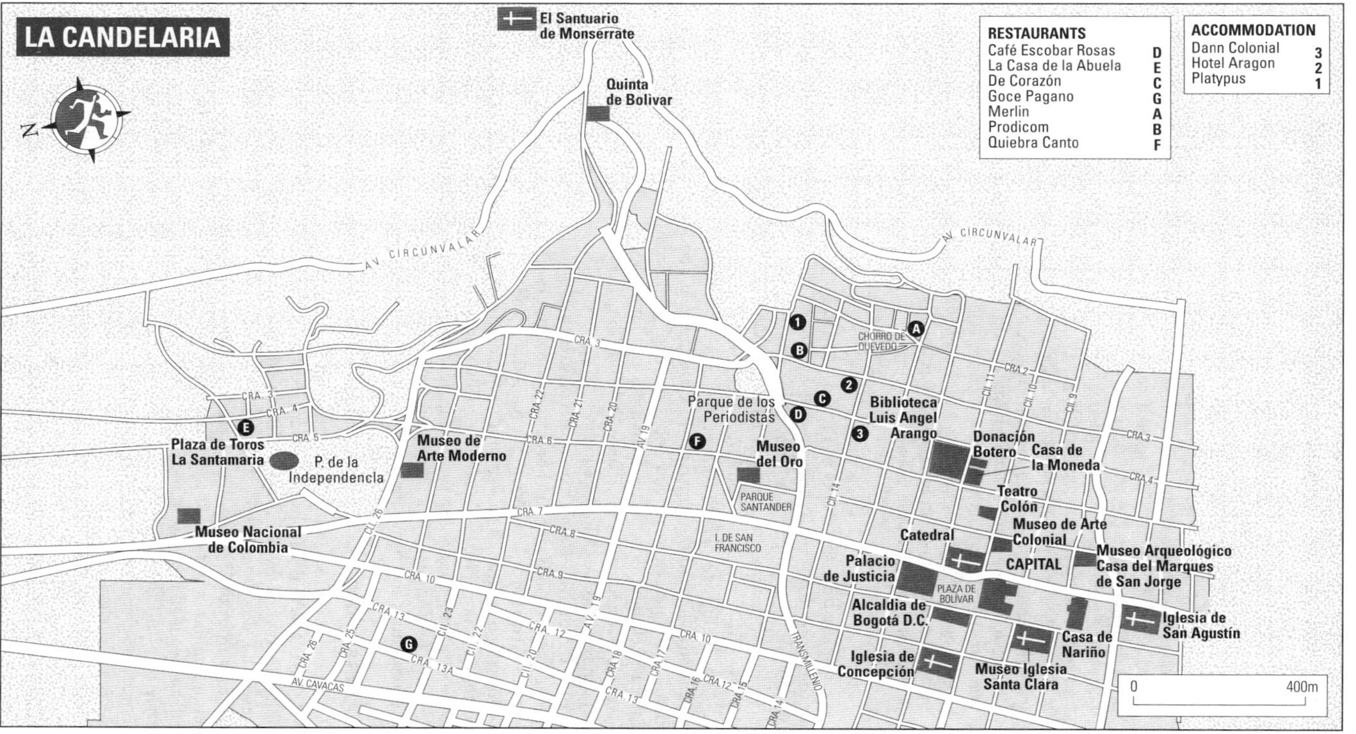
LA CANDELARIA
RESTAURANTS
Café Escobar Rosas D
La Casa de la Abuela E
De Corazón C
Goce Pagano G
Merlin A
Prodicom B
Quiebra Canto F
ACCOMMODATION
Dann Colonial 3
Hotel Aragon 2
Platypus 1
El Santuario de Monserrate
Quinta de Bolivar
AV. CIRCUNVALAR
Plaza de Toros La Santamaria
P. de la Independencia
Museo Nacional de Colombia
Museo de Arte Moderno
Parque de los Periodistas
Museo del Oro
PARQUE SANTANDER
I. DE SAN FRANCISCO
CHORRO DE QUEVEDO
Biblioteca Luis Angel Arango
Donación Botero
Casa de la Moneda
Teatro Colón
Museo de Arte Colonial
Catedral
CAPITAL
Museo Arqueológico Casa del Marques de San Jorge
Palacio de Justicia
PLAZA DE BOLÍVAR
Alcaldía de Bogotá D.C.
Iglesia de San Agustín
Casa de Nariño
Iglesia de Concepción
Museo Iglesia Santa Clara
TRANSMILENIO
AV. CAVACAS
0
400m

The churches of La Candelaria

In addition to its cathedral, La Candelaria is teeming with some of the best-preserved colonial-era **churches** and convents found in Latin America. Overlooking Palacaio Nariño at Cra 8 No. 8–91, the austere exterior of the **Iglesia Museo de Santa Clara** (Tues–Fri 9am–1pm and 2–5pm, Sat–Sun 10am–4pm), formerly part of the convent of Clarissa nuns, contrasts sharply with its gaudy, gold-plated interior. The single-nave church looks much the same as when it was built in the early part of the seventeenth century. The **Iglesia de San Francisco** (Mon–Fri 7am–7.30pm, Sat–Sun 7am–1.30pm & 5.15–7.30pm), appropriately facing the Museo del Oro (see below) on Parque Santander, is noted for its ornate golden altar, while the soaring vault at **Iglesia de La Concepción** (Mon–Sat 6.30am–6.30pm, Sun 6.30am–1pm) at C 10, No. 9–50 is a fine example of the Moorish-influenced Mudéjar style popular in the sixteenth century. Two other noteworthy colonial-era churches are the recently restored **Iglesia de San Agustín**, on Cra 7 and C 7 (Mon–Fri 7am–noon & 4–6pm, Sun 8am–11am), which is noted for its woodcarvings and frescoes, and the domed **Iglesia de San Ignacio**, on C 10, No. 6–35 (Mon–Fri, 9am–noon & 3–7pm, Sat 9am–noon & 6–7pm, Sun 9am–noon), which was begun in 1605 and became the first Jesuit church in Nueva Grenada.

those displayed are the works of Picasso, Monet, Renoir and Dali; eclipsing them are the more than one hundred pieces by Botero himself, which offer a satirical take on human plumpness. In front of the Donación Botero stands the thoroughly modern **Biblioteca Luis Angel Arango** (Mon–Sat 8am–8pm, Sun 8am–4pm; ⓣ1/286-4610), reputedly South America's largest library. Inside is the free **Museo de Arte Religioso**, which contains the largest collection of tabernacles and sacred goblets anywhere in the Americas. Recitals are held periodically in a concert hall; there's also a peaceful café and bookstore here with English-language paperbacks. Take a peek next door at the banknotes on display at the adobe and stone-built **Casa de Moneda**, or mint (Tues–Sat 10am–7pm, Sun until 6pm; free), one of the city's most elaborate colonial edifices.

After walking La Candelaria's narrow streets, cool your heels in the museums devoted to Colombia's past. For an overview of pre-Columbian cultures visit the **Museo Arqueologico** (Mon–Sat 8am–noon and 1–4pm; US$1), at Cra 6 No. 7–43, which is housed in yet another restored colonial townhouse. Two blocks north, on Cra 6 No. 9–77, is the equally impressive **Museo de Arte Colonial** (Mon–Fri 9am–5pm & Sat 10am–4pm; US$0.50), a former schoolhouse that boasts the city's first fountain. The 3000 items on display include fine colonial-era paintings, sculptures and furniture.

Monserrate

Perched above La Candelaria is the rocky outcrop known as **CERRO DE MONSERRATE** an obvious landmark from almost anywhere in the city. The hilltop, crowned by **El Santuario de Monserrate** church, offers spectacular views back down on the city. It is easily reached by a cable car (US$2 each way) up the road from the Quinta de Bolívar (see below). Alternatively it's a gruelling, but rewarding, hour-and-a-half trek along a stoned path that begins at the base of the hill and leads all the way to the summit 600 metres above. If you go on foot, depart early to avoid the harsh midday sun and leave all but essentials at the hotel as tourists are frequently robbed here; indeed, crime has got worse since 2002, when the Alcaldía cleared the mountain of dozens of illegal dwellings, some belonging to families who'd called Monseratte home for centuries. The **safest time** to go is Sunday, when you'll be accompanied by thousands of pilgrims hoping for miracles from the church's dark-skinned Christ. Atop are snack bars and a few pricey restaurants, including the French-inspired *Casa San Isidro* (ⓣ1/281-3909).

At the foot of Monserrate is the **Casa Museo Quinta de Bolívar** (Tues–Sat 9am–5pm, Fri & Sat 10am–4pm; US$0.60; ⓣ1/284-6819, ⓦwww.quintabolivar.gov.co), a spacious colonial mansion where Simon Bolívar lived from 1820 to 1829. The informative museum retells the story of Bolívar's final, desperate days in power before being banished by his political rivals. One object you won't find among the plethora of "El Libertador" paraphernalia is the sword he used to free the continent from four centuries of Spanish rule. It was stolen in 1974 from the collection containing his bedpan, military medals and billiard table in what is the now legendary debut of urban guerrilla group **M-19**. When they handed in its arsenal in 1991, the sword was quickly shuttled into the vaults of the Banco Republica for fear of another embarrassing burglary. Several of the trees in the garden were planted by Bolívar himself.

Downtown Bogotá

Beginning north of Avenida Jiménez de Quesada, **DOWNTOWN BOGOTÁ** continues roughly until Calle 60. On the northeast corner of **Parque de Santander**, at Cra 6 and C 16, is the must-see **Museo del Oro**, or Gold Museum (Tues–Sat 9am–4.30pm, Sun 10am–4.30pm; US$1; ⓣ1/343-2222, ⓦwww.banrep.gov.co/museo). Most of Colombia's gold was hauled away by its Spanish plunderers, but the leftover scraps were still sizeable enough to assemble the world's largest collection of auriferous ornaments, some 35,000 pieces strong, only a third of which are on exhibition. A maze of informative displays on Colombia's indigenous cultures culminates in the **Salon Dorado**, where 8000 gold objects dazzle in an otherwise pitch-dark bank vault brought to life by Andean pipe music and moody jungle sounds. Be sure to check out the **poporo quimbaya**, a gourd that indigenous cultures used to hold the lime that sweetened their hourly dose of coca. Self-guided audio tours in English are available for US$0.50. Next to the Gold Museum there's a permanent **Feria Artesanal**, where you can buy handicrafts – hammocks, *mochilas* or woven handbags, and *ruanas*, or ponchos.

As exhaustive as the Museo de Oro, **The Museo Nacional de Colombia** (Tues–Sat 10am–8pm, Sun 10am–4pm; US$1; ⓣ1/334-8366, ⓦwww.museonacional.gov.co), Cra 7 at C 28, affords a detailed look at the country's tumultuous history. The converted jailhouse's most impressive exhibits relate to the conquest and the origins of the beguiling El Dorado myth that so obsessed Europe. The recently remodelled third floor houses an extensive collection of paintings by modern Colombian artists, including Fernando Botero. Nearby, the **Museo de Arte Moderno**, C 24 at Cra 6 (Tues–Sat 10am–6pm & Sun 10am–3pm; US$0.50), contains six rooms of contemporary Colombian art, the largest collection in the country; there's also a *cinemeteca* here that projects art films. Two blocks north on Carerra 6, the **Plaza de Toros La Santamaria** is the Moorish-style bullring where the *fiesta brava* takes place each January and February with the enthusiastic support of well-heeled *cachacos*. If the blood-spattered spectacle seems repugnant, you can join the loud protesters that gather beyond the police barricades before each "match". Tours of the impressive complex are given on weekdays 8–11am.

North Bogotá

North of Calle 60, the museums peter out and are replaced by leafy neighbourhoods comprising of gourmet restaurants, lively bars and modern shopping malls. An exception is the cobblestoned *barrio* of **Usaquen**, which was a small village before being swallowed up by the capital's expansion. On weekends the central plaza hosts an antiques fair.

Eating, drinking and nightlife

The traditional highlander diet consisted of vegetables and starch. The city's specialty, which no visitor should leave without trying, is the *ajiaco de pollo*, a chicken stew blended with maize, three types of highland potatoes, avocado and, crucially, capers. For the most part, middle class *cachacos* prefer the same food as their counterparts in London or New York and the wide variety of ethnic offerings – Thai, Japanese, Arabic – is a reflection of the city's cosmopolitan habits. But, unlike Europe, dining out at a nice restaurant is incredibly affordable, costing on average about US$10-15 for a full meal with drinks.

Armadillo Cra 5 No. 71A–05, North Bogotá ⓣ1/345-9992/9994. This top top-notch steak and seafood restaurant caters to the business and embassy crowd.

Café and Crèpes Diag 108 No. 9A–11, North Bogotá ⓣ1/214-5312. A meeting place for mountaineers, this hard-to-find rustic lodge serves excellent *empanadas.*

La Casa de la Abuela C 27 No. 4–75, Downtown Bogotá ⓣ1/243-0831. This simple diner serves Bogotá's best – and cheapest – *ajiaco* on Friday's.

El Corral Gourmet C 81 No. 13–05 in Atlantis Shopping Centre, North Bogotá ⓣ1/530-7309. Judging from its chain-eatery decor there's nothing to distinguish El Corral from Friday's or any other American after work bars. But after you try its beefy burgers you'll know why it's so popular.

De Corazón Cra 4 No. 14–83, La Candelaria ⓣ1/282-6218. This stand-up pizza and pastry shop is open late in the heart of the historic centre. The piled-high vegetarian slice is unforgettable.

Plaza de los Nieves C 19 and 20 between Cra 8 and 9, Downtown Bogotá. A covered, outdoor market with several colourful, mom and pop stalls serving inexpensive but filling *comida corriente* and fresh fruit juices. Popular with regular Colombians.

Lina's Cra 7A No. 72–71, North Bogotá ⓣ1/310-7806/7631. Ideal for lunch, *Lina's* is a good option for suffering vegetarians or anyone craving a New York-style deli sandwich. The service is excellent.

Secretos del Mar Cra 5 No. 13–20, Downtown. Informal restaurant that's popular among locals for its fresh seafood at reasonable prices. Open at lunch.

Luna C 83 No. 12–20, North Bogotá ⓣ1/257-2088. Italian pastas and meat dishes that are pricey but so good it'll have you howling at the moon. Request the table inside the brick chimney.

Merlin Cra 2 No. 12–84, La Candelaria ⓣ1/284-9707. The house speciality of this candle-lit poets' café and restaurant, a quaintly refurbished colonial residence, is anything concocted with mushrooms.

Prodicom C 15A and Cra 3, La Candelaria ⓣ1/337-4325. This no-frills worker's co-op serves inexpensive, nutritious breakfasts. Quiet dining room ideal for reading a book but not socializing.

Wok Cra 13 No. 82–74, North Bogotá ⓣ1/218-9040. Trendy, but moderately priced sushi bar popular with the young and beautiful. All-white modern decor and electronic music add to the cosmopolitan appeal. There's also a branch located at Parque de 93.

Nightlife

Rumbear, literally to dance the rumba, is how *cachacos* refer to a night's partying, which invariably involves heavy doses of dancing. **Bars** and **discos** in La Candelaria attract a somewhat bohemian crowd and are very lively until 3am, when they shut down. Their fluorescent-lit counterparts in the Zona Rosa in North Bogotá around Calle 83 and Carerra 13, appealing to the city's beautiful people, get around the early curfew by declaring themselves social clubs. One-time membership dues can be paid at the doors.

Andrés Carne de Res C 3 No. 11A–56 in the suburb of Chia. Colombia's party central is a destination in itself. On weekends, more than a thousand people pay top dollar for the privilege of dining and dancing salsa in this rustic *rancho*, decorated with eccentric knick-knacks rescued from a junkyard. The long schlep is well worth the effort and the US$8 cover.

Café Escobar Rosas C 4 No.15–01, La Candelaria. The infectious funk music spun at this pea-sized former pharmacy makes it nearly impossible not to dance and intermingle with locals. Cheap cover.

Café Libro C 81 No. 11–92, North Bogotá. Despite its bookish-sounding name, scholars should stay away from this raucous salsa joint, which fills up after 1am. There's a string of similarly high-priced clubs nearby.

Goce Pagano Cra 13A No. 23–97. Downtown. Less is more in this legendary watering hole, which boasts a barebones dancefloor and Bogotá's largest rack of golden-era salsa LPs. Sapient owner Gustavo is a throwback to the era when the revolution was fought listening to salsa. Open Thurs–Sat only. Don't expect huge crowds but the ambience is unforgettable. No cover.
Invitro C 59 No. 6–38 North Bogotá. Popular with locals, this aquamarine-lit lounge changes moods with the hour, from quiet cocktail bar early on to late-night dance joint embracing diverse musical styles.
Quiebra Canto Cra 5, No. 17–76, Downtown. Salsa like it was meant to be – hot and sticky. Its two dance floors fill up on Wednesday for funk night. Cheap cover.

Listings

Banks and exchanges ATMs are available throughout the city. Several currency exchanges, charging 2–3 percent commission, can be found near the Museo de Oro, at most shopping centres, hotels and the city's airports. Avoid exchanging bills on the street.
Car rental Most car rental agencies have offices at the airport and in northern suburbs locations Hertz ⓣ1/541-7643 is the best bargain, costing about US$40 a day for unlimited mileage. Also try Dollar ⓣ1/691-4700 and Arrendautos ⓣ1/345-1878/1879.
Embassies Australia Cra 18 No. 90–38 ⓣ1/636-5247; Brazil C 93 No. 14-20 8th floor ⓣ1-218-0800; Canada Cra 7 No. 115–33 14th floor ⓣ1/657-9800; Ecuador C 89 No. 13–07 ⓣ1/635-0322; New Zealand Cra 7 No. 73–55 Office 401 ⓣ1/312-1231; Peru Cra 10 No. 93–48 ⓣ1/257-6292; UK Cra 9 No. 76–49 9th floor ⓣ1/317-6690; US Cra 50 Av El Dorado southeast side ⓣ1/315-1566; Venezuela Cra 13 No. 87–51 ⓣ1/640-1213.
Immigration For 30-day VISA extension (they cost US$18) visit the DAS (Departamento Administrativo de Seguridad) at their Dirección de Extranjería office C 100 No. 11B–27 between 7.30am and 4pm Mon–Fri.
Medical Call ABC Ambulancias ⓣ1/226-9365 or 481-0333 for on ambulance. Clinica Marly at C 50 No. 9–67 ⓣ1/570-4424 or 572-5011 is a modern medical facility accustomed to attending foreigners.
Police Headquarters of the tourist police is at Cra 13 No. 26–62 ⓣ1/337-4413. In an emergency dial ⓣ112 from any phone.
Taxis Always best to call at night. Try Radio Taxi ⓣ1/288-8888, Taxi Real ⓣ1/333-3333 or Taxi Express ⓣ1/411-1111. There's a small surcharge.
Tour agencies Ecoguías Cra 7 No. 57–39 Of 501 (call first for appointment) ⓣ1/212-6049 or 345-0197, ⓦwww.ecoguias.com; **Vitramar** Cra 14 No. 95–69 ⓣ1/616-1484, ⓦwww.vitramar.com.

Zipaquirá

High on the list for anyone staying more than a few days in Bogotá is a visit to the magnificent salt cathedral of **Zipaquirá** (Tues–Sun 9am–5pm; US$0.50), some fifty kilometres north of the city. Inaugurated in 1995 to great fanfare, the cathedral lies completely underground, topped by a huge mountain that was mined by local Indians even before the Spaniards started salting away its hidden treasures in the seventeenth century. It replaced an earlier chapel that was built in the 1950s and closed in 1990 after it was deemed at risk of collapse. As you descend 180 metres into the earth, you'll pass **fourteen chapels** built entirely of salt that glow like marble in the soft light. The main nave is a sublime feat of modern engineering, complete with the world's largest subterranean cross and a baptism carved from a natural waterfall of stalagmites. Above ground, there's a museum (same hours as cathedral) explaining the history of salt extraction.

Mass is held on Sundays at 12.30pm and, on religious holidays, concerts are held here. Informative tours are available in English for US$3.50. From Bogotá take the Transmilenio to the Portal del Norte station at the end of the #2 or #3 line and from there a *buseta* (US$0.75) to Zipaquirá. From the centre of Zipaquirá, it's a short cab ride or fifteen-minute walk to the entrance.

5.2

North to Venezuela

Just a few kilometres from Bogotá the smog and busy streets quickly give way to a rolling spread of rustic farming hamlets and resplendent piedmonts. The Central Andean departments of Boyacá, Cundimarca and Santander are both geographically and historically the epicentre of Colombia. First inhabited centuries ago by the gold-worshipping Muisca Indians, the area played a pivotal role in forging Colombia's national identity. Near **Tunja**, one of Colombia's oldest cities, stands the bridge where Bolívar defeated the Spanish army in 1819, clearing the way for independence. An hour by bus from Tunja is one of Colombia's best-preserved colonial towns, the sleepy **Villa de Leyva**, whose savoury restaurants and refined B&Bs help maintain the city's aristocratic air. Beyond the reaches of the weekend Bogotá crowd, **Barichara**, while lacking Villa de Leyva's genteel atmosphere, is even more peaceful and just as comely, while further north the thoroughly modern city of **Bucaramanga** makes a pleasant enough midway point if you're heading to the coast. On the border with Venezuela lies **Cúcuta**, where the tripartite federation of Gran Colombia between Colombia, Ecuador and Venezuela was born in 1821. All these destinations are easily accessed **by bus**.

Tunja

Capital of Boyacá department, **TUNJA** is one of the foremost preserves of the country's colonial heritage. It was founded in 1539 on the ruins of the ancient Muisca capital of Hunza, and its architectural treasures make a worthwhile few hours' detour for anyone visiting the more popular Villa de Leyva. It is also the most convenient base from which to visit **El Puente de Boyacá** (see box below). Two early homes have been converted into museums exhibiting colonial artwork. On Plaza Bólivar, the **Casa del Fundador Suárez Rendón** (Wed–Sun 8.30am–12.30pm & 2–6pm; free), home of the town's founder, dates from 1540 and was built in the Moorish Mudéjar style; it's also the site of the local tourism office. At C 20 and Cra 8 the 1590 **Casa de Don Juan de Vargas** (daily 8am–noon & 1–6pm; US$0.50) stands out for its eighteenth-century interior frescoes as well as its garden, which suggests an Andalusian landscape.

Like much of the town's architecture, Plaza Bólivar's **Catedral**, built in 1569, contains Islamic motifs. More ornate are the **Santo Domingo** and **Santa Clara** churches; the former, on Calle 11 between Carerra 19 and 20, is known for its

El Puente de Boyacá

About sixteen kilometres south of Tunja on the main road back to Bogotá is a reconstructed colonial-era **El Puente de Boyacá** bridge commemorating the Battle of Boyacá of August 7, 1819, which cleared the way for Bólivar and his freedom fighters to march triumphantly into Bogotá. The trickling river's trivial girth lends a new perspective to the popular myth of Bólivar's bravery – perhaps during the battle it formed a more substantial natural barrier. There's also a monument to El Libertador here, as well as a restaurant and small museum.

Rosario Chapel which exhibits religious paintings and woodwork by Gregorio Váquez de Arce y Ceballos, while the latter, on Cra 7 and C 19, was the first convent in the region.

If you need a **place to stay**, the family-run *Saboy* (☎8/742-3492; ❶), at C 19 No. 10–40, maintains a nice covered patio and is very clean. They also serve breakfast. For Carefully prepared regional **cuisine** in a fine-dining environment, try *Brasas de Oro* at Av Norte 33–06.

Villa de Leyva

Just four hours by bus from Bogotá and an hour from Tunja, the scenic and near spotless **VILLA DE LEYVA** is rightfully the hub of tourism in the high Andes heartland. Whether you're hunting for fossils or just sitting around the 400-year-old plaza drinking sangria, the town's untroubled ambience penetrates everything.

Founded in 1572, the town is a showcase of colonial architecture and was declared a national monument in 1954, one of a few attributes that brings people to visit; it's also a centre for the arts, and the municipal government sponsors frequent cultural events with the city's numerous working artists. Posh *cachacos* typically descend in droves on weekends, though during the rest of the week, the town of 4500 is relatively peaceful. The **tourist office** at Cra 9 No. 13–04 is helpful in pointing out what's going on.

Accommodation

Villa de Leyva has a wide range of quality **hotels**, many of them former colonial residences. Discounts of up to thirty percent are often available during the week; book early for weekends.

Dino's Cra 9 No. 12–52 ☎8/732-0803. Colonial house on main plaza converted to a youth hostel, *Dino's* nice lounge and pizzeria look out on to an internal courtyard. Rooms feature private bath. ❶

El Marqués de San Jorge C 14 No. 9–20 ☎8/732-0480/240. Colonial mansion with cosy, clean rooms overlooking a beautiful courtyard. The friendly English-speaking owner offers discounts during the week. ❹

Plaza Mayor Cra 10 No. 12–31 ☎8/732-0425/832. Centrally located on the main plaza, the hotel is surprisingly quiet. Its large, decorative rooms are ideal for romantic couples on a budget. ❺

El Portal de la Candelaria C 18 No. 8–12 ☎8/732-1953. Tranquil hotel five blocks from centre with rooms on the smallish side; there's also a colourful restaurant decorated with antiques on site. ❹

The Town

Villa de Leyva's patrimony is immaculately preserved. The impressive **Plaza Mayor** is one of the largest in Colombia, completely paved over in large cobblestones, surrounded by whitewashed colonial buildings and centred on a stone well hailing from the colonial era. Dominating the plaza is the huge stone portal of the seventeenth-century **Catedral**, rebuilt after an 1845 earthquake. Directly in front across the plaza, the **Casa-Museo Luis Alberto Acuña** (daily 9am–5pm; US$0.50) houses sculptures and large murals by the early avant-garde twentieth-century artist it is named after. A block along north along Carerra 10, the **Iglesia del Carmen** is noted for its high, pointed bell tower, which overlooks a tiny, secluded plaza. Facing the simple church is one of Colombia's largest religious art museums, the **Monasterio de las Carmelitas** (Sat & Sun & holidays only, 10am–1pm & 3–5pm; US$0.50), containing large numbers of wooden icons from the Church's early years of proselytizing in the New World. A few blocks east, at Cra 8 and C 15, the **Casa de Antonio Ricaurte** was home to a national hero who fought for Bólivar. Operated by the Colombian armed forces since 1970, the attractive house contains military objects pertaining to one of the country's most noteworthy patriots.

The arid desert highlands surrounding Villa de Leyva are now a magnet for trekkers, but 120 million years ago the huge flood plain would have been better suited to scuba diving. The ocean waters have since retreated and in their wake they've left the country's largest repository of **fossils**. To the delight of avid palaeontologists, as well as the simply curious, much of the area's fossil-rich soil has barely been sifted. What has been discovered is on display at the well-maintained **Palaeontological Museum**, a kilometre north of the town along Carerra 9 (Tues–Sat 9am–noon & 2–5pm, Sun 9am–3pm; US$0.75). Further afoot, about an hour's pleasant walk from the Plaza Mayor, **El Fósil** (daily 9am–5pm; US$0.75) is a small museum built around the fossil remains of a Kronosaurus, a prehistoric marine lizard found by a *campesino* here in 1977. The 12.8 metre-long lizard, whose head exceeds that of North America's Tyrannosaurus Rex, is one of only two in the world excavated in its entirety. Two kilometres further along the road from El Fosil, you'll find **El Infiernito**, a Muisca observatory made famous in tourist photos because of its large, phallic stone monoliths.

Eating and drinking

Stiff competition among quality **restaurants** means that even backpackers can eat like gourmands. Although Villa de Leyva attracts large numbers of visitors on weekend the **nightlife** tends to be subdued though a few pubs with live guitar music are always open around the main plaza.

Casa Blanca C 13 No. 7–16. This austere eatery serves up cheap *comida corriente* as well as a range of good fruit juices. It is very popular with locals.

La Dicha Buena Cra 9 No. 13–41. At this hole-in-the-wall restaurant just off the plaza, you'll be warmly welcomed by its friendly owner, who also doubles as cook and waitress. *La Dicha Buena* serves excellent breakfasts with hot chocolate as well as good *empanadas* for moderate prices.

Sazón & Sabor next to *Plaza Mayor* hotel on Cra 10. This candle-lit, late-night pub features low-key guitar music.

Los Tres Caracoles C 13 No. 9–82. Traditional restaurant serving Spanish paella and beef. Live music and good-humoured staff makes for a fun atmosphere.

Towards Bucaramanga

With its undulating brick roads, clay-tiled *tejas* roofs draped in bougainvillaea flowers and single-story adobe homes, the quiet alpine hamlet of **BARICHARA**, population 10,000, looks and feels much like it did when it was founded some 250 years ago. Although it lacks the obvious attractions of more affluent Villa de Leyva, the town is just as well preserved, which is why it was declared a national monument in 1978. Barichara is also a lot less crowded, making it an ideal resting spot for weary travellers on the way to Venezuela. Indeed, the town's name comes from an Indian word, *Barachala*, meaning "a good place to rest". Check out the striking **Catedral de la Inmaculada Concepeción** on the Parque Central, which stands on fluted, sandstone columns. At the time of writing, there are plans to convert the restored colonial house of the former president **Casa de Aquileo Parra Gómez** on Cra 2 between calles 5 and 6 into a museum.

If you're looking for a **place to stay**, try *Rosari García*, on C 10 No. 7–46 (ⓣ7/267-225; ❶), a *casa de familia* that offers home stays.

Bucaramanga

Founded in 1622, **BUCARAMANGA** has since shed much of its colonial heritage and evolved into one of Colombia's largest, most modern cities. There's little to detain visitors, but the capital of Santander department makes a convenient stopover point for anyone travelling to the coast of Venezuela. If you're lucky enough to make it here during Easter Week, be sure to try the local delicacy – *hormigas culonas*, or fried ants, which are available in local markets and food stalls along main highways into town.

For a short while in 1828, El Libertador lived in the **Casa de Bolívar** (Tues–Sat 9am–noon & 2–5pm; free), which now contains a small historical museum and research centre. It's near Parque García Rovira, the city's administrative centre, on Calle 37 between Carerras 12 and 13. Across the street another colonial mansion houses the **Casa de la Cultura** (Mon–Sat 9am–5pm; US$0.50), with a museum on regional handicrafts. If you need a break from this historical fare, head out to the **Jardín Botánico Eloy Valenzuela** (weekends 8am–11am & 2–5pm; US$0.25) in the Bucarica suburb, which belongs to the agency representing the tobacco industry that has a strong presence here. The Río Frío runs through the verdant gardens.

Practicalities

If you want **accommodation** in Bucaramanga, *Meliá Confort Chicamocha*, on C 34 No. 31–24 (☎7/634-3000; ❻), offers all the comfort and services expected from an international chain, including swimming pool, sauna and cable TV. *La Hormiga*, on Cra 17C No. 55–56 ☎7/644-9010; ❷), is an affordable, clean hotel with restaurant, bar and swimming pool, while *Tayrona*, on C 13 No. 19–39 ☎7/630-4832; ❷), is a budget hotel for backpackers.

For **local cuisine** try *La Puerta del Sol* at Cra 30 No. 65-08, whose speciality is a heaping dish of regional favourites such as *arepas santandereanas*, baked goat and jerked beef. A less expensive option is the 24-hour *El Viejo Chiflas* at Cra 33 and C 34, while *DiMarco* on Cra 28 No. 54–21 specializes in beef.

Crossing into Venezuela: Cúcuta

The only reason to visit **CÚCUTA**, capital of Norte de Santander department, is if you're heading overland to Venezuela, as the city offers precious few tourist attractions and the outlying area has been the focus of intense guerrilla and paramilitary activity in recent years. If you do spend time in the city, take a peek inside the ornate Neoclassical **Palacio de la Gobernación**, the department's main administrative building on Av 5 between calles 13 and 14 and the **Casa de la Culutra**, at C 13 No. 3–67, which contains a museum recounting the city's history. Just eight kilometres away is the small colonial town of **Villa del Rosario**, where a municipal park houses the ruins of the temple where Gran Colombia's independence was declared in 1821.

Several basic *residencias* are situated along Av 7, though the area can be somewhat dangerous at night. One of the few not doubling as a love hotel is *Imperial* at Av 7 No. 6–28 ☎7/572-3321; ❷), while *Amaruc* at Av 5 No. 9–73 ☎7/571-7625; ❹) costs more but offers rooms with air conditioning and TVs. Visitors should move with utmost **caution** and think twice before crossing into Venezuela from here. At the **Venezuelan consulate** (Mon–Fri 8am–noon & 1–4pm; ☎7/713-983 or 781-034), at Av 0 and C 8, you can purchase a tourist visa for US$30. You will need to present a photo and a passport valid for at least six more months; they may ask to see an onward ticket. Entering into Venezuela from Cúcuta, the first town you reach is San Antonio, but it's advisable to take the bus (US$2) directly to the larger **San Cristóbal** if you want to make connections to **Caracas** (see p.1022).

5.3

Cartagena and the Caribbean

Ever since Rodrigo de Bastidas became the first European to touch Colombian soil in Santa Marta in 1525, there's been a long history of foreigner fascination with the country's Caribbean coastline, and hundreds of thousands of outsiders follow in his footsteps annually. Indeed, if it weren't for Colombia's reputation for violence **Cartagena** would be even more of a tourist gold mine than it already is. In addition to hot weather and cool breezes, there are the architectural treasures remaining from the town's splendorous past as the main conduit for the Spanish crown's imperial plundering. For its extensive fortifications and colonial legacy, the walled city was declared a Unesco World Heritage site in 1984. But Cartagena occupies just a small fraction of the country's 1600-kilometre Caribbean coastline. From the dense jungles of the **Darien Gap** on the border with Panama to the arid salt planes of the **Guajira Peninsula**, there's a wider variety of things to see and do here than anywhere else in the country. If it's tropical paradise you're after, head to the white, jungle-fringed beaches of **Tayrona National Park** near Santa Marta. The translucent waters around **Santa Marta** are also one of the most inexpensive places in the world to learn to scuba dive. Inland, the most mesmerizing part about the six-day trek to the archeological ruins of **Ciudad Perdida** is the chance to cross paths with the coca-chewing Kogis, who live almost as primitively as they did centuries ago.

The Andean highlands may be Colombia's sober-minded nerve centre, without which the wheels of business and government wouldn't churn, but the low-lying Caribbean is definitely its heart and soul, in which all Colombians would choose to dwell if it were not for life's more mundane considerations. Everyone, of course, except the affable *costeños* (those who live on the coast), who take to the pursuit of leisure with commensurate ease.

Cartagena de Indias and around

Without a doubt one of the Caribbean's hottest and most beautiful cities, **CARTAGENA DE INDIAS** offers all-night partying, photogenic colonial architecture, gourmet dining and beachcombing; the question isn't whether to come but how long to stay.

Founded in 1533, it was one of the first Spanish cities in the New World and served as the main port through which the continent's riches were salted away to the mother country. Indeed, the Spanish galleon *San José*, still lying fifty kilometres from the harbour at a depth of 750 metres, is purported to have been carrying a booty worth more than US$3 billion when it was sunk by an English convoy in 1708.

Not surprisingly, the city proved an appetizing target for English pirates prowling the Caribbean, and it suffered several dreadful sieges in the sixteenth century. Sir Francis Drake led the most famous raid in 1586, setting fire to the cathedral and holding the town hostage for more than a hundred days before extracting a hefty ransom. After "the Dragon" withdrew, the Spaniards began construction on the elaborate network of fortifications that are now the city's hallmark and source of its timeless beauty. In total there are some eleven kilometres of heavy, stone ramparts encircling the city.

Since independence, however, the city's fortunes have declined precipitously. Other than the horse-drawn carriages locals call *huelepedos* (or farties) that shepherd tourists (and odorous fumes) around the city, little of the city's aristocratic ways remain. Instead, the overcrowded city has the crumbling look and feel of Old Havana. Along cobblestone streets laundry hangs from carved wood balconies while shirtless men plays dominoes in the plazas and shuffle their feet to a radio playing a Cuban *son* or Colombian *cumbia*.

Arrival, information and city transport

Cartagena's **Rafael Nuñez International Airport** is located in the *barrio* of Crespo, a ten-minute (US$2.50) taxi or bus (US$0.20) ride from the centre. The city's large **bus terminal** is some 45 minutes away by bus from the centre; a taxi will set you back US$4.

Despite the huge numbers of visitors Cartagena receives, official information is hard to come by, and the two main tourist offices are both outside the city centre. **Proturismo** (☎5/665-1843) is located at the Muelle Turistica and is dedicated primarily to selling excursions to the outlying beaches. A short walk away, the **Cartagena Convention & Visitor Bureau** (☎5/660-2418) inside the convention centre on Cra 8 in Getsemaní supplies old maps during weekday office hours.

The best way to get around the Old City is **by foot** as streets are narrow and usually congested. To get **to Bocagrande** it's a twenty-minute walk from the Old City, or a taxi ride (US$1.50). Almost as quick, the more colourful city **buses** cost about US$0.25. When walking around at night, especially in Getsemaní, it's best to take a **taxi** as streets are poorly lit and the likelihood of being robbed greater. Reputable companies include Telecomsa ☎5/653-2222 and Capilla del Mar ☎5/665-1930.

Accommodation

Finding comfortable **accommodation** at an affordable price is next to impossible in the Old City and only slightly easier in Bocagrande. At the other end of the price range, charming hotels converted from colonial-era buildings abound. Prices during the summer high season from December to February usually surge thirty to fifty percent.

Capilla del Mar Cra 1 No. 8–12, Bocagrande ☎5/665-1666, 665-1140. Every room is large and has a balcony overlooking the beach. Top floor *bar giratorio* spins while you enjoy cocktails. There's a pool, and breakfast is included. ❼

Casa Viena C San Andrés 30–53, Getsemaní ☎5/664-6242 or 660-2311. Full service backpackers hostel with kitchen just beyond Puerta del Reloj outside Old City. Dorm or private rooms are available with bath and a/c, and the staff is friendly. Be careful walking streets at night. ❶

Charleston Cartagena Cra 3A No. 31–23 Plaza Santa Teresa, the Old City ☎5/664-9494/9547. An architectural delight, this restored seventeenth-century convent has graceful rooms, while its fifth-floor pool with public bar offers panoramic views of the city. ❾

Hostal Tres Banderas C Cochera del Hobo 38–66, the Old City ☎5/660-0160. A small B&B a block from Plaza San Diego, *Hostal Tres Banderas* offers good value and quiet, air-conditioned rooms. Its lovely patio features caged parakeets and a cooling fountain. ❺

San Martín Av San Martín 8–164, Bocagrande ☎5/665-4142/6884. Pleasant and reasonably priced rooms with a/c and sun-filled lounge. A block away from the beach. ❺

Santa Clara Hotel C del Torno, the Old City ☎5/664-8040. Magnificently restored seventeenth-century convent converted into twenty-first-century love palace. This elegant boutique hotel figures prominently in Gabriel García Márquez's 1994 novella *Of Love and Other Demons*. Even if you can't afford a room here, the bar in the catacombs is worth a visit. ❾

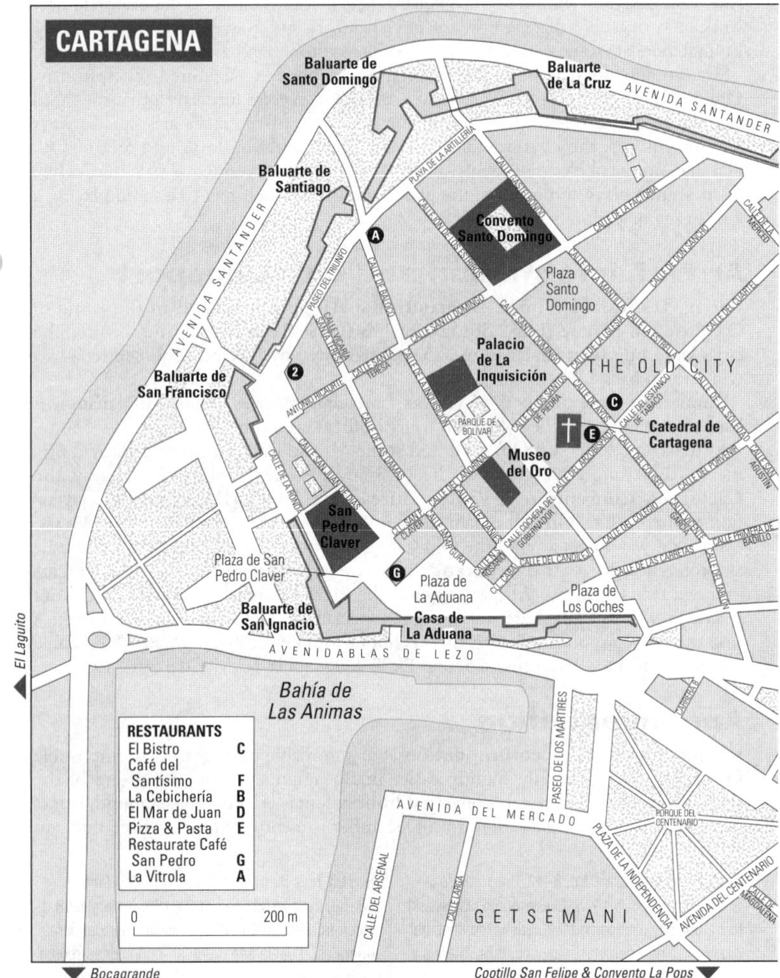

The City

While Cartagena has grown into a city of almost a million inhabitants, the **Old City**, at least architecturally, is virtually unchanged from the colonial era. With its shadowy, narrow streets and heavy stonework, it has an uncanny medieval feel – fertile ground for a young journalist by the name of Gabriel García Marquez to hone the arts of magical realism in the 1940s. **Bocagrande**, a ten-minute walk south of the Old City, is Cartagena's commercial centre, an L-shaped peninsula dotted by touristy hotels and fast-food restaurants. Although a thin strip of sand here faces the Caribbean, the beach tends to be overcrowded and dirty. Although these are popular with locals, most tourists will prefer to take a boat from the Muelle Turistica to the **Islas del Rosario** or **Playa Blanca** on Barú island, some of the most isolated

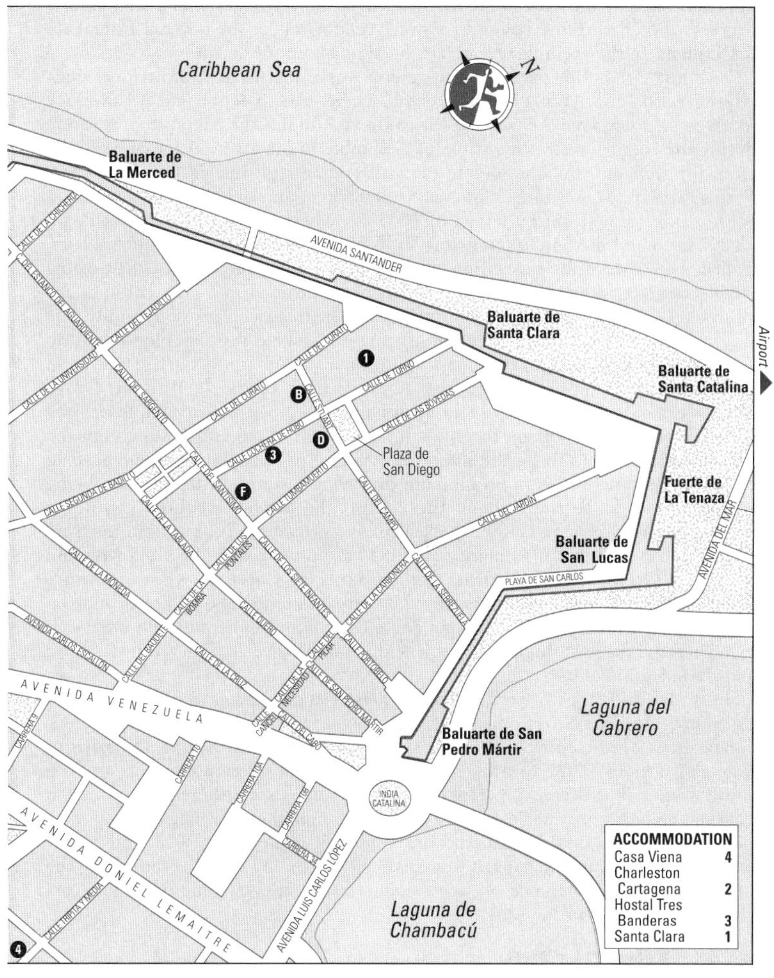

ACCOMMODATION	
Casa Viena	4
Charleston Cartagena	2
Hostal Tres Banderas	3
Santa Clara	1

and scenic beaches anywhere in the Caribbean. Less scenic but more accessible, by bus, **Marbella** and **La Boquilla** are two quieter beaches preferred by locals that are northeast of Cartagena.

The Old City

Bursting with history and buzzing with Caribbean devil-may-care spirit, Cartagena's walled **Old City** is where the bulk of the sightseeing is. The city's main entranceway is the three-arched **Puerta del Reloj**, which gives way to the **Plaza de los Coches**, a former slave-trading square. Today, it's the area where horse-drawn carriages can be hired at night for romantic tours around the city and the stage for a variety of street performances. In one dark yet irrefutably Colombian spectacle, a toy poodle feigns death after being shot by his owner's finger pistol only miraculously to come back to life moments later. Equally entertaining are the local dandies who chat up the voluptuous sweet vendors under the covered **Portal de los Dulces**. In the evening, several bars open up above the arcade.

Once inside the Old City, expect to get lost – as if the labyrinth of narrow, winding streets isn't disorienting enough, each block bears a different name. A half-block south of the Puerta del Reloj is the **Plaza de la Aduana**, the administrative centre during the colonial era, with a statue of Columbus in the centre. A few steps in the same direction and you'll bump into the dank and decrepit **Iglesia Convento San Pedro Claver** (daily 8am–5.30pm; US$1.50 for museum only), on the quiet plaza of the same name. Built by Jesuits in 1603, it's where Spanish-born priest Pedro Claver lived and died, in 1654, before his canonization some two centuries later. Called the "slave of the slaves" for his door-to-door fundraising on behalf of the city's slaves, the ascetic monk's skull and bones – guarded in a glass coffin at the church's altar – is an important pilgrimage site for the local black community. The well-preserved church has a religious art museum, where you can plop down on the same throne Pope John Paul II sat in during his 1986 visit to Cartagena.

A popular meeting place for locals is the tree-lined **Plaza de Bolívar**. On its west side stands the **Palacio de la Inquisición**, a block-long example of late-colonial architecture, perhaps the city's finest remnant of the era. It was completed in 1776 and believed to be the site where at least 800 people were sentenced to death. At the time of writing, a museum displaying torture instruments was being renovated inside. To the right of the Palacio, the **Museo de Oro** (Mon–Fri 8.30am–noon & 2–6pm; US$0.75) specializes in ornaments hailing from the Sinú culture and is well worth seeing if you don't have time to visit the Gold Museum in Bogotá. On the northeast corner of the plaza is the **Catedral**, whose construction began in 1575, was almost destroyed by cannon fire in 1586 by Drake and was not completed until 1612. Its baroque dome dates from this century, but otherwise it respects the original three-nave form with an impressive altar carved from wood and shrouded in gold.

Head a block west past a series of nicely preserved balustrades to the lively **Plaza de Santo Domingo**. In front of Fernando Botero's satirical *La Gorda* sculpture is Cartagena's oldest church: the **Iglesia y Convento de Santa Domingo**. Completed in 1579, the fortress-like structure's austere interior shows its age. On the Baroque altar there's a Christ carved from the sixteenth century which is believed to perform miracles. In front of the church, there's a neighbourhood of sidewalk cafes and outdoor bars that are popular in the evening. While the plaza's environs are virtually unchanged since the city's birth, the mood is spoiled by the otherwise harmless presence of street vendors hawking everything from gold earrings to imitation Cuban cigars.

East of the Old City

For a bird's-eye view of Cartagena walk up 150 metres to the **Convento de la Popa** (daily 8am–5pm; US$0.75) on the hillock of the same name just outside the city's walls. Hiring a guide at the base of the hill is recommended if you propose to make the ascent. The restored whitewashed chapel, built in 1608, is clearly visible from almost anywhere in the city. On February 2, when the city celebrates the day of its patron saint, the **Virgin of Candelaria**, protector against pirates and the plague, a candle-lit procession of pilgrims storms the hill.

More than a single, uniform wall, Cartagena is surrounded by a series of impressive fortresses, most of which are still standing. The largest and most important was **Castillo de San Felipe de Barajas** (daily 8am–6pm, US$2.50), a maze of tunnels, underground chambers and drawbridges just east of the walled city along Avenida Pedro de Heredia. Built between 1536 and 1657, the castle is an ideal spot from which to watch the sunset. Most of Cartagena's other remaining defences were built much later than San Felipe, during the dawning of the Spanish Empire in the

△ Ancient indigenous statue, Parque Arqueológico

late eighteenth century. Visible on excursions to Islas del Rosario (see opposite), the **Fuerte de San Fernando** on **Tierrabomba Island** was built to seal off Bocachica, which, after a sandbar blocked Bocagrande in 1640, was the only access to the city's harbour. As part of the complex engineering feat, a heavy metal chain was dangled across the entrance to the restored **Fuerte San José** on Barú Island.

Bocagrande and city beaches

A cab ride (US$1.50) south of the Old City is **Bocagrande**, Cartagena's modern sector, a thin isthmus dotted with high-rise hotels and timeshare apartments catering to Colombian vacationers. Other than its overcrowded and dirty beach, the closest one to the Old City, there's little reason to visit Bocagrande unless you're somehow craving a hamburger or movie. For a more peaceful tan, take a bus or cab north along the coast to **Marbella**, which is also good for swimming. Twenty minutes past the airport, the quaint fishing village of **La Boquilla** features a quiet beach, where it's possible to eat fish under the shade of a palm tree.

Eating

Among Cartagena's greatest charms is its array of fine **restaurants** – nowhere else in Colombia is the urge to splurge so intense. However, be sure to choose wisely before settling on where to dine as many restaurants are overpriced and mediocre. The outdoor **cafés** surrounding Plaza Santa Domingo, though inviting, are better for an after-dinner cigar then for a gourmet meal. Better choices exist on adjacent streets and near the less central Plaza San Diego, and cheaper alternatives are found in Getsemaní, just beyond the walled city.

El Bistro C de Ayos No. 4–42/46, the Old City. German-owned bistro serving moderately priced pastas and sandwiches made with home-made bread.

La Bonga del Sinú C del Arsenal and C Larga, Getsemaní. *La Bonga del Sinú* specializes in local, Caribbean cuisine, especially beef dishes, at low prices. Close to some of the city's hottest rumba spots.

Café del Santísimo C de Santísimo No. 8–19, the Old City ⓣ5/664-3316. The seafood served in this quiet, leafy patio is spiced with Caribbean-flavoured salsas. Pricey; reservations are recommended.

La Cebichería C Stuart next to *Hotel Santa Clara*, the Old City. Moderately priced *cebiche* topped with mandarins and other tropical fruit sauces. Good for a quiet lunch.

El Mar de Juan Plaza de San Diego, the Old City ⓣ5/664-5862. Outdoor dining in the plaza provides unbeatable ambience for the moderately priced Thai-inspired seafood dishes. Live music is sung by the owner, a local soap-opera celebrity.

Pizza & Pasta C del Arzobispado and C del Coliseo, the Old City Cheap and quick, this is one of the better quality inexpensive restaurants.

Restaurate Café San Pedro Plaza San Pedro Clave No. 30, the Old City. Expensive, but tasty seafood is on offer here, as is good sushi.

La Vitrola C Baloco No. 2–01, the Old City ⓣ5/660-0711or 664-8243. The long-time standard bearer of haute cuisine in Cartagena is pricey but well worth it. Enjoy excellent seafood and beef dishes accompanied by live, unintrusive Cuban music. Reservations recommended.

Drinking and nightlife

When the hot sun sinks into the ocean Cartagena gets its second wind. "The hour of mysterious flourishing" poet Guillermo Valencia called the peaceful twilight hour, start of one of Colombia's liveliest Caribbean **nightlife** centres. There's a large concentration of tourist bars and dance clubs **above the Portal de los Dulces** overlooking the Plaza de los Coches. Depending on business and the season, most will charge a small cover. Locals tend to flock to the cheaper but no less rowdy clubs in **Getsemaní**.

Antigua Bar Plaza de los Coches, the Old City. Each of the new, modern-looking night club's four floors plays a different music – salsa, disco or merengue. Fills up on weekends.

Mr Babilla C 24 No. 8B–137, Getsemaní. It's impossible not to dance in this club, where the party usually extends until dawn with people dancing on the bar.

Quiebra Canto Cra 8B No. 25–10, Getsemaní. A local legend where old-school salsa mixes with bottomless shot glasses of locally distilled *ron*. The second-floor balcony offers a great view of Puerta del Reloj and the Old City. Great atmosphere for revellers and wall urchins alike.

Tu Candela Above the Portal de los Dulces, the Old City. Cartagena's wildest and most popular salsa club is frequented by tourists and Colombian jetsetters, who dance the night away packed tightly in this second-floor club. It is possible to enjoy a quiet beer early in the evening.

Listings

Banks and exchange Several banks with 24-hour ATMs and *casas de cambio* are on the Plaza de la Audana and adjoining streets as well as along Avenida San Martín in Bocagrande.

Car rental There's a concentration of rental agencies at the airport and along Avenida San Martín in Bocagrande. Upscale hotels in the Old City also have representatives in their foyers. Try Hertz ⓣ5/665-3359, National ⓣ5/665-3336 or Alquilautos ⓣ5/665-8459.

Embassies and consulates Canada Cra 3 No. 8–129 ⓣ5/665-5838

Immigration For visa extensions DAS has an office in Calle Gastelbondo near the Ramparts. Otherwise dial ⓣ153 for any immigration-related emergencies.

Medical Hospital Bocagrande ⓣ5/665-5270 on C 5 and Cra 6.

Police Dial ⓣ112 for the Policía Nacional.

Taxis Telecomsa ⓣ5/660-0006 and La Matuna ⓣ5/660-0000 both have 24-hour pick-up service.

Islas del Rosario and other beaches

About forty kilometres out to sea from Cartagena lies an archipelago of small coral islands known as the **ISLAS DEL ROSARIO**. In total there are more than seventy islands, many of them private islets barely large enough for a bungalow. The forested **Isla Grande** is the largest settlement, site of several exclusive resorts and a two-hour nature trail. The islands are surrounded by coral reefs sunk in transparent waters that form every possible hue of turquoise. The entire area is protected by the **Corales del Rosario National Park**.

The carnaval at Barranquilla

Despite being Colombia's fourth largest city and main port, **Barranquilla**, on the mouth of the Río Magdalena, about three hours by bus from Cartagena, would be all but overlooked if it were not for its annual **Carnaval** (ⓦwww.carnavaldebarranquilla.com). For four days at the start of each March, this miserably hot, industrial city drapes itself in a salmagundi of vibrant colours, playful costumes and pulsating music – salsa, *cumbia*, *vallenato* and African drumming. Preparations begin much earlier, in mid-January, with the public reading of a municipal diktat ordering residents to have fun. Once the festivities begin, the town converts into one huge street party, kicked off by traditional parades like the "Battle of the Flowers" and "Dance of the Caiman". Parallel to the festivities, the city-sponsored gay Carnaval, though less publicized, is equally bacchanalian. Although barely known outside Latin America, Barranquilla's festivities are second only to Rio's Carnaval (see p.339) in size.

Be sure to arrange **accommodation** well in advance if you visit during Carnaval. Options range from *Canadiense*, on C 45 No. 36–142 (ⓣ5/341-5391; ❷), a no-frills budget hotel two blocks from bus station, to *El Prado*, at Cra 54 No. 70–10 (ⓣ5/368-0111, ⓦwww.cotelco.org/hotelprado; ❼), Barranquilla's most traditional and upscale hotel, which has a pool, business centre and tennis courts. *Hotel Dorado*, on Cra 42F No. 79–38 (ⓣ5/360-2251, 356-8101; ❹), is a good-value modern establishment, with a swimming pool.

Cruises to the islands depart early in the morning from Cartagena at the Muelle de los Pegasos, commonly called Muelle Turistica. Most day-trips cost around US$12 and include admission to the national park, a visit to an open-air aquarium showing off some of the Islas' 2500 plant and animal species, including stingrays, giant sea turtles, sharks and hoop-jumping dolphins and beach time after a meal. The *Alcatraz*, operated by Cocoliso (Ⓣ665-9339) in Av San Martín No. 8–19, Bocagrande, provides economical daily service throughout the year. Cocoliso also run a kitschy but peaceful resort for honeymooners starting at US$70 a night for a small junior suite. On Isla Grande, *San Pedro de Majagua* is an upscale resort renting luminous *cabañas* (❽) and offering scuba diving courses. It's run by the *Santa Clara Hotel* in Cartagena (see p.613). All bookings must be made on the mainland.

Facing the Islas del Rosario and at the opposite end of the comfort spectrum is the wonderfully remote **Playa Blanca**, on Barú Island. By road or ferry, Playa Blanca is less than an hour away from Cartegena, and once here all vestiges of civilization – electricity, telephones, even proper plumbing – give way to raw nature. A few hermit-like fishermen will rent you hammocks on the porches of their shacks for as little as US$1.50 a day, an extra US$2 for meals.

Santa Marta and around

Although Colombia's oldest city, founded in 1525, **SANTA MARTA**'s colonial heritage was all but swept away at the hands of English and Dutch pirates. The result is a drab, featureless place of overly congested streets and sand-blasted buildings – more the setting for a Graham Greene novel than the pearl of the Americas that it claims to be. But while the city is no Cartagena, it compensates with its proximity to fine natural beauty. Nearby are some of Colombia's most placid beaches, particularly the upscale **Rodadero** resort four kilometres south of the city, as well as the quiet fishing village of **Taganga**. The city is also the hub for organizing hikes to the ruins of **Ciudad Perdida** and trips to **Parque Nacional Tayrona**, Colombia's version of a Caribbean paradise.

That Santa Marta has developed a reputation as a haven for drug smugglers and itinerant hippies is largely the fault of *The Fruit Palace*, Charles Nicholl's flippant exploration of Colombia's cocaine underworld in the early 1980s. The fruit stand on Calle 10C that gave the book its title has since been shut down.

Accommodation

Santa Marta, especially Calle 10C, seems like Colombia's epicentre for dirty, backpacker dens. In general, modern, reasonably priced lodging are hard to come by. In January and February, prices can double and reservations are recommended. Pricier holiday **hotels** are located mostly in Rodadero.

Hospedeía Casa Familiar C 10C No. 2–14 Ⓣ5/421-1697. The cleanest and best serviced of the backpacker lodges. Large rooms have private bath, and the fifth-floor terrace affords views of harbour. The Cabrera Torres family, proprietors of the hotel, can organize excursions, including trips to Ciudad Perdida. ❶

Hostería Tima Uraka C 18 No. 2–59 Ⓣ5/422-8433. Attractive youth hostel in Rodadero near beach. Laundry services and kitchen facilities. ❶

Hotel Miramar C 10C No. 1C–59 Ⓣ5/421-4756. By far Santa Marta's cheapest hotel – just US$0.75 to hang a hammock – the *Hotel Miramar* often gets overcrowded with dazed hippies clipping overgrown toenails on the patio. But its charm lies in its sordid atmosphere, and it has good tourist info. ❶

Hotel Tamacá Cra 2 No. 11A–98 Ⓣ5/422-7015. On the beach in Rodadero, the *Tamacá* features a swimming pool, casino and spacious rooms. ❼

La Sierra Cra 1 No. 9–47 Ⓣ5/422-8521. Modern rooms on the beach in Rodadero with seafront views. It has a café on the boardwalk, but no pool. ❻

Sol Arhuaco Cra 2 No. 6–49 Ⓣ5/422-7166. Located on the beach and offering a nice terrace, swimming pool and restaurant. ❻

The Town

Although better known for drawing sun worshipers, Santa Marta does boast a few worthwhile museums. A striking building with wooden garrets underneath a pitched tile roof, the well-maintained **Casa de la Aduana** (Customs House), on the corner of C 14 and Cra 2, is the city's oldest building, dating from 1531, and an important historical landmark the nation over. Simon Bolívar stayed here briefly, and his body lay in state in an upstairs gallery after his death. On its first floor, the **Museo Antropoógico y Etnológico** (Mon–Fri 8am–noon & 2–6pm; free) has extensive displays on ancient Tayrona culture and its modern day descendants – the Kogis, Arhuacos and Arsarios. An oversized replica of Ciudad Perdida provides a valuable introduction for anyone planning to visit the ruins (see p.622).

The sun-bleached **Catedral**, at Cra 4 and C 17, is the oldest church in Colombia but has received successive facelifts. The current structure, with its bulky bell tower and stone portico, dates mostly from the seventeenth century. Bolívar's remains were kept here until 1842, when they were sent off to his native Venezuela.

An obligatory stop for history buffs is the **Quinta de San Pedro Alejandrino** (daily 9.30am–4.30pm; US$2.50), the sugar plantation five kilometres south of town, where Bolívar spent his last agonizing days. The hacienda's peaceful grounds and exotic gardens are alone worth a visit, yet the displays are more an exercise in Libertador fetishism – medical vials, military badges, a lock of hair – than they are biographical. For the uninitiated, guided tours (in Spanish) are included in the price of admission. There's also a museum on the premises with contemporary art donated from the six countries Bolívar liberated. Buses leaving the waterfront for the Mamatoco suburb will drop you off at the Quinta, if you ask the driver.

While boasting no historical attractions **Rodadero**, four kilometres south of Santa Marta, draws tourists with its palm-lined boardwalk and white-sand beaches. An invasion of high-rise apartments and tacky tourist shops has rubbed away Rodadero's exclusivity of late, yet it remains the cleanest and safest place to bathe near Santa Marta. In the evening, it's also popular with clubbers. Local buses from Santa Marta cost US$0.35 and a taxi will set you back about US$2.

Eating, drinking and nightlife

Many of the resort hotels in Rodadero have quality **restaurants** serving international cuisine. Along the waterfront in Santa Marta are several fast-food eateries. Most of the **clubs** can be found in Rodadero.

China Town Cra 1 No. 18–47. Abundant and inexpensive Chinese fare featuring plenty of vegetables.

Café del Parque C 14 between Cra 1 and 2. Leafy park and outdoor café next to Casa de la Aduana. It offers excellent pastries and iced cappuccinos but closes at 8.30pm.

La Escollera C 5 No. 4–107. The pioneer of Rodadero's nightclub scene this giant-sized disco plays salsa music, sometimes featuring live acts.

El Pibe C 6A No. 1–26. Low-key Rodadero eatery serving moderately priced steak and Argentine meat dishes on a shaded patio.

Parque Nacional Tayrona

Colombia's most unspoilt tropical area, **TAYRONA**, about 25km east of Santa Marta, comprises 15,000 hectares of jungle-fringed beaches, archeological ruins and lush forest with howling spider monkeys and falling coconuts. Silhouettes of swaying palm trees set against sunsets complete the cinematic image.

The park gets its name from the Tayrona Indians, one of South America's greatest pre-Columbian civilizations. This area was a major trading centre for the Tayrona, as many as one million of whom inhabited it at one point. However, with the arrival of the Spanish, their peaceful existence came to an end. The Spanish governor ordered their annihilation in 1599 on the trumped-up charges that the Tayrona men practised sodomy; the brutal massacre that followed forced the remaining

Tayronas to seek refuge high into the Sierra Nevada de Santa Marta, whose foothills flank the park to the south. Rising from sea level, these snowcapped sierras reach their apex just 42 kilometres from the coast, at the 5775-metre **Cristóbal Colón**, Colombia's tallest peak.

Buses (US$1) leave the market in Santa Marta every half-hour for El Zaino, 35 kilometres from Santa Marta, where you'll need to take a (US$2) taxi – prices are negotiable – or walk the four-kilometre road to the main entrance at **Cañaveral**. After paying your US$7 entrance fee, take a quick look at the visitor's centre (8am–6pm), where it's possible to buy a map. From here, it's a 45-minute walk through alternating patches of forest to the crowded **Arrecifes Beach**, where a hammock will set you back US$2 a day, limited *cabañas* US$10–20. Although stunningly beautiful, Arrecifes isn't recommended for swimming because of the strong tide that claims a few overconfident tourists every year. Another 45 minutes west along the beach lies the more tranquil **Cabo San Juan**, where the swimming is safer and the forest touches the tiny spit of beach carved from the headland. From here a clear, uphill path after ninety minutes arrives at the archeological site of **Pueblito**, a former Tayrona village with a large number of terrace dwellings, the reason why it's sometimes called a mini-Ciudad Perdida. Although it's possible to complete a Cañaveral–Arrecifes–Cabo San Juan–Pueblito circuit in one long, strenuous day, most people will want to drop out of the world for as long as their itinerary permits.

Ciudad Perdida

With good reason, **CIUDAD PERDIDA**, the Lost City of the Tayronas, ranks among South America's most magical spots. More than a lost city, it's a lost world. Although its archeological ruins are less spectacular than those found at Macchu Picchu, thanks to its geographic isolation the once teeming city perched high in the Sierra Nevada de Santa Marta effortlessly preserves all the natural allure that the overrun Incan capital lost years ago to tourism. While steadily climbing the sierras' luxuriant foothills, you'll get a chance to bathe under idyllic waterfalls, visit inhabited indigenous villages and marvel at the swarms of monarch butterflies and abundant jungle wildlife. In September 2003, eight tourists hiking to Ciudad Perdida were kidnapped by terrorists. **Extreme caution** is advised, and visitors should consult local officials before planning excursions here.

Built sometime after 500 AD, the Tayrona capital is less than fifty kilometres southeast of Santa Marta. But, despite its importance and short distance from the Colombian coast, it wasn't discovered until 1975 when a few of the more than 10,000 *guaqeros*, or tomb raiders, from Santa Marta chanced upon it while scavenging for antiquities. Perched atop a steep slope 1300m high in the vast jungle, the site consists of more than a thousand circular **terraces** – only ten percent of which have been uncovered – that once served as foundations for Tayrona homes. Running throughout the city and down to the Buritaca River Valley is a complex network of paved footpaths and steep, stone steps – over 1350 if you're counting – purportedly added later to obstruct the advance of Spanish horsemen.

Although now uninhabited, Ciudad Perdida is in many respects a living monument. It's surrounded by villages of **Kogi Indians**, who call the revered site Teyuna. By far the biggest highlight of any visit is the chance to interact with the Kogis as they drift on and off the trail. Easily one of South America's most primitive surviving indigenous groups, the men are recognizable by their long, ragged hair, cream-coloured smocks and trusty *poporo*, the saliva-coated gourd holding the lime that activates the coca leaves they constantly chew. About 9000 Kogis are believed to inhabit the Sierra Nevada.

When flower power was in full bloom in the US in the 1970s, the Sierra Nevada became a major marijuana factory, and an estimated seventy percent of its native forests were burned to clear the way for untold amounts of the lucrative Santa Marta Gold strand. As the forest's prime inhabitants, the Kogis suffered dearly from the arrival of so many fast-buck farmers, one of the reasons why they're so sceptical of the outside world. Although some Kogis are friendly, and a few even speak Spanish, you'd be begging for a machete whip if you take a picture without their permission. This is very much their territory. To make quick friends, present them with some seashells, which they grind to extract the lime for their *poporos*.

Hiking practicalities

While the hills around Ciudad Perdida are considered safe by Colombian standards, it's easy to lose the trail and hiring a **guide** is a must. Prices for the six-day-long hike start at around US$125 and include all meals, hammock lodging at farmhouses, the entrance fee to the ruins and transportation to and from the trailhead. The most knowledgeable guides are Wilson, Edwin and Frankie Rey (one of the repentant *guaqueros* who discovered the site), who can be found sharing photos with prospective customers at the youth hostels on Calle 10C in Santa Marta (see p.620). Paying more, it's also possible to book a tour in advance from Bogotá with Ecoguías or in Santa Marta through the Turcol Travel Agency (Ⓣ5/421-2256) at Cra 1C No. 20–15. The hike can be done all year round, though during the wet months from May to November the trail can get quite muddy. In any case, expect to get and stay wet any time of the year – the steamy jungle pardons no one.

Taganga

Although no longer as pristine as it used to be, **TAGANGA** retains much of the spirit of the quiet fishing village it was before being absorbed last decade by Santa Marta's expansion. A Kogi legend holds that when Tayrona priests came down from the mountains they found Taganga populated by beautiful women with long hair who taught them to fish using nets. Today, it's the men with long hair, as Taganga has gained the reputation of being a resort for foreign beach bums. Although only fifteen minutes from Santa Marta by frequent public buses along the boardwalk on Carerra 1C, Taganga offers a wholly different vibe. Built on the side of a mountain, the town has an uncanny Mediterranean feel. For budget travellers, it's an ideal base for exploring the surrounding area's attractions, though you'll need to backtrack to Santa Marta for most excursions. Another worthwhile option is learning to **scuba dive**. Poseidon (Ⓣ5/421-9224), at C 18 No. 1–69, is Taganga's only dive centre offering PADI certification. Its five-day open watercourse, in English, starts at US$170. Also be sure to talk with locals; usually a curious stare is enough for obliging fishermen to invite you out on a sunset trawl.

Practicalities

For **accommodation**, *Casa Blanca*, Cra 1 No. 18–161 (Ⓣ5/421-9232; ❷), is right on the beach, with clean rooms overlooking the ocean. It offers shared kitchen facilities and hammocks on the terrace for the all-night partying crowd. Also on the beach, *La Ballena Azul* (Ⓣ5/421-9005; ❹) is Taganga's only traditional resort hotel and fills up on weekends with Colombian families. Its rooms have air conditioning and TV. *Casa de Felipe* (Ⓣ5/421-9101, Ⓦwww.lacasadefelipe.com; ❷), three blocks uphill from the beach, has rustic decorated rooms with private terraces, an outdoor **dining area** and (slow) Internet service.

Riohacha

Founded in 1539 by German explorer Nicolás de Federmán, **RIOHACHA** is the capital of the little explored Guajira Peninsula, an arid spit that juts into the Caribbean to form the northern tip of South America. The city itself offers few attractions other than its fine white beaches, but makes a comfortable base from which to explore the surrounding badlands.

Guajira Peninsula's hostile, desert climate has kept it largely isolated since colonial times. As a result it's one of those special places where independent travellers can still feel as if they're leaving fresh tracks. Some 150 miles long and no more than thirty miles wide, the barren peninsula is empty except for the semi-Nomadic Wayúu, or Guajiro, Indians – and drug smugglers. The infinite number of sheltered coves from which drugs leave for the US has earned Guajira Peninsula the reputation of being Colombia's contraband capital. Most illicit activity, however, is kept hidden, and, as in any frontier area, the absence of the law doesn't pose any risks so long as you don't seek out trouble.

Practicalities

Twice-daily buses make the three-hour trip along the northern coast from Riohacha to **Manaure**, where traditionally dressed Wayúu extract salt manually and pile it in mounds against a stark white background. Otherwise, the beautifully

San Andrés and Providencia

Dropped like rocks in the southwestern corner of the Caribbean the coral islands of **San Andrés** and **Providencia** are Colombian territory in name only. Closer to Nicaragua (230 kilometres west) than to the Colombian mainland (750 kilometres), these two islands are the largest in a small archipelago discovered by Columbus on his fourth trip to the New World before they quickly passed into British hands. At the same time English puritans were establishing themselves in New England, a far less egalitarian Plymouth Rock, built on slavery and pirating, sprouted up in the tropics. In contrast with its North American sister, these colonies were a huge failure and, when the British left in 1641, the Spanish crown quickly seized on the opportunity to take them into their colonial fold. Even so, the **English presence** survived in its influence on language, religion, architecture and music.

Surrounded by a turquoise sea, extensive coral reefs and rich sea life, both islands are ideal, albeit expensive, for **scuba diving** and **snorkelling**. San Andrés, with a population of 100,000 on an eleven-kilometre-long mostly flat terrain, is the larger of the two (12.5 kilometres long and 3.5 wide) and the preferred playground for the Colombian upper class. The invasion of so many tourists has led to a construction boom that has contributed to the Spring Break feel that envelopes San Andrés year-round. By contrast Providencia, or Old Providence as its 6000 residents still call it, is largely unspoiled by tourism and retains much of the traditional island lifestyle of the original English and *patois*-speaking black, Jamaican settlers. The far fewer tourists that arrive on Providencia tend to be more eco-oriented.

Although almost every travel agency in Bogotá or elsewhere offers **packaged deals** to the islands, it's possible to arrive on your own and, if it's off-season, probably cheaper. Flights from Bogotá start at US$150 and from Cartagena US$100. Cheap **accommodation options on San Andrés** are hard to come by since most budget travellers skip the island anyway. *La Posada de Lulu* on Av Antioquia No. 2–18 (☎8/512-5669; ④) is one of the cheapest, at under US$20. At the other end of the scale, *Cocoplum Beach* on Carretera San Luis No. 43–39 (☎8/513-2421; ⑦), is a resort hotel with a private beach, pool and air-conditioned rooms. **Hotels on Providencia** tend to be more rustic and luxuries taken for granted on San Andrés – pools, bars and televisions, for example – are almost nonexistent here. *Hotel Miss Elma* (☎8/514-8229; ⑥) has four rooms overlooking Freshwater Bay (Agua Dulce) starting at US$50, extra for cheap meals.

On San Andrés, Sharky's Dive Shop (☎8/513-0420) at the *Sun Set Hotel* on Carretera Circunvalar km 13 offers night **diving** and PADI-certified courses. The diving in Providencia is more extensive than it is in San Andrés, and quality guides from Sonny's Dive Shop in Freshwater Bay (☎8/514-8112) can take you to the more than thirty dive spots around the island.

remote **Cabo de la Vela** is famous for its large flamingo population and long sunsets, while at the peninsula's northern tip, six hours from Riohacha, the **Parque Nacional La Macuira** is home to an elfin cloudforest that rises 500 metres straight up like a lush, island habitat amid the otherwise scorching desert. The heat and lack of good roads can make travelling in La Guajira hazardous so you'll probably want to contract a **tour agency** in Riohacha; two options are Guajira Viva at Cra 8 No. 1–27 Local 3 (Ⓣ5/727-0607) and Guajira Tours C 3 No. 6–47 (Ⓣ5/727-3325).

If you wish to **stay** in Riohacha, *Arimaca*, on Av 1A No. 8–75 (Ⓣ5/727-3481; ❺), is the town's plushest lodge, with rooms overlooking the sea, a swimming pool, disco and restaurant. *Gimaura*, on Av La Playa (Ⓣ5/727-2266; ❹), is a peaceful if somewhat decadent resort on the beach just a short walk from downtown. It has a pool and allows camping.

5.4

Tierra Paisa

Nominally a slang term to describe anyone from the region of Antioquio, **paisas** are alternately the butt of jokes and the object of envy for many Colombians. What makes them stand out is their rugged individualism and reputation for industriousness. They're fame dates back to the early nineteenth century, when they cleared Colombia's hinterland for farming in exchange for the government's carrot of free land. The rapid progress over the next century earned the mostly European colonists a reputation for hard work, exaggerated frugality and an unequalled skill at turning a profit from any enterprise, legal or otherwise. Perhaps the biggest *paisa* contribution to Colombia is its role in the spread of coffee.

The heart of *paisa* country is the burgeoning metropolis of **Medellín**, which has made a remarkable turnaround since its days as Colombia's murder capital in the early 1990s. The picturesque coffee-growing *fincas* near the modern cities of **Manizales** and **Pereira** were almost all established by *paisa* homesteaders. With the collapse in international coffee prices, many growers have opened their estates to tourists, who during harvest time can partake in the picking process. Unknown even to Colombians just a few years ago, the so-called **zona cafetera**, or "Coffee Zone", is Colombia's newest and fastest growing tourist attraction. The zone is also the base for exploring one of Colombia's most postcard-perfect national parks, the **Parque Nacional Natural Los Nevados**.

Coffee and cocaine

It's hard to say which of Colombia's two cash crops garner more international attention, the white or the black one. One thing is for certain: whether or not it contains the seal of approval of Juan Valdez or Pablo Escobar, both are synonymous with quality.

The country's first bumper crop was **coffee**. Colombia is the world's leading producer of mild Arabica coffee and its twenty percent overall share of the world's coffee market is second only to Brazil's. Although originally from East Africa – where legend holds it was discovered by a shepherd when his flock reacted strangely after feeding on the wild berry – it's Mother Nature's gift of high temperatures, heavy rainfall and a cool evening breeze that makes Colombia the bean's ideal habitat.

Cocaine was perceived as an equally innocuous stimulant until the twentieth century. Two US presidents, several European monarchs, even a pope were early addicts (and vocal advocates) of Vin Tonique Mariani, a nineteenth-century liqueur made from coca extract. The "real thing" Coca-Cola initially pushed on its customers – and drug company Parke-Davis spiked its throat lozenges and cigarettes with – was cocaine. For Sigmund Freud, a spoonful of coke each day was the cure for depression.

As supplier of eighty percent of the world's cocaine, Colombia is responsible for an estimated US$4 billion each year, the equivalent of a third of its legal exports. The profits are largely a result of simple economics: a gram of coke that fetches US$2 in Colombia can bring in as much as US$80 abroad because of the risks along the supply chain.

Medellín

It's hard to think of a city, apart from Baghdad, more in need of a public relations makeover than **MEDELLÍN**. When turf wars between rival **drug gangs** became public in the 1980s and 1990s, Colombia's second largest city was rampaged by teenage hitmen, called *sicarios*, who, for as little as US$30, could be hired to settle old scores. The blood thirst earned Medellín the world's highest murder rate, 5000 per year – eight times greater than the most dangerous cities in the US.

But when cocaine kingpin **Pablo Escobar** (see box p.629) was snuffed out in 1993, Medellín began to bury its sordid past. While most foreigners still stay away, those who do visit will be surprised to find an inviting, modern city of two million, with a vibrant urban life resembling Bogotá's. The friendliness of its residents can be disarming – despite it's big city size, Medellín still preserves a small-town atmosphere. Even more alluring, the self-proclaimed "City of Eternal Spring", capital of Antoquio department, boasts one of Colombia's best climates, with average year-round temperatures of 24°C.

Dramatically perched 1538 metres high in the **Central Cordillera** overlooking the **Aburrá Valley**, the city was founded in 1675, purportedly by so-called "New Christian" Jews escaping the Spanish Inquisition. Today's descendants of these immigrant roots, **paisas**, as residents of Antoquia are known, are alternately scoffed

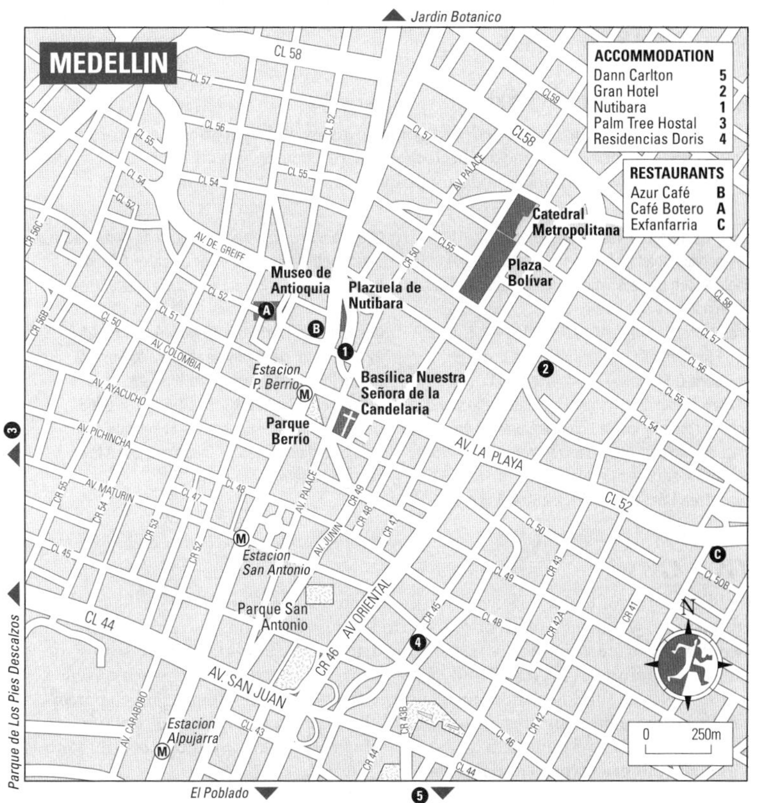

at and admired by Colombians for their rigid work ethic. Such is the experience, at least, of the country's most famous *paisa*, Colombian President Alvaro Uribe, who's routinely satirized for his 5am cabinet meetings. In any case, the *paisa* myth has been used to explain everything from the city's strong economy to the incredible success of its metro system, among the cleanest and most efficient in the world.

Arrival, information and city transport

Medellín's futuristic **José María Córdova airport** lies a hilly 28 kilometres from the city along a scenic new highway. Taxis to the city cost around US$11 but you can get a seat on a chartered minibus for US$1.50. Depending on which part of the country you're arriving from, long-distance **buses** arrive either at the Terminal del Norte or Terminal del Sur, both almost equidistant from the centre. A taxi to the centre costs about US$2 from either.

Despite its size and apparent organization, tourism is still not yet a priority for Medellín. Other than an informational stand at the airport, the only other **tourist office** (Mon-Sat 7.30am–12.30pm & 1.30–5.30pm; ⓣ4/232-4022) is tucked away on the second floor at the Placio de Exposiciones, C 41 No. 55–35, a long (and ultimately worthless) hike from the centre.

While most sightseeing in the centre can be done on foot, visitors to El Poblado will want to take a **taxi** (try Tax Individual ⓣ4/331-1111 or Coodetaxi ⓣ4/311-7777); better yet, try the city's excellent **metro** system (US$0.25, less if you buy a ten-trip pass). The safety and efficiency of the metro has rendered **buses** mostly redundant, but at US$0.25 a ride they're a cheap – though not recommended – option after the metro closes at 11pm.

Accommodation

Like any big city, **hotels** in Medellín come in many different varieties. More run-down but cheaper ones tend to be located in the centre, which becomes a ghost town at night. More modern lodging can be found closer to the night time action in **El Poblado**.

Dann Carlton Cra 43A No. 7–50 ⓣ4/312-4141. Full-service hotel featuring sauna and Jacuzzi in El Poblado. It has a spinning bar on the top floor with commanding views of city. ❼

Gran Hotel C 54 No. 45–92 ⓣ4/513-4455. Good value for centrally located hotel with pool. ❺

Nutibara C 52 No. 50–46 ⓣ4/511-5111, ⓦwww.hotelnutibara.com. This stately Old World hotel is centrally located on noisy, downtown Plazuela Nutibara. Its rooms are large, and the pool and sauna are open to outsiders for US$3.50. ❺

Palm Tree Hostal Cra 67 No. 48D–63 ⓣ4/260-2805, ⓦwww.palmtreeMedellín.com. Comfortable, quiet youth hostel with Internet, cable TV and kitchen facilities. Private or shared rooms. Three blocks from Suramericana metro stop. ❶

Residencias Doris Cra 45 No. 46–23 ⓣ4/251-2245. Cheap, clean private rooms close to the centre though otherwise uninviting. ❶

Plaza Rosa Cra 32D No. 9–17 ⓣ4/312-0005. One of the cheapest options in El Poblado, with rooms starting at US$30. Clean and just a few years old. Breakfast included.

The City

Unlike the rest of Colombia, Medellín came into its own at the start of the twentieth century, when the coffee boom spurred industrialization. The city's organized layout and architecture mostly dates from that period. The most impressive is the **Palacio Nacional**, on Cra 52 and C 48, an Art Nouveau-inspired work unveiled in 1937. Now a rundown shopping centre, it's brass-coloured dome can be appreciated from the metro. Another treasure from the steel era is the restored **Palacio de la Cultura**, on Cra 51 and C 52, a Neo-Gothic palace (now a cultural centre) with a gingerbread brickwork facade and marble interior.

Pablo Escobar's grave

Much to the displeasure of the well-intentioned tourist board, the former stomping grounds of **Pablo Escobar** – his homes, the modern buildings he built, the country-club mountain jail he was ambushed at – are becoming a minor draw for curious tourists. The former godfather of the Medellín cartel is still very much venerated for his extensive philanthropy by the city's poorer residents, who've even named a *barrio* after him. To make your own pilgrimage, visit his austere gravestone at the **Jardines Montenegro cemetery** near the Itaguí metro station.

Despite its younger blood, a few churches from the late colonial era survive. The most important is the **Basílica Nuestra Señora de la Candelaria**, whose Baroque interior dates from 1776. The whitewashed, flat-naved chapel, which overlooks the centrally located **Parque Berrío**, was Medellín's Cathedral until 1931. Today that honour is held by the more recent, but no less fanciful, **Catedral Metropolitana**, four blocks away, along a pedestrian walkway, at Plaza Bolívar. The fortress-like structure was constructed between 1875 and 1931 and claims to be the largest church in the world built entirely of bricks – 1.2 million, if you're counting.

Medellín is the birthplace of sculptor and painter **Fernando Botero**, known for his satirical representation of all things fat – oranges, priests, even Mona Lisa. Although Medellín residents felt miffed by Botero's recent donation of his extensive European art collection to a Bogotá museum (see Donación Botero, p.602), the largest collection of his works is housed in the modern **Museo de Antioquia** at Cra 52 No. 52–43 (Mon & Wed–Fri 9.30am–5pm, Sat–Sun 10am–4pm; US$1.50). Another twenty sculptures are on display outside the museum in the busy **Plaza Botero**. If your appetite for the artist isn't sated, be sure to walk ten minutes southeast to check out his *Pajaró de Paz* (Bird of Peace) sculpture at **Parque San Antonio**, on Carerra 46 between calles 44 and 46. When a guerrilla bomb destroyed the bronze sculpture in 1996, Botero ordered the skeleton to be left in its shattered state and placed alongside it a replica of the original as an eloquent protest against violence.

The geographical limitations of so many people living in a narrow valley has forced residents to live in overcrowded conditions, with many homes literally running up 45 degree angle slopes. At the same time, within the city itself there's a huge shortage of open recreational spaces. An exception is Pueblito Paisa, a replica of a typical Antioquian village found atop Cerro Nutibara, a hilly outcrop downtown offering panoramic views of the city. The city's other diminutive green space is the **Jardín Botánico Joaquín Antonio Uribe** (Mon–Sat 8am–5pm, Sun 9am–6pm; US$1.25), located ten minutes by metro in the city's northern sector. The Jardín is one of Colombia's oldest botanical gardens, dating from 1913. A symbol of Medellín's renaissance is the new **Parque de los Pies Descalzos**, a Zen-inspired playground where children of all ages are encouraged to take off their shoes and tread barefoot through a series of sand, water and pebble mazes.

Eating, drinking and nightlife

Paisa cuisine, among Colombia's most distinctive, is heavy on the *frijoles* (black beans), grilled meat, plantains and rice. Perhaps no dish is more characteristic of the region than the *bandeja paisa*, a large bowl filled with ground beef, *chorizo* sausage, *frijoles*, rice, fried green bananas, a fried egg, avocado and fried pork. Around the leafy Parque Llera a trendy Zona Rosa of bars, **restaurants** and clubs has developed, most of them catering to young clientele. Most of Medellín's **nightlife** has migrated to the upscale suburb of El Poblado, ten minutes south of the centre by metro.

La Aguacatala Cra 43A No. 7 Sur–130. Old country house in El Poblado, specializing in typical *paisa* and Colombian cuisine including *arepas* and *bandeja paisa*. The serenading band ensures a peaceful ambience.
Azur Café Cra 51 No. 52–03. Located in the gingerbread-looking Palacio de la Cultura, built in 1925, the *Azur Café* features cafeteria-style lunches for around US$2 in a shaded outdoor plaza.
Café Botero inside Museo de Antoquio. Excellent salads and international cuisine, popular with business lunch crowd.
Exfanfarria Cra 40 No. 50B–32. This high-ceilinged and wooden-floor bohemian poet's café and underground theatre serves cheap beer. Popular with locals.
Leboncafe C 9 No. 39–09. Excellent pastries and 18 types of coffee are on offer at this El Poblado café, which has several other locations throughout city.
Al Rojo C 9 No. 38–09. Pasta and pizza are the fare in this fun, outdoor patio in El Poblado, which attracts a big crowd when the rumba starts after 11.
Sanyori Cra 38 No. 10A–27. Traditional Japanese food, particularly sushi, is the mainstay in this intimate El Poblado dining room.

Manizales and around

Founded in 1849 by migrating *paisas*, **MANIZALES** developed in the late nineteenth century with the growth of coffee as Colombia's main industry. One legacy is the numerous Neoclassical buildings from the era found in the city centre, which has been declared a national monument. The high-mountain city of 362,000 sits at the base of the snowcapped Nevado del Ruiz volcano (see opposite), which, on a clear day, can be seen burping vapour from the bridge in front of the Teatro Los Fundadores. The town owes its hilly topography – most streets are steep and windy – to the fact that the earth below it is geologically volatile, which is why earthquakes are a frequent, and sometimes devastating, occurrence. This capital of Caldas department is a university town – there are seven in all here – and the large student population gives the city a festive air that other large cities in the region lack. It is an ideal base for exploring the surrounding **coffee farms** and the **Parque Nacional Natural Los Nevados**.

Accommodation

Hotel California C 19 No. 16–37 ☎6/847-720. True to its Tequila Sunrise-evoking name, this otherwise no-frills hotel is cheap and clean – and right in front of the bus terminal for a quick getaway when the thrill is gone. Includes cable TV. ❷
Hotel Escorial C 21 No. 21–11 ☎6/884-7696. One of Manizales' most traditional hotels gets high marks for Old World ambience, but its central location can make for a noisy night's sleep. It has a good restaurant and includes breakfast. ❺
Hotel Yaripa Av Centenario No. 24–121 ☎6/883-7928/32/33. Recently renovated, this quality hotel a ten-minute walk from downtown is probably the best bang for your buck in Manizales. Some of the rooms have views of mountains. Includes breakfast. ❹

The Town

While the bulk of your stay in the Manizales area will be spent outside the city, there are a few buildings worth checking out around the **Plaza de Bolívar**, on Cra 21 and C 22. Linger on the north side of the square and appreciate the Romanesque facade of the departmental government building, the **Palacio de La Gobernación**, which was built in 1925. Opposite it stands the Gothic-style **Catedral**, built entirely of reinforced concrete in 1928. A helpful tourist office (weekdays 7.30am–noon & 2–6.30pm; ☎6/884-6211), with English-language brochures and a cinema functions out of the **Teatro de los Fundadores**, on Cra 22 and C 33, about a five-minute cab ride from the centre.

In the northwest suburb of Chipre, on a high bluff at the end of Av 12 de Octubre, the new **Monumento a Los Colonizadores** is a 25-tonne bronze sculpture reliving the trials and triumphs of the Antioquian mule drivers who founded the city. At the other end of the city, in the well-manicured Cable neighbourhood, you'll find the **Estación del Cable Aéreo**, the well-conserved end station for the 73-kilometre suspended funicular (once the world's longest), which linked Manizales with the Magdalena River port of Honda (and hence the Atlantic Ocean) from 1910 to 1961. This incredible monument to *paisa* ingenuity, with a little help from migrant Australian engineers, can be found at Cra 23 (also called Avenida Santander) and C 65.

Eating and drinking

The city centre clears out at night and most **eating** and **drinking** is done in the suburbs. The liveliest area, popular with students, is between calles 60 and 75 along Carerra 23, El Cable's main drag, where you'll find a nice selection of pubs and discotheques.

101 Perros C 51 No. 22A07. This nondescript hot dog and hamburger stand makes some of the best patties you'll try anywhere in Colombia. Open late.

Atlantis Cra 23 No. 63122. This darkly lit disco specializes in salsa music.

La Carbonera Cra 23C No. 6266. Quality Argentine *parilla*-style steaks in a relaxed, family environment.

Wok & Thai Torre Casa Luker on Cra 23 and Cl 64. Exquisite Thai cuisine (for Colombia at least) in a modern, chic setting, at moderate prices.

Parque Nacional Natural Los Nevados

Indisputably one of the crown jewels in Colombia's national parks system, the 58,300-hectare **PARQUE NACIONAL NATURAL LOS NEVADOS**, forty kilometres from Manizales, protects some of the last surviving snowcapped peaks in the tropics. In total, there are five volcanoes covered in white stuff year-round, the tallest being the 5321m **Nevado del Ruiz**. The majority of the peaks are now dormant, but Nevado del Ruiz remains an active threat, having killed 22,000 people and buried the now extinct town of Armero when it erupted in 1985. Sadly, though, for a park whose name, Nevado, implies perpetual snow, global warming has lifted the snow line to almost 5000 metres on most peaks.

Though it's of little compensation, because of the severe melt, it's now possible for even moderately fit armchair adventurers to reach the peak's summit in a long day's journey from Manizales. Although not technically difficult – with good weather you can climb in regular hiking shoes – a **guide** is required to steer you clear of the toxic fumaroles drifting from the volcano's core. Your easiest option is to contract Bioturismo (☎6/884-4037) at Centro Comercial Parque Caldas PB #45, which runs a ten-hour trip daily from Manizales, including transport, the ascent of Ruiz and a visit to the thermal baths at the park entrance for around US$20 (more for English-speaking guides). The park entrance fee is an additional US$7.

Most visitors, though, will want to spend at least a couple nights inside the park exploring the boggy *páramo* landscape, an important freshwater reserve dominating the high massifs. Inexpensive mountain **refugios** of varying comfort can be found at the park's entrance and visitors' centre at Las Brisas, at the base of Ruiz and several other strategic locations spread throughout the park. There's also a campsite and upscale hotel being built at El Cisne, the base for exploring the park's less visited interior, including the hidden mountain pond **Laguna Verde** and the cloud-covered **Nevado de Satna Isabel**. Unfortunately, the park's dramatic southern end, where a dense wax palm tree forest slowly metamorphoses into *páramo* near **Laguna del Otún**, was off limits to visitors after four fishermen and a local guide were found dead, presumably killed by guerrillas, in 2002. The violence, however, hasn't ever affected the park's touristy northern end, and at the time of writing authorities pledged that Ruiz was safe to visit.

Staying on a coffee farm

Although coffee remains the planet's heaviest traded commodity after oil, a worldwide glut that's triggered record low prices – currently about US$0.50 a pound versus US$1.30 in 1998 – has made earning a living from it virtually impossible for Colombia's 300,000 growers. Desperate to supplement their incomes, savvier farmers are increasingly turning to tourism. Instead of harvesting rich berries, some 300 **coffee fincas** near Manizales exploit their heritage to curious tourists whose only previous contact with Arabica roast is at Starbucks.

No two *fincas* are alike – they range from traditional estates still attended by their owner to deceptively modern rural hotels where the only coffee you'll find comes served with breakfast. Most, however, are small estates of a few hectares, as coffee's labour-intensive picking process conspired against the concentration of large land holdings. Scenically, the farms look out on lush slopes, overgrown with the shiny-leaved coffee shrubs and interspersed with banana plants and bamboo-like *guadua* forests. Most *fincas* will also arrange horseback riding, walks and guided visits to traditional *paisa* hamlets. Indeed, for those with a more flexible budget, *fincas* make an ideal base to explore the region's many attractions.

Your best hope in locating the best *finca* for your needs is to ask other travellers or a trusted travel agency like Ecoguías in Bogotá (see "Listings" p.607). You can also inquire at the local tourist offices in Manizales or Pereira (see pp.630 and 633), but be sure to see photos and inquire thoroughly about accommodation to make sure you get the *finca* you want. There's also a stand at the **Parque Nacional del Café** (see opposite), which helps arrange visits.

Although it no longer grows coffee, the history of **La Pequeña Granja de Mamá Lulú** is intimately linked to the social and economic impact the crop's bust-boom cycle has caused in the region. A model ecological farm and guest lodge, where everything from animal manure to rainwater is recycled, it's owned by a family of *campesinos* who had the vision some fifteen years ago to reject monocultivation and dependence on consumerism and return to the self-sufficient roots of their ancestors. In recent years, Mamá Lulú and her children have started warmly receiving tourists in a comfortable and modern guesthouse built entirely of *guada*. Double rooms cost US$15, extra for their excellent organic meals. For non-guests, a fascinating guided tour of the tiny, two-acre patch by one of the family members costs US$1.50. Access is via a local bus or taxi to Vereda Palermo from the quaint coffee village of Quimbaya, 31 kilometres south of Pereira. For inquiries and transportation instructions try ⓣ6/752-1260 or 310/435-6607 (mobile).

For further information, a map and good logistical advice on camping or hiking, talk with Nelson Carvajal at the **park office** (ⓣ6/886-4104) in Manizales, at C 76B No 18–14. When he's not off climbing in the Himalayas, Nelson will also rent equipment and help more experienced alpinists plan ascents of the more challenging **Nevado del Tolima**.

Pereira

Just 56 kilometres south of Manizales, **PEREIRA** makes an equally suitable base for exploring the *zona cafetera*. The region's largest city, with 433,000 inhabitants, it shares Manizales' history as a centre for the coffee industry but lacks its sister's city's youthful energy. However, it's closer to many of the region's coffee *fincas* and the Parque Nacional del Café.

Pereira's **Plaza de Bolívar** is unique among the uniformly named central plazas of Colombia for its modern sculpture of the El Libertador nude on horseback, a controversial pose when it was unveiled in 1963 but now a beloved city symbol.

Also on the plaza is the town's magnificent **Catedral**, built in 1875. Otherwise nondescript from the outside, the single-nave interior is supported by an elaborate latticework of 12,000 wooden beams forming a spider's web-like canopy. The **tourist office** (Mon-Fri 9am–5pm), at Cra 7 No. 18–55, 2nd Floor, is very helpful.

Pareira's most traditional **hotel**, the Art Deco *Gran Hotel*, at C 19 No. 9–19 (☎6/333-9838 or 335-9500; ❺), is centrally located one block from Plaza de Bolívar and includes breakfast. Part of the Dann Hotel chain, *Soratama*, at Cra 7A No. 19–20 (☎6/335-8650; ❺), features clean and modern rooms with views overlooking the plaza and a nice café in the lobby. If you want more substantial **meals**, try *Punto Rojo*, on Cra 8 No. 19–17, for buffet-style food and a good salad bar open 24 hours. *Le Gascon*, at Cra 7A bis No. 18B–09, is an outdoor French bistro and café on the pedestrian walkway near Plaza de Bolívar, while nearby *El Mesón Español* offers good Spanish cuisine. *Mama Flor* at C 11 No. 15–12 specializes in local cuisine like *arepas*, *bandeja paisa* and *chorizo*.

Parque Nacional del Café

Some 30 kilometres southwest of Pereira, Juan Valdez meets Disney World at the **PARQUE NACIONAL DEL CAFÉ** (daily 9.30am–6pm; admission starts at US$3.25; ☎6/753-6095, Ⓦwww.parquenacionaldelcafe.com). The park occupies a former coffee *finca* whose main house has been barely touched. During the two-hour interpretative walk through the park's manicured grounds, you'll pass a wide range of exotic coffee shrubs, a Quimbaya Indian cemetery, a model *paisa* village – even a rollercoaster. As in any theme park, kitsch comes first – witness the singing orchid show – but beyond the frivolity, there's an astonishingly well-organized museum that retraces the history of coffee, its marketing and its importance in Colombia's development.

To get here, take a bus from Pereira to Montenegro taxi from Armenia where you can grab a seat on any Willy Jeep marked "Parque" for US$1.

Salento

In the heart of coffee country, the quaint hamlet of **SALENTO** is one of the region's earliest settlements, and its slow development has barely altered the original lifestyle or buildings of the *paisa* journeymen who settled here in 1842. Rural workers clad in cowboy hats and *ruanas*, the name for Colombian, are a common sight. Although there are no monumental buildings as there are in Manizales or Pereira, the colourful, one-storey homes of thick adobe and clay-tile roofs that surround the plaza are as authentic as it gets. Soaking in Salento's unpretentious treasures – the Danubi cowboy billiard bar, the multicoloured Jeep Willy's around the plaza and the courtyard gardens of so many open-door residences – gets better with time. Although an afternoon visit is worthwhile, one could easily spend a few, relaxing days here or use it as a base to explore the rest of the *zona cafetera*.

Salento sits atop the Corcora Valley, which contains a thick forest of the skyscraper wax palm, Colombia's national plant. Though a trail through the forest leads to the snowcapped peaks of Parque Nacional Natural Los Nevados (see p.631), visible from the town, because of guerrilla activity in the area, it's strongly recommended that you enter the park from Manizales. You can still spend a few days hiking the numerous trails closer to town; enquire at Trocha y Montaña Expediciones, at Cra 6 and C 2, for information. On Sundays, the main plaza hosts a handicrafts fair catering to the day-trippers. During the rest of the week, though, the town is as sleepy as ever.

Salento's other great charm is its peaceful **B&Bs**. At the upper end of the scale, *La Posada del Café*, at Cra 5 No. 3–08 (☎6/967-593-012; ❹), has a beautiful garden and rustic decorated rooms with wooden floors. *Calle Real* Cra, at 6 No. 2–20, (☎6/749-3118; ❷), is a nice colonial house offering a few more luxuries, like a TV. Rooms are a little dark, but the open porch and economical price more than make up for it.

5.5

The southwest

Leaving the snowy white caps of the "Coffee Zone" behind, the Cauca River Valley descends south and widens until you reach Cali, gateway to Colombia's southwest and the self-proclaimed world capital of salsa music. Further south the Pan American Highway stretches past steamy fields of sugar cane to the serene, colonial town of Popayán, Colombia's *joya blanca*, or white jewel, known for its blindingly white rococo colonial architecture. The hilly, multi-hued scenery behind Popayán is some of Colombia's finest, and the hippies who flock here say it's also endowed with an otherworldly aura emanating from the enigmatic stone monoliths, twice the size of humans, found at the archeological sites of Tierradentro and San Agustín. Heading further south from the overlooked town of Pasto one ascends a ridge dominated by volcanoes all the way to Ecuador.

Cali

Colombia's third largest city, with a population of 1.9 million, **CALI** was founded in 1536 but only shed its provincial backwater status in the early 1900s, when the profits brought in by its sugar plantations prompted industrialization. Today it's one of Colombia's most prosperous cities, in part because of its central role in the drug trade since the dismantling of the rival Medellín cartel in the early 1990s.

The low-lying and extremely hot city (with temperatures routinely surpassing 40°C) saddles the **Río Cali**, a tributary of the Río Cauca from which the marshy valley of sugar plantations surrounding Cali derives its name. The large numbers of African slaves brought to work the sugar mills left a notable impact on Cali's culture, no more so than in its music. The city stakes a powerful claim to being Colombia's party capital, and if you walk its steamy streets any time of the day or night and you'll hear Cuban-style **salsa** music blaring from the numerous clubs.

Arrival, information and city transport

The best way into town from Cali's **Palmaseca airport**, twenty kilometres north-east of the city, is to hire a minibus, which takes about a half-hour and costs US$1.50. The city's gigantic **bus terminal**, at C 30N No. 2AN-29, is a 25-minute walk following the river along Av 2N.

The city's main **tourist office**, the Fondo Mixto de Promoción del Valle de Cauca, at C 8 No. 3–14, 13th floor (Mon–Fri 9am–5pm; ⓣ2/886-1300), offers information about excursions outside the city.

Most local sightseeing can be done on foot; go by **bus** (US$0.25) to leave the centre, local . At night, however, be sure to call a **taxi**. Try Taxi Libre ⓣ2/444-4444 or Taxis Valcali ⓣ2/443-0000.

Accommodation

Calidad House C 17N No. 9AN–39 ⓣ2/661-2338. British-run youth hostel with dorm rooms, kitchen and laundry facilities. Rooms are bare but the atmosphere is friendly. ❶

Iguana C 21N No. Av 9N–22 ⓣ2/661-3522. Swiss-run youth hostel with laundry service and

Internet access. They can arrange salsa classes as well as excursions. ❶

Imperial C 9 No. 3–93 ☎2/889-9571. Old World elegance meats modern comfort at the *Imperial*, which offers an open-air swimming pool and rooms with a/c for great value. ❹

Windsor Plaza C 17N No. 4N–65 ☎2/660-6390. *Windsor Plaza* features clean, newly furnished rooms and friendly staff. Adjacent Italian restaurant makes for relaxed lounge. ❻

The City

The city's centre is **Plaza de Caicedo**, which has a statue of independence hero Joaquín de Caycedo y Cuero in the middle. On the plaza's south end is the nineteenth-century **Catedral**, which stands out for its elaborate stained-glass windows. Walking north along Calle 12 and you'll run into the Río Cali. On your right, at Cra 1 and C 13, impossible to miss with its tall spires and striking powder-blue facade, is the Gothic-style **Iglesia de la Ermita**. To your right is the Neoclassical **Colombia de Tobaco** building, now an office building, which is a fine example from the city's early twentieth-century economic boom.

While few make a special trip to Cali besides partygoers and salsa fans, it offers several splendid colonial churches. The oldest is the **Iglesia de la Merced**, on the corner of Cra 4 and C 7, built from adobe and stone shortly after the city's founding. In the adjoining monastery, the **Museo de Arte Colonial y Religioso** (Mon–Sat 9am–1pm & 2–6pm; US$0.75) exhibits an extensive collection of New World religious relics. Cali residents are also proud of their **Zoológico** (Mon–Sun 9am–5pm; US$2), where you can get so close to the animals it's almost dangerous. It's located on spacious grounds on the south bank of the Río Cali, on Cra 2A West and C 14, about 3km from the city centre.

If you have time for just one excursion, be sure to visit **El Paraiso** (Tues–Sun 9am–4.30pm; US$1), the colonial hacienda that served as the backdrop for Jorge Isaacs's *María*, considered the apogee of nineteenth-century Latin American literary romanticism. The well-maintained house is decorated as it would have been when Isaacs lived here, with bedpans, candlestick chandeliers and a working aqueduct that delivers water and a pleasant, fresh breeze throughout the estate. But even more amazing is its location, on a gentle slope halfway between a verdant mountain chain rising directly from the backyard and an immense spread of sugarcane fields. To get to El Paraiso take any bus from Cali north that passes El Cerrito, forty kilometres away, from where you can share a taxi to the estate for US$4. Alternatively, on Sundays, *busetas* shuttle picnickers every two hours between El Paraiso and Palmira, eighteen kilometres from Cali, for US$1.

Eating, drinking and nightlife

Cauca Valley cuisine consists of heavy portions of chicken and pork. Food stalls around town often sell *mazorcas*, baked corn on the cob, as well as fresh fruit. *Manjar blanco*, made from sugar and served with a biscuit, is a highly popular desert.

Cali's reputation as Colombia's **salsa capital** suffered a setback in late 2002 with the implementation of a municipal ordinance ordering clubs to shut down at midnight to help curb night-time violence. As a result, the party has moved to clubs just beyond the city limits, in suburbs like Menga and Juanchito. The cheaper, traditional clubs along Avenida 6 get started early in the afternoon, but really pullulate with revellers on the weekends.

Cali Viejo Parque El Bosque near the Zoológico. Fine restaurant with lovely, flowered garden. Specializes in local Cauca Valley cuisine.

La Casa de la Cerveza Av 8N No. 10N–18. Serving cheap beer in boot-size glasses, this rustic pub has an excellent ambience for kicking off any night. If you're still here after 10pm, you'll find up to 300 people crowding the dancefloor.

Changó Vía Cavasa Km 2 ⓦwww.chango.com.co. Named after the African god of virility and leisure, *Changó* overlooks the Río Cauca at the entrance to Juanchito. It features two dancefloors and a relaxed environment.

La Flor de la Canela Av 6 Bis Norte No. 27–50. The Peruvian chef-owner serves excellent *ceviche* at this reasonably priced restaurant.

Grill Tropicali Av 6N No. 15N–66. One of Avenida Sexta's classic salsa joints, *Grill Tropicali* serves good cocktails.

Panadería Kuty Av 6N No. 27N–03. This is a great place for sidewalk dining on the weekends when the city centre clears out. Try the excellent omelettes or fruit juices.

Tajamares Av 9N No. 10–81. Decorated with the colours and spirit of Carnaval, this upscale restaurant specializes in Caribbean cuisines. Try the *tairona acocado*, a lobster wrapped in beef dish. Nice Latin jazz sets relaxed atmosphere.

Popayán

Although less illustrious than Cartagena, Colombia's other open-air colonial museum, **POPAYÁN**, has little reason to envy its more celebrated rival. Founded in 1537 by Sebastián de Belalcazár on his march northward from Quito, the town was a powerful counterweight to Bogotá's dominance during the colonial era and a bastion of Spanish loyalty during the wars of independence. Unlike Cartagena, which saw its influence wane after independence, Popayán's aristocrats remained very active in politics, and no fewer than eleven presidents have emerged from their ranks.

Civic pride runs high in Popayán. When a disastrous earthquake destroyed most of the historic centre in 1983 residents banded together to rebuild, and the result is one of the most attractive cities in Colombia, with cobblestone streets and whitewashed mansions that in many ways look better and more uniformly conserved than before the earthquake. In addition to its architectural splendour, the city of 232,000 is uniquely tranquil and traditional for a city of its size. Not a single traffic light pervades the quiet city centre, which still comes to a complete standstill during the midday siesta. During Easter week the city is cordoned off to make way for thousands of parading worshipers brandishing candles and colourful flowers.

Accommodation

It's almost impossible not to have an incredible **hotel** room in Popayán. The town boasts a plethora of colonial residences tastefully converted into hotels and small B&Bs, many of which are ridiculously inexpensive.

Camino Real C 5A No. 5–59 ☎2/824-3595/0685. Colonial house with charming restaurant. Breakfast is included and the service is friendly service. ❺

Casa Familiar El Descanso Cra 5 No. 2–41 ☎2/822-4787. The very clean but small rooms here look out on a luminous lounge shared with the family. The owner is highly knowledgeable, but there is no kitchen service. ❶

Casa Familiar Turistica Cra 5 No. 2–11 ☎2/824-4853. On a quiet street, the *Casa Familiar Turistica* is a nice colonial house whose friendly owner offers shared rooms with bath. This is the closest thing to a youth hostel in Popayán. ❶

Santo Domingo C 4A No. 5–14 ☎2/824-0676/1607. Each of the seven rooms at Popayán's most elegant B&B look down upon a brick courtyard and are decorated with eighteenth-century furniture. The service is very personable. ❺

The City

There are so many **churches** in Popayán that it's almost impossible not to run into one every two or three blocks. The whitewashed **Catedral** overlooks **Parque Caldas**, the town's main square. Although the biggest and most frequently used, architecturally it's the least important having been built around 1900 on the site where two earlier structures stood. Four blocks east, on C 2 and Cra 5, the city's oldest standing church, **La Ermita**, features an austere single-naved chapel comprised of wooden ribbing and a golden altar dating from 1564. Three blocks away, on C 4 and Cra 5, the **Iglesia de Santo Domingo**'s, Baroque stone portal is an excellent example of Spanish New World architecture. Equally ornate is the staircased pulpit of **Iglesia de San Francisco**, situated on a quiet plaza on C 4 and Cra 9, where several of Popayán's patrician families are buried.

The best way to appreciate Popayán's Rococo riches is to wander aimlessly the streets radiating from Parque Caldas. Several colonial homes have been donated to the government and converted into museums, offering a rare glimpse into the salon society of the colonial and early independence era. One of the best maintained is the **Museo Mosquera** (8am–noon & 2–6pm; US$0.50) on C 3 No. 5–14, which was the childhood residence of Tomás Cipriano de Mosquera, four times Colombia's president. There's a room dedicated to General Carlos Albán, who died a hero resisting Panama's secession from Colombia. The **Museo Negret** (8am–noon & 2–6pm; US$0.50) on C 5 No. 10–23, was the home of modernist sculptor Edgar Negret and is now a museum exhibiting his work. Next door the **Museo Iberoamericano de Arte Moderno** (8am–noon & 2–6pm; US$0.50) exhibits Negret's private collection of works by Picasso and other important artists from Spain and Latin America. The **Museo Casa Valencia** (8am–noon & 2–6pm; US$0.50) is an eighteenth-century home belonging to the city's most famous bard, Guillermo Valencia. The well-conserved, two-story mansion contains a vast collection of colonial paintings and furniture as well as the burial remains of the poet's son, Colombian President Guillermo León Valencia.

Well worth a detour is the nearby rural village of Silvia, which fills up with Guambiano Indians in colourful blue and fuchsia dress every Tuesday for market day. Buses (US$1) leave every hour from Popayán's bus terminal a fifteen-minute walk from the centre along Autopista Norte to Cali. The scenery during the two-hour ride is breathtaking.

Eating, drinking and nightlife

Most of Popayán's finer **restaurants** occupy the colonial patios of some of the town's choicer hotels, an ideal setting for a quiet, slow meal. Although subdued, Popayán's **cafés and bars** are a great place to converse with locals. Popayán's peacefulness is its biggest charm and as expected its **nightlife** is sedate. But if you've come south from Cali you'll probably need a break anyway. The historic centre boasts several appealing spots ideal for settling in with a book, meeting locals and soaking in the town's heritage.

La Cave Cra 7 No. 2–71. A candle-lit bistro started by two Frenchmen, *La Cave* serves sumptuous sandwiches during the day and affordable, freshly prepared haute cuisine like wild mushroom chicken marsala at night.

La Iguana Afro Club C 4 No. 9–67. Knowledgeable owner Diego Velásquez spins records from his extensive Latin Jazz and 1970s salsa collection in this low-key, rustic pub.

Kaldivia Café C 5 No. 5–63. This inviting café serves gourmet grinds, by the cup or in bulk ,in decorative, airtight pouches that make excellent gifts. Closes early.

Pizzería Italiana C 4 No. 8–83. A good meeting place, this Swiss-owned pizzeria serves good pasta as well as fondue and more exotic, European dishes.

La Viña C 4 No. 7–79. *La Viña* does a good breakfast complemented by fresh fruit juices. Otherwise serves fast but good Colombian dishes at economical prices.

San Agustín and the Parque Arqueológico

The thoroughly laid-back little town of **SAN AGUSTÍN** 140 kilometres southeast of Popayán has everything a hippie could want – awesome landscape, cryptic ruins and bargain-basement prices. If that's not enough, there's also the San Isidro mushroom, a powerful hallucinogenic that grows especially well in the surrounding area's perennially green pastures. But even if you're not part of the rainbow culture there's still plenty to discover here. The town is home to one of the continent's most important archaeological sites. Some 3300 years ago the jagged landscape around the town was inhabited by masons whose singular legacy is the hundreds of monumental stone statues comparable in size and detail to the more famous Maoi statues found on Chile's Easter Island (see p.580).

Much mystery still surrounds the civilization that built the monoliths, though the surreal imagery of sex-crazed monkeys, serpent-headed humans and other disturbing zoomorphic glyphs suggest that San Isidro may have already been working its magic when the statues were first created. What is known, at least, is that the priestly culture disappeared before the Spanish arrived, probably at the hands of the Incas, whose empire stretched into southern Colombia. The statues weren't discovered until the middle of the eighteenth century.

Parque Arqueológico

The nearest archeological sites are 2.5 kilometres west of San Agustín in the **PARQUE ARQUEOLÓGICO** (daily 8am–4pm; US$2), declared a UNESCO Heritage Site in 1995. About 2.5 kilometres outside town, the park contains over a hundred statues – some as tall as seven metres – the largest concentration of statues in the area. Many of them are left as they were found, and others, like the ones in the sector of the park known as the **Bosque de las Estatuas**, are rearranged and linked by an interpretative trail. There's also a museum in the park that displays Indian earthenware. To tour the park you'll need at least three hours, and if you don't want to spend up to US$20 for the price of a guide be sure to buy an English-language guidebook for about US$3.50.

Hundreds more statues are littered across the colourful hillside on either side of the Río Magdalena, the source of which can be visited in a strenuous five-day hike. For most visitors, walking or horseback riding through the steep, unspoiled landscape is more impressive than the ruins themselves. The numerous trails could keep you busy for more than a week but the most popular destinations, none of which requires a guide and many of which are within a day's return hike from town, are **La Chaquira**, **La Pelota** and **Alto de los Idolos** (US$1.50 entrance fee). If you do venture into the hills bring along rain gear and good boots as the weather near San Agustín often changes throughout the day. If you do hire a guide – don't worry, they'll find you first – be sure they're accredited by the **tourism office** inside the town hall, C 3 and Cra 12 (Mon–Fri 8am–noon & 2–6pm; ⓣ8/837-3061) and not overcharging. If in doubt, check with rates at your hotel, as they can usually arrange cheaper packages.

Practicalities

In February 2003, the FARC dynamited a bridge over the Río Mazamorras thus doubling the travel time to San Agustín. It's now a full-day, twelve-hour journey from Popayán via La Plata, but the long haul and bumpy road is redeemed by being able to look out of the bus window at the beautiful scenery. You'll probably be stopped at **army and guerrilla roadblocks** separated a short distance from one another; in general, the extent of the harassment reported is the occasional stolen camera or payment of a minimal road toll, but it is best to leave all valuables in Popayán. For those going on to Bogotá, or coming from the capital, it makes sense to exit San Agustín via the paved road to Neiva rather than backtrack to Popayán.

While budget **accommodation** in San Agustín abounds, more modern hotels are harder to come by. *Casa de Francois*, 1km along Via El Tablón (ⓣ8/837-3847; ❶) offers cheap lodging and an easy-going but sociable environment. The French owner of this colourful shack on a bluff overlooking the city is so laid back he's horizontal most of the time. It is popular with backpackers and serves home-made bread and free coffee. Also on the outskirts of town, *Casa de Nelly* (☎8/8373-221), on Via la Estrella 1.5 kilometres along Av 2, is a peaceful and attractive lodge catering to backpackers, while *Osoguiaco* (☎8/837-3069; ❸), 1.5km along Av Parque Arqueológico, has a large swimming pool on spacious grounds and allows camping.

For **restaurants**, *Brahama*, on C 5 No. 15–11, serves *comida tipica* and vegetarian dishes, while the *Tea Rooms*, near *Casa de Nelly,* is great for economical, hearty meals. The more expensive *La Brasa*, one kilometre along the road to the Parque Arquelógico, is a great place for steaks.

Tierradentro

After San Agustín, **Tierradentro** is Colombia's most treasured archeological complex. Its hallmarks are a hundred-odd circular burial caverns – some as deep as seven metres – decorated with elaborate geometric iconography. Monumental statues have also been found here, indicating a cultural influence from San Agustín, yet, like the latter, little is known about the Tierradentro civilization other than that it flourished around 1000 AD.

Surprisingly, considering its complex burial rituals, no large population centres have been discovered here, lending credence to the belief that the original inhabitants belonged to a dispersed group of loosely related farmers. The tomb dwellers' modern descendants are the **Paez Indians**, 25,000 of whom live in the surrounding hillside. During the colonial era, the Paez were known as a ruthless warrior tribe, a reputation that allowed them to remain free of Spanish subjugation well into the seventeenth century.

Tierradentro means "Inner Land", an appropriate nickname to describe the rugged countryside of narrow valley and jagged summits. Less touristy than San Agustín, the wide variety of hikes to outlying Indian villages, cascading waterfalls and high altitude *paramos* are enough to easily keep walkers busy for more than a week.

Most tourists to the area stay in **San Andrés de Pisimbalá**, four kilometres from *El Cruce* on the main Popayán–La Plata road. The tiny village is within walking distance of most burial sites. It has a picturesque thatched roof chapel that dates from the seventeenth-century mission. You should start your visit at the **Tierradentro Museum** (daily 8am–5pm; US$1.50), halfway on the road to El Cruce, which contains pottery urns and other ossuary artefacts. There's also information on the Paez and a useful model of the surrounding region. Your ticket to the museum is valid for entry into the archeological park, which contains four **cave sites** – Segovia, El Duende, Altod de San Andrés and El Aguacate – spread across a sublime landscape. Be sure to bring your own torch when exploring the tombs, as most are unlit.

Practicalities

Getting to Tierradentro has become a logistical nightmare of late. Sporadic fighting between the guerrillas and the army has effectively cut off all direct links with Popayán, 113 kilometres away on a rough mountain road. The best alternative from Popayán is to take a bus (there's at least one a day) for US$5 to La Plata, about six hours away, and then transfer to another heading towards Belalcazar, another five hours along a scenic road. If the bus does not continue to El Cruce outside San Andrés, there are frequent *chivas* that do. In general, when travelling in this area be prepared for long waits, even overnight stays, as delays are frequent. From La Plata you can also make connections to San Agustín but be prepared for another full day of travel.

As in San Agustín, the **accommodation** in Tierradentro is cheap. The most modern spot in town, *El Refugio* (☎8/252-904; ❹), is still a bargain. It is close to the museum, offers a restaurant and a swimming pool and has camping available.

Pasto

Capital of Nariño department and home to some 325,000 residents, **PASTO** is the commercial hub of southern Colombia. Although the surrounding foothills of the Galeras Volcano are attractive, the bustling town is devoid of major sights and likely to be visited only in passing on the way to Ecuador, 88 kilometres further south along the Pan American highway. The southern stretch of the highway between Pasto and Popayán is notoriously unsafe, and all overland travelling at night should be avoided.

Founded in 1537 by Sebastían de Belalcázar on his march from Quito, Pasto sided with Spain during the wars of independence and later tried to fuse with Ecuador when Bolívar's Nueva Granada confederation split up in 1830. Successive earthquakes have destroyed most of its colonial architecture but a few churches still recall its past glory. The **Cristo Rey** at C 20 and Cra 24, noted for its stained-glass windows, is the best-preserved church in town, while the pulpit at the city's oldest church, **San Juan Bautista**, on C 18 and Cra 25, was built in the Arabesque Mudéjar style. The **Museo de Oro** (Mon–Fri 9am–7pm, Sat 9am–1pm; US$0.25), at C 19 No. 21–27, exhibits art from the region's pre-Columbian cultures.

Each early January, the politically incorrect **Carnaval de Blancos y Negros** presents one of Colombia's most traditional celebrations. The festival's racist roots date from the colonial period when, once a year, slaves would paint themselves white and their masters, in approval, would parade the next day in blackface. Pasto is also known for its handicrafts, especially the *barniz de pasto*, a china-like finish to decorate wooden objects. Examples can be bought at the Mercado de Bomboná, an artisan market on C 14 and Cra 27.

If you need a **place to stay**, *Don Saul*, on C 17 No. 23–52 (☎2/723-0618; ❹), has comfortable rooms with gym, sauna and **restaurant**. The *Koala Inn*, on C 18 No. 22–37 (☎2/722-1101; ❶) is a typical travellers' hostel with hot water and a **cafeteria**. The English-speaking owner is friendly, and the fridge is stacked with beer.

Crossing into Ecuador

The Colombian town of **Ipiales**, a three-hour bus ride (US$3) from Pasto, is two kilometres from the **Rumichaca Bridge**, which crosses into Ecuador at the town of Tulcán (see p.689). An Ecuadorian consulate is located in the DAS immigration complex where your passport is stamped before leaving. The heavily crossed border is open daily from 6am to 9pm.

5.6

Amazonia

Although Colombia's portion of the Amazon River basin occupies a third of its total territory, it remains only loosely integrated with the rest of the country. The region's staggering biodiversity – more than 6000 bird and animal species – is safeguarded in a half-dozen national parks. However, owing to the boggy terrain and thick forest, which makes road building impossible, only one, **Parque Nacional Amacayacú**, is at all accessible from the port city of **Leticia**, where most tourism is concentrated. Despite the fact that the region's difficult topography and isolation make travelling expensive, one silver lining is that it's not riddled like other areas by political violence. You'd be hard-pressed to find a safer "safe hole" than Leticia in Colombia.

Leticia and around

A stone's throw from Brazil and Peru, the end of the world settlement of **LETICIA** is a superb, if until recently overlooked, gateway to the Amazon. With 25,000 residents, it's the largest and most modern of Colombia's Amazon colonies, but still barely a shadow of the river's two other, rapidly growing tourist centres, Iquitos in Peru and Manaus in Brazil. The pint-sized town was settled by Peruvians in the mid-nineteenth century but passed into Colombian hands when the region's irregular border was redrawn in the 1930s to quell a series of skirmishes between Colombia, Peru and Brazil sparked by the rubber boom. Despite past tensions, relations with their neighbours couldn't be better today. The town has all but fused with the Brazilian port of **Tabatinga**, 4km down the road, for which no entry visa is required.

Carved, as it were, from the otherwise impenetrable jungle, you don't need to venture very far to experience the region's wildlife. Indeed, the town's main plaza, **Parque Santander**, is a symphony of sound and colour, especially when exotic parrots flock there at sunset. Leticia is landlocked and the only way out is via daily air connection to Bogotá available via Aero Republica. Several small **hotels** and *residencias* catering to tourists offer cheap lodging in Leticia, notably *Colonial*, at Cra 10 No. 7–08 (Ⓣ8/27164; ❺), which has air-conditioned rooms and a pool, and *Anaconda*, on Cra 11 No. 7–34 (Ⓣ8/27119, Ⓦwww.hotelanaconda.com.co; ❺), a full-service resort hotel with pool, cable TV, **restaurant** and a good terrace. It also runs jungle tours.

Parque Nacional Amacayacú

Most visitors to Letitica will want to take a jungle tour two hours up the Amazon by boat to **PARQUE NACIONAL AMACAYACÚ** (entrance fee US$7), a 293,000-hectare preserve created in 1975. The park, only a small part of which is open to the public, is home to some 500 bird species and 150 mammals, including pink river dolphins and the world's smallest monkey, the *tití leoncito.* Tours of the park are led by indigenous guides from the **ticuna** tribe still living in virtual isolation in the park's interior. The highlight is a walk on a rope bridge built above the forest canopy from which you can see the virgin jungle stretch off into the horizon. There are also visits to several indigenous settlements where you can buy handicrafts made before your eyes by the villagers. Boats to the park can be hired along the riverfront in Leticia (US$10.50). A restaurant and affordable lodging in beds or hammocks are available. Be sure to bring cash, as there are no places to get money.

Crossing into Brazil and Peru

Three days a week there are **flights** to Manaus from the Brazilian town of Tabatinga, just across the border. Minibuses leaving Leticia for the Tabatinga airport cost US$0.60. Although flights occasionally operate to **Iquitos** (see p.951) and **Lima** (see p. 000), don't count on that being the case when you're there. Otherwise, your only way to cross into Peru is by **river cruise** on the Amazon. Speedboats **to** Iquitos leave daily for about US$50. For a more adventurous, if somewhat primitive, experience you can hang a hammock between dead fish and live chickens on the deck of one of the slow barges (about US$15) that follow the same route in three days. Food is provided, but be sure to bring water and plenty of insect repellent. Several boats of varying standards also leave Tabatinga for **Manaus** (see p.401), a journey of no more than four days. Even if you leave Colombia overland you'll have to go to the airport in Leticia to have your passport stamped.

6

Ecuador

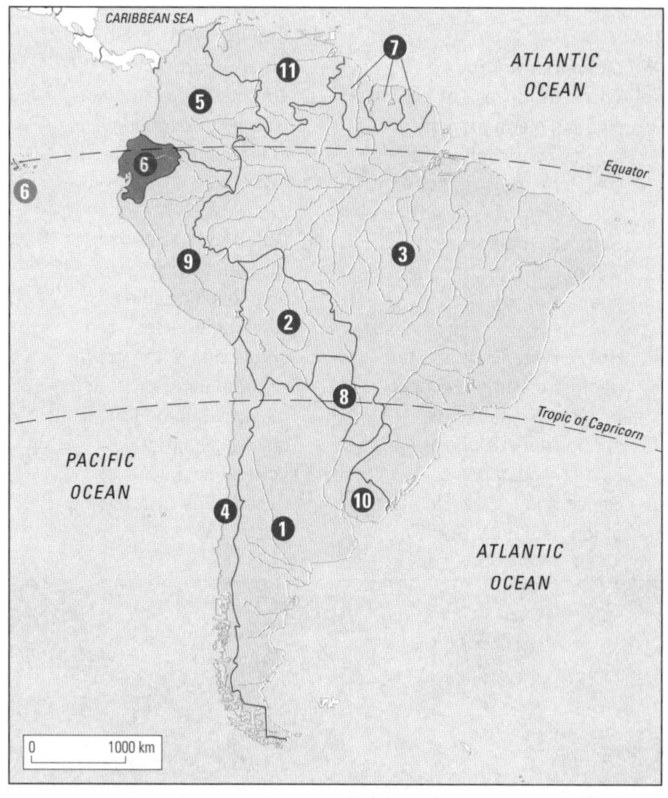
CARIBBEAN SEA
ATLANTIC OCEAN
Equator
PACIFIC OCEAN
Tropic of Capricorn
ATLANTIC OCEAN
0 1000 km

Ecuador highlights

* **Quito Old Town** A World Heritage site with a beautifully preserved historic centre packed with elegant squares, churches and monasteries. See p.668

* **Otavalo market day** There are dozens of fascinating sierra markets, but for handicrafts and weavings the size, colour and energy of Otavalo's Saturday market are without rival on the continent. See p.678

* **Hot springs** In an active geothermal area, Ecuador boasts dozens of hot springs set in stunning scenery, but those at Baños and Papallacta are among the best. See p.691

* **Cuenca** Ecuador's finest colonial city, of stately architecture and cobbled streets, imbued with a relaxed and cultivated air. See p.697

* **Staying with an indigenous community in the Oriente** There's no better way to experience life in the rainforest. See p.705

* **Galápagos Islands** Unique, humbling and awe-inspiring, the "Enchanted Isles" constitute one of the greatest wonders of the natural world, home to fearless wildlife that provoked humankind to question its own origins. See p.736

Introduction and basics

Sitting on the equator between Colombia and Peru, **Ecuador** is the smallest of the Andean nations, covering an area no bigger than Nevada. For all its diminutive size, however, the country is packed with the most startling contrasts of scenery, where you can find yourself in steaming tropical rainforests amongst clouds of neon-coloured butterflies one day, and in a highland market beneath ice-capped volcanoes, mixing with scarlet-ponchoed *indígenas* the next. It's also a country of astounding **biodiversity**, boasting 1600 species of bird (more per area than any other South American country), and over 3500 species of orchid, to cite just two examples.

Nowhere is this spectacular and unique wildlife more apparent than in the Galápagos Islands, where Charles Darwin first developed his theories on evolution.

Geographically, Ecuador's mainland divides into three distinct regions. Running down its centre is the **sierra**, formed by the eastern and western chains of the Andes, joined by a series of high plateaux at around 2800m above sea level, which form the agricultural and indigenous heartland of Ecuador. East of the sierra, the **Oriente** is a large, sparsely populated area extending into the upper Amazon basin, much of it covered by dense tropical rainforest. West of the sierra, the **coastal region** is formed by a fertile alluvial plain, used for growing tropical crops, which borders the Pacific in a string of beaches, mangrove swamps, shrimp farms and ports.

All this provides a home to some fourteen million people, a largely **mestizo** (mixed) population, but with a strong **indigenous** component, particularly among the Quichua-speaking communities of the rural sierra, and the various ethnic groups of the Oriente and northern coast, where there's also a significant black population.

Where to go

The capital **Quito**, the common point of arrival and base between excursions, offers a modern district, featuring good services, hotels, restaurants and travel agents, and a gorgeous colonial centre with narrow streets, stately plazas, and exquisite monasteries and churches. Within a few hours to the north, **Otavalo**, the focus of a region famed for its *artesanías*, hosts the country's largest and most famous **market**, while to the northwest there are a number of excellent **cloudforest reserves**, misty, otherworldly havens of gnarled and vine-draped trees teeming with wildlife.

South of Quito, the so-called **Quilotoa loop**, west of Latacunga, passes through some of the best scenery of the **central sierra**: remote indigenous villages, vertiginous patchwork fields, haunting paramo and the dazzling crater lake of **Laguna Quilotoa**. More established attractions of this region include the **Parque Nacional Cotopaxi**, the spa town of **Baños**, and the train ride down the **Nariz del Diablo** ("the Devil's Nose") from **Riobamba**, a base for hikes and attempts on **Chimborazo**.

In the **southern sierra** you'll find Ecuador's most captivating colonial city, **Cuenca**, declared a UNESCO World Heritage Site, and a convenient base for visiting **Ingapirca** – the country's only major Inca ruins – and **Parque Nacional El Cajas**, a starkly beautiful protected area.

The **Oriente** holds one of Ecuador's greatest wildernesses – dense Amazonian **rainforests**. **Jungle lodges** make for the most comfortable way of experiencing the world's most exciting habitat, but **guided tours** or stays **with an indigenous community** are inexpensive and straightforward to arrange in **Tena**, **Misahuallí** and **Puyo**, while the grittier centres of the oil industry, **Lago Agrio** and **Coca**, are the gateways to the remotest forests and reserves.

On the **coast**, steamy **Guayaquil**, the country's largest and wealthiest city, is fast

emerging as a tourist destination, but is usually sidelined for dozens of popular **beach** resorts, such as the boisterous **Atacames**, laid-back **Canoa**, surf-mad **Montañita**, or prestigious **Salinas** and **Bahía de Caráquez** which are filled with smart high-rise condos. **Puerto López** is a good place to arrange whale-watching trips, hikes into the **Parque Nacional Machalilla**, or tours to see the birdlife on the **Isla de la Plata**.

Finally, Ecuador's showpiece, the **Galápagos Islands**, is for many the initial lure to the country, and arguably the most compelling nature spot in the world.

When to go

In the **sierra**, the warmest and driest months tend to be June to August and December, otherwise you can expect sunny, clear mornings and cloudy, often wet, afternoons; temperatures greatly depend on altitude, with Quito seeing daytime highs of around 25°C and lows of 8°C. In the **Oriente**, it will be warm (daytime average being about 25°, with the range occasionally topping 35°C in some lowland areas), humid and rainy throughout the year, though there may be more frequent let-ups in the daily rains between December and February. The **coast** has the most clearly defined wet and dry seasons, though even here there are variations, with generally drier weather seen in the south. It's hottest and wettest from December to May, with bursts of rain and bright clear skies, but for the rest of the year it can be overcast and cool, with very little rainfall on the southern coast. The **Galápagos** climate sees hot, sunny days interspersed with the odd heavy shower from January to June, and dry and overcast weather for the rest of the year, when the *garúa* mists are also prevalent and the sea is choppier.

Red tape and visas

Citizens of the EU, and North American and Australasian countries, do not need a visa to enter Ecuador, and only require a passport valid for more than six months, a return ticket and proof of having enough money for the duration of the stay. You'll be issued with a **T-3 tourist card** on arrival, which you should keep with your passport – it will be collected when you leave the country. The tourist card can allow up to ninety days' stay, though it's up to the official whether you're allocated thirty, sixty or ninety days on arrival.

You can get **extensions** for $10 at the Jefatura Provincial de Migración in provincial capitals, often at the same address as the police headquarters; and in Quito it's at Isla Seymour N44-174 and Río Coca, Sector Jipijapa (Mon–Fri 8am–12.30pm & 3–6.30pm; ☎02/224-7510). You can't be granted an extension until the day on which your tourist card runs out and there's a small fine if you renew it after it's expired. Extensions are given at the discretion of the relevant official in batches of thirty days, up to a maximum of 180 days per twelve months.

Once in Ecuador, you have to report to the Dirección de Extranjería at 10 de Agosto and General Murgeon in Quito (Mon–Fri 8am–1pm; ☎02/223-1022) within thirty days of arrival in order to get a **censo** (identity card); the procedure is bureaucratic and may take a couple of days with plenty of paperwork and visits to more than one authority. The officials often neglect to tell you this, but you'll also need **permission to leave** the country (*permiso de salida*). You can use it for multiple exits during the course of one year. Please note that visa regulations and procedures change regularly.

Note that for international flights, you must pay **departure tax** in cash at the airport: $25 when leaving Quito and $10 from Guayaquil.

Costs and money

In 2000, the **US dollar** became the official currency of Ecuador. Dollar bills are those issued from US banks and the coinage is a mixture of familiar US-minted cent pieces and Ecuadorian-minted coins that cannot be used outside the country. Bills come in denominations of $1, $5, $10, $20, $50 and $100. There is also a $2 bill, but it's uncommon. Coins come in 1, 5, 10, 25, 50 cent pieces (centavos), plus there are $1 coins only minted in the US. Be warned that $100 and $50 bills are rarely accepted at most shops and restaurants, and small change is often in short supply.

Despite price rises brought about by dollarization, Ecuador is still one of the **cheaper South American countries**. Those on a tight budget should be able to get by on $15–20 per day, with the occasional treat, less if travelling in a group and buying most food from markets. Spending $30–40 daily will get you accommodation in more comfortable hotels, better food and the occasional guided tour.

Overland from neighbouring countries

Overland entry into Ecuador is possible **from Peru and Colombia**, its only land neighbours. Details on border crossings are given at the relevant places in the chapter but, briefly, from Peru, there are three crossing points: Aguas Verdes north of Tumbes to **Huaquillas** in Ecuador (see p.731); Piura to **Macará**, southwest of Loja (see p.703); and Pantoja to **Nuevo Rocafuerte** (see p.710). From Colombia, the safest recommended crossing is from Ipiales to **Tulcán** (see p.685), but you should always check with the authorities for the latest security information in this area.

Watch out for **IVA** (*Impuesto al Valor Agregado*), a tax of twelve percent which is added to most goods and services in better-than-average hotels and restaurants, often in tandem with a further ten percent service charge.

The practice of charging foreigners much higher prices than Ecuadorian residents is becoming increasingly common for tourist attractions, museums, national parks and domestic flights. Some hotels and tour operators are also adopting this policy, but if you have a **censo** (see p.649), you can usually pay the national rate. Note that this two-tier system is not in operation for taxis and fbuses; you should be paying the same for them as anyone else.

Money-changing facilities and **ATMs** are generally scarce except in medium-sized towns. Visa cards and those using the Plus system are accepted at many ATMs in branches of Banco del Austro and Banco de Guayaquil; MasterCard and Cirrus or Maestro-related cards can be used at the machines owned by Banco del Pacífico and some branches of the Banco de Guayaquil and Produbanco. A smaller number of machines also accept American Express and Diners Club cards. For store purchases, Visa and MasterCard are the most widely accepted (note that in the Galápagos, MasterCard is just about the only option), followed by Diners Club and American Express. You may have to pay a surcharge of around ten percent on purchases in some places. Standard hotels, restaurants and shops are unlikely to accept credit cards even when they have stickers on the door; check first.

Take a reasonable proportion of your money in US dollars **travellers' cheques** – other currencies are rarely exchanged – preferably American Express ones, currently the most widely accepted brand. You can change them at some branches of Banco de Guayaquil, Produbanco, Banco del Pichincha and Banco del Pacífico. *Casas de cambio* (exchange bureaus) offer longer opening hours and swifter service, but have all but disappeared since dollarization.

Information and maps

In Ecuador there's a Ministry of Tourism **information office** in every provincial capital and the main tourist centres, having rudimentary maps, lists of hotels and restaurants, leaflets and probably basic information on any sites of interest in the area. Many regional centres also have tourist offices run by the municipality, which can be as good or better than their government counterparts.

Another good source of information is **South American Explorers** (**SAE**) (ⓦwww.samexplo.org), a non-profit organization that provides the latest information on travel, research and adventure sports in Central and South America. Membership is $50 per year ($80 per couple), which entitles you to use the clubhouse in Quito (see p.665) – plus two others in Peru at Lima and Cusco – where you have access to detailed country information and trip reports on everything from a Galápagos cruise to climbing Cotopaxi, a large range of maps, a lending library, bag storage and book exchange.

The widest selection of **maps** covering Ecuador in a range of scales is published by the Instituto Geográfico Militar in Quito, at Senierges and Paz y Miño (you'll need to bring your passport or ID along). The best internationally available general map of Ecuador is the 1:1,000,000 International Travel Maps Ecuador map (530 W Broadway, Vancouver, BC V5Z 1E9, Canada, ⓦwww.itmb.com). It also produces a map of the Galápagos Islands and Quito.

Accommodation

Accommodation in Ecuador comes in a variety of different guises; generally, in increasing order of comfort they are: *pensión*, *residencial*, *hostal*, *hotel* and *hostería* – terms that will often help give you some idea what to expect of the place. Note that a **motel** is the sort of place that charges guests by the hour. Some **hoteles** are as bad as the worst **pensiones**, however, and there's no substitute for having a good look round the rooms yourself before you sign in. In the highlands, you can hope for **hot water** in all but the cheapest places, but in the lowlands, where people largely consider it unnecessary, only the more exclusive hotels will offer such a luxury. Conversely, **air conditioning** and fans are more common at a cheaper level in the lowlands than in the highlands. **Mosquito nets** are usually – but not always – only in evidence on the coast and in jungle lodges; consider bringing one from home if you plan to spend time in remote lowland areas.

Prices are typically around the $7–12 mark for a standard bottom-end double room, falling to as little as $3–5 in the really basic places. For $15 a double you'd expect a clean room with private bath and decent plumbing. Greater comfort and more facilities such as cable TV and phone are more likely the more you pay, while anything over $40 a double is likely to be pretty smart and in many provincial places will get you the best room in town. At the top end, usually costing over $80, you'll find beautiful colonial haciendas, luxurious international hotels and jungle lodges near pristine forest.

Electricity is supplied at 110V/60Hz, and sockets are for two flat prongs. Fluctuations in the supply are common so you need to use a surge protector if you're plugging in expensive equipment.

With so few designated campsites and so much budget accommodation, not many people bother with **camping**, unless they're out exploring Ecuador's wildernesses. Generally, you'll be allowed to pitch a tent inside most parks and reserves, where you can sometimes use the facilities of a nearby guardpost or refuge but, on the whole, you'll have to be entirely self-sufficient. A few hotels mentioned in the chapter allow you to camp on their grounds and use their facilities at cheap rates.

Getting around

Ecuador's inexpensive and generally reliable **buses** are the country's most useful and preferred form of public transport, trundling along just about everywhere there's a road. The **Panamericana** (Pan American Highway) forms the backbone of the country's road network, linking all major highland towns and cities. The network's biggest problem has always been the **weather** – floods and landslides are common – while the rough nature of the terrain means that travelling in the country's highland regions is much slower than small-scale maps suggest.

By bus

Hundreds of bus companies ply the country's roads, with anything from fleets of non-stop air-conditioned buses with TV, toilet and on-board snacks, to beaten-up old monsters with cracked windows, growling gears and belching exhausts. The further into the backwaters you go, the more the standards of comfort are likely to drop. At the margins of the bus network, pick-up trucks (**camionetas**), minibuses (**busetas**) and open-sided trucks converted to hold wooden benches (**rancheras**, **chivas**) often fill the vacuum. **Avoid travelling on buses at night.**

Larger towns usually have a main **bus terminal** (*terminal terrestre*), where all the long-distance bus companies are based. In smaller towns, company offices and departure points may be scattered around, though they're usually never very far from the central square or main thoroughfare. You can buy your **fare** from the conductor (*ayudante*) on board, or from the ticket office at the terminal. If you can, bring your **luggage** inside the bus with you and keep it in sight. Local **city buses** in the larger towns generally carry a board in the window showing their route, with a list of street names and key landmarks.

By car

Bus coverage is such that you'll only need to **rent a car**, if you intend to zoom around the country in a short space of time, or want to get to really off-the-beaten-track destinations. Expect to pay around $35 a day or $230 a week for a small hatchback, and from around $60 a day or $450 a week for a mid-sized 4WD, including insurance and tax. You will need to be at least 25 years old and have a major credit card for the deposit. An international licence isn't necessary, but certainly useful at Ecuador's many police checkpoints. The national **speed limit** is 100km per hour on highways (or less if indicated), and usually around 50km per hour in towns or urban areas. Note that there are draconian penalties (rarely enforced) for minor motoring offences.

Four-wheel-drive definitely comes in handy on unpaved roads, especially in the rainy season, but isn't necessary for the busier and better-maintained parts of the road network. Excesses on insurance, known as *el deducible*, or *la franquicia*, are usually frighteningly high – around $1000 in the case of damage to the vehicle, and around $3000 for theft or "total destruction", as the rental companies alarmingly put it.

Never drive at night if you can avoid it, as this is when most accidents occur, in part owing to the absence of decent road markings and the lack of signs alerting drivers to hazards. Never leave valuables in your car at any time, or your car on the street overnight; try only to stay in hotels with a garage, or else leave your vehicle overnight in a securely locked parqueqadero.

By train

Ecuador's rail system once stretched from Guayaquil and Cuenca in the south to San Lorenzo near the Colombian coast in the north, but lack of funding, the rise of road-building and a string of disruptions caused by landslides and El Niño events has effectively finished it off as a means of public transport, and relegated it to a tourist curiosity. At the time of writing, there were only a few services in operation, notably the **Nariz del Diablo** (see box on p.693) from Riobamba to Durán.

By air

Flying within Ecuador is a quick, convenient and relatively inexpensive way of getting around; you could cut an all-day bus journey down to a 30-minute hop – and enjoy wonderful aerial views of volcanoes and rainforests while you do so. There are two main domestic carriers, **Tame** (Ⓦwww.tame.com.ec) and **Icaro** (Ⓦwww.icaro.com.ec), plus a number of small-scale and local charter companies, particularly on the coast and in the Oriente. Tame offers the most extensive service, flying to most of the country's major centres, with ticket **prices** between $30 and $60 one-way, apart from flights to the Galápagos Islands, which are disproportionately expensive. Busier routes should be booked days, if not weeks, in advance and it's important to reconfirm, as overbooking is not uncommon.

By boat

The most likely place you'll end up in a boat is in the **Oriente**, where the best of the jungle is often a boat ride away. On the **coast**, the repaired coastal highway which now runs the entire length of the Ecuadorian seaboard, means you're less likely to need to travel by boat, though a few communities in the northern Pacific lowlands are still only reachable by river boat. Travel around the Galápagos Islands is almost exclusively by boat. A **chartered boat** (*flete*) is always much more expensive than going on a public one, though you can reduce costs by gathering a group; the fare is usually fixed for the journey regardless of the number of passengers. Be prepared for intense sun, torrential rain and hard wooden seats.

Mail and communications

Letters and postcards **sent from Ecuador** can take anything from five days to a month to reach their destination, though they're often faster to North America than anywhere else. If you need to send something of value, you're probably better off using a courier.

You can receive **poste restante** at just about any post office in the country. In Quito, Lista de Correos mail usually ends up at the main office on Espejo and Guayaquil in the old town; if marked "Correo Central", it could well go to the head office on Eloy Alfaro 354 and Avenida 9 de Octubre. **American Express** cardholders can make use of AmEx offices for mail services, and some **embassies** also do poste restante. The **SAE** will take mail, phone messages (during club hours) and fax messages for members.

The telephone service is currently split

between three state-run arms: **Andinatel**, serving the sierra and the Oriente; **Pacífictel** for the coast and Galápagos; and **Etapa** for Cuenca. The system is slowly modernizing, with more phone offices opening, and far cheaper prices for international calls, though the service can still be erratic in rural areas. Even small towns and some villages have a **telephone office** (daily 8am–10pm, except in remoter places), which are generally the cheapest and most straightforward places for conventional calls. The phone companies are also beginning to install **public phone boxes**, but far more prevalent at the moment are the cellular public phones maintained by Porta and Bell South, which use prepaid phone cards specific to each company, usually sold at a nearby shop or kiosk (look for a sign).

Calling North America costs $0.47 a minute, Europe $0.58 and the rest of the world $0.73 (except South American countries). Many offices will now let you dial direct without questions, but a few places may still want to know how long you wish to speak for, or ask for a deposit, and cut you off if you overstep either.

You can now get **Internet access** in small towns, villages and even some remote backwaters. Quito is the national centre of Internet activity, with a huge number of cafés, mostly focused in the Mariscal area, and fierce competition which keeps prices as low as $0.50–0.70 for an hour online. Even in areas further afield where national phone rates are needed to link to a server, it's rare to be charged more than $2–3 per hour.

Food and drink

Eating out can cost less than $2 per head if you stick to set menus; at **lunch** this is called *almuerzo* and at **dinner** *merienda*, which consist of two or three courses and a drink. À la carte and individual **main courses** (*platos fuertes*) are typically $2–5 – you're probably in a smart place if it's much more than $7.

In the **highlands**, a typical meal might start off with a *locro*, a delicious **soup** of potato, cheese and corn with half an avocado tossed in for good measure. Other soups might be *caldo de patas*, cattle hoof soup; *caldo de gallina*, chicken soup; or even *caldo de manguera*, which literally means "hose pipe soup", a polite name for bull's penis soup. For a **main course** you might go for *llapingachos*, cheesy potato cakes or *mote*, a hard corn that is peeled with calcium carbonate solution and then boiled in salt water – cheese, corn and potatoes are big in the highlands – perhaps served with *fritada*, seasoned pork deep-fried in lard, and *hornado*, pork slow-roasted in the oven, *lomo* (steak) or *pollo* (chicken) and fried eggs. The famous *cuy*, **guinea pig** roasted whole, has remained for centuries a speciality of the indigenous highlanders, and is rather good, if a bit expensive.

Coastal delicacies, unsurprisingly, centre on **seafood.** The classic *ceviche* is prepared by marinating raw seafood in lime juice and chilli, and serving with raw onion. On the north coast, *encocados* are fantastic fish dishes with a Caribbean flavour, cooked in a sauce of coconut milk, tomato and garlic and often served with a huge mound of rice. Bananas and plantain often replace the potato, appearing in many different forms on the side of your plate. *Patacones* are thick-cut plantains fried up in oil and served with plenty of salt, while *chifles* are thinly cut plantains cooked the same way.

The **Oriente**, being originally composed of many disparate indigenous groups, has rather less well-defined specialities, but you can count on *yuca* (a manioc similar to yam) making an appearance, alongside rice, bananas and fish (including the scrawny piranha) caught in the rivers. As a guest of a forest community, you may eat game such as wild pig or *guanta*, a large rodent not that different to *cuy*.

There's no shortage of **vegetarian food** in the main tourist centres, but away from those, the cry of "*soy vegeteriano*" ("*vegeteriana*" for a woman), "I'm a vegetarian", will sometimes be met with offers of fish or chicken. A quick discussion with the staff usually ends with them finding something appropriate for you, even if it's just egg, chips and rice – and even the blandest food can be enlivened by *ají*, the chilli sauce found on most restaurant dining tables.

Drinking

Bottled **mineral water** can be bought throughout the country in still (*sin gas*) or sparkling (*con gas*) varieties, which you should drink instead of tap water.

Ecuador has more types of fruit than you can imagine, certainly far more than there are English names for, and just about all of them are made into mouthwatering **juices** (*jugos*). Juices can come pure (*puro*) or mixed with water – make sure it's purified water. When they're mixed with milk they're called *batidos*.

Considering that Ecuador is a major **coffee**-producing country, it's a shame there's not more of the real stuff about. You'll get a cup of hot milk if you ask for *café con leche*, and hot water for black coffee if you specify *café negro*. **Tea** (*té*) is served without milk and usually with a slice of lemon. Asking for *té con leche* is likely to get you a cup of hot milk and a teabag. For just a dash of milk, it's best not to say anything until your (milkless) tea arrives, and then ask for a little milk. **Herbal teas** (*aromáticas* or *mates*) come in a variety of flavours, some of which are familiar, while others are made from native plants.

Beer essentially comes in three forms: Pilsener is the people's beer, weak and light and in big bottles; Club is a bit stronger, a bit more expensive and comes in small bottles or cans; and Biela, from the slang word short for "*bien helada*" ("well chilled"). Ecuadorian **wine** isn't common, but you'll find good Chilean and Argentinian vintages in the smarter restaurants for less than you'd pay at home. The local tipple, especially in the sierra, is **chicha**, a fermented corn drink of which there are many varieties. Buckets – literally – of the stuff do the rounds at all highland fiestas. In the Oriente, the *chicha* is made from *yuca*, which is chewed up, spat in a pot and allowed to ferment. **Aguardiente** (also called *caña* or *punta*) is a sugarcane spirit, sharper than rum (*ron*), that will take off the roof of your mouth. In fiestas they might mix it with fruit juices, or in the sierra drink it as *canelazo*, adding sugar, cinnamon (*canela*) and hot water to make a traditional highland warmer.

Safety and the police

Opportunistic and **sneak theft** are the main problems in Ecuador, usually aided by carelessness and lack of awareness, but another concern are the **con-artists** who employ an array of tricks to distract your attention away from your belongings. Note too that often the people involved are smartly dressed and seem implausible thieves. Walk briskly away from them with firm hold of your gear, and ignore them entirely.

Armed robbery is unusual, but does happen – sadly with increasing frequency in the Mariscal hotel district **in Quito**. Other danger spots are parts of the old town, the walk up to El Panecillo (always take a cab), Rucu Pichincha and Cruz Loma volcanoes, and Parque Carolina. You shouldn't go into any city park outside full daylight hours. Security **in Guayaquil** has greatly improved, but nevertheless you should be extra vigilant in the downtown areas, the dock and the airport.

In the big cities, especially Quito, always **take a taxi at night** rather than wandering the streets; staff at restaurants and hotels will be happy to call you one. Also take a taxi whenever you're weighed down with all your gear, no matter what time of day it is. You will need to go to the police as soon as

Carry identification at all times

By law you are required to carry proper identification at all times – for foreigners this means a passport. Visa holders will also need to carry their *censo* and any other relevant documentation. Most of the time photocopies of the stamps and important pages are sufficient, so that you can keep the original in a safe place. In the Oriente and border areas, however, only the originals will do. If you're stopped by the authorities and can't produce identification you can be detained.

Emergency phone numbers

Police ☎101
Fire ☎102

possible **if you are robbed**, in order to make a report (*denuncia*) for insurance purposes.

Travelling at night, whether in your own vehicle or on public transport, is a bad idea whatever part of the country you're in, but especially in Guayas province, where hold-ups have been an ongoing problem, as well as Esmeraldas province and the border regions with Colombia.

The **possession of drugs** is a very serious offence in Ecuador, one that can end in fifteen years in jail. Don't take any chances with drugs or drug dealers – set-ups have happened. Drug smuggling and Colombian guerrilla activity in the northern border areas have made certain areas of Sucumbíos (capital Lago Agrio), Carchi (capital Tulcán) and Esmeraldas (capital Esmeraldas) provinces unsafe. On the southern border, the Cordillera del Cóndor, southeast of Zamora, a region long involved in a border dispute with Peru, still contains unmarked minefields and should be avoided altogether.

Demonstrations (*manifestaciones*) and strikes (*paros* or *huelgas*) form a common and normal part of political expression in the country. Violence is rare, but you should steer clear in case trouble breaks out. When there's widespread discontent, roadblocks, particularly on the Panamericana, are common, so make allowances for delays in your itinerary.

Opening hours, public holidays and fiestas

Most **shops** are open Monday to Saturday from 9am to 6pm. Many occupy the family home and, outside the biggest cities, open every day for as long as someone is up.

Calendar of public holidays

Note that on public holidays just about all shops and facilities are closed all day.

January 1 New Year's Day (*Año Nuevo*).

January 6 Epiphany (*Reyes Magos*). Celebrated mainly in the central highlands, but also in Montecristi on the coast.

February/March Carnival (*Carnaval*). The week before Lent marked by nationwide high-jinx, partying and water-throwing.

March/April Holy Week (*Semana Santa*). The big processions in Quito are on Good Friday. Public holidays for Maundy Thursday and Good Friday.

May 1 Labour Day (*Día del Trabajo*).

May 24 Battle of Pichincha (*La Battala del Pinchincha*).

June 21 and onwards *Inti Raymi* ("Festival of the Sun"). A pre-conquest festival celebrated on the solstice at important ancient sites such as Cochasquí.

June 24 San Juan. John the Baptist's saint day, celebrated particularly heartily in the Otavalo region.

June 28–29 San Pedro and San Pablo. Celebrated across the country, though particularly in Cayambe and the northern sierra.

Last Friday in June Bank holiday.

July 24 Birthday of Simón Bolívar.

August 10 Independence Day (*Día de la independencia*).

October 9 Independence of Guayaquil.

October 12 Columbus Day (Día de la Raza).

November 2 All Souls' Day or Day of the Dead (*Día de los Muertos*).

November 3 Independence of Cuenca.

December 6 Foundation of Quito.

December 25 Christmas Day (*Navidad*).

December 31 New Year's Eve (*Nochevieja*). *Años viejos.*

Opening hours of **public offices** are generally from 9am to 5 or 6pm Monday to Friday, with an hour or so for lunch. In rural areas, the working day often starts earlier, say at 8am, and a longer lunch of a couple of hours is taken. **Banks** do business from 8am or 9am to 1.30pm, Monday to Friday, often closing at 1pm on Saturdays. Some banks extend business to 6pm during the week, though with reduced services – usually this means you can't change travellers' cheques after 1.30pm. **Post offices** are open Mondays to Fridays from 8am to 7pm, closing at noon on Saturdays, and **telephone offices** are open daily from 8am to 10pm; in rural regions and smaller towns, expect hours to be shorter for both services. **Museums** are usually closed on Mondays.

Most **national holidays** mark famous events in post-conquest history and the standard festivals of the Catholic church. Whether public holiday or fiesta, Ecuadorians love a party and often go to much trouble and expense to ensure everyone enjoys a great spectacle lubricated with plenty of food and drink.

Outdoor activities

Having so much untamed wilderness within easy striking distance of major population centres, Ecuador is among the world's prime destinations for outdoor enthusiasts.

Climbing

Boasting ten volcanoes over 5000m, including the beautifully symmetrical volcano Cotopaxi, and the point furthest from the centre of the Earth, the summit of Chimborazo, Ecuador offers numerous **climbing** opportunities, from relatively easy day-trips for strong hill-walkers to challenging technical peaks for experienced climbers. The most popular **snow peaks**, requiring full mountaineering equipment, include **Cotopaxi** (5897m), **Chimborazo** (6310m) and **Cayambe** (5790m).

Not all of the higher peaks require previous mountaineering **experience**: many beginners make it up Cotopaxi, for instance, which demands physical fitness, stamina and sheer determination rather than technical expertise. It is, of course, essential that climbers with limited mountaineering experience are accompanied by an experienced and utterly dependable **guide**, whose first concern is safety. Ecuador's best-trained mountain guides are those certified by an organization called ASEGUIM (Asociación Ecuatoriana de Guías de Montaña), whose members have to pass exams and take courses spread over a three-year period before receiving the Diploma de Guía.

December and January are generally regarded as the **best months** to climb, followed by the dry summer months of June to August. March to May are considered the worst months, but because of the topography and microclimates of the land, several mountains, such as Cotopaxi, are more or less climbable throughout the year.

You must **acclimatize** before attempting the higher peaks (see Basics, p.28, for details on the risks of **altitude sickness**). Remember also that several popular climbs are on **active volcanoes** – particularly Guagua Pichincha, Reventador, Sangay, Cotopaxi and Tungurahua – and you should be fully aware of the current situation before you ascend.

Hiking

The widest choice of hikes is found in the sierra, where numerous mule paths lead into the mountains and up to the paramo, providing access to stunning views and exhilarating, wide-open spaces. Rewarding possibilities include day-hikes in the area around **Laguna Quilotoa**. **Cotopaxi** (see p.686) and **Machalilla** (see p.734, national parks also present good hiking possibilities, as do many areas of open country throughout the highlands. Again, a good way of getting around logistical difficulties is by **hiring a guide**, usually through a local tour operator. Typical **rates** for guided hikes are $20–40 per person per day, often with a minimum of three to four people per group. For a selection of Quito-based companies see "Listings", p.675–6, while provincial guides and tour operators are detailed throughout the chapter.

Rafting and kayaking

White-water rafting combines the thrill of riding rapids with the chance to reach some spectacular landscapes that simply can't be visited by other means. A small number of rafting and **kayaking** companies, mainly based in Quito, Tena and Baños, organize trips to dozens of rivers. Not far from Quito, on the way to Santo Domingo, the **Ríos Blanco and Toachi** offer a selection of popular runs suitable for beginners and old hands alike. Around Tena, among the most popular is the **Upper Napo**, a typical beginner's run, while the nearby **Río Misahuallí** is suitable for more advanced paddlers, weaving through a stunning canyon in a remote section of rainforest. Other options from Tena include the **Río Hollín**, **Río Anzu** and the **Río Quijos**, and tributaries give up a range of possibilities. In the southern Oriente, the **Río Upano** is one of the most talked about runs, involving a trip through the spectacular Namangosa Gorge.

Only go rafting with a reputable company, those that have fully trained guides who know first aid, can supply good-quality life jackets and helmets, and employ a safety kayak to accompany the raft on the run. Check too that your guide is accredited with **AGAR** (Asociación de Guías de Aguas Rápidas). For rafting companies operating out of Tena, refer to box on p.713; for runs around Quito, try Yacu Amu rafting (see "Listings" p.676. Note that rafting companies in Baños are not as highly regarded as those listed in Tena and Quito.

Diving, snorkelling and surfing

Ecuador's top **scuba-diving** spots are in **the Galápagos**, where there are good chances to see large sea fish as well as a number of spectacular endemic reef fish. Most people arrange **diving tours** before arrival, but there are several operators on the islands who can arrange trips for you there and then. Note that the Galápagos is not the easiest place for novices to learn to dive – mainly owing to strong currents and cold temperatures – but it is possible.

Snorkelling is likely to be an important part of a Galápagos cruise: bring your own gear if you have it; even though most boats can provide it, there may not be enough to go around and what there is may not fit. A **wetsuit** is recommended between July and December. On the mainland, there's not a lot of scuba or snorkelling, apart from tours arranged in Puerto López for dives around the Isla de la Plata.

The coasts of Manabí and Guayas provinces are the country's most popular places for **surfing**, and laid-back Montañita in Guayas province has the reputation of being the leading surf centre, though quieter **Canoa** to the north also has a loyal, less hippieish following. There are some keen surfers on the Galápagos Islands too, particularly at **Puerto Baquerizo Moreno** on San Cristóbal island, where you'll find several places to hire a board and even get a lesson. You won't need to take a wetsuit if you're surfing on the mainland, but the water in the Galápagos can get cold in the dry season. The best time to surf is from December to February, when the waves are usually at their fiercest, but conditions are good up until May.

History

The earliest evidence of human presence in Ecuador, discovered east of Quito at the El Inga archeological site, dates back to 10,000 BC. The Inca invasion was followed by the Spanish invasion, and post-independence Ecuador was marked by an often brutal schism between Liberals and Conservatives. The spectre of violence is still present today, and the country endured a brief military coup in 2000.

The Incas

By the time **the Incas** invaded from the south around 1460, the region was composed of dozens of highly stratified and interrelated indigenous cultures, each with its own territory and some with a sophisticated knowledge of astronomy (such as the **Cara**, responsible for the large ceremonial complex, Cochasquí). **Tupac Yupanqui** led a force of 200,000 men but met savage resistance and it was left to Tupac's son, **Huayna Capac**, to finish the job of securing this most northern expanse of the great Inca Empire (known as **Tahuantinsuyo**), ending a seventeen-year war with the Cara with a terrible massacre at Laguna Yahuarcocha in 1495. Considering that the Incas were rulers in what is now southern Ecuador for no more than seventy years, and the north for only thirty years, they had an enormous impact on the region. New urban and ceremonial centres were built, such as **Tomebamba** (now buried beneath Cuenca) and **Quito**, with roads connecting them to the rest of the empire, and fortresses were erected at strategic points across the country, as at **Ingapirca**. The language of the Incas, **Quechua**, was imposed on the defeated population and it's still spoken in various forms (as Quichua) by the majority of Ecuador's *indígenas*.

The Spanish conquest

When **the Spanish** appeared in 1532, it couldn't have been at a worse time for the Incas. A succession crisis, precipitated by the sudden death of Huayna Capac and his likely heir, erupted into a bloody civil war between two of his sons based in the northern and southern halves of the empire. **Atahualpa**, ruling from Quito, had only just emerged as the victor when – in a fatal miscalculation – he invited the small band of unusual-looking foreigners to a meeting at **Cajamarca**, letting them past countless guard posts and strongholds and over mountainous terrain that would have been too steep for cavalry attacks. The Spanish leader, **Francisco Pizarro**, took Atahualpa hostage, massacring thousands of Inca soldiers and nobles in just a few hours. Fearing for his life, Atahualpa offered a huge **ransom** of gold and silver in return for his liberty and his kingdom at Quito but, having fulfilled his part of the bargain, he was betrayed by Pizarro and executed. Within a year, the key cities of the empire had fallen to the Spanish. In August 1534, **Sebastián de Benalcázar** founded the city **San Francisco de Quito** on the charred remains of the Inca capital. Through war, forced labour and, above all, Old World **diseases** such as smallpox, measles, plague and influenza, the native population of Ecuador was cut down from 1.5 million to just 200,000 by the end of the sixteenth century.

The colonial era

The Spanish were quick to consolidate their victories, with the Crown parcelling out land to the conquistadors in the form of **encomiendas**, grants that entitled the holders, the **encomenderos**, to a substantial tribute in cash, plus produce and labour from the *indígenas* that happened to live there. The *encomenderos* became the elite of the region, the **Audiencia de Quito**, a basically autonomous area that was part of the Viceroyalty of Peru, which roughly corresponded to modern-day Ecuador. While about half the indigenous population worked on the *encomiendas*, a quarter were rounded up and resettled in purpose-built "Indian towns", or **reducciones**, where the colonists could more easily collect tribute and exploit their labour through a corruption of the **mita**, an Inca institution which effectively made debt-slaves of them. The last quarter of the indigenous population escaped the rule of the Spanish altogether by living in the inaccessible tropical forests of the Oriente or the north coast.

The Audiencia de Quito was an essentially peaceful colony given over to agriculture and textile production, but slowly the **criollos** – Spanish people born in the colonies – began to resent the high taxes, continual interference from Spain, and the fact that all the best jobs still went to the **peninsulares**, or Spanish-born newcomers.

The birth of the republic

After a couple of failed attempts to throw off the Spanish yoke, it wasn't until 1820 that the movement regained momentum. Guayaquil declared its **independence** on October 9 and sent urgent requests for assistance to the El Libertador, **Simón Bolívar**, and **José de San Martín**, who were sweeping in from Venezuela and Argentina respectively, crushing the Spanish armies as they went. Bolívar quickly sent his best general, the 26-year-old **Antonio José de Sucre**, who eventually won the decisive **Battle of Pichincha**, outside Quito, on May 24, 1822. Five days later the old *audiencia* became the Department of the South in a new nation, **Gran Colombia**, more or less covering the combined territories of present-day Ecuador, Colombia, Panama and Venezuela. This huge country didn't last and, in 1830, Quito representatives seceded and declared their own republic, naming it **Ecuador**, after its position on the equator.

The new nation didn't gel at all well. In the sierra, the **Conservative** land-owning elites were happy enough to keep the colonial system in operation while, on the coast, the **Liberal** merchant classes, rich on the country's sole export commodity, cacao, wanted free trade, lower taxes and a proper break with the old order. This conflict has coloured the politics and history of the country ever since. Rivalries between the regions became increasingly bitter, and in 1859 – what came to be known as the **Terrible Year** – the strain between the regions finally shattered the country. Quito set up a provisional government; Cuenca declared itself autonomous; Loja became a federal district; and Guayaquil signed itself away to Peruvian control. Peru invaded and blockaded the port, while Colombia hungrily eyed the rest of Ecuador for itself.

Conservative rule: 1861–95

It took a determined leader to set the republic right, and **Gabriel García Moreno** was the man, a fierce Conservative and devout Catholic, who quashed the various rebellions and seized power in 1861. He quickly strengthened the position of the Church, establishing it as the state religion, signing control over to the Vatican, and made **Catholicism** a prerequisite for citizenship. He was also ruthless with his many opponents, crushing them and several coup attempts with savage efficiency. His presidency did, however, help foster growth in agriculture and industry, initiating a much-needed programme of road-building and beginning the Quito–Guayaquil railway.

After García Moreno's death, Conservative control began to wane while Liberal power and influence strengthened, thanks in large part to a phenomenal growth in Ecuador's coastal **exports**. For a time the country was the world's leading producer of **cacao**, while coffee, tagua nuts and Panama hats – products that were all based on the coast around Guayaquil – were also doing well. Money began flooding into Liberal coffers.

The Liberal era: 1895–1925

The Conservatives' nemesis was the revolutionary Liberal, **Eloy Alfaro**, who was brought to power in 1895 by a military coup funded by cacao lords. Fervently anti-clerical, Alfaro immediately set about undoing García Moreno's work by secularizing the state and education, expelling the foreign clergy, instituting civil marriage and divorce and cutting the links with the Vatican. He was under heavy attack, however, from both the Conservatives and hostile factions within the Liberal Party, and when his chosen successor died suddenly just after his inauguration in 1911, the country slipped into a bloody **civil war**. A year later, Alfaro and his supporters was defeated and transported on the new railway to Quito (whose completion he oversaw), where they were murdered, dragged through the streets and burnt in the Parque Ejido. After the civil war, power shifted from the cash-strapped government to **la argolla**, a "ring" of Ecuador's wealthiest cacao merchants and bankers, all underpinned by the private Banco Comercial and Agrícola in Guayaquil, which provided loans to a succession of ailing administrations at the expense of rocketing inflation rates.

In the 1920s, Ecuador descended into an **economic crisis**, a symptom of the political arrangement and a catastrophic slump in cacao production, caused by a devastating blight. Matters came to a head in the bloodless **Revolución Juliana** of 1925, which effectively marked the end of the old Liberal–Conservative tug-of-war and ushered in a disoriented era of coups and overthrows.

Political crisis: 1925–47

After two swift juntas, in 1926 the military handed power to **Isidro Ayora**, who embarked on a programme of reforms, including the creation of the Banco Central in Quito to smash the influence of *la argolla*. However, the new bank couldn't temper high inflation, and popular discontent forced Ayora's resignation in 1931, ushering in a period of extreme political instability fuelled by a perilous national economy and the Great Depression. In the 1930s, a total of fourteen men took the presidency, and from 1925 to 1948 Ecuador had 27 governments.

Out of the turbulence of this era emerged a figure whose strident populism, firebrand rhetoric and magnetic charisma gave him unprecedented appeal across the political spectrum, and a career that was to last into the 1970s. The first of **José María Velasco Ibarra**'s five presidential terms, however, began in 1934 and lasted less than a year, before his removal by the military when he tried to assume dictatorial powers.

In 1941, amid the confusion, **Peru invaded** and seized 200,000 square kilometres of Ecuador's Amazonian territory – almost half of the country at the time. The loss was a huge blow to pride in a country that had identified itself with the Amazon since its navigation by Francisco de Orellana 400 years earlier.

Prosperity and decline: 1948–72

After World War II, the debilitating political volatility was tempered by **Galo Plaza Lasso**, a fair and popular president who was the first since 1924 to complete his term of office. The stability of his administration was greatly aided by the **banana boom**, which soon made the country the world's largest exporter of bananas, a position that it retains today. In the late 1950s and early 1960s, however, the banana crop was all but destroyed by the "Panama" fungal disease. Multinationals effectively packed up shop, sacked employees or severely cut wages, leaving the banana industry and thousands of its workers in a parlous state; the industry didn't recover until well into the 1970s.

Meanwhile, the repercussions of the Cuban revolution were felt in Ecuador, when Velasco exploited its popularity, lacing his speeches with anti-US rhetoric. Fearing Ecuador might have its own revolution, the military intervened. To their credit, they passed the **1964 Agrarian Reform Law**, ending an oppressive system of debt peonage that highland *indígenas* had been subjected to since the late seventeenth century. Elections in 1968 brought Velasco, now aged 75, back to power by the slenderest of margins; with a weak power base and a poor economy, he clung to power by assuming dictatorial powers until his overthrow by the military in 1972, which brought his epic political career to a close.

Military control and the oil boom: 1972–87

When large **oil reserves** were found near Lago Agrio by Texaco in 1967, dozens of international companies swarmed to the Oriente, on the scent of a fortune. Seeing themselves as the most reliable custodians of this new-found national treasure, the military, led by **General Guillermo Rodríguez Lara**, took control and adopted aggressively nationalist policies, renegotiated contracts with the foreign companies, set up a state-owned petroleum company and joined OPEC. Money flooded into the public sector, stimulating employment, industrialization, growth of the domestic economy and urbanization. Ecuador was also anxious to populate the Oriente, lest Colombia or Peru should get ideas about the oil-rich lands, and colonists, especially military conscripts, were encouraged into the region in their thousands. The huge **environmental impact** of colonization and the oil industry's successes, however, is still being felt throughout the region.

Even with the extraordinary increases in revenues and booming economy, the government racked up some serious **debts** and clumsy attempts to redress the balance – a sixty percent duty on luxury imports – sparked a failed coup that claimed 22 lives. Rodríguez Lara's position was weakened enough for a second, bloodless coup in 1976 to be successful, which returned the government to civilian rule after three years.

Return to democracy: 1979–98

Between 1979 and 1996 there were alternate center-left and "neo-liberal" governments. None was able to extricate the economy from rising inflation, vulnerability to fluctuations of the oil price and spiralling foreign debt, inevitably leading to strikes, widening public disenchantment and the rise of the indigenous movement represented by the **Confederación de Nacionalidades Indígenas del Ecuador** (CONAIE). This at last gave a voice to peoples marginalized for centuries.

In 1998, the country turned to **Jamil Mahuad**, the Harvard-educated mayor of Quito. He showed early promise by securing a peace treaty with Peru, resolving a border dispute that had soured relations between the two countries for decades, but before long he found himself in the middle of Ecuador's worst **economic crisis** in seventy years. Gross domestic product shrank by over seven percent, strikes and blockades gripped the country; inflation went out of control; banks started to collapse; and the government defaulted on its foreign debt payments. Mahuad implemented **austerity measures** in a desperate bid to save the economy, most controversially by freezing over $3 billion in private bank deposit assets; there was instant outrage when Ecuadorians found they couldn't withdraw more than a couple of hundred dollars from their accounts and more banks started to fold. The freeze couldn't stop the freefalling sucre, the national currency, from devaluing further, so Mahuad decreed that it would have to be replaced by the more stable US dollar.

The new millennium

In January 2000, thousands of indigenous protesters stormed Congress and, supported by some mid-ranking army officers, installed the "**Junta of National Salvation**", ousting Mahuad. The junta only lasted a few hours before it was agreed that **Gustavo Noboa**, the vice-president, should take the helm.

The portly, one-time university rector forged ahead with the **dollarization** process, steering the country towards stability and averting the threat of hyperinflation – at the price of rising costs and worsening conditions for the ever-increasing poor. In November 2002, **Lucio Gutiérrez**, one of the colonels who led the January 2000 coup, was elected president of Ecuador on an anti-corruption ticket backed by the indigenous vote and the left. In addition to rampant corruption, Gutiérrez will have to contend with the country's huge foreign debt and chronic lack of foreign investment, social inequality that has 60 to 80 percent of the population living in poverty, and deteriorating security on the Colombian border caused by the infiltration of paramilitaries and guerrillas. These problems will need an exceptional leader to resolve them.

Books

With the possible exception of the Galápagos Islands, foreign writers have paid less attention to Ecuador than to its South American neighbours, and few Ecuadorian works are ever translated into English. That said, there's a reasonable choice of books available in English, covering subjects as diverse as archeology, exploration, travel and cookery.

Demetrio Aguilera Malta *Don Goyo* (Humana). A spellbinding novel, first published in 1933, dealing with the lives of a group of *cholos* who eke out a living by fishing from the mangrove swamps in the Gulf of Guayaquil, which are in danger of being cleared by white landowners.

John Hemming *The Conquest of the Incas* (Papermac/Harcourt Brace). Marrying an academic attention to detail with a gripping narrative style, Hemming's book is widely regarded as the best account of this devastating conquest. His earlier work, *The Search for El Dorado* (UK: Michael Joseph), covers the Spaniards' unquenchable desire for gold that fuelled the Conquest.

Alexander von Humboldt *Personal Narrative of Travels to the Equinoctial Regions of the New Continent during the Years 1799–1804* (o/p). Written by perhaps the greatest of all scientist-explorers, who composed 29 volumes on his travels across South America. A heavily edited version of *Personal Narrative* is available as well (Penguin).

Joe Kane *Savages* (Pan/Vintage). An affecting and sensitive book on the protests of the Huaorani against the monolithic multinational oil industry and its supporting agencies. It's sprinkled with a poignant humour generated from the gap in cultures between the author and his subjects.

Henri Michaux *Ecuador* (o/p UK and US; Gallimard, France). Beautifully written – and sometimes ether-induced – impressions of Ecuador, based on the mystical Belgian author's travels through the country in 1977, and presented in a mixture of prose, poetry and diary notes.

Robert S. Ridgely and Paul J. Greenfield *The Birds of Ecuador* (Cornell University). Long-awaited, monumental two-volume book (each available separately) including a field guide with glorious colour plates of Ecuador's 1600 bird species. The country's definitive bird guide, and an indispensable resource for anyone interested in South American avifauna.

Andy Swash and Robert Still *Birds, Mammals and Reptiles of the Galápagos Islands* (Yale). Excellent compact field guide with colour photos and sketches, including a fin guide to aid the identification of dolphins and whales.

Moritz Thomsen *Living Poor* (Eland/University of Washington). An American Peace Corps volunteer writes lucidly about his time in the fishing community of Río Verde in Esmeraldas during the 1960s, and his mostly futile – sometimes farcical – efforts to haul its people out of poverty.

John Treherne *The Galápagos Affair* (Pimlico). Excellent overview of the extraordinary events on Floreana in the early 1930s that led to unexplained deaths and disappearances, including a large appendix detailing the author's own theories.

Edward Whymper *Travels Amongst the Great Andes of the Equator* (o/p). Exploits of the pioneering mountaineer at the end of the nineteenth century who managed to rack up a number of first summits, including Chimborazo, Cayambe and Antisana. Climbing stories and engaging travelogue are mixed with observations on insects and pre-Columbian pottery.

6.1

Quito

High in the Andes, Ecuador's capital, **QUITO**, unfurls in an implausibly long north–south ribbon, more than 30km long and just 5km wide. To the west, the city is dramatically hemmed in by the steep green walls of **Volcán Pichincha**, the benign-looking volcano which periodically sends clouds of ash billowing into the sky and over the streets. Eastwards, Quito abruptly drops away to a wide valley known as the **Valle de los Chillos**, marking the beginning of the descent towards the Amazon basin. It's a superb setting, but outside July and August it can be bone-chillingly cold, with its much-vaunted "spring-like climate" all too often giving way to grey, washed-out skies that somewhat undermine the beauty of the surroundings.

Founded by invading Spaniards in 1534 on the site of an important Inca city, Quito quickly grew into a major colonial centre, boasting some of the grandest and most dazzling buildings on the continent – chiefly churches, monasteries and convents. Today, it's this stunning colonial architecture, beautifully preserved in the compact historical quarter known as the **Old Town**, that makes Quito so special. With its colourful markets and narrow, cobbled streets thronged with *indígenas* and *mestizos*, the Old Town has a great atmosphere by day but is perceived as a dangerous place after dark, and most tourists stay in the adjacent **New Town** – bland and modern, but featuring a convenient concentration of hotels, restaurants and such. But street theft against tourists has been on the rise there too, so use taxis at night and don't take valuables onto the streets at any time.

Arrival and information

The **Aeropuerto Internacional Mariscal Sucre** (Ⓣ02/243-0555), serving both national and international flights, is about 6km north of the New Town's main hotel district, known as **La Mariscal**. There's a *casa de cambio* in the international terminal and several ATMs in the wall outside, midway between the international and domestic terminals. Taxis lined up outside the arrivals gate charge around $2–3 to anywhere in the New Town (about $1 more at night), or you can pay a fixed fare of $4 at the dedicated taxi desk in the airport just beyond customs, the best guarantee you won't be ripped off outside. Many hotels offer a free pick-up service with prior reservation.

Quito's main **bus terminal**, the Terminal Terrestre de Cumandá at Avenida Maldonado on the southern edge of the Old Town is not a great place to arrive, especially at night. As with the airport, there's an information desk (Mon–Fri 8.30am–5.30pm), an ATM and plenty of taxis waiting right where buses arrive. You'll have to agree a price with the driver before you get in as most will refuse to use the meter from here; you shouldn't pay more than a couple of dollars to get to La Mariscal. Alternatively, the terminal is a stone's throw from the Cumandá trolley stop (see "City Transport", opposite), but you should beware of pickpockets in the few minutes it takes to walk there and on crowded trolleys too.

The **Ministerio de Turismo** (Mon–Fri 8.30am–5pm, with an irregular lunch break; Ⓣ02/250-7555, Ⓦwww.vivecuador.com) is in the north end of town at Avenida Eloy Alfaro N32-300, opposite Parque Carolina; take any bus north along Amazonas and get off at Eloy Alfaro, then walk east down the avenue for about ten minutes. Once there, you'll find a number of glossy brochures, fold-out maps of Quito and some general information on the rest of Ecuador. The ministry also runs a 24-hour information service (Ⓣ1800/004887).

More conveniently located at Jorge Washington 311 and Leonidas Plaza, the US-run travellers' club **South American Explorers** (Mon–Fri 9.30am–5pm & Sat 9am–noon, open till 8pm Thurs; Ⓣ02/222-5228, Ⓦwww.saexplorers.org) is a gold mine of information on Quito and the whole of the country. Non-members can pick up information on accommodation, restaurants, Internet access, climbing guides, outdoor equipment suppliers and more, while members can access a vast number of trip reports (mainly recommendations or warnings) filed by other members.

City transport

Most visitors use public transport to shuttle between the New Town and the Old Town (the alternative is a 45min walk). The modern trolley-bus system, **El Trole** (Mon–Fri 6am–midnight, Sat & Sun 6am–10pm; flat fare of $0.20 per ride), runs along a north–south axis formed mainly by Avenida 10 de Agosto; stops are easy to spot with their green metal waiting areas sitting on raised platforms. Unless you're travelling out to the suburbs it makes no difference which trolley-bus you take. One thing to watch out for, though, is the one-way system through the Old Town: buses running south go along Guayaquil, while those returning north use Flores and Montúfar.

The **Ecovía** (same hours and fare as El Trole) is made up of a fleet of deep-crimson *buses ecológicos*, low-emission buses that run between Plaza La Marín in the Old Town (usually known simply as La Marín) and the Río Coca transfer station in the north every ten or fifteen minutes, mainly along Avenida 6 de Diciembre. In contrast, Quito's **ordinary buses** are for the most part ancient, decrepit affairs. Most ply up and down main arterial avenues like 12 de Octubre, Amazonas, 10 de Agosto and Colón, with their stops and final destination marked on the front window. Buses charge a flat **fare** which varies according to type: smarter, more modern ones charging a little more ($0.25) than the older ones ($0.18).

Alternatively, **taxis** are plentiful and cheap; make sure you pick one with a four-digit code on the doors and windscreen of the vehicle, signifying a registered taxi. Quito is the only city in the country where taxis use a meter (*taxímetro*); check that your driver resets the meter when you get in. Note that taxi drivers don't use their meters at night when fares can be as much as double the daytime rate; agree a price before you set off. If you want to book a taxi, try the taxi companies given in "Listings" on p.675.

Accommodation

Nearly all visitors to Quito stay in the **New Town**, in the downtown zone of **La Mariscal**, which is lively after dark, and convenient for changing money, booking tours, sorting out laundry and the like. Be warned that many streets are very noisy so it's always worth asking for a back room. Staying in the **Old Town** is by no means unthinkable – you just need to choose your hotel carefully. Wherever you intend to stay, if you'll be arriving at night it's a good idea to book ahead and take a taxi to the hotel.

New Town

Amazonas Inn Joaquín Pinto E4-325 Ⓣ02/222-5723. Modern hotel with a pleasant street-level café. Some rooms are small, but they're all spotless and have private bath and cable TV. ❹

La Casa Sol Calama 127 Ⓣ02/223-0798, Ⓦwww.lacasasol.com. Lovely, cosy guesthouse with comfortable en-suite rooms set around a pretty courtyard; good breakfasts included. ❻

Cayman Hostal Juan Rodríguez 270 and Reina Victoria Ⓣ02/256-7616, Ⓔhcayman@uio.satnet.net. Beautifully renovated old house with polished floors, attractive decor and a huge fireplace in the sitting room. ❺

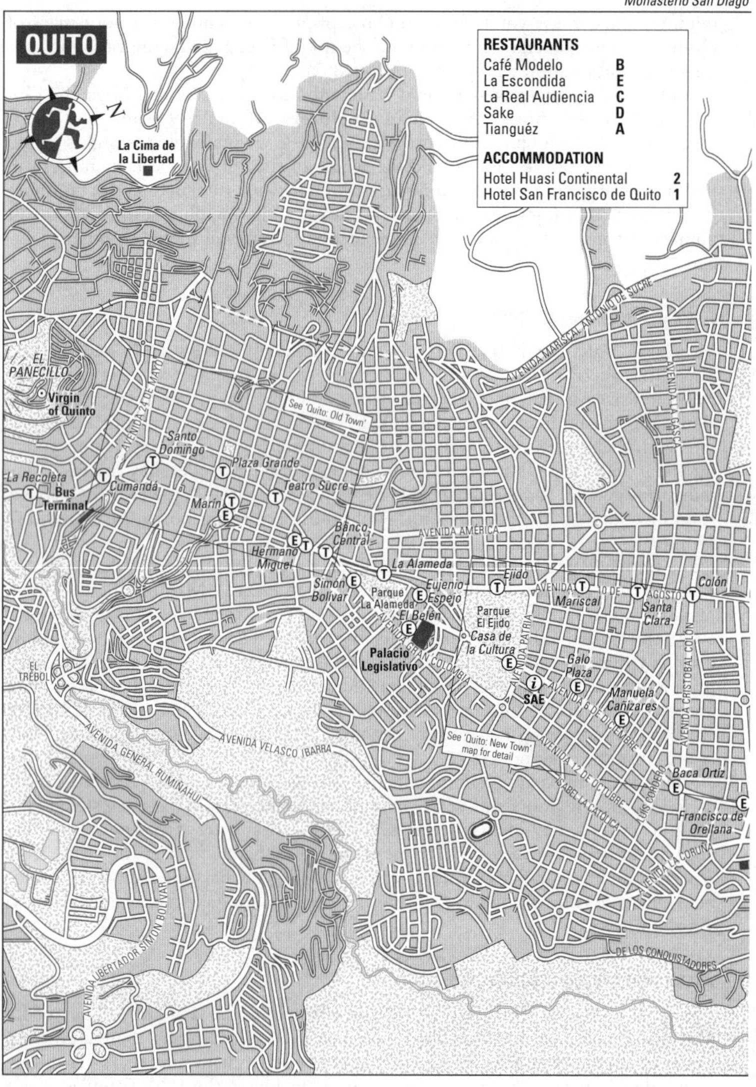

Crossroads Foch E5-23 ⓣ02/223-4735, ⓦwww.crossroadshostal.com. American-run *hostal* with a range of dorm and private rooms (some en suite) with good showers, a small café, TV room with VCR, kitchen and storage facilities. Dorm $5–6, doubles ❹

La Galería Hostal Calama 233 y Diego de Almagro ⓣ02/250-0307, ⓔhostallagaleria@hotmail.com. Friendly, family-run hotel with a range of different-sized en-suite rooms – some are a bit dog-eared, but it's still decent value. ❷

Hostal Bask Lizardo García E7-56 ⓣ02/250-3456. Welcoming place with a mix of small dorms and private rooms painted in cheery pink tones. Guests have access to a kitchen and lounge with a huge cable TV. ❶–❷

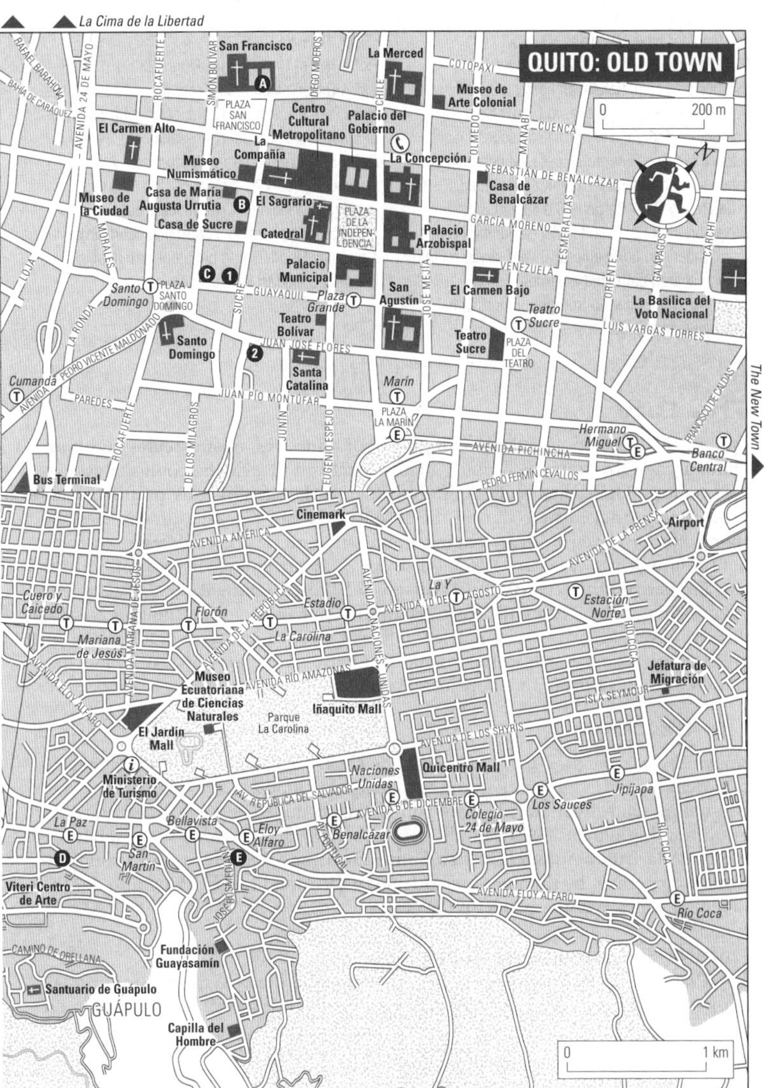

Hostal Calama José Calama E7-49 ⓣ02/223-7510. Popular budget hotel offering neat, square rooms with white walls, clean floors and private bath; functional and good value. ❸

Hostal Centro del Mundo Lizardo García 569 and Reina Victoria ⓣ02/252-29050, ⓔcentrodelmundo@hotmail.com. Characterful old house with 8- to 12-bed dorms plus some doubles. Also offers free breakfast, laundry facilities and use of a kitchen. Dorms $3–5, doubles ❷–❹

Hotel Café Cultura Robles 513 and Reina Victoria ⓣ02/222-4271, ⓦwww.cafecultura.com. Exuberantly decorated old house with high ceilings, stone fireplaces and frescos on the walls. ❼

Hotel Lafayette Baquedano 358 ⓣ02/222-4529. A little threadbare, but the en-suite rooms are neat, comfortable and very good value. Those on the top floor have balconies. ❷–❸

El Taxo Foch 909 ⓣ02/222-5593, ⓦwww.hostaleltaxo.com. Bohemian hostel, offering dorms and private rooms with shared bath, plus a bamboo-roofed patio with "holistic sound stage". Kitchen facilities, Internet access, laundry and tattoo services available; breakfast included. ❷–❸

Villa Nancy B&B Carrión E8-158 and 6 de Diciembre ⓣ02/256-3084, ⓔvilla_nancy@yahoo.com. Quiet and agreeable B&B with seven rooms, all with shared bath, and a garden with a hammock. Free pick-up from the airport with advance booking. ❹

Old Town

Hotel Huasi Continental Flores 332 ⓣ02/295-7327. Doesn't look much from the outside but the rooms are pleasant and light, some with polished parquet floors and clean, en-suite bath. ❷–❸

Hotel San Francisco de Quito Sucre 217 and Guayaquil ⓣ02/228-7758, ⓔhsfquito@andinanet.net. Modest but cared-for en-suite rooms around a charming courtyard with a gurgling fountain, in a beautiful historical building. Breakfast included. ❹

The City

Quito's chief attraction is the dazzling array of **churches**, **monasteries** and **convents** of the **Old Town**, occupying a fairly small area that can be comfortably covered on foot. The capital is also famous for the wealth of **religious paintings** and **sculpture** produced here during the seventeenth and eighteenth centuries and abundantly displayed in many churches and museums. The **New Town** has fewer sights, though it does boast a handful of museums including the best one in the city, and perhaps the country, in **El Museo del Banco Central**.

Something to bear in mind as you try to find your way around the Old Town is that many streets have two completely different **street names**: the official one on green plaques, and the historical name painted on ceramic tiles. Note also that churches are most likely to be open 8–11am and 3–6pm.

The Old Town

Known by *quiteños* as *el Centro Histórico*, the **OLD TOWN** is compact enough to be covered in a day. However, trying to take in old Quito's thirty-odd churches and assorted museums will quickly leave you feeling swamped and exhausted, so single out a few highlights. These should definitely include the three main squares – **Plaza de la Independencia**, **Plaza Santo Domingo** and **Plaza San Francisco** – followed perhaps by the short taxi-ride up to the summit of **El Panecillo**, for the sweeping views over the whole of the city.

Plaza de la Independencia and around

The **Plaza de la Independencia**, also known as the **Plaza Grande**, was first laid out with a string and ruler in 1534, and still preserves its original dimensions almost five hundred years down the line. Surrounded by the city's most important civic and religious buildings – the Catedral, the Government Palace, the Archbishop's Palace and the City Hall – the plaza has always formed the city's focal point. The south side of the square is dominated by the sturdy horizontal outline of the **Catedral**, with its gleaming white walls, grey-stone portals and terracotta-tiled roof; it was first completed in 1678 and then heavily restored in 1806. Adjoining the cathedral (and entered just off the square, on Calle García Moreno) is **El Sagrario**, a seventeenth-century church topped by a conspicuous pale blue dome, with a brightly painted interior.

At right angles to the Catedral, spreading across the west side of the square, the **Palacio de Gobierno** (Government Palace) is a white-stuccoed, perfectly symmetrical building fronted by a long row of columns supporting an upper balcony. Both the seat of government and the presidential palace, the Palacio is guarded by a couple of ineffectual-looking soldiers decked out in antiquated gold-and-blue uniforms; entrance is not allowed. Just off the northwest corner of the square are the thick, white walls of **La Concepción** – Quito's oldest convent, dating from 1577 – while opposite, stretching across the plaza's north side, is the dazzlingly white **Palacio Arzobispal** (Archbishop's Palace), a two-storey Neoclassical building. Finally, completing the circle, the east side of the square is taken up by the 1970s concrete **Palacio Municipal** (City Hall), which blends in surprisingly well with the neighbouring colonial buildings, thanks to its low, horizontal design and white-painted walls.

One block east of the Plaza de la Independencia, on Calle Chile, stands the imposing **Iglesia San Agustín**, dominated by its massive 37-metre bell tower crowned by a statue of St Augustine. The church dates from the sixteenth century but was substantially rebuilt in 1880, following an earthquake. Its dark, Gothic interior contains a series of enormous paintings by the distinguished seventeenth-century artist Miguel de Santiago, depicting the life of St Augustine. The adjoining **Convento de San Agustín** has survived intact since its completion in 1627 and contains a very fine cloister. On the second floor of the convent, a **museum** (Mon–Fri 9am–noon & 3–5.30pm, Sat 9am–noon; $2) houses a large, dusty collection of religious paintings attributed to artists of the Quito School (see below).

Also on Calle Chile, a couple of blocks west of the Plaza de la Independencia, the **Iglesia de La Merced** sports a wonderfully over-the-top Baroque interior. Its ceilings and walls are a confection of white, lace-like plaster relief against a sugary pink background, looking like icing on a cake, while the main altar and two side altars are resplendent with gold leaf. You can also visit the adjoining **convent**, built around a huge central patio enclosed within beautiful arched cloisters.

Directly behind La Merced, on the corner of Cuenca and Mejía, is the **Museo Nacional de Arte Colonial** (Tues–Fri 10am–6pm, Sat 10am–2pm; $1; closed for refurbishment and due to reopen in 2004; its collection has been moved temporarily to the Casa de la Cultura; call ⓣ02/2282297 for information), inside a handsomely restored sixteenth-century colonial house arranged around a colonnaded courtyard with a fountain. The museum is dedicated almost exclusively to religious art (mainly oil paintings and carved, polychrome statuary) and contains some impressive examples of work produced by the **Quito School** (1660–1765), whose artists are noted for their decorative colouring and exuberant decoration, particularly of their carvings of Mary, Christ and numerous saints, made out of cedar or red oak. If the prospect of six rooms full of Baroque religious imagery seems overwhelming, head round the corner to the **Casa de Benalcázar** (Mon–Fri 9am–1pm & 2–5.30pm; free) on Sebastián de Benalcázar and Olmedo, for a bite-sized chunk of the same thing. You'll find a splendid colonial mansion with a gorgeous courtyard and a small collection of religious paintings and statues in one room on the ground floor.

La Compañía and around

On the west side of the Plaza de la Independencia, Calle García Moreno runs south towards El Panecillo past a string of churches and other points of interest. The most opulent of these is **La Compañía**, Garcia Moreno and Sucre, half a block from the Plaza (apart from church services, Mon–Fri 10am–1pm & 2–5pm, Sat 10am–1pm; $2 with guide), built by Jesuits between 1605 and 1765 and completed just two years before Spain expelled the order from the continent. Boasting an extraordinary Baroque facade of carved volcanic stone, the church is piled high with twisted columns, sacred hearts, cherubs, angels and saints. Inside, any thoughts of restraint vanish amidst the wild extravagance of gold leaf gone mad, with a reputed seven tonnes of the stuff covering the altars, galleries and pulpit.

For more shows of old wealth, cross over the street to the corner of García Moreno and Sucre and enter the new **Museo Numismático** (Tues–Fri 9am–1pm & 2–5pm, Sat–Sun 10am–1pm & 2–4pm; $1, free Sun), a museum outlining the history of the country's money, currency and coinage with some fascinating exhibits. Diagonally opposite stands the **Casa de María Augusta Urrutia**

(Tues–Sun 9am–5pm; $2.50), a fine nineteenth-century mansion built around three internal patios. Guided tours are offered around the house where Doña María – widowed at an early age – lived alone with her 24 servants until her death in 1987. Continuing south down García Moreno for a couple of blocks you'll reach the dynamic **Museo de la Ciudad** (Tues–Sun 9.30am–5.30pm; $3 or $4 with guide) whose innovative replicas, scale models, mannequins, friezes and sound effects bring Quito's developmentto life.

Plaza San Francisco

A couple of blocks northwest of the Museo de la Ciudad lies the vast, grey, cobbled **PLAZA SAN FRANCISCO**, one of Quito's most beautiful squares. Stretching across the whole of its western side is the monumental outline of the sixteenth-century **Iglesia and Monasterio de San Francisco**, whose horizontal, white-washed walls are dominated by the twin bell tower and carved-stone portal of the church's main entrance. Hidden behind this facade are the extensive buildings and seven courtyards that make San Francisco the largest religious complex in South America. From the square, a broad flight of stone steps leads up to the **church**, whose interior is heavily embellished with gilt, almost rivalling the theatricality of La Compañía. Next door, the **Museo de San Francisco** (Mon–Sat 9am–6pm, Sun 9am–noon; $2.50; free guides available) displays an impressive collection of religious sculpture, paintings and furniture in a gallery off the monastery's main cloister.

Plaza Santo Domingo and La Ronda

From the Plaza San Francisco, a short walk east along Simón Bolívar brings you to Quito's third major square, the **PLAZA SANTO DOMINGO**, dominated by the graceful **Iglesia Santo Domingo**, built by Dominican friars during the sixteenth century. Unfortunately, an ill-conceived remodelling of the interior took place in the nineteenth century, leaving the church with an altar that looks more like a miniature gothic castle, surrounded by dozens of flickering candles. The adjoining monastery houses the **Museo Fray Pedro Bedón** (daily 9am–1pm & 2–4pm; $2) which contains a large collection of Dominican religious art from the sixteenth to eighteenth centuries, including a series of remarkable life-size sculptures of various saints, with moving arms and hands.

A stone's throw from the square, branching downhill from Guayaquil, is the narrow, pedestrianized section of Calle Morales still known by its original name of **LA RONDA**. Lined with thick-walled, whitewashed houses with tiny windows and brightly painted balconies, this picturesque alley is one of Quito's oldest streets, and one of the few remaining stretches of eighteenth-century working-class housing. It's also, however, notorious for **pickpockets** so be alert and only come during daylight hours.

El Panecillo

Rising over the southern edge of the Old Town is the hill known as **El Panecillo** (the "little bread loaf"), crowned by a magnificent, thirty-metre high statue of the **Virgin of Quito**. Walking up isn't safe, so be sure to take a taxi (about $3 round-trip, including waiting time, or $7 from the New Town and back). From the summit, you're treated to exhilarating views down to the city, as well as a dizzying close-up view of the colossal winged Virgin. At weekends a bus service (45min; $0.75) runs every fifteen minutes between El Panecillo and the country's other famous landmark, the Mitad del Mundo (see p.676).

Basílica del Voto Nacional

Perched on a small hill on Calle Venezuela, some eight blocks north of the Plaza de la Independencia, the **Basílica del Voto Nacional** (towers open daily 9am–5pm; $2; church open Mon–Fri 7–9am & 6–7pm, Sat 6am–6.30pm; free) is the tallest church in Ecuador thanks to its two imposing 115-metre towers plainly visible from many parts of the city. It's a flamboyant concoction of neo-Gothic spires, pinnacles, flying buttresses, turrets, parapets, arches and gables, all the more striking for being built largely in concrete – this is a modern construction, begun in 1892 and still not entirely completed. Don't miss the fantastic **views** from two vantage points unnervingly accessed by lift and steep metal ladders.

The New Town

About 1km north of the Basílica del Voto Nacional, your arrival in the **New Town** is signalled by **Parque El Ejido**, a pleasant park that is the site of a large art market on Sunday mornings. Quito's New Town sprang up in the 1940s, when the city's wealthy elite abandoned their old-town mansions and moved north. The heart of this district is an area called **Mariscal Sucre** – known by locals as **La Mariscal** – whose main commercial artery is **Avenida Amazonas**, lined by banks, *cambios*, tour operators, restaurants and souvenir shops. La Mariscal is no longer particularly new-looking, with its peculiar mixture of colonial-style town houses, Art Deco villas and 1970s blocks, nor could it be described as attractive, but it's where the vast majority of visitors base themselves, thanks to the convenient facilities.

The Casa de la Cultura

Standing adjacent to the Parque El Ejido, on 6 de Diciembre, the **Casa de la Cultura** (Ⓣ02/290-2262, Ⓦwww.cce.org.ec) is a landmark oval building clad in mirrored plates. As well as a cinema, theatres and auditoriums, the complex houses two notable museums: the Museo de Artes Visuales e Instrumentos Musicales and the Museo del Banco Central.

Walking along the outside of the Casa de la Cultura counterclockwise from its main entrance, you'll first come to the **Museo de Artes Visuales e Instrumentos Musicales** (MAVIM; Tues–Fri 10am–5pm, Sat 10am–2pm; $1), which was closed for restoration in 2003. Formerly built around a long, echoing hall blighted by terrible lighting, a low ceiling, dowdy decor and zero atmosphere, the museum's new look may help considerably to showcase its wide-ranging collections. Among them are striking **portraits**, like that of the malevolent Padre Vicente Solano, with his black robes, hooked nose and steely eyes; **watercolours** of Ecuadorian landscapes; fine *indigenismo* **paintings** by Eduardo Kingman; and an array of three thousand **musical instruments**, including wonderfully crafted guitars and a charango made out of an armadillo shell.

Heading clockwise around the Casa de la Cultura from the main entrance, you'll come to the impressive **Museo del Banco Central** (Tues–Fri 9am–5pm, Sat & Sun 10am–4pm; $2), Ecuador's premier museum, housing an outstanding collection of pre-Columbian ceramics and gold artefacts, as well as colonial, republican and contemporary art.

The Museo Jacinto Jijón y Caamaño and the Museo Amazónico

From the Casa de la Cultura, a five-minute walk up Avenida 12 de Octubre will bring you to another couple of museums. On the corner with Roca, the **Museo Jacinto Jijón y Caamaño** (Mon–Fri 8am–4pm; $0.60), inside the library of the Universidad Católica, is a sort of small-scale version of the Museo del Banco Central, with some well-presented pre-Hispanic ceramics, seventeenth-century religious art and beautiful inlaid colonial furniture.

For something a little different, continue three blocks up 12 de Octubre to the Abya Yala building, whose first floor houses the **Museo Amazónico** (Mon–Fri 8.30am–5pm, Sat–Sun 9am–1pm; $1), dedicated to the indigenous peoples of the Oriente region. It's not a big-budget museum, but the exhibits – which include vibrantly coloured feather headdresses, textiles, a long dugout canoe, musical instruments and fabulous beaded skirts and belts – are absorbing and well displayed.

QUITO: NEW TOWN

RESTAURANTS

Le Arcate	B
La Bodeguita de Cuba	G
Café Sutra	E
El Cafecito	F
Grain de Café	C
El Maple	D
Sugar Mamma's	A

ACCOMMODATION

Amazonas Inn	2
La Casa Sol	12
Cayman	11
Crossroads	5
La Galeria	7
Hostal Bask	10
Hostal Calama	8
Hostal Centro del Mundo	9
Hotel Café Cultura	3
Hotel Lafayette	4
El Taxo	1
Villa Nancy B&B	6

Parque La Carolina
Guápulo
Old Town
Old Town
Mariscal
Santa Clara
Colón
Colón
Parque Julio Andrade
Parque El Ejido
Casa de la Cultura (Museo del Banco Central & MAVIM)
Police Station
SAE
CAPTUR
Vivarium
Museo Jacinto Jijón y Caamaño (Universidad Católica)
Museo Amazónico
Avenida 10 de Agosto
Ulpiano Páez
9 de Octubre
Robles
Avenida Amazonas
Juan León Mera
Reina Victoria
Avenida Patria
Avenida 6 de Diciembre
18 de Septiembre
Jorge Washington
Veintimilla
Avenida General Ignacio de Veintimilla
General Baquedano
Leonidas Plaza
Ramón Roca
Jerónimo Carrión
Presidente Wilson
Joaquín Pinto
José Calama
Foch
Diego de Almagro
Mariscal
Juan Rodríguez
Alfredo Baquerizo Moreno
Luis Cordero
Lizardo García
Avenida Colón
Santa María
Avenida Francisco de Orellana
Berlín
La Rábida
La Pinta
La Niña
Yánez Pinzón
José Luis Tamayo
Avenida 12 de Octubre
España
Diego Ladrón de Guevara
Queseras del Medio
0 250 m

The Vivarium

At the northern end of La Mariscal, at Reina Victoria 1576 and Santa María, you'll find one of Quito's most unusual attractions. The **Vivarium** (Tues–Sat 9am–12.45pm & 2.30–5.45pm, Sun 11am–5.45pm; $2) consists of two rooms full of snakes – including a five-metre cobra – and other reptiles and amphibians, kept in large glass cabinets. If you're feeling up to it, staff will obligingly place a boa around your neck while you have your photo taken – many such photos of nervously grinning tourists are stuck on the wall.

The Museo Fundación Guayasamín, the Capilla del Hombre and Guápulo

Up in the hilltop barrio of Bellavista Alto and best reached by taxi, the **Museo Fundación Guayasamín** (Mon–Fri 9am–1.30pm & 3–6.15pm; $2) at Bosmediano 543, houses one of Quito's most compelling collections of art. There's an excellent display of pre-Columbian ceramics and colonial carvings and paintings here, but the real attraction is the permanent retrospective of the work of Oswaldo Guayasamín himself, Ecuador's most famous contemporary artist, who died in 1999. Standing out, in particular, are his famous moon-faced, round-eyed women and children, and the powerful series of giant, clenched hands and skeletal figures. A ten-minute walk away at Mariano Calvache and Lorenzo Chávez, you'll find more of Guayasamín's work on display at his **Capilla del Hombre** (Tues–Sun 10am–5pm; $3), a secular "chapel" commemorating the suffering of the oppressed and the tortured, and celebrating Latin American identity.

The outdoor terrace of the Fundación Guayasamín gives great views down to the picturesque village-like district of **Guápulo**, perched on the steep slopes flanking the east side of town. Its narrow, cobbled streets and terracotta-roofed, whitewashed houses have the look of a Mediterranean village, and feel far removed from the hurly burly of the capital. In fact, it's less than 2km from the New Town, and shouldn't cost more than $2–3 to reach by taxi. Besides the pretty streets and houses, the principal attraction down here is the magnificent **Santuario de Guápulo**, a beautiful seventeenth-century church and monastery housing the **Museo Franciscano Fray Antonio Rodríguez** (daily 9am–6pm; $2), with its impressive collection of Quito School paintings and elegantly carved ecclesiastical furniture.

Eating

Quito boasts by far the best choice of **restaurants** in the country, covering a huge range of cuisines from Thai to Italian – a real treat when you've just come back from a stint in the sierra or Oriente. The vast majority of them are in the **New Town**, with **Old Town** options much thinner on the ground. Where advance **reservations** are advisable, we've included the relevant telephone numbers.

Snacks and light meals

Books & Coffee Juan León Mera 1227, the New Town. Peaceful café offering good coffee and a range of cakes and snacks, plus comfy armchairs, English magazines, a book exchange, table football and chess sets.

Café Modelo Sucre 391, the Old Town. Quito's oldest café, where customers are shoehorned into the small room to take their coffees, beers, sandwiches, *empanadas* and pastries.

El Cafecito Luis Cordero 1124, the New Town. Lovely café with an open fire, creaking wooden floors and great coffees and home-made cakes. Also does bargain vegetarian lunches, light evening meals and yummy breakfasts.

Grain de Café General Baquedano 332, the New Town. Cheerful café-restaurant serving great-value set lunches, always with a vegetarian option, as well as quiches, croques monsieur, salads and desserts. Closed Sun.

The Magic Bean Foch E5-08, the New Town. Hugely popular café-restaurant with a little garden where you can sit out until late, warmed by hot coals. Great for moderately priced breakfasts, brownies, strudels, pancakes, toasted sandwiches and more.

Sugar Mamma's Juan León Mera N24-19 and Wilson, the New Town. Great little snack and juice bar, with a boggling range of speciality juices, as well as good set lunches and dinners for under $3. Student and SAE discounts. Closes Sat 1pm & Sun.

Restaurants

Le Arcate Baquedano 358, the New Town. Quito's best pizzeria, offering no fewer than 59 pizzas cooked in a huge wood-fired oven. Snappy service and reasonable prices add to the appeal. Closed Mon.

La Bodeguita de Cuba Reina Victoria N26-105, the New Town ☎02/254-2476. Well-prepared mid-priced Cuban food with live Cuban music on Thursday nights (reservations essential), when locals come to eat, drink and dance until 2am. Closed Mon.

Café Sutra Calama 380 and Juan León Mera (upstairs), the New Town. Cosy bar-restaurant serving good-value hearty meals of a mainly Middle Eastern flavour, such as falafel, pita and hummus.

La Escondida General Roca N33-29 and Bosmediano, the New Town ☎02/224-2380. Excellent if pricey Californian cuisine prepared by a young American chef. Tucked away at the end of a cul-de-sac. Closed all day Sat & Sun pm.

Hotel La Real Audiencia Bolívar 220, the Old Town ☎02/295-0590. Uninspiring if inexpensive food, but the views over the Plaza Santo Domingo are superb, especially at night when the church is floodlit. Worth booking a window seat in advance. Closed Sun.

El Maple Calama N10-5 and Juan León Mera, the New Town. Trendy vegetarian restaurant offering reasonably priced dishes from around the world, from curries to burritos and stir-fries. Breakfast here gets you free time on their Internet terminals.

Sake Paul Rivet N30-166 and Whymper, the New Town ☎02/252-4818. Seriously good, super-smart sushi restaurant, with a massive (and expensive) menu including eel, octopus and sea urchin. Out of the way, but a taxi won't cost more than $1.50 from La Mariscal.

Tianguéz Plaza San Francisco, the Old Town. Lively café-restaurant under the stone portals of the Iglesia de San Francisco. The snacks and main meals are a little pricey, but the tables and chairs on the plaza can't be beaten for atmosphere.

Drinking and nightlife

Quito's **nightlife** is, on the whole, a little parochial, with only a small number of really good bars and nightclubs, and not a lot of live music around. The main happening street is Santa María, between Juan León Mera and Diego de Almagro – mainly crammed with small, steamy disco-bars pumping out loud techno music. Most places tend to be fairly quiet through the week, but packed from Thursday to Saturday. In general, bars usually open around 8pm and close around 2am, while clubs stay open until around 4am or longer. Remember to take a taxi at night.

Bars, pubs and late-night cafés

Bogarín corner of Reina Victoria and Lizardo García. Stylish bar hosting excellent live music, popular with a slightly older age group. Closed Sun & Mon.

El Cafecito Luís Cordero 1124. This café (see p.673) is also good for a relaxing evening drink, to a background of soothing music from the likes of Billie Holiday. Closes at 10pm Mon–Thurs, midnight Fri & Sat.

Café Sutra Calama 380 and Juan León Mera (upstairs). A popular drinking hole with a huge cocktail list as well as a good place to have a meal or snack (see above). Always buzzing in the evenings.

Kings's Cross Underground Bar Reina Victoria 1781 and La Niña. Cosy little bar, popular with an older crowd, serving a decent range of imported beers plus a large, smoky, outdoor BBQ every night except Sun.

El Pobre Diablo Isabel La Católica and Galavis. Very appealing, atmospheric bar with good music (often live acts Thurs and Sat) and a young studenty crowd. Closed Sun.

La Reina Victoria, Reina Victoria 530 and Roca. Surprisingly authentic British-style pub with a roaring log fire, decent pub food (with BBQ nights on Sat) and beers, bitters and darts. Closed Sun.

The Turtle's Head La Niña E4-57 and Juan León Mera. Bawdy Scottish-owned pub featuring its own microbrewery that produces some excellent draught beer including bitters and Guinness-style creamy stout. Lots of fun.

Latin music and salsatecas

La Bodeguita de Cuba Reina Victoria 1721 ☎02/254-2476. Actually a restaurant (see above), but on Thursday nights fills with people of all ages dancing to the live Cuban music. Great atmosphere.

Seseribó Edificio El Girón, Veintimilla and 12 de Octubre. Thursday night at *Seseribó* is a Quito institution – a good mixture of students in jeans and gyrating devotees.
Varadero Reina Victoria 1751 and La Pinta. Unpretentious bar-restaurant with live Cuban music (Wed, Fri & Sat), a great atmosphere and knock-out *mojito cubano*, a cocktail of mint with rum and soda. Closed Sun.

Listings

Airlines Alitalia, Eloy Alfaro N32-541 and Shyris, Edificio Nuevola ☎02/227-2802; American Airlines, Amazonas and Av Naciones Unidas, Edificio Puerto del Sol ☎02/226-0900; Austro Aéreo, Amazonas and río Curaray ☎02/227-1536; Avianca, Twin Towers building, República de El Salvador 780 and Portugal ☎02/226-4392; Continental Airlines, World Trade Centre, Tower B, 12 de Octubre and Luis Cordero ☎02/255-7170; Iberia, Amazonas 239 and Jorge Washington ☎02/256-6009; Icaro, Palora 124 and Amazonas ☎02/244-8626; KLM, 12 de Octubre N26-97 and A Lincoln, Torre 1492 ☎02/298-6828; LanChile, Pasaje Río Guayas E3-131 and Amazonas ☎1800/526-328; Lufthansa, 18 de Septiembre N20-705 and Reina Victoria ☎02/250-8396; Tame, Amazonas 1354 and Colón ☎02/250-9375; Varig, Porto Lisboa building, Portugal 794 and República de El Salvador ☎02/225-0126.
Banks and exchange Most facilities are in the New Town and are generally open from Mon–Fri 8.30am–4/5pm and Saturday mornings. Try Banco de Guayaquil on Reina Victoria and Colón or Banco del Pacífico, on Amazonas N22-94 and Veintimilla, or Benalcázar 619 and Banco Chile in the Old Town.
Car rental All the main car rental companies have offices just outside the international terminal of the airport, including Avis ☎02/244-0270; Budget ☎02/245-9052; Ecuacars ☎02/224-7298; Expo ☎02/243-3127; Hertz ☎02/225-4258; and Localiza ☎1800/562254.
Embassies and consulates Argentina, Amazonas 477 and Robles, Edifico Río Amazonas ☎02/2562292; Bolivia, Eloy Alfaro 2432 and Fernando Ayarza ☎02/224-4830; Brazil, Amazonas 1429 and Colón, Edificio España ☎02/256-3086; Canada, 6 de Diciembre 2816 and Paul Rivet, Edificio Josueth González ☎02/223-2114; Chile, Juan Pablo Sanz 3617 and Amazonas ☎02/224-9403; Colombia, Colón 1133 and Amazonas, Edificio Arist ☎02/222-8926; Ireland, Antonio de Ulloa 2651 and Rumipamba ☎02/245-1577; Peru, República de El Salvador 495 and Irlanda ☎02/246-8389; UK, Naciones Unidas and República de El Salvador, Edificio Citiplaza, 14th floor ☎02/297-0800, Ⓦwww.britembquito.org.ec; US, 12 de Octubre and Patria ☎02/256-2890, Ⓦwww.usembassy.org.ec; Venezuela, Cabildo 115 and Quito Tenis ☎02/226-8635.
Emergencies ☎911, police ☎101, fire ☎102, ambulance ☎131.
Hospitals Hospital Metropolitano, Av Mariana de Jesús and Av Occidental ☎02/226-1520, emergency and ambulance ☎02/226-5020.
Internet facilities Quito is reputed to have the largest concentration of Internet cafés in South America, and prices are very low at around $0.50–1 per hour. A few places to try are: Choclo Net, Juan León Mera N26-153 and La Niñaa; Pizza Net, Calama 354; Planeta Net, Calama 414, between Juan León Mera and Amazonas; Pool Net, Calama 233 and Diego de Almagro; Tomato Net, Juan León Mera and Calama; Café Web, Amazonas 333 and Jorge Washington.
Police Dirección Nacional de la Policía Judicial, cnr of Roca 582 and Juan León Mera ☎02/250-3945.
Post offices The main office is at Eloy Alfaro 354 and 9 de Octubre, but the most convenient branch for La Mariscal is on the corner of Reina Victoria and Colón, in the Edificio Torres de Almagro. Mon–Fri 8am–7pm, Sat & Sun 8am–noon.
Taxis Reliable 24hr radio taxis include: Central Radio Taxis ☎02/250-0600; City Taxi ☎02/263-3333; Cooperativa Colón 10 ☎02/254-3621; and Teletaxi ☎02/222-2222.
Telephones Andinatel is in the process of privatizing, and phone offices are appearing all over Quito, including: Colón E4-284 and Amazonas; Reina Victoria 1225 and Lizardo García (collect calls not allowed); and Eloy Alfaro and 9 de Octubre. In the Old Town, head for Benalcázar and Mejía. You can buy Porta and Bell South phonecards from shops displaying their signs.
Tour guides Safari Tours, at Calama 380 and Juan León Mera (☎02/255-2505, Ⓦwww.safari.com.ec), offers a wide choice of climbing and adventure day-tours from Quito, including women-only tours; Ecuadorian Alpine Institute, at Ramírez Dávalos 136 and Amazonas, office 102 (☎02/256-5465, Ⓦwww.volcanoclimbing.com), has guides up all the main peaks as well as a climbing school; Biking Dutchman, at Foch 714 and Juan León Mera (☎02/256-8323, Ⓦwww.biking-dutchman.com), is the original bike-tour operator in Ecuador, offering

a wide range of mainly downhill biking tours; Enchanted Expeditions, at Foch 726 and Amazonas (☎02/256-9960, ⓦwww.enchantedexpeditions.com), is a very professional tour operator with an enormous choice of programmes including trekking, birding and archeological tours; and Yacu Amu at Foch 746 and Juan León Mera (☎02/290-4054, ⓦwww.yacuamu.com), is the longest-established white-water rafting and kayaking specialist in Ecuador.

Travel agents Delgado Travel, Amazonas 1226 and Foch ☎02/252-0229; Ecuadorian Tours, Amazonas 329 and Jorge Washington ☎02/256-0488; Polimundo, Amazonas 2374 and Eloy Alfaro ☎02/250-9619; Turismundial, Amazonas 657 and Ramírez Dávalos ☎02/250-6050.

Around Quito

Just over 20km north of Quito lies the purpose-built colonial-style complex of whitewashed buildings, gift shops, snack bars and museums known as **Ciudad Mitad del Mundo** (Middle-of-the-World City; $0.50), straddling the line that divides the earth's northern and southern hemispheres and gives the country its name – the **equator** (latitude of 0° 0' 0"). It's permanently packed with day-trippers making their way along the paved streets up to the main square, where they take snaps of each other standing astride the **equatorial line** painted across it, overlooked by a monolithic 30m-high monument. Of the on-site attractions, the best are the **Ethnographic Museum** (Mon–Thurs 9am–6pm, Fri–Sun 9am–7pm; $3), inside the monument, with fine displays on Ecuador's indigenous populations; the **Museo Quitsa To**, southeast of the monument (entrance by donation), devoted to pre-Columbian astronomy; and the **Fundación Quito Colonial** near the entrance south of the main avenue (daily 9am–5pm; $1), containing miniature models of Quito, Guayaquil and Cuenca that are saturated with detail.

To get to the complex from Quito, catch a pink-and-white "Mitad del Mundo" **bus** (every few minutes, 40min; $0.35) from Avenida América and Colón. At weekends a special bus service (every 15min, 45min; $0.75) runs between the complex and El Panecillo (see p.670). A **taxi** from the New Town will cost around $15 one-way, or $20 return including waiting time.

A visit to the Mitad del Mundo is commonly combined with a trip up to the rim of the extinct volcano of **PULULAHUA**, whose 3400-hectare **crater** – one of the continent's largest – supports rich cultivated land on the valley floor, as well as cloudflorests, 260 plant species and a large variety of orchids. Outlooks on the rim offer fabulous **views** over bucolic scenery within the crater, beautiful networks of fields and small settlements squeezed around the two volcanic cones of Pondoña and Chivo, all cradled by the thickly forested and deeply gullied crater walls. It's best to get up here early in the morning as thick cloud engulfs the crater later in the day. From the Mitad del Mundo, a **taxi** will take you to a **viewpoint** and back for about $5, or a little more if you want the driver to wait while you follow the steep **trail** down towards the crater settlements below (about 30min down, 1hr back up). Alternatively, Calimatours (☎02/239-4796), which has an office inside the Mitad del Mundo complex, arranges **tours** up to the crater from around $4 per person.

6.2

The northern sierra

The **northern sierra**, a magnificent sequence of volcanoes, sparkling crater lakes and crumpled patchwork scenery, extends northeast from Quito to the Colombian border for 140km as the crow flies. On the ground, however, the **Panamericana** – the main transport artery – must pick its way for over 250km through the region's cracked topography, as it skirts cloud-piercing peaks and coils up and down between windblown hilltop passes across the fruit orchards and flower plantations of warmer valley bottoms. Buses regularly ply the Panamericana, making light work of getting to the main attractions from Quito, but wander off this busy route and you will soon find yourself in seldom-visited territory, where tourism has yet to make a significant mark.

Leaving the capital, the first town of any size is **Cayambe**, set in rich pastureland at the foot of **Volcán Cayambe**, the country's third-highest volcano. Close by are the pre-Inca ruins of **Cochasquí** and the hot springs of **Oyacachi**, an idyllic village nestled in the high forests of the Reserva Ecológica Cayambe-Coca. The great magnet of the region, however, is the splendours of **Otavalo**'s colourful Saturday market. One of the continent's most famous, it is bursting with an irresistible array of weavings, textiles, handicrafts, carvings, jewellery and all manner of assorted knick-knacks.

Ibarra, the "*ciudad blanca*" 30km north of Otavalo, is the largest city in the northern sierra, which charms with its relaxed atmosphere and elegant, whitewashed buildings. The transport hub of the region, the town is also the departure point for the beautiful descent to the isolated north coast, a journey once made only by a hair-rising train ride, now only over the top fraction of the trip. Between Ibarra and **Tulcán**, a jittery town on the Colombian border and the unlikely location for some remarkable topiary gardens, are a few little-visited attractions including the bleak páramo of the **Reserva Ecológica El Ángel**, the huge grotto-shrine of **La Paz**, and the **Reserva Guandera**, which protects one of the last pockets of high-altitude cloudforest in the country.

Cayambe and around

Lying 57km north of Quito in a fertile valley that shimmers with greenhouses for the cut-flower industry, **CAYAMBE** has been compared unfavourably with nearby Otavalo for its lack of *artesanía* tradition. The town does serve as a base for visiting the ruins of **Cochasquí** (daily 8.30am–4.30pm; $3), one of the country's most significant pre-Inca excavations of what was probably a kind of celestial observatory. Consisting of fifteen grassy flat-topped pyramids commanding awesome views, Cochasquí was constructed from blocks of compressed volcanic soil. There are no direct **buses** to Cochasquí, but you can take a bus from Cayambe 8km west towards Tabacundo and get off at the Cochasquí turning from where it's an eight-kilometre uphill **walk** (2hr 30min–3hr 30min; take water); a **taxi** from Tabacundo or Cayambe costs about $8–10 return, including waiting time. Cayambe is also a means of access to the **Reserva Ecológica Cayambe-Coca** ($10, though this is often overlooked), which protects over 4000 square kilometres of land spilling down the eastern Andean cordillera and holding ten life zones, a vast number of recorded plant and animal species and 900 species of birds. Inside the reserve,

Volcán Cayambe (5790m), Ecuador's third-highest mountain and the world's highest point on the equator, is a dangerous climb with crevices and the risk of ice-fall; the basic **refuge** ($17), at about 4700m, is reached by a 25km dirt track leading southeast from Cayambe.

Practicalities

Many **buses** travelling between Quito and Otavalo stop in Cayambe at the two roundabouts next to the bullring (about 40min from Otavalo and 1hr 20min from Quito). The best cheap **hotel** nearest the park (four blocks to the north of it) is the *Hotel Crystal* (ⓣ02/236-1460; ❷) but, at the southern edge of town on Avenida Natalia Jarrín, marginally better rooms at this price are available at *Hostal Mitad del Mundo* (ⓣ02/236-1607; ❷). About 5km south of Cayambe on the road to Cangahua, the distinguished *Hacienda Guachalá* (ⓣ02/236-3042, ⓦwww.haciendaguachala.com; ❻), built in 1580 beyond a flank of rustling eucalyptus trees, is the most charming place to stay in this area. **Restaurants** aren't plentiful in Cayambe town, but in the centre, try the popular *Café Aroma* (closes 8pm & all day Wed), on Bolívar near the park, or, on the same block, the pleasant *Café Encuentro* (closed Mon) for hams, sandwiches and ice creams.

Otavalo

A two-hour bus ride north of the capital, **OTAVALO** is one of Ecuador's top attractions, thanks largely to its world-renowned **Saturday market**, arguably the largest, most colourful *artesanía* market on the continent, with a boggling range of handicrafts, carvings, clothing, crafts, musical instruments and many other oddities for sale. Above all though, Otavalo is famous for its **weavings** and the **Plaza de Ponchos** at the heart of the tourist market, becomes a dizzying labyrinth of colour, its winding makeshift passageways lined with countless tapestries and clothes. During the week Otavalo settles into a quiet provincial town, but trips to the nearby lakes, mountains or the weaving villages are enough to keep you busy for days. Fiestas around June 24 and 29 for San Juan and San Pedro, and the Fiesta del Yamor in the first two weeks of September, see parades, bonfires, bullfights, music, dance and traditional food.

Arrival and information

The **bus station** is on Atahualpa and Neptali Ordoñez, at the northeastern edge of the town. Make sure your bus goes to the terminal (from Quito, Trans Otavalo and Trans Los Lagos do), rather than dropping you off at the Panamericana, at the far southern end of Atahualpa, from where it is a walk of more than six blocks north to the nearest accommodation. This is unsafe and best avoided, especially at night. From the bus terminal, the **Plaza de Ponchos**, the focus of the weaving market, is about a five-minute walk to the southwest. For **information** and **maps**, try the Ministerio de Turismo office (ⓣ06/920-460; Mon–Fri 8.30am–12.30pm & 2–5.30pm) in the Edificio Unaimco above the post office on the corner of Sucre and Salinas.

Accommodation

Otavalo probably has more **hotels** per inhabitant than any other town in the country, despite most of them being virtually empty during the week. Even so, things can get busy on Friday night when you should arrive early or reserve in advance in high season.

Hotel Ali Shungu Quito and Quiroga, Casilla No. 34 ⓣ06/920750, ⓦwww.alishungu.com. The best place to stay in Otavalo, run by a hospitable US couple and a helpful and dedicated local staff. Lavishly decorated with plants and fine weavings, the hotel and rooms overlook a colourful garden towards Volcán Imbabura beyond. Good hot showers, excellent service, maps and tourist information, no check-out time, and a superb restaurant (see p.681) top it all off. Two luxury

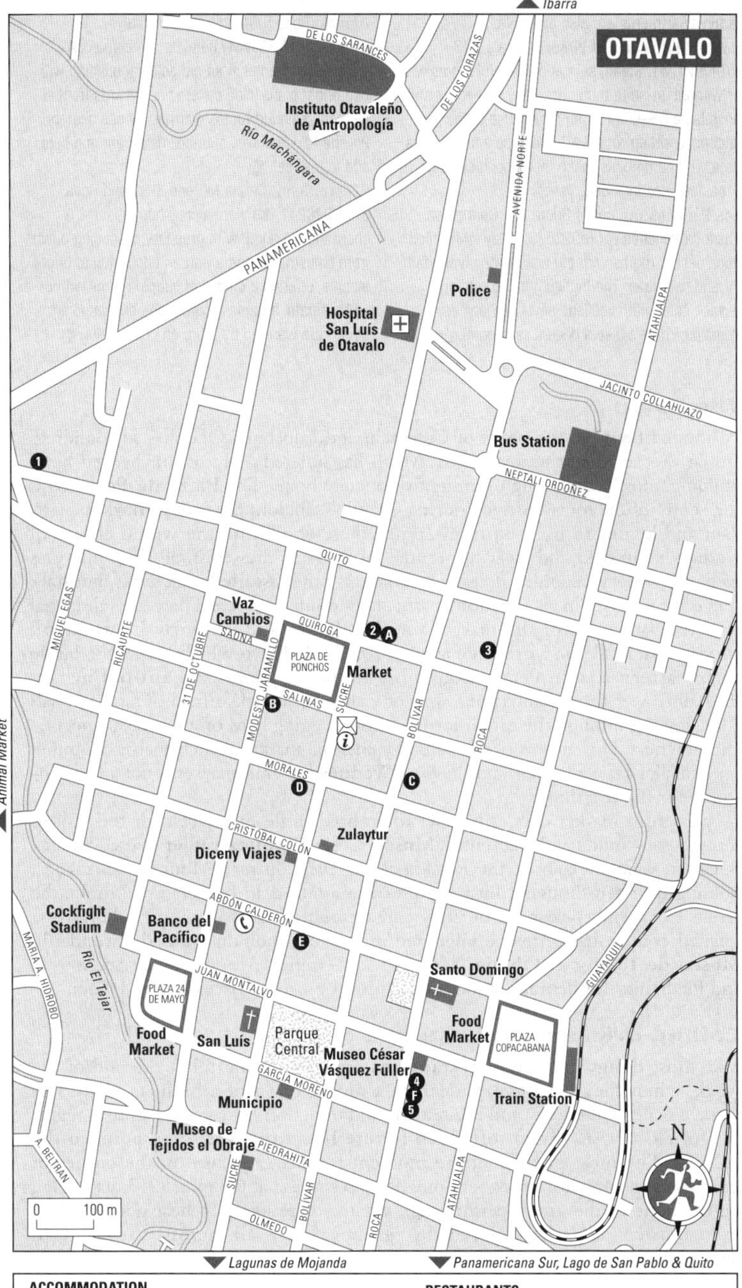

ACCOMMODATION				RESTAURANTS			
Ali Shungu	1	Los Ponchos Inn	2	Café Sahara	A	Pizza Siciliana	D
Hostal Eincón Viajera	3	Riviera Sucre	5	Café Shanandoa	B	Quino	F
Otavalo	4			Café Sol y Luna	C	SISA	E

family apartments are also available. ❺

Hostal El Rincón del Viajero Roca 10-17 ⓣ06/921741. Clean, safe and peaceful rooms with or without en-suite bath offered by a cheerful and hospitable US–Ecuadorian family. Use of the kitchen, a sitting room with fireplace and a games area with hammocks make this a good choice. Breakfast also included. ❸–❹

Los Ponchos Inn cnr of Sucre and Quiroga on Plaza de Ponchos ⓣ06/923575. Glitzy white-tiled floor, decent rooms with big windows, private bath, TV and hot water. The highlight is the rooftop terrace café with excellent views of Plaza de Ponchos. There's also a decent restaurant. ❷

Otavalo Roca 5-04 and Juan Montalvo ⓣ06/920416, ⓦwww.hotelotavalo.com.ec. A distinguished hotel in an old colonial building with two bright plant-filled covered courtyards fronted by high-ceilinged rooms warmed by gas heaters. Polished floorboards, a smart restaurant and café add to the feel. ❹

Riviera Sucre Garcia Moreno 3-80 and Roca ⓣ06/920241, ⓔrivierasucre@hotmail.com. A charming old hotel, with greenery cascading down from balustrades and a garden chock-full of bright blooms, offering a choice of simple rooms with or without bath, a games room, book exchange and small café warmed by a fire on cold nights. ❸–❹

The Town

Positioned between the peaks of Cotacachi and Imbabura, Otavalo's surroundings are far prettier than the town itself, which has suffered a glut of unchecked hotel building, mostly consisting of unsightly concrete boxes. The **Plaza de Ponchos** is the centre of the tourist activity during Otavalo's fabulous **Saturday market** (starts 7am and begins to pack up from 3pm), where you'll find the widest choice of clothes, hammocks and weavings touted by *indígenas* dressed in all their finery, as well as jewellery, ceramics, dolls and numerous other assorted craftworks, but stalls spill off the square in all directions, particularly south on Sucre. There are substantial non-touristy parts of the market too: **hardware** and everyday items are on Modesto Jaramillo, and **produce** at the Plaza 24 de Mayo which has all the bustle of an eastern bazaar. Perhaps the most authentic part is the **animal** market (5–10am) over the Panamericana west of Calderón, a packed field of farm animals all bellowing through the early morning mists, tugging hard on their busily negotiating owners. The success of the Saturday *artesanía* market is such that it continues on a smaller scale all week, and the busy **Wednesday** craft market is not a bad substitute for the real thing.

Apart from market days, this quiet town holds little of interest for the visitor, though you could try the eccentric **Museo César Vásquez Fuller** (closed Sun; $2 donation welcome), above the *Residencial Los Andes* on Juan Montalvo and Roca, holding over ten thousand Inca and pre-Inca artefacts in one cramped room, the results of an eighty-year life of study and accumulation by its owner who gives a spirited commentary. Anyone interested in weaving shouldn't miss the wonderful **Museo de Tejidos el Obraje** (Mon–Sat 9am–1pm & 3–5pm; $2) on Sucre 6-08 and Piedrahita, for demonstrations of traditional processes of textile production.

Eating, drinking and nightlife

Like most things in Otavalo, **restaurants** are more colourful at the end of the week, when they have live Andean folk music, often of a high standard. The market-generated energy and excitement find outlet on Friday and Saturday nights at Otavalo's *peñas*, several of which feature **live music** at some point in the evening. The most popular of the moment is *Peña La Jampa* on the corner of Jaramillo and Morales (Fri & Sat 8pm–3am, live music at 9.30pm; $2–3 depending on the fame of the group performing), where you're likely to hear good Andean folk music (*folklórica*) played by groups from all across the Andean region. Occasionally there are Cuban musicians and mariachi bands.

Café Sahara Quiroga between Bolívar and Sucre. Lounge on cushions at floor level and enjoy Middle Eastern food served on low tables. You can even order a hookah pipe plugged up with fruit-flavoured tobacco.

Café Shanandoa Salinas and Modesto Jaramillo;

also known as *The Pie Shop*. Juices, milkshakes, sandwiches and, above all, tasty home-baked pies with several fruity fillings are on offer at this Plaza de Ponchos stalwart.

Café Sol y Luna Bolívar and Morales. Popular, brightly painted café and art gallery with a shaded patio set back from the street, serving sandwiches, organic salads, veggie burgers, breakfast and a range of bar snacks. Closed Mon and Tues.

Hotel Ali Shungu Quito and Quiroga ⓣ06/920750. Otavalo's best restaurant, where the excellent food, including plenty of vegetarian dishes, is made with local organic produce – the tomatoes in the lasagne, for example, are heavenly. It's a good idea to reserve on Fridays, when there's live music around 8–9pm. Last orders 8.30pm, Fri 9.30–10pm.

Il de Roma Juan Montalvo 4-44. Attractive and atmospheric pizzeria at the *Hostal Doña Esther*, featuring a large clay oven and good pizzas.

Pizza Siciliana Morales and Sucre. The town's most popular pizzeria, notable for its excellent live music on Fridays and Saturdays and occasionally during the week too. The pizzas run $4–14 depending on size and toppings, which include vegetarian options.

Quino Roca and García Moreno. Colourful restaurant specializing in seafood dishes, including fish stew, trout and shrimp for around $4–6 a main course.

SISA Abdón Calderón 4-09 and Sucre. Part of an arts complex that includes bookshop, gallery, café and art workshop. Upstairs is a classy, but moderately priced restaurant serving tasty meals, such as trout and large salads. Live music Friday and Saturday.

Ibarra

Some 125km north of Quito, the Panamericana passes around the base of Volcán Imbabura and into a broad, sunny valley to reveal **IBARRA**, known as the *ciudad blanca* (white city), its low, whitewashed and tiled buildings gleaming with stately confidence, interrupted only by the occasional church spire. Founded in 1606 to oversee the region's forced-labour textile workshops, only a few of Ibarra's original colonial buildings survived the great earthquake of 1868, from which the town eventually recovered to become the commercial and transport hub of Imbabura province. By far the largest highland city north of Quito, Ibarra's population of more than 100,000 comprises an unusual blend of *mestizos*, *indígenas* and Afro-Ecuadorians from the Chota valley and Esmeraldas province, and the city boasts an enjoyably slow pace and easygoing charm.

Arrival, information and getting around

Arriving by **bus**, you'll have to contend with seven terminals servicing the different routes, all in the downtown area west of the obelisk and within a few blocks of the principal hotels. At night, it's worth getting a **taxi** to your hotel from the downtown area (the blocks south and west of the obelisk), which is unsafe after dark. Also stay alert at the train station if you're carrying all your gear. For **onward travel** by bus, Aerotaxi and Expreso Turismo have the best services to Quito, Trans Otavalo for Otavalo; Valle del Chota and Espejo for San Lorenzo; Expreso Turismo and Flota Imbabura for Tulcán; Espejo for El Ángel; and Trans La Esperanza for La Esperanza. **Local buses** leave from the obelisk and service the main thoroughfares such as Avenida Mariano Acosta and Oviedo, or from Bolívar and Mosquera heading south to Caranqui and costing around $0.20 per journey. The well-staffed **tourist office**, García Moreno on Parque La Merced (Mon–Fri 8.30am–1pm & 2–5pm; ⓣ06/955711) can supply free maps and general information.

Accommodation

If you're looking for the really rock-bottom budget joints, there are several in the rougher downtown areas around the train station, but be warned that these are pretty insalubrious places and generally not worth the few saved cents.

Hostal Imbabura Oviedo 9-33 and Chica Narváez ⓣ06/950155 or 958522, ⓔhotel_imbabura@hotmail.com. The best and most popular budget choice in town, boasting large, high-ceilinged

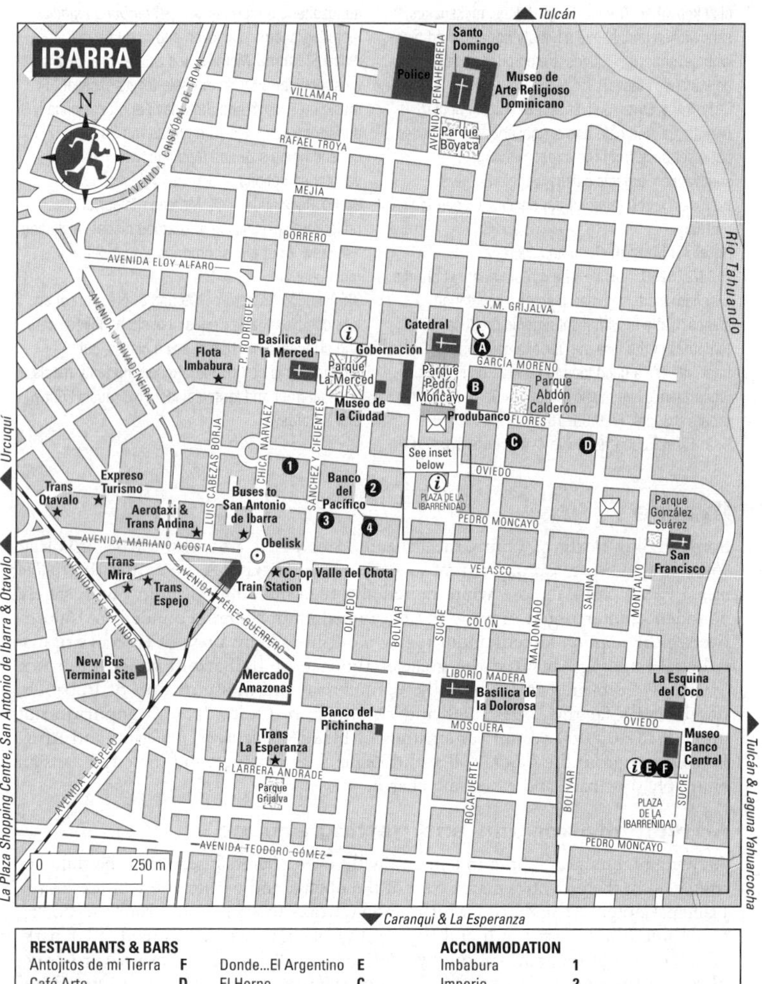

RESTAURANTS & BARS

Antojitos de mi Tierra	F	Donde...El Argentino	E
Café Arte	D	El Horno	C
Café Floralp	A	Mr Peter's	B

ACCOMMODATION

Imbabura	1
Imperio	2
Madrid	3
Royal Ruiz	4

rooms around a pretty courtyard and fountain; the spotless shared bathrooms have strong showers and 24hr hot water. The café on the patio offers good breakfasts, and drinks throughout the day. Other facilities include laundry, Internet access, and trips to the Reserva El Ángel (see p.684). ❷

Hostal Imperio Olmedo 8-62 and Oviedo ☎06/952929. Good-value place with simple, clean en-suite rooms, some decked out with office-type furniture, and all having cable TV. Owns the disco (free) downstairs too. ❷

Hotel Madrid Pedro Moncayo 7-41 and Sánchez y Cifuentes ☎06/956177. Comfortable rooms with private bath, phone and cable TV, though avoid those without a window. Internet service and parking. ❸

Hotel Royal Ruiz Olmedo 9-40 and P. Moncayo ☎06/641999. Upmarket hotel with clean, comfortable and carpeted rooms with private bath, phone and cable TV. Extras include a sauna, steam room and parking. ❹

The Town

Ibarra's sedate atmosphere is manifested in several attractive parks replete with tall flowering trees and surrounded by elegant old buildings. The **Parque La Merced**, fronted by the imposing, grey **Basílica La Merced**, features stalls selling Ibarra's sweet specialities, including *nogadas* and *arrope de mora*, as well as the **Museo de la Ciudad** (not yet open at the time of writing), which will showpiece the traditions and culture of Ibarra, and house temporary exhibitions. A block east, the grander **Parque Pedro Moncayo** has neatly clipped lawns and lofty palms, flanked on the north side by the **Catedral** adorned with a golden altar, portraits of the disciples by Rafael Troya, one of the country's greatest artists, who was born in Ibarra in 1845. The **Museo Banco Central**, a block to the south on Sucre and Oviedo (Mon–Fri 8.30am–1.30pm & 2.30–4.30pm; $0.50), houses a well-presented exhibition covering general Ecuadorian archeology from prehistory to Inca times, as well as exhibits on more localized regional history, including a gold funeral mask from the nearby village of Pimampiro. At the northern end of Bolívar the **Museo de Arte Religioso Dominicano** (daily 8am–noon & 2–6pm; $0.50), around the side of the **Iglesia Santo Domingo**, which itself features some flamboyant paintings inside, holds a small collection of good eighteenth- and nineteenth-century canvases by Ecuadorian greats including Troya, Reyes and Salas among others.

Eating and drinking

Ibarra has countless cheap **restaurants** where you can get perfectly good *almuerzos* and *meriendas* for a dollar or two; other budget options include the cluster of **chifas** along Olmedo between Flores and Velasco, serving much the same Chinese food at much the same low prices. Ibarra is famous for its delicious **helados de paila**, a smooth and flavoursome sorbet prepared in great copper pans (*pailas*), kept cool on a bed of straw and salted ice. The *Heladería Rosalía Suárez*, on the corner of Oviedo and Olmedo, is an Ibarra institution, the oldest and most famous place to scarf a cone or two and watch the stuff being made. For a **drink**, a couple of good bars are *El Barbudo* on the Plaza de la Ibarreñidad and *El Encuentro* on Olmedo 9-59 and Velasco.

Antojitos de mi Tierra Plaza de la Ibarreñidad. Excellent and very friendly little place specializing in Ecuadorian dishes, such as delicious *humitas*, *bonitísimas* and *quimbolitos*, which make the perfect accompaniment to a cup of coffee enjoyed at their outdoor tables.

Café Arte Salinas 5-43 and Oviedo. Owned by an artist, this café-cum-art gallery has a classy wooden interior and outside sculpture yard. Intellectual flourishes abound, from the mock triptych menu to the Frida Kahlo cocktail. Concerts Fri or Sat. Mon–Sat from 4pm.

Café Floralp García Moreno 2-42 and Rocafuerte. Has its own dairy in Caranqui and serves up fantastic cheeses, yogurts, milkshakes and ice creams. Moreover, it's Swiss-owned, so expect great fondue and *raclette* ($3.50–5) as well as other tasty meals. Smart and a little more expensive than other cafés, but worth it.

Donde...El Argentino Plaza de la Ibarreñidad. Friendly Argentinian-owned steak and grill house with outdoor seating offering moderately priced meat-dominated meals, best devoured with a jar of their Argentine wine ($5). Closed Mon.

El Horno Rocafuerte and Flores. Excellent pizzas (from $2.50 according to size) cooked in a big clay oven that dominates the restaurant. Vegetarian options and wine available. Tues–Sun 6pm–midnight.

Mr Peter's Sucre and García Moreno. Wide-ranging, inexpensive but mostly meat-based menu of traditional dishes, tacos and Italian cuisine at this popular Ibarra institution. Often buzzing weekday lunchtimes when their good *almuerzos* are snapped up for $1.50 ($3 at weekends).

North to Tulcán

Some 33km north of Ibarra, at **Mascarilla**, the **old road** to Colombia branches north heading past **Mira** to **El Ángel**, a small highland town with an interesting Monday market and a couple of **places to stay** – try *Hostal Los Faroles*

(☎06/977144; ❷), on the corner of Parque Libertad, or the more comfortable *Hostería El Ángel*, Panamericana Norte and Av Espejo 1302 (☎06/977584; ❺) – that's also the main base for getting to the **RESERVA ECOLÓGICA EL ÁNGEL** This paramo reserve is a wind-blown wilderness of rolling grassland hills peppered with trout-filled lakes and *frailejones*, an endemic plant of the northern Andes region; for information on visiting the reserve and guides, go to the Ministerio del Ambiente office in El Ángel on Salinas and Esmeraldas, upstairs in the Sindicato de Choferes building (☎06/977597).

While the road north of El Ángel to Tulcán is in poor condition and seldom used, back at Mascarilla, you can pick up the **Panamericana**, which continues on a more easterly route to the border, passing **Bolívar** and then **LA PAZ**. Famous for its huge **grotto**, an important religious shrine which attracts pilgrims throughout the year, La Paz is especially crowded in early July for the festival day of the Virgen de la Paz.

Tulcán

TULCÁN, the provincial capital of Carchi, is a skittish frontier town, shifting people with ruthless efficiency in and out of Ecuador via the **Colombian border** just 7km away. At 3000m, the morning sun struggles to warm Tulcan's grey-concrete buildings and dusty streets, something that intensifies the cold and bleak atmosphere, though the busy textile and produce **markets** on Thursdays and Sundays, when the central street is draped in billowy cloth, lend the town some colour. Most travellers don't linger in Tulcán, but if you have time, don't miss the splendid **topiary gardens** in the town cemetery near the Parque Ayora, about a fifteen-minute walk northeast of the centre, where fragrant cypresses have been snipped with meticulous care into well over a hundred different figures, shapes and patterns. The central district feels similarly elongated, contained around the length of the two central streets, **Bolívar** and **Sucre**, which is where you'll find most of the hotels, restaurants and shops. For personal **safety**, try to avoid walking the streets after about 10pm, always make sure you carry your passport with you, and don't travel in the border regions off the Panamericana without checking thoroughly that it is safe to do so.

Practicalities

Buses from within Ecuador deposit you at the large terminal on Bolívar, from where it's a twenty-minute walk (1.5km) uphill northeast to the city centre and most of the hotels; take a taxi (about $1) to the centre rather than a town bus at night or if weighed down with luggage. Regular **vans from the Colombian border** stop at the Parque Ayora, but will take you on to the bus terminal for a little extra. The Cámara de Turismo office (Mon–Fri 9am–12.30pm & 2.30–6pm; ☎06/986606), upstairs in the Edificio Muñoz on Bolívar and Ayacucho, has basic **tourist information** and will help you where they can. The **Colombian Consulate** is on Bolívar and Junín (Mon–Fri 8am–1pm & 2–3pm); to **exchange** dollars to pesos, try the Casa de Cambio on the corner of Ayacucho and Bolívar, or the official moneychangers carrying ID on the Plaza de la Independencia (the main square), but check all calculations before handing money over. The Banco del Austro on Ayacucho and Bolívar and the Banco del Pichincha on the Plaza de la Independencia both have Visa ATMs.

For **places to stay**, competition for the town's many through-travellers means that there are plenty of inexpensive places, most with private bath, hot water and even cable TV. *Hotel Alejandra* (☎06/981784; ❷) on Sucre and Quito and *Hotel Lumar* (☎06/980402; ❸–❹) on Sucre and Pichincha have such facilities, as does *Hotel Los Alpes* (☎06/982235; ❷) on Av J.R. Arellano and Veintimilla, the best option by the bus station. The comfortable *Hotel Sara Espindola* (☎06/986209; ❸), on the corner of Sucre and Ayacucho, has all this plus a sauna, steam room, disco and laundry service. Several very good Colombian **restaurants** exist, all within a block of each other on Bolívar and 10 de Agosto; try *La Fonda Paisa*. *Extrapan*, down on Bolívar and Boyaca, is a good bakery that also serves inexpensive standards such as chicken and rice until midnight.

Crossing into Colombia

Seven kilometres east of Tulcán, the **Rumichaca Bridge** marks the busy **Colombian border**. Customs controls on both sides are modern, efficient facilities (daily 6am–10pm, planned 24hr if border security improves), and there's even a **telephone office** and **restaurant** in the vicinity.

To cross the border, you'll need an **exit stamp** from Ecuadorian customs, in the building marked *Migración*, and an **entry stamp** from the Colombians on the other side of the bridge (both stamps free). The Colombians will give you up to ninety days on entry, but ask to make sure you get the full amount if you need it, and note that stamps are always required, even if only visiting Ipiales for the day. If you're arriving from Colombia, the Ecuadorians will also give you up to ninety days and a tourist card, which you should retain until you leave the country.

Colectivos to the border leave when full from the corner of Venezuela and Bolívar, on the Parque Ayora (10min; $0.70), while a **taxi** costs about $3.50 from there, or $4 from the bus station. From the border *colectivos* to **Ipiales**, a town with plenty of hotels 3km inside Colombia, cost about $0.40, while taxis are around $1.50; add a few hundred pesos (dimes) if you're heading straight for the Ipiales bus terminal. *Colectivos* to **Tulcán** ($0.70) from the frontier usually stop at the Parque Ayora, though if you're in a hurry to get to the bus station, the driver will usually take you there for a little extra. Official **moneychangers** throng the border on both sides, offering acceptable rates for cash dollars and pesos, but always check the calculations and money you receive before handing anything over.

6.3

The central and southern sierra

South of Quito, the two parallel chains of the Andes running the length of Ecuador rise to their most dramatic and spectacular in the central sierra, forming a double row of snowcapped peaks that the nineteenth-century German explorer Alexander Von Humboldt memorably christened "the avenue of volcanoes". Eight of the country's ten highest summits are found here, including Chimborazo (6310m) and Cotopaxi (5897m), towering over a series of inter-montane basins that separate the two ranges. Sitting in these basins, at an altitude of around 2800m, are the region's principal towns – Latacunga, Ambato and Riobamba, which provide convenient bases for visiting the region's main attractions.

The most popular are **Parque Nacional Cotopaxi**, dominated by the perfect cone of the eponymous volcano, and the little town of **Baños**, whose warm climate, spectacular setting and thermal springs have made it a magnet for Ecuadorians and foreigners. Another favourite with gringos is the famous train ride from Riobamba: it no longer runs all the way to Guayaquil, on the coast, but the hundred-kilometre stretch as far as the dramatic incline known as the **Nariz del Diablo** ("Devil's Nose") is maintained as a tourist service, offering fantastic views and a thrilling ride.

South down the Panamericana, the snowcapped peaks and rumbling volcanoes give way to the southern sierra's softer and gentler landscape of lower elevations and warmer, drier climates. The region's main urban centre – and only large city – is **Cuenca**, famed for its magnificent colonial architecture and graceful churches and monasteries. Easily the country's most captivating city, it was raised on the site of the ruined Inca city of Tomebamba. Virtually nothing remains of Tomebamba, but you can get an idea of the remarkable stonework the Incas were famous for at the ruins of **Ingapirca**, Ecuador's only major Inca remains, within easy striking distance of Cuenca.

South of Cuenca, the sense of remoteness increases towards the small provincial capital of **Loja**, hemmed in by jagged, deep-green hills that soar over the town. It serves as a good jumping-off point for the trip south to the laid-back gringo hangout of **Vilcabamba**, nestled in an idyllic mountain valley.

Parque Nacional Cotopaxi

About 60km, south of Quito, the perfectly symmetrical **Volcán Cotopaxi** (5897m) forms the centrepiece of Ecuador's most-visited mainland national park, **PARQUE NACIONAL COTPAXI** (daily 8am–5pm, last entrance 3pm; $10), covering 33,000 hectares of the eastern cordillera. With its broad, green base and graceful slopes tapering to the lip of its crater, Cotopaxi is the most photogenic of the country's thirty or so volcanoes, and on a clear day makes a dizzying backdrop to the stretch of highway between Quito and Latacunga. One of the highest active volcanoes in the world, it's also one of Ecuador's most destructive, with at least ten

Climbing Cotopaxi

It's possible **to climb Cotopaxi** with little or no technical mountaineering experience, but you'll need to be fit, strong, fully acclimatized and have a good, reliable guide, preferably certified by ASEGUIM (Asociación Ecuatoriana de Guías de Montaña). Many climbing and tour companies in Quito and Latacunga offer guided climbs up Cotopaxi, and can rent equipment to solo climbers – see "Listings" p.675 and p.688 for a list of recommended companies. Typical costs are around $200 to $250 per person, including all equipment, transport and food.

The ascent takes, on average, six to eight strenuous hours, and involves negotiating several crevices and climbing on snow and ice. From the top, you're treated to exhilarating views onto all of Ecuador's major peaks, just after sunrise, and down to the wide crater, steaming with sulphurous fumes. The descent normally takes three to four hours, and the importance of acclimatizing properly beforehand cannot be stressed enough. Cotopaxi can be climbed all year round, but December and January are regarded as the best months, with February to April a close second. The late summer (Aug–Sept) can also be good, but is likely to be windier.

major eruptions since 1742 responsible for repeatedly destroying the nearby town of Latacunga. It's been fairly quiet since its last burst of activity in 1904, and today Cotopaxi is the most popular climb in Ecuador. Most day-visitors head here to simply admire the volcano and get a close-up view of its dazzling form before turning home – though another attraction is the wild and starkly beautiful paramo setting, with its rolling moorland streaked by wispy clouds and pockets of mist. At an altitude of some 3500–4500m, the air up here is thin and crisp, and the tundra-like vegetation is made up principally of cropped *pajonales* (straw-like grass) and shrubs, lichens and flowers adapted to harsh climates. Over ninety species of birds inhabit the park, including the tury hummingbird, Andean hillstar and Andean lapwing, while mammals include white-tailed deer, rabbits, Andean foxes and pumas.

Practicalities

Unless you're on a guided tour from Quito (see "Listings" p.675), the easiest way to get here is to take a bus down the Panamericana to the village of Lasso and hire one of the Cooperativa de Camionetas de Lasso pick-up trucks (Ⓣ03/719493) outside the train station. They charge about $25 per group to go up to the parking area below the refuge, and $40 for the round trip, including waiting time of a couple of hours. Often, there are also pick-ups waiting on the Panamericana by the turn-off to the park, charging similar prices. If you're staying in a hotel near the park (see below), staff should be able to arrange transport for you, but if you want to go all the way up to the refuge parking area make sure they've got a 4WD vehicle. Note that it takes about forty minutes to get from the Panamericana to Laguna Limpiopungo, and just over an hour to get to the parking area below the refuge.

By far the best **camping** option is at the Tambopaxi mountain lodge (Ⓣ09/9448223 or in Quito 02/2224241, Ⓦwww.tambopaxi.com; camping $5.60 per person, dorm mattress $16.80) near the northern edge of the park (hire a truck in the small town of Machachi on the Panamericana, 35km south of Quito, or in Lasso), which also has a good restaurant and runs guided hikes and horse rides. There are also a number of **hotels and haciendas** just outside the park. Only a few hundred metres along the main-entrance turn-off is the friendly *Hostal Quinta Huagra Corral* (Ⓣ09/9801122; ❹ including breakfast) which has a few simple double rooms, one with private bath, and a restaurant. Some 5km south of this is the glorious *Hacienda San Agustín de Callo* (Ⓣ03/719160, or in Quito Ⓣ02/2906157, Ⓦwww.incahacienda.com; ❾), a superb colonial hacienda with luxurious rooms.

Latacunga and around

A further 30km south of the turn-off to Cotopaxi – and 91km south of Quito – **LATACUNGA** is a charming, mid-sized market town of narrow, cobbled streets and whitewashed, clay-roofed houses, huddled on the east bank of the Río Cutuchi. Its centre looks distinctly colonial, but most buildings date only from the early twentieth century – a fact owed to Cotopaxi's repeated and devastating eruptions, which have seen the town destroyed and rebuilt five times since its foundation in 1534, most recently in 1877. After a couple of hours' wandering, there's little to occupy you in town, but the vibrant indigenous Thursday market at **Saquisilí** is an easy twenty-minute bus ride northwest, while the sparkling crater lake of **Quilotoa** can be visited on a long day-trip, or as part of a circuit, often called the Quilotoa loop.

Latacunga's focal point is the **Parque Vicente León**, a wide, leafy square dominated by the plain, whitewashed **Catedral** on one side and the austere **Municipio** on the other. A couple of blocks north, the large, twin-towered Iglesia Santo Domingo is the most impressive of the town's churches, with its Grecian pillars and extravagantly painted interior covered with swirling blue, green and gold designs. Right in front of it, on the little Plazoleta de Santo Domingo, you'll find a small *artesanía* **market** (daily except Thurs & Sun), selling knitwear, *shigras* and other souvenirs. The town's daily main market is a huge, outdoor affair spreading over Plaza El Salto (also known as Plaza Chile), off Avenida Amazonas and at its liveliest on Saturdays. Just off the market, on the corner of Vela and Padre Salcedo, is the **Museo de la Casa de la Cultura** (Tues–Fri 8am–noon & 2–6pm; $0.50), where you'll find a collection of effigies that are paraded through the streets during local festivals, as well as some textiles and ceramics.

Practicalities

Latacunga's large **bus station** is on the Panamericana, on the opposite side of the river from the town. While you're here, you can pick up basic **tourist information** and maps from the small municipal tourist office before heading into the centre by **taxi** (no more than $1) or on foot over the 5 de Junio bridge. In town, *Residencial Amazonas*, Félix Valencia 4-67 (☎03/812673; ❷), is the best of a grubby bunch of bottom-dollar **hotels** around the noisy market square, though for a few more dollars you'll find more comfortable rooms with private bath at friendly *Hotel Central*, Sánchez de Orellana and Padre Salcedo (☎03/802912; ❸). *Hotel Makroz* at Félix Valencia 8-56 and Quito ☎03/800907, ⓔhotelmakroz@latinmail.com; ❹) is the smartest choice in town, offering comfortable rooms with cable TV, private parking and a decent restaurant. Other **eating** options include *Los Copihues*, Quito 70-83 (closed Sun), a large restaurant serving mid-priced steaks and grills; great-value Los Sabores de Italia, Quito and Guayaquil, with its delicious pizzas and hot sandwiches; and cheap and cheerful *Chifa China*, Antonio Vela and 5 de Junio 76-85, an Ecuadorian–Chinese restaurant that's usually still open when everywhere else has closed for the night.

Several tour companies offer guided treks around or **climbs up Cotopaxi** and elsewhere, including Neiges, at Guayaquil 5-19 and Belisario Quevedo (☎03/811199); Tobar Expeditions on Guayaquil and Quito (☎03/811333), run by an ASEGUIM guide; and Expediciones Volcanroute on Quito and Padre Salcedo (☎03/812452). In addition, several hotels offer guided day-trips up to Cotopaxi (around $20 per person, including lunch) and to Laguna Quilotoa ($30), including the Estambul, Central and Cotopaxi (see p.686). You'll find **camionetas** for hire (☎03/802625) just off the Plaza El Salto at the corner of Valencia and Antonio Vela; they charge around $30 one-way or $40 for a return trip to Cotopaxi, including waiting time, and around $40 to Laguna Quilotoa and back.

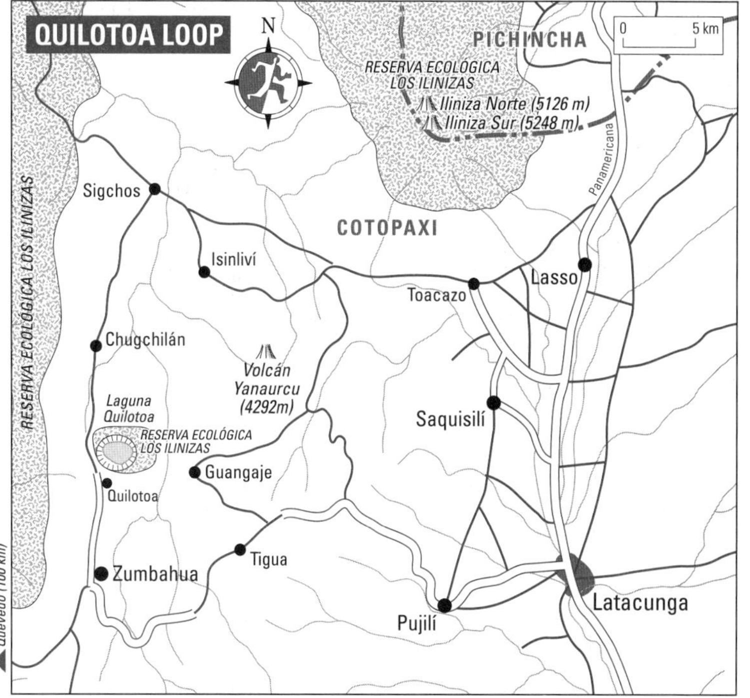

The Quilotoa loop

A popular and highly rewarding excursion from Latacunaga is 90km west to **Laguna Quilotoa**, a spectacular crater lake filled with emerald waters, in one of the most beautiful parts of the sierra. You can squeeze it into a long day-trip from Latacunaga, but it's more enjoyable to do it as a two- or three-day circular trip, taking a different road back to Latacunga – a route that is commonly known as the **QUILOTOA LOOP**.

From Latacunga, Transportes La Iliniza runs a daily bus to Quilotoa (2hours 30min) at noon. As you climb the steep hills of the sierra, the temperature drops noticeably and soon you're in wild, starkly beautiful countryside. The first major stop is **TIGUA**, a prosperous little village famous for the distinctive naive art style it developed, featuring vibrantly coloured peaks, fields and village scenes painted on sheep hide. You'll find a good selection of works for sale at an art gallery co-operative on the hillside above the road. If you want to **stay the night**, *Hostería Samana Huasi* (❹), near the art gallery, offers simple rooms and meals, but most travellers push on for another 30km to **ZUMBAHUA**, a lonely, windswept village set against a stunning backdrop of sharp peaks covered with chequered, tawny fields. Buses to Quilotoa make a stop here, or you can take an hourly bus to Quevado from Latacunga – ask the driver to set you off by the turn-off into the village, a ten-minute walk away. Try to time your visit with Zumbahua's dazzling Saturday-morning **market**, when its large square is crammed with traders, buyers and mountains of fresh produce. A convenient overnight stop before visiting Laguna Quilotoa, Zumbahua has a few very simple **places to stay**, including clean and tidy *Hostal Cóndor Matzi* on the square (❷), with kitchen facilities, and, just round the corner, the *Oro Verde* (❷) with a modest **restaurant**.

About 13km north of Zumbahua, the remote and isolated **LAGUNA QUILOTOA** ($0.50 visitor's fee) is a breathtaking lake lying in the crater of an extinct volcano, surrounded by sleep slopes and jagged cliffs. It's possible to walk down to the lake from the crater's edge in about half an hour, following the path that starts at a muddy chasm just left of the parking area as you face the lake. It's steep, but the solitude and views at the bottom more than repay the effort. Getting back up involves either a stiff one-hour climb, or a 45-minute mule ride (around $4), which you can organize in the parking area before walking down to the lake. There are a few very basic **places to stay** (bring your own sleeping bag) in nearby Quilotoa hamlet, including *Hostal Sunrise* (Ⓔjose_guamangate@latinmail.com; ❷), whose owners offer mule trips and guided hikes.

North of Quilotoa hamlet, a hair-raising 22km drive takes you through dramatic scenery to **CHUGCHILÁN** (daily bus from Quilotoa, 2.30pm). Although one of the poorest villages in the region, it has some comfortable places to stay on its outskirts: notably the lovely *Black Sheep Inn* (Ⓣ03/814587, Ⓦwww.blacksheepinn.com; ❻ including two meals), with cosy rooms and fantastic views, and the more modest *Mama Hilda's* (Ⓣ03/814814, Ⓔmama_ilda@hotmail.com; ❹ including breakfast and dinner), with neat, simple rooms and great food. Moving on from Chugchillán, you can catch a bus back to Latacunga (daily 3am, Thurs 2pm, Saturday late morning, Sun noon; 3hr 45min), via the small town of Sigchos, or else hire a truck to Sigchos (around $15), from where there are plenty of buses (last one 2.30pm) to Latacunga.

Ambato

Continuing down the Panamericana, the next major town you reach is **AMBATO**, 47km south of Latacunga. Although an important commercial centre with a bustling downtown core, there's little here to hold your interest for more than an afternoon or so, and many travellers choose to press straight on to Baños or Riobamba. On the **Parque Juan Montalvo**, the humble, whitewashed **Casa de Montalvo** (Mon–Fri 9am–noon & 2–6pm, Sat 10am–1pm; $1) was the former home of the distinguished nineteenth-century writer Juan Montalvo, and displays a moderately interesting collection of photos, manuscripts and personal effects. More compelling, on the Parque Cevallos three blocks northeast, is the **Museo de Ciencias Naturales** (Mon–Fri 8.30am–12.30pm & 2.30–6.30pm; $1), an old-fashioned natural history museum. Home to numerous stuffed animals including a jaguar, elephant, spectacled bears, iguanas, monkeys and condors, it is rounded off by a stomach-churning display of preserved freak animals.

Practicalities

Ambato's **bus station** is a couple of kilometres northeast of the centre; taxis line up outside (no more than $1 into town), or catch a local bus to downtown Parque Cevallos from Avenida de las Americas, directly behind the station. Most of the town's cheap **hotels** are on or near the slightly rundown Parque 12 de Diciembre, including scrubbed and tidy *Residencial San Andrés*, 12 de Noviembre and Montalvo (Ⓣ03/821604; ❷), and good-value *Hotel del Sol*, Luis A. Martínez and 12 de Noviembre (Ⓣ03/825258; ❸), with modest but clean en-suite rooms. As for **eat**

Volcán Tungurahua

Owing to the unpredictable condition of **Tungurahua Volcano**, which towers over Baños to the south, it's important to check on its current state of activity before visiting the town, either from the daily reports in all the national newspapers, from the SAE in Quito (see p.665) or from the Instituto Geofísico's (Spanish) website Ⓦwww.igepn.edu.ec.

ing, you'll find delicious, inexpensive pizzas at cosy *La Fornace*, Av Cevallos 17-28; tasty grills at *Parrilladas El Gaucho*, Bolívar and Quinto (closed Sun), and classic, mid-priced *comidas típicas* (along with international fare) at comfortable *El Álamo Chalet*, Cevallos and Montalvo.

Baños

Some 44km southeast of Ambato, the thriving little town of **BAÑOS** is one of the most popular tourist destinations in Ecuador. A good 1000m lower than most sierra towns, at 1820m above sea level, Baños enjoys a warm, subtropical climate, but the real pull is its spectacular location, nestled among soaring green hills streaked with waterfalls. Add to this the **thermal baths** that give the town its name and an excellent choice of hotels and restaurants, and it becomes clear why it's so easy to spend time here – especially between November and April, when the weather's at its best.

Enclosed by such dramatic, verdant scenery, there's little to catch your eye in the town itself, with the exception of the massive **Basílica de Nuestra Señora del Rosario de Agua Santa** on Calle Ambato, dominated by a pair of 58-metre spires. The church attracts thousands of pilgrims each year, who come to worship Nuestra Señora de Agua Santa, a supposedly miraculous icon credited with rescuing

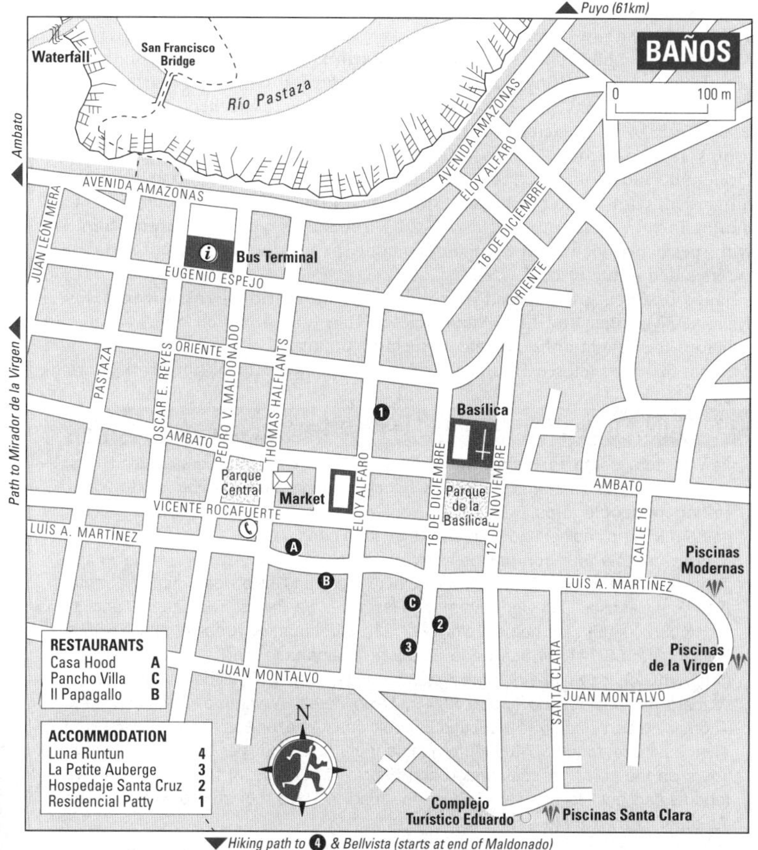

Baños and its citizens from countless calamities over the years. You can admire the Señora's processional wardrobe in a **museum** upstairs from the cloisters (daily 8am–5pm; $0.50), along with a bizarre assortment of objects including a shrunken head from the Oriente, pickled snakes in jars and a collection of stuffed Ecuadorian wildlife put together by someone with a very poor grasp of anatomy.

Once you've visited the basilica and museum there's nothing to detain you from taking a plunge in one of the town's six thermal baths. Most appealing are the **Piscinas de la Virgen** (4.30am–5pm & 6–10pm; $2) at the eastern extreme of Avenida Martínez, sitting at the foot of a waterfall which tumbles down a rocky cliff, floodlit at night to spectacular effect. About 1.5km west of the town, sitting in a gorgeous spot at the foot of Volcán Tungurahua, the **Piscinas El Salado** (daily 4.30am–5pm; $2) are also recommended, with six small pools at various temperatures, plus an ice-cold river for a cool dip; you can get here on the frequent town buses that leave from the corner of Vicente Rocafuerte and Eloy Alfaro, or walk it in about 25 minutes.

Practicalities

Buses drop passengers inside or right next to the bus terminal, three blocks north of the central square, just off the main Ambato–Puyo road. While you're here you can pick up maps and other information at the municipal **tourist office** (Mon–Fri 8am–12.30pm & 2–5.30pm, ⓣ03/740483), on the upper level of the bus terminal. Taxis are parked just outside, but it's an easy walk to most hotels from the terminal.

Baños offers a huge choice of **accommodation**. Best of the cheapies is the basic but clean *Residencial Patty,* a real backpackers' institution at Eloy Alfaro 556 and Oriente (ⓣ03/740202; ❶). For a few dollars more there's excellent-value *Hospedaje Santa Cruz*, 16 de Deciembre and Montalvo (ⓣ03/740648; ❷), with neat en-suite rooms around gardens. For a step up in comfort, try *La Petite Auberge*, 16 de Deciembre and Montalvo ⓣ03/740936; ❹–❺), a delightful hotel in its own peaceful garden, with a good restaurant, or, for real luxury, Swiss-run *Luna Runtun*, a mountain retreat 8km east of town (ⓣ03/740882, ⓦwww.lunaruntun.com; ❾) with spectacular views and a range of fantastic spa treatments; breakfast and dinner are included in the price.

Baños boasts a great spread of good-value international **restaurants**: try *Il Papagallo*, Martínez and Eloy Alfaro (closed Tues lunch), which offers a range of delicious fresh pasta dishes, or the enduringly popular *Casa Hood* at Martínez and Thomas Halflants (closed Tues), with an extensive international (mostly vegetarian)

Activities and tours around Baños

Few visitors come to Baños without wanting to explore the surrounding hills, ravines, rivers and waterfalls, either by **hiking**, **cycling**, **horse riding, white-water rafting** or **jungle trips**. Make sure your guide is qualified (AGAR for rafting; ASEGUIM for climbing) and your gear is in good condition.

A few reliable **tour companies** to try are Aventura Travel Agency, Montalvo and Thomas Halflants (ⓣ03/740566), for guided horse and bike rides and bike rental ($16–22); Caballos Con Christián at the *Hostal Isla de Baños*, Thomas Halflants 1-31 (ⓣ03/740609), for horse treks ($22–25); Geotours at Ambato and Thomas Halflants (ⓣ03/741344) and Río Loco at Maldonado and Luis A. Martínez (ⓣ03/740929) for white-water rafting ($30 half-day, from $60 full day); Rain Forestur Ambato and Maldonado (ⓣ03/740743), Deep Forest Adventure, Rocafuerte and Thomas Halflants (ⓣ03/741815) and Expediciones Amazónicas, Oriente 11-62, and Thomas Halflants (ⓣ03/740506) for jungle tours (from $25 per day); and Córdova Tours on the corner of Maldonado and Espejo (ⓣ03/740923) for trips on a *chiva* (open-sided bus) to the waterfalls on the road to Puyo ($8) and to watch Volcán Tungurahua by night (9–11pm; $3).

menu that takes in Indian, Chinese, Indonesian and Thai dishes. *Pancho Villa*, 16 de Diciembre and Martínez, is a cheerful Mexican restaurant complementing its tasty food and good margaritas. There's plenty of **nightlife** on offer, as well: a couple of good places to catch live music, usually *folklórica*, are *Peña Ananitay*, 16 de Diciembre and Espejo, and *Peña Canela y Clavo*, Rocafuerte and Maldonado.

Riobamba and around

Sitting on the Panamericana 52km south of Ambato, **RIOBAMBA** is a handsome and lively city made up of stately squares, flaking, pastel-coloured buildings, cobbled streets and sprawling markets – an enjoyable place to visit in itself, but also the starting point of the famous "Devil's Nose" train ride (see box below). The town's centre is marked by the **Parque Maldonado**, a wide square lined by the most impressive of Riobamba's nineteenth-century architecture, including the colonnaded, peach and white **Municipio**, and other flamboyant colonial buildings trimmed with elaborate stucco mouldings. On the northeast side of the square, the delicately carved stone facade of the **Catedral** is Riobamba's only survivor of a devastating earthquake in 1797, painstakingly transported and reassembled here when the ruined town was rebuilt in a new location. A couple of blocks north, the **Monasterio de las Conceptas** houses one of the best museums of religious art outside Quito (entrance on Argentinos, Tues–Fri 9am–noon & 3–6pm, Sat 9am–6pm; $4), with a fine collection of carvings and paintings, as well as some richly embroidered robes, silver lecterns and crowns, and – the museum's pride – a gold, jewel-encrusted **monstrance**, believed to be one of the most valuable in South America.

If you're in town on a Saturday you can catch Riobamba's immense **market** bulging out of the streets bounded by calles España, 5 de Junio, Guayaquil and Argentinos, where you'll find a staggering range of goods from squawking chickens to rubber boots. And, if you're around on a very clear day, wander out to the **Parque 21 de Abril**, a small, landscaped hill about eight blocks north of Parque Sucre, offering fine views over the town and across to Volcán Chimborazo.

Practicalities

Riobamba's main **bus terminal** (☎03/962005) is a couple of kilometres from the centre at the intersection of avenidas Daniel León Borja and De La Prensa; taxis

The Devil's Nose train ride

Riobamba is the starting point of the train ride that takes in the famous **Nariz del Diablo** ("Devil's Nose") – a series of tight switchbacks carved out of the mountainside, taking you down an 800m descent. It was originally part of the Guayaquil–Quito service – Ecuador's first railway, completed in 1905 – but the only section still running is the 100km stretch from Riobamba west to Sibambe, operated as a tourist service by the state railway company. It's quite fun, with most travellers piled onto the roof where they trundle along admiring the splendid sierra views.

The train leaves Riobamba on Wednesdays, Fridays and Sundays at 7am, taking around five hours to get to **Sibambe**; tickets ($11) are available at Riobamba's train station (daily 8am–noon & 2–6pm, also the morning before departure from 6am; ☎03/961909). An alternative is to take a bus to the small town of Alausí (every 30min; 2hr), where you can join the train for the last hour, which includes the descent down the Nariz del Diablo. Coming back, many passengers get off at Alausí to take a bus back to Riobamba, or on to Cuenca (4hr 30min); otherwise the train will finally get you back to Riobamba around 6–7pm. Note that it's very cold travelling on the roof for the first couple of hours, so bring plenty of layers; also, it can be pretty uncomfortable up there, so bring a sleeping bag to sit on, or buy one of the cushions for sale by the tracks (about $0.50).

RIOBAMBA

ACCOMMODATION
Hotel Ecuador 1
Hotel Metro 2
Hotel Montecarlo 3

RESTAURANTS
Che Carlitos B
Café Concerto El Delirio A
San Valentín Club C

0 100 m

Terminal Oriental
Bus Terminal

La Basílica
Catedral
Municipio
La Concepción
Monasterio de las Conceptas
Colegio Maldonado
Mercado San Francisco
Mercado La Merced
Mercado La Condamine
Train Station
Plaza de Toros
Parque de la Libertad
Parque Maldonado
Parque Sucre
Parque 21 de Abril
PLAZA SAN FRANCISCO
PLAZA LA CONCEPCIÓN

MORONA
ALVARADO
BENALCÁZAR
MARIANA DE JESÚS
VELASCO
TARQUI
5 DE JUNIO
ESPEJO
COLÓN
LARREA
ESPAÑA
GARCÍA MORENO
PICHINCHA
ROCAFUERTE
M. DÁVALOS
CARABOBO
JUAN MONTALVO
ESPECTADOR
JUAN LAVELLE
V. TORRES
MIGUEL ANGÉL LEÓN
FRANCIA
DIEGO DE IBARRA
URUGUAY
BRASIL
CAPITÁN ALLENDE
C. JIMÍNEZ
MAYOR RUÍZ
AYACUCHO
JUNÍN
ARGENTINOS
OROZCO
VELOZ
PRIMERA CONSTITUYENTE
10 DE AGOSTO
GUAYAQUIL
OLMEDO
VILLARROEL
CHILE
COLOMBIA
ESMERALDAS
AVENIDA DANIEL LEÓN BORJA
AVENIDA UNIDAD NACIONAL
AVENIDA LA INDEPENDENCIA

into town cost $0.80, or you can take a bus down Daniel León Borja as far as the centrally located **train station**. If you're arriving from Baños or the Oriente you'll pull in at the smaller **Terminal Oriental** (Ⓣ03/960766) on the corner of Espejo and Luz Elisa Borja, about 1km northeast of the centre and served by plenty of taxis, as well as city buses going to the train station. You'll find tourist information and maps at the very helpful **Ministerio de Turismo** (Mon–Fri 8.30am–1pm & 2.30–6pm; Ⓣ03/941213) in the Centro de Arte y Cultura on Avenida Daniel León Borja and Brasil.

If you're arriving in Riobamba the night before the "Devil's Nose" train departs (see box on p.695), it's worth phoning ahead to book your **accommodation**. If you're on a tight budget, try bottom-dollar (but reasonably clean) *Hotel Ecuador*, Espectador 22-32 (Ⓣ03/940800; ❷), though, for a little more, nearby *Hotel Metro*, Av Daniel León Borja and Lavalle (Ⓣ03/961714; ❷) is a better bet with its spick-and-span rooms (many with cable TV) and en-suite bath. You'll find more character at colonial-style *Hostal Montecarlo*, 10 de Agosto 25-41 (Ⓣ03/960557; ❺), with a lovely flower-filled courtyard. **Restaurants** to try include the appealing *Café Concerto El Delirio*, Primera Constituyente 28-16 (Ⓣ03/960029), serving tasty meat and fish dishes (pricier than average) in a beautiful colonial house, and *Che Carlitos*, Colón 22-44, a down-to-earth Argentine steakhouse (closed Sun). The cheerful *San Valentín Club*, Av Daniel León Borja 22-19 is a lively, diner-style **café-bar** serving pizzas, burgers, tacos and burritos, washed down by plenty of beer (evenings only; closed Sun).

Volcán Chimborazo

Some 30km northwest of Riobamba, 6310m-high **VOLCÁN CHIMBORAZO** is the highest peak in Ecuador. An extinct volcano, thought to have last erupted some 10,000 years ago, it is a giant of a mountain, its base spanning approximately 20km and its upper elevations permanently covered in snow and ice. Its summit was once imagined to be the highest in the world, and still enjoys the distinction of being the furthest point from the centre of the earth, thanks to the bulge around the equator.

With a good access road and two mountain refuges perched on its lower slopes, Chimborazo can easily be visited on a day-trip from Riobamba: several hotels there offer good-value trips to the volcano's lower refuge (4800m), from where you can walk up to the second refuge (5000m) in thirty to sixty strenuous minutes. For experienced mountaineers wanting to climb to the summit, a number of dedicated **climbing companies** and **guides** will take you for around $200, including Alta Montaña, Av Daniel León Borja 35-17 and Diego Ibarra (Ⓣ03/950601, Ⓔaventurag@laserinter.net); Andes Trek, Colón 22-25 and 10 de Agosto (Ⓣ03/940964, Ⓦwww.andes-trek.com); Expediciones Andinas, Km 3.5 along the road to Guano from Riobamba (Ⓣ03/940820, Ⓦwww.expediciones-andinas.com); and Veloz Coronado Expediciones, Chile 33-21 and Francia (Ⓣ03/960916, Ⓔivoveloz@yahoo.com). The best months for climbing Chimborazo are November to May; between June and October it can be windy.

Ingapirca

South of Riobamba and Alausí, the Panamericana leaves the central sierra behind and winds its way into the southern sierra. The first important attraction on the route is **INGAPIRCA** (daily 8am–6pm; $6), Ecuador's only major Inca ruins. Though not as dramatic or well preserved as the Inca remains of Peru, it's nonetheless an impressive site. Perched on a breezy hill commanding fine views over the surrounding countryside, Ingapirca was built during the Inca expansion into Ecuador towards the end of the fifteenth century, on a site that had been occupied by the Cañari people for over 500 years. Originally a large, elaborate complex that

△ The streets of Quito's Old Town

probably functioned as a place of worship, a fortress, and a *tambo*, or way-station, the only part that remains substantially intact is the central structure known as the **Adoratorio**, or Temple of the Sun – an immense oval-shaped platform whose slightly inward-tapering walls are made of exquisitely carved blocks of stone, fitted together with incredible precision. The rest of the site consists mainly of low foundation walls, possibly the remains of storehouses, dwellings and a great plaza, among other things; there's not a great deal left, but guides (some English spoken) can explain various theories about what once stood where. There's also a small but well-laid-out **museum** just inside the entrance to the site, displaying some Cañari and Inca pots, tools, jewellery and a skeleton found here, there is a shop next to it.

The easiest way to **get to Ingapirca** is on the Transportes Cañar bus from Cuenca (9am & 1pm; 2hr), which runs directly to the site entrance (coming back 1pm & 4pm). Note that on Saturday and Sunday there's only one bus in each direction (9am there, 1pm back). If you want to stay overnight, you'll find comfortable **rooms** in *Posada Ingapirca* (ⓣ07/215116; ❻), a lovely 120-year-old farmhouse, a stone's throw from the ruins, or more basic accommodation at *Hostal Hinti Huasi* (ⓣ07/215171; ❸) over in Ingapirca village, a five-minute walk from the site.

Cuenca

CUENCA is Ecuador's most seductive, and possibly its most beautiful colonial city. A classic example of a planned Renaissance town in the Americas, Cuenca shares many architectural features with Old Quito, such as its narrow, cobbled streets, harmonious, balconied houses with interior courtyards, and an abundance of flashing white **churches** and diverse **museums**. Here, however, they're presented without the pollution, noise and overbearing crowds of the capital, in a relaxed, provincial and altogether more enjoyable atmosphere.

Founded by the Spaniards on April 12, 1557, Cuenca was not the first dazzling city to be erected on this site: the city of **Tomebamba** had been founded here by the Inca Tupac Yupanqui around 1470, and was said to have rivalled Peru's Cuzco with its splendour. Its glory was short lived, however, as the city was destroyed during the Inca civil war that broke out during the second decade of the sixteenth century, prompted by rival claims to the throne by the brothers Atahualpa and Huascar. These days, Cuenca's Inca legacy has all but vanished, hinted at only by the foundation stones of some its buildings, and some modest ruins excavated in the twentieth century.

Arrival and information

Cuenca's **airport** (ⓣ07/862203) and **bus terminal** are both east of the city centre, on Avenida España; taxis into town cost around $2, or you can pick up a bus on Avenida España to Calle Vega Muñoz, on the northern edge of downtown.

For information, you'll find the **Ministerio del Turismo** office on the main square at Sucre and Benigno Malo (Mon–Fri 9am–1pm & 2.30–5pm; ⓣ07/839337, ⓔmturaustro@ec-gov.net); the The Travel Center at Hermano Miguel 4-46 and Calle Larga (closed Sun in low season; ⓣ07/823782) has general information in English, including bus, train and flight times as well as advice on tours.

Accommodation

Cuenca boasts a wealth of **hotels** to suit all budgets, many of them in charming old colonial-style houses built around little courtyards. It's a good idea to book ahead if you're arriving on a Friday as Cuenca is a popular weekend destination with Ecuadorians and places fill quickly.

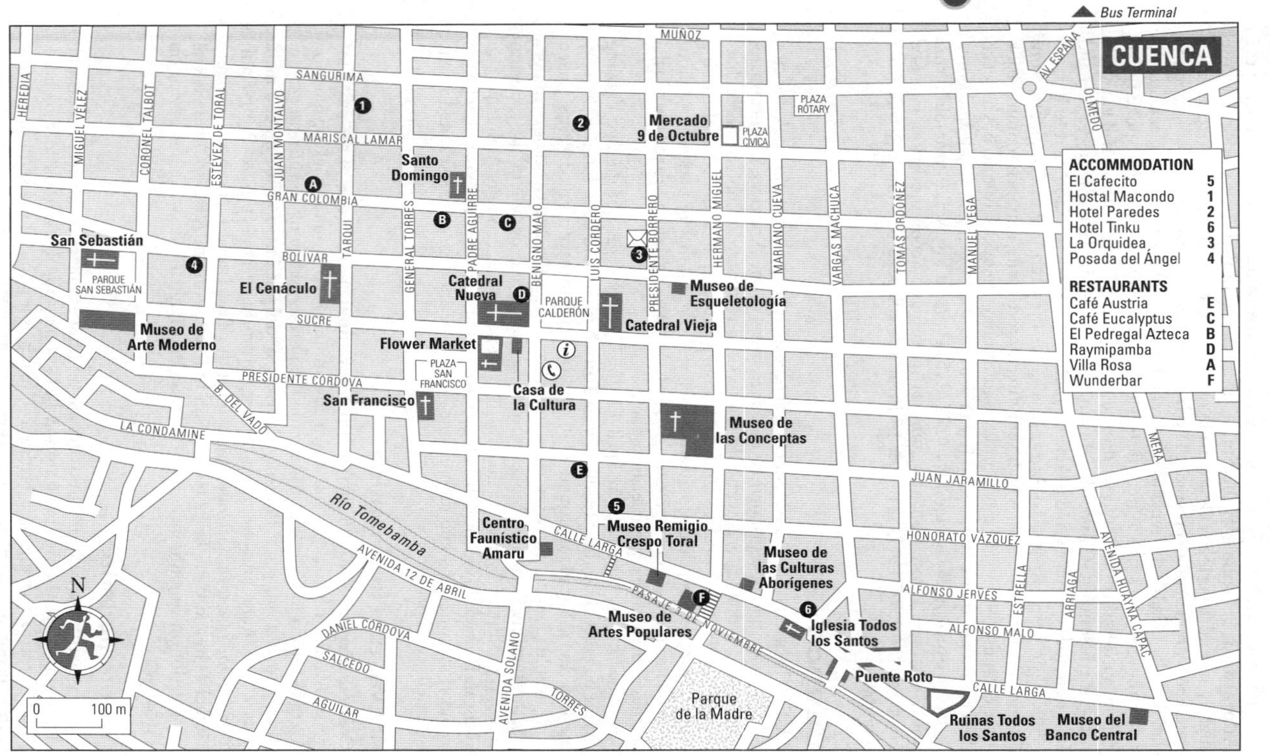
CUENCA
Bus Terminal
ACCOMMODATION
El Cafecito 5
Hostal Macondo 1
Hotel Paredes 2
Hotel Tinku 6
La Orquidea 3
Posada del Ángel 4
RESTAURANTS
Café Austria E
Café Eucalyptus C
El Pedregal Azteca B
Raymipamba D
Villa Rosa A
Wunderbar F
Mercado 9 de Octubre
PLAZA CÍVICA
PLAZA ROTARY
Santo Domingo
San Sebastián
PARQUE SAN SEBASTIÁN
El Cenáculo
Catedral Nueva
PARQUE CALDERÓN
Catedral Vieja
Museo de Esqueletología
Museo de Arte Moderno
Flower Market
PLAZA SAN FRANCISCO
San Francisco
Casa de la Cultura
Museo de las Conceptas
Centro Faunístico Amaru
Museo Remigio Crespo Toral
Museo de las Culturas Aborígenes
Museo de Artes Populares
Iglesia Todos los Santos
Puente Roto
Ruinas Todos los Santos
Museo del Banco Central
Parque de la Madre
Río Tomebamba
MUÑOZ
SANGURIMA
MARISCAL LAMAR
GRAN COLOMBIA
BOLÍVAR
SUCRE
PRESIDENTE CÓRDOVA
B. DEL VADO
LA CONDAMINE
CALLE LARGA
PASAJE 3 DE NOVIEMBRE
AVENIDA 12 DE ABRIL
DANIEL CÓRDOVA
SALCEDO
AGUILAR
AVENIDA SOLANO
TORRES
HEREDIA
MIGUEL VÉLEZ
CORONEL TALBOT
ESTÉVEZ DE TORAL
JUAN MONTALVO
TARQUI
GENERAL TORRES
PADRE AGUIRRE
BENIGNO MALO
LUIS CORDERO
PRESIDENTE BORRERO
HERMANO MIGUEL
MARIANO CUEVA
VARGAS MACHUCA
TOMÁS ORDÓÑEZ
MANUEL VEGA
AV. ESPAÑA
OLMEDO
MERA
JUAN JARAMILLO
HONORATO VÁZQUEZ
ALFONSO JERVÉS
ALFONSO MALO
ESTRELLA
ARRIAGA
AVENIDA HUAYNA CAPAC
N
0 100 m

El Cafecito Honorato Vásquez 7-36 ⓣ07/832337, ⓔelcafec@cue.satnet.net. Popular budget rooms with and without private bath, set around an attractive courtyard that also functions as a café-bar (can be noisy Thurs, Fri & Sat nights). The quietest rooms are out at the back. ❷–❸.

Hostal Macondo Tarqui 11-64 ⓣ07/840697, ⓔmacondo@cedei.org. Quiet, beautiful old house with simple but spotless rooms (shared and private bath) and a delightful garden. Guests can use the kitchen in the afternoon. ❹

Hostal Tinku Calle Larga and Jervés ⓣ07/814373. An old house reinvented as a funky backpacker's hangout, featuring private and shared rooms and a ten-bed dormitory (all with shared bath), kitchen facilities, and a comfy lounge with cable TV. Also has a good café and bar. ❷

Hotel Paredes Luis Cordero 11-29 ⓣ07/835674. Large mostly en-suite rooms in an extravagantly decorated old mansion with lots of bric-a-brac lying around, and a resident parrot. A little rundown, but with lots of character. ❷–❸

La Orquidea Presidente Borrero 9-31 ⓣ07/824511. Attractive hotel in a renovated old building, offering twelve simply furnished but stylish rooms with lots of natural wood, pale walls and good-quality en-suite bathrooms. ❹

Posada del Ángel Bolívar 14-11 ⓣ07/840695, ⓔhdaniel@cue.satnet.net. Comfortable rooms with cable TV and private bath in this old building featuring two brightly painted covered courtyards. Breakfast and 30min free Internet included. ❺

The City

Despite being Ecuador's third-largest city, Cuenca has a very manageable downtown. If possible, try to coincide your visit with a Friday or Saturday evening, when the city's **churches** are illuminated to stunning effect, or Sunday during the day, when traffic is kept out of the main square. Note that most churches are open between 7am and noon and from 6pm to 8pm.

Parque Calderón and around

Start exploring around flower-filled central square, **Parque Calderón**, dominated by the immense twin-towered facade and sky-blue domes of the nineteenth-century **Catedral Nueva**. The cathedral's grand scale and self-confidence stand in marked contrast with the modest eighteenth-century **Catedral Vieja** across the square, with its low, horizontal outline, simple, whitewashed walls, clay-tiled roof and central bell tower.

Just off the Parque Calderón, on Calle Sucre, the Plazoleta del Carmen – a tiny square more commonly known as the **Plaza de las Flores** – is home to a daily flower market, presided over by chola women wearing blue- or pink-checked aprons, long black plaits and Panama hats. One block south of here, on Córdova and Padre Aguirre, you'll find another market square, the **Plaza San Francisco**, this one selling a diverse mix of chunky knitwear, wall hangings and cheap clothes. It's overlooked by the **Iglesia San Francisco**, rebuilt in the early twentieth century in a Neo-colonial style – take a look inside at the splendid eighteenth-century gold-leaf pulpit. Three blocks north, on Gran Colombia and Padre Aguirre, the grey-blue, twin-towered **Iglesia Santo Domingo** is another early twentieth-century church built in the colonial style, sporting a colourful interior painted with intricate geometric motifs.

Iglesia San Sebastián and Museo de Arte Moderno

Six blocks west of the Parque Calderón, the **Iglesia San Sebastián** marks the western limit of Cuenca's *centro histórico*. Built in the seventeenth century, this is one of the city's oldest churches and features a single bell tower over the right side of the entrance, giving the church a slightly lopsided appearance. Opposite, the municipal **Museo de Arte Moderno** (Mon–Fri 8.30am–1pm & 3–6.30pm, Sat & Sun 9am–1pm; free) puts on temporary exhibitions of national and Latin American artists, displayed in a series of rooms around a large, beautiful courtyard.

Museo de las Conceptas and the Museo de Esqueletología

A couple of blocks southeast of the Parque Calderón, the Monasterio de las Conceptas, founded in 1599, hides behind the thick, white walls that separate its occupants from the outside world. Part of the convent is open to the public as the **Museo de las Conceptas** (Mon–Fri 9am–3.30pm, Sat 10am–1pm; $2.50; entrance on Hermano Miguel 6-33), which presents a large collection of religious paintings and sculpture from the seventeenth to nineteenth centuries, as well as a roomful of nineteenth-century toys, brought here by novices entering the convent. While you're here, check out the attached **Iglesia de las Conceptas**, giving onto Presidente Córdova, which features a flamboyant steeple, some finely carved wooden doors and an impressive gold-leaf altar inside. For something different, walk two blocks north to Bolívar 6-57 and Presidente Borrero, where the little **Museo de Esqueletología** (Mon–Fri 10am–1pm & 4–7pm, Sat 10am–2pm; $1) houses an unusual collection of skeletons from the tiny frames of a hummingbird and foetus skulls to the rather larger condor, llama and elephant calf.

Along the Río Tomebamba

Backing onto the Río Tomebamba, Calle Larga is home to a couple of good little museums: at No. 7-07 the **Museo Remigio Crespo Toral** (Mon–Fri 8.30am–1pm & 3–6pm, Sat 10am–noon; free) houses a small but noteworthy collection of pre-Columbian ceramics, documents dating from the city's foundation, and religious paintings and sculpture in a beautifully restored nineteenth-century house. A couple of blocks east, at no. 5-20, the **Museo de las Culturas Aborígenes** (Mon–Fri 8.30am–6pm, Sat & Sun 9am–1pm; $2) has an excellent collection of pre-Columbian ceramics and artefacts, beginning with Stone Age tools and dinosaur teeth and ending with accomplished Inca earthenware (it also has a good café). Midway between the two museums, a set of stone steps leads down to the riverside – "*el barranco*" – giving wonderful views onto the back parts of Calle Larga's grand houses, hanging precipitously over the steep riverbank. At the bottom of the steps is the excellent Centro Interamericano de Artesanías y Artes Populares (CIDAP), whose **Museo de Artes Populares** (Mon–Fri 9.30am–1pm & 2.30–6pm, Sat 10am–1pm; free) brings together arts and crafts from all over Latin America.

About 1km east along the river bank, the **Museo del Banco Central** (Mon–Fri 9am–6pm, Sat 9am–1pm, last entry an hour before closing; $1) is Cuenca's most polished and absorbing museum – highlights include some fine Inca artefacts and a series of excellent displays on Ecuador's indigenous cultures, including an extraordinary collection of **Shuar tsantsas** (shrunken heads) from the southern Oriente. Entrance to the Museo del Banco Central also includes access to the **Pumapungo archeological** site (same hours), directly behind the museum, which is where the most important religious buildings of Tomebamba were located. The site has been reworked as an archeological park, combining the ruins with botanical displays of important Andean plants and a bird rescue centre.

Mirador de Turi

The best spot for a panoramic view of the whole city is the **Mirador de Turi**, a lookout point in front of the Iglesia de Turi, perched high on a hill some 4km south of the centre (about $1.50 each way by taxi). The views are particularly theatrical on Friday and Saturday evenings when the city's churches are floodlit.

Eating and nightlife

Cuenca offers the best choice of **restaurants** south of Quito, offering everything from cheap lunches to fine international cuisines and high-quality *comida típica*. Cuenca's **nightlife** only really takes off on Thursday, Friday and Saturday nights, when the city's disco-bars and *salsatecas* fill with teenagers and twenty-somethings; bars tend to close around 1am, with disco-bars and nightclubs open until 3am.

Café Austria Benigno Malo 5-95 and Juan Jaramillo. Excellent cakes, ice creams and specialities such as *apfelstrudel* in this delightful Austrian-run café. Closed Mon.

Café Eucalyptus Gran Colombia and Benigno Malo. Excellent English–US restaurant offering a huge international menu ranging from Vietnamese *Chaotom* to English bakewell tart, plus a bar serving good wines and beers.
El Pedregal Azteca Gran Colombia 10-29. Large, lively, mid-priced restaurant serving excellent Mexican food like enchiladas, tacos and *quesadillas*. Great atmosphere on Friday nights, when there are live *mariachis*. Closed Sun.
Raymipamba Benigno Malo and Bolívar, Parque Calderón. Always-busy café-restaurant under the colonnaded arcade of the New Cathedral, serving inexpensive crepes, pastas, stir-fries, meats and much more.
Villa Rosa Gran Colombia 12–22 ⓣ07/837944. Classy restaurant favoured by Cuenca's bourgeoisie, offering well-executed international dishes like *coquilles Saint Jacques* and wild trout. Closed Sat and Sun.
Wunderbar Escalinata, off Calle Larga. This café-bar is a nice place for lunch on a sunny day, when you can eat in the little garden among the trees and flowers. Serves tasty sandwiches, salads and light meals. Closed Sat and Sun mornings.

Listings

Airlines Aerocontinente, Bolívar 12-60 and Tarqui ⓣ07/840196; American Airlines, Hermano Miguel 8-63 and Bolívar ⓣ07/841172; Austro Aéreo, Hermano Miguel 6-86 ⓣ07/832677, for Quito, Guayaquil and Macas; Avianca, represented by Importadora Román, Av Huayna Cápac 7111 ⓣ07/835916; Continental, Padre Aguirre 10-96 and Mariscal Lamar ⓣ07/847374; Ecuatoriana, Bolívar 820 and Luis Cordero ⓣ07/832220; Icaro, Av España 11-14 at airport ⓣ07/802700; Tame, Benigno Malo 5-08 and Calle Larga ⓣ07/843222.
Banks and exchange Banco de Guayaquil (Visa/MasterCard/Cirrus ATM and changes travellers' cheques), on Sucre, between Hermano Miguel and Presidente Borrero; Banco del Austro (Visa ATM), on Sucre and Presidente Borrero; Banco del Pacífico (MasterCard/Cirrus ATM, changes travellers' cheques), Benigno Malo and Gran Colombia; Vazcambios, at Gran Colombia and Luis Cordero (changes TCs and currency).
Car rental At the airport: Localiza, Av España 1485 and Granada (ⓣ07/863902); and Internacional, Av España 10-50 (ⓣ07/801892).
Consulates US, Centro Abraham Lincoln, Presidente Borrero 5-18 (ⓣ07/823898).
Hospitals Hospital Santa Inés, Av Daniel Córdova Toral 2-113 ⓣ07/817888.
Post office The main post office is at Presidente Borrero and Gran Colombia.
Taxis Radio taxis include: Atenas ⓣ07/826464; Paisa ⓣ07/863774; and Transvista ⓣ07/818182.
Telephone office Etapa is at Benigno Malo and Presidente Córdova, and Pacífictel is more or less opposite. You can make cheap international calls at most Internet cafés.
Tour operators Expediciones Apullacta, Gran Colombia 11-02 and General Torres (ⓣ07/837815; ⓦapullacta.cedei.org), and Río Arriba Expeditions, Hermano Miguel 7-14 (ⓣ07/830116, ⓔnegro@az.pro.ec) for day-trips to Parque Nacional El Cajas (see below). Also, the very helpful Travel Center, Hermano Miguel 4-46 and Calle Larga (ⓣ07/823782, ⓦwww.terradiversa.com) for horse riding, mountain biking, trekking in Parque Nacional El Cajas and much more.

Parque Nacional El Cajas

Only 35km northwest of Cuenca, **PARQUE NACIONAL EL CAJAS** is one of the most compellingly beautiful wilderness areas in Ecuador: a wild, primeval landscape of craggy hills and glacier-scoured valleys studded with a breathtaking quantity of lakes, glinting like jewels against the mottled earth and rock that surround them. Spread over a large tract of high páramo (3000–4500m), the park offers superb **hiking** and **trout fishing** opportunities and – despite sitting on the doorstep of a major city – a tremendous sense of solitude, with visitors kept at bay by the inhospitable rain and fog that so frequently plague the area. The easiest way to explore the park is on an organized **tour** from Cuenca (about $35 per person; see "Listings" above for recommended operators), which normally involves a three- to five-hour hike accompanied by an English-speaking naturalist guide, who'll point out the paramo flora and birds to you.

Otherwise, buses from Cuenca to Molleturo (Transportes San Luis from the bus station, or Transportes Occidental from Plaza San Sebastián at 6.30am, 10am, 2pm & 5pm) can drop you at the **Centro de Informaciones** (daily 7am—5pm) in the middle of the park, where you need to register your visit and pay a $10 entrance fee. The wardens here can furnish you with a basic map and point out **trails**; a popular and easy option is walking around the shimmering **Laguna Toreadora**, right next to the information centre. For any kind of hiking in El Cajas, it's crucial to come properly prepared, with waterproof clothing, warm layers, emergency food and a compass. The park is driest between June and August, but it might rain, hail or snow at any time of the year.

Loja

From Cuenca, the Panamericana winds its way through increasingly remote and isolated countryside, passing only a handful of villages on its way to the thriving little city of **LOJA**, 204km south. Loja's centre is a curious mix of the concrete and the colonial but, while it lacks the architectural harmony of Cuenca, it preserves enough handsome old eighteenth- and nineteenth-century buildings to lend its **centro histórico** a graceful colonial look, with much charm and appeal. The city's focal point is the large, palm-filled **Parque Central**, lined by an eclectic collection of buildings including the ugly, concrete **Municipio**; the flamboyant **Catedral**, sporting a towering white facade trimmed in yellow and gold; and the former **Casa de Justicia**, a traditional early eighteenth-century mansion with whitewashed adobe walls, a clay-tiled roof and an overhanging upper floor leaning on thick wooden posts. Inside, the **Museo del Banco Central** (Mon–Fri 9am–1pm & 2–4.30pm; $0.40) displays a modest collection of pre-Columbian ceramics and religious sculptures in rooms off a creaking wooden veranda.

A couple of streets off the square are dotted with elegant nineteenth-century houses sporting painted balconies, shutters and eaves, particularly 10 de Agosto, between Bolívar and 18 de Noviembre, and Bolívar, from the Parque Central towards Calle Lourdes. A couple of blocks south along Bolívar, you'll pass the imposing **Iglesia Santo Domingo**, crammed with over a hundred biblical-themed oil paintings hanging amid swirling floral motifs covering the walls and ceilings. Continuing down Bolívar you'll reach the **Plaza de la Independencia**, the city's most beautiful square, enclosed by colonial-style buildings that look like outsized dolls' houses with their brightly painted walls, balconies, shutters and doors, and the cheerful, blue and white **Iglesia San Sebastián**.

Practicalities

Flights from Quito and Guayaquil land at the **Aeropuerto La Toma**, some 33km west of Loja; shared taxis into town cost around $3 per person, while a private taxi costs $10–12. Loja's **bus terminal** is 2km north of the centre on Avenida Cuxibamba, served by plenty of taxis and local buses to the centre. For **tourist information**, head to the excellent municipal office on the central square, at J. A. Eguiguren and Bolívar (Mon–Fri 9–11am & 3–7pm, Sat & Sun 9am–5pm; ⓣ07/584018), or the Ministerio de Turismo office, in the Edificio Banco de Fomento on the corner of J.A. Eguiguren and Sucre (Mon–Fri 8.30am–1pm 3–5.30pm; ⓣ07/572964).

Loja offers a decent spread of generally good-value **hotels**. The best budget choice is friendly *Hostal Londres* at Sucre 07-51 (ⓣ07/561936; ❷), offering spacious rooms with shared bath in a well-maintained old house with lots of plants and flowers. You'll find more comfort at *Hotel Podocarpus*, José A. Eguiguren 16-15 (ⓣ07/581428, ⓔhotelpod@hotmail.com; ❺), which comes with modern rooms with cable TV and spotless en-suite baths (the back rooms are quietest), or *Hotel Libertador*, Colón 14-30 (ⓣ07/560779; ❻), Cuenca's smartest hotel, offering well-furnished rooms (the best ones are in the new block) plus a small pool, sauna and steam bath. There are plenty of good **restaurants** in Loja, too. Try friendly *Parrillada Uruguay*, Juan de Salinas and Avenida Universitaria (evenings only) for delicious steaks and grills; *José Antonio's*, upstairs at J.A. Eguiguren 12-24 and Olmedo, for excellent, great-value fish and seafood; or *Rincón de Francia*, Valdivieso and J.A. Eguiguren, for a reasonably priced international menu in an intimate setting.

Vilcabamba

Just over 40km south of Loja, sitting in a beautiful valley enfolded by crumpled, sunburnt hills, **VILCABAMBA** is a relaxing, chilled-out resort perfect for recharging your batteries. There's not much else to do in the village itself, a sprawling collection of mostly unpaved streets spreading out from a leafy **Parque Central**. The only real attraction here is the **Centro Recreacional Yamburara** (daily 8am–5pm; $0.30), the site of a swimming pool ($0.50), a small zoo and an impressive orchid garden (closed at lunchtime), a 1.5km walk southeast down Calle Diego Vaca de la Vega. Striking a little further afield, you could hike up **Cerro Mandango** for fabulous, panoramic views over the valley. The hill rises over the southeast side of the village; the tourist office can give you a map with instructions on finding the path, which can be tricky. The best months to visit Vilcambamba are June to September, while October to May can often be rainy.

Practicalities

Buses and minibuses from Loja's bus terminal drop passengers off at the **bus terminal** every fifteen minutes on the main road running into town, the Avenida de la Eterna Juventud, a couple of blocks from the central square. As some hotels are a good fifteen- to twenty-minute walk away from the terminal, you may wish to hop in one of the loitering pick-up trucks that act as **taxis**, charging about $1 per ride. For tourist info, head for the municipal **tourist office** opposite the church on the Parque Central (daily except Tues & Fri 8am–noon & 2–6pm; ⓣ07/580890).

For such a small place, there's an enormous amount of **accommodation** to choose from: central options include the *Hidden Garden*, on Sucre, just north of Parque Central (ⓣ07/580281; ❷), offering simple budget rooms with shared or private bath around a beautiful walled garden with a pool and hammoks; friendly *Hostería Paraíso*, Av Eterna Juventud, two blocks north of Parque Central (ⓣ07/580266; ❸); with spotless *cabañas* in a pretty garden with a pool, whirlpool, steam baths and sauna; and, a little further out, across the bridge on the road to Yamburara, *Las Ruinas de Quinará* (ⓣ07/580314, ⓔruinasqui@hotmail.com; ❹ including dinner and breakfast), a slick operation offering shared rooms (four beds) with cable TV, a pool, steam baths, Jacuzzi, volleyball court and evening movies on a giant TV.

Most hotels offer food as well as rooms, sometimes as a package with the room rate, but if you fancy a change you'll find plenty of decent, inexpensive **restaurants** and cafés in the village. Three to try on the Parque Central are colourful and popular *La Terraza*, serving well-prepared Mexican, Thai and Italian dishes (closed Mon); *Che*, a little Argentine-owned restaurant known for its substantial and tasty steaks; and *Cafetería Solomaco*, offering delicious home-baked cakes, pastries, donuts and wholemeal bread (closed Tues).

Crossing into Peru

By far the most convenient border **crossing into Peru** from the southern sierra is on the direct bus service **from Loja** (see opposite) to **Piura**, near **Tumbes** (see p.945) in Peru, via the small frontier town of Macará, 190km southeast of Loja – an infinitely faster and more straightforward alternative to the larger and more frenetic border control at Huaquillas, on the coast. The service is operated by Cooperativa Loja Internacional (ⓣ07/579014), which has offices at the bus terminal in Loja, and close to the bus terminal and taxi rank in Vilcabamba. Tickets cost $8 and should ideally be bought the day before travelling, either directly from the bus company or from one of the *hostales* in Vilcabamba that acts as a ticket agent, including *Las Ruinas de Quinará* (see p.703). There are daily departures from Loja's bus terminal at 7am, 1pm and 10.30pm, and the journey takes around eight hours. When you arrive at the border (5hr), the bus drops you off to get your **exit stamp** at the Migración office, which is open 24hr. You then walk across the bridge over the Río Macará – which forms the border between Ecuador and Peru in this area – and get your entry stamp on the other side, before hopping back on your bus. It's all extremely simple and hassle-free.

6.4

The Oriente

Ecuador's slice of the Amazonian basin, **THE ORIENTE**, occupies almost half of the country, but is home to less than five percent of the population, around 480,000 people. Consisting of six provinces and nine nature reserves including the two largest mainland protected areas, **Parque Nacional Yasuní** and the **Reserva Faunística Cuyabeno**, the Oriente drops from the highest peaks of the eastern Andean flank at well over 5000m down to the sweltering lowland rainforests at around 300m that in places stretch for more than 250km to the borders of Colombia and Peru. This vast emerald wilderness, under constant stress from commercial pressure from outside, harbours a bewildering diversity of **flora and fauna**, one of the many reasons that it's among the country's most thrilling destinations.

In the north the most pristine areas are best reached from the pioneer oil towns **Lago Agrio** and **Coca**, respectively, and demand at least four or five days to enjoy properly; these tours are usually arranged from Quito. Closer to Quito, and favoured by those with limited time on their hands, **Tena** and **Puyo** are near smaller, more accessible patches of forest. Visits to or stays with **indigenous communities** are also likely to figure in tours from Tena and Puyo. Generally speaking, the tourism infrastructure is much less developed in the far southern Oriente, though **Macas** is home to a handful of operators and projects.

The **oil industry** has nevertheless given the region an **infrastructure** that makes Ecuador's rainforests among the most easily accessed in the continent. From the capital the fastest route descends into the Amazon basin from the Papallacta Pass, splitting at Baeza, north to Lago Agrio and south to Tena. In the southern sierra, lesser routes enter the Oriente from Cuenca and Loja, and a road is also being built between Guamote (south of Riobamba) directly to Macas, though at the time of writing it was not complete.

Visiting the jungle

Unguided travel in the lower Oriente is frowned upon by Ecuadorian authorities, conservation groups and indigenous communities, and is not recommended for your own safety. Taking a **guided tour** is the cheapest way to visit the jungle, usually costing from $25 to $50 per person per day, depending on the type of tour and the number of people in your group. The best places to meet people looking to share a jungle tour in roughly descending order are Quito, Baños, Tena, Misahuallí, Puyo and Macas. Make sure your guide can produce a permit from the Ministerio de Turismo; it's always a good idea to meet them before parting with your cash.

Staying in a **jungle lodge** is more expensive and offers the most comfortable way to experience the rainforest, but even the most well-appointed lodge still falls short of some people's idea of luxury. Stays usually last from three to five days and all the logistical problems are taken care of, from river transport from the nearest town to permits and multilingual guides. Most lodges are on or near the Río Napo.

Indigenous-community stays give a glimpse of life in the rainforest and access to some of the most knowledgeable guides in the Oriente. Furthermore, money raised provides a sustainable source of income while strengthening the case for the

conservation of the forests within an economic framework, and reasserting cultural identities. The main centres for organizing visits to an indigenous community are Tena, Puyo and Lago Agrio. The bare **essentials** for visiting the jungle include insect repellent, long-sleeve shirt and trousers, torch and waterproofs; rubber boots are usually provided. See "Basics" p.31 for information on malaria prophylaxis and yellow fever vaccinations. You will need to have your **passport** to hand to show at the regular military checkpoints.

The road to Lago Agrio

The fastest and most direct route from Quito to the northern Oriente is the road to Lago Agrio and Tena via Baeza. At about 60km from Quito, the winding road reaches the quiet highland town of **PAPALLACTA** famous for its **hot springs**, including arguably the best and most luxurious thermal baths in the country at **Las**

Jungle tour operators in Quito

Emerald Forest Expeditions Joaquín Pinto E4-244 and Amazonas ⓣ02/254-1543, ⓦwww.emeraldexpeditions.com. Runs four-, five- and seven-day tours to their lodge on the Pañayacu river in the Bosque Protector Pañacocha, off the Río Napo. One of their best guides, Luís García, speaks excellent English and is based in Coca. Around $60 per person per day, with discounts for SAE members.

Kem Pery Tours Pinto 539 and Amazonas ⓣ02/2226583 or 226715, ⓦwww.kempery.com. Offers trips to the Huaorani reserve where they have the *Bataburo Lodge*, under a special agreement with the Huaorani. A four-day tour costs $225, plus there's a $20 donation per tourist to the Huaorani. Trips also available to the Huaorani community of Conanaco near the Peruvian border, and Siona and Secoya communities in the Cuyabeno area.

Magic River Tours of Lago Agrio represented in Quito by Positiv Turismo, Voz Andes N41-81 and Mariano Echeverría ⓣ02/244-0698, ⓦwww.magicrivertours.com. Specializes in non-motorized kayaking trips down the quiet tributaries of the Cuyabeno reserve, in a five-day package to the Cuyabeno lakes ($275), or an eight-day package to the remote Lagartococha lakes ($480).

Nuevo Mundo Av Coruña N26-207 and Orellana ⓣ02/256-4448, ⓦwww.nuevomundotravel.com. Operates the new *Manatee Amazon Explorer*, a luxurious river cruiser, equipped with air-conditioned cabins for thirty people, that navigates the lower Napo on regular four- or five-nightly excursions, including visits to the Yasuní reserve, an observation tower and a parrot lick. From $460 per person in a double cabin.

Tropic Ecological Adventures Av República 307 and Almagro, Edif Taurus ⓣ02/225-907 or 223-4594, ⓦwww.tropiceco.com. Ecologically minded agency that works alongside community-based eco-tourism projects throughout the Oriente. Good people to talk to for advice on an indigenous community stay. They also offer jungle kayaking tours down the Shiripuno river with Huaorani guides.

Termas de Papallacta, a stiff 1km, twenty-minute uphill slog from La Y de Papallacta junction at the north end of the town. You can stay at this complex (ⓣ06/320620, ⓦwww.termaspapallacta.com) in comfortable rooms with private bath (❼) private Jacuzzi (❽) or fancy two-storey cabins, sleeping up to six with fitted kitchen, sunken bath and private outdoor Jacuzzi ($125 the cabin).

Lago Agrio and around

LAGO AGRIO, the hot and bustling capital of Sucumbíos province 250km from Quito, was founded only a few decades ago by Lojanos looking for a new life in the Oriente (its official name is Nueva Loja). In the late 1960s, it was used by Texaco as a base for oil exploration, and took its nickname from Sour Lake in Texas, the company's original headquarters. Oil is still Lago Agrio's *raison d'être*, but the hotels, paved roads and transport links that arrived with the industry have given tourism a foothold here, though the town itself is of very little interest.

Note that the Colombian border areas around Lago Agrio have been infiltrated by **guerrilla** and paramilitary units and are **extremely dangerous**; do not venture into these areas, and **do not cross the Colombian border** here (21km north of town).

Practicalities

The town's centre runs along **Avenida Quito**, which is also the main road connecting Coca and Quito to Lago Agrio, and this is where you'll find most hotels,

Jungle tours around Lago Agrio

Indigenous community stays

A good place to get information on indigenous-community stays in or near the Cuyabeno reserve, with the Cofán, Siona or Secoya people, is **La Dirección Bilingüe de Sucumbíos** on Av Quito and 20 de Junio (☎06/832681).

Comuna Cofán Dureno Contact through the FEINCE office on the third floor of La Dirección Bilingüe de Sucumbíos on Av Quito and 20 de Junio ☎06/832681, or through ⓦwww.cofan.org. A 300-strong community stands on the south bank of the Río Aguarico about 25km east of Lago Agrio.

Siona Tours 12 de Febrero 277 and 10 de Agosto, Lago Agrio ☎06/831875, or try at the FEPP office upstairs (☎06/830232). Tours to the Siona communities of Orahuëayá on the Río Shushufindi, Biaña on the banks of the Río Aguarico, or Puerto Bolívar in the Cuyabeno reserve.

Zábalo Fundación Sobrevivencia Cofán, Domingo Rengifo N74-96, Carcelén Alto, Quito ☎02/247-0946, ⓦwww.cofan.org. Randy Borman, the son of American missionaries, grew up in Dureno, married a Cofán, and established a new community at Zábalo, where he's a leader, running this well-organized foundation and eco-tourist project, located on the Río Aguarico, in the pristine heart of the Cuyabeno reserve.

Lago tour operators

Magic River Tours 18 de Noviembre and Guayaquil ☎06/831003, ⓦwww.magicrivertours.com. A German-owned company specializing in non-motorized canoe trips on small tributaries in the Cuyabeno reserve.

Pioneer Tours no address, but on a dirt road off Av Amazonas to the south in Barrio Colinas Petroleras ☎06/831845. Run by Galo Sevilla, who has eighteen years' guiding experience and takes tours to a basic campsite by the Laguna de Cuyabeno with local Siona and Secoya guides.

restaurants and tourist agencies. There's a **bus station** 2km northeast of the centre on Calle del Chofer, but most buses still pass along Avenida Quito anyway, where you can also jump on. The **airport** is 4km east of the centre, and Tame and Icaro fly here from Quito. A taxi there from the centre will cost a few dollars. You can get tourist **information** at the Cámara de Turismo (☎06/832502) and the Ministerio del Ambiente office on Eloy Alfaro and Av Colombia (☎06/830139) can provide information on the Cuyabeno reserve and some eco-tourism projects. **Taxis** – white and yellow pick-up trucks – cost $1.25–1.50 between any two points in town; they are plentiful on Avenida Quito, particularly around the market area.

As far as **accommodation** is concerned, a little extra cash will let you can trade in a grimy, musty room for something bright and clean with air conditioning, cable TV and fridge, such as the popular *Hotel D'Mario* (☎06/830172; ❹–❺), which also has a pool, or *Hotel Gran Colombia* (☎06/830601; ❸–❹), both on Avenida Quito. The rival next-door **restaurants** belonging to the *D'Mario* and *Gran Colombia* hotels serve good food. Over the road *Oroaz* dishes up ample portions of Colombian specialities at low prices as does the *Pedacito de Colombia* also on Avenida Quito.

Reserva Faunística Cuyabeno

East of Lago Agrio, the **Reserva Faunística Cuyabeno** (entrance $20 per day) encompasses over 6000 square kilometres of rainforest, protecting the Río Cuyabeno basin and much of the watershed of the lower Río Aguarico as far as the Peruvian border, including areas with species that survived the last ice age. This has made for a staggering level of biodiversity; Cuyabeno harbours 228 tree species per hectare, where for the same area in a British forest you'd be struggling to count ten. The reserve also contains a huge network of lakes and lagoons, including fourteen major interconnected bodies of water, large areas of inundated forest, and black-water lake systems, such as the **Cuyabeno Lakes** and **Lagartococha**. Some people come to the reserve specifically to see its **aquatic wildlife**, such as pink freshwater dolphins, turtles, black caiman, anaconda, manatee and giant otters.

Coca

Up till the 1970s, **COCA** was a forgotten outpost in the midst of virgin jungle, but since the oil industry came to town it has quickly mutated into an urban nightmare, with filthy, pot-holed streets lined with ramshackle houses; there's no main park in town, as if no one had time to plan one. Money has recently been spent on improving the town's appearance, but with nothing much to see or do, it's still not a place you'll want to linger. After all, its only real attraction as the last major town on the Río Napo is as a gateway to the primary rainforest of the vast **Parque Nacional Yasuní** and the neighbouring Huaorani Reserve downstream or south across the river along the Vía Auca. Following Ecuador's improved relations with **Peru** since 1999, Coca is also emerging as the gateway to **Iquitos** in the Peruvian Amazon (see p.951) via the newly opened border crossing at **Nuevo Rocafuerte**; talk to the Jefetura Provincial de Migración (on Napo opposite *El Auca*) about border conditions and travel requirements.

Practicalities

Coca's **bus terminal** is on Napo and Sergio Saenz, twelve blocks north of the waterfront, but most major bus companies have other offices on the same street a few blocks from the river, also serviced by their buses; most tour agencies, hotels and restaurants are also on and around Napo near the waterfront. Trans Baños has

Tours from Coca

If you're looking to make a group to bring down the price of a tour, bear in mind that other travellers can be thin on the ground in Coca, especially during the low season. Always make it clear that essential equipment and transport is included; note that the first and last days of the tour may largely be spent in transit.

Tour operators and guides

Emerald Forest Expeditions Napo and Espejo ⓣ06/882285. Their tours to Pañacocha are usually arranged in Quito (see box, p.707), but you may be able to graft yourself onto a trip from Coca. Their best guide is Luís García.

River Dolphin Expeditions Napo 432 and García Moreno ⓣ06/881563 or 880489, ⓦwww.aamazon-green-magician.com. Led by Randy Smith, a Canadian author with ten years' experience of rainforest eco-tourism and conservation in Ecuador, giving tailor-made trips into any part of the Oriente. From $70 to $200 per person per day, depending on itinerary.

Wimper Torres ⓣ06/880336 or 881196, or contact through Mady Duarte in Quito on ⓣ02/2659311. Enthusiastic guide offering tours of various lengths to the ríos Tiputini and Shiripuno south of Coca, and the Pañacocha area off the Napo. Spanish speaking only. Around $40 per person per day.

Indigenous community stays

Amasanga Ask at the FCUNAE headquarters (Federación de Comunas Unión de Nativos de la Amazonia Ecuatoriana) opposite *La Misión* hotel. Owned by the Quichua community of San Luis de La Armenia, 13km west of Coca. Tours to Quichua communities down the Río Napo, south to the Río Tiputini and the Yasuní reserve, or west up the Río Payamino to the Sumaco park. $35–40 per person per day.

the most regular service to Quito (7 daily; 9–11hr). White pick-up trucks – the town's **taxis** – usually can take you to any destination in town for $1. The entrance to the **airport** is about 1km down the Lago Agrio road from the town centre. Go to the Capitanía by the dock for information on downstream **boats**; the only regular public service is to Nuevo Rocafuerte ($25; 2 weekly; 13hr). The **Ministerio del Ambiente** on Amazonas and Bolívar (Mon–Fri 8am–12pm & 2–6pm; ⓣ06/880171) can answer questions about Parque Nacional Yasuní and nearby reserves and any new eco-tourism initiatives.

For **accommodation**, *El Auca*, on Napo and García Moreno (ⓣ06/880127; ❺), pleasant cabins and rooms set in a peaceful garden, is the most popular hotel and your best bet if you're looking to make up a tour group, even though its prices have shot up without noticable change in its rooms. The town's cheapest passable place is *Oasis* (ⓣ06/880206; ❸–❹), east of Napo, on the waterfront at Padre Camilo Torrano, which has decent rooms with private bath and battered fans.

There's no shortage of cheap and unattractive **restaurants** dishing up fried chicken and beer to oil workers, but few to be excited about. *El Auca* hotel has a good air-conditioned restaurant patronized by tourists and better-off locals, while *Ocaso*, on Eloy Alfaro and Napo, is very popular with locals and serves up hearty portions at a decent price. *Parrilladas Argentinas* on Cuenca and Inés serves up good char-grilled steaks, chicken and chops. The *Emerald Forest Blues Bar*, on Espejo and Napo, is a good place to meet travellers, check your **email** and have a drink.

Parque Nacional Yasuní

By far Ecuador's largest national park, **Yasuní** ($10) protects just under 10,000 square kilometres of tropical rainforest around the basins of the ríos Tiputini, Yasuní, Nashiño and Curaray, which harbours almost sixty percent of Ecuador's mammal species and over 520 bird species, while one recent botanical study found 473 **tree species** in only one hectare, which is thought to be a world record. Most of the reserve consists of dry upland humid tropical forest (*tierra firme*), but other life zones include **seasonally flooded forest** (*várzea*) and permanently flooded *igapó* **swamp forest**. Even today, scientists believe they've only scratched the surface of identifying all life here, with hundreds of species yet to be discovered. Because of Yasuní's importance, UNESCO was quick to declare it an International Biosphere Reserve in 1979, two months before the park's official creation but, despite this, there is still interference from oil companies and prospectors, and even a road, the Vía Maxus, which cuts through the northern arm of the park.

Several tour operators arrange adventure tours into the park, but if they are visiting Huaorani villages, make sure that they have permission. You can **stay inside the park** at the *Napo Wildlife Center* near Añangu, in its northwestern reaches, or at the *Bataburo Lodge* operated by Kem Pery Tours (see box, p.707) inside the Reserva Huaorani. You might also try the **Tiputini Biodiversity Station** (in the US ⓣ512/263-0830, ⓔtiputini@aol.com or ⓔtbs@mail.usfq.edu.ec), built primarily for research, education and conservation by Quito's San Francisco University and Boston University, which is on the Río Tiputini at the northern fringes of the park in an area excellent for wildlife. A typical week-long workshop costs around $1500 per person.

Crossing into Peru: Nuevo Rocafuerte

Thirteen hours downstream of Coca, **NUEVO ROCAFUERTE** is about as far as you can go along the Río Napo before the Peruvian border. The only reason you're likely to come here is if you're travelling between Ecuador and **Peru**, a crossing made possible by improved relations between the countries since 1999. International traffic is still light, but tourist services are likely to pick up over the coming years as the crossing becomes more established – there is even talk of a boat being built to travel between Coca and Santa Rosa on the Peruvian border with Brazil. Note that border formalities can change swiftly and dramatically; keep yourself informed and check with the authorities in Coca about current conditions before coming here.

From Nuevo Rocafuerte, **boats** go over the border to **Pantoja** in Peru (2hr–2hr 30min; $6, likely to be more for foreigners), where you get an **entry stamp**. There are a couple of very cheap, basic hotels here. From Pantoja, boats leave for Iquitos. Deck space is cramped and often shared with animals; you'll be sleeping in a hammock that you made need to purchase beforehand. The journey takes four or five days: it's a four-day journey (around $20) if you get off at **Mazán**, and take a moto-taxi short-cut across a huge river bend, followed by another two-hour boat trip (around $3) to **Iquitos** (see p.951); staying on the Pantoja boat and navigating the bend will add thirteen hours (effectively another day) to your journey. Iquitos is a major Amazon town, with plenty of hotels, restaurants and tourist facilities, as well as onward transport by boat or air. Those coming **into Ecuador** at Nuevo Rocafuerte can pick up the boat returning to **Coca** on Thursday and Sunday mornings (departs around 5am, 15hr, usually broken en route for the night).

Tena and around

TENA is by far the most agreeable of the three big towns in the northern Oriente, thanks to its slightly cooler climate, cleaner streets, friendlier people, better facilities, the rushing rivers and lush backdrop of forested hills around town, and the complete absence of the oil industry. Tena is both one of the best places in the Oriente to arrange a **indigenous-community stay** with a Quichua group, mostly in villages easily reached by road or river – though the wildlife will not be as forthcoming as in the more pristine forests reached from the oil towns – and a centre for river sports, especially **white-water rafting** and **kayaking**, on the huge number of tributaries that converge around the town at the head of the Napo basin.

Although pleasant, there's not a great deal to do in town. Locals – a mixture of *mestizos* and Quichuas – can often be found relaxing on the city's **river beaches** or ambling around the verdant **Parque Amazónico La Isla** (daily 8.30am–5pm; $2), reached by a wooden footbridge over the Río Pano about 200m south of the main pedestrian bridge, where paths meander through the greenery past caged animals recovering from injury and abuse, to swimming spots along the river and a high observation tower overlooking the treetops and town.

Practicalities

The bus terminal, 1km south of the centre, is where all **long-distance buses** stop except those from Archidona, which arrive at the corner of Amazonas and Bolívar in the northern part of town. For **maps** and **information** about Tena and Napo province, head to the tourist office on the western riverfront between the two bridges (Mon–Fri 8.30am–5pm). White pick-up trucks operate as the town's **taxis**, and will take you to any in-town destination for a fixed price of $1. The Banco del Austro on the corner of Av 15 de Noviembre and Dias de Pineda has a Visa **ATM**. Access to the **Internet** is available at Selva Selva on Avenida 15 de Noviembre and Pano.

Tena's best **hotel**, the *Hostería Los Yutzos* on Agusto Rueda 190 and Av 15 de Noviembre (ⓣ06/886717 or 886769, ⓦwww.geocities.com/losyutzos; ❺), has smart, comfortable rooms with hot water, cable TV, minibar, fans or a/c; there's a courtyard garden too. The *Hostal Indiyana*, on Bolívar between Amazonas and García Moreno (ⓣ06/886334; ❸), is a family-run hotel offering a handful of big, light rooms with polished wooden floors, cable TV, private bath and hot water, and a laundry service. A good meeting place, *Hostal Travellers Lodging*, on Av 15 de Noviembre 438 and 9 de Octubre (ⓣ06/886372; ❸–❹), has a tour agency, a restaurant and a pizzeria next door, laundry service, and rooms with private bath and hot water. The top floors (more expensive) have cable TV and city views.

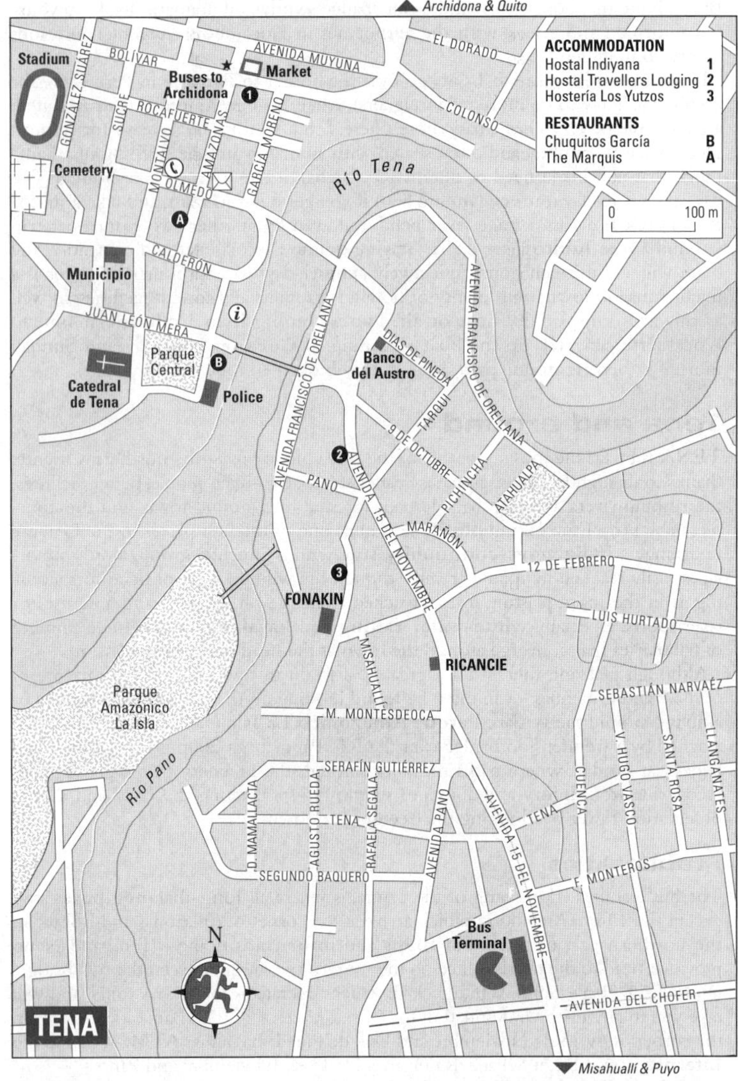

Inexpensive **restaurants** are two-a-penny. *Chuquitos* García, on Moreno near the footbridge, is a popular choice owing to its excellent riverside position. The meals are a bit hit and miss, but there's a huge menu ranging from *guatita* to frogs legs to kidneys, plus all the usual staples. *Cositas Ricas*, on Av 15 de Noviembre and 9 de Octubre, caters to the international crowd, with several vegetarian dishes on top of the usual beef, chicken, pasta and fish *platos*, while *The Marquis,* on Amazonas and Olmedo, is the classiest restaurant in town by some margin, run by a chef who specializes in Latin American food, particularly steaks and *parrilladas*.

Tours and activities from Tena

As well as several conventional operators, Tena has a number of **community eco-tourism projects**. These schemes are co-ordinated by two local organizations. The **Unión Huacamayos** consists of eleven Quichua communities who have developed the AACLLAC *cabañas* (Ⓣ06/888608; $45 per day), only fifteen minutes from Tena, from where you can arrange visits to the other communities in the forests of the Cordillera de los Huacamayos. Contact AACLLAC through Benito Nantipa in the mornings at FONAKIN, Agusto Rueda 242, Casilla Postal 217 (Ⓣ06/886288) or afternoons at the Museo Mundos Amazónicos in Archidona on Ⓣ06/889324. **RICANCIE**, Av 15 de Noviembre 774 (Ⓣ06/887953, Ⓔricancie@ecuanex.net.ec), co-ordinates nine indigenous-community eco-tourism projects in the upper Napo region around Misahuallí and Ahuano. Circuits are available whereby you visit a series of neighbouring communities as part of one package, and prices depend on group size but are usually around $30–40 per person per day including food, accommodation, transport, guides and excursions.

Tour operators

Most tour operators offer rafting trips, but be sure to check safety standards first. There should be a safety kayaker to accompany you, and the guide should have accreditation, ideally from AGAR.

Runa Ñambi Av 15 de Noviembre 7–23, also at Av Orellana and Pano Ⓣ06/886301 or 886318. Jungle, rafting and kayaking trips, and jungle tours to the Runa Huasi community or the Sinchi Sacha lodge. $35–40 per person.

Sacharicsina Tour Montesdeoca 110 and Pano Ⓣ06/886839, Ⓔsacharicsina-tour@yahoo.com. Run by a Quichua family, who have some rustic *cabañas* on the Río Illoculín, southwest of Tena. Rafting, horse riding, waterfalls and jungle walks are on the agenda for $30–40 per day.

Puyo and around

Seventy-nine kilometres south of Tena, **PUYO** is the capital of Pastaza, by far the largest province in Ecuador, with one of the smallest populations. True to its name – derived from the Quichua word for "cloudy" – Puyo seems to be permanently suffused with a grey, insipid light that gives the town a gloomy air. Founded in 1899 by Dominican missionaries, very little remains of its traditional timber architecture, and these days most of the city's buildings are modern and concrete. There's little to grab your attention in town, but Puyo does boast several attractions on its outskirts. Most notable is the fabulous **Jardín Botánico Las Orquídeas**, a five-minute taxi ride ($1) southeast of the centre in the suburb of Intipungo (daily 8am–6pm; advance reservations essential on Ⓣ03/884855 or 884854; $5), an outstanding private botanical garden, with over two hundred species of native Amazonian orchids poking out of a lush tangle of vegetation spread over a couple of hills. You can also get access to a bite-sized chunk of native forest laced with paths, a medicinal-plants nursery and several examples of typical indigenous dwellings at the **Parque Pedagógico Etno-Botánico Omaere** (daily 8am–6pm; $2) at the north end of 9 de Octubre, a ten-minute walk from the city centre, and across a rickety suspension bridge.

Practicalities

The **bus station** is 1km west of the centre on the road to Baños, from where it's a short taxi ride ($0.80) or fifteen-minute walk into town. For **tourist information**, head for the helpful Oficina de Turismo (9am–12.30pm & 2.30–6pm; Ⓣ03/885122) on the first floor of the Municipio, on the corner of 9 de Octubre and Francisco de Orellana. For **places to stay**, the *Hostal Araucano*, on Ceslao Marín 576 (Ⓣ03/883834; ❸–❹), is popular with backpackers and has a choice of

Tours from Puyo

Puyo has an amazing diversity of indigenous groups currently operating tours out of town, in many cases to very remote communities deep in the rainforest which are most easily reached by light aircraft (the airport is at Shell around 10km to the west). These are more expensive than local tours ($60–100 per person including flight).

Papangu 27 de Febrero and Sucre ⓣ03/883875. Representatives of OPIP, an indigenous organization that controls the bulk of Pastaza. They offer tours to nearby primary forest inhabited by five Quichua families, and to Sarayacu (ⓦwww.sarayacu.com/tourism) involving an exciting canoe journey down the Río Bobonazo returning by light aircraft ($60 per person per day for a minimum group of four), or the even remoter community of San José de Curaray ($100), a short plane-ride away on the Río Curaray.

Iari Inti Travel Ceslao Marín, upstairs in the Centro Comercial Zúñiga ⓣ03/886747, ⓣ09/971-6820, ezapara@punto.net.ec. Tours to the Záparo communities of Llanchamacocha (35min flight) on the Río Conambo and Cuyacocha (45min), a tiny settlement near the Peruvian border; both can boast fantastically rich forests and lagoons where the communities have prohibited hunting and cultivation (around $80 per person including flights).

Fundación Yawa Jee Ceslao Marín, upstairs in the Eva Zúñiga building (ⓣ03/883782, eyawajee@andinanet.net), which organizes inexpensive trips to Santana and Arútam ($35 per day), Shuar villages a car ride away, and Pakintsa, an Achuar settlement deep in the forests of Morona-Santiago province, near a salt lick, great for birdwatching, with waterfalls and forest trails.

rooms with and without bath, but water is only available on request in the dry season. More secluded, the *Hostería Turingia* further west on Ceslao Marín 294 (ⓣ03/885180, ⓦwww.hosteriaturingia.com; ❹), is a secure German-owned hotel of long standing featuring modern and older bungalows with private and shared bath, respectively, set in pleasant gardens with pool, Jacuzzi and spa complex. There's not a huge selection of **places to eat** in Puyo, though several hotels have reasonable restaurants. For pizza, try *Pizzeria Buon Giorno* in the small shopping centre on 9 de Octubre and Francisco de Orellana or the *Rincón de Suecia* near the park on 9 de Octubre and Sucre, which also does Swedish goulash and chicken curry

Macas and around

South of Puyo, the dusty, potholed road crosses two wobbly suspension bridges – strong enough to take light vehicles, but where buses deposit passengers, who cross on foot and pick up a connection waiting at the other side – on its way to **MACAS**, 129km down the road. Smaller, cleaner and quieter than Puyo, Macas is the most appealing town in the southern Oriente, mainly for its pleasant climate, laid-back atmosphere and beautiful views onto the surrounding countryside. A good place to take in the lie of the land is on the steps of the modern, concrete **Catedral**, on the Parque Central, giving views across the low roofs of the town onto the eastern flanks of the sierra, but for the best views eastwards head five blocks north from the cathedral to the **Parque Recreacional**, a park with a *mirador* looking down to the seemingly endless blanket of vegetation, stretching into the horizon in a fuzzy green haze. While you're up in the Parque Recreacional, take a look inside the **Museo Arqueológico Municipal** (Mon–Fri 8am–noon & 1.30–4.30pm; free), sitting by the entrance, which has a poorly presented but fascinating display of Shuar artefacts, including a replica of a *tsanta* (shrunken head).

Tours around Macas

If your tour includes a visit to a Shuar community, make sure it is with their permission; you can check at the **Federación Shuar** on Domingo Comín 17-38 (ⓣ07/740108) in Sucúa, 23km south of Macas, who will also have information on other indigenous eco-tourism projects. **Costs**, based on a group of two people, are generally around $35 per person per day on tours that don't involve flights; bear in mind that much of the final day of the tour may be taken up by a lengthy bus journey returning to town.

Cabañas Yuquipa Contact the Pancesa bakery at Soasti and 10 de Agosto ⓣ07/700071. Near the Shuar community of San Vicente, 12km north of town and an hour's walk from the highway, these rustic cabins with composting toilet are built by the Río Yuquipa near forest. Packages from around $30 a day include meals and guided jungle walks.

Kujáncham Expeditions 24 de Mayo and Domingo Comín ⓣ07/700299, ⓔkujancham_expeditions@yahoo.com. Flexible trips from one to seven days to local Shuar and Quichua communities, involving guided jungle hikes and exposure to indigenous culture.

Orientravel 10 de Agosto and Soasti ⓣ07/700371, ⓔortravel@c.ecua.net.ec. Offers a range of three- to six-day tours, most frequently to their cabins in the Buena Esperanza area, an hour northeast of town. Doubles up as an ordinary travel agent for booking flights, etc.

Winia Sunka the kiosk on Amazonas and Domingo Comín ⓣ07/700088, ⓔwisunka@juvenilemedia.com. Three- to six-days tours, usually to the Buena Vista area, where they have their own *cabañas*, as well as tours further into the jungle.

Practicalities

Arriving in Macas by **bus**, you're dropped at the centrally located bus station on the corner of Avenida Amazonas and 10 de Agosto. **Flights** from Quito land on Mondays and Thursdays at the tiny airport on Amazonas and Cuenca, four blocks north of the bus terminal. There's no official **tourist office** in town, but you can pick up a glossy brochure listing attractions and tourist services in Macas at the Municipio on the plaza (ⓣ07/700143). Of Macas' dozen or so **hotels**, none could be described as upmarket, but there are plenty of comfortable, good-value options, most offering similar rooms at similar prices. The best is probably the newly built *Casa Blanca* at Soasti 14-29 (ⓣ07/700195; ❹), offering spacious, clean rooms with tiled floors, private hot-water showers, cable TV and breakfast. As for **restaurants**, the best in town by a long shot is the classy *Pagoda China*, with large modern windows, bright decor and an extensive Chinese menu, a little pricier than most here but worth it. For Oriente specialities, head for the bargain canteens clustered on Domingo Comín between Soasti and 24 de Mayo, where you'll find *ayampaco* (meat or fish wrapped in palm leaves) and the occasional *guanta* cooking over charcoal grills on the pavement.

6.5

The northern lowlands and coast

The **northern lowlands and coast** comprise the entire lowland region west of the Andes and north of the road from Manta to Quevedo. As opposed to the dry and scrubby southern coast, the north is typified by lush vegetation and high levels of rainfall, especially during the wet season (Dec–May), when the monthly average is around 300m and can reach 600mm, even though this is also the time of year when you'll get the hottest, sunniest days. The main attractions of the region are its **beaches** and its **forests**, the latter of which fall into the Chocó bioregion, one of the planet's few "biodiversity hotspots" holding hundreds of unique plant and animal species.

From Quito there are two main **routes** to the lowlands: one leaves the capital to the north and descends towards La Independencia (on the Santo Domingo–Esmeraldas highway) via the town of Calacalí. The main arterial road leaves Quito to the south, and winds down the Andes from Aloág towards **Santo Domingo de los Colorado**s, an unattractive transport hub from where fast roads continue to the coast at **Esmeraldas**. Another road to the lowlands descends from Ibarra in the northern sierra to **San Lorenzo**, an isolated port on the northwestern tip of the country and access to little-visited Afro-Ecuadorian and Chachi communities.

The string of **beach resorts** south of Esmeraldas are among Ecuador's most popular, with the noisiest and brashest of them by some margin being **Atacames**, an hour's bus ride down the coast from the provincial capital. Beyond **Muisne**, the resorts largely peter out until **Canoa** a laid-back surfers' hangout over 130km to the south. Nearby **Bahía de Caráquez** is an elegant peninsula town, from where you can visit mangroves and tropical dry forests, while the bustling port of **Manta** is the region's lively economic powerhouse with its own beaches.

Mosquitoes can be a problem on the northern coast in the wet season, and Esmeraldas province has one of the highest incidences of **malaria** in the country. Take plenty of insect repellent and, if not supplied, ask your hotel for a mosquito net (*toldo* or *mosquitero*) during problem times.

Santo Domingo de los Colorados

As befits a major transport hub, getting to and from **SANTO DOMINGO DE LOS COLORADOS** is far easier than finding anything to do while you're actually there. Its narrow, crowded and polluted streets hold few attractions to sightseers, but fast arterial roads serviced by dozens of bus companies radiate out from Santo Domingo: to Quito via Alóag; to Esmeraldas; west to Pedernales; southwest to Manta, Bahía de Caráquez and Portoviejo; and south to Guayaquil via Quevedo. The **bus terminal** is 1.5km north of the town centre along Avenida de los Tsáchilas; take a **taxi** (about $1) or one of the **town buses**, many of which go to the terminal. If you get caught out at the terminal, your best bet for **accommodation** is the secure *Hotel Sheraton* (Ⓣ02/751988; ❷) directly opposite, which has decent, clean rooms, hot water and a popular restaurant downstairs. Otherwise, in town you'll find a glut of cheap hotels on and around the noisy 29 de Mayo, such as the *Hotel Covi Center*, 29 de Mayo and Cuenca (☎02/275-4237; ❷), which has clean rooms with private bath, phone and cable TV, and, perhaps the best bet in town, the *Grand Hotel Santo Domingo* on Río Toachi and Galápagos (☎02/276-7947; ❻ with breakfast), with smart and comfortable rooms and a fine **restaurant**. The *Hotel Zaracay*, Avenida Quito Km1.5, and the less expensive *Hotel La Siesta*, on Avenida Quito and Yambo, have reasonable restaurants, and of several *chifas*, the smart *Chifa China*, on 29 de Mayo and Latacunga, tucked in the courtyard of *Hotel Jennefer* is the best.

San Lorenzo

The final destination on the spectacular railway from Ibarra in the highlands (sadly, now largely defunct), **SAN LORENZO** is a small, run-down town in the far northwestern tip of the country, surrounded by sea inlets and mangrove swamps. This northernmost coastal town has little to recommend it, with its ramshackle houses and muddy, pot-holed streets, but it is at the end of the fastest road from the highlands to the Pacific, and as such is a possible access point to the beach resorts to the south. The high proportion of Afro-Ecuadorians gives San Lorenzo a distinct cultural flavour, one of the manifestations of which is **marimba** music; the Federación Cultural Afro, on Imbabura opposite the *Hotel Continental*, will have the latest information. The town is also surrounded by the **Reserva Ecológica Manglares Cayapas-Mataje** which holds beaches at San Pedro and Palma Real, and archeological sites at **La Tolita**, in addition to its knotted **mangrove swamps**; talk to Coopseturi (☎06/780161) at the dock about exploring by motorized canoe.

There are nine daily buses for Ibarra (3hr 30min), and hourly services to Esmeraldas (5hr) until around 4pm. Boats run to Limones, San Pedro and the **Colombian border**, but please note that this is **not a safe area to cross the border**, and you should make extensive enquiries about the security situation before attempting to do so. The best of a fairly uninspiring bunch of **hotels** is the *Continental*, on Imbabura and Isidro Ayora (☎06/780125 or 780304; ❸-❹), offering clean rooms with private bath, hot water and the option of air conditioning. San Lorenzo's **restaurants** are basic and few, but *La Red* on Isidro Ayora and Imbabura cooks up good seafood despite being a bit grimy.

Esmeraldas

A rough industrial town, **ESMERALDAS** is the largest port on the north coast, where bananas, cocoa, citrus fruits and coffee from the lowlands are shipped away, and to where oil from the Oriente is pumped for refining and export. For all this economic activity, it is a poor town and the provincial capital of a poor province (of the same name). Apart from the **Museo del Banco Central** (Mon–Sat 9am–4.30pm; $0.25) by the Colegio Sagrado Corazón, on Espejo between Colón and Olmedo, housing a superb little collection of pre-Columbian artefacts mainly from the Esmeraldas region, there is nothing to see, and you're only likely to come into town to catch a connecting bus to one of the several coastal resorts nearby. The town has a pretty bad reputation for **crime**, and you should be particularly wary on the Malecón Maldonado, from where coastal bus services depart.

Practicalities

Local **bus services** are run by Trans Esmeraldas, on main square, which has a good connection to Quito, and Trans La Costeñita and Trans Pacífico, both of which operate buses up and down the coast, including to Atacames and Muisne. The **airport**, served by flights from Quito, is at Tachina across the Río Esmeraldas estuary, about 25km by road (a 45min taxi drive, costing around $5). The helpful **tourist office** (Mon–Fri 8.30am–12.30pm & 2.30–5.30pm; ☎06/711370), upstairs on the Avenida Libertad opposite the *Apart Hotel Esmeraldas*, can give you information and handouts on Esmeraldas' few attractions.

The city's better **hotels** and restaurants, as well as bars and discos, are found at Las Palmas, an upmarket suburb 3km north of the centre ($0.20 by city bus on Avenida Libertad). The *Hotel Cayapas*, on Kennedy and Valdez (☎06/721318; ❺), has nice rooms with a/c, hot water and a neatly pruned garden, while the *Hotel Suites Costa Verde*, on Luís Tello 809 and Hilda Padilla (☎06/728714; ❻), offers comfortable suites with kitchenette, dining space and satellite TV. Five blocks north of the parque central, the *Apart Hotel Esmeraldas* at Libertad 407 and Ramón Tello (☎06/728700 or 728701; ❻) is the best hotel in Esmeraldas proper, frequented mainly by businessmen. The best of the city's **restaurants** are at the more expensive hotels listed above, but downtown Esmeraldas is home to a number of cheap and cheerful eateries, such as *Chifa Asiático* on Cañizares and Sucre, which boasts a spacious and air-conditioned interior and dishes out cheap and reliable Chinese nosh, and the nearby *Las Vegas* (closed Sun), on Cañizares and Bolívar, which serves large portions of fried chicken, meat and pasta at low prices.

Atacames and around

ATACAMES, 33km down the coast from Esmeraldas, is one of Ecuador's favourite beach resorts, relaxed by day and brash, noisy and fun at night. It's always crowded during holidays, and at Carnaval (the days leading up to Lent) it's so popular that it's literally standing room only on its dusky beach. The town is cleft in two by the tidal waters of the Río Atacames, which run parallel to the shore for about 1km, leaving a slender peninsula of sand connected to the mainland by a footbridge and, further upstream, a road bridge. Most of the bars, hotels, restaurants and the beach are on the peninsula, while the town's shops and services are in the other half, along the main road from Esmeraldas and around the little *parque central*. The **Malecón**, by the **beach**, is where you'll find the night-time action: salsa, merengue, pop and techno pummel the air from rival speakers only metres apart while revellers dance – or stagger – to the counter to order another fruity cocktail. On weekdays and throughout the low season the crowds evaporate, but you can still count on a smattering of open bars to keep you entertained and a steady supply of international travellers for company. Be aware that the sea has a strong **undertow** here that has claimed its victims, despite the occasional volunteer lifeguard. **Crime** is also an unfortunate feature of the quieter beach areas, so stay near the crowds, avoid taking valuables onto the beach and stay off it at night. The beachside **market**, mostly stocked with trinkets and sarongs, sometimes has black-coral jewellery for sale, which is a species under threat and it is illegal to take it out of the country. During the season between June and September you can watch **humpback whales** off the coast; contact Atacames Ecology Tours at *Le Castell* hotel on the Malecón (☎06/731476 or 731442) or get **information** from the *municipio*, 1km out of town towards Esmeraldas (Mon–Fri 8am–5pm; ☎06/731395). **Diving** trips are also offered by Gina Solórzano who can be reached through *Hotel Tahiti* or *Villas Arco Iris*.

Practicalities

Bus company offices are in central locations near the *parque central*, but for movement up and down the coast, hop on Trans La Costeñita and Trans Pacífico buses, which call at the central bus stop (*parada*) every twenty to thirty minutes. Trans Esmeraldas on Juan Montalvo and Luis Vargas Torres has five daily buses and two to Guayaquil (8hr), while Trans Occidentales, not far from the footbridge, has five to Quito and a night bus to Guayaquil (8hr). Tricycles are the town's **taxis** ($0.50) and can be picked up all over town, especially by the bus stop and on the Malecón.

Inexpensive **accommodation** options include *La Casa de Manglar* on 21 de

Noviembre, just over the footbridge to the left (☎06/731464; ❸), run by a friendly family offering simple rooms, mostly with bunks and shared bath, and a peaceful terrace overlooking the river strung with hammocks and gnarled-wood furniture, and the *Cabañas Caída del Sol* on the Malecón del Río (☎06/731479; ❸), having clean and roomy cabins equipped with private bath, fan, TV, fridge and kitchen sink. More comfortable and upmarket is *Villas Arco Iris* at the northern end of the Malecón (☎06/731069, Ⓦwww.villasarcoiris.com; ❺), featuring a palm-shaded avenue of attractive air-conditioned cabins, porch-side hammocks and a swimming pool. An abundance of **restaurants** along the Malecón serve up near-identical fish dishes for $3–4; *Marco's*, *Pelicano* and *Galería* are reliable options. The traditional Atacames breakfast, also reputed to be a great hangover cure, is *ceviche*, freshly prepared at the street stalls on Calle Camarones. The *Restaurant No Name*, overlooking the Malecón, helps stave off seafood overload with tasty pizzas and pastas.

Same

Of all the resorts around Atacames, **SAME** is the most exclusive and the least prone to overcrowding. A beautiful soft **beach** of clean, grey sand shaded by rows of palms and caressed by a warm sea has made land here hot property and there are strings of white holiday villas cresting the hills around the village. But strip away the trappings of the burgeoning tourist industry and Same is a tiny village with little more than a couple of basic shops. There's very little rock-bottom **accommodation** in Same – one reason why it's quieter than elsewhere. The cheapest choice, on the main road at the south end of town, is *Azuca* (no phone; ❷), which has three large and simple rooms in a pleasant house and a good Colombian restaurant. The *Hostal Seaflower* (☎06/733369), over the bridge on the left, rents four pleasant rooms sleeping two to five for $25 a night, each decorated with artistic flourish; the German-run **restaurant** here is one of the best in the region, offering delicious seafood for around $8–13 a main course. On the beach to the left, *La Terraza* (☎06/733320; ❹) comprises a series of attractive beach cabins looking out to sea and furnished with porches, hammocks and private bath. Its restaurant serves moderately priced pasta and seafood dishes.

Same's beach stretches 3km down to Tonchigüe, passing several other expensive *cabañas* and villas on the way, the best of which is the gorgeous German-run *El Acantilado* (☎06/733466; ❺, discounts for Rough Guide users) comfortable cabins – some with astounding views – in beautiful gardens perched on a high sandy cliff 1km south of Same.

Muisne

Some 48km down the coast from Atacames, **MUISNE** seems to exist just outside the radius of the main tourist exodus from the highlands. Nevertheless the town's laid-back and friendly air draws a reasonable stream of travellers down to this unusual, rather exotic place, sitting on a seven-kilometre palm-fringed sandbar lurking in mangrove swamps just off the mainland and connected to it only by boat ($0.15) from the small town of **El Relleno**, across the Río Muisne. As you dock, first impressions are not promising. The salty breeze, equatorial sun and high humidity bring buildings out in an unsightly rash of peeling paint and mouldy green concrete, giving the town a dilapidated appearance – but across the island at the end of **Isidro Ayora**, a boulevard running 2km from the docks, serviced by armies of competing *tricicleros*, you'll find crashing breakers and a broad, flat **beach** at low tide, fronted by a handful of inexpensive hotels, restaurants and the odd bar, all shaded by a row of palms. For personal **safety**, you should stick to the busier beach areas, stay off it altogether at night, and avoid carrying valuables on it.

Practicalities

Buses and camionetas arrive at and depart from El Relleno, also known as Nuevo

Muisne, on the mainland opposite Muisne. There are regular services to Esmeraldas (2hr 30min) passing all the resorts to the north on the way, and south via El Salto to Chamanga (45min), from where there's frequent transport to Pedernales (1hr). Long-distance buses depart nightly for Quito (8hr) and Guayaquil (9hr). The best **hotels** are by the beach, including the *Hostal Playa Paraíso* (☎06/480192; ❷), about 150m south of the entrance, which has a lounging area with comfy chairs and hammocks and bright, fresh rooms kitted out with large mosquito nets, with clean shared bathrooms and the appealing *Hotel Calade* (☎06/480279; ❷–❸), the last hotel on the beachfront as you walk south, featuring colourful balustrades, hammocks, Internet access and decent rooms, some with private bath which cost more. For **places to eat**, the *Restaurant Suizo-Italiano* on Isidro Ayora, 100m back from the beach, is a friendly place in which to polish off delicious pizza and spaghetti dishes. The *Coral Restaurant* at the *Hotel Calade* also does fine seafood and vegetarian dishes. The beachfront itself is graced with several good seafood restaurants around the entrance area, *Las Palmeras* and *Santa Martha* being among the most popular.

Canoa

CANOA sits at the top end of a huge surf-beaten beach extending 17km south to San Vicente, a fantastic natural attraction that has helped cement its transition from sleepy fishing village to laid-back beach resort. It's a quiet little place, with a single paved street linking its shaded square at one end to the sea at the other, accompanied by a few sandy side streets branching off, and what low-level hubbub there is seems to be blanched away by the continuous roar of the breakers rising and falling on the shore. Unsurprisingly, it's a lovely place to relax, with long, empty expanses of beach and ample waves for **surfing** (best in Jan and Feb, but good from Dec to May). At low tide **horse rides** and **walks** are possible to the sandy cliffs rising up through the haze in the north, where there are a couple of **caves** to explore; there used to be nine in total, but seven collapsed in an earthquake in 1998.

Buses between Pedernales and San Vicente pass through Canoa every thirty minutes or so and stop at the main square. As for **places to stay**, *Hotel Bambú* (☎05/616370; ❷–❹), on the beach at the north end of the village, has the best rooms in town, bright and breezy, with little balconies overlooking a garden and the sea, or less expensive cabins with shared bath. You can sleep in a hammock or **camp** here for a couple of dollars, and longboards and bodyboards are available for rent. By the square, 150m back from the beach, *La Posada de Daniel* (☎05/616373, ⓦwww.posadadaniel.com; ❸) has cabins with private bath, fan, mosquito nets and balconies affording views of village and shore, plus a communal lounge area. Daniel himself, once a junior champion, gives **surfing lessons**. There are several good seafood **restaurants** in town, including *Torbellino* (closes 5.30pm), down from the square, *Costa Azul* and *Jixsy*, opposite each other at the beach. The restaurant at *Hotel Bambú* is good, more expensive and reliable, and *Arena Bar* on the beachfront, south of the main street does good pizzas, snacks, juices and drinks.

Bahía de Caráquez

One of Ecuador's most agreeable coastal resort towns, **BAHÍA DE CARÁQUEZ** occupies a slender peninsula of sand extending out into the broad mouth of the Río Chone. Clusters of spotless, white high-rise apartment blocks, well-presented avenues and leafy parks immediately mark Bahía, as it's often called, as a town that's a cut above the rest. In 1998 the town suffered a double disaster in the form of unrelenting El Niño rains that demolished roads and washed away entire hills triggering landslides, and a double earthquake that sent over two hundred buildings tumbling. A strong Green movement arose from the ashes of the destruction, culminating in the declaration of Bahía de Caráquez as a *ciudad ecológica*, or **eco-city**, with active recycling, reforestation, conservation and environmental education schemes underway. It's a pleasant town to stroll about – or get a *triciclero* to ferry you around ($2 per hour) – and there are a few distractions including the **Museo Banco Central** (Tues–Fri 10am–5pm, Sat–Sun 11am–3pm; $1) housing a well-displayed collection of pre-Columbian artefacts, such as a Valdivian belt of the highly prized *spondylus* (thorny oyster) shells from 3000 BC and a replica balsa raft. For a fascinating insight into the more recent past, don't miss the **Museo Casa Velázquez** (Tues–Sun 9am–noon & 3–7pm; $1 low season, $5 high season), a beautiful wood-panelled 1900s house on Mejía and Eloy Alfaro, filled with turn-of-the-century antiques and furniture.

Practicalities

Bahía de Caráquez has a straightforward layout, with its main avenues running north–south parallel to the estuary on the east side. **Buses** to Bahía will drop you at the obelisk at the junction of Malecón Alberto Santos and Ascázubi – close to the cheaper hotels and the **car ferry** to San Vicente (every 30min, 6.30am–8.30pm; $2 cars; foot passengers free) – and depart from the Malecón, south of the *Hotel Bahía*. **Boats** from San Vicente leave the municipal docks into the night. There are plenty of **taxis** and tricycles around the obelisk, costing under a dollar for a trip in town, though the cheaper hotels are within easy walking distance. Maps and general **tourist information** can be obtained at the Ministerio de Turismo office on Bolívar and Checa (Mon–Fri 9am–5pm, with a break for lunch; ⓣ05/691124).

Most of the smarter **hotels** are found on the northwest side of the peninsula, while cheaper places tend to be back from the obelisk but, wherever you stay, it can be difficult to find a room on spec in high season and during national holidays. You're probably best off at *Hostal La Querencia* on Velasco Ibarra and Eugenio Santos, south of the Capitanía (ⓣ05/690009; ③), a friendly, family-run hotel offering some rooms with private bath but without hot water, or the *Bahía Bed & Breakfast* on Ascázubi and Morales (ⓣ05/690146; ③–④).

There are several very good **places to eat**, especially on the Malecón around the docks, such as *El Muelle Uno* serving big, tasty fish and barbecue lunches and dinners, plus basic veggie options like baked potatoes and cheese, all at reasonable prices, *La Terraza*, which offers inexpensive seafood and grills, and *La Chozita* specializes in *parrilladas* (barbecues). Moving back from the Malecón, *Columbio's* on Bolívar and Ante has a large, delicious and well-priced menu of Colombian and Ecuadorian dishes, good seafood and grills.

Manta

Around 50km south of Bahía de Caráquez, **MANTA**, a city of around 170,000 people, is Ecuador's largest port after Guayaquil. Divided by the Río Manta between the throbbing commercial and administrative centre to the west, and **Tarqui**, a poorer residential area to the east, the city is the centre of a thriving processing and seafood industry, as well as a US air base for drug surveillance operations. Although the US presence has been criticized for unnecessarily drawing Ecuador into the drug war with Colombia, it has brought money and a vibrant international flavour to the city.

Arrival and information

The port has a straightforward street numbering system: Manta starts at Calle 1, and Tarqui at Calle 101, heading west and east respectively from the river; avenues run parallel to the shore and follow a similar system starting from the coastline. Note that the area east of Calle 110 is regarded as unsafe. The **bus station** is on Calle 7 and Avenida 8, and the **airport** is a few kilometres east of Tarqui, a taxi ride costing a few dollars. Tourist **information** and maps can be obtained at the helpful municipal tourism office on Calle 9 and Avenida 4 (ⓣ05/611471, ⓔmimm@systray.net; Mon–Fri 9am–5pm), or try the student-run Centro de Información Turística (ⓣ05/624099) by the Playa Murciélago.

Accommodation

There's plenty of choice of good **accommodation** in Manta, with most of the more expensive hotels positioned at the smarter northwest end of town near the beach, while cheaper places tend to cluster around downmarket Tarqui.

Cabañas Balandra Av 8 and C 20 ⓣ05/620316, ⓦwww.hotelbalandramanta.com. Attractive and commodious cabins sleeping four to five, set amidst garden walkways of fig tree and colourful verbena arches. Rooms are also available, and all accommodation comes with a/c, fridge, phone, cable TV and private bath with hot water. Swimming pool. ❽

Hostal Miami Av 102 and C 107 ⓣ05/622055. This friendly place abounds with replicas of artefacts from the Manteño culture and has decent, if slightly dog-eared, rooms with private bath around a courtyard. Some have balconies and are the same price as less impressive interior rooms. One of the town's few passable budget choices. ❷

Hotel Oro Verde Malecón and C 23 ⓣ05/629200, ⓦwww.oroverdehotels.com. This immaculate five-star hotel on Playa Murciélago has all you could desire – including supremely comfortable rooms, a pool, sports and sauna facilities, a casino, a delicatessen and an excellent restaurant. Breakfast included. ❾

The Town

In addition to its roles as maritime centre and military air base, Manta is also known as a lively, popular holiday destination with good hotels and restaurants, and its main **beach**, the **Playa Murciélago** 1.5km north of the town centre, has recently been improved with large injections of cash and is fronted by a strip of restaurants and bars at the **Malecón Escénico**. The beach is popular for swimming and surfing but note that there's an undertow, and that the police advise against wandering west of the *Oro Verde* to undisturbed spots where robberies are frequent. The **Playa Tarqui**, with its calm waters, is the town's second beach, though it's dirtier, more dangerous than Murciélago, and not a recommended place to spend the day. At Calle 7, between the Malecón and Avenida 8, the **Museo del Banco Central** (Tues–Sat 9am–5pm, Sun 10am–3pm; $1, free Sun) keeps an interesting collection (Spanish labels only) of locally found artefacts from the Valdivia and Manteño cultures, including fish-shaped ocarinas and beautiful zoomorphic jugs and flasks.

Eating

The two beaches are replete with inexpensive seafood **restaurants** and bars, and fish fans should also try the popular *El Marino*, on Malecón Tarqui and Calle 110, though the menu is short and the place shuts up at 5.30pm, and the well-presented *El Cormorán* on Avenida 24 and Calle M-2 (beyond the *Oro Verde*). Breaking the shackles of seafood monotony, the best Chinese restaurant is at *Hotel Lun Fun*, while the international restaurant at the *Oro Verde* is very good for a treat. *El Ejecutivo*, on the eleventh floor of Edificio Banco Pichincha, Avenida 2 and Calle 12 (closed Sat & Sun), has great views of the city and bay, and the food and service are excellent, but even smarter is *Riviera*, Calle 20 and Avenida 12, an elegant Italian restaurant offering excellent food that ranges from lobster in saffron sauce to fresh pasta, gnocchi, and risotto ($6–12) and less expensive pizzas.

6.6

Guayaquil and the southern coast

The nucleus of the southern coast is the port of **Guayaquil**, Ecuador's biggest city and economic powerhouse, handling most of the country's imports and exports. Traditionally considered loud, frenetic, dirty and dangerous, Guayaquil is in reality much less overwhelming and intimidating than its reputation bears out and its upbeat urban tempo makes an exciting change of pace from rural Ecuador.

South of Guayaquil, the coastal highway slices its way to **Machala**, the provincial capital of **El Oro** province. Famous as the "banana capital" of Ecuador, Machala is low on sights and ambience, but handy as a staging post on the way to the border crossing at **Huaquillas**. West of Guayaquil the **beaches** start, a long, golden string of them dotted up the coast towards Manta and the north, though apart from flash, high-rise **Salinas** most are fairly undeveloped. Few places see many gringos along here, with the exception of **Montañita**, a laid-back, grungy surfing hangout and the dusty, tumbledown port of **Puerto López**, used as a base for **whale-watching** from June to September or visiting **Parque Nacional Machalilla** year-round. This park is the southern coast's most compelling attraction, taking in stunning, pristine beaches, dry and humid **tropical forests** and, most famously, the **Isla de la Plata**, an inexpensive alternative to the Galápagos for viewing boobies, frigates and albatrosses.

The **best time to visit** the coast is between December and April, when bright blue skies and hot sunshine more than compensate for the frequent showers. This **rainy season** has the added advantage of bringing the coastal vegetation to life, making the dry tropical forests luxuriant and moist. Outside these months, during the dry season, the weather is still warm (averaging 23°C), but the skies are often depressingly grey. Another consideration is the irregular and unpredictable **El Niño** weather phenomenon, when unusually heavy storms can leave the coast severely battered, washing away roads and disrupting communications.

Guayaquil

For years, **GUAYAQUIL** was regarded as one of Ecuador's most dangerous cities, dogged by high crime rates and suffering from a general breakdown in law and order. However, after a recent period of night-time curfews and clean-up campaigns, and following a major redevelopment of key downtown areas, the nation's largest city (with a population of over two million), has started to shake off its old notoriety; the central district is now an unthreatening and surprisingly likeable place. Indeed, if you've just come down from the sierra, the city's energy, intensity and heat can be quite exhilarating, and the sophisticated big-city shops and restaurants make a real treat. Outside the well-to-do areas, and the sparkling and heavily patrolled attractions of the waterfront and city centre, Guayaquil quickly loses its charms – its dynamism turns to chaos, its heat and humidity become oppressive, and its litter-strewn streets aren't safe enough to wander.

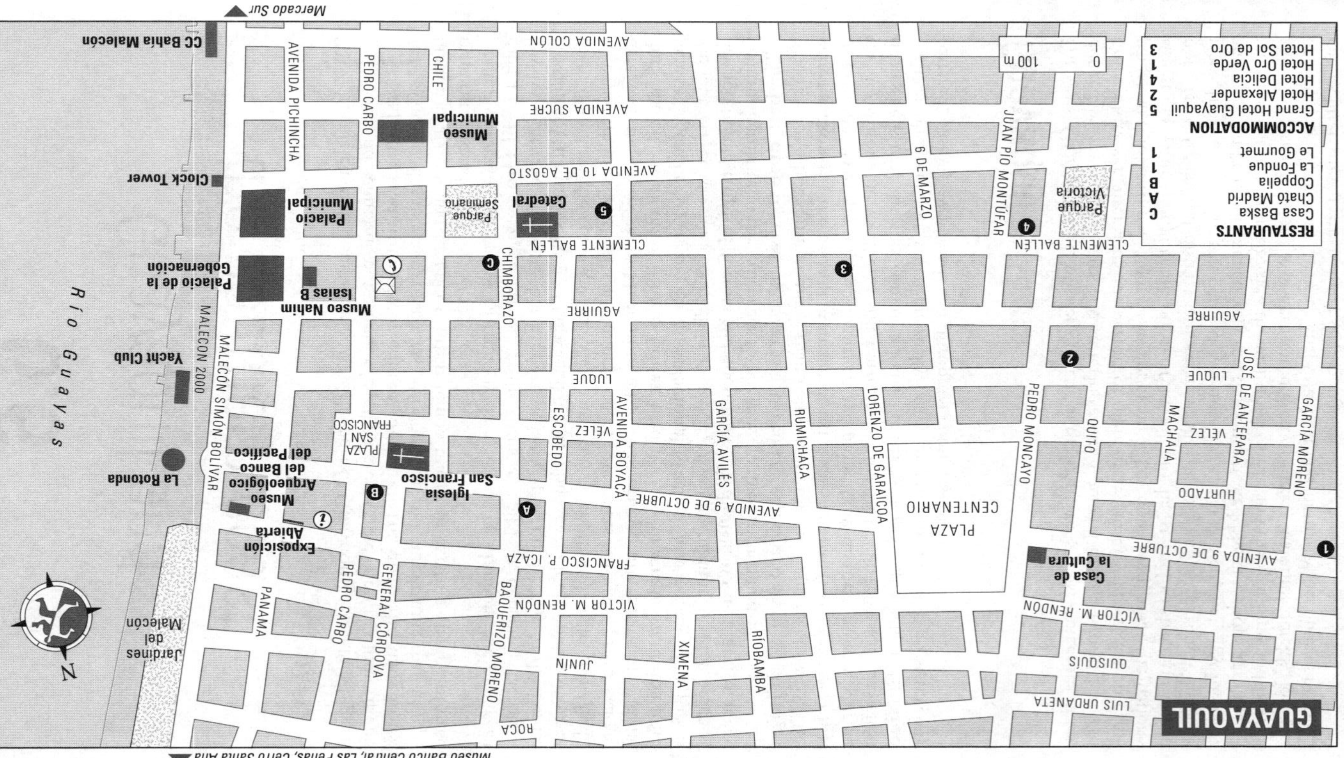

GUAYAQUIL
RESTAURANTS
Casa Baska C
Cható Madrid A
Coppelia B
La Fondue 1
Le Gourmet 1
ACCOMMODATION
Grand Hotel Guayaquil 5
Hotel Alexander 2
Hotel Delicia 4
Hotel Oro Verde 1
Hotel Sol de Oro 3
0 100 m
Museo Banco Central, Las Peñas, Cerro Santa Ana
Mercado Sur
Río Guayas
Jardines del Malecón
La Rotonda
Yacht Club
Clock Tower
CC Bahía Malecón
Palacio de la Gobernación
Palacio Municipal
Museo Municipal
Museo Nahim Isaias B
Exposición Abierta
Museo Arqueológico del Banco del Pacífico
Iglesia San Francisco
PLAZA SAN FRANCISCO
Parque Seminario
Catedral
PLAZA CENTENARIO
Casa de la Cultura
Parque Victoria
MALECÓN 2000
MALECÓN SIMÓN BOLÍVAR
AVENIDA PICHINCHA
PEDRO CARBO
CHILE
CHIMBORAZO
ESCOBEDO
AVENIDA BOYACÁ
GARCÍA AVILÉS
RUMICHACA
LORENZO DE GARAICOA
PEDRO MONCAYO
QUITO
MACHALA
JOSÉ DE ANTEPARA
GARCÍA MORENO
AVENIDA COLÓN
AVENIDA SUCRE
AVENIDA 10 DE AGOSTO
CLEMENTE BALLÉN
AGUIRRE
LUQUE
VÉLEZ
AVENIDA 9 DE OCTUBRE
FRANCISCO P. ICAZA
VÍCTOR M. RENDÓN
JUNÍN
ROCA
HURTADO
QUISQUÍS
LUIS URDANETA
PANAMA
GENERAL CÓRDOVA
BAQUERIZO MORENO
XIMENA
RÍOBAMBA
6 DE MARZO
JUAN PÍO MONTÚFAR
N

Some history

Guayaquil – or **Santiago de Guayaquil**, to give it its full name – was **founded** by the Spanish conquistador Francisco de Orellana on July 25, 1537. Its name is said to have been given in honour of the local Huancavilca chieftain, **Guayas**, and his wife, **Quil**, who killed themselves rather than be captured by the approaching Spaniards. From its earliest years it was the most important point of entry into Ecuador (at that time known as the Presidency of Quito) and quickly grew into a flourishing little port.

On October 9, 1820, it became the first city in Ecuador to declare its **independence** from Spain, and it was from here that **General Sucre** conducted his military campaign that culminated in the liberation of Quito on May 24, 1822. Shortly afterwards, Guayaquil was the site of the famous meeting between the two great liberators of South America, **Simón Bolívar** and **José de San Martín**, whose campaigns from opposite ends of the continent were now drawing together in the middle (see p.659). In the decades following independence, Guayaquil continued to grow rapidly and to assert its role as a major cog of the new republic. The country's first bank was founded here in 1859, soon followed by a major public library and university. The tide of optimism and success, however, came crashing to the ground when, in 1896, the worst **fire** in its history wiped out seventy percent of the city in 36 hours.

Arrival, information and getting around

Finding your feet in Guayaquil takes a little longer than in other Ecuadorian cities, what with the hustle and bustle, the noise and the general sense of disorder. With the risk of **petty theft**, it's important to be on your guard when arriving in town and getting your bearings; don't wander the streets with your valuables, and always get a taxi at night.

Guayaquil's huge, chaotic **bus terminal** is about 7km north of the city centre. Near the main exit, a Banco del Pacífico ATM accepts MasterCard and Cirrus cards. The road that loops around the terminal is used only by **local buses**, which call here in their hundreds; several will take you into the centre (#2, for example), but it's a huge challenge trying to work out which buses go where, and infinitely easier to take a **taxi** to your hotel for around $4 – they rank in a large parking area at one end of the terminal (ask anyone to point you in the right direction).

The busy **airport** – Aeropuerto Internacional Simón Bolívar – is a couple of kilometres south of the bus terminal. It also has a couple of ATMs and a *casa de cambio*. **Taxis** (around $4 to the centre) are easily available from outside the arrivals gate; alternatively, walk out to the main avenue in front of the terminal, Avenida de las Américas, where you can flag down a cab (and where you should be able to negotiate a slightly cheaper rate) or a **local bus** heading south into the centre (again, try #2); always take a taxi from within the airport complex at night, however. If you're leaving Ecuador from the airport, note that you're required to pay a **$10 international airport departure tax** in cash.

The **Ministerio de Turismo** office, at Pedro Icaza 203 (Mon–Fri 9am–5pm; ⓣ04/256-2544, ⓔinfotour@telconet.net), is quite a small affair, though they do have a decent collection of up-to-date **maps** and brochures, and the staff are friendly. The regional **Ministerio del Ambiente** office can be found at Av Quito 402 and Padre Solano (Mon–Fri 8.30am–4.30pm; ⓣ04/256-0870).

Getting around

Most sights are no more than a ten- or fifteen-minute walk from the **Parque Seminario**; to get further afield, your best bet is to take a **taxi**, rather than attempt to negotiate the chaotic and confusing local bus network. Note that taxis are not metered in Guayaquil; ask in your hotel what the local going rate is for short journeys around the city (it shouldn't be more than $1), and be sure to agree the price with your driver before you set off. It's safest to avoid the privately owned "freelance" taxis and take one belonging to a cooperative whose name and phone number is displayed on the side of the car – you should be able to flag one down easily on most city-centre streets. Alternatively, call one of the following 24-hour companies: Aeropuerto (Ⓣ04/229-4944); Carrousel (Ⓣ04/225-0610); Radio Taxi El Paraíso (Ⓣ04/22-1877); and Servitaxis Ecuador (Ⓣ04/230-1393).

Accommodation

Guayaquil is packed with **hotels**, but few of them are geared towards tourists. Top-end hotels fill mainly with corporate clients and nearly all have separate, much higher, rates for foreigners; single rooms are also hard to come by. Note that many of the cheaper hotels only have cold-water showers, while air conditioning is offered in all the expensive and many mid-priced hotels. Also bear in mind that Guayaquil's streets are extremely noisy, so it's always worth asking if there are any back rooms available.

Grand Hotel Guayaquil Boyacá and Clemente Ballén Ⓣ04/232-5127. Large, upmarket hotel boasting a gorgeous outdoor pool with a waterfall cascading into it. Good standard of rooms and furnishings, as well as a roof deck, sauna, massage rooms, steam baths and a 24-hour café that's also open to non-guests. Breakfast and 30min Internet use included. ❽

Hotel Alexander Luque 1107 Ⓣ04/253-2000. Very polished little hotel with well-furnished rooms, all with a/c and cable TV. All the doubles are quiet but dark interior rooms, while the suites overlook the street. ❺

Hotel Delicia Clemente Ballén 1105 Ⓣ04/232-4925. Dozens of rather bare, box-like rooms with shared or private bath, and fan or a/c; very modest but super-clean, friendly and safe. Popular with backpackers. ❷–❸

Hotel Oro Verde 9 de Octubre and García Moreno Ⓣ04/232-7999, Ⓔov_gye@oroverdehotels.com. Guayaquil's premier city-centre hotel, this is modern, impeccably decorated and enormous, with restaurants, a pleasant outdoor pool, and stylish, contemporary rooms. ❾

Hotel Sol de Oro Lorenzo de Garaicoa 1243 Ⓣ04/253-2067. Friendly hotel with well-furnished, rooms with cable TV and a/c. The suites on the top floor (extra) are huge; excellent views over the city make this a good mid-price choice. Also has its own garage and breakfast is included. ❺–❻

The City

The most impressive part of town by a long shot is the **Malecón 2000** riverside development, which includes the new **Museo Banco Central**, leading towards the regenerated **Cerro Santa Ana** and its spectacular viewpoint. Other potential targets include the enjoyable **Museo Municipal** and a few other private **museums**, showcasing a wealth of pre-Columbian artefacts and religious art. All these museums have air conditioning, providing delicious relief from the heat. The tiny but attractive district of **Las Peñas** is also worth a look-in, for its turn-of-the-century architecture and string of art galleries. One worthwhile excursions out of town is to the **Parque Histórico Guayaquil**.

The Malecón

Guayaquil's riverside avenue – officially the Malecón Simón Bolívar but referred to by everyone as just the **Malecón** – skirts the western bank of the wide, yellow-brown Río Guayas, which empties into the Pacific at the Gulf of Guayaquil, some 60km downstream. The road itself is always heaving with traffic but the long pedestrianized stretch lining the waterfront is by far the most pleasant place to stroll in the city – especially following its massive face-lift as part of the multimillion-dollar **Malecón 2000** project, which has transformed it into the best conceived and executed, most diligently maintained, and most beloved modern public space in Guayaquil. It's a large, paved esplanade filled with trees, immaculate botanical gardens, contemporary sculpture and architecture, shopping malls, cafés and restaurants, as well as several of the city's best-known monuments. The whole promenade, regularly patrolled by security guards, is enclosed by railings and accessed only at entrance gates, which are manned by further guards, so it's also one of the safest places to spend a day in Guayaquil.

The Malecón's centrepiece is the **Plaza Cívica**, reached by gates at the end of 9 de Octubre and 10 de Agosto. As you enter by the former gate you're faced with **La Rotonda**, the imposing statue of South America's two great liberators – José de San Martín and Simón Bolívar – shaking hands against a background of tall marble columns and billowing South American flags. The monument, which looks stunning when illuminated at night, commemorates the famous meeting between the two generals in Guayaquil on July 26 and 27, 1822, which was ostensibly to discuss the emancipation of Peru, but was used by Bolívar as an opportunity to annex Ecuador to his fledgling nation of Gran Colombia (see p.659). The monument is designed in such a way that two people whispering into the two end pillars can hear each other, though the din of the traffic somewhat undermines the effect.

From La Rotonda walking south, you'll pass four sculptures dedicated to the four elements; fire and earth double up as a couple of timber-and-metal **lookout towers** topped by sail-like awnings. The views from the top are quite striking: on one side is the vast urban sprawl stretching to the horizon; on the other is the low, fuzzy vegetation across the river, completely free of buildings. Beyond the sculptures, past the Yacht Club, stands the slender, cream-coloured Moorish **Clock Tower**, decorated with Islamic geometric designs at its base and long Arabic-style windows around the column. The 23-metre tower marking the southern end of the Plaza Cívica, was originally constructed in 1842, but its present version, following a relocation and several rebuilds, dates to 1931.

After a commerical area of fast-food joints and a compact subterranean shopping centre, the CC Bahía Malecónm, you'll reemerge at the stately **Plaza Olmedo**, dedicated to the statesman and poet, José Joaquín de Olmedo (1780–1847), the first mayor of Guayaquil and a key agitator in the movement towards the city's independence on October 9 1820. At the southern end of the promenade, the glass and wrought-iron **Mercado Sur** (daily 9am–10pm; $1), floodlit at night to dazzling effect, houses an art gallery for temporary exhibitions.

To the north of the Plaza Cívica is a magnificent sequence of sumptuous **botanical gardens**, fountains, ponds and walkways. Each garden is themed on a historical period or represents one of Ecuador's many habitats, such as the Plaza de las Bromelias, a lavish concoction of trees swathed in mosses and bromeliads in the manner of a cloudforest. At the northern end of the Malecón 2000 is the new Museo Banco Central, more accurately called the **Museo Antropológico y de Arte Contemporáneo** (MAAC), with a collection of fine pre-Columbian ceramics, ritualistic paraphernalia and gold objects.

Las Peñas and Cerro Santa Ana

At its northern end, the Malecón stops at the picturesque *barrio* of **Las Peñas**, overlooking the river. There's little more to it than a single dead-end street – **Numa Pompilio Llona** – that takes about five minutes to walk up and down, but the once-grand old houses leaning against the hillside, the narrowness of the street and the uneven, century-old cobblestones make it one of the prettiest corners of Guayaquil. Stick to Numa Pompilio Llona, as the neighbouring alleys have a reputation for being dangerous.

Rising above La Peñas, the **Cerro Santa Ana** was a very dangerous slum until a recent regeneration project turned some ramshackle buildings into an eye-catching sequence of brightly painted houses, restaurants, bars, cafés and shops. These ascend a winding 456-step staircase to a viewpoint at the top of the hill, the grandly titled **Plaza de Honores**, where a new chapel (in colonial Latin-American style) and lighthouse (after Guayaquil's first lighthouse of 1841) have been built. The spectacular **views** from the summit and the top of the lighthouse are well worth a visit in themselves, particularly enjoyable after a day on the Malecón as the suns dips on the seething city below. Just below the Plaza de Honores, the **Museo Abierto** holds the foundations of the Fortress of San Carlos, built in 1629 to defend the city from pirate attacks.

Parque Seminario and around

Three blocks behind the Palacio Municipal, you'll find Guayaquil's central square, the **Parque Seminario** (also known as Parque Bolívar), famous for the iguanas that make occasional appearances out of the trees and shrubs where they live. The west side of the square is dominated by the huge, gleaming-white **Catedral**, a Neo-Gothic confection of spires, arches and tall pointy windows. The first cathedral built on this site was back in 1547; since then it and several other incarnations have been destroyed by various fires, with the current one, made of concrete, dating from 1948. The rest of the square is overlooked mainly by hotels and the monolithic Pacifictel building.

One block southwest, on Sucre and Chile, is the **Museo Municipal** (Tues–Sat 9am–5pm; free), dedicated to the history of the city and the region. One of its most stunning pieces greets you in the entrance lobby – an enormous **tree trunk** embellished with dozens of carvings of human figures, produced about six hundred years ago by the Manteño-Huancavilca culture, the seafaring group that was the first in Ecuador to have any contact with the Spaniards. Other highlights include the 10,000-year-old tooth of a mastodon, scale models of the fledgling town and docks of Guayaquil and a diorama of the great fire of 1896. It's all very polished and well laid out with good information panels, though unfortunately these are only in Spanish.

Parque Histórico Guayaquil

Northeast of the city at La Puntilla in the Entre Ríos district on the highway to Samborondón, the **Parque Histórico Guayaquil** (Tues–Sun 9am–4.30pm; $3, or $3.50 on Sun, holidays and for special events; Ⓦwww.parquehistorico.com) is a well-designed and slickly operated historical park – one of the key planks in the city's quest to bolster tourism. The park is divided into three zones: a **forest-life zone** with walkways through mangroves, spacious enclosures holding tapirs, caiman, ocelots, spider monkeys, sloths and a harpy eagle, and an observation tower for bird spotting; the **traditions zone** representing coastal culture and the *montuvio* way of life by means of a traditional farmstead (*granja*), with crops of cacao, banana, coffee, rice, paja toquilla and mate, as well as a reconstructed cacao plantation hacienda dating to 1883; and the **urban architecture zone**, where some of the last fragments of Guayaquil's late nineteenth-century buildings have been reassembled and restored, overlooking the "Malecón 1900". City **buses** #97 and #4 pass near the park entrance, but it's probably easier to get a **taxi** from downtown for $3–4.

Eating

Despite its reputation as the "last port on the Caribbean", Guayaquil is no Havana, and its eating scene is less vibrant than you might expect. Many of the city-centre **restaurants** are attached to hotels, which makes some of them rather impersonal – though the best ones serve excellent high-quality food. There are fantastic night-time views onto the illuminated Malecón, and you can buy tasty *platos típicos* like *seco de gallina* (chicken stew), *humitas* and *empanadas*.

Casa Baska Clemente Ballén 422, Parque Seminario. Informal Spanish restaurant with bare brick walls and a long list of mouthwatering tapas chalked up on a blackboard – manchego cheese, *serrano* ham, croquettes, sardines in olive oil, seafood broth and lots more. It's all delicious, but quite pricey. Closed Sun.

Cható Madrid Baquerizo Moreno 1118 and 9 de Octubre. Smart but compact restaurant offering fairly expensive but good Spanish food, such as manchego cheese, stuffed squid, crab in green sauce and *crema catalán*, as well as a decent international wine list. Closed Sun.

Coppelia 9 de Octubre and Pedro Carbo. Small, bargain café-restaurant overlooking the Plaza San Francisco. Serves simple but well-prepared Ecuadorian food like *humitas*, *empanadas* and *ayacas* (chicken tamales).

La Fondue *Hotel Oro Verde*, 9 de Octubre and García Moreno. Small restaurant mocked up as a Swiss chalet interior, with the help of dangling cowbells and waitress dressed as Alpine milkmaids. Despite the gimmicks, not bad fondues, raclettes and Swiss cuisine is on offer for around $8 a main course.

Le Gourmet *Hotel Oro Verde*, 9 de Octubre and García Moreno. Rather formal award-winning restaurant with a French head chef and a very sophisticated French-based menu. Expensive, but not a bad place to have a blowout.

Parilladas Columbus Las Lomas 206 and Estrada, Urdesa. One of the best grill houses in Guayaquil, with excellent steaks and cuts in handsome portions.

Nightlife

There's a more concentrated collection of restaurants, **bars** and **nightclubs** lining the main drag, Estrada, out in the affluent suburb of **Urdesa**, which can be reached by buses #52 and #54 from the Malecón, #10 from Parque Centenario or a twenty-minute taxi ride ($2) – which is fine if you're on for a night on the town, but quite an effort if you just want to wind down your day over a good meal. In town, by far the best place for an evening drink is *Artur's Café*, at Numa Pompilio Llona 127 in Las Peñas, a tall old house on the riverbank with several little patios where you can sit and chat while romantic balladeers strum their guitars.

Listings

Airlines Air Canada, represented by Transinversiones, office 301, Icaza 407 and Córdova ⓣ04/256-4050; Air France, Edificio Torres del Norte, Av Miguel H. Alcívar, Urbanización Kennedy Norte ⓣ04/268-7149; American Airlines, Edificio San Francisco 300, Córdova 1021 and 9 de Octubre ⓣ04/256-4111; airport ⓣ04/228-2082; Continental, Edificio Banco La Previsora, 9 de Octubre 100 and Malecón ⓣ04/256-7241; airport ⓣ04/228-7311; Copa, 9 de Octubre and Malecón, Edificio Banco La Previsora ⓣ04/230-3227, airport 228-6336; Iberia, 9 de Octubre 101 and Malecón ⓣ04/232-9558; airport ⓣ04/228-4151; Icaro, airport ⓣ04/229-4265; KLM, Galerías Colón, office 10, next to *Hotel Hilton Colón* ⓣ04/269-2876; airport ⓣ04/269-10252; Tame, Edificio Gran Pasaje, 9 de Octubre 424 ⓣ04/256-0776; airport ⓣ04/228-1182; United, Miguel Alcívar, Torres del Norte B ⓣ04/268-7600; Varig, Aguirre 116 y Pichincha ⓣ04/232-7082.

Banks and exchange The most convenient downtown banks are Banco del Pacífico on Pedro Carbo and Icaza (TCs and MasterCard, Cirrus ATM); Banco de Guayaquil on Icaza 105 and Pichincha (Amex TCs, Visa cash advance, Visa and MasterCard ATM); Banco del Austro, Boyacá and 9 de Octubre (Visa ATM and cash advance).

Car rental Most car-rental outfits have offices just outside the airport, and some also have a downtown branch. Branches include: Avis, Avenida de las Américas, CC Olímpico ⓣ04/228-5498; Budget, at the airport ⓣ04/228-8510; Ecuacars, at the airport ⓣ04/228-5533; Expo, at the airport ⓣ04/228-2467; Localiza, Av J Taca Marengo Km2.5, and at the airport ⓣ1800/562254; Hertz, *Hotel Oro Verde*, 9 de Octubre and García Moreno ⓣ04/232-7895, and at the airport ⓣ04/229-3011; Sicorent, at the airport ⓣ04/269-0633; and Super-Rent, at the airport ⓣ04/228-4454.

Consulates Australia, San Roque and Av Francisco de Orellana, Ciudadela Kennedy Norte ⓣ04/268-0823; Canada, Edificio Torres de la Merced, General Córdova 800 ⓣ04/256-3580; UK, General Córdova 623 and Padre Solano ⓣ04/256-0400; US, 9 de Octubre and García Moreno ⓣ04/232-3570.

Hospital Clínica Kennedy on Av del Periodista ⓣ04/228-6963.

Police and immigration Av Río Daule, Prolongación de Av de las Américas ⓣ04/229-7004.

Post office The main office is on Pedro Carbo and Ballén, just off the Parque Seminario.

Telephone office Pacifictel, in the big building off Parque Seminario, at the corner of Ballén and Chile.

Travel agents Carlson Wagonlit Travel, 4th floor, Edificio El Fortín, Padre Aguirre 104 and Malecón ⓣ04/231-1800; Delgado Travel, 3rd floor, Edificio San Francisco, Córdova 1021 and 9 de Octubre; or Metropolitan Touring, José de Anteparra 915 and 9 de Octubre ⓣ04/232-0300, ⓦwww.metropolitan-touring.com.

Machala

About 60km south of Guayaquil, the coastal town of **MACHALA** is often the last or first stopping point for people travelling the coast between Ecuador and Peru. Like Guayaquil, however, the place is a good deal wealthier than outward appearances would suggest, and Machala prides itself on its position at the centre of Ecuador's banana industry, dubbing itself "Banana Capital of the World". There's plenty of hustle and bustle here, but little in the way of tourist attractions – the only time you might want to make a special trip here is during the **annual World Banana Festival**, a huge commercial fair accompanied by festivities and events like the World Banana Queen beauty competition, spread over the last ten days of September.

Practicalities

Arriving by **bus**, you'll be dropped at your bus company's depot; most are a few blocks southeast of the central square – mainly on and around Tarqui and Colón which are parallel to Junín – an easy walk to hotels. The Tame office is at Juan Montalvo and Bolívar (ⓣ07/930139, airport ⓣ07/964865). There's a very helpful (but unsigned) **Ministerio de Turismo** information office (Mon–Fri 8.30am–5pm; ⓣ 07/932106), upstairs in the Almacen Galarza, at 9 de Octubre and 9 de Mayo. The city centre is entirely walkable on foot, but if you need a **taxi** you'll be able to flag one down around the central square, or on any of the main arteries such as 9 de Octubre or Vicente Rocafuerte; journeys within the central core cost around $0.80.

Accommodation in Machala is pricey for what you get, with not a great choice on offer. One of the most attractive hotels in the country, the *Oro Verde*, at Circunvalación Norte and Calle Vehicular V-7 (ⓣ07/933140: ❾), resembles an old timber-clad plantation manor, with beautiful gardens and a pool. A short taxi ride 3km from the centre, they sometimes offers rooms at the national rate (a third of the foreign rate) if you beg hard enough Otherwise, *Hotel Inés*, on Juan Montalvo 1509 (ⓣ07/932301; ❹), has small, rather old but perfectly fine rooms, most with a/c and cable TV, in a whitewashed house set back from a busy market area inside a secure courtyard with private parking, while the best mid-priced rooms in town can be found at *Oro Hotel*, at Sucre and Juan Montalvo (ⓣ07/937569; ❺), which has good quality bedding, new carpets, clean bathrooms, a/c and cable TV (more channels than you usually get).

There's not exactly a surplus of **restaurants** in Machala, but there are a couple of inviting places among the more pedestrian options. If you feel like a splurge, *Oro Mar* at *Hotel Oro Verde* is the place to do it – fairly pricey ($6 or more for a main course) but delicious international food served in a dining room overlooking the pool. *Don Angelo*, on 9 de Mayo and Rocafuerte, is an unassuming local canteen that's been going for years, serving cheap and reliable *comida típica* like *locro de papa* and *seco de chivo*, plus staples like spaghetti and fried chicken and fish, while *Mesón Hispano*, on the corner of Av Las Palmeras and Sucre, serves delicious charcoal-grilled meat in a bright, attractive dining room.

Huaquillas and the Peruvian border

Some 73km southwest of Machala, **HUAQUILLAS** is a chaotic, jerry-built, mosquito-ridden border town that most people ensure they spend as little time in as possible. Its main commercial street is lined by hundreds of hectic market stalls selling cheap clothes, shoes, bags, food, electrical goods and much more besides, while enormous, attention-grabbing shop signs hang over their canopies from the dilapidated buildings either side. Most people avoid staying over in Huaquillas by spending the night in Machala before crossing the border, but if you need a place to stay here you'll find clean, modest rooms with private bathroom, a/c and cable TV at the friendly *Hotel Vanessa*, on 1 de Mayo 323 and Hualtaco (☎07/907263; ❸), and the *Grand Hotel Hernancor* next door (☎07/995467; ❸). There are a number of cheap canteens, but a good restaurant is *La Habana* on T. Córdovez and Santa Rosa, for inexpensive seafood and grills, as well as breakfast and *almuerzos*, while *El Flamingo*, at Avenida de la República and Costa Rica, serves cakes, shakes and ice creams. **Internet facilities** are available at Hot Net on Avenida de la República and Santa Rosa.

For those arriving in Ecuador, **buses** from Huaquillas leave from company depots within a few blocks from the international bridge. Co-op CIFA, on Santa Rosa and Machala, has the most regular service to **Machala** (every 10–20min; 1hr), the biggest nearby city, with banking facilities and onward transport connections; CIFA also services **Guayaquil** (5 daily; 4hr 30min) as do Ecuatoriano Pullman on T. Córdovez and Rutas Orenses on R. Gómez. Panamericana at T. Córdovez and Santa Rosa has seven comfortable buses daily to **Quito** (12hr), one of which (departs 4.30pm) continues to Tulcán (17hr) on the Colombian border, while Trans Occidentales on R. Gómez runs five buses a day to Quito. For **Cuenca** (5hr) use Trans Azuay, on T. Córdovez and Santa Rosa, which has eight daily buses.

Crossing into Peru

The **border** itself is formed by the Río Zarumilla, hugging the southwestern edge of Huaquillas, and crossed by the international bridge leading to the small town of **Aguas Verdes** in Peru. Before crossing it, you need to get your **exit stamp** at the **Ecuadorian immigration** office (open 24hr; ☎07/996755), located 2km north of Huaquillas on the road from Machala, a $1.50 taxi ride away. If you're heading here straight from Machala, your bus driver will drop you at the office on the way into Huaquillas (remind them as they sometimes forget), but won't wait for you while you get your exit stamp sorted out, which is usually a fairly fast and painless process. From here, hop on a bus or take a taxi ($1.50) to the bridge, which you have to cross on foot, then get your passport checked by Peruvian officials on the other side, though **entry stamps** are usually obtained at the main **Peruvian immigration office** at **Zarumilla** a couple of kilometres away; mototaxis will take you for less than a dollar. It's quite a stressful experience, with a multitude of moneychangers, bus touts, bag carriers and taxi drivers jostling for your business, and plenty of thieves around as well – keep your wits about you, and don't lose sight of your bags for a second. Change as little **money** as possible, as the rates aren't good unless you bargain hard. Official moneychangers in Ecuador wear ID; always check calculations and cash received before handing anything over. You'll have no problem finding a direct **bus** to Tumbes, Piura, Trujillo or Lima. **Tumbes** (see p.945), 27km south, can also be reached by **taxi** for around $5–6 (firm bargaining required), or by *colectivo* for about $0.70, though they are not so good at stopping and waiting at the Zarumilla immigration complex while you get your passport stamped.

Santa Elena Peninsula

West of Guayaquil, the E-40 highway heads to the westernmost tip of the mainland, marked by the **SANTA ELENA PENINSULA**. It's a busy route, especially on Friday evenings when droves of Guayaquileños flee the uncomfortable heat of the city for the cooling westerly breezes of the Pacific. A further 45km west, a side road branches south to the easy-going, somewhat shabby little town of **Playas**, the closest beach resort to Guayaquil and always heaving with visitors on summer weekends (Dec to April). Continuing west along the main road you enter increasingly drier, scrubbier terrain as you approach the peninsula, best known for its **beaches**, the star attraction being the glitzy resort of **Salinas**, whose golden sands draw thousands of visitors each summer.

Salinas

About 170km from Guayaquil, the E-40 ends its course at **SALINAS**, Ecuador's swankiest beach resort. The **beach** boasts clean, powdery sand, warm, calm waters and safe swimming. The best time to enjoy it is December, early January or March, avoiding weekends. Around Carnaval it gets unbearably packed, along with weekends throughout the summer, while from April to November it can be overcast and dreary. If you get bored with the beach, check out the **Museo Salinas Siglo XXI**, on the Malecón and Calle Guayas y Quil (Wed–Sun 9am–1pm & 3–7pm; $2), a very well-presented museum offering an excellent overview of pre-Columbian cultures on the peninsula and a section on naval history displaying – among other things – items from the hoard recovered from the galleon *La Capitana*, which hit a submerged reef and sank off the coast near Punta Chanduy in 1654, taking down with it over two thousand silver bars and 216 chests of coins.

Practicalities

CLP **buses** from Guayaquil arrive in Salinas via the Malecón and continue to the avenue's western end (heading out of town, you need to catch one returning along Avenida General Enríquez Gallo). There's no shortage of **accommodation** in Salinas. The small and elegant *Hostal Francisco* at General Enríquez Gallo and Rumiñahui (C 20) (Ⓣ04/277-4106; ❹–❼ depending on season) is superb, with its immaculate air-conditioned rooms giving onto a patio with a small pool. For a sea view, try the upmarket *Hotel El Carruaje* at Malecón 517 (Ⓣ04/277-4282; ❻ including breakfast), whose rooms are smartly furnished and come with cable TV and air conditioning.

The *Colón Miramar*, the premier hotel in town at Malecón and Galápagos (Ⓣ04/277-1610, Ⓦwww.barcelo.com; ❾), is one of the most stylish (and expensive) **places to eat** in Salinas, serving everything from local seafood to national *comida típica* and elaborate international dishes. *Amazon*, on the Malecón and Lupercio Bazán Malave (C 23), is an attractive and moderately priced pizzeria and grill, also offering seafood, salads and vegetarian dishes. On the Malecón, you'll find a cluster of cheap *cevicherías*, known as "Cevichelandia" – of which *Don Kleber's* stands out for quality and good value – around the municipal market at General Enríquez Gallo and Las Palmeras (C 16).

The Ruta del Sol

From La Libertad, a paved road runs 137km up the coast to Punta de Cayo – promoted by the tourist authorities as the **Ruta del Sol** – offering fantastic views of long, empty beaches and passing a string of unpretentious fishing villages, occasionally swinging back from the shore to negotiate the forested hills of the Chongón-Colonche range. Most visitors head straight for laid-back **Montañita**, popular with surfers and rapidly growing into a backpackers' beach hangout. A little further north, the dishevelled town of **Puerto López** serves as a base for **whale-watching** trips (June–Sept), and visits to the **Parque Nacional Machalilla**, which takes in a major tract of tropical dry forest, some fabulous beaches and the **Isla de la Plata**, favoured by bird lovers as a cheaper alternative to the Galápagos Islands.

From Guayaquil's bus terminal, Transportes CLP runs six **daily services** directly to Montañita and Olón between January and April, and Cooperativa Jipijapa buses leave for Jipijapa every thirty minutes.

Montañita

Just 4km north of Manglaralto, **MONTAÑITA** is like nowhere else on the southern coast. Crammed into the centre are straw-roofed, bamboo-walled *hostales* and pizzerias, advertised by bright wooden signs, while tanned, chilled-out gringos lounge around in bikinis and shorts, and surfers stride up the streets, board under arm. Its transformation from isolated fishing village to backpackers' hang-out has been brought about by some of the best **surfing** conditions in Ecuador, offering strong, consistent waves ranging from one to three metres in height, and a long right break off the northern end of the beach by the rocky promontory known as **La Punta**. The best waves fortuitously coincide with the hottest time of year, from January to April, when the water temperature averages 22–25°C. Every Februrary surfing fever reaches a peak during the international surfing competition held here over Carnaval, which attracts contestants from the USA and Australia.

Boards (*tablas*) can be rented for $5 a day at the Tsunami Surf Shop opposite *Hotel Montañita* and at DMCA on Chiriboga opposite *Hotel Casa Blanca*; Montañita's waves are best suited to experienced surfers, but beginners can get in on the action by taking one-to-one **lessons** at DMCA ($10 for 1hr 30min lesson, plus board hire and wetsuit for the whole day).

Practicalities

In the centre, a popular budget **hotel** choice is the *Hostal El Centro del Mundo* (no phone), a tall bamboo house on stilts, right by the ocean, offering simple wooden rooms with ($4) or without ($3 per person) en-suite bathrooms. On the hill just off the main road, *Cabañas Nativa Bambú* (Ⓦwww.nativabambu.com; ❺ including breakfast and dinner) are very attractive cabins with varnished floors, well-presented shared or private bathrooms, mosquito nets and terraces overlooking the village and sea. Four-person tents are also available for $10 including breakfast. Out at **La Punta**, where the atmosphere is calmer and quieter, appealing choices include *Hostal Casa del Sol* (Ⓣ04/290-1302, Ⓦwww.casasol.com; ❹), offering agreeable rooms with private bath or cheaper dormitory bunks ($8 per person) in a cosy, straw-roofed wooden building with balconies, terraces, hammocks, a TV room and restaurant. There's a wide choice of café-**restaurants** in the centre, all of them cheap and most offering a fish-based menu, often supplemented by pizzas, pastas, pancakes and tropical fruit juices: standing out are *Doña Elena*, on the main street, who serves great sea bass caught by her fisherman husband.

Puerto López

About 5km north of Salango, the coast road cuts across the brow of a hill to give you a sudden, splendid view down to **PUERTO LÓPEZ**, a small fishing town strung along a wide, crescent-shaped bay. The town enjoys an undeniably picturesque setting, its golden beach set off by the turquoise waters of the ocean and the green hills rising either side of the bay. At close quarters, however, Puerto López turns out to be an untidy place with potholed streets, crumbling buildings and a litter-strewn beach. All the same, the surge of morning activity provided by fishermen busying to and from the beach, and the swarm of children playing in the breakers after school, give it a spirited atmosphere and it's by far the most convenient base for visiting **Parque Nacional Machalilla**, whose headquarters and information centre are based in the town at García Moreno and Eloy Alfaro, where there's a small interpretation centre. Indeed, most visitors are here not for the town but to explore the park's beaches, forests and offshore island, **Isla de la Plata**.

Practicalities

Puerto López is well served by **buses** running along the coastal road to La Libertad in the south (every 30min; 3hr) and Manta in the north (hourly; 2hr), as well as north to Jipijapa inland (every 30min; 1hr 30min) where there are onward connections to Guayaquil. There are three direct buses to Quito (5am, 9am & 6.30pm; 10hr), and two daily services from Quito at 7am and 10pm. Buses drop passengers on the main road, General Córdova, by the church and the market building; there should be plenty of *tricicleros* ($0.50) offering to cycle you to your hotel, while *camionetas* linger around the market for longer journeys.

Of the town's plentiful **accommodation**, *Hostal Los Islotes* (☎05/604108 or 604128; ❷–❹), down on the seafront, at the corner with General Córdova, is a tidy little hotel with spacious en-suite rooms, while at the far north of the Malecón the friendly Swiss–Italian-owned *Hostería Mandála* (☎05/604181; ❹) offers thatched-roof cabins with private bath and hot water set in lavish botanical gardens, and a lovely restaurant overlooking the ocean. Back in town, the best **place to eat** is *Carmita's* on the Malecón and General Córdova, a friendly restaurant run by the same family for thirty years, serving fresh-as-it-comes fish and seafood at great prices. Especially recommended are the *pescado al vapor* (steamed sea bass in tomato, onion and herb sauce) and *spaghetti con mariscos*.

Parque Nacional Machalilla

Parque Nacional Machalilla is Ecuador's only coastal national park, created in 1979 to protect the country's last major tract of tropical dry forest, which since the 1950s has been reduced to a mere one percent of its original size. What really stands out about this forest is the remarkable contrast between the vegetation at sea level and that covering the hills rising from the coastline to around 800m. The **dry forest**, panning in from the shore, is made up of scorched-looking trees and shrubs adapted to scarce water supplies and saline soils, including many different cactuses, gnarled ceibas, algarobbo (able to photosynthesize through their green bark) and barbasco trees. Also common down here are the highly fragrant *palo santo* trees, whose bark is burned as incense in churches. A short hike east into the hills brings you into a wholly different landscape of **coastal cloudforest**, moistened by rising sea mist that condenses as it hits the hills. Here, you'll find a dense covering of lush vegetation taking in ferns, heliconias, bromeliads, orchids and bamboos, inhabited by howler monkeys, *guantas*, anteaters and over 350 species of birds. You can observe the two different habitats on a 10km trail leading from the community of **Agua Blanca**, north of Puerto López, up to an area of cloudforest known as **San Sebastián**. Agua Blanca also sits near one of the most important **archeological sites** on the coast: the former settlement known as Sangólome, once an important civic and ceremonial centre of the Manteño culture. Furthermore, the park takes in a number of pristine **beaches**, of which the most spectacular is **Playa Los Frailes**, a virgin, white-sand beach framed by dramatic cliffs and forested hills. Offshore areas include the tiny **Isla Salango** and the famous, bird-rich **Isla de la Plata**, the most popular destination within the park.

The park's administration and **visitor centre** (daily 8am–noon & 2–6pm; ☎05/604170) are based in Puerto López, in the brown and white thatched building opposite the market, just off the main road running through town. This is where you pay your **entrance fee**. There are three types of ticket: for the mainland only ($12), for the Isla de la Plata only ($15), and a combined ticket for $20; all are good for five days. **Getting to the park** is easy on any of the buses running north along the coast road, (see "Practicalities" p.733–4). The **weather** is typically rainy, hot and sunny from January to April, and dry, slightly cooler and overcast during the rest of the year, with average temperatures hovering around 23–25°C year-round.

Playa Los Frailes

Ten kilometres north of Puerto López, a signed dirt track branches west from the coast road just south of the rundown village of Machalilla to **Playa Los Frailes**, one of the most beautiful beaches on the entire Ecuadorian coast, enclosed by rocky cliffs at each end and backed by a tangle of forest. Despite its popularity, this still feels like a wild, unspoiled place, particularly if you arrive early in the morning when you're almost guaranteed to have it all to yourself. To get to Playa Los Frailes, hop on any of the **buses** heading north from Puerto López and ask to be dropped at the turn-off to the beach, about fifteen minutes out of town. Just off the road there's a national park kiosk where you have to present your ticket or buy one if you haven't already paid your entrance fee. From here, a footpath leads directly to Los Frailes in thirty minutes (the left fork), or you can follow a 4km circular trail (the right fork), via the tiny black-sand cove known as **La Payita**, followed by **Playa La Tortiguita**, where spiky rock formations rise out of the turquoise waters. From La Tortiguita, continue on the main footpath to Los Frailes, or follow the fork leading through dry forest dotted with fragrant *palo santo* trees up to a wooden **lookout point**, giving spectacular views up and down the coast. This longer approach, via La Playita, La Tortiguita and the *mirador*, is by far the more rewarding and takes about a couple of hours to complete, taking your time.

Isla de la Plata

Thirty-seven kilometres out to sea from Puerto López, and visitable through one of the tour companies there, **Isla de la Plata** is a small, scrubby island covering just eight square kilometres, of some fame for its large population of **marine birds**, which are relatively fearless and allow close observation. Such accessibility has given it the sobriquet of "poor man's Galápagos", though this hackneyed phrase doesn't do the island justice. Notably, the island is the only place in Ecuador, including the Galápagos, where blue-footed, red-footed and Nazca boobies are found together at the same site.

From the landing point in **Bahía Drake**, two circular **footpaths** lead around the island, each one taking around three to four hours to complete, including time spent watching the birds and listening to your tour guide's explanation. The most numerous bird species on the island is the **blue-footed booby**, but – as well as the red-footed and Nazca varieties – you can also see **frigate birds**, **red-billed tropicbirds** and **waved albatrosses** (the breeding season for albatrosses on the island is April–Oct), as well as sea lions which are colonizing the island in small numbers. Visits are usually rounded up with some **snorkelling** as well, when you'll see a fabulous array of colourful fish. You might also spot dolphins and manta rays on the boat ride there and back, as well as **humpback whales** between June and September.

6.7

The Galápagos Islands

It's quite humbling to think that thirteen scarred volcanic islands, flung across 45,000 square kilometres of ocean, 960km adrift from the Ecuadorian mainland and defying permanent human colonization until the twentieth century, should have been so instrumental in changing humanity's perception of itself. Yet it was the forbidding **Galápagos Islands** that spurred **Charles Darwin** to formulate his theory of evolution by natural selection, catapulting science into the modern era and colouring the values and attitudes of the Western world ever since. Three years before Darwin's arrival in 1835 Ecuador had claimed sovereignty over the islands, which swiftly took root in the country's consciousness, not as the forsaken land of unearthly creatures and lava wastes that the rest of the world saw, but as a source of great national pride, bolstered still further by Darwin's discoveries. When the islands became desirable to foreign powers as a strategic military base from which to protect the entrance to the Panama Canal, the Ecuadorian government – even after a string of unsuccessful colonization attempts – resisted several enticing offers for territorial rights over them. In fact, it wasn't until World War II, when it became clear that just such a strategic base was necessary, that the US was allowed to establish an airforce base on Baltra. When the war ended, the base was returned to Ecuador and became the principal point of access to the islands for a steadily increasing flow of immigrants and tourists.

Today, the Galápagos Islands' matchless wildlife and natural history pulls in around 70,000 tourists a year to the archipelago, most of which can only be seen on expensive boat tours. Its population of 16,000 live in just eight main settlements on the four inhabited islands. In the centre of them all lies **Santa Cruz**, site of **Puerto Ayora**, the islands' most developed town and serviced by the airstrip on Baltra, where the majority of tourists begin a visit to the islands. **San Cristóbal**, to the east, holds the provincial capital, **Puerto Baquerizo Moreno**, less developed than Puerto Ayora but with the archipelago's other major runway. Straddling the equator to the west of Santa Cruz is the largest and most volcanically active of all the islands, **Isabela**, whose main settlement, the tiny **Puerto Villamil**, keeps the archipelago's only other airport. South of Santa Cruz, **Floreana**, with its population of about eighty people, has very little infrastructure and a bizarre history of settlement.

The settled sites, however, represent a mere three percent of the total land area of the archipelago. In response to the damage caused to flora and fauna populations by centuries of human interference, the rest of it – almost 7000 square kilometres – has been protected as a **national park** since 1959, with tourists restricted to the colonized areas and over fifty designated **visitor sites** spread across the archipelago. Most of them are reached by cruise boats only, or far less comprehensively by day-trips from the colonized areas, and visitors must be accompanied by a licensed guide to see them. Despite the restrictions, each site has been chosen to show off the full diversity of the islands, and in a typical tour you'll be encountering different species of flora and fauna every day, many of them endemic (not found anywhere else on the planet). It's worth noting, however, that while sites close to Santa Cruz tend to be the more crowded, several of the most unusual ones are in remoter places.

It was also in 1959, the centenary of the publication of Darwin's *Origin of the Species*, that the **Charles Darwin Foundation** (CDF) was created and set about

Galápagos time

Galápagos time is GMT minus 6 hours, 1 hour behind the Ecuadorian mainland.

building the **Charles Darwin Research Station** (CDRS) in Puerto Ayora, whose vital work includes boosting the threatened populations of unique Galápagos species. Its position was further strengthened in 1986 with the creation of the **Reserva Marina de Galápagos**, now the second largest marine reserve in the world (after the Great Barrier Reef in Australia). It's mainly thanks to the huge conservation effort that the tourists who flock to the islands are privy to such incomparable experiences as swimming with hammerhead sharks and turtles, and walking beside the nests of frigate birds and boobies as unique species of finches hop on to their shoes.

When to visit

Although wildlife spotting is good throughout the year, the Galápagos have a two-season **climate** governed by the strong **ocean currents** swirling around them. The **Humboldt Current** (or Peru Current) is particularly prevalent in the cool season, helped on by brisk southeast winds. It cools the sea and forms the **garúa mist**, hanging at 300m to 600m where the cool, moist air over the water meets the warm air above that's heated by the sun. In the warm season, the winds fall off, allowing warm currents from Panama to displace the Humboldt current. Sea temperatures rise, the mist dissipates, and normal rain clouds can form.

The islands are relatively dry all year, but during the **warm wet season** (Jan–June) sunny skies are broken by short and heavy bursts of rain while temperatures nudge 30°C. You can also expect sea temperatures to be between 20°C and 26°C, reaching perhaps as high as 29°C around the northeastern islands. In the

Galápagos essentials

Galápagos **prices** are higher than on the mainland, and you'll also have to pay at least ten percent extra on credit-card transactions here, so take plenty of **cash**. Note also that only **MasterCard** is accepted at the banks and at many hotels.

For daytime **clothing**, you'll be fine in shorts, a T-shirt, a hat and sunglasses; in the evenings, sea breezes make trousers and a long-sleeved top necessary. A lightweight raincoat is adequate for the odd rain shower and *garúa* drizzle. You'll need sturdy boots or shoes for the jagged lava wastes and sandals for the beaches. A torch comes in handy for visiting lava tunnels, or for the remoter settlements, which don't have 24-hour electricity.

For health-related matters, take plenty of **sunscreen** and, particularly for the highlands and during the wet season, **insect repellent**. If you wear contact lenses, you may need **eyedrops** as the islands can also be hot, windy and dusty. On board, **earplugs** will help block out the engine noise of your tour boat at night, while **seasickness tablets**, or patches, are a must for sufferers.

Most of the time you'll be watching wildlife from close quarters, but occasionally **binoculars** are essential. Your **camera equipment** should include a zoom or telephoto lens and a polarizing filter to prevent the colours being bleached by the fierce sun; remember, too, to bring something to protect it from sea spray and rain. If you're planning on **swimming** with marine wildlife, your **snorkelling gear** should include a mask, snorkel and fins, as they may not be supplied by your tour operator or may not fit if they are. You can also rent snorkelling equipment at several places in Puerto Ayora (see "Listings" p.746). From July to December a **wetsuit** or jacket is a good idea for the cold water. If you're going **scuba diving** and have your own equipment, bring as much of it along as is practical.

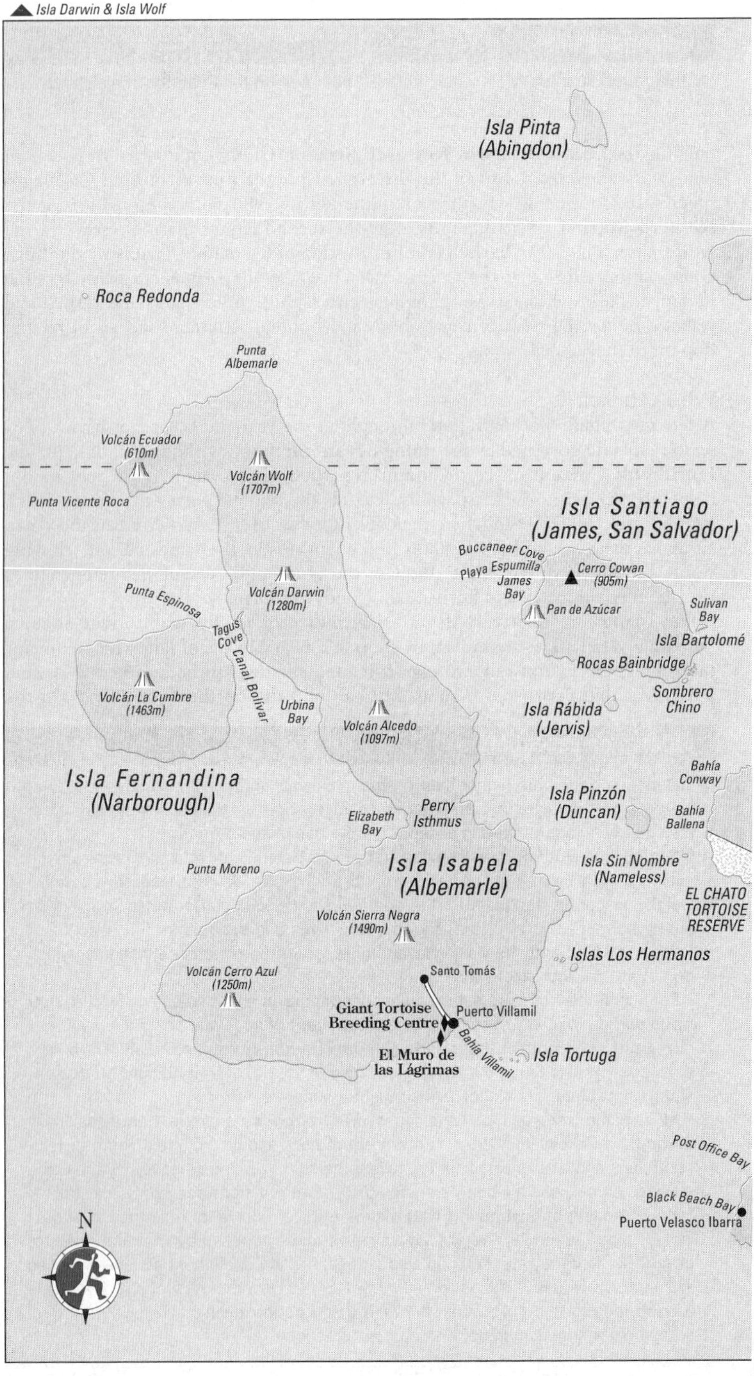

Isla Darwin & Isla Wolf

Isla Pinta (Abingdon)

Roca Redonda

Punta Albemarle

Volcán Ecuador (610m)

Volcán Wolf (1707m)

Punta Vicente Roca

Isla Santiago (James, San Salvador)

Buccaneer Cove

Playa Espumilla

James Bay

Cerro Cowan (905m)

Pan de Azúcar

Sulivan Bay

Isla Bartolomé

Rocas Bainbridge

Sombrero Chino

Volcán Darwin (1280m)

Punta Espinosa

Tagus Cove

Canal Bolívar

Volcán La Cumbre (1463m)

Urbina Bay

Volcán Alcedo (1097m)

Isla Rábida (Jervis)

Bahía Conway

Isla Fernandina (Narborough)

Isla Pinzón (Duncan)

Bahía Ballena

Elizabeth Bay

Perry Isthmus

Isla Isabela (Albemarle)

Isla Sin Nombre (Nameless)

Punta Moreno

EL CHATO TORTOISE RESERVE

Volcán Sierra Negra (1490m)

Islas Los Hermanos

Volcán Cerro Azul (1250m)

Santo Tomás

Giant Tortoise Breeding Centre

Puerto Villamil

El Muro de las Lágrimas

Bahía Villamil

Isla Tortuga

Post Office Bay

Black Beach Bay

Puerto Velasco Ibarra

N

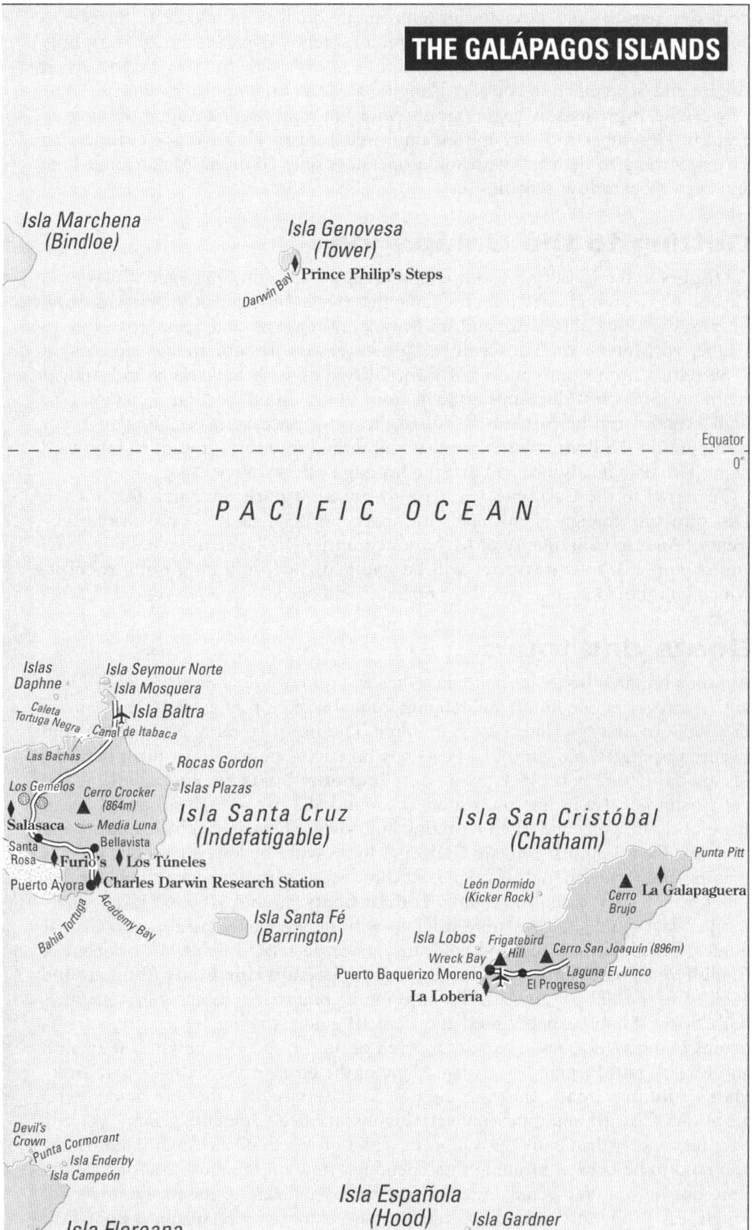

THE GALÁPAGOS ISLANDS

Isla Marchena
(Bindloe)

Isla Genovesa
(Tower)

Darwin Bay

Prince Philip's Steps

Equator
0°

PACIFIC OCEAN

Islas
Daphne

Isla Seymour Norte

Isla Mosquera

Isla Baltra

Caleta
Tortuga Negra

Canal de Itabaca

Las Bachas

Rocas Gordon

Islas Plazas

Los Gemelos

Cerro Crocker
(864m)

Isla Santa Cruz
(Indefatigable)

Salasaca

Media Luna

Bellavista

Santa
Rosa

Furio's

Los Túneles

Puerto Ayora

Charles Darwin Research Station

Academy Bay

Bahía Tortuga

Isla Santa Fé
(Barrington)

Isla San Cristóbal
(Chatham)

Punta Pitt

León Dormido
(Kicker Rock)

Cerro
Brujo

La Galapaguera

Isla Lobos

Frigatebird
Hill

Cerro San Joaquín (896m)

Wreck Bay

Puerto Baquerizo Moreno

Laguna El Junco

El Progreso

La Lobería

Devil's
Crown

Punta Cormorant

Isla Enderby

Isla Campeón

Isla Floreana
(Charles, Santa María)

Isla Española
(Hood)

Isla Gardner

Gardner Bay

Punta Suárez

0 20 km

cool dry season (July–Dec), the air temperature drops to around 22°C, the oceans become choppier, and the skies are more consistently overcast, though very little rain falls on the lowlands. Sea temperatures can dip as low as 16°C, especially in August and September, so consider bringing a wet suit if you plan to snorkel.

Pricewise, **high season** begins around mid-June and lasts till August, starting up again in December and carrying on until mid-January. However, exact times can vary according to demand, with some operators only counting May to mid-June and September as **low season**.

Getting to the Galápagos

All **flights** to the Galápagos (a 3hr trip in total) depart from Quito and stop over in Guayaquil for around forty minutes. Tame flies twice daily to Baltra, a bus ride from Puerto Ayora on Santa Cruz; and on Monday, Wednesday and Saturday to Puerto Baquerizo Moreno on San Cristóbal. Wherever you fly into, **prices** are fixed at $389 return from Quito and $374 from Guayaquil, with low-season and student (with an ISIC card) discounts at $334 from Quito and $294 from Guayaquil. In high season it can be particularly difficult to get a place, so make sure you're not being put on the waiting list. Note that you should reconfirm inward and outward flights two days in advance and that the **luggage allowance** is 20kg.

On arrival in the Galápagos you have to pay $100 **park entrance fee** in cash. **Discounts** for foreigners only apply for under-12s ($50), under-2s (no charge), citizens of Andean Community or Mercosur countries ($50), and those holding a visa and *censo* ($25). Your **passport** will be stamped and you'll be given a **receipt**, which you should keep as your boat operator will need it.

Boats and tours

Almost a hundred **boats** currently have licences to tour the Galápagos, divided into several categories of comfort and ranging from converted fishing boats for a handful of people to luxury cruisers for a hundred. The majority carry between ten and twenty passengers, and almost all boats rely on engine power to get them between islands, but several boost speed with sails. **Economy boats** can cost as little as $60 per person per day in the low season or around $85 in the high season. Many of these boats are poky and often have tiny bunk-bed cabins, shared bath, uninspiring food and Class I guides, who are Galápagos locals with the lowest level of naturalist training and a fair amount of English. If the weather's bad, these are the boats that suffer most from rocking and rolling. **Tourist boats** (around $100 to $150 per person per day) should be a bit more spacious with slightly better facilities and Class II guides, Ecuadorians with good education, often in related fields, who can speak English and French or German fluently. **Tourist-superior boats** (from around $150 to over $300 per day) usually have more comfortable cabins still, sometimes with air conditioning, better food and Class III guides, the highest level of accreditation, who have degrees in biology, tourism or similar, and can speak fluent Spanish and English plus French or German. Many of the boats in the Galápagos are **first-class** or **luxury boats**, enjoying the best food, service, comfort and guides, who are always Class III and invariably very highly qualified naturalists. Cabins typically have beds rather than bunks, private bath with hot water and air conditioning. They also tend to be faster – meaning they spend less time on the move and often more time on the remoter islands – and a few have stabilizers to lessen the effects of rough seas. While the largest boats tend to have extra facilities, such as a pool, bear in mind that they take longer to disembark, giving you less time on shore. Tours on first-class and luxury boats are most often arranged in your home country (see "Basics", p.13, 16 & 18 for details of specialist operators); for an eight-day cruise, costs start at around $1500 and can rise to over $3500 excluding flights and entrance fees.

Galápagos tour operators in Quito

This list is not comprehensive but gives a good selection of boat owners rather than general operators, and includes prices for an eight-day cruise in high season, per person, based on two sharing a cabin. Agencies with offices in the Galápagos are listed under the relevant island. A good general operator is the Galápagos Boat Company, Calama 380 and Juan León Mera in Quito (☎02/255-2505), which can arrange tours on most boats, keep customer reports on good and bad boats, and help with last-minute deals, but you'll pay a $45 commission if you book through them.

Andando Tours Av Coruña N26-311 and Orellana, Quito ☎02/255-0952, ⓦwww.angermeyercruises.com. They have three good-looking first-class sailing yachts, *Sea Cloud*, *Sagitta* and *Heritage*, and also represent the owners of *Samba* and *The Beagle*. From $1500.

Ecoventura Almagro N31-80, Edificio Venecia ☎02/229-06898 or in the US or Canada ☎1800/633-7972, ⓦwww.ecoventura.com operates three first-class motor yachts, *Eric*, *Flamingo I* and the specialist diving boat, *Sky Dancer*. From $2195.

Enchanted Expeditions Foch 726 and Amazonas, Quito ☎02/256-9960, ⓦwww.enchantedexpeditions.com. A reliable and recommended operator running the luxury *Beluga* motor yacht and the first-class *Cachalote I*, an attractive 96-foot schooner for sixteen people. A good standard of service and guiding is complemented by some excellent cooking.

Kem Pery Joaquín Pinto 539 and Amazonas ☎02/222-6583, ⓦwww.kempery.com. Owns *Angelique*, a tourist-superior motor-sailer with capacity for sixteen people, which has a good reputation for inexpensive four-, five- or eight-day cruises. Special deals can be arranged combining a Galápagos trip with a stay at their jungle lodge in the Huaorani reserve. From $900.

Quasar Nautica Brasil 293 and Granda Centeno, Edificio IACA, 2nd floor, Quito ☎02/244-6996, ⓦwww.quasarnautica.com. A well-respected company offering tours on six first-class and luxury yachts. Guiding, service and accommodation are excellent and the boats *Alta*, *Parranda* and *Eclipse* are among the most comfortable in the islands (from $2660); less expensive boats *Mistral* and *Diamante* are still very well appointed (from $2100). Quasar also offers specialist diving cruises, notably on the exquisite trimaran *Lammer Law* (from $2750).

Note that if you're travelling alone, you may be asked to pay a hefty **supplement** for your cabin, unless you're prepared to share. Other hidden costs include alcohol, which isn't included in the price, and the **tip** at the end of the tour for the guide and crew – this will depend on the service you've received and what you can afford but, as a general rule, an economy guide and crew will each expect around $25 per cabin per week, while luxury boats suggest as much as $100 per person per week for the crew and $40 per person per week for the guide. If you can give the tip directly to the deserving, so much the better, as this avoids the possibility of unfair distribution of a general tip by an unscrupulous captain or guide.

Problems can occur: overbooking, petty theft, annoying engine noise and smells, food and water supplies running out, changes of itinerary, breakdowns and, unfortunately, sexual harassment from guide or crew. One trick of operators is to downgrade boats at the last moment; your contract should stipulate a refund if the category of boat changes. Even so, getting a **reimbursement** can be hard work: if you feel wronged, report the operator to the Ministerio de Turismo and Capturgal (see p.743), and the Capitanía in Puerto Ayora. You can also tell the SAE in Quito (see p.665). In rare cases irresponsible guides have disobeyed park rules, perhaps erring from the path, touching animals, bringing food onto the islands, disturbing nests, or encouraging the crew to fish for food (an illegal activity). This kind of behaviour should be reported to the Galápagos National Park Service.

Scuba-diving trips and tours

While the Galápagos Islands are one of the best **scuba-diving** spots in the world, diving here isn't easy and at times you'll have to contend with strong currents, surge, low visibility and cold water. With this in mind, the islands are not considered a suitable place to learn to scuba dive, even though training courses are offered here.

Several companies organize **day-trip dives** from Puerto Ayora to a variety of sites for $80–120, including all equipment and a guide (see "Listings" p.746 for details). **Diving boat tours** cruise the islands, mixing one to four dives per day with land visits, and you may even get to dive around islands such as Wolf and Darwin, where land visits are prohibited. On such tours, you'll need to be an experienced diver with a certificate, and to bring most of your own equipment, usually with the exception of tanks (and air), weights and weight belts; in the cool season, your wetsuit should be 6mm thick. Prices for eight-day diving tours start at around $1300 and rise to $3000, depending on the level of luxury and standard of guiding: reservations should be made well in advance.

Day-trips and independent travel

An inexpensive way to see the islands is to arrange **day-trips**, especially from Puerto Ayora. Costing around $60 per person, these usually include a guide, lunch and a visit to one island. They're easy to organize as they're offered by many of the travel agencies in town, though you'll be limited to a handful of islands within striking distance of the port, namely Plaza Sur, Seymour Norte, Santa Fé and Floreana (if the boat leaves from Baltra, you may get to visit Bartolomé also).

Independent travel between the islands is most efficient by **flying** with EMETEBE (☎05/526177, see relevant town accounts for details). Their nine-seater light aircraft flies from San Cristóbal to Baltra and then to Isabela, Monday to Saturday, returning by the same route on the same day ($120 one-way, $210 return; each leg around 30min). Buy your ticket at least two days in advance and stick to the luggage allowance – just 13.5kg (30lbs).

If you've got plenty of time, you could try getting around on the fortnightly **ferry** (one-way $40) operated by the Instituto Nacional Galápagos, or INGALA (☎05/526199), which runs from Puerto Ayora (Santa Cruz) to Puerto Villamil (Isabela) every other Friday, returning on Sunday, before continuing to Puerto Baquerizo Moreno (San Cristóbal) in the afternoon, returning back to Puerto Ayora on Monday. If demand is high enough it makes another trip back to San Cristóbal every other Tuesday, returning on Thursday. A more convenient option is to take one of several **fibras** (fibreglass motorboat) that make daily trips between Puerto Ayora, Puerto Baquerizo Moreno and Puerto Villamil ($30). Piloted by local fishermen, these are faster and more frequent than the INGALA ferry, but the ride can be rough and uncomfortable, and there are no scheduled trips. Ask about outgoing boats at the Capitanía, local travel agents, or the *Salvavidas* restaurant.

Isla Santa Cruz and around

The archipelago's centre and tourist hub, **SANTA CRUZ** is a conical island of just under 1000 square kilometres, whose luxuriant southeastern slopes are cloaked each year in *garúa* drizzle. Reaching an altitude of 864m, the island supports all the Galápagos vegetation zones (see p.737), from cactus-strewn deserts around the coast, to tangled *scalesia* and *miconia* forests wreathed in cloud in the highlands, and sodden grassy pampas at the summit. Many of its endemic plants, however, have become increasingly threatened by a number of introduced species. Its proximity to the airport on Baltra has conspired to make it the most heavily populated island in the Galápagos, having the archipelago's largest town, **Puerto Ayora**, and is also the nerve centre of the conservation programme, headquarters of the **Charles Darwin Research Station** and the **Parque Nacional Galápagos**. Home to more boats, tour brokers, hotels and restaurants than anywhere else in the islands, it's also the best place for budget travellers to find last-minute places on cruises.

Puerto Ayora and around

Lying around the azure inlets of Academy Bay's rocky shore, **PUERTO AYORA**, on the southern coast of Santa Cruz, was home to fewer than a couple of hundred people until the early 1970s. Now, laden with souvenir shops, travel agents, restaurants and hotels, the town supports a population of around 11,000 people who enjoy a standard of living higher than any other province in the republic, giving the port a distinct aura of well-appreciated privilege. There's a relaxed atmosphere to the place, with tourists meandering down the waterfront in the daytime, browsing while fishermen work across the street in little **Pelican Bay**, building boats and sorting through their catches, watched by hungry pelicans. As it gets darker, the bars fill with locals, tourists and research scientists, a genial mix that ensures Puerto Ayora has the best **nightlife** of all Galápagos towns.

Arrival and information

Flights arrive on the island of Baltra, from where municipal **buses** (no charge) take you either to the dock where your cruise boat will be waiting, or to the Canal de Itabaca, the narrow stretch of water between Baltra and Santa Cruz. Here a passenger **ferry** ($0.70) connects with more buses ($1.50) on the other side taking you over the highlands to Puerto Ayora, ending up on Darwin. The buses only connect with incoming flights from the mainland, so at other times you'll have to get a **camioneta** or taxi to Puerto Ayora ($8–10). Once in town, **taxis** cost around $1 for most in-town destinations, and about $4 for a trip to Santa Rosa. **Water taxis**, yellow dinghies with blue awnings, are useful for trips across the bay, or for day-and-night runs between the shore and your tour boat ($0.50–1 per person).

In town, you're spoilt for choice as far as **information** goes. The traditional source, the Ministerio de Turismo on Avenida Charles Darwin, stocks simple **maps** of the islands and population centres for free, and Capturgal (Camera Provincial de Turismo de Galápagos), next door, sells large glossy maps of towns and islands for $2; these include the locations of all the boat operators' offices if you're set on seeing the islands by a particular vessel. The Charles Darwin Research Station (see p.745) can furnish you with all the nitty-gritty facts and figures of Galápagos wildlife and natural history, while the Capitanía, near the dock, keeps tabs on boat arrivals and departures.

Accommodation

Like everything in the Galápagos, the price of **accommodation** is higher than on the mainland. The thriftiest backpackers, however, should find something to suit them, and in the low season you may be able to bargain down to the rate nationals pay, though many hotels insist on one price throughout the year. The higher-end hotels can quickly fill up in the high season, so reserve rooms at these well in advance. Hot water is generally only available in such establishments.

Estrella de Mar 12 de Febrero ⓣ05/526427. Overlooking the bay, this is a good choice for its attractive rooms (those with bay views cost extra), with private bath and hot water, and blue floors inlaid with red starfish and dotted with "Happy Hanukkah" foot mats. ❸–❹

Lobo de Mar 12 de Febrero and Av Charles Darwin ⓣ05/526188, ⓦwww.lobodemar.com.ec. Remodelled to include courtyard, swimming pool and a range of rooms, some with gorgeous sea views, some with a/c and all with hot water. Internet and laundry services are available. ❹–❻

Pensión Gloria Av Charles Darwin, down the side street next to *Pizza Media Luna* (no phone). The cheapest place in town and fantastic value if you can get the room with lava walls, fireplace and eccentric cave-like bathroom. Most others are dreary prefab affairs, but all have private bath. You can use the kitchen or camp for a dollar or so in the garden too. ❷

Red Mangrove Inn Av Charles Darwin ⓣ 05/526564 ⓦwww.redmangrove.com. At the water's edge amidst mangroves, this secluded bohemian hotel was designed and built by its artist owners and has many idiosyncratic flourishes. Rooms are bright with bay views and have hot water, and there's a whirlpool on the veranda. Day-trips, windsurfing, kayaking, horse riding and mountain biking can all be arranged. Breakfast included. ❽–❾

Residencial Los Amigos Av Charles Darwin and 12 de Febrero ⓣ05/526265. Popular, friendly and inexpensive place, where the cheapest rooms are upstairs, divided by thin plywood and mosquito screening (not the best sound insulators) and have shared bath and tepid water. Rooms downstairs come with private bath and better walls. ❷

The Town

It's easy to find your way around the port. The main thoroughfare is named, predictably, **Avenida Charles Darwin**; it runs along the **waterfront**, from the municipal dock at its southern end to the Charles Darwin Research Station at its

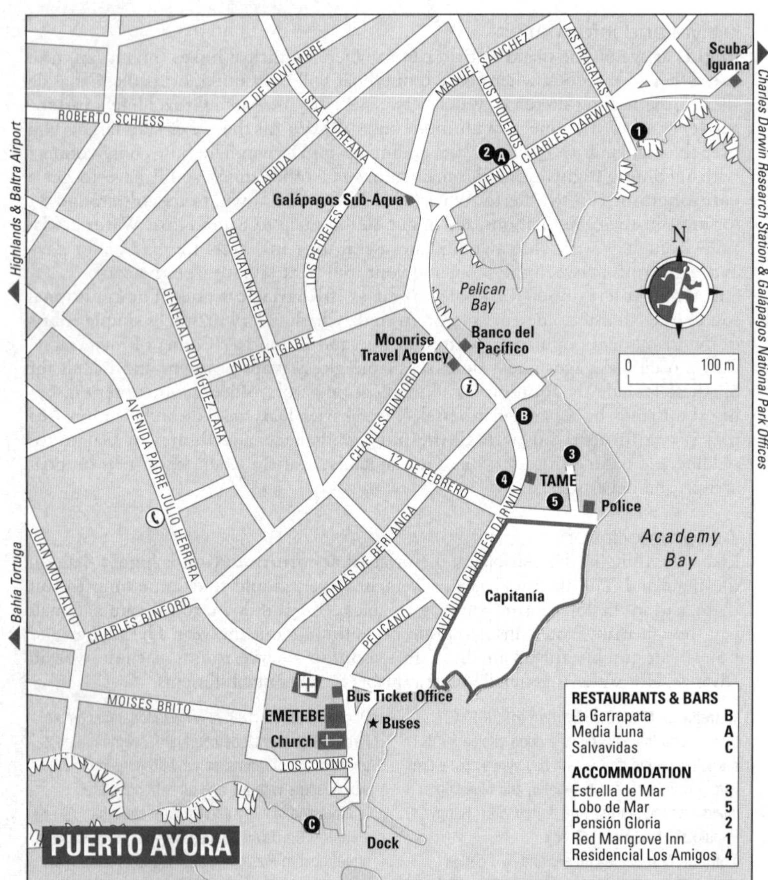

northern. Just about everything you'll need is on Darwin: hotels, restaurants, the bank, travel agents, bars, discos, information, plus a number of less indispensable souvenir shops. The town's other important road is **Avenida Padre Julio Herrera**, running inland from Darwin and the dock to become the main road to the highlands and the link to the airport on Baltra.

For a spot of peace and quiet, you can't do better than head to one of the local beaches, such as the glorious **Bahía Tortuga**, a short walk southwest of town through a cactus forest, or the **Playa de los Alemanes** and the nearby swimming hole, **Las Grietas**, reached by water taxi. The Santa Cruz highlands also holds a number of natural attractions, including lava tunnels, craters and a tortoise reserve, which can be visited on day tours through many local agencies.

Charles Darwin Research Station

Even though it is first and foremost a science and conservation facility, just about every visitor to the islands sooner or later washes up at the **Charles Darwin Research Station**, twenty-minutes' stroll from the town centre at the northern end of Avenida Charles Darwin. Past the **information booth** at the entrance, a path leads between some giant cacti to the **Van Straelen interpretation centre** (daily 7am–5pm; no charge) exhibiting information on geology, climate, conservation and many related aspects of Galápagos nature, including a seismograph that etches the islands' subterranean rumblings. A short video about the CDRS and the islands, introduced by a member of staff, can be seen on request (daily 8am–noon & 2–4pm), and details are available here about joining Galápagos conservation organizations. Walking on from the visitor centre, you'll come to the **tortoise-rearing pens**, where predator-proof enclosures hold batches of miniature giant tortoises divided by age; the creatures are best seen when the covers are off (Mon–Fri 7am–4pm). From the pens, a raised boardwalk weaves through the trees, scrub and cacti past the **tortoise corrals**, where you can see fully grown giant tortoises. The most famous resident is **Lonesome George** (*Solitario Jorge*), the last surviving tortoise of the Pinta Island subspecies, thought to be around seventy years old with about eighty more years to look forward to. From 1906 until 1971, when George was found, it was thought that the Pinta tortoises were extinct; since then, however, the search has been on to find him a Pinta partner, with a $10,000 reward on offer. He's quite a shy animal, and the best time to see him is when he's being fed on Mondays, Wednesdays and Fridays at 9am.

At the end of the walkway, you can enter an enclosure with half-a-dozen friendly tortoises, mostly former-pets donated to the station. This is the best place to get up close and take photos, but be careful not to touch them or walk on their feeding area. Near the exit, you'll pass the CDRS kiosk, selling T-shirts, videos and souvenirs; this is the only place on the islands you can buy CDRS logo clothing, the proceeds of which go straight to the station. Near the exit you'll see a sign for a little **beach**, a hidden spot for lazing about and looking across the bay.

Eating

There are plenty of **restaurants** along Avenida Darwin, including a good proportion aimed squarely at tourists, which are expensive by local standards, as well as a number of cheaper places filled with locals, such as *El Rincón del Alma* with serves bargain **almuerzos** and *meriendas*. To get the best of local **seafood** head to Charles Binford of an evening, where a string of *kioscos* (kiosks) simmer up cauldrons of *encocados* and other *mariscos*, mostly from the cuisines of the mainland coast. Of these, *William* (closed Mon) and *Tia Juanita* (closed Tues) are the best, but anywhere you can see a crowd of satisfied customers washing down their rice and fish with a glass of cold beer is also likely to be good.

Angermeyer Point An $0.80 water-taxi ride from the dock. Elegant first-class restaurant serving excellent but pricey international food, including good seafood and fillet steaks, freshly baked bread and great cocktails. It's built on decks over a rocky promontory, home to cormorants and marine iguanas, looking back over Academy Bay. Open for dinner every night except Mon, and Sunday brunch.

La Garrapata Av Charles Darwin and Tomás de Berlanga. Highly regarded open-air restaurant with candlelit tables and a good ambience, serving good seafood and grills. A little costlier than most places.

Media Luna Av Charles Darwin. Of all the pizza venues, this offers the best value, the friendliest service and the tastiest food too. A favourite of locals and tourists alike, it also does thick sandwiches. Closed Tues.

Salvavidas Muelle Municipal. A decent seafood joint overlooking the dock. While you tuck into an ample portion of fish and chips for around $5 or $2 an *almuerzo*, you can watch the herons getting their own nightly feed.

Drinking and nightlife

At *Limón y Café*, Avenida Charles Darwin and 12 de Febrero (daily until 1am), a dedicated beer-swilling following brings a good atmosphere to this thatched **bar** where you can shoot pool, sip a blue-footed booby cocktail or relax in a hammock. Food is also served up to 8pm. The disco at *La Panga*, on Avenida Charles Darwin (Mon–Thurs 8.30pm–2am, Fri & Sat 8.30pm–3am), tends to fill up quite late in the evening. Upstairs is the *Bongo Bar*, a rooftop drinking hole offering open-air seating, pool table, a small dancefloor. For good live *folklórica* music, ask a taxi driver to take you to *La Taberna del Duende* (Thurs–Sat), in a residential area towards the back of town, a *peña* done up in bamboo and straw matting that's popular with locals.

Listings

Airlines Tame is on Charles Darwin and 12 de Febrero (☎05/526527) and at Baltra airport (☎05/520111). The EMETEBE office is above the post office, on Darwin (☎05/526177).

Banks and exchange Banco del Pacífico, on Av Charles Darwin and Charles Binford, has an ATM for MasterCard and Cirrus. Several souvenir shops accept travellers' cheques, including Peer Galápagos, at the traffic triangle on Darwin.

Boats and ferries To buy ferry tickets (see "Independent travel" p.742 for service details), you must visit the INGALA ticket office in person (☎05/526199; Mon–Fri 7am–noon & 1–4pm), a 20min walk from the waterfront, 50m before the petrol station as you head out of town on Av Padre Julio Herrera. A taxi there will cost about $1. Talk to the Capitanía about the *Estrella del Mar* service to Isabela, and for details on departure times for *fibras*.

Diving operators Galápagos Sub-Aqua on Darwin (☎05/526350, ⓦwww.galapagos_sub_aqua.com.ec) is a long-established outfit offering introductory dives at Academy Bay, day-trips and longer live-aboard tours, plus PADI and NAUI training courses for beginners and divemasters. Scuba Iguana on Darwin near the *Hotel Galápagos* (☎05/526330 or 526296, ⓦwww.scubaiguana.com) has a similar range of services, and can give certified training programmes for beginners, divemasters and instructors. English is spoken at both agencies. Rates are fairly standard with day-trips usually costing around $120 per person (or $80 for introductory dives), while five-day open-water certification courses start at $400.

Hospital Protesub (☎05/526911 or 09/985-5911) on 18 de Febrero and General Rodríguez Lara.

Post office Darwin, next to the Proinsular Supermarket.

Telephone office Pacifictel, on Av Padre Julio Herrera and Española, can be chaotic. Write your name and number on the list and wait from 15 minutes to an hour for your turn. Calls can also be made from cellular phones operated by Porta and Bell South. Daily 7am–11pm.

Travel agents and day-trip operators Most of the boats based in Puerto Ayora have a corresponding office somewhere in town; if you're interested in a particular boat ask for the office location at Capturgal (see "Arrival and information", p.743). Moonrise Travel Agency, on Av Charles Darwin, opposite the Banco del Pacífico (☎05/526403 or 526402, ⓔsdivine@pa.ga.pro.ec), has a reputation for finding last-minute places on the more reliable tour boats quickly, and they run day-trips to the nearby islands and tours of the highlands. Galasam (☎05/526126) on Darwin and Av Herrera, offers tours of four, five, or eight days on any of its seven boats, including several budget options. Ensugal, on Binford and Juan Montalvo (☎05/526593), runs daily tours on the *Santa Fé II* to Seymour Norte, Plaza Sur, Bartolomé, Floreana and Santa Fé. Aqua Tours (☎05/526632) has a glass-bottomed boat, leaving the dock at 8.30am and 2.30pm for a 4hr tour, subject to demand.

△ The Inca ruins of Ingapirca

Isla Seymour Norte and Isla Daphne Mayor

Getting around a dozen visitor groups a day, **SEYMOUR NORTE**, directly north of Baltra, a low, flat island, just under two square kilometres in size, created by geological uplift, makes frequent appearances on tour-boat itineraries. Pangas put passengers ashore on black lava, where a trail leads past large colonies of **blue-footed boobies**, and both types of **frigate bird** – it's one of the best places in the islands to see the magnificent frigate bird. Along the shore you'll find barking **sea lions** and **marine iguanas**: take care where you put your feet as they nest here. An endemic variety of the *palo santo* tree borders the inland loop of the trail, smaller than its relative with hairier, greyer leaves, and occasionally **land iguanas** (brought here from Baltra) tucked away in the vegetation.

Visible about 10km to the west of Baltra and Seymour, **DAPHNE MAYOR** (the larger of the two Daphnes) is composed of a tuff cone embedded with two craters. Since the early 1970s it's been the focus of research into **Darwin's finches** by two British scientists, Peter and Rosemary Grant, who have weighed, ringed, measured and photographed every finch on the island – about 25,000 altogether. Only small yachts are allowed to call at the islands, and even then only a limited number of times per year. The dry landing is quite hairy, involving a leap onto a cliff, from where a slender trail leads up to the rim of the island; here you can gaze down into the craters. Colonies of **blue-footed boobies** nest here in the furnace heat of these natural cauldrons, and **red-billed tropicbirds** tenant the crevices in the cliff walls.

Isla Plaza Sur

Less than a kilometre from the eastern coast of Santa Cruz, the two tiny Plaza islands were formed by seismic uplift, flat islands dramatically tilted to form sheer cliffs on the southern side. Only **PLAZA SUR**, the larger of the two at less than 1.5km long and under 250m at its widest point, is open to visitors. Being within range of the Puerto Ayora day-trippers, the little island can get crowded, so a dock has been built to prevent tourists causing erosion on landing. Vociferous members of the thousand-strong colony of **sea lions** here see this as a territorial boundary, so take care boarding and disembarking; snorkelling and swimming is also better around Plaza Norte, out of the war zone. A rather more subdued group of elderly bachelors holds a corner of smooth lava (polished by the defeated over the years) up on the cliffs, a tortuous climb over the rocks away from the macho action of the main colony.

The island has striking vegetation, a covering of juicy *Sesuvium* plants that turn crimson in the dry season, punctuated by chunky *Opuntia* cactus trees. When their succulent pads fall to the ground, **land iguanas** wriggle out of their torpor for a bite to eat. Before the park rules were in place, the iguanas were often fed fruit by visitors, and subsequently learned to dash to the dock whenever a party landed. As a hangover from those lax days, you'll often see them lurking around newly arrived groups, trying their luck for a banana or orange.

A trail leads up to sheer cliffs, an excellent vantage point to spot **noddy terns**, **swallow-tailed gulls**, **Audobon shearwaters** and **red-billed tropicbirds** as well as the occasional **blue-footed and Nazca boobies**, **frigate birds** and **pelicans**. Looking down into the swell, you may see **yellow-tailed mullet**, **surgeonfish**, **manta rays** and **dolphins**.

Isla Santa Fé

Visitors to **SANTA FÉ**, about 25km southeast of Puerto Ayora, disembark for a wet landing on the northeastern side of the island, at a stunning cove with brilliant-blue water and white sand that's protected by a partly submerged peninsula. The bay is good for swimming – though give the bull sea lions here a wide berth – and snorkelling may yield up spotted **eagle and stingrays**, **white-tipped reef sharks** and a number of colourful reef fish.

There are two trails. The first is short and easy, circling through a forest of giant *Opuntia* **cacti** (a variety found only on the island), many reaching 10m in height with trunks 4m in circumference. The second is more strenuous, heading up a steep hill which affords spectacular views of the island. On both, you have a fair chance of seeing a species of **land iguana** unique to Santa Fé, having a paler colour and longer spines on its back than its counterparts on the other islands. You might also be lucky enough to see one of the three surviving endemic species of **rice rat** rustling in the scrub – unlike on Fernandina, the only other island where they are found, this species often appears in the daytime. This is a good island to spot several other endemic species, including the **Galápagos hawk**, **Galápagos dove** and **Galápagos snake**.

Islas Bartolomé and Sombrero Chino

BARTOLOMÉ, positioned a few hundred metres off the east coast of Santiago, holds the best-known landmark of the Galápagos, the teetering dagger of **Pinnacle Rock**, a jagged remnant of an old tuff cone overshadowing a streak of pale sand at the southwestern end of the island. The many tours that come here usually combine a hike to the island's summit (114m) and a refreshing swim beneath the Rock, where you'll get some fine snorkelling around the submerged rocks, and perhaps catch a glimpse of **Galápagos penguins** zipping by schools of colourful fish. If you don't see them here, you've a better chance of spotting them on the shaded cliffs each side of the bay.

The **trail to the summit** begins at the man-made dock on Bartolomé's northern point, before crossing a parched landscape relieved only by a scant covering of silvery *Tiquilia* – just about the only plant that can survive such dry, ashy soil – and the infrequent slitherings of a **Galápagos snake**. The trail then loops round to the east and climbs up several hundred wooden steps to reach the top of the hill, to give you the famous view of Pinnacle Rock. On the opposite side a stunning moonscape vista unfolds, with large spatter cones and **lava tunnels** dropping to the southeast to reveal the Daphnes, Baltra, Seymour Norte and Santa Cruz in the distance. Bartolomé's second trail begins at the beach and leads through the mangroves and dunes across the island's isthmus to a second beach, patrolled by sharks and rays and out of bounds for swimmers. **Marine turtles** nest here at the outset of the warm wet season.

Barely 100m from the southeastern tip of Santiago, the volcanic cone of tiny **SOMBRERO CHINO** does indeed bear more than a passing resemblance to a Chinese hat. Boats moor in the blazing-blue channel between the islands, a terrific spot for some snorkelling where **Galápagos penguins** are occasionally seen. A trail here follows a white-coral beach, past a **sea lion** colony to a vantage point surrounded by scuttling **Sally lightfoot crabs** and **marine iguanas**, overlooking a cliff battered by the swell. The pockmarked lava is dashed with brighter blotches of **lava cactus**, while around the beach you'll find **saltbush** and colourful **Sesuvium**.

Isla San Cristóbal

Out on the eastern side of the archipelago, **SAN CRISTÓBAL** is the administrative seat of the Galápagos and, at 558 square kilometres, the fifth largest island in the archipelago. **Wreck Bay**, at its western tip, is the site of the provincial capital, **Puerto Baquerizo Moreno**, a peaceful town that has been slowly awakening to the rustle of tourist dollars since the opening of the airport on the island in 1986, though it's still a way behind Puerto Ayora. In its favour though, you can visit the excellent new **Centro de Interpretación**, which concentrates on the human and natural history of the islands, plus the nearby islets such as **León Dormido** (Kicker Rock) and **Isla Lobos**. On the rest of the island, points of interest include the highland town of **El Progreso**, a peaceful village of wooden, stilted houses, banana plants and fruit trees, as well as the **Laguna El Junco**, a caldera lake at about 650m that is often shrouded in mist and surrounded by ferns, *miconia*, brambles and guava bushes.

The southwestern half of the island is dominated by the slopes of the **Cerro San Joaquín** (measurements of its summit range from 730m to 896m), its windward slopes covered in vegetation and farmed by the island's agricultural community. The northeastern area has the characteristic volcanic landscape of the archipelago, a collection of lava flows, spatter cones and other volcanic features, which rise to a couple of hundred metres at **Cerro Pan de Azúcar**.

Puerto Baquerizo Moreno

Founded by the colonist General Villamil in the mid-nineteenth century (see p.736), **PUERTO BAQUERIZO MORENO** was named after the first Ecuadorian president to visit the islands, in 1916. Despite being the capital of the Galápagos, it's a sleepy town, virtually lifeless in the heat of the early afternoon, only coming alive fully when the sun sets over the bay. It may not get as many visitors as Puerto Ayora, but there is a burgeoning industry here: along the waterfront, a glut of travel agents, cafés, restaurants and souvenir shops all show a town keen to cut itself a larger slice of the tourist pie. Puerto Baquerizo Moreno is a bit short of things to do, but there's enough on the island to keep visitors busy for a few days. Just outside the port, the **Centro de Interpretación** has great displays of the archipelago's human and natural history, while spots on the coast nearby, such as **Tongo Reef** west of town, have become the focus of the Galápagos' growing reputation among South Americans as a **surfing** hotspot, with the best waves at the beginning of the warm wet season (Dec–Feb), when the water is also much warmer.

Arrival, information and transport

From the **airport** you can pick up a taxi or truck to the town centre for $1; it's within walking distance too, only being about 15–20 minutes southwest of the centre along Avenida Alsacio Northia. **Ferries** and **fibras** from Santa Cruz arrive on Friday at the town's dock.

There's an **information** booth by the dock too, identifiable by the giant cement whale on the roof. They can give you **maps**, but opening hours are erratic, so you're better off trying the national park offices for information, north of Alsacio Northia, about a fifteen-minute walk from the town centre.

Pick-up trucks and **taxis** can be caught on the Malecón and charge a minimum fare of $1, and around $2 to El Progreso, $10 to El Junco (return) or about $4 to hire per hour. Island **buses** to El Progreso pick people up on Avenida 12 de Febrero, though the service is irregular so ask locals for details. If you want to go beyond El Progreso, for example to El Junco, catch the bus from the market at 12 de Febrero and Juan José Flores (Wed & Sat at 2pm). Tell the driver you want the lagoon and check what time it'll be passing back, usually about ninety minutes later.

Accommodation

Puerto Baquerizo Moreno has enough **hotels** to keep its modest flow of tourists sheltered throughout the year. The cheaper, funkier places can fill out with South American surfers during the December to February season, when you'll need to book in advance. The town was recently equipped with 24-hour electricity, but water shortages and feeble water pressure remain a problem for many of the less expensive hotels. Some locals also rent out **rooms** for short- and long-stay visitors, usually park volunteers, and advertise in the port's bars. **Campers** can get the latest information on permissible sites at the national park offices at the north end of Alsacio Northia.

Cabañas Don Jorge a 15min walk north of town along Alsacio Northia, near a small beach ⓣ05/520265, ⓔcterana@ga.pro.ec. Four red-roofed cabins with private bath and hot water, slotted between the rocks and cacti in a secluded garden with sea views. One has two floors and kitchen facilities. Reservations advised. ❹

Hotel Mar Azul Alsacio Northia and Av Armada

Nacional ⑦05/520139, Ⓔseaman1@andinanet.net. Clean and spacious rooms with private bath and electric showers, set around two tranquil, leafy courtyards. ❹

Residencial San Francisco Malecón Charles Darwin and Española ⑦05/520304. A quiet, inexpensive place popular with surfers, in a central location offering rooms with private bath, fans and television. Pipes going all over the cheerfully daubed indoor courtyard reflect the rather erratic plumbing, however. ❷

The Port and around

Puerto Baquerizo Moreno has three main streets. On the waterfront, the Malecón Charles Darwin is where you'll find several tour agencies, restaurants, souvenir shops and the odd hotel; running parallel to it, a couple of blocks to the east, is the main thoroughfare servicing the length of the town, from the national park offices (and interpretation centre) in the north to the airport in the south; while Avenida 12 de Febrero links the town to the rest of the island, heading uphill to the east from the centre.

The **Centro de Interpetación**, the Galápagos National Park's excellent exhibition centre (daily 8am–noon & 1–5pm; donation), about twenty-minutes' walk north of the centre along Alsacio Northia, covers everything from geology, climate and conservation, to attempts at colonization in the 1920s; it has detailed explanations in Spanish and English. Talks, lectures and concerts are regularly held at the open-air theatre and audiovisual projection room within the complex.

Behind the last exhibition room at the centre, a path leads up to **Cerro de Las Tijeretas**or **Frigatebird Hill**. It's only twenty minutes' walk through fragrant *palo santo* forests to the top to a viewpoint, where you'll have a fine panorama of the yachts in Wreck Bay, Isla Lobos to the north, and León Dormido to the northeast. Below you a rocky cove echoes with jockeying **sea lions** while **frigate birds** circle in the air above. They nest here in March and April, and are seen less frequently during the cool dry season. A series of paths network around the hill, so you can do a circuit; it's relatively easy to stay oriented. One trail leads to the cove where you can snorkel, others go down to the road back to town past the interpretation centre. Heading away from town to the north, you'll come to a secluded beach.

At the weekends, **surfing** crowds make their way to the shoreline west of town to catch the waves. **Tongo Reef** is one of the more popular places, a twenty-minute walk past the Capitanía, but others include Punta Carola and El Cañón. You'll need to leave identification at the entrance, as this is a military area, then cross the runway through the scrub to the rocky shore. Bring sandals that you don't mind getting wet, as the volcanic rocks somehow combine extreme sharpness with extraordinary slipperiness. It's best to go with someone who knows the place as currents can be strong; ask at local travel agents about board hire and guides or instructors.

A good place near town to spot wildlife is **La Lobería**, thirty-minutes' walk to the southwest. Here, a trail leads along a rugged coast of pitted black lava buffeted by ocean spray to a small beach, where you'll find sea lions, marine iguanas and many shore birds. Locals take the shortcut to La Lobería, via the airport along to the southern end of the runway and down the steep embankment at the end. Make sure there are no imminent air arrivals if you follow their example. Otherwise continue on from the southern end of Alsacio Northia down a dirt road heading to the shore. Taxis ($2.50) or bikes are alternatives to the walk.

Eating, drinking and nightlife

It's easy to get a cheap feed in town, with a number of **restaurants** and **cafés** offering two-course set-lunch *almuerzos* for around $2. Menus are rather samey, though, concentrating mainly on seafood, with the usual chicken and meat courses as back-up. The booming teenage population surfs in the afternoons and spend their nights enjoying the port's **nightlife**. *Scuba Bar*, on the Malecón is a popular hangout, while *Neptunus*, above *Casablanca* at the north end of the Malecón, is a disco with an energetic, youthful crowd.

Albacora Av Alsacio Northia and Española. Popular for its cheap *almuerzos* and *meriendas*, the decor comprises cane walls, gravel floor and wicker lights flitting with finches. At night it twinkles with fairy lights.

Bambú Villamil and Ignacio de Hernández. In addition to the inexpensive *almuerzo*, you'll also find pizza and pasta dishes with vegetarian options.

Miconia Av Armada Nacional, by the Capitanía. The best restaurant in town overlooks the bay and offers a range of à la carte goodies, from tapas to *ceviche*.

Rosita Cnr of Ignacio de Hernández and Villamil. Long-standing restaurant, with a patio shaded by a thatched awning. English names on the menu betray the place's success with the tourists, so expect to pay a little more for fish, meat and a range of *ceviche* dishes.

Listings

Airlines Tame have an office at the airport (☎05/521089), as do EMETEBE (☎05/520036).

Bank Banco del Pacífico, on the promenade by Malecón Charles Darwin, has an ATM for Cirrus and MasterCard.

Ferries and fibras For advance ferry tickets go to the INGALA office, a 20min walk out of town on the way to El Progreso (a taxi costs around $1), or you can buy tickets on board. The ferry departs every other Mon for Santa Cruz, and again the Thurs after if demand is high enough. Ask at the Capitanía for upcoming *fibra* departures.

Hospital Alsacio Northía and Quito (☎05/520118 in emergencies).

Post office Malecón Charles Darwin and Manuel Cobos.

Telephone office Pacifictel, Av Quito and Juan José Flores.

Travel agents Chalo Tours, on Malecón Charles Darwin and Española (☎05/520953); Galparadise, Teodoro Wolf and Charles Darwin (☎05/520618, ©galparadise@hotmail.com); and Biological Expeditions, Av Quito and Alsacio Northía (☎05/520933, ©bxgalapagos@hotmail.com), all offer bay tours and various expeditions.

Isla Isabela

Straddling the equator, **ISABELA** is the largest island in the Galápagos at 4558 square kilometres, accounting for well over half the total land surface of the archipelago. It comprises six **volcanoes**, fused together over time: from north to south, **Ecuador** (610m), **Wolf** (1707m), **Darwin** (1280m) and **Alcedo** (1097m) make up a narrow volcanic chain that tapers into the inaccessible lava flow of the Perry Isthmus, on the other side of which **Sierra Negra** (1490m) and **Cerro Azul** (1250m) compose the squat base of the island. Several of the volcanoes are still active, the last eruption being in September 1998, when Cerro Azul spurted molten lava into areas populated by two subspecies of giant tortoise, including the endangered *Geochelone elephatopus guntheri*, of which there are fewer than one hundred left. The threatened tortoises were airlifted by helicopter or hauled to safety over the unforgiving terrain by ground crews.

Much of Isabela's huge land mass is impassable, riven by fissures, blocked by jagged lava flows, or clothed in tangled thickets of vegetation. The rocky shores mean that there are few landing places on the island. Three of the visitor sites – **Urbina Bay**, **Elizabeth Bay** and **Tagus Cove** – are on its far western side, putting them in range only of the longer tours. Volcán Alcedo, the only visitor site on the eastern site, is closed for the eradication of goats, which are seriously disrupting the largest **giant tortoise** colony in the Galápagos. The upwelling of cold waters off the coast make for a nutrient rich zone, supporting such oddities as the **Galápagos penguin** and the **flightless cormorant**, more usually spotted on nearby Fernandina. Plentiful stocks of fish also attract **whales**, large schools of **common dolphins** and gregarious **bottle-nosed dolphins** – an unexpected highlight of the western islands.

Puerto Villamil, the island's first town on its southeastern coast, is far less developed than either Puerto Ayora or Puerto Baquerizo Moreno, but there are several interesting places that you can see without much difficulty; you can go by horse through the verdant highlands up to the awesome crater of **Sierra Negra**.

Puerto Villamil and around

PUERTO VILLAMIL, sitting under the cloud-draped slopes of the huge Sierra Negra volcano, was founded at the beginning of the nineteenth century and named after the general who annexed the islands for Ecuador in 1832. Now home to around a thousand settlers who fish or farm coffee and fruit in the highlands, the quiet port isn't well developed for tourism, and visitors are infrequent enough to stick out here. Just a small town of sandy roads and simple houses with fences of woven branches and cactus, fronted by a beautiful palm-fringed **beach**, it is nevertheless one of the most pleasant off-the-beaten track places to stay on the islands, boasting several good attractions nearby, which can be seen without guides.

Arrival, information and transport

EMETEBE **flights** arrive daily from San Cristóbal via Baltra when there is sufficient demand, and return the same day. Their office is on Conocarpus, opposite the Capitanía (☎05/529155). The airport is 3km outside town; there's no bus service, and taxis ($2) rarely wait here, so try and get a lift with someone. The hour walk along the road across the lava wastes is hot and uncomfortable. The INGALA **ferry** arrives from Santa Cruz every other Friday and returns on Sunday morning, while the *Estrella del Mar* runs weekly to Puerto Ayora, though it is currently being renovated; enquire at the *municipio* for the latest. For **fibras**, ask about availability at the Capitanía.

You can buy **maps** of town in Puerto Ayora, or pick up a thin guide to the island with a fold-out map of the town, by Jacinto Gordillo in *La Ballena Azul* hotel (see below) for about $5. The only travel agent is Isabela Travel (☎05/529207), on Conocarpus, opposite the Capitanía, who can arrange local **tours**, but don't believe claims that you need a guide to visit any of the places around Puerto Villamil; hotel owners are just as good at arranging tours and are often cheaper. There are no banks, but the *Ballena Azul* will **exchange** a small amount of low denomination travellers' cheques.

Accommodation

Although it's a small town, the **hotels** are generally of a good standard and cater to a range of budgets. Shaded by palms on a gorgeous stretch of beach at the east end of town, the attractive *Casa de Marita* (☎05/529238, ⓦwww.galapagosisabela.com) offers an array of tasteful colour-coded rooms, all bright, comfortable and spacious with lovely views of the bay, costing around the $50–90 mark, and coming with air conditioning, mini-fridge, private bath and hot water. The cosy "*habitación arlequín*" is a bit smaller and darker, but is a bargain at $12 a night. A fine complimentary breakfast is served around the kitchen table and other meals are available by arrangement in an attractive third-floor dining room with a lovely view of the sea. Bicycles and snorkelling equipment can be rented, and horse rides can be arranged.

Heading west along the beach from here you'll see the cabins of *Hostería Isabela de Mar* (☎05/529030, ⓦwww.hosteriaisabela.com.ec; ❹), which are lined by flowery borders and have large, plain rooms with private bath and hot water. Walk through the group of cabins, away from the beach, and you come to *La Ballena Azul* (same contact details) across the road, which is where you'll find the Swiss owner, plus a few budget rooms with shared bath and a restaurant serving tasty international food in a large dining room (by prior arrangement).

The Port and around

There's not a whole lot going on around the port, but Avenida Antonio Gil, the road heading west out of the port, passes small, secluded **lagoons** (*pozas*) – where you can spot waders, shore birds and sometimes flamingos – before a signposted track branches off north to the **Giant Tortoise Breeding Center**, about twenty minutes from the town centre. Work is ongoing here to breed the island's five unique tortoise subspecies, each based around the five largest volcanoes. On show are the rearing pens for the tiny hatchlings, and corrals for adult tortoises taken from the wild.

The westward road along the coast (ignoring the turn-off to the tortoise centre) continues past several peaceful beaches, including the **Playa de Amor**, where there are some scenic trails perfect for local wildlife spotting. After about two hours' walk, you'll come to **El Muro de las Lágrimas** (The Wall of Tears), a testament to the suffering of three hundred prisoners who toiled here in the 1940s and 1950s. They had the task of building their own prison, using the only material to hand – sharp-edged lava boulders. Driven on by guards, they made a wall some 190m long, 9m high and 6m wide at the base, but many died in the process. The prison colony was closed down after a revolt in 1959, the wall unfinished.

The best place to see marine life in the area is at **Las Islas de los Tiburones** (also known as **Las Tintoreras**), a handful of ragged black-lava grottoes poking out of the sea, a short boat ride from the port ($15–20). From the natural dock a trail leads past scuttling **marine iguanas** up to a lagoon and a narrow channel, where a "viewing gallery" allows you to see the sleek shapes of white-tipped **reef sharks** cruising back and forth. You can swim and snorkel in the lagoon – though don't swim in the channel itself as it's not big enough for both you and the sharks – or back at the landing site. If you're lucky you may see **rays** and **marine turtles**.

Sierra Negra

If you have a day to spare in Puerto Villamil, you can't do much better than go to the summit of **SIERRA NEGRA** (1490m), a monstrous **caldera**, some 10km in diameter and 200m deep, best reached by horse from **Santo Tomás**, a highland farming community 14km northwest of the port. The muddy trail leads over rugged terrain as you climb, and in the cool dry season, about all you'll make out in the thick mist are the introduced guava bushes dominating the slopes. Once on the rim, however, the thick clouds that you've been battling through curl dramatically over the southern lip before evaporating, leaving the gaping black crater stretching out in front of you. On the north side of the rim, you can walk to **Volcán Chico**, a collection of hissing volcanic cones that last erupted in 1963 and 1979. This side is almost always in the sun and gives stupendous views of Fernandina and the four volcanoes beyond the Perry Isthmus. It's an utterly barren landscape around Chico: red and black lava coloured by wispy sulphur deposits and, for vegetation, only the odd candelabra cactus and a few hardy shrubs clinging to the walls of the fumaroles to suckle on the volcanic steam.

The **bus** for Santo Tomás (a 1hr 30min trip) leaves on weekdays at 7am and noon, and on weekends at 6am and noon, returning at around 8.30am and 2.30pm. Getting to the crater from there takes about ninety minutes by horse or about three hours on foot, and a further thirty minutes walk to Volcán Chico. A **horse** and **guide** cost upwards of $12 for the day, though going in a group can work out cheaper; most hotel owners in town can arrange things for you. You don't need a qualified guide, but do go with someone who knows their way around, as it's very easy to get lost in the mist. Wear long trousers for the horse ride and take a long-sleeved top and rain jacket to keep warm.

Eating and nightlife

In addition to the fine international food on offer at *La Casa de Marita* and *La Ballena Azul*, both of which require arrangement in advance, other **eating** options include the *Costa Azul*, on the plaza, while on the west side of the square, and *La Choza*, across the street from the Capitanía, which are fairly pricey but serve good food. Better value is the *Kiosco El Caracol*, between the Capitanía and the police station, which does *almuerzos* for $2 and good, inexpensive seafood. *El Encanto de Pepa*, on Conocarpus, also does good fish (and more expensive chicken) in a comfortable little restaurant with plenty of character, that has the *Peña La Playita* at the back of it, a small bar and **disco**, which only gets going if there are enough people. On the beach near the *Cormorant Beach House*, *Beto's Bar* has lively music and does barbecues when there's a big enough crowd.

Isla Floreana

Arriving at the beginning of the nineteenth century, the deranged Patrick Watkins was the first in a long line of colonists to **FLOREANA**. As the sixth-largest island in the Galápagos (173 square kilometres), and just some 50km south of Santa Cruz, it was favoured as a potential colony for its good supply of fresh water up in the hills and tortoise meat. General Villamil began Ecuador's first official colony on the islands, the "**Asilo de la Paz**" ("Haven of Peace"), using convict labour in 1832, but he gave up after five years, handing the settlement over to the brutal Colonel José Williams. The colonel kept a pack of vicious dogs to keep his unruly charges at bay, and the Haven of Peace soon acquired the nickname of the "Kingdom of the Dogs", but the hounds weren't protection enough and Williams fled the island for his life after a rebellion in 1841. Almost thirty years later, José de Valdizán sought to rekindle the ill-fated venture, but after eight years his desperate settlers took to arms and fought each other. Valdizán and several others were killed, and the settlement fell apart. All this human interference has not been without effect on Floreana: its tortoise population is extinct, and the **Charles mockingbird** has been so severely predated by feral cats that it's now only found on the islets Enderby and Campeón off its northeastern shore.

Today, there's a small settlement on the western coast of the island, **Puerto Velasco Ibarra**, home to fewer than a hundred people. There's just one **place to stay**, the *Pensión Wittmer* (Ⓣ05/520150; ❻). Apart from this, it's a very quiet island, with little to see and do, but an unbeatable place to get away from it all. The port is not well connected: the INGALA **boat** passes by for a few hours once every month on a Sunday on its way from Isabela to Santa Cruz. Otherwise, you'll have to arrange a **fibra**; they leave from the other islands only infrequently.

7

The Guianas

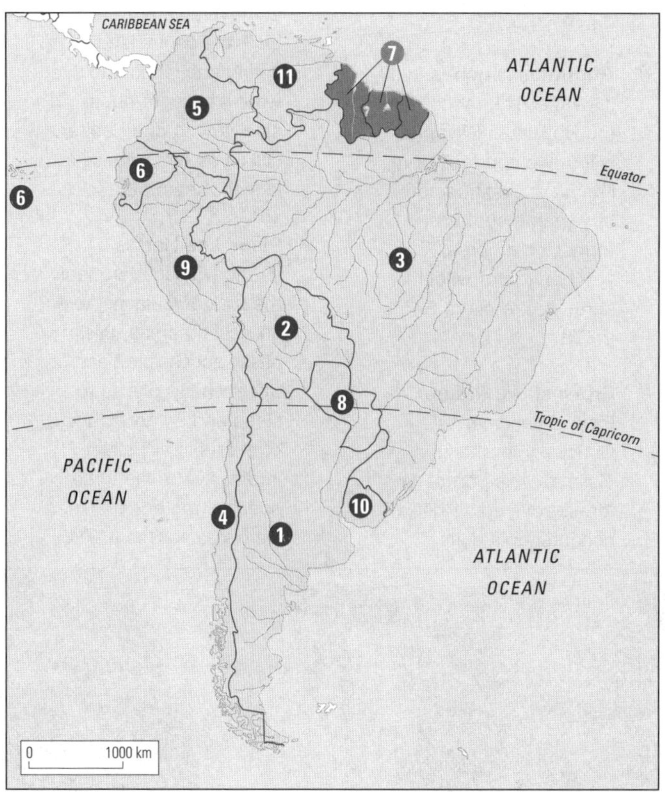

The Guianas highlights

* **Kaieteur Falls** (Guyana) Fly in for a fantastic view of the world's highest single drop waterfall – or walk there to get a sense of their isolation. See p.776

* **Rupununi ranches** (Guyana) The ranches of the Rupununi Savanna will make you feel more like an apprentice cowboy than a sunburnt tourist on a horse. If you can't spot wildlife here, you're blind. See p.778

* **Brownsberg Nature Park** (Suriname) Unusually for the Guianas, this part of its forest-covered, wildlife-rich interior is quite accessible for travellers of all budgets. See p.793

* **Centre Spatial Guyanais** (French Guiana) High technology in the middle of the jungle – the centre is fascinating enough just to see what it takes to put a satellite into orbit; better still if you can witness a launch. See p.803

* **Plage Les Hattes** (French Guiana) Arguably the pick of Guianas' turtle-nesting areas, this easily accessible beach offers cheap places to sleep and an abundance of the most visually impressive of the turtle species, the huge leatherback. See p.804

Introduction and basics

The **GUIANAS**, which comprise the independent nations of **Guyana** and **Suriname** and the French overseas *département* of **French Guiana**, are in some ways very un-South American. The official languages in the three countries are English (Guyana), Dutch (Suriname) and French (French Guiana) as opposed to Spanish, the continent's *lingua franca*, the result of the historical legacy of **English**, **Dutch** and **French colonizers**. This legacy has spawned an ethnically diverse population, with indigenous peoples, descendants of European colonizers and the slaves who manned their plantations, East Indians, Indonesians, South East Asian refugees and Haitians present across the region. The region's linguistic and ethnic diversity gives travelling in the Guianas a rather Caribbean feel, especially in the low-lying alluvial plain along the Atlantic Coast, where most of the population lives.

Tucked between Brazil's Amazonian region and the continent's northeast coast, the Guianas are as lush and verdant a place as you will find in South America. Between eighty and ninety percent of the area is covered by dense tropical forests, and rivers run through it in abundance (indeed, the Indian word *guiana* means "land of water"). Jaguar, pumas, caimans, iguanas, ocelots, tapirs and other diverse wildlife thrive in this environment, making the Guianas an excellent destination on any sort of eco-tourist itinerary you might have – it's not likely to be the cities, pleasant though they might be, that lure you here.

Where to go

With its mostly muddy beaches and murky waters (the result of silt deposits from the mouths of the region's many rivers), the Guianas' main attraction is their stunning interior of **pristine rainforest**. Although eco-tourism in this part of the world does not come cheaply, it's well worth trying to sample the nature either by staying at a **jungle lodge** or taking a **river trip**; you will have missed the region's finest asset if you don't. Aside from the rainforest, the greatest natural wonder comes in the form of the world's highest single-drop waterfall, **Kaieteur Falls**, made all the more dramatic by its isolated location in a tree-covered mountain range in southwestern Guyana. Eco-tourism also holds sway along the coast, where **Shell Beach** (Guyana), **Galibi Beach** (Suriname) and **Plage Les Hattes** (French Guiana) are three of the best sites in the world to observe various species of sea turtle laying their eggs. Visitors entering Guyana from Brazil should definitely take a day or two to explore the **Rupununi Savanna**: vast tracts of flatlands dotted with cowboy ranches and easy-to-spot wildlife.

While the towns take a backseat to the nature in the Guianas, **Georgetown**, the capital of Guyana, is a charming, if somewhat dilapidated, architectural gem, well worth exploring for a day or two. **Paramaribo** and **Cayenne**, the capitals of Suriname and French Guiana respectively, will probably not detain you long.

Perhaps the most unexpected thing in this land of rivers, trees, and chirping, slithering and screeching creatures is the **Centre Spatial Guyanais** at Kourou in French Guiana, where rocket-launch towers, silos and high-tech machinery help to send satellites into orbit from a clearing in the jungle.

When to go

Temperatures in the Guianas vary little from one country to another and from one month to the next: generally 20°C to 33°C, with a mean temperature of around 26°C (slightly hotter in the interior owing to the absence of the cooling coastal trade winds). This makes deciding when to plan a trip much more dependent on the vagaries of the dry and wet seasons. While the nature is undeniably lush and verdant during the **wet season**, road travel can be extremely difficult (if not impossible) along the many unsealed roads that govern land access to the interior. The big rains fall in French Guiana from mid-April to the end of June and, although drier in comparison, from April or May to around August in Guyana and Suriname. November to January or February can also be wet, but the rains are light compared with the periods mentioned above. Therefore, late winter and early spring are the optimum times for a visit – the more so because this is when the various **carnival** celebrations take place.

Red tape and visas

Visitors from Australia, Canada, Ireland, New Zealand, UK and the US do not need visas to enter **Guyana**. Where visas are necessary, make sure that you have a **passport** with at least six months' validity and two or three passport photos for the visa application; and note that occasionally proof of sufficient funds and tickets for onward travel will be required. The same immigration rules that apply in metropolitan France apply in **French Guiana**: Western Europeans, Canadians, Americans, Australians and New Zealanders do not require a visa, and are normally permitted to stay for up to three months; other nationals should consult their local French embassy.

Suriname is the most bureaucratic country in the Guianas – only nationals of Brazil, Chile, Israel, Japan, Malaysia, Philippines, Singapore, South Korea, Switzerland and CARICOM countries can enter without a visa. Overland travellers can obtain **visas** for Suriname in Cayenne, French Guiana and Georgetown, Guyana (see p.773 and 802). The cost of a tourist visa depends on your nationality and where it is issued – budget on US$30 and up for a single-entry visa. Multiple-entry visas are often only issued to those visiting Suriname on business – although rules differ from one mission to another. Irrespective of the stated validity of your visa (usually two months), your passport will be stamped for only a few days' stay at the point of entry. You must then make your way to the Immigration Office at van't Hogerhuysstraat, Nieuw Haven, Paramaribo (☎403101 or 403609) to get a **second stamp** in your passport authorizing you to remain in the country for a longer period. It is very important that you do not forget to get your passport stamped on entry from French Guiana – the immigration office at Albina (see p.795) is easy to miss if you do not take the ferry; those without an entry stamp in their passports will have problems trying to leave Suriname.

In Guyana, a **permit** may be necessary should you wish to visit an Amerindian village, and if you are on an organized excursion, the tour operator will have done all of the necessary paperwork. Independent travellers, however, should contact the Ministry of Amerindian Affairs in Georgetown (☎226-5167) to find out whether or not a permit is required.

Arrival

While overland travel between the three countries is relatively straightforward, the

Health

The three Guianas are included in the list of nations where **yellow fever** is endemic, and to travel from one to another will require (theoretically, at least) the presentation at border posts of a valid International Certificate of Vaccination or Revaccination Against Yellow Fever. For more details on yellow fever and its prevention, see Basics, p.30.

Depending on exactly where you will be travelling, **malaria** can be a risk in all three of the Guianas. In Guyana, the greatest risk is in the interior, while the danger on the coastal belt is much less. Likewise, in Suriname malaria is present in the southern part of the country, but not in Paramaribo and points north of latitude 5°N; you can really catch the disease anywhere in French Guiana. For more information on malaria and its prevention, see Basics, p.31.

Guianas are not the easiest – or the cheapest – region to reach in South America. The main **international gateways** are Georgetown (Guyana), Paramaribo (Suriname) and Cayenne (French Guiana). See "Arrival" sections of each country for details.

North American travellers will find the widest choice and best deals on flights to Georgetown, and those combining travel to the Guianas visits to the Caribbean should consider **BWIA's Caribbean airpass** (US$450), which includes Georgetown among its other destinations. The pass lasts for thirty days; you have to plan your itinerary at the time of booking, start in one of the airline's Caribbean destinations and not visit any place more than once (unless making a connection).

Visitors from Europe will find it easier to get to Suriname and French Guiana. Suriname's national carrier, Surinam Airways or SLM, has four direct flights a week to Paramaribo from Amsterdam, while French Guiana is linked to Paris by two or three flights daily on Air France, either directly or via the other overseas *départements* of Martinique and Guadeloupe.

Within South America, you can fly to the Guianas from Caracas, Venezuela (a useful option given that the border between Guyana and Venezuela is closed owing to a longstanding border dispute between the two countries), and Belém, Brazil. Flights also operate between Georgetown, Paramaribo and Cayenne. BWIA and Surinam Airways are the main carriers.

Travellers **arriving overland** from Brazil can enter Guyana at the town of Lethem, about 130km northeast of the Brazilian town of Boa Vista, or by crossing the Oyapok River to Saint-Georges-de-l'Oyapok in French Guiana (there is no border crossing between Brazil and Suriname). You can then continue by public transport to Georgetown and Cayenne respectively.

Getting around

Borders between the Guianas are marked by imposing rivers, and crossing involves taking a **ferry**. From Guyana to Suriname, cross the Corentyne River from Moleson Creek to South Drain near Nieuw Nickerie (see p.781); from Suriname to French Guiana, you will need to cross the Maroni River from Albina to Saint-Laurent-du-Maroni (see p.795).

For details on negotiating your way around each country, see the relevant "Getting around" section.

Accommodation

In Guyana and Suriname, accommodation in the main towns will normally consist of **hotels** and **guesthouses**, the difference between the two often being ambiguous. The former are generally larger and pricier, while the latter are sometimes in private homes and can be quite basic. No matter how luxurious or lamentable your lodgings, almost all rooms will come equipped with running water, mosquito nets and fans.

There are a number of **resorts** in Guyana – several of them on islands in the Essequibo River and in the interior not far from Georgetown – and **tourist ranches** in the Rupununi Savanna. Suriname also has several resorts around Paramaribo, primarily along the Suriname River, and **lodges** in the nature parks and reserves. Staying at these types of accommodation will usually be on an all-inclusive basis, and bookings are best made through tour operators, who will also arrange transfers; these are tricky if attempted independently.

Accommodation in French Guiana is tailored to businesspeople and package tourists, and somewhat limited in extent and variety. The few budget options are hopeless dives – and not cheap for travellers used to prices elsewhere in South America. The ever-so-French *gîte* (inexpensive lodgings typically in a rural setting) is available, though more commonly referred to as **carbets**; makeshift wooden huts on the beach or in the forest with hammocks slung to the rafters and adjacent ablution blocks. While it may only cost e10 or so for hammock space (sometimes hammock rental is extra), note that few are conveniently located, and the expense of getting to them will probably negate any savings made on sleeping costs.

Opening hours and public holidays

General opening hours don't differ too much across the three countries. In **Guyana**, banks are usually open Mon–Fri 8am–2pm, with an additional couple of hours Fri 3–5pm. This, at least, is the rule; some branches, particularly those outside Georgetown, could be closed during the week and open at weekends. Opening hours for government offices are Mon–Thurs 8am–noon & 1–4.30pm, Fri 8am–noon & 1–3.30pm; and for shops and other businesses, Mon–Fri 8am–4pm, Sat 8am–noon. In **Suriname**, banks are open Mon–Fri 9am–2pm; government offices Mon–Thurs 7am–3pm, Fri 7am–2.30pm; and shops and businesses Mon–Fri 9am–4.30pm, Sat 9am–1pm, although almost all close for at least a couple of hours' siesta in the afternoons. Apart from those in Paramaribo, it often seems that they never reopen. Meanwhile, in **French Guiana** most shops and businesses are open Mon–Sat 9am–noon & 4–7pm. Supermarkets usually stay open until later in the evenings (around 9.30pm) and sometimes do business Sun 9am–12.30pm. You may find that the mainly Chinese-owned convenience stores or *libre service* stay open during the afternoon siesta period.

Calendar of public holidays

January 1 New Year's Day
February 23 (Guyana) Republic Day
Early April, but varies, (French Guiana) Ash Wednesday
Early April, but varies, Good Friday
Early April, but varies, Easter Monday
May 1 Labour Day
May 5 (Guyana) Indian Heritage Day
May 29 (French Guiana) Ascension Day
June 9 (French Guiana) Whit Monday
June 10 (French Guiana) Slavery Day
July 1 National Union Day
July 7 (Guyana) Caribbean Day
July 14 (French Guiana) National Day
August 4 (Guyana) Freedom Day
November 11 (French Guiana) Armistice Day
November 25 (Suriname) Independence Day
December 25 Christmas Day

Guianas map

International Travel Maps, at 345 West Broadway, Vancouver V5Y 1P8 (☎604/879-3621, ⓦwww.itmb.com), produces a convenient Guianas map, which includes Guyana, Suriname and French Guiana in about as much detail as most visitors will require. The same company also has good individual maps of Guyana, Suriname and French Guiana (US$7.95 each).

The best plan of Georgetown is Georgetown "The Garden City" Tour Map and Business Guide, a foldout map which can be purchased from Rainforest Tours (see box on p.767) in the Hotel Tower lobby. The free map distributed by the tourist office in Paramaribo, Suriname (see p.782), has a plan of the capital (and Nieuw Nickerie) on one side and a basic overview of the country and its main points of interest on the other. Upon arrival in French Guiana, visit any tourist office to pick up one of several free country maps and street plans of major towns such as Cayenne, Kourou and Saint-Laurent-du-Maroni.

Books

Henri Charrière *Papillon*. Famous story based on the experiences of the author in the penal colonies of French Guiana. Wrongly convicted of murder in 1931 and sent to French Guiana to see out the rest of his days, Charrière finally escaped in the late 1940s.

Marc Herman *El Dorado: A Journey into the South American Rainforest on the Tail of the World's Largest Gold Rush*. Recently published story of adventure and commercialism in post-colonial Guyana. The book wonders how a country so rich in natural resources can remain so impoverished.

Steven Hilty et al *Birds of Venezuela*. Revamped version of the landmark 1978 publication. Very relevant to birders in Guyana and Suriname.

Deborah Layton *Seductive Poison*. Of the several books on the Jonestown massacre, this one tells the story from the perspective of one of its survivors.

History

The different cultures and loyalties of the Guianas make it hard to generalize about a shared history; instead, brief individual histories of each country can be found on p.768, p.785 & p.799.

7.1

Guyana

English-speaking, cricket-loving, rum-drinking **GUYANA** has rather more in common with the Caribbean than South America. Indeed, **Georgetown**, the capital city of the Guianas' largest and most populous country, offers wooden architecture and a cosmopolitan mix of black, white, East Indian and Asian faces, a testament to a colonial legacy and cultural diversity typical of Caribbean countries. The first giveaway, though, occurs when you stroll along Georgetown's sea wall and see a muddy stretch of beach and a murky brown sea where white sand and emerald waters should be sparkling under the sun's rays – this is no tropical paradise.

Yet while the coastal belt of Guyana, a fertile land of rice paddies, sugar plantations and most of the country's population, is culturally more akin to the islands to the north than the continent to the south, Guyana's real appeal lies firmly in the wonderful natural attractions in the interior. Here the country's vibe is unmistakably Amazonian. The vast expanse of tropical rainforest contains the world's highest single-drop waterfall, **Kaieteur Falls**, as well as the **Iwokrama Rainforest**, where the sustainable use of the forest for eco-tourism is a priority. To the far south of the country, the **Rupununi Savanna** offers a flat landscape, contrasting with the several highland regions in the interior, where you can stay at working ranches, play cowboy and stare at birds, caimans and giant river otters for days.

Information and websites

In the absence of an official tourist office, the **Tourism and Hospitality Association of Guyana** (THAG), 157 Waterloo St, Georgetown (Ⓣ225-0807, Ⓦwww.exploreguyana.com, Ⓔthag@networksgy.com), does its best to make as much information available to visitors as possible. Their best publication is *Explore Guyana*, a free yearly magazine that contains articles on the country's various attractions and up-to-date practical information. One of the best Guyana-related **websites**, Ⓦlanic.utexas.edu/la/sa/guyana, offers links to anything and everything to do with the country, while Ⓦwww.sdnp.org.gy/gallery/travel_guyana/index features specific information on various places in Guyana's nine regions. For news, politics, investment and official government information (including red tape and visas), Ⓦwww.guyana.org is essential.

Costs and money

Your greatest expense in Guyana will be travel. Few of the country's many wonderful natural attractions are on the bus routes and you will need to take internal flights and charter boats and 4WD vehicles to get to them. Budget travellers content on seeing Guyana from the back of a minibus and bypassing the more expensive eco-trips will find prices are quite reasonable. You can generally get a room in a guesthouse for around US$15, a standard restaurant meal for US$5, and travelling anywhere along the coastal belt will rarely cost more than US$10.

The currency of Guyana is the **dollar (G$)**, which comes in 20, 100, 500 1000, notes and 1, 5, 10 coins. While you can change cash and travellers' cheques at the major banks, the *cambios* in and around Georgetown's Stabroek Market are often a

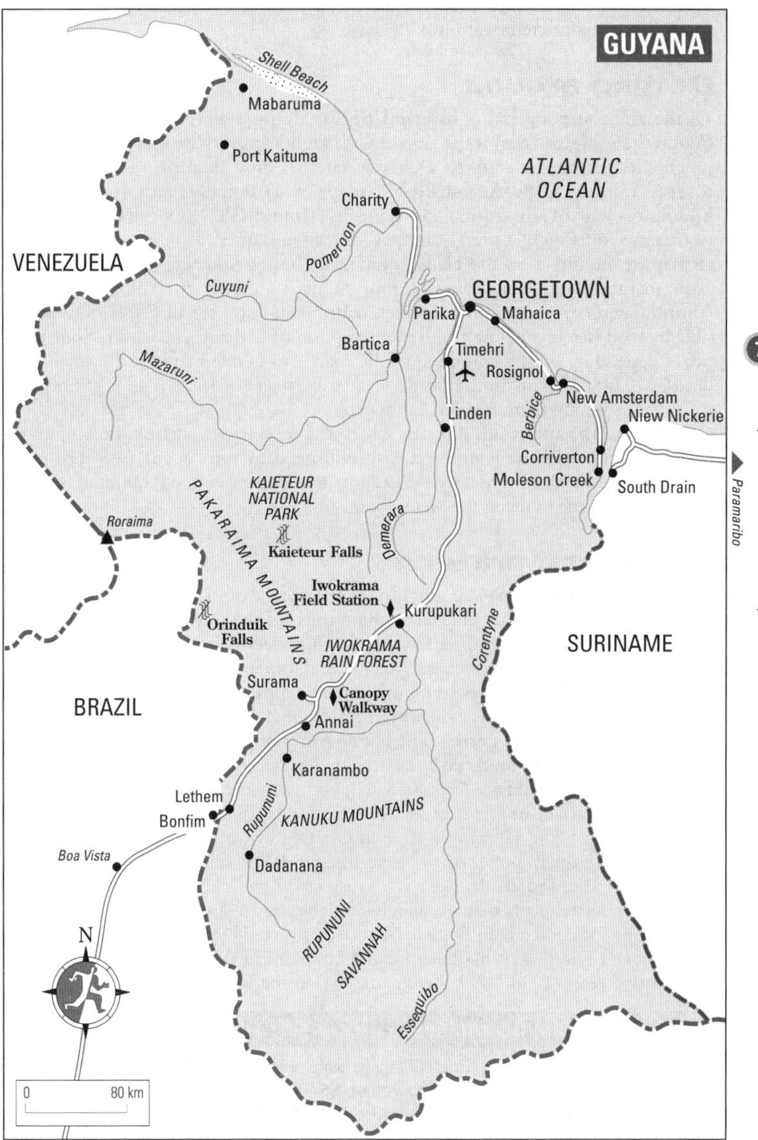

more convenient – and better value – for cash transactions. US dollars are the most widely accepted foreign currency; pounds sterling and euros are the next best, although try to carry at least some US dollars for places where other currencies are not accepted. **ATM machines** are appearing in Georgetown and other main towns, although none as yet accept credit cards. Scotiabank in Georgetown will give you a cash advance on your credit card, while tour operators and several of the more upscale hotels and restaurants accept plastic. Generally, however, you should not rely too much on your credit card in Guyana

Getting around

Of the companies operating **internal flights**, Transguyana Airways (Ⓣ222-2525, Ⓦwww.transguyana.com) is the largest, with flights to every imaginable hamlet and jungle clearing in the country. One-way fares to most destinations of interest to tourists from the **Ogle Aerodrome**, Georgetown's domestic airport about seven kilometres east of the capital, are typically around G$21,000. Planes are small (sometimes only eight-seaters), and you can often request to be dropped off at an airstrip in the direction the plane is going (although you will still pay full fare). Note that the baggage allowance on most flights is a measly nine kilograms.

From Georgetown's Stabroek Market, **minibuses** leave for all destinations accessible by road (see box below), with the exception of Lethem. The eleven-hour journey – depending on the condition of the road – to Lethem and the Brazilian border (G$10,000) departs from outside *Rockies International Hotel* at 43 Light St daily at 7pm – assuming there is sufficient demand.

To explore the attractions through which the road passes, such as the Rupununi Savanna and Iwokrama Rainforest, you will need to **rent a car** (see "Listings", p.773, for agencies); be sure it's a 4WD. Note that driving in the Rupununi Savanna is severely impeded during the wet season.

Eating and drinking

Guyanese cuisine is varied enough in style (a result of its ethnic diversity), if not in the ingredients it uses. Chicken is ubiquitous – fried in the typical Creole way, curried to suit East Indian palates or with ginger, lemon or some other Chinese accompaniment. Rice is never very far behind, boiled with beans (usually black-eye beans), okra and perhaps some other meat to make a traditional Creole *cook-up*, or fried in the Chinese style. Other staples include *chow mein* and *roti*, a fried pancake used to mop up curries. The lasting Amerindian contribution to Guyanese cuisine is *pepperpot*, a blood-red meat stew made with cassava juice or *casareep* and served mainly for breakfast. *Tomapot*, which you will only find in Amerindian communities, is a variant of *pepperpot* that uses fresh *casareep* as opposed to the recycled stuff in *pepperpot*. The *Georgetown Club* in Georgetown has apparently had a pot of *casareep*, known for its preservative properties, on the go for over a hundred years.

The locally brewed Banks Beer is a satisfactory and cheaper alternative to the range of imported beers that are widely available, but if you can get your hands on it, the tipple of choice is El Dorado Special Reserve fifteen-year-old rum. Brewed by Demerara Distillers, it has been judged best rum in the world for a record four consecutive years (1998, 1999, 2000 and 2001) at the International Wine and Spirit

Minibuses from Georgetown

Mahaica (Ogle Aerodrome) Route #44, opposite clock tower, 20min (another 15min-walk from the main road to the aerodrome), G$40.
Moleson Creek (Suriname border) Route # 63, Ave of the Republic, at Robb, 3hr, G$1000.
Parika (for Bartica) Route #32, catch ferry across the Demerara River from next to the clock tower, 1hr, G$200 including ferry crossing.
Rosignol (for New Amsterdam) Route #50, Ave of the Republic, at Robb, 1.5hr, G$500.
Timehri (for Cheddi Jagan International Airport) Route #42, opposite clock tower, 1hr, G$160.

Tour operators

The simplest – and in the long run often the most economical – way of getting to see the interior is by booking an excursion with a **tour operator**. Wilderness Explorers, Cara Suites, 176 Middle St, Georgetown (☎227-7698, Ⓦwww.wilderness-explorers.com), is a supremely well-organized outfit, which can arrange trips to virtually all of the country's places of interest. Rainforest Tours, Hotel Tower, 74–75 Main St, Georgetown (☎227-5632, Ⓦwww.rainforesttoursgy.com), is run by an extremely knowledgeable former miner and is the place to go if you are interested in overland treks to Kaieteur Falls. For the turtles at Shell Beach, get in touch with Shell Beach Adventures, *Le Meridien Pegasus*, Georgetown (☎225-4483, Ⓦwww.sbadventures .com). Rates to the most accessible destinations are not usually less than US$100 a day, which includes transportation, food, lodging and guides. They can be considerably more if internal flights and the like are required.

Competition. The five- and ten-year-old stuff is not nearly the same. The main brands of soft drinks are sold everywhere, along with regional offerings such as the multiflavoured Busta (from Trinidad and Tobago) and Guyana's very own, perfectly drinkable I-Cee. Despite its off-putting brown coloration, tap water is drinkable; fragile stomachs, however, will prefer bottled water such as Tropical Mist.

Mail, telecommunications and media

Sending letters and postcards from Guyana is cheap (G$20 to anywhere in the world), but delivery times can be slow. There are **post offices** in most towns, although not always in the most obvious of places.

You can make local, national and international **telephone calls** with phone cards issued by the Guyana Telephone and Telegraph Company. There are phone booths in Georgetown for making collect calls to the UK, US and Canada. Many of the Internet cafés in Georgetown (see "Listings", p.774) give you the option of making overseas calls via the Internet. These calls can work out considerably cheaper than using cards and making collect calls. Typical rates to North America, Western Europe, Australia and New Zealand are 30–40¢ per minute.

Georgetown is awash with **Internet cafés**. Not all of them have great connections, but they are cheap and quite satisfactory for keeping in touch by e-mail. Outside the capital there may be one or two places to get online, but obviously not in towns where there are no telephone lines.

The three daily **newspapers**, *Stabroek News*, *Chronicle* and *Kaieteur News*, are all good for keeping in touch with local goings-on. Twenty-plus **television** stations mainly show imported US and Indian programmes, while the main **radio** stations are the government-run Voice of Guyana, Radio Roraima and 98.1FM, which is good for music.

Festivals

Various festivals are celebrated in Guyana. **Mashramani**, a colourful, carnival-style celebration with float parades, calypsos, steel bands and dancing in the streets, is usually held on Republic Day. The Hindu festivals of **Holi Pagwah** and **Divali** are also celebrated (usually in March and October or November respectively), along with various Muslim holidays such as **Id al-Fitr** (the end of Ramadan) and **Yum an-Nabi** (the birth of the Prophet).

Crime and personal safety

While the police struggle to cope with the almost daily incidents in Georgetown and the built-up areas along the coast west and particularly east of the capital, it must be pointed out that Guyana is hardly a war zone. **Serious crime** is along this relatively short stretch of the coast – an area of the country not greatly visited by tourists – and at no time have the bandits specifically targeted foreigners. Guyana is essentially a very safe country with honest, welcoming people, and the current problem is the exception rather than the rule. Even in Georgetown, a friendly city with a bad reputation, you should have no major problems provided that you act with common sense and a certain amount of caution. Avoid displaying your wealth for everyone to see, take taxis after dark and, most importantly, seek local advice about where not to go.

History and culture

Long before European settlers arrived in Guyana, tribes of **Warrau**, **Arawak** and **Carib** inhabited the highlands. While the Spanish were the first to lay claim to the land, sighted by Christopher Columbus in 1498 it was the Dutch who started to build settlements and trading posts in the interior in around 1580. Over the course of the next century, they imported African slaves to work on the sugarcane plantations, and the colonists gradually moved their settlements towards the more fertile coastal plains. The Dutch lost de facto control of the colony to the more powerful British in 1796, who then formally purchased Essequibo, Demerara and Berbice in 1814 and united them in 1831 as the colony of **British Guiana**. A few years later, slavery was abolished, and emancipated blacks left the plantations and moved to the towns, primarily on the coastal plain. To fill the labour shortage on the plantations, thousands of indentured workers from India (and to a lesser extent Portugal and China) were brought to Guyana, a practice which continued until 1917. As a result, much of the rural population is of East Indian or Asian origin, while in the urban areas the majority is black.

These ethnic divisions were to play a considerable role in the shaping of post-colonial Guyana. The first elections under universal suffrage were held in 1953 and won by the **People's Progressive Party** (PPP) led by **Cheddi Jagan**. However, five months later the British suspended the constitution that had permitted these elections and sent troops to Guyana, fearing Jagan was about to establish a communist state. This intervention led to a split in the PPP along racial lines: Jagan and his largely East Indian supporters led the PPP, while **Forbes Burnham** drew support from the African-descended population to form the **People's National Congress** (PNC). Elections under a new system of proportional representation were held in 1964 as a prelude to Guyanese independence, and although the PPP won the largest number of seats, it was the PNC in coalition with a smaller party who led the country to independence in May 1966. Guyana was proclaimed a cooperative republic within the Commonwealth on February 23, 1970.

Through a series of dubious elections and mounting political violence Burnham and the PNC remained in power until his death in 1985, his rule marked by ultra-socialist policies aimed at making Guyana self-sufficient. Imports of basic foodstuffs such as wheat were stopped, and long queues were common at shops, petrol stations and the like. In 1992, after the first Guyanese election since 1964 to be internationally recognized as free and fair, Jagan and the PPP finally got their chance to rule after 28 years of PNC government. Since Jagan's death in 1987, Samuel Hinds, Janet Jagan (Cheddi's American-born wife) and most recently the 39-year-old **Bharrat Jagdeo** have continued the PPPs market-orientated policies, although opposition parties continue to gripe about electoral fraud. The 2001 election, monitored by an international team of observers and won by Jagdeo, was declared generally free and fair, though the familiar political tensions between PPP-favouring East Indians and pro-PNC blacks were evident in street demonstrations in Georgetown. Jagdeo and his PNC counterpart, **Desmond Hoyte**, established joint committees after the election to restore public confidence in the political process and tackle some of the country's problems, of which the steady rise in violent crime and the decline of the bauxite industry are two of the more serious. Hoyte died in December 2002, to be replaced as leader of the PNC by **Robert Corbin**. Time will tell how he and Jagdeo get along.

Culture

Guyana's **cultural life** is driven by its ethnic diversity and colonial past. Just over half of the population of "the land of six peoples" is of East Indian origin, around forty per cent is African, seven per cent Amerindian and one per cent Portuguese or Chinese. Hinduism, Islam and Christianity all have their places in Guyanese society and, although relatively small and apolitical, the Amerindian communities, who inhabit the country's interior, are generally given a great deal of cultural recognition and protection. Politically, relations between Guyana's dominant ethnic groupings are often strained; day-to-day life, however, is relatively harmonious given the diversity of Guyana's cultural composition.

The official **language** in Guyana is English. Most people also speak Guyanese Creole – Afro-Guyanese in the case of the blacks and Indo-Guyanese for the East Indians. Various Amerindian languages – notably Macushi, Patamona and Akawaio – can be heard on visits to indigenous villages in the interior.

Georgetown

Set on the east bank of the Demerara estuary, **GEORGETOWN**, easily the country's largest city with around 200,000 inhabitants, was designed largely by the Dutch in the eighteenth century when they held sway in the town, then called Stabroek. When the British took over in 1796, it was renamed Georgetown.

Most travellers who visit the city are in transit between Brazil and Suriname and tend not to stay longer than they have to – which is a mistake. For all the talk – legitimate as it may be – about rising crime rates, Georgetown remains the most attractive of the Guianas' three capital cities by quite a wide margin. While the city's epithet of the "Garden City of the Caribbean" is slightly misleading, there are enough green spaces to provide an antidote to the hectic pace that prevails in the main market, the soul of the city. However, the real draw of Georgetown is its magnificent colonial wooden architecture, much of it in a dilapidated state but enchanting nonetheless.

Arrival and getting around

The main airport **Cheddi Jagan International** lies in Timehri about forty kilometres south of Georgetown (for information on getting into the city, see p.766). Be aware that there is a **departure tax** of G$2500 (or the US$ equivalent), which can be paid either at the airport or when reconfirming your ticket in Georgetown at least three days before departure. Domestic flights arrive at the **Ogle Aerodrome**, about seven kilometres east of the capital. You can catch a minibus into the centre (see box on p.766) or take a taxi for around G$800.

Safety in Georgetown

Provided you take **sensible precautions**, the central parts of Georgetown, where the majority of shops, services and attractions are concentrated, are safe to explore on foot by day. After dark, you are well advised to take taxis to avoid potential problems. Parts of town that can get a bit edgy include the Seawall Road after dark, the Tiger Bay area (on the banks of the Demerara, north of the market) and the ghetto of Albouystown (south of the centre). While tourists might realistically consider taking a stroll along the sea wall after dark, it is unlikely that they would find any reason for going to Tiger Bay and Albouystown – unless they are looking for trouble.

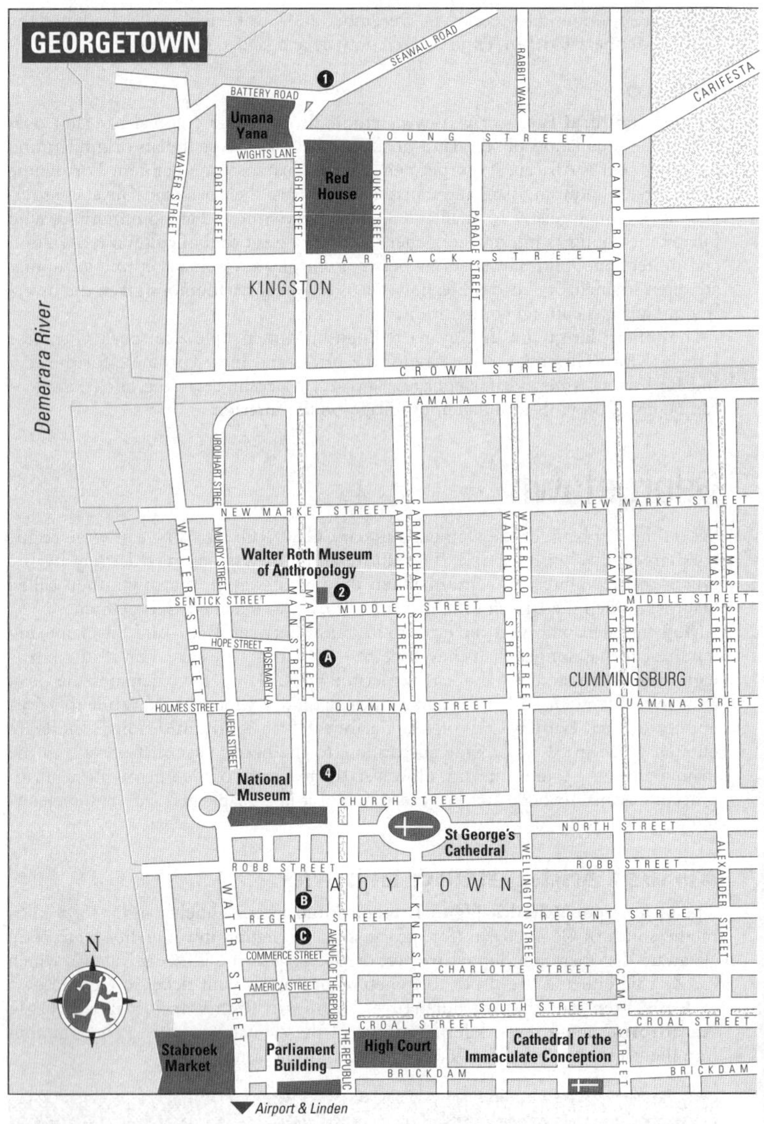

Getting around Georgetown is easy and cheap. Minibuses leave from Stabroek Market for the city's various neighbourhoods and suburbs (around G$30), while taxis are easily found outside the main hotels, in the market and at many other locations. For short trips around town expect to pay G$200–220.

Accommodation

There is no lack of **accommodation** in Georgetown for all types of budget. The

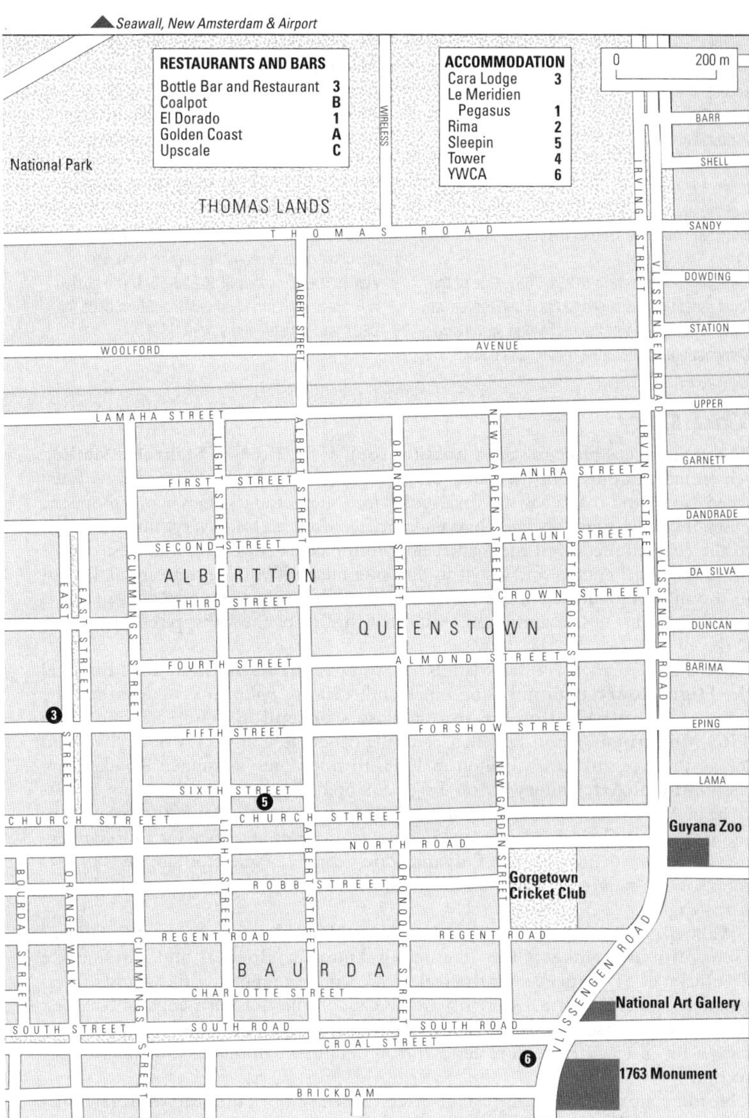

choices can basically be broken down into hotels and guesthouses, the former being generally larger and more expensive than the latter.

Cara Lodge 294 Quamina St ⓣ225-5301, ⓦwww.carahotels.com/cara_lodge. A hotel with character in a city where the accommodation options can be somewhat monotonous, the *Cara Lodge* offers spacious rooms with a/c and attractive wooden floors in an illustrious house that was once the focal point of high-society events in Georgetown. ❽

Le Meridien Pegasus Seawall Rd ⓣ225-2853, ⓦwww.lemeridien-pegasus.com. The only business hotel of a truly international standard in Guyana. Some of the perks for which you will pay handsomely are the gourmet restaurant, a large swimming pool, tennis courts, a fitness centre and access to the nearby Lusignan Golf Club. ❾

Rima 92 Middle St ⓣ225-7401, ⓔrima@networksgy.com. The self-proclaimed "cleanest guesthouse in town" does indeed have fresh, tidy rooms. A central location and homely feel are also good reasons for staying here, although note that none of the rooms are en suite. ❹

Sleepin 151 Church St ⓣ231-7667. One of the most recent guesthouses to open in Georgetown *Sleepin* is also one of the best value for money. Compact but comfortable rooms, all en suite, the cheapest with fans and TV, the more expensive with a/c. ❹

Tower 74–75 Main St ⓣ227-2011, ⓦwww.hoteltowerguyana.com. The oldest and second largest hotel in Georgetown still enjoys an unbeatable location a few minutes' walk from many of the city's major attractions. Comfortable rooms, a large swimming pool – access costs G$1000 a day for non-guests – and friendly staff are other good reasons for staying here. ❼

YWCA 106 Brickdam St ⓣ226-5610 The hostel welcomes both men and women. Dorm beds for US$7 and private rooms from US$20.

The City

The most logical place to start a **walking tour** of the city is at **Stabroek Market**, which radiates out from the banks of the Demerara River. Dominated by a four-faced clock, the market is the focal point for Georgetown's merchants, shoppers, buses, moneychangers, beggars and pickpockets. You can find everything here – go to the covered section of the market next to the clock tower for your best chance of finding local crafts – and lose it in the same breath if you are not careful. Busiest in the morning and uncomfortably hot during the early afternoon, the market is best visited in the late afternoon. Note that this is not the safest place to be after dark.

Leaving the market via Brickdam Road, you pass the **Parliament Building** and the **High Court**, both imposing nineteenth-century colonial structures, and the rather dour **Cathedral of the Immaculate Conception** before arriving at the **1763 Monument**, a not altogether flattering tribute to Cuffy, an African slave who led an unsuccessful slave rebellion in 1763. Turn left onto Vlissingen Road, where the **National Art Gallery** (Mon–Fri 10am–5pm, Sat 2–6pm; free) offers exhibitions of Amerindian art and sculpture. A little further on, you'll find the entrance to the **Botanical Garden** (daily 6am–5.30pm; free), a pleasant place for a more relaxing stroll. On its grounds, the **Guyana Zoo** (daily 7.30am–5.30pm; G$100) features a wide range of South American birds and mammals, including the massive harpy eagle.

Walk back towards the city centre along North Road, passing the famous **Georgetown Cricket Club** (commonly known as Bourda), and you'll arrive eventually at **St George's Cathedral**, at 43.5 metres reputedly the world's tallest wooden building. Further down North Road, on the northern edge of Stabroek Market, the **National Museum** (Mon–Fri 9am–5pm, Sat 9am–noon; free) contains a bit of everything, from historical and cultural exhibits to a natural history section.

Heading north now along Main Street, another museum, the **Walter Roth Museum of Anthropology** (Mon–Thurs 8am–4.30pm, Fri 8am–3.30pm; free), is also worth a look for its Amerindian artefacts. Main Street eventually becomes High Street and bends to the right when it reaches the Atlantic coast. On your right is the **Red House**, former home of Cheddi Jagan (see p.768), famous for its bright red wallaba shingles, and to the left **Umana Yana** is a somewhat incongruous Amerindian thatched hut, or *benab*, built in the 1970s as a "meeting place for the people". Following the coastal road or Seawall Road, you will get your first glimpse of the Dutch-built dyke or **sea wall** that protects Georgetown from flooding and continues for some 450 kilometres along the Atlantic coast of Guyana and Suriname. While this is a popular spot for jogging and kite flying, it should be avoided after dark.

Eating and drinking

Head to the enclosed part of Stabroek Market for cheap, tasty curry and *roti* lunches at the many **cook shops**. Along with the places listed below, Georgetown has its share of **fast-food** restaurants, including international chains. **Liquor restaurants** (local watering holes) are dotted all over town and are the place to go should you crave drunken conversations about cricket; most close after the last drinker has stumbled out of the door. It's best to get a taxi if going out after dark.

Bottle Bar and Restaurant Cara Lodge ⓣ225-5301. The real attraction here is the attractive, airy dining room bedecked with plants and the hundreds of bottles from which the restaurant takes its name. The pricey house specials include salsa snapper, prawns *thermidor* and tropical chicken curry, which are ever popular with tourists and expats alike.

Coalpot 17 Hincks St ⓣ225-8556. Lovely little dining room with wicker chairs, plants and a/c. Well-balanced and copious meals featuring standard Guyanese fare from around G$600. Friendly service to boot.

El Dorado in *Le Meridien Pegasus* ⓣ225-2856. The swankiest of the *Pegasus'* several eateries serves up *confit de canard*, beef tenderloin and other gourmet dinners. Main dishes start at around G$2000.

Golden Coast 62 Main St ⓣ231-7360. One of the more recent additions to the city's wealth of Chinese restaurants, *Golden Coast's* menu goes way beyond the standard chow mein and fried rice to include favourites such as lemon chicken, sweet and sour pork, and various meat and seafood dishes in black bean sauce.

Upscale 32–33 Regent St, at Hincks ⓣ225-4721. At first glance, it looks chic and, well, upscale. On closer inspection, the fancy drapes cover plastic chairs and main dishes of chow mein, curry and the like cost a mere G$400. A good place to escape the chaos of the market and pretend to be dining in real class.

Nightlife and entertainment

The crime problems do not seem to have dampened Georgetown's party spirit. The **bars** and **clubs** along Sheriff Street, the city's most famous place for nightlife, continue to be busy with drinkers, dancers and pool players, while several other nightspots are worth checking out, especially at weekends when they are at their liveliest. The two most popular clubs on Sheriff Street are *Buddy's Pool Hall and Nightclub* (cover charge G$1000) and *Sheriff* (G$500). *Buddy's* attracts a mainly East Indian clientele of beautiful people, who come to strut their stuff on a flashy, air-conditioned dancefloor, safe in the knowledge that a metal detector at the entrance ensures that no guns, knives or other offensive weapons will interrupt their revelries. There are no such guarantees at *Sheriff*, the club of choice for blacks who enjoy bumping and grinding to Afro-Caribbean sounds – a raw and raucous place in comparison to the somewhat rarefied atmosphere at *Buddy's*. Elsewhere, try the *Sidewalk Café and Jazz Club*, 176 Middle St, where afternoon tea with fashion shows and stand-up comedy on Wednesdays, live jazz on Thursdays and karaoke on Fridays have made it a firm fixture on the Georgetown entertainment circuit.

Listings

Banks and cambios Try Swiss House Cambio, 25A Water St or Confidential Cambio, 29 Lombard St. The only bank in Georgetown which gives cash advances on credit cards (Visa and MasterCard) is Scotiabank, Robb Street, at Avenue of the Republic. ATM machines only accept cards issued by local banks.

Car rental Saloon cars are available for US$40 a day from Budget Rent-A-Car, 75 Church St, Georgetown (ⓣ225-5595).

Embassies and consulates Brazil, 308 Church St ⓣ225-7970; Canada, Young St, at High ⓣ227-2081, ⓦwww.dfait-maeci.gc.ca/guyana; France, 7 Sheriff St ⓣ226-5238; Netherlands, 61 Ave of the Republic ⓣ227-4085; Suriname, 171 Peter Rose St, at Crown ⓣ226-7844, ⓔsurnemb @gol.net.gy (consular section Mon, Wed & Fri 8am–3pm; visa issued in the afternoon if application submitted in the morning); UK, 44 Main St ⓣ226-5881, ⓦwww.britain-in-guyana.org; USA, Young St, at Duke ⓣ225-4900, ⓦgeorgetown.usembassy.gov; Venezuela 296 Thomas St ⓣ226-6749.

Resorts near Georgetown

Good for day-trips or overnight stays away from the city, several **resorts** lie a short distance from Georgetown on the banks of pleasant creeks in jungle settings. All offer swimming, watersports, nature walks and other eco-related activities.

Arrowpoint c/o Roraima Airways, 101 Cummings St, Georgetown ⓣ225-9648, ⓦwww.roraimaairways.com/arrowpoint. A 35min boat trip from the international airport up the Demerara River to Kamuni Creek, *Arrowpoint* is situated in the Amerindian reservation of Santa Mission. Some of the activities on offer are visits to the village of Santa Mission as part of a guided mountain-bike tour, canoeing and walks in the jungle (by day and night). All-inclusive day-trips around US$60 per person; US$120 per person overnight.

Emerald Tower 74–75 Main St, Georgetown ⓣ227-2011, ⓦwww.hoteltowerguyana.com/emeraldtower. About 45min from Georgetown on Madewini Creek, this resort features a long sandy beach, swimming in the black-water creek and accommodation in wooden cabins intelligently constructed for maximum shade amongst the trees of the surrounding rainforest. Doubles from US$85, day-trips from US$5 (without meals), lunch and dinner US$10 each.

Timberhead Le Meridien Pegasus Seawall Rd, Georgetown ⓣ225-2853, ⓦwww.lemeridien-pegasus.com/timberhead. Located, like *Arrowpoint*, in the Amerindian reserve of Santa Mission, the resort overlooks savanna land bordering Pokerero Creek and offers three wooden cabins with a total of seven rooms. *Timberhead* has played host to notables such as Queen Elizabeth II and former US President Jimmy Carter. All visits are inclusive of transportation, meals, drinks and activities. Day-trips US$55 per person; US$105 per person overnight.

Internet cafés *Central Net Surf*, Central Garage, Avenue of the Republic, allows you to buy Internet time that does not have to be used all in one go; or the Internet café attached to *Upscale Restaurant*, 32–33 Regent St, at Hincks (Mon–Sat 8am–11pm).

Post office on North Road at the northern end of the market.

Telephone services Booths on Church Street next to the National Library, where you can make collect calls to the UK, US and Canada.

West toward Venezuela

While most travellers leave Georgetown on the southeast road for the Suriname border, there are several worthwhile things to see and do in the other direction. Minibuses frequently travel the forty kilometres or so to Parika, from where you can catch a river-taxi to the mining town of **Bartica**. However, the most obvious attraction between Georgetown and the Venezuelan border is **Shell Beach** in the extreme northwest of the country, the best place in Guyana to observe egg-laying turtles. Shell Beach is accessible from the town of **Mabaruma**, which in turn can only be reached by flying or taking the ferry from Georgetown. There is no legal border crossing to Venezuela.

Bartica

The crime wave on the coast, ethnic tensions, drug wars and the country's various other deterrents to tourism seem very far removed from **BARTICA**, Guyana's most enjoyable town. One of the country's oldest settlements, situated on the confluence of the Essequibo, Mazaruni and Cuyuni rivers, it remains an important hinterland mining town. The town's population, a gritty mix of gold and diamond miners and lumberjacks, is rough, raucous (witness the preponderance of bars and nightclubs) but extremely friendly. The bandits are in Georgetown; Bartica is as safe and welcoming as you could hope for.

Apart from strolling along the town's streets and avenues soaking up the laid-back atmosphere, most of the things to see are on and around the Essequibo and Mazaruni rivers. All that remains of **Kyk-Over-Al** (See-Over-All), the seventeenth-century, Dutch-built fort on one of the 365 islands in the Essequibo, is an arch. After defeat by the English in 1676, the Dutch moved from the fort to a site on the banks of the Mazaruni River, which is now occupied by **Mazaruni Prison**. Further upstream, on the banks of the Mazaruni River, **Marshall Falls** (G$1000 entrance fee; G$6000 overnight in hammocks with meals) is a reasonably pleasant waterfall, where, despite the wine-coloured water (the result of leaves and mineral deposits), there is good swimming at all times of the year. To visit these and other river attractions try Bartica-based Bhagwandas Balkarran, Lot 2, Triangle St (☎455-2544 or 621-0469), who gives guided tours in his boat for G$15,000 (the boat seats around six people).

Practicalities

Getting to Bartica from Georgetown involves catching minibus #32 (45min, G$200 including the Demerara River crossing) from Georgetown to Parika, from where river-taxis (1hr; G$1000) leave when full to Bartica. There is also a ferry that takes five or six hours, leaving Parika on Thursdays and Saturdays and returning from Bartica on Fridays and Sundays.

The two **places to stay**, one next to the other at the end of First Avenue, cater to the prince and pauper of travellers. The posh *Hotel Castillo* (☎455-3042; ❹) offers air-conditioned rooms, phones and hot and cold water; the cheaper option, *Modern Hotel* (☎455-2301; ❷), has all the basics, but no air conditioning. Both have large and noisy **bars** downstairs. For **restaurants**, try *D'N'I Restaurant* on Second Avenue (☎455-3088) for Chinese and Creole dishes, as well as good pastries, or *Kool Breeze*, the popular tourist hang-out overlooking the river, which is also a good spot for a sundowner.

Mabaruma

The main reason for coming to **MABARUMA**, a one-hour flight from Georgetown, is to visit the nearby turtle-nesting site at Shell Beach. This said, you

The Jonestown massacre

The chilling events of November 18, 1978, when over nine hundred members of a sect died in an apparent mass suicide in a jungle clearing in northwestern Guyana, have been the subject of many books and theories. What is undisputed is that **Reverend Jim Jones**, the leader of a sect called **The People's Temple**, had, in 1974, chosen Guyana to establish a self-sufficient community of about 1100 based on utopian socialist ideals and which he had humbly named Jonestown. Continually referring to an unnamed enemy that would come to destroy Jonestown and all it represented, he would tell his flock that "revolutionary suicide" was the only way to combat this threat.

When Congressman Leo Ryan and a party of journalists and concerned family members came to Jonestown in November 1978 to investigate alleged human rights abuses, the enemy had apparently arrived. Ryan was shot and killed at Port Kaituma airstrip as he tried to leave, while at about the same time back at Jonestown the men, women and children of The People's Temple were drinking poison. A total of 913 people died in the mass suicide, although a Guyanese coroner's report suggested that as many as seven hundred of the victims had been forcibly killed. Indeed, many, including Jones himself, died as a result of gunshot wounds, leading to doubts as to whether the charisma of one man had been enough to persuade so many people to commit suicide. Nowadays the Jonestown site is covered by forest, and there is no monument or other reminder of its existence.

could quite easily spend a day or two relaxing in this quiet town pleasantly situated on a hill overlooking the rainforest and Kaituma River. Mabaruma is the administrative centre of Region 1, and around ninety per cent Amerindian.

There are basically two ways of **getting to** Mabaruma from Georgetown: fly or take the boat. Transguyana Airways has four flights a week (Mon, Wed, Fri & Sat; G$12,500 one-way). The ferry *Kimbia* (one-way G$1,500) leaves Georgetown fortnightly on Wednesdays at 1pm, taking roughly 24 hours to reach Kumaka, Mabaruma's river port. The return to Georgetown is on Saturdays at 8am, subject to delays.

Practicalities

Accommodation options also boil down to two choices. The *Government Guest House*, in the centre of town (Ⓣ777-5091; ❷), has only eight basic but comfortable rooms and fills up quickly with civil servants, so making a reservation is a good idea. *Broomes Guest House*, halfway between the town centre and Kumaka (Ⓣ777-5006; ❸), is a good alternative, with pleasant, self-contained rooms, the east-facing ones with balconies and good views of the forest and Kumaka.

Finding something to **eat** can be a problem in Mabaruma. Apart from a few snackettes in Kumaka and *Broomes Shop*, about 400 metres before *Broomes Guest House*, where you can get boxes of chicken and fried rice, the pickings are thin.

Shell Beach

Strictly speaking, **SHELL BEACH** extends from the mouth of the Pomeroon River to the Venezuelan border, a distance of around 160 kilometres. The part that visitors will be interested in, however, is the dozen or so beaches, composed of seashells rather than sand, a short boat-ride from Mabaruma. From around March to August, four species of turtle – leatherback, green, olive ridley and hawksbill – come to these beaches at night to lay their eggs. During the day, there is good birdwatching, for such species as corri-corris, scarlet ibises, egrets, herons and the occasional flamingo.

The Guyana Marine Turtle Conservation Society has a field station at Almond Beach, where there is basic **accommodation** in tents. The simplest way to arrange a visit is to organize it all with a tour operator such as Shell Beach Adventures, *Le Meridien Pegasus*, Georgetown (Ⓣ225-4483, Ⓦwww.sbadventures.com). If you are intent on going it alone, you must look in Kumaka, Mabaruma's river port, for a boat to take you to Shell Beach and back. You might be lucky and find transport carrying provisions upriver to the beach communities; otherwise, count on paying at least G$20,000 return to charter your own boat.

South to Brazil

Connecting Georgetown to the Brazilian border crossing in the southwest of the country is a stretch of mostly unsealed road that traverses pristine rainforests and wide-open plains. Guyana's most famous attraction, the dramatically isolated **Kaieteur Falls**, lies southwest of Georgetown, deep in the interior – you will have to either fly or spend a few days trekking through the forest. The other places most worth exploring before crossing into Brazil at **Lethem** are the **Iwokrama Rainforest**, a good example of the country's efforts to promote sustainable eco-tourism, and the **Rupununi Savanna**, an area of wooded hills and dry grassland strewn with cattle ranches and providing excellent possibilities for bird and animal spotting.

Kaieteur Falls

Even waterfall aficionados will find **KAIETEUR FALLS**, the centrepiece of the ancient Pakaraima mountain range in southwestern Guyana, more special than anything they have seen before. Not only is it the world's highest single-drop waterfall at 226 metres (almost five times the height of Niagara), but it also enjoys a location equal to the grandeur of the falls themselves. It stands in a cavernous gorge surrounded by the forests of the **Kaieteur National Park**, which encompasses an area of eight square kilometres around the falls, with the nearest gift shop and ice-cream seller a one-hour flight away in Georgetown. Kaieteur's isolation and trickle of visitors – there are usually only about two planeloads a week – give it an aura not found at many of the world's other great waterfalls. The high chance of spotting **wildlife**, including the brilliant orange cock-of-the-rock bird and golden frogs that reside in giant bromeliads and produce a toxin 160,000-times more potent than cocaine, is an additional reason for forking out the money to visit Kaieteur.

Seeing Kaieteur Falls does not come cheap. Day-trips from Georgetown, including the flight from Ogle, park entrance fees and lunch, start at US$165. (For an additional US$45 or so you can take another twenty-minute flight to **Orinduik Falls**, a series of mini-falls and pools on the Ireng River bordering Brazil, which are ideal for swimming.) The best time to visit Kaieteur is really in the wet season when the falls are at their widest (while high, they are relatively narrow when compared with the likes of Niagara, Iguaçu, Angel and other well-known waterfalls). The problem here is that planes often have trouble landing on the airstrip owing to mist. Most tour operators in Georgetown offer Kaieteur trips (see box, p.767).

While flying in will give you a panoramic view of the falls, Kaieteur Gorge and the Pakaraima Mountains, trekking there is the more rewarding experience – provided you have the time and money. Rainforest Tours, Hotel Tower, 74–75 Main St, Georgetown (Ⓣ227-5632, Ⓦwww.rainforesttoursgy.com), offers five-day **overland tours** to Kaieteur, which involve driving to the Potaro River and continuing by boat and on foot to the falls, sleeping at basic camp sites en route. At Kaieteur itself, there is a **guesthouse** with hammocks – but no running water – for G$1000 a night. Be sure to bring your own food.

Iwokrama Rainforest

The road south of Georgetown passes through **Linden**, Guyana's second largest town with little of interest for visitors. It gets increasingly bumpier as it approaches the **Essequibo River crossing** (G$9000 for 4WD vehicles; G$25,000 for trucks; you only pay if you are coming from Georgetown, since prices are for a return), roughly 160km south.

A short way downriver is the Iwokrama Rainforest Field Station, the focal point of an ambitious, internationally funded project to promote sustainable development of the rainforest. The forest in question, the pristine, 400,000-plus square hectare **IWOKRAMA RAINFOREST**, is home to 474 bird species, 130 different mammals, 420 types of fish and 132 species of reptile – subjects of the ongoing scientific research at the field station and the basis of Iwokrama's other main activity: eco-tourism. Tourists staying at the field station share lodgings and meals with biologists, botanists and other researchers engaged in projects aimed at conserving and developing the forest in a sustainable way for economic and social ends. The eco-tourism-side of things involves natures walks, nocturnal caiman spotting and visits to a nearby Amerindian village, all conducted by very knowledgeable, well-trained guides.

Don't miss the opportunity to visit the rainforest's newest tourist attraction, the **Canopy Walkway** (US$12), approximately one kilometre off the road to Lethem, about a 45-minute drive south from the Essequibo River. This 140-metre network of aluminium suspension bridges in the treetops has four observation platforms, the highest of which is some thirty metres above the forest floor, an excellent vantage point to spot birds, monkeys and various fauna on the forest floor. The bridges wobble, but are very solid and have high ropes to hang on to; even so, vertigo sufferers might find the experience challenging.

A few kilometres further south is the turn-off for **Surama Village** at the southern end of the Iwokrama Rainforest. A small Amerindian settlement of some 226 people, it rests on a patch of savanna land in the forest. Of all the native villages in Guyana, Surama has been one of the most proactive in preparing for the arrival of tourists: there is a small guesthouse (G$1500 for a bed, G$1000 for a hammock) and local guides conduct nature walks and mountain hikes. One of the most popular excursions is a night spent on the banks of the nearby Burro River, where you can enjoy (be kept awake by) the sounds of the forest.

Practicalities

The main **accommodation** in the Iwokrama Rainforest is available in three cabins overlooking the river with five beds and a bathroom (US$27.50). There is also a user fee of US$27.50 per person. Budget travellers who just want to spend the night without visiting the forest can sling a hammock at the field station for G$220 (they don't pay the user fee). **Meals** cost US$5.50 each and transport is a hefty US$79.50 per day, plus 17¢ per 1.6km. Contact the Iwokrama International Centre for Rainforest Conservation and Development, 67 Bel Air, Georgetown (Ⓣ225-1504, Ⓦwww.iwokrama.com) for information and reservations.

Rupununi Savanna

A few kilometres further south of the turn-off for Surama Village, the dense vegetation on either side of the road suddenly disappears as you enter the flatlands that stretch across the whole of southern Guyana, or about one-third of the whole country. The **RUPUNUNI SAVANNA,** provides a welcome break from the typical rainforest-and-river experience offered in all three of the Guianas. Here, you'll find a land of vast cattle ranches, cowboys, Amerindian settlements and wildlife much easier to spot than it is under the forest canopy.

Rupununi ranches

Visitors to the Rupununi Savanna stay at the cattle ranches, which have incorporated a range of activities for the eco-tourist into the day-to-day operation of running a ranch. These activities have the feel of being complimentary to – rather than the purpose for – the ranch, so when you accompany a *vacqueiro*, or cowboy, to round up cattle, for example, you really do feel more like a fly-on-the-saddle than a tourist being taken for a (horse) ride. The ranches constitute the lifeblood of the

Getting to and around the Rupununi Savanna

Travel in the Rupununi Savanna is expensive for those without their own transportation. It is easy enough to get to the savanna's main settlements such as Lethem, Annai and Karanambo by **air** from Georgetown. Transguyana Airways have flights to all of these destinations for G$21,000 one-way, G$36,000 return. If you then want to fly from one Rupununi destination to another, you will have to pay another G$21,000 for a confirmed seat. A stand-by fare of only around G$4000 is also possible, assuming that there is space on the flight and the plane is scheduled to stop at your desired destination (while Lethem is always a scheduled stop, landings at Annai and Karanambo are by request only).

Arranging **land** transfers by 4WD is more expensive than flying. Typical one-way prices are as follows: Lethem–Annai G$27,000; Annai–Karanambo G$27,000, Annai–Surama G$9000; Annai–Iwokrama G$25,000. Apart from the infrequent public transport between Lethem and Georgetown (see opposite), there are no passenger services to the various places of interest in the Rupununi. Note that during **wet season** driving becomes difficult, if not impossible, since much of the savanna is under several metres of water.

small Amerindian settlements – **Annai**, **Karanambo** and **Dadanawa** – which have formed around them.

The *Rock View Lodge*, c/o Evergreen Adventures (Ⓣ226-5412, Ⓦwww.rockviewlodge; ❻ room only, ❽ with meals, ❾ with meals and activities, ❷ for hammock), in **ANNAI** is the only ranch accessible by public transport, lying as it does a short way from the Lethem–Georgetown road. It is also the logical base from which to explore the other attractions of the North Rupununi such as Karanambo, as well as nearby Surama Village and Iwokrama. The lodge provides comprehensive bird lists and maps of the local area for birders and trekkers, has comfortable, self-contained rooms, probably one of the only swimming pools outside of Georgetown, and excellent food.

A couple of hours' drive southwest across the savanna from Annai, *Karanambo*, c/o Wilderness Explorers (Ⓣ227-7698, Ⓦwww.wilderness-explorers.com/karanambu; ❾ including meals and most activities), is the largest ranch in the North Rupununi and the first to offer nature-based tourism in the region – if not the whole country. **KARANAMBO**, which also has a small village, is known for its wildlife, much of it easily spotted during boat trips on the nearby Rupununi River. The highlight for many is the giant river otters, the rehabilitation of which is close to the heart of *Karanambo*'s owner, Diane McTurk. Accommodation is in five twin-bedded *cabañas* with verandas, hammocks and a bewildering selection of toiletries, creams and repellents. Note that during wet season, *kaboura* flies, sandflies and mosquitoes can be a problem in this part of the savanna.

Dadanawa, c/o Wilderness Explorers (Ⓣ227-7698, Ⓦwww.wilderness-explorers.com/dadanawa; ❽ including meals and most activities), is the largest and most isolated – and therefore the most difficult to access – ranch in the country, a three-hours' drive southeast of Lethem and the Kanuku Mountains in the tiny settlement of **DADANAWA.**

Lethem

Apart from an airstrip and one or two administrative buildings and hotels, there is not much to detain you in **LETHEM**, a relaxing Guyanese town on the Brazilian border, unless you are breaking your journey either on your way to or from Boa Vista in Brazil.

Those wanting to get a **vehicle to Georgetown** should contact Peter (Ⓣ772-2033), who operates 4WD passenger services more or less daily, from the blue and white building at the turn-off before the roundabout in the town centre. The daily departure is scheduled for 10pm, and his friendly mother will let you sleep for free in hammocks until the vehicle is ready to leave. The trip to Georgetown takes around eleven hours and costs G$10,000.

For good **accommodation**, try *Savannah Inn* (Ⓣ772 2035, Ⓔsavannahinn@futurenetgy.com; ❹), which has comfortable rooms and cabins, or the friendly and good value *Takatu Guest House* (Ⓣ772 2034; ❸), with its clean rooms, patio and garden for barbecues. Both of these places offer meals, but another **place to eat** is *Kanuku View Restaurant and Snackette* next to the roundabout, which boasts a menu of Chinese, Indian and Brazilian specialities (rice is pretty much guaranteed at all times).

Crossing into Brazil

Lethem is separated from the Brazilian town of Bonfim by the Takutu River. The official crossing is about 1.5 kilometres north of Lethem (pick-ups from the airstrip to the crossing G$300), although Guyanese **immigration formalities** should be completed either at the airstrip, when there are flights, or at the Lethem immigration office in a nondescript house in a residential part of town – ask at the Chinese restaurant at the first turning on the left when entering town from the river crossing for directions. Dug-outs transport foot passengers across the river (G$200), while a pontoon carries vehicles. You can get your passport stamped on the Brazilian side of the border before making your way to Bonfim, from where you can get buses to Boa Vista. **Moneychangers** on the Lethem side of the river will change Guyanese dollars for Brazilian reals and vice-versa (US dollars are harder to sell); make sure that you have enough reals to get you to Bonfim, if not Boa Vista.

East to Suriname

Most travellers leave Georgetown on the road that runs southeast, parallel to the Atlantic coast, cutting through the sugarcane plantations of the populous region of East Demerara. Many small towns and settlements line the road between Georgetown and Rosignol on the west bank of the Berbice River, including that of **Buxton**, the focal point of much of the violent crime that has ravaged the country in recent years. The beautiful villas along this stretch of road – there is a surprising number of them – were probably not all built from sugarcane money. Crossing the Berbice River brings you to quiet, laid-back **New Amsterdam**, the country's third largest town. A little over an hour from New Amsterdam lies **Corriverton** on the banks of the Corentyne River, on the other side of which is Suriname.

New Amsterdam

While hardly a highlight of Guyana, the compact town of **NEW AMSTERDAM**, just over 100 kilometres from Georgetown, is worth breaking your journey between Georgetown and Paramaribo – certainly a better place to rest your head than rowdy Corriverton or soulless Nieuw Nickerie in Suriname. An important port town for the export of bauxite, New Amsterdam's points of interest are limited to a rather sad looking wooden church at the end of Main Street, a municipal park and some grand old wooden buildings around the market on Strand Street.

Practicalities

Getting to New Amsterdam (often referred to as "Berbice" by minibus drivers) from Georgetown is simple: take a #50 bus to Rosignol (1.5hr; G$500), then cross the Berbice River by ferry to New Amsterdam (roughly every half-hour; G$40). Minibuses to Corriverton (1hr 10min; G$400) and the Suriname ferry at Moleson Creek (1hr 30min; G$500) leave from the road leading to the New Amsterdam ferry stelling.

Good, central **accommodation** options include *Hotel Astor*, 7 Strand St (☎333-3578; ❸), in an attractive wooden building with a veranda 100 metres or so from the ferry stelling, and *Parkway Hotel*, 4 Main St (☎333-3928; ❹), which has self-contained rooms with fan and TV. Considerably more expensive than the rest is *Little Rock Hotel*, 67 Vryman's Erven (☎333-4758 or 3758; ❻), in a quiet residential part of town about a ten-minute walk from the centre (follow the signs from Backdam Road).

For good Chinese **food**, try *Lim Kang*, 12 Chapel St (☎333-2755), where large portions of sweet and sour pork and fried rice are served up while Indian music plays in the background. *Jokwesan's*, 7 Charlotte St (☎333-2464), is the place to go for Creole dishes such as *cook-up* and *channa*. The best restaurant in the region, serving local and international cuisine, is the upscale and expensive *Caribbean Cuisine*, about two kilometres out of New Amsterdam on the road to Corriverton.

Corriverton

From New Amsterdam, the road continues to run parallel to the Atlantic coast, bending evermore southward towards its terminus at the mouth of the Corentyne River. Before reaching **CORRIVERTON** (actually comprised of Springlands and

Skeldon), facing Suriname across the river, you will pass the Guyana Sugar Corporation at **Albion**, which – for now at least – is the largest sugar estate in the country. The main reason for coming here, however, is the cricket ground on the estate that plays host to international matches. About ten kilometres before Corriverton, **No. 63 Beach** in Village 63 is arguably Guyana's most popular beach; a muddy stretch of coast, it is more suitable for cricket than sunbathing.

Corriverton itself is an uninspiring strip of service stations and hardware shops, full of moneychangers and the interrogating glances typical of small border towns. If you have to **stay the night**, *Mahogany Hotel*, 50 Public Rd, Village 78 (Ⓣ339-2289; ❹), is the best choice by virtue of its pleasant, compact, clean rooms and veranda overlooking the Corentyne River. A more expensive option is *Paraton Inn*, next to the Esso Service Station (Ⓣ339-2248; ❺). *The Train*, also next to the Shell Service Station, is a popular **place to eat** a curry and *roti* breakfast before crossing the border.

Crossing into Suriname

The ferry that crosses the Corentyne River to South Drain in Suriname (about forty kilometres southwest of **Nieuw Nickerie**, see p.792) leaves from **Moleson Creek**, around fifteen kilometres south of Corriverton. If you are not on a through-bus to Moleson Creek from Georgetown or New Amsterdam, you will have to arrange transport from Corriverton on local buses known as *tapirs*, which run regularly to Crabwood Creek (G$60), the last settlement of any note before the ferry crossing. The driver will probably take you the further seven kilometres to Moleson Creek for G$200–300.

There is only one **ferry crossing** a day, leaving Moleson Creek at 11am. Fares are G$1,500 or US$8 one-way; G$2,900 or US$15 return valid 21 days; G$2,850 or US$15 one-way with car; G$5,700 or US$30 return with car. Note that no change is given when purchasing ferry tickets. Immigration formalities are carried out at the ferry stelling. Illegal speedboats also cross the river regularly, and although it is tempting to take one if you have missed the ferry, there will be nowhere to get your passport stamped either when leaving Guyana or entering Suriname if you do. **Moneychangers** will latch on to you at Corriverton and are also present at Moleson Creek. Rates when buying Surinamese guilders are slightly lower than in Nieuw Nickerie and Paramaribo, although the difference is small. Be aware that there are no moneychangers at South Drain, so be sure to have enough guilders to pay for the bus to either Nieuw Nickerie or Paramaribo (see p.792 & 786 for details on those cities).

7.2

Suriname

Most visitors to **SURINAME** are Dutch, spending a week or two in the former colony to remind them their country was once a great colonial power. The vestiges of Dutch colonialism, not least of which are the language and some attractive wooden architecture in the capital, **Paramaribo**, make Suriname a quirky place to include on a pan-South American trip. For serious eco-tourists, meanwhile, the fact that nearly thirteen per cent of the country's land surface area is under official environmental protection has led to the creation of a number of nature parks and reserves offering good opportunities for hiking and observing wildlife. **Brownsberg Nature Park** is the most easily accessible from Paramaribo; the **Central Suriname Nature Reserve** is one of the largest of its kind in the world; and olive ridley turtles can be seen laying their eggs in **Galibi Nature Reserve**.

Information and websites

The **Suriname Tourism Foundation**, Dr J.F. Nassylaan 2, Paramaribo (Ⓣ410357, Ⓦwww.mhw.org/tourism), is responsible for promoting tourism in Suriname, and its **tourist office** in Paramaribo at Waterkant 1 (Mon–Fri 9am–3.30pm; Ⓣ479200) is eager to help and has enough material to cover your stay in Paramaribo. No trip to the nature parks and reserves should be contemplated without first having touched base with **STINASU**, at Cornelis Jongbawstraat 14, Paramaribo (Ⓣ476597, Ⓦwww.stinasu.sr), which manages the country's protected areas.

A considerable amount of research can also be done on the **web**. Ⓦourworld.compuserve.com/homepages/OPKemp is good for those with a particular interest in Suriname's natural resources, topography and infrastructure, while Ⓦwebserv.nhl.nl/~ribot/english/introd is a great site for birders, with photos, check lists and distribution tables for the bird species present in Suriname. Ⓦwww.parbo.com is devoted to Paramaribo; Ⓦwww.surinam.net offers news, current affairs and Suriname-related message boards; and Ⓦwww.surinfo.org/indexeng is an attractive site aimed specifically at tourists (with a good photo page).

Costs and money

Generally more expensive than Guyana, Suriname is not nearly as costly as French Guiana. Budget **accommodation** in Suriname costs around US$20; mid-range options can be had for US$40; and nothing much will cost over US$100 or so. **Eating** at local restaurants is affordable at around US$5 for a reasonable meal; and the cost of travelling by public transport – where available – is within the means of the budget traveller.

The currency of Suriname is the **guilder** (**Sf**), which comes in the following notes and coins: (notes) 5, 10, 25, 100, 500, 1000, 2000, 5000, 10,000 and 25,000; (coins) 1 and 2,50 guilders, and 1, 5, 10 and 25 cents. The **exchange rate** at the time of writing was roughly US$1 = G$2,700.

You can change cash and travellers' cheques at the major banks, occasionally for a commission of around five per cent. The *cambios* (*wisselkantoor*) at Paramaribo, Nieuw Nickerie and Albina sometimes offer slightly better rates and more convenient opening hours than the banks. Changing money on the black market is offi-

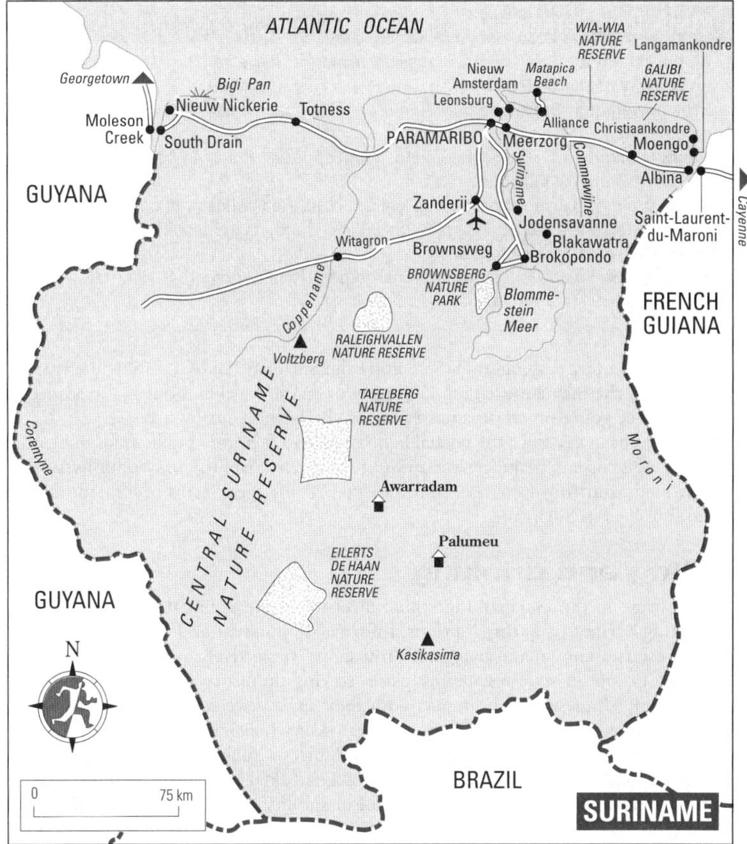

cially illegal and not worth the risk. **US dollars** are the most widely accepted foreign currency, while **euros** are also popular. Your credit card will be useful to pay for hotel bills and organized excursions with tour operators, but not for withdrawing money from ATM machines, which only accept cards from local banks.

Getting around

As there are no scheduled **internal flights** in Suriname, tour operators charter planes to visit the parks and reserves in the interior, a practice obviously dependent on having a minimum number of people for a particular tour. You can also charter your own planes from SLM, Coppenamestraat 136, Paramaribo (☎465531), and Gum Air, Doekhieweg oost 3 (☎432057), or a helicopter from Hi-Jet, Doekhieweg oost 1 (☎432577). The airport for internal flights is called **Zorg en Hoop**, situated in a southeastern suburb of the city.

You can travel by land from Paramaribo to the borders of Guyana and French Guiana. State-run **buses** ply certain routes (see box on p.784) at fixed times; **minibuses** cover the same routes and others not served by state buses, leaving when full and costing slightly more.

Buses from Paramaribo

Albina (for French Guiana border crossing) minibuses leave from the Central Market on Waterkant, 2hr, Sf15,000.
Brownsweg (for Brownsberg Nature Park) Saramacastraat, at Ladesmastraat, before 9am.
Nieuw Nickerie Dr Sophie Redmondstraat, opposite *Hotel Ambassador*, 3.5hr, Sf7,500 minibus, Sf4000 state-run bus.
South Drain (for Guyana border crossing) Dr Sophie Redmondstraat, opposite Hotel Ambassador, one a day at 5–6am, Sf25,000, call Bobby Taxi Bus Service (℗491277 or 08/838779) for more information.
Zanderij (for Johan Pengel International Airport) Knuffelsgracht, 1–1.5hr, Sf1,400 minibus, Sf850 state-run bus.

Apart from a few passenger services along the Suriname and Commewijne rivers (operated by the Suriname Sailing Company or SMS), travel by **boat** is also a question of either going on an organized tour or chartering your own vessel

Be aware that away from the coastal belt, roads (and therefore public transport) are virtually nonexistent, making river and ultimately air travel the only options. With so few roads, **renting a car** (see "Listings", p.790, for agencies) is of limited interest to travellers in Suriname.

Eating and drinking

As elsewhere in the Guianas, the ethnic diversity of the population has led to an interesting variety of **eating** options. Informal Indonesian and Hindustani (East Indian) eateries known as *warungs* and "roti shops" respectively are juxtaposed with gourmet, European-style restaurants, places serving up hearty Creole fare, and the ever-present Chinese establishments with their exhaustive menus and ultra-rapid service. One of the most typically Surinamese dishes is *moksie alesie*, a filling mix of rice, beans, chicken and various vegetables and spices. Chicken (*kip*) features in several other local specialities, such as *pom* – chicken baked with a root of the cassava family – and *saoto* – chicken soup with bean sprouts, potatoes and a boiled egg. Chicken is also the star performer in other offerings, including Hindustani curries (eaten with a *roti* pancake rather than a knife and fork) and Indonesian *saté*. Other common Indonesian dishes are *bami* and *nassie goreng* – fried noodles and fried rice respectively. *Pindasoep* and *petjil* are two tasty peanut soups, the former made with *tom-tom* (plantain noodles), the latter with vegetables.

While beer – both imported and local brands such a Parbo – spirits, soft drinks and bottled water are widely available, *dawet*, a local concoction of coconut milk and lemongrass is worth a try. The tap water in Paramaribo is safe to drink, although it could upset fragile stomachs to begin with.

Tour operators

If you want to visit the nature parks and reserves of Suriname, at some time or another you will have to deal with STINASU, the organization charged with protecting and studying these areas. STINASU can arrange transport, accommodation and tours to Brownsberg, Raleighvallen, Galibi and Matapica. The other main player is METS (see page 790), which operates its own jungle lodges in the far south of the country, as well as selling tours to virtually every other point of interest from the resorts south of Paramaribo to Bush Negro villages and Jodensavanne. As a guideline, day-trips don't usually cost under US$50, and you can easily blow around US$750 if you want to visit all of the country's nature parks and reserves.

Mail, telecommunications and the media

Letters, postcards and the like are franked at the **post office** rather than being sent with stamps. Surpost (Ⓦwww.surpost.com) provides a reasonably reliable service, and airmail rates are Sf1000 to anywhere in the world.

As public **telephone** booths in Suriname do not accept coins, you must purchase a phonecard issued by Telesur in denominations of US$3, 5 and 10, and sold at shops and street stands everywhere. Telesur cards work with PIN numbers and can be used to make local, national and international calls.

Internet cafés are common enough in Paramaribo, but much less so elsewhere. All of the Surinamese newspapers, television and radio stations are in Dutch. This said, you can sometimes read the news in English on the website of *De Ware Tijd* (Ⓦwww.dwt.net), the main daily **newspaper**. The principal **radio** stations include Radio 10, Radio Paramaribo – which both have news bulletins in English – ABC, Apintie and SRS. Some of the **television** stations also show programmes in English.

Festivals

In addition to Christmas and Easter, the Hindu festival of **Holi Pagwah** is celebrated, usually in March, as well as the Muslim holiday of **Id al-Fitr** (the end of Ramadan), the exact date of which is dependent on sightings of the moon (the 2003 date is November 26). From mid-December to the first week in January there are several happenings in and around Paramaribo – cultural shows, street parties, firework displays – generically known as **Surifesta** (Ⓦwww.surifesta.com) and designed to make the bringing in of the new year in Suriname a tourist attraction in its own right.

History and culture

The earliest inhabitants of Suriname were the **Surinen**, although by the time Christopher Columbus first sighted the Surinamese coast in 1498 other Amerind tribes such as the Arawak and Carib were dominant. Indeed, the strong resistance of these tribes disrupted various Spanish, British, Dutch and French attempts to build settlements during the first half of the seventeenth century before Suriname became **Dutch Guiana** in 1667, when it was formally exchanged with the British for Nieuw Amsterdam (now New York). During the course of the next couple of centuries, the colony's sugarcane plantations thrived thanks to the importation of thousands of West African slaves. Many of these slaves managed to escape to the interior, where they established the five major Bush Negro, or *maroon*, tribes in existence today: the Djuka, Matuwari, Paramaccaner, Quinti and Saramaccaner. After the abolition of slavery in 1863, indentured workers were imported from India, China and Java to work on the plantations, although agricultural production would soon be overtaken by the mining of the country's newly discovered reserves of bauxite.

The first step on the road to Surinamese independence was the granting of autonomy in the running of its internal affairs by the Netherlands in 1954. Suriname's political parties, most of them formed along ethnic lines, took shape during this period of autonomy, and a coalition of several of the most important ones governed the country when it won **independence** on November 25, 1975. In the few years immediately after independence, the economy was stagnant, unemployment high and wages low. In this climate, the military coup that toppled the government in 1980 was generally well received by the majority of the population, yet the new regime was dictatorial, oppressive and ineffective in halting the economic decline. Civilian governments were installed by the military, but to all intents and purposes the country was run by Lieutenant Colonel **Dési Bouterse**.

One of the most serious challenges to Bouterse's grip on power occurred when the Surinamese Liberation Army, a guerrilla group made up mainly of Bush Negroes, started to attack economic targets in the interior in 1986. The National Army responded by killing many Bush Negro civilians, and many more fled to neighbouring French Guiana. In 1991, international pressure forced Bouterse to hold elections, won by a coalition of parties called the **New Front**. The candidate of the party representing the light-skinned Creole elite, **Ronald Venetiaan**, was elected president and set about trying to improve the Surinamese economy by re-establishing relations with the Dutch in the hope that financial aid would follow. The new government also settled the Bush Negro insurgency by signing a Peace Accord in 1992. Despite these efforts, the New Front coalition lost popularity to such an extent that the rival **National Democratic Party**, founded by Bouterse in the early 1990s, was able to win the 1996 elections; however, Venetiaan and the New Front coalition won back the presidency in 2000 with further promises of fixing an economy that had deteriorated even further during four years of chaotic National Democratic Party rule.

So far the government has introduced various corrective measures to reduce inflation, stabilize the exchange rate and bring down the budget deficit. Although in 2001 inflation did fall and the Dutch approved a €137.7 million loan, Venetiaan's greatest challenge is arguably keeping his fragile, ethnically diverse coalition together in the face of such problems, the latest of which is international concern over Suriname's role in drug trafficking.

Culture

With so many different ethnic groupings, Surinamese **culture** is a patchwork of different influences, each ethnic group preserving its own cultural traditions in isolation from the rest; even in public spheres such as politics racial allegiances die hard. Just over thirty-five per cent of the population is Hindustani (the local term to describe East Indians), around thirty per cent is Creole (people of African or mixed European and African origins), fifteen per cent is Javanese, ten per cent Bush Negro and the remainder Amerindian, Chinese, Portuguese and Jewish.

The official **language** in Suriname is Dutch, but in reality this is used by many as a second tongue. Hindustani and Sranan Tongo (Surinamese Creole) are the first languages of over sixty per cent of the population, while other ethnicities have clung to their own linguistic traditions. Several *maroon* languages, the principal of which are Saramaccan and Aukan, as well as Javanese and Amerindian languages such as Carib are also spoken in Suriname.

Paramaribo

Arriving in **PARAMARIBO**, it is hard to imagine that Suriname is one of the world's leading destinations for eco-tourism. Ugly development, a serious traffic problem and other offshoots of urbanization have spoiled a once beautiful city, and these days you cannot see the flowers for the weeds. Pleasant streets with fine colonial architecture do survive, but you have to fight your way through car fumes, shopping malls and traffic jams to get to them. This struggle makes Paramaribo a tiring, disappointing city, redeemed only slightly by the refreshing **Suriname River**, upon whose west bank Paramaribo sprawls, some twelve kilometres from the point where the river spills into the Atlantic ocean.

Arrival and getting around

The **Johan Pengel International Airport** is 45 kilometres south of Paramaribo in the town of Zanderij; visitors should remember that there is a **departure tax** of US$15. For internal flights, **Zorg en Hoop airfield** is in a southeastern suburb of

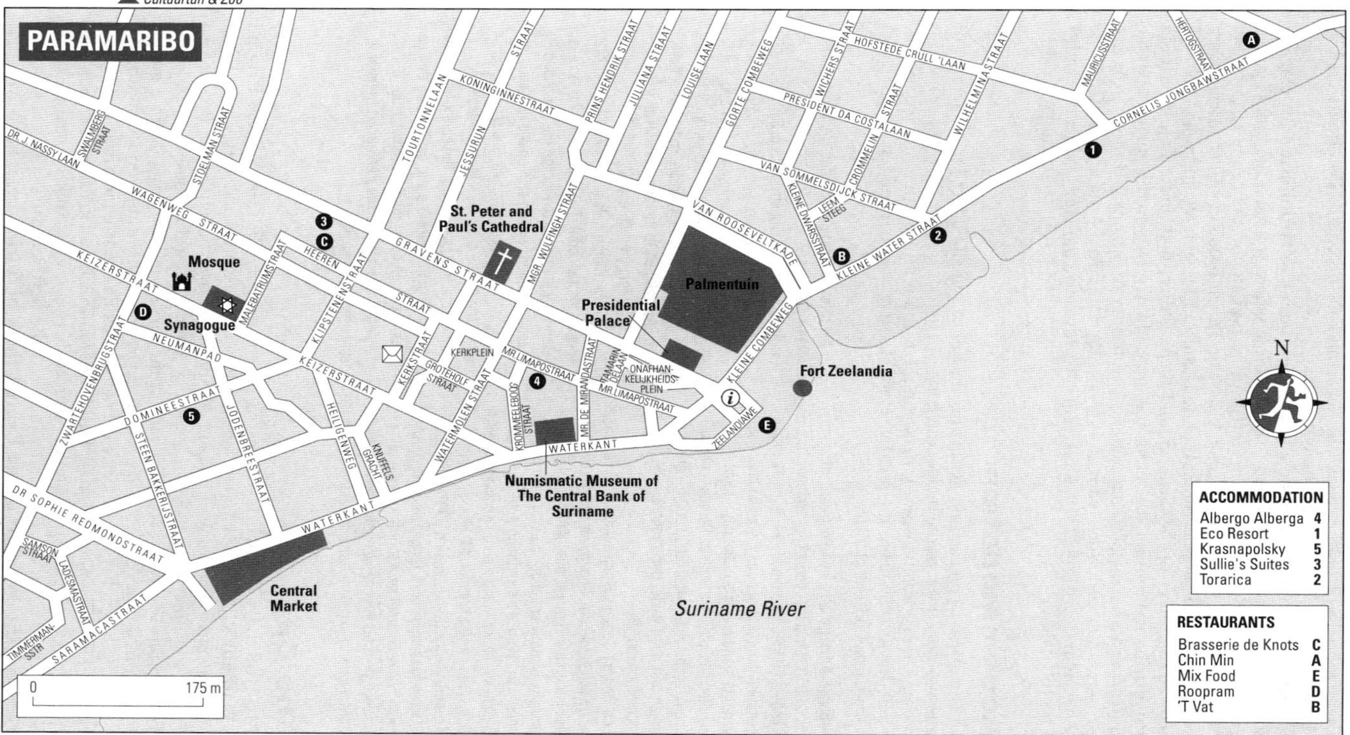
Cultuurtun & Zoo
PARAMARIBO
Immigration Office, Meerzorg, Albina & Nieuw Nickerie
St. Peter and Paul's Cathedral
Mosque
Synagogue
Presidential Palace
Palmentuin
Fort Zeelandia
Numismatic Museum of The Central Bank of Suriname
Central Market
Suriname River
N
0
175 m
ACCOMMODATION
Albergo Alberga 4
Eco Resort 1
Krasnapolsky 5
Sullie's Suites 3
Torarica 2
RESTAURANTS
Brasserie de Knots C
Chin Min A
Mix Food E
Roopram D
'T Vat B
HOFSTEDE CRULL 'LAAN
HERTOGSTRAAT
MAURICIUSSTRAAT
CORNELIS JONGBAWSTRAAT
WILHELMINASTRAAT
PRESIDENT DA COSTALAAN
WICHERS STRAAT
CROMMELIN STRAAT
VAN SOMMELSDIJCK STRAAT
KLEINE DWARSSTRAAT
LEEM STEEG
KLEINE WATER STRAAT
VAN ROOSEVELTKADE
KLEINE COMBEWEG
GORTE COMBEWEG
LOUISE LAAN
JULIANA STRAAT
PRINS HENDRIK STRAAT
KONINGINNESTRAAT
JESSURUN
TOURTONNELAAN
MGR. WULFINGH STRAAT
GRAVENS STRAAT
HEEREN STRAAT
KLIPSTENENSTRAAT
KERKSTRAAT
KERKPLEIN
GROTEHOLF STRAAT
MR.LIMAPOSTRAAT
MR. DE MIRANDASTRAAT
TAMARIN DELAAN
ONAFHANKELIJKHEIDSPLEIN
ZEELANDIAWE
WATERKANT
KROMMEELEBOOG STRAAT
WATERMOLEN STRAAT
KNUFFELS GRACHT
HEILIGENWEG
KEIZERSTRAAT
JODENBREESTRAAT
MALEBATRUMSTRAAT
NEUMANPAD
DOMINEESTRAAT
STEEN BAKKERIJSTRAAT
ZWARTEHOVENBRUGSTRAAT
WAGENWEG STRAAT
STOELMAN STRAAT
SWALMBERG STRAAT
DR. J. NASSY LAAN
DR SOPHIE REDMONDSTRAAT
SAMSON STRAAT
LADESMASTRAAT
SARAMACASTRAAT
TIMMERMAN-SSTR

Paramaribo. To get to the town centre, take minibus #8 or #9. SMS **boats** dock at the wharf next to the market on Waterkant.

Getting around Paramaribo and its suburbs using the **minibuses** that clog the streets is easy enough provided that you know where you (and the bus) is going. Expect to pay Sf3000 or so for short trips by **taxi** around the centre of town and Sf4000 from the centre to *Torarica Hotel*. The Dutch residents of Paramaribo cling proudly to their bicycle-riding traditions and can be seen cycling round the city blissfully ignorant of the chaos around them. Others will find riding bicycles in Paramaribo too stressful, dangerous and unhealthy. Cycling on the other side of the Suriname River in the much quieter and fresher Meerzorg is a more attractive proposition, and **bike rental** is available at Cardy Adventures, Cornelis Jongbawstraat 31 (Ⓣ422518, Ⓔbikerental@cardytours.com), for US$5 a day with a US$100 deposit.

Accommodation

In Paramaribo, you can find **accommodation** to suit all budgets; and a number of guesthouses – even in the budget category – have rooms every bit as comfortable as the mid-range hotels. Most of the accommodation is found either in the busy, polluted downtown area or the holiday resort-like strip of hotels and restaurants east of Onafhankelijkheidsplein.

Albergo Alberga Mr Lim A Postraat 13B, Ⓣ520050, Ⓔsabina_florida@yahoo.com. Arguably the best budget accommodation in town, this beautiful nineteenth-century wooden house with veranda stands on one of the city's most aesthetically pleasing streets. Rooms – which should all be self-contained by 2004 – are clean, bright and good value. Reservations recommended. ❹

Eco Resort Cornelis Jongbawstraat 16 Ⓣ425522, Ⓦwww.ecores.com. Slightly smaller rooms than its sister hotel *Torarica*, but just as comfortable and significantly cheaper. You also have free access to *Torarica's* swimming pool and other facilities – as well as the same annoying check-in time. Free airport transfer. ❼

Krasnapolsky Domineestraat 39 Ⓣ475050, Ⓦwww.krasnapolsky.sr. Large, six-storied, 87-room business hotel smack in the centre of downtown. It features a swimming pool on the third floor and excellent buffet breakfasts (included in the rates) served in the hotel's restaurant, *The Atrium*. ❼

Sullie's Suites Gravenstraat 53 Ⓣ520522, Ⓔsulliessuites@sr.com. Superbly equipped rooms with kitchens, toasters, microwaves, video recorders, CD players and even windows with one-way glass. The most expensive room has a full-size Jacuzzi next to the bed. Look at all rooms before making your choice. ❺

Torarica Mr Rietbergplein 1 Ⓣ471500 or 477432, Ⓦwww.torarica.com. The swimming pool here is a favourite gathering place for the city's sizeable Dutch contingent, which also enjoys its tennis courts, a fitness centre, sauna, Jacuzzi and the small zoo on the grounds. The hotel itself is comfortable, but overpriced. The check-in time of 5pm is incomprehensible and could mean that you miss out on enjoying many of the facilities if staying just one night. The free airport transfer is some recompense. ❽

The City

Most of the worthwhile things to see in Paramaribo are clustered round **Onafhankelijkheidsplein**, the small green with a statue of a very portly Johan Adolf Pengal, the former president of Suriname, overlooked by the Presidential Palace and other attractive state buildings. **Fort Zeelandia** houses the Suriname Foundation Museum (Tues–Fri 9am–2pm, Sun 10am–2pm; Sf6000; free guided tours Sun 11am & 12.30pm), which, apart from affording good views of the Suriname River, has an unspectacular range of exhibits related to Surinamese history. The few remaining **colonial buildings** for which Paramaribo was once celebrated can be found on a handful of streets between Onafhankelijkheidsplein and Kerkplein. Mr Lim A Postraat, which has the best selection, also contains the **Numismatic Museum of the Central Bank of Suriname**, at no. 7 (Mon–Fri

8am–2pm; free), a treat for those interested in Surinamese coins and banknotes dating from the seventeenth century. The other attraction around Onafhankelijkheidsplein, behind the Presidential Palace, is a park full of lofty palm trees known as the **Palmentuin** (to be avoided at night).

To the west of Onafhankelijkheidsplein lies downtown Paramaribo, full of shopping malls, ugly buildings and traffic. For all the ugliness of downtown Paramaribo, there are but a few buildings of note. Made entirely of wood and almost as large as St George's Cathedral in Georgetown (see p.772), the **St Peter and Paul's Cathedral** on Gravenstraat is closed for renovation; however, guided tours in Dutch (Mon & Wed 10am–noon) include a climb up one of the towers for fine views over Paramaribo. Various other religions are represented on Keizerstraat, running parallel to Gravenstraat, where a **mosque** sits next to a **synagogue**, with the golden arches of *McDonald's* just a few doors down.

Eating

The ethnic diversity of Suriname makes Paramaribo a good place for **eating**. At least once during your stay head to the neighbourhood of Blauwgrond (past Residence Inn) to eat at one of the many *warungs* (Javanese restaurants) found in abundance in this part of the city. There are also several worthy food stands by the Suriname River that are good for late night snacks – try *Uncle Ré*, which specializes in Creole food.

Brasserie de Knots Heerenstraat 42 ⓣ520291. Recently opened, this Dutch-owned sandwich bar and coffee shop offers a good selection of salamis, cold meats, cheeses and other Dutch-style delicatessen items as well as fine imported coffee.

Chin Min Cornelis Jongbawstraat 83 ⓣ412155. Probably the most popular Chinese restaurant in town, *Chin Min* has a vast menu (with English translations), including several tofu-based dishes as part of a good selection for vegetarians. It has an ornate dining room with a/c upstairs and takeaway service at street level.

Mix Food Zeelandiaweg 1 ⓣ420688. Generous portions of Creole and Indonesian food, including the Surinamese dish *moksie alesie*, served at tables next to the Suriname River. The absence of traffic adds to the pleasant dining experience.

Roopram Zwartehovenbrugstraat (another one on Watermolenstraat) ⓣ410388. Piping hot plates of chicken curry and *roti* appear before you have uttered the final syllable of your order at this popular place. Eat with your fingers. Fried chicken upstairs.

'T Vat Kleine Waterstraat 1A. Popular Dutch hang-out. Well known for its *saté* and shady sidewalk terrace – sometimes a venue for live music and shows. For all this, the portions are small and the service slow.

Nightlife and entertainment

The **bars and clubs** of Paramaribo start to get going at around midnight. This is especially true for the city's most popular discotheque, *Club Touché*, Dr Sophie Redmondstraat, at A L Waaldijkstraat (Fri–Sat; Sf7000), which is the place to go for a weekend boogie. *Dance Pub Millennium*, Petrus Donderstraat 2 (Wed–Sun) is busy on Wednesday nights (Ladies' Night), while *Grand Café Rumors* at the *Krasnapolsky* has live jam sessions on Fridays. Another good place to go is *Waaggebouw* (otherwise known as *Bodeco*), Waterkant 5 (Wed–Sat until 3am), which also has jam sessions (Wednesdays) and often live bands at the weekends. This is the place of the moment with the Dutch crowd, and Friday evenings are particularly busy. For something a little different (at least in conservative Suriname), try *XPO*, Gemenelandsweg 158, a "straight-friendly" **gay bar**.

Listings

Banks Branches of most of the main banks (RBTT, Surinaamsche Bank, Landbouwbank) can be found on and around Kerkplein. Travellers' cheques can be changed for around a five per cent commission. Multitrack Exchange (Mon–Sat 8.30am–11.30pm, Sun 10am–11.30pm) is a good alternative place to change money should you be staying in one of the hotels near *Torarica* (an area devoid of banks). There is also a Western Union office here.

Car rental Companies include Hertz, at van't Hogerhuysstraat 23 (☎400409); Avis, Fred O'Kirkstraat 11 (☎450447); and SPAC, Verl Gemenelandsweg 139A (☎490877), with saloon cars costing from US$30 a day and 4WD vehicles from US$60.

Embassies and consulates Brazil, Maratakastraat 2 ☎494509; Canada, Waterkant 90–94 ☎481222; France, Gravenstraat 5–7 ☎476455; Guyana, Gravenstraat 82 ☎475209 (Mon–Fri 7.30–1pm; visa issued in 1–2 days); UK, van't Hogerhuysstraat 9–11 ☎472558; USA, Dr Sophie Redmondstraat 129 ☎477828.

Internet access available at Carib Computers, Heerenstraat 22 (Mon–Sat 9am–10pm, Sun 2–9pm; Sf1,800 for 30min). The Internet café at the post office is slightly cheaper and has the advantage that tickets are valid for one month, but the opening hours are the same as at the post office and thus less convenient. There is also a small Internet place opposite *Torarica* called Green Tone (Mon–Sat 9am–10pm, Sun 2–9pm).

Post office Located on Kerkstraat (Mon–Fri 7am–3pm, Sat 8am–noon).

Around Paramaribo

All **day-trips from Paramaribo** are most easily accomplished – and sometimes only possible – if you have your own transport or join an organized tour (see box on p.784), the majority of which offer trips to many of the following places for US$40–60.

LEONSBERG, eight kilometres northeast of Paramaribo on the banks of the Suriname River, is a good base from which to visit the largely Javanese, eighteenth-century fortified town of **NIEUW AMSTERDAM**. There is a museum with a limited selection of exhibits in the fortress on the other side of the river, as well as the several colonial plantations in the area, including the one at **Marienburg**, the oldest sugarcane plantation in Suriname. Should you wish to **spend the night** in Leonsburg, *Hotel Stardust*, Condorstraat 1 (☎451544, Ⓦwww.hotelstardust.com; ❺), has a choice of 135 rooms with a full range of other facilities including swimming pool, tennis court, fitness centre and even a miniature-golf course.

Seventy kilometres south of Paramaribo on the east bank of the Suriname River lies **JODENSAVANNE**, named after the Jews who settled in this savanna area in around 1650. Have a look at the ruins of the synagogue – the oldest in the Americas – and the graveyard. While nothing remains of the rest of the village, there is a small museum to give you some sense of its historical importance of the place.

Continue about five kilometres east to the recreation resort of **BLAKAWATRA**, where you can splash about in the dark, mineral-rich waters of the creek. Another resort five kilometres from the international airport **Colacreek** (reservations through METS, Dr J.F. Nassylaan 2, Paramaribo; ☎477088, Ⓦwww.metsresorts.com) is a busy place at weekends by virtue of its proximity (50km) to Paramaribo. The daily entrance fee is Sf3000, overnight accommodation costs from Sf15,000 in tents and Sf50,000 in a self-catering cabin with water and electricity (bring your own bed linen).

West to Guyana

The drive along the coastal belt **west of Paramaribo** is a scenic one, even if there are few reasons to stop en route. Around 140 kilometres from Paramaribo, the road passes through **Totness**, once a Scottish settlement, as it continues towards the district of Nickerie, where salt ponds, Dutch-style *polders* (land reclaimed from water) and, most notably, rice paddies start to appear. **Nieuw Nickerie** is the largest town in these parts – and the second largest in the country – and the obvious place to break your journey to Guyana. The ferry crossing the Corentyne River into Guyana is at **South Drain**, about an hour's drive southwest of Nieuw Nickerie on an unsealed and potholed track.

△ Sea turtle, Plage Les Hattes

Nieuw Nickerie

If you have just arrived on the ferry from Guyana and your first taste of Suriname is **NIEUW NICKERIE**, the country's second largest town, you will not see the type of compact, lively town that predominates in Guyana. A sprawling place with an ill-defined centre and an atmosphere which is at times sleepy, at others completely comatose, Nieuw Nickerie is 237 kilometres west of Paramaribo along a good stretch of paved road and about an hour's drive north from the ferry stelling at South Drain. The best thing to do in Nieuw Nickerie is leave town and spend the day at **Bigi pan**, a mangrove-ridden stretch of swampy coast with excellent bird-watching. Day-trips can be organized at *Residence Inn*.

Practicalities

Buses for Paramaribo depart from the market. Minibuses leave when full (3.5hr, Sf7000–15,000 depending on the size of the minibus), while state-run buses operate to a fixed schedule, the first leaving at 6am (Sf4,500). Transport to South Drain for the ferry to Guyana takes about one hour and costs Sf10,000. Note that it will be difficult to find buses going anywhere after around 1pm. In this case, a taxi (about Sf200,000 to Paramaribo) will be the only option.

The most expensive **hotel** is the centrally located *Residence Inn*, R.P. Bharosstraat 84 (Ⓣ210950, Ⓦwww.metsresorts.com/index3-en; ❼), featuring comfortable, air-conditioned rooms, while a good, clean budget option exists nearby in the form of *Hotel Concord 2000*, Wilhelminastraat 3 (Ⓣ232345; ❷), for those who don't mind sharing a bathroom and having a fan instead of air conditioning.

For good Indonesian **food**, go to *Restaurant Mellissa's* at *Hotel Concord 2000*, while the best Chinese place in town is *Thien Thien Restaurant* on West Kanalstraat. The terrace at *Residence Inn* is a pleasant place to have a **drink**.

There are several **banks** around *Residence Inn*, including Surinaamsche Bank, where you can get a cash advance on your MasterCard. For cash transactions, however, the rates are better at the town's *cambios*. One of the more central is Eurora Exchange, a hundred metres or so up the road from *Residence Inn* on West Kanalstraat.

Crossing into Guyana

There is normally only one bus a day from Paramaribo to South Drain, connecting with the ferry service to **Moleson Creek** in Guyana (see p.781). There is also only one **ferry crossing** a day, leaving South Drain at 10am. Fares are US$8 one-way; US$15 return (valid 21 days); US$15 one-way with car; US$30 return with car. **Immigration** formalities are carried out at the ferry stelling.

There are **moneychangers** at Moleson Creek with whom you can change Guyana dollars, Suriname guilders and US dollars; on the Suriname side, the only place to change money is 40 kilometres away in Nieuw Nickerie.

South into the interior

You will not have seen the real Suriname until you venture south of Paramaribo into the interior. The country's natural riches are easy to reach either by day-trips (see "Around Paramaribo", p.790) or by visiting **Brownsberg Nature Park.** However, seeing the more isolated areas such as **Raleighvallen** in the sprawling **Central Suriname Nature Reserve** and one or two **privately owned resorts** in the far south of the country will take more time and money. Although still on the tourist circuit, these resorts are as far away from civilization as you can get without crash-landing in the middle of the Amazon Rainforest.

Brownsberg Nature Park

About 130 kilometres south of Paramaribo on the 500-metre high Mazaroni Plateau, **BROWNSBERG NATURE PARK** (US$5) is the only protected area in Suriname that can be easily visited from Paramaribo using public transport. STINASU operates a lodge on the plateau (from US$15 per person or US$12,50 to camp), and maintains several hiking trails to the impressive waterfalls, which, given the unpredictability involved in spotting much of the wildlife, constitute the park's main attractions. Among the animals you might run into on a lucky day are howler and spider monkeys, deer, agouti and birds such as woodpeckers, macaws and parrots. There are also fine views of the Van Blommestein Lake and rainforest from your elevated position on the plateau.

The simplest way to visit Brownsberg is on an **all-inclusive tour** arranged by STINASU (US$45 for the day, US$115 overnight). Even if you choose to go it alone, you will still have to rely on STINASU for certain things – accommodation at the lodge, for instance, should be paid for at the STINASU office in Paramaribo before you leave. **Public transport** runs as far south as Brownsweg, the generic name for seven villages some thirteen kilometres from the plateau, buses leaving from Paramaribo (see box on p.784) before 9am. Once in Brownsweg, you can arrange for a STINASU bus to pick you up (Sf10,000 return). Getting to Brownsberg by public transport is fine provided you are planning to spend the night; day-trippers, however, will not be able to get back to Paramaribo in the same day if relying on the buses.

The Central Suriname Nature Reserve

Created in 1998 by amalgamating the nature reserves of Raleighvallen, Tafelberg and Eilerts de Haan, the **CENTRAL SURINAME NATURE RESERVE** occupies a 1.6 million-hectare chunk of southwestern Suriname, some nine per cent of the country's total surface area. Most tourist trips are to **Raleighvallen**, where STINASU has a lodge located on Foengoe Island on the upper Coppename River (from US$30 per person or US$12,50 to camp). Other than bathing in the river (the island has the odd sandy beach), the main thing to do is hike to and up the **Voltzberg**, a 375-metre granite mountain affording good views of the surrounding forest canopy. It takes about three hours to get to the base of the mountain (where there is a jungle camp with hammocks); it is another 240 metres or so to the summit. The Voltzberg is a good place to see the world's largest-known species of cock-of-the-rock.

STINASU runs **four-day tours** to Raleighvallen for US$395, whereby you fly one way (50min from Paramaribo) and travel overland the other. The overland journey involves a five-hour drive to a *maroon* village called Witagron and then a three-hour boat trip up the Coppename River to Foengoe Island. There is an entrance fee of US$5 to visit Raleighvallen; note that having a guide is obligatory.

East to French Guiana

It only takes two hours to cover the 141 kilometres between Paramaribo and **Albina**, the last town in Suriname before crossing into French Guiana. You could, however, spend considerably longer exploring the stretch of coast parallel to which the road to Albina runs, the location of the country's two coastal nature reserves: the wild and little-explored **Wia-Wia Nature Reserve**, access to which is from **Matapica Beach** and **Galibi Nature Reserve** with its population of nesting turtles and nearby Amerindian villages of **Christiaankondre** and **Langamankondre**.

Wia-Wia Nature Reserve

Although geographically close to Paramaribo, **WIA-WIA NATURE RESERVE**, which occupies a 36,000-hectare swathe of coast halfway between the Surinamese capital and the French Guiana border, is perhaps the least visited of the country's protected areas. Indeed, the reserve itself has no tourist facilities and will be of most interest to researchers. The tourists who do venture out this way stay at the small and basic STINASU camp (US$35 for a room sleeping up to eight or US$7.50 to camp) at **Matapica Beach** (US$2). This is just west of Wia-Wia, at the end of a channel linking it to the Commewijne River, where turtles come to lay their eggs.

Overnight **tours** to Matapica cost US$105 with STINASU. To get there independently either drive to Alkmaar on the south bank of the Commewijne River, where a STINASU boat will pick you up for the two-hour ride to Matapica, or catch an SMS **boat** (leaves Fri & Sun 7.30am, returns from Alliance 3.30pm; Sf7000 one-way, Sf14,000 return) from Paramaribo to Alliance at the mouth of the Matapica Channel – passing old Dutch plantations en route – then get a STINASU boat up the channel to Matapica. Note that the tide is only high enough for boats to get through the channel twice a day.

Galibi Nature Reserve

Situated in the northeastern corner of Suriname at the mouth of the Maroni River, the 4000-hectare, 13km-long, 1km-wide **GALIBI NATURE RESERVE** (US$2) is one of the Guianas' most famous nesting areas for sea turtles. Unlike Shell Beach in Guyana (see p.776) and Plage Les Hattes in French Guiana (see p.804), where leatherbacks predominate, Galibi Beach is the most important nesting area in the western Atlantic region for the much smaller olive ridley. Leatherbacks, greens and, to a much lesser extent, hawksbills are also present. The nesting season is generally from March to July. The peak time for olive ridleys is mid-May to the end of July, leatherbacks April to June, greens April to May and hawksbills May to July.

The STINASU-run **lodge** (US$50 per room sleeping up to four people) is on the beach itself. The alternative is to base yourself in the Amerindian villages of **Christiaankondre** and **Langamankondre** on the banks of the Maroni Estuary and walk the few hours to Galibi Beach. As Amerindian villages go, these are relatively large (approximately 750 inhabitants) and used to having tourists pop in on them en route to Galibi (visits to the villages are included in most Galibi tours offered by tour operators). Indeed, so comfortable are the villagers with foreigners that they organize and host the annual **Galibi Beach Festival** in September, where you can listen to traditional and not-so-traditional music and witness the election of Miss Galibi.

Overnight **tours** to Galibi, whether organized by STINASU or other tour operators, generally cost US$150. Travellers can do the trip independently – costing at least as much as an organized tour – by going by minibus from Paramaribo to Albina (2hr; Sf15,000), then finding a boat to take you down the Maroni River to Galibi. If you are lucky, a boat carrying provisions might be prepared take you for around Sf40,000 one-way. Of course, you will then have to find another vessel for the return to Albina. Chartering a boat specially for the purpose of carrying you to Galibi is obviously going to be more expensive. The owner of *The Creek Guesthouse* in Albina (see below) has various contacts; alternatively, try calling Galibi Tours (☎08/814577).

Albina

Travellers end up in **ALBINA**, the poor brother of Saint-Laurent-du-Maroni across the Maroni River in French Guiana, for one of three reasons: they are either crossing to or from French Guiana, on a day-trip from Saint-Laurent or trying to find a boat to take them down the Maroni to see the turtles at Galibi Beach.

The town itself has nothing to detain you for more than the briefest of moments. If you are obliged to **spend the night**, you can get a self-contained room with fan at *The Creek Guest House*, Verlengdewilhelminastraat (☎342031 or 342039; ❹). Albina also has several simple Chinese **restaurants** and a *roti* shop.

Crossing into French Guiana

The actual crossing of the border between Suriname and French Guiana is so easy, visitors are tempted to get straight on a motorized dug-out to cross to Saint-Laurent-du-Maroni in French Guiana (Sf10,000) or board a minibus for Paramaribo (2hr; Sf15,000). Be sure, however, to walk past the market and follow the road for about 500 metres to the **immigration office** (7am–6pm) to get your passport stamped. Many travellers report having had problems when either trying to leave or re-enter Suriname because they have failed to get this stamp. There is little reason to wait for the **ferry**, unless of course you have a car. Sailing times from Albina are Mon–Tues & Thurs–Fri 8am, 10am, 3pm & 5.30pm, Wed 7.30am & 5.30pm, Sat 8.30am & 9.30am, Sun 4pm & 5.30pm. The one-way fare is e3,50 (or the guilder equivalent) for a foot passenger, e23 with a car.

Another good reason for going to the immigration office is to change your excess Suriname guilders for euros at the **cambio** located there. The rates are slightly poorer than when buying guilders, but you will not be able to change Surinamese money easily in French Guiana. On the other hand, the rates are good if buying guilders with euros or US dollars.

7.3

French Guiana

Until around fifty years ago, **FRENCH GUIANA**'s muggy, oppressive climate, malaria-ridden forests and inhospitable terrain were considered an ideal way to punish criminals and social misfits of Mother France. After penal colonies were found not to work all that well, some bright spark pointed out that French Guiana was an excellent place to put satellites into orbit, and the European Space Agency duly cleared a patch of jungle and built a space centre. Now, as the number of rocket launches dwindles, French Guiana may need to find a new niche – and why shouldn't this be tourism? The French *département d'outre mer* already attracts a considerable number of visitors from metropolitan France, the majority interested in taking a look at the **space centre at Kourou** and the infamous penal colony on the isolated but beautiful **Iles du Salut**. Both attractions are within easy access of the *département's* capital **Cayenne**, where mosquitoes and a distinct lack of things to do will probably not keep you for too long. As with Guyana and Suriname, eco-tourism is big here. Pirogue trips along **rivers** such as the Maroni, Approuague and Oyapok and treks in the **Amazonian interior** are popular, but the eco-highlight remains **Plage Les Hattes**, one of the finest places in the world to observe huge leatherback turtles laying their eggs on the beach.

Information and websites

While tourist information can be hard to come by in Guyana and Suriname, it flows plentifully in French Guiana. The **Comité du Tourisme de la Guyane** has an office at 12 rue Lallouette, BP 801–97338, Cayenne (Ⓣ0594/296500, Ⓦwww.tourisme-guyane.com), though it was undergoing extensive renovations at the time of writing. The **Office de Tourisme**, at 19 rue L G Damas (Mon–Fri 8am–1pm & 3–6pm, Sat 8am–noon; Ⓣ0594/312919), is the place to go for brochures and maps. Elsewhere in the *département*, you will normally find either a tourist office or a *syndicat d'initiative* with relevant local information. Most of the documentation is in French, and the English-speaking skills of the staff are generally quite limited.

Unsurprisingly, most **websites** on the *département* are also in French. Detailed descriptions of the major attractions with insider tips are available at Ⓦguyane.lutinmalin.com/index, while Ⓦlaguyane.free.fr offers good general information – including in-depth coverage of the space centre at Kourou – with an English version promised for the future. Ⓦwww.outremer.com/GF/Guyindex is one of the better resources for French-speaking visitors, with good tourist and background information and Ⓦwww.terresdeguyane.fr/guyane features news, politics, history, nature and has some helpful links.

Costs and money

If you are arriving in French Guiana from Suriname or Brazil, it will take a moment to acclimatize yourself to the **costs**, which are at least as expensive as metropolitan France. While the food served in the restaurants is generally worth the price, the accommodation and in particular the transportation can be very bad value for money. If you are travelling by land between Suriname and Brazil, expect

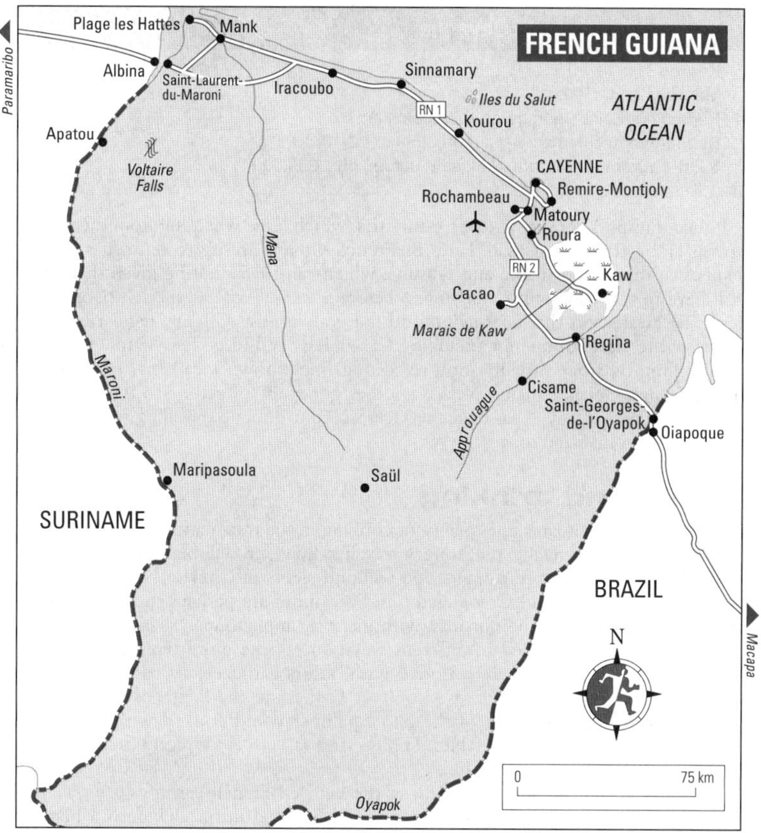

to pay over US$80 in public transportation costs to traverse French Guiana. Independent, budget-conscious travellers who are able to split costs with travel companions should budget on around e40 a day for food and lodging – double this if you plan to be on the move each day and visit every museum and tourist trap.

The currency of French Guiana is, as in metropolitan France, the **euro** (€). Perhaps nowhere else in South America will your **credit card** be as useful as it will be in French Guiana. You can pay for most goods and services with plastic, and **ATM** machines at the major banks and the post office (La Poste) normally accept Visa, MasterCard, Eurocard – but rarely American Express. Banks do not always have foreign exchange facilities (indeed, in Cayenne you will have to go to a *bureau de change* if you want to exchange dollars, pounds sterling, other major currencies and travellers' cheques for euros).

Getting around

With the exception of reaching small towns in the interior, you can get to most of the main attractions **by car** (see "Listings", p.802, for agencies). However, for Saül, Maripasoula and Saint-Georges-de-l'Oyapok (if you don't fancy going by land), Air Guyane (℡0594/293630 at the airport or buy tickets in Cayenne at Takari Tours ℡0594/311960) operates **flights** from Cayenne.

Taxis collectifs from Cayenne

Kourou 1hr; €10.
Matoury 20min; €2.
Regina (for Saint-Georges-de-l'Oyapok) 2hr; €23.
Rochambeau (international airport) 25min; €3,10.
Saint-Laurent du Maroni (Suriname border) 3hr; €30,50.

Public transport consists of **taxis collectifs**, which leave when full from the main towns along the coastal road. Fares in French Guiana are up to ten times more expensive than in Suriname and Guyana, which can be frustrating given that you still have to wait (sometimes for hours) before a *taxi collectif* has enough people to leave. Be aware, also, that *taxis collectifs* do not go – at least with any regularity – to many of the places of interest, including Cacao, Kaw and Plage Les Hattes.

Travelling by **boat** (usually motorized dug-outs known locally as "pirogues") along French Guiana's many rivers is another good way of getting to the interior. There are few – if any – passenger services, so your pirogue travelling will usually be part of an organized tour.

Eating and drinking

By lofty French standards, the quality of cooking in the restaurants of this far-flung *département* is only average; the hungry traveller, however, will be more than satisfied. Along with French restaurants, you will find plenty of Chinese, North African, Indonesian, Brazilian and Creole eateries. Fish dishes are perhaps more common here than elsewhere in the Guianas, with giant shrimp, grouper, shark and several freshwater varieties cooked in different ways, one of the more typical being the *blaff*: a stock (*bouillon*) heavily seasoned with onion, garlic, celery, basil and other spices. Another popular stock, used only at Easter and the Pentecost, is *bouillon d'awara*, made from the fruit of the *awara* palm tree and cooked with chicken, shrimp, crab and various vegetables. *Fricassée* and *colombo* are typical Creole stews, the latter with a strong curry taste.

The most authentic thing to **drink** at the beloved French *aperitif* is a *ti' punch*: lime, sugarcane syrup and rum – sans ice and downed in one. There is a better selection of wines in French Guiana than you will find in most of the rest of South America, and every now and then you will stumble across a café that would not look out of place in Montmartre, serving short, sharp espressos and shots of pastis. The tap water is generally safe to drink, although most people guzzle bottled water (as they do in metropolitan France).

Tour operators

Virtually the only way of getting off the beaten track and out into nature is to join an excursion run by a **tour operator**. Adventurous types should definitely check out Couleurs Amazone, 2bis Ave Pasteur, Cayenne (☎0594/287000, Ⓦwww.couleursamazone.fr), whose young, dynamic owners make a conscious effort to appeal to young, dynamic customers. Their most challenging trip involves being air-dropped by helicopter into a remote part of the jungle and trekking for six days back to civilization. More destination-specific operators, such as Maroni Club, 1 Esplanade Laurent Baudin, Saint-Laurent-du-Maroni (☎0594/347373), and Oyapock Evasion, Thierry Beltan, Village Bambou, Saint-Georges-de-l'Oyapok (☎0594/370259 or 0594/416001), are good if you want to get a glimpse of the Maroni and Oyapok rivers respectively. Many attractions are most easily visited by seeking the services of a tour operator. Prices range from around e40 for day-trips to nearly e1000 for twelve-day adventures to the interior.

Mail, telecommunications and media

The postal system is integrated with that of metropolitan France, which makes deliveries to Europe quick and cheap. There is at least one **post office** (La Poste) in each town, and some have ATM machines that accept major international credit cards (though not American Express).

Public **telephone** booths do not take coins, but cards issued by France Telecom are OK for making local calls. However, they are not good value for calling abroad, and it is better to buy phone cards that work with PIN numbers. A good selection is usually available from the convenience (or *libre service*) stores found all over town.

Internet cafés are harder to find in French Guiana than they are in Guyana and Suriname. There is (an expensive) cybercafé in Cayenne and one or two less formal places elsewhere where you can get online if you have to. The main daily **newspaper** is the French *La Presse de la Guyane*. French **television** is beamed by satellite to most homes in French Guiana.

Festivals

The major festival in French Guiana is **carnival**, which lasts from the first week in January to Ash Wednesday, the last five days of which feature street parades. On Saturday nights during carnival you can witness at certain dance clubs the tradition of *Touloulou*, when the women or *Touloulou*, heavily disguised and wearing masks, are given the sole, non-reciprocal right to ask the men to dance; guys are not allowed to refuse. For more information (in French) on the *Touloulou* and the other institutions of carnival in French Guiana, visit Ⓦwww.carnaval.gf.

History and culture

The inhospitable climate and resistance from Arawak and Carib Indians thwarted early European attempts to establish settlements in what is now French Guiana. By 1624, however, French merchants from Rouen had opened a trading centre in Sinnamary, and Cayenne was founded in 1643. The territory was officially awarded to France in 1667 under the Treaty of Breda, and thereafter all of its inhabitants became French citizens. The colony operated a fragile plantation economy, which collapsed after the abolition of slavery in 1848, after which the French used the place as a penal colony. From 1852 until the colony's abolition in 1947 some 70,000 French convicts were sent to French Guiana, some serving their time on the notorious Iles du Salut. In more recent times, French Guiana is better known for being the European Space Agency's rocket-launching base, which was constructed at Kourou during the 1960s.

French Guiana became an overseas *département* of France in 1946; and in 1974 each overseas *département* also became a *région* with its own Conseil Régional, enjoying a certain amount of autonomy in social and economic matters. French Guiana's recent history has been marked by a rise in pro-independence feeling, starting in the mid- to late 1970s when the strongest political party, the Parti Socialiste Guyanais, demanded greater autonomy for the *département*. Several bomb attacks in 1980 by extremist groups prompted the French government to devolve more power over local affairs to the Conseil Régional. However, social and political tensions between the *département* and metropolitan France continued to simmer. In 1996, rioting and looting broke out after a boycott of classes by secondary school pupils demanding improved conditions, while in 2000 riots occurred in Cayenne following an organized march calling for greater autonomy for French Guiana. Discussions with the French government followed these disturbances, culminating in the publication by local officials in June 2001 of a series of proposals for increased autonomy, which included a request that the territory be given legislative authority on issues concerning French Guiana alone. The French gave these proposals tentative approval and promised to discuss them further after national elections in the spring of 2002.

Culture

Amerindian tribes and ethnic blacks maintain their own **cultural traditions**, as do other groups – notably the immigrant population of Laotians in towns such as Cacao and Javouhey. However, the majority of the population is Creole, and a mixed-Creole culture is dominant in the metropolitan areas. This is typified by the carnival (see p.799), when much of the population dresses up in colourful costumes and performs dances with French, African and East Indian overtones.

The official and most widely spoken **language** in French Guiana is obviously French. A significant proportion of the population also speaks a French-based patois or Creole, with Chinese, Bush Negro (*neg maron*) and Amerindian languages spoken in certain areas.

Cayenne

French Guiana is not blessed by a wealth of beautiful towns, and **CAYENNE** is perhaps the best of a rather average bunch. The administrative capital of the *département* is compact and easy to walk around. There is an attractive central *place*, several good spots from which to gaze out over the Atlantic Ocean, a colourful market and some decent beaches a few kilometres south of town. However, all of this can be seen in a day or two, after which Cayenne quickly loses its lustre. The capital is enjoyable in small doses, and should be treated as a base for excursions into the interior rather than an end in itself.

Arrival and getting around

Aéroport de Rochambeau (☎0594/350300) is about sixteen kilometres south of Cayenne near the town of Matoury. *Taxis collectifs* run to Cayenne from the airport.

The best way to **get around** Cayenne is on foot. **Local buses** to the city's suburbs are run by SMTC (€1,10; ☎0594/254929), most of them leaving from Place du Coq opposite the market. Expect to pay a minimum fare of around €5 for **taxi** trips around town, €25 and more to the airport; good places to find taxis are opposite Canal Laussat with the *taxis collectifs* and Place des Palmistes.

Accommodation

Expensive, limited, rarely very good value and quite often daylight robbery – that just about sums up the bleak **accommodation** options in Cayenne, particularly for those on a tight budget. If you have your own transport, you might consider staying slightly out of town in or around Rémire-Montjoly – no cheaper, but sometimes the surroundings are more pleasant – and you are pretty much guaranteed to have a swimming pool.

Amandiers Place Auguste Horth ☎0594/289728. With only nine rooms (some with sea views), *Amandiers* is one of the more intimate Cayenne hotels and has a well-regarded restaurant. ❻

Amazonia 28 Ave du Général de Gaulle ☎0594/310000, ⓦwww.amazonia-hotel.com. Reliable, if unspectacular, accommodation at this Best Western hotel right in the centre of town. The small swimming pool is the major selling point. ❼

Bodéga 42 Ave du Général de Gaulle ☎0594/302513, ⓦwww.labodega.fr. The only place within the means of the solo budget traveller, with beds in a dorm that has not been cleaned for weeks for €20. Private rooms are slightly better, and more expensive – unless you have people to share with. ❺

Ket Tai 72 Blvd Jubelin ☎0594/289777. Works out a little cheaper than a dorm bed at *Bodéga* if you can share a triple. The rooms do have private bathrooms, a/c and TV, although the cigarette butts on the floor and walls stained with God-knows-what will be the abiding memories of your stay. ❻

Novotel Route de Montabo ☎0594/303888, ⓔh0677@accor-hotels.com. In a lush tropical garden by the beach 3km from the city centre, the *Novotel* is not exactly cheap, but given its relatively short distance from Cayenne, good facilities, comfortable rooms and aesthetic surroundings, one of the more attractive packages. ❽

The City

Before doing anything else, climb the hill to **Fort Céperou** (owned by the Ministry of Defence, but not subject to any great security controls), which affords a **good view** over Cayenne and the ocean. The fort, of which little remains today, was the first building to appear in Cayenne after the Compagnie de Rouen purchased the hill upon which it stands from an Indian Chief named Céperou in 1643. Descending the hill, you will pass the Jesuit-built **Hôtel de la Préfecture** and the **Fontaine de Montrard**, a popular place for the homeless to take an afternoon bath, before arriving at **Place des Palmistes**. This three hectares of green space covered with palms imported from the Approuage region, one of the rare places in French Guiana where they grow, is where much of Cayenne's activity is centred: banks, cinemas, the tourist office, restaurants and at times a small fairground are all on or around the *place*. Next to it is the library and **Musée Départemental**, 1 Ave du Général de Gaulle (Mon, Wed & Fri 8am–1.15pm, Mon & Thurs 3–5.45pm, Sat 8.30am–12.45pm; €2.29), with its exhibits highlighting the cultural and natural riches of the *département*, including paintings by local artists and an impressive butterfly collection. Turn right from the museum and follow the road down the hill to the **fruit and vegetable market**, a colourful place where most of the fruits and vegetables on sale comes from the Laotian farmers in Cacao (see p.808).

The **beaches** in Cayenne itself are not up to much – although there are some good places to watch the ocean sunsets, notably **Place des Armandiers** (officially known as Place Auguste Horth). The coastline a few kilometres south of Cayenne has the best opportunities for sunbathing and swimming. **Plage Montjoly** in Rémire-Montjoly is the longest stretch of beach in these parts: a pleasant-enough spot spoiled slightly by stiff breezes and constant rumours of shark-infested waters. *Taxis collectifs* go to Rémire-Montjoly from opposite Canal Laussat in Cayenne.

Eating and drinking

Anyone on an extended South American trip whose stable diet has been beans, rice and chicken for longer than they care to remember will find the dining options in Cayenne, while not cheap, a refreshing change. Note that most **restaurants** are closed on Sundays.

Amandiers Place Auguste Horth ⓣ0594/289728. Popular restaurant with a terrace that, although not exactly on the coast itself, is close enough to benefit from its refreshing sea breezes. Main dishes from €15; fish is generally cheaper than meat.

Crêp'in 5 rue Lieutenant Becker ⓣ0594/302806. Cayenne's most popular *crêperie* – a good compromise between a fast-food establishment and a more formal restaurant – offers a good selection of sweet and savoury crêpes, as well as salads and freshly squeezed juices.

Mini 3 rue Adjudant Pindard ⓣ0594/300952. Busy little place next to the fruit and vegetable market, *Mini* serves generous portions of Indonesian and Creole lunches for €7.

Palmistes 12 Ave du Général de Gaulle ⓣ0594/300050. On Place des Palmistes in one of Cayenne's most famous buildings, this nineteenth-century bourgeois house contains a lovely wooden-beamed dining room. Traditional French duck and snail dishes (€15 and up) share the menu with not-so-traditional pizzas and the like.

Paris-Cayenne 59 rue de Lallouette ⓣ0594/317617. One of Cayenne's most prestigious, longstanding and expensive restaurants, this is the place to splurge on such dishes as atipa ravioli with ginger or salmon with sea urchin coral, rounded off by passion fruit tart with mango coulis.

Nightlife

One of the city's more relaxing **bars** (even on busy nights), *Harry's Bar* on 20 rue Rouget de l'Isle offers a great selection of whiskeys, beers and cocktails as well as a/c and jazz. A livelier place that's open even when the rest of Cayenne is asleep,

Bodéga, on 42 Ave du Général de Gaulle, is a godsend for those who fancy a *Cuba libre* and a bit of company – and a curse for those trying to get some sleep in the hotel upstairs. The few **nightclubs** in Cayenne tend to be rather low-key and expensive. You will pay a cover charge of around €15 at the likes of *Club 106* and *Number One*, both on Avenue du Général de Gaulle at nos. 106 and 5 respectively. More interesting – though certainly more daring – would be to venture out to **La crique**, a cluster of local bars on the north bank of Canal Laussat, where white faces are as rare as the fast women and barroom brawls are common. In the couple of months preceding carnival, from the first Saturday after Epiphany to Ash Wednesday, *Polina*, the large discotheque at the intersection of the roads to Kourou and Matoury, is the place to go to experience the *Touloulou* tradition unique to carnival in French Guiana, (see p.799).

Listings

Banks Credit Agricole, Crédit Mutuel, Banque Populaire on Place des Palmistes all allow cash withdrawals from ATM machines using Visa and MasterCard – but not American Express. There are also four ATM machines at the post office (see below). If you want to change cash or travellers' cheques, however, you will have to go to a bureau de change such as Change Caraïbes, 64 Ave du Général de Gaulle, which changes most major currencies.

Car rental Companies include Avis (℡0594/302522), Budget (℡0594/313132), and Hertz (℡0594/296930), each with offices along Boulevard Jubelin and at the airport. Expect to pay around e50 a day for the cheapest saloon car.

Foreign consulates Brazil, 23 Chemin Saint Antoine ℡0594/296010; Netherlands, Bâtiment Sogudem Zi, Dégrad de Cannes, 97354 Rémire ℡0594/354931, ©consulat-pays-bas @wanadoo.fr; Suriname, 38 ter rue Christophe Colomb ℡0594/300461; UK 16 Ave Gaston Monnerville ℡0594/311034.

Internet access Information Jeunesse Point Cyb, rue Schoelcher, at 14 Juillet (Mon–Thurs 8am–1pm & 3–6pm, Fri 8am–1pm & 3–5pm; ℡0594/378539), offers an hour's worth of surfing completely free but requires reservations; otherwise try *Restaurant Les Palmistes*, 12 Ave du Général de Gaulle, fifteen minutes online will set you back e4 and thirty minutes e6.

Post office, just off Place des Palmistes opposite Hôtel de la Préfecture (Mon–Fri 7.30am–1.30pm, Sat 7.30–11.45am).

West to Suriname

If much of French Guiana's eco-style tourism takes place to the south of Cayenne, the *département's* most visited attractions are strung along the coast between Cayenne and the border with Suriname. Prime among these is the **Centre Spatial Guyanais** in **Kourou**, the focal point of the European space programme, and **Iles du Salut**, home during the nineteenth century to the most notorious convict settlements. The road (RN1) continues west to the turtle-nesting beach at **Plage les Hattes**. Continuing along RN1, you will arrive eventually at **Saint-Laurent-du-Maroni**, the last town in French Guiana before crossing the Maroni River into Suriname.

Kourou

There was not a great deal to **KOUROU**, about sixty kilometres northwest of Cayenne, before the late 1960s, when the decision was made to clear a patch of the forest and build a rocket-launching site. All of a sudden, Kourou – the only place in the world where both polar and equatorial synchronous orbits can be achieved – became home to thousands of technicians and servicemen imported from metropolitan France. The development of Kourou has not exactly been with the tourist in mind: it is a hopelessly sprawling place with no defined centre, difficult to get around on foot and aesthetically uninspiring. The overwhelming majority of the

20,000-strong population have something or other to do with the Centre Spatial Guyanais, and most people who visit Kourou come for the rockets or because Kourou is the access point for Iles du Salut.

Centre Spatial Guyanais

While hardly set up for tourism in the same way that the Kennedy Space Center is, the **Centre Spatial Guyanais** or CSG is every bit as rewarding as a visit to NASA's Florida-based operation. The sight of rocket launch towers and state-of-the-art technology surrounded by tropical forest could be something out of a James Bond film, and makes a visit to the CSG as surreal as it is educational.

The CSG occupies a total area of 85,000 hectares and has sent over 500 rockets (most of them carrying satellites) into orbit since *Véronique* was the first to blast off on April 9, 1968. Nowadays *Ariane 5* does the trip roughly once every two months, although the schedule is hard to predict (check the website ⓦwww.csg-spatial.tm.fr for updates on the next launch date). The CSG welcome centre is about four kilometres from the centre of Kourou; the actual launch site is a further fifteen kilometres up the road. There is no public transport.

Three-hour **guided tours** of the CSG (Mon–Thurs 7.45am & 12.45pm, Fri 7.45am; compulsory reservations by phone ⓣ0594/326123, ⓔvisites.csg @wanadoo.fr; must be over eight years of age; ID required; free) include a film charting the history of the centre and a visit to the Jupiter Control Centre. *Ariane 5* gives off more light than its predecessor *Ariane 4*, which makes **watching a launch** quite possible from almost anywhere in Kourou. Of course, the experience is enhanced considerably if you get invited to one of the official observation sites. To get an invitation, write including your full name, age and contact details to: CNES, Centre Spatial Guyanais, Relations Publiques, BP 726, 97387 Kourou Cedex. For more information try ⓣ0594/334200 or ⓔcsg-accueil@cnes.fr.

The sites Toucan, Kikiwi, Colibri and Agami are between 4.5 and 6.5 kilometres from the launch pad and usually reserved for clients of the launch (you also have to be over sixteen). The Ibis site is twelve kilometres away (no one under eight), while Carapa, just before the CSG welcome centre, is free for anyone to use. A résumé of the CSG and space exploration in general is available at the **Musée de l'Espace** (Mon–Fri 8am–1pm & 2–6pm, Sat 2–6pm; e6,10, Sat and weekdays if attending a guided tour of the CSG €3,80; ⓣ0594/335384) next to the CSG welcome centre.

Practicalities

You can **get to** Kourou easily enough by *taxi collectif* from either Cayenne (1hr; e10) or Saint-Laurent du Maroni (2hr; €23). However, to leave Kourou, there is no central place where *taxis collectifs* depart, let alone any fixed times (although very early in the morning is often a safe bet). A good place to wait for them is at the bus stand opposite the Gendarmerie in Place de l'Europe. It's best to call the companies directly on ⓣ0594/326093 or ⓣ0594/322800 to arrange a ride. Hitchhiking is a realistic option, especially to Cayenne where traffic is regular.

Point Information Tourisme, 30 Ave du Général de Gaulle (ⓣ0594/322540), dispenses tourist information on the CSG, Iles du Salut and other attractions in the Kourou area.

The two best **places to stay** are the Accor hotels on Lac du Bois Diable at the northern edge of town. *Mercure Ariatel*, Avenue St Exupéry (ⓣ0594/328900, ⓔh1592@accor-hotels.com; ❾), has bungalow-style suites (which include an excellent breakfast), while *Mercure Atlantis*, Lac Bois Diable (ⓣ0594/321300, ⓔh1538@accor-hotels.com; ❽), has smaller – though equally comfortable – hotel rooms rather than suites. Both have swimming pools and various other facilities, including access to bicycles – extremely useful in sprawling Kourou. At the completely opposite end of town next to Kourou's most popular **beach**, Plage des Roches, *Hotel des Roches*, Avenue des Roches (ⓣ0594/320066; ❼), benefits greatly from its attractive, coastal location. The more expensive rooms have views of the sea and, in some cases, Iles du Salut. The most economical option, especially if you are travelling in a group of four, is *Residence Hôtelière Le Gros Bec*, 56 rue du Dr Floch (Ⓣ0594/323523; ❻), where all rooms have a kitchen and a mezzanine with an additional double bed.

There is no shortage of **places to eat** in Kourou. The menu at *Latina Café* at *Mercure Atlantis* (Ⓣ0594/321300) features French, Creole, Surinamese and Brazilian cuisine as well as an excellent club sandwich, which you have to ask for specially since it is not on the menu. *Le Créolia* on Avenue des Roches, next to *Hotel des Roches* (0594/320066), has dishes such as grilled shark fillet and *magret de canard* and a pleasant, beachfront setting. Otherwise, you could do worse than head to Avenue du Général de Gaulle where there is a cosmopolitan selection of eateries, such as *L'Abreuvoir* at no. 5 (Ⓣ0594/321845), which does Provençal dishes for around e15 and *Cupuacu* at no. 27 (Ⓣ0694/423752), a Brazilian *churrascaria* that offers *feijoada, vatapa* and other such dishes.

Iles du Salut

Fifteen kilometres north of Kourou lie the **ILES DU SALUT** (Salvation Islands), infamous for their use as a penal colony from 1852 to 1953. **Ile Royale**, the island visited by tourists today, was used for administration and housing common law criminals. **Ile Saint-Joseph** was where the "incorrigible" convicts and those who tried to escape were sent; while the virtually inaccessible **Ile du Diable** was reserved for political prisoners, most famously Alfred Dreyfus. While Ile Royale has been restored, the ruins of the penal colony on Ile Saint-Joseph are overgrown with vegetation and arguably offer a more authentic and atmospheric experience.

Popularised by the book entitled *Papillon* – and later the Steve McQueen film of the same name – in which former prisoner Henri Charrière recounts the horrors of life in the colony and his various attempts at escape (which finally succeeded), the Iles du Salut have become a major tourist attraction. This has led to the somewhat incongruous presence of an upscale **hotel**, *Auberge des Iles du Salut* on Ile Royale (Ⓣ0594/321100, Ⓦwww.ilesdusalut.com; ❾ full board, ❻ double room or ❹ for hammock space), where you can get comfortable, albeit somewhat austere, rooms and good meals. Another rather contradictory aspect of the Iles du Salut given their gruesome past is their natural beauty. Unlike the Guiana's coastline, the islands are surrounded by clear blue water, and the vegetation is green and lush. There is nothing to stop you slinging a hammock or camping anywhere on Ile Royale and Ile Saint-Joseph (assuming that you can get there), but note that Ile du Diable is off-limits to the public. Although you can purchase basic supplies at the hotel, bring your own food and water if you are considering the camping option.

You should be at the boat jetty in Kourou, at the end of Avenue du Général de Gaulle, at 7.50am to catch the daily **ferry** (Ⓣ0594/320995, reservations necessary; €35 round-trip) to Ile Royale. The trip takes around one hour each way, and the return from Ile Royale leaves at 5pm. The alternative is aboard a **private yacht** such as *La Hulotte* (Ⓣ0594/323381, Ⓔlahulotte@terresdeguyane.fr) or *Albatros* (Ⓣ0594/321612 or 0694/263954), which offer one- or two-day tours (around €45 and €70 respectively; children under twelve half-price). Both include visits to Ile Royale and Ile Saint-Joseph, and on the two-day tour you usually end up spending the night on Saint-Joseph's small beach.

Plage les Hattes

From roughly April to July, **PLAGE LES HATTES**, at the mouth of the Maroni River a few kilometres from the Suriname border is French Guiana's best place to view leatherback turtles laying their eggs on the beach at night. Compared with Galibi Beach in Suriname (see p.794) and Shell Beach in Guyana (see p.776), Plage

Les Hattes is relatively accessible, lying a mere four kilometres from Awala-Yalimapo. There is also an abundance of **accommodation** in the vicinity – unusually for French Guiana, much of it is quite affordable. In Awala-Yalimapo, you can rent a hammock 100 metres from the beach at *Chez Judith et Denis*, Avenue Paul Henri (☎0594/342438 or 0694/263327; ❺) – where breakfast is included – while *Chez Jeanne* (☎0594/342982; ❹ per person) is a mere fifty metres from the beach. Mana has more varied options, ranging from the three basic rooms rented by the *Soeurs de Saint-Joseph de Cluny*, 1 rue Bourguignon (☎0594/348270; ❸ per person; collect keys 3–5pm) to the ten rooms with air conditioning available at *Le Bougainvilliers* 33 rue Frères (☎0594/348062 or 0694/238044; ❺). The **eating** options in Awala-Yalimapo basically boil down to the Creole–Amerindian *Au Paradis des Acajous* (☎0594/343708) and *Yalimale* (☎0594/34 34 32), which has refreshing shrimp salads with coconut milk and *fricassée*. Creole food also predominates in Mana, although there are alternatives such as the French restaurant *Le Buffalo*, 36 rue A.M. Javouhey (☎0594/348036) – even if its dishes are "adapted" from local produce and eaten in a cowboy-themed dining room.

Saint-Laurent-du-Maroni

Now one of French Guiana's larger towns with a population of around 25,000, **SAINT-LAURENT-DU-MARONI** on the east bank of the Maroni River some 260 kilometres from Cayenne is quiet and down at heel. It was originally conceived as an agricultural penal colony, where convicts were put to cultivating bananas and sugarcane, and managing forests. The old **Camp de la Transportation** (guided tours Mon–Sat 8am, 9.30am, 11am, 3pm & 4.30pm, Sun & public holidays 9.30am & 11am July–Aug also 3pm & 4.30pm; e4) is on a bend in the Maroni River. Though you can walk round the grounds and check out the permanent exhibition of photos in the camp's former kitchen for free, tours of the detention cells and other installations put everything into its chilling context and should not be missed. Buy tickets for the tour at the **Office du Tourisme**, 1 Esplanade Laurent Baudin (Mon–Fri 7.30am–6pm, Sat 7.45am–12.45pm & 2.45–5.45pm, Sun 9am–1pm; ☎0594/342398), which also provides plenty of documentation (in French) on the history of the camp and Saint-Laurent-du-Maroni, as well as details of excursions up the Maroni River (see below).

Practicalities

Taxis collectifs will be waiting where dug-outs from Suriname arrive – and at the ferry terminal to meet boats – to take passengers to Kourou (2hr; €23) and Cayenne (3hr; €30.50). Unless there is a wave of arrivals from Suriname, these vehicles can take some hours to fill up. With this in mind, hitchhiking becomes an increasingly attractive – and feasible – option. You can also **rent a car** at Maroni Rent-A-Car, 6 rue Jean-Jacques Rousseau (☎0594/341430) for €107 a day.

The most comfortable **hotel**, *Le Relais des Trois Lacs*, 19–21 Domaine du Lac Bleu (☎0594/340505, ©r3lacs@nplus.gf; ❼), is actually three kilometres from the centre of town in an attractive lake and forest setting. All 23 rooms are air conditioned and have satellite TV, and the hotel boasts a huge swimming pool. More central, but still with air conditioning and swimming pools, are *La Tentiaire*, 12 rue Roosevelt (☎0594/342600; ❻), and the more downmarket *Star Hotel*, 109 rue Thiers (☎0594/341084; ❺). If you prefer the more intimate *gîte* or guesthouse experience, try the six-room *Chez Julienne*, rue Gaston Monnerville (☎0594/341153; ❻), which still has comfortable rooms with all the mod cons. Five kilometres south of Saint-Laurent-du-Maroni you can rent hammock space for e14 per person (hammock not included) at *Maroni Club*, 1 Esplanade Laurent Baudin (☎0594/347373), a jungle camp at Balaté Creek.

For **food**, try *Chez Felicia*, 23 Blvd du Général de Gaulle (☎0594/343087), a small, bustling place (at least at lunchtimes) serving *fricassé* and other Creole dishes.

Excursions from Saint-Laurent-du-Maroni: Maroni River

Almost all of the tour operators in French Guiana (see box on p.798) offer Pirogue trips up the **Maroni River**, and you should shop around for the most suitable itinerary. The attraction of the Maroni River compared to others in the *département* – such as the Approuague and Oyapok – is its relatively large Amerindian and Bush Negro populations (on both the French Guiana and Suriname sides of the river). As a result, excursions are based much more on visits to native villages along the banks of the river than wildlife spotting and the like. A number of tour operators in Saint-Laurent-du-Maroni offer day-trips and even shorter excursions for those just wanting to get out on the water for a few hours and take in an "authentic" village, with a traditional dance performance and local craft hawking thrown in for good measure. Try Maroni Club, 1 Esplanade Laurent Baudin next to the Office du Tourisme (☎0594/347373).

An alternative to going on an organized tour is to make your own way to the Bush Negro village of **Apatou**, about seventy kilometres upriver from Saint-Laurent-du-Maroni. A pirogue leaves daily (€12 one-way) from the Glacière in Saint-Laurent-du-Maroni at 11am, arriving in Apatou at around 2pm. The return from Apatou is the following morning at 7am from in front of *Restaurant Célia*, next to the riverbank in the village centre. You can **sleep** in a hammock at *Célia* for €12.20 per person (including hammock rental). Forty-two kilometres east of Apatou are the **Voltaire Falls**, plummeting waters with nearby facilities for picnics and lodging – *L'Auberge des Chutes Voltaire*, Route de Paul Isnard (closed Tues–Wed; ❻ or €13 per person for a hammock).

Le Mambari, 13 rue Jean-Jacques Rousseau (☎0594/343590), where you can eat *moules frites* or pizza before a game of billiards or table football, has a Franco-American feel to it. *Le Toucan*, Blvd du Général de Gaulle (☎0694/406029), has salads and daily menus for e9.50.

If you have just crossed over from Suriname and need to **change money**, you can do so at BFC on Avenue F. Eboué. The post office on Boulevard du Général de Gaulle has ATM machines that accept Visa and MasterCard.

Crossing into Suriname

The quickest and easiest way to cross the Maroni River to **Albina** (see p.794) in Suriname is by taking a motorized dug-out (Sf10,000) from the end of rue Ho-Kong-You in the Village Chinois, not forgetting to get your passport stamped at the **immigration office** (6am–7pm) at the ferry terminal about 500 metres south from where the dug-outs leave. There is no real reason to wait for the **ferry**, unless of course you have a car. Sailing times from Saint-Laurent-du-Maroni are as follows: Mon–Tues & Thurs–Fri 7am, 9am, 2pm & 5pm; Wed 7am & 5pm; Sat 8am & 9am; Sun 3.30pm & 5pm. The one-way fare is e3.50 for a foot passenger, e23 with a car.

There is a **cambio** at the ferry terminal in Albina (see p.795) which gives good rates when buying Suriname guilders with euros and US dollars. Indeed, these rates are better than you will get in Paramaribo.

The Amazon: Maripasoula and Saül

The remoteness of Maripasoula and Saül, the two main settlements in French Guiana's Amazon Rainforest interior, has been promoted by the tour operators to such an extent that both of them have ceased to become particularly off-the-beaten-track destinations. OK, so getting to them will involve flying or spending several days on the river (and sometimes on foot), but once there you will likely be surrounded by fellow tourists and the odd local inhabitant trying a little too hard to be as authentic as the brochures promised. This said, being this far into the Amazon while still having a reasonably comfortable place to lay your head is good recompense for the company.

MARIPASOULA, nearly 300 kilometres up the Maroni River, is the logical starting or finishing point for pirogue trips (for more on the Maroni River, see box opposite); while **SAÜL**, an old gold-mining town 150 kilometres from Cayenne, in the geographical centre of the *département*, is the base for exploring the ninety kilometres of marked jungle trails maintained by the New York Botanical Garden.

Practicalities

Air Guyane has **flights** to both Maripasoula and Saül from Cayenne. For Saül, flights depart Tues–Fri 2pm, Mon & Sat 10am; €52.92 one-way, €98,18 return; for Maripasoula, they leave Mon–Thurs & Sat 10.15am, Fri & Sun 2.15pm; €67,10 one-way, €126.54 return. **Tour operators** such as Takari Tours, 8 rue du Caitaine Bernard (Ⓣ0594/311960, Ⓔtakari.tour@wanadoo.fr), offer several intrepid alternative ways of reaching these towns. A four-day trip up the Maroni to Maripasoula, visiting Saramaca, Bonis and Wayana villages en route, will set you back around e450. And to Saül, a twelve-day adventure on the Maroni River from Saut Sabbat to Degrad Blanc followed by a 25-km hike, is a mere e930. For excursions in and around Saül, contact Explorando, Christain Baur (Ⓦexplorando.free.fr/pages/menu, Ⓔexplorando@wanadoo.fr). Rates are around e70 a day**,** and there must be a minimum of four people.

Contact the *mairies* (town halls) in Maripasoula (Ⓣ0594/372150) and Saül (Ⓣ0594/374500) for information on **accommodation**. In Maripasoula, two tourist camps on the Inini River (a tributary of the Maroni) offer comfortable, hammock-based lodgings with all meals and river transfers from Maripasoula included in the price. *Saut Sonnelle*, Crique Inini (Ⓣ0594/314945; €85 per person), is closer – about 30min from Maripasoula – and cheaper than the more remote *Tolenga* (Ⓣ0594/294894, Ⓔlodge.tolenga@wanadoo.fr; €99 per person). Saül also has a tourist camp a seven-kilometre walk from the village next to the water: *Les Eaux Claires – Horizons Secrets* (Ⓣ0594/415379; ❻ per person full board, ❷ per person in a hammock). Accommodation in Saül itself is in *carbets* equipped with hammocks. Rates at the *Gïte municipal* are around €11 per person.

South to Brazil

The traffic on the road **south from Cayenne** thins considerably once you have cleared the city's several satellite towns and the airport. The settlements in the southern part of the *département* are few and far between compared with the relatively populous north coast, and tourism here is mainly nature oriented. Interesting side-trips – but only if you have your own transport – can be made to the Hmong (Laotian) village of **Cacao** and the *marais* or swamp of **Kaw**, but most will venture this way on the way to Brazil. At the end of the paved section of RN2, **Regina** is the departure point for excursions on the **Approuague River**, but the road continues on the opposite bank of the river as an unsealed track all the way to **Saint-Georges-de-l'Oyapok** on the Brazilian border.

Kaw

Just past Matoury, instead of continuing along RN2 towards Regina, take the turn-off on the left, which leads eventually to Kaw. This 60km stretch of road is surely one of the most scenic in the Guianas, winding its way up and across the heavily forested Kaw Hills. The picturesque town of **ROURA** is nestled on the banks of the Orapu River, its church spire poking out through the trees. You can get

accommodation (two air-conditioned rooms) and traditional Creole **food** at *Restaurant Creola* in the nearby Laotian village of Dacca (Ⓣ0594/280715; ❺), and **tourist information** at the Syndicat d'Initiative de Roura (Ⓣ0594/311104).

Some fifty kilometres further on, the road ends abruptly at the Everglades-style swamp known as the **Marais de Kaw**. The small village of **KAW** is on an island in the middle of the swamp – but is not the main reason for coming out this far. The swamp covers some 100,000 hectares, and the presence of surrounding hills complete with mists during the wet season makes for some stunning vistas. Kaw is an excellent place to observe many species of water birds including buzzards and flamingos, and organized tours make a great deal of the after-dark pirogue trips to spot black caiman (rarer than red caiman). You can **spend the night** on a floating *carbet* in the middle of the swamp. There are enough hammocks and bunk beds for around twenty people, although half this number is preferable if the swamp's serenity is not to be completely shattered by screaming kids and disgruntled tourists from Paris. JAL Voyages, 26 Ave du Général de Gaulle (Ⓣ0594/316820, Ⓦwww.jal-voyages.com), specializes in one-day and overnight **trips** to the Marais de Kaw. Somewhat surprisingly, mosquitoes are not a problem on the swamp itself; there are considerably more on the banks and in the hills around it.

Cacao and the Approuague River

The paved section of RN2 continues for some one hundred kilometres after the Kaw turn-off, terminating at the small town of Regina on the north bank of the Approuague River. Forty kilometres before Regina is the turn-off for **CACAO**, a village created in 1977 for the express purpose of accommodating a group of Laotian refugees of Hmong ethnicity no other town in French Guiana wanted. Since then, Cacao has become the fruit and vegetable basket of the *département*. You can **sleep** in hammocks at *Quimbé Kio* on a wooded hill next to the village (Ⓣ0594/270122; e10 per person; reservations necessary), or opt for a room at *L'Auberge des Orpailleurs* on RN2 near the turn-off (Ⓣ0594/270622; closed Sun evening & Mon; ❺). The best Laotian **restaurant** in Cacao is *Chez By et Daniel* (Ⓣ0594/270998), which has a shady terrace to go with its pork steamed in a banana leaf and chicken with Laotian caramel lunches.

Don't be mislead by the numerous Renaults, Peugeots and Citroens often seen parked next to the small river jetty in **Regina** – there is little to see in the town itself, and the cars belong to tourists who have come to Regina to join pirogue trips up the **APPROUAGUE RIVER**. A good number of these tourists have booked a **stay** at *Cisame*, a 1.5-hour journey upriver – make bookings through Couleurs Amazone, 2bis Ave Pasteur (Ⓣ0594/287000, Ⓦwww.couleursamazone.fr). Arguably the most comfortable of French Guiana's jungle camps (you still sleep in hammocks, but not cheek by jowl, and there are good sanitary facilities, constant electricity and tasty meals), *Cisame* also offers other activities such as river swims, panning for gold and extremely informative nature walks (provided you understand French). Two-day visits departing from Regina every Tuesday, Thursday and Saturday irrespective of the number of people cost €149 including all transport, meals and activities.

Taxis collectifs run from Cayenne to Regina (2hr; €23). You will be left at the river jetty. If you are continuing on to Saint-Georges-de-l'Oyapok and the Brazilian border, you should take a pirogue across the river (€5) where *taxis collectifs* will be waiting (1–1.5hr; €20).

Saint-Georges-de-l'Oyapok

No one is expecting **SAINT-GEORGES-DE-L'OYAPOK**, the last town in French Guiana before crossing the Oyapok River to Brazil, to become a firm fixture on the South American travel circuit now that it is possible to get there by public road transportation from Cayenne. Apart from excursions on the Oyapok organized by tour operators, there is not a great deal to do but get your passport stamped and hightail it to Brazil. If you do feel like sticking round for a while, check out the **Saut Maripa** rapids, the longest in French Guiana, about thirty minutes upstream past the Brazilian town of Oiapock. Oyapock Evasion (Ⓣ0594/370259 or 0694/416001) can organize day-trips from €54; Couleurs Amazone, 2bis Ave Pasteur (Ⓣ0594/287000, Ⓦwww.couleursamazone.fr) have five-day excursions on the Oyapok for €435.

Practicalities

Air Guyane has daily **flights** between Cayenne and Saint-Georges (departing Mon–Sat 8am, Fri & Sun 4.45pm; €52.82 one-way, €98.18 return). The road from Regina to Saint-Georges is unsealed, but easily navigable – at least during the dry season – in 4WD vehicles and sturdy *taxis collectifs,* which do the trip in an hour or two for €20. While cheaper to **spend the night** across the border in Brazil, there are lodgings in Saint-Georges. In the town itself, *Caz Calé*, rue E Elfort (Ⓣ0594/370054; ❻), has fifteen rooms, some with air conditioning, and dancing on Saturday evenings. *Chez Modestine* on the main square (Ⓣ0594/370013; ❻) offers pretty much the same thing, as well as **meals** for around €12. If you prefer a room overlooking the river, go to *Le Tamarin* (Ⓣ0594/370884; ❻). On the river itself, occupying a small islet facing Saint-Georges, *Ilha do Sol* has hammocks for negotiable prices. On Ilet Sophia about thirty minutes upstream you can also sleep in hammocks for around €5 per person (contact *Chez Modestine* for information).

Crossing into Brazil

Taxi collectifs from Regina will drop you on the eastern edge of town where boats cross the Oyapok River to Oiapoque in Brazil (15min; €4 or 10 real). The **immigration office** can also be found here. Once in Brazil you should go to the **Federal Police** to get your passport stamped. With the river on your right, follow the main street until you see a road to your left with a church in its middle. The Federal Police can be found on the right side of this road past the church.

Moneychangers operate on the Brazilian side of the river, but not in Saint-Georges.

8

Paraguay

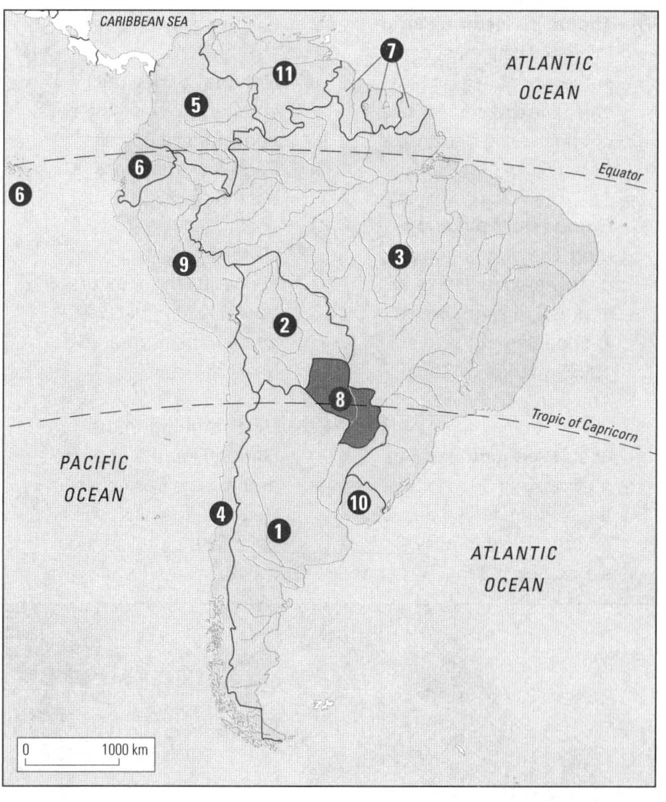

CARIBBEAN SEA
ATLANTIC OCEAN
Equator
PACIFIC OCEAN
Tropic of Capricorn
ATLANTIC OCEAN
0 1000 km
11
5
7
6
6
9
3
2
8
10
4
1

Paraguay highlights

✱ **Panthéon de los Heroes** Get a sense of Paraguay's brutal history at this monument in Asunción's magnificent Plaza de los Heroes. See p.825

✱ **The Itaipú Hydroelectric Project** The largest dam in the world, Itaipú presents an extraordinary feat of engineering design. See p.833

✱ **Ciudad del Este shopping** The duty-free bargains here are almost as impressive as the frenetic shopping at the "Supermarket of South America". See p.832

✱ **Jesuit reducciónes** Get a glimpse of Jesuit life at the well-preserved Jesús and the Trinidad missions. See p.837

✱ **Caacupé Basilica de Nuestra Señora de los Milagros** At the Día del Virgen procession every December 8th, the entire town comes alive for the festivities around the basilica. See p.830

✱ **National parks** The country's eleven national parks show unspoilt Paraguay at its very best. See p.839

✱ **Tereré** A Paraguayan speciality, this ice-cold herbal tea is truly welcome in the oppressive heat. See p.817

✱ **Birdwatching in the Chaco** Home of the rare and elusive Burmeister's Seriema, the Chaco is a twitcher's paradise. See p.840

△ caption

Introduction and basics

Landlocked in the centre of the continent and hemmed in by much bigger, more exotic locales, Paraguay is primarily rural and largely unspoilt. Relatively untouched by tourism, it is strongly influenced by its Guaraní heritage and by a turbulent history of dictatorship and oppression. Guaraní is still taught in schools and, outside the cities, it often replaces Spanish as the spoken tongue.

As a result of the unsavouriness of the country under Stroessner's rule (see pp.819–20), Paraguay has generally been omitted from many South American travel itineraries, and the country has acquired an undeserved reputation as boring and uninteresting amongst the travelling community. Because of a relative lack of demand, not much of a tourist infrastructure has been put in place, and there's little commercial buildup, especially compared with that of neighbouring countries like Argentina and Brazil; indeed, areas devoted to tourism concerns tend to be right at border crossings, like Ciudad del Este, which you'll hit coming from Brazil. Nevertheless, if you make the the journey you'll be rewarded with a sense of exploration and taste of a very unvarnished South America in the small villages and relatively untrammelled national parks that dot the land.

Where to go

Despite its more than 1.2 million inhabitants, the capital and largest city **Asunción** is relaxed and friendly and retains the atmosphere of a large provincial town. With a compact centre easily navigable on foot, its numerous squares and gardens afford a peaceful, pleasant atmosphere, while a series of impressive monuments are testament to violent episodes of days gone by.

To the east, a tourist circuit runs out from Asunción around the resorts of **Lago Ypacarai**, via the religious centre of **Caacupé**, to the duty-free haven of **Ciudad del Este** on the Brazilian border. Commonly known as "The Supermarket of South America" the latter is a tacky place, with bargains galore, especially in duty free goods and electronics. Nearby, the **Itaipú Hydroelectric Project** is the largest of its kind in the world, a remarkable engineering achievement that has to be seen to be believed.

South of the capital, the ruins of **Jesús** and **Trinidad** are the finest examples of the unique social experiments conducted by the **Jesuit missions** in the seventeenth and eighteenth centuries. The friendly city of **Encarnación** on the border with Argentina makes an excellent base for exploring them and their surroundings.

Paraguay's biggest asset, however, is its natural beauty, and the increased interest in **eco-tourism** is opening up more and more of the country to visitors. The vast wilderness of **the Chaco** with its scattered **Mennonite colonies** is one of the last great frontiers on the continent. Home to the *tagua*, a pig-like creature thought extinct for many years, the Chaco's wildlife is abundant and it is a haven for **birdwatchers.** With eleven **national parks** to choose from, visitors looking for natural beauty will be spoilt for choice in Paraguay. Though remote and occasionally difficult to reach, the stunning scenery and idyllic surroundings will make any trip well worth the effort.

When to go

Notorious for its extremes of climate, Paraguayan weather can be unbearable at times. Temperatures **in the Chaco** can be uncomfortably high in the summer (December to February), with an average of 40°C and very little rainfall. **Southern Paraguay** is rather more humid, with rain likely to fall throughout the year, though lowest in winter (June though August). Here, summer temperatures average around 35°C, although the humidity can make it feel

unpleasant. Winter temperatures are rather more variable, averaging around 22°C, though occasionally dipping to freezing point. Perhaps the best times to visit are the spring (March to May) and autumn (September to November) when temperatures are rather more amenable. During this time of year, however, cold fronts blowing in from the Argentine pampas can cause sudden drops of temperature from hot to near freezing in a matter of hours. If visiting outside the summer months it is only sensible to prepare for any eventuality.

Red tape and visas

A **passport** valid for six months after entry is required by all nationals, except those of other Latin American countries who can use their **national identity documents**. Australian, Canadian, Irish and US citizens require a visa for entry, which is granted for three months; other Western European, UK and Japanese citizens do not (see ⓦwww.columbusguides.com for a full list of countries not requiring visas). **Visas** cost US$56 for single entry and US$81 for multiple entries, and are available from consulates or consular sections of each country's embassy. Two passport photographs, proof of adequate funds and an exit ticket are necessary for applications. There is a US$18 **departure tax** payable on leaving the country by air.

Costs and money

Recent economic difficulties in South

America have affected Paraguay as badly as Argentina and Uruguay, but the currency was in a state of turmoil long before that. Devaluation and high inflation are common features of the Paraguayan economy and it remains one of the most unpredictable currencies on the continent. It is also among the cheapest countries in South America, and it is possible to live comfortably on US$10–15 per day.

The local currency is the **Guaraní**, (noted in the text as **G**), and notes are issued in denominations of 1000, 5000, 10,000, 50,000 and 100,000. Coins are becoming increasingly worthless but are still in wide circulation, in denominations of 50, 100 and 500. It is almost impossible to change the Guaraní outside Paraguay, and you should attempt to get rid of any spare currency before crossing the border. **Credit cards** are not widely accepted outside the capital and incur a charge of five to ten percent. Many ATMs accept foreign cards such as Visa and MasterCard but, if not, it is possible to withdraw money over the counter with the presentation of a valid passport. **Travellers' cheques** can be more troublesome and some banks refuse to cash them if you cannot produce a bill of sale.

Banks are open from 8am to 2pm and invariably closed at weekends. Most of the larger towns feature several *casas de cambio* for **changing money**, but the unpredictability of the currency means it is unwise to withdraw large amounts at any one time.

Information, websites and maps

Tourism is not well developed in Paraguay, and even in Asunción it can be difficult to find information. The headquarters of the **Direccion General de Turismo** is at Palma y Alberdi in Asunción, but staff do not give out leaflets or city maps. (There is, however, an excellent website at Ⓦwww.senatur.gov.py). Permits, required to visit many of the **national parks**, are available from Dirección de Parques Nacionales y Vida Silvestre at Franco y Ayolas in Asunción (Ⓣ021/445214). There is not much information on Paraguay on the Internet, but prospective eco-tourists will find Ⓦwww.ecotour.com.py, which also gives information about estancias, helpful, while the Spanish-language Ⓦwww.mundolatino.com/paraguay offers an excellent general overview of the country. Birders may find the Ⓦwww.birdlist.org/paraguay of some use when looking for information about what they can expect to see.

Good national and local **maps** are available from the Servicio Geografico Militar in Asunción at Artigas 920.

Accommodation

On the whole accommodation in Paraguay represents excellent value for your money, though away from bigger towns it can sometimes be difficult to find. It is not usually necessary to book in advance, although it is a must in **Caacupé** during the weeks surrounding the feast of the Día del Virgen (December 8th), and in Filadelfia during the Trans-Chaco Rally (September–October) when both towns are flooded with people.

While all but the very cheapest of **hotel rooms** are en suite, **aparthotels**, self-contained mini-apartments including kitchen, bathroom and living area are particularly worth seeking out. In most places, it is possible to get a decent double room for as little as 35,000–50,000G, usually with TV and breakfast. Budget travellers should have no problem finding a good deal, and should not be scared off by very cheap rooms – though it always pays to inspect a room before handing over any cash. Generally even the most basic accommodation comes with an en-suite bathroom. There are **no youth hostels** in Paraguay, but **campsites** can be found in almost every town. Beware, however, that very few boast running water or electricity and in many cases they are little more than a cordoned-off area, frequently close to a river. In winter, heavy rains and strong winds can put many camps out of action and those on riverbanks are liable to flood at any time.

Should you fancy getting your hands dirty, a stay on an **estancia**, a country ranch estate, is worth looking into. Comfortable but occasionally basic accommodation is offered alongside a number of outdoor pursuits to give you an enjoyable taste of the country life. Most are very isolated and difficult to access without your own transport, and many are out in the Chaco, but several Asunción tour companies offer all-inclusive packages that include a stay on an estancia (see Asunción listings).

Getting around

With the exception of the Chaco in the north, travelling around Paraguay is, like in much of South America, generally cheap and easy. There are currently no **train** services in Paraguay, although there is some talk of a privatized service running in the future.

By car

The Paraguayan **road network** is good, with major roads (*rutas*) in the majority of the country being well paved. In the Chaco, however, roads are poor and seasonally unpassable. Even in major Chaco towns such as Filadelfia most roads are dust tracks that quickly turn to mud in wet weather. **Car hire** is rather expensive ($US40–60 per day), and most companies charge for extra kilometres, making it difficult to see the country cheaply. On the other hand, petrol costs are very low. Remember that an International or Inter-American Driving Permit is required.

By bus

By far the easiest way of getting around Paraguay is by **bus**. Asunción is the main transport hub with very regular services to all major national destinations, although the large number of independent bus companies (see "Listings", p.827) can make it difficult to get to grips with timetables. You will be approached by ticket touts at the terminal, but do not be afraid to ask their assistance as this can save time and they do not expect to be tipped. It is important to make the distinction between direct buses (*directo*) and those that stop along the way (*removido*), as the latter can almost double the journey time.

City buses are also cheap, with a fixed fare of around 1500G. There are few night services even in the biggest towns.

By air

The main domestic carrier is Arpa, which flies between Asunción and the main cities including Ciudad del Este and Concepción. **Flights** are moderately expensive and often infrequent, and you can expect to pay up to US$80 for a single from Asunción to Ciudad del Este. There are regular flights with non-Paraguayan carriers from Asunción to Buenos Aires, Santiago de Chile, Montevideo and Brazilian destinations. Costs for international flights can be saved with a Mercosur Airpass. Valid for thirty days travel to Argentina, Brazil, Chile, Paraguay and Uruguay, it is available to customers living outside South America from participating airlines.

Mail and telecommunications

Postal services are occasionally unreliable, and important mail should always be sent registered or by international courier companies.

Telephone services are provided by ANTELCO, with an increasing number of private cabins offering satellite connections. There are very few payphones on the streets and none outside the capital.

Internet access is widespread, remarkably cheap (around 4000G per hour) and by far the easiest way to keep in touch. Besides cybercafés, most shopping malls also have access. Connections are generally good, but can be a little slower at peak times.

Food and drink

If you're coming from Argentina or Brazil you are likely to be disappointed by the standard of **Paraguyuan cuisine**. Outside the capital, the majority of restaurants serve up a depressingly similar and rather bland menu of junk food, and it is only in Asunción and the larger cities that you will find any real variety.

While *parrilladas* (large open grills) are not uncommon, it is rare for them to reach the

Language and culture

Paraguay is highly influenced by its strong **Guaraní heritage**. The native population is estimated at three percent of the total population – two-thirds of whom live in the Chaco, where they are employed mainly as agricultural labourers – and the Guaraní language predominates in rural areas; **Spanish** is the language of towns and cities.

Oddly, despite the influence of the Spanish being less obvious than in other South American countries, the **music** of Paraguay is almost entirely European in origin. The Jesuits of the seventeenth and eighteenth centuries swamped the native music with the establishment of their missions, and today the guitar and the harp are the main instruments. Paraguayan **dance** shows strong Argentinean influences. Major dances include the *galopa*, the *polca Paraguaya* and the *danza de la botella,* during which female performers balance a tower of bottles on their heads as they swirl their multi-coloured skirts.

Woodcarving and engraving featured heavily in the Jesuit period, leading to the highly ornate building works seen at sites such as Trinidad and Jesús. Among Paraguay's most famous artists are Pablo Alborno, Juan Anselmo Samudio and Carlos Colombo.

same level of choice or the quality of meat that is found in Argentina or Brazil. Roast chicken (*pollo asado*) is excellent, however, particularly from take-away stalls, where it is served with *mandioca* (manioc) and a cut of meat. *Milanesas* (meat escalopes) are popular but often stringy and sometimes inedible, while pizza is sold just about everywhere and can be very good; *pizza común* is a pizza without cheese. By far the most common fish on the menu is *surubí*, usually grilled and a little more expensive than meat dishes.

Drinks

Undoubtedly the most widely consumed drink is **tereré**, ice-cold *yerba mate*, a herbal tea that is surprisingly refreshing and addictive. Paraguayans are not averse to experimenting with their *yerba mate* in the search for new flavours, and local children will even drink the herb mixed with Coca-Cola. *Mosto* is a sickly sweet juice made from sugarcane, while **caña** is a distilled alcoholic spirit from the same source. **Beer** is usually imported from Brazil and Argentina, but *Pilsen Dorada* and *Baviera* are good local brands. Although usually served in litre bottles, a *chopp* is a draft beer. Paraguayan **wines** are not widely available, and most are imported. Local wines are not to everybody's taste, but brands to look out for are Rey Baco and La Copa.

Safety and the police

Paraguay is generally a safe country to visit, and what few problems you are likely to have will probably only be encountered in Asunción or Ciudad del Este. However, the usual precautions regarding personal safety and the safety of belongings should be taken, and it is unwise to wander alone after dark in unpopulated areas of the capital. In border towns, overcharging is common particularly in duty-free stores, and it is advisable to compare prices before buying.

The Chaco, a vast, largely unpopulated wilderness, is an extremely desolate and hostile environment, and you should not go off the beaten track without a local guide or substantial preparation and supplies. The High Chaco, north of Filadelifa, is particularly harsh, and every year expeditions north to the Bolivian border come to grief because of insufficient planning. **Political tension** can also render the larger cities unsafe – several people died during violent anti-government demonstrations in Asunción during 2002. For up to date information on safety, check the British Foreign Office website Ⓦwww.fco.gov.uk/travel/countryadvice or the US State Department's Ⓦtravel.state.gov /travel_warnings.

Opening hours and public holidays

Opening hours are generally from 9am until 6pm from Monday to Friday, with half day closing on Saturday. Most businesses are closed all day Sunday.

In addition to the **national holidays** listed below, some local anniversaries or **saints' days** are also public holidays when everything in a given town may close down, taking you by surprise.

Calendar of public holidays

January 1 New Year's Day (*Año Nuevo*)

February 3 San Blas Day, Patron Saint of Paraguay (*Día de San Blas*)

March 1 Death of Mariscal Francisco Solano López (*Cerró Corà*)

March/April Easter and Holy Week (*Pascua y Semana Santa*)

May 1 Day of the Worker (*Dia del Trabajador*)

May 15 Independence Day (*Dia de la Independencia Patria*)

June 12 Commemoration of the end of the Chaco War (*Paz del Chaco*)

August 15 Founding of Asunción (*Fundación de Asunción*)

August 25 Victory in the Battle of Boquerón (*Victoria del Boquerón*)

December 8 Immaculate Conception (*Día del Virgen*)

December 25 Christmas Day (*Navidad*)

Sport and outdoor activities

Like most South American countries, **soccer**, or *fútbol*, is the main sporting obsession. Although the national league is not considered as strong as those of neighbouring countries, this did not prevent Club Olímpia of Asunción from winning the *Copa Liberatdores* (South American Championship) in 2002, the year of their 100th anniversary.

The Chaco is home to the **Trans-Chaco Rally** – usually held in September or October – one of the most demanding motor races on earth. **Fishing** is becoming increasingly popular, with *surubí* and *pacu* popular game species. Undoubtedly the biggest prize for any angler in Paraguay though is the *dorado* of the Rios Paraguay, Paranà and Tebicuary, a monster fish of up to 30kg (68 pounds).

Visitors with an interest in nature will find the vast unpopulated areas of the country to their liking. There are a total of eleven national parks, and the animal life is spectacular and easy to see, particularly the **birdlife** of the Chaco. **Mammal** species worth looking out for include the capybara (the world's largest rodent), the elusive jaguar and the endangered *tagua*, a pig-like creature from the Chaco once thought extinct. **Ecotourism** is becoming increasingly popular, and some tour companies, notably Ecotour (Ⓦwww.ecotour.com.py), organize visits to areas of natural beauty from the capital. Perhaps the best way to see the country though is to hire a car and explore for yourself, although this can be pricey. For more information on national parks contact the Dirección de Parques Nacionales y Vida Silvestre (Ⓣ021/615812).

History

Paraguayan history has, for the most part, been shaped by a series of crazed, despotic dictators, each determined to leave their mark on the record books. From the valiant efforts in the War of the Triple Alliance under the insane Francisco Solano López, right through to the brutal and oppressive regime of Alfredo Stroessner, life in Paraguay has frequently been hard. It is only over the last decade or so that the country has finally begun to embrace democracy.

Colonial Paraguay

The Spanish explorer **Alejo García** first encountered the **Guaraní** tribes of the upper Paraguay and Paraná rivers in the early sixteenth century. The Spanish founded Asunción in 1537 and, as the city grew, it became an important base for the conquest of Bolivia, Argentina and Paraguay.

In 1609, **Jesuit missionaries**, operating independently of the Spanish, arrived to convert and "civilize" the natives through nonviolent means. They offered financial and religious inducements to the Indians to settle in *reducciones*, where they assisted in the building of magnificent churches, the remains of which can still be seen today. At their height, the *reducciones* covered most of the Alto Parana of what is now Southern Paraguay and Northern Argentina in a series of thriving, self-sufficient communities, but their success was short-lived. After the expulsion of the Jesuits in 1767, the Indians were reduced to virtual slavery for their colonial masters.

A lack of valuable resources and precious metals led to the neglect of Paraguay by the colonial authorities, and the hated **encomienda** system of land distribution caused widespread unrest throughout the seventeenth and eighteenth centuries. Under this system, land and any inhabitants of it became the property landowners appointed by the colonists. Tensions were exacerbated by popular demands for the free trade of *yerba mate* and tobacco, and when the Spanish Governor in Asunción refused to cede he was soon ousted. With the Spanish Empire's attention focused elsewhere, **independence** was declared in May 1811.

Independence and war

Independence brought political turmoil, and an ensuing series of military dictatorships led the country into a number of costly and catastrophic wars. Most notable was the **War of the Triple Alliance** (1865–70), in which the crazed dictator **Francisco Solano López**, who considered himself the Napoleon of South America, declared war on Brazil. When Argentina refused to assist him, he promptly declared war on them as well, thereby dragging their allies Uruguay into the conflict. The war ended with the death of López at Cerro Corá in 1870, by which time Paraguay's population had been halved to 200,000, only 28,000 of whom were male. The situation became so bad that, during the war, children as young as 10 were routinely drafted into battalions and sent out to the front line, often armed with nothing more than farm implements.

Political upheaval and economic catastrophes consumed the country in the years after the war, with political instability and economic crisis typical, a period of unrest that the Bolivians capitalized upon by beginning to occupy areas of the Chaco. This was largely ignored until the discovery of oil in the region in the 1920s gave the area a new importance. In the resulting **Chaco War** (1932–37), **Mariscal Estigarribia** led the Pargauayans to victory, at the cost of a further 36,000 lives.

The Stroessner dictatorship

After the war, turbulence continued, with civilian and army factions launching bids for power. In the 31 years before 1954, no fewer than 22 presidents had held office. There was a brief civil war in 1946, before a military coup in 1954 brought **General Alfredo Stroessner** to power. With control over the army and the main political party, the Colorados, he maintained power for 34 years, winning eight rigged elections and brutally purging the country of political opponents. A network of informants meant that any evidence of infraction was rapidly and mercilessly crushed, while leaders of opposition parties were hand-picked under a policy known as "guided democracy" to ensure that he emerged victorious in elections. One of the few positive features of his rule was heavy investment in the infrastructure of the country and the joint completion of the **Itaipú Hydroelectric Project** with Brazil in 1982 was perhaps his finest achievement.

Present-day Paraguay

After a military coup in 1989 finally ousted Stroessner, its leader, **General Andrés Rodriguez**, became the first new president in over a third of a century and immediately set about liberalization measures. Free elections were held in May 1993, won by the quasi-liberal Colorado Party, but the unpopular economic reforms they implemented led to a general strike the following year.

In 1996, the deteriorating economic situation caused a split within the Colorado Party, and the controversial **General Lino Cesar Oviedo** was chosen as the man to lead them in the 1998 elections. Oviedo had often spoken out against corruption at the highest level of government, but before the elections could take place he was jailed for ten years for his part in an attempted coup two years earlier. Oviedo's running mate **Raúl Cubas Grau** stood in his place and duly won the election, yet immediately created a constitutional crisis when he freed General Oviedo within a week of assuming power. However, the supreme court ruled that Oviedo should serve his sentence and, when it sought to impeach Cubas Grau just six months after taking charge, succeeded in driving him into exile in Brazil. He was followed by **Luis González Macchi**, who survived an unsuccessful coup in May 2000, but continues to battle against social unrest, an unpredictable economy and massive unemployment.

Books

The most renowned Paraguayan author is Augusto Roa Bastos (*I The Supreme, Son of Man*), winner of the Cervantes Prize in 1989, the highest literary award in Spanish, while the nation's poets are Josefina Pla, Elvio Romero and Herib Campos.

Paraguay (Cultures of the World) by Leslie Jermyn is a good introduction to the country; *Paradise with Serpents* by Robert Carver is an account of travel through Paraguay; and *Indians of the Paraguayan Chaco* by Renshaw provides a good overview of the native population. Paraguay's colourful history has led to the appearance of a large number of political and historical texts. An excellent study is *Socialism, Liberalism and Dictatorship in Paraguay* by Paul Lewis; while *Rule by Fear*, published by Human Rights Watch, covers the period of Stroessner's rule. *The Chaco War* by Bruce Farcau deals specifically with the conflict with Bolivia from 1932 to 1935. *Paraguay: An Informal History* is one of a number of books on the history of the country by Harris Gaylord Warren. *Forgotten Fatherland* by Ben MacIntyre is an interesting investigation into the life of Elisabeth Nietzsche and her attempt to establish "pure" colonies in Paraguay. There is no specific guide for birdwatchers, but *The Illustrated Checklist to the Birds of Southern South America and Antarctica* by Martin de la Pena illustrates all species that are recorded in the country.

8.1

Asunción

Perched on the Bahia de Asunción and overlooking the Río Paraguay, **ASUNCIÓN** is the only city of any real size in the country. Once the historic centre of governance for the Spanish colonies of Rio de la Plata, the city declined in importance with the founding of Buenos Aires, while the impenetrable Chaco prevented it from becoming the envisioned gateway to Peru. For the Paraguayan economy, however, the capital retains its significance, and its population of 1.2 million represents almost 25 percent of the figure for the whole country.

At first glance, Asunción doesn't appear to offer much to the visitor. Many of its finest colonial buildings were demolished shortly after independence in a misguided attempt to improve the city's infrastructure, while high volumes of traffic have raised pollution in the centre to unpleasant levels. Nevertheless, anybody prepared to commit some time here should find it to be one of South America's more pleasant capital cities. Large areas of parkland and tree-lined avenues give the days a laid-back, almost sleepy ambience. During the evening, the city springs to life thanks to a friendly populace and vibrant nightlife. As well, the proximity of nearby resort towns and the city's excellent transport connections prove Asunción to be the ideal base from which to begin your exploration of the country.

Arrival and information

The international **airport**, Aeropuerto Internacional Silvio Pettirossi, is 15km northeast of the city along Avenida España. From the airport, bus #30A runs to the bus terminal, from where you can catch a **bus** to the centre (1500G); however, buses are often very busy and rather slow when traffic is bad, and a **taxi** to the centre for around 50–60,000G is a better bet.

The two-tiered **intercity bus terminal** (☎021/551740) at Argentina y Fernando de la Mora lies in the south of the city. A plethora of companies run regular services across the country from the upper tier, while the lower tier (*subsuelo*) serves shorter journeys to Lago Ypacarai and the surroundings. A taxi from the terminal to the centre will cost around 20,000G.

There is very little in the way of tourist provision in Paraguay, and it can be difficult to obtain even the most basic information. Small kiosks at the airport and bus terminals will answer questions, but **maps** can be hard to come by. In town, a limited **tourist information office** (☎021/441530) can be found on the ground floor of the Direccion General de Turismo building at Palma y Alberdi. One of the best free city maps is produced by National Car Rental (see "Listings", p. 827); pop into their office to pick one up.

City transport

The centre of the city is compact and easily walkable, and once you are there it is unlikely you will need to use public transport to see any of the main sights. **Taxis**,

however, are cheap, and most congregate around the Plaza Uruguaya and a journey in the city streets shouldn't come to more than about 10,000G, although prices rise at night. City **buses** stop at all street corners, and while you may be initially overwhelmed by the sheer number of them, it won't take you long to work out those that are of most use to you. Destinations are advertised on the front of the buses and there is a flat fare of 1500G for most journeys. Buses #28 and 31 run from Cerro Corá to the bus terminal.

Accommodation

Accommodation in Asunción is generally good and very affordable, and all the establishments listed below are found in the centre of the city. While some of the plushest establishments quote their prices in American dollars during times of economic uncertainty, those that do not can be exceptionally cheap. The best areas for cheap accommodation are in the streets around the two main plazas, de los Heroes and Uruguaya, in the north of the city, and are also ideally located for the main sights.

Camping is available at the attractive Jardín Botaníco, entrance Av Artigas (no phone; ❶), 6km east of the centre. Facilities are basic but the site is safe. Take bus #44B marked Artigas from the centre.

Amalfi Caballero 877 y Fulgencio Moreno ☏021/494154. Sleek and modern with bright, colourful rooms and efficient service. Situated five blocks south of Plaza Uruguaya. ❺

Aparthotel Manduará Mexico 554 y Azara ☏021/490223. Various standards of self-contained apartments with kitchen and living area. Internet access and room service included. Handily located a block south of Plaza Uruguaya. ❻

Atlantico Mexico y Azara ☏021/449919. Next to *Manduará* and in stark contrast to it, the *Atlantico* is spacious but with rather bare rooms and thin mattresses. Nonetheless, this is an acceptable budget option. ❸ with TV and a/c, ❷ without

City NS de Asunción y Humaitá ☏021/491418. Classy but pricey with superb location three blocks south of Plaza de los Heroes. Rooms have TV and room service, and there's a decent on-site restaurant. ❺

Itapua Fulgencio Moreno y EEUU ☏021/445121. Despite the palatial colonial design of the exterior of the building, the interior rooms are rather sparsely decorated. Nevertheless, *Itapua* is perhaps the best budget option in Asunción, and the friendly owners will hand out useful city maps that can be hard to find elsewhere. ❷ with a/c, ❶ with fan

La Española Herrera 142 ☏021/449280. Modern, bright and airy, *La Española* features a restaurant and bar. The rooms are small but clean and comfortable, and it is ideally located three blocks south of Plaza de los Heroes. ❺

Plaza Ayala y Paraguari ☏021/444196. Great location overlooking Plaza Uruguaya and next to the old railway station. The rooms are well equipped, with minibars and cable TVs. ❹

Preciado Azara 840 ☏021/447661. Modern and spotless, the *Preciado* has a friendly, helpful staff and offers plush rooms, with cable TV, a/c and marble bathrooms. Price includes an excellent buffet breakfast and use of a swimming pool. Three blocks southeast of Plaza Uruguaya and handily placed for the city's best nightlife. ❺

Rivera Aparthotel Franco 261 ☏021/497311. Friendly, self-contained apartments with kitchen, living area and cable TV at a very reasonable price and just a block from Plaza de los Heroes. Rooms are large and dark, but do not have a/c. ❸ per person

The City

It is near the **waterfont** that you will find the best of Asunción's architecture, the finest examples of which date mainly from the late nineteenth century and the regime of President Carlos López. The approximate centre of town is the area around **Plaza Uruguaya** and **Plaza de los Heroes**, and the main attractions are nearby. The Plaza de los Heroes contains the city's – and possibly the country's – most instantly recognizable monument, the cathedral-like **Panteón de los Heroes**, erected in memory of the great names in Paraguayan history.

Beyond the centre the roads become gridlocked and sights are few and far between. Don't miss the **Jardín Botanico** at the end of Avenida General Artigas, the main road north out of the city. Of historic importance as the former López family estate, it is also a great place to spend the day relaxing in the sunshine.

The waterfront and Plaza de la Independencia

Paraguayo Independiente, and its continuations, Avenidas República and Mariscal López, run along **THE WATERFRONT**, taking in the majority of the city's sights. At the eastern end, set among highly coiffeurred gardens, the stunning, marble president's residence, the **Palacio de Gobierno**, was completed in 1892 on a design based on the Palace of Versailles. It was once decreed that anybody caught looking at the building and its arched porticoes and windows would be "shot in the act". Fortunately, the approach is rather more relaxed today – though armed guards are still on hand should you step out of line.

One block east, Avenida República begins to branch north to the **PLAZA DE LA INDEPENDENCIA**. Marked largely by balding lawns, the northern end is dominated by the ageing, pink **Palacio Legislativo** (Mon–Fri 7am–3pm; free), while the western edge houses the **Antiguo Colegio Militar** (Mon–Fri

9am–3pm; free), a former Jesuit College. The latter, the main recruitment centre of the Paraguayan army, also houses a small museum of military artefacts celebrating the triumphs and failures of the nation's armed forces. A block south of here, along 14 de Mayo, the 1772 **Casa de la Independencia** (Tues–Fri 7am–noon & 2–6pm, Sat & Sun 7am–noon; free) is one of the oldest buildings in the country. It was here the architects of Paraguayan independence met to discuss their plans, though today it houses a historical museum, largely devoted to the fight for independence. Worth checking out are the displays associated with the Jesuit Missions, especially if you don't plan to visit any of the *reducciones* yourself. On the southeastern corner of the plaza stands the Neoclassical **Catédral**, a rather disappointing, plain structure which, despite its gaudy lemon colour, fails to capture the imagination.

Plaza de los Heroes

Two blocks south of the Catédral, the **PLAZA DE LOS HEROES** is a huge and verdant square encompassing four blocks. The square itself is immense and filled with *lapacho* trees that bloom a dramatic pink in July and August. A lively and vibrant place, it attracts tourists and peddlers alike, mostly for the **Panteón de los Heroes** (daily 8am-6pm; free) in the northwest corner. This great domed memorial to Paraguayan heroes was begun in 1863, but the building was not completed until 1937 and the end of the Chaco War. Permanently guarded by foot soldiers, it suffers somewhat from the close proximity to the surrounding modern buildings, which make it difficult to view and photograph from the outside.

The Panteón contains the remains of former presidents Carlos Antonio López and his son Mariscal Francisco Solano López as well as Chaco War hero Mariscal Estigarribia. Towards the end of the War of the Triple Alliance (1865–70), when the male population had been severely depleted, children as young as 12 years old were routinely drafted. Their deaths are marked by **La Tumba a los Soldaditos Desconocidos** (the tomb of the unknown child soldiers). The interior of the Panteón is like a mini-cathedral, with statues and busts adorning the walls, while the tombs are viewed from a raised balcony in the centre of the building. Changing of the guards takes place every few hours, involving much pomp and ceremony, as well as some blatant flag-waving.

West of here, you'll find the busy commercial and shopping street of **Palma**, where high-street shops and boutiques rub shoulders with street traders peddling counterfeit wares at apparently bargain prices.

Plaza Uruguaya and around

Head two blocks east along Mariscal Estigarribia to the **Museo de Bellas Artes** (Tues–Fri 8am–6pm, Sat & Sun 8am–noon; free). Minor works by Tintoretto and Courbet, as well as numerous pieces by Paraguayan artists including Pablo Alburno and Juan Samudio, figure in this large collection of fine arts, though some of the displays are rather disappointing.

The Paraguayan flag

The only national banner whose front and reverse sides are different, the **Paraguayan flag** has undergone several changes through the years. Though the main theme has always remained the same – three horizontal stripes of red, white and blue forming the background – the central emblems have had their designs altered. The current flag has been in existence since 1991, with the Paraguayan coat of arms on the front, featuring a gold star and wreath, and the seal of the treasury on the reverse side, identified by a gold lion carrying a pole bearing a Jacobean cap and featuring the motto *"Paz y Justicia"* (Peace and Justice).

Another two blocks east is the leafy but rather charmless **PLAZA URUGUAYA**. With patchy lawns and prostitutes touting their wares freely among the trees, it can be a little intimidating after dark, but the surrounding streets boast some excellent restaurants and hotels. On the northern edge is the dilapidated **Estación de Ferrocarril**, the city's railway station, which was in use until the abandonment of the railroads. The old steam engine *Sapucai*, made in 1861, is still visible through the door and until recently would still ferry tourists around the country.

Outside the city centre

Outside its compact city centre, Asunción is a sprawling metropolis, and departing from the city by road can be a lengthy and frustrating process. Beyond some picturesque residential suburbs, there is little to warrant extended exploration, but a few sights might capture your attention if you have time on your hands.

The **Cementario de la Recoleta**, 3km east of the centre along Avenida Mariscal López, is an atmospheric and attractive cemetery of ornate tombs and mausoleums built in a host of architectural styles, from Spanish colonial and Neoclassical through to Art Deco. Colourful and far less morbid than you may imagine, it is a fascinating historical journey through Asunción high society. Several hours can be wasted simply wandering around and reading the inscriptions. Perhaps the most distinguished occupant is **Eliza Lynch**, the Irish mistress of Mariscal Francisco Solano López, who gained notoriety for her lavish lifestyle while the people starved. She is buried near to the tomb of their baby daughter.

Winding its way north from the centre around the bay, Avenida General Artigas arrives at the **Jardín Botanico** (daily 7am-darkness; 5000G) 6km east (bus #24 or 35 from Cerro Corá). Once the grounds of the López family estate, today the gardens are open to the public. Set around the banks of the river, there are suggested walks through the trees and a small, if rather distressing zoo of exotic wildlife. The gardens' **Museo de Historia Natural** (Mon–Sat 8am–6pm, Sun 8am–1pm; free) presents a patchy collection of natural history housed in the attractive colonial-style former home of Carlos Antonio López; the nearby house of his son, Solano López, is an altogether grander affair housing the **Museo Indigenista** (same hours; free).

Eating

Some of Paraguay's best cuisine can be found in the streets of the capital, where the menus take on a more cosmopolitan feel than in the rest of the country. The best **restaurants** are found in the colourful streets of the centre around plazas **de los Heroes** and **Uruguaya**. Food in shopping malls can often be good, offering a wide range of choices in a small area. The top floor of *Shopping Excelsior* has a particularly good selection of eateries including a *parrillada*, an Austrian-style pub, a Spanish *taverna* and a Brazilian *por kilo* joint.

Café Literario Mariscal Estigarribia. Just off Plaza Uruguaya, this atmospheric, bohemian café offers a small but interesting snack menu. Try the *sopa paraguaya* – not a soup as the name suggests, but a sort of corn cake.

Le Saint-Tropez 25 de Mayo y Paraguari. Pleasant and friendly French restaurant, with unusual seaside decor on Plaza Uruguaya. Good cheap *menu del día* for 5000G served until 3pm and several French specialities. Try the steaks, which are thick and juicy – but be sure to ask for them well done if you don't like the sight of blood.

Munich Eligio Ayala y Independencia Nacional. One of the best restaurants around with great steaks and large portions. German specialities and pleasant, shaded courtyard add to the experience.

Oliver's Independencia Nacional y Azara. Hot and cold buffet of meats and salads from 15,000G (22,000G including drink and dessert) served until 3pm. The evening menu is limited and rather pricey but the food is excellent.

Rodizio Palma 591 y 15 de Agosto. Brazilian-style buffet *rodizio* with price dependent on weight. Grill, salad bar and pizzas from around 7000G make this a very popular choice among those wanting as much as possible for as little as possible.

San Roque Eligio Ayala y Tacuary. Excellent fish and a wide-ranging menu of meats at surprisingly reasonable prices.

Talleyrand Estigarribia 932. Rustic French farmhouse interior with overbearing service but the international menu is well prepared and portions are ample. Rather more expensive than most (30–40,000G for a main course) but well worth it if you are looking for silver service without the usual bill. Try the *brochette mixta*.

Drinking and nightlife

Asunción has a thriving **nightlife**, especially on weekends. Things only really get going after midnight and many revellers begin their journey home in the early morning sunshine. The blocks east of **Plaza Uruguaya** are where most of the action is, but it is not unusual for a bar that is jam-packed with people one night to be totally deserted the next. Ask around to keep your finger on the pulse or check out the listings guide *Tiempo Libre*, sporadically available throughout the city.

Africa Eligio Ayala y 14 de Mayo. A slightly upmarket disco bar with dress code, the *Africa* plays Latin and international pop.

Asunción Rock Mariscal Estigarribia y Tacuary. Wacky rock hang-out, packed with revellers at weekends. With rest areas and an ample dance floor, you will hardly notice the unusual choice of decor, which includes a car apparently crashing out of a wall.

Bavaria Estados Unidos y Cerro Corá. Small, but friendly German-style bar with bizarre surrealist paintings adorning the wall. Great place for a quiet beer.

Brittania Cerro Corá y Tacuary. Ever popular with travellers and locals alike, *Brittania* serves English pub grub and beer well into the early morning hours. The place tends to be busiest on week nights, acting more as a meeting place at weekends. Pleasant outdoor courtyard and bar, but the indoor seating is limited. Closed Mon.

K2 Mariscal Estigarribia y Tacuary. Trendy hang-out with open-air courtyard and stage for live rock and pop performances.

Listings

Airline offices Few airlines operate out of Asunción, and those that do have offices at the airport. Aerolíneas Argentinas ☎021/491011; Aerolíneas Paraguayas, Oliva 761 ☎021/491040; American Airlines ☎021/443330; Iberia ☎021/214246; LanChile, 15 de Agosto 588 ☎021/490782; Lloyd Aéreo Boliviano, 14 de Mayo 586 ☎021/441586; Varig ☎021/448777

Banks ABN-Amro, Eusebio Ayala 4215 ☎021/514167; Aleman, Mariscal López ☎021/391660; Banco do Brasil, Olivia y NS de Asunción ☎021/490121; Citibank, Chile y Estrella ☎021/418200; Continental, Artigas ☎021/294228; Lloyds TSB, Palma y O'Leary ☎021/419369; Multibanco, Ayolas 482 ☎021/498466

Bus companies The following bus companies all operate out of the main bus terminal and are listed here in alphabetical order with their major route destinations – Buenos Aires (BA), Ciudad del Este (CDE), Concepción (CON), Encarnación (ENC), Filadelfia (FIL), Pedro Juan Caballero (PJC), Villarrica (VIL).

Alborada, ENC; Carreta del Amambay, PJC, CON; Concepcionera, CON; El Tigre, FIL; Fecha de Oro, ENC; Guareña, VIL; Golondrina, PJC, CON, FIL; La Encarnacena, BA, ENC; La Ovetense, CON, PJC; La Santaníana, CON; Libertador, PJC; Lions, CDE, ENC; Nasa, CON, PJC, FIL; Nuestra Señora de Asunción, ENC; Pycasu, ENC, CDE; Rapido Caaguazu, CDE; San Luis, CDE; Rysa, ENC, CDE, PJC; San Juan, ENC; Yacyreta, ENC, BA.

Car rental National, Yegros 501 ☎021/491848; Nauticar Sacramento y Cespedes ☎0981/522935; Only, 15 de Agosto 520 ☎021/492731; Rem Car, Padre Cardozo 452 ☎0981/457764.

Crafts Folklore, Palma y Iturbe, sells a wide-ranging collection of local arts and crafts, with woodcarvings particularly noteworthy. Street stalls on the Plaza de los Heroes also sell limited traditional crafts of variable quality and price. The Pettirossi market, at the intersection of Pettirossi and de Francia, is a claustrophobic but enthralling mass of crafts, agricultural products, foodstuffs and junk.

Embassies Argentina, España y Boqueron ⓣ021/212320; Bolivia, América 200 ⓣ021/203656; Brazil, General Díaz 521 ⓣ021/444088; Canada, Profesor Ramírez y Juan de Salazar ⓣ021/227207; UK, Av Boggiani 5848 ⓣ021/612611; USA, Mariscal López 1776 ⓣ021/213715.

Emergencies Fire ⓣ132; police ⓣ130; general emergencies ⓣ911.

Exchange Money can be changed in most of the major bank branches and there are a number of *casas de cambio* along Palma. Several street moneychangers operate in the area around the Panteón de los Heroes, but be sure you know the exchange rate before dealing with them, and be prepared to negotiate.

Hospitals Central, Sacramento ⓣ021/206896; Francés Privado, Brasilia 1194 ⓣ021/295250.

Internet access Internet access is very easy to find, especially in and around shopping malls. Prices start at around 40–60,000G per hour. Cyber SPC, Chile 677; Excelsior Shopping, NS de Asunción y Dominguez; Cyberking, Olivia y 14 de Mayo, very large with over thirty terminals.

Post office International mailings are expensive and sometimes unreliable. Artigas 749 ⓣ021/200788.

Tour companies VIP's Tour, Mexico 782 ⓣ021/441199, ⓔvipstour@uninet.com.py organizes a series of guided tours of the capital and Paraguay as a whole from US$20 per day. Lion's Tour, Alberdi 456 ⓣ021/490591 and Intertours, Peru 436 ⓣ021/211747 visit the mission lands and the *circuito central*.

Travel agents Asunción Tours, Alberdi 456 ⓣ021/490711; Skytours, España 2220 ⓣ021/662843; and Turismo Latino, Eligio Ayala 1820 ⓣ021/205386.

8.2

East of Asunción

Respite from the urban jungle of Asunción is easier than you might imagine, and just a short distance from the city limits the pace of life slows to a more typically Paraguayan tempo. The lushness of the area is immediately striking, the greenness of the vegetation contrasting with the brick-red clay soils to create a textbook image of fertile South America, which the smoky streets of the capital may have pushed to the back of your mind.

Ruta 2 heads east out of Asunción passing the cool waters of **Lago Ypacaraí** and its surrounding resort towns. Famed for their crafts and laid-back atmosphere, they are the perfect places to begin your exploration of the country. Check out **Itaguá** for its *nanduti* lace, **Aregua** for its ceramics or, if you are seeking spiritual enlightenment, **Caacupé**, the country's main religious centre. The road continues on to the crossroads of **Coronel Oviedo**. A major transport centre and meeting point of four main *rutas*, it is depressingly bereft of interest and not somewhere to be stranded. From here take Ruta 8 a short distance south to the well-kept town of **Villarrica**, or Ruta 7 east to the consumer-driven mayhem of **Ciudad del Este**. Ruta 3, the northerly connection with **Pedro Juan Caballero** (see p. 840) on the Brazilian border, is a long and arduous road through a largely deserted no man's land, but teeming with wildlife.

Lago Ypacaraí and around

In the absence of a usable coastline, the watery expanse of **LAGO YPACARAÍ**, 30km east of Asunción, has been adopted by holidaymakers as a popular **water-sports** and **beach resort**. Varying pollution levels occasionally make swimming unsafe, and you should always seek local advice before taking the plunge. Easily accessible from the capital as a day-trip or weekend destination, the lake features several towns around its shores that are worth the visit, though not necessarily an overnight stay.

Surprisingly picturesque, despite straddling the main *ruta* east of Asunción, **ITAGUÁ** (platform 35 from Asunción bus terminal) is a small town near the lake whose centrepiece is a serene plaza with a sprawling church. Home of *nandutí* spiderweb lace, fine early examples of it can be seen at the **Museo San Rafael** (daily 8am–6pm; free) in the old town, which was founded in 1728. In the surrounding streets, the nondescript box-like dwellings with their red roofs and pillars closely resemble eighteenth-century Jesuit settlements. Three blocks to the east of the plaza is the **Mercado Municipal**, the best place to buy quality lace at competitive prices. If you want to see the lace being made before you buy it, **Mutuales Tejedoras** (Mon–Sat 7am–6pm, Sun 7am–1pm) a couple of kilometres out of town is recommended, although prices are slightly higher than elsewhere.

AREGUA is a pleasant town on the cool mountain slopes above the lake, 7km north of Ruta 2 at km20. Noted for its ceramics, it is the choice destination for Asunción day-trippers, and during the peak season (December to February) it can become rather crowded. Should you wish to stay, *Hospedaje Ozli*, Av del Lago 860 (☎0291/2380; ❷) has comfortable rooms with fans and communal bathrooms.

Nearby are **cerros Koí** and **Chorori**, unique mountains that command glorious views over the lake and its surroundings. The pattern of horizons and columns in the rock is usually confined to igneous rocks of South Africa and Canada, but the two represent the only place on earth where the pattern is present in sedimentary rocks. You'll pass them on the road north from the main *ruta* to Aregua.

From Aregua boat trips run at weekends to the shady village of **SAN BERNARDINO** on the eastern shore of the lake. Favoured by Asunción's mega-rich, prices are much higher than in nearby towns, but the surrounding mix of valleys and wooded mountain slopes makes for some fantastic walking. The cheapest place to stay is *Hotel Balneario*, Nuestra Senora de la Asunción y Yegros (☎0512/2252; ❷), with small, but comfortable rooms and breakfast included. Simple meals will also be served in the evening on request. South of San Bernardino, near the junction with Ruta 2, a sign for **La Gruta** marks the trail to a series of caves and grottoes with rippling pools and moss-covered cliffs.

Caacupé

The self-styled religious capital of Paraguay, **CAACUPÉ**, 54km east of Asunción, is for most of the year a quiet, unassuming, provincial town. Despite its divine calling, the marketing potential of religious paraphernalia isn't lost on the locals, and many make a healthy living peddling iconoclastic trinkets to the steady stream of pilgrims and interested tourists that pass through the town almost daily.

It is on December 8th that Caacupé really comes alive, though, with the **Día del Virgen** (Feast of the Immaculate Conception). Candlelit processions lead a statue of the sacred virgin through the town streets, while celebrations involve fireworks and bottle dancers, transforming the town from a quiet site of pilgrimage into the focus of the country's religious fervour. The prelude to the celebration is a period of prayer in the modern, but glorious **Basilica de Nuestra Señora de los Milagros**. Consecrated by the Pope in 1988, the copper-domed roof dominates the skyline and the whole structure is completely at odds with the rest of the town's rather bland architecture. Most of what you will want to see is contained in or around the cobbled main plaza, said to hold 300,000 worshippers on feast days, but more often occupied by traders and beggars hoping to capitalize on the guilt of the penitents as they approach the Basilica.

Practicalities

Frequent **buses** from the *subsuelo* in Asunción (platforms 33 and 34) make the journey east to Caacupé, prolonged by frequent and seemingly pointless stops along the way. Get off as soon as you see the Basilica's domed roof. Buses back to the capital run from along Mariscal Estigarribia, one block from the Basilica. **Accommodation** is plentiful but fills quickly in early December, when it is essential to book ahead. Good budget options in view of the Basilica include the basic *Virgen Serrana* on Eligio Ayala 1577 (☎0511/2366, ❷), with some rooms having cable TV at no extra cost; and *Katy Maria*, around the corner on Dr Pino (☎0511/42860, ❸), which is perhaps the better option and contains a good **restaurant** serving the usual Paraguayan menu. Prices are likely to rise during the Día del Virgen, when competition for rooms is great.

Villarrica and around

From Caacupé, Ruta 2 continues east to the transport crossroads of Coronel Oviedo, from where it is 42km south to the pretty, once prosperous town of **VILLARRICA**. Small, friendly and relaxed, it sits in a forested landscape among lush green hills and is a good base for visiting the nearby German colonies, notably **Colonia Independencia**, and boasts a few attractions of its own.

Buses arrive and depart from the grubby **bus terminal** at Talavera y Colón, two blocks northeast of the Plaza de los Heroes. All intercity buses run via Coronel Oviedo, while there are local services to the nearby German colony of Colonia Independencia. A **taxi** (☎0541/42475) to Colonia Independencia will cost around 35,000G one-way. Taxis are most easily located at the bus terminal or, occasionally, around the plazas. There is no **tourist information** centre, and maps are very hard to come by. The Intendencia Municipal, an impressive colonnaded building on the plaza, may have some otherwise the nearby *Libreria* can provide you with a very poor photocopy for 2000G, although it omits major street names.

The Town

The **Plaza de los Heroes** is a good place to start your exploration of the town, with monuments, busts and statues in honour of the fallen in the Chaco War against Bolivia. Plaques give battle by battle descriptions of the main encounters, detailing the appalling number of lives lost on both sides and the extraordinary odds the Paraguayans overcame on their way to their costly victory. A block south, the **Plaza Libertad** is site of the bright and airy **Catédral**. A covered walkway around the outside of the building is supported by pillars and is a typical feature of Paraguayan churches, while the bright, airy interior is almost spartan in appearance, save for a decorative altarpiece. Around the back of the cathedral, the **Museo Fermin López** (Mon–Fri 7.30am–1pm; donations suggested) is dedicated to a schoolteacher born in Villarrica in 1801, who led two battalions of schoolchildren in the disastrous War of the Triple Alliance. One of the young troops' main achievement was the defence of the main plaza in Piribebuy against invading Brazilian forces. The varied collection of arts, military memorabilia and numismatics is small but nicely displayed, especially the collection of Paraguayan and South American bank notes from throughout history.

Practicalities

Accommodation isn't bad in Villarrica, and prices are low. *Plaza* (☎0541/42096; ❷) is a good cheap option with bags of character. Run by an eccentric old lady, it has a small bar and was once frequented by the notorious Nazi war criminal Dr Josef Mengele. *Guaira* near the bus terminal on Talavera y Mariscal Estigarribia (☎0541/42369; ❷) is family run, with no-frills rooms and space for parking, although it can get noisy. There are several **places to eat** around the plaza, most serving a standard menu of uninspiring fare, including *Paris,* notable solely for its large portions. Two blocks east of the plaza on Carlos Antonio López, *Asaje* offers hot and cold food for 12,000G per kilo. *Miami Bar*, also on Carlos Antonio López, is a popular **nightspot** serving burgers and the like.

Colonia Independencia

From the village of Mbocaytay, 7km north of Villarrica, a road runs 23km east to **COLONIA INDEPENDENCIA**, a picturesque but sprawling German cooperative and agricultural town, easy to miss on the drive through. Probably of particular interest to German visitors, there is little to actually do here except enjoy the relaxing atmosphere and stunning scenery of lush forested hillsides and river beaches. Should you wish **to stay**, *Tilinski* (☎054/8240, ❺) with a pool, bar and restaurant boasts a good location but is expensive, while *Panorama* (no phone; ❺) on the road in has chalet-style accommodation with fantastic views of the surroundings. For **food** you can do a lot worse than eat at *El Mangal*, a shaded beer garden with a pleasant mix of Latin and German hospitality. It is well signposted off the main road.

Ciudad del Este and around

Glitzy, commercial, tacky, frequently intimidating and occasionally sordid, **CIUDAD DEL ESTE** is a shock to the system for many visitors entering Paraguay from Brazil for the first time, leading some to turn round and head straight back again. Founded in 1957 as Ciudad Presidente Stroessner (the city dropped the link to the hated dictator almost as soon as he fell from power), it grew rapidly, both as a centre of control for the Itaipú damming project and as "The Supermarket of South America". Capitalizing on its position on the Brazilian border, the town provides cheap duty free – and occasionally contraband – goods to a public hungry for bargains. Though the growth has slowed since the completion of the hydroelectric dam, the commercial aspect continues to thrive, and Ciudad del Este is one of the best places on the continent for purchasing cheap electric goods. It does have a darker side, though, with crime rates among the highest in the country and dishonesty among dealers rife. Care should be taken before any transaction takes place – especially with street dealers – and always insist on trying out goods before purchasing them; be aware that there is always a mark-up for gringos.

The Town

Shoppers will not stray far from the **Microcentro**, a maze of shops and stalls on either side of the main *ruta*, near the border with Brazil. It is here that the bulk of the bargains are to be found but the area also attracts petty thieves like bees to a honey-pot. Electronics, alcohol and perfumes provide the best deals, but beware of substandard goods passed off as genuine and do not be afraid to haggle or barter, it is expected. It is also sensible to compare prices among several stalls or dealers before completing any transaction.

Its relative modernity ensures that Ciudad del Este has little in the way of sights, although the **Plaza China** at the southeastern corner of the Microcentro is home to some attractive mock-Oriental pagodas. The surrounding area, however, contains some of Paraguay's biggest attractions and, with its transport connections and lively nightlife, Ciudad del Este is perhaps the best place to base yourself when viewing them.

Practicalities

The **bus terminal** (☎061/510421) is some way south of the centre on Chaco Boreal y Capitan del Puerto, adjacent to the **Estadio Club 3 de Febrero** soccer stadium. Regular services run west to the capital and south to Encarnación. A local bus (4500G) runs to Foz do Iguacu every quarter of an hour, for visits to the falls. The airport, 30km west of town on Ruta 7, has regular flights to Asunción, as well as nearby destinations in Brazil and Argentina. **Taxis** (☎061/510180) and are a relatively inexpensive and convenient way of making day-trips. For example, a trip to the Itaipú dam complex 20km away is around 25,000G one way.

A **tourist office** (daily 10am–8pm) at the Friendship Bridge is helpful and you should make full use of it as it is likely to be one of the only functioning tourist offices that you will encounter during your time in Paraguay. It can provide a map of the city as well as information regarding day-trips to the Itaipú Dam and other nearby attractions.

Accommodation is plentiful and on the whole of a high quality. A cluster of good hotels align Emilio Fernandez, two blocks north of the *ruta* near the bridge. The cheapest and most basic is the cheerful and friendly *Caribe* (no phone; ❶ with a/c, a little less without) with a sun-trap courtyard but shady rooms. Opposite, the *Austria* (☎061/500883, ❸) has excellent rooms with TV, minibar and a spacious terrace with views out over the river. German is spoken here, and the price includes a breakfast so mammoth it has to be seen to believed. A little further along, *Munich*

(☎061/500347; ❸) is another good option with parking facilities, cable TV and minibar. For **restaurants** you could do a lot worse than eating at *Hotel Austria*, whose astonishingly cheap menu consists largely of Austrian and German specialities. *Patussi Grill* on Monseñor Cedzich south of the centre is a typical *churrasqueria* with live weekend shows and a menu of over seventy dishes. *Doli Bar* at Jara y Abay is one of the best snack bars in the city and besides the usual menu of *milanesas* and burgers has a buffet option from 8000G. For **nightlife**, *Shopping Mirage* on Pampliega off Adrian Jara, contains several restaurants of varying quality, a cinema, casino, bowling alley and karaoke bar. *Buskers Discoteca*, west of the Microcentre (taxi 25,000G) on Avenida Mariscal López, is popular at weekends.

Around Ciudad del Este

No visit to Ciudad del Este is complete without a trip to the **Itaipú Hydroelectric Project** 20km north of the city (taxi 25,000G one-way or take bus marked Hernandarias). A vast project, producing more than twice the output of America's Grand Coulee Dam, and almost fifty percent more than the world's second largest HEP project, Venezuela's Guri Dam, it supplies all of Paraguay's and most of southern Brazil's national grid with its electricity requirement. With a maximum height of 195m and generating up to 75,000GWh of energy per year, it has been called one of the seven wonders of the modern world. The first of four phases of construction began in 1975, and it was finally completed in 1991, although work to install extra turbines continues. Visits are by guided tour only (Mon–Fri 8am, 9.30am, 1.30pm & 3pm, Sat mornings only; free but a passport is required) and last about an hour and a half. Tours begin with a rather boring half-hour video of facts and figures before the visit to the dam itself. The highlight of the trip is undoubtedly the opportunity to see the inside of the dam and the colossal 1km long machine room.

The erection of the dam flooded much of the surrounding area, including the Sete Quedas, a set of waterfalls comparable to those at Iguassu. As a result, the project's backers were forced to invest heavily in ecological damage limitation projects including relocation of wildlife, replanting of forests and habitat enrichment schemes. Part of this entailed the setting up of the **Flora and Fauna Itaipú Binacional** (9am–5pm; free), a zoo housing animals – including jaguar rescued from the flooding – in pens that tend to resemble the natural habitats. A few kilometres south of the dam's entrance, it also contains excellent **natural history** and **archeological museums**.

Though smaller than the Iguassu Falls, the waterfalls at **Salto de Monday** 10km south of the city are worth a visit. At 80m high, they are a stunning natural feature, although they suffer from being so close to their more famous and spectacular neighbours just across the border. The 20km taxi ride to the falls shouldn't cost more than about 50,000G return.

Crossing into Brazil

The Puente de la Amistad (Friendship Bridge) at the eastern end of the Microcentro marks the border with the Brazilian town of **Foz do Iguaçu**. Immigration formalities take place at opposing ends of the bridge. As the falls (see p.450) are just across the border, this is Paraguay's busiest border crossing, and there are frequently huge queues of traffic waiting to cross in either direction. Crossing on foot is quicker, but be sure to obtain all necessary entrance and exit stamps. Traffic police do not help matters by putting pressure on pedestrians to speed up their crossing, occasionally directing them away from the customs checkpoint.

8.3

South of Asunción

The main road south of the capital is Ruta 1, following a rather convoluted route to the Argentine border city of **Encarnación**. Along the way it passes a number of small towns, some with colourful histories, though none worthy of an extended stay. Ruta 1 meets Ruta 4 at **San Ignacio Guazu**, the latter running west to Pilar, which has little to detain you beyond the crossing to Argentina. The far south of the country, particularly the area around Encarnación, is the heart of the Jesuit mission lands, with several sites of historic and archeological importance to explore, notably the *reducciones* at **Jesús** and **Trinidad**.

South to Encarnación

Several towns align the road to Encarnación from Asunción, each worth stopping for without warranting a stay. The attractive citrus-growing town of **YAGUARÒN** is the first real point of interest south of the capital. Founded in 1539, it is noted for the church of **San Buenaventura**, which dates from a time when the town was at the centre of the Franciscan missions. Although heavily reconstructed, parts of the original building still remain, including sections of the facade and some interior pillars and walls. The **Museo del Doctor Francia** (Mon–Fri 7am–11am & 2–5pm; free) commemorates the life of the Paraguayan dictator known as "El Supremo" with a series of portraits depicting his life.

Fifteen kilometres further south at km63 stands **PARAGUARÍ**, site of a church notable for its two free-standing bell towers, while a few kilometres northeast of here is the historically important town of **PIRIBEBUY**. Capital of the country during the War of the Triple Alliance, it played a pivotal role in the conflict. Then, as now, it was a small, largely rural farming town, but its stand in 1869 against the invading Brazilians with an army consisting largely of children will live long in the nation's memory. The **Museo Histórico Comandante Pedro Juan Caballero** (Tues–Fri 8am-noon & 1-6pm; 1500G) at Estigarribia y Yegros details much of this history, although many of the displays are beginning to decay somewhat. At the small town of **Carapeguà** a road branches off, east to the **Parque Nacional Ybycuì** (see box on p.839).

Ruta 1 continues south to the popular resort town of **VILLA FLORIDA** on the Río Tebicuary, which once formed the border between the Franciscan mission

Itá

Famed for its local pottery, the little town of **ITÁ** was the centre of a media storm in the mid-1990s when it was claimed to be the burial site of former Nazi Party leader Martin Bormann. The official story was that Bormann committed suicide in Berlin in 1945, and a body unearthed on a German building site in the 1970s seemed to support that view, but rumours that he had fled Germany after the war persisted. The discovery at Itá attracted the world's attention and prompted DNA tests to be carried out on the Berlin body, later proving that the original theory had been right all along.

lands of the north and Jesuit missions of the south. There is a good river beach here and excellent fishing. At **San Ignacio Guazu**, a **Jesuit Museum** (daily 8–11.30am & 2–5.30pm; free) exhibits rare Guaraní carvings and Jesuit relics, while the town itself retains period buildings. It was the site of the first Jesuit *reducción* (see box on p.837) in the region. From here, two roads run to the Argentine border: Ruta 1 continuing southeast to Encarnación and Ruta 4 heading west to Pilar.

Encarnación

Situated on the Alto Paraná, the friendly city of **ENCARNACIÓN** is perhaps the best place to base yourself for visiting the nearby Jesuit ruins, not to mention crossing the border into Argentina. The city itself is relatively modern, much of the older area having been flooded during the construction of the Yacyretá Dam complex, but what remains of the old town is a bustling conglomeration of market stalls and duty-free shops designed to entice Argentine visitors from across the border in Posadas.

In the new town, the **Plaza Central** is the hub of most of the activity. Large and leafy it contains a Japanese garden and a series of monuments to, among other people, the famously prolific Paraguayan poet Emiliano R. Fernandez (1894–1949), who produced more than 1800 poems in his life, as well as assorted German settlers in the region.

Practicalities

Buses terminate in and depart from the **bus terminal** (☎071/203527) in a plaza between Memmel and Estigarribia, some six blocks south of the Plaza Central. The main transport links are northwest to Asunción and northeast along Ruta 6 to Ciudad del Este, with regular services in both directions. **Taxis** congregate around the Plaza and bus terminal. A small **tourist office** (no set hours) at the customs checkpoint near the Puente San Roque opens very occasionally, but maps can be obtained from another branch next to the Universidad Católica (8am–noon).

Accommodation options are numerous, with the best bets found in the area just north of the Plaza Central. *Nelly,* two blocks north at 25 de Mayo y Estigarribia (☎071/204737; ❷), has cool, shaded rooms with cable TV and a large courtyard for parking. Around the corner at Mallorquín 1559 y Villarrica, *Acuario* (☎071/202676; ❷) features cable TV, minibar, breakfast and access to a magnificent indoor swimming pool and bar. Closer to the bus terminal, *Viena*, Pedro Juan Cabellero 568 (☎071/203486; ❶), is the cheapest and most basic option in town; the price includes a simple bread and jam breakfast. *Germano,* at Cabañas y CA López (☎071/203346; ❷) directly opposite the bus terminal, is small, welcoming and the best option in the immediate area.

There are several excellent **restaurants** in Encarnación. The rustic *Juana la Sabrosa,* Mallorquin y Pereira, is the most upmarket in town, though prices are still reasonable. Try the *cazuela de mariscos* or house speciality *rana Provençal* (frogs' legs). *Ajisai,* Villarrica 547, is a hugely popular Japanese restaurant serving sushi and other specialities in huge portions. *La Boehme*, Estigarribia y 25 de Mayo, is good for steaks and has an excellent grill option for groups of up to six people, while *Piccola*, Avenida Caballero, is an Italian restaurant with tasty pizzas and decent pasta. Good pizzas are also available 24 hours a day from the restaurant below the *Hotel Cuarajhy* on Estigarribia y 25 de Mayo.

Nightlife is good but limited. The most popular disco is *Avenue* (weekends only, entrance 10,000G), an unmissable purple building on Avenida Caballero, while *La Estación* at Villarrica y Francia has occasional live shows. Opposite is *Polux*, a pool bar-cum-disco.

△ The Itaipú Hydroelectric Project

Jesuit missions

The arrival in 1609 of the **Jesuit missionaries** from the order of the Company of Jesus, sparked the beginning of one of the most daring social experiments of its time. Establishing a cultural, social and political order of its own, the company invited the native Guaraní peoples to join them and attempted to create a written vocabulary of the Guaraní tongue for the first time. Although the natives weren't accorded equal rights, they were trained in agricultural methods and a select few were given a classical education. The colonies, which totalled thirty missions in the eighteenth century (fourteen in Paraguay and sixteen in what today is Argentina), thrived until King Carlos III of Spain expelled the Jesuits in 1767, leaving their grand building projects to decay gracefully.

There are a total of seven missions in Paraguay and their architecture combines European and native elements in a style known as Hispano-Guaraní Baroque, being heavy on religious icons and murals. Perhaps the most famous is at **Trinidad** (daily: summer 7am–7pm, winter 7am–5.30pm; 2000G), 28km northeast of Encarnación along Ruta 6. A hilltop settlement and UNESCO World Cultural Heritage Site, the partially restored church will immediately capture the attention. Fantastically ornate stone carvings of religious figurines fill the church (which is for the most part roofless) and have survived well despite their exposure to the frequently harsh climate, while the pulpit and font are also worth checking out. Should you wish to stay, the German-owned *Hotel Leon* (☎0985/777341; 50,000G) has comfortable rooms and a good restaurant immediately adjacent to the ruins. A dirt track turn-off, a few hundred metres north of Trinidad, runs 13km to **Jesús** (same times and price), fully restored to its original state and superficially more impressive. For two years, 3000 natives worked on the construction of the vast church here, which was left uncompleted and roofless when the Jesuits were expelled. To the west, a turn-off at Ruta 1 km306 runs south to the ruins of **San Cosme Y Damiàn**. Here another grand church project was also left incomplete, but has been finished according to the original plans.

While the sites are undoubtedly impressive, they suffer from a lack of tourist facilities. There are no marked paths, maps or information placards, and guided tours tend to be in Spanish only. Interested readers should consult *They Built Utopia: The Jesuit Missions in Paraguay 1610–1768* by Frederick Reiter for a full background on the history of the Jesuits in Paraguay.

Crossing into Argentina

The **Puente San Roque** to the south of the town links the two countries, with border formalities taking place at opposite ends of the bridge. **Local buses** to Posadas across the Argentine border run every half an hour or so from marked stops on the streets of Encarnación, and you will have to disembark at either end of the bridge to obtain entrance and exit stamps should you require them. The bus will not wait.

8.4

North of Asunciòn

Crossing the Río Paraguay, the main route north from the capital is Ruta 1, via the town of **Villa Hayes**. Named after the otherwise forgettable US president Rutherford B Hayes, who's decision to support Paraguay's bid to keep the Chaco after the War of the Triple Alliance was influential in thwarting Argentine claims, the town is peppered with monuments to him. From here it is a long and uneventful journey to the crossroads of **Pozo Colorado** at the gateway to the Chaco. If you are heading north to Bolivia and did not get a Paraguayan exit stamp in Asunción, Pozo Colorado represents your last chance to obtain one or you will risk being turned back at the border. Ruta 9 continues north to **Filadelfia** and the **Mennonite colonies**, the dramatic and beautiful Ruta 5 heads east through glorious countryside in which wildlife abounds. The main towns along here are **Concepción** on the Río Paraguay and **Pedro Juan Caballero** on the border with Brazil.

Concepción

A pretty port town on the eastern bank of the Río Paraguay, **CONCEPCIÓN** is the main trading centre in the north of the country. The town is bisected north to south by **Avenida Agustín Pinedo**, its central reservation filled with a mixed bag of industrial and agricultural machinery – the **Museo al Aire Libre**. Two blocks east of here along Don Bosco is the **Mercado Municipal**, a dingy warren of tiny, cramped stalls selling all manner of merchandise.

West of the Avenida is where most of the interest is, centred on the balding **Plaza Libertad**, six blocks along. An eclectic, almost Venetian-style, **Catédral** (access after 5pm) overlooks the plaza, and adjacent to it is the **Museo Diocesano** (Mon–Sat 7.30–11.30am; free), displaying all manner of religious paraphernalia. Two blocks east of here along Estigarribia is a series of charming **mansion houses** that now operate as municipal buildings. A pastel blue mansion dating from 1898 houses the Intendencia (council headquarters), while the delightful honey-coloured **Mansión Otaño** (1940) houses the public works department.

On the western outskirts of town, the strange, pyramidal **Monumento al Indio** commemorates the indigenous population, while the unnecessarily steep **bridge** over the Río Paraguay, 9km southwest, provides exceptional views along the river's course.

Practicalities

The **bus terminal** is on the northern edge of town, eight blocks from the centre along Garal. There is no **tourist office**, but staff at the Intendencia Municipal can occasionally be persuaded to part with town maps if you are persistent. **Banks** are a problem, as no ATMs accept foreign cards. Visa and MasterCard transactions can be carried out over the counter at Banco Amambay (Mon–Fri 7am–1pm) at Pinedo y Franco, but they are not accepted at other banks and it is safer to ensure that you have sufficient funds on arrival. **Internet** access costs 5000G at *Cyber C@t* at Franco y Garal.

The best place to look for **accommodation** is along Franco, west of Avenida Pinedo. *Victoria*, Franco y Pedro Caballero (☎031/42256; ❸), is a handsome old whitewashed building with spacious communal areas. Cable TV, breakfast and air conditioning are all included, and there is also dormitory accommodation at a slightly cheaper rate. *Center*, Franco y Yegros (☎031/42360; ❶), is a real cheap option but rather unappealing. Good, filling **food** can be had at the restaurant under *Hotel Francès* where chicken dominates the menu. *Quincho del Victoria* opposite the hotel of the same name also serves a decent menu of similar fare in a pleasant open-air setting. A number of *pollerias* specializing in BBQ chicken dot Franco and serve basic, but succulent fare. *Camilla's Burguer* on Pinedo does cheap fast food, and is also a popular drinking den for a younger clientele.

Paraguay's national parks

With eleven national parks within its borders, Paraguay is ideal for those who love the wilderness. Though spectacular, the majority are unfortunately difficult to reach without transport, and many require a permit to visit, but if you are willing to make the effort you will not be disappointed. Free permits are available from Dirección de Parques Nacionales y Vida Silvestre at Franco y Ayolas in Asunción (☎021/445214), where you will also find information about local guides and tours. Some of the most spectacular and accessible of the parks are covered below.

Among the most easily visited of the national parks is the **Parque Nacional Cerro Corrà** 35km west of Pedro Juan Caballero. This 22,000-hectare park is the site of Paraguay's final defeat in the War of the Triple Alliance and the place were Francisco Solano López finally met his end, it is of historical importance as well as intense natural beauty. The site of **López's death** is marked by a monument set above a small wooded brook, at one end of a long line of busts of the war leaders, while at the opposite end is an abstract **monument to the war dead** featuring commemorative plaques from groups as diverse as the Uruguayan Rotary Club and Brazilian Air Force. There is an administrative office with a small museum and information centre where you can ask about **camping**.

Approximately 120km southeast of Asunción, there is a turn-off from Ruta 1 at Carapeguá to a beautiful forested reserve, the 5000-hectare **Parque Nacional Ybycui**. Noted for its forested hills, creeks, waterfalls and limpid pools, it contains one of the last remaining tracts of rainforest in the country. Popular with day-trippers at weekends, during the week it retains a sense of isolation and you may almost have the place to yourself. Several nature trails are available and a visitors centre will provide you with information about what to look out for. Keep an eye out for *tinamous*, partridge-like birds, which are occasionally glimpsed crossing the forest tracks, while a myriad of coloured butterflies are always visible. There is a campsite near to the pretty **Salto Guaraní** waterfalls, but you will need to bring your own supplies.

Paraguay's largest reserve is the remote 780,000-hectare **Parque Nacional Defensores del Chaco**, near to the Bolivian border in the far north of the country. The park's most distinctive natural landmark is the 500m **Cerro León**, but it is for the animals that most people make the journey. **Birdlife** is spectacular here, especially the magnificent six-foot tall *jabiru* stork, but other wildlife, though rarely seen, is well worth waiting for. The last of Paraguay's jaguars are found here, along with puma, tapir and peccary, but visiting the park can be exceptionally difficult and permission is required. A rough dirt road heads 350km north of Filadelfia, the last town of any real size you will encounter, and it is passable only by four-wheel-drive vehicles in good weather. It is strongly advised that you do not attempt to make the journey without a trained guide. Dirección General de Protección y Conservación de la Biodiversidad (☎021/615812) represents the best bet, putting you in touch with park rangers that regularly visit Asunción.

Pedro Juan Caballero

A major border crossing to the Brazilian Pantanal, **PEDRO JUAN CABALLERO** has, like so many border towns, been consumed by a shallow and often tawdry consumerism. The **Avenida Internacional** marks the border with **Ponta Pora** in Brazil, but it is on the Paraguayan side that you will find most of the duty free shops and stalls. Electronics and alcohol are both cheap, but the abundance of street salesman, more aggressive and intimidating than elsewhere, gives the town an unfriendly feel. To cross the border for any length of time you will need to obtain a Paraguayan exit stamp from immigration (Mon–Fri 7am–6pm, Sat 7am–3pm) at Naciones Unidas y Francia and a Brazilian entrance stamp from the same building, or the office at Presidente Vargas 70 in Ponte Pora.

There's little in the town to detain you but it's a good base for visiting the nearby **Parque Nacional Cerro Corá** (see box on p.839). **Accommodation** is expensive; among the cheapest and best is *Eiruzú*, at Mariscal López y Estigarribia (T036/431306; ❹). Now rather dated, but clearly once very grand, its 1970s furniture and decor give it the appearance of a place stuck in a time warp. There is a small pool and the price includes breakfast at the excellent restaurant below. Opposite the hotel on Mariscal López is a cybercafé with **Internet access** for 6000G per hour.

The Chaco

After the Amazon jungle, **THE CHACO** is probably the last great wilderness on the continent. A mysterious and remote place, it is known as the "desert of Paraguay" and makes up almost the entire northern half of the country's land area, yet accounts for less than three percent of the total population. Ignored by colonists until the early twentieth century, it was the German-speaking **Mennonites** who first began to settle it (see box on p.842), using advanced farming techniques to cultivate the land with the help of native labour. As the settlements thrived, they set up a number of colonies, with their administrative centres being the only towns of any size for hundreds of square kilometres. Such towns (with **Filadelfia** being the largest) are few and far between and the roads that connect them are poor and frequently impassable, making exploration of the Chaco a difficult and frequently hazardous pastime. For those with an interest in nature, though, it gives a unique insight into how Paraguay was before the arrival of the Europeans. The Chaco can be broadly split into three sections, low, middle, and high, based around the changing natural habitats or biomes.

Characterized by palm savannah and seasonally flooded grassland, the **LOW CHACO** is a comparatively gentle introduction to the area. Cattle ranching is the main source of income for the people, but tourists are more likely to be attracted by the astonishing variety of birdlife. Birds of prey fill the skies and scavenge for roadkill, while waterside ponds throng with waterbirds like the enormous *jabiru* stork and associated wildlife such as the caiman, the South American alligator.

Featuring the main settlements, including Filadelfia, the **MIDDLE CHACO** is where most tourists will spend their time. Made up largely of scrub forest and semi-desert, it tends towards hardwoods in the far north. It is here that the *quebracho* tree abounds, a rich-source of tannin, as well as the bizarrely teardrop-shaped *palo borracho* with a trunk that stores water.

As you head towards Bolivia through the **HIGH CHACO** the vegetation becomes increasingly savage and impenetrable. Fire-resistant thorn forest is the order of the day, and the broken branches of the vegetation mean that most journeys will involve at least one tyre change before reaching completion. Closer to the border, the increasing dryness has formed something akin to a cactus desert, where rain rarely falls.

Trans-Chaco Rally

Since its initiation in 1970, the **Trans-Chaco Rally** has developed a reputation as one of the toughest competitions in world motorsport. Held over three days in September in some of the planet's harshest driving conditions, it is famed for its ability to push drivers to their limits. Since Peña-Federer guided his Toyota to victory in the inaugural race, the Japanese car manufacturers have dominated the team table, winning 13 of the 29 races to date (the race was not held between 1984 and 1986 owing to political unrest), while the most wins by an individual drive are the three claimed by Volkswagen's Orlando Penner in 1989, 1992 and 1994. For more information see ®www.transchacorally.com.py.

Filadelfia

The Chaco's most highly populated town, and administrative headquarters of Fernheim Colony (see box on p.842), **FILADELFIA** is little more than a small conglomeration of houses, farms and shops. It is a hot and dusty town in the Middle Chaco, and most of the action centres around the dual-laned **Avenida Hindenburg**, which runs right through the centre of town. The main interest lies in absorbing the colonial lifestyle of the people, a simple and almost puritanical existence built largely around dairy farming and cooperation with native populations. Those looking for a little historical enlightenment may want to visit the **Unger Museum** (ask at *Hotel Florida* opposite for access; 5000G) for a clearer idea of the difficulties that faced the first pioneers.

In the absence of a **bus terminal**, buses arrive and depart from the company offices along Chaco Boreal, off Hindenburg. There are several daily services south to Asunción, all via Pozo Colorado, where it is possible to change for buses to Concepción. If you are in a hurry be sure to take a direct service, as indirect services stop seemingly every few kilometres and can take up to fifty percent longer.

There are several good **accommodation** options, but you will need to book ahead in September when the town is gripped by **Trans-Chaco Rally** (see box above) fever and becomes uncharacteristically lively. Perhaps the best bet is *Florida* (©0491/32151; 40,000–120,000G) at Hindenburg 984 opposite the Unger Museum. Attractively laid out with a great pool and garden, the hotel has a range of rooms: at the higher end are spacious rooms with cable TV and minibar, while the cheapest rooms consist of little more than four walls and a bed. Its restaurant is also excellent. *Safari* (©0491/32218; 180,000G), around the corner on Industrial 149E, is a plusher option. Attractive, if rather retro, rooms boast cable TV and air conditioning. There are no **banks**, so be sure that you bring enough currency with you.

Around Filadelfia

Buses north from Asunción routinely call in at **Loma Plata** administrative centre of Menno Colony, before heading 25km west to Filadelfia. The oldest of the Mennonite settlements, it is not as large as Filadelfia but is arranged along very similar lines, with a collection of buildings arranged around a sandy main street. Should you feel compelled to stay, *Hotel Loma Plata* is the only accommodation option in town. Heading 33km south of Filadelfia you reach the third of the Mennonite centres, **Neu-Halbstadt**, associated with Neuland Colony. Founded in 1947 it is close to **Fortín Boquerón** where trenches from the Chaco War can still be seen. With several Lengua and Nevaclé Indian settlements in the area around, Neu-Halbstadt has become an important centre for local people to sell traditional arts and crafts.

About 40km west of Filadelfia is **Fortín Toledo**, with a Paraguayan military cemetery and other remnants of the war. A small reserve, **Proyecto Taguá** is home

The Mennonites

During the 1920s a series of pioneering **Anabaptist refugees** set about colonizing what had, until then, been viewed as an inhospitable wilderness – the Chaco. Seeking freedom for beliefs ranging from pacifism to adult baptism, they were attracted to Paraguay by the vast tracts of uninhabited land in the north where they could practise their beliefs free from persecution. They proved to be hardy settlers, overcoming the extreme climate and Bolivian military attacks of the Chaco War to establish a series of thriving agricultural and industrial settlements.

Unsurprisingly, they also had to contend with a suspicious and frequently aggressive native population. Groups of nomadic Indians, resentful of their intrusion, took every opportunity to try and drive them out of their lands, while those that assimilated with the Mennonites soon became angry with their treatment as labourers and second-class citizens and soon openly rebelled. Things settled down and today there are three main Mennonite colonies – **Menno**, **Fernheim** and **Neuland**, each with an administrative centre – which run the 120 separate villages; there is a population of around 12,000 Mennonites matched by a similar number of indigenous peoples. **Plattdeutsch** (Low German) is the first language of the area, but Spanish and Guaraní are also widely understood. Peanuts, citrus fruits and cotton are the main crops, while dairy farming accounts for almost half of Paraguay's milk supply.

With traditional views becoming diluted with every generation in favour of a more materialistic approach, the Mennonite way of life is gradually becoming more of an ideal than a practice. Much to the chagrin of the older generations, the youth are developing an interest in modern technology and shunning traditional dress and decorum. Pressure from the Paraguayan authorities has also led to many Mennonites seeking to invest or relocate abroad.

to a population of the Chaco peccary, a pig-like creature thought extinct for over fifty years until it was rediscovered in 1975.

North to the Bolivian border

Beyond Filadelfia, Ruta 9 deteriorates badly as it heads north. At km540, the small military settlement of **Mariscal Estigarribia** is likely to represent the last glimpse of civilization you will see until you are well into Bolivia. Much of this area is under military jurisdiction, and it pays to have photo identification handy in case of military checkpoints. Consequently, so few tourists venture this far north that your mere presence alone is enough to arouse suspicion.

There are few opportunities to buy petrol or supplies after leaving Mariscal Estigarribia, but if you are planning a lengthy trip you should stock up in Filadelfia. From here a rough road runs 250km north to the **Parque Nacional Defensores del Chaco** (see box on p.839), while the main route continues northwest via **Estancia la Patria** (122km from Mariscal Estigarribia), which has a tiny supermarket, to the border. The border is approximately 304km from Filadelfia, but the poor state of the roads means that the journey may take much longer than expected.

Crossing into Bolivia

If visiting **Bolivia**, it is essential that you obtain an exit stamp from Asunción or the small town of Pozo Colorado at the gateway to the Chaco. There are currently no immigration facilities in the entire Chaco, and failure to display all the necessary stamps at the Bolivian border may lead to you being turned back and facing a rather lengthy journey back to the capital.

9

Peru

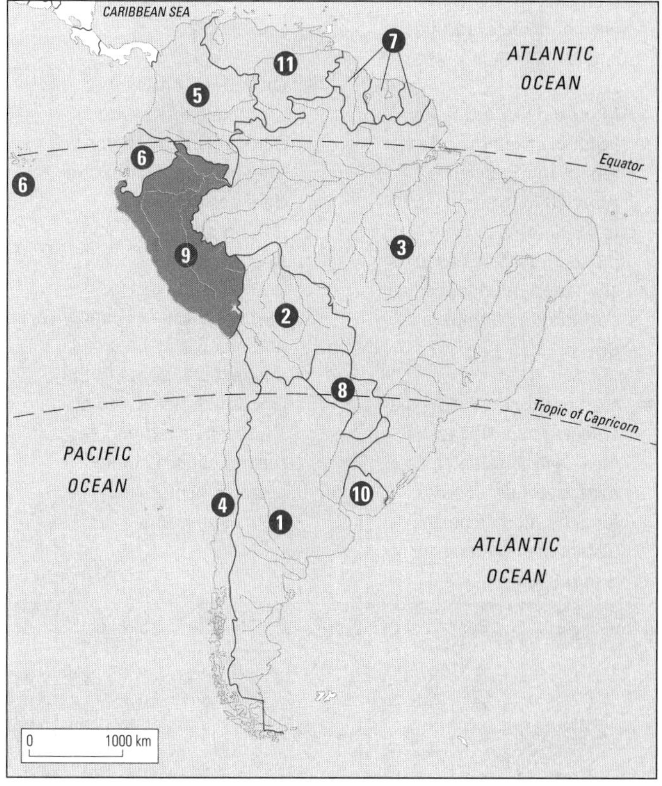

CARIBBEAN SEA
ATLANTIC OCEAN
Equator
PACIFIC OCEAN
Tropic of Capricorn
ATLANTIC OCEAN
0 1000 km
1
2
3
4
5
6
6
7
8
9
10
11

Peru highlights

* **Ceviche** Savour this classic Peruvian seafood dish consisting of fish, shrimp, scallops or squid, marinated in lime juice and chilli peppers, then served raw with corn and sweet potato and onions. **See p.853**

* **Museo de la Inquisición** Formerly the headquarters of the Spanish America Inquisition (1570 to 1820), this Livna museum features requisite creepy dungeons and torture chambers. **See p.869**

* **Machu Picchu** Follow the stunning Inca Trail to these awe-inspiring Inca ruins, set against spiky, forested mountains and distant glacial summits. **See p.892**

* **Nazca Lines** Fly over these dazzling geometric figures and complex animal designs, which are etched, seemingly impossibly, into a massive the desert pampa. **See p.909**

* **Cruz del Condor** A breathtaking viewing point in Colca Canyon, offering sightings of condors sailing below, around and above you. **See p.920**

* **Pacaya Samiria** Remote and stunningly beautiful, this reserve, home to the Cocoma tribe, is one of the least visited and yet the largest protected areas of rainforest in Peru. **See p.956**

Introduction and basics

The land of gold and of the sun-worshipping Incas, Peru was sixteenth-century Europe's major source of treasure, and once the home of the largest empire in the world. While the riches of the Incas have since fuelled the European imagination, the country's real appeal lies in the sheer beauty of its various landscapes, the abundance of its wildlife, and the strong and colourful character of the people – newly recovered after a period of political upheaval, from the 1980s until the early 1990s, that was as bloody and unpredictable as any during the country's history.

Peru is the most varied and exciting of all the South American nations. Most people visualize the country as mountainous, and are aware of the great Inca relics, but many are unaware of the splendour of the immense **desert coastline** and the vast tracts of **tropical rainforest**. Dividing these contrasting environments, chain after chain of breathtaking peaks, **the Andes**, over seven thousand metres high and four hundred kilometres wide in places, ripple the entire length of the nation. So distinct are these three regions that it is very difficult to generalize about the country, but one thing for sure is that Peru offers a unique opportunity to experience an incredibly wide range of spectacular scenery, a wealth of heritage, and a vibrant living culture.

In the more rural parts of Peru, native life can have changed little in the last four centuries. However, "progress" is gradually transforming much of Peru – already the cities wear a distinctly Western aspect, and roads and tracks now connect almost every corner of the Republic with the industrial *urbanizaciones* that dominate the few fertile valleys along the coast. Only the Amazon jungle – nearly two-thirds of Peru's landmass but with a mere fraction of its population – remains beyond modernization's reach, and even here oil and lumber companies, cattle ranchers, cocaine producers and settlers, are taking an increasing toll.

Always an exciting place to visit, and frantic as it sometimes appears on the surface, the laid-back calmness of the Peruvian temperament continues to underpin life even in the cities.

Where to go

With each region offering so many different attractions, it's hard to generalize about the places you should visit first. Apart from **Lima**, where you are most likely to arrive, the beautiful and busting colonial city of **Cusco**, surrounded by some of the most spectacular mountain landscapes and palatial ruins in Peru, is perhaps the most obvious place to start. From here, you can head northwest into the **Sacred Valley** featuring the Inca ruins of **Pisac** and **Ollantaytambo**, and follow the **Inca Trail** up to the justly famous citadel of **Machu Picchu**.

Along the coast, too, there are fascinating archeological sites, notably the bizarre **Nazca Lines** south of Lima. Heading east of Nazca brings you to **Arequipa**, featuring the impressive Santa Catalina Monastery, and **Lago Titicaca**, home to the floating islands.

The **jungle** provides startling opportunities for close and exotic encounters with Peruvian wildlife. From the comfort of tourist lodges in **Iquitos** to exciting river excursions around the **Manu** reserved areas or **Puerto Maldonado**, the fauna and flora of the world's largest tropical forest can be experienced first-hand perhaps more easily than in any other quarter of the Amazon.

When to go

Picking the **best time to visit** Peru's various regions is complicated by the country's physical characteristics. The **desert coast** is extremely hot and sunny between December and March (especially in the north), cooler and with a frequent hazy mist

QUITO
ECUADOR
Guayaquil
Rio Pastaza
Rio Putumayo
COLOMBIA
Rio Napo
Pevas
Rio Amazonas
Iquitos
Caballococha
Letica
Tabatinga
Ramon Castilla
Manaus, Belém & the Atlantic
Tumbes
Mancora
Talara
Piura
Catacaos
Sechura
Oimos
Lambayeque
Chiclayo
Cajamarca
Pacasmayo
San Pedro de Lloc
Trujillo
Chimbote
Caraz
HUASCARÁN NATIONAL PARK
Rio Morona
Boria
Orellana
Puerto América
Barranca
Rio Marañon
Jaen
Bagua Grande
Bagua Chica
Rioja
Moyobamba
Chachapoyas
Tingo
Leimebamba
Celendin
Huamachuco
Lamas
Tarapoto
Yurimaguas
Lagunas
Santa Cruz
PACAYA-SAMIRIA NATIONAL RESERVE
Nauta
Requena
Rio Ucayali
Juanjui
DANGEROUS ROUTE (JUANJUI - TINGO MARIA)
Rio Huallga
Contamana
Pucallpa
BRAZIL
N

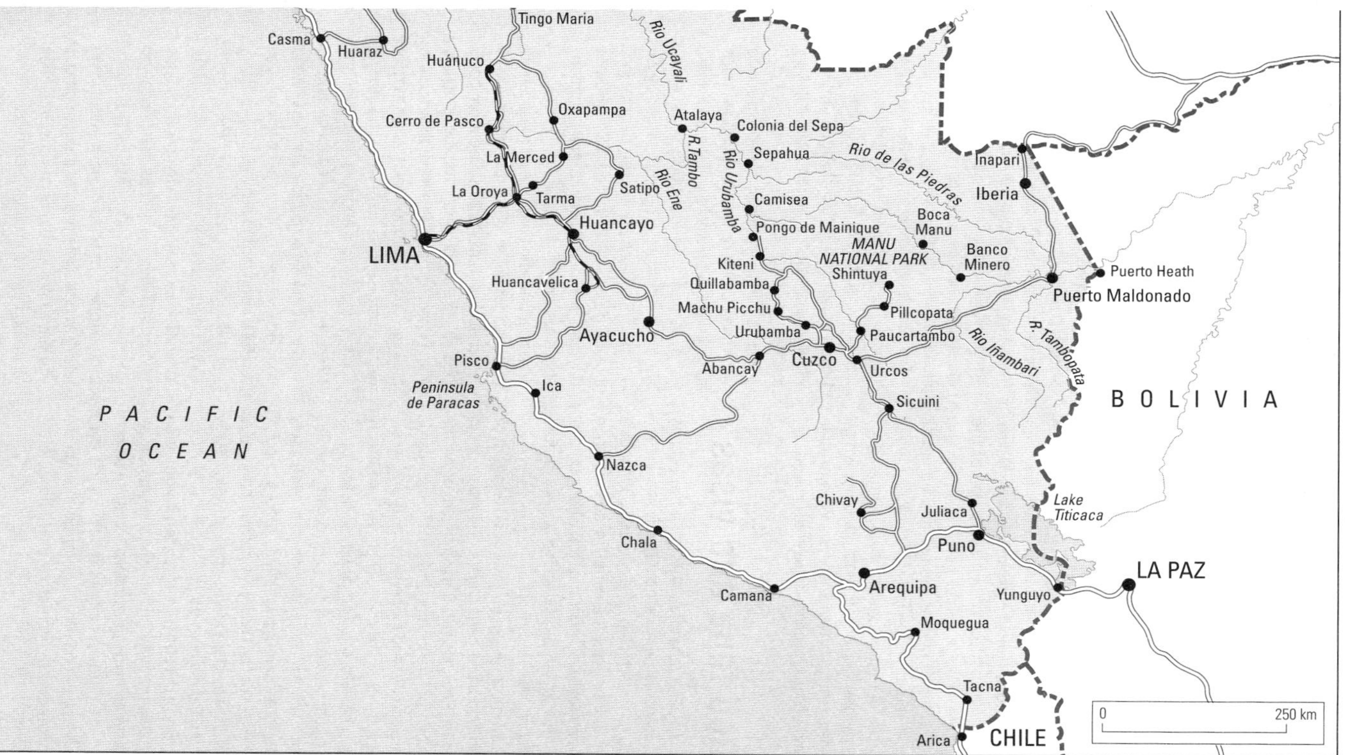

Tingo Maria
Casma
Huaraz
Huánuco
Rio Ucayali
Oxapampa
Atalaya
Colonia del Sepa
Cerro de Pasco
R.Tambo
Rio Urubamba
Sepahua
Rio de las Piedras
Inapari
La Merced
Rio Ene
Satipo
La Oroya
Tarma
Iberia
Camisea
Huancayo
Boca Manu
Pongo de Mainique
MANU NATIONAL PARK
LIMA
Banco Minero
Kiteni
Shintuya
Puerto Heath
Huancavelica
Quillabamba
Puerto Maldonado
Machu Picchu
Pillcopata
Ayacucho
Urubamba
Paucartambo
Rio Iñambari
R. Tambopata
Pisco
Abancay
Cuzco
Urcos
Peninsula de Paracas
Ica
B O L I V I A
P A C I F I C
O C E A N
Sicuini
Nazca
Chivay
Juliaca
Lake Titicaca
Chala
Puno
LA PAZ
Arequipa
Camana
Yunguyo
Moquegua
Tacna
0
250 km
Arica
CHILE

between April and November. Apart from the occasional shower over Lima it hardly ever rains in the desert. The freak exception, every ten years or so, is when the shift in ocean currents of **El Niño** (which last hit Peru in 1998) causes torrential downpours, devastating crops, roads and communities all down the coast.

In **the Andes** the seasons are more clearly marked, with heavy rains from December to March and a relatively dry period from June to September, which, although it can be cold at night, is certainly the best time for **trekking** and most outward-bound activities. A similar pattern dominates much of **the jungle**, though rainfall here is heavier and more frequent, and it's hot and humid all year round. In the lowland rainforest areas around Iquitos water levels are higher between December and January, which offers distinct advantages for spotting wildlife and access by canoe to remote creeks.

Red tape and visas

EU, US, Canadian, Australian and New Zealand citizens can all currently stay in Peru as tourists for up to ninety days without a visa. However, the situation does change periodically, so always check with your local Peruvian embassy some weeks before departure.

All nationalities, however, need a **tourist or embarkation card** (*tarjeta de embarque*) to enter Peru, issued at the frontiers or on the plane before landing in Lima. Tourist cards are usually valid for between sixty and ninety days – only sixty for US citizens. In theory you have to show an outbound ticket (by air or bus) before you'll be given a card, but this isn't always checked. For your own safety and freedom of movement keep a copy of the tourist card and your passport on you at all times – particularly when travelling away from the main towns.

Should you want to **extend your visa** (between thirty and sixty additional days), there are two basic options: either cross one of the borders and get a new tourist card when you come back in; or go through the bureaucratic rigmarole at a Migraciones office.

Student visas (which last 12 months) are best organized as far in advance as possible through your country's embassy in Lima, your nearest Peruvian Embassy and the relevant educational institution.

Costs and money

Although more under control since the 1980s, devaluation is a regular occurrence, leading to two major currency switches in the past couple decades. The current Peruvian currency, the **nuevo sol**, whose symbol is S/, is still simply called a "Sol" on the streets and has so far remained relatively steady against the US dollar.

Despite being closely tied to the US dollar, the value of the nuevo sol still varies from day to day, so **prices throughout this section are quoted in US dollars**, against which costs have so far remained relatively stable.

Peru is certainly a much cheaper place to visit than Europe or the US, but how much so will depend on where you are and when. As a general rule low-budget travellers should – with care – be able to get by on around US$10–20 per person per day (not including transport), while US$40–60 per day can provide you with a more comfortable experience.

In most places in Peru, a good **meal** can still be found for under US$3, **transport** is very reasonable, a comfortable double **room** costs US$10–35 a night, and **camping** is usually free. Expect to pay a little more than usual in the larger towns and cities, and also in the jungle, as many supplies have to be imported by truck. In the villages and rural towns, on the other hand, things come cheaper – and by roughing it in the countryside, and buying food from local villages or the nearest market, you can live well on next to nothing.

In the more popular parts of Peru, costs vary considerably with the seasons. Cusco, for instance, has its best weather from June to August, when many of its hotel prices go up by around 25–50 percent. The same thing happens at fiesta times. It's also worth taking along an international **student card**, if you have one, for the occasional reduction (up to 50 percent in some museums).

Information, maps and websites

You'll find some sort of **tourist office** in most towns of any size, which can help with information and occasionally free local maps. Quite often, though, these are simply fronts for tour operators, and are only really worth bothering with if you have a specific question – about fiesta dates or local bus timetables, for example. A *Peru Guide* booklet is available free from hotels and travel agencies in most major cities; it has a few good city maps and gives recommendations for hotels and restaurants plus other useful information for Lima, Arequipa, Cusco, Huaraz, Chiclayo, Ica/Nazca/Paracas and Iquitos.

Explorers' Club

The nonprofit **South American Explorers' Club** is your best bet for getting relevant, up-to-date information both before you leave home and when you arrive in Lima (membership starts at around US$50 a year). It has clubhouses in Lima (see p.863) and Cusco (Ⓣ084/254-484), and a main office in the US at 126 Indian Creek Road, Ithaca, NY 14850 (Ⓕ607/277-0488, Ⓦwww.samexplo.org). The Club offers a variety of **maps** as well as brochures.

Peru is surprisingly switched on to electronic communications, with **Internet cafés** in all towns of any size and in many small, out-of-the-way places. Some of the best websites devoted to Peru are the excellent Ⓦwww.andeantravelweb.com/peru, which links to a whole range of travel-related features and listings; Ⓦwww.enjoyperu.com, information and pictures of travel, restaurants, accommodation, local events, fiestas and ceremonies; Ⓦwww.perulinks.com, which has English pages on a range of Peruvian topics like art, entertainment, and travel; and Ⓦwww.peruonline.net, a great source of general background information. Finally, Ⓦwww.virtualperu.net covers Peruvian geography, history and people with satellite photos, maps and other information.

Accommodation

Peru has the typical range of Latin American accommodation, from top-class international hotels at prices to compare with any Western capital. Virtually all upmarket accommodation will call itself a **hotel** or, in the countryside regions, a **posada**. In the jungle, **tambo lodges** can be anything from quite luxurious to an open-sided, palm-thatched hut with space for slinging a hammock. Technically, something that calls itself a **pension** or **residencial** ought to specialize in longer-term accommodation, and while they may well offer discounts for stays of a week or more, they are just as geared up for short stays.

Hotels

The **cheaper hotels** are generally old – sometimes beautifully so, converted from colonial mansions with rooms grouped around a courtyard – and tend to be within a few blocks of a town's central plaza, general market, or bus or train station. At the low end of the scale, which can be fairly basic with shared rooms and a communal bathroom, you can usually find a bed for between US$5 and US$10, and occasionally even less. For a few dollars more you can find a good, clean single or double room with private bath in a **mid-range hotel**, generally for somewhere between US$15 and US$45. A little haggling is often worth a try, and if you find one room too pricey, another, perhaps identical, can often be found for less: the phrase "*Tiene un cuarto más barato?*" ("Do you have a cheaper room?") is useful.

Hotels de Turistas, a privatized chain of formerly state-run hotels, tend to be among the best **upmarket accommodation** options in all towns outside of Lima. Out of season some of these can be relatively inexpensive (from around US$15–20 per person), and if you like the look of a place it's often worth asking. Note that all luxury hotels in Peru charge eighteen percent **tax** and often ten percent **service** on top of this again; always check beforehand whether the quoted price includes these extras.

One point of caution – it's not advisable to pay tour or travel agents in one city for accommodation required in the next town. By all means ask agents to make reservations but do not ask them to send payments; it is always simpler and safer to do that yourself.

Youth hostels and camping

There are currently 28 **youth hostels** (*hostals*) spread throughout Peru. They are not the standardized institution found in Europe, but are relatively cheap and reliable; expect to pay US$4–10 for a bed, perhaps slightly more in Lima. All hostels are theoretically open 24 hours a day and most have cheap cafeterias attached. Many of the hostels don't check that you are a member, but if you want to be on the safe side, you can join up at the Associación Peruana de Albergues Turísticos Juveniles, Casimiro Ulloa 328 Miraflores ⓣ01/446-5488 or 242-3068, ⓦwww.limahostell.com.pe. You can get a full list of all the country's hostels here, and they can also make advance bookings for you.

Camping is possible almost everywhere in Peru, and it's rarely difficult to find space for a tent. Camping is free since there are only one or two organized campsites in the whole country. It's also the most satisfactory way of seeing Peru, as some of the country's most fantastic places are well off the beaten track: with a tent – or a hammock – it's possible to go all over without worrying if you'll make it to a hostel.

It's usually OK to set up camp in fields or forest beyond the outskirts of settlements, but ask **permission** and advice from the nearest farm or house first. Apart from a few restricted areas, Peru's enormous sandy coastline is open territory, the real problem not being so much where to camp as how to get there; some of the most stunning areas are very remote. The same can be said of both the mountains and the jungle – camp anywhere, but ask first, if you can find anyone to ask.

Getting around

With the distances in Peru being so vast, many Peruvians and travellers are increasingly **flying** to their destinations, as all Peruvian cities are within a two-hour flight of Lima. Most get around the country by **bus**, as these go just about everywhere and are extremely good value. However, wherever possible, visitors tend to use one of the country's **trains** – an experience in itself – despite being considerably slower than the equivalent bus journey.

By bus

Peru's privately operated **buses** offer remarkably low **fares** – you can travel the length of the country (over 2000km) for under US$30. Long-distance bus journeys cost from around US$1.50 per hour on the fast coastal highway, and are even cheaper elsewhere. The condition of the buses ranges from the efficient and relatively luxurious Cruz del Sur fleet that runs along the coast, to the scruffy old ex-US schoolbuses used on local runs throughout the country. If you don't want to miss the scenery, you can hop relatively easily between the smaller towns, which usually works out to be not much more expensive. Cruz del Sur now operates an excellent website (ⓦwww.cruzdelsur.com.pe) with timetables and ticket purchase option (credit cards accepted).

At least one **bus depot** or **stopping area** can be found in the centre of any town. Peru is investing in a series of **terminal terrestres**, or **terrapuertos**, centralizing the departure and arrival of the manifold operators, but it's always a good idea to doublecheck where the bus is leaving from, since in some cities, notably Arequipa, bus offices are in different locations from the bus terminal. For intercity rides, it's best to buy **tickets** in advance direct from the bus company offices; for local trips, you can buy tickets on the bus itself. On long-distance journeys, try to avoid getting seats right over the jarring wheels, especially if the bus is tackling mountain or jungle roads.

By taxi, mototaxi and colectivo

Taxis can be found anywhere at any time in almost every town. Any car can become a taxi simply by sticking a taxi sign up in the front window; a lot of people, especially in Lima, take advantage of this to supplement their income. Whenever you get into a taxi, always fix the **price** in advance since few of them have metres, even the really professional firms. Relatively short journeys in Lima generally cost around US$1.50, but it's cheaper elsewhere. Radio taxis, minicabs and airport taxis tend to cost more. Taxi drivers in Peru do not expect tips.

In many rural towns, you'll find small cars and motorcycle rickshaws – known variously as **mototaxis** or **motokars** – all competing for customers. The latter are always cheaper if slightly more dangerous and not that comfortable, especially if there are more than two of you or if you've got a lot of luggage.

Colectivos (shared taxis) are a very useful way of getting around that's peculiar to Peru. They connect all the coastal towns, and many of the larger centres in the mountains, and tend to be faster than the bus, though often charge twice as much. Most *colectivo* **cars** manage to squeeze in about six people plus the driver and can be found in the centre of a town or at major stopping-places along the main roads. Colectivo **minibuses**, also known as **combis**, can squeeze in twice as many people, or often more.

In the cities, particularly in Lima, *colectivos* (especially *combis*) have an appalling reputation for **safety**. They frequently crash, turn over and knock down pedestrians. Equally dangerous is the fact that the driver is in such a hurry that he does not always wait for you to get in.

By train

Peru's spectacular **train** journeys are in themselves a major attraction, and you should aim to take at least one long-distance train during your trip. The **Southern Railway** runs passenger services inland from Puno on Lake Titicaca north to Cusco, from where another line heads out down the magnificent Urubamba Valley as far as Machu Picchu (see p.900). The trains move slowly, and are often much bumpier than buses. However, trains generally allow ample time to observe what's going on outside, but you do have to keep one eye on events inside, where the carriages – often extremely crowded – are notorious for **petty thefts**. Wherever possible **tickets** should be bought in advance by at least a day.

By plane

Some places in the jungle can only sensibly be reached by **plane** and Peru is so vast that the odd flight can save a lot of time. **Tickets** can be bought from travel agents or airline offices in all major towns. The most popular routes, such as Lima–Cusco, cost upwards of US$50 and usually need to be booked at least a few days in advance (more during the run-up to and including major fiestas). Other, less busy routes tend to be less expensive.

On all flights it's important to **confirm your booking** two days before departure. Flights are often cancelled or delayed, and sometimes they leave earlier than scheduled – especially in the jungle where the weather can be a problem. If a passenger hasn't shown up twenty minutes before the flight, the company can give the seat to someone on the waiting list.

There are also **small planes** (6- and 10-seaters) serving the jungle and certain parts of the coast. The companies that fly out of Lima have reputations for being dangerous and poorly maintained. Small **air colectivo** companies operate scheduled services between larger settlements in the jungle, at quite reasonable rates. An *expresso* **air taxi** will take you to any landing strip in the country whenever you want for over US$200 an hour.

All the Peruvian domestic airlines offering **flight passes** went bust in the late 1990s, and airline companies are still in a state of flux in Peru. As new ones arrive and competition for passengers increases, passes are likely to become available again, and it's worth checking what the status is with your travel agent or with the major airlines on arrival in Peru.

By car

Cars can be very handy for reaching remote rural destinations or sites, though, as stated before, not for exploring Lima.

If you bring a car into Peru that is not registered there, you will need to show (and keep with you at all times) a *libreta de pago por la aduana* (proof of customs payment) normally provided by the relevant automobile association of the country you are coming from. **Spare parts**, particularly tyres, will have to be carried as will a tent, emergency water and food. The chance of **theft** is quite high – the vehicle, your baggage and accessories are all vulnerable when parked.

Renting a car costs much the same as in Europe and North America. The major rental firms all have offices in Lima, but outside the capital you'll generally find only local companies are represented. You may find it more convenient to reserve a car in advance from your own country – expect to pay around US$35 per day, or US$200 per week, for the smallest car. In the jungle it's usually possible to **hire motorbikes** or **mopeds** by the hour or by the day; this is a good way of getting to know a town or to be able to shoot off into the jungle for a day.

International driving licences are generally valid for thirty days in Peru, after which a permit is required from the Touring y Automovil Club del Peru, Cesar Vallejo 699, Lince, Lima (Mon–Fri 9am–4.45pm; ⓣ01/440-3270, ⓦwww.touringperu.com.pe).

What few **traffic signals** there are are either completely ignored or obeyed at the drivers' "discretion". The pace is fast and roads everywhere are in bad shape: only the Panamerican Highway, running down the coast, and a few short stretches inland, are paved.

By boat

There are no coastal **boat** services in Peru, but in many areas – on **Lake Titicaca** and especially in the **jungle regions** – water is the obvious means of getting around. From Puno, on Lake Titicaca, there are currently no regular services to Bolivia, but there are plenty of smaller boats that will take visitors out to the various islands in the lake for a small fee.

In the jungle areas **motorized canoes** come in two basic forms: those with a large outboard motor and those with a Briggs and Stratton *peque-peque* engine. The outboard is faster and more manoeuvrable, but it costs a lot more to run. Though hitching is possible, it is more practical to **hire a canoe** along with its guide or driver for a few days. This means searching around in the port and negotiating, but you can often get a *peque-peque* canoe from around US$40–50 per day, which will invariably work out cheaper than taking an organized tour, as well as giving you the choice of guide and companions. Obviously, the more people you can get together, the cheaper it will be per person.

Mail and communications

Communictions in Peru have improved dramatically with the widespread availability of Internet cafés. The phone service, too, has improved in the last seven years since being taken over by a Spanish company. Postal services are slow but quite acceptable for normal letters and postcards.

You can have mail sent to you **poste restante** care of any main post office (Correo Central) and, on the whole, the system tends to work quite smoothly. Have letters addressed: full name (last name in capitals), Poste Restante, Lista de Correos, Correo Central, city or town, Peru. To pick up mail, you'll need your passport, and you may have to get the files for the initials of all your names (including Ms, Mr, etc) checked.

An alternative to the official *lista* is to use the **American Express** mail collection service. Their main offices in Peru are in Lima at Pardo y Aliaga 698, San Isidro (ⓣ441-4744). Officially, American Express charges for this service unless you have one of their cards or use their travellers' cheques (though they rarely seem to). The **South American Explorers Club** (see box on p.849) offers members a postal address service.

With a little patience you can make **international calls** from just about any town in the country. All Peruvian towns have a Teléfonica del Peru or Locutorio Teléfonico office, which offers an operator service; give the receptionist your destination number and they will allocate you to a numbered phone booth when your call is put through (you pay afterwards); or, just dial direct from the booth. These offices also have phones taking cards (see below). In Lima, the central Teléfonica del Peru office (see "Listings", p.876) is often crowded, so a better option is to phone from your hotel or from the street telephone kiosks.

All phone kiosks are operated by coins or **tarjetas telefonicas** – phone cards – which are available in a variety of denominations, and nuevo sol coins. You can buy cards from corner shops, *farmacias* or on the street from cigarette stalls in the centres of most towns and cities. There are currently two main phone outfits, Telefonica del Peru and Telepoint, each of which produce their own cards for use in their phones only. Other companies, such as Nortek, offer cards with greater discounts, particularly on international calls from most types of street phone kiosks.

If you need to contact the **international operator**, dial ⓣ108. **Collect calls** are known either simply as *collect* or *al cobro revertido* and are fairly straightforward. Calls are cheaper at night. Most shops, restaurants or corner shops in Peru have a phone available for public use, which you can use for calls within Peru only.

Peru has good **Internet** connections, with cybercafés and Internet cabins in the most unlikely of small towns. Lima and Cusco have abundant Internet facilities, closely followed by Arequipa, Huaraz, Puno, Iquitos and Trujillo; beyond that it gets a little patchy, but the odd public access office or café does exist and many hotels now offer access too. The general rate is 50¢ to US$1 an hour, though thirty- and fifteen-minute options are often available.

Food and drink

Guinea pig (*cuy*) is the traditional dish most associated with Peru, and indeed, you can find it in many parts of the country, but especially in the mountain regions, where it is likely to be roasted in an oven and served with chips. In the past twenty years, however, the wave of North American interests in the country has made fast food very commonplace, and hamburgers, as well as the ubiquitous pizza, have been adopted with enthusiasm and are now more readily available than the traditional guinea pig.

All larger towns in Peru have a fair choice of **restaurants**, most of which offer a varied menu. Among them there's usually a few *chifa* (**Chinese**) places, and nowadays a fair number of **vegetarian** restaurants too. Often places will offer a *cena*, or **set menu**, from morning through to lunchtime and another in the evening. Ranging in price from US$1 to US$3, these most commonly consist of three courses: soup, a main dish and a cup of tea or coffee (which appears to count as a course) to follow.

Depending on the very different ingredients available locally, food in each of the three major areas of Peru is essentially a *mestizo* creation, combining indigenous Indian cooking with four hundred years of European – mostly Spanish – influence. **Along the coast**, not surprisingly, fish is the speciality. **Ceviche** is the classic Peruvian seafood dish and has been eaten by locals for over two thousand years. It consists of fish, shrimp, scallops or squid, or a mixture of all four, marinated in lime juice and chilli peppers, then served "raw" with corn and sweet potato and onions. *Ceviche de lenguado* (soul fish) and *ceviche de corvina* (sea bass) are among the most common, but there are plenty of other fish and a wide range of seafoods served on most menus.

Mountain food is more basic – a staple of potatoes and rice with the meat stretched as far as it will go. One speciality is the **Pachamanca**, a roast prepared mainly in the mountains but also on the coast by digging a large hole, filling it with stones and lighting a fire over them, then using the hot stones to cook a wide variety of tasty meats and vegetables.

In the **jungle**, **bananas** and **plantains** figure highly, along with *yuca* (a manioc rather like a yam), rice and plenty of fish. There is **meat** as well, mostly chicken supplemented occasionally by **game** – deer, wild pig or even monkey.

Drinking

Beers, **wines** and **spirits** are served in almost every bar, café or restaurant at any time, but there is a deposit on taking beer bottles out (canned beer is one of the worst inventions to hit Peru this century – some of the finest beaches are littered with empty cans).

Most Peruvian **beer** – except for *cerveza malta* (black malt beer) – is bottled lager almost exclusively brewed to five percent, and extremely good. In Lima the two main beers are *Cristal* and *Pilsen*. *Cuzqueña* (from Cusco) is one of the best and by far the most popular at the moment, but not universally available; you won't find it on the coast in Trujillo, for example, where they drink *Trujillana*, nor are you likely to encounter it in every bar in Arequipa where, not surprisingly, they prefer to drink *Arequipeña* beer. **Fruit juices** (*jugos*), most commonly papaya or orange, are prepared fresh in most places, and you can get **coffee** and a wide variety of herb and leaf **teas** almost anywhere. Surprisingly, for a good coffee-growing country, the coffee served in cafés and restaurants leaves much to be desired, commonly prepared from either *café pasado* (previously percolated coffee mixed with hot water to serve) or simple powdered Nescafé.

Peru has been producing **wine** for over four hundred years, but with one or two exceptions it is not that good. Among the better ones are *Vista Alegre* (*tipo familiar*) and *Tacama Gran Vino Blanco Reserva Especial.*

As for spirits**,** Peru's main claim to fame is **Pisco**. This is a white grape brandy with a unique, powerful and very palatable flavour – the closest equivalent elsewhere is probably tequila. The jungle regions produce *cashassa*, a sugarcane rum also called **aguardiente**, which has a distinctive taste and is occasionally mixed with different herbs, some medicinal. While it goes down easily, it's incredibly strong stuff and leaves you with a very sore head the next morning.

Safety and the police

While **pickpockets** are remarkably ingenious in Peru, this country no longer deserves such a poor reputation when compared with Venezuela, Colombia and even Ecuador or Brazil. As far as violent attacks go, you're probably safer in Peru than in New York, Sydney or London; nevertheless muggings do happen in certain parts of Lima (such as in the Centro main shopping areas and also in the parks of Mirflores), Cusco, Arequipa and, to a lesser extent, Trujillo. And as for terrorism – as the South American Explorers' Club once described it – "the visitor, when considering his safety, would be better off concentrating on how to avoid being run over in the crazed Lima traffic".

The dangers of **robberies** cannot be over emphasized, though the situation does seem to have improved since the dark days of the late 1980s. Although you don't need to be in a permanent state of paranoia and constant watchfulness in busy public situations, common sense and general alertness are still recommended.

You'd need to spend the whole time visibly guarding your luggage to be sure of keeping hold of it; even then, though, a determined team of thieves will stand a chance. However, a few simple **precautions** can make life a lot easier. The most important is to keep your ticket, passport (and tourist card), money and travellers' cheques on your person at all times (under your pillow while sleeping and on your person when washing in communal hotel bathrooms). **Money belts** are a good idea for travellers' cheques and tickets, or a holder for your passport and money can be hung either under a shirt, or from a belt under trousers or skirts.

Terrorism is much less of a problem in Peru these days than it was in the 1980s and 1990s. You can get up-to-date information on the situation in each region from the South American Explorers' Club (see box on p.849), Peruvian embassies abroad or your embassy in Lima. There are two main **terrorist groups** active in Peru – the Sendero Luminoso (the Shining Path) and Tupac Amaru (MRTA), though they are both definitely on the wane.

Most of your contact with the **police** will, with any luck, be at frontiers and *controls*. Depending on your personal appearance and the prevailing political climate the police at these posts (*Guardia Nacional* and *Aduanas*) may want to search your luggage. This happens rarely, but when it does the search can be very thorough. Occasionally, you may have to get off buses and register documents at the police *controls* that regulate the traffic of goods and people from one *departmento* of Peru to another. Always stop, and be scrupulously polite – even if it seems that they're trying to make things difficult for you.

In general the police rarely bother travellers but there are certain sore points. The possession of (let alone trafficking in) either soft or hard **drugs** (basically grass or cocaine) is considered an extremely serious offence in Peru – usually leading to at least a ten-year jail sentence. There are many foreigners languishing in Peruvian jails after being charged with possession, some of whom have been waiting two years for a trial – there is no bail for serious charges.

If you find yourself in a tight spot, don't make a statement before seeing someone from your embassy, and don't say anything without the services of a reliable translator. It's not unusual to be given the opportunity to pay a **bribe** to the police (or any other official for that matter), even if you've done nothing wrong.

If you're unlucky enough to have anything stolen, your first port of call should be the **tourist police** (*policia de turismo*), from whom you should get a written report Bear in mind that the police in popular tourist spots, such as Cusco, have become much stricter about investigating reported thefts, after a spate of false claims by dishonest tourists. This means that genuine victims may be grilled more severely than expected, and the police may even come and search your hotel room for the "stolen" items. For **emergency services**, call ⓣ105.

Opening hours, public holidays and fiestas

Most **shops** and **services** in Peru open Monday to Saturday 9am–5pm or 6pm. Many are open on Sunday as well, if for more limited hours. Peru's more important **ancient sites** and ruins usually have opening hours that coincide with daylight – from around 7am until 5pm or 6pm daily.

Peruvians love any excuse for a celebration and the country enjoys a huge number of **religious ceremonies**, **festivals** and **local events**. **Carnival** time (generally late Feb) is especially lively almost everywhere in the country, with fiestas held every Sunday – a wholesale licence to throw water at everyone and generally go crazy. It's worth noting that most hotel prices go up significantly at fiesta times and bus and air transport should be booked well in advance.

Calendar of public holidays

January 1 New Year's Day.

February Carnival. Wildly celebrated immediately prior to Lent, throughout the whole country.

March/April Easter Semana Santa (Holy Week). Superb processions all over Peru (the best are in Cusco and Ayacucho).

June 24 Inti Raymi Cusco's main Inca festival.

July 28–29 National Independence Day. Public holiday with military and school processions.

August 13–19 Arequipa Week. Processions, firework displays, plenty of folklore dancing and craft markets.

September end of the month Festival of Spring. Trujillo festival involving dancing, especially the local Marinera dance and popular Peruvian.

October 18–28 Lord of Miracles. Festival featuring large and solemn processions (the main ones take place on October 18, 19 and 28).

November 2 Diá de los Muertos (All Souls Day).

December 25 Christmas Day.

Outdoor activities

Few of the world's countries can offer anything remotely as varied, rugged, remote and stunningly beautiful as Peru when it comes to exploring the wilderness.

Hiking

Hiking – whether in the desert, mountains or jungle – can be an enormously rewarding experience, but you should go properly equipped and bear in mind a few of the **potential hazards**. Never stray too far without food and water, something warm and something waterproof to wear. The weather is renowned for its dramatic changeability, especially in **the mountains**, where there is always the additional danger of *soroche*, or altitude sickness (see p.877). In **the jungle** the biggest danger is getting lost. If this happens, the best thing to do is follow a water course down to the main stream, and stick to this until you reach a settlement or get picked up by a passing canoe. If you get caught out in the forest at night, build a leafy shelter and make a fire or try sleeping in a tree.

In the mountains it's often a good idea to hire a **pack animal** to carry your gear. Mules can be hired from upwards of US$5 per day, and they normally come with an *arriero*, a muleteer who'll double as a guide. It is also possible to hire mules or horses for **riding** but this costs a little more. With a guide and beast of burden it's quite simple to reach even the most remote valleys, ruins and mountain passes, travelling in much the same way as Pizarro and his men over four hundred years ago.

Canoeing and white-water rafting

Again, Peru is hard to beat for these adventurous activities. The rivers around Cusco and the Colca canyon, as well as Huaraz and, nearer to Lima, at Lunahuana can be exciting and demanding, though there are also sections ideal for beginners.

Cusco is one of the top **white-water rafting and canoeing** centres in South America, with easy access to a whole range of river grades, from 2, 3, 4 and 5 on the Río Urubamba (shifting up grades in the rainy season) to the most dangerous white-water on the Río Apurimac. On the Vilcanota, some 90km south of Cusco, at Chukikahuana there's a 5km section of river which, between December and April, offers a constant level 5 (just about the highest rating you can reasonably expect to raft on). One of the most amazing trips from Cusco goes right down into the **Amazon Basin**.

Mountain biking

In Peru, **cycling** is a major national sport, as well as one of the most ubiquitous forms of transport available to all classes in towns and rural areas virtually everywhere. Consequently, there are bike shops and bicycle repairs workshops in all major cities and larger towns. Perhaps more importantly, a number of tour companies offer **guided cycling tours** which can be an excellent way to see the best of Peru. Huaraz and Cusco are both popular destinations for bikers.

For **mountain-biking tours**, Ecomontana, Calle Garcilaso 265, Of. 3, is a professionally run company operating thirty different circuits; and Vision Trek, at Portal de Harinas 181 (ⓣ243039, ⓦwww.quia.happy.com) can organize mountain biking.

History

The vestiges of Peruvian history are visible in its ruins, which are better preserved than anywhere in South America. The first Peruvians were descendants of the nomadic tribes, which had crossed into the Americas from Asia during the last Ice Age (40,000–15,000 BC). Many of the tribes made their way south, through Central America, and down along the Andes, into the Amazon, and the Peruvian and Ecuadorian coast, while others found their niches en route.

Pre-Inca times

While archeological evidence of human occupation in the **Ayacucho Valley** dates back to around 20,000–15,000 BC, the first real evidence of significant craft skills – stone blades and knives for hunting – can be traced to the north in the **Chillon Valley** (just above modern Lima) around 12,000 BC. Several millennia later, **migratory bands** of hunters and gatherers alternated between camps in the lowlands during the harsh mountain winters and highland summer "resorts". Around 5000 BC saw the first **cultivation** of seeds and tubers, followed over the next two millennia by squashes, peanuts, and eventually cotton. Towards the end of this period a climatic shift turned the coast into a much more arid belt and forced those living there to try their hand at **agriculture** in the fertile riverbeds, a process to some extent paralleled in the mountains.

The earliest signs of a complex Peruvian civilization can be found at the recently uncovered site of **Caral**. Radiocarbon dating proves that the site was fully functioning for around 500 years, from around 2600 BC, growing into a major trading and administrative centre housing thousands of people before being inexplicably abandoned – perhaps owing to a lack of water.

The next really significant cultural and architectural development came around 1500 BC to 200 AD – the **Formative Era** – when agriculture and village life became established and many isolated regions came into contact with each other mainly because of the widespread dispersal of the **Chavín Cult**. Remarkable in that it seems to have spread without the use of military force, the cult was based on a conceptualization of nature spirits, and an all-powerful feline creator god and was responsible for a ubiquity of temples and pyramids.

A diverse period – and one marked by intense development in almost every field – the **Classical Era** (200–1100 AD) saw the emergence of numerous distinct cultures, both on the coast and in the sierra. The best documented are the **Moche** and **Nazca** cultures as well as the **Tiahuanuco**, all forebears of the better-known Incas.

The Incas

With the **Inca Empire** (1200–1532) came the culmination of the city-building phase and the beginnings of a kind of Peruvian unity. Although originally no more than a tribe of around forty thousand, the Incas gradually took over each of the separate coastal empires.

Historically, little definite is known about Inca developments or achievements until the accession in 1438 of **Pachacuti**, and the onset of their great era of expansion.

Within three decades, Pachacuti had consolidated his power over the entire sierra region from Cajamarca to Titicaca, defeating in the process all main imperial rivals except for the Chimu. At the same time the capital at **Cusco** was spectacularly developed, with the evacuation and destruction of all villages within a ten-kilometre radius, a massive programme of agricultural terracing, and the construction of unrivalled palaces and temples.

At the end of the fifteenth century the Inca Empire was thriving, vital as any civilization before or since. Its politico–religious authority was finely tuned, extracting what it needed from its millions of subjects and giving what was necessary to maintain the status quo – be it brute force, protection or food. At this point in history, the Inca Empire was probably the largest in the world even though it had neither horse nor wheel technology. The empire was over 5500km long, stretching from southern Colombia right down to northern Chile, with Inca **highways** covering distances of around 30,000km in all. This overextension may have led to the civil war that started in 1527 and was still simmering when the Spanish arrived.

The Spanish conquest and the colonial era

In 1532 **Francisco Pizarro** (who had stumbled upon and named the Pacific Ocean about two decades earlier) led a small band of Spaniards, totalling less than 170 men to the Inca city of **Cajamarca** to meet the leader of what they were rapidly realizing was a mighty empire.

Although ridiculously outnumbered, the Spaniards had the advantages of surprise, steel, cannon and, above all, mounted cavalry. The day after their arrival, in what at first appeared to be a lunatic endeavour, Pizarro and his men massacred thousands of Inca warriors and captured the Inca ruler **Atahualpa**. The decisive battle was over in a matter of hours. It's likely that European-introduced smallpox, which had been ravaging the area for years, played a factor in Spain's easy victory.

Queen Isabella of Spain indirectly laid the original foundations for the political administration of Peru in 1503 when she authorized the initiation of an **encomienda system**, which meant that successful Spanish conquerors could extract tribute for the Crown and personal service in return for converting the natives to Christianity. This system essentially enslaved the indigenous population of Peru.

The **foundation of Lima** in 1535 began a multilayered process of satellite dependency that continues even today. The fat of the land (originally mostly gold and other treasures) was sucked in from regions all over Peru, processed in Lima, and sent on from there to Spain.

Meanwhile Peruvian society was being transformed by the growth of new generations: **Creoles**, descendants of Spaniards born in Peru, and **mestizos**, of mixed Spanish and native blood, created a new class structure. In the coastal valleys where populations had been decimated by European diseases, **slaves** were imported from Africa. There were over 1500 black slaves in Lima alone by 1554.

Despite the evangelistic zeal of the Spanish, **religion** changed little for the majority of the native population. In return for the salvation of their souls the native population was expected to surrender their bodies to the Spanish. The most feared form of service was the *mita de minas* – **forced work in the mines** – where millions of Indians were literally worked to death. Two major rebellions against Spanish rule were initially successful but eventually repressed, in 1571 and later in 1781.

Independence

After **José de San Martín** liberated Chile by force in 1817, it was only a matter of time before one of the great liberators – San Martín in the south or **Simon Bolívar** in the north – reached Peru. San Martín was the first to do so. Having already liberated Argentina and Chile, he entered Lima without a struggle and proclaimed Peruvian **independence** on July 28, 1821.

Ramon Castilla was the first president to bring any real strength to his office. On his assumption of power in 1845 the country began to exploit one of Peru's major resources – guano (birdshit) fertilizer. In the 1872 elections, an attempted military coup was spontaneously crushed by a civilian mob, and Peru's first civilian president – the laissez-faire capitalist **Manuel Pardo** – assumed power.

The War of the Pacific

By the late nineteenth century Peru's foreign debt, particularly to England, had grown enormously. Even though interest could be paid in guano, there simply wasn't enough. To make matters considerably worse, Peru went to war with Chile in 1879.

Lasting over four years, this "**War of the Pacific**" was basically a battle for the rich nitrate deposits located in Bolivian territory. Victorious on land and at sea, Chilean forces had occupied Lima by the beginning of 1881 and the Peruvian president had fled to Europe. By 1883 Peru "lay helpless under the boots of its conquerors" and only a diplomatic rescue seemed possible. The **Treaty of Anco**, possibly Peru's greatest national humiliation, brought the war to a close in October 1883.

Peru was forced to accept the cloistering of an independent Bolivia high up in the Andes, with no land link to the Pacific, and the even harder loss of the nitrate fields to Chile. The country seemed in ruins: the guano virtually exhausted and the nitrates lost to Chile, the nation's coffers were empty and a new generation of *caudillos* prepared to resume the power struggle all over again.

Modern Peru

In the early years of the twentieth century Peru was run by an oligarchical clan of big businessmen, the most powerful being **Augusto Leguia**, who acted as de facto dictator. During Leguia's long dictatorship, the **labour movement** began to flex its muscles. A general strike in 1919 had established an eight-hour day, and ten years later the unions formed the first National Labour Centre. The worldwide Depression of the early 1930s hit Peru particularly badly and demand for its main exports (oil, silver, sugar, cotton and coffee) fell off drastically. Finally, in 1932, the Trujillo middle class led a violent uprising against the sugar barons and the primitive conditions of work on the plantations. Suppressed by the army, nearly five thousand lives are thought to have been lost, many of the rebels being taken out in trucks and shot among the ruins of Chan Chan.

The rise of **APRA** – the American Popular Revolutionary Alliance – which had instigated the Trujillo uprising, and the growing popularity of its leader, **Haya de la Torre**, kept the nation occupied during World War II. Allowed to participate for the first time in the 1945 elections, APRA controlled 18 out of 29 seats in the Senate and 53 out of 84 in the Chamber of Deputies.

Post-war euphoria was short-lived, however, as the economy spiralled into ruin, and a military junta took control from 1948 to 1956. The primary problem facing Peru in the 1960s was **land reform**, which even the army believed was a prerequisite for building a successful economy. On October 3, 1968, General Velasco and the army seized power, deporting President **Fernando Belaunde**. The new government, revolutionary for a **military regime**, gave the land back to the workers in 1969. The great plantations were turned virtually overnight into producer's co-operatives, in an attempt to create a genuinely self-determining peasant class. At the same time guerrilla leaders were brought to trial, political activity was banned in the universities, indigenous banks were controlled, foreign banks nationalized, and diplomatic relations established with East European countries. By the end of military rule, in 1980, the land reform programme had done much to abolish the large capitalist landholding system.

Belaunde was re-elected to the presidency in 1980. His government increased the pace of industrial development, and in particular emulated the Brazilian success in opening up the

Amazon – building new roads and exploiting the untold wealth in oil, minerals, timber and agriculture. But inflation continued as an apparently insuperable problem, and Belaunde fared little better in coming to terms with either the parliamentary Marxists of the United Left or the escalating guerrilla movement.

The Maoist **Sendero Luminoso** (the Shining Path), founded in 1970 and led by **Abimael Guzman**, persistently discounted the possibility of change through the ballot box. Sendero was very active during the late 1980s and early 1990s, when they carried out attacks on anything regarded as interference with the self-determination of the peasantry. By 1985, new urban-based terrorist groups like the Movimiento Revolutionario Tupac Amaru (**MRTA**) began to make their presence felt in the shantytowns around Lima.

Belaunde lost office in the April **1985 elections** to an APRA government led by **Alan Garcia**. The once young and popular President Alan Garcia eventually got himself into a financial mess and was chased by the Peruvian judiciary from Colombia to Peru, having been accused of high-level corruption and stealing possibly millions of dollars from the people of Peru.

Fujimori and Toleda

Elections in 1990 proved to be a turning point for Peru, the real surprise coming in the guise of a young college professor of Japanese descent, **Alberto Fujimori**, who just barely beat renowned author **Mario Vargas Llosa**. Fujimori managed to turn the nation around and gain an international confidence in Peru reflected in a stock exchange that was one of the fastest growing and most active in the Americas.

However, the real turning point, economically and politically, was the capture of Sendero's leader Guzman in September 1992. Soon, the international press no longer described Peru as a country where terrorists looked poised to take over. Despite many aid organizations confirming widespread poverty and unemployment in Peru, and despite the nation being hit hard by the **El Niño of 1998**, the economy stayed buoyant and Fujimori was re-elected in 2000. Shortly after, though, stunning revelations of corruption and bloody misdeeds forced Fujimori to resign and go into exile in Japan. Fujimori's 2000 rival, **Alejandro Toledo**, was elected president in 2001, Peru's first full-blooded Indian leader since the arrival of the Spanish.

Toledo's first few years have been rocky: in June 2002, riots broke out in Arequipa over attempts to privatize the city's electric utility, followed a month later by paralyzing transportation strikes in the northern *ceja de selva* region.

One good sign for Peru is that it seems so far to have withstood the recent economic downturns suffered by both Argentina and Brazil, largely because of its booming mining sector. Indeed, the economic growth rate in 2002 was the highest five years – despite more than half the population still living in poverty.

Books

There are few books published exclusively about Peru and very few Peruvian writers ever make it into English. Many of the classic works on Peruvian and Inca history are now out of date, though frequently one comes across them in libraries around the world or bookshops in Lima and Cusco.

Hiram Bingham *Lost City of the Incas* (Greenwood Publishing, US). The classic introduction to Machu Picchu; the exploration accounts are interesting but many of the theories should be taken with a pinch of salt.

Eduardo Calderon *Eduardo El Curandero: The Words of a Peruvian Healer* (North Atlantic Books). Peru's most famous shaman – El Tuno – outlines his teachings and beliefs in his own words.

John Hemming *The Conquest of the Incas* (Papermac). The authoritative narrative tale of the Spanish Conquest, very readably brought to life from a mass of original sources.

Thor Heyerdahl, Daniel Sandweiss and Alfredo Navárez *Pyramids of Túcume*. (Thames & Hudson). A relatively recently published description of the archeological site at Túcume plus the life and society of the civilization which created this important ceremonial and political centre around 1000 years ago. Widely available in Peruvian bookshops.

Richard Keatinge (ed) *Peruvian Prehistory* (Cambridge University Press). One of the most up-to-date and reputable books on the ancient civilizations of Peru – a collection of serious academic essays on various cultures and cultural concepts through the millennia prior to the Inca era.

Dervla Murphy *Eight Feet in the Andes* (Flamingo). An enjoyable account of a rather adventurous journey Dervla Murphy made across the Andes with her young daughter and a mule. It can't compare with her Indian books, though.

David Scott Palmer (ed) *Shining Path of Peru* (C. Hurst & Co, UK; St Martin's Press, US). A modern history compilation of meticulously detailed essays and articles by Latin American academics and journalists on the early and middle phases of Sendero Luminoso's civil war in Peru.

Starn, Degregori and Kirk (ed) *The Peru Reader: History, Culture, Politics* (Latin American Bureau, UK; Duke University Press, US). One of the best overviews yet of Peruvian history and politics, with writing by characters as diverse as Mario Vargas Llosa and Abimael Guzman (imprisoned ex-leader of Sendero Luminoso).

Hugh Thomson *The White Rock* (Phoenix, 2002). One of the best travelogue books on Peru for some time, focusing mainly on the archeological explorations and theories of an English Peruvianist.

Cesar Vallejo *Collected Poems of Cesar Vallejo* (Penguin). Peru's one internationally renowned poet – and deservedly so. Romantic but highly innovative in style, it translates beautifully.

Mario Vargas Llosa *Death in the Andes* (Faber & Faber), *A Fish in the Water* (Farrar, Straus and Giroux), *Aunt Julia and the Scriptwriter* (Picador), *The Time of the Hero* (Picador), *Captain Pantoja and the Special Service* (Faber), *The Green House* (Picador), *The Real Life of Alejandro Mayta* (Faber), *The War of the End of the World* (Faber), *Who Killed Palomino Molero?* (Faber). The best-known and the most brilliant of contemporary Peruvian writers, Vargas Llosa is essentially a novelist but has also run for president, presided over his own TV current affairs programme in Lima and even made a (rather average) feature film.

Ronald Wright *Cut Stones and Crossroads: A Journey in the Two Worlds of Peru* (Penguin). An enlightened travel book and probably the best general travelogue writing on Peru over the last few decades, largely owing to the author's depth of knowledge on his subject.

9.1

Lima

Once one of the most beautiful cities in Spanish America, Peru's sprawling capital **Lima** is now home to more than eight million people, over half of whom live in relative poverty without decent water, sewage or electricity. This is not to say you can't enjoy the place, but it's important not to come here with false expectations. There is still a certain elegance to the old **colonial centre**, and the city hosts a string of excellent and important **museums**, but polluted and traffic-choked Lima is not exotic, though the central areas have been cleaned up in recent years. Nevertheless, with its numerous facilities and firm footing as a transport and communications hub, Lima makes a good base from which to explore Peru and furnishes a good introduction to the county.

Some history

Francisco Pizarro founded **Spanish Lima**, "City of the Kings", in 1535, only two years after the invasion. By the 1550s, the town had grown up around a large plaza with wide streets leading through a fine collection of mansions, all elegantly adorned by wooden terraces and well-stocked shops run by wealthy merchants. Since the very beginning, Spanish Lima has always looked out, away from the Andes, towards the Pacific, as though seeking contact with the world beyond.

Lima rapidly developed into the **capital of a Spanish viceroyalty** including Ecuador, Bolivia and Chile. By 1610 its population had reached a manageable 26,000 and the town's centre was crowded with stalls selling silks and furniture from as far as China. In the nineteenth century Lima expanded far into the east and south, creating poor suburbs, while above the **beaches**, at Miraflores and Barranco, the wealthy developed new enclaves. An early twentieth-century renovation programme modernized the city and boosted the city's **explosive population growth**. Lima's 300,000 inhabitants of 1930 became 3.5 million by the mid-1970s and many of its current 8 million are rural peasants who escaped the theatre of civil war that raked many highland regions between the early 1980s and 1993.

Today the city is as cosmopolitan as any other in the developing world, with a thriving middle class enjoying living standards comparable to or better than those of the West and an elite riding around in chauffeur-driven Cadillacs and flying to Miami for their monthly shopping. The vast majority of Lima's inhabitants (or **limeños**), however, have somehow to scrape together meager incomes and food with no access to land and no real jobs, just their ingenuity and grit.

Arrival and information

From **Jorge Chavez Airport**, 7km northwest of the city centre, the quickest way to get into the city is by taxi, which will take around 45 minutes to Lima Centro or downtown Miraflores. It is simplest is to go to the taxi kiosk inside the terminal where you can book an official taxi to most parts of Lima for US$9. If you don't use this service, remember to fix the price with the driver before getting in. A cheaper and very efficient alternative is to take the **airport express** bus (US$5–6) that usually leaves from outside domestic arrivals doors, some heading for Miraflores, others for Lima Centro via Tacna.

If you arrive in Lima by **bus**, you'll probably come in at one of the **terminals** or offices between the *Hotel Sheraton* and Parque Universitario, or in the district of La Victoria along Avenida 28 de Julio and Prolongación Huanuco. However, many operators have depots out in the suburbs, in an attempt to avoid the Lima Centro traffic jams. One of the most reliable operators, Cruz del Sur, has its busy depot at Javier Prado Este 1109 (Ⓕ424-9772, Ⓦwww.cruzdelsur.com.pe) on the edge of La Victoria and San Isidro. For full details of Lima bus companies and their terminals, see "Listings", p.876. Whichever terminal you arrive at, your best bet is to hail the first decent-looking taxi you see and fix a price – about US$3 to anywhere in the central area, or US$5 for anywhere else in Lima.

Driving into the city is really only for the adventurous, as the roads are highly congested with sometimes frustrating traffic levels plus the general madness of fellow drivers, which will either send you insane or turn you into an equally skilful but unpredictable road hog. Wherever you arrive, it can be a disorienting experience as there are few landmarks to register the direction of the centre of town.

Information and tours

Tourist information offices in Lima are plentiful if dispersed. The *municipalidad* office of Informacion Turistica, C Los Escribanos 145, Plaza Mayor (Mon–Fri 9am–6pm, Sat 10am–5pm; Ⓣ01/427-6080), in **Lima Centro**, provides good information and occasionally maps. In **Miraflores** there's a small tourist information point, based in the central Parque 7 de Junio (daily 9am–9pm); the Central de Informacion y Promocíon Turística, Av Larco 770 (Mon–Fri 8.30am–5pm; Ⓣ01/446-2649 or 446-3959 x114), usually has leaflets, information and some maps of Lima and around. The South American Explorers' Club, at C Piura 135, Miraflores (Mon–Sat 9.30am–5pm; Ⓣ445-3306, Ⓔlimaclub@saexplorers.org, Ⓦwww.saexplorers.org), has good information, including maps, listings and travel reports, available to its members. The office of Informacion y Asistencia al Turista, run by i-Peru from Jorge Basadre 610 in San Isidro (Ⓣ01/421-1227 or 421-1627, Ⓔiperulima@promperu.gob.pe), also has a range of information sheets on regions and cities of Peru.

Some of the commercial tour companies are also geared up for offering good tourist information, notably Fertur Peru, which also offers good **city tours**, and Lima Vision, which also does tours. The *PERU Guide*, published in Peru monthly by Lima Editora S.A., Av Benavides 1180 (Ⓣ01/444-3849), gives up-to-date information on most things in Lima; it's readily available in hotels, tour and travel agents and information offices.

City transport

It's a fairly simple matter to find your way around the rest of this huge, spread-eagled city. Almost every corner of it is linked by a regular **municipal bus service**, with flat-rate tickets (around 15¢) bought from the driver as you board. In tandem with these public buses are the much more ubiquitous, privately owned **microbuses**, some older and some smaller than others, more colourful and equally crowded, but again with flat rates (25¢). Quickest of all Lima transport, **combi colectivos** race from one street corner to another along all the major arterial city roads. *Colectivos* dash dangerously fast (frequently crashing), and speeding off before their passengers have got both feet into the vehicle; wave one down from the corner of any major street and pay the flat fare (around 20¢) to the driver or fare collector. You can catch *colectivos* or buses to most parts of the city from Avenida Abancay; for routes and destinations covered in this chapter you'll find the number or suburb name (written on the front of all buses). **Taxis** can be hailed on any street, and cost US$2–4 to most central parts of the city; try Taxi Seguro

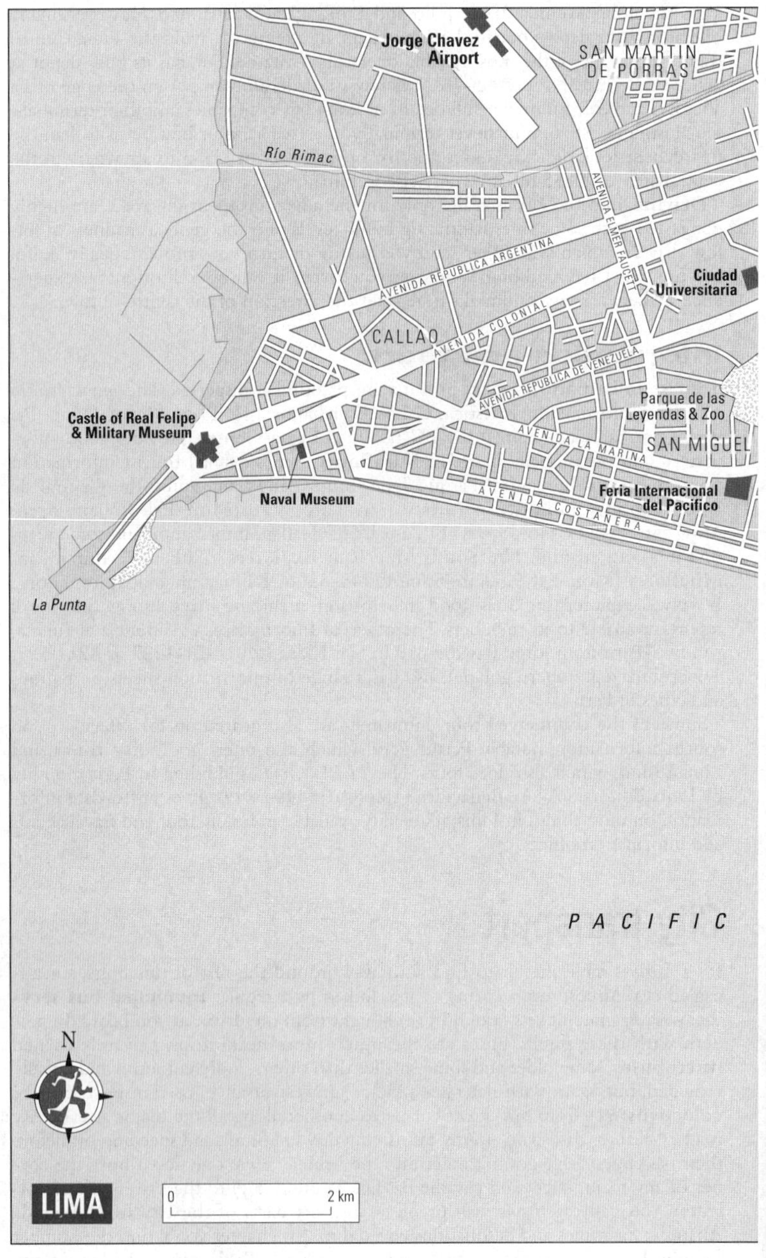
Jorge Chavez Airport
SAN MARTIN DE PORRAS
Río Rimac
AVENIDA ELMER FAUCETT
AVENIDA REPUBLICA ARGENTINA
Ciudad Universitaria
CALLAO
AVENIDA COLONIAL
AVENIDA REPUBLICA DE VENEZUELA
Parque de las Leyendas & Zoo
Castle of Real Felipe & Military Museum
AVENIDA LA MARINA
SAN MIGUEL
Naval Museum
AVENIDA COSTANERA
Feria Internacional del Pacifico
La Punta
PACIFIC
N
LIMA
0
2 km

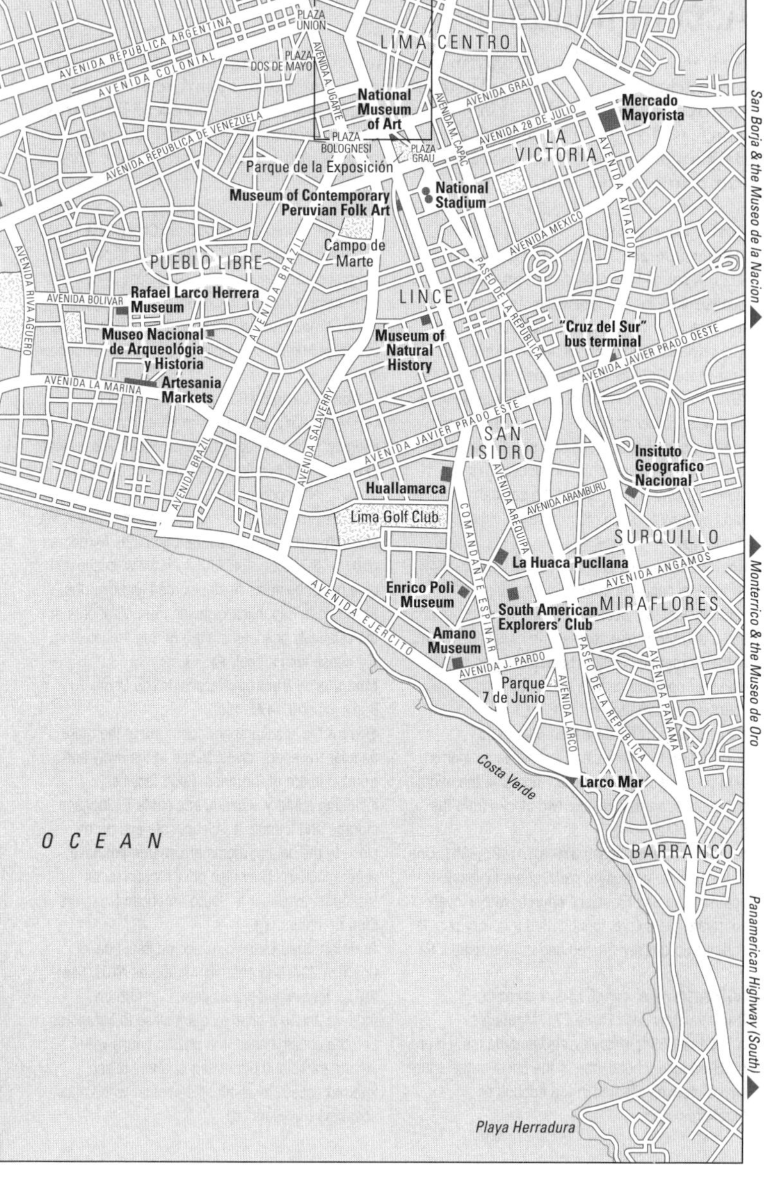
RIMAC
Río Rimac
See 'Lima Centro' map
Plaza de Acho (Bull Ring)
LIMA CENTRO
PLAZA UNION
PLAZA DOS DE MAYO
AVENIDA PERU
AVENIDA REPUBLICA ARGENTINA
AVENIDA COLONIAL
AVENIDA REPUBLICA DE VENEZUELA
AVENIDA A. UGARTE
National Museum of Art
PLAZA BOLOGNESI
PLAZA GRAU
AVENIDA GRAU
AVENIDA 28 DE JULIO
AVENIDA M. CAPAC
Mercado Mayorista
LA VICTORIA
Parque de la Exposición
Museum of Contemporary Peruvian Folk Art
National Stadium
AVENIDA AVIACION
AVENIDA MEXICO
Campo de Marte
PUEBLO LIBRE
AVENIDA BRAZIL
LINCE
PASEO DE LA REPUBLICA
AVENIDA RIVA AGUERO
AVENIDA BOLIVAR
Rafael Larco Herrera Museum
Museo Nacional de Arqueológia y Historia
Museum of Natural History
"Cruz del Sur" bus terminal
AVENIDA JAVIER PRADO OESTE
AVENIDA LA MARINA
Artesania Markets
AVENIDA SALAVERRY
AVENIDA JAVIER PRADO ESTE
SAN ISIDRO
Insituto Geografico Nacional
Huallamarca
AVENIDA AREQUIPA
AVENIDA ARAMBURU
Lima Golf Club
COMANDANTE ESPINAR
SURQUILLO
La Huaca Pucllana
AVENIDA ANGAMOS
Enrico Poli Museum
South American Explorers' Club
MIRAFLORES
AVENIDA EJERCITO
Amano Museum
AVENIDA J. PARDO
Parque 7 de Junio
AVENIDA LARCO
AVENIDA PANAMA
Costa Verde
Larco Mar
OCEAN
BARRANCO
Playa Herradura
San Borja & the Museo de la Nacion
Monterrico & the Museo de Oro
Panamerican Highway (South)

(ⓣ01/275-2020); San Borja Taxis (ⓣ01/476-8945), or; P&P Transport Turistico (ⓣ01/424-9556). Always agree on a price beforehand. If you want to **rent a car** to take out of the city (the city's anarchic driving is best avoided), see "Listings" p.876.

Accommodation

Even more so than most Peruvian cities, modern hotels in the capital tend to be very exclusive and expensive. There are three main areas of Lima to stay – **Lima Centro**, which boasts hotels in just about every category imaginable, **Miraflores**, which is close to most of Lima's nightlife, culture and commercial activity, and **Barranco**, which is popular as a less modern and more stylish centre. There are no **campsites**, official or otherwise.

Lima Centro

El Balcon Dorado Jr Ucayali 199 ⓣ01/427-6028, ⓔbalcondorado@hotmail.com. Really well located, close to the Plaza Mayor, this colonial-style hotel is a very reasonable option. All rooms with private bath. Price includes breakfast. ❹

Gran Hotel Bolivar Jr de la Union 958 ⓣ01/427-7672. This old, very luxurious hotel dominating the northwest corner of the Plaza San Martín has certainly seen better times and usually has more staff than guests. It's probably not worth the money to stay, but check out the cocktail lounge and restaurant, which often have live music on Sat nights. ❽

Hostal España Jr Azángaro 105 ⓣ01/428-5546, ⓔhotel_espana@hotmail.com. Popular and centrally located, *Hostal España* is very secure and has a dormitory, plus rooms with or without private bath, Internet connection, book exchange and its own tour operator service, all based around a nice courtyard and rooftop patio. ❷–❸

Hostal La Estrella de Belen Belen 1051 ⓣ01/428-6462. Very clean and pleasant rooms with private baths in a friendly hostel in the middle of Lima's busiest zone, just two blocks from the Plaza San Martín. ❹

Hotel Europa Jr Ancash 376 ⓣ01/427-3351. One of the best-value budget pads, centrally located opposite the San Francisco church, with a lovely courtyard. Be aware, though, that it is very popular and fills up quickly. Shared and private rooms. ❷

Miraflores and Barranco

Boulevard Av Jose Pardo 771, Miraflores ⓣ01/444-6564, ⓔboulevard@amauta.rcp.net.pe. A full-on luxury hotel, one of the finest in the entire city. Quite well situated in the hubbub of Miraflores. ❽

Casa del Mochilero Jr Cesareo Chacallana 130a, 2nd floor, Miraflores ⓣ01/444-9089, ⓔpilaryv@hotmail.com. Close to block 10 of José Pardo, this safe place is remarkably good, with hot water, cable TV and kitchen facilities. It's not right at the centre of Miraflores's action, but it's close enough. ❷

Hostal El Carmelo Bolognesi 749, Miraflores ⓣ01/446-0575, ⓔcamelo@amauta.rcp.net.pe. Friendly, safe and popular, *Hostal El Carmelo* is close to the heart of Miraflores, one block from the sea front. Clean, modern rooms with private bath; there's a small bar, caféteria and parking spaces. ❻

Lima Youth Hostel Casimiro Ulloa 328, Miraflores ⓣ01/446-5488 or 242-3068, ⓦwww.limahostell.com.pe. Unbeatable hostel located just over the Paseo de la Republica highway from Miraflores in the relatively peaceful suburb of San Antonia, in a big house with a pool. ❷–❸

Mochileros Backpackers Pedro de Osma 135, Barranco ⓣ01/477-4506, ⓦwww.backpackersperu.com. One of the more popular travellers' dives, based in the lively and trendy suburb of Barranco. Good facilities, including laundry, kitchen, bar, cable TV, luggage storage and lounge. It's clean, safe and pretty close to the beach; rooms are shared but have secure lockers. They also offer bicycle rental. Discounts available to South American Explorers' Club members. ❸

Pension Jose Luis Francisco de Paula de Ugarriza 727, San Antonio, Miraflores ⓣ01/444-1015, ⓦwww.hoteljoluis.com. Comfortable, modern and in a good location close to Miraflores and the ocean, based in a private house with private baths and hot water; phone, fax and Internet access available. It's popular with English-speaking travellers. ❹

The City

Laid out across a wide, flat alluvial plain, Lima fans out in long, straight streets from its heart, **Lima Centro**. The old town focuses on the colonial **Plaza Mayor** and the more modern **Plaza San Martín**, which are separated by some five blocks of the **Jirón de la Unión**, Lima Centro's main shopping street.

From Lima Centro, the city's main avenues stretch out into the sprawling suburbs. The two principal routes are **Avenida Colonial**, heading out to the harbour area around the suburb of **Callao** and the airport, and, perpendicular to this, the broad, tree-lined **Avenida Arequipa**, extending to the old beach resort of **Barranco**. Some 7 or 8km down Avenida Arequipa, the suburb of **Miraflores** is the modern, commercial heart of Lima, where most of the city's businesses have moved during the last thirty years.

Lima Centro

Since its foundation, Lima has spread steadily out from the **Plaza Mayor** – virtually all of the **Río Rimac**'s alluvial soil has now been built on and even the sand dunes beyond are rapidly filling up with migrant settlers. When Pizarro arrived here, he found a valley dominated by some 400 temples and palaces, most of them pre-Inca, well spread out to either side of the river. The conquistador founded Lima on the site of an existing palace belonging to Tauri Chusko, the local chief who had little choice but to give up his residence and move away.

The Plaza Mayor

Today the heart of the old town is around the **Plaza Mayor** – until a few years ago known as the Plaza de Armas, or "armed plaza" (Plaza Armada) as the early conquistadores called it. There are no remains of any Indian heritage in or around the square; standing on the site of Tauri Chusco's palace is the relatively modern Palacio de Gobierno, while the cathedral occupies the site of an Inca temple once dedicated to the Puma deity, and the Municipal Building lies on what was originally an Inca envoy's mansion. The **Palacio de Gobierno** – also known as the Presidential Palace – was Pizarro's house long before the present building was built in 1938. It was here that he spent the last few years of his life, until his assassination in 1541. The **changing of the guard** takes place outside the palace (Mon–Sat starts 11.45am) – it's not a particularly spectacular sight, though the soldiers look splendid in their scarlet and blue uniforms. There are free **guided visits** (daily 10am–12.30pm) in English and Spanish, which include changing of the guard; to get on one you have to register with the Departmento de Actividades, office 201, Jr de la Union, Plaza Pizarro (☎01/311-3908) at least 48 hours before the tour.

On the eastern corner of the plaza stands the squat and austere Renaissance-style **Catedral** (Mon–Sat 10am–4.30pm; US$1.50). It is primarily of interest for its **Museum of Religious Art and Treasures** (daily 10am–4.30pm; US$1.50), which contains seventeenth- and eighteenth-century paintings and a collection of human remains thought to be Pizarro's body. Although gloomy, the interior retains some of its appealing Churrigueresque (highly elaborate Baroque) decor.

Directly across the square, the brilliantly white **Municipal Building** (Mon–Fri 9am–1pm; free) is a typical example of a half-hearted twentieth-century attempt at something neocolonial. Inside, the **Pinacoteca Museum** (same hours) houses a selection of Peruvian paintings, notably those of Ignacio Merino from the nineteenth century. In the library you can also see the city's Act of Foundation and Declaration of Independence.

East of the Plaza Mayor

Jirón Ancash leads away from the Palacio de Gobierno towards one of Lima's most attractive churches, **San Francisco** (daily 9.30am–5.30pm; US$1.80). A large

LIMA CENTRO

Convento de los Descalzos & Plaza de Acho

0 200 m

RIMAC
JULIAN PINÉYRO
Río Rima
Puente de Piedra
Train Station
San Francisco
Casa Aliaga
Santo Domingo
Casa de Osamblea
JIRÓN ANCASH
Casa Pilatos
JIRÓN AYACUCHO
Palacio de Gobierno
JIRÓN JUNIN
Museo de la Inquisicíon
JIRÓN LIMA (CONDE DE SUPERUNDA)
Sancturio de Santa Rosa de Lima
Municipal Building
PLAZA MAYOR
Catedral
JIRÓN HUALLAGA
JIRÓN CALLAO
Torre Tagle Palace
JIRÓN UCAYALI
AVENIDA TACNA
JIRÓN CAYLLOMA
JIRÓN CAMANÁ
JIRÓN DE LA UNION
JIRÓN CARABAYA
JIRÓN LAMPA
AVENIDA ABANCAY
JIRÓN ICA
Municipal Theatre
San Augustin
Casa de Riva-Aguero
San Pedro
JIRÓN MIRO QUESADA
HUANCAVELICA
La Merced
Las Nazarenas
JIRÓN RUFINO TORRICO
AVENIDA EMANCIPACION
AVENIDA CUSCO
JIRÓN AZÁNGARO
JIRÓN PUNO
MOQUEGUA
Jesus Maria
JIRÓN OCOÑA
PLAZA SAN MARTIN
AVENIDA NICOLAS DE PIEROLA (LA COLMENA)
AVENIDA NICOLAS DE PIEROLA
Parque Universitario
MONZON
AVENIDA GARCILASO DE LA VEGA
JR. RUFINO TORRICO
Lima Tours
BELÉN
PACHITEA
COTABAMBAS
AVENIDA ABANCAY
JIRÓN QUILCA
Buses & Colectivos to Miraflores
PLAZA FRANCIA
AVENIDA ROOSEVELT
Cruz del Sur
Tepsa
PASEO DE LA REPUBLICA
PASEO DE LA REPUBLICA
AVENIDA BOLIVIA
AVENIDA ESPAÑA
Parque Neptuno
Museo de Arte Italiano
PLAZA GRAU
PASEO COLÓN
Museo de Arte
Avenida Arequipa
Chinatown & Central Market
Buses to Pachachamac & Lurin
Ormeño & Mariscal Caceres buses
N

ACCOMMODATION	
El Balcon Dorado	3
Gran Hotel Bolivar	4
Hostal España	2
Hostal La Estrella de Belen	5
Hotel Europa	1

RESTAURANTS & BARS	
Cordano Café	A
De Cesar	B
El Estadio	D
Machu Picchu	B
Natur	C

seventeenth-century construction with an engaging stone facade and towers, San Francisco's vaults and columns are elaborately decorated with Mudéjar (or Moorish-style) plaster relief. It's a majestic building that has withstood the passage of time and the devastation of successive earth tremors. The San Francisco **Monastery** also contains a superb library and a room of paintings by (or finished by) Pieter Paul Rubens, Jordaens and Van Dyck. You can take a forty-minute guided tour of the monastery and its **Catacombs Museum** (daily 9.30am–5pm; US$1.80), both of which are worth a visit. The museum is inside the church's vast **crypts**, only discovered in 1951 and containing the skulls and bones of some seventy thousand people.

A couple of blocks south, the **Museo de La Inquisición**, Jr Junin 548 (daily 9am–5pm; free but by guided tour only), faces out onto Plaza Bolivar near the Congress building. Behind a facade of Greek-style columns, the museum contains the original tribunal room with its beautifully carved mahogany ceiling. This was the headquarters of the Inquisition for the whole of Spanish-dominated America from 1570 until 1820 and, beneath the building, you can look round the dungeons and torture chambers, which contain a few gory, life-sized human models. The few blocks behind the museum and Avenida Abancay are taken over by the **central market** and **Chinatown**. Perhaps one of the most fascinating sectors of Lima Centro, Chinatown is now swamped by the large and colourful (if also smelly and rife with pickpockets) daily market. An ornate Chinese gateway, crossing over Jirón Huallaya, marks the site of Lima's best and cheapest *chifa* (Chinese) restaurants.

Heading from Chinatown back towards the Plaza Mayor along Ucayali, you'll pass **San Pedro** (Mon–Sat 10am–noon & 5–6pm; free) on the corner of Jirón Azángaro. Built by the Jesuits and occupied by them until their expulsion in 1767, this richly decorated colonial church dripping with art treasures is worth a brief look around. However, just over the road, you'll find the far more spectacular **Torre Tagle Palace**, at Ucayali 358 (Mon–Fri 9am–5pm; free), pride and joy of the old city. Now the home of Peru's Ministry for Foreign Affairs and recognizable by the security forces with machine guns on the roof and top veranda, Torre Tagle is a superb, beautifully maintained mansion built in the 1730s. Originally, mansions such as Torre Tagle served as refuges for outlaws, the authorities being unable to enter without written and stamped permission – now anyone can go in (afternoons are the quietest times to visit).

North of the Plaza Mayor: Rimac

Heading north from the Plaza Mayor along Jirón de la Unión, you pass the **Casa Aliaga**, at no. 224, an unusual mansion, reputed to be the oldest in South America, and occupied by the same family since 1535. It's one of the most elaborate mansions in the country, with sumptuous reception rooms full of Louis XIV mirrors, furniture and doors. You need to call Lima Tours in advance to arrange a visit (☎01/424-5110 or 241-7751; US$3).

Continuing up Jirón de la Unión, it's a short walk to the **Puente de Piedra**, the stone bridge that arches over the Río Rimac – usually no more than a miserable trickle – behind the Palacio de Gobierno. Initially a wooden construction, today's bridge was built in the seventeenth century to link the centre of town and the district of San Lazaro, known these days as **Rimac**, or Bajo El Puente ("below the bridge"). This zone was first populated in the sixteenth century by African slaves, newly imported and awaiting purchase by big plantation owners; a few years later, Rimac was plagued by outbreaks of leprosy. Although these days its status is much improved, Rimac is still one of the most run-down areas of Lima and can be quite an aggressive place at night – unfortunate, since some of the best *peña* folklore nightclubs (see pp.874–51, for details) are down here. However, a one-hour guided **tour** (Sat & Sun 10am–9pm, departing every 15min) through old Rimac and up to the top of San Cristobal departs from outside the Santo Domingo monastery and is a good and safe way to see many of Rimac's rather dilapidated sites. Take one in the afternoon, when the visibility is generally better.

Rimac is also home to the **Plaza de Acho**, on Hualgayoc 332, Lima's most important bullring, which also houses the **Museo Taurino de Acho**, or Bullfight Museum (Mon–Sat 9am–6pm, Sun 10am–6pm; US$1.80; ⓣ01/482-3360), containing some original Goya engravings, several interesting paintings and a few relics of bullfighting contests. At the far end of the Alameda a fine 1592 Franciscan monastery, **El Convento de los Descalzos** (Mon–Sat 9.30am–1pm & 3–6pm; ⓣ01/481-0441; US$1.80, usually including a forty-minute guided tour), houses a collection of colonial and Republican paintings from Peru and Ecuador. Its Chapel of El Carmen possesses a beautiful Baroque gold-leaf altar.

West of the Plaza Mayor

Two interesting sanctuaries can be found on the western edge of old Lima, along Avenida Tacna. The **Sanctuario de Santa Rosa de Lima** (daily 9.30am–12.30pm & 3.30–6.30pm; free), on the first block of Tacna, is a fairly plain church named in honour of the first saint canonized in the Americas. The construction of Avenida Tacna destroyed a section of the already small seventeenth-century church, but in the patio next door you can visit the fascinating **Museo Etnografico**, containing crafts, tools, jewellery and weapons from jungle tribes, plus some photographs of early missionaries.

At the junction of Avenida Tacna and Huancavelica, the church of **Las Nazarenas** (daily 6am–noon & 5–8pm; free) is again small and outwardly undistinguished but it has an interesting history. After the severe 1655 earthquake, a mural of the crucifixion, painted by an Angolan slave on the wall of his hut, was apparently the only object left standing in the district. Its survival was deemed a miracle – the cause of popular processions ever since – and it was on this site that the church was founded. The widespread and popular processions for the Lord of Miracles, to save Lima from another earthquake, take place every autumn (Oct 18, 19, 28 & Nov 1), based around a silver litter which carries the original mural. Purple is the colour of the procession and many women in Lima wear it for the entire month.

South of the Plaza Mayor

The stretch between the Plaza Mayor and Plaza San Martín is the largest area of old Lima. Worth a quick look here is the church of **San Augustin** (daily 8.30am–noon & 3.30–5.30pm; free), founded in 1592 and located on the corner of Ica and Camana. Although severely damaged by earthquakes (only the small side chapel can be visited nowadays), the church retains a glorious facade, one of the most complicated examples of Churrigueresque architecture in Peru.

Perhaps the most noted of all religious buildings in Lima is the **Iglesia de La Merced** (daily 8am–1pm & 4–8pm; free), just two blocks from the Plaza Mayor on the corner of Jirón de la Unión and Jirón Miro Quesada. Built on the site where the first Latin mass in Lima was celebrated, the original church was demolished in 1628 to make way for the present building. Its most elegant feature, a beautiful colonial facade, has been adapted and rebuilt several times – as have the broad columns of the nave – to protect the church against tremors. But by far the most lasting impression is made by the **Cross of the Venerable Padre Urraca**, whose silver staff is smothered by hundreds of kisses every hour and witness to the fervent prayers of a constantly shifting congregation.

Plaza San Martín and around

The **Plaza San Martín** is a grand, large square with fountains at its centre which is virtually always busy by day, with traffic tooting its way around the square, and buskers, mime artists and soapbox politicos attracting small circles of interested faces. The Plaza San Martín has seen most of Lima's political rallies in the last century and one sometimes still sees rioting office workers and attendant police with water cannons and tear gas.

The wide Avenida Nicolas de Pierola (also known as La Colmena) leads off the plaza, west towards the **Plaza Dos de Mayo**, which sits on the site of an old gate dividing Lima from the road to Callao and hosts a great street market where some fascinating bargains can be found. Built to commemorate the repulse of the Spanish fleet in 1866 (Spain's last attempt to regain a foothold in South America), the plaza is probably one of the most polluted spots in Lima and is markedly busier, dirtier and less friendly than Plaza San Martín. East of Plaza San Martín, Avenida Nicolas de Pierola runs towards the **Parque Universitario**, site of South America's first university, San Marcos. Nowadays, the park itself is base for *colectivo* companies and street hawkers, and is almost permanently engulfed in crowds of cars and rushing pedestrians.

South of Plaza San Martín, Jirón Belén leads down to the Paseo de la República and the shady **Parque Neptuno**, home to the pleasant **Museo de Arte Italiano**, Paseo de la República 250 (Mon–Fri 10am–5pm; ⊕01/423-9932; US$1). Located inside an unusual Renaissance building, the museum exhibits contemporary Peruvian art as well as reproductions of the Italian masters and offers a very welcome respite from the hectic modern Lima outside. Just south of here at Paseo Colón 125 is the **Museo de Arte** (Thurs–Tues 10am–5pm; ⊕01/423-5149; US$2), housed in the former International Exhibition Palace built in 1868. It contains interesting, small collections of colonial art and many fine crafts from pre-Columbian times, and also hosts frequent temporary exhibitions of modern photography and other art forms, as well as lectures and film screenings.

Miraflores

MIRAFLORES, with its streets lined with cafés and flashy shops, is the major focus of Lima's action and nightlife, as far as most of the capital's residents are concerned. Although still connected to Lima Centro by the long-established Avenida Arequipa, another road – Paseo de la República (also known as the Via Expressa) – now provides the suburb with an alternative approach. The fastest way to get here is by yellow bus marked "Via Expressa" from Avenida Abancay to Benavides bridge.

Once there, make for the **Huaca Pucllana** (Tues–Sun 10am–5pm; US$1), a vast pre-Inca adobe mound which continues to dwarf most of the houses around and has a small site museum, craft shop and restaurant. It's just a two-minute walk from Avenida Arequipa, on the right as you come from Lima Centro at block 44. One of a large number of *huacas* – sacred places – and palaces that formerly stretched across this part of the valley, little is known about the Pucllana, though it seems likely that it was originally named after a pre-Inca chief of the area.

The suburb's central area focuses on the attractive, almost triangular **Parque 7 de Junio** (Miraflores Park) at the end of the Avenida Arequipa, which has a good craft and antiques market set up in stalls every evening (6–10pm). The streets around the park are filled with flashy cafés and bars and crowded with shoppers, flower-sellers and young men washing cars. **Larco Mar**, the popular, flash clifftop development at the bottom of Avenida Larco, which has done an excellent job of integrating the park with what was previously a rather desolate point, is home to several decent bars, ice-cream parlours, eating establishments, cinemas and nightclubs.

Miraflores' only important mansion open to the public is the **Casa de Ricardo Palma**, at General Suarez 189 (Mon–Fri 10am–12.30pm & 4–7pm, Sat 10am–noon; free), where Palma, probably Peru's greatest historian, lived for most of his life. There are two museums worth visiting: the **Enrico Poli Museum**, Lord Cochrane 466 (hours by appointment; ⊕01/422-2437; US$10 per person for a minimum of 5), contains some of the finest pre-Inca archeological treasures in Lima, including ceramics, gold and silver. The private **Amano Museum**, on C Retiro 160, off block 11 of Angamos Oeste (Mon–Fri, hours by appointment;

☎01/441-2909; entry by donation), also merits a visit for its fabulous exhibition of Chancay weavings, as well as bountiful ceramics.

Barranco

BARRANCO, a quieter place than Miraflores, is easily reached by taking any bus or *colectivo* along Diagonal. Overlooking the ocean, and scattered with old mansions as well as fascinating smaller homes, this was the capital's seaside resort during the last century and is now a kind of *limeño* Left Bank, with young artists and intellectuals taking over many of the older properties. There's little to see specifically, though you may want to take a look at the clifftop remains of a funicular rail-line, which used to carry aristocratic families from the summer resort down to the beach; also there's a pleasant, well-kept municipal park, where you can while away the afternoon beneath the trees. Worth a browse is the **Museum of Electricity**, Pedro Osma 105 (daily 9am–5pm; free), which displays a wide range of early electrical appliances and generating techniques. Otherwise the main joy of Barranco is its bars, clubs and cafés clustered around the small but attractive **Plaza Municipal de Barranco**, which buzz with frenetic energy after dark while retaining much of the area's original charm and character.

Callao

Still the country's main commercial harbour, and one of the most modern ports in South America, **CALLAO** lies about 14km west of Lima Centro. It's easily reached on bus #25 from Plaza San Martín, which runs all the way there – and beyond to La Punta – or by taking or buses (marked "La Punta") from Avenida Arequipa west along either Avenida Angamos or Avenida Javier Prado. The suburb is none too alluring a place – its slum zones, infamous for prostitution and gangland assassins, are considered virtually no-go areas for the city's middle classes – but if you're unworried by such associations, you will find some of the best *ceviche* restaurants anywhere in the continent.

Further along, away from the rougher quarters and dominating the entire peninsula, you can see the great **Castle of Real Felipe** (Mon–Fri 9am–2pm), on the Plaza Independencia. Built after the devastating earthquake of 1764, which washed ships ashore and killed nearly the entire population of Callao, this is a superb example of the military architecture of its age, designed in the shape of a pentagon. The fort's grandeur is marred only by a number of storehouses, built during the late nineteenth century when it was used as a customs house. Inside, the **Military Museum** (Mon–Fri 9.30am–4pm; free) houses a fairly complete collection of eighteenth- and nineteenth-century arms and has various rooms dedicated to Peruvian war heroes. Also in Callao is the **Naval Museum**, Av Jorge Chavez 121, off Plaza Grau (Mon–Fri 9am–2pm; free), displaying the usual military paraphernalia, uniforms, paintings, photographs and replica ships.

San Borja and the Museo de La Nacion

The **Museo de la Nacion**, Javier Prado Este 2465 in the suburb of **San Borja** (Tues–Sun 9am–6pm; US$1, US$3 extra for exhibitions; ☎01/476-9875 or 476-9897), is Lima's largest modern museum and contains permanent exhibitions covering most of the important aspects of Peruvian archeology, art and culture; there's also a café (daily 10am–6pm). The exhibits, displayed mainly in vast salons, include a range of traditional, regional peasant costumes from around the country and life-sized and miniature models depicting life in pre-Conquest times. The museum can be visited by taking a *colectivo* along Avenida Javier Prado east from Avenida Arequipa; after ten to fifteen minutes you'll see the vast, concrete building on the left.

Eating

Predictably, Lima boasts some of the best **restaurants** in the country, serving not only traditional Peruvian dishes, but cuisines from all parts of the world. Seafood is particularly good here, with **ceviche** – raw fish or seafood marinated in lime juice and served with onions, chillis, sweet corn and sweet potatoes – being the speciality. Many of the more upmarket restaurants fill up very quickly, so it is advisable to reserve in advance; where this is the case we have included the phone number.

Bar/Restaurant Machu Picchu Ancash 312, Lima Centro. A busy place opposite San Francisco church in Lima Centro, serving inexpensive snacks; a good spot for meeting up with other travellers. Daily 8am–11pm.

Las Brujas de Cachiche Av Bolognesi 460, Barranco ⓣ01/447-1883. An interestingly conceived, top-class restaurant and bar, which serves conventional Peruvian dishes as well as a range of pre-Columbian meals using only ingredients available more than 1000 years ago. Very trendy and expensive, its theme is traditional Peruvian healing and magic.

Café Haiti Diagonal 160, Miraflores ⓣ01/446-3816. The most popular meeting place for middle-class *limeños*, based by the Cinema El Pacifico in the heart of Miraflores; excellent snacks and drinks but expensive. Daily 8am–midnight.

Cevicheria El Pezon Honorío Delgado 106, La Victoria ⓣ01/226-0614. Located between blocks 13 and 14 of Av Canada, this moderately priced restaurant is another brilliant and unpretentious *cevichería*; very friendly and the owner speaks English. Call to book in advance.

Chifa Capon Ucayali 774, Lima Centro. An excellent and traditional Chinese restaurant, the best of many in this block of Chinatown, close to the centre. It offers a range of authentic *chifa* dishes, but doesn't stay open very late.

Chifa Chun Yion C Union 126, Barranco ⓣ01/477-0550. An excellent, cheap and very busy Chinese restaurant, quite traditional with some private booths in the back room.

Cordano Jr Ancash 202, Lima Centro ⓣ01/427-0181. Beside the Palacio de Gobierno in Lima Centro this is one of the city's last surviving traditional bar-restaurants – very resonably priced, with old-fashioned service. Worth visiting if only to see the decaying late nineteenth- and early twentieth-century decor. Mon–Sat 8am–11pm.

De Cesar Ancash 300, Lima Centro ⓣ01/428-8740. Great little café-cum-restaurant and bar right in the heart of old Lima; food is fine and cheap, service friendly, decor pleasant and the range of breakfasts quite endless.

El Estadio Restaurant Bar Nicholas de Pierola 926, Lima Centro ⓣ01/428-8866, ⓦwww.Estadio.com.pe. The theme is strongly football and the walls on several floors are covered in murals and paraphernalia fascinating even for those only remotely interested in the sport; plus you can have your picture taken next to a lifesize bust of Pele while you're here. Both the reasonably priced food and bar are decent and there are sometimes disco evenings in the basement.

Natur Moquegua 132, Lima Centro. A surprisingly good vegetarian restaurant, caters to vegans as well and, perhaps because of the generous portions, is a very popular Lima Centro lunchtime meeting place, just a couple of blocks from the Plaza San Martín. Mon–Fri 10am–5pm.

Naturista Av Petit Thouars 4747, Miraflores. An excellent vegetarian restaurant with a pleasant atmosphere and set lunches for under US$2.

Restaurant Huaca Pucllana Gral. Borgoño, block 8, Miraflores ⓣ01/445-4042. Tasty modern Peruvian cuisine in elegant surroundings with excellent service. Mon–Sat 12.30pm–midnight, Sun 12.30–4pm.

Restaurant Naturista El Paraiso Alcanfores 416–453, Miraflores. An inexpensive but very good vegetarian restaurant; convenient place to shelter from the hustle and bustle of the Miraflores streets.

La Vieja Taberna Av Grau 268, Barranco ⓣ01/247-3741. A fascinating, historic place built in 1903 and the venue where the political party APRA was created. It's very stylish, with views over the Barranco plaza and often has music weekend evenings. Particularly good for tasty traditional *limeño* cuisine.

Drinking and nightlife

The daily *El Comercio* provides the best **information** about music events and its Friday edition carries a comprehensive supplement guide to Lima's nightlife, which is easy to understand, even if your Spanish is limited. The suburb of **Barranco** is now the trendiest and liveliest place to hang out.

Live music and dance

All forms of **Peruvian music** can be found in Lima, some of them, like salsa and Peruvian black music, better here than anywhere else in the country. Even Andean folk music is close to its best here (though Puno, Cusco and Arequipa are all contenders). As far as the **live music scene** goes, the great variety of traditional and hybrid sounds is one of the most enduring reasons for visiting the capital. Things are at their liveliest on Friday and Saturday nights, particularly among the folk group **peñas** and the burgeoning **salsadromos** (clubs dedicated to all night salsa and other Latin beat dancing). Most places charge around US$5–10 entrance fee, which often includes a drink and/or a meal.

Peñas

Las Brisas del Titicaca Jr Wakulski 168, Lima Centro. One of the liveliest and cheapest of the city's *peñas*.

La Estacion de Barranco Av Pedro de Osma 112, Barranco. Just across the road from the suburb's main plaza, this established *peña* regularly varies its flavour between folklore, criolla and even Latin jazz at times; it has a very good atmosphere most Fridays and Saturdays.

Manos Morenas Av Pedro de Osma 409, Barranco. This club usually hosts criolla gigs, often with big names like Eva Ayllon and internationally renowned dance groups such as Peru Negro; excellent food and shows, though the atmosphere can be a little constrained.

Peña Sachún Av del Ejercito 657, Miraflores. Very lively and popular tourist restaurant with a good reputation for live folklore music and criolla dancing at weekends, usually till at least 2am.

Salsadromos

Fiesta Latina Federico Villareal 259, Miraflores. A lively place to get a feel for popular salsa music. Thurs–Sat 10pm–2am.

Kimbala Av Republica de Panama 1401, La Victoria. A very frenetic nightspot, with vibrant salsa music.

Tropical Plaza Av Manco Capac 618, La Victoria. An inexpensive, no frills place with great music at weekends.

Jazz, rock and Latin jazz

Bar La Parada San Martín 587, Miraflores. Live rock music every night, with open jam sessions on Wednesdays.

La Casona de Barranco Av Grau 329, Barranco. Very popular club with Lima's trendy under-40s and has particularly good live jazz most weekends.

El Ekeko Av Grau 266, by the municipal plaza in Barranco. Often has Latin jazz at weekends, though also hosts Peruvian Andean and coastal music, mainly criolla.

Media Cuadra San Martín, half a block from Av Larco, Lima Centro. An excellent live music venue with an ever-changing variety of sounds; best from Thursday to Saturday.

Bars and clubs

Lima boasts a wide range of exciting **clubs**, with the vast majority of its popular **bars** and discos out in the suburbs of **San Isidro** and **Miraflores**. Most open Thursday to Saturday 10pm–2am or 3am. Many clubs have a members-only policy, though if you can provide proof of tourist status, such as a passport, you usually have no problem getting in. There are no specifically **gay** meeting places in Lima but, in general, the Parque Kennedy and Larco Mar centre in Miraflores are a bit cruisy in the evenings.

Bars

Brenchley Arms Atahualpa 174, Miraflores. A bar trying hard to replicate a typical English pub, with a pleasant atmosphere, good beer and music; also dart board and English taped music.

Juanito's Av Grau 687, Barranco. Probably the most traditional of the area's bars; facing onto the Parque Municipal, it is small and basic and offers an excellent taste of Peru as it used to be. It has no pop music and the front bar is designated for couples only during weekend evenings.

O'Murphy's Irish Pub C Shell 627, Miraflores. Mon–Sat all day and until late, it's a spacious, modern looking joint and a good meeting place in the heart of the neighbourhood.

The Old Pub San Ramon 295 Miraflores. The most authentic of the English-style pubs in Lima; it's actually run by an Englishman, and also plays good music. Easy to find just a block or two from the park, at the far end of San Ramon.

Clubs

Avenida 13 Manuel Segura 270, Lince. Located off block 15 of the Avenida Arequipa, this gay-friendly disco is popular at weekends and is the only club to have a ladies-only night (Fridays).

Bar Kitsch Bolognesi 243, Barranco. A mixed straight and gay crowd come here for the floral wallpaper, sequined mermaids and generally kitsch decor. Plays disco and is pretty crowded at weekends. No entry fee.

Discoteca Gotica Larco Mar, Miraflores. Music is excellent and the service, too; a popular, locally famous, Lima club.

Heaven Av Larco 481 Miraflores Ⓦwww.heavenentraffic.com. A clever club that plays Latin, US and European music; sometimes live sets. Very popular and easy to find. Entrance generally US$10.

La Noche Av Bolognesi 307, El Boulevard, Barranco. Right at the top end of the Boulevard, this gets really packed at weekends. Small entry fee when there's live music and free jazz sessions on Monday evening. Fine decor, arguably the top nightspot in the neighbourhood and one of the best places for meeting people.

Strokers Av Benavides' 325, Miraflores. Low-key, traditional disco, with pool tables and bars as well as dance spaces.

Shopping

All types of Peruvian **artesanía** are available in Lima, including woollen goods, crafts and gemstones. Some of the best in Peru are on Avenida Petit Thouars, which is home to a handful of markets between Avenida Ricardo Palma and Avenida Angamos, all well within walking distance of Miraflores centre. Artesania Gran Chimu, Av Petit Thouars 5495, has a wide range of jewellery and carved wooden items, as does Mercado Artesanal, Av Petit Thouars 5321. More places selling artesania are listed below.

Slightly cheaper are the *artesanía* **markets** on blocks 9 and 10 of Avenida La Marina in Pueblo Libre and the good craft and antique market, which takes place every evening (6–9pm) in the Miraflores Park between Diagonal and Avenida Larco. In Lima Centro the Artesania Santo Domingo, at Jr Conde de Superunda 221–223 which is a little square pavement area just a stone's throw from the Correo central, is a good for beads, threads and other *artesanía* components or completed items.

For **jewellery**, Casa Wako, Jr de la Unión 841, is probably the best place in Lima Centro, specializing in reasonably priced Peruvian designs in gold and silver, while Plateria Pereda, Jr Venecia 186a, Miraflores, stocks fine silver jewellery to suit most tastes. Nazca, Av La Paz 522, has a nice range of offerings, much of it in silver.

Listings

Airlines Aero Condor, Juan de Arona 781, San Isidro Ⓣ442-5663; Aero Continente, Av José Pardo 605, Miraflores Ⓣ01/242-4260, Ⓔaerocont@aerocontinente.com; Aeroparacas, Ⓣ01/271-6941, Ⓔaeroparacas@wayna.rcp.net.pe; LanChile, Av Jose Pardo 269, Miraflores Ⓣ01/213-

8200 or 213-8300; Lan Peru, Av Los Incas 172, eighth floor, San Isidro or Av José Pardo 269, Miraflores ⓣ213-8200 or 213-8300; TACA Peru Av Comandante Espinar 331 Miraflores ⓣ01/213-7000, ⓦwww.taca.com; TANS, C Belen 1015, Lima Centro and Av Arequipa 5200 Miraflores ⓣ01/241-8510, for reservations call ⓣ01/213-6000.

Airport Lima airport applies a flat US$25 departure tax on international flights, paid on departure at the airport. For domestic flights the departure tax is around US$4. The airport boasts lots of shops, cafés, Internet facilities, a post office and a rather expensive left luggage deposit in the international departure area.

American Express Based at Lima Tours, Belen 1040, near Plaza San Martín Mon–Fri 9.15am–4.45pm ⓣ 426-1765 or 424-0831.

Banks Banco de la Nacion, Av Nicolas de Pierola 1065 and Av Abancay 491; Banco de Credito, Jr Lampa 499, Av Larco 1099, Miraflores (well run and with small queues), and on the corner of Rivera Navarrete and Juan de Arona, San Isidro, both of which offer good rates on traveller's cheques; Banco Continental, Av Larco, Miraflores.

Bus companies Always check which terminal your bus is departing from when you buy your ticket. Cial Av Abancay 947 and Terminal Paseo de la República 646 ⓣ01/330-4225 for the north coast including Mancora, Cajamarca and Huaraz. Cruz del Sur, the best choice (if not the cheapest) for most destinations, has several terminals: in Lima Centro it's Jr Quilca 531 ⓣ01/427-1311 and the corner of Zavala with Montevideo ⓣ01/428-2570, for the coast, Huaraz, Huancayo, Cusco, Arequipa and Puno; for international services it's at Av Javier Prado at the corner with Nicolas Arriola (ⓣ01/225-6200 or 225-6163, tickets can be booked and paid for on their website (ⓦwww.cruzdelsur.com.pe); for their Ideal service, which includes the coast, Cusco, Arequipa, Puno, Cajamarca, Huancayo and Huaraz it's Paseo de La Republica 809, La Victoria ⓣ01/332-4000. Emtrafasa, Jr Humbolt 109 (ⓣ01/423-0046) for the whole north coast and also Cajamarca. Transportes Rodriguez, Av Roosevelt 354 (ⓣ01/428-0506), for Huaraz, Caraz and Chimbote. Tepsa, Av Paseo de la República 129 (ⓣ01/427-5642 or 4271233); ticket office at Jr Lampa 1237, Lima Centro (ⓣ01/427-5642).

Car rental Budget, at Av La Paz 522 ⓣ444-4546 in Miraflores, ⓣ01/575-1674 at the airport; (24hr) and at Av Canaval y Moreyra 569, San Isidro ⓣ01/441-9458, ⓦwww.budget.tci.net.pe; Dollar, La Paz 438, Miraflores ⓣ01/444-4920; at the airport ⓣ01/452-6741; National, Av España 453, Lima Centro ⓣ433-3750.

Embassies and consulates Australia, Av Victor Belaúnde 147, Via Principal 155, building 3 of 1301 San Isidro ⓣ01/222-8281; Bolivia, Los Castaños 235, San Isidro ⓣ01/442-8231; Brazil, Av Jose Pardo 850, Miraflores ⓣ01/421-5650; Canada, C Libertad 130, Miraflores ⓣ01/444-4015; Chile, Javier Prado Oeste 790, San Isidro ⓣ01/221-2818 or 2212817; Ecuador, Las Palmeras 356, San Isidro ⓣ01/221-2880; Ireland, Angamos Este 340, Miraflores ⓣ01/446-3878; UK Torre Parque Mar, Av Larco 1301 third floor Miraflores ⓣ01/617-3050; US, La Encalada, block 17, Monterrico ⓣ01/434-3000.

Exchange *Cambistas* gather on the corner of Ocoña, at the back of the *Gran Hotel Bolivar*. Alternatively, you can change cash and travellers' cheques in the smaller hostels and the many *casa de cambios* around Ocoña. Universal Money Exchange, Av José Pardo 629, Oficina 16, Miraflores or Koko's Dollar, Av Ricardo Palma 437, Stand 21, Comercial Las Estaciones, in Miraflores, are both OK.

Internet services Dragon Fans, C Tarata 230, Miraflores, open 24 hours ⓣ01/446-6814; Inter Palace, Diez Canseco 180, Miraflores ⓣ01/242-2070, fast, private cabins, coffee; Mondonet, Av Ancash 412 ⓣ01/427-9196, Internet and telephone service; Phantom Internet Café Bar, Av Diagonal 344, Miraflores ⓣ01/242-7949, ⓦwww.phantom.com.pe; Plazanet, Av 28 de Julio 451, Miraflores ⓦwww.plazanet.com.pe, which is open 24hr and has a café and TV.

Police Tourist Police are at the Museo de La Nacion, Javier Prado Este 2465 ⓣ01/225-8699.

Postal services The main post office is at Pasaje Piura, Jirón Lima, block 1 near the Plaza Mayor, with other branches on Av Nicolas de Pierola, opposite the *Hotel Crillon* and, in Miraflores, at Petit Thouars 5201, a block from the corner of Angamos.

Telephones Phone kiosks are found all around the city. In Lima Centro the main Teléfonica del Peru office is near the corner of Wiese and Carabaya 933, on Plaza San Martín.

Travel agents and tour operators Fertur Peru, Jr Junin 211, Lima Centro ⓣ01/427-1958, ⓔfertur@terra.com.pe; Lima Tours, Belén 1040, near Plaza San Martín ⓣ01/424-7560 or 424-5110, ⓦwww.limatours.com.pe; Lima Vision Jr Chiclayo 444, Miraflores ⓣ01/447-0482 or 447-5323, ⓦwww.limavision.com, which does a variety of city tours and visits, Pachacamac, Nazca and Cusco. Rainforest Expeditions, Aramburu 166-4b, Miraflores ⓣ01/221-4182 or 9638759, ⓦwww.perunature. com.

Visas Migraciones, corner of Prolongacion Av España and Jr Huaraz.

9.2

Cusco and around

Known to the Incas as the "navel of the world", modern **CUSCO** is an exciting and colourful city, built by the Spanish on the solid remains of Inca temples and palaces. Enclosed between high hills and dominated in equal degree by the imposing ceremonial centre and fortress of **Sacsayhuaman** and the nearby white Christ figure, it's one of South America's biggest tourist destinations, with its thriving culture, substantial Inca ruins and architectural treasures from the colonial era attracting visitors from every corner of the world. Yet despite its massive pull, this welcoming city remains relatively unspoiled, its whitewashed streets and red-tiled roofs home to a wealth of traditional culture, lively nightlife and a seemingly endless variety of museums, walks and tours.

Once you've acclimatized – and the altitude here, averaging 3500m, has to be treated with respect – there are dozens of enticing destinations within easy reach. For most people the **Sacred Valley** of the Río Urubamba is the obvious first choice, with the citadel of **Machu Picchu** as the ultimate goal, and with hordes of other ruins – **Pisac** and **Ollantaytambo** in particular – amid glorious Andean panoramas on the way. The mountainous region around Cusco boasts some of the country's finest trekking, and beyond the **Inca Trail** to Machu Picchu are hundreds of lesser-known, virtually unbeaten paths into the mountains, including the **Salcantay** and **Ausungate** treks, which begin less than a day's train ride northwest and a bus ride south of Cusco respectively. Further afield you can explore the lowland **Amazon rainforest** in Madre de Dios, such as the Tambopata and Candamo Reserved Zone, or the slightly nearer Manu Reserved Zone, among the most accessible and bio-diverse wildernesses on Earth.

The **best time to visit** the area around Cusco is during the dry season (May–Sept), when it's warm with clear skies during the day but relatively cold at night. During the wet season (Oct–April) it rarely rains every day or all week, but when it does, downpours are heavy.

Cusco

Although actually inhabited first by the Killki between 700 and 800 AD, legend has it that Cusco was founded by **Manco Capac** and his sister **Mama Occlo** about four centuries later. Over the next two hundred years, the **Cusco Valley** was home

Mountain sickness

Soroche, or mountain sickness, is a reality for most people arriving in Cusco by plane from sea level. It's vital to take it easy, not eating or drinking much on arrival, even sleeping a whole day just to assist acclimatization. Coca tea is a good local remedy. After three days at this height most people have adjusted sufficiently to tackle moderate hikes at similar or lesser altitudes. Anyone considering tackling the major mountains around Cusco will need time to adjust again to their higher base camps. *Soroche* needs to be treated with respect.

to the Inca tribe, one of many localized warlike groups then dominating the Peruvian *sierra*. A series of chiefs led the tribe after Manco Capac, but it wasn't until **Pachacuti** assumed power in 1438 that Cusco became the centre of an expanding empire. Of all the Inca rulers, only **Atahualpa**, the last, never actually resided in Cusco, and even he was en route there when the conquistadores captured him at Cajamarca. In his place, **Francisco Pizarro** reached the native capital on November 15, 1533, after holding Atahualpa to ransom, then killing him anyway. The Spaniards were astonished: the city's beauty surpassed anything they had seen before in the New World, the stonework was better than any in Spain and precious metals were used in a sacred context throughout the city. As usual, they lost no time in plundering its fantastic wealth.

Today Cusco possesses an identity above and beyond the legacy left in the andesite stones carved by the Incas. Like its renowned art, Cusco is dark, yet vibrantly coloured. It's a politically active, left-of-centre city where street demon-

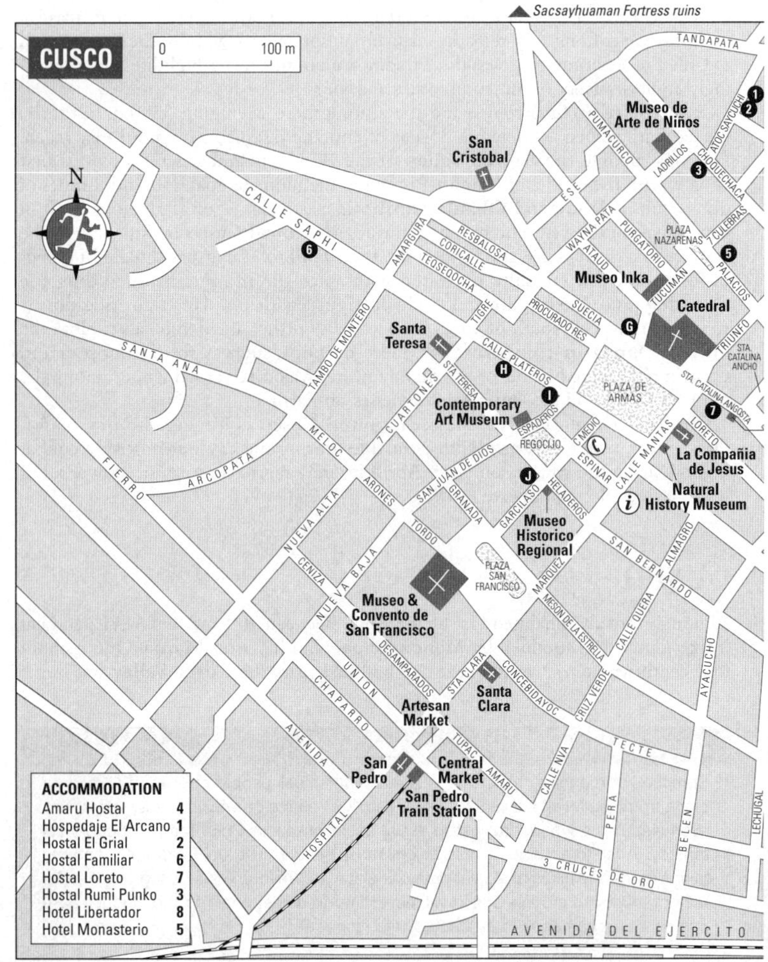

strations organized by teachers, lecturers, miners or some other beleagured profession are commonplace.

Arrival and information

Cusco **airport** (ⓣ084/222611 or 222601 for information) is 4km south of the city centre. You can either take a taxi from outside the arrivals hall (US$2–3 to the city centre), or a *colectivo combi* (frequent departures), from outside the airport car park, which goes to Plaza San Francisco via Avenida Sol and Plaza de Armas. If you're coming in from Puno by **train**, you'll arrive at the Huanchac **station** in the southeast of the city. From here you can hail a taxi on the street outside (around US$1 to the centre), catch the airport *colectivo* mentioned above, or walk the eight or nine blocks up a gentle hill to the Plaza de Armas.

Apart from Cruz del Sur, which has its own independent depot at Avenida

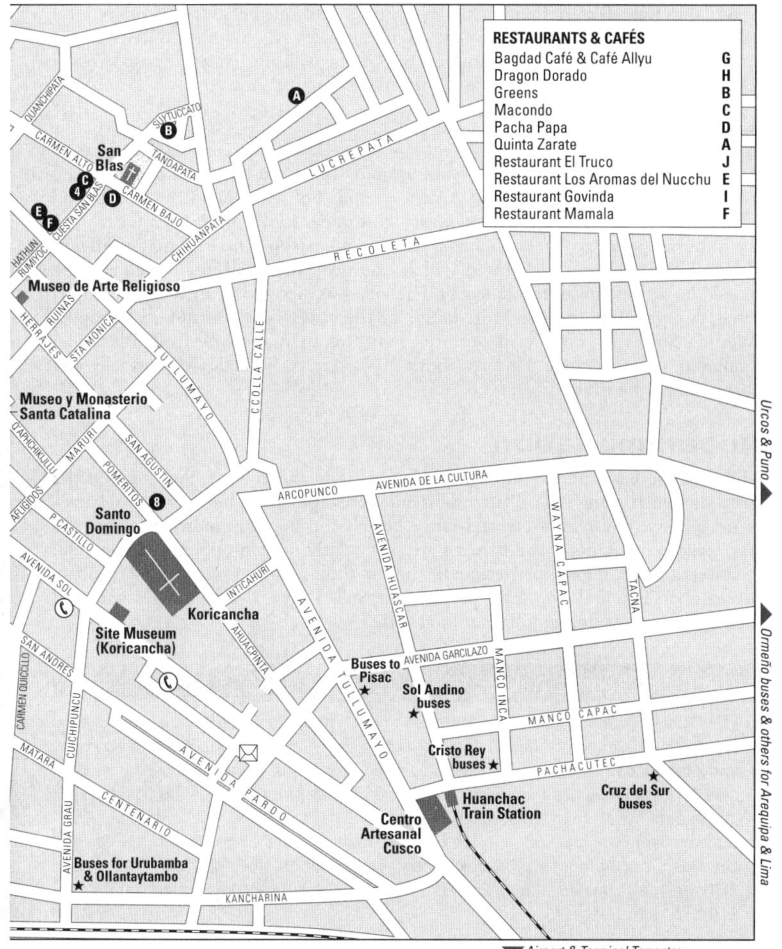

Pachacutec, a few blocks east of Huanchac railway station and Avenida Sol, **inter-regional and international buses** arrive and depart from the rather scruffy Terminal Terrestre, southeast of the centre, close to the Pachacutec monument and roundabout (*ovalo*). Taxis from here to the city centre cost US$1–2, or you can walk to the Pachacutec *ovalo* and catch a *colectivo* uphill to either the Plaza San Francisco or the Plaza de Armas; otherwise, it's about a half-hour walk. **Regional buses** from the Sicuani, Urcos and Paucartambo areas stop around blocks 15 and 16 of Avenida de la Cultura, from where it's a bit of a hike, so you'll almost certainly want to take a taxi (US$1–2) or bus or *combi colectivo* (30¢) to the centre. Almost all Sacred Valley buses come and go from Av Grau 525 (for Pisac, Urubamba, Chincheros, and Ollantaytambo), near Puente Grau or Tullumayu 207 (for Pisac),

The main **tourist office**, operated by the Direccion Regional de Industria y Turismo (DRIT) at Mantas 117-A (Mon–Fri 8am–7pm, Sat 8am–2.30pm; ⓣ084/263176) is a short block from the Plaza de Armas and operates a kiosk at the airport and the Terminal Terrestre. The downtown office is well staffed, spacious and offers a friendly service with sound advice on where to go and how to get there as well as maps and brochures. The English-language *Cusco Weekly* newspaper is available free all over Cusco from bookshops and on the streets; it offers local information and interesting up-to-the-minute articles on cultural and news events and operates one of the more interesting Cusco websites (ⓦwww.cuscoweekly.com), which is also a good source of information on the city.

City transport

Cusco's centre is small enough to **walk** around. **Taxis** can be waved down on any street, particularly on the Plaza de Armas, Avenida Sol and around the market end of Plaza San Francisco; rides within Cusco cost under US$1 or US$2–3 for trips to the suburbs or up to Sacsayhuaman and Quenko (some *taxistas* may prefer to charge US$5 and wait for you, in which case give them half in advance and the remainder at the end of the journey). The city **bus** network is incredibly complicated, though cheap and fast. More useful are the **colectivos** that run up and down Avenida Sol every couple of minutes, many of them starting from Plaza San Francisco; these charge a flat fare (about 20¢) and can be hailed on virtually any corner along the route

Accommodation

Much of the city's budget **accommodation** is in the zone to the north of the Plaza de Armas along calles Plateros, Procuradores and Saphi, but there are relatively inexpensive and reasonable mid-range hostels and hotels in most corners of the city. Calles Procuradores and Plateros are particularly noisy at night; more peaceful locations, though slightly pricier, are further up Calle Saphi, around Plaza Regocijo, towards San Blas and, if you are prepared to walk a little, along Choquechaca and Tandapata, further up the hill from the centre.

The Cusco Tourist Ticket

The **Cusco Tourist Ticket** (US$10 for ten days, students US$5; a one-day ticket costs only US$6, no discounts) is a vital purchase for most visitors. The only key to entry for sixteen of the city and region's main attractions, it includes useful maps plus opening times. It's theoretically available from all of the sites on the ticket, but in practice only from two main offices in Cusco and at the entrances to Sacsayhuaman or the Catedral. The Cusco Tourist Ticket offices are in the Casa Garcilaso, on the corner of Garcilaso and Heladeros (Mon–Fri 7.45am–6pm, Sat 8.30am–4pm, Sun 8am–noon), and at Av Sol 103, office 106 (Mon–Fri 8am–6pm, Sat 8.30am–1pm).

Amaru Hostal Cuesta San Blas 541 ⓣ084/225933, ⓔamaru@telser.com.pe. There's a pleasant colonial feel here, with a lovely garden patio and another out back with views over town. There are laundry, safety deposit and left-luggage facilities, plus bottled oxygen for those in need. Good rooms, with or without private bath. ❹

Hospedaje El Arcano Carmen Alto 288 ⓣ084/244037. A pleasant family-run hostel on the edge of the pleasant San Blas area, *Hospedaje El Arcano* has a good hot-water system, a laundry, family rooms and a comfortable lounge. Rooms come with or without private bath. ❷

Hostal El Grial Atoqsayk'uchi 594 ⓣ084/223012, ⓔgrial_celta@yahoo.com. A pretty central place with a nice energy, clay oven fireplace and pleasantly furnished. Rooms are modernized, spotless and pleasant, with or without private bathroom; Spanish lessons are available and there's a pleasant lounge as well as a TV room. Hot water is both solar and electric and there's a balcony with views over the city. ❷–❸

Hostal Familiar C Saphi 661 ⓣ084/239353. Quiet, safe and one of Cusco's best budget options (it's best to reserve in advance). Rooms are spartan but cool, clean and nicely furnished, with or without private bath (in which case showers are communal) and there's usually hot water in the mornings. ❷–❸

Hostal Loreto C Loreto 115 ⓣ084/226352. An interesting old place on the corner of an Inca stone-lined alleyway connecting Plaza de Armas with Koricancha. The best rooms incorporate the original Inca masonry of the Temple of the Virgins of the Sun, and all have private bath and hot water. Prices vary according to the room you choose and the number of people in it. ❺

Hostal Rumi Punku Choquechaca 339 ⓣ084/221102, ⓦwww.rumipunku.com. A friendly family establishment on an old Inca temple site and in one of Cusco's nicest streets. The rooms have private hot showers, are stylish for the price, plus there's access to kitchens, a patio, a *comedor* and a small sitting room with a fireplace. Best booked in advance in high season. Price includes breakfast. ❺

Hotel Libertador Plazoleta Santo Domingo 259 ⓣ084/231961, ⓦwww.libertador.com.pe. One of the most luxurious hotels in Peru, set in a thoroughly modernized old mansion close to Koricancha, just a few blocks from the Plaza de Armas. ❽

Hotel Monasterío C Palacio 136, Plazoleta Nazarenas ⓣ084/241777, ⓔreserlima@peruhotel.com. Cusco's newest luxurious establishment, charging over US$200 for a double. It's a rather fantastic place, set around massive sixteenth-century monastery cloisters, and there are tables in the courtyard, where you can sip drinks and eat delicious food from the plush bar and restaurants. ❽

The city centre

The city divides into several distinct zones based around various squares, temples and churches, with the **Plaza de Armas** at the heart of it all.

The broad **Avenida Sol** runs southeast from the corner of the plaza by the university and Iglesia de La Compañía towards the Inca sun temple at **Koricancha**, Huanchaq train station and on to the airport in the south. Running southwest from the top of Avenida Sol, Calle Mantas leads uphill past **Plaza San Francisco** and the Iglesia di Santa Clara, then on towards the Central Market and San Pedro train station. Just one block west of the central plaza lies **Plaza Regocijo** and from the northeast corner of Plaza de Armas, Calle Triunfo leads uphill through some classic Inca stone-walled alleys towards the artisan *barrio* of **San Blas**, passing near **Plaza Nazarenas**, northeast of the centre. Calle Plateros heads northwest from Plaza de Armas, leading to Calle Saphi and Calle Suecia, both of which run uphill through quaint streets and on towards **Sacsayhuaman Fortress** above the city.

Each of these zones is within easy walking distance of the Plaza de Armas and their main features can be covered easily in half a day, allowing for a little extra time for browsing in the bars and shops en route. As you wander around, you'll notice how many of the important Spanish buildings were constructed on top of Inca palaces and temples, often incorporating the exquisitely constructed walls and doorways into the lower parts of churches and colonial structures.

Around the Plaza de Armas

Cusco's ancient and modern centre, the **Plaza de Armas**, corresponds roughly to the ceremonial *Huacapata*, the Incas' ancient central plaza, and is the obvious place to get your bearings. With the unmistakable ruined fortress of **Sacsayhuaman** towering above, you can always find your way back to the plaza simply by locating Sacsayhuaman, or, at night, the illuminated white figure of Christ that stands beside the fortress on the horizon. The plaza is always busy, its northern and western sides filled with shops and restaurants. The **Portal de Panes** is a covered cloister pavement hosting processions of boys trying hard to sell postcards, and waiters and waitresses competing for customers, trying to drag passing tourists into their particular dive.

The plaza's exposed northeastern edge is dominated by the squat **Catedral**, (Mon–Sat 10am–noon & 2–5pm, Sun 2–5pm; entry by Cusco Tourist Ticket, see box on p.880), which sits solidly on the foundations of the Inca Viracocha's palace. Its massive lines look fortress-like in comparison with the delicate form of the nearby Iglesia de la Compañía de Jesús, with its impressive pair of belfries, which sits at the southeastern end of the plaza. Check out the cathedral's finely carved granite altar and huge canvas depicting the terrible 1650 earthquake, before moving into the main cathedral to see an intricately carved Plateresque pulpit and beautiful, cedar-wood seats, as well as a Neoclassical high altar made entirely of finely beaten embossed silver. Ten smaller chapels surround the nave, including the **Chapel of the Immaculate Conception** and the **Chapel of El Señor de los Temblores** (The Lord of Earthquakes), the latter housing a 26-kilo crucifix made of solid gold and encrusted with precious stones.

North of the cathedral, slightly uphill beside the **Balcon de Cusco**, you'll find one of the city's most beautiful colonial mansions, **El Palacio del Almirante** (The Admiral's Palace). Commanding superb views down onto the Plaza de Armas from the Calle Cuesta del Almirante, this palace now houses the **Museo Inka** (Mon–Sat 8am–5pm; US$1.70). The museum itself has been recently renovated and is one of the best places in Cusco to see exhibits of mummies, trepanned skulls, Inca textiles and a range of Inca wooden *quero* vases.

Looking downhill from the centre of the plaza, the **Iglesia de la Compañía de Jesús** dominates the skyline. First built in the late 1570s, it was resurrected after the earthquake of 1650, in a Latin cross shape, over the foundations of Amara Cancha –

The Cusqueña school

While the **Cusqueña art** movement, which worked mainly in oils and blended indigenous and Spanish iconography, was limited to the Cusco region in the sixteenth century, during the seventeenth century, it spread to Titicaca and Bolivia, after which much of its technique was developed and elaborated. By the eighteenth century, the style had disseminated as far afield as Quito, Santiago and even into Argentina, making it a truly South American art form and one of the most distinctive indigenous to the Americas.

The most famous Cusqueña artists were the sixteenth-century **Bernardo Bitti**; the seventeenth-century **Diego Quispe Tito Inca**, an artist of mixed blood who was influenced by the Spanish Flamenco school and whose paintings were vital tools of communication used by priests attempting to convert Indians to Catholicism; and the eighteenth-century **Mauricio Garcia**, who helped to move the form into a fuller *mestizo* synthesis, mixing Spanish and Indian artistic forms. Many of the eighteenth- and nineteenth-century Cusqueña-*mestizo* works display bold composition and use of colour. In terms of its look, the Cusqueña school is best known for portraits or religious scenes, with dark backgrounds, serious-looking, almost tortured characters and plenty of gold leaf decoration. Today, they are sought-after pieces fetching many tens of thousands of dollars in the right markets.

originally Huayna Capac's Palace of the Serpents. Cool and dark, with a grand gold-leaf altarpiece, a fine wooden pulpit displaying a relief of Christ, high vaulting and numerous paintings of the Cusqueña school, its transept ends in a stylish Baroque cupola.

South to Koricancha

Leading away from the Plaza de Armas, Callejón Loreto separates La Compañía from the tall, stone walls of the ancient **Acclahuasi**, or Temple of the Sun Virgins, where the Sun Virgins used to make *chicha* beer for the Lord Inca. Today, the Acclahuasi building is occupied by the **Convent of Santa Catalina**, built in 1610, with its small but grand side entrance half a short block down Calle Arequipa; just under thirty sisters still live and worship here. Inside the convent is the **Museo de Arte y Monasterio de Santa Catalina** (Mon–Thurs & Sat 9am–5.30pm, Fri 9am–3pm; entry by Cusco Tourist Ticket, see box on p.880), with a splendid collection of paintings from the Cusqueña school – a seventeenth- and eighteenth-century Peruvian art movement that often emphasized themes of inter racial mixing – as well as an impressive Renaissance altarpiece and several gigantic seventeenth-century tapestries depicting the union of Indian and Spanish cultures.

Koricancha

The Convento de Santo Domingo rises imposingly but rudely from the impressive walls of the **Koricancha** complex at the intersection of Avenida El Sol and Calle Santa Domingo (Mon–Sat 8am–5pm; US$1), which the conquistadores laid low to make way for their uninspiring Baroque seventeenth-century church. The tightly interlocking blocks of polished andesite abut the street as firmly rooted as ever, but before the Spanish set their gold-hungry eyes on it, the temple must have been even more breathtaking, consisting of four small sanctuaries and a larger temple set around the existing courtyard, which was encircled by a cornice of gold (Koricancha means "golden enclosure"). Some of the inner walls, too, were hung with beaten sheets of gold. Below the temple was an artificial garden in which everything was made of gold or silver and encrusted with precious jewels, from llamas and shepherds to the tiniest details of clumps of earth and weeds, including snails and butterflies. Unsurprisingly, none of this survived the arrival of the Spanish.

To reach the **Koricancha Site Museum** (daily 9.30am–6pm; entry by Cusco Tourist Ticket, see box on p.880), or Museo Arqueologico de Qorikancha, it's a three-minute walk downhill from the complex reception to the underground museum entrance on block 3 of Avenida Sol. There are five rooms here, each containing a number of interesting archeological pieces.

Plaza San Francisco and the Central Market

Ten minutes' walk southwest along Calle Mantas from the Plaza de Armas, then a left turn along Calle San Bernardo, brings you to the **Iglesia y Convento de La Merced** (Mon–Sat 8.30am–noon & 2.30–5pm; 50¢), sitting peacefully amid the bustle of one of Cusco's more interesting quarters. Founded in 1536 by Brother Sebastian de Trujillo y Castañeda, it was rebuilt some 25 years after the 1650 earthquake in a rich combination of Baroque and Renaissance styles by such artisans as the native master builders Alonso Casay and Francisco Monya. The facade is exceptional and the roof is endowed with an unusual Baroque spire, while inside there's a beautiful star-studded ceiling, a finely carved chair and a huge silver cross, which is adored and kissed by a shuffling crowd. Its highlight, however, is a breathtaking 1720s **monstrance** standing a metre high and crafted by Spanish jeweller Juan de Olmos, using over 600 pearls, more than 1500 diamonds and upwards of 22kg of solid gold. The monastery also possesses a fine collection of Cusqueña school paintings, particularly in the cloisters and vestry, but it is the exceptional beauty of the white-stone cloister here that really catches the eye.

△ The Inca Trail

Continue another block south and you'll come to the **Plaza San Francisco**, frequently filled with food stalls that couldn't be squeezed into the Central Market or along Calle Santa Clara. The square's southwestern side is dominated by the simply decorated **Museo y Convento de San Francisco** (Mon–Sat 2–5pm; 30¢), founded in 1645 and completed in 1652 and incorporating two facades and a tower. Inside, two large cloisters boast some of the better colonial paintings by such local masters as Diego Quispe Tito, Marcos Zapata and Juan Espinosa de los Monteros, who was responsible for the massive oil canvas measuring some 12m by 9m. There's also an unusual candelabra made out of human bones.

In the area around the **Central Market** (daily 8am–5pm), street stalls sell excellent alpaca goods, while the shops around the indoor market building sell antique textiles. At its top end, the Central Market itself is full of stalls selling colourful Andean foods, with a few interesting herb stalls, and magic kiosks displaying everything from lucky charms to jungle medicines.

Around Plaza Regocijo

Only a block southwest of the Plaza de Armas, the **Plaza Regocijo**, a pleasant garden square sheltering a statue of Bolognesi, was originally the Inca *cusipata*, an area cleared for dancing and festivities beside the Inca's ancient central plaza. Regocijo is dominated on its northwestern side by an attractively arched municipal building housing the Contemporary Art Museum, with a traditional Inca rainbow flag flying from its roof. Opposite this is the *Hotel Cusco*, formerly the grand, state-run *Hotel de Turistas*, while on the southwest corner of the plaza lies an impressive mansion where more Inca stones mingle with colonial construction, home to the Museo Histórico Regional y Casa Garcilaso. Leading off from the top of Regocijo, **Calle Santa Teresa** is home to the House of the Pumas and leads to the Iglesia de Santa Teresa.

Museo Histórico Regional y Casa Garcilaso

Once the residence of a prolific half-Inca, half-Spanish poet and author, the **Museo Histórico Regional y Casa Garcilaso** (Mon–Sat 8am–5.30pm; entry by Cusco Tourist Ticket, see box on p.880) is home to significant regional archeological finds and much of Cusco's historic art. Fascinating **pre-Inca** ceramics from all over Peru are displayed, plus a Nasca mummy in a foetal position and with typically long (1.5m) hair, embalming herbs and unctures, black ceramics with incised designs from the early Cusco culture (1000–200 BC), and a number of **Inca** artefacts such as bolas, maces, architects' plumb lines and square water dishes for finding horizontal levels on buildings. The museum also displays gold bracelets discovered at Machu Picchu in 1995, some gold and silver llamas found in 1996 in the Plaza de Armas when reconstructing the central fountain, and golden pumas and figurines from Sacsayhuaman. From the **colonial** era there are some weavings, wooden *quero* drinking vessels and dancing masks.

The main exhibition rooms upstairs house mainly period furniture and a multitude of Cusqueña paintings, which cross the range from the rather dull (religious adorations) to the more spectacular (like the famous eighteenth-century *Jacob's Ladder*). As you progress through the works you'll notice the rapid intrusion of cannons, gunpowder and violence throughout the 1700s, something which was reflected in Cusco art as a microcosm of what happened across the colonial world.

Calle Santa Teresa

On **Calle Santa Teresa** you'll find the **House of the Pumas** (no. 385), though this isn't as grand as it sounds and is now a small café; the six pumas above its entrance were carved during the Spanish rebuilding of Cusco. Turn right at the end of this street and you pass the **Iglesia de Santa Teresa** (daily 6am–6pm; free), an attractive but neglected church with stone walls, the upper half of which have paintings featuring St Teresa. Inside, the small brick ceiling is finely domed and there's a gold-leaf altar inset with paintings. There's a small **chapel** next door with intricately painted walls (featuring yet more of St Teresa), usually beautifully candle-lit.

Around Plaza Nazarenas and San Blas

Calle Cordoba del Tucman runs northeast from Plaza de Armas along the northern edge of the cathedral, past the Museo Inka (see p.882) and up to the small, quiet **Plaza Nazarenas**. At the top of this square, the unmistakable **Casa Cabrera** (Mon–Fri 8am–5.30pm, Sat 10am–noon & 3–5pm; free) has a fine open courtyard and some exhibition rooms displaying interesting nineteenth- and twentieth-century and indigenous photography, usually presenting many exhibits by renowned photographer, the late Martín Chambi, plus unusual period artefacts. Once part of Cancha Inka, a busy Inca urban centre prior to the Spanish Conquest, it was occupied by Jeronimo Luis de Cabrera, mayor of Cusco, in the seventeenth century and has been owned by the Banco Continental since 1981.

On the northeastern side of Plaza Nazarenas, the ancient, subtly ornate **Chapel of San Antonio Abad** was originally connected to a religious school before becoming part of the university in the seventeenth century. It's not open to the public, but you can usually look around the courtyard of the **Nazarenas Convent**, virtually next door and home to the plush *Hotel Monasterio*.

Just around the corner you come to the narrow alley of **Hathun Rumiyoq**, the most famous Inca passageway of all. Within its impressive walls lies the celebrated Inca **stone**, perhaps best known through its representation on bottles of Cusqueña beer. The twelve-cornered block fits perfectly into the lower wall of the Inca Roca's old imperial palace, but you may have to look carefully to find it as it's often hidden behind Quechua women selling crafts.

Walking up the Cuesta de San Blas, which continues from the far end of Hathun Rumiyoq, you come to the tiny **Chapel of San Blas** (Mon–Wed, Fri & Sat 10–11am & 2–5.30pm; entry by Cusco Tourist Ticket, see box on p.880). The highlight here is an incredibly intricate pulpit, carved from a block of cedar wood in a complicated Churrigueresque style; its detail includes a cherub, a sun-disc, faces and bunches of grapes. Outside, along Calle Plazoleta (also called Suytuccato), there are a few art workshops and galleries, the most notable of which is Galeria Olave, at no. 651. The **Museo de Ceramica**, Carmen Alto 133, is worth checking out for its pottery, while on the plazoleta is the quaint **Museo Taller Hilario Mendivil**, containing a number of Cusqueña paintings, some interesting murals and religious icons.

Eating and drinking

Cusco **restaurants** range from cheap and cheerful to top quality fine dining establishments. Many serve international cuisine but the *quintas*, basic local eating houses, serve mostly traditional **Peruvian fare**, full of spice and character in a typical Cusco ambience. Generally speaking trout is plentiful, reasonably priced and usually excellent, and roast guinea pig (*cuy*) can usually be ordered, but **pizza** seems to lead in the local popularity stakes. The more central **cafés and restaurants** accommodate most tastes, serving anything from a toasted cheese sandwich to authentic Andean or *criolla* dishes (a Peruvian form of Creole).

Bagdad Café Portal de Carnes 216, Plaza de Armas. A popular location not least because it has tables on a colonial balcony overlooking the plaza. Serves good pizzas, breakfasts, sandwiches, some pasta dishes and cool drinks.

Café Ayllu Portal de Carnes 208, Plaza de Armas. Serves one of the best breakfasts in Peru, including fruit, yogurt and toasted sandwiches, though it's not cheap. Centrally located with downstairs views across the plaza, it's Cusco's most traditional meeting place and the service is fast.

Dragon Dorado C Plateros 373 ⓣ084/245192. A small Chinese restaurant near the Plaza de Armas with good, ample portions and quick service; try the delicious *kamlu wantan*, crispy meatballs in a tamarind sauce.

Greens Tandapata 700 ☎084/243820. A Peruvian–British partnership, this brilliantly run albeit pricey restaurant has a very good reputation for Sunday roasts among other more exotic dishes like fettuccini or curries. It is well-situated in San Blas; reservations are advised.

Macondo Cuesta San Blas 571 ☎084/229415. A gay-friendly restaurant with wacky decor and serving some of the best nouveau Andean and Amazonian cuisine you'll find anywhere; try the *yuquitas* stuffed with *chimbivalcano* cheese, the vegetarian curry or the Alpaca mignon *a la parmesana*. Best in evenings when it's a good idea to book in advance, but serves meals, a menu and sandwiches during the day.

Pacha Papa Plaza San Blas 120 ☎084/241318. A great, inexpensive restaurant set around an attractive courtyard, serving a range of hard-to-find Andean dishes, from a *gulash de alpaca* to the highly nutritious *sopa de quinoa*. Reservations recommended.

El Pie Shop Carmen Alto 254a San Blas. Has arguably the best espresso coffee in Cusco and serves a daily selection of freshly baked sweet and savoury pies; very friendly place, sometimes up for a game of cards or backgammon.

The Quinta Zarate Totora Paccha 763 ☎084/245114. Excellent traditional food and atmosphere, close to the San Blas plazoleta, though it's difficult to find without a taxi.

Restaurant El Truco Plaza Regocijo 261 ☎084/235295. Delicious but expensive traditional Cusco food in one of the city's flashiest restaurants, with fine beef and fish dishes. Music and Andean folk dancing is usually performed during the evenings.

Restaurant Los Aromas del Nucchu Choquechaca 130. Featuring possibly the best value set menus in central Cusco, *Los Aromas del Nucchu* tends to be busy at lunch times. Pleasant enough space but no frills.

Restaurant Govinda C Espaderos 128. The original vegetarian eating house in Cusco, serving simple healthy food which is generally adequate, the fruit and yogurt breakfasts are very good and the set lunches excellent value. If you get the chance, eat upstairs where there's more atmosphere and more room. Daily 8.30am–7pm

Restaurant Mamala Choquechaca 509 ☎084/246090. Exceptionally good and very cheap set lunches in a nice ambience, conveniently located between San Blas and the Plaza de Armas. Also serves decent pizzas and burgers.

Nightlife and entertainment

Apart from Lima, no Peruvian town has as varied a **nightlife** as Cusco. The corner of Plaza de Armas, where Calle Plateros begins, is a hive of activity until the early hours, even during the week. Most nightspots in the city are simply **bars** with a dancefloor and sometimes a stage, but their styles vary enormously, from Andean folk joints with panpipe music through to reggae or jazz joints and more conventional **clubs**. Most places are within staggering distance of each other, and sampling them is an important part of any stay in Cusco. Many open around 9pm and keep going until 2 or 3am, so it shouldn't be too difficult to manage.

Pubs and bars

The Cross Keys Pub first floor, Portal Confituras 233. One of the hubs of Cusco's nightlife, this classic drinking dive has the feel of a London pub, with good music, football scarves adorning the walls and pool tables. Food is available and there are often English-language newspapers and magazines.

Los Perros Teqsecocha 436. Billing itself as "the original couch bar", *Los Perros* is a trendy hang-out where travellers snack, drink and play board games or read from the wide-ranging library and magazines (books can be part-exchanged – give two, take one). There's often jazz music at weekends.

The Muse Bar Café Art Gallery Tandapata 682. On the terrace above the Plazoleta San Blas. It has a cosy atmosphere, good drinks and food all day with tables outside; also plays live music from 10ish most weekends and sometimes during the week.

Norton Rats Tavern 2nd floor, C Loreto 115. Just off the Plaza de Armas, with great views over the square, by Iglesia La Compañia. Best known as a drinking establishment, it serves special jungle cocktails, is spacious, plays rock, blues, jazz and Latin music and features a pool table and dartboard and cable TV for sports. There's also a café serving grills.

Clubs and dance bars

KamiKase Bar Portal Cabildo 274, Plaza Regocijo. One of Cusco's best-established nightspots, with modern Andean rock-art decor and basic furnishings. Drinks are quite cheap, though when it hosts live music (most weekends), there's usually a small entrance fee, but it's worthwhile if you're into rock and Andean folk. Happy hour 8.30–9.30pm; live music usually starts around 10pm.

Mama Africa Portal Belen 115, Plaza de lArmas, upstairs. A good, very buzzing dance bar with a small entrance fee, popular with an under-thirties crowd of locals and gringos. Drinks are a bit pricey, but they also do food. The music, including reggae, is pretty loud. Daily 9pm–2am or later. Often shows videos in the afternoons and sometimes offers dance classes in salsa and samba.

Ukuku's Bar C Plateros 316, down the alley and upstairs. A highly popular venue with one of the best atmospheres in Cusco, thronging with energetic revellers most nights by around 11pm, when the live music gets going. There's a small dancefloor and a long bar, with music ranging from live Andean folk with panpipes, drums and *charangos* (small Andean stringed instruments) to taped rock.

White.vinyl Espaderos 135, 2nd floor. Aiming to change the face of nightlife in Cusco, *White.vinyl* is the trendiest club playing mainly cool music and laying on special events at any excuse. It has two main spaces, the main bar approached by a long black catwalk amid white vinyl lounge furniture and chill out areas, almost "Clockwork Orange", but definitely fun; the main dancefloor has another bar. There are periodic performances of dance, acrobatics and creative body art as well as fashion shows.

Xcess Portal de Carnes 298. One of Cusco's most popular dance bars with great decor and lighting, playing a wide range of music, from Latin pop to reggae. Free drinks 10–11.30pm with the pass handed out on the street outside.

Shopping

The main concentration of touristy *artesanía* and jewellery **shops** is in the streets around the Plaza de Armas and up Triunfo, though Calle San Agustin (first right off Triunfo as you head towards San Blas), has slightly cheaper but decent shops with leather and alpaca work. You'll find shops selling photographic film, postcards and books in the same zone. It's worth heading off the beaten track to find other outlets hidden in the backstreets, and even in the smarter shops it's quite acceptable to bargain a little. In the markets and at street stalls you can often get up to twenty percent off.

Listings

Airlines Aero Condor, Av Sol 789a ⓣ084/225000, 252774 or 624005; Aero Continente, Portal de Carnes 245, Plaza de Armas ⓣ084/235666, 243031 or 263978, ⓦwww.aerocontinente.com.pe; Imperial Air, corner of Garcilaso and Plaza San Francisco ⓣ084/238000; TACA Peru, Av Sol 226 ⓣ084/249921, ⓔqtacuz@gruptaca.com.pe, for Lima (from about US$70 standard, including tax); TANS, C San Agustin 315 ⓣ084/242727 or ⓣ251000. Departure tax is US$10 for international departures, US$4 for domestic flights.

American Express Lima Tours, Av Machu Picchu D-6, Urbina. Manuel Prado ⓣ084/228431 or 235241.

Banks and exchange Interbank, Av Sol 380 (also has ATM at airport) is good for travellers' cheques, cash exchange and credit card extraction and has an ATM compatible with MasterCard, Visa, Cirrus and Amex Mon–Fri 9am–6pm, Sat 9am–12.30pm; Banco Continental, Av Sol 366, changes cash and most traveller's cheques. For faster service and better rates than banks, try Cambio Cusco, Portal Comercio 177, Oficina B (daily 9am–10pm; ⓣ084/238861), one of the better and more central money changing offices; street *cambistas* can be found on blocks 2 and 3 of Av Sol, around the main banks, but as usual take great care here.

Bus companies Inter-regional and international buses depart from Terminal Terrestre, Sector Molino Pampa, right side Río Huatanay, in the district of Santiago ⓣ084/224471; except for those run by Cruz del Sur, which leave from Av Pachacutec 510 ⓣ084/221909 5.30am–8pm for tickets, Imperial or Economico services to Arequipa (US$15 or US$8) and Puno (US$15 or US$5), daily. At the Terminal Terrestre there is an embarkation tax of 30¢, which you pay before alighting. Recommended operators include: CIVA for Puno and Arequipa; Cruz del Sur ⓣ084/221909 or 233383 for Arequipa and Desaguadero; Ormeño

(Ⓣ084/233469) for Espinar, Tintaya, Arequipa, Lima, Copacabana and La Paz.

Camping equipment Gregory's Tours, at Portal Comercio 177, has tents, sleeping bags, bed mats, stoves and gas to rent. Inkas Trek, at C Medio 114, offers all the gear you'll need, which is available to rent.

Car hire Aventurismo Cusco, San Borja K-1 Wanxhaq Cusco (Ⓣ084/227730, Ⓦwww.4x4cusco.com), has 4WD cars for rent as do Inka Planet Belen C-25 (Ⓣ084/240507); and AVIS Av El Sol 808 (Ⓣ084/248800).

Consulates Bolivia, Av Pardo, Pasaje Espinar Ⓣ084/231412; UK, Av Pardo 895 Ⓣ239974; US, contact the Instituto de Cultura Peruana Norte Americana, Av Tullumayo 125 Ⓣ084/224112.

Post office The main office is at Av Sol 800 Ⓣ225232

Taxis Alo Cusco Ⓣ084/222222; Llama taxi Ⓣ084/222000; Reynaldo Gamarra Ⓣ084/621854.

Telephones Telesur, C del Medio 117 (Ⓣ084/242222) is right by the Plaza de Armas and has a fast service with Internet facilities too; Telefonica, Av Sol 608, Mon–Sat 8am–9pm, Sun 10–6pm, is good for international calls and has private cabins.

Tourist police C Saphi 581 Ⓣ249654 and also Monumemto Pachacutec Ⓣ084/211961.

Tourist protection service Servicio de Protecion al Turista, Portal de Carrizos 250, Plaza de Armas (Mon–Fri 8am–8pm; Ⓣ084/252974).

Train tickets The Estacion Huanchac ticket office (Mon–Fri 7am–noon & 2–5pm, Sat 7am–noon, Sun 8–10am; Ⓣ084/238722 or for reservations 221992, Ⓦwww.perurail.com) sells Puno and Machu Picchu tickets. For Machu Picchu it's best to buy in advance from here though, if available, the remainder can be bought on the day by queuing at San Pedro station (daily 5–7am & 3–4pm; Ⓣ084/238722 for reservations and sales).

Travel agents America Tour, Portal de Harinas 175 Ⓣ084/227208, mostly books and sells air tickets; Orellana Tours, C Garcilaso 206 Ⓣ084/263455, Ⓔorellanotours@terra.com.pe, sells air tickets and organises some tours; Milla Turismo, Av Pardo 689 Ⓣ084/231710, Ⓦwww.millaturismo.com will organize travel arrangements, tours, study tours and cultural tourist related activities.

Visas Migraciones, Av Sol, 620 (Mon–Fri 9am–5pm; Ⓣ084/222741).

Inca sites outside Cusco

The megalithic fortress of **Sacsayhuaman**, which looks down from high above the city onto the red-tiled roofs of Cusco, is the closest and most impressive of several historic sites scattered around the Cusco hills, but there are four other major Inca sites. Not much more than a stone's throw beyond Sacsayhuaman lies the great *huaca* of **Qenko**. A few kilometres further on, at what almost certainly formed the outer limits of the Incas' home estate, you come to the small, fortified hunting lodge of **Puca Pucara** and the nearby stunning imperial baths of **Tambo Machay**.

All these sites are all an energetic day's **walk** from Cusco, but you'll probably want to devote a whole day to Sacsayhuaman and leave the other sights until you're more adjusted to the rarefied air. If you'd rather start from the top and work your way downhill, it's possible to take one of the regular **buses** to Pisac and Urubamba, run by Empressa Caminos del Inca (from C Huascar 128) and Empressa Urubamba (from Inti Cahuarina 305, 200m from Koricancha, just off Tullumayo). Ask to be dropped off at the highest of the sites, Tambo Machay, from where it's an easy two-hour walk back into the centre of Cusco, or at Qenko, which is closer to Sacsayhuaman and the city. Alternatively, you can take a **horseback tour** incorporating most of these sites, though you will have to get to Sacsayhuaman or Qenko first (a US$1–2 taxi ride from the centre of Cusco).

Sacsayhuaman

Although it looks relatively close to central Cusco, it's quite a steep forty-minute, two-kilometre climb up to the ruins of Sacsayhuaman from the Plaza de Armas. The simplest route is up Calle Suecia, then first right (up a few steps) and along the narrow cobbled street of Huaynapata until it meets the even narrower lane of Pumacurco going steeply up (left) to a small café-bar with a balcony commanding superb views over the city; here the lane meets the road coming up from Calle

Tours in and around Cusco

Tours in and around Cusco range from a half-day city tour to an expedition by light aircraft or a full-on adventure down to the Amazon. **Prices** range from US$20 to over US$100 a day, and service and facilities vary considerably, so check exactly what's provided, whether insurance is included and whether the guide speaks English. The main agents are strung along three sides of the Plaza de Armas, along Portal de Panes, Portal de Confiturias and Portal Comercio, up Procuradores and along the calles Plateros and Saphi and, although prices vary, many are selling places on the same tours and treks, so always hunt around.

Standard tours around the city, Sacred Valley and to Machu Picchu range from a basic bus service with fixed stops and little in the way of a guide, to luxury packages including guide, food and hotel transfers. The three- to six-day **Inca Trail** is the most popular of the **mountain treks**, with thousands of people hiking it every year; many agencies offer trips with guides, equipment and fixed itineraries; but it's important to remember (see p.897) that entry to the Inca Trail is restricted and requires tourists to travel with a guide or tour as well as to be registered with the Unidad de Gestion (your tour company does this) at least two days before departure. In selecting the right Inca Trail tour option it's a good idea to check with at least two or three of those listed before deciding which to go with; prices vary considerably between US$60 & US$300 and a higher price doesn't always reflect genuine added value. Check exactly what's provided: train tickets (which class), quality of tent, roll mat, sleeping bag, porter to carry rucksack and sleeping bag, bus down from ruins, exactly which meals, transport to start.

Other popular hikes are around the snowcapped mountains of Salcantay (6264m) to the north and Ausangate (6372m) to the south, a more remote trek, which needs at least a week plus guides and mules. Less adventurous **walks** or **horse rides** are possible to Qenko, Tambo Machay, Puca Pucara and Chacan, in the hills above Cusco and in the nearby Sacred Valley. You can also rent out **mountain bikes** for trips to the Sacred Valley and around, and some outfits arrange guided tours (or contact Renny Gamarra Loaiza, a good biking guide; ⓣ0841/231300). Many **jungle trip** operators are based in Cusco, and those that also cover the immediate Cusco area are listed oppoite.

Saphi, via the **Iglesia de San Cristobal**, a fine adobe church next to the even more impressive ruined walls of Kolkampata, the palace of the expansionist emperor Manco Capac, a good diversion to take on your way back down. It's only another ten minutes from the café, following the signposted steps all the way up to the ruins.

Because **SACSAYHUAMAN** (daily 7am–5.30pm; entry by Cusco Tourist Ticket, see box on p.880) was protected by such a steep approach from the town, it only needed defensive walls on one side, and three massive, parallel walls zigzag together for some 600m. Little of the inner structures remain, yet these enormous ramparts stand 20m high, quite unperturbed by past battles, earthquakes and the passage of time. The strength of the mortar-less stonework – one block weighs more than 300 tonnes – is matched by the brilliance of its design: the zigzags, casting shadows in the afternoon sun, not only look like jagged cat's teeth, but also expose the flanks of any attackers trying to clamber up.

It was the Emperor Pachacuti who began work on Sacsayhuaman in the 1440s, although it took nearly a century of creative work to finish it. The chronicler Cieza de León, writing in the 1550s, estimated that some twenty thousand men had been

Cusco tour operators

Apumayo C Garcilaso 265, Oficina 3, Cusco ⓣ084/246018, ⓔapumayo@terra.com.pe. Expert operator offering trekking in the Sacred Valley region, mountain biking around Cusco and the Sacred Valley, historic and archeological tours, tours for disabled people (with wheelchair support for visiting major sites), horse riding, and rafting on the ríos Urubamba and Apurimac. Apumayo can customize trips to suit your agenda, though note that they usually only work with the following:

Explorandes Av Garcilazo 316-A, Wanchaq ⓣ084/238380, ⓦwww.explorandes.com or San Fernando 320, Miraflores, Lima ⓣ01/4450532 or 4458683. A long-established company with a range of tours, including the Inca Trail and to Cordillera Vilcanota.

Manu Nature Tours Av Sol 582, Cusco ⓣ084/224384, ⓔpostmaster@mnt.com.pe. Good, nature-based adventure travel in the jungle (see p.963), plus longer tours, mountain biking, birdwatching and rafting.

MAYUC Portal Confiturias 211, Cusco ⓣ084/232666, ⓦwww.mayuc.com. Highly reliable outfit with the experience to organize any tour or trek of your choice, from an extended Inca Trail to visiting the Tambopata-Candamo area. White-water rafting is their speciality with standard scheduled 4 day/3 night excursions involving grade 2, 3, 4 and 5 rapids from about US$230.

Mountain Bike & Trekking C Plateros 364 ⓣ084/635259. Bike tours and treks to a variety of locations, including Laras, ruins around Cusco, Manu cloud forest run, the Pongo de Mainique, the Cordillera Urubamba and Choquequirao.

Peruvian Andean Treks Av Pardo 705, Cusco ⓣ084/225701, ⓔpostmaster@patcusco.com.pe. Expensive but top-quality options for the Inca Trail, plus treks in Cusco and the Peruvian Andes. Worth contacting in advance for their brochure.

United Mice C Plateros 351, Cusco and a second office at C Triunfo 392, # 218 ⓣ084/221139, ⓔunitedmi@terra.com.pe. The top specialists in guided tours of the Inca Trail and reasonably priced (4 days, 3 nights for US$220 including tax, discounts for students), with good guides, many of whom speak English. Food is of a high standard and their camping equipment is fine. If anything, their popularity is a drawback, since groups are largish in high season.

involved in its construction: four thousand cutting blocks from quarries, six thousand dragging them on rollers to the site, and another ten thousand working on finishing and fitting them into position. According to legend, some three thousand lives were lost while dragging one huge stone.

Originally, the inner "fort" was covered in buildings, a maze of tiny streets dominated by three major towers. In front of the main defensive walls, a flat expanse of grassy ground – the esplanade – divides the fortress from a large outcrop of volcanic diorite. Intricately carved in places and scarred with deep glacial striations, this rock, called the **Rodadero** ("sliding place"), was the site of an Inca throne and, most likely, ceremonial gatherings at fiesta times. Today the most colourful time to be at this site is during the **Inti Raymi festival** in June held here annually at the summer solstice. However, throughout the year, you may stumble across various **sun ceremonies** being performed by mystics from the region.

Qenko

An easy twenty-minute walk from Sacsayhuaman, the large limestone outcrop of **QENKO** (daily 7am–5.30pm; entry by Cusco Tourist Ticket, see box on p.880) was another important Inca *huaca*. Head towards the Cusco–Pisac road along a track from the warden's hut on the northeastern edge of Sacsayhuaman, and Qenko is just over the other side of the main road; the route is straightforward but poorly signposted.

This great stone, carved with a complex pattern of steps, seats, geometric reliefs and puma designs, illustrates the critical role of the Rock Cult in the realm of Inca cosmological beliefs, and the surrounding foothills are dotted with carved rocks and elaborate stone terraces. The name of the temple derives from the Quechua word *quenqo* meaning "labyrinth" or "zigzag" and refers to the patterns laboriously carved into the upper, western edge of the stone. At an annual festival priests would pour *chicha* or sacrificial llama blood into a bowl at the serpent-like top of the main zigzag channel; if it flowed out through the left hand bifurcation, this was a bad omen for the fertility of the year to come. If, on the other hand, it continued the full length of the zigzag and poured onto the rocks below, this was a good omen.

Puca Pucara

Although a relatively small ruin, **PUCA PUCARA** (daily 7am–5.30pm; entry by Cusco Tourist Ticket, see box on p.880), meaning "Red Fort", is around 11km from the city, impressively situated overlooking the Cusco Valley and right beside the main Cusco–Pisac road. Between one and two hour's cross-country walk, uphill from Sacsayhuaman and Qenko (longer if you keep to the sinuous main road), this area is dotted with cut rocks. The zone was well populated in Inca days, and many of these may have been worked to obtain stones for building. Although in many ways reminiscent of a small European castle, Puca Pucara is more likely to have been a hunting lodge, or out of town lodgings (a *tambo*, as the Incas would have called this) for the emperor than simply a defensive position. Thought to have been built by the Emperor Pachacutec, it commands views towards glaciers to the south of the Cusco Valley.

Tambo Machay

TAMBO MACHAY (daily 7am–5.30pm; entry by Cusco Tourist Ticket, see box on p.880), less than fifteen minutes' walk away along a signposted track that leads off the main road just beyond Puca Pucara, is one of the more impressive Inca baths, or temple of the waters, evidently a place for ritual as well as physical cleansing and purification. Situated at a spring near the Incas' hunting lodge, its main construction lies in a sheltered gully where some superb Inca masonry again emphasizes the Inca fascination with, and adoration of, water.

The ruins basically consist of three tiered platforms. The top one holds four trapezoidal niches that may have been used as seats, but have been suggested to represent the four cardinal directions; on the next level, underground water emerges directly from a hole at the base of the stonework, and from here cascades down to the bottom platform, creating a cold shower just about high enough for an Inca to stand under. On this platform the spring water splits into two channels, both pouring the last metre down to ground level. Clearly a site for ritual bathing, the quality of the stonework suggests that its use was restricted to the higher nobility, who perhaps used the baths only on ceremonial occasions.

The Sacred Valley and Machu Picchu

The **SACRED VALLEY**, known as Vilcamayo to the Incas, traces its winding, astonishingly beautiful course to the northwest of Cusco. As a river valley it starts much further upstream to the south and also flows on right down into the jungle to merge with the other major headwaters of the Amazon, but the section known as the Sacred Valley lies just between Pisac and Ollantaytambo. Standing guard over the two extremes of the Sacred Valley road, the ancient **Inca citadels** of Pisac and Ollantaytambo hang high above the stunning Río Vilcanota-Urubamba and are among the most evocative ruins in Peru.

Pisac itself is a small, pretty town just 30km from Cusco, close to the end of the Río Vilcanota's wild run from Urcos. Further downstream is the ancient village of **Urubamba**, which has the most facilities for visitors plus a developing reputation as a spiritual and meditative centre, yet it retains its traditional Andean charm and has a bustling market and one or two good eating houses. At the far end of the Sacred Valley, the magnificent ancient town of **Ollantaytambo** is overwhelmed by the great temple-fortress clinging to the sheer cliffs beside it.

Beyond Ollantaytambo the route becomes too tortuous for any road to follow, the valley closes in around the rail tracks, the Río Urubamba begins to race and twist below **Machu Picchu** itself, the most famous ruin in South America and a place that – no matter how jaded you are or how commercial it seems – is never a disappointment.

Getting to the Sacred Valley and Machu Picchu

The classic way to arrive at Machu Picchu is to do the three- to five-day **hike** along the stirring Inca Trail, which you can do with an official guide or by taking one of the guided tour treks offered by the many operators in Cusco (see box on pp.890–1). By road, you can follow the Sacred Valley only as far as Ollantaytambo, from where it cuts across the hills to Chaullay, just beyond Machu Picchu. Buses for Ollantaytambo leave from the Terminal Terrestre and in the afternoons from a depot at Av Grau 525 at 4pm, 5pm and 5.30pm (US$1.80); outside here, near the Puente Grau you'll sometimes find *colectivos* taking people in minibuses to Ollantaytambo for US$3 (1hr 10mins). Once in the valley, there are plenty of pick-up points in Pisac, Calca and Urubamba. Of the **bus** companies, the best departs from Av Grau 525 ⓣ084/805639, with buses leaving for Urubamba (US$1) via Chincheros (50¢) every 15 minutes from about 5am daily; some buses from here marked for Puputi pass by Tambo Machay and Pisac. Smaller buses leave every thirty minutes for Pisac and Calca via Tambo Machay from Tullumayu 207 most mornings, less frequently in afternoons. **Taxis** to Pisac cost more – about US$10 one-way. Once you're in the Sacred Valley, hail one of the many cheap buses or *colectivos* that travel constantly up and down the main road. From Ollantaytambo, afternoon buses to Cusco (US$2) leave regularly from the small yard just outside the railway station, often coinciding with the train timetable. In the mornings they mostly depart from Ollantaytambo's main plaza.

The **train** also connects Cusco with Ollantaytambo as well as Machu Picchu and recently a new piece of line has been reopened from Urubamba (only used in high season). The train trip from Cusco all the way to Machu Picchu is almost as spectacular as walking the Inca Trail. There are three tourist classes, each departing Cusco at least once a day and ranging from US$58 to US$86 return trip. All the Cusco departures for Machu Picchu leave from San Pedro station; it's sometimes possible to queue from 5am to buy tickets for the same day but it's less stressful and a more sure bet if you book and buy in advance from the PeruRail office at Huanchac Station, Avenida Pachacutec ⓣ084/238722 or 221992, ⓦwww.perurail.com.

A much more expensive alternative (though even more dramatic) means of transport direct to Machu Picchu is to fly into the valley **by helicopter**; Helicusco, Calle Triunfo 379 (ⓣ243635, ⓦwww.rcp.net.pe/HELICUSCO), offers the 25-minute flight there from Cusco for US$85 (US$150 return). Fears have been voiced about detrimental effects large helicopters might have on both the stone fabric of ancient Machu Picchu and its reputed mystical energies. However, the helicopters never venture nearer than a couple of kilometres from the most important Inca ruins.

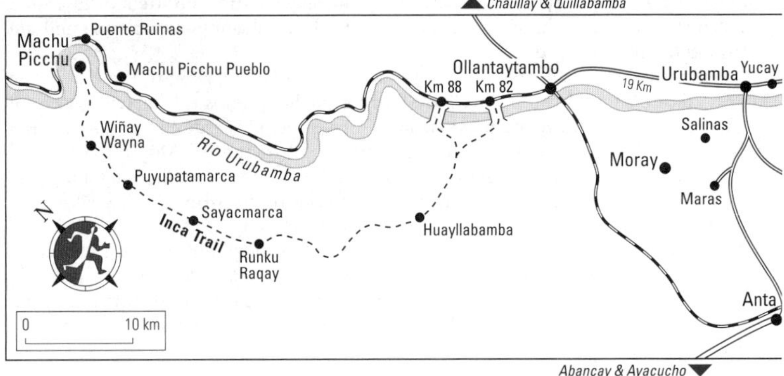

Pisac

A vital Inca road once snaked its way up the canyon that enters the Sacred Valley at **PISAC**, and the ruined citadel which sits at the entrance to the gorge controlled a route connecting the Inca Empire with Paucartambo, on the borders of the eastern jungle. Nowadays, less than an hour by bus from Cusco, the village is best known for its good Tuesday, Thursday and Sunday morning **market**, held on the town's main square, the Plaza Constitución, where you can buy hand-painted ceramic beads and pick up the occasional bargain. The main local **fiesta** – Virgen del Carmen (July 16–18) – is a good alternative to the simultaneous but more remote Paucartambo festival of the same name, with processions, music, dance groups, the usual fire-cracking celebrations, and food stalls around the plaza.

It takes a good ninety minutes to climb directly to the **citadel** (daily 7am–5.30pm; entry by Cusco Tourist Ticket, see box on p.880), heading up through the agricultural terraces still in use at the back of Plaza Constitución. Alternatively, you can catch a bus (20¢) from the end of Calle Mariscal Castilla, or take a taxi, *colectivo* or pick-up (US$3–5) from the main road, on the corner of Calle Bolognesi. Set high above a valley floor patchworked by patterned fields and rimmed by centuries of terracing amid giant landslides, the stonework and panoramas at the citadel are magnificent. On a large natural balcony, a semicircle of buildings is gracefully positioned under row upon row of fine stone terraces thought to represent a partridge's wing (*pisac* meaning "partridge"). In the upper sector of the ruins, the main **Temple of the Sun** is the equal of anything at Machu Picchu and more than repays the exertions of the steep climb. Reached by many of the dozens of paths that crisscross their way up through the citadel, it's poised in a flattish saddle on a great spur protruding north–south into the Sacred Valley and was built around an outcrop of volcanic rock, its peak carved into a "hitching post" for the sun. Above the temple lie still more ruins, largely unexcavated, and among the higher crevices and rocky overhangs several ancient burial sites are hidden.

Practicalities

The only time when accommodation may be hard to find is in September, when the village fills up with pilgrims heading to the nearby sanctuary of Huanca. The most luxurious **place to stay** is the *Hotel Royal Inca* (ⓣ084/203064, ⓦwww.royalinkahotel.com; ❸), which has a pool and all mod cons, though it's 2km out of the village on the long road that winds up towards the ruins. About 1km out of Pisac towards Calca on the main road just before the first bend there's also the pleasant *Inti Wasi* (ⓣ084/203047, ⓔintiwasi@latinmail.com; ❺), which has a restaurant and offers bungalow-style accommodation. In Pisac itself there's a good

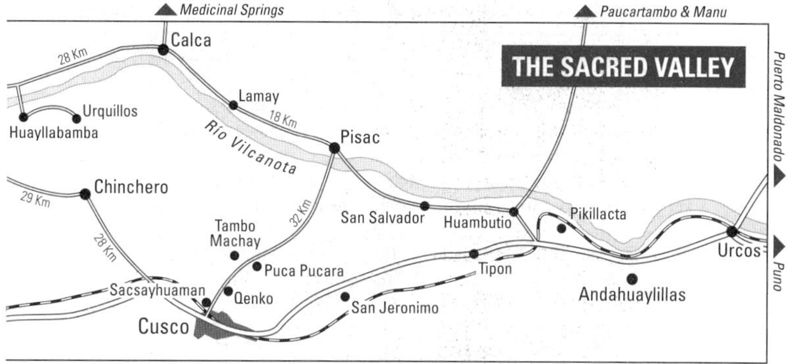

selection of lodgings and some pleasant restaurants. By far the most agreeable is the *Hotel Pisac*, Plaza Constitución 333 (☎084/203058; ❸), with lavishly decorated bedrooms (with or without private bath) and there's also a rock-heated sauna, plus good breakfasts and lunches, including vegetarian food (available to non-residents). There are a few decent **restaurants** in Pisac, but it's hard to better the excellent *Restaurant Samana Wasi*, on the corner of Plaza Constitución 509, with a pleasant little courtyard out the back and very tasty trout, salad and fried potatoes. The *Restaurant Pisac* is a dingy but friendly family run place back down on the main road by the taxis at #147, which also serves generous portions of other standard basic Peruvian fare.

Urubamba and around

URUBAMBA, about 80km from Cusco via Pisac or around 60km via Chinchero, is only a short way down the main road from Yucay's Plaza Manco II, and here the Río Vilcanota becomes the Río Urubamba (though many people still refer to this stretch as the Vilcanota). Although it has little in the way of obvious historic interest, the town is well endowed with tourist facilities and is situated in the shadow of the beautiful Chicon and Pumahuanca glaciers.

The attractive Plaza de Armas is laid-back and attractive, with palm trees and a couple of pines surrounded by interesting topiary. At the heart of the plaza is a small fountain topped by a maize corn, but it is dominated by the red sandstone **Iglesia San Pedro** with its stacked columns below two small belfries; the cool interior has a vast three-tier gold-leaf altarpiece. At weekends there's a large **market** on Jirón Palacio, which serves the local villages.

Because of its good facilities and position, Urubamba makes an ideal base from which to explore the mountains and lower hills around the Sacred Valley, which are filled with sites. The eastern side of the valley is formed by the **Cordillera Urubamba**, a range of snowcapped peaks dominated by the summits of Chicon and Veronica. Many of the ravines can be hiked, and on the trek up from the town you'll have stupendous views of Chicon. **Moray**, a stunning Inca site, part agricultural centre part ceremonial, lies about 6km north of Maras village on the Chinchero side of the river, within a two- to three-hour walk from Urubamba.

Regular **buses** connect Urubamba with Cusco, Pisac, Calca and Ollantaytambo. Buses for Ollantaytambo, Cusco and Chinchero leave regularly from Terminal Terrestre, on the main road more or less opposite the *Hotel Incaland*. The *Neuvo Mundo Café* (see below) has some local **tourist information**.

The two most upmarket **accommodation** options in town are *Hotel San Augustin*, Km 69, Panamerican Highway (☎084/201025; ❼), twenty minutes' walk down the main road towards Cusco, just beyond the bridge over the Río

Urubamba, which boasts a small pool and a popular restaurant (delicious buffet lunches served Tues, Thurs & Sun), and the *Hotel Incaland*, on Avenida Ferrocarril (Ⓣ084/201071 or 201126, Ⓦwww.enperu.com; ❽), a large Best Western hotel and conference centre with Internet access, a pool and tennis courts. The basic but friendly *Hostal Urubamba*, Jr Bolognesi 665 (no phone; ❶), lies behind the police station, one and a half blocks from the Plaza de Armas. There is a surprising range of good **places to eat** in and around Urubamba. *La Casa de la Abuela*, in Bolognesi around the corner from the plaza, to the left of the church and one block up on the left, is a very friendly restaurant with a lovely courtyard full of flowers and trees; they serve excellent pizzas and very good lasagna. Or try the *Restaurant Pub Che Mary* on Plaza de Armas at the corner of Jirón Comercial and Jirón Grau, serving alpaca steaks, *ponche de leche*, juices, drinks and food such as trout and *ceviche*.

Ollantaytambo

On the approach to **OLLANTAYTAMBO** from Urubamba, the river runs smoothly between a series of fine Inca terraces that gradually diminish in size as the slopes get steeper and rockier. Just before the town, the rail tracks reappear and the road climbs a small hill into the ancient plaza. Built as an Inca administrative centre rather than a town, it's hard not to be impressived by the foundations that abound in the backstreets radiating up from the plaza, especially in Calle Medio. Laid out in the form of a maize corncob – and one of the few surviving examples of an Inca grid system – the plan can be seen from vantagepoints high above it, especially from the hill opposite the fortress.

The main focuses of activity in town are the main **plaza**, the heart of civic life and the scene of traditional folk dancing during festive occasions, the Inca fortress and the train station. The useful **Ollantaytambo Heritage Trail** helps you find the most of the important sites with a series of blue plaques around town. Close to the central plaza there's the recently refurbished **CATCCO Museum** (Tues–Sun 10am–1pm & 2–4pm; US$1.75), a small but very interesting museum containing interpretative exhibits in Spanish and English about local history, culture, archeology and natural history. It also has a ceramic workshop and you can buy some good pottery here.

Downhill from the plaza, just across the Río Patacancha, is the old Inca **Plaza Mañya Raquy**, dominated by the fortress. There are a few *artesanía* shops and stalls in here, plus the town's attractive church, the Templo Santiago Apóstal, built in 1620 with its almost Incaic stone belfry containing two great bells supported on an ancient timber. The church's front entrance is surrounded by simple yet attractive and stylized *mestizo* floral relief painted in red and cream. Climbing up through the **fortress** (daily 7am–5.30pm; US$4.50, or by Cusco Tourist Ticket, see box on p.880), the solid stone terraces, jammed against the natural contours of the cliff, remain frighteningly impressive.

High up over the other side of the Río Patacancha, behind the town, are rows of **ruined buildings** originally thought to have been prisons but now believed to have been granaries. To the front of these it's quite easy to make out a gigantic, rather grumpy-looking profile of a face carved out of the rock, possibly an **Inca sculpture** of Wirraccochan, the mythical messenger from Wiraccocha, the major creator god of Peru.

Practicalities

The **train station** is a few hundred metres down the track to the left just before the town's traditional little church, which itself is surrounded by *artesanía* shops; by **road**, you'll arrive at the main plaza. **Tourist information** can be obtained from the CATCCO Museum, or call Ⓣ084/204024. The **telephone** and **post offices** are on the main plaza. Ollantaytambo is something of a centre for **river rafting**, with a Rafting Adventure office on the main plaza; see box on p.891. The river around Ollantaytambo is class 2–3 in dry season and 3–4 in the rainy period (Nov–March).

There are several **hotels**, but the best option is the attractive *El Albergue Ollantaytambo*, Casilla 784, Cusco (☎084/204014; ❸), right next to the river and the train station at the bottom end of town, and offering discounts to families. (Contact well in advance in high season.) The hospitable *Hostal La Ñusta*, on Carretera Ocobamba (☎084/204035 or 204077; ❷), has simple rooms, a *comedor*, and a patio offering excellent views across to the mountains. The owner also rents out horses at US$10 a day (Pumamarca is reachable in about 2hr). Similar, but slightly more comfortable for the same price, there's the *Choki Wasi*, on Calle de Medio some two blocks from the plaza; breakfast is available and its nicely furnished ❷. For a decent **meal**, it's hard to beat *El Albergue* (see above), though there are a couple of reasonable cafés in the main plaza, notably the *Bar Ollantay*, often serving superb *quinoa* soup as part of its set-lunch menus. The plaza is home to a few gringo-orientated cafés, all with similar menus and most with vegetarian options.

The Inca Trail

The world-famous **Inca Trail** is set in the **Sanctuario Histórico de Machu Picchu**, an area of over 32,000 hectares set apart by the Peruvian state for the protection of its flora, fauna and natural beauty. Acting as a bio-corridor between the Cusco Andes, the Sacred Valley and the lowland Amazon forest, the National Sanctuary of Machu Picchu possesses over 370 species of birds, 47 mammals and over 700 butterfly species. Specialities include the cock-of-the-rock (*rupicola peruviana*) known as *tunkis* here, spectacled bear (*tremarctos ornatus*) and condor (*vultur gryphus*).

Although just one of a multitude of paths across remote areas of the Andes, what makes the Inca Trail so popular is the fabulous treasure of **Machu Picchu** at the end. It's important to choose your **season** for hiking the Inca Trail. Local tradition dictates that the perfect time is around the full moon, though May is the best month, with clear views, fine weather and verdant surroundings. Between June and September it's usually a pretty cosmopolitan stretch of mountainside, with travellers from all over the globe converging on Machu Picchu the hard way, but from mid-June to early August it's overly busy (and the campsites are noisy), especially on the last stretch. From October until April, in the rainy season, it's far less crowded but also, naturally, very wet.

In its wisdom, the sanctuary authority, the Unidad de Gestion del Sanctuario Histórico de Machu Picchu, has now imposed a **limit of up to 500 trekkers a day** on the Inca Trail. Names and passport or identity numbers need to be registered in Cusco at least 36 hours before departure by your tour company, in effect this means at least three days and some of the better companies recommend a minimum of five days advance booking.

It's no longer possible to do the trail on your own, you have to go with a tour or a licensed guide through one of the **tour companies** (see box on pp.890–1); that guide will be expected to register your details with the Unidad de Gestion, Garcilaso 233, two days or more prior to your departure date. It's a good idea to check the precise details of exactly what you are paying for and what, if anything, is not included in the price (such as sleeping bags, tips for porters, roll mats, cooks). It is best to organize all this by email well in advance. As far as **preparations** go, the most important thing is to acclimatize, preferably allowing at least three days in Cusco if you've flown straight from sea level.

Setting off

There are two **trailheads** for the Inca Trail. Organized tours usually approach the trail by road via Ollantaytambo and then take a dirt track from there to **Chilca**,

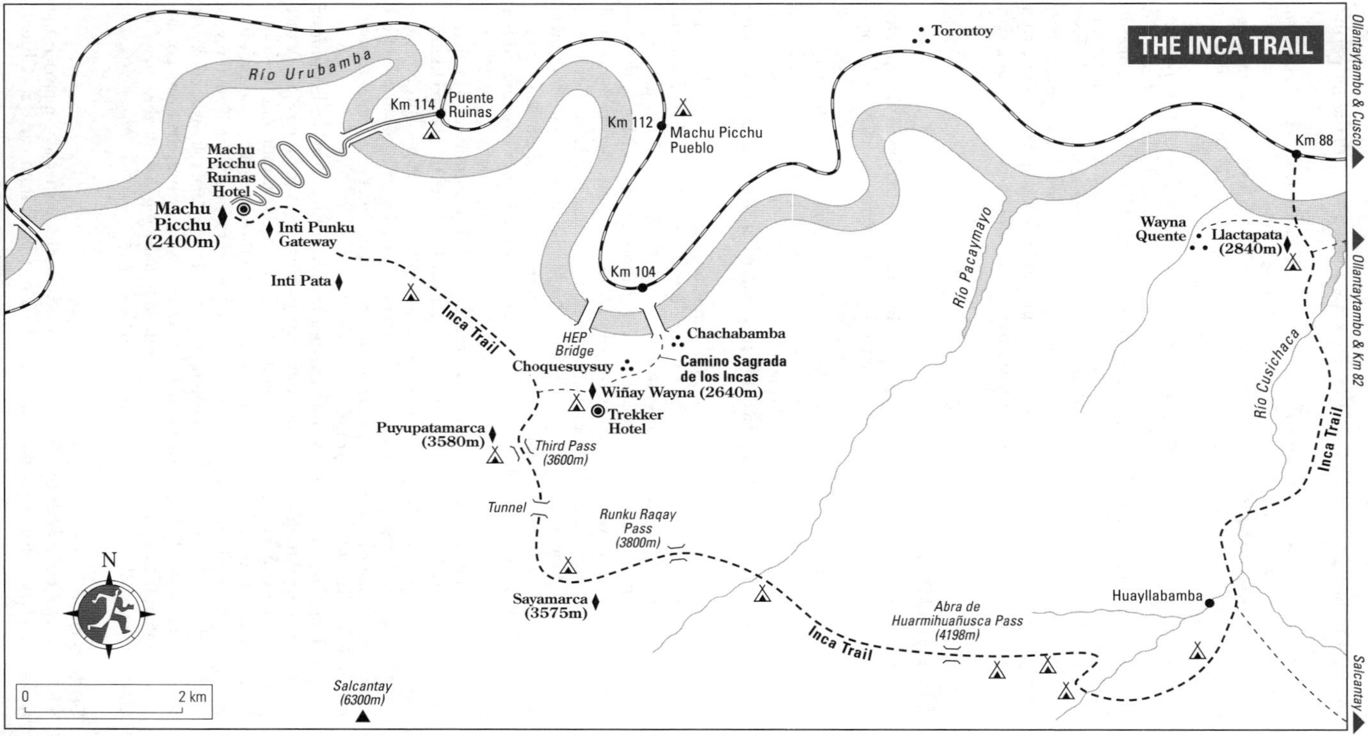
THE INCA TRAIL
Ollantaytambo & Cusco
Ollantaytambo & Km 82
Salcantay
Chaullay & Quillabamba
Torontoy
Río Urubamba
Km 114
Puente Ruinas
Km 112
Machu Picchu Pueblo
Km 88
Machu Picchu Ruinas Hotel
Machu Picchu (2400m)
Inti Punku Gateway
Inti Pata
Km 104
Río Pacaymayo
Wayna Quente
Llactapata (2840m)
Inca Trail
HEP Bridge
Chachabamba
Choquesuysuy
Camino Sagrada de los Incas
Wiñay Wayna (2640m)
Trekker Hotel
Puyupatamarca (3580m)
Third Pass (3600m)
Río Cusichaca
Inca Trail
Tunnel
Runku Raqay Pass (3800m)
N
Sayamarca (3575m)
Abra de Huarmihuañusca Pass (4198m)
Huayllabamba
Inca Trail
0
2 km
Salcantay (6300m)

which adds a few hours to the overall trek but forms the **road trailhead**. Minibuses from Ollantaytambo to Chilca cost US$1. For independents and groups arriving by train, however, the **rail trailhead** is at Km88 along the tracks from Cusco, at a barely noticeable stop announced by the train guard. Have your gear ready to throw off the steps, since the train pulls up only for a few brief seconds and you'll have to fight your way past sacks of grain, flapping chickens, men in ponchos and women in voluminous skirts.

The recent hike in entrance fees to the trail (US$50, or US$25 for students, including Machu Picchu) caused an outcry by Peruvians since it effectively banned all but the very wealthy. Proponents of the new scheme say, however, that higher fees and greater restrictions are necessary to halt deterioration and overuse of the trail.

From the station, a footbridge sees you across the Río Urubamba. Once over the bridge the main path leads to the left, through a small eucalyptus wood, then around the base of the Inca ruins of Llactapata (worth a visit for archeology enthusiasts, though most people save their energy for the trail and other archeological remains ahead) before crossing and then following the Río Cusichaca upstream along its left bank. It's a good two hours' steep climb to **Huayllabamba**, the only inhabited village on the route and the best place to hire horses or mules for the most difficult climb on the whole trail, the nearby **Dead Woman's Pass**. This section of the valley is rich in Inca terracing, from which rises an occasional ancient stone building. To reach Huayllabamba you have to cross a well-marked bridge onto the right bank of the Cusichaca. Many groups spend their first night at Huayllabamba **campsite**.

The Camino Sagrado de los Incas

The **Camino Sagrado de los Incas**, a truncated Inca Trail, starts at Km104 of the Panamerican Highway, 8km from Machu Picchu. The footbridge here (US$25 entry, free to under 12s, includes Machu Picchu) leads to a steep climb (3–4hr) past Chachabamba to reach Wiñay Wayna (see p.900), where you join the reminder of the Inca Trail.

The first and second passes

The next five hours or so from Huayllabamba to the Abra de Huarmihuañusca, **the first pass** (4200m) and the highest point on the trail, is the hardest part of the walk – leave this (or at least some of it) for the second day, especially if you're feeling the effects of the altitude. There are three possible places to camp between Huayllabamba and Huarmihuañusca. The first and most popular, known as **Three White Stones**, is at the point where the trail crosses the Río Huayruro, just half a kilometre above its confluence with the Llullucha stream. The next camp, just below the **Pampa Llullucha**, has toilets and space for several tents. Another twenty minutes further up, there's plenty more camping space on the pampa within sight of the pass – a good spot for seeing rabbit-like viscachas playing among the rocks.

The views from the pass itself are stupendous, but if you're tempted to hang around savouring them, it's a good idea to sit well out of the cutting wind (many a trekker has caught a bad chill here). From here the trail drops steeply down, sticking to the left of the stream into the Pacamayo Valley where, by the river, there's an attractive spot to **camp**, where you can see playful **spectacled bears** if you're very lucky, or take a break before continuing up a winding, tiring track towards the **second pass** – Abra de Runkuracay – just above the interesting circular ruins of the same name. About an hour beyond the second pass, a flight of stone steps leads up to the Inca ruins of **Sayacmarca**. This is an impressive spot to **camp**, near the remains of a stone aqueduct that supplied water to the ancient settlement (the best spots are by the stream just below the ruins).

From the third pass to Machu Picchu

From Sayacmarca, make your way gently down into increasingly dense cloud forest where delicate orchids and other exotic flora begin to appear among the trees. By the time you get to the **third pass** (which, compared with the previous two, has very little incline) you're following a fine, smoothly worn flagstone path where at one point an astonishing tunnel, carved through solid rock by the Incas, lets you sidetrack an otherwise impossible climb. The trail winds down to the impressive ruin of **Puyupatamarca** – "Town Above the Clouds" – where there are five small stone baths and in the wet season constant fresh running water. There are places to **camp** actually on the pass (above the ruins), commanding stunning views across the Urubamba valley and, in the other direction, towards the snowcaps of Salcantay (Wild Mountain); this is probably one of the most magical camps on the trail (given good weather) and it's not unusual to see deer feeding here.

It's a very rough, two- or three-hour descent along a non-Inca track to the next ruin, a citadel almost as impressive as Machu Picchu, **Wiñay Wayna** – "Forever Young" – another place with fresh water. These days there's an official *Trekker Hotel* here (no phone; US$8 a bed, US$3 floor space, US$1 for a hot shower) and restaurant too – nothing splendid, but with a welcome supply of cool drinks.

Wiñay Wayna was a companion site for Machu Picchu, just two hours walk away. Comprising of only two major groups of architectural structures – a lower and an upper sector – it's most visible features are stone baths with apparently as many as nineteen springs feeding them all set amidst several layers of fine Inca terracing. Nearby there's also a small waterfall created by streams coming down from the heights of Puyupatamarca. As it's used today, Wiñay Wayna was probably used as a washing, cleansing and resting point for travellers before their arrival at the grand Machu Picchu citadel.

This is usually the spot for the last night of camping and, especially in high season, the crowds mean that it's a good idea to pitch your tent soon after lunch, but don't be surprised if someone pitches their tent right across your doorway. To reach Machu Picchu for sunrise the next day you'll have to get up very early with a flashlight to avoid the rush.

A well-marked track from Wiñay Wayna takes a right fork for about two more hours through sumptuous vegetated slopes to **Intipunku**, for your first sight of Machu Picchu – a stupendous moment, however exhausted you might be. Aim to get to Machu Picchu well before 9.30am, when the first train hordes from Cusco arrive, if possible making it to the "hitching post" of the sun before dawn, for an unforgettable sunrise that will quickly make you forget the long hike through the pre-dawn gloom – bring a torch if you plan to try it.

Machu Picchu

The most dramatic and enchanting of the Inca citadels lies suspended on an extravagantly terraced saddle between two prominent peaks. The beautiful stone architecture is enhanced by the Incas' exploitation of local 250 million-year-old rocks of grey-white granite with a high content of quartz, silica and feldspar among other minerals. **MACHU PICCHU** (daily 6.30am–5pm; US$10) is one of the greatest of all South American tourist attractions, set against a vast, scenic backdrop of dark-green forested mountains that spike up from the deep valleys of the Urubamba and its tributaries. The distant glacial summits are dwarfed only by the huge sky.

With many legends and theories surrounding the position of Machu Picchu, most archeologists agree that the sacred geography and astronomy of the site were auspicious factors in helping the Inca Pachacuti decide where to build this citadel here at 2492m. The name "Machu Picchu" apparently means simply Old or Ancient Mountain. It's thought that agricultural influences as well as geo-sacred indicators prevailed and that the site secured a decent supply of sacred coca and maize for the Inca nobles and priests in Cusco. However, it is quite possible to enjoy a visit to

Machu Picchu without knowing too much about the history or archeology of the site or the specifics of each feature; for many it is enough just to absorb the atmosphere.

Some history

Unknown to the Spanish conquerors, for many centuries the site of Machu Picchu lay forgotten, except by local Indians and settlers, until it was rediscovered by the US explorer **Hiram Bingham** who, on July 24, 1911, accompanied by a local settler who knew of some ruins, came upon a previously unheard-of Inca citadel.

It was a fantastic find, not least because it was still relatively intact, without the usual ravages of either conquistadores or tomb robbers. Accompanied only by two locals, Bingham continued across a bridge so dodgy that he crawled over it on his hands and knees before climbing a precipitous slope. After resting at a small hut, he received hospitality from some local peasants who described an extensive system of terraces where they had found good fertile soil for their own crops. Bingham was led to the site by an 11-year-old local boy, and it didn't take long for him to see that he had come across some important ancient Inca terraces – over a hundred of which had recently been cleared of forest for subsistence crops. After a little more exploration Bingham found the fine white stonework and began to realise that this might be the place he was looking for. Bingham's theory was that Machu Picchu was the lost city of Vilcabamba, the site of the Incas' last refuge from the Spanish conquistadores. Not until another American expedition surveyed the ruins around Machu Picchu in the 1940s did serious doubts begin to arise over this assignation, and more recently the site of the Inca's final stronghold has been shown to be Espiritu Pampa in the Amazon jungle (see p.908).

Meanwhile, Machu Picchu began to be reconsidered as the best preserved of a series of agricultural centres which served Cusco in its prime. The city was conceived and built in the mid-fifteenth century by Emperor Pachacuti, the first to expand the empire beyond the Sacred Valley towards the forested gold-lands. With crop fertility, mountains and nature so sacred to the Incas, an agricultural centre as important as Machu Picchu would easily have merited the site's fine stonework and temple precincts. It was clearly a ritual centre, given the layout and quantity of temples; but for the Incas it was usual not to separate out things we consider economic tasks from more conventional religious activities. So, Machu Picchu represents to many archaeologists the most classical and best preserved remains of a citadel which the Incas used as both a religious temple site and an agricultural (perhaps experimental) growing centre.

Arrival and accommodation

If you arrive **by train**, you'll get off at **Machu Picchu Pueblo station**, at the nearest town to the ruins, which has experienced explosive growth over the last decade or so and is occasionally still referred to by its older name, Aguas Calientes. You walk down the steps from the station and over the bridge where you can catch one of the **buses** to the ruins (the first buses leave at 6.30am and continue until there's no demand upto 7.30; after that they leave hourly 9.30am–12.30pm, returning continually 12.30–5.30pm; US$9 return, US$4.50 one-way, children under 4 half price). The ticket office is to the right of the bridge; buses leave from the street lined with *artesanía* stalls that leads down to the left of the bridge towards the river. Tickets are stamped with the date, so you have to return the same day. It's possible to walk from Machu Picchu Pueblo to the ruins, but it'll take between one-and-a-half and three hours, depending on how fit you are and whether you take the very steep direct path or follow the more roundabout paved road. **Helicopters** land at the small helipad on the opposite side of Machu Picchu Pueblo from the ruins, from where it's a short walk to catch a bus up to the site.

Train journey to Machu Picchu

The new, improved service offered by PeruRail between Cusco and Machu Picchu – one of the finest mountain train journeys in the world – enhances the thrill of riding tracks through such fantastic scenery even further by offering very good service and comfortable, well-kept carriages.

Rumbling out of **Cusco** around 6am, the wagons zigzag their way through the back streets, where little houses cling to the steep valley slopes. It takes a while to rise out of the teacup-like valley, but once it attains the high plateau above, the train rolls through fields and past highland villages before eventually dropping rapidly down into the Urubamba Valley using several major track switchbacks, which means you get to see some of the same scenery twice. It reaches the Sacred Valley floor just before getting into **Ollantaytambo**, where from the windows you can already see scores of impressively terraced fields and, in the distance, more Inca temple and storehouse constructions. The train continues down the valley, stopping briefly at Km88, where the Inca Trail starts, then following the Urubamba river as the valley gets tighter (that's why there's no road!) and the mountain more and more forested as well as steeper and seemingly taller. The end of the line these days is usually the new station at **Machu Picchu Peublo** (also known as Aguas Calientes), a busy little town crowded into the valley just a short bus ride from the ruins themselves.

A **cable car** planned to carry visitors straight to the ruins from Pueblo Machu Picchu has caused considerable debate, not least because engineers would have to blast away a section of the Incas' sacred mountain of Putukusi to site a supporting tower, and while the views from the cable car would no doubt be spectacular, the increased volume in visitors could well prove damaging to the site. So far the project has been kept at bay.

The local *consejo*-run **campsite** (US$2, collected every morning), is just over the Río Urubamba on the railway side of the bridge, from where the buses start their climb up to the ruins of Machu Picchu. The *Machu Picchu Sanctuary Lodge* hotel (Ⓣ084/241777, Ⓦwww.monasterio.orient-express.com; ❽) located right at the entrance to the ruins, is something of a concrete block, but it's comfortable and has a restaurant, and staying here allows you to explore the site early in the morning or in the afternoons and evenings when most other people have left. Also, it's the only hotel in the immediate area. In the main, however, travellers tend to stay at Machu Picchu Pueblo (see p.904).

Next to the entrance to the ruins there's a **left-luggage office** (no backpacks or camping equipment are allowed inside, price per item US$1.20), toilets, a shop and the **ticket office** (daily 6am–5.30pm; US$20, US$10 students or US$5 at night), where you can also hire a guide (US$3.50 per person, for a minimum of 6) and buy a **map**.

The ruins

Though it would take a lot to detract from Machu Picchu's incredible beauty and unsurpassed location, it is a zealously supervised place, with the site guards frequently blowing whistles at visitors who have deviated from one of the main pathways. The best way to enjoy the ruins – and avoiding the guards' ire – is to hire a guide, or buy the map and stick to its routes.

Though more than 1000m lower than Cusco, Machu Picchu seems much higher, constructed as it is on dizzying slopes overlooking a U-curve in the Río Urubamba. More than a hundred flights of steep stone steps interconnect its palaces, temples, storehouses and terraces, and the outstanding views command not only the valley below in both directions but also extend to the snowy peaks around Salcantay. Wherever you stand in the ruins, spectacular terraces (some of which are once again being cultivated) can be seen slicing across ridiculously steep cliffs, transforming mountains into suspended gardens.

Entering the main ruins, you cross over a dry moat. The first site of major interest is the **Temple of the Sun**, also known as the *Torreon*, a wonderful, semicircular, walled, tower-like temple displaying some of Machu Picchu's finest stonework. Its carved steps and smoothly joined stone blocks fit neatly into the existing relief of a natural boulder, which served as some kind of altar and also marks the entrance to a small cave. A window off this temple provides views of both the June solstice sunrise and the constellation of the Pleiades, which rises from here over the nearby peak of Huayna Picchu. The Pleiades are still a very important astronomical Andean symbol relating to crop fertility; locals use the constellation as a kind of annual signpost in the agricultural calendar giving information about when to plant crops and when the rains will come. Below the Temple of the Sun is a cave known as the **Royal Tomb**, despite the fact that neither graves nor human remains have ever been found there. In fact, it probably represented access to the spiritual heart of the mountains, like the cave at the Temple of the Moon (see below).

Retracing your steps 20m or so back from the Temple of the Sun and following a flight of stone stairs directly uphill, then left along the track towards Intipunku (see p.904), brings you to a path on the right, which climbs up to the thatched **guardian's hut**. This hut is associated with a modestly carved rock known as the **funerary rock** and a nearby graveyard where Bingham found evidence of many burials, some of which were obviously royal.

Back down in the centre of the site, the next major Inca construction after the Temple of the Sun is the **Three-Windowed Temple**; part of the complex based around the **Sacred Plaza**, and arguably the most enthralling sector of the ruins. Dominating the southeastern edge of the plaza, the attractive Three-Windowed Temple has unusually large windows looking east towards the mountains beyond the Urubamba river valley. From here it's a short stroll to the **Principal Temple**, so-called because of the fine stonework of its three high main walls, the most easterly of which looks onto the Sacred Plaza. Unusually (as most ancient temples in the Americas face east), the main opening of this temple faces south, and white sand, often thought to represent the ocean, has been found on the temple floor, suggesting that it may have been allied symbolically to the Río Urubamba, water and the sea.

A minute or so uphill from here along an elaborately carved stone stairway brings you to one of the jewels of the site, the **Intihuatana**, also known as the "hitching post of the sun". This fascinating carved rock, built on a rise above the Sacred Plaza, is similar to those created by the Incas in all their important ritual centres, but is one of the very few not to have been discovered and destroyed by the conquistadores. This unique and very beautiful survivor, set in a tower-like position, overlooks the Sacred Plaza, the Río Urubamba and the sacred peak of Huayna Picchu. Intihuatana's base is said to have been carved in the shape of a map of the Inca Empire, though few archeologists agree with this. Its main purpose was as an astro-agricultural clock for viewing the complex interrelationships between the movements of the stars and constellations. It is also thought by some to be a symbolic representation of the spirit of the mountain on which Machu Picchu was built – by all accounts a very powerful spot both in terms of sacred geography and its astrological function. The Intihuatana appears to be aligned with four important mountains. The snowcapped mountain range of La Veronica lies directly to the east, with the sun rising behind its main summit during the equinoxes; directly south, though not actually visible from here, sits the father of all mountains in this part of Peru, Salcantay, only a few days' walk away; to the west, the sun sets behind the important peak of Pumasillo during the December solstice; while due north stands the majestic peak of Huayna Picchu.

Following the steps down from the Intihuatana and passing through the Sacred Plaza towards the northern terraces brings you in a few minutes to the **Sacred Rock**, below the access point to Huayna Picchu. A great lozenge of granite sticking out of the earth like a sculptured wall, little is known for sure about the Sacred Rock, but its outline is strikingly similar to the Inca's sacred mountain of Putukusi, which towers to the east.

The prominent peak of **Huayna Picchu** juts out over the Urubamba Valley at the northern end of the Machu Picchu site, and is easily scaled by anyone reasonably energetic. The record for this vigorous and rewarding climb is 22 minutes, but most people take about an hour. Access to this sacred mountain (daily 7am–1pm, last exit by 3pm) is generally controlled by a guardian from his kiosk just behind the Sacred Rock. From the summit, there's an awe-inspiring panorama and it's a great place from which to get an overview of the ruins suspended between the mountains among stupendous forested Andean scenery.

About two-thirds of the way back down, another little track leads to the right and down to the stunning **Temple of the Moon**, hidden in a grotto hanging magically above the Río Urubamba, some 400m beneath the pinnacle of Huayna Picchu. Not many visitors make it this far and it's probably wise to have a guide (and if you've already walked up Huayna Picchu, you might want to save this for another day because it's another 45min each way at least). The guardian by the Sacred Rock will often take people for a small fee (around US$1 per person, provided there are two or more). Once you do get there, you'll be rewarded by some of the best stonework in the entire site, the level of craftmanship hinting at the site's importance to the Inca. The temple's name comes from the fact that it is often lit up by the moonlight, but some archeologists believe the temple was most likely dedicated to the spirit of the mountain. The main sector of the temple is in the mouth of a natural cave, where there are five niches set into an elaborate white granite stone wall. There's usually evidence – small piles of maize, coca leaves and tobacco – that people are still making offerings at these niches. In the centre of the cave there's a rock carved like a throne, beside which are five cut steps leading into the darker recesses, where you can see more carved rocks and stone walls, nowadays at least inaccessible to humans. Immediately to the front of the cave is a small plaza with another cut stone throne and an altar. Outside, steps either side of the massive boulder lead above the cave, from where you can see a broad, stone-walled room running along one side of the cave-boulder. There are more buildings and beautiful little stone sanctuaries just down a flight of steps from this part of the complex.

If you don't have the time or energy to climb Huayna Picchu or visit the Temple of the Moon, simply head back to the guardian's hut on the other side of the site and take the path below it, which climbs gently for thirty minutes or so, up to **Intipunku**, the main entrance to Machu Picchu from the Inca Trail. This offers an incredible view over the entire site with the unmistakable shape of Huayna Picchu in the background.

Machu Picchu Pueblo (Aguas Calientes)

Many people who want to spend more than just a day at Machu Picchu base themselves at the settlement of **MACHU PICCHU PUEBLO** (previously known as Aguas Calientes), which is connected to the ruins by bus and has good accommodations, restaurants and shops. Its warm, humid climate and surrounding landscape of towering mountains covered in cloud forest make it a welcome change to Cusco, but the main attraction (apart from Machu Picchu itself) is the natural **thermal bath** (daily 6am–8.30pm; US$2), which is particularly welcome after a few days on the Inca Trail or a hot afternoon up at Machu Picchu. You can find several communal baths of varying temperatures right at the end of the main drag of Pachacutec, around 750m uphill from the town's small plaza.

There is also a recently restored **trail** (90min each way) up the sacred mountain of Putukusi, starting just outside of the town, a couple of hundred yards down on the left if you follow the railway track towards the ruins. The walk offers stupendous views of the town and across to Machu Picchu, but watch out for the small poisonous snakes reported to live on this mountain.

By now, Machu Picchu Pueblo's explosive growth has reached the limits of the valley; there's very little flat land that hasn't been built on or covered in concrete. Not surprisingly, this boomtown has a lively, bustling feel and enough restaurants and bars to satisfy a small army. For **tourist information**, maps of local walks, money exchange, or credit card cash, go to Avenida Imperio de los Inca 119, the shop front with the telephones on the old railway platform, which is the office for Rikuni Sacred Experience Tours (Ⓣ084/211036). It's also worth checking out a couple of dedicated websites: Ⓦwww.machupicchu.com and Ⓦwww.machupicchuhostals.com. INRENA, responsible for the Sanctuario Nacional de Machu Picchu administration, has two offices in town, one in the Centro Cultural Machu Picchu, near the school, just above the plaza; their other, more useful, location can be found back along the railway tracks towards Cusco, only 100m or so, on the right just beyond the post office. The train ticket office on the tracks of Avenida Imperio de Los Incas is open 5–6am and again from 8.30am–5.30pm.

Accommodation

Although there is an overwhelming choice of **places to stay** in Machu Picchu Pueblo, there can be a lot of competition for lodgings during the high season (June–Sept), when large groups of travellers often turn up and take over entire hotels. Coming to town on an early train will give you some increased choice in where to stay, but for the better places try and book at least a week or two, if not months, in advance. **Camping** is also possible at a safe and secure site with evening campfires, just ten minutes' walk from Machu Picchu Pueblo at *Campamento Intiwasi* Las Orchideas M-23 (US$5 per tent); contact via Rikuni Tours, Imperio de los Incas 119 (Ⓣ084/211036 or 211151, Ⓔhanan65@latinmail.com or ask in the *Café Internet Restaurant* for details). The other camping option is the *consejo*-run site (see p.902).

Gringo Bill's Colla Raymi 104 Ⓣ084/211046, Ⓔgringobills@yahoo.com, Ⓦwww.machupicchugringobills.com. Also known as the *Hostal Q'oni Unu*, this is the best mid-range choice in town, offering moneychanging, laundry, lunch packs, ample hot water, a relaxed environment, breakfasts included, grilled meats in the evening, rooms with interesting decor, and a book exchange. ❸–❹

Hostal la Cabaña Pachacutec M20-Lot 3 Ⓣ084/211048, Ⓔlacabana_mapi@latinmail.com. Price unusually includes breakfast in this safe and friendly hostel. Other features include comfy, stylish rooms with fresh flowers, open lounge areas, a laundry and library (one of the owners is also a local guide). ❹

Hostal Don Guiller Pachacutec 136 Ⓣ084/211128. This well-run hostel features clean, comfortable rooms, hot water in private bathrooms and breakfast included. ❸

Hostal Pachacuteq at the top end of Pachacutec Ⓣ084/211061, Ⓔpachacuteq@hotmail.com. It has plain but nice enough rooms, a café, laundry service and will help with train or bus tickets if required. ❹

Hostal Quilla Ⓣ084/211009, Ⓔquillalex@hotmail.com. A very friendly hostel offering breakfasts and good tourist information. Rooms have private bath. ❸

Pueblo Hotel Km110 on the railway line Ⓣ084/211122, Ⓦwww.inkaterra.com; Lima sales office: Andalucia 174, Miraflores Ⓣ01/422-6574. The most elegant and interesting hotel around, its almost hidden entrance is on the left just beyond the edge of town as you walk up the rail track towards Cusco. The Pueblo has its own swimming pool, extensive gardens and five hectares of cloud forest. ❼–❽

Eating and drinking

As well as the **foodstalls** specializing in excellent herb teas and fruit juices, which can be found near the little market by the police station, just over the tracks, there are plenty of full-fledged **restaurants** in Machu Picchu Pueblo. *Restaurant Aiko*, Imperio de los Incas 153 (Ⓣ084/211001), is one of the closest restaurants to the

Machu Picchu end of the tracks in the pueblo. It features good service in a cool interior and dishes out reasonably priced meals including trout, soups, pastas, burgers and serve delicious falafels (unfortunately not always on the menu). *Restaurant Inti Killa*, Avenida Imperial de los Incas 147 (☎084/211012), serves very good pizzas and trout with tables outside and local new age paintings inside along with Incaic relief murals; nearby the *Restaurant Pizzeria Pachamama*, at Imperio de los Incas 143 (☎084/212231), opposite the small market, specializes in pizzas, pancakes, breakfasts and lomo steak in mushroom sauce. On the other side of the railway tracks you'll find the *Café Internet Restaurant*, which has fast access and a good, friendly service for coffees, omelettes, pizzas, trout, spaghetti; this place is also a contact for the campsite Inti Wasi, less than ten minutes' walk from here).

On the plaza, the *Inka's Pizzeria Restaurant* is very popular, with a large space and fine murals; as well as the obvious it serves soups, trouts, chicken and juices. For a proper **vegetarian** meal, there's the ubiquitous *Govinda* at the top end of Pachacutec, on the left. *Donofrio's* ice-cream shop, Pachacutec 120, does reasonable lunch menus. *El Indio Feliz*, Lloque Yupanqui Lote 4m-12 (☎084/211090), serves exceptional three- or four-course meals of French and local cuisines at remarkably inexpensive prices; try to reserve a table as far in advance as possible. *Restaurant El Manu*, on Pachacutec, has a nice open dining area (sometimes doubling up as a dance space, quite lively at night), and specializes in trout and pizzas. *Totos House Restaurant*, Avenida Imperio de los Incas (☎084/211020), is a vast restaurant with great views and some tables at the front by the railway tracks; they offer buffet lunch daily for US$10, expensive but quite good.

For **drinking**, the *Blues Jazz Bar*, at the top end of Pachacutec towards the entrance to the Thermal Springs, is a sexy little café with a dark interior, good drinks, groovy music, decent food, money exchange and occasionally shows movies. *Wasicha Pub*, Calle Lloque Yupanqui, Lote 2, M-12 (☎084/211157), is the town's loudest, hottest nightspot, with a vibrant dancefloor, a good bar and a spacious restaurant attached, as well. *Waki's Pub Bar* on Capac Yupanqui 2 (☎084/227699) is a jungle-themed pizzeria with a dancefloor that sometimes has live bands on Saturdays and shows movies most days.

Listings

Exchange Available in the pool room and café next to *Hostal Los Caminantes*.
INRENA Instituto Nacional de Cultura offices, responsible for management of the Nacional sanctuary of Machu Picchu, is on the railway line, just passed the post office, towards the Pueblo Hotel end.
Internet services Café Internet Restaurant, corner of Avenida Imperios de los Incas next to the old railway station; decent service plus cakes, snacks and drinks 6.30am–10pm; Bar El Toldo Internet, Avenida Imperio de los Incas 115, six computer connections and great views from the back over the river. Café Internet World Net, Avenida Pachacutec 147-b, seems to have a good link; Inkanet, Avenida Contisuyo 101.
Police Avenida Imperio de los Incas, next to the small market just down from the old railway station (☎084/211178).
Post office On the railway tracks, right-hand side, towards Pueblo Hotel.
Telephones Centro Telefonica, Avenida Imperio de los Incas 132 (☎084/211091). The post office (see above) also has a public phone.
Tour operators Rikuni Tours, Imperio de los Incas 119 (☎084/211036 or 084/211151, Ⓔrikuni@mixmail.com or rikunis@yahoo.com.ai). They offer a wide range of local outings, including Machu Picchu by night, the Temple of the Moon, Chaskapata ruins, Wiñay Wayna and Chacabamba ruins.

Beyond Machu Picchu: into the jungle

The area along the Río Urubamba from Machu Picchu onwards is a quiet, relatively accessible corner of the Peruvian wilderness. As you descend by road from Ollantaytambo, over a pass and then down to Chaullay and the jungle beyond, the vegetation along the valley turns gradually into jungle, thickening and getting greener by the kilometre and the air gets steadily warmer and more humid. Most people going down here get as far as the town of Quillabamba, but the road continues deeper into the rainforest where it meets the navigable jungle rivers at Kiteni. Some people come to the region to explore the mountains, cloudforest and rainforest areas of this zone either to check out known Inca ruins or to search out more new ones.

It is relatively easy to visit the hilltop ruins of the palace at **Vitcos**, a site of Inca blood sacrifices, and possible, though an expedition of six days or more, to explore the more remote ruins at **Espiritu Pampa**, now thought to be the site of the legendary lost city of Vilcabamba. The easiest way to see the ruins is on a guided tour with one of the adventure tour companies listed on p.890–1. If you'd rather travel independently, at least book a local guide through one of the companies in Cusco before setting off.

Major Inca sites are still being discovered in this region. In April 2002, Hugh Thomson and Gary Zeigler, following rumours of a lost city, led an expedition that discovered an Inca city in the virtually inaccessible valley bottom at the confluence of the ríos Yanama and Blanco in the Vilcabamba region. Apparently seen briefly by Bingham nearly 100 years ago, its coordinates were never recorded and this settlement of forty main buildings set around a central plaza hadn't been spotted since. Although very difficult to access – owing to river erosion – there appears to have been an Inca road running through the valley, probably connecting this site to the great Inca citadel of Choquequirao. This settlement is believed to have been Manco Inca's hideout during his rebellion against the conquistadores, which lasted until his execution in Cusco in 1572.

Pukyura

If you want to visit the ruins at Vitcos or Espiritu Pampa independently, it's best to go via the villages of **PUKYURA** and **Huancacalle**, in the Vilcabamba river valley. They are reached in six hours by truck which are usually easily picked up (small fee charged) at Chaullay on the Ollantaytambo–Quillabamba road. Pukyura has a long history of guerrilla fighting and a tradition of willful anti-authoritarian independence. Chosen by Manco Inca as the base for his rebel state in the sixteenth century, this area was also the political base for land reformer and Trotskyist revolutionary **Hugo Blanco** in the early 1960s. When the economy was in dire straits, with domestic prices soaring and strikes and serious riots breaking out all over the country, a much more radical feeling was aroused in the provinces by **Blanco**. He was a charismatic *mestizo* from Cusco who had joined a Trotskyist group – the Workers Revolutionary Party. Blanco created nearly 150 syndicates, mainly in the Cusco region, whose peasant members began to work their own individual plots while refusing to work for the hacienda owners. Many landowners went bankrupt or opted to bribe workers back with offers of cash wages. The second phase of Blanco's "reform" was to take physical control of the haciendas, mostly in areas so isolated that the authorities were powerless to intervene. Blanco was finally arrested in 1963 but the effects of his peasant revolt outlived him: in future, Peruvian governments were to take agrarian reform far more seriously. In 2002 Blanco was hospitalized, victim of a brain haemorrhage while visiting the peasant communities of this region. He managed to get to Mexico City, where he was being treated in hospital during 2003.

Camping at Pukyura is possible and you can usually arrange independently for an *arriero* here to take you over the two- or three-day trail to Espiritu Pampa. Narcisco Huaman is recommended (US$10 per day, including 2 horses), contactable through Genaro, the Instituto Nacional de Cultura representative in Huancacalle. The hour-long walk uphill to Vitcos from Pukyura is easy to do independently, however. If you're seriously interested in exploring this region, you should also check on the prevailing **political and access rights** situation with the Instituto Nacional de Cultura (☎ 084/236061) before attempting what is a very ambitious journey.

Vitcos and Espiritu Pampa

In 1911, after discovering Machu Picchu, Hiram Bingham set out down the Urubamba Valley to Chaullay, then up the Vilcabamba valley to the village of Pukyura, where he expected to find more Inca ruins. What he found – **VITCOS** (known locally as Rosapata) – was a relatively small but clearly palatial ruin, based around a trapezoidal plaza spread across a flat-topped spur. Down below the ruins, Bingham was shown by local guides a spring flowing from beneath a vast, white granite boulder intricately carved in typical Inca style and surrounded by the remains of an impressive Inca temple. This fifteen-metre-long and eight-metre-high sacred white rock – called Chuquipalta by the Incas – was a great oracle where blood sacrifices and other religious rituals took place. According to early historical chronicles, these rituals had so infuriated two Spanish priests who witnessed them that they exorcized the rock and set its temple sanctuary on fire.

Within two weeks Bingham had followed a path from Pukyura into the jungle as far as the Condevidayoc plantation, where he found some more "undiscovered" ruins at **ESPIRITU PAMPA** – "Plain of the Spirits". After briefly exploring some of the outer ruins at Espiritu Pampa, Bingham decided they must have been built by Manco Inca's followers and deduced that they were post-Conquest Inca constructions since many of the roofs were Spanish-tiled. Believing that he had already found the lost city ofVilcabamba in Machu Picchu, Bingham paid little attention to these newer discoveries. Consequently, and in view of its being accessible only by mule, Espiritu Pampa remained covered in thick jungle vegetation until 1964, when serious exploration was undertaken by US archeological explorer Gene Savoy. He found a massive ruined complex with over sixty main buildings and some three hundred houses, along with temples, plazas, wells and a main street. Clearly this was the largest Inca refuge in the Vilcabamba area, and Savoy rapidly became convinced of its identity as the true site of the last Inca stronghold. More conclusive evidence has since been provided by the English geographer and historian John Hemming who, using the chronicles as evidence, was able to match descriptions of Vilcabamba, its climate and altitude, precisely with those of Espiritu Pampa. Getting to these sites really requires expedition type preparation, the hire of local guides (best done through Cusco tour agents) and possibly even mules. You'll need a week or more even to cover the nearer sites. There are no services or facilities as such at any of the sites, none of which are staffed by permanent on-site guardians, so they are free and open as long as you have permission from the Instituto Nacional de Cultura.

9.3

Nazca and the south coast

The south has been populated as long as anywhere in Peru – for at least nine thousand years in some places – but until the twentieth century no one guessed the existence of this arid region's unique cultures, whose enigmatic remains, particularly along the coast, show signs of a sophisticated civilization. With the discovery and subsequent study, beginning in 1901, of ancient sites throughout the coastal zone, it now seems clear that this was home to at least three major cultures: the **Paracas** (500 BC–400 AD), the influential **Nazca** (500–800 AD) and finally, contemporaneous with the Chimu of northern Peru and the Cuismancu around Lima, the **Ica Culture**, or **Chincha Empire**, overrun by and absorbed into Pachacutec's mushrooming Inca Empire around the beginning of the fifteenth century.

The Nazca Lines

One of the great mysteries of South America, the **NAZCA LINES** are a series of animal figures and geometric shapes, none of them repeated and some up to 200m in length, drawn across some five hundred square kilometres of the bleak, stony Pampa de San José. Each one, even such sophisticated motifs as a spider monkey or a hummingbird, is executed in a single continuous line, most created by clearing away the brush and hard stones of the plain to reveal the fine dust beneath. They were probably a kind of agricultural calendar to help regulate the planting and harvesting of crops, while perhaps at the same time some of the straight lines served as ancient sacred paths connecting *huacas*, or power spots. Regardless of why they were made, the Lines are among the strangest and most unforgettable sights in the country.

Getting to the Lines

The road to Nazca from Ica crosses a large strip of desert named the **Pampa de Gamonal** after the unfortunate man who, as the local story goes, found a vast

Flying over the Nazca Lines

A pricey but spectacular way of seeing the Lines is to **fly** over them. Flights leave from Nazca airstrip, about 3km south of Nazca, and cost US$30–50 a person depending on the season, the size of the group, and how long you want to spend buzzing around – they can last from ten minutes to a couple of hours. The usual package costs between US$35 and US$45, lasting from 30–45min. **Flight operators** include Aero Ica, C Lima 103 ⓣ034/522434 or via the *Hotel la Maison Suisse* (ⓣ034/522434) in Nazca; Aero Nazca, C Lima 165, Nazca (ⓣ034/522297, ⓔaeroNazca@Latinmail.com); Aeroparacas, Jr Lima 185, Nazca (ⓣ034/521027, ⓦwww.nascatravel.com), or at Km447 Nazca airport ⓣ034/522699, ⓔaeroparacas @wayna.rcp.com.pe); Alas Peruanas, Jr Lima 168 (ⓣ 034/522444, ⓔalasperuanas@nazcaperu.com). Both Aero Montecarlo and Aero Palpa have offices at the airstrip.

amount of treasure here, buried it, and then promptly developed amnesia as to its whereabouts. Winds here frequently achieve speeds of up to 45km per hour, bringing sandstorms in their wake. The Lines begin on the tableland above the village of **PALPA** about 70km south of Ica on the Panamerican Highway, where amid orange groves, cherry plantations and date farms are a couple of small **hostels**, the basic *Hostal Palpa* (❶) and the simple but clean *Hostal San Francisco* (❷) and the **restaurant** *Monterrey*, Av Grau 118 (Ⓣ034/404062).

It's still another 20km until you can see the Lines, at Km420 of the Panamerican Highway, where a tall metal **viewing tower** (or *mirador*; 30¢) has been built above the plain. Unless you've got the time to climb up onto one of the hills behind, or take a **flight** over the Lines (see box on p.909), this is the best view you'll get.

Nazca and around

Some 20km south of the viewing tower, the colonial town of **NAZCA** spreads along the margin of a small coastal valley. Although the river is invariably dry, Nazca's valley remains green and fertile through the continued application of an Incaic subterranean aqueduct. It's a small town – slightly at odds with its appearance on maps – but an interesting and enjoyable place to stay. Indeed, these days it has become a major attraction, boasting, in addition to the Lines, the excellent **Museo Antoni/Centro Italiano Archaeologico**, adobe Inca ruins of **Paredones** only a couple of kilometres to the south, the **Casa Museo Maria Reiche** about 1km beyond the *mirador*, with access to several of the Nazca desert's animal figures, and two or three important **archeological sites** within an easy day's range.

Arrival, information and getting around

Roughly halfway between Lima and Arequipa, Nazca is easily reached by frequent bus, *colectivo*, or even by small **plane** from Lima with Aero Condor (see box on p.909 for details); *colectivos* link the airstrip with *jiróns* Bolognesi and Grau in town. Cruz del Sur **buses** drop off opposite the Alegria Tours office, C Lima 168; Lima–Arequipa service and Ormeño buses arrive at Avenida de Los Incas 112 several times weekly; most other buses stop around the start of Jirón Lima, by the *ovalo* on Avenida Los Incas.

Colectivos to and from Ica arrive at and leave close to the presently closed *Hotel Montecarlo*, Jr Callao 123, on the corner of Avenida Los Incas and Micaelo Bastidas; those from Vista Alegre leave from the corner of Bolognesi and Grau. Most people use the noisy, beeping little *tico* **taxis** or **motorcycle-rickshaws**, which can be hailed anywhere and compete to take you in or around town cheaply – you shouldn't pay more than US$2 for any destination in town. Buses leave every hour for the Nazca airstrip, from the corner of Grau with Jirón Bolognesi, and are normally marked *B-Vista Allegre*. For **tourist information** the best places are Nazca Trails, Bolognesi 550, on the Plaza de Armas (Ⓣ034/522858, Ⓦwww.nascalinesperu.com), or Alegria Tours, C Lima 168 (Ⓣ034/522444, Ⓦwww.nazcaperu.com).

Accommodation

Finding a **hotel** in Nazca is simple enough, with an enormous choice for such a small town; most places are along Jr Lima or within a few blocks of the Plaza de Armas.

Hostal Alegria Jr Lima 166 Ⓣ034/522702, Ⓦwww.nazcaperu.com. Popular with travellers, it has rooms with or without private bath set around an attractive garden, as well as a number of newer, plusher chalet-style rooms with fans and bath. It also has a café that serves good and good value set lunches, and their travel agency can arrange tours and bus connections to Lima or Arequipa. Camping is sometimes allowed. ❷–❺

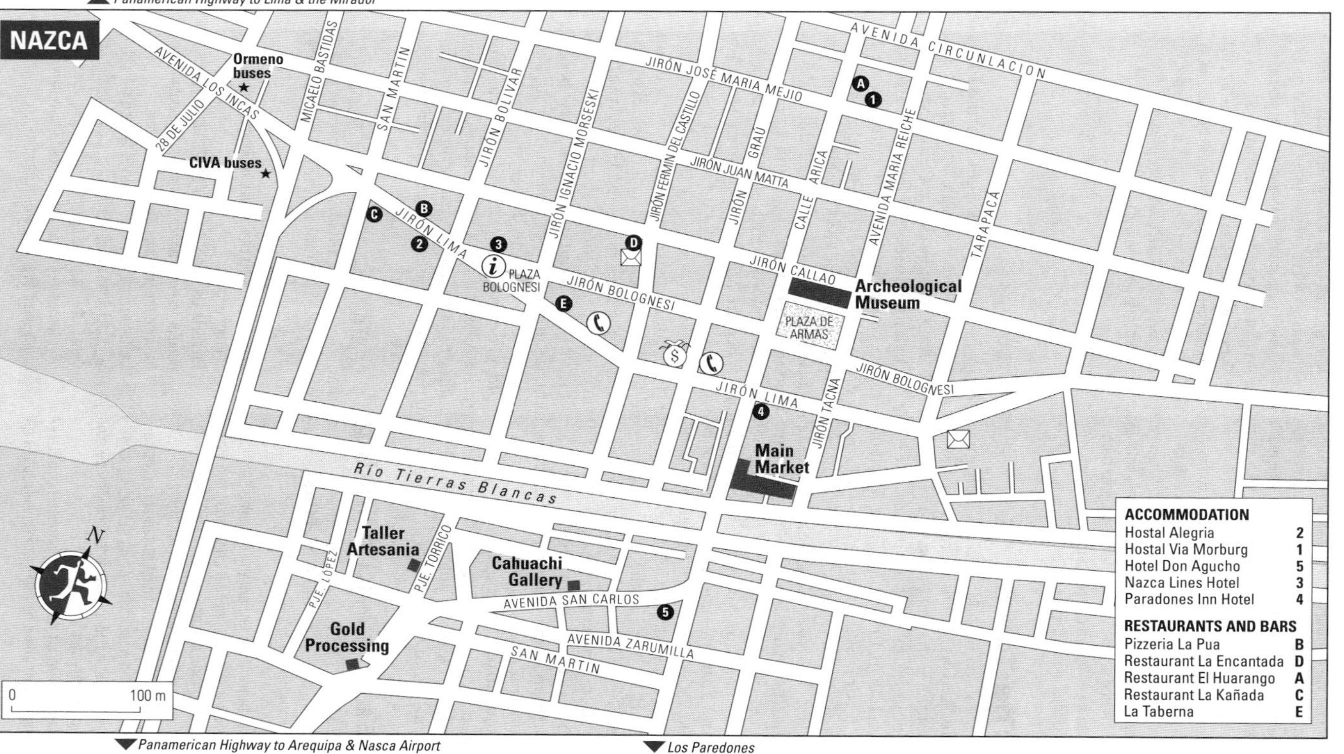

NAZCA
Panamerican Highway to Lima & the Mirador
Panamerican Highway to Arequipa & Nasca Airport
Los Paredones
AVENIDA CIRCUNLACION
JIRÓN JOSÉ MARIA MEJIO
JIRÓN JUAN MATTA
JIRÓN CALLAO
JIRÓN BOLOGNESI
JIRÓN LIMA
AVENIDA LOS INCAS
28 DE JULIO
MICAELO BASTIDAS
SAN MARTIN
JIRÓN BOLIVAR
JIRÓN IGNACIO MORSESKI
JIRÓN FERMIN DEL CASTILLO
JIRÓN GRAU
CALLE ARICA
AVENIDA MARIA REICHE
TARAPACA
JIRÓN TACNA
Ormeno buses
CIVA buses
PLAZA BOLOGNESI
PLAZA DE ARMAS
Archeological Museum
Main Market
Río Tierras Blancas
Taller Artesania
Cahuachi Gallery
Gold Processing
PJE. LÓPEZ
PJE. TORRICO
AVENIDA SAN CARLOS
AVENIDA ZARUMILLA
SAN MARTIN
N
0
100 m
ACCOMMODATION
Hostal Alegria 2
Hostal Via Morburg 1
Hotel Don Agucho 5
Nazca Lines Hotel 3
Paradones Inn Hotel 4
RESTAURANTS AND BARS
Pizzeria La Pua B
Restaurant La Encantada D
Restaurant El Huarango A
Restaurant La Kañada C
La Taberna E

Hostal Via Morburg Jr Jose Maria Mejia 108 ☎034/522566. A modern, secure place in a quiet part of town, the hostel offers comfortable rooms with private bath, reliable hot water, and a small pool. Very reasonably priced. ❸

Hotel Don Agucho Av Paredones, at corner with Av San Carlos 100 ☎034/522048. One of the nicest options in and around Nazca, this hacienda-style place has comfortable rooms, with bath and TV, based around cactus-filled passages. There's also a pool and a bar-restaurant; breakfast included in price. ❺

Nazca Lines Hotel Jr Bolognesi ☎034/522293. Luxurious, with its own well-kept pool and an excellent restaurant. Non-residents can also use the pool for approximately US$5 a day. ❼

Paradones Inn Hotel C Lima 600 ☎034/522181, Ⓔparedoneshotel@terra.com.pe. A brand new hotel in the heart of Nazca's small commercial area; smart and clean, with TVs, private bathrooms, hot water. ❹

The Town

As you come into town, Jr **Bolognesi**, the main street, leads straight into the **Plaza de Armas** where there are a few restaurants, bars and a couple of hotels. If you continue straight across the plaza and head along Avendia de La Cultura you soon come to the new town museum – the fascinating **Museo Didattico Antonini**, an Italian Pre-Columbian Archeological Research and Study Centre, Av de la Cultura 600 (☎034/523444, Ⓦwww.digilander.iol.it/MDAntonini; daily 9am–7pm). Opened in 1999, the museum stretches for six long blocks from the Plaza de Armas along Bolognesi and presents excellent interpretative exhibits covering the evolution of Nazca culture, a good audiovisual show and scale model reconstructions of local remains such as the Templo del Escalonado at Cahuachi. The museum complex extends to almost a hectare and includes an archeological park that contains the *bisambra* aqueduct (fed by the Bisambra reservoir higher up the valley) and some burial reconstructions.

Heading along Calle Arica from the Plaza de Armas, south, the town's **main market**, offering the usual food and electronic goods, is based in a ramshackle collection of huts and stalls, on the left just before the river bridge on Calle Arica. The **Taller Artesania**, Pasaje Torrico 240, in Barrio San Carlos, a short walk south of the plaza over the bridge, is worth a visit for its wonderful ceramics; if a few people turn up at the same time, they'll demonstrate the process of ceramic-making from moulding to polishing. San Carlos suburb also boasts the **Taller de Ceramica Juan Jose**, at Pasaje Lopez 400, and a **gold processing** operation, both located on the right-hand side about 500m down the Avenida San Carlos from the market bridge. Don't be put off by the fact that they're in someone's back garden – it's fascinating to watch them grind rocks into powder and then extract gold dust from it.

Eating and drinking

Eating in Nazca offers more variety than you might imagine given the town's small size. What little **nightlife** exists is mainly based around **restaurants** and **bars**, particularly on Jirón Lima, Plaza de Armas and Jirón Bolognesi.

Restaurant La Encantada Jr Callao 592 ☎034/522930. Excellent *criolla* food in a nice atmosphere, though pricey.

Restaurant El Huarango C Arica 602 ☎034/521287. The finest restaurant in Nazca, with a solid reputation among the locals, it has a rooftop patio and a great ambience. The delicious food is very well priced.

Restaurant La Kañada Jr Lima 160 ☎522917. Nice decor and a pleasant atmosphere, often full of gringos eating their great seafood; also offers Internet access.

Pizzeria La Pua Lima 169 ☎522990. A very popular trattoria and snackbar, located out of the town centre opposite the *Hostal Alegria*.

La Taberna Jr Lima 321. Serves a good selection of local and international dishes, plus a variety of drinks; its walls are covered with graffiti scrawled over the years by passing groups of travellers. Lively most evenings until midnight.

Archeological sites around Nazca

Chauchilla and **Cahuachi**, after the Lines the most important sites associated with the Nazca culture, are both difficult to reach by public transport, and unless your energy and interest are pretty unlimited you'll want to take an organized tour.

Roughly 30km south of Nazca along the Panamerican Highway, then out along a dirt road beside the Poroma riverbed, **Chauchilla Cemetery** certainly rewards the effort it takes to visit. Once you reach the atmospheric site, you realize how considerable a civilization the riverbanks must have maintained in the time of the Nazca culture. Scattered about the dusty ground are literally thousands of graves, most of which have been opened by grave robbers, leaving the skulls and skeletons exposed to the sun, along with broken pieces of pottery, bits of shroud fabric and lengths of braided hair, as yet unbleached by the desert sun. Further up the track, near Trancas, there's a small ceremonial **temple** – Huaca del Loro – and beyond this at Los Incas you can find Quemazon **petroglyphs**. These last two are not usually included in the standard tour, but if you hire your own guide you can negotiate with him to take you there – expect to pay US$5 extra.

Tours around Nazca

Some well-established companies arrange **tours** to the major sites around Nazca, all offering similar trips to Los Paredones, Cantalloc, Cahuachi, Chauchilla and the Lines. Tours around Chauchilla Cemetery last two and a half hours for about US$10 a person; a trip to the viewing tower and the Casa Museo Maria Reiche also takes two and a half hours and costs around US$10. Tours out to the ruined temple complex in the desert at Cahuachi (see above) last four hours and cost in the region of US$50 for a party of four or five; these need to be arranged in advance. The best **tour operators** are Nazca Trails, Bolognesi 550, Plaza de Armas (Ⓣ034/522858, Ⓔnazca@correo.dnet.com.pe); Alegria Tours, C Lima 168 (Ⓣ034/522444, Ⓦwww.nazcaperu.com). Otherwise try Tour Peru, C Arica 285, Of 1 (Ⓣ034/522481), an established agency specializing in Nazca flights and local tours; NaNazca Tours and Souvenirs, C Lima 160 (Ⓣ034/522917, Ⓔnanazcatours@yahoo.com); Huarango Travel Agency, C Lima 165 (Ⓣ034/522297); and Viajes Nazca, Jr Lima 185 (Ⓣ034/521027).

9.4

Arequipa and Lago Titicaca

Arequipa, second city of Peru and a day's journey from Lima, sits in a dramatic setting, poised at the edge of the Andes against an extraordinary backdrop of volcanic peaks. The major centre of the south, Arequipa is an enjoyable place to take it easy for a while, distinguished by its architecture (including the magnificent **Santa Catalina Monastery**) and for several spectacular, if tough-going, excursions into the surrounding countryside where you can explore the **Colca Canyon**, one of the deepest in the world, and watch condors glide gracefully against the backdrop of ancient Inca mountain terraces. The Arequipa region is also the last place to merit a stop before continuing on south to the Chilean border.

Heading inland, you'll probably want to spend time in the **Lago Titicaca** area, getting to know its main town and port – **Puno**, a high, quite austere city with a cold climate and incredibly rarefied air. Alternatively you might fancy a break on one of the huge lake's islands where life has changed little in the last five hundred years. The Titicaca region is renowned for its folk dances and Andean music and, along with Puno, makes an interesting place to break your journey from Arequipa to Cusco or into Bolivia.

Arequipa

An active city, some 2400m above sea level, and with a relatively wealthy population of over three-quarters of a million, **AREQUIPA** maintains a rather aloof attitude toward the rest of Peru. Most Arequipans feel themselves distinct, if not culturally superior, and resent the idea of the nation revolving around Lima, and with **El Misti**, the 5821-metre dormant volcano poised above, the place does have a rather legendary sort of appearance. But besides its widespread image as the country's second biggest and arguably, after Cusco, most attractive city, Arequipa has some very specific historical connotations for Peruvians. Developing late as a provincial capital, and until 1870 connected only by mule track with the rest of Peru, it has acquired a reputation as *the* centre of **right-wing political power**: while populist movements have tended to emerge around Trujillo in the north, Arequipa has traditionally represented the solid interests of the oligarchy. Arequipa typifies the social extremes of Peru more than any other of its major cities, with a huge increase in recent years in the number of street beggars, despite the tastefully ostentatious architecture and generally well-heeled appearance of most townsfolk.

One of the best times to visit is around August 15, when there's a **festival** celebrating the city's foundation with processions, music and poetry. There's also a folklore festival in the first week of July.

Arrival, information and city transport

Arequipa is the hub of most journeys in the southern half of Peru and is generally an almost unavoidable stopping-off point between Lima and the Titicaca, Cusco and Tacna regions. **Flights** land at Arequipa airport, 7km northwest of the town. A

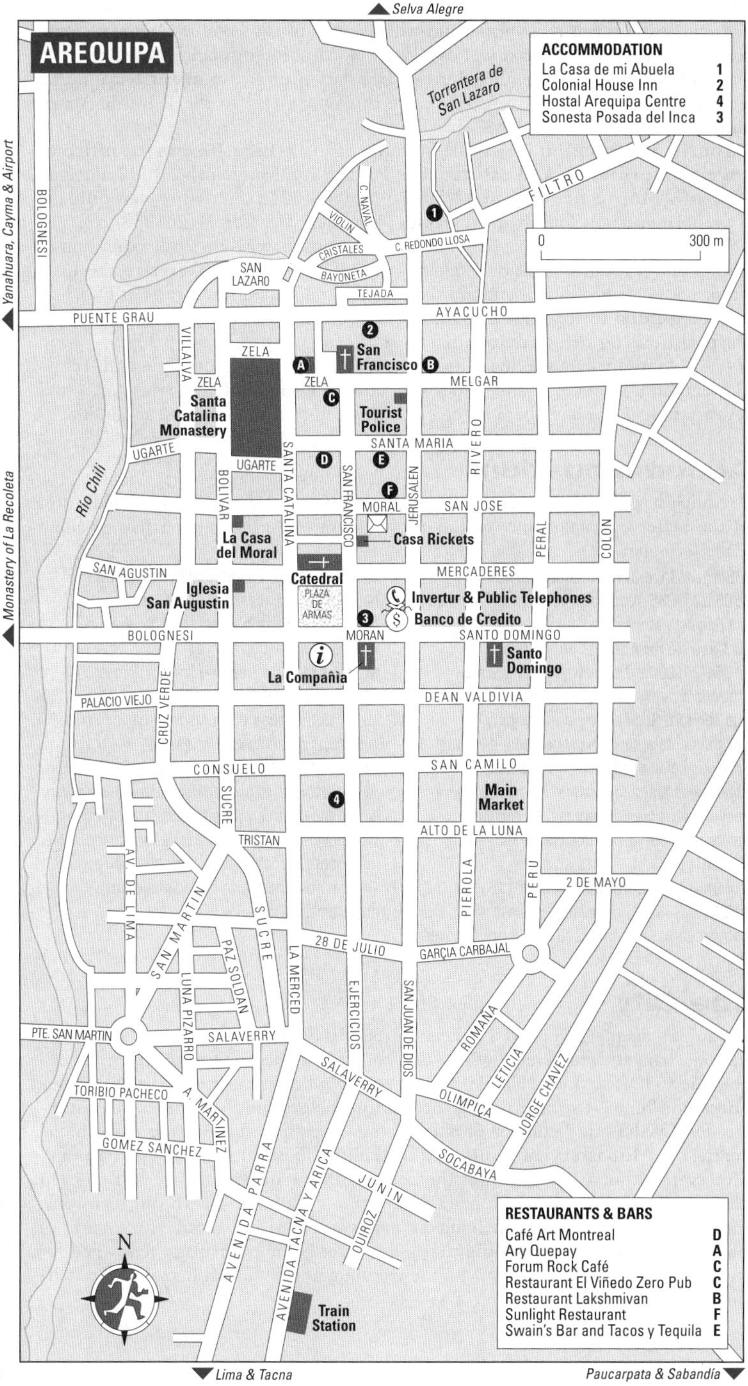

AREQUIPA

ACCOMMODATION

La Casa de mi Abuela	1
Colonial House Inn	2
Hostal Arequipa Centre	4
Sonesta Posada del Inca	3

RESTAURANTS & BARS

Café Art Montreal	D
Ary Quepay	A
Forum Rock Café	C
Restaurant El Viñedo Zero Pub	C
Restaurant Lakshmivan	B
Sunlight Restaurant	F
Swain's Bar and Tacos y Tequila	E

Selva Alegre
Yanahuara, Cayma & Airport
Monastery of La Recoleta
Lima & Tacna
Paucarpata & Sabandía

Torrentera de San Lazaro
Río Chili
0 300 m
N

Santa Catalina Monastery
San Francisco
Tourist Police
La Casa del Moral
Casa Rickets
Catedral
Plaza de Armas
Iglesia San Augustin
Invertur & Public Telephones
Banco de Credito
La Compañia
Santo Domingo
Main Market
Train Station

Puente Grau, Ayacucho, Zela, Melgar, Ugarte, Santa Maria, San Jose, Moral, Mercaderes, San Agustin, Bolognesi, Moran, Santo Domingo, Palacio Viejo, Dean Valdivia, Consuelo, San Camilo, Tristan, Alto de la Luna, 2 de Mayo, 28 de Julio, Garcia Carbajal, Salaverry, Pte. San Martin, Toribio Pacheco, Gomez Sanchez, Socabaya, Junin, Olimpica, Filtro, C. Redondo Llosa, Cristales, Bayoneta, Tejada, Violin, C. Naval, San Lazaro, Villalva, Bolivar, Santa Catalina, San Francisco, Jerusalen, Rivero, Peral, Colon, Cruz Verde, Sucre, Av. de Lima, San Martin, Paz Soldan, Luna Pizarro, La Merced, Ejercicios, San Juan de Dios, Pierola, Peru, Romaña, Leticia, Jorge Chavez, A. Martinez, Avenida Parra, Avenida Tacna y Arica, Quiroz

red shuttle bus meets most planes and will take you to any hotel in the town centre for US$1; alternatively, a taxi will cost US$3–4. Most long-distance **buses** arrive at the modern, concrete Terminal Terreste bus station or at the newer Terrapuerto, next door, around 4km from the centre of town; a taxi to the Plaza de Armas should cost no more than US$2.

Tourist information is available from the official **i-Peru Promperu office of tourist information and assistance** at Portal de La Municipalidad 112, Plaza de Armas (Mon–Sun 8.30am–7.30pm; ⓣ054/221228, ⓔiperuarequipa@promperu.gob.pe); The **Tourist Police**, Jerusalen 315 (ⓣ054/201258), are also particularly helpful with maps and information, plus they have a small exhibition of photos and postcards of major local attractions. The **Terminal Terrestre** also has a kiosk with details of hotels and tour companies, and sometimes maps. For information on **guided tours** of the city and the surrounding area, see the box on p.920. **i-Peru** also has an **information office at the airport** (6.30am–6.30pm, 7 days; ⓣ054/444564) where they have maps of the city, information on sights and cultural events and can recommend guides, tour companies and hotels. If you want a **taxi** it's easy to hail one anywhere in the city; rides within the centre cost about 80¢.

Accommodation

Arequipa has a good selection of **accommodation** in all price ranges, with most of the better options mainly within a few blocks of the Plaza de Armas or along Calle Jerusalen.

Albergue Juvenil Ronda Recoleta 104 ⓣ054/257085. Arequipa's youth hostel, out near the Recoleta Monastery. Simple, but it suffices. ❷

La Casa de mi Abuela Jerusalen 606 ⓣ054/241206, ⓔlperezwi@ucsm.edu.pe. Innovative family-run hostel, combining elegance and comfort. Rooms are set in a variety of environments around lovely gardens; there are spacious colonial quarters, chalets, family apartments and a fine swimming pool. It's very secure, has a good library and an excellent cafétería. Reserve well in advance during high season. ❹–❺

Colonial House Inn Puente Grau 114 ⓣ054/223533, ⓔcolonialhouseinn@hotmail.com. Pleasant place with a pretty covered courtyard, electric heated showers, private bathrooms and access to TV and Internet facilities. Well worth it, not least for the nice rooftop breakfast option. ❸

Hostal Arequipa Centre Alvarez Thomas 305 ⓣ054/496169. Central, simple but spotlessly clean, with a range of rooms from basic to suites with Jacuzzis and cable TV. ❷–❹

Sonesta Posada del Inca Portal de Flores 116 ⓣ054/215530, ⓔposada@sonestaperu.com. Very smart and central, with a top-class restaurant, views over the plaza, conference rooms and, more importantly, a rooftop pool and patio with superb views across the city to the southeastern mountains. ❼

The City

Arequipa's deeply ingrained architectural beauty comes mainly from the colonial period, characterized here by white *sillar* stone and arched interior ceilings. In general, the style is stark and almost clinical, except where Baroque and *mestizo* influences combine, as seen on many of the fine sixteenth- to eighteenth-century facades. Of the huge number of religious buildings spread about the old colonial centre, the **Monastery of Santa Catalina** is the most outstanding and beautiful. However, within a few blocks of the colonial **Plaza de Armas** are half a dozen churches well deserving of a brief visit, and a couple of superb old mansions. Further out, but still within walking distance, you can visit the attractive suburbs of **San Lazaro**, **Cayma** and **Yanahuara**, this latter being particularly renowned for its dramatic views of the valley with the volcanos, notably El Misti, patiently watching the city from high above.

The Plaza de Armas and around

The **Plaza de Armas**, one of South America's grandest and the focus of social activity in the early evenings, comprises a particularly striking array of colonial architecture, dotted with palms, flowers and gardens. At its heart sits a newly renovated bronze fountain, topped by an angel fondly known as *turututu* because of the trumpet it carries, but it's the arcades and elegant white facade of the seventeenth-century **Catedral** (daily 6–11am & 5–7pm; free) that grab your attention, even drawing your sight away from El Misti towering behind. There are two bronze medallions in the facade symbolizing the Peruvian–Bolivian confederation, and the whole thing looks particularly beautiful when lit up in the evenings.

On the southeast corner of the plaza, opposite side from the cathedral, and rather more exciting architecturally, is the elaborate **La Compañía** (Mon–Fri 9–11.30am & 3–5.30pm; 30¢), with its extraordinary zigzagging *sillar* stone doorway. Built over the last decades of the seventeenth century, the magnificently sculpted doorway, with a locally inspired Mestizo-Baroque relief, is curiously two-dimensional, using shadow only to outline the figures of the frieze. Inside, by the main altar hangs a *Virgin and Child* by Bernardo Bitto, which arrived from Italy in 1575. In what used to be the sacristy (now the Chapel of San Ignacio), the polychrome cupola depicts jungle imagery alongside warriors, angels and the Evangelists. Next door to the church are the fine **Jesuit Cloisters** (Mon–Sat 8am–10pm & Sun noon–8pm), superbly carved back in the early eighteenth century. In the first cloister the fine squared pillars support white stone arches and are covered with intricate reliefs showing more angels, local fruits and vegetables, seashells and stylized puma heads. The second cloister is, in contrast, rather austere.

Santo Domingo (daily 7–11am and 3–6pm; free), two blocks east of La Compañía, was built in the seventeenth century but was badly damaged by earthquakes in 1958 and 1960. It was originally built in 1553 by Gaspar Vaez, the first master architect to arrive in Arequipa, though most of what you see today started in 1650 and was finished in 1698, while the towers were constructed after the 1960 quake. It has been well restored, however, and on the main door you can make out an interesting example of Arequipa's *mestizo* craftsmanship – an Indian face amid a bunch of grapes, fine leaves and even cacti. North of the plaza, at Santa Catalina 101, the **Casa Arróspide** (also known as the Casa Iriberry) is home to the Complejo Cultural Chavez de la Rosa (Mon–Sat 10am–6pm; free). This attractive colonial house, built in 1743, belongs to the Law Faculty of the University of San Augustin and hosts changing selections of modern works by mostly Peruvian artists.

Santa Catalina Monastery

Just two blocks north of the Plaza de Armas, the vast protective walls of **Santa Catalina Monastery** (daily 9am–4pm, last entrance at 4pm; US$7.50; guides are optional at around US$3) housed almost two hundred secluded nuns and three hundred servants until it opened to the public in 1970. The most important and prestigious religious building in Peru, its enormous complex of rooms, cloisters and tiny plazas takes a good hour or two to wander around. Some 30 nuns still live here today, spanning between 18 and 90 years of age, but they're restricted to the quarter bordered by calles Bolivar and Zela, worshipping in the main chapel only outside visiting hours.

Originally the concept of Gaspar Vae in 1570, though only granted official licence five years later, it was funded by the Viceroy Toledo and the wealthy Maria de Guzmán, who later entered the convent with one of her sisters and donated all her riches to the community. The most striking feature of the architecture is its predominantly Mudéjar style, adapted by the Spanish from the Moors, but which rarely found its way into their colonial buildings. The quality of the design is emphasized and harmonized by a superb interplay between the strong sunlight, white stone and brilliant colours in the ceilings and in the deep blue sky above the maze of narrow interior streets. You notice this at once as you enter, filing left along the first corridor to a high vaulted room with a ceiling of opaque *huamanga* stone imported from the Ayacucho valley. Beside here are the **locutorios** – little cells where on holy days the nuns could talk, unseen, to visitors.

The **Novices Cloisters**, beyond, are built in solid *sillar*-block columns, their antique wall paintings depicting the various qualities to which the devotees were expected to aspire and the Litanies of the Rosary. Off to the right, the **Orange Tree Cloister**, painted a beautiful blue with birds and flowers over the vaulted arches, is surrounded by a series of paintings showing the soul evolving from a state of sin to the achievement of God's grace. In one of the side rooms, dead nuns were mourned, before being interred within the monastic confines.

A new convent, where the nuns now live, is on the right off Calle Cordoba. **Calle Toledo**, a long, very narrow street that's the oldest part of the monastery and connects the main dwelling areas with the *lavandería*, or communal washing sector, is brought to life with permanently flowering geraniums. There are several rooms off here worth exploring, including small chapels, prayer rooms and a kitchen. The **lavandería** itself, perhaps more than any other area, offers a captivating insight into what life must have been like for the closeted nuns; open to the skies and city sounds yet bounded by high walls, there are twenty halved earthenware jars alongside a water channel. It also has a swimming pool with sunken steps and a papaya tree in the lovely garden.

Monastery of La Recoleta

Over the Río Chili is the large Franciscan **Monastery of La Recoleta** (Ⓣ054/270996; Mon–Sat 9am–noon & 3–5pm; US$1.80), standing conspicuously on its own on Callejón de la Recoleta, Ronda Recoleta 117, just 10–15 minutes walk east of the Plaza de Armas. Founded in 1648 by the venerable Father Pedro de Mendoza and designed by Father Pedro de Peñaloza, in 1651 the stunning major and minor cloisters were built, then in 1869 it was converted to an Apostolic Mission school administered by the Barefoot Franciscans.

The suburbs: San Lazaro and Yanahuara

The oldest quarter of Arequipa – the first place the Spaniards settled in this valley – is the *barrio* **San Lazaro**, an uncharacteristic zone of tiny, curving streets stretching around the hillside at the top end of Calle Jerusalen, all an easy stroll from the plaza. If you feel like a walk, and some good views of El Misti, you can follow the streambed from here to Puente Grau – a superb vantage point. From here, a longer stroll takes you across to the west bank of the Chili, along Avenida Ejercito and out to suburbs of Yanahuara (1–2km) and Cayma (3–4km), quite distinct villages until the railway boom of the late nineteenth century, which brought peasant migrants to Arequipa from as far away as Cusco. Both are built up now, though they still command stunning views across the valley, above all from their **churches**. There are also one or two fine restaurants in these sectors, particularly Yanahuara. Buses and *colectivos* to these areas leave from avenidas Ayacucha and Puente Gran.

The municipal plaza at **Yanahuara** possesses a **viewing point** (*mirador*), whose view of the city, with Misti framed behind by the *mirador's* white stone arches, has been made famous by postcards. Buses and *colectivos* to Yanahuara's *mirador* can be caught from the corner of Grau with Santa Catalina (near the *Hostal Santa Catalina*), or it's a fifteen-minute walk from Puente Grau, between blocks 2 and 3 of Avenida Ejercito. The small **Iglesia Yanahuara** on the tranquil main plaza dates to the middle of the eighteenth century, and its Baroque facade, with a stone relief of the tree of life incorporating angels, flowers, saints, lions and hidden Indian faces, is particularly fine.

Eating and drinking

Arequipa boasts all sorts of **restaurants** dotted about the town serving a wide variety of foods, but is particularly famous for a dish called *ocopa*, a cold appetizer made with potatoes, eggs, olives and a fairly spicy yellow chilli sauce. As it's not too far from the Pacific, the town's better restaurants are also renowned for their excellent fresh seafood. **Picanterias** – traditional Peruvian eating houses serving spicy seafood – are particularly well established here. Unless otherwise indicated, all the places below open daily from 11am to 11pm. It's often hard to distinguish between **bars**, restaurants and **nightclubs** (or **discos**, as most are referred to), as many restaurants have a bar and live music while many bars and clubs also serve food.

Restaurants

Ary Quepay Jerusalen 502. A large restaurant space serving local food, such as alpaca steaks, as well as international dishes, vegetarian options and fine pisco sours; frequently busy at night, service is good and there's sometimes live folk music.

Complejo Turistico Bob Gourmet Alameda Pardo 123 ⓣ054/270528. Combining two of the finest restaurants in the city, this complex overlooks the city from the western banks of the Río Chili. *El Montonero* is its excellent lunchtime restaurant which is attempting to rescue some traditional regional dishes such as *senca* meat balls and *pesque*, which is made from quinoa, with a cheese and steak topping. *Che Carlitos* is its Argentinian grill and bar which is quite fancy, but also caters for vegetarians as well as serving excellent beef and alpaca cuts.

Restaurant Lakshmivan Jerusalen 402. A very popular lunchtime vegetarian café at the back of a small patio, which also sells a range of healthfood products, yogurts and wholemeal bread; it plays classical music and has a pleasant ambience.

Restaurant El Viñedo San Francisco 319 ⓣ054/205053. Quite a large posh place offering quality service. Pricey but worth it for arguably the best Argentinian style steaks and grills in Southern Peru.

Sunlight Restaurante Moral 205. A very small but excellent and inexpensive Asian vegetarian restaurant which set lunch menus at give away prices.

Tradicion Arequipeña Av Dolores 111 ⓣ054/426467. Opened in 1991 and situated several blocks east of the city centre, this is probably the best *picanteria* restaurant in town. It has a pleasant garden, covered and indoor spaces and is usually bustling with locals enjoying the extremely fresh and tasty food.

Bars and nightclubs

Café Art Montreal Ugarte 210. Although open for breakfasts and lunches, this attractive place set around a fine stone courtyard really comes to life at night (Wed–Sat, 10pm–2am) when excellent foods are served up to live local rock and Latino ballad bands. This is a *peña* but certainly isn't folkloric. The cocktails here are very interesting.

Forum Rock Café San Francisco 317. The liveliest and funkiest scene in the city, with live music on Friday and Saturday. Also has a café, a decent bar and serves snacks.

Restaurant Peña Las Quenas Santa Catalina 302 ⓣ054/206440. One of the better and larger venues in town, dishes out authentic Andean music, food and good pisco sours; music most weekends and also during the week from June to Sept. Closed on Sundays, but open all other days from 10am for breakfast.

Swain's Bar Ugarte 106a ⓣ054/454462 or 602337. Run by a friendly young Englishman and his Peruvian wife, this bar offers a decent range of drinks, some snacks, frequent fun and games as well as a darts board and cable TV to access European sports events. Football is a dominant theme, with Liverpool paraphernalia being particularly prevalent.

Around Arequipa

The spectacular countryside around Arequipa rewards a few days' exploration, with some exciting and adventurous possibilities for trips. Climbing **El Misti** is a demanding but rewarding trek, while the Inca ruins of **Paucarpata** at the foot of the volcano offer excellent scenery, great views and a fine place for a picnic. The attractive village of **Chapi** makes a good day-trip, and just a few hours' drive away from Arequipa, the **Sumbay caves**, on the road towards Caylloma via the austere

Tours, trekking and climbing in Arequipa and around

Taking a guided tour is the easiest way to get around this otherwise quite difficult region. All operators tend to offer similar packages. Most companies offer one- to three-day trips out to the **Colca Canyon** for US$20–80 (sometimes with *very* early morning starts) or to the petroglyphs at **Toro Muerto** for US$20–40. Trips to the **Valley of the Volcanos** are only offered by a few companies. Specialist adventure activities, eg rafting in the Colca Canyon, mountaineering or serious trekking can cost anything from US$55 up to US$350 for a three- to six-day outing. Competition between companies is high, so check out all the options and determine exactly what you're getting.

Campamento Base and Colca Trek Jerusalen 401b ⓣ054/206217, 224378 (24hr) or 600170, ⓦwwwcolcatrek.com. An excellent tour, trek, climbing, mountain biking and canoeing company which specializes too in customized tours permitting a mix of the above.

Giardino Agencia de Viajes Jerusalen 606a ⓣ054/241206 or 226416, ⓦwww.giardinotours.com. A well-organized outfit with excellent two-day tours to Colca, trekking and climbing trips, plus the usual city and countryside trips.

Peru Expeditions Av Arequipa 5241–504, Miraflores, Lima ⓣ01/4472057, ⓦwww.peru-expeditions.com. Highly professional and helpful Lima-based company, offering environmentally sound adventure travel in the Arequipa region.

Santa Catalina Tours Santa Catalina 223 ⓣ054/284883 or 216994, ⓔsantacatalina@rh.com.pe. City tours, local and Colca Canyon trips, plus ascents up El Misti and occasional rafting on the Río Chili, all at reasonable prices. Good, reliable guides.

but stunning Lake Salinas, are hard to reach independently but contain hundreds of unique prehistoric cave paintings.

Further out, 200km to the north, is the **Colca Canyon**, one of Peru's major attractions, second only to Machu Picchu and developing fast as a trekking and canoeing destination (best in the dry season, May–Sept). Called the "Valley of Marvels" by the Peruvian novelist Marío Vargas Llosa, it is nearly twice the size of Arizona's Grand Canyon and one of the country's most extraordinary natural sights. Around 120km west of Arequipa, you can see the amazing petroglyphs of **Toro Muerto**, perhaps continuing on to hike amid the craters and cones of the **Valley of the Volcanos**.

Chivay and the Colca Canyon

The entry point for the Colca Canyon is **CHIVAY**, 150km north of Arequipa and just three to four hours by bus from there, set amongst fantastic hiking country, surrounded by some of the most impressive and intensive ancient terracing in South America. Today, it is notable as the market town dominating the head of but not the best place to see the canyon from. These days Chivay is ever more bustling with gringos eager to use the town's growing range of accommodation, restaurants and bus services, making it a reasonable place to stay while you acclimatize to the high altitude, before going further.

The sharp terraces of the **COLCA CANYON**, one of the world's deepest canyons at more than 1km from cliff edge to river bottom, are still home to more or less traditional Indian villages, despite the canyon's rapidly becoming one of Peru's most popular tourist attractions. To the north of Colca sits the magestic Nevado Mismi, a snowcapped peak that, according to the *National Geographic*, is the official source of the Amazon. The Mirador Cruz del Condor is the most popular viewing point for looking into the depths of the canyon – it's around 1200m deep at this point – and where you can almost guarantee seeing several condors circling up from the depths against breathtaking scenery (best spotted 7–9am, the earlier you get there the more likely you are to have fewer other spectators around). The small but growing town of **Cabanaconde** (3300m), which offers a good option for lodgings as a base to descend into the canyon, is about 10km further down the road.

You'll need a couple of days to begin exploring the area and three or four to do it any justice, but several tour companies offer one-day tours as well as extended trips with overnight stops in either Chivay, a posada en route, in Cabanaconde itself, or one of the other campsites and small villages dotted around the edges of the canyon.

Crossing into Chile

The **border with Chile** (daily 9am–10pm) is about 40km south of Tacna. Regular buses and *colectivos* to **Arica** (see p.528) leave from the modern bus terminal, on Hipolito Unanue in Tacna, and three trains a day depart from the station, on Calle Coronel Albarracin (at 7am, 8.30am and 3pm). At around US$3.50, the **train** is the cheapest option, but it's slow and you have to visit the Passport and Immigration Police, on Plaza de Armas, and the Chilean Consulate, Presbitero Andia, just off Coronel Albarracin, beforehand. You will already have cleared Peruvian customs control on your way into Tacna, along the Panamerican Highway.

Coming back into Peru from Arica is as simple as getting there. *Colectivos* run throughout the day and the train leaves at the same times as the one from Tacna. Night travellers, however, might be required to have a *salvoconducto militar* (safe-conduct card), particularly in times of tension between the two countries. If you intend to travel at night, check first with the tourist office in Arica, C Prat 305, on the second floor.

East from Arequipa to Puno

Heading **east from Arequipa**, you cross the 4500m-high Meseta del Collao through some of the most stunning yet bleak Andean scenery in southern Peru. It's not a particularly comfortable journey by bus, usually between seven and nine hours long, travelling at very high altitudes for many long and weary hours. Many buses these days go to the Titicaca area via Moquegua and the new sections of road which connect with Desaguaderos for the Bolivian frontier or Puno at the northern end of the lake. Alternatively, some buses still follow the largely dirt road that runs to the south of the railway line – crossing the *pampa* at Toroya (4693m) and passing the spectacular **Lake Salinas**, in the shadow of Peru's most active volcano, Ubinas. This icy-blue lake is frequently adorned with thousands of flamingos and the surrounding landscape is dotted with herds of llamas, alpacas and the occasional flock of fleet-footed vicuñas. Passenger trains between Arequipa and Puno are only available for charter bookings by groups of forty or more. See Ⓦwww.perurail.com.

Puno and Lago Titicaca

An immense region both in terms of its history and the breadth of its magical landscape, the **Titicaca Basin** makes most people feel as if they are on top of the world. The skies are vast and the horizons appear to bend away below you. The high altitude ensures that recent arrivals from the coast take it easy for a day or two, though those coming from Cusco will already have acclimatized.

The first Spanish settlement at **Puno** sprang up around a silver mine discovered by the infamous Salcedo brothers in 1657, a camp that forged such a wild and violent reputation that the Lima viceroy moved in with soldiers to crush and finally execute the Salcedos before things got too out of hand. At the same time – in 1668 – he created Puno as the capital of the region and from then on it developed as the main port of Lago Titicaca and an important town on the silver trail from Potosi.

The arrival of the railway, late in the nineteenth century, brought another boost, but today it's a relatively poor, rather grubby sort of town, even by Peruvian standards, and a place that has suffered badly from recent drought and an inability to manage its water resources.

On the edge of the town spreads the vast **Lago Titicaca** – enclosed by white peaks and dotted with unusual **floating islands**, basically huge rafts built out of reeds and home to a dwindling and much-abused Indian population. Densely populated since well before the arrival of the Incas, the lakeside Titicaca region is also home to the curious and ancient tower tombs known locally as **chullpas**, which are rings of tall, cylindrical stone burial chambers, often standing in battlement-like formations.

Puno

With a dry, cold climate – frequently falling below freezing in the winter nights of July and August – **PUNO** is just a crossroads to most travellers, en route between Cusco and Bolivia or Arequipa and maybe Chile. In some ways this is fair, for it's a breathless place (at 3870m above sea level), with a burning daytime sun in stark contrast to the icy evenings, and a poor reputation for pickpockets, particularly at the bus and train terminals. Yet the town is immensely rich in traditions and has a fascinating ancient history with several stone *chullpas* nearby. Puno's port is a vital staging point for exploring the northern end of Lago Titicaca, with its floating islands and beautiful island communities of Amantani and Taquile just a few hours away by boat. Perhaps more importantly, though, Puno is famed as the folklore capital of Peru, particularly relevant if you can visit in the first two weeks of February for the **Fiesta de la Candelaria**, a great folklore dance spectacle, boasting incredible dancers wearing devil masks; the festival climaxes on the second Sunday of February. If you're in Puno at this time it's a good idea to reserve hotels in advance (though hotel prices can double).

Arrival and information

However you arrive in Puno, you'll immediately be affected by the altitude and should take it easy for at least the first day, preferably for the first two, although if you arrive from Cusco or Bolivia, the chances are you will already be accustomed to the altitude. Arriving **by bus** you are most likely to end up somewhere central on Jirón Tacna or a few blocks east towards the lake, along Avenida Titicaca or Jirón Melgar; see "Listings" p.925 for details of the different companies and their terminals. *Colectivos* to and from Juliaca and **Juliaca Airport** (Aeropuerto Manco Capac) also use Jirón Tacna. If you're coming in Cusco by train, you'll arrive at the **train station** (information on ⓣ054/351041) on Avenida la Torre. Taxis and motorcycle rickshaws leave from immediately outside the station and will cost less than US$2 to anywhere in the centre of town. The main **port**, used by boats from Bolivia (contact Capital del Puerto, Av El Sol 725, for information), as well as the Uros Islands, Taquile and Amantani, is a fifteen- to twenty-minute walk from the Plaza de Armas down, straight up Avenida El Puerto, crossing over Jirón Tacna, then up Jirón Puno.

The helpful and friendly staff at the **tourist information office**, Jr Lima 585 (Mon–Fri 7.30am–7pm, Sat 8am–1pm), and can provide photocopied town plans, leaflets and other information. The **tourist police**, Jr Deusta 538, are very helpful and also give out free maps. And the Direccion Regional de Industria and Turismo has an office on Jirón Ayacucho (ⓣ054/356097).

Accommodation

There is no shortage of **accommodation** in Puno for any budget, but the town's busy and narrow streets make places hard to locate, so you may want to make use of a taxi or motorcycle rickshaw.

Hostal Europa Jr Alfonso Vgarte 112 ⓣ054/353023. Good rates, friendly, secure (with safe luggage

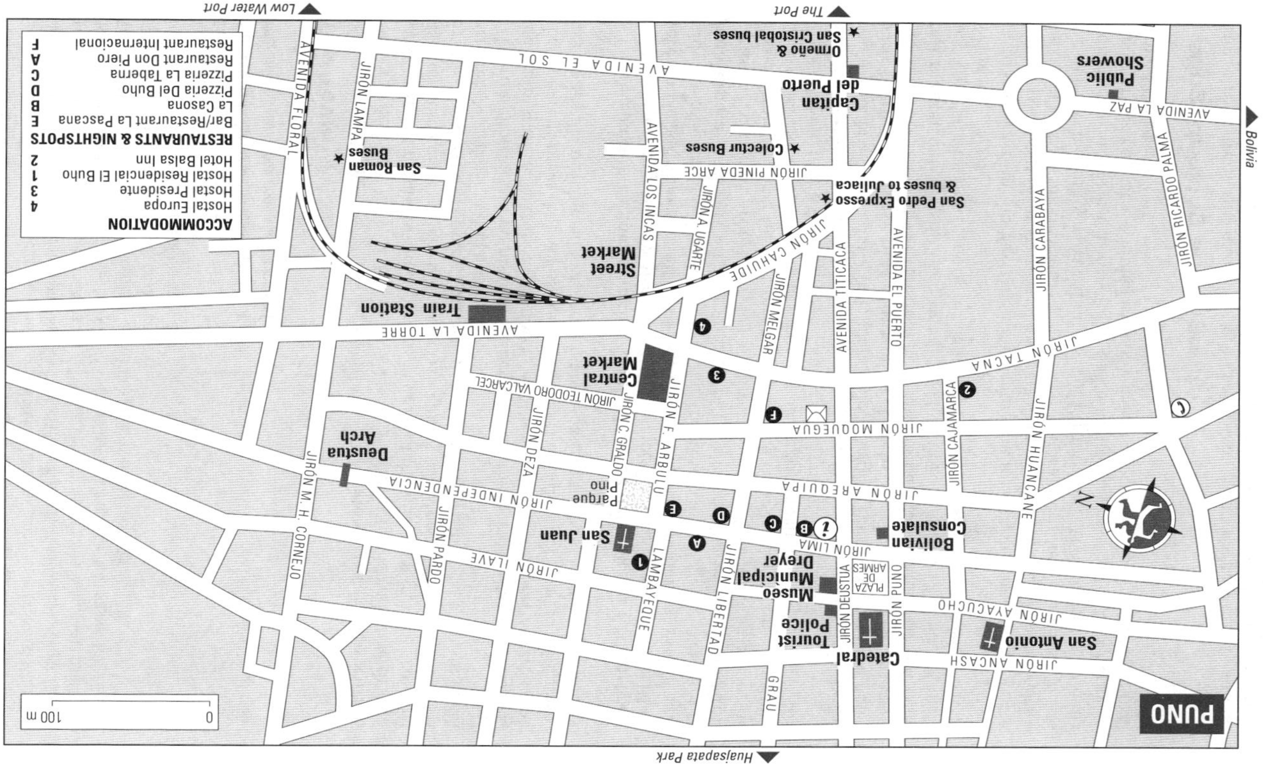

PUNO
Huajsapata Park
Bolivia
The Port
Low Water Port
0 100 m
San Antonio
Catedral
Tourist Police
Museo Municipal Dreyer
Bolivian Consulate
San Juan
Parque Pino
Deustua Arch
Central Market
Train Station
Street Market
San Pedro Expresso & buses to Juliaca
Colectur Buses
San Roman Buses
Capitan del Puerto
Ormeño & San Cristobal buses
Public Showers
PLAZA DE ARMES
JIRÓN ANCASH
JIRÓN AYACUCHO
JIRÓN PUNO
JIRÓN DEUSTUA
GRAU
JIRÓN LIBERTAD
LAMBAYEQUE
JIRÓN ILAVE
JIRÓN PARDO
JIRÓN M. H. CORNEJO
JIRÓN LIMA
JIRÓN AREQUIPA
JIRÓN INDEPENDENCIA
JIRÓN HUANCANE
JIRÓN CAJAMARCA
JIRÓN MOQUEGUA
JIRÓN F. ARBULU
JIRÓN C. GRALDO
JIRÓN DEZA
JIRÓN TEODORO VALCARCEL
JIRÓN TACNA
AVENIDA LA TORRE
AVENIDA EL PUERTO
AVENIDA TITICACA
JIRÓN MELGAR
JIRÓN CAHUIDE
JIRÓN A. UGARTE
AVENIDA LOS INCAS
JIRÓN PINEDA ARCE
JIRÓN RICARDO PALMA
JIRÓN CARABAYA
AVENIDA LA PAZ
AVENIDA EL SOL
JIRÓN LAMPA
AVENIDA FLORAL
ACCOMMODATION
Hostal Europa 4
Hostal Presidente 3
Hostal Residencial El Buho 1
Hotel Balsa Inn 2
RESTAURANTS & NIGHTSPOTS
Bar/Restaurant La Pascana E
La Casona B
Pizzeria Del Buho D
Pizzeria La Taberna C
Restaurant Don Piero A
Restaurant Internacional F

store) and very popular with travellers, with 24hr hot water but few private bathrooms. ❷

Hostal Presidente Tacna 248 ⓣ054/351421. Excellent value with a lot of character; hot water most evenings, all rooms with private baths. Has a nice, small café on the first floor for breakfast. ❷

Hostal Residencial El Buho Lambayeque 142 ⓣ054/366122, ⓔzuluqv@mix.mail.com. A pleasant and comfortable place with private baths in all rooms and hot water much of the time; also has its own tour company. ❸–❹

Hotel Balsa Inn Jr Cajamarca 555 ⓣ054/363144, ⓦwww.hotelbalsainn.com. A pleasantly modern hotel conveniently located about one block from the plaza; it has some 20 comfortable rooms, most with cable TV, all with private baths and heating. ❺

Hotel Sillustani Lambayeque 195 ⓣ054/351881 or 352641, ⓔhtl-sill@unap.edu.pe. A bright, airy place that's excellent value, with private bath, TV, fridge-bar and telephone in all rooms. There's also a pleasant dining room. ❼

The Town

Puno is one of the few Peruvian towns where the motorized traffic seems to respect pedestrians. Busy as it is, there is less of a sense of manic rush here than in most coastal or mountain cities, perhaps because of the altitude. It lacks the colonial style of Cusco or the bright glamour of Arequipa's *sillar* stone architecture, but it's a friendly town, whose sloping corrugated iron roofs reflect the heavy rains that fall between November and February.

There are three main points of reference in Puno: the spacious **Plaza de Armas**, the **train station** several blocks north, and the vast strung-out area of old, semi-abandoned docks at the ever-shifting **Titicaca lakeside port**. It all looks impressive from a distance but, in fact, the real town-based attractions are few and quickly visited.

The seventeenth-century **Catedral** on the Plaza de Armas (daily 7.30am–6pm; free), is surprisingly large with an exquisite Baroque facade and, unusually for Peru, very simple and humble inside, in line with the local Aymara Indians' austere attitude to religion. High up, overlooking the town and Plaza de Armas, the **Huajsapata Park** sits on a prominent hill, a short but steep climb up Jirón Deustua, right into Jirón Llave, left up Jirón Bolognesei, then left again up the Pasaje Contique steps. Often crowded with young children playing on the natural rock-slides and cuddling couples, Huajsapata offers stupendous views across the bustle of Puno to the serene blue of Titicaca and its unique skyline.

In the northern section of town, at the end of the pedestrianized Jirón Lima, you'll find an attractive busy little plaza called **Parque Pino**, dominated in equal parts by the startlingly blue **Church of San Juan** and the scruffy, insistent shoeshine boys. Two blocks east from here, towards the lake, you find the **old central market**, which is small and very dirty. Head from here down Avenida los Incas and you'll find a much more substantial **street market**, whose liveliest day is Saturday.

Moored down in the port, the nineteenth-century British-built steamship, the **Yarari** (Wed–Sun 8am–5pm; free; for guided tours call ⓣ054/622215), provides a fascinating insight into maritime life on Lago Titicaca over a hundred years ago and the military and entrepreneurial mindset of Peru in those days. Delivered by mule from the coast of Peru in over 1300 different pieces, it started life as a Peruvian navy gunship complete with bulletproof windows, but ended up delivering the mail around the lake.

Eating, drinking and nightlife

Puno's **restaurant** and **nightlife** scene is fairly busy and revolves mainly around Jirón Lima, but bear in mind that places shut relatively early – not much happens after 11pm on a weekday. The city's strong tradition as one of the major Andean folklore centres in South America means that you're almost certain to be exposed to at least one live band an evening. The food in Puno is nothing to write home about, but the local delicacies of trout and kingfish (*pejerey*) are worth trying and are available in most restaurants.

Restaurants

Bar/Restaurant La Pascana Jr Lima 339–341. Particularly good for evening meals, with a fine selection for vegetarians and interesting murals on the walls.

La Casona Jr Lima 517. The best restaurant in town, particularly for evening meals, serving excellent *criolla* dishes in an attractive traditional environment. It is also something of a museum, with antique exhibits everywhere, and is very popular with locals.

Pizzeria La Taberna Jr Lima 453. A lively evening spot serving warming alcoholic drinks and scrumptious pizzas; the garlic bread baked in a real-fire oven is particularly good.

Restaurant Don Piero Jr Lima 364. A favourite with travellers, it's relatively inexpensive, has good breakfasts, a fine selection of cakes and a magazine rack for customer use.

Restaurant Internacional Corner of Libertad and Moquegua. Popular with locals for lunch and supper; they come for its good range of reasonably priced meals. Upstairs has the best atmosphere.

Bars and nightlife

Apu Salcantay Jr Lima 425. Good drinks and food at this bar, and the disco is accompanied by the latest Latin and European pop videos.

Casa del Abuelo On the corner of Tarapaca and Libertad. A folklore *peña* at its most lively on Sat nights.

Pizzeria Del Buho Libertad 386 and Jr Lima 347. Probably the best pizzas in Puno and a warm, pleasant environment to boot; a crowded and popular spot with travellers on Puno's cold, dark evenings; serves delicious mulled wines and often has good music.

Listings

Airline Faucett, Libertad 265 (☎054/355860 or 351301).

Banks and exchange Banco Continental, Lima 400; Banco de La Nacion, on the corner of Grau and Ayacucho 269; Banco de Credito, on the corner of Lima with Grau; and Banco del Sur, Arequipa 459. *Cambistas* hang out at the corner of Jr Tacna near the central market. There are *casas de cambios* at Tacna 232, Lima 440, and at Vilca Marilin, Tacna 255.

Bus companies Jr Tacna, Jr Melgar and Av Titicaca are the main areas for buses, but always check who is leaving for where and when. Companies and their terminals include: Altiplano, Av Titicaca 270 (☎054/369592), for Moquegua and Ilo; Cruz del Sur, Av Sol 668 (☎054/352451) for Cusco, Arequipa, the coast, Desaguaderos and La Paz; Dur Oriente, Av Titicaca 254 (☎054/368133), for Moquegua and Tacna; Expreso San Ramon, Jr Lampa 301 (☎054/352121), for Arequipa; Huanca, Melgar 250 (☎054/364335), for Cusco and Arequipa; Latino Tours, Av Titicaca 238 (☎054/364260), for Deasaguaderos, Moquegua, Tacna and Ilo; Ormeñol, Melgar 338 (☎054/352321) for Lima and Arequipa; Porvenir, Av Titicaca 258 (☎054/363627), for Moquegua and Tacna; Rodriguez, Melgar 328 (☎054/363741) for Lima and Arequipa; San Cristoval, Melgar 338 (☎054/352321) for Lima and Arequipa; San Martín, Av Titicaca 210 (☎054/363326), for Juliaca, Moquegua and Puno; Señor de Los Milagros, Melgar 308 (☎054/351481), for Lima; and Tranzela, Melgar 300 (☎054/364192), for Cusco and Arequipa.

Consulate Bolivia, Jr Arequipa 120 (☎054/351251).

Police The Tourist Police are at Jr Deusta 538 (☎054/357100).

Post office Moquegua 269.

Taxis ☎054/351616 or 332020.

Telephones and faxes Telefonica del Peru, corner of Federico More and Moquegua (daily 7am–11pm); and Mabel Telecommunications, Jr Lima 224 (Mon–Fri 7am–noon & 2–7pm).

Tour operators All Ways Travel, Jr Tacna 234 (☎054/355552, Ⓔawtperu@mail.cosapidata.com.pe); Lake Country Treks, Lima 458 (☎054/355785 or 352259); Tur Puno, Lambayeque 175 (☎054/352001, Ⓔturpuno@via_expresa.com).

Visas Migraciones Libertad 403 ☎054/357103 or 352801.

Tours around Puno

The streets of Puno are full of touts selling guided tours and trips, but don't be swayed, always go to a respected, established **tour company**, such as one of those listed below. There are four main local tours on offer in Puno, all of which will reward you with abundant bird and animal life, immense landscapes and genuine living traditions. The trip to **Sillustani** normally involves a three- or four-hour tour by minibus and costs US$5–8 depending on whether or not entrance and guide costs are included. Most other tours involve a combination of visits to the nearby **Uros Floating Islands** (half-day tour; US$5–10) and **Taquile and the Uros Islands** (full day from US$7, or from US$12 overnight). Of the independent tour **guides** operating in Puno, Andres Puelino Arucutipa Inta (☎054/353847 or 689775) is reliable and knowledgeable about the sites around Puno and Titicaca, while Andres Lopez is good and can be contacted through any of the town's hotels.

Lago Titicaca

An undeniably impressive sight, **Lago Titicaca**'s skies are vast, almost infinite, and deep, deep hues of blue; below this sits a usually placid mirror-like lake reflecting the big sky back on itself. A national reserve since 1978, the lake has over sixty varieties of birds, fourteen species of native fish and eighteen types of amphibians. It's also the world's largest high-altitude body of water, at 284m deep and more than 8500 square kilometres in area, fifteen times the size of Lake Geneva in Switzerland and higher and slightly bigger than Lake Tahoe in the US. It's often seen as three separate regions: curious Inca-built **Chullpa burial tombs** circle the lake and its man-made **Uros Floating Islands**. These islands have been inhabited since their construction centuries ago by Uros Indians who were retreating from more powerful neighbours like the Incas. More powerful and self-determined are the communities who live on the fixed islands of **Taquile** and **Amantani**, often described as the closest one can get to heaven by the few travellers who make it out this far into the lake. There are, in fact, more than seventy islands in the lake, the largest and most sacred being the **Island of the Sun**, an ancient Inca temple site on the Bolivian side of the border which divides the lake's southern shore. Titicaca is an Aymara word meaning "Puma's Rock", which refers to an unusual boulder on the Island of the Sun. The island is best visited from Copacabana in Bolivia, or through trips arranged by one of the tour companies in Puno (see box above).

Crossing into Bolivia

The most popular routes to Bolivia involve overland road travel, crossing the frontier either at **Yunguyo** or at the river border of **Desaguaderos** (this latter route is little frequented these days owing to the poor condition of the road). En route to either you'll pass by some of Titicaca's more interesting colonial settlements, each with its own individual styles of architecture. Several **bus companies** run services from Puno over these routes: Empresa Los Angeles has twice weekly buses to Desaguaderos (US$1.50, a 3hr trip); Tour Peru runs daily to Copacabana (US$1.50, also 3hr) and La Paz (US$6, a 7hr trip); Altiplano Buses go most days to La Paz (US$6); Colectur runs to Copacabana and La Paz daily for around US$5; and San Pedro Express runs daily to Yunguyo, Desaguaderos and Copacabana (US$8). From Yunguyo some buses connect with a minibus service to **Copacabana** (see p.232), then a Bolivian bus on to **La Paz** (see p.218), though many go straight on to both places, especially between June and August.

9.5

Huaraz and the Cordillera Blanca

Sliced north to south by parallel ranges of high Andean peaks, the Departmento of **Ancash**, some 200–300km north of Lima, unfurls along an immense desert coastline, where pyramids and ancient fortresses are scattered within easy reach of several small resorts linked by vast, empty Pacific beaches. Behind range the barren heights of the Cordillera Negra, and beyond that the spectacular backdrop of the snowcapped **Cordillera Blanca**; between the two the Huaraz Valley, known locally as the **Callejón de Huaylas**, around 3000m above sea level, offers some of the best hiking and mountaineering in the Americas.

Nestling in the valley, the *Departmento's* capital, **Huaraz** – six or seven hours by car from Lima – makes an ideal base for exploring some of the best mountain lakes, ruins, glaciers and remote trails in the Andes. Over the last twenty years or so this region has become a major focus for mountaineers, and Huaraz, the vital centre of this inland region, is the place to stock up, hire guides and mules, and relax after a breathtaking expedition. The city is close to scores of exhilarating mountain trails, as well as the ancient Andean treasure, **Chavín de Huantar**, an impressive stone temple complex which was at the centre of a culturally significant puma-worshipping religious movement just over 2500 years ago.

Huaraz

Less than a century ago, **HUARAZ** – some 400km from Lima – was still a fairly isolated community, barricaded to the east by the dazzling snowcapped peaks of the Cordillera Blanca and separated from the coast by the dry, dark Cordillera Negra. Between these two mountain chains the powerful Río Santa has formed a valley, the **Callejón de Huaylas**, a region with strong traditions of local independence and a history of revolt, led by native leader, the charismatic Pedro Pablo Atusparia, and thirteen other village mayors, who protested over excessive taxation and labour abuses. Today the town has a lively atmosphere and is an ideal springboard for exploring the surrounding mountains.

Arrival, information and city transport

Most people arrive in Huaraz by **bus** from Lima, which takes eight or nine hours (US$8–12). Cruz del Sur, Jr Lucar y Torré 585 (☎044/722491), is, as usual, the safest and most comfortable option, closely followed by Movil Tours, Av Raimondi 730 (☎044/722555). Companies coming from and going to Trujillo (8–10hr; around US$8) include Cruz del Sur and Turismo Chimbote, Av Raimondi 815 (☎044/721984). Coming from or going to Chimbote (5–7hr; US$7) or Caraz (6–8hr; US$7), you'll probably travel with Turismo Chimbote, or Empressa Huandoy, Av Fitzcarral 261 (☎044/722502).

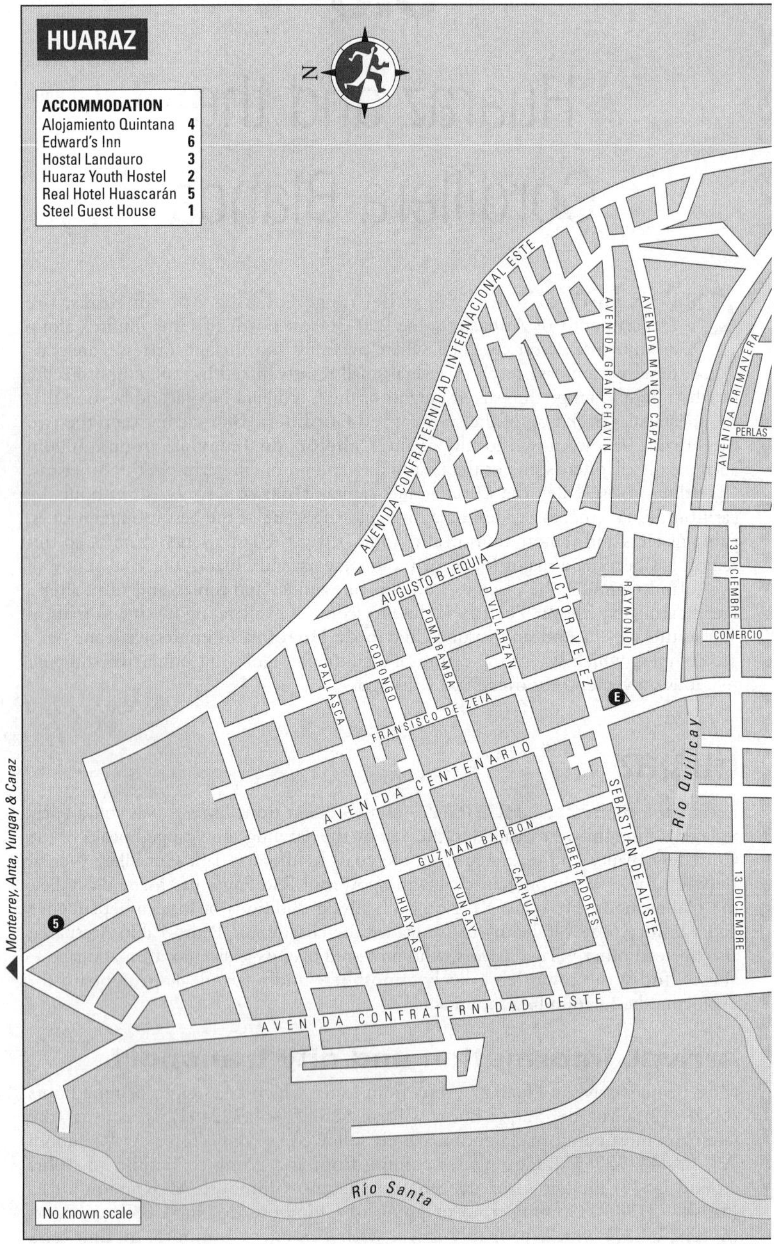

HUARAZ

N

ACCOMMODATION

Alojamiento Quintana	4
Edward's Inn	6
Hostal Landauro	3
Huaraz Youth Hostel	2
Real Hotel Huascarán	5
Steel Guest House	1

AVENIDA CONFRATERNIDAD INTERNACIONAL ESTE
AVENIDA GRAN CHAVIN
AVENIDA MANCO CAPAT
AVENIDA PRIMAVERA
PERLAS
13 DICIEMBRE
COMERCIO
RAYMONDI
VICTOR VELEZ
D VILLARZAN
AUGUSTO B LEQUIA
POMABAMBA
CORONGO
PALLASCA
FRANSISCO DE ZEIA
AVENIDA CENTENARIO
SEBASTIAN DE ALISTE
Río Quillcay
GUZMAN BARRON
LIBERTADORES
CARHUAZ
YUNGAY
HUAYLAS
13 DICIEMBRE
AVENIDA CONFRATERNIDAD OESTE
E
5
Monterrey, Anta, Yungay & Caraz
Río Santa
No known scale

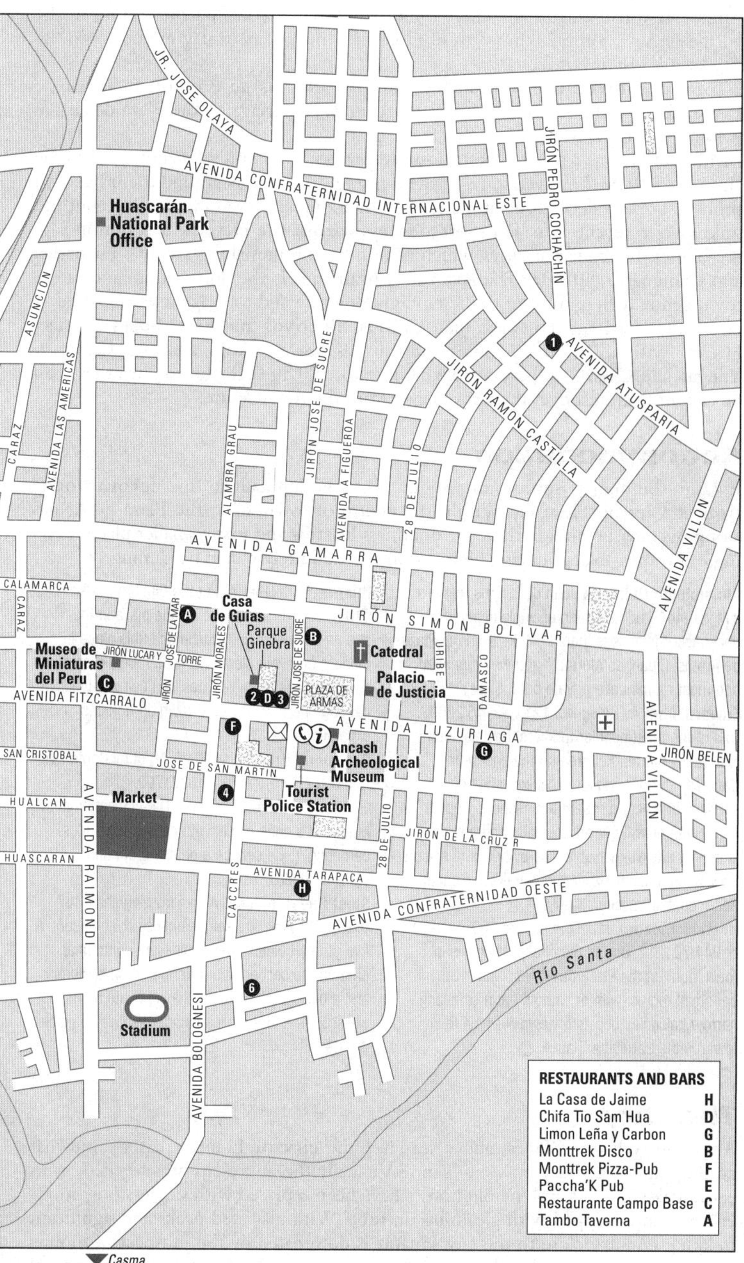

Mirador de Rataquena
JR. JOSE OLAYA
AVENIDA CONFRATERNIDAD INTERNACIONAL ESTE
JIRÓN PEDRO COCHACHÍN
Huascarán National Park Office
ASUNCION
AVENIDA LAS AMERICAS
CARAZ
AVENIDA ATUSPARIA
JIRÓN RAMON CASTILLA
JIRÓN JOSE DE SUCRE
AVENIDA A FIGUEROA
28 DE JULIO
ALAMBRA GRAU
AVENIDA GAMARRA
AVENIDA VILLON
CALAMARCA
Casa de Guias
Parque Ginebra
JIRÓN SIMON BOLIVAR
Museo de Miniaturas del Peru
JIRÓN LUCAR Y TORRE
JIRÓN JOSE DE LA MAR
JIRÓN MORALES
JIRÓN JOSE DE SUCRE
Catedral
URIBE
DAMASCO
Palacio de Justicia
PLAZA DE ARMAS
AVENIDA FITZCARRALO
AVENIDA LUZURIAGA
Ancash Archeological Museum
SAN CRISTOBAL
JOSE DE SAN MARTIN
JIRÓN BELEN
Tourist Police Station
HUALCAN
Market
AVENIDA RAIMONDI
JIRÓN DE LA CRUZ R
HUASCARAN
CACCRES
AVENIDA TARAPACA
AVENIDA CONFRATERNIDAD OESTE
Río Santa
Stadium
AVENIDA BOLOGNESI
Casma
RESTAURANTS AND BARS
La Casa de Jaime H
Chifa Tio Sam Hua D
Limon Leña y Carbon G
Monttrek Disco B
Monttrek Pizza-Pub F
Paccha'K Pub E
Restaurante Campo Base C
Tambo Taverna A

Few people arrive in the Callejón de Huaylas **by air** since there is no regular service, though Aero Condor fly from Lima around once a week between June and August. If you do arrive by air, you're dropped off at a small airstrip close to the village of Anta, some 23km north of Huaraz; from here it's thirty minutes into the city by *colectivo* or bus.

Tourist information is available from the Oficina de Promocion Turistica, Pasaje Alfonso Martel Oficina 1, just off Avenida Luzuriaga by the Plaza de Armas (Mon–Fri 9am–1pm & 5–8pm, Sat 9am–1pm).

Much of Huaraz town can be negotiated on foot once you've acclimatized to the altitude (3091m); however, some of the more remote sectors around the urban area should not be walked alone at night since mugging and even rape are rare but not unknown in recent years. For short journeys **within the city**, the best option is to use one of the regular *colectivos*, which run on fixed routes along avenidas Luzuriaga and Centenario (40–60¢). The **Avenida Luzuriaga is** the north–south axis of the town centre, where most of the restaurants, nightlife and tour agencies are based. A city centre **taxi** ride costs less than US$1. **Colectivos** and **local buses** connect Huaraz with all the main towns and villages north – Anta, Marcara, Carhuaz, Yungay and Caraz – at very reasonable rates (US$0.50–2 for up to 2hr); these can be caught from just over the river bridge from the town centre.

Accommodation

Even in the high season, around August, it's rarely difficult to find **accommodation** at a reasonable price. Within the centre of town, from the Plaza de Armas along Avenida Luzuriaga, there are countless **hostels** and many smaller places renting out rooms; except during high season it is definitely worth bargaining.

Alojamiento Quintana Juan de la Crus Romero 411 ⓣ044/726060. An increasingly popular backpacker joint, less than 3 blocks from the Plaza de Armas. Clean, comfortable and well managed, and most rooms have private bath. ❸–❹

Edward's Inn Av Bolognesi 121 ⓣ044/722692. One of the most popular trekkers' hostels, found just below the market area (at the end of Jr Caceres) and offering an excellent range of services in a very pleasant atmosphere. Rooms come with or without private bath, and hot water is almost always available. The owner, who speaks English, is a highly experienced trekker, climber and mountain rescuer. ❷–❸

Hostal Landauro Jr José de Sucre 109 ⓣ044/721212. One of the cheapest places in town, right on the Plaza de Armas, with pleasant but small rooms (with or without bath) set along narrow balconies boasting views over the town towards the Cordillera Blanca. ❷

Huaraz Youth Hostel Parque Ginebra 28-G ⓣ044/721811. On a quaint little plaza in the streets behind Avenida Luzuriaga, this place is modern and very clean, with communal rooms and showers at reasonable rates. You can safely leave baggage here while out of town on trekking expeditions. ❷

Real Hotel Huascarán Block 10 of Av Centenario ⓣ044/721640, 722821 or 721709, ⓔjezquerra@infotex.com.pe. The biggest hotel in Huaraz. It's quite plush, with cabins and suites, carpeting, good service a games room and pleasant bedrooms. ❼

Steel Guest House C Alejandro Maguina 1467 ⓣ044/729709, ⓔsteelguesthouse@yahoo.com. A five-storey building with a pleasant communal area on the second floor offering TV, small library and a billiard table. Rooms have private baths, hot water 24hr and there's a laundry service available. ❸–❹

The City

Although well over 3000m above sea level, the **city of Huaraz** has a somewhat cosmopolitan and very busy city centre. Virtually the entire city was levelled by an earthquake in 1970, and the old houses have been replaced with single-storey modern structures topped with gleaming tin roofs. With glaciated peaks and significant trekking country close to the city, Huaraz is dominated by the prospect of mountaineering, and the city's only real tourist attraction is the **Ancash Archeological Museum**, Av Luzuriaga 762, facing the modern Plaza de Armas (Mon–Sat

8.30am–6.30pm & Sun 9am–noon; US$1.50). Fronting attractive, landscaped gardens, this small but interesting place contains a superb collection of Chavín, Chimu, Wari, Moche and Recauy ceramics, as well as some expertly trepanned skulls. On the other side of the Plaza de Armas from the museum is the **Catedral** (daily 7am–7pm; free). Completely rebuilt after being destroyed in the 1970 earthquake, it has nothing special to see inside, but its vast blue-tiled roof makes a good landmark and, if you look closely, appears to mirror one of the glaciated mountain peaks, the Nevado Huanstán (6395m), behind.

Eating, drinking and entertainment

There's no shortage of **restaurants** in Huaraz, though they do vary considerably in value and quality. There's also a lively nightlife scene, with several **peñas** hosting traditional Andean music, as well as a few **clubs** where locals and tourists can relax, keep warm and unwind during the evenings or at weekends.

Restaurants

La Casa de Jaime A Gridilla 267, four blocks west of the Plaza de Armas. An inexpensive and very friendly place where they serve a mix of Peruvian meals and tasty snacks. You're also likely to meet other travellers, trekkers and climbers.

Chifa Tio Sam Hua In the passage at block 8 of Av Luzuriaga. The most traditional and arguably the best *chifa* in Huaraz, they offer a broad selection of Chinese and Peruvian meals in a friendly environment.

Limon Leña y Carbon Luzuriaga 1002 ⓣ044/693360. A really good seafood resaurant which has fresh fish delivered from Chimbote; they also serve local trout, meat dishes and pizzas in the evening. Daily 9am–midnight.

Monttrek Pizza-pub Luzuriaga 646 ⓣ044/721124, ⓔmonttrek@terra.com.pe. A spacious, very popular place with trekkers and a great meeting place with a useful noticeboard for contacting like-minded backpackers. Serves delicious food and plays good music. Has a climbing wall, maps and aerial photos of the region.

Restaurante Campo Base Av Luzuriaga 407 ⓣ044/725772, ⓔandeway@terra.com.pe. A good pizzeria that also serves local and international dishes well aimed at the trekking and climbing crowd. Excellent food and drinks, often hosting live folk music at weekends. It's the best place in the city for *cuy a la Huaracina* (guinea pig, Huaraz style); open 4.30–11pm daily.

Pubs, music bars and clubs

Monttrek Disco By the Plaza de Armas on Jr José de Sucre. One of the better discos in town; large and quite exciting music especially at weekends.

Paccha'K Pub Centenario 290. A good trekkers' joint with a noticeboard for messages that hosts lively Andean folk music shows most weekends.

Tambo Taverna Jr José de la Mar 776. A restaurant-cum-*peña* serving good drinks, with occasional live music after 10pm – one of Huaraz's best nightspots.

Hiking in the Huaraz region

You don't have to be a mountaineer to enjoy the high Andes of Ancash, and there is plenty of scope for trekking as well in the two major mountain chains accessible from Huaraz. The closest is the **Cordillera Blanca**, detailed on p.933. The **Cordillerra Huayhuash**, about 50km south of the Cordilerra Blanca, is still relatively off the beaten tourist trail. About 31km long it is dominated by the Yerupajá glacier, and *Andinistas* claim it to be one of the most spectacular trekking routes in the world. Wherever you end up, be sure to pay heed to the rules of **responsible trekking**: carry away your waste, particularly above the snow line, where even organic waste does not decompose (if you can pack it in the first place, you can pack it back up). Note too that you should always use a camping stove – campfires are strictly prohibited in Huascarán National Park, and wood is scarce anyway. Just as important, though, is to realize that the solar irradiation in this art of the Andes is stronger than that found in the north American Rockies, the Alps or even the Himalayas. This creates unique glacier conditions, making the ice here less stable and consequently the addition of an experienced local guide essential for the safety

Tours and activities in and around Huaraz

Most of the tour agencies in Huaraz can be found along Avenida Luzuriaga and offer guided **city tours**, including stopping at all the major panoramic viewpoints (4hr; US$8). For the surrounding area the most popular outings are to the **Llanganuco Lakes** (8hr; US$10–15 per person), **Chavín de Huantar** (9–11hr; US$10–15 per person), including lunch in Chavín before exploring ruins, and to the edge of the **Pastoruri Glacier** at 5240m (8hr; US$10 per person). Most agents can also arrange trips to the thermal baths at **Chancos** (4hr; US$8) and **Caraz** (6hr; US$10), and some offer **adventure activities** in the area. Always check if the guide leading your tour speaks English.

Baloo Tours Av Julian de Morales 605, Huaraz ⓣ044/723928, ⓔnilocamp@hotmail.com. Expeditions throughout the Cordillera Blanca and Huayhuash, with mountaineering equipment for rent, including tents.

Mountain Bike Adventures Castilla Postal 111, Jr Lucre y Torre 530, Huaraz ⓣ044/724259, ⓔjulio.olaza@terra.com.pe. Customizable guided bike tours with mountain bikes to rent. They also have English speaking guides and offer a book exchange in their office.

Pablo Tours Av Luzuriaga 501, Huaraz ⓣ044/721145, ⓔpablot@net.telematic.com.pe. One of the best agencies for standard tours and good for organized treks, though they get booked up very quickly.

Pony Expeditions Sucre 1266, Caraz ⓣ044/791642, ⓔponyexp@terra.com.pe. A very professional organization that provides outfits and guides expeditions in the area.

of any serious climbing or ice-walking expedition. It's also vital to be fit, particularly if you are going it alone.

If you intend to hike at all, it's essential to spend at least a couple of days **acclimatizing** to the altitude beforehand; if you intend high mountain climbing, this should be extended to at least five days. Although Huaraz itself is 3060m above sea level, most of the Cordilleras' more impressive peaks are over 6000m. If you're going to trek in Huascarán National Park, register beforehand with the **Park Office**, at the top end of Avenida Raymondi (ⓣ044/722086), and at the **Casa de Guias**, Parque Ginebra 28-G (Mon–Fri 9am–1pm & 4–8pm, Sat 9am–1pm; ⓣ044/721811, ⓦclientes.telematic.com.pe/agmp), where there's also a good contact noticeboard, worth checking to see if there are any groups about to leave on treks that you might want to join. The National Police (ⓣ044/793327, ⓔusam@pnp.gob.pe) have a mountain rescue team.

Ideally you should have detailed maps and one or other of these excellent **guidebooks**: *Backpacking and Trekking in Peru and Bolivia*, *Trails of the Cordillera Blanca and Huayhuash* or *The High Andes: A Guide for Climbers*. **Maps**, too, are available there, or from the Casa de Guias, where there's also a list of official local mountain guides, as well as lots of local expertise and the Andean Mountain Rescue Corp on hand. For additional information on trekking in the region, try the tourist information office (see p.930).

There are three levels of guides available: certified mountain guides, who cost from US$60 a day; mountain guides undergoing the one year trial period after training, from US$40 a day; and trekking guides, who cost from US$30 a day. Note that these costs don't include transport or accommodation. For local tour operators offering guided treks, see the box above. Porters, mule drivers (*arrieros*) and cooks will each cost you US$5–20 a day, not to mention extra charges for pack-carrying mules or llamas.

North to Caraz and the Cordillera Blanca

No one should come to the **Callejón de Huaylas** without visiting the northern valley towns, and many travellers will want to use them as bases from which to explore one or more of the ten snow-free passes in the Cordillera Blanca. Simply combining any two of these passes makes for a superb week's trekking. Further along the valley north from Huaraz are the distinct settlements of **Yungay** and **Caraz**. Physically they have little in common but both are popular bases from which to begin treks into the **Cordillera Blanca**. The highest range in the tropical world, the Cordillera Blanca consists of around 35 peaks poking their snowy heads over the 6000m mark, and until early in the twentieth century, when the glaciers began to recede, this white crest could be seen from the Pacific. Above Yungay, and against the sensational backdrop of Peru's highest peak, **Huascarán** (6768m), are the magnificent **Llanganuco Lakes**, whose waters change colour according to the time of year and the sun's daily movements, and are among the most accessible of the Cordillera Blanca's three hundred or so glacial lakes.

Fortunately, most of the Cordillera Blanca falls under the auspices of the **Huascarán National Park**, and the habitat has been left relatively unspoiled. Among the more exotic **wildlife** that hikers can hope to come across are the viscacha (Andean rabbit-like creatures), vicuña, grey deer, pumas, foxes, the rare spectacled bear and several species of hummingbirds.

Hiking in the Cordillera Blanca

There are a multitude of excellent hikes in the Cordillera Blanca, almost all of which require acclimatization to the rarified mountain air, a certain degree of fitness, good camping equipment, all your food and good maps. Hiking in this region is a serious affair and you will need to be properly prepared. Bear in mind that for some of the hikes you may need guides and mules to help carry the equipment at this altitude. One of the most popular routes, the **Llanganuco to Santa Cruz Loop**, is a well-trodden trail offering spectacular scenery, some fine places to camp and a relatively easy walk that can be done in under a week even by inexperienced hikers. There are shorter walks, such as the trails around the **Pitec Quebrada**, within easy striking distance of Huaraz, and a number of other loops like the **Llanganuco to Chancos** trek.

Caraz and around

The attractive town of **CARAZ** is little less than 20km down the Santa Valley from Yungay and sits quietly at an altitude of 2285m well below the enormous Huandoy Glacier. Palm trees and flowers adorn a classic colonial **Plaza de Armas**, while the small daily **market**, three blocks north of the plaza, is normally vibrant with activity, good for fresh food, colourful basketry, traditional gourd bowls, religious candles and hats. Nearby there are the interesting archeological ruins of **Tunshucayco**, a couple of kilometres northeast of town along 28 de Julio, close to the Lago Parón turnoff; probably the largest ruins in the Callejón de Hualyas they apparently date back to the pre-Chavín era.

One of the best **places to stay** is the modern *Hostal Perla de Los Andes,* Plaza de Armas (Ⓣ044/792007; ❸) – spic, span and thus completely out of character with the rest of Caraz – offering comfortable rooms with hot water, private bath and TV; it also has a very nice restaurant. Also near the plaza, the efficient and clean *Hostal Chavín*, Jr San Martín 1135 (Ⓣ044/791171; ❷), offers some rooms with private bath. The cheapest place in town is the **youth hostel**, *Los Pinos* at Parque San Martín 103 (Ⓣ044/7791130, Ⓔlospinos@terra.com.pe; ❶), which also offers camping spaces for US$2 a person and has reasonable Internet facilities. One other rather unusual hostel is the *Hostal Chamanna*, a little out of town down 28 de Julio, at Av Nueva Victoria 185 (☎044/682802, Ⓦwww.welcome.to/chamanna; ❹), which is set in a lovely labyrinth of gardens, streams and patios.

For **places to eat**, the *Café Oasis*, Jr Raymondi 425 (☎044/791785) just a small stone's throw from the plaza is good and also has four pretty, cheap rooms. Also on the plaza, the *Polleria El Mirador* does reasonably priced lunches and evening meals of Peruvian and international food. The *Restaurant Esmeralda*, Jr Alfonso Ugarte 404, does fine simple breakfasts. The helpful **tourist information** office (Mon–Sat 7.45am–1pm & 2.30–5.30pm), with maps and brochures covering the attractions and some of the hikes (the relatively demanding 6–8hr Patapata walk) in the immediate area, is on the Plaza de Armas, while the **telephone office** is at Raimondi 410. For trekking **guides**, local information or help organizing or fitting out an expedition, the excellent Pony Expeditions (see box on p.932) can't be beaten. Most of the **bus** offices are along calles Daniel Villar and Cordova, within a block or two of the Plaza de Armas. **Colectivos** for Huaraz leave from just behind the market more or less every thirty minutes.

Chavín de Huantar

Only 30km southeast of Huari, or a three- to four-hour journey from Huaraz, the magnificent temple complex of **CHAVÍN DE HUANTAR** is the most important site associated with the Chavín cult, and a fascinating place for anyone even vaguely interested in Peruvian archeology. The religious cult that inspired Chavín's construction also influenced subsequent cultural development throughout Peru, right up until the Spanish Conquest some 2500 years later, and the temple complex of Chavín de Huantar is equal in importance, if not grandeur, to most of the sites around Cusco.

The vast majority of people approach the temple complex from Huaraz. **Buses** leave Huaraz daily around 10am (US$4; a 3–4hr trip) for Chavín, while all the tour companies in Huaraz (see box on p.932) offer a slightly faster though more expensive service (US$10–15; a 3hr trip). A more adventurous way to reach Chavín is by following the two- to four-day **trail** over the hills from **Olleros**. *Colectivos* leave daily every thirty minutes from the end of Jirón Caceres, for Olleros (US$1), from where the hike is fairly simple and clearly marked all the way. It's quite a walk, so take maps and, ideally, arrange a guide and pack-llamas in Huaraz.

The temple complex

North of Lima, the magnificent temple complex of **Chavín de Huantar** (daily 8am–5pm; US$1) evolved and elaborated its own brand of religious cultism during the first millennium BC. By 300 BC, Chavín was at the height of its power and one of the world's largest religious centres, with about three thousand resident priests and temple attendants. Most archeologists agree that the U-shaped temples were dedicated to powerful mountain spirits or deities, who controlled meteorological phenomena, in particular rainfall that was vital to the survival and wealth of the people. These climatic concerns became increasingly important as the ancient Peruvians became increasingly dependent on agriculture rather than hunting.

The complex's main building consists of a central rectangular block with two wings projecting out to the east. The large, southern wing, known as the **Castillo**, is the most conspicuous feature of the site: Massive, almost pyramid shaped, the platform is built of dressed stone with gargoyles attached, though few remain now. Some way in front of the Castillo, down three main flights of steps, is the **Plaza Hundida**, or sunken plaza, covering about 250 square metres with a rectangular, stepped platform to either side. Here, the thousands of pilgrims thought to have worshipped at Chavín would gather during the appropriate fiestas. Standing in the Plaza Hundida, facing towards the Castillo, you'll see on your right the **original temple**, now just a palatial ruin dwarfed by the neighbouring Castillo. Among the fascinating recent finds from the area are bone snuff tubes, beads, pendants, needles, ceremonial shells (imported from Ecuador) and some quartz crystals associated with ritual sites. One quartz crystal covered in red pigment was found in a grave, placed after death in the mouth of the deceased.

Practicalities

The pretty village of **Chavín de Huantar**, with its whitewashed walls and traditional tiled roofs, is just a couple of hundred metres from the ruins and has a reasonable supply of basic amenities. The best **accommodation** is at the relatively new and very good-value *Hotel La Casona de JB*, Wiracocha 130 (Ⓣ044/754020; ❸), just next door to the town hall on the plaza, with hot showers. There's also a friendly family lodging at the *Casa del Senor Chapaco* (❷), while *Hotel Inca* (❷), at Wiracocha 160, has hot water most evenings but shared bathrooms, or try the basic but clean *Hotel Monte Carlo*, at C 17 de Enero 1015 (❷), on the plaza. Alternatively, you can **camp** by the Baños Quercos thermal springs (daily 7am–6pm; 50¢) some twenty minutes' stroll from the village, 2km up the valley. For **places to eat** the best bets are the *Restaurant Chavín Turistico*, 17 de Enero Sur 439, or the *Restaurant La Ramada*, a few doors further up the same road at 17 de Enero 577. Getting back to Huaraz or Catac, there are buses daily from Chavín, more or less on the hour from 3 to 6pm. There's a **post and telephone office** at C 17 de Enero 365 (6.30am–10pm), plus a small **tourist information** office on the corner of the Plaza de Armas, next to the market, though it doesn't have regular hours.

9.6

Trujillo and the north

Peru's northern capital, **Trujillo** is small enough to get to know in a couple of days, and has the feel of a lively, cosmopolitan regional city. The pleasant coastal **climate** here is warm and dry without the fogs you get around Lima, but not as hot as the deserts further north.

North of Trujillo, but largely beyond the scope of this chapter on Peru, the vast desert stretches all the way to the Ecuadorian frontier at Tumbes, passing two major cities – Chiclayo and **Piura** – en route as well as Peru's trendiest beach at **Mancora**. Around Chiclayo, for those with sufficient time, there are scores of wonderful pre-Inca pyramids, tombs and temple sites, many very rich in gold and other precious grave goods which can now be seen in the excellent new **museums at Lambayeque and Ferreñafe**, both within half an hour's drive of Chiclayo city centre. In the Andes to the east of Trujillo and Chiclayo lies the city of **Cajamarca**, a town and region full of fine Inca remains and astonishing pre-Inca relics and the place where Pizarro captured and eventually put to death the Inca Emperor, Atahualpa. Further east from here, but easier to access from Chiclayo, was once the domain of the cloud people, or Chachapoyas culture whose fantastic stone walled citadel – Keulap – still stands as symbol of Peru's non-Inca heritage in the cloud-forests close to the modern town of Chachapoyas and in a region full of unique tombs on cliffs and scattered ancient communities.

Trujillo

Pizarro, on his second voyage to Peru in 1528, sailed by the site of ancient Chan Chan, then still a major city and an important regional centre of Inca rule. He returned to establish a Spanish colony in the same valley, naming it **TRUJILLO** in December 1534 after his birthplace in Estremadura, and officially founding it in March 1535. A year later, in 1536, the town was besieged by the Inca Manco's forces during the second rebellion against the conquistadores. Many thousands of Conchuco Indian warriors, allied with the Incas, swarmed down to Trujillo, killing Spaniards and collaborators on the way and offering their victims to Catequil, the tribal deity. Surviving this attack, Trujillo grew to become the main port of call for the Spanish treasure fleets, sailors wining and dining here on their way between Lima and Panama.

Trujillo continued to be a centre of popular rebellion, declaring its independence from Spain in the Plaza de Armas in 1820, long before the Liberators arrived, and rising in bloody revolt after the APRA (American Popular Revolutionary Alliance) was outlawed in 1931. Revolutionary land reform of the 1960s gave way to the violence of the Sendero Luminoso during the mid-1980s and early 1990s. Nowadays the city, just eight hours north of Lima along the Panamerican Highway, looks every bit the oasis it is, standing in a relatively green, irrigated valley bounded by arid desert at the foot of the brown Andes mountains. It hardly seems a city of nearly a million inhabitants – walk twenty minutes in any direction and you're out in open fields, hedged by flowering shrubs.

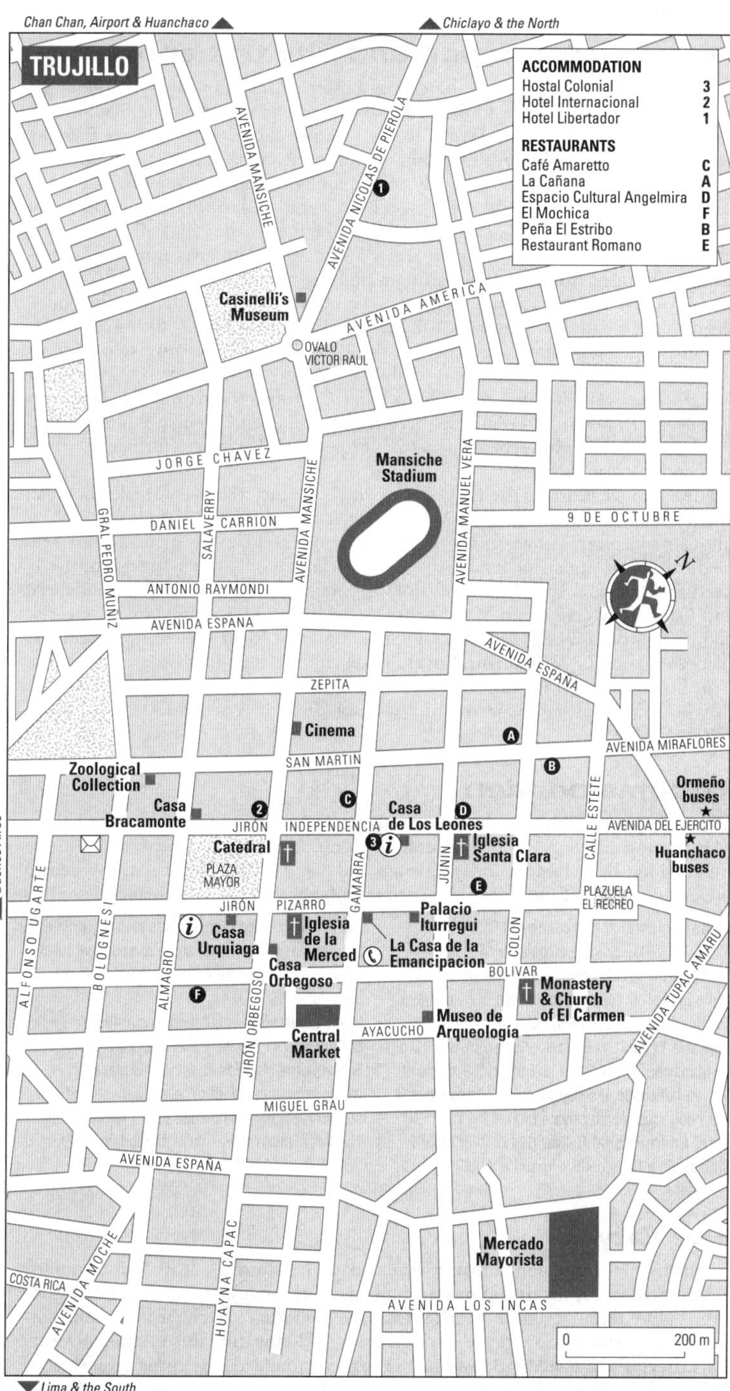
TRUJILLO
Chan Chan, Airport & Huanchaco
Chiclayo & the North
ACCOMMODATION
Hostal Colonial 3
Hotel Internacional 2
Hotel Libertador 1
RESTAURANTS
Café Amaretto C
La Cañana A
Espacio Cultural Angelmira D
El Mochica F
Peña El Estribo B
Restaurant Romano E
AVENIDA MANSICHE
AVENIDA NICOLAS DE PIEROLA
Casinelli's Museum
AVENIDA AMERICA
OVALO VICTOR RAUL
JORGE CHAVEZ
Mansiche Stadium
AVENIDA MANUEL VERA
9 DE OCTUBRE
DANIEL CARRION
SALAVERRY
GRAL PEDRO MUÑIZ
ANTONIO RAYMONDI
AVENIDA ESPANA
ZEPITA
Cinema
AVENIDA MIRAFLORES
SAN MARTIN
Zoological Collection
Casa Bracamonte
Casa de Los Leones
Ormeño buses
JIRÓN INDEPENDENCIA
AVENIDA DEL EJERCITO
Catedral
Iglesia Santa Clara
CALLE ESTETE
Huanchaco buses
Buenos Aires
PLAZA MAYOR
JUNIN
GAMARRA
PLAZUELA EL RECREO
ALFONSO UGARTE
BOLOGNESI
JIRÓN PIZARRO
Palacio Iturregui
Casa Urquiaga
Iglesia de la Merced
La Casa de la Emancipacion
COLON
AVENIDA TUPAC AMARU
ALMAGRO
Casa Orbegoso
BOLIVAR
Monastery & Church of El Carmen
JIRÓN ORBEGOSO
Central Market
AYACUCHO
Museo de Arqueología
MIGUEL GRAU
AVENIDA ESPAÑA
HUAYNA CAPAC
Mercado Mayorista
COSTA RICA
AVENIDA MOCHE
AVENIDA LOS INCAS
0
200 m
Lima & the South

Arrival, information and city transport

You're most likely to arrive in the city by bus or *colectivo* from Lima. Most of the **buses** have terminals close to the centre of town near the Mansiche Stadium, on avenidas Daniel Carrion or España to the southwest, or east of it along Ejercito. **Colectivos** also mostly leave from and end up on Avenida España. If you're arriving by day it's fine to walk to the city centre, though at night it's best to take a taxi (US$2–3). If you **fly** into the city, you'll arrive at the airport (information on ⓣ044/246000 or 252301), near Huanchaco. Taxis into the city will cost around US$5, or you can get a bus, which leaves every twenty minutes from the roundabout just outside the airport gates, for around 30¢.

For **tourist information** and photocopied city maps, go to the very helpful i-Peru office at Jr Pizarro 402 (Mon–Fri 9am–5pm; ⓣ044/294561, ⓔiperutrujillo@promperu.gob.pe) on the Plaza Mayor. The **tourist police**, at POLTUR, Jr Independencia 630 (daily 9am–1pm & 4–7pm; ⓣ044/291705 or 200200) are very helpful, too. The official **Camara Regional de Turismo** (Mon–Fri 9am–1pm & 4–8pm, Sat 9–1pm), also useful and friendly, is next door to the Tourist Police at Independencia 628 (ⓣ044/203718) where further information and maps are available.

The colonial heart of the city consists of about fifty relatively small bocks, all encircled by the Avenida España. More or less at the centre of the circle is the ubiquitous main plaza, known as the Plaza Mayor or the Plaza de Armas. From here begin the main streets of Pizarro, Independencia; the only other streets you really need to know are San Martín and Bolivar, parallel to Pizarro and Independencia, and Gamarra, where many of the banks are to be found. Getting around the city and its environs is cheap and easy, using the numerous **local buses** and **colectivos** (flat rates around 30¢) and **minibuses**. **Taxis** cost less than US$1 for a ride within Trujillo and can be hailed anywhere, but if you need to call one, Taxi Seguro (ⓣ044/253473) is best. **Car rental** is available from Jr Ayacucho 414, Oficina 11 (ⓣ044/234985).

Accommodation

The majority of Trujillo's **hotels** are within a few blocks of the central Plaza Mayor: most of them are to the south, but a number of reasonable ones are to be found along Jirón Pizarro, Independencia and San Martín. However, many people prefer to stay out of the city centre, at the nearby beach resort of Huanchaco.

Hostal Colonial Jr Independencia 618 ⓣ044/268261, ⓔhostalcolonialtruji@hotmail.com. An attractive, central place, where some English is spoken. Rooms are fine and have TV, plus there's a patio and café. ❺

Hosteria El Sol Los Brillantes 224, off block 12 of Av Mansiche ⓣ044/231933. Built in the shape of a Bavarian castle, it's slightly out of the way but has good rooms with private bath. ❸

Hotel Internacional Bolivar 646 ⓣ044/245392. Situated in a fairly central, grand old building, with clean, if very basic rooms. It's reasonably priced but not that comfortable; some rooms have toilets but no showers, while a few have full private bathrooms. ❷

Hotel Libertador Jr Independencia 485 ⓣ044/232741, ⓦwww.libertador.com.pe. Formerly the *Hotel de Turistas*, this place is particularly grand, with excellent service and a superb restaurant renowned for its *criolla* dishes. The large, plush rooms have all mod cons. ❼

The City

From the graceful colonial mansions and Baroque churches at its heart, Trujillo's grid system gives way to commercial buildings, light industry and shantytown suburbs, before thinning out into rich sugar-cane fields that stretch far into the neighbouring Chicama Valley. At the city's centre is its dominating force – the university **La Libertad**, founded by Bolivar in 1824, and surrounded by elegant, Spanish-style streets, lined with ancient green ficus trees and overhung by long wooden-railed balconies. **Gamarra** is the main commercial street, dominated by ugly, modern, brick and glass buildings, shops, hotels and restaurants. The other main street, older and more attractive, is **Jirón Pizarro**, where much of the city's nightlife can be experienced and which has been pedestrianized from block 8 to the pleasant **Plazuela El Recreo**. Life for most Trujillanos still revolves around the old town, centered on **Plaza Mayor** and bounded roughly by San Martín, Ayacucho, Almagro and Colón.

Around Plaza Mayor

Trujillo's **Plaza Mayor** (also known as the Plaza de Armas) is packed with sharp-witted shoeshine boys around the central statue – the *Heroes of the Wars of Independence*. Besides a couple of beautiful colonial mansions, Plaza Mayor is also home to the city's **Catedral** (daily 6–9am & 5–9pm; free), built in the mid-seventeenth century, then rebuilt the following century after earthquake damage. Known locally as the Basilica Menor, it's plain by Peruvian standards but houses some colourful Baroque sculptures and a handful of paintings by the Quiteña school (a style of painting that originated in eighteenth-century Quito). Inside the cathedral, a **museum** (daily 8am–2pm; US$2) exhibits a range of mainly eighteenth- and nineteenth-century religious paintings and sculptures. Just behind the plaza at San Martín 368, is a **zoological collection** (Mon–Fri 7am–7pm; 70¢), full of dozens of bizarre stuffed animals from the coastal desert and Andean regions as well as a large bird display and lots of amazing sea creatures (including a now extinct crab some 70cms across) and a number of reptiles.

From Plaza Mayor to the Central Market

Just off the plaza, the **Iglesia de La Merced**, Jr Pizarro 550 (daily 8am–7pm; free), built in 1636, is worth a look for its unique priceless Rococo organ, plus its attractive gardens. Around the corner from here, between the Plaza de Armas and the Central Market, stands the most impressive of Trujillo's colonial houses – the **Casa Orbegoso**, at Jr Orbegoso 553 (Mon–Sat 9am–4pm; free). This old mansion was the home of Orbegoso, former president of Peru, and houses displays of period furniture, glass and silverware amid very refined decor. Trujillo's main market, the **Central Market**, is 100m from here, on the corner of Ayacucho and Gamarra. From the market, head along Ayacucho until you reach the corner of Junin, and you'll find University's **Museo de Arqueología y Antropología**, Jr Junin 602 (Mon 9.30am–2pm, Tues–Fri 9.15am–1pm & 3–7pm, Sat & Sun 9.30–4pm; US$1.50; ⓣ044/249322 ⓦwww.unitru.edu.pe/arq/indice.html), which is pretty good, specializing in ceramics, early metallurgy, textiles and feather work.

East of Plaza Mayor

East of the plaza, on the corner of Jirón Pizarro and Gamarra, stands another of Trujillo's impressive mansions, **La Casa de la Emancipacion**, at Jr Pizarro 610 (Mon–Sat 10am–8pm; free). The building was remodelled in the mid-nineteenth century by the priest Pedro Madalengoitia (which is why it is also sometimes known as the Casa Madalengoitia), and is now head office of the Banco Continental. The main courtyard and entrance demonstrate a symmetrical and austere design, while the wide gallery has some impressive marble flooring. Inside, there are a couple of interesting late eighteenth-century murals depicting peasant life, and paintings or historical photographs are usually exhibited in at least one of its rooms.

Further down the same road, two blocks east of the Plaza Mayor, is the **Palacio Iturregui**, Jr Pizarro 688 (Mon–Fri 8.30–10.30am; free), a striking mid-nineteenth-century mansion. The highlight of the building is its pseudo-classical courtyard, with tall columns and an open roof. The courtyard is encircled by superb

△ A *caballitos del mar* fishing boat

galleries, and gives a wonderful view of the blue desert sky. At the eastern end of Jirón Pizarro, five blocks from the Plaza Mayor, there's a small but attractive square known as the restored **Plazuela El Recreo** where, under the shade of some vast 130-year-old ficus trees, a number of bars and foodstalls present a focus for young couples in the evenings. A couple of minutes' walk south from the Plazuela, on the corner of Colón and Bolivar, stands the most stunning of the city's religious buildings, the **Monastery and Church of El Carmen** (Mon–Sat 9am–1pm; US$1). Built in 1759 but damaged by earthquake in the same year, its two brick towers were then reconstructed of bamboo for safety. Inside you can see the single domed nave, with exquisite altars and a fine gold-leaf pulpit. The processional and recreational cloisters, both boasting fine vaulted arches and painted wooden columns, give access to the **Pinacoteca** (picture gallery), where Flemish works include a *Last Supper* (1625) by Otto van Veen, one of Rubens' teachers. There are also some interesting figures carved from *huamanga* stone and a room showing the process of restoring oil paintings.

Eating and drinking

There's no shortage of **bars** or **restaurants** in Trujillo. Some of the liveliest are along Jirón Independencia, Jirón Pizarro, Bolivar and Ayacucho, to the east of Plaza Mayor. A speciality of the city is good, reasonably priced **seafood**, which is probably best appreciated on the beach at the nearby resorts of Buenos Aires or Huanchaco (see p.942).

Restaurants and cafés

Café Amaretto Gamarra 368. Great coffee and good cakes, breakfast and snacks.

Espacio Cultural Angelmira on the corner of Independencia with Junin ☎044/297200. A plush and fascinating little café and bar with the associated Museo del Juguette (Toy Museum) in the same building as well as an art gallery and library.

El Mochica Bolivar 462. A superb, smart restaurant that offers reasonably priced seafood and exquisite *criolla* dishes.

Restaurant Romano Jr Pizarro 747 ☎044/252251. Small, friendly restaurant specializing in good Peruvian and Italian dishes. Good-sized portions, and exceptional value with its *economico familia* or *turistico* set menu, but it gets very busy in the evenings, so reservations are advised.

Clubs and peñas

Burbujas Night Club Av Tupac Amaru 340, Urbino H. Grande. A classic drinking and dancing club, popular with most age groups.

La Canana San Martín 791 (☎044/232503). A highly popular restaurant-*peña* as well as a *discoteca*, serving excellent meals, with a great atmosphere and good danceable shows that generally start after 10pm and carry on into the early hours.

Peña El Estribo San Martín 810. A large, newly restored and very lively dance and music venue with great weekend shows of coastal folklore and *musica negra*.

Listings

Airlines Aero Condor, Bolivar 613 (☎044/256794 or 232865); Aero Continente, Av España 307 (☎044/244592); Air Lider (☎044/204470); TANS, Av España 106 (☎044/255722); VARIG, Independencia 533 (☎044/254763). All flights out of Trujillo airport are liable to US$4 airport tax.

Banks and exchange Banco de Credito, Jr Gamarra 562; Banco Wiese, Jr Pizarro 314; Banco Latino, Jr Gamarra 574; Banco de La Nacion, Jr Almagro 297. America Tours, Jr Pizarro 470, Casa de Cambio, Jr Pizarro 336, or the Casa de Cambios Martelli, Jr Bolivar 665, give the best rates in town for dollars cash, or try the numerous *casas de cambio* found on block 6 of Pizarro.

Buses Alto Chicama, José Sabogal 305, Urbino Palermo (☎044/203659), for Chicama; Cruz del Sur, Amazonas 437 (☎044/261801), for all coastal destinations, Cajamarca and Huancayo; El Aguila, Nicaragua 220 (☎044/243211), for Lima, Chimbote and Huaraz; Linea, Av Carrion 140 for Chiclayo and Piura or from Av America Sur 2857 for Cajamarca, Huaraz or Lima; Ormeño, Av Ejercito 233 (☎044/259782), for the coast and international destinations; Transportes Chiclayo, Av

America Norte 2404 (ⓣ044/243341) for Chiclayo, Piura and Tumbes; Turismo Chimbote, Jr Nicaragua 194–198 (ⓣ044/245546), for Chimbote, Casma, Huaraz and Caraz.

Consulates UK, Av Jr Nazareth 312 ⓣ044/235548.

Internet facilities There are several Internet cafés along Pizarro (Macrochips at 183a, Masterdata at 197, Megaltel at 510, Net@House at 551) between the Plaza Mayor and Gamarra. A 24hr service is available at Interc@ll, Zepita 728 (ⓣ044/246465); otherwise, there's also Vizzio Internet at Ayacucho 496.

Post office Serpost (8am–7.45pm Mon–Sat) is based at Independencia 286, a block and a half southwest of the plaza.

Telephones Telefónica del Peru, Bolivar 658 (daily 7am–11pm). There's also a telephone and fax office at Bolivar 611.

Tour operators and guides Most companies offer tours to Chan Chan for US$15–20 (including the site museum, Huaca Arco Iris and Huaca Esmeralda), and to *huacas* del Sol and Luna from US$8. For Chicama sites, expect to pay US$20 plus. Recommended operators include Clara Brava's Tours, Cahuide 495 (ⓣ044/243347, ⓦwww.xanga.com/CasadeClara) who speak good English; Guia Tours, Independencia 580 (ⓣ044/234856); and Trujillo Tours, Diego de Almagro 301 (ⓣ044/257518, ⓔttours@pol.com.pe). Good English-speaking guides for Trujillo and around include Clara Brava (ⓣ044/243347), Takanga López Edith (ⓣ044/222705), Soto Ríos José (ⓣ044/251489), and Fajardo Linares Luis (ⓣ044/248917).

Tourist police ⓣ044/200200.

Visas Imigraciones Av Larco 1220, Urbanizacion Los Pinos.

Huanchaco

Although no longer exactly a tropical paradise, **HUANCHACO** is still a beautiful and relatively peaceful resort, 12km west, or twenty minutes by bus, from Trujillo. Until the 1970s, Huanchaco was a tiny fishing village, quiet and little known to tourists. Today it is one of the fastest growing settlements in Peru, and is slowly spreading back towards Trujillo as half-finished adobe houses, concrete hotels and streets appear beside the main road. However, it still makes an excellent base for visiting many of the sites around the region, in particular the nearby ruins of Chan Chan, and the development hasn't entirely diminished its intrinsic fishing village appeal. There is a long jetty (18¢) which has been recently renovated, where you can jostle with fishermen for the best positions for fishing or simple watching the fishermen surfing on the sea with their *caballitos del mar* – the ancient seagoing rafts designed by the Mochicas. Just at the entry to the pier is a small *artesanía* market. Some of the fishermen offer 10–15 minute boat trips (US$1.50) on the back of their *caballitos*.

The best time to visit Huanchaco is during its June **fiesta** week, at the end of the month when a large *tortora* raft comes ashore accompanied by a smaller flotilla of *caballitos*. But even out of season the town is always lively, with people on the beach, others fishing, and a few travellers hanging around the restaurants. To get to Huanchaco from Trujillo, taxis cost around US$4–5, or it's easy enough to take the frequent orange and yellow **microbus** from Avenida España block 13 (on far side of road from the town centre), by the corner with Independencia, or pick up a bus or one of the white *colectivos* marked Empresa *Caballitos de Tortora* (30¢) from the Mobil or Shell petrol stations at Ovalo Victor Raul.

Accommodation

The town is well served by the kind of accommodation range you'd normally expect at a popular beach resort. *Hospedaje Sunset*, Ribera 600 (ⓣ044/461863; ❶) is where most of the visiting surfers hang out, while *Hospedaje Familiar La Casa Suiza*, Los Pinos 451 (ⓣ044/461285, ⓦwww.casasuiza.com; ❷), offers friendly budget accommodation. Many local families also put people up in **private rooms**; just look out for the signs reading "Alquila Cuarto" on houses, particularly in the summer (Dec–Feb). It's also possible to **camp** here, in the grounds of the very welcoming *Hostal Bracamonte*, Los Olivos 503 (ⓣ044/461162, ⓦwww.welcome.to/hostal_ bracamonte; ❹).

Eating and nightlife

There are seafood **restaurants** all along the front in Huanchaco, one or two of them with verandas extending to the beach. Not surprisingly, seafood is the local speciality, including excellent crab. The fishermen can also be seen returning usually around 3–4pm on their *caballitos*. A kilo of fresh fish can be bought for just US$1–2, but the catches these days aren't huge. Anyone looking for **nightlife** should check out *Sun Kella Bar*, at the southern end of the beach.

Club Colonial at Grau 272 ⓣ044/461015. A beautifully restored colonial house with paintings, old photos and fine stained-glass work adorning it. The food is sumptuous, with an extensive menu of traditional dishes, but it's not cheap. The garden is the residence of some penguins and a couple of rare Tumbes crocodiles.

Huanchaco Beach Restaurant Malecón Larco 602. Very tasty fish dishes, and excellent views across the ocean and up to the clifftop Iglesia Soroco.

El Pescadito C Grau 482 ⓣ044/461484. Actually located in the new block 5, and one block back from the ocean, this is one of the smaller, less expensive restaurants in the back streets of Huanchaco; the views are not so good as those from along the seafront, but the seafood is just as fresh and well prepared.

Restaurant El Caribe Atahualpa 100. Really close to, but just around the corner from the seafront to the north of the pier, this place has great *ceviche* and is very popular with locals.

Restaurant Estrella Marina Malecón Larco 594. Very good, fresh *ceviche* served in a seafront restaurant, which often plays loud salsa music and is popular with locals.

Ancient sites around Trujillo

One of the main reasons for coming to Trujillo is to visit the numerous archeological sites dotted around the nearby Moche and Chicama valleys. There are three main zones of interest within easy reach, first and foremost being the massive adobe city of **Chan Chan** on the northern edge of town. To the south, standing alone beneath the Cerro Blanco hill, you can find the largest mud-brick pyramids in the Americas, the **Huaca del Sol** and **Huaca de la Luna**.

The Chan Chan complex

The huge, ruined city of **CHAN CHAN** stretches across a large sector of the Moche Valley, beginning almost as soon as you leave Trujillo on the Huanchaco road, and ending just a couple of kilometres from Huanchaco. Chan Chan was the capital city of the **Chimu Empire**, an urban civilization which appeared on the Peruvian coast around 1100 AD. By 1450, when the Chimu Empire stretched from the Río Zarumilla in the north to the Río Chancay in the south and covered around 40,000 square kilometres, Chan Chan was the centre of a chain of provincial capitals. They were all gradually incorporated into the Inca Empire between 1460 and 1480.

Of the three main sectors specifically opened up for exploration, the **Tschudi temple-citadel** is the largest and most frequently visited. Not far from Tschudi, **La Huaca Esmeralda** displays different features, being a ceremonial or ritual pyramid rather than a citadel. The third sector, the **Huaca El Dragon** (or **Arco Iris**), on the other side of this enormous ruined city, was similar in function to Esmeralda but has a unique design which has been restored with relish if not historical perfection. Entrance to all three sectors of the ruins and the Museo de Sitio (daily 9–4.30pm, closed Christmas week & May; US$3, or US$1.50 for students with ID cards, including the Museo de Sitio) is included on the same **ticket**, called the *Talon Visitante*, which is valid for only one day (but you can try asking for an extension if you need more days). **Guided tours** are easily arranged (around US$3 for the museum); guides for the Tschudi complex (US$6 an hour) usually hang around at Tschudi entrance and, if you want, will also take you round the *huacas* too. The **Museo de Sitio** (daily 9am–4pm), a few hundred metres before the entrance to the Tschudi temple-citadel. It has an interesting eight-minute multimedia show in

Spanish, but the museum itself is quite small. Getting there is the same as for Huanchaco, only you have to get off well before the *ovalo* where the road divides, one way to Huanchaco and the other to the airport; the Museum is easy to spot, but it is best to ask the driver to drop you at the Museo de Sitio when you jump on board.

Huaca del Sol and Huaca de la Luna

Five kilometres south of Trujillo, beside the Río Moche in a barren desert landscape, are two temples that really bring ancient Peru to life. The stunning **Huaca del Sol** (Temple of the Sun) is the largest adobe structure in the Americas, and easily the most impressive of the many pyramids on the Peruvian coast. Its twin, **La Huaca de la Luna** (Temple of the Moon), is smaller, but more complex and brilliantly frescoed. This complex is believed to have been the capital, or most important ceremonial and urban centre, for the Moche culture, at its peak between 400 and 600 AD. Collectively known as the Huacas del Moche, these sites make a fine day's outing and shouldn't be missed. To get there from Trujillo take one of the golden coloured **colectivos**, marked Campina de Moche (30¢), which run every thirty minutes from the corner of Suarez with Los Incas, near the market.

The **Huaca del Sol** is presently off limits to visitors, but it's an amazing sight from the grounds below or even in the distance from the Huaca de La Luna which is very much open. Clinging to the bottom of Cerro Blanco, just 500m from the Sun Temple, is another Mochica edifice, the **Huaca de la Luna** (9am–4pm; US$3; ⓣ044/291894), a fascinating ritual and ceremonial centre that was constructed and used in the same era as the Huaca del Sol.

Máncora and Tumbes

About 30km from the Ecuadorean border and 287km north of Piura, **Tumbes** is usually considered a mere pit-stop for overland travellers. However, the city has a significant history and, unlike most border settlements, is a surprisingly warm and friendly place. On top of that, it's close to some of Peru's finest **beaches** and the country's only serious mangrove swamp, **Los Bosques de Manglares**. In the rural areas around the city, nearly half of Peru's tobacco leaf is produced. The most popular beach, **Máncora**, is only a couple of hours south of Tumbes where the sea is still warm and the waves often near perfect.

Máncora

Easily the trendiest beach in Peru these days, even attracting the young surf crowd from Ecuador, **MÁNCORA** (ⓦwww.vivamancor.com) is also a highly welcome and very enjoyable stopover when travelling along the north coast. Though spread out along the Panamerican Highway, Máncora is parallel to a beautiful sandy beach, well served by public transport and still retains its charm. Swimming is safe and the surfing can be pretty good.

In fact it's the north coast's current major **surfing** centre, rivalling Chicama near Trujillo at least in its popularity if not quite for its waves. You can hire gear from several places, including the Soledad Surf Company (ⓣ01/983-0425 in Lima), which sells and rents equipment as well as offering surf and Spanish lessons, or from *Godwanaland* restaurant for around US$1.50 each per hour.

At the north end of the main drag, there's a plaza and just beyond this there's sometimes a street market, though only the usual clothing, shoes and food. Between here and the south end you'll find most of the hotels and restaurants, a promenade with hippie *artesanía* stalls, selling sea-inspired crafts and jewelry.

Practicalities

All the main hotels are located between the bridge at the south entrance to town and the plaza towards the north end, though there are several cheaper basic **hostels** strung out along the southern end of the Panamerican Highway, such as the comfortable *Hostal Sausalito* (☎074/858058, ©jcvigoe@terra.com.pe; ❹). The *Hostal Sol y Mar* (☎074/858106 and 858088, ©hsolymar@hotmail.com; ❷) is very popular with the surfing crowd; it is right on the beach, has a good swimming pool and games courts, plus a decent restaurant and bar, private baths, and its own little shop and Internet café. The *Hostal El Mar* (❺) overlooks the sea, has smart cabin-like rooms, private baths, hammocks and meals are included.

For eating, there's a surplus of **restaurants** in the centre of town, mainly along the Panamerican Highway. One of the best is the *Restaurant Arplan*; opposite this are the *Espada*, at Av Piura 655 (☎074/858097) and the *San Pedro*, Av Piura 657 (☎074/858083) all among the best in town offering a range of fish dishes, including surprisingly affordable lobster. Generally speaking, though, their prices are not that cheap. The *Restaurant Las Gemelitas,* is the best and cheapest in town for seafood dishes, *Restaurant Jugeria Regina's*, in the centre, is good for fruit salads and breakfasts; and, opposite, the *Jugeria Mi Janet*, Carretera Panamericana, Av Piura 682, is also good. There's a hectic **nightlife** scene, especially during Peruvian vacation times, but the only club as such is *Las Terrazas*, on the main drag, backing onto the beach. Apart from this place, many of the cafés turn into nightspots when there's the demand.

The **bus companies** are all in the main street, Avenida Piura, where you can buy tickets for their selection of daily and nightly services up or down the coast, connecting Tumbes with Lima and the major cities in between. Transportes EPPO runs five buses between here and Piura (US$3; a 3hr journey) from its office just north of the plaza, towards the northern end of Máncora. Other bus companies include the quality service of Civa, Av Piura 656 (☎074/858026), and Ormeño, Av Piura 499 (☎074/858334), going daily to Piura, Chiclayo, with connections for Cajamarca (and also buses for Ecuador). El Dorado, Av Grau 111 (an extension of Piura), runs south to Piura, Chiclayo and Trujillo daily and nightly. **Colectivos** depart from near the EPPO office for Los Oreganos (50¢; a 30min trip), from where there are other **combis** to Talara (US$1; a 1hr trip).

Tumbes

TUMBES was the first town to be "conquered" by the Spanish and has maintained its importance ever since – originally as the gateway to the Inca Empire and more recently through its strategic position on the controversial **frontier with Ecuador**. Despite three regional wars – in 1859, 1941–42 and 1997–98 – the exact line of the border remains a source of controversy. The traditional enmity between Peru and Ecuador and the continuing border dispute mean that Tumbes has a strong Peruvian army presence and consequently a strict ban on photography anywhere near military or frontier installations. Most of the city's hundred thousand inhabitants are engaged in either transport or petty trading across the frontier, and are quite cut off from mainstream Peru, being much nearer to Quito than Lima, 1268km to the south.

Arrival, city transport and information

Most **buses** coming to Tumbes arrive at offices along Avenida Tumbes Norte (also known as Avenida Teniente Vasquez), or along Piura, although a new Terminal Terrestre is planned for the near future. Ormeño and Continental buses from Ecuador stop at Av Tumbes Norte 216 (see "Listings" p.946 for more bus details). Comite **colectivos** also pull in on Tumbes Norte at no. 308 (☎074/525977). If you're **flying** in from Lima, note that Tumbes airport is often very quiet, particularly at night, when there's no access to food or drink. A taxi into town should cost around US$5; it is about a twenty-minute journey.

Tumbes is quite pleasant and easy to get around **on foot**, or you can hail down one of the many **motorcycle rickshaws**, which will take you anywhere in the city for around 50¢. **Tourist information** is available from the first floor of the Centro Civico, on the Plaza de Armas (8am–1pm & 2–6pm).

Accommodation

Central Tumbes is well endowed with **places to stay**. Some of the better budget options are strung out from the Plaza de Armas along Calle Grau, an attractive old-fashioned hotchpotch of a street, lined with wooden colonial buildings.

Hostal Chicho Av Tumbes Norte 327 ⓣ074/522282. This new *hostal* has some rooms with private bath and TV. Note that the ones at the back are quieter. ❸
Hostal Gandolfo Bolognesi 118 ⓣ074/522868. Small, budget rooms are decent for the price. ❶
Hostal Sol del Costa Av San Martín 275 ⓣ074/523991, ⓦwww.costadelsolperu.com. It has a nice pool, very comfortable rooms with air conditioning and private baths, TV cable; close to the Plaza de Armas. ❻
Hostal Tumbes C Grau 614 ⓣ074/522203. Very pleasant rooms with showers that are excellent value, but the ones upstairs have better light. ❷
Hotel Costa del Sol San Martín 275 ⓣ074/523991. A smart, revamped hotel on the Plazuela Bolognesi; all rooms have TV, minibar, a/c and private bath with hot water. ❽

The City

Although it has very few real sights, Tumbes is a surprisingly elegant city, at least in the centre where its broad **Plaza de Armas** is bounded by the **Biblióteca Municipal** and the plain **Catedral**, dating from 1903. An attractive pedestrian precinct, the **Paseo de la Concordia**, decorated with colourful tiles and several large sculptures and statues, leads off the plaza between the cathedral and the *biblióteca* to the Plazuela Bolognesi. Older and slightly grubby is the long **Malecón** promenade that runs along the high banks of the Río Tumbes, a block beyond the southern end of the Plaza de Armas.

Eating and drinking

Tumbes has some excellent **restaurants** and is the best place in Peru to try *conchas negras* – the black clams found only in these coastal waters, where they grow on the roots of mangroves. The *Pub-disco Keops*, Bolivar 121, on the plaza, has a rustic style **bar** at the front with a music scene going on behind it; at weekends they sometimes have live music.

Cevichería El Sol Ñato Bolivar 608. The best place in town for a wide range of seafood, but only open for lunches; try a *ceviche* with *conchas negras* or a huge steaming dish *of sudado de pescado.*
Pollos a la Brasa Venecia Bolivar 237. Does exactly what it says in its name – a great place for chicken.
Restaurant Latino C Bolivar 163. Right on the Plaza de Armas, this old-fashioned eatery specializes in excellent Continental and American breakfasts.
Restaurant Si Señor C Bolivar 119. Serves mostly beer and seafood, right on the Plaza de Armas.

Listings

Airlines Aero Continente, Tumbes Norte 217 (ⓣ074/522350).
Banks and exchange Banco de Credito, C Bolivar 227, and Banco de la Nacion, on the corner of calles Grau and Bolivar, by the Plaza de Armas. *Cambistas* are at the corner of Bolivar with Piura.
Bus companies CIAL, Av Tumbes Norte 586, for Lima; Cruz del Sur, Av Tumbes Norte 319 (ⓣ074/522350), for Lima and the coast; El Dorado, Piura 454, for Máncora; Emtrafesa, Av Tumbes Norte 397 (ⓣ074/525850), for Chiclayo and Trujillo; Ormeño and Continental, Av Tumbes Norte 319, for Trujillo; Santa Rosa, Av Tumbes Norte, for Piura, to Piura and Máncora; Tepsa, Tacna 216 (ⓣ074/522428), for Lima; and Transportes Chiclayo, Av Tumbes Norte 466 (ⓣ074/525260), for Chiclayo.
Post office San Martín 240. Mon–Sat 7am–7pm.
Telephones The Telefónica del Peru office is on San Martín in the same block as the post office. Ravitel telephone is at Av Tumbes Norte 322.
Tour operators Tumbes Tours, Av Tumbes Norte 341 (ⓣ074/522481), runs a number of tours including a 4-day/3-night trip exploring the nearby Puerto Pizarro mangrove swamp and beaches from US$20 per person per day, depending on size of group. Manglares Tours, Av Tumbes Norte 313 (ⓣ074/522887), can organize local tours with guides, though it specialises in air tickets.

Crossing into Ecuador

Crossing the border is relatively simple in either direction. Two kilometres before the busy frontier settlement of **Aguas Verdes**, you'll find the **Peruvian immigration office** (daily 9am–noon & 2–5pm) where you get an exit or entry stamp and tourist card for your passport. Once past these buildings, it's a fifteen-minute walk or a short drive to Aguas Verdes. **Combis** for the border leave Tumbes from block 3 of Tumbes Norte, but ensure that it's going all the way to the border; some continue to Zarumilla or Aguas Verdes. A **taxi** from Tumbes costs US$4–5. From Aguas Verdes, you just walk over the bridge into the Ecuadorian border town of **Huaquillas** (see p.730) and the **Ecuadorian immigration office** (daily 8am–1pm & 2–6pm), where you'll get your entry or exit stamps and tourist card. If coming from Ecuador to Peru, Tumbes is the nicer place to stay close to the border. If going north, frequent buses depart to all the major destinations in Ecuador from Huaquillas. The best bet is to go on to Cuenca (5hr), an attractive, small Ecuadorian city and a major cultural centre, although Machala is nearer (75km) and has some accommodation and other facilities.

If you're coming into Peru from Ecuador, it's simply a reversal of the above procedure, though there is one other option which is to take a bus direct from the frontier to Sullana (2–3hr; US$5) from where there are buses and *colectivos* regularly to Piura (45min; 50¢). In both directions the authorities occasionally require that you show an onward ticket out of their respective countries. Unless you intend to recross the border within a week or two, it's not worth taking out any local currency; the best policy is to change as little money as possible, because of the poor exchange rates.

The **Peruvian customs** point is a concrete complex in the middle of the desert between the villages of Cancas and Máncora more than 50km south of the border. Occasionally inactive, when it is operating, however, most buses are pulled over and passengers have to get out and show documents to the customs police while the bus and selected items of luggage are searched for contraband goods.

9.7

The jungle

Whether you look at it up close, from the ground or from a boat, or fly over it in a plane, the Peruvian **jungle** seems endless, even though it is actually disappearing at an alarming rate. Even so, well over half of Peru is covered by dense tropical rainforest, with its eastern regions offering unrivalled access to the world's largest and most famous jungle, the **Amazon**. Of the Amazon's original area, around four million square kilometres (about 80 percent)

Indigenous jungle tribes

Outside the few main towns, there are hardly any sizeable settlements, and the jungle population remains dominated by between 35 and 62 **indigenous tribes** – the exact number depends on how you classify tribal identity – each with its own distinct language, customs and dress. After centuries of external influence (missionaries, gold seekers, rubber barons, soldiers, oil companies, anthropologists, and now tourists), many jungle Indians speak Spanish and live pretty conventional, Westernized lives, preferring jeans, football shirts and fizzy bottled drinks to their more traditional clothing and manioc beer (the tasty, filling and nutritious *masato*). But while many are being sucked into the money-based labour market, others, increasingly under threat, have been forced to struggle for their cultural identities and territorial rights, or to retreat as far as they are presently able beyond the new frontiers of so-called civilization. In 1996, for instance, oil workers encountered some previously uncontacted groups while clearing tracts of forest for seismic testing in the upper Río de Las Piedras area of Madre de Dios, northwest of Puerto Maldonado. In this region it appears that some of the last few uncontacted tribal communities in the Amazon – Yaminahua, Mashco Piro and Amahuaca Indians – are keeping their distance from outside influences.

In 2002, these same remote groups came out of the forest en masse to prevent further intrusion by aggressive **illegal loggers** in their last remaining territory at the headwaters of the Río de Las Piedras. In August of that year some 400 naked Indians appeared on the riverbanks as a flotilla of illegal logging launches made its way upstream from Puerto Maldonado. Shaking and rattling their bows and arrows, the Indians raised long vines as a barrier across the river and then attacked the boats, badly injuring several loggers.

For most of the traditional or semi-traditional tribes, the jungle offers a **semi-nomadic** existence and, in terms of material possessions, they have, need and want very little. Communities are scattered, with groups of between 10 and 200 people, and their sites shift every few years. For subsistence they depend on small, cultivated plots, fish from the rivers and game from the forest, including wild pigs, deer, monkeys and a great range of edible birds. The main species of edible jungle fish are *sabalo* (a kind of oversized catfish), *carachama* (an armoured walking catfish), the feisty piranha (generally not quite as dangerous as Hollywood makes out), and the giant *zungaro* and *paiche* – the latter, at up to 200kg, being the world's largest freshwater fish. In fact, food is so abundant that jungle dwellers generally spend no more than three to four days a week engaged in subsistence activities.

remain intact, fifteen percent of which lie in Peru, where they receive over 2000mm of rainfall a year and experience average temperatures of 25–35°C. Considered as *El Infierno Verde* – "the Green Hell" – by many Peruvians who've never been here, it's the most biodiverse region on Earth, and much that lies beyond the main waterways remains relatively untouched and often unexplored. Jaguar, anteaters and tapirs roam the forests, huge anaconda snakes live in the swamps, and trees like the giant Shihuahuaco, strong enough to break an axe head, rise from the forest floor. Furthermore, there are over fifty indigenous tribes scattered throughout the Peruvian section alone, many surviving primarily by hunting, fishing and gathering, as they have done for thousands of years.

Getting into the jungle

Given the breadth and quality of options, it's never easy to decide which bit of the jungle to head for. Your three main criteria will probably be budget, ease of access, plus the depth and nature of jungle experience you're after. Flying to any of the main jungle towns is surprisingly cheap and, once you've arrived, a number of **excursions** can be made easily and cheaply, though the best experience comprises a few nights at one of the better **jungle lodges**. For more intimate (but often tougher) travel, it's easy enough to arrange a **camping expedition** and a guide, travelling in canoes or speedboats into the deeper parts of the wilderness. A further, costlier, though rewarding, option, mainly restricted to a few operators based in Iquitos, is to take a **river cruise** on a larger boat.

Iquitos, the capital of the **NORTHERN SELVA**, is the Peruvian jungle's only genuinely exciting city. Much easier to access by air from Lima or to arrive by boat from Brazil, the Northern Selva is also accessible from the northern Peruvian coast via an adventurous, increasingly popular four- to five-day boat journey up the Río Huallaga. Cusco is the best base for trips into the jungles of the **SOUTHERN SELVA**, with road access to the frontier town of **Puerto Maldonado**, itself a good base for budget travellers. The nearby forests of **Madre de Dios** boast the **Tambopata-Candamo Reserved Zone** and the **Bahuaja-Sonene National Park**, an enormous tract of virgin rainforest close to the Bolivian border. An expedition into the **Manu Reserved Zone** (part of the larger **Manu National Biosphere Reserve**), will also bring you into one of the more exciting wildlife regions in South America, but for a quicker and cheaper taste of the jungle, you can go by bus from Cusco via Ollantaytambo to **Quillabamba**, on the Río Urubamba. Flowing north along the foot of the Andes, through the dangerous and unforgettable white-water rapids of the **Pongo de Mainique**, the Urubamba merges with the Ucayali in the Central Selva.

The northern selva: Iquitos and Río Amazonas

Most people visit Iquitos briefly with a view to moving on into the rainforest but, wisely, few travellers actually avoid the place entirely. A busy, cosmopolitan tourist town with a buzzing population of about 300,000, connections to the rest of the world are by river and air only – Yurimaguas, the end of the road from the Pacific coast, is the nearest road to Iquitos. It's the kind of place that lives up to all your expectations of a jungle town, from its elegant reminders of the rubber boom years to the atmospheric shantytown suburb of **Puerto Belén**, where you can buy just about anything.

When to come

Unlike most of the Peruvian *selva*, the **climate** here is little affected by the Andean topography, so there is no rainy season as such; instead, the year is divided into "high water" (Dec–May) and "low water" (June–Nov) seasons. The upshot is that the weather is always hot and humid, with temperatures averaging 23–30°C and with an annual rainfall of about 2600mm. Most visitors come between May and August, but the high-water months are perhaps the best time for **wildlife**, because the animals are crowded into smaller areas of primary forest and dry land. Perhaps the best time to visit Iquitos, however, is at the end of June (supposedly June 23–24, but actually spread over three or four days), when the main **Fiesta de San Juan** takes place.

Iquitos

IQUITOS began life in 1739 when Jesuit José Bahamonde established settlements at Santa Barbara de Nanay and Santa Maria de Iquitos on the Río Mazán. By the end of the nineteenth century, it was, along with Manaus in Brazil, one of *the* great rubber towns. A number of structures survive from that era of grandeur, but during the last century Iquitos has vacillated between prosperity – as far back as 1938, the area was explored for oil – and the depths of depression. However, its strategic position on the Amazon, which makes it accessible to large ocean-going ships from the distant Atlantic, has ensured its importance. **Expeditions around Iquitos** are the most developed in the Peruvian jungle, offering a wide and often surprising range of attractions. As usual, anything involving overnight stays is going to cost a fair bit, though there are also cheap day-trips. With all organized visits to Indian villages in this area, expect the inhabitants to put on a quick show, with a few traditional dances and some singing, before they try to sell you their handicraft (occasionally over-enthusiastically).

Arrival, information and getting around

If you've come by boat from Yurimaguas (5 days), Pucallpa (6–7 days), Leticia or Tabatinga (both 3 days), you'll arrive at **Puerto Masusa**, some eleven blocks northeast of the Plaza de Armas. Flights land at Iquitos **airport**, Aeropuerto Internacional de Francisco Secada Vignetta (Ⓣ094/260147), 5km southwest of town and connected by taxis (US$3–4) and cheaper *motokars* (US$2). **Buses** pull in on the Plaza de Armas and on calles Huallaga and La Condamine.

The very helpful and friendly main tourist office is in the City Hall building on the Plaza de Armas at Napo 226 (Ⓣ094/235621, Ⓦwww.siturismo.org.pe). It has brochures and maps, and staff can advise on hotels; they keep a list of registered tour operators and guides, and can help book accommodation. The monthly English-language *Iquitos Review* is also a good source of information.

For **getting around** Iquitos you'll probably want to make use of the rattling **motokars** again; alternatively, **motorbikes** can also be rented – try the shop near the Ferretaria Union (block 2 of Raymondi), or one at Yavari 702. Expect to pay around US$2 an hour or US$10 for twelve hours (you'll need to show your passport and licence), and remember to check the brakes before leaving. For getting around town by **car**, try the office at Tute Pinglo 431 (Ⓣ094/235857). If you want to get onto the river itself, **canoes** can be rented very cheaply from the port at Bellavista (see p.955).

For **changing money**, it's best not to do it on the street with the *cambistas* who have a bit of a reputation (particularly at the corner of Prospero with Morona) for ripping tourists off, especially after around 8pm. Use one of the *casa de cambios* on Sargento Lores or the banks (see "Listings" p.954).

Accommodation

Like every other jungle town, Iquitos is a little expensive, but the standard of its **hotels** is very good and the range allows for different budgets. Even a room in an average sort of place will include a shower and fan, and many others offer cable TV and minibars.

Hobo Hideout – The Great Amazon Safari and Trading Company Putumayo 437 Ⓣ094/234099, Ⓦwww.safarisareus.net. A unique and special backpackers hostel right in the heart of Iquitos, offering superb food and a range of different rooms, some with own bathrooms. Lots of character. ❷–❸

Hostal la Libertad Arica 361 Ⓣ094/235763. A fine backpackers' place, rooms have private bathrooms, hot water and cable TV, plus there's a restaurant. It's also home to a good tour company. ❷–❸

Hostal Lima Prospero 549 Ⓣ094/235152. Rooms have private bath and fans; it doesn't look much from the outside but is surprisingly pleasant, possessing a certain jungle flavour, with parrots on the patio. ❷

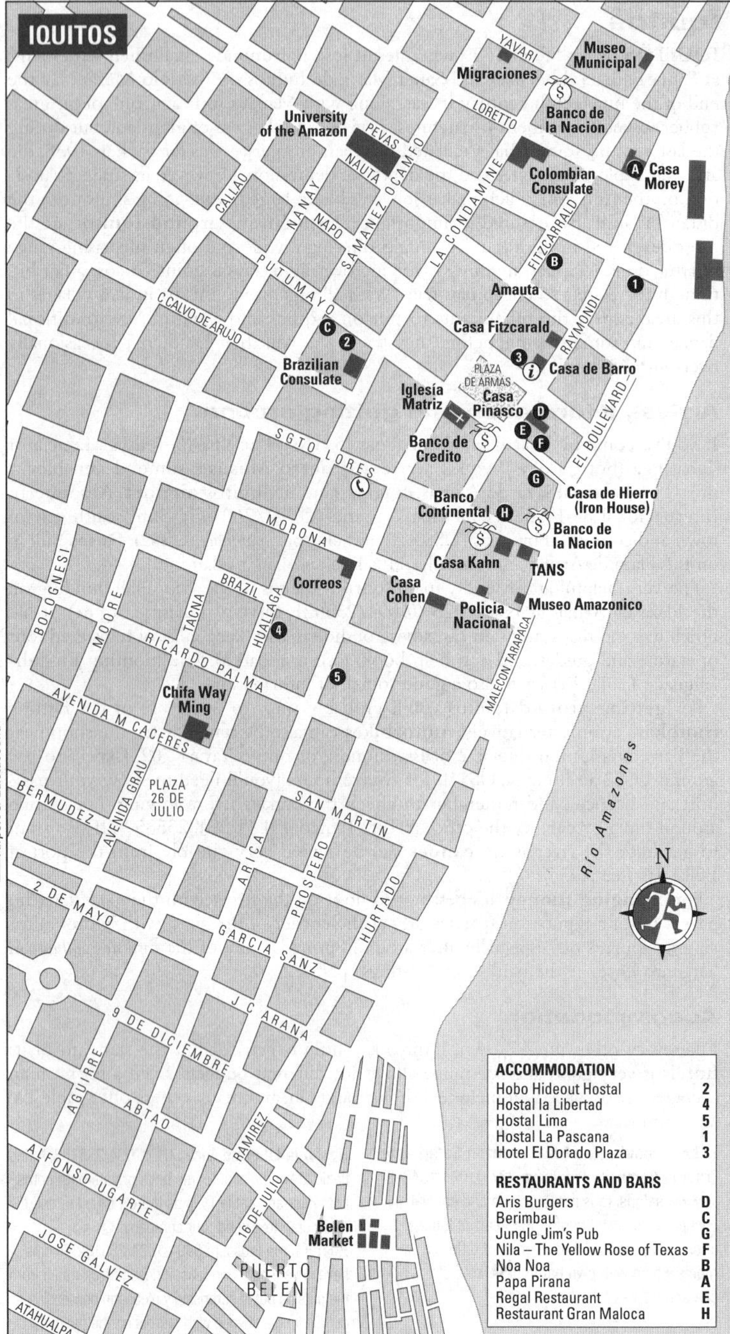
IQUITOS
Puerto Masusa (Brazil), Leticia (Colombia), Pucallpa & Yurimaguas
Airport & Quistacocha
Museo Municipal
Migraciones
YAVARI
LORETTO
Banco de la Nacion
University of the Amazon
PEVAS
NAUTA
Casa Morey
Colombian Consulate
CALLAO
NANAY
NAPO
SAMANEZ OCAMPO
LA CONDAMINE
FITZCARRALD
PUTUMAYO
Amauta
C CALVO DE ARUJO
Casa Fitzcarald
RAYMONDI
Brazilian Consulate
PLAZA DE ARMAS
Casa de Barro
Iglesía Matriz
Casa Pinasco
EL BOULEVARD
Banco de Credito
SGTO LORES
Banco Continental
Casa de Hierro (Iron House)
Banco de la Nacion
MORONA
Casa Kahn
TANS
BOLOGNESI
BRAZIL
Correos
Casa Cohen
Policia Nacional
Museo Amazonico
MOORE
TACNA
HUALLAGA
RICARDO PALMA
MALECON TARAPACA
Chifa Way Ming
AVENIDA M CACERES
AVENIDA GRAU
PLAZA 26 DE JULIO
BERMUDEZ
SAN MARTIN
Río Amazonas
ARICA
PROSPERO
HURTADO
N
2 DE MAYO
GARCIA SANZ
J C ARANA
9 DE DICIEMBRE
AGUIRRE
ABTAO
RAMIREZ
ALFONSO UGARTE
16 DE JULIO
Belen Market
JOSE GALVEZ
PUERTO BELEN
ATAHUALPA
ACCOMMODATION
Hobo Hideout Hostal 2
Hostal la Libertad 4
Hostal Lima 5
Hostal La Pascana 1
Hotel El Dorado Plaza 3
RESTAURANTS AND BARS
Aris Burgers D
Berimbau C
Jungle Jim's Pub G
Nila – The Yellow Rose of Texas F
Noa Noa B
Papa Pirana A
Regal Restaurant E
Restaurant Gran Maloca H

Hostal La Pascana Pevas 133 ⓣ094/231418, ⓔhs_pascana@lima.business.com.pe. Appealing doubles based around a small courtyard close to the river, less than two blocks from the Plaza de Armas. Clean, friendly, has book exchange and travel service; popular with travellers, it offers a ventilated, quiet haven from Iquitos's sometimes hectic street life. It is best to book in advance ❸

Hotel El Dorado Plaza Napo 258, Plaza de Armas ⓣ094/222555, ⓦwww.eldoradoplaza.com. A superb hotel, arguably the best anywhere in the Amazon, this is the first ever 5-star in Iquitos. There's great service, a nice pool, a *maloca*-style bar, and quality restaurant and some fantastic rainforest-inspired art. ❽

The Town

Much of Iquitos's appeal is derived from the fact that it's the starting point for excursions into the rainforest, but the town is an interesting place in its own right. Like Manaus, Iquitos is world famous for its architecture, mainly created during the rubber boom. Many of the late eighteenth- and early nineteenth-century buildings are decorated with Portuguese *azulejo* tiles, some of which are brilliantly extravagant in their Moorish inspiration, and the **Casa Kahn**, on block 1 of Sargento Lore, is a particularly fine example.

On the southeast conrer of the **Plaza de Armas**, you'll find the unusual, majestic **Casa de Fierro** (Iron House), now home to a restaurant, but originally created by Eiffel for the 1889 Paris exhibition and shipped out to Iquitos in pieces by one of the rubber barons to be erected here in the 1890s. On the southwest side of the plaza is the **Iglesía Matriz**, the main Catholic church, whose interior paintings depicting biblical scenes are by the Loretano artists Americo Pinasco and Cesar Calvo de Araujo.

One block southeast of Plaza de Armas are the two best sections of the **old riverfront**, El Boulevard and Malecón Tarapaca. **El Boulevard** is the busiest of the two areas, especially at night, full of bars and restaurants and with a small **amphitheatre** where some kind of entertainment occurs most nights, from mini-circuses to mime, comedy and music. The **Malecón Tarapaca** boasts some fine old mansions, one of which, at Tarapaca 262, with lovely nineteenth-century *azulejos*, is presently one of the town's better bakeries. Also on Malecón Tarapaca is the Prefectura de Loreto mansion, home to the municipal museum **Museo Amazonico** (Mon–Fri 8am–1pm & 3–7pm, Sat 8am–noon; US$1, 60¢ students), devoted to the region's natural history and tribal culture.

Puerto Belén

The most memorable area, **Puerto Belén**, looms out of the main town at a point where the Amazon, until recently, joined the Río Itaya inlet. Consisting almost entirely of wooden huts raised on stilts, it has earned fame among travellers as the Venice of the Peruvian jungle. Actually more Far Eastern than Italian in appearance, it has changed little over its hundred years or so of life, remaining a poor shanty settlement and continuing to trade in basics like bananas, manioc, fish, turtle and crocodile meat. While filming *Fitzcarraldo* here, **Werner Herzog** merely had to make sure that no motorized canoes appeared on screen: virtually everything else, including the style of the *barriada* dwellings, looks like an authentic slum town of the last century. Wandering through the streets market is the highly atmospheric route into the backstreets, dirty but somehow beautiful, of Belén. Ask for directions to *Pasaje Paquito*, the busy herbalist alley in the heart of the frenetic Amazon River economic community, which synthesizes the very rich flavour of the place.

Eating and drinking

Food in Iquitos is exceptionally good for a jungle town, specializing in fish dishes but catering these days pretty well for any taste. While mainly an extension of eating out and meeting friends in the main streets, the **nightlife** in Iquitos is pretty good, and there are a number of highly charged discos, clubs and bars worth knowing about.

Restaurants

Aris Burgers Prospero 127 ⓣ094/231479. Actually serving more than burgers (though these are quite delicious), including plates with a variety of river fish and even caiman meat, plus the best french fries in town. It's the most popular meeting spot in Iquitos and a bit of a landmark for taxi and *motokar* drivers.

Jungle Jim's Pub Putumayo 168 ⓣ094/235294. Very central, with tables inside and out on the street, this is newest English pub in town. *Jungle Jim's* serves a superb range of drinks as well as great regional cuisine (an excellent place to eat alligator if that's what you feel like after a jungle trip). Will accept most major credit cards and stays open as late as customers want.

Nila – The Yellow Rose of Texas Putumayo 180 ⓣ094/241010. Very tasty local dishes and reasonably priced menu; good location near the plaza with tables outside on the street. Great coffee.

Regal Restaurant Putumayo 282 ⓣ094/222732. Upstairs in the Casa de Fierro, this is a busy place with a very pleasant, almost colonial ambience, run by the British Consul and his wife. The food, mainly traditional local dishes, is great, plus there are ceiling fans, fine views over the Plaza de Armas from Eiffel's iron balcony, and a large pool table inside. *Paiche* fish is a speciality.

Restaurant Gran Maloca Flores 170 ⓣ094/233126, ⓔmaloca@tvs.com.pe. One of Iquito's finest restaurants, lavishly decorated, with jungle paintings adorning the walls and a high-ceiligned, cool interior. Food is excellent (nice jungle ice creams).

Nightlife

Berimbau Putumayo 467. One of the newest and flashiest nightclubs in Iquitos; very central and pretty hectic. It plays good rock and Latin dance music most nights, serves cool drinks at several bars on different levels by different dancefloors. Good air conditioning, which is pretty important here.

Noa Noa Fitzcarrald 298 (ⓣ094/242310). Easily identified after 11.30pm by the huge number of flashy motorbikes lined up outside, this is the most popular and lively of Iquitos' clubs, attracting young and old, gringo and Iquiteño alike. It has three bars and plays lots of Latino music, including the latest technocumbia. Mon–Sat 10pm–late; US$6 entrance.

Papa Pirana Loreto 220 ⓣ094/242333. This club has the biggest dancefloor and frequently presents live shows of music, dance and comedy; very popular with locals and tourists alike. One of he hottest scenes in town at weekends. Tues–Sun opens 10pm.

Listings

Airlines AeroContinente, Prospero 232 ⓣ094/235990, flies daily to Lima, with connections for Cusco and other main Peruvian destinations; TANS, for Pucallpa, Tarapoto and Lima, Sargento Lores 127 (ⓣ094/234632); for very reasonably priced flights to Requena, Angamos and Santa Rosa there's Grupo 42 whose office is at Prospero 215 (094/ⓣ221071 or 221086).

Banks and exchange Banco de Credito, Putumayo 201; Banco Wiese, Prospero 282, for MasterCard; Banco de la Nacion; Interbanc, Prospero 336; Banco Latino, Prospero 332; and the Banco del Trabajo, block 1 of Prospero, has an ATM taking Visa. *Casa de Cambio* corner of Sargento Lores with Prospero. The only place said to be reasonably safe for changing with *cambistas* (especially OK with Genaro Sullo, Fernando Echegalier and Danilo Melendez) on the street is at the corner of Morona with Arica, by the post office.

Consulates Brazil, Morona 238 ⓣ094/232081; Colombia, corner of Nauta with Calloa ⓣ094/231461; UK, Putumayo 182 ⓣ094/222732.

Jungle supplies Mad Mick's Trading Post, Putumayo 184b. Provides everything you need, for purchase or rental, for a jungle trip, including rubber boots, rainproof ponchos, sunhats, fishing tackle etc.

Pacaya Samiria National Reserve Office Ricardo Palma 113, third floor ⓣ094/233980. Good for maps, information on the National Reserve and permission to enter it.

Police Policia de Turismo, Sargento Lores 834 ⓣ094/242801.

Post office SERPOST, Arica 482. Mon–Sat 8am–7.30pm.

Telephones Sargento Flores 321. Daily 7am–11pm.

Visas Migraciones Block 4 of Nauta (Mon–Fri 8am–1pm & 1.30–4.30pm; ⓣ094/235371).

Short trips and tours from Iquitos

The closest place you can get to from Iquitos without a guide or long river trip is **Padre Isla**, an island opposite town in the midst of the Amazon, over 14km long and with beautiful beaches during the dry season. It's easily reached by canoe from Belén or the main waterfront. Alternatively, some 4km northeast of the centre of Iquitos, just fifteen minutes by bus, is the suburb of **Bellavista** on the Río Nanay. From Bellavista you can set out by canoe ferry for **Playa Nanay**, the best beach around Iquitos, where bars and cafés are springing up to cater for the weekend crowds. Be aware that currents here are pretty strong and, although there are life-guards, drownings have occurred.

On the western edge of Iquitos, an affluent of the Nanay forms a long lake called **Moronacocha**, a popular resort for swimming and water-skiing; some 5km further out (just before the airport) another lake, **Rumococha**, has facilities on the Río Nanay for fishing and hunting. Beyond this, still on the Nanay, is the popular weekend beach and white sands of **Santa Clara**. The village of **Santo Tomas** is only 16km from here; a worthwhile trip and well connected by local buses, this agricultural and fishing village, on the banks of the Río Nanay, is renowned for its jungle *artesanía*, and has another beach, on the **Lago Mapacocha**, where you can swim and canoe.

Short tours in the area include a boat trip that sets out from Bellavista and travels up the Río Momón to visit a community of Yaguar or Bora Indians at **San Andres**, then goes downriver to visit **Serpentario las Boas**, an anaconda farm near the mouth of the Momón. Here you can see and touch anacondas and more (boas, sloths and monkeys to name a few), slithering around in what is essentially someone's backyard. The whole trip lasts around two hours and costs about US$5–10 per person (including a US$2 tip at Serpentario las Boas), depending on the size of group.

Moving on

From Puerto Masusa, **speedboats** go downstream to Santa Rosa, Tabatinga and Leticia (all on the three-way frontier, see p.958) several times a week, taking up to ten hours there and twelve hours back, for around US$40. The main companies have their offices on Raymondi, just a few blocks from the Plaza de Armas. Larger **riverboats** go upstream from Puerto Masusa to Lagunas (3 days), Yurimaguas (5 days), Pucallpa (6–7 days), or downstream to Pevas (about 1 day), Leticia and Tabatinga (both 3 days). Take along a good book, plenty of extra food and drink, a hammock, a sweater and one or two blankets; it's usually possible to sling your hammock up and sleep free of charge on the larger boats in the days leading up to the unpredictable departure. It's also advisable to secure your baggage with a chain to a permanent fixture on the deck and also keep bags locked, as **theft** is quite common.

Around Iquitos

The massive river system around Iquitos offers some of the best access to Indian villages, lodges and primary rainforest in the entire Amazon. You can go it alone with the *colectivo* boats that run more or less daily up and down the Río Amazonas, but it's usually best to travel with one of the lodge and tour companies (see p.957).

A long day's ride (130km) **upstream from Iquitos** lies **Nauta**, at the mouth of the Río Marañon. There are excellent organized tours to be had from **LAGUNAS**, close to the Pacaya Samiria Reserve and some three days upstream from Nauta (US$10–25 depending on whether you take hammock space or a shared cabin). There are a couple of **hostels** in Lagunas: the *Hostal Montalban* (❷), on the Plaza de Armas, is basic and small but suffices, as does the slightly cheaper *Hostal La Sombra* (❶) at Jr Vasquez 1121.

Lagunas is the main starting-point for trips into the huge **Pacaya Samiria National Reserve**, which comprises around two million hectares of virgin rainforest (about 1.5 percent of the landmass of Peru). The reserve is a swampland during the rainy season (Dec–March), when the streams and rivers all rise. This region is home to the Cocoma tribe, whose main settlement is Tipishca. You should of course be well prepared with mosquito nets, hammocks, insect repellent and all the necessary food and medicines (see p.27). It's possible to arrange the **guides** here (about US$10 a day per person, less if you're in a group) and to spend as long as you like in the national reserve. Officially you should obtain permission from the National Reserve office (see "Listings" p.954) to get into the Reserve, but not everyone does. The Reserve office also provides maps and information on the region, when available.

Downstream from Iquitos lies **PEVAS**, some 190km to the east and reached in a day by riverboat *colectivo* or in a few hours by speedboat. An attractive, largely palm-thatched settlement, it's the oldest town in the Peruvian Amazon. The economy here is based primarily on fishing (visit the *mercado*, where produce is brought in by boat every day), and dugout canoes are the main form of transport, propelled by characteristically ovoid-bladed and beautifully carved paddles, which are often sold as souvenirs, sometimes painted with designs. The nearby Witoto and Bora Indians, relocated here in the 1930s from the Columbian Amazon, are now virtually in everyday contact with the riverine society of Pevas, producing quality artefacts for sale to passers-by. The nearby Bora village of Puca Urquillo is a good example, a large settlement based around a Baptist church and school, whose founders moved

here from the Colombian side of the Río Putumayo during the hardships of the rubber era rather than be enslaved.

For a good **place to stay**, try the *Casa de la Loma* (write to PO Box 555, Iquitos; ⓣ094/221184, ⓦwww.greentracks.com), also contactable in the US (write to 10 Town Plaza 231, Suite 231, Durango, CO 81301; ⓣ1-800-9-Monkey). Set on a small hill close to Pevas, the lodge was set up by two nurses from Oregon who operate a free clinic here for the two thousand or so local inhabitants. They have five large bedrooms with shared bathrooms, and there's electricity, a refrigerator and a kitchen. Costs are from US$60 per person per day, extra for their speedboat transport from Iquitos.

Lodges, cruises and guides

If you're planning an expedition beyond the limited network of roads around Iquitos, you'll have to take an organized trip with a **lodge operator**, a **river cruise** or hire a **freelance guide**. The larger local entrepreneurs have quite a grip on the market, and even the few guides who remain more or less independent are hard to bargain with since so much of their work comes through the larger agents. That said, they mostly have well-worked-out itineraries, though you should always deal with an established office – check out which companies are registered at the tourist office in Iquitos – and insist on a written contract and receipt. Be aware that there's no shortage of con-artists among the many **touts** around town, some of whom brandish brochures that have nothing to do with the established offices. Under no circumstances should you hand them any money.

Before approaching anyone it's a good idea to know more or less what you want in terms of time in the forest, total costs, personal needs and comforts, and things you expect to see. If Iquitos is your main contact with the Amazon and you're unlikely to return here, you can rent a boat for an overnight trip from upwards of US$40–50 per person.

Guided tours require some kind of camp set-up or tourist **lodge** facilities. There are two main types of jungle experience available from Iquitos – what Peruvian tour operators describe as "conventional" (focusing on lodge stays) and what they describe as "adventure trips" (going deeper into the jungle). Prices given are per person.

Amazon Explorama CEIBA TOPS Contact Explorama, Av la Marina 340, Iquitos ⓣ094/253301, ⓦwww.explorama.com, or Box 445, Iquitos; toll-free in the US ⓣ1-800-707-5275. Explorama is the top operator in the region; not cheap but worth it. Explorama also now has its own very well equipped river ferryboat – the *Amazon Queen*. Some 40km from Iquitos, this is the most luxurious Amazon lodge of all, with a fantastic jungle swimming pool, bars and dining areas, surrounded by 40 hectares of primary forest and 160 hectares of *chacra* and secondary growth. Accommodation is in smart conventional bungalows with a/c and flushing toilets, or in simpler bungalow huts. There are 75 rooms and a superb pool. Can be visited in conjunction with other Explorama lodges; US$100–400 per day, depending on size of group, length of trip and the number of lodges visited.

Cocoma Lodge Piura 1072 ⓣ094/251185. Operated by the Cocoma Indian community in the Pacaya Samiria Reserve, it offers adventure and shamanic trips as required; plenty of wildlife including dolphins, howler and black monkeys. Pretty good value from around US$40 a day.

Cumaceba Lodge Putumayo 184 ⓣ094/232229 or 610656, ⓔcumaceba.lodge@mailcity.com. A highly recommended budget option on the Río Yanayacu, some 40km downriver from Iquitos (45min by speedboat), with accommodation in private rustic bungalows with individual bathrooms. It takes visitors to the local Yagua village and on jungle walks; bird- and dolphin-watching also form part of their programmes. It also runs an explorer camp downriver. Around US$120 for three days.

The Great Amazon Safari and Trading Company Putumayo 437 ⓣ094/234099 ⓦwww.safarisareus.net. Run by the North American Jimmy Ford, this company has its own speedboat and offers customized jungle trips; from US$25 a day for local trips or from US$50 a day for longer expeditions. The five-day or longer trips offer genuine jungle expedition options.

Crossing into Colombia or Brazil: the three-way frontier

Leaving or entering Peru via the Amazon is often an intriguing adventure; by river this inevitably means experiencing the **three-way frontier**. The cheapest and most common route is by river from Iquitos, some twelve hours in a *lancha rapida* or three to four days downriver in a standard *lancha* riverboat (see p.955 for details on companies operating boats from Iquitos for downriver). Some services go all the way to Leticia, Colombia or Tabatinga (Brazil), but many stop at one of the two small Peruvian frontier settlements of Santa Rosa or Islandia; at Chimbote, a few hours before you get to Santa Rosa and on the right as you head towards the frontier, is a small police post, the main **customs checkpoint** (*guarda costa*) for river traffic.

SANTA ROSA is your last chance to complete formalities with Migraciones if you haven't already done so at the Iquitos office (see "Listings" p.954) – essentially obtaining an **exit stamp** from Peru, if you're leaving, or getting an **entry stamp and tourist card** if arriving, which can take up to an hour. On larger boats, you often don't have to disembark here, as the Migraciones official may board the vessel and do the paperwork there and then. There are few hostels, but the small *La Brisa del Amazonas* (❸) is also a **restaurant** whose owner is a useful contact for local **information**. However, there are several cafés, and ferries connect the town with Tabatinga and Leticia.

The only other way of crossing these three borders is by **flying** – a much less interesting approach, though not necessarily a more expensive one (though there's an airport departure tax of US$2). Flights from Iquitos to Santa Rosa are operated by TANS, and both Varig and Rico fly to Manaus via Tabatinga at least three times a week. TANS tickets can be bought from Señor Teddy, who operates out of one of the restaurants in this tiny town – just ask anywhere for him. From Leticia, Avianca flies to a few major Colombian cities, including Bogota, several times a week.

The southern selva: Madre de Dios

A large, forested region, with a manic climate (usually searingly hot and humid, but with sudden cold spells – *friajes* – between June and August, owing to icy winds coming down from the Andean glaciers), the **southern selva** regions of Peru have only been systematically explored since the 1950s and were largely unknown until the twentieth century, when rubber began to leave Peru through Bolivia and Brazil, eastwards along the rivers.

Named after the broad river that flows through the heart of the southern jungle, the still relatively wild *departmento* of **Madre de Dios** is changing rapidly with a recent influx of agribusinesses moving in to clear mahogany trees and prospectors panning for gold dust along the riverbanks. Nearly half of Madre de Dios *departmento*'s 78,000 square kilometres are accounted for by national parks and protected areas such as **Manu Biosphere Reserve**, **Tambopata-Candamo Reserved Zone** and **Bahuaja-Sonone National Park**, between them encompassing some of the most exciting jungle and richest flora and fauna in the world. Taken together, these comprise some 1.5 million hectares, almost the size of Manu (15,000 square kilometres).

The **Río Madre de Dios** is fed by two main tributaries, the **Río Manu** and the **Río Alto Madre de Dios**, which roll off the Paucartambo Ridge (just north of Cusco), which divides the tributaries from the **Río Urubamba** watershed and delineates Manu Biosphere Reserve. At Puerto Maldonado, the Madre de Dios meets with the **Río Tambopata** and the **Río de las Piedras**, then flows on to Puerto Heath, a day's boat ride away on the Bolivian frontier. From here it continues through the Bolivian forest into Brazil to join the great Río Madeira, which eventually meets the Amazon near Manaus. Madre de Dios is still very much a frontier zone, centred on the rapidly growing river town of **Puerto Maldonado**, near the Bolivian border, supposedly founded by legendary explorer and rubber baron **Fitzcarrald**.

Puerto Maldonado and around

A remote settlement even for Peru, **PUERTO MALDONADO** is a frontier colonist town with strong links to the Cusco region and a great fervour for bubbly jungle *chicha* music. With an economy based on goldpanning and Brazil-nut gathering from the rivers and forests of Madre de Dios, it has grown enormously over the last twenty years. From a small, laid-back outpost of civilization to a busy market town, it has become the thriving, safe (and fairly expensive) capital of a region that feels very much on the threshold of major upheavals, with a rapidly developing tourist industry.

In town, the main street, **León de Velarde**, immediately establishes the town's stage-set feel, lined with bars, hardware shops, and a poolroom. At one end is the **Plaza de Armas**, with an attractive if bizarre Chinese pagoda-style clock tower at its centre, and along another side a modern **Municipalidad** – where, not much more than ten years ago, a TV was sometimes set up for the people to watch an all-important event like a game of *futbol*. These days there are satellite TV dishes all over town and the youth of Puerto Maldonado are as familiar with computer software as they are with jungle mythology. If you're considering a river trip, or just feel like crossing to the other side for a walk, follow Jirón Billingshurst, or take the steep steps down from the Plaza de Armas to the **main port**, situated on the Río Madre de Dios – one of the town's most active corners. A regular bus and *colectivo* (US$5) service now connects Puerto Maldonado with **Laberinto** (leaving from the main market on Ernesto Rivero), some ninety minutes away – most boats going upstream start here, though if you're planning to visit Manu Biosphere Reserve you should set out from Cusco (see p.877).

Arrival, information and getting around

If you arrive by plane, the blast of hot, humid air you get the moment you step out onto the **airport**'s runway is an instant reminder that this is the Amazon Basin. Aero Continente operates daily jets from Lima via Cusco, while Aero Condor and Aero Santander offer cheaper, daily propeller planes from Cusco. Military Grupo Ocho planes also jet in from Cusco several times weekly, but you need to check their schedule at Cusco airport. There are also two or three flights weekly to other jungle destinations in Madre de Dios, such as Iberia; check with travel agents or the new airline companies on arrival in Peru. Unless you're being picked up as part of an organized tour, **airport transfer** is simplest and coolest by *motokar*, costing around US$2.50 for the otherwise very hot eight-kilometre walk.

The quickest way of **getting around town** and its immediate environs is to hail a *motokar* (75¢ in-town flat rate, but check before getting on) or passenger-carrying motorbikes (30¢, also a flat rate). If you fancy doing a bit of running about on your own, or have a lot of ground to cover in town, moped rental is a useful option; you'll find a reasonable place at Av Gonzalez Prada 321, by the *Hotel Wilson* (US$1 for 1hr, US$10 for 12hr; no deposit, but passports and driving licences required). Make sure there's ample petrol in the tank.

Puerto Maldonado has two main **river ports**, one on the Río Tambopata, at the southern end of León de Velarde, the other on the Río Madre de Dios, at the northern end of León de Velarde; from the former, there's a very cheap **ferry** service across the river to the newish road to Brazil. From either it's possible to hire a **boatman and canoe** for a river trip; prices usually start at US$25 per person for a day journey, for a minimum of two people; this rises to US$35 for trips of two to four days. Boats are equipped with a *peque-peque* or small outboard motor, and usually take up to twelve people. If you're prepared to pay significantly more (from US$100 a day per person, again for a minimum of two), you can find boatmen with speedboats and larger outboard motors.

However you get here, you have to go through a yellow fever **vaccination checkpoint** at Puerto Maldonado's small but clean, modern and air-conditioned airport, where there's also a **tourist information** kiosk and *artesanía* shops. For entry and exit stamps, the **immigration office** is at 26 de Diciembre 356, one block from the Plaza de Armas.

Accommodation

Puerto Maldonado has a reasonable range of **hotels**, most of them either on or within a couple of blocks of León de Velarde. All the better hotels offer protection against mosquitos and some sort of air conditioning.

Cabaña Quinta Cusco 535 ⓣ084/571863 or 571045. This is a very comfortable establishment, with rooms surrounded by an attractive garden, plus there's an excellent bar-restaurant. ❹–❺

Moderno Billingshurst 357 ⓣ084/571063. A brightly painted and well-kept hotel, with something of a frontier-town character, all at extremely reasonable rates. ❶

Wasai on Billingshurst ⓣ084/571355, ⓔwasai@telematic.edu.pe, or in Cusco ⓣ084/572290, The best of the more expensive options, offering fine views over the Río Madre de Dios, and a swimming pool with a waterfall and bar set among trees, overlooking a canoe-builder's yard. All rooms are cabin-style with TV and shower, and staff here also staff organize local tours and run the *Wasai Lodge* (see p.962). ❺

Eating, drinking and nightlife

You should have no problem finding a good **restaurant** in Puerto Maldonado. Delicious river fish are always available, even in *ceviche* form, and there's venison or wild pig fresh from the forest (try *estofado de venado*). The restaurant at the *Cabaña Quinta* (see above) is hard to beat for its excellent three-course set lunches, often including fresh river fish and fried manioc. The cosy *Pizzeria Chez Maggy*, on the Plaza de Armas, is very popular with travellers and locals alike; there are no exotic toppings, but it's hard to imagine how they can produce such good **pizzas** in this jungle environment. If you like grilled **chicken**, you're spoiled for choice; try *Pollos a la Brasa La Estrella*, Velarde 474 for the tastiest. Along León de Velarde are a number of **cafés and bars**, one or two of which have walls covered in typical *selvatico*-style paintings, developed to represent and romanticize the dreamlike features of the jungle – looming jaguar, brightly plumed macaws talking to each other in the treetops, and deer drinking water from a still lake. There's very little **nightlife** in this laid-back town, especially during the week – most people just stroll around, stopping occasionally to sit and chat in the Plaza de Armas or in bars along the main street.

Around Puerto Maldonado

Madre de Dios boasts spectacular virgin lowland rainforest and exceptional wildlife. Brazil-nut tree trails, a range of lodges, some excellent local guides and ecologists, plus indigenous and colonist cultures are all within a few hours of Puerto Maldonado. There are two main ways to explore: firstly, by arranging your own boat and boatman; and secondly, though considerably more expensive, by taking an excursion up to one of the lodges.

Less than one hour downriver from Puerto Maldonado (90min on the return upriver) is **LAGO SANDOVAL**, a large lake where the Ministry of Agriculture has introduced the large *paiche* fish. At its best on weekday mornings (it gets quite crowded at other times), there are decent opportunities for spotting wildlife, in particular **birds** similar to those at Lago Valencia. It's also possible to walk to the lake (about 1hr), and once here boatmen and canoes can usually be obtained by your guide for a couple of hours, as can food and drink.

It takes the best part of a day by canoe with a *peque-peque*, or around two hours in a *lancha* with an outboard, to reach the huge lake of **LAGO VALENCIA** from Puerto Maldonado. Easing onto the lake itself, the sounds of the canoe engine are totally silenced by the weight and expanse of water. Up in the trees around the channel lie hundreds of hoatzin birds, or *gallos* as they are called locally – large, ungainly creatures with orange and brown plumage, long wings and distinctive spiky crests.

Another good trip, if you've got at least three days to spare (two nights minimum), is up to the **Río Heath**, a national rainforest sanctuary, though while the **Pampas del Heath** are excellent for macaws they don't have the primary forest necessary for a great variety of wildlife. A shorter trip – five hours up and about two hours down – is to **Tres Chimbales**, where there are a few houses belonging to the Infierno community on the Río Tambopata; it's possible to spend two or three days watching for wildlife, walking in the forest and fishing. From here you can visit **Infierno** village itself – spread out along the river, you can see glimpses of thatched and tin-roofed huts.

Organized tours

Compared with independent travel, an **organized excursion** saves time and adds varying degrees of comfort. It also ensures that you go with someone who knows the area, who probably speaks English and, if you choose well, can introduce you to the flora, fauna and culture of the area. It's also worth noting that you are less likely to get ripped off with a registered company with a fixed office and contact details, especially if you should need redress afterwards. Most people book a trip in Cusco before travelling to Puerto Maldonado, though it is possible to contact most of the operators in Puerto itself, either at the airport or through one of the offices (see below), or through the cafés on León de Velarde. Flying from Cusco is the quickest way to reach Puerto Maldonado, and most Cusco agencies will organize plane tickets (US$40–50) for you if you take their tours. The cheapest option is a two-day and one-night tour, but on these you can expect to spend most of your time travelling and sleeping. Frankly, the Amazon deserves a longer visit, and you're only looking at US$25–50 more for an extra day.

Of the ever-increasing number of **lodges** and **tour operators** around Puerto Maldonado, mainly on the ríos Madre de Dios and Tambopata, all offer a good taste of the jungle, but the quality of the experience varies from area to area and lodge to lodge – all lodges tend to offer full board and include transfers, though always check the level of service and ask to see photos at the lodges' offices in Cusco or Lima. It's also worth checking out what costs will be once you're there; complaints are common about the price of drinks (soft drinks and beer), although given the distance they've travelled, the mark-up is hardly surprising. Remember, too, that even the most luxurious place is far removed from normal conveniences, and conditions – from toilets to sleeping arrangements – tend to be extremely rustic and relatively open to the elements.

Lodges and tour operators

Cusco Amazonico Lodge Pasaje J. C. Tello C-13, Urbanización Santa Monica, Cusco ⓣ084/235314, ⓔkoechlin@inkaterra.com.pe; in Lima ⓣ01/422-6574, ⓔreservas@inkaterra.com.pe. Set up by a French–Peruvian venture in 1975, comforts here include a cocktail bar and good food (often a buffet). The main excursion is to Lago Sandoval, some 20min upriver, and guides speak several languages. The lodge owns 10,000 hectares of forest surrounding it and has recently established a monkey island. From US$160 per person for three days and two nights (US$25 supplement for a single).

Eco Amazonia Lodge Portal de Panes 109, Oficina 6, Cusco ⓣ084/236159, ⓔecolodge@chasqui.unsaac.edu.pe; Av Larco 1083, Oficina 408, Miraflores, Lima ⓣ01/242-2708; ⓦwww.unsaac.edu.pe/CUSCO/TURISMO/Agencia/EcoAmazonia. Less than two hours downriver from Puerto Maldonado, this large establishment offers basic bungalows and dormitories. Packages usually include visits to Lago Sandoval, about 30min upriver, and organized visits can be made to the Palma Real community, though this is often anticlimactic and of dubious value to both tribe and tourist. There's also a monkey island. From US$40–60 per person per night according to length of stay.

Posada Amazonas Lodge and Tambopata Research Centre Contact through Rainforest Expeditions, Aramburu 166, 4B, Lima 18 ⓣ01/421-8347 or 221-4182, ⓦwww.perunature.com. *Posadas* is probably the region's best lodge for its relationship with locals – it's owned by the Ese Eja community of Infierno (though mainly non-native members work here) – and for its wildlife research. Resident researchers act as guides (different languages available), and most packages include a visit to Lago Tres Chimbadas; additional trips to the Tambopata macaw *colpa* (6–8hr upriver) can be arranged, involving a night at the remote Tambopata Research Center (TRC); a minimum of six days is recommended for complete tours. The lodge itself features large, stylish doubles with shared bath, set in three native-style buildings, plus a central dining-area-cum-bar and lecture room. From US$90 per day per person.

Wasai Lodge Owned by the *Wasai* hotel in Puerto Maldonado, C Arequipa 242, or in Cusco at Solo Selva, Plateros 364 ⓣ084/228590, ⓦwww.soloselva.com. Four hours upriver from Puerto Maldonado is this relatively new and smallish lodge set in the forest, with a pleasant jungle bar and dining area. Spanish- and English-speaking guides are available, with 15km of trails in the vicinity plus trips to the Chuncho *colpa* on request. Usually from US$340 per person for 4 days and 3 nights, but sometimes offers promotional discounts at around US$175, including a visit to Lago Sandoval plus the last night at the *Wasai* (avoiding the early morning start); US$500 for 7 days/6 nights, including a visit to the *colpa*.

Manu Biosphere Reserve

Encompassing almost two million hectares (about half the size of Switzerland) on the foothills of the eastern Andes, the **Manu Biosphere Reserve** features a uniquely varied environment of pristine rainforest, from crystalline cloudforest streams and waterfalls down to slow-moving, chocolate-brown rivers in the dense lowland jungle. For **flora and fauna**, the Manu is pretty much unbeatable in South America, with over 5000 flowering plants, 1200 species of butterfly, 1000 types of bird, 200 kinds of mammal and an unknown quantity of reptiles and insects. Rich in macaw salt licks, otter lagoons, prowling jaguar, there are also thirteen species of monkey and seven species of macaw in Manu.

Accessible only by boat, any expedition to Manu is very much in the hands of the gods, thanks to the changeable jungle environment; the region experiences a rainy season from December to March, but is best visited between May and August when it's much drier, although at that time the temperatures often exceed 30°C.

The highlight of most organized visits to Manu is the trail network and lakes of **Cocha Salvador** (the largest of Manu's oxbows, at 3.5km long) and **Cocha Otorongo**, bountiful jungle areas rich in animal, water and bird-life. Cocha Otorongo is best known for the family of **giant otters** who live here; because of this, canoeing is not permitted, but there is a floating platform which can be manoeuvred to observe the otters fishing and playing from a safe distance. Other wildlife to look out for includes – the plentiful **caimans** – the two- to three-metre white alligators and the rarer three- to five-metre black ones, and you can usually see several species of **monkey** (dusky titis, woolly monkeys, red howlers, brown capuchins and the larger spider monkeys – known locally as *maquisapas*). Sometimes big mammals such as **capybara** or **white-lipped peccaries** (called *sajinos* in Peru) also lurk in the undergrowth.

The flora of Manu is as outstanding as its wildlife. Huge cedar trees can be seen along the trails, covered in hand-like vines climbing up their vast trunks (most of the cedars were taken out of here between 1930 and 1963, before it became a protected area). The giant Catahua trees, many over 150 years old, are traditionally the preferred choice for making dugout canoes – and some are large enough to make three or four – though second choice is the lagarto tree.

Organized tours

There are quite a few **organized tours** competing for travellers who want to visit Manu. Many are keen to keep the impact of tourism to a minimum, which means limiting the number of visits per year (it's already running well into the thousands). However, they do vary quite a bit in quality of guiding, level of comfort and price range. If you go with one of the companies listed below, you can generally be confident that you won't be doing anything that might have lasting damage.

Manu Expeditions Av Pardo 895, PO Box 606, Cusco ⓣ084/226671, ⓔAdventure@ManuExpeditions.com. One of the best and the most responsible companies, run by a British ornithologist. It offers three- to nine-day camping expeditions into Zone B and to the Manu Wildlife Centre, with solar-powered radio communications and a video machine. Thoroughly recommended, the guides and service are top quality, good English is spoken, they offer air and overland transfers to Boca Manu (they have their own overland transport), and food, beds (or riverside campsite) and bird-blinds are all included. US$688–1595, discounts available to South American Explorers' Club members.

Manu Nature Tours Av Pardo 1046, Cusco ⓣ084/252721, ⓦwww.manuperu.com; Portal Comercio, 195 Plaza de Armas, Cusco ⓣ084/252526. A highly professional company that operates *Manu Lodge*, one of only two within Zone B, where you can join their four- to eight-day programmes. It also runs three-day trips to *Manu Cloud Forest Lodge* in its private reserve by the southeast boundary of Zone A, where torrent ducks, *gallos* and even woolly monkeys are often seen. US$268–299 for *Manu Cloud Forest Lodge*, US$1040–2065 for four- to eight-day programmes; discounts available to South American Explorers' Club members.

Pantiacolla Tours Plateros 360, Cusco ⓣ084/238323, ⓦwww.pantiacolla.com. A company with a growing reputation for serious eco-adventure tours. Its cheapest option is also the longest, a nine-day tour that takes groups in and out by bus and boat, while the more expensive five- to seven-day trips go in by road and out by plane from Boca Manu. It has an excellent lodge on the Río Alto Madre de Dios at Itahuania, and its tours into Zone B are based in tents at prepared campsites. US$675–795, discounts available to South American Explorers' Club members.

10

Uruguay

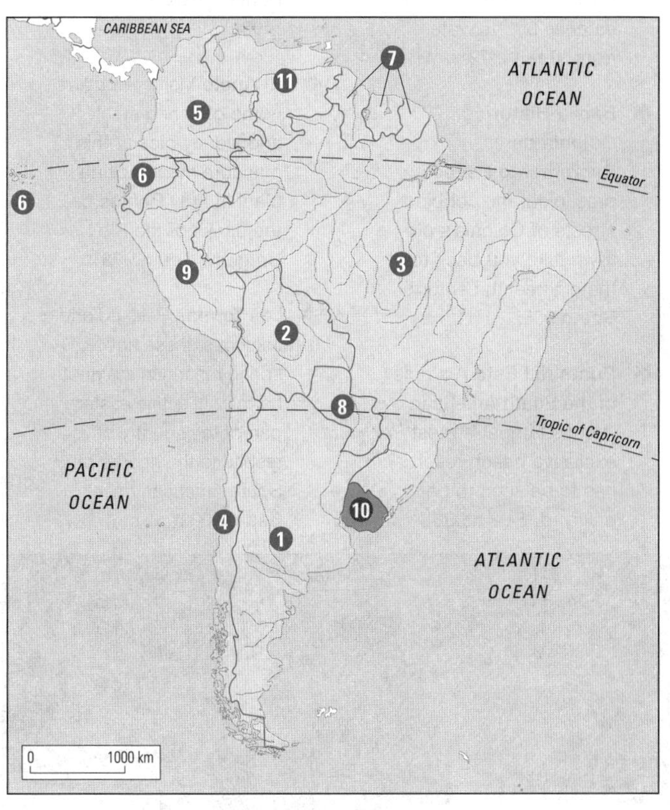

CARIBBEAN SEA
ATLANTIC OCEAN
Equator
PACIFIC OCEAN
Tropic of Capricorn
ATLANTIC OCEAN
0 1000 km
1
2
3
4
5
6
6
7
8
9
10
11

Uruguay highlights

* **Mercado del Puerto** After a day negotiating the sights of the capital, visitors will be spoilt for choice in this atmospheric treasure chest of eateries by the waterfront. See p.979

* **Barrio Histórico, Colonia del Sacramento** Perfectly preserved, the cobbled streets of Colonia's old town take you back to the eighteenth century. See p.995

* **Punta del Este** A staple of the South American jetset, Uruguay's most exclusive beach resort has to be seen to be believed. See p.988

* **Isla de los Lobos** Take a boat trip to this island, one of the world's largest sea lion colonies, just off the coast of Punta del Este. See p.988

* **El Anglo** Visit the bizarre home of tinned steak and kidney pies at this macabre meatpacking plant in Fray Bentos on the banks of the Río Uruguay. See p.998

* **Las Termas** Relaxed and luxurious, these hot spring resorts in the geothermically active eastern part of the country offer a respite to the rigours of South American travel. See p.1002

Introduction and basics

Unfortunately, most visitors to South America see Uruguay as a mere stepping stone between Brazil and Argentina, stopping only along the south coast at the capital Montevideo, the historic Colonia del Sacramento or the exclusive resort of Punta del Este. While it surely lacks the obvious appeal of its larger neighbours, Uruguay does merit an extended visit; not only is its capital city, Montevideo, one of the more agreeable around, but the coast is larded with unspoilt beaches and attractive fishing villages.

The interior of the country is ideal for those who like their nature raw and anyone looking to be pampered can head to one of the multiple thermal resorts. Economic crisis means that travelling around the country – traditionally one of the more expensive in South America – has never been more affordable, and there is an extensive and efficient transport system in operation, as well as numerous border crossings to Brazil and Argentina.

Where to go

Intensely likeable, the capital, **Montevideo**, is of an easily manageable size, and it doesn't take long to feel at home. The city boasts some magnificent architecture, less high-rise and oppressive than Buenos Aires, while retaining a relaxed atmosphere. From the capital, main roads (*rutas*) run like spokes to all corners of the country. The stretch east of the city contains magnificent beaches, among the best on the continent. **Punta del Este** is the most famous resort, popular with rich Argentines and Brazilians, but beyond here quiet bays, forested hillsides and sand dunes enable you to enjoy the surroundings without the crowds.

West of Montevideo, **Colonia del Sacramento** is one of the prettiest towns in the country. Beautifully set on the River Plate, it too boasts some magnificent beaches and a quaint old town of historic importance. Beyond it are **Mercedes**, the "city of flowers", and **Fray Bentos**, site of the famous canning factory. The now deserted El Anglo plant makes one of the most unusual, if slightly macabre, day-trips in the whole of South America. Further north the twin cities of **Paysandú** and **Salto** are well placed for visiting nearby **thermal spa resorts**, an ideal way of relaxing after a few days on the road.

Much of the interior of Uruguay is taken up by farming and ranch land, and it is possible to drive for kilometres without seeing another soul, although isolated **estancias**, or working ranches, offer visitors the opportunity to test their skills as a gaucho. In the centre of the country the Río Negro has been dammed to create **Lago Rincón del Bonete**, sparking the development of watersports and encouraging the growth of towns like **Paso de los Toros**. North of here the landscape changes dramatically, becoming hillier, more forested and a deeper green as grassland gives way to subtropical forest at the Brazilian border.

When to go

Uruguay has a temperate climate, mild throughout most of the year, though influenced by prevailing conditions in the Atlantic. The hottest temperatures are during the **high season** (November to March) when it averages 28°C on the coast, while in winter (June to August), or **low season**, a maximum of around 15°C can be expected. In the interior temperatures can be more extreme and summer days can occasionally be stiflingly hot and dry, while coastal temperatures are tempered by Atlantic breezes. **Rainfall** is comparatively constant throughout the year, with 50 to 100 millimetres falling in most months.

Red tape and visas

A **passport** valid for six months after entry is required of all nationals, except those of

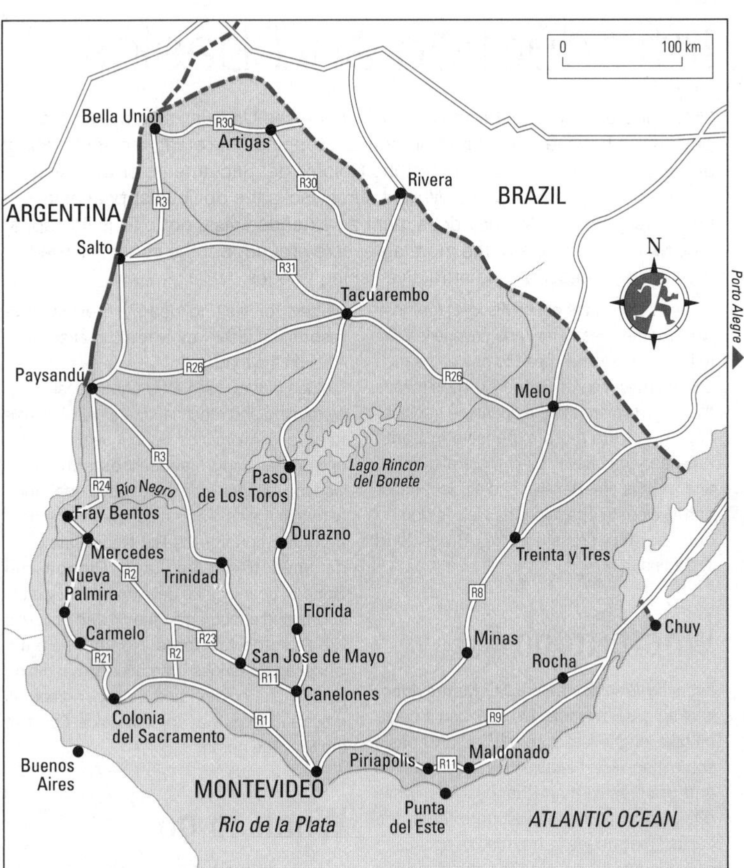

other Latin American countries, who can use their national identity documents. Australians, Canadians, UK nationals, Western Europeans and US citizens do not require a **visa** for entry (see Ⓦwww.columbusguides.com for a full list of countries not requiring visas). Visas cost US$42, and a passport photograph and exit ticket are necessary for applications. Three months entry is granted initially for all visitors, with the option to extend for a further three months if required, on production of the same documentation as for visa applications.

For **extensions**, visit the Direccion Nacional de Migración at Misiones 1513 in Montevideo. There is a charge of UR$183 if you renew before the expiry date of your previous entry card, or UR$280 if you do so afterwards. Alternatively, leaving and re-entering the country will see you supplied with a new three month stay free of charge. There is a US$12 **departure tax** payable on leaving the country by air.

Costs and money

As Uruguay's economy is heavily dependent upon its neighbours, recent **economic problems** in the region have had knock-on effects for the country. Traditionally one of the more expensive South American countries, a catastrophic economic crash in 2002, originating in Argentina, now makes it one of the cheapest to visit – budget travellers can comfortably get by on US$10–15 a day, while US$25–50 a day guarantees a pretty high standard of living.

Bank notes are issued in 10, 50, 100, 200, 1000, 5000 and 10,000 **pesos** (represented by the symbol **UR$** throughout this chapter), although anything over 100 can have shop owners running along the street searching for change. Dollars are more widely accepted since the economic difficulties arose and many hotels have taken to quoting their prices in dollars to preserve their profit margins.

There is no limit to how much currency you can take out of the country, but beyond Brazil and Argentina the peso can be very difficult to change and rates are unfavourable. **Changing money** is rarely difficult, and *casas de cambio* are abundant in the bigger towns. Moneychangers on the street may offer slightly better rates, but be careful that your dealings with them are in a public place and that you know the exchange rate before you talk business. **Travellers' cheques** are difficult to change, but those in US dollars are more readily accepted than those in other currencies. **Credit cards** are not widely accepted outside Montevideo and incur a commission charge of ten percent. Most towns have at least one ATM that accepts VISA or MasterCard, but if not some banks will let you draw against the card on producing your card and a valid passport for identification. Transactions can be made for pesos or dollars, but this is a lengthy process involving a lot of waiting around.

Information, websites and maps

Despite the paucity of foreign visitors to the country, Uruguay's **Ministry of Tourism** is extremely well developed. Offices are located in every main town, and each is well stocked with a variety of leaflets and information to assist the traveller. The headquarters of the Ministry (Ⓦwww.turismo.gub.uy) is located on Plaza Fabini in Montevideo.

Useful facts can also be gleaned from the **Internet** at Ⓦwww.uruguaytotal.com, Ⓦwww.visit-uruguay.com and Ⓦwww.eltimon.com. A list of tourist offices with their contact details is at Ⓦwww.chasque.net/guambia/turismo/oftur, and Uruguay's nineteen government departments each have individual websites (such as Ⓦwww.salto.gub.uy or Ⓦwww.rocha.gub.uy), which offer up-to-date guides to what is happening within their sphere of influence. While much of the information is of local interest only, they generally have a section for tourist information that can be a good starting point.

Good **maps** are available from the Geográfico Militar (Ⓣ02/801-6868) at 8 de Octubre 3255 in Montevideo. A limited number of maps are available online through Maptown (Ⓦwww.maptown.com/uruguaymaps).

Accommodation

The standard of **accommodation** in Uruguay is generally good in comparison with other South American countries, though off the main tourist tracks places to stay can be rather thin on the ground. Tourist offices usually have a list of hotels and, in smaller towns, a list of private rooms, although you may have to request them specifically. Outside the largest resorts it is not usually necessary to book in advance, and in the low season, when prices fall dramatically, rooms are easy to come by.

The vast majority of **hotel rooms** are en suite, and in most places it is usually possible to find decent quality double rooms for as little as UR$300, some including breakfast. While more upmarket establishments charge almost European prices for rooms, this does not necessarily guarantee a vastly improved level of service, and many two- and three-star hotels are remarkably cheap for the facilities they provide. If possible, ask to see the room before paying, and remember that in winter it is well worth paying a little more to get a room with heating. Budget travellers should have no problem finding a good deal, but should beware of being tempted by astoundingly cheap **hospedajes** and **pensiones**. With a few exceptions, these are of very poor quality, unsafe and located in the seediest areas of town.

Should you fancy getting your hands dirty, a stay on an **estancia**, a country ranch estate (see box on p.1004) is worth the extra expense. Comfortable, and often luxurious, accommodation is offered alongside a number of outdoor pursuits to give you an enjoyable taste of the country life. Most are very isolated and difficult to access without your own transport, but several Montevideo tour companies offer all-inclusive packages involving a stay on an estancia. For more information visit Ⓦwww.turismo.gub.uy/estancias and www.lares.com.uy.

Hostels and campsites

There are **youth hostels** in the largest towns and cities. While facilities are usually good, often including free Internet access, prices are frequently comparable to hotels. Rooms are usually dormitories, with a few doubles, and they are always a good place to meet fellow travellers. YHA membership is not compulsory, although members do receive a slight reduction. **Campsites** can be found in almost every town, but very few boast running water or electricity, and in many cases they are little more than a cordoned off area of land, frequently close to a river. More comfortable are **cabañas** (self-catering cabins), which are a pleasant break from the norm, although they fill rapidly in summer. Prices vary as much as quality, but as a general rule US$20 per person will get you the top of the range.

Getting around

Uruguay is very compact, and it is rarely more than a few hours by car, bus or plane from A to B. Passenger **train** services no longer operate, although there has been talk of restoring some routes for several years.

By car

Car hire is very reasonable (around US$20–30 a day) and a great way of seeing the country, but remember that an **International or Inter-American Driving Permit** is required. The main *rutas* are little used and speed limits may seem overly cautious (90kmh) – be warned, however, that arbitrary stops by traffic police are not unusual and many solicit bribes for minor violations. While roads along the south and east coasts are excellent, away from the most well-trodden areas the quality deteriorates dramatically and many roads are full of potholes. Remember that the law states that headlights must be illuminated at all times on the main roads.

By bus

Several daily **buses** connect the main towns and cities and on the whole these are fast, efficient and cheap. All the larger towns have central bus terminals, but for the smaller ones that do not, the offices of the bus companies (see p.985) are invariably located on or around the main plaza. The maximum duration of a single journey is unlikely to be more than six hours, while the average journey time will be around one or two hours.

By plane

A network of **internal flights** connects the main population centres from around US$50 one-way. The main internal airlines are Aeromas (Ⓦwww.aeromas.com) and the national airline Pluna (Ⓦwww.pluna.com.uy), which is also the main international airline operating out of the country. A **Mercosur Airpass** (see p.39), valid for thirty days' travel to Argentina, Brazil, Chile, Paraguay and Uruguay is available to customers resident outside South America from participating airlines.

By taxi

Taxis are generally cheap, although a little pricier in resorts like Punta del Este where large numbers of tourists congregate. Where possible agree a fee in advance, and if metered ensure that the meter is at zero before starting the journey. The majority of drivers are honest, fair and friendly, but there will always be a few looking to make some easy cash out of unsuspecting travellers.

Mail and telecommunications

Postal services are notoriously unreliable and it is recommended that all items of importance are sent by registered mail or a private mail company such as DHL or FedEx.

Telephone services are provided by ANTEL, with offices in all major towns. Payphones are operated by phone card only, available in denominations up to UR$500 from ANTEL offices or kiosks. Increasingly private satellite cabins are appearing which are more convenient, do not require a card, but are frequently more expensive. Phone calls are cheaper at weekends and after 9pm. To call Uruguay from any other country, dial the country code (00) 598 followed by the area code (without the first number) and the number.

Internet access is now much more widely available in Uruguay than previously and is very reasonably priced (around UR$30 per hour). Most towns have at least one cybercafé, and in Montevideo particularly there should be no problem in getting online. Although most Internet cafés close in the afternoon between 2 and 5pm, the majority open early in the morning and do not close until around 11pm.

Food and drink

Breakfast is often little more than toast and jam in Uruguay, but *crepes* (pancakes) sometimes figure, usually with fruit and syrup, as do pastries such as *media lunas* (croissants).

While the average Uruguayan menu will horrify vegetarians, meat eaters will be salivating at the prospect of tucking in at lunch or dinner. As in Argentina, **beef** dominates and a good steak is astonishingly cheap. Worth checking out are **parrilladas**, huge grills where the food is cooked in front of your eyes. Servings are immense, filling and often dangerously loaded with calories, but they ensure that even those on the tightest of budgets will never go hungry.

Entrecote is a thick steak, while *lomo* is a fillet steak, although these terms are sometimes interchangeable. *Costillas* are chops (not ribs as they are in Spain). The average *parrillada* menu is large and complex and frequently features large amounts of offal, so be sure to ask what things are before you order to avoid a nasty surprise. Two to look out for, or avoid, are *mondongo* (tripe) and *choto* (intestine wrapped with tripe). **Sausages** in Uruguay are excellent, from spicy *chorizo* to the delicious *morcilla dulce*, a type of black pudding sweetened with orange peel that should not be missed. *Morcilla salada* is a savoury black pudding more akin to those served in Europe, while *panchos* are hot dogs and *húngaros* are spicy hot dogs. A typically Uruguayan dish is the *chivito*, a thin steak served *al plato* (on a plate) or *al pan* (in a sandwich). *Chivito Canadiense* has ham, bacon and cheese melted over the beef, often with a fried egg, salad and chips.

For a break from beef, **milanesas** (veal in breadcrumbs) are ubiquitous, as is *pollo asado* (roast chicken), which is best when cooked on roadside spits. The Italian influence on Uruguayan cuisine can be seen in **pizzas** (a *pizzeta* is a small pizza for one person) and pasta, although the latter is frequently overcooked to a gooey pulp.

For **dessert**, *chajá de Paysandú* is the speciality. A sickly-sweet sponge cake stuffed with apricot jam, coated with cream and rolled in powdered meringue, one portion of it is often enough for two people. *Masas,* available from *confiterias*, are bite-size cakes sold by weight. Incredibly cheap and irresistibly delicious, these are often the best way to sample a range of desserts.

Drinks

Uruguayan **coffee** is excellent and English **tea** is widely available, but you should not miss the opportunity to try *maté*. A national obsession, it is a herbal tea drink around which a whole social culture has developed. It is hard to miss people walking along the street with their flasks of hot water under their arm, or groups of friends passing around the mug and straw as they share their beverage. **Milk** and **yoghurt** are sold in rather inconvenient plastic bags that make storage very difficult.

Uruguayan **beer**, usually sold in litre bottles, is good and very cheap. Among the best brands are Prinz and Zillerthal, while Pilsen, the most popular brand, has a stronger flavour that might not appeal to some tastes. Foreign beers are also widely available, although a little more expensive. **Wines** are also of a high standard, the best local products being easily the equal of anything produced by Chile or Argentina. Good brands to look out for are Pisano and Juanico. Local **spirits** like *caña* (from sugarcane) and *grappa* (from grapes) are only for hardened drinkers, while a *medio medio* is a mind-blowingly strong mixture of *caña* and cheap whiskey (note that in Mercado del Puerto, Montevideo, a *medio medio* is a much more palatable mixture of still and sparkling white wine).

Safety and the police

On the whole, Uruguay is one of the safest South American countries to visit, and the presence of **tourist police** on the streets of Montevideo has had a profound effect on reducing crime. Petty theft and pickpocketing do still occur, although simple avoidance measures like appearing confident and avoiding unfamiliar areas after dark can almost eliminate the possibility. Outside the capital you are unlikely to encounter anything more threatening than mild curiosity from the locals – however, it is important that you apply the same common sense measures to personal safety as you would anywhere else. Overt displays of wealth are especially likely to attract opportunistic thieves who would otherwise let you pass in peace, particularly during times of economic instability. Minor crimes can be reported to police officers on the streets, but in case of emergency use the numbers below.

Useful numbers

Ambulance ☎109
Fire ☎104
Police ☎109
General emergency operator ☎911

Opening hours, public holidays and fiestas

Most establishments are open from 8.30am to noon and from 2.30 to 7pm. **Banks** generally open in the afternoon only between 1 and 5pm. They are usually closed at weekends.

Calendar of public holidays

January 1 New Year's Day (*Año Nuevo*)

January 6 Epiphany (*Epifanía*)

March/April Easter and Holy Week (*Pascua y Semana Santa*)

April 19 Commemoration of the return of the 33 (*Desembarco de los 33)*

May 1 Day of the Worker (*Dia del Trabajador*)

June 19 Birthday of General Artigas (*Natalicio de Artigas*)

July 18 Constitution Day (*Jura de la Constitución*)

August 24 Nostalgia Night (*Noche de Nostalgia*)

August 25 Independence Day (*Dia de la Independencia*)

October 12 Columbus Day (*Dia de la Raza*)

November 2 All Soul's Day (*Dia de los Muertos*)

December 8 Start of official summer holidays

December 25 Christmas Day (*Navidad*)

Sport and outdoor activities

Soccer, or *fútbol*, is without doubt the number one sport among most Uruguayans. The country was the host and first winner of the inaugural FIFA World Cup in 1930, but despite winning it again in 1950 the standard of domestic football has declined and most of the better players now ply their trades abroad. However, the Uruguayan league is still very competitive and the bigger matches guarantee a fantastic, if slightly intimidating atmosphere. Nacional versus Peñarol, the Montevideo derby, is the biggest match of the season. **Rugby Union** is also on the up, with the national team qualifying for the World Cup in 2003 for the first time.

Water sports, although beyond the budget of most Uruguayans, are an attraction for many visitors. Punta del Este is the main centre for surfing, scuba diving and yachting, but recent attempts have been made to develop the gargantuan man-made lake at Rincón del Bonete for these purposes. Still in its infancy in Uruguay, **eco-tourism** (try Ⓦwww.eco-uruguay.com and aventuras@mundoturismonatural.com) takes the form of organized hiking in most areas, with the far north and southeast of the country providing the most spectacular landscapes. **Fishing** for game fish like *dorado* (golden bass) and, at the right time of year, **whale-watching** are becoming increasingly popular on the south coast, especially around Punta del Este; visits to nearby sea lion colonies rarely disappoint. **Birdwatchers** can choose from a potential 400 species native to Uruguay, although most of the spectacular land mammals have long since disappeared. The rhea (*nandú*), a type of South American ostrich, is still relatively easy to see in the north, while the lagoons of Maldonado and Rocha departments are home to large numbers of flamingos and graceful black-necked swans.

History

Largely neglected by the colonial Spaniards owing to its lack of mineral wealth and hostile native population, Uruguay did not gain its independence until 1828. Sandwiched between the great landmasses of Argentina and Brazil, it initially acted as something of a buffer between the two larger powers, and it wasn't until the twentieth century that Uruguay really achieved prominence in its own right, developing a reputation as one of South America's most stable economies.

The colonial period

Home to the **Charrúa Indians**, a hunter-gatherer people hostile to strangers, the area known today as Uruguay was largely ignored by colonial powers because of the absence of gold and silver. The Spanish began to show an interest in the late sixteenth century, and the wild cattle introduced by them had a massive influence on the early history of the region. The Charrúa adapted to hunting of the cattle, bringing them into closer contact with Europeans, and mixed marriage soon gave rise to the gaucho lifestyle of cattle ranching and hunting. But despite the Spanish influence, it was the Portuguese who founded **Colonia del Sacramento**, the first major colony in Uruguay in 1680. Viewed as a trade rival to Buenos Aires across the River Plate, the Spanish responded – some 46 years later – by founding the defensive citadel of Montevideo. Friction between the two powers defined the following century, with attack and counter-attack launched as both struggled for dominance over the important River Plate trade routes that gave access to the wealthy interior of the continent. The importance of the area was not lost on other world powers, either, and Montevideo was briefly taken by the British in 1807 as part of their campaign to take Buenos Aires. Their failure to secure the Argentine capital forced them to withdraw entirely from the region, indirectly leading to the first declaration of **independence** the following year.

Independence

Hoping to capitalize on the instability of the fledgling nation, Brazil invaded in 1811, only to be repelled with Argentinean help by **General José Artigas**, who took up arms as a freedom fighter. Peace didn't last long, though, as Uruguay's former allies Argentina invaded just a year later, finally taking Montevideo in 1814. The Uruguayans, or **Orientales**, regained Montevideo the following year, but the turmoil continued until 1820, when Brazil marched into Montevideo, forcing Artigas, by now a senior figure, to seek sanctuary in Paraguay, where he remained until his death.

In 1825 **General Juan Lavalleja** led the legendary **Treinta y Tres Orientales** (a group of 33 freedom fighters driven into exile by the Brazilian reconquest of 1820) in a bid to drive out the occupiers, vanquishing the Brazilians on February 20 1827. A year later, Argentina and Brazil relinquished their claims on the territory allowing Uruguay finally to achieve its independence.

Civil War and the War of the Triple Alliance

Civil War (the Guerra Grande) racked the new republic as two rival leaders fought for control. **José Fructuoso Rivera**, leader of the **Colorados** (liberals), eventually defeated Manuel Oribe of the **Blancos** (nationalists) to become the first president of the country, and the two groups remain the two main political parties today. The disputes between the two factions continued until 1865 when Uruguay found itself dragged into the **War of the Triple Alliance**, joining with Brazil and Argentina against Paraguay. Once Paraguay was defeated and there was no further common cause to distract the factions, civil unrest, political corruption and dictatorship soon became the norm.

The twentieth century

Early in the twentieth century, the two presidential terms of the controversial Colorado **José Batlle y Ordoñez** (1903–07 and 1911–15) went some way to making Uruguay Latin America's first and only welfare state, and the country entered an era of prosperity. **Immigration** increased (see box below), especially into Montevideo, and rapid urbanization ensued forming a large liberal middle-class educated in Europeanized state schools. Exports grew, and the country enjoyed a healthy trade balance surplus during the World War II years, supplying meat and meat products to the warring nations. However, inflation and corruption were never far away, and during the 1950s the industrial sector stagnated irreversibly.

During the 1960s, Uruguay reverted to **military rule** and, although there was a verbal commitment to spending more money on the poor, the dire economic situation meant that poverty increased considerably. The **Tupamaros National Liberation Movement** fought against military rule from 1968 until they were effectively wiped out by 1972; around the same period, left-wing political activity was outlawed. Over time, the welfare state, though not officially abolished in theory, ceased to exist in practice, and mass emigration ensued. With political repression and public unrest increasing through the 1970s, the military elected to hand back power to the politicians, and free elections were held again in 1984. **Dr Julio Sanguinetti** of the Colorado Party was the eventual victor, holding office until 1989.

Uruguay today

In the mid-1990s there was a resurgence in leftist politics and Tabare Vazquez of the left-wing coalition **Encuentro Progresista** (EP) was only just pipped to the presidency by a rejuvenated Sanguinetti in 1994. Sanguinetti's retirement in 1999 saw the Colorados and Blancos (under the banner of the **Partido Nacional**) form a centre-right coalition to keep the EP from power, despite the latter dominating the National Assembly elections. Incoming president **Jorge Batlle** planned to bring economic growth by diversifying exports away from the traditional wool and beef, but his plans were seriously hampered by a continuing recession that struck in 1999, caused largely by economic stagnation in neighbouring Argentina, a fellow member of the Mercosur trade pact. By 2002, economic crisis had affected all the Mercosur countries, and Uruguayan unemployment was up as high as fifteen percent. With the Uruguayan economy so dependent on those of other Mercosur countries, the chances of an economic revival being seen in Uruguay before Brazil and Argentina are slim, and the immediate future does not look promising.

A nation of immigrants

Uruguayan culture is predominately of **Spanish** origin with a strong **Italian** influence, both clearly represented in the music and food. Although black slaves were widespread in the River Plate area during colonial times, today only three percent of Uruguay's population is of **African** origin. Prior to independence, Montevideo was a small town of 20,000 people, but over the next hundred years almost 650,000 European immigrants made their home there. More recently, **Jewish** and **Chinese** immigrants have brought a more cosmopolitan feel to the capital. Close to the Brazilian border there is a strong **Portuguese** flavour to the language, music and lifestyle.

Books

Uruguay's most renowned novelists are Juan Carlos Onetti (*The Shipyard*) and Mario Benedetti (*The Truce, Blood Pact*). *Uruguay (Cultures of the World)* by Leslie Jermyn is a good introduction to the country and *The Purple Land* by William Henry Hudson is a classic nineteenth-century text. Christopher Empson's *Thirty Years Amongst the Gauchos of Uruguay* is a fascinating account of gaucho life, while *Voices of the River Plate* by Clark Zlotchew contains interviews with Argentinean and Uruguayan writers. For a discussion of the political history of the country *Uruguay: South America's First Welfare State* by George Pendle covers the early twentieth century, while *The Politics of River Trade* by Thomas Whigham is a discussion of tradition and development from 1780 to 1870.

Birdwatchers will find *The Illustrated Checklist to the Birds of Southern South America and Antarctica* by Martin de la Pena to be the most complete guide to the region.

10.1

Montevideo

With a population of around 1.3 million, **MONTEVIDEO** is the only city of any real size in the country, thirteen times larger than Paysandú, the second largest. Initially founded in 1726 as a fortress city on the northern shore of the **River Plate**, it was in a strong trade position and, following a turbulent and often violent early history, its growth was rapid. The nineteenth century saw mass immigration from Europe resulting in a vibrant mix of architectural styles and cultures, giving the city a cosmopolitan atmosphere that persists to this day.

Visitors arriving from Buenos Aires – a likely first stop before a venture into Uruguay – will be immediately struck by the contrast between the hectic pace of life of the Argentine capital and the relaxed atmosphere here. Less affluent than its neighbour across the river, the Uruguayan capital seems happy with its lot, and while regional economic disasters have hit the city harder than most, it remains a friendly and welcoming place, with enough low-key museums, crumbling churches and high-quality restaurants to merit a couple of days' exploration.

Arrival and information

Domestic and international flights arrive at **Carrasco International Airport** 25km east of the city centre. Regular buses (UR$17) depart every fifteen minutes or so from outside the arrivals building to the city centre, a journey of approximately an hour. The buses do not hang around, so be alert and be sure to inform the driver of your destination to avoid missing it; buses only stop if asked. Taxis, which take about thirty minutes to reach the city centre, cost around UR$230, twenty percent more on Sundays.

Ferries from Buenos Aires (see box on p.986) arrive at the port terminal in the Ciudad Vieja, a ten-minute walk north of the Plaza Independencia, the hub of most of the city's activity. If arriving after dark, it is advisable to take a taxi (which shouldn't cost more than UR$30) as the area can be intimidating at night. Despite a very grand old railway building close to the port, public rail services no longer run out of Montevideo.

All intercity buses operate out of **Tres Cruces bus station**, 2km northeast of the centre. From here take bus #186 or #187 (UR$11) for the main sights, or buses marked "Aduana" for the Ciudad Vieja. Alternatively it is a very short and cheap taxi ride to Plaza Independencia.

The main **tourist office**, in the Ministry of Tourism building on Plaza Fabini (Mon–Fri 10am–6pm; ⓣ02/908-9105), will provide you with maps, a useful city walks leaflet and a copy of *Pimba*, the monthly events magazine. There are also information kiosks at the airport (daily 10am–7pm; ⓣ02/604-0396) and at Tres Cruces bus station (daily 10am–7pm; ⓣ02/409-7399). A new, well-stocked tourist information centre is located on Avenida 18 de Julio in front of the Intendencia Municipal (Mon–Fri 10am–7pm, Sat–Sun 11am–6pm; ⓣ02/903-0649) and is open on weekends, when the other central office is closed.

City transport

Most of the points of interest in the city are within **walking distance** of Plaza Independencia, but those a little further out are easily reached by public transport. The city is covered by an exhaustive, if rather daunting, network of **buses** and although no route maps are available, destinations are clearly displayed on the front of the buses and at major stops. Most buses visiting tourist sights depart from along **Avenida 18 de Julio**, the major thoroughfare into the centre of the city. For **Pocitos** and the outskirts the most direct bus is #14. To get back to the centre, take any bus marked "Aduana". Buses are very cheap (UR$13.50), yet often slow. If you are in a hurry, **taxis** may be a better option, with journeys within the confines of the city rarely amounting to more than UR$50. Beware of overcharging and ensure that metered taxis reset their meters before starting a journey.

Accommodation

Accommodation in Montevideo is, on the whole, very reasonably priced and even budget travellers should have no problem finding a good room near the centre. As a general rule *pensiónes* and *hospedajes* are best avoided, despite the tempting tariffs. Unlike their namesakes in Europe, they hire rooms by the month, have very lax security and are frequently filled with transient labourers. There are several cheap options in the Ciudad Vieja, but the area can be unsafe at night and the area around the port is notorious as a red light district. For the best combination of value and location try the area immediately south of **plazas Fabini** and **Independencia**, where there are a number of budget hotels with good facilities.

There are **no camping facilities** within the boundaries of the city currently in operation.

Hospedaje del Centro Soriano 1128 ⓣ02/900-1419. Very cheap and a little shabby, this is still cleaner than most *hospedajes*. Excellent location, though rooms at the front can be rather noisy. ❶

Hotel Europa Colonia 1341 ⓣ02/902-0045, ⓦwww.hoteleuropa.com.uy. Luxury option with spacious rooms, minibar, TV, bathroom and breakfast buffet included. Room service and secure parking are available. ❻

Hotel Florida Uruguay 808 ⓣ02/900-3667. Airy rooms with central heating, vital in winter. Rooms also boast cable TV and bathrooms. Friendly service. ❷

Hotel Nuevo Ideal Soriano 1073 ⓣ02/908-2913, ⓔmlage@adinet.com.uy. Bright, airy and pleasant in summer with a suntrap courtyard, the *Nuevo Ideal* is somewhat cold and damp in winter. Rooms are large and washing facilities are available. ❷

Hotel Palacio Bartolomé Mitre 1364 ⓣ02/916-3612, ⓔfpalaez@internet.co.uy. Grand old-style hotel in an excellent location. The rooms have TVs, bathrooms and balconies, while the slightly more expensive ones on the top floor also feature terraces with pleasant river views. ❹

Hotel Royal Soriano 1120 ⓣ02/908-3115. With smartly decorated rooms with bathroom and TV, the *Royal* provides the best value for money of all the cheaper options and is in an excellent location. ❷

Hotel Solis Bartolomé Mitre 1314 ⓣ02/915-0279, ⓔhotelsolis@hotmail.com. Though expensive, the large rooms here have bathroom and cable TV. Well located just off Plaza Independencia, in front of the Teatro Solis and in walking distance of some of the city's best nightlife. ❹

Hotel Windsor Michelini 1260 ⓣ02/901-5080. Good budget option, although the decor is a little dated, with comfortable rooms and en-suite bathrooms. The very friendly owners will hand out useful city maps. ❷

YHA Canelones 935 ⓣ02/908-1324. Superbly equipped hostel with 4–6 bedroom dormitories. The price includes breakfast and bedclothes, while a kitchen, laundry, table tennis table, Internet and bicycle hire are also available. Members ❷, non-members ❸

The City

Montevideo is an eclectic yet easily negotiable city, and mass migration in from the provinces ensures the capital evokes the country's regions within its streets. For many visitors the arrival point is the **Ciudad Vieja**, the old port town, decaying and rundown for the most part, yet bursting with historical character along its tight grid of streets. Here you will find the **Plaza de la Constitución**, the oldest square in the country, flanked by buildings of colonial grandeur that reflect the wealth of Uruguay's past. The main tourist centre is **Plaza Independencia**, site of the original citadel of Montevideo and burial place of freedom fighter and national hero **General Artigas**, while the surrounding streets contain most of the sights of architectural interest. East of here, the main commercial street **Avenida 18 de Julio** and its continuations run towards the affluent suburbs of **Pocitos** and **Carrasco** with their exclusive, sandy beaches. The seemingly endless, right-angled **Boulevar General Artigas** provides the main thoroughfare into and out of the city, as well as an arbitrary boundary between the city centre and its outskirts.

Ciudad Vieja

Although years of neglect have allowed much of the **CIUDAD VIEJA** to fall into disrepair, it is still home to some of the city's most historical monuments. The port marks the northern edge, defined by the impressively colossal but grimly monolithic **Dirección General de Aduana** building. Opposite the port entrance at the top end of Calle Pérez Castellano stands **Mercado del Puerto**, a former meat market dating from 1868. Built in the style of a nineteenth-century British railway station, complete with a station clock, it remains operational as a market, its grills and restaurants the most atmospheric spots to eat in the city (see p.983). Two blocks east, along Calle Piedras, the gargantuan Italian Neoclassical **Banco de la Republica**, one of the most impressive buildings in the entire country, dwarfs its surroundings. Built in 1938, its attractive colonnaded facade gives way to a gaping vault-like interior. On the opposite corner of Calle Solis y Cerrito is the decaying **Iglesia de San Francisco**, most notable for the unusual font made from the shell of a giant clam. From here it is two blocks south to **Plaza Zabala**, the former site of the Governor's mansion, which has as its centrepiece a horseback statue of Zabala, founder of the city. On the north side of the plaza stands the **Palacio Taranco**, home to the **Museo de Arte Decorativo** (Tues–Sat 11am–5pm, Sun 2–6pm; free), a beautifully displayed collection, particularly remarkable for the pottery and glassware that used to grace the palaces of the Uruguayan aristocracy.

On and around Calle 25 de Mayo are a number of small but interesting **museums**. On 25 de Mayo itself, the **Casa de Garibaldi** (Mon–Fri 11am–7pm, Sat noon-6pm; free), once occupied by Italian hero Giuseppe Garibaldi, houses a small collection of artefacts associated with him. The **Museo Romantico**, at 25 de Mayo 428 (same hours; free with tour in English), gives a unique and valuable insight into the opulent lifestyles of the wealthy at the end of the nineteenth century, including the rather egotistical practice of having the owner's initials inscribed onto every possession of value. The **Casa General Lavalleja** (Mon–Fri 11am–7pm, Sat noon–6pm; free), former home of the exalted General, at Zabala 1469, contains a neat museum of largely military items from the struggle for independence. But the pick of the bunch is the **Casa de Rivera** (same hours; free) at Rincón 437, which traces a fascinating journey through Uruguay's history from prehistoric times to modern day. Of particular interest are the bizarre *rompecabecas* (head-breakers), worked stones resembling 3D starfish used by indigenous peoples as weapons some 7000 years ago. Two blocks further east is the **Plaza de la Constitución**.

Plaza de la Constitución and around

Built in 1726, the **PLAZA DE LA CONSTITUCIÓN** (commonly known as the **Plaza Matriz**) is the oldest square in Uruguay, dominated by the **Catedral Metropolitana**, itself often referred to as the Iglesia Matriz. Hewn from a warm brown stone, the twin-towered, Neoclassical cathedral contains the ornate marble tombs of Mariano Soler, the first Archbishop of Montevideo, and Jacinto Vera, the first Bishop of Montevideo. The altarpiece centres upon the Virgin Mary, flanked by St Philip and Santiago and watched over by an Angel of the Faith. Right across the plaza stands the **Cabildo** (Mon–Fri & Sun 2–6.30pm, Sat 11am–5pm; free), once the town hall and prison, but now operating as a museum and national archive. It houses temporary exhibition rooms on the ground floor and an attractive collection of period furniture on the second, but for many visitors the main interest lies in the Spanish Neoclassical building itself, which dates from 1804. A grandiose, whitewashed structure, its airy courtyards with fountains and arches, and spacious, high-ceilinged rooms are typical of the colonial period. On the south side, the decadent and decaying **Club Uruguay** building deserves a quick visit if you can find someone willing to show you around. A sort of Uruguayan Rotary Club, down to its last 130 members, they are particularly proud of an old grandfather clock presented to them by Club England in 1912, that now adorns the bridge room.

On the south side of the Plaza de la Constitución, **Sarandí** heads east through a pedestrianized bohemian sector with a high concentration of bars and cafés and site of the understated **Museo Torres Garcia** (Mon–Fri 10am–7pm, Sat–Sun 10am–6pm; donation suggested). Former home of Uruguayan artist Joaquin Torres Garcia, modern art pioneer and founder of "La Escuela del Sur", the South American modern art movement, the museum is dedicated to his work. On the second floor, a fascinating display entitled "Men, Heroes and Monsters" features a collection of Torres Garcia's portraits of historical figures, such as Columbus, Mozart and Velázquez, with the natural proportions of the face altered. The viewer is left to decide which are the men, the heroes or the monsters. Sarandí terminates at the **Puerta de la Ciudadela**, gateway to the original Citadel of Montevideo and now standing at the western end of **Plaza Independencia**.

Plaza Independencia and around

Marking the original site of the Citadel of Montevideo, **PLAZA INDEPENDENCIA** commemorates the emergence of Uruguay as a sovereign nation. Impressively massive, it is the largest square in the city and in its concrete-paved centre stands the marble-based **mausoleum of General José Gervasio Artigas**, housing the remains of the nationally revered man who did most to bring about that independence. With a horseback statue of Artigas standing 17m high above ground, a set of steps lead down to his tomb below, permanently under the watchful eye of an armed guard.

The area around the plaza contains some of the city's most architecturally exciting buildings, not least of which is the **Teatro Solis** in the southwest corner. Although recent financial difficulties have forced the closure of the interior to the public, its torch-lit colonnaded facade is still impressive when viewed from the outside, despite being surrounded by a temporary and rather unsightly corrugated iron fence.

Built in Italian Neoclassical style with colonnaded facade, the **Casa de Gobierno** (Mon–Fri 10am–5pm; free) on the south side of the plaza is an almost palatial government building now used largely for ceremonial purposes. The second floor contains a fascinating museum dedicated to the men who have led Uruguay. Unusual items of interest include a horse-drawn coach belonging to the first president, Fructuoso Rivera (1830–34), and the embalmed body of Coquimbo, trusted canine companion of Venancio Flores, who was briefly president from 1854 to 1855. **Avenida 18 de Julio** heads out from the eastern end of the plaza splitting the centre of the modern city in two. Facing each other across the avenue at its most westerly end are the Art Deco facade of the **Palacio Rinaldi**, now an office building, and the bizarrely eclectic **Palacio Salvo**. Superficially resembling an immense space rocket, Palacio Salvo is a major landmark and operates as an upmarket hotel.

East of Plaza Independencia along Avenida 18 de Julio

The lengthy **AVENIDA 18 DE JULIO** is central Montevideo's main thoroughfare. An important stopping point for the majority of the city's buses major routes, it is a paradise for shoppers, with its pavements constantly crammed with bargain-hunters looking for the latest deals in one of the many malls. Five blocks east of Plaza Independencia along Avenida 18 de Julio, **Plaza Fabini** is a pleasant, verdant square featuring a statue of combative gauchos, one of the last major pieces from the renowned Uruguayan sculptor José Belloni whose work is dotted around the city. To the north of the Plaza, Avenida General Lavalleja, runs for over a kilometre to the immense **Palacio Legislativo**, a gargantuan structure built from 55 different colours of marble. Construction was completed in 1925, seventeen years after work began, and today the decadent building operates largely as an awe-inspiring exhibition centre, with every room dripping with opulence, from ornate chandeliers to elegant marble.

Retrace your steps to Plaza Fabini and follow Avenida 18 de Julio east, passing through **Plaza de Cagancha**, home to an excellent **arts and crafts market** and a rather disappointing, columnar **Statue of Liberty**. Soon you reach the colossal and somewhat ugly **Intendencia Municipal** building on Soriano between Ejido and Santiago de Chile. Free **elevators** accessed at the back of the Intendencia building give magnificent panoramas of the surroundings as they climb the main tower, but they operate inconsistent opening hours and there's nothing in the building itself worth seeing. In the basement of the building, the excellent **Museo Historia del Arte** (Tues–Sun 2.30–8pm; free) explores the history of art from prehistoric times, through Egyptian to Greek and Roman. Although many of the pieces are replicas of originals housed abroad, they still don't fail to appeal. On the lowest floor a display of pre-Columbian American art gives a fascinating perspective and overview of the times.

From the Intendencia the road forks at a statue of **El Gaucho**, with Avenida 18 de Julio continuing northeast to meet **Boulevar General Artigas** at the **Obelisco**, and Avenida Constituyente heading southeast towards the affluent suburb of **Pocitos**.

Boulevar General Artigas and around

From Ruta 1 and western Uruguay, the enormously long **BOULEVAR GENERAL ARTIGAS** is the main point of entry and exit for road traffic. It runs west to east as far as the **Edificio Libertad** and the wishbone-shaped **Monumento al Presidente Batlle**, before turning abruptly south, past **Tres Cruces bus station** to the **Obelisco**, a monument dedicated to the constituents of 1830 and inscribed "Ley, Libertad, Fuerza" (Law, Liberty, Power). A few blocks east of here along Avenida Dr Morquio is the spacious, leafy **Parque Batlle y Ordoñez** featuring several statues by José Belloni, the most famous being "La Carreta", a sculpture of a wagon drawn by oxen. Nearby, the 70,000 capacity **Estadio Centenario**, Uruguay's ageing national football stadium, features a small free museum (Mon–Fri 10am–1pm & 4–6pm) and plaques on the wall commemorating World Cup winning sides. Venue of the first World Cup Final in 1930, it has been declared an international monument of world soccer by FIFA. South of the park on Avenida General Rivera lies the small **Parque Zoo Pereira de Rossell** (Wed–Sun 9am–5pm; UR$10, under 12s free; bus #60 from Avenida 18 de Julio), which, despite some archaic enclosures, is making efforts to modernize and is on the whole pretty good. A small **planetarium** on site gives two daily shows that are usually free.

From the Obelisco, Boulevar General Artigas continues south to **Punta Carretas**, an exclusive resort complete with lighthouse, golf course and a massive shopping complex. Just to the north of Punta Carretas is **Parque Rodó**, a popular picnic spot for families with a boating lake (UR$15 per person for 30 minutes), open-air theatre and amusement park. From Punta Carretas, **Rambla Naciones Unidas**, which adopts the names of various nations along its length, runs east along the coast through the suburbs of Pocitos and Carrasco, past some excellent **beaches** (bus #14 and 104 from Avenida 18 de Julio). Despite the colour of the water, the beaches are clean and safe, though be aware that lifeguards are only on duty in the high season. Particularly recommended are the sheltered **Playa de los Pocitos** in Pocitos, and the lengthy **Playa Miramar** in eastern Carrasco.

Eating

Café culture isn't well developed in Montevideo, and away from the squares and pedestrian areas traffic pollution can make sitting on outdoor tables an unpleasant experience. However, Uruguayan coffee is excellent and pastries are cheap, delicious and filling. Try **media lunas** (literally "half moons") croissants stuffed with ham and cheese, which are available in most cafés.

Montevideo is awash with good **restaurants**, with beef featuring heavily on most menus. Look out for the *parrilladas*, huge open charcoal grills affording a selection of meats and offal, usually at very reasonable prices. Avoid *choto* if you are squeamish – it is grilled intestine wrapped with tripe. The Italian influence is also apparent with pizza and pasta widely available, although the quality varies considerably. Some of the best value eats can be found in and around **San José**, just behind Plaza Fabini, but don't miss eating at **Mercado del Puerto**, an unforgettable experience for true carnivores.

Away from the centre, restaurants are a little thinner on the ground, but those that are available tend to be more upmarket and of high quality. In Pocitos, the areas around Parque Punta Carretas and Avenida Brasil are worth a look, while in Carrasco P.D. Murillo off Avenida Italia offers several good restaurants.

City centre

Las Brasas San José 909. An upmarket, pricey *parrillada* specializing in seafood. The king prawns here are particularly excellent.

Danubio Azul Colonia 835. Hugely popular *parrillada* with takeaway option. Comfortable, if a little hectic at times and very reasonably priced. Try the *cazuelas* (stews) for wholesome, filling meals that won't do too much damage to your wallet.

El Fogón San José 1080. Always busy, but the huge menu is complemented by good, quick service. Try the *Filet Fogón* from the *parrilla* for one of the thickest and juiciest steaks you will ever see.

Gran Buffet Río Negro 1376. All you can eat Chinese and international buffet for UR$85. Good selection of vegetarian dishes and mouthwatering desserts on offer as well as the usual Chinese favourites.

La Paella San José 1242 y Yi. Seafood restaurant specializing, as its name suggests, in delicious paella. Portions are wholesome and the smell of the grilling fish is a treat.

Mercado del Puerto A mouthwatering collection of grills and restaurants that will leave you spoilt for choice. Meat dominates most menus, but don't miss out on the grilled seafood. *El Palenque Roldos* and *La Pradera* are particularly recommended but the quality is generally high throughout (see p.971). Don't forget to ask for a *medio medio*, an unusual mixture of still and sparkling wine unique to the Mercado del Puerto, which will round your meal off nicely.

Morini Ciudadela 1229. Famed for its good value steaks, this is a first class restaurant with service to boot.

Rufino San José 1164. Specializes in Italian foods; the pizzas are delicious and very reasonably priced. Typically Italian in character and decor, stepping through the doors you could be forgiven for momentarily forgetting you are in Uruguay.

La Silenciosa Ituzaingó 1426. High quality French and international cuisine served in a historic building that was once a Jesuit convent. A little pricier than many places, but the steaks are exceptional.

El Torero 18 de Julio 1251. Diverse and sumptuous all you can eat buffet of meat, salads and desserts for UR$79. High quality table service means this place gives real value for money.

Viejo Sancho San José 1229. The understandably popular *Viejo Sancho* features a wide range of meats, chicken, pasta and seafood available at reasonable prices.

Pocitos and Carrasco

El Balcon de Lobo Zorilla de San Martin, Pocitos. Offering a delicious menu of meats and fish, *El Balcon de Lobo* is worth visiting for the fantastically ornate Art Nouveau bathrooms alone.

Posta del Viejo Pancho Viejo Pancho y Libertad, Pocitos. Rabbit is the unusual house speciality at this colourful restaurant, decked out in contrasting and occasionally ill-advised colour schemes.

Vegetariana Brasil 3086, Pocitos. Part of a chain of restaurants and one of the only meat-free menus you are likely to find in the city, *Vegetariana* offers a self-service buffet. There is another, more central branch on Sarandí between Plaza Independencia and Plaza Constitución.

Drinking

There are a number of good **bars** in the area between Plaza Independencia and Plaza Constitución, the most lively area being on and around Bartolomé Mitre. Venturing beyond there into the Ciudad Vieja, things become a little seedy after dark and potentially unsafe. The area around Punta Carretas shopping centre, south-east of the centre, is popular with younger drinkers, particularly on Thursday nights. More authentically Uruguayan, *Boliches* are traditional folk pubs that often offer live music.

△ Mercado del Puerto, Montevideo

Cabildo Bartolomé Mitre. Disco bar and popular nightspot opposite the *Hotel Palacio*.
Cerveceria Pasiva A great place to enjoy a beer in the sun with branches on Plaza Fabini and Plaza Constitución.
Clave de Fu 26 de Marzo 1125, Pocitos. Atmospheric *boliche* with regular live folk music on Friday and Saturday nights. Closed Sun–Tues.
Concierto in a former prison opposite Punta Carretas shopping. This is an atmospheric place with a model train set in perpetual motion. Whiskey happy hour from 6 to 8pm Monday to Thursday, (2 for 1).
Pizza Sing Schroeder 6411, Carrasco. Visiting this karaoke pizza bar is a unique, if slightly bizarre, experience.
Shannon Irish Pub Bartolomé Mitre. Every city needs one.
Taj Mahal Andes 1255. A typical *boliche*, with live music and good food.

Nightlife

Most of Montevideo's **discos** are outside the centre but can be reached cheaply and easily by taxi. The *W Lounge* (daily 1am–6am) on Rambla Wilson, Parque Rodó, is the city's main nightspot for all ages, featuring a complex of restaurants and discos with live shows. *Millennium* on Juncal in the Ciudad Vieja is popular with a younger crowd for its mixture of pop and dance music from midnight on, while *Montevideo News* (Thurs–Sat 11pm–7am) on Avenida Luis Giannattasio in Carrasco is another favourite, if a long way from the centre. *Flannagan's* Luis Cavia 3082, Pocitos, is an ever popular rock and pop disco.

Listings

Airline offices Numbers are for the airport offices unless an address is given. Aerolineas Argentinas, Convención 1343 ⓣ02/901-9466; Aerolineas Uruguayas ⓣ02/601-1425; American Airlines, Sarandí 699 ⓣ02/916-9876; British Airways, Río Negro 1354 ⓣ02/903-1760; Iberia, ⓣ02/604-0235; LanChile, Colonia 993 ⓣ02/900-3791; Lloyd Aéreo Boliviano, ⓣ02/604-0224; Lufthansa, Buenos Aires 618 ⓣ02/915-7591; Pluna, 02/604-0306; United Airlines, Plaza Independencia 831 ⓣ02/902-3080; Varig, Río Negro 1362 ⓣ02/902-4676.
Banks Banks are usually only open 1–5pm on weekdays only. ABN Amro, 25 de Mayo 501 ⓣ02/903-1747; AmEx, Rincón 477 8th Floor ⓣ02/916-0000; Boston, Zabala 1463 ⓣ02/916-0127; Centro Hispano, 18 de Julio 1119 ⓣ02/901-3734; Citibank, Cerrito 455 ⓣ02/915-0374; Comercial, Cerrito 400 ⓣ02/924-0740; Intercontinental, Colonia 999 ⓣ02/902-8864; Lloyds TSB, Zabala 1500 ⓣ02/916-0976; Montevideo, Av D Fernandez 2450 ⓣ02/924-3300.
Bus companies All numbers are for the offices at Tres Cruces bus station. Agencia Central, ⓣ02/902-1064 for all major destinations in the west and centre including Tacuarembó, Fray Bentos, Mercedes; CITA, ⓣ02/902-5466 for Libertad, Canelones, Florida; COPSA, ⓣ02/408-668 for Maldonado, Punta del Este, Piriapolis; COT, ⓣ02/400-9767 for Punta del Este, La Paloma, Maldonado, Chuy, Colonia, Piriapolis; COTMI, ⓣ02/401-7443 for San José, Libertad; CUT ⓣ02/288-6653 for Fray Bentos, Mercedes, Rivera, Minas; Emdal ⓣ02/409-7098 for Minas, Chuy; Minuano ⓣ02/402-2768 for Minas, Treinta y Tres; NOSSAR ⓣ02/409-1880 for Durazno, Tacuarembó, Rivera, La Paloma, Colonia; Nuñez ⓣ02/508-4758 for Paysandú, Tacuarembó, Rocha, Treinta y Tres; Rutas del Sol ⓣ02/402-5451 for Rocha, Chuy; Turil ⓣ02/622-3396 for Colonia, Rivera, Artigas, Tacuarembó; Turismar ⓣ02/409-0999 for Durazno, Melo, Sarandí.
Car rental Car hire on the whole is rather cheap, and don't be afraid to barter. Avis, Uruguay 1417 ⓣ02/903-0093 and airport ⓣ02/604-0334; Budget, General Flores 2211 ⓣ02/203-7080 and airport ⓣ02/604-0189; Econo Rent-a-car, La Paz 1280 ⓣ02/902-8943; Hertz, Río Negro 1354 ⓣ02/908-5887 and airport ⓣ02/604-0006.
Embassies Most are situated in the suburbs around Pocitos and Carrasco. Full listings of embassies to Uruguay can be found at ⓦwww.embassyworld.com. Argentina, Cuareim 1470 ⓣ02/902-8166; Bolivia, Dr P De Pena 2469 ⓣ02/707-0862; Brazil, Blvr Gral Artigas 1328 ⓣ02/707-2119; Canada, Plaza Independencia 749

☎02/902-2030; Chile, Andes 1365 ☎02/900-9273; South Africa, Echevarriarza 3335 ☎02/623-0161; UK, Marco Bruto 1073 ☎02/622-3630; US, Dr L Muller 1776 ☎02/418-7777.

Emergencies Police officers are prevalent on most city streets to report minor crimes. Ambulance ☎109, fire ☎104, police ☎109, general emergency ☎911.

Exchange Money can be exchanged in most of the major bank branches, but *casas de cambio* are in evidence throughout the city especially along 18 de Julio and offer reasonable rates.

Hospital Britanico, Italia 2400 ☎02/487-1020; Central de las FFAA, Centenario 3057 ☎02/487-2307; Italiano, Blvr Gral Artigas 1632 ☎02/487-0515; Pereira Rossell, Blvr Gral Artigas 1550 ☎02/708-7741.

Internet access Internet access is widely available throughout the city, especially along major city centre roads such as 18 de Julio. ANTEL, San José, operated by telephone cards but rather expensive at UR$50 per hour; Ciber Center, San José 1084, UR$30 per hour; Cyber Cassinoni, Peatonal Tres Cruces adjacent to the bus terminal UR$30 per hour; Cybergate, Galeria del Virrey Locutorio 41, 18 de Julio 1268 UR$15 per hour, UR$25 for two hours.

Markets Artesano Market on Plaza de Cagancha has a good selection of local crafts and artwork. Mercado Piedras Blancas at the northern end of Av Gral Flores on Sundays from 8.30am – known locally as the Feria de los Ladrones (Thieves Market). Mercado Tristan Narvaja on Calle Tristan Narvaja, opposite the Universidad de la Republica, is a big Sunday morning market.

Post office International mailings are expensive and frequently unreliable. The main office is at Buenos Aires 451 ☎02/916-0200.

Travel agents Austral, Blvr Gral Artigas 280 ☎02/711-4161; Jetmar, Plaza Independencia 725 ☎02/902-0793; Jorge Martinez, De La Herrera 1196 ☎02/622-1136; Orientur, Río Negro 1284 ☎02/604-0119; Thomas Cook, 25 de Mayo 732 ☎02/902-0930.

Ferries to Buenos Aires

Buquebus **ferries** (Ⓦwww.buquebus.com) link Buenos Aires with Montevideo and Colonia del Sacramento. Though convenient, the trip is expensive (US$27–32) and, with the exception of the approach into Colonia, not especially picturesque. Four daily ferries (three on Sunday) depart from Colonia for Buenos Aires (though none between 9.15am and 5.30pm), and two leave from Montevideo (at 11.31am and 7.01pm), with returns to Colonia at 12.30am, 9am, 11am and 7pm, and returns to Montevideo at 8am and 3.30pm. If you're in a hurry, make sure you take the faster *Atlantic 3* boat, which crosses in 55 minutes, and not the slower *Eladia Isabel* and *Juan Patricio*, which take two hours longer. **Customs** formalities for both countries take place only at the departure terminal, not at the arrival point.

10.2

East of Montevideo

The area east of Montevideo is notable for some of South America's finest and most unspoilt beaches. The exclusive resort of **Punta del Este** and nearby **Maldonado** are obvious destinations, but if you have access to your own transport a series of tiny coastal fishing villages are worth checking out, where you shouldn't have too much trouble finding a secluded beach all to yourself. Towards the **Brazilian border** there is less urban development, and nature abounds. A number of shimmering *lagunas* (lagoons) are home to flocks of pink flamingos and rare black-necked swans, while the Atlantic coast is a great place to see whales in season.

Montevideo to Punta del Este

East of Montevideo, the Ruta Interbalnéario runs along the coast of the River Plate towards the extravagant resort of **Punta del Este**. Along the way, you'll pass a landscape of rugged rocky bays, sandy beaches, wooded hillsides and coastal lagoons, where a few smallish resort towns make for pleasant stop-offs. While **Atlántida**, with golden beaches, casinos and discos attracting a young crowd, is closest to Montevideo, the pick of the bunch is **Piriápolis**, 98km east of the capital. Situated among lush forests of acacia and eucalyptus, it has become a popular alternative to the more expensive Punta del Este. A **tourist information office** on the seafront at Rambla de los Argentinos y Armenia ⓣ043/22560 produces a booklet of maps of all of the nearby beach resorts. Superb views of the magnificent Piriápolis beach can be gained from the forested **Cerro Pan de Azucar**, 5km north of town along Ruta 37.

A little further east, Ruta 37 intersects Ruta 93 inland which continues east between Laguna del Sauce and the coast to **Portezuelo**, a peaceful beach town with seemingly endless views along the bay. Three kilometres inland you'll find **Arboreto Lussich** (daily 10am–5pm; free), a vast forest of tropical trees planted by the poet-revolutionary Antonio Lussich, which makes for a pleasant stroll. Maps and tree identification guides are handed out to visitors and periodic viewpoints provide unique panoramas through the tree canopy. The spectacular promontory of **Punta Ballena** lies 8km west of Punta del Este and 3km south of the Arboreto. A looped road leads down to a rocky headland with great fishing and a number of stalls selling souvenirs plundered from the sea. Just before the road meets the Ruta is a turn-off for the bizarre, sprawling Moorish mansion that is the **Museo Casapueblo Paéz Villaro** (daily 9.30am–6.30pm; UR$60). Almost Gaudíesque in appearance, it is home to the Uruguayan artist Carlos Paéz Villaro, one-time friend of Picasso. His ongoing work is displayed in several exhibition rooms, but the full extent of the building is best enjoyed by seeing it from the beach below.

Punta del Este and around

Exclusive, luxurious and often prohibitively expensive, **PUNTA DEL ESTE** is second only to Rio de Janeiro as the place to be seen among the South American jetset. Yet while thriving and crowded in the summer months, it is cold, deserted and largely closed in winter. Situated on a narrow peninsula 140km east of Montevideo, Punta del Este is a jungle of high-rise hotels, expensive restaurants and casinos, bordered by some of the finest beaches on the coast. The calmer waters on the bay side are preferred by recreational bathers, while the more turbulent Atlantic coast is a mecca for surfers and water-sports enthusiasts.

The **bus station** (☎042/489467) at the top end of Avenida Gorlero at the neck of the peninsula is the arrival point for intercity buses and provides connecting services with the airport. COPSA and COT provide over thirty daily services west to Montevideo (2–3hrs) via Maldonado, and two daily to Chuy (3hr 20min) in the east. Regular local buses to Maldonado run from Rambla General Artigas. Punta del Este **airport** handles three to four daily flights to and from Buenos Aires, while the bus station houses a **tourist information office** and offices of several **tour companies**, but shop around for a good price. There are other tourist information offices at Plaza Artigas (daily 8am–8pm in season, varies out of season; ☎042/446519) and a private office one block south of the bus station at Calle Inzaurraga (31) that also has **Internet** access for UR$40 per hour. Other cybercafés can be found at Calle Los Meros and Calle Los Arrecifes y Golero.

The beaches and the peninsula

The **beaches** attract most visitors to Punta del Este, and two of the best are on either side of the neck of the peninsula. **Playa Mansa** on the bay side is a huge arcing stretch of sand, with excellent views out to the wooded **Isla de Gorriti**. Formerly heavily fortified by the Spanish, and once visited by Sir Francis Drake, the isla now forms a popular day-trip for bathers trying to escape the crowds on the mainland. Boats (UR$70) run hourly from the yacht marina on the southwest tip of the peninsula. On the Atlantic side, the equally beautiful **Playa Brava** is marked by a fantastic statue of a giant hand, which appears to be emerging from the sand. The ocean here is considerably more aggressive, ideal for water sports such as surfing, windsurfing and jet-skiing, but frequently too dangerous for swimming. Eight kilometres off the coast lies the fantastic **Isla de los Lobos**, one of the largest sea lion colonies in the world, which can be visited by expensive guided tours only (see opposite). Cruises leave from the marina, but if you wish to see sea lions more cheaply they are often visible in and around the port, especially during the early morning when fishing boats are preparing to set sail.

If beach lifestyle doesn't grab you, there are a few sights of interest here. Within the peninsula itself, the most attractive area is the less-developed southern tip around the **El Faro** (lighthouse) on Calle 2 de Febrero (10). Constructed entirely from volcanic red brick imported from Rome, it is a distinctive structure and towers above its surroundings, in compliance with old laws that decree that no building in the vicinity may exceed its 43m of height. It is not open to the public. From here, the Rambla General Artigas circuits the peninsula, bypassing the confusing grid of numbered one-way streets in the centre. On the Atlantic side of the peninsula, at the eastern end of Calle Arrecifes (25) is a rocky outcrop just to the south of **Playa El Emir** (a popular spot for surfers). Here a small shrine to the **Virgen de la Candelaria** marks the site of the first mass said by conquistadores on their arrival on February 2, 1515. Two blocks west is **Plaza Artigas**, home to a seasonal arts and crafts market.

Practicalities

Accommodation is on the whole overpriced and rapidly fills in summer, when you should book in advance to avoid paying through the nose; indeed, budget travellers may prefer to commute from nearby Maldonado (see p.990), where accommodation is much more reasonable. In winter, when Punta del Este resembles something of a ghost town, many of the hotels close down completely, but those that remain open often slash their prices dramatically. Punta del Este boasts an astounding number of hotels, and the websites ⓦwww.puntaweb.com and www.apuntadoor.com are very useful for comparing prices. *Embajador*, Risso, Parada 1 (ⓣ042/448757; ❼) is conveniently located near to the bus terminal and boasts comfortable, luxurious rooms, many with great views over Playa Mansa; it is one of the few large hotels that remains open out of season. Of the cheaper options, a good bet is *Marbella*, Calle Inzaurraga (ⓣ042/441814; ❻), near the bus station and tourist office, with small but comfortable rooms and including breakfast and TV. *Amsterdam*, El Foque 759, near Playa Ingleses (ⓣ042/444170, ⓦwww.hotelamsterdampunta.com; ❼, although as low as US$20 in the off season) boasts an excellent location in the heart of the peninsula. The only cheap option in town is the **youth hostel** *El Castillo* (ⓣ094/409799; ❷ per person) which has poor facilities and can be cold in winter. Dormitories and double rooms are available.

If you are looking for something more substantial to eat than pizzas or burgers, you will have to be prepared to pay top prices in **restaurants**. There are good options down by the marina including *El Mejillon*, Rambla de Circunvalación, which has nice views of Isla de Gorriti and does excellent *chivitos*; *El Viejo Marino*, 739 Calle 11 (ⓣ042/443565), an ever popular seafood restaurant with a good wine list; and the relaxed *Los Caracoles*, El Remanso y Los Meros, with a reasonably-priced, international menu.

For **nightlife**, Punta del Este is one of the most happening places in Uruguay, but discos can be very expensive (US$20–25 for entrance alone). If you fancy a dance but the entrance fee puts you off, there are several disco-pubs on the peninsula including *Mercury*, Gorlero 1045, and *Moby Dick*, General Artigas 650, which may be a better bet. These have a far more laid-back atmosphere and allow you to let your hair down without inflicting too much damage on your wallet.

Tours of Isla de los Lobos are available through Crucero Samoa (ⓣ042/446166; US$50) and Don Quico (ⓣ042/443963; US$50), the latter also running fishing trips and excursions. Eco-tours (ⓣ042/493512, ⓦwww.eco-uruguay.com; US$35-55) runs themed nature trips to local sites of ecological interest including Cabo Polonio and Laguna Negra, the latter famous for its flocks of flamingos. For those with an interest in whales, the Organización para la Conservación de Cetáceos (ⓔballenato@adinet.com.uy, ⓦwww.whalestime.com) accepts a small number of unpaid volunteers and has assisted in the erection of twelve whale-watching posts along the coast. **Water-sports** equipment can be hired from I'Marangatu, Parada 13.5 Playa Mansa (ⓣ094/435100), and Punta Surf School (ⓣ042/493440, ⓦwww.sunvalleysurf.com) provides surfing lessons for all abilities.

East of Punta del Este: La Barra de Maldonado and José Ignacio

Rambla Lorenzo Batlle Pacheco, a continuation of Rambla General Artigas, runs 8km east of Punta del Este along the coast to the mouth of the Arroyo Maldonado, where an unusual M-shaped bridge crosses the river to **LA BARRA DE MALDONADO**. Sandwiched between forested hills on one side and golden beaches on the other, it is becoming an increasingly fashionable place to stay for those tired of the crowds of Punta del Este. The new **Museo del Mar** (summer daily 10am–8.30pm, winter weekends only 10am–6pm; UR$50) is a response to this increased tourism, displaying an intriguing collection of marine artefacts, including a 19m whale skeleton and a 2.6m long ocean sunfish that washed up on a nearby beach. An excellent **place to stay** is the homely *La Ballanera Bed and Breakfast* (Ⓣ042/771079, Ⓦwww.vivapunta.com/laballenera; ❹ per person) at Km162, which will also organize excursions such as fishing trips, birdwatching and whale watching in season (Aug–Nov).

From La Barra the coastal Ruta 10 heads east 30km to the tiny fishing village of **JOSÉ IGNACIO**, renowned for its seafood and its **lighthouse**. Should you wish to stay there is a small **tourist office** between Calles Los Teros and Las Garzas that holds details of private rooms, although there is little available out of season. Beyond José Ignacio Ruta 10 is unpaved, and Ruta 9, which runs inland, is the main route east towards Brazil.

Maldonado

Capital of the department, but now little more than a dormitory town supplying labour to Punta del Este, **MALDONADO** lacks the pretensions of its more illustrious neighbour. Sacked by the British in 1806, today it is a peaceful and laid-back place that retains a number of sights of colonial interest. Maldonado is considerably cheaper than Punta del Este and close enough to it to make commuting far more economical.

The **bus terminal** (Ⓣ042/220847) is eight blocks south of the centre. Green buses and yellow buses head towards Punta del Este from the same stop. **Taxis** (Ⓣ042/229090) to Punta del Este should cost no more than UR$150. The helpful **tourist office** (daily 9am–9pm; Ⓣ042/220847, Ⓦwww.maldonado.gub.uy) in the Intendencia Municipal building on the south side of Plaza San Fernando can provide you with city maps and information booklets. **Internet** access on the corner of Florida and Jose Dodera, one block west of the plaza, costs UR$30 per hour.

The Town

The main focus lies around **Plaza San Fernando**, with the Neoclassical **Catedral San Fernando** on the west side. A charming, rose-coloured building with three *azulejo* domes, it was inaugurated in 1895, 94 years after building commenced, and features an altar, with images of the Virgen del Santander, designed by Antonio Veija. One block north of the plaza on the corner of 18 de Julio y Ituzaingó, the **Museo Mazzoni Regional** (Mon–Fri 1–6pm; free) exhibits a broad collection of items reflecting the history of the region, with colonial pieces of indigenous, Spanish, Portuguese and even British influence on display, as well as an exhaustive art gallery featuring works by local artists. Just south of the plaza along 18 de Julio stands the **Cuartel de Dragones**. Built between 1771 and 1797 from *piedra de silleria* its parade ground and surrounding buildings are now an unusually atmospheric exhibition centre containing a small museum dedicated to the military campaigns of General Artigas. Three blocks west of here along Perez del Puerto, the **El Vigia Watchtower** was once, at 13m, the tallest building in the town. Built between 1797 and 1799, it bears the inscription "Protector of Land and Sea", harking back to the days when it gave unrivalled views across the estuary. A kilometre or so southeast of the centre, along 3 de Febrero, is the **Cachimba del Rey**, an ancient water source that supplied the city until 1873. Legend has it that those who drink from the Cachimba will never leave Maldonado, although today that is probably a reflection of how contaminated the water is.

Practicalities

Accommodation is on the whole much better value than in Punta del Este, although it too can be crowded during the summer, mainly with tourists commuting to the peninsula. Particularly recommended is the friendly, central and comfortable *Hotel Catedral*, Florida 830 (☎042/242513, ⓔhotel_catedral@yahoo.com; ❸), one block from the plaza, which includes cable TV and breakfast. *Hospedaje Isla de Gorriti*, Zelmar Michelini 884 (☎042/245218; ❷ with TV, less without) is more basic, but represents a safe and secure budget option and has a pleasant courtyard. *Le Petit*, Sarandí y Florida (☎042/223044; ❸), is above a noisy shopping centre with rooms at the front having good views of the plaza, although those at the back are rather dingy.

Restaurants are thin on the ground, but *Al Paso* one block north of the plaza at 18 de Julio y Ituzaingó is just about the best in town; try *brochete agridulce*, a delicious pork and fruit kebab. Five blocks further north, *Piano Bar JR Pizzetas* on Rincon y Gutierrez Ruiz specializes in pizzas and pasta, and provides activities for children.

San Carlos, Rocha and La Paloma

The little town of **SAN CARLOS** lies 16km north of Maldonado along Ruta 39. Peaceful and serene, it represents a change of pace from the hectic commercialism of Punta del Este, and a series of sights make it worth the short trip. The Plaza Mayor is home to the attractive Romanesque **Iglesia San Carlos Borromeo**. The church dates from 1722 but has been heavily reconstructed and is considerably more impressive from the outside than the inside. Here the whitewashed, bare brick interior walls are a real disappointment after the grandiose, domed, twin towers of the exterior. On the south side of the same plaza is the **Museo Historico Regional** (Tues–Sun 1–6pm; free), a former Spanish prison that now houses a small collection of indigenous figures, and colonial arms and coins. East of town, approximately 1km beyond the Puente San Carlos, is the **Zoo Parque Medina** (daily 10am–6pm; free) containing an array of indigenous wildlife, as well as more spectacular species such as big cats.

From Maldonado, local **buses** (UR$16 one-way) running every fifteen minutes make the journey to San Carlos, arriving from the plaza on Avenida Jacinto M Alvariza, from where it is six blocks east to the Plaza Mayor. While it is unlikely that you would want to stay overnight, cheap, if basic, accommodation is available at *Hospedaje Uruguay* (no phone; ❶) on 25 de Agosto near the bus stop.

Rocha and La Paloma

From San Carlos, Ruta 9 runs east, through the palm-filled department of Rocha, to the Brazilian border. Approximately halfway it meets the departmental capital **ROCHA**, an ugly little town with good travel connections to La Paloma (8 daily buses) and Chuy (3 daily buses) on the border. Bus offices can be found on and around the Plaza Independencia, which also has a church dating from 1793. If you need a **place to stay** in Rocha while waiting to make a connection, *Hotel Aguate* on the plaza (☎0472/6756; ❸) is a large, airy hotel, although some rooms are rather cramped and uncomfortable; the price includes breakfast. The tourist office (☎0472/8202, ⓦwww.rocha.gub.uy) is inconveniently located 2km outside of town.

Due south of Rocha, 22km along Ruta 15, the easy-going port and beach town of **LA PALOMA** boasts some of the finest **beaches** on the coast and is surrounded by sand dunes, forests and wetlands that are perfect for walking. The town also has a **casino** and **cinema** at the bottom end of Avenida Solari, the main street. The **Faro Cabo Santa Maria** (lighthouse) at the end of **Calle del Faro** near the beach merits a look, but it is the beach lifestyle that attracts most visitors. Fishing is popular here and the sea is also good for swimming, especially off the **sheltered Playa la Balconada**, although swimming is inadvisable on the Atlantic beaches owing to a heavy swell.

Practicalities

If arriving by bus you will be deposited at the **bus terminal** five minutes north of town on Calle Paloma. Local buses connect with Avenida Solari (UR$9) and continue on to the quieter, nearby towns of **La Pedrera** and **La Aguada**. The **tourist office** at the top end of Avenida Solari (Mon–Fri 2–5pm, Sat–Sun 10.30am–12.30pm & 3–5.30pm; ☎0479/6088) can inform you of other companies, but be warned that price and quality vary considerably.

Accommodation is expensive on the whole, although there are several good options. *La Tuna*, Neptuno y Juno (☎0479/6083; ❻), includes a TV and great views of the beach from many rooms, while *Viola*, Solari (☎0479/6020, ⓔhviola@adinet.com.uy; ❼), offers large rooms with cable TV and some apartments. *Bahia*, on del Sol just off Solari (☎0479/6029, ⓔhbahia@montevideo.com.uy; ❼), is friendly with a good location, and its rooms have good views; the price includes breakfast. Groups may also wish to hire **cabañas** (cabins) in the shady, pine-forested **Parque Andresito** at the top end of Avenida Solari near to the bus station. The cheapest can be hired through *Tio Con* (☎0479/6175; ❼ for 4 people), although a better standard is available from *Complejo Anaconda* (☎0479/7007; ❽ for four people). For food, the **restaurant** below the *Hotel Bahia* is excellent, with an unusual speciality of *Nandú* (rhea); while *La Marea* near the tourist office is renowned for its seafood.

East to the Brazilian border

A series of charmingly quaint beach villages, including **La Pedrera** and **Cabo Polonio**, run east along the coast from La Paloma to **Aguas Dulces**. From here Ruta 16 runs north to **Castillos**, where it meets the inland Ruta 9, 55km east of Rocha. Castillos has good travel connections to surrounding villages and is a good place for organizing tours to local sites of interest including **Punta del Diablo** (34km east), an attractive fishing village, **Parque Nacional Santa Teresa** (51km east) with its spectacular imposing fortress, **Laguna Castillos** and the **Bosque de Ombues**, a woodland consisting largely of Uruguay's national tree - the *ombu*. *La Barra Grande* at Km249 (☎0470/5158) is one of the best tour companies, with trained guides. From Castillos it is 75km east along the continuation of Ruta 9 to **Chuy** on the Brazilian border.

Chuy and the Brazilian border

A duty-free haven and frontier with the Brazilian town of **Chui** (see p.461), with which it straddles the border, **CHUY** has little to detain you. **Buses** terminate on the main plaza between Avenida Artigas and Calle Olivera, and the offices of the main bus companies are scattered in the streets around. COT and CITA run regular services to Rocha, Maldonado and Montevideo. At the end of the western continuation of Avenida Brasil, 7km from town, lies the **Forte San Miguel** (1752) overlooking the Laguna Merin. Set in a park, with a small collection of animals, it makes for a relaxing day-trip to escape the hectic commercialism of the town.

Accommodation in the town is rather cheap, but standards vary. Among the best places to stay are the friendly *Vitoria* at Numancia 143 off Avenida Brasil (☎0474/2280, ❷), and *Internacional*, Avenida Brasil, a couple of blocks west of the main plaza (☎0474/2055, ❸), with good spacious rooms, if a little oddly decorated. There is an excellent, if expensive, hotel, the *Fortin San Miguel* (☎0474/2207; ❼) at the Forte San Miguel; it has a good restaurant.

Internet access is available at *Nemar* next to Hotel Vitoria on Numancia for UR$40 per hour. For **food**, *Parrillada Jesus* opposite the COT office on Calle Olivera is perhaps the best option on the Uruguayan side, with hearty steaks and excellent *chorizo*.

Crossing into Brazil

The **border crossing** is by no means simple. The frontier runs along the centre of Avenida Brasil/Uruguay, but the Uruguayan customs post is 2km away on the approach to town along Ruta 9. Buses from Rocha do not stop at the customs checkpoint unless asked and, although it is possible to visit Chui without a Brazilian entrance stamp, it is essential that you receive all necessary entrance and exit stamps before entering Brazil proper, to avoid problems later. A helpful **tourist office** (Mon–Sat 8am–8pm; ⓦwww.chuynet.com) opposite the Uruguayan customs can provide you with maps and, if necessary, will assist with information regarding crossings.

10.3

West of Montevideo

Ruta 1 runs west of Montevideo towards the historic city of **Colonia del Sacramento**, an arrival point for ferries from Buenos Aires near the mouth of the Río Uruguay. North of here, the west of the country is still relatively unexplored by visitors, yet it yields some hidden delights. Unspoilt riverside cities like **Salto** and **Mercedes**, convenient ferry and bridge crossings to Argentina and the unmissable **thermal spa** resorts, all deserve attention, while the town of **Fray Bentos** is home to one of the world's most gruesome tourist attractions.

Colonia del Sacramento

COLONIA DEL SACRAMENTO, often referred to simply as "Colonia", is one of the most picturesque towns in the whole of Uruguay. Founded in 1680 by the Portuguese, it soon became an important centre for smuggling goods into the Spanish colonies. Today, despite an increasing number of tourists visiting the town (many crossing over from Buenos Aires on day-trips), it retains a sleepy indifference to the outside world and it is well worth spending a few days to get to know it better.

Arrival and information

Ferries run between Buenos Aires and Colonia although departures from Colonia are at inconvenient times (see box on p.986). The terminal is three blocks south of Avenida General Flores (the main street) along Calle Rivera. **Buses** arrive at the new terminal a few hundred yards from the port entrance, with regular services arriving from Montevideo and the northern cities of Mercedes, Paysandú and Salto. A small **airport** 17km out of town on Ruta 1 has one daily flight to and from Buenos Aires Aeroparque. There is a good **tourist office** (daily 9am–7pm; ⓣ052/22182, ⓦwww.colonia.gub.uy) on Av Gral Flores y Rivera which can supply you with maps and details of organized tours.

Accommodation

Prices for **accommodation**, although rising, are on the whole very reasonable in Colonia, and the comparatively compact nature of the city means that most boast a convenient location.

Bahia Playa Rambla de las Americas 1606 ⓣ052/25089, ⓔhotelbahiaplaya@netgate.com.uy. Upmarket rooms right on the beach, halfway between the town and Real de San Carlos resort. *Bahia Playa* has excellent facilities, including a swimming pool and minibar. Price includes breakfast. ❺

Beltran Av Gral Flores 311 ⓣ052/22955, ⓔhotelbeltran@netgate.com.uy. This high quality establishment has spacious, comfortable, if a little floral, rooms with cable TV and telephones. The hotel is above a good restaurant. ❼, less for cash

Colonial Av Gral Flores 440 ⓣ052/30347, ⓔhostelling_colonial@hotmail.com. Conveniently located next to an excellent ice-cream parlour, the YHA-affiliated *Colonial* is first choice with most backpackers. Accommodation is in twin rooms or four-bed dorms. Friendly and comfortable, they offer free Internet, free bike hire and a communal kitchen and TV room. ❷ per person

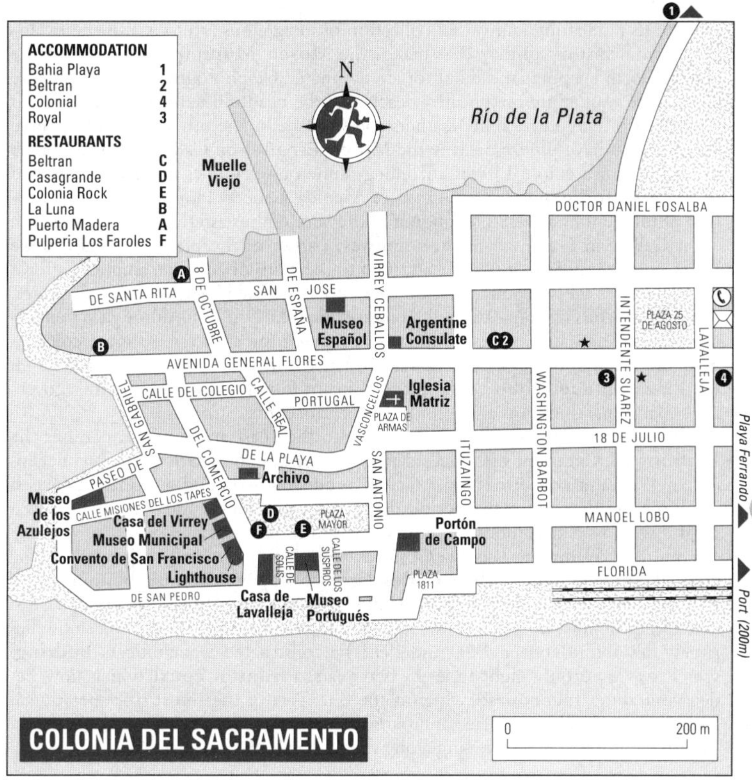

Royal Av Gral Flores 340 ☎052/22169. The *Royal* is in an ugly building, some of whose rooms are better than others, though all have TV, bathroom and telephone. The back rooms have good views across the bay. ❹ with breakfast, a little cheaper without

The Town

The highlight of any trip to Colonia is undoubtedly the atmospheric **Barrio Histórico** (the old quarter). Formerly the colonial port area, a fascinating warren of cobbled streets and honey-coloured buildings radiate out from the delightful **Plaza Mayor**, where screeching parakeets nest in the palm and orange trees. The plaza is seldom peaceful, but the shade can be welcome on hot days. The remains of the old city gates, the **Puerta del Campo**, lie at the bottom end of Calle Manuel Lobo, where they were once charged with protecting the important trade centre from invading forces; now they are permanently open to tourists and separate old Colonia from the new city. The Barrio Histórico was declared a site of cultural importance by UNESCO, and just strolling around the streets will spirit you into the past.

Dotted around the Barrio Histórico is a series of seven **museums** (all open Mon–Sun 11.45am–4.45pm). These can all be visited on a single UR$10 ticket available from the **Museo Municipal**, on the west side of Plaza Mayor, where they will also furnish you with a map showing the locations of the other museums.

Despite its fascinating and varied collection of indigenous artefacts, it is the extensive natural history display that makes the **Museo Municipal** the pick of the bunch. Worth keeping an eye out for are the incredible photographs of an immense blue whale washed up on a nearby beach, and the beautiful natural history collages made up from colourful birds' feathers and snail shells. The other museums deserve a peek if you have time, especially the **Museo Español** on Calle de España, which exhibits Spanish colonial items, including numerous examples of period dress, and the **Museo Indigena** at the bottom of Avenida General Flores, a private collection of indigenous artefacts belonging to the very enthusiastic Roberto Banchero.

On Calle San Francisco, at the southwest corner of the plaza, the **lighthouse** (Mon–Sun 10am–5pm; UR$15), attached to the ruins of a former nunnery, affords great views of the surroundings from the cupola. A few blocks north of the plaza, the **Iglesia Matriz** claims to be the oldest church in Uruguay. Although systematically demolished and rebuilt by various occupying forces, it retains some columns from the original Portuguese building constructed in 1730. Adjacent to the church the **Plaza Manuel Lobo** contains the remnant foundations of the former governor's mansion, which was also a mid-eighteenth century structure.

Follow Virrey Cavallos two blocks north to the coast and you'll encounter the **Bastion del Carmen**, with walls dating from the time of Governor Vasconcellos (1722–49). Later converted into a factory producing soap and gelatine products, a red brick chimney from the period dated 1880 still stands. Today it operates as a theatre with a small outdoor museum dedicated to its history.

From the Bastion, the Rambla Costanera runs along a wide-arcing beach to the unusual resort of **Real de San Carlos** (accessible by bus from the bottom end of Av Gral Flores). Originally the brainchild of millionaire Nicolas Mihanovic, who conceived the idea of an exclusive tourist complex for rich Argentines, it now lies largely deserted. Between 1903 and 1912, he constructed a magnificent **bullring**, which was used only eight times in two years, a **fronton court** which now lies decaying and a **racecourse**, which is the only part of the resort still operational. Regular horse races take place approximately every second Sunday, and the horses can frequently be seen exercising along the nearby beach.

Eating and drinking

A number of excellent restaurants can be found in the old town, particularly around the Plaza Mayor. Although some are rather pricey, the quality on the whole is excellent and the ambience of the surroundings is hard to beat in Uruguay.

Beltran Av Gral Flores 311. Beneath the *Beltran* hotel, this is a good place for breakfast.

Casagrande Plaza Mayor. Arguably the best in town, with an interesting and unusual menu. The steaks are fantastic, beef medallions in port sauce hard to beat and the desserts are irresistible.

Colonia Rock Misiones de los Tapes 157 on Plaza Mayor. Very popular grill, pizzeria and pub, with frequent live shows at weekends. The food is not always up to the standard of some of the other restaurants, but it is always full and the atmosphere is second to none.

La Luna Av Gral Flores. At the bottom end near the waterfront, this is more of a pub than a restaurant, although the food isn't bad. Spacious roof terrace gives great views out over the river.

Puerto Madera Santa Rita Mercado del Puerto. Friendly, all-you-can-eat *parrillada* with outdoor tables in front of the grill. Great value for money for just UR$120.

Pulperia Los Faroles Plaza Mayor. Rustic venue with delicious menu. Great steaks and chicken in pineapple sauce is worth a try. Occasional live weekend shows.

Around Colonia del Sacramento

A number of charming towns and villages are located on the eastern approach to Colonia del Sacramento from Montevideo. These are best visited by day-trips, and organized tours from Colonia del Sacramento can be arranged, although you may prefer to do it yourself with your own transport.

Just before Colonia Valdense, on the turn-off to Ruta 2, the small town of **Rosario** is noted for its murals, which cover a host of topics from bullfighting to the struggle for independence. Beyond here, **Colonia Valdense**, at Km121 on Ruta 1, was founded as a colony by followers of Pedro Valdo's religious cult. Persecuted in France they fled to Uruguay in 1857 and the **Museo Valdense Sudamericano** (Mon–Fri 10am–6pm; free) on Avenida Armand details their history. Further European heritage is on view after following the road north to the nearby Swiss settlement at **Colonia Suiza**, with its typically Swiss buildings. The **El Surco** monument dated April 25, 1862, is dedicated to the settlers.

West of Colonia del Sacramento, **Carmelo**, 77km away along Ruta 21, is the point of departure for extremely picturesque **ferry crossings into Argentina**. Approached by a magnificent avenue of trees, you reach the first swing bridge ever built in Uruguay. Before the bridge, a left turn leads down to the excellent **Playa Seré** river beach, with views across to Argentina and the forested islands of the Río Uruguay. The road continues round to the expensive *Hotel Casino Carmelo* (Ⓣ0059/8542, Ⓔairemar@adinet.com.uy; ❼), with its **Reserva de Fauna**, a fenced-off area containing indigenous species of animals such as capybara and black-necked swans. A **tourist office** (Mon–Sat 12.45–5.30pm) is located in the Casa de Cultura on 19 de Abril (the main road into town) and two daily **ferries** to Tigre in Argentina depart from the port in the south of town. The crossing, between the forested islands, is a particularly picturesque one. Day-trips to the **Isla San Martin**, a beautiful wooded island with nature reserve and camping facilities, are available through *Cacciola* based in Tigre (Ⓣ0054 11 4393/6100, Ⓔinfo@cacciolaviajes.com). Should you wish to **stay** in Carmelo, *Oriental*, 19 de Abril 284 (Ⓣ0542/2404; ❷ with bath, ❶ without), is the cheapest option, although many rooms are windowless. Rather better, the *Centro*, Uruguay 370 (Ⓣ0542/4488; ❹ with breakfast, ❸ without), sports a bar and restaurant.

The west coast

From Colonia del Sacramento, Ruta 21 heads north up the coast of the Río Uruguay to the attractive town of **Mercedes** and on to **Fray Bentos** of meat pie fame. Further north the bigger cities of **Paysandú** and **Salto** are convenient crossing points into northern Argentina, and excellent bases for visiting the **thermal spa resorts** in the area. Beyond here the quality of the roads deteriorates dramatically, and although the scenery is frequently spectacular, drivers are more likely to be preoccupied with avoiding potholes and looking for sporadic road signs than enjoying the view.

Mercedes

Known locally as "La Ciudad de las Flores" (The City of Flowers), **MERCEDES** is a pretty, well-kept little town on the Río Negro. Spanish colonial buildings are the order of the day, while the tranquil riverside gives ample opportunity for enjoying water-based activities such as fishing, boating and swimming. Capital of Soriano department, it is also an excellent place for transport connections between Montevideo and the cities of the west.

The **bus terminal** is in the shopping mall on Plaza Artigas, eight blocks south of the Plaza Independencia along Colón. It is a long walk from here to the centre, but a taxi should cost no more than UR$25. The **tourist office** on the Plaza Independencia (Mon–Thurs 12.30–6.30pm, Fri–Sun 8am–7pm) is very helpful, and maps and information are displayed in the windows. There are several **banks** in the streets around the Plaza Independencia, although withdrawing money out of hours can be difficult, as cash machines do not accept foreign cards. **Internet** access on Artigas y Independencia, opposite the marble Sociedad Italiana, costs UR$40 per hour.

The Town

The nicest part of the town is the broad riverside *costanera* just to the north, with its ornate squares, tree-lined banks, floral gardens and slow pace of life. Away from the river, the **Plaza Independencia**, shaded by palm and *espinilla* trees, is the hub of most activity, its south side dominated by the impressive **Catedral Nuestra Señora de las Mercedes**. Dating from the eighteenth century, its bell towers are adorned with carved figurines of angels. One block south of the plaza on Roosevelt y Artigas a small plaque on the wall marks the birthplace of Pedro Blanes Viale (1879–1926), one of Uruguay's most famous painters.

Five kilometres west of town, the **Castillo Mauá** deserves a quick look. Built under the orders ofViscount Evangelisto de Souza in 1853, it is supposedly haunted, and legend has it that you can hear the sound of rattling chains at night. A wine *bodega* now occupies most of the building, as well as the **Museo Palaentologico Alejandro Berro** (daily 11am–6pm; free) with a nice collection of national and international remains. The gardens, peppered with acacia trees, stretch down to the river and contain a small **zoo** (daily 1–6pm; free).

Practicalities

Some of the best cheap **accommodation** in Mercedes can be found at the *Club de Remeros* (☎0532/2534; ❶–❷) on the riverfront, a sort of sports-hostel-cum-yacht-club with fantastic facilities including clay tennis courts. Dormitory-style accommodation is available in huge rooms, marginally more expensive with private kitchens and bathrooms. *Colón*, Colón 169 (☎0532/4720; ❺) just off the main plaza, has more upmarket rooms, with minibar and breakfast included. *Marin*, 18 de Julio (☎0532/2987; ❷), is a fair mid-range option in a good location, although some rooms are a little dingy. There is **camping** on the Isla del Puerto, a river island just off the coast, but beware that the island frequently floods following periods of heavy rain.

Sadly, there is a shortage of good **places to eat** in Mercedes. The restaurant at *Club de Remeros* isn't bad and is convenient if you are staying there, but in town *Parrillada Volver*, 18 de Julio y Giménez, serves good, solid fare from the grill.

Fray Bentos

Once the centre of the world's meatpacking industry, **FRAY BENTOS** is today a sad and rather dull place. Nonetheless, the remnants of the meatpacking factory, a few kilometres south of the town and now called the **Museo de la Revolución Industrial** (2 daily tours in Spanish at 10am & 3pm; UR$10), are one of the most unusual and macabre tourist attractions in South America. The vast plant, known as "El Anglo", was founded by the Leibig Meat Extract Company in 1865 and at its height employed one-quarter of the population of Fray Bentos. Tour guides speaking in English show you around the whole site, where rusted, blood-stained meat hooks still litter the floor and an eerie silence pervades, but perhaps the most fascinating parts are the administrative offices, left exactly as they were when they were vacated for the last time, and the machine rooms, that once generated the electricity for the entire town.

The main road into town from Ruta 2 is Avenida 18 de Julio, and it is here that the **bus terminal** is located. The **tourist office** (daily noon–6pm) is on the Plaza Constitución, where most of the interest lies, 11 blocks west of the terminal. A second tourist office in the bus terminal does not have any printed information and is useless. **Taxis** (☎056/22217) are relatively easy to find around the plazas and are generally very cheap. **Internet** access at *LA Cyber*, 18 de Julio 1106, one block from the plaza, costs UR$45 per hour.

There is little of interest in the town itself, although the **Museo Luis Solari** (Tues–Sun 2–6pm; free) on the Plaza Constitución might entice you. Housed in a grand old building, it displays the often bizarre work of Luis Solari, famed for his paintings of human figures with animal heads and born in Fray Bentos in 1918. In the centre of the plaza is a Victorian-style bandstand, presented to the town by English investors in the El Anglo plant at the turn of the twentieth century. If you fancy a bit of relaxation, the tourist complex of **Las Cañas** with good beaches, swimming pools, sporting and camping facilities is 8km south. However, it can be crowded during the holiday season.

Practicalities

Accommodation is limited, often pricey and not always of the highest quality. One of the cheapest options is *Colonial*, 25 de Mayo y Zorilla (☎056/22260; ❷). It is friendly enough, although the brown windowless rooms are rather depressing. *Plaza* on the Plaza Constitución (☎056/22363; ❺) is more upmarket, has cable TV and an adjacent casino, but this is reflected in the higher price. Although there are a number of fast-food eateries around the Plaza Constitución, there is a real shortage of decent **restaurants**. *El Angel*, Avenida Brasil y 18 de Julio, is a hot and cold buffet open until 4pm only, while *Wolves* in the Barrio Histórico near El Anglo does good food, even if the pasta is best avoided. The *Enigma* **discotheque** is also located in the old town and is very busy at weekends.

Crossing into Argentina

Nine kilometres north of Fray Bentos, the **San Martín Bridge** is one of the more popular crossing points into Argentina. Customs formalities take place at opposite ends of the bridge, and there is a toll of around UR$100 for each car. The **Argentine consulate** in Fray Bentos is located at Sarandí 3195.

Paysandú

With its sweltering summer temperatures and profusion of mosquitoes, **PAYSANDÚ**, Uruguay's second largest city, is not everybody's cup of tea. However, for those willing to give it a chance, there is enough to see in the town itself and a number of worthwhile excursions into the surrounding areas.

Intercity buses arrive at the **bus terminal** (☎072/23225) at Zorilla de San Martin y Artigas, eight blocks south of the Plaza Constitución, with regular service between here and Montevideo as well as north via Salto to Rivera on the border with Brazil. There is a **tourist office** (daily 8am–6pm) on the plaza at 18 de Julio 1226, which can provide you with a good city map and an excellent folder-guide to the city. A few doors along at 18 de Julio 1250, **Internet** access is available for UR$50 per hour.

The Town

The effective centre of town is the **Plaza Constitución**, site of the magnificent **Basilica Nuestra Señora del Rosario**, one of Uruguay's finest cathedrals outside the capital. Completed in 1879, its gold-gilded frescoes are quite unlike anything found in the rest of the country, while its pipe organ is notable for its sheer size. Adjacent to the Basilica, the **Campana Misionera** is a huge bell dating from 1698, donated to the church by Fructuoso Rivera, first president of the republic of Uruguay. Beneath the shady plaza, a set of steps lead down to the **Mausoleo al General Leandro Gomez**, containing the remains of the great defender of Paysandú. With only limited ammunition and supplies, his force of 1500 men held out for 33 days against 5000 invading, well-armed Brazilians before finally surrendering on New Year's Day 1865. Despite being a prisoner of war, he was executed by the Brazilians, along with three of his most senior officers. Above ground, the site is marked by a statue of him calling his troops into action.

Three blocks south of the plaza, the **Museo Histórico Municipal** (Mon–Fri &

Sun 8am–4.45pm, Sat 8–11.45am; free) is a superbly displayed collection of largely military items dating from Uruguay's struggle for independence. If your interest in Paysandú's past has peaked, six blocks further south near to the bus terminal the **Monumento a la Perpetuidad** marks the gateway to a fascinating, once grand, and now gracefully decaying cemetery. In the far northwest of town on the river bank the **Museo de la Tradición** (9am–6pm; free) is beautifully set next to the 20,000 capacity **Anfiteatró del Río Uruguay**. Its collection is largely junk, although the gaucho articles repay consideration.

Practicalities

Most of the cheap **places to stay** are found along Avenida 18 de Julio, and are conveniently located for most of the main attractions. *Hospedaje Victoria*, 18 de Julio 979 (☎072/24320; ❷), is secure, friendly and has plenty of character. Opposite is *Nuevo Hotel Concordia*, 18 de Julio 949 (☎072/22417; ❷), which has rather old-fashioned decor, although rooms do have cable TV. The YHA-affiliated *La Posada* (☎072/27879; ❸) is located well south of the plaza near the bus terminal at José Pedro Varela 566. More of a hotel than a hostel, it is comfortable and modern, although there are no cooking facilities. **Camping** is possible at several designated sites along the Río Uruguay, such as the Balnéario Municipal near the Anfiteatró, but facilities are poor.

Paysandú is the birthplace of the sickly sweet cake-like dessert *chagá*, popular throughout Uruguay. Should you feel like something more substantial to eat, there is a good selection of reasonable **restaurants**. The homely *Artemio*, near the tourist office at 18 de Julio 1248, boasts the "best food in town" but IVA is not included in the price and meals can end up being rather costly. Nevertheless, you are guaranteed a good feed if your wallet is up to it, and surroundings that give the impression that you are eating in the owner's front room. *Don Diego*, Av España 1474, is a typical *parrillada*. For **nightlife** try *Zeus* on Avenida Brasil y Ledesma, the continuation of 18 de Julio, five blocks west of the port.

Crossing into Argentina

Eight kilometres north of town the **José Artigas Bridge** crosses the river to Colón, Argentina, with customs formalities taking place at opposite ends of the bridge. There is a toll of around UR$100 for each car.

Salto

The picturesque port city of **SALTO** lies 120km north of Paysandú along Ruta 3, in the midst of the thermal resort area (see box on p.1002). The town itself, a central player in the cultivation and export of citrus fruits, is a neat, tidy, attractive place with two large parks and two fine plazas.

Buses arrive and depart from the new, modern **bus terminal** (☎073/37200) at Avenida Blandengues y Diego Lamas in the northwest of town. It is some way from the centre but taxis are relatively cheap. The **tourist office** at Uruguay 1052 (Mon–Fri 7am–8pm, Sat 7am–7pm; ☎073/25194, ⓦwww.salto.gub.uy) will organize tours to the Salto Grande dam and HEP power plant, while tours to thermal resorts are available through *Argentur* (☎073/29931).

The Town

The main street, **Calle Uruguay**, runs east to west through the centre of town, connecting the two plazas **Treinta y Tres** and, six blocks further east, the **Plaza Artigas**. Here the ornate **Catedral San Juan Bautista**, built in the domed, twin-towered style so typical of Uruguayan churches, dominates its surroundings. The two **parks** are found at opposite ends of town, the leafy **Parque Solari** in the north and **Parque Harriague**, with a zoo and open-air theatre, in the south. The city also boasts a number of good museums, the pick of the bunch being the excellent **Museo del Hombre y la Technologia** (2–7pm; free), two blocks north of Plaza Treinta y Tres on the corner with Calle Brasil. Beautifully displayed (despite a leaky roof), the recreations of a gaucho bar and early twentieth-century Art Nouveau tearoom are fascinating. An archeology section downstairs is currently closed for renovation. The somewhat pretentious **Museo Bella Artes**, opposite the tourist office at Uruguay 1067 (3–8pm; free), is set in an old French-style mansion, while the dusty **Museo Historico** (Tues–Sun 1–5pm; free) in the north of town adjacent to Parque Solari offers an interesting, if jumbled, collection of artefacts from the late nineteenth and early twentieth centuries.

Outside the city lie a number of minor attractions. The **Salto Grande Dam**, 20km north, is perhaps the most popular destination, with organized tours visiting the interior and explaining the workings of the bi-national damming project. If you are not part of a tour, the outside of the dam can still be viewed at any time as it forms the **crossing point** to Concordia in Argentina. Customs formalities for Uruguay and Argentina take place in the same office at the Argentine end of the bridge. Buses make obligatory stops at the customs points.

Should you feel in need of relaxation, Salto is in the middle of an area famous for its **hot springs (las termas)** (see box on p.1002) and there are several resorts nearby that can be visited for a day-trip or longer. The excellent **Termas del Daymán** is located 10km to the south and the family-orientated **Termas del Arapey** 61km north, both off Ruta 3.

Practicalities

There is a good selection of **accommodation** for all budgets. The best of the cheaper options is *Tia*, Brasil 566 (☎073/26574; ❷), recently renovated with modern marble rooms and some family rooms available. *Gran Hotel Concordia*, Uruguay 749 (☎073/32735; ❸), is a once grand establishment with a good restaurant where once the great tango musician Carlos Gardel stayed on an occasion. Nearer to the bus station, *Danaly* (☎073/35784; ❷), owned by the same people as *Tia*, is at Agraciada 2060. Rooms are rather shabby but it is a convenient choice if arriving late at night. Salto has a number of good **restaurants**, especially along Uruguay, and it shouldn't be too difficult to eat well on a budget. The stylish *Alzabache*, Sarandí y Uruguay, and the rustic *La Caldera* at Uruguay 22 both have extensive menus of fish and salads. *Las Mil y Una*, Uruguay 906, is an ever-popular pizzeria and *Salto Uruguay*, Uruguay 457 on Plaza Treinta y Tres, gives good cheap eats such as *chivitos* and *milanesas* in basic surroundings.

North to the Brazilian border

Ruta 3 continues 144km north of Salto to the border town of **BELLA UNIÓN**. Frequently unpaved on the approach to town, progress can be painfully slow, and as a result the border crossing has become a very minor one. At the northern edge of town an international bridge connects Bella Unión to the Brazilian town of **Barra del Cuaraim**. Should you wish to cross, regular bus services to Brazil depart from the Plaza 25 de Agosto in Bella Unión.

Thirty kilometres or so south of Bella Unión, there is a turn-off for Ruta 30, which heads east to the more important border town of **ARTIGAS**. However, this route is also largely unpaved and poorly signposted, and approaching from the east of town via Ruta 5 is quicker and easier. Known for its amethysts, Artigas has a very pleasant plaza and a bridge across the Río Cuareim to the Brazilian town of **Quarai**. Customs formalities take place at either side of the bridge, but if crossing by bus do not forget to obtain all the necessary entry and exit stamps, as buses seldom stop.

Las Termas thermal resorts

Among the highlights of any trip to Uruguay, **Las Termas** are relaxed – and frequently luxurious – hot spring resorts located in the geothermically active eastern part of the country. While many of the thermal resorts take on the air of a health farm, prices are often surprisingly cheap for the level of facilities, and it is well worth staying a night or two to reap the full benefits. Should time be limited, however, most resorts can be visited on a day-trip for a small fee, where you might enjoy a hydro-massage, an afternoon in a water park or merely lounge around in the naturally heated spa pools.

For those seeking a holiday-resort feel, the best is **Termas del Daymàn**, 8km south of Salto. Site of the first thermal aquapark in South America (daily noon–6pm; UR$145) and with waters reaching 46°C there is plenty to occupy visitors of all ages. For accommodation *Posada del Siglo XIX* (ⓣ073/69955; ❸ including breakfast) cannot be highly recommended enough. With several heated pools, sauna, gym and hydro-massage facilities, not to mention enormous, fully fitted rooms, it is exceptional value for money. **Termas del Arapey**, 60km north of Salto off Ruta 3, is rather more family orientated. Set in a secure, peaceful, wooded site, with indoor and outdoor pools, it is the perfect place to relax. Accommodation varies from cheap double cabins (❶) through to self-catering bungalows for two to four people (❷–❹). Day-trippers can use the pools for UR$50. There is also an excellent restaurant, *Parrillada Paradise*, which does a delicious grill of fresh meats and a very reasonable *menú turístico* (UR$50). The only salt-water springs are at **Termas del Almirón**, 85km east of Paysandú along Ruta 90, while **Termas de Salto Grande**, 10km north of Salto near the dam, features delightful riverside pools and an expensive hotel and casino complex.

10.4

North of Montevideo

There are two main routes north of Montevideo. Ruta 8 via **Minas** radiates out to the northeast and terminates at the border with Brazil. Ruta 5 heads due north through wine-growing country to **Durazno** and **Tacuarembó**. In its later stages it passes through some of the finest countryside that Uruguay has to offer, while its earlier stages consist largely of flat ranching land, with little of interest to the tourist. However, there are always a few places that merit stopping off, and a stay at an estancia is a good way to feel part of the surroundings.

Minas

Birthplace of Juan Lavalleja, leader of the revered Treinta y Tres Orientales (see p.974), peaceful **MINAS** will always have a special place in Uruguay's history. Set among rolling wooded hills just 120km north of Montevideo, the town's main attraction lies in its sleepy indifference to the outside world. An ideal place to escape the hustle of the capital, it features a number of sights in the surrounding area that make it worth a few days stopover.

Intercity buses arrive and depart from the **terminal de omnibuses** (☎0442/9796) three blocks west of Plaza Libertad on Calle Treinta y Tres. There is a small but very helpful **tourist office** here (daily 7am–7pm; Ⓔturismoiml@hotmail.com), which can provide you with a map and details about how to visit the surrounding attractions. **Internet** access is available at *Cyber Idim* three blocks northeast on the corner of Sanchez and Batlle y Ordoñez.

The Town

The approximate centre of town is the **Plaza Libertad**, graced by a horseback statue of Lavalleja. One block east along Calle Roosevelt, the main road through town, is the **Catedral**, a white, twin-towered structure with a five-arched portico. From here it is three blocks north to the **Teatro Lavalleja Museo Humor y Historieta** (Mon–Fri 1–5pm summer only; free) on Calle Batlle y Ordoñez. A red-brick edifice, it looks out of place amongst the soft pastel-coloured buildings of the rest of the town and houses a small rather nondescript museum. In the far south of town lies a pleasant riverside **Rambla** with picnic tables, wooded park and children's adventure playground that captures the serenity of the town nicely.

Minas provides an excellent base for visiting a number of attractions in the surrounding area. At 18m high, 9m wide and weighing 150 thousand kilos, the horseback **statue of Artigas**, on top of the Cerro Artigas just outside town, is supposedly the largest equestrian statue in the world. The **Parque Salus** 8km south of town has a brewery and mineral spring. The **Cascada del Penitente waterfalls** are 11km east of town along Ruta 8, but there is no public transport and it can be difficult to reach them, especially in the low season (taxi UR$350 one-way).

Estancias Turisticas

No visit to the interior of the country would be complete without a stay on an **Estancia Turistica**, a working ranch. Dotted throughout the country, most estancias offer a high level of accommodation coupled with the opportunity to get closely involved with the day-to-day running of the ranch. Many organize tours for visitors, usually with an ecological theme and often involving **birdwatching** and **horse riding**. The ranches are split into broad categories: *quintas y chacras* (country estates); *granjas* (farming ranches); *serranos* (highland estates); and *llanuras* (prairie estates), each a subtly different take on the ranch lifestyle. For a full list of the estancias in the country with photographs and reservation details visit ⓦwww.turismo.gub.uy/estancias/operadores_s. The official travel agent of SUTUR (Sociedad Uruguaya de Turismo Rural) is LARES (ⓣ02/901-9120, ⓦwww.lares.com.uy), which organizes a series of themed tours involving stays on ranches. Tours and day-trips can also be arranged through other companies in Montevideo such as *Estancias Gauchas*, Bacacay 1334 (ⓣ02/915-7308).

Practicalities

In terms of **accommodation** you could do a lot worse than stay at *Posada Verdun*, Avenida Beltran 715 (ⓣ0442/4563; ❷ with bath and cable TV, ❶ without), and *Las Sierras*, Avenida 18 de Julio 486 (no phone; ❶ including breakfast). More upmarket, but still quite reasonable, is *Plaza* on Plaza Lavalleja (ⓣ0442/2328, ⓔhplaza@adinet.com.uy; ❺ with balcony, ❹ without), which has great facilities including a swimming pool, Jacuzzi and cable TV. For **food** there are a number of decent eating places around the plaza, including *Ki-joia*, a *parrillada* that does excellent *chorizo* and *morcilla* (blood sausage).

From Minas to the Brazilian border

Beyond Minas, Ruta 8 passes through **Treinta Y Tres**, the departmental capital named in honour of the country's founders, the 33 Orientales. The only sight worth stopping for around here is the magnificent **Quebrada de los Cuervos** outside town, a stunning, forested valley, 12km in length, named after the large numbers of vultures that congregate to take advantage of the thermals it generates. The road continues on to **Melo**, where it meets the direct road from the capital (Ruta 7) and Ruta 26 north to Tacuarembó. From here it is a short distance to the border town of **Río Branco**, a bridge crossing to **Jaguarão** in Brazil.

Durazno and the north

Founded in 1821, ten years after General Artigas launched the fight for independence from here, **DURAZNO** lies 182km north of Montevideo. Seldom visited by tourists, one's first impressions are of a pleasant, if rather uninspiring, provincial town. The **Museo Historico Casa del General Rivera** (Tues–Fri 9am–noon & 2–7pm, Sat–Sun 9am–1pm & 4–8pm; free) on the Plaza Independencia features original photos of important figures from nineteenth-century society, notable largely for their bizarre moustaches. There is a very helpful **tourist office** 2km south of town on the Ruta, and next door is a small **zoo** (10am–5pm; UR$5). Should you wish to stay overnight Señora Chola (ⓣ0362/9008; ❷) rents homely private rooms from her house on 19 de Abril y Artigas. A better bet is to stay in an estancia, and there are several in the vicinity including *La Cueva del Tigre* 18km north of Durazno, (ⓣ0360/2329; ❻), with a swimming pool and facilities for children, and *Los Galpones* 4km further north(ⓣ0362/5770; ❻), with horse riding and fishing opportunities.

Paso de los Toros

On the shores of the man-made **Lago Rincón del Bonete**, **PASO DE LOS TOROS** 66km north of Durazno, is a small, lively town that is becoming increasingly popular with tourists. The lake was formed by the damming of the Río Negro as part of the **Central Hidroeléctrica Dr Gabriel Terra** project, and the resultant flooding formed an immense, irregular reservoir – the first of its kind in Uruguay – which almost splits the country in two. The outside of the dam, reached by taking the first right after the church, going under a bridge and continuing 12km east can be visited at any time, although to see the inside you will need to make arrangements at the guard house to visit (2–6pm; free although tipping is expected). Paso de los Toros's unusual **church** is in an odd mixture of gothic and traditional styles, although it is rather disappointing inside. At the entrance to town on Boulevar José Artigas, a **tourist office** (Mon–Fri 10am–5pm; ⓦwww.pasoweb.8k.com) holds information about walking in the surrounding countryside, sporting activities associated with the nearby lake and a list of potential **places to stay**. A good cheap option is the run-down but well-equipped *Sarandí*, Avenida Sarandí 777 (ⓣ0623/3963; ❷), while the campsite at *El Sauce* (ⓣ0664/3503) has excellent facilities and *cabañas* for four to six people (❶–❷). For **food** *Pizzeria Pingui*, 18 de Julio 757 does surprisingly good steaks, as well as the expected pizzas.

Tacuarembó

The major transport centre of the north, **TACUAREMBÓ**, 142km north of Paso de los Toros, is an industrial town at the confluence of three major *rutas* linking Salto, Paysandú, Melo and Montevideo with the Brazilian border towns of Artigas and Rivera. The **tourist office** (Mon–Fri 7am–7pm; ⓣ0632/4671) on the Plaza 19 de Abril can provide a rather limited city map, and while they have little in the way of printed information, the staff is knowledgeable and helpful if your Spanish is good enough. The **bus terminal** is on the eastern edge of town close to the turn-off for Ruta 5. From here there are regular services to Montevideo and north to Rivera on the Brazilian border.

The town comes alive during the annual **gaucho festival** in March, with displays of horsemanship and celebrations of the gaucho lifestyle, but throughout the rest of the year there is enough to make a stopover worthwhile. The **Plaza 19 de Abril** marks the centre of town, with the unusual mixed-colonial style **Catedral San Fructuoso** on one side. The streets around the plaza harbour a few small museums, the one-room **Museo Geociencias** (daily 1–6.30pm; free) on the plaza, with an unusual mineral collection, and the **Museo del Indio y Gauchos** (daily 1–7pm; free) one block south, with its gaucho paraphernalia, being the best.

Outside town, seven kilometres to the north, there is an excellent swimming pool and campsite at **Balnéario Iporá**, from where there are magnificent views over Tacuarembó and the forested hills surrounding it. A little further afield, **Valle Edén**, 25km south of the centre off Ruta 5, is set in intensely beautiful, lush countryside. It incorporates a museum (daily 9am–6pm; UR$15) dedicated to the famous tango star Carlos Gardel, born in Tacuarembó.

Perhaps the best **hotel** in Tacuarembó is the central *Tacuarembó*, 18 de Julio 133 (ⓣ0632/2104; ❸), but rather cheaper is *Hospedaje Bertis* (ⓣ0632/3324; ❶), Ituzaingo 211, which has small, old-fashioned rooms but is nonetheless comfortable. The town suffers from having very few quality **restaurants**, although *Parrilla La Rueda* at Beltran 251 will satisfy those needing a meat fix.

Crossing into Brazil

RIVERA is a lively and busy border crossing to the town of **Santana do Livramento** in Brazil (see p.463). Modern and somewhat tacky, it is a hive of commercial activity from the numerous duty-free shops that line the streets to the hordes of street vendors that seem to appear from nowhere. In the north of town is an attractive **park**, swamped at one edge by a huge and growing **arts and crafts market** selling everything but the kitchen sink.

Crossing the border can be a complex affair, and the Uruguayan immigration office is located at the **Complejo Turistíco** at Sarandí y Viera, 2km from the frontier. Exit stamps must be obtained before attempting to cross. The Brazilian **consulate** is at Calle Caballos 1159 (☎0622/244-3278). There is also a small **tourist office** (Mon–Fri 1–7pm; ☎0622/5899) here that can provide advice on crossing to Brazil. A good cheap **hotel** is the friendly *Sarandí* (☎0622/3521; ❷) at Sarandí 777, which is well located in the centre of town a few blocks from the Plaza Internacional. For **eating**, *Cambalache*, also on Sarandís, is a fantastic *parrillada* with a good house wine.

11

Venezuela

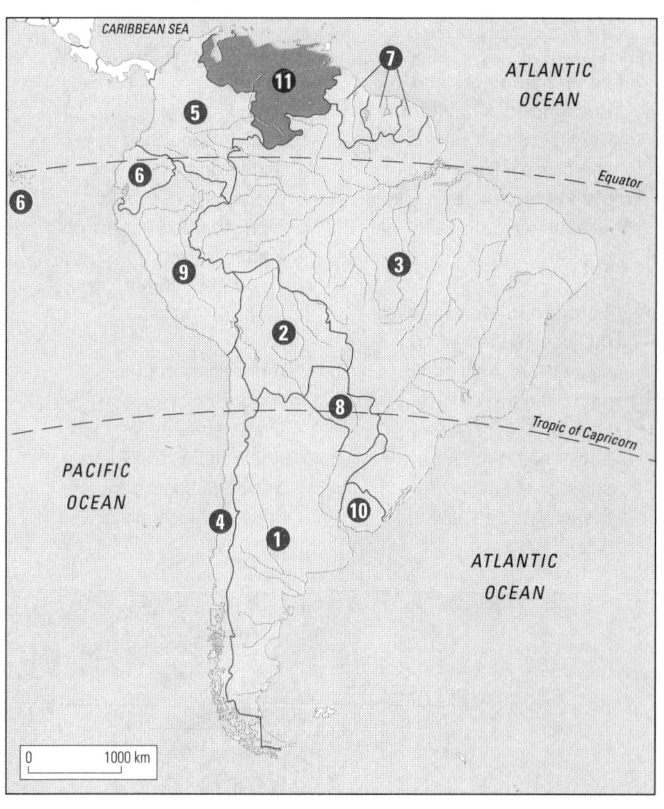

Venezuela highlights

✱ **Parque Nacional Morrocoy** The pristine beaches of this national park are among the most unspoilt in South America – for now. See p.1034

✱ **The mansions of Coro** Recognized as a World Heritage Site, Venezuela's finest colonial town is exceptionally well preserved. See p.1036

✱ **Teleférico in Mérida** Take the world's longest and highest-climbing cable car to the top of Pico Espejo, 4765 metres above sea level, for a stirring view of the surrounding Sierra Nevada. See p.1042

✱ **Angel Falls** The Río Churún falls dramatically off the edge of the enormous Auyantepui table-top mountain in the Parque Nacional Canaima into the verdant jungle below. See p.1063

✱ **Delta lodges** Stay at a lodge on the Orinoco Delta and visit indigenous Warao villages, go canoeing and try your hand at piraña fishing. See p.1066

✱ **Snorkelling in Los Roques** The crystal clear water surrounding the 42 islets of this archipelago, now a national park, are ideal for snorkelling. See p.1075

Introduction and basics

Venezuela's location on the Caribbean coast makes the flight there one of the shortest – and often cheapest – from most parts of Europe and the US. Not that hordes of foreign visitors tend to take advantage of that. Despite packing nearly every natural environment on the continent into a relatively small place – Caribbean beaches, snowcapped mountains, wildlife-rich wetlands, desert, Amazonian jungle, fertile river valley – the country has historically been one of the least-visited in South America; even war-torn Colombia receives five times more tourists annually than Venezuela.

In any case, as the world's fourth largest **oil** producer, Venezuela has not had a pressing need for additional sources of revenue, and the country has done very little to promote itself abroad. Moreover, until recently its oil wealth translated into extremely high prices, making dining and accommodation rather expensive in comparison with the rest of South America.

However, changes may be on the horizon. President **Hugo Chávez** has looked to increase development, and falling oil prices have led to a severe currency devaluation in the past several years, making travel within Venezuela considerably less expensive than before. And much is in place already: an extensive highway system makes internal travel easy, while a countrywide guesthouse network provides ample accommodation options. Ironically, many tourists now avoid Venezuela because of the political instability that has accompanied Chávez's rise to power, overthrow and return to power (see p.1021). Although most of the country is safe except for Caracas, international headlines have served as a powerful deterrent to would-be visitors.

Where to go

Venezuela's prime attractions lie outside its major cities, and few travellers spend any more time than necessary in **Caracas** – a good strategy given the capital's security problems and lack of major tourist draws.

With 43 **national parks** and many private nature reserves, the country is well suited to outdoors-oriented visitors. Most visitors explore at least part of Venezuela's over 2600km of Caribbean coastline, which contains some of South America's finest and most diverse **beaches**. With postcard-like white sand and crystal-clear water, Venezuela's most pristine beaches are found in the over forty keys that make up the **Los Roques Archipelago**, but building restrictions and lack of maritime access make it a rather exclusive destination. However, there are several national parks that are easily accessible by bus from Caracas. Several hours east of the capital, **Parque Nacional Mochima** boasts red-sand beaches with emerald water and backdrops of rocky hills and cactuses, while **Parque Nacional Henri Pittier**, about three hours west, offers a number of beaches with stunning backgrounds of palm trees and verdant mountains. Just two hours to the west is **Parque Nacional Morrocoy**, which features picturesque white-sand keys, but is more financially accessible than Los Roques.

An overnight bus ride from Morrocoy or Pittier will take you to **Mérida**, in the heart of the Andes Mountains. It might be the only city in which you want to spend more than a few days, given its pretty setting, impressive and inexpensive tourist facilities. Mérida is also the best place to arrange trips to **Los Llanos**, the extensive plains that provide some of the best wildlife and birdwatching opportunities on the continent.

The enormous region of **Guayana**, which encompasses most of the south and west portions of the country, contains a number of adventurous attractions. In the south, near the border with Colombia, **Puerto Ayacucho** is the only town in the Amazon region with accommodation and tour operator offices. To the northeast, the picturesque, historical town of **Ciudad Bolívar** is the most economical base from which to explore **Parque Nacional**

CARRIBBEAN SEA
Archipiélago Los Roques
CARACAS
Coro
Chichiriviche
Maracaibo
Choroní
Colonia Tovar
Maracay
Lago Maracaibo
Mucuchíes
Trujillo
Apartaderos
Tabay
Mucuchíes
Merida
Barinas
Río Apure
San Fernando de Apure
Cúcuta
San Cristobal
Los Llanos
Puerto Ayacucho
COLOMBIA

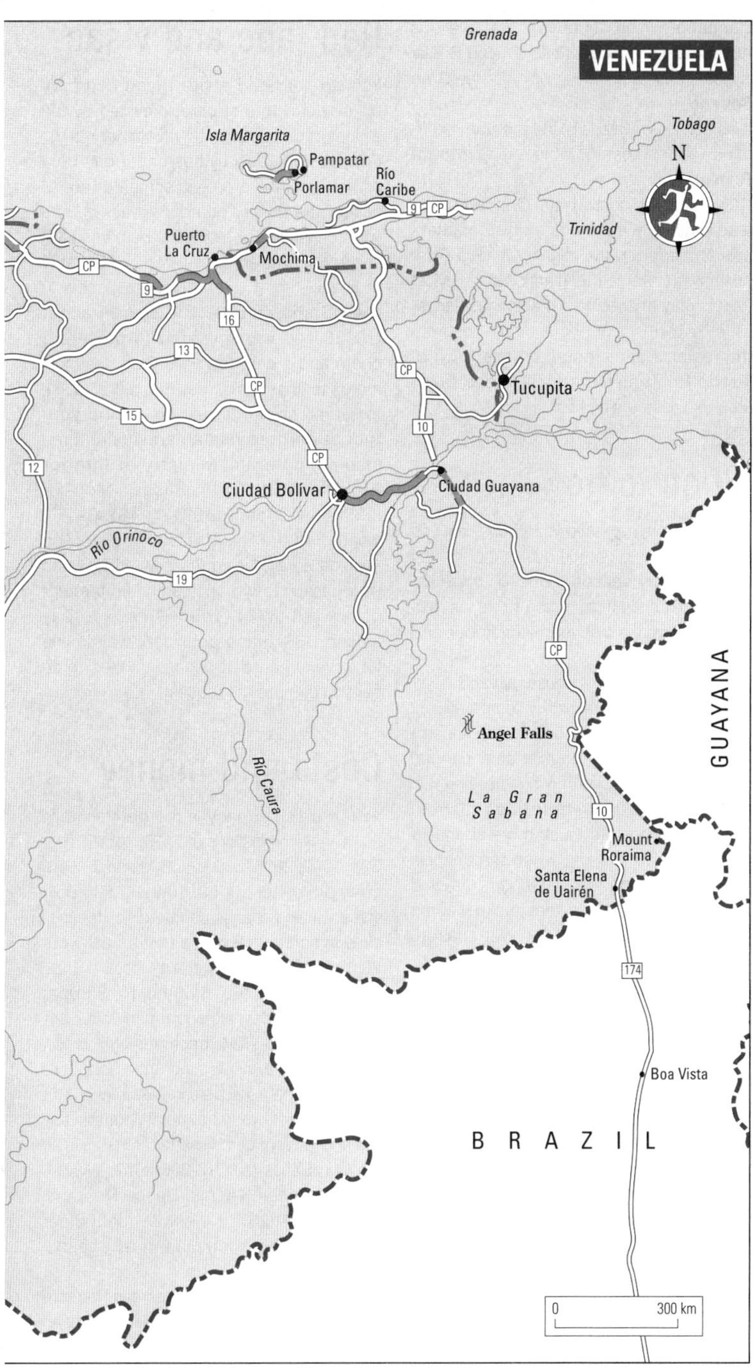

11

VENEZUELA | Basics

Canaima, which contains the marvellous **Auyantepui** and **Angel Falls**. Ciudad Bolívar is also the ideal launching point for the **Gran Sabana**, a magical and vast area that contains countless waterfalls and tabletop mountains – the most notable being **Mount Roraima**.

Guayana also contains the **Orinoco Delta**, a labyrinth of marshlands and water channels formed from the mighty Orinoco River on its way towards the Atlantic Ocean. Most visitors stay at one of several lodges accessible by two-to eight-hour boat rides from the region's unmemorable base town of **Tucupita**. The return to Caracas takes around nine hours by bus.

When to go

Venezuela can be visited year-round, but you are most likely to get the best out of visiting during the **dry season**. Although there are slight differences from region to region, this generally means between November and May.

On **the coast**, there is less rain and fewer mosquitoes, if slightly higher temperatures. In **the Andes**, it is more difficult and uncomfortable to climb the popular snowcapped peaks in the wet season, when freezing rain and snow are frequent. In **Los Llanos**, wildlife spottings are much more abundant during the dry season, when the animals congregate at the few watering holes, and hordes of pesky mosquitoes make walking very unpleasant during the wet season. Travel in the **Guayana** region is more comfortable during the dry season, though Angel Falls tends to be fuller and therefore more spectacular during the wet season.

It is probably best to avoid the national vacation periods of Easter, Carnaval (beginning at the end of February or beginning of March), Christmas vacation (December 15–January 15) and summer vacation (July 15–September 15), when beaches are considerably more crowded and prices significantly higher.

Red tape and visas

You do not need a visa if you come by plane, just a **tourist card**, provided by the airlines, that lets you stay for ninety days. Entry to Venezuela by bus or car can be a bit more complicated – in some but not all cases, the border guards will ask to see your tourist **visa**, which must be purchased at the Venezuelan consulates in Colombia or Brazil – they're not always available in the US and Europe. The cost is about US$30 and you will need to present a photo and a passport valid for at least six more months. Sometimes they will also ask to see an onward ticket. **To extend your tourist card or visa** an additional three months, go to the **Ministry of Interior Affairs (DIEX)** in Caracas (Mon–Fri 8.30am–4.30pm; ⓣ0212/ 482-0977), located off the Capitolio subway stop on Avenida Baralt, facing Plaza Miranda. Bring your passport, two photos and your return or onward ticket. You will have to pay around US$70 and potentially wait in line for several hours. It generally takes three days to process the request.

Costs and money

Venezuela's currency is the **bolívar**. Bills come in denominations of 5, 10, 20, 50, 100, 500, 1000, 2000, 5000, 10,000 and 20,000; coins are of 10, 20, 50, 100 and 500 bolívares. Getting change can be difficult, especially in smaller towns, so try to break your 20,000 bills when you get a chance.

Bank hours are 8.30am to 3.30pm Monday to Friday, although many offer 24-hour access to **ATM machines**, which can be problematic, depending upon your card type. Most banks advertise that they are on the cirrus and maestro systems, but still may not accept your card. The two most reliable are CorpBanca (ⓣ0212/206-2677, ⓦwww.corpbanca.com.ve) and Banco Mercantil (ⓣ0212/206-2677, ⓦwww.bancomercantil.com), both found in most sizeable towns.

Cashing **travellers' cheques** can be more difficult, and cheques other than American Express are often not accepted. CorpBanca does not charge commission, but its queues are often unbearable and some branches have bizarre requirements such as for fingerprints. Usually it is best to go to exchange houses, most of which accept travellers' cheques but at varying rates and commission levels – always ask before exchanging. Italcambio, found in most urban centres, is reliable and does not charge a commission for exchanging American Express travellers' cheques.

In terms of exchanging cash, the US dollar is by far the most reliable currency. Finding someone to exchange US dollars is easy, even in small towns. Although you do not want to carry too many dollars, it is a good idea to save some for when there are no other options. **Prices in this section are given in US dollars**.

After nearly one hundred percent **devaluation** in the past few years, prices are far more reasonable for visitors. A typical, moderately priced meal should set you back US$3–4, while a double room will cost around US$25–35. One-way plane tickets cost US$30–100.

Information, maps and websites

The **Viceministerio de Turismo**, the federal government's official tourism organization, has two offices in Caracas. The one that deals most directly with the public is in the national terminal of the Maiquetia airport (daily 8am–noon; ⓣ0212/355-2598), and its friendly attendants, many of whom speak English, offer maps, brochures and help finding accommodation. For more extensive information you can visit the headquarters, in the Torre Oeste of Parque Central, on the 35th floor (Mon–Fri 8.30am–12.30pm & 2–5pm). Each state also has a tourism office in its capital.

Venezuela does not have an official website and, in general, there are few sources of information about Venezuela on the **Internet**. Of those that exist, the most useful include ⓦwww.discovervenezuela.com, ⓦwww.think-venezuela.net and ⓦwww.venezuelatuya.com.

While a variety of **maps** are available, the *Guia Vial de Venezuela/Atlas de Carreteras*, available in most bookshops, covers Venezuela's major places.

Accommodation

The quality of accommodation varies widely from place to place. The best options are almost always the **posadas**, or guesthouses, of which there are over 1600. Often in restored or newly built colonial-style houses, they tend to offer attractive and authentic surroundings with more personalized attention. They range from very economical to extremely luxurious, and most of the upper-end posadas were built or opened within the last six years. **Hotels** generally offer more in the way of service and amenities, but tend to be older and lacking in character.

Many hotels have mosquito screens on the windows, but often with holes in them. Check the screens before you take the room, since few rooms have mosquito nets and, contrary to what most hotel owners say, air conditioning does not always deter hungry mosquitoes.

Many places on the coast and other popular tourist areas have separate rates for high and low season. Prices are often flexible, so don't be afraid to negotiate, especially during the low season. Some places include breakfast in the price of the room, so be sure to ask.

Youth hostels and camping

There are no **youth hostels** in Venezuela, but there are a few scattered dorm-style places to stay. Budget lodging is not hard to find, but for a little more money you can generally find significantly better accommodation. Lower-end hotels and posadas generally have fans but for a few extra dollars you can often get air conditioning and television. Many have rooms with private bathrooms, but no hot water middle- and upper-end accommodation usually has rooms with private bathrooms, hot water, air conditioning and televisions with cable.

Camping is not very popular among Venezuelans, so there are few designated sites. The most common camping areas are on the beaches, often in national parks (where it is technically illegal). In general, camping is not recommended because of robberies, even on isolated beaches and keys. The safest time to camp is on weekends and during national holidays, when there are likely to be a number of Venezuelan youths camping.

Getting around

Travellers are best off using the generally convenient and inexpensive public transport system of **buses** and **por puesto** vans. To avoid extremely long rides, it is sometimes necessary to take internal **flights**, which are reasonably priced but unreliable. There are no trains in Venezuela.

By car

Although there is an extensive system of paved highways, driving is difficult because roads are not well marked and speed limits are not enforced. **Renting a car** is extremely expensive (at least US$80 per day), primarily because insurance costs are so high. The one exception is on Isla Margarita, where rates start at US$50 per day and roads are very well marked.

Because of safety concerns, **hitching** is neither recommended nor particularly successful.

By bus and por puesto

Most cities and towns have **bus** terminals offering frequent service to most major destinations. A few have a general information desk, but generally you will have to walk around to each bus company's individual booths to figure out departure times. Upon entering the bus terminal, you will often be approached by aggressive salespeople asking you where you are going. Before letting them take you to the bus, check first at the mini-offices to make sure there aren't buses with better departure times, prices or conditions.

Economical buses, or **servicio normal** (roughly US$1 per hour), are often cramped and have no bathrooms or air conditioning. Executive buses, often called **servicio ejectivo**, have bathrooms, air conditioning and more comfortable seating. They run longer routes and generally cost about US$1.50–2 per hour. Some, called *bus camas*, even have almost fully reclinable seats. These are often available for overnight rides over eight or so hours, especially to and from Caracas.

Cars or vans that leave as soon as they fill up their seats, **por puestos**, generally wait in the bus terminals or on designated streets and have much more frequent departures than buses. Five people are squeezed into each car before it departs, and you rarely have to wait more than half an hour. They generally cost about twice as much as a typical bus, or about US$2 per hour. Most are beat-up cars from the 1970s whose drivers take them at often frightening speeds. They are much more common in the eastern half of the country, especially along the coast.

By plane

There are ten domestic **airlines** in Venezuela. In general, they are not reliable and delays are more the rule than the exception. Larger airlines such as Aeropostal (T 0800/237-6252 and 1-888/912-8466 in the US, W www.aeropostal.com) and Avensa (T 0212/976-5353, W www.avensa.com.ve) are a bit more dependable and marginally more expensive than smaller companies like Avior (T 0212/202-5811, W www.avior.com.ve) and Aserca (T 0212/951-0787). Confirm and reconfirm your reservations and check your receipt to make sure they haven't overcharged you.

Routes between major tourist destinations are generally frequent, although it is common to switch planes in Caracas, sometimes with long layovers. Schedules often change so make sure you have the most current information.

By boat and ferry

On the coast, there are many keys and beaches accessible only by **boat**. Motorboats usually congregate at the town's dock and can be hired either by individual groups or *por prestos*. Most will drop you off and arrange a pick-up time, although some can be rented for a half- or full-day tour of the local beaches or keys. Expect to pay between US$20 and US$50, depending upon the distance. Prices are generally fixed, but bargaining occasionally pays off.

Ferries are used to access Isla Margarita and Trinidad (ferries to Aruba and Curacao no longer run). Several ferries leave daily from Cumana and Puerto La Cruz to Margarita. They vary in speed, comfort and price (US$5 to US$15).

Mail and communications

The Venezuelan **postal service** is at best slow and often unreliable, so if you have an important letter or package, send it through one of the **international carriers**, who have offices in all major cities, but do not expect deliveries to occur as quickly as they claim.

Both domestic and international **phone** calls are quite easy to make, either from telephone **cabañas** or public phones. Most cities and towns have CANTV offices with *cabañas* that allow you to pay for the exact amount of the call. Alternatively, you can buy public phone cards of various denominations at nearly any corner store or magazine stand. Either way, local calls will cost less than US$0.10 per minute, long-distance national calls about US$0.20 per minute, and international calls about US$1 a minute to the US and US$1.25 to most of Europe. To place an international call, first dial 00 and then the code of the country you are calling.

The **Internet** is easy to access cheaply. Internet cafés are commonplace and in some places, like Mérida, it seems there is one on every block. Most charge around US$1 an hour and in some cities you can even get high-speed connections. Small towns without Internet cafés generally have **Infocentros**, Internet offices built by Chávez as part of a programme to give access to all Venezuelans.

Food and drink

Huge cattle ranches produce high quality beef; the Caribbean waters and mountain lakes are home to dozens of fish varieties; and fertile farms allow cultivation of countless vegetables and grains. Moreover, periods of mass immigration have given Spanish, Italian, Chinese and Middle Eastern cooking a lasting impact on Venezuelan cuisine.

Breakfast almost always includes *arepas,* round pieces of fried cornmeal that are probably Venezuela's biggest staple. They are often accompanied by fresh fruit, ham and *perico* (scrambled eggs with diced tomatoes and onions). **Lunch** is generally lighter – a good economic choice is the *menú del día*, which many restaurants offer. **Dinner** is generally a bit more expensive. While the major cities have a decent variety of cuisines, which almost certainly include Spanish, Italian and Chinese outside of the cities the majority of the restaurants have nearly identical menus. There are very few **vegetarian** restaurants. **Markets** have fresh, tasty food at low prices, yet *panaderias*, or bakeries, often disappoint in terms of variety and quality. Fast food is quite common, served by large American chain restaurants as well as simple to elaborate mobile stands open most evenings. Fortunately, Venezuelan food presents few health problems for visitors.

The Venezuelan national dish is the **pabellón criollo**, which consists of *carne mechada* (shredded beef), avocado, *tajadas* (sliced plantains), cheese, rice and beans. *Arepas* are found nearly everywhere, although in the mountains they are made of wheat instead of cornmeal, while *cachapas* are similar to the cornmeal *arepas*, but larger and sweeter. Another ubiquitous food is the *empanada*, a deep-fried turnover made of cornmeal and filled with *carne mechada*, cheese, chicken or *cazón* (shark meat). In areas with indigenous populations you will probably find *casaaba*, a dry flat bread made from the yucca plant.

The ocean, abundant rivers and mountain lakes afford **fresh fish**, the most common varieties being *mero* (grouper), *dorado* (dolphin fish), *pargo* (red snapper), *trucha* (trout), *corvina* (sea bass) and *corocoro* (grunt). **Beef** is also found throughout the country, although it is especially delicious in Los Llanos, where the grass is ideal for cow grazing. Meats are often served with *guasacaca*, a spicy green sauce made of avocado, peppers, onions and spices.

Common **desserts** are strawberries and cream, *quesillo* (similar to flan), *dulce de leche* (caramel) and sweets made from guava or plantains. Venezuelan *cacao* (cocoa) is considered among the best in the world but, as nearly all is exported to Europe, Venezuelan chocolate is difficult to find.

Drinking

Fruit **juices**, or *jugos,* are delicious, inexpensive and safe to drink. The most common are *lechosa* (papaya), *parchita* (passion fruit), mango, *piña* (pineapple), melon, *guayaba* (guava) and *tamarindo* (tamarind). Another sweet, refreshing drink is *papelón con limón* (lemonade made with unrefined brown sugar). Bottled water is inexpensive and available everywhere, and the locally grown coffee is quite good.

Venezuelans are extremely fond of their **beer**. The two major brands are Polar and Regional, each with light and stronger ice versions. The liquor of choice is **rum**, and the better quality varieties, such as Ron Cacique and Ron Añejo Aniversario Pampero, are aged several years and therefore darker.

Crime and safety

In recent years, crime rates have risen to alarming levels in Caracas. High unemployment rates and increasing poverty have combined with less police enforcement to create conditions that make even locals very uncomfortable. Walking alone at night is not considered safe anywhere and some places, such as the city centre, are considered dangerous even during the day. For this reason a special unit of the police called the **tourist brigade** was created to escort tourists through town – look for policemen with red berets outside major sites and ask them to accompany you on your tour. Buses and non-official taxis are not recommended, but the metro is generally safe.

Outside Caracas, security issues are not as common. Notable exceptions are a few towns near the Colombian border, such as San Cristobal and Puerto Ayacucho, considered dangerous because of occasional kidnappings by Colombian rebel groups. Beware, too, that some beach areas have high levels of robbery and petty crime, but little violent crime.

For **insurance claims** you will need to report any incidents of theft to the police. They will write up the claim and give you a copy of the statement, but otherwise are of little assistance. When travelling by road, make sure you carry identification, which you will occasionally have to present at one of the many police stops. Carrying **drugs** is strongly discouraged, since narcotics laws in Venezuela are extremely strict.

Useful numbers

Ambulance ☎171
Fire ☎161
Police ☎169

Opening hours, public holidays and fiestas

Most **shops** are open from 8am until 6pm on weekdays; outside Caracas they generally close during midday, from around 12.30pm until 2 or 3pm. **Shopping malls**, however, generally stay open until 9 or 10pm. Typical **museum hours** are 9am to noon and 2 to 5pm Tuesday to Sunday. Nearly all are closed on Mondays.

Festivals, most with a religious basis, seem to occur constantly. Some are national, while others are local, as each town celebrates its patron saint. The country's most famous **Carnaval** celebrations are in Carupano and El Callao, where there are processions of costumed revellers, as well as the requisite dancing, eating and heavy drinking. **Semana Santa** celebrations are most elaborate in several small towns in the state of Mérida, as well as El Hatillo, just outside Caracas, when large processions involve re-enactments of Jesus' last days and resurrection; most Venezuelans, however, celebrate by heading to the beach. The major **Corpus Christi** festivals, called Diablos Danzantes (Dancing Devils), occur in San Francisco de Yare (Miranda state), Chuao (Aragua state), Patanemo (Carabobo state) and Naiguatá (Federal District). The celebrations are characterized by large parades and performances by the garishly dressed "dancing devils".

Caracas celebrates the anniversary of its foundation every year from July 21 to July 29 with a series of cultural events that include theatre presentations, painting and sculpture exhibits, concerts and sporting events.

Calendar of public holidays

January 1 New Year's Day

Monday and Tuesday before Ash Wednesday Carnaval

Thursday to Saturday of Holy Week Semana Santa

April 19 Declaration of Independence

May 1 Labour Day

June 24 Battle of Carabobo

July 5 Independence Day

July 24 Bolívar's Birthday

October 12 Discovery of America

December 25 Christmas

The media

Above all else, Venezuela is a **TV** culture. Its penetration rate is extremely high and many Venezuelans use it as their only news source. The three major national networks are Televen, RCTV and Venevision. Televen is considered the most reputable, consistently providing the most complete news coverage. The other two feature second-tier **telenovelas**, or soap operas, as well as some fairly seedy programming. The government-owned ValeTV airs cultural events, documentaries and other educational programes.

The country's most influential news **radio** station is *Unión Radio Noticias* (1098 AM in Caracas). For English-language news, BBC World News (SW 5975, 6195, 15190 KHz) and Voice of America (SW 5995, 7405, 9455 KHz) can be accessed by short-wave radio.

Venezuela's two most influential daily **newspapers** are *El Universal* (US$0.50) and *El Nacional* (US$0.50). There is also the English-speaking *Daily Journal* (US$0.75), featuring Venezuelan and international news, which can be found at newsstands in cosmopolitan Caracas neighbourhoods such as Altamira and Sabana Grande, as well as at large international hotels. You can also find the *New York Times*, the *International Herald Tribune* and many major international magazines at several of these same newsstands.

History

Venezuela was neither home to any of the more advanced pre-Columbian cultures nor considered an important colony by the Spanish. However, it has achieved fame as the first and only place that **Christopher Columbus** landed in South America and as the birthplace of **Simon Bolívar**, the celebrated liberator of the continent.

Pre-Columbian Venezuela

On the eve of Columbus's arrival, there were an estimated 500,000 indigenous people in what is now know as Venezuela, belonging to three principal ethno-linguistic groups: **Carib**, **Arawak** and **Chibcha**. While the Carib are best known for practising cannibalism and their expert basketweaving, the Arawak were community-dwelling tribes that subsisted through agriculture and fishing. The third group, the Chibcha, lived in the Andes and were therefore geographically separated from the other tribes.

On August 4, 1498, **Christopher Columbus** arrived at the eastern tip of the Paria Peninsula, thinking it was an island, until he proceeded south and came upon the mighty Orinoco Delta. His stay was short, but in the following year, **Alonso de Ojeda** and the Italian **Amerigo Vespucci** received financing for a return journey to explore further west. In 1502, Vespucci saw the Arawak houses on wooden stilts in Lake Maracaibo and called the place, perhaps sarcastically, Venezuela, or "little Venice".

Colonial Venezuela

Ojeda found an abundance of **pearls** off the coast of Venezuela and, needing a workforce to harvest them, began to enslave the indigenous population. The first settlement was created in 1500 on the island of **Cubagua**, and 21 years later the first permanent mainland settlement was established at **Cumaná**, on the northeast coast. It served as a base for Catholic missionaries and further exploration of the mainland.

Finding no silver or gold, but a native population difficult to subjugate, the Spanish crown had limited interest in Venezuela. In 1528 King Carlos V of Spain, trying to alleviate some of his debts, leased exploration and colonization rights for much of the western part of Venezuela to **Welser**, a German banking house. Above all else, Welser was hoping to find gold and other riches of the famed El Dorado. Its efforts failed and, after massacring much of the indigenous population, it left in 1556.

While **Caracas** – strategically located at the midpoint of the colony's coastline and protected against pirate attack by surrounding mountains – became an important commercial centre, by the late sixteenth century it and the rest of the colony were governed by officials in Santo Domingo and Bogotá. In this vacuum, the **Creoles** – Spanish descendants born in the New World – attained a large degree of autonomy. Owning huge plots of land on which they raised cattle and cultivated tobacco, cacao, indigo and sugar, they relied heavily upon African **slave labour**. Many Creoles also amassed great wealth through illegal trade with the Dutch, British and French.

Precursors to independence

In 1728 the Spanish crown granted a tax-fee trading monopoly to the Basque Compañia Guipozcoana and forbade all trade with other European nations. The Creoles, whose wealth was threatened, protested and eventually revolted in

1749 under the leadership of **Juan Francisco de León**. The revolt was put down by the royal soldiers and de León was exiled, but the rift between the Spanish and the Creoles widened. In 1781 the Guipozcoana monopoly ended, but the idea of independence had been implanted in the Creoles' minds and, in the following years, a number of unsuccessful insurrections took place.

In 1806 the Creole **Francisco de Miranda**, having successfully fought in the American and French revolutions, invaded Venezuela with a group of mercenaries. His attack against the Spanish was rebuffed, but he returned in 1810, taking advantage of Napoleon's occupation of Spain, and led the Creoles from Caracas and six other provinces in ousting their Spanish governors and declaring independence. However, their efforts were thwarted less than a year later when the Spanish were aided by the mixed-blood **pardos**, who distrusted the wealthy Creoles.

El Libertador: Simon Bolívar

In 1813 a wealthy Creole landowner from Caracas named **Simon Bolívar** took the reins of the revolution. Able to capture the support of the *pardos* by promising land and social benefits, his initial campaigns were successful enough to prompt King Fernando VII to send 10,000 troops and 59 ships to Venezuela. However, with aid from the British and the new republic of Haiti, Bolívar furthered his success with several decisive naval victories. He then crossed the Andes and liberated the territory of Colombia.

Upon his triumphant return in 1819 he proclaimed the new **Republic of Gran Colombia**, an independent nation formed by the territories of Venezuela, Colombia and Ecuador. On June 24, 1821, Bolívar secured Venezuelan independence with a victory over the Spanish in the **Battle of Carabobo**. He then set his sights on the territories of Ecuador, Peru and Bolivia. After liberating all three, however, he returned to find Gran Colombia's existence threatened by internal conflicts over the new nation's political structure. He desperately attempted to resolve these disputes, but his efforts were in vain and the nation disbanded in 1829. Bitterly disappointed, he resolved to live in Europe, but died of tuberculosis before his voyage there.

Post-independence and the Federal War

The first seventy years of independence were marked by power struggles, corruption and violence. The first leader was the war hero General **José Antonio Paez** (1830–48), a military dictator who worked in cooperation with the Conservative Party. The stability he brought ended in 1846 when **José Tadeo Monagas** was elected as a Conservative, but soon switched to the newly formed Liberal party and replaced all of his Conservative ministers. He abolished slavery in 1854, but his list of achievements was otherwise limited; when he tried to extend his term to six years, he was overthrown in a rebellion. The ensuing power vacuum between the Conservatives and Liberals led to the bloody **Federal War** from 1859 to 1863. While the Liberals ultimately won and retained control until the turn of the century, for the most part their governments were poorly run and unsuccessful at alleviating the financial woes that plagued the country. The Liberals also altered the balance of power by weakening the church and strengthening the military, which resulted in 59 years (1899–1958) of tyrannical military rule by five successive strongmen from the Andean state of Táchira.

Gómez and the Andeans

The first of the five Andean dictators was **Ciprano Castro**, who seized control in 1899 after leading a victorious revolution aimed at centralizing government power. He immediately amassed great personal wealth while neglecting the mounting foreign debt, and England and Germany responded by forming a naval blockade around Venezuela. They threatened to seize land as payment, but were ultimately deterred when the US threatened to intervene. When Castro went to Europe for medical treatment in 1908, power was seized by **General Juan Vicente Gómez**, who went on to become one of Venezuela's most infamous leaders. A brutal dictator, he took over control of the press, eliminated all personal liberties and murdered all political dissidents. His economic policies were aided tremendously by the discovery of oil in 1918; by 1928 Venezuela had became the world's largest oil producer. Although most of the profits were taken by the international petroleum companies, Gómez was still able to pay off all foreign debts and build an impressive infrastructure of roads, ports and public buildings. Nevertheless, most of the country remained poor as the oil wealth was distributed among an elite few. When Gómez died in 1935 people throughout the country took to the streets in massive celebrations.

The succeeding governments allowed for more personal freedoms, but were terribly corrupt and failed to address the social problems plaguing the majority of the population. These conditions gave rise to two new political parties, **Acción Democratica** (AD) and **Partido Social Cristiano** (COPEI), which would dominate Venezuelan politics for the next fifty years. In 1945 **Rómulo Betancourt** of the AD seized power and created a new constitution with sweeping reforms. However, he was overthrown 28 months later by a military coup led by **Carlos Delgado Chalbaud** and **Marcos Pérez Jimenez**. Chalbaud took power but was assassinated two years later, at which point Pérez Jimenez began his tyrannical dictatorship, eliminating free speech and other civil liberties. He spent most of the country's oil profits on modernizing Caracas and lining his own pockets. Finally, in 1958, the navy and air force ousted him, thereby officially ending the reign of the Andean dictators.

That year also marked the end of one of Venezuela's largest **immigration** movements – over a million foreigners had entered the country over a ten-year period during Venezuela's first open-immigration policy, put in place to attract skilled labour and boost agricultural production. Most of the immigrants came from Portugal, Spain, Italy and Colombia.

Democracy

In 1958 leaders from AD and COPEI signed the **Pact of Punto Fijo**, which ensured that the two parties would share power based on peaceful and democratic elections. The AD's Betancourt won the elections of 1959 but suffered from a poor economy and several coup attempts. In 1968, when COPEI founder **Rafael Caldera** won the 1968 election, it marked the first time in Venezuelan history that a government peacefully surrendered power to an opposition party. When **Carlos Andrés Pérez** of the AD won in 1973, he governed Venezuela through one of its most prosperous periods. He **nationalized the petroleum industry** and quadrupled the price of oil after the Arab–Israeli War of 1973. Money poured in and the nation's wealthy embarked upon spending sprees of epic proportions.

The oil bust

In the late Seventies, the **oil boom ended** when increased production in other countries sent prices spiralling downwards. Through the Eighties, inflation and unemployment increased as foreign capital dropped off significantly. To pay off its debts, Venezuela had to resort to selling off much of its precious oil reserves. Pérez was elected for a second term in 1989, but his attempts to reduce the debt were met with violent protests. In 1992, a mid-level military officer named **Hugo Chávez** launched an unsuccessful coup attempt, which resulted in his imprisonment. Another coup attempt was also put down, but not before the government palace at Miraflores was partially destroyed by a bomb. Soon after, Pérez was indicted and later found guilty on corruption charges after two years of house arrest.

The Chávez era

The 1998 presidential election featured two unlikely candidates. **Irene Sáez**, a former Miss Universe who had success as mayor of a municipality in Caracas, and the populist Chávez, who had been pardoned in 1994 for his coup attempt. Chávez won in a landslide and, taking advantage of his popularity, was able to pass, through a **national referendum**, a new constitution that dismantled the Senate, increased state control over the oil industry and granted the military greater autonomy. The new constitution also extended the presidential term from five to six years, which Chavez exercised after calling for and winning a new presidential election in 2000.

However, Chavez's popularity waned in the following years with the passage of controversial reform laws and a weakening national economy. On April 11, 2002, a large rally in Caracas broke out into violence as ten protesters were killed and over a hundred injured by members of the national guard. On the following day, what appeared to be a successful coup attempt ended with Chavez being taken into military custody. Two days later the interim government collapsed, and Chavez regained control, which he has tenuously maintained up to the time of writing.

Books

Simón Bolívar *El Libertador: Writings of Simón Bolívar* (Oxford University Press). One of the most influential figures in Venezuelan – if not Latin American – history, Bolívar produced plenty of letters, addresses and the like, all found in this fine volume.

Fernando Coronil *The Magical State: Nature, Money and Modernity in Venezuela* (University of Chicago). An academic's political and ethnographical study of the latter twentieth century in the country, through democracy, oil-boom times and its developmental struggles.

Richard Gott *In the Shadow of the Liberator: The Impact of Hugo Chavez on Venezuela and Latin America* (Verso). This strong firsthand analysis covers Chavez's rule over turbulent times.

Stephen Hilty The Birds of Venezuela (Princeton University Press). Extensive and lavishly illustrated self-explanatory volume, essential for real enthusiasts.

11.1

Caracas and around

Though its concrete and glass skyscrapers juxtaposed with the lush mountains of El Ávila make for a rather attractive skyline, the capital **Caracas** is a dangerous, chaotic city without probably enough major tourist attractions to merit much of a stopover. Unlike most other Latin American capitals, it offers few noteworthy remnants of its Spanish colonial period, and any time spent here means less time to explore the country's natural gems; there are a few worthy day-trips in the mountains that surround the city.

Home to nearly six million people, Caracas holds almost a quarter of Venezuela's population and is the political and economic centre of the country. It does contain many of Venezuela's finest museums and restaurants, although few are remarkable by European or American standards. Most of its museums are in the city centre, where an armed tourist brigade (see p.1016) was created to protect foreign visitors. Restaurants tend to be in more affluent suburbs, often accessible by the efficient and relatively safe subway system, which primarily runs from east to west. Those off the subway line can be often difficult to reach by bus, so you will most likely need to spring for a taxi (US$5–10) and experience firsthand the city's constant gridlock.

Caracas

Founded by Captain Diego de Losada in 1567 after a brutal battle with its indigenous inhabitants, **Santiago de León de Caracas** was named for Spain's patron saint Santiago, the provincial governor Don Pedro Ponce de León and the area's original inhabitants, the Caracas Indians. Soon it became Venezuela's most important city, its status cemented by its location in the centre of the Venezuelan coast, which was reasonably well protected from pirate attacks by the mountains of El Ávila, its access to freshwater, its relatively cool climate and cacao. In 1577 **CARACAS**, as it came to be known, became the provincial capital and continued to grow in size and power, despite an attack from British pirates in 1595 and devastating earthquakes in 1755 and 1812. Because of Spain's lack of interest in Venezuela, however, it never attained the colonial splendour of other Latin American cities such as Lima, Potosí, Bogotá or Santo Domingo.

Caracas's most famous native, **Simon Bolívar**, was born to an influential family in 1783. After several years abroad he returned in 1813 and captured the city from the Spanish, at which time he was deemed "El Libertador". When Venezuela became fully independent in 1830, Caracas was made the capital of the new nation. In 1870 President Antonio Guzmán Blanco started the urbanization of Caracas based on the layout and architecture of Paris, where he spent most of his time. But the leader with the most influence on Caracas was the dictator **Marcos Pérez Jiménez**, who used the tremendous influx of oil money in the 1950s to modernize the town with superhighways and high-rise buildings. Most of the infrastructure he built remains, along other major constructions from the oil boom era that lasted until the late 1970s.

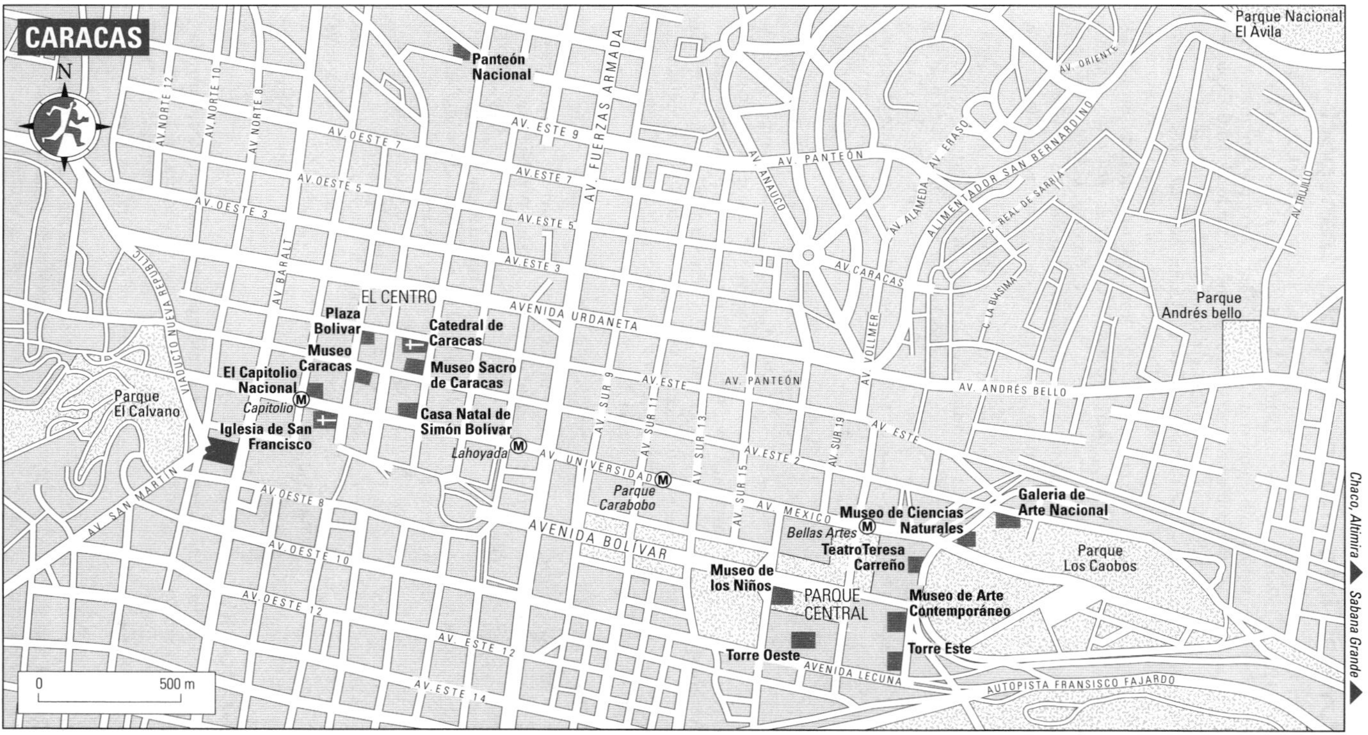

CARACAS
N
Panteón Nacional
Parque Nacional El Ávila
AV. ORIENTE
AV. NORTE 12
AV. NORTE 10
AV. NORTE 8
AV. OESTE 7
AV. OESTE 5
AV. OESTE 3
AV. ESTE 9
AV. ESTE 7
AV. ESTE 5
AV. ESTE 3
AV. FUERZAS ARMADA
AV. PANTEÓN
AV. ANAUCO
AV. ALAMEDA
AV. ERASO
ALIMENTADOR SAN BERNARDINO
C. REAL DE SARRIA
AV. TRUJILLO
AV. CARACAS
C. LA BIASIMA
AV. VOLLMER
Parque Andrés bello
AV. BARALT
VIADUCTO NUEVA REPUBLIC
EL CENTRO
AVENIDA URDANETA
Plaza Bolivar
Catedral de Caracas
Museo Caracas
Museo Sacro de Caracas
El Capitolio Nacional
Capitolio
Casa Natal de Simón Bolívar
Parque El Calvano
Iglesia de San Francisco
Lahoyada
AV. UNIVERSIDAD
AV. SUR 9
AV. SUR 11
AV. SUR 13
AV. SUR 15
AV. SUR 19
AV. ESTE
AV. PANTEÓN
AV. ANDRÉS BELLO
AV. ESTE
AV. ESTE 2
Parque Carabobo
AV. SAN MARTIN
AV. OESTE 8
AVENIDA BOLÍVAR
AV. MEXICO
Bellas Artes
Museo de Ciencias Naturales
Galeria de Arte Nacional
Parque Los Caobos
AV. OESTE 10
Teatro Teresa Carreño
Museo de los Niños
PARQUE CENTRAL
Museo de Arte Contemporáneo
AV. OESTE 12
AV. ESTE 12
Torre Oeste
Torre Este
AVENIDA LECUNA
AUTOPISTA FRANSISCO FAJARDO
AV. ESTE 14
0
500 m
Chaco, Altimira
Sabana Grande

Arrival, information and city transport

Both international and domestic flights arrive at the **airport** in Maiquetía (☎0212/355-2598), 26km west of Caracas. A **taxi** to Caracas takes around 35 minutes (depending upon traffic) and costs around US$15. Don't pay attention to the many people who offer you taxis – go directly to the official black Ford Explorers waiting directly outside the exit. Although it is not recommended because of safety concerns, you can also take the blue and white Ucam **bus** that takes you to the Gato Negro metro stop or Parque Central, two blocks from the Bellas Artes metro stop. The bus leaves every twenty minutes daily from 6am to 8pm and costs US$2.

At the international terminal, there are numerous *casas de cambio* to exchange money, ATM machines (your best bet is Banco Mercantil), a CANTV office to make phone calls or buy telephone cards, tour operator stands and car rental companies. There is also an **information** booth run by the Viceministerio de Turismo (daily 8am to midnight; ☎0212/355-2598 or 355-1060).

Caracas has two major bus terminals. **Terminal La Bandera** has buses that go to the west and southwest, while **Terminal de Oriente** has buses that go to the east and southeast. Terminal La Bandera is two blocks from the metro station of the same name, while Terminal de Oriente is to the east of the city – the best way to get there is to take the metro to the Petare station and then take a fifteen-minute taxi ride to the terminal (US$3). There is a local bus that runs between the metro station and terminal, but it is considered dangerous; exercise extreme caution in and around both bus stations, as robberies are common.

There are also several bus companies that do not leave from the bus terminals. **Expreso Ormeño** (☎0212/471-7205) has a route that runs through much of South America – Colombia, Ecuador, Peru, Bolivia, Chile and Argentina – and leaves twice weekly from its own terminal near the La Paz metro station. **Aereoespresos Ejecutivos** (☎0212/266-2321) offers a very comfortable, but slightly more expensive service to Valencia, Maracaibo, Puerto La Cruz and several other cities. The buses leave from a safe location on Avenida Bellos Campo, a few blocks from the Altamira metro station.

City transport

The best way to get around the city is the efficient and fairly safe **metro** system. There are three lines, but the most useful for tourists is Line 1, which runs east to west. Lines 2 and 3 run southwest from the line 1 transfer stations of Capitolio/El Silencio and Plaza Venezuela, respectively. The metro runs daily from 5am to 11pm, although a few stations close at 9 or 10pm. Tickets cost about US$0.40, but you can buy a ten-trip pass for about US$2. There is also a system of multicoloured **metrobuses** that run to and from the various metro stations between 5.30am and 11pm daily. They cost around US$0.20 and do not accept metro tickets.

Taxis are useful when you are heading somewhere not near a metro stop. Take one of the modern-looking white taxis with placards at the top. No taxis have meters, so you will have to bargain first. Try to ask a local what the proper price should be; most taxi rides within the city will cost between US$3 and US$8.

Accommodation

Few good budget options exist in Caracas; most of the inexpensive **accommodation** is in Sabana Grande, an increasingly dangerous neighbourhood that should not otherwise inspire a visit. The nicer hotels are more or less scattered about, with some clusters in the wealthier eastern suburbs of Altamira, Las Mercedes and Chacao.

Best Western Hotel CCT Centro Ciudad Comercial Tamanaco ☎0212/700-8000, Ⓦwww.bwhotelcct.com. Extremely well-run hotel with all the services and amenities a demanding traveller could ask for, such as tennis courts, swimming pool, exercise room, restaurants, and a lounge. Located inside one of the city's largest shopping malls, it's convenient for those who don't want to venture out at night. ❽

Hotel Ávila Av Washington, San Bernardino ⓣ0212/555-3435, ⓔhÁvila@cantv.net. Built by Rockefeller in the 1940s, this colonial-style hotel has retained much of its original charm and splendour. Rooms show some sign of wear, but the hotel remains a favourite of frequent travellers for its tranquil setting, beautiful pool and excellent prices. ❻

Hotel Continental Altamira Av San Juan Bosco, Altamira ⓣ0212/261-0644, ⓕ261-0131, ⓦwww.hotel-continental.org. Business-oriented hotel with good service and spacious rooms. Excellent location in safe neighborhood, just two blocks from metro. ❽

Hotel Crillon Av Libertador at intersection of Av Las Acacias, Sabana Grande ⓣ0212/761-4411. This remodelled all-suite hotel near the Plaza Venezuela metro station is one of the best values in town. The 79 rooms have mini-fridges and terraces. ❺

Hotel Jolly Inn Av Francisco Solano next to Galerias Bolívar, Sabana Grande ⓣ0212/762-3665. Surly reception clerks make this a bit of a misnomer, but this is a decent budget option. Rooms, while unattractive, are for the most part clean and well equipped, with hot water, a/c, phones and TV (no cable). ❸–❹

Hotel Plaza Palace C Los Mangos between Av Libertador and Av Francisco Solano, Sabana Grande ⓣ0212/762-4821. Good mid-range option on a quiet block of Sabana Grande. Rooms are very clean, with a/c, TVs and private bathrooms. ❺

Hotel Tanausu Final Av de Atlántida, Catia la Mar ⓣ0212/312-6518. With excellent service and clean, pretty rooms, this is the best moderately priced option near the airport. ❺

Intercontinental Tamanaco Final Av Principal de las Mercedes ⓣ0212/909-8830, ⓦwww.interconti.com. Despite its age, this remains one of the most luxurious and expensive hotels in Caracas. It has a safe location away from the city centre plus a large pool, extensive fitness room/spa, and Internet access. ❾

Lincoln Suites Av Francisco Solano between C San Jerónimo and Av Los Jabillos, Sabana Grande ⓣ0212/762-8575, ⓦwww.lincoln-suites.com.ve. All-suite hotel with very large, comfortable rooms. It's often full so book in advance. Buffet breakfast included. ❻

Nuestro Hotel Calle El Colegio, Sabana Grande ⓣ0212/761-5431. This self-proclaimed "backpacker's hostel" is a favourite among budget-minded visitors. Reasonably clean rooms have fans and private bathrooms. Call in advance, as it is often full. ❸

The City

The two main areas to visit within Caracas are El Centro and Parque Central, though neither is particularly safe – the former has specially trained policemen, donning red berets, to accompany visitors. The bustling **El Centro**, which was the original town centre, contains a few sites of moderate interest: the cathedral, several churches, numerous government buildings and several museums dedicated to Simon Bolívar. Unfortunately, little of the city's original colonial architecture remains because of several devastating earthquakes and modernization efforts in the past fifty years.

Just three metro stops to the east at the Bellas Artes station, **Parque Central** contains many art museums and cultural centres. The architecture and open spaces between buildings are hardly awe-inspiring, but the museums together offer many of Venezuela's finest art works.

El Centro

While most sights in **EL CENTRO** are within close walking distance of each other, walking around is a bit challenging because of the hundreds of street vendors that have monopolized most of the sidewalk space. As with all Venezuelan towns, the **Plaza Bolívar** is the main square, and Caracas's version, two blocks east and one block north of the Capitolio/El Silencio metro station, is a good starting spot for the walking tour. The south side of the square features the **Museo Caracas** (Tues–Fri 9am–4.30pm, Sat & Sun 10am–4.30pm; free), on the ground floor of the **Concejo Municipal** (Municipal Council). This visually bland, but historically important, museum contains paintings and documents related to the quest for independence and other significant events in the city's past. On the east side of the plaza, the colonial-style **Catedral de Caracas** was originally built in 1575 but reconstructed in 1666 after the earthquake of 1641. Rather modest compared with the cathedrals of most other Latin American capitals, it reflects the relatively small value the Spanish accorded the city and territory. Bolívar's parents and wife are buried inside, where you'll also find Rubens' *Resurrection of Christ*. More religious paintings and sculptures are on offer at the **Museo Sacro de Caracas** (Tues–Sun 9am–4.30pm; Ⓦwww.cibernetic.com/sacro; US$0.50), just next door to the south. The museum also contains remains from the days when the original construction functioned as a convent and prison. The pretty *Café del Sacro* makes for a good place to grab coffee or a quick bite to eat.

The best place to learn about Bolívar is at the **Casa Natal de Simón Bolívar** (Mon–Fri 9am–noon & 2–5pm, Sat & Sun 10am–1pm & 2–5pm; free), one block south and then one east on Avenida Universidad. Built in 1680, the large, colonial-style house contains some of its original furniture as well as numerous portraits of El Libertador, who only lived here until the age of 9. If you're as fascinated with Bolívar as most Venezuelans, you may also want to visit his final resting place in the **Panteón Nacional**, five blocks north of Plaza Bolívar. Otherwise, continue two blocks west along Avenida Universidad, where the golden-domed Neoclassical **El Capitolio Nacional** (Tues–Sun 9am–noon & 2–5pm) is the current home to the Venezuelan congress. Step inside to see the impressive **Salón Elíptico**, which contains portraits of every former Venezuelan leader, as well as enormous depictions of the Batalla de Caradobo.

The one church to visit in Caracas is the **Iglesia de San Francisco** on the south side of Avenida Universidad, opposite the Capitolio Nacional. One of Venezuela's oldest churches, its rich Baroque interior contrasts with its Neoclassical facade, which was remodelled during the eighteenth century. Its principal claim to fame is as the place where Bolívar was proclaimed "El Libertador" in 1813. Notice the many people praying at the altar of San Onofre, the saint responsible for miracles related to work and health.

Parque Central

Not really a park, **PARQUE CENTRAL** is a long concrete strip filled with hundreds of street vendors, selling everything from pirated CDs to miracle herbs. This is the most easily identifiable part of city, thanks to the twin glass and concrete structures right above the **Bellas Artes metro station**. At 53 stories, the octagonal **Torre Oeste** and **Torre Este** are the country's tallest buildings, though neither is open to the public.

It is Parque Central's museums, however, that draw you here. Just one block east from the Bellas Artes station lies the entrance to the sparsely decorated **Parque Los Caobos**, which contains a cluster of three museums and two cultural centres. The **Galeria de Arte Nacional** (Tues–Fri 9am–5pm, Sat & Sun 10-5; free; Ⓦwww.wtfe.com/gan) is connected to the **Museo de Bellas Artes** (same hours, Ⓦwww.museodebellasartes.org). While the former is a handsome Neoclassical edifice containing a vast collection of paintings and sculptures exclusively by national artists, the latter, an imposing concrete structure, primarily houses temporary exhibits of Venezuelan and international artists. With the exception of a fascinating exhibit that helps trace the evolution of the Cubist movement, the Museo de Bellas Artes' small permanent collection does not warrant more than a quick look, but its roof has great views of the city. If you are with children or have an active interest in natural sciences, it is certainly worth crossing the oval plaza in front of the museums to make for the well-designed **Museo de Ciencias Naturales** (Tues–Fri 9am–5pm, Sat & Sun 10.30am–6pm; US$2). The small space contains bones of crocodiles and sabre-tooth tigers millions of years old.

A two-minute walk south brings you to the 1973 **Teatro Teresa Carreño** (Tues–Sat 9am–1pm & 1pm–5pm; US$0.50; Ⓣ0500/67372 or Ⓦwww.teatro

teresacarreno.com for events information), the third-largest theatre in Latin America and the sixth largest in the world. A great source of pride to residents, it is a daunting concrete and black-glass structure counterbalanced by extensive greenery in the open spaces that surround the theatre. Across the road is the **Museo de Arte Contemporáneo** (Tues–Sun 10am–6pm; ⓦwww.maccsi.org.ve; free), the gem of the Parque Central area. A five-storey museum, it houses works by Venezuelans, such as Jesús Soto, a kinetic artist of some world renown, as well as international artists. Take a few hours to see the museum whose highlights include Matisse's *Odalisque in Pants*, Miró's *Ski Lesson*, Chagall's *Night Carnival* as well as a number of works by Picasso. Further west, next to the Torre Oeste, is the **Museo de los Niños** (Tues–Fri 9am–5pm, Sat & Sun 10am–5pm; US$3) a highly interactive, and quite extensive, children's museum.

Eating

Caracas is without a doubt Venezuela's premier city for **food**. Several generations of heavy immigration from Europe and other Latin American countries have contributed to the town's wide array of international cuisine, and added to some attractive offerings of local cooking, the result is an almost overwhelming choice of dining options. While the top restaurants are primarily in the affluent suburbs of Altamira, Las Mercedes and La Castellana, some of the town's more traditional establishments can be found in Sabana Grande.

Café del Sacro Plaza Bolívar. This attractive café in the Museo Sacro is one of few palatable options in El Centro. Its delicious salads and sandwiches make for a perfect lunch.

Café L'Attico Av Luis Roche, Altamira. A true Caracas establishment, this classy café doubles as a pub and sports bar, with barstools and large-screen TVs. The reasonably priced Sunday morning brunch features a combination of American and Venezuelan favourites.

Da Guido Av Francisco Solano, Sabana Grande. Pictures of national celebrities on the walls attest to this forty-year-old establishment's storied past. *Da Guido* serves delicious Italian meat and pasta dishes for US$3–7.

Delicatesses Indú C Villaflor, Sabana Grande. One of few Indian restaurants in Caracas, it serves savoury, inexpensive vegetarian dishes from the south of India. Closed on Sundays.

Helena de Ibarra Ground floor of Paseo las Mercedes (shopping centre) ⓣ0212/991-6570. This new restaurant opened by famed chef of the same name offers creative, exquisite versions of typical Venezuelan dishes. Excellent prices (US$8–15 per entree) have contributed to its popularity, so reserve at least a day in advance. Closed Mondays.

Tantra Top level of Centro Comercial Los Naranjos. Absolutely stunning restaurant with beautiful views of Caracas and El Ávila on an open-air terrace. Skilfully prepared international dishes and excellent prices (US$8–10 per entree) more than justify the long taxi ride. The pan-seared tuna is exquisite.

Tarzilandia 10a transversal de Altamira and Av San Juan Bosco. This popular Caracas establishment on the edge of El Ávila offers a serene ambience with lush vegetation and chirping birds. If the sounds don't make you averse to eating poultry, try the *pato con salsa de parchita* (duck with passion fruit sauce).

Tasca Rías Gallegas Av Francisco Solano, Sabana Grande. Of the many Spanish-style *tascas* in town, this is one of the most consistently recommended. You can get a huge cut of steak (*churrasco*) for US$5 or fresh fish for slightly more. The paella is quite good.

Drinking and nightlife

Caracas has **bars and clubs** for virtually anyone, and at any time. Many of the establishments are open every day of the week, often until 4 or 5am. Most of the real hotspots are in Las Mercedes and a few of the other eastern suburbs such as La Castellana and Altamira; few establishments have cover charges.

One of the most enduring clubs is *El Maní es Así*, on Calle El Cristo in Sabana Grande, a disco with live salsa music. Another is an enormous, bi-level disco named *Da Dío*, which is on Avenida Principal in Las Mercedes. Two clubs that are more upscale and popular with an older crowd are *Vog a Bar*, on Calle Trinidad in Las Mercedes, and *Le Club*, on Avenida Principal in La Castellana. Both play mostly international music pop from the 1980s and 1990s. *Greenwich*, on 1a Avenida in Altamira, is a small but spirited Irish pub that has live pop and alternative music Thursday through Sunday.

Unsurprisingly, given its size and relative cosmopolitanism, Caracas has the largest **gay and lesbian community** in the country. Most of the city's gay bars are in Sabana Grande, one of the most well known being *Tasca Pullman*, on Avenida Francisco Solano. Open every day, it plays primarily house music.

Listings

Airlines Air France, Av Fco de Mirando, Edif Parque Cristal in Los Palos Grandes ☎0212/285-3887; Alitalia, Av Andrés Bello, Edif Atlantic in Los Palos Grandes ☎0212/951-3005; American Airlines, Av Principal de la Castellana, Centro Letonia ☎0212/209-8111; Aserca Airlines, Av Guaicaipuro, Torre Taeca in El Rosal ☎0212/905-5333; Avensa, Av Río Caura, Torre Humboldt in Urbanizacíon Parque Humboldt ☎0212/907-8222; British Airways, Centro San Ignacio in Las Castellana ☎0212/266-0122; Continental Airlines, Av Fco de Miranda, Centro Lido in El Rosal ☎0212/953-3107; Iberia, Av San Juan Bosco, Edif Centro Altamira in Altamira Norte ☎0212/267-8666; KLM Av Rómulo Gallegos, Torre KLM in Santa Eduvigis ☎0212/285-3333; LanChile, Av Fco de Miranda, Edif Mene Grande in Los Palos Grandes ☎0212/284-1211; United Airlines, Av Fco de Miranda, Torre Seguros Caracas in Los Palos Grandes ☎0212/355-1120; Varig, Av Principal de Los Ruices, Edif Centro Empresarial Los Ruices ☎0212/237-7311.

Banks and exchange Banks usually have slightly better exchange rates than the exchange houses, but also less convenient hours and longer queues. Italcambio exchanges AMEX travellers' cheques at no commission. They have offices in the airport and more than ten other locations in town. CorpBanca also exchanges AMEX travellers' cheques at no commission. It has many locations, including on Plaza Castellana, two blocks from the Altamira metro station.

Car rental Avis, Final Av Libertador and Av Principal de Bello Campo ☎0212/261-5556; Budget Rent a Car, Av Rómulo Gallegos and Av Las Palmas, Edif Centro Gerencial Los Andes in Boleita Norte ☎0212/263-4359; Dollar Rent a Car, Av Fco de Mirando, Torre Mene Grande in Los Palos Grandes ☎0212/285-4433; Hertz, Av Principal del Bosque and Av Francisco Solano ☎0212/952-1603.

Embassies and consulates Australia, Av Luis Roche between 6ta and 7ma Transv in Altamira ☎0212/263-4033; Brazil, Av Mohedano and C Los Chaguaramos in La Castellana ☎0212/261-4481; Colombia, C Guaicaipuro in El Rosal ☎0212/951-3631; Guyana, Av El Paseo, Quinta Roraima in Prados del Este ☎0212/977-1158; UK, Av La Estancia, Torre Las Mercedes in Chuao ☎0212/993-4111; US, Av C F and C Soapure in Colinas de Valle Arriba ☎0212/977-2011.

Immigration office Dirección de Identificación y Extranjería (DIEX), Av Baralt in front of Plaza Miranda, two blocks south of El Silencio metro station (Mon–Fri 8.30am–4.30pm; ☎0212/482-0977).

Medical care A highly recommended clinic is Hospital de Clinicas Caracas, on Av Panteón at Av Alameda in San Bernardino. Another good option is Clinica Ávila, on Av San Juan Bosco at 6ta Transversal in Altamira.

Post office The principal Ipostel office on Av Urdaneta at Carmelitas, three blocks north of the Capitolio metro station, is open on weekdays from 8.30am to 4.30pm.

Travel agents Candes ☎0212/571-0987 in the Caracas Hilton on Av Sur at Av Mexico; Club de Trotamundo ☎0212/283-7235 in Centro Comercial Centro Plaza in Los Palos Grandes, and Perez Travel & Turismo ☎0212/762-8575 in the Lincoln Suites Hotel on Av Francisco Solano in Sabana Grande.

Around Caracas

For a quick escape from the hustle and bustle of Caracas, ride the recently restored cable car that ascends the slopes of **Parque Nacional El Ávila**, with its spectacular view of the capital. If you've got more time consider visiting **Colonia Tovar**, a scenic mountain village inhabited for over 150 years by German descendants.

Parque Nacional El Ávila

Separating Caracas from the coast, **PARQUE NACIONAL EL ÁVILA** is based more or less around a mountain whose highest point is 2765 metres. From here, visitors have stunning views – on clear days – of Caracas on one side and the Caribbean Sea on the other.

There are several ways to explore the park. Four well-marked and safe hiking trails lead into the park from Caracas, all reachable via Avenida Boyacá. It is also possible to drive to the top in a four-wheel-drive vehicle. However, the most popular option nowadays is the recently built **Teleférico** (Mon–Thurs, Sat & Sun 10am–8pm, Fri noon–8pm; US$8), a high-speed cable car that leaves the station at the intersection of Avenida Principal de Maripérez and Avenida Boyacá and climbs to the top of the mountain. Several government-run *teleféricos* have been built and closed in the past fifty years owing to poor management, but this most recent one was built in 2002 by a Swiss company and is privately run. Its dramatic 1200m ascent takes only ten minutes, letting you off at a 600m walkway leading to Pico El Ávila. Along the way are small food stands, telescopes to view Caracas and the sea and a playground.

A trail from the pathway leads down to the small village of **Galipán** and excellent views of the sea, coloured by the many flowers grown along the mountain slopes. A perfect spot to stop for lunch is *El Restaurante Caney Entreverao Galipanero*, across from La Escuela San Isidro. Hearty meals on the terrace are accompanied by live music and, of course, wonderful vistas. If you want to explore the park further, contact **Akanan Tours** (Ⓣ0212/234-2103, Ⓦwww.akanan.com), a reputable tour operator that offers day-long hiking (US$15 per person), rappelling (US$20 per person) and jeep tours (US$30 per person).

Colonia Tovar

Founded by German immigrants in 1843, the small mountain village of **COLONIA TOVAR**, 60km west of Caracas, is still inhabited by their ancestors. Because of its geographic isolation, there was almost no interaction with other Venezuelans for over a century, until a highway connecting the town with Caracas was built. Though many of the village's inhabitants have since assimilated into Venezuelan culture, it is still common to find blonde haired, blue-eyed people speaking in German. Most of the houses have been reconstructed or built in the traditional style of the Black Forest, where the original settlers came from, and restaurants selling German sausages and local strawberries and cream line the main roads of the village.

Colonia Tovar is a popular weekend destination, primarily for day-trippers but also for visitors who stay over in the charming German-style inns. In addition to the architecture and food, the **Museo de Historia y Artesania** (Sat & Sun 9am–6pm; US$0.40) features a small but interesting collection of documents, clothes, tools, guns and other relics of the village's early days; the museum's founder, anthropology professor Nestor Rojas, is on hand to answer any and all questions. **Cerveceria Tovar** (Mon–Fri 8am–5pm, Sat & Sun 10am–4pm), next to the *Sonnengarten* restaurant 100m below the church, offers free tours of their new microbrewery, explaining the brewing process, which you can see in action on weekdays. At the end, you can sample the delightful finished product for US$0.50.

Practicalities

To get to Colonia Tovar from Caracas take the metro to La Yaguara, switching at Capitolio/Silencio from Line 1. Across the street from the station, a bus (US$0.50) heads to El Junquito, dropping you off on the side of the road to catch an hour-long bus (US$1) to Colonia Tovar. Alternatively, you can take a taxi from Caracas and have it wait for you for about US$40–50.

Most of the **hotels and inns** in town are mid-priced, although a few good budget options exist. *Cabañas Silberbrünnen* (☎0244/355-1490; ❹–❺), a block below the church, is a great economical option. Small, but tidy *cabañas* have TVs, refrigerators, hot water and nice views – some even have mini-kitchens. The cosy *Posada Don Elicio* (☎0244/355-1254; ❺), on the outskirts of town, offers a romantic ambience with fireplaces and flowers. There is a two-day minimum stay on weekends. *Hotel Selva Negra* (☎0244/355-1415; ❻), on the right-hand side of the church, is a Black Forest-style building that appears to have changed little since its construction in 1936. Its **restaurant** is one of the town's finest, serving a fine selection of international cuisine and traditional German dishes. Reserve a week in advance for weekend stays. For something more casual, try a German sausage at the cheap, tasty *Luncheria Schmuk*, about 100 metres uphill from the church.

Venezuela's beauty queens

Venezuela's dominance in the realm of international beauty competition is legendary. Since the inception of the Miss World and Miss Universe pageants in 1951 and 1952, Venezuelan women have captured a total of nine titles, matched only by the US, a nation with a population that is nearly twelve times larger. The importance of physical beauty is instilled early in Venezuela, as children choose Carnaval queens for nearly every grade of school, fuelling the machinery of a system that stages competitions at the local, state, regional and national levels. Training, dieting and the nips and tucks of cosmetic surgery are typical rigours in the lives of would-be beauty queens, and victories on the global stage cause intense national pride. So much so that in a sensational market research study published in 1999, 65 percent of Venezuelan women and 47 percent of Venezuelan men claimed that they think about their physical appearance "all the time". Despite the fact that some 80 percent of the population lives below the poverty line, Venezuelans spend an average of 20 percent of household income on cosmetics and personal care products (tops per capita in the world), and the country is a global leader in plastic surgery.

11.2

The northwest coast

Venezuela's underrated **NORTHWEST COAST** gets much less press than the offshore Caribbean islands of Aruba, Bonaire and Curaçao, but offers similarly spectacular beaches alongside some of the Caribbean's prettiest colonial towns and two fine national parks.

The **Parque Nacional Henri Pittier**, roughly 150km from Caracas, sports beautiful, palm-lined sands, striking mountain-range backdrops and four vegetation zones housing a tremendous array of birds and plant life. More popular than Pittier, the **Parque Nacional Morrocoy**, a few hours to the west, is best known for its gorgeous white-sand keys surrounded by crystalline water.

Three hours west of Morrocoy, the well-preserved colonial town of **Coro**, Venezuela's only UNESCO World Heritage city, serves as a good break from the surrounding parks. Most head directly from Coro into the Andes, but you might consider passing through the marginally interesting **Maracaibo**, Venezuela's second city, bordering on **Lago Maracaibo**, South America's largest lake.

Parque Nacional Henri Pittier and around

Created in 1937, **PARQUE NACIONAL HENRI PITTIER** was Venezuela's first national park, named for a famous Swiss geographer and botanist who classified more than 30,000 plants in Venezuela. Despite the park's great biodiversity, the vast majority of visitors come for its **beaches**. In fact, on weekends it can be totally overrun, but it is generally quiet during the week.

Pittier's wide array of flora and fauna is a result of the relatively short distance within which it climbs from sea level to 2430 metres, for the changes in altitude create numerous distinct **vegetation zones**. From 1500 metres and above, Pittier is a humid tropical forest, containing several types of palms, ferns, orchids and bromeliads. From 800 to 1500 metres, it is a cloudforest that contains several species of ficus, and *gunnera pittierana,* a type of grass with gigantic leaves that is endemic to the area. Descending to the coast, you will also see deciduous forest, savanna vegetation, shrubby forest, xerophytic vegetation and mangroves.

The park is also renowned among birdwatchers, containing 520 species in just over a thousand square kilometres – 41.6 percent of the **bird species** in Venezuela and 6.5 percent of the bird species in the world. Noteworthy species include the orange-winged parrot, the black and white owl, the lance-tailed manakin and the white hawk. Besides the multiple vegetation zones, another major reason for the spectacular bird diversity here is that many migratory birds enter the South American continent through the relatively low 1128m Portachuelo Pass, in the southwestern portion of the park.

The park can be explored through several **hiking trails**. Informal paths link the coastal towns, but the best place from which to explore the park is the Rancho Grande Biological Station (☎0213/550-7065), used for university research but also offering rustic facilities for overnight stays. Some trails are not always well maintained, so it is best to inquire about the current options at the station.

The only two roads into Pittier form a "V", with Maracay at the vertex and **Choroní** and **Ocumare** at the two ends. While most visitors stay in or near the colonial towns of Choroní and Puerto Colombia in the eastern portion of the park, Ocumare, which is less picturesque, makes an equally good base.

Arrival

From Terminal La Bandera in Caracas, take the hour and a half **bus** (US$3 round-trip) to Maracay and, at the chaotic outdoor bus terminal there, ask around for the bus to Choroní; the wait could be five minutes or over an hour. The subsequent two-hour ride is an incredible experience as the driver navigates the extremely narrow two-way road that winds its way through the mountains. Alternatively, a **taxi** from Caracas costs around US$50, and from Maracay about US$20. There are no **banks** in Choroní. You can change dollars at some hotels, but don't count on being able to change travellers' cheques.

Accommodation

Excellent **posadas** in all price categories can be found in Puerto Colombia. The town of Choroní only has a few options, but there are several mid-range and upscale posadas in the 2km corridor between the two. Be sure to ask for midweek discounts.

Hacienda El Portete Calle Cementerio, 100m from entrance to main Choroní–Puerto Colombia road ⓣ0243/991-1255, ⓦwww.elportete.com. Beautifully restored, 130-year-old colonial mansion set on a coffee plantation halfway between Choroní and Puerto Colombia. Excellent facilities include a pool, basketball court and game room with table tennis and pool tables. Rooms are large and comfortable, with hammocks in front. ❻

Hostal Casa Grande Av Principal de Puerto Colombia in front of the church ⓣ0243/991-1251, ⓦwww.hostalcasagrande.com. This meticulous reconstruction of an 1830s colonial house, with beautiful antiques and pretty courtyard garden, offers the town's classiest and most romantic accommodation. Handsomely decorated rooms have hand-carved wooden bed frames and candelabras. Price includes breakfast. ❼

Hostal Colonial Av Prinipal de Puerto Colombia next to *Posada Lemontree* ⓣ0243/991-1087. The best of the budget options, despite poor service and lack of amenities. Most rooms have private bathrooms, but with cold water. All are spacious and clean. ❸

Hostería Río Mar Main road near entrance of Choroní ⓣ0243/991-1038, ⓔriomar@cantv.net. Set in one of the town's oldest houses, this is the nicest posada in the town of Choroní, with colourful, clean and spacious rooms with high ceilings. Perfect if you want to escape the commotion of Puerto Colombia. ❹

Posada Lemontree Av Principal de Puerto Colombia next to *Hostal Colonial* ⓣ0243 991-1123. One of most economical options in town, this basic posada with a communal kitchen and bathrooms is only slightly grungy. There are two *Lemontrees* in town – this is the cheaper of the two. ❷

Posada Pittier Main road just before Puerto Colombia ⓣ0243/991-1028. You can find great midweek deals at this pleasant eight-room posada. Rooms are small but attractive, with interesting paintings by the artist owner. ❺

Posada Puerto Escondido ⓣ0243/241-4645. This colonial house is set on a cacao plantation about 200m from the beach in Playa Cepe. Prices include transfer from Puerto Colombia and excellent meals – you can also arrange to snorkel or dive with the owner, who is a dive master. ❻

Choroní and the beaches

Choroní actually consists of the colonial town of **Choroní** and **Puerto Colombia**, a beach town two kilometres away. The former won't hold your interest too long, but a walk through its narrow, winding streets filled with colourful houses, some well over 200 years old, is mildly diverting. Head to Puerto Colombia to experience the liveliness of the **malecón**, where all of the fishing boats dock; at night, people congregate here, while on weekends it is common to see *tambores*, a coastal tradition of drum playing, singing and dancing that is fun to observe, if not join in.

The one **beach** easily reached on foot is **Playa Grande**. Just 500 metres east of Puerto Colombia, it becomes mobbed with weekend visitors, who leave tons of trash. That aside it is a very picturesque beach with palm trees, aquamarine water, tan sand and lush mountains in the background. About the same distance to the west, but harder to reach (and thus less crowded) **Playa El Diario** is about a 45-minute walk from Puerto Colombia via Calle Cementerio – the entrance is near a bridge around the midpoint of the main Choroní–Puerto Colombia road. Follow Calle Cementerio past the cemetery and bear left at the split.

To access the other area beaches you will need to take a *lancha*, which can be arranged at the *malecón* in Puerto Colombia. The boat ride costs about US$20 round-trip, but can be split among five or six people. To the east, the closest beach is **Playa Valle Seco**, which has some coral reefs and decent snorkelling. While you're at it, pick up food because there are no restaurants or food stands.

Continuing east, **Playa Chuao** offers tranquil water, good shade provided by palm trees and a few food stands that prepare fresh fish. The colonial town of the same name, a few kilometres inland, is famous for producing some of the world's best cacao, as well as the Diablos Danzantes festival in May or June. The boat ride from Puerto Colombia costs about US$25 round-trip. Still further to the east and about a US$30 boat ride away is **Playa Cepe**, a palm-lined, white-sand beach that is the prettiest in the entire park. A fine lodging option here is *Posada Puerto Escondido* (see opposite).

Eating and drinking

There are surprisingly few **dining options** in Choroní. At *Restaurant Mora*, in Puerto Colombia, you can get tasty, but somewhat overpriced fish dishes, while *Restaurant Del Alemán*, just after crossing the bridge to Playa Grande, offers delicious fish dishes and nice views of the little river that passes by; it's closed on Fridays. On weekends, *Hacienda El Portete* has an excellent dinner buffet with a wide selection of local seafood and meat dishes for around US$10 per person. There are no real **bars** or **clubs** in Choroní – the best bet is to buy a few beers and drink them on the *malecón*.

Ocumare de la Costa and the surrounding beaches

The colonial town of **Ocumare de la Costa** is set a few kilometres from the beach village, **El Playón**. Neither is as nice as their Choroní counterparts nor has much of interest, and the beach itself, used primarily by fishermen, is a bit dirty. However, there are some secluded snorkelling spots, narrow mangrove inlets, small waterfalls and swimming holes and hiking trails around the Rancho Grande research station.

Five kilometres east of El Playón is one of the area's best-known beaches, **Playa Cata**. Despite two horrible concrete apartment buildings right on the beach, it is otherwise attractive, with palm trees lining the white-sand beach. It is accessible by road and buses (US$0.75) run from El Playón hourly. A short boat ride or hike away, **Playa Catita** is smaller and less crowded; boats on the west side of the bay can be hired for a US$1 round-trip fare. Further east, **Playa Cuyagua** has become very hip among Venezuela's surfers and rich young bohemians. Its waves can get fairly large, so caution should be exercised when swimming. Two buses (US$0.75) leave daily from El Playón – or you can take a *lancha* for about US$25.

La Cienaga, a beautiful lagoon several kilometres to the west of Ocumare and accessible only by boat, is well worth exploring. Its crystalline waters offer some of the park's best snorkelling and a little river inlet called *cueva de amor* allows for entrance into the mangrove forest. There are also a few strips of sand for sunbathing. Boats found at La Boca, on the east side of El Playón, cost around US$27 round-trip or, for about US$30 per person, you can take a highly enjoyable tour with knowledgeable, English-speaking Viktor Gorodeckis from *De La Costa Eco-Lodge* (see below). Included in the price are snorkel equipment, beach chairs, lunch and beverages.

Practicalities

There are not many **accommodation** options in the town or on El Playón. The best is *Posada María Luisa* (☎0243/993-1073, ⓦwww.posadamarialuisa.com; ❹), a pink, 125-year-old colonial-style house filled with antiques and a pretty garden in the centre. The value is excellent, with hot water and a swimming pool. Another good reason to come to this side of the park is *De La Costa Eco-Lodge* (☎0243/993-1986, ⓦwww.ecovenezuela.com; ❺–❻), 23 Calle California across from the beach in El Playón. The four-storey lookout tower, which looks like a pagoda from the sea, has incredible views of the surrounding area, and at night you can barbecue in the plant-filled gravel courtyard. Rooms are basic, but comfortable and well equipped.

Right next door is *Tasca Restaurant Terraza Mar*, a good place to **eat** tasty, moderately priced seafood dishes; it's only open Thursday through Monday in the low season.

Estación Biológica Rancho Grande

On the highway between Maracay and Ocumare, the **Estación Biológica Rancho Grande** was formerly a grand hotel, but after being abandoned for many years was turned into a research station for the Universidad Central de Venezuela. At about 1100 metres, it has a multitude of hiking trails from which visitors are likely to see an incredible variety of birds and perhaps some howler monkeys.

Rustic **accommodation** consists of a room with ten bunk beds but no linen, so bring sheets or a sleeping bag. Also bring food to cook in the communal kitchen. The cost is around US$5 per person per night – call Carlos on ☎0243/550-7065 to let him know of your arrival. To get here, just ask the bus driver to let you off at Rancho Grande.

Parque Nacional Morrocoy

Gorgeous white-sand keys surrounded by crystalline water are the highlights of **PARQUE NACIONAL MORROCOY**, one of the most popular national parks in Venezuela. The 30,000-hectare park, spread primarily over water, was created in 1974, but today it doesn't feel much like a national park. There are huge developments in several areas, no restriction on the large numbers of tourists that enter and little enforcement of litter or camping laws. Worst of all, there is no enforcement of water-pollution laws, even after an unknown contaminant killed nearly forty percent of the coral several years ago.

Fortunately, for the time being the **beaches** are still relatively pristine, snorkelling and scuba diving is still quite good and the park is still home to nearly four-fifths of Venezuela's aquatic **bird species**. Among the park's more notable birds are the great egret, the American flamingo, the brown pelican and several species of hummingbirds. The park also contains numerous types of mammal, such as red howler monkeys, crab-eating foxes, opossums and deer.

There is a principal tourist base at each end of the park, both of which have had sporadic safety problems. Tucacas, to the south, is overdeveloped and does not have many good accommodation options; it is better to hit the slightly nicer **Chichiriviche**, to the north. The best posadas are scattered along the corridor between the two.

The keys

There are a total of 22 **keys**, or *cayos*, in the park. Most only differ in terms of size and facilities. **Cayo Punta Brava**, which is connected to Tucacas by bridge, is the most developed key, with camping facilities, food stands and watersports equipment rental, but gets extremely crowded and littered on weekends. **Cayo Paiclás**, to the south, is a large key with several very popular beaches such as Playuela, Playuelita and Playa Paiclás. There are small food stands or restaurants, as well as shower facilities, but no water for campers. On the east end of the key is the more secluded, very pretty beach **Playa Mero**.

Dotted with shade-producing palms, **Cayo Sombrero**, halfway between Chichiriviche and Tucacas, is one of the larger and most frequently visited of the keys, although some parts are less crowded. It has two small restaurants, permits camping and has good snorkelling – but the best places for snorkelling and scuba diving are probably further north, around **cayos Sal** and **Norte**. The former is also good for bathing, although unpleasant odours sometimes emanate from the small salt lake in the middle of the key. The northernmost island, **Cayo Borracho**, is the park's most beautiful, yet it is often not possible to visit because of sensitive turtle nesting areas.

Keep in mind that some but not all beaches are lined with palms, so be sure to bring a hat and or strong suntan lotion. Also, some have small mangrove forests, which are best explored wearing mosquito repellent.

Chichiriviche

Proximity to a number of keys and quality accommodation make **CHICHIRIVICHE** (chee-chee-ree-vee-chay) the preferred choice for most visitors to Morrocoy. The town is quite small, with essentially nothing to see. It has a few beaches on the north end, in the Playa Norte area, but they don't compare to those on the keys. Round-trip **boat rides** to the most of the keys cost US$10–15.

As with the trip to Tucacas, take a bus to Valencia. From there, you shouldn't have to wait more than a half-hour for the two-and-a-half-hour bus to Chichiriviche. Buses do not run after 6pm. There are no information booths or offices here. To access the Internet, head to *Bit Manía* (daily 8.30am–12.30pm & 2–9pm) on Paseo Bolívar.

Practicalities

There is a mixture of **hotels** and **posadas**, although the latter tend to be better. Some of the nicest are at the north end of town, at Playa Norte. The seaside *Posada Morrukue* (ⓣ0259/818-6492, ⓦwww.morokkue.com; ❼–❽), 2km from the city centre on Av Principal de Playa Norte, offers various packages that include transport to keys and meals in romantic, open-air restaurant. Another winner a bit further down on Av Principal de Playa Norte is *Posada Kanosta* (ⓣ0259/818-6246, ⓦwww.kanosta.com; ❼). Italian owner Patrizia Barsanti runs a tight ship and cooks stupendously at this four-room guesthouse across the street from the beach. Rooms are spacious and comfortable. The posada is 3km from the centre, but Patrizia can often pick you up at the bus terminal – reservations only. In town, the small *Posada El Profe* (ⓣ0414/336-3808; ❸–❹), just off C Mariño and one block from sea, is a good option for budget travellers, and has a mini-gym and its own sea kayaks, which are ideal for exploring nearby keys. Walls of the communal kitchen serve as the guestbook. Another good deal in town is *Villa Gregoria* (ⓣ0259/818-6359; ❸) on C Mariño. The Spanish-owned, Mediterranean-style guesthouse has simple but spacious and tidy rooms with private bathrooms and fans. There is nowhere in or around town to camp.

Places to eat in Chichiriviche are fairly basic. *Brisas del Mar* is your best bet for inexpensive seafood. Just off the *malecón*, it is right in front of where fishermen return from sea, so it is no surprise that the fish and lobster here are fresh and delicious. Also on the waterfront area, *Casamare* is a good, Italian-owned pizza and seafood restaurant with a wide selection and decent prices. Views from the covered sidewalk are pleasant when there aren't parked cars in the way. *El Buen Sabor*, on Avenida Zamora, is a local favourite for fresh *empanadas*. Choose among shark, cheese, ground beef, shredded beef and chicken – all cost about US$0.40. Fresh juices cost about the same. It's only open from 7 to 11am. You may want to consider skipping desert and instead paying a visit to the *Gelatería Roma*, on Av Zamora near the town entrance. Try one of 36 flavours of delicious, authentic gelato made by its Italian owners.

Coro

Venezuela's prettiest colonial town, **CORO** makes for a great one- or two-day stop-over between the coast and mountains. Named a national monument in 1950 and a World Heritage Site in 1993, the town has made considerable efforts to restore and maintain the relics of its rich history.

One of South America's first towns and Venezuela's first capital, it was founded by the Spanish in 1527 to suppress the slave hunting in the area. Later that year, it became the base of exploration for Welser, the German banking house to which Carlos I of Spain leased much of western Venezuela. When Welser's attempts to find El Dorado failed, it abandoned Coro in 1546 and over the next few centuries, the town's importance diminished and it was subjected to terrible looting from repeated pirate attacks. However, in the eighteenth century, it regained much of its old wealth and splendour by being the main supply centre for the Dutch colonies of Curacão and Bonaire. Most of the colonial structures present in the historic centre hail from that era.

Arrival and information

Flights arrive several times daily from Caracas, and the airport is right at the edge of the small city centre, so you can either walk or take a taxi ride (US$1) to your hotel. By **bus**, it takes about seven hours from the capital, arriving at the terminal on Avenida Los Médanos, 2km east of town; from Chichiriviche, frequent buses take about three and a half hours. Coro's bus terminal lies about two kilometres from the town centre and shouldn't cost more than US$2 to reach in a taxi. There are also cheaper city buses.

Tourists can get **information** and maps at the *Secretaría de Turismo* (weekdays 8am–6pm; ⓣ0268/251-8033), on Paseo Alameda between Calle Falcón and Calle Palmasola. The employees are generally helpful and several speak English. There are a number of places in town to access the **Internet**, including one in the Centro Comercial Punta del Sol on Avenida Manaure and Calle Falcón.

Accommodation

Coro's **hotels** are generally old, poorly maintained and overpriced, but the city does have its fair share of posadas with tons of character and very reasonable rates.

La Casa de los Pajaros C Monzón, #74, between C Ampiés and C Comercio ⓣ0268/252-8215, ⓔrstiuv@cantv.net. The owners, specialists in old building restoration, have done a tremendous job of mixing old and new in this three-room guesthouse. About five blocks from the historical centre, it's not easy to find, but good prices and a fun atmosphere make the search worthwhile. ❹

Hotel Miranda Cumberland Av Josefa Camejo across from airport ⓣ0268/252-3344, ⓦwww.hotelescumberland.com. The most luxurious hotel in town, the *Miranda Cumberland* is geared towards business travellers. The three-storey white concrete building was constructed in 1958 and shows some signs of age. It has all major conveniences, as well as a large pool with sauna. ❻

Posada el Gallo C Federación, #28 ⓣ0268/252-9481, ⓔposadaelgallo2001@hotmail.com. Very popular with backpackers, especially French, it is sometimes difficult to find a room or a bed in one of the two dorm rooms. The lovely colonial house in the historic centre has beautiful gardens, communal bathrooms and barbecue area and a gift shop in front. ❷–❸

Posada Villa Antigua C Comércio between C Churuguara and Callejon Tocuyito ⓣ0414/683-7433. Restored colonial house a few blocks from the historic centre, featuring bi-level, colourful rooms. Often full in high season. ❸

Taima Taima C Falcón, Paseo Manaure ⓣ0268/252-1215, ⓔhospedajetaimataima@hotmail.com. New posada/hotel with exceptional service from its English-speaking owner. The rooms are a bit small, but well equipped and comfortable. Ask for special backpacker price. ❸

The City

Coro's most impressive churches, museums and colonial mansions lie within the **casco histórico**, or historic centre, replete with colonial architecture and cobblestone roads. The five-square-block area can be easily explored in a day or even a morning.

The centre of the *casco histórico* is not surprisingly the Plaza Bolívar. On the east end stands the unassuming, colonial-style **Catedral**. Venezuela's oldest, its construction began in 1583, was not finished until 1634 and was almost entirely rebuilt in 1790. A block and a half to the northeast on Avenida Talavera, the **Museo de Arte Coro** (Tues–Sat 9am–noon & 3–7.30pm, Sun 9am–4pm; free) has temporary exhibits set in a beautiful colonial mansion. An ideal spot for a quick rest is **Plaza Falcón**, just a half-block further down Paseo Talavera. The trees of the pleasant, shady square are home to a family of sloths, whose proximity to the state parliament building, also on the square, is the source of numerous comparisons and jokes.

Another square that warrants a visit is the **Plaza San Clemente**, two blocks to the north of Plaza Bolívar. Its main draw is the **Iglesia San Clemente**, which was originally built in 1538 by the town's founder, Juan de Ampies. Totally rebuilt in the eighteenth century in a combination of Spanish Baroque and the Dutch Nordic architectural styles, San Clemente is one of three churches in Venezuela built in the shape of a cross. Beside it, a small monument contains the **Cruz de San Clemente**, the wooden cross used during the first mass after the town was founded.

One of Coro's highlights is its splendid colonial mansions. A block to the west on Calle Zamora, the **Casa de las Ventanas de Hierro** (Tues–Fri 9am–noon & 3–6pm, Sat 9am–1pm & 3–6pm, Sun 9am–1pm; free) is notable for its iron window frames and grilles. Imported from Santo Domingo, these extravagant fittings were some of the first to arrive to Venezuela. Inside, the **Museo de Tradicion Familiar** exhibits clothes and furniture from the colonial era. At the **Casa del Tesoro** (Tues–Sat 9am–noon & 3–6pm, Sun 9am–3pm; free), another stately mansion just across Calle Colón, the work of local artists can be seen.

During the nineteenth century, Coro was home to a sizeable Jewish community, which had initially come over from Curacão. The Jews of Coro thrived here through commerce with the Dutch Antilles but were expelled in 1855; when invited back three years later, most did not return. Their history is explored in the **Museo de Arte Alberto Henríquez** (Tues–Sun 9am–noon & 3–6pm; free), across from the Museo de Arte Coro. It contains the oldest synagogue in Venezuela, constructed in 1853 and one of the first synagogues on the continent. Its seats are on sand, symbolic of the era when Jews were in the Sinai desert. Another vestige of the Jewish community, the **Cementerio Judío**, on Calle Zamora at Calle 23 de Enero, was built in 1830 and is the oldest of all South American Jewish cemeteries still in use. The cemetery is locked, but the tour operator La Colmena (☎0268/251-1446), on Calle Comercio between Paseo Talavera and Calle Garcés, will take you there for around US$5. The *Hotel Miranda Cumberland* also has keys, which it sometimes lends to guests.

The perfect way to end your day in Coro is a trip to the desert. Just at the northern city limits is an entrance into **Parque Nacional Médanos de Coro** (daily 7am–7.30pm; free), an 80-square-kilometre park covering one of Venezuela's few desert areas. Large dunes up to 30m high make it especially picturesque. There is not a whole lot to do there – especially after the transplanted camels died – but it's worth a stroll among the dunes. A late afternoon visit is ideal, so as to avoid the heat and catch the sometimes stunning sunsets. Be sure to leave immediately after sunset, since the area is not considered safe in the evening. The 1km taxi ride from the *casco histórico* should not set you back more than US$2.

Eating

While there are no spectacular **restaurants** in Coro, there is a number of fair and moderately priced ones.

La Barra de Jacal C Unión at Av Manaure. Popular with both locals and tourists, this colonial-style complex has a patio seating area with a wood-burning pizza oven, a more elegant restaurant upstairs, a bar inside and even a small kiddie-park. The food is on the expensive side, but good. Closed Monday.

Caribe Criollo Restaurant C González between C Urdaneta and C Zamora. This pleasant indoor restaurant offers a nice mix of local meat and seafood dishes. Portions are big, but prices are quite reasonable. If hungry, a good choice is the *pollo Puerto Rico* (grilled chicken with cheese, avocado and plantains).

La Colmena C Comércio between Paseo Talavera and C Garcés. This centrally located café, set in the patio of an old colonial house, is an excellent place to stop for a snack or lunch. Desserts such as *quesillo* and *dulce de plátano* are recommended.

Il Ristorante da Vicenzo Av Josefa Camejo next to airport. This moderately priced restaurant, specializing in pasta dishes and crepes, is a local favourite. The ambience is very 80s Italian, with checkered tablecloths and wine racks.

Maracaibo

Despite its importance as the seat of the oil industry and the country's second most populous city (1.4 million), **MARACAIBO**, southwest of Coro, receives very few tourists. Though founded in 1574, it has few colonial relics, and those that survive tend to be in marginal neighbourhoods. Neighbouring Lago Maracaibo is the continent's largest lake at 12,800 square kilometres, but oil pollution prevents its use for recreation. Overall, the city is not particularly easy to navigate, and the heat is often unbearable – temperatures rarely dip below 35°C – but it is the safest place to catch a bus into **Colombia**, and it is fairly convenient to get to Coro, 254km to the east.

Whether entering or leaving Maracaibo, you will inevitably cross the **Rafael Urdaneta Bridge**. A source of tremendous pride for the local *maracuchos*, this 8679m bridge across Lago Maracaibo is the longest in South America. If you do spend time on Lago Maracaibo, visit the **Santa Rosa de Agua**, a small lakeside village built on stilts, which holds a number of good fish restaurants. It's best to go during the day, as the area is dangerous at night; a taxi will charge about US$5 for the five-kilometre ride. A larger and more famous version of Santa Rosa, **Sinamaica**, is the site where Vespucci was inspired to name the new land "Venezuela", but the area is quite dangerous and the trip takes a few hours in either direction.

Practicalities

If you need a **place to stay**, one of the best options is the somewhat upscale *Gran Hotel Delícias* (ⓣ0261/797-6111, ⓔhoteldelicias@telcel.net.ve; ❺) on Av 15 at C 70. It shows some signs of wear and tear, but it's good value and having a pool in Maracaibo is a real plus. *Hotel Victoria* (ⓣ0261/722-9697; ❷–❸), Av 6 on Plaza Baralt, is a good budget spot in the centre of the historic district. Beds are not in great condition and lighting is dim, but the rooms have a/c, private bathrooms and balconies with good views of the square. For **eating**, try *Bambi Café*, which has remained in style for more than fifty years. It serves quality breakfasts, sandwiches and pasta dishes at reasonable prices. It has four locations, the most central being on C 71 and Av 20. *Pastelería Jeffrey's* on Calle 36 across from Plaza Republica is a superb bakery owned by a pastry expert from New Jersey.

Crossing into Colombia

If you are heading **to Colombia** from Maracaibo, you should take Bus Ven, which has morning and afternoon departures for the six-hour trip to **Santa Marta** (see p.620) and ten-hour trip to **Cartagena** (see p.612), from the bus terminal in the southwest of the city. You will have to stop at the border town of Paraguachón, pass through customs, pay a US$15 exit tax in bolívars, and then switch buses; book as early as possible.

11.3

Mérida and the Andes

The mountainous state of **MÉRIDA** finds it way onto nearly all visitors' itineraries, regardless of how long they are spending in Venezuela. The raw beauty of the carved, green slopes and snowcapped peaks of the **ANDES** is not to be missed – even if the mountains are not at their most spectacular here. Plus, the facilities in Mérida are by far Venezuela's finest: impressive posadas, gourmet restaurants, the world's largest cable car and even major theme parks. Also, taking advantage of their privileged surroundings, locals have developed an impressive array of mountain sport facilities for hiking, ice climbing, canyoning, rafting, mountain biking and paragliding.

With over 300,000 inhabitants, the state capital of the same name is the region's principal gateway and largest city. Yet it is safe, tranquil and easy to navigate. To the south and east of the city, the **Parque Nacional Sierra Nevada** offers some of the finest hiking opportunities in the region. It is dominated by the country's most famous snowcapped peaks, **Pico Bolívar** (5007m) and **Pico Humboldt** (4920m). To the northwest of Mérida, the Carretera Transandina, or the Trans-Andean Highway, passes several charming mountain towns such as **Muchuchíes** and **Apartaderos**. There are numerous hiking trailheads along the way, many of which pass through pretty mountain lakes.

Mérida and around

From the bottom of a deep valley, the city of **MÉRIDA** enjoys stunning views of the surrounding mountains without ever becoming uncomfortably cold. Its storied past has left a wealth of colonial architecture and culture, yet, unlike many other mountain towns in South America, it is also quite modern and progressive. A base for tours to Los Llanos, the city attracts a lot of visitors, and it is also home to close to 40,000 college students who come from throughout the country to study at La Universidad de los Andes, one of the country's most prestigious universities. To accommodate the two groups, there is an impressive array of Internet cafés, restaurants, bars that would normally only be found in large cities – there are even three **theme parks** in the city's vicinity. Yet, Mérida enjoys many of the privileges of smaller cities: low prices, safe streets and a small enough downtown that you can walk nearly everywhere. The only real problem is the traffic near the city centre.

Some history

Mérida was founded in 1558 by Juan Rodríguez Suárez, a captain from the Spanish territory of Nueva Granada (present-day Colombia), who named it "Mérida" in homage to the Spanish city where he was born. This angered the governors of Nueva Granada because colonial laws dictated that towns could only be founded by royal decree. Captured and taken to Bogotá, the territory's capital, he was sentenced to death but managed to escape to the territory of Venezuela, where he was granted asylum.

Mérida remained part of Nueva Granada until 1777, when it was transferred to Venezuela. Geographically isolated, it was never a major colonial centre, and much

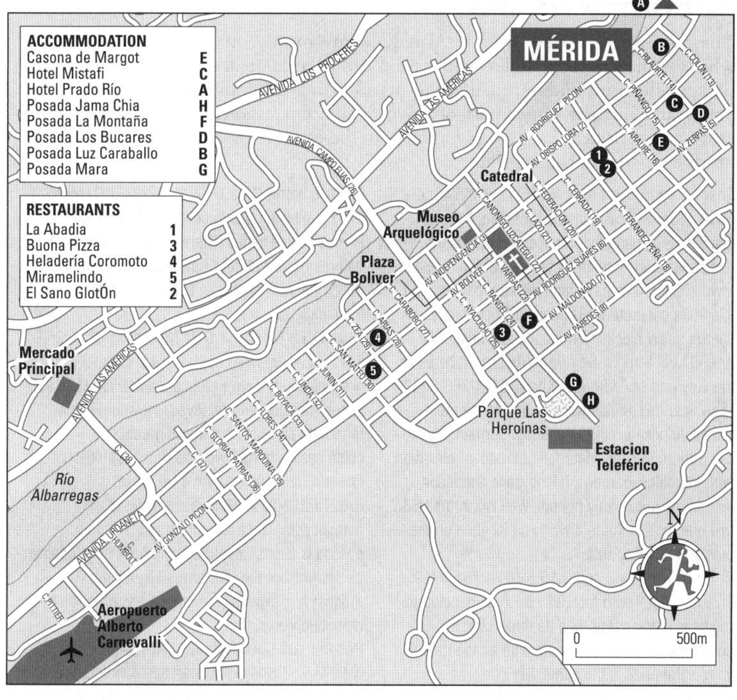

of it was destroyed during the devastating earthquake of 1812. However, its importance increased in the middle of the eighteenth century as its isolation made it a safe haven for refugees of the Federal War. The city's population continued to rise as better roads and transport made it more accessible from the rest ofVenezuela. Today its population is estimated at over 300,000.

Arrival, information and city transport

There are at least ten daily flights from Caracas, one from Coro, and two from Maracaibo. The **airport** is only two kilometres from the city centre, on Avenida Urdaneta. From here, there are city buses (US$0.50) going to Plaza Bolívar but taxis shouldn't cost more than US$2.

The **bus terminal** is about a kilometre beyond the airport, on Avenida Las Américas. There are half a dozen night buses from Caracas (twelve hours), several daily from Maracaibo (six hours) and two daily from Coro (eleven hours). City buses go to Plaza Bolívar, but taxis are inexpensive.

The state tourism board, Cormetur, has **information** booths in several locations including the bus station, the airport and the Mercado Principal on Avenida Las Américas. You can also stop by their main office right next to the airport, open on weekdays from 8am until noon and 2 until 6pm.

Getting around within the city is generally quite easy. Usually, your best bet is walking, as the distances are short and traffic can get heavy. Taxis are plentiful and only cost about US$1.50 to any destination within the city. City buses are also an option.

Accommodation

The few luxury **hotels** are a bit dated and are mostly on the outskirts of town, which is inconvenient unless you have a car. Mérida's real strength is its posadas, which offer outstanding quality and prices. Most are conveniently found in the pretty and historic upper part of town, which corresponds to lower numbered cross-streets, or near Parque Las Heroínas to the east. There are also some wonderful upscale posadas outside town.

Casona de Margot Av 4 No 15-17 ⓣ0274/252-3312, ⓦwww.lacasonademargot.com. Although quality has apparently dropped in recent years, this popular guesthouse is still one of the nicest in town. Cosy rooms have high wooden ceilings and igloo-like concrete walls. Ideal location in city centre, a few blocks from hustle and bustle. ❹

Hosteria & Spa La Sevillana Av Los Próceres at the very end of Pedregosa Alta ⓣ0274/266-3227, ⓦwww.andes.net/lasevillana. One of the most attractive posadas in the country. German owner Ilse Gudrun Gasser offers the ultimate in relaxation with fountains, gardens, hiking trails and a spa (extremely reasonably priced). Well worth the US$5 taxi ride or 30-minute drive to its location on the outskirts of a city suburb. ❻

Hotel Mistafi Av 3 and C 15 ⓣ0274/251-0729. This new hotel with tastefully decorated, colourful rooms is better value than its three-star counterparts. Request a room with a mountain view – the price is the same. ❺

Hotel Prado Río Av Universidad, Hoyada de Milla ⓣ0274/252-0633, ⓦwww.hotelpradorio.com.ve. Most luxurious hotel in town, despite being run by the government. Rooms in oddly designed main building have balconies overlooking pool and mountains. For same price, you can stay in larger *cabañas*. Facilities also include volleyball court, Internet café and nail/massage parlour. ❻

Posada Jama Chia C 24 No 8-223 ⓣ0274/252-5767. Well-run posada conveniently located on Parque Las Heroínas. There are only communal bathrooms, but all four have hot water. For about US$5, you can sleep in a shared room or hammock. ❷

Posada La Montaña C 24 No 6-47 ⓣ0274/252-5977, ⓦwww.andes.net/lamontana. Usually the first posada in town to fill up, *La Montaña* has a superb design that employs local wood, brick, terracotta tiles, and extensive greenery. Owners could easily charge twice as much. ❸–❹

Posada Los Bucares Av 4 No 15-05 ⓣ0274/252-2841, ⓔlosbucarespos@hotmail.com. The front part of this 16-room posada is almost identical to its neighbour *Casona de Margot*, but the rear offers slightly more modern and expensive rooms, a few of which have mountain views. ❹

Posada Luz Caraballo Av 2 No 13-80 ⓣ0274/252-5441, ⓔluzcaraballo@hotmail.com. One of the best deals in town, this restored colonial house fills up quickly – reserve a few weeks in advance in high season. The lobby is extremely attractive, with coloured glass ceilings and a chimney. ❹

Posada Mara C 24 No 8-215 ⓣ0274/252-5507. Very basic, but adequate accommodation in ten-room posada on Parque Las Heroínas. Rooms with bathrooms cost slightly more. No English spoken. ❷

The City

Although the environs of Mérida offer a great variety of entertainment and sporting options, the city itself has a limited number of sights. In fact, Mérida's top attraction, the world's longest-travelling, highest-climbing cable car, actually takes you out of the city. From its base station in Parque Las Heroínas in the south of the city, the **Teleférico** (daily July–Sept 7am–noon, daily Oct–June Wed–Sun 7am–noon; US$15 round-trip; ⓣ0274/252-5080, ⓦwww.telefericodemerida.com) journeys 12.6 kilometres, rising over 3000 metres to the top of **Pico Espejo**, 4765 metres above sea level. There are three intermediate stations, La Montaña (2436m), La Aguada (3452m) and Loma Redonda (4045m), and you should pause at the last before ascending to Pico Espejo, since the dramatic climb, made in less than an hour, can cause mild **altitude sickness**. From the Loma Redonda station you can also follow hiking trails thirteen kilometres to the small Andean town of Los Nevados, which contains several posadas and places to eat.

Back in town, walking the streets of the old **old town** to admire its colonial houses and pretty parks will only take a few hours. Right on the Plaza Bolívar, the somewhat nondescript **Catedral** grew out of plans for a seventeenth-century cathedral that wasn't actually started until 1803 and not completed until 1958. There are several decent museums in the area, most with rotating exhibitions. Of particular note is the **Museo Arquelógico** (Tues–Fri 8am–noon & 2–6pm, Sat–Sun 3–6pm) on Avenida 3, in the Universidad de los Andes building. It presents pre-Columbian artefacts from the region, augmented by thorough historical descriptions.

Of the city's many squares, **Plaza Beethoven** has a clock that plays a different tune by the composer each hour – it's a few kilometres away from the old town, so take a US$2 taxi or the Santa María bus that runs along Avenida 5. Far less placid is the **Mercado Principal** (Sun 7am–2pm, Tues 7am–1pm, Mon & Wed–Sat 7am–6pm), a three-storey, tourist-oriented market about a kilometre southwest of the old town on Avenida Las Américas. The first floor offers fruits and vegetables, the second artisan works and other souvenirs and the third an eating area with a number of delicious restaurants (see below).

The theme parks

The three **theme parks** in the vicinity of Mérida were created by Alexis Montilla, deemed the Walt Disney of Venezuela. Although La Montaña de los Sueños, Los Aleros and Venezuela de Antier have a few rides, their main emphasis is on experiencing history and culture.

Forty-five kilometres southwest of Merida, **La Montaña de los Sueños** (2–11pm; US$13) is dedicated to last century's major forms of entertainment: movies, radio, television, theatre and photography. Visitors can produce their own radio shows, learn how to make their own movies and develop pictures taken from crude cameras that they create. The grounds contain most of the set of the acclaimed 1995 film *Una vida y dos mandados*, a fifty-year retrospective of Alexis Montilla's life. A taxi ride there will cost about US$26.

Los Aleros (daily 8am–6pm; US$12), 17km northeast of Mérida past the town of Tabay, was Montilla's first theme park. A recreation of a 1930s Andean village, its attractions include music, typical Andean food and theatre productions of local folktales, and workers are in full costume to make the experience seem more authentic. The park also features a few excellent restaurants. A taxi will set you back US$10–15; otherwise, you can take a *por puesto* from Av 4 and C 19 in Mérida.

Some 12km southwest of Mérida on the road to Jají, **Venezuela de Antier** (daily 8am–6pm; US$15) showcases all of Venezuela's greatest heroes, historical moments, traditions and tourist attractions in the form of replicas and live reproductions. It's particularly good for recent arrivals to Venezuela or those who do not have time to see much of the country. You can get there for about US$10 in a taxi or take a *por puesto* from Calle 26 between Avenida 3 and Avenida 4.

Eating and drinking

The **cuisine** from Mérida and the Andes region is famous throughout the country. Some specialities include *arepas de trigo* (*arepas* made from wheat flour, as opposed to corn flour), *queso ahumado* (smoked cheese), *trucha* (trout) prepared in a variety of ways, *pizca andina* (a stew made with potatoes, eggs, onions and cheese) and *dulces* (sweet candies made from bananas, figs, papaya and caramel). Typical drinks include *tizana* (juice served with fruit chunks in the cup), *vino de fresa* or *mora* (wine made from strawberries or blackberries) and *calentaito* (a reputed aphrodisiac consisting of sugarcane liquor with an infusion of local herbs). Mérida also has some classy restaurants serving various international cuisines.

La Abadía Av 3 between C 17 and 18. Spectacular restaurant and Internet café set in a beautifully restored convent. Romantic dining in three settings – second-floor terrace, lower-level garden area and cellar – is accentuated by live music on weekends. The menu is fairly typical of the region, with a wide variety of trout, pasta and grilled meat dishes.

Buona Pizza Av 7 between C 24 and 25. Great deep-dish pizza with a variety of toppings – a large costs US$3–5. Attractive restaurant has colourful paintings, glass roof and brick walls.

Heladería Coromoto Av 3 between C 28 and 29. *Guinness Book of World Record* holder for most ice-cream flavours with nearly 800, although only around 100 are available at any given time. Wacky flavours include smoked tuna, calamari, garlic, beans and spaghetti with meatballs. It's truly impressive how well they reproduce flavours, although some are rather disgusting. Closed Mondays.

Mercado Principal Av Las Américas and Viaduto Miranda. Great food, huge portions and reasonable prices make it one of best places to sample local favourites. Seating area on the third floor contains tables from eight nearly identical restaurants – some have pushy representatives that try to bring you to their area.

Miramelindo Av 4 and C 29, in the *Hotel Chama*. One of the town's finest restaurants, it is not excessively expensive considering the level of service and quality of the Basque specialities. Try the *merluza* (or sea bass) *con salsa verde*.

Mogambo Café next to Miramelindo. Elegant, jazz-themed restaurant serving a variety of Mexican and Spanish dishes at terrific prices. A favourite is the honey and ginger-marinated smoked salmon sandwich, served with wasabi and alfalfa.

El Sano Glotón Av 4 between C 17 and 18. Bi-level vegetarian restaurant with nice offering of sandwiches, lasagnas, salads, falafel and juices.

Nightlife

In large part because of the immense student population, Mérida enjoys a rather active **nightlife**. Sunday and Monday are dead, but things pick up Tuesday and Wednesday and get quite lively the rest of the week. Because of their proximity to the university, many of the hot spots are in town, especially on Avenida 4 between calles 18 and 20. *El Hoyo de Queque*, on Av 4 and C 19, is a small but lively bar that is constantly packed with both locals and tourists. *Alfredo's,* just across the street, is a bar and disco that becomes extremely loud and raucous on weekends and tends to have a somewhat younger crowd. On Av 2 and C 24, another widely frequented bar and disco, *Birosca Carioca*, is known for its strong *caipirinhas* and Brazilian music. One of Mérida's oldest nightspots, *La Cucaracha*, is outside the city, in the Centro Comericial Las Tapias on Avenida Urdaneta. The large but always crowded disco has two floors, one with techno and the other with salsa and merengue.

Listings

Airlines Aeropostal ☎0274/263-0775; Avior ☎0274/262-1530; Lai ☎0274/263-7815; and Santa Barbara ☎0274/263-2723.

Banks and exchange Italcambio (Mon–Fri 8.30am–5pm, Sat 9am–1pm; ☎0274/263-3643) has an office at the airport. Another good place to exchange travellers' cheques or cash is CorpBanca (☎0274/262-0411), on Avenida Las Américas just above the Mercado principal.

Car rental The two major operations, both at the airport, are Budget Car Rental (☎0274/263-1697) and Davila (☎0274/263-4510).

Internet cafés are on nearly every block. Most have high-speed connections and charge about US$1 per hour.

Medical Care A reputable clinic with some English-speaking doctors is Clinica Mérida (☎0274/263-6395) on Av Urdaneta next to the airport.

Police The main station is on Avenida Urdaneta, adjacent to Parque Gloria Patrias (☎0274/263-0462). The emergency number is 171.

Tour operators Arassari Trek (☎0274/252-5879, ⓦwww.arassari.com) specializes in adventure sports, especially canyoning and rafting. Guamanchi Expeditions (☎0274/252-2080, ⓦwww.guamanchi.com) offers nearly all hiking, biking and water sports options. Natoura (☎0274/252-4075, ⓦwww.natoura.com) runs excellent hiking and climbing trips and rents top of the line equipment. They are also a travel agency, so they can make flight bookings or put together Venezuela tour packages. All three operators are located on Parque Las Heroínas.

Parque Nacional Sierra Nevada

Looming above Mérida to the south and east, the Sierra Nevada runs northeast along the Carretera Transandina and through the 276,000-hectare **PARQUE**

Mountain sports

Outdoor activity is the principal attraction in the state of Mérida, owing to its natural endowment as well as the efforts of several excellent tour operators. Nearly all who visit the area go **hiking** on the infinite trails in the area, but two of the most popular routes are up Venezuela's highest peaks, Pico Bolívar (5007m) and Pico Humboldt (4942m). To ascend to the top, **ice climbing** is necessary for both, although it is more technical on some routes up Pico Bolívar. Ascents can get quite hairy in the wet season, but some do it anyway. Three very reputable operators in the Plaza Heroínas area of Mérida will furnish guides, transport and equipment (even warm clothes) at roughly the same prices: **Natoura** (Ⓣ0274/252-4075, Ⓦwww.natoura.com), **Guamanchi Expeditions** (Ⓣ0274/252-2080, Ⓦwww.guamanchi.com) and **Arassari Trek** (Ⓣ0274/252-5879, Ⓦwww.arassari.com). They charge between US$45 and $75 per person for each day, depending upon the size of the group. For porters, add on an additional US$20 per person. Other operators may be a bit cheaper, but are not necessarily to be trusted.

Mountain biking is an excellent way to discover the area and the limits of your endurance. A number of shops, including the three above, rent quality bikes. They will also be able to indicate some of the best routes. If you're looking for something more extreme, there are several options. Some of the surrounding mountains provide the ideal setting for **paragliding**. For about US$60, you can go on an absolutely thrilling yet safe 24-minute ride with a certified pilot guide, arranged through any of the above operators. Be sure to bring a jacket or sweater and don't eat before going. Another adrenaline sport that has become very popular recently is **canyoning**, which involves rappelling alongside and under waterfalls. Proceed at your own risk, as broken noses and chipped teeth are not uncommon. The cost is about US$45 for a full day. The most experienced canyoning operator is Arassari Trek, which also specializes in **rafting**. The three rivers they use, in Mérida and Barinas states, have class three to five rapids. Trips range from one to several days and cost about $60 per day. Rafting season is from June to December.

NACIONAL SIERRA NEVADA. The park features the country's highest mountains as well as its best mountain sports activities (see box above). Given the park's altitude, which ranges as high as 5000 metres, it is not surprising that there is great diversity in flora and fauna here; the most famous inhabitant is the endangered Andean condor.

Pico Bolívar

At 5007 metres, **PICO BOLÍVAR** is the country's highest and most hiked peak. There are multiple routes up, varying in difficulty and length of ascent. Many get off at the last Teleférico station, Pico Espejo, and make the five-hour ascent along the Ruta Weiss, which is not very technical in the dry season (December–May). However, guides (see Mérida tour operators listing opposite) are recommended year-round, and climbers should spend at least a few days in the mountains acclimatizing themselves before going up. The Ruta Sur Este and North Flank are two more challenging routes, which involve ice climbing. Views from the top are spectacular – on a clear day, you can see the city of Mérida, the Colombian Andes and the vast expanse of Los Llanos.

Pico Humboldt

A strenous four-day trip to and from the peak to **PICO HUMBOLDT** and back is worthwhile if you have the time and energy. Starting at the entrance of Parque Nacional La Mucuy, about 10km to the northeast of Mérida, the first day's ascent is

1000 metres; after the six-hour, nine-kilometre walk, most camp around the picturesque Laguna Coromoto. The ascent on the second day is shorter but steeper as you get into the rocky terrain above the tree line. Most camp around another pretty lake, Laguna Verde. The final day's ascent to the peak and return to the campsite usually takes at least eight hours, depending upon your ice-climbing ability. During the wet season, it is often snowing or raining towards the top, complicating the climb significantly. Caution should also be exercised if feeling the effects of high altitude. The fourth day is for the descent back to La Mucuy.

Northeast of Mérida

The region **northeast of Mérida** is best known for its quaint Andean towns, which have, for the most part, structured themselves to accommodate their numerous visitors. The majority are right along the Carretera Transandina, with beautiful views of the Sierra Nevada range to the south and the Sierra Culata range to the north. Mountain lakes are dotted throughout the region – many offer excellent trout fishing. Exploring the region is easy, as there are buses passing back and forth along the Carretera Transandina every half-hour.

Tabay

A tiny town ten kilometres from Mérida, **TABAY** makes for a nice day excursion or as a base for exploring Parque Nacional La Mucuy. Founded in 1689, it became one of the country's largest coffee-producing towns and also the scene of several battles in the Federal War of the mid-nineteenth century. One of its principal attractions today is the **aguas termales** (daily 8.30am–5pm; US$1.50), or hot springs, just outside town. In reality, they are not that spectacular, since the water is just pumped into a concrete pool.

In terms of **accommodation**, a good budget option on the Plaza Bolívar is *Posada Tabay* (ⓣ0274/283-0025, ⓦwww.andes.net/posadatabay; ❸). It offers an attractive locale with clean, fully equipped rooms and professional service (but no English spoken). Heading steeply up the price scale is *Cabañas de Xinia y Peter* (ⓣ0416/874-7698, ⓦwww.andes.net/cabanasxiniaypeter; ❾) about a half kilometre away in the town of Mucuy. It is easily one of the country's top ten posadas, offering marvellously decorated "suites" and slightly more spacious *cabañas* with full kitchens. Packages include airport pick-up, three splendid meals, and day-trips. The **restaurant**, open to the public, is highly recommended.

Mucuchíes

Fifty-two kilometres to the northeast of Mérida, **MUCUCHÍES** is another authentic, picturesque mountain town along the Carretera Transandina. Meaning "place of the waters" in the indigenous dialect, Mucuchíes was founded by the Spanish in 1586. The town has since given its name to a famous Venezuelan dog breed, a type of Great Pyrenees, which you will likely see often in the town and area – there's even a statue of one in the Plaza Bolívar. It stands alongside the Indian boy Tinjaca, a local hero who loyally served Simon Bolívar after he passed through town in 1813. Both Tinjaca and his Mucuchíes died in the decisive battle of Boyacá.

Just a few kilometres further along the Carretera Transandina, in the tiny village of San Rafael de Mucuchíes, is a small grey **chapel** that has become one of the most famous emblems of the region. Local artist Juan Félix Sánchez built the chapel himself, using thousands of uncut stones.

Probably the most interesting sight in the town of Mucuchíes is a hotel. **Hotel Castillo San Ignacio** (ⓣ0274/872-0021; ❺), a half kilometre outside the centre on Avenida Cardobo, is actually an Italian-style castle. Hardly what you'd expect to find in the middle of the Andes, this impressive brick and stone construction is decorated with medieval items such as shields and suits of armour. The Italian restaurant is open to the public. A more economical option is the *Posada Los Andes* (☎0274/872-0151; ❸), a block and a half from the Plaza Bolívar on Calle Independencia. The historic house has five clean, colourful rooms and two communal bathrooms. It's often full, which is not surprising given its location and prices. Room 6 has the best views.

For **dining**, *Restaurant Carillón* on Avenida Caradobo is easily the town's finest. Fortunately, the prices of the skilfully prepared, predominantly lamb dishes (around US$5–7) are not consistent with the ambience.

Apartaderos and around

Continuing along the Carretera Transadina brings you to **APARTADEROS**, little more than a strip of houses and accommodation. It's not a traditional Andean town – in fact, it doesn't even have a Plaza Bolívar. However, its proximity to several prominent sights attracts numerous visitors. Ten kilometres from Apartaderos is the **Estación Biológica Juan Manuel Paz** (open all day; free; ☎0274/262-2979), home to the well-known Andean condor conservation and research project. Of the eight condors that are currently in the region, two are protected in the station. The others have been tagged and are being studied. Visitors are shown an instructional ten-minute video, in English or Spanish. Also nearby, the **Observatorio Astronómico Nactional** (open daily during high season, Sat during low season; US$2; ⓦwww.cida.ve) is one of the highest observatories in the world (3600 metres). Its four domed structures house an enormous telescope – the Schmidt telescope being the world's fourth largest. In 2000 scientists used it to discover Plutino, a celestial body slightly too small to be considered the tenth planet.

Apartaderos is also just a few kilometres from the entrance to the northern section of **Parque Nacional Sierra Nevada**. Just inside the entrance is **Laguna Mucubají**, where camping is allowed; you will need to permission and pay the US$1 camping fee at the Inparques office near the entrance. A good hiking trail connects Laguna Mucubají with **Laguna Negra**, a good fishing lake with dark water, as the name suggests. The beautiful hike takes an hour and a half to two hours – you'll probably need to take frequent stops because of the high altitude (3600 metres). You can continue another hour and a half to the pretty **Laguna Los Patos**. In the wet season, it is best to leave early to avoid rain and fog that could limit visibility considerably.

Practicalities

Apartaderos has numerous **accommodation** choices, varying considerably in quality and price. *Casa Solar* (☎0416/674-5653, ⓔcasasolar@hotmail.com; ❺), up the road towards the observatory, is a newly opened posada in a restored colonial house. The six attractive guestrooms have spectacular views, heat and private bathrooms with hot water. Price includes delicious breakfasts. At the lower end of the price scale is *Posada Viejo Apartaderos* (☎0274/872-0658, ⓔposadaviejoapartaderos@cantv.net; ❸). Right before Apartaderos on the Carretera Transandina, this old but well-maintained posada has rooms with hot water and cable TV. For about US$4 more per person, you can get breakfast and dinner. During the day you can get a very typical **meal** just up the road towards Apartaderos at *El Antojo*. They serve inexpensive *cachapas* with cheese and tasty *cochino frito* (fried pork), and have a nice selection of teas to warm you up.

Southwest of Mérida

For the most part, the area to the **southwest of Mérida** does not draw many visitors. It offers no major peaks, its altitudes are generally lower and the views are not quite as spectacular. Nevertheless, there are some rather pleasant towns and scenic areas to hike or bike, and all are easily accessible by car, bus or *por puesto*.

Jají

Owing to its accessibility from Mérida, **JAJÍ** is the one town in the region that does receive large quantities of tourists during high season and weekends, though it is quite sleepy otherwise. The 38-kilometre trip takes less than an hour, and buses (US$1) leave the Mérida terminal regularly. Jají was founded in 1610, but most of what tourists see today is totally reconstructed in typical Andean colonial style. The visually appealing Plaza Bolívar is full of posadas, restaurants and artisan shops; it is clear that the small town of 3000 inhabitants is almost entirely given over to tourism.

However, there's little to do or see beyond the Plaza Bolívar area, and for this reason many make it just a day-trip. Nevertheless, Jají has some decent **accommodation**. Places tend to be reasonably priced, but with substandard service, as most owners live in Mérida. One of the best options in town is *Posada Aldea Vieja* (Ⓣ0414/471-8380, Ⓦwww.andes.net/posadaaldeavieja.com; ❹), set right off Plaza Bolívar on the site of an old coffee plantation. All seven rooms in this handsome posada have balconies with great views of the church and valley below. In front there's a small lookout tower and a cement slide good for a ten-second thrill. *Posada Araguaney* (Ⓣ0416/775-9388; ❷) is in a pretty colonial house right on the main square. It is not particularly well run or maintained, but the price is right. Most **restaurants** in town are decent, but for the most part carbon copies of each other. A nice quick option is the shop up the hill just a block from the Plaza Bolívar – the sign out front simply says "*pasteles/arepas*". The *pasteles*, basically just small *empanadas*, are delicious and cost about US$0.15 each.

La Mesa de los Indios

Although not much further from Mérida than Jají, the small village of **LA MESA DE LOS INDIOS** has considerably fewer visitors. The name of the town refers to its position on a table-top overlooking an expansive valley. The town is totally authentic, with many charming colonial houses. Its Plaza Bolívar, filled with palm trees and colourful flowers, is atypical of the region – because the town's altitude is just under 1500 metres, the vegetation here is lusher than in other Andean towns. To get to La Mesa de los Indios from Mérida, take the *por puesto* at calle 26 in front of Lourdes stadium.

The only **hotel** in town is a particularly good one. *Posada Turistica Papá Miguel* (Ⓣ0274/252-2529, Ⓔpapamiguel@hotmail.com; ❹) is a well-run, colonial-style guesthouse 500m from the Plaza Bolívar – just follow the signs. The owners arrange hiking and biking trips to nearby mountains and hot springs.

11.4

Los Llanos

Taking up nearly a third of the country, the immense plains of **LOS LLANOS** are one of the continent's premier wildlife viewing areas. Some of the most abundant species are alligators and capybara, the world's largest rodent with a length of over one metre. Other common species are river dolphins, jaguar, pumas, howler and capuchin monkeys, anteaters and anacondas. However, the livelihood of the region's inhabitants, the Llaneros, is most closely linked with domesticated animals. Like the cowboys of the Old American West, they have a reputation for being extremely skilled horsemen. Most work on **hatos**, enormous ranches with cattle often numbering in the tens of thousands (see p.1051).

This huge region comprises Barinas, Apure, Portuguesa, Cojedes and much of the Guárico and Anzoátegui states. To the north lies the coastal region, to the west the Andes, and to the south and east the jungle, separated by the Río Orinoco. The Río Apure bisects the region horizontally, separating the **Llano Alto** (upper plains) and **Llano Bajo** (lower plains).

Los Llanos has two very pronounced **seasons**. During the wet season, from May to November, much of the land becomes flooded and extremely verdant. In the dry season, the land becomes parched and dusty, with most vegetation turning brown and yellow. While the scenery is more picturesque in the wet season, wildlife sightings are far fewer – the best viewing comes when water is scarce, causing animals to concentrate at the few watering holes.

Visiting during the dry season is preferable; it rains nearly every day during the wet season, limiting visibility and making for rough conditions, and mosquitoes are numerous and voracious. The rain can, however, offer a break from the searing heat – the average high temperature is around 27°C during both seasons.

Some history

The region was first settled by the Spanish in the middle of the sixteenth century. The first settlement, Calabozo, served as a base for expeditions in search of the famed El Dorado. The explorers were followed by Catholic missionaries, aiming to convert the local indigenous population. The region had a fairly quiet history until the War of Independence, when the Llaneros played an instrumental role. Of mixed blood, the Llaneros distrusted the wealthy Creoles and therefore fought on the side of the Spanish. They quickly earned a reputation as formidable fighters and were able to thwart Bolívar's early attempts at independence. However, in one of the main turning points of the war, Bolívar convinced them to join forces with the Creoles by offering them economic and social benefits, including grants of land seized from the Spanish. After victory was achieved, the leaders of the new government did not fulfil Bolívar's promises, instead granting the Creole officers huge parcels of land that largely coincide with the present day hatos. The Llaneros were for the most part relegated to the position of ranch hands on the hatos. It appears that not much has changed since then.

Barinas

There is little to capture your attention in **BARINAS**, and you're likely only to be passing through on the way to the hatos. It is hard to believe that this provincial, run-down city is the largest and arguably most important urban area in Los Llanos. Even more surprising is that during the colonial period it was the second largest and wealthiest city in the country after Caracas. Founded in 1567, Barinas became an important agricultural and ranching centre almost immediately, and in the early 1600s, it was granted Venezuela's only licence to grow tobacco. The city also thrived from such crops as sugarcane, cacao and bananas, yet during the civil wars of the nineteenth century, much of the architecture was destroyed and many of the city's inhabitants fled.

The discovery of oil nearby has led to some repopulation – the town now has about 250,000 inhabitants – and increased wealth, yet it still lacks sights or places of interest. The sole attraction is the odd-looking **Palacio del Gobierno**, a long, blue-glass structure with strange pipes and ironwork. Right on the Plaza Bolívar, it was recently constructed by the father of Hugo Chávez (who became governor soon after his son became president). Nearly all buildings in the city are low and elongated, much like the region itself, and few are taller than one storey.

Practicalities

There are about ten daily flights from Caracas – flight time is about an hour. The **airport** is 1.5 kilometres from the centre of town, and a taxi should cost around US$3. **Buses** to Mérida (four to five hours) leave about every two hours from the terminal, about two kilometres from the town centre. There are also several evening buses going to Caracas, and the trip takes twelve hours. For **information**, there is a Cormetur stand at the bus station, but their hours are erratic and they are not particularly well organized.

If you need a **place to stay**, the best option is *Hotel Internacional* (☎0273/552-1749; ❹) on Calle Arzobispo Méndez in front of Plaza Zamora. The half-century-old hotel has spacious rooms with a/c, TV, hot water and antique phones that actually work. Ask for rooms in the garden area. A cheaper option right in front of the bus terminal is *Hotel El Palacio* (☎0273/552-6947; ❷), which offers decent-sized rooms with a/c, plus TVs for US$3 extra. If you will be **eating** in Barinas, you may want to try the famous Llanero beef. *El Estribo* on Calle Apure has some of the best beef in town, served with fresh cheese and salad.

San Fernando de Apure

With 135,000 inhabitants, **SAN FERNANDO DE APURE** is the largest city in the Llano Bajo. Founded as a missionary outpost in the seventeenth century, it is now the capital of the state of Apure and one of the region's most important trading centres. There is very little to detain tourists, but some pass through on the way to the southern hatos. The only vaguely interesting site is the **Palacio Barbarito**, a nineteenth-century palace built by Italians involved in the lucrative trade of cayman leather. Once grand, the palace, which is just off the Paseo Libertador, the main thoroughfare that runs along the banks of the Río Apure, has deteriorated considerably.

Practicalities

San Fernando has a small airport that receives two daily flights from Caracas. The airport is three kilometres from the town centre, and a **taxi** should not cost more than US$2. There are also several **buses** that run daily to Caracas (about eight hours). Buses leave every two hours or so to Barinas (about eight hours). The bus terminal is less than a kilometre from the town centre. If you have to **stay** the night, consider the *Nuevo Hotel Apure* (☎0247/341-4759; ❺) on Av María Nieves. One of the nicest hotels in town, it has decent-sized rooms and reasonable rates. A less expensive option is *La Torraca* (☎0247/342-3557; ❸–❹), in the town centre on Paseo Libertador, whose rooms have a/c, TVs, private bathrooms, and balconies. A good place to **eat** is *Taberna de Don Juan*, on Avenida Carabobo at Calle Negro Primero. A Spanish *tasca*, it serves delicious paellas and has live music some evenings. It is closed on Sundays.

The hatos

Ironically, the evolution of **THE HATOS** into important wildlife sanctuaries owes much to their owners' attempts to prevent costly cattle theft (and, more recently, kidnappings). It was only after employing tight security measures to keep out poachers that some began to realize the value of their wildlife stocks in terms of eco-tourism. Consequently, several major hatos have built accommodation and other facilities for tourists, but these stays are fairly expensive, and backpackers and more budget-conscious travellers usually go on tours organized by most major companies in Mérida (see "Listings", p. 1004).

The cattle ranches themselves are certainly the best places to experience the region's wildlife and culture. Most offer similar activities that include truck rides through the property, canoe trips and hikes and they tend to have trained guides who speak at least some English. Accommodation on the ranches tends to be rustic, but comfortable, and while prices tend to be fairly steep, many ranches offer lower rates for the wet season, when the wildlife is not abundant and some can only be accessed by river. Accommodation arranged **by tours** are in campsites, and the areas they arrange for you to explore are generally not the private hatos, so the wildlife viewing is not quite the best. Such trips often include a day of rafting, which you cannot book through tour operators in Los Llanos.

For the most part, the hatos are not easily accessible to each other or to the major cities of Venezuela. Visitors must either have their own transport (in some cases it must be four-wheel drive) or arrange for expensive transport. The following are the four hatos that receive nearly all the visitors.

Hato El Cedral

With its excellent reputation for conservation and research activities, **HATO EL CEDRAL** is a good ranch for the curious visitor – there are often lectures by international scientists open to the public. Fifteen comfortable *cabañas* have air conditioning and private bathrooms. Quality facilities also include a swimming pool, which cannot be found at any of the other hatos. In addition to its 20,000 head of cattle, Hato El Cedral's wildlife includes stocks of capybara (between 10,000 and 20,000) and caymans (around 5000), which are probably the largest population of all the hatos. It also has 340 species of birds that include scarlet ibises and pygmy kingfishers. During the day, you can take guided tours on foot, in trucks or by boat; evening activities include searching for caymans, watching educational videos and listening to live Llanero music.

The ranch is in the southern state of Apure, about three hours from San Fernando de Apure. Transfers can be arranged from Barinas or San Fernando de Apure. Prices are between US$120 and 145 per person each day. Reservations are required (☎0212/781-8995, Ⓦwww.hatocedral.com).

△ Beach on the Archipiélago Los Roques

Los Llaneros

Many comparisons have been drawn between **Los Llaneros** and the cowboys of the American West. Known for being tough and independent, both are portrayed as embodying the spirit of their countries. Other similarities include their legendary penchants for drinking, gambling and singing sad ballads.

The mixed-blood Llaneros captured the nation's imagination during the **War of Independence** as word of their ferocity spread. Their role in the struggle was integral, and their switch of allegiance in the middle of the war was one of the principal reasons for Bolívar's victory. Life has changed little for them since then, as they continue to work almost exclusively on the enormous cattle ranches.

Typically, the Llaneros work hard all week at the ranches, where they are not allowed to drink, and return to their small villages on weekends to more than make up for their abstinence. During bouts of singing, dancing and betting on cockfights, it is not uncommon for drunken skirmishes to occur – a frightening prospect since a Llanero never goes anywhere without his machete.

Los Llaneros participate in a number of other somewhat less dangerous competitions that allow them to showcase their machismo. One of the most popular is **toros coleados**. Riding horseback, each of the contestants has to take down a bull by pulling its tail in a certain way; the one who does it quickest wins. Another common competition is the **conrapunteo**, during which two Llaneros face off in a verbal sparring contest hurling improvised insults at one other to the beat of *piropa*, a musical form pioneered by the Llaneros.

Hato Doña Barbara

Also known as Hato La Trinidad de Arauca, **HATO DOÑA BARBARA** is a 36,000-hectare ranch offering simple accommodation and good wildlife viewing. It has 21 guestrooms with fans and private bathrooms. Activities include horseback rides, visits to nearby dunes and wet-season trips to observe anacondas, some more than six metres long. With a stone boat filled with Orinoco turtles and a statue of Christ surrounded by angels, the ranch has acquired a somewhat quirky reputation.

Hato Doña Barbara is accessible by four-wheel drive during the dry season from the state capital of San Fernando de Apure; in the wet season, it is only accessible by boat. Reservations and transport must be arranged in advance (ⓣ0247/341-3463, ⓔdbarbara@cantv.net). The cost is US$110 per person each day.

Hato El Frío

One of the largest and also most accessible ranches, **HATO EL FRÍO**'s 80,000 hectares of land are home to 45,000 head of cattle and over 1000 horses. Located in Apure, it is just 90km west of San Fernando de Apure. In 1974, a group of Spanish scientists formed a biological station on the ranch, and it has since been an important research centre and often works with UNESCO and other international organizations. The ranch protects many endangered species, including the manatee, arrau turtle, giant river otter and the Orinoco crocodile, for which it has created a breeding station. Howler monkeys, pumas, jaguar, river otters, capybaras, river dolphins and anteaters are also visible. The 270 bird species include hoatzins, odd, primitive-looking birds found only in a few South American lowland areas.

Accommodation is in the form of ten simple but nicely decorated double rooms with fans and private bathrooms. Buses going from San Fernando de Apure to Caracas and Mérida pass by the gate on the San Fernando de Apure–Mantecal road. From there it's a twenty-minute walk. Stays cost between US$100 and US$130 per person each day. Reservations (ⓣ0414/743-5329, ⓦwww.elfrioeb.com) are preferable but they generally accept walk-ins.

Hato Piñero

A pioneer in conservation and eco-tourism efforts, **HATO PIÑERO** began wide-scale conservation forty years ago and started to accept guests in 1986. It has 80,000 hectares of land, but only 13,000 head of cattle because seventy percent is forestland set aside for wildlife. The hato contains 340 species of birds, including egrets, herons, osprey, macaws, hawks, hummingbirds and storks, as well as forty species of reptiles and fifty species of mammals, the most notable of which are the large populations of pumas and jaguar, although they are difficult to spot. It is also one of the most picturesque of hatos, with four rivers and rolling hills that mark the edge of the central plains.

The guest quarters are perhaps the finest of all the hatos. The eleven handsome guestrooms are very comfortable, with private bathrooms and fans. One downside is that the hato is not easily accessed, although it is one of the closest to Caracas (five hours). It is an equal distance from Barinas, but either way it is very difficult to arrive with public transport or a car that does not have four-wheel drive. Transport can be arranged, but it will cost about US$100 each way from Caracas or Barinas. Stays cost US$120–150 per person each day. Reservations (Ⓣ0212/992-4413, Ⓦwww.hatopinero.com) are required – be sure to reconfirm them before coming because security at the gate is very tight.

11.5

Guayana

Covering the southeastern half of Venezuela, **GUAYANA** comprises of just three states – Amazonas, Bolívar and Delta Amacuro – and has only about 1.5 million inhabitants. Most of them are concentrated in the region's only two real cities, **Ciudad Guayana** and **Ciudad Bolívar**, while roughly 150,000 live in indigenous communities, belonging to the Yanomami, Pemón, Warao and Piaroa. While some of these groups barely resemble their ancestors, others have had limited contact with "civilization" and have therefore retained many of their customs.

Despite its lack of inhabitants, the region is extremely important economically, containing a tremendous wealth of such natural resources as gold, iron ore, bauxite and diamonds. It also supplies hydroelectricity for the entire country and even exports it to Venezuela's neighbours.

One of the region's important natural resources is nature itself. Many of the country's main tourist attractions are in Guayana, including the **tropical rainforests** of the Amazon, the breathtaking **Angel Falls**, the magnificent *tepuis*, or tabletop mountains, of **Canaima** and the **Gran Sabana** and the **Orinoco Delta**. But the tremendous distances and lack of major tourism facilities mean there are fewer visitors than you might expect.

Amazonas

The second largest state in Venezuela after Bolívar, **AMAZONAS** has its smallest population. Half of its 120,000 inhabitants live in its capital, **Puerto Ayacucho**. Almost completely covered in tropical rainforest, the state contains hundreds of rivers and is even the birthplace of the mighty **Orinoco River**. Amazonas is known to contain over 8000 plant species, although there are certainly many more that have not yet been identified. To protect the unique flora, as well as the abundant fauna, numerous national parks have been created here. Despite the government's progressive conservation efforts, tourism here is not nearly as common as it is in the Amazonian regions of Brazil, Ecuador or Peru, and because public transport tourist facilities are limited, visitors invariably have to make arrangements through tour operators.

Puerto Ayacucho and around

A sleepy capital city of 60,000, **PUERTO AYACUCHO** is the state's only major town. Founded along the Orinoco River in 1924 primarily as a port for shipping timber, its position **near the Colombian border** makes it a convenient place to cross but has also created safety concerns. Puerto Ayacucho is also the only true entry point for the Amazon region.

The town itself has limited tourist appeal, but a few decent attractions and places to stay are nearby. The **Museo Etnológico de Amazonas** (Tues–Fri 8.30–11.30am & 2.30–6pm, Sat 9am–noon & 3.30–7pm, Sun 9am–1pm; US$1) on Avenida Río Negro has a number of well-elaborated exhibits showcasing clothing and other objects pertaining to the region's indigenous Guajibos, Arawak, Yanomami, Yekuanas and Piaroas. The museum also explains the history of the missionaries that came to the area. In front of the museum is a market where locals sell all types of handicrafts.

The hills around town provide some excellent vistas of the surrounding area. **Cerro Perico**, to the southwest of town, has views of the town and the Orinoco, while **Cerro el Zamuro**, to the south, looks out over the wild, unnavigable Ature Rapids; both can be reached on foot. About eighteen kilometres south of town, **Cerro Pintado** is a large rock with impressive pre-Columbian **petroglyphs** that are an estimated to be three to five thousand years old. It is best to go on a sunny day, as the markings can be difficult to see without proper light. There is no public transport, but a taxi from town should set you back no more than US$10. **Parque Tobagán de la Selva**, a nice though often-crowded park area, contains a natural waterslide – a smooth rock with the water of the River Maripures running over it. The park is thirty kilometres south of town and costs around US$15 by taxi – make sure you arrange for pick-up.

Two daily **flights** go between Puerto Ayacucho and Caracas – flight time is an hour and a half. The airport is six kilometres southeast of town. **Buses** go fairly regularly to Ciudad Bolívar (ten hours) and San Fernando de Apure (eight hours), and several times daily to Caracas (twelve hours). The bus terminal is six kilometres east of town.

Practicalities

Hotel selections in town are generally quite modest. Perhaps the nicest is *Guacharo's Amazonas Resort* (☎0248/521-0328, ©turismoamazonas@cantv.net; ❺) on Calle Evilio Roa. Built in 1949, it was abandoned and more recently renovated. It has gardens, large communal areas, and the town's only pool. *Campamento Genesis* (☎0248/521-1378; ❹), also known as *Campamento Tucan,* is a pleasant, well-run camp on an unnamed street behind the bus terminal. Rooms are comfortable and modern – some have a/c. *Residencias Miramar* (☎0248/521-4521; ❸), at the southern end of Avenida Orinoco, is a new and highly recommended guesthouse. Rooms are spacious and clean with private bathrooms, a/c and TVs. Each also has a small garden in front. On Avenida Aguerrevere, *Residencias Internacional* (☎0248/521-0242; ❷–❸) is a basic hotel popular with foreign backpackers. Some rooms have a/c and TVs, but all have private bathrooms.

A **restaurant** to please all tastes, *Fuente de Soda El Capi*, on Avenida Evilio Roa, serves locals and tourists who appreciate its wide variety of Venezuelan dishes at reasonable prices. Tasty Llanos-style meat and roasted chicken can be found at *El Tranquero* on Avenida Perimetral, while the small, simple *La Arepita* on Calle Amazonas offers delicious *arepas*. It is closed Sundays.

Tours of Amazonas

Compressing all of the wonders of the Amazon into three days is impossible. However, if you just want a quick taste of the best the Venezuelan jungle has to offer, take a boat trip up the Sipapo and Autana rivers to the **Autana Tepui**, a stunning 1200-metre-high tabletop mountain with views of the jungle below. If you have more time, you can take what is known as the **Ruta Humboldt**, following in the footsteps of the famous explorer, an eight- to ten-day trip that takes tourists up many of the region's most important rivers. White-water rafting and fishing trips are also possible.

Several reputable companies in Puerto Ayacucho offer these tours, and most have their own jungle lodges. All-inclusive prices per day tend to be around US$50. **Turismo Yutajé** (☎0248/521-0604), at 31 Barrio Monte Bello, is one of the oldest but most expensive operators in the area. Its high-end campsite offers some of the highest quality accommodation in the area. **Cacao Expediciones** (☎0248/521-

3964, ®www.amazonasvenezuela.com/cacao), on Calle Piar, is a relatively new but very well-run operator with two jungle lodges. The Orinoquía Lodge, an attractive construction near Puerto Ayacucho, receives the majority of their customers, while the Ventuari Lodge, on the Ventuari River, is used primarily for serious fishing excursions. For independent travellers, the best option may be the reasonably priced **Coyote Expediciones** (®0248/521-4583) on Avenida Aguerrevere. **Aguas Bravas** (®0248/521-0541), on Avenida Río Negro, specializes in one-day or multi-day white-water rafting trips.

Crossing into Colombia

To get **to Colombia** from Puerto Ayacucho, there are two possible routes. From the port you can catch a frequently departing ferry (US$2), which crosses the Orinoco and leaves you in the small Colombian village of **Casuarito**. From there you can take a high-speed boat (US$10) to the larger city of **Puerto Carreño**, from where there are three weekly flights to **Bogotá** (see p.598) as well as other large cities.

Alternatively, you can take the San Fernando de Apure bus (US$3) from Puerto Ayacucho and get off after about two hours in the town of Puerto Páez. From there, you can take a quick boat ride to Puerto Carreño (US$2). In either case, it is good to get a **Venezuelan exit stamp** in your passport beforehand. This can be done at the DIEX office (Mon–Fri 8am–noon & 2–5pm) in Puerto Ayacucho, on Avenida Aguerrevere.

Bolívar

BOLÍVAR is the country's largest state and one of its richest too, thanks to abundant natural resources – gold, diamonds, iron, bauxite, manganese, quartz and titanium. Its three huge dams also produce 85 percent of the country's hydroelectric energy.

Much of the southeast part of the state is made up of the **Gran Sabana**, long plains punctuated by incredible *tepuis*. The Gran Sabana was formed by the Guayanese Massif, which, at 1.8 billion years, is claimed to be the oldest geographic formation on earth. Within the Gran Sabana is **Parque Nacional Canaima**, home to the celebrated Auyantepui, which spawns **Angel Falls**, and **Roraima**, another notable *tepui* in the southeastern corner of the state. The only two sizeable cities are **Ciudad Bolívar**, a pretty colonial town with a very rich history, and **Ciudad Guayana**, a characterless city recently created to be one of the country's primary industrial centres.

Ciudad Bolívar

CIUDAD BOLÍVAR, a colonial city of 350,000, is the ideal jumping-off point for exploring the state of Bolívar, especially for those who are budget conscious. The pleasant city contains some excellent museums as well as sights that afford visitors an insight into its storied past. The city was founded in 1764 and given the name Santo Tomé de Guayana de Angostura del Orinoco. For obvious reasons, most just called it Angostura, which refers to its position at the narrowest part of the Orinoco River. Ciudad Bolívar is perhaps best known for the pivotal role it played in the War of Independence. In 1817, Simon Bolívar came to reorganize his forces and plan what ended up being the final phase of the war. After winning the Battle of Boyacá, in which independence was gained for Colombia, he returned in 1819 to convene the Angostura Congress. The outcome was the founding of Gran Colombia, one nation consisting of Ecuador, Venezuela and Colombia. In 1846, the town was renamed Ciudad Bolívar to honour "El Libertador".

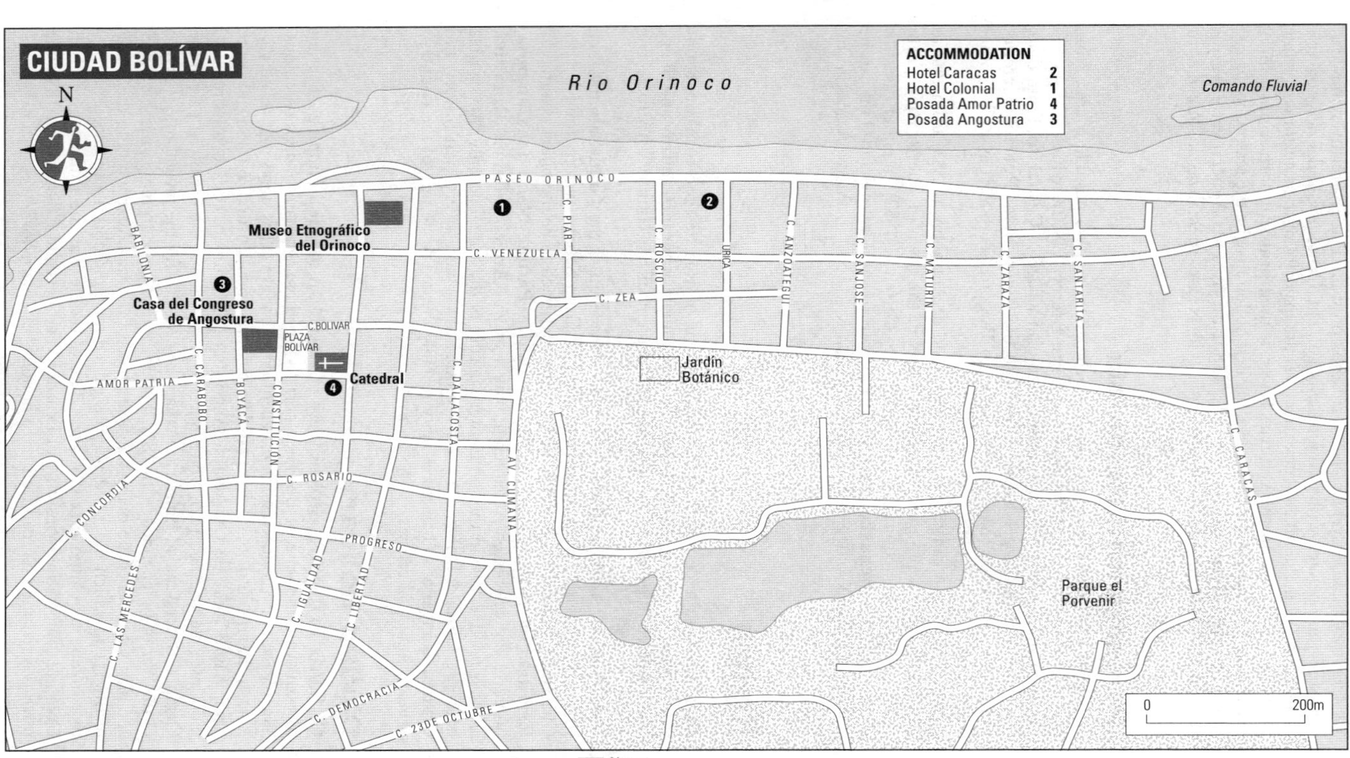
CIUDAD BOLÍVAR
N
ACCOMMODATION
Hotel Caracas 2
Hotel Colonial 1
Posada Amor Patrio 4
Posada Angostura 3
Rio Orinoco
Comando Fluvial
Mercado la Carioca
Bus Terminal and Punte de Angustura
Airport
PASEO ORINOCO
C. VENEZUELA
C. ZEA
C. BOLIVAR
C. PIAR
C. ROSCIO
URICA
C. ANZOATEGUI
C. SANJOSE
C. MATURIN
C. ZARAZA
C. SANTARITA
C. CARACAS
BABILONIA
C. CARABOBO
BOYACÁ
CONSTITUCIÓN
C. DALLACOSTA
AV. CUMANA
AMOR PATRIA
C. ROSARIO
PROGRESO
C. IGUALDAD
C. LIBERTAD
C. CONCORDIA
C. LAS MERCEDES
C. DEMOCRACIA
C. 23DE OCTUBRE
Museo Etnográfico del Orinoco
Casa del Congreso de Angostura
PLAZA BOLÍVAR
Catedral
Jardín Botánico
Parque el Porvenir
0
200m

Arrival and information

Owing to the relatively long distance between Ciudad Bolívar and many of the country's other attractions, most visitors arrive by air. There are three daily flights to and from Caracas, with a flight time of an hour and ten minutes. The **airport** is at the southeastern edge of town, at the intersection of Avenida Táchira and Avenida Aeropuerto. A **taxi** into town will only cost a dollar or two.

The **bus terminal** stands at the southern end of the city, at the intersection of Avenida Republica and Avenida Sucre. Most buses to Caracas (ten hours) leave between 6 and 11 in the evening, while those bound for Puerto Ayacucho (eleven hours) and Puerto La Cruz (four hours) run every hour or two. Buses to Ciudad Guayana (one hour) leave every half-hour. To Boa Vista, Brazil, there is generally only one bus, which leaves in the evening. The trip takes about fourteen hours, with a stopover in Santa Elena. There is no bus to Tucupita – you must go through Ciudad Guayana.

For general **information**, head to the Dirección de Turismo (Mon–Fri 9am–5pm; ⓣ0285/632-2362) on Av Bolívar at Av Táchira; its staff are among the most knowledgeable and helpful of all the tourism boards in the country. To get money from ATMs or exchange travellers' cheques, there is a Banco Mercantil on Paseo Orinoco and a CorpBanca at the intersection of avenidas Aeropuerto and Andrés Bello. The only **exchange** house in town is in the lobby of the *Hotel Laja Real*, also on Andés Bello.

Accommodation

While there are no luxury **hotels in** Ciudad Bolívar, there are some very good low-end and mid-range options in town.

Hotel Caracas Paseo Orinoco ⓣ0285/632-8512, ⓔexpediciones_dearuna@hotmail.com. Basic but colourful accommodation at outstanding prices. It's very backpacker-friendly with a pool table, football table, a bar, a terrace restaurant overlooking the Paseo Orinoco, and a good in-house tour operator (see Expediciones Dearuna below). ❷

Hotel Colonial Paseo Orinoco ⓣ0285/632-8390. The fifty-year-old *Hotel Colonial* is certainly past its prime, but has a good location and reasonable prices. Spacious rooms have a/c and hot water, and half have views of the Paseo Orinoco and the river (though some of the windows are cracked). ❸

Hotel La Cumbre Av 5 de Julio ⓣ0285/632-7709, ⓔlacumbre@cantv.net. Modern and innovative resurrection of a former top hotel, whose hilltop location gives its restaurant and rooms the best view of the city. Rooms have no TVs, phones or curtains – so be prepared to get up early and enjoy the beautiful sunrise. It's great value so reservations are recommended. ❹–❺

Posada Amor Patrio C Amor Patrio, n.30 ⓣ0285/632-8819, ⓔplazaBolívar@hotmail.com. This German-run posada in a 250-year-old house brimming with personality is a terrific budget option. All five rooms have distinct, attractive designs. Or for US$4, you can sleep in a hammock on the open-air top level. Communal kitchen and four communal bathrooms. ❷

Posada Angostura C Boyacaln.8 ⓣ0414/851-295, ⓦwww.cacaotravel.com. The new, upscale *Posada Angostura* is in a totally reconstructed colonial house two blocks from the Plaza Bolívar. Often full since owner Cacao Travel uses it for package tours. ❹

The City

Unsurprisingly, much of the city's colonial architecture is found within the **casco histórico**, a roughly ten-block area on the southern bank of the Orinoco River centred on the **Plaza Bolívar**. On the east side of the plaza, the imposing 1840 **Catedral** has a light, airy interior, which, while not particularly ornate, makes for a good escape from the midday heat. To the west of the plaza, the **Casa del Congreso de Angostura** (Tues–Sun 9am–5pm; free) is the site where the Angostura Congress founded Gran Colombia; Bolívar also lived here briefly in 1817. A quick peek reveals paintings of the original congressmen, an old printing press and archives of documents pertaining to Bolívar.

Plaza Bolívar may be the heart of the city, but the Ciudad Bolívar's pulse is best felt along the **Paseo Orinoco**. Two blocks to the north of the plaza, this bustling riverside thoroughfare is lined with stores and fishermen. The **Museo Etnográfico del Orinoco** (Tues–Sun 9am–noon & 2–5.30pm; free), at the Paseo's intersection with Calle Igualdad, is a decent museum containing information about local indigenous groups as well as aquariums with a number of Orinoco fish species. It is inside a building that formerly served as the governor's mansion and later as a prison. Heading west on Paseo, you'll come to the **Puente de Angostura**, notable for being the sole bridge that crosses the Orinoco River. It is prohibited to walk across, but you can hire a taxi to bring you back and forth. You may wish to stay in the taxi and head straight to the **Museo de Arte Moderno Jesús Soto** (Tues–Sat 9.30am–5.30pm, Sat & Sun 10am–5pm; free), just outside town on Avenida Germania. One of the city's highlights, the museum contains the fascinating works of Soto, generally regarded as Venezuela's most famous contemporary artist. Many of his paintings and sculptures make use of optical illusions, and you can ask to be accompanied by one of the guides, who will point out the visual tricks.

Towards late afternoon, as the heat subsides, consider a stroll through the well-maintained **Jardín Botánico** (Mon–Fri 8am–noon & 2–5pm; free) on Av Bolívar and C Caracas. The gardens contain plant species from all over the world, as well as a good restaurant and Internet café.

Eating and drinking

Ciudad Bolívar is not particularly noted for its **food**, but a few decent options exist. Local fish such as dorado, palometa and sapoara are usually fresh and tasty, but the meat varies in quality.

Canela Café C José Mendez and Av Andrés Bello. This small and simple café serves good, inexpensive breakfasts and has a large selection of lunches.

Mercado La Carioca East end of Paseo Orinoco. This is the ideal place to get a large and satisfying meal without spending much money. It has a number of small restaurants – locals prefer *Rincón de los Papillos* on the second floor.

Restaurant La Gran Fraternidad C Amor Patrio and C Dalla Costa. A peaceful vegetarian restaurant with large portions and good prices. They only serve lunch and are closed on weekends.

Ristorante Mezza Luna Av Tachira and Av Bolívar. One of the pricier restaurants in town, with elegant indoor and outdoor seating areas. They serve a variety of savoury Italian specialities and have a *gelato* cart on the patio.

Tasca La Traviata C Maracay and Av Táchira. This tastefully decorated restaurant-café-bar-disco serves an eclectic mix of delicious Mexican, American and Japanese dishes. The service is top-notch and prices are not as high as they should be.

Nightlife

The town's **nightlife** is hardly overwhelming and few of the options could avoid being classified as tacky. Little happens before Thursday. One of the more aesthetically and rhythmically pleasing places to dance is *Tasca La Traviata* (see above), while *La Noche*, on Avenida Bolívar in front of the *Hotel Jardín*, is a small bar-club that caters to a somewhat older, more affluent crowd. They have decent live music, but also a US$5 cover charge. *Baja*, in the *Hotel Laja Real*, is the only large dance club in town, and just after midnight on weekends it starts filling up with boisterous young revellers. *La Rumba*, on Avenida República, has live salsa and meringue music. It generally has a somewhat older crowd and is only open on weekends.

Tour operators

Ciudad Bolívar is the best place to book trips to Parque Nacional Canaima and the Gran Sabána (operators in Ciudad Guayana charge more and are accustomed to working with package groups). There are a number of operators, all with fairly similar products. Two very reputable companies can be found at the airport: **Bernal Tours** (☎0414/852-3293, ©bernaltours@terra.com.ve) and **Turismo Gekko**

(0285/632-6883, ⓔgekkotours@hotmail.com). Another very professional and well-priced operator is **Expediciones Dearuna** (ⓣ0285/632-6054, ⓔexpediciones_dearuna@yahoo.com) in the *Hotel Caracas*. All three offer a number of different options and combinations for Canaima and the Gran Sabana, as well as trips to the Río Caura region and the Orinoco Delta. Typical prices are US$270 for a three-day/two-night trip to Canaima, US$210 for a three-day/two-night trip to the Gran Sabana, and US$300 for the six-day/five-night climb up Mount Roraima. Expediciones Dearuna has the most economical option to Canaima because they are the only ones that go by land and boat (they return by plane). However, they need at least ten people to run the trip. For private city tours and transport you can call the bilingual and knowledgeable **Rodrigo Torres** (ⓣ0416/485-7244).

Ciudad Guayana

Though Ciudad Bolívar is a better jumping-off spot for the main attractions in Bolívar, **CIUDAD GUAYANA** still receives some visitors, mostly through pre-arranged package tours to Canaima. Lacking in history, culture and visual appeal, the city was founded in 1961 expressly as a major industrial centre, and has great economic importance for the country as a major iron, aluminium and hydroelectric energy producer. High wages have attracted workers from throughout the country and world, causing the population to jump to 600,000 in little over forty years.

Of the few attractions, the most interesting is a two-hour boat ride that takes visitors near one of the hydroelectric dams to the confluence of the Orinoco and Caroní rivers, and to two parks, Parque La Llovizna and Parque Cachamay, that feature nice waterfalls. The trip is arranged at the *Inter-Continental Guayana* through **Piraña Tours** (ⓣ0286/922-7748, ⓦwww.piranatours.com; US$36), one of the oldest and most respected operators in town. Otherwise, head for the **Ecomuseo de Caroní** (Tues–Sun 10am–9pm; free), next to the 23 de Enero dam. This modern building has a number of temporary exhibits of varied educational and entertainment value, and there is a large window through which you can see the dam's gargantuan generators.

There are three daily flights to and from Caracas, as well as daily flights to Barcelona, Valencia, Maracaibo, Barquisimeto and Porlamar. The **airport** is on the western edge of the city, on the road to Ciudad Bolívar. It has an Italcambio for exchanging money and travellers' cheques. The town's two **bus terminals** – Puerto Ordaz on Avenida Guayana, about ten minutes from the town centre, and San Felix on Avenida Gumilla, about five minutes from the centre – run most of the same routes, except that buses to Tucupita leave only from San Felix – twice daily and taking four hours. Other frequent routes are to Caracas (nine hours) and Puerto La Cruz (five hours). Buses to Ciudad Bolívar leave every half-hour and take an hour.

Practicalities

By far the nicest **hotel** in the area is the *Inter-continental Guayana* (ⓣ0286/920-1111, ⓦwww.interconti.com; ⑧), fifteen minutes east of Puerto Ordaz, with an extremely privileged position right across the Caroní River from the Salto Llovizna waterfalls. Rooms with views of the falls are slightly more expensive, and facilities include a pool, tennis court, gym and the city's only casino. *Residencias "Tore"* (ⓣ0286/923-0679, ⓔtore@cantv.net; ⑤), on Calle Cristóbal at Calle Los Andes, is a well-run, tour-group haven with fifty immaculate and well-equipped, but bland rooms. It's a bit far from the airport and bus terminal, but they offer free transfers.

Given the amount of money in the city, it's not surprising that there are some upscale **restaurants**. One of the best is *Restaurant La Romanina*, on Carrera Ciudad Piar, which specializes in pasta and fish dishes. For some typical Guayanese food – large helpings of barbecued beef, fried pork, *cachapas* with *queso guayanese* and yucca – a good bet is *Rinconcito*, on Avenida Las Americas behind Centro Comercial Santo

Tome 4. A large, open-air restaurant, it becomes more crowded and festive on weekends, when they have live music.

Parque Nacional Canaima

PARQUE NACIONAL CANAIMA, one of the world's largest national parks, receives surprisingly few visitors. Those that do come usually head to **Angel Falls**, the world's highest waterfall, and **Auyantepui**, the 700-square-kilometre *tepui* from which it falls, without taking full advantage of the breathtaking landscapes created by the many other *tepuis*, waterfalls and rivers. But you'll be well rewarded by spending more than just a day or two here, seeing some of the small villages and exploring the unique surroundings.

Said to be along one of the world's major energy meridians, which also passes through Macchu Picchu and Stonehenge, the park has induced many reports of visitors having extremely lucid dreams, experiencing spiritual rejuvenations and even seeing UFOs. Some believe the parks' mystical nature is related to its being one of the oldest places on Earth, for the *tepuis* date back to the Precambrian period (1.5 to 2 billion years ago). Indeed, seen from above, they appear very otherworldly, each an island unto itself with many endemic species of flora and fauna.

The park is inhabited by roughly 20,000 Pemón Indians, made up of three major tribes: Kamakoto, Arekuna and Taurepan. Most live in small villages with one to two hundred people. While some rely upon tourism, many still live on slash and burn farming and hunting. The majority have been converted by Catholic and Protestant missionaries, but still practise many of their traditional customs. They are extremely hospitable hosts and genuinely seem to enjoy receiving tourists from around the world; many speak Spanish and a few even speak English. Tour operators often suggest that visitors bring an extra T-shirt or hat to leave with the Pemóns.

To get beyond Angel Falls and **Canaima**, the village that provides easiest access to the falls, it's best to make arrangements through tour operators. One such operator is Angel Eco-Tours (Ⓦwww.angel-ecotours.com), which offers customized itineraries and very high quality service.

Canaima

The most visited village in the park, **CANAIMA** is generally favoured as a base for trips to Angel Falls. It has a population of 1200, the park's only paved airstrip and about ten different places to stay. Just beside the village are four postcard-worthy waterfalls – **Salto Hacha**, **Salto Ucaima**, **Salto Galondrina** and **Salto Guadima** – that emanate from the Río Carrao and empty into the picturesque **Laguna de Canaima**, which has small sand beaches along its banks. Tour packages generally include a short boat trip to another waterfall, **Salto El Sapo**, which you can actually walk right behind. The pathway through the falls was created by a Peruvian hermit Tomás Bernal, who carved it out of rock; be prepared to get a bit wet. After crossing behind the falls, continue walking a few minutes until you reach **Salto El Sapito**, a smaller but equally picturesque waterfall.

Practicalities

The only way to arrive in Canaima is by air, and **flights** leave regularly from Ciudad Bolívar and Puerto Ordaz. The airstrip is right on the edge of the village. **Accommodation** in the village ranges from semi-luxurious complexes to simple campsites with hammocks. A favourite among celebrity visitors is the attractive *Campamento Ucaima* (Ⓣ0286/962-2359, Ⓔucaima@etheron.net; ⑨). Founded over fifty years ago, it is still cosy and intimate and offers packages that include transfer from the airport and food – tours are optional. The same family owns *Campamento Parakaupa* (Ⓣ0286/961-4963, Ⓔparakaupa@etheron.net; ⑨), created as a somewhat more basic and economical option. Rooms are decorated with local artisan work and have great views of Salto Hacha. The meals, included in the package price are quite good. *Campamento Tomás Bernal* (☎0414/852-3293, ⓔbernaltours@terra.com.ve; ❹) is a rustic camp on the Isla Anatoly, in the Laguna de Canaima. Many guests have booked tours through the owner, Bernal Tours, in Ciudad Bolívar. Everyone sleeps in hammocks and shares communal bathrooms, and transfer from the airport is provided. One of the cheapest options in town is *Posada Kusari* (☎0286/962-0443; ❷). It has twelve simple rooms with private bathrooms and fans. If they are full, you can go next door to the equally basic *Posada Kaikuse* (☎0414/884-0931; ❷).

One stand-alone **dining** option is *Imawari*, also known as *Simón*, on the south side of the village. A large, simple restaurant, it serves typical Venezuelan fish, chicken and meat dishes at decent prices.

Angel Falls and Auyantepui

Officially discovered in 1935 by daredevil American pilot Jimmie Angel, **ANGEL FALLS** was of course already well known to the Pemón, who called it *Kerapukai-merú*, or "falls from the deepest place". They believed that at the top lived *mawari*, or spirits in human form, who were able to steal the souls of the living, and for that reason never ascended the *tepui*.

At 980 metres, Angel Falls is the world's highest waterfall – over twenty times the height of Niagara Falls and fifteen times the height of Iguazà Falls (see pp.130 & 448). It is created by the Churún River, which makes a dramatic free fall off the edge of the enormous Auyantepui and into the verdant jungle below. The result is an extremely long and thin stream of water that some describe as a silver braid.

Seeing the falls from the air is an unforgettable experience. Some of the smaller planes will fly right above the **Auyantepui**, following the Churún River until it drops off the precipice. The flight not only affords a tremendous view of the falls, but also a sense of the incredible dimensions and unique landscapes of Auyantepui. On the surface of the 700-square-kilometre tabletop mountain, shrouded in mist, are eerie rock formations reminiscent of Stonehenge.

Seeing the falls from below is also a must. If you do not come to Canaima, a tour operator can arrange the roughly US$100 day-trip through any of the *campamentos* or posadas in the village. The first leg of the trip is a three-hour, seventy-kilometre boat ride from Canaima; the second leg is an hour-and-a-half hike through the jungle, ending at the falls' principal vantage point. The falls themselves are generally fuller, and therefore more spectacular, during the rainy season; the trade-off is less visibility as the top of the falls is often covered in clouds during those months.

Gran Sabana

Although the 35,000-square-kilometre **GRAN SABANA** technically includes Angel Falls and most of Parque Nacional Canaima, trips to Gran Sabana do not. Rather, they go to the vast area that extends southeast to the Brazilian border. Just before the border is where one of the principal attractions lies: the beautiful and climbable *tepui* **Mount Roraima**. But the entire region is filled with magnificent *tepuis* and waterfalls, separated by vast expanses of grasslands. One of the most famous waterfalls is **Quebrada de Jaspe**, noted for its bright red jasper rock. Other well-known waterfalls in the region include the 105-metre-high **Salto Aponguao**, which has natural pools to swim in at its base, and **Quebrada Pacheco**, two pretty waterfalls with natural pools and waterslides at its base.

The region has only one road, which was not fully paved until 1990. Because travel without your own means of transport is impossible, most visitors come with tour companies based in Ciudad Bolívar (see p.1060). While the region also has only one town, Santa Elena de Uairén, which offers easy access to Mount Roraima, there are over 200 settlements inhabited by Pemón Indians scattered across the territory.

Santa Elena de Uairén

SANTA ELENA DE UAIRÉN grew significantly when the paved road connecting it with the rest of the country was completed, but it's still a rather quiet town, with a population of only 15,000. Many of its inhabitants are originally from Brazil, whose border is just fifteen kilometres south of town, and a number of the Brazilians contribute to what is a fairly impressive array of reasonably priced lodging and dining options. The town also has a number of tour operators that specialize in trips through the Gran Sabana and up Mount Roraima (see below).

Practicalities

The town is accessible by **air**, although routes are limited and the planes tend to be very old and very small. Daily flights leave from Ciudad Bolívar and weekly flights leave from Puerto Ordaz. A **bus** leaves Ciudad Bolívar and takes around ten hours to reach Santa Elena. From Puerto Ordaz, five or six buses leave daily and generally take about eight or nine hours.

The town has its fair share of decent **accommodation**. Towards the high end, *Villa Fairmont* (Ⓣ0289/995-1022, Ⓔinfo@posadaturistica.com; ❺) is a group of thatched-roof houses at the end of the divided boulevard in the Akurimá area. Each comfortable, attractive room is named after, and has a photo of, a Gran Sabana waterfall. Amenities include a/c, hot water, cable TV and a small refrigerator. *Cabañas Friedenau* (Ⓣ0289/995-1353, Ⓔfriedanau@cantv.net; ❹), on Av Principal Urbanización Cielo Azul) is a compound with *cabañas* for up to six and also "mini-suites" for two to three people. The prices are quite good considering the personalized service and more than adequate facilities. *Casa de Gladys* (Ⓣ0289/995-1171, Ⓔcasadegladys@cantv.net; ❷) at 187 C Urdaneta is a popular backpacker's refuge with Internet access and a communal kitchen. Guests can sleep in simple rooms with private baths or in a dormitory-type room. At the cheaper end of the spectrum is the *Hospedaje Michelle* (Ⓣ0289/995-1415; ❶), on C Urdaneta at Av Perimetral, which has six very basic, but for the most part clean, rooms and one shared bathroom.

One of the most popular **restaurants** in town is *Venezuela Primero*, on Avenida Perimetral, not surprising given the quantity and quality of food offered. *Café Madrigal* on Calle Bolívar is a beautifully decorated café with a nice variety of sandwiches and natural juices. Another good café, which has the added bonus of Internet access is *Café Goldfieber*, on Calle Urdaneta. The German owners offer some tasty specialities from their homeland. If in the mood for pizza or hamburgers, the name *Pizzas Texas* says it all; it's on Avenida Perimetral.

While there are a number of **tour operators**, two of the best established are Ruta Salvaje Tours (Ⓣ0289/995-1134, Ⓦgeocities.com/rutagransabana) and Frontiers Adventure Tours (Ⓣ0289/995-1584, Ⓦwww.newfrontiersadventures.com). Both offer two- and three-day Gran Sabana jeep tours for US$25–50 per day, but generally do not leave with fewer than four people, which can make matters complicated if you are in a smaller group. Hiking trips up Mount Roraima generally last six days and cost around US$250.

Crossing into Brazil

If you are **crossing into Brazil**, you will need a visa, and the Brazilian consulate (weekdays 8am–noon), near the intersection of Av Gran Mariscal and Av Perimetral on the northeast end of town, generally takes at least a day to process the request. Two daily buses make the four-hour trip from Santa Elena to **Boa Vista** in Brazil, from where you can make the twelve-hour connection to **Manaus** (see p.401).

Mount Roraima

Around 150 years ago, European explorers in the area were entranced by **MOUNT RORAIMA**. Tales of this over 2700-metre high *tepui* swirled around Europe, and many climbers grew obsessed with the idea of being the first to reach the top, a feat first achieved in 1884 by Everard Im Thorn and Harry Perkins, who were financed by the Royal Geographic Society of London. Nowadays, the rewarding six-day climb is undertaken by many foreigners, some of who consider it one of the best hikes in all of South America. Although not technically difficult, it is physically demanding, especially with packs full of camping equipment and food. Porters as well as guides are available in town, although some come with tour groups.

Once atop the *tepui*, few regret making the time and effort. You'll see mist-shrouded rock formations that have been carved into striking shapes by the passage of wind and water; crystal clear ponds and odd-looking vegetation, including many endemic species. When there is no cloud cover, views from the top are even more remarkable, as you can see down upon much of the Gran Sabana.But be sure to bring rain gear and a plastic bag or cover for your backpack year-round, as the weather is never predictable.

Delta Amacuro

DELTA AMACURO is best known for the Orinoco Delta, one of the world's largest river deltas. In fact, the state's entire landmass was formed by sediment left behind by the Orinoco River on its way out to sea. Besides the Orinoco, the state has many other rivers and over 300 *caños*, which are small waterways that often link the rivers. From above, the entire area looks like an enormous labyrinth.

Created in 1991, Delta Amacuro is Venezuela's newest state; it is also one of the poorest. Economic activity is for the most part limited to farming, cattle ranching and some oil drilling. The population of the entire state is only 135,000, more than half of which lives in the state capital and only real town, **Tucupita**. A large population of Warao Indians lives primarily along the Orinoco and other rivers. The area is not heavily visited despite its unique ecosystem.

Tucupita

There's really no reason to come to dreary **TUCUPITA** unless you're passing through on the way to one of the delta's river lodges. Nothing seems to work and the selection of hotels is dismal. Not surprisingly, plane routes to Tucupita were recently cancelled. From San Felix, two **buses** leave daily, but *por puestos* leave fairly regularly. The whole trip takes around three hours. Four or five buses go back and forth between Caracas daily – the trip takes about nine hours. If you must **stay** over an evening, the only really good deal is the *Pequeño Hotel* (☎0287/721-0523; ❷) on 32 C La Paz. This eleven-room hotel, run by cordial owner Roselia Marcano, feels more like a guesthouse. Rooms are plain, but clean with private bathrooms, and doors close at 10pm. One of the best budget **dining** options in town is *Mi Tasca*, on Calle Dalla Costa between C La Paz and Av Arismendi. It's long on variety, but short on ambience. Try the *lau-lau al ajillo*, a local fish cooked in garlic sauce.

Trips to the delta

Several operators in Tucupita have **delta lodges**, ranging from very rustic to relatively luxurious. Activities are generally the same no matter where you go and encompass visiting indigenous **Warao villages** to see and buy crafts, **canoeing** through the small *caños*, **piraña fishing**, exploring the tropical forest areas to see local flora and fauna and night trips to catch cayman. The operators offer package tours that include river transport to and from Tucupita, accommodation, food and all daily excursions. Most visitors stay two or three evenings, but for those who stay more, some of the operators have smaller lodges further downriver. Using these remote lodges as a base, visitors are likely to see a bit more wildlife, meet Waraos who have had less contact with the outside world, and even travel out to where the *caños* empty out into the sea. Packages cost between US$60 and US$110 per person per day. The following four operators are the most reliable. A few other smaller lodges seem to go in and out of business frequently.

Aventura Turistica Delta C Centurión, no. 62 ⓣ0287/721-0835. Because it takes walk-ins and is relatively inexpensive, this operator is popular with backpackers. The French owners have two camps in the northern part of the delta. Both are fairly rustic – visitors sleep in hammocks. Packages cost US$60–75 per day, depending upon group size.

Delta Surs C Pativilca at C Mariño ⓣ0287/721-3840. This is one of the few operators to have lodges in the southern part of the delta, which is considered to be more "virgin". Its principal lodge, *Maraisa*, is about eight hours by boat from Tucupita. It contains ten fairly rustic *cabañas*, which have beds and hammocks. The three-day, two-night package costs US$180–220 per person, depending upon group size. Delta Surs was the first to build a lodge and is also the only locally owned operator. Unfortunately, it is not very well organized and can be hard to contact before arriving in Tucupita.

Mis Palofitos in front of the Plaza Bolívar in the Centro Comercial Delta Centre ⓣ0287/721-5166, ⓔmispalofitos@cantv.net. Mis Palofitos's lodge of the same name caters to tour groups that come from Isla Margarita. One of the most expensive lodges, costing US$300 for a three-day, two-night package, it is in the northern part of the delta, two-and-a-half hours from Tucupita by speedboat. Built in local Warao style, its 39 attractive *cabañas* all have beds and private bathrooms. It also has a number of pets, including a capybara and an otter. Greek owner Alexis Marmonides also runs the *Hotel Saxxi* (see listing above).

Tucupita Expeditions C Las Acacias across from the hospital ⓣ0287/721-1953, ⓦwww.orinoco delta.com. The *Orinoco Delta Lodge* is similar to *Mis Palofitos* in terms of quality, size, price and location. The only real difference is that the *cabañas* are a bit larger and more attractive. Tucupita Expeditions also has a more remote lodge generally used for sportfishing. The tour guides, some of whom speak English, are wholly good. Pets include a jaguar, otter, howler monkey and porcupine.

11.6

The northeast coast and islands

The **NORTHEAST COAST** sports some of the country's most popular and secluded beaches. To the far east, in the state of Sucre, the **Paria Peninsula**, centred on **Rio Caribe**, is far enough from the urban centres to remain largely undeveloped, and the lack of crowds, along with the stark beauty of the verdant mountain backdrops, lead some connoisseurs to pronounce its beaches Venezuela's finest.

To the west, the frequently visited **Parque Nactional Mochima National Park** is split between the states of Sucre and Anzoátegui. Like Morrocoy (p.1034), it has a number of uninhabited keys for visitors to explore in chartered boats. However, the landscapes are quite distinct. Instead of Morrocoy's lush vegetation, the keys here are characterized by rocky terrain with little vegetation besides cacti.

Isla Margarita is one of two well-known island areas off the coast. Built in the style of some of the Caribbean's most famous (or infamous) mega-resort areas, it is a huge magnet for Venezuelans and international package tourists. In direct contrast, **Los Roques** is a protected archipelago made up of small pristine islands. The immaculate beaches are never crowded, as the number of visitors is restricted to the privileged few who can afford the plane ticket and expensive accommodation, not to mention the exclusive yacht tours.

Río Caribe and around

In the early 1900s, pleasant **RÍO CARIBE** was one of the country's major cacao-exporting centres, and seeing the pastel-coloured colonial buildings from its heyday, it seems that little of this small fishing village of only 15,000 inhabitants has changed. Indeed life seems to move very slowly here, making it ideal for some relaxation time. The impulse to stay is furthered by the town's wonderful accommodation, nearby beaches and easy day-trips to cacao and water buffalo ranches.

As Río Caribe has no airport or bus terminal, you will have to pass through the larger and less interesting town of Carúpano, a cheap, twenty-minute ride away by *por puesto*. The Carúpano **airport** receives three daily flights from Caracas and the **bus terminal** receives hourly arrivals from Caracas (nine hours) and Puerto La Cruz (three hours) and four daily arrivals from Maturín (three hours) and San Felix (eight hours). Changing money in Río Caribe is difficult, so you are best off doing so in Carúpano. There's also no official **tourism office**, but you can find out everything you need to know at the *Pariana Café* on Avenida Bermúdez. Friendly owner Támara Rodgriguez is very knowledgeable and can help you find great day tours.

Practicalities

Quality **accommodation** can be found in several price ranges. At the top end is the *Caribana* (☎0294/696-1242, ⓔcaribanainn@cantv.net; ❺), owner Gonzalo Denis's stylish restoration of an old colonial house on Avenida Bermúdez, with ample and attractive rooms. They also offer a wide range of day-trips at decent prices. *Villa Antillana* (☎0294/646-1413, ⓔantilla99@cantv.net; ❹) on Calle Rivero is a stunning, colonial-style posada with excellent service and great prices. Painted in pastels, its rooms are large and beautifully decorated. *Pensión Papagayos* (☎0294/646-1868; ❷) on Calle 14 de febrero is one of the best budget hotels in the country. It has four tastefully decorated rooms and two even nicer communal bathrooms. Reserve at least a week in advance during high season. A more basic and slightly less expensive budget option is *Posada Doña Eva* (☎0294/646-1465) on the Plaza Bolívar. Its four rooms are clean, with private bathrooms but limited furniture.

The *Pariana Café* (see p.1067), which serves a variety of local dishes, is also the best **restaurant** and bar in town. It is closed on Sundays. Another good dining option is *Mi Cocina* on Calle Juncal. The atmosphere is a bit tacky, but the fried fish and other plates are ample and inexpensive.

Around Río Caribe

There are two **buffalo ranches** within an hour of Río Caribe, both owned and run by Germans who came to the area many years ago to employ innovative sustainable development practices. Typical visits involve education tours of the premises, canoeing in water channels amongst water buffalo and birdwatching. *Hato Río de Agua* (☎0416/894-4122, ⓔwilfried@telcel.net.ve), owned by Wilfried Merle, is a 540-hectare ranch home to over 500 water buffalo. *Hacienda Vuelta Larga* (☎0294/666-9052) is owned by Klaus Muller, whose son Daniel gives excellent tours in English or Spanish. The ranch is home to 450 water buffalo and 230 species of birds.

Between the two buffalo ranches, about 45 minutes from Río Caribe, the *Hacienda Termales Aguasana* (☎0212/265-9150; ❺) is situated right on a geographic fault, with seventeen small **thermal baths** of varied temperatures. The water and mud are reputed to have therapeutic properties, and it is best to go in the early evening when it's a bit cooler outside. Day visits costs about US$2, but some choose to spend the evening there. The hacienda features six basic but attractive rooms, each with fans and a private bathroom. Massages are also available.

Hacienda Bukare (☎0294/808-1509, ⓔbukare@cantv.net; ❺) is a pretty, early twentieth-century **cacao plantation** that offers hour-long tours and overnight stays. Tours, which cost around US$2, take participants through the whole chocolate producing process – from fruits growing in the garden to scrumptious bonbons they offer as samples. The colonial-style house has four gorgeous guestrooms ideal for honeymooners. Outside the rooms are gardens and a small, circular pool.

Of course, most visitors come to the northeast coast for its picturesque **beaches**, several of which are to the east of Río Caribe. **Playa de Uva** is a private, secluded beach with a stunning posada of the same name (☎0416/781-3705, ⓔcaribanainn@cantv.net; ❻), built by the owner of the *Caribana*. Packages including transfer and meals cost about US$35 per person. Further east is **Playa Medina**, which has achieved fame for its white sand, towering palms, and lush mountain backdrop. Lying in a protected cove, it is ideal for swimming yet rarely crowded. On weekends and holidays, local vendors offer delicious fried fish for around US$3. The only accommodation on the beach is *Cabañas de Playa Medina* (☎0294/331-5241, ⓔplayamedina@cantv.net; ❺–❻). Each of the attractive, bi-level *cabañas* has two bedrooms, a comfortable living room, and a small kitchen. It is best to reserve a few weeks ahead of time during high season. The most economical option near the beach is the *Posada El Milagro* (☎0416/794-5291; ❹), 2km before the beach, just before the split in the road. It has nice, simple rooms with floor fans and decent private bathrooms. But they are not mosquito-proof, so enter at your own risk between May and September. Eight kilometres beyond Playa Medina along a pock-marked road is **Playa Pui-Puy**, whose currents make it popular with surfers, but swimming is not advisable.

Parque Nacional Mochima

The 95,000-hectare **PARQUE NACIONAL MOCHIMA** was created in 1973 to protect 36 uninhabited keys and the surrounding coastal area. The seaside cliffs and keys have rugged landscapes with little vegetation, and much of the park's beauty lies in the stunning contrast between the red earth tones of the rocks and the emerald green water. While the beaches are not as conventionally beautiful as those of Morrocoy and Pittier national parks, which have lighter sand, clearer water and more vegetation, the snorkelling and scuba diving is just as good, if not better here. Extensive coral reef formations can be found around the rocky, deserted Islas Caracas, Isla Chimana Grande and Islas Borrachas; this last also features underwater caves.

The most popular beach in the park is easily accessible **Playa Colorada**. It has extensive facilities including a few good accommodation options within walking distance. More accommodation can be found in **Mochima**, a small village that has decent, locally owned facilities but no beach. **Santa Fe** is a backpacker haven with inexpensive lodging right on a unremarkable beach. One final option for stays is **Puerto La Cruz**, a high-rise hotel, fast-food paradise geared towards the Venezuelan mass market. At each location there are a number of boats that offer day tours of the keys. These generally include several snorkelling opportunities and brief stopovers at a few ditto beaches.

Mochima

A former fishing village now almost entirely dedicated to tourism, **MOCHIMA** did not exist until 1979, when the road connecting the town to the main coastal highway was built. Now, nearly every house in town rents out rooms to tourists – most of whom are Venezuelan – although few actually have signs posted. Many former fishermen use their boats to take tourists to the keys of the national park. The town has no beach – just a dock from which boat trips leave.

To reach Mochima, you will need to pass through Cumaná, around 20km to the northeast. On Avenida Arismendi, just off the Redoma El Indio, you will see a *por puesto* stand. They leave regularly and cost about US$1. While in Cumaná you can change money at several banks on Avenida Bermúdez, since there is no place to change in Mochima.

Practicalities

Accommodation is generally more expensive than that in Santa Fe. *Posada Gaby* (☎0414/773-1104; ⑤) is the town's top **hotel**, although the service is substandard and the bright yellow and lime green walls, rainbow-coloured couches and plastic flowers are more than a little tacky. Nevertheless, it's a decent deal considering that the price includes breakfast and boat trips to the keys. *Villa Vicenta* (☎0293/416-0916; ③–④) is a three-storey guesthouse with good views and attractive stonewall rooms. Interiors vary a bit so look around – room 5 is a good choice. Air conditioning costs US$2 extra. The cheapest option in town is *Posada Beatriz* (☎0414/773-2262; ②), which has three simple but clean rooms with decent private bathrooms. Two recommended **restaurants** with tasty local dishes and nice sea views are *El Puerto Viejo* (closed Wednesdays) and *El Guayacan* (closed Mondays).

For **diving** and **rafting** trips, head to Mochima Divers (Ⓣ0212/961-2531, Ⓔfaverola@cantv.net). English-speaking Rodolfo Plaza, a very experienced diver, offers two-tank trips for US$50–70 per person. He also offers rafting trips on class 1–4 rapids in the Río Neverí for about US$30 per person. Those taking trips can stay for about US$5 per night in humble accommodation at his house.

Santa Fe

Like Mochima, **SANTA FE** was also once predominantly a fishing village. Now, through hospitality training and beach conservation efforts led by an ex-journalist, it has become a magnet for foreign backpackers. Ten small posadas, most charging around US$9 per night, line the thin beach. Santa Fe is in fact one of the few locations in Venezuela where you can actually stay on the beach. Ordinances prevent building on the beach, but most of the posadas here are remodelled houses that used to belong to fishermen. The beach is not particularly attractive, but the weak current allows for easy swimming and kayaking. **Dolphin sightings** occur year-round and whale sightings generally occur from November to May.

Despite the good prices and beach location, some tourists are deterred by reports of **security problems** related to widespread drug use and robberies. Visitors who exercise caution, however, can generally avoid problems. Changing money in Cumaná may be a good idea, since there is nowhere to do so here. The only place to access the Internet is in *La Sierra Inn* (see below).

Practicalities

By far the top **accommodation** in the area can be found 7km east of Santa Fe on highway to Cumaná. *Villa Majagual* (Ⓣ0293/433-2120, Ⓔmajagul V@aol.com; ❽) has an impeccable reputation based on excellent service, world-class food, terrific snorkelling off a private beach and beautiful seaside *cabañas* with sea views. Back in town, the posadas are very similar in terms of size, quality and price. All are have fans and private bathrooms and are all practically right next to each other on the beach. They fill up very quickly in the high season, so it is a good idea to reserve in high season. Luxury accommodation exists at *Playa Santa Fe Resort & Dive Centre* (Ⓣ0414/840-1055, Ⓦwww.santaferesort.com; ❹–❻), where the top-end rooms are beautifully decorated, with sea views and all major amenities. Budget rooms aren't nearly as nice. For that, it's better to head to a posada like *La Sierra Inn* (Ⓣ0293/231-0042, Ⓔplayacochaimaposadasierrainn@hotmail.com; ❷). Run by English-speaking tourism pioneer José Vivas, this is the best deal on the beach. Rooms in Andes-style stone building are decorated with furniture and paintings from Mérida. *Posada Bahia del Mar* (Ⓣ0293/231-0073; ❷) is a simple, pleasant place towards the end of the beach. It's almost always full, so reserve a few weeks in advance – ask for one of the rooms with a sea view.

Eating options in Santa Fe are limited. Certainly the best and priciest restaurant is *El Club Nautico* (closed Wed), right on the beach. Before opening the restaurant, owner Anibal Lozano was a renowned chef in Caracas. One of his specialities is paella, which must be ordered a day in advance. The place for cheap, hearty breakfasts is the *Posada Cochaima* (see above). *Café y Posada del Mar* also has decent food, with a covered seating area right on the beach.

Day-trips and water sports

Day-trips to some of the park's keys leave every morning in front of *Café y Posada del Mar*. They charge around US$5 per person and provide snorkelling equipment, but no food or drinks. These can be purchased at the nearby market. Sea **kayaks** can be rented at several posadas for about US$4 per hour. *Kayak Playa Cochaima* (Ⓣ0416/681-4678, Ⓔkayakplayacochaima@hotmail.com) offers kayak trips either in the surrounding sea or though class 1 or 2 rapids on the Río Neverí for around

US$15 per person. *Playa Santa Fe Resort and Dive Centre* (see opposite) offers scuba-diving trips for US$65 (two tanks) and water skiing for US$45 per hour.

Playa Colorada

Lying in a protected cove lined with swaying palm trees, **PLAYA COLORADA** has blue-green water and a swathe of tan, almost red sand from which it derives its name. Unfortunately, it is also riddled with innumerable beach chairs and aluminium food stands with Coca-Cola logos. On weekends and holidays, when the crowds can be unbearable and blasting radios vie with one another in a total cacophony, just walking along the beach is like going through an obstacle course. Consequently, Playa Colorada only merits a visit during weekdays or low season. Directions for arriving are the exact same as for Santa Fe – the *por puesto* in Cumana goes to both destinations.

For those who want a **place to stay** there are a few possibilities about a half kilometre behind the beach. *Hotel Villas Turisticas Playa Colorada* (☎0416/681-6365; ❺), otherwise known as *Tucusito*, is a somewhat luxurious, but plain hotel on the Avenida Principal, whose rooms are very large, with rather dated furniture. Facilities include a restaurant, nice pool, and a boat for key tours. *Posada Nirvana* (☎0414/803-0101; ❸–❹), on Calle Merchant, is a nice guesthouse with seven rooms that vary in size, design and amenities. Find one you like and then negotiate the price with Swiss owner Rita. Across the street is *Posada Jaly* (☎0416/681-8113; ❷), a terrific bargain. The five-room posada is ideal for foreigners, with a multilingual French–Canadian owner, a book exchange and a communal kitchen/barbecue. It is also possible to camp on the beach for about US$1.50 per tent. As in most parts of the country, it is not recommended to camp during the week or when there are few others around.

Most visitors eat the fried fish and other food at the stalls on the beach. But locals say the best **meals** are served at *Café Las Carmitas*, a small, inexpensive restaurant less than five minutes from the beach. It is just off the Avenida Principal on the tercera transversal, or third cross street.

Puerto La Cruz

It's hard to imagine that the modern, bustling city of **PUERTO LA CRUZ** is not long removed from being a small fishing village. Venezuelans come here for its proximity to Parque Nacional Mochima and the **ferry to Isla Margarita** (see p.1072); the fast-food restaurants and fifteen-storey hotels certainly don't make it an overly attractive place to spend much time. However, the city has torn down hotels directly on the beach to creating a wide pedestrian walkway along Paseo Colón and make it more palatable to those coming for cruise stops.

From Santa Fe, Mochima or Playa Colorada, take a *por puesto*, which should take a half-hour to forty minutes and cost around US$1.50. It will let you off near the beach or at the **bus terminal**, just a few blocks from the Plaza Bolívar, on Calle Democracia at Calle Concordia, though at the time of writing there is talk of it moving.

Practicalities

Bargain seekers will find few good **accommodation** options; those seeking luxury accommodation will be a bit more pleased. *Hesperia* (☎0281/265-3611, ⓦwww.hoteles-hesperia.es; ❾) on the Paseo Colón is a well-run, five-star hotel with tennis courts, a large pool, a private beach, and the area's only casino. *Cristal Park* (☎0281/267-0744; ❺), on Calle Libertad at Calle Buenos Aires, is a relatively new hotel just a few blocks from the Paseo Colón. Rooms are rather large and tastefully decorated. One of the better low-end options is *Hotel Comercio* (☎0281/265-1429; ❹), on Calle Maneiro at Calle Libertad. It is a 1970s hotel that looks every bit the part, but the rooms have cable TV, phones, a/c and hot water.

Most of the town's **restaurants** are found along the Paseo Colón. *O Sole Mio* is a fairly upscale restaurant serving delicious pizzas and pastas. *Café Piccolo*, open 24 hours, serves above average breakfasts and sandwiches. To exchange money, go to the Italcambio in the Centro Comercial Paseo del Mar on Paseo Colón. It's open 8.50am–5pm during the week and 9am–1pm on Saturday.

For **diving** and other **water sports**, head to Aquatic Adventures (☎0281/267-3256) at the northeast end of Paseo Colón. To explore the islands of Mochima, go to one of the two *embarcaderos* (docks), which are on both ends of Paseo Colón. They leave every half-hour or so and charge about US$4 per person.

Isla Margarita

On the ferry to **ISLA MARGARITA** from the mainland, you're unlikely to see more than one or two backpacks, as the 940-square-kilometre island is primarily visited by well-to-do Venezuelans and European tourists who come over on relatively cheap package deals. While the main draws here are the beaches, duty-free shopping and nightlife, the beaches are not as spectacular as many on the mainland, few foreigners will find the shopping all that inexpensive and the nightlife does not really warrant the journey. Prices are higher here than on the mainland, but the quality of service is much better. Finding any traces of cultural authenticity can be a challenge, as the mega-resorts have mushroomed at a steady pace for over twenty years, supplanting some of the more traditional structures.

While most of this development has been centred on **Porlamar**, the island's largest city, visitors may prefer staying at the smaller and better preserved town of **Pampatar**, which has a few small posadas in town and large resorts on the outskirts. Near the most visited beach on the island, **Playa El Agua**, you can also find hotels of varying sizes.

Three different **ferries** go to Isla Margarita. The Conferry two-hour express, which costs around US$15 whether you are with car or without, leaves three times daily from its terminal, about a kilometre west of the Puerto La Cruz town centre. A second option is the Conferry five-hour conventional ferry, which costs as little as US$5 and makes three daily departures from the Conferry terminal. The two-hour Gran Cacique Express (US$13) is just a passenger boat that makes three departures from its own dock right next door to the Conferry terminal. No matter which ferry you choose, you must go to the terminal to buy tickets beforehand; the wait could be anywhere from ten minutes to four hours.

Porlamar

For better or worse, **PORLAMAR**, a town of close to 100,000, is the commercial centre of the island, featuring most of its duty-free shopping, the principal places lining Avenida Santiago Mariño. The town is simply not attractive, has little in the way of tourist attractions and has become a bit dangerous, especially after dark. Most of the new, upscale hotels, therefore, have been built outside town, primarily in the Costa Azul suburb, which is the island's nightlife epicentre.

Arrivals in Margarita are by ferry or plane. **Ferries** arrive from Puerto La Cruz and Cumana at Punta Piedras, 29km southwest of Porlamar; *por puestos* are usually available. **Flights** from all over the country arrive regularly into the airport, 20km to the southwest of Porlamar, where you can hail taxis or *por puestos*. Margarita is easily the best place in the country to **rent a car** because of its well-marked roadways and much lower prices. Rentals start at around US$40 per day and can be done through one of the many agents at the airport. To book in advance, you can contact Budget (☎0295/269-1047); to **exchange money**, head to the Italcambio in the Ciudad Comercial Jumbo.

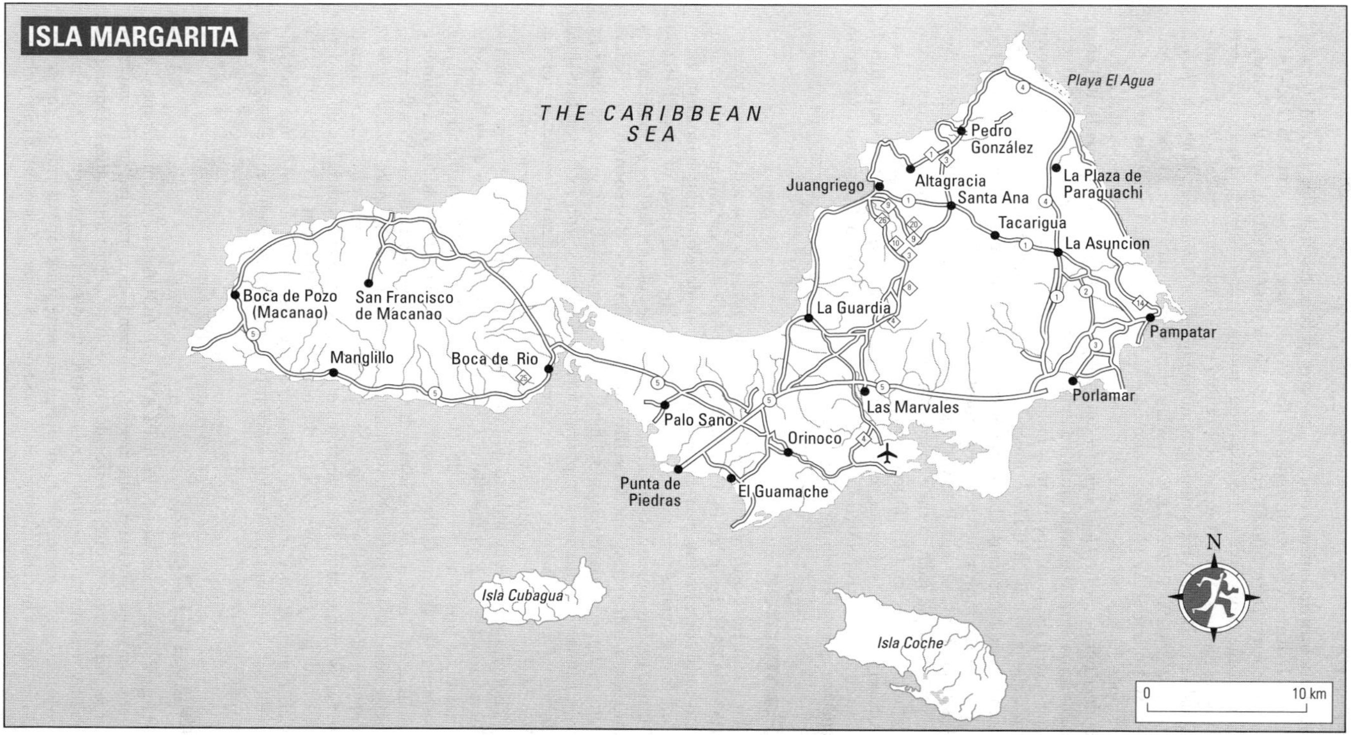

ISLA MARGARITA

THE CARIBBEAN SEA
Playa El Agua
Pedro González
La Plaza de Paraguachi
Juangriego
Altagracia
Santa Ana
Tacarigua
La Asuncion
La Guardia
Pampatar
Porlamar
Las Marvales
Orinoco
Palo Sano
Punta de Piedras
El Guamache
Boca de Pozo (Macanao)
San Francisco de Macanao
Manglillo
Boca de Rio
Isla Cubagua
Isla Coche
N
0
10 km

Practicalities

Most **accommodation** comes in the form of large resorts, often owned by international chains. One such option is the *Best Western Dynasty* (℡0295/262-1411, Ⓦwww.bestwestern.com; ❼), on Calle los Uveros in Costa Azul, with the best deals of the large chain hotels. It has spacious rooms with kitchens and balconies overlooking the large pool. Reserve at least two weeks in advance to get special promotional rates. Better is the stunning boutique hotel *La Samanna de Margarita Hotel & Thalasso* (℡0295/262-2222, Ⓦwww.lasamannademargarita.com; ❽), in Costa Azul on Av Bolívar at Av Gomez. Rooms are stylishly decorated, with handsome furnishings. It's not on the beach, but it has two pools and an impressive spa. A good budget option is the *Hotel Imperial* (℡0295/261-6420; ❹), on Avenida Raúl Leoni right across from the beach; fully equipped rooms come with sea views. At the very low end of the price spectrum is *Hotel Malecón* (℡0414/786-9973; ❷), downtown on Calle la Marina at Calle Arismendi. It's a bit dingy, but has decent-sized rooms with private bathrooms. The neighbourhood is not considered safe after 10pm.

Perhaps the most renowned **restaurant** on the island is *Cocody Restaurant*, on Av Raúl Leoni at C Ortega. It serves elegant French cuisine and, unsurprisingly, is fairly pricey. *Utopia Café*, in the Centro Comercial Costa Azul, offers Internet access, delicious coffee and hamburgers with over forty toppings. A good, economical Italian restaurant is *Alinsuca*, on C Cedeño and Av 4 de Mayo. As far as **nightlife** is concerned, most is centred in the Costa Azul neighborhood. Bars and clubs go in and out of business almost seasonally.

Pampatar

Ten kilometres north of Parlamar lies the much more peaceful and pleasant town of **PAMPATAR**. Founded in 1530, it was one of the first settlements in Venezuela, and today, despite the ever-encroaching tourism developments emanating from Porlamar, it retains some of its colonial charm. The small town of around 15,000 inhabitants has a pretty waterfront area with some colonial buildings, shady squares and even a fortress, the **Castillo de San Carlos Borromeo** (weekdays 8am–5.30pm, weekends 9am–5.30pm). Completed in 1684, it was considered by the Spanish to be the most important fort on the island. With its typical five-sided shape and rusted cannons it does not really look very different from other forts in Venezuela – but the turquoise-water backdrop makes it rather photogenic.

Though there's really little to do in Pamapatar, it serves as a nice respite from the more crowded areas of the island. Consistent with this are a few small, somewhat charming **posadas**. *Posada de Aleja* (℡0295/262-7044, Ⓔlaposadadealeja@hotmail.com; ❹), on Calle Nueva Cadiz next to the Circulo Militar, is a fourteen-room guesthouse run by the island's hotel school. The service is excellent, the prices are reasonable and the sea views from five of the rooms are quite nice. *Posada La Bufonera* (℡0295/262-9977; ❹), three blocks from the castle on Calle Almirante Brion, is another attractive offer. Each of the fully equipped rooms has a back door that leads to a terrace overlooking the beach. One **restaurant** that stands out is the *Café Trattoria Casa Caranta*, an Italian spot in a beautiful colonial house on Calle Principal de Pampatar, serving fresh fish and delicious home-made pastas with imaginative sauces.

Playa El Agua

Margarita's most renowned beach, **PLAYA EL AGUA** is three uninterrupted kilometres of white sand and palm trees. The beach is not protected so the waves are large and current strong, but that doesn't seem to deter most bathers. During the holiday season, the water and beach are utterly overrun with tourists.

Most come from Porlamar, about a 45-minute drive or bus ride to the south. Others stay at **hotels** near the beach, most of which are smaller than their Porlamar counterparts. One of the most appealing is *Hotel Costa Linda Beach* (☎0295/249-1303, Ⓦwww.hotelcostalinda.com; ❻), a colonial-style establishment a hundred metres from the beach on Avenida 31 de Julio. It features a pretty pool and 24 attractive, immaculate rooms. *Hotel Miramar Village* (☎0295/249-1797, Ⓦwww.miramarvillage.com; ❺) is a handsome, Mediterranean-style hotel just across from the beach on Avenida 31 de Julio. Rooms are large, with nice bathrooms and mini-fridges. Across Avenida 31 de Julio is one of the best places on the islands: *Posada Miragua* (☎0295/249-1593, Ⓔjrussian@ne.udo.edu.ve; ❸–❹). Given the quality of accommodation and great location, the owners could easily charge twice the price. Ten *cabañas*, each with two separate room units, are spread across a well-manicured garden area. The posada also has two good **restaurants** that are open to the public. *Café Margarita* has delicious breakfasts and some memorable desserts. *Restaurant Miragua*, right on the beach, serves excellent pasta and seafood.

Archipiélago Los Roques

Surrounded by crystal clear water, the white-sand beaches on the 42 islets of **ARCHIPIÉLAGO LOS ROQUES** are among Venezuela's finest. They are also the country's most pristine and exclusive, largely because of tight building restrictions imposed when the archipelago was made a national park in 1972. The park was created in large part to protect the 24-kilometre coral-reef system, which is home to a tremendous diversity of aquatic life, including barracudas, octopi, manta and eagle rays, sea urchins, lobsters and crabs – excellent for snorkelling and scuba diving.

Besides the plane ticket from Caracas, accommodation and boat tours are costly. However, several companies in Caracas, such as LTA (☎0212/761-6231, Ⓦwww.tuy.com), offer package **tours**, which are in some cases cheaper. Day tours cost between US$100 and US$150 per person and include round-trip air tickets, food and boat rides to a few of the keys. Two-day tours generally cost at least US$300 per person.

Arrival and information

All visitors fly into the **airstrip** on Gran Roque, a forty-minute journey from Caracas, 166km due south. Upon arrival, visitors must pay the US$10 park admission fee. The airstrip is within easy walking distance of all posadas on Gran Roque, and although there is no tourism office you can get **information** at *Oscar's Shop*, just in front of the airstrip. They will help you find accommodation, economical boat tours, windsurfing lessons and **snorkel equipment** rental.

Accommodation

All visitors **stay** on Gran Roque, the only inhabited island. It has around sixty posadas, most with four to eight guestrooms. All were formerly fishermen homes, since new building is not allowed here, but most have been renovated by their wealthy Venezuelans or foreigner owners. There are very few budget options yet even those are not cheap. Although there are no street names, finding posadas is quite easy on the tiny islet.

Acuarela ☎0212/781-9635, Ⓦwww.posadaacuarela.com. Recently renovated posada with eleven handsome rooms, five of which have a/c and an appealing terrace. Reception area and terrace. Unlike at some other posadas, the restaurant is open to the public. Price does not include boat trips. ❾

La Cigala Posada ☎0414/200-4357, Ⓔposadacigala@cantv.net. Pleasant Italian-run posada with simple bi-level rooms and outstanding food. The patio is lined with palms and has a Zen-like garden containing smooth rocks and whalebones. ❾

Malibu Lodge ⓣ0414/906-1929, ⓔaprmalibu@unete.com.ve. This elegant, thoughtfully decorated posada has ample rooms with pretty bathrooms. Colourful plants are scattered among fine furnishings in the ground floor social area. ❾

Posada Gremary ⓣ0414/314-5194, ⓔpollon24@hotmail.com. One of the better budget options, the *Posada Gremary's* rooms are neat, with high ceilings and a/c. The back entrance leads to a nice rooftop terrace. ❽

Posada Mediterraneo ⓣ0237/221-1130, ⓦwww.posadamediterraneo.com. This upscale, Mediterranean-style posada with a gorgeous rooftop terrace offers cosy rooms with white moulded concrete and white ceramic tiles; you'll feel like you're in an igloo. Many guests come on fishing packages offered by owner. ❾

Turismo Doña Carmen ⓣ0414/938-2284. One of the most affordable options, this old posada boasts the most desirable location – right on the beach and main square. Three of the nine spacious rooms are in front of the beach – call to reserve them at least two weeks in advance. ❻

Gran Roque and the zona recreativa

Although the Spanish discovered Los Roques in 1529, the first real settlers were actually the Dutch, who came in the nineteenth century but were, for the most part, displaced in the early twentieth century by fishermen from Isla Margarita, who built simple houses on archipelago's principal key, **Gran Roque**. Around twenty years ago, the archipelago started to become a vacationing spot for wealthy families who would sail in their yachts from Caracas. Today, planes run several times daily from Caracas, yet Los Roques is not for budget travellers. As prices have risen dramatically, increasingly few of the island's original inhabitants remain.

Besides houses and posadas, there is little else on Gran Roque – the **beaches** are not nearly as spectacular as those on other keys, so chartering a boat is quite necessary. Many of the keys, however, are protected and therefore off limits. The popular keys in the *zona recreativa*, where visitors are allowed, are **Nordisquí**, **Madrisquí Francisquí** and **Crasquí**. They do not vary greatly in appearance, each featuring postcard-perfect white sand and clear water. All are surrounded by coral, which makes for great snorkelling and diving, and Nordisquí has the added bonus of a few shipwrecks, in which large numbers of lobsters take refuge. Francisquí and Crasquí are the only ones with restaurants, while Madrisquí has a few houses built by rich Caracas families before Los Roques was declared a national park.

Eating and drinking

Most visitors **eat** at their posadas, which tend to have excellent food. Only a few, however, are open to the public. *Acuarela* is one of the finest, with a wide variety of food, desserts and coffee; reservations are required. For packed lunches, *Posada Aquarena* offers sandwiches, fruit juice as well as brownies and carrot cake. One of the few stand-alone restaurants on Gran Roque is *La Chuchera*, a large and colourful establishment that serves pizzas, hamburgers, pastas and fried fish.

Language

Language

Spanish

Although there are dozens of indigenous tongues scattered throughout South America – some thirty in the Peruvian Amazon alone – this is, with the exception of Brazil, a Spanish-speaking continent (see pp.1085–8 for a Portuguese primer). However, the Spanish you will hear in South America does not always conform to what you learn in the classroom or hear on a cassette, and even competent Spanish-speakers will find it takes a bit of getting used to. In addition to the odd differences in pronunciation – discussed in detail below – words from native languages as well as various European tongues have infiltrated the different dialects of South American Spanish, giving them each their own unique character.

For the most part, the language itself is the same throughout the continent, while the pronunciation varies slightly. In parts of Argentina, for example, the **ll** and **y** sound like a soft j (as in "Gigi"), while the final **s** of a word is often not pronounced.

Spanish itself is not a difficult language to pick up and there are numerous books, cassettes and CD-ROMs on the market, teaching to various levels – *Teach Yourself Latin American Spanish* is a very good book-cassette package for getting started. You'll be further helped by the fact that most South Americans, with the notable exception of motormouthed Chileans, speak relatively slowly (at least compared with Spaniards) and that there's no need to get your tongue round the lisping pronunciation. Of the many **dictionaries** available, you should try the *Dictionary of Latin American Spanish* (University of Chicago Press), while *Spanish: A Rough Guide Phrasebook* is an extremely concise and handy **phrasebook**.

Pronunciation

The rules of Spanish **pronunciation** are pretty straightforward and, once you get to know them, strictly observed. Unless there's an accent, words ending in d, l, r, and z are **stressed** on the last syllable, all others on the second last. All **vowels** are pure and short.

A somewhere between the "A" sound of back and that of father.

E as in get.

I as in police.

O as in hot.

U as in rule.

C is soft before E and I, hard otherwise: **cerca** is pronounced "serka".

G works the same way: a guttural "H" sound (like the ch in loch) before E or I, a hard G elsewhere – **gigante** becomes "higante".

H is always silent.

J is the same sound as a guttural G: **jamon** is pronounced "hamon".

LL sounds like an English Y: **tortilla** is pronounced "torteeya".

N is as in English unless it has a tilde (accent) over it, when it becomes NY: **mañana** sounds like "manyana".

QU is pronounced like an English K.

R is rolled, RR doubly so.

V sounds more like B, **vino** becoming "beano".

X is slightly softer than in English – sometimes almost SH – except between vowels in place names where it has an "H" sound – for example México (Meh-Hee-Ko) or Oaxaca.

Z is the same as a soft C, so **cerveza** becomes "servesa".

There is a list of a few essential words and phrases below, though if you're travelling for any length of time a dictionary or phrase book is obviously a worthwhile investment – some specifically Latin American ones are available (see above).

Words and phrases

The following will help you with your most basic day-to-day language needs.

Basic expressions

Yes, No **Sí, No**
Please, Thank you **Por favor, Gracias**
Where, When **Dónde, Cuándo**
What, How much **Qué, Cuánto**
Here, There **Aquí, Allí**
This, That **Este, Eso**
Now, Later **Ahora, Más tarde/luego**
Open, Closed **Abierto/a, Cerrado/a**
Pull, Push **Tire, Empuje**
Entrance, Exit **Entrada, Salida**
With, Without **Con, Sin**
For **Para/Por**
Good, Bad **Buen(o)/a, Mal(o)/a**
Big, Small **Gran(de), Pequeño/a**
A little, A lot **Poco/a, Mucho/a**
More, Less **Más, Menos**
Another **Otro/a**
Today, Tomorrow **Hoy, Mañana**
Yesterday **Ayer**
But **Pero**
And **Y**
Nothing, Never **Nada, Nunca**

Greetings and responses

Hello, Goodbye **Hola, Adios**
Good morning **Buenas dias**
Good afternoon/night **Buenas tardes/noches**
See you later **Hasta luego**
Sorry **Lo siento/Disculpeme**
Excuse me **Con permiso/Perdón**
How are you? **¿Como está (usted)?**
What's up? **¿Qué pasa?**
I (don't) understand **(No) Entiendo**
Not at all/You're welcome **De nada**
Do you speak English? **¿Habla (usted) inglés?**
I don't speak Spanish **(No) Hablo español**
My name is... **Me llamo...**
What's your name? **¿Como se llama usted?**
I am English/American **Soy inglés(a)/Americano(a)**
Cheers **Salud**

Asking directions, getting around

Where is...? **¿Dónde está...?**
...the bus station **...la estación de autobuses**
...the train station **...la estación de ferrocarriles**
...the nearest bank **...el banco más cercano**
...the post office **...el correo**
...the toilet **...el baño/sanitario**
Is there a hotel nearby? **¿Hay un hotel aquí cerca?**
Left, right, straight on **Izquierda, derecha, derecho**
Where does the bus to ... leave from? **¿De dónde sale el autobús para...?**
How do I get to...? **Por dónde se va a...?**
I'd like a (return) ticket to... **Quiero un pasaje dos (de ida y vuelta) para...**
What time does it leave? **¿A qué hora sale?**

Accommodation

Private bathroom **Baño privado**
Shared bathroom **Baño compartido**
Hot water (all day) **Agua caliente (todo el día)**
Cold water **Agua fría**
Fan **Ventilador**
Air-conditioned **Aire-acondicionado**
Mosquito net **Mosquitero**
Key **Llave**
Check-out time **Hora de salida**
Do you have...? **¿Tiene ...?**
... a room **...una habitación**
... with two beds/double bed **...con dos camas/cama matriomonial**
It's for one person **Es para una persona** (two people) **(dos personas)**
...for one night **...para una noche**
(one week) **(una semana)**
It's fine, how much is it? **¿Está bien, cuánto es?**
It's too expensive **Es demasiado caro**
Don't you have anything cheaper? **¿No tiene algo más barato?**

Numbers and days

1 **un/uno/una**
2 **dos**
3 **tres**
4 **cuatro**
5 **cinco**
6 **seis**
7 **siete**
8 **ocho**
9 **nueve**
10 **diez**
11 **once**
12 **doce**
13 **trece**
14 **catorce**
15 **quince**
16 **dieciséis**
20 **veinte**
21 **veitiuno**
30 **trienta**
40 **cuarenta**
50 **cincuenta**
60 **sesenta**
70 **setenta**
80 **ochenta**
90 **noventa**
100 **cien(to)**
200 **doscientos**
500 **quinientos**
1000 **mil**
Monday **lunes**
Tuesday **martes**
Wednesday **miércoles**
Thursday **jueves**
Friday **viernes**
Saturday **sábado**
Sunday **domingo**

A Spanish menu reader

While menus vary by country and region, these words and terms will help negotiate most menus.

Basic dining vocabulary

Almuerzo Lunch
Carta (la)/Lista (la) Menu
Cena Dinner
Comida típica Typical cuisine
Cuchara Spoon
Cuchillo Knife
Desayuno Breakfast
La cuenta, por favor The bill, please
Merienda Set menu
Plato fuerte Main course
Plato vegetariano Vegetarian dish
Tenedor Fork

Frutas (fruit)

Cereza Cherry
Chirimoya Custard apple
Ciruela Plum
Fresa/frutilla Strawberry
Guayaba Guava
Guineo Banana
Higo Fig
Limón Lemon or lime
Manzana Apple
Maracuyá Passion fruit
Melocotón/durazno Peach
Mora Blackberry
Naranja Orange
Pera Pear
Piña Pineapple
Plátano Plantain
Pomelo/toronja Grapefruit
Tomate de arból Tree tomato

Legumbres/verduras (vegetables)

Aguacate Avocado
Alachoafa Artichoke
Cebolla Onion
Champiñón Mushroom
Choclo Maize/sweetcorn
Coliflor Cauliflower
Espinaca Spinach
Frijoles Beans
Guisantes/arvejas Peas
Hongo Mushroom
Lechuga Lettuce
Lentejas Lentil
Menestra Bean/lentil stew
Palmito Palm heart
Patata Potato
Papas fritas French fries
Pepinillo Gherkin
Pepino Cucumber
Tomate Tomato
Zanahoria Carrot

Carne (meat) y aves (poultry)

Carne Meat (frequently beef)
Carne de chancho Pork
Cerdo Pork
Chicharrones Pork scratchings, crackling
Chuleta Pork chop
Churrasco Grilled meat with sides
Conejo Rabbit
Cordero Lamb
Cuero Pork crackling
Cuy Guinea pig
Jamón Ham
Lechón Suckling pig
Lomo Steak
Pato Duck
Pavo Turkey
Res Beef
Ternera Veal
Tocino Bacon
Venado Venison

Menudos (offal)

Chunchules Intestines
Guatita Tripe
Hígado Liver
Lengua Tongue
Mondongo Tripe
Patas Trotters

Mariscos (fish) y pescado (seafood)

Anchoa Anchovy
Atún Tuna
Bonito Bonito (like tuna)
Calamares Squid
Camarón Prawn
Cangrejo Crab
Ceviche Seafood marinated in lime juice with onions
Concha Clam; scallop
Corvina Sea bass
Erizo Sea urchin
Langosta Lobster
Langostina King prawn
Lenguado Sole
Mejillón Mussel
Ostra Oyster
Trucha Trout

Cooking terms

A la parilla Barbequed
A la plancha Lightly fried
Ahumado Smoked
Al ajillo In garlic sauce
Al horno Oven-baked
Al vapor Steamed
Apanado Breaded
Asado Roast
Asado al palo Spit roast
Crudo Raw
Duro Hard boiled
Encebollado Cooked with onions

Encocado In coconut sauce
Frito Fried
Picante Spicy hot
Puré Mashed
Revuelto Scrambled
Saltado Sautéed
Secado Dried

Bebidas (drinks)

Agua (mineral) Mineral water
Con gas Sparkling
Sin gas Still
Sin hielo Without ice
Aguardiente Sugarcane spirit
Aromática Herbal tea
Hierba luisa Lemon verbena
Manzanilla Camomile
Menta Mint
Batido Milkshake
Café Coffee
Café con leche Milk with a little coffee
Caipirinha Cocktail of rum, lime, sugar & ice
Cerveza Beer
Chicha Fermented corn drink
Cola Fizzy drink
Gaseosa Fizzy drink
Jugo Juice
Leche Milk
Limonada Fresh lemonade
Mate de coca Coca leaf tea
Ron Rum
Té Tea
Vino blano White wine
Vino tinto Red wine
Yerba (hierba) mate Paraguayan tea

Food glossary

Aciete Oil
Ají Chilli
Ajo Garlic
Arroz Rice
Azucar Sugar
Galletas Biscuits
Hielo Ice
Huevos Eggs
Mantequilla Butter
Mermeleda Jam
Miel Honey
Mixto Mixed seafood/meats
Mostaza Mustard
Pan (integral) Bread (wholemeal)
Pimienta Pepper
Queso Cheese
Sal Salt
Salsa de tomate Tomato sauce

Soups

Caldosa Broth
Caldo de gallina Chicken broth
Caldo de patas Cattle-hoof broth
Crema de espárragos Cream of asparagus
Locro Cheese and potato soup
Sopa de bolas de verde Plantain dumpling soup
Sopa del día Soup of the day
Yaguarlocro Blood sausage (black pudding) soup

Bocadillos (snacks)

Bolón de verde Baked cheese and potato dumpling
Chifles Banana chips/crisps
Empanada Cheese/meat pastry
Hamburguesa Hamburger
Humitas Ground corn and cheese
Omelet Omelette
Palomitas Popcorn
Patacones Thick cut dried banana/plantain
Salchipapas Sausage, fries and sauces
Sanwiche Sandwich
Tamale Ground maize with meat/cheese wrapped in leaf
Tortilla de huevos Firm omelette
Tostada Toast
Tostado Toasted maize

Postres (dessert)

Cocados Coconut candy
Ensalada de frutas Fruit salad
Flan Crème caramel
Helado Ice cream
Manjar de leche Very sweet caramel made from condensed milk
Pastas Pastries
Pastel Cake
Torta Tart

Portuguese

The great exception to the Spanish-speaking rule in South America is, of course, **Portuguese**-speaking Brazil (that is, putting the Guianas to the side). Unfortunately, far too many people – especially Spanish-speakers – are put off going to Brazil solely because of the language, while this should actually be one of your main reasons for going. Brazilian Portuguese is a colourful, sensual language full of wonderfully rude and exotic vowel sounds, swooping intonation and hilarious idiomatic expressions.

The best **dictionary** currently available is the *Collins Portuguese Dictionary*. There is a pocket edition, but you might consider taking the fuller, larger version, which concentrates on the way the language is spoken today and gives plenty of specifically Brazilian vocabulary. For a **phrasebook**, look no further than *Portuguese: A Rough Guide Phrasebook*, with useful two-way glossaries and a brief and simple grammar section.

Pronunciation

Although its complex pronunciation is far too difficult to be described in detail here, for the most part, Brazilian Portuguese is spoken more slowly and clearly than its European counterpart. The neutral vowels so characteristic of European Portuguese tend to be sounded out in full; in much of Brazil outside Rio the slushy "sh" sound doesn't exist; and the "de" and "te" endings of words like *cidade* and *diferente* are palatalized so they end up sounding like "sidadgee" and "djiferentchee".

Words and phrases

You'll also find that Brazilians will greatly appreciate even your most rudimentary efforts, and every small improvement in your Portuguese will make your stay in Brazil much more enjoyable.

Basic expressions

Yes, No **Sim, Não**
Please **Por favor**
Thank you **Obrigado (men)/ Obrigada (women)**
Where, When **Onde, Quando**
What, How much **Que, Quanto**
This, That **Este, Esse, Aquele**
Now, Later **Agora, Mais tarde**
Open, Closed **Aberto/a, Fechado/a**
Pull, Push **Puxe, Empurre**
Entrance, Exit **Entrada, Saída**
With, Without **Com, Sem**
For **Para/Por**
Good, Bad **Bom, Ruim**
Big, Small **Grande, Pequeno**
A little, A lot **Um pouco, Muito**
More, Less **Mais, Menos**
Another **Outro/a**
Today, Tomorrow **Hoje, Amanhã**
Yesterday **Ontem**
But **Mas (pronounced like "mice")**
And **E (pronounced like "ee" in "seek")**
Something, Nothing **Alguma coisa, Nada**
Sometimes **Às vezes**

Greetings and responses

Hello, Goodbye **Oi, Tchau (like the Italian "ciao")**
Good morning **Bom dia**
Good afternoon/night **Boa tarde/Boa noite**
Sorry **Desculpa**
Excuse me **Com licença**
How are you? **Como vai?**
Fine **Bem**
I don't understand **Não entendo**
Do you speak English? **Você fala inglês?**
I don't speak Portuguese **Não falo português**
My name is... **Meu nome é...**
What's your name? **Como se chama?**
I am English/American **Sou inglês/americano**
Cheers **Saúde**

Asking directions, getting around

Where is...? **Onde fica...?**
...the bus station **...a rodoviária**
...the bus stop **...a parada de ônibus**
...the nearest hotel **...o hotel mais próximo**
...the toilet **...o banheiro/sanitário**
Left, right, straight on **Esquerda, direita, direto**
Where does the bus to... leave from? **De onde sai o ônibus para...?**
Is this the bus to Rio? **É esse o ônibus para Rio?**
Do you go to...? **Você vai para...?**
I'd like a (return) ticket to... **Quero uma passagem (ida e volta) para...**
What time does it leave? **Que horas sai?**

Accommodation

Do you have a room? **Você tem um quarto?**
...with two beds **...com duas**
...with double bed **...camas/cama de casal**
It's for one person/two people **É para uma/pessoa duas pessoas**
It's fine, how much is it? **Está bom, quanto é?**
It's too expensive **É caro demais**
Do you have anything cheaper? **Tem algo mais barato?**
Is there a hotel/campsite nearby? **Tem um hotel/camping por aqui?**

Numbers and days

1 **um, uma**
2 **dois, duas**
3 **três**
4 **quatro**
5 **cinco**
6 **seis**
7 **sete**
8 **oito**
9 **nove**
10 **dez**
11 **onze**
12 **doze**
13 **treze**
14 **quatorze**
15 **quinze**
16 **dezesseis**
17 **dezesete**
20 **vinte**
21 **vinte e um**
30 **trinta**
40 **quarenta**
50 **cinquenta**
60 **sesenta**
70 **setenta**
80 **oitenta**
90 **noventa**
100 **cem**
200 **duzentos**
300 **trezentos**
500 **quinhentos**
1000 **mil**
Monday **segunda-feira (or segunda)**
Tuesday **terça-feira (or terça)**
Wednesday **quarta-feira (or quarta)**
Thursday **quinta-feira (or quinta)**
Friday **sexta-feira (or sexta)**
Saturday **sábado**
Sunday **domingo**

A Brazilian menu reader

For more information on the regional cooking of Bahia and Minas Gerais, see the boxes on p.375 and p.355.

Basic dining vocabulary

Almoço/lonche Lunch
Café de manhã Breakfast
Cardápio Menu
Colher Spoon
Conta/nota Bill
Copo Glass
Entrada Hors d'oeuvre
Faca Knife
Garçon Waiter
Garfo Fork
Jantar Dinner, to have dinner
Prato Plate
Sobremesa Dessert
Sopa/Caldo Soup
Taxa de serviço Service charge

Frutas (fruit)

Abacate Avocado
Abacaxi Pineapple
Ameixa Plum, prune
Caju Cashew fruit
Carambola Star fruit
Cerejas Cherries
Côco Coconut
Fruta do conde Custard apple (also *ata*)
Goiaba Guava
Graviola Cherimoya
Laranja Orange
Limão Lime
Maçã Apple
Mamão Papaya
Manga Mango
Maracujá Passion fruit
Melancia Watermelon
Melão Melon
Morango Strawberry
Pera Pear
Pêssego Peach
Uvas Grapes

Legumes (vegetables)

Alface Lettuce
Arroz e feijão Rice and beans
Azeitonas Olives
Batatas Potatoes
Cebola Onion
Cenoura Carrot
Dendê Palm oil
Ervilhas Peas
Espinafre Spinach
Macaxeira Roasted manioc
Mandioca Manioc/cassava/yuca
Milho Corn
Palmito Palm heart
Pepinho Cucumber
Repolho Cabbage
Tomate Tomato

Carne (meat) and aves (poultry)

Bife Steak
Bife a cavalo Steak with egg and *farinha*
Cabrito Kid (goat)
Carne de porco Pork
Carneiro Lamb
Costela Ribs
Costeleta Chop
Feijoada Black bean, pork and sausage stew
Fígado Liver
Frango Chicken
Leitão Suckling pig
Lingüíça Sausage
Pato Duck
Peito Breast
Perna Leg
Peru Turkey
Picadinha Stew
Salsicha Hot dog
Veado Venison
Vitela Veal

Frutos do mar (seafood)

Acarajé Fried bean cake stuffed with *vatapá* (see below)
Agulha Needle fish
Atum Tuna
Camarão Prawn, shrimp
Caranguejo Large crab
Filhote Amazon river fish
Lagosta Lobster
Lula Squid
Mariscos Mussels
Moqueca Seafood stewed in palm oil and coconut sauce
Ostra Oyster
Pescada Seafood stew, or hake
Pirarucu Amazon river fish
Pitu Crayfish
Polvo Octopus
Siri Small crab
Sururu A type of mussel
Vatapá Bahian shrimp dish, cooked with palm oil, skinned tomato and coconut milk, served with fresh coriander and hot peppers

Cooking terms

Assado Roasted
Bem gelado Well chilled
Churrasco Barbecue
Cozido Boiled, steamed
Cozinhar To cook
Grelhado Grilled
Mal passado/Bem passado Rare/well done (meat)
Médio Medium-grilled
Milanesa Breaded
Na chapa/Na brasa Charcoal-grilled

Temperos (spices)

Alho Garlic
Canela Cinnamon
Cheiro verde Fresh coriander
Coentro Parsley
Cravo Clove
Malagueta Very hot pepper, looks like red or yellow cherry

Bebidas (drinks)

Água mineral Mineral water
Batida Fresh fruit juice (sometimes with *cachaça*)
Cachaça Sugarcane rum
Café com leite Coffee with hot milk
Cafézinho Small black coffee
Caipirinha Rum and lime cocktail
Cerveja Bottled beer
Chopp Draught beer
Com gás/sem gás Sparkling/still
Suco Fruit juice
Vinho Wine
Vitamina Fruit juice made with milk

Food glossary

Açúcar Sugar
Alho e óleo Garlic and olive oil sauce
Arroz Rice
Azeite Olive oil
Farinha Dried manioc flour beans
Manteiga Butter
Molho Sauce
Ovos Eggs
Pão Bread
Pimenta Pepper
Queijo Cheese
Sal Salt
Sorvete Ice cream

Glossary

Common Spanish terms

Adobe Sun-dried mud
Allyu Kinship group, or clan
Altiplano High plateau region in the Andes
Apu Mountain god
Arriero Muleteer
Arroyo Stream or small river
Artesanía Traditional handicraft
Asada Barbecue
Barrio Suburb, or sometimes shantytown
Burro Donkey
Cacique Headman
Callejón Corridor, or narrow street
Campesino Peasant, country dweller, someone who works in the fields
Carretera Route or highway
Ceja de la selva Edge of the jungle
Cerro Hill, mountain peak
Chacra Cultivated garden or plot
Chaquiras Pre-Columbian stone or coral beads
Chicha Maize beer
Colectivo Collective taxi/bus
Combi Small minibus that runs urban routes
Cordillera Mountain range
Criollo "Creole": a person of Spanish blood born in the American colonies
Curaca Chief
Curandero Healer
Empresa Company
Encomienda Colonial grant of land and native labour
Entrada Ticket (for theatre, football match, etc)
Estancia Ranch, or large estate
Extranjero A foreigner
Farmacia Chemist
Flacoa Skinny (common nickname)
Gaucho The typical Argentinian "cowboy", or rural estancia worker
Gordo(a) Fat (common nickname)
Gringo Foreigner, Westerner (not necessarily a derogatory term)
Hacienda Large estate
Huaca Sacred spot or object
Huaco Pre-Columbian artefact
Huaquero Someone who digs or looks for **huacos**
Huaso Chilean "cowboy", or mounted farm worker
Jirón Road
Junta A ruling council; usually used to describe small groups who've staged a coup d'état
Malecón Coastal or riverside avenue
Mestizo Person of mixed Spanish and indigenous blood
Micro City bus
Mirador Viewpoint
Municipalidad Municipality building or town hall
Pampa Plain
Peña Nightclub with live music
Plata Silver; slang for "cash"
Playa Beach
Poblado Settlement
Pueblos jovenes Shanty towns
Puna Barren Andean heights
Quebrada Stream, or ravine
Ruta Route or road
Sala Room or hall
Selva Jungle
Selvatico A jungle dweller
Serrano Mountain dweller
Sierra Mountains
Soroche Altitude sickness
Tambo Inca highway rest-house
Tienda Shop
Tramites Red tape, bureaucracy
Unsu Throne, or platform

Common Portuguese terms

Aldeia Originally a mission where Indians were converted, now any isolated hamlet
Amazônia The Amazon region
Artesanato Craft goods
Azulejo Decorative glazed tiling
Bairro Neighbourhood within town or city
Barraca Beach hut
Batucada Literally, a drumming session music-making in general, especially impromptu
Boîte Club or bar with dancing
Bosque Wood
Caboclo Backwoodsman/woman, often of mixed race
Candomblé African-Brazilian religion
Capoeira African-Brazilian martial art/dance form
Carimbó Music and dance style from the North
Carioca Someone or something from Rio de Janeiro
Carnaval Carnival
Cerrado Scrubland
Choro Musical style, largely instrumental
Convento Convent
Correio Postal service/post office
Dancetaria Nightspot where the emphasis is on dancing
Engenho Sugar mill or plantation
EUA USA
Ex voto Thank-offering to saint for intercession
Favela Shantytown, slum
Fazenda Country estate, ranch house
Feira Country market
Ferroviária Train station
Forró Dance and type of music from the northeast
Frescão Air-conditioned bus
Frevo Frenetic musical style and dance from Recife
Gaúcho Person or thing from Rio Grande do Sul; also southern cowboy
Gringo/a Foreigner, Westerner (not derogatory)
Ibama Government organization for preservation of the environment; runs national parks and nature reserves
Igreja Church
Largo Small square
Latifúndios Large agricultural estates
Leito Luxury express bus
Litoral Coast, coastal zone
Louro/a Fair-haired/blonde – Westerners in general
Maconha Marijuana
Marginal Petty thief, outlaw
Mata Jungle, remote interior
Mercado Market
Mirante Viewing point
Mosteiro Monastery
Movimentado Lively, where the action is
Nordeste Northeastern Brazil
Paulista Person or thing from São Paulo state
Pelourinho Pillory or whipping-post, common in colonial town squares
Planalto Central Vast interior tablelands of central Brazil
Posto Highway service station, often with basic accommodation popular with truckers
Praça Square
Praia Beach
Prefeitura Town hall, and by extension city governments in general
Quebrado Out of order
Rodovia Highway
Rodoviária Bus station
Samba Type of music most associated with Carnaval in Rio
Selva Jungle
Senzala Slave quarters
Sesmaria Royal Portuguese land grant to early settlers
Sobrado Two-storey colonial mansion
Umbanda African–Brazilian religion especially common in urban areas of the south and southeast
Vaqueiro Cowboy in Brazil's north
Visto Visa

Index

and small print

Index

map entries are in colour

Abbreviations

Argentina (A)
Bolivia (Bo)
Brazil (Br)
Chile (Ch)
Colombia (Co)
Ecuador (E)
French Guiana (FG)
Guyana (G)
Paraguay (Pa)
Peru (Pe)
Suriname (S)
Uruguay (U)
Venezuela (V)

A

B

C

INDEX

D

E

F

G

H

I

J

K

L

Q

R

INDEX

S

T

U

V

W

Z

A rough guide to Rough Guides

In the summer of 1981, Mark Ellingham, a recent graduate from Bristol University, was travelling round Greece and couldn't find a guidebook that really met his needs. On the one hand there were the student guides, insistent on saving every last cent, and on the other the heavyweight cultural tomes whose authors seemed to have spent more time in a research library than lounging away the afternoon at a taverna or on the beach.

In a bid to avoid getting a job, Mark and a small group of writers set about creating their own guidebook. It was a guide to Greece that aimed to combine a journalistic approach to description with a thoroughly practical approach to travellers' needs – a guide that would incorporate culture, history and contemporary insights with a critical edge, together with up-to-date, value-for-money listings. Back in London, Mark and the team finished their Rough Guide, as they called it, and talked Routledge into publishing the book.

That first *Rough Guide to Greece*, published in 1982, was a student scheme that became a publishing phenomenon. The immediate success of the book – with numerous reprints and a Thomas Cook prize shortlisting – spawned a series that rapidly covered dozens of destinations. Rough Guides had a ready market among low-budget backpackers, but soon also acquired a much broader and older readership that relished Rough Guides' wit and inquisitiveness as much as their enthusiastic, critical approach. Everyone wants value for money, but not at any price.

Rough Guides soon began supplementing the "rougher" information about hostels and low-budget listings with the kind of detail on restaurants and quality hotels that independent-minded visitors on any budget might expect, whether on business in New York or trekking in Thailand.

These days the guides – distributed worldwide by the Penguin group – offer recommendations from shoestring to luxury and cover more than 200 destinations around the globe, including almost every country in the Americas and Europe, more than half of Africa and most of Asia and Australasia. Our ever-growing team of authors and photographers is spread all over the world, particularly in Europe, the USA and Australia.

In 1994, we published the *Rough Guide to World Music* and *Rough Guide to Classical Music*, and a year later the *Rough Guide to the Internet*. All three books have become benchmark titles in their fields – which encouraged us to expand into other areas of publishing, mainly around popular culture. Rough Guides now publish:

- Travel guides to more than 200 worldwide destinations
- Dictionary phrasebooks to 22 major languages
- History guides ranging from Ireland to Islam
- Maps printed on rip-proof and waterproof Polyart™ paper
- Music guides running the gamut from Opera to Elvis
- Restaurant guides to London, New York and San Francisco
- Reference books on topics as diverse as the Weather and Shakespeare
- Sports guides from Formula 1 to Man Utd
- Pop culture books from Lord of the Rings to Cult TV
- World Music CDs in association with World Music Network.

Visit **www.roughguides.com** to see our latest publications.

Rough Guide credits

Text editor: Richard Koss
Layout: Tanya Hall and Helen Prior
Picture research: Jj Luck
Proofreader: Susannah Wight

....

Editorial: **London** Martin Dunford, Kate Berens, Helena Smith, Claire Saunders, Geoff Howard, Ruth Blackmore, Ann-Marie Shaw, Gavin Thomas, Polly Thomas, Richard Lim, Lucy Ratcliffe, Clifton Wilkinson, Alison Murchie, Fran Sandham, Sally Schafer, Alexander Mark Rogers, Karoline Densley, Andy Turner, Ella O'Donnell, Andrew Lockett, Joe Staines, Duncan Clark, Peter Buckley, Matthew Milton; **New York** Andrew Rosenberg, Richard Koss, Yuki Takagaki, Hunter Slaton, Chris Barsanti, Thomas Kohnstamm, Steven Horak
Design & Layout: **London** Helen Prior, Dan May, Diana Jarvis; **Delhi** Madhulita Mohapatra, Umesh Aggarwal, Ajay Verma
Production: Julia Bovis, John McKay, Sophie Hewat
Cartography: **London** Maxine Repath, Ed Wright, Katie Lloyd-Jones; **Delhi** Manish Chandra, Rajesh Chhibber, Jai Prakesh Mishra, Ashutosh Bharti, Rajesh Mishra, Animesh Pathak
Cover art direction: Louise Boulton
Picture research: Sharon Martins, Mark Thomas, Jj Luck
Online: **New York** Jennifer Gold, Cree Lawson, Suzanne Welles; **Delhi** Manik Chauhan, Amarjyoti Dutta, Narender Kumar
Marketing & Publicity: **London** Richard Trillo, Niki Smith, David Wearn, Chloë Roberts, Demelza Dallow; **New York** Geoff Colquitt, David Wechsler, Megan Kennedy
Finance: Gary Singh
Manager India: Punita Singh
Series editor: Mark Ellingham
PA to Managing Director: Julie Sanderson
Managing Director: Kevin Fitzgerald

Publishing Information

This first edition published January 2004 by
Rough Guides Ltd,
80 Strand, London WC2R 0RL
345 Hudson St, 4th Floor,
New York, NY 10014, USA
Distributed by the Penguin Group
Penguin Books Ltd,
80 Strand, London WC2R 0RL
Penguin Putnam, Inc.
375 Hudson Street, NY 10014, USA
Penguin Books Australia Ltd,
487 Maroondah Highway, PO Box 257,
Ringwood, Victoria 3134, Australia
Penguin Books Canada Ltd,
10 Alcorn Avenue, Toronto, Ontario,
Canada M4V 1E4
Penguin Books (NZ) Ltd,
182–190 Wairau Road, Auckland 10,
New Zealand
Typeset in Bembo and Helvetica to an original design by Henry Iles.

Printed in Italy by LegoPrint S.p.A

1146pp includes index
A catalogue record for this book is available from the British Library.

ISBN 1-85828-907-6

The publishers and authors have done their best to ensure the accuracy and currency of all the information in **The Rough Guide to South America**, however, they can accept no responsibility for any loss, injury, or inconvenience sustained by any traveller as a result of information or advice contained in the guide.

1 3 5 7 9 8 6 4 2

Help us update

We've gone to a lot of effort to ensure that the first edition of **The Rough Guide to South America** is accurate and up to date. However, things change – places get "discovered", opening hours are notoriously fickle, restaurants and rooms raise prices or lower standards. If you feel we've got it wrong or left something out, we'd like to know, and if you can remember the address, the price, the time, the phone number, so much the better.

We'll credit all contributions, and send a copy of the next edition (or any other Rough Guide if you prefer) for the best letters. Everyone who writes to us and isn't already a subscriber will receive a copy of our full-colour thrice-yearly newsletter. Please mark letters: "**Rough Guide South America Update**" and send to: Rough Guides, 80 Strand, London WC2R 0RL, or Rough Guides, 4th Floor, 345 Hudson St, New York, NY 10014. Or send an email to **mail@roughguides.com**

Have your questions answered and tell others about your trip at **www.roughguides.atinfopop.com**

Acknowledgements

Editorial acknowledgments

Heartfelt thanks go to Tanya Hall, Helen Prior and Diana Jarvis for their diligent typesetting; Jj Luck for her assiduous photo research; Maxine Repath, Manish Chandra and company, and Stratigraphics for their mapmaking acumen; Susannah Wight for her vigilant proofreading; Anja Mutic for the fine index; Chris Barsanti for his Peruvian expertise; and, as ever, to Andrew Rosenberg, without whom the ship wouldn't float.

Author acknowledgements

Harry Adès: Christopher Sacco and Dominique Allen for their invaluable additional research; Melissa for her support and crucial editorial help; and Fernando Luque of the Ecuadorian Embassy in London. Special thanks to my friends and family for everything, and to Shahla who was great company away and a pillar of strength at home.

Andrew Benson: in Chile– Ingrid Hamdorf, Raúl Wünkhaus, David Muller, Iris Fernández, Nicholas, Jeremy, Charlie, Edda, Anthony, Carolyn, Clark, Manuela, Paty, Jorge and Melissa; in Argentina –Pablo, Frédéric, Carlos, Gustavo, Julia, Frank, Rubén, Ignacio, Sergio, Carolina, Omar, Raphael, Gaby, Alberto, Juan Pablo and the Pasqualinis; the staff at tourist offices up and down Chile and Argentina; Marjan, Walter and Max; and Martín Gambarotta for his info on latest political developments.

Jonathan Franklin: Felipe Pumarino, Sernatur, Macarena Velasco and Fundacion Chile

Joshua Goodman: German Escobar from Platypus Hostel; Naia George; Luis and Camilo Camargo from OpEpa; Ricardo Corredor and Jaime Abello from the Fundación Nuevo Periodismo; Bernardo Gutierrez, Medios por la Paz; Kirk Semple; Alex Campuzano; Claudia Steiner; and Eli Winkler.

Dilwyn Jenkins would like to thank Carlos Montenegro; Aiden, Tess and Bethan; Dora Lucio Meza Ortiz; Antonio and Jorge Montenegro; Rosana Correa Alamo; Susie and Martin Cannon; Alberto Cafferata (Pony Expeditions); Rafael Belmonte (Peru Expeditions); Peter Jenson and Jaime Acevedo (Explorama); Henry Aguilar; Peter and Leo Frost; John Forrest; Katia Fabiola Cerna Rivera; Edilson, Cecilia and Nina; Chris Barsanti, Yuki Takagaki and Richard Koss; Howard Davis; Mark at Swallows and Amazons; Alex at Ecological Expeditions; and last most importantly Claire, Tess, Bethan Max and Teilo.

Oliver Marshall: Richard Koss; the many municipal and state tourist offices and convention and visitors bureaux (CVBs) throughout Brazil; Margaret and Anneliese Doyle and Chris Pickard; Alicia and Kevan Prior; Karin Luize de Carvalho; Graça Salgado, Eduardo Silva, Isaura Silva and Karin Hanta; and Darién Davis.

Anja Mutic: The miners of Koala Tours in Potosí (special thanks to Efrain); Carolina Udovicki; Agustin Echalar; Brian Morgan and Beatriz Martinez; everyone at Fremen Tours,

Turismo Sucre and Candelaria; Richard Koss, Andrew Rosenberg and the Rough Guides Online team.

Paul D Smith: Val Isaacs at British Embassy in Uruguay, Maby and Veró in Encarnacion, Richard James, Florian (RIP), Richard Koss (for often going beyond the call of duty!), Mum, Dad, Joe and Carol (I love you!).

Ross Velton: in Guyana – Tony Thorne, Suria (Teri) Ramnarain, Nicole Correia, Mohamed Bandoo, Colin Edwards, Dianne McTurk, Colette McDermott, Franky Singh, Indira Anandjit and Bernard Lee Yong; in Suriname – Jerry R. A-Kum, Kathlyn Craig, Sabina Floridia, Karen Tjon Pian Gi and Bradley R. Fräser; and in French Guiana – Karl Joseph, Jacques Leizerovici, Veronique Cybulski, Couleurs Amazone and Jean-Louis Antoine.

Brad Weiss: Orimar Morón at the Viceministerio de Turismo; Paul Stanley and Antonio Pestana at Angel Eco-tours; Alexandra Tellez and Andrés Branger at discovervenezuela.com; Berthapaula García at El Solar de la Luna; José Luis Troconis at Natoura; Viktor Gorodeckis at De la Costa Eco-lodge; Lara Lorenzo at Taima Taima; Javier Cubillos at Expediciones Dearuna; and Tamara Rodriguez at the Pariana Café.

Photo Credits

Cover Credits
Main front: Train to Cuzco © Robert Harding
Small front top picture: Patagonia © Robert Harding
Small front lower picture: Barbudo © Monkey Image Bank
Back top picture: Iguassu Falls © Getty
Back lower picture: Buenos Aires © Getty

Colour Introduction
Christ the Redeemer on Corcovado mountain, Rio © Jason P Howe/South American Pictures
Fitz Roy Massif and Cerro Poincenot © Kathy Jarvis/South American Pictures
Oruro Carnival, Bolivia © Eric Lawrie
Laguna del Diario nr Punta del Este, Uruguay © Tony Morrison/South American Pictures
Toucan © Tony Morrison/South American Pictures
Amazon – the meeting of R. Negro and R. Solimoes © Tony Morrison/South American Pictures
Jungle trip, Lago Sandoval, Peru © C. Caldicott, Axiom
Patchwork fields, Ecuador © Paul Harris
Fiesta de San Felipe, Amarete © Eric Lawrie

36 Things not to miss
01. Boat trip down the Amazon © Ricardo Azoury/CORBIS
02. Mountain biking in Bolivia © Mark A. Johnson/CORBIS
03. Colca Canyon – condors © Johan Elzenga/Alamy
04. Football – Maracaná Stadium © Jason P Howe/South American Pictures
05. Ceviche © Tony Morrison/South American Pictures
06. Parque Nacional Torres del Paine © Paul Harris
07. The Amazon © Tony Morrison/South American Pictures
08. The architecture of Brasília © Tony Morrison/South American Pictures
09. Plaza de los Héroes © Tony Morrison/South American Pictures
10. Galápagos wildlife – sealion © Harry Adès
11. Rocket launch © Guyana Space Centre/South American Pictures
12. Andean festivals © Tony Morrison/South American Pictures
13. Sugar Loaf mountain © Peter Wilson
14. Iguazú Falls © Tony Morrison/South American Pictures
15. Buenos Aires café culture, San Telmo © Reinaldo Vargas
16. Scenic wintersports © Jeff Curtis/CORBIS
17. Kogi village huts © Josh Goodman
18. Nazca Lines – outline of hands © Kevin Schafer/CORBIS
19 Tango © Jason P Howe/South American Pictures
20. Volcán Cotopaxi © Tony Morrison/South American Pictures
21. Angel Falls © Chris Sharp/South American Pictures
22. Floating Totora Reed Islands of Lago Titicaca © Peter Wilson
23. La Paz's Mercado de Hechiceria © Kathy Jarvis/South American Pictures
24. Tiwanaku © Eric Lawrie
25. Capybara © Theo Allofs/CORBIS
26. Copacabana © Jason P Howe/South American Pictures
27. Parilla © Robert Frerck/Robert Harding
28. Mercado del Puerto, Montevideo © Tony Morrison/South American Pictures
29. Carnaval, Olinda © Tony Morrison/South American Pictures
30. Salar de Uyuni © Jerry Callow
31. Salsa club © Jeremy Horner/CORBIS
32. Trekking (Volcan Villarica) © Robert Francis/South American Pictures
33. Machu Picchu © Peter Wilson
34. Otavalo market – colorful weavings © Sue Mann/South American Pictures
35. Glaciar Perito Moreno © Frank Nowikowski/South American Pictures
36. Chilean wine © Charles O'Rear/CORBIS

Black and whites
Banks of River Paraná © Lucy Phillips p.66
A gaucho on horseback © Tony Morrison/South American Pictures p.132
The pampa plains © Tony Morrison/South American Pictures p.183
Rooftops, Potosí © Jerry Callow H p.198
The highway to Coroico © Kimball Morrison/South American Pictures p.257
The Arbol de Piedra, © Eric Lawrie p.290
Crocodile in the Pantanal © Tony Morrison/South American Pictures p.296
The Teatro Amazonas, Manaus © Tony Morrison/South American Pictures p.353
The Museu de Arte Contemporânea, Rio © Oliver Marshall p.384
A capoiera display © Karen Ward/South American Pictures p.446
Mercado Central, Santiago © Robert Francis/South American Pictures p.466
An *ascensor* funicular, Valparaiso © Paul Harris p.505
A *moai* statue, Easter Island © Sue Mann/South American Pictures p.562
Colonial shot © Joshua Goodman p.586
Ancient indigenous statue, San Augustin © Tony Morrison/South American Pictures p.617
Land Iguana © David Forman/Travel Ink p.646
The streets of Quito's Old Town © Tony Morrison/South American Pictures p.696
The Inca ruins of Ingapirca © Kathy Jarvis/South American Pictures p.747
Kaieteur Falls © Tony Morrison/South American Pictures p.758
Sea turtle, Plage Les Hattes © Jan Baks/Alamy p.791
Stone carving of head, Trinidad © Tony Morrison/South American Pictures p.812
The Itaipú Hydroelectric Project © Tony Morrison/South American Pictures p.836
Adobe walls, Chan Chan Complex © Jamie Marshall p.844
The Inca Trail © Doug McKinlay/Axiom – Scan# b/w9 p.884
A *caballito* fishing boat © Tony Morrison/South American Pictures p.940
Thermal Springs, Guayaviu © Tony Morrison/South American Pictures p.966
Mercado del Puerto, Montevideo © Tony Morrison/South American Pictures p.984
Thatched house/Warau © Tony Morrison/South American Pictures p.1008
Beach on the Archipiélago Los Roques © Johnathan Smith; Cordaiy Photo Library Ltd./CORBIS p.1052

stay in touch

roughnews

Rough Guides' FREE full-colour newsletter

News, travel issues, music reviews, readers' letters and the latest dispatches from authors on the road

If you would like to receive roughnews, please send us your name and address:

Rough Guides, 80 Strand,
London WC2R 0RL, UK

Rough Guides, 4th Floor, 345 Hudson St,
New York NY10014, USA

newslettersubs@roughguides.co.uk

...music & reference

Africa & Middle East
Cape Town
Egypt
The Gambia
Jerusalem
Jordan
Kenya
Morocco
South Africa, Lesotho & Swaziland
Syria
Tanzania
Tunisia
West Africa
Zanzibar
Zimbabwe

Travel Theme guides
First-Time Around the World
First-Time Asia
First-Time Europe
First-Time Latin America
Gay & Lesbian Australia
Skiing & Snowboarding in North America
Travel Online
Travel Health
Walks in London & SE England
Women Travel

Restaurant guides
French Hotels & Restaurants
London
New York
San Francisco

Maps
Algarve
Amsterdam
Andalucia & Costa del Sol
Argentina
Athens
Australia
Baja California
Barcelona
Boston
Brittany
Brussels
Chicago
Crete
Croatia
Cuba
Cyprus
Czech Republic
Dominican Republic
Dublin
Egypt
Florence & Siena
Frankfurt
Greece
Guatemala & Belize
Iceland
Ireland
Lisbon
London
Los Angeles
Mexico
Miami & Key West
Morocco
New York City
New Zealand
Northern Spain
Paris
Portugal
Prague
Rome
San Francisco
Sicily
South Africa
Sri Lanka
Tenerife
Thailand
Toronto
Trinidad & Tobago
Tuscany
Venice
Washington DC
Yucatán Peninsula

Dictionary Phrasebooks
Czech
Dutch
Egyptian Arabic
European
French
German
Greek
Hindi & Urdu
Hungarian
Indonesian
Italian
Japanese
Mandarin Chinese
Mexican Spanish
Polish
Portuguese
Russian
Spanish
Swahili
Thai
Turkish
Vietnamese

Music Guides
The Beatles
Cult Pop
Classical Music
Country Music
Cuban Music
Drum'n'bass
Elvis
House
Irish Music
Jazz
Music USA
Opera
Reggae
Rock
Techno
World Music (2 vols)

100 Essential CDs series
Country
Latin
Opera
Rock
Soul
World Music

History Guides
China
Egypt
England
France
Greece
India
Ireland
Islam
Italy
Spain
USA

Reference Guides
Books for Teenagers
Children's Books, 0–5
Children's Books, 5–11
Cult Football
Cult Movies
Cult TV
Digital Stuff
Formula 1
The Internet
Internet Radio
James Bond
Lord of the Rings
Man Utd
Personal Computers
Pregnancy & Birth
Shopping Online
Travel Health
Travel Online
Unexplained Phenomena
The Universe
Videogaming
Weather
Website Directory

Also! More than 120 Rough Guide music CDs are available from all good book and record stores. Listen in at www.worldmusic.net